THE ROUGH GUIDE TO

Southeast Asia

D0569198

There are more than one hundred a~~~ ~~~, ~~~~~~
covering destinations from Amsterdam to Zimbabwe

Forthcoming titles include
Alaska • Copenhagen • Ibiza & Formentera • Iceland

Rough Guide Reference Series
Classical Music • Country Music • Drum 'n' bass • English Football
European Football • House • The Internet • Jazz • Music USA • Opera
Reggae • Rock Music • Techno • Unexplained Phenomena • World Music

Rough Guide Phrasebooks
Czech • Dutch • Egyptian Arabic • European Languages • French • German
Greek • Hindi & Urdu • Hungarian • Indonesian • Italian • Japanese
Mandarin Chinese • Mexican Spanish • Polish • Portuguese • Russian
Spanish • Swahili • Thai • Turkish • Vietnamese

Rough Guides on the Internet
www.roughguides.com

ROUGH GUIDE CREDITS

Text editor: Ruth Blackmore
Series editor: Mark Ellingham
Editorial: Martin Dunford, Jonathan Buckley, Jo Mead, Kate Berens, Amanda Tomlin, Ann-Marie Shaw, Paul Gray, Helena Smith, Judith Bamber, Orla Duane, Olivia Eccleshall, Geoff Howard, Claire Saunders, Gavin Thomas, Alexander Mark Rogers, Polly Thomas, Joe Staines, Lisa Nellis, Andrew Tomičić, Richard Lim, Duncan Clark, Peter Buckley, Sam Thorne, Lucy Ratcliffe (UK); Andrew Rosenberg, Mary Beth Maioli, Don Bapst, Stephen Timblin (US)
Production: Susanne Hillen, Andy Hilliard, Link Hall, Helen Ostick, Julia Bovis, Michelle Draycott, Katie Pringle, Robert Evers, Mike Hancock, Robert McKinlay, Zoë Nobes

Cartography: Melissa Baker, Maxine Repath, Ed Wright
Picture research: Louise Boulton, Sharon Martins
Online: Kelly Cross, Anja Mutić-Blessing, Jennifer Gold (US)
Finance: John Fisher, Gary Singh, Edward Downey, Mark Hall, Tim Bill
Marketing & Publicity: Richard Trillo, Niki Smith, David Wearn, Jemima Broadbridge, Chloë Roberts, Birgit Hartmann (UK); Simon Carloss, David Wechsler (US)
Administration: Tania Hummel, Demelza Dallow, Julie Sanderson

PUBLISHING INFORMATION

This first edition published November 2000 by Rough Guides Ltd, 62–70 Shorts Gardens, London WC2H 9AH.

Distributed by the Penguin Group:

Penguin Books Ltd, 27 Wrights Lane, London W8 5TZ

Penguin Putnam, Inc. 375 Hudson Street, NY 10014, USA

Penguin Books Australia Ltd, 487 Maroondah Highway, PO Box 257, Ringwood, Victoria 3134, Australia

Penguin Books Canada Ltd, 10 Alcorn Avenue, Toronto, Ontario, Canada M4V 1E4

Penguin Books (NZ) Ltd, 182–190 Wairau Road, Auckland 10, New Zealand

Typeset in Linotron Univers and Century Old Style to an original design by Andrew Oliver.

Printed in England by Clays Ltd, St Ives PLC

Illustrations in Part One and Part Three by Edward Briant

Illustrations on p.1 & p.449 by Louise Boulton

Illustrations on p.55, p.185, p.819 & p.959 by Link Hall

Illustrations on p.71, p.551, p.669 & p.773 by Katie Pringle

Illustrations on p.141 & p.531 by Robert Evers

© Rough Guides, in part under licence from the authors of the Rough Guides to China, Indonesia, Laos, Malaysia, Singapore & Brunei, Thailand and Vietnam.

No part of this book may be reproduced in any form without permission from the publisher except for the quotation of brief passages in reviews.

1104pp – Includes index

A catalogue record for this book is available from the British Library

ISBN 1-85828-553-4

THE ROUGH GUIDE TO

Southeast Asia

written and researched by

Jeremy Atiyah, Stephen Backshall, Jeff Cranmer,
David Dalton, Jan Dodd, Paul Gray, Jonathan Knight,
Charles de Ledesma, David Leffman, Mark Lewis,
Simon Lewis, Steven Martin, Lesley Reader,
Lucy Ridout, Pauline Savage and Henry Stedman.

With additional contributions by

David Atkinson, Arnold Barkhordarian, Samantha Coomber,
Sophy Fisher, Robert Snodgrass, Thomas Vater.

ROUGH
GUIDES

TRAVEL GUIDES • PHRASEBOOKS • MUSIC AND REFERENCE GUIDES

 We set out to do something different when the first Rough Guide was published in 1982. Mark Ellingham, just out of university, was travelling in Greece. He brought along the popular guides of the day, but found they were all lacking in some way. They were either strong on ruins and museums but went on for pages without mentioning a beach or taverna. Or they were so conscious of the need to save money that they lost sight of Greece's cultural and historical significance. Also, none of the books told him anything about Greece's contemporary life – its politics, its culture, its people, and how they lived.

So with no job in prospect, Mark decided to write his own guidebook, one which aimed to provide practical information that was second to none, detailing the best beaches and the hottest clubs and restaurants, while also giving hard-hitting accounts of every sight, both famous and obscure, and providing up-to-the-minute information on contemporary culture. It was a guide that encouraged independent travellers to find the best of Greece, and was a great success, getting shortlisted for the Thomas Cook travel guide award, and encouraging Mark, along with three friends, to expand the series.

The Rough Guide list grew rapidly and the letters flooded in, indicating a much broader readership than had been anticipated, but one which uniformly appreciated the Rough Guide mix of practical detail and humour, irreverence and enthusiasm. Things haven't changed. The same four friends who began the series are still the caretakers of the Rough Guide mission today: to provide the most reliable, up-to-date and entertaining information to independent-minded travellers of all ages, on all budgets.

We now publish more than 150 titles and have offices in London and New York. The travel guides are written and researched by a dedicated team of more than 100 authors, based in Britain, Europe, the USA and Australia. We have also created a unique series of phrasebooks to accompany the travel series, along with an acclaimed series of music guides, and a best-selling pocket guide to the Internet and World Wide Web. We also publish comprehensive travel information on our web site:

www.roughguides.com

HELP US UPDATE

We've gone to a lot of effort to ensure that the first edition of *The Rough Guide to Southeast Asia* is accurate and up-to-date. However, things change – places get "discovered", opening hours are notoriously fickle, restaurants and rooms raise prices or lower standards. If you feel we've got it wrong or left something out, we'd like to know, and if you can remember the address, the price, the time, the phone number, so much the better.

We'll credit all contributions, and send a copy of the next edition (or any other Rough Guide if you prefer) for the best letters. Please mark letters: "Rough Guide Southeast Asia Update" and send to:
Rough Guides, 62–70 Shorts Gardens, London WC2H 9AH, or Rough Guides, 4th Floor, 345 Hudson St, New York, NY 10014.
Or send email to: mail@roughguides.co.uk
Online updates about this book can be found on Rough Guides' Web site at www.roughguides.com

ACKNOWLEDGEMENTS

The editor would like to thank Lucy Ridout for her hard work and commitment throughout the editing stages, Jo Mead and Martin Dunford for expert guidance, Gerrard Kennedy and Narrell Leffman for extra basics research, Maxine Repath and Stratigraphics for the maps, Katie Pringle for typesetting and Laurence Larroche for proofreading.

The authors and researchers would like to thank the following:

David Atkinson: Liem, Phuong and Huong at *Love Planet*; Aaron and Max at *Kangaroo Café*; the guys at *TF Handspan*; Bret Zastera and Hong Anh; Hoai Linh; Deborah and Hugh at *The Guide*; Tom Greenwood; Digby Greenhalgh; Mirjam Huizinga; Jacobi Leaver; Jimmy Pham and the KOTO guys; Adam McCarty; Christophe; Vy and Uyen in Hoi An; Mr Da in Ninh Binh; the staff of the *Camellia 2* for looking after me when I was sick; and, most of all, Thuong for being a good friend.

Arnold: Ms Khoo Sien Wah at the tourist centre in the Komtar Building in Georgetown and all the staff at the tourist office in Melaka.

Sam: Colm; Mark and Carol Coomber; Andrea and Jane for all their continuing support; Nhut, Dung and Kim; Eric, Liem Nguyen, Tony Nong, Loc and Virginie for help in Ho Chi Minh City; Anh (AKA Tony) for his imput on Phu Quoc Island; Su, Benjamin, Mr Lang and all in Nha Trang for their wealth of information; Huynh in Kontum for the truly awesome motorbike-rides; Hai in Pleiku and Tung in Qui Nhon for their whistle-stop motorbike tours; and Vietnam itself and its people, to whom I am forever indebted.

David Dalton: above all, my wife Giselle for checking the Tagalog, helping with the travel arrangements and generally being wonderful in every respect; John Walsh, Anne Parton, Matthew Brooker and Kelly Noel-Smith for their constant emails; Lynne Palma and the team at *Go!* magazine; Kristine and Noel Matta for introducing us to Popototan; and all the staff at ABC Divers in Coron for their help with some memorable trips, particularly on board the *MV Maribeth*. Finally, thanks to Zoë Barber and Max "Nodge" Barber for the fun in Palawan.

Charles: in Malaysia, Stevie and Vincent at the *Backpackers Travellers Lodge* for the best lodging and help around town; David Nathan, KL's club guru; and Professor Khoo Kay Kim for insights into the rich history of the region. In Sarawak, thanks to the Kuching duo of Wayne Tarman and Mike Reed, the perfect hosts for any thirsty traveller; and Audrey Wan Ullock at *Telang Usan Hotel*, the perfect hostess. Further north, thanks to Gracie Geikie at Seridan Mulu tours. In Brunei, thanks to Leslie Chiang and Anthony Chieng at Sunshine Borneo Tours for helping to open up the country.

Sophy: Michael Sheridan, Chantal Hooper, Finnoula McHugh and the HKTA.

Jonathan: David Smyth at the University of London School of Oriental and African Studies for valuable assistance with the language section; the staff at the Center for Advanced Study in Phnom Penh; Em Sarun in Phnom Penh for information and advice; Nareoun for accompanying me on trips all over the Southwest; Kim Lee; Multan; Senf Vanna; Deu Sophoeun for her help in Mondolkiri; Sam in Krong Koh Kong; Tra You in Siem Reap; Sam Din in Kompong Cham; Narin, and the entire Smiley gang all over Cambodia; Ben "Jamin" Wilkes and Ross "Fat-boy" Gearing for hospitality in Bangkok; and all the travellers who shared their experiences with me or accompanied me on adventures, especially Sanlina Yu, Tracy D'Souza, Clint McLean, Josie Scerri, the Nella contingent, the Sihanoukville nightlife crew, the Siem Reap nightlife crew, Nick Malloni, Dougal, Amanda, George, and anyone else I've missed out. Hello to Sa the travelling doris and sidekick Ra, wherever you may be. Finally, thanks to my family and friends for not forgetting me after being away for so long.

Mark: my wife and family for their continued love and support.

Robert: Thanks to Sorn at Suan Keo Guest House for her help on Louang Phabang and for nursing me back to health; P'Wat at Tamila Guest House for his great stories and useful tips. Big hugs to Dao for the loan of the fantastic "plastic" typing machine and continual support; Gene for his friendly smile and companionship amidst adverse travelling conditions and finally to Steve for the late-night chat sessions and for convincing me I could do it in the first place.

Thomas: Aroon Taewchatturat (Kasetsart University); Carissa Hine; Sontharee Wechanon; Yves and Ning Barbry; Mark Read (Khao Yai); Krissana Intharasook; Tuangsuang Sakunkonchak and the rest of the crew from Chulalongkorn University; Sarah, Gavin and Kevin; Goona; Katya Myllymaki; Tawan; Duunung; Ko-Yang and all other Moken; Stephano, his wife and Yai and the Urak Lawoy; Anie; Zora5; Peter Weber; Dennis; Graham "Sponge" Franklin; Simon Jenkins and all at Blue Moon; Sam Murphy; Dr Janet Topp Fargion (British Library); Tony Engle (Topic); Simon Foster; Lucy Ridout.

CONTENTS

Introduction xvi

● CHAPTER 3: HONG KONG 140

● CHAPTER 4: INDONESIA 185

• CHAPTER 5: LAOS 449

• CHAPTER 6: MACAU 531

● CHAPTER 7: MALAYSIA 551

● CHAPTER 8: THE PHILIPPINES 669

● CHAPTER 9: SINGAPORE 773

• CHAPTER 10: THAILAND 819

● CHAPTER 11: VIETNAM 963

LIST OF MAPS

MAP SYMBOLS

═══	Main road	⊼	Lighthouse
──	Road	⊠—⊠	Gate
◄──	One-way street	⚲	Golf course
──■──	Railway	〰	Surfing beach
------	Footpath	✗	Airport
── ──	Ferry route	★	Public transport stop
■■-■■	International boundary	⛽	Petrol station
────·	Chapter division boundary	◉	Hotel
♦	Point of interest	⛺	Campsite
✚	Temple	■	Restaurant or bar
▲	Khmer Temple	ⓘ	Information centre
⊠	Mosque	ⓒ	Telephone
♥	Museum	⊠	Post Office
⊙	Statue	Ⓗ	Hospital
🏛	Monument	■	Building
♔	Fort	▨	Park
〽	Mountains	▨	National park
▲	Mountain peak	░	Beach
◖	Cave	✚	Church
𝄞	Waterfall	⊹	Cemetery
〜	Spring	⊻	Muslim cemetery
⊼	Gardens		

INTRODUCTION

Bordered by the Indian subcontinent to the west, and by China and Japan to the north and east, **Southeast Asia** is a tropical region of volcanoes, rainforest, ricefields and coral reefs, whose constituent countries – **Brunei, Cambodia, Indonesia, Laos, Malaysia, the Philippines, Singapore, Thailand and Vietnam** – together make one of the most stimulating and accessible regions for independent travel in the world. Here you can spend the day exploring thousand-year-old Hindu ruins, and the night at a rave on the beach; attend a Buddhist alms-giving ceremony at dawn and go whitewater rafting in the afternoon; chill out in a bamboo beach hut for a fortnight or hike energetically through the jungle looking for orang-utans. In short, there is enough diversity here to keep anyone hooked for months, and the average cost of living is so low that many Western travellers find they can actually afford to be here for months. In addition, the tourist infrastructure is sufficiently developed to make travel reasonably comfortable and straightforward, and there are recognizable tourist trails that span the region. We have also included in this Guide sections on Southeast Asian neighbours **Hong Kong** and **Macau**, which are useful gateways to the region; we have excluded **Burma** (Myanmar), respecting the boycott on tourism requested by Aung San Suu Kyi, the democratically elected leader of the country.

The most popular destination in Southeast Asia is **Thailand**, and the vast majority of travellers begin their journey through the region in Bangkok, tempted both by the number of cheap flights from the West, and by the well-established backpackers' scene there. Thailand offers some of the best beaches in the world, as well as many moderate hilltribe treks, and has fast, inexpensive road and rail links to neighbouring Malaysia and Laos. Conveniently, Bangkok is also the easiest place in the world to get hold of a visa for Laos, Vietnam and Cambodia. The most popular trans-Southeast Asia route takes travellers down to one of the beaches in south Thailand, from where they get a train or bus into Malaysia. Slightly less trendy than Thailand, but a similarly straightforward place to get around, **Malaysia** boasts equally nice beaches, particularly on the east coast, good diving, and some rewarding national park hikes. East Malaysia, which shares the large island of Borneo with Indonesia's Kalimantan province and the little kingdom of Brunei, is much more off the beaten track and offers adventurous (if costly) travel by river through the jungle and nights in tribal longhouses. Marooned in the middle of Malaysian Borneo, the tiny independent kingdom of **Brunei** is expensive and dull, so most people stop here only when obliged to by plane sched-

THE BEST OF SOUTHEAST ASIA

The beaches of Thailand	see p.821
The Khmer temples of Angkor, Cambodia	see p.105
The sunrise climb up Mount Bromo, Indonesia	see p.260
The Buddhist temple of Borobodur, Indonesia	see p.244
Overnighting in the Iban longhouses of Sarawak, Malaysia	see p.640
Diving in the Philippines	see p.679
Surfing in Indonesia	see p.200
Travelling by boat along the Mekong River to Louang Phabang, Laos	see p.508
Banaue rice terraces, Philippines	see p.724
Hué's Imperial City and seven royal mausoleums, Vietnam	see p.1030
Keli Mutu's three-coloured lakes, Indonesia	see p.383
The dramatic architecture and strange burial rituals of Torajahland, Indonesia	see p.420
Bizarre karst seascapes of Ha Long Bay, Vietnam	see p.1054

TOP TEN BEACHES OF SOUTHEAST ASIA			
Boracay, Philippines	see p.749	Kuta, Lombok, Indonesia	see p.372
Ko Chang, Thailand	see p.936	Palawan, Philippines	see p.752
Ko Phi Phi, Thailand	see p.947	Pulau Perhentian, Malaysia	see p.614
Ko Samui, Thailand	see p.925	Pulau Tioman, Malaysia	see p.628
Ko Tarutao, Thailand	see p.951	Romblon Island, Philippines	see p.752

ules. Overland travellers with plenty of time might stop off for a couple of days in hi-tech **Singapore**, which sits at the southern tip of Peninsular Malaysia, but as it's relatively pricey and has no unmissable sights, Singapore's main appeal is the boat service across to Sumatra, the northernmost island of Indonesia (travellers who don't fancy Singapore generally opt for the boats from Melaka or Penang to Sumatra). **Indonesia** vies with Thailand as the region's most visited destination, with fantastic volcanic landscapes, plenty of hiking opportunities, an unparalleled diversity of tribal cultures, decent beaches and diving, and lots of arts and crafts. There are so many islands in Indonesia that it could take you a lifetime to explore the whole archipelago, but the classic itinerary takes you through Sumatra, across to Java and then on to Bali and Lombok. With extra time, you could continue east as far as Flores, from where it's just a few hours' flight to northern Australia.

The less common route out of Thailand heads northeastwards, across the Mekong River and into Laos, with the possibility of continuing overland into Vietnam and Cambodia. Laos, Vietnam and Cambodia are sometimes collectively referred to as **Indochina**, a legacy of the time when all three countries came under French rule. For many, **Laos**'s main appeal lies in the fact that it's a lot less developed and much less touristed than neighbouring Thailand. Accommodation here is generally basic, and road transport can be tiresome, but there are memorable long-distance boat journeys, some fine old temples, and the chance to experience traditional rural culture. Neighbouring **Vietnam** offers many more famous sights, including some impressive old Chinese towns, plenty of sobering memorials from the American (Vietnam) War and one or two passable beaches. It's a more popular destination than Laos, but less mainstream than Thailand. Until recently, a dangerous and rarely visited country owing to bandits, guerrillas and mines, **Cambodia** now figures on an increasing number of itineraries, mainly because of the fabulous temple ruins at Angkor, and because it's a new frontier. Cambodia has two legal border crossings with Thailand, which makes it possible to complete the entire Indochina circuit overland.

Stuck way out beyond both Thailand loops, the **Philippines** is often omitted from Southeast Asia trips because it has no overland access – most people fly there via Hong Kong. Once you have made the commitment though, the Philippines archipelago boasts some of the best beaches and most dramatic diving in the whole region, along with good volcano hikes, plus some exceptionally exuberant festivals.

The highlights

The **beaches** of Southeast Asia are some of the finest in the world, and you'll find the cream of the crop in Thailand, the Philippines and Malaysia, all of which boast postcard-pretty white-sand bays, complete with azure waters and wooden beach shacks dotted along their palm-fringed shores. The clear tropical waters also offer supreme **diving** opportunities, with particularly rich reefs off **Boracay, Moalboal, Bohol** and **Palawan** in the Philippines, off **Pulau Tioman** and **Pulau Sipadan** in Malaysia, near **Phuket** and **Ko Tao** in Thailand, and at **Pulau Bunaken, Pulau Menjangan** and **Tulamben** in Indonesia.

Almost every visitor to Indonesia makes an effort to get up before dawn and climb Java's spectacular volcano **Mount Bromo** in time for sunrise; further east, on the more remote Indonesian island of Flores, the famous three-coloured crater lakes of **Keli Mutu** are anoth-

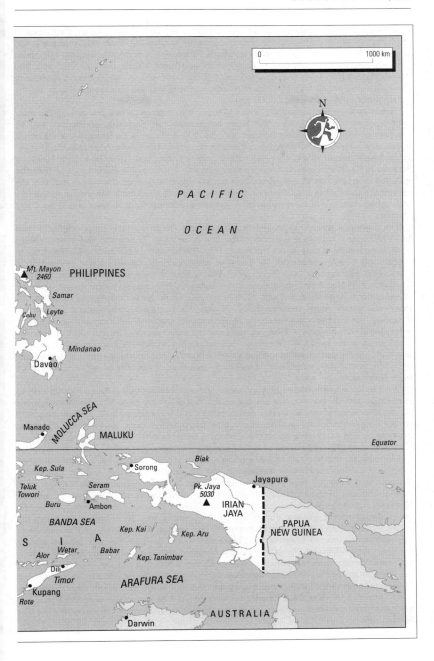

er must-see. East Malaysia (Borneo) is also off the main trail, but here you get the chance to explore parts of the largest cave system in the world, in **Gunung Mulu national park**, and to climb the 4101-metre-high **Mount Kinabalu**. There are similarly challenging mountains awaiting you in the Philippines, most popularly at **Mount Mayon**, an active volcano, and **Mount Apo**, which takes four days to conquer. The much shorter hikes around **Banaue** in the Philippines are classics of a different order, drawing you through breathtakingly beautiful amphitheatres of sculpted rice terraces.

Tribal culture is a highlight of visits to many less explored areas, and among the most approachable communities are the **Iban longhouses of Sarawak**, which can only be reached by taking a boat along the river systems of East Malaysia, the **Torajans of Sulawesi** in Indonesia, known for their intriguing architecture and ghoulish burial rituals, the **Dani of Irian Jaya's** Baliem Valley, who hunt with arrows and wear penis gourds, and the **Igorot of Sagada** in the Philippines, famous for their hanging coffins and burial caves. The **hilltribe villages of northern Thailand** are now such a major feature on the tourist trail that the experience can feel akin to visiting a human zoo – you'll have more rewarding encounters with other branches of these same tribal groups at **Muang Sing** in Laos and at **Sa Pa** in Vietnam.

The dominant threads of mainstream **Southeast Asian culture** came originally from India and China, and since the start of the first millennium, Hindu and Buddhist practices have had a lasting impact across the region. The Hindu Khmers of Cambodia left a string of magnificent temple complexes, the finest of which can still be seen today at **Angkor** in Cambodia, with smaller scale versions at **Wat Phou** in Laos and at **Phanom Rung** in Thailand. The Buddhists' most impressive legacy is the colossal ninth-century stupa of **Borobudur** in Indonesia, but with Buddhism still one of the main religions in the region there are plenty more modern Buddhist temples to admire, particularly in **Louang Phabang**, the Lao city of golden spires. In Vietnam, the eighteenth-century Imperial City and seven Royal Mausoleums of **Hué** rate as some of the finest examples of traditional Chinese architecture in the world. For Western visitors it is often not just the monuments to faith that fascinate, but the daily devotions still practised across the region – be it Thai Buddhist monks collecting food at their neighbours' doors every morning, or Balinese housewives setting out daily offerings for the spirits.

With religion and tradition playing such overt roles in Southeast Asian life, it's easy to over-emphasise the picturesque and the quaint. In reality, the region has its share of banal fast-food outlets and standard-issue urban sprawl, and there are pockets of extreme poverty too. Very few cities are as charming as Hué, but most are great places to absorb all that is engaging and depressing about contemporary Asian culture. The heaving sidewalks and choking fumes of **Bangkok** can be a daunting prospect for a new arrival, but there are plenty of grandiose temples and museums to keep you off the streets, not to mention cybercafés and cutting-edge clubs. **Jakarta** is another fearsome sprawl, but an undeniably dynamic one, while the view of sky-scrapered **Hong Kong** Island, across the harbour from Kowloon, is one of the most stunning urban panoramas on earth. With the exception of Thailand, every Southeast Asian nation has lived under Western colonial rule for a significant span of recent history, and there are particularly well preserved relics from the region's colonial past in **Penang**, a former British trading post, on the cobbled streets of the old Spanish town of **Vigan** in the Philippines, and in the grand French facades of civic buildings across **Phnom Penh** and **Hanoi**. Vietnam, Cambodia and Laos are also littered with reminders of more recent encounters with the West – the war between America and the communists of Indochina that dominated the 1960s and 70s has left thousands of bomb craters and unexploded mines and a large population of amputees. Many visitors are curious to descend into the 250-kilometre network of **Cu Chi tunnels**, where the Viet Cong guerrillas lived for many years, and to see for themselves a chunk of the legendary **Ho Chi Minh Trail**.

TOP TEN PLACES TO HANG OUT

Bukittinggi, Indonesia	see p.290	Mae Hong Son, Thailand	see p.891
Cherating, Malaysia	see p.618	Sagada, Philippines	see p.723
Danau Toba, Indonesia	see p.278	Ubud, Indonesia	see p.324
Gili Islands, Indonesia	see p.368	Vang Viang, Laos	see p.484
Ko Pha Ngan, Thailand	see p.930	Yogyakarta, Indonesia	see p.234

Despite all the obvious highlights in Southeast Asia, there usually comes a point on any longish journey when you tire of ticking off sight after sight and just want to stop moving for a while. What you want is somewhere nice to **hang out** for a week or more – on a beach, at the foot of a mountain, in the heart of a happening city – a place where the accommodation is cheap and the banana juices plentiful, where you can impress other travellers with your adventures and catch up on your postcards. There are scores of great places to do this in Southeast Asia: the list in the box above will introduce you to a few, and you'll find more ideas in the introductions to each chapter.

Whether you stick to the cities or venture out into the sticks, you'll find sampling the local **food** an unexpected pleasure. There are countless different regional specialities across Southeast Asia, most famously in Thailand, whose mouthwatering national dishes are pungently laced with lemongrass, sweet basil and a fiery dose of chillis; Vietnam is also a foodie's paradise, with liberal use of fresh herbs in spring rolls and noodle soups, while Malaysian and Indonesian specialities appeal to the milder palate, mixing in plenty of coconut milk and peanut sauce. Half the fun of Southeast Asian food is in the eating experience: picking up a stick of sizzling chicken satay from a street-corner handcart, constructing a three-course feast from the stalls at a night-market, or simply honing your chopstick technique at a neighbourhood noodle shop.

Inevitably, this book focuses on the most rewarding and most visited destinations in Southeast Asia. Because of their overwhelming popularity, some of the more developed tourist **hot spots**, like Ko Samui in Thailand or Bali's Kuta beach for example, can isolate travellers almost completely from authentic local culture. If you confine yourself to these places it's quite possible never to take a local bus, eat a typical meal, or utter so much as a greeting in the local language. While some travellers appreciate this cushioning, many find that a little mollycoddling goes a long way. Generally, the most memorable encounters with local people happen away from the beach resorts and tourist restaurants, and for most tourists it is these meetings that stand out as the greatest highlights of a Southeast Asian trip. No guidebook can set these up for you, but we can at least supply a useful springboard.

TOP FIVE FESTIVALS

Ati-Atihan Mardi Gras-style costumed parades and street dancing (Kalibo, Philippines; Jan). See p.748.

Thaipusam Hindu penitents skewer themselves with steel objects (KL, Malaysia; Jan/Feb). See p.563.

Buddhist New Year Nationwide public water fights (Chiang Mai, Thailand; Louang Phabang, Laos; April). See pp.830 and 462.

Gawai Dayak Raucous free-for-all harvest festival parties in Iban longhouses (Sarawak, Malaysia; June). See p.640.

Elephant roundup Working elephants play soccer and dress up (Surin, Thailand; Nov). See p.830.

PART ONE

THE
BASICS

CLIMATE AND WHEN TO GO

Southeast Asia sits entirely within the tropics and so is broadly characterized by a hot and humid climate that varies little throughout the year, except during the two annual monsoons ("seasonal winds"). The **southwest monsoon** arrives in west-coast regions at around the end of May and brings daily rainfall to most of Southeast Asia by mid-July (excepting certain east-coast areas, explained on p.4). From then on you can expect overcast skies and regular downpours across the region till October or November. This is not a great time to travel in Southeast Asia, as west-coast seas are often too rough for swimming, some islands become inaccessible, and less well maintained roads may get washed out. However, rain showers often last just a couple of hours a day and many air-

AVERAGE MAXIMUM DAILY TEMPERATURES (°C) AND AVERAGE MONTHLY RAINFALL (MM)												
	Jan	Feb	March	April	May	June	July	Aug	Sept	Oct	Nov	Dec
Bandar Seri Begawan												
(°C)	30	30	31	32	32.5	32	31.5	32	31.5	31.5	31	31
(mm)	133	63	71	124	218	311	277	256	314	334	296	241
Bangkok												
(°C)	28	28	29	30	31	31	30	31	31	30	29	28
(mm)	66	28	33	36	58	112	147	147	170	178	206	97
Hanoi												
(°C)	17	18	20	24	28	30	30	29	28	26	22	19
(mm)	18	28	38	81	196	239	323	343	254	99	43	20
Hong Kong & Macau												
(°C)	18	17	19	24	28	29	31	31	29	27	23	20
(mm)	33	46	74	137	292	394	381	367	257	114	43	31
Jakarta												
(°C)	29	29	30	31	31	31	31	31	31	31	30	29
(mm)	300	300	211	147	114	97	64	43	66	112	142	203
Kuala Lumpur												
(°C)	32	33	33	33	33	32	32	32	32	32	31	31
(mm)	159	154	223	276	182	119	120	133	173	258	263	223
Manila												
(°C)	28	28	30	31	32	30	29	29	29	29	29	28
(mm)	35	25	25	35	130	260	415	415	340	210	145	80
Phnom Penh												
(°C)	25	27	28	29	29	29	29	29	29	28	27	26
(mm)	10	10	45	80	120	150	165	160	215	240	135	55
Singapore												
(°C)	31	32	32	32	32	32	31	31	31	31	31	30
(mm)	146	155	182	223	228	151	170	163	200	199	255	258
Vientiane												
(°C)	28	30	33	34	32	32	31	31	31	31	29	28
(mm)	5	15	38	99	267	302	267	292	302	109	15	3

lines and guesthouses offer decent discounts during this low-season period. The **northeast monsoon** brings drier, slightly cooler weather to most of Southeast Asia (east-coast areas excepted) between November and February, making this period the best overall time to travel in the region. The main exceptions to the above pattern are the east-coast regions of Vietnam, Peninsular Thailand and Peninsular Malaysia, which get rain when the rest of tropical Asia is having its driest period, but stay dry during the southwest monsoon. If you're planning a long trip to Southeast Asia, this means you can often escape the worst weather by hopping across to the other coast. Indonesia and Singapore are hit by both monsoons, attracting the west-coast rains from May through October, and the east-coast rains from November to February. The **climate chart** on p.3 lists average maximum daily temperatures and average monthly rainfall for the capital cities of Southeast Asia. Bear in mind however, that each country has myriad micro-climates, determined by altitude and proximity to the east or west coast amongst other factors; for more detail consult the introduction to each chapter.

GETTING THERE FROM THE UK AND IRELAND

The cheapest way of getting to Southeast Asia **from the UK and Ireland** is to buy an inexpensive **one-way flight** to one of the region's major gateways – Bangkok, Singapore, Bali, Kuala Lumpur or Hong Kong – and make onward travel arrangements from there, by air, road, rail or sea. If you want to visit India and China en route to Southeast Asia, you should consider a **stopover** or an **open-jaw** ticket, which flies you into one country and out of another, with a long overland sector in between. Popular alternatives to this are the air tickets that take you via two or more Asian cities en route; these are generally known as **Circle Asia** tickets, or **Round-the-World** (RTW) tickets if they include Australia, and are offered by all long-haul travel agents. There's also the possibility of following one of the world's classic overland trips, by **Trans-Siberian Railway** through Russia and Mongolia to China, and from there continuing by road or rail into Indochina.

TICKETS AND FARES

Booking a scheduled ticket direct with the airline is the most expensive way to fly. Generally, you're best off booking through an established **discount agent**, which can usually undercut airline prices by a significant amount. See the box on pp.6–7 for a list of recommended agents, or check the adverts in national Sunday papers and major regional newspapers and listings magazines. The **Internet** is also a fertile source of cheap flights, and *www.cheapflights.com* and *www.deckchair.com* are useful places to start looking.

The biggest factor affecting the price of a ticket is the time of year you wish to travel. **Peak season** for many Asian destinations is over Christmas, when much of Asia is experiencing its driest period of the year, and during the UK summer holidays when many people want to travel. It's best to book well in advance for a ticket in high season.

Some airlines charge more than others, as do some travel agents, so it's always good to shop around. And it's usually more expensive to fly nonstop than to change planes in Europe or Asia en route. If you are a **student** or **under 26**, you may be able to get special discounts on flights, especially through agents like Usit Campus or STA Travel. Some European airlines offer competitive fares to Asia from **regional airports** such as Glasgow, Manchester, Dublin and Belfast, otherwise you'll need to go via London, adding the relevant return fare.

ONE-WAY TICKETS TO GATEWAY CITIES

Flying into Southeast Asia on a one-way ticket is inexpensive and gives you plenty of options for onward travel, but it can cause **problems at Immigration**. Many officials like to see proof of onward or return transport, fearing that you may stay illegally in their country. Some will be happy if you show proof of sufficient funds to keep you going (about £1350), others will be more satisfied if you can give details of a convincing onward route, with dates. Some travellers get round all this by buying the cheapest return flight available and then cashing in the return sector, but read the small print before going for this option.

In some countries, you may have to apply for a **visa** in advance if arriving on a one-way ticket, rather than being granted one automatically at Immigration, so always check with the relevant embassy before you leave. If you are continuing overland, you need to research visa requirements at the border crossings before leaving home (see p.20). Details on **overland transport from neighbouring Southeast Asian countries** are given at the beginning of each chapter.

One of the cheapest and most useful gateways to Southeast Asia is **Bangkok**. London–Bangkok flights start at £245 one-way, £350 return, rising to at least £330/420 during peak times (July, August, December), and take a minimum of twelve hours. Once in Bangkok, you can choose to travel overland to Laos or Cambodia, or head south by road or rail into Malaysia and Singapore and then across to Sumatra in Indonesia. Or you can buy one of the good-value flights to Southeast Asian destinations offered by many Bangkok travel agents, eg Bangkok–Bali for about £95, or Bangkok–Phnom Penh for £80. Visit the Web site *www.thaifare.com* for a fuller list of current fares from Bangkok to destinations in Southeast Asia. If you're planning to fly direct from London to either Vientiane or Phnom Penh, you will have to change planes in Bangkok or Singapore anyway, as there are currently no long-haul flights to these destinations. It's also much faster and easier to get visas for Laos, Vietnam and Cambodia in Bangkok than in London (see "Entry requirements" in the introduction to each country), so it's worth building in a stopover just for that.

Another inexpensive and popular gateway city is **Singapore**. London–Singapore flights start at £260 one-way, £390 return, or £350/470 during peak times (mid-July to September), and take at least thirteen hours. Locally bought flights from Singapore are generally a little more expensive than from Bangkok (Singapore–Bali £120), but you can fly direct from Singapore to Lombok or Sulawesi for £145. Few travellers stay long in Singapore itself, but it's just half an hour's bus ride into southern Malaysia, from where you could continue north to Thailand and Indochina, or make a short ferry ride across to Sumatra, and then island-hop across the Indonesia archipelago.

If you're keen to see China as well as Southeast Asia, consider buying a flight to **Hong Kong**. London–Hong Kong flights start at £239 one-way, £350 return or £430/£650 during peak times (mid-June to Sept, Christmas, Chinese New Year, and Easter), and take twelve hours. Hong Kong gives you easy and inexpensive local transport options into Guangdong province, from where you could continue west into Vietnam, and on into Laos, then Thailand and down to Malaysia and Indonesia. It's also a good place from which to buy a cheap local flight: from Hong Kong to Vietnam costs £120, to the Philippines £95.

Sample low-season fares from London to other Southeast Asian cities include **Bali** £280 one-way, £450 return; **Ho Chi Minh City** £330/450; **Kuala Lumpur** £250/380; **Manila** £280/410; and **Phnom Penh** £400/530. For high-season fares, add at least an extra 35 percent.

If you do decide to buy a single or return flight to a gateway city, ask your travel agent about the **Circle Asean deals** offered as a joint package by the national airlines of Brunei, Indonesia, Malaysia, the Philippines, Singapore, Thailand and Vietnam. You choose which of the above countries you would like to start from and you then buy a return ticket, with stopovers in any two, three, four, five or six of the other countries. There's a minimum stay of three nights and a maximum of three months for each stopover. Prices vary according to your departure point, and how many stopovers you require: a circle Asean beginning and ending in Vietnam or Indonesia costs £315 with two stopovers, £385 with three stopovers and £455 with four, five or six stopovers; if you begin and end your tour in the Philippines you're looking at £350/420/450.

STOPOVER RETURNS AND OPEN-JAW TICKETS

If you're only visiting a couple of countries in Asia, buying a ticket with a **stopover** option may be your best deal. You can fly London–Singapore return with a stopover in Bangkok for about £420 for example, or London–Hong Kong return via Manila for £540. Most airlines allow stopovers for up to three months, which gives you plenty of time to explore.

On some airlines, it's possible to buy an **open-jaw** ticket that flies you into one country (eg

Thailand) and out of another (eg Singapore); in this way you get to organize your own transport in between and don't have to backtrack. A more challenging route might take in India and Pakistan en route to China and Indochina, perhaps buying an open-jaw plane ticket from London that flies you into **Delhi** and then takes you out of Bangkok or Singapore a few months later, giving yourself the option of buying some internal flights en route if necessary. From India, you can either cross into **Pakistan** overland (via Amritsar) or fly to Karachi from Delhi or Bombay, or to Lahore from Delhi. From Pakistan buses run along the spectacularly scenic Karakoram Highway into northwest **China**, and you can then continue into **Vietnam** and on into Laos, Thailand, Malaysia and **Singapore**. Another variation would be to exit China via Hong Kong and fly on to the **Philippines**, then take a cargo boat to Indonesia, from where you could overland to Thailand and on into Indochina. Open-jaws are usually more expensive than standard or stopover

returns: prices are generally calculated by halving the return fares to each destination and then adding the two figures together.

CIRCLE ASIA AND RTW TICKETS

Multi-stop **Circle Asia and RTW (Round-the-World) tickets** are good value, and with all your major travel expenses sorted out in advance, you can budget realistically for your trip, and don't have to waste time organizing onward travel when you're there. It also eliminates the hassle that Immigration officials sometimes give travellers with no onward or return tickets. Circle Asia and RTW tickets are in fact a whole series of tickets, generally put together by a travel agent using the cheapest flights they can find to construct a trans-Asia route via a series of key cities chosen by you. Once you've bought your ticket the route cannot be changed, though dates can be altered at any point along the way; tickets are generally valid for one year.

DISCOUNT FLIGHT AGENTS

Apex Travel, 59 Dame St, Dublin 2 (☎01/671 5933). Flights to Australia and the Far East.

Austravel, 50 Conduit St, London (☎020/7734 7755); 12 The Minories, Temple Court, Birmingham (☎0121/200 1116); 45 Coulston St, Bristol (☎0117/ 927 7425); 33 George St, Edinburgh (☎0131/226 1000); 16 County Arcade, Victoria Quarter, Leeds (☎0113/244 8880); 3 Barton Arcade, Deansgate, Manchester (☎0161/832 2445). *www.austravel.com* Very good deals on flights to Australia and New Zealand via Indonesia, also on RTW tickets.

Bridge the World, 47 Chalk Farm Rd, London NW1 (☎020/7911 0900, *www.bridgetheworld. com*). Specializing in RTW tickets, with good deals aimed at the backpacker market.

Cheap Flights *www.cheapflights.co.uk* Online service that lists the day's cheapest flight deals available from subscribing UK flight agents.

Co-op Travel Care, 35 Belmont Rd, Belfast 4 (☎028/9047 1717). Budget fares agent.

Destination Group, 14 Greville St, London EC1 (☎020/7400 7000, *www.destination-group.com*). Budget-fares agent, especially good for Garuda flights.

Flightbookers, 177–178 Tottenham Court Rd, London W1 (☎020/7757 2444); Gatwick Airport,

South Terminal (☎01293/568300; daily 7am–10pm); 34 Argyle Arcade, off Buchanan Street, Glasgow (☎0141/204 1919). *sales@flightbookers.co.uk* Low fares on an extensive offering of scheduled flights.

Joe Walsh Tours, 69 Upper O'Connell St, Dublin 2 (☎01/872 2555); 8–11 Baggot St, Dublin 2 (☎01/676 3053); 117 St Patrick St, Cork (☎021/277959). Budget fares agent.

The London Flight Centre, 131 Earls Court Rd, London SW5 (☎020/7244 6411); 47 Notting Hill Gate, London W11 (☎020/7727 4290); Shop 33, The Broadway Centre, Hammersmith tube, London W6 (☎020/8748 6777). Long-established agent dealing in discount flights.

North South Travel, Moulsham Mill Centre, Parkway, Chelmsford, Essex (☎01245/608 291). Travel agency that supports projects in the developing world, especially sustainable tourism.

Quest Worldwide, 10 Richmond Rd, Kingston, Surrey (☎020/8547 3322). Specialists in RTW and Australasian discount fares.

STA Travel, 86 Old Brompton Rd, London SW7; 117 Euston Rd, London NW1; 38 Store St, London WC1; 11 Goodge St, London W1 (☎020/7361 6262); 25 Queens Rd, Bristol (☎0117/929 4399); 38 Sidney St, Cambridge

The cheapest and most popular Circle Asia and RTW routes include one or more "surface sectors" where you have to make your way between point A and point B by road, rail or sea or by a locally bought flight. A typical **Circle Asia** from London to Bali and back, for example, would include a flight from London to Bangkok, then a surface sector from Bangkok to Singapore, followed by flights from Singapore to Bali, then Bali to London; total cost from £480. Similarly, for £660 you could fly from London to Hong Kong and then on to Manila, then go overland to Cebu, from where you fly to Singapore and then on to London. For help with planning surface sectors, see the sections on overland travel at the beginning of each chapter.

An **RTW** ticket is similar but includes stops in Australia and the Pacific, North America or South Africa. For example, a one-year open RTW ticket from London taking in Bangkok, Singapore, Perth, Sydney, Auckland and Los Angeles starts for as little as £630, rising to around £1200 if you add stops in India or China and the South Pacific. The cheapest

time to begin your RTW trip is usually April through June.

OVERLAND TO HONG KONG VIA THE TRANS-SIBERIAN

The **Trans-Siberian Railway** is *the* classic overland route into Asia. All trains begin in Moscow (you can take the train from London to Moscow as well if you want), and there are two possible routes into Asia. The Trans-Mongolian route and the Trans-Manchurian route both end up in **Beijing**, take about six days to get there, and start at £295 from Moscow; it's then another 24 hours by rail to **Hong Kong**, or about five days by train to **Hanoi**. Providing you arrange relevant visas, you can stop off anywhere en route. The cheapest tickets are for intolerably uncomfortable four-berth hard-sleeper accommodation, so it's well worth upgrading for an extra £100. For a full rundown of everything you need to know about visas, life on the train and ideas for stopoffs, see the *Trans-Siberian Handbook*, pub-

(☎01223/366966); 75 Deansgate, Manchester (☎0161/834 0668); 88 Vicar Lane, Leeds (☎0113/244 9212); 78 Bold St, Liverpool (☎0151/707 1123); 9 St Mary's Place, Newcastle (☎0191/233 2111); 36 George St, Oxford (☎01865/792 800); 27 Forrest Rd, Edinburgh (☎0131/226 7747); 184 Byres Rd, Glasgow (☎0141/338 6000); 30 Upper Kirkgate, Aberdeen (☎0122/465 8222) and on many university campuses. *www.statravel.co.uk* Worldwide specialists in low-cost flights for students and under-26s, though other customers welcome. Also over two hundred offices abroad.

Trailfinders, 194 Kensington High St, London W8 (☎020/7938 3939); 48 Earls Court Rd, London W8 (☎020/7938 3366); 1 Threadneedle St, London EC2 (☎020/7628 7628); 58 Deansgate, Manchester (☎0161/839 6969); 254–284 Sauchiehall St, Glasgow (☎0141/353 2224); 22–24 The Priory Queensway, Birmingham (☎0121/236 1234); 48 Corn St, Bristol (☎0117/929 9000); 4–5 Dawson St, Dublin 2 (☎01/677 7888). *www.trailfinders.co.uk* One of the best-informed agents for independent travellers.

Travel Bag, 52 Regent St, London W1 (☎020/7287 5558); 373–375 The Strand, opposite the *Savoy Hotel*, London WC2 (☎020/7497 0515); 12 High St, Alton, Hants (☎01420/80828).

www.travelbag.co.uk Discount flights, with good deals on Qantas and BA flights.

The Travel Bug, 125 Gloucester Rd, London SW7 (☎020/7835 2000); 597 Cheetham Hill Rd, Manchester (☎0161/721 4000). *www.flynow.com* Large range of discounted tickets.

Travel Cuts, 295a Regent St, London W1 (☎020/7255 2082). *www.travelcuts.co.uk* Specializes in budget, student and youth travel and RTW tickets.

Usit Campus, national call centre ☎0870/240 1010; 52 Grosvenor Gardens, London SW1 (☎020/7730 8111); Fountain Centre, College St, Belfast (☎028/9032 4073); 541 Bristol Rd, Selly Oak, Birmingham (☎0121/414 1848); 61 Ditchling Rd, Brighton (☎01273/570 226); 37–39 Queen's Rd, Clifton, Bristol (☎0117/929 2494); 5 Emmanuel St, Cambridge (☎01223/324 283); 10–11 Market Parade, Patrick St, Cork (☎021/270 900); 19 Aston Quay, Dublin 2 (☎01/602 1700); 53 Forest Rd, Edinburgh (☎0131/225 6111); 122 George St, Glasgow (☎0141/553 1818); 166 Deansgate, Manchester (☎0161/ 273 1721); 105–106 St Aldates, Oxford (☎01865/242 067). *www.usitcampus.co.uk* Student/youth travel specialists, with branches also in YHA shops and on university campuses all over Britain.

Williames, 18–20 Howard St, Belfast (☎028/9023 0714). Long-haul specialists.

lished by Trailblazer. Or talk to an experienced agent like Regent Holidays (☎0117/921 1711, *www.regent-holidays.co.uk*) or China Travel Service (☎020/7836 9911), who can organize all tickets, visas and stopovers.

COURIER FLIGHTS

A number of **courier** companies offer heavily discounted international flights to travellers willing to accompany documents and/or freight to the destination for them. These flights can be up to fifty percent cheaper than advertised rates, but are only available to certain destinations (chiefly Hong Kong, Singapore and Malaysia). Most have considerable restrictions attached: you will probably have to come back within a month, you will have to travel alone, and you might only be allowed to take carry-on luggage. Courier deals are advertised in the press and sold through special agents; contact Flight Masters, 83 Mortimer St, London W1 (☎020/7462 0022) or Bridges Worldwide, Old Mill Road House, West Drayton, Middlessex TW3 (☎01895/465 065); or the International Association of Air Travel Couriers, c/o International Features, 1 Kings Rd, Dorchester, Dorset DT1 (☎01305/264 564, *www.aircourier.co.uk*) who are agents for lots of courier companies.

ORGANIZED TOURS AND PACKAGE HOLIDAYS

Dozens of tour operators organize trips to Southeast Asia, offering **packages** that cover the whole range of options, from beach holidays to cultural tours, from

SPECIALIST TOUR OPERATORS

Asian Journeys, 32 Semolong Rd, Northampton NN2 6BT (☎01604/234855,*www.asianjourneys. com*). Escorted small-group tours across the region, including "Following the Mekong" – 21 days, through Thailand, Laos, Cambodia and Vietnam (£2787).

Earthwatch Institute, Belsyre Court, 57 Woodstock Rd, Oxford OX2 6HU (☎01865/311600, *info@uk.earthwatch.org*). Volunteer work on projects in Indonesia, including assisting archeologists, biologists and community workers. You stay with local people. Around £1000 for two weeks.

Exodus, 9 Weir Rd, London SW12 0LT (☎020/8675 5550, *www.exodus.co.uk*). Overland trips aimed at 18–45-year olds, including "Indochina Overland" from Hong Kong to China, Laos, Thailand, Malaysia and Singapore (£1290); and Grand Asia Overland (26 weeks; £4550), in which the London–Islamabad–Hong Kong legs are also done by local transport.

Explore Worldwide, 1 Frederick St, Aldershot, Hants GU11 1LQ (☎01252/760000); Maxwells Travel, D'Olier Chambers, 1 Hawkins St, Dublin 2 (☎003531/677 9479). *www.explore.co.uk* Heaps of options throughout Southeast Asia, including "Indochina Highlights" (22days; £2155) featuring Vientiane, Louang Phabang, Hanoi and Hué; and "East Indies Seatrek" (fifteen days; £1360) from Bali by boat to Lombok, Sumbawa and Komodo.

Guerba Expeditions, Wessex House, 40 Station Rd, Westbury, Wiltshire BA13 3JN (☎01373/858956, *www.guerba.co.uk*). Small-group, walking, trekking and discovery holidays throughout the region, including "Indonesia Overland" from Jakarta to Bali (two weeks; £750 excluding flight).

Imaginative Traveller, 14 Barley Mow Passage, London W4 4PH (☎020/8742 8612, *www.imaginative-traveller.com*). Broad selection of tours to less-travelled parts of Asia, including walking, cycling, camping, cooking and snorkelling. Also "The Great Indo-China Loop" – thirty days overland from Bangkok via Laos, Vietnam and Cambodia (£1355); and "Bali to Bangkok Overland", 29 days in either direction (£895).

Silverbird, 4 Northfields Prospect, Putney Bridge, London SW18 1PE (☎020/8875 9090, *www.silverbird.co.uk*). A Southeast Asia specialist, who can arrange tailor-made holidays, including a sixteen-day "Total Indochina" package, which starts at Vientiane and takes in Hanoi, Saigon and Phnom Penh.

Symbiosis, 113 Bolingbroke Grove, London SW11 1DA (☎020/7924 5906, *www.symbiosis-travel.co.uk*). Environmentally aware outfit that offers specialist interest holidays in Southeast Asia, including an island-hopping trip through the Philippines, via North Palawan and Boracay, plus Easter celebrations at Bulacan (15 days; £1653); a Kelabit Highlanders' Trek through jungles and longhouse communities of Sarawak and Sabah (fourteen days; £1228).

city breaks to overland expeditions through several countries. Most operators give you the option of buying your own flights and joining the tour on the ground. A selection of specialist operators are listed in the box opposite, but any travel agent will be able to furnish you with a bigger selection of brochures.

GETTING THERE FROM NORTH AMERICA

There's no way around it, **flights from North America** to Southeast Asia are long. With the exception of non-stop service to Hong Kong from the US's West Coast, all flights, including so-called "direct flights", will require a stop somewhere along the way. This however, offers a good chance for travellers to take advantage of the **stopovers** offered by many airlines. **Open-jaw** tickets, where you fly into one country and out of another, also give you some flexibility. Popular alternatives to this are **Round-the-World tickets** or **Circle Pacific** tickets, which will take you to a series of destinations, pre-determined before you leave American or Canadian soil. There's also the possibility of following one of the world's classic overland trips, by **Trans-Siberian Railway** through Russia and Mongolia to China, and from there continuing on by road or rail into Indochina.

TICKETS AND FARES

You'll find the cheapest flights are not through the airlines themselves, but with a **discount flight agent**. See the box on p.10 for a list of recommended agents, or check the adverts in national Sunday papers. The **Internet** is also a useful resource. Try *www.cheaptickets.com* or *www.lastminute.com* for deals or just to compare prices quoted to you by agents. In addition to offering discounted flights, discount travel agents may also offer a range of other travel-related services such as travel insurance, rail passes, car rentals, tours and the like. Bear in mind, though, that penalties for changing your plans can be stiff. Remember too that these companies make their money by dealing in bulk – don't expect them to answer lots of questions. If you travel a lot it is worth getting in contact with discount travel clubs, where, for an annual fee, they will offer a number of savings on air tickets and car rental.

What will most affect the price of your ticket is the time of year you choose to travel. Air fares from the US and Canada to Southeast Asia are highest between June and August, and then again over the Christmas period (early December to early January). The **price difference between high and low** season is about US$300/CAN$450 on a typical round-trip fare. It is also worth noting that reservations in high season should be made further in advance, as tickets get booked up quickly.

There are also good deals if you are a **student or youth** under 26 with discount agents such as Council Travel, STA and Travel CUTS (a passport or driving licence is sufficient proof of age), though these tickets are subject to availability and can have eccentric booking conditions.

GATEWAY CITIES

If you're keen to see China as well as Southeast Asia, consider flying to **Hong Kong**. The cheapest low-season fare from the US's West Coast is around US$730 round-trip. Flying time from the West Coast is approximately fourteen hours. From the East Coast it's a different story, with most flights to Hong Kong stretching to 22 hours, and all include a connection, most commonly in Vancouver, Tokyo, or Singapore. The cheapest published fares from New York are around US$870. The best options for flights **from Canada** to Hong Kong include non-stop flights from Vancouver (13hr) and direct flights from Toronto and Montréal (21hr). Fares from Canada's West Coast start at around CAN$1410. Hong Kong gives you easy and inexpensive local transport options into Guangdong province, from where you could continue west into Vietnam, and on into Laos, then Thailand and down to Malaysia and Indonesia. Alternatively, you could buy a flight from Hong Kong to Vietnam for US$180 or to the Philippines for US$140.

Singapore is another popular gateway city, with flights from New York, Los Angeles, and San Francisco. Flying eastbound is more direct and a bit faster at about 21 hours travelling time. Most consolidators consistently offer the best deals on tickets, with prices starting at around US$1175 from

New York. If you're travelling from Washington, Miami, or Chicago expect to pay from US$1275; from Houston US$1200; from Los Angeles, San Francisco or Seattle $1000. From Toronto or Montréal prices start at CAN$1275 and from Vancouver CAN$1200. From Singapore you can fly direct to Lombok or Sulawesi for US$215. Few travellers stay long in Singapore itself, but it's just half an hour's bus ride into southern Malaysia, from where you could continue north to Thailand and Indochina, or make a short ferry ride across to Sumatra, and then island-hop across the Indonesia archipelago. It's also possible to get a ferry direct from Singapore to Indonesia.

Plenty of airlines run daily flights to **Bangkok** from major East-and West-coast cities, usually mak-

DISCOUNT FLIGHT AGENTS IN THE USA AND CANADA

Air Brokers International, 150 Post St, Suite 620, San Francisco, CA 94108 (☎415/397 1383 or 1-800/883 3273, *www.airbrokers.com*). Consolidator and specialist in RTW and Circle Pacific tickets.

Council Travel, 205 E 42nd St, New York, NY 10017 (☎1-800/226 8624, *www.counciltravel. com*), and branches in many other US cities. Student/budget travel agency.

Educational Travel Center, 438 N Frances St, Madison, WI 53703 (☎1-800/747 5551 or 608/256 5551, *www.edtrav.com*). Student/youth and consolidator fares.

High Adventure Travel, 442 Post St, Suite 400, San Francisco, CA 94102 (☎1-800/350 0612 or 415/912 5600, *www.airtreks.com*). RTW and Circle Pacific tickets. The extensive Web site features an interactive database called "Farebuilder" that lets you build your own RTW itinerary.

Now Voyager, 74 Varick St, Suite 307, New York, NY 10013 (☎212/431 1616, *www. nowvoyagertravel.com*). Courier-flight broker and consolidator.

STA Travel, 7810 Hardy Drive, Suite 109, Tempe, AZ 85284 (☎1-800/777 0112 or 1-800/781 4040, *www.sta-travel.com*), with branches in most major US cities, including: 10 Downing St, New York, NY 10014 (☎212/627-3111); 7202 Melrose Ave, Los Angeles, CA 90046 (☎323/934-8722); 51 Grant Ave, San Francisco,

CA 94108 (☎415/391-8407); 297 Newbury St, Boston, MA 02115 (☎617/266 6014); 429 S Dearborn St, Chicago, IL 60605 (☎312/786 9050); 3701 Chesnut St, Philadelphia, PA 19104 (☎215/382 2928); 317 14th Ave SE, Minneapolis, MN 55414 (☎612/615 1800). Worldwide discount travel firm specializing in student/youth fares; also student IDs, travel insurance, car rental, rail passes, etc.

Travel Avenue, 10 S Riverside Plaza, Suite 1404, Chicago, IL 60606 (☎1-800/333 3335 or 312/876 6866, *www.travelavenue.com*). Full-service travel agent that offers discounts in the form of rebates.

Travel CUTS, 187 College St, Toronto, ON M5T 1P7 (☎1-800/667 2887 [Canada only] or ☎416/979 2406, *www.travelcuts.com*), and other branches all over Canada – also associated with Adventure Travel in San Francisco (☎415/247 1800). Organization specializing in student fares, IDs and other travel services.

UniTravel, 11737 Administration Dr, Suite 120, St Louis, MO 63146 (☎1-800/325 2222 or 314/569 2501, *www.flightsforless.com*). Consolidator offering international and domestic discounted fares, which are not necessarily the lowest, but they have helpful customer service and are a good starting point.

Worldtek Travel, 111 Water St, New Haven, CT 06511 (☎1/800-243 1723, *www.worldtek.com*) Discount travel agency for worldwide travel.

ing only one stop. Flying time from the West Coast via Asia is approximately eighteen hours, and from New York via Europe it's around nineteen hours. From Canada, if you are travelling via Japan, you can expect to spend something like sixteen hours from Vancouver or 21 from Toronto. From the US West Coast expect to pay from US$800. From the East Coast prices start at about $900. For Canadians coming from Toronto, you'll most likely have stops in Vancouver and Osaka, although at certain times of the year there are non-stop flights from Toronto to Osaka. Barring special promotions you can expect to pay from around CAN$1645 from Vancouver, and CAN$2045 from Toronto.

Some **sample low-season round-trip fares** from the US to other Asian cities include US$950 from New York to Bali; from Los Angeles to Ho Chi Minh City US$950; from New York to Kuala Lumpur US$1100; from San Francisco to Manila US$800; from Los Angeles to Phnom Penh US$1000. Canadian prices start at CAN$1600 from Toronto to Bali; CAN$1400 from Vancouver to Kuala Lumpur; CAN$1400 from Toronto to Manila.

STOPOVER RETURNS AND OPEN-JAW TICKETS

To allow yourself some freedom in travelling you might consider buying an **open-jaw ticket**, offered by most major airlines. This allows you to fly into one country and out of another. You might choose to fly into Bangkok and out of Jakarta a few months later, allowing you to decide how you want to make your travel arrangements once inside Asia. Open-jaws are usually more expensive than standard round-trip flights: prices are generally calculated by halving the round-trip fares to each destination and then adding the two figures together.

Another useful option is to buy a ticket with a **stopover**, which allows you to spend up to three months in a city before heading out again. For example, a ticket from New York to Singapore with a stopover in Hong Kong would only be an extra US$100.

RTW AND CIRCLE PACIFIC TICKETS

Round-the-World (RTW) tickets or **Circle Pacific** tickets can be very good value if you are planning a multi-stop trip. Some travel agents can sell you an "off-the-shelf" RTW/Circle Pacific ticket that will have you touching down in about half a dozen cities (the capital cities of all major Southeast Asian destinations are available on many

itineraries); other travel agents will assemble one for you, which can be tailored to your needs, but is apt to be more expensive. An example of a RTW itinerary is San Francisco–Bali–Singapore surface to Bangkok–Cairo–Athens surface to London–San Francisco for under US$1600. A typical Circle Pacific ticket might be New York–Hong Kong–Bangkok–Jakarta–Bali–Los Angeles–New York for under US$1500.

Another option is Cathay Pacific's **All-Asia Pass**, which allows you to fly into Hong Hong and then gives you thirty days of flights to a choice of sixteen different cities with prices starting from just US$999.

COURIER FLIGHTS

If you are prepared to forgo a few creature comforts for a cheaper airfare then you might consider **courier flights**. In exchange for an inexpensive airline ticket you will most likely be expected to take a package through customs and/or give up your luggage allowance entirely. This type of travel is best suitable for single travellers who are travelling lightly and have a flexible schedule. Courier flights to Hong Kong, Malaysia, and Singapore are the easiest to come by and from there you might be able to arrange another courier flight. To arrange a flight contact Air Courier Association, 15000 W 6th Ave, Suite 203, Golden, CO 80401 (☎303/279 3600 or 1-800/282 1202, *www.aircourier.org*); Now Voyager, 74 Varick St, Suite 307, New York, NY 10013 (☎212/431 1616, *www.nowvoyagertravel.com*) or the International Association of Air Travel Couriers, 220 S Dixie Hwy, #3, PO Box 1349, Lake Worth, FL 33460 (☎561/582 8320, *www.courier.org*).

PACKAGES AND ORGANIZED TOURS

The scope of **packages and tours** that are available in Southeast Asia is vast. It won't be hard to find something that suits your needs, be it trekking, ecotourism, or a five-star hotel on the beaches of Bali. In addition, tours can offer an excellent opportunity to take in regions you might not otherwise see or more importantly have access to as an independent traveller. On the other hand, while package tours do take care of a lot of the leg work, they also take away some of the spontaneity of travelling on your own – although you could do a bit of both, exploring on your own until you meet up with your tour group. Either way, the box overleaf will give you ideas of what is on offer.

Another option to bear in mind is a trip on the **Trans-Siberian Express** from Moscow to Beijing, then on to Hong Kong. Train tickets can be purchased from agents in the US, and package tours including overnight stays in Beijing and Moscow are available.

Mir Corp in Seattle (see below) offers a wide range of packages – a fourteen-night trip from Moscow to Hong Kong, for example, costs around $1600. See "Getting there from the UK and Ireland", p.7, for more information on the route.

SPECIALIST TOUR OPERATORS IN THE USA AND CANADA

Here are just a few specialists offering good-value tours of Southeast Asia. Unless stated otherwise, all prices quoted below exclude taxes and are subject to change, and international flights are extra. Where applicable, round-trip flights are from the West Coast, and accommodation is based on single person/double occupancy. All prices below are in US dollars.

Abercrombie & Kent, 1520 Kensington Rd, Suite 212 Oak Brook, IL 60523 2141 (☎800/323 7308, *www.abercrombiekent.com*). "The Lost Kingdom of the Mekong" is a basic fifteen-day tour which starts in Bangkok, moving on to track the course of the Mekong through Chiang Rai, carrying on to Laos and back to Bangkok ($4260 plus $535 for internal flights). "Images of Indochina" is a sixteen-day tour of Vietnam and Cambodia (with optional four-day extension to Laos) departing from Hong Kong, and visits Hanoi, Hué, Da Nang and Ho Chi Minh City (basic tour $6120 – land only – plus $1180 internal air fares).

Adventure Center, 1311 63rd St, Suite 200, Emeryville, CA 94608 (☎1-800/227 8747, *www.adventurecenter.com*). Offering extremely affordable Southeast Asian tours. Their "Malay Peninsula Southbound" is a fifteen-day tour travelling from Bangkok, down to southern Thailand, through the jungles of Malaysia, with a stop in Kuala Lumpur and over to Singapore for $950 (international flights not included). "The Limestone Trail" is a sixteen-day tour of Hong Kong, Hanoi, and Vietnam and costs $1150. "The Philippines Island of Adventure" comprises ten days of island-hopping from Manila to Palawan, Puerto Princesa, Sabang, and El Nido and then back again to Manila, for $745.

Adventures Abroad, 2148-20800 Westminster Hwy, Richmond, BC V6V 2W3 (☎1-800/665 3998, *www.adventures-abroad.com*). Specializing in small-group tours, such as a twenty-day tour of Laos/Vietnam for $3450. Their four-week Laos/Vietnam/Cambodia tour runs at $3990. Three weeks on Sumatra, Java, Lombok and Bali from US$3796. A forty-five day tour of Thailand, Burma, Laos and Cambodia costs $7231.

Geographic Expeditions, 2627 Lombard St, San Francisco, CA 94123 (☎800/777 8183 or 415/922 0448, *www.geoex.com*). Specialists in "responsible tourism" with a range of customized tours and/or set packages. Their trips are perhaps a bit more demanding of the traveller than the average specialist, although each tour is rated from easy to rigorous. "Asia's Hidden Jewel Boxes" is a 24-day exploration of Burma, Thailand and Laos for $4795, which includes international flights and land travel (rigorous). "Indochina Unveiled" is a less demanding twenty-day tour through Vietnam, Cambodia and Laos for $4600 (international flights and land included.

Himalayan Travel, 110 Prospect St, Stamford, CT 06901 (☎1-800/225 2380, *www.gorp.com/himtravel.htm*). Customized tours plus "Grand Indochina Tour", which combines Laos with Vietnam and Cambodia, costing $1815. The "Philippines Discovery Tour" is a fifteen-day tour of the islands of the Philippines costing $1750.

Mir Corp, ☎1-800/424 7289, *www.mircorp.com* Trans-Siberian-Express trips.

Mountain Travel-Sobek, 6420 Fairmount Ave, El Cerrito, CA 94530 (☎888/MTSOBEK; US ☎1-800/227 2384; Canada ☎1-800/282 8747). Tours to Laos, Vietnam, Thailand and Cambodia.

Pacific Holidays, 2 West 45th St, Suite 1101, New York, NY 10036 (1-800/355-8025). Inexpensive tour group. "Best of Southeast Asia" sightseeing tour of Bangkok, Bali, Singapore, Hong Kong for fifteen days for $1995 (including flights from the West Coast and internal flights).

TEI Tours, (☎1-800/435 4334). Trans-Siberian-Express packages and customized tours.

GETTING THERE FROM AUSTRALIA AND NEW ZEALAND

The fastest and most reliable way to get to Southeast Asia **from Australia or New Zealand** is to fly, and the cheapest is to buy a one-way flight to one of the region's gateways such as Kupang, Denpasar, Jakarta, Singapore, Kuala Lumpur, Bangkok or Hong Kong and carry on from there by air, sea or overland. There's no shortage of direct flights to major Southeast Asia gateways, although it's well worth taking advantage of a **stopover** en route or considering an **open-jaw** ticket that allows you to fly into one country and out of another and travel overland in between. Other options are **Circle Asia** tickets – which can be a little complicated, as each sector needs to be costed separately – and **Asean Air Passes** that take you via two or more Asian cities en route, or **Round-the-World** (RTW) tickets if you're taking in Southeast Asia as part of a wider trip.

TICKETS AND FARES

Tickets purchased direct from the airlines are usually expensive – more than likely you'll be quoted the published rate. You'll get a much better deal with a **discount travel agent**. Fares are very competitive, so whatever kind of ticket you're after it's best to shop around. The travel agents listed in the box overleaf can fill you in on all the latest deals and any special limited offers. If you're a student or under 26, you may be able to get a discounted fare; STA is a good place to start. Fares are seasonally rated, with prices for flights usually higher during Christmas and New Year and mid-year periods; generally, high season is mid-May to end-August and December to mid-January, shoulder March to mid-May and September to mid-October and low the rest of the year – with a

difference of around A/NZ$200 between each. Airfares from east-coast **Australian gateways** are all pretty much the same (common rated on most airlines, with Ansett and Qantas providing a shuttle service to the point of departure). Perth and Darwin are around A$100–200 cheaper. **From New Zealand** you can expect to pay about NZ$150–300 more from Christchurch and Wellington than from Auckland. Fares to Indonesia, Malaysia, the Philippines and Brunei start at roughly A$599/NZ$799 for a single and A$899/NZ$1299 for a return, while to Thailand, Indochina and Hong Kong you can expect to pay from A$799/NZ$999 single and A$1199/NZ$1499 return.

ONE-WAY TICKETS TO GATEWAY CITIES

See "Getting there from the UK and Ireland", p.5, for information on flying to gateway cities.

STOPOVER RETURNS AND OPEN-JAW TICKETS

In a region the size of Southeast Asia it's well worth taking advantage of a **stopover** en route, often a little cheaper than flying non-stop. All Asian airlines fly via their home base giving you a perfect opportunity to explore a bit more of the area. Alternatively, **open-jaw** tickets are a good idea if you want to travel overland between gateways; for example into Kuala Lumpur and out of Bangkok (or vice versa), won't cost you much more than a straight-through fare to Bangkok – from A$1099/NZ$1199.

CIRCLE ASIA AND RTW TICKETS

If you intend to visit the region as part of a wider trip then tickets that are put together by an alliance of airlines such as **Circle Asia**, that allow you to travel via two or more Asian cities en route, and **RTW (Round-the-World)** tickets offer greater flexibility than a straightforward return flight. For example, an RTW ticket from Sydney to Singapore, taking in London, New York, Los Angeles and Auckland, starts at around A$2399/NZ$2999; a round-trip to Brunei from Singapore or Kuala Lumpur will add an extra A$450/NZ$530 to the basic price. Another good-value option is a **Circle Asean Pass** which is put together by the national airlines of Brunei, Indonesia, Malaysia, the Philippines, Singapore, Thailand and Vietnam. Prices depend on which country you choose to start from and the number of stopovers you want to make. Stopovers are allowed in any two to six of the other countries with a minimum stay of three

Anywhere Travel, 345 Anzac Parade, Kingsford, Sydney (☎02/9663 0411, *anywhere@ozemail. com.au*). Worldwide fare discount agent close to the airport.

Budget Travel, 16 Fort St, Auckland, plus branches around the city (☎09/366 0061 or 0800/808 040). Discount/budget fares and holidays.

Destinations Unlimited, level 7 FAI Building, 220 Queens St, Auckland (☎09/373 4033). Worldwide fare discounts plus a good selection of tours and holiday packages.

Flight Centres, Australia: 82 Elizabeth St, Sydney, plus branches nationwide (☎02/9235 3522, nearest branch ☎13 1600). New Zealand: 350 Queen St, Auckland (☎09/358 4310), plus branches nationwide. Friendly service with competitive discounts on air fares plus a wide range of package holidays on offer. *www.flightcentre.com.au*

Northern Gateway, 22 Cavenagh St, Darwin (☎08/8941 1394, *oztravel@norgate.com.au*). Specialists in discount fares to Southeast Asia.

STA Travel, Australia: 855 George St, Sydney; 256 Flinders St, Melbourne; other offices in state capitals and major universities (nearest branch ☎13 1776, fastfare telesales ☎1300/360 960). New Zealand: 10 High St, Auckland (☎09/309 0458, fastfare telesales ☎09/366 6673), plus

branches in Wellington, Christchurch, Dunedin, Palmerston North, Hamilton and at major universities. Fare discounts for students and under 26s, plus visa, student cards and travel insurance. *www.statravel.com.au*

Student Uni Travel, level 8, 92 Pitt St, Sydney (☎02/9232 8444) plus branches in Brisbane, Cairns, Darwin, Melbourne and Perth. Student/youth discounts and travel advice.

Thomas Cook, Australia: 175 Pitt St, Sydney (☎02/9231 2877); 257 Collins St, Melbourne; plus branches in other state capitals (nearest branch ☎13 1771; Thomas Cook Direct telesales ☎1800/801 002); New Zealand: 191 Queen St, Auckland (☎09/379 3920). Discounts on fares, travellers' cheques, bus and rail passes. *www.thomascook.com.au*

Trailfinders, 8 Spring St, Sydney (☎02/9247 7666); 91 Elizabeth St, Brisbane (☎07/3229 0887); Shop 3, Hides Corner, Lake St, Cairns (☎07/4041 1199). Independent travel advice, good discounts on fares.

Travel.com.au, 76–80 Clarence St, Sydney (☎02/9262 3555, *www.travel.com.au*). Online worldwide fare discounter.

Usit Beyond, cnr Shortland St and Jean Batten Place, Auckland (☎09/379 4224 or 0800/788 336), plus branches in Christchurch. Student/youth travel specialists.

nights and a maximum of three months for each one: a Circle Asean beginning and ending in Malaysia or Brunei costs from A$820/NZ$1025 with two stopovers, A$1000/$1245 with three stopovers and A$1170/NZ$1470 with four, five or six stopovers. For more information on Circle Asia and RTW tickets, see "Getting there from the UK and Ireland" p.6.

OVERLAND ROUTES

Many travellers from Australia and New Zealand fly to **Indonesia** and overland from there. The main onward routes are from Kupang in West Timor or Bali to Bangkok via Java, Sumatra and the Malaysian Peninsula (of course this can be extended to Indochina), and Kupang or Bali to the Philippines via Java, and either Borneo or Suluwesi.

There are regular direct **flights to Denpasar** on Qantas, Ansett and Garuda from eastern Australian gateway cities (from A$599 one-way, A$999 return) and on Garuda (NZ$799 one-way, NZ$1299 return)

and Air New Zealand (NZ$899 one-way, NZ$1399 return) from Auckland. The cheapest fares are to **Kupang** in West Timor from Darwin with Merpati Airlines (A$144 one-way/A$396 return) flying every Saturday; if you're thinking of entering Indonesia on a one-way fare make sure you have a valid onward ticket (air or ferry) out of the country. From Kupang, it takes around a month to **island-hop through Nusa Tenggara** by ferry and bus to Bali where you can either pick up a flight to another gateway at Denpasar, a ferry to Makassar or carry on through Java to either Malaysia and Thailand, or to Surabaya where there are flights and ferries to Banjamasin in Kalimantan and Makassar in Sulawesi. From Banjamasin you can bus it through Kalimantan to Sarawak or Sabah and then island-hop through the Philippines to Manila. Alternatively, fly or take the ferry from Surabaya to Makassar in Sulawesi, then bus it to the ferry port of Bitung in the north of the island where there's a regular ferry service (36 hr) to

Davao on the southern Philippine island of Mindanao. Make sure you plan your route well, allowing at least two weeks longer than you think your trip will take, as local transport doesn't always leave at the time or on the day specified.

ORGANIZED TOURS AND PACKAGE HOLIDAYS

Package holidays to Southeast Asian destinations are numerous and good value. As well as flights and

SPECIALIST TOUR OPERATORS

Adventure Specialists, 1/69 Liverpool St, Sydney (☎02/9261 2927). Overland and adventure tour agent for numerous companies, including Exodus' "Indochina Overland" (six weeks A$3350/NZ$4100) from Hong Kong through SW China and onto Laos, Thailand, Malaysia and Singapore).

The Adventure Travel Company, 164 Parnell Rd, Parnell, Auckland (☎09/379 9755). NZ's one-stop shop for adventure travel are agents for Intrepid, Perigrine, Guerba Expeditions, Encounter Overland and a host of others including Geko's "Southern Ramble"; with an emphasis on flexibility this tour takes you to the beaches and rainforest of southern Thailand.

Adventure World, 73 Walker St, North Sydney (☎02/9956 7766 or 1800/221 931), plus branches in Adelaide, Brisbane, Melbourne and Perth; 101 Great South Rd, Remuera, Auckland (☎09/524 5118, *www.adventureworld.com.au*). Agents for a vast array of international adventure travel companies including Explore's "Java, Bali & Tribal Sumatra" (22-day A$2195/NZ$2799 land only) which focuses on the islands' popular highlights; travel is by local transport.

Always Padi Travel, 4/372 Eastern Valley Way, Chatswood, Sydney (☎1800/259 297, *www.padi.com*). All-inclusive dive package holidays to prime dive sites in Indonesia, Malaysia, Thailand and the Philippines.

Earthwatch, 126 Bank St, South Melbourne, Vic 3205 (☎03/9682 6828, *earth@earthwatch.org*). Volunteer work on projects in Indonesia and Thailand.

Intrepid Adventure Travel, 12 Spring St, Fitzroy, Melbourne (☎1300/360 667, *info @intrepidtravel.com.au*). Small-group tours to China and Southeast Asia with an emphasis on cross-cultural contact and low-impact tourism such as their "Philippines Adventure" (21 days A$1790/NZ$2330 land only) which takes you through scenic Luzon in the north and to the superb beaches in the south.

Peregrine Adventures, 258 Lonsdale St, Melbourne (☎03/9662 2700, *www.peregrine.net.au*), plus offices in Brisbane, Sydney, Adelaide and Perth. Small-group adventure travel company and agent offering a range of graded trips such as their challenging "Cycle Vietnam" (seventeen days A$2350/NZ$3125 land only) from Ho Chi Minh City and Da Lat, through Nha Trang, the Central Highlands, Hoi An and finally to Hanoi, and their more sedate "Hidden Laos" (seven days A$1220/NZ$1625 land only) round-trip from Vientiane to Louang Phabang, Phonsavan and the Plain of Jars.

Pro Dive Travel, Dymocks Building, 428 George St, Sydney (☎02/9232 5733). Shore and boat dive trips on Bali and Flores (A$100 for two shore dives, A$130 for two boat dives).

San Michele Travel, 81 York St, Sydney (☎02/9299 1111 or 1800/222 244), plus branches in Melbourne and Perth. Customized rail tours throughout Southeast Asia. A favourite is their Singapore–Bankok journey (A$1620/NZ$2100 including accommodation).

Silke's Travel, 263 Oxford St, Darlinghurst, Sydney (☎1800/807 303, 1800/807 860, or 02/9380 5835, *www.silkes.com.au*). Specially tailored packages for gay and lesbian travellers.

The Surf Travel Co., 2/25 Cronulla Plaza, Cronulla Beach, Sydney (☎02/9527 4722 freecall 1800/687 873); 7 Danbury Drive, Torbay, Auckland (☎09/4738388, *www.surftravel.com .au*). A well established surf travel company that can arrange airfares, accommodation and yacht charter in Indonesia, as well as give the lowdown on the best surf beaches.

Travel Indochina, 403 George St, Sydney (☎1300 362 777 or 02/9244 2133, *travindo@ travelindochina.com.au*). Offers low-impact tour packages, using mid- to top-range hotels, such as their Bangkok-to-Hanoi tour (fourteen days from A$2025), exploring the remoter regions of Thailand, Laos and Vietnam.

accommodation, most companies also offer a range of itineraries that take in the major sights and activities. Bookings are usually made through travel agents who carry a wide selection of brochures for you to choose from. An organized tour is worth considering if you're after a more energetic holiday, have ambitious sightseeing plans and limited time, are uneasy with the language and customs or just don't like travelling alone. The specialists listed on p.15 can also help you get to more remote areas and orga-

nize activities that may be difficult to arrange yourself, such as extended overland tours that take in several countries, white-water rafting, diving, cycling and trekking, for example Intrepid's 22-day "Borneo Traverse", from Pontianak to Balikpapan starting with a demanding seven-day trek through Kalimantan's jungle-covered central highlands, sleeping in jungle camps along the way, and finishing with a more leisurely cruise along the Mahakam River. Most organized tours don't include airfares from Australasia.

GETTING AROUND SOUTHEAST ASIA

Local transport across Southeast Asia is uniformly good value compared to public transport in the West, and is often one of the highlights of a trip, not least because of the chance to fraternize with local travellers. Overland transport between neighbouring Southeast Asian countries is also fairly straightforward – a variety of trains, buses, share-taxis and ferries shuttle across most of the region's international borders and are available to foreigners, so long as they have the right paperwork; full details on cross-border transport options are given at the beginning of each chapter.

LOCAL TRANSPORT

Not surprisingly, the ultra-modern enclaves of Singapore and Hong Kong boast the fastest, sleekest and most efficient transport systems in the region. Elsewhere, **trains** are generally the most comfortable way to travel any distance, if not always the fastest or most frequent. Thailand and Malaysia both have decent train networks, while Indonesia, Vietnam and Cambodia only have limited systems. Faster and more frequent, but often a lot more nerve-wracking, **long-distance buses** are the chief mode of travel in Southeast Asia. Drivers tend to race at dangerous speeds and are sometimes high on amphetamines to keep them going through the night. Seats are usually

cramped and the whole experience is often uncomfortable, so wherever possible try to book a pricier but more comfortable air-conditioned bus for overnight journeys – or take the train. Shorter bus journeys can be very enjoyable however and are often the only way to get between places. Buses come in various shapes, many of them quite novel to Western eyes. In small towns and rural areas in particular, **local buses** are often either minivans or even small pick-up trucks fitted with bench seats, while in parts of east Malaysia and Laos, riverboats function as buses; full details of all these idiosyncrasies are given in each chapter. On many buses, you just shout out when you want to get off, though the larger government-run buses tend to have busboys who issue tickets and tell the driver where you're going. **Taxis** also come in many unrecognizable forms, including three-wheeled buggies with deafening two-stroke engines, elegant rickshaws powered by a man on a bicycle, or simply a bloke on a motorbike (usually wearing a numbered vest); none of these have meters, so all prices must be bargained for and fixed before you set off. In many riverine towns and regions, it's also common to travel by taxi boat. Regular **ferries** connect all major tourist islands with the mainland, and often depart several times a day, though some islands become inaccessible during the monsoon. In some areas, **flying** may be the only practical way to get around. Tickets are reasonably priced considering the distances involved, and there's a surprising number of interesting regional routes.

In most countries **timetables** for any transport other than trains and planes are vague at best and sometimes don't exist at all; the vehicle simply leaves when there are enough passengers to make it worthwhile. The best strategy is to turn up early in the morning when villagers travel to market. For an idea of frequency and duration of transport services between the main towns, check the **travel details** at

THE MEKONG RIVER

The **Mekong** is one of the great rivers of the world, the third longest in Asia, after the Yangtse and the Yellow River. From its source 4920m up on the east Tibetan Plateau it roars down through China's Yunnan province, where it's known as Lancang Jiang, the Turbulent River, then snakes its way a little more peaceably through Laos, by way of the so-called Golden Triangle, where Burma, Thailand and Laos touch. From Laos it crosses Cambodia and continues south to Vietnam, where it splinters into the many arms of the Mekong Delta before flowing into the South China Sea, 4184km from where its journey began.

For the adventurous traveller, it may be possible to travel almost the entire length of this great waterway by boat, though the uppermost reaches are characterized by steep descents and fierce rapids and the Yunnan stretch is only served by the occasional barge that rumbles down from Jinghong. Once in **Laos**, however, river transport becomes the norm, and the two-day trip by cargo boat from Houayxai to Louang Phabang is one of the highlights of Southeast Asia. Laos is truly a country of the Mekong: the river is the lifeline of this country, its highway and its rice basket, and for 750km it also defines the Lao–Thai border. Laos's two most important cities were built on the banks of the Mekong, and both the ancient royal city of **Louang Phabang** and the modern capital **Vientiane** make the most of their riverside settings – there's no denying the charm of the myriad waterside guesthouses, or the pleasure of watching from a beer garden as the sun sets over the Mekong. Laos's other big Mekong draw is the riverine archipelago in the far south known as Si **Phan Don**, or Four Thousand Islands, where the fourteen-kilometre-wide Mekong is dotted with tiny islands inhabited by fishing communities and freshwater dolphins.

Across in **Thailand**, the Mekong attractions are more low-key, with a string of laid-back guesthouses making the most of the views from the west bank, and a few of them, like those at Chiang Khan and Sri Chiangmai, offering short trips up or downriver to see local caves and waterfalls. Here too you can try the local delicacy, the giant catfish, found only in the Mekong and, at up to three metres long, the world's largest freshwater fish. **Chiang Khong** is one of the most popular Mekong-side stops in Thailand,

chiefly because of its shuttle boats to Houayxai on the Lao bank of the river, where you can pick up a boat down to Louang Phabang. **Nong Khai** is the main transport hub on the Thai side of the Mekong, linked to Laos by the Australian Friendship Bridge that spans the great river close to Vientiane.

As in Laos, **Cambodia**'s greatest cities have also been shaped by the Mekong. The Cambodian capital **Phnom Penh** is one of the most important ports along the whole course of the river, and sits at the confluence of the Mekong and the Tonlé Sap River. The 100-kilometre-long **Tonlé Sap River** is quite extraordinary, as it changes its direction of flow according to the level of the Mekong. During the rainy season, instead of flooding the Phnom Penh valley, the Mekong forces the waters of the Tonlé Sap River to back up, sending them northwards to fill the enormous Tonlé Sap lake at its head. By the climax of the rainy season, this very shallow lake covers 8000 square kilometres, spawning hundreds of tonnes of freshwater fish and irrigating vast plains of rice. It was the bounty of this natural reservoir that fuelled the ancient Khmer empire, enabling it to prosper, to expand its territories across Southeast Asia, and to construct the magnificent temples at nearby Angkor. When the Mekong waters subside, in early November, the Tonlé Sap River changes direction and drains once more into the Mekong. This is marked in Phnom Penh by an exuberant **Water Festival**, which draws crowds from all over the area.

The Mekong saves its most spectacular dramas for its final act, when it separates into the many tributaries known as **Cuu Long** or Nine Dragons to water the vast alluvial plains of **Vietnam's Mekong Delta**. This agricultural powerhouse near Ho Chi Minh City is one of the greatest rice-growing areas of the world and has always been crucial to Vietnam's economy; it is also densely populated, and was the scene of some of the most intense fighting of the Vietnam War. These days, however, the region is more tranquil and there are boats and sampans aplenty to ferry travellers to the floating markets at Can Tho and the delta villages of My Tho and Ben Tre, where the views of emerald paddies, coconut palms and conical-hatted farmers make a fitting climax to any Southeast Asian journey.

the end of each chapter. **Security** is an important consideration on public transport. On buses, never fall asleep with your bag by your side, and never leave belongings unattended at a food-stop. On trains, be especially vigilant when the train stops at stations and takes on hawkers, ensure your money-belt is safely tucked under your clothes before going to sleep and that your luggage is safely stowed (preferably padlocked to an immovable object). See "Crime and Personal Safety" on p.42 for more advice.

Throughout Southeast Asia it's possible to rent your own transport. **Cars** are available in all major

OVERLAND ROUTES AND INTER-ASIA FLIGHTS

The following information provides an overview of those **land and sea crossings** that are both legal and straightforward ways for tourists to travel between the countries of Southeast Asia. The information is fleshed out in the accounts of relevant border towns within the Guide. There are so many **flights** between Southeast Asian countries, that we have only singled out the most exceptional (outstanding routes or prices); you can make inter-Asia flights to and from every capital city in Southeast Asia, and from many other major airports besides.

TO BRUNEI

From Malaysia Boats to Brunei depart daily from Lawas and Limbang in northern Sarawak, and from Pulau Labuan, itself connected by boat to Kota Kinabalu in Sabah. From Miri in Sarawak, several **buses** travel daily to Kuala Belait, in the far western corner of Brunei. The overland route from Sabah to Brunei necessitates taking a bus to the Temburong District, from where it's only a short boat trip to Bandar.

TO CAMBODIA

From Vietnam By bus from Ho Chi Minh via Moc Bai to Phnom Penh.

From Thailand By **bus and boat** from Trat to Sihanoukville, via Ban Hat Lek and Krong Koh Kong. By **bus and/or train** from Aranyaprathet to Sisophon, via Poipet. Daily Bangkok Airways **flights** from Bangkok to Phnom Penh and Siem Reap.

From Laos The Laos border remains officially closed for now.

TO HONG KONG AND MACAU

From China The **train** journey from Beijing to Hong Kong (via Guangzhou in Canton) takes 34 hours by express train and costs from around $75.

TO INDONESIA

From Malaysia and Singapore By **ferry or speedboat** from Penang to Medan in northern Sumatra; from Melaka to Dumai in northern Sumatra; from Johor Bahru in far southern Malaysia; from Singapore to Batam, Bintan and Karimun islands, in Indonesia's Riau Archipelago; and from Kuala Lumpur to Tanjung Balai in Sumatra. By **bus** from Kuching (Sarawak) via Entikong to Pontianak (Kalimantan). By **ferry** from Tewau (Sabah) to Pulau Nunukan in north-eastern Kalimantan. There are direct **flights** from Kuala Lumpur to Makassar in southern Sulawesi, and from Singapore to Mataram on Lombok and Manado in northern Sulawesi.

From the Philippines: Every week or so a **cargo boat** leaves General Santos for Bitung in Northern Sulawesi.

TO LAOS

From Thailand Five legal border crossings (by various combinations of **road, rail and river** transport): Chiang Khong to Houayxai; Nong Khai to Vientiane; Nakhon Phanom to Thakhek; Mukdahan to Savannakhet; and Chong Mek to Pakse. Many travellers also **fly** from Bangkok to Vientiane or from Chiang Mai to either Louang Phabang or Vientiane.

From Vietnam There are two **border points**. The Lao Bao Pass, 80km southwest of Dong Ha, is about 240km from Savannakhet, and there's also an international **bus** link between Da Nang and Savannakhet. The Kaew Nua Pass (known as Nam Phao in Lao), links Vinh with Lak 20, and is reasonably convenient for Vientiane and Thakhek. Both Vietnam Airlines and Lao Aviation **fly** from Hanoi to Vientiane (1 hr).

From China By **bus** from Kunming in China's southwestern Yunnan province to Vientiane; from Jinghong to Oudomxai or Louang Namtha; from Mengla via Mo Han to Boten. Lao Aviation operates **flights** from Kunming to Vientiane, via Louang Phabang.

From Cambodia Western tourists are currently not allowed to cross into Laos at the far southern tourist centres, and range from flimsy Jimnys to air-conditioned 4x4s; you will need your international driver's licence. If you can't face the traffic yourself, you can often hire a **car with driver** for a small extra fee. One of the best ways to explore the countryside is to rent a **motorbike**. They vary from small 100cc Yamahas to more robust trail bikes and can be rented from guesthouses, shops or tour agencies. Check the small print on your insurance policy, and buy extra cover locally if necessary. **Bicycles** are also a good way to travel, and can be rented from guesthouses or larger-scale rental places.

---

end of Champasak province along Route 13 (banditry is not uncommon in this area), although this may change. Lao Aviation operates **flights** between Phnom Penh and Vientiane via Pakxe.

TO MALAYSIA AND SINGAPORE

From Thailand By direct **train** from Bangkok to: Penang, Kuala Lumpur via Hat Yai, or Singapore via Penang. By **bus** or share-taxi from the southern Thai terminal of Hat Yai to Penang or Singapore. By share-taxi from Betong on route 410 to Butterworth via Keroh; by road from Ban Taba to Kota Bharu. By frequent **ferry** from Satun to Kuala Perlis and Langkawi. From Phuket, you can **fly** to Penang, KL and Singapore; while from Hat Yai, there are services to KL and Singapore.

From Indonesia By **ferry** from Medan in northern Sumatra to Penang; from Dumai (northern Sumatra) to Melaka; from Pulau Batam in the Riau Archipelago to either Johor Bahru or Singapore; and from Tanjung Balaito Kukup, just to the southwest of JB. From Kalimantan, you can take a **bus** from Pontianak to Kuching in Sarawak, or walk across the border at Nanga Badau then take a bus to Kuching. Alternatively, you can cross into Sabah on a two-hour ferry from Pulau Nunukan to Tawau, two days' bus ride southeast of Kota Kinabalu.

From Brunei Direct **boats** from Bandar to Lawas (for Sabah), Limbang, and Pulau Labuan (just off Sabah). Also, **buses** from Bandar to Miri in Sarawak (via Seria and Kuala Berait) and Kota Kinabalu in Sabah.

From the Philippines There are several weekly sailings from Zamboanga to Sandakan, in Sabah.

TO THE PHILIPPINES

From Hong Kong Cathay Pacific has five flights a day to the Philippines, and Philippine Airlines has three. British Airways, Emirates and Gulf Air all fly to Manila through Hong Kong and it is possible to get good fares because they are keen to fill seats for the last leg of the journey.

From Indonesia Every week or so a **cargo boat** leaves Bitung in Northern Sulawesi for General Santos.

From Malaysia Boats sail from Sandakan in Sabah to Zamboanga twice weekly.

TO THAILAND

From Malaysia and Singapore By **train** to Hat Yai and Bangkok from Singapore, Johor Bahru and Kuala Lumpur. By **bus** to the southern Thai town of Hat Yai from Singapore, Kuala Lumpur and Penang. Also, long-distance buses and minibuses to Bangkok, Krabi, Phuket and Surat Thani from Kuala Lumpur, Penang and Singapore. By **boat** from Kuala Perlis and Langkawi to Satun in south Thailand. Bangkok Airways operates daily **flights** between Singapore and Ko Samui.

From Laos By **bus** and/or **boat** from Houayxai to Chiang Kong; Vientiane to Nong Khai; Thakhek to Nakhon Phanom; Savannakhet to Mukdahan; and Pakxe to Chong Mek. Lao Aviation operates a handy **flight** between Vientiane and Chiang Mai.

From Cambodia By **bus** or private minibus and train from Sisophon, Siem Reap (for Angkor) and Phnom Penh to Bangkok, via Poipet and Aranyaprathet. By **bus and boat** from Sihanoukville via Krong Koh Kong and Ban Hat Lek to Trat in east Thailand. Daily Bangkok Airways **flights** between Phnom Penh and Bangkok and Siem Reap and Bangkok.

TO VIETNAM

From Laos There are now two border crossings, at Lao Bao, some 80km southwest of Dong Ha, and at Cau Treo, 100km west of Vinh. Both are accessible by **bus**.

From Cambodia By **bus** from Phnom Penh to Moc Bai, and from there on to Ho Chi Minh City.

From China The Beijing–Nanning–Hanoi **train** enters Vietnam at Dong Dang, north of Lang Son, where there's also a road crossing known as Huu Nghi Quan. Trains from Kunming cross the border further west at Lao Cai and terminate at Hanoi.

TRANSPORT BETWEEN COUNTRIES IN SOUTHEAST ASIA

Except for Burma, all countries in Southeast Asia open some of their land borders to travellers with the right **visa**, which means you can explore the region without backtracking. Most countries demand that you specify the exact land border when applying – see the section on "Entry requirements and visa extension", at the beginning of each chapter, for more advice on this.

Travelling between countries by bus, train or boat is obviously more time-consuming than flying, but it's also cheaper and can be more satisfying. The permutations for overland travel are endless, and worth investigating before you buy your initial flight from home, but by far the most common place to start is Bangkok, as it gives easy access to Laos and then on into Vietnam and Cambodia, as well as to Malaysia and by extension Singapore and Indonesia. From Australia, however, it makes sense to begin in eastern Indonesia.

RED TAPE AND VISAS

Country-specific advice about **visas**, entry requirements, border formalities and visa extensions is given in the section at the beginning of each chapter. As a broad guide, the only countries in Southeast Asia for which citizens of the EU, USA, Canada, Australia and New Zealand need to buy a visa in advance if arriving by air and staying less than thirty days are: Laos (15 days maximum on arrival), the Philippines (21 days maximum on arrival) and Vietnam (no entry without advance visa). However, as all visa requirements, prices and processing times are subject to change, it's always worth double-checking with embassies. Also, different rules usually apply if you're staying more than thirty days or arriving overland. Nearly every country requires that your passport be valid for at least six months from your date of entry. Some also demand proof of onward travel (such as an air ticket) or sufficient funds to buy a ticket.

SOUTHEAST ASIAN EMBASSIES AND CONSULATES ABROAD

It's usually straightforward to get visas for your next port of call while you're on the road in Southeast Asia. Details of **neighbouring Southeast Asian**

embassies are given in the "Listings" section of each capital city within the Guide.

BRUNEI
www.brunet.bn/homepage/gov/bruemb/govemb.htm
Australia 16 Bulwarra Close, O'Mally ACT 2606, Canberra (☎02/6290 1801).
Canada Contact the embassy in the US.
New Zealand Contact the embassy in Canberra.
UK and Ireland 19/20 Belgrave Square, London SW1X 8PG (☎020/7581 0521).
USA 3520 International Court NW, Washington DC 20008 (☎202/342 0159).

CAMBODIA
www.embassy.org/cambodia/
Australia 5 Canterbury Court, Deakin, ACT 2600 (☎02/6237 1259).
Canada Contact the embassy in Washington.
France 11 Ave Charles Floquet, 75007 Paris (☎01/40 65 04 70).
New Zealand Contact the embassy in Canberra.
UK and Ireland Contact the embassy in France.
USA 4500 16th St, Washington DC 20011 (☎202/726 7742); 53–69 Alderton St, Rego Park, New York 11374 (☎718/830 3770).

HONG KONG
Contact your nearest Chinese embassy.
www.chinese-embassy.org.uk
Australia 15 Coronation Drive, Yarralumla, ACT 2600 (☎02/6273 4783); 539 Elizabeth St, Surry Hills, Sydney (☎02/9698 7929); plus offices in Melbourne (☎03/9822 0607/4) and Perth (☎08/9321 8193).
Canada 515 St Patrick's St, Ottawa, Ontario K1N 5H3 (☎613/789 9608).
Ireland 40 Ailesbury Rd, Dublin 4 (☎01/269 1707).
New Zealand 588 Great South Rd, Greenland, Auckland (☎09/525 1588).

UK 31 Portland Place, London W1 (visa line
☎0891/880808).
USA 2300 Connecticut Ave NW, Washington DC
20008 (☎202/328 2500).

INDONESIA
www.kbri.org/
Australia 8 Darwin Ave, Yarralumla, Canberra, ACT
2600 (☎02/6250 8600); 20 Harry Chan Ave, Darwin,
NT 5784 (☎089/41 0048); 72 Queen Rd, Melbourne,
VIC 3004 (☎03/9525 2755); 134 Adelaide Terrace, East
Perth, WA 6004 (☎08/9221 5858); 236–238 Maroubra
Rd, Maroubra, NSW 2035 (☎02/9344 9933).
Canada 55 Parkdale Ave, Ottawa, Ontario K1Y 1ES
(☎613/724 1100).
New Zealand 70 Glen Rd, Kelburn, Wellington, PO
Box 3543 (☎04/475 8697).
UK and Ireland 38 Grosvenor Square, London W1X
9AD (visa line ☎0891/171210).
USA 2020 Massachusetts Avenue, NW,
Washington DC 20036 (☎202/775 5200).

LAOS
It's much easier to apply for a visa in Bangkok (takes
less than a week) than in the West (about two
months), as all visa applications must be sent to Laos
for approval.
www.laoembassy.com
Australia 1 Dalman Crescent, O'Malley, Canberra
(☎02/6286 4595).
Canada Contact embassy in Washington.
France 74 Ave Raymond Poincaré, Paris (☎01/45
53 02 98).
New Zealand Contact embassy in Canberra.
UK and Ireland Contact embassy in France or
Thailand.
USA 2222 S Street, NW, Washington DC 20008
(☎202/332 6416).

MACAU
Contact your nearest Chinese embassy, listed under
"Hong Kong", opposite.

MALAYSIA
Australia 7 Perth Ave, Yarralumla, Canberra, ACT
2600 (☎02/6273 1543).
Canada 60 Boteler St, Ottawa, Ontario K1N 8Y7
(☎613/241 5182)
New Zealand 10 Washington Ave, Brooklyn,
Wellington (☎04/385 2439).
UK and Ireland 45 Belgrave Square, London SW1X
8QT (☎020/7235 8033).
USA 2401 Massachusetts Avenue, NW,
Washington DC 20008 (☎202/328 2700).

THE PHILIPPINES
www.philemb.demon.co.uk/
Australia 1 Moonah Place, Yarralumla, Canberra,
ACT 2600 (☎02/6273 2535); Philippine Centre, Level
1 27–33 Wentworth Ave, Sydney, NSW, 2000 (☎02/
9262 7377).
Canada 130 Albert St, Suite 606–608, Ottawa,
Ontario K1P 5G4 (☎613/233 1121).
New Zealand 50 Hobson St, Thorndon, Wellington
(☎04/4729 848); 8th Floor, 121 Beach Rd, Auckland
1 (☎09/303 2423).
UK and Ireland 9a Palace Green, London W8 (visa
line ☎0891/171244).
USA 1600 Massachusetts Ave, NW, Washington
DC 20036 (☎202/467 9300).

SINGAPORE
www.gov.sg/mfa/consular/
Australia 17 Forster Crescent, Yarralumla,
Canberra, ACT 2600 (☎02/6273 3944).
Canada 999 West Hastings St, Suite 1305,
Vancouver, BC V6C 2W2 (☎604/669 5115).
New Zealand 17 Kabul St, Khandallah, Wellington,
PO Box 13-140 (☎04/479 2076). Visas on entry.
UK and Ireland 9 Wilton Crescent, London SW1X
8SA (☎020/7245 0273).
USA 3501 International Place, NW, Washington DC
20008 (☎202/537 3100).

THAILAND
Australia 111 Empire Circuit, Yarralumla, Canberra
ACT 2600 (☎02/6273 1149); consulates in Adelaide,
Brisbane, Melbourne, Perth and Sydney.
Canada 180 Island Park Drive, Ottawa, Ontario K1Y
0A2 (☎613/722 4444).
New Zealand 2 Cook St, PO Box 17–226, Karori,
Wellington (☎04/4768 618).
UK and Ireland 30 Queens Gate, London SW7 (visa
line ☎0891/600150, *www.thaiconsul-uk.com*).
USA 1024 Wisconsin Avenue, NW, Suite 401,
Washington DC 20007 (☎202/944 3600,
www.thaiembdc.org/).

VIETNAM
www.vietnamembassy-usa.org
Australia 6 Timbarra Crescent, O'Malley, Canberra,
ACT 2606 (☎02/6286 6059); 489 New South Head
Rd, Double Bay, NSW 2025 (☎02/9327 1912).
Canada 226 MacLaren St, Ottawa, Ontario K2P 0L9
(☎613/236 0772).
New Zealand Contact embassy in Canberra.
UK and Ireland 12–14 Victoria Rd, London W8 5RD
(☎020/7937 1912).
USA 1233 20th Street NW, Suite 400, Washington
DC 20037 (☎202/861 0737).

MONEY AND COSTS

Western tourists have always found Southeast Asia an extremely **cheap place to travel**, with accommodation, food and transport costing a fraction of what it does in the West. In the last few years, the region has become even more of a bargain for Western travellers as a result of the financial crisis of 1997/98, which hit the whole of Southeast Asia very hard, sending local currencies into freefall against the US dollar, and giving foreigners a lot more for their money. Local people suffered horribly, however, with prices for daily necessities such as rice and fuel shooting up, but no corresponding hike in wages. At the time of writing, most Southeast Asian economies seem to have stabilized, with the dollar still fetching a higher rate than it did before the crisis, but nothing like as much as it did at the height of the crash.

COSTS

Your **daily budget** in Southeast Asia depends both on where you're travelling and on how comfortable you want to be. You can survive on £7/US$10 a day in most parts of Cambodia, Laos, Indonesia, Thailand and Vietnam, or on around £10/US$14 a day in Malaysia, Singapore and the Philippines, but for this money you'll be sleeping only in the most basic accommodation, eating every meal at simple food stalls, and travelling only on local non-air-conditioned buses. You should carry extra funds to cover more expensive places such as capital cities and major tourist resorts, as well as for other occasional outlays like tourist buses, air-conditioned rooms, the odd taxi or hire car, a few classier meals and the occasional beer. Fairly regular indulgence in all these small luxuries cranks up the daily budget to £15/US$20 and £20/US$28. More specific budgets for different styles of travel are given at the beginning of each chapter.

Travellers soon get so used to the low cost of living in Southeast Asia that they start **bargaining** at every available opportunity, much as local people do. Pretty much everything is negotiable, from cigarettes and woodcarvings to taxi-hire and accommodation rates. Most buyers start their counterbid at about 25 percent of the vendor's opening price, and the bartering continues from there. If your price is way out of line, the vendor's vehement refusal should be enough to make you increase your offer: never forget that the few pennies you're making such a fuss over will go a lot further in a local person's hands than in your own.

Price tiering also exists in some parts of Southeast Asia, with foreigners paying more than locals for services such as public transport, hotels, and entry fees to museums and historical sites. Be cautious about causing a scene until you've established the cost of things, and remember prices vary within individual countries, especially when you enter more remote areas. In some countries, prices for tourist accommodation and foreigners' restaurants are quoted in **US dollars**, though the local equivalent is always acceptable. There are very few **student discounts** offered on entry prices, tours and airfares in Southeast Asia, but if you have an ISIC card it's worth bringing just in case. It's very easy to buy fake ISIC cards in Bangkok, which is one of the reasons why they're rarely accepted in the region. Most tourist sights give discounts for **children** under 14 years old, and many hotels don't charge for children sharing their parents' room. **Tipping** isn't a Southeast Asian custom, although some upmarket restaurants expect a gratuity, and most expensive hotels add service taxes.

CHANGING MONEY

In Laos and Cambodia you will need to carry a reasonable amount of US dollars cash, but throughout the rest of the region the safest way to carry the bulk of your money is in **travellers' cheques**, which can be cashed at banks, exchange booths and upmarket hotels in most sizeable Southeast Asian towns, and are refundable if stolen. The best cheques to take are those issued by the most familiar names, particularly American Express and Visa, ideally in US dollars, though pounds sterling are widely accepted and many other currencies are fine in the largest resorts. Small-denomination cheques are generally less economical than larger ones as you get a lower rate per cheque, though it might be advisable to take a few for exchange in smaller banks that don't keep large stocks of cash. Some outlets offer better rates for cheques than for straight cash and most charge commission, either per cheque or per transaction. Hold on to the **receipt** (or proof of purchase) that you get when you buy your travellers' cheques, as some exchange places require to see it before cashing your cheques.

Most **international airports** have exchange counters that open for arriving passengers, which is useful, as you can't always buy Southeast Asian currencies before leaving home. Wherever you change your money, ask for a mix of denominations, as in some backwaters bigger bills can be hard to split. Refuse really dog-eared banknotes, as you'll have difficulty getting anyone else to accept them. If you're staying in a developed tourist centre, you'll probably find that the money **exchange counters** are the most convenient places to cash your cheques. Many of these open daily from around 8am to 8pm, and rates generally compare favourably with those offered by the banks, but always establish any **commission** before signing cheques – the places that display promising rates may charge a hefty fee. Always count your money carefully, as it's not uncommon for moneychangers to short-change tourists in a variety of ways, including by miscalculating amounts (especially when there are lots of zeros involved), using a rigged calculator, folding over notes to make the amount look twice as great, and invisibly removing a pile of notes after the money's been counted. In some **banks** the foreign exchange counter only opens for a few hours, and in some small towns, banks won't accept travellers' cheques at all, so get into the habit of carrying a **few dollars cash** with you to allow for unforeseen circumstances. Banking hours and other local idiosyncrasies are described in the introduction to each country. Details of **local currencies** and **exchange rates** are also given at the beginning of each chapter, but for the up-to-the-minute **exchange rate**, visit the Oanda online currency converter (*www.oanda.com/cgi-bin/ncc*), which gives you the day's Interbank rate for 164 currencies.

Keep a record of cheque serial numbers safe and separate from the cheques themselves. All travellers' cheque issuers give you a list of numbers to call in the case of **lost or stolen cheques** and will refund you if you can produce the original receipts and a note of your cheque numbers. Instructions in cases of loss or theft vary, but you'll usually have to notify the police first and then call the issuing company collect who will arrange a refund, usually within 24 hours.

CREDIT CARDS, ATMS AND CASH ADVANCES

American Express, Visa, MasterCard and Diners Club **credit cards** and **charge cards** are accepted at top hotels and by a growing number of posh restaurants, department stores, tourist shops and travel agents, but surcharging of up to five percent is rife, and theft and forgery are major industries – always demand the carbon copies and destroy them immediately, and never leave cards in baggage storage.

Except in Cambodia and Laos, many of the biggest tourist centres and cities have a useful number of **ATMs** that accept international debit and credit cards such as MasterCard, Cirrus and Visa; see individual accounts for details. For an up-to-date list of ATM locations in Southeast Asia, check the relevant Web sites (*www.mastercard.com* and *www.visa.com*). All banks charge a handling fee of about 1.5 percent per transaction when you use your debit card at overseas ATMs. Don't rely on plastic alone, however, which is more tempting to thieves and less easy to replace than the trusty travellers' cheque. In countries without ATMs (such as Laos), you can obtain **cash advances** on Visa cards, and less frequently MasterCard, in major urban centres, but you will most likely be required to withdraw a minimum of $100 at a rate of 2.5 to 3 percent commission.

WIRING MONEY

Wiring money through a specialist agent (see box overleaf) is a fast but expensive way to send and receive money abroad. The money wired should be available for collection, usually in local currency, from the company's local agent within twenty minutes of being sent via Western Union or Moneygram; both charge on a sliding scale, so sending larger amounts of cash is better value.

It's also possible to have money wired **directly from a bank in your home country** to a bank in Southeast Asia, although this is somewhat less reliable because it involves two separate institutions. Most banks will allow account holders to nominate almost any branch of any bank as a collection point, though if this is not the central bank that they usual-

---

WIRING MONEY

FROM THE UK
Moneygram ☎0800/8971 8971.
Western Union ☎0800/833 833.

FROM IRELAND
Moneygram: contact your nearest Bank of Ireland.
Western Union ☎1800/395 395.

FROM NORTH AMERICA
Moneygram ☎1-800/543 4080.
Western Union ☎1-800/325 6000.

FROM AUSTRALIA
Moneygram ☎1800/230100.
Western Union ☎1800/649565.

FROM NEW ZEALAND
Moneygram ☎09/379 8243 or 0800/262263.
Western Union ☎09/270 0050.

---

ly deal with, it will take longer than normal. It's therefore a good idea to check with your bank before travelling to see which branch of which bank they have reciprocal arrangements with. Your home bank will need the address of the branch where you want to pick up the money and the address and telex number of the head office, which will act as the clearing house; money wired this way will take at least two working days to arrive, and costs around £25/US$40/A$25 per transaction.

HEALTH MATTERS

The vast majority of travellers to Southeast Asia suffer nothing more than an upset stomach, so long as they observe basic precautions about food and water hygiene, and research pre-trip vaccination and malaria prophylactic requirements.

The standard of **local health care** varies across the region, with Laos having the least advanced system (best to get across the border and go to a Thai hospital) and Singapore boasting world-class medical care. If you have a minor ailment, it's usually best to head for a pharmacy – most have a decent idea of how to treat common ailments and can provide many medicines without prescription. Otherwise, ask for the nearest doctor or hospital. Details of major hospitals are given throughout the Guide and there's an overview of local health care under "Medical care and emergencies" in the introduction to each country. If you have a serious accident or illness, you may need to be evacuated home or to Singapore, so it's vital to arrange **health insurance** before you leave home (see p.31).

When planning your trip, **visit a doctor** at least two months before you leave, to allow time to complete any recommended courses of vaccinations. Most general practitioners in the UK can give advice and certain vaccines on prescription, though they may not administer some of the less common immunizations. For up-to-the-minute **information**, call the Travellers' Health phone lines or visit a travel clinic (listed on pp.26–27), although immunizations at these clinics can be costly. In the UK, pick up the Department of Health's free publication, *Health Advice for Travellers*, available at the post office, or by calling ☎0800/555777. The content of the booklet, which contains immunization advice, is constantly updated on pages 460–464 of CEEFAX (or you can consult it on *www.open.gov.uk/*). It's also advisable to have a trouble-shooting dental check-up before you leave – and remember that you generally need to start taking **anti-malarial tablets** one week before your departure.

INOCULATIONS

There are no compulsory vaccinations required for entry into any part of Southeast Asia, but health professionals strongly recommend that travellers to all

Some of the illnesses you can pick up in Southeast Asia may not show themselves immediately. If you become ill within a year of returning home, tell your doctor where you have been.

Southeast Asian destinations get **inoculations** against the following common and debilitating diseases: typhoid, hepatitis A, tetanus and polio (you may be up-to-date with polio and tetanus anyway). In addition, you may be advised to have some of the following vaccinations, for example if travelling during the rainy season or if planning to stay in remote rural areas: rabies, hepatitis B, Japanese encephalitis, diphtheria, meningitis and TB. If you're only going to Hong Kong and Macau, you may not have to get any inoculations. All shots should be recorded on an **International Certificate of Vaccination** and carried with your passport when travelling abroad; some immigration officials levy fines for those without a certificate, in particular at the Thai/Cambodian border in Poipet (see p.843). If you've been in an area infected with yellow fever during the fourteen days before your arrival in Southeast Asia, you will need a certificate of vaccination against the disease.

GENERAL PRECAUTIONS

Bacteria thrive in the tropics, and the best way to combat them is to keep up standards of personal hygiene. Frequent **bathing** is essential and hands should be washed before eating, especially in countries where food is traditionally eaten with the hands. Cuts or scratches can become infected very easily and should be thoroughly cleaned, disinfected and bandaged to keep dirt out.

Many countries in Southeast Asia have significant **AIDS** problems. Using latex condoms during sex reduces the risks. Bring a supply of them with you, take special care with expiry dates and bear in mind that condoms don't last as long when kept in the heat. Blood transfusions, intravenous drug use, acupuncture, dentistry, tattooing and body piercing are high-risk. Get a dental checkup before you leave home, and carry a sterile needles kit for medical emergencies.

Ask locally before **swimming** in freshwater lakes and rivers, including the Mekong River, as tiny worms carrying diseases such as bilharzia infect some tracts of freshwater in Southeast Asia. The worm enters through the skin and may cause a high fever after some weeks, but the recognizable symptoms of stomach pain and blood in the urine only appear after the disease is established, which may take months or even years. At this point some damage to internal organs may have occurred.

MALARIA AND DENGUE FEVER

The whole of Southeast Asia lies within a **malarial zone**, although in many urban and developed tourist areas there is little risk (see overleaf). Most health professionals advise that travellers on a multi-country trip through Southeast Asia should take full precautions against malaria – it's essential to take medical advice on this as malaria can be fatal and comes in a variety of strains, some of which are resistant to the most common anti-malarial drugs (prophylactics). Information regarding malaria is constantly being updated, and pregnant women and children should seek specialist advice.

Malaria is caused by a parasite in the saliva of the anopheles mosquito which is passed into the human when bitten by the mosquito. There are various prophylactic drug regimes available, depending on your destination, all of which must be taken according to a strict timetable, beginning one week before you go and continuing four weeks after leaving the area. If you don't do this, you are in danger of developing the illness once you have returned home. One drug, Mefloquine (sold as Larium) has received some very critical media coverage; in some people it appears to produce disorientation, depression and sleep disturbance, although it suits other people very well. If you're intending to use Larium you should begin to take it two weeks before you depart to see whether it will agree with your metabolism. Anyone planning to **scuba-dive** should discuss the use of Larium very carefully with their medical advisers, as there has been some indication of an increased risk of the "bends".

None of the drugs is one hundred percent effective and it is equally important to the **prevention of malaria** to stop the mosquitoes biting you. Malarial mosquitoes are active from dusk until dawn and during this time you should wear trousers, long-sleeved shirts and socks and smother yourself and your clothes in mosquito repellent containing the chemical compound DEET: shops all over Southeast Asia stock it. DEET is strong stuff, and if you have sensitive skin a natural alternative is citronella (called Mosi-guard in the UK), made from a blend of Eucalyptus oils. At night you should either sleep under a mosquito net sprayed with DEET or in a room with screens across the windows. Accommodation in tourist spots nearly always provides screens or a net (check both for holes), but if you're planning to go way off the beaten track, you can either take a net with you or buy one locally from department stores in capital cities. Mosquito coils – widely available in Southeast Asia – also help keep the insects at bay.

The **symptoms** of malaria are fever, headache and shivering, similar to a severe dose of flu and often coming in cycles, but a lot of people have additional symptoms. Don't delay in seeking help fast: malaria can be fatal. You will need a blood test to confirm the illness and the doctor will prescribe the most effective treatment locally. If you develop flu-like symptoms any time up to a year after returning home, you should inform a doctor and ask for a blood test.

DENGUE FEVER

Another important reason to avoid getting bitten is **dengue fever**, a virus carried by a different species of mosquito, which bites during the day. There is no vaccine or tablet available to prevent the illness, which causes fever, headache and joint and muscle pains, as well as possible internal bleeding and circulatory-system failure. There is no specific drug to cure it, and the only treatment is lots of rest, liquids and Panadol (or any other acetaminophen painkiller, not aspirin), though more serious cases may require hospitalization. Reports indicate that the disease is on the increase across Asia and it can be fatal. It is vital to get an early medical diagnosis and get treatment.

MALARIAL OR NOT?

BRUNEI – Not malarial.

CAMBODIA – Malarial in all forested and hilly rural areas, but Phnom Penh, Sihanoukville and Battambang are malaria-free and transmission is very low in Siem Reap.

HONG KONG – Not malarial.

INDONESIA – Malarial, except on Bali.

LAOS – Very malarial.

MACAU – Not malarial.

MALAYSIA – Malarial, but low risk on the Peninsula.

PHILIPPINES – Malarial only in the southern tip of Palawan and in the Sulu Archipelago.

SINGAPORE – Not malarial.

TRAVEL CLINICS AND INFORMATION LINES

BRITAIN

British Airways Travel Clinic Provides vaccinations, tailored up-to-the-minute advice and travel healthcare products. There are 28 regional clinics in the UK (call ☎01276/685040 for the one nearest to you or consult *www.britishairways.com*). In London, visit 156 Regent St, London W1 ☎020/7439 9584, no appointment necessary, or call in advance for appointments at 101 Cheapside, London EC2 ☎020/7606 2977; and at the BA terminal in London's Victoria Station ☎020/7233 6661.

Hospital for Tropical Diseases, 2nd Floor, Mortimer Market Centre, off Copper St, London WC1E 6AU (☎020/7388 9600). Travel clinic and recorded message service (☎0839/337733; 50p per min) which lists appropriate immunizations.

Malaria Helpline 24-hr recorded message (☎0891/600 350; 60p per minute).

MASTA (Medical Advisory Service for Travellers Abroad), London School of Hygiene and Tropical Medicine. Pre-recorded 24-hour Travellers' Health Line (☎0906/822 4100; 60p per min), giving written information tailored to your journey by return of post. Or consult *www.masta.org*

Nomad Pharmacy Tailored information and vaccinations at 40 Bernard St, London WC1, and 3–4 Turnpike Lane, London N8 (Mon–Fri 9.30am–6pm, ☎020/7833 4114 for appointments). Telephone helpline ☎0891/633 414 (60p a minute).

Trailfinders No-appointments-necessary immunization clinics at 194 Kensington High St, London (Mon–Fri 9am–5pm, Thurs to 6pm, Sat 9.30am–4pm; ☎020/7938 3999).

Yahoo! Health Web site
http://health.yahoo.com Gives information about specific diseases and conditions, drugs and herbal remedies, as well as advice from health experts.

IRELAND

All of these places offer pre-trip advice.

Travel Medicine Services, PO Box 254, 16 College St, Belfast 1 (☎028/9031 5220).

Tropical Medical Bureau, Grafton St Medical Centre, 34 Grafton St, Dublin 2 (☎01/671 9200).

Tropical Medical Bureau, Dun Laoghaire Medical Centre, 5 Northumberland Ave, Dun Laoghaire, Co. Dublin (☎01/280 4996, *www.iol.ie/-tmb*).

THAILAND – Malarial, but only high-risk along the Burma and Cambodia borders, including in northern Kanchanaburi Province, and in parts of Trat Province including Ko Chang.

VIETNAM – Very malarial in the highlands and rural areas, but low risk in Hanoi, Ho Chi Minh, northern Red River delta and coastal regions of the south and centre.

FOOD AND WATER

Most health problems experienced by travellers are a direct result of **food** they've eaten. Avoid eating uncooked vegetables and fruits that cannot be peeled, and be warned that you risk ingesting worms and other parasites from dishes containing raw meat or fish. Cooked food that has been sitting out for an undetermined period of time should also be treated with suspicion. Avoid sharing glasses and utensils. The amount of money you pay for a meal is no guarantee of its safety; in fact, food in top hotels has often been hanging around longer than food cooked at roadside stalls. Use your common sense – eat in places that look clean, avoid reheated food and be wary of shellfish.

Most **water** that comes out of taps in Southeast Asia has had very little treatment, and can contain a whole range of bacteria and viruses (local water conditions are described in the section on "Food and drink" at the beginning of each chapter). These micro-organisms cause diseases such as diarrhoea, gastroenteritis, typhus, cholera, dysentery, poliomyelitis, hepatitis A and giardia, and can be present even when water looks clean and safe to drink. Therefore, you should stick to bottled, boiled or sterilized water; fortunately, except in the furthest-flung corners of Southeast Asia, **bottled water** is on sale everywhere. Be wary of salads and vegetables that have been washed in tap water, and bear in mind that **ice** is not always made from sterilized water.

USA AND CANADA

Canadian Society for International Health, 1 Nicholas St, Suite 1105, Ottawa, ON K1N 7B7 (☎613/241 5785). Distributes a free pamphlet, "Health Information for Canadian Travellers", containing an extensive list of travel health centres in Canada.

Centers for Disease Control, 1600 Clifton Rd NE, Atlanta, GA 30333 (☎404/639 3311, www.cdc.gov). Publishes outbreak warnings and suggested inoculations. International Travelers Hotline on ☎1/888-232 3228.

International Association for Medical Assistance to Travellers (IAMAT), 417 Center St, Lewiston, NY 14092 (☎716/754 4883, www.sentex.net/~iamat) and 40 Regal Rd, Guelph, ON N1K 1B5 (☎519/836 0102). Provides a list of local English-speaking doctors and leaflets on inoculations.

International SOS Assistance, PO Box 11568, Philadelphia, PA 19116 (☎1-800/523 8930). Members receive pre-trip medical info, as well as overseas emergency services to complement travel insurance coverage.

Travel Medicine, 369 Pleasant St, Suite 312, Northampton, MA 01060 (☎1-800/872 8633, www.travmed.com). Sells health-related travel products.

Travelers Medical Center, 31 Washington Square West, New York, NY 10011 (☎212/982 1600). Consultation service on immunizations and treatment of diseases for travellers to developing countries.

AUSTRALIA AND NEW ZEALAND

Travellers' Medical and Vaccination Centre (www.tmvc.com.au) has Vaccination Centres throughout Australia, New Zealand and Southeast Asia, plus general information on travel health. Branches include Adelaide, 27–29 Gilbert Place (☎08/8212 7522); Auckland, 1/170 Queen St (☎09/373 3531); Canberra, Mezzanine Level, City Walk Arcade, 2 Mort St (☎02/6257 7156); Christchurch, 147 Armagh St (☎03/379 4000); Perth, 5 Mill St (☎08/9321 1977); Sydney, 7/428 George St (☎02/9221 7133); Wellington, Shop 15, Grand Arcade, Willis St (☎04/473 0991).

Travellers' Immunization Service, 303 Pacific Hwy, Sydney (☎02/9416 1348).

Travel-Bug Medical and Vaccination Centre, 161 Ward St, North Adelaide (☎08/8267 3544).

MEDICAL KIT

Some of the items listed below can be purchased more easily and cheaply in local pharmacies; Imodium and dental/sterile surgical kits will need to be bought before you leave home. Condoms are available at pharmacies throughout Southeast Asia, though quality is not always reliable; oral contraceptives are only available at pharmacies in Brunei, Malaysia and Singapore. Tampons are available only in the major cities, so it's advisable to bring your own supplies.

Antiseptic cream
Insect repellent
Antihistamine
Plasters/band aids
Water sterilization tablets or water purifier
Sunscreen
Lint and sealed bandages
A course of flagyl antibiotics
Anti-fungal/athletes-foot cream

Imodium (Lomotil) for emergency diarrhoea treatment
Paracetamol/aspirin
Anti-inflammatory/Ibuprofen
Multivitamin and mineral tablets
Rehydration salts
Emergency dental kit with temporary fillings
Hypodermic and intravenous needles, sutures and sterilized skin wipes
Condoms and other contraceptives

The only time you're likely to be out of reach of bottled water is trekking into remote areas when you'll be relying on **boiled water**. Boiling for ten minutes gets rid of most bacteria in water but at least twenty minutes is needed to kill amoebic cysts, a cause of dysentery. To be safe, you may wish to use some kind of **chemical sterilization**. Iodine purification tablets or solutions are more effective than chlorine compounds, though still leave a nasty aftertaste – using a filter afterwards makes the water slightly more palatable. Note that iodine products are unsuitable for pregnant women, babies and people with thyroid problems. **Purification**, a two-stage process involving both filtration and sterilization, gives the most complete treatment. Consider taking a portable purifier with you, such as the ones made by Pre-Mac (*www.pre-mac.com*); call ☎01732/460333 for **UK** stockists, or ☎01/466 0133 in Ireland. In the **US** try Travel Medicine, 351 Pleasant St, Suite 312, North Hampton, MA 01060 (☎1-800/872 6833); in **Canada** call Outbound Products (☎604/321 5464). Even if you are in areas where bottled water is available, still consider purifiying or sterilizing water, since drinking bottled water generates more rubbish. In **Australia**, purifiers are available from Mountain Equipment, 491 Kent St, Sydney (☎02/9264 3146), and in **New Zealand**, from Bivouac, 5 Fort St, Auckland 1 (☎09/366 1966).

HEAT PROBLEMS

Travellers who are unused to tropical climates regularly suffer from **sunburn** and **dehydration**. Limit your exposure to the sun in the hours around midday, use high-factor sunscreen and wear dark glasses and

a sunhat. You'll be sweating a great deal in the heat, so the important thing is to make sure that you drink enough. If you are urinating very little or your urine turns dark (this can also indicate hepatitis), increase your fluid intake. When you sweat you lose salt, so you may want to add some extra to your food. A more serious result of the heat is **heatstroke**, indicated by high temperature, dry red skin and a fast, erratic pulse. As an emergency measure, try to cool the patient off by covering them in sheets or sarongs soaked in cold water and turn the fan on them; they may need to go to hospital, though. **Heat rashes**, **prickly heat** and **fungal infections** are also common: wear loose cotton clothing, dry yourself carefully after bathing and use medicated talcum powder.

STOMACH PROBLEMS AND VIRUSES

If you travel in Asia for an extended period of time, you are likely to come down with some kind of stomach bug. For most, this is just a case of **diarrhoea**, caught through bad hygiene, unfamiliar or affected food, and is generally over in a couple of days if treated properly; **dehydration** is one of the main concerns if you have diarrhoea, so rehydration salts dissolved in clean water provide the best treatment. **Gastroenteritis** is a more extreme version, but can still be cured with the same blend of rest and rehydration. You should be able to find a local brand of **rehydration salts** in pharmacies in most Southeast Asian towns, but you can also make up your own by mixing three teaspoons of sugar and one of salt to a litre of water. You will need to drink as many as three litres a day to stave off dehydration. Eat non-spicy, non-greasy **foods** such as young coconut, unbuttered toast, rice, bananas and noodles, and steer away from alcohol, coffee, milk and most fruits. Since diarrhoea purges the body of the bugs, taking blocking **medicines** such as Lomotil and Imodium, or charcoal tablets, is not recommended unless you have to travel. Antibiotics are a worse idea, as they can wipe out friendly bacteria in the bowel and render you far more susceptible to future attacks.

The next step up from gastroenteritis is **dysentery**, diagnosable from blood and mucus in the (often blackened) stool. Dysentery is either amoebic or bacillary, with the latter characterized by high fever and vomiting. Serious attacks will require antibiotics, and therefore must always be treated, preferably in hospital.

Giardia can be diagnosed by foul-smelling farts and burps, abdominal distension, evil-smelling stools that float, and diarrhoea without blood or pus. Don't be over-eager with your diagnosis though, and treat it as normal diarrhoea for at least 24 hours before resorting to flagyl antibiotics.

TROPICAL FRUITS OF SOUTHEAST ASIA

One of the most refreshing snacks in Southeast Asia is **fruit**, and you'll find it offered everywhere – neatly sliced in glass boxes on hawker carts, blended into delicious shakes at night-market stalls, and served as dessert in restaurants. The fruits described below can be found in all parts of Southeast Asia, though some are seasonal. The region's more familiar fruits are not listed here, but include forty varieties of banana, dozens of different mangoes, three types of pineapple, coconuts, and watermelons. To avoid stomach trouble, peel all fruit before eating it, and use comon sense when buying it pre-peeled on the street, avoiding anything that looks fly-blown or has been sitting in the sun for hours.

Custard apple (soursop) Inside the knobbly, muddy green skin you'll find creamy, almond-coloured blancmange-like flesh and many seeds. Described by Margaret Brooke, wife of Sarawak's second Rajah, Charles, as "tasting like cotton wool dipped in vinegar and sugar".

Durian Southeast Asia's most prized, and expensive, fruit has a greeny-yellow, spiky exterior and grows to the size of a football. Inside, it divides into segments of thick, yellow-white flesh that give off a disgustingly strong stink that's been compared to a mixture of mature cheese and caramel. Not surprisingly, many airlines and hotels ban the eating of this smelly delicacy on their premises. Most Southeast Asians consider it the king of fruits, while most foreigners find it utterly foul in both taste and smell.

Guava The apple of the tropics has green textured skin and sweet, crisp flesh that can be pink or white and is studded with tiny edible seeds. Has five times the vitamin C content of orange juice and is sometimes eaten cut into strips and sprinkled with sugar and chilli.

Jackfruit This large, pear-shaped fruit can weigh up to 20kg and has a thick, bobbly, greeny-yellow shell protecting sweet yellow flesh. Green, unripe jackfruit is sometimes cooked as a vegetable in curries.

Mangosteen The size of a small apple, with smooth, purple skin and a fleshy inside that divides into succulent white segments which are sweet though slightly acidic.

Papaya (paw-paw) Similar in size and shape to a large melon, with smooth green skin and yellowy-orange flesh that's a rich source of vitamins A and C. It's a favourite in fruit salads and shakes, and sometimes appears in its green, unripe form in vegetable salads.

Pomelo The pomelo is the largest of all the citrus fruits and looks rather like a grapefruit, though it is slightly drier and has less flavour.

Rambutan The bright red rambutan's soft, spiny exterior has given it its name – *rambut* means "hair" in Malay. Usually about the size of a golf ball, it has a white, opaque fruit of delicate flavour, similar to a lychee.

Salak (snakefruit) Teardrop-shaped, the *salak* has a brown, scaly skin like a snake's and a bitter taste.

Sapodilla (sapota) These small, brown, rough-skinned ovals look a bit like kiwi fruit and conceal a grainy, yellowish pulp that tastes almost honey-sweet.

Star fruit (carambola) A waxy, pale-green fruit with a fluted, almost star-like shape. It resembles a watery, crunchy apple and is said to be good for high blood pressure. The yellower the fruit, the sweeter its flesh.

Hepatitis A or E is a waterborne viral infection spread through water and food. It causes jaundice, loss of appetite and nausea and can leave you feeling wiped out for months. Seek immediate medical help if you think you may have contracted hepatitis. The Havrix vaccination lasts for several years, provided you have a booster the year after your first jabs. **Hepatitis B** is transmitted by bodily fluids, during unprotected sex or by intravenous drug use.

Cholera and typhoid are infectious diseases, generally spread when communities rely on sparse water supplies. The initial symptoms of **cholera** are a sudden onset of watery, but painless diarrhoea. Later, nausea, vomiting and muscle cramps set in. Cholera can be fatal if adequate fluid intake is not maintained. Copious amounts of liquids, including oral rehydration solution, should be consumed and medical treatment should be sought immediately. Although there is a vaccine against cholera, few medical professionals recommend it, as it is only about fifty percent effective. Like cholera, **typhoid** is also spread in small, localized epidemics. Symptoms can vary widely, but generally include headaches, fever and constipation, followed by diarrhoea. Vaccination against typhoid is recommended for all travellers to Southeast Asia.

THINGS THAT BITE OR STING

The most common irritations for travellers come from tiny pests whose most serious evil is the danger of infection to or through the bitten area, so keep bites clean and wash with antiseptic soap. **Fleas, lice** and **bed bugs** adore grimy sheets, so examine your bedding carefully, air and beat the offending articles and then coat yourself liberally in insect repellent. Visitors who spend the night in hilltribe villages where hygiene is poor risk being infected by **scabies** which cause severe itching by burrowing under the skin and laying eggs.

Ticks are nasty pea-shaped bloodsuckers which usually attach themselves to you if you walk through long grass. A dab of petrol, alcohol, tiger balm or insect repellent, or a lit cigarette, should convince them to leave; if not, then grab hold of their head with tweezers and twist them off. Bloodsucking **leeches** can be a problem in the jungle and in fresh water. The best way to get rid of them is to run them with salt, though all the anti-tick treatments also work. **DEET** is an effective deterrent, and applying it at the tops of your boots and around the lace-holes is a good idea.

Southeast Asia has many species of both land and sea **snakes**, so wear boots and socks when hiking. Most snakes will get out of your way long before you know they are there, but if you're confronted, back off. If **bitten**, the number one rule is not to panic. Try to stay still in order to slow the venom's entry into the bloodstream. Wash and disinfect the wound, apply a pressure bandage as tightly as you would for a sprain, splint the affected limb, keep it below the level of the heart and get to hospital as soon as possible. Tourniquets, cutting open the bite and trying to suck the venom cause more harm than good. **Scorpion** stings are very painful but not fatal; swelling usually disappears after a few hours.

If stung by a **jellyfish** the priority treatment is to remove the fragments of tentacles from the skin – without causing further discharge of poison – which is easiest done by applying vinegar to deactivate the stinging capsules. The best way to minimize the risk of stepping on the **toxic spines** of sea urchins, sting rays and stone fish is to wear thick-soled shoes, though these cannot provide total protection; sea-urchin spikes should be removed after softening the skin with a special ointment, though some people recommend applying urine to help dissolve the spines; for sting-ray and stone-fish stings, alleviate the pain by immersing the wound in very hot water – just under 50°C – while waiting for help.

Rabies is transmitted to humans by the bite of carrier animals, who have the disease in their saliva; **tetanus** is an additional danger from such bites. All animals should be treated with caution, but particularly monkeys, cats and dogs. Be extremely cautious with wild animals that seem inexplicably tame, as this can be a symptom. If you do get bitten, scrub the wound with a strong antiseptic and then alcohol and get to a hospital as soon as possible. Do not attempt to close the wound. The incubation period for the disease can be as much as a year or as little as a few days; once the disease has taken hold it will be fatal.

TRAVEL INSURANCE

If you're unlucky enough to require hospital treatment in Southeast Asia, you'll have to foot the bill, so make sure you have adequate **travel insurance** before you leave. A typical travel insurance policy should also provide cover for the loss of baggage, tickets and – up to a certain limit – cash or cheques, as well as cancellation or curtailment of your journey. Most policies exclude so-called **dangerous sports** unless an extra premium is paid: in Southeast Asia this can mean scuba-diving, whitewater rafting and bungee jumping, though probably not trekking. Read the small print and benefits tables of prospective policies carefully; coverage can vary wildly for roughly similar premiums.

With many policies you can exclude coverage you don't need, but for Southeast Asia you should definitely take **medical coverage** that includes both

hospital treatment and medical evacuation; be sure to ask for the 24-hour medical emergency number. Keep all medical bills and, if possible, contact the insurance company before making any major outlay. Very few insurers will arrange on-the-spot payments in the event of a major expense – you will usually be reimbursed only after going home, so a credit/debit card could be useful to tide you over. When securing **baggage cover**, make sure that the per-article limit – typically under £500 equivalent – will cover your most valuable possession. If you have anything stolen, get a copy of the **police report**, otherwise you won't be able to claim. Always make a note of the policy details and leave them with someone at home in case you lose the original.

Before buying a policy, check that you're not already covered. Your home insurance policy may cover your possessions against loss or theft even when overseas, or you can extend cover through your household contents insurer. Many bank and charge accounts include some form of travel cover, and insurance is also sometimes included if you pay for your trip with a credit card (though it usually only provides medical or accident cover).

In **North America**, Canadian provincial health plans usually provide some overseas medical coverage, although they are unlikely to pick up the full tab in the event of a mishap. Holders of official student/teacher/youth cards are entitled to meagre accident coverage and hospital in-patient benefits. Students will often find that their student health coverage extends during the vacations and for one term beyond the date of last enrolment.

ROUGH GUIDES TRAVEL INSURANCE

Rough Guides now offer their own **travel insurance**, customized for our readers by a leading UK broker and backed by a Lloyds underwriter. It's available for anyone, of any nationality, travelling anywhere in the world.

There are two main Rough Guides insurance plans: **Essential**, for effective, no-frills cover, starting at £23.03 for two weeks; and **Premier**, for more extensive benefits, starting at £28.79 for two weeks. Each can be supplemented with a "Hazardous Activities Premium". Unlike many poli-

cies, the Rough Guides schemes are calculated by the day, so if you're travelling for 27 days rather than a month, that's all you pay for. You can alternatively take out annual **multi-trip insurance**, which covers you for all your travel throughout the year (with a maximum of sixty days for any one trip).

For a **policy quote**, call the Rough Guides Insurance Line on UK freefone ☎0800/015 0906, or if you're calling from outside Britain on ☎ (44) 1243 621 046. Alternatively, you can book online at *www.roughguides.com/insurance*

INFORMATION: TOURIST OFFICES, ONLINE RESOURCES AND BOOKS

Although some Southeast Asian countries have no dedicated tourist information offices abroad, there's plenty of **information** available on the Internet, as well as in guidebooks and travelogues.

TOURIST OFFICES ABROAD

Local **tourist information** services are described at the beginning of every chapter.

BRUNEI

Contact your nearest Bruneian embassy or consulate (see p.20).

CAMBODIA

Contact your nearest Cambodian embassy or consulate (see p.20).

HONG KONG

www.hkta.org
Australia Level 4, 80 Druitt St, Sydney, NSW 2000 (☎02/9283 3083).
Canada 3rd Floor, 9 Temperance St, Toronto, ON M5H 1Y6 (☎416/599 6636).
New Zealand representative: PO Box 2120 Auckland (☎09/307 2580) or contact Sydney office.
UK and Ireland 6 Grafton St, London W1 (☎020/7533 7100).
USA 401 N Michigan Ave, Suite 1640, Chicago, IL 60611 (☎312/329 1828); 10940 Wilshire Blvd, Suite 1220, Los Angeles, CA 90024 (☎310/208 4582).

INDONESIA

www.tourismindonesia.com
Australia and New Zealand Contact the Indonesian Consulate General, 236–238 Maroubra Rd, Maroubra, NSW 2035, Australia (☎02/9344 9933).
UK and Ireland Contact the embassy.
USA and Canada Contact the embassy.

LAOS

No tourist offices abroad. Contact embassies if desperate, but the most useful information is to be found online; see p.35.

MACAU

www.macautourism.gov.mo
If your country has no representation, contact the relevant Portuguese National Tourist Office for information.
Australia Level 17, 456 Kent St, Sydney, NSW 2000 ☎02/9285 6856; local call-rate ☎1300/300236.
Canada Contact the US office listed below.
New Zealand c/o 101 Great South Rd, Remuera, Auckland ☎09/309 8094.
UK and Ireland 1 Battersea Church Rd, London SW11 (☎020/7771 7006).
USA 5757 W. Century Blvd, Suite 660, Los Angeles, CA (☎1-8776 22280).

MALAYSIA

www.visitmalaysia.com
Australia 65 York St, Sydney, NSW 2000 (☎02/9299 4441); 56 William St, Perth, WA 6000 (☎09/481 0400).
Canada 830 Burrard St, Vancouver, BC V6Z 2KA (☎604/689 8899).
New Zealand Contact the embassy.
UK and Ireland 57 Trafalgar Square, London WC2 (☎020/7930 7932).
USA 818 West 7th St #804, Los Angeles, CA 90017 (☎323/689 9702); 120 E 56th St, Suite 810, New York, NY 10022.

THE PHILIPPINES

www.tourism.gov.ph
Australia Level 1, Philippine Centre, 27–33 Wentworth Ave, Sydney, NSW, 2000 (☎02/9283 0711).

Canada Contact offices in the USA.
New Zealand Contact the Sydney office or the consulate in Auckland.
UK and Ireland 146 Cromwell Rd, London SW7 (☎020/7835 1100).
USA 30 North Michigan Ave #913, Chicago, IL 60602 (☎312/782 2475); 556 Fifth Ave, New York, NY 10036 (☎212/575 7915); 447 Sutter St, Suite 507, San Francisco, CA 94108 (415/956 4060).

SINGAPORE

www.stb.com.sg
Australia 111 Empire Circuit, Yarralumla, Canberra ACT 2600 (☎02/6273 1149).
Canada 2 Bloor St West, Suite 404, Toronto, Ontario M4W 3E2 (☎416/363 8898).
New Zealand 2 Cook St, PO Box 17–226, Karori, Wellington (☎04/476 8618).
UK and Ireland 1st Floor, Carrington House, 126–130 Regent St, London W1 (☎020/7437 0033).
USA 8484 Wilshire Blvd #510, Beverly Hills, CA 90211 (☎323/852 1901); 260 Fifth Ave, 12th Floor, New York, NY 10036 (☎212/302 4861).

THAILAND

www.tat.or.th
Australia Level 11, AWA Building, 47 York St, Sydney NSW 2000 (☎02/9290 2888); Unit 2, 226 James St, Perth, WA 6000 (☎08/9228 8166).
Canada Representative – Mr Diderich, 116 Alvwych Ave, Toronto, Ontario M4J 1X6 (☎416/465 5620).
New Zealand 3rd Floor, 43 High St, Auckland (☎09/358 1191).
UK and Ireland 49 Albemarle St, London W1 (☎020/7499 7679).
USA 611 N Larchnont Blvd, 1st Floor, Los Angeles, CA 90004 (☎213/382 2353); 1 World Trade Center, Suite 3729, New York, NY 10048 (☎212/432 0433).

VIETNAM

www.vietnamtourism.com
Australia and New Zealand No offices.
UK and Ireland 12 Victoria Rd, London W8 (☎020/7937 3174).
USA and Canada No offices.

SOUTHEAST ASIA ONLINE

There's plenty of **online information** about Southeast Asia. For details of Internet access within the region, see p.39.

GENERAL SOUTHEAST ASIAN TRAVEL

Accommodating Asia *www.accomasia.com* Heaps of good traveller-oriented stuff on nearly all parts of Southeast Asia, with especially interesting links to travellers' homepages, under "travellers notes".

AsianDiver *www.asiandiver.com/themagazine/index.html* Online version of the divers' magazine, with good coverage of Southeast Asia's diving sites, including recommendations and firsthand diving stories.

Excite Travel's City Net *www.excite.com/travel/regions/asia* Features geopolitical and tourist information for every country in Southeast Asia, with detailed links plus hotel bookings, sightseeing and weather forecasts.

Geocities *www.geocities.com/cgi-bin/search/isearch* Heaps of links to interesting Asian travel sites, including travellers' reports, virtual tours, and a forum for travel companions.

Internet Travel Information Service *www.itisnet.com* Specifically aimed at budget travellers, this site is a really useful resource of current info on many Southeast Asian countries, regularly updated by travellers and researchers. Up-to-the-minute info on airfares, border crossings, visa requirements and hotels.

1000 Travel Tips *www.1000traveltips.org* Useful site that gathers travellers' practical reports on fairly recent trips through Indonesia, Singapore, Vietnam, Thailand, Laos and Cambodia.

Online tourist information *www.efn.org/~rick/tour* Exhaustive online travel resource, with links for more than 150 other countries to both official Web sites and travellers' homepages.

Open Directory Project *www.dmoz.org/Recreation/Travel/Budget_Travel/Backpacking/* Scores of backpacker-oriented links, including a lot of Asia-specific ones, plus travelogues, web rings and message boards.

Rec. Travel Library *www.travel-library.com* Highly recommended site, which has lively pieces on dozens of travel topics, from the budget travellers' guide to sleeping in airports to how to travel light. Good links too.

Tourism Concern *www.tourismconcern.org.uk* Web site of the British organization that campaigns for responsible tourism. Plenty of useful links to politically and environmentally aware organizations across the world, and a particularly good section on the politics of tourism in Burma.

Weather *www.usatoday.com/weather* Five-day forecasts from capital cities across the world.

TRAVELLERS' FORUMS

Fielding's adventure forum *www.fieldingtravel. com/blackflag* Travellers' forum on adventurous and "dangerous" places to travel. Especially useful on the less travelled routes across borders.

Lonely Planet Thorn Tree *http://thorntree.lonely-planet.com/thorn* Very popular travellers' bulletin boards, divided into regions (eg islands of Southeast Asia). Ideal for exchanging information with other travellers and for starting a debate, though it does attract an annoying number of regular posters just itching for an argument.

Rec. Travel Asia *news:rec.travel.asia* This Usenet forum deals specifically with travel in Asia, and gets a lot of traffic.

Rough Guides *www.roughguides.com* Interactive site for independent travellers, with forums, bulletin boards, travel tips and features, plus online travel guides.

COUNTRY-SPECIFIC SITES

BRUNEI : Brunei Net *www.brunet.bn/homepage/ tourism/tourhome.htm* Not a riveting site, but there are only a handful of tourist-oriented Brunei sites out there. Gives a reasonable introduction to the country.

CAMBODIA: Cambodia Information Center *www.cambodia.org* Topics include basic tourist information and a chat forum, plus links to other Cambodia-related sites.

HONG KONG: Hong Kong Tourist Association *www.hkta.org* Provides one of the most detailed and up-to-date sites, featuring festivals, weekly events, shopping, food and entertainment listings, plus full visa and visitor information.

INDONESIA: The Ultimate Indonesia Homepage *http://indonesia.elga.net.id* As good as its word – masses of links to sites covering the whole archipelago, plus a fruitful travel section too.

TRAVEL BOOKSHOPS AND MAP OUTLETS

UK AND IRELAND

Blackwell's Map and Travel Shop, 53 Broad St, Oxford (☎01865/792792, *bookshop. blackwell.co.uk*).

Daunt Books, 83 Marylebone High St, London W1M 3DE (☎020/7224 2295); 193 Haverstock Hill, London NW3 (☎020/7794 4006).

Easons Bookshop, 40 O'Connell St, Dublin 1 (☎01/873 3811).

Hodges Figgis Bookshop, 56–58 Dawson St, Dublin 2 (☎01/677 4754).

Heffers Map and Travel, 19 Sidney St, Cambridge (☎01223/568467, *www.heffers.co.uk*). Also at 20 Trinity St.

John Smith and Sons, 57–61 St Vincent St, Glasgow (☎0141/221 7472, *www.johnsmith.co.uk*).

The Map Shop, 30a Belvoir St, Leicester (☎0116/2471400).

National Map Centre, 22–24 Caxton St, London SW1 (☎020/7222 2466, *www.mapsworld.com*).

Newcastle Map Centre, 55 Grey St, Newcastle (☎0191/261 5622, *nmc@enterprise.net*).

Stanfords, 12–14 Long Acre, London WC2 (☎020/7836 1321, *sales@stanfords.co.uk*). Also at Campus Travel, 52 Grosvenor Gardens, London SW1 (☎020/7730 1314), at British Airways, 156 Regent St, London W1 (☎020/7434 4744), and at 29 Corn St, Bristol (☎0117/929 9966).

The Travel Bookshop, 13–15 Blenheim Crescent, London W11 (☎020/7229 5260, *www.thetravelbookshop.co.uk*).

USA

Adventurous Traveler Bookstore, 245 S Champlain St, PO Box 64769, Burlington, VT 05406-4769 (☎1-800/282 3963, *www .adventuroustraveler.com*).

Book Passage, 51 Tamal Vista Blvd, Corte Madera, CA 94925 (☎415/927 0960).

The Complete Traveller Bookstore, 199 Madison Ave, New York, NY 10016 (☎212/685 9007).

Map Link, 30 S La Petera Lane, Unit #5, Santa Barbara, CA 93117 (☎805/692 6777, *www.maplink.com*).

The Map Store Inc., 1636 1st St, Washington DC 20006 (☎202/628 2608).

Phileas Fogg's Books & Maps, #87 Stanford Shopping Center, Palo Alto, CA 94304 (☎1-800/533-FOGG, *www.foggs.com*).

LAOS: Internet Travel Guide *www.datacomm.ch/ pmgeiser/laos/index.html* A general introduction to the country, plus pages on sights, visas, forthcoming events and transport options.

MACAU: Macau Government Tourist Office *www.macautourism.gov.mo* Lively general site, including useful links to 3-, 4-, and 5-star hotels, plus a roundup of sights and special events.

MALAYSIA: Fascinating Malaysia *www. fascinatingmalaysia.com/index.html* Recent tourism and travel news, an interesting emphasis on eco-travel, plus standard introductions to the country and its culture.

PHILIPPINES: Tanikalang Ginto *www. filipinolinks.com* Links to over thirty topics about travel in the Philippines, including airport info, unusual destinations, books and hotels.

THAILAND: **René Hasekamp's Homepage** *www. hasekamp.demon.nl/thaiindex.htm* Constructed by a Dutch man who is married to a Thai woman, this site lists practical tips, dos and don'ts, info on certain sights, and an especially handy list of FAQs for travellers to Thailand.

VIETNAM: Vietnam Adventures Online *www. vietnamadventures.com* This general site looks at customs and culture, as well as featuring tourist destinations around the country.

BOOKS AND MAPS

Recommended **maps** of individual countries are detailed in the section at the beginning of each chapter, but the clearest and most detailed map of the whole region is the Southeast Asia 1:4,000 000, published by GeoCenter. For **books** specific to each country, see the relevant chapter; only general introductions to the region and books that cover more than one country are reviewed below. The abbreviation o/p means out-of-print. Where a book is pub-

Rand McNally, 444 N Michigan Ave, Chicago, IL 60611 (☎312/321 1751); 150 E 52nd St, New York, NY 10022 (☎212/758 7488); 595 Market St, San Francisco, CA 94105 (☎415/777 3131); call ☎1-800/333 0136 (ext 2111) for other locations, or for maps by mail order. *www.randmcnally.com*

Sierra Club Bookstore, 6014 College Ave, Oakland, CA 94618 (☎510/658 7470).

Travel Books & Language Center, 4437 Wisconsin Ave NW, Washington, DC 20016 (☎1-800/220 2665).

CANADA

International Travel Maps and Books (ITMB), 552 Seymour St, Vancouver, BC V6B 3J5 (☎604/687-3320, *www.itmb.com*).

Open Air Books and Maps, 25 Toronto St, Toronto, ON M5R 2C1 (☎416/363 0719).

Ulysses Travel Bookshop, 4176 St-Denis, Montréal (☎514/843 9447, *www.ulyssesguides.com*).

AUSTRALIA AND NEW ZEALAND

Mapland, 372 Little Bourke St, Melbourne (☎03/9670 4383).

The Map Shop, 16a Peel St, Adelaide (☎08/8231 2033).

Mapworld, 173 Gloucester Street, Christchurch (☎03/374 5399, *www.mapworld.co.nz*).

Perth Map Centre, 1/884 Hay St, Perth (☎08/9322 5733).

Specialty Maps, 58 Albert St, Auckland (☎09/307 2217).

Worldwide Maps and Guides, 187 George St, Brisbane (☎07/3221 4330).

ONLINE TRAVEL BOOKSTORES

Adventurous Traveler *www.adventuroustraveler.com*

Amazon *www.amazon.co.uk* and *www.amazon.com*

Literate Traveller *www.literatetraveller.com*

lished in the UK and the US, the UK publisher is given first, followed by the US one.

BOOKS ABOUT SOUTHEAST ASIA

Nigel Barley (ed.) *The Golden Sword: Stanford Raffles and the East* (British Museum Press, UK). An excellent, well-illustrated introduction to the man, his life, work and the full extent of his fascination with all the countries he explored.

Hans-Ulrich Bernard with Marcus Brooke, *Insight Guide to Southeast Asian Wildlife* (APA). Adequate introduction to the flora and fauna of the region, full of gorgeous photos, but not very useful for identifying species in the field.

Russell Braddon, *The Naked Island* (Penguin/ Simon & Schuster, o/p). Southeast Asia under the Japanese: Braddon's disturbing yet moving first-hand account of the POW camps of Malaya, Singapore and Siam displays courage in the face of appalling conditions; worth scouring secondhand stores for.

Ian Buruma, *God's Dust* (Vintage; Noonday). Modern portraits of various Southeast and East Asian countries, full of sharp, stylish observations.

Michael Carrithers, *The Buddha* (Oxford University Press). Clear, accessible account of the life of the Buddha, and the development and significance of his thought.

Joseph Conrad, *Lord Jim* (Penguin). Southeast Asia provides the backdrop to the story of Jim's desertion of an apparently sinking ship and subsequent efforts to redeem himself; modelled upon the sailor, AP Williams, Jim's character also yields echoes of Rajah Brooke of Sarawak.

Alfred W McCoy, *The Politics of Heroin: CIA Complicity in the Global Drug Trade* (Lawrence Hill Books). Exhaustively researched, revised and expanded version of McCoy's landmark *The Politics of Heroin in Southeast Asia*.

Henri Mouhot, *Travels in Siam, Cambodia, and Laos* (White Lotus, Bangkok). The account of the final journey of the legendary "discoverer of Angkor Wat", filled with characteristically blunt observations.

Philip Rawson, *The Art of Southeast Asia* (Thames & Hudson, UK). Attractive glossy volume, crammed with colour plates.

Lucy Ridout & Lesley Reader, *First-Time Asia: A Rough Guide Special* (Rough Guides). Easy-to-digest book aimed at backpackers planning their first ever trip to Asia. It fills in the gaps that guidebooks don't cover, addressing common pre-departure fears, advising on which countries to avoid, and giving heaps of practical tips. Also includes cartoons and anecdotes from other travellers.

Stan Sesser, *The Lands of Charm and Cruelty: Travels in Southeast Asia* (Picador/Vintage Departures). Superb book of insightful essays and well-observed accounts based on articles Stesser originally wrote for *The New Yorker*.

Liesbeth Sluiter, *The Mekong Currency* (International Books). An excellent, earthy account of green issues along the Mekong corridor, in Laos, Cambodia and Thailand.

John Tenhula, *Voices from Southeast Asia: The Refugee Experience in the United States* (Holmes & Meier). A moving collection of oral histories of Indochinese refugees, many of whom have relocated to the USA.

ACCOMMODATION

You'll rarely have a problem finding inexpensive accommodation in Southeast Asia, particularly if you stick to the main tourist areas. In most parts of the region, **electricity** is supplied at 220 volts, though socket type varies from country to country, so you should bring a travel plug with several adapters. Specific details are given in the "Accommodation" section at the beginning of each chapter. Power cuts are common, so bring a **torch**. There are hardly any coin-operated **laundries** in Southeast Asia, but nearly every guesthouse and hotel will wash your clothes for a reasonable price. Every guesthouse and hotel will **store luggage** for you, though sometimes only if you make a reservation for your anticipated return; major train stations and airports also have left-luggage facilities.

GUESTHOUSES AND HOTELS

The mainstay of the travellers' scene in Southeast Asia are the **guesthouses** (also known as bungalows, homestays or backpackers'), which provide inexpensive, basic accommodation specifically aimed at Western travellers and are usually good places to meet other people and pick up information. They are found in all major tourist centres and can be anything from a bamboo hut to a three-storey concrete block. A standard guesthouse room will be a simple place with one or two beds, hard mattresses, thin walls and a fan – some, but not all, have a window (usually screened against mosquitoes), and the cheapest ones share a bathroom. Always ask to see several rooms before opting for one, as standards can vary widely within the same establishment. For a **basic double room** with shared bathroom in a guesthouse that's in a capital city or tourist centre, rates start at about US$3 in Indonesia, US$4 in Laos, US$5 in Thailand and Cambodia, US$6 in the Philippines, US$7 in Malaysia and Vietnam; the highest prices are in Singapore (from US$12 a double) and Hong Kong (from US$25). In smaller towns and beach resorts, rates can be significantly lower, and prices everywhere are usually negotiable during low season. **Single rooms** tend to cost about two-thirds the price of a double, but many guesthouses also offer dormitory beds, which can cost as little as US$1 a night. More specific costings for accommodation are given in the introduction to each chapter. Some guesthouses also offer more comfortable rooms, with private bathroom, extra furnishings and even air-conditioning. In addition, the most clued-up places provide useful **facilities**, such as restaurants, travellers' noticeboards, safes for valuables, baggage-keeps, tour-operator desks and their own postes restantes. At most guesthouses **check-out time** is noon, which means that during high season you should arrive to check in at about 11.30am to ensure you get a room: few places will draw up a "waiting list", and they rarely take advance bookings unless they know you already.

ACCOMMODATION PRICE CODES

All **accommodation** reviewed in this guide has been graded according to the following price codes, in US dollars, which represent the cost of the cheapest double room available in high season. Where a price range is indicated, this means that the establishment offers rooms with varying facilities – as explained in the write-up. In cases where an establishment charges per bed the actual price is given.

① under $5	④ $15–20	⑦ $40–60
② $5–10	⑤ $20–25	⑧ $60–80
③ $10–15	⑥ $25–40	⑨ $80 and over

If you venture to towns that are completely off the tourist circuit, the cheapest places to stay are usually the bland and sometimes seedy **cheap urban hotels** located near bus and train stations. These places are designed for local businesspeople rather than tourists and often double as brothels; they tend to be rather soulless places, but are usually inexpensive and clean enough.

For around US$15–30 almost anywhere in Southeast Asia except Singapore and Hong Kong, you can get yourself a comfortable room in an upmarket guesthouse or small, **mid-range hotel**. These places are often very good value, offering pleasantly furnished rooms, with private hot-water bathroom, and quite possibly air-conditioning, a fridge and a TV as well. Some of these places also have a swimming pool. And for $60 you'll get the kind of **luxury** you'd be paying over $100 for in the West.

BATHROOMS

Many budget guesthouses and cheap hotels, and all mid-range accommodation in Southeast Asia will provide bathrooms with Western-style facilities such as sit-down toilets and showers (only the more expensive rooms have hot water and bathtubs). But in rural areas, on some beaches, and in some of the cheapest accommodation, you'll be using a **traditional Asian bathroom**, where you wash using the scoop-and-slosh method, sometimes known as a **mandi**, after the Indonesian word for "bath". This entails dipping a plastic scoop or bucket into a huge vat or basin of water (often built into the bathroom wall) and then sloshing the water over yourself. The basin functions as a water supply only and not a bath, so never get in it; all washing is done outside it and the basin should not be contaminated by soap or shampoo. If you're really far off the beaten track,

you may have to pump your own water from a well or even bathe in a stream. **Toilets** in these places will be Asian-style squat affairs, flushed manually with water scooped from the pail that stands alongside, so you'll have to provide **toilet paper** yourself.

VILLAGE ACCOMMODATION

In the more remote and rural parts of Southeast Asia, you may get the chance to stay in **village accommodation**, be it the headman's house, a family home, or a traditional longhouse. Accommodation in these places usually consists of a mattress on the floor in a communal room, perhaps with a blanket and mosquito net, but it's often advisable to take your own net and blanket or sleeping bag (which you may be able to rent locally). As a sign of appreciation, your hosts will welcome gifts, and a donation may be in order too.

CAMPING AND YOUTH HOSTELS

Because accommodation is so inexpensive in Southeast Asia, few travellers bother to take a tent with them, and anyway, there are hardly any campsites. The only times when you may need to **camp** are in the national parks or when trekking, and you may be able to rent gear locally – check the Guide for details. In theory you could also camp on most beaches, though almost no-one does as there are generally appealing bamboo huts to rent nearby.

As a rule, it's not worth becoming an HI member just for your trip to Southeast Asia, as there are so few **youth hostels** in the region, and prices don't necessarily compare favourably with other budget options. The one exception is Hong Kong, whose seven youth hostels offer the cheapest accommodation in the territory.

COMMUNICATIONS

Country-specific information on phone, mail and Internet facilities is given at the beginning of each chapter. What follows is general advice about **communications** across the region.

POSTE RESTANTE

Travellers can receive mail in any country in Southeast Asia via **poste restante**. The system is universally fairly efficient, but tends only to be available at the main post office in cities and backpackers' centres, not in small towns and villages. Most post offices hold letters for a maximum of one month, though some hold them for up to three. Mail should be addressed: Name (family name underlined or capitalized), Poste Restante, GPO, Town or City, Country. It will be filed by family name, though it's always wise to check under your first initial as well. To collect mail, you'll need to show your passport and may have to pay a tiny fee per item received. The poste restante system works best if you have given friends and relatives an outline of your itinerary, so that they can send mail in time for your anticipated arrival. Mail takes three to fourteen days to get from Europe, North America or Australia to Southeast Asia, depending on the destination. For a small fee you can arrange for poste restante mail to be forwarded from one GPO to another, though you usually have to apply for this service in person.

In certain major cities and upmarket resorts, holders of Amex credit cards or travellers' cheques can also make use of the **American Express** poste restante facility, which holds mail for up to sixty days: see individual city "Listings" in the Guide for details.

EMAIL

Email can make a good alternative to post office postes restantes, as Internet access is becoming increasingly widespread in Southeast Asia, and there are now cybercafés in even the poorest nations such as Cambodia and Laos, while backpackers' areas such as Thanon Khao San in Bangkok and Kuta in Bali have dozens of them. Fees are nearly always very low. Most travellers use the **free web-based email accounts** offered by Hotmail (*www.hotmail.com*) or Yahoo (*www.yahoo.com*), and all Internet cafés have these bookmarked. This is easy enough as all you have to do is log on to the sites and they basically hold your hand from there. You are very unlikely to be able to access your own home-based email account owing to the difficulty in getting an international line to your local ISP; even if you can get a line, the cost will be phenomenal. Some international ISPs, such as AOL and IBM, do have local numbers in Asian capital cities so you may get lucky if you're at a cybercafé in Bangkok or Singapore for example, but it's far less complicated and more efficient to organize a forwarding service from your home email account to your Hotmail or Yahoo account for the duration of your trip. For a list of useful Web sites, see "Southeast Asia online" on p.33.

PHONES

You should be able to **phone** home from any city or large town in Southeast Asia. The cheapest method is to make an **IDD call** (International Direct Dialling) from the national telecommunications office or post office, some of which are open 24 hours. You can also make IDD calls from private telephone offices and guesthouses – these places charge higher rates than the public phone offices, but are often more conveniently located. IDD calls from rooms in expensive hotels are usually subject to huge surcharges. In some countries, it's also possible to make IDD calls from public phone boxes, using high-value phone cards.

In phone centres where there's no facility for reverse-charge calls you can almost always get a "**call-back**". Ask the operator for a minimum (one-minute) call abroad and get the phone number of the place you're calling from; you can then be called back directly at the phone centre.

In addition to IDD, some big hotels, national telephone offices and airports also have **home-country**

IDD CODES

To phone abroad from the following countries, you must first dial the international access code, then the IDD country code, then the area code (usually without the first zero), then the subscriber number:

International access codes when dialling from:

Australia ☎0011	Ireland ☎010	Singapore ☎001
Brunei ☎01	Laos ☎00	Thailand ☎001
Cambodia ☎00	Macau ☎00	UK ☎00
Canada ☎011	Malaysia ☎007	USA ☎011
Hong Kong ☎001	New Zealand ☎00	Vietnam ☎00
Indonesia ☎00	Philippines ☎00	

IDD country codes

Australia ☎61	Indonesia ☎62	Philippines ☎63
Brunei ☎673	Ireland ☎353	Singapore ☎65
Cambodia ☎855	Laos ☎856	Thailand ☎66
Canada ☎1	Macau ☎853	UK ☎44
China ☎86	Malaysia ☎60	USA ☎1
Hong Kong ☎852	New Zealand ☎64	Vietnam ☎84

direct phones. With these, you simply press the appropriate button for the country you're ringing, and you'll be put through to the international switchboard of that country. You can **call collect** (reverse-charge calls), or the operator will debit you and you can settle with the cashier. Home-country direct phones are also useful if you have a chargecard. They do, however, cost more than IDD phones.

Many telephone companies offer **telephone chargecards** for use while travelling abroad. Using access codes for the particular country you are in, and personal PIN numbers, you can make calls from most hotel, public and private phones that will be charged to your own account. These cards are useful for minimizing hotel phone surcharges but rates aren't necessarily cheaper than calling from a public phone and can't compete with local off-peak rates. Not all phone cards work in all Southeast Asian countries, so contact the companies first: BT Charge Card, British Telecom (☎0800/345600 or 0800/345144, *www.charge-card.bt.com/*); Global Calling Card, AT&T (Dial ☎0800/890 011, then 888 641 6123 when you hear the AT&T prompt to be transferred to the Florida Call Centre); Global Calling Card, Cable & Wireless (☎0500/100505).

FAXES

Most telephone centres, major post offices and clued-up guesthouses and hotels offer a domestic and international **fax service**. Many of these places also do "fax restante". As with phone calls, the post offices usually offer the cheapest rates.

SHORT-WAVE RADIOS

With a shortwave radio, you can pick up the **BBC World Service**, **Radio Australia**, **Voice of America** and various other international stations on a variety of bands (depending on the time) right across the region. Times and wavelengths change frequently, so get hold of a recent schedule just before you travel. The BBC World Service Web site (*www.bbc.co.uk/worldservice*) carries current frequency details in a useful format that's designed to be printed out and carried with you.

CULTURAL HINTS

Although the peoples of Southeast Asia come from a huge variety of ethnic backgrounds and practise a spread of religions, they share many **social practices and taboos**, most of which are unfamiliar to Westerners. You are unlikely to get into serious trouble if you flout local mores, though you will get a much friendlier reception if you do your best to be sensitive, particularly when it comes to dress. Social and religious customs specific to each country are dealt with in the relevant chapters.

DRESS

Appearance is very important in Southeast Asian society, and dressing neatly is akin to showing respect. Clothing – or the lack of it – is what bothers Southeast Asians most about tourist behaviour. You need to **dress modestly** whenever you are outside a tourist resort, and in particular when entering temples, mosques, churches, important buildings and peoples' homes, and when dealing with people in authority, especially when applying for visa extensions. For women that means below-knee-length skirts or trousers, a bra and sleeved tops, for men, long trousers. "Immodest" clothing includes thongs, shorts, vests, and anything which leaves you with bare shoulders. Always take your **shoes** off when entering temples, pagodas, mosques and private homes. Most Southeast Asian people find **topless** and nude bathing extremely unpalatable. True, villagers often bathe publicly in rivers and pools, but there's an unspoken rule of invisibility under these circumstances; women wear sarongs, and men shorts or underwear, often using segregated areas. If you bathe alongside them, do as they do. If you wash your own clothes, hang out your **underwear** discreetly – women should take particular care, as women's undergarments are believed to have the power to render certain tattoos and amulets powerless.

VISITING TEMPLES, MOSQUES AND SHRINES

Besides dressing conservatively there are other conventions that must be followed when visiting **Buddhist temples**. Theoretically, **monks** are forbidden to have any close contact with women, which means, as a female, you mustn't sit or stand next to

a monk, even on a bus, nor brush against his robes, or hand objects directly to him. When giving something to a monk, the object should be placed on a nearby table or passed to a layman who will then hand it to the monk. All **Buddha images** are sacred, and should never be clambered over. When sitting on the floor of a monastery building that has a Buddha image, never point your feet in the direction of the image.

When visiting a **mosque**, women should definitely cover their shoulders and may also be asked to cover their heads as well (bring a scarf or shawl).

Many religions prohibit **women** from engaging in certain activities – or even entering a place of worship – during menstruation. If attending a **religious festival**, find out beforehand whether a dress code applies.

SOCIAL PRACTICES AND TABOOS

In Buddhist, Islamic and Hindu cultures, various parts of the body are accorded a particular status. The **head** is considered the most sacred part of the body and the **feet** the most unclean. This means that it's very rude to touch another person's head – even to affectionately ruffle a child's hair – or to point your feet either at a human being or at a sacred image. Be careful not to step over any part of people who are sitting or lying on the floor (or the deck of a boat), as this is also considered rude. If you do accidentally kick or brush someone with your feet, apologize immediately and smile as you do so. That way, even if the words aren't understood, your intent will be. On a more practical note, the **left hand** is used for washing after defecating, so Southeast Asians never use it to put food in their mouth, pass things or shake hands.

Public displays of sexual affection like kissing or cuddling are frowned upon across the region, though friends (rather than lovers) of the same sex often hold hands or hug in public. Most Asians dislike **confrontational behaviour**, and will rarely show irritation of any kind. Arguing, raising one's voice and showing anger are all considered extremely bad form. However bad things become, try to keep your temper, as tourists who get visibly rattled for whatever reason will be derided, and even baited further, rather than feared.

CRIME AND PERSONAL SAFETY

For the most part, travelling in Southeast Asia is safe and unthreatening, though, as in any unfamiliar environment, you should keep your wits about you. The most common hazard is opportunistic theft, which can easily be avoided with a few sensible precautions. Occasionally, political trouble flares in the region, as it has done recently in parts of Indonesia, so before you travel you may want to check the official government advice on international troublespots (see box below). Most experienced travellers find this official advice less helpful than that offered by other travellers – the online travellers' forums listed on p.34 are a particularly useful resource. In some countries, there are particular year-round dangers such as banditry (parts of Laos), kidnapping (southern Philippines), and unexploded ordnance (Laos, Cambodia, Vietnam); details of these and how to avoid them are described in the introduction to the relevant country.

THEFT AND HOW TO AVOID IT

As a tourist, you are an obvious target for opportunistic **thieves** (who may include your fellow travellers), so don't flash expensive cameras or watches around. Most people carry travellers' cheques, the bulk of their cash and important documents (airline tickets, credit cards and passport) under their clothing in an invisible **money belt** – the all-too-obvious bum-bags are easy to cut off in a crowd. It's a good idea to keep $100 cash, photocopies of the relevant pages of your passport, insurance details and travellers' cheque receipts separate from the rest of your valuables.

Ensure that **luggage** is lockable (gadgets to lock backpacks exist), and never keep anything important in outer pockets. A **padlock** and chain, or a cable lock, is useful for doors and windows at inexpensive guesthouses and beach bungalows, and for securing your pack on **buses**, where you're often separated from your belongings. If your pack is on the top of the bus, make sure it is attached securely, and keep an eye on it whenever the bus pulls into a bus station. Be especially aware of pickpockets on buses, who usually operate in pairs: one will distract you while another does the job. On **trains**, either cable lock your pack or put it under the bottom bench-seat, out of public view. Be wary of accepting food and drink from strangers on long overnight bus or train journeys: it may be drugged so as to knock you out while your bags are stolen.

Don't hesitate to check that doors and windows – including those in the bathroom – are secure before accepting **accommodation**. Some guesthouses and hotels have **safe-deposit boxes** or lockers, which

OFFICIAL ADVICE ON INTERNATIONAL TROUBLESPOTS

FCO Travel Advice Unit, Consular Division, 1 Palace St, London SW1E SHE (☎020/7238 4503, *www.fco.gov.uk*).

US State Department Travel Advisory Service, 2201 C St NW, Room 4811, Washington, DC 20520 (☎202/647 5225, *www.travel.state.gov*).

Canadian Department of Foreign Affairs and International Trade, 125 Sussex Drive, Ottawa, Ontario K1A 0G2 (☎1-800/387 3124, *www. dfait-maeci.gc.ca*).

Australian Department of Foreign Affairs and Trade, The RG Casey Building, John McEwan Crescent, Barton, Canberra, ACT 2600 (☎02/6261 9111, *www.dfat.gov.au*).

New Zealand Department of Foreign Affairs, Stafford House, 40 The Terrace, Wellington, Private Bag 18 901 (☎04/494 8500, *www.nz -high-com.org.sg*).

solve the problem of what to do with your valuables while you go swimming. The safest lockers are those which require your own padlock, as valuables sometimes get lifted by hotel staff. Padlock your luggage when leaving it in hotel or guesthouse rooms.

OTHER HAZARDS

Violent crime against tourists is not common in Southeast Asia, but it does occur. If you're unlucky enough to get **mugged**, never resist and, if you disturb a thief, raise the alarm rather than try to take them on – they're unlikely to harm you if you don't get in their way. Obvious precautions for travellers of either sex include locking accessible windows and doors at night, preferably with your own padlock, and not travelling alone at night in an unlicensed taxi, tuk-tuk or rickshaw. Think carefully about motorbiking alone in sparsely inhabited and politically sensitive border regions. If you're going hiking on your own for a day, inform hotel staff of your route, so they can look for you if you don't return when planned.

Con-artists try their luck with tourists all over Southeast Asia, but are usually fairly easy to spot. Always treat **touts** with suspicion – if they offer to take you to a great guesthouse/jewellery shop/untouristed village, you can be sure there'll be a huge commission in it for them, and you may end up being taken somewhere against your will. A variation on this theme involves taxi drivers assuring you that a major sight is closed for the day, so encouraging you to go with them on their own special tour.

Some, but by no means all, **travel agencies** in the backpackers' centres of Southeast Asia are fly-by-night operations. When you buy an airline ticket in Southeast Asia, don't hand over any money to the agent until you've contacted the airline directly to check that you're on the passenger list.

SEXUAL HARASSMENT

Southeast Asia is generally a safe region for **women** to travel around alone. Most people will simply be curious as to why you are on your own and the chances of encountering any threatening behaviour are rare. That said, it pays to take the normal precautions, especially **late at night** when there are few people around on the streets; after dark, take licensed taxis rather than cycle rickshaws and tuk-

tuks. It's as well to be aware that the Asian perception of Western female travellers is of sexual availability and promiscuity. This is particularly the case in the traditional Muslim areas of Indonesia, Malaysia, and the southern Philippines, where lone foreign women can get treated contemptuously however decently attired. Most Southeast Asian women **dress** modestly and it usually helps to do the same, avoiding skimpy shorts and vests, which are considered offensive. Some Asian women travelling with a white man have reported cases of serious harassment, from verbal abuse to rock throwing – something attributed to the tendency of Southeast Asian men to automatically label all such women as prostitutes.

REPORTING A CRIME

If you are a victim of theft or violent crime, you'll need a **police report** for insurance purposes. Try to take someone along with you to the police station to translate, though police will generally do their best to find an English speaker. Allow plenty of time for any involvement with the police, whose offices often wallow in bureaucracy; you may also be charged "administration fees" for enlisting their help, the cost of which is open to sensitive negotiations. You may also want to contact your **embassy** – see the "Listings" section of the nearest capital city for contact numbers. In the case of a medical emergency, you will also need to alert your **insurance company**: see p.31 for more details on this.

DRUGS

Drugs penalties are tough throughout the region – in many countries there's even the possibility of being sentenced to death – and you won't get any sympathy from consular officials. Beware of drug scams: either being shopped by a dealer or having substances slipped into your luggage – simple enough to perpetrate unless all fastenings are secured with padlocks. Drug enforcement squads in some countries are said to receive 25 percent of the market value of seized drugs, so are liable to exaggerate the amounts involved. If you are arrested, or end up on the wrong side of the law for whatever reason, you should ring the consular officer at your embassy immediately: see the "Listings" section of the nearest capital city for details.

GAY TRAVELLERS

Homosexuality is broadly accepted in Southeast Asia, if not always positively embraced. Most gay Asian men and women are private and discreet about being gay, generally pursuing a "don't ask, don't tell" understanding with their family. But, as it's more acceptable in Asia to show a modest amount of physical affection to friends of the same sex than to lovers of the opposite sex, gay couples generally encounter less hassle about being seen together than they might in the West.

Thailand has the most public and developed **gay scene** in Southeast Asia, and gay travellers are generally made to feel welcome there, with plenty of gay bars in Bangkok and other major tourist destinations. The Philippines, Indonesia, Cambodia, Laos and Vietnam all have less obvious gay communities, but they do exist and homosexuality is not illegal in any of them. The situation is less rosy in Malaysia, where Islamic laws can be used to punish gay sexual activity and travellers should be especially discreet – despite this there are gay bars and meeting places in Kuala Lumpur and Penang. You should also be careful in Singapore, where the government follows a repressive line on homosexuals, and sodomy is illegal.

A lot of gay visitors and expats have affairs with Asian men, and these **liaisons** tend to fall somewhere between holiday romances and paid sex. Few gay Asians in these circumstances would classify themselves as rent boys – they wouldn't sleep with someone they didn't like and most don't have sex for money – but they usually expect to be financially cared for by the richer man (food, drinks and entertainment expenses, for example), and some do make their living this way. The tourist-oriented gay sex industry is a tiny but highly visible part of Southeast Asia's gay scene, and is most obvious in Thailand.

For detailed **information** on the gay scene in Southeast Asia, check out the **Web site** created by Bangkok's Utopia gay and lesbian centre (*www.utopia-asia.com*), which is an excellent resource for gay travellers to all regions of Asia and has travellers reports on gay scenes across the region. Another worthwhile Web site is *www.viajartravel.com* which also carries reports from gay and lesbian travellers, and has a useful forum.

TRAVELLERS WITH DISABILITIES

Most Southeast Asian countries make few provisions for their own disabled citizens, which clearly affects **travellers with disabilities**. Pavements are usually high, uneven, and lacking dropped kerbs, and public transport is not wheelchair-friendly. On the positive side, however, most disabled travellers report that help is never in short supply, and wheelchair users with collapsible chairs may be able to take cycle rickshaws and tuk-tuks, balancing their chair in front of them. Also, services in much of Southeast Asia are very inexpensive for Western travellers, so you should be able to afford to hire a car or minibus with driver for a few days, stay at better equipped hotels, and even take some internal flights. You might also consider hiring a local tour guide to accompany you on sightseeing trips – a native speaker can facilitate access to temples and museums. Or perhaps book a package holiday – see the box opposite for useful contacts.

The two most-clued up destinations in Southeast Asia are **Hong Kong** and **Singapore**, both of which have some wheelchair-accessible public transport. Both countries publish brochures listing all amenities for people with disabilities: *A Guide for Physically Handicapped Visitors to Hong Kong* is distributed by the Hong Kong Tourist Association (see p.32); and *Access Singapore* is produced by the Singapore Council of Social Service, 11 Penang Lane, Singapore.

Before you travel, read your **insurance** small print carefully to make sure that people with an existing medical condition are not excluded. And use your travel agent to make your journey simpler: airlines can provide a wheelchair at the airport, for example. A **medical certificate** of your fitness to travel, provided by your doctor, is also extremely useful; some airlines or insurance companies may insist on it. Take a backup prescription including the generic name of

CONTACTS FOR TRAVELLERS WITH DISABILITIES

UK AND IRELAND

Access Travel, 6 The Hillock, Astley, Lancashire M29 7GW (☎01942/888844). Tour operator that can arrange flights, transfer and accommodation.

Disability Action Group, 2 Annadale Ave, Belfast BT7 3JH ☎028/9049 1011. Information about access for disabled travellers abroad.

Holiday Care, 2nd Floor, Imperial Building, Victoria Road, Horley, Surrey RH6 7PZ (☎01293/774535, Minicom ☎01293/776943, *www.freespace.virgin.net/hol-care*). Provides free lists of accessible accommodation.

Irish Wheelchair Association, Blackheath Drive, Clontarf, Dublin 3 (☎01/833 8241, *iwa@iol.ie*). A national voluntary organization.

RADAR (Royal Association for Disability and Rehabilitation), 12 City Forum, 250 City Rd, London EC1V 8AF (☎020/7250 3222, Minicom ☎020/7250 4119, *www.radar.org.uk*). A good source of advice on holidays and travel abroad. They produce *Getting There* on travel abroad (£5 inc p&p).

Tripscope, Brentford Community Resource Centre, Alexandra House, Brentford High Street, Brentford, Middlesex TW8 0NE (☎08457/585 641, *www.justmobility.co.uk/tripscope*). This registered charity provides a national telephone information service offering free advice on international transport.

NORTH AMERICA

The First Access Travel Group, 239 Commercial St, Malden, MA 02148 (☎1/800 557 2047, TTY 617/397 8610). Current information for disabled travellers.

Directions Unlimited, 123 Greenlane, Bedford Hills, NY 10507 (☎914/241 1700). Travel agency specializing in custom tours for people with disabilities.

Mobility International USA, PO Box 10767, Eugene, OR 97440 (Voice and TDD: ☎541/343-1284, *www.miusa.org*). Information and referral services, access guides, tours and exchange programs. Annual membership $35.

Society for the Advancement of Travel for the Handicapped (SATH), 347 5th Ave, Suite 610, New York, NY 10016 (☎212/447 7284, *sath-travel@aol.com*). Non-profit travel-industry referral service that passes queries on to its members as appropriate; allow plenty of time for a response.

Travel Information Service (☎215/456 9603). Telephone information and referral service.

Twin Peaks Press, Box 129, Vancouver, WA 98666 (☎360/694 2462 or 1-800/637 2256). Publisher of the *Directory of Travel Agencies for the Disabled*, listing more than 370 agencies worldwide; *Travel for the Disabled*; the *Directory of Accessible Van Rentals* and *Wheelchair Vagabond*, loaded with personal tips.

AUSTRALIA AND NEW ZEALAND

ACROD (Australian Council for the Rehabilitation of the Disabled), PO Box 60, Curtin ACT 2605 (☎02/6282 4333); 24 Cabarita Road, Cabarita NSW 2137 (☎02/9743 2699). Provides lists of travel agencies and tour operators for people with disabilities.

Barrier Free Travel, 36 Wheatley St, North Bellingen, NSW 2454 (☎02/6655 1733).

Independent consultant – draws up individual itineraries for people with disabilities for a fee.

Disabled Persons Assembly, PO Box 10, 138 The Terrace, Wellington (☎04/472 2626). Also provides lists of travel agencies and tour operators for people with disabilities.

ONLINE RESOURCES

Access-able Travel Source (*www. access-able.com*) and **Global Access** (*www.geocities.com/Paris/1502/index*). Useful sites with links to travel agents and tour operators in the US, a bulletin board where travellers swap information and advice, and a section for travellers' tales.

any drugs in case of emergency, and carry spares of any equipment that might be hard to find.

Make sure that you take sufficient supplies of any **medications**, and – if they're essential – carry the complete supply with you whenever you travel (including on buses and planes), in case of loss or theft. Carry a doctor's letter about your drug prescriptions with you when passing through airport customs, as this will ensure you don't get hauled up for narcotics transgressions. If your medication has to be kept cool, buy a thermal insulation bag and a couple of freezer blocks before you leave home. That way you can refreeze one of the two blocks every day while the other is in use; staff in most hotels, restaurants and bars should be happy to let you use their freezer compartment for a few hours. You may also be able to store your medication in hotel and guesthouse refrigerators.

WORK AND STUDY

As Southeast Asia is such an inexpensive region to travel through, most travellers on longish trips save enough money to get them as far as Australia, where temporary jobs are both more plentiful and more lucrative. **Casual work** in Southeast Asia tends to be thin on the ground and is unlikely to improve your bank balance much – though it's quite possible to earn enough to keep yourself ticking over for a few extra weeks. The most common jobs are listed below, of which only teaching English may require some qualifications. Depending on the job, and the employer, you might get away with working on your tourist visa for a month or two; to work any longer entails regular "visa runs" across the nearest border. For more official employment you'll need a working visa; contact the relevant embassy, listed on pp.20–21.

For long-term **volunteer placements** in Southeast Asia, apply to VSO (Voluntary Service Overseas; ☎0181/780 2266) in the UK; Australia's Overseas Service Bureau (☎03/9279 1788); or CARE Australia (☎1800/020046), which employs people on a contract basis for long-term development work in areas including agriculture and natural resources, healthcare and business development.

It's also possible to do short, traveller-oriented **courses** in local arts, crafts and cuisines, of which the most popular are: traditional music and dance (Indonesia); batik (Indonesia and Malaysia); cookery (Thailand and Indonesia); massage (Thailand); and meditation (Thailand and Indonesia). Most capital cities and some other big towns and travellers' centres also offer short- and long-term language courses. Details of all these are given in the relevant chapters of the Guide.

SHORT-TERM JOBS

For short-term casual work in any country, look in the local English-language press and on guesthouse noticeboards, or ask at language schools and in bars.

Teaching English If you have teaching qualifications, you could try the British Council and American University (AUA) schools, as well as the universities. Cambodia (Phnom Penh); Hong Kong; Indonesia (Bali and Jakarta); Singapore; Thailand (Bangkok, Chiang Mai and Sukhothai); Vietnam.

Bar and restaurant work Particularly in Australian and English pubs. Anyone can do this, but the pay and conditions are likely to be poor. Hong Kong; Singapore.

Film extra Often just a question of being in the right place at the right time. Usually advertised on lampposts in backpackers' areas.

Hostess, modelling and escort work It helps if you have a portfolio with you – and if you're exceptionally attractive. Hong Kong.

Dive instructor You will need relevant experience and certificates from one of the internationally accredited dive organizations. Alternatively, you could take your dive instructor or dive master course while you're on the road. Indonesia; Malaysia; the Philippines; Thailand.

Import/export To make any significant money from this involves a lot of time and patience, as well as a local contact to oversee packing and shipping. However, things oriental continue to be very popular in the West, so you can be sure there's a market there somewhere. Indonesia; Thailand.

Smuggling Guesthouse noticeboards sometimes advertise for people to take items – electronic gear and the like – to other countries, where it can be sold at a premium. You'll get the air ticket, and maybe paid too, but if customs stamp the gear in your passport you'll be expected to have it when you leave the country you've brought it into – and if you don't know exactly what it is you're taking, or haven't checked the goods, it could well be drugs. Not at all recommended.

RELIGIONS OF SOUTHEAST ASIA

Religion pervades every aspect of life in most Southeast Asian communities, dictating social practices to a much greater extent than in the West. All the world's major faiths are represented in the region, but characteristic across much of Southeast Asia is the syncretic nature of belief, so that many Buddhists, Hindus and Muslims incorporate animist rituals into their daily devotions as well as occasional elements of other major faiths.

BUDDHISM

Buddhists follow the teachings of Gautama Buddha who, in his five-hundredth incarnation, was born in present-day Nepal as **Prince Gautama Siddhartha,** to a wealthy family some time during the sixth century BC. At an early age Siddhartha renounced his life of luxury to seek the ultimate deliverance from worldly suffering and strive to reach **Nirvana,** an indefinable, blissful state. After several years, Siddhartha attained enlightenment while sitting under the famous riverside bodhi tree at Bodh Gaya in India, and then devoted the rest of his life to teaching the Middle Way that leads to Nirvana.

His **philosophy** built on the Hindu theory of perpetual reincarnation in the pursuit of perfection, introducing the notion that desire is the root cause of all suffering and can be extinguished only by following the eightfold path or Middle Way. This **Middle Way** is essentially a highly moral mode of life that includes all the usual virtues like compassion, respect and moderation, and eschews vices such as self-indulgence and anti-social behaviour. But the key to it all is

an acknowledgement that the physical world is impermanent and ever-changing, and that all things – including the self – are therefore not worth craving. Only by pursuing a condition of complete detachment can human beings transcend earthly suffering.

In practice most Buddhists aim only to be **reborn** higher up the incarnation scale rather than set their sights on the ultimate goal of Nirvana. Each reincarnation marks a move up a kind of ladder, with animals at the bottom, women figuring lower down than men, and monks coming at the top. The rank of the reincarnation is directly related to the good and bad actions performed in the previous life, which accumulate to determine one's **karma** or destiny – hence the obsession with "**making merit**". Merit-making can be done in all sorts of ways, from giving alms to a monk to attending a Buddhist service or donating money to the neighbourhood temple, and most festivals are essentially communal merit-making opportunities. For a Buddhist man, temporary ordination is an important way of accruing merit not only for himself but also for his mother and sisters.

SCHOOLS OF BUDDHISM

The Buddha himself passed into Nirvana at the age of eighty in 543 BC, after which his doctrine spread relatively quickly across India. His teachings, the *Tripitaka*, were written down in the Pali language – a derivative of Sanskrit – in a form that became known as **Theravada** or "The Doctrine of the Elders". Sometimes referred to as the "southern school" of Buddhism owing to its geographic spread via Indian trade routes, the Theravada school of Buddhism is prevalent in **Thailand, Laos and Cambodia** as well as in Sri Lanka and Burma. In essence, Theravada Buddhism is an ascetic form of the faith, based on the principle that each individual is wholly responsible for his or her own accumulation of merit or sin and subsequent enlightenment.

The other main school of Buddhism practised in Southeast Asia is **Mahayana Buddhism** (or "northern school"), which is current in **Vietnam**, and in **ethnic Chinese communities** throughout the region, as well as in China itself, and in Japan and Korea. The ideological rift between the Theravada and Mahayana Buddhists is as vast as the one that divides Catholicism and Protestantism. Mahayana Buddhism attempts to make Buddhism more accessible to the average devotee, easing the struggle towards enlightenment with a pantheon of Buddhist saints or **bodhisattva** who have postponed their own entry into Nirvana in order to work for the salvation of all humanity. The most well-known *bodhisattva* is Avalokitesvara, usually worshipped as the Goddess of Mercy, variously known as Quan Am, Kuan Im, Kuan Yin and Kwun Yum.

CHINESE RELIGIONS

The **Chinese communities of Singapore, Hong Kong, Macau, Malaysia, Vietnam and Thailand** generally adhere to a system of belief that fuses Mahayana Buddhist, Taoist and Confucianist tenets, alongside the all-important ancestor worship.

ANCESTOR WORSHIP

One of the oldest cults practised among both city dwellers and hilltribespeople who migrated into Southeast Asia from China is that of **ancestor worship**, based on the fundamental principles of filial piety and of obligation to the past, present and future generations. Practices vary, but all believe that the spirits of deceased ancestors have the ability to affect the lives of their living descendants, rewarding those who remember them with offerings, but causing upset if neglected. At funerals and subsequent anniversaries, paper money and other **votive offerings** (including television sets and cars) are burnt, and special food is regularly placed on the ancestral altar. Traditionally, it is the responsibility of the oldest, usually male, member of the family to tend the altar and keep the ancestors abreast of all important family events.

CONFUCIANISM

The teachings of **Confucius** provide a guiding set of moral and ethical principles based on piety, loyalty,

humanitarianism and familial devotion, which permeate every aspect of Chinese life. Confucius is the Latinized name of K'ung-Fu-Tzu, who was born into a minor aristocratic family in China in 551 BC and worked for many years as a court official, where he observed the nature of power and the function of government at close quarters. At the age of 50, Confucius packed it all in and for the next twenty years wandered the country spreading his ideas on social and political reform. His central tenet was the importance of **correct behaviour** and **loyal service**, reinforced by ceremonial rites whereby the ruler maintains authority through good example rather than force. Important qualities to strive for are selflessness, respectfulness, sincerity and non-violence, and great emphasis is placed on observing ancient rituals such as making offerings to heaven and to ancestors. Confucian **teachings** were handed down in the Analects, but he is also credited with editing the Six Classics, among them the Book of Changes (*I Ching*) and the Book of Ritual (*Li Chi*).

After the death of Confucius in 478 BC the doctrine was developed further by his disciples, and by the first century AD, Confucianism had absorbed elements of Taoism and evolved into a **state ideology** whereby kings ruled under the Mandate of Heaven. Social stability was maintained through a fixed hierarchy of interdependent relationships encapsulated in the notion of filial piety. Thus children must obey their parents without question, wives their husbands, students their teacher, and subjects their ruler.

TAOISM

Taoism is based on the **Tao-te-ching**, the "Book of the Way", traditionally attributed to **Lao Tzu** ("Old Master"), who is thought to have lived in China in the sixth century BC. A philosophical movement, it advocates that people follow a central path or truth, known as *Tao* or "The Way", and cultivate an understanding of the nature of things. The Tao emphasizes effortless action, intuition and spontaneity; it cannot be taught, nor can it be expressed in words, but can be embraced by virtuous, compassionate and nonviolent behaviour. Central to the Tao is the duality inherent in nature, a tension of complimentary opposites defined as **yin** and **yang**, the male and female principles. Yang is male, the sun, active and orthodox; yin is female, the earth, flexible, passive and instinctive. Harmony is the balance between the two, and experiencing that harmony is the Tao.

In its pure form Taoism has no gods, but in the first century AD it corrupted into an organized religion venerating a deified Lao Tzu, and developed highly complex **rituals**, incorporating magic, mysticism, superstition and the use of geomancy ("feng shui") to ensure harmony between man and nature. Ancient spirit worship, the cult of ancestors and the veneration of legendary or historic figures all fused happily with the Taoist idea of a universal essence. The vast, eclectic pantheon of Taoist **gods and immortals** is presided over by the Jade Emperor, who is assisted by three ministers: the southern star, the north star, and the God of the Hearth. Then there is a collection of immortals, genies and guardian deities, including legendary and historic warriors, statesmen and scholars. Confucius is also honoured as a Taoist saint.

ISLAM

Islam is the youngest of all the major religions, and in Southeast Asia is practised mainly in **Indonesia, Malaysia, Singapore and Brunei**. It all started with **Mohammed** (570–630AD), an illiterate semi-recluse from Mecca in Arabia, who began, at the age of 40, to receive messages from Allah (God) via the Archangel Gabriel. On these revelations Mohammed began to build a new religion: Islam or "Submission", as the faith required people to submit to God's will; his followers were known as the Muslims, or "Surrendered Men". Islam quickly gained in popularity not least because its revolutionary concepts of equality in subordination to Allah freed people from the feudal Hindu caste system which had previously dominated parts of the region.

The Islamic religion is founded on the **Five Pillars**, the essential tenets revealed by Allah to Mohammed and collected in the **Koran**, the holy book which Mohammed dictated before he died. The first is that all Muslims should profess their faith in Allah with the phrase "There is no God but Allah and Mohammed is his prophet". It is this sentence that is intoned by the muezzin five times a day when calling the faithful to prayer. The act of praying is the second pillar. Praying can be done anywhere, and not just in a mosque, though Muslims should always face Mecca when praying, cover the head, and ritually wash feet and hands. The third pillar demands that the faithful should always give a percentage of their income to charity, whilst the fourth states that all Muslims must observe the fasting month of **Ramadan**. This is the ninth month of the Muslim lunar calendar, when the majority of Muslims fast from the break of dawn to dusk, and also abstain from drinking and smoking. The reason for the fast is to intensify awareness of the plight of the poor and to identify with the hungry. The fifth pillar demands

that every Muslim should make a pilgrimage to Mecca at least once in their lifetime. To many Westerners, it comes as something of a surprise to find how close the Islamic faith is to Christianity: the ideas of heaven and hell and the creation story are much the same, and many of the prophets – Abraham, Noah, Moses – appear in both faiths. Indeed, Jesus is an Islamic prophet too, although Muslims believe that Mohammed is the only true prophet.

HINDUISM

Hinduism was introduced to Southeast Asia by Indian traders more than a thousand years ago, and spread across the region by the Khmers of Cambodia who left a string of magnificent castle-temples throughout northeast Thailand, Laos and most strikingly at Angkor in Cambodia. The most active contemporary Hindu communities live in **Singapore** and **Malaysia**, and the Indonesian island of **Bali** is also a very vibrant Hindu enclave, though the Hinduism here is a very particular blend of Hindu doctrine and local animist practices.

The central tenet of Hinduism is the belief that life is a series of rebirths and reincarnations that eventually leads to spiritual release. The aim of every Hindu is to attain **enlightenment** (*moksa*), which brings with it the union of the individual and the divine, and liberation from the endless painful cycle of death and rebirth. *Moksa* is only attainable by pure souls, and this can take hundreds of lifetimes to attain. Hindus believe that everybody is reincarnated according to their **karma**, this being a kind of account book which registers all the good and bad deeds performed in the past lives of a soul. Karma is closely bound up with caste and the notion that an individual should accept rather than challenge their destiny.

A whole variety of **deities** is worshipped, the most ubiquitous being Brahma, Vishnu (Wisnu) and Shiva, each of whom has different roles and is associated with specific colours and animals. **Brahma** is the Creator, represented by the colour red and often depicted riding on a bull. As the Preserver, **Vishnu** is associated with life-giving waters; he rides the garuda (half-man, half-bird) and is honoured by the colour black. Wisnu also has several avatars, including Buddha – a neat way of incorporating Buddhist elements into the Hindu faith – and Rama, hero of the Ramayana story. **Siwa**, the Destroyer or, more accurately, the Dissolver, is associated with death and rebirth, and with the colour white. He is sometimes represented by a phallic pillar or lingam. He is the father of the elephant-headed deity **Ganesh**, gener-

THE RAMAYANA

The epic poem known as the **Ramayana** is essentially a morality tale, a dramatization in around 24,000 verses of the eternal conflict between the forces of good and the forces of evil. It was originally written in India in the fourth century BC, from where it spread to all the Hindu-influenced countries of Southeast Asia (namely Thailand, Cambodia, Laos, Malaysia and Indonesia), inspiring countless interpretations by local writers, artists, dramatists, theologians and sculptors. Even in countries where Buddhism has since become the dominant faith, the *Ramayana* still provides moral and practical lessons, and continues to be the most popular subject for traditional dance performances and shadow-puppet shows, as well as being turned into films and comic strips.

The forces of good in the *Ramayana* are represented by Rama and his friends. **Rama** is the hero of the piece, a refined and dutiful young man, handsome, strong and courageous, who also happens to be an avatar of the god Vishnu. Rama's wife **Sita** epitomizes the Hindu ideals of womanhood – virtue, fidelity and love – while Rama's brother **Laksmana** (also known as Lakshaman) is a symbol of fraternal loyalty and youthful courage. The other important member of the Rama camp is **Hanuman**, the general of the monkey army, a wily and athletic ape who is unfailingly loyal to his allies. On the opposing side, the forces of evil are mainly represented by the demon king **Ravana**, a lustful and devious leader whose retainers are giants and devils.

The **story** begins with Rama, the eldest son of the king, being banished to the forests for thirteen years, having been cheated out of his rightful claim to the throne by a scheming stepmother.

Sita and Laksmana accompany him, and together the trio have various encounters with sages, giants and seductresses.

The most crucial event in the epic is the **abduction of Sita** by Ravana, a crime that inspires the generally easy-going and rather unwarlike Rama to wage battle against his avowed enemy. A favourite subject for dance performances, puppet shows, paintings and carvings, the episode starts with Sita catching sight of a beautiful golden deer and imploring her husband Rama to catch it and bring it back for her. The golden deer turns out to be a decoy planted by Ravana, and the demon king duly swoops down to abduct Sita as soon as Rama and Laksmana go off to chase the animal. The distraught Rama determines to get Sita back and, together with Laksmana, he sets off in the direction of Ravana's kingdom. En route he meets Hanuman, the monkey general, who agrees to help him by sneaking into Sita's room at Ravana's palace and **giving her Rama's ring** (another popular theme of pictures and dramas). Eventually, Rama, Laksmana, Hanuman and his monkey army all arrive at Ravana's palace and, following a big battle, Sita is rescued and Ravana done away with.

There's a fabulous series of painted Ramayana **murals** in the compound of the Grand Palace in Bangkok (see p.853), featuring some very lively illustrations of the magic tricks and fantastical beings involved in the story. Many of the same episodes appear in sculptural reliefs at the magnificent Khmer temples in Angkor (see p.110), and along the walls of the massive Prambanan temple complex near Yogyakarta in Indonesia (see p.246). Epic performances of the Ramayana ballet are regularly staged at Prambanan too.

ally worshipped as the remover of obstacles. Hindu gods and legends live on in the popular arts like *wayang kulit* (shadow plays), and in the epic Ramayana story, which continues to inspire countless dances, paintings and sculptures throughout Southeast Asia.

ANIMISM

Animism is the belief that all living things – including plants and trees – and some non-living natural features such as rocks and waterfalls, have **spirits**.

It is practised right across Southeast Asia, by everyone from the Dayaks of Sarawak and the hilltribes of Laos, to the citydwellers of Bangkok and Singapore, though rituals and beliefs vary significantly. As with Hinduism, the animistic faiths teach that it is necessary to live in harmony with the spirits; disturb this harmonious balance, by upsetting a spirit for example, and you risk bringing misfortune upon yourself, your household or your village. For this reason, animists consult, or at least consider the spirits before almost everything they do, and you'll often see small offerings of flowers or food left by a tree or river to appease the spirits that live within. Spirits can also be called upon for favours: to cure sickness, for example, or to bring rain or guarantee a fine harvest. In villages, witch doctors traditionally act as the go-between linking the temporal and spirit world.

GLOSSARY OF RELIGIOUS TERMS

Ancestral Hall main room or hall in a Chinese temple complex where the ancestral records are kept, and where devotions take place.

apsara a female divinity, commonly portrayed in Khmer temple architecture.

bodhisattva in Mahayana Buddhism, an inter-mediary who has chosen to forgo Buddhist nir-vana to work for the salvation of all humanity.

bot main sanctuary of a Buddhist temple in Thailand.

Brahma one of the Hindu Trinity: "the Creator".

Cao Daism indigenous Vietnamese religion, essentially a hybrid of Buddhism, Taoism and Confucianism.

chedi reliquary tower in Thai Buddhist temple.

devaraja god-king; a Khmer concept of divine kingship.

dvarapala guardian divinities at doors and gate-ways of Khmer ruins.

feng shui literally "wind and water", the Chinese art of geomancy.

Ganesh Hindu elephant-headed deity.

garuda mythical Hindu creature, half-man and half-bird.

gopura a large and elaborate Khmer temple doorway.

Indra Hindu king of the gods.

jataka mythological tales of the Buddha's previ-ous 500 lives.

lingam phallic-shaped stone representation of Shiva.

Mahabharata lengthy Hindu epic describing the battles between good and evil.

makara a mythical water beast, commonly depicted in Khmer temples.

mesjid mosque.

mondop small, square temple building in Thailand, housing minor images or religious texts.

naga a benevolent mythical water serpent in Buddhism and Hinduism.

Pha In Hindu god Indra.

phi spirit or ghost.

Prang central tower in a Khmer temple.

prasat Khmer temple complex or central shrine.

preah pertaining to anything sacred or holy.

Ramayana Hindu epic about the battles between good and evil.

Shivalinga see *lingam*.

sim building in a monastery housing the main Buddha image.

stupa a Buddhist structure built to contain holy relics.

that the Lao word for "stupa".

viharn Buddhist temple assembly hall for the laity.

wat Buddhist temple.

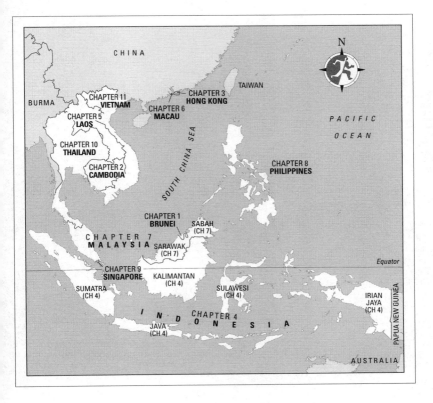

CHAPTER ONE

BRUNEI

Introduction

The tiny but thriving Islamic Sultanate of **Brunei** perches on the northwestern coast of Borneo, completely encircled by the East Malaysian state of Sarawak. It has a population of 323,000, nearly seventy percent of which is made up of Malays and indigenes from the larger ethnic groups like the Murut and Dusun; the rest are Chinese, Indians, smaller indigenous tribes and expats. They enjoy a quality of life that is quite unparalleled in Southeast Asia, with the literacy rate a staggering 93.7 percent of the population. Education and healthcare are free; houses, cars, and even pilgrimages to Mecca are subsidized; taxation on personal income is unheard of; and the average per capita salary is around US$19,000. The explanation is simple: oil, first discovered in 1903 at the site of what is now the town of Seria.

The sultanate's full name is *Negara Brunei Darussalam*, the "Country of Brunei, the Abode of Peace", and peaceful is a fair, if rather polite, description of the state. Nightlife is almost nonexistent, and liquor extremely hard to get hold of since a ban in 1991. Until recently, the Sultan viewed the development of a **tourist industry** as unnecessary, and there's been little for visitors to do in Brunei. However, things are gradually changing. Brunei is becoming **less introspective** and looking more to the West. You can see the results in the building of smart plazas with their requisite coffee bars in the capital Bandar. The authorities are starting to promote Brunei's natural resources, and sections of pristine rainforest like **Ulu Temburong National Park** in eastern Brunei are opening up to visitors. The lack of accommodation outside the capital is being tackled by the recently formed **homestay programme** – where travellers overnight in Malay and Murut kampungs (villages) and Iban longhouses. This opportunity to share in rural life is gaining popularity. Add to this the fact that the capital **Bandar Seri Begawan** is an attractive city, with two exquisite mosques and the fascinating **Kampung Ayer stilt village**, and a stop-off in Brunei is a more appealing proposition than ever before.

That said, the problem remains that Brunei is more **expensive** than neigbouring Malaysia or even Singapore – hotel prices in the capital are at least double those in nearby Kota Kinabalu or Miri. Most travellers still end up in Brunei either because of an enforced stopover on a Royal Brunei Airlines flight, or as a stepping stone to either Sabah or Sarawak. In the latter case, however, it can work out cheaper to take an internal MAS flight between Miri and Labuan rather than bussing it through Brunei.

Brunei's **climate**, like that of neighbouring Sabah and Sarawak, is hot and humid, with average temperatures in the high twenties throughout the year. Lying 440km north of the equator, Brunei has a tropical weather system, so even if you visit outside the official wet season (usually November to February) there's every chance that you'll see some rain.

Overland and sea routes into Brunei

Boats to Brunei depart daily from Lawas (see p.649) and Limbang (see p.653) in northern Sarawak, and from Pulau Labuan (see p.660), itself connected by boat to Kota Kinabalu in Sabah. From Miri (see p.648) in Sarawak, several **buses** travel daily to Kuala Belait, in the far western corner of Brunei. The overland route from Sabah to Brunei necessitates taking a bus to Lawas and on to Bangar in the Temburong District, from where it's only a short boat trip to Bandar.

Entry requirements and visa extension

British nationals, Singaporeans and Malaysians don't need a **visa** for visits of up to thirty days; US citizens can stay up to three months without a visa; Canadian, French, Dutch, German, Swedish, Norwegian, Swiss and Belgian citizens can stay for fourteen days without a visa; all other visitors require visas, which can be obtained at local Brunei diplomatic missions (see p.20) or, failing that, at a British consulate. Visas are normally valid for two weeks, but renewable in Brunei. Officials may ask to see either an onward ticket, or proof of sufficient funds to cover your stay, when you arrive.

Although Brunei is a **dry state**, all non-Muslim travellers are permitted to bring in twelve cans of beer or two bottles of liquor (wine or spirits).

AIRPORT DEPARTURE TAX

Bruneian airport departure tax is B$5 for flights to East Malaysia; and B$12 to West Malaysia and Singapore and all other destinations.

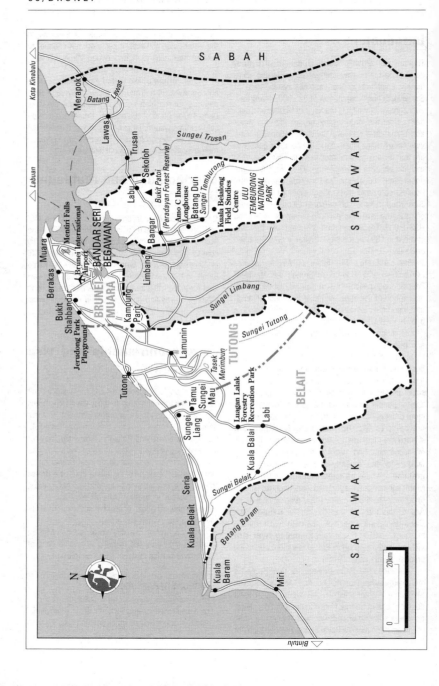

Money and costs

Brunei's **currency** is the Bruneian dollar, which is divided into 100 cents; you'll see it written as B$, or simply as $. The Bruneian dollar has parity with the Singapore dollar and both are legal tender in either country. Notes come in $1, $5, $10, $50, $100, $500, $1000 and $10,000 denominations; coins come in denominations of 1, 5, 10, 20 and 50 cents. The current **exchange rate** is B$3 to the pound or B$4.50 to the US dollar. There are two Malaysian ringgit to one Bruneian dollar.

Sterling and US dollar **travellers' cheques** can be cashed at banks, licensed moneychangers and some hotels. Major **credit cards** are accepted in most hotels and large shops. Banks will **advance cash** against major credit cards, and with American Express, Visa and Mastercard, you can withdraw money from automatic teller machines (ATMs). You can get **money wired** to you (see "Basics" p.23) via any of the major banks in the capital.

There's only one budget place to stay in the capital and if you can't get in there, you're looking at around £20/US$30 minimum per night in a hotel, which means an average **daily budget** in Brunei is likely to start at around £25–30/US$37–45.

Information and maps

As Brunei still doesn't have a Ministry for Tourism you won't see any **tourist offices** in Bandar, apart from a small information booth at the airport. This leaves **local tour operators** as the city's – and country's – sole source of information. Sunshine Borneo Tours and Travel, 2nd Floor, Unit 1, Block C, Abdul Razak Complex, Gadong, Bandar (☎02/441791), has dozens of leaflets on attractions in the city and around the state. They also run numerous tours, including a three-day excursion to Brunei's Temburong District (B$200). Owner Anthony Chieng can offer good insights into travelling in the state. Borneo Outdoors (☎02/454764), 3b Kiarong Apts, Simpang, also organizes trips, while AJ Wildman Tours, PO Box, Salambigar (☎02/786987), has information on the homestay programme at Iban longhouses in Temburong.

Nelles East Malaysia **map** includes the best country map of Brunei, while the Bruneian government publication, *Explore Brunei*, includes a reasonable map of Bandar city centre.

Getting around

If you intend to explore Brunei in some depth, you've got little option but to **rent a car**. South of the main coastal roads, bus services are nonexistent, while taxis are expensive. Apart from short hops across Sungei Brunei in Bandar's water taxis, the only time you're likely to use a boat is to get to Temburong District (see p.69.), which is cut off from the rest of Brunei by the Limbang area of Sarawak.

Accommodation

Accommodation in Brunei is much more expensive than in Sabah and Sarawak. On the whole, you can expect to pay double what you would pay in Malaysia. Accommodation outside Bandar is limited, although recently, the government has launched a **homestay programme**, where travellers stay in Malay and Murut villages and Iban longhouses. **Electricity** in Brunei is supplied at 220 volts.

Food and drink

The **food** in Brunei is very similar to that of Malaysia; see the Malaysia "Food and drink" section for further details. Alcoholic **drink** is illegal.

ACCOMMODATION PRICE CODES

All **accommodation** reviewed in this guide has been graded according to the following price codes, in US dollars, which represent the cost of the cheapest double room available in high season. Where a price range is indicated, this means that the establishment offers rooms with varying facilities – as explained in the write-up. In cases where an establishment charges per bed the actual price is given.

① under $5	④ $15–20	⑦ $40–60
② $5–10	⑤ $20–25	⑧ $60–80
③ $10–15	⑥ $25–40	⑨ $80 and over

Communications

Postcards to anywhere in the world cost 30c, aerogrammes 45c; overseas **letters** cost 90c for every 10g. Local calls cost 10c from phone boxes and are free from private **phones**. International (IDD) calls can be made through hotels, in booths at Bandar's Telekom office (see p.68) or from card phones. Phone cards (B$5, B$10, B$20 or B$50) can be bought from the Telekom office and post offices. To **phone abroad** from Brunei, dial ☎01 + IDD country code (see p.40) + area code minus first 0 + subscriber number. There are a number of **cybercafés** around Bandar. Charges are generally B$5 per minute.

TIME DIFFERENCES
Brunei is eight hours ahead of London (GMT), sixteen hours ahead of Los Angeles, thirteen ahead of New York, and two hours behind Sydney.

Opening hours and festivals

Government offices in Brunei **open** Mon–Thurs & Sat 7.45am–12.15pm & 1.30–4.30pm; shopping centres open daily 10am–10pm. **Banking hours** are Mon–Fri 9am–3pm and Sat 9–11am. **Post offices** are open Monday to Thursday and Saturday 7.45am–4.30pm; see p.68 for details of the GPO in Bandar.

Most of Brunei's **festivals** have no fixed dates, but change annually according to the lunar calendar,

---

PUBLIC HOLIDAYS
January 1: New Year's Day
January/February: Chinese New Year
February/March: Hari Raya Haji
February 23: National Day
March/April: First Day of Hijrah
May/June: Birthday of the Prophet Mohammed
June 1: Armed Forces' Day
July 15: Sultan's Birthday
October: Israk Mikraj
November: First day of Ramadan
November/December: Anniversary of Revelation of the Koran
December: Hari Raya Aidilfitri
December 25: Christmas Day

---

so check with the tourist office. During **Ramadan**, Muslims spend the ninth month of the Islamic calendar (Jan–April) fasting in the daytime; during this time it is culturally sensitive for tourists not to eat or smoke blatantly in public during daylight hours. The festival celebrations of most interest to tourists include **Brunei National Day** (Feb 23), when the Sultan and 35,000 other Bruneians watch parades and fireworks at the Sultan Hassanal Bolkiah National Stadium, just outside Bandar Seri Begawan; **Hari Raya Aidilfitri**, the end of the Ramadan fasting period (March/April), which is marked by the annual opening of Brunei's royal palace to the public; **Brunei Armed Forces Day** (June 1), when Bandar's square hosts parades and displays; and His Majesty the **Sultan of Brunei's Birthday Celebrations** (July 15), which kicks off a fortnight of parades, lantern processions, traditional sports competitions and fireworks.

Cultural hints

Brunei broadly shares the same attitudes to dress and social taboos as other Southeast Asian cultures; see "Basics", p.41 for details.

Crime and safety

There's very **little crime** in Brunei and travellers rarely experience any trouble. Note that the possession of **drugs** – whether hard or soft – carries a hefty prison sentence and trafficking is punishable by the death penalty. If you are caught smuggling drugs into or out of the country, at the very best, you are facing a long stretch in a foreign prison; at worst, you could be hanged.

Medical care and emergencies

Medical services in Brunei are excellent; staff speak good English and use up-to-date techniques. See p.68 for details of hospitals in Bandar. Oral **contraceptives** and condoms are available at pharmacies.

EMERGENCY PHONE NUMBERS
Police ☎993
Ambulance ☎991
Fire Brigade ☎995

History

Contemporary Brunei's modest size belies its pivotal role in the formative centuries of **Bornean history**. China was probably trading with Brunei as long ago as the seventh century, and Brunei later benefited from its strategic position on the trade route between India, Melaka and China, exercising a lucrative control over merchant traffic in the South China Sea. It became a staging post, where traders could stock up on local supplies such as beeswax, camphor, rattan and brasswork, which was traded for ceramics, spices, woods and fabrics. For a brief period in the fourteenth century it was taken over by the **Majapahit Empire**, but by the end of the century it had become **independent** and was governed by the first of a long line of sultans.

By the mid-fifteenth century, as the sultanate courted foreign Muslim merchants' business, **Islam** began to make inroads into Bruneian society. This process was accelerated by the decamping to Brunei of wealthy Muslim merchant families after the fall of Melaka to the Portuguese in 1511. In the first half of the sixteenth century, Brunei was Borneo's foremost kingdom, its influence stretching along the island's northern and western coasts, and even as far as territory belonging to the modern-day Philippines. Such was the extent of Bruneian authority that Western visitors found the sultanate and the island interchangeable: the word "Borneo" is thought to be no more than a European corruption of Brunei. But by the close of the sixteenth century, things were beginning to turn sour. Trouble with **Catholic Spain**, now sniffing around the South China and Sulu seas with a view to colonization, led to a sea battle off the coast at Muara in 1578; the battle was won by Spain, whose forces took Brunei Town, only to be chased out days later by a cholera epidemic. The threat of piracy caused more problems, scaring off passing trade. Worse still, at home the sultans began to lose control of the noblemen, as factional struggles ruptured the court.

Western entrepreneurs arrived in this self-destructive climate, keen to take advantage of gaps in the trade market left by Brunei's decline. One such fortune-seeker was **James Brooke**, whose arrival off the coast of Kuching in August 1839 was to change the face of Borneo for ever. For helping the sultan to quell a Dyak uprising, Brooke demanded and was given the governorship of Sarawak; Brunei's contraction had begun. Over subsequent decades, the state was to shrink steadily, as Brooke and his successors used the suppression of piracy as the

excuse they needed to siphon off more and more territory into the familial fiefdom. This trend culminated in the cession of the Limbang region in 1890 – a move which literally split Brunei in two.

Elsewhere, more Bruneian land was being lost to other powers. In January 1846, a court faction unsympathetic to foreign land-grabbing, seized power in Brunei and the chief minister was murdered. British gunboats quelled the coup and Pulau Labuan was ceded to the British crown. A treaty signed the following year, forbidding the sultanate from ceding any of its territories without the British Crown's consent, underlined the **decline of Brunei's power**. Shortly afterwards, in 1865, American consul Charles Lee Moses negotiated a treaty granting a ten-year lease to the **American Trading Company** of the portion of northeast Borneo that was later to become Sabah. By 1888, the British had declared Brunei a protected state, which meant the responsibility for its foreign affairs lay with London. The turn of the twentieth century was marked by the discovery of **oil**: given what little remained of Bruneian territory, it could hardly have been altruism that spurred the British to set up a Residency here in 1906. By 1938, oil exports, engineered by the British Malayan Petroleum Company, had topped M$5 million.

The **Japanese invasion** of December 1941 temporarily halted Brunei's path to recovery. While Sabah, Sarawak and Pulau Labuan became Crown Colonies in the early postwar years, Brunei remained a **British protectorate** and retained its British Resident. Only in 1959 was the Residency finally withdrawn and a new constitution established, with provisions for a democratically elected legislative council. At the same time, Sultan Omar Ali Saifuddien (the present sultan's father) was careful to retain British involvement in matters of defence and foreign affairs – a move whose sagacity was made apparent when, in 1962, an **armed coup** was crushed by British Army Gurkhas. The coup was led by Sheik Azahari's pro-democratic Brunei People's Party (PRB) in response to Sultan Omar's refusal to convene the first sitting of the legislative council. Despite showing interest in joining the planned Malaysian Federation in 1963, Brunei suffered a last-minute attack of cold feet, choosing to opt out rather than risk losing its new-found oil wealth and compromising the pre-eminence of its monarchy. Brunei remained a British Protectorate until January 1, 1984, when it attained full **independence**. Ever since the 1962 coup, Brunei has been ruled by the decree of the sultan, who fulfils the dual roles of (non-elected) prime minister and defence minister, while the posts of minister of foreign affairs and minister of finance are held by his brothers. Political parties were countenanced for three years in the mid-1980s, but outlawed again in 1988. The sultan is quoted in Lord Chalfont's biography, *By God's Will*, as saying, "When I see some genuine interest among the citizenry, we may move towards elections." The government's emergency powers have also remained in place since 1962, which include provisions for the detention, without trial, of citizens.

Meanwhile, oil reserves have fulfilled all expectations, particularly in the 1970s, the decade that saw oil prices shoot through the ceiling, when money really began to roll in. Oil has made Bruneians rich, none more so than Brunei's twenty-ninth sultan, **Hassanal Bolkiah** (his full title is 31 words long). The *Guinness Book of Records* and *Fortune Magazine* have both credited the present sultan as the richest man in the world, with assets estimated to be as high as US$37 billion. The sultan himself disputes such claims, asserting that he doesn't have unlimited access to state funds. Nevertheless, he has managed to acquire hotels in Singapore, London and Beverly Hills; a magnificent residence, the US$350-million Istana Nurul Iman; a collection of three hundred cars and a private fleet of aircraft; and over two hundred fine polo horses, kept at his personal country club.

Although Brunei can only grow richer with its oil reserves and massive global investements, in recent years the Sultan has decided that the economy should **diversify** into hi-tech industries, the service sector and ecotourism – evidence of a less isolationist and self-contained outlook. Bruneians themselves want to feel part of a larger world – many pop over to Miri in Sarawak on the weekends, where they see the benefits of a tourist infrastructure, such as cheaper goods, and where they encounter less restrictive traditions.

Ecotourism is viewed as appropriate for a religiously conformist state like Brunei. It certainly plays to the State's strengths – with logging almost nonexistent, southern parts of the country consist mostly of pristine rainforest and are a delight to travel in, now that a basic infrastructure has been put in place.

Religions of Brunei

The overwhelming majority of Bruneians are **Muslim**. See p.49 for an introduction to Islam.

Books

James Bartholomew, *The Richest Man in the World* (Penguin, UK). Despite an obvious (and admitted) lack of sources, Bartholomew's study of the Sultan of Brunei makes fairly engaging reading – particularly the mind-bending facts used to illustrate the sultan's wealth.

C Mary Turnbull, *A Short History of Malaysia, Singapore & Brunei* (Graham Brash, Singapore). Decent, informed introduction to the region.

Language

The national language of Brunei is **Bahasa Malaysia**, as spoken in Malaysia; see p.572 for an introductory vocabulary. English is also widely spoken.

BANDAR SERI BEGAWAN

BANDAR SERI BEGAWAN, or Bandar as it's known locally, is the capital of Brunei and the sultanate's only settlement of any real size. Straddling the northern bank of a twist in the Sungei Brunei, the city is characterized by its unlikely juxtaposition of striking modern buildings (the latest and most impressive being the twin malls of the Yayasan Sultan Haji Hassanal Bolkiah shopping complex) and traditional stilt houses. These stilt houses make up the water village, or **Kampung Ayer**, Brunei's original seat of power and still home to half the city's population. Indeed, as recently as the middle of the last century, Brunei's capital was little more than a sleepy water village, but with the discovery of oil came its evolution into the attractive, clean and modern waterfront city of today. Large-scale urbanization took place north of the Sungei Brunei, resulting in housing schemes, shopping centres and, more obviously, the magnificent **Omar Ali Saifuddien Mosque**, which dominates the skyline of Bandar. First-time visitors are pleasantly surprised by a sense of space that's rare in Southeast Asian cities. However, Bandar isn't somewhere you're likely to stay for long: most of its sights can be seen in a day or two. You might end up staying a bit longer if you use it as a base to explore outlying attractions such as Temburong and Tutong. Tourism in Brunei is still in its infancy and is not yet seen as a moneyspinner, so you'll find that many sites in the capital have no entrance charge.

Arrival

Flying into Bandar, you'll arrive at plush **Brunei International Airport** (Lapangan Terbang Antarabangsa; ☎02/331747). If you need to book a room on arrival, there are free public phones to your right beyond passport control. To the left, as you walk out of the arrivals concourse and into the car park, is a **tourist information** booth. Taking a **taxi** to cover the 11km into Bandar costs B$15–20, but if you bear right as you exit arrivals, into the free parking zone, you can catch a **bus** (every 15min; 8am–8pm; B$1) into town. You can get change for the fare at the airport branch of the **Islamic Bank of Brunei** (Mon–Thurs 9am–noon & 2–3pm, Fri 8–11am & 2.30–3.30pm, Sat 9–11am).

Boats from Limbang dock centrally, beside the Customs and Immigration Station at the junction of Jalan Roberts and Jalan McArthur. Boats from Pulau Labuan and Lawas dock at Serasa Wharf in **Muara**, 25km northeast of the city; regular buses run from here to Bandar. Buses from Miri in Sarawak (via Seria and Kuala Belait) arrive at the **bus station** below Jalan Cator.

City transport

With as much as half of Bandar's population living in the villages that make up Kampung Ayer, the most common form of city transport are **water taxis**, nicknamed "flying coffins" because of their shape and speed; they charge B$2 for a short hop. The jetty below the intersection of Jalan Roberts and Jalan McArthur is the best place to catch a water taxi, though it's also possible to hail one from Jalan Residency.

Local buses to points north, east and west of the city centre leave from the bus station, underneath the multistorey car park just south of the eastern end of Jalan Cator (every 15–20min; 6.30am–6pm; B$1). Central Line buses run between the airport and the Brunei Museum, crossing the city en route; while the Circle Line loops up to the new Jame 'Asr Hassanil Bolkiah Mosque and Gadong. Of the Northern Line's three routes, #1 and #2 run from Bandar northwards to the airport and Berakas, and #3 to the Technology Museum. One infuriating thing about Bandar's local bus system is that it shuts down around 6pm, after which you have no option but to take taxis which can be few and far between.

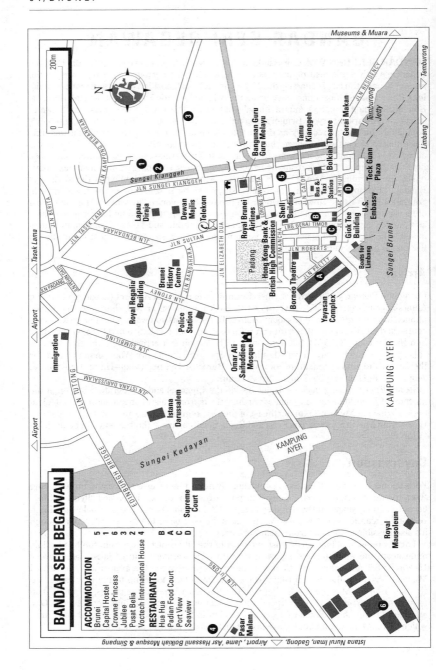

BANDAR SERI BEGAWAN

ACCOMMODATION

Brunei	5
Capital Hostel	1
Crowne Princess	6
Jubilee	3
Pusat Belia	2
Voctech International House	4

RESTAURANTS

Hua Hua	B
Padian Food Court	A
Port View	C
Seaview	D

MOVING ON FROM BANDAR SERI BEGAWAN

Times and frequency of boats and buses are given in the "Travel Details" p.70.

By plane

Travelling to the **airport** from central Bandar, take any Central Line or Northern Line bus #1 or #2 (every 15min; 6.30am–6pm; B$1) from the bus station below Jalan Cator. For flight information call ☎02/331747.

By boat

Boats to Limbang leave from beside the Customs and Immigration Station at the junction of Jalan Roberts and Jalan McArthur. For **Pulau Labuan** and **Lawas** boats you have to go to the Serasa Ferry Terminal at **Muara**, a small village 25km northeast of Bandar and pass through immigration there. To get to Muara, go to the main bus terminal below Jalan Cator (B$2).

Tickets for Labuan (B$20) and Lawas (B$15) are sold by New Island Shipping, 1st Floor, Giok Tee Building, Jalan McArthur (☎02/243059), and Halim Tours, Lorong Gerai Timor, off Jalan McArthur (☎02/226688); tickets for Limbang (B$10) are sold at the open stalls opposite Lorong Gerai Timor, on Jalan McArthur. From Labuan, there are daily connections on to Kota Kinabalu and Menumbok in Sabah, though to ensure you catch one, it's wise to leave Bandar early in the day.

Boats to **Bangar** in Temburong (B$7) depart from the wharf at Jalan Residency, 2km east of the centre. Tickets are sold beside the jetty. From Bangar, it's possible to travel overland to both Lawas and Limbang in Sarawak (see p.70).

By bus

Buses to Miri in Sarawak (via Seria and Kuala Belait) leave from the bus station below Jalan Cator: for details see p.70.

Fares for regular, metered **taxis** start at B$4; from the city centre to the Brunei Museum costs B$5–7. A night-time surcharge applies between 9pm and 6am, there's a B$5 charge on trips to the airport, and each piece of luggage loaded in the boot costs a further B$1. The new PPP taxi service (purple cars) charge a flat fare and run as far afield as the outlying districts of Gadong and Batu One – but not, infuriatingly, to either the museums or the airport.

Accommodation

Brunei is almost bereft of budget **accommodation**, with the *Pusat Belia* (youth hostel) and *Voctech International House* the only real options. Some visitors have resorted to taking a bus to the coast and sleeping on the beach, though this is hardly advisable. Otherwise, most double rooms start at B$70.

Brunei, 95 Jalan Pemancha (☎02/242372). Comfortable and well appointed, this is Bandar's most central commercial hotel. ⑥.

Capital Hostel, Jalan Kampung Berangan (☎02/223561). A budget option by Bruneian standards, and a useful standby if you can't get into the neighbouring *Pusat Belia*. ④.

Crowne Princess, Jalan Tutong (☎02/241128). 117 well-appointed rooms, situated a little way out of town over the Edinburgh Bridge, connected to the city centre by regular shuttle bus. ⑤.

Jubilee, Jubilee Plaza, Jalan Kampung Kianggeh (☎02/228070). East of Sungei Kianggeh, a well-groomed, mid-range hotel set opposite a patch of traditional kampung houses. ④.

Pusat Belia, Jalan Sungai Kianggeh (☎02/222900). Brunei's youth hostel, and by far the cheapest option in town, providing you can get in. You'll need an ISIC or IH card. Rooms are shared with three others, and there's a pool (B$1) downstairs. B$10 per person for one to three nights and B$5 for further nights.

Voctech International House, Jalan Pasar Baharu, Gadong (☎02/447992). Slightly out of the centre (bus #22 from the station) on the way to Gadong, this massive, comfortable place has quite transformed accommodation options in Bandar. Ostensibly set up for international educational groups, it is now increasingly used by tour groups and independent travellers. It's got a well-priced café, a kitchen which can be used by guests and a library with Internet access. Rooms are large with bathrooms attached. Five minutes' walk away there's the excellent *pasar malam* (night market) with cheap and tasty food available. ③.

The City

Downtown Bandar is hemmed in by water. To the east is Sungei Kianggeh; to the south, the wide Sungei Brunei; and to the west, Sungei Kedayan, which runs up to the Edinburgh Bridge. The Omar Ali Saifuddien Mosque, overlooking the compact knot of central streets, is Bandar's most obvious point of reference, sitting in a cradle formed by Kampung Ayer, which spreads like water lilies on a pond across large expanses of the river.

The Omar Ali Saifuddien Mosque

At the very heart of both the city and the sultanate's Muslim faith is the magnificent **Omar Ali Saifuddien Mosque** (Mon–Wed, Sat & Sun 8am–noon, 1–3.30pm & 4.30–5.30pm, Thurs closed to non-Muslims, Fri 4.30–5.30pm). Built in classical Islamic style, it was commissioned by and named after the father of the present sultan, and completed in 1958 at a cost of US$5 million. It makes splendid use of opulent yet tasteful fittings – Italian marble, granite from Shanghai, Arabian and Belgian carpets, and English chandeliers and stained glass. Topping the cream-coloured building is a 52-metre-high golden dome whose curved surface is adorned with a mosaic comprising over three million pieces of Venetian glass. It is sometimes possible to obtain permission to ride the elevator up the 44-metre-high minaret, and look out over the water village below. The usual dress codes – modest attire, and shoes to be left at the entrance – apply when entering the mosque.

Kampung Ayer

From the mosque, it's no distance to Bandar's **Kampung Ayer**, or water village, whose sheer scale makes it one of the great sights of Southeast Asia. Stilt villages have occupied this stretch of the Sungei Brunei for hundreds of years, and today, an estimated thirty thousand people live in the scores of sprawling villages that compose Kampung Ayer, their dwellings connected by a maze of wooden promenades. These villages have their own clinics, mosques, schools, a fire brigade and a police station; the homes have piped water, electricity and TV. Its waters, however, are distinctly unsanitary, and the houses are susceptible to fire. Even so, a strong sense of community has meant that attempts to move the inhabitants onto dry land and into housing more in keeping with a state that has the highest per capita income in the world have met with little success.

The meandering pathways of Kampung Ayer make it an intriguing place to explore on foot. For a real impression of its dimensions though, it's best to charter a water taxi: a half-hour round trip will cost B$15–20 per person. A handful of traditional cottage industries continue to turn out copperware and brassware (at Kampung Ujong Bukit) and exquisite sarongs and boats (Kampung Saba Darat); the boatmen should know the whereabouts of some of them.

The Brunei Museum and Malay Technology Museum

The **Brunei Museum** (Tues–Thurs 9am–5pm, Fri 9.30–11.30am & 2.30–5pm, Sat & Sun 9am–5pm; free), about 5km east of Sungei Kianggeh on Jalan Residency, has several outstanding galleries. The undoubted highlight is its superb **Islamic Art Gallery**, where, among the riches on display are beautifully illuminated antique Korans from India, Iran, Egypt and Turkey, exquisite prayer mats, and quirkier items like a pair of ungainly wooden slippers. In the inevitable **Oil and Gas Gallery**, exhibits, graphics and captions recount the story of Brunei's oil reserves, from the drilling of the first well in 1928, to current extraction and refining techniques. Also interesting, though tantalizingly sketchy, is the **Muslim Life Gallery**, whose dioramas allow glimpses of social traditions, such as the sweetening of a new-born baby's mouth with honey or dates, and the disposal of its placenta in a *bayung*, a palm-leaf basket which is either hung on a tree or floated downriver. At the back of the gallery, a small collection of early photographs shows riverine hawkers trading from their boats in Kampung Ayer.

Steps around the back of the museum drop down to the riverside **Malay Technology Museum** (Mon, Wed, Thurs, Sat & Sun 9am–5pm, Fri 9–11.30am & 2.30–5pm; free), whose three galleries provide a mildly engaging insight into traditional Malay life, including examples of Kedayan, Murut and Dusun dwellings.

The Jame 'Asr Hassanil Bolkiah Mosque

Many people reckon that the **Jame 'Asr Hassanil Bolkiah (State) Mosque** (Mon–Wed, Sat & Sun 8am–noon, 1–3.30pm & 4.30–5.30pm; Thurs & Fri closed to non-Muslims), set in harmonious gardens in the commercial suburb of Gadong, has a distinct edge over the Omar Ali Saifuddien Mosque both in style and grandeur. With its sea-blue roof, golden domes and slender minarets, this is Brunei's largest mosque, constructed to commemorate the silver jubilee of the sultan's reign in 1992. It's also referred to as the Kiarong Mosque. Circle Line buses skirt the grounds of the mosque en route to Gadong.

The Istana Nurul Iman

The **Istana Nurul Iman**, the official residence of the sultan, is sited at a superb riverside spot 4km west of the capital. Bigger than either Buckingham Palace or the Vatican, the istana is a monument to self-indulgence. Its design, by Filipino architect Leandro Locsin, is a sinuous blend of traditional and modern, with Islamic motifs such as arches and domes, and sloping roofs fashioned on traditional longhouse designs, combined with all the mod cons you'd expect of a house whose owner earns an estimated US$5 million a day.

James Bartholomew's book, *The Richest Man in the World*, lists some of the mind-boggling figures relating to the palace. Over half a kilometre long, it contains a grand total of 1778 rooms, including 257 toilets. Illuminating these rooms requires 51,000 light bulbs, and simply getting around the building requires 18 lifts and 44 staircases. The throne room is said to be particularly sumptuous: twelve one-tonne chandeliers hang from its ceiling, while its four grand thrones stand against the backdrop of an eighteen-metre arch, tiled in 22-carat gold. In addition to the throne room, there's a royal banquet hall that seats 4000 diners, a prayer hall where 1500 people can worship at any one time, an underground car park for the sultan's hundreds of vehicles, a state-of-the-art sports complex, and a helipad. Unfortunately, the palace is rarely open to the general public, though the sultan does declare open house every year during Hari Raya. Otherwise, nearby Taman Persiaran Damuan, a kilometre-long park sandwiched between Jalan Tutong and Sungei Brunei, offers the best view, or you can fork out for a boat trip and see the palace lit up at night from the water. All westbound buses travel along Jalan Tutong, over the Edinburgh Bridge and past the istana.

Eating

Fortunately, Bandar's **restaurants** are more reasonably priced than its hotels. If you're on a tight budget, head for the night stalls situated in the car park of the main market across the road from *Voctech* on the way to Gadong. Here, Malay favourites are laid out buffet-style, though there are no tables and chairs. Gadong, with its numerous Malay cafés, is a very good place to eat in the day. Unfortunately, there is no public transport to the suburb after 6pm, and the area closes down quite early anyway. Another cheap, more accessible, option is the cluster of stalls behind the Temburong jetty on Jalan Residency, serving good and cheap *soto ayam*, *nasi campur* and other Malay staples.

Hasinah Restoran, Block 1, Unit 9, Abdul Razak Complex, Gadong. Quite fabulous and inexpensive Malay and South Indian daytime café. Serves nine types of *dosai* and a mouthwatering *nasi campur* spread.

Hua Hua, 48 Jl Sultan. Steamed chicken with sausage is one of the highlights in this hole-in-the-wall Chinese establishment, where B$15 feeds two people. Daily 7am–9pm.

Padian Food Court, 1st Floor, Yayasan Complex, Jl Kumbang Pasang. Air-con food court whose stalls serve Thai, Arabic, Japanese, Indian and other regional cuisines. Daily 9am–10pm.

Port View, the jetty, western end of Jl McArthur. Western and Malay food in relaxing setting overlooking harbour and Kampung Ayer. Main courses are around B$15. Bands play at weekends 10pm–2am. Midweek open 6pm–midnight.

Sarasaya, Block C, Abdul Razak Complex, Gadong. Excellent Japanese restaurant. Reckon on around B$30 a head. Open 6–11pm daily.

Listings

Airlines MAS, 144 Jl Pemancha (☎02/224141); Philippine Airlines, 1st Floor, Wisma Haji Fatimah, Jl Sultan (☎02/222970); Royal Brunei Airlines, RBA Plaza, Jl Sultan (☎02/242222); Singapore Airlines, 49–50 Jl Sultan (☎02/227253); Thai Airways, fourth floor, Komplek Jl Sultan, 51–55 Jl Sultan (☎02/242991).

American Express Unit 401–03, 4th Floor, Shell Building, Jl Sultan (Mon–Fri 8.30am–5pm, Sat 8.30am–1pm; ☎02/228314).

Bookshops English-language books at Best Eastern Books, G4 Teck Guan Plaza, Jl Sultan, and Times Bookshop, 1st Floor, Yayasan Complex.

Car rental Sukma, Lot 26, 69 Jl Kiarong (☎02/427238); Sykt Yuran Rent-A-Car, 144a Jl Pemancha, PO Box 119 (☎02/224054).

Embassies and consulates Australia, 4th Floor, Teck Guan Plaza, Jl Sultan (☎02/229435); Indonesia, Simpang 528, Lot 4498, Sungei Hanching Baru, Jl Muara (☎02/330180); Malaysia, Lot 27 & 29, Simpang 396–39, Kampong Sungai Akar, Jl Kebangsaan (☎02/3456520); Philippines, 4th & 5th Floor, Badi'ah Building, Mile 1, Jl Tutong (☎02/241465); Singapore, 5th Floor, RBA Plaza, Jl Sultan (☎02/227583); Thailand, no. 1, Simpang 52-86-16, Kampung Mata-Mata, Jl Gadong (☎02/229653); UK, Unit 2.01, Block D, Complex Yayasan Sultan Hassanal Bolkiah (☎02/222231); USA, 3rd Floor, Teck Guan Plaza, Jl Sultan (☎02/229670).

Exchange There are many cash-only moneychangers on Jl McArthur.

Hospital The Raja Isteri Pengiran Anak Saleha Hospital (RIPAS) is across Edinburgh Bridge on Jl Putera Al-Muhtadee Billah (☎02/222366); or there's the private Hart Medical Clinic at 47 Jl Sultan (☎02/225531).

Immigration The Immigration Office (Mon–Thurs & Sat 7.45am–12.15pm & 1.45–4.30pm) is on Jl Menteri Besar (☎02/383106).

Internet access FS School of Computing, Unit 1, 1st Floor, Block C, Abdul Razak Complex, Gadong; *Cyber Café*, 8 Block A, Kiarong Complex, Kiulap, opposite State Mosque.

Laundry Superkleen, opposite *Brunei Hotel*, Jl Pemancha.

Pharmacies Khong Lin Dispensary, G3A, Wisma Jaya, Jl Pemancha; Sentosa Dispensary, 42 Jl Sultan.

Police Central Police Station, Jl Stoney (☎02/222333).

Post office The GPO (Mon–Thurs & Sat 8am–4.30pm) is at the intersection of Jl Elizabeth Dua and Jl Sultan. Poste restante/general delivery is at the Money Order counter.

Taxis ☎02/222214/226/853.

Telephone services IDD calls at Telekom (daily 8am–midnight), next to the GPO on Jl Sultan.

Jerudong Park Playground

An evening spent enjoying the free funfair rides at **Jerudong Park Playground** (grounds open daily 2pm–2am; games and rides Mon, Tues & Wed 5pm–midnight, Thurs & Sat 5pm–2am, Fri & Sun 2pm–midnight; during Ramadan daily 8pm–2am; free), about 20km northwest of Bandar on the road to Tutong, is the only activity close to the capital worth considering. The park is a cracking funfair/adventure park whose scores of rides – all completely free – make it that rarest of treats, a Bruneian must-see. The park was conceived as a lasting testimony to His Majesty's generosity to his *rakyat* ("people"), and, though daily gates average two thousand, there's very little queuing for rides, which include a rollercoaster, a giant drop, supakarts, shooting galleries, boat rides, space-ride simulators, bumper cars and carousels. Jerudong Park Playground is tricky to reach, and trickier to get back from once buses have stopped in the early evening, so taking a taxi is your best bet – a return fare shouldn't exceed B$50, but you'll have to haggle.

Bangar and the Temburong District

Brunei's main ecotourism effort is focused on the **Temburong District**, a sparsely populated part of the state which is only accessible by boat from Bandar. It has been isolated from the rest of Brunei since 1884, when the strip of land to the west was ceded to Sarawak. The area's chief attractions are the superb **Ulu Temburong National Park** and the chance to stay in **Malay and Murut kampungs** or **Iban longhouses**. The starting point for both of these is the district's only town of any size, Bangar.

BANGAR stands on the Sungei Temburong in the hilly Temburong District. Bangar can only be reached by a hair-raising speedboat journey from Bandar (B$7). The boats scream through narrow mangrove estuaries that are home to crocodiles and proboscis monkeys, swooping around corners and narrowly missing vessels travelling the opposite way, before shooting off down Sungei Temburong. After such a lead-up, the town of Bangar is something of a disappointment; its main street, which runs west from the jetty to the town mosque, is lined only with a handful of coffee shops and provision stores. Across the bridge is Bangar's grandest building, its new District Office, whose waterfront café is the town's best place to eat. There are no places to stay in Bangar.

From Bangar it's a twenty-minute drive south to the jetty at the small kampung, **Batang Duri**. There's no public transport to this spot; you'll either have to hitch a lift (quite a safe practice in Brunei) or take a taxi (B$15). From here you will have to charter a longboat (B$50; 90min) to Ulu Temburong Park Headquarters. This upstream stretch of Sungei Temburong is very shallow and when the water level is low you may have to get out and help pull the boat over rocks. Dense jungle cloaks the hills on either side and birds and monkeys abound in the trees. At the headquarters it is possible to stay in cabins (④), but you will have to bring your own provisions, as a cafeteria is still in the process of being built, due to be finished in 2001.

The main attraction of the park, one hour's walk over a hanging bridge and along a wooden pathway, is the **canopy walkway**, a near-vertical aluminium structure, a climb which tests your nerves to the limit. It is the highest of its type in Borneo and the view from the top is breathtaking: you can see Brunei Bay to the north and Gunung Mulu Park in Sarawak to the south. Other activities in the park include chartering a small longboat (around B$50 for two hours) to go further upstream to a tree house, passing the Kuala Belalong Field Studies Centre along the way. The centre is the site of a scientific research project examining the unique fauna of the park.

Iban homestays

From Bangar, take a taxi (20min; B$15) to Amo C, a five-door Iban longhouse on the Batang Duri road (no telephone, just turn up), where the people offer their longhouse as a "homestay" for independent travellers. There are always people around to welcome you and invite you in; many of them speak some English. It's always best to take some small gifts for the children – not expected but you'll make friends. Guests sleep on the veranda. You will have to pay for the meals and give something for your stay, but this doesn't amount to much – the Iban are very hospitable and rather embarrassed to ask for money, since traditionally they invite people to stay for free. A rough framework is B$3 for breakfast, B$6 for lunch and dinner and B$5 for staying the night. Around the longhouse there are some pleasant trails into the forest that the Ibans use for hunting. You will need a guide (B$20–30 per person for a daytrip; B$50 overnight). If you choose an overnight trip, take your own gear and ask the people at the longhouse to take food for you too.

Malay and Murut homestays

Twenty kilometres east of Bangar on the road to Lawas is the Labu region of Temburong. Again, the only way to get here is by taxi from Bangar. Rice paddies line the road on one side, while thick forest lines the other – this used to be largely rubber plantations until the bottom dropped out of the rubber market in the Fifties. Fifteen kilometres further along this road you come to the Perdayan Forest Reserve. There are no facilities here, but the small park includes a strenuous three-hour trek on a wooden pathway up Bukit Patoi. From the top of the hill there are great views across Brunei's spectacular, largely undisturbed rainforests south towards Sarawak. Five kilometres further on take a road to the right. This leads to **SEKOLOH**, a Malay and Murut village comprising a few dozen elevated dwellings (see pp.569–570 for more on the Malay and Murut peoples). Visitors are welcome here – just ask around to find out which is the house you can stay in. The villagers take turns putting people up, thereby sharing the "fun" of having foreigners in their isolated kampung. Prices are about the same as at the Iban longhouse (see p.69). Besides walking around the kampung, meeting people, eating and relaxing, there's little to do. Nevertheless, a visit to a homestay like this one gives you a rare insight into the lifestyle of traditional, rural Bruneians. It's well worth making the effort to go for that alone.

Crossing the Malaysian border to Limbang and Lawas

If you're planning to **cross into Sarawak** – either to Limbang or to Lawas – you'll first have to make for the immigration post beside the turning for Kampung Puni, 5km west of Bangar. **Limbang** is easiest and cheapest to reach: after a B$5–10 taxi ride from Bangar, take a ferry (B$1) across the river at Kampung Puni, which marks the border with Malaysia, and then catch one of the connecting buses (B$2) which run into Limbang until 5pm. The only way to get to **Lawas** is to catch the Lawas express, which starts in Limbang, reaches Bangar around 9am and pulls into Lawas at 1pm. Coming the other way towards Limbang, it arrives at Bangar around 3pm.

Kuala Belait and on to Miri

It's a little under 85km from Bandar to Brunei's second biggest town, **KUALA BELAIT**. There's nothing very enticing here, but it's the main transit point for buses to and from **Miri** in **Sarawak**. Buses to Sarawak leave from the **bus station** on the intersection of Jalan Bunga Raya and Jalan McKerron (B$10.20); the fare includes the ferry across Sungei Belait and the connecting Sarawakian bus over the border. The town's taxi stand is across the road from the bus station: drivers charge around B$100 for a full car to Miri, though you should be able to haggle them down substantially. To get to Kuala Belait from Bandar, you have to go via Seria, 20km east (see "Travel Details", below).

Jalan McKerron houses several good **restaurants** – the best of which are the *Buccaneer Steakhouse* at no. 94, whose mid-priced international food is aimed squarely at the expat market; and the *Akhbar Restaurant*, at no. 99a, with a Malay and North Indian menu. *Raya's Orchid Room*, on Jalan Bunga, does good-value three-course Western set lunches (Mon–Fri; B$5). Next door to the *Buccaneer Steakhouse* at no. 93, *Hotel Sentosa* (☎03/331345; ⑤) offers well-appointed and welcoming **rooms**. You can **change money** at the Hong Kong Bank.

travel details

Buses

Bandar Seri Begawan to: Muara (every 30min; 30min); Seria (hourly until 2pm; 1hr 45min).

Kuala Belait to: Miri (5 daily 7.30am–3.30pm; 1hr 30min); Seria (every 30min until 6.30pm; 45min).

Seria to: Bandar Seri Begawan (every 45min until 2pm; 1hr 45min); Kuala Belait (every 30 min; 45min).

Boats

Bandar Seri Begawan to: Bangar (every 45min 6.30am–4.30pm; 50min); Limbang (at least 8 daily; 30min);

Muara to: Lawas (1 daily at 11.30am; 2hr); Pulau Labuan (4 daily; 1hr 30min).

CHAPTER TWO

CAMBODIA

Introduction

Cambodia was largely out of bounds to tourists until recently, but now, areas that were unsafe because of Khmer Rouge guerrillas and bandit groups have been returned to the control of the Cambodian army, and virtually the whole of the country has become accessible. For many travellers, lured by the prospect of little explored and unspoilt regions, Cambodia has become a top destination on Southeast Asia's otherwise well-trodden tourist trail.

The Kingdom of Cambodia, with a population of ten million, occupies a modest wedge of land, almost completely hemmed in by its neighbours, Vietnam, Laos and Thailand. Its glory days began in the early ninth century, when the rival Indian-influenced Chenla kingdoms united under King Jayavarman II to form the **Khmer Empire**, a powerful and visionary dynasty, which, at its peak, stretched from Vietnam in the east, to China in the north and Burma in the west. Recent history has been less kind to the country. French colonization was followed by an extended period of turbulence and instability, culminating in the devastating Kampuchean holocaust instigated by Pol Pot's Khmer Rouge in 1975. The brutal regime lasted four years before invading Vietnamese forces reached the capital in 1979 and overthrew the Khmer Rouge. Pol Pot and his supporters fled to the jungle bordering Thailand, from where they continued to wage war on successive governments in Phnom Penh. Pol Pot's death in 1998 finally signalled the demise of the Khmer Rouge, and their subsequent surrender has given Cambodia a real chance for peace for the first time in thirty years. There are indeed many signs that Cambodia is at last shaking off the shadows of its past and looking to the future with a cautious confidence. International investors are beginning to back business ventures, there is increasing evidence of development and modernization in urban areas and foreign aid is flowing in.

Most visitors to Cambodia head for the stunning **Angkor** ruins, a collection of over one hundred temples dating back to the ninth century. Once the seat of power of the Khmer Empire, Angkor is royal extrav-

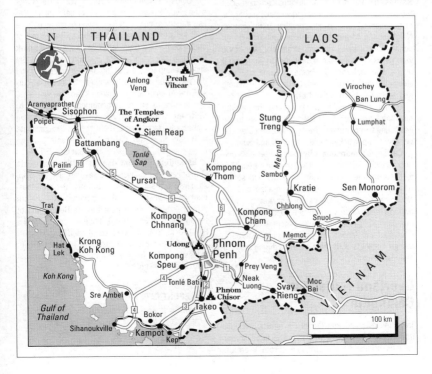

agance on a grand scale, its imposing features enhanced by the dramatic setting of lush jungle greenery and verdant fields. The complex is acknowledged as the most exquisite example of ancient architecture in Southeast Asia, and has been declared a World Heritage Site by UNESCO.

The flat, sprawling capital of **Phnom Penh** is also an alluring attraction in its own right. Wide, sweeping boulevards, and elegant, if neglected, French colonial-style facades lend the city a romantic appeal. However, there's also stark evidence of great poverty, a reminder that you're visiting one of the world's poorest countries.

Those enterprising travellers who look beyond the standard itinerary of Angkor and Phnom Penh will be rewarded with a rich variety of experiences. Miles of unspoilt beaches and remote islands offer sandy seclusion along the **southern coastline**. Although **Sihanoukville** is the main port of call, it's easy enough to commandeer transport to nearby hidden coves and offshore islands, with only the odd fisherman or smuggler to interrupt your solitude. **Ratanakiri** province in the northeastern corner of the country, with its hilltribes and volcanic scenery, is also becoming increasingly popular with visitors. Neighbouring **Mondolkiri** is less well known, but equally impressive, offering dramatic alpinesque woodlands, villages and mountains. In the central plains, **Battambang**, Cambodia's second city, is a sleepy provincial capital, and the gateway to the old Khmer Rouge stronghold of **Pailin**.

Getting to Cambodia's attractions can be half the fun. "Infrastructure" is not a word well known to the locals and **travel** outside the main tourist routes can be slow and punishing, facilities less than luxurious.

Cambodia's **monsoon climate** creates two distinct seasons. The southwesterly monsoon from May to October brings heavy rain, humidity and strong winds, while the northeasterly monsoon from November to April produces dry, hot weather, with average temperatures rising from 25°C in November to around 32°C in April. The best months to visit are December and January, as it's dry and relatively cool, though Angkor is at its most stunning during the lush rainy season.

Overland routes into Cambodia

Travelling overland into Cambodia is now possible from both Vietnam and Thailand. The **Laos** border remains officially closed for now. **From Vietnam**

there is only one border crossing open to foreigners, northwest of Ho Chi Minh City at Moc Bai (see p.951).

From Thailand there are two entry points: the border crossing at Poipet (see p.843), east of Bangkok, and the coastal border near Krong Koh Kong, known as Ban Hat Lek (see p.905) on the Thai side.

Entry requirements and visa extension

All foreign nationals, except Malaysians, need a **visa** to enter Cambodia. Tourist visas are valid for thirty days and cost $20. A business visa costs $25 and is valid initially for thirty days. Tourist visas are issued on arrival at Pochentong airport in Phnom Penh; one passport photo is required. It's also possible to obtain a visa on arrival at the Thai overland border crossing at Poipet, but not as yet at the other overland crossings – Ban Hat Lek on the Thai border, and Moc Bai, the border crossing with Vietnam. For these border points, you'll need to obtain a visa beforehand. You can either organize this before you leave home (see p.20 for a list of Cambodian Embassy addresses) or obtain one at the Cambodian Embassy in **Bangkok** (see p.861) – you'll need a passport photo and the visa takes up to two working days to process. If you don't want the hassle of queuing at the embassy yourself, travel agencies on Thanon Khao San will organize the visa for you for an additional charge of $5. **In Vietnam**, you can get visas from the Cambodian Embassy in Hanoi (see p.1049) or from the consulate in Ho Chi Minh City (see p.993), but note that the latter charges $30 instead of the standard $20.

Extending a tourist visa is a painless process in Phnom Penh, but impossible elsewhere in Cambodia, so if you're planning a long trip into the provinces, think about whether you'll need an extension before you go. Extensions are issued at the Department of Immigration, 5 Street 200, Phnom Penh (Mon–Fri 8–10.30am, 2.30–4.30pm); you'll need two passport photos. Next-day service costs $40 for a one-month extension or $75 for three months. A tourist visa can only be extended once.

AIRPORT DEPARTURE TAX

Cambodian Airport Tax is currently $20 for international departures, and $10 for domestic departures. Tax on flights from Siem Reap is slightly cheaper.

Money and costs

Cambodia's unit of currency is the **riel**, abbreviated to "r". **Notes** come in denominations of 100, 200, 500, 1000, 2000, 5000, 10,000, 20,000, 50,000 and 100,000, although the bigger notes are seldom seen, as dollars tend to be used for larger transactions. **American dollars** are accepted everywhere; indeed, you'll be expected to pay in dollars rather than riel at guesthouses, restaurants and for most entrance fees to tourist sites. In fact, it's possible to get by in Cambodia without actually changing any foreign currency into riel, but there are times when riel notes are useful – lower priced items such as street food and motos are normally paid for in riel, and bargaining in riel for crafts at a market, for example, gives you more room for manoeuvre. Changing up to say $10 worth will give you a chunky pile of riel, enough to last you a few days. **Thai baht** are also widely used in the border areas, and on the main trade routes from Thailand.

It's best to change your currency into dollars before you enter Cambodia if possible, although banks in Phnom Penh and Siem Reap will exchange most currencies. Travellers' cheques can be changed at most banks for a small commission. **Credit-card cash advances** are available in Phnom Penh, Siem Reap, Sihanoukville and Battambang. ATMs haven't yet arrived in Cambodia.

To **exchange** dollars into riel, don't bother with the banks – they issue riel at a low rate, if at all. Head instead for the nearest market, where money-changers display bundles of riel in their glass cabinets. At the time of writing, a dollar in Phnom Penh's central market was worth 3800r.

On the whole, food and accommodation is slightly more expensive in Cambodia than in its neighbouring countries. However, it's possible to live quite **cheaply**: if you stay in the cheapest guesthouses, eat only at the markets and street stalls and travel on trains or on the back of pick-ups, you'll be able to scrape by on £5/$8 a day, not including entrance fees to museums and other sights. However, eating a few guesthouse or restaurant meals, and staying in en-suite accommodation will quickly increase daily costs to around £10/$15. For decent air-con accommodation, three good meals a day, and a bit of nightlife, reckon on spending around £20/$30. At present there is **no two-tier pricing system** as in Vietnam, though there are signs that this may be changing. The fast boat between Siem Reap and Phnom Penh attracts a foreigner price, and it seems the other boat routes are

catching on. On the whole, however, accommodation and food are charged at the Khmer price.

The easiest way to get money **wired** to you in Cambodia (see "Basics" p.23) is via the branches of Western Union in Phnom Penh and Siem Reap. See the "Listings" sections of these towns for details.

Information and maps

Cambodia is beginning to recognize the importance of tourism to its economy, and is establishing a network of basic **tourist offices**. These offices, however, are desperately starved of resources and generally don't have much information. Better information can usually be found at popular **guesthouses**.

The easiest **map** to use is the 1:1,100,000 Periplus Travel Map of Cambodia. It's a handy size and also has plans of Phnom Penh and Angkor. International Travel Maps also publishes a useful 1:800,000 map. If you're travelling around the region, you could try the 1:2,000,000 regional map of Vietnam, Cambodia and Laos published by UBD or Bartholomew. Bear in mind, however, that all these maps are based on dated surveys. Many of the older roads featured no longer exist, and new roads are not shown.

Getting around

Transport in Cambodia is all part of the adventure. The roads are in a terrible state, boats can only operate when the water is high enough, and the packed trains travel at walking speed. Fortunately, Cambodia's not a big country.

■ By train

Until 1999, **train** travel was considered too dangerous for tourists, but with the improved security situation, increasing numbers of visitors are choosing the rail option. Travel is, however, tediously slow and pretty uncomfortable – the only seating is hard wooden benches. There are no reservations, so you'll need to turn up early to stand a chance of a seat, though don't expect the train to leave on time. Some trains consist only of cargo carriages, so a hammock can be useful. Men usually sit on the roof of busy trains.

There are two narrow-gauge **railway lines** in Cambodia: one from Phnom Penh to Sihanoukville, the other from Phnom Penh to Sisophon via Battambang. Trains are a good place to meet and talk to locals. You'll probably be the centre of attention, as foreigners on trains are still very much a novelty. It's a good idea to take food and water, although hawkers will be selling food along the way. **Fares** are extremely cheap: Phnom Penh to Battambang and Phnom Penh to Sihanoukville each cost 4500r.

■ By road

Buses and coaches of the conventional sort are a rarity in Cambodia, the exceptions being on the routes from Phnom Penh to Sihanoukville and Kompong Cham, which are in a state of good repair. Elsewhere, the roads vary from dodgy to impassable, and the usual mode of public transport is a **pick-up truck** – often scarcely adequate two-wheel-drive Toyotas. The journeys are long and uncomfortable, but reasonably cheap. **Prices** vary, depending on whether you sit in the cab or out in the open in the back. Many travellers prefer sitting **in the back**, as it's cheaper and there's generally more space to get comfortable. You'll need to protect yourself from the sun, though; as for the dust, there's little you can do about that. For half a seat in the cab you'll pay up to twice the price of a seat in the back; for the luxury of a whole seat you'll pay double again. Prices given in the guide text refer to travel in the back. **Timetables** don't exist for pick-ups. They tend to leave early in the morning as soon as they're full, around 6 or 7am.

■ By boat

Boats are an easy way to travel to areas on the Tonlé Sap River, Mekong River and south coast. On the whole, Malaysian-made fast boats are used – a cross between an old school bus and a torpedo. The ride is more comfortable (and much faster) than pick-ups or trains, but conditions are still fairly cramped, so don't expect the luxury that the foreigner prices imply. Many tourists opt to sit on the roof for the views. Some routes may not be navigable in the dry season when the water level drops.

■ By plane

There are three domestic **airlines** in Cambodia. Royal Air Cambodge runs a fairly slick operation. President Airlines and Phnom Penh Airways are cheaper, but their planes tend to be older. Prices are very reasonable: a one-way ticket from Phnom Penh to Battambang costs $45, a return $90. During the rainy season, flying is the only way to get to the remoter areas.

■ Vehicle rental

Renting a **motorbike** is the most practical self-drive option for Cambodia's poor provincial roads. At the rental shops in Phnom Penh, you can pick up a fairly good 250cc trials bike, which should be able to handle most terrain. **Cars** tend to come with a driver. They're almost exclusively white Toyota Camrys, and cost a reasonable $20–25 per day. A small number of guesthouses have their own jeeps which they may rent out (self-drive).

Bicycles and **motorbikes** are available to rent cheaply. Although in Phnom Penh the traffic is intimidating, especially at rush hour, most other towns in Cambodia are not particularly dangerous places to explore on two wheels.

If you do intend to **self-drive** any vehicle in Cambodia, bear in mind that road conditions are unpredictable. Your journey may take much longer than you anticipate, you should never travel alone and it's a good idea to carry food and water.

Officially, vehicles drive on the right, but **traffic regulations** in Cambodia are flexible and you may encounter people driving on the left. Driving on the roads to Sihanoukville and Kompong Cham can be dangerous, as the traffic is heavy and hectic, but elsewhere, traffic is much lighter.

■ Local transport

Motorcycle taxis, commonly called motodops or **motos**, are the most convenient way of getting around town and are inexpensive – short journeys cost between 500 and 2000r. The baseball-capped drivers are highly skilled at spotting customers before they even realize they need a moto. English-speaking drivers can usually be found outside hotels, guesthouses and other tourist spots, though they may well charge a small premium for being able to communicate. Non-English-speaking drivers will often nod enthusiastically in a show of understanding, only to proceed to the nearest guesthouse or tourist site.

Three-wheeled **cyclos** are a more relaxing way to trundle around cities, but are only practical for shorter trips. Cyclo fares are subject to negotiation, usually between 500 and 1000r, perhaps a little more in the midday heat. With both motos and cyclos it's best to agree a fare in advance unless you know what you should be paying.

Taxis aren't really used for short hops around town. There is one metered taxi service in Phnom Penh, which you must book in advance. Otherwise, cars are booked by the day, or by the journey.

Accommodation

Cambodia's **hotel** industry kicked into gear when UNTAC descended on the country in 1991. United Nations officials and soldiers were in need of half-decent accommodation, so hotels sprung up in every provincial capital, offering en-suite rooms with TV and air-con. When the UN disappeared, the prices dropped. The standard price for a basic provincial hotel room is now a bargain $5, although most of these places are way past their prime.

Budget guesthouses are found only in the main tourist areas of Phnom Penh, Siem Reap and Sihanoukville. It's possible to get a bed for $2 or even $1 if you don't mind basic facilities. Most establishments offer a range of rooms, from the very basic to those with air-con or fan and bathroom. Many have cheap single rooms available, too. You'll also find a number of **mid-range guesthouses** in the main towns, offering better and cleaner facilities for $7–15. It's always worth negotiating at these, especially in low season (May–Oct). At the other end of the scale, there's now a number of **luxury international hotels** in Phnom Penh, Siem Reap and Sihanoukville charging upwards of $120.

ADDRESSES

Many roads in Cambodia have no names and those that do are often known by a number rather than a name, so for example, 50 Street 125 means building number 50 on Street 125. Throughout the chapter, where street names are non-existent, we have located places by describing their location or giving a nearby landmark.

Electricity is usually supplied at 220 volts. Plugs are the two-round-pin variety. Power cuts and power surges are common, and hotels and guesthouses often have back-up generators.

There are no official campsites in Cambodia, but **camping** is a possibility in many places, for example on the beaches and islands of the south coast. In the dry season, all you need is a mosquito net and hammock for a comfortable night's sleep.

Food and drink

Khmer **food** is similar to Thai cuisine, but not as spicy. Chilli is usually served on the side rather than blended into the dish. Even the curry dishes, such as the delicious coconut milk and fish *amoc*, tend to be served very mild. Rice is the staple food for mealtimes, while noodles are more of a snack. Hygiene standards are not high, especially at street stalls, so make sure the food is fresh and piping hot, and make for the busiest places if possible.

■ Where to eat

The cheapest Khmer cuisine is to be found at **street stalls** and **markets**. There are usually one or two dishes on offer at each stall, perhaps pigs' organ soup, fried noodles or a tasty filled baguette. If you're ordering soup, you can pick and choose the ingredients to taste. These stalls are dirt cheap – you can certainly get a meal for less than 2000r – though the portions tend to be on the small side.

Khmer restaurants are the next step up, recognizable by their beer signs outside. In the evenings, the better ones fill up early on and most places close soon after 9pm. Buying a selection of dishes to share is the norm at Khmer restaurants. Each dish costs around 5000–10,000r and there's also a small cover charge. In these restaurants, as in beer gardens, drinks are purchased from "beer girls" (see "Drinks" on p.79).

Western restaurants are plentiful in Phnom Penh, Siem Reap and Sihanoukville, though standards vary enormously. Most places cost roughly the same as eating at a Khmer restaurant, with meals at

---

<table>
<tr><td colspan="3">**ACCOMMODATION PRICE CODES**</td></tr>
</table>

All **accommodation** reviewed in this guide has been graded according to the following price codes, in US dollars, which represent the cost of the cheapest double room available in high season. Where a price range is indicated, this means that the establishment offers rooms with varying facilities – as explained in the write-up. In cases where an establishment charges per bed the actual price is given.

① under $5	④ $15–20	⑦ $40–60
② $5–10	⑤ $20–25	⑧ $60–80
③ $10–15	⑥ $25–40	⑨ $80 and over

FOOD AND DRINK GLOSSARY

See language box on pp.86–87 for pronunciation guide.

GENERAL TERMS AND REQUESTS

How much is it?	*t'lai bpon maan?*	I don't eat meat or fish	*k'nyom meun hoap*
Cheers!	*lek gai-o*		*saich dt'ray*
Only vegetables	*dtai bon-lai*	I'd like...	*k'nyom jong...*
		Could I have the bill?	*kOOt loo-ee?*

RICE AND NOODLES

mee sOOp	noodle soup	*goo-ee dtee-o*	white rice noodles
mee sOOp saich goa	noodle soup with beef	*bai*	cooked rice
mee chaa	fried noodles	*bai chaa*	fried rice
mee	yellow noodles	*bor bor*	rice porridge

FISH, MEAT AND VEGETABLES

bong-gorng	shrimp/prawn	*dom-loang*	potato	*moa-un*	chicken
bon-lai	vegetables	*dt'ray chaa*	fried fish	*saa-lut*	salad
bpayng boh	tomato	*dt'ray*	fish	*saich goa*	beef
bpoat	corn	*dtee-a*	duck	*saich j'rook*	pork
chaa bon-lai	stir-fried	*dtray-meuk*	squid	*saich*	meat
	vegetables	*g'daam*	crab	*spay-ee k'daop*	cabbage

BASICS

ber	butter	*dtao-oo*	tofu	*plai cher*	fruit
bporng moa-un	omelette	*m'tayh*	chilli	*s'gor*	sugar
ch'rop bol		*nOOm*	cake	*sout*	egg
bporng moa-un	fried eggs	*nOOm-bpung*	bread		
chien		*om-beul*	salt		

DRINKS

bee-yair	beer	*dteuk om pao*	sugar cane juice
dteuk dtai	tea	*dteuk*	water
dteuk groatch bpoa-sut	orange juice	*gaa-fay dteuk doh goa*	coffee with milk
dteuk groatch ch'maa	lemon juice	*gaa-fay gdao*	hot coffee
dteuk groatch doang	coconut milk	*gaa-fay*	coffee (black)
dteuk k'nai choo	palm wine	*k'mien dteuk goa*	no ice
dteuk moo-ay dorp	bottle of water		

$2–4, although the more upmarket restaurants charge around $5–10.

Many **guesthouses** also do meals – typically noodles, rice and pasta – for about the same price as Khmer restaurants. It's easy to make do with guesthouse food after a hard day's sightseeing, but for authentic Cambodian culinary colour, you'll need to be more adventurous.

■ Khmer food

A standard **meal** in Cambodia consists of rice, a fish or beef dish, and a steaming bowl of soup. Flavours are dominated by fish sauce, lemongrass (particularly in soup), coconut milk and tamarind.

If you only try one Khmer dish, it should be *amoc*, a delightful fish curry with a rich coconut-milk sauce. Freshwater fish from the Tonlé Sap are abundant and turn up in popular dishes, such as *dt'ray chorm hoy* (steamed fish), *dt'ray aing* (grilled fish) and *dt'ray chean neung spey* (sour fish soup).

For **snacks**, try *un som chroo*, (sticky rice, soy beans and pork served in a bamboo tube) or *un som che* (sticky rice and banana). Baguettes are always a handy snack food, especially when travelling. Vendors have a selection of fillings, including pâté, sardines, pork and salad.

There are some surprisingly tasty **desserts** to be found at street stalls, markets and some restaurants, many of them made from rice and coconut milk. They're very cheap, so you could try a selection. Succulent **fruits** are widely available at the markets. Rambatan, papaya, pineapple, mangosteen and dragonfruit are all delicious and cheap. Durians grow in abundance in Memot and Kampot, apparently some of the world's finest − if you like that sort of thing.

■ Drinks

If you want to avoid stomach problems, don't drink the **water**, and don't take **ice**. Bottled, sealed water is available everywhere. Other thirst-quenchers are the standard international **soft drinks** brands, available in bottles or cans, and a few local variants. Freshly squeezed sugar-cane juice is another healthy roadside favourite, although the tastiest Khmer beverage has to be *dteuk rolok*, a sweet, milky fruit shake, to which locals add an egg for extra nutrition.

Coffee is usually served iced and black, unless requested otherwise. Milk is of the sweet, condensed variety. Chinese-style **tea** is commonly drunk with meals, and is served free in most restaurants.

The **local brew** is Angkor beer, a fairly good drop, owing in part to the use of Australian beer technology at the Sihanoukville brewery. International brands, such as Tiger, Fosters and Heineken, are also on offer at restaurants and beer gardens and are purchased from so-called **beer girls**. Each brand has its own beer girls, so if you want a particular brand you have to order from the corresponding beer girl. Once you've ordered, a tray of cans is brought to your table and a beer girl will keep coming back to open the cans and top up your glass.

Communications

To send anything by **mail** it's best to use the main post office in Phnom Penh, as it's the only place in Cambodia where you can post letters and be more or less sure that they'll arrive at their destination. A stamp for a letter to Europe or Australia costs 2300r, and for a postcard 1800r. Letters to the US cost 2500r, postcards 2100r. International post is often delivered in around a week, but can take up to a month, depending on the destination. Post offices are open every day from 7am until at least 5pm, sometimes later. **Poste restante** is also available at the Phnom Penh post office.

Domestic and **international calls** can be made from guesthouses, hotels, post offices and public phone booths. Phonecards are usually on sale at the shop nearest to the phone booth. Making a phone call in Cambodia, however, is expensive, about double the amount you'd pay in Bangkok, for example. International calls cost from $3 per minute in Phnom Penh, while calls from the provinces are generally more expensive. To **phone abroad** from Cambodia, dial ☎00 + IDD country code (see p.40) + area code minus first 0 + subscriber number. For domestic **directory enquiries** phone ☎1211-5, for international directory enquiries ☎1201-5.

The cost of **Internet access** has been sent tumbling by an influx of Internet cafés. It's now possible to surf for as little as $4 an hour in Phnom Penh (see "Listings", p.102) and it's also worth looking out for special promotions around town. Internet access is also available in Sihanoukville, Siem Reap and Battambang, although it costs more than three times as much as in Phnom Penh.

TIME DIFFERENCES

Cambodia is seven hours ahead of London (GMT), fifteen hours ahead of US Pacific Standard, twelve hours ahead of US Eastern Standard, one hour behind Perth, and three hours behind Sydney.

Opening hours and festivals

Opening hours vary. Even when "official" opening times are posted, these tend to be flexible, as many people juggle more than one job. In theory, office hours are Monday to Saturday, 7.30am to 5.30pm, with a siesta of at least two hours from around 11.30am. **Banking hours** are generally Mon–Fri 8am–3pm, and many banks are also open on Saturday morning. **Post offices**, markets, shops, travel agents and many tourist offices open every day. Museums may close on a Monday.

■ Festivals

P'chum Ben, "Ancestors' Day", in late September, marks the beginning of **festival** season, which continues through until Cambodian New Year in April. In between, the highlight is **Bon Om Dteuk**, the "Water Festival"– celebrated every year when the current of the Tonlé Sap River reverses and flows into the Mekong River. The centre of festivities is Phnom Penh's riverbank, where everyone, including the royal family, gathers to watch boat racing, an illuminated boat parade and fireworks. At this time, Phnom Penh's population swells massively, as thousands of country workers head to the capital for the occasion. Festivals tend to be fixed by the lunar calendar, so dates vary from year to year. Offices may shut on national holidays, but everything else continues much as normal.

PUBLIC HOLIDAYS

January 7: Liberation Day, celebrating the fall of the Khmer Rouge

February: Chinese New Year

March 8: Women's Day

mid-April: Cambodian New Year

May 1: International Labor Day

May: Chat Preah Nengkal, the "Royal Ploughing Ceremony"

late September: P'chum Ben Day, "Ancestors' Day" (offerings made to deceased relatives)

September 24 Constitution Day

November 1: King Sihanouk's Birthday

November 9: Independence Day

early November: Bon Om Dteuk, "Water Festival"

Cultural hints

Cambodia shares the same attitutudes to dress and social taboos as other Southeast Asian cultures; see "Basics" p.41 for details.

Crime and safety

The **security situation** in Cambodia has improved significantly over the last few years. Areas that were once plagued with bandit activity or by the threat of unpredictable Khmer Rouge factions, are now pretty safe to travel in. However, there is a huge number of guns in Cambodia, and there have been incidents of armed robbery against tourists. All areas covered in this book are safe to travel to overland, with the exception of Stung Treng and Ratanakiri, which have been subject to infrequent bandit attacks. Even in these areas, most overland travellers do not have any problems. Check the current situation before you travel. It's also a good idea not to take anything of value to the remoter provinces and to take the minimum of cash.

Gun crime is actually more frequent in Phnom Penh than anywhere else in the country, and reaches a peak at festival times, most notably Khmer New Year. Even so, the threat is small, so it shouldn't stop you enjoying the nightlife. Taking a few simple precautions can reduce the risk further:

Do not go out alone after dark.

Do not carry your passport or other valuable items; lock them in your hotel safe.

Carry only a small amount of cash.

Use a moto or taxi rather than walk.

Use a trustworthy moto-driver, preferably someone recommended by your hotel or guesthouse.

If you are robbed, do not resist and do not run.

There are plenty of civilian and military **police** hanging around, whose main function appears to be imposing arbitrary fines or tolls. Of the two, the **civilian police**, who wear blue or khaki uniforms, are more helpful. Military police wear black-and-white armbands.

■ Landmines

The war has ended, but the killing continues. Years of guerrilla conflict have left Cambodia the most densely mined country in the world. The statistics are horrendous – up to eight million **landmines** in the country; 50,000 amputees; a further 2000 mine victims every year. The worst affected areas are the province of Battambang and the border regions adjacent to Thailand in the northwest, namely Banteay Meanchey, Pailin and Preah Vihear provinces.

Slow progress is being made by mine-clearance organizations, such as the British-based Mine Action Group (MAG) and The Halo Trust, but resources are extremely limited compared to the scale of the problem.

Although the risk is very real for those who work in the fields, the threat to tourists is minimal. The main **tourist areas** are clear of mines, and even in the heavily mined areas the towns and roads are safe. The main danger occurs when striking off into fields or forests, so the simple solution is to stick to known safe paths. If you must cross a dubious area, try to use a local guide, or at least ask the locals "mian min dtay?" ("Are there mines here?"). Look out for the red mine-warning signs, and do not remove them.

Medical care and emergencies

For serious **medical emergencies** consider flying to Bangkok, although clinics and hospitals in Phnom Penh are equipped to deal with most ailments (see "Listings", p.102, for addresses). Sihanoukville and Siem Reap have limited facilities, but generally medical facilities outside Phnom Penh are poor. If you are stuck in the provinces and require emergency evacuation to Phnom Penh, contact AEA International on ☎023/216911. General emergency telephone numbers are listed in the box below, but whatever the emergency, it's probably best to contact the English-speaking operators (see box below), available 24 hours.

Street-corner **pharmacies** throughout Cambodia are well-stocked with basic supplies diverted from NGOs, and money rather than a prescription gives easy access to anything available, though beware of out-of-date medication. Standard shop hours apply at most of these places, but some stay open in the evening. More reputable operations with English- and French-speaking pharmacists can be found in Phnom Penh, where a wider variety of specialized drugs are available. Some even offer 24-hour service (see "Listings", p.102).

EMERGENCY PHONE NUMBERS

Police ☎117
Fire ☎118
Ambulance ☎119
Police Assistance (English, French and Italian spoken) ☎017/816601 or 018/811542
Police Assistance for expats ☎023/724793, 023/366841 or 023/366842

History

Little is known about the **early history** of Cambodia. Archeological evidence suggests that the area was occupied and cultivated from at least 4000BC. These early dwellers lived in buildings similar to those

inhabited by today's Khmers, indicating that they may be direct ancestors, but the origin of these first settlers and the date of their arrival in Cambodia is unknown.

It wasn't until the first century AD that the indigenous population began to adopt advanced concepts of rice cultivation, religious beliefs and social structure and to establish themselves as a civilization worthy of note. This transformation owes much to the visiting Indian traders, en route to China, who brought ideas as well as goods to the region. Thus, the area to the west of the Mekong Delta began establishing itself as an important commercial settlement centred around the port of Oc Eo (now in Vietnam). The civilization became known by the Chinese as Funan.

The Indianized **Funan** port community enjoyed prosperity for several centuries, but gradually declined in importance from the sixth century, as farmers began to move away and cultivate the fertile areas around the Mekong and Tonlé Sap. From this time, the Chinese referred to the inhabitants as the **Chenla**. Although this term implies a cohesive culture, the Chenla actually consisted of small, disparate fiefdoms operating independently. It took the foresight and inspirational guidance of Jayavarman II, recently returned from Indonesia, to guide these rival factions towards a prosperous unification.

■ Angkorian period

Cambodia's heyday, the **Angkorian period**, started in the early ninth century when the rival Chenla kingdoms united under King Jayavarman II as their universal monarch. Forging alliances through marriages and offerings of land, and gaining territory through military campaigns, he created the beginnings of the mighty Khmer Empire. Jayavarman II also introduced the religious cult of Devaraja god-king, a belief system which continued with his successors. In total, 39 successive kings reigned over the Angkor Empire (known at the time as Kambuja-desa) from various capitals to the northeast of the Tonlé Sap; the temples of Angkor remain as a legacy of these cities. The last major king, Jayavarman VII, embarked on a massive programme of construction, culminating in the creation of the magnificent walled city of Angkor Thom.

For most of the Angkorian period, the biggest military threat came from the **Champa Kingdom**, located in central Vietnam. It was at the hands of the Chams that the Khmers suffered their worst defeat: sailing their fleet up the Mekong Delta and into the

Tonlé Sap, the Chams devastated the capital and occupied Cambodia for four years. It was Jayavarman VII who eventually pushed them out, annexing Champa in the process.

Thailand was a further threat to the supremacy of the Khmer Empire, and by the fourteenth century, the Siamese army had become a formidable force, mounting raids on Cambodian territory, and virtually destroying Angkor Thom. It was probably due to the proximity of Angkor to the hostile Thai-occupied areas that the capital was abandoned in favour of more southerly locations by the middle of the fifteenth century. By this time, repeated wars had taken their toll, in both human and financial terms, and Jayavarman VII's royal excesses had further depleted the coffers. The Khmer Empire was in irreversible decline.

■ From empire to protectorate

The **Thai** army continued to grow in strength during the fifteenth century. Conversely, the Khmers were in a state of disarray and could not mount an effective defence. In 1594, their capital fell to the Thais. From that point on, Cambodian fortunes looked decidedly bleak. As different factions of the Cambodian royal family looked to either Thailand or Vietnam for military and financial assistance, vast swathes of land were lost in tribute payments to both nations. Had the French not arrived in the 1860s, Cambodia may have been entirely swallowed up by Thailand and Vietnam.

■ French control

By 1863, the **French** already had a strong foothold in the area, with the Mekong Delta in Vietnam under their control, and missionaries already in residence in Cambodia. The then monarch King Norodom saw an opportunity to use the French as a way of reducing Thai control, and securing his own position against other claims to the throne. In August 1863, he exchanged timber concessions and mineral exploitation rights for military protection, ushering in an era of French control that would last until 1941. When the French pushed for more control in Cambodian affairs, a vicious rebellion erupted across the country that ended only when the French agreed to revert to the older agreement. Despite the insurrection and subsequent agreement, French control tightened, and after King Norodom's death in 1904 the following three kings were selected by the French. In 1941, eighteen-year old Prince Norodom Sihanouk was chosen to succeed King Monivong, but before the

French had a chance to manipulate the impressionable young monarch, the Japanese marched into Cambodia, and World War II interrupted French control.

■ Independence

Following the Japanese surrender in 1945, King Sihanouk stunned the French by campaigning for **independence**. As international support for Sihanouk grew, and conflict in Vietnam occupied French troops and resources, France was left with no option but to grant independence. This was formally recognized by the Geneva Conference in May 1954, with a stipulation that elections should follow. As communism was gaining popular support across Southeast Asia, King Sihanouk embarked on a drastic course of action to retain control of Cambodia. He abdicated from the throne, installing his father Norodom Suramarit as king, and formed a political party to fight in the 1955 elections. Incredibly, his party, The People's Socialist Community, won every seat in the newly-formed parliament, and 99 percent of the vote in the subsequent 1958 elections. But the power-crazed monarch-turned-politician ruled with an iron hand, and political opposition was ruthlessly smothered. Communist elements, termed "Khmers Rouges" by Sihanouk, fled to the countryside to avoid arrest. When, in 1960, his father died, he appointed himself Chief of State, in a further gesture of despotic power.

■ The Vietnamese factor

Meanwhile, things were beginning to heat up in **Vietnam**, and Sihanouk was being pressured into taking sides in the conflict. Despite publicly declaring neutrality, he allowed the Vietcong to shelter from American bombings on Cambodian soil, and tolerated deliveries of arms and supplies through the port of Sihanoukville to Vietcong encampments. But in a policy u-turn in 1969, Sihanouk began negotiating with the US, and allowed American planes to start bombing Cambodia's Eastern provinces, where **Vietcong** guerrillas were hiding. Hundreds of Cambodian civilians were killed or maimed in these raids, and left-wing disquiet began to grow. General Lon Nol and Prince Sisowath Matak seized an opportunity to depose Sihanouk while he was away in France in 1970, and ordered the Vietcong to leave Cambodian soil. Instead, they pushed deeper into Cambodia, pursued by US and Southern Vietnamese troops, transforming Cambodia into a savage battlefield. Thousands of war refugees fled the fighting and headed to Phnom Penh. With the country in complete disarray under a weak and ineffective leadership, the communist Khmer Rouge regrouped, and began taking control of large areas of the provinces.

■ The Khmer Rouge regime

Khmer Rouge forces marched into Phnom Penh on 17 April 1975 to the cheers of the Cambodian people. The war was over, and peace would prevail, they assumed. Unfortunately, this was not to be. From the very day that the Khmer Rouge arrived in Phnom Penh, a systematic process of communist re-engineering was ordered, presumably by Communist Party leader Saloth Sar, or **Pol Pot** as he was subsequently known. The deranged attempt to transform the country into an agrarian collective, inspired by Maoist ideology, proved a monumental human disaster and caused international outrage, but little action. The entire population of Phnom Penh and other provincial capitals was forcibly removed to the countryside to begin their new lives as peasants working on the land. They were the lucky ones. Pol Pot ordered the mass extermination of intellectuals, teachers, writers, educated people, and their families. Even wearing glasses was an indication of intelligence, a "crime" punishable by death. The brutal regime lasted four years before invading **Vietnamese forces** reached the capital in 1979; by this time, at least one million, perhaps three million Khmers had died as a result of the Kampuchean holocaust. Pol Pot and his supporters fled to the jungle bordering Thailand, from where they continued to wage civil war on successive governments in Phnom Penh.

■ Vietnamese occupation

The **Vietnamese-backed government** installed in Phnom Penh was led by Hun Sen and Heng Samrin, both Cambodians who had served in the Khmer Rouge, but defected to Vietnam. Meanwhile, a Chinese-backed coalition government-in-exile was being created to unify opposition to the Vietnamese government. It was dominated by the Khmer Rouge, and headed by Sihanouk. For Cambodian people, Vietnamese occupation was by no means the perfect solution, but compared to the suffering and death of the previous four years, it was a welcome change. The international community, however, came down on the side of a Khmer Rouge-dominated coalition, and refused to recognize the new government. After all, the new Vietnamese occupation could be the start of communist expansionism, whereas the

Khmer Rouge, despite being communists, only killed their own and didn't pose a threat to the capitalist world. So Thailand, Britain and the US colluded to train the genocidal rebels, shelter them on Thai soil, provide money, arms and food, and offered them the Cambodian seat in the United Nations.

However, in 1985, there was a transformation in the international communist landscape. Mikhail Gorbachev rose to power in the Soviet Union, and in the face of harsh economic pressures, cancelled aid to Vietnam. Vietnam in turn could no longer support the Cambodian occupation, and in 1987, negotiations began between the Hun Sen government and the coalition led by Sihanouk. Finally, after intense fighting between rival factions of the coalition in Cambodia, the Paris Peace Accords were signed in 1991.

■ UNTAC

Under the Paris Peace Accords, sweeping powers were granted to the **United Nations Transitional Authority in Cambodia (UNTAC)**, who were to implement and oversee free and fair elections in 1993, at that point the largest UN operation in history. But the demobilization and disarmament that was essential for free and fair elections never occurred. Hun Sen's troops remained in charge, able to intimidate voters, so the Khmer Rouge refused to participate in the election process. The elections took place amid assassinations, intimidation tactics, bribery, corruption and the shelling of some polling stations. Despite this, a huge turnout of voters supported the royalist FUNCINPEC party, led by Prince Norodom Ranariddh, who won 58 seats. The Cambodian People's Party (CPP) led by Hun Sen gained 51 seats, and eventually a fragile coalition was agreed. Prince Ranariddh was named First Prime Minister and Hun Sen was named Second Prime Minister. Sihanouk was reinstated as monarch in August 1993.

■ The end of the Khmer Rouge

Khmer Rouge guerrilla activity intensified after the 1993 elections. An amnesty for Khmer Rouge soldiers had already begun to attract some defections to the Royal Cambodian Armed Forces (RCAF), and in 1996, the government scored a coup; Ieng Sary, Pol Pot's trusted Number Two, defected with 10,000 troops. This signalled a major split in the Khmer Rouge ranks, and isolated the ageing Pol Pot. Further defections looked likely, and a paranoid Pol Pot ordered the murder of his defence minister and his entire family. Another senior Khmer Rouge military

commander, the notorious Ta Mok, turned on his former master. He arrested Pol Pot, and sentenced him
to life imprisonment. More defections followed, and
as the RCAF troops began a final push into the last
Khmer Rouge stronghold in April 1998, the infamous
Pol Pot supposedly died in his sleep.

■ Recent history

Hun Sen has been consolidating his powerful position since UNTAC left. In 1997, he accused Prince
Ranariddh of planning a military coup after arms
apparently bound for Ranariddh's private army were
found at Sihanoukville port. Ranariddh fled in fear of
his life, but was arrested, tried and eventually par-
doned, to participate in another round of elections in
July 1998. This time, Hun Sen's CPP came out on top,
gaining 64 of the 122 seats. FUNCINPEC won fifteen
seats, and the newly formed Sam Rainsy Party also
won fifteen. Again, an alliance was negotiated, this
time with Hun Sen as sole Prime Minister. Hun Sen
continues to be the most powerful man in Cambodia.
Although he stands accused of nepotism, corruption
and human rights violations, he remains popular, particularly among those benefitting financially from the
current economic climate.

Religions of Cambodia

The state religion in Cambodia is **Theravada
Buddhism** (see "Basics", p.47), though historically,
Hinduism was also a major influence. There is also
a significant number of Cambodian **Muslims**, often
referred to as Chams. The Chams were the medieval
inhabitants of the Hindu Champa kingdom, on the
coast of what is now Vietnam. In the fifteenth century, as the Vietnamese began to extend their territory,
the Chams were forced to flee south seeking refuge
amongst the Hindu Khmers and settling in fertile
areas north of Phnom Penh, primarily in the area
known today as Kompong Cham. Soon after, the
Chams converted to Sunni Islam as the religion
swept through the region. Khmer Muslims tend to
live in their own villages or in small neighbourhoods
within the larger cities. Marriage outside the Muslim
community is prohibited, so the community has
retained a strong identity over the years. There are
thought to be more than 300,000 Khmer Muslims in
Cambodia.

All religions suffered **persecution** from 1975 to
1979; monks and priests were murdered, temples,
wats and mosques destroyed. Buddhism has still not
fully recovered, and you'll notice less emphasis on

religion in Cambodia than in other Southeast Asian
nations.

The architecture of ancient Cambodia

While its form is unmistakably rooted in India, the
wealth of **architecture** that the ancient Khmer left
scattered across Southeast Asia has no Indian parallel. This is largely due to the uniquely Khmer cult
known as *devaraja*, literally "god-king". Founded on
the belief that Khmer kings were earthly incarnations
of Shiva, Vishnu or the Buddha, the cult inspired
dizzying heights of architectural megalomania as
each successive king endeavoured to construct a
temple to his own greatness that would eclipse the
efforts of all his predecessors. The monuments from
Cambodia's glorious past rival those of ancient Egypt
and Mesoamerica in size and grandeur, and like their
counterparts on far-off continents, the ancient Khmer
suffused their imposing stone architecture with religious symbolism.

Many **Khmer temples** are actually scale models
of the Hindu–Buddhist universe. Moats and walls
symbolize oceans and mountain ranges that encircled the five-peaked Mount Meru, the lofty home of
the gods. The majority of these temples face east to
catch the rays of the rising sun, symbolic of life. The
exception is **Angkor Wat**, which faces west, the
direction of the setting sun and death. While the
mathematical equations that dictated the dimensions
of Khmer temples are no longer understood, it is
known that the ancient Khmer placed great stock in
the auspiciousness of such precise measurements.
This can be discerned in the lay-out of Khmer temples, most of which possess a severe symmetry.

The building materials used by the ancient Khmer
changed over time. **Early Angkor-period temples**
were constructed of brick. Using a now-forgotten
technique to cement the bricks together, the Khmer
built towers that were similar in style to those built
by the Cham in what is present-day central Vietnam.
Examples of these early towers can be seen at
Roluos, but the most impressive brick temple is
Prasat Kravan, the interior of which has bas-reliefs
carved right into the brick. A type of stucco made
from such esoteric ingredients as pounded tamarind
and the soft earth of termite mounds was used as a
medium to sculpt ornamentation for the brick structures. Laterite, a porous stone that resembles lava
rock, was utilized for foundations and walls. The use
of **sandstone** was, of course, what set Khmer tem-

ples apart from religious architecture constructed by the ancient Cham, Thai and Burmese, all of whom worked almost exclusively in brick and stucco. As a medium for decoration, sandstone also allowed the wondrous talent of Khmer sculptors to shine through.

While the extent of **sculpted motifs** varies from temple to temple, two portions of Khmer edifices were always lavishly decorated: lintels and pediments. The lintel, a rectangular stone block fixed over doorways, became an important element in Khmer architecture when the Khmer began carving ornate designs into them several centuries before the Angkor period. Early prototypes have been found dating to the seventh century and indicate that the designs were influenced by pre-Angkor kingdoms such as Funan. As the styles and motifs have evolved over the centuries, experts on Khmer art are able to date lintels by comparing them to known works. A motif commonly found on **lintels** is Kala, an ogre-like temple guardian usually depicted with two stylized garlands spewing from the corners of his mouth. Often a deity or divinity is perched atop Kala's head. **Pediments**, the triangular space just above doorways and lintels, were also favourite spots for lavish adornment. Often these depict elaborate scenes from Hindu or Buddhist legends – the pediments at Angkor Wat and Banteay Srei being particularly fine examples. Framing the pediments are usually the undulating forms of **nagas**, long, multi-headed water serpents, issuing forth from the gaping mouths of **makaras**, another type of water beast. So popular was this particular architectural detail that it has survived to this day, and cobra-like nagas can be seen framing the pediments of modern temples in Cambodia as well as in neighbouring Thailand and Laos. Other images found in the vicinity of doorways are **dvarapalas**, standing male guardians usually depicted wielding a club or spear, and **devatas**, guardian female divinities. The realistically portrayed guardian images at Banteay Srei are thought by experts to be pinnacles of Khmer art. To many modern visitors, the most easily admired of the mythical representations are the **apsaras**, the celestial nymphs who seem to dance upon the smooth sandstone walls. Angkor Wat has by far the most sensitively rendered collection of *apsaras* and it is readily apparent that the artisans who sculpted these sublime images spent much time ensuring that no two were alike.

Apart from the images carved in bas-relief described above, **"story telling" bas-reliefs** were used to striking effect by the Khmer. Illustrating historical events, mythology (such as the Ramayana and Mahabharata) and exploits of the kings who had them commissioned, they cover over a thousand square metres of gallery walls in Angkor Wat alone. Depending on how they were executed, the bas-reliefs could be "read" like pages from a giant comic book, from panel to panel. Sometimes the bas-reliefs on a wall were divided into several levels, such as the depiction of the levels of heaven and hell found at Angkor Wat. Often though, a story or event was illustrated in a single large panel. As in Egyptian art, an image's importance is illustrated by its size in relation to the images around it. Thus the bas-reliefs at Angkor Wat depict grand images of the Hindu god Vishnu, his vehicle Garuda, and Vishnu's incarnations as Krishna, Rama and Kurma – evidence that Suryavarman II, the *devaraja* who had Angkor Wat commissioned, believed himself to be an incarnation of Vishnu on earth.

To Suryavarman II goes the credit for erecting ancient Cambodia's greatest architectural masterpiece, the silhouette of which graces the Cambodian national flag. Yet not long after his death, the Cham sacked Angkor and the empire fell into disarray. Not until a young prince, Jayavarman VII, took the throne and drove out the invaders was building to begin again in earnest. But major changes came with Jayavarman VII's reign that would affect Khmer architecture. The king's embrace of Buddhism caused the ascendancy of **Mahayana Buddhism** over Hinduism as the official religion. This is most readily seen in the mixed Buddhist and Hindu iconography of temples such as Ta Phrom and Preah Khan, where bas-reliefs depicting meditating Buddhas are found alongside the usual Hindu deities and demigods. At least, this would have been more apparent before Jayavarman VII's death. Following the Buddhist king's demise there was a backlash against Buddhism, and many of the carvings of meditating Buddhas at Ta Phrom and Preah Khan were defaced or recarved to resemble meditating Hindu ascetics.

Jayavarman VII's reign was also a time of vast territorial gains. Owing mainly to Jayavarman VII's rush to plant monuments across his newly expanded empire, the artisans and architects of the **Bayon period** have been accused by modern art historians of producing crude, hurried works. **Laterite blocks** were used in place of sandstone in the construction of many of Jayavarman VII's temples outside of the Angkor region. Because it was more easily quarried, laterite made it possible for Jayavarman VII to erect edifices in the more far-flung corners of his empire in a relatively short time. Unfortunately, the rough surface of laterite makes it impossible to carve reliefs upon.

KHMER LANGUAGE

Khmer is the national language of Cambodia. Unusually for this region, it is not a tonal language, which theoretically makes it easier to master. However, the difficulty lies with pronunciation, as there are both vowels and consonant clusters that are pronounced unlike any sounds in English. That makes it difficult to represent accurately in romanized form, and what follows here is a phonetic approximation widely used for teaching Khmer. (People and places throughout this chapter follow the commonly used romanized spellings rather than the phonetic system used below.)

CONSONANTS

Most consonants follow English pronunciation, except the following;

bp	a sharp 'p' sound, between the English 'b' and 'p'	dt	a sharp 't' sound, between the English 'd' and 't'
		n'y/ñ	as in 'canyon'

VOWELS

-a	as in 'ago'	-ee	as in 'see'	-oa	as in 'moan'
-aa	as in 'bar'	-eu	as in the expression of	-oo	as in 'shoot'
-ai	as in 'Thai'		disgust 'uugh'	-ou	similar to 'cow'
-ao	as in 'Lao'	-i	as in 'fin'	-OO	as in 'look'
-ay	as in 'pay'	-o	as in 'long'	-u	as in 'fun'

GREETINGS AND BASIC PHRASES

Hello	*soo-a s'day*	What's your name?	*loak ch'moo-ah ay?*
How are you?	*sok sa- bai jee-a dtay?*	My name is...	*k'nyom ch'moo-ah...*
Fine, thanks	*sok sa-bai jee-a dtay*	Can you speak	*loak jeh ni-yee-ay pee-a-*
Goodbye	*lee-a hai-ee*	English?	*saa ong-klayh reu dtay?*
Good night	*ree-a-dtree soo-a s'day*	I don't understand	*k'nyom s'dup meun baan*
	sewesedai		*dtay*
Excuse me	*soam dtoah*	Yes (male)	*baht*
Please	*soam*	Yes (female)	*ja*
Thank you	*or-gOOn*	No	*dtay*

EMERGENCIES

Are there any mines here?	*mee-un meen dtay?*	Please call an ambulance	*soam hao lamphet mok*
Can you help me?	*joo-ay k'nyom baan dtay*	Hospital	*moo-un dtee bpairt*
Accident	*kroo-ah t'nuk*	Police station	*s'taa-nee dtom-roo-ut*
Please call a doctor	*soam hao kroo bpet moak*		

GETTING AROUND

Where is the?	*... noo-ee-naa?*	I'd like to go to...	*k'nyom jong dtou...*
How many kilometres	*dtou... bpon-maan*	Ticket	*som-bot*
is it to...?	*ogee-loa-mait?*	Aeroplane	*yoo-un hoh*
How long does it take?	*joom-nai bpayl bpon-maan?*	Airport	*jom nort yoo-un hoh/aa-gaah-sa-yee-un-taan*

Boat	*dtook*	Motorbike taxi	*moto*
Bus/coach	*laan ch'noo-ul/laan krong*	Pick-up	*laan ch'noo-ul*
Train station	*staa-nee a-ya-s'mai yien*	Restaurant	*poa-cha-nee-ya-taan*
Taxi	*dtuk-see*	Please stop here	*soam chOOp dtrong neung*
Car	*laan*		*hai-ee*
Gas station	*staa-nee*	Left/right	*ch'wayng/s'dum*
Bicycle	*bprayng sung gong*	North	*kaang jerng*
Bank	*tor-nee-a-gee- a*	South	*kaang t'boang*
Post office	*bprai-sa-nee*	East	*kaang gart*
Passport	*li-keut ch'lorng dain*	West	*kaang leuch*
Hotel	*son-ta-gee-a*		

ACCOMODATION

Do you have any rooms?	*tan'y mee-un bon-dtOOp dtay?*	Double room	*bon-dtOOpsom-rup bpee nay-uk*
How much is it?	*t'lai bpon maan?*	Air-conditioner	*maa-seen dtra-jay-uk*
Can I have a look?	*soam merl baan dtay?*	Electric fan	*dong-hul*
Do you have...	*mee-un...*	Mosquito net	*mOOng*
Room with bathroom	*bon-dtOOp mee-un bon-dtOOp dteuk*	Toilet paper	*gra-daah som-rup bong-goo-un*
		Telephone	*dtoo-ra-sup*
		Laundry	*boak-oot*
Cheap/expensive	*taok/t'lai*	Blanket	*poo-ay*
Single room	*bon-dtOOpdtai moo-ay*	Open/closed	*bark/beut*

TIME

What's the time?	*maong bpon-maan?*	Day	*t'ngai*	Yesterday	*m'serl meun~*
		Week	*aa-dteut*	Now	*ay-lou nih*
Noon	*t'ngai dtrong*	Month	*kai*	Morning	*bpreuk*
Midnight	*aa-tree-ut*	Year	*ch'num*	Afternoon	*ra-see-ul*
Minute	*nee-a-dtee*	Today	*t'ngai nih*	Evening	*l'ngee-ich*
Hour	*maong*	Tomorrow	*t'ngai sa-aik*	Night	*yOOp*

NUMBERS

1	*moo-ay*	30	*saam seup*
2	*bpee*	40	*sai seup*
3	*bay*	50	*haa seup*
4	*boo-un*	60	*hok seup*
5	*bprum*	70	*jeut seup*
6	*bprum-moo-ay*	80	*bpait seup*
7	*bprum bpee/ bprum bpeul*	90	*gao seup*
8	*prum bay*	100	*roy*
9	*bprum boo-un*	101	*roy moo-ay*
10	*dop*	200	*bpee roy*
11	*dop moo-ay/moo-ay don dop*	1000	*bpoa-un*
12	*dop bpee/bpee don dop*	10,000	*meun*
13	*dop bay/bay don-dop*	100,000	*sain*
20	*m'pay*	1,000,000	*lee-un*
21	*m'pay moo-ay*		

Stucco was used to decorate some of these laterite temples but the effect could never match the intricate bas-reliefs of carved sandstone. In the same vein, the bas-reliefs at the Bayon, Jayavarman VII's grandest monument, seem rather primitive when compared to the delicate intricacies of those at Angkor Wat. Despite the inferior quality of Jayavarman VII's works, there is one unique design innovation from his reign that many agree is the Khmers' most striking contribution to architecture: the **colossal stone faces** that gaze with blissful detachment from the towers of the Bayon and the gates of Angkor Thom. Thought to depict the Bodhisattva Lokeshvara, the Mahayana Buddhist 'Lord of Compassion', the faces can also be seen adorning gates at Banteay Kdei and Ta Phrom, as well as the towers of Banteay Chhmar in western Cambodia. Not surprisingly, this powerful visual theme – stone visages smiling enigmatically as the roots of mammoth banyan trees threaten to topple them into jumbled heaps – has been used extensively by modern artists, including several Hollywood film makers, to symbolise ancient civilizations lost to the ravages of time.

While the architecture of the ancient Khmer manages to inspire awe even in its ruined state, it is important to remember that when we look at the monuments today, we see only what did not perish with the centuries – stone, brick and stucco. What we don't see are the ornately carved pavilions of golden teak that housed troupes of court dancers, minstrels, high priests and the god-kings themselves. Gone are the decorative embellishments that would have brought the monuments to life: the sheets of gilded copper that covered unadorned stone walls and towers, the parasols, banners and tapestries of delicate silk that gave colour to dimly-lighted galleries and antechambers, the finely woven mats of aromatic grasses that covered rough stone causeways. Important elements which, when combined with the grandeur of bold stones rising up to dominate the jungle canopy, would surely have evoked paradise on earth.

Books

Most **books** about Cambodia concentrate either on Angkor or the Khmer Rouge atrocities – travelogues and fiction are virtually non-existent. If you can't find the following books before you leave home, you should be able to get them in Bangkok or Cambodia itself. Where a book is published in the UK and the US, the UK publisher is given first, followed by the US one. The abbreviation o/p means "out of print".

David Chandler, *A History of Cambodia*; *Brother Number One* (both Westview Press). In *A History of Cambodia* Chandler, the acknowledged authority on Cambodian history, examines the changing fortunes of the country during the two thousand years of its existence. His considered biography, *Brother Number One*, serves to shed some light on the enigma of Pol Pot, a man with mild manners, but a genocidal bent.

Amit Gilboa, *Off the Rails in Phnom Penh – Into the Dark Heart of Guns, Girls and Ganja* (Asia Books, Bangkok). A shallow, seedy, sensational account of expat life in Phnom Penh. Gilboa sets out to shock rather than to create a literary masterpiece.

Claude Jacques, *Angkor* (Konemann). One for the library rather than the suitcase, this generous volume tracks the rise and fall of the great Khmer civilization. Bright, readable history and thorough technical descriptions of the temples are interspersed with stunning photographs and detailed temple plans.

Henry Kamm *Cambodia – Report from a Stricken Land* (Arcade, US). The truth of contemporary Cambodian history laid bare – an informed and authoritative narrative of the complex international manoeuvres which destroyed Cambodia's chances of an early recovery.

Norman Lewis, *A Dragon Apparent* (Picador/ Transatlantic-Pubns Inc). Now only available as part of the *Norman Lewis Omnibus: A Dragon Apparent; Golden Earth; A Goddess in the Stones*, Lewis's colourful travelogue describes his journey through Indochina during the last years of French rule.

Dith Pran, *Children of Cambodia's Killing Fields* (Yale University Press). A moving compilation of memoirs from those who experienced the Cambodian holocaust first-hand.

Dawn Rooney, *Angkor* (Odyssey, Hong Kong). A comprehensive introduction to the temples of Angkor, with the benefit of detailed plans and a monument-by-monument guide to the main temples.

Vittorio Roveda, *Khmer Mythology* (Thames and Hudson/Weatherhill). Roveda explains the legends and histories behind Angkor's incredible carvings, bringing numerous reliefs to life.

David Smyth, *Colloquial Cambodian* (Routledge). An easy-to-use introduction to written and spoken Cambodian.

Chou Ta-Kuan, *The Customs of Cambodia* (Siam Society, Bangkok). A translation of the intriguing accounts of thirteenth-century Chinese Mandarin Chou Ta-Kuan. His detailed chronicles offer an amazing insight into daily life at Angkor, at the peak of the Khmer Empire.

Usha Welaratna, *Beyond the Killing Fields* (Stanford University Press, US). As fearful Cambodians fled the country in 1979, thousands of refugees were left without homes. Welaratna's perceptive book examines the experiences of nine Cambodian refugees who settled in the United States to rebuild their lives.

Ray Zepp, *The Cambodia Less Traveled* (o/p). Part travelogue, part dated guide book, this rare edition is worthy of a read if a copy can be found. Reveals the wonders, limitations and frustrations of travelling through Cambodia in the mid-1990s.

PHNOM PENH

Cambodia's capital, **PHNOM PENH**, sprawls west from the confluence of the Mekong and Tonlé Sap rivers. At first glance, the city is a confusing mess with no obvious landmarks. The main boulevards are choked with motos and other traffic and lined with generic low-rise concrete blocks, crying out for repairs. The unsealed back streets look identical, with only the varying pattern of potholes and piles of building debris to distinguish them.

Despite initial impressions, however, the heart of Phnom Penh, immediately west of the river, has a strong appeal. The French influence is particularly evident, from the colonial shophouses lining the boulevards to the cheese-filled baguettes, and here and there a majestic Khmer building animates the cityscape. The Phnom Penhois are open and friendly, and the city itself is small enough to get to know quickly. Phnom Penh may not have much in the way of tourist attractions – the majority of sights can be covered in a day or two – but many visitors end up lingering, if only to soak up the unique indolent atmosphere of this neglected city.

Phnom Penh's **history** began in 1372, when a local widow, Lady Penh, stumbled across a floating trunk containing four bronze Buddha statues and another in stone, washed up by the Mekong River. She saw them as bearers of good fortune and had a small temple built for them high above the water level to guard against flooding. This hill became known as Penh's hill – Phnom Penh – a name adopted by the town that grew up around the site. Phnom Penh was briefly made the capital in the fifteenth century, sacked and destroyed by the invading Thais in 1834, then reinstated as capital again in 1866 under the French. The city flourished during the Indochina years, but the departure of the French signalled the beginnings of political in-fighting in Cambodia, with Phnom Penh at the centre. Then came the Khmer Rouge whose experimental ideology rejected an urban existence, and the city was completely emptied, many of its buildings destroyed. It wasn't until 1979 and the Vietnamese victory over the Khmer Rouge that people began drifting back to the devastated city. From a low of around fifteen thousand during the Pol Pot era, the population now stands at around one million.

Prosperity has also been slowly returning, and mobile phones, land cruisers, and glitzy karaoke joints are much in evidence. Although not a modern, developed capital by any means, it's still a huge contrast to the rest of the country, where the majority of Khmers live a simple, rural existence, earning an average weekly wage of less than $5.

Arrival and information

Pochentong Airport, Cambodia's international gateway, lies 6km west of the city centre. The terminal has a tourist information desk (opening hours variable), with a list of hotels and travel agents. There's a post office, where you can make domestic and international calls and send faxes; and a Foreign Exchange Bank kiosk (Mon–Fri 8.30am–3.30pm). Licensed taxis are operated from a counter directly outside the terminal building; these charge a flat fee of $7 for the journey into the city centre. If you want to get straight down to some haggling, head out to Pochentong Boulevard, outside the airport, where you're free to negotiate your own fare – reckon on around $4 for a taxi, $1 for a moto.

Trains pull into Phnom Penh station, a crumbling art-deco delight situated centrally at the corner of Pochentong and Monivong Boulevards. Most **buses** draw up near the southwest corner of the central market. **Pick-ups** will either draw up here or drop you off somewhere in town. Express **boats** dock at the terminal north of Friendship Bridge.

For **tourist information**, don't expect much joy at either the Phnom Penh Tourist Office at 313 Sisowath Quay (Mon–Fri 7–11.30am & 2–5.30pm; ☎023/724059) or the Ministry of Tourism on Monivong Boulevard at the corner of Street 232 (Mon–Fri 8–11.30am & 2.30–5.30pm; ☎023/426876). Most guesthouses and hotels have more reliable information. *Capitol Guesthouse* (see opposite) has set itself up as the tourist guru in the absence of official information, though, naturally, they will try and pedal their own tours.

City transport

Motorcycle taxis, or **motos**, are the most convenient way of getting around the city and are inexpensive. Expect to pay 500–1000r for a short hop, or up to 2000r for a longer journey. Prices go up after dark – a 500r surcharge is fair, but drivers will invariably ask for more. You can also hire a moto-driver for a day – explain to the driver exactly where you want to go and negotiate a price beforehand. A good English-speaker will charge around $7 per day for his services as driver and guide. If you're not in a hurry, **cyclos** are handy for short trips. Fares are subject to negotiation, usually between 500r and 1000r.

A number of useful **bus services** connect the city with the suburbs and beyond. Ho Wah Genting operates buses along National Routes 1, 2, 4 and 5 daily, leaving from the southwest corner of the central market. You can jump on or off anywhere along the route; wave the bus down to get on, and to get off, just shout at the driver. The fare varies, depending on distance, but is usually 1000–3000r; tickets are bought on board.

Taxis are not hailed on the street – you can either book them over the phone (see "Listings", p.103, for numbers) or pick one up at Monivong Boulevard near the central market, where they tend to gather. Negotiate the fare in advance. Taxis are also available for hire for the day: you can expect to pay around $20–25, excluding petrol. Most hotels and guesthouses also have cars with driver available.

Accommodation

Phnom Penh has plenty of rooms in all price ranges, and the competition has led to some of the lowest **accommodation** prices in Cambodia. There is a cluster of budget guesthouses around Boeng Kak Lake, offering beds for as little as $1. Other budget options are scattered throughout town, the most popular being *Capitol Guesthouse* and *Narins*, recently joined by newer alternatives. Many of these budget places also have cheap single rooms. Mid-range hotels are plentiful, and more are being opened, so it's worth negotiating on price, particularly in the low season. In addition to those mentioned here, there is a concentration of mid-range hotels on Monivong Boulevard running south from the station. This is a good place to shop around for a bargain if you have the time and energy. Phnom Penh also has its share of international hotels, with the refurbished *Hotel Le Royale* setting the standard.

Guesthouses

Apsara, 24 Street 47 (☎012/824370). A newcomer to the Phnom Penh guesthouse scene, this place offers good-sized rooms for the price, some with sitting areas and desks. The attentive management aims to please, and can organize anything, including breakfast in bed. ③.

Boddhi Tree, 50 Street 113 (☎012/893138). You'll feel more like a friend of the family than a tourist at this new, well decked-out little guesthouse opposite Tuol Sleng Museum. Immaculate, homely rooms with shared bath and decent meals in the leafy courtyard. ③.

Café Freedom, left at the mosque, last guesthouse on the lake (☎012/807345). Attractive lakeside wooden bungalow-style accommodation, including some rooms with balconies right on the lake. ①–③.

Capitol, 14 Street 182 (☎023/364104). The *Capitol* empire is the Phnom Penh equivalent of Bangkok's Khao San Road, comprising *Capitol Guesthouse* and nearby clones *Capitol 2*, *Happy* and *Hello*. Backpackers arrive here by the bus-load for the cheap accommodation, food and tours. Indeed, it offers the most comprehensive selection of inexpensive tours in Phnom Penh, and can help arrange onward transport. If minibussing all the central sights in one day is your bag, sign up here. Rooms are clean and come with varying facilities. ①–②.

Dara Reang Sey, 45 Street 118 (☎023/428181). Family-run establishment in busy Khmer neighbourhood, not far from the downtown action, offering clean rooms, a roof terrace and good restaurant. The third-floor rooms are particularly nice. ③.

Lakeside/Number 10 Guesthouse, 10 Street 93 (☎012/851652). A guesthouse offering budget rooms in a spectacular spot, with a large terrace overlooking Boeng Kak Lake. Free snooker, videos, hammocks and sunset views. ①.

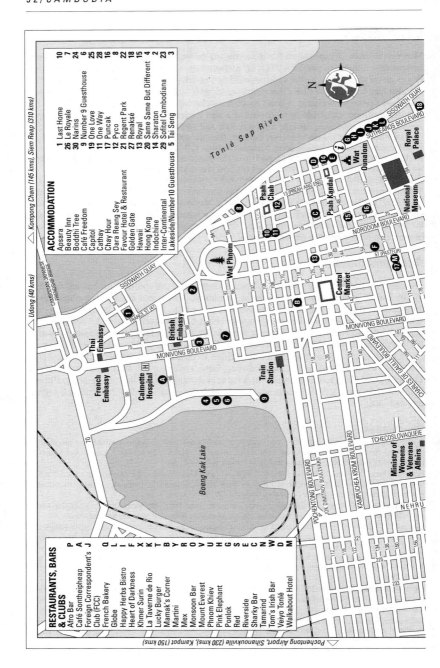

△ Udong (40 kms)   △ Kompong Cham (145 kms), Siem Reap (310 kms)

ACCOMMODATION

Apsara	1	Last Home 10
Beauty Inn	26	Le Royale 7
Boddhi Tree	30	Narins 24
Café Freedom	9	Number 9 Guesthouse 6
Capitol	19	One Love 25
Cathay	11	One Way 28
Chay Hour	17	Puncak 16
Dara Reang Sey	12	Pyco 8
Favour Hotel & Restaurant	21	Regent Park 22
Golden Gate	27	Renaksé 18
Hawaii	13	Royal 15
Hong Kong	20	Same Same But Different 4
Indochine	14	Sharaton 2
Inter-Continental	29	Sofitel Cambodiana 23
Lakeside/Number10 Guesthouse	5	Tai Seng 3

RESTAURANTS, BARS & CLUBS

Afro Bar	P
Café Sontheipheap	A
Foreign Correspondent's	J
Club (FCC)	Q
French Bakery	L
Globe	I
Happy Herbs Bistro	F
Heart of Darkness	X
Khmer Surin	K
La Taverne de Rio	T
Lucky Burger	B
Mamak's Corner	Y
Martini	R
Mex	O
Monsoon Bar	V
Mount Everest	U
Phnom Khiev	H
Pink Elephant	G
Ponlok	S
Red	E
Riverside	C
Sharky Bar	N
Tamarind	W
Tom's Irish Bar	D
Veiyo Tonlé	M
Walkabout Hotel	

Tonlé Sap River

Wat Phnom

British Embassy

French Embassy

Thai Embassy

Calmette Hospital

Train Station

Boeng Kak Lake

Central Market

Psah Chah

Psah Kandal

Wat Ounalom

National Museum

Royal Palace

Ministry of Womens & Veterans Affairs

SISOWATH QUAY
FRANCE ST (4)
MONIVONG BOULEVARD
NORODOM BOULEVARD
MONIVONG BOULEVARD
CHARLES DE GAULLE BOULEVARD
POCHENTONG BOULEVARD
KAMPUCHEA KROM BOULEVARD
TCHECOSLOVAQUEIE
NEHRU
SOTHEAROS BOULEVARD
SISOWATH QUAY
CAMBODIAN-JAPANESE FRIENDSHIP BRIDGE

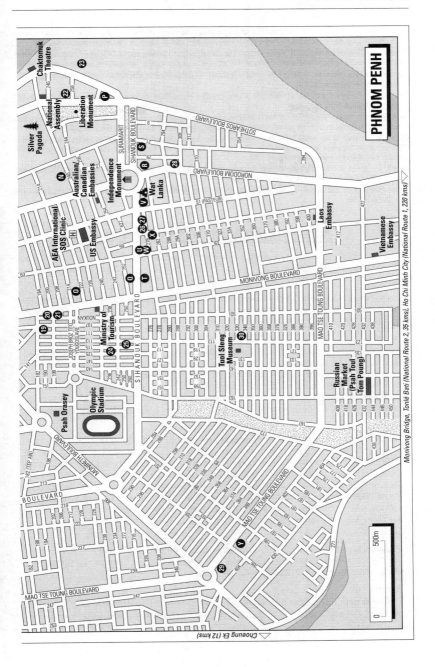

PHNOM PENH

Last Home, 47 Street 108 (☎023/724917). Quirky little guesthouse near the main post office. Rooms come in all shapes and sizes, including a large room with balcony and glimpes of Wat Phnom and river. ①.

Narins, 50 Street 125 (☎023/213657). One of the nicer budget guesthouses in Phnom Penh, with a reputation for friendly service and secure rooms. It's a popular place, with a pleasant restaurant terrace. ①–②.

Number 9 Guesthouse, 9 Street 93 (☎023/300331). Cheap lakeside chilling. Popular with budget travellers and mosquitoes. ①.

One Love, 74 Street 115 (☎012/864735). Cosy wooden house just around the corner from *Narins*, but smaller and quieter. ①.

One Way, 136 Street 308 (☎023/212443). Homely four-room guesthouse, tucked away in the southern end of town. TV, bathroom, air-con, good restaurant, breakfast included. Long-term rates available. ⑤.

Pyco, 79 Sisowath Quay (☎012/862289). Run by a Cambodian Army doctor, *Pyco* occupies a prime spot, a little way from the main drag on the river. The nicest rooms are on the top floor. Plans are afoot to turn the first-floor roof terrace into a restaurant. ②.

Royal, 91 Street 154 (☎023/360298). Average rooms, but good facilities for the price. Cable TV, mini-bar, and en-suite in all rooms, optional air-con. ②–③.

Same Same But Different, 11 Street 93 (☎012/879620). Another lakeside retreat, recently moved from over the road. ①.

MOVING ON FROM PHNOM PENH

For addresses and telephone numbers of embassies, airlines and travel agents in Phnom Penh, see "Listings", p.101.

By plane

Even some of the most die-hard overlanders are resigned to travelling by **air** during the wet season. Schedules of the three domestic airlines change regularly, so it's best to talk to a travel agent or directly to the airline.

By train

Two **train** services depart from Phnom Penh station: one eases northwards to Pursat, Battambang and Sisophon, the other rumbles south towards Kampot and Sihanoukville. There's only one train on the Sihanoukville line and it leaves Phnom Penh every two days, with the return leg on the other days. The train is scheduled to leave at 6am, and takes twelve hours. The Battambang train leaves every day at 6am, and also takes twelve hours. If you are continuing on to Sisophon, you'll need to overnight in Battambang.

By bus

The only regular service by conventional **bus** out of Phnom Penh is to Sihanoukville. Three companies compete for business: GST, Ho Wa Genting and DH Cambodia. All offer a similar service, with seat reservations and free water, and there are regular departures from 7am until 1.30pm; fares are 8000–10,000r. Buses leave from the Ho Wa Genting terminal at the southwest corner of the central market. The other decent road out of Phnom Penh connects with Kompong Cham – the route is covered by a minibus service, with regular departures from the northwest corner of the central market every day from 6am until around 4pm.

By taxi

Share **taxis** can be commandeered from the stand on Monivong Boulevard, just south of the central market. Prices are negotiable, but bear in mind that the cost of a car and driver for a day is about $20–25 excluding petrol.

By pick-up

Pick-ups depart from the northwest corner of the central market once they are full to bursting, and not before. For longer journeys, get here early (6–7am); pick-ups to near-

Hotels

All **hotels** listed here include en-suite bathroom, cable TV, fridge and air-con. Many also run tours.

Beauty Inn, 100 Sihanouk Blvd (☎023/211515). Full room facilities, restaurant and room service. ⑤.

Cathay, 123–125 Street 110 (☎023/722471). Huge, spotless rooms with armchairs and desk; the bathrooms alone are bigger than some hotel rooms in Phnom Penh. ④.

Chay Hour, 39 Street 174 (☎023/725822). Not a bad deal if you can handle the fake wood panelling and brown tiled floors. ⑤.

Golden Gate, 9 Street 278 (☎023/721161). A variety of rooms available in two buildings, but the impressive lobby outclasses the rooms themselves. Similar rooms are available next door at the smaller *Golden Bridge* and *Golden Sun* hotels. ⑤.

Hawaii, 18 Street 130 (☎023/426652). Popular hotel, with good Chinese/Thai restaurant. All rooms have the same facilities, but you'll pay more for the larger rooms. ⑤.

Hong Kong, 419 Monivong Blvd (☎023/211891). Clean, well-run hotel with good-sized rooms. In vogue with Chinese businessmen. ⑤.

er destinations usually run until early afternoon. There are daily departures to Battambang (for Poipet, Pailin and Sisophon), Kompong Cham, Kompong Chhnang, Kampot (for Kep), Pursat, Sihanoukville (for Krong Koh Kong), Siem Reap, Sre Ambel (for Krong Koh Kong), Takeo and Udong.

By boat

Express **boats** leave from the terminal just north of Friendship Bridge. Daily services to Siem Reap ($25) leave at 7am and take four to five hours. Slow boats (36hr) occasionally make the journey, so it's worth enquiring if you have plenty of time. Boats also leave here for Kompong Cham; Kratie, the overland staging post for Mondolkiri; and less frequently, Stung Treng, the gateway to Ratanakiri. All boats are at the mercy of water levels, so services trail off come February.

Organized tours

If the trials of the public transport system prove too much, you could opt for the easy life with an **organized tour**; call into any travel agent. Tours are limited to the major tourist spots, though.

Crossing the border into Vietnam

The one **border crossing between Cambodia and Vietnam** open to tourists is at Moc Bai, 160km from Phnom Penh. The 245-kilometre trip from Phnom Penh to Ho Chi Minh in Vietnam has become easier and cheaper over the last few years, as guesthouses in these cities are teaming up to offer hassle-free public transport all the way. It's now possible to get a minibus for $8. Check the prices at *Narins* and *Capitol*. With prices so cheap, it doesn't make sense to suffer the alternative public transport. For more flexibility, a shared taxi will cost around $20 to the border, and the same again from the border to Ho Chi Minh. Bargain hard for this price on the Vietnam side.

However you get to the border, allow plenty of time to clear immigration, as it can take two hours or more. The border closes at 6pm. The city-to-city trip takes about eight or nine hours, including immigration formalities. Visas are available from the Vietnamese Embassy in Monivong Boulevard, Phnom Penh (Mon–Fri 8–11am, 2–4pm) for $50. Guesthouses can usually organize this for slightly less.

Favour Hotel & Restaurant, 429 Monivong Blvd (☎023/219336). Chinese-style hotel, heavy on the white tiling, with very popular Khmer/Chinese restaurant downstairs. ⑤.

Indochine, 251 Sisowath Quay (☎023/427292). Friendly Khmer-owned hotel right on the river, offering spacious good-value en-suite rooms. ⑤.

Inter-Continental, 296 Mao Tse Toung Blvd (☎023/424888). Business-class hotel with international restaurants, bars, gym and swimming pool. ⑨.

Le Royale, corner of Monivong Boulevard and Street 92 (☎023/981888). Fully restored to colonial glory by the Raffles group, and now the most luxurious hotel in Phnom Penh. Fine dining, cocktail bars, conference facilities, spa and swimming pool. ⑨.

Puncak, 115–155 Street 172 (☎023/213205). Modern, clean and comfy, with all the trimmings and a reasonably priced restaurant. ⑥.

Regent Park, 58 Sotheros Blvd (☎023/427131). At the classy end of the mid-rangers, more of a business-oriented hotel. Modern, comfortable, fully equipped rooms. ⑦.

Renaksé, 40 Sotheros Blvd (☎023/722457). This old colonial nugget commands a superb location between the Royal Palace and the river. Prices are worth it for the free terrace breakfast buffet alone, which is just as well, because the standard rooms are a tad grotty for the price, despite cable TV, minibar, air-con and bathroom. ⑥.

Tai Seng, 56 Monivong Blvd (☎023/427220). Well-established, clean mid-range hotel, though rooms fronting the boulevard are very noisy. ⑤.

Sofitel Cambodiana, 313 Sisowath Quay (☎023/426288). Huge international-class hotel overlooking the river. Restaurants, bars, swimming pool, tennis courts, business and conference facilities. ⑧.

Sharaton, Street 47, North of Wat Phnom (☎023/426773). Not quite up to the standard of its almost-namesake, but a good-value place, with restaurant, swimming pool and nightclub. ⑦.

The City

Phnom Penh city centre can be loosely defined as the area between Monivong Boulevard and the Tonlé Sap River, stretching as far north as Friendship Bridge, and as far south as Sihanouk Boulevard. Its tourist hub is the scenic Sisowath Quay, from where most of the sights and monuments are easily accessible.

Sisowath Quay and around

The heart of Phnom Penh life is a small, fairly nondescript square of land at the junction of **Sisowath Quay** and Street 184, in front of the Royal Palace. It's here that Cambodians used to congregate to listen to declarations and speeches from the monarch, and where Khmer families still gather in the evenings and at weekends. Picnics, games, kite flying, and perhaps a cup of *dteuk k'nai choo* are the order of the day. Running to the north and south of here is the scenic Sisowath Quay, lined with tall palms on one side, and bars, cafés and restaurants on the other. In the middle of the day the area is deserted, save for the odd tourist, but as evening draws in, the quay is transformed into a popular and lively social centre – the Phnom Penhois enjoy the simple pleasures of the fine river views from the riverbank, the expats, tourists and well-to-do locals do the same from the luxury of the bars across the road.

The Royal Palace and Silver Pagoda

Behind the park, set back from the riverbank on Sotheros Boulevard, stand the Royal Palace and adjacent Silver Pagoda (daily 7.30–11am, 2.30–5pm; $3, additional $2 charge for cameras; entrance at Silver Pagoda). These are Phnom Penh's principal tourist sights and its finest examples of twentieth-century Khmer-influenced architecture. Both are one-storey structures – until the Europeans arrived, standing above another's head (the most sacred part of the body) was strictly prohibited.

You'll catch glimpses of the glistening, golden Royal Palace buildings behind the high daffodil-yellow perimeter walls with their white-painted castellations. The buildings are at once simple and ornate – the main building structures follow uncomplicated geometry, but are crowned with highly decorative roofs. Naga finials ripple and curl towards the heavens. The multi-gabled golden-yellow roofs finished with wide green borders, draw the eye to the central wedding-cake spires which in turn climb skywards to the hot Cambodian sun.

The **Royal Palace** itself is strictly off-limits, but it's possible to visit several buildings within the compound, even when the king is around – a blue flag flies when he is in residence. The original palace on this site was built in 1866 during the reign of King Norodom, great-grandfather to the present king. Norodom decided to move his residence from the then capital, Udong, to Phnom Penh, presumably on the advice of his colonial masters. In 1913, work began to replace the deteriorating wood-and-brick structures with the current concrete buildings, remaining faithful to the original designs.

Visitors enter via the Silver Pagoda and are directed to the palace compound first, an oasis of order and calm, its perfect gardens and well maintained buildings strangely at odds with the chaos of the city outside. Head straight for the main building in the centre of the compound, the exquisite **Throne Hall**, guarded on either side by statues of naga. The cambered ornamental curves that adorn the tiered roof are also likenesses of naga, their flowing tails peeling upwards into the air, as if trying to prise open the layered roof. The hall is crowned by a spire with four heads carved around its base, a modern-day rendering of the ancient carved faces at Bayon (see p.85). Inside, the ceiling is adorned with colourful murals recounting the Hindu legend of Ramayana. The throne itself, watched over by busts of past monarchs, only sees action at coronations.

Leaving the Throne Hall via the main stairs, on your left you'll see the **Elephant Pavilion** where the king's elephants were kept. A similar building on the right, the **Royal Treasury**, once housed the crown jewels, royal dress and other valuable items. In front and to the left, bordering Sothearos Boulevard, is the Chan Chaya Pavilion, from where the king used to address his subjects. Classical dancing also used to be a regular event at this podium, but it's little used nowadays.

Back towards the Silver Pagoda stands the quaint grey **Pavilion of Napoleon III**, originally erected at the residence of Empress Eugénie in Egypt, then packed up and transported to Cambodia as a gift to King Norodom. It was reassembled on this site in 1876, and now contains royal portraits, dresses for the royal ballet, and other royal paraphernalia. From the balcony it's possible to view the ornate detail of the roof of the neighbouring Royal Offices.

The internal wall of the **Silver Pagoda** is decorated with a faded mural, another depiction of the Ramayana myth, painted in 1903–4 by forty Khmer artists. A Polish project to restore the fresco ran out of money, so it remains in a state of disrepair. The Silver Pagoda takes its name from the floor of the temple, completely covered with silver tiles – 5329 to be exact. The temple is also known as Preah Vihear Keo Morakot ("Temple of the Emerald Buddha"), after the famous **Emerald Buddha** image kept here. Made from baccarat crystal, the Buddha image was a gift from France in 1885. Near the central dais stands another Buddha, a solid-gold life-size statue, decorated with over nine thousand diamonds and precious stones.

Returning to the stupa-filled courtyard, seek out the artificial Mount Meru to see one of the Buddha's footprints – with feet that size, buying shoes must have been a problem. Notice also the statue of King Norodom in front of the pagoda, a gift from France in 1875. The body and horse actually belonged to a statue of Napoleon that was surplus to requirements. The French simply knocked up a Norodom head and stuck it on Napoleon's shoulders.

National Museum

Just north of the Royal Palace on Sothearos Boulevard, the grand red-painted structure that houses the **National Museum** (daily except Mon 8–11am & 2.30–5pm; $2) is a collaboration of French design and Cambodian craftsmanship. Opened in 1920, the museum houses the country's most important collections of ancient Cambodian culture. The museum's four galleries, set around a tranquil courtyard, shelter an impressive array of ancient relics, art and sculpture, and general craftsmanship covering Cambodian history from the sixth century to the present day. Angkor buffs will not be disappointed – in addition to numerous Angkor relics and sculptures, some of the sculpted heads from the bridge at Angkor Thom are exhibited, as is the original statue of Yama the Leper King from the Terrace of the Leper King in Angkor. The catalogue of exhibits continues to grow as treasures hidden from the Khmer Rouge are rediscovered. Some ten thousand pieces of art found in the basement are currently being cleaned and restored. The statues and images are arranged chronologically, becoming fatter and happier with the increasing prosperity of the Angkor kingdom. An interesting exhibit from more recent history is the king's boat cabin, a portable wooden room used by the king for travelling on the Tonlé Sap. Closer inspection of the intricate wooden carvings reveals images of birds, dogs, monkeys, crocodiles and dragons.

If you have time, it's worth exploring the **streets around the museum**. Street 178 is dotted with art-and-craft shops, selling paintings, woodcarvings and silverware, while Street 184 west of the National Museum is home to a plethora of language schools. Occasionally referred to as English Street, this area comes alive after class, with students only too happy to trade colloquial Khmer for conversational English.

The National Assembly and around

Back on Sothearos Boulevard, just south of the Royal Palace, you'll come to the **National Assembly**. You'll know if the Assembly is in session by the excessive police presence and a row of black limousines. Just beyond, on the other side of the road, there's a park, in the middle of which stands the **Liberation Monument**, sometimes called the Cambodia–Vietnam Monument, commemorating the defeat of the Khmer Rouge by the invading Vietnamese troops. Designed by the Vietnamese and crafted by Phnom Penh's own School of Fine Arts, it was erected in 1979. The southern tip of the park is crossed by Sihanouk Boulevard, lined with colonial-era buildings. Following Sihanouk Boulevard west brings you to **Independence Monument**, at the roundabout at the junction of Norodom Boulevard. Built in 1958 to celebrate Cambodian independence from France, the curious muddy-brown tower now serves as a war memorial.

Tuol Sleng Museum (S21)

As the Khmer Rouge were commencing their reign of terror, Tuol Svay Prey Secondary School, in a quiet Phnom Penh neighbourhood, was commandeered and converted into a primitive prison. Corrugated iron and barbed wire were installed around the perimeter, and classrooms were divided into individual cells, or housed rows of prisoners secured by shackles. During the four years from 1975 to 1979, an estimated twenty thousand victims were imprisoned in **Security Prison 21**, or S21 as it became known. Teachers, students, doctors, monks and peasants suspected of anti-revolutionary behaviour were brought here, often with their spouses and children. They were subjected to horrific tortures, and then killed or taken to extermination camps outside the city.

The prison is now a **museum** (daily 7–11.30am & 2–5.30pm; $2) and a monument to the thousands of Khmers who suffered at the hands of the Khmer Rouge. It's been left almost exactly as it was found by the liberating Vietnamese forces – the fourteen victims found hideously disfigured in the individual cells have been buried in the school playground. It's a thoroughly depressing sight, and it's not until you see the pictures of the victims, blood stains on the walls and instruments of torture that you get any idea of the scale of suffering endured by the Cambodian people.

Wat Phnom

The most popular of Phnom Penh's temples, **Wat Phnom** ($1 donation), atop the city's only hill, was originally founded by Lady Penh in 1372 (see p.90). The current construction, dating from 1927, sees hundreds of Cambodians converge daily for elephant rides, photos and perhaps a prayer or two. Weekends and holidays are especially busy.

At the eastern entrance, lions and naga images beckon the visitor to the top of the staircase, where a gold-painted bas-relief depicts the victory of King Jayavarman VII over the

Cham army in the twelfth century. Apsara images flank the mural. Inside the temple, a resplendent Maitreya Buddha ("Buddha of the Future") looks down from the central dais. Some of the paintings adorning the walls and ceiling are barely visible – years of incense burning have taken their toll – but you can just about make out tales of the Buddha's life and the Ramayana. Behind the main sanctuary, King Punyayab's stupa remains the highest point in Phnom Penh, a fact not lost on the French, who commandeered the shrine as a watch-tower. Rumour has it that Lady Penh's original Buddhas are entombed here and there's a small shrine to her between the temple and the stupa.

On the northern side of the hill nestles a temple to the spirit **Preah Chau**, popular among the Chinese and Vietnamese communities. Gifts of raw meat and eggs are offered to the stone lions outside in return for protection from enemies. The empty, half-finished construction on the western side of the hill was intended to house the Buddha relics currently enshrined in the small blue stupa outside Phnom Penh railway station. However, financial and engineering problems have caused the project to be abandoned.

Wat Ounalom

Set back slightly from the river at the junction of Sothearos Boulevard and Sisowath Quay, **Wat Ounalom** ("Eyebrow Temple") is the centre of modern-day Khmer Buddhist teaching, led by Supreme Patriarch Taep Vong, respectfully referred to by the novices as "The King Of Monks". The main temple building, built in 1952, is a modern reincarnation of the original, built in the fifteenth century. The building to the right is the main residence for the monks, and the five-hundred-year-old stupa behind the temple encases one of the Buddha's eye-brows, after which the temple is named. Just in front stands an UNTAC monument to those killed during the Pol Pot regime. It's pleasant to stroll around the complex – many of the monks are learning English, and are happy to tell you what they know about the temple and its history. The best time to visit is at 6pm, when the monks congregate in the main sanctuary to chant their prayers.

Eating

Street stalls will keep shoestring travellers happily fed on noodle dishes or filled baguettes for 2000r or less. Stalls spring up in different places at various times of day: markets are a good place for a daytime selection, and the riverside in the early evening. Next up in the price range, guesthouses tend to serve a standard selection of local and Western dishes for $1–3. Khmer street-corner **restaurants**, with plastic garden chairs, charge around the same for standard local fare. This is the fulcrum of evening social activity for moderately well-off Khmers, so it's often difficult to find a table in the more popular of these restaurants. The more fashionable options are concentrated at the southern end of Monivong Boulevard. For a slightly more upmarket variation on the same theme, make for the cluster of popular Khmer joints on the other side of Friendship Bridge. Finally, there are innumerable reason-ably priced restaurants aimed at expats and tourists; expect to pay $3–5. Most restaurants open from around 11am until 9pm, although places catering to a mainly Western clientele stay open until 11pm.

Cafés and restaurants

Café Sontheipheap, Street 86, halfway between Monivong and the lake. Good food, generous portions and backpacker-friendly.

Capitol Guesthouse Restaurant, 14 Street 182. Cheap and cheerful travellers' fare at this busy street-cor-ner café.

Favour Restaurant, 429 Monivong Blvd. One of the most popular of the early-evening Monivong Khmer/Chinese restaurants. Get here early for a table.

Foreign Correspondents' Club (FCC), 363 Sisowath Quay (☎023/724014). Fine dining in this famous riverside colonial building. Bar snacks also available, or just pop in for a soothing ale.

French Bakery, 99 Sihanouk Blvd. Continental cakes and pastries, washed down with good coffee.

Globe, First Floor, 389 Sisowath Quay (☎023/215923). Great views of the river and the Royal Palace from this pleasant fan-cooled restaurant. Check out the daily specials – fish and chips on Friday, and Sunday roast. Good service, and the barbecue's a winner.

Happy Herbs Bistro, 345 Sisowath Quay. Cheap pizza and pasta. A large Special pizza will get you nicely full – the extra Happy topping will get you nicely stoned.

Khmer Surin, 9 Street 57 (☎023/363050). A very popular restaurant serving authentic Khmer and Thai cuisine to hungry expats. Thai-style seating upstairs.

Mamak's Corner, 118 Street 114. Nasi Goreng, Roti Pratha, Satay and other Malaysian delights for $2 a plate, tasting as good as anything you'd buy at a KL street stall.

Mex, 115 Norodom Blvd. Air-con restaurant serving generous portions of burritos, nachos, tacos and other Mexican favourites.

Mount Everest, 98 Sihanouk Blvd. An indoor, air-con restaurant serving Indian and Nepalese cuisine from $2. Does top-notch lassies.

Phnom Khiev, 138 Sihanouk Blvd. Wide selection of French and Khmer dishes for $2–4, served in a pleasant outside seating area.

Lucky Burger, 160 Sihanouk Blvd. Phnom Penh's attempt at American burgers and fries.

Ponlok, 319 Sisowath Quay. Illustrated menus in English and French make ordering good Khmer food here easy. Attentive service and a busy, breezy balcony.

Red, 56 Sihanouk Blvd (☎023/360676). This French–Canadian-owned restaurant with a leafy balcony is the place to splash out on a succulent steak, a large goblet of red wine and if you've still room, a slice of *Red*'s famous chocolate cheesecake. Expect to pay around $10 per head.

Riverside, 273 Sisowath Quay. Pavement terrace partially shielded from the passing shoe-shine boys by a jungle of potted plants. Reasonably priced European, Khmer and Russian dishes; Cuban cigars; and a pool table.

Tamarind, 31 Street 240 (☎023/721478). The best Sunday brunch in town. Try out traditional Khmer breakfast dishes alongside European favourites on the roof terrace for a bargain $3. The food is excellent, and $4 daily lunchtime specials are very good value.

Veiyo Tonlé, 237 Sisowath Quay. This relaxed, family-run, riverside restaurant serves Khmer and international cuisine. Try a Happy Gourmet Pizza from the charcoal burning oven, or get there early in the day for an authentic Khmer breakfast.

Entertainment and nightlife

Unfortunately, cultural events in Phnom Penh are few and far between. The ancient tradition of Cambodian **classical dance**, which originated in the twelfth century, was all but wiped out in the 1970s. It is slowly beginning to resurface, but lack of funding means that performances at the Chaktomuk Theatre on Sisowath Quay are infrequent – check the listings in the Friday edition of the *Cambodia Daily*. The theatre is also the venue for occasional Khmer **plays** and **musical shows**.

If you're in Phnom Penh during one of the big festivals, there may be a live Khmer **pop music** concert at the Olympic Stadium. Tickets are reasonably priced, so it's worth popping along for an hour or two to see Cambodia's answer to Tom Jones.

A popular Phnom Penh Sunday-afternoon outing is a trip to the **kick-boxing**. Much like Muay Thai, it's a no-holds-barred experience, but the crowds tend to be more subdued than at the average Bangkok event. It's a snip at 2000r for the stands, 3000r for ringside. Moto-drivers will know where to go (ask for "boxer" or "gay-laa bpra-dul") or head straight to the Ministry of Women's and Veteran's Affairs on Street 169 and follow the crowds. The fun is usually over by 5 or 6pm, depending on the number of KO's.

You can see films at the International Youth Club (Daun Penh Street, West of Wat Phnom; ☎023/722722) in the evenings. Admission is free and non-members are welcome. The French Cultural Centre (Street 184, just east of Monivong) screens French films with English subtitles. Check local listings for details. There's a very small cineplex at 262 Monivong Blvd, playing mainly Western and Chinese action movies, or select your own laser disc movie at Movie Street Video Centre, 116 Sihanouk Blvd, and watch it in their comfortable screening rooms for $5.

For most Khmers, **nightlife** centres around an early evening meal out, followed by a tuneful burst of karaoke. The southern end of Monivong Boulevard has a particular concentration of the larger, glitzy joints, but KTV can be found all over town. Just follow your ears. Western nightlife tastes are more than catered for, and an oversupply of bars and clubs means that many are less than full, especially during the low season. However, you'll always find a crowd in established favourites such as *FCC* (see p.99), *Heart of Darkness*, *Sharky* and *Martini*.

Bars and clubs

Afro Bar, 112 Sothearos Blvd. Small bar with an African theme, and a social centre for the local football fraternity.

Casa, at the *Sharaton Hotel*, Street 47. Late-night club, with Asian/Western crossover and live band. Good fun at 2am after a tour of Phnom Penh's other nightspots.

Heart of Darkness, 26 Street 51. This atmospheric bar is a long-running favourite. Good place to shoot some pool, meet expats and other tourists, and buy the T-shirt. 7pm–late.

La Taverne de Rio, 371 Sisowath Quay. Fun riverside joint with Brazilian cocktails and occasional live music. Food available, including South American specialities. Lunchtime till late.

Martini, 402 Mao Tse Toung Blvd. Western-style disco and bar, with movies on the big screen, inexpensive food on the menu, and girls on the game. 7pm–3am.

Monsoon Bar, 36 Street 214. A bar by week, nightclub at weekends, housed in a smart French colonial building. 5pm–late.

Pink Elephant, 343 Sisowath Quay. Relaxed, backpacker-oriented bar on the river, with cheap drinks, free pool, and board games. Popular after a Happy Herbs pizza next door. 9am–late.

Sharky Bar, 126 Street 130. Busy nightspot, with large bar and balcony. 5–7pm happy hour deals, pool tables, and sports TV. The girls will leave you alone if you ask them politely. Open until 2am.

Tom's Irish Pub, 163 Street 63. Relaxed expat drinkery, with occasional live bands. 3pm–midnight.

Walkabout Hotel, corner of 51 & 174 streets. Twenty-four-hour bar with pool table, restaurant and sports TV. Popular with ageing long-termers, probably because of proximity of nearby bordellos.

Markets

Phnom Penh may not be world-renowned as a shopping destination, but there are certainly bargains to be had. A trip to one of the capital's numerous **markets** is essential, if only to buy the red-checked *krama* (traditional Khmer scarf) popular with Khmers and visitors alike. The markets all open early, and wind down by 5pm. They are liveliest in the morning, and many vendors have a snooze at midday for a couple of hours.

Although the drugs, guns and ammunition have been quietly removed from prominent display, a stroll around the **Russian Market** (Psah Tuol Tom Poung) remains a colourful experience. Situated in the southern end of town at the junction of 163 Street and 440 Street, it's a good balance of tourist-oriented curios and stalls for locals. Jewellery, gems, CDs, food stalls, souvenirs, furniture and motorbike parts are all grouped in their own sections. Don't expect an easy bargain – you'll have to work hard to pay the locals' price.

Vendors at the central market are also wise to the limitless funds that all "barangs" ("foreigners") apparently possess, and will price their wares accordingly. Electronic goods, T-shirts, shoes and wigs are all in abundance here. Confusingly, its name in Khmer (Psah Thmei) means New Market, and there is in fact another central market, but most moto drivers will correctly assume you want the larger market at the eastern end of Street 128.

The other markets around town are less tourist-friendly, but are good places to pick up cheap toiletries, clothes, food and alcohol. For convenience of location, you might try Psah Kandal, Psah Chah or Psah Orasey (see map on pp.92–93).

Listings

Airlines Air France, 389 Sisowath Quay (☎023/426426); Bangkok Airways, 61 Street 214 (☎023/426624); Lao Aviation, 18B Sihanouk Blvd (☎023/216563); Phnom Penh Airways, 209 Street 19 (☎023/217419);

President Airline, 50 Norodom Blvd (☎023/212887); Royal Air Cambodge, 206 Norodom Blvd (☎023/428891); Silk Air, 219B Monivong Blvd (☎023/364545); Thai Airways, 19 Street 106 (☎026/722335); Vietnam Airlines, 41 Street 214 (☎023/363396).

Banks and exchange Travellers' cheques can be cashed at virtually any bank around town for a commission of two per cent. For credit-card cash advances, either the Cambodian Commercial Bank or the Foreign Trade Bank of Cambodia can assist. Most banks are open Mon–Fri 8.30am–3.30pm, and a few are open until 11.30am on Saturday. The best rates for changing dollars into riel can be found at the moneychangers in and around the central market.

Cambodian Commercial Bank, 26 Monivong Blvd (☎023/426145); Canadia Bank, 265–269 Street 110 (☎023/724672); First Commercial Bank, 263 Street 110 (☎023/210026); First Overseas Bank, 20 Street 114 (☎023/213023); Foreign Trade Bank of Cambodia, 26 Norodom Blvd (☎023/724466); Standard Chartered Bank, 89 Norodom Blvd (☎023/216685).

Western Union Money transfer is available at FCC and at Sampan Tour (48 Street 240).

Bicycle rental *Capitol Guesthouse* (see p.91); $1.

Bookshops The FCC stocks a wide range of English and French books, including novels and bestsellers, as well as books on Cambodia and Angkor. Monument Books (155 Monivong Blvd; ☎023/723020) has a large collection of new books. Second-hand books are sold at The London Book Centre (65 Street 240; ☎023/214258), which has over 5,000 titles in English, French and German.

Dentists Dr Leo Phiv, 74 Street 108 (☎012/850311); European Dental Clinic, 195A Norodom Blvd (☎023/362656). Both are English-speaking.

Embassies and consulates Australia, 11 Street 254 (☎023/213470); Belgium, 1 Street 21 (☎023/360877); Canada, 11 Street 254 (☎023/213470); China, 256 Mao Tse Toung Blvd (☎023/720922); France, 1 Monivong Blvd (☎023/430020); Germany, 76 Street 214 (☎023/216381); India, 777 Monivong Blvd (☎023/210912); Indonesia, 90 Norodom Blvd (☎023/216148); Japan, 75 Norodom Blvd (☎023/217161); Laos, 15–17 Mao Tse Toung Blvd (☎023/983632); Malaysia, 161 Street 51 (☎023/216176); Poland, 767 Monivong Blvd (☎023/720916); Russia, 213 Sothearos Blvd (☎023/210931); Singapore, 92 Norodom Blvd (☎023/360855); Thailand, 4 Monivong Blvd (☎023/363869); UK, 27–29 Street 75 (☎023/427124); USA, 27 Street 240 (☎023/216436); Vietnam, 426 Monivong Blvd (☎023/362531).

Hospitals and clinics For any travel-related illness, tests or vaccinations, head for AEA International/SOS Clinic at 161 Street 51 (☎023/216911) or the Tropical & Traveller's Medical Clinic, 88 Street 108 (☎023/366802). The Naga Medical Centre at 108 Sothearos Blvd (☎011/811175) also has English and French-speaking doctors. The main hospital is Calmette Hospital, 3 Monivong Blvd (☎023/426948).

Immigration department For visa extensions and other immigration queries, go to the Department of Immigration, 5 Street 200, near the Norodom Boulevard intersection. The office is open Mon–Fri 8–10.30am, 2.30–4.30pm.

Internet access Khmer Web, 150 Sihanouk Blvd (☎012/846467), offers Internet access for $5 an hour, or a monthly email account for $14. Underneath the FCC, Café Asia, 365 Sisowath Quay (☎023/217041), offers internet access by the hour for $5 7–10pm, or $6 at all other times. The cheapest place ($4/hour) is the Public Internet Centre at the Lidée Khmer, 5 Street 53 (Mon–Sat 8am–6pm, Sun 9am–5pm; no phone), but there's often a wait for the terminals.

Motorbike rental New! New! Motorcycle Rentals at 417 Monivong Blvd (☎012/855488) will let you loose on a clapped-out old Honda from $3 per day or a more impressive trials bike from $6 per day. Two doors up, Lucky! Lucky! Motorcycle Rentals (☎023/212788) charges similar prices. It's worth paying the 300r to park in the many moto compounds around the city – thieves are rather partial to unattended Hondas.

Newspapers and magazines The FCC stocks a few international newspapers and magazines, but a wider selection can be found at the *Hotel Sofitel Cambodiana*, the *Inter-Continental* or *Le Royale*.

Pharmacies The Naga Pharmacy (Hong Kong Center, 108 Sothearos Blvd; ☎023/361225) offers English- and French-speaking pharmacists. Open daily 7am–8pm.

Post office The Main Post Office is east of Wat Phnom, at the corner of Street 102 and Street 13 (Ang Eng Street). It's open daily 6.30am–9pm, and the staff are helpful. Poste Restante pick-up is at the far left-hand counter. A PO Box service is also available.

Sports Taillal Fitness Center (53 Street 178; ☎023/215063) has a gym available to non-members for $5 per session, or two sessions for $6. The International Youth Club (Duan Penh Street, West of Wat Phnom, ☎023/722722) has a swimming pool, gym, squash, badminton and tennis courts. There are also two tennis courts at the *Hotel Sofitel Cambodiana*. At the *Hotel Inter-Continental*, the Clark Hatch Fitness Center (☎023/424888) has a fully equipped gym with aerobics, sauna & pool access. The outdoor swimming pool at the *Sharaton Hotel* is free of charge if you're buying their drinks. If the heat doesn't deter you from a good run, the Hash House Harriers meet every Sunday afternoon, 2.45pm at the Railway Station, intersection of Monivong Boulevard and Street 184.

Supermarkets Bayon Supermarket, 135 Monivong Blvd (7am–7.30pm); Lucky Supermarket, 160 Sihanouk Blvd (8am–6.30pm); Pencil Supermarket, 15 Street 214 (7am–9pm); Thai Hout, 92 Monivong (7am–7.30pm).

Taxis Baileys Taxi Service, 8 Street 308 (☎023/300808, mobile 012/853179) offers a 24-hour taxi service with experienced, reliable English-speaking drivers.

Telephone services International phone and fax services are available at the Main Post Office or any sizeable hotel. Public phones can only be used with a pre-paid phonecard, available at shops everywhere.

Travel agencies Diethelm Travel, 65 Street 240 (☎023/219151), also new branch office at the FCC, 363 Sisowath Quay (☎023/214059); Intra, 2–3 Street 118 (☎023/428596); Mittapheap Travel & Tours, 262 Monivong Blvd (☎023/216666); Transpeed Travel, 19 Street 106 (☎023/723999).

Around Phnom Penh

Escaping into Phnom Penh's surrounding countryside for some peace and fresh air is very easy – it doesn't take long to get out past the shanty-town suburbs, and the majority of roads that extend from the capital are in fairly good condition, making the excursions listed here an easy day- or even half-day trip.

Mekong Island Tour

Oknhatey Island in the **Mekong River**, an hour's boat ride north of Phnom Penh, has been developed as a tourist attraction. An all-day tour here is organized by *Hotel Sofitel Cambodiana* and most travel agents, and costs $32 per person. It's billed as an experience of traditional Khmer culture, and does indeed include dancing, music and handicrafts. There's also a zoo, model village and elephant rides. Alternatively, to experience real Mekong River life, simply hire a boat from Sisowath Quay for a few hours ($5–10).

Choeung Ek (The Killing Fields)

A visit to **CHOEUNG EK** (daily except Mon 8.30am–4.30pm; $2), 15km southwest of Phnom Penh, signposted from Monireth Boulevard, is a sobering experience. It was here in 1980 that the bodies of 8985 people, victims of Pol Pot and his Khmer Rouge comrades, were exhumed from 86 mass graves. A further 43 graves have been left untouched. Many of those buried here had suffered prolonged torture at S21 prison in Phnom Penh, before being led to their deaths at Choeung Ek. Men, women and children were beaten to death, shot, beheaded, or tied up and buried alive.

At the entrance, a hand-written sign in Khmer and English outlines the Khmer Rouge atrocities, a period described as "a desert of great destruction which overturned Kampuchean society and drove it back to the stone age". A tall, white, hollow stupa commemorates all those who died from 1975 to 1979, displaying thousands of unearthed skulls, demographically arranged on glass shelves. A pile of the victims' ragged clothing lies scattered underneath. Although Choeung Ek is by far the most notorious of the killing fields, scores of similar plots can be found all over Cambodia, many with no more than a pile of skulls and bones as a memorial. **Transport** to Choeung Ek can be arranged at *Capitol Guesthouse* (see p.91) for $2, or take a moto for $3 return.

Royal Tombs of Udong

The ancient capital of **UDONG**, 40km to the northwest of Phnom Penh, served for over two hundred years as the seat of power for successive Cambodian kings, until, in 1866, it was sacked by King Norodom, who transferred his court to Phnom Penh. Nowadays, visitors come to see the hill of Phnom Udong, dotted with stupas harbouring the ashes and spirits of bygone royalty along its east–west ridge. A long line of food and drink stalls marks your arrival. Continue to the end of the road, where a staircase will lead you up to the larger of two ridges. You can then descend via the staircase at the eastern end of the ridge to complete the circuit.

At the top of the staircase, at the western edge of the hill, sits what's left of Vihear Preah Ath Roes, also known as **Wat Preah Thom**, built by the Chinese in around the thirteenth century to house a giant stone Buddha. The buildings and Buddha were badly damaged by the Khmer Rouge in the 1970s. Continuing eastwards along the ridge, you come to a series of viharas containing statues of the sacred bull Preah Ko, his younger brother Preah Keo, a naga-guarded Preah Prak Neak, and the strong and powerful Preah Boun Dai. The **royal stupas** themselves are higher on the ridge to the northeast. The first you'll see is the decorative, yellow stupa built by King Monivong for King Sisowath, who died in 1927. Elephants, garudas and lotus flower motifs make this the most interesting of the stupas. The adjacent Tray Troeng chedi, said to house the ashes of Ang Duon and his wife, is weather-beaten and neglected, but bright-painted tiles can still be seen. The third stupa, Dam Rei Sam Poan, now rather overgrown, was built by King Chey Chetar II for the former King Soriyopor. At the end of the ridge, a further stupa is under construction, designed to house Buddha relics currently contained in Preah Sack Kyack Moni Chedi, outside Phnom Penh railway station.

From the Royal Stupas, the eastern staircase descends to a small, dusty monument in memory of those killed at a nearby **Khmer Rouge detention centre**. Bones and skulls of the victims were exhumed from mass graves in the early 1980s, and are displayed here.

To get to Udong by rented Honda or bicycle follow Route 5 northwards from Phnom Penh for about 37km, turn left at a large Angkor Beer-sponsored picture of Udong, and follow the road for a few kilometres to the western staircase. Guesthouses and hotels in Phnom Penh organize tours for $5. A taxi here and back costs $20, a moto around $9. Local transport is also available, with buses (4500r) and pick-ups (3000r) leaving from the central market throughout the morning.

Tonlé Bati

If, for some reason, you can't make it to Angkor, you might consider a trip to **TONLÉ BATI** (daily 8am–4pm; $2), some 40km south of Phnom Penh and the nearest Angkorian site to the capital. The site consists of two temples located near Tonlé Bati's lake, Ta Prohm and Yeay Peau. The temples are small by ancient Cambodian temple standards, but impressive nonetheless. Many legends surround their construction, but it is thought King Ta Prohm had them built in the twelfth century. **Ta Prohm** is set in a garden of palms and tamarind trees. Approaching from the eastern entrance, don't miss the carved stones either side of the path, one depicting The Churning of The Ocean of Milk, the other an episode from the Ramayana. Inside, there is only one intact Buddha image, the Khmer Rouge having destroyed most of the other artefacts. You'll need to take a torch to examine the bas-reliefs in the smoky darkness, and to find the upright *lingam* phallic symbol in the central chamber. In the southern chamber a headless Vishnu statue presides over a local fortune-teller who will tell you what you want to hear for a few thousand riel.

The smaller temple of **Yeay Peau** is to the north of Ta Prohm, dwarfed by the new, colourful buildings of Wat Tonlé Bati. Inside, a headless Madame Peau (Ta Prohm's mother) stands next to a seated Buddha. The **lakeside** to the northwest of the temples is a popular spot for lunch and a swim. You can rent a platform (*p'deh tdeuk*) for the whole day for 3000r, or 2000r just for lunchtime. There's a restaurant and food stalls nearby. Inflatable tyres are available to splash around in the lake for 500r each.

To **get to Tonlé Bati by moto** ($7) take the smooth National Route 2, and after about 32km turn right onto a bumpy track, then right again for the temples. A **taxi** for the day will cost about $25. **Buses** from the central market cost 2500r each way, or *Capitol* (see p.91) organizes a day tour for $5. It's quite feasible to combine the trip with a visit to Phnom Chisor (see below), further south on Route 2.

Phnom Chisor

Originally known as Suryaparvata in honour of the monarch Suryavarman I, the eleventh-century temple of **Phnom Chisor**, around 17km south of Tonlé Bati just off National Route

2, looks east from its hilltop vantage point, across the green palm and paddy plains of Takeo province. There are two routes to the top of the hill, both of which are best climbed in the cooler early-morning temperatures. The track which skirts around the hill is an easier climb and gets you to the top in about twenty minutes.

The modern pagodas and preahs that surround Phnom Chisor are of little interest. Make straight for the main courtyard of the ancient temple. Eight edifices surround the main sanctuary tower dedicated to Shiva. Although the buildings were badly damaged by American bombing raids in the 1970s, you can still see some of the sculptural reliefs. The most impressive of these is to be found in the former library, where there is a pediment carved with a dancing Shiva figure set above a lintel, showing Indra riding a three-headed elephant. Looking down from the eastern edge of the complex, you'll see a long causeway, interrupted by temple ruins, stretching to the lake of Tonlé Om, the former gateway to Phnom Chisor.

The site lies off National Route 2 – a few kilometres along a dirt track that bears left at Prasat Neang Khmau. You can **hire a moto** for around $10 in Phnom Penh, or a **taxi** for about $25 – a side-trip to Tonlé Bati should be included in the price. *Capitol* (see p.91) runs a **tour** to both destinations for $8.

ANGKOR

The world-renowned temples of **Angkor**, in northwest Cambodia, stand as an impressive monument to the greatest ancient civilization in Southeast Asia. Spiritually, politically and geographically, Angkor was at the heart of the great Khmer Empire. During the Angkorian period, the ruling god-kings (*devarajas*) built imposing temples as a way of asserting their divinity. As successive kings came and went, so new temples were built, and cities were created around them. What remains today are the stone-built monuments of that period – a legacy of more than one hundred temples built between the ninth and fifteenth centuries.

The nearest town to the temples is **Siem Reap**, which has established itself as the base from which to explore Angkor, a tradition begun by American Frank Vincent Jr, who borrowed three elephants from the governor of Siem Reap in 1872 to explore the ruins. These days, there are plenty of motos and taxis on hand for the journey.

Siem Reap

SIEM REAP is Cambodia's most touristy town, and has sacrificed much of its charm and authenticity as a result. However, Western luxuries are freely available, and there are plenty of English-speaking locals. **Arriving** in Siem Reap by **pick-up**, you'll probably be dropped at the large central market to the east of the city, a hectic, noisy transport hub, knee-deep in mud for most of the rainy season. Boats cruise into the **pier**, 11km south of Siem Reap – the approach is a tranquil introduction to the area, passing hundreds of floating houses, children splashing about in the water, and families going about their daily chores. At the pier, guesthouse reps will be keen to offer a free ride into town, so it's a good idea to decide beforehand where you want to stay. Guesthouse touts also meet the planes at the **airport**, 8km west of town; the other option is a moto ($1) or a taxi ($5).

There is a **tourist information office** (daily 7–9.30am & 2.30–4pm; ☎063/963996), opposite the *Grand Hôtel d'Angkor*, on Tosamut Boulevard, but as usual you'll find the guesthouses are better sources of information. **Transport** around town is limited to motos. Short hops are 500r, a trip out to the central market will cost around 1000r.

Accommodation

Guesthouse **accommodation** is largely concentrated in three areas – just east of the river, off Route 6; on the sidestreets west of Sivatha Street; and around the junction of Route 6 and Sivatha Street. Most accommodation in these areas is aimed at budget travellers. There's not

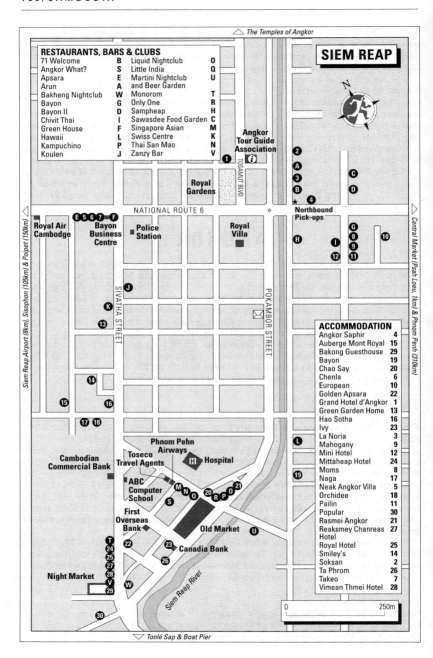

△ The Temples of Angkor

SIEM REAP

RESTAURANTS, BARS & CLUBS

71 Welcome	B	Liquid Nightclub	O
Angkor What?	S	Little India	Q
Apsara	E	Martini Nightclub	U
Arun	A	and Beer Garden	
Bakheng Nightclub	W	Monorom	T
Bayon	G	Only One	R
Bayon II	D	Sampheap	H
Chivit Thai	I	Sawasdee Food Garden	C
Green House	F	Singapore Asian	M
Hawaii	L	Swiss Centre	K
Kampuchino	P	Thai San Mao	N
Koulen	J	Zanzy Bar	V

Angkor Tour Guide Association

Royal Gardens

TOSAMUT BLVD

NATIONAL ROUTE 6

Northbound Pick-ups

Royal Air Cambodge

Bayon Business Centre

Police Station

Royal Villa

SIVATHA STREET

POKAMBOR STREET

ACCOMMODATION

Angkor Saphir	4
Auberge Mont Royal	15
Bakong Guesthouse	29
Bayon	19
Chao Say	20
Chenla	6
European	10
Golden Apsara	22
Grand Hotel d'Angkor	1
Green Garden Home	13
Hao Sotha	16
Ivy	23
La Noria	3
Mahogany	9
Mini Hotel	12
Mittaheap Hotel	24
Moms	8
Naga	17
Neak Angkor Villa	5
Orchidee	18
Pailin	11
Popular	30
Rasmei Angkor	21
Reaksmey Chanreas Hotel	27
Royal Hotel	25
Smiley's	14
Soksan	2
Ta Phrom	26
Takeo	7
Vimean Thmei Hotel	28

Phnom Pehn Airways

Toseco Travel Agents

Hospital

Cambodian Commercial Bank

ABC Computer School

First Overseas Bank

Old Market

Night Market

Canadia Bank

Siem Reap River

Siem Reap Airport (8km), Sisophon (105km) & Poipet (150km)

Central Market (Psah Leou, 1km) & Phnom Penh (310km)

0 — 250m

▽ Tonlé Sap & Boat Pier

much to choose between these places, though an increasing number of guesthouses are adding newer annexes with mid-range facilities. Mid-range establishments with TV, air-con and en-suite facilities charge $15–20 and are concentrated on Sivatha Street. The *Grand Hôtel d'Angkor* is Siem Reap's first international-standard hotel, but more are under construction.

GUESTHOUSES

Auberge Mont Royal, behind Sivatha Street (☎063/964044). One of the nicest mid-range options, tucked away in a discreet corner of town. Very nice fully furnished rooms with all facilities. ⑨.

Bakong Guesthouse, Sivatha Street (☎063/963419). Well-kept, modern en-suite rooms, with TV and air-con. ⑨.

Chao Say, Old Market (☎063/964029). Immaculate, good-value rooms, including en-suite, cable TV, and optional air-con. ③.

Chenla, junction of Route 6 and Sivatha Street (☎015/630046). A popular guesthouse, recently extended with a brand-new building, including deluxe rooms with all facilities. Older rooms ①. Deluxe rooms ⑨.

European, east of the river (☎012/890917). Large and extremely clean rooms at this new guesthouse, tucked away in a quiet street. Good-value evening set menu available. ①.

Green Garden Home, just off Sivatha Street. Friendly guesthouse with a variety of ample-sized rooms, run by a budding photographer. Pleasant terrace area. ③.

Hao Sotha, Sivatha Street (☎015/633154). Newer, comfortable rooms, some on the large side, in this cosy, family-run guesthouse. ②.

Ivy, Old Market (☎012/800860). Tastefully renovated guesthouse with homely touches and friendly management, but music from the bar floats up through the floor, so can be noisy. Shared bath. ②.

MOVING ON FROM SIEM REAP

By plane

Royal Air Cambodge, Phnom Penh Airways and President all fly from Siem Reap Airport to Phnom Penh. Some **flights** stop in Battambang. Schedules of the three domestic airlines change regularly, so check with a travel agent in Siem Reap. Bangkok Airways operates the only international flight from Siem Reap: the flight to Bangkok ($155 one-way).

A very old military **helicopter** occasionally makes the trip to Phnom Penh. You can jump aboard for $40. Ask at your guesthouse for information, but it's not generally known in advance when the flights will be made. The helicopter usually flies around in circles above the town to announce impending departure.

By road

Northbound pick-ups leave from the east side of the National Route 6 bridge over the Tonlé Siem Reap, near the Sokimex petrol station, between 6 and 7am. After 7am, they tend to cluster around the central market. The market is also the place for all **southbound** departures. Get there early to bag a good seat, and expect to drive around town touting for passengers for an hour or so. Pick-ups to Battambang cost around $4, to Poipet $4, and to Sisophon $2.

Note that the **road north** to Sisophon and Thailand begins to disintegrate a few kilometres out of Siem Reap, then stops altogether, and is replaced by a potholed track. During the wet season, the trip becomes an adventure, with mud and water filling the six-foot-deep potholes. There's a major industry in roadside assistance: locals charge for building temporary bridges, directing vehicles through the shallower water or through paddy fields, and for pulling pick-ups out of the quagmire with tractors.

By boat

Boat tickets are best booked through your guesthouse proprietor, who can usually arrange free transport to the pier, and a discount off the foreigner fare. Boats leave daily for Phnom Penh ($25) and Battambang ($15), water levels permitting.

Mahogany, one block east of the river, off Route 6. Relaxed and friendly budget guesthouse with comfortable old sofas on the terrace and cheap breakfast. Some en-suite rooms. ②.

Moms, one block east of the river. An old favourite, especially popular with French visitors. Basic rooms in the characterful old wooden house are reasonable, but the new building with en-suite rooms for $20–40 is overpriced. ②–⑥.

Naga, west of Sivatha Street, near Sokimex petrol station (☎063/963439). Justifiably popular guesthouse. Clean, friendly and helpful, free pool table, cheap restaurant, but not renowned for good security, so don't leave valuables in your room. ①.

Neak Angkor Villa, junction of Route 6 and Sivatha Street (☎063/964903). A dependable mid-range option including TV and en-suite. ③.

Orchidee, west of Sivatha Street, near Sokimex petrol station (☎012/898178). Quiet guesthouse in an attractive older building, run by friendly, helpful staff. Cheap restaurant. ②.

Pailin, one block east of the river, off Route 6. Small, quiet, friendly budget shack with unlimited free coffee. ②.

Popular, south of the night market (☎015/917377). The older rooms here are a bit small and smelly, but the new en-suite rooms are good value. ①.

Rasmei Ankgor, on the riverbank, near the Old Market (☎015/834264). It's a shame these rooms are so shabby, because the French colonial building is superb, with a terrace overlooking the river. There is talk of refurbishment, however. ②.

Soksan, east bank of the river, north of Route 6 (☎012/880764). Characterful wooden house near the river, with a small, cheap restaurant and a balcony for stringing up your hammock. Some rooms have views of the crocodile farm next door. ①.

Smiley's, just off Sivatha Street (☎012/852955). A firm favourite with budget travellers for good-value food and accommodation. Sociable courtyard and helpful staff. ②.

Takeo, junction of Sivatha Street and Route 6 (☎012/821604). Small, cheap hole-in-the-wall guesthouse, popular with Japanese tourists. One-dollar dinners are a bargain. ①.

HOTELS

Angkor Saphir, Route 6, east of the river (☎063/963566). Good, clean rooms in this well-located mid-range hotel. All rooms come with telephone, TV, en-suite and fridge, but more expensive rooms are larger. ⑥.

Angkor Village, one block east of *Bayon* (☎063/963563). Luxurious wooden bungalow-style eco-accommodation in a jungle setting. Includes telephone, air-con, en-suite and fridge. $75 per bungalow.

Bayon, on the riverbank, in the south of town (☎015/631769). Huge rooms with river views, sparse 1980s decor, strangely appealing in an ageing, retro kind of way. TV, en-suite with bath tubs. ⑥.

Golden Apsara, north of the night market (☎063/963533). Good, clean rooms, including some with a huge terrace area. Very helpful management. ③.

Grand Hôtel d'Angkor, opposite tourist information, Tosamut Boulevard (☎063/963888). Refurbished colonial splendour fit for upmarket tourists and visiting dignitaries. Superior international-standard accommodation; facilities include spa, swimming pool and tennis court. ⑧.

Mini Hotel, one block east of the river, north of Route 6 (☎011/817818). Despite its name, more of a guesthouse than a hotel. Has basic, clean rooms with en-suite bathroom, some with air-con. ②.

Mittapheap Hotel, Sivatha Street (☎063/964375). Clean, if slightly musty, rooms, with TV and air-con. ④.

La Noria, east bank of the river, north of Route 6 (☎063/964242). Mid-range villa-style accommodation frequented mainly by French guests. All rooms are en suite, with either fan or air-con. ⑥.

Ta Phrom, south of the Old Market. Very nice rooms with all the usual refineries of a top-end hotel. Favoured by tour groups. Breakfast included. ⑧.

Eating

Siem Reap boasts a huge selection of **restaurants** catering to tourist tastes, but if you want something more authentic, it's best to head for the markets and the cheap stalls on the eastern side of the river, near Route 6. In the evenings, more impromptu stalls set up all over town, with the culinary epicentre being the night market. Out at the temples, you're never far from food, although the choice is a bit limited, and the prices reflect their location. Restaurants in Siem Reap tend to open for breakfast and stay open until around 11pm.

71 Welcome, east bank of the river, north of Route 6. Cheap local food at this riverside eatery, with plenty of dishes for under a dollar.

Arun, a few doors down from *71 Welcome*. Reasonable food, great service, and a handy spot to listen to the Khmer music wafting across the river from the nightly traditional dancing at the nearby *Grand Hôtel d'Angkor*.

Apsara, near junction of Route 6 and Sivatha Street. Cheap Khmer food, popular with the local moto set.

Bayon, one block east of the river, south of Route 6 (☎012/855219). It's a good idea to book a table during peak season at this popular, atmospheric garden restaurant. Good-value Khmer and Western dishes are priced $1–3, and there's an extensive wine list.

Bayon II, one block east of the river, north of Route 6. Owned by the extended family of *Bayon Restaurant* fame with a similar standard of good food, but more geared up for tour groups, so less authentic ambience.

Chivit Thai, opposite *Bayon*. More than just the usual Thai and Khmer menu at a reasonable $2–4. Relaxed veranda, Thai-style seating.

Continental Café, *Rasmei Angkor*, on the river, near Old Market. Sophisticated European chic at sophisticated European prices. Good selection of Western meals and drinks. Happy hour 5–8pm includes Tiger draught for $1.

Green House, junction of Sivatha Street and Route 6. A good selection of Chinese, Khmer, Thai and European cuisine for around $2, served in an atmospheric garden setting. Vegetarian menu available.

Hawaii, on the riverbank, north of *Bayon* hotel. Fantastic food at a good price, mixed up by the ex-chef of the FCC in Phnom Penh. Cambodian cuisine, Italian and salads are all on the menu. Free pool table.

Kampuchino, near Old Market. High-class pizza and pasta joint near the river with main courses at $3–5.

Koulen, Sivatha Street, near police station. Pleasant, modern Khmer restaurant with good food. Cheap breakfasts priced in riels, main courses cost from $3. Guides often bring people here for lunch.

Little India, north of Old Market. Popular curry house with the full selection of lassis.

Monorom, Sivatha Street, north of night market. Khmer restaurant with limited menu but good food. Try the round fried egg for breakfast, or the frog specials. Closes at 9pm.

Only One, Old Market. This restaurant serving Western food used to be the only one in Siem Reap. Main courses cost $5–6.

Sampheap, near the river, south of Route 6. A mix of tour groups and local visitors enjoying Khmer foods from $2 to $5 at this riverside location.

Sawasdee Food Garden, one block east of the river, north of Route 6. Fantastic Thai food in a relaxed garden setting. Dishes around $1–4.

Singapore Asian, north of Old Market. A popular place serving Western and Asian dishes for $1–3 in a relaxing roof-top garden. Service, however, leaves a lot to be desired.

Swiss Centre, Sivatha Street. A pleasant veranda bar and garden restaurant offering Khmer and Western cuisine. Mains $3–6.

Thai San Mao, north of Old Market. Some cheap rice and noodle dishes, but most dishes $3–4. Offers a good selection of pizzas.

Entertainment and nightlife

Several hotels around town host performances of **traditional dance and music** on certain nights of the week. The *Ta Phrom Hotel* puts on a show of Cambodian classical dance on Tuesday, Thursday and Sunday at 7pm. Tickets are $5–6. A more upmarket version is staged at the *Grand Hôtel d'Angkor*, incorporating dinner and show for $22. For later entertainment there are a handful of tourist/expat bars and the usual Khmer clubs, but on the whole, nightlife in Siem Reap is pretty tame, and most places shut around midnight.

Angkor What?, one block northwest of Old Market. Quiet, chilled-out bar, good for a relaxing drink. 2pm–late.

Bakheng Nightclub, night market. The dance floor is packed full with line-dancing Khmer youngsters by 10pm every night.

Liquid Nightclub, on the river, near Old Market. Futuristic-looking nightclub, completely out of place in provincial Siem Reap. Open 11am–late; happy hour 5–9pm.

Martini Nightclub and Beer Garden, across the river from Old Market. The beer garden is *the* place to be seen for an evening drink, and to enjoy some live Khmer music. The disco is a bit racier than the others in town.

Zanzy Bar, Sivatha Street, near night market. Small, popular expat bar, with $1.50 beers and free pool table.

Listings

Airlines Phnom Penh Airways office, just north of the Old Market; Royal Air Cambodge, west of town towards the airport on National Route 6.

Banks and exchange Cambodian Commercial Bank, Sivatha Street, north of the night market, offers credit-card cash advances and travellers' cheques. Other banks offer only travellers' cheques at the standard two-percent commission. Western Union (☎012/846517), opposite the hospital, can organize money transfers from overseas.

Hospital north of the Old Market.

Internet access ABC Computer School, opposite the Cambodian Commercial Bank, offers Internet connection at $5 for ten minutes; *Angkor Internet Café*, opposite the National Bank, charges $15 for one hour, and can whip up a tasty Café Lao. They also offer an email address facility for $25 per month.

Police junction of Sivatha Street and Route 6.

Post office The main post office is on the western bank of the river, 500m north of the Old Market. Open daily 7am–5pm for stamps, telephone, fax, postcards and souvenirs.

Supermarkets Stock up on bottles of spirits, Rizlas and a scattering of Western luxuries at Lotus Market, opposite the Old Market in town.

Telephone services Bayon Business Centre, near junction of Route 6 and Sivatha Street (☎063/964914), offers fax, telephone, travel-agent services and exchange; Lotus Temple (☎063/964029) at the *Chao Say Guesthouse* near the Old Market has similar services, with additional email facilities; The Swiss Centre, Sivatha Street (☎015/638808), can organize telephone, fax, email, computer rental, typing and translation services.

Travel agents Neak Kror Horm Travel and Tours, near the Old Market (☎063/964924); Toseco Travel Agents, 103 Svay Dongkum (☎063/964929); VLK Royal Tourism, near Cambodian Commercial Bank (☎063/963556).

The temples of Angkor

In 802, Jayavarman II united the warring Chenla factions and worked towards building a magnificent and prosperous kingdom. He declared himself universal god-king, and became the first of a succession of 39 kings to reign over the most powerful kingdom in Southeast Asia at that time. So the **Angkor era** was born, a period marked by imaginative building projects, the design and construction of inspirational **temples** and palaces, the creation of complex irrigation systems and the development of magnificent walled cities. However, as more resources were channelled into ever more ambitious construction projects, Angkor became a target for attack from neighbouring **Siam**. Successive invasions by the Siamese army culminated in the sacking of Angkor in the fifteenth century and the city was abandoned to the jungle. Although Khmers knew of the lost city, it wasn't until the West's "discovery" of Angkor in the nineteenth century that international interest was aroused. A French missionary, Father Bouillevaux, first reported on the "pagoda of Angcor and the ruins of Angcor-Thom", overgrown and camouflaged with jungle greenery. Soon after, in 1858, the famous botanist **Henri Mouhot** led a journey of exploration that began years of continuing archeological work to restore the temples.

More than one hundred Angkorian monuments are spread over some 3000 square kilometres. The best-known monuments are the vast Hindu temple of **Angkor Wat** and the walled city of **Angkor Thom**. Jungle-ravaged **Ta Phrom** and exquisitely decorated **Banteay Srei** are also popular sites. The **Roluos** ruins are significant as the site of the first capital city and as a point of comparison with the later architectural styles of **Banteay Kdei** and **Takeo**. A visit to Angkor wouldn't be complete without the compulsory late-afternoon sunset trip to **Phnom Bakeng**, with its stunning views of Angkor Wat and the surrounding countryside. For more background on the art and architecture of Khmer temples, see pp.84–88.

Many of the artefacts on display at the temples of Angkor are not originals. **Thefts** of the valuable treasures have been common since the 1970s, but have accelerated since the peace process began in 1993, when access to the temples became easier. Attempts have been made to protect the most valuable artefacts by moving them to the National Museum in Phnom Penh, or to the Angkor Conservation Office in Siem Reap, and replacing them with copies.

Practicalities

Visitors to Angkor need to buy a **pass**. There are three different kinds, valid for varying lengths of time: a one-day pass costs $20, a three-day pass $40 and a seven-day pass $60. It is not possible to upgrade passes, so decide before buying one how long you want to spend. Realistically, one day isn't enough. Three days gives you enough time to see the main temples and a few others at a leisurely pace. With a seven-day pass, there's enough time to see everything and return to your favourites at different times of day. The temples are open daily and there are no set opening times. Entry is free after 4.30pm, so if you arrive in Siem Reap in the afternoon, you can hot-foot it over to Phnom Bakheng or Angkor Wat for sunset. There have been stories of ticket scams, and although the authorities have clamped down, it's probably safer to buy your pass at the official entrance booth rather than from your driver or guesthouse.

You'll need to hire a local driver to visit the temples; visitors are not allowed to drive themselves. **Motos** cost around $6 per day, with a surcharge for a visit to Banteay Srei. A few two-seater motorized cyclos have appeared around town, charging $10 per day. A car for the day costs around $20, and is a more comfortable option for three people. A South Korean company has put forward a proposal to transport tourists around in electric cars to reduce pollution, but the plan has met with strong resistance from locals. As yet, no decision has been made. English-speaking **guides** are available for $20 a day from the Angkor Tour Guide Association (☎063/964347), located in the tourist information office in Siem Reap (see p.105).

Angkor Wat

Built in the twelfth century as a mausoleum and temple for King Suryavarman II, **Angkor Wat** represents the height of inspiration and perfection in Khmer art, combining architectural harmony, grand proportions and detailed artistry. Your first close-up view of Angkor Wat is likely to be a memorable sight. Approaching along the sandstone causeway across a broad moat and through the western gate, you're teased with glimpses of the central towers, but it's not until you're through the gate that the full magnificence of the temple comes into view. At once, its size and scale becomes apparent – a truly stunning sight. The causeway, extending 300m across the flat, open compound, directs the eye to the proud temple and its most memorable feature, the distinctive conical-shaped towers, designed to look like lotus buds. Four smaller towers surround a taller central one. The temple is made up of three platforms, linked by stairways, and long, columned galleries extend outwards from the central gopura. If you can resist the urge to head straight for the main temple building, the entry gopura at which you're standing is worth exploring, both inside and out, for its exceptional carvings and an eight-armed Vishnu image with a Buddha head, an interesting marriage of Buddhism and Hinduism. Originally built as a Hindu temple dedicated to Vishnu, Angkor Wat was later converted to a Buddhist monument.

Continuing east along the causeway, you'll pass between the wat's library buildings and two ponds, and mount a flight of steps, guarded by a set of four crouching lions, to the **Terrace of Honour**, where the king would no doubt have stood, looking down on his subjects, perhaps enjoying some festivities or receiving dignitaries. The terrace is the gateway to the extraordinary **Gallery of Bas Reliefs**, a covered gallery which extends around the perimeter of the first level, and the inner wall of which is carved with sandstone reliefs. The carvings cover almost the entirety of the wall, 700m long, 2m in height, and depict religious narratives, battle scenes and Hindu epics such as the Ramayana. The best-known carving, *The Churning of the Ocean of Milk*, in the East Gallery, depicts the myth of creation: gods (*devas*) and evil spirits (*asuras*) churn the ocean for a thousand years to produce the elixir of immortality, and to create order out of chaos. The detail and sharpness of the images make this one of the greatest stone sculptures ever created.

As you approach the central chamber, you'll pass through the cruciform galleries that link the first and second levels. On the right-hand side is the **Gallery of One Thousand Buddhas**, though only a handful of figures now remain. Steps take you up to the next level and into a courtyard, the walls of which are carved with numerous detailed *apsaras*, celestial nymphs. There are a total of 1850 *apsara* figures in Angkor Wat, each individually carved with unique features. The final steep climb to the third level, best approached from the south-

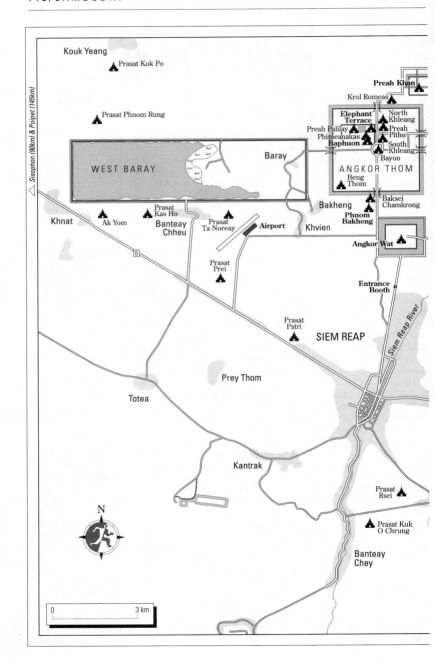

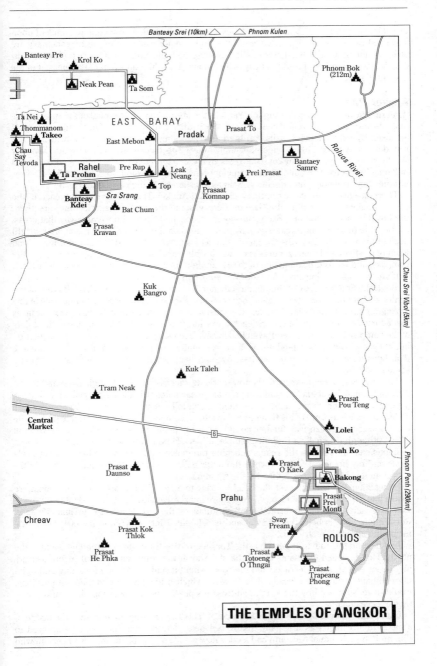

Banteay Srei (10km) △   △ Phnom Kulen

Banteay Pre   Krol Ko

Phnom Bok
(212m)

Neak Pean   Ta Som

Ta Nei
Thommanom
Takeo

EAST   BARAY

East Mebon   Pradak   Prasat To

Roluos River

Chau
Say
Tevoda

Rahel   Pre Rup
Ta Prohm   Leak
Neang   Prei Prasat

Bantaey
Samre

**Banteay
Kdei**   *Sra Srang*   Top

Bat Chum   Prasaat
Komnap

Prasat
Kravan

Chau Srei Vibol (5km) △

Kuk
Bangro

Kuk Taleh

Tram Neak   Prasat
Pou Teng

**Central
Market**   Lolei

Phnom Penh (290km) △

6

Preah Ko

Prasat
Daunso   Prasat
O Kaek   **Bakong**

Prahu   Prasat
Prei
Monti

Chreav   Svay
Pream   **ROLUOS**

Prasat Kok
Thlok   Prasat
Totoeng
O Thngai

Prasat
He Phka   Prasat
Trapeang
Phong

THE TEMPLES OF ANGKOR

ern side, is rewarded with magnificent views of the countryside, framed in the ancient doorways and carved pillars. The *apsaras* carved on the outer walls of the central sanctuary are so sharp and unweathered, that even the tiny fingernails and cuticles of the nymphets are visible. Inside, a number of Buddha images look down from this vantage point at the seat of the ancient Khmer empire.

Angkor Thom

Angkor Thom, 2km north of Angkor Wat, was the last and greatest capital of the Angkor era, built during the late twelfth century and early thirteenth century. The immense city is enclosed by four defensive walls, 8m high and 3km long on each side. This in turn is surrounded by a moat, 100m wide. Certainly more spectacular and extravagant than any Western city at the time, Angkor Thom was an architectural masterpiece, home to perhaps a million inhabitants. The buildings were mainly constructed of wood, so have weathered away, but the stone religious monuments remain as a testament to the city's grand scale.

There are five gateways set in the walls around Angkor Thom, four covering each of the cardinal points and the fifth, the Gate of Victory, set in the east wall and leading directly to the Royal Palace compound. Each gateway is approached via a **stone causeway** that crosses the wide moat. On each causeway, 54 god images on the left and 54 demons on the right depict the myth Churning the Ocean of Milk, as featured in the East Gallery of Angkor Wat. Each of the five sandstone gopuras is crowned with four large heads, facing the points of the compass, and flanked by an image of the Hindu god Indra riding a three-headed elephant.

If you're approaching from Angkor Wat, your entrance to Angkor Thom will probably be through the South Gate. Continuing directly northwards will bring you to **The Bayon**, at the centre of Angkor Thom. Despite its poor workmanship and haphazard sculpting, this is one of Angkor's most endearing temples, its unusual personality created by large carved faces that adorn the sides of its 54 towers; each tower has four heads, each facing one of the points of the compass. The celebrated Bayon heads have been subject to much scholarly conjecture, but they are widely accepted to be a representation of Jayavarman VII. These smiling guardians have aged over time, so that now, each face is unique with weathering, war damage and weeds.

The temple is pyramid-shaped, the towers rising successively to the highest central tower. Although small, it's actually a confusing temple to navigate, owing in large part to its complex history. It was built on top of an earlier monument, follows an experimental layout, and was added to at various times. It is thought to have been completed in the early thirteenth century, but its chaotic plan was further complicated by damage from the Siamese invasion in 1431. Although originally a Buddhist temple, it has a Hindu history too, and themes of both religions can be found in the reliefs adorning the galleries. The inner gallery displays religious and mythological themes, while the outer gallery, added later, is decorated with historical motifs, including the fight with the Chams in 1181.

Lying 200m to the northwest, the neighbouring temple of **Baphuon**, though now no more than a pile of rubble, was, at its peak, even more impressive than the Bayon. Baphuon's tower was originally covered in bronze, and writings of the era testify to its magnificence. Restoration work is being carried out and is scheduled for completion in 2004, but in the meantime access is restricted.

Just beyond the gate to Baphuon is the **Terrace of the Elephants**, extending 300m to the north. Three-headed elephants guard the stairway at the southern end, but before ascending, be sure to view the terrace from the road, where a sculpted frieze of hunting and fighting elephants adorns the facade. The terrace, which originally housed wooden pavilions, would have been used by the king to address his public and as a viewing platform on ceremonial occasions.

Immediately north of here is the **Terrace of The Leper King**, named after the statue of a naked figure that was originally discovered here. The original has been transferred to Phnom Penh's National Museum and a copy now stands on the platform; it is uncertain who the Leper King was or even where the name originates from. An inscription on the statue suggests that it may represent Yama, the god of death or judgement. This would also bear out the theory that the terrace was used as a royal crematorium. Superb sculptures of a variety of figures and sea creatures grace the sides of the terrace. The existing outer wall is in fact a later extension to the terrace. The original wall, also adorned with beautiful carvings, can be accessed via a viewing passageway. You'll need a torch to see the detail.

The two terraces mark what would have been the western edge of the Royal Palace. The timber buildings have since disintegrated, leaving just the temple mountain of **Phimeanakas** and the king's and queen's **bathing pools**. Now little more than a pyramid of stones, Phimeanakas was the palace chapel, crowned with a golden tower and probably completed in the early eleventh century. The western staircase has a hand rail to aid the short, steep climb to the upper terrace. From the top, there's a good view of Baphuon to the south through the trees, and to the north, the royal baths. Feel free to join the bathing monks if the heat gets too much.

Phnom Bakheng

The hilltop temple of **Phnom Bakheng**, south of Angkor Thom, is the earliest building in this area, following Yasorvarman's move westwards from Roluos. The state temple was built from the rock of the hill on which it stands. Upon its completion in the early tenth century it boasted 108 magnificent towers, set on a spectacular pyramid. Only part of the central tower now remains. The five diminishing terraces rise to the central sanctuary, adorned with female divinities, and once housing the *lingam* of the god Yashodhareshvara. Bakheng, however, is visited less for its temple than for the view from the hilltop – Angkor Wat soars upwards from its jungle hideout to the east. At sunset, the best time to visit for great views of Angkor, it becomes a circus crowded with tourists and vendors, with elephant rides on offer and one-dollar drinks and souvenir T-shirts piled up on the ancient stones.

Preah Khan

Just beyond the northeast corner of the perimeter wall around Angkor Thom stands **Preah Khan**, a tranquil, jungle-ravaged temple, surrounded by dense foliage on all sides. The twelfth-century temple served as the temporary residence of King Jayavarman VII while he was rebuilding Angkor Thom, damaged in an attack by the Siamese. A systematic tour of the temple is impossible, as routes are blocked with piles of fallen stones, trees or archeological excavation. Most people enter from the western entrance, but it's worth continuing all the way to the eastern edge of the temple. Here you'll find an unusual two-storey structure, with circular columns supporting the second floor of square columns and windows, unique in Khmer architecture. Not far from here, at the southern end of the east gopura, a photogenic battle of wood and stone is being fought as an encroaching tree grows through the ruins. The tree appears to be winning. Preah Khan can be visited in the hotter hours of the day, as it's largely in shade.

Takeo

About 2km east of the Bayon, this towering replica of Mount Meru scores well on the height points but is awarded nothing for decoration. **Takeo** is bereft of the usual Angkor refineries; perhaps they were to be added later, as the temple was never finished. The sandstone pyramid, although imposing and architecturally significant, is hard to get really excited about, especially as there's so much else on offer at Angkor.

Ta Phrom

The stunning twelfth-century temple-monastery of **Ta Phrom**, 1km southeast of Takeo, has a magical appeal. Rather than being cleared and restored like most of the other Angkor monuments, it's been left to the ravages of the jungle and appears roughly as it did to the

Europeans who rediscovered these ruins in the nineteenth century. Roots and trunks intermingle with the stones and seem almost part of the structure. The temple's cramped corridors reveal half-hidden reliefs, while valuable carvings litter the floor.

Jayavarman VII originally built Ta Phrom as a Buddhist monastery, although Hindu purists have since defaced the Buddhist imagery. The temple was once surrounded by an enclosed city. An inscription found at the site testifies to the importance of Ta Phrom: it records that there were over 12,000 people at the monastery, maintained by almost 80,000 people in the surrounding villages.

Banteay Kdei

Southeast of Ta Phrom and one of the quieter sites in this area, **Banteay Kdei** is a huge twelfth-century Buddhist temple, constructed under Jayavarman VII. It's in a pretty poor state of repair, but the crumbling stones create an interesting architecture of their own. Highlights are the carvings of female divinities and other figures in the niches of the second enclosure, and a frieze of Buddhas in the interior court. Opposite the east entrance to Banteay Kdei are the **Srah Srang** or "royal bath", a large lake, which was probably used for ritual ablutions, and its landing stage, decorated with lions and nagas.

Roluos Group

Not far from the small town of **Roluos** are three of Cambodia's oldest temples: **Bakong**, **Preah Ko** and **Lolei**. Signposts mark the route from National Route 6, about 13km east of Siem Reap; the temples are a couple of kilometres further on. The relics date from the late ninth century, the dawn of the Angkorian era. With the emphasis on detail rather than size, the period is characterized by innovative construction methods, architecture and ornamentation, evident in all three temples.

Cambodia's earliest temple mountain, **Bakong** is made up of five tiers of solid sandstone surrounded by brick towers. Entering from the east across the balustraded causeway, you'll come to some newer temple buildings and a school just before the inner compound. Continuing through the almost completely ruined gopura to the inner compound, you'll see a number of square towers at ground level. Originally eight towers surrounded the central sanctuary, of which only five remain standing today. The towers are of stucco-faced brick opening to the east, with false doors on the other side. Guardian figures decorate the niches, and exquisite carvings adorn the sandstone lintels. Turning to the central five-tiered pyramid, you'll see a number of carved elephants looking out into the surrounding forests from the corners of the first three platforms. At the fourth tier, twelve sandstone towers surround the central sanctuary, while on the fifth tier, a few panels remain of the frieze that originally adorned all four walls surrounding the central sanctuary. The sanctuary itself is a later addition; you can see the newer stones resting on the original base, and the lotus spire betrays its twelfth-century origins.

On the western side of the road to Bakong stands **Preah Ko**, built by Indravarman I as a funerary temple for his ancestors. It was originally surrounded by three enclosure walls, now in a state of ruin. The highlight are the six brick towers of the central sanctuary, approached through a pile of rubble, once an imposing gopura, entry tower and galleries. The carved window balusters remain standing. Passing through the foundations of the galleries, you'll see on your left a square brick structure of unknown purpose, possibly some kind of storeroom. Before the central sanctuary, three ruined sculptures of the sacred bull *Ko* face westwards. Pass through any of the small lion-flanked staircases to reach the raised platform of the central sanctuary: much of the original decorative stucco remains on the towers and is exceptionally elegant, especially on eastern towers. Male figures flank the three eastern towers and those behind are female.

The sanctuary of **Lolei**, 1km north of Preah Ko, was built by Yashovarman I on an artificial island, and consists of four brick-and-sandstone towers opening to the east. The stucco has all but disappeared, but the excellent decorative sandstone lintels of *makaras* and the bulbous-eyed Kala hint at the previous intricate splendour of these towers.

Banteay Srei

The pretty tenth-century temple of **Banteay Srei** is unique amongst its Angkorian peers. Its miniature proportions, unusual pinkish colour and intricate ornamentation create a surreal effect, enhanced by its astonishing state of preservation. The journey to the site, about 30km northeast of Angkor Wat, takes about an hour. Tour groups start arriving en masse from 8.30am, and because of its small size, it gets crowded quickly. If you can arrive here an hour or so beforehand, you'll have the temple to yourself.

The sharp and detailed carving above the doorway of the east gopura is a prelude to the delights within. The roseate tones here and throughout the temple are caused by the quartz arenite sandstone used in construction. A paved causeway flanked by rows of sandstone markers takes you to the entry tower. From here, across the moat, the tops of the three intricate central towers and two libraries are visible over the low enclosure wall. The reddish sandstone against the green backdrop of the jungle is a magnificent sight, as if you've stumbled across a fairytale city. Inside the enclosure wall, there's a riot of intricate decoration and architecture with elegant pillars and exquisite frontons; walls are covered with carved foliage and guardian divinities, and panels are extravagantly decorated with scenes from Hindu mythology. It's like a magical, miniature fantasy land; the central towers have midget doors barely a metre tall, and the shrines have Lilliputian internal dimensions, making entry impractical for all but the shortest people.

WESTERN CAMBODIA

The flat stretch of land that fans out from Phnom Penh to the border with Thailand is sandwiched between the **Cardamom Mountains** in the southwestern corner of the country, and the **Dangrek Range** in the north. A perfect hideout, these frontier hills were home to the Khmer Rouge guerrillas for nearly twenty years from 1979. Until the defections of the late 1990s, the Khmer Rouge had a tight grip over these upland regions. However, government control has now been officially restored, and travellers are returning to areas that were previously off-limits. The towns within the former occupied territories, such as the remote frontier outpost of **Pailin**, are not attractive places, as you might expect after twenty years of war and isolation, but the countryside is stunning in places and has a Wild West appeal. Many of the residents are ex-soldiers who have spent most of their lives living in the jungle. Sticking to the roads and paths is essential, as this is the most densely mined area in the world. Stretching across the vast central plain is the country's largest lake, the **Tonlé Sap**, which swells to 8000 square kilometres during the rainy season, and is the region's primary focus of transport, livelihood and leisure. The area's commercial hub is **Battambang**, an agreeable town, bearing traces of its French colonial days. Its northern neighbour, **Sisophon** makes a convenient stopping-off point on the route into Thailand.

Sisophon

SISOPHON has emerged from the shadows of the Khmer Rouge to become an increasingly important staging post for Thai–Cambodian trade. Thai goods are trucked into the town and transferred to trains for the slow journey to Phnom Penh. Travellers, too, are passing through in increasing numbers from the Poipet border crossing (see p.118), though they don't tend to hang around – Sisophon is a pretty nondescript town, but it's a handy place to break your journey, especially if you get delayed owing to bad road conditions between Sisophon and Siem Reap (see box on p.107). From here you can either tackle the last and worst stretch of road to Siem Reap in daylight or detour via Battambang.

The **train station** is in the southwest of town. A cargo train leaves Sisophon station at 2pm daily, arriving in Battambang at 6pm (1400r). Few, if any, of the carriages have seats, so you could do what the locals do and take a hammock to lie in. Rice sacks are fairly comfortable

POIPET BORDER CROSSING

From Sisophon it's a relatively painless two-hour pick-up ride to the border crossing at Poipet (daily 8am–5pm). Services operate regularly throughout the day. Thai visas can be arranged on the spot. From the border take a tuk-tuk to Aranyaprathet, where there are regular buses and trains to Bangkok and elsewhere.

Coming **into Cambodia**, it's now possible to obtain a visa on arrival at the Poipet border crossing. You'll need $20 and two photos. The border officials will also ask to see a medical card to check your vaccinations. It's a scam of course, but if you don't have your card, you'll be forced to swallow unidentified pills and pay 200B for the "medication". Many people travelling from Bangkok opt for an all-in trip to Siem Reap, but bear in mind this doesn't give you the flexibility of staying overnight in Sisophon if road conditions are bad.

to sit on, but if the train is loaded with pineapples you're in for an uncomfortable ride. Currently, Sisophon is the nearest train station to the Thai border, but plans to refurbish the line onwards to Thailand have already been tabled.

Pick-ups stop either at the northern edge of town or in the centre; motos (10B) will be on hand to ferry you to a guesthouse or hotel. **Accommodation** in Sisophon is nothing to write home about. The best option is the sleepy *Santapheap Hotel* (②), which has small, cute rooms overlooking the river with bathroom and TV. There are two places to stay on the road into town from Poipet, next to the silver Apsara statue: the *Rong Roeng Hotel* and neighbouring *Phnom Svay Hotel* (both ②), offering a variety of rooms, all with bathroom and TV. Nearby, on the same road, is a surprisingly good, inexpensive **restaurant**, *Pkay Proeuk* (daily 6am–9pm). **Nightlife** is limited to the *Sereisophon Nightclub*, near the train station. While dollars and riel are accepted in Sisophon, most transactions are in **baht**.

Battambang

BATTAMBANG, 71km south of Sisophon, is Cambodia's second city, but it's a world apart from Phnom Penh's urban bustle, enjoying an unhurried, pedestrian pace and noted for its friendliness and pleasant atmosphere. The city, however, is keen not to get left behind in the country's recent surge of development and modernization. French-colonial-era terraces on the riverside are rapidly filling with private English-language schools and mobile-phone shops. The busiest Battambang gets, however, is at the central market, where gem stones from the town of Pailin, southwest of Battambang, are cut and traded. Don't expect to pick up a bargain unless you know what to look for – the better stones are shipped straight to Thailand.

The daily **train** from Sisophon trundles into the station at the western edge of town. **Pick-ups** arrive at the central market, and a few blocks north is the **port**, where boats to and from Siem Reap dock. **Planes** land in a field of cows to the east of the city. A **taxi** into town will cost $3–5, depending on the number of people.

When you're ready to **move on**, pick-ups for Phnom Penh leave from the central market and charge according to road conditions, generally around 8000–10,000r. A taxi will cost around 25,000r. Pick-ups to Sisophon (4000r) leave from the stand in the northwest corner of town. For Pailin, join a pick-up in the south of town, near the start of Route 10. Again, costs vary according to conditions, around 5000–7000r. When the river is high enough, **boats** depart daily at 7am for Siem Reap. The foreigner price is $15 for the three-hour trip. **Planes** fly frequently to Phnom Penh. Check the latest schedules. Phnom Penh Airways and President Airways offices are both on Street 3, south of the market. Phnom Penh Airlines charge $40 one way.

The **post office** on the riverside (daily 8am–7pm) has stamps and a national telephone facility, charging 2000r per minute to Phnom Penh. **Internet access** is available at ABC

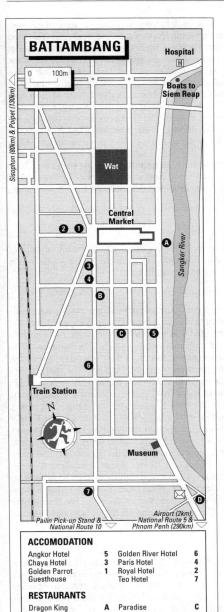

ACCOMODATION

Angkor Hotel	5	Golden River Hotel	6
Chaya Hotel	3	Paris Hotel	4
Golden Parrot	1	Royal Hotel	2
Guesthouse		Teo Hotel	7

RESTAURANTS

Dragon King	A	Paradise	C
Neak Poan	D	Paris Hemling	B

Computer on the riverbank, south of the central market. The **provincial hospital**, at the northern end of the riverside, has some English- and French-speaking doctors, although facilities aren't great. The **Soksan Clinic** (☎012/897405) is the private alternative.

Accommodation

An abundance of **hotels** makes for competitively priced accommodation in Battambang. This doesn't mean that you'll find much below $5 per night, but you'll get more for your money. All accommodation here includes cable TV, en-suite and fan, unless otherwise stated.

Angkor Hotel, on the riverside, south of the market (☎053/952310). River views and balconies justify the higher than average prices. Indifferent staff. ③.

Chaya Hotel, Street 3. Popular, but shabby and past its prime. No longer the best deal in town compared to the newer competition. ②.

Golden Parrot Guesthouse, western end of the market (☎015/530201). The cheaper rooms are a bit dingy, so it's worth paying the extra dollar for larger, brighter rooms. ①–②.

Golden River Hotel, Street 3, south of the market (☎053/952158). Good location enjoyed by this friendly, helpful place, run by an Australian/Khmer family, though some of the single rooms are a bit small. ②.

Paris Hotel, Street 3, south of the market. Average rooms in a good central location. ②.

Royal Hotel, western end of the market (☎015/912034). This refurbished hotel is now the best value in Battambang, offering huge modern rooms with cable TV, fridge and en-suite facilities. Cheap singles are also available and some rooms have balconies. ②.

Teo Hotel, Street 3, on the southern edge of town (☎053/952288). The top-end hotel in Battambang, not as expensive as it looks from the outside and a bit of a distance from the town-centre action. Double rooms include a telephone in addition to the usual facilities. ③.

Eating, drinking and entertainment

The best **place to eat** is a little way south of the town centre on Street 3: *Phkay Pruek Restaurant* serves outstanding food in its popular courtyard restaurant. Its mainstay is MSG-laced

Khmer food, but there are Western alternatives. Back in town, on Street 3, south of the market, *Paris Hemling Restaurant* is not the most atmospheric of places, but has reasonable food and a limited menu in English; most dishes are 5000r. *Chip Sreng* north of the train station, is a good alternative, although the Sparrow Casserole might be too alternative for some tastes. Meals are 5000–10,000r in the pleasant beer-garden restaurant. *Neak Poan Restaurant*, near the post office, is a favourite place for an early-evening beer, followed by the Steam Boat speciality. Dodgy live music is an added bonus. A shantytown of **food and drinks stalls** appears on the riverbank outside the restaurant in the evening. Other food stalls can be found at the market, and there are a number of cheap restaurants between the *Angkor Hotel* and *Paradise Nightclub*. If you're missing home luxuries, *Chea Neang Drink Shop* opposite the western end of the market, sells all kinds of Western goodies, including French cheeses and wines.

Battambang offers nothing like the variety or scope of **nightlife** available in Phnom Penh, but there are a few nightclubs. Popular are the *Dragon King* on the riverside by the market, and the seedier *Paradise*, two blocks south. If you fancy a yodel, make for the Karaoke joints on the road between the station and the market.

Around Battambang

Two popular day-trips, a bumpy moto-drive from Battambang, are the artificial lake of **Kamping Pouy** and the hilltop temple of **Wat Sampeau**. Both can be visited easily in one day, with a moto costing $5 for the round-trip from Battambang.

Wat Sampeau

Around 25km along the road that heads west from Battambang, you'll see two lopsided hills rising from the plain. Supposedly, they resemble a sinking boat, Phnom Sampeau being the broken hull, and Phnom G'daong the broken sail bobbing around in the water. An unshaded ten-minute climb up the northeast side of Phnom Sampeau takes you to **Wat Sampeau**. The site was used to great advantage by the government forces in their skirmishes with the Khmer Rouge. A legacy of the conflict, two Russian-made guns stand near the wat; it's best to steer clear of these, as locals claim that mines could still be lurking there. Across the ridge are the temple of Prasat Brang, built in 1964, and a small brown decorative stupa. If your moto-driver doesn't know it, ask children in the area to show you the complex of **caves**, known as Lang L'kaon, nearby. The caves were the site of atrocities committed by the Khmer Rouge – smashed skulls are piled up on a wooden makeshift memorial to victims who were thrown into the deep cave from a hole above. An adjacent cave, trailing eerily downwards into the darkness, is apparently still full of the scattered bones of victims. It's thought that more than 10,000 people died in these caves at the hands of the Khmer Rouge. A smaller cave nearby houses a primitive cage full of more bones and skulls, with victims' clothes hanging from the vines. This was allegedly the torture chamber. In previous times, these caves had a pleasanter role: the larger cave was used for plays and theatrical productions, its approaching slope providing the seats for the audience. The smaller caves off to the side were used as dressing rooms and props storage.

Kamping Pouy Lake

The vast **Kamping Pouy Lake**, around 35km west of Battambang, is an artificial lake, formed by a dam built during the Pol Pot era as part of an irrigation project to enable the farming of three rice crops a year. The dam was built entirely by hand, at a cost of many thousands of lives. People now come here to picnic and cool off in the fast-flowing waters. Inflatable tubes can be rented for 500r from the side of the road at the dam. Make sure you stick to the roads – the countryside all around has been heavily mined, and is not yet cleared.

Pailin

Some 85km southwest of Battambang, **PAILIN** may not appeal to everyone. Remote and isolated, its only link with the rest of Cambodia is the long and arduous road from Battambang. Once you finally arrive at Pailin, there's really no reason to be here: there's not much to see, and nowhere else to go – the border crossing to Thailand is not open to Westerners, so the only option is to retrace your steps to Battambang. However, the very fact that tourists have no business here is precisely the attraction of Pailin. It's a down and dirty **frontier town**, the heart of old **Khmer Rouge** Cambodia, and a roughneck **gem-mining** outpost. It's easy to get the feeling that you've stumbled into guerrilla territory, that you're somewhere you shouldn't be. In reality, the wild and edgy atmosphere owes more to the history of the place than to the outward appearance of modern-day Pailin. The town, high up and surrounded by jungle, was long a Khmer Rouge stronghold, supplied with food and weapons from the nearby Thai border. The highly organized, well-disciplined group of guerrilla soldiers was led by **Ieng Sary**, Brother Number Two to Pol Pot in the old Khmer Rouge government. In 1994, government forces launched a sustained attack, and pushed all the way to Pailin. Celebrating their victory, the forces ran riot in the town, pillaging and looting, without a thought for securing the area. Meanwhile, the Khmer Rouge regrouped and counterattacked, driving the Cambodian Army eastwards to within six miles of Battambang. However, in an unexpected move in 1996, Ieng Sary and the soldiers under his command defected to the government, and struck a deal. In return for ending his revolutionary struggle, Ieng Sary was spared the death penalty, and Pailin was to become a semi-autonomous region. In reality, however, central government still holds little sway over this border outpost; its lucrative gem mines and timber concessions are now run like a business by the warlords of old. Although Ieng Sary has officially retired, the current Governor of Pailin is his former Khmer Rouge commander Ei Chhien, and the Deputy Governor is his son Ieng Vuth. You might be surprised to learn that Pailin has the lowest crime rate in Cambodia: the reason for this is that in Khmer Rouge tradition, criminals are executed without trial, often on the spot.

Forget French terraces and colonial mansions; Pailin is a worn and shabby collection of timber shacks and concrete blocks, with the odd incongruous glamorous chalet, recently erected by the old warlords, now Pailin's nouveaux riches. All over town, there's evidence of **gem mining**. Bulldozers dig up every available square inch of earth, and machines sift through the heaped piles. Outside nearly every shop is a man sitting behind a rickety table, ready to hand over cash for rough, uncut stones pulled from the ground. Rubies are commonly found, but sapphires are more prized.

A carving of the legend The Churning of The Ocean of Milk covers the outer wall of **Wat Kong Kang** on the way into town. Inside, the unusual three-story temple is decorated with tales from the Buddha's life, and two curious-looking, strangely proportioned Buddha images can be seen on the ground floor. In a room of their own on the roof of the wat are two intricately carved four-faced wooden figures, at one time set with gems. The adjacent hill of **Phnom Yath** houses a smaller pagoda, its outer wall decorated with startling images of people being tortured in hell. Tongues are pulled out with pliers, women drowned, people stabbed with forks, heads chopped off; it's all X-rated stuff. The main buildings have been repaired and restored, but its strategic hilltop position meant that the pagoda took a beating, and there are bullet holes everywhere. Large artillery shells are painted yellow and are used to house incense sticks and offerings to Ta Dom Don Dai. From the hill, there's a great view of Pailin and the mountains around.

It's an interesting twenty-kilometre moto ride out of town to the **Thai border**, Pailin's Wild-West frontier. The road winds past neglected coffee plantations originally established by the French, but nothing more than a few derelict buildings remain. The bumpy track continues past abandoned military vehicles and climbs gradually through the forest, where areas are illegally logged. The timber is often fashioned into desirable furniture at workshops on the spot before being whisked away to Thailand. Big, heavy beds, tables and chairs can all be seen on the backs of trucks. At 20km, a few food stalls mark the border area, and a huge white casino comes into view, where the Thais arrive to lose their money.

Practicalities

There are plenty of small **guesthouses** near the market, the pick of which is the *Pailin Punleu Pich Motel* (①), with reasonable rooms, although its proximity to karaoke bars and brothels may keep you up late. Downhill from the market, on a road to your left is *Meas Sam Oeun* (①), a pleasant, quiet, cheap guesthouse. On the same road, but in a different world, is the upmarket *Hang Meas Pailin Hotel* (⑤), frequented by visiting Thai businessmen and assorted high-rollers.

Of the many **restaurants** around the market one worth trying is *Sinyee's Restaurant*, offering pots of bubbling soup and where some English is spoken. For a more Western-influenced menu, the restaurant at the *Hang Meas Pailin Hotel* offers dishes at 50–70B; try the Modern Lettuce, or the Glorious Porridge. Note that **baht** is the favoured currency in Pailin.

The only way to **get to Pailin** is by pick-up from Battambang. Pick-ups leave until mid-afternoon from Pisar Loeu, in the south of the town. The journey takes four to five hours and costs 5000–7000r.

The road out to Pailin and beyond to Thailand is safe to travel, but is surrounded by mine-fields. To the south lies the most **heavily mined** area in Cambodia. Do not think about leaving the road. Even around Pailin, it's prudent to stick to paths, although most of the mines have been cleared from the town.

THE SOUTHWEST

To the southwest of Phnom Penh, a series of mountain ranges, known as the Cardamom and Elephant mountains, rise up imposingly from the plains, as if shielding Cambodia's only stretch of coast from the world. Indeed, only a few places along the coast are accessible by road or rail. The most popular destination is the beach resort of **Sihanoukville**, whose sandy shores are the launching point for remote and sparsely populated islands in the Gulf of Thailand. Further east along the coast, the city of **Kampot** makes a good base for exploring **Bokor** ghost-town hill station and the quaint coastal village of **Kep**. On Cambodia's western border, **Krong Koh Kong** serves as an interesting transit point for visitors arriving from Thailand.

The accessible areas of the southwest are well served by public **transport**. National Routes 2, 3 and 4 all in a fairly good state of repair and passable all year round, while comfortable Malaysian-mad speedboats ply the sea routes.

Sihanoukville

The closest that Cambodia gets to a full-blown beach resort, **SIHANOUKVILLE** is overrun with locals on weekends and holidays, enjoying the sandy beaches, well-stocked seafood restaurants and slow-paced ambience. It's a friendly, prosperous town, thanks to the soothing influence of the sea and the healthy local economy, based on port trade, fishing and tourism. It may not be able to compete with the best of the **beaches** in neighbouring countries – the vistas are pleasant rather than stunning, and facilities, though improving, are not exactly up to international standards – but the town does have a certain charm and is proving a popular stop with travellers, not just those en route to or from Thailand, but also Phnom Penh visitors looking for an easy excursion. The resort is certainly a good place to relax and unwind, especially if you've been travelling hard on the provincial Cambodian roads. Moreover, lazy days on the beach can be complemented by an evening of partying at one of the town's vibrant nightspots.

Sihanoukville came into being just after the dissolution of Indochina. The French-occupied Mekong Delta reverted to Vietnamese possession, depriving Cambodia of a maritime port.

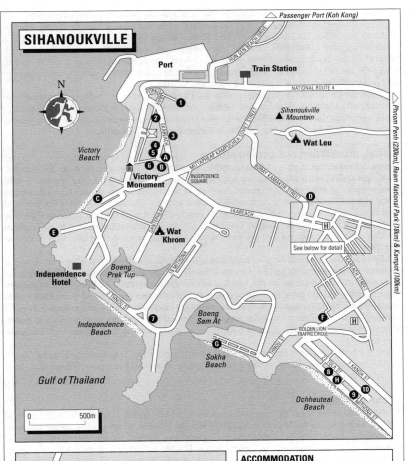

SIHANOUKVILLE

Passenger Port (Koh Kong)

Port

Train Station

NATIONAL ROUTE 4

Sihanoukville
▲ Mountain

♦♦ Wat Leu

Victory
Beach

Victory
Monument

INDEPEDENCE
SQUARE

See below for detail

Phnom Penh (230km); Ream National Park (18km) & Kampot (100km)

♦ Wat
Khrom

Independence
Hotel

Boeng
Prek Tup

GOLDEN LION
TRAFFIC CIRCLE

Independence
Beach

Boeng
Sam Ất

Gulf of Thailand

Sokha
Beach

Ochheuteal
Beach

0   500m

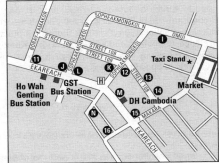

SOPHEAKMONGKOL N

SOPHEAKMONGKOL W

STREET 108

OMUI

BORAY KAMAKOR

STREET 109

Taxi Stand ★

EKAREACH

GST
Bus Station

Ho Wah
Genting
Bus Station

DH Cambodia

Market

MAKARA

EKAREACH

ACCOMMODATION			
Caledonian	14	Royal Hotel	16
Chez Mari-yan	6	Sampovmeas	12
Da-Da	4	Sea Breeze	7
Kohtakeiv	3	Seaside Hotel	8
Mealy Chenda	5	Singapore Hotel	13
Moon	2	Star Paris	11
Orchidee	10	Susaday	9
Peak Hotel	1	Thmor Tep	15

RESTAURANTS, BARS & CLUBS			
Anchor Arms	L	Melting Pot	B
Angkor Beer	D	Mick and Craig's	J
Discotheque		Nasa Disco	F
Apsara	K	Red Snapper Bar	N
Hawaii Seaview	C	Sam's Restaurant	A
Koh Pos	E	Sea Dragon	H
Lucky Beer Garden	I	Restaurant	
Marlin Bar & Grill	M	Sokha	G

The Cambodians decided to build a new one at Kompong Som, as Sihanoukville was then known, with work beginning in 1955. Sihanoukville has since been used to supply arms to Vietcong guerrillas, Nationalist troops and Khmer Rouge soldiers, depending on prevailing political conditions. A small amount of humanitarian aid managed to make its way through the port during the famines of 1979–81, but its primary trade seems to be in arms; as recently as 1998, containers of illegal arms heading for Prince Ranarridh's soldiers were discovered here, allegedly evidence of a proposed coup against Hun Sen.

Sihanoukville sprawls over a large peninsula. The **town centre** is roughly equidistant from the port and its four beaches. Located here are the markets, most of the nightspots and many of the mid-range hotels. A satellite town of sorts, a couple of kilometres to the west, near to the port and Victory Beach, has become a budget travellers' favourite.

Arrival, information and getting around

Buses arrive in the centre of Sihanoukville, on Ekareach Road, not far from the market. **Pick-ups** and **taxis** usually terminate opposite the market. Most town-centre hotels are within easy walking distance, but if you're heading to any of the beach suburbs, you'll need to invest around 2000r in a moto. Sihanoukville **train station** is located just east of the port and Hun Sen Beach Drive on National Route 4. Trains from the capital are scheduled to take twelve hours, but often take longer. The fare is a bargain 4500r. **Boat** arrivals from Thailand via Krong Koh Kong speed into the passenger port to the northwest of the town centre on Hun Sen Beach Drive.

Motos are the principal form of **local transport** in Sihanoukville, but have a tendency to overcharge foreigners. Negotiate the fare beforehand, and aim for no more than 2000r for a town-to-beach trip. If lazing on the beach isn't enough excitement, and you want to explore Sihanoukville and the area, the best option is to rent a **motorcycle**. Good Luck Motorcycle Rental (☎015/850411) next to the GST bus depot on Ekareach Road, has a selection from $6 per day. A **car** with driver can be arranged for around $20 through most hotels and guesthouses or at the taxi stand. A self-drive army jeep is available at the *Caledonian Guesthouse* (see below).

For the latest **tourist information**, track down a copy of *The Sihanoukville Visitors' Guide*, a comprehensive, regularly updated tourist guide available from guesthouses and bars around town.

Accommodation

Sihanoukville is not short of hotels, which tend to fill up quickly at weekends and holidays. During midweek, it's fairly easy to haggle down the price at all types of **accommodation**. Most of the places listed here have cheap single rooms. Budget accommodation tends to be concentrated in the streets above Victory beach. In addition, many local families with a spare room or two, will put up a "Guesthouse" sign to attract the tourist over-spill at peak times. You'll find them all over town, with a small concentration in Ekareach Street. The rooms are a standard $5, regardless of position, facilities or cleanliness, so it's worth shopping around. Depending on where you end up, it's a rare opportunity to spend some time with a Khmer family, though bear in mind that these families are unlikely to speak any English, standards of cleanliness will be fairly low, and you're unlikely to be able to sleep in past sunrise.

GUESTHOUSES

Caledonian, Street 108, towards 7 Makara Street (☎034/933840). The cheapest option in the town centre, this is a small, friendly guesthouse with a comfortable restaurant, serving travellers' fare. Share bathroom only. ①.

Chez Mari-yan, near the Victory Monument (☎034/933709). Mid-range bungalows overlooking Victory beach, with tasty food on the classy restaurant deck.

Da Da, next door to *Mealy Chenda* (☎012/879527). Friendly, family-run place, with ocean views, offering six large, clean en-suite rooms. Close to budget eateries. ②.

MOVING ON FROM SIHANOUKVILLE

Buses

Three competing private companies, GST, Ho Wah Genting, and DH Cambodia run **buses to Phnom Penh**. There's little to choose between them except departure times, which cluster around 7am–8.45am and 12–1.30pm. The trip takes about four hours and costs 8000–10,000r. The buses leave from the respective bus depots on Ekareach Road (see map p.123) and tickets can be booked direct or through some guesthouses.

Share taxis and pick-ups

Share taxis and pick-ups to **Phnom Penh** can be joined at the rank opposite Sihanoukville central market or at the junction of Route 4 and the road to Independence Square. Most leave before 10am, with pick-ups costing 6000r, and a place in a taxi 10,000r. If you want to avoid the usual cramped conditions, get a few friends together and hire a whole taxi – you can sometimes negotiate a bargain in the afternoon if a Phnom Penh-based driver wants to get back home in time for tea. **Taxis** at the rank opposite the market also go to **Kampot** for around 8000r and take about two hours, depending on road and weather conditions.

Trains

The **train** that leaves Sihanoukville station at 6am is scheduled to take twelve hours to the capital for a bargain 4500r, but often takes longer. The train is also a good way to get to Kampot, Kep, Kompong Trach and Takeo.

Boats to Thailand

The sea route from Sihanoukville **into Thailand** is proving an increasingly popular alternative to the Poipet border crossing (see p.118), as it avoids the bad roads and border scams. It's faster, easier, but more expensive, as the boat operators have recently introduced foreigner prices. The fast boat leaves from the passenger ferry terminal on Hun Sen Beach Drive daily at noon and takes just over four hours to reach Krong Koh Kong, just inside the Cambodian border, with stops at Koh S'dach (2hr) and Pak Long (4hr). The foreigner price is 600B to either Pak Long or Krong Koh Kong. To Koh S'dach everybody pays 300B.

If you want to hurry straight on to Thailand the same day, you'll need to disembark at Pak Long, where small boats will be waiting to ferry you to the border at Ban Hat Lek (40B per person) before it shuts at 5pm. The alternative, less frantic route is to stay on board until Krong Koh Kong, where you can stay the night, and cross the border at leisure the next day. From Krong Koh Kong, you'll need to take a boat (20B) across the Dong Tong River, then a moto (20B) to the border.

You can get a **visa on arrival** at the border post. Once you've completed the formalities and crossed into Thailand, you'll be able to pick up a minibus for the hour's journey to Trat (80–100B). From Trat, frequent public buses run to Bangkok and elsewhere, but if you miss the 6pm Bangkok bus, the next bus doesn't leave until 11pm, arriving in Bangkok at 4.30am. If you're in a hurry to get to Bangkok, a minibus leaves from the Ban Hat Lek Casino at the border crossing at 5pm each day, going directly to Bangkok for 450B.

Kohtakeiv, Ekareach Street (☎034/933611). Don't be put off by the tacky green-and-gold facade: this well maintained guesthouse beats the average town-centre hotels on price, homeliness and cleanliness. Usual mid-range luxuries and close to budget restaurants. ④.

Mealy Chenda, west of Ekareach Street, above Victory beach (☎034/933472). Legendary on the budget circuit, and still popular despite increasing competition. Accommodation is en-suite. A limited number of rooms have sea views, as does the restaurant, which has better food than service. ②.

Moon, near the post office, on Victory beach (☎012/863091). Small, friendly, chilled-out wooden shack on a quiet road near Victory beach. Share bathroom. ①.

Orchidee (☎015/920771). Fully equipped, spacious rooms one block back from Ochheuteal beach, with pleasant breakfast terrace. Ask here about the annexe nearer the beach, with clean en-suite rooms at a bargain $5. ⑤

Sea Breeze, Independence beach (☎034/320217). The only accommodation option on Independence beach. Large, clean rooms with chunky wooden double beds. All facilities, with a terrace overlooking the sea. ⑤.

Susaday, Ochheuteal beach (☎034/320156). Within a towel's throw of the beach, this guesthouse offers spotless, secure rooms, all with fan and bathroom. ②.

HOTELS

Sihanoukville has an abundance of **hotels**, all offering en-suite bathroom, cable TV, fridge and air-con.

Peak Hotel, Porkombar Street, overlooking the port (☎034/320301). Sihanoukville's newest top-range hotel with tennis courts, swimming pool, zoo, casino and rooftop restaurant. ⑦.

Royal Hotel, 7 Makara Street (☎034/320046). Nice clean rooms with all facilities. ③.

Seaside Hotel, Ochheuteal beach (☎034/933641). At the upper end of the Sihanoukville accommodation spectrum, popular with conferences. Trees have been chopped down for unhindered sea views. ⑥.

Singapore Hotel, Street 108, near 7 Makara Street (☎034/9338347). Brand-new, clean hotel in good central location. ③.

Sampovmeas, corner of Street 108 and Sopheakmongkol E Street (☎034/933700). Clean rooms above a popular restaurant. ③.

Star Paris, Ekareach Street, corner of Boray Kamakor Street (☎034/933608). Best-value mid-range hotel in the town centre, with clean, en-suite rooms and a cheap restaurant downstairs. ③.

Thmor Tep, corner of Ekareach Street and 7 Makara Street (☎034/933635). Run by friendly English-speaking staff. Rooms with all facilities. ③.

The City

Sihanoukville's main attraction is its four beaches. **Victory beach** is the nearest to most of the budget accommodation, but its small size and its proximity to the port, about 3km north of the downtown area, render it the least attractive. You're more likely to find a few fishermen working on their boats than tourists soaking up the sun on this quiet beach. It's worth making the trip to **Sokha** and **Ochheuteal beaches**, the most impressive of Sihanoukville's seaside offerings. Ochheuteal, about 1km south of the town centre, has the most facilities and accommodation, all concentrated at the western end of the three-kilometre beach. Sokha, west of Ochheuteal, is often the busiest beach, with plenty of palm-tree shade, drinks stalls, snorkelling, and rockpools to explore. The entire area, however, is slated for redevelopment in the near future. **Independence beach**, the next beach along, is named after a seven-storey 1960s monstrosity, the *Independence Hotel*, at the western end of the beach, now derelict and possibly facing demolition. The beach itself is a gently curved bay, with a line of drinks stalls and shaded huts. As the beach sweeps round, rocks and small secluded bays allow some privacy. As at the other beaches, deckchairs and inner tubes are available for 1000r.

The town's handful of sights include Independence Square with a crumbling naga-roofed monument at its centre. The town's main temple, **Wat Leu**, atop Sihanoukville Mountain, north of the town, is a worthy excursion for the panoramic views and the colourful temple interior. To get there take the turning off from National Route 4 at the brewery. The town's other prominent temple, **Wat Khrom**, on Santepheap Street, is set in a tranquil spot among Boddhi trees, with views across the sea and surrounding countryside.

Boat trips to Sihanoukville's offshore islands are intermittently organized by the *Melting Pot* (see opposite). A day-trip, including barbecue, costs around $10 per head, and takes in Koh Koang Kang, or the larger and more picturesque Koh Rong Samloem. Both islands have beaches, snorkelling, and diving action.

Eating, drinking and entertainment

It's a shame that many visitors hardly venture out of the Victory beach budget enclave when in fact there's so much on offer downtown. A variety of **eateries** and nightspots are all within walking distance, and although the majority of popular hangouts are tourist-oriented, there are beer gardens and other local establishments, especially around the market, where you can mix it up with some local flavour. The night market at the corner of Ekareach Street and Sopheakmongkol Street is a good place for the late-night munchies on the way home. For **nightlife**, *Nasa* is the most popular Khmer-style disco, but like most places in town, it's shut by midnight. The *Red Snapper* is often the busiest traveller-oriented hang-out, and stays open later than most. Other **entertainment** options include a few karaoke bars and casinos.

RESTAURANTS AND CAFÉS

Apsara, corner of Street 109 and Sopheakmongkol E Street. Locals swear by this town-centre eatery, specializing in Khmer and Chinese food. Open for lunch and dinner. Turn up early.

Hawaii Seaview. Seafood restaurant right on Victory beach. Open all day, but popular early evening for sunset views of Koh Pos Island.

Koh Pos, south of Victory beach. Actually a rundown, over-priced hotel, but with a gem of a restaurant on its own small, secluded beach, ideal for watching the sunset. Average food at reasonable prices. Open for lunch and dinner.

Melting Pot, Victory beach. A good popular budget café and meeting place. Tourist information available, and boat trips can be arranged. Open all day.

Mick and Craig's, Sopheakmongkol Street, near Ekareach Street. Choice Western scram for the discerning budget traveller. Serves sandwiches, quiches and other standard fare. Open all day.

Sampovmeas, corner of Street 108 and Sopheakmongkol Street. Popular mid-priced restaurant serving Khmer and Chinese dishes inside and outside. Open for lunch and dinner.

Sam's Restaurant, Victory beach. Excellent, inexpensive food from these well-established Sihanoukville veterans, who know everything there is to know about the area. Open all day.

Sea Dragon Restaurant. Nice spot on Ochheuteal beach, with very reasonably priced seafood specials. Serves breakfast, lunch and dinner.

Sokha. The only restaurant option on Sokha beach serves mainly seafood for lunch and dinner.

BARS AND CLUBS

All **bars** and **clubs** are open daily and close at midnight unless otherwise stated.

Anchor Arms, corner of Ekareach Street and Sopheakmongkol E Street. The nearest thing you'll find to an English pub in Sihanoukville. Good selection of beers, Western food, and sports events on the cable TV.

Angkor Beer Discotheque, Boray Kamakor Street. Teenage Khmers giving it the large to Techno and Europop.

Biba Nightclub, Hun Sen beach Drive, Dom Thmei Village. Popular Khmer disco, a little way out of town.

Lucky Beer Garden, Omui Street. Inexpensive draught beer in a pleasant outdoor setting.

Marlin Bar & Grill, Ekareach Street. Western food, sports on the cable TV, but not much in the way of atmosphere. Diving trips can be arranged here.

Nasa Disco, Ekareach Street. Live-music disco packed full of up-for-it holidaying Khmers at weekends. Lots of popular Khmer hand dancing and fancy footwork. Study the form of each dance before blundering onto the floor. There's no entry fee, but you'll pay slightly more for your drinks and peanuts.

Red Snapper Bar, Sopheakmongkol Street, opposite Caltex gas station. Legendary rooftop nightspot, above the *Kim Chantha Guesthouse*. Good tunes and atmosphere. Open until the last customer leaves.

Listings

Banks and exchange Canadia Bank, Ekareach Street, east of 7 Makara St (☎034/933490); Cambodian Commercial Bank, Ekareach Street, junction of Boray-Kamakor Street (☎034/933537); First Overseas Bank, Ekareach Street, west of 7 Makara Street (☎034/933489); Union Commercial Bank, on the corner of Ekareach and Sopheakmongkol streets (☎034/933833).

Hospitals and Clinics The best option is Chuan Min Hospital, on the corner of Ekareach and Sopheakmongkol streets (☎034/933751); Sihanoukville Public Hospital, on Ekareach Street, between the town centre and Ochheuteal beach, has very limited facilities.

Internet access ABC Computer, Boray-Kamakor St; *Marlin Bar & Grill*, Ekareach Street (☎034/320169). From 40 cents per minute.

Police The Police Station is on Ekareach Street between Independence Square and the town centre.

Post office The main post office is one block behind Krong Street, off Victory beach. It's not particularly easy to find, and not worth it when you get there. Post Restante is available, but not advisable. You may well be directed to the smaller branch opposite the market for stamps and other services.

Sports For diving, talk to Steve at the *Marlin Bar & Grill* (☎034/320169) or Claude at *Chez Claude* (☎013/824870) to arrange a trip. The Hash House Harriers organize regular runs; ask Craig at *The Melting Pot*.

Supermarkets Samudera Market, 7 Makara St, 50m from Ekareach Street (☎034/933441); Star Mart at the Caltex gas station, Ekareach Street.

Telephone services Calls are expensive from Sihanoukville, as there is no landline connection with the rest of the country. Calls can be made from hotels, the post office or from the Camintel office, Ekareach Street, just west of Boray-Kamakor Street.

Ream National Park

Ream National Park, also known as Preah Sihanouk National Park, located 18km east of Sihanoukville, is one of the most accessible national parks in Cambodia. Its 50,000 acres include evergreen and mangrove forests, sandy beaches, coral reefs, offshore islands and a rich diversity of flora and fauna. It's a great place to explore some of Cambodia's unique, unspoilt natural environment. To get to the **park headquarters** you'll need to take a taxi or moto from Sihanoukville along National Route 4 to Ream village and then turn right down the track next to the airport. The rangers at the park headquarters (☎015/914174) are extremely helpful, and can arrange boat trips ($20) along the Prek Toek Sap estuary, to the fishing village of Koh Kcchang, and perhaps on to the islands of Koh Thmei and Koh Ses. They can also organize guided walks and basic guesthouse accommodation at Ream beach for $5 per room (two beds per room, bring your own food).

If you want to visit the park independently, continue along National Route 4 through Ream until the next village of Bot Koki, where the park will be signposted to the right. Follow the dirt road to Koh Kcchang fishing village, where some hard-nosed negotiation in pidgin Khmer should secure a fishing boat to the islands for about $6, depending on the number of people in your group. It's possible to stay overnight on the islands, but as always you'll need to bring supplies, including mosquito net, and make it clear to the boatman when you want to be picked up.

Koh S'dach

The small island of **KOH S'DACH** (population 2306) is the fishing capital of Cambodian waters, just off Koh Kong province in the Gulf of Thailand. If you're rushing between Sihanoukville and Thailand, there's little here to warrant an overnight stop, but if you've time on your hands, the area is worth exploring. Koh S'dach itself (King's Island) takes its name from the legend of a visiting monarch who sheltered here with his soldiers in ancient times. They had been fighting off invaders from across the sea, but were low on supplies and in desperate need of fresh water. Finding no source of fresh water on the island, the King summoned the powers of the gods and miraculously fresh water began gushing forth from an undiscovered spring. The **royal spring** can be found near the passenger boat port. The island's other attractions include the friendly monks at **Wat Koy Koh**, and the tiny beach from where it's possible to swim to Koh K'maoch (Ghost Island). Locals will tell you that a few lucky officials from Lon Nol's administration fled here to escape the Khmer Rouge. A US navy ship then ferried them to safety. It is not clear whether they took the time to snorkel around the nearby **coral**. They would have needed the foresight to bring their own snorkels and masks, as none are available on the island.

The real reason for stopping in Koh S'dach is to get out in a boat to explore the cluster of **islands** and the **mainland** nearby. Koh Samai, Koh Samot, Koh Chan and Koh Totang are all within a boat's row. The remote mainland village of Boy Japon, named after the Japanese logging concession located here, is easily reached from here. The Japanese have long since gone, taking with them most of the primary forest, but a long narrow beach stretches out from the village, and a small waterfall can be found a short walk along the inland path, a cool spot for a dip. A boat to the mainland is 20B each way, while a fishing boat to the islands is open to negotiation. Guesthouse **accommodation** can only be found on Koh S'dach, although it is possible to camp on any of the beaches if you have a hammock, mosquito net, food and water. Make it clear to the fisherman when you want to be picked up. *Koh S'dach Guest House* (①) on the main path from the port has rooms with comfortable double beds or dorm beds for 100B. Further down the path, a small blue sign in Khmer points left down an alleyway to a rustic guesthouse (①) over the water. Note that all transactions on the island are in **baht**. The pathway from the port to the small market area is the centre of activity on the island. Fishermen gather to gamble at street-side games of cards, dice, or playing-card pool. There are also plenty of places to buy simple food here, and of course the fresh seafood is fantastic.

The only way **to get here** is by one of the speedboats, which stop briefly as they surge between Krong Koh Kong and Sihanoukville or Sre Ambel. The fare is a flat 300B to or from any of these destinations and takes about two hours.

Krong Koh Kong

Boat schedules and border opening times conspire to make an overnight stop in **KRONG KOH KONG** (Koh Kong town) a necessity for many, but tourists tend not to loiter as they hurry onwards to Thailand or Sihanoukville, so the town remains largely unaffected by the steady stream of *barangs*. Krong Koh Kong is not an island as commonly assumed, but the principal mainland town of Koh Kong province, which in turn takes its name from the largest island off its coast. Situated on the eastern bank of the Dong Tong River, where it empties into the Gulf of Thailand, the town was historically a remote and insular outpost, its small economy based on fishing and prostitution. As the logging and smuggling industries began to flourish, so the town grew, trebling in size during the 1990s to a current population of around 22,000.

Despite the fact that much of the rich sandalwood forests has been transported to Thailand, the area around the town remains beautiful and unspoilt. This remote outpost owes its identity more to **Thai** influences than Khmer culture: most people speak Thai, **baht** is the favoured currency and Beer Chang is the drink of choice. Even the Governor of the province sends his children to school in Thailand.

The locals consider the **Royal Palace** to be a tourist site of sorts, but it's not. Looking like a deserted 1980s Spanish time-share villa, it sits empty and decaying on the northern-most point of the riverside. Wat enthusiasts might want to make the short trip out to **Wat Chotgneau**, named after Supreme Monk Chuom Nat Chotgneau, who died in 1972. In 1972, Lon Nol used his forces to begin the construction of a building to distribute food to the poor. On becoming Army General in 1968, he built the Buddhist temple nearby, although this was all but destroyed in the late seventies. Despite its renovation, it still has the air of a crumbling, neglected temple. An interesting feature is the statue of Bpray-ah K'mao setting off on a journey of discovery with a big blue umbrella, a kettle and a walking stick.

A popular spot with locals is the jungle **waterfall**, sometimes known as **Chros Srei** (Charming Stream) waterfall, around 20km from the town. A moto costs 100B for the return trip. The interesting journey to the falls takes you past cashew-nut-trees, with the Cardamom Mountains rising to the left. Very quickly, the countryside turns to forest, and then to dense jungle. After thirty minutes on a moto, you arrive at a picnic spot, from where it's an enjoyable trek through the foliage and across streams to the waterfall, best in the wet season. It's only a smallish waterfall, but there's a fast-churning plunge pool for an exhilarating swim. With a local guide and time on your hands, it might be possible to trek further upstream where allegedly the falls are more impressive. There is no shortage of waterfalls in the area around Koh Kong, the most impressive of which is reputed to be **Tatai Waterfall**, around

50km from the town. Access is a problem; the only way to get there is to charter a boat for the hour-long journey.

There are several **islands** near to the town, the largest of which is **Koh Kong** itself. However, an easier excursion is **Koh Kapi**, where you'll find some of the nicest beaches in the district. A small speedboat will cost around 200B each way for the thirty-minute trip. No guesthouse accommodation is available on the island, but it's possible to buy seafood and water at the small village, and camping is an option if you want to explore the island. Nearer to home, it takes just twenty minutes to cover the 17km on a moto to **Love beach**, although the beach isn't as good as those at Koh Kapi and can get overcrowded.

Practicalities

Unless you've hitched on a logging truck from Pursat, you'll **arrive by boat** at Krong Koh Kong port, at the eastern edge of town, from where it's a five-minute walk to Dong Tong Market in the town centre. When it comes to **moving on**, a speedboat leaves for **Sihanoukville** at 8am every day, costing 600B, and taking four hours. If you're simply heading for **Phnom Penh**, the quickest way is to get the 7.15am speedboat to **Sre Ambel** (500B), a smuggling town not far from Route 4 and then get a pick-up or taxi on to the capital. Both speedboats stop at **Koh S'dach** en route (300B; 2hr). There is a little-known cheaper option, which is the **slow boat** to Sre Ambel, leaving most days at 3pm from the same pier as the speedboats. The sixteen-hour overnight voyage costs 200B, but it's not much fun in rainy season storms, and a hammock, food and water are essential. Get there early to bag a good spot. To **Thailand**, take the smaller speedboats from the port across the river for 20B. A moto to the border is then 20B. See the box on p.125 for more information on this border crossing.

A road exists overland **to Pursat**, passable in the dry season, but it's difficult to hitch, as very few vehicles make the journey. A trials motorbike would be the best option, but if you decide to undertake this journey, do not go alone, and do not leave the track, as mines are a problem in this area.

There is a **tourist office** on the port road, virtually opposite the speedboat terminal, and although it keeps irregular hours, it's usually open most weekday mornings. Koh Kong town is not a large place, so you can get around **on foot**, which is just as well, as most of the **moto** drivers do not speak English.

ACCOMMODATION

There is no outstanding **accommodation** among the dreary options in town. If you take a moto from the port, you'll probably end up at *Penh Chet Guesthouse* (①), as they pay the best commission to drivers. The rooms are good value and include bathroom. You'll get the same deal at the *Sovann Angkor* and the *Phkaousaphea Hotel*, while nearby *Poy Sian Guesthouse* (①) is slightly cheaper. The best bargain in town is the nameless guesthouse (①) on the port road between the Sihanoukville landing pier and the Had Lek jetty. There's no sign in English, just a blue sign in Khmer, but if you can find it, basic, cosy rooms with shared bathroom facilities are very cheap. Don't expect English to be spoken at any of these places. For a bit more luxury, head just out of town to either the *Koh Pich Hotel* or to the *Rasami Hotel* (both ④), where you'll get you a room with cable TV, fridge and air-con.

EATING, DRINKING AND NIGHTLIFE

None of the guesthouses offers **food**, so your stomach will probably lead you to the eateries grouped around the port and market. There's a good choice of stalls in the evenings, one block north of the eastern edge of the market. This is also the western boundary of the red light district, home to the most popular evening entertainment for locals. It's worth noting that Krong Koh Kong has one of the highest incidences of Aids in Cambodia, so if you're out for some exciting **nightlife**, stick to dancing which can be found at two nightclubs: *Mohasako* down by the port, or the more lively *Koh Pich Nightclub* at the hotel of the same name.

Kampot

Despite its riverside location and French terraces, **KAMPOT**, on the south coast, isn't as attractive as it might be. However, it's a handy stepping stone to nearby Bokor, Kep and Kampong Trach, and is a pleasant place to spend an afternoon, browsing round the markets, strolling along the Tuk Chhou River, or heading out to nearby Tuk Chhou Waterfalls. The river marks the northern boundary of the town, with the new market at the eastern end and the roundabout in the centre of town.

The **train station** is near the new market in the eastern part of town. **Taxis** and **pick-ups** will drop you at the stand just south of the roundabout on the road to Kep. Taxis to either Phnom Penh or Sihanoukville will cost around 8000r, while a pick-up to Phnom Penh will cost 5000r. Most places around Kampot are walkable, but **motos** are readily available to take the weight off tired feet.

The best **place to stay** is the *Borey Bokor Hotel* (☎033/932826; ④), between the round-about and the river, with brand-new en-suite rooms, equipped with cable TV and air-con. A cheaper option, at the roundabout, is *Phnom Khieu Hotel* (②). Cheaper still is the friendly *Ta Eng Guesthouse* (①), on the road towards Kep, with no-frills rooms. The curiously named *National Bank Guest House and Karaoke* (①), tucked away at the western end of the river-bank, has basic, clean rooms with two double beds in each.

Two of the local **restaurants** in Kampot do outstanding Khmer cuisine, particularly seafood dishes, but note that they usually close at 9pm or soon after: *Phnom Penh Thmey* and *Prochum Mith Restaurant* at the roundabout. Opposite, the restaurant at *Phnom Kamchay Hotel* serves up cheap Cambodian food in a canteen-like setting. The food isn't as good as its competitors', but it stays open a bit later in the evenings. More upscale, *Restaurant Marco Polo* (☎015/330166), south of the roundabout, offers fine Italian dining with main courses for around $6. The manager David can help organize excursions and boat trips and is a walking library of information about the area.

Kampot isn't known for its **nightlife**, but there is a club, the *Bopha Yaya* (over the bridge, turn right), which stays open until midnight. You can escape the painfully bad live music by taking drinks onto the riverside balcony.

Kep

Some 25km southeast of Kampot, **KEP** is a gem, with its agreeable tropical atmosphere, palm-shaded walks and delicious, inexpensive seafood freshly plucked from the clean waters. The beach, unfortunately, is tiny and grubby, but serves its purpose as a place to soak up some rays, and forms part of an indisputably pretty bay. Kep is also a province in its own right, the second smallest after Pailin, although it's really no more than a fishing village dur-ing weekdays. At weekends, however, hordes descend on the seaside resort from the capital, and the pace picks up a notch.

Approaching Kep from Kampot, you'll see the remains of magnificent **colonial villas** and holiday homes half-hidden in the shrubs. These bombed-out shells hint at Kep's distin-guished past, when Kep-sur-Mer was a highly exclusive coastal resort. No one knows for sure whether the resort was destroyed on principle by the Khmer Rouge, caught in the crossfire, or looted by locals – it was probably a combination of all three, leaving Kep the poor neigh-bour of prosperous Sihanoukville.

The large Vietnamese island of **Phu Quoc** rises offshore in the Gulf of Thailand. The sov-ereignty of the island has long been in dispute, however, and the white statue of a woman at Kep beach looks out towards the island, yearning for the day when it will be returned to Cambodia. At the other end of the bay from the white statue, the old **Royal Palace** occupies a fine sunset vantage point atop the cliff.

One of the highlights of a trip to Kep is a boat tour to one of the nearby islands, such as quaint **Koh Tonsay** (Rabbit Island), with its three good beaches and five welcoming families.

Nicer still is the beautiful **Koh Poh** (Coral Island), with blue water and white beaches, and of course great coral for snorkelling. Boat trips can be arranged at *Le Bout Du Monde Guesthouse* (see below) in Kep, or back in Kampot at *Marco Polo Restaurant* (see p.131). A boat to Koh Tonsay costs about $15, or $40 to Koh Poh. Overnight stays are possible.

If you happen to be in Kep on a Saturday, the Especa Orphanage opposite the *Seaside Guesthouse* puts on a show of **traditional dance and music**. Ask locally for details.

Practicalities

The usual way to travel the 25km from Kep from Kampot is by **moto**, costing around 6000r, or 5000r going the other way. Alternatively, negotiate a **share taxi** from the Kampot stand. **Accommodation** in Kep is limited. Just behind the main beach at Kep, *Le Bout Du Monde* (①) is a popular guesthouse and restaurant, with simple rooms. It's a nice place to chill out, but a lack of electricity makes for early nights. There's talk of a move to larger premises, but the name will stay. On the way into Kep from Kompot you'll pass the *Seaside Guesthouse* (②) on your right, with nice, modern rooms, including bathroom. If these two places are full, continue along the coast past the decrepit, overpriced concrete block of *Krong Kep Hotel* (②), until you reach *Krong Kep Guesthouse* (②), about 1km further on, just past the hospital, which has large, bright rooms with electricity and fan.

Kep is heaven for the **seafood** connoisseur. The Crab Market towards the *Seaside Guesthouse* is the place for crab bisque. *Le Bout Du Monde* also does very tasty food with generous portions, but meals need to be ordered in advance.

Bokor

Unable to cope with the Cambodian heat during the hottest months of the year, the French searched for cool relief among the higher elevations of the Elephant Mountains. Thus the hill station of **BOKOR**, 40km northwest of Kampot, was born, combining the requirements of a milder climate at its elevation of just over 1000m, and magnificent views across the Gulf of Thailand. As in Kep, the villas, King Sihanouk's former royal palace and casino were abandoned in the 1970s, but here the buildings, while still derelict, remain somewhat more intact. It's a ghost town that feels as if the last guests left just recently. In fact, the last people to stay in the empty hotel were UNTAC officials helicoptered in during the early 1990s.

Bokor, however, has been given a new lease of life as **Bokor National Park** (daily; $2), nearly 350,000 acres of prime forest. Park Rangers claim that tigers, leopards, pythons and more than sixty elephants roam the park, but they keep well away from the touristed areas, so your most exciting brush with nature is likely to be a dive-bomb attack by exotic butterflies.

The rangers have also recently opened **Popokvil Waterfall**, a magnificent sight that has been virtually inaccessible for the last twenty years. It's now an easy twenty-minute walk to the falls on a well marked path. Four streams converge just before the rocks to push the discoloured jungle water over two giant steps of more than ten metres each, flanked on both sides by dense vegetation.

One of Bokor's neglected buildings that has seen better days is the **Bokor Palace Hotel**. It's safe to explore the upper stories of the structure, but the best views are from the terrace, looking out towards the Vietnamese island of Phu Quoc, and the smaller islands of Ream National Park on the right. As you walk to the edge of the terrace, and look over the sheer drop into the dense jungle, a concert of jungle calls rises up from the foliage. Legend has it that high-rollers who lost big at the casino would throw themselves over this steep ledge in despair.

Practicalities

Bokor can be reached by **share taxi**, **moto** or hire transport from Kampot. The turning to the town is signposted to the right on the road towards Sihanoukville. The track that twists up the mountain through banana and pineapple plantations, followed by lush, green jungle-scape has been upgraded as part of the National Park project. About 15km up the hill, the strange-shaped rock that juts out from the left is known locally as Kabal Barang, or The French Head. Past some rainy-season waterfalls, the trees begin to thin out as you approach the summit. The first house to be seen is part of Sihanouk's old palace. Take the right fork here for the Bokor Palace Hotel and casino. At the next junction, Bokor is to the left, while Popokvil Falls are to the right.

The large green-roofed building sitting proudly in the centre of Bokor is the National Park Research and Training Centre, where you can **stay** in large, comfy bunk beds for $5 per person. If you're planning on staying, though, bring your own food as none is available.

EASTERN CAMBODIA

The further east you travel from the Mekong to the Vietnamese border, the poorer the people and the more basic the infrastructure. The Mekong River is the overland gateway to this region, punctuated by the three very different towns of **Kompong Cham**, **Kratie** and **Stung Treng**. Travellers are beginning to make the journey here and beyond to the remote hilly provinces of **Ratanakiri** and **Mondolkiri**, populated by hilltribes and dotted with spectacular waterfalls.

During the **American War**, the eastern provinces were heavily bombed by the Americans in their attempt to flush out the Vietcong from the Ho Chi Minh Trail. These attempts proved largely unsuccessful, however, and thousands of Cambodian civilians were killed, wounded or left homeless by these attacks. It was during this period that the Khmer Rouge began gathering strength and momentum in the area. Pol Pot was using the remote northeastern provinces to hide from Sihanouk's troops, while receiving support from his communist brothers in the Vietcong. Recruiting countrymen for the cause was not difficult – they were happy to join the fight against the systematic destruction of the region.

Nowadays, the Mekong towns, Kompong Cham in particular, are forward-looking and relatively prosperous, having integrated well with modern-day Cambodia. But striking off eastwards, you'll see a different story, as the remote uplands remain stuck in their own isolated world, largely untouched by the march of modernization and development.

Kompong Cham

Cambodia's third-largest city and the capital of the province of the same name, **KOMPONG CHAM**, 120km northeast of Phnom Penh, is a busy port and transport hub, though with little atmosphere. The current construction of the Japanese-funded bridge across the Mekong, scheduled for completion in 2002, will improve access to Cambodia's northeastern provinces, but in the meantime, the project has turned the town into an unattractive building site.

If you do find yourself in Kompong Cham for a few hours, be sure to explore **Wat Nokor**, about 2km north of town, just off Route 7, an unusual fusion of ancient and modern Khmer religious architecture, with new preahs built in and around the eleventh-century ruins. Approaching the main preah through the darkness of the crumbling east gate highlights the juxtaposition of old and new: luminous blues, pinks, oranges and greens from the paintings on the walls, columns and ceilings are framed by the ancient monochrome gopura. Elsewhere around the complex, though, the modern buildings sit rather more incongruously with their older, ornate predecessors, the newer facades less inspired in composition.

About 12km further out of town past Wat Nokor rise up the twin temple hills of **Phnom Pros** and **Phnom Srei**, Man and Woman Mountains. The legend goes that, in ancient times, it was the women who had to ask the men to marry them. Getting fed up with this, the women invited the men to compete against them to see who could build the best temple by daybreak – the winners would also win the right to be proposed to in future. They set to work, building their temples on adjacent hills. The women, realizing that they were lagging behind their male counterparts, built a huge fire, which the men took to be the rising sun. Exhausted, they headed for bed, while the women carried on building; they produced a magnificent temple, thereby winning the right to receive marriage proposals. Both Phnom Pros and Phnom Srei afford fine views – of Lake Boeng Tom to the west, and Kompong Cham town and the Mekong River in the east.

Practicalities

Fast **boats** stop at the port near the *Mekong Hotel*. The fast boat from Phnom Penh leaves at around 7am and takes three hours (10,000r). **Buses** and taxis arrive at the market. A bus from Phnom Penh is 6000r, a minibus or share taxi is 4000r for the easy two-hour trip.

Guesthouses abound on the riverside, though most are overpriced and fairly grotty. The best-value accommodation can be found on the river, just north of Rue Pasteur, at the *Mekong Hotel* (②), which has spotless, sizeable rooms with TV, some with air-con. Good-value guesthouses are grouped around the market. Best of the bunch is *Nava Guesthouse* (②), offering clean, smallish twin-bed rooms, with bathroom and TV. If you're short of cash, there's a cluster of basic guesthouses on the same road. The *Bopharik Guesthouse* (②) across the way has large rooms with bathroom, and its balcony is a good place to escape the frantic activity of the market below. Another recommended option in town is the spanking-new *Ponleu Rasmei Hotel* (③) on Rue Pasteur, offering spotless rooms with all facilities.

The best **food** can be found on Rue Pasteur, running down from the river. *Prayong Restaurant* does a good selection of Thai and Khmer dishes for $2–3, while opposite, *Ginga* offers flavoursome Japanese food for around $6, and Western breakfasts from $2. *Hao An Restaurant* at the corner of Pasteur and Monivong has a vast selection of delicious food from $2 and easy ordering from the full-colour picture menu. The riverside and market areas are home to cheaper drink stalls and Khmer fast-food places.

Kratie

Life ticks by slowly in **KRATIE**. This tiny town on the Mekong is an unexpected delight, with a relaxing, indolent atmosphere. Away from the blemish of the modern market, Kratie is a wonderful hotchpotch of colonial terraces and traditional old Khmer buildings – sturdy wooden structures, with dark-red roof tiles and often a decorative flourish. There's not much for visitors to do in Kratie, but it makes a good base for exploring the surrounding countryside. About 11km north of Kratie, **Phnom Sampo** is set in a grotto of lush-green vegetation on a twin-peaked hill. The dense trees hide a meditation commune on the first level, and a small temple on the higher summit. Around 10km further north on Route 7, a sign marks your arrival at **Kampai**, the best riverside vantage point from which to view the rare freshwater **Irrawaddy dolphins**. Around thirty dolphins live in this area, and can usually be seen in the morning and late afternoon – consult your guesthouse or moto-driver for the best viewing times. Heavy boat traffic and destructive fishing practices are threatening the ongoing existence of this rare species, and it's thought that no more than a hundred of these snub-nosed dolphins remain in the Mekong. The only way to visit these places is to hire a moto from Kratie. If you're negotiating the price for a day, you could also include a visit to **Sambor**, some 35km north of Kratie, the site of an ancient pre-Angkorian capital.

Practicalities

The 7am fast **boat** from Phnom Penh to Kratie takes around six hours and costs 30,000r. A boat leaves Kompong Cham at 10am daily, arriving at 1pm (20,000r). You could also get a **pick-up** from Kompong Cham (6000r), but it's a circuitous journey of five to six hours.

For **accommodation**, the new *Santapheap Hotel* (②), with clean rooms, is handily located just opposite the port, though the karaoke rooms make it noisy. A better deal is the *Heng*

Heng Guesthouse (②), a short walk south from the boat – try and get the first-floor corner room, with a balcony overlooking the Mekong. *Hotel December 30* (①) – the date Kratie was liberated by the Vietnamese – also on the river between the port and *Heng Heng*, has basic rooms with two beds and shared facilities. Best value in town, however, is newcomer *Star Guesthouse* (①) – to get there take the road towards the market at *Heng Heng Guesthouse*. The staff are incredibly helpful, have lots of information and can organize trips to the surrounding sights.

Food and drinks stalls proliferate by the riverside and at the market. The restaurant at *Hotel December 30* can knock up a good rice or noodles dish, while next door, the *Mekong Restaurant* has a menu in English.

Stung Treng

STUNG TRENG is a riverside town like Kratie, but without its charm and atmosphere. It's bigger, noisier and is essentially a staging post on the overland trek to Ratanakiri. Most people do not stay any longer than they need to, with an afternoon arrival and an early-morning departure providing sufficient time for a quick look around. A border crossing with Laos, just 50km north from here, is officially closed to foreigners.

Boats from Kratie dock here daily when the river is high enough (25,000r), but by the height of the dry season, a **pick-up** from Kratie is the only option (15,000r). Virtually opposite the boat terminal and taxi stand is the cheapest **place to stay** in town, the *Amatak Hotel* (①), offering rustic rooms with shared facilities. A notch up in price is the *Sekong Hotel* (③), a five-minute walk west along the riverside, though its en-suite fan rooms look rather neglected. If it's luxury you're after to recover from a long journey, look out for the brand-new *Sok Sambath Hotel* (⑤) at the eastern end of the market. Other than the usual stalls at the market, the best **food** in town can be found at the *Sokhapeap Restaurant*, a few blocks west of the market, with some of the menu in English.

Ratanakiri

Tucked away in the remote northeastern corner of Cambodia is hilly **Ratanakiri** province, bordered by Vietnam to the east and Laos to the north. If you like nature and wildlife, this is the place to be. The rainy season leaves the area dripping with greenery and alive with exotic animals and rushing waterfalls. The rich and fertile lands are covered with plantations; rubber, coffee, sugar cane, bananas, cashew nuts and pineapples all grow in abundance. The upland forests are also home to around twelve distinct hilltribes, known collectively as **chunchiets**. It's thought that more than eighty percent of Ratanakiri's population consists of these ethnic groups, although nowadays most ethnicities speak Khmer and have forgone traditional dress for modern clothing. Ratanakiri's principal town is **Ban Lung**, elevated to provincial capital status after its predecessor Lumphat was devastated by American bombs. Ban Lung is a good base for trips into the countryside to see chunchiets and waterfalls. It's also a short hop to **Voen Sai**, one of the most accessible villages in the region, and the gateway to the **Virachey National Park**.

Isolated Ratanakiri is one of the least developed provinces, with a mere five percent of households having access to safe drinking water. **Malaria** is also a huge problem, and has wiped out whole villages. The **best time to visit** is in December just after the rains.

Ban Lung and around

The sprawling town of **BAN LUNG**, approximately 600km northeast of Phnom Penh, has been the capital of Ratanakiri Province since 1979. The town's centre is its **market**, especially lively in the early morning when hilltribe people set up an unofficial market outside its walls.

Chunchiets aside, the town is chiefly known for **Yeak Laom Lake** (daily; 1000r), 4km east of town, created by a volcanic eruption many thousands of years ago and the centrepiece of a government Protected Area project, covering around 12,000 acres. The lake's eight-hundred-metre circumference is lined with dense green forest, its remarkable tranquillity interrupted only by the occasional birdcall. A swim in the clean, turquoise waters is a good way to cleanse yourself of the dust from Ban Lung's unsealed roads. The committee responsible for managing the lake and surrounds is comprised of Tampuan villagers, the indigenous inhabitants of the area; they are currently constructing a Chunchiet Cultural Centre in traditional Tampuan style at the lake.

About 14km from Ban Lung is a bizarre clearing in the forest covered by an almost circular area of flat stone. The area is known in English as Field of Stone, and in Khmer as **Veal Rum Plang**. Rum Plang, so the legend goes, was a young boy who fell to his death from a tree onto the black volcanic rock while trying to retrieve his kite. His spirit is believed to live on, protecting the plateau and surrounding trees.

There are a number of **waterfalls** around Ban Lung, the most impressive of which are Kanchan and Chaa Ong. At Chaa Ong, water sprays from a rock overhang into a small jungle clearing. It lacks a decent pool for a swim, but brave visitors shower under the smaller column of water. Be careful, though, as it's slippery. To get there follow the Stung Treng road past the airport for about 2km. A small road to the right leads to Chaa Ong, and the one on the left goes to Kanchan. It's best to go with a guide, as you need to navigate your way through about 5km of forest.

An easy ten-minute climb up **Eisey Patamak Mountain**, behind the town's wat, is well worth it for the glorious views of the O Traw Mountains. Locals even claim it's possible to see the mountains of Laos to the north, and Vietnam to the east. All this is lost on the five-metre-long Reclining Buddha, which lies at the summit, its eyes closed. If you've time to spare, you could ask about **elephant rides** at your guesthouse. Nearby villagers are only too happy to give these animals a break from hard work and let them stroll around for a day with tourists on board.

PRACTICALITIES

Labansiek Airport, in the centre of Ban Lung, is served by all three domestic airlines. **Planes** are met by moto-drivers and guesthouse reps. **Pick-ups** from Stung Treng to Ban Lung are 30,000r, a little more in bad weather. The road is shocking, and is often impassable during the rainy season, although from December till April/May, the road trip is covered daily. Ban Lung is small enough to walk around, but **motos** are available at 500r a go if the heat gets too much. Aside from backtracking, your options for **moving on** from Ban Lung are pretty limited. All three of Cambodia's **airlines** operate flights out, though flights tend to be infrequent; you'll need to check with the airlines. Phnom Penh Airways is near the market (☎075/974147), President Airlines can be found on the road between the market and the central roundabout (☎075/974059), while Royal Air Cambodge is opposite the *Long Sok San Guesthouse* (☎075/974067). There is a **road from Ban Lung to Sen Monorom** (see opposite) in the south, but public transport is non-existent. Travellers on trials bikes have taken this route and reported a passable, but very bad road. You'd also need to make an overnight stop.

The most popular **place to stay** in Ban Lung is *Long Sok San Hotel* (②), just north of the airstrip, offering rooms with shared facilities. Previously of the *Intercontinental Hotel* in Phnom Penh, the proprietor knows about service, speaks English and can act as a tour guide. A pleasant alternative, the wooden *Mountain Guesthouse* (②), on the road to the airport, has a balcony overlooking the landing strip and rooms with fan and shared facilities. A block north from the *Mountain Guesthouse*, the owner Mrs Kim also has larger rooms at the quieter *Mountain 2 Guesthouse* for the same price, but with better views. Staff at *Ban Lung Guesthouse* (②), on the road to the airport, are very helpful, and offer en-suite rooms, some with air-con.

There's not much choice for **food** in Ban Lung. Besides the usual stalls around the market and limited menus at the guesthouses there's only one restaurant in town, known variously as *The American Restaurant* and *Ratanakiri Restaurant*. Fortunately, it does good, though simple, food, with a three-course set menu for only 3000r. The local speciality is fish from the Sre Pok River at Lumphat – ask for Pasaii or Kya.

The provincial **bank** opposite *Hotel Labansiek* cannot change travellers' cheques or give cash advances, so make sure you bring a supply of money. Telephone, fax and postal facilities are available at the **post office**, on the right-hand side of the road out towards the lake.

VOEN SAI AND VIRACHEY NATIONAL PARK

The road north of Ban Lung winds its way past numerous chunchiet villages until, after around 38km, it reaches the village of **VOEN SAI**, located on the Tonlé Se San River, the headquarters of **Virachey National Park**. The park headquarters are on the left as you enter the village. Covering over 800,000 acres, the park is a haven for a variety of endangered species, including tigers, deer, rare hornbills, and kouprey, the almost extinct jungle cow. Rangers have made real progress in the reduction of logging and slaughtering of rare animals, although it would be impossible to halt these activities altogether, as they have been the livelihood of generations of indigenous people.

Voen Sai itself is home to an unusual mix of **ethnic minorities**, predominantly Lao and Chinese, but also Kreung and Khmer. A small boat (200r) connects Voen Sai with villages on the opposite bank – to the right, there is a small Lao settlement, and to the left a Chinese community. It's best to visit these places with a local guide, as you'll need someone to act as an interpreter and smooth the way.

As yet, organized treks within the park are not available, but it's possible to take a three-hour boat trip upstream (ask at the park headquarters) to the hilltribe village of **Oh Lalay**, or further on to **Chort Preas**, inhabited by Kavet chunchiets and site of a high waterfall.

The easiest way to **get to Voen Sai** is to rent a moto from Ban Lung ($US5–10), or you could ask at your guesthouse. Theoretically, it's also possible to get to Voen Sai via boat from Stung Treng.

Mondolkiri

The province of **Mondolkiri** is Ratanakiri's forgotten southern neighbour, in the far east of the country. Although less visited than Ratanakiri, Mondolkiri can claim similar attractions: a high proportion of ethnic minorities, waterfalls and beautiful landscapes. Forested highlands are interrupted occasionally by grassy fields and gentle hills that would look more at home in rural England. Indeed, the climate is not dissimilar either: the temperature is a mere 18°C on average in dry season, with chilly nights. The provincial capital, **Sen Monorom**, makes a good base for excursions into the countryside. The best way to access Sen Monorom and the region is from Phnom Penh.

Sen Monorom and around

Provincial capitals don't get more remote or inaccessible than **SEN MONOROM**, 420km from Phnom Penh. The town extends for a short way down either side of a low hill, atop which is an airport. It's not a very appealing place, but it makes a good base from which to explore surrounding hilltribe villages. The only point of interest in the town itself is the Office of Women's Affairs, where you can watch the women **weaving** *kramas* on intricate machines.

Locals will direct you to **Damnak S'dach**, also known as **Monorom Falls**, a peaceful nook on the edge of the jungle, where an eight-metre-high cascade of water drops into a swirling plunge pool. At the time of writing, they were upgrading the road to the falls, so access should now be easy. You can either walk the few kilometres here or hire a moto. The path ends at the top of the waterfall, where brave souls jump into the deep water during the rainy season. The less brave scramble down through the foliage for a refreshing swim. Waterfall enthusiasts might also seek out the spectacular **Bon Sra Falls**, about 40km northeast from Sen Monorom. It's a dramatic two-tiered affair, with more than fifty metres of vertical gushing water.

The solemn-looking **hilltribes** like to keep themselves to themselves and some villages are not keen on foreign visitors, so it's best to take a local to act as a guide and interpreter. There are hundreds of minority villages around Sen Monorom, one of the largest and easiest to access being **Phlung** village inhabited by Phnong chunchiets. The curious huts have woven wooden walls and thatched roofs almost to the floor. Three or more families often live in just one hut, but you'll be lucky to see more than a handful of people during daytime, as they're all out working in the fields.

PRACTICALITIES

Although Sen Monorom is served by domestic airlines, the **airport** regularly closes for months on end. Overland transport from Phnom Penh has become a viable option, however, since the recent completion of the logging **road** from Schlong to Sen Monorom. From Phnom Penh, take the 7am fast boat to Kratie, alighting at Schlong (25,000r) then join one of the regular pick-ups to Snuol (10,000r). You may be lucky to get a pick-up (30,000r) to Sen Monorom on the same day – ask at the market. If not, you'll have to stay overnight at one of the guesthouses in Snuol, and move on the next day. Returning to Phnom Penh, it's sometimes possible to get a truck all the way for 50,000r, although this route is long and tedious, with some rough stretches.

To see most sights, you'll need to employ the help of a guide or moto driver. **Guides** with motos are available at the **tourist office**, behind the post office (the white building just off the airstrip), but they don't come cheap at a starting price of $20 per day.

The best **accommodation** in town is at the well-maintained *Pich Kiri Hotel* (②), on the left as you enter the town from Snuol. Remaining on the market side of the airstrip, two guesthouses (①) in the "town centre" area, one with a sign in English, the other at the pharmacy, have partitioned rooms with splash-and-dash washing facilities outside. Sen Monorom has a surprisingly good **restaurant**: it's through a small door, opposite the guesthouse with the sign in English. There's no menu, so take a phrase book, and they'll cook to order. Bear in mind that the cost of transport to this remote region means that goods are more expensive than elsewhere in Cambodia.

travel details

Pick-ups and buses

For more information on pick-ups and buses in Cambodia see "Getting around", p.75. It's almost impossible to give the frequency with which pick-ups leave, but generally, they depart early in the morning as soon as they're full, so it's best to get there around 6 or 7am.

Battambang to: Pailin (4hr); Phnom Penh (7–10hr); Sisophon (2hr).

Kampot to: Kep (1hr); Sihanoukville (2hr).

Kompng Cham to: Kratie (5–6hr).

Kratie to: Stung Treng (8hr).

Phnom Penh to: Battambang (7–10hr); Ho Chi Minh City (8–9hr); Kampot (6 hr); Kompong Cham (frequent departures 6am–4pm; 2hr); Siem Reap (8hr); Sihanoukville (frequent departures 7am–1.30pm; 4hr); Vietnam border at Moc Bai (4–5hr).

Poipet to: Battambang (4hr); Siem Reap (6–8 hr); Sisophon (2hr).

Schlong to: Snuol (2hr).

Sen Monorom to: Phnom Penh (infrequent; 12–14hr).

Siem Reap to: Phnom Penh (8hr); Poipet (6–8hr); Sisophon (4–6hr).

Snuol to: Sen Monorom (4–5hr).

Stung Treng to: Ban Lung (8–10hr).

Trains

Battambang to: Phnom Penh (1 daily; 12hr); Sisophon (1 daily; 4hr).

Phnom Penh to: Battambang (1 daily; 12hr); Sihanoukville via Kampot and Kep (1 every other day; 12hr).

Sihanoukville to: Phnom Penh via Kampot and Kep (1 every other day; 12hr).

Sisophon to: Battambang (1 daily; 4hr).

Boats

Battambang to: Siem Reap (1 daily at 6.30am; 3–4hr).

Kratie to: Phnom Penh (1 daily; 5 hr); Stung Treng (1 daily; 6hr).

Krong Koh Kong to: Sihanoukville (1 daily at 8am; 4hr).

Phnom Penh to: Kompong Cham (1 daily; 3hr); Kratie (1 daily; 6hr); Schlong (1 daily; 5hr); Siem Reap (1 daily; 6hr).

Siem Reap to: Battambang (1 daily at 6.30am; 3–4hr).

Sihanoukville to: Krong Koh Kong (1 daily at noon; 4hr).

Flights

Plane schedules change frequently. There are usually three flights daily between Phnom Penh and Siem Reap, but most other destinations might only be served by one or two flights per week. Check locally with the airlines or travel agents.

CHAPTER THREE

HONG KONG

Introduction

Hong Kong works as a useful gateway into Southeast Asia and into China. It is also an interesting place in its own right – an extraordinary, complex territory of seven million people that's a repository of traditional Chinese culture, a recently relinquished British outpost, and one of the key economies of the Pacific Rim. The view of sky-scrapered Hong Kong Island, across the harbour from Kowloon, is one of the most stunning urban panoramas on earth, but Hong Kong also holds some surprises for the traveller – alongside the myriad shopping possibilities (not all of them such a bargain as they used to be), are a surprising number of inviting beaches, rewarding hiking trails and some surviving bastions of Chinese village life, most of them in the New Territories. An excellent infrastructure, an efficient underground system and all the other facilities of an international city make this an extremely soft entry into the Chinese world.

Some visitors dislike the speed, the obsessive materialism and the addiction to shopping, money and brand names in Hong Kong. Downtown is certainly not a place to recover from a headache, but it's hard not to enjoy the sheer energy of its street and commercial life. Hong Kong's per capita **GNP** has doubled in a decade, overtaking that of the former imperial power, and the territory is currently the largest trading partner and largest source of foreign investment for the People's Republic of China, a country of 1.2 billion people. Yet the inequality of incomes is staggering: the conspicuous consumption of the few hundred super-rich (all Cantonese), for which Hong Kong is famous, tends to mask the fact that most people work long hours and live in crowded, tiny apartments.

Since the **handover** to China in 1997 the people of Hong Kong have found themselves in a unique position: subject to the ultimate rule of Beijing, they live in a semi-democratic capitalist enclave – a "Special Administrative Region of China" – under the control of an unaccountable communist state. This is not to say that the people of Hong Kong were not glad to see the end of colonialism – an overwhelming majority supported the transfer of power, and a huge majority speak only the Cantonese dialect, eat only Cantonese food, pray in Chinese temples and enjoy close cultural and blood relations with the Cantonese population that lives just over the border, in the southern provinces of mainland China. Indeed, it is hard to overstate the symbolic importance that the handover had for the entire Chinese population, marking the end of the era of foreign domination. However, worrying questions remain, notably whether the One Country/Two Systems policy created by Deng Xiaoping will work in the longer term, especially if China's own economic progress begins to falter.

Hong Kong's **climate** is subtropical. The pleasantest time to visit is between October and April. The weather is cooler, humidity and pollution levels drop,

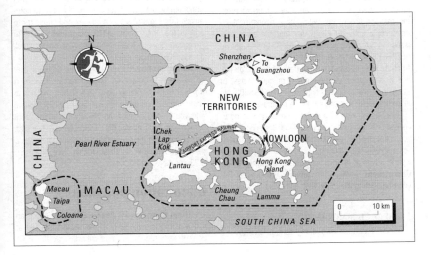

and the flowers are in bloom. In January and February it can get quite rainy and cold – you'll need a light jacket and sweater. The temperature and humidity start to pick up in mid-April, and between late June and early September readings of 30°C and 95 percent humidity or more are the norm. Walking and other physical activities become unpleasant and sleeping without air-con difficult. May to September is also the peak typhoon season, when ferry and airline timetables are often disrupted by bad weather.

Overland and sea routes into Hong Kong

The main land route into Hong Kong is by **train**. Both express trains and cheaper local trains leave daily from Guangzhou on the Chinese mainland. There are also regular daily **bus** services from Guangzhou and Shenzhen. **Sea routes** from China include ferries from Shanghai, Xiamen, Guangzhou, Shekou and Zhuhai. Frequent ferries also run from Macau. For details on all these routes see the box on p.156.

Entry requirements and visa extension

Most nationalities need only a valid passport to enter Hong Kong, although the length of time you can stay varies. Citizens of the **United Kingdom**, **Eire**, **Australia** and **New Zealand**, nearly all other Commonwealth passport holders and citizens of most European countries can stay for up to three months; and Americans and South Africans for thirty days. For a sixty- or ninety-day multiple-entry visa, issued in two days, visit CTS at 78–83 Connaught Rd or 27–33 Nathan Rd. Note that these visas are active from the date of issue, not the date of entry. You can get a six-month multiple-entry business visa at Shoestring Travel (27–33 Nathan Rd) for HK$600. No invitation letter is required, just a business card.

The easiest way to **extend your stay** is to go to Macau or China for the weekend and come back, and you'll get another period stamped in your passport. For a longer stay, though, you'll need to apply for a visa in advance of your visit from the **Immigration Department**, Immigration Tower, 7 Gloucester Rd, Wanchai, Hong Kong ☎2824 6111, as you will if

---

AIRPORT DEPARTURE TAX

Airport departure tax in Hong Kong is HK$50.

---

you're intending to work in the territory; allow at least six weeks for most visa applications.

Money and costs

Hong Kong's unit of **currency** is the Hong Kong dollar (HK$), divided into one hundred cents. Bank notes are issued by the Hongkong and Shanghai Banking Corporation, the Standard Chartered Bank and the Bank of China, and are of slightly different design and size, but they're all interchangeable. **Notes** come in denominations of HK$10, HK$20, HK$50, HK$100, HK$500 and HK$1000; there's a nickel-and-bronze HK$10 coin; **silver coins** come as HK$1, HK$2 and HK$5; and **bronze coins** as 10c, 20c and 50c. The current **exchange rate** is around HK$12–13 to the pound sterling, and it's pegged at HK$7.78 to the US dollar. There's no black market, and money, in any amount, can be freely taken in and out of the territory.

Food and accommodation are more expensive in Hong Kong than most other Southeast Asian destinations, so you will need to give yourself a bigger **daily budget** here. The cheapest dorm beds will set you back £7/US$10.50 a night, while it's hard to come by a decent double room for under £60/US$90. Staying at cheap lodgings and eating simply from noodle stalls will cost you about £20/US$35 a day, up to £23/US$35 with a mid-range restaurant meal thrown in. For more comfort and classier food, budget from £80/US$120 and up.

All major **credit cards** are accepted in Hong Kong, but watch out for the three to five percent commission that lots of travel agencies and shops try to add to the price. Some **ATM machines** will take American Express, Mastercard and Visa cards; check details from the companies direct.

Wiring money to Hong Kong is no problem. Any of the major international banks here can organize a transfer from your home bank to a specific branch in Hong Kong. It will take the best part of a day, though, and you'll be charged a handling fee. International companies, such as Western Union Money Transfer, can also handle the transaction for you and charge a percentage of the sum transferred. See "Basics", p.23, for more details.

Information and maps

The **Hong Kong Tourist Association** (HKTA) has an office in the arrivals area of the airport (staffed at peak times, information and cyberlink available 24 hours), at the Star Ferry Terminal in Tsimshatsui (daily 8am–6pm) and on the ground floor of The Centre, 99 Queen's Rd, Central (daily 8am–6pm). There's also an HKTA multilingual **telephone service** (Mon–Fri 8am–6pm, Sat & Sun 9am–5pm; ☎2508 1234).

HKTA **maps** and the maps in this guide should be enough for most purposes, though more detailed versions such as the paperback *Hong Kong Guide*, which includes all major bus routes, can be bought from English-language bookstores (see "Listings", p.182).

Accommodation

Hong Kong boasts some of the most luxurious **hotels** in Asia – if not the world – as well as some of the seediest guesthouses. **At the top end** of the spectrum, a suite or room with the classic harbour view will set you back thousands of dollars a night. For that, guests – mostly business people – get considerable luxury in the room, plus five-star service and all the other facilities of international hotels. These hotels also function as meeting and dining places for the local business and social elite, and it's worth hanging out in their lobbies to see the world go by.

All these hotels – the *Mandarin*, the *Grand Hyatt* and the *Regent* among others – will be packed when a big trade fair or conference is on, as will the three- and four-star places. However, when business is quieter, for example, in the rainy summer season, these **mid-range hotels** can offer some interesting bargains, particularly those in areas like north Kowloon, away from the main business districts. They usually charge by the room rather than the person and include breakfast in the rate as well as extras like free airport transfers, but beware of service charges and taxes which can add up to 17 percent to the bill. If you're interested, check travel agents' offers before you get to Hong Kong, or ask the Tourist Authority at the airport.

Sky-high property prices mean that cheaper accommodation is not nearly as plentiful as in other Asian cities, or generally as good value. **Guesthouses** are almost all in Tsimshatsui and Kowloon, and the majority are crammed into a couple of huge, warren-like blocks, *Mirador Mansions* and *Chungking Mansions*. Both have poor fire safety standards. Inside, quality and cleanliness varies greatly from guesthouse to guesthouse, but all the rooms will be small, and some will have no windows. Often, very little English is spoken. These two blocks are also crammed with shops, travel agents and restaurants, and the noticeboards are focal points for travellers' information. If you want something a bit better, try heading north up the Kowloon peninsula or to the **new towns** such as Shatin, where land prices, and so room rates, are lower. An alternative is to stay at a **Youth Hostel**, where rates are as low as HK\$35 for members or HK\$55 for non-members. These are usually packed out at weekends but empty during the week, although as most are some way out of town you should ring to check availability first. Expect to bring your own food. Another budget option is to stay on one of **the islands**, like Lamma or Lantau. During the week, hotel rates are around HK\$300–500 for a double – half the weekend price. Guesthouses are less, around HK\$200 mid-week, but the rooms can be very basic, as most are used by local couples for getaway weekends. **Electricity** throughout the territory is usually supplied at 200 volts.

Food and drink

As one of the great culinary capitals of the world, Hong Kong can boast not only a superb native cuisine – **Cantonese** – but also perhaps the widest range of **international restaurants** of any city outside Europe or North America. This is due in part to the cosmopolitan nature of the population, but perhaps more importantly, to the incredible seriousness attached to dining by the local Chinese.

As well as the joys of *dim sum* – another Hong Kong speciality – the city offers the full gamut of

---

ACCOMMODATION PRICE CODES

All **accommodation** reviewed in this guide has been graded according to the following price codes, in US dollars, which represent the cost of the cheapest double room available in high season. Where a price range is indicated, this means that the establishment offers rooms with varying facilities – as explained in the write-up. In cases where an establishment charges per bed the actual price is given.

① under \$5	④ \$15–20	⑦ \$40–60
② \$5–10	⑤ \$20–25	⑧ \$60–80
③ \$10–15	⑥ \$25–40	⑨ \$80 and over

FOOD AND DRINK GLOSSARY

The following lists should help out where you can't make yourself understood – and, if they're written clearly, in deciphering the characters on a Chinese menu. If you know what you're after, try sifting through the staples and cooking methods to create your order, or sample one of the everyday or regional suggestions. Don't forget to tailor your demands to the capabilities of where you're ordering, however – a street cook with a wok isn't going to be able to whip up anything much more complicated than a basic stir-fry. Remember to note whether dishes are priced per order or per hundred grams – common for seafood.

ORDERING

Bill/cheque	买单	*mǎidān*
Chopsticks	筷子	*kuàizi*
House speciality	拿手好菜	*náshǒuhǎocài*
How much is that?	多少钱?	*duōshǎo qián?*
I'm Buddhist/I'm vegetarian	我是佛教徒/我只吃素	*wǒ shì fójiàotú/wǒ zhǐ chī sù*
I would like...	我想要....	*wǒ xiǎng yào...*
Menu/set menu/English menu	菜单/套菜/英文菜单	*càidān/tàocài/yīngwén càidān*
Small portion	少量	*shǎoliàng*
Spoon	勺	*sháo*
Waiter/waitress	服务员/小姐	*fúwùyuán/xiǎojiě*

DRINKS

Beer	啤酒	*píjiǔ*
Coffee	咖啡	*kāfēi*
Tea	茶	*chá*
(Mineral) water	(矿泉)水	*(kuàngquán) shuǐ*
Wine	葡萄酒	*pútáojiǔ*

STAPLE FOODS

Bamboo shoots	笋尖	*sǔnjiān*
Beans	豆	*dòu*
Bean sprouts	豆芽	*dòuyá*
Beef	牛肉	*niúròu*
Black bean sauce	黑豆豉	*hēidòuchǐ*
Buns (plain)	馒头	*mántou*
Buns (filled)	包子	*bāozi*
Cashew nuts	坚果	*jiānguǒ*
Chicken	鸡	*jī*
Chilli	辣椒	*làjiāo*
Crab	蟹	*xiè*
Dog	狗肉	*gǒuròu*
Duck	鸭	*yā*
Eel	鳝鱼	*shànyú*
Fish	鱼	*yú*
Garlic	大蒜	*dàsuàn*
Ginger	姜	*jiāng*
Green vegetables	绿叶素菜	*lǜyè sùcài*
Lotus root	莲心	*liánxīn*
MSG	味精	*wèijīng*
Mushrooms	磨菇	*mógū*
Noodles	面条	*miàntiáo*
Pancake	摊饼	*tānbǐng*
Peanut	花生	*huāshēng*

Pork	猪肉	zhūròu
Potato	土豆	tǔdòu
Prawns	虾	xiā
Preserved egg	皮蛋	pídàn
Rice, boiled	白饭	báifàn
Rice, fried	炒饭	chǎofàn
Rice porridge congee	粥	zhōu
Salt	盐	yán
Snake	蛇肉	shéròu
Soup	汤	tāng
Sugar	糖	táng
Tofu	豆腐	dòufu

COOKING METHODS

Boiled	煮	zhǔ
Casseroled	焙	bèi
Fried	炒	chǎo
Poached	白煮	báizhǔ
Roast	烤	kǎo
Steamed	蒸	zhēng
Stir-fried	清炒	qīngchǎo

EVERYDAY DISHES

Braised duck with vegetables	炖鸭素菜	dùnyā sùcài
Chicken and sweetcorn soup	玉米鸡丝汤	yùmǐ jīsī tāng
Chicken with cashew nuts	坚果鸡片	jiānguǒ jīpiàn
Crispy aromatic duck	香酥鸭	xiāngsūyā
Egg fried rice	蛋炒饭	dànchǎofàn
Fish ball soup with white radish	萝卜鱼蛋汤	luóbo yúdàn tāng
Fish casserole	焙鱼	bèiyú
Fried shredded pork with garlic and chilli	大蒜辣椒炒肉片	dàsuàn làjiāo chǎoròupiàn
Hotpot	火锅	huǒguō
Kebab	串肉	chuànròu
Noodle soup	汤面	tāngmiàn
Prawn with garlic sauce	大蒜炒虾	dàsuàn chǎoxiā
Roast duck	烤鸭	kǎoyā
Sliced pork with yellow bean sauce	黄豆肉片	huángdòu ròupiàn
Steamed eel with black beans	豆豉蒸鳝	dòuchǐ zhēngshàn
Stewed pork belly with vegetables	回锅肉	huíguōròu
Stir-fried chicken and bamboo shoots	笋尖炒鸡片	sǔnjiān chǎojīpiàn
Sweet and sour spare ribs	糖醋排骨	tángcù páigǔ
Sweet bean paste pancakes	赤豆摊饼	chìdòu tānbǐng
Wonton soup	馄饨汤	húntun tāng

VEGETABLES AND EGGS

Aubergine with chilli and garlic sauce	大蒜辣椒炒茄子	dàsuàn làjiāo chǎoqiézi
Braised mountain fungus	炖香菇	dùnxiānggū
Fried beancurd with vegetables	豆腐素菜	dòufu sùcài
Fried bean sprouts	炒豆芽	chǎodòuyá
Spicy braised aubergine	香茄子条	xiāngqiézitiáo
Stir-fried bamboo shoots	炒冬笋	chǎodōngsǔn
Stir-fried mushrooms	炒鲜菇	chǎoxiānggū
Vegetable soup	素菜汤	sùcài tāng

continued overleaf

FOOD AND DRINK GLOSSARY CONTINUED

REGIONAL DISHES

Northern

Mongolian hotpot	蒙古火锅	*ménggǔ huǒguō*
Peking duck	北京烤鸭	*běijīng kǎoyā*
Shark's fin soup	鱼翅汤	*yúchìtāng*

Eastern

Crab soup	蟹肉汤	*xièròu tāng*
Drunken prawns (steamed in wine)	醉虾	*zuìxiā*
Shark fin and crabmeat soup	蟹肉鱼翅汤	*xièròuyúchì tāng*
Steamed sea bass	清蒸鲈鱼	*qīngzhēnglúyú*

Sichuan and western China

Deep-fried green beans with garlic	大蒜刀豆	*dàsuàn dāodòu*
Gongbao chicken (with chillis and peanuts)	宫爆鸡丁	*gōngbào jīdīng*
Green pepper with spring onion and black bean sauce	豆豉青椒	*dòuchǐ qīngjiāo*
Hot and sour soup	酸辣汤	*suānlà tāng*
Wind-cured ham	火腿	*huǒtuǐ*
Stuffed aubergine slices	馅茄子	*xiànqiézi*

Southern Chinese/Cantonese

Baked crab with chilli and black beans	辣椒豆豉焙蟹	*làjiāo dòuchǐ bèixiè*
Casseroled beancurd stuffed with pork mince	豆腐煲	*dòufubāo*
Crisp-skinned pork on rice	脆皮肉饭	*cuìpíròufàn*
Fish-head casserole	焙鱼头	*bèiyútóu*
Fish steamed with ginger and spring onion	清蒸鱼	*qīngzhēngyú*
Fried chicken with yam	芋头炒鸡片	*yùtóu chǎojīpiàn*
Honey-roast pork	叉烧	*chāshāo*

Dim sum (Yum cha)

Barbecue pork bun	叉烧包	*chāshāo bāo*
Crab and coriander dumpling	蟹肉虾饺	*xièròu xiājiāo*
Custard tart	蛋挞	*dàntà*
Doughnut	炸面饼圈	*zhá miànbǐngquān*
Fried taro and mince dumpling	蕃薯糊饺	*fānshǔ hújiāo*
Jiaozi (steamed pork dumplings)	饺子	*jiǎozi*
Lotus paste bun	连蓉糕	*liánrónggāo*
Moon cake (sweet bean paste in flaky pastry)	月饼	*yuèbǐng*
Pork and prawn dumpling in ornate wrapping	烧麦	*shāomài*
Prawn crackers	虾片	*xiāpiàn*
Prawn dumpling	虾饺	*xiājiǎo*
Prawn paste on fried toast	芝麻虾	*zhīmaxiā*
Shanghai fried meat and vegetable dumpling	锅帖	*guōtiē*
Spring roll	春卷	*chūnjuǎn*

Chinese restaurants, from Beijing to Shanghai to Sichuan (and many smaller localities). It also offers excellent curry houses from the Indian subcontinent, surprisingly reasonable Japanese sushi bars, British pub-style food and endless cheap **street stalls** (*dai pai dongs*), which are often the best value for money of all. You'll also find the local Chinese fast-food chains, *Café de Coral* and *Maxim's*, alongside *McDonald's*, *Pizza Hut* and *KFC*. The choice is endless, and all budgets are catered for. English **menus** are widely available. Nearly all restaurants will add a ten percent **service charge** to your bill, and if there are nuts and pickles on your table you'll often pay a small cover charge too.

■ What to eat

The kind of **snacks** you'll find at the *dai pai dongs*, or street stalls, include fish, beef and pork balls, stuffed buns, grilled chicken wings, spiced noodles, fresh and dried squid, spring rolls, *congee* (rice gruel served with a greasy, doughnut-type stick), cooked intestines, tofu pudding and various sweets. Some *dai pai dongs* have simple tables and chairs and serve slightly more elaborate food, such as seafood, mixed rice and noodle dishes, stews and soups, and bottled beer. A meal here will cost around HK$50–60.

The most common Chinese food in Hong Kong is **Cantonese**, from China's southern Guangdong province. Dishes consist of extremely fresh food, quickly cooked and only lightly seasoned. Popular ingredients are fruit and vegetables, fish and shellfish, though the cuisine is also known for its more unusual ingredients – things like fish maw, snake liver, dog and guinea pig – which most Westerners would baulk at eating. Cantonese restaurants also have the best selection of **dim sum** ("little eats"), a midday meal consisting of small flavoured buns, dumplings and pancakes, washed down with copious amounts of tea (see opposite for a list of the most common dishes). The food is wheeled in trolleys through the restaurant: they'll come to your table and you select what you want. Most things cost the same, around HK$30–40 each, and you'll find it hard to spend more than HK$90–120 a head. Restaurants that specialize in *dim sum* open early in the morning, from around 7am, and serve right through lunch up until around 5pm; many regular Cantonese restaurants also serve *dim sum*, usually 10–11am until 3pm. It's best to go in a group so that you can order a number of items to share.

Beijing food is heavier than Cantonese cooking, based around a solid diet of wheat and millet buns, noodles, pancakes and dumplings, accompanied by the savoury tastes of dark soy sauce and bean paste, white onions and cabbage. The north's cooking has also been influenced by neighbours and invaders: Mongols brought their hotpots and grilled roast meats, and Muslims a taste for mutton and chicken. Combined with exotic items imported by foreign merchants, these rather rough ingredients were turned into sophisticated marvels such as Peking duck and bird's nest soup.

Shanghainese cuisine delights in seasonal fresh seafood and river fish. Dried and salted ingredients feature too, pepping up a background of rice noodles and dumplings. The cuisine is characterized by little, delicate forms and light, fresh, sweet flavours, sometimes to the point of becoming precious – tiny meatballs are steamed in a rice coating and called "pearls" for example.

Szechuan (Sichuan) food is the antithesis of Shanghainese cuisine. Here there's a heavy use of chillies and pungent, constructed flavours – vegetables are concealed with "fish-flavoured" sauce, and even normally bland tofu is given enough spices to lift the top off your head. Yet there are still subtleties to enjoy in a cuisine which uses dried orange peel, aniseed, ginger and spring onions, and the cooking methods themselves – such as dry frying and smoking – are refreshingly unusual.

In most Chinese restaurants, the usual **drink** with your meal is **jasmine tea**, often brought to your table as a matter of course. **Beer** and wine are also popular, though the latter is expensive. The **water** is fit for drinking everywhere in Hong Kong, though bottled water tastes nicer.

Communications

Airmail takes three days to a week to reach Britain or North America. Letters sent **poste restante** will arrive at the GPO building in Central (see p.182 for details). To send **parcels**, turn up at the post office with the goods you want to send and the staff will help you pack them. You can either bring your own paper and tape or buy boxes at the post office. You'll also need to fill out a customs declaration form. Parcels go by surface mail unless you specify otherwise.

Local calls from private phones are free; most shops and restaurants will let you use theirs for nothing. There are no area codes. Public **phones** cost HK$1 for five minutes, and every pay- and cardphone has instructions in English. **Phone cards** come in units of HK$50, HK$100, HK$200 and HK$300, and are available from HK Telecom Service Centres, tourist offices and convenience stores.

You can make **international calls** from International Direct Dialling (IDD) phones or one of the several **Hong Kong Telecom Service Centres** in the territory (see p.182 for addresses). Collect or reverse-charge calls and home-direct calls can be made free of charge from these centres. They also have fax services. To phone abroad from Hong Kong, dial ☎001 + IDD country code (see p.40) + area code minus first 0 + subscriber number. For directory enquiries in English call ☎1081.

Internet and **email access** are available at the main public library in Central, at most branches of the *Pacific Coffee Company* and other cybercafés (see "Listings" p.182) or in the business centres of major hotels.

Opening hours and festivals

Generally, **offices** are open Monday–Friday 9am–5pm, and some open Saturday 9am–1pm; **shops**, daily 10am–7/8pm, though later in tourist

areas. **Banking hours** are Monday–Friday 9am–4.30pm, Saturday 9am–12.30pm. **Post office** opening hours are Monday–Friday 8am–6pm, Saturday 8am–2pm (the main post offices in Central and Tsimshatsui are also open 8am–2pm on Sunday). All government offices close on **public holidays** and some religious festivals. As the Chinese use the **lunar calendar** and not the Gregorian calendar, many of the festivals fall on different days, even different months, from year to year; for exact details contact the Hong Kong Tourist Association (see p.144).

With roots going back hundreds (even thousands) of years, many of Hong Kong's **festivals** are highly symbolic and are often a mixture of secular and religious displays and devotions. On these occasions, there are dances and Chinese opera displays at the temples, plenty of noise and a series of **offerings** left in the temples – food and paper goods which are burned as offerings to the dead. The most important is **Chinese New Year** (Jan/Feb), when the entire population takes time out to celebrate. The **Mid-Autumn (Moon Cake) Festival** in September is almost as popular, and celebrations are more public. Festivals particular to Hong Kong rather than the whole of China include the **Tin Hau Festival** (late April or May), in honour of the Goddess of Fishermen, when large seaborne festivities take place at Joss House Bay on Sai Kung Peninsula (see p.174); the **Tai Chiu (or Bun) Festival**, which is held on Cheung Chau island in May; and the **Tuen Ng (Dragon Boat) Festival** in early June, with races in various places around the territory in long, narrow boats.

Cultural hints

Generally speaking, Hong Kong people are not as worried as other Southeast Asian cultures about covering the skin – girls often wear skirts as short as those in the West. Having said that, however, don't think of **bathing topless** on any of Hong Kong's beaches: you'll draw a lot of attention to yourself, offend some people, and in any case it's illegal. Hong Kong residents tend to be less polite and courteous than other Asian cultures and indeed than most Western cultures. They also talk more openly about money – it's quite common for people to ask you what you paid for things.

Crime and safety

You're very unlikely to encounter any trouble in Hong Kong. The main thing to look out for is **pickpockets**:

it's best to keep money and wallets in inside pockets, carry handbags around your neck and be careful when getting on and off packed buses and trains. The only other problems you might encounter are in bars where the emphasis is on buying very expensive drinks for the "girls": if you get drunk and refuse or are unable to pay, the bar heavies will soon make sure you find your wallet.

On the street, **police** officers who speak English wear a red flash under their shoulder number. In Hong Kong, everyone is required to carry some form of **identification** at all times: anything with your photograph will do, or your driving licence.

Medical care and emergencies

Pharmacies (daily 9am–6pm) can help with minor injuries or ailments and will prescribe basic medicines. Contraceptives and antibiotics are also available over the counter. All pharmacies are registered and are usually staffed by English speakers.

For a **doctor**, look in the local phone directories' Yellow Pages under "Physicians and Surgeons". Large hotels also have a clinic for guests offering diagnosis, advice and prescriptions. You'll have to pay for a consultation and any medicines that are prescribed; be sure to get a receipt so that you can make an insurance claim when you get home.

Hospital treatment is very expensive, making it important to have some form of medical insurance. Casualty visits are free, however, and public hospitals have 24-hour casualty departments. See p.182 for hospital addresses. Note that both doctors and **dentists** are known as "doctor" in Hong Kong.

EMERGENCY PHONE NUMBERS

Dial ☎999 for fire, police and ambulance.

History

While the Chinese argue that Hong Kong has always been Chinese territory, the development of the city only began with the **arrival of the British** in Guangzhou in the eighteenth century. The **Portuguese** had already been based at Macau, on the other side of the Pearl River Delta, since the mid-sixteenth century, and as Britain's sea power grew, so its merchants, too, began casting covetous eyes over the Portuguese trade in tea and silk. The initial difficulty was to persuade the Chinese authorities that there was any reason to want to deal with them, though a few traders did manage to get permission to set up their warehouses in Guangzhou – a remote southern outpost, from the perspective of Beijing – and slowly trade began to grow. In 1757, a local Guangzhou merchants' guild called the **Co Hong**, won the exclusive rights to sell Chinese products to foreign traders, who were now permitted to live in Guangzhou for about six months each year.

In the meantime, it had not escaped the attention of the foreigners that the trade was one-way only, and they soon began thinking up possible products the Chinese might want to buy in exchange. It did not take long to find one – **opium** from India. In 1773, the first British shipload of opium arrived and an explosion of demand for the drug quickly followed, despite an edict from Beijing banning the trade in 1796. Co Hong, which received commission on everything bought or sold, had no qualms about distributing opium to its fellow citizens and before long the balance of trade had been reversed very much in favour of the British.

The scene for the famous **Opium Wars** was now set. Alarmed at the outflow of silver and the rising incidence of drug addiction among his population, the emperor appointed Lin Zexu as Commissioner of Guangzhou to destroy the opium trade. Lin, later hailed by the Chinese communists as a patriot and hero, forced the British in Guangzhou to surrender their opium, before ceremonially burning it. Such an affront to British dignity could not be tolerated, however, and in 1840, a naval expeditionary force was dispatched from London to sort the matter out once and for all. After a year of gunboat diplomacy – blockading ports and seizing assets up and down the Chinese coast – the expeditionary force finally achieved one of their main objectives, through the **Treaty of Nanking** (1842), namely the ceding to Britain "in perpetuity" of a small offshore island. The island was called Hong Kong. This was followed eighteen years later, after more blockades and a forced march on Peking, by the **Treaty of Peking**, which granted Britain the Kowloon peninsula, too. Finally, in 1898, as the Qing dynasty was entering its terminal phase, Britain secured a 99-year lease on an additional one thousand square kilometres of land to the north of Kowloon, which came to be known as the New Territories.

During the twentieth century, Hong Kong grew from a seedy merchants' colony to a huge international city, but progress has not always been smooth. The drug trade was voluntarily dropped in 1907 as the Hong Kong merchants began to make the transfer from pure trade to manufacturing. Up until World War II, Hong Kong prospered, as the growing threat of both civil war and Japanese aggression in mainland China increasingly began to drive money south into the apparently safe confines of the British colony. This confidence appeared glaringly misplaced in 1941 when **Japanese forces** seized Hong Kong along with the rest of eastern China, though after the Japanese defeat in 1945, Hong Kong once again began attracting money from the mainland, which was in the process of falling to the communists. Many of Hong Kong's biggest tycoons today are people who escaped from mainland China, particularly from Shanghai, in 1949.

Since the beginning of the **communist era**, Hong Kong has led a precarious existence, quietly making money while taking care not to antagonize Beijing. Had China wished to do so, it could have rendered the existence of Hong Kong unviable at any moment, by a naval blockade, by cutting off water supplies, by a military invasion – or by simply opening its border and inviting the Chinese masses to stream across in search of wealth. That it has never wholeheartedly pursued any of these options, even at the height of the Cultural Revolution, is an indication of the huge **financial benefits** that Hong Kong brings to mainland China in the form of its international trade links, direct investment and technology transfers.

For the last twenty years of British rule, the spectre of **1997** loomed large in people's minds. In 1982, negotiations on the future of the colony began, although during the entire process that led to the **Sino-British Joint Declaration** nerves were kept on edge by the public posturings of both sides. The eventual deal, signed in 1984, paved the way for Britain to hand back sovereignty of the territory – something the Chinese would argue they never lost – in return for Hong Kong maintaining its capitalist system for at least fifty years.

Almost immediately the deal sparked controversy. It was pointed out that the lack of democratic institutions in Hong Kong – which had suited the British – would in future mean the Chinese could do what they liked. Fears grew that repression and the erosion of freedoms such as travel and speech would follow the handover. The **Basic Law**, which was published by the government in 1988, in theory answered some of those fears. It served as the constitutional framework, setting out how the One Country/Two Systems policy would work in practice. However, it failed to restore confidence in Hong Kong, and a brain-drain of educated, professional people to other countries began to gather pace.

The **1989 crackdown in Tian'anmen Square** seemed to confirm the Hong Kong population's worst fears. In the biggest demonstration seen in Hong Kong in modern times, a million people took to the streets to protest at what had happened. Business confidence was equally shaken, as the Hang Seng index, the performance indicator of the Stock Exchange, dropped 22 percent in a single day.

The 1990s were a roller-coaster ride of domestic policy dramas: the arrival of tens of thousands of Vietnamese boat people (ironically, refugees from communism), the rise of the **democracy movement** and arguments about whether Britain would give passports to the local population. When Chris Patten arrived in 1992 to become the last Governor, he walked into a delicate and highly charged political situation. By means of a series of reforms, Patten quickly made it clear that he had not come to Hong Kong simply as a make-weight: first, much of the colonial paraphernalia was abandoned, and then – much to the fury of Beijing – he broadened the voting franchise for the 1995 **Legislative Council elections** (Legco) from around 200,000 to 2.7 million people. Even though these and other changes he introduced guaranteed that the run-up to the 1997 handover would be a bumpy ride, they won the Governor significant popularity among ordinary Hong Kong people, although the tycoons and business community had far more mixed feelings.

After the build-up, the **handover** itself was something of an anticlimax. The British sailed away on HMS Britannia, Beijing carried out its threat to disband the elected Legco and reduce the enfranchised population, and Tung Che Hwa, a shipping billionaire, became the first Chief Executive of the Hong Kong Special Administrative Region (SAR). But if local people had thought that they would be able to get on with "business as usual" post-handover, they were wrong. Within days the **Asian Financial Crisis** had begun, and within months Hong Kong was once again in the eye of a storm. While the administration beat off attempts to force a devaluation of its currency, the stock and property markets suffered dramatic falls, tourism collapsed, unemployment rose to its highest levels for fifteen years, and the economy officially went into recession. While the administration characterized these as temporary setbacks – part of a global economic downturn – there was undoubted dismay amongst official circles in both Hong Kong and Beijing at the increasing – and unprecedented – level of criticism of officials and their policies in newspapers, on radio phone-ins and among ordinary people. Just as alarming to the powers-that-be has been the enduring and not unrelated popularity of the democratic parties. As the economy recovers, local people are unlikely to lose their new taste for expressing their opinions and criticizing authority.

Religions of Hong Kong

The most prevalent religions in Hong Kong are **Taoism**, **Confucianism** and **Buddhism**; see "Basics" p.47 for an introduction to these. Importance is also attached to **superstition** and **ancestor worship**, and things are further complicated by the way in which deities from various religions are worshipped in each other's temples – it's common for Buddhist deities to be worshipped in Taoist temples, for example. The **Catholic** community is also prominent – because of their schooling many leading government and business figures are Catholic, as of course are the tens of thousands of Filipina amahs.

Books

In the selection of books below, where a book is published in the UK and the US, the UK publisher is given first, followed by the US one; o/p signifies out of print.

Jonathon Dimbleby, *The Last Governor* (Little Brown, UK & US). Charts Chris Patten's struggle to introduce more democracy and the run-up to the handover. The author was given unprecedented access to Government House, though critics say that the book – a TV tie-in – does a poor job of fully recording what went on in the last crucial years of Britain's rule.

Jan Morris, *Hong Kong: Epilogue to an Empire* (Penguin/Vintage). A great introduction to Hong Kong by one of travel writing's most incisive observers. Morris mixes history, storytelling and colour in an easy-to-read style which ignites one's curiosity to visit.

John Le Carré, *The Honourable Schoolboy* (Coronet/Bantam). Perhaps not Le Carré's best novel, but the usual George Smiley mix of spooks, moles and traitors is a good, racy read. The Hong Kong scenes capture the atmosphere of the dying years of colonialism well – paranoia, money, drink and politics mixed together.

Christopher Patten, *East and West* (Random House, UK & US). The last British Governor's views not just of his controversial years in Hong Kong, but more broadly of the Asian "miracle", democracy, and the region's future. Thoughtful, with as much relevance to Asia's future as its most recent past.

Sally Blyth and Ian Wotherspoon, *Hong Kong Remembers* (Oxford University Press, o/p). A collection of views and reminiscences of life in Hong Kong from the 1930's to the handover. Chinese and British, famous and obscure, their stories give a true picture of what it was like to live through some of Hong Kong's most turbulent times.

Edward Stokes, *Exploring Hong Kong's Countryside, a visitor's companion* (Hong Kong Tourist Authority; price HK$80). This guide contains all you need to explore Hong Kong's most popular country-park walks and hikes, and see another – green – side to the city, which most visitors never discover. Stokes has been photographing and writing about Hong Kong's countryside for years, and few know more about this subject.

HONG KONG

The territory of **HONG KONG** comprises an irregularly shaped peninsula abutting the Pearl River Delta to the west, and a number of offshore islands, which cover in total more than a thousand square kilometres. The bulk of this area, namely the land in the north of the peninsula, as well as most of the islands, is semi-rural and is known as the **New Territories** – this was the land leased to Britain for 99 years in 1898. The southern part of the peninsula, known as **Kowloon**, and the island immediately south of here, **Hong Kong Island**, are the principal urban areas of Hong Kong. They were ceded to Britain in perpetuity, but were returned to China at midnight on June 30, 1997, since when it has been the **Hong Kong Special Administrative Region** (SAR) of China.

The island of Hong Kong offers not only traces of the old colony – from English place names to ancient trams trundling along the shore – but also superb modern architecture and bizarre cityscapes, as well as unexpected opportunities for **hiking** and even bathing on the **beaches** of its southern shore. Kowloon, in particular its southernmost tip, **Tsimshatsui**, boasts more shops offering a greater variety of goods per square kilometre than anywhere in the world, and is also the budget accommodation centre of Hong Kong. North of Tsimshatsui, Kowloon stretches away into the **New Territories**, an area of so-called New Towns as well as ancient villages, secluded beaches and rural tranquillity. In addition, there are the **offshore islands**, including **Lamma** and **Lantau,** which are well worth a visit for their fish restaurants, scenery and, if nothing else, for the experience of chugging about on the inter-island ferries.

> **Hong Kong phone numbers** have no area codes. From outside the territory, dial the normal international access code + ☎852 (country code) + the number. However, from Macau you need only dial ☎01 + the number.

Orientation

Orientation for new arrivals in the main urban areas is relatively easy: if you are "**Hong Kong-side**" – on the northern shore of Hong Kong Island – **Victoria Harbour** lies to your north, while to your south the land slopes upwards steeply to the **Peak**. The heart of this built-up area on Hong Kong Island is known, rather mundanely, as **Central**. Just across the harbour, in the area known as **Tsimshatsui**, you are "**Kowloon-side**", and here all you really need to recognize is the colossal north–south artery, **Nathan Road**, full of shops and budget hotels, that leads down to the harbour, and to the phenomenal view south over Hong Kong Island. Two more useful points for orientation on both sides of Victoria Harbour are the **Star Ferry Terminals** where the popular cross-harbour ferries dock, in Tsimshatsui (a short walk west of the south end of Nathan Road) and in Central.

Arrival

Public **transport** is so convenient and efficient that even first-time arrivals are unlikely to face any particular problems in reaching their destination within the city – apart from the difficulty of communicating with taxi drivers or reading the destinations on minibuses.

By plane

Hong Kong's new **Chek Lap Kok airport** (known officially as Hong Kong International Airport) is some way from downtown areas, 34km west of Central, on the north coast of Lantau Island, but it's connected to the urban areas by excellent rail and road links. The high-speed **Airport Express (AER)** rail service can be accessed directly from arrivals (every

8min; 6am–1am), whisking you to Central on Hong Kong island in 23 minutes (HK$150), via Tsing Yi (12min; HK$60) and Kowloon (19min; HK$90). There are taxi ranks, bus stops and hotel-shuttle bus stops at the AER stations, plus a left-luggage service at the Central and Kowloon AER stations (6am–1am).

There are six **Airbus** routes from the airport (frequent 6am–midnight); the airport customer-service counters sell tickets (exact money only if you pay on the bus). The #A11 and #A12 go to Causeway Bay on Hong Kong Island via Sheung Wan, Central, Admiralty and Wanchai; the #A12 continues to Fortress Hill, North Point, Quarry Bay, Tai Koo and Shau Kei Wan. Bus #A21 goes to Kowloon KCR Station in Hung Hom via Tsimshatsui, Jordan, Yau Ma Tei and Mongkok; #A22 to Kowloon and Lam Tin MTR Station via Kwung Tong, Ngau Tau Kok, Kowloon Bay, To Kwa Wan, Hung Hom and Jordan; #A31 and #A41 go to the New Territories, with #A31 calling at Tsuen Wan MTR Station, Kwai Chung Road, Kwai Fong, Tsing Yi Road, and #A41 going to Sha Tin.

Taxis into the city are metered and reliable, but get the tourist office in the Buffer Hall, in the arrivals area of the airport, to write down the name of your destination in Chinese characters, so that you can show it to the taxi driver. It costs roughly HK$290 to get to Tsimshatsui, about HK$350 for Hong Kong Island. The journey should take thirty to fifty minutes to Hong Kong Island and twenty to thirty minutes to Tsimshatsui, depending on the time of day. There may be extra charges for luggage and for tunnel tolls – on some tunnel trips the passenger pays the return charge too. Rush-hour traffic can slow down journey times considerably.

By train

The main land route into Hong Kong is by **train**. Express trains from Guangzhou (4 daily; 3hr) arrive at **Hung Hom railway station**, also known as the **Kowloon–Canton railway station, or KCR** (☎2602 7799), east of Tsimshatsui. Signposted walkways lead from here to an adjacent bus terminal, taxi rank and – ten minutes around the harbour – the Hung Hom Ferry Pier. For Tsimshatsui, take bus #5C to the Star Ferry; for Hong Kong Island, take the cross-harbour ferry to Wanchai or Central.

A cheaper alternative is to take a **local train** from Guangzhou to the Chinese border city of Shenzhen, from where you walk across the border to Lo Wu on the Hong Kong side and pick up the regular KCR trains to Kowloon (50min). There are now regular daily **bus** services from Guangzhou and Shenzhen operated by CTS and Citybus; these take about one hour longer than the direct train and arrive in downtown Tsimshatsui.

By ferry

Arriving by sea is a great way to approach Hong Kong for the first time. There are two important long-distance ferry terminals, one for Macau ferries and one for ferries from other Chinese ports. The Macau Ferry Terminal is in the Shun Tak Centre, on Hong Kong Island, from where the Sheung Wan MTR station is directly accessible; Macau ferries run frequently throughout the day and take an hour. The China Hong Kong Ferry Terminal, where ferries from Shanghai (60hr), Xiamen (20hr), Guangzhou (3–9hr), Shekou (45min) and Zhuhai (1hr 10min), and a few from Macau dock, is in the west of Tsimshatsui, just ten minutes' walk from Nathan Road. There is also a berth for international cruise liners at Ocean Terminal in Tsimshatsui.

Information

For **Hong Kong Tourist Association** (HKTA) outlets, see p.144. HKTA **listings magazines** include the useful *Hong Kong Now!* and *Essential: The Official Hong Kong Guide*, both of which cover all events for the current month. Among the unofficial listings magazines, the free *HK Magazine*, published every Friday, contains excellent, up-to-date

MOVING ON TO CHINA FROM HONG KONG

To enter China, you'll need a **visa** – easily obtainable in Hong Kong. Any travel agency and most hotels, even the cheapest hostels, offer this service, though you can do it yourself slightly more cheaply by going to the visa office of the **Ministry of Foreign Affairs** of the PRC, 5th Floor, Lower Block, China Resources Building, 26 Harbour Rd, Wanchai (Mon–Fri 9am–12.20pm & 2–5pm, Sat 9am–12.20pm; ☎2827 1881 or 2585 1794). The fee varies according to whether you want a single- or multiple-entry, one-month or three-month visa, and whether you want fast (same-day) processing or the normal two to three days. Most people pay around HK$200, though same-day visas can cost up to HK$500. Depending on your nationality and passport, it's now also possible to make brief trips to Shenzhen without a pre-arranged visa (you get a temporary one at the border), but check with the Ministry of Foreign Affairs as to whether you qualify – British passports don't.

By train and bus

The simplest route into China is by **direct train to Guangzhou** (4 daily; 2hr 40min; HK$230). Tickets are obtainable in advance from CTS offices (see "Listings", p.183), or on the same day from the Kowloon-Canton Railway Station in Hung Hom. As a cheaper alternative, ride the KCR up to Lo Wu (frequent; 50min; HK$33), walk into Shenzhen and pick up one of the hourly trains to Guangzhou – tickets can be easily purchased in Hong Kong dollars and cost about HK$100. The other land route is by **bus**. Citybus, 13th Floor, 9 Des Voeux West (☎2873 0818), runs frequent services to Shenzhen (1hr; HK$60–100) and Guangzhou (3hr 30min; HK$100).

By boat

By **boat**, you can travel to several Chinese cities, all from the China Hong Kong ferry terminal in Tsimshatsui, where tickets can be bought in advance from a branch of CTS. There is a daily overnight ferry service to **Guangzhou** (9hr) as well as a daily jetcat (3hr); both cost about the same as the train. Local departures to nearby destinations such as **Macau** (frequent; 1hr), **Shenzhen** (6 daily; 1hr), **Shekou** (4 daily; 45min) and **Zhuhai** (daily; 1hr 10min) are also available. There are also less frequent long-distance departures for **Zhaoqing**, **Zhongshan**, **Xiamen** (4 weekly; 20hr), **Shanghai** (weekly; 60hr) and **Wuzhou**, on the way to Guilin (daily; 10hr). These long-distance ferries are generally clean and comfortable and represent the most stress-free way of approaching mainland China for the first time. Ticket prices vary according to class but are not expensive – Shanghai starts from around HK$1000, Xiamen from around HK$500.

By plane

Finally, you can **fly** from Hong Kong into virtually all major Chinese cities on regional Chinese carriers such as China Southern and China Northwest, or to a more restricted number on the Hong Kong-based Dragonair. It's always worth shopping around since prices can vary sharply, and even on the major airlines, special seasonal deals and discounts are often attractively priced. Destinations include Beijing (several daily; 4hr); Chengdu (daily; 2hr 30min); Fuzhou (3–4 daily; 1hr 30min); Guangzhou (4 daily; 50min); Guilin (2 daily; 1hr 10min); Haikou (2 daily; 1hr 10min); Hangzhou (2 daily; 2hr); Kunming (daily; 2hr 30min); Nanjing (2 daily; 2hr); Ningbo (daily; 2hr); Shanghai (10 daily; 2hr); Shengyang (4 weekly; 3hr 40min); Tianjin (daily; 3hr); Wuhan (daily; 1hr 40min); Xiamen (3 daily; 1hr); Xi'an (daily; 2hr 45min).

information on restaurants, bars, clubs, concerts and exhibitions, as does the less frequent *Where* magazine.

City transport

Hong Kong's public transport system is efficient, comfortable, extensive and cheap, although it can be extremely crowded in rush hours. The MTR system and the main bus routes are easy to use and most signs are in English as well as Chinese, although don't expect staff to speak much English. The same is true with the drivers of taxis and minibuses. It's a good idea to get someone to write down your destination (and where you've come from for the return) in Chinese characters. If you get stuck, the tourist maps also print the Chinese characters for the main tourist places.

Trains and trams

The **MTR** (Mass Transit Railway) is Hong Kong's **underground train system**, comprising four lines, which operate from 6am to 1am. The Island Line (marked blue on maps) runs along the north shore of Hong Kong Island, from Sheung Wan in the west to Chai Wan in the east, taking in important stops such as Central, Wanchai and Causeway Bay. The Tsuen Wan Line (red) runs from Central, under the harbour, through Tsimshatsui, and then northwest to the new town of Tsuen Wan. The Kwun Tong Line (green) connects with the Tsuen Wan Line at Mongkok in Kowloon, and then runs east in a circular direction, eventually coming back down south under the harbour to join the Island Line at Quarry Bay. Finally, the Tung Chung Line (yellow) follows much of the same route as the Airport Express, linking Central and Tung Chung. You can buy single-journey **tickets** (HK$4–11) from machines in the stations, or a rechargeable stored-value **Octopus Card** (☎2266 2266 for information) for travel on the MTR, KCR, LRT, the Airport Express and some ferries and buses. You pay a deposit of HK$50 to get the plastic card, then add value to it by feeding it and your money into machines in the MTR. Your fare is electronically deducted each time you use the ticket – just swipe it over the yellow sensor pad on the top of the entry barrier.

The **KCR** (Kowloon–Canton Railway) is Hong Kong's main **overground train line**, running from Kowloon station in East Tsimshatsui, north through the New Territories to the border with China at Lo Wu. Apart from the direct trains running through to Guangzhou, there are frequent local trains running between Kowloon and Lo Wu, though you are not allowed to travel beyond the penultimate station of Sheung Shui unless you have documentation for crossing into China. There is an interchange between the KCR and MTR at Kowloon Tong station. A third transport system, the **LRT** (Light Rail Transit) runs between towns in the western New Territories, though tourists rarely use it.

Trams are a great way to tour the north shore of Hong Kong Island (outside the crowded rush hour). They run between Kennedy Town in the west and Shau Kei Wan in the east, via Central, Wanchai and Causeway Bay (some going via Happy Valley). You board at the back, and drop the money in the driver's box (HK$2; no change given) when you get off.

Buses, minibuses and maxicabs

The single- and double-decker **buses** that run around town are not fast, but they're comfortable enough, and essential for many destinations, such as the south of Hong Kong Island and parts of the New Territories not served by trains. You pay as you board and exact change is required; the amount is often posted up on the timetables at bus stops. HKTA issues useful up-to-date information on bus routes, including the approximate length of journeys and cost. The **main bus terminal** in Central is at Exchange Square, a few minutes' walk west of the Star Ferry Terminal, though some buses also start from right outside the ferry terminal, or

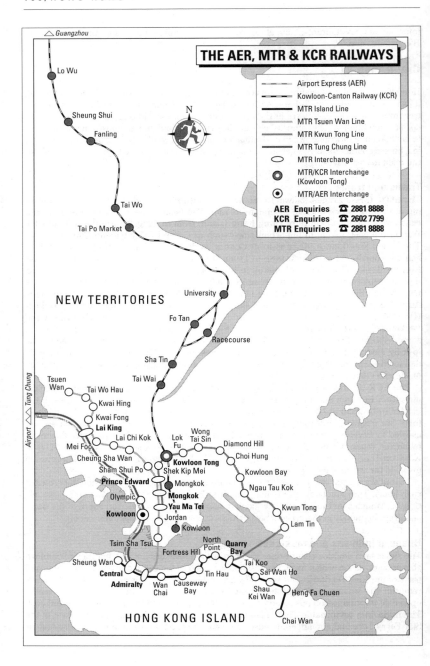

△ Guangzhou

THE AER, MTR & KCR RAILWAYS

Lo Wu

Sheung Shui

Fanling

N

Airport Express (AER)
Kowloon-Canton Railway (KCR)
MTR Island Line
MTR Tsuen Wan Line
MTR Kwun Tong Line
MTR Tung Chung Line
○ MTR Interchange
◎ MTR/KCR Interchange (Kowloon Tong)
⊙ MTR/AER Interchange

AER Enquiries ☎ 2881 8888
KCR Enquiries ☎ 2602 7799
MTR Enquiries ☎ 2881 8888

Tai Wo

Tai Po Market

NEW TERRITORIES

University

Fo Tan

Racecourse

Sha Tin

Tai Wai

Tsuen Wan

Tai Wo Hau

Kwai Hing

Kwai Fong

Lai King

Lai Chi Kok

Mei Foo

Cheung Sha Wan

Sham Shui Po

Prince Edward

Olympic

Kowloon

Wong Tai Sin

Lok Fu

Diamond Hill

Choi Hung

Kowloon Tong

Shek Kip Mei

Mongkok

Mongkok

Yau Ma Tei

Jordan

Kowloon

Tsim Sha Tsui

North Point

Quarry Bay

Fortress Hill

Sheung Wan

Central

Admiralty

Wan Chai

Causeway Bay

Tin Hau

Tai Koo

Sai Wan Ho

Shau Kei Wan

Heng Fa Chuen

Chai Wan

Kowloon Bay

Ngau Tau Kok

Kwun Tong

Lam Tin

Airport ◁◁ Tung Chung

HONG KONG ISLAND

A FEW IMPORTANT LOCAL BUS ROUTES	
From Central:	**From Tsimshatsui Star Ferry:**
#6 and #6A to Stanley via Repulse Bay	#8A and #5C to Hung Hom KCR station
#15 to the Peak	#1 and #1A to Mongkok
#70 to Aberdeen	#6A to Lei Cheng Uk Han Tomb Museum
#90 to Ocean Park	#1, #1A, #2, #6, #6A, #7 and #9 to Temple Street Night Market

from the Outlying Islands Piers, west of the Star Ferry. In Tsimshatsui, Kowloon, the main bus terminal is right in front of the Star Ferry Terminal.

Ubiquitous cream-coloured **minibuses** and **maxicabs** can be stopped almost anywhere on the street (not on double yellow lines), though these often have the destination written in Chinese only. They cost a little more than regular buses, and you usually pay the driver as you disembark; small amounts of change are given on the minibuses only (which have a red stripe, while the maxicabs have green ones). The drivers of any of these buses are unlikely to speak English.

Taxis

Taxis in Hong Kong are not expensive, though they can be hard to get hold of in rush hours. Note that there is a toll to be paid (around HK$20) on any trips through a tunnel, and drivers often double this – as they are allowed to do – on the grounds that they have to get back again. Many taxi drivers do not speak English, so be prepared to show the driver the name of your destination written down in Chinese. If you get stuck gesture to the driver to call the dispatch centre on the two-way radio; someone there will speak English.

Ferries

One of the most enjoyable things to do in Hong Kong is to ride the **Star Ferry** between Kowloon and Hong Kong Island. The views of the island are superb, particularly at dusk. You'll also get a feel for the frenetic pace of life on Hong Kong's waterways, with ferries, junks, hydrofoils and larger ships looming up from all directions. You can ride upper deck (HK$2.20) or lower deck (HK$1.70). Ferries run every few minutes between Tsimshatsui and Central (daily 6.30am–11.30pm; 8min), and between Tsimshatsui and Wanchai. There are also similarly cheap and fun ferry crossings between Hung Hom, Central and Wanchai. For ferries to the **outlying islands**, see p.175.

Accommodation

Hong Kong boasts a colossal range of **hotels and guesthouses**, particularly in the Tsimshatsui area of Kowloon, and it's always worth checking for good package deals in middle-market hotels before you arrive. At the lower end, most of the options are squeezed into one or two giant blocks on Nathan Road, principally *Chungking Mansions* and the slightly more salubrious *Mirador Mansions*. Even budget hotel accommodation is not that cheap, however – you'll be lucky to find a room for less than HK$200, and dorm beds cost HK$70–80 a night. Among the cheapest options are Hong Kong's seven official **youth hostels**, all of which offer very reasonable dormitory accommodation at around HK$35–65 if you've got an IYHF membership card, slightly more if you don't.

Kowloon

Most of the accommodation listed below is within fifteen minutes' walk of the Tsimshatsui Star Ferry Terminal – conveniently central, though very touristy.

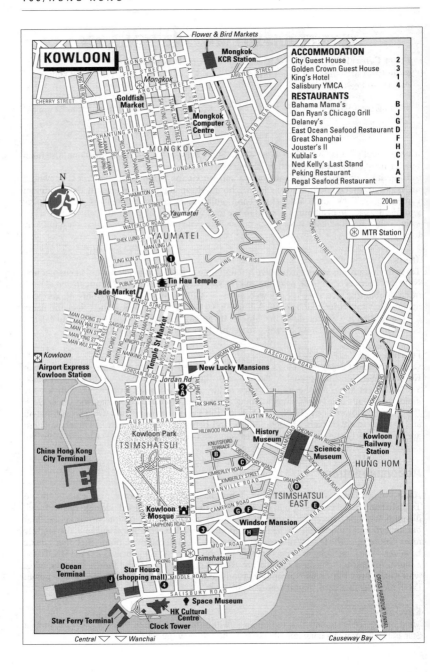

KOWLOON

△ Flower & Bird Markets

Mongkok
KCR Station

ACCOMMODATION
City Guest House — 2
Golden Crown Guest House — 3
King's Hotel — 1
Salisbury YMCA — 4
RESTAURANTS
Bahama Mama's — B
Dan Ryan's Chicago Grill — J
Delaney's — G
East Ocean Seafood Restaurant — D
Great Shanghai — F
Jouster's II — H
Kublai's — C
Ned Kelly's Last Stand — I
Peking Restaurant — A
Regal Seafood Restaurant — E

Mongkok

Goldfish
Market

Mongkok
Computer
Centre

MONGKOK

0 — 200m

⊗ MTR Station

Yaumatei

YAUMATEI

Tin Hau Temple

Jade Market

Temple St Market

Kowloon
Airport Express
Kowloon Station

New Lucky Mansions

Jordan Rd

China Hong Kong
City Terminal

Kowloon Park

TSIMSHATSUI

History
Museum

Science
Museum

Kowloon
Railway
Station

HUNG HOM

Kowloon
Mosque

Windsor Mansion

TSIMSHATSUI
EAST

Tsimshatsui

Ocean
Terminal

Star House
(shopping mall)

Space Museum

HK Cultural
Centre
Clock Tower

Star Ferry Terminal

CROSS HARBOUR TUNNEL

Central ▽ ▽ Wanchai

Causeway Bay ▽

City Guest House, 6th Floor, Cumberland House, 227 Nathan Rd (☎2730 0212). A wide variety of reasonably priced rooms, overseen by a friendly, helpful and chatty manager. ⑦.

Golden Crown Guest House, 5th Floor, Golden Crown Court, 66–70 Nathan Rd (☎2369 1782). A very friendly, clean, if rather cramped, place in one of the better Nathan Road blocks. Bathrooms are mostly communal. Dorms HK$50. ⑥.

King's Hotel, 473–475A Nathan Rd, Yaumatei (☎2780 1281). Immediately south of the Yaumatei MTR. Probably the cheapest "real" hotel in town. Ask for a room at the back, as the others can be noisy. Single and double rooms. ⑦.

Salisbury YMCA, 41 Salisbury Rd, Tsimshatsui (☎2369 2211). Great location with views over the harbour and Hong Kong Island. Facilities include pools and a fitness centre. Book early. Four-bed dorms with attached shower are also available, but cannot be reserved in advance. Open to both men and women. A ten-percent service charge is added to all room rates. Dorms HK$190. ⑨.

CHUNGKING MANSIONS

Occupying one of the prime sites towards the southern end of Nathan Road, **Chungking Mansions** looks fit for demolition. The arcades on the lowest two floors are a warren of tiny shops and restaurants, while the remaining sixteen floors are crammed with budget guesthouses. Above the second floor, the building is divided into five blocks, lettered A to E, each served by two tiny lifts, usually attended by long queues. Most of the guesthouses are pleasant and cheap, but the whole building is a fire and safety hazard.

Chungking House, 4th floor, A Block (☎2366 5362). The most upmarket place in the whole building, just like a proper hotel, with carpets, air-con, TV and even bathtubs. ⑦.

Fortunate Guesthouse, Flat 2, 11th Floor, A Block (☎2366 5900). Passable English spoken here, and the rooms are quite a decent size. Doubles, triples and quads available; the doubles have air-con and TV, but shared bathrooms. ⑥.

New Carlton Guesthouse, 15th Floor, B Block (☎2721 0720). Friendly, with good English spoken and clean rooms on offer. ⑤–⑥.

Payless Guesthouse, Flat 2, 7th Floor, A Block (☎2723 0148). Quite friendly, with English spoken. Has clean, tiny doubles with bath. ⑤.

Rhine Guest House, Block A, 11th & 13th Floors (☎2367 1991 or 2721 6863). Very friendly, family-run place, offering two singles and basic doubles with and without bath. ⑤.

Tom's Guesthouse, Flat 5, 8th Floor, A Block (☎2722 4956). Run by friendly management, the double and triple rooms here are reasonably bright and very good value. *Tom's* has another branch at Flat 1, 16th Floor, C Block (☎2722 6035), where the rooms are positively salubrious. ⑤ and ⑥ respectively.

Travellers' Hostel, 16th Floor, A Block (☎2368 7710). A time-worn, shabby retreat for backpackers with mixed six-bed dorms and some singles, with or without air-conditioning. Shared bathrooms. Dorms ③, rooms ⑤.

Welcome Guest House, Block A, 7th Floor (☎2721 7793). A recommended first choice, offering air-con doubles, with and without shower. Nice clean rooms, luggage storage, laundry service and China visas available. ⑥.

Yan Yan Guest House, Block E, 8th Floor (☎2366 8930). Helpful staff renting out doubles with all facilities; you could sleep three in some at a squeeze, making them pretty good value. ⑤–⑥.

MIRADOR MANSIONS

This is the big block at 54–64 Nathan Rd, on the east side, in between Carnarvon Road and Mody Road, right next to the Tsimshatsui MTR station. Dotted around in among the residential apartments are large numbers of guesthouses. The advantage of **Mirador** over the *Chungking Mansions* is that the stairwells and corridors are a lot cleaner and quieter, and there's no queue for lifts.

Garden Hostel, Flat F4, 3rd Floor (☎2311 1183). A scruffy but friendly travellers' hangout, with washing machines, lockers and even a patio garden. Mixed and women-only dorms; discounts for long stays. Dorms HK$60.

Kowloon Hotel, Flat F4, 13th Floor (☎2311 2523). Offers a range of immaculately clean singles and doubles. Discounts for long stays. ⑦.

Man Hing Lung, Flat F2, 14th Floor (☎2722 0678 or 2311 8807). Run by a helpful, friendly man with good English, this is a clean and recently refurbished place, offering both singles and doubles, although the rooms are very small. ⑥.

Mei Lam Guesthouse, Flat D1, 5th Floor (☎2721 5278). The helpful English-speaking owner has very presentable singles and doubles, all spick-and-span, with full facilities. Worth the higher-than-usual prices. ⑥.

Hong Kong Island

Accommodation on the island is nearly all upmarket, with just one budget option for walk-ins, though you may be able to get a good package deal in advance.

Garden View International House, 1 Macdonnell Rd, Central (☎2877 3737). This YWCA-run place is just off Garden Road, south of the Zoological and Botanical Gardens. Bus #12A from the Central Bus Terminal runs past. Very salubrious, and the cheapest place in this area of Central. ⑧–⑨.

Harbour View International House, 4 Harbour Rd, Wanchai (☎2802 0111). Very close to the Wanchai Ferry Terminal, and next door to the Arts Centre, this is an excellent place to stay, with good-value rooms starting at the bottom of this category. ⑨.

Mount Davis Youth Hostel (Ma Wui Hall), Mt Davis Path, Mt Davis (☎2817 5715). Perched on top of a mountain, this place has superb views over the harbour and is unbelievably peaceful. Conditions are excellent, though all guests have to do one small cleaning task daily. YHA members pay less. Unfortunately, getting here is a major expedition: take bus #47A from Admiralty, or minibus #54 from the Outlying Islands Ferry Terminal in Central and get off near the junction of Victoria Road and Mt Davis Path; walk back 100m from the bus stop and you'll see Mt Davis Path branching off up the hill – a long, hot forty-five-minute walk. Otherwise, get off the bus in Kennedy Town and catch a taxi (around HK$50 plus HK$5 per item of luggage). A hostel shuttle bus (HK$10) departs from the bus terminal next to the Shun Tak Centre at the Macau Ferry Terminal at 9.30am, 7pm, 9pm, 10.30pm; the return service leaves Ma Wui Hall at 7.30am, 9am, 10.30am, 8.30pm. Dorms HK$75, doubles/family rooms ⑤–⑥.

Noble Hostel, 7th Floor, Patterson Building, 37 Paterson St, Causeway Bay (☎2576 6148). A good place to stay, right in the middle of Causeway Bay. Immaculately clean and good-sized rooms, with air-con. Singles, doubles, triples and quads are available. ⑦.

The Wesley, 22 Hennessy Rd (☎2866 6688). A quiet and comfortable modern hotel, cheap for its location. ⑨.

The New Territories and outlying islands

These tranquil outer regions are a good place to stay if you want to escape the noise and bustle. The best time to visit is during the week, when rooms may be discounted by forty percent or more. At weekends, many will be booked solid, so advance planning is essential. Six of Hong Kong's seven official **youth hostels** are here, two on Lantau Island, and four in the New Territories. Don't imagine, however, that you can use them as a base for exploring the rest of Hong Kong – they are far too remote, and you are even advised to take your own food with you.

Babylon Villa Hotel, 29 Cheung Sha Lower Village, Lantau Island (☎2980 3145). With a pretty terrace overlooking Hong Kong's longest beach, this quiet hotel has only three rooms, but bags of character. Weekend rates include a three-course dinner, and there's a sixty percent discount during the week. ⑨.

Bradbury Lodge, Tai Mei Tuk, Tai Po, New Territories (☎2662 5123). Of all the hostels this is about the easiest to get to. Take the KCR train to Tai Po, then bus #75K to Tai Mei Tuk Terminal. Walk south a few minutes, with the sea on your right. Lots of boating, walking and cycling opportunities right by the scenic Plover Cove Reservoir. Dorms HK$75.

Concerto Inn, Hung Shing Ye Beach, Lamma Island (☎2982 1668). Lamma's best hotel – all rooms have a TV and fridge, some have a small kitchen, too. ⑦.

Lamma Vacation House, 29 Main St, Yung Shue Wan, Lamma Island (☎2982 0427). A few minutes' walk from the ferry pier, its small rooms offering a very cheap way of staying on the island. ④–⑤.

Man Lai Wah Hotel, Yung Shue Wan, Lamma Island (☎2982 0220 or 2982 0600). Right in front of the pier where ferries from Hong Kong dock. Has pleasant doubles with private baths. ⑦.

Mui Wo Inn, Silvermine Bay, Mui Wo, Lantau Island (☎2984 8597). A few minutes' walk from the Mui Wo ferry pier. It's a small place with a range of rooms, some with seafront views and balconies. ⑦.

Pak Sha O Hostel, Pak Sha O, Hoi Ha Road, Sai Kung, New Territories (☎2328 2327). Take bus #94 from Sai Kung (see p.174). Get off at Ko Tong, walk 100m farther on and take Hoi Ha Road on the left – from here it's a forty-minute walk. Close to Hong Kong's cleanest, most secluded beaches. Dorms HK$55.

S G Davis Hostel, Ngong Ping, Lantau Island (☎2985 5610). From Mui Wo (see p.177) take bus #2 to the Ngong Ping Terminal and follow the paved footpath south, away from the Tian Tan Buddha and past the public toilets (10min). A great base for hill-walking on Lantau, and you can eat at the nearby Po Lin Monastery. It's cold on winter nights, though – bring a sleeping bag. Dorms HK$55.

Hong Kong Island

As the oldest colonized part of Hong Kong, its administrative and business centre, and site of some of the most expensive real estate in the world, **Hong Kong Island** is naturally the heart of the whole territory. Despite its tiny size, just 15km from east to west and 11km from north to south at the widest points, and the phenomenal density of development on its northern shore, the island offers a surprising range of mountain walks and attractive beaches, as well as all the attractions of a great city.

Central

On the northern shore of Hong Kong Island, overlooking Victoria Harbour and Kowloon on the mainland opposite, lies the territory's major financial and commercial quarter, known as **Central**. The area takes in the core of the old city, which was originally called Victoria, after the Queen, and in the last two decades has sprouted several of Asia's tallest and most interesting skyscrapers. It extends out from the Star Ferry Terminal a few hundred metres in all directions, east to the Admiralty MTR, west to the Central Market and south, up the hill, to the Zoological and Botanical Gardens.

Inland from the shore, the main west–east roads are Connaught Road, Des Voeux Road and Queen's Road respectively, though pedestrians are better off concentrating on the extensive system of **elevated walkways**. To get to this system from the Star Ferry Terminal, climb the stairs to the west (right as you come out). Before reaching the entrance to the International Finance Centre (on the ground floor of which is the Airport Express Station), you take the walkway to the left and follow it inland, you'll pass right between Jardine House (the tall building full of portholes) on your left and **Exchange Square** on your right; the three gloriously opulent marble-and-tinted-glass towers here house the Hong Kong Stock Exchange. The Exchange Square bus station is located underneath the square. A further branch of the elevated walkway runs northwest from here, parallel with the shore and along the northern edge of Connaught Road, past Exchange Square and all the way to the Macau Ferry Terminal and Sheung Wan MTR; follow this for some great views over the harbour. Otherwise, continue across Connaught Road into the heart of an extremely upmarket shopping area, around Des Voeux Road.

Easily recognizable from the tramlines that run up and down here, **Des Voeux Road** used to mark Hong Kong's seafront before the days of reclamation, hence the name of the smartest shopping mall in the area, the **Landmark**, on the corner with Pedder Street. Of all the shops around here, one definitely worth a visit is **Shanghai Tang**, across Pedder Street from the Landmark, selling kitschy communist memorabilia and superb designer garments influenced by traditional Chinese wear.

The stretch of Des Voeux Road running west from the Landmark is connected by a series of lanes running south to the parallel Queen's Road. Two of these, Li Yuen Street East and Li Yuen Street West, are **markets**, packed out with clothes and fabric stalls. About 300m from the Landmark, you'll reach the **Central Market** – worth dropping in on in the morning (if you're not squeamish) to see poultry, fish and meat being hacked about on a huge scale. Just southwest of Central Market, leading uphill from Queen's Road Central, is **Graham Street**, one of the great fruit-and-vegetable markets which still manage to survive in downtown Hong Kong. Also leading uphill from Queen's Road, immediately south of Central Market, is the fantastic **Mid-Levels Escalator Link**, basically a giant series of escalators which runs 800m straight up the hill as far as Conduit Road, servicing the expensive **Mid-Levels** residential area, as well as the blossoming restaurant district of **SoHo** (short for south of Hollywood Road). During the morning rush hour (6am–10am), when people are setting out to work, the escalators run downwards only; from 10.20am to midnight they run up, offering a convenient way to explore some of Central's most interesting and historic streets.

In the opposite direction from the Landmark, east along Des Voeux Road, you'll find Statue Square on your left towards the shore, and, immediately south, the magnificently hi-tech

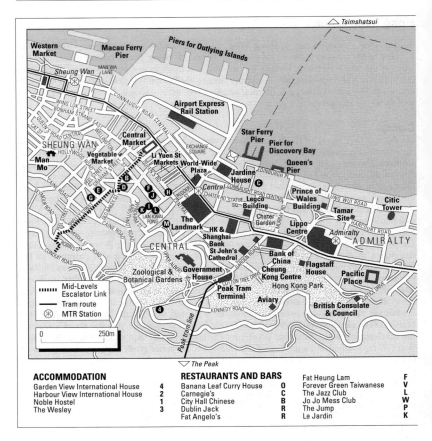

Hong Kong Bank and Shanghai Bank building, designed by Norman Foster. At the time of its construction it was reputedly one the most expensive buildings ever. The whole building is supported on giant pillars, and it's possible to walk right under the bank and come out on the other side – a necessity stipulated by the old feng shui belief that the centre of power on the island, Government House, which lies directly to the north of the bank, should be accessible in a straight line by foot from the main point of arrival on the island, the Star Ferry. From under the bank the building's insides are transparent, and you can look up, through the colossal glass atrium, into the heart of the building.

A couple of hundred metres east of the Hong Kong and Shanghai Bank, is the three-hundred-metre-high blue glass **Bank of China**, designed by a team led by the internationally renowned architect I M Pei, who was also responsible for the National Gallery of Art in Washington, DC, and the pyramid in the forecourt of the Louvre in Paris. Although under instructions from Beijing, the designers of this bank had no hesitation in by-passing all the normal feng shui sensitivities, and this knife-like structure is accordingly feared and disliked in Hong Kong. In between these two architectural landmarks is the equally tall **Cheung**

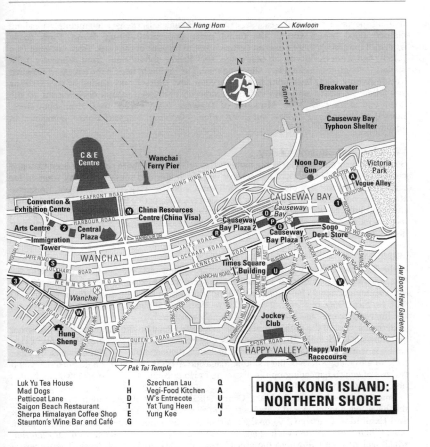

Luk Yu Tea House   I   Szechuan Lau   Q
Mad Dogs   H   Vegi-Food Kitchen   A
Petticoat Lane   D   W's Entrecote   U
Saigon Beach Restaurant   T   Yat Tung Heen   N
Sherpa Himalayan Coffee Shop   E   Yung Kee   J
Staunton's Wine Bar and Café   G

**HONG KONG ISLAND:
NORTHERN SHORE**

Kong Centre. Its undistinguished design – compared to its two neighbours – has led it to be known locally as "the box the Bank of China came in".

SOUTH OF QUEEN'S ROAD
South of Queen's Road the land begins to slope seriously upwards, and walking can become extremely laborious in hot weather. Head south up D'Aguilar Street (just west of Pedder Street) from Queen's Road, and you'll enter the **Lan Kwai Fong** area, the main focus for eating and, particularly, drinking in Central. One of the most interesting places here for visitors is the **Luk Yu Tea House** on Stanley Street, a delightfully traditional Chinese tea house (see p.178). Just above (south) Lan Kwai Fong is Hollywood Road, the centre of Hong Kong's antique and curio trade. Follow the road west to where the escalator crosses it, and you'll find yourself on the edge of the SoHo restaurant area.

In a general southerly direction from Lan Kwai Fong – a short but steep walk along Glenealy Street and under the flyover – are the **Hong Kong Zoological and Botanical Gardens** (daily 6am–7pm; free), originally opened in 1864 and still a pleasant refuge, though nothing spectacular. From the eastern exit of the Botanical Gardens, a ten-minute walk along Garden Road brings you to the rather more impressive **Hong Kong Park** (daily 6.30am–11pm; free); there's also an entrance just to the east of the Peak Tram terminal (see p.168), and from the north, on Supreme Court Road – follow signs from Admiralty MTR station, through the Pacific Place shopping mall. The highlight here is the excellent **Edward Youde Aviary** (daily 9am–5pm; free), where you find yourself surrounded by rare birds as you follow the raised walkways inside the superbly re-created natural environment. At the north end of the park is the **Museum of Teaware** (daily except Wed, 10am–5pm; free), housed in Hong Kong's oldest surviving colonial building, Flagstaff House, completed in 1846.

Wanchai and Causeway Bay

Stretching away east of Central, the built-up area on the north shore runs for at least 6km and comprises a number of localized centres, of which the two most visited by tourists for nightlife, dining and shopping are **Wanchai** and **Causeway Bay**. The main street, Hennessy Road, is a continuation of Queensway from Central, and carries the tramlines right through the whole area. MTR trains and trams connect Central with both Wanchai and Causeway Bay, as do numerous buses, including #2 and #11. Wanchai is additionally accessible by ferry from Tsimshatsui.

WANCHAI

In the 1950s and 1960s, **Wanchai** was known throughout east Asia as a thriving red-light district, catering in particular for US soldiers on leave from Korea and Vietnam. Hong Kong's most famous fictional character, Suzy Wong, a prostitute from Richard Mason's novel *The World of Suzy Wong*, resided and worked here. Wanchai has since lost most of its raunchy air, but the **restaurants** and **bars** are still certainly worth a visit.

In the far west of the area, just north of Gloucester Road on the corner of Fenwick Street and Harbour Road, is the **Hong Kong Arts Centre** (ten minutes' walk from Wanchai MTR), which is worth dropping in on for its art galleries, films and other cultural events. You can pick up a free copy here of the monthly magazine *Artslink*, which has a detailed diary and reviews of what's happening on the art scene in Hong Kong. There are also two good cafés here, both with harbour views.

Immediately to the east of the Arts Centre stands a vast set of gleaming modern buildings that have changed the face of Wanchai beyond all recognition. The **Hong Kong Convention and Exhibition Centre** (CEC) on the seafront is probably the biggest and best of its kind in Asia. When there are no events going on, you can visit the centre's extraordinary interior, which includes the hall where the official handover ceremonies took place. There's also a cybercafé in the foyer. You can reach the CEC by following raised walkways from Wanchai MTR station, or from the ferry terminal immediately in front.

On Queen's Road East, south of the tramlines on Johnston Road, is the little **Hung Sheng Temple**, built into the hillside. This old brick building, smoke-blackened and hung with ancient draperies, was once a shrine by the sea; now, rather sadly, it has been marooned far inland by reclamation. There's a tiny flower and bird market opposite the temple, on Tai Wong Street West. A short walk east on Stone Nullah Lane is the **Pak Tai Temple**, where you can see craftsmen making fantastic burial offerings out of bamboo and coloured paper, including cars, houses and aeroplanes.

CAUSEWAY BAY

Causeway Bay is a colourful district packed with shops and restaurants centred between the eastern end of Lockhart Road and the western edge of Victoria Park. Trams run just to the south of here along Yee Wo Street, a continuation of Hennessy Road from Wanchai. Causeway Bay has an MTR station and is also the point of arrival of the original **cross-harbour tunnel** which carries vehicle traffic over from Kowloon.

The main activity in Causeway Bay is shopping. Within a few of minutes of the MTR station you'll find a couple of ultra-modern Japanese department stores, while slightly to the north is **Vogue Alley**, a covered mall running north–south, parallel to Paterson Street. As the name suggests, it comprises fashion boutiques, as well as some restaurants and bars. On the shore, in front of the *Excelsior Hotel* on Gloucester Road, stands the **Noon Day Gun** – immortalized in Noel Coward's song *Mad Dogs and Englishmen* – which is fired every day at noon. The eastern part of Causeway Bay is dominated by **Victoria Park**, which contains a swimming pool and other sports facilities. In recent years, this has become the location for the annual candle-lit vigil held on June 4 to commemorate the victims of Tian'anmen Square.

One last sight in the hills to the south of Causeway Bay is the **Aw Boon Haw Gardens**, otherwise known as the Tiger Balm Gardens (daily 9.30am–4pm; free). This bizarre land-scaped garden was built in the 1930s by a Hong Kong millionaire, Mr Aw Boon Haw, who had made his fortune out of **Tiger Balm**, a pain-killing ointment still widely available and sold in tiny red tins. Weirdly painted rockeries, statues of animals in suits, caves, a pagoda and, above all, a statue of Mr Aw Boon Haw himself make up a genuinely Chinese theme park, but the gardens have recently been sold to a major property developer and are unlikely to survive. Bus #11 from Central or from Yee Wo Road in Causeway Bay passes the park.

HAPPY VALLEY

The low-lying area extending inland from the shore south of Wanchai and Causeway Bay and known as Happy Valley means only one thing for the people of Hong Kong: horse-racing, or more precisely, gambling. The **Happy Valley Racecourse**, which dates back to 1846, was for most of Hong Kong's history the only one in the territory, until a second course was built at Shatin in the New Territories. Hong Kong is gripped by serious gambling fever during the racing season, which runs from September until June, with meetings once or twice a week at Happy Valley. Entrance to the public enclosure is just HK$10. There's a racing museum (Tues–Sun 10am–5pm, race days 10am–12.30pm; free), and HKTA (see p.144) runs a "Come Horse-racing Tour" (HK$490), which includes transport to and from the track, entry to the Members' Enclosure and a buffet meal at the official Jockey Club – plus tips on how to pick a winner. Happy Valley can be reached from Central or Causeway Bay on a spur of the tram-line, or on bus #1 from Central.

Western District

West of Central lies a district rather older and more traditional in character than other parts of Hong Kong. An almost entirely Chinese-inhabited area, its crowded residential streets and traditional shops form a characterful contrast to Central, though the atmosphere has been somewhat diluted by the building of the road network for the **Western Harbour Crossing**, the third cross-harbour road tunnel from Kowloon.

Sheung Wan, immediately adjacent to Central, spreads south up the hill from the seafront at the modern Shun Tak Centre, which houses the Macau Ferry Terminal and the Sheung Wan MTR station, the last stop on this line. The Shun Tak Centre is a pleasant fifteen-minute walk along the elevated walkway from Exchange Square in Central, though you'll get more flavour of the district by following the tramlines along Des Voeux Road, west from Central Market. A number of interesting lanes extend south from this stretch of Des Voeux Road, such as Man Wa Lane, very near the Sheung Wan MTR, where **Chinese character chops** (name stamps) are carved from stone or wood. Another couple of minutes along Des Voeux Road from here brings you to the back end of **Western Market** (daily 10am–7pm), a brick Edwardian building, where you'll find shops selling fabric and kitsch, plus a couple of cafés.

A short walk south, up the hill from the harbour, is **Bonham Strand**, which specializes in Chinese medicinal products, teas and herbs. This is a fascinating area for poking around, with shop windows displaying snakes (alive and dead), snake-bile wine, birds' nests, shark fins, antlers and crushed pearls, as well as large quantities of expensive ginseng root. You'll find medicinal shops scattered along an east–west line extending from Bonham Strand to the small **Ko Shing Street** – the heart of the trade – which is adjacent to, and just south of, Des Voeux Road West. This section of Des Voeux Road specializes in every kind of dried food, including sea slugs, starfish, shark fins, snakes and flattened ducks.

A short but stiff walk uphill from Bonham Strand leads to **Hollywood Road**, running west from Wyndham Street in Central (immediately south of Lan Kwai Fong; see p.165) as far as the small Hollywood Park in Sheung Wan, where it runs into Queen's Road West. Bus #26 takes a circular route from Des Voeux Road in Central to the western end of Hollywood Road, then east again along the whole length of the road. The big interest here is the array of **antique and curio shops**, and you can pick up all sorts of oddities, from tiny embroidered women's shoes to full-size traditional coffins. The antique shops extend into the small alley, Upper Lascar Row, commonly known as **Cat Street**, which is immediately north of the western end of Hollywood Road and due south of the Sheung Wan MTR. Here you'll find wall-to-wall curiosity stalls with coins, ornaments, jewellery and chops all on sale. If you want to buy, healthy scepticism and hard bargaining are useful tools.

Another attraction in the Cat Street area is **Ladder Street**, which runs north–south across Hollywood Road and is, almost literally, as steep as a ladder. This is a relic from the nineteenth century when a number of such stepped streets existed to help sedan-chair carriers get their loads up the steep hillsides. On Hollywood Road, adjacent to Ladder Street, the 150-year-old **Man Mo Temple** (daily 7am–5pm) is notable for its great hanging coils of incense suspended from the ceiling. The two figures on the main altar are the Taoist gods of Literature (Man) and the Martial Arts (Mo). Located as it is in a deeply traditional area, this is one of the most atmospheric small temples in Hong Kong.

The Peak

The uppermost levels of the 550-metre hill that towers over Central and Victoria Harbour have always been known as **the Peak**, and, in colonial days, the area was populated by upper-class expats. Meanwhile, most of the population lived down below, where the climate was hotter and less healthy. The story of the colonization of what was originally a barren, treeless rock is an extraordinary one. Before 1859, when the first path up to the Peak was carved out, it was barely possible to get up here at all, let alone put houses on it. And yet, within twenty years, a number of summer homes had been built, with everything – from human beings to building materials – carried laboriously up the hill by coolies. In 1888, the opening of a **funicular railway**, known as the Peak Tram, allowed speedy and regular connections to the harbour. By 1924, when the first road to the Peak was built, permanent homes had begun to appear on it. Aside from its exclusive residential area, the Peak is still a cool, peaceful retreat and a vantage point offering some extraordinary panoramic views over the city and harbour below.

Ascending the Peak is half the fun, assuming you plan to ride the **Peak Tram**, which climbs 373 vertical metres to the terminus in eight minutes. To find the Peak Tram terminal in Central, catch the free shuttle bus (daily 9am–7pm) from outside the Star Ferry Terminal or take bus #15C (HK$3). On foot it's on Garden Road a little way up the hill from St John's Cathedral. The Peak Tram itself (daily 7am–midnight; HK$20 single, HK$30 return) runs every ten to fifteen minutes, and you can also use the shuttle bus back to the Star Ferry afterwards. You can also catch **minibus** #1 or bus #15 to the Peak from City Hall car park and Exchange Square respectively.

ON AND AROUND THE PEAK

The Peak Tram drops you at the **Peak Tower**. This building and the **Peak Galleria** across the road are full of souvenir shops and pricey bars and restaurants, some with spectacular views. Just next door is the historic **Peak Café**, a traditional place with rattan chairs and a great outdoor terrace. From the Peak Tram terminal area, Mount Austin Road leads up to the very top of the Peak where you'll find the Victoria Peak Garden, formerly the site of the Governor's residence. But it's more interesting to follow Harlech Road, due west of the terminal area, for a delightful rural stroll through trees; after half an hour the road runs into Lugard Road, which heads back towards the terminal around the northern rim of the Peak, giving magnificent views over Central and Kowloon. The fourth road from the terminal area, Old Peak Road, leads down to the May Road tram station.

An excellent way to descend the Peak is to walk, the simplest route being to follow the sign pointing to Hatton Road, from opposite the picnic area on Harlech Road. The **walk** is along a very clear path all the way through trees, eventually emerging after about 45 minutes in Mid-Levels, near the junction between Kotewall Road and Conduit Road. Catch bus #13 or minibus #3 from Kotewall Road to Central, or you can walk east for about 1km along Conduit Road until you reach the top end of the Mid-Levels Escalator (see p.163), which will also take you into Central. Another good route down is to take a road leading from Peak Road, not far from the Peak Tram, signposted to **Pokfulam Reservoir**, a very pleasant spot in the hills. Beyond the reservoir, heading downhill, you'll eventually come out on Pokfulam Road, from where there are plenty of buses to Central, or south to Aberdeen.

Hong Kong Island: the southern and eastern shores

On its south side, Hong Kong Island straggles into the sea in a series of dangling peninsulas and inlets. The atmosphere is far quieter here than on the north shore, and the climate reputedly sunnier. You'll find not only separate towns such as **Aberdeen** and **Stanley** with a flavour of their own, but also beaches, such as that at **Repulse Bay**, and much farther east, at the remote little outpost of **Shek O**. Buses are plentiful to all destinations on the southern shore, and Aberdeen is linked to Central by a tunnel under the Peak. Nowhere is more than an hour from Central.

ABERDEEN

Aberdeen is the largest separate town on Hong Kong Island, with a population of more than sixty thousand, a dwindling minority of whom still live on **sampans and junks** in the narrow harbour that lies between the main island and the offshore island of Ap Lei Chau. The boat people who live here are following a tradition that certainly preceded the arrival of the British in Hong Kong, though, sadly, it now seems that their ancient way of life is facing extinction. In the meantime, a time-honoured and enjoyable tourist activity in Aberdeen is to take a **sampan tour** around the harbour. From the bus stop just head towards the ornamental park by the waterfront until you reach a sign advertising "Water Tours" (HK$50 per head for a thirty-minute ride). The trip offers great photo opportunities of the old houseboats jammed together, complete with dogs, drying laundry and outdoor kitchens. Along the way you'll also pass boat yards and the floating restaurants, which are especially spectacular when lit up at night. To reach Aberdeen, catch **bus** #7 or #70 from Central, or #72 from Causeway Bay (30min). There's also a **boat** connection between here and nearby Lamma Island (see p.175).

OCEAN PARK

Ocean Park, a gigantic theme and adventure park (daily 10am–6pm; HK$140, children HK$70 including all rides), covers an entire peninsula to the east of Aberdeen. You could easily spend the best part of a day here, though make sure you arrive early in summer to avoid queues. The latest attraction is a pair of Giant Pandas, An-An and Jia-Jia, for whom a special complex has been created, complete with fake slopes, bamboo groves and misting machines. Other highlights include one of the fastest and longest roller coasters in the world, a Water World fun park, an aquarium with sharks, dolphins and whales, and the Middle Kingdom, which aims to re-create five thousand years of Chinese history through architecture, crafts, theatre and opera. A special **bus** service, the #629 Citybus Tour, runs from Central and from Admiralty MTR to Ocean Park (daily every 15min 9am–6.30pm); the ticket includes the entrance fee. Otherwise, a number of regular services cover the route, including the #6 minibus (Mon–Sat) and buses #70, #75, #90, #97, #260, #262 and #590 from Central; #72, #92,

#96 and #592 from Causeway Bay, and #973 from Tsimshatsui. Get off immediately after the Aberdeen Tunnel and follow the signs. On Sundays, buses #90 from Central and #73 from Stanley/Repulse Bay stop right by the park.

REPULSE BAY AND BEYOND

Two bays with names ringing of adventure on the high seas, Deep Water Bay and **Repulse Bay**, the more popular of the two, line the coast east of Ocean Park. Unfortunately, the water in this area can be quite polluted, while on summer weekends the beaches are jam-packed with tens of thousands of people. Repulse Bay has a Tin Hau Temple (dedicated to the goddess of the sea), with a longevity bridge, the crossing of which is said to add three days to your life. South of Repulse Bay, you'll find the more secluded but narrower beaches of **Middle Bay** and **South Bay**, fifteen and thirty minutes' walk respectively farther along the coast. You can reach Repulse Bay on **buses** #6, #61 or #260 from Central. Between Aberdeen (to the west) and Stanley (to the east) there are frequent buses that pass all of the bays mentioned above.

STANLEY

Straddling the neck of Hong Kong's southernmost peninsula, **Stanley** is a moderately attractive, tiny residential village, of which perhaps the main draw is the number of pubs and restaurants catering to expatriates. A little way to the north of the bus stop is **Stanley Beach**. Walk downhill from the bus stop and you'll soon find **Stanley Market** (selling a mish-mash of cheap clothes and tourist souvenirs). To the west, on Stanley Main Road, there are some great seafront restaurants and bars. If you continue walking beyond the restaurants, you'll come to another **Tin Hau Temple**, built in 1767, on the western side of the peninsula. Inside, there is a large tiger skin, the remains of an animal shot near here in 1942 – a poignant symbol of how the area has changed. Stanley is accessible on **buses** #6 and #260 from Central, or #73 from Aberdeen or Repulse Bay.

SHEK O

In the far east of the island, **Shek O** is Hong Kong's most remote settlement and still has an "undiscovered" feel about it, if such a thing is possible in Hong Kong. There's a strong surf beating on the wide, white **beach** and, during the week, it's more or less deserted. Come for sunbathing and lunch at one of the cheap local restaurants. The beach is just a few minutes' walk east from the bus stop, beyond a small roundabout. For a small detour through the village, however, stop at the excellent Thai restaurant with outdoor tables that you see on your left just before the roundabout. If you take the small lane left running right through the restaurant area, you'll pass first the local temple and then a variety of shops and stalls.

Reaching Shek O in the first place is one of the best things about it. First you need to get to **Shau Kei Wan** on the northeastern shore of Hong Kong Island, either by tram or MTR. From the bus terminal outside the MTR station, catch bus #9 to Shek O, a great journey over hills (30min) during which you'll be able to spot first the sparkling waters of the Tai Tam Reservoir, then Stanley (far to the southwest) and finally Shek O itself, appearing down below like a Mediterranean village on the shore.

Kowloon

A four-kilometre strip of the mainland grabbed by the British in 1860 to add to their offshore island, **Kowloon** was part of the territory ceded to Britain "in perpetuity" and was accordingly developed with gusto and confidence. With the help of land reclamation and the diminishing significance of the border between Kowloon and the New Territories at Boundary Street, Kowloon has over the years just about managed to accommodate the vast numbers of people who have squeezed into it. Today, areas such as Mongkok, jammed with soaring tenements, are among the most densely populated urban areas in the world.

While Hong Kong Island has mountains and beaches to palliate the effects of urban claustrophobia, Kowloon has just more shops, more restaurants and more hotels. It's hard to imagine that such a relentlessly built-up, crowded and commercial place as this could possibly have any cachet among the travelling public – and yet it does. The **view** across the harbour to Hong Kong Island, wall-to-wall with skyscrapers, is one of the most unforgettable city panoramas you'll see anywhere, especially at night.

Tsimshatsui and beyond

The tourist heart of Hong Kong, **Tsimshatsui**, is an easy place to find your way around. The **Star Ferry Terminal**, for ferries to Hong Kong Island, is right on the southwestern tip of the peninsula. East of here, along the southern shore, facing Hong Kong Island, are a number of hi-tech, modern museums and galleries built on reclaimed land, while **Salisbury Road**, just to the north, is dominated by the magnificently traditional *Peninsula Hotel*. Running south to north right through the middle of Tsimshatsui, and on through the rest of Kowloon, is Hong Kong's most famous street, **Nathan Road**, jammed with shoppers at all hours of the day and night.

The distinctive ski-slope roofline of the **Hong Kong Cultural Centre**, which occupies the former site of the Kowloon Railway Station, about 100m east of the Star Ferry Terminal, is unmissable. Inside there are concert halls, theatres and galleries, including, in an adjacent wing, the **Museum of Art** (Mon–Wed, Fri & Sat 10am–6pm, Sun 1–6pm; HK$10), which is definitely worth a visit. As well as calligraphy, scrolls and an intriguing selection of paintings covering the history of Hong Kong, the museum has a good Chinese antiquities section. Immediately to the east, the domed **Hong Kong Space Museum** (Mon & Wed–Fri 1–9pm, Sat & Sun 10am–9pm; HK$10) houses some highly user-friendly exhibition halls on astronomy and space exploration. The highlight here, however, is the planetarium, known as the **Space Theatre**, which presents amazing wide-screen space shows for an additional fee (HK$32, concessions HK$16; call ☎2721 0226 for show times).

Immediately east of the *Peninsula Hotel*, running north from Salisbury Road, neon-lit **Nathan Road** dominates the commercial heart of Kowloon and boasts Hong Kong's most concentrated collection of electronics shops, tailors, jewellery stores and fashion boutiques. The variety of goods on offer is staggering, but the southern section of Nathan Road, known as the Golden Mile for its commercial potential, is by no means a cheap place to shop these days, and tourist rip-offs are all too common. One of the least salubrious, but most exotic, corners of Nathan Road is the gigantic **Chungking Mansions**, 200m north of the junction with Salisbury Road. The shopping arcades here on the two lowest floors are a steaming jungle of ethnic shops, curry houses and dark corners, which seem to stretch away into the impenetrable heart of the building, making an interesting contrast with the antiseptic air-conditioned shopping malls that fill the rest of Hong Kong. The upstairs floors are packed with guesthouses (see p.161) – the mainstay of Hong Kong's backpacker accommodation.

A few hundred metres north of Chungking Mansions, **Kowloon Park** (daily 6am–midnight) is marked at its southeastern corner by the white-domed Kowloon Mosque (not open to tourists). There's also an indoor and outdoor swimming-pool complex in the park, with Olympic-size facilities (daily 6.30am–9.30pm; ☎2724 3577).

Yaumatei and Mongkok

In some ways, the part of Kowloon north of the tourist ghetto of Tsimshatsui is more rewarding to walk around, with more authentic Chinese neighbourhoods and interesting markets. **Yaumatei** is jammed with high-rise tenements and busy streets and begins north of Jordan Road, with most of the interest lying in the streets to the west of Nathan Road. You can walk here from Tsimshatsui in about twenty minutes, otherwise take the MTR.

Temple Street, running north off Jordan Road, a couple of blocks west of Nathan Road, becomes a fun-packed **night market** after around 7pm every day, although the market actually opens in the early afternoon. As well as buying cheap clothing, watches and souvenirs, you can get your fortune told here, eat some great seafood from street stalls, and sometimes listen in on impromptu performances of Chinese opera. Just to the north of here is the local **Tin Hau Temple**, off Nathan Road, tucked away between Public Square Street and Market Street, a couple of minutes' walk south of Jordan MTR. Surrounded by urban hubbub, this old little temple, devoted to the sea, sits in a small concreted park, usually teeming with old men playing mahjong under the banyan trees. A couple of minutes' walk east of the Tin Hau Temple, just under the Gascoigne Road flyover, the **Jade Market** (daily 10am–3.30pm) has hundreds of stalls in two different sections offering an amazing variety of items from trinkets to family heirlooms in jade, crystal and quartz.

To the east of Nathan Road, at the corner of Nelson Street and Fa Yuen Street, is a specialist market of a rather different flavour, the **Mongkok Computer Centre**, where some incredible bargain software can be picked up, though, as much of this is pirated and, strictly speaking, illegal, you should exercise caution when importing such material into your own country. Around the corner, the electronics shops on Sai Yeung Choi Street are also worth checking out. A few hundred metres north of here in the direction of Prince Edward MTR, are three delightful markets. The Goldfish Market (daily 10am–6pm) is on Tung Choi Street, and just to the north of Prince Edward Road are the **Flower Market** (daily from 7am), in Flower Market Road, and the **Bird Market** (daily 7am–8pm), at the eastern end of the same street, where it meets the KCR flyover. The flower market is at its best on Sundays and in the run-up to Chinese New Year, when many people come to buy narcissi, orange trees and plum blossom to decorate their apartments with in order to bring good luck. The bird market is set in a Chinese-style garden, with trees, seats and elegant carved marble panels. As well as the hundreds of birds on sale here, along with their intricately designed bamboo cages, there are live crickets – food for the birds. Many local men bring their own songbirds here for an airing, and the place gives a real glimpse into a traditional area of Chinese life which is spiritually a thousand miles from Tsimshatsui.

Outer Kowloon

Head a few hundred metres north of Mongkok and you reach **Boundary Street**, which marks the border between Kowloon and the New Territories – though these days this distinction is pretty meaningless. By far the busiest tourist attraction in this area is well to the northeast at **Wong Tai Sin Temple** (daily 7am–5.30pm; small donation expected), a huge, thriving place packed with more worshippers than any other temple in Hong Kong. Big, bright and colourful, it's interesting for a glimpse into the practices of modern, popular Chinese religion: vigorous kneeling, incense-burning and the noisy rattling of fortune-telling sticks in canisters, as well as the presentation of food and drink to the Taoist deities. Large numbers of fortune-tellers, some of whom speak English, have stands to the right of the entrance and charge around HK$200 for palm-reading, about half that for a face-reading. The temple can be reached directly from the Wong Tai Sin MTR station.

Northwest from Mongkok, in the opposite direction from Wong Tai Sin, are a couple of places worth a visit. The **Lei Cheng Uk Branch Museum** (Mon–Wed, Fri & Sat 10am–1pm & 2–6pm, Sun 1–6pm; free), part of the main Museum of History, has been constructed over a two-thousand-year-old Han-dynasty tomb which was unearthed by workmen in 1955. By far the oldest structure discovered in Hong Kong, the tomb offers some rare proof of the ancient presence of the Chinese in the area. What is really interesting, however, is to compare photos of the site from the 1950s (paddy fields and green hills) with the high-rises that surround the area today. You can reach the museum from Chang Shan Wan MTR; take exit A2, walk for five minutes along Tonkin Street and the museum is on your left.

The New Territories

Comprising some 750 square kilometres of land abutting the southern part of China's Guangdong Province, **the New Territories** include some of the most scenic and traditionally Chinese areas of Hong Kong – complete with country roads, water buffalo, old villages, valleys and mountains – as well as booming New Towns. The highlights are the designated country parks, offering excellent **hiking trails** and secluded beaches. Frequent **buses** connect all towns in the New Territories, while the MTR reaches as far as Tsuen Wan and the KCR runs north through Shatin, the Chinese University and Tai Po. There are also a number of boats from Central, including the fast hoverferries that connect with Tuen Mun in only thirty minutes. Tuen Mun is the terminus of the LRT rail line that runs north to Yuen Long. By public transport, a satisfying do-it-yourself **tour** can be made in a few hours along the following route, starting from the Jordan Road bus terminus in Kowloon (accessible by bus #8 from Tsimshatsui): take bus #60X to Tuen Mun bus terminal, then from here ride the LRT north to its terminus at Yuen Long. From Yuen Long, take bus #76K to Sheung Shui KCR station in the north. Finally ride the KCR train south back to Kowloon. If you are coming from Hong Kong Island you can take the #960 or #961 from Des Voeux Road in Central directly to Tun Mun.

The west

Tsuen Wan in the west of the New Territories is one of Hong Kong's **New Towns** – a satellite town, built from scratch in the last 25 years, and easily reached by MTR or by hoverferries from Central. Virtually in the middle of Tsuen Wan is the **Sam Tung Uk Museum** (daily except Tues 9am–5pm; free), which is essentially a restored two-hundred-year-old walled village of a type typical of this part of southern China. The village was founded in 1786 by a Hakka clan named Chan, who continued to live here, incredibly, until the 1970s. Now, the houses have been restored with their original furnishings, and there are various exhibitions on aspects of the lives of the Hakka people. Follow signs out of Tsuen Wan MTR station – it's about a five-minute walk.

From the bus terminal opposite the Tsuen Wan MTR catch bus #51 north to Kam Tin. The ride is spectacular, running right past Hong Kong's highest peak, **Tai Mo Shan**, which at 957m is nearly twice the height of Victoria Peak. If you want to climb up to the top, there's a bus stop on a pass right under the peak – get off here and follow a signposted path up to the top. The excellent **MacLehose Trail** runs right through here, and this is as good a place as any to join it. Every autumn there is a charity race along the trail – the record time is 13 hours 18 minutes. For detailed information on the trail, which in all runs 100km across the New Territories from Tuen Mun in the west to the Sai Kung Peninsula in the east, contact the HKTA, who publish a guide for walkers, *Exploring Hong Kong's Countryside* (HK$80), or the Country and Marine Parks Branch on the 14th Floor, 393 Canton Rd, Tsimshatsui, Kowloon (Mon–Fri 9am–5pm, Sat 9am–noon; ☎2733 2211).

The small town of **Kam Tim** is famous in Hong Kong as the site of **Kat Hing Wai**, one of Hong Kong's last inhabited walled villages. Dating back to the late seventeenth century when a clan named Tang settled here, the village (HK$1 donation) still comprises thick six-metre-high walls and guard towers, although most traces of the moat have gone. Inside the walls, there's a wide lane running down the middle of the village, with tiny alleys leading off it. A few souvenir sellers pester visitors for more donations, but the atmosphere is very different from the rest of Hong Kong. The village is on your left, a few minutes' walk from the Kam Tin bus stop.

North: the KCR route

There is a whole series of possible outings to be made from the stops dotted along the **Kowloon–Canton Railway** as it wends its way north from Kowloon to the border with mainland China. The first important stop is at the booming New Town of **Shatin**, best known to Hong Kongers as the site of the territory's second racecourse, but also the location of the forty-year-old **Ten Thousand Buddhas Monastery** (daily 9am–5pm; free), which is probably the single most interesting temple in the whole of the New Territories, if not in all Hong Kong. To reach it from the KCR station, follow the signs saying "buses", and exit the station on the side facing the green hilly area – it's a few minutes' walk north along the road from here. Head towards the larger white-and-green complex of Chinese buildings, which house the **Po** (or Bo) **Fook Ancestral Worship Halls** (9am–5pm; free). Turn right just before the Halls entrance and the path will take you up the side of that complex – a stiff climb of around 400 steps – until you emerge on the terrace of the monastery. The "Ten Thousand Buddhas" – actually more like thirteen thousand – are stacked on shelves filling the inside walls of the main temple hall, surrounding the central Buddha. The terrace outside, which commands some great views, also contains a quite bizarre array of giant statues, including an elephant and a dragon. Overall, the mixture of jungle, panoramic views and colourful statuary makes this an excellent spot. From the monastery you can also follow a path farther up the mountain to another terrace containing some smaller temples, although recently this has been closed by landslides caused by monsoon rain.

The east

The eastern part of the New Territories, around **Clearwater Bay** and the **Sai Kung Peninsula**, is where you'll find the most secluded beaches and walks in Hong Kong, though at weekends they do begin to fill up. The starting point for buses into both areas is Choi Hung Hill MTR station.

CLEARWATER BAY

The forty-minute ride on bus #91 from Choi Hung MTR to Clearwater Bay already gives an idea of the delightful combination of green hills and sea that awaits you. Around the terminus at **Tai Au Mun**, overlooking Clearwater Bay, are a couple of excellent, clean **beaches**, and to the south is the start of a good three-to-four-hour walk around the bay. First, follow the road south along the cliff-top, as far as the Clearwater Bay Golf and Country Club car park, from where signposts lead you to the wonderfully located **Tin Hau Temple** in **Joss House Bay**. There is thought to have been a temple to the Taoist goddess of the sea here for more than eight hundred years, and although today's temple dates back only to its last major restoration in 1962, there is a venerable feel about the place. As one of Hong Kong's few Tin Hau temples actually still commanding the sea, it's of immense significance, and on the 23rd day of the third lunar month each year (Tin Hau's birthday) a colossal seaborne celebration takes place on fishing boats in the bay.

Heading back up the slope, you can take another path which starts from the same car park outside the Golf and Country Club down past **Sheung Lau Wan**, a small village on the western shore of the peninsula. The path skirts the village and continues on, forming a circular route around the headland back to the Clearwater Bay bus terminal.

SAI KUNG PENINSULA

Some way to the north of Clearwater Bay, the jagged Sai Kung Peninsula, with headlands, bluffs and tiny offshore islands, is one of the least developed areas in the whole of Hong Kong, and a haven for hikers and beach-lovers. The only sizeable town in the area, **Sai Kung Town**, accessible on minibus #1 from Choi Hung MTR, is the jumping-off point for explorations of Sai Kung.

Sai Kung's highlights are the **country parks** that cover the peninsula with virgin forest and grassland leading to perfect sandy beaches. Although it is possible to see something of these on a day-trip, the best way really to appreciate them is to bring a tent or consider staying at the youth hostel on Sai Kung. Access to the parks is by hourly bus #94 from Sai Kung Town and #96R (Sundays only) from Diamond Hill MTR to **Pak Tam Chung visitors' centre** (daily except Tues 9.30am–4.30pm; ☎2792 7365), which supplies hikers with maps and trail information. Of the many possible hikes, the MacLehose Trail, liberally dotted with campsites, heads east from here, circumventing the **High Island Reservoir** before heading west into the rest of the New Territories. If you want to follow the trail just part of the way, the **beaches** at Long Ke, south of the reservoir, and Tai Long, to the northeast, are Hong Kong's finest, though to walk out to them and back from Pak Tam Chung takes several hours. The last bus back from Pak Tam Chung is at 9pm.

The outlying islands

Officially part of the New Territories, the outlying islands of Hong Kong offer a delightful mix of seascape, old fishing villages and relative rural calm, almost entirely free of motor vehicles, except for the taxis and buses on Lantau Island. The islands are conveniently connected to Central by plentiful ferries and other boats. By comparison with other areas, development has been relatively restrained, although the opening of the new Chek Lap Kok airport and the development of the new Hong Kong Disneyland on the northern shore of the largest island, Lantau, means that this is likely to change. Although most tourists come on day-trips, there is some accommodation on the islands (see p.162).

Lamma

Lying just to the southwest of Aberdeen, **Lamma** is the closest island to Hong Kong Island, with a population of less than ten thousand, no cars, some nice green hills and sandy beaches, and lots of cheap, interesting restaurants. There are two possible crossing points, either by **ferry** from Central to Yung Shue Wan, or to Sok Kwu Wan from Central or from Aberdeen. By far the best way to appreciate the island is to take a boat to either Yung Shue Wan or Sok Kwu Wan, then walk to the other and catch the boat back from there.

Yung Shue Wan is a pretty little tree-shaded village, with one or two hotels and a cluster of small grocery stores, bars and eating places. There's a very relaxed feel to the place in the

---

FERRIES TO THE ISLANDS

The following is a selection of the most useful island ferry services. Schedules differ slightly on Saturdays and Sundays, when prices also rise:

To Cheung Chau
From Outlying Islands Ferry Piers – first boat out 6.15am, last boat back 11.45pm (at least hourly; 1hr).

To Sok Kwu Wan, Lamma Island
From Outlying Islands Ferry Piers – first boat out 7.20am, last boat back 11.40pm (11 daily; 50min).

To Yung Shue Wan, Lamma Island
From Outlying Islands Ferry Piers – first boat out 6.35am, last boat back around 11.30am (at least hourly; 40min).
From Aberdeen (via Pak Kok Tsuen)– first boat out 6.30am, last boat back 7.30pm (9 daily; 30min).

To Discovery Bay, Lantau Island
(hoverferries)

From Central (the pier just east of the Star Ferry) – 24-hour departures (at least every 30min between 6.50am and 12.30am; 25min).

To Mui Wo (Silvermine Bay), Lantau Island
From the Outlying Islands Ferry Piers – first boat out 6.10am, last boat back 11.30am (at least hourly; 30–50min). Some sailings go via Peng Chau.
From Peng Chau – first boat out 5.40am, last boat back 11.20am (approximately every 2hr 30min; 25min).

To Peng Chau
From the Outlying Islands Ferry Piers – first boat out 7am, last boat back 11.30am (approximately hourly; 50min).

evening, when people sit out under the banyan trees. To walk to Sok Kwu Wan from here (1hr), follow the easy-to-find cement path that branches away from the shore by the *Light House Pub*, shortly before the Tin Hau Temple. Make your way through the rather grotty apartment buildings on the outskirts of the village and you'll soon find yourself walking amid butterflies, long grass and trees. After about fifteen minutes you'll arrive at **Hung Shing Yeh Beach**, nicest in its northern half. The *Han Lok Yuen Restaurant* here is well known for its roast pigeon. On from the beach, the path climbs quite sharply up to a little summit, with a pavilion commanding views over the island. Thirty minutes' walk further on will take you to **Sok Kwu Wan**, which basically comprises a row of seafood restaurants with terraces built out over the water. The food and the atmosphere are good, and consequently the restaurants are often full of large parties. Some of the larger places also operate their own boat services for customers. Many people get the ferry over to Sok Kwu Wan in the evening for dinner, but, if you're not taking a restaurant service, make sure you don't miss the last scheduled boat back at 10.40pm, because there's nowhere to stay here – your only option would be to hire a sampan back to Aberdeen.

Cheung Chau

Another great little island where you can spend a couple of hours strolling around and then have dinner, **Cheung Chau** is just south of Lantau and an hour from Hong Kong by ferry. Despite its minuscule size of 2.5 square kilometres, Cheung Chau is nevertheless the most crowded of all the outer islands, with a population of some twenty thousand. Historically, the island is one of the oldest settled parts of Hong Kong, being notorious as a base for pirates who enjoyed waylaying the ships that ran between Guangzhou and the Portuguese enclave of Macau. Today, it still gives the impression of being an economically independent little unit, with the narrow strip between its two headlands jam-packed with tiny shops, markets and seafront restaurants. As well as romantic dinners and late-night ferry rides home, the island offers some nice **walks** around the old fishing ports and views of traditional junk building. It also has some interesting temples, the most important being the two-hundred-year-old **Pak Tai Temple**, a few hundred metres northwest of the ferry pier, along the interesting Pak She Street, lined with old herbalists and shops selling religious trinkets. Fishermen come to the temple to pray for protection, and beside the statue of Pak Tai, the god of the sea, is an ancient iron sword, discovered by fishermen and supposedly symbolizing good luck. For a few days in late April or early May the temple is the site of one of Hong Kong's liveliest and most spectacular festivals, the so-called **Tai Chiu (Bun) Festival**.

The main beach on the island, the scenic but crowded **Tung Wan Beach**, is due west of the ferry pier. Windsurfers are available for rent at the southern end of the beach from a centre run by the family of Hong Kong's Olympic medal-winning windsurf champion, Lee Lai Shan, who won a gold at the 1996 Atlanta games. If you catch a small sampan from the ferry pier across the bay to the small pier of **Sai Wan** – a five-minute ride – you can then follow marked trails to the nearby **Tin Hau Temple** and on to the **Cheung Po Tsai Cave**, supposedly used as a pirates' hide-out in the early nineteenth century. The walk back from the cave area to the main ferry pier is an attractive one that takes about an hour.

Lantau

With wild countryside, monasteries, old fishing villages and seriously secluded beaches, Lantau Island – twice the size of Hong Kong Island – offers the best quick escape from downtown Hong Kong; more than half the island is designated as a "country park". However, this tranquillity is unlikely to last, at least along the northern and northeastern shores, as Hong Kong's airport at Chek Lap Kok and its associated transport links are spawning a range of new commercial and residential developments, and the building work for the new Hong Kong Disneyland – scheduled to open in 2005 – gets underway.

Hopefully, the tranquillity of other parts of the island won't be fatally disturbed, and serious hikers might want to take advantage of the seventy-kilometre **Lantau Trail**, which links up the popular scenic spots on the island and is dotted along its length by campsites and youth hostels. The main point of arrival for visitors to Lantau Island is **Mui Wo**, otherwise known as **Silvermine Bay**, about one hour from Central. Some of the Mui Wo boats stop at the small island of Peng Chau en route. There are also a few ferries daily which connect Mui Wo with Cheung Chau. The other point of arrival is **Discovery Bay**, a residential development connected by frequent high-speed ferries from Central that run 24 hours a day. The Discovery Bay pier in Central is a few steps to the east of the Star Ferry Terminal.

FROM MUI WO TO DISCOVERY BAY

Mui Wo itself is not much to speak of, and having disembarked at the ferry pier, most people head straight for the bus station right outside. There are, however, some excellent walks that can be made directly from Mui Wo, one of which, the trail to Discovery Bay (2hr), is reasonably straightforward. Head northwest from the pier towards the attractive, curving, sandy bay you saw from the ferry. Continue around the bay until you reach a small river flowing down from the hills. Immediately after the river take the path that goes left. The path climbs up through virtual jungle, heading in a generally easterly direction for just over an hour, until you reach the **Trappist Monastery**. There's not much to see here apart from rushing streams, hills and trees, because most of the buildings are closed to the public, but it's a pleasant, cool spot. The monastery can also be reached by an infrequent boat service from nearby Peng Chau Island: the boat stops at the pier, about fifteen minutes' walk from the monastery, on the broad path that leads down the hill. If you want to go on from the monastery to **Discovery Bay** (known as "Disco Bay" to the locals), follow the same road down towards the pier, and a little way down on your left you'll see a flat-topped, derelict building; the path begins immediately opposite here. After about thirty minutes, walking north, with the sea on your right, you'll arrive at a beach, a shanty town and then Discovery Bay itself, which has a slightly Orwellian atmosphere, with condominiums, shopping malls and blonde families riding around in golf buggies. This is the main settlement on the island, largely inhabited by expatriate families. From Discovery Bay you can catch ferries back to Mui Wo, direct to Central, or to the airport and from there on to Tun Mun.

WESTERN LANTAU

The road west from Mui Wo passes along the southern shore, which is where Lantau's best beaches are located. **Cheung Sha Beach**, with a couple of cafés and a hotel, is the nicest, and buses #1, #2, #4 and #5 all pass by here.

Beyond the beaches, there are a couple of more interesting sights in the western part of the island that can also be reached by direct bus from Mui Wo. The first of these is the **Po Lin Monastery** (daily 10am–6pm; free), which is by far the largest temple in the whole territory of Hong Kong. Located high up on the Ngong Ping Plateau, this is not an ancient site; indeed, it was only established in 1927. Nevertheless, it is very much a living, breathing temple, and busloads of locals arrive here by the hour, in particular to pay their respects to the bronze **Tian Tan Buddha**, the largest seated bronze outdoor Buddha in the world, and to eat in the huge vegetarian **restaurant** (11.30am–5pm; meal tickets HK$60 for the "deluxe" meal, HK$25 for a "snack"; tickets from the office at the bottom of the steps to the Buddha). The Po Lin Monastery is often referred to in bus schedules as Ngong Ping and is reached by bus #2 from Mui Wo. It's a spectacular forty-minute ride through the hills. The last bus back to Mui Wo leaves at 7.20pm.

Right on the far northwestern shore of Lantau is the interesting little fishing village of **Tai O**. This remote place, constructed over salt flats and a tiny offshore island, has become a popular tourist spot (the government has plans for further development) particularly at weekends, but still retains much of its old character. There are some interesting local temples, wooden houses built partially on stilts, caged animals, and a big trade in dried fish. You can reach it by bus #41 from Mui Wo (last bus back 12.10am) and also by the relatively infrequent bus #21 from the Po Lin Monastery (last service at 3pm).

Eating

Menus in all but the cheapest restaurants should be in English as well as Chinese. The busiest, brightest restaurants of all are often those serving **dim sum** for breakfast or lunch (see pp.148–149, for an introduction to *dim sum*). The streets around D'Aguilar Street in Central, just a couple of minutes' walk south from the MTR, are particularly popular with young people and yuppie expatriates. Known as **Lan Kwai Fong**, after the small lane branching off D'Aguilar Street to the east, this area is choc-a-bloc with bars and restaurants. Five minutes' walk away is the newest restaurant area, known as **SoHo**, which, with its traditional streets and shophouses, has a less frenetic character. Generally, **prices** are comparable to those in the West: a full dinner without drinks is unlikely to cost less than HK$150 per head, although set-price lunches can offer a good-value alternative.

Central

Café Deco Bar & Grill, Level 1 & 2, Peak Galleria, 118 Peak Rd, The Peak (☎2849 5111). Superbly located, with unrivalled views and a stylish Art-Deco interior. The menu includes gourmet pizzas, curries, Thai noodles, grilled meats, as well as afternoon tea. Prices are not too high and they don't mind if you just go for a drink. Kitchen closes around 11.30pm.

City Hall Chinese Restaurant, 2nd Floor, City Hall Low Block (☎2521 1303). A short walk east of the Star Ferry Pier. Some of the best *dim sum* in Hong Kong, served in enormous crowded halls. Come for breakfast around 10am.

Fat Heung Lam, 94 Wellington St (☎2593 0404). A Cantonese-style vegetarian restaurant of excellent quality, where prices are reasonable.

Luk Yu Tea House, 24–26 Stanley St, just west of D'Aguilar St (☎2523 5464). A living museum with spittoons, sixty-year-old staff and authentically rude staff, this is possibly the most atmospheric restaurant in Hong Kong. Tea and *dim sum*, as well as full meals, are available, though the prices are tourist-inflated.

Peak Café, 121 Peak Rd (☎2849 7868). A long-standing local favourite, with traditional colonial-style fittings. South-facing views from the terrace are superb, and the food has an Asian–Indian slant; around HK$230 per head for a full meal.

Sherpa Himalayan Coffee Shop, 11 Staunton St, SoHo (☎2973 6886). Friendly restaurant with an interesting range of tasty dishes and beers to go with them. Food is good for veggies too. The *Nepal* opposite is under the same management.

Yung Kee, 32–40 Wellington St, on the corner with D'Aguilar St (☎2522 1624). An enormous place with bright lights, scurrying staff and seating for a thousand, this is one of Hong Kong's institutions. Roast meats (often served cold) are a speciality, and the *dim sum* is also good. Highly recommended.

Wanchai and Causeway Bay

Banana Leaf Curry House, 440 Jaffe Rd, Wanchai (☎2573 8187). One of a number of branches of this highly popular Malaysian–Singaporean restaurant, offering great mild curries full of cream and coconut.

Fat Angelo's, 414 Jaffe Rd (☎2574 6263). Homely Italian–American place serving vast portions of pasta and rich, sinful deserts. Popular and well priced.

Forever Green Taiwanese Restaurant, 93 Leighton Rd, Causeway Bay (☎2890 3448). Despite the OTT decor and traditionally dressed staff, there's more than just curiosity-value at this late-opening Taiwanese restaurant, with an interesting and comparatively cheap menu.

Jo Jo Mess Club, 1st Floor, 86–90 Johnston Rd, Wanchai (☎2527 3776). Entrance on Lee Tung St. Deservedly popular spot for tandoori dishes and street views. They also have a branch specializing in Tandoori at Shop D, G/F, Towning Mansions, 50–56 Paterson St, Causeway Bay (☎2894 9722).

Saigon Beach Restaurant, 66 Lockhart Rd, Wanchai (☎2529 7823). Good little restaurant that's a draw with young travellers and locals because it sticks to the basics and cooks them well.

Szechuan Lau, 466 Lockhart Rd, Causeway Bay (☎2891 9027). Some of the best szechuan food in Hong Kong, serving all the most famous dishes such as chilli prawns in cosy, old-style surroundings. It is, however, noisy, crowded and quite expensive.

Vegi-Food Kitchen, 8 Cleveland St, Causeway Bay (☎2890 6663). A couple of blocks east of Paterson Street at its northern end. Classy, strictly vegetarian Chinese food.

W's Entrecote, 13th Floor, Times Square, 1 Matheson St, Causeway Bay (☎2506 0133). For meat aficionados, this is the perfect place, with variations on steak, chips and salad the only thing on the menu.

Yat Tung Heen, 2nd Floor, Great Eagle Centre, 23 Harbour Rd (☎2878 1212). Busy, large, inexpensive restaurant, popular with local office workers. The noodles are excellent.

Hong Kong Island: South Side

Jumbo Floating Restaurant, Aberdeen Harbour (☎2553 9111). This famous floating restaurant serves *dim sum* from breakfast onwards, as does its neighbouring sister ship, the *Jumbo Palace*. Shuttle boats carry customers to and from the quayside. Unfortunately, both restaurants are horribly touristy, and the food quality reflects that – few locals eat here. Open 7am–5pm.

Lucy's, 64 Stanley Main St, Stanley (☎2813 9055). Cheaper than the European restaurants on the seafront, with food that is virtually as good. Friendly staff and reasonably priced wine (for Hong Kong) make it popular with locals.

Chungking Mansions

African Food Palace, 11th Floor, Block E, 36–44 Nathan Rd (☎2366 2563). Tasty African dishes in a friendly place.

Delhi Club, 3rd Floor, C Block (☎23681682). A curry house par excellence; the ludicrously cheap set meal would feed an army.

Everest Club, 3rd Floor, D Block (☎2316 2718). Reasonable Nepali–Indian food; very clean and friendly.

Khyber Pass, 7th Floor, E Block (☎2721 2786). Consistently good food, with friendly and efficient service. One of the best in Chungking Mansions.

Sher-E-Punjab, 3rd Floor, Block B (☎2368 0859). Excellent food with friendly service in clean surroundings. Slightly more expensive than its neighbours.

Taj Mahal Club, 3rd Floor, B Block (☎2722 5454). Quality Indian food and good value if you avoid the relatively expensive drinks.

Tsimshatsui

Dan Ryan's Chicago Grill, 1st Floor Ocean Terminal (☎2736 6111). If you're craving American-size portions the salads, hamburgers, steaks and puddings here will hit the spot. Friendly, noisy and consistent. There's also a bar where you can get something smaller. There's a second branch in Pacific Place, Admiralty.

East Ocean Seafood Restaurant, 3rd Floor, East Ocean Centre, 98 Granville Rd (☎2723 8128). Noisy basement dining, with excellent seasonal cooking and approachable waiters.

Great Shanghai, 26 Prat Ave (☎2366 8158). One of the most reliable of Hong Kong's Shanghai restaurants, with especially fine fish and seafood; a good choice for a first Shanghai meal.

Kublai's, 55 Kimberly Rd (☎2722 0733); another branch at 3rd Floor, One Capitol Place, 18 Luard Rd, Wanchai (☎2529 9117). Mongolian-style barbecue restaurant where you fill a bowl with your selection of meat, fish, vegetable and sauce, then hand it over to be stir-fried. At only HK$50 for the set lunch – including one refill – this is excellent value, though the food tends to the greasy.

Peking Restaurant, 227 Nathan Rd, Jordan MTR (☎2730 1316). Despite its glum decor, this place serves some of the best Beijing food in Hong Kong. The Beijing Duck is particularly good.

Peninsula Hotel Lobby, *Peninsula Hotel*. The set tea served in the lobby comes to around HK$150 plus ten percent service. As well as a lot of food, you also get a chance to sit in Hong Kong's most beautiful lobby, serenaded by live music.

Regal Seafood Restaurant, *Regal Kowloon Hotel*, 71 Mody Rd (☎2722 1818). Hideous French–Chinese decor, but great food and helpful staff.

Sweet Basil Thai, 73 Kai Tak Rd, Kowloon City (☎2718 8077); 1st Floor 1 Lyndhurst Terrace, Central (☎2530 0068). The Kowloon branch used to be a favourite with travellers at the old airport, and it's still a great place to eat, with good, spicy Thai food served in a friendly atmosphere. The Central branch is a more recent addition, but is just as good. You could get away with about HK$100 a head.

Bars, pubs and clubs

The most concentrated collection of bars is in the **Lan Kwai Fong** area on Hong Kong Island. Just up the hill, the bars of **SoHo** are also becoming increasingly popular, and are slightly less raucous. **Wanchai** is another busy area after dark, though not so convenient for browsing, as the various locations are more thinly scattered. **Tsimshatsui** is not generally known for its nightlife, though in fact there is something of a scene here, too, catering for both travellers and expats. Hart Avenue and Prat Avenue, west from Chatham Road South, are the best places to look for a drink, with several alternatives very close together. For up-to-the-minute listings consult the latest issue of *HK Magazine* or other listings publications (see p.155).

Hong Kong Island

Carnegie's, 53–55 Lockhart Rd (☎2866 6289). Noise level means conversation here is only possible by flash cards, and once it's packed hordes of punters fight for dancing space in the bar. Regular live music.

Dublin Jack, 37 Cochrane St, SoHo (☎2543 0081). Reliable Irish-style pub, just under the escalator exit for Lyndhurst Terrace. Draught Guinness, Irish food, reasonable prices, and well over a hundred different varieties of whiskey.

Le Jardin, 10 Wing Wah Lane (☎2526 2717). One of the few places where you can sit and drink al fresco, this friendly bar is on a small raised terrace at the end of the lane. Watch out for the Elvis impersonator.

The Jazz Club, 2nd Floor, 34–36 D'Aguilar St (☎2845 8477). The narrow bar is open to non-members. Live jazz on Friday and Saturday nights (up to HK$100).

The Jump, 7th Floor, Plaza Two, 463 Lockhart Rd, Causeway Bay (☎2832 9007). Mildly notorious bar with a small dance floor and boisterous bar tenders. Lie back in the dentist's chair and have drink poured straight down your throat. Popular with office parties.

Mad Dogs, 1 D'Aguilar St, Central (☎2810 1000). A few metres south of Stanley Street. Always packed out with expats, who can get fairly riotous by the late evening. Occasionally has live bands.

Petticoat Lane, 1 Tung Wah Lane (☎2973 0642). Stylish wine bar under the escalator just above Lyndhurst Terrace. Baroque hangings, topiary and candles give it a great atmosphere. Patronized by the local gay community.

Post '97, 9 Lan Kwai Fong, Central (☎2810 9333). A disco downstairs and a vaguely arty atmosphere in the bar upstairs; strong gay presence on Fridays.

Staunton's Wine Bar and Café, 10–12 Staunton St, SoHo (☎2973 6611). Right by the escalator, this rather cavernous bar quickly fills up in the evening, as this is a popular place to gather before moving on to neighbouring restaurants.

Vong, *Mandarin Oriental Hotel*, 5 Connaught Rd, Central (☎2522 0111). If you want to join Hong Kong's chic set for an hour or so, this is the place. Impossibly stylish black-and-gold bar, with sensational views. The staff are charming. Prices as you would expect.

Kowloon

Bahama Mama's, 4–5 Knutsford Terrace, just north of Kimberly Rd (☎2368 2121). A good atmosphere with plenty of space for pavement drinking. There's a beach-bar theme and outdoor terrace that prompts party crowd antics.

Delaney's, 3–7A Prat Ave (☎2301 3980). Friendly Irish pub with draught beers, Guinness and Irish pub food; features Irish folk music most nights. Also at 2nd Floor, 18 Luard Rd, Wanchai (☎2804 2880).

Jouster's II, 19–23 Hart Ave (☎2723 0022). Ludicrous, mock-medieval interior, with loud rock music and a mix of Chinese and expats. Cheap drinks until 9pm.

Ned Kelly's Last Stand, 11A Ashley Rd (☎2376 0562). Very popular with both travellers and expats. Features excellent nightly ragtime jazz.

Shopping

Visitors are still coming to Hong Kong to go **shopping** despite the fact that the cost of living in the territory has risen above that of most other countries in the world. The famed **electronic goods** of Nathan Road, for example, are by no means cheap any more and when you consider the high possibility of some form of rip-off, you are probably best advised to buy your gadgets at home, although the secondhand camera shops in Stanley Street are worth a look if you know your business. But some things are indeed cheap, particularly **clothes, silk, jewellery, Chinese arts and crafts**, some **computer accessories** and **pirated goods**. In Tsimshatsui, Causeway Bay and Wanchai, opening hours are generally 10am–9.30pm; in Central it's 10am–7pm.

Arts and crafts

For Chinese **arts and crafts**, including fabrics, porcelain and clothes, visit Chinese Arts and Crafts, which has branches at the China Resources Building, 26 Harbour Rd, Wanchai; 230 The Mall, Pacific Place; 88 Queensway, Admiralty; and Star House, 3 Salisbury Rd, Tsimshatsui. Other good outlets include Mountain Folkcraft, 12 Wo On Lane (off D'Aguilar St), Central, which has beautiful folk crafts from Southeast Asia; Shanghai Tang, Pedder Building, Pedder Street, Central, which does upmarket gifts and clothes, including the ever-popular Mao and Deng watches; and Wah Tung China Ltd, 59 Hollywood Rd, Central, which offers high quality ceramics and can ship and make to order.

Clothes

Clothes can be good value in Hong Kong, particularly the local fashion brand names such as Gordiano, U2, 2000 and Bossini, which have branches all over the city, but big-name foreign designer clothes are often more expensive than back home. Good places to browse include Granville Road in Tsimshatsui, Hing Wai Centre in Aberdeen, the Pedder Building on Pedder Street in Central, and just round the corner, Wyndham Street and D'Aguillar Street. Beware of size labels – they're often way out.

  Tailor-made clothes are a traditional speciality of the Hong Kong tourist trade and wherever you go in Tsimshatsui you'll be accosted by Indian tailors. However, you may find better work elsewhere – in residential areas and locations like hotels or shopping arcades, where the tailors rely on regular clients. Don't ask for something in 24 hours – it either won't fit or will fall apart, or both. The best-known tailor in town is probably Sam's Tailors, at 94 Nathan Rd, Tsimshatsui. Sam is famous as much for his talent for self-publicity as for his clothes. Others include the well-established ladies' tailors, Linva Tailor, 38 Cochrane St, Central; Margaret Court Tailoress, 8th Floor, Winner Building, 27 D'Aguilar St, Central; and Shanghai Tang, 12 Pedder St, Central, which does glamorous Chinese-style garments for men and women. All tailors can supply fabric, though if you want more choice go to the Western Market. For **shoes and leather goods** try Wong Nai Chung Road in Happy Valley. For **clothing repairs** there are many shops in World-Wide Plaza, Des Voeux Road, Central, including Perfect Fashion Alteration on the 3rd Floor.

Computers

Both hardware and software can work out very cheap in Hong Kong, though you'll need to make sure you get an international warranty. Check special offers in Tuesday's *South China Morning Post*. **Pirated computer software** is also big business, though these days it's more discreet. Some recommended outlets include Asia Computer Plaza, 2nd Floor, Star House, Salisbury Road, Tsimshatsui; Computer Zone, 298 Hennessy Rd, Wanchai; Golden Shopping Arcade, 156 Fuk Wah St, Sham Shui Po, Kowloon; and Mongkok Computer Centre, at the corner of Nelson and Fa Yuen streets, Mongkok.

Department stores

Some of Hong Kong's longest established **department stores** include the typically Chinese CRC Department Store, Chiao Shang Building, 92 Queen's Rd, Central; and Lok Sing Centre, 31 Yee Wo St, Causeway Bay; Wing On, 111 Connaught Rd, Central (and other branches); and Yue Hwa Chinese Products Emporium, 301–309 Nathan Rd, Yau Ma Tei (and other locations). For an upmarket Western-style store, check out Lane Crawford, 70 Queen's Rd, Central; Levels 1–3, The Mall, One Pacific Place, 88 Queensway, Admiralty.

Jewellery

There are literally thousands of **jewellers** in Hong Kong, and prices are relatively low. Some places to start include Gallery One, 31–33 Hollywood Rd, Central, which has a huge selection of semi-precious stones and beads. For precious stones and gold try Johnson & Co, 44

Hankow Rd, Kowloon; New Universal, 23rd Floor, Diamond Exchange Building, 8–10 Duddell St, Central, and Peter Choi Gems & Jewellery, Shop 224A, *Hong Kong Hotel*, 3 Canton Rd, Kowloon, just inside the main entrance to Ocean Terminal.

Listings

Airlines Air India, Rm 3008–9, The Centre, 99 Queen's Rd, Central (☎2522 1176); British Airways, 30th Floor, Alexandra House, 25 Chater Rd, Central (☎2868 0303); Cathay Pacific, 10th Floor, Peninsula Office Tower, 10 Middle Rd, Tsimshatsui (☎2747 1888); Dragonair, 46th Floor, Cosco Tower, 183 Queen's Rd, Sheung Wan (☎2590 1188); JAL, 20th Floor, Gloucester Tower, The Landmark, Pedder St, Central (☎2523 0081); KLM, Rm 2201–03, World Trade Centre, 280 Gloucester Rd, Causeway Bay (☎2808 2111); Korean Air, Ground Floor, Tsimshatsui Centre, 66 Mody Rd, Tsimshatsui East (☎2368 6221); Malaysia Airlines, Central Tower, 28 Queen's Rd, Central (☎2521 8181); Qantas, Rm 3701, Jardine House, 1 Connaught Place, Central (☎2842 1438); Singapore Airlines, 17th Floor, United Centre, 95 Queensway, Admiralty (☎2520 2233); Thai International, 24th Floor United Centre, 95 Queensway, Admiralty (☎2876 6888); United Airlines, 29th Floor, Gloucester Tower, The Landmark, 11 Pedder St, Central (☎2810 4888).

American Express 1st Floor, Henley Building, 5 Queen's Rd, Central (Mon–Fri 9am–5pm, Sat 9am–12.20pm; ☎2801 7300/2277 1010; report stolen cheques on ☎2885 9331).

Bookshops The Swindon Book Company is the largest central English-language bookstore at 13–15 Lock Rd, Tsimshatsui; it has another branch at the Star Ferry concourse, Tsimshatsui. Dymock's bookshop at the Star Ferry, Central and 1st Floor Prince's Building, Central, is good for paperbacks and travel guides. Also try Page One in Festival Walk, Kowloon Tong, in Times Square, Causeway Bay, and Kelly and Walsh, Shop 304, Pacific Place, Admiralty.

Embassies and consulates Australia, 23rd Floor, Harbour Centre, 25 Harbour Rd, Wanchai (☎2827 8881); Britain, 1 Supreme Court Rd, Admiralty (☎2901 3000); Canada, 14th Floor, 1 Exchange Square, Central (☎2810 4321); China, 5th Floor, China Resources Bldg, Lower Block, 26 Harbour Rd, Wanchai (☎2285 1794); India, 504 Admiralty Centre, Tower One, 18 Harcourt Rd, Admiralty (☎2527 2593); Japan, 46th Floor, One Exchange Square, Central (☎2579 8216); Korea, 5th Floor, Far East Financial Centre, 16 Harcourt Rd, Central (☎2529 4141); Malaysia, 23rd Floor, Malaysia Building, 50 Gloucester Rd, Wanchai (☎2527 0921); New Zealand, Rm 2705, Jardine House, Connaught Rd, Central (☎2877 4488); Philippines, 6th Floor, United Centre, 95 Queensway, Admiralty (☎2823 8500); Taiwan, 4th Floor, East Tower, Lippo Centre, 89 Queensway, Admiralty (☎2525 8315); Thailand, 8th Floor, Fairmont House, 8 Cotton Tree Drive, Central (☎2521 6481); USA, 26 Garden Rd, Central (☎2523 9011); Vietnam, 15th Floor, Great Smart Tower, 230 Wanchai Rd, Wanchai (☎2591 4510).

Hospitals Government hospitals have 24-hour casualty wards, where treatment is free. These include the Princess Margaret Hospital, Lai King Hill Rd, Lai Chi Kok, Kowloon (☎2990 1111) and the Queen Mary Hospital, Pokfulam Rd, Hong Kong Island (☎2855 3111). For an ambulance dial ☎999.

Internet access Free Internet access at most branches of *Pacific Coffee Company* cafés: Ground Floor, Bank of America Tower (Mon–Sat 7.30am–6pm); Basement, Pacific Place II, Admiralty (Mon–Sat 7.30am–1pm, Sun 8am–9pm); Star Ferry Piers, Central and Kowloon (Mon–Fri 8am–8pm, Sat & Sun 8am–10pm). The Public Library, Star Ferry, Central, also offers access (Mon–Fri 10am–7pm), as does the British Council, 3 Supreme Court Rd, Admiralty.

Laundry On the ground floor of Golden Crown Court, Nathan Rd (one block north of Mirador Mansions; red entrance). Also at *Mirador Mansions*, 13th Floor. Dry cleaners are everywhere; if you get stuck try in the concourse of an MTR station. Some also do laundry.

Left luggage In the departure lounge at the airport (daily 6.30am–1am), at the Central and Kowloon stations for the Airport Express, and in the Hong Kong China international ferry terminal in Tsimshatsui.

Police Crime hotline and taxi complaints ☎2527 7177. For general police enquiries call ☎2860 2000.

Post office The general post office is at 2 Connaught Place, Central (Mon–Fri 8am–6pm, Sat & Sun 8am–2pm; ☎2921 2222), just west of the Star Ferry and north of Jardine House (the tower with porthole windows). Poste restante mail is delivered here (you can pick it up Mon–Sat 8am–6pm), unless specifically addressed to "Kowloon". The Kowloon main post office is at 10 Middle Rd, Tsimshatsui (☎2366 4111).

Telephone services For IDD calls, use a payphone (which take coins or stored value cards) or go to the Hong Kong Telecom offices at Hermes House, 10 Middle Rd, Tsimshatsui (24hr), 3 Gloucester Rd, Wanchai (Mon–Fri 8am–9pm, Sat 8am–3pm), or at the airport.

Travel agents Hong Kong is full of budget travel agents including Shoestring Travel Ltd, Flat A, 4th Floor, Alpha House, 27–33 Nathan Rd (☎2723 2306), China Touring Centre (HK), 703 Stag Building, 148–150 Queen's Rd, Central (☎2545 0767) and Hong Kong Student Travel Ltd, 608, Hang Lung Centre, Paterson St, Causeway Bay (☎2833 9909). For train tickets, tours, flights and visas to mainland China, try the Chinese state travel agency, CITS, Rm 1213–15, 13th Floor, Tower A, New Mandarin Plaza, 14 Science Museum Rd, Tsimshatsui East (☎2732 5888), or the more friendly CTS, whose main office is on the 4th Floor, CTS House, 78–83 Connaught Rd, Central (☎2853 3888).

CHAPTER FOUR

INDONESIA

Introduction

The **Indonesian** archipelago spreads over 5200km between the Asian mainland and Australia, all of it within the tropics, and comprises between 13,000 and 17,000 islands. Its ethnic, cultural and linguistic diversity is correspondingly great – around 500 languages and dialects are spoken by its 200 million people, whose fascinating customs and lifestyles are a major attraction.

Much of the **recent news** about Indonesia has emphasized the fragility of the state. The horrifying chaos that followed the East Timor elections in 1999 highlighted the dangerous role played by the Indonesian military, and riots in many parts of the archipelago have pitched Muslims against their Christian neighbours. The Indonesian economy remains on the point of collapse and further turmoil can be expected, though realistically this is unlikely to affect the islands' major tourist destinations. One area that is still badly affected, however, is the **Maluku islands** – travel here remains unsafe, and for that reason they have been omitted from this edition.

Because Indonesia encompasses such a diversity of cultures, it can be very difficult to decide where to go. However, there is a well-worn overland travellers' route across the archipelago, which begins by taking a boat from Penang in Malaysia to **Medan** on **Sumatra**'s northeast coast. From here the classic itinerary runs to the **orang-utan sanctuary** at Bukit Lawang, the nippy little hill resort of **Berastagi**, the chilled-out lakeside resorts of **Danau Toba** and the surfers' mecca of **Pulau Nias**. Further south, the area around **Bukittinggi** appeals because of its flamboyant Minangkabau architecture and dances. Many travellers then hurtle through the southern half of Sumatra in their headlong rush to **Java**, probably bypassing the exhaustingly overpopulated capital **Jakarta**, but perhaps pausing at the relaxed beach resort of **Pangandaran** in West Java. Next stop is always the ancient capital of **Yogyakarta**, a cultural centre which hosts daily performances of traditional dance and music and offers batik courses for curious travellers. Yogya also makes a good base for exploring the huge **Borobodur** (Buddhist) and **Prambanan** (Hindu) temples. Java's biggest natural attractions are its volcanoes: the **Dieng plateau**, with its coloured lakes and ancient Hindu temples and, most famously, **Gunung Bromo**, where most travellers brave a sunrise climb to the summit.

Just across the water from East Java sits **Bali**, the longtime jewel in the crown of Indonesian tourism, a tiny island of elegant temples, verdant landscape and fine surf. The biggest resorts are the party towns of **Kuta** and adjacent **Legian**, with the more subdued beaches at **Lovina** and **Candi Dasa** appealing to travellers not hell-bent on raging nightlife. Most visitors also spend time in Bali's cultural centre of **Ubud**, whose lifeblood continues to be painting, carving, dancing and music-making. The islands east of Bali – collectively known as Nusa Tenggara – are now attracting bigger crowds, particularly neighbouring **Lombok**, with its beautiful beaches and temples. East again, the chance of seeing the world's largest lizards, the **Komodo dragons**, draws travellers to **Komodo** and then it's an easy hop across to **Flores** which has great surfing, and the unforgettable coloured crater lakes of **Keli Mutu**. South of Flores, **Sumba** is famous for its intricate fabrics, grand funeral ceremonies and extraordinary annual ritual war, the *pasola*. To the east, the divided island of **Timor** is just a two-hour flight from Darwin in Australia.

North of Flores, **Sulawesi** is renowned for the intriguing culture of the highland Torajans, whose idiosyncratic architecture and impressively ghoulish burial rituals are astonishing. West of Sulawesi, the island of Borneo is divided into the Malaysian districts of Sabah and Sarawak, the independent kingdom of Brunei, and the Indonesian state of **Kalimantan**. For the overland traveller short on time, there's not much here that can't be experienced more rewardingly across the border in Sarawak, but Tanjung Puting national park offers guaranteed close contact with orang-utans, and there are opportunities for river travel in remote jungle. East of Sulawesi, **Irian Jaya** is expensive and time-consuming to reach, but is worth considering for the remote **Baliem Valley**, home of the Dani people, who hunt with arrows and wear penis gourds.

The whole archipelago is tropical, with **temperatures** at sea level always between 21°C and 33°C, although cooler in the mountains. In theory, the year divides into a wet and dry season, though it's often hard to tell the difference. Very roughly, in much of the country, November to April are the wet months (January and February the wettest) and May through to October are dry. However, in northern Sumatra, this pattern is effectively reversed. The **peak tourist season** is between mid-June and mid-September and again over the Christmas and New Year season. This is particularly relevant in the major resorts, where prices rocket and rooms can be fully booked for days, and sometimes weeks, on end.

Overland and sea routes into Indonesia

Indonesia has good ferry connections with Malaysia and Singapore, and there are frequent cargo boats from the Philippines.

■ From Malaysia and Singapore

A variety of ferries and speedboats depart from Penang (see p.593), on the west coast of Peninsular Malaysia, to **Medan** and from Melaka (see p.623), south of Medan, in southern Malaysia, to **Dumai**. You can also take ferries from Johor Bahru (see p.627), in far southern Malaysia; from Singapore (see p.789) to the Sumatran islands of **Batam** and **Bintan**; and from Port Klang (see p.575), near Kuala Lumpur, to **Tanjung Balai** in Sumatra.

There are two entry points between **East Malaysia and Kalimantan**. You can catch a bus between the capital of Malaysian **Sarawak** at Kuching (see p.637) to Kalbar's capital, Pontianak; alternatively, you can cross from the East Malaysian state of **Sabah** by catching a two-hour ferry (see p.666) to **Pulau Nunukan** from Tawau, two days' bus ride southeast of Kota Kinabalu.

■ From the Philippines

Every week or so a cargo boat leaves General Santos in the Philippines for Bitung in Northern **Sulawesi**.

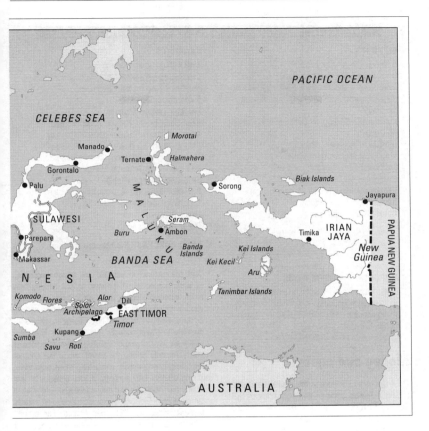

It's a rough ride shorn of any sort of comfort, but at around US$30 one-way, it's a lot cheaper than flying. See p.433 for details.

Entry requirements and visa extension

Citizens of Britain, Ireland, most of Europe, Australia, New Zealand, Canada and the USA **do not need a visa** to enter Indonesia if intending to stay for less than sixty days, and if entering and exiting via a designated gateway. There are currently around forty of these air and sea **gateways** into Indonesia (see the box overleaf), at which you can get a free, non-extend-

able sixty-day visa on arrival; "sixty days" includes the date of entry. You'll be fined US$20 for every day you **overstay your visa**, up to a maximum of fourteen days. After that you'll get blacklisted from Indonesia for two years. The best way to get yourself a **new sixty-day visa** is to leave the country for a few hours and then come straight back in through a designated port of entry (Singapore is the most popular for this).

If you want to stay more than two months, or are **entering via a non-designated gateway**, then you must get a visa from an Indonesian consulate (listed on p.21) before travelling. **Tourist visas** are initially valid for four weeks, and cost US$25. They can be extended for up to six months at **immigration offices** (*kantor immigrasi*) in Indonesia, but this is never easy.

OFFICIAL IMMIGRATION GATEWAYS INTO INDONESIA

AIRPORTS
Bali Ngurah Rai, Denpasar.
Irian Jaya Frans Kaisiepo, Biak.
Java Husein Sastranegara, Bandung; Sukarno-Hatta, Jakarta; Adi Sumarmo, Solo; Juanda, Surabaya.
Kalimantan Sepinggan, Balikpapan; Soepadio, Pontianak.
Lombok Selaparang, Mataram.
Riau Hang Nadim, Pulau Batam.
Sulawesi Sam Ratulangi, Manado; Hasanuddin, Makassar.
Sumatra Polonia, Medan; Simpang Tiga, Pekanbaru; Tabing, Padang.
Timor El Tari, Kupang.

SEAPORTS
Bali Benoa, Sanur; Padang Bai.
Java Tanjung Priok, Jakarta; Tanjung Perak, Surabaya; Tanjung Mas, Semarang.
Kalimantan Nunukan.
Lombok Lembar, Mataram.
Riau Batu Ampar, Batam Island; Nongsa Terminal Bahari, Batam Island; Sekupang, Batam Island; Sri Bay Intan, Selat Kijang & Tanjung Pinang, Bintan Island; Tanjung Balai, Karimun; Teluk Senimba, Batam Island.
Sulawesi Bitung, Manado.
Sumatra Belawan, Medan; Dumai; Lhok Seumawe; Malahayati, Aceh; Sultan Iskandar Muda, Aceh.
Timor Tebau, Kupang.

LAND BORDERS Kalimantan Entikong.

AIRPORT DEPARTURE TAXES
These vary from airport to airport, but are approximately Rp30,000–50,000 on international flights, and Rp10,000–20,000 for domestic flights.

Money and costs

The Indonesian currency is the **rupiah** (abbreviated to "Rp"). **Notes** come in denominations of Rp100, Rp500, Rp1000, Rp5000, Rp10,000, Rp20,000, Rp50,000 and Rp100,000; **coins**, mainly used for public telephones and bemos (minibuses), come in Rp25, Rp50, Rp100, Rp500 and Rp1000 denominations. Officially, rupiah are available outside of Indonesia, but the currency's volatile value means that very few banks carry it. The current exchange rate is Rp7,500 to US$1 and Rp13,000 to £1.

There were severe price hikes for daily necessities after the **rupiah devalued** by 600 percent in the twelve months from August 1997 and, as wages haven't increased proportionately, hotels, restaurants and services aimed primarily at Indonesians have been slow to raise their rates for fear of pricing out customers. Strictly tourist businesses, however, have responded by charging for their goods and services in **US dollars**. Even where prices are displayed in US dollars, though, you're usually given the option of paying with cash, travellers' cheques, credit card or rupiah.

With the currency in free fall, and prices responding at varying speeds, it's difficult to say exactly how much Indonesia **costs** on a daily basis. However, you'll keep all costs to a minimum if you concentrate on Java, Sumatra, Bali and Nusa Tenggara where it's possible to travel cheaply. In Kalimantan, Sulawesi and Irian Jaya, flying or cruising between places is often the only option for travel, while the cost of importing goods makes everything more expensive. Taking all this into account, if you're happy to eat where the locals do, use public transport and stay in simple accommodation, you could manage on a **daily budget** of £6.50/US$10 per person. For around £20/US$30 a day (less if you share a room), you'll get hot water and air-conditioning in your accommodation, bigger meals and a few beers.

You'll find **banks** capable of handling foreign exchange in provincial capitals and bigger cities throughout Indonesia, with privately run **money-changers**, who sometimes offer better rates, in major tourist centres. You may be asked to supply a **photocopy** of your passport, or the **receipt** (or proof of purchase) that you get when you buy your travellers' cheques. Always count your money carefully, as unscrupulous dealers can rip you off, either by folding notes over to make it look as if you're getting twice as much, or by distracting you and then whipping away a few notes from your pile.

In less-travelled regions, provincial banks won't cash travellers' cheques, but will take **US dollar notes**. **Credit cards** are beginning to set exchange-rate ceilings of around Rp7500 to the US dollar, irrespective of the official value, and over-the-counter **cash advances** on Visa can be used for obtaining the full international rate. A growing number of bank **ATMs** across the country also have Cirrus-Maestro connections. For details on getting **money wired** to you, see "Basics" p.23.

Information and maps

There's a range of **tourist offices** in Indonesia, including government-run organizations, such as Kanwil Depparpostel offices, and the province-oriented **Dinas Pariwisata** (Diparda). Though they can lack hard information, staff often speak some English, and may advise about local transport options or arrange guides. Many **private tour operators** are also excellent, if sometimes partisan, sources of information. In remote locations, you can try asking the local **police**.

Good all-round **maps** include GeoCentre's 1:2,000,000 series and the Nelles Indonesia series. In the same league is Periplus' growing range of user-friendly city and provincial maps.

Getting around

Delays are common to all forms of **transport** – including major flights – caused by weather, mechanical failure, or simply not enough passengers turning up, so you'll save yourself a good deal of stress if you keep your schedule as flexible as possible. For an idea of the duration and frequency of journeys between major destinations, see "**Travel Details**" on p.442.

■ Buses and minibuses

Buses are cheap, easy to book and leave roughly on time. But they're also slow, cramped and often plain terrifying: accidents can be devastating. Where there's a choice of operators on any particular route, ask local people which bus company they recommend. **Tickets** are sold a day or more in advance from the point of departure or bus company offices – which are not necessarily near the relevant **bus station** (*terminal*). Where services are infrequent it's a good idea to buy tickets as early as possible. Tell the driver your exact destination, as it may be possible to get delivered right to the door of your hotel. The average **long-distance bus** has padded seats but little leg- or headroom; it's worth forking out for a luxury bus, if available, which costs twice as much but will have reclining seats. You'll get regular meal stops at

roadhouses along the way. On shorter routes you'll use minibuses, widely known by their Balinese tag, **bemo**, along with **kijang**, a jeep lookalike. Once on their way they are faster than buses and cheaper; fares are handed over on board, and rarely advertised. You may also have to pay for any space your luggage occupies. In resort areas such as Bali, a more pleasant option are **tourist shuttle buses** – though far more expensive than local services, these will take you between points as quickly as possible. The longest established firm on Bali and Lombok is **Perama**. They have offices in most major tourist destinations and produce a useful leaflet outlining their routes.

■ Planes

In some areas, **flying** may be the only practical way to get around. State-operated **Garuda** handles international flights (though you might use them for transport within Indonesia), and **Merpati** is the domestic operator. Provincial services are supplemented by **Mandala** and **Bouraq**. The quantity and quality of services is very uncertain at present, however, and some marginal routes have closed. It's essential to **reconfirm** your seat, as waiting lists can be huge and the temptation for airline staff to bump you off in favour of a benefactor is enormous; get a computer printout of the reconfirmation if possible. Arrive at the airport **early**, as seats on overbooked flights are allocated on a first-come, first-served basis. At other times, "fully booked" planes can be almost empty, so if you really have to get somewhere it's always worth going to the airport to check.

■ Boats and ferries

Most Indonesians choose to travel between islands by boat, either on the state shipping line, Pelni, or on anything from cargo freighters to tiny fishing vessels. **Pelni** currently operates about twenty **passenger liners**, which run on two-week or monthly circuits and link Java with ports on all the main island groups between Sumatra and Irian Jaya; see pp.192–193 for a chart of the Pelni routes.

The vessels carry 500 to 1600 passengers each, are well maintained, as safe and punctual as any form of transport in Indonesia can be, and the only widespread form of public transport that offers any luxury. Comprehensive **timetables** for the whole country can be picked up from their head office in Jakarta; provincial offices should have complete timetables of all the ferries serving their ports, which you can copy or take away. **Tickets** are available

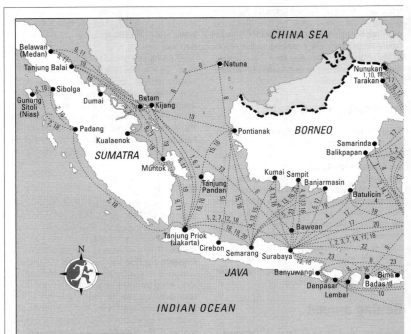

PELNI FERRIES

All **Pelni ferries**, with a couple of minor exceptions, follow the same routes on their outward and return legs, calling in at the same ports on both journeys. The exceptions are *KM Lawit* and *KM Tidar*, nos. 15 and 17 in the list below, which sail between northern Java and Kalimantan without doubling back on themselves, and *KM Kelud* and *KM Sinabung* (nos. 9 and 11), which both follow a circular route between Belawan, near Medan, and Jakarta's Tanjung Priok harbour.

The following table gives the departure and destination ports for each ship, along with a broad summary of the islands visited en route (the chart shows the exact route of each ferry).

	Name of ship	Departure port	Destination	Via
1.	*KM Kerinci*	Dumai	Nunukan	Kijang, Jakarta, Java, Balikpapan, W. Sulawesi
2.	*KM Kambuna*	Gunung Sitoli (Nias)	Bitung	Padang, Jakarta, Balikpapan, W. Sulawesi
3.	*KM Rinjani*	Surabaya	Jayapura	S. Sulawesi, Ambon, Tual
4.	*KM Binaiya*	Surabaya	Samarinda	Bawean, Semarang, S. Kalimantan
5.	*KM Kelimutu*	Surabaya/Semarang	Banjarmasin	–
6.	*KM Bukit Raya*	Surabaya	Natuna	S. Kalimantan, Tanjung Priok, Kijang,
7.	*KM Bukit Siguntang*	Dumai	Dobo/Kaimana	Kijang, Jakarta, Java, Sulawesi, Banda, Ambon, Tual
8.	*KM Tatamailau*	Merauke	Banyuwangi	Maluku, S. Sulawesi, N. Tenggara, Bali, Flores
9.	*KM Sinabung*	Tanjung Priok (Jakarta)	Belawan (Medan)	Clockwise via Tanjung Balai, Batam

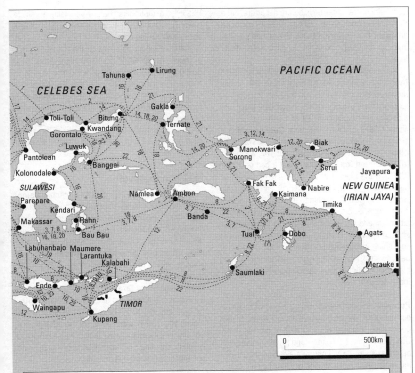

Name of ship	Departure port	Destination	Via
10. *KM Awu*	Kalabahi	Nunukan	N. Tenggara, Bali, E. Sulawesi, E. Kalimantan
11. *KM Kelud*	Tanjung Priok	Belawan	Same route as KM Sinabung above, but anti-clockwise
12. *KM Dobonsolo*	Tanjung Priok	Jayapura	N. Java, Bali, Flores, Ambon, N. Irian Jaya
13. *KM Leuser*	Pontianak	Sampit	N. Java, Kumai
14. *KM Umsini*	Surabaya	Jayapura	Sulawesi, Kalimantan, Ternate, N. Irian Jaya
15. *KM Lawit*	Cirebon/Semarang	Pontianak	–
16. *KM Tilongkabila*	Pontianak	Lirung	Java, S. Kalimantan, Bali, N. Tenggara, E. Sulawesi
17. *KM Tidar*	Surabaya	Nunukan	W. Sulawesi, Balikpapan
18. *KM Lambelu*	Sibolga	Ternate	Jakarta, N. Java, S. Sulawesi, Ambon, N. Sulawesi
19. *KM Sirimau*	Tanjung Balai	Kupang	Jakarta, Batulicin, S. Sulawesi, N. Tenggara
20. *KM Ciremai*	Tanjung Priok	Jayapura	Semarang, S. Sulawesi, E. Sulawesi, Ternate
21. *KM Pangrango*	Bitung	Merauke	W. Irian Jaya
22. *KM Sangiang*	Gorontalo	Surabaya	Flores, Timor, Tual, Ambon, Luwuk
23. *KM Wilis*	Semarang	Kupang	Surabaya, Sumbawa, Flores, Sumba

from Pelni offices three days before departure, but as there's a big demand for cabin berths it's best to pay an **agent** to reserve you these as early as possible. You can only buy tickets for services which depart locally.

Accommodation on board is usually divided into two or four classes. All are good value, and include **meals**; cabins also have large **lockers** to store your luggage. **First class** consists of a private cabin with a double bed, washroom, TV and air-conditioning – about US$15 a day is standard. **Second class** is similar, but with four bunks and no TV (US$10); **third class** is a six-bunk cabin without the washroom (US$7.50); and **fourth class** is just a bed in a dorm (US$5). If the fourth class is full, which it usually is, then the only option is to sleep in the corridors, stairwells or on deck; if you plan to travel in this class, it's a good idea to buy a rattan mat before boarding to sit/lie on, and get to the port early to stake out your spot on the floor. Lock luggage shut and chain it to something immovable. Fourth-class food is edible at best, so stock up in advance with instant noodles and biscuits. It's always possible to upgrade after boarding, if space is available.

Where Pelni don't venture, you'll find that **Perentis** (Pioneer) **freighters** do, along with numerous local craft. While these are always willing to rent deck space to passengers for next to nothing – say US$1 for 24 hours – comfort and privacy aboard will be nonexistent. Bring your own sleeping mat, drinking water and snacks, though you may be able to buy rice and fish heads on board. Guard your gear and don't flash anything around. **Schedules** for these services are posted at ports.

■ Rental vehicles

Local operators offer a range of **cars**, most frequently 800cc Suzuki Jimneys (US$25 per day), and larger, more comfortable jeep-like 1600cc Toyota Kijangs (US$40). The rates drop if you rent for a week or more; one day means twelve hours, and the above prices exclude fuel. You'll need to produce an **international drivers' licence** before you rent. Rental **motorbikes** vary from small 100cc Yamahas to trail bikes. Prices start at US$5 per day without insurance. If you don't have a valid international motorbike **licence**, you may be able to get one by taking a test (Rp100,000). Conditions are not suitable for inexperienced drivers, with heavy traffic on major routes; there are increasing numbers of accidents involving tourists, so don't take risks. A few rental outfits offer **insurance** for an extra US$5 a day for a car and

US$3 for a motorbike. Before you take a vehicle, check it thoroughly, and get something in writing about any existing damage.

Traffic in Indonesia drives on the left and there is a maximum speed limit of 70kmph. **Fuel** costs Rp1000 a litre. Drivers must always carry an international driving licence and the vehicle registration documents. All motorcyclists must wear a **helmet**. In some places certain roads change from two-way to one-way during the day, not publicized in any way that is comprehensible to foreigners. The **police** carry out regular spot checks and you'll be **fined** for any infringements.

■ Urban transport

In cities, colour-coded or numbered minibus **bemos** might run fixed circuits, or adapt their routes according to their customers. Rides usually cost a few hundred rupiah, but **fares** are never displayed, and you'll get overcharged at first. Other standbys include **ojek** (single-passenger motorbikes) and **becak** (cycle-rickshaws), which take two passengers. Jakarta and Banjarmasin also have motorized becak, called **bajaj**. Negotiating **fares** for these vehicles requires a balance of firmness and tact; try for around Rp1000 for ojek and Rp500 a kilometre for bajaj or becak, though you'll have to pay more for the latter if there are any hills along the way. They are also notoriously tough customers – never lose your temper with one unless you want a serious fight.

Accommodation

Prices for the simplest double room start at around US$1, but in all categories are at their most expensive from mid-June through August, and in December and January. Single rooms are a rarity, so lone travellers will get put in a double at about 75 percent of the full price. Check-out time is usually noon. The cheapest accommodation has shared **bathrooms**, where you wash using a *mandi* (see "Basics" p.38). **Toilets** in these places will be squat affairs, flushed manually with water scooped from the pail that stands alongside, so you'll have to provide toilet paper yourself.

The bottom end of Indonesia's accommodation market is provided by **homestays** and hostels. *Penginapan*, or homestays, are most often simply spare bedrooms in the family home, though there's often not much difference between these and *losmen*, *pondok* and *wisma*, which are also family-run operations. Rooms vary from whitewashed concrete

ADDRESSES

A recent law banning the use of foreign words for business names, including those for accommodation and restaurants, has caused a few problems. Some hotels have circumvented the new rule by just adding the word "Hotel" in front of their name (this is an Indonesian as well as an English word), but others have had to start over. Street names are another cause of confusion, many having been renamed as historical or political figures fall in and out of fashion. Where relevant, we have included both new and old names for hotels and streets, as many people still refer to them by the old name, though the sign will show the new version.

cubes to artful bamboo structures – some are even set in their own walled gardens. Hard beds and bolsters are the norm, and you may be provided with a light blanket. Most losmen rooms have fans and cold-water bathrooms.

Almost any place calling itself a **hotel** in Indonesia will include at least a basic breakfast in the price of a room. All but the cheapest add a service-and-tax surcharge of up to 22 percent to your bill, and upmarket establishments quote prices – and prefer foreigners to pay – in dollars, though they accept plastic or a rupiah equivalent. In popular areas such as Bali and Tanah Toraja, it's worth booking ahead during the peak seasons; some hotels will also provide transport to and from transit points if requested in advance. Bland and anonymous, cheap urban hotels are designed for local businesspeople rather than tourists, with tiny rooms and shared squat toilets and mandi. Moderately priced hotels often have a choice of fan or air-conditioned rooms, almost certainly with hot water. Expensive hotels can be very stylish indeed, particularly in Bali.

In rural Indonesia, you may end up **staying in villages** without formal lodgings, in a bed in a family house. First ask permission from the local police or the *kepala desa* (village head). In exchange for accommodation and meals, you should offer cash or useful gifts, such as rice, salt, cigarettes or food, to the value of about US$2. The only bathroom might be the nearest river, with all bodily functions performed in the open. With such readily available and inexpensive alternatives, **camping** is only necessary when trekking.

Usually, **electricity** is supplied at 220–240 volts AC, but outlying areas may still use 110 volts. Most outlets take plugs with two rounded pins.

Food and drink

Compared to other Southeast Asian **cuisines**, Indonesian meals lack variety. Coconut milk and aromatic spices at first add intriguing tastes to the meats, vegetables and fruits, but after a while everything starts to taste the same – spiced, fried and served with rice. Be particularly careful about food **hygiene** in rural Indonesia, avoiding poorly cooked fish, pork or beef, which can give you flukes or worms.

Rice (*nasi*) is the favoured staple across much of the country, an essential, three-times-a-day fuel. Noodles are also widely popular. The seafood is often superb, and chicken, goat and beef are the main meats in this predominantly Muslim country. **Vegetarians** can eat well in Indonesia, though restaurant selections can be limited to *cap cay* – fried mixed vegetables. There's also plenty of tofu and the popular *tempe*, a fermented soya-bean cake.

ACCOMMODATION PRICE CODES

All **accommodation** reviewed in this guide has been graded according to the following price codes, in US dollars, which represent the cost of the cheapest double room available in high season. Where a price range is indicated, this means that the establishment offers rooms with varying facilities – as explained in the write-up. In cases where an establishment charges per bed the actual price is given.

① under $5	④ $15–20	⑦ $40–60
② $5–10	⑤ $20–25	⑧ $60–80
③ $10–15	⑥ $25–40	⑨ $80 and over

■ Indonesian food

The backbone of all Indonesian cooking, **spices** are ground and chopped together, then fried to form a paste, which is either used as the flavour base for curries, or rubbed over ingredients prior to frying or grilling. **Chillies** always feature, along with *terasi* (also known as *belacan*), a fermented shrimp paste. Meals are often served with *sambal*, a blisteringly hot blend of chillies and spices.

Light meals and snacks include various rice dishes such as **nasi goreng**, a plate of fried rice with shreds of meat and vegetables and topped with a fried egg, and **nasi campur**, boiled rice served with a small range of side dishes. Noodle equivalents are also commonly available, as are **gado-gado**, steamed vegetables dressed in a peanut sauce, and **sate**, small kebabs of meat or fish, barbecued over a fire and again served with spicy peanut sauce. Indonesian **bread** (*roti*) is made from sweetened dough, and usually accompanies a morning cup of coffee.

Sumatran **Padang restaurants** are found right across Indonesia, the typically fiery food pre-cooked – not the healthiest way to eat – and displayed cold on platters piled up in a pyramid shape inside a glass-fronted cabinet. There are no menus; you either select your composite meal by pointing, or wait for the staff to bring you a selection and pay just for what you consume. You may encounter boiled *kangkung* (water spinach); *tempe*; egg, vegetable, meat or seafood curry; fried whole fish; potato cakes; and fried cow's lung.

■ Where to eat

The cheapest places to eat in Indonesia are at the **mobile stalls** (*kaki lima*, or "five legs"), which ply their wares around the streets and bus stations during the day, and congregate at night markets after dark. You simply place your order and they cook it up on the spot. **Warung** are the bottom line in Indonesian restaurants, usually just a few tables, and

---

A FOOD AND DRINK GLOSSARY

GENERAL TERMS

Menu	*Daftar makanan*	Drink	*Minum*	I am	*Saya seorang*
Cold	*Dingin*	Hot (temperature)	*Panas*	vegetarian	*vegetaris*
Delicious	*Enak*	Hot (spicy)	*Pedas*	I don't eat	*Saya tidak*
Fork	*Garpu*	Plate	*Piring*	meat	*makan daging*
Glass	*Gelas*	Knife	*Pisau*	Spoon	*Sendok*
Fried	*Goreng*	I want to pay	*Saya injin*		
To eat	*Makan*		*bayar*		

MEAT, FISH AND BASIC FOODS

Anjing	Dog	*Ikan*	Fish	*Sapi*	Beef
Ayam	Chicken	*Itik*	Duck	*Soto*	Soup
Babi	Pork	*Jaja*	Rice cakes	*Tikkus*	Rat
Bakmi	Noodles	*Kambing*	Goat	*Telur*	Egg
Buah	Fruit	*Kare*	Curry	*Udang*	Prawn
Es	Ice	*Kepiting*	Crab	*Udang karang*	Lobster
Garam	Salt	*Nasi*	Rice		
Gula	Sugar	*Sambal*	Hot chilli sauce		

EVERYDAY DISHES

Ayam bakar	Fried chicken	*Cap cay*	Mixed fried vegetables
Bakmi goreng	Fried noodles mixed with	*Es campur*	Fruit salad and shredded ice
	vegetables and meat	*Fu yung hai*	Seafood omelette
Bakso	Soup containing meatballs	*Gado-gado*	Steamed vegetables served
Botok daging sapi	Spicy minced beef with tofu,		with a spicy peanut sauce
	tempe and coconut milk	*Ikan bakar*	Grilled fish

offering much the same food as *kaki lima* for as little as 50c a dish. **Rumah makan** are bigger, offer a wider range of dishes and comfort, and may even have a menu. Anything labelled as a **restaurant** will probably be catering to foreigners, with fully fledged service and possibly international food; many close by 8 or 9pm. Tourist restaurants will charge from three times as much for the same dish you'd get in a warung. Where restaurants are reviewed in the Guide, inexpensive means you will get a satisfying main dish for less than US$2, moderate means it'll be US$2.50–5, and expensive is US$5.50 and over. In addition, many of the moderate and all of the expensive establishments will add up to 21 percent service tax to the bill.

■ Drinks

Most **water** that comes out of taps in Indonesia has had very little treatment, and can contain a whole range of bacteria and viruses (see p.27). Drink only bottled, boiled or sterilized water. Boiled water (*air putih*) can be requested at accommodation and restaurants, and dozens of brands of **bottled water** (*air minum*) are sold throughout the islands. Indonesian **coffee** is amongst the best in the world, and drunk with copious amounts of sugar, or occasionally condensed milk.

Alcohol can be a touchy subject in parts of Indonesia, where public drunkenness may incur serious trouble. There's no need to be overly paranoid about this in cities, however, and the locally produced **beers**, Anker and Bintang Pilsners, are good, and widely available at Chinese restaurants and bigger hotels. In non-Islamic regions, even small warung sell beer. **Spirits** are less publicly consumed, and may be technically illegal, so indulge with caution. Nonetheless, home-produced brews are often sold openly in villages. *Tuak* (also known as *balok*) or palm wine is made by tapping a suitable tree for its alcoholic sap, comes in plain milky-white or pale red vari-

Krupuk	Rice or cassava crackers	Pisang goreng	Fried bananas
Kue tiaw	Singaporean stir-fry of flat rice noodles and meat	Rendang	Dry-fried beef and coconut-milk curry
Lalapan	Raw vegetables and sambal	Rijsttaffel	Dutch/Indonesian dish made up of six to ten different meat, fish and vegetable dishes with rice
Lawar	Balinese raw meat paste		
Lontong	Steamed rice in a banana-leaf packet		
Lumpia	Spring rolls	Rujak	Hot spiced fruit salad
Murtabak	Thick, dough pancake, often filled with meat	Rujak petis	Vegetable and fruit in spicy peanut and shrimp sauce
Nasi ayam	Boiled rice with chicken	Tahu goreng telur	Tofu omelette
Nasi campur	Boiled rice served with small amounts of vegetable, meat, fish and sometimes egg	Sate	Meat or fish kebabs served with a spicy peanut sauce
		Soto ayam	Chicken soup
		Sayur bening	Soup with spinach and corn
Nasi goreng	Fried rice	Sayur lodeh	Vegetable and coconut-milk soup
Nasi gudeg	Rice with jackfruit and coconut milk curry		
Nasi putih	Plain boiled rice	Urap-urap/ urap timum	Vegetables with coconut and chilli
Nasi soto ayam	Chicken-and-rice soup		

DRINKS

Air jeruk	Orange juice	Brem	Local rice beer	Tolong tanpa es	Without ice, please
Air jeruk nipis	Lemon juice	Kopi	Coffee		
Air minum	Drinking water	Kopi susu	White coffee	Tolong tanpa gula	Without sugar, please
Arak	Palm or rice spirit	Sopi	Palm spirit		
		Susu	Milk	Tuak	Palm wine
Bir	Beer	Teh	Tea		

eties, and varies in strength. Far more potent are rice wine (variously known as *arak* or *brem*), and *sopi*, a distillation of *tuak*, either of which can leave you incapacitated after a heavy session.

Communications

Most **post offices** (*Kantor pos*) open Mon–Thurs 8am–2pm, Fri 8–11am & Sat 8am–1pm; aside from the usual services some also offer email and fax facilities. Indonesia's **poste restante** system is fairly efficient, but only in the cities; poste restante is officially held for a maximum of one month, though often it's held for much longer. See p.39 for general advice on poste restante. **Overseas letters** to Western Europe and America take between seven and ten days to arrive.

In larger post offices, the **parcels** section is usually in a separate part of the building and sending one is expensive and time-consuming. The cheapest way of sending mail home is by surface (under 10kg only). Don't seal the parcel before staff at the post office have checked what's inside it; in the larger towns there's usually a parcel-wrapping service near the post office. A parcel weighing up to 3kg airmailed to Europe takes about three weeks and costs around Rp170,000; a 5–10kg parcel costs Rp425,000 (by sea it will cost Rp170,000 and takes three months).

There are two types of **telephone** office in Indonesia: the ubiquitous government-run **Telkom** offices (open 24hr), and privately owned **wartels** (usually 7am–midnight), which tend to be slightly more expensive, but are often conveniently located. Both also offer fax services, though the wartels rarely have a collect-call service.

Public **payphones** are useful for local calls and take Rp100 and Rp500 coins. Put the coins in only after someone picks up the phone and starts speaking. Many payphones now take telephone cards only (*kartu telefon*), available in various denominations from 20 units (Rp2000) to 680 units (Rp68,000). Cards

can be bought from most local corner stores. In the big cities there are also new *kartu cip* phones that take the new microchip cards. Long-distance domestic calls (*panggilan inter-lokal*) are charged according to a zone system, with different rates; it's cheaper between 9pm and 6am.

Rates for **international IDD calls** are fixed, though the premium charged by the private wartels varies: Australia, Japan, New Zealand and the USA cost Rp8500 per minute; Canada and the UK, Rp9300; Alaska and Western Europe, Rp10,500. You get 25 percent discount between midnight and 6am and at weekends. To **call abroad** from Indonesia, dial ☎00 + IDD country code + area code (minus the first 0) + number. For international directory enquiries call ☎102; the international operator is ☎101. Some Telkom offices and airports also have home-country direct phones, from which you can **call collect** (reverse-charge calls), or settle up after the call; they cost more than IDD phones.

Internet access is becoming increasingly widespread in Indonesia, and there are now tourist-friendly Internet offices and cybercafés in many towns and cities; prices vary widely from Rp3500 to Rp40,000 per hour. **Email** can make a good alternative to post office postes restantes – even if you're not on the Internet at home; see "Basics" p.39 for details.

Opening hours and festivals

As a rough outline, **businesses** such as airline offices open Mon–Fri 8am–4pm & Sat 8am–noon. **Banking hours** are Mon–Fri 8am–3pm & Sat 8am–1pm, but banks may not handle foreign exchange in the afternoons or at weekends. Moneychangers usually keep shop rather than bank hours. **Post offices** operate roughly Mon–Thur 8am–2pm, Fri 8–11am & Sat 8am–12.30pm. Muslim businesses, including **government offices**, may also close at 11.30am on Fridays, the main day of prayer, and **national public holidays** see all commerce compulsorily curtailed.

TIME DIFFERENCES

The Indonesian archipelago is divided into **three time zones**. Sumatra, Java, Kalimantan Barat and Kalimantan Tengah are on **Western Indonesian Time** (7hr ahead of GMT, 15hr ahead of US Pacific Standard, 12hr ahead of US Eastern Standard, and 3hr behind Sydney); Bali, Lombok, the Nusa Tenggara islands, Sulawesi and South and East Kalimantan are on **Central Indonesian Time** (8hr ahead of GMT, 16hr ahead of US Pacific Standard, 13hr ahead of US Eastern Standard, and 2hr behind Sydney); and Irian Jaya is on **Eastern Indonesian Time** (9hr ahead of GMT, 17hr ahead of US Pacific Standard, 14hr ahead of US Eastern Standard, and 1hr behind Sydney).

PUBLIC HOLIDAYS

Most of the **national public holidays** fall on different dates of the Western calendar each year, as they are calculated according to Muslim or local calendars.

December/January *Idul Fitri*, the celebration of the end of Ramadan.

January 1 New Year's Day (*Tahun Baru*).

March/April *Nyepi*, Balinese *saka* New Year.

March/April Good Friday and Easter Sunday.

May *Idul Adha* (*Hajh*), Muslim Day of Sacrifice.

May *Waisak* Day, anniversary of the birth, death and enlightenment of Buddha.

May/June Ascension Day.

June/July *Muharam*, Muslim New Year.

July/August *Maulud Nabi Muhammad*, the anniversary of the birth of Mohammed.

August 17 Independence Day (*Hari Proklamasi Kemerdekaan*) celebrates the proclamation of Indonesian Independence in 1945 by Dr Sukarno.

December Ascension Day of Mohammed.

December 25 Christmas Day.

Ramadan, a month of fasting during daylight hours, falls during the ninth Muslim month (starting in November/December/January). Even in non-Islamic areas, Muslim restaurants and businesses shut down during the day, and in staunchly Islamic parts of rural Lombok, Sumatra or Kalimantan's Banjarmasin, you should not eat, drink or smoke in public at this time. **Idul Fitri**, also called *Hari Raya* or *Lebaran*, marks the end of Ramadan and is a two-day national holiday of noisy celebrations.

■ Local festivals

In addition to national public holidays, there are frequent **religious festivals** throughout Indonesia's Muslim, Hindu, Chinese and indigenous communities. Each of Bali's 20,000 temples has an anniversary celebration, for instance, and other ethnic groups may host elaborate marriages or funerals, along with more secular holidays. Many of these festivals change annually against the Western **calendar**. The *Calendar of Events* booklet, produced annually by the Directorate General of Tourism, should be available in tourist offices in Indonesia and overseas.

Erau Festival, Tenggarong, Kalimantan Timor. September. A big display of indigenous Dayak skills and dancing.

Funerals, Tanah Toraja, Sulawesi. Mostly May to September. With buffalo slaughter, bullfights, and *sisemba* kick-boxing tournaments.

Galungun, Bali. Takes place for ten days every 210 days to celebrate the victory of good over evil.

Kasada, Bromo, East Java. Offerings are made to the gods and thrown into the crater.

Nyepi, throughout Bali. End of March or beginning of April. The major purification ritual of the year. In the lead-up, religious objects are paraded from temples to sacred springs or the sea for purification. The night before *nyepi*, the spirits are frightened away with drums, cymbals, firecrackers and huge papier-mâché monsters. On the day itself, everyone sits quietly at home to persuade any remaining evil spirits that Bali is completely deserted.

Pasola, West Sumba. Held four times in February and March, the exact dates being determined by local priests, this festival to balance the upper sphere of the heavens culminates with a frenetic and lethal pitched battle between two villages of spear-wielding horsemen.

Sekaten, Central Java. The celebration of the birthday of the prophet Mohammed, held in the royal courts of Central Java, includes a month-long festival of fairs, gamelan recitals, wayang kulit (Javanese shadow puppet performances) and wayang orang (a form of Javanese ballet) performances, culminating in a procession.

Cultural hints

Indonesia shares the same attitudes to dress and social taboos as other Southeast Asian cultures, described in "Basics" on p.41. In addition, Indonesians are generally very sociable, and dislike doing anything alone. It's normal for complete strangers engaged in some common enterprise – catching a bus, for instance – to introduce themselves and start up a friendship. **Sharing cigarettes** between men is in these circumstances a way of establishing a bond, and Westerners who don't smoke should be genuinely apologetic about refusing; it's well worth carrying a packet to share around even if you save your own "for later".

Diving, surfing and trekking

Indonesia has many of the world's best **diving sites**, one of the finest of which is Pulau Bunaken off

Sulawesi, where the vast diversity of tropical fish and coral is complemented by visibility that can reach over 30m. **Bali** has many good sites including the famous *Liberty* wreck, and reputable tour operators at all major beach resorts; **Lombok**'s operators are limited to Senggigi and the Gili Islands; and in **Kalimantan** there's fine diving off Pulau Derawan. The best time for diving is between April and October. Most major beach resorts have dive centres, but once you get further afield you'll probably have to rely on live-aboard cruises or even on having your own gear. A day's diving with two tanks, lunch and basic equipment costs anything from $30 to $100. Be sure to enquire about the reputation of the dive operators before signing up, check their PADI or equivalent accreditation and, if possible, get first-hand recommendations from other divers. Be aware that it is down to you to **check your equipment**, and that the purity of an air tank can be suspect, and could cause serious injury. Also check your guide's credentials carefully, and bear in mind that you may be a long way from a decompression chamber.

■ Surfing

Indonesia is also one of the world's premier **surfing** destinations, with an enormous variety of class waves and perfect, uncrowded breaks. The best-known waves are found on **Bali**, **G' Land** (Grajagan) on Java, and **Nias** off Sumatra. Sumbawa's **Hu'u** and **Pulau Roti** have been hot spots for a few years now, and **Sumba**, **Savu** and the **Mentawi Islands** are the destinations of the future. In June and July, during the best and most consistent surf, you can expect waves to be crowded, especially in Java and Bali. For all-in **surf safaris** on luxury yachts, try STC (*surftrav@ozemail.com.au*), who have boat trips around all major destinations. Try to bring your own **board**, and a padded board-bag; most public transport charge extra for boards. Also pack high-strength sun block; plenty of iodine, a helmet and thin suit are advisable too.

■ Trekking

There are endless **trekking** opportunities in Indonesia. The most popular volcano treks include **Batur** on Bali and **Bromo** on Java; more taxing favourites include **Gunung Rinjani** on Lombok, **Kerinci** on Sumatra and **Semeru** on Java. In Sumatra, the **Gunung Leuser** national park is Southeast Asia's largest, and includes the famous Bukit Lawang orang-utan sanctuary. Many routes need **guides**, and not just to find the paths: turning up at a remote village unannounced can cause trouble, as people may mistrust outsiders, let alone Westerners. Guides are always available from local vilages and tourist centres.

Crime and safety

Foreign fatalities resulting from the suppression of independence movements in Irian and Timor, and the urban violence which surrounded the political and religious upheavals of the last couple of years, all undermine the idea that Indonesia is a safe place to travel. However, it's also true that serious incidents involving Westerners are rare. **Petty theft**, however, is a fact of life, so don't flash around expensive jewellery or watches. Don't hesitate to check that doors and windows – including those in the bathroom – are secure before accepting **accommodation**; if the management seems offended by this, you probably don't want to stay there anyway. Some guesthouses and hotels have safe-deposit boxes.

If you're unlucky enough to get **mugged**, never resist and, if you disturb a thief, raise the alarm rather than try to take them on. Be especially aware of **pickpockets** on buses or bemos, who usually operate in pairs: one will distract you while another does the job. Afterwards, you'll need a **police report** for insurance purposes. In smaller villages where police are absent, ask for assistance from the headman. Try to take along someone to translate, though police will generally do their best to find an English speaker. You may also be charged "administration fees", the cost of which is open to sensitive negotiations. Have nothing to do with **drugs** in Indonesia. The penalties are tough, and you won't get any sympathy from consular officials. If arrested, ring your embassy immediately.

> **EMERGENCY PHONE NUMBERS**
> Police ☎110
> Ambulance ☎118
> Fire ☎113

Medical care and emergencies

If you have a minor ailment, head to a **pharmacy** (*apotik*), which can provide many medicines without prescription. Condoms (*kondom*) are available from pharmacists. Only in the main tourist areas will assistants speak English; in the village health posts, staff are generally ill-equipped to cope with serious illness. If you need an English-speaking **doctor** *(doktor)* or dentist (*doktor gigi*) seek advice at your hotel (some of the luxury ones have an in-house doctor) or at the local tourist office. You'll find a public **hospital** (*rumah sakit*) in major cities and towns, and in some places these are supplemented by private hospitals, many of which operate an accident and emergency department. If you have a serious accident or illness, you will need to be evacuated home or to Singapore, which has the best medical provision in Asia. It is, therefore, vital to arrange health insurance before you leave home (see "Basics" p.31).

History

Until the Dutch subsumed most of the islands under the title the "Dutch East Indies" towards the end of the nineteenth century, the Indonesian archipelago was little more than a series of unrelated kingdoms, sultanates and private fiefdoms with distinct histories.

■ Beginnings

Hominids first arrived in Indonesia about eight hundred thousand years ago. Excavations uncovered parts of the skull of *Pithecanthropus erectus*, since renamed *Homo erectus erectus* – or **Java Man** – in Sangiran near Solo.

Homo sapiens first made an appearance in about 40,000 BC, having crossed over to the Indonesian archipelago from the Philippines, Thailand and Burma, using land bridges exposed during the Ice Ages. Later migrants brought knowledge of rice irrigation and animal husbandry, sea navigation and weaving techniques, and from the seventh or eighth centuries BC, the **Bronze Age** began to spread south from Southern China.

■ Early traders and kingdoms

One of the methods of rice growing brought by the early migrants was wet-field cultivation, which required substantial inter-village co-operation and so gave rise to the first **kingdoms** in the archipelago.

Merchants from India brought **Hinduism** to the archipelago, which spread quickly. By the fifth century, a myriad of small Hindu kingdoms peppered the archipelago, the most successful being the **Srivijaya** kingdom, based in Palembang in South Sumatra. For approximately four hundred years, beginning in

around the seventh century AD, Srivijaya controlled the Melaka Straits – and the accompanying lucrative trade in spices, wood, camphor, tortoise shell and precious stones – and extended its empire as far north as Thailand and as far east as West Borneo. Srivijaya was also a seat of learning and religion, with over a thousand **Buddhist** monks living and studying within the city.

Whilst the Srivijayans enjoyed supremacy around the coasts of Indonesia, small kingdoms began to flourish inland. In particular, the rival **Saliendra** and **Sanjaya** (the latter sometimes known as Mataram) kingdoms began to wield considerable influence on the volcanic plains of Central Java, constructing spectacular monuments such as the magnificent temple at **Borobodur**, built by the Buddhist Saliendras, and the manifold temples of **Prambanan**, built by the Hindu Sanjayas. But by the twelfth century things had begun to change: the Cholas of southern India destroyed the Srivijayan empire, and the influence of the Saliendras and Sanjayas was declining in the face of new empires emerging in the east of Java.

■ The Majapahit Empire and the arrival of Islam

The **Majapahit Empire,** a Hindu kingdom based in East Java, enjoyed unrivalled success from 1292 to 1389, boasting at least partial control over a vast area covering Java, Bali, Sumatra, Borneo, Sulawesi, Lombok and Timor. This was the first time the major islands of the Indonesian archipelago had been united under one command. As well as economic prosperity, the Majapahit empire also saw the first flowering of Indonesian culture, in particular certain courtly traditions still extant. However, the arrival of Islam on Java and a massive revolt in the north of the island eventually left the empire weak and in disarray, although it managed to survive for over a hundred years longer on its new home in Bali.

Islam first gained a toehold in the archipelago as early as the fifth century AD, during the rule of the Buddhist Srivijaya Empire. Merchants from Gujarat in India who called in at Aceh in northern Sumatra were the first to bring the message of Mohammed, followed soon after by traders from Arabia. From Sumatra, Islam spread eastwards, first along the coast and then into the interior of Java and the rest of Indonesia (Bali, Flores and Irian Jaya excepted), where it syncretized with the Hindu, Buddhist and animist faiths that were already practised throughout the archipelago. The first Islamic kingdoms in the archipelago emerged on Java, where small coastal sultanates grew in the vacuum left by the Majapahit.

■ The spice trade and the Dutch conquest of Indonesia

Portuguese ships began appearing in the region in the early sixteenth century and soon established a virtual monopoly over the archipelago's lucrative spice trade. They took control of the Moluccas (Maluku), which became known as the **Spice Islands**, because of their wealth of pepper, nutmeg, cloves, mace, ginger and cinnamon.

Dutch forays into the Indonesian archipelago began at the very end of the 16th century, and by 1600 they had become the supreme European trading power in the region. In 1602, they founded the **United Dutch East India Company (VOC)**, with monopoly control over trade with the Moluccas. They then invaded and occupied the Banda Islands, part of the Moluccas, in 1603 – the first overtly aggressive act by the Dutch against their Indonesian hosts. Two years later, the VOC successfully chased the Portuguese from their remaining strongholds on Tidore and Ambon, and the Dutch annexation of Indonesia began in earnest. Trading vessels were now being replaced by warships, and the battle for the archipelago commenced.

By the end of the first decade of the seventeenth century, the VOC had begun to build a loose but lucrative **empire**, becoming the Dutch government's official representatives in the archipelago. At the helm of the VOC was the ruthless Jan Pieterzoon Coen, who set about raising the prices of nutmeg and clove artificially high by destroying vast plantations on the island, thus devastating the livelihood of Banda's already decimated population.

Coen then turned his attention to Java, and in particular Jayakarta (now Jakarta), which he wanted to become the capital of the ever-expanding VOC territories. When he built a fortress there, the local population responded angrily, upon which the Dutch retaliated by razing the city and renaming it **Batavia**. Further strategically important territories were acquired soon after, including Melaka (in modern-day Malaysia) and Makassar.

The plains of Central Java and the northern shores were by this time in the grip of the influential Islamic **Mataram Empire** (different from the Mataram, or Sanjaya, empire, which was Hindu), whose rulers were treated almost as deities by their subjects. However, the royal house was often riven with squabbles and during the early years of the eighteenth century the region was paralyzed by **Three Wars of Succession**. The last of these (1746–57) brought about the division of the empire into three separate sultanates, two at Solo and one at Yogyakarta, aided and abetted by the politically astute Dutch who then subjugated the entire territory.

Though they were now the first rulers of a united Java, the VOC began to see their fortunes dwindle in the face of huge competition from the British and French. In 1795 the Dutch government, investigating the affairs of the company that for 99 years had represented their interests in the Far East, found mismanagement and corruption on a grand scale. The VOC company was bankrupt, and eventually expired in 1799. The Netherlands government took possession of all VOC territories, and thus all of the islands we regard as Indonesia today formally became part of the **Dutch colonial empire**.

■ The arrival of the British

In 1795, the French, under Napoleon, invaded and occupied Holland, and Herman Willem Daendels was made governor-general of the East Indies. He ruled for just three years, but was unable to fend off attacks by the **British** who, under the leadership of Sir Thomas Stamford Raffles, picked off the islands one by one, eventually landing at Batavia in 1811.

Raffles' tenure lasted for just five years before he was forced to hand back the territories to the Dutch. But he left a lasting impact, having ordered surveys of every historical building, and conducted extensive research into the country's flora and fauna.

■ The return of the Dutch

The **Dutch** returned to Indonesia in 1816 and were soon embroiled in a couple of bloody disputes against opponents of their rule. But, having finally regained control over their old colonies, the rest of the nineteenth century and the beginning of the twentieth saw the Dutch attempting to expand into previously independent territories. Their early efforts met with limited success: the **Balinese** only surrendered in 1906, a full sixty years after the Dutch had first invaded, whilst the war in Aceh, which the Dutch had first tried to annex in 1873, dragged on until 1908, costing thousands of lives on both sides. By 1910, however, following the fall of **Banjarmasin** in 1864, **Lombok** in 1894 and **Sulawesi** in 1905, the Dutch had conquered nearly all of what we today call Indonesia; the only major exception, **Irian Jaya**, finally accepted colonial rule in 1920.

Following the debilitating battles in Java and Sumatra, the Dutch in Indonesia were facing bankruptcy, so they devised the **Cultural System** in 1830, under which Javanese farmers had to give up a significant portion of their land to grow lucrative cash crops that could be sold in Europe for a huge profit. Java became one giant plantation and Indonesia evolved into a major world exporter of indigo, coffee and sugar. But indigenous farmers suffered hugely, some of them starving to death.

The **Liberal System** (1870–1900) aimed to rectify the injustices of the Cultural System and end the exploitation of the local population, but unfortunately coincided with some devastating natural and economic disasters, including widespread coffee-leaf disease and a sugar blight. A vocal, altruistic minority in the Dutch parliament began pressing for more drastic policies to end the injustices in Indonesia, giving rise to what is now called the **Ethical Period**. During this time, radical irrigation, health care, education, drainage and flood control programmes were started, and **transmigration** policies, from Java to the outlying islands, were introduced. But transmigration, as is still seen today, while temporarily alleviating over-population on Java, brought its own set of problems, with the displaced often ending up as the victims of ethnic violence in their new homelands.

■ The Independence movement

Though education amongst Indonesians was still the preserve of a rich minority, it was from this minority that the leaders of the **Independence movement** would emerge. The Partai Nasional Indonesia (PNI), founded in 1927 by Achmed Sukarno, grew to become the biggest of the independence organizations. It aimed to achieve independence through non-co-operation and mass action, and quickly became a major threat to Dutch domination, so much so that the Dutch outlawed the party four years after its foundation, throwing its leaders, Sukarno included, in prison, and later exiling them. But when Hitler invaded Holland on May 10, 1940, the Dutch government fled to London, and the issue of Indonesia's independence was put on ice.

The Japanese made no secret of their intention to "liberate" Indonesia and when they did finally invade, in January 1942, most Indonesians saw them as liberators, rather than just another occupying force. On March 8, 1942, the Dutch on Java surrendered, and a three-and-a-half-year **Japanese occupation** began. Though every bit as ruthless as the

Dutch, the Japanese did at least encourage the nationalist movement, and by 1945 were negotiating with Sukarno and others. Sukarno came up with his constitutional doctrine of **Pancasila**, the "five principles" by which an Independent Indonesia would be governed: belief in God, nationalism, democracy, social justice and humanitarianism.

On August 17, 1945, two days after the Japanese surrender to the Allied forces, Sukarno read a simple, unemotional **Declaration of Independence** to a small group of people outside his house in Menteng. The Republic of Indonesia was born, with Achmed Sukarno as its first president.

■ The Revolution

However, under the terms of the surrender agreed with the Allies, the Japanese actually had no right to hand over Indonesia to the Indonesian people. Lord Louis Mountbatten arrived in mid-1945 with several thousand **British** troops to accept the surrender of the Japanese occupying force. The Japanese tried to retake towns that they'd previously handed over to the local people and some intense, short-lived battles occurred. The British tried to remain neutral, withdrawing only when the Dutch were in a position to resume control in November 1946.

The **war with the Dutch** continued for the next three years. But the world was turning against the Dutch campaign, finding their colonial activities anachronistic in the twentieth century. The Dutch finally withdrew in December 1949, and sovereignty was handed over to the new **Republic of Indonesia**.

■ The Sukarno years

Sukarno introduced the concept of **guided democracy**, an attempt to create a wholly Indonesian political system based on the traditional, hierarchical organization of Indonesian villages. Decisions were to be made with the consent of everyone, and not simply the majority; the various political factions would all have their say, though Sukarno would now play the part of village chief, with all the power that entailed.

In reality, guided democracy was the first step on the road to **authoritarian rule**, removing power from the elected cabinet and investing it instead with the presidency and a non-elected cabinet. Unsurprisingly, many people, both within and outside government, were suspicious of Sukarno's real motives, and lengthy protests in Sulawesi and Sumatra marred the early years of guided democracy.

Meanwhile, Sukarno began to forge strong ties with the **Soviet Union**, who appreciated his Marxist leanings and anti-Western foreign policy. They began financing the **Konfrontasi** ("Confrontation"), Sukarno's bid to wrest the northern Borneo states of Sabah, Sarawak and Brunei from neo-colonial Malaysia, which he saw as a puppet of the British. However, Sukarno was unwilling to commit too many troops to the jungles of Kalimantan and his ambition to bring Sabah, Sarawak and Brunei into the Indonesian republic failed.

Sukarno's ties with the Soviet Union made him more sympathetic towards the views of Indonesia's **communist party**, the PKI, and openly sided with them against the increasingly powerful **Indonesian army**. This led to the polarization of the entire parliament, with Sukarno and the communists on one side, and the army and its unlikely allies – including the Islamic NU and nationalist PNI – on the other. The political fighting in parliament was mirrored by pitched battles between the various factions on the streets of the capital, and law and order began to break down.

■ The Communist coup, 1965

In 1965, Sukarno's demise was accelerated by the still not completely explained events of September 30, 1965, when a number of leading generals were taken from their homes at gunpoint to Halim airport; their bodies were later discovered down a nearby well. Their abductors were a group of **communist** and other leftist sympathizers, who later claimed that they were only preventing an army-led coup. Of more significance, however, was the presence of President Sukarno at Halim. Although the rebels claimed he was only taken there for his own safety, it was hard not to see Sukarno as being in cahoots with them, fabricating the idea of an army coup as an excuse for getting rid of senior army personnel.

The communist rebels managed to occupy **Medan Merdeka** in the middle of Jakarta, and thus controlled the telecommunications centre and the presidential palace situated nearby. Their success was shortlived, however. General Suharto, a senior member of the Indonesian army, rounded up those generals who weren't kidnapped and eventually took control of Medan Merdeka.

■ Suharto takes control, 1965–67

Though he lived until 1970, Sukarno's grip on power had almost completely slipped by the end of 1965, and for the remaining year of his presidency he ruled in name only, as **General Suharto** manoeuvred himself to the top of the political ladder. Communists throughout the archipelago became the victims of a massive Suharto-led purge, with the **slaughter of communist sympathizers** continuing until the early months of 1966. It was the bloodiest episode in Indonesia's history: most experts today reckon that at least 500,000 people lost their lives, although the official figure was a more modest 160,000. The army was now the dominant force in Indonesian politics.

On returning to power, Sukarno tried desperately to weaken the power of the armed forces but Suharto's response was to encourage a renewed outbreak of violence. On March 11, 1966, Sukarno was informed that unidentified troops were surrounding his palace, and in panic he fled to Bogor. Once there, Sukarno was persuaded to give Suharto full authority to restore order and protect the president by whatever means necessary.

The following year, pro-Suharto Adam Malik was made minister for foreign affairs, and quickly set about restoring **relations with the West** and loosening existing ties with communist China. Soon aid began pouring back into Indonesia, rescuing the ailing economy and providing essential relief to thousands of the poorest in Indonesian society. Suharto now had popular support to go with his burgeoning political power and, in the new bourgeoisie, he found a powerful and secure foundation for his regime. On March 12, 1967, Sukarno was stripped of all his powers and Suharto was named **acting president**.

■ The New Order

Suharto dubbed his new regime the **New Order**. His first few years in power were seen as a brave new dawn, as the economy improved beyond all recognition and he managed to create a pluralistic society where religious intolerance had no place; providing people belonged to one of the five main faiths, their religious beliefs were respected.

But this was not matched by political tolerance, and people were forced to live under a suffocating **dictatorial regime**, taking part in the charade of the so-called "festivals of democracy", the "elections" that took place every five years. Where beforehand there had been a multitude of **political parties**, Suharto reduced them to just three: the PPP (United Development Party) made up of the old Islamic parties; the PDI (Indonesian Democratic Party) made up largely of the old nationalist party, the PNI; and the government's own political vehicle, Golkar. The re-election of Suharto was a foregone conclusion, and critics were jailed and tortured. A huge underclass developed in rural areas and in slum districts on the outskirts of large cities. There was also widespread corruption throughout society, from the president down.

East Timor, independent since a revolution in Portugal had emancipated the tiny former colony in 1974, collapsed into civil war the following year as various factions failed to agree on whether the territory should become part of Indonesia. In the event, the decision was taken out of their hands by the Indonesians themselves, who invaded on Suharto's orders in December 1975. Despite strong condemnation from the United Nations, and regular Amnesty International reports of human rights abuses in East Timor, the US and Europe were unwilling to upset their new Southeast Asian ally. East Timor was incorporated into the republic of Indonesia the following year.

The oil crisis of the 1970s raised the price of oil, then Indonesia's most lucrative export, significantly. This windfall lasted until 1983, allowing the government to use the **oil revenue** to create a sound industrial base founded on steel and natural gas production, oil refining and aluminium industries. Welfare measures were introduced, with 100,000 new schools built, and the 1980s also saw an increase of fifty percent in agricultural production. Yet the beneficiaries of Suharto's economic miracle were a small minority who lived in air-conditioned luxury in the big cities, while the majority continued to eke out a meagre existence in the rural areas of the country.

■ Suharto's downfall

Resentment against Suharto's regime grew throughout the 1990s, but he would probably have survived for a few more years if it hadn't been for the **currency crisis** that hit the region in the latter part of 1997, a crisis triggered by a run on the Thai baht. In a few dramatic months, the rupiah slipped in value from Rp2500 to the US dollar to nearly Rp9000. Prices of even the most basic of goods such as fuel and food rose five hundred percent.

The **IMF** promised to help Indonesia out of the crisis only after certain conditions had been met, including the removal of Suharto's family and friends from a number of senior and lucrative posts. Foreign investors lost all confidence in Suharto, and the rupiah went into freefall.

Pressure on Suharto was also growing from his own people, as many took to the streets to protest against his incompetence and demand greater political freedom. These **demonstrations**, initially fairly peaceful, grew more violent as the people's frustration increased, until a state of lawlessness ensued. For over a week, riots took place in all the main cities, buildings were set on fire and shops looted. The **Chinese community**, long resented in Indonesia for their domination of the economy and success in business, were targeted by the rioters for special persecution. Over 1200 people died in the mayhem that followed the May elections, until, on May 21, 1998, Suharto stepped down and his vice-president, BJ Habibie, took over.

■ The future

Despite promises to introduce sweeping reforms, many believed **Habibie** was dragging his feet over a number of issues, and, in early November 1998, more rioting occurred. The cry for **"Reformasi"**, first heard in May, grew more voluble by the day as the rioters – largely students – demanded the removal of the army from parliament, an end to corruption within government, the bringing to trial of Suharto on charges of mismanagement and corruption, and a return to democracy. Ordinary people began to openly express their support for reform and, just as importantly, their dissatisfaction with the government. Even the press is enjoying a freedom of expression it has never enjoyed before.

Nobody expected Indonesia's transition to democracy to be an easy one and the country is currently in the grip of a mixture of fear, intrigue and hope. Occasionally this manifests itself in the form of **religious intolerance**: a number of Christians have been killed in a series of attacks, prompting revenge killings by Christian gangs, and almost two hundred Muslim clerics have also been murdered, though nobody knows by whom.

Despite the widespread mistrust of Habibie, he did lay the ground for the first **free and democratic elections** ever to be held in Indonesia, keeping a promise that he made during his first few days in power. In the elections, the Indonesian Democratic Party of Struggle, led by **Megawati Sukarnoputri**, the daughter of the country's first president, Sukarno, scored an easy victory. However, Indonesia's parliament, the People's Consultative Assembly, decided she couldn't be trusted to lead, a decision that led to widespread rioting on the streets of Jakarta. In the vote that followed, parliament chose **Abdurrahman Wahid**, the leader of the Islamic National Awakening Party, which came third in the elections, to be the country's first democratically elected president. To placate the rioters, Megawati was installed as vice-president.

Though almost totally blind and physically very frail following two strokes, Gus Dur, as Abdurrahman is affectionately known, has been very busy since taking office. In his bid to reduce the influence of the army in Indonesian politics, many top generals were sacked, including **General Wiranto**, the man who directed operations in East Timor in 1999 when that territory finally won independence from Indonesia after 24 years under occupation. Many believe Wiranto was behind the atrocities and violations of human rights that occurred on the island at that time, an accusation the UN is currently investigating. The **army**, though shorn of much of its power, still remains a credible threat to Abdurrahman's leadership, and whispers of an imminent coup circulate constantly.

The president also has his hands full trying to restore the faith of the international community in the **Indonesian economy**. His frequent overseas trips aimed at achieving his goal have drawn criticism too, particularly from those who feel he should be spending more time sorting out affairs closer to home: in **Maluku and Ambon**, over two thousand people have died recently in Muslim–Christian fighting, and in Aceh, north Sumatra, pro-independence rebels are waging a bloody campaign against the authorities. Abdurrahman's efforts to curb the cancer of corruption and resolve the current banking crisis have also met with limited success.

Indonesia's first experience of democracy has been a difficult and often bloody time. But if the ambitions of Abdurrahman for his country bear fruit, the future of the new democratic republic of Indonesia may not be so bleak as many had originally feared.

Religions of Indonesia

Indonesia has a predominantly Muslim population, though with significant Buddhist (the Chinese populations in the large cities and in West Kalimantan), Hindu and animist minorities (in Bali, Irian Jaya, Sumatra, Kalimantan and other remote outposts). The Batak of North Sumatra, the Ambonese, Florinese and a few tribes in Irian Jaya and Kalimantan are the only pockets of Christianity. For an introduction to all these faiths, see "Basics" p.47. Yet the major faiths in the archipelago bear striking differences to their counterparts in other parts of the world because religion in Indonesia is dynamic, not dogmatic, adapted over the centuries to incorporate

rituals and beliefs of existing faiths, in particular indigenous animism.

Indonesia is the largest **Islamic** nation in the world. The northernmost province of Aceh, which received Islam directly from India, is still the most orthodox area, whereas Muslims in the rest of the archipelago follow a style of Islam that has been syncretized with animism, Buddhism and Hinduism. Nearly all Indonesian Muslims are followers of the Sunni sect. Women in veils or full purdah are a rare sight in Indonesia, and men are only allowed two wives, as opposed to four in Arabian countries, though just one wife is the norm.

Animism is still the predominant faith in some of the villages of the outlying islands, particularly Sumatra, Kalimantan and Irian Jaya. The rituals and beliefs vary significantly between each of these islands. Many of these ancient animist beliefs permeate each of the five major religions, and many Indonesian people, no matter what faith they profess, still perform animist rituals.

Despite certain obvious similarities, Balinese **Agama Hinduism** differs dramatically from Indian and Nepalese Hinduism. At its root lies the understanding that the natural and supernatural world is composed of opposing forces, such as good and evil, order and disorder, gods and demons – and that these forces need to be balanced. Positive forces, or *dharma*, are represented by the gods and need to be honoured with offerings, dances, paintings and sculptures, fine earthly abodes (temples) and rituals. The malevolent forces, *adharma*, which manifest themselves as earth demons and cause sickness, death and volcanic eruptions, need to be neutralized with elaborate rituals and special offerings. All Balinese gods are manifestations of the supreme being, Sanghyang Widi Wasa, a deity who is only ever represented by an empty throne-shrine, that stands in the holiest corner of every temple. Sanghyang Widi Wasa's three main aspects manifest themselves as the Hindu trinity: Brahma, Wisnu and Siwa. Siwa's consort is the terrifying goddess Durga, whose Balinese personality is the gruesome widow-witch Rangda, queen of the demons.

Traditional dance and music

Given the enormous cultural and ethnic mix that makes up Indonesia, it's hardly surprising that the range of traditional music and dance across the archipelago is so vast. Best-known are the highly stylized and mannered **classical dance performances** in Java and Bali, accompanied by the gamelan orchestra. Every step of these dances is minutely orchestrated, and the merest wink of an eye, arch of an eyebrow and angle of a finger has meaning and significance. The tradition remains vibrant, passed down by experts to often very young pupils. **Ubud** on Bali and **Yogyakarta** on Java are the centres for these dances, with shortened performances staged in several venues every night for Western visitors. Yogya is also the main place in Indonesia to catch a performance of shadow puppet plays, **wayang kulit**.

■ Gamelan

A **gamelan** is an ensemble of tuned percussion, consisting mainly of gongs, metallophones and drums. Gamelan instruments may be made of bronze, iron, brass, wood or bamboo, with wooden frames, which are often intricately carved and painted.

The largest bronze gamelans in Indonesia are found in **Central Java**. A complete Javanese gamelan is made up of two sets of instruments, one in each of two scales – the five-note *laras slendro* and the seven-note *laras pelog*. The two sets are laid out with the corresponding instruments at right angles to each other. Various hanging and mounted gongs are arranged at the back and provide the structure and form of the music. In the middle, the metallophones play the central melody. At the front are the more complex instruments, which lead and elaborate the melody. These include metallophones, a wooden xylophone, spike fiddle, bamboo flute and zither. The full ensemble also includes vocalists – a male chorus and female solo singers – and is led by the drummer in the centre of the gamelan. Although a large gamelan may be played by as many as thirty **musicians**, there is neither a conductor nor any visual cues, as the players all sit facing the same way. Gamelan musicians learn all the instruments and so develop a deep understanding of the music plus great flexibility in ensemble playing. It is a communal form of music-making – there are no soloists or virtuosos. Most village halls and neighbourhoods in Central Java have a gamelan for use by the local community, and the majority of schoolchildren learn basic gamelan pieces.

Most villages in Bali boast several gamelans owned by the local music club. The club members meet in the evenings to rehearse, after earning their living as farmers, craftsmen or civil servants. Gamelan playing is traditionally considered a part of every man's education, as important as the art of rice growing or cooking ceremonial food. When the Dutch took control of Bali in the early twentieth century, the island's courts all but disappeared. The court gamelans were sold or taken to the villages where they were melted down to make new gamelans for the latest style that was taking Bali by storm: **kebyar**, a fast, dynamic music, full of dramatic contrasts, changes of tempo and sudden loud outbursts. It is this dynamic new virtuoso style that makes much Balinese gamelan music today sound so different from the Javanese form. The rhythmic vitality of Balinese music comes from lively interlocking patterns played on the bronze gangsas (similar to the Javanese gender but struck with hard wooden mallets), a pair of drums and the reong (a row of small kettle-gongs in a frame, played by four people). The various pairs of instruments are tuned slightly "out" with each other, so that when two instruments are played together, there is a "harmonic beating". This gives the sound of the Balinese gamelan its characteristic shimmering quality.

The sound of Sundanese (West Javanese) **degung** is arguably the most accessible of all gamelan music to Western ears. Its musical structures are clear and well-defined, and the timbres of the instruments blend delicately with one another without losing any of their integrity or individuality. The ensemble is small, consisting only of a few instruments, but includes the usual range of gongs and metallophones found in all gamelan.

By Jenny Heaton and Simon Steptoe

Books

In the selection of books below, where a book is published in the UK and the US, the UK publisher is given first, followed by the US one; the abbreviation "o/p" means "out of print".

David Attenborough *Zoo Quest for a Dragon* (o/p). A youthful Attenborough's travels through the archipelago during the 1950s as a wildlife collector and filmmaker, peaking with the capture of a Komodo dragon.

Nigel Barley *Not a Hazardous Sport* (Penguin). Humourous, double-sided culturê-shock tale, as the anthropologist author persuades craftsmen from Sulawesi to return to London with him in order to build a traditional Torajan rice barn in the Museum of Mankind.

Lawrence and Lorne Blair *Ring of Fire* (Bantam). Possibly the definitive account of a tour around the Indonesian archipelago. The photos are great, the tales are occasionally tall and certainly not lacking in genuine passion for the country and its inhabitants.

LANGUAGE

The national language of Indonesia is **Bahasa Indonesia**, although there are also over 250 native languages spoken throughout the archipelago. Bahasa Indonesia is a form of Bahasa Malay and, because it's written in Roman script, has no tones and uses a fairly straightforward grammar, it's relatively easy to learn.

If you need more help, try *Indonesian: A Rough Guide Phrasebook*.

PRONUNCIATION

a as in a cross between f**a**ther and c**u**p

e sometimes as in **a**long; or as in p**ay**; or as in g**e**t; or sometimes omitted (*selamat* pronounced "slamat")

i either as in bout**i**que; or as in p**i**t

o either as in h**o**t; or as in c**o**ld

u as in b**oo**t

ai as in f**i**ne

au as in h**ow**

Most consonants are pronounced as in English, with the following exceptions:

c as in **ch**eap

g always hard as in **g**irl

k hard, as in English, except at the end of the word, when you should stop just short of pronouncing it.

GREETINGS AND BASIC PHRASES

If addressing a **married woman**, it's polite to use the respectful term *Ibu* or *Nyonya*; if addressing a **married man** use *Bapak*. *Mau ke mana*? (literally "want to where") is the usual opening gambit in any conversation, and means "**where are you going**?" The proper reply is *mau ke...* (want to go to...) followed by your intended destination. Other good answers are *saya jalan jalan* (I'm just walking) or *saya makan angin* (literally "I'm eating the wind"). When asked **if you can speak Indonesian**, *bisa berbicara bahasa Indonesia?*, the usual response is *saya belum lancar* (I'm not yet fluent) or *sedikit sedikit* (just a little); the less confident should go for *ma'af tidak bisa* (sorry not at all).

Good morning (5–11am)	*Selamat pagi*	Not (with verb)	*Tidak* (sometimes pronounced "tak")
Good day (11am–3pm)	*Selamat siang*		
Good afternoon (3–7pm)	*Selamat sore*	What is your name?	*Siapa nama anda?*
Good evening (after 7pm)	*Selamat malam*	My name is...	*Nama saya...*
Good night	*Selamat tidur*	Where are you from?	*Dari mana?*
Goodbye	*Selamat tinggal*	I come from...	*Saya dari...*
See you later	*Sampai jumpa lagi*	Do you speak English?	*Bisa bicara bahasa Inggris?*
Have a good trip	*Selamat jalan*		
Enjoy your meal	*Selamat makan*	I don't understand	*Saya tidak mengerti*
Cheers/Enjoy your drink	*Selamat minum*	Do you have...?	*Ada...?*
How are you?	*Apa kabar?*	I want/would like...	*Saya mau...*
I'm fine	*Bagus/Kabar baik*	I don't want it/No thanks	*Tidak mau*
Please (requesting)	*Tolong*	What is this/that?	*Apa ini/itu?*
Please (offering)	*Silakan*	When?	*Kapan?*
Thank you (very much)	*Terima kasih (banyak)*	Where?	*Dimana?*
You're welcome	*Sama sama*	Boyfriend or girlfriend	*Pacar*
Sorry/Excuse me	*Ma'af*	Foreigner	*Turis*
No worries/Never mind	*Tidak apa apa*	Friend	*Teman*
Yes	*Ya*	Men/women	*Laki-laki/perempuan* or *wanita*
No (with noun)	*Bukan*		

ADJECTIVES

Another	*Satu lagi*	Expensive/ inexpensive	*Mahal/murah*	Hot (spicy)	*Pedas*
Beautiful	*Cantik*			Ill	*Sakit*
Big/small	*Besar/kecil*	Good/bad	*Bagus/buruk*	Married/single	*Kawin/bujang*
Clean/dirty	*Bersih/kotor*	Hot (water/ weather)	*Panas*	Open/closed	*Buka/tutup*
Cold	*Dingin*			Very much/a lot	*Banyak*

GETTING AROUND

Where is the...?	*dimana...?*	Car	*Mobil*
I would like to go to the...	*Saya mau pergi ke...*	Entrance/exit	*Masuk/keluar*
... airport	*... lapangan terbang*	Ferry	*Ferry*
... bank	*... bank*	Motorbike	*Sepeda motor*
... beach	*... pantai*	Taxi	*Taksi*
... bemo/bus station	*... terminal*	Ticket	*Karcis*
... city/downtown	*... kota*	To come/go	*Datang/pergi*
... hospital	*... sakit*	How far?	*Berapa kilometre?*
... hotel	*... losmen*	How much is	*Berapa harga karcis ke...?*
... market	*... pasar*	the fare to...?	
... pharmacy	*... apotik*	Where is this bemo	*Kemana bemo pergi?*
... police station	*... kantor polisi*	going?	
... post office	*... kantor pos*	Stop!	*Estop!*
... shop	*... toko*	Here	*Disini*
... telephone office	*... wartel/kantor telkom*	Right	*Kanan*
Bicycle	*Sepeda*	Left	*Kiri*
Bus	*Bis*	Straight on	*Terus*

ACCOMMODATION AND SHOPPING

How much is...?	*Berapa harga...?*	...breakfast	*...makan pagi*
...single room	*...kamar untuk satu orang*	...fan	*...kipas*
...double room	*...kamar untuk dua orang*	...hot water	*...air panas*
Can I look at the room?	*Boleh saya lihat kamar?*	...mosquito net	*...kelambu nyamuk*
Is there...?	*Apakah ada...?*	...toilet	*...kamar kecil/wc*
...air-conditioning	*...AC*		(pronounced "way say")
...bathroom	*...kamar mandi*		

NUMBERS

Zero	*Nol/kosong*	Eleven	*Sebelas*	Two hundred,	*Duaratus,*
One	*Satu*	Twelve,	*Duabelas,*	three hundred, etc	*tigaratus, etc*
Two	*Dua*	thirteen, etc	*tigabelas, etc*	One thousand	*Seribu*
Three	*Tiga*	Twenty	*Duapuluh*	Two thousand,	*Duaribu,*
Four	*Empat*	Twenty one,	*Duapuluh satu,*	three thousand,	*tigaribu,*
Five	*Lima*	twenty two,	*duapuluh dua,*	etc	*etc*
Six	*Enam*	etc	*etc*	Ten thousand	*Sepuluhribu*
Seven	*Tujuh*	Thirty, forty,	*Tigapuluh,*	One hundred	*Seratusribu*
Eight	*Delapan*	etc	*empatpuluh,*	thousand	
Nine	*Sembilan*		*etc*	One million	*Sejuta*
Ten	*Sepuluh*	One hundred	*Seratus*	Two million	*Dua juta*

TIME AND DAYS OF THE WEEK

What time is it?	*Jam berapa?*	Today/tomorrow	*Hari ini/besok*
It's three o'clock	*jam tiga*	Yesterday	*Kemarin*
... ten past four	*jam empat lewat sepuluh*	Monday	*Hari Senin*
... quarter to five	*jam lima kurang seperempat*	Tuesday	*Hari Selasa*
... six-thirty	*jam setengah tujuh*	Wednesday	*Hari Rabu*
	(literally "half to seven")	Thursday	*Hari Kamis*
... in the morning	*... pagi*	Friday	*Hari Jumat*
... in the afternoon	*... sore*	Saturday	*Hari Sabtu*
... pm/in the evening	*... malam*	Sunday	*Hari Minggu*

Guy Buckles *Dive Sites of Indonesia* (New Holland). Exhaustively researched, attractive, up-to-date guide with strong practical details.

Vern Cook (ed.) *Bali Behind the Seen: Recent Fiction from Bali* (Darma Printing, Australia). Interesting collection of short stories by contemporary Balinese and Javanese writers.

Cubitt & Whitten *Wild Indonesia* (New Holland). Plenty of good pictures and text in this overview of Indonesia's natural history, including coverage of national parks.

Jacques Dumarcay *The Temples of Java* (OUP Asia). Slim but entertaining rundown of all the major historical temple complexes in Java.

Fred B Eisemann Jr *Bali: Sekala and Niskala Vols 1 and 2* (Periplus, Singapore). The fascinating and admirably wide-ranging cultural and anthropological essays of a contemporary American, thirty years resident in Bali. His pieces encompass everything from the esoteric rituals of Balinese Hinduism to musings on the popularity of the clove cigarette.

Anna Forbes *Unbeaten Tracks in Islands of the Far East* (OUP Asia). Island life in remote corners of Maluku and Nusa Tenggara as observed by the resourceful wife of nineteenth-century naturalist Henry Forbes.

John Gillow and Barry Dawson *Traditional Indonesian Textiles* (Thames & Hudson). Beautifully photographed and accessible introduction to the *ikat* and batik fabrics of the archipelago.

Rio Helmi and Barbara Walker *Bali Style* (Thames & Hudson). Sumptuously photographed glossy volume celebrating all things Balinese, from the humblest bamboo craftwork to the island's most fabulous buildings.

Paul Jepson and Rosie Ounsted *Birding Indonesia: A Bird-watcher's Guide to the World's Largest Archipelago* (Periplus, Singapore). Excellent introduction to the subject with plenty of photographs and practical detail.

Garret Kam *Perceptions of Paradise: Images of Bali in the Arts* (Yayasan Dharma Seni Neka Museum, Bali). One of the best introductions to Balinese art, with helpful sections on traditions and practices, and plenty of full-colour plates.

Hugh Mabbett *The Balinese* (January Books, New Zealand). Accessible collection of anecdotal essays on contemporary Balinese life, from the role of women to the impact of tourism.

Anna Matthews *Night of Purnama* (o/p). Evocative and moving description of village life and characters of the early 1960s, focusing on events in Iseh and the surrounding villages from the first eruption of Gunung Agung until 1963.

Jean McKinnon *Vessels of Life: Lombok Earthenware* (Saritaksu). Fabulously photographed and exhaustive book about Sasak life, pottery techniques and the lives of the women potters.

George Monbiot *Poisoned Arrows: An Investigative Journey Through Indonesia* (Joseph). The author travels through some of the less well known areas of Irian Jaya, researching the effects of the Indonesian government's transmigration policy.

Kal Muller *Underwater Indonesia: A Guide to the World's Best Diving* (Periplus, Singapore). This is the must-have handbook for anybody planning to dive in Indonesia. Exquisitely photographed, with useful maps.

Sri Owen *Indonesian Regional Cooking* (St Martin's Press, US). Relatively few recipes, but plenty of background.

M C Ricklefs *A History of Modern Indonesia Since c.1300* (Macmillan). Acknowledged as the most thorough study of Indonesian history, but probably best dipped into rather than consumed from start to finish.

Neville Shulman *Zen Explorations in Remotest New Guinea: Adventures in the Jungles and Mountains of Irian Jaya* (Summersdale). Not a drop of rain escapes without some obscure explanatory proverb or quotation, but even if you find his determination to find the zen in everything irritating, you can't escape the author's genuine enthusiasm for his journey.

Tara Sosrowardoyo, Peter Schoppert and Soedarmadji Damais *Java Style* (Thames and Hudson). Sumptuous volume, evocatively photographed, with illuminating descriptions of buildings and design all across the island.

John G Taylor *Indonesia's Forgotten War: The Hidden History of East Timor* (Zed Books/ Humanities Press). Clear and incisive account of the disastrous events in East Timor, from the fifteenth century to present.

Adrian Vickers *Bali: A Paradise Created* (Periplus, Singapore). Detailed, intelligent and highly readable account of the outside world's perception of Bali, the development of tourism and how events inside and outside the country have shaped the Balinese view of themselves.

Alfred Russell Wallace *The Malay Archipelago* (OUP o/p). A thoroughly readable account of the eight years that British naturalist Wallace spent in Indonesia collecting and studying wildlife during the mid-nineteenth century.

JAVA

One of the most populous places in all of Asia, **Java** is still characterized by great natural beauty. Its central spine is dominated by hundreds of volcanoes, many of which are still very evidently active, and their fertile slopes support a landscape of glimmering ricelands spotted with countless small villages. To the south of this mountainous backbone is the homeland of the ethnic Javanese and the epicentre of their arts, culture and language, epitomized by the royal courts of **Yogyakarta** and **Solo**. Still steeped in traditional dance, music and art, these two cities are the mainstay of Java's tourist industry and offer first-rate facilities for travellers. They also provide excellent bases from which to explore the giant ninth-century Buddhist temple **Borobudur**, and the equally fascinating **Prambanan complex**, a contemporary Hindu site. To the east, the huge volcanic massif of **Gunung Bromo** is the other major stop on most travellers' itineraries, not least for the sunrise walk to its summit. But there are plenty more volcanic landscapes to explore, including the coloured lakes of the windswept **Dieng** plateau, the stunning crater lake and sulphur mines of the **Ijen Plateau,** and the world's most famous – and destructive – volcano, **Krakatau** off the coast of west Java. And when it's time to chill out, most travellers opt for a spell in **Pangandaran**, which boasts crashing surf, endless expanses of sand, superb seafood and a national park on its doorstep. Aside from Yogya, Java's cities are not that enticing, but **Jakarta**, the chaotic sprawl that is Indonesia's capital, does boast several worthwhile museums. And once you've exhausted the pleasures of Java you can move easily on to neighbouring islands – Sumatra is just ninety minutes' ferry ride from Merak in the west; Bali a mere half hour from Banyuwangi in the east.

Jakarta

Bounded to the north by the Java Sea and the south by the low Bogor Hills, Indonesia's overwhelming capital, **JAKARTA**, is one of the fastest growing cities in the world. From a mere 900,000 inhabitants in 1945, the current population is well over ten million and continues to grow at a rate of 200,000 every year. The capital currently sprawls over 656 square kilometres of northern Java. Unfortunately, few foreign visitors find the city as alluring as the local population, and down the years Jakarta has been much derided. Yet the suburb of **Kota** in the north, the former heart of the old Dutch city, still retains a number of beautiful historic buildings, as does the neighbouring port of **Sunda Kelapa**. The capital also has some of the country's finest museums, including the **Maritime Museum**, the **Wayang Museum** and the **National Museum**.

The site of modern-day Jakarta first entered the history books in the twelfth century, when the Pajajarans, a Sundanese kingdom based in West Java, established a major trading port at Sunda Kelapa and held on to it for over 300 years. In the early sixteenth century, the Islamic Sultanate of Banten, 50km to the west, invaded the city and renamed it **Jayakarta**, "City of Victory"; the date of their invasion, June 22, 1527, is still celebrated as the city's birthday today. By 1619 the Dutch had won control of the city and the newly named **Batavia** became the administrative centre of their vast trading empire; it was also given a facelift, with a new network of canals and a host of imposing civic buildings. When the Japanese invaded Batavia on March 5, 1942, the city was once again retitled Jayakarta, or **Jakarta** for short. Dutch power declined, and many of their buildings were pulled down. In 1949, Sukarno entered Jakarta, amid scenes of wild jubilation, to become the first president of the Republic of Indonesia. In the following two decades, ugly, Soviet-style monuments sprouted like warts on the face of the city and huge shantytowns emerged on the fringes to house economic migrants from across the archipelago, a population shift that continues to this day. Since then, Jakarta has continued to be the focus of Indonesia's changing political face, most recently and dramatically with the **demonstrations** against Suharto in May 1998, during which time the

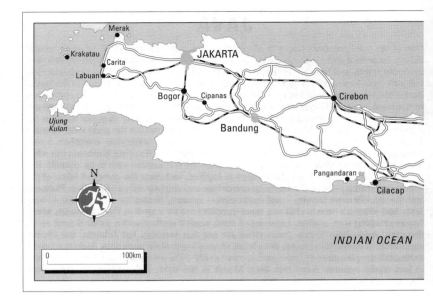

city was looted and set alight by angry mobs. The city is less tense at the moment, though the armed forces still maintain a large presence on the streets.

Arrival

BY AIR
Both international and domestic flights into Jakarta land at **Sukarno-Hatta airport**, 13km west of the city centre. The baggage reclamation area has currency exchange booths, hotel booking desks and a small **yellow board** which lists taxi fares into town and the DAMRI bus timetable. Through customs, there's a small **tourist office** and more exchange booths, most of which close at 10pm; rates are 25 percent lower than in the city centre. If you need a **hotel** at the airport, head for the *Aspac* (☎021/5590008; ⑤) at terminal 2E.

DAMRI buses run from the airport every thirty minutes from 3am to 10pm (45 min; Rp5000) to the central Gambir station, a fifteen-minute walk from the backpackers' enclave of Jalan Jaksa, and then south towards Blok M, Rawamangun and Kemayoram. With **taxis**, in addition to the metered fare, passengers must also pay the toll fees (about Rp7000) plus another Rp2500 guaranteed service fee, all of which means a taxi ride from the airport to Jalan Jaksa costs approximately Rp35,000. Recommended taxi firms include Steady Safe, Kosti, Blue Bird and President.

BY TRAIN
There are four central train stations (and dozens of minor suburban ones), of which **Gambir** station is the most popular and convenient, being just a fifteen-minute walk from Jalan Jaksa, or Rp1500 by *bajaj* (motorized rickshaw).

Of the other stations, **Kota**, near old Batavia, is the busiest. Although Kota is on the same line as Gambir, some of the trains departing from Kota do not stop at Gambir, and many start their journey at Gambir and miss out Kota. To reach Jalan Jaksa from Kota, catch bus #P1,

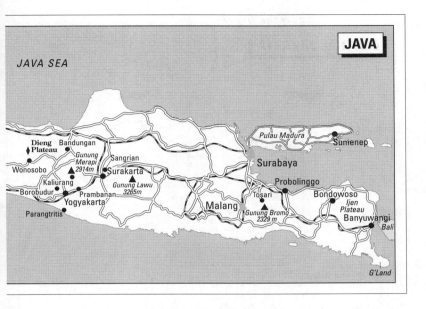

#P10, #P11 or #AC01 to the Sarinah department store, about a ten-minute walk away. From there the buses continue south to the Welcome Monument.

A third train station, **Tanah Abang**, serving Merak, for Sumatra, lies to the west of Jalan Thamrin (bus #P16 to Sarinah and Gambir), and a fourth station, **Pasar Senen**, is situated 1km east of Gambir (bus #15 or #P15 to Jalan Jaksa), though you are unlikely to arrive at either of these.

BY BUS

Jakarta's three major **bus stations** are all inconveniently situated. Each serves different destinations, although there are overlaps: buses to and from Sumatra, for example, arrive at both Kalideres and Pulo Gadung stations.

Most buses from Central Java, East Java and Bali pull into **Pulo Gadung** station, 12km to the east of the city. To get to the centre of town, catch bus #507, which passes the southwestern corner of Medan Merdeka by the fountain. Buses from West Java use **Rambutan Kampung** station, 18km south of the city centre near Taman Mini. Buses #P10, #P11, #P16 and #AC70 all ply the route between Rambutan and the Sarinah department store, taking ninety minutes. Buses from the west of Sumatra arrive at a third station, **Kalideres**, 15km west of the city centre. Buses #78 and #64 run from here to Sarinah.

BY FERRY

All Pelni ferries dock at **Tanjung Priok harbour**, 500m from the bus station of the same name. For Jalan Jaksa, catch **bus** #P14 from the harbour bus station and alight at the junction of Jalan Siri Timur and Jalan HA Salim. A taxi to Jalan Jaksa should cost Rp11,000. Travelling by ferry from Borneo, the chances are you'll arrive at the Sunda Kelapa harbour, near the Kota district. Walk to the Kota bus station and catch bus #P1, #P10, #P11 or #AC01.

The **Kapuas Express ferry** runs from Godown 2 at the Sunda Kelapa harbour near the Kota district to Pontianak in Kalimantan (2 weekly; 19hr). Tickets can be bought from PT

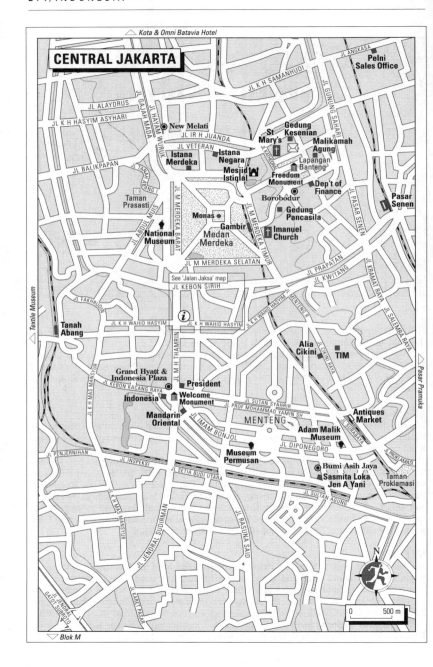

MOVING ON FROM JAKARTA

By plane

All scheduled **flights**, both domestic and international, currently use Sukarno-Hatta airport (☎021/5505000). DAMRI buses depart for the airport from Gambir station every thirty minutes from 3am to 10pm (45min; Rp5000). A taxi from town to the airport costs from Rp20,000.

By train

Most of the trains travelling to West and Central Java destinations begin their journeys at **Gambir** station, including those to Yogya, Solo and Bandung. There are two special offices (daily 7.30am–7pm) selling tickets for the luxury trains, such as the Parahiyangan express to Bandung and the Argolawu express to Yogya and Solo. There's also a tourist-only window on the main concourse.

Of the other stations, **Kota**, near old Batavia, is the busiest. Although Kota is on the same line as Gambir, some of the trains departing from Kota do not stop at Gambir, and many start their journey at Gambir and miss out Kota. To reach Jalan Jaksa from Kota, catch bus #P1, #P10, #P11 or #AC01 to the Sarinah department store, about a ten-minute walk away. From there the buses continue south to the Welcome Monument. The other two train stations, **Tanah Abang** and **Pasar Senen**, are further out of town, have fewer services and rarely see tourists.

By ferry

Pelni **ferries** sail from Tanjung Priok harbour. **Bus** #P14 runs from Tanah Abang via Jalan Kebon Siri, at the northern end of Jalan Jaksa, before continuing on to Tanjung Priok bus station, 500m from the harbour. Allow at least 75 minutes for your journey from Jalan Jaksa. Tanjung Priok is on the circuits of **Pelni** boats *KM Bukit Raya, KM Bukit Siguntang, KM Dobonsolo, KM Kambuna, KM Kelud, KM Kerinci, KM Lambelu, KM Lawit, KM Sirimau, KM Sinabung, KM Leuser, KM Ciremai* and *KM Tilongkabila*. For details see "Getting around" p.191 and "Travel Details" p.442. For the latest timetable, call in at the fifth floor of the Pelni head office at Jl Gajah Mada 14. The Pelni **booking office** is at Jl Angkasa 18 (Mon–Thurs 8am–noon & 1–2.30pm, Fri 8–11.30am & 1–2.30pm); catch bus #15 or #P15 to Pasar Senen then bus #10 to Angkasa.

The **Kapuas Express ferry** runs from Godown 2 at the Sunda Kelapa harbour to Pontianak in Kalimantan. Tickets can be bought from PT Egel Tripelti, Rajawali Condominium Edelweiss Tower, Jl Rajawali Selatan 1/1b (☎021/6409288). The harbourmaster's office is on the second floor of the Departemen Perhubungan at the end of Baruna III in Sunda Kelapa.

By bus

The capital has good **bus** connections to all points in Java, and many cities on neighbouring islands too. There is usually a range of prices for every destination, depending on the type of bus you're travelling in. Tickets bought from an agency in town are more expensive, but as some of the buses leave from outside the agency, you're saved a trip to the bus station. If your bus does depart from the station, leave at least an hour and a half to get from downtown to your terminal.

Most buses to Central Java, East Java and Bali depart from Pulo Gadung station. Buses to West Java, including Bogor and Bandung, use Rambutan Kampung station, 18km south of the city centre near Taman Mini. The third station, Kalideres, is 15km west of the city centre, and serves destinations to the west of Sumatra, including Merak and Padang, but rarely sees tourists.

Egel Tripelti, Rajawali Condominium Edelweiss Tower, Jl Rajawali Selatan 1/1b (☎021/6409288). The harbourmaster's office is on the second floor of the Departemen Perhubungan at the end of Baruna III in Sunda Kelapa.

Getting around and information

City buses operate a set-fare system, regardless of distance, but prices depend on the type of bus. The cheapest are the small, **pale-blue minivans**, which operate out of Kota bus station (their numbers are always preceded by the letter "M") and charge Rp400–500; the **large coaches** found all over the city charge the same, except those with a "P" prefix, which charge Rp700. The small, battered orange **micro-minibuses** all charge Rp500; the large, **double-deckers** charge Rp750; and the **air-con buses** cost Rp1800–2300.

Now that the traditional cycle-rickshaws, or becak, have been banned from Jakarta, the two-stroke motorized rickshaws, or **bajaj** (pronounced "ba-jais"), have monopolized Jakarta's backstreets. Be sure to bargain very, very hard and remember that bajaj are banned from major thoroughfares such as Jalan Thamrin, so you might get dropped off a long way from your destination. A sample fare, from Jalan Jaksa to the post office, would be Rp2000.

Jakarta's **taxis** are numerous and, providing you know your way around the city, inexpensive. Rates are usually around Rp6000 per kilometre, with a standard flag-fall of Rp1500. Drivers generally expect a tip from foreigners and may be very reluctant to hand back all your change.

Tourist information can be found in the Jakarta Theatre building, opposite Sarinah department store on Jalan Wahid Hasyim (Mon–Fri 9.30am–5pm, Sat 9.30am–noon; ☎021/3142067), and at the southern entrance of Gambir station.

Accommodation

Jakarta has relatively few budget hotels, so they fill up fast and should be booked ahead – prices start at Rp7000 for a dorm bed. Nearly all budget places are located on or around **Jalan Jaksa**, the city's travellers' enclave to the south of Medan Merdeka in the heart of the city. **Jalan Wahid Hasyim**, at the southern end of Jalan Jaksa, plays host to a number of mid-priced places, while the best and most expensive hotels in the city huddle around the Welcome Monument on **Jalan Thamrin**, to the southwest of Sarinah's department store.

JALAN JAKSA AND AROUND

Arcadia, Jl Wahid Hasyim 114 (☎021/2300050). Unique, state-of-the-art hotel, characterized by clean lines, natural light and conversation-piece furniture. Worth looking around and having a drink in the bar (happy hour 5–7pm), even if you're not staying here. ⑥.

Batavia Brothers, Jl Kebon Sirih Barat Gg X/5 (☎021/3917492). Poky but friendly little losmen tucked away down the odorous alley opposite the *Borneo Hostel*. ②.

Bloemsteen, Jl Kebon Siri Timur I/174 (☎021/323002). Perfectly acceptable hostel, with spacious rooms, good bathrooms, and a pleasant, sunny balcony. ①.

Borneo, Jl Kebon Siri Barat 35–37 (☎021/3140095). Large, ramshackle hostel-cum-brothel with the cheapest dorms in town. Avoid the filthy west wing. Rp10,000 for a dorm bed. ①.

Delima, Jl Jaksa 5 (☎021/337026). The oldest and one of the best value of the city's hostels, though some rooms could be cleaner. Often full in high season. ①.

Djody Hostel, Jl Jaksa 27 (☎021/3151404). Not to be confused with its slightly more expensive sister down the road, the rather gloomy Djody Hostel comprises 24 rooms, all watched over by a 24hr security guard. Rp27,500 for a dorm bed.

Djody Hotel, Jl Jaksa 35 (☎021/3151404). Pricier version of the *Djody Hostel*, though with no real difference in quality. ②.

Indra Internasional, Jl Wahid Hasyim 63 (☎021/3152858). Light, airy hotel, with clean air-con rooms (all with TV) and friendly service. ⑤.

Karya, Jl Jaksa 32–34 (☎021/3907119). One of a growing number of mid-priced hotels on Jl Jaksa. All rooms have air-con, TV and hot-water showers. ⑤.

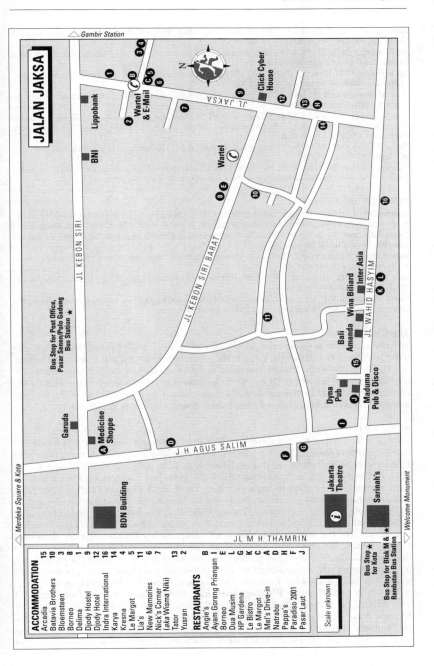

JALAN JAKSA

△ Gambir Station

Merdeka Square & Kota △

JL KEBON SIRI

Bus Stop for Post Office,
Pasar Senen/Pulo Gadung
Bus Station ★

Garuda

Medicine Shoppe

BDN Building

JL KEBON SIRI BARAT

JL H AGUS SALIM

Jakarta
Theatre

Sarinah's

JL M H THAMRIN

▽ Welcome Monument

Lippobank

BNI

Wartel
& E-Mail

Click Cyber
House

JL JAKSA

Wartel

Dyna
Pub

Maduma
Pub & Disco

Bali
Amanda

Wina Biliard

Inter Asia

JL WAHID HASYIM

Bus Stop ★
for Blok M

Bus Stop for Blok M &
Rambutan Bus Station

ACCOMMODATION

Arcadia	15
Batavia Brothers	10
Bloemsteen	3
Borneo	8
Delima	1
Djody Hostel	9
Djody Hotel	12
Indra International	16
Karya	14
Kresna	4
Le Margot	5
Lia's	11
New Memories	6
Nick's Corner (aka Wisma Niki)	7
Tator	13
Yusran	2

RESTAURANTS

Angie's	B
Ayam Goreng Priangan	I
Borneo	E
Dua Musim	L
HP Gardena	G
Le Bistro	K
Le Margot	C
Mel's Drive-in	A
Natrabu	D
Pappa's	H
Paradiso 2001	F
Pasar Laut	J

Scale unknown

Kresna, Jl Kebon Siri Timur I/175 (☎021/325403). Acceptable budget hotel with tiny and dank downstairs rooms but brighter ones upstairs; good showers. ②.

Le Margot, Jl Jaksa 15 (☎021/3913830). Average mid-priced hotel with some rather poky rooms and a basement air-con dorm. Dorm Rp11,500. ④.

Lia's, Jl Kebon Siri Barat Gg VIII/47 (☎021/3162708). Recommended little hostel with reasonable-value, clean, basic rooms and a pleasant front garden. ①.

New Memories Café, Jl Jaksa 17 (no phone). Two beautiful double rooms secreted away behind the *Memories Café*. Great value. ②.

Nick's Corner (aka **Wisma Niki**), Jl Jaksa 16 (☎021/3107814). Large, popular hostel offering a variety of budget and not-so-budget rooms. The two mixed-sex dormitories are reasonable, though they have no windows. Rp15,000 for a dorm bed. ②.

Tator, Jl Jaksa 37 (☎021/323940) Many people's favourite, this spotless hotel has friendly staff, hot water and breakfast is included. ②.

Yusran, Jl Kebon Siri Barat Dalam VI/9 (☎021/3140373). Surprisingly pleasant budget hotel at the end of Gang 6 to the west of Jaksa. Doubles are spotless and comfortable; try bargaining. ①.

THE REST OF THE CITY

Borobudur, Jl Lapangan Banteng Selatan (☎021/3805555). Once the best in the city, this grand hotel is set in lovely gardens with a pool and has sumptuous rooms, as well as some at the cheaper end. ③–⑨.

Bumi Asih Jaya, Jl Solo 4 (☎021/3860839). Small and relaxing fifteen-room hotel set round a garden in a suburb to the south of Jl Diponegoro. ③.

Grand Hyatt, Jl Thamrin (☎021/3901234). Massive complex in the centre of town with luxurious rooms, a pool and several restaurants. ⑨.

New Melati, Jl Hayam Wuruk 1 (☎021/3841943). Indonesian-owned hotel where all rooms have TV, air-con, telephone, mini-bar and bath. ④.

Omni Batavia, Jl Kali Besar Barat 46 (☎021/6904118). Beautiful place with a spectacular stained-glass facade and the full set of plush facilities, including a pool. ⑨.

The City

To head from north to south through the centre of Jakarta is to go forward in time, from the pretty, old Dutch city of Batavia, **Kota**, in the north, to the modern golf courses and amusement parks in the south. **Medan Merdeka**, the giant, threadbare patch of grass marks the spiritual centre of Jakarta, if not exactly its geographical one, bordered to the west by the city's major north–south thoroughfare. The main commercial district and the budget accommodation enclave of **Jalan Jaksa** lie just a short distance to the south of Merdeka.

KOTA (OLD BATAVIA)

Located in the north of the city, the quaint old district of **Batavia** used to serve as the administrative centre of the great Dutch trading empire, stretching from South Africa all the way to Japan. Plenty of buses head north from Thamrin to Kota, including #P1, #P11 and air-con #P17. All these buses drive north along Jalan Gajah Mada past the impressive facade of **Kota train station**, a good place to begin your tour. Head north from Kota station along Jalan Lada, past the Politeknik Swadharma, and enter the boundaries of what was once the walled city of Batavia. The centre of Batavia, **Taman Fatahillah**, lies 300m to the north of the train station, an attractive cobbled square hemmed in on all four sides by museums and historical monuments. On the south side is the largely disappointing **Jakarta History Museum** (Tues–Thurs & Sun 9am–3pm, Fri 9am–2pm, Sat 9am–1pm; Rp1500), which sets out to describe (in Indonesian only) the history of the city from the Stone Age to the present day, but unfortunately only really gets as far as the seventeenth century. Upstairs is more interesting, with many of the rooms furnished as they would have been two hundred years ago.

The more entertaining **Wayang Museum** (Tues–Thurs & Sun 9am–3pm, Fri 9am–2.30pm, Sat 9am–12.30pm; Rp1500), to the west of the square, is dedicated to the Javanese art of puppetry and housed in one of the oldest buildings in the city. Exhibits display puppets from right across the archipelago, and every Sunday between 10am and 2pm some of them perform in a free **wayang show**. Continuing clockwise around the square, next to *Café Batavia* you'll come to the ornate **Cannon Si Jagur**, built by the Portuguese to defend the city of Melaka. On the side is the Latin inscription *Ex me ipsa renata sum* – "Out of myself I was reborn" – and the whole thing is emblazoned with sexual imagery, from the clenched fist (a suggestive gesture in Southeast Asia) to the barrel itself, a potent phallic symbol in Indonesia.

To the east of the square, the **Balai Seni Rupa** (Tues–Thurs & Sun 9am–3pm, Fri 9am–2pm, Sat 9am–1pm; Rp1500), Jakarta's fine arts museum, and accompanying **Ceramics Museum** house some works by Indonesia's most illustrious artists, including portraits by Affandi and sketches of the capital by Raden Saleh.

SUNDA KELAPA

About 1km north of Taman Fatahillah lies the historic harbour of **Sunda Kelapa** (Rp350), which, established during Pajajaran times, grew to become the most important in the Dutch empire. Although the bulk of the sea traffic docks at Tanjung Priok today, a few of the smaller vessels, particularly some picturesque wooden schooners, still call in at this 800-year-old port. You can either walk here from Taman Fatahillah (about 20min) or hail an *ojek* (motorcycle taxi).

From the port, cross over the bridge to the west of the harbour and turn right at the nineteenth-century watchtower, the Uitkijk, originally built to direct shipping traffic to the port. Here, buried in the chaotic Pasar Ikan (fish market) that occupies this promontory, you'll find the entrance to the excellent **Museum Bahari**, or **Maritime Museum** (Tues–Thurs & Sun 9am–3pm, Fri 9am–2.30pm, Sat 9am–12.30pm; Rp1500), housed in a warehouse that was built in 1652 for spice, pepper, tea, coffee and cotton. The highly informative museum charts the relationship between the Indonesian archipelago and the sea that both divides and surrounds it, beginning with the simple early fishing vessels and continuing through the colonial years to the modern age. All kinds of sea craft, from the Buginese *pinisi* to the *kora-kora* war boat from the Moluccas can be seen here.

Head south, keeping the Kali Besar canal on your left, until you come to the ornate 200-year-old wooden drawbridge, **Jembatan Pasar Ayam**. The streets south of here were once the smartest addresses in Batavia, and the grand Dutch terrace houses still stand, the most famous being the Chinese-style **Toko Merah** (Red Shop) at no. 11 Jalan Kali Besar Barat – the former home of the Dutch governor general Van Imhoff. The Batavia bus station lies on the eastern side of the canal, from where you can catch bus #938 back to Jalan Thamrin.

MEDAN MERDEKA

The heart and lungs of Jakarta, **Medan Merdeka** is a square kilometre of sun-scorched grass in the centre of the city. It was here in the 1940s that Sukarno whipped his supporters up into a revolutionary frenzy, and here that the biggest demonstration of the May 1997 riots took place. At the centre of the square stands the **Monas**, a soaring 137-metre marble, bronze and gold torch, commissioned by Sukarno in 1962 to symbolize the indomitable spirit of the Indonesian people, and known to ex-pats as "Sukarno's last erection". You can take a lift up to its top for a city view (daily 8am–5pm; Rp3000); the ticket includes entry to the **National History Museum** (daily 8am–5pm; Rp500) in Monas's basement, a series of 48 dioramas that depict the history of Jakarta.

The **National Museum** (Tues–Thurs & Sun 8.30am–2.30pm, Fri 8.30–11.30am, Sat 8.30am–1.30pm; Rp750), on the western side of Medan Merdeka, is a fabulous place and a great introduction to Indonesia; the Indonesian Heritage Society conducts tours in English (Tues–Thurs 9.30am). The eclectic range of items from all over the archipelago are grouped together into categories such as musical instruments, costumes and so on. Many of the country's top ruins have been plundered for their statues, which now sit, unmarked, in the museum courtyard. Other highlights include huge Dongson kettledrums, the skull and thighbone of Java Man, found near Solo in 1936 (see p.251), and the cache of golden artefacts discovered at the foot of Mount Merapi in 1990.

The dazzling white, if rather unprepossessing, **Mesjid Istiqlal** looms over the northeastern corner of Medan Merdeka. Completed in 1978, it is the largest mosque in Southeast Asia and can hold up to 250,000 people. For a donation, and providing you're conservatively dressed, the security guards will take you on an informal tour. At the foot of the minaret sits a 2.5-tonne wooden drum from east Kalimantan, the only traditional feature in this otherwise state-of-the-art mosque.

THE OUTSKIRTS

Jakarta's **Textile Museum** (Tues–Thurs &Sun 9am–4pm, Fri 9am–3pm; Rp1000) stands to the west of the Tanah Abang train station at Jalan Aipda KS Tubun 4. Catch bus #P16 heading north from Thamrin to the Tanah Abang market, then walk west for five minutes over the bridge. Housed in a spacious old Dutch villa, the well presented collection displays over three hundred **indigenous textiles** from every part of the archipelago.

Eighteen kilometres south of Medan Merdeka, the **Taman Mini Indonesia Indah** (daily 8am–5pm; Rp4000) is a huge theme park celebrating the rich ethnic and cultural diversity of the archipelago. At its centre is a man-made lake, around which are 27 houses, each built in the traditional style of Indonesia's 27 provinces. The park also contains several **museums** (Rp1000–2000 each), including the Science Museum, the Asmat Museum, housing woodcarvings from Irian Jaya, and the Museum of Indonesia, with displays on the country's people, geography, flora and fauna. Neighbouring **Museum Purna Bhakti Pertiwi** (daily 9am–4pm; Rp4000) displays a fabulously opulent collection of stunning gifts presented to President Suharto. Highlights include a whole gamelan orchestra made of old Balinese coins, a series of carved wooden panels depicting Suharto's life story, and an enormous rubber-tree root decorated with the nine gods of Balinese Hinduism. To get to all these attractions, catch **bus** #P10, #P11 or #P16 to Rambutan bus station, then minibus #T19 or #M55 to the Taman Mini entrance (1hr total).

Eating

Food is more expensive in the capital than anywhere else in Indonesia: *nasi goreng* can cost twice as much here. Local **street food** thrives in the city, particularly along Jalan HA Salim, (also known as Jalan Sabang).

JALAN JAKSA

Angie's, Jl Jaksa 15. One of the better-value places in Jaksa, this budget restaurant serves the usual Indonesian staples and Western fare; their tahu telor pancake is great value.

Borneo, Jl Kebon Siri Barat 35–37. Popular budget restaurant serving some of the best Western food in Jaksa – try their burgers (Rp7500).

Le Margot, Jl Jaksa 15. Very popular open-sided bar (with MTV), that does tasty but overpriced meals, including a good ginger beef (Rp7000).

New Memories, Jl Jaksa 17. Large menu of somewhat overpriced Western and local dishes, but the Szechwan chicken (Rp11,000) is terrific.

Pappa's, Jl Jaksa 41. A popular but overpriced restaurant that specializes in Indian curries (Rp9000–15,000), with "paper dums" (Rp1000) optional. A good place for lunch.

JALAN HA SALIM (JALAN SABANG)

Ayam Goreng Priangan, Jl Sabang 55a. Fairly inexpensive Indonesian fried-chicken restaurant. Try *ayam bakar*, chicken cooked in coconut milk and grilled in a sweet soya sauce, for Rp7700.

HP Gardena, Jl Sabang 32a. Unusual "hot pot" restaurant, where you choose the ingredients – ranging from fish cakes (Rp4500) to meatballs (Rp4500), salads and spicy sauce dips.

Mel's Drive-in, Jl Sabang 21. Inexpensive fast-food shack which does a good-value Rp18,500 breakfast, and two beers (including Guinness) for the price of one during happy hour (3–5pm).

Natrabu, Jl Sabang 29a. Flashy but excellent mid-priced Minang restaurant serving Padang-style food from West Sumatra and live Minang music every evening (7–9.30pm).

Paradiso 2001, Jl Sabang 30. Excellent, cheapish little vegetarian joint, hidden down an alley next to the *Gardena Restaurant*. Closed from Fri at 5pm until Sun at 6pm.

JALAN WAHID HASYIM AND ELSEWHERE

Akbar Palace, Wijaya Grand Centre, Kebayoran. Excellent north Indian restaurant, which serves some wonderful tandoori dishes.

Café Batavia, Taman Fatahillah, Kota. One of the city's best and most popular places, serving delicious Chinese, Indonesian and Western dishes, and over sixty cocktails. Nightly live jazz and soul. Pricey. Open 24 hours.

Dua Musim, Jl Wahid Hasyim 71a. Huge and trendy fresh-fish restaurant with equally vast selection of seafood, including lobster (Rp19,500) and crabs.

Le Bistro, Jl Wahid Hasyim 71. Classy French restaurant hidden behind a wealth of foliage and serving terrific French food; main courses around Rp30,000.

Oasis, Jl Raden Saleh 47 (☎021/3150646). Jakarta's finest, this historic restaurant is housed in a 1920s Dutch villa in Cikini, complete with crystal chandeliers and enormous stained-glass window. The menu ranges from steak tartare to *rijsttaffel* and is expensive but worth it.

Pasar Laut, Jl Wahid Hasyim 125. Mid-priced seafood restaurant where you select your seafood from tanks as you walk in. The *kepiting* (crabs), at about Rp16,000 per crab, are especially good.

Nightlife and entertainment

Most travellers don't even leave Jalan Jaksa in the evening, preferring to hang out in one of the many **bars** that are strung along the road: *Le Margot* at no. 15, which has MTV, and the newly revamped *New Memories Café*, are currently the most popular. The expensive *Hard Rock Café*, in the Sarinah building, is by far the most popular **live-music venue**, particularly with Jakarta's teenyboppers, but *Café Batavia* on Fatahillah Square in Kota, is more salubrious, with jazz and soul groups performing most evenings (see above). After 10.30pm, the long-established *Jaya* pub, opposite the *Sari San Pacific* hotel at Jl Thamrin 12, starts filling up with locals, and Westerners come to listen to the jazz and soft-rock sounds of the resident band. The small *Dyna Bar*, down an alley off Jalan Wahid Hasyim to the west of Jalan Jaksa, is also popular with expats and has an early-evening happy hour.

If you're after a huge night out, head for **Blok M**, which has a wealth of bars and Irish- and English-style pubs. A good place to start a crawl is the *Sportsman Bar & Grill*, Jl Palatehan 6–8, which offers beers from around the world. There are plenty of bars nearby, including the *King's Head*, Jl Iskadarasyah I 9, and the *Top Gun Bar*, just opposite the *Sportsman*. You can round off your evening at the *Prambors Café* in Basement II of the Blok M shopping centre, which holds regular live-music evenings. The most interesting place to rave is the **Tanamur Disco** (Rp15,000), at Jl Tanah Abang Timur 14, where the music is a fairly mainstream mix of European and American house, and the clientele includes expats, pimps, prostitutes, ladyboys, junkies and the occasional traveller; up to 1500 revellers on Friday and Saturday nights. Next door is *JJ's*, a smaller and quieter disco which survives on the overspill (free from 2am until 5am closing).

Jakarta isn't great for indigenous **cultural performances**, and if you're heading off to Yogya and Solo you're better off waiting. If you're not, the **Gedung Kesenian**, at Jl Kesenian 1 (☎021/3808283), just north of the GPO, stages classical music, ballet and *wayang orang*, and the **Bharata Theatre** at Jl Kalilio 15, Pasar Senen (bus #15 from Jalan Kebon Siri), holds traditional *wayang orang* and *ketoprak* performances every night at 8pm. If you're in Jakarta on a Sunday, check out the Wayang Museum on Fatahillah Square in Kota (see p.218), which holds a free four-hour **wayang kulit** performance at 10am.

Shopping

While Jakarta has no particular indigenous craft of its own, the capital isn't a bad place to go **souvenir shopping**. The antiques market on Jalan Surabaya, one block west of Cikini station in Jakarta's Menteng district, sells fine silver jewellery, and traditional Javanese wooden trunks and other pieces of furniture, as well as old records. The entire third floor of the Sarinah department store is given over to souvenirs, with wayang kulit and wayang golek puppets, leather bags and woodcarvings a speciality. A similar selection of souvenirs can be found at Ancol's Pasar Seni, alongside paintings and woodcarvings. Hadi Handicraft in the

Indonesia Plaza specializes in good-quality, reasonably priced, wooden statues and ornaments, mainly from Central Java. There are three reasonable souvenir shops on Jalan Pasar Baru, north of the GPO: Toko Bandung at no. 16b, the Ramayana Art Shop at no. 17, and the Irian Art Shop at 16a. The fourth floor of Sarinah's is devoted to good-quality **batik** clothes. A similar selection can be found at the branch of Batik Kris in the Indonesia Plaza, the most exclusive store of its kind in the capital.

For new **books**, the Times Bookshop in the Indonesia Plaza (under the *Hyatt*) has the widest selection, and the fifth floor of the Sarinah department store is also worth a browse. For secondhand books, visit Cynthia's bookshop on Jl Jaksa, or the small store in the corner of *New Memories Café*.

Listings

Airlines Aeroflot, *Hotel Sahid Jaya*, Jl Jend Sudirman, Kav 24 (☎021/5702184); Air China, ADD Building, Tamara Centre, Suite 802, Jl Jend Sudirman (☎021/5206467); Air France, Summitmas Tower, 9th Floor, Jl Jend Sudirman (☎021/5202262); Air Lanka, Wisma Bank Dharmala, 14th Floor, Jl Jend Sudirman (☎021/5202101); Balkan Air, Jl K H Hasyim Ashari 33b (☎021/373341); Bourag, Jl Angkasa 1–3, Kemayoran (☎021/6288815); British Airways, World Trade Centre, Jl Jend Sudirman Kav 29–31 (☎021/5703747); Cathay Pacific, Gedung Bursa Efek, Jl Jend Sudirman Kav 52–53 (☎021/5151747); China Airlines, Wisma Dharmala Sakti, Jl Jend Sudirman 32 (☎021/2510788); Emirates, *Hotel Sahid Jaya*, 2nd Floor, Jl Jend Sudirman 86 (☎021/5205363); Eva Air, Price Waterhouse Centre, 10th Floor, Jl Rasuna Said Kav C3 (☎021/5205828); Garuda, Jl Merdeka Selatan 13 (☎021/2311801), and at the BDN Building, Jl Thamrin 5; Japan Airlines, MID Plaza, Ground Floor, Jl Jend Sudirman Kav 28 (☎021/5212177); Kuwait Airways, behind the BNI building, Jl Sudirman; Lufthansa, Panin Centre Building, 2nd Floor, Jl Jend Sudirman 1 (☎021/5702005); Malaysian Airlines, World Trade Centre, Jl Jend Sudirman Kav 29 (☎021/5229682); Myanmar Airways, Jl Melawai Raya 7, 3rd Floor (☎021/7394042); KLM, New Summitmas, 17th Floor, Jl Jend Sudirman Kav 61–62 (☎021/5212176 or 5212177); Korean Air, Wisma Bank Dharmala, 7th Floor, Jl Jend Sudirman Kav 28 (☎021/5782036); Mandala, Jl Garuda 76 (☎021/4246100), also Jl Veteran I 34 (☎021/4246100); Merpati, Jl Angkasa 7, Blok B15 Kav 2 & 3 (☎021/6548888) and 24hr city check-in at Gambir station; Philippine Airlines, Plaza Mashil, 11th Floor suite 1105, Jl Jend Sudirman Kav 25 (☎021/3810949, 3810950 or 5267780); Qantas Airways, BDN Building, Jl Thamrin (☎021/327707); Royal Brunei Airlines, World Trade Centre, 11th Floor, Jl Jend Sudirman Kav 29–31 (☎021/2300277); Sabena, Ground Floor, Wisma Bank Dharmala, Jl Jend Sudirman Kav 28; Saudi Arabian Airlines, Wisma Bumiputera, 7th Floor, Jl Jend Sudirman Kav 75 (☎021/5710615); Silk Air, Chase Plaza, 4th Floor, Jl Jend Sudirman Kav 21 (☎021/5208018); Singapore Airlines, Chase Plaza, 2nd Floor, Jl Jend Sudirman Kav 21 (☎021/5206881/5206933); Swissair, Plaza Mashil, 6th Floor, Jl Jend Sudirman Kav 29 (☎021/5229912); Thai International, BDN Building, Ground Floor, Jl Thamrin (☎021/330816 or 3140607).

Banks and exchange Many of the banks, Sarinah, the post office and Gambir have their own ATM machines, which offer a better rate than any bank or moneychanger. Otherwise, the Bank BNI and Lippobank, just west of the northern end of Jl Jaksa on Jl Kebon Siri, offer the best rates in town, with the latter also offering credit-card advances. The AMEX office is at Graha Aktiva, Jl Rasuna Said, Kuningan (catch bus #11 heading south from Sarinah) and is currently the only place that accepts Australian dollar travellers' cheques (AMEX only). The InterAsia moneychanger at Jl Wahid Hasyim 96a is reasonable for cash exchanges, but offers poor rates for travellers' cheques.

Embassies and consulates Australia, Jl H Rasuna Said Kav 10–11 (☎021/5227111); Britain, Jl H Agus Salim 128 (☎021/3907448); Canada, Metropolitan Building 1, Jl Jend Sudirman Kav 29 (☎021/5250709); China, Jl Jend Sudirman Kav 69 Kebayoran Baru (☎021/7243400); Germany, Jl Thamrin 1 (☎021/3901750); India, Jl Rasuna Said S-1, Kuningan (☎021/5204150); Japan, Jl Thamrin 24 (☎021/5212177); Malaysia, Jl Rasuna Said 1–3, Kuningan (☎021/5224947); Netherlands, Jl Rasuna Said S-3, Kuningan (☎021/5251515); New Zealand, Jl Diponegoro 41 (☎021/330680); Singapore, Jl Rasuna Said 2, Kuningan (☎021/5201489); South Africa, Wisma GKBI Jl Sudirman (☎021/7193304); Thailand, Jl Imam Bonjol 74 (☎021/3904055); US, Jl Medan Mereka Selatan 5 (☎021/360360).

Hospitals and clinics The MMC hospital on Jl Rasuna Said in Kuningan is the best in town (☎021/5203435). The private SMI (Sentra Medika International) clinic at Jl Cokroaminoto 16 in Menteng (☎021/3157747), is run by Australian and Indonesian doctors.

Immigration office At Jl Teuku Umar 1, 5min east of the southern end of Jl Wahid Hasyim (Mon–Thurs 8am–3pm, Fri 8am–noon).

Internet access Most efficiently at the GPO (Mon–Fri 8am–8pm, Sat 8am–7pm, Sun 9am–3pm; Rp2000 for 15min). Also at the Wartel, Jl Jaksa 17 (daily 8am–9pm; Rp15,000 for 1hr), and Snapy on Jl Thamrin to the north of the *President Hotel* (Rp14,000 for 1hr).

Maps The best map of the city is the one published by Periplus.

Post office The GPO lies to the north of Lapangan Benteng (Mon–Sat 8am–8pm, Sun 9am–5pm), north-east of Medan Merdeka (catch bus #15 or #P15 from Jl Kebon Siri, to the north of Jl Jaksa). Poste restante is currently at counter no. 55.

Telephone services There is no main government-run communications centre in the city. The Indosat building at 21 Jl Medan Merdeka Barat has IDD and HCD on its ground floor (cash only), as do the RTQ warpostel at Jl Jaksa 17 (8am–midnight) and the wartel on Jl Kebon Siri Barat.

Travel agents Good travel agencies on or near Jalan Jaksa include PT Robertur Kencana at no. 20b, Lipta Marsada Pertala at no. 11 (☎021/326291), and PT Bali Amanda at Jl Wahid Hasyim 110a, which can book Pelni ferry tickets on the Internet.

Merak and ferries to Sumatra

At the extreme northwestern tip of Java, **MERAK** is the port for ferries across the Sunda straits to Bakauheni on Sumatra. **Ferries** to **Sumatra** leave about every thirty minutes and take about two hours and thirty minutes; crowds of buses connect with the ferries to take you on to Bandar Lampung, Palembang or destinations further north in Sumatra. If you get stuck at Merak, the *Hotel Anda* at Jl Florida 4 has basic rooms with fan and mandi (☎0254/71041; ①).

Carita

CARITA boasts one of the most sheltered stretches of sea in Java and is the best spot to arrange **tours to Krakatau** (day-trips $30–50); those by Black Rhino (☎0253/81072), across from the marina, are recommended, but don't fall for the unqualified guides who approach you on spec. Carita also makes quite an easy escape from the capital; a bus from Kalideres bus station in Jakarta, usually changing to a colt at Labuan, will take just over three hours. If you do have to change at Labuan terminal, don't get conned into taking transport round to the stop for colts to Carita, just walk two minutes towards the seafront and round to the right. Try to avoid coming to Carita at a weekend though, when the bay reverberates with the constant roar of jet skis and accommodation prices shoot up.

All **accommodation** is on or close to the main seaside road, known as Jalan Carita Raya or Jalan Pantai Carita. There are no building numbers, so all are listed here in the order they appear along this road heading north from Labuan town. *Pondok Bakkara* (☎0253/81260; ①) is one of the cheapest places here, though the en-suite rooms are not especially clean and often full. Friendly staff, clean rooms and interesting decor make *Sunset View* (☎0253/81075; ①) one of the best-value places on the west coast. *Carita Krakatau* (☎0253/83027; ①), behind the restaurant of the same name, is also recommended and offers spotless rooms with mandi, fan and breakfast. *Lucia Cottages* (☎0253/81262; ②) has bungalows and rooms around a pool and some of the comfiest beds in Carita.

The public parts of the beach are lined with **food** carts selling *murtabak*, sate and soto. Other good options include the plush and fairly pricey *Café de Paris*, at the 14km Anyer marker, which does European and Chinese dishes and seafood; *Carita Krakatau*, 30m towards Anyer from the marina, which cooks a good fish steak for Rp15,000; and *Diminati*, opposite the entrance to the marina, which boasts the cheapest cold beer in town (Rp7500), and does an excellent *kakap* fish steak meal for Rp15,000.

Labuan

LABUAN is a dull and dirty port town, but it has good transport connections (3hr by frequent bus from Jakarta's Kalideres terminal) and is the best place to arrange **independent trips to Krakatau**, and to get the essential park permits (Rp5000). These are available from the **PHPA parks office**, which is quite far out along Jalan Perintis Kemerdekaan, heading towards Carita, almost opposite the *Rawayan* hotel. The BRI bank on the south side of the bus terminal will change cash and travellers' cheques. The post office is on Jalan Perintis Kemerdekaan heading towards Carita.

The best budget **accommodation** is *Telaga Biru*, just off Jl Raya Carita, about 2km from Labuan, across the road from the sea (no phone; b); all the quiet rooms have mandi inside. The more central *Hotel Citra Ayu*, Jl Perintis Kemerdekaan 27 (☎0253/81229; ➀), is basic but clean. The nicest place in Labuan is *Rawayan*, out on the road towards Carita at Jl Raya Carita 41 (☎0253/81386; ➃–➄), with quaint bungalows and private rooms, all en-suite.

Krakatau

At 10am on August 27, 1883, an explosion equivalent to 10,000 Hiroshima atomic bombs rent **Krakatau** island; the boom was heard as far away as Sri Lanka. As the eruption column towered 40km into the atmosphere, a thick mud rain began to fall over the area, and the temperature plunged by 5°C. Tremors were detected as far away as the English Channel and off the coast of Alaska. One single *tsunami* (pressure wave) as tall as a seven-storey building, raced outwards, erasing 300 towns and villages and killing 36,417 people; a government gunboat was carried 3km inland and deposited up a hill 10m above sea level. Once into the open sea, the waves travelled at up to 700kph, reaching South Africa and scuttling ships in Auckland harbour. Two-thirds of Krakatau had vanished for good, and on those parts that remained not so much as a seed or an insect survived.

Today, the crumbled caldera is clearly visible west of the beaches near Merak and Carita, its sheer northern cliff face soaring straight out of the sea to nearly 800m. But it is the glassy black cone of **Anak Krakatau**, the child of Krakatau volcano, that most visitors want to see, a barren wasteland that's still growing and still very much active. It first reared its head from the seas in 1930, and now sits angrily smoking amongst the remains of the older peaks. To get here requires a **motorboat trip** (4–6hr) from Labuan or Carita, then a half-hour walk up to the crater, from where you can see black lava flows, sulphurous fumaroles and smoke. The easiest way to visit Krakatau is with the Black Rhino **tour** company in Carita (see p.223) or through the *Beringin Hotel* in Kalianda on Sumatra (see p.306). If you have your own group, inquire at the PHPA parks office in Labuan (see p.223) and see if they can fix you up with a boat, which should cost around Rp500,000 for the day. Bring lots of water and some food (include emergency supplies).

Bogor

Located 300m above sea kevel and just an hour's train journey south of Jakarta, **BOGOR** enjoys a cool, wet climate and famously lush **Botanical Gardens** (daily 8am–5pm; Rp1500), which were founded by Sir Stamford Raffles in 1811. In the gardens, pathways wind between towering bamboo stands, climbing bougainvillea, a small tropical rainforest, and ponds full of water lilies and fountains. Perhaps the garden's best-known occupants are the giant rafflesia and *bungu bangkai*, two of the world's hugest (and smelliest) flowers. Near the gardens' main entrance, the rather dilapidated **zoological museum** (daily 8am–4pm; Rp1000) houses some 30,000 specimens, including a complete skeleton of a blue whale, a stuffed Javan rhino and a Komodo dragon. **Wayang golek puppets** are made at a workshop to the northeast of the gardens; ask for Pak Dase's place. If you're interested in **gamelan** and Javanese gongs, visit Pak Sukarna's factory on Jalan Pancasan to the southwest of the gardens. Here the instruments are forged using traditional methods, and are also for sale.

Practicalities

The **train station** is about 500m northwest of the Botanical Gardens and close to the budget accommodation; trains from Jakarta take 90 minutes. Buses from Jakarta's Rambutan terminal arrive at the **bus terminal** about 500m southeast of the gardens. There are also frequent buses to and from Bandung. The main bemo stop is behind the bus terminal, but the best place to pick up bemos is on the main road that borders the southern edge of the gardens. There is a small **tourist information** centre (Mon–Fri 9am–4pm) at the southern entrance to the gardens.

Pensione Firman, Jl Palendang 48 (☎0251/323246; ①) has long been the budget travellers' favourite **accommodation** and has neat and basic rooms, as well as doing various tours around West Java. With excessively friendly staff, river views and excellent breakfasts, *Abu Pensione*, Jl Mayur Oking 15 (☎0251/322893; ①), is probably the best budget losmen in Bogor; the pricier rooms here have hot water and air-con. *Wisma Karunia*, Jl Serupur 35–37 (☎0251/323411; ①) is friendly and quiet, with a range of rooms and breakfast included; the owners run a door-to-door bus service to Bandung. *Hotel Mirah*, Jl Pangrango 9a (☎0251/328044; ②) has an inviting pool (open to non-guests for Rp10,000) and air-con en-suite rooms, and *Wisma Bogor Permai*, Jl Sawajajar/Jend Sudirman 23a (☎0251/321115; ③), is a delightful establishment with hot water and large beds, plus a good Indonesian breakfast.

One of the best places to try genuine Sundanese **food** is in the garden at *Restoran Si Kabayan*, Jl Bina Marga I 2, where *ikan mas* is a speciality. *Jongko Ibu*, Jl Juanda 36, also does good, cheap Sundanese food, including steamed carp in banana leaf. *Bogor Permai*, on the corner of Jalan Jend Sudirman and Jalan Sawojajar, is a small food complex housing a fine delicatessen, the best bakery in Bogor and a stand selling tasty pizza slices (Rp2000). The *Bogor Permai* restaurant in the back of the building serves quality seafood and steaks from Rp25,000. Near the bus station on Jalan Raya Pajararan, *Cahaya Bari, Simpang Rayu* and *Trio Permai* are three of the flashiest, cleanest Padang restaurants you will ever see. Along Jalan Pengadillan, near the Telkom and train station, are bunches of **night stalls**, which set up after 6pm.

Bandung and around

Set high above sea level, and protected by a fortress of sullen volcanoes 190km southeast of Jakarta, **BANDUNG** is the third largest city in Indonesia and a centre of industry and traditional Sundanese arts – with plenty of cultural performances for tourists – though it suffers from traffic pollution and uninteresting modern developments. Sundanese culture has remained intact here since the fifth century when the first Hindu Sundanese settled in this part of West Java. Modern Bandung's main tourist attraction is nearby **Tangkbuhan Prahu volcano**, and there's a very pleasant two-hour forest walk down to the city too.

The Dutch spotted the potential of this lush cool plateau and its fertile volcanic slopes in the mid-seventeenth century, and set about cultivating coffee and rice here. But it wasn't until the early nineteenth century that the planters decided to settle in the area, at Bandung, rather than commute from Batavia. Several relics from the city's colonial era remain, including some of the elegant shops along Jalan Braga, and some fine buildings on Jalan Asia-Afrika.

Arrival and city transport

Bandung's **train station** is located within walking distance of most budget accommodation, fairly close to the centre of town. **Bus** services to Bandung run from every major town in Java, including Jakarta, but many tourists use the **minibus** services organized by losmen in Pangandaran, Bogor and Yogya; they're at least twice the price of public transport and not that much quicker, but can save you a lot of hassle when you arrive in Bandung, as they drop you off at your chosen hotel. The main Leuwi Panjang **bus terminal** for buses from the west is 5km south of the city; the Cicaheum terminal for those from the east is at the far eastern edge of town. Local DAMRI buses serve both stations. The **airport** is 3km northwest of the train station, served by plenty of taxis.

Bandung's white-and-blue **DAMRI buses** cost Rp250 a journey, and ply routes between the bus terminals through the centre of town. Red **angkots** (minibuses) also run a useful circular route, via the train station and square, to the Kebun Kelapa bus terminal, which services Cicaheum bus terminal, Dago and Ledeng.

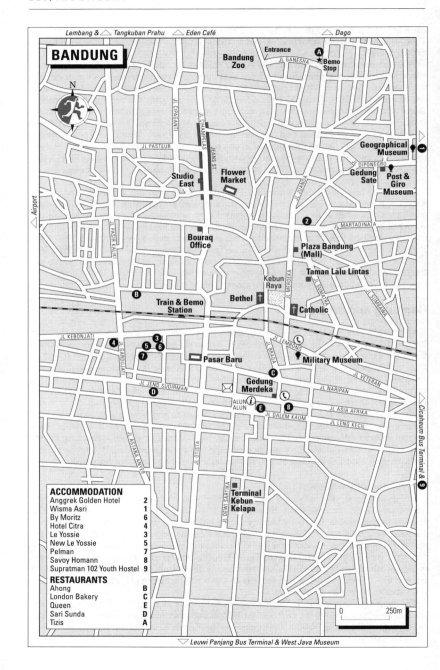

BANDUNG

Lembang & △ Tangkuban Prahu △ Eden Café △ Dago

Bandung Zoo

Entrance

★ Bemo Stop Ⓐ

JL GANESHA

JL CIPAGANTI

JL CIHAMPELAS

JEANS ST

JL PASTEUR

Studio East

Flower Market

Geographical Museum ①

DIPONEGORO

Gedung Sate

Post & Giro Museum

Airport

JL PASIR KALIKI

Bouraq Office

JL JUANDA

②

JL MARTADINATA

Plaza Bandung (Mall)

Taman Lalu Lintas

Kebun Raya

JL MERDEKA

JL SUMATRA

JL SUMBAWA

Ⓑ

Train & Bemo Station

Bethel †

† Catholic

JL KEBONJATI

③
⑤ ⑥
④
⑦

JL GARDUJATI

Pasar Baru

JL BRAGA

JL LEMBONG

☎

Military Museum

Ⓒ

JL VETERAN

JL JEND SUDIRMAN

Ⓓ

Gedung Merdeka

JL NARIPAN

ALUN ALUN

ⓘ

Ⓔ

JL DALEM KAUM

☎ ⑧

JL ASIA AFRIKA

JL LENG KECIL

JL ASTANA ANYER

JL OTISTA

Circaheum Bus Terminal & ⑨

JL DEWI SARTIKA

Terminal Kebun Kelapa

ACCOMMODATION
Anggrek Golden Hotel	2
Wisma Asri	1
By Moritz	6
Hotel Citra	4
Le Yossie	3
New Le Yossie	5
Pelman	7
Savoy Homann	8
Supratman 102 Youth Hostel	9

RESTAURANTS
Ahong	B
London Bakery	C
Queen	E
Sari Sunda	D
Tizis	A

0   250m

▽ Leuwi Panjang Bus Terminal & West Java Museum

Information

The **tourist information** office (Mon–Sat 9am–5pm; ☎022/4206644) is on the *alun-alun* ("town square"). The two Golden Megacorp moneychangers, at Jl Juanda 89 opposite the Telkom building and at Jl Otista 180, have excellent rates. The GPO is at Jl Asia-Afrika 49 at the corner of Jalan Banceuy (Mon–Sat 8am–9pm), and has the best Internet connection in town (Rp1900 for 15min; Rp125 per minute thereafter), while the main Telkom office is on Jalan Lembong (24hr). There is a 24hr clinic with English-speaking doctors at Jl Cihampelas 161. Garuda's airline offices are inside the *Hotel Preangher Aerowista* at Jl Asia-Afrika 81; Merpati is at Jl Kebonjali 62, and the Bouraq office is at Jl Naripan 44.

Accommodation

Coming into town from the airport or bus terminals, it's best to get dropped off at the train station, which is close to all the cheap **hostels**.

Anggrek Golden Hotel, Jl Martadinata 15 (☎022/4205537). Immaculate rooms with air-con, phone and hot water. ④.

Wisma Asri, Jl Merak 5. A charming, quiet place with comfortable, clean rooms. The large rooms with shared mandi are a little overpriced, but those with air-con are reasonable. ③.

By Moritz, Jl Belakang Pasar/Luxor Permai 35 (☎022/4205788). A popular travellers' hangout, with dorms (Rp12,500), singles and doubles, some en-suite. ①.

Hotel Citra, Jl Gardujati 93 (☎022/6005061). Close to the train station, and one of the best bargains in Bandung. Sparkling new rooms with mandi, TV, fan and air-con. ①.

Le Yossie, Jl Kebonjati 35 (☎022/4204543) and **New Le Yossie**, Jl Belakang Pasar 112 (☎022/4266036). Twin hostels charging the same rates. *Le Yossie* is reasonable but often deserted; *New Le Yossie* is quieter and built around a central courtyard, but the hostel itself is not quite as well kept as some of the others here. ①.

Pelman, Jl Belakang Pasar 117 (☎022/436277). Smart, clean and friendly hotel in central location. All rooms come with television, and rates include breakfast. ②.

Savoy Homann, Jl Asia-Afrika 112 (☎022/432244). If you want colonial flavour then this is the place. Sizeable rooms, some with views of the courtyard gardens. ⑧.

Supratman 102 Youth Hostel, Jl Supratman 102 (☎022/473204). Cheap and cheerful youth hostel that's a good place to hook up with Indonesian travellers. Dorms are adequate. ①.

The City

Heading east down Jalan Asia-Afrika, along the northern edge of the alun-alun, you come to the **Gedung Merdeka building**, which hosted the first Asia-Afrika Conference in 1955 and is known as the Asia-Afrika or Liberty building. Inside, a small museum commemorates the conference. Many of the delegates stayed at the nearby Art Deco *Savoy Homann* hotel, which opened in 1939 and is still one of Bandung's premier hotels. Slightly west of here is the beginning of **Jalan Braga**, the chic shopping boulevard of 1920s Bandung. There's still one bakery here that's tried to hang on to its history, and a few of the facades maintain their stylish designs. The side streets that run off Jalan Braga were notorious for their raucous bars and brothels – at night a lot of the seediness remains.

North of Jalan Braga, to the east of Kebun Raya park, off Jalan Sumatra, is the bizarre Taman Lalu Lintas, the "**Traffic Park**". Designed to educate kids in the way of the highway, it has a system of miniature cars, roads and street signs. A twenty-minute walk to the northeast, the impressive **Gedung Sate** building at Jl Diponegoro 22, is known as the Sate Building because the regular globules on its gold-leaf spire resemble meat on a skewer. It was built in the 1920s and now houses local government offices. The excellent **Geographical Museum** (Mon–Thurs 9am–2pm, Fri 9–11am, Sat 9am–1pm; free) is nearby at Jl Diponegoro 57, and displays mountains of fossils, as well as several full dinosaur skeletons, a four-metre mammoth skeleton and a replica of the skull of the famous Java man.

About 750m west of the museum, Jalan Cihampelas, known to Westerners as **Jeans Street**, is lined with shops selling cheap T-shirts, bags, shoes and jeans (though these are no longer such a bargain). The shopfronts themselves are adorned with a kitsch kaleidoscope of colossal plaster superheroes, including Rambo, straddling spaceships and fluffy stucco clouds.

Eating

There are **food** courts in the numerous shopping centres, and side streets near the square serve some of the best warung **food**.

Ahong, Jl Kebon Kawang. Chinese place serving *kangkung* (water spinach) and *sapi* (beef) hotplate (Rp9500).

London Bakery, Jl Braga. Specializing in a range of coffees and teas, this is a modern European-type place with newspapers and books in English.

Penineungan Indah, Jl Tubagus Ismail Raya 60. One of the best Sundanese restaurants there is; each table is in a private room around gardens and ponds from which your dinner is fished. The *ikan mas* steamed in banana leaves is a speciality.

Queen, Jl Dalem Kaum 79. Superb Cantonese food and a great value set menu: for Rp15,000 you get soup, sweet-and-sour pork, chicken soy, shrimps in a nut sauce, veggies, rice and fruit.

Sari Sunda, Jl Sukarno Hatta 479 and Jl Jenderal Sudirman 103–107. Two branches, both serving superb Sundanese food: tofu baked with chilli is excellent.

Tizis, Jl Kidang Pananjung 3, off Jl Juanda, just north of the large bemo stop. An expat haven serving possibly the best homemade bread, sausages and pastries in Java.

Nightlife

On weekdays, you're best off heading for the **bars** like *Fame Station*, 11th floor, Lipo Building, Jl Gatot Subroto (11am–2am; Rp15,000), which draws a young crowd and often features live music. Expats tend to gravitate towards *Laga Pub*, Jl Junjungan 164, which has live music, cheapish beer (Rp9000) and a Rp5000 cover charge, or the seedier *Duta Pub* at Jl Dalem Kaum 85.

CULTURAL PERFORMANCES

Bandung is the capital of Sundanese culture; pick up the *Bandung Kini* magazine from the tourist information office to find out about special performances. The *Sindang Raret* restaurant at Jl Naripan 9 puts on **wayang golek** performances (Sat 8pm) for diners, and the *Panghegar* hotel, Jl Merdeka 2, stages Sundanese cultural performances in its restaurant (Wed & Sat). On Saturday evenings, *Sakadarna* homestay, Jl Kebonjati 50/7b, features Banten's **Debus players**, who perform feats of self-mutilation, such as eating glass and setting red-hot coals upon their heads. On Sunday mornings there are often shows at Bandung Zoo in the north of town, usually either the Indonesian martial art **pencak silat**, or **puppet shows**. Probably the most spectacular local event is the **ram fighting** (*adu domba*), held every other Sunday at 10am near the Sari Ater hot spring, 30km from the city. Take a minibus from the train station to Lembang terminal, then a second minibus to Ciater (Rp2500). To the sound of Sundanese flutes and drums, the rams lunge at each other until one of them fades; there's no blood, just flying wool and clouds of dust.

Around Bandung: Tangkuban Prahu volcano and the Dago Tea House walk

The mountainous region to the north of Bandung is the heart of the Parahyangan Highlands – the "Home of the Gods" – a highly volcanic area considered by the Sundanese to be the nucleus of their spiritual world. A very pleasant day out from Bandung on public transport takes you first to the 1830-metre-high **Tangkuban Prahu volcano**, the most visited volcano in West Java, 29km north of Bandung. Although it hasn't had a serious eruption for many years, the volcano still spews out vast quantities of sulphurous gases and at least one of its ten craters is still considered to be active. To get there from Bandung, take a Subang **minibus** from the train station (30min; Rp1500) and ask to be put down at the turn-off for the volcano, where there's a Rp1250 entrance fee. From here you can either charter an ojek or minibus up the asphalt road to the summit (10min; Rp5000) or walk up – it's about 4km up the road, or there's a good footpath via the Domas Crater, which starts just over 1km up the road from the guard post, to the right by the first car park. The **information booth** at the summit car park has details about crater walks; lots of guides will offer their services, but it's pretty obvious where you should and shouldn't go – just be sure to wear strong hiking boots. The main crater is called **Kawah Ratu** and is the one you can see down into from the end of the summit road, a huge dull grey cauldron with a few coloured lakes. From the summit you can trek down to **Domas Crater**, site of a small working sulphur mine.

On the return journey from Tangkuban Prahu to Bandung you'll pass through Lembang, where you should change on to a minibus for the resort of **MARIBAYA** (4km; Rp500). There are waterfalls near the entrance gate and hot springs, which have been tapped into a public pool. Further down is the largest **waterfall**, which you have to pay extra to see. An ugly iron bridge has been built right across the lip of the falls, and this is the starting point for a wonderful **walk down to the Dago Tea House** on the edge of Bandung (6km; 2hr). The path winds downhill through a gorge and forests – just before the teahouse are tunnels used by the Japanese in World War II and the Dago waterfall, which lies amongst bamboo thickets. At the end of your walk is the teahouse, with private tables under their own thatched roofs, and superb views over Bandung city. From here there are plenty of minibuses heading back into the centre of town (15min; Rp500).

Cipanas

The quiet spa village of **CIPANAS**, at the foot of Gunung Guntur, around two hours' journey southeast of Bandung, makes a delightful place to witness a picture-postcard idyll of Javanese rural life. The plentiful rice paddies are punctuated by glassy ponds, palm trees and flowering bushes, and local villagers supplement their living with fish-rearing. In the background looms the volcanic peaks of Gunung Guntur, Galunggung, Papandayan and the perfect cone of Cikurai. There are walks to nearby waterfalls and you can climb Gunung Guntur in a hard five-hour trek. To get to Cipanas, you must first take a **bus** from Bandung to Garut bus station (2hr; Rp2000), from where you should walk round to the next-door bemo terminal and take the brown bemo #4 to Cipanas (6km; 15min; Rp500).

All **accommodation** here is along the road that runs into Cipanas from the main Bandung–Garut road; every place features piped-in hot-water baths. *Kurina*, at no. 131 (①), is the best deal in Cipanas; the similar *Pondok Melati*, no. 133 (①), is also pleasant. *Pondok Wulandari*, Jl Raya Cipanas 99 (☎0262/234675; ①), has good-value rooms with fan and TV, and *Tirta Merta*, the first hotel on the left as you pass through the gateway, offers reasonably upmarket rooms (③). There are a few **warung** on the main street.

The Pangandaran peninsula

Lashed by huge, impressive waves that are for the most part too rough for swimming, the resort town of **Pangandaran** runs either side of a narrow isthmus connecting the mainland with a forested national park. Now virtually deserted owing to the recent economic and political turmoil in the country, Pangandaran has gone into virtual hibernation: many of the losmen have closed, as has the local cinema and even the town's only disco. Nevertheless, Pangandaran's beaches are still impressive, and the surrounding countryside offers a dizzying wealth of trips. The beach to the west is rent by powerful wind and waves, the eastern cove sheltered and quiet. There are a number of souvenir stalls on the seafront, many selling carcasses and shells from the once-abundant local population of turtles and monitor lizards. Every July and August, there's a **kite-flying festival** at the beach, with plenty of kite-fights: strings are treated with glue and ground glass so that they can sever rivals' lines.

About eighty percent of Pangandaran **national park** is secondary rainforest, and its most famous resident is the enormous **Javanese rafflesia** flower, which can grow to be the diameter of a car tyre. It's actually a parasite, flowering during the rainy season, and is pollinated not by bees but by a fly. Its relative, the Sumatran rafflesia, is the largest flower in the world and can grow up to 1m in diameter. Other occupants include Banteng oxen, mouse- and barking deer, armadillos, civets, flying lemurs, several species of primates and horn-

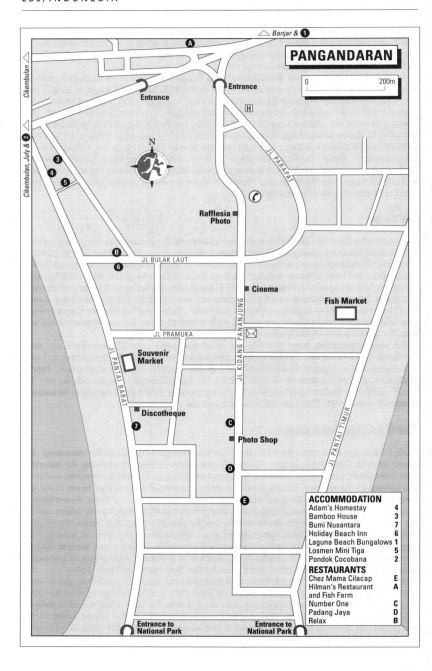

PANGANDARAN

0   200m

△ Banjar & ❶

◁ Cikembulan

◁ Cikembulan, July & ❷

Entrance

Entrance

H

JL PARAPAT

N

❸
❹
❺

Rafflesia ■
Photo

ℂ

B
❻ JL BULAK LAUT

■ Cinema

Fish Market

JL KIDANG PANANJUNG

JL PRAMUKA

✉

JL PANTAI BARAT

Souvenir
Market

■ Discotheque

❼

ℂ

■ Photo Shop

D

JL PANTAI TIMUR

E

Entrance to
National Park

Entrance to
National Park

ACCOMMODATION
Adam's Homestay	4
Bamboo House	3
Bumi Nusantara	7
Holiday Beach Inn	6
Laguna Beach Bungalows	1
Losmen Mini Tiga	5
Pondok Cocobana	2

RESTAURANTS
Chez Mama Cilacap	E
Hilman's Restaurant and Fish Farm	A
Number One	C
Padang Jaya	D
Relax	B

bills; the beaches are good places to spot turtles, coming ashore both to lay their eggs and bask in the sun. You can see the recreational area of the park by yourself, though to venture into the interior you must join a guided **tour** from one of the operators in town. Get your guide to show you the magnificent limestone caves and the fifty-metre waterfall that tumbles straight into the sea; there's a good pool for swimming at the top. **Surfing** off the park can be exceptional – there's a reef break on the Western border, though you are not, strictly speaking, supposed to be there. The coral here is razor-sharp, so bring a helmet and lots of iodine.

Buses into Pangandaran town stop at the terminal just beyond the isthmus on the mainland, and outside the town gates. The nearest **train** station on the main line is at **BANJAR**. Banjar is two hours away by bus (Rp2000–Rp15,000). One of the most popular ways of getting between Pangandaran and **Yogya** is by a memorably picturesque **riverboat trip**. From Pangandaran, take a bus to the town of Kalipucang (45min; Rp1000), 15km east. Here, a regular ferry (7am, 9am and 1pm; 4hr; Rp3000) runs across the Segara Anakan Lagoon to Cilacap, from where there are buses on to Yogya and beyond; to get to Yogya or Wonosobo in one day, you'll need to catch the first boat. Many places in Pangandaran sell the whole bus/river/bus trip as a package. Otherwise, when the ferry stops at Cilacap harbour you'll need to catch a becak, bemo or ojek to the terminal, and then catch a bus on from there.

Pangandaran has most essentials for tourists, but is short of a **bank**. The BRI in town has lousy rates for exchanging foreign currency and is only open until lunchtime. At the time of writing, the best rates were to be found at the *Chez Mama Cilacap*. The **tourist information** booth next door is refreshingly impartial and can help with trips out of Pangandaran and into the national park. The twenty-four-hour **Telkom office** is on Jalan Kidang Panunjang as you head from town towards the gates. The **post office** is also on Jalan Kidang Panunjang, closer to the centre of town (Mon–Sat 8am–2pm, Fri & Sun 8am–11am).

Accommodation

The Pangandaran peninsula still has plenty of losmen and **hotels**; prices can triple at weekends, and you'll need to book in advance. The ojek/becak mafia have organized a system where losmen have to pay them as much as Rp10,000 commission for each guest, so you may be charged more for your first night in a place, or have to stay more than one night. Most of the accommodation is in the town. A couple are located further along the beachfront in Cikembulan, 4km from the centre. To reach Cikembulan from the bus station, follow the road running west parallel to the shore; most public buses will carry on down this road past the village.

Adam's Homestay, Jl Pamugaran Bulak Laut (☎0265/639164). A kind of traveller's guesthouse for those with a little extra cash, featuring a library, a small pool and bike and car rental. Accommodation is pristine, ranging from basic rooms to fully appointed family bungalows. ③.

Bamboo House, Jl Bulak Laut 8 (☎0265/639419). The best budget place in town: quiet and well kept, with en-suite rooms and two detached bungalows. ①.

Bumi Nusantara, Jl Pantai Barat (☎0265/639032 or 639031). A variety of rooms, some with delightful balconies, air-con and hot water. Huge discounts when quiet. ⑥–⑨.

Delta Gecko Village, Cikembulan. Attractive, comfortable losmen. ①.

Holiday Beach Inn, Jl Bulak Laut 50 (☎0265/639285). One of the cheapest places, offering a choice of rooms with mandi. Two nights minimum stay. ①.

Kristina's, Cikembulan. Attractive and comfortable bungalows run by a gregarious Aussie character. ①.

Laguna Beach Bungalows, Jl Pengadilan Kebon–Carik RT3/RW12, Desa Babakan (☎0265/639761). Stunning, superb-value set of bungalows built around a small pond 4km to the east of Pangandaran. Rates include twice-daily taxis into town, breakfast and dinner and free coconuts from the garden. ①–②.

Losmen Mini Tiga, Jl Pamugaran Bulak Laut (☎0265/639436). Colourful losmen offering cool rooms with mosaic bathrooms, breakfast and fan. ①.

Pondok Cocobana, Jl Pantai Barat (☎0265/630510). Clean, quiet rambling little guesthouse located down a gang (alley) off Jl Pantai Barat, on the way to Cikembulan. Rooms, all en-suite, are extremely comfortable. ②.

Eating

The **restaurants** near the fish market off Jalan Pantai Timur should not be missed. The small square is surrounded by warung where you simply look through the iceboxes until you find your fish and then barter for it: Rp5000 max.

Chez Mama Cilacap, Jl Kidang Pananjung 187. Popular place whose specialities include black-rice pudding, lychees, longon and crêpes suzettes.

Hilmans Restaurant and Fish Farm, Jl Merdeka 312. Outside the gates to Pangandaran town, but worth the trip. There's live music every night and the menu includes lobster tails (Rp130,000), sandwiches (Rp12,000) and Bintang (Rp10,000).

Holiday Beach Inn, Jl Bulak Laut 50. Deserves a mention simply because of its wonderful pizzas (Rp10,000–12,000), the best in West Java.

Number One, Jl Kidang Pananjung. Has a few Sundanese dishes such as *nasi timbel* (rice, chillies and vegetables) for Rp7500 as well as pizzas for Rp10,000; the *arak* cocktails are also an attraction.

Padang Jaya, Jl Pamugaran 37, right on the corner with Jl Pantai Barat. A typical Padang restaurant which serves very spicy fish curries; you'll have a job to spend more than Rp8000.

Relax, Jl Bulak Laut 74. Probably the swishest café/restaurant in town, *Relax* is well-known for its excellent but expensive home-baked bread, milkshakes and ice cream.

Around Pangandaran

The most famous site in the Pangandaran area is the unmissable **Green Canyon**. Groups of tourists take noisy motorboats, or infinitely more appealing rowing boats up Sungai Cijulang to the entrance to a narrow gorge, from where you clamber over the rocks and swim through the pools upriver into the canyon. Wear a swimsuit and sun block. **Boats** take about six people and can be haggled down to Rp75,000. To get to the jetty, take a bus west from Pangandaran and ask to be let off at Green Canyon or Cukang Taneuh, which is right by the turn-off for Batu Keras. Alternatively, Pangandaran tour operators do packages for Rp40,000 per person; try Dastina Holidays, Jl Bulak Laut 2 (☎0265/630239).

The **Cituman Dam** is a place of stunning beauty with several waterfalls, distinctive limestone shapes and caves, and surrounded by thick forest. Either rent a motorbike, or take a minibus 8km west of town to the easily missed signpost, at the turn-off for Cituman Dam (on the right-hand side of the road), then hire an ojek to take you the remaining 3km (15min; Rp1500). Nearby **Gunung Tiga** park also has great views, bat caves and a beautiful river and cavern system. Take the same route as for Cituman, but ask for an ojek to Gunung Tiga. For the waterfalls, walk up the hill at the end of the rough road, and continue for about 500m. Just before the peak, there's a tiny path to the right down through the coconut palms – follow this all the way downhill to the river. The water has several glorious blue pools and, upstream, there's a magnificent cave you can swim into.

Down the coast to the west of Pangandaran, you can watch giant green, hawksbill, loggerhead and brown **sea turtles** feeding near the flat rock bed in front of the beach of Sindang Kerta village. To get there catch a minibus to Cijulang (30min; Rp750), then another bus to Cikalong (morning only; 1hr 30min–2hr; Rp2000), before catching an ojek for the seven-kilometre ride to Sindang Kerta (Rp1500).

Batu Keras is a popular beach spot and **surfers' enclave** 35km west of Pangandaran. From September to February there's a good right-handed reef break here. Sharks are very regular visitors to this bay and it's not uncommon to see a long black fin as it cruises around the point. There are several **places to stay** at Batu Keras. The *Dadang* homestay on Jalan Genteng Parakan (①) is a lovely, clean place, run by a young surfie couple. *Alanas* losmen is on the beachfront at Jl Legok Pari 336 (☎0811/230442; ①) and is an unashamed surfers' hangout: they rent out surfboards at Rp25,000 a day.

Cilacap

The biggest city on Central Java's southern coast, **CILACAP** is 170km west of Yogya and sees plenty of tourists, most passing through on their way to and from Pangandaran. The

Pangandaran ferry docks at Lomanis port in the northwest corner of the city. The **bus station** is 1km east of the port. To get between the two, take *angkuta* #C2 (city minibus). There's an infrequent **train** service from Cilacap to Jakarta and Surabaya. The train station is just to the north of the town centre. If you need to stay, the *Losmen Tiga*, Jl Mayor Sutoyo 61 (☎0282/33415; ①), has inexpensive, cell-like rooms.

Wonosobo

If you're travelling to the Dieng Plateau you'll almost certainly have to change buses at the sleepy hilltop village of **WONOSOBO**. **Buses** from the lowlands pull into the southern terminus. If you wish to travel straight on to Dieng, walk up the hill to the junction with Jalan Kyai Muntang: Dieng buses run past here before calling in at the Dieng terminus to the west of town; it's a one-hour journey. An *andong* (horse-drawn carriage) between the two stations costs Rp1000. There's a helpful **tourist office** on the alun-alun on the hill (Mon–Thurs 7am–2pm, Fri 7–11am, Sat 7am–12.30pm). If you need to stay, *Duta* at Jl RSU 3 (☎0286/21674; ①), 200m south of the Dieng bus station, is the most popular with backpackers, and the en-suite rooms are extremely comfortable.

Dieng

The **Dieng plateau** lies in a volcanic caldera 2093m above sea level and holds a rewarding mix of multicoloured sulphurous **lakes**, craters that spew pungent gases, and some of the oldest **Hindu temples** in Java. The volcano is still active – in 1979 over 150 people died after a cloud of poisonous gas bled into the atmosphere – and the landscape up on this misty, windswept plain is sparse and largely denuded. Although travel agents run day-trips from Yogya, these involve eight hours' travelling for just one hour on the plateau, so it's better to spend a night up here, in the damp and isolated village of **DIENG**, just across the road from the plateau's main temple complex; bring warm clothes and waterproofs. To get to Dieng **from Yogya** you need to change **buses** twice, going first to **MAGELANG** from the Jomber terminal (Rp1500), then to Wonosobo, and then to Dieng (Rp1500).

The tiny village of Dieng lines Jalan Raya Dieng, the road that runs along the plateau's eastern edge, and has a **tourist office** (random hours), a small kiosk that sells tickets to the Arjuna temples, and some fairly grim **accommodation**, the best of which is *Gunung Mas Hotel* (☎0286/92417; ②), at the northern end, which at least has hot water and TV. The rooms at the *Dieng Homestay*, Jl Raya Dieng 16 (☎0286/92823; ①), are basic and full of flies, and the mandi are excruciatingly cold; this is, however, the best of the budget bunch. *Bu Djono,* next door (no phone; ①), has shabbier rooms but superior food. Two hundred metres to the south at Jalan Telaga Warna 117–119 stands the smarter but less welcoming *Asri Losmen* (①).

The temples

It is believed that the Dieng plateau was once a completely self-contained **retreat** for priests and pilgrims. Unfortunately, it soon became completely waterlogged, and the entire plateau was eventually abandoned in the thirteenth century, only to be rediscovered, drained and restored in the nineteenth century. The eight temples left on Dieng today are a tiny fraction of what was once a huge complex built by the Sanjayas in the seventh and eighth centuries.

Of these temples, the five that make up the **Arjuna complex** (daily 6.15am–5.15pm; Rp3000 fee payable at the village kiosk), standing in fields opposite Dieng village, are believed to be the oldest. They have been named after heroes from the *Mahabharata* tales, although these are not the original names. Three of the five were built to the same blueprint: square, with two storeys and a fearsome *kala* head above the main entrance. The northernmost of these two-storey temples, the **Arjuna temple**, is the oldest on Java (c680 AD). Dedicated to Shiva, the temple once held a giant *lingam* (phallic-shaped stone), which was washed by worshippers several times a day; the water would then drain through a spout in the temple's north wall. Next to Arjuna stands **Candi Srikandi**, the exterior of which is adorned with reliefs of Vishnu (on the north wall), Shiva (east) and Brahma (south).

Candi Gatutkaca overlooks the Arjuna complex 300m to the southwest, and twenty minutes' walk (1km) south of here stands the peculiar-looking **Candi Bima**, named after the brother of Arjuna. Rows of faces stare impassively back at passers-by from the temple walls, a design based on the temples of southern India.

The coloured lakes

Telaga Warna (Coloured Lake), 2km along the main road heading south from the village, is the best example of Dieng's coloured lakes, where sulphurous deposits shade the water blue, from turquoise to azure. The lake laps against the shore of a small peninsula which holds a number of meditational caves. It was in one of these caves, **Gua Semar**, that Suharto and Australian prime minister Gough Whitlam decided the future of Timor in 1974. A visit to the lakes and caves can be combined with a visit to the Arjuna complex and Candi Bima, which makes for an interesting day's hiking.

Of the other lakes on the plateau, **Telaga Nila** and **Telaga Dringo**, 12km west of Dieng village, are the prettiest and can be combined with seeing **Sumur Jalatunda**, a vast, vine-clad well just off the main road – for a fee, small boys will show you a little-used path from the well to the two lakes. Just 250m further along the road is the turn-off to **Kawah Candradimuka**, one of a number of *kawah* (mini-craters) dotted around the plateau. The crater is a twenty-minute walk up the hill from the road; five minutes along its length a small path on the left heads west to Telaga Nila. The sulphurous smell can be nauseating, and the steaming vents may obscure your view of the bubbling mud pools below. Further east along the road, an extremely overgrown path leads up to **Gua Jimat**, where the sulphurous emissions are fatal to anyone and anything who stands too close. To get to all these lakes and caves involves a fairly tortuous route by public transport, so you might prefer to hire an **ojek** from Dieng village (Rp10,000 per day) or join a **tour** from *Dieng Homestay* (Rp5000). Otherwise, take a Batur-bound **bus** from Dieng to **Pasurenan** (7km; Rp500), and then an ojek (Rp1000) up the hill to the Sumur Jalatunda. Note that place-name spellings change frequently on the signposts, but Dieng and Tieng really are two different places.

Yogyakarta

YOGYAKARTA (pronounced "Jogjakarta" and often just shortened to "Jogja") ranks as one of the best preserved and most attractive cities in Java, and is a major centre for the classical **Javanese arts** of batik, ballet, drama, music, poetry and puppet shows. At its heart is Yogya's first family, the Hamengkubuwonos, whose elegant palace lies at the centre of Yogya's quaint old city, the **Kraton**, itself concealed behind high castellated walls. Tourists flock here, attracted not only by the city's courtly splendour but also by the nearby temples of **Prambanan** and **Borobudur**, so there are more hotels in Yogya than anywhere else in Java and, unfortunately, a correspondingly high number of touts, pickpockets and con artists.

Yogyakarta grew out of the dying embers of the once-great Mataram dynasty. In 1752, the Mataram empire, then based in nearby Solo, was in the throes of the Third Javanese War of Succession. The reigning *susuhunan*, **Pakubuwono II**, had been steadily losing power in the face of a rebellion by his brothers, Singasari and Mangkubumi, and the sultan's nephew, Mas Said. To try to turn the tide, Pakubuwono persuaded Mangkubumi to swap sides and defend the court, offering him control over three thousand households within the city in return. Mangkubumi agreed, but the sultan later reneged on the deal. In fury, Mangkubumi headed off to establish his own court. Thus Yogyakarta was born, and Mangkubumi crowned himself **Sultan Hamengkubuwono I**. He spent the next 37 years building the new capital, with the Kraton as the centrepiece and the court at Solo as the blueprint. By the time he died in 1792, his territory exceeded Solo's. After his death, however, the Yogya sultanate went into

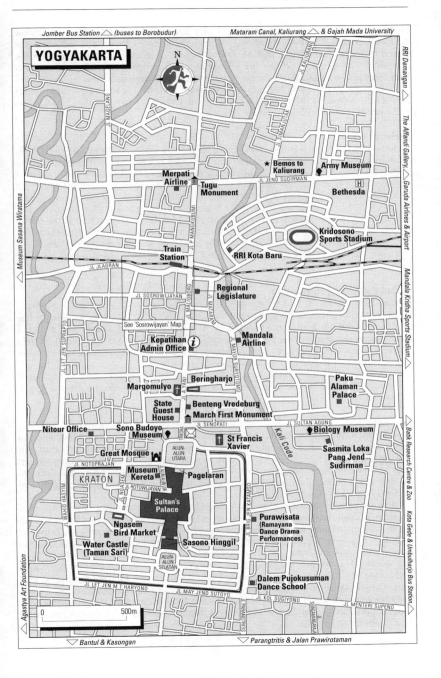

YOGYAKARTA

Jomber Bus Station △ (buses to Borobudur)

Mataram Canal, Kaliurang △ & Gajah Mada University

N

JL MAGELANG

Museum Sasana Wiratama

RRI Demangan ▷

The Affandi Gallery, ▷ Garuda Airlines & Airport

Merpati Airline

Tugu Monument

★ Bemos to Kaliurang

Army Museum

Bethesda [H]

JL JEND SUDIRMAN

JL P MANGKUBUMI

Train Station

Kridosono Sports Stadium

RRI Kota Baru

JL JLAGRAN

Mandala Kridha Sports Stadium ▷

JL SOSROWIJAYAN

Regional Legislature

JL MATARAM

See 'Sosrowijayan' Map

Kepatihan Admin Office (i)

Mandala Airline

JL MAYOR SURYOTOMO

JL LET JEN SUPARTO

Beringharjo

Margomulyo

JL A YANI

Paku Alaman Palace

State Guest House

Benteng Vredeburg

March First Monument

JL SULTAN AGUNG

Nitour Office

Sono Budoyo Museum

JL SENOPATI

St Francis Xavier

Kali Code

Biology Museum

Great Mosque

ALUN-ALUN UTARA

Sasmita Loka Pang Jend Sudirman

JL NOTOPRAJAN

Museum Kereta

Pagelaran

KRATON

JL NGASEM

JL ROTOWIJAYAN

JL WAHID HASYIM

Sultan's Palace

JL BRIG JEN KATAMSO

Purawisata (Ramayana Dance Drama Performances)

Ngasem Bird Market

Water Castle (Taman Sari)

Sasono Hinggil

ALUN-ALUN SELATAN

Dalem Pujokusuman Dance School

Agastya Art Foundation

JL LET JEN M T HARYONO

JL MAY JEND SUTOYO

JL KOL SUGIYONO

JL MENTERI SUPENO

Batik Research Centre & Zoo   Kota Gede & Umbulharjo Bus Station ▷

0   500m

▽ Bantul & Kasongan

▽ Parangtritis & Jalan Prawirotaman

freefall and spent most of the nineteenth century concentrating on artistic pursuits rather than warmongering. In 1946, the capital of the newly declared Republic of Indonesia was moved to Yogya from Jakarta, and the Kraton became the unofficial headquarters for the republican movement. With the financial and military support of **Sultan Hamengkubuwono IX**, Yogya became the nerve centre for the native forces. Today, over fifty years on from the War of Independence, the royal household of Yogya continues to enjoy almost slavish devotion from its subjects and the current sultan, Hamengkubuwono X, is one of the most influential politicians in the country.

Arrival

Arriving at **Adisucipto Airport**, 10km east of the city centre, walk 200m south of the terminal on to Jalan Adisucipto, where you can flag down any **bus** (Rp500) heading west to Yogya. A taxi costs Rp8000. The **train station** (Tugu Station) lies just one block north of Jalan Sosro, on Jalan Pasar Kembang. A becak to Jalan Prawirotaman costs Rp3000, a taxi, Rp5000; or catch southbound bus #2 (Rp500) from Jalan Mataram, one block east of Jalan Malioboro. All inter-city buses arrive at the **Umbulharjo bus station**, 3km east of the city centre. If you're arriving in Yogya from Borobudur, Magelang, or elsewhere in the north, you can alight at **Jomber Terminal**, around 3km north of the city centre, from where you can catch bus #5 (Rp500) to the GPO. From the **local bus station** adjacent to Umbulharjo there are regular services into town, including bus #2 (Rp500), which travels via Jalan Prawirotaman.

Orientation and information

Most of the interest for visitors is focused on the two-kilometre-wide strip of land between the two westernmost rivers, Kali Winongo and Kali Code – this is the site of the **Kraton**, the historic heart of the city. A kilometre north of the Kraton walls, the budget travellers' mecca of **Jalan Sosrowijayan** (known as Jalan Sosro) runs west off Malioboro to the south of the train station. There's a second, more upmarket cluster of tourist hotels and restaurants on **Jalan Prawirotaman**, in the suburbs to the southeast of the Kraton.

The **tourist office** is at Jl Malioboro 16/175 (Mon–Thurs & Sat 8am–7pm, Fri 8am–1pm & 3–6pm; ☎0274/566000) and keeps plenty of information on local events, language and meditation courses.

City transport

All **city buses** charge a set Rp500 and begin and end their journeys at the Umbulharjo bus station. Most buses stop running at about 6pm, although the #15 runs to the GPO until 8pm (see box opposite). The most useful buses for travellers are the #4, which runs south down Jalan Malioboro before heading to Kota Gede and the Umbulharjo bus station; and the #5 running between Umbulharjo and Jomber via Jalan Sosrowijayan (when heading north) and the GPO (when returning to Umbulharjo).

There are literally thousands of **becak** in Yogya, and they are the most convenient form of transport. It should cost no more than Rp500 from Jalan Sosro to the GPO (Rp1500 from Jalan Prawirotaman), although hard bargaining is required. The horse-drawn carriages, known as **andong**, which tend to queue up along Jalan Malioboro, are a little cheaper. **Taxis** are good value (Rp800, plus Rp400 per km). You can usually find them hanging around the GPO, or ring either Jas (☎0274/373388), Setia Kawan (☎0274/522333) or Sumber Rejo (☎0274/514786). Yogya is a flat city, so you might want to rent a **bicycle**: try Bike 33 in Jl Sosro Gang I (Rp5000 per day). Orange-suited parking attendants throughout the city will look after your bike for Rp100. You can rent a Honda Astrea **motorbike** for Rp40,000 per day from Fortuna 1 and 2 near the train station at Jl Jlagran Lor 20–21 and Jl Pasar Kembang 60 (☎0274/564680 or 589550).

USEFUL BUS ROUTES

#2 Umbulharjo bus station–Jalan Sisingamangaraja (for Prawirotaman)–Jalan Brig Jen Katamso (along the eastern wall of the Kraton)–Jalan Mataram–Kridono sports centre –Gajah Mada University–Jalan Simanjutak (for minibuses to Prambanan)–Jalan Mataram–Jalan Sisingamangaraja–Umbulharjo.

#4 Umbulharjo–Jalan Sultan Agung–Jalan Mataram–Prambanan minibus station on Jalan Simanjutak–Jalan Malioboro–Jalan Ngeksigondo (Kota Gede)–Umbulharjo.

#5 Umbulharjo–Jalan Parangtritis (western end of Jalan Prawirotaman)–Jalan Wahid Hasyim (along the western wall of the Kraton)–Jalan Sosro (western end)–train station–Jomber (for buses to Borobudur, Magelang and Semarang)–Jalan Pringgokusuman (west of Sosro)–Jalan Let Jen Suprapto–Jalan Ngasem (bird market)–Jalan Parangtritis–Umbulharjo.

#15 Umbulharjo–Jalan Sisingamangaraja (for Prawirotaman)–Jalan Brigjen Katamso–GPO–Gaja Mada University–Umbulharjo.

Accommodation

Most of Yogya's 150 **hotels** and losmen are concentrated around Jalan Sosrowijayan and Jalan Prawirotaman. Jalan Sosro, in the heart of the business district, is busy and downmarket; Jalan Prawirotaman is a lazier, leafier street.

JALAN SOSRO AND AROUND

Bagus, Jl Sosro Wetan GT1/57 (☎0274/515087). Small, inexpensive but adequate rooms and clean bathrooms make this very good value, though breakfast is not included. ①.

Bladok, Jl Sosro 76 (☎0274/523832). Friendly, efficient and impeccably clean hotel built round a central courtyard. All rooms are en suite. ②.

Citra Anda, Jl Sosro Wetan GT1/144 (no phone). While the exterior resembles a maximum-security jail, the interior is much more homely; all rooms are en suite and breakfast is included. ①.

Dewi I, Jl Sosro (☎0274/516014). Largish losmen offering decent-sized, spotless rooms at reasonable prices. Good value, despite the moody manager. ①.

Ella, Jl Sosrodipuran GT1/487 (☎0274/582219). One of the best. Clean fan-cooled rooms, friendly staff and good info. Students get a small discount and breakfast is included. ①.

Kota, Jl Jlagran Lor 1 (☎0274/515844). A colonial feel pervades this lovely hotel, even though it was only established in the 1950s. Fifteen beautiful en-suite rooms. The best on the street. ④.

Lita, Jl Sosro Wetan GT1 (☎0274/512878). Decorated with work by local artists, this losmen offers large, spotless rooms at reasonable prices. Very good value indeed. ①.

Lotus, Jl Sosro Wetan GT1/167 (☎0274/515090). Light, airy and clean losmen, popular with Yogya's adolescents, who congregate in the lounge to watch the TV. Fine rooftop balcony. ①.

Royal Batik Palace, Jl Pasar Kembang 29 (☎0274/587012). Good outdoor swimming pool, bar and restaurant, and salubrious, en-suite, air-con rooms. ③.

Selekta, Jl Sosro (☎0274/566467). Rivalling *Ella* as the best of the budget bunch, this very welcoming losmen has a good atmosphere and capacious, clean rooms; breakfast is included. ①.

Superman I and **II**, Jl Sosro Gang I (☎0274/515007). *Superman I* was once the travellers' favourite, but is clearly being wound down now in favour of the newly built and pristine *Superman II*, which offers good-value accommodation, with fine rooms. ①.

Supriyanto Inn, Jl Sosro Wetan GT1/59 (no phone). Another very popular choice. Good location in central Sosro, away from the mosque and hubbub of *Gang ll*. ①.

Suryo, Jl Sosro Wetan GT1/145 (no phone). Jauntily decorated little homestay run by an energetic octogenarian. Free tea and coffee. ①.

Yogya Moon, Jl Kemetiran 21 (☎0274/582465). Sparkling hotel in a rather run-down area west of Sosro. The rooms (all en suite) have air-con and TV. Economy singles (Rp40,000) are terrific value. ④.

The map shows streets including Train Station, Fortuna Car Hire, JL JLAGRAN LOR, JL PASAR KEMBANG, Borobudur Bar, Natour Garuda Hotel, Cheap Food Stall, JL JOYOREGARAN, GANG II, GANG I, JL SOSROWIJAYAN, JL SOSRODIPURAN GTI, JL MALIOBORO, JL DAGEN, Apotik 21, N compass, 0 100m scale.

ACCOMMODATION

Bagus	3
Bladok	13
Citra Anda	6
Dewi I	12
Ella	15
Kota	1
Lita	10
Lotus	9
Royal Batik Palace	2
Selekta	11
Superman I	4
Superman II	8
Supriyanto Inn	7
Suryo	5
Yogya Moon	14

RESTAURANTS

33	G
Anna's	D
Chaterina	I
FM Café	H
Lily Pudding	B
Mama's	A
Murni	F
N.N.	C
Superman II	E

SOSROWIJAYAN

JALAN PRAWIROTAMAN AND AROUND

Asli, Jl Prawirotaman MGIII/510 (no phone, fax ☎0274/371175). Less a hotel than an acid flashback. Psychedelic pictures on the walls and music courtesy of Jimi Hendrix. Laid-back. ①.

Duta, Jl Prawirotaman I 26 (☎0274/372064). Big hotel that comes highly recommended by all who stay here; it has a good pool and does huge breakfasts. ②.

Duta Garden, Jl Timuran MGIII/103 (☎0274/373482). Exceptionally beautiful cottage-style hotel smothered in bougainvillea. Rooms are exquisite. Bargain for low-season discounts. ⑤.

Metro II, Jl Sisingamangaraja 21 (☎0274/376993). Reasonable hotel, 200m south of eastern end of Jl Parangtritis. Most of the rooms are very homely, but avoid the rodent-infested basement. ①–②.

Rose, Jl Prawirotaman I 28 (☎0274/377991). The best value in Prawirotaman. Hearty breakfasts, a swimming pool and some great bargains to be had, particularly in the low season. ①–②.

Yogya Village Inn, Jl Menukan 5 (☎0274/373031). Excellent, stylish little place combining homely hospitality with classy accommodation. Includes a library and games pavilion. ⑥–⑨.

The Kraton

The layout of Yogya reflects its character: modern and brash on the outside, but with a very ancient and traditional heart in the **Kraton**, the walled city designed by Yogya's first sultan, Mangkubumi. *Kraton* means "royal residence" and originally referred just to the sultan's palace, but today it denotes the whole of the walled city (plus Jalan Malioboro), which includes not only the palace but also an entire town of some ten thousand people. The Kraton has changed little in the two hundred years since Mangkubumi's time; both the palace, and the 5km of crenellated icing-sugar walls that surround the Kraton, date from his reign.

ALUN-ALUN UTARA

Most people enter the Kraton through the northern gates by the GPO, beyond which lies the busy town square, Alun-alun Utara. As is usual in Java, the city's grand mosque, **Mesjid Agung** (visit outside of prayer times), built in 1773 by Mangkubumi, stands on the western side of the alun-alun. It's designed along traditional Javanese lines, with a multi-tiered roof on top of an airy, open-sided prayer hall. A little to the north of the mosque, just by the main gates, stands the **Sono Budoyo Museum** (Tues–Thurs 8am–1.30pm, Fri 8–11.15am, Sat & Sun 8am–noon; Rp750), which houses a fine exhibition of the arts of Java, Madura and Bali. The intricate, damascene-style wooden partitions from Northern Java are particularly eye-catching, as are the many classical gold and stone statues dating back to the eighth century. Just outside the entrance, a small puppet workshop supplies the characters for the regular wayang kulit shows (see p.241).

NGAYOGYOKARTO HADININGRAT — THE SULTAN'S PALACE

On the southern side of the alun-alun lies a masterpiece of understated Javanese architecture, the elegant collection of ornate kiosks and graceful *pendopos* (open-sided pavilions) that comprises the **Sultan's Palace**. It was designed as a scale model of the Hindu cosmos, and every plant, building and courtyard is symbolic; the sultans, though professing the Islamic faith, still held on to many of the Hindu and animist superstitions of their forefathers and believed that this particular design would ensure the prosperity of the royal house.

The palace is split into two parts. The first section, the **Pagelaran** (Mon–Thurs, Sat & Sun 8am–1pm, Fri 8–11.30am; Rp1000) lies immediately to the south of the alun-alun and is bypassed by most tourists, as there is little to see save for two large, drab pendopos and an extremely mediocre display of regal costumes.

Further down Jalan Alun-alun Lor stands the entrance to the main body of the **palace** (Mon–Thurs, Sat & Sun 8.30am–2pm, Fri 8.30am–1pm; Rp75000 including optional guided tour). Shorts and revealing clothes are frowned upon here, so you may have to rent a batik shirt from the ticket office (Rp1000). The palace has been the home of the sultans ever since Mangkubumi arrived here from Solo in 1755, and little has changed. The hushed courtyards, the faint stirrings of the gamelan drifting on the breeze and the elderly palace retainers, still dressed in the traditional style with a kris (traditional dagger) tucked by the small of their back, all contribute to a remarkable sense of timelessness. You enter the complex through the palace's outer courtyard or **Keben**, where the sultan used to sit on a stone throne and pass sentence on lawbreakers. Two pendopos stand on either side of a central path in the next courtyard, each sheltering an antique gamelan orchestra; the eastern pendopo also houses royal curios including an early royal playpen.

Two silver-painted *raksasa* (temple guardian statues) guard the entrance to the largest and most important palace courtyard, the Pelataran Kedaton. On your right, the yellow-painted **Gedung Kuning** contains the offices and living quarters of the sultan. This part of the palace is out of bounds to tourists, as the current sultan (Hamengkubuwono X), his wife and five daughters still spend much of their time here. A covered corridor joins the Gedung Kuning with the Golden Throne Pavilion, or **Bangsal Kencono**, the centrepiece of the Pelataran Kedaton. In the imagery of the Hindu cosmos, the pavilion represents Mount Meru, the sacred mountain at the very centre of the universe. Its intricately carved roof is held aloft by hefty teak pillars, whose carvings neatly sum up the syncretism of the three main religions of Indonesia, with the lotus leaf of Buddhism supporting a red-and-gold diamond pattern of Hindu origin, while around the pillar's circumference runs the opening line of the Koran: "There is no God but Allah and Mohammed is his prophet." A large, arched gateway flanked by two huge drums connects the Pelataran Kedaton with the

Kesatrian courtyard, home to both another gamelan orchestra and a collection of royal portraits.

THE TAMAN SARI

A five-minute walk to the west of the palace, along Jalan Rotowijayan and down Jalan Ngasem and Jalan Taman, is the unspectacular **Taman Sari** (Water Garden) of Mangkubumi (daily 9am–3pm; Rp1000). This giant complex was designed in the eighteenth century as an amusement park for the royal house, and features a series of swimming pools and fountains, an underground mosque and a large boating lake. Unfortunately it fell into disrepair and most of what you see today is a concrete reconstruction. The main entrance gate is about the most attractive part of the ruins; you can still wander through the cobwebbed underground passages, where the shell of the sultan's underground mosque is visible.

Jalan Malioboro

The two-kilometre stretch of road heading north from the alun-alun is as replete with history as it is with batik shops and becak. Originally this was designed as a **ceremonial boulevard** by Mangkubumi, along which the royal cavalcade would proceed on its way to Mount Merapi. The road changes name three times along its length, beginning as Jalan JA Yani in the south before continuing as Jalan Malioboro, and then finally Jalan Mangkubumi. At the southern end of the street, at the junction of Jalan JA Yani and Jalan Senopati, stands the **Benteng Vredeburg** (Tues–Thurs 8.30am–1.30pm, Sat and Sun 8.30–noon; Rp750), a fort ordered by the Dutch, and built by Mangkubumi in the mid-eighteenth century. This relic of Dutch imperialism has been restored to its former glory, and now houses a series of well made and informative dioramas which recount the end of colonialism in Indonesia. Nearby, the raucous, multi-level market complex **Pasar Beringharjo** buzzes noisily throughout the day, selling mass-produced batik (with a small, quality selection in the southeastern corner on the ground floor).

The rest of the city

Yogyakarta's second court, **Paku Alaman** (Tues, Thurs & Sun 9.30am–1.30pm; free), lies 50m to the east of the Biology Museum on the north side of Jalan Agung. As is traditional, the minor court of the city faces south as a mark of subservience to the main palace. The royal household of Paku Alam was created in 1812 by the British in a deliberate divide-and-rule tactic. The current prince, the octogenarian Paku Alam VIII, is by far the longest-reigning ruler of all Central Java's royal courts, having been in place for over sixty years. The part that is open to general view – by the southeastern corner of the courtyard – houses a motley collection of royal artefacts, including a room filled with the prince's chariots, which unfortunately appear to be permanently shrouded in dust sheets.

Two kilometres east along Jalan Adisucipto, on the west bank of the Kali Gajah Wong, you'll find the **Affandi Gallery** (Mon–Fri & Sun 8.30am–4pm, Sat 8.30am–1pm; Rp1250). Heralded by the *New Statesman* in 1952 as the most important post-war painter in the world, Affandi was born in Cirebon in 1907, but spent most of his life in Yogya, in the unusual house-cum-studio that still stands on stilts above the river near the galleries. During the 1920s and 1930s Affandi developed his idiosyncratic style, preferring to apply the paint to the canvas directly from the tube, forming thick swirls of colour; many of the paintings were completed in just one hour. The galleries were built after his death in 1990 and contain over a hundred of his greatest works, including several self-portraits.

One of Yogya's best museums lies 7km east of town on Jalan Raya Yogya (take a Wonosari-bound bus from the bus station for 10min; Rp300). The excellent **Museum Wayang Kekayon** (Wayang Museum; daily except Mon 8am–3pm; Rp1000) covers the development of puppeteering and explores the many different forms of wayang today, including some seldom-seen treasures.

Eating and drinking

Yogya's specialities are *ayam goreng* and *nasi gudeg* (rice and jackfruit), and many foodstalls serve nothing else. Every evening a **food market** sets up on Jalan Malioboro, and by 8pm the entire street is thronged with diners. Beware of being overcharged, and note that in many of the larger **lesehan** places (where you sit on the floor by low tables), particularly those by the end of Jalan Sosro, diners pay restaurant prices. The stalls by the train station and on the top floor of the Malioboro Mall are cheaper. Jalan Sosro and Jalan Prawirotaman are chock-full of good-quality **restaurants** asking reasonable prices (about Rp3000 for nasi goreng). Most of these restaurants open from midday until about 10pm.

If you're looking for a drink, try the *Laba Laba* on Jalan Prawirotaman, an over-priced restaurant and **bar**, with weird cocktails a speciality. The *Borobudur Bar*, on Jalan Pasar Kembang by the northern end of Sosro Gang I, is one of the few places that stays open beyond midnight, attracting locals, expats and tourists.

JALAN SOSRO

33, Gang I. A cross between a restaurant and a warung, this tiny two-tabled restaurant serving Indonesian standards and pancakes ranks as the cheapest in Sosro. Unpredictable hours.

Anna's, Gang II. Popular little family-run restaurant proffering some wonderful, genuinely Javanese food. Their *nasi gudeg* (Rp9000) is one of the best feasts in town.

Chaterina, Jl Sosro. Very reasonably priced restaurant with *lesehan* seating at the rear, serving some of the best food in Sosro. Let down a little by hassle from the batik touts. Internet access available.

FM Café, Jl Sosro. Poky little eatery on the main drag that's proving increasingly popular with both local youths and travellers. Serves good, cheap, large portions.

Lily Pudding, Jl Jlagran Lor, 50m to the west of the train station. This place turns out a treasure trove of treacle treats. Try their nine-inch caramel pudding for Rp4500.

Mama's, Jl Pasar Kembang. Most popular of all the cheap eateries by the train station, serving huge portions of tasty Indonesian food.

Murni, Gang I. Busy little alcohol-free budget restaurant serving huge portions of delicious food. Probably the best value in Sosro. Closes for a couple of hours in the early evening.

N.N., Gang II. A family-owned place with hearty food (particularly the delicious soups), and good service. Very cheap too.

Superman II, JL Sosro Gang I. *Superman II* continues to be the most popular restaurant in Sosro, with ice-cold beer, regular screenings of European football and Internet facilities compensating for the rather bland, overpriced food.

JALAN PRAWIROTAMAN

Going Bananas, Jl Prawirotaman 48. Café/souvenir shop at the eastern end of the street. Good coffees and sandwiches.

Griya Birjana, Jl Prawirotaman. Hugely popular restaurant on the main drag, serving Indonesian and Western fare and ice-cold beer. Lively atmosphere in the evenings, and good value.

Lotus Garden, Jl Prawirotaman MG3/593a. Mid-priced restaurant specializing in producing high-quality, healthy local dishes. Good vegetarian selection. Classical and modern dance and puppet performances throughout the week (8pm; Rp3000).

Mercury, Jl Parawirotaman II MG3/595. Beautiful, colonial-style restaurant serving surprisingly afford-able mid-priced Indonesian and Western dishes.

Nusa Dua, Jl Prawirotaman. Highly recommended inexpensive restaurant with a large menu of Indonesian, Chinese and Western dishes served by very professional, friendly staff.

Via Via, Jl Prawirotaman 24b. Serves a different menu of inventive and excellent dishes every day. Has a couple of good "travellers' tips" books, plus current editions of *Time* and *Newsweek*.

Traditional cultural performances

Wayang kulit is the epitome of Javanese culture and shows are well worth catching, although **wayang golek**, where wooden puppets are used, tends to be easier to follow. Most wayang performances are designed with tourists in mind, being only two hours long. The **Ramayana dance drama** is a modern extension of the court dances of the nineteenth cen-tury and is most popularly seen at the moonlit performance, which takes place every summer in the open-air theatre at Prambanan temple (see p.245 for details). Note that most performances stop during Ramadan.

Agastya, Jl Gedongkiwo 996. Tucked away in the city's southwestern suburbs, this institute was founded to prevent wayang kulit from dying out. Stages wayang kulit (daily except Sat; 3pm) and wayang golek performances (Sat; 3pm) for Rp4000.

Ambar Budaya (aka **Dewi Sri**), Jl Adisucipto 66. Daily wayang kulit performance (8pm; Rp2500) at this governement craft centre opposite *Ambarrukmo Palace Hotel*.

Ambarrukmo Palace Hotel, Jl Adisucipto 66. This former palace has a marvellous floating restaurant where you can sit and watch traditional Javanese dancing (every evening at 8pm) and wayang golek (Mon at 8pm).

Hanoman's Forest, Jl Prawirotaman 9 (☎0274/372528). Nightly cultural entertainments – wayang kulit (Wed 7pm; Rp3000), Javanese ballet and live bands.

Lotus Garden Restaurant, Jl Prawirotaman II. Selection of dance styles from the archipelago (Tues, Thurs & Sat, 8pm; Rp3000).

Nitour, Jl KHA Dalan 71 (☎0274/376450). This centre, outside of the northern walls of the Kraton, puts on a wayang golek performance of the *Ramayana* tales. Daily 11am–1pm; Rp3000.

Ndalem Pujokusirman, Jl Brig Jen Katamso 45. A two-hour performance of classical Javanese dance at this illustrious dance school (Mon, Wed & Fri 8pm; Rp10,000).

Purawisata Theatre, Jl Brig Jen Katamso (☎0274/374089). Every night for the last twenty-odd years, the Puriwisata Theatre has put on a 90min performance of the *Ramayana*. The story is split into two episodes, with each episode performed on alternate nights. On the last day of every month the whole story is performed. Free transport (8pm; Rp20,000 or Rp32,000).

Sasana Hinggil, Alun-alun Selatan. Yogya's only full-length wayang kulit show runs from 9pm to 5.30am on the second Saturday of every month, and on alternate fourth Saturdays (Rp3000).

Sonobudoyo Museum, Jl Trikora 1. The most professional and popular wayang kulit show, performed daily for 2hr (8pm; Rp4000).

Sultan's Palace Holds regular wayang golek, wayang kulit and wayang orang performances. Ask at tourist office or palace for current timetable.

Shopping

Yogya is Java's souvenir centre, and you'll find crafts from all over the archipelago here. **Jalan Malioboro** is the place to come for inexpensive souvenirs like batik pictures, leather bags, woodcarvings and silver rings. The more upmarket **souvenir emporiums** which sell tasteful local craft items include Sosro's Going Bananas and Something Different in Prawirotaman. Another good place is the Desa Kerajinan, the government's craft centre opposite the *Ambarrukmo Palace Hotel* at Jl Adisucipto 66. Harto has several specialist outlets around Jalan Tirtodipuran, including one selling woodcarvings and another dealing in **wayang kulit puppets**. There are also a couple of puppet shops on Jalan Prawirotaman, and two at the northern end of Malioboro. Shops on Jalan Malioboro and at the Beringharjo market sell both traditional indigo-and-brown **batik** clothing, as well as tourist-oriented chocolate-box batik painting. If your knowledge of batik is shaky, start off at the Balai Penelitian Kerajinan dan Batik (Batik and Handicraft Research Centre) at Jl Kusumanegara 2 (Mon–Thurs 9–11.30am, Fri 9–10.30am). From here, head west to the galleries in the Kraton, most of them in the grounds of the old Taman Sari. For top quality batiks in town, head to Jalan Tirtodipuran, west of Jalan Prawirotaman, home of renowned artists Tulus Warsito (at 19a) and Slamet Riyanto (61a). The suburb of Kota Gede is the home of Central Java's **silver industry**. It's famous for its fine filigree work and some workshops, such as the huge Tom's Silver at Jl Ngeksigondo 60 (daily 8.30am–7.30pm), allow you to watch the smiths at work. Borobudur Silver on the way to Kota Gede at Jl Menteri Supeno 41 (daily 8am–8pm) gives discounts to HI and ISIC card-holders.

Listings

Airlines Bouraq, Jl Mataram 60 (☎0274/562664); Garuda, *Ambarrukmo Palace Hotel* (☎0274/565835), and at the airport (☎0274/563706); Merpati, Jl Diponegoro 31 (☎0274/514272); Mandala, Jl Mayor Suryotomo 573 (☎0274/520603).

Batik courses The *Via Via Café* on Jl Prawirotaman runs a one-day batik course for Rp30,000, and a one-week course for US$150. At the entrance to the Taman Sari, Dr Hadjir Digdodarmodjo (☎0274/377835), runs a more serious three- to five-day course (from US$25 for three days).

Bookshops The Lucky Boomerang at Jl Sosro Gang I/67 stocks English-language novels and books on Indonesia; also try Gramedia Bookshop in the Malioboro shopping centre.

Cookery courses The *Via Via Café* on Jl Prawirotaman runs afternoon courses (Rp30,000).

Dance and gamelan courses Mrs Tia of the Ndalem Pujokusirman school at Jl Brig Jen Katamso 45 (☎0274/371271) invites foreigners to join her 2hr group dance lessons beginning at 4pm. At the northern end of the same street, the Puriwisata (☎0274/374089) holds Javanese dance courses for Rp50,000 per 3hr session. They also run a school for gamelan (Rp50,000 per session). The *Via Via Café* on Jl Prawirotaman runs intensive one-week courses for US$150.

Internet access Most of the Internet places around Jl Sosro are way overpriced (Rp15,000 per hour). You're better off visiting either the Wasantara-Net in the GPO (Mon–Sat 8am–9pm, Sun 9am–8pm; Rp45000 for 30min); or, the best in town, *Pointers* at Jl Mangkubumi 73, which charges the same, but has much better, faster equipment. Opposite the western end of Jl Prawirotaman, on Jl Parangtritis, *Uninet* also charges Rp4500 per hour.

Language courses Puri (☎0274/583789), just to the east of the RRI auditorium at the Kompleks Kolombo 4 on Jl Cendrawasih, offers a two-week intensive course for US$390 (payable in dollars only), or a 10hr version for US$30. Puri Bahasa Indonesia (☎0274/588192) at Jl Bausasran 59, two blocks east of Jl Malioboro, runs similar language courses (Rp15,000–25,000). The *Via Via Café* on Jl Prawirotaman holds a 3hr course for Rp20,000. The Wisma Bahasa, Jl Rajawali Gang Nuri 6 (☎0274/520341) does a 30hr "travellers" course over five days (US$100).

Hospitals and clinics The Gading Clinic, south of the Alun-alun Selatan at Jl Maj Jen Panjaitan 25, has English-speaking doctors (☎0274/375396). Yogya's main hospital is in Bethes Da, Jl Sudirman 81 (☎0274/81774).

Immigration office Jl Adisucipto Km10, on the way to the airport near the *Ambarrukmo Palace* hotel (Mon–Thurs 8am–2pm, Fri 8–11am, Sat 8am–1pm; ☎0274/514948).

Massage and massage courses Gabriel at *Anna's Restaurant* provides a highly-recommended traditional Javanese one-hour massage for Rp30,000. They also run courses, charging Rp350,000 for four days, or Rp200,000 for two days (3hr per day). The *Via Via* café also offers a traditional massage as part of their tour to a herb market and jamu traditional medicine factory (Rp30,000).

Post office Jl Senopati 2, at the southern end of Jl Malioboro (Mon–Sat 7am–9pm, Sun 8am–8pm). The parcel office is on Jl Maj Jen Suryotomo (Mon–Sat 8am–3pm, Sun 9am–2pm).

Telephone services The main Telkom office at Jl Yos Sudarso 9 is open 24hr and has Home Direct phones too. There's a wartel office at no. 30 Jl Sosro and another on Jl Parangtritis, south of Jl Prawirotaman Gang II.

Gunung Merapi and Kaliurang

Symmetrical, smoke-plumed **Gunung Merapi** is an awesome 2911-metre presence in the centre of Java, visible from Yogyakarta, 25km away. This is Indonesia's most volatile volcano, and the sixth most active in the world; as recently as 1994 an entire mountain village was incinerated by lava, killing 64 people. But the Javanese worship the mountain as a life-giver, its lava providing Central Java with its agricultural fecundity.

Nearly a kilometre up on Merapi's southern slopes is the village of **KALIURANG**, a tatty but popular hill station. A bus from Yogya's Umbulharjo station costs Rp700; it's Rp1000 by bemo from behind the Terban terminal on Jalan Simanjutak. In Kaliurang, you can join a **trekking** group to the summit, a fairly arduous five-hour scramble through snake- and spider-infested forest. During Merapi's dormant months, usually March to October, it is possible to climb all the way to the top, but at other times you may have to settle for a distant view from the observation platform. All treks begin at 3am, when the lava, spilling over the top and tracing a searing path down the mountainside, can be seen most clearly. Bring warm clothes, a torch and sturdy boots (against poisonous snakes). Treks cost Rp7500 including breakfast and are organized by *Vogel's Hostel* in Kaliurang, Jl Astya Mulya 76 (☎0274/395208; ①), which also happens to be one of the best budget **hostels** in Java. The owner is the head of the rescue team in Kaliurang.

Borobudur and around

Forty kilometres west of Yogya, surrounded on three sides by volcanoes and on the fourth by jagged limestone cliffs, is the largest monument in the southern hemisphere. This is the temple of **Borobudur**, the number one tourist attraction in Java and the greatest single piece of classical architecture in the entire archipelago. The temple is actually a colossal multi-tiered Buddhist stupa lying at the western end of a four-kilometre-long chain of temples (one of which, the nearby **Candi Mendut**, is also worth visiting), built in the ninth century by the Saliendra dynasty. At 34.5m tall, however, and covering an area of some 200 square metres, Borobudur is on a different scale altogether, dwarfing all the other *candi* in the chain.

The world's largest Buddhist stupa was actually built on Hindu **foundations**, which began life in 775 AD as a large step pyramid. Just fifteen years later, however, the construction was abandoned as the Buddhist Saliendras drove the Sanjayas eastwards. The Saliendras then appropriated the pyramid as the foundation for their own temple, beginning in around 790 AD and completing the work approximately seventy years later. Over 1.6 million blocks of a local volcanic rock (called andesite) were used in Borobudur's construction, joined together without mortar. Sculpted reliefs adorned the lower galleries, covered with stucco and painted. Unfortunately, the pyramid foundation proved to be inherently unstable, cracks appeared, and the hill became totally waterlogged. After about a century, the Saliendras abandoned the site and for almost a thousand years Borobudur lay neglected. The English "rediscovered" it in 1815, but nothing much was done until 1973, when UNESCO began to take the temple apart, block by block, in order to replace the waterlogged hill with a concrete substitute. The project took eleven years and cost US$21million.

Practicalities

Most people choose to see the **site** (daily 6am–5.30pm; US$5 or equivalent in rupiah) on a day-trip from Yogya. Plenty of agencies offer **all-inclusive tours**, or you can catch one of the regular buses from Yogya's Umbulharjo station, which calls in at Jomber terminal (handy for Jalan Sosro; bus #5) before heading off to Borobudur village bus station (90min; Rp2000), though you may have to change one more time in Muntilan. The entrance to the temple lies 500m southwest of the bus stop.

The most popular budget **accommodation** in the village is the *Lotus Guesthouse* at Jl Medang Kamulan 2 (✆0293/88281; ①), opposite the entrance to Borobudur park, but rooms are awful and beds filthy. Though it looks scruffier, *Losmen Borobudur*, on the road that runs alongside the eastern edge of the temple grounds, at Jl Pramudya 1 (✆0293/88258; ①), is cleaner and better value. Round the back of the temple, the *Manohara* (✆0293/788680; ⑦) is by a long way the plushest place in town, and the room charge includes breakfast and the entrance fee into Borobudur.

The ruins

Borobudur is pregnant with symbolism, and precisely oriented so that its four sides face the four points of the compass; the **entrance** lies to the north. Unlike most temples, it was not built as a dwelling for the gods, but rather as a representation of the Buddhist cosmic mountain, Meru. Accordingly, at the base is the real, earthly world, a world of desires and passions, and at the summit is nirvana. Thus, as you make your way around the temple passages and slowly spiral to the summit, you are symbolically following the path to enlightenment.

Every journey to enlightenment begins in the squalor of the real world, and at Borobudur the first five levels – the square terraces – are covered with three thousand **reliefs** representing man's earthly existence. As you might expect, the lowest, subterranean level has carvings depicting the basest desires, best seen at the southeast corner. The reliefs on the **first four levels above ground** cover the beginning of man's path to enlightenment. Each of the ten series tells a story, beginning by the eastern stairway and continuing in a clockwise direction. Follow all ten stories, and you will have circled the temple ten times – a distance of almost 5km. Buddha's own path to enlightenment is told in the upper panels on the inner wall of the first gallery. As you enter the **fifth level**, the walls fall away to reveal a breathtaking view of the surrounding fields and volcanoes. You are now in the Sphere of Formlessness, the realm of enlightenment: below is the chaos of the world, above is nirvana, represented by a huge empty stupa almost 10m in diameter. Surrounding this stupa are 72 smaller ones, each occupied by a statue of Buddha.

Candi Mendut

Originally Borobudur was part of a chain of four temples joined by a sacred path. Two of the other three temples have been restored and at least one, **Candi Mendut** (daily 6.15am–5.15pm; Rp100), 3km east of Borobudur, is worth visiting. Buses between Yogya and Borobudur drive right past Mendut (Rp800 from Yogya for the 80min journey, Rp300 for the 10min from Borobudur). Built in 800 AD, Mendut was restored at the end of the nineteenth century. The exterior is unremarkable, but the three giant **statues** sitting inside – of Buddha and the Bodhisattvas Avalokitesvara and Vajrapani – are exquisitely carved and startling.

The Prambanan Plain

Nourished by the volcanic detritus of Mount Merapi and washed by innumerable small rivers, the verdant **Prambanan Plain** lies 18km east of Yogya, a patchwork blanket of sun-spangled paddy-fields and vast plantations sweeping down from the southern slopes of the volcano. As well as being one of the most fertile regions in Java, the plain is home to the largest concentration of ancient ruins on the island. Over thirty **temples** and **palaces**, dating mainly from the eighth and ninth centuries, lie scattered over a thirty-square-kilometre area, a number of which have been fully restored. The temples were built at a time when two rival kingdoms, the Buddhist Saliendra and the Hindu Sanjaya dynasties, both occupied Central Java. In 832 AD, the Hindu Sanjayas gained the upper hand and soon the great Hindu Prambanan temple complex was built, perhaps in commemoration of their return to power. It seems that some sort of truce followed, with temples of both faiths being constructed on the plain in equal numbers.

Practicalities

Most people visit the Prambanan temples on a day-trip from Yogya. Although many tour companies in Yogya offer all-inclusive packages to Prambanan, it is easy enough to get there by local **bus** from Yogya or Solo. Public buses drop passengers off in **Prambanan village**, a tiny huddle on the southern side of Jalan Adisucipto, a five-minute walk from the eastern entrance to the temple complex. The only disadvantage to coming by bus is that you can't then get to the other ruins on the plain, which is why many visitors choose to **cycle** here from Yogya. Fume-choked Jalan Adisucipto is the most straightforward route, but there's a quieter alternative that begins by heading north along Yogya's Jalan Simanjutak and Jalan Kaliurang until you reach the Mataram Canal, just past the main Gajah Mada University compound. Follow the canal path east for 12km (1hr), and you'll come out eventually near Candi Sari on Jalan Adisucipto. Prambanan village is 4km east of Candi Sari, along Jalan Adisucipto. You can **stay** in the village at the rudimentary *Losmen NY Muharti*, Jl Tampurnas Ngangkruk 2–3 (☎0274/496103; ②).

Ramayana ballet peformances

The highlight of the dancing year in Central Java are the phenomenal *Ramayana* ballets held during the summer months at the **Prambanan Open-Air Theatre**, to the west of the complex. The *Ramayana* story is performed just twice monthly from May to October, spread over the two weekends closest to the full moon. The story is split into four episodes, each evening from Friday to Monday (7–9pm). The second night is the best, with most of the characters making an appearance, and the action is intense. Tickets cost Rp5000–30,000; plenty of agents in Yogya organize transport. Yogya's tourist office also organizes taxis to and from the theatre.

Throughout the year, Prambanan's **Trimurti Theatre**, an indoor venue to the north of the open-air arena, performs the *Ramayana* ballet (Tues–Thurs 7.30–9.30pm; Rp10,000–15,000). Tickets are available on the door or from agencies.

The Prambanan complex

As you drive east along Jalan Adisucipto from Yogya, your eye will be caught by three giant, rocket-shaped temples, each smothered in intricate narrative carvings, that suddenly loom up by the side of the highway. This is the **Prambanan complex** (daily 6am–5pm; US$5 or its equivalent in rupiah), the largest Hindu complex in Java and a worthy rival to the Buddhist masterpiece at Borobudur.

The Sanjayas began work on the three giants around 832 AD, finishing them 24 years later. Their choice of location, just a few hundred metres south of the once mighty Buddhist **Candi Sewu**, is of great significance. Not only was it a reminder to the Saliendras that the Hindus were now in charge but, by leaving Sewu unharmed, it also gave a clear message to the Buddhists that the Sanjayas intended to be tolerant of their faith. The three Prambanan temples were in service for just fifty years before they were abandoned. Restoration work finally began in the 1930s.

The temple complex itself consists of six temples in a raised **inner courtyard**, surrounded by **224 minor temples**, which now lie in ruins. The three biggest temples in the courtyard are dedicated to the three main Hindu deities: Shiva, whose 47-metre temple is the tallest of the three, Brahma (to the south of the Shiva temple) and Vishnu (north). Facing these are three smaller temples housing the animal statues – or "chariots" – that would always accompany the gods: Hamsa the swan, Nandi the bull and Garuda the sunbird.

The **Shiva Temple** is decorated with exceptional carvings, including a series along the inner wall of the first terrace walkway, beginning at the eastern steps and continuing clockwise around the temple, that recounts the first half of the Ramayana epic. At the top of the steps is the inner sanctuary of the temple, whose eastern chamber contains a statue of Shiva himself, while in the west chamber is Shiva's elephant-headed son, Ganesh. A beautiful sculpture of Nandi the Bull stands inside the temple of Shiva's chariot. Though smaller than the Shiva Temple, the other two temples are just as painstakingly decorated. The first terrace of the **Brahma Temple** takes up the Ramayana epic where the Shiva Temple left off, whilst the carvings on the terrace of Vishnu's temple recounts stories of **Krishna**, the eighth of Vishnu's nine earthly incarnations.

Other temples on the Prambanan Plain

The other ancient sites on the Prambanan Plain (dawn–dusk; free) are not as spectacular as the Shiva Temple, but you are almost certain to be the only person on site. Only the three temples immediately to the **north of Prambanan** are within easy walking distance of the Shiva Temple, reached via the children's park next to the museum. All three date from the late eighth century, just predating Borobudur. **Candi Lumbung** consists of sixteen small, crumbling temples surrounding a larger, but equally dilapidated, central temple. Buddhist **Sewu** once consisted of 240 small shrines surrounding a large, central temple, but has been severely looted. A ten-minute bike ride or thirty-minute walk to the east of Candi Sewu, **Candi Plaosan** is also surrounded by building debris, but the two-storey building still houses two stone Bodhisattvas.

The other worthwhile ruins (US$5) lie to the **south of Prambanan** and are best tackled by bicycle. From the village, cycle down the path which begins by the small graveyard to a small village school on the left-hand side (10min). Turn left and after five minutes you reach **Candi Sojiwan**, a plain, square temple, sparingly decorated with *Jataka* scenes. Return to the main path and head south towards the foot of the Shiva Plateau. The path to the summit of the plateau and **Kraton Ratu Boko** is unsuitable for bicycles, so ask to leave them at the house at the bottom. The ruins are in two parts: a series of bathing pools and, 400m to the west, the ceremonial gate that adorns many tourist posters. The views from the kraton are wonderful, as they are from **Candi Barong**, to the south – to get there, head west towards the main road, Jalan Raya Piyungan, where you turn left (south) and cycle for 1.5km until a signpost on your left points to Barong, 1km to the east. This *candi* is actually two hillside Buddhist temples mounted on a raised platform on the southern slopes of the plateau. A little way back along this path and to the south is **Banyunibo**, a pretty Buddhist shrine dedicated to Tara. From there, head back onto the main road and turn right; Prambanan village lies 2km away.

Surakarta (Solo)

Sixty-five kilometres northeast of Yogya stands quiet, leafy low-rise **SURAKARTA**, or, as it's more commonly known, **SOLO**. This is the older of the two royal cities in Central Java, and its ruling family can lay claim to being the rightful heirs to the Mataram dynasty. Like Yogya, Solo has two **royal palaces** and a number of museums, yet its tourist industry is nowhere near as developed. The city's main source of income is from textiles, and Solo has the biggest **batik market** on Java. Solo also makes an ideal base from which to visit the home of Java Man at Sangiran, as well as the intriguing temples Candi Ceto and Candi Sukuh.

Up until 1744, Solo was little more than a quiet backwater village, 10km east of Kartasura, the contemporary capital of the Mataram kingdom. But in that year the Mataram *susuhunan* (king), **Pakubuwono II**, backed the Chinese against the Dutch, and the court at Kartasura was sacked as a result. Pakubuwono II searched for a more auspicious spot to rebuild his capital, and in 1745 the entire court was dismantled and transported in a great procession to Surakarta, on the banks of the Kali Solo. However, the decline continued, and in 1757 a rival **royal house of Mangkunegoro** was established right in the centre of Solo. Thereafter, Solo's royal houses wisely avoided fighting and instead threw their energies into the arts, developing a highly sophisticated and graceful court culture. The gamelan pavilions became the new theatres of war, with each city competing to produce the more refined court culture – a situation that continues to this day.

Arrival, orientation and information

Adisumaryno Airport is 10km west of Solo and 2km north of Kartasura. A half-hourly **minibus** drives along the main road beside the runway to Kartasura (Rp300), from where you can catch a double-decker to Solo (Rp400). A **taxi** costs Rp10,000. All buses to Solo use the **Tirtonadi bus station** in the north of the city. Just across the crossroads by the north-eastern corner of Tirtonadi is the **minibus terminal**, Gilingan. To get into the town centre from here, take orange angkuta (minibus) #6 from the front of the *Hotel Surya*, which goes via Ngapeman, the junction of Jalan Gajah Mada and Jalan Riyadi. Heading to the bus station from the town centre, catch a BERSERI bus (Rp400) from the bus stop on Jalan Riyadi, 100m east of Jalan Dahlan. A becak from the bus station to Jalan Dahlan costs Rp3000. Most home-stays and travellers' restaurants sell door-to-door bus tickets to popular tourist destinations, as does Niki Tours (☎0271/53278) on Jl Yos Sudarso. **Balapan train station** is 300m south of Tirtonadi. Niki tours also has details of **Pelni** ferries.

Solo's **double-decker buses** all charge a flat Rp200 and travel along the same route: from Kartasura in the west, down Jalan Riyadi, past the post office and on to Palur, where you can catch buses to Tawangmangu. Because of the one-way system on Slamet Riyadi, they head west along Jalan Veteran instead. Many homestays rent **bicycles** (Rp5000).

Nearly all of the hotels, sights and facilities are either on, or within walking distance of, the main road through the city, **Jalan Brig Jen Slamet Riyadi** (hereafter called simply Jalan Riyadi). The centre of the travellers' scene is **Jalan Dahlan**, a smallish road heading north

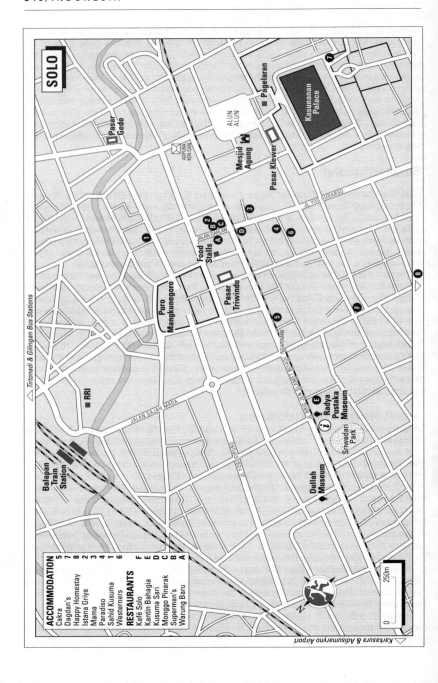

SOLO

Tirtonadi & Gilingan Bus Stations

Pasar Gede

ADIPURA KEN GAAI

ALUN ALUN

Pagelaran

Kasunanan Palace

Mesjid Agung

Pasar Klewer

JL YOS SUDARSO

Food Stalls

JALAN DAHLAN

Puro Mangkunegoro

Pasar Triwindu

JL BRIG JEN SLAMET RIYADI NGAPEMAN

RRI

JALAN GAJAH MADA

Balapan Train Station

JL YOSODIPURO

Dullah Museum

Radya Pustaka Museum

Sriwedari Park

Karksura & Adisumaryno Airport

0   250m

ACCOMMODATION
Cakra   5
Dagdan's   7
Happy Homestay   8
Istana Griya   2
Mama   3
Paradiso   4
Sahid Kusuma   1
Westerners   6

RESTAURANTS
Kafé Solo   F
Kantin Bahagia   E
Kusuma Sari   D
Monggo Pinarak   C
Superman's   B
Warung Baru   A

off Jalan Riyadi. The **tourist office** is behind the Radya Pustaka Museum at Jl Riyadi 275 (Mon–Sat 8am–4pm; ☎0271/711435).

Accommodation

Most of the **budget hotels** are hidden in the kampung to the south of Jalan Riyadi, and can be difficult to find. The simplest solution is to hire a becak to take you there, although, as usual, the driver's commission will result in a higher room rate.

Cakra, Jl Riyadi 201 (☎0271/45847). With its swimming pool, billiard room and air-con rooms, this is one of the best-value hotels in this category. ⑥.

Dagdan's, Baluwerti Rt II/7 42 (☎0271/54538). The only accommodation within the kraton walls is attractive and has smart rooms sharing a bathroom. Highly recommended. ②.

Happy Homestay, Jl Honggowongso, Gang Karagan 12 (☎0271/712449). Also known as *Hotel Bahagia*, this is a friendly, scruffy and popular homestay with both basic and spacious rooms. ①.

Istana Griya, Jl Dahlan 22 (☎0271/632667). Quiet and highly recommended homestay down a *gang* behind *Superman's*; smart, good-value rooms. ①.

Mama, Kauman Gang III/49, Jl Yos Sudarso (☎0271/52248). One of the best places to come for a batik course, a bicycle tour, or simply good, clean economical rooms with large breakfasts. Upstairs rooms are cheaper and noisier. ①.

Paradiso, Jl Riyadi 335 (☎0271/54111). Hidden behind huge white walls and tastefully festooned with statues and baubles, the reception rooms of the Paradiso look sumptuous. The 32 bedrooms can't quite maintain this standard, however, and the cheaper ones are a little grotty. ①.

Sahid Kusuma, Jl Sugiopranoto 20 (☎0271/46356). Once a royal court, this place is stylishly set in landscaped gardens with a pool. Air-con, TV and fridge come as standard. ⑧.

Westerners, Jl Kemlayan Kidul 11 (☎0271/633106). Cramped, plant-filled hangout that accepts foreign travellers only. Inexpensive rooms and Rp6000 dorms. ①.

The City

Brought from Kartasura by Pakubuwono II in one huge day-long procession in 1745, the **Kasunanan Palace** (daily except Fri 9am–2pm; Rp2500) is Solo's largest and most important royal house. It stands within the kraton, just south of the alun-alun; guides are available free of charge and are definitely worth taking. Non-royals must enter the main body of the palace by the eastern entrance. This opens out into a large courtyard whose surrounding buildings house the palace's **kris collection**, as well as a number of chariots, silver ornaments and other royal knick-knacks. An archway to the west leads into the susuhunan's living quarters; the current sultan, the septuagenarian Pakubuwono XII, is still in residence, along with a few of his 35 children and two of his six wives. Many of the buildings in this courtyard are modern copies, the originals having burnt down in 1985.

The second royal house in Solo, the **Puro Mangkunegoro** (guided tours only Mon–Thurs 8.30am–2pm, Sun 8.30am–1pm; Rp5000) stands 1km west of the kraton and, like Yogya's court of Paku Alam, faces south towards the Kasunanan Palace as a mark of respect. With its fine collection of antiques and curios, in many ways the Puro Mangkunegoro is more interesting than the Kasunanan palace. It was built in 1757 to placate the rebellious Prince Mas Said (Mangkunegoro I), a nephew of Pakubuwono II, whose relations with Mangkubumi deteriorated after the latter founded Yogya and was recognized as its sultan. Exhausted by fighting wars on three fronts, Mas Said eventually accepted a peace deal which gave him a royal title, a court in Solo and rulership over four thousand of Solo's households. The palace hides behind a high white wall, entered through the gateway to the south. The vast **pendopo** (the largest in Indonesia) which fronts the palace, shields four gamelan orchestras underneath its rafters, three of which can only be played on very special occasions. Be sure to look up at the vibrantly painted roof of the pendopo, with Javanese zodiac figures forming the main centrepiece. A portrait of the current resident, Mangkunegoro IX, hangs by the entrance to the **Dalam Agung**, or living quarters, whose reception room has been turned into an extremely good museum, displaying ancient coins, ballet masks and chastity preservers.

Just south of Puro Mangkunegoro, the three-storey Pasar Klewer (daily 9am–4pm), by the southwest corner of the alun-alun, claims to being Java's largest **batik market**, and designs from all over Java can be found here. Another kilometre west along Jalan Riyadi brings you to the **Radya Pustaka Museum** (Mon–Thurs & Sun 8am–1pm, Fri & Sat 8–11am; Rp500). Built by the Dutch in 1890, this is one of the oldest and largest museums in Java, housing a large Dutch and Javanese library as well as collections of wayang kulit puppets, kris, and scale models of the mosque at Demak and the cemetery at Imogiri. Another 500m further west, at Jl Dr Cipto 15, the paintings and sculptures by the prolific artist Pak Dullah are on show in the **Dullah Museum** (currently closed for restoration).

Eating and drinking

Solo's warung are renowned for local **specialities** such as *nasi liwet* – chicken or vegetables and rice drenched in coconut milk and served on a banana leaf – and *nasi gudeg*, a variation on Yogya's recipe. For dessert, try *kue putu* (coconut cakes) or *srabi*, a combination of pancake and sweet rice served with a variety of fruit toppings. Most of these delicacies can be purchased along Jalan Teuku Umar, one block west of Jalan Dahlan, and around the Sriwedari Park at night.

Kafe Solo, Jl Dr Rajiman 87. Stylish mid-priced restaurant with an excellent selection of beef and chicken steaks, salads and other Western dishes.

Kantin Bahagia, Pujosari Market, Jl Musium. Tiny bar and restaurant just to the south of Jalan Riyadi in the Pujosari Market, serving good-value Indonesian staples and cheap beer. Stays open till 1am.

Kusuma Sari, Jl Yos Sudarso 75. Large and spotless but lacking atmosphere, this restaurant sells good-value local dishes and Indonesian versions of Western food.

Monggo Pinarak, Jl Dahlan 22. This inexpensive restaurant/book and batik shop is owned by a well-travelled Bangladeshi and serves dishes from the subcontinent. Highly recommended.

Superman's, Jl Dahlan. Mid-price travellers' place specializing in steaks. Their nasi goreng special, with the rice wrapped inside an omelette, is a tasty twist on an Indonesian staple. Also serves *arak*.

Warung Baru, Jl Dahlan. Popular travellers' restaurant serving good, inexpensive food, including delicious homemade bread. Also organizes tours and batik courses.

Performing arts

For the last two centuries, the royal houses of Solo have developed highly individual styles for the traditional Javanese arts of gamelan and wayang. The Puro Mangkunegoro's performances of **wayang orang** (Wed 10am–noon) are more rumbustious and aggressive than the graceful, fluid style of the Kasunanan Palace (Sun 9–11am). Another option is the three-hour performance at Sriwedari Park (Mon–Sat 8pm). **Gamelan** is also something of a Solonese speciality. The *Sahid Kusuma Hotel* gamelan orchestra plays every afternoon and evening in the reception hall, and the Puro Mangkunegoro stages a ninety-minute performance on Saturday evening (9pm).

The **radio station** Radio Republik Indonesia (RRI) regularly records performances of Solo's traditional arts, including wayang orang (every first and third Tuesday of the month), gamelan (every second and fourth Thursday), and wayang kulit (third Saturday); performances generally start around 9pm and tickets should be bought in advance from the RRI Building just to the south of the Balapan train station.

Listings

Airlines Garuda, *Cakra Hotel*, Jl Riyadi 201 (☎0271/630082).

Batik courses Solo is a better place to study batik than Yogya. The course at *Warung Baru* on Jl Dahlan is very popular (Rp10,000–20,000).

Hospital Rumah Sakit Panti Kosala (aka Rumah Sakit Dr Oen), Jl Brig Jen Katamso 55.

Immigration office Jl Adisucipto, on the way to the airport (☎0271/48479).

Internet access Rp70 per minute at the *Warposnet* by the post office. Also at *Aloha*, at the *Hotel Sahid Kusuma* (daily 8am–11pm; Rp3600 per hour).

Post office Jl Jend Sudirman (daily 6am–10pm). The poste restante counter closes in the evening.

Telephone services Just behind the Telkom offices on Jl Sumoharjo, at Jl Mayor Kusmanto 3, there's a 24hr wartel office, and a number of other wartels on Jl Riyadi.

Sangiran

The unassuming little village of **SANGIRAN**, 18km north of Solo, ranks as one of the most important archeological sites in Central Java. One million years ago, Sangiran was the home of **Pithecantropus Erectus**, or **Java man** as he's more commonly known. A few fragments of his jawbone were discovered in 1936 and, until the Rift Valley finds in Kenya, were the oldest hominid remains ever found, and the first to support Darwin's theory of evolution. Many scientists of the day even suggested that Java man might have been the so-called "missing link", the evolutionary connection between the anthropoid apes and modern man. Replicas of Java man's cranium (the real skulls are in Bandung) are housed in Sangiran's single-room **museum** (daily 8am–5pm; Rp1000), where a life-size diorama tries to bring to life Java man's world, but none of the captions is in English. To get to Sangiran, take a Damri or BERSERI **bus** from Solo's Jalan Riyadi to Kalijambe (Rp500), then either wait for a yellow angkuta (Rp200) or hire an ojek (Rp1500) to take you to the village.

Gunung Lawu

Pine-crowned **Gunung Lawu** (3265m), a two-hour drive due east of Solo, is one of the largest – and least active – volcanoes on Java, and its forested slopes are dotted with temples, of which two, **Sukuh** and Ceto, have been restored to their former glory. The temples are usually visited on a day-trip from Solo, but the mountain provides perfect conditions for hikers, not least because of the gentle gradients and cool air. The main transport hub is **Karangpandan**, 45 minutes (Rp2000) by bus from Solo. From here there are frequent buses to the temples, and expensive ojek too.

The best place to stay up here is **TAWANGMANGU**, a hill resort on the southwestern slopes, 12km on from Karangpandan. The village spreads over one square kilometre from the **bus station** in the south up to the forty-metre waterfall, Grojogan Sewu (8am–4.30pm; Rp1500), at its northern end; catch an angkuta (Rp200) between the two. Below the bus station, at the bottom of the hill, the *Balaistirahat Dana* at Jl Lawa 47 (①) is the cheapest **losmen** in the village. Fifty metres up from the bus station stands the slightly better *Pak Amat*, Jl Raya Tawangmangu 117 (☎0271/97022; ①), which also has a recommended restaurant. All room rates double at the weekends.

Candi Sukuh and Candi Ceto

Situated 910m up the forested western slopes of Gunung Lawu, **Candi Sukuh** (daily 6.15am–4.30pm; Rp300) is one of the most interesting of Java's classical temples. Catch a Kubening-bound bus from Karangpandan and hop off at **Nglorok** village (Rp300), where you buy your ticket for the temple. From here you can hire an ojek (Rp2500) for the steep two-kilometre journey. West-facing, pyramid-shaped Sukuh was built in around 1430, and seems to have been linked to a **fertility cult**. Although the temple is unadorned, there's an orgy of semi-explicit statuary lying nearby, with a few displaying impressive genitalia. There are also plenty of grotesque bas reliefs, many of them depicting scenes from the life of Bima, an incarnation of Shiva in the *Mahabharata*, who became the centre of a religious cult in the fifteenth century. The temple itself is fronted by the remains of a small ceremonial gateway, and three large turtles, their backs flattened to form three circular dais, stand on the third terrace, guarding the entrance to the temple proper.

Candi Ceto, the youngest classical temple on Java, was built 1400m up on the northern flanks of Gunung Lawu in around 1470. Catch a bus from Karangpandan to Kalbening (Rp500), from where it's a steep two-hour climb (5km) up the mountainside. Isolated and frequently shrouded in mist, Candi Ceto has a mystical, almost eerie atmosphere. It was built on ten narrow terraces stretching up the mountainside, beyond a large monumental gateway, similar in style to those found on Bali. The first few terraces beyond the gate are bereft of decoration, though a giant bat has been carved on the paving on the fourth level. The bat carries on its back a large turtle, which in turn carries crabs, lizards and frogs on its shell. On the top three terraces, small kiosks shelter a variety of icons, including one of Bima, and yet another large lingam. The main temple, with the same pyramidal shape as Sukuh, stands on the very top terrace.

Walking on Lawu
It is possible to walk all the way from Candi Ceto to Candi Sukuh, and from there to the waterfall at Tawangmangu in around five hours. There is not enough time to do this as a day-trip from Solo, however, as it can take up to four hours just to get to Ceto, and the last bus back to Solo leaves Tawangmangu at 5pm. Day-trippers should miss out Candi Ceto and join the trail at Candi Sukuh for the final leg to the waterfall. The walk **between Ceto and Sukuh** is a pleasant three-hour ramble, passing first through large fields, then through the pine forest shrouding the summit of Gunung Lawu. The path begins 200m below Ceto, where a small track branches left from the road towards the fields. This path is very difficult to follow, and you will probably need to ask the workers in the field for directions. After about an hour you arrive at the forest, where again you will probably need help in finding the correct path. Once you have, following the trail is straightforward. The two-hour stroll **from Sukuh to the waterfall** at Tawangmangu, over gently undulating fields and foothills, is the most rewarding walk on Lawu and fairly easy to follow.

Surabaya and around

Polluted, noisy and sprawling, **SURABAYA** is the second largest city in Indonesia, and the major port of East Java. With time and effort the city is comprehensible and even somewhat enjoyable, but for most tourists Surabaya is nothing more than a transport hub. If you do want to linger, the **Chinese** and **Arab quarters** to the north of the city centre and the **zoo** and **museum** to the south are the most interesting sights.

Arrival
Surabaya is a visa-free entry point for international arrivals by air; all **flights** arrive at Juanda International Airport (☎031/8667642), 18km south of the city, where there's a tourist office. No public bus service connects with the town centre, but there's a rank for fixed-price **taxis** (Rp12,500). If you arrive by sea, probably by Pelni ferry, you'll dock at **Tanjung Perak port** in the far north of the city, served by C, P and PAC buses.

Surabaya has three main **train stations. Gubeng station** is in the east of town with exits on Jalan Gubeng Mesjid and Jalan Sumatera. It has a hotel reservation desk (daily 8am–8pm), but only for expensive places. **Kota station** is towards the north of the city centre and exits onto the junction of Jalan Semut Kali and Jalan Stasiun, while **Pasarturi station** is in the west of the city centre on Jalan Semarang.

The main **bus terminal** is Bungusarih (also known as Purabaya), 6km south of the city. All long-distance and inter-island buses start and finish here, plus many of the city buses and bemos. **Local buses** into the city leave from the far end of the Bungusarih terminal: follow the signs for "Kota". Many of the C, P and both PAC buses serve Bungusarih. There's also a huge **taxi rank** here: expect to pay about Rp10,000 to anywhere in town.

City transport and information
Three types of public buses operate in the city, with routes indicated by letters. They stop only at designated places, which are often signified by blue bus-stop signs. The most useful **ordinary bus service** (Rp300) is the "C" route, which runs from Bungusarih past

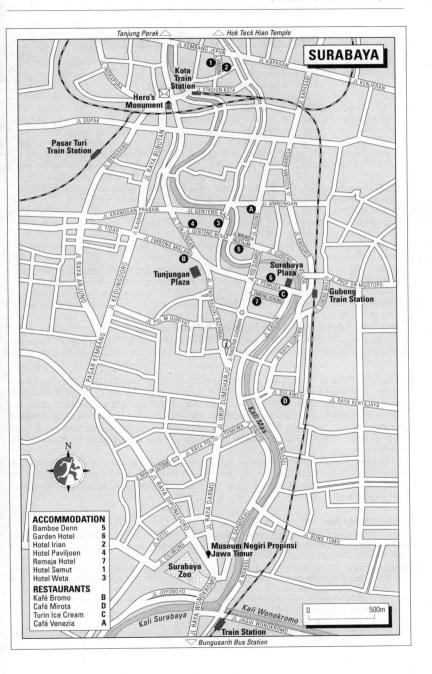

Tanjung Perak △   △ Hok Teck Hian Temple

SURABAYA

JL KEMBANG JEPUN
❶ ❷
JL KAPASAN
JL INDRAPURA
JL KENJERAN

Kota Train Station
JL STASIUN KOTA

Hero's Monument 🏛

JL DUPAK

Pasar Turi Train Station

JL RAYA BUBUTAN
JL SEMARANG
JL KUSUMA BANGSA
JL KAPASARI

JL KRANGGAN PRABAN
JL GENTENG KALI
JL AMBENGAN
JL BLAURAN
JL GENTENG BESAR
JL TIDAR
❹ ❸ Ⓐ
JL TUNJUNGAN
JL EMBONG MALANG
JL WALIKOTA MUSTAJAR
❺ Ⓑ
JL KEDUNGDORO

Tunjungan Plaza
JL GUBENG
Surabaya Plaza
❻ Ⓒ
JL PROF DR MUSTOPO

JL PEMUDA
Gubeng Train Station
JL RAYA ARJUNO
JL EMBONG KENONGO
❼
JL POL M DURIYAT

JL PASAR KEMBANG
ⓘ
JL URIP SUMOHARJO
JL PANGLIMA SUDIRMAN
JL RAYA GUBENG

JL SULAWESI
Ⓓ
JL RAYA KERTAJAYA

Kali Mas

JL RAYA POLISI ISTIMEWA
JL RAYA DR SUTOMO
JL RAYA DIPONEGORO
JL NGAGEL

Ⓝ
N

JL RAYA DARMO
JL BUNG TOMO

ACCOMMODATION

Bamboe Denn	5
Garden Hotel	6
Hotel Irian	2
Hotel Paviljoen	4
Remaja Hotel	7
Hotel Semut	1
Hotel Weta	3

RESTAURANTS

Kafé Bromo	B
Café Mirota	D
Turin Ice Cream	C
Café Venezia	A

JL KUTEI
JL CILIWUNG

Museum Negiri Propinsi Jawa Timur

Surabaya Zoo

JL JOYOBOYO
JL RAYA WONOKROMO
JL NGAGEL

Kali Wonokromo

0   500m

Kali Surabaya
JL RAYA WONOKROMO
Kali Wonokromo
JL JAGIH WONOKROMO

Train Station

▽ Bungusarih Bus Station

MOVING ON FROM SURABAYA

Surabaya is the main air, sea, rail and road hub for East Java and has excellent connections across Indonesia and internationally. Some international **flight** destinations are reached direct, while others have connections via Jakarta or Denpasar; see "Listings", p.256, for airlines offices in Surabaya, and p.443 for flight details. There are numerous domestic flights. Taxis from Gubeng station taxi rank to the airport are fixed at Rp25,000.

Tanjung Perak port is the major port in East Java, and no fewer than fifteen of the fleet of twenty-three **Pelni ferries** call here on their routes through the archipelago: *KM Binaiya, KM Bukit Raya, KM Bukit Siguntang, KM Dibonsolo, KM Kambuna, KM Kelimutu, KM Kerinci, KM Lambelu, KM Leuser, KM Pangrango, KM Rinjani, KM Tidar, KM Tilongkabila, KM Wilis* and *KM Umsini*. For details see "Getting around" p.191 and "Travel Details" p.443. The main Pelni office is at Jl Pahlawan 112 (Mon–Thurs 9am–noon & 1–3pm, Fri–Sat 9am–noon; ☎031/3523462), and there's another one at Tanjung Perak, at Gedung Gapura Surya, Jl Zamrut Utara 5 (☎031/3293197).

Trains from Gubeng station go to Banyuwangi, Malang, Yogyakarta, Solo and Jakarta via the southern route across Java – some but not all of these trains also pass through Kota station, which is towards the north of the city centre. The entrance to Kota is at the junction of Jalan Semut Kali and Jalan Stasiun. Pasarturi station serves destinations along the northern route across the island to Jakarta via Semarang.

For **bus** journeys **within East Java**, just buy your ticket on the bus, but be wary of overcharging. You will pay Rp100 to get into the departure area – the bays are clearly labelled. **Long-distance journeys** are completed by night buses (departing 2–6pm) from Bay 8 – the ticket offices for all the night-bus companies are in the bus station; book ahead. If you can't bear the slog out to the bus station, central **minibus** companies run more expensive daily trips to the main Javan destinations, leaving from their offices. Try Tirta Jaya, Jalan Jend Basuki Rachmat 64 (☎031/5468687) for Yogya and Solo.

Tunjungan Plaza, in through the centre of the city and up to Tanjung Perak, passing conveniently close to the post office on the way; the more luxurious P1 and P2 buses (Rp500–700) cover the same route; as do deluxe **air-con buses** PAC1 and PAC2 (Rp1000). There are also plenty of **metered taxis**: a trip within the city centre will cost Rp2000–3000. **Crossing the road** in Surabaya is so hair-raising that there are special long poles with red dots on them at some traffic lights – you hold them high towards the traffic to let drivers know you're there.

The most useful **tourist office** is at Jl Jend Basuki Rachmat 119–121 opposite the *Hyatt* (Mon–Thurs & Sat 7am–2pm, Fri 7–11am; ☎031/5344710). One of the best places to get **information** is the losmen *Bamboe Denn* (see below), which gives guests up-to-date transport timetables.

Accommodation

Much of the less expensive **accommodation** is slightly out of the centre, in the area north of Kota station, which isn't good either for buses (you'll need to figure out the bemos around here) or the central sights.

Bamboe Denn, Jl Ketabangkali 6a (☎031/5340333). This is the main backpacker accommodation in the city. It isn't easy to find, about 30min walk from Gubeng station (Rp2500 by becak), but local people will help you. Accommodation is very basic in tiny singles, doubles and dorms, all with shared bathrooms, but there's a pleasant sitting room and good information available. Rp10,000 per dorm-bed. ①.

Garden Hotel, Jl Pemuda 21 (☎031/5321001). Showing its age, but comfortable and convenient. Guests can use the *Garden Palace Hotel* pool. ⑨.

Hotel Irian, Jl Samudra 16 (☎031/3554937). A pleasant old-style bungalow, cool and with a choice of rooms, some en suite. ①.

Hotel Paviljoen, Jl Genteng Besar 94–98 (☎031/5343449). Spotlessly clean rooms in an old colonial bungalow, all with cold-water mandi and some with verandahs and air-con. Southbound buses P1 and P2 stop at the end of the street on Jl Tunjungan. ②.

Remaja Hotel, Jl Embong Kenongo 12 (☎031/5341359). Central but quiet, this place is adequate and utilitarian without much character; all rooms have air-con and hot showers. ③.

Hotel Semut, Jl Samudra 9–15 (☎031/352478). In the area north of Kota station. All rooms have air-con and attached bathroom, and there's a garden. ②.

Hotel Weta, Jl Genteng Kali 3–11 (☎031/5319494). Good-value place with clean, attractive rooms with air-con and hot-water. Discounts possible. ④.

The City

Surabaya's **Chinese quarter** hums with activity, an abundance of traditional two-storey shophouses lining narrow streets, and minuscule red-and-gold altars glinting in shops and houses. The area centres on Jalan Slompretan, Jalan Bongkaran and the part of Jalan Samudra southwest of the 300-year-old **Hok Teck Hian temple** on Jalan Dukuh. The temple itself is a vibrant place with several tiny shrines spread over two floors, and Buddhist, Confucian and Hindu effigies. Upstairs, at the altar to Kwan Im Poosat, the "Valentine Angel", pregnant women come to pray for the sex of their child.

The oldest and most famous mosque in Surabaya is **Mesjid Ampel**, located in the Arab area, the **kampung Arab** or **Qubah**, to the north of the Chinese quarter. The whole kampung, bounded by Jalan Nyanplungan, Jalan KH Mas Mansur, Jalan Sultan Iskandar Muda and Jalan Pabean Pasar, was originally settled by Arab traders and sailors who arrived in Kali Mas harbour. It's a maze of tidy, well-kept alleyways crammed with flowers, beggars and shops selling Muslim hats, perfumes, dates and souvenirs. Mesjid Ampel, built in 1421, is the site of the grave of Sunan Ampel, one of the nine *wali* credited with bringing Islam to Java in the sixteenth century, and as such, a site of pilgrimage and reverence. The area isn't particularly tourist-friendly, and women will have to dress extremely conservatively and take a scarf to cover their heads.

In the far north of the city, **Kalimas harbour**, a two-kilometre length of wharves and warehouses at the eastern end of the main port, lies just north of the Arab Quarter on Jalan Kalimas Baru; take bus C, P1 or P2 or either PAC bus to Tanjung Perak and walk around to the east. It's fantastically atmospheric, the traditional Sulawesi schooners loading and unloading cargoes which are either unsuitable for containerization, or destined for locations too remote for bigger ships. You need permission to take photographs; ask at the police post by the harbour entrance.

One of the best places to visit in the city, **Surabaya Zoo** (Kebun Binatang Surabaya), Jl Setail 1 (daily 7am–6pm; Rp3000), lies 3km south of the city centre; take buses C, P1, P2 or either PAC bus. Spacious, and with over 3500 animals, it's surprisingly pleasant and, at least in parts, less distressing for animal-lovers than many Indonesian zoos. Highlights include the orang-utans and Komodo dragon.

A few minutes' walk from the zoo, the **Museum Negiri Propinsi Jawa Timur**, MPU Tantular, Jl Taman Mayangkara 6 (Tues–Thurs 8am–2.30pm, Fri 8am–2pm, Sat 8am–12.30pm, Sun 8am–1.30pm; Rp500), is crammed with crafts and artefacts, including a fine collection of shadow puppets and *topeng* masks.

Eating and drinking

Kafé Bromo, *Sheraton Surabaya Hotel*. Probably the best of the top-class hotel restaurants, although it's fairly informal. The fabulous Rp30,000 lunchtime buffet and Rp37,500 dinner buffet features Indonesian, Western, Chinese and Japanese options and a whole counter of desserts.

Kafé Excelso This Indonesian chain has branches on the ground floor of Surabaya Plaza and a couple in Tunjungan Plaza, and has an excellent choice of expensive Indonesian coffees plus iced coffee, salads, snacks, cakes and ice creams.

Café Mirota, Jl Sulawesi 24. Attached to the souvenir shop of the same name, this café serves snacks and light meals of soup, rice and noodles.

Tunjungan Plaza Food Court Huge seventh-floor food court, featuring *McDonald*'s, Singaporean noodles, Cajun grills, ice cream, crêpes and kebabs.
Turin Ice Cream, Jl Kayun 10a. The address is a bit misleading: the entrance is at the east end of Jl Embong Kenongo. They have a small menu of moderately priced Indonesian and Chinese food, but the speciality is their own ice cream, which ranges from vanilla through durian.
Café Venezia, Jl Ambengan 16. Comprehensive mid-priced menu of Indonesian, Chinese, Japanese, Korean and Western food, plus plenty of ice creams and sundaes.

Entertainment

With a large student population in the city there are plenty of **live-music** venues. Try *Tequila Willies*, Jl Kayon 62 (daily 6pm–5am), or *News Café*, Jl Raya P Sudirman 47–49 (daily 11pm–1am). RRI Surabaya, Jalan Pemuda, stages free **wayang kulit** shows every Saturday at 10pm, and during the dry season (July–Nov) there are free fortnightly open-air performances of traditional **dance** and **drama** at Pandaan, 45km from Surabaya; enquire at the tourist offices in Surabaya for a schedule, or at the travel agent's there if you want to arrange an inclusive tour.

Shopping

The most modern and popular **shopping centres** are the Surabaya Plaza (daily 10am–9.30pm) on Jalan Pemuda, and Tunjungan Plaza, Jl Jend Basuki Rachmat 8–12 (daily 10am–10pm) – and both places have branches of Toko Gunung Agung, which stocks English-language books; Tunjungan Plaza has designer outlets, and a branch of the well-known Batik Keris, which specializes in textiles and souvenirs. The Siola department store and supermarket, Jalan Tunjungan 1, is also good. For a more traditional shopping experience, try **Pasar Atum**, a two-storey concrete local market, packed with stalls selling pretty much everything; bemo M will get you here from the east end of Jalan Genteng Kali in the city centre. Other recommended **bookshops** include those at the *Sheraton Surabaya Hotel* and *Hyatt Regency*, which have the best selection of English-language titles in town, and *Gramedia*, Jl Jend Basuki Rachmat 95. Mirota, Jl Sulawesi 24, sells secondhand books, and it is also a great **souvenir** outlet for carvings, basketware, leatherwork, furniture, paintings, batik and silver. Sarinah, Jl Tunjungan 7, has a souvenir department on the second floor with a huge range of textiles, woodcarvings and assorted craft items. Lastly, don't miss Pinguin, at Jl Taman Naviton 45, a multi-room antique/junk shop and the most rewarding place for a rummage in Surabaya.

Listings

Airline offices The following airlines are found in the Skyline Office Building, *Hyatt Regency*, Jl Jend Basuki Rachmat 106–128: Brunei (☎031/5326407); Cathay Pacific, 1st floor (☎031/5317421); Eva Air, 5th floor (☎031/5465123); Garuda (☎031/5457747); Lufthansa, 5th floor (☎031/5316355, fax 5322290); Malaysia, 1st floor (☎031/5318632); Qantas, 5th floor (☎031/5452322); Thai, 5th floor (☎031/5340861). Elsewhere are: Bouraq, Jl P. Sudirman 70–72 (☎031/5452918), and Jl Genteng Kali 63 (☎031/5344940); KLM, World Trade Centre, Jl Pemuda 27–31 (☎031/5315096); Mandala, Jl Diponegoro 73 (☎031/5687157); Merpati, Jl Raya Darmo 111 (☎031/5688111); Singapore Airlines, 10th floor, Menara BBD Tower, Jl Jend Basuki Rachmat 2–6 (☎031/5319217); Trans Asia Airways Regency, Jl Jend Basuki Rachmat 106–128 (☎031/5463181).
Cash advance At Bank Duta, Jl Pemuda 12 (Mon–Fri 8.30am–2pm).
Consulates Australia, World Trade Centre, Jl Pemuda 27–31 (☎031/5319123); Belgium, Jl Raya Kupang Indah III/24 (☎031/716423); CIS Denmark, Jl Sambas 7 (☎031/5675047); France, Jl Darmokali 10–12 (☎031/5678639); Germany, Jl TAIS Nasution 15 (☎031/5343735); Great Britain, c/o Hong Kong and Shanghai Bank, 3rd floor, Skyline Office Building, *Hyatt Regency*, Jl Jend Basuki Rachmat 106–128 (☎031/5326381); India, Jl Pahlawan 17 (☎031/5341565); Japan, Jl Sumatra 93 (☎031/5344677); Netherlands, Jl Pemuda 54 (☎031/5311612 ext 558); Sri Lanka (☎031/715732); USA, Jl Dr Sutomo 33 (☎031/5676880).
Hospitals The following have doctors who speak English, Dutch and German: RS St Vincentius A Paula, Jl Diponegoro 51 (☎031/5677562), and RSUD Dr Soetomo, Jl Dharamahusada 7–9 (☎031/5501111). Otherwise, contact your hotel for recommended hospitals or doctors.
Immigration office Jl Jend S Parman 58a (☎031/8531785).

Internet access Digidagidu at the Plaza Surabaya, 2nd floor. Rp6000 per hour. Also at the main post office (Mon–Thurs 8am–8pm, Fri & Sat 8am–3pm; Rp1500 for 15min).

Post office The main post office (Mon–Thurs 8am–3pm, Fri & Sat 8am–1pm), is at Jl Kebonrojo 10. To get there from the city centre take a C, P1, P2, PAC1 or PAC2 bus from outside Tunjungan Plaza to the junction of Jl Kebonrojo and Jl Bubutan; to get back to the city go along to the other end of Jl Kebonrojo and pick up the same buses on Jl Pahlawan. Poste restante is at the philatelic counter; get mail addressed to you at Poste Restante, Post Office, Jl Kebonrojo 10, Surabaya 60175, Java Timur. The parcel office (Mon–Thurs 8am–3pm, Fri 8–11am & 12.30–3pm, Sat 8am–1pm) is to the right of the main building. A more central post office is at Jl Taman Apsaril 1 (Mon–Thurs 8am–12.30pm, Fri 8–11am, Sat 8am–noon), just off Jl Pemuda.

Telephone services Jl Genteng Besar 49 (daily 5am–11pm); on the ground floor of Tunjungan Plaza, just behind *Kafé Excelso* (daily 24hr); and Jl Walikota Mustajab 2 (24hr).

Pulau Madura

Located just 3km across the Madura Strait, **Pulau Madura** is a restful and totally rural place, where village life continues in timeless fashion. Although a quiet backwater for much of the year, the island bursts into activity during the exciting **kerapan sapi (ox races)**, held every August and September. The races originated as a way of toughening up the oxen and, these days, individual and village pride can be boosted considerably by having a prizewinning pair of 600kg beasts (a good racing ox can fetch Rp20 million). The oxen are yoked together and adorned with highly decorated bridles, and the rider half-stands and half-sits very precariously on a long pole that is dragged behind; together they charge over a course just over 100m long, reaching speeds up to 50km per hour. The finals take place in September or October in Pamekasan, accompanied by ceremonies, parades, dancing and gamelan orchestras. Check in tourist offices in Surabaya for exact dates.

Stretching 160km from west to east and around 35km from north to south, Madura is mostly flat, although there is a low range of hills across the centre. The main towns are **Bangkalan** in the west, **Pamekasan** and **Sampang** in the centre and **Sumenep** in the east. The main road on the island links the major settlements along the south coast, and there is a quieter road along the north coast. **Ferries** operate from Tanjung Perak in Surabaya across the Madura Strait to **KAMAL** in the west of Madura around the clock (every 30min; 30min; Rp500). From Kamal there are **minibuses** to Sumenep (3hr 30min–4hr), Sampang (1hr 30min–2hr) and Pamekasan (2hr 30min); local transport covers the villages in between. There's also a daily ferry (4hr) from Tanjung Jangkhar in the far east of Java, 60km north of Banyuwangi, to **KALIANGET** in the east of Madura. Local minibuses operate from Kalianget to Sumenep, or you can stay at *Baitul Kamal* (①).

Camplong and the west

One of the nicest places to stay on the island is **CAMPLONG**, a small market town and beach resort situated on an attractive river estuary 35km east of Sampang. Here, the appealing *Pondok Wisata Camplong* (☎0323/21586; ①–②) has nice en-suite bungalows set in pleasant grounds. There's a good beach, a fair-sized pool, and an inexpensive restaurant. All public transport between Pamekasan and Bangkalan passes the entrance.

The capital of Madura and its largest town, **PAMEKASAN** lies in the middle of the island, but has little charm and not much to interest visitors. The main shopping area, Pasar Kampung Arab, is just off Jalan Diponegoro, west of the alun-alun. The main **bus terminal**, just east of the town centre, provides regular direct services to Surabaya, Bandung, Jakarta and Banyuwangi. The long-distance buses (beyond Surabaya) leave at around midday, others operating throughout the day. Amongst the town's limited **accommodation**, try *Hotel Garuda*, Jl Masgit 1 (☎0324/22589; ①–②), on the alun-alun, with very basic rooms.

Sumenep

SUMENEP in the far east of the island is the most attractive town, with worthwhile sights and the best choice of accommodation. The centrepiece of the town is the eighteenth-century **Mesjid Agung** (also known as Mesjid Jam'q), a large, cool, white-tiled edifice with wonderfully carved wooden doors and an attractive interior of rich gold decoration and blue-and-white Chinese tiles; women should cover arms and legs, but a scarf isn't necessary. **Museum Daerah** and the neighbouring kraton (Mon–Fri 7.30am–5pm, Sat & Sun 8am–4pm; Rp300) are two intriguing sights, located at Jl Dr Sutomo 8, which leads from the east side of Taman Adipura Kota Sumenep gardens directly opposite the mosque. The two-part museum houses an enormous collection of old photographs of the Madurese royal family, carriages, textiles, furniture and weapons – frustratingly, there are no labels in English, but museum staff will show you round. Far better is the **kraton**, the old palace, which dates from 1762, was designed by a Chinese architect and is the only remaining palace in East Java. The Pendopo Agung (Grand Hall) has lovely gold-painted woodcarving, old lanterns and a cool tiled floor. The wonderfully lively local market, **Pasar Anom**, is just north of the bus terminal.

PRACTICALITIES

The main **bus terminal**, Wiraraja, is 1.5km south of the town centre. Jalan Trunojoyo leads from the terminal into the town centre, which is just north of Mesjid Agung. All long-distance buses, as well as buses from Pamekasan and points west, arrive at Wiraraja; take a becak or local bemo into the town centre. There are two other terminals: Giling for bemos to Lombang, and Kegongagong for bemos to Kalianget. Leaving Madura, there are direct buses from Sumenep back to Surabaya (5hr), departing from Wiraraja and going via Kamal. Get tickets on the bus or at the ticket offices on Jalan Trunojoyo just north of the terminal.

Hotel Wijaya 1, Jl Trunojoyo 45–47 (☎0328/21433; ①–②), is central and has a range of **rooms**, some with air-con. *Hotel Wijaya 2*, Jl Wahid Hasyim 3 (☎0328/21532; ①–②), about 200m away, sits in a quieter road and is of a similar standard. In the evening on the Jalan Trunojoyo side of Taman Adipura Kota Sumenep, a small **night market** mushrooms; there are several pleasant Padang places on Jalan Trunojoyo: *Do'a Bundo* at 10a or *Megajus* next door.

The **post office** is at Jl Urip Sumoharjo 5 (Mon–Thurs 8am–2pm, Fri 8–11am, Sat 8am–noon), 1km east of the town centre. The most convenient wartel is at Jl Raya P Sudirman 55 (daily 24hr) and the 24hr **telephone office** is 1km beyond the post office at Jl Urip Sumoharjo 41. You can **exchange** cash and travellers' cheques at BCA, Jl Trunojoyo 196.

Lombang and the north coast

The beach at **LOMBANG**, 43km northeast of Sumenep, is long and lovely, with white sand in all directions and a few warung located in the trees behind. There are some direct minibuses from Sumenep at the weekends and on public holidays, but otherwise you'll have to get a minibus to Legung, from where it's 3km to the gate, and then 1km to the beach. On the track down to the beach, *Lombang Homestay* (①) offers very simple **accommodation** in the family house, with shared mandi.

There is no long-distance public transport along the north coast, only minibuses between villages. Located 20km northwest of Sumenep, the pretty beach at **SLOPENG**, several kilometres long and backed by big dunes, spreads away from the small village whose residents specialize in *topeng* mask production. The village of **PASONGSONGAN**, 10km west of Slopeng, is attractive and has a good place to stay: the *Coconut Rest House* (①; ask for Pak Taufik), on the road down to the new fish auction building on the coast. Minibuses operate direct to Pasongsongan from Sumenep. One of the island centres of batik is **TANJUNG BUMI**, 25km west of Ketapang, where all the families are involved in the work. They don't get many visitors up here and are generally happy to show you what they do. From here it is 60km to Kamal via Bangkalan.

Malang and around

The second largest city in East Java, **MALANG**, 90km south of Surabaya, is a busy city with a population in excess of 600,000. Situated at an altitude of 450m and circled by attractive volcanoes, it is cool, tree-lined and much more tourist-friendly in all respects than Surabaya. The city's **commercial centre** is the alun-alun to the south of Sungai Brantas, with the main shopping and market area along or near Jalan Agus Salim, which runs off the south side. Jalan Mojopahit runs across Sungai Brantas and links this commercial sector with the Tugu area to the north, in which most government offices are located.

The most attractive and evocative **colonial area** is Jalan Ijen, with renovated bungalows in wide, palm-lined boulevards. It's a rich and refined area, with fabulous iron railings that guard the privacy of the wealthy of the city. To get there, take bemo GL (which goes along Jalan Ijen), or MM (along Jalan Kawi nearby). **Museum Brawijaya**, Jl Ijen 25a (daily 8am–2pm; donation), is a military museum fronted by tanks and full of military memorabilia – a rather chilling celebration of Indonesian military might, including artefacts connected with the suppression of Irian Jaya. A fascinating **bird market** can be found in the Pasar Sengkol/Jalan Brawijaya area; head down towards the river from Jalan Mojopahit on the south side of the river. Birds change hands for Rp2–3 million for good singers, and up to Rp7 million for exceptional ones. The **flower market** is slightly further north of the bird market – it ranges down the riverbank of Sungai Brantas and you can walk to it from Jalan Brawijaya.

Arrival

The Arjosari **bus terminal** is 7km northeast of the city centre on Jalan Ratu Intan and served by blue city bemos to the city. **City bemos** (4am–11pm; flat fare Rp500) run between two of the three Malang bus terminals and are labelled by the two letters of the relevant terminals. "A" refers to Arjosari, "G" is Gadang, 5km south of the city centre on Jalan Kolonel Soegiono, and "L" is for Landung Sari on Jalan Majen Haryono, 6km northwest of the city centre. So, for example, LA operates between Landung Sari and Arjosari. GA and AG are not the same route, worth noting if you're heading to an intermediate point. The **train station** is a short walk east of Jalan Tugu.

When it comes to moving on, you could consider getting a minibus instead of the usual bus to Surabaya, Solo or Yogyakarta; expect to pay around three times the express bus price. Several places also sell night-bus tickets which include a hotel pick-up. **Agents** are: *Helios Hotel*, Jl Pattimura 37 (☎0341/362741); Haryono, Jl Kahuripan 22 (☎0341/367500), who can book Pelni and flight tickets; Tuju Transport, Jl Kertanegara 5 (☎0341/368363), who also book Pelni and flight tickets; Toko Oen Travel Service, Jl Jend Basuki Rachmat 5 (☎0341/364052); Juwita, Jl KH Agus Salim 11 (☎0341/362008); and Harapan Transport, Jl Surapati 42 (☎0341/353089), close to *Helios Hotel*.

Information and tours

There is no government-run tourist office in Malang, though a number of private companies can offer help with arranging tours and car rental. The best of these is PD Jasa Yasa (daily 8am–3pm; ☎0341/364111) at Jl Basuki Rahmat 11, which arranges city tours (US$14.50 for two people), as well as tours to nearby sights, such as **Mount Bromo** (US$22.50). The **national park office**, Taman Nasional Bromo-Tengger-Semeru, Jl Raden Intan 6 (Mon–Thurs 8am–2pm, Fri 8–11am, Sat 8am–1pm; ☎0341/491828), close to Arjosari terminal, issues permits for climbing Semeru, but it's probably more convenient to buy them in Ranu Pane (see p.262).

There are several popular **day-trip destinations** close to Malang, many of which feature on the backpacker-oriented tours run by *Helios Hotel*. Popular local sights include **Candi Singosari**, a grand but incomplete fourteenth-century temple 12km north of Malang, and the fine south-coast **beaches of Sendangbiru, Balekambang** and **Ngliep**, all with impressive scenery and lovely sand.

Accommodation

There is some excellent **accommodation** in Malang, and, although there are no really cheap places, value is generally good, which makes it an attractive place to stay.

Gress Homestay, Jl Kahayan 6 (☎0341/491386). A GA or AL bemo will drop you off at Jl Mahakan; get off at Apotik Mahakan. This is a real homestay with spotless en-suite rooms and help with trekking, fishing and local tours. ②.

Helios Hotel, Jl Pattimura 37 (☎0341/362741). The best budget choice in the city: clean rooms, some en suite, set round a garden. Tours, bus tickets and transport rental. ①–②.

Montana Hotel, Jl Kahuripan 9 (☎0341/362751). Conveniently close to Tugu. All rooms have a hot-water bath and some have air-con. Good value. ③–⑤.

Hotel Santosa, Jl KH Agus Salim 24 (☎0341/366889). In the middle of the main shopping area, but quiet. Plain but spotless rooms, some with hot water and air-con. ①–⑥.

Hotel Splendid Inn, Jl Mojopahit 4 (☎0341/366860). All rooms have hot-water bathrooms and there is a small pool; this is an old-fashioned, pleasant maze of a place. ③.

Hotel Tosari, Jl KH Ahmad Dahlan 31 (☎0341/326945). In a central location with clean, tiled rooms, some en suite. ①–⑥.

Eating

There is an excellent **night market** on Medan Merdeka on Saturday evenings and every night during Ramadan.

Amsterdam Restaurant, Jl Terusan Kawi 2. Huge menu with steak as the speciality but also many Indonesian staples. Moderate to expensive.

Asri Dua, Jl Brig Jen Slamet Riadi 14. Has a small menu of good-value Indonesian and Chinese food plus steak and sandwiches in clean, attractive surroundings.

Gloria café, Jl KH Agus Salim 21–23. Huge Chinese-run eatery serving a wide variety of inexpensive Indonesian and Western dishes.

Rindu, Jl KH Agus Salim 29. Centrally located Padang restaurant with a big selection of attractively prepared and displayed food.

Toko Oen, Jl Jend Basuki Rachmat 5. This has been a restaurant and ice-cream parlour since 1930 and is a Malang institution. The menu is substantial, with sandwiches, salads, steaks, seafood and Chinese food, all at moderate prices.

Listings

Airline offices Garuda, Jl Merdeka Timur 4 (☎0341/369494); Merpati, Jl Basuki Rahmat 1 (☎0341/361909).

Banks and exchange BNI, Jl Jend Basuki Rachmat 75–77; and BCA, Jl Jend Basuki Rachmat 70–74 (on the corner of Jl Kahuripan) do currency exchange.

Bookshops English-language books at Gramedia, Jl Jend Basuki Rachmat 3; Jl Mojopahit, just south of the bridge across Sungai Brantas, is lined with secondhand bookshops.

Car rental From PD Jasa Yasa, Jl Basuki Rahmat ll (☎0341/364111); Rp120,000 per day for a car with driver.

Hospital Rumah Sakit Umum Daerah Dr Saiful Anwar, Jl Jaksa Agung Suprapto 2 (☎0341/366242); Rumah Sakit Umum Lavalette, Jl WR Supratman 10 (☎0341/362960).

Immigration office Jl Jend A Yani Utara (☎0341/491039).

Internet access At the post office, Jl Merdeka Selatan 5 (Rp1500 for 15min); Primanet, Jl Basuki Rahmat, near the telephone office (Rp4000 per hour).

Pharmacy Kima Farma 53, Jl Kawi 22a (☎0341/326665), is large, well-stocked and open 24hr.

The Bromo region

The **Bromo region** is best-known for its awesome scenery; at its heart is a vast, ancient volcanic crater with sheer walls over 300m high. Within this crater, a host of picturesque mountains, including the dramatic, still-smoking Gunung Bromo (2392m), rises up from the "Sea of Sand", the sandy plain at the crater's base. Hundreds of thousands of visitors come here each year to climb Bromo for the sunrise – a stunning sight, and less strenuous than many other Indonesian peaks.

APPROACHES TO GUNUNG BROMO

One hypothesis for the formation of the area is that Gunung Tengger, then the highest mountain in Java at over 4000m, erupted to form a caldera of between 8km and 10km in diameter and crater walls between 200m and 700m high. This is now the main outer crater rim with the Sea of Sand in the bottom. However, eruptions continued to occur, forming the smaller inner peaks such as Bromo, Batok and Widodoren that rise up from the Sea of Sand.

This unique landscape now comprises the Bromo-Tengger-Semeru National Park, whose highlights are the dramatic smoking crater of **Gunung Bromo**, **Gunung Penanjakan**, on the outside crater's edge and one of the favourite sunrise spots, and **Cemoro Lawang**, with its brilliant panoramic view of the crater, where most visitors stay. The park also contains the highest mountain in Java, **Gunung Semeru**, which can be climbed by experienced trekkers. Views are best in the dry season but, whatever time of year, you should bring warm clothes.

There are two main approaches to the Bromo region. The most popular is to head inland from **Probolinggo**, on the north coast, to the crater's edge at Cemoro Lawang, where most people stay in order to make the dawn trip to Gunung Bromo as easy as possible. Alternative access is from **Pasuruan**, also on the north coast, inland to the villages of Tosari and

Wonokitri. These villages are linked by road to Gunung Penanjakan, so they offer an excellent approach for the sunrise from there.

Gunung Bromo, Gunung Penanjakan and Gunung Semeru

There are a variety of excursions possible from Cemoro Lawang, the most popular being the climb to the top of **Gunung Bromo** (2392m); if you are lucky with the clouds, there may be an absolutely spellbinding sunrise. To get to the base of Gunung Bromo, you can walk (1hr; bring a torch), get a horse (Rp10,000 from Cemoro Lawang, Rp15,000 return), or hire a car or ojek. However you get there, you'll still have to manage the 249 concrete stairs (30min) up to the crater rim, from where there are great views down into the smoking crater and back across the Sea of Sand.

The best spot for the sunrise across the entire Bromo area is **Gunung Penanjakan** (2770m). Leave Tosari or Wonokitri at around 4.30am to get to the lookout in time. The whole crater area lies below, Bromo smoking and Semeru puffing up regular plumes while the sun rises dramatically in the east. You can **camp** up here if you wish, but you'll be invaded before dawn by the hordes. To see the sunrise, either organize return transport from Wonokitri or Tosari (Rp60,000 per jeep, Rp25,000 motorcycle); do a loop to Penanjakan for the sunrise, across the Sea of Sand to Bromo and then back to Wonokitri or Tosari after you've climbed to the top; or (less popular) go to Penanjakan and Bromo and then on to Cemoro Lawang – it's Rp90,000 per jeep, Rp30,000 per motorcycle for either of the final two.

Essentially a dry-season expedition (from June to September or possibly October), the climb up **Gunung Semeru** (3676m), Java's highest mountain, is for fit, experienced trekkers only and requires good preparation and equipment. It takes at least three full days. The volcano is still active, with over 20,000 seismic events recorded in a typical year; in 1997, two climbers were killed by a big eruption which sent boulders flying out of the crater, so it is vital to take a guide and heed local advice. The path starts at the village of **RANU PANE**, to the north of the mountain, accessible by microlet and chartered jeep from Malang or Tumpang, or via a path across the Sea of Sand. In the village you need to check in at the **PHPA office** and get your **permit** (Rp2100). The PHPA office will also recommend porters (one per person at Rp30,000 each). Bring your own sleeping bag and tent, and rent a cooking stove in Ranu Pane. In the village, trekkers can stay in the *Forest Guest House* (①), where you'll need to cook for yourself, or there's a **campsite** near the PHPA office. If you don't want to make your own arrangements, a **package trip** from the *Helios Hotel* in Malang will run to about Rp500,000 (2–4 people) excluding transport and porters from Ranu Pane, but including a guide and equipment.

Probolinggo

PROBOLINGGO is 38km east of Pasuruan. The **train station** is on the northern side of the alun-alun. The **bus terminal** is 6km southwest of town; yellow microlets run to the town centre. **Minibuses** for Cemoro Lawang leave from the terminal, and there are two buses daily – they are labelled "Sukapura" and "Ngadisari" on the front but also serve Cemoro Lawang.

The best **accommodation** is *Hotel Bromo Permai*, Jl Raya P Sudirman 237 (☎0335/427451; ①–②), where staff can arrange chartered transport to Cemoro Lawang and have train information. To get here from the bus station take a G or F yellow microlet and, from here to the terminal or station, a G. For **eating**, *Rumah Makan Sumber Hidup*, Jl Dr Moch Saleh 2, at the junction with Jalan Raya P Sudirman, has an extensive menu of rice, sate, soup, juices and ices. The banks on Jalan Suroyo do **foreign exchange**: Bank Bumi Daya at no. 23, BCA at no. 28, BRI at no. 30, or BNI at no. 46. All have ATMs. The **post office**, Jl Suroyo 33 (Mon–Sat 7am–8pm), has public Internet access (daily 9am–8pm). The **wartel** (daily 7am–11pm), next to the main Telkom administration office, is at Jl Suroyo 37.

Cemoro Lawang

The small village of **CEMORO LAWANG**, 46km from Probolinggo, is perched on the crater's edge and is the easiest place from which to set off on the pre-dawn excursion to Gunung Bromo itself. From the crater's edge in Cemoro Lawang there are brilliant views of the entire area – best at the end of the road from the north coast and in front of *Lava View Lodge*. **Minibuses** from Probolinggo run up to the crater rim from 6am to 5.30pm; they do the return journey from 8am till 4pm. Several places advertise minibus and express-bus tickets, which are more expensive but more convenient.

There is a **national park post** on the Probolinggo–Cemoro Lawang road where you pay admission to the park at Ngadisari (Rp2500). The **national park office** (Kantor Taman Nasional Bromo Tengger Semeru; daily 7.30am–4pm) in Cemoro Lawang has displays about the area. *Hotel Yoschi* is the best place for local information, especially if you want to trek. The postal agent at the *Hotel Bromo Permai* charges a lot, so bring stamps with you. There's a wartel (daily 3am–10pm) on the left as you reach the top of the road, and a **health centre** in Ngadisari, Jl Raya Bromo 6, just by the checkpost.

ACCOMMODATION IN AND AROUND CEMORO LAWANG

There is plenty of **accommodation** in Cemoro Lawang, Ngadisari (3km from the rim), Wonokerto (5km) and Sukapura (18km). You can **camp** anywhere: Penanjakan is popular, although you will get disturbed at sunrise, and there's a good site 200m along the rim from the *Lava View Lodge*. There are plenty of **places to eat** in the vicinity of Cemoro Lawang, and many of the hotels have restaurants.

Hotel Bromo, Jl Wonokerto 5, Wonokerto (☎0335/541022). If you're on a very tight budget, this place is worth considering. Small rooms, with cold-water mandi. ①.

Café Lava Hostel (aka **Puri Lava**) (☎0335/541020). A justly popular travellers' choice, close to the crater rim, on the main road into Cemoro Lawang. Cheaper rooms share cold-water mandi, more expensive ones have garden sitting areas. ①–②.

Cemoro Indah (☎0335/541019). On the crater's rim around to the right from the *Hotel Bromo Permai*. The main road into Cemoro Lawang forks about 200m before it reaches the crater rim. The left fork goes to the centre of the village, and the right fork to the *Cemoro Indah*. There's a big choice of rooms, including stunningly positioned bungalows with hot water. ①–⑤.

Hotel Cik Arto (☎0335/541014). Just below the terminal in Ngadisari. This is a new place, with a range of en-suite rooms in a pleasant garden setting. ②.

Lava View Lodge (☎0335/541002). About 500m left along the crater's edge from the centre of Cemoro Lawang; go through the concrete area between the row of shops and *Hotel Bromo Permai* and follow the main track. It doesn't look too great from the outside, but rooms are comfortable and en suite, and the views are brilliant. ②.

Hotel Yoschi, Jl Wonokerto 1, Wonokerto (☎0335/541018). A great place with many options: the cheaper rooms share bathrooms, while the top-priced ones are actually cottages. Good information, hiking maps, book exchange, local guides and warm jackets for rent. ①–⑤.

Pasuruan

Located 60km southeast of Surabaya, the port town of **PASURUAN** is a convenient stopping-off spot close to Bromo on the way to or from Tosari and Wonokitri; buses run every few minutes throughout the day between Surabaya and Pasuruan (1–2hr), and there are daily trains (1hr 30min) from Gubeng station in Surabaya. The main north-coast road is Jalan Raya, with the **bus terminal** at its eastern end, about 1.5km from the alun-alun. **Microlets** run direct to Tosari, although there is no sign at the terminal. The **train station** is just north of Jalan Raya, on Jalan Stasiun.

Hotel Pasuruan, Jl Nusantara 46 (☎0343/424494; ②), has a range of **rooms**, including some with air-con and hot-water, as does *Wisma Karya*, Jl Raya 160 (☎0343/426655; ①). You can **eat** at the small night market around the alun-alun, or try the inexpensive Indonesian and Chinese food at *Rumah Makan Savera*, on Jl Raya 92a. The **tourist office**, Jl Hayam Wuruk 14 (☎0343/429075), is in the district government offices, Kantor Kapeputan Pasuran. The post office (Mon–Thurs 7.30am–2pm & 3–8pm, Fri 7.30–11.30am & 1–8pm, Sat 7.30am–1pm & 2–8pm), Jl Alun-alun Utara 1, provides **Internet** access (Rp2500 for 15min). There's a 24hr **wartel** at Jl Stasiun 11 and **exchange** facilities at BNI, Jl A Yani 21 and BCA, Jl Periwa 200, 200m west of the terminal.

Tosari and Wonokitri

Just over 40km south from Pasuruan, the small villages of Tosari and Wonokitri sit 2km apart on neighbouring ridges of the Bromo massif foothills. These are excellent choices for early access to **Gunung Penanjakan** and are less tourist-oriented than Cemoro Lawang. Microlets that go to one also go to the other, and both villages have accommodation. The road from Pasuruan divides 500m before Tosari: the right fork leads up to the market area of that village, and the left fork twists up to the next ridge and Wonokitri. Wonokitri is a compact, shabby town with good views, while Tosari is more spread out, with an attractive ridge to the northeast that leads to the *Hotel Bromo Tosari*. It's better to take a minibus direct from Pasuruan, rather than changing at **Pasrepan**, though that's also possible.

In **TOSARI**, *Penginapan Wulun Aya*, Jl Bromo Cottage 25 (☎0343/57011; ②), is small and clean with good views. *Mekar Sari*, Jl Raya 1 (no phone; ②), is a small rumah makan and has a few simple rooms and a good roof terrace.

WONOKITRI features several places to stay. At the time of writing, the only place that was signed was *Pondok Wisata Surya Nuta* (②), a concrete, charmless building. Far better choices are *Kartiki Sari* (no phone; ③) with simple rooms, and *Bromo Surya Indah* (☎0343/571049; ②), which is just before the Balinese-style village meeting hall, about 300m before the national park checkpost at the far end of the village; rooms have attached bathroom, clean bedding and good views. At the **national park checkpost** and information centre at the southern end of Wonokitri you pay the **admission fee** to the park (Rp2100).

Bondowoso

Attractively situated between Gunung Argopuro to the southwest and Gunung Beser to the north, **BONDOWOSO**, is a small, relaxed town, useful for access to the Ijen Plateau. There's good **access** by road or rail; the **train station** is 2km southeast of the alun-alun. The **bus station** is 500m beyond the train station. Coming from Banyuwangi, you'll need to change at Situbondo or Jember. **Becak** wait at the bus terminal and station to ferry arrivals around town.

The centre of town is the **alun-alun**, less manicured than many, but still attractive, and surrounded by the main administration buildings. The main shopping street, Jalan Raya P Sudirman, runs from the northeast corner of the square.

The **hotel** most used to travellers is *Hotel Anugerah*, Jl Mayjen Sutoyo 12 (☎0332/21870; ②), with lots of options including top-end rooms with air-con – all have attached mandi and outside sitting areas. The owner can help with chartering transport (Rp120,000 with driver to Ijen). The most atmospheric **place to eat** is the extensive night market along Jalan Martadinata, which heads east off the southeast corner of the alun-alun.

The **post office** is at Jl Jaksa Agung Suprapto 9 (Mon–Thurs 7.30am–noon & 1–4pm, Fri 7.30–11.30am, Sat 7.30am–1pm, Sun & hols 8–11am). There's a 24hr **Telkom office** at Jl Mayjen Panjaitan 6; the road is left off Jalan A Yani about 500m south of the alun-alun. You can only **exchange** cash, not travellers' cheques, at BNI, Jl A Yani 26.

The Ijen Plateau

The **Ijen Plateau** is a large upland area southeast of Bondowoso, which includes the peaks and foothills of Gunung Ijen, Gunung Raung (3332m), Gunung Suket (2950m) and Gunung Merapi (2800m), plus several smaller peaks. The entire area is rural, coffee plantations and vegetable gardens blending into the forested uplands, with a few widely dispersed villages. The highlight is the dramatic lake, **Kawah Ijen**, in the crater of the dormant volcano from which dozens of miners dig sulphur by hand.

The usual access to the crater lake is a three-kilometre (90min) hike from **PAL TUDING**, where there's a campsite, dorm (①; bring a sleeping bag), café, and national park office (Rp1000 park entrance fee). From Pal Tuding, the **path** heads steeply uphill through the forest and is easy to follow. After 45 minutes it passes a building, and the climb steepens. Just above here the path splits; the right fork, leads to the best route, to the crater rim and the left fork to the dam at the end of the lake. After a while you find yourself 200m above the lake in a dramatic, austere landscape of almost bare rock sloping down into the crater. You can walk along the top of the crater, or descend to the edge of the lake along the narrow path that the sulphur miners use – allow 30 to 45 minutes to get down, and twice that to get back up. The **sulphur miners** come up to Kawah Ijen daily; they set off from the Banyuwangi area before dawn, walk up to the lake from Licin, hack out a full load of sulphur (50–70kg) by hand, which they bring up to the crater rim and back down to Licin where they receive around Rp125 per kilo. It's dangerous work, and sudden eruptions and sulphur fumes have been known to kill miners.

From Bondowoso there are four **buses** daily to **SEMPOL**, the main village on the plateau (66km; 3hr); from Sempol you have to hitch or use an ojek (Rp10,000 one-way) to get to Pal Tuding. The most convenient **place to stay** is at the national park office area in Pal Tuding, but it's also possible to stay near Sempol, 1km from the main road in the hamlet of **Kalisat**, at the guesthouses, *Jampit II* and *III* (no phone; ②), which are signposted "Penginapan Kaliasat" from the centre of Sempol. Staff here can arrange excursions to Kawah Ijen, local guides, transport and inexpensive food.

Banyuwangi and ferries to Bali

The town of **BANYUWANGI** has excellent transport links and is 8km south of **KETAPANG**, from where ferries run to Gilimanuk in **Bali** (every 30min; 30min; Rp1000) 24hr a day. There is a helpful East Java **tourist office** (daily 8am–7pm) inside the terminal building. There is a convenient **Pelni** agent on the main road opposite the Ketapang ferry terminal: Hariyono NPPS, Jl Gatot Suproto 165 (☎0333/22523). The Pelni office is at Jalan Raya Situbondo (☎0333/510325). Pelni ship *KM Tatamailou* calls at Banyuwangi every two weeks (see "Getting around" p.191 and "Travel Details" p.443). You can also book tickets for the *KM Dibonsolo*, which calls at Benoa on Bali.

There are several **bus terminals** serving Banyuwangi. The main long-distance terminal is **Sri Tanjung**, 2km north of Ketapang. If you're heading to Surabaya, you can either go around the north coast via Situbondo, or via Jember (further but more scenic); travel time on both routes is similar, at five to seven hours.

On the northern edge of the town centre is the **Blambangan** microlet terminal and, 3km from the city centre on the southwestern edge, **Brawijaya** terminal. Microlets numbered 1, 2, 4 and 5 ply between Brawijaya and Blambangan, and yellow microlets 6 and 12 link Blambangan and Sri Tanjung, as do blue Kijang. They are known locally as Lin 1, Lin 2, and so on.

There are several **train stations** serving Banyuwangi, the main one being **Ketapang**, just 500m from the ferry terminal. Book onward tickets here (9.30am–3pm). Trains run to and from Malang (daily; 5–6hr), Probolinggo (daily; 5–6hr), Surabaya (3 daily; 7hr) and Yogyakarta (daily; 15hr). The others are **Argopura**, near the Blambangan microlet terminal (get off here if you plan to stay in town), and **Karangasem**, which is on the western outskirts of town on the way up to Licin.

The best **places to stay** are the popular *Hotel Baru*, Jl M.T. Hariyono 82–84 (☎0333/21369; ③), in a quiet central location, ten minutes' walk from the post office, and the more spacious *Hotel Berlin Barat*, Jl MT Hariyono 93 (☎0333/21323; ①), which is owned by the same people. There is a **night market** along Jalan Pattimura, otherwise try the *Rumah Makan Hotel Baru*, opposite *Hotel Baru*, or the *Wina Restaurant*, on the street side of Blambangan terminal at Jl Basuki Rachmat 62.

For **exchange**, go to BCA at Jl Jend Sudirman 85–87 or BNI at Jl Banetrang 46. The **post office**, Jl Diponegoro 1 (Mon–Thurs 8am–3pm, Fri 8–11am, Sat 8am–1pm, Sun & hols 8am–noon), is on the west side of the sports field and has public **Internet** access. Just around the corner, off the southwest corner of the sports field, the 24hr **Telkom office** is at Jl Dr Sutomo 63 and there are plenty of wartels around town, including Jl Jaksa Agung Suprapto 130.

Grajagan surf: G' Land

In the far southeastern corner of Java, the fishing village of **GRAJAGAN** has become famous for the world-class surf in Grajagan Bay, whose awesomely long left-handers, promising endless tubes and walls, are known as **G' LAND**. The beach, Pantai Coko, is signed from the village: it's 300m to the gate (admission Rp1050) and then another 2km through the forest to the black-sand beach. Due to the surf, take local advice from the forestry office about safe swimming spots, and never swim near the rocks. There is **accommodation** at *Wisma Perhutani* (no phone; ①) in basic rooms (bring your own sheet sleeping bag. To get to Grajagan, take a **minibus** from Banyuwangi's Brawijaya terminal to **PURWOHARJO**, and then a microlet for the final 14km to Grajagan. To get to **PLENGKUNG**, 15 km east across the bay, where a surf camp caters for surfers from April to October, you can charter boats from Grajagan – you'll start bargaining at US$200 for a boat for ten people. Book Plengkung accommodation through PT Wadasari Wisata Surf, Jl Pantai Kuta 8b, Denpasar, Bali (☎0361/7555588) or Plengkung Indah Wisata, Andika Plaza Blok A 22/23, Jl Simpang Dutah 38–40, Surabaya (☎031/5315320). Several tour operators on Bali and Lombok run all-inclusive surfaris which feature G' Land in their itineraries.

SUMATRA

North Sumatra now receives more tourists than any other Indonesian province except Bali and Yogyakarta, and the main interest lies in the rugged central highlands, the homelands of the **Batak** who arrived over four thousand years ago and evolved almost completely in isolation from the rest of the island, developing languages and cultures that owe little to any outside influences. The Batak are divided into six distinctive ethnolinguistic groups, each with its own rituals, architectural style, mode of dress and religious beliefs. Many Batak have been exposed to Western education since Dutch missionaries arrived in the early 1800s, and as a result the Toba Batak people in particular are amongst the most educated, powerful and richest minorities in the country today.

The hill station of **Berastagi**, part of the Karo Batak territory, and the many waterside resorts around beautiful **Danau Toba** – Southeast Asia's largest lake and the spiritual home of the Toba Batak – throng with tourists every summer. The province also features the hugely popular Orang Utan Rehabilitation Centre at **Bukit Lawang**, just a couple of hours' drive from the provincial capital of **Medan**, an entry point from Malaysia, as well as the surfer's mecca of **Pulau Nias**. Bukit Lawang, Berastagi, Danau Toba and Nias form such a perfect diagonal route across the centre of Sumatra that most tourists bypass Aceh province to the north, but here you'll find **Gunung Leuser national park**, the largest in Indonesia, and the picture-perfect beaches of **Pulau Weh**.

Major gateways into Indonesia are also provided by the west-coast port of **Padang** and the islands of **Batam** and **Bintan** in the Riau Archipelago, between the Sumatran mainland and Singapore. Travellers entering Sumatra through the Riau Islands can transit in the prosperous city of **Pekanbaru** before heading north to Medan and Danau Toba, south to Bandar

Lampung, or west to picturesquely located **Bukittinggi**, the heartland of Minang culture and a major tourist destination with a thriving travellers' scene. Nearby, **Danau Maninjau** is developing plenty of low-key lakeside guesthouses. Most travellers rush between Bukittinggi and Java, with perhaps an overnight stop in the city of **Bandar Lampung** or, better, in smaller, quieter **Kalianda** nearby, but in between sprawls the **Kerinci-Seblat national park**, with plenty of scope for trekking and the isolated **Mentawai Islands**, 100km off the west coast of Sumatra, and home to some very traditional groups of people.

Getting around Sumatra on **public transport** can be gruelling – distances are huge, the roads tortuous and the driving hair-raising. There are plenty of road connections on to Java from even the smallest towns, but if you intend to use sea or air to make your trip less stressful, you'll need to plan carefully as only the large cities have airports, and ferry connections are generally irregular. For all major Pelni ferry connections and inter-city flights, see "Travel Details" on p.443.

Medan

MEDAN, Indonesia's fourth largest city, occupies a strategic point on Sumatra's northeast coast and is a major entry point for boats and flights from Malaysia. It has acquired a reputation for being filthy and chaotic, but also holds some glorious examples of nineteenth-century colonial architecture, built by the Dutch gentry, who grew rich on the back of the vast plantations that stretch up the slopes of the Bukit Barisan to the west of the city. The boom was started by the entrepreneurial Jacob Nienhuys, who saw the potential for tobacco plantations, prompting even the local royalty to migrate to the city to be nearer the action.

Arrival

Thanks to a local superstition that noise drives away evil spirits, Medan's **Polonia Airport** lies near the town centre at the southern end of Jalan Imam Bonjol. A taxi from the airport to the main square, Lapangan Merdeka, should cost Rp4000.

Belawan Harbour is 25km to the north of the city. A complimentary bus service is laid on to meet the hydrofoil ferries from Penang; the yellow "Morina" *angkuta* (mini-vans) #811 or #122 (Rp1500) also ply the route.

Medan has two main **bus stations**. The huge **Amplas terminal**, 5km south of the city centre, serves buses arriving from points south of Medan. White "Medan Raya" minibuses (Rp750) leave from the bemo station next door to Amplas, travel past Mesjid Raya and on to Lapangan Merdeka via Jalan Brig Jend A Yani. The **Pinang Baris** bus station, 10km west of the city centre, is where buses from the north or west of the city arrive. A DAMRI bus leaves from Pinang Baris to Lapangan Merdeka every twenty minutes (Rp500). Medan is connected by **train** to just a couple of minor towns in North Sumatra, and the station is on the eastern side of Lapangan Merdeka.

Information and city transport

Medan's knowledgeable **tourist office** is at Jl Brig Jend A Yani 107 (Mon–Thurs 7.30am–4pm, Fri 7.30am–noon; ☎061/538101), 200m south of Lapangan Merdeka near the *Tip Top Kafé*.

Angkuta mini-vans are the mainstay of the city transport network; they are numbered, and many have names too. The main angkuta station is at **Sambu**, west of the Olympia Plaza and the Central Market on Jalan Sutomo.

Accommodation

Medan has no distinct travellers' centre, although some cheap **hotels** cluster around Mesjid Raya. The Grand Education Centre, Jl Kapten Muslim (☎061/852872), invites travellers to teach English in exchange for food and accommodation

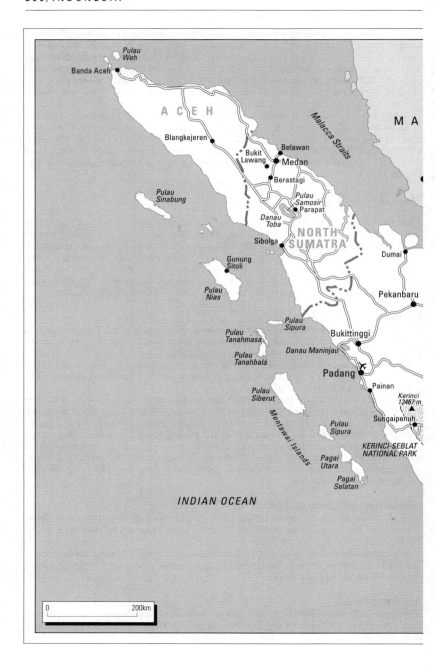

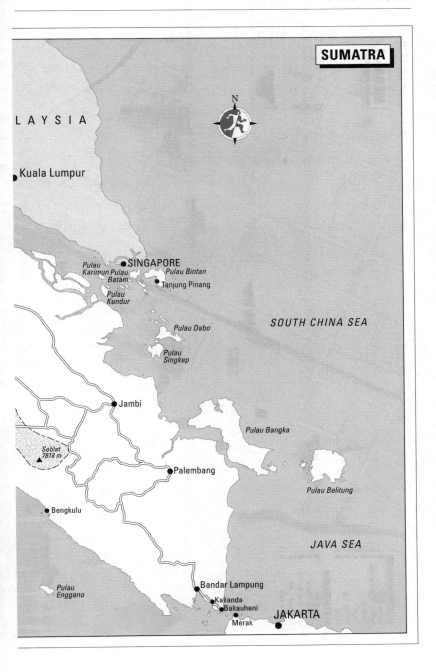

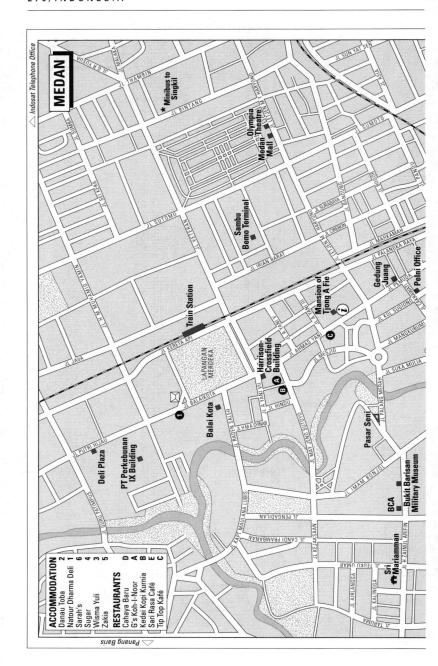

△ Indosat Telephone Office

MEDAN

★ Minibus to Singkil

JL BINTANG

Olympia
Medan Theatre
Mall

Sambu
Bemo Terminal

Train Station

Mansion of
Tiong A Fie

Gedung
Juang

Pelni Office

Harrison-
Crossfield
Building

LAPANGAN
MERDEKA

Balai Kota

Deli Plaza

PT Perkebunan
IX Building

Pasar Seni

Bukit Barisan
Military Museum

BCA

Sri
Mariamman

ACCOMMODATION
Danau Toba   2
Natour Dharma Deli 1
Sarah's   6
Sugar   4
Wisma Yuli   3
Zakia   5

RESTAURANTS
Cahaya Baru   D
G's Koh-I-Noor   A
Kedai Kopi Kurnia B
Sari Rasa Café   E
Tip Top Kafé   C

▽ Penang Baris

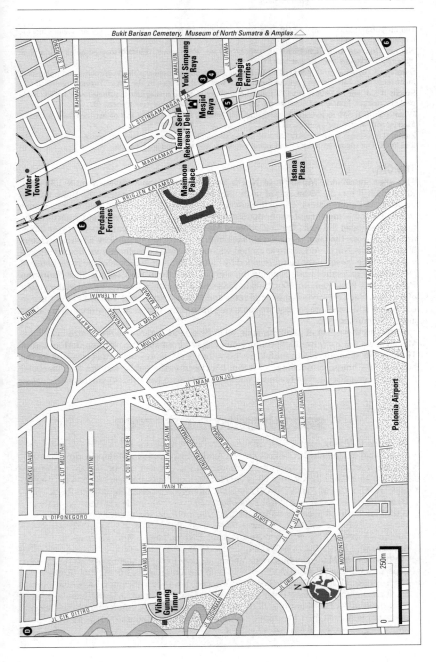

Bukit Barisan Cemetery, Museum of North Sumatra & Amplas

JL SORISNO
JL RAHMADSYAH
JL PURI
JL AMALUN
Yuki Simpang Raya
JL UTAMA
Bahagia Ferries
JL SISINGAMANGARAJA
Mesjid Raya
Taman Seri Rekreasi Deli
JL MAHKAMAH
Water Tower
Istana Plaza
JL BRIGJEN KATAMSO
Maimoon Palace
Perdana Ferries
JL PADANG GOLF
JL TERATAI
JL MAWAR
JL KENANGA
JL LETJEN SUPRAPTO
JL MELATI
JL ALMIN
JL MULTATULI
JL IMAM BONJOL
JL K H A DAHLAN
JL AMIR HAMZAH
JL R H JUANDA
Polonia Airport
JL TENGKU DAUD
JL CUT MEUTIAH
JL R A KARTINI
JL HAJI AGUS SALIM
JL CUT NYAK DIEN
JL LETJEN JENDERAL SUDIRMAN
JL H A TARMIZI
JL RIVAI
JL DIPONEGORO
JL HANG TUAH
JL SURYO
JL R H JUANDA
JL MONGINSIDI
Vihara Gunung Timur
JL SYODIRMAN
JL URIP
JL CIK DITIRO
N
0   250m

Danau Toba, Jl Imam Bonjol 17 (☎061/557000). The liveliest of the luxury hotels, whose facilities include a pool, a pub and a disco. ④.

Natour Dharma Deli, Jl Balai Kota 2 (☎061/547744). Prestigious, centrally located hotel with a pool, where all 180 rooms have air-con and TV. ④.

Sarah's, Jl Pertama 10/4 (☎061/743783). Decent, quiet budget option with clean rooms and good food, inconveniently located in the south of the city, just west of Jl SM Raja by the large "Toyota" signboard. ③.

Sugar, Jl SM Raja 59 (☎061/743507). Small hotel under German management aiming to corner the backpackers' market. Rooms and facilities are very basic, but the bar serves cheap beer. ③.

Wisma Yuli, Jl SM Raja, Gang Pagaruyung 79b (☎061/719704). One of the oldest travellers' places in Medan, with dorms and doubles. ③.

Zakia, Jl Sipisopiso 10–12 (☎061/722413). Unexceptional but hugely popular guesthouse with very persistent touts. The rooms are pretty good value, but noisy, and the beds are hard. ③.

The City

The large, informative **Museum of North Sumatra** (Tues–Sun 8.30am–noon & 1.30–5pm; Rp3500), at Jl Joni 51, 500m east of Jalan SM Raja on the southern side of the Bukit Barisan cemetery, tells the history of North Sumatra, and includes a couple of Arabic gravestones from 8AD and some ancient stone Buddhist sculptures. Eight hundred metres north of the museum on Jalan SM Raja, the black-domed **Mesjid Raya** (9am–5pm, except prayer times; donation) is one the most recognizable buildings in Sumatra. Designed by a Dutch architect in 1906, it has North African-style arched windows, blue-tiled walls and vivid stained-glass windows. The mosque was commissioned by Sultan Makmun Al-Rasyid of the royal house of Deli and, 200m further west, opposite the end of Jalan Mesjid Raya, stands their **Maimoon Palace** (daily 8am–5pm; Rp1000), built in 1888 with yellow walls (the traditional Malay colour of royalty), black crescent-surmounted roofs and Moorish archways. The brother of the current sultan still lives here so only two rooms are open to the public, but they are dull and don't justify the entrance fee.

At the northern end of Jalan Pemuda, Jalan Brig Jend A Yani was the centre of colonial Medan and a few early twentieth-century buildings still remain. The weathered **Mansion of Tjong A Fie** at no. 105 is a beautiful, green-shuttered, two-storey house that was built for the head of the Chinese community in Medan. It's closed to the public, but the dragon-topped gateway is magnificent, with the inner walls featuring some (very faded) portraits of Chinese

---

MOVING ON FROM MEDAN

Belawan Harbour serves both passenger ferries to Malaysia and local Pelni ferries to other parts of Indonesia. Tickets for the ferries to Penang in **Malaysia** (Rp165,000) include free transport between the harbour and the city and can be bought from the Perdana agent at Jl BI Katamso 35 (☎061/545803), or the Bahagia agent, Sukma Tours and Travel, at Jl SM Raja 92 (☎061/706500), one block south of the Mesjid Raya. The **Pelni** ships *KM Sinabung* and *KM Kelud* both call in every four days at Belawan on their way to Jakarta (42hr), and as they don't offer free transport to the city, you'll need to use the yellow "Morina" *angkuta* (mini-vans) #811 or #122 (Rp1500). The Pelni office is at Jl Sugiono 5 (☎061/518899), opposite the blue BNI building (Mon–Fri 9am–3pm, Sat 8–10.30am).

When leaving Medan by **bus**, remember that buses to points north and west of Medan depart from Pinang Baris (DAMRI bus #2 from the tourist office, or angkuta "Koperasi" #64 from Jalan Katamso). Travellers **to Berastagi**, however, will find it much quicker to catch an angkuta to Padang Bulan (#60 from the Istana Plaza on Jalan RH Juanda, or #1 from the tourist office), in the southwestern corner of the city, from where buses leave every ten minutes (2hr). The Amplas terminal (angkuta "Soedarko" #3 or #4 from the tourist office) serves all other destinations.

gods. The fine 1920s **Harrison-Crossfield Building**, at Jalan Brig Jend A Yani's northern end, was the former headquarters of a rubber exporter and is now the home of the British Consulate. Continuing north along Jalan Balai Kota, you reach the grand, dazzlingly white headquarters of **PT Perkebunan IX** (a government-run tobacco company), which was commissioned by Jacob Nienhuys in 1869; it's on narrow Jalan Tembakau Deli, 200m north of the *Natour Dharma Deli* hotel.

In the west of the city, on Jalan H Zainul Arifin, the **Sri Mariamman Temple** is Medan's oldest and most venerated Hindu shrine. It was built in 1884 and is devoted to the goddess Kali. The temple marks the beginning of the Indian quarter, the **Kampung Keling**, the largest of its kind in Indonesia. Curiously, this quarter also houses the largest Chinese temple in Sumatra, the Taoist **Vihara Gunung Timur** (Temple of the Eastern Mountain) which, with its multitude of dragons, wizards, warriors and lotus petals, is tucked away on tiny Jalan Hang Tuah, 500m south of Sri Marriamman.

Eating

Medan has its own style of alfresco **eating**, where a bunch of stall-owners gather in one place, chairs are put out, and a waitress brings a menu listing the food available from each of the stalls. The best of these is the *Taman Rekreasi Seri Deli*, which encircles the small pond to the north of Mesjid Raya. Amongst the many Western-style **bakers** in town are the *French Baker* at Jl Pemuda 24c, and three on Jalan Tuama opposite the northern end of Jalan Cik Ditiro: the *Tahiti*, *Suans* (which does good ice cream) and the *Royal Holland*.

Nightlife

For such a big city, Medan's **nightlife** is surprisingly subdued. *Lyn's*, at Jl Jend A Yani 98, is one of the few karaoke-free joints in town. With a dartboard, a piano and a well-stocked bar, it's the closest you'll come to a British pub in Medan. The *Tavern Pub*, part of the *Danau Toba* complex, offers draught beer and live music. The *Ari Kink Kink Disco*, also in the grounds of the *Hotel Danau Toba*, has an excellent sound system, and is, by quite some distance, the trendiest and most popular in town. You need to buy a drink at the door (beers cost Rp12500), though there is no extra entry charge. The same entrance policy is enforced by the *Haus Musik Nightclub* on Jalan Sutoyo, just 50m east of the bridge, which draws a younger crowd and is also the club of choice for Medan's **gay** community.

Listings

Airline offices Bouraq, Jl Brig Jend Katamso 411 (☎061/552333); Cathay, Tiara Building, Jl Cut Mutiah (☎061/537008); Garuda, Jl Suprapto 2 (☎061/516066; includes city check-in), also at the *Hotel Dharma Deli*, Jl Balai Kota (☎061/516400), and the Tiara building, Jl Cut Mutiah (☎061/538527); Mandala, Jl Brig Jend Katamso 37e (☎061/513309); MAS, *Hotel Danau Toba*, Jl Imam Bonjol 17 (☎061/519333); Merpati, Jl Brig Jend Katamso 71d (☎061/321888); Silk Air, 6th floor, Bank Umum Servitas Building, Jl Imam Bonjol (☎061/537744); SMAC, Jl Imam Bonjol 59 (☎061/564760); Thai, *Hotel Dharma Deli*, Jl Balai Kota (☎061/510541).

Banks and exchange Best rates at BCA, corner of Jl Pangeran Diponegoro/ H Zainul Arifin (10am to noon).

Consulates Australia, Jl Kartini 32 (☎061/557810); Denmark, Jl Hang Jebat 2 (☎061/323020); Germany, Jl Karim MS (☎061/537108); Japan, Jl Suryo 12 (☎061/510033); Malaysia, Jl Pangeran Diponegoro 11 (☎061/25315); Netherlands, Jl A Rivai 22 (☎061/519025); UK, Jl Brig Jend A Yani 2 (☎061/518699).

Hospital Dewi Maya Hospital, Jl Surakarta 2 (☎061/519291).

Internet access At Indonet, Jl Brig Jend Katamso 32l (Rp10,000 per hour); the faster *Novonet Café*, on the third floor of the Hong Kong Plaza (9am–midnight); Infosinet, Jl Brig Jend Katamso 45J, on the corner opposite the palace.

Poste restante At counter 11 in the GPO on Jl Balai Kota (Mon–Fri 7.30am–8pm, Sat 7.30am–3pm).

Telephone services Overseas calls from Indosat (7am–midnight), on Jl Jati at the intersection with Jl Thamrin (Rp500 by becak from the GPO). The *Tip Top Kafé*, *Wisma Yuli* and the *Losmen Irama* all have Home Country Direct telephones.

Bukit Lawang

Tucked away on the easternmost fringes of the Bukit Barisan range, 78km north of Medan, the **Orang-Utan Rehabilitation Centre** at **BUKIT LAWANG** is one of the most enjoyable places in North Sumatra and has become a major tourist attraction. The setting for the village, on the eastern banks of the Sungai Bohorok, opposite the forest-clad slopes of Gunung Leuser, is idyllic. The village also contains some of the most charming and inexpensive losmen in Sumatra, with balconies overlooking the river and macaques on the roof looking for food.

Practicalities

Bukit Lawang village is little more than a kilometre-long, hotel-lined path running along the eastern side of Sungai Bohorok; it charges a one-off Rp1000 entrance fee. **Buses** from Medan's Pinang Baris terminal and Berastagi (daily tourist bus; 5hr) stop at the southern end of the path in a square dominated by souvenir stalls, a wartel (7am–7pm) and an uninformative **tourist office** (Mon–Sat 7am–2pm). There is no bank, but the travel agencies all change money.

You'll need a **permit** to watch the feeding sessions at the rehab centre, costing Rp4500 per day and available from the **PHPA Permit Office** (daily 7am–5pm) that overlooks the square to the east. Separate trekking permits (Rp4000 per day) are also available here. The permit office is part of the excellent **WWF Bohorok Visitor Centre** (daily 8am–3pm), which is packed with information about the park and shows a documentary about the Rehabilitation Centre (Mon, Wed & Fri at 8pm).

ACCOMMODATION AND EATING

Most of the larger **hotels** lie at the southern end of the path near the bus stop, whilst the **losmen** line the path up to the crossing by the Rehabilitation Centre. Most places have attached restaurants.

Anggrek Leuser (☎061/545559). Large, quiet hotel on the western side of the Bohorok with some good-value rooms. The restaurant is recommended. ①.

Ariko Inn Set in a lovely forest clearing a 30min walk north from the bus stop, the *Ariko's* 24 bungalows are clean and pleasant, the restaurant serves hearty meals, and there's a good atmosphere. Remember to bring a torch if you head out at night. ①.

Bukit Lawang Indah (☎061/575219). Large hotel built on similar lines to the neighbouring *Leuser Sibayak*, with nicer rooms but less friendly staff. ①.

Eden Inn (☎061/575341). One of the best-value places in Bukit Lawang, a five-minute walk north of the bus station. The rooms are spacious and clean and have pleasant balconies overlooking the river, and the food is excellent. ①.

Farina 53 Impressive guesthouse up on the slopes away from the river. The rooms are good value, though the disco (Wed & Sat 10pm) can be noisy. ①.

Jungle Inn, about 100m down from the canoe crossing. Popular losmen with some of the most spacious and comfortable rooms in this price range; serves good curries and cakes too. ①.

Leuser Sibayak. Large, attractive and long-established wisma situated at the bend of Sungai Bohorok opposite the bus station. Prices start at less than US$1 in the low season for a big en-suite double, and the new luxury rooms have TV. ①.

The Orang-Utan Rehabilitation Centre

The **Bukit Lawang Orang-Utan Rehabilitation Centre** was founded in 1973 by two Swiss women, Monica Borner and Regina Frey, with the aim of returning captive and orphaned orang-utans into the wild. The wild orang-utan population had been pushed to the verge of extinction by the destruction of their natural habitat, and the apes themselves had become extremely popular as pets, fetching up to US$40,000. Here, apes who have spent most of their lives in captivity are retaught the art of tree climbing and nest building before being freed into the nearby forest.

Though the Rehabilitation Centre is normally closed to the public, visitors are allowed to watch the twice-daily (8am & 3pm), hour-long **feeding sessions** that take place on the hill behind the centre. All visitors must have a permit from the PHPA office (see opposite). The centre is reached by a small pulley-powered canoe that begins operating approximately thirty minutes before feeding begins. All being well, you should see at least one orang-utan during the session, and to witness their gymnastics is to enjoy one of the most memorable experiences in Indonesia.

Trekking

Bukit Lawang is the most popular base for organizing **treks** into the Gunung Leuser national park (see p.287). The park around Bukit Lawang is actually a little over-trekked, and most serious walkers now prefer to base themselves in Ketambe in southern Aceh (see p.286). But if you only want a short day-trek, a walk in the forest around Bukit Lawang is fine, and your chance of seeing monkeys, gibbons, macaques and, of course, orang-utans is very high. If you do decide to do a **long trek** from Bukit Lawang, the five- to seven-day walk to Ketambe is pleasant and passes through some excellent tracts of primary forest. The three-day hike to Berastagi is also very popular.

You must have a **permit** for every day that you plan to spend in the park. The PHPA office at Bukit Lawang recommends three local **guides**: Pak Nasib, Pak Mahadi and Pak Arifin. Their fees are higher than average, at approximately US$15 including lunch and permit for a one-day trek, but you can be certain that they know the forest well. Most of the other guides charge about Rp30,000 per day. Whoever you decide to hire, they shouldn't feed the orang-utans.

There are a couple of **minor walks** around Bukit Lawang that don't actually cross into the park, so permits and guides are unnecessary. The short, forty-minute walk to the **Gua Kampret**, Black Cave (Rp1000), is the simplest. It begins behind the *Bukit Lawang* cottages, across from the wartel on the north side of the river, and heads west through the rubber plantations, and, though it's easy, you'll need good walking shoes and a torch if you're going to scramble over the rocks and explore the single-chamber cave.

By contrast, the path to the **Panorama Point**, in the hills to the east of Bukit Lawang, is difficult to follow. Most people take the path that begins behind the *Back to Nature Guesthouse*, though this can be tricky. A slightly easier route to follow – though much longer – is the path behind the Poliklinik near the visitor centre. It passes through cocoa and rubber plantations and, if you're successful, ninety minutes after setting out you should be able to gaze upon the valley of Bohorok.

Tubing

Despite the risks involved, at some stage during your stay in Bukit Lawang you might be tempted to have a go at **tubing** – the art of sitting in the inflated inner tube of a tyre as it hurtles downstream, battered by the wild currents of the Bohorok. The tubes can be rented from almost anywhere for about Rp2000 per day, or your losmen may supply them for free. There is a bridge 12km downstream of the village, where you can get out, dry off and catch a bus back. If you're not a strong swimmer, consider tubing on a Sunday, when lifeguards are dotted along the more dangerous stretches of the river around Bukit Lawang.

The Karo Highlands

Covering an area of almost five thousand square kilometres, from the northern tip of Danau Toba to the border of Aceh, the **Karo Highlands** comprise an extremely fertile volcanic plateau at the heart of the Bukit Barisan mountains. The plateau is home to over two hundred farming villages and two main towns: the regional capital, Kabanjahe, and the popular market town and tourist resort of **Berastagi**.

According to local legend, the Karo people were the first of the Batak groups to settle in the highlands of North Sumatra, and, as with all Batak groups, the strongly patrilineal Karo have their own language, customs and rituals, most of which have survived, at least in a modified form, to this day. These include convoluted wedding and funeral ceremonies, both of which can go on for days, and the **reburial ceremony**, held every few years, where deceased relatives are exhumed and their bones are washed with a mixture of water and orange juice.

When the Dutch arrived at the beginning of this century they assumed, mistakenly, that the Karo were cannibals. The now-defunct Karonese tradition of filing teeth, combined with a fondness for chewing betel nut that stained their mouths a deep red, gave the Karo a truly fearsome and bloodthirsty appearance. In fact, the Karo, alone amongst the Batak tribes, abhorred cannibalism, though their traditional **animist religion** was as rich and complex as any of the other Batak faiths. Today, over seventy percent of the Karo are Christian, fifteen percent Muslim and the rest adhere to the traditional Karo religion. Every member of Karonese society is bound by obligations to their clan, of which there are five, and seen as more important than any religious duties.

Berastagi

Lying 1330m above sea level, 70km southwest of Medan and 25km due north of the shores of Toba, **BERASTAGI** is a cold, compact little hill station in the centre of the Karo Highlands. It was founded by the Dutch in the 1920s as a retreat from the sweltering heat of Medan, and has been popular with tourists ever since. The town is set in a gorgeous bucolic landscape bookended by two huge but climbable **volcanoes**, Gunung Sibayak and Gunung Sinabung, and provides a perfect base for **trekking**. It's little more than a one-street town, with nearly all accommodation running north of the bus station on Jalan Veteran.

There are a number of attractions in the town itself, including three markets: the photogenic **general market**, which takes place five times a week (not Wed or Sun) behind the bus station; the daily **fruit market**, which also sells souvenirs, to the west of the roundabout, and the **Sunday market**, which takes place every other week on top of Gundaling Hill and attracts such novelty acts as the teeth-pulling man (Rp200 per tooth) and the snake charmer.

The **post office** (Mon–Thurs 8am–2pm, Fri 8–11am) and **Telkom office** stand together by the war memorial, just off Jalan Veteran on the road that leads to Gundaling Hill. The **tourist office** (daily 8am–7pm) is just over the road; but the losmen are much better sources of advice. The BNI bank at Jl Veteran 53 offers poor rates; to change US dollars, contact Toko Mas Gemilang, the jeweller at no. 139.

ACCOMMODATION

Because of the altitude, thick blankets are vital, and most **losmen** offer hot showers at Rp1000 a time. Nearly all the losmen and hotels have restaurants.

Bukit Kubu, Jl Sempurna 2 (☎0628/91533). The best-looking hotel in Berastagi, built by the Dutch in the 1930s and set in its own golf course. The old part of the hotel, with its polished-wood floors and open fireplaces, is a delight. Book ahead. ⑨.

Ginsata, Jl Veteran 27 (☎0628/91441). Quiet, unfussy hotel overlooking the main roundabout that's good if you want solitude. Rooms are basic but adequate and inexpensive. ①.

Ikut, Jl Gundaling 24 (☎0628/91171). Housed in an old Dutch cottage just to the north of Jl Veteran, this losmen's rooms are a little scruffy, though the draughty dorm beds are cheap. ①.

Losmen Sibayak, Jl Veteran 119 (☎0628/91122). Reasonable standard of rooms and a few added features such as a book exchange, a Pelni ticket office and a pizza restaurant. ①.

Sibayak Multinational Guesthouse, Jl Pendidikan 93 (☎0628/51031). Set in gardens to the north of town on the way to Sibayak. Even the cheapest rooms have terraces and hot showers. ①.

Wisma Sibayak, Jl Udara 1 (☎0628/91104). South of the bus station, this is one of Sumatra's best and longest-established hostels: the walls are smothered with good information, the travellers' comments books are very useful, and the beds are clean and cheap. ①.

The Karo villages

During the Dutch invasion of 1904, most of the larger villages and towns in the Karo Highlands were razed by the Karonese themselves to prevent the Dutch from appropriating them. But there are villages where you can still see the **traditional wooden houses**, built on thick, metre-high stilts and home to eight to ten families. Their most striking feature are the palm-frond gables, woven into intricate patterns and topped by a set of buffalo horns. Inside, there are no partitions, save for the sleeping quarters, and family life is carried out in full view of the neighbours.

The most accessible of the Karo villages is **PECEREN** (Rp1000 entrance fee), just 2km northeast of Berastagi. Coming from the town, take the road to Medan and turn down the lane on your right after the *Rose Garden* hotel. There are six traditional houses here, but although some are in good condition, the village itself is probably the least picturesque in the region.

There are three more villages to the south of Berastagi that, when combined, make a pleasant day-trek from town: it takes about three hours to cover all three. The villages tend to be extremely muddy, and many of the villagers, especially the women, are very shy, so always ask before pointing your camera at them. The first village, **GURUSINGA**, lies about an hour due south of Berastagi. From the southern end of Jalan Veteran, take the road running southwest alongside the *Wisma Sibayak*. After about twenty minutes you'll come to a path signposted "Jl ke Koppas", which heads off through fields dotted with family graves to Gurusinga, home to several huge traditional thatched longhouses. The path continues along the western edge of Gurusinga to the village of **LINGGA TULU**, before passing through a bamboo forest. At the end of the path, turn left and head down the well-signposted road to **LINGGA**. Three hundred metres before Lingga village itself, is the one-room Karo Lingga Museum (7am–5pm; donation). Lingga has some of the best traditional houses in the area, many of which are over 150 years old. Unfortunately, the village has also become something of a tourist trap: you have to pay Rp1000 just to enter and guides have to accompany you into the houses (Rp500). Once you've finished wandering around the village, head back to the main road and catch a **minibus** to Kabanjahe (last bus 5pm; Rp250), from where you can catch a bemo back to Berastagi (last bus 7pm; Rp500).

Volcanoes around Berastagi

There are two active **volcanoes** more than 2000m high in the immediate vicinity around Berastagi. **Sibayak**, to the north of town, is possibly the most accessible volcano in the whole of Indonesia, and takes just four hours to climb up and down, while the hike up **Sinabung**, to the southwest of town, is longer and tougher. The lists of missing trekkers plastered all around Berastagi prove that these climbs are not as straightforward as they seem. The tourist office urges climbers always to take a guide, whom you can hire from them or from your losmen, though for Sibayak a guide is unnecessary providing you're climbing with someone. Before departing, pick up one of the *Wisma Sibayak*'s free **maps**, and read their information books too. For both volcanoes, set off early in the morning, and take bananas and chocolate for energy, and warm clothing.

GUNUNG SIBAYAK

The path up **Sibayak** (2094m) begins fifteen minutes' walk beyond the *Sibayak Multinational Guest House* at the northern end of town. A wide, muddy track branches off from the road and up the mountain; having registered at the bottom and donated Rp500, follow it for over ninety minutes until you come to a set of concrete steps heading straight up to the summit on your left. At the top are a number of sulphuric fissures and an attractive turquoise lake. The most difficult part about this trek is trying to find the path back down. Having reached the rim of the crater, walk around the path in an anticlockwise direction until the stone hut in the crater stands between you and the lake. From this point scramble up and over the top of the crater and with any luck you should see the first few broken steps of the path down. The steps are in a terrible condition, but the path that continues through the forest to the Sibayak Geothermal plant at the bottom is clear enough. Behind the plant are some hot springs (Rp1500), where you can soak your tired calf muscles. From the spring you can catch a bemo back to Berastagi (Rp1000).

GUNUNG SINABUNG

At 2452m, **Gunung Sinabung** is only slightly higher than Sibayak, but the ascent takes at least three hours and is a lot harder. A guide is recommended for this trek, as the trail is difficult to follow. The path begins by the side of a restaurant to the north of tiny Danau Kawar, and continues through cabbage fields for approximately an hour, before entering fairly thick jungle. The walk becomes relentlessly tough soon after; having left the jungle you soon find yourself scrambling up some steep and treacherous rocky gullies. All being well, a couple of hours later you'll be standing on the edge of a cliff looking down into Sinabung's two craters.

Danau Toba

Lying right in the middle of the province, jewel-like **Danau Toba** is Southeast Asia's largest freshwater lake, and (at 525m) possibly the world's deepest too. It was formed about eighty thousand years ago by a colossal volcanic eruption: the caldera which was created eventually buckled under the pressure and collapsed in on itself, the high-sided basin that remained filling with water to form the lake. A second, smaller volcanic eruption, 50,000 years after the first, created an island the size of Singapore in the middle of the lake. This island, **Samosir**, is the cultural and spiritual heartland of the **Toba Batak** and the favoured destination for foreign travellers. Ferries leave regularly from **Parapat** – the largest and most convenient gateway for Samosir – and other lakeside towns to the tiny east-coast peninsula of **Tuk Tuk** and neighbouring **Ambarita**, the most popular resorts on Samosir. The **resorts**, with their bookshops, bars and magic mushroom omelettes (illegal but ubiquitous), make Danau Toba the perfect spot to chill out after the rigours of travel in Sumatra. From these resorts you can go trekking in the deforested hills in the centre of Samosir, or cycle around the coastline, calling in at the tiny Batak villages with their flamboyant tombs and distinctive concave-roofed houses.

Getting there

Most tourists catch a **ferry** from the Tigaraja Harbour in the resort of **Parapat** (see opposite), with hourly ferries during the day to Tuk Tuk (Rp1500) and Ambarita (Rp1000). The

---

MOVING ON FROM DANAU TOBA

Most travel agents in Tuk Tuk can sell through-tickets to your next destination, with the ferry crossing to Parapat included in the price. Ferries leave every hour from Ambarita and Tuk Tuk to Parapat. The first bus to Pangururan from Tomok (via the Tuk Tuk turn-off and Ambarita) leaves Tomok at 8am. From Pangururan buses leave every hour up to 2pm for Sidikalang, two hours away.

The trip from Toba **to Berastagi** involves two bus changes and takes four to six hours from Parapat. Firstly, you'll have to catch a bus to Pematangsiantar from Parapat (1hr; Rp1000), and from there a bus to Kabanjahe (3hr; Rp2000) and then a bemo to Berastagi (15min; Rp500). An alternative is to catch the daily tourist bus (4 hr; Rp25,000), which takes in a couple of sights en route.

The first bus to Pangururan from Tomok (via the Tuk Tuk turn-off and Ambarita) leaves Tomok at 8am. From Pangururan buses leave every hour up to 2pm for Sidikalang, two hours away.

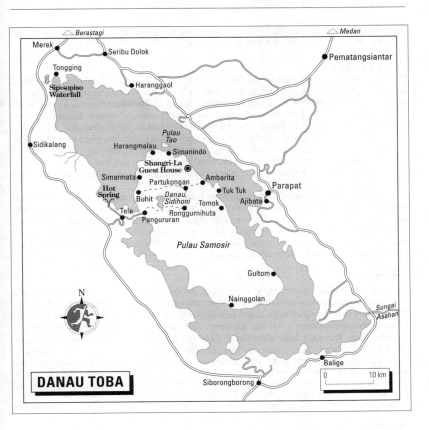

DANAU TOBA

market town of **Haranggaol**, 40km north of Parapat, has infrequent ferries to Ambarita and Simanindo, while **Tongging** has just one to Tuk Tuk, via Ambarita. You can stay in Tongging at *Wisma Sibayak Guesthouse* (①), but check that it's open before you arrive by contacting the *Losmen Sibayak* in Berastagi (☎0628/91122), which is run by the same family. You can also get to Samosir by **bus**: there are services from Sidikalang to Pangururan (2hr), useful if you're coming from the west coast of Aceh.

Parapat

Situated at the point where the Trans-Sumatran Highway touches the eastern shore of Toba, **PARAPAT** is a town split in two. There's the rather tawdry **resort**, crammed with hotels, restaurants, karaoke bars and souvenir shops and, set on the hills away from the lake, the area where you'll find the bus station, bank and telephone office. Buses arriving in Parapat drive through the resort to the ferry terminal before heading back to the bus station.

Nearly all the hotels in Parapat are geared towards Asian tourists rather than Westerners, who tend to head straight for the resorts on Samosir instead. Before leaving though, change money at **Bank BNI** on Jalan Sisingamangaraja, and make any necessary international calls from the **Telkom office**, on the back road between the bus station and the quay – both much better value than in the resorts. The best budget **accommodation** is the clean and welcoming *Charley's*, right by the ferry terminal at Jl Pekan Tiga Raja 7 (☎0625/41277; ②).

Pulau Samosir

Pulau Samosir is the spiritual heartland of the Toba Batak people, and one of the most fascinating, pleasant and laid-back holiday resorts in Indonesia. Most travellers stay on the touristy eastern shores of Toba, where there's a string of enjoyable resorts, from **Tomok** in the south, to **Tuk Tuk**, **Ambarita** and the island's cultural centre, **Simanindo**, on Samosir's northern shore. Despite the vast number of hotels and restaurants, the tourist infrastructure on Samosir is actually fairly poor and you can only change money and make international calls at private places charging ridiculous fees. The only place with an **Internet** connection, the *Tabo Guesthouse*, charges Rp100,000 per hour. It's a great place for shopping though, with dozens of places selling Batak woodcarvings, weavings and other souvenirs.

In general, the **accommodation** on Samosir is excellent value, and it can be even better if you're good at bargaining, especially in the low season. Choose your accommodation carefully, as in most cases the hotel owner will insist that you eat in their restaurant every evening. Public **buses** run throughout the day from Pangururan to Tomok (5.30am–5.30pm) and vice versa (8am–9pm), a ninety-minute journey (Rp2000) round the north coast via Ambarita and Simanindo. None of the buses drive through Tuk Tuk.

TUK TUK

Over thirty losmen and hotels, numerous restaurants, bars, bookshops, travel agents and souvenir stalls stand cheek by jowl on the **Tuk Tuk** peninsula. If you plan to stay here, tell the ferryman which hotel you plan to go to and he'll drop you off on the nearest quay. In general, the cheapest accommodation is on the northern side of the peninsula. For entertainment, *Brando's Blues Bar* has a large selection of CDs, and *Roy's Pub* has its own disco and sometimes hosts live bands. *Saza's*, near *Leo's* and *Brando's*, has a number of decent pool tables.

Bagus Bay Homestay (☎0625/41481). Clean and basic bungalows set in large grounds, near the first ferry port, with a pool table, board games, bar, videos and a twice-weekly Batak dancing display. Variable food. ③.

Carolina's (☎0625/41520). On the southern tip of the peninsula. One of the classiest complexes in the area: huge, Batak-style bungalows, each with a lakeside view and its own little section of beach. ④.

Hariara's One of the most charming spots on Tuk Tuk: four spacious, tasteful en-suite rooms situated in wonderful gardens on the eastern side of the peninsula, near the Gokhon Library. Ask at the *Boruna*, 100m along the road, for the key. ③.

Lek Jon's (☎0625/41578). Budget losmen with 38 plain but pleasant rooms, located to the south of *Hariara's*. The staff are a lot of fun – until, that is, you decide to eat elsewhere. ③.

Linda's Long-established travellers' favourite, to the east of Bagus Bay, with both spartan and more luxurious accommodation. One of the few places that doesn't mind if you eat elsewhere. ③.

Romlan's A few hundred metres north of *Carolina's*. Hugely popular, exquisite little guesthouse whose traditional-style bungalows are probably the best of their kind despite their unfavourable location behind a rubbish dump. ③.

Samosir Cottages (☎0625/41050). At the northern end of Tuk Tuk. Good mid-range accommodation, ranging from basic rooms to luxury bungalows (complete with hot water and a bathtub) overlooking the lake. ②–③.

Tony's Simple, basic but popular losmen on the northwestern side of the peninsula. ③.

AMBARITA

The **Ambarita resort** actually lies 2km north of Ambarita town. Unfortunately, boats have stopped calling at the resort, and now terminate in the town harbour before returning back to Parapat. Buses heading north often call in at the harbour to see if there's a ferry arriving, though you may have to wait a while for one. You could also try booking your accommodation in advance, as many hotels lay on a free transfer service from the harbour to the hotel.

Barbara's (☎0625/41230). The most popular hotel in Ambarita, thanks to its excellent and well-deserved reputation for friendly service and comfortable rooms. ③.

Kings I and II (☎0625/41421). Formerly known as *Gordon's*, *Kings I* and *II* are a long-established and popular pair of inexpensive homestays. *Kings II* has some smart Batak bungalows (with hot showers), and is a more upmarket version of the busier, budget-orientated *Kings I*, a fairly nondescript place redeemed by its restaurant which serves some great vegetarian dishes. ③.

Shangri-La. Lying an awkward 6km to the north of the main Ambarita resort, this excellent homestay is a perfect hideaway from the Tuk Tuk hordes. The rooms are smart and comfortable, the restaurant serves large portions, and the owner is very helpful. ②.

Thyesza (☎0625/41443). One of a string of fairly similar-looking places, with simple neo-Batak bungalows and pricier rooms in the main building that come with hot water. ③.

AROUND THE ISLAND

TOMOK, 2km south of Tuk Tuk, is the most southerly of the resorts on the east coast and a good place to begin a tour of this side of the island. A chain of stalls leads all the way up the hill to the early nineteenth-century stone **sarcophagus of Raja Sidabutar**, the chief of the first tribe to migrate to the island. The coffin has a Singa face – a part-elephant, part-buffalo creature of Toban legend – carved into one end, and a small stone effigy of the king's wife on top of the lid. Halfway up the hill on the right is the small **Museum of King Soribunto Sidabutar** (Mon–Sat 9am–5pm; Rp500), with a collection of tribal artefacts, stuffed animals and fading photographs.

In **AMBARITA** itself there is a curious collection of stone chairs (dawn to dusk; Rp1000), one of which is mysteriously occupied by a stone statue. Most villagers will tell you that these chairs acted as the local law courts two hundred years ago, where defendants were tried and the guilty executed. Others say that the chairs are actually less than fifty years old.

SIMANINDO lies at the northern end of the island, 15km beyond the town of Ambarita and 9km beyond the *Shangri-La Hotel*. The **Simanindo Museum** (daily 12.30–5pm; Rp1000) is housed in the former house of Raja Simalungun, the last Batak king, who was assassinated in 1946 for colluding with the Dutch and has some mildly diverting spears and magical charms. The large *adat* houses in the **traditional village**, through the stone archway, are unexceptional save for their thatched roofs – a rarity on Samosir. The museum and village also hold traditional Batak dancing performances every morning (10.30–11.10am at the museum, 11.45am–12.30pm in the village), though the performances at the **Gokasi cultural centre** (10–11am & 11.15am–12.15pm; Rp3000), 1.5km further along the highway, are said to be better.

Continuing round to the western side of the island, **Simarmata**, halfway between Simanindo and Pangururan, is one of the best-preserved Batak villages on Samosir, though sadly all of the houses have lost their thatched roofs. There's little to see in **PANGURURAN** itself, though there's a **hot spring** (Rp1500) across the bridge in the village of **Tele**.

TREKKING ACROSS SAMOSIR

The hills in the centre of Samosir tower 700m above the lake and, on a clear day, afford arresting views. At the heart of the island is a large plateau and pond-sized Danau Sidihoni. It is possible, just, to walk from one side of the island to the other in one day – it takes ten hours or more – but a stopover in one of the villages on the plateau is usually necessary, so take overnight gear and a torch.

Many trekkers start by catching the first bus to Pangururan (8am from Tomok), arriving at about 9.30am. This account, however, begins in Ambarita on the eastern shore, on the uphill path that starts to the north of the Ambarita petrol station. It's a stiff climb, but after two hours you should find yourself in the tiny hilltop village of **Partukongan** – aka Dolok or "summit" – the highest point on Samosir. There are two hostels here, *John's* and *Jenny's*, in fierce competition not only with each other, but also with the three losmen in the next village on the trail, **Ronggurnihuta**. The villagers can be a bit vague when giving directions, so take care and check frequently with passers-by. All being well, you'll find Ronggurnihuta is a three- or four-hour walk away, with **Panguruan** three to fours hours further on at the end of a tortuously long downhill track (18km) that passes **Danau Sidihoni** on the way. Arrive in Pangururan before 5pm and you should be in time to catch the last bus back to the eastern shore; otherwise, you'll have to stay in one of Pangururan's rather soulless hostels, such as the *Wartel Wisata* (✆0626/20558; ②) at Jl Dr TB Simatupang 42, by the bus stop.

Pulau Nias

Though the journey is long and arduous, and involves passing through the unlovely town of **Sibolga**, most visitors agree that any effort expended to get to Nias is worth it. An island the size of Bali, with a rich tribal culture, wonderful beaches and some of the best surfing in the country, **PULAU NIAS** is a microcosm of almost everything that's exciting about Indonesia. The north of Nias is largely swampland and unappealing save for the capital, **Gunung Sitoli**. The south, however, plays host to a number of fascinating hilltop villages, such as Orahili, Bawomataluo and the spiritual heartland of Gomo, where the last few remnants of Nias's famed megalithic culture survive. The south also has the best and most popular beaches, such as the surfer's paradise at **Lagundri Bay**. The island is **malarial**, and chloroquine-resistant strains have been reported. Take the correct prophylactics and bring repellent and a mosquito net.

Lying 125km southwest of Sibolga, the island's reputation as a land of malarial swamps and bloodthirsty natives succeeded in keeping visitors at bay for centuries, leading to the development of a culture free from the influences of India, Arabia, Europe and, indeed, the rest of Indonesia. The 600,000 **Niasans** speak a distinct language, one that has more in common with Polynesian than any Indonesian tongue, and their sculptures resemble closely those of the Nagas in the eastern Himalayas. Their traditional class system depended on slaves – usually people captured from nearby villages in raids – which eventually attracted slave-traders from as far afield as Europe, including the Dutch, who arrived in 1665 and remained on the island for most of the next 250 years. During this time, nearly all of the Nihas' animistic totems and megaliths were either destroyed or shipped to Europe. Today, over 95 percent of Nias is, nominally at least, Christian, and the last recorded instance of headhunting, an essential component of Niha animism, occurred way back in 1935.

Approaching Pulau Nias: Sibolga

SIBOLGA is the main port for ferries to Gunung Sitoli on Nias. All **buses** and bemos call in at the terminus on Jalan Sisingamangaraja, at the back of the town away from the coast. The port for **ferries to Nias** – as well as the occasional Pelni boat from Padang – is about 1.5km south of here at the end of Jalan Horas. Three companies run ferries to Gunung Sitoli: Jambo Jet (KM Cucit/Poncan Moale; and Sumber Rezeki. Tickets for Jambo Jet are available from the counter by the harbour gate (✆0631/22370); tickets for the two slow ferries should be bought from PT Simeulue at Jl S Bustami Alamsyah 9 (✆0631/21497), near the Bank BNI. The **Pelni agent**, PT Sarana Bandar Nasional, is near the market by the bus terminus at Jl Patuan Anggi 39 (✆0631/22291) and sells tickets for the fortnightly *KM Kambuna* and *KM Lambelu*; see "Getting Around" pp.192–193 and "Travel Details", p.442. At the moment, Gunung Sitoli is the only place on Nias that passenger boats stop at, though there are hopes that the direct ferry from Sibolga to Teluk Dalam in southern Nias will begin sailing again soon.

If you're going to Nias, **change money** in Sibolga at the BNI bank on Jl Parman 3 (Mon–Fri 8am–4.15pm). Budget travellers should head to one of the Chinese-run **hotels**, such as the friendly and efficient *Pasar Baru*, on the junction of Jalan Raja Djunjungan and Jalan Imam Bonjol (②) or the *Indah Sari* at Jl Jend A Yani 29 (✆0631/21208; ②), which is a tad scruffier but still acceptable. The best **restaurants** are *Hebat Baru* at Imam Bonjol 79, and the slightly cheaper *Restoran Restu* opposite at no. 58c; both serve excellent Chinese food.

Gunung Sitoli

The capital of Nias, **GUNUNG SITOLI** is a fairly charming little seaside town and has the best facilities on Nias. The **Nias Museum** (daily 8.30am–5pm; free), halfway between the town and the harbour, houses the most complete set of Niha antiquities in Indonesia, including leather shields and tunics from the last century.

The town is little more than two streets – Jalan Gomo and Jalan Sirao – running parallel to the shore, and a number of roads running off them. All ferries currently dock at Gunung Sitoli's **harbour**, 2km north of the town; bemos (until 6pm; Rp500) and becak (Rp2000) run to the **bus station** at the southern end of town, from where frequent buses leave for Teluk Dalam (every 30min until 4pm; 4hr), where you can get onward connections to Lagundri. Those who take advantage of SMAC airlines' reasonably priced **flights** from Medan to Gunung Sitoli, arrive at the tiny airstrip to the southeast of town; the fifteen-kilometre jeep ride to the town centre is included in the flight price.

Two of the ferries to Sibolga – the *Poncan Mo'ale* and *KM Cucut* – share a **ticket office** on the main road by the port, while PT Simeulue, Jl Sirao 23, and Jambo Jet, Jl Gomo 41, are right in the centre of town. The **Pelni** office is to the east of Jalan Sirao, one block back from the coast at Jalan Lagundri 38 (☎0639/21846). Nias's only **tourist office** is behind the green square on Jalan Gomo, at Jalan Sukarno 6 (Mon–Thurs 8am–4pm, Fri 8am–noon; ☎0639/21545). The **post office** stands across the green at Jl Hatta 1, next to the **Telkom office**. One block further south, at Jl Imam Bonjol 40, the **Bank BNI** offers poor rates.

The better-value **accommodation** is on the southern side of town, near the bus station and across the river bisecting Gunung Sitoli. These include the *Marja* (☎0639/22812; ①), at Jl Diponegoro 128, and the slightly grimier *Laraga* (☎0639 /21760; ①), at no. 135. Sitoli's most popular **restaurant**, the excellent Padang food specialist *Rumah Makan Nasional*, is at Jl Gomo 87.

Lagundri

The horseshoe bay of Lagundri lies 12km west of Teluk Dalam, the largest town in southern Nias, served by **buses** from Gunung Sitoli. From Teluk Dalam, frequent buses run to **LAGUNDRI** (Rp500), stopping by the small bridge at the Jamborai/Botohili junction, where the Trans-Nias highway starts. (This is also the place to wait for buses out of Lagundri.) Lagundri has been famous among surfers since the 1970s, though it's at neighbouring **Jamborai**, on the western edge of the bay, that the waves actually break. In July and August the waves are over 4m high and travel for up to 150m – fantastic for experienced surfers, but not a good place for beginners. The **accommodation** at Lagundri Bay consists almost entirely of simple wooden beachside bungalows. There are over fifty of them stretching out all along the bay, with a particularly high concentration at Jamborai. Most have electricity now, cost next to nothing (usually Rp1000 per night, or free if you stay for a fortnight or more), though you'll be expected to eat there too. Tales of pickpockets and robbers are numerous.

Bawomataluo

BAWOMATALUO (Sun Hill) is the most impressive of the hilltop villages in south Nias. It's an hour's walk uphill from the turn-off on the Teluk Dalam–Lagundri road; taxis from Lagundri to the turn-off charge Rp1000, and ojek cost Rp2000 (or Rp3000 all the way to Bawomataluo). Bawomataluo has been exposed to tourism for too many years now, and touts are persistent. The old village consists of an east–west road and a wide cul-de-sac that branches off due south from opposite the Chief's House. The stonework, particularly on the tables and chairs outside the Chief's House, is exceptional. These chairs once held the corpses of the recently deceased, who were simply left to decay in the street before being buried. In the centre of the village you'll find the two-metre tall **jumping stone** (*fahombe*), which once would have been topped by sharp sticks and thorns. The custom was for teenage boys to jump over this stone to show their bravery and agility; you can see a picture of a *fahombe* ceremony on the back of a Rp1000 note. This quality of craftsmanship is continued inside the nineteenth-century **Chief's House** (9am–5pm; donation), where the walls are decorated with carvings of lizards, monkeys, and a depiction of an early European ship. A pair of carved royal seats for the chief and his wife share the same wall. Other notable features of the house are the plethora of pig's jaws hanging from the rafters, and the huge hearth at the back of the room.

WALKS TO NEARBY VILLAGES

Bawomataluo can be seen as part of a larger **trek** around the southern hills. Take waterproof clothing, plenty of food and a torch, and aim to reach a main road by mid-afternoon at the latest in order to catch a bus back. Buses from Teluk Dalam to Lagundri along the south coast road cease running at about 4pm, and along the Trans-Nias Highway to Lagundri they stop at about 5pm.

Behind the Chief's House in Bawomataluo, a scenic path leads to **Siwalawa**, one hour away. The village stretches along the path for at least 500m, though the oldest part actually lies at the very end, up some steps to the left of the main path. At the end of this old quarter a path heads downhill and divides: turn right and you eventually arrive at Hilifalago; turn left and you pass through Onoltondo and, twenty minutes further on, the large village of **Hilinawalo**. The old part of the village has some good examples of traditional housing. After Onoltondo the path descends to a large stream and continues for an hour, via Hilinawalo, to **Bawogosali**, a small village with some recent stone carvings lining the path. The village is dominated by the large church, behind which a path leads up to the crest of a hill and along to **Lahuna**. This village lies at an important crossroads: continue past the end of the village and you'll reach, 45 minutes later, Bawomataluo, or turn right, and after a steep descent you arrive at the lovely village of **Hilisimaetano**, which is in an excellent state of preservation, and many of the paving stones have been carved with reliefs of lizards, ships and signs of the zodiac. At the very end of the path, twenty minutes beyond Hilisimaetano, the Trans-Nias Highway thunders by, from where you can catch an ojek back to Lagundri (Rp2500–3000).

Banda Aceh

BANDA ACEH, often just shortened to **BANDA**, is the capital of Aceh, the most staunchly Islamic province of Indonesia. After Independence, the Acehnese, unhappy with the new government's attempts to incorporate them into the North Sumatran province with Medan as the capital, broke away in 1953 and declared themselves part of the Islamic World (Dar Islam). Central government troops quelled the rioting that followed in the cities, though the Acehnese terrorists continued to launch attacks from the countryside. Finally, in 1967, Suharto granted **Aceh** the status of Daerah Istimewa (Special District). This entitled the Acehnese to a certain amount of autonomy over matters of religion, education and *adat* (customary law) – which in Aceh is largely a watered-down version of the Islamic law of the Middle East: steal something in the province, for example, and your hand will be broken, rather than amputated.

As with the rest of Aceh, however, those who are willing to obey the dress code will find Banda a laid-back and pleasant city of impressive white mansions. The most breathtaking sight, though, is the seven coal-black domes and three minarets of **Mesjid Raya Baiturrahman**; ask the guards for permission to go inside. Banda's other major sight is the dull **Aceh Museum** (Tues–Thurs, Sat & Sun 8am–6pm, Fri 8–11am & 2.30–6pm; Rp200) on the eastern banks of Sungai Assyiqi, 300m southeast of the mosque along Jalan Sultan Alauddin Mahmudsyah.

Just 13km west of Banda, **LAMPU'UK BEACH** is a glorious sandy arc that's both a popular day-trip and a pleasant alternative base for travellers, chiefly because of the excellent *Aceh Bungalows* (①) on the beach here. Catch *labi-labi* (bemo) #4 from Jalan Diponegoro and ask the driver to stop at MNS Balee, a small school and council office that's a fifteen-minute walk from the bungalows.

Practicalities

The **bus station** is in the southern part of town on Jalan Teuku Umar. **Labi-labi** (Rp350) – the local name for a bemo – leave from outside the station to the Central Market, south of the river by the Mesjid Raya Baiturrahman. The **tourist office** is at Jl Chik Kuta Karang 3 (Mon–Thurs 7.30am–2pm, Fri 7.30am–noon, Sat 8am–2pm; ☎0651/23692). The Garuda airline office is in the *Sultan Hotel* (☎0651/31811) and the Pelangi agent is Indomatha Wisata Tours and Travel, Jl Panglima Polem 3 (☎0651/23706). There are **flights** to Kuala Lumpur and Medan from **Kreung Raya**, 16km to the east of town (Rp25,000 by taxi).

The **post office** on Jalan Nyak Arief (Mon–Thurs & Sat 8am–7pm, Fri 8–11am & 2–7pm) also has email and poste restante counters. **Bank BCA**, Jalan Panglima Polem (10am–noon only), has rates comparable to the BCA in Medan, though it accepts Malaysian and US dollar travellers' cheques only.

The city has little in the way of budget **accommodation**, with many of the cheapest places refusing to take foreigners. A small knot of hotels lies to the north of the river along Jalan Khairil Anwar, where most visitors stay. The prettiest budget losmen here is *Aceh Barat*, at no. 16 (☎0651/23250; ③), comprising basic rooms with shared bathrooms. At no. 51, *Palembang* (☎0651/22044; ③) is one of the more bizarre of budget places, its walls plastered with Disney characters and a monkey chained up in the back yard. The small, cramped *Ujong Kalak*, Jl St Johan 7 (☎0651/31146; ②), has the cheapest rooms in town, tucked down an alley to the west of Jalan TP Aceh; some come with bath and fan. *Sri Budaya*, Jl Prof A Majid Ibrahim-III 25e (☎0651/21751; ③), is a welcoming losmen housing twenty simple fan-cooled rooms. At the western end of Jalan Khairil Anwar is Banda's excellent **night market**.

Pulau Weh

A mountainous outcrop of dark green rising sharply from the azure waters of the Indian Ocean north of Banda Aceh, **Pulau Weh** is yet another gorgeous Indonesian paradise, with excellent diving and snorkelling possibilities and white sandy beaches. Weh's airport has been closed since 1985, though currently the runway is being extended and it is hoped that flights to the island should begin soon. Until they do, the twice-daily **ferry** crossing from Kreung Raya harbour, 35km west of Banda Aceh, is the only connection from the mainland (2hr 30min; Rp4250). Labi-labi from Banda Aceh to Kreung Raya leave regularly during the morning from outside the Pasar Ikan (fish market), and also from Jalan Diponegoro (Rp1500). The ferries dock on Weh at **Balohan**, on the southeastern corner of the island, from where it's a fifteen-minute bemo ride to Sabang (Rp1500).

Sabang

SABANG is a compact and pretty little town with plenty of quaint colonial architecture. On the main street, Jalan Perdagangan, there's a small **post office**, a Telkom office next door (with Home Dialling Direct phones), a BRI bank and exchange, four losmen, a hotel and some restaurants. There's also Weh's only **diving shop**, the Stingray Dive Centre, Jl Teuku Umar 3 (☎0652/21265), which does diving courses and an underwater photography workshop (US$100), sells secondhand books and rents **motorbikes** (Rp20,000 per day).

Of the **losmen**, the *Irma* (☎0652/21148; ②) and *Pulau Jaya* (☎0652/21344; ②), at nos. 3 and 17 on Jalan Teuku Umar, are the two most popular choices with travellers, though they are both basic and noisy. The *Sabang Marauke* (☎0652/21928; ②), on Jalan Seulawah, a side road opposite the *Irma*, is cheaper, friendlier and quieter. All lie within 200m of the bus stop in Sabang, opposite the *Irma*. The *Dynasty*, Jl Perdagangan 54, serves the best **food** – try their *cumi goreng* (fried squid) for Rp6500. *Harry's*, the café below the *Irma*, is the main travellers' café in Sabang and serves excellent pancakes.

Weh resorts

For most visitors, Sabang is just a temporary stop on the way to the **beaches** on Weh's north-western promontory. The most popular of these is **IBIOH**, 45 minutes by bemo from Sabang; the service runs three times a day (10am, 1pm & 6pm, returning at 6am, noon & 4pm). Ibioh is a tiny fishing village, at the end of which lies the tourist resort (Rp1000 one-off entry fee), actually little more than a collection of simple tourist bungalows and restaurants stretched along a forested hillside running down to the shore. The main attraction here is the excellent **snorkelling** – gear can be rented from Stingray's office in Ibioh (Rp2000–5000). The coral starts just a few metres from Ibioh beach and continues all the way to Pulau Rubiah, 200m away, a tiny islet that's the focus of a large nature reserve. **Accommodation** in Ibioh is mainly in simple A-frame bungalows and, at the moment, guests have to wash at the well in the middle of the resort. There are over fifty bungalows in the resort now, though from June to August it can still be very difficult finding a room. Try to get one with a mosquito net, as malaria is a problem on Weh. Most of the bungalows are pretty similar, though *Patimah's* (①) and *Oong's* (①) are recommended.

The island features two other beaches with accommodation. **GAPANG** is an attractive, horseshoe-shaped beach, 2km south of Ibioh, with its own family of five hawksbill turtles. There is a small selection of bungalows here, with prices similar to those at Ibioh. In the off season most of them close down, and those that stay open often turn their electricity off. The best (②) are owned by the *Barracuda Restaurant*.

The third beach, **LHONG ANGEN**, lies on the western side of the island. It's one of the best, although for six months of the year it completely disappears – swept away by the sea in November, returning again in May. The *Flamboyan Bungalows* (①) at the northern end of the beach provide the best-value accommodation on the island, and *Manta Ray Bungalows* (①), 500m away, offer healthy competition: contact the *Losmen Irma* in Sabang if you wish to stay here.

Kutacane

Coming from the south, the first major town on the highland road is **KUTACANE**, a typical Acehnese one-street town, that's mainly used as a place to change buses. There are **bus** services to and from Berastagi, Blangkejeren, Ketambe and Takengon. If you get stuck, you can **stay** at *Wisma Marron* (②) at Jl Jend A Yani II 15–17, or the nearby travellers' favourite *Rindu Alam*, Jl Jend A Yani 7 (☎0629/21289; ②), which is a bit grimy.

Ketambe

KETAMBE (aka Gurah) is little more than six hotels and a sprinkling of houses at the very edge of the Gunung Leuser national park, a ninety-minute bus ride north of Kutacane. There's nothing to do here except plan a trek in the park (see opposite), or recover from one. At the northern end of Ketambe is a small kiosk, where you can pick up a **permit** (Rp2000) for the park. All the travel agencies in Ketambe organize **rafting** trips down Sungai Alas, lasting between one and five days, averaging about US$100 per day including food and permit. It's a very good idea to inspect your raft before you go to make sure it's riverworthy; life jackets are a must too.

Two of Ketambe's **homestays**, the *PHPA Guest House* (②) and the *Gurah Bungalows* (⑤), are actually inside the park beyond the entrance gates. The *Gurah Bungalows* have the best accommodation, with spotless doubles. South of the gates, the *Sadar Wisata* (☎0629/21406; ②) offers attractive wooden bungalows on the banks of the Alas; the en-suite bungalows at *Pondok Wisata Ketambe* (☎0629/21289; ①) are similarly charming; and *Pondok Cinta Alam* (①), nearest the park entrance, is older and scruffier but has the cheapest rooms.

The Gunung Leuser national park

Straddling the border between the provinces of Aceh and North Sumatra, the **Gunung Leuser national park**, at over eight thousand square kilometres, is the largest wildlife reserve in Indonesia, with over 300 bird species and 132 different mammals. The park's most famous residents are the sixty or so Sumatran tigers – but you're very unlikely to see them – or the equally elusive and just as endangered Sumatran rhinoceros. You may well, however, see **orang-utans**, as well as Thomas leaf monkeys, white-handed gibbons, black siamang, and rhinoceros- and helmeted **hornbills**.

There are two main **entrance points** into the Gunung Leuser national park: Ketambe (see opposite) and Bukit Lawang (p.274). Ketambe is a good base for longer treks, as the jungle here is more varied and less explored. But Bukit Lawang has superior facilities, is more accessible and offers the greatest chance of spotting wildlife. All visitors to the park must buy a permit, available at the entrance (Rp2000 per day), and be accompanied by a registered **guide** (at least Rp20,000 per day). Choosing the right guide is very important: there are over two hundred licensed guides operating out of Bukit Lawang alone; read the comments books at the hostels in Ketambe and Bukit Lawang, and ask other travellers. In Ketambe, Daniel and Syamsul of the PT Intan Leuser Tour and Travel Agency are recommended. One of the keys to an enjoyable trek is to take as little as possible; tents are usually provided by the guides. It's probably best to avoid the rainy seasons (April, May & Oct–Dec), when some rivers are impassable.

There are a number of established **treks** through the park, one of the most popular being the six-day route between the two entrances, Ketambe and Bukit Lawang. If you just want to make a one-day trail from Ketambe, consider the walk to the nearby **sulphurous springs**, which are popular with the local wildlife. To really experience the park, however, it's much better to spend at least one night out in the jungle. The four-day trek to **Danau Marpunga** (aka Danau Tiga Sagi) runs to a small lake near a flat sulphurous gully, where many animals – including elephants – come to feed.

Blangkejeren

The busy rural town of **BLANGKEJEREN**, 72km from Ketambe, stands at an important crossroads and has connections with both the west and east coasts; **buses** to and from Kutacane run hourly (3hr). Blangkejeren also lies at the heart of a marijuana-growing region; the locals use it in their cooking. As most buses leave Blangkejeren in the morning, you may have to stay overnight: *Rahmat*, Jalan Besar, Gang Tengah 200 (☎0642/21023; ①), 250m south of the bus station, has the best and cheapest accommodation, with huge clean rooms, and *Juli*, Jl Kong Bur 53 (☎0642/21036; ①), is another popular option.

Padang

A bustling port and university town, attractive **PADANG** is an important transport hub and famed throughout Indonesia for its spicy local cuisine, *Makanan Padang* (Padang food). Its climate is equally extreme: hot and humid and with the highest rainfall in Indonesia at 4508mm a year (in the top ten of rainiest inhabited spots in the world). Most tourists pause only briefly here, before aiming for the nearby hill town of Bukittinggi, the Mentawai Islands, the Kerinci-Seblat national park, or more distant Bengkulu. The city's main sight is the very pleasant **Adityawarman Museum** (Tues–Sun 9am–4pm; Rp300), housed in a traditional Minang house and specializing in Minangkabau culture, with textiles, kris and finely worked basketware. For a good local shopping experience, ignore the large new shopping centres and head instead for Pasar Raya in the city centre, a terrific general **market**. There's a **tourist office** at Jl Sudirman 43 (☎0751/34232).

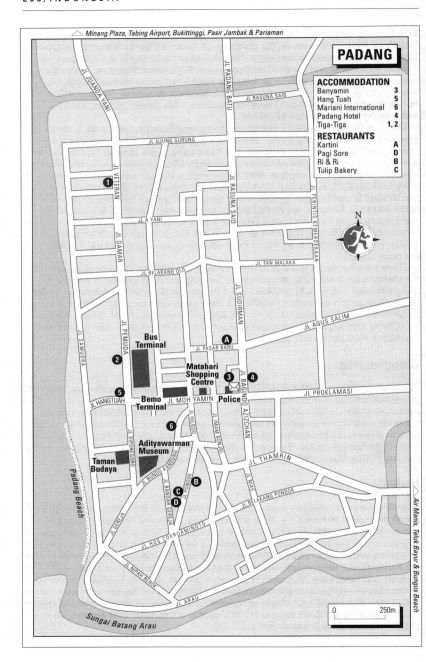

Minang Plaza, Tabing Airport, Bukittinggi, Pasir Jambak & Pariaman

PADANG

ACCOMMODATION

Benyamin	3
Hang Tuah	5
Mariani International	6
Padang Hotel	4
Tiga-Tiga	1, 2

RESTAURANTS

Kartini	A
Pagi Sore	D
Ri & Ri	B
Tulip Bakery	C

Bus Terminal

Matahari Shopping Centre

Bemo Terminal

Police

Adityawarman Museum

Taman Budaya

Padang Beach

Air Manis, Teluk Bayur & Bungus Beach

Sungai Batang Arau

0   250m

Practicalities

Padang is a **visa-free entry point** to Indonesia (see p.190). All domestic and international flights – including those to and from Kuala Lumpur and Johor Bahru – use **Tabing Airport**, 9km north of the city centre, which has exchange counters in international arrivals. For a taxi into town (Rp12,000—15,000), collect the fixed-price ticket from the taxi office and pay the driver at your destination. The alternative is to walk 200m from the terminal and catch bus #14a or #14b (Rp250) from outside the airport gates: those heading to the left go into the city. Small white bemos also stop here and will take you to the bemo terminal in town (Rp500). If you're heading straight up to **Bukittinggi** from the airport, cross the road and hail a long-distance bus going in the opposite direction (every 20min, 6am–7pm; 2hr 30min).

Pelni boats dock at the port of Teluk Bayur, 7km south of town, served by white bemos #432, #433 and #434 to the city centre. The port is on the fortnightly circuit of *KM Lambelu* and *KM Kambuna* (see "Getting around" pp.192–193 and "Travel Details" p.442). The Pelni office is also here, at Jl Tanjung Priok 32 (☎0751/33624).

The **local and long-distance bus terminals** (Rp300 entrance) are side by side on Jalan Pemuda, 200m north of the junction with Jalan Moh Yamin. When it comes to moving on, you'll find most of the ticket offices are here, and as all bus companies operate their own schedule with their own fares, it's worth shopping around. There are daily departures (6am–7pm) to destinations throughout Sumatra, Java, Bali and Nusa Tenggara (see "Travel Details", p.444).

The **bemo terminal** is on Jalan Moh Yamin, in the market area. Local buses (flat fare Rp250) and bemos (Rp500) run from 6am to 10pm. Buses only stop at the designated stops, but you can flag down bemos anywhere.

ACCOMMODATION

With the increasing use of Padang as a gateway into Indonesia, the number of tourist **hotels** is growing. But Bukittinggi (see p.290) is only two and a half hours' drive away on the frequent bus service.

Benyamin, Jl Pasar Baru IV (☎0751/22324). In an alleyway that runs along side *Femina Hotel*, served by buses #14a and #14b. Clean, en-suite fan rooms, but noisy in the early morning. ①.

Hang Tuah, On the corner of Jl Pemuda and Jl Hang Tuah (☎0751/26556). The best and most popular hotel near the bus terminal. Basic but adequate en-suite rooms, plus some air-con. ①.

Mariani International, Jl Bundo Kandung 35 (☎0751/25466). Centrally located, with comfortable en-suite air-con rooms. Motorbike rental is available. ②.

Padang Hotel, Jl Bagindo Azizchan 28 (☎0751/22563). Convenient, recently refurbished bungalows and pleasant atmosphere. Served by buses #14a and #14b. ③.

USEFUL BUS AND BEMO ROUTES IN PADANG

Local **bus routes #14a** and **#14b** complete circular routes around Padang from north of the airport into the city and out again. They both head south into the city past the airport via Jalan Prof Hamka to the Minang Plaza, Jalan S Parman and the Jalan Khatib Sulaiman junction. The #14a then heads along Jalan Khatib Sulaiman towards the city centre. The #14b continues south to Jalan S Parman, Jalan Raden Saleh and Jalan Padang Baru; it then joins #14a and they both head straight into the city down Jalan Rasuna Said, Jalan Sudirman, Jalan Bagindo Azizchan, across the main junction with Jalan Moh Yamin and Jalan Proklamasi, Jalan Thamrin, Jalan Nias, Jalan Belakang Pondok, Jalan HOS Cokroaminoto, the beach entrance, Jalan Gereja, Jalan Diponegoro, the Adityawarman Museum, Jalan Moh Yamin, Jalan Hilgoo, Jalan Thamrin, Jalan Bagindo Azizchan and north out of the city on the route they have come in.

White bemos #416, #419, #420, #422, #423 and #424 run north from Jalan Pemuda out to Minang Plaza and towards the airport.

Tiga-Tiga, Jl Pemuda 31 (☎0751/22633). The older of the two hotels in town with this name is opposite the bus terminal. Airier rooms on the upper floors; the cheapest ones share facilities and have no fan. ①.

EATING

While here, you should try a typical **Padang restaurant**, distinguishable by their window display of dishes. There's no menu: up to a dozen small plates are placed in front of you (see p.196 for details) and you pay for whatever you eat. Generally, the redder the sauce, the more explosive it is to the taste buds: the yellow, creamy dishes are often less aggressive. At the southern end of Jalan Pondok, due south of the market area towards the river, you'll find a small **night market** of sate stalls; another one sets up on Jalan Imam Bonjol, south of the Moh Yamin junction.

Kartini, Jl Pasar Baru 24. The most popular of the many Padang-style restaurants along this street. They are unfazed by tourists and the food is fresh and well cooked.

Matahari Foodcourt, 2nd floor, Matahari Shopping Centre. Air-con, with a wide range of Indonesian options such as soup, gado-gado, sate, *murtabak*, drinks and juices.

Pagi Sore, Jl Pondok 143. A popular and good-value Padang restaurant with plenty of choice, one of the nicest of the many restaurants on this road.

Ri & Ri, Jl Pondok. Pleasant and relaxed, this is both a Padang place (10am–2pm) and a slightly more upmarket restaurant in the evening, offering frog, chicken, squid and goat dishes.

Tulip Bakery, Jl Pondok 139. Stretching back from the road, with high ceilings, this is a cool place to take a rest. Basic fried rice and noodles are on offer as well as bakery items.

LISTINGS

Airline offices Garuda, *Hotel Istana Pangeran*, Jl Veteran 79 (☎0751/58489); Mandala, Jl Pemuda 29a (☎0751/32773); Merpati, Jl Gereja 34 in the grounds of the *Natour Muara Hotel* (☎0751/32010); Pelangi, Jl Gereja 34, in the grounds of the *Natour Muara Hotel* (☎0751/38103); Silk Air, Jl Hyam Wuruk 16 (☎0751/38122).

American Express representatives Pacto Tours and Travel, Jl Tan Malaka 25 (☎0751/37678); red bemos heading north outside the post office on Jl Bagindo Azizchan pass the office. American Express customers can use this office to receive mail and faxes.

Exchange Bank of Central Asia, Jl H Agus Salim 10a; Bank Dagang Negara, Jl Bagindo Azizchan 21; Bank Negara Indonesia, Jl Dobi 1. There are several moneychangers near the bus station: PT Citra Setia Prima, Jl Diponegoro 5 (Mon–Sat 8am–noon & 1–4.30pm); PT Enzet Corindo Perkasa, Jl Pemuda 17c (Mon–Fri 8am–4pm, Sat 8am–2pm).

Hospitals Rumah Sakit Umum Padang, Jl Perentis Kemerdekan (☎0751/25181); Rumah Sakit Selasih, Jl Khatib Sulaiman 72 (☎0751/51405).

Immigration office Jl Khatib Sulaiman (☎0751/55113).

Post office Reasonably efficient poste restante at the GPO, Jl Bagindo Azizchan 7.

Telephone services The most convenient 24hr wartel are at Jl Imam Bonjol 17 and Jl Belakang Tangsi 3, which isn't far from the Matahari Shopping Centre and the bus terminal; it's signed south from Jl Moh Yamin. There's also a 24hr warpostel on the ground floor of the Minang Plaza.

Bukittinggi and the Minang highlands

The gorgeous mountainous landscape, soaring rice terraces and easily accessible traditional culture make the Minang highlands a justly popular stop on any trip through Sumatra. The highlands consist of three large valleys, with **BUKITTINGGI**, a bustling hill town, the administrative and commercial centre of the whole district. The surrounding area holds plenty of attractions, including craft villages, a rafflesia reserve, the beautiful Harau Canyon, and some fine examples of Minang culture. Located to the west of the main highland area, **Danau Maninjau** is rapidly developing as an appealing travellers' destination.

The highlands around Bukittinggi are the cultural heartland of the **Minangkabau** (Minang) people. The Minang are staunchly matrilineal, one of the largest such societies extant, and Muslim. The most visible aspect of their culture is the distinctive architecture of

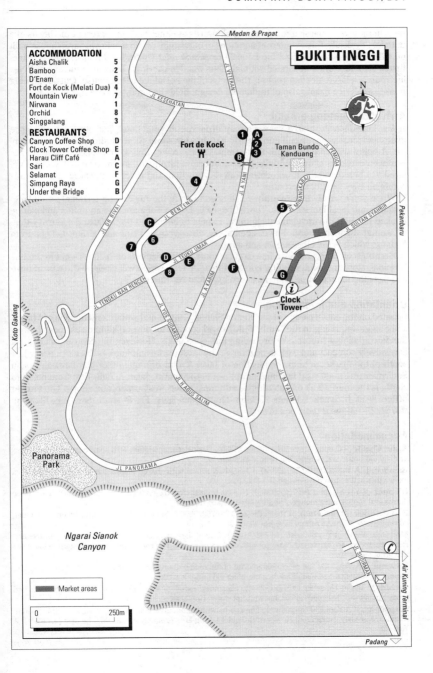

△ Medan & Prapat

BUKITTINGGI

N

ACCOMMODATION
Aisha Chalik	5
Bamboo	2
D'Enam	6
Fort de Kock (Melati Dua)	4
Mountain View	7
Nirwana	1
Orchid	8
Singgalang	3

RESTAURANTS
Canyon Coffee Shop	D
Clock Tower Coffee Shop	E
Harau Cliff Café	A
Sari	C
Selamat	F
Simpang Raya	G
Under the Bridge	B

JL VETERAN

JL KESEHATAN

Fort de Kock

Taman Bundo Kanduang

JL PEMUDA

JL A YANI

JL MINANGKABAU

JL SULTAN SYAHRIR

△ Pekanbaru

JL BENTENG

JL DR RIVAI

JL TEUKU UMAR

JL A KARIM

JL TENGKU NAN RENCEH

JL YOS SUDARSO

Clock Tower

JL M YAMIN

JL H AGUS SALIM

△ Koto Gadang

Panorama Park

JL PANORAMA

Ngarai Sianok Canyon

JL SUDIRMAN

△ Air Kuning Terminal

Market areas

0   250m

Padang ▽

their homes, with massive roofs soaring skywards at either end (to represent the horns of a buffalo). Typically, three or four generations of one family would live in one large house built on stilts, the *rumah gadang* ("big house") or *rumah adat* ("traditional house"), a wood-and-thatch structure often decorated with fabulous wooden carvings. In front of the line of sleeping rooms, a large meeting room is the focus of the social life of the house. Outside the big house, small rice barns, also of traditional design, hold the family stores.

Arrival and getting around

A few long-distance tourist services may drop you at your hotel, but other long-distance buses and local services pull into the **Air Kuning terminal**, 3km southeast of the town centre. A bemo will take you from the terminal to the town. Buses from Padang stop on the southern outskirts of town on Jalan Sudirman before turning off for the terminal; you can get a red #14 bemo into the town centre from this junction, and much of the accommodation is within an easy walk of the route.

When you're ready to **move on**, you'll need to go to the Air Kuning terminal for all long-distance and local bus services. Tourist buses to Danau Toba are also an option and can be booked through the travel agents in town. Expect to be quoted Rp27,000 and a journey time of around thirteen hours. Travel agents can also arrange Pelni and airline tickets from Padang, which is the closest port and airport.

Bemos scurry around town in a circular route, with a flat fare of Rp300. To get to the bus terminal, stop any bemo heading north on Jalan A Yani, which will circle to the east of town and pass the main post office before turning left to Air Kuning.

Orientation and information

Situated on the eastern edge of the Ngarai Sianok Canyon and with the mountains of Merapi and Singgalang rising to the south, **Bukittinggi** spreads for several kilometres in each direction into adjoining suburbs, before fading into open fields. However, the central part of town is relatively compact and easy to negotiate. The most useful landmark is the clock tower just south of the market area at the junction of Jalan A Yani (the main thoroughfare) and Jalan Sudirman (the main road leading out of town to the south). Jalan A Yani, 1km from north to south, is the tourist hub of Bukittinggi, with most hotels, restaurants and shops. The **tourist office** is at Jl Syech Bantam 1 (Mon–Thurs 8am–2pm, Fri 8–11am, Sat 8am–12.30pm; ☎0752/22403), near the clock tower.

Accommodation

Aisha Chalik, Jl Cinduo Mato 101 (☎0752/35260). Basic accommodation with shared facilities in a characterful old house with a quiet but central location. ③.

Bamboo, Jl A Yani 132 (☎0752/23388). Basic, dark rooms with shared mandi, but the small sitting area makes this better than the average Jl A Yani place. ①.

D'Enam, Jl Yos Sudarso (☎0752/21333). Not far from the centre on a quiet road, with airy, good value dorms and rooms and a lounge. Laundry service next door. ③.

Fort de Kock (Melati Dua), Jl Yos Sudarso 33 (☎0752/33005). Small hotel with pleasant rooms in a quiet, convenient location. All rooms have hot water. ②.

Mountain View, Jl Yos Sudarso (☎0752/21621). One of the few places to take advantage of the scenery. However, rooms are extremely basic, all with cold-water mandi. The road is quiet and the garden has seats and great views. ①.

Nirwana, Jl A Yani 113. The most characterful of the rock-bottom places at the northern end of this road. Rooms without attached mandi are in a rambling old bungalow. ①.

Orchid, Jl Teuku Umar 11 (☎0752/32634). Gleaming, excellent value place with attractively furnished rooms, many with balconies and some with hot water. Breakfast included. ①.

Singgalang, Jl A Yani 130 (no phone). The rooms without mandi are adequate but variable; the en-suite rooms are grossly overpriced. However, the quiet sitting area probably makes this the best place on Jl A Yani. ①.

The Town

A few hundred metres to the north of the Clock Tower, **Fort de Kock** (daily 8am–7pm; Rp1500, plus Rp350 for the museum) was built by the Dutch in 1825 and is linked by a foot-bridge to the park, Taman Bundo Kanduang, on the hill on the other side of Jalan A Yani; there's little left of the original fort but some old cannons and parts of the moats. From here you can see Gunung Merapi, on the left, and the much more dramatic cone-shaped Gunung Singgalang to the right. The park's **museum** is housed in a traditional *rumah gadang*, and features clothing, musical instruments, textiles and models of traditional houses. En route you'll pass through the abysmally inhumane zoo.

Much more pleasant is a trip to **Panorama Park** (daily 7am–7pm; Rp500), perched on a lip of land overlooking the sheer cliff walls down into Ngarai Sianok Canyon, the best Bukittinggi sight by far. Beneath the park stretch 1400m of Japanese **tunnels** (Rp500) and rooms built with local slave labour during World War II as a potential fortress. You can venture down into these dank, miserable depths, although there's nothing really to see. The **Ngarai Sianok Canyon** is part of a rift valley that runs the full length of Sumatra – the canyon here is 15km long and around 100m deep with a glistening river wending its way along the bottom.

Eating

A small **night market** sets up near the Jalan A Yani/Teuku Umar junction.

Canyon Coffee Shop, Jl Teuku Umar 18b. An inexpensive and popular travellers' place with a friendly atmosphere. The menu includes seventeen varieties of toast and eight coffees.

Clock Tower Coffee Shop, Jl Teuku Umar 7d. Pleasant furnishings and a good menu of Western and Indonesian favourites including steak, spaghetti and tacos.

Harau Cliff Cafe, Jl A Yani. Extremely good value place (steak is Rp7000 and sate, gado-gado and cap cay under Rp2000) with a relaxed atmosphere.

Sari, Jl Yos Sudarso 31. Large place with an expensive menu (fried rice and noodles are over Rp6000, vegetable dishes Rp10000–12000), and an outside area giving good views of the canyon.

Selamat, Jl A Yani 19. One of the best Padang restaurants in town, they usually have eggs in coconut sauce, which is especially good for vegetarians.

Simpang Raya, Jl Muka Jam Gadang. This large, popular restaurant has good-quality Padang food plus a basic Indonesian menu with soup, rice or noodle dishes.

Under the Bridge Restaurant, Jl A Yani. A slightly upmarket travellers' restaurant serving steaks, pasta, pizza, apple pie and chocolate cake.

Traditional entertainment

Local dance troupes stage recommended **Minangkabau dance shows** (8.30pm; Rp7500) nightly in a hall just behind *Hotel Jogya* on Jalan Moh Yamin; head up the small road on the left of the hotel and the hall is on the right. The dancing is accompanied by *talempong pacik*, traditional Minang music performed by a gamelan orchestra similar to those of Java and Bali, with gongs, drums and flutes. Most shows also include a demonstration of *silek*, the Minang martial art taught to both young men and women, and the *tari piriang*, a dance that originated in the rice fields after harvest time when young people danced with the plates they had just eaten from: piles of crockery shards are trodden and even rolled in by the dancers.

Animal-lovers may balk at the idea of watching **buffalo fights**, a popular local event, but the reality is rarely gory and usually good fun. Regular contests take place in villages near Bukittinggi: the most accessible of which is Batagak, 9km south on the way to Padangpanjang; the entrance is through a set of white gates just above the road and contests are held here on Wednesdays. Either arrange a Rp10,000 ticket through a travel agent or the tourist office, or go independently and pay Rp1000 at the gate. There are usually three bouts, starting at around 4pm. The massive buffalo are led towards each other and enticed to lock horns. They then push and heave against one another until one turns tail and runs away. At this point the hilarity begins, the crowding spectators diving for cover.

Listings

Bookshops Anyone heading into central and southern Sumatra, an English-language book desert, should stock up in the new and secondhand bookshops on Jl Teuku Umar and Jl A Yani.

Cash advance At Tigo Balai Indah, Jl A Yani 100 (daily 8am–8pm; ☎0752/31996), and other travel agents.

Car and motorbike rental Inquire at your accommodation or any travel agent. Rp100,000 for a 12hr car rental; Rp25,000–40,000 for a motorbike.

Hospital Rumah Sakit Dr Achmad Mochtar is on Jl Dr A Rivai (☎0752/21013). The tourist information office will advise on English-speaking doctors.

Internet access at the post office.

Post office The main post office is inconveniently far from the town centre on Jl Sudirman. Poste restante here is reasonably secure and organized. More convenient postal agents near the clock tower, and at Tilas bookshops on Jl Teuku Umar and Jl A Yani.

Shopping Lively Pasar Atas (Upper Market), just south of the clock tower, is lined with stalls and shops selling everyday goods and souvenirs. Nearby, Sumatera, Jl Minangkabau 19, has a huge range of textiles from Sumba and Irian Jaya and king sticks from North Sumatra.

Telephone services The main telephone office is on Jl M Syafei towards the southern end of town, around the corner from the post office. There's a wartel at Jl A Yani 111 (8am–7.30pm) but a much better value 24hr one at Jl Yos Sudarso 1.

Tours Many places offer one-day local tours to traditional villages, the Pagaruyung palace and the Harau Canyon (Rp25,000 per person). Travel agents do longer tours, involving three or more days trekking, camping and/or nights in local villages (US$22.50 per person per day). The most widely publicized tour is a trip to Siberut in the Mentawai islands; see p.296 for more details.

Koto Gadang

KOTO GADANG is a small, attractive village situated on the western edge of the Ngarai Sianok Canyon, with plenty of small silver workshops and shops. Though you can get local transport to the village, many people try to find the route from Bukittinggi by foot that starts off down Jalan Tengku Nan Renceh, and then heads along a footpath to the footbridge across the river and up the steps on the other side of the canyon. Be aware that there's a well-orchestrated scam, with local people refusing to point the way and hapless tourists being led by young lads on a two-hour rough trek through the canyon, for which they expect payment.

Batang Paluh

Rafflesia arnoldi is the largest flower in the world – up to 90cm across – has remarkable red-and-white colouring, and an appalling smell like rotting meat. One of the most accessible places in Sumatra to see this rare and extraordinary flower is at **BATANG PALUH**, 13km north of Bukittinggi; take a local bus (Rp900) and ask in the village. Inquire at the tourist office in Bukittinggi first as it generally flowers for a couple of weeks between August and December – but even in bud the plant is quite something.

Climbing Gunung Merapi

Access to 2890-metre **Gunung Merapi** (Fire Mountain) is from Koto Baru, 12km south of Bukittinggi. Typically, the climb, which is strenuous rather than gruelling if you are reasonably fit, takes five hours up and four down; most people climb at night to arrive at the top for the sunrise. The first four hours or so are through the forest and then across bare rocks leading to the summit. The top is actually a plateau area with the still smoking crater in the middle. You may spot bats, gibbons and squirrels in the forest, but the main reason to go is the view across to Gunung Singgalang. Engage an experienced local guide through your losmen (US$15 per person) and take enough water and energy food, plus warm clothes for the top and sturdy footwear.

Batusangkar and Pagaruyung

Accessed via Padangpanjang, the largest town in the Tanah Datar Valley is **BATU-SANGKAR**, 39km southeast of Bukittinggi and served by frequent buses (90min). The Minang court of the fourteenth to nineteenth centuries was based in the valley, the gold and iron mines of ancient times the source of its riches. The entire area is awash with cultural relics, megaliths and places of interest, and to explore it fully takes more than the limited time available on the one-day Minangkabau tours from Bukittinggi. The most worthwhile tourist destination in the area is **Pagaruyung** (daily 7am–6pm; Rp1000), the reconstructed palace of the last Raja Alam of the Minangkabau, Sultan Arifin Muning Alam Syah. The palace was reconstructed using traditional techniques some twenty years ago, the woodcarving alone taking two years to complete. The building comprises the traditional three storeys – the first for official visitors, the second for unmarried daughters and the third for meetings; the rice barn at the front would traditionally have held food to help the poor and the palace mosque is in the garden, with the kitchen at the back.

Batusangkar's **tourist office** is at Jl Pemuda 1 (Mon–Thurs 8am–2pm, Fri 8–11am & Sat 8am–noon; ☎0752/71300), and the **accommodation** all clustered fairly close together on the same street: *Pagaruyung*, Jl Prof Hamka 4 (☎0752/71533; ②); *Yoherma*, Jl Prof Hamka 15 (☎0752/71130; ②); and *Parma*, Jalan Hamka (☎0752/71330; ②), all have a range of basic but adequate rooms and restaurants attached.

Danau Maninjau

Rapidly developing a reputation as a pleasant and hassle-free area for rest and relaxation on the way to or from Danau Toba, **Danau Maninjau** is situated 15km due west of Bukittinggi, although public transport on the road takes a long-winded 37km (90min) to get there. At an altitude of 500m, the lake is 17km long and 8km wide and set 600m below the rim of an ancient volcanic crater, with jungle-covered walls, almost sheer in places, providing a picturesque backdrop. The area of interest for tourists, and all the facilities, centres on the village of **MANINJAU**, just where the road from Bukittinggi reaches the lakeside road, and, to a lesser extent, the village of **Bayur** 4km to the north.

The **tourist office** is located at Jl Rasuna Said 15 (daily 8am–5pm; ☎0752/61056), just north of the main junction, and the post office isn't far from the main junction on Jalan Telaga Biru Tanjung Raya; the 24hr Telkom office is on the main street, as is the bank. There are a couple of secondhand bookshops. Moving on, there are regular **buses** back to Bukittinggi and two direct buses daily to Padang; book ahead at your guesthouse or the tourist office. Otherwise, the lakeside bemos go to Lubukbasung, where you can pick up Padang buses during the day. Daily direct buses run to Pekanbaru (8hr) and you can also book through to Batam with a few hours halt in Pekanbaru – allow two days and a night.

Accommodation

Simple **accommodation** is ranged along the east side of the lake, from about 500m south of the junction of the lakeside road with the road from Bukittinggi, to just north of the five kilometre marker.

Alam Guest House (☎0752/61242). Up on the hillside away from the lake, the slog up the hill is worth it and this is the only place in the area to take advantage of the lake scenery. Offers a range of rooms, some en suite. ②.

Bamboo House (no phone). The best of a clutch of simple, basic homestays just north of the *Pasir Pangang Permai*. Lovely views across the lake. ①.

Beach Guest House (☎0752/61082). Large, bustling and popular place in a great location on the lakeside, with a small beach and hammocks. Range of rooms, including some en suite. ①.

Febby (☎0752/61586). Smaller and quieter than the *Beach Guest House* nearby, this is right on the lakeside but still convenient for Maninjau village. ①.

Pillie (☎0752/61048). Towards the southern end of Maninjau village, this lakeside place is clean, cool and tiled, with simple rooms and a pleasant upstairs balcony. ①.

Rizal Beach (no phone). Basic bamboo bungalows with mosquito nets, set back from their own white-sand beach just over 4km north of Maninjau village. Good views of the lake and a restaurant. ①.

Eating and drinking

A good variety of **restaurants** are situated on or close to the lakeside road; much of the fun of a stay in Maninjau is trying them out.

Alam Maninjau Restaurant Just off the road at the start of the track up to the *Alam Guest House*, this open-sided *bale* has magazines to read and a good range of meals: around Rp7500 for chicken, sirloin and *teriyaki*; baked potatoes with cauliflower cheese cost Rp3000.

Maransy Beach This is the place for a special meal or a sunset beer. The restaurant is set on stilts over the lake and offers an excellent range of cocktails (Rp3000 upwards), beer and white wine, plus classy appetizers, goulash and beef escalope.

Srikandi Café At the southern end of Maninjau village. A slightly grander dining experience than many, with a varied menu including soups (pumpkin, curried apple, Thai tom yam), stir-fries, sate, fish, steak, pizzas and burgers (Rp5500–9000).

Three Tables Coffee Shop (Gondang Ria). Just across the road from the louder, more assertive *Bodo's* south of the main junction, this is a tiny place with a good balcony, serving inexpensive Padang food plus the usual travellers' fare.

The Mentawai Islands

The enticing rainforest-clad **Mentawai Islands**, 100km off the west Sumatran coast, are home to an ethnic group who are struggling to retain their identity in the modern world. There are over forty islands in the chain, of which the four main ones are Siberut, Sipora, North Pagi and South Pagi. Only **Siberut**, the largest island, at 110km long by 50km wide, is accessible to tourists; all visitors must be registered by the authorities. The islanders' **traditional culture** is based on communal dwelling in longhouses (*uma*) and subsistence agriculture, their religious beliefs centring on the importance of coexisting with the invisible spirits that inhabit the world. With the advent of Christian missionaries and the colonial administration in the early twentieth century, many of the islanders' religious practices were banned, but plenty of beliefs and rituals have survived and some villages have built new *uma*. However, the islanders are still under threat, not least from an Indonesian government seeking to integrate them into mainstream life.

Siberut

The island of **Siberut** is the best-known, largest and most northerly of the Mentawai chain and the only one with anything approaching a tourist industry. Access to the island is by overnight ferry from Padang and, whilst it's possible, still, to visit the island independently, the vast majority of visitors go on tours arranged from Bukittinggi by young men from West Sumatra rather than Mentawai people.

The main town of **MUARASIBERUT** is in reality a sleepy little shanty-style village on the coast and around the mouth of the river. Small, unstable "speedboats" ferry passengers and cargo around. The only **accommodation** in Muarasiberut is the *Syahruddin Hotel* (☎0759/21014; ①) on the coast at the mouth of the river. It's light and airy, but at low tide looks straight onto stinking mud flats; rooms have no mosquito nets, and unattached mandi.

There's an excellent coffee shop across the road. The post office and Telkom offices are just behind the mosque, but there are no exchange facilities on the island.

TAKING A TOUR

The **tours** of Mentawai are loudly marketed in Bukittinggi as a trip to see the "primitive" people and "stone-age" culture. Generally, Mentawai people welcome tourism as a way of validating and preserving their own culture, although they get little financial benefit from it. Be sure to read and obey guidelines about behaviour that are given to you, as the people have a complex system of taboo behaviour. Be aware that on a five-day trip, Day One usually means a 3pm departure from Bukittinggi and Day Five may well end at 10am when you get back to Bukittinggi. Most tours centre on the southeast of the island, where you'll be able to watch and join in with people going about their everyday activities, such as farming, fishing and hunting. The ceremonies of Siberut are something of a draw for tourists, but many are actually staged for them. Malaria is endemic on the island, so take your own net or borrow one from the tour company.

VISITING INDEPENDENTLY

To visit Siberut **independently**, you'll need to get a **permit** in Padang from PT Mentawai Wisata Bahari, Jl Sumatera X5, Wisma Indah 1 (Mon–Sat 8am–5pm; ☎0751/52335): you won't be sold a boat ticket without one. Go to the office at least a day in advance (for travel on Monday, apply on Friday), with a photocopy of your passport, including the Indonesian entry stamp, and immigration card. You should approach the Siberut Guide Association (☎0759/21064) to find a **guide**. An all-inclusive five-day guided tour/trek will cost Rp600,000 for one person or Rp350,000 each for three people.

Two companies run **ferries** between Padang and the island: PT Rusco Lines, Jl Bt Arau 88 D/11 (☎0751/21941; Mon & Wed to Siberut and Sikabulan; return Tues & Thur) and PT Semeleue, Jl Bt Arau 7h (Sat to Siberut; return Mon). Tickets are Rp10,000, plus Rp1000 port tax for deck class or Rp15,000 plus tax for a cabin. The lower decks are close to the extremely noisy, exhaust-belching engine. In a cabin you'll get one of the four bunks on the next deck up.

The Kerinci-Seblat national park

Kerinci-Seblat national park, Sumatra's largest, is named after its two highest mountains, Gunung Kerinci (3805m), north of Sungaipenuh, and Gunung Seblat (2383m), much further south. It's a brilliant destination for nature-spotting and trekking, and the scenery is particularly lush. It's also said to harbour the terrestrial primate *orang pendek* (short man), apparently a little over 1m high, which is well-known to local people but has never been photographed. Scores of **treks** are possible, ranging from easy one- and two-day walks along well-used trails between villages where traditional longhouses and magic ceremonies still survive, to forest treks of a week or more. The national park office in Sungaipenuh has plenty of informnation about the myriad options and can recommend guides. Two of the more popular treks are those up **Gunung Kerinci** and to **Danau Gunung Tujuh**, both of which begin in the town of Kersik Tua.

Park practicalities: Sungaipenuh

The most popular access point into the park is **SUNGAIPENUH**, a small, attractive town, located 277km southwest of Padang in a high fertile valley of rice, tea, coffee and clove plantations. You can get all necessary information and hire national park guides here at the **national park office**, Mitra Kerja, on the edge of town at Jl Basuki Rahmat 11 (Mon–Thurs 7am–2pm, Fri 7–11am, Sat 7am–12.30pm; ☎0748/22250): look for a white gateway with red lettering. Fees for non-English-speaking deep-forest village **guides** are around US$6.50 per day and for porters US$5 per day, but rates vary. Trekkers pay for their guide's food and transport, and it's traditional to provide in addition a daily packet of cigarettes. The park office also issues **permits** (Rp1500 for Gunung Kerinci or Danau Gunung Tujuh), as do offices closer to each place.

The **bus terminal** is in the market area between Jalan Prof J Amin and Jalan H Agus Salim; waiting *dokar* (horse-carts) ferry arrivals around town. The most luxurious **accommodation** in town is *Aroma*, Jl Imam Bonjol 14 (☎0748/21142; ②), conveniently central and with some hot water. *Matahari* on Jalan Basuki Rahmet (☎0748/21061; ①) offers large rooms in a big old house, some en-suite, and a huge amount of local information. Slightly more central, *Yani*, Jl Muradi 1 (no phone; ①), feels less spacious and is on a busier road, but offers similar accommodation. For **eating**, *Soto Minang*, Jl Muradi 4, serves good, inexpensive Padang food, as does *Simpang Tiga*, on Jalan H Agus Salim in the market area: the brains in coconut sauce are particularly renowned. The BNI bank, opposite *Matahari*, has **foreign exchange** facilities, the 24hr Telkom office is on Jalan Imam Bonjol, and the post office is at Jl Sudirman 1a.

Gunung Kerinci and Danau Gunung Tujuh

The departure point for climbs up Gunung Kerinci is the attractive highland village of **KERSIK TUA**, 48km north of Sungaipenuh. The entire region is beautiful, with brilliant green-tea plantations on gently rolling hillsides as far as the eye can see. To get to Kersik Tua, catch a local **bus** from Jalan H Agus Salim in Sungaipenuh (the bus conductors yell "Kayuaro", which is the local name for the entire district); it takes about ninety minutes. If coming **from Padang**, the long-distance buses to Sungaipenuh pass through Kersik Tua. *Darmin Homestay* (no phone; ①) is on the main road, several hundred metres north of the sideroad to Gunung Kerinci and is clean and welcoming, with fine views. They will help you arrange local **trips**; expect to pay Rp20,000–25,000 per day for a porter and Rp25,000–40,000 for a guide.

CLIMBING GUNUNG KERINCI

The highest active volcano in Sumatra, **Gunung Kerinci** (3805m) is a tough climb with uncertain rewards at the top; the views can be stunning early in the morning, but the weather is very changeable. The crater, over 500m across, belches poisonous gases, so a great deal of care is necessary: there's no path around the edge. The mountain is famous for the white-flowered Javanese edelweiss (*Anaphalis javanica*), which is found only on volcanoes, can grow to 4m and looks remarkably striking on the bare volcanic soil. The Kerinci trail is one of the best **birding** areas in the park: expect babblers, thrushes, mesias and fantails as well as warblers, woodpeckers, minivets and the rare Sumatran cochea, plus several species of hornbill. You can also hope to spot gibbons, macaques and leaf-monkeys.

To tackle the summit you need to be properly prepared. Temperatures regularly plummet to 5°C, so take a sleeping bag, and a tent if possible, plus a stove and rain gear. A spring above Shelter 2 provides fresh drinking water, but check this before you set off. Hiring a guide is very highly recommended, as a number of climbers have come to grief up here – the descent can be easy to miss. The route goes from a side road in Kersik Tua, 5km to the PHPA office, where you buy a **permit** (Rp1500). From here it takes about two hours' climbing through cultivated fields and then into the forest to Shelter 1, then a further two to three hours to Shelter 2, where most people aim to spend the night. You'll need to get up between 3am and 5am to get to the top for dawn. The slippery volcanic rock gets steeper and steeper as you go up above the treeline. Most people make the descent back to Kersik Tua in one day.

Danau Gunung Tujuh

The trek to **Danau Gunung Tujuh** (Seven Mountains Lake), the highest volcanic lake in Southeast Asia at an altitude of 1996m, is a much less gruelling excursion and extremely picturesque, with plenty of wildlife and heaps of birds. The lake is surrounded by mountains, the seven of the name, and dominated by Gunung Tujuh on the far side, with densely forested slopes right down to the water's edge. This scene is particularly lovely in the early morning, when wisps of mist rise off the surface and the siamang gibbons start to call but, as long as you leave early, it's a relatively straightforward day-trip from Kersik Tua.

The walk starts from the village of **PELOMPEK**, 7km north of Kersik Tua, which is the last place to buy supplies for the trek, and there are a couple of *rumah makan*. The only major turning in the village to the right (east) leads 2km to the small village of Ulujernih; just under 1km beyond Ulujernih, the national park office is amongst a small huddle of concrete houses at the far end of the valley. At the office you can book in, buy a **permit** (Rp1500), get information, arrange accommodation at the PHPA guesthouse and, if necessary, a **guide** (Rp25,000/day). A 1.5km track from the office leads to the park **guesthouse**, which costs Rp6000 per night and includes the use of a cooking stove and a bathroom, though there's no electricity. Bring your own food and lots of warm clothes. It's a great setting and good spot to start the walk from. The **path to the lake** passes to the left of the wooden building and on into the forest, where it climbs relentlessly to Shelter 2, between one and two hours' hike through the forest from the guesthouse, which is on the crater rim above the lakeside. From here, the steep descent to the lakeside takes about thirty minutes. Down on the lakeside there's a fairly sizeable shelter, but you'll be more comfortable in a tent.

Dumai and into Malaysia

Sumatra's major east-coast port is **Dumai**, 189km north of Pekanbaru and just across the Straits of Melaka from the Malaysian city of Melaka. Dumai recently became a **visa-free entry point**, and a fast ferry runs daily to and from Melaka (2hr 30min). Regular buses run between Dumai and Pekanbaru, but if you get stranded you can stay at the *City Hotel*, Jalan Sudirman (☎0765/21550).

Pekanbaru

The booming oil town of **PEKANBARU** is a major gateway into Indonesia from Singapore, via Pulau Batam and Pulau Bintan. Most travellers head straight through but it's worth considering a journey break here – it's six hours west to Bukittinggi and another nine or ten hours east to Singapore. Pekanbaru's main street is Jalan Sudirman, which runs north–south from the river through the centre of town to the airport. Most hotels, restaurants and shops are within easy reach of this thoroughfare. However, the **tourist information office** is inconveniently sited at Jl Diponegoro 24 (Mon–Thurs 8am–2pm, Fri 8–11am, Sat 8am–12.30pm; ☎0761/31562). The one must-see in town is **Yayasan Sepena Riau**, Jl Sumatera 7 (Mon–Sat 10am–4pm), a small private museum and souvenir shop. It's an absolute treasure trove of artefacts collected by one family over many years, including items connected with traditional Riau weddings. The **markets** are fun too: Pasar Pusat is the food and household-goods market, and Pasar Bawah and Pasar Tengeh in the port area have an excellent range of Chinese goods, including ceramics and carpets.

Practicalities

All domestic and international **flights** (Singapore, KL, Melaka) touch down in Simpang Tiga airport, 9km south of the city centre. The closest public transport is 1km away on the main highway, where you can catch public buses into the Pasar Pusat terminal in the city centre. Otherwise, fixed-price taxis charge Rp10,000.

Long-distance buses arrive at the terminal on Jalan Nangka, about 5km south of the river, from where you can catch a blue bemo to the city centre. Most **express ferry** services from Pulau Batam and Pulau Bintan dock at **BUTON**, connected to Pekanbaru by a three-hour bus journey; buses arrive at the express-ferry offices at the northern end of Jalan Sudirman or at the bus terminal. **Slow ferries** come into the main port area at the northern end of Jalan Saleh Abbas in the Pasar Bawah market area, a couple of hundred metres west of Jalan Sudirman.

City buses (6am–9pm; Rp300) run the length of Jalan Sudirman and beyond, between the Pasar Pusat terminal near the Jalan Imam Bonjol junction with Jalan Sudirman and Kubang terminal, which is 3km beyond the turning to Simpang Tiga airport. Colour-coded **bemos** (Rp250) operate to and from the main bemo terminal, Sekapelan, which is situated just west of the main market area behind Jalan Sudirman; most have their destinations marked on them.

Moving on from Pekanbaru, you'll find there are extremely good sea, land and air connections with the rest of the island, as well as the rest of the archipelago. Long-distance buses to destinations throughout **Sumatra** and in **Java** depart from the terminal on Jalan Nangka. Many of the bus offices are in the terminal itself but others are spread along Jalan Nangka, up to about 500m west of the terminal and also at the very start of Jalan Taskurun. Shop around and book ahead.

High-speed ferry services for Pulau Batam and Pulau Karimun leave from the ticket offices at the northern end of Jalan Sudirman. Although located near the river and with adverts conspicuously picturing speedboats, most services actually involve a three-hour bus trip to Buton, where you transfer to the high-speed ferry for the trip to the islands. Prices vary from Rp30,000 to Rp35,000, and ticket sellers make all sorts of dramatic claims for the length of the trip from Pekanbaru, but it will take six to eight hours travelling time, plus up to a two-hour wait for a ferry at Buton. Some companies also sell tickets straight through to Tanjung Pinang on Pulau Bintan, but check whether you have to change boats in Batam. If you're planning to go straight through to **Singapore**, take the earliest departure from Pekanbaru. For the daily slow-ferry sailing at 9pm for the 25-hour trip **to Pulau Batam** via Tanjung Pinang and Tanjung Balai, enquire at PT Lestari Polajaya Sakti, Jl Saleh Abbas 8 (☎0761/37627).

ACCOMMODATION

There isn't much **accommodation** under Rp20,000 for a double. Most places are either close to Jalan Sudirman, or in the bus terminal area, about 5km south. In the bus terminal area, steer clear of the noisy and poor-value places on Jalan Nangka itself and aim for the quieter Jalan Taskurun and Jalan Cempaka.

Afri, Jl Dr Setiabudhi 5 (☎0761/33190). On the corner of Jl Sudirman about 200m south of the speedboat ferry dock, this is a clean, multi-storey setup with some air-con and en-suite rooms. ②.

Anom, Jl Gatot Subroto 3 (☎0761/22636). Located centrally, about 100m from Jl Sudirman, this has spotlessly clean rooms, some with hot water. Prices include breakfast. ②.

Wisma Gemini, Jl Taskurun 44 (☎0761/32916). A pleasant garden and a range of rooms, including some with air-con and hot water. ②.

Hotel Linda, Jl Nangka 145 (☎0761/36915). A big white house with a pleasant atmosphere on a quiet alleyway off Jl Nangka, opposite the bus terminal, about 50m west of *Penginapan Linda* – don't get these places confused. Offers a big range of decent rooms, all en-suite. ②.

Muara Takus, Jl Cempaka 17 (☎0761/21045). Set back slightly from the road and convenient for the bus terminal, this place offers very good value, with simple en-suite rooms. ①.

EATING

Even if you stayed in the city for a month, you could have every meal at the brilliant Pasar Pusat **night market** (located in the market area near Jalan Bonjol) and not eat the same thing twice. *Sederhana*, Jl Nangka 121–123, is one of many Padang-style **restaurants** that offer good value but spicy eating in the area near the bus terminal. *New Holland*, Jl Sudirman 153, is a very popular fast-food place which veers towards the upper end of the price range (steaks for Rp16,000), but also offers burgers, pizza, juices and drinks at moderate prices.

Listings

Airline offices Garuda, *Mutiara Merdeka* hotel, Jl Yos Sudarso 12a (☎0761/32526); Mandala, Jl Sudirman 308 (☎0761/28390); Merpati, Jl Sudirman 343 (☎0761/41555); Pelangi, Jl Pepaya 64c (☎0761/28896); Silk Air, *Mutiara Merdeka* hotel, Jl Yos Sudarso 12a (☎0761/28175).

Hospitals Rumah Sakit Santa Maria, Jl A. Yani 68 (☎0761/20235); Rumah Sakit Umum Pusat Pekanbaru, Jl Diponegoro 2 (☎0761/36118).

Immigration office Jl Singa (☎0761/21536).

Post office The main post office is at Jl Sudirman 229 and poste restante should be sent here. There's a more convenient post office at Jl Sudirman 78, the northern end.

Telephone services The Telkom office is at Jl Sudirman 117 and there are wartel all over town.

Pulau Karimun and ferries to Malaysia

Pulau Karimun, at the southern end of the Melaka Straits, is of most interest to travellers as a gateway to **Malaysia**. Boats leave six days a week from the busy port of **TANJUNG BALAI** for Port Klang, just outside Kuala Lumpur. The busy port of Tanjung Balai lies on the south coast and its ferry terminal is at the eastern end of town. All the ferry ticket offices are located just inside the gates. The Pelni agent is CV Putra Karimun Jaya, Jl Kesatria 1a (☎0777/22850). **Guesthouses** include the slightly ramshackle, though characterful,*Wisma Gloria* (②), Komplek Gedung Putih (☎0777/21133), at the far eastern end of Tanjung Balai; to get here come out of the ferry terminal car park, turn right along the coast past *Wisma Karimun* and it's about 300m walk up on the hill at the end of the road. A cheaper option and well placed for the night market, *Harmoni* (①), Jl Pelabuhan 55, offers very basic fan-rooms with outside bathroom.

Pulau Batam and ferries to Singapore

Apart from its proximity to Singapore, just 20km at the closest point, and usefulness as a major staging post on to Indonesia, there's little to recommend **Pulau Batam** to travellers, and nothing to make staying overnight worthwhile. Most travellers arrive at the port of **SEKUPANG**, from where boats run to Singapore (see below).

The international terminal at Sekupang runs boats to and from **Singapore's** World Trade Centre (7.30am–7pm; to 8pm on Mon & Wed), and the domestic terminal (200m away) operates services to and from Sumatran destinations like **Pekanbaru** and Dumai. The port for Tanjung Pinang on **Pulau Bintan** is **TELAGA PUNGGUR** on the east coast, accessible only by taxi (Rp15,000 from Nongsa, Rp15,000–20,000 from Nagoya and Rp30,000 from Sekupang).

There are several other ferry terminals on the island. The international ferry terminal at **NONGSA** (☎0778/761777) runs services to and from Tanah Merah terminal in Singapore. The Waterfront ferry terminal, **TELUK SENIMBA**, has services to the World Trade Centre in Singapore (8.45am–8.30pm). There's also a ferry service (8am–8pm) from **BATU AMPAR** to Singapore's World Trade Centre. The **Pelni** boats *KM Kelud* and *KM Sinabung* operate from Batam (see "Getting around" pp.192–193 and "Travel Details" p.444); booking is through Andalan Aksa Tour, Komplek New Holiday, Block B, 9 (☎0778/454181).

If you get stuck on Pulau Batam, you can **stay** in the island's main town, **NAGOYA** (also known as Lubuk Baja), on the northeast coast of the island, though it is inconvenient for all transport points and the room charges are extortionate, with nothing below Rp40,000. The scruffy *Peningapan Gajah Mada* (☎0778/425270; ②), Komplek Windsor Square Blok B, 77–78, is one such place, though at least it is central and has some helpful staff. *Wisma Bougenville*, Komplek Nagoya Business Centre, Block 11, 28/29 (☎0778/426682; Rp55,000) is a little more expensive but better value; rooms are en-suite and some have hot water and air-con.

Pulau Bintan and beyond

Situated less than 10km from Batam at the closest point, **Pulau Bintan** is about two and a half times the size of Singapore, which seems to have left plenty of room for traditional culture to survive alongside the plush tourist development. Not only is it more attractive than other nearby islands, but there's much more of an Indonesian feel about the place and things are reasonably priced. **Tanjung Pinang**, the main town on Pulau Bintan, has been largely untouched by the tourist influx, and the low-key guesthouses of **Trikora** on the east coast continue to cater for those who want a few days of sun and sand.

The **international and domestic ferry terminals** are on the coast at Tanjung Pinang, with the ticket offices ranged in the terminal area and along Jalan Merdeka. There are connections to Pulau Batam, Pekanbaru and Jakarta, as well as to Singapore and Johor Bahru (see "Travel Details", p.444). For **ferry tickets** to Singapore contact New Oriental, Jl Merdeka 61 (☎0771/521614), or Osaka, Jl Merdeka 43 (☎0771/21829), both in Tanjung Pinang.

There are several **Pelni sailings** to and from Pulau Bintan, which give access to the entire archipelago: *KM Bukit Siguntang, KM Kerinci, KM Sirimau, KM Bukit Raya* are all on a two-weekly cycle and operate out of Kijang on the southeast corner of the island; see "Getting around" pp.192–193 and "Travel Details" p.444. The Pelni agent in Tanjung Pinang is Netra Service Jaya, Jl Pos 1 (☎0771/21384).

Flights to Jakarta and Pekanbaru leave from Kijang airport, 15km southeast of Tanjung Pinang. Book tickets through PT Pinang Jaya, Jl Bintan 44 (☎0771/21267).

Tanjung Pinang

Lying on the southeast coast of the island, the traditional capital of the Riau Islands, **TANJUNG PINANG**, is an attractive bustling port town with good tourist facilities and useful transport links throughout Indonesia. There are a few sights in the town itself, although **Pasar Baru**, between Jalan Merdeka and the harbour, is undoubtedly the gem. This is a terrific traditional Indonesian market: tiny alleyways are lined with shops and stalls selling mountains of exotic food, household goods, textiles, tools and religious artefacts. The town has a large Chinese trading population and there are plenty of red-and-gold **temples** with smoking incense, fierce dragons and serene statues of Chinese goddesses. One of the most atmospheric – with Kuan Yin, the goddess of mercy, in pride of place – is on the harbourfront at the end of the most easterly jetty, Jl Pelantar II.

The Tanjung Pinang **tourist office** is at Jalan H Agus Salim (Mon–Thurs 8am–1.30pm, Fri 9–11am & Sat 9–12.30pm; ☎0771/25373) and the main **post office** is at Jl Brigjenkatamso 122; poste restante should be sent here. The **Telkom office** is at Jl Hang Tuah 11 (7am–midnight). **Immigration** is at Jl Jend A Yani 31 (☎0771/21034) and on the ferry pier. The island's **hospitals** are Rumah Sakit Umum, Jl Sudirman 795 (☎077121733), and Rumah Sakit Angkatan Laut, Jalan Ciptadi (☎0771/25805).

The **bus terminal** is Batu Tujuh (Stone Seven) on the outskirts of town; bemos ply between the town centre and the terminal (Rp300) from 6am to 10pm and public buses operate to Kijang (1hr), Trikora (1–2hr) and Tanjung Uban (2hr) during daylight hours, but are irregular and infrequent.

ACCOMMODATION AND EATING

The budget mainstays are the **homestays** on Jalan Lorong Bintan II, which connects Jalan Samudera and Jalan Bintan. Here you'll find *Bong's, Johnny's* and *Rommel's*, Jl Lorong Bintan II (no phones; ①), all very similar basic homestays with rooms in family houses. On Jl Bintan itself, *Surya* (☎0771/21811; ①) is a good budget choice with just a few fan rooms, some en suite, set around a small garden. More upmarket, *Furia*, Jl Merdeka 6 (☎0771/29922; ⑤) is a clean place just opposite the harbour exit, where all rooms have hot water and air-con (⑤).

There are several **night markets** in town: there's a convenient little one at the entrance to the harbour area on Jalan Hang Tuah, but the biggest is at **Bintan Mall** (daily 5pm–2am), on the outskirts of town next to the *Paradise Hotel* and near the main post office. During the day you can eat here too at *Ayam Goreng 88*, an air-con, fast-food place offering moderately priced fried chicken, fish and fries and Indonesian staples. *Suka Ramai*, Jl Merdeka 18, on the second floor above a shop, serves a varied mid-priced menu of Indonesian favourites, fish and steaks.

The beaches

At **TRIKORA**, on the east coast of Pulau Bintan, the beach area covers around 30km of coastline comprising bay after palm-fringed bay. The disadvantage is that, when the tide goes out, it goes quite a long way, leaving dull-looking flats.

The accommodation begins 5km north of the small, attractive village of **KAWAL**, situated at the point where the main trans-island road reaches the east coast, and where many of the houses are built over the river on stilts. Heading north from Kawal, you'll first come to *Bukit Berbunga Cottages* (no phone; ①), where a hundred-metre track leads down to the wood-and-thatch cottages with attached mandi, mattresses on the floor and electricity at night. Just 200m north, *Yasin's Guest House* (☎0771/26770; ①) has three types of wood-and-thatch chalets on offer, all with verandahs, and some with mandi. Another kilometre north, *Trikora Beach Resort* (☎0771/24454; ⑥–⑧) is the most upmarket place on this coast, with attractive gardens, good views, and comfortable bungalows with verandah, air-con and hot water. One of the best beaches on the coastline, **TRIKORA TIGA**, is about 13km further north and boasts several kilometres of glorious white sand, gently lapped by turquoise waters. At the weekends, several warung open up for day-trippers, but during the week it's pretty much deserted.

Pulau Penyenget

Out in the bay, clearly visible from Tanjung Pinang, small **Pulau Penyenget** is well worth a trip for its peaceful atmosphere, lovely old buildings and lingering sense of ancient glories. In the early nineteenth century, Penyenget became a major centre for Muslim religion and literature – scholars from Mecca came to teach in the mosque and many works of Malay literature were written here. Many of the ruins date from that time, an era regarded as a "Golden Age".

Just 2500m long by 750m wide, the island is reached by small **ferry** (daylight hours; 15min; Rp500) from Pelantar I, at the end of Jalan Pos, just around the corner from the post office in the centre of Tanjung Pinang. Allow three or four hours to explore the island, and take plenty of water and some snacks, as there are only a few shops. From the western jetty, the road leads straight to **Mesjid Raya Sultan Riau**, which was completed in 1844, and is now restored to its turreted and domed glory. The floor is covered with richly patterned prayer mats, fabulously carved old cupboards hold an Islamic library, and in the glass case there's a stunning nineteenth-century Koran. Outside the mosque, a right turning along Jalan YDMR Abdurrahman takes you south across the island to **Istana Raja Ali**, the palace of the raja who ruled from 1844 to 1857. The path goes through the palace grounds and, continuing out the other side, leads across to the south side of the island. Down on the south coast, turn left, and after a couple of hundred metres follow Jalan Nakhoda Ninggal to **Tungku Bilek** (Lady Room), the ruined two-storey house by the sea. It was once inhabited by the sister of one of the sultans and was so named because she was said never to leave her room.

On the north side of the island, about 200m east of the mosque, is the **grave of Raja Hamidah**, also known as Engku Puteri, who died in 1844 and is revered as the original owner of the island. This is a place of pilgrimage for Muslims, who believe it to be *keramat* ("able to bring about miracles"). Of all the graves on the island it's the most lovely, set in a restored compound with a central mausoleum.

Bandar Lampung

Occupying a stunning location in the hills overlooking Lampung Bay, from where you can see as far as Krakatau, **BANDAR LAMPUNG** is an amalgamation of Teluk Betung, the traditional port, and Tanjung Karang, the administrative centre on the hills behind. Local people continue to talk about Teluk Betung and Tanjung Karang, and when you're coming here from other parts of Sumatra your destination will usually be referred to as Rajabasa, the name of the bus terminal. There are few sights in town. The **Krakatau monument**, set in a small park on Jalan Veteran, is a huge metal buoy which was washed up here from Lampung Bay in 1883 in the tidal waves that followed the eruption of Krakatau, killing over 35,000 people on both sides of the straits (see p.224). The **Museum Negeri Propinsi Lampung**, 1km south of Rajabasa terminal at Jl Abdin Pagar Alam 64 (Tues–Thurs 8am–1.30pm, Fri 8–10.30am, Sat & Sun 8am–noon; Rp200), houses a good collection of artefacts, including drums, kris, statues, jewellery and masks, plus some megalithic figures, unfortunately not labelled in English.

Practicalities

Buses from all destinations north of Bandar Lampung pull into the **Rajabasa terminal**, 7km north of the city, one of the busiest in Sumatra. Follow the signs towards the main road for "*microlet*" (bemos), where you can either get a light-blue bemo as far as Pasar Bawah, just south of Jalan Kotoraja, or catch the bus that goes to Pasar Bawah but then continues its circular route down Jalan Raden Intan, along Jalan A Yani and Jalan Kartini before going out to Rajabasa again. If you stay on past Pasar Bawah it counts as two journeys, so you'll pay double.

Buses from Bakauheni and Kalianda arrive at **Panjang terminal**, about 1km east of Panjang market, to the east of the city on the coast. Some terminate here, while others go on to Rajabasa. Orange bemos run between Panjang terminal and Sukaraja terminal in the heart of Teluk Betung; depending on where you want to stay in town it may be better to get off at Panjang or stay on to Rajabasa.

The **train station** is on Jalan Kotoraja, about 100m from Pasar Bawah. The local **high-speed ferry terminal** from Jakarta is at Sukaraja, just next to the bemo and bus terminal. **Branti airport** is 25km north of the city; walk 200m onto the main road and catch a Branti–Rajabasa bus to Rajabasa (Rp250) and take connections to the city from there. Fixed-price taxis from the airport into town will cost Rp20,000. Merpati is at Jl A Yani 88b (☎0721/258046).

USEFUL BEMOS

Dark purple – between Tanjung Karang and Sukaraja via Jalan Diponegoro, Jalan Salim Batubara, the southern end of Jalan KHA Dahlan and Jalan Yos Sudarso. Coming back up, they run along Jalan Yos Sudarso, Jalan Malahayat, up Jalan Ikan Tenggiri, Jalan Pattimura, Jalan Diponegoro, Jalan A Yani, Jalan Kartini and around to Pasar Bawah.

Light blue – between Rajabasa terminal and Tanjung Karang.

Orange – Sukaraja and Panjang terminals.

Green – Tanjung Karang and Garuntang (Jalan Gatot Subroto) via Jalan Sudirman and Jalan KHA Dahlan, which is useful for the post office.

Dark red – Tanjung Karang and Kemiling (Langka Pura) on the western edge of the city.

Grey – Tanjung Karang and Sukarame on the eastern edge of the city.

The easiest way to **get around** the city are the DAMRI **bus services** that operate from 6am to 6pm and only call at designated stops. The **Rajabasa–Karang service** runs from Rajabasa along Jalan Teuku Umar into the city and left into Jalan Kotoraja to Pasar Bawah where it terminates. Its return route to Rajabasa is down Jalan Raden Intan, along Jalan A Yani and up Jalan Kartini before going out to Rajabasa again. The bus labelled **Karang–Betung** operates from the Pasar Bawah area down Jalan Raden Intan, Jalan Diponegoro and Jalan Salim Batubara, the southern end of Jalan KHA Dahlan and Jalan Yos Sudarso to Sukaraja terminal. Coming back up they run along Jalan Yos Sudarso, Jalan Ikan Kakap, up Jalan Ikan Tenggiri, Jalan Pattimura, Jalan Diponegoro, Jalan A Yani, Jalan Kartini and around to Pasar Bawah.

The buses are supplemented by small colour-coded **bemos** (flat fare Rp350; 5am–9pm) which often have their routes printed on the back (see box opposite).

INFORMATION

There are two helpful **tourist offices** in town: at Jl WR Supratman 39 (Mon–Thurs 7am–3pm, Fri 7am–noon & 1–3pm; ☎0721/482565), and the Depparpostel, above the main post office at Jl KHA Dahlan 21 (same times; ☎0721/251900).

The **post office** is at Jl KHA Dahlan 21; the main Telkom office is at Jl Kartini 1 and there's also a 24hr wartel at Jl Majapahit 14. The Immigration Office is at Jl Diponegoro 24 (☎0721/482607). Local **hospitals** include Rumah Sakit Bumi Waras, Jalan Wolter Moginsidi (☎0721/263851), Rumah Sakit Immanuel Way Halim, Jalan Sukarno Hatta B (☎0721/704900), and Rumah Sakit Abdul Muluk, Jalan Kapten Rivai (☎0721/702455).

ACCOMMODATION

Bandar Lampung has good-value mid-range hotels, but budget **accommodation** is poor value, so you may prefer to commute from Kalianda (see p.306).

Cilamaya, Jl Imam Bonjol 261 (☎0721/263504). Basic, centrally located place that's popular and unfortunately often full. ②.

Gading, Jl Kartini 72 (☎0721/255512). Large setup on a quiet alleyway near the market area with a variety of rooms. A short walk from the bus route from Rajabasa. ②–⑤.

Kurnia Perdana, Jl Raden Intan 114 (☎0721/262030). A small, friendly and pleasant setup, all rooms offering air-con and TV, and some with hot water. Price includes breakfast. ④.

Mini 1, Jl Dwi Warna 71 (☎0721/2555928). This is a small setup in a quiet alley off Jl Kartini; it's opposite *Hotel Gading* and offers clean, basic rooms with no frills but attached mandi. ②.

Rarem, Jl Way Rarem 23 (☎261241). Tucked away behind Jl KHA Dahlan, not far from the green bemo route (get off at the junction of Jl Dr Susilo and Jl KHA Dahlan), this small place is super-clean. Some en-suite rooms and some air-con. ②–⑤.

Tambakaya, Jl Imam Bonjol, Gang Beringin 60 (no phone). Follow the sign that is about 50m from *Cilamaya* towards the town centre, fork right at the nursery school just inside the alleyway, go over the stream and it's a small compound on the left. Basic but adequate. ②.

EATING

The **night market**, at the southern end of Jalan Hassanudin, operates from dusk until about 11pm and offers a huge range of food, including Chinese and seafood.

Garuda, Jl Kartini 31. Just north of Tanjung Karang Plaza, this is part of a popular chain, serving all the Indonesian staples at moderate prices in relaxed surroundings.

Gembira, Jl Pangkhal Pinang 20. Popular place serving a huge range of inexpensive local dishes including *pempek*, soups, chicken dishes and ice confections.

Marcopolo Restaurant at the *Marcopolo Hotel*. The view from the terrace makes this a great place for a meal or a drink. Chinese and Indonesian food from Rp10,000, steak Rp35,000, plus tax.

Moro Seneng, Jl Diponegoro 38. Good-value Indonesian and Chinese food at Rp7500–12,000, up to shrimp, *gurame* and squid at Rp22,500.

Pemplek 56, Jl Salim Batubara 56. Just one of a huge range of *pempek* places along this road, all serving the Palembang speciality of grilled or fried sago and fish balls.

Kalianda

Situated just under 60km south of Bandar Lampung, the small coastal town of **KALIANDA** is a great alternative to the hassles and expenses of the city, and an excellent stopping-off point whether you're entering or leaving Sumatra. It's served by public transport from the Bakauheni ferry terminal and from the Panjang and Rajabasa terminals in Bandar Lampung Kalianda. Public transport in Kalianda arrives at Terminal Pasar Impress in front of the main market; wander the alleyways here to enjoy the sights, sounds and smells.

The best travellers' **accommodation** is in the *Beringin Hotel*, Jl Kesuma Bangsa 75 (☎0727/2008; c), in a large, colonial-style bungalow with big rooms, an airy lounge and a garden. To get here from the terminal, go back onto the road, turn right for about 400m to a junction where a large road joins from the right; head down here past the local school and the hotel is at the far end on the left. Alternatively, hire an ojek. The hotel organizes local trips, including excursions to Krakatau (see p.224). The **post office** is at Jalan Pratu M Yusuf and the **telephone office** on the main street is open 7am to midnight. The main shopping street is Jalan Serma Ibnu Hasyim, a short walk from the *Beringin Hotel*.

Bakauheni and ferries to Java

Around 30km south of Kalianda, lies **Bakauheni**, the departure point for **ferries** to Merak, on Java's northwest tip. There's no reason to stay in Bakauheni itself. The town is served by regular **buses** from Rajabasa terminal and Panjang terminal in Bandar Lampung, and by bemos from Kalianda. There's also a 24hr wartel and a couple of shops. Ferries from Bakauheni operate round the clock for the two-and-a-half-hour crossing to Merak, leaving every thirty minutes during the day and less frequently at night. High-speed ferries also depart hourly from 7.40am to 5pm (40min).

BALI

With its fine beaches, pounding surf, emerald-green rice terraces and exceptionally artistic culture, the small volcanic island of **Bali** – the only Hindu society in Southeast Asia – has long been Indonesia's premier tourist destination. As a result, it has become very much a mainstream destination and suffers the predictable problems of congestion and commercialization. However, Bali's original charm is still much in evidence, its stunning Hindu temples and spectacular festivals set off by the gorgeously lush landscape of the interior.

Bali's most famous and crowded resort is **Kuta** beach, a six-kilometre sweep of golden sand, with plenty of accommodation, shops and nightlife. Nearby **Sanur** is much quieter, but most backpackers prefer the beaches of peaceful east-coast **Candi Dasa** and traveller-oriented **Lovina** on the north coast. The island's other major destination is the cultural centre of **Ubud**, a still charming but undeniably commercialized overgrown village, where traditional dances are staged every night of the week and the streets are full of arts-and-crafts galleries. In addition, there are numerous elegant Hindu temples to visit, particularly at **Tanah Lot** and **Besakih**, and a good number of volcano hikes, the most popular being the route up **Gunung Batur**, with **Gunung Agung** only for the very fit. **Transport** to and from Bali is extremely efficient: the island is served by scores of international and domestic flights, which all land at **Ngurah Rai Airport** just south of Kuta beach, as well as round-the-clock ferries to Java, thirty minutes' west across the sea from **Gilimanuk**, and frequent ferries to Lombok, two- to four hours' east of **Padang Bai** and Benoa. The Pelni ferry *KM Dibonsolo* also calls fortnightly at Benoa Harbour; see "Getting around" pp.192–193 and "Travel Details" p.445. Prices throughout Bali rocket during the **peak tourist seasons** from mid-June to mid-September and over Christmas, when rooms can be fully booked for days, if not weeks, in advance.

Bali was a more or less independent society of Buddhists and Hindus until the fourteenth century when it was colonized by the strictly **Hindu** Majapahits from neighbouring Java.

Despite the subsequent Islamicization of nearly all her neighbours, Bali has remained firmly Hindu ever since. In 1849, the Dutch started to take an interest in Bali, and by January 1909 had wrested control of the whole island. Following a short-lived Japanese occupation in World War ll, and Indonesia's subsequent declaration of Independence in 1945, Bali became an autonomous state within the Republic in 1948. But tensions with Java have continued: following the 1965 Gestapu affair in Java, some 100,000 actual or suspected members of the Communist Party on Bali were killed in reprisals. More recently, there has been growing concern about the number of wealthy entrepreneurs from Jakarta who have exploited Bali's considerable attractions for their own ends, with the Balinese starting to lose control of their own homeland.

Denpasar

Bali's capital city, **DENPASAR** (formerly known as Badung, and still sometimes referred to as such), has lost some of its charm to the roaring motorbikes and major traffic congestion that now dog much of south Bali. However, it remains a pleasantly small-town city at heart, dominated by family compounds grouped into traditional *banjar* (village association) districts, with just a few major shopping streets crisscrossing the centre. It feels nowhere near as hectic as Kuta but, as there's no nightlife (and no beach), few tourists spend long here.

Denpasar's central and most convenient landmark is Puputan Square, marking the heart of the downtown area. Overlooking its eastern edge on Jalan Mayor Wisnu, the **Bali Museum** (Tues–Sun 8am–3pm; Rp750; turquoise Kereneng–Ubung bemo route) is Denpasar's most significant attraction, prettily located in a series of traditional courtyards. The Main Building, at the back of the entrance courtyard, houses items from Bali's prehistory, and upstairs, there's a fine exhibition of traditional household utensils. The compact First Pavilion displays Balinese textiles, the Second Pavilion, which resembles an eighteenth-century Karangasem-style palace, contains all manner of religious paraphernalia, and the Third Pavilion exhibits theatrical masks and puppets.

The biggest and best of Denpasar's traditional markets is **Pasar Badung**, which stands at the heart of the downtown area, set slightly back off Jalan Gajah Mada, in a three-storey covered *pasar* beside Sungai Badung. Trading takes place here 24 hours a day: clothes, batik and ceremonial gear are on the top floor. You may get landed with one of the market's official guides, who hang out around the entrance. Across on the west bank of the narrow river, also a few meters south off Jalan Gajah Mada, the four-storey **Pasar Kumbasari** is dedicated to handicrafts, souvenirs and clothes, many of them much cheaper than in the shops of Kuta and Ubud.

In the eastern part of town, on Jalan Nusa Indah, fifteen minutes' walk from the Kereneng bemo station, or direct on a Sanur-bound bemo, the **Taman Budaya Cultural Centre** (daily 8am–3pm; Rp250) houses a moderately interesting art museum covering the development of Balinese painting and woodcarving. From mid-June to mid-July it also hosts the annual Arts Festival.

Practicalities

If you're **arriving** in Bali by air, you'll land at **Ngurah Rai Airport**, which is not in Denpasar as sometimes implied, but just beyond the southern outskirts of Kuta (all information on the airport is given on p.313). Arriving in Denpasar by bemo or public bus from another part of the island, you'll almost certainly be dropped at one of the four main **bus and bemo stations**. Bemos run from these stations into town; see box on p.312 for main routes. Getting from one bemo station to another is fairly easy, but connections can be time-consuming.

When you're ready to **move on**, destinations south of Denpasar, including Kuta, Ngurah Rai Airport and Sanur, are served by **Tegal** bemo station. **Kereneng** bemo station runs services to Sanur. Batubulan station in the village of Batubulan (see p.324) runs bemos to Ubud and the east coast, including Candi Dasa, Padang Bai and Singaraja. Ubung bemos run to the

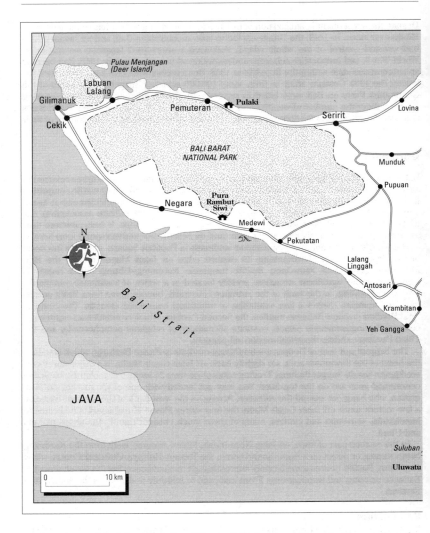

north and west of the island, including Gilimanuk, Bedugul and Singaraja. Buses to Java also use Ubung: Jakarta, Solo, Surabaya and Yogya.

Denpasar's **city transport** system relies on the fleet of colour-coded public bemos that shuttle between the city's bemo terminals. Only certain routes are covered, and the complex one-way system often means that the bemos take different routes on each leg of their journey; see the City Bemo Routes box on p.312. Prices are fixed, but tourists are often obliged to pay more – generally between Rp500 and Rp1000 for a cross-city ride.

The **tourist office** is just off Puputan Square, at Jl Surapati 7 (Mon–Thurs 7am–2pm, Fri 7–11am, Sat 7am–1pm; ☎ 0361/223602).

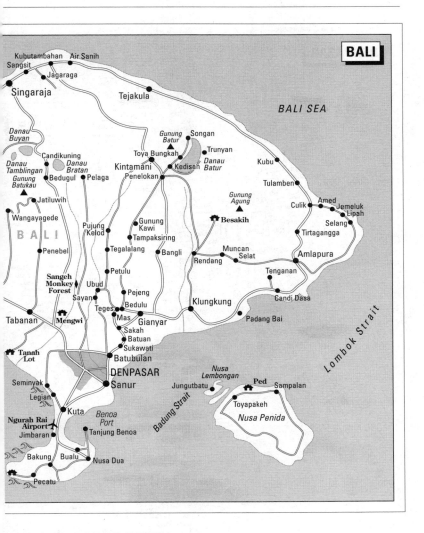

ACCOMMODATION AND EATING

Very few backpackers **stay** in Denpasar, but those who do, usually head for *Adi Yasa*, Jl Nakula 23 (☎0361/222679; ①–②), a friendly, family-run losmen that's slightly run-down and not all that secure. Yellow/turquoise Tegal–Kereneng bemos pass the front door; from Kereneng, take an Ubung-bound bemo to the Pasar Seni market at the Jalan Abimanyu/Jalan Veteran junction. Across the road is the less popular but more comfortable *Nakula Familiar Inn*, Jl Nakula 4 (☎0361/226446; ②), which has modern, clean en-suite rooms (bemo access as above).

One of the most rewarding **places to eat** in Denpasar is *Betty*, Jl Sumatra 56, which has a big, cheap menu that includes an imaginative vegetarian selection (closes at 9pm). *Depot*

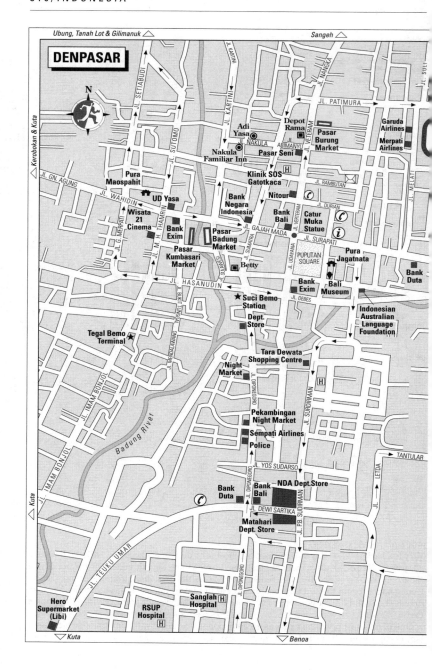

DENPASAR

Ubung, Tanah Lot & Gilimanuk △

Sangeh △

Kerobokan & Kuta ◁

JL. SETIABUDI
JL. KARTINI
JL. SUTOMO
JL. PATIMURA
JL. MANGKA
JL. SULI

N

Adi Yasa
Depot Rama
JL. NAKULA
Garuda Airlines
Merpati Airlines
JL. ABIMANYU
JL. VETERAM

Nakula Familiar Inn
Pasar Seni
Pasar Burung Market

Pura Maospahit
Klinik SOS Gatotkaca
JL. RAMBUTAN
JL. GN. AGUNG
JL. WAHIDIN
UD Yasa
Bank Negara Indonesia
Nitour
JL. DURIAN
JL. MELATI

Wisata 21 Cinema
Bank Exim
Bank Bali
Catur Muka Statue
JL. MERPATI
JL. G. GALUH
JL. M. H. THAMRIN
Pasar Badung Market
JL. GAJAH MADA
JL. VETERAN
JL. SURAPATI

Pasar Kumbasari Market
Betty
JL. SUMATRA
JL. SULAWESI
JL. UDAYANA
PUPUTAN SQUARE
Pura Jagatnata
Bank Duta

JL. HASANUDIN
Bank Exim
Bali Museum

★ Suci Bemo Station
Dept. Store
JL. DEBES

JL. BUKIT TUNGGAL
JL. MANDALAWANG
Tegal Bemo Terminal

Indonesian Australian Language Foundation

Tara Dewata Shopping Centre

Badung River

JL. DIPONEGORO
Night Market

Pekambingan Night Market
Sempati Airlines
Police
JL. SURDIRMAN

JL. IMAM BONJOL
TANTULAR

JL. YOS SUDARSO

JL. IMAM BONJOL
Bank Duta
Bank Bali
NDA Dept.Store
JL. DIPONEGORO
JL. DEWI SARTIKA
JL. P.B. SURDIRMAN
LETDA

◁ Kuta
Matahari Dept. Store

JL. TEUKU UMAR

Hero Supermarket (Libi)
RSUP Hospital
Sanglah Hospital
JL. DIPONEGORO

▽ Kuta
▽ Benoa

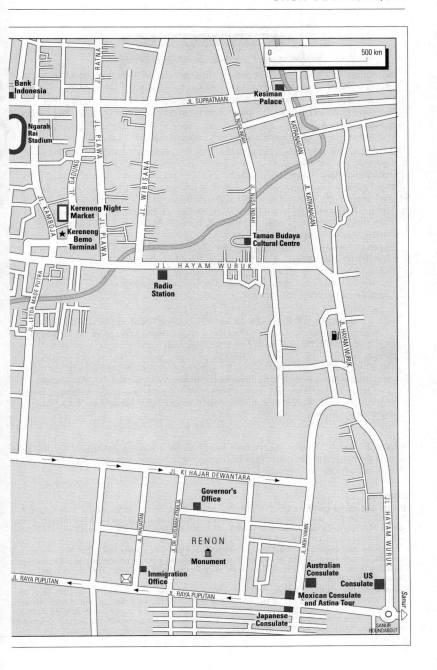

CITY BEMO ROUTES

Unless stated, all routes are identical in reverse.

Kereneng – Jl Plawa – Jl Supratman – Jl Gianyar – corner Jl Waribang (for barong dance) – Kesiman – Government Handicraft Centre – Tohpati – **Batubulan**.

Ubung (grey-blue) – Jl Cokroaminoto – Jl Gatot Subroto – Jl Gianyar – corner Jl Waribang (for barong dance) – Government Handicraft Centre – Tohpati – **Batubulan**.

Kereneng (dark green) – Jl Hayam Wuruk – corner Nusa Indah (for Taman Budaya Cultural Centre) – Sanur roundabout (for Renon consulates) – Jl Raya Sanur – **Sanur**.

Kereneng (turquoise) – Jl Surapati (for Tourist Information, Bali Museum and Pura Jagatnata) – Jl Veteran (alight at the corner of Jl Abimanyu for short walk to Jl Nakula losmen) – Jl Cokroaminoto – **Ubung**.

Tegal (yellow or turquoise) – Jl Gn Merapi – Jl Setiabudi – Ubung – Jl Cokroaminoto – Jl Subroto – Jl Yani – Jl Nakula (for budget hotels) – Jl Veteran – Jl Patimura – Jl Melati – Kereneng – Jl Hayam Wuruk – Jl Surapati – Jl Kapten Agung – Jl Sudirman – Tiara Dewata Shopping Centre – Jl Yos Sudarso – Jl Diponegoro – Jl Hasanudin – Jl Bukit Tunggal – **Tegal**.

Kereneng (beige) – Jl Raya Puputan (for GPO) – Jl Dewi Sartika (for Matahari and NDA department stores) – Jl Teuku Umar – Hero Supermarket – junction with Jl Imam Bonjol (alight to change onto Kuta bemos) – **Tegal**.
Because of the one-way system, the return Tegal–Kereneng route runs along Jl Letda Tantular instead of Jl Raya Puputan.

Tegal (dark blue) – Jl Imam Bonjol – Jl Teuku Umar – Hero Supermarket – junction with Jl Diponegoro (alight for Matahari and NDA department stores) – Jl Yos Sudarso – Jl Sudirman – Jl Letda Tantular – junction with Jl Panjaitan (alight for 500m walk to Immigration and GPO) – Jl Hajar Dewantara – Jl Moh Yamin – Sanur roundabout – **Sanur**.
The return Sanur–Tegal route goes all the way along Jalan Raya Puputan after the round-about, passing the entrance gates of the immigration office and the GPO, then straight along Jalan Teuku Umar, past Hero Supermarket to the junction with Jalan Imam Bonjol (where you should alight to pick up Kuta-bound bemos) before heading north up Jalan Imam Bonjol to Tegal.

Rama, Jl Veteran 55, is an inexpensive neighbourhood warung convenient for the Jalan Nakula losmen. After dark, the huge Kereneng Night Market sets up just off Jalan Hayam Wuruk and adjacent to Kereneng bemo station.

Listings

Banks and exchange There are ATMs for Visa, MasterCard and Cirrus Maestro at Bank Central Asia (BCA), Jl Sudirman 1 and Jl Diponegoro 183. Visa cash advances are available at Bank Bali diagonally opposite the Matahari department store on Jl Dewi Sartika (☎0361/261678), or at Jl Sulawesi 1 (☎0361/261684), and at Bank Duta, Jl Hayam Wuruk 165 (☎0361/226578).

Embassies and consulates Most foreign embassies are based in Jakarta (see p.222), but residents of Australia, Canada, Great Britain, Ireland and New Zealand should apply for help in the first instance to Bali's Australian consulate, which is at Jl Moh Yamin 51 in Renon (☎0361/235092). The US consulate is at Jl Hayam Wuruk 188 in Renon (☎0361/233605).

Hospitals and clinics Sanglah Public Hospital, at Jl Kesehatan Selatan 1, Sanglah (five lines ☎0361/227911–5; bemos from Denpasar's Kereneng bemo station), is the main provincial public hospital, with the island's most efficient emergency ward and Bali's only divers' decompression chamber. Kasih Ibu at Jl Teuku Umar 120 (☎0361/223036) is a private hospital and fine for minor ailments, but not equipped for emergencies. Klinik SOS Gatotkaca at Jl Gatotkaca 21 (☎0361/223555) is open 24hr and staffed by English-speakers.

Immigration office At the corner of Jl Panjaitan and Jl Raya Puputan, Renon (Mon–Thurs 8am–3pm, Fri 8–11am, Sat 8am–2pm; ☎0361/227828; Sanur–Tegal bemo).

Internet access The cheapest and fastest place in Bali is Wasantara Net (Mon–Sat 8am–8pm), at the back of the GPO compound in Renon (Sanur–Tegal bemo route).

Pharmacies Inside Tiara Dewata department store on Jl Sutoyo, Matahari department store on Jl Dewi Sartika, and Hero Supermarket on Jl Teuku Umar. Also, Apotik Kimia Farma at Jl Diponegoro 123.

Police There are police stations on Jl Pattimura and Jl Diponegoro.

Post offices Denpasar's poste restante (Mon–Sat 8am–8pm; Sanur–Tegal bemo) is at the GPO on Jl Raya Puputan in Renon. The Jl Rambutan PO, near Puputan Square, is more convenient.

Telephone services Telkom offices at Jl Teuku Umar 6, and on Jl Durian. IDD phones in the Tiara Dewata Department Store on Jl Sutoyo; Home Country Direct phone at the Bali Museum.

Kuta-Legian-Seminyak

The biggest, brashest, least traditional beach resort in Bali, the **KUTA-LEGIAN-SEMI-NYAK** conurbation is just 10km southwest of Denpasar. Packed with hundreds of hotels, restaurants, bars, clubs and shops, the six-kilometre strip plays host to several hundred thousand visitors a year and yet, for all its hustle, it remains a very good-humoured place, almost completely unsleazy. The beach is quite possibly the most beautiful in Bali, with its gentle curve of golden sand stretching for 8km, lashed by huge breakers. These waves make Kuta a great beach for surfers, but less pleasant for swimming, with a strong under-tow: always swim between the red- and yellow-striped flags. Poppies 2 is the centre of Kuta's surf scene, and the best place to buy boards or get them repaired; you can also rent boards on the beach (about Rp25,000). Monthly tide charts are compiled by Tubes bar on Poppies 2 and you can learn to surf at the Cheyne Horan School of Surf (mobile ☎081/835-7690; US$55/day). Wanasari Wisata, inside the G-Land surf shop at Jl Pantai Kuta 8b (☎0361/755588,), organizes four-to-seven-day surfing tours to the mega-waves off Sumbawa, East Java, West Java, Lombok and West Timor (US$200 to US$425), and Bali Surfing (☎0361/730184) does surfing packages to Bali, Lombok, Sumbawa and Nusa Lembongan (US$325–750 inclusive).

Arrival

All international and domestic flights use **Ngurah Rai Airport** (☎0361/751011), in the district of Tuban, 3km south of Kuta. There are 24hr currency exchanges here, several ATMs, accepting Visa, Cirrus and MasterCard, and a hotel desk. The domestic terminal is in the adjacent building. The easiest transport from the airport is by **prepaid taxi**: rates are fixed (Rp11,000 to Kuta's Bemo Corner; Rp16,500 to Legian; Rp17,500 to Seminyak; Rp25,000 to Sanur; Rp65,000 to Ubud) and payable just beyond the customs exit doors. **Metered taxis** are cheaper, but you have to walk out of the airport compound to hail one. Cheaper still are the dark-blue **public bemos** (6am–6pm; Rp1000 to Kuta/Legian), whose route takes in the big main road, Jalan Raya Tuban, about 700m beyond the airport gates. The northbound bemos (heading left up Jalan Raya Tuban) go via Kuta's Bemo Corner and Jalan Pantai Kuta as far as Jalan Melasti, then travel back down Jalan Legian and on to Denpasar's Tegal terminal. If you want to go straight from the airport to **Ubud**, **Candi Dasa** or **Lovina**, the cheapest way is to take the bemo to Denpasar's Tegal bemo station (Rp2000) and then continue by bemo from there.

Arriving in Kuta by **shuttle bus**, you could be dropped almost anywhere, depending on your shuttle-bus operator. The two biggest operators both have drop-offs in south Kuta: Perama buses terminate at their office on Jalan Legian, about 100m north of Bemo Corner, while Simpatik buses make two stops, at Kuta Square (west end of Jalan Singo Sari), and at Kuta Centre (Jalan Dewi Sartika).

Public bemos have a number of drop-off points in the Kuta area. Coming from Denpasar's Tegal terminal, the most convenient option is the dark-blue Tegal-Kuta-Legian service that

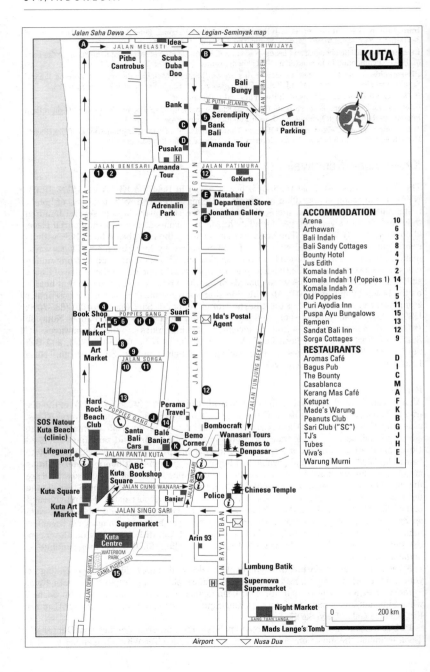

KUTA

ACCOMMODATION

Arena	10
Arthawan	6
Bali Indah	3
Bali Sandy Cottages	8
Bounty Hotel	4
Jus Edith	7
Komala Indah 1	2
Komala Indah 1 (Poppies 1)	14
Komala Indah 2	1
Old Poppies	5
Puri Ayodia Inn	11
Puspa Ayu Bungalows	15
Rempen	13
Sandat Bali Inn	12
Sorga Cottages	9

RESTAURANTS

Aromas Café	D
Bagus Pub	I
The Bounty	C
Casablanca	M
Kerang Mas Café	A
Ketupat	F
Made's Warung	K
Peanuts Club	B
Sari Club ("SC")	G
TJ's	J
Tubes	H
Viva's	E
Warung Murni	L

goes via Bemo Corner, west and then north along Jalan Pantai Kuta, east along Jalan Melasti before heading north up Jalan Legian only as far as Jalan Padma before turning round and continuing south down Jalan Legian as far as Bemo Corner; for anywhere north of Jalan Padma, you're better off getting a taxi.

Orientation and information

Although Kuta, Legian and Seminyak all started out as separate villages, they've now merged together so completely that it's impossible to recognize the borders. Kuta stretches north from the Patra Jasa hotel to Jalan Melasti; Legian runs from Jalan Melasti as far as Jalan Arjuna (aka Jalan Double Six); and Seminyak goes from Jalan Arjuna up to the Bali Oberoi hotel in the north. The resort's main road, Jalan Legian, runs north–south through all three districts, a total distance of 6km, and a lot of businesses give their address as nothing more than "Jalan Legian". Kuta's other main landmark is Bemo Corner, the tiny roundabout at the southern end of Kuta that stands at the Jalan Legian–Jalan Pantai Kuta intersection.

The most helpful government **tourist office** is the Bali and Java Tourist Information Centre at JlBunisari 36b (Mon–Sat 8am–8pm). Amanda Tour in the Century Plaza complex at JlBenesari 7 (daily 9am–8pm; ☎0361/754090) has good long-distance travel information, and sells shuttle bus tickets, domestic flights and bus and train tickets to Java; they also store luggage and act as a postal agent. The North Sulawesi Tourist Office is also in this building.

MOVING ON FROM KUTA

Flights

Many Kuta hotels provide transport to the **airport** (Rp20,000), though metered taxis are cheaper (Rp7500 from Kuta). Tourist shuttle buses run to the airport regularly throughout the day from every tourist centre on the island (Rp8000 from Sanur, Rp10,000 from Ubud, Rp15,000 from Candi Dasa, and Rp20,000 from Lovina). During daylight hours, you can also take the dark-blue Tegal (Denpasar)–Kuta–Tuban bemo from Denpasar or Kuta, which will drop you just beyond the airport gates.

Shuttle buses and transport to other islands

If you're going from Kuta to anywhere beyond Denpasar, it's always quicker – although more expensive – to take a tourist **shuttle bus** rather than public transport. Every one of the hundred or more tour agencies in Kuta–Legian–Seminyak offers "shuttle bus services" to tourist destinations on Bali, and some do transport to Lombok and Java as well. **Perama Travel** (☎0361/751551), located 100m north of Bemo Corner at Jl Legian 39, is the biggest operator and does several daily runs to Sanur, Ubud, Kintamani, Lovina, Bedugul, Padang Bai, Candi Dasa, Tirtagangga, Tulamben, Culik and Yeh Sanih, as well as to Jakarta, Yogya, Senggigi, Kuta (Lombok) and the Gili Islands. Their main competitor is **Simpatik**, whose Kuta agent is at *Millertime Café* (☎0361/755663), next to *Paddy's Bar* on Jalan Legian. Or try Amanda Tour, in the Century Plaza complex at Jl Benesari 7 (☎0361/754090).

Bemos

To get from Kuta to most other destinations in Bali by **bemo** almost always entails going via Denpasar. Dark-blue bemos to Denpasar from Kuta run throughout the day and terminate at Denpasar's Tegal terminal (25min; Rp1500–2000). The easiest place to catch them is at the Jalan Pantai Kuta/Jalan Raya Tuban intersection, about 50m east of Bemo Corner. For destinations further afield, you'll need to get a cross-city bemo from Tegal to another bemo station.

LEGIAN-SEMINYAK

Bali Oberoi, Bintang Lima, Kerobokan, Canggu

0   200 m

N

JALAN DHYANA PURA (JALAN GADO-GADO)

Scandal Disco

Deva Internet

Banjar Seminyak

Krakatoa

JALAN ABIMANYU

JALAN SEMINYAK

Biasa

Talismans of Power

In Touch

Mini Market

ATM

A J Hackett Bunjy

Mahogany Bookstore
Oxo Gallery

Batik Shops

JALAN DOUBLE SIX (JALAN ARJUNA)

Batik Shops

JALAN WERK UDARA

JALAN LEGIAN

Swiss & Austrian Consulate

Banjar Legian Kaja

PURA BAGUS TARUNA

Rusty's Surfwear

(RUM JUNGLE)

Bali Cyber Café

Patola Ratu

Legian Clinic 7

Balé Banjar

Oasis

Balé Banjar

Rudyana

ATM

Kerta Books

GANG THREE BROTHERS

JALAN PADMA UTARA

JALAN PADMA

Legian Cyber Café

JALAN SAHADEWA

Banjar Legian Kelod

Sumba Shop

Art Market

JALAN MELASTI

Jalan Benesari   see 'Kuta map'

RESTAURANTS, BARS & CLUBS

Bali Too	L
Bulongo	H
Bruna Reggae Bar	C
Double 6	D
Gado-Gado	B
Glory	I
Goa 2001	E
Gosha Seafood	M
Hulu Café	K
Jaya Pub	F
Made's Warung 2	A
Soda Club	G
Warung Kopi	J

ACCOMMODATION

Ayodia Beach Inn	11
Bali Coconut Hotel	8
Hotel Kumala	5
Legian Beach Bungalow	14
Lumbung Sari	10
Mesari Beach Inn	3
Puri Cendana	1
Puri Mangga Bungalows	4
Raja Gardens	2
Rum Jungle Road	7
Sri Ratu Cottages	9
Sri Ratu Cottages	12
Suri Wathi	15
Su's Cottages	6
Three Brothers Inn	13

AIRLINE OFFICES IN BALI

International

Most airline offices open Mon–Fri 8.30am–5pm, Sat 8.30am–noon. Garuda has offices and city check-ins inside the *Sanur Beach Hotel* in southern Sanur (24-hour ☎0361/270535), and at the *Natour Kuta Beach Hotel* in Kuta (☎0361/751179).

The following international airlines all have their offices inside the compound of the *Grand Bali Beach Hotel* in Sanur: Air France ☎0361/288511 extn 1105; Ansett Australia ☎0361/289636; Cathay Pacific ☎0361/286001; Continental Micronesia ☎0361/287774; JAL ☎0361/287576; Northwest Airlines ☎0361/287841; Qantas ☎0361/288331; Thai International ☎0361/288141.

Air New Zealand has offices in Ngurah Rai Airport (☎0361/756170), as do ANA (☎0361/761101), Eva Air (☎0361/751011), and Malaysia Air (☎0361/764995). Singapore Airlines/Silk Air is on the 3rd Floor of the Bank Bali building at Jl Dewi Sartika 88 in Denpasar (☎0361/261666); Lauda Air is at Jl Bypass Ngurah Rai 12 (☎0361/758686), and British Airways is in Jakarta on ☎021/521 1500.

Domestic

Air Mark, Ngurah Rai airport (☎0361/759769); Bouraq, Jl Sudirman 19a, Denpasar (☎0361/223564), Natour Bali hotel compound, Jl Veteran, Denpasar (☎0361/241397); Garuda, Jl Melati 61, Denpasar (☎0361/263523); Merpati, Jl Melati 51, Denpasar (☎0361/263918).

Getting around

Public transport in Kuta-Legian-Seminyak is less than ideal, as the dark-blue public Tegal-Kuta-Legian **bemos** (6am–8.30pm) only cover a clockwise loop around Kuta, leaving out most of Legian and all of Seminyak (see box on p.312). You can flag them down at any point along this route; the standard fare for any distance within this area is Rp500, but tourists are sometimes obliged to pay up to Rp1000. The easiest alternative is the resort's **metered taxis**, which all charge Rp2000 flagfall and Rp900/km, day and night. The informal taxi service offered by the ubiquitous transport touts involves tiresome bargaining and is rarely cheaper.

Most **car rental** places offer 800cc Suzuki Jimnys as well as larger, more comfortable 1600cc Toyota Kijangs (from Rp80,000/day). At the most reputable outlets, insurance is included, though usually with a US$500 excess. You can also rent **motorbikes** (Rp35,000) and **bicycles** (Rp15,000) from many of the same places.

Accommodation

The inexpensive **losmen** are mainly concentrated in the Kuta area, particularly along Poppies 1 and the gang (alleys) running off it, and along Poppies 2 and Jalan Benesari. (In the rainy season, from late October through March, some losmen on the middle stretches of Poppies 1, Jalan Sorga and Poppies 2 get flooded, so you may have to upgrade a little.) Legian has particularly good-value accommodation in the ③–⑤ bracket, often with a pool and air-con.

KUTA

Kuta is the most congested and hectic part of the resort, with the bulk of the bars, restaurants, clubs and shops. The beach gets crowded, but has clean, fine sand.

Arena, off Poppies Gang 1 (☎0361/752974). Good-value, modern place about 5min from the beach, with hotel rooms, bungalows, traditional cottages, some air-con and a pool. Most bemos and taxis will only drop off at the Maharani hotel on Jl Pantai Kuta, from where you'll have to walk. ②–③.

Arthawan, Poppies 2 (☎0361/752913). Decent, inexpensive budget losmen right in the heart of Kuta's surfers'/travellers' hub. Rooms are quiet, if a bit faded, and breakfasts are huge. ①–②.

Bali Indah, between Poppies 2 and Jl Benesari (☎0361/752509). Slightly shabby rooms in a block, and a bit of a trek from the beach, but rates are low. If full there are three similar options next door. ②.

Bali Sandy Cottages, off Poppies 2 (☎0361/753344). Excellent-value, prettily furnished rooms set round a huge lawn. Quiet location, 3min from the beach and 5min from Poppies 2. ③.

Bounty Hotel, Poppies 2 (☎0361/753030). Large, extremely good-value terraced air-con bungalows set in a garden. Two pools and big discounts. ⑦.

Jus Edith, south off Poppies 2 (☎0361/750558). Basic rooms, but exceptionally cheap for the location, which is close to the action. Extremely popular. ②.

Komala Indah 1 (Jl Benesari), Jl Benesari (☎0361/753185). A range of terraced bungalows set in a pretty garden. Some hot water. ①–③.

Komala Indah 1 (Poppies 1), Poppies 1 (☎0361/751422). Compact square of terraced bungalows that's conveniently located and one of the cheapest places to stay in Kuta. ①.

Komala Indah 2 (Jl Benesari), Jl Benesari (☎0361/754258). Simply furnished, inexpensive losmen rooms located on a quiet part of Jl Benesari that's just thirty seconds' walk from the beach. ①–②.

Old Poppies, Poppies 2 (☎0361/751059). Attractive traditional-style cottages set in a beautiful garden, with use of the pool at *Poppies Cottages* on Poppies 1. ⑥.

Puri Ayodia Inn, Jl Sorga (☎0361/754245). Well-furnished, inexpensive losmen rooms in a convenient but quiet location between Poppies 1 and Poppies 2. Fills up fast. ①.

Puspa Ayu Bungalows, Gang Puspa Ayu, off Jl Dewi Sartika (☎0361/756721). The cheapest and most popular accommodation in this area, with decent bungalows 50m off the main road. ③–④.

Rempen, off Poppies 1 (☎0361/753150). Well-kept rooms, some in a three-storey tower, others in terraced garden bungalows. Directions as for Arena, p.317. ②.

Sandat Bali Inn, Jl Legian 120 (☎0361/753491). Right in the heart of the action, just a few metres from *Paddy's Bar*, with reasonable losmen rooms in a garden. ②.

Sorga Cottages, Jl Sorga (☎0361/751897). Recommended, good-value, comfortable rooms (some air-con) in a three-storey block. Pool. ③–⑤.

LEGIAN

Significantly calmer than Kuta, **Legian** attracts the resort's more laid-back travellers as well as long-stay surfers.

Ayodia Beach Inn, Gang Three Brothers (☎0361/752169). Shabby, inexpensive terraced rooms in a garden. ①.

Bali Coconut Hotel (aka *Kelapa Hotel*), Jl Padma Utara (☎0361/754122). This bargain seafront hotel has 36 good rooms, all with air-con and TV, and there's a pool. ⑤.

Hotel Kumala, Jl Werk Udara (☎0361/732186). Huge complex of nicely furnished air-con rooms and cottages. Two pools. Good value. ⑥.

Legian Beach Bungalow, Jl Padma (☎0361/751087). Average but pleasant enough bungalows set in a garden with a swimming pool. Close to the shops and near the beach. ③.

Lumbung Sari, Gang Three Brothers (☎0361/752009). Huge, good-value two-storey bungalows, with kitchen, plus some cheaper rooms in a block. Pool. ④–⑦.

Puri Mangga Bungalows, Jl Arjuna (☎0361/730447). Good-value rice barn-style bungalows with kitchen, for two to four people. Also losmen rooms. Discounts for weekly rental. 1min from the beach. ②–⑥.

Rum Jungle Road, Jl Bagus Taruna (☎0361/764947). Exceptionally good value small, if rather compact hotel, with smart, air-con rooms and a pool. Some cheaper fan rooms too. ③–⑤.

Sri Ratu Cottages, Gang Three Brothers (☎0361/751722). Set in a pretty garden away from the main drag, with good-value bungalows and a pool. ③–⑥.

Suri Wathi, Jl Sahadewa 12 (☎0361/753162). Friendly, family-run losmen with good-value bungalows, some smaller rooms and a pool. ③–④.

Su's Cottages, Jl Bagus Taruna/Jl Werk Udara 532 (☎0361/730324). Spotless, nicely furnished rooms in a small, family-run losmen. Some air-con, and a tiny pool. ④–⑤.

Three Brothers Inn, Jl Three Brothers (☎0361/751566). Rambling garden complex that stretches all the way from Jl Padma Utara to Jl Three Brothers and holds dozens of large, attractive bungalows and a pool. It's efficiently run, good value and popular. Recommended. ⑤–⑥.

SEMINYAK

You'll need transport if staying in **Seminyak**, as eating and entertainment options are limited, and Legian's shops and restaurants are at least 1km away.

Mesari Beach Inn, Jl Abimanyu, south off Jl Dhyana Pura (☎0361/730401). Exceptionally cheap semi-detached cottages, plus some two-storey cottages with kitchens. Direct access to the beach. ②–④.

Panca Jaya, Jl Abimanyu, south off Jl Dhyana Pura (☎0361/730458). Simple but comfortable enough losmen, offering some of the cheapest rooms in the area. ②.

Puri Cendana, Jl Dhyana Pura (☎0361/730869). Balinese-style two-storey cottages with air-con in a gorgeous garden with swimming pool just 30m from the beach; good value. ⑦–⑧.

Raja Gardens, Jl Abimanyu, south off Jl Dhyana Pura (☎0361/730494). Six nicely furnished bungalows, a 2min walk from the beach. Family-run and good value, with a pool. ⑥.

Eating

There are hundreds of **places to eat** in Kuta-Legian-Seminyak, and the range is phenomenal, from tiny streetside Balinese warungs to plush international restaurants in the smartest hotels. In general, the most sophisticated and interesting restaurants are located in the northern reaches of Legian and in Seminyak, but they are relatively expensive at around Rp30,000 for a main course. The main night market sets up on Gang Tuan Langa at the southern edge of Kuta.

KUTA

Aromas Café, Jl Legian. Outstanding and imaginative vegetarian food served in large portions. Menu includes Lebanese, Indian and Indonesian dishes. Mid-priced.

Bamboo Corner, Poppies 1. Small, inexpensive restaurant that serves especially delicious *fu yung hai* (fluffy Chinese omelettes stuffed with seafood or vegetables).

Kerang Mas Café, corner of Jl Pantai Kuta and Jl Melasti. Great location right on the beach – ideal for beers at sunset. Inexpensive pizzas, sandwiches and juices.

Ketupat, behind the Jonathan Gallery jewellery shop on Jl Legian. Superb menu of exquisite Indonesian dishes based around fish, goat and chicken, plus some vegetarian options. Upmarket in both style and quality. Moderate to expensive.

Made's Warung 1, Jl Pantai Kuta. Long-standing Kuta favourite whose table-sharing policy encourages sociability. Mainly standard Indonesian fare, plus cappuccino and cakes.

TJs, Poppies 1. Popular, efficiently run Mexican restaurant with tables set around a water garden. Mid-priced menu of tacos, enchiladas and burritos.

Viva's (Gemini) Restaurant, Jl Legian 135. Excellent mid-priced Chinese and seafood dishes, where specialities include crab and salted vegetables.

Warung Murni, Jl Pantai. Exceptionally cheap, old-style travellers' warung where the nasi goreng costs a bargain Rp4000 and there are just five formica tables.

LEGIAN AND SEMINYAK

Bali Too, Jl Melasti, Legian. Popular, inexpensive place serving recommended spicy Thai soup and some less interesting Indonesian and Western standards. Good-value set breakfasts.

Bintang Lima, Jl Lasmana 5a, at the head of the road down to the Oberoi (mobile ☎082/361 4905). Highly recommended, unpretentious and cheap but very unusual Balinese restaurant that's well worth the taxi-ride from Kuta; it's only got six tables, so call ahead. Closed Sun.

Bulongo, Jl Legian between Jl Bagus Taruna and Jl Arjuna, Legian. Modern take on a Masakan Padang café, where you assemble your own meal from the display of cold Sumatran dishes.

Glory, 200m north of Jl Yudisthira (aka Jl Padma) on Jl Legian, Legian. Hearty all-you-can-eat buffet breakfasts ($2) and Saturday-night Balinese buffets. ☎0361/751091 for free transport.

Goa 2000, Jl Legian, Seminyak. Stylish, barn-like restaurant with a huge, moderately priced menu spanning several national cuisines plus a range of cocktails.

Gosha Seafood, Jl Melasti, Legian. The most popular seafood restaurant in Legian and reasonably priced; lobster a speciality.

Made's Warung 2, 100m north of Jl Dhyana Pura on Jl Raya Seminyak. More stylish offshoot of the long-running Kuta eatery, with a surprisingly good Indonesian and European menu. Prices are moderate to expensive.

Soda Club, beachfront, off the west end of Jl Arjuna. Trendy, split-level seafront bar/restaurant whose imaginative, moderately priced menu covers everything from seafood to beef stroganoff.

Warung Kopi, Jl Legian 427, Legian. Delicious and imaginative mid-priced menu of Indonesian and Western dishes, with the emphasis on wholefood and plenty of veggie options.

Bars and clubs

Kuta boasts the liveliest and most diverse nightlife on the island, with most **bars and clubs** staying open till at least 1am. The clubs and bars here are friendly enough towards lone drinkers – male or female – but if you can't stand the prospect of drinking alone, you could join the twice-weekly Peanuts Pub Crawl, which starts at *Casablanca* and progresses north up Jalan Legian to the *Peanuts* disco-bar (☎0361/754149; every Tues & Sat, departs hotels from 6.30pm; Rp5000). Kuta's gay scene is becoming more developed, with a dedicated gay bar in Legian at *Hulu Café*, and a strong gay presence at most Seminyak venues.

Bagus Pub, Poppies 2, Kuta. Large and loud tourist restaurant and video bar, popular with Australians and surfers.

The Bounty, just north of Jl Benesari on Jl Legian, and The New Bounty, between Poppies 1 and Poppies 2 on Jl Legian. Two identical novelty buildings, built to resemble Captain Bligh's eighteenth-century galleon, with heaving dance floors after 10pm. Both close at 2am.

Bruna Reggae Bar, Jl Legian, between Jl Arjuna and Jl Dhyana Pura, Seminyak. Nightly sets from local reggae bands (starting around 10.30pm); free.

Casablanca, south of Bemo Corner on Jl Buni Sari, Kuta. Lively enough drinking spot, with live music at least twice weekly, when the Peanuts Pub Crawl rolls in.

Double Six ("66"), off the beachfront end of Jl Arjuna, Seminyak (☎0361/731266). Current club hits and European DJs attract a fashion-conscious local and expat crowd. Opens midnight to 6am every Mon, Thurs & Sat, but call first. Admission Rp30,000–50,000.

Gado-Gado, Jl Dhyana Pura (aka Jl Gado-Gado), Seminyak (☎0361/730955). Huge, stylish beachfront club, with a trendy atmosphere very similar to *Double Six*. Admission Rp30,000–50,000. Open midnight–6am, closed Mon & Thurs, but call first.

Goa 2001, Jl Legian, Seminyak. Sophisticated restaurant that serves drinks after midnight and gets packed with the trendy pre-clubbing crowd. Closes around 3am.

Hard Rock Café, Jl Pantai. Part of the international chain, this place has a good reputation and attracts a huge crowd from around 11pm when the nightly band comes on stage. Drinks are expensive. Shuts at 2am (3am weekends).

Hulu Café, Jl Sahadewa, Legian. Bali's only exclusively gay venue attracts a mix of Indonesians, expats and tourists and stages regular drag shows. Admission Rp10,000. Open Tues–Sun 4pm till late.

Jaya Pub, Jl Legian, Seminyak. Fairly sedate live-music venue and watering-hole for older tourists and expats. Twenty or so tables; no real dance floor.

Paddy's Pub, Jl Legian, between Poppies 1 and Poppies 2. Loud music and reasonably priced beer make this Kuta's liveliest venue; the dance floor is always packed with young tourists and gigolos. Stays open till at least 2am.

Peanuts Club, just south of the Jl Melasti intersection on Jl Legian, Kuta. Large disco and bar with low-grade live music in the streetside section, and a classic rock sound system inside. Pool table, karaoke and reasonably priced drinks; closes at 2am.

Sari Club ("SC"), Jl Legian, Kuta. Hugely popular bar and club which attracts a young crowd of drinkers and clubbers. Friendly, party atmosphere and no cover charge. Closes about 3am.

Tubes, Poppies 2, Kuta. The surfers' hangout in Kuta, with notice boards and surfing videos, plus a bar and pool tables. No food or dancing. Closes around 2am.

The Villas, off Jl Raya Seminyak at Jl Kunti 118, 50m north of Made's Warung 2, Seminyak. Holds regular all-night parties and raves on Thurs, Fri & Sat nights from midnight to sunrise; check lamppost flyers for details. Attracts the trendy Seminyak expats.

Listings

Airline offices see box on p.317.

Banks and exchange There are Visa, MasterCard and Cirrus ATMs at branches of Bank Central Asia (BCA) on the ground floor of the Matahari department store in Kuta Square; in the Kuta Centre, Jl Dewi Sartika; at Jl Raya Kuta 121, Jl Legian 200 and Jl Seminyak 42. The Bank Bali opposite The Bounty at Jl Legian 118 offers Visa cash advances, as do several banks in Kuta Square. Be very careful about being ripped-off at exchange counters in Kuta: always work out exactly how much you should receive, and always be the last person to count your own money.

Batik classes Batik artist Heru gives workshops at his studio on Gang Kresek 5a, off Jl Singo Sari (☎0361/765087). Three-day workshops from Rp250,000.

Hospitals and clinics Tourist-oriented 24hr clinics with English-speaking doctors and emergency call-out facilities include: Legian Clinic 1, on Jl Benesari, north Kuta (☎0361/758503); Legian Clinic 7, on Jl Legian, 100m north of Glory restaurant, in Legian (☎0361/752376); SOS Natour Kuta Beach, next to the Natour Kuta hotel on Jl Pantai Kuta (☎0361/751361). Nearly all the big hotels have an in-house doctor. The nearest hospitals are in Denpasar, see p.312 for details.

Internet access Kuta is awash with places offering Internet access; the cheapest rate is Rp300/min, but Rp500/min is standard. Some of the most efficient cybercafés include *Bali @ Cyber Café and Restaurant* at Jl Pura Bagus Taruna 4 in Legian (daily 8.30am–11pm; ☎0361/761326); *Legian Cyber C@fe* at Jl Sahadewa 21, Legian (daily 8am–10.30pm; ☎0361/7621804); and *Krakatoa* at Jl Raya Seminyak 56, Seminyak, opposite Jl Dhyana Pura (Mon–Fri 8am–10pm, Sat & Sun 8am–8pm; ☎0361/730849).

Left luggage At Amanda Tour, Century Plaza, Jl Benesari 7, north Kuta (☎0361/754090); office hours are daily 8am–9pm, but luggage is accessible 24hr; Rp2000/day per piece.

Pharmacies You'll find a pharmacy on every major shopping street, as well as Legian Clinic 1, on Jl Benesari, north Kuta; next to Bemo Corner on JL Legian, south Kuta; and inside the Matahari Department Store in Kuta Square.

Police The police station is at the intersection of Jl Raya Tuban and Jl Singosari, and there's a tourist police booth on the beachside stretch of Jl Pantai, just north of Poppies 2.

Post office Kuta's GPO and poste restante is on a small gang between Jl Raya Tuban and Jl Tanjung Mekar (Mon–Thurs 8am–2pm, Fri 8am–noon, Sat 8am–1pm). Ida's Postal Agent opposite the Poppies 2 intersection at Jl Legian 61, Kuta, is more central and keeps longer hours (Mon–Sat 8am–8pm); services here include poste restante and fax receiving (fax 0361/751574). Poste/fax restante also at Amanda Tour in Century Plaza at Jl Benesari 7, Kuta (fax 0361/754146), and at Asthini Yasa Postal Agent, opposite Glory restaurant on Jl Legian, Legian (Mon–Sat 8am–8pm; fax 0361/752883). All the email centres also offer fax services.

Swimming pools Waterbom Park on Jl Dewi Sartika, south Kuta (☎0361/755676; daily 9am–6pm; US$13, 5–12 year olds US$7) is an aquatic adventure park with water slides and helter-skelters. The Hard Rock swimming pool on Jl Pantai Kuta (daylight hours; adults Rp50,000, family Rp150,000) is hundreds of metres long, with water chutes, a sandy beach area and poolside food.

Telephone services The government wartel is inconveniently sited down at the airport, but there are dozens of private wartels in the resort, most of them open 8am–midnight.

Sanur

Stretching down the southeast coast just 18km northeast of Ngurah Rai Airport, **SANUR** is an appealing, more peaceful alternative to Kuta, with a long, fairly decent white-sand beach, plenty of attractive accommodation in all price brackets and a distinct village atmosphere. There are plenty of restaurants and some bars, but the nightlife is pretty tame. A huge expanse of shore gets exposed at low tide and the reef lies only about 1km offshore at high tide. The currents beyond the reef are dangerously strong, which makes it almost impossible to swim here at low tide, but at other times of day swimming is fine and watersports are popular. You'll find Sanur's **best sand** in front of the *Grand Bali Beach* in north Sanur, where non-guests can rent sun-loungers for a small fee.

Many of south Bali's **watersports** facilities are centred in Sanur. In general, prices are higher at the hotels than at the independent places on the beachfront and along the main roads. All these places rent out canoes, windsurfers and jet skis, and most offer parasailing as well. Sanur is quite a good place to learn to dive, as the local diving sites are close by. All Sanur dive centres run certificated diving courses and one-day diving excursions (including tanks and weights only) for US$60–80.

Practicalities

Sanur is an eighteen-kilometre, Rp25,000 taxi-ride from the **airport**. The fastest and most direct way of getting to Sanur from most other places on Bali is by **tourist shuttle bus**. The two biggest operators, Perama and Simpatik, both have agents in Sanur, and run several buses a day between Sanur and Kuta, Ubud, Kintamani, Lovina, Bedugul, Padang Bai, Candi Dasa, Tirtagangga, Tulamben, Culik, Yeh Sanih, Senggigi, and Kuta in Lombok. Perama's agents are at *Si Pino* restaurant on Jalan Hang Tuah in north Sanur, Nagasari Tours opposite

Gazebo hotel on central Jalan Danau Tamblingan, and Tunas Tour on southern Jalan Danau Tamblingan. The Simpatik agent is Sinar VCD Rental, just south of the Alas Alarum supermarket on south-central Jalan Danau Tamblingan.

The only direct **bemos** to Sanur leave from Denpasar. Dark-green bemos from Denpasar's Kereneng terminal take fifteen minutes to north Sanur (Rp1500–2000), where they will drop passengers just outside the *Grand Bali Beach* compound at the Ngurah Rai Bypass/Jalan Hang Tuah junction only if asked; otherwise, they usually head down Jalan Danau Beratan and Jalan Danau Buyan, before continuing down Jalan Danau Tamblingan to the *Trophy Pub Centre* in south Sanur. Direct dark-blue bemos from Denpasar's Tegal terminal run via Jalan Teuku Umar and Renon (30min; Rp2000) and then follow the same route as the green Kereneng ones, depending on passenger requests.

The Sanur–Tegal and Sanur–Kereneng public bemos are also useful for **getting around** Sanur if you're sticking to the main streets; they cost Rp500 for any journey within Sanur. Otherwise, flag down a metered taxi (Rp2000 flagfall, then Rp900/km), or bargain hard with a transport tout. The touts also **rent cars** (Rp100,000) and motorbikes (Rp35,000), and most hotels rent bicycles (Rp10,000).

ACCOMMODATION

Sanur has less budget **accommodation** than Kuta, but mid-priced hotels are particularly good here, often offering air-con, hot water and a pool.

Bali Wirasana, Jl Danau Tamblingan 138, central Sanur (☎0361/288632). Large, clean and central, if unexciting, rooms; some air-con. Guests can use next door's pool. ③–④.

Baruna Beach, Jl Sindhu, north-central Sanur (☎0361/288546). Tiny beachfront complex of pleasant air-con bungalows. Friendly and good value. ⑥.

Coco Homestay, Jl Danau Tamblingan 42, central Sanur (☎0361/287391). Archetypal homestay offering some of the cheapest accommodation in Sanur. ②.

Hotel Kesumasari, Jl Cemara 22, south Sanur (☎0361/287492). Very good-value bungalows, with spacious rooms, a pool and some air-con. ⑥–⑦.

Hotel Segara Agung, Jl Duyung 43, south Sanur (☎0361/288446). Attractive place with twenty bungalows (some air-con) and a pool, set in a very quiet spot close to the beach. ④–⑥.

Keke Homestay, Gang Keke 3, off Jl Danau Tamblingan 96, central Sanur (☎0361/287282). Tiny losmen that's basic but friendly and offers simple fan rooms with cold-water mandi. ②.

Luisa Homestay, Jl Danau Tamblingan 40, central Sanur (☎0361/289673). One of three similar losmen clustered together in family compounds behind streetside businesses. Basic but cheerful. ②.

Respati Bali, Jl Danau Tamblingan 33, central Sanur (☎0361/288427). Smart, pristine bungalows in a rather compact compound that runs down to the sea. Pool and restaurant. ⑥–⑧.

Simon Homestay, down a tiny gang at Jl Danau Tamblingan 164d (☎0361/289158). Small, sparklingly clean family losmen with nicely furnished, well maintained rooms. ②–④.

Swastika, Jl Danau Tamblingan 128, central Sanur (☎0361/288693). Deservedly popular place, with good, comfortable rooms in a garden. Two pools and some air-con. Named after the Buddhist symbol, not the Nazi emblem. ⑥–⑦.

Watering Hole (Agung & Sue), Jl Hang Tuah 37, north Sanur (☎0361/288289). The cheapest rooms in this part of Sanur, only 250m from the beach; some air-con. Very handy for boats to Nusa Lembongan, and there's luggage storage and a restaurant. ②–④.

Yulia Homestay, Jl Danau Tamblingan 38, central Sanur (☎0361/288089). Friendly, family-run losmen, the best of the three similar outfits in this cluster. ②.

EATING

Sanur has plenty of **restaurants**, most of them located either on the main road through the resort, Jalan Danau Tamblingan, or along the beachfront walkway between La Taverna and Jalan Sindhu (north-central Sanur) and between Jalan Kesumasari and Jalan Duyung (south Sanur). The **night market** sets up at the Jalan Danau Tamblingan/Jalan Sindhu intersection.

Bonsai Café, beachfront walkway just north of *La Taverna* hotel, access off Jl Danau Tamblingan, central Sanur. Breezy seafront café, restaurant and bar (open till 2am) whose expansive views make it a relaxing place to eat and drink any time of day.

Café Batu Jimbar, Jl Danau Tamblingan, central Sanur. Mexican and Italian favourites, plus salads, home-baked cakes, breads and herbal teas.

Café Bawana, Jl Hang Tuah, north Sanur. Alternative eatery serving wholesome and unusual dishes (most of them vegetarian). Has a small library and Internet access.

Kafé Tali Jiwa, in front of the *Santai Hotel*, Jl Danau Tamblingan 148, central Sanur. Sanur's best vegetarian menu, plus traditional Balinese dishes.

Le Pirate, seafront, north-central Sanur. Large, mid-priced menu of pasta and pizza, plus some Indian and Thai food. Seaside location; attached to Segara Village.

Segara Agung, on the beachfront next to Segara Village, north-central Sanur (☎0361/288574). Ideally located restaurant with a huge choice of dishes, including lots of seafood. Run as a cooperative with all profits going to local schools; call for free transport.

Sri Bundo, Jl Danau Poso. Typical 24hr Masakan Padang place serving cheap Sumatran dishes.

Warung Aditya, Jl Danau Tamblingan, central Sanur. Homely, popular warung serving refreshingly cheap Indonesian and tourist favourites.

Warung Blanjong, Jl Danau Poso 78. Recommended cheap restaurant that serves only Balinese dishes, both veggie and non-veggie specialities.

BARS AND CLUBS

There are plenty of **bar-restaurants** on Sanur's beachfront, most of which stay pretty lively till around 1am, but only a few rather uninteresting **clubs**.

Banjar, beachfront end of Jl Duyung, south-central Sanur. Shoreside bar and restaurant, with occasional club nights fronted by local and international DJs. Check flyers for details.

Bali Janger, Jl Danau Tamblingan 21, central Sanur. Flashy, cavernous disco frequented by young professional couples from Denpasar. Opens from midnight till 5am.

Jazz Bar & Grille, inside the Sanur Raya complex at the Jl Ngurah Rai Bypass/Jl Hang Tuah crossroads, north Sanur. In the mellow downstairs bar, some of Bali's best jazz and blues bands play live sets every night from about 9.30pm. The upstairs restaurant serves quality seafood and there's a pool table. Daily 8am till about 1am.

Madés Pub, opposite *Gazebo* hotel on Jl Danau Tamblingan, central Sanur. Streetside bar with young, trendy staff who keep the punters plied with beers and cocktails until about 1am.

Mango Bar and Restaurant, beachfront end of Jl Sindhu, north-central Sanur. Beachfront bar and restaurant which features live reggae on Monday and Friday nights (9pm), a local band on Wednesdays (8pm) and children's traditional legong dance every Monday and Friday (8pm).

Matahari Beach Bar, beachfront end of Jl Sindhu, north-central Sanur. Breezy beachfront bar and restaurant with a pool table and a well-stocked bar. Shuts around 1am.

The Trophy, in the Trophy Pub Centre at Jl Danau Tamblingan 49, south Sanur. Typical expat pub with a darts board, pool table and satellite TV. Live music every night.

Listings

Banks and exchange American Express, Room 1111 inside the *Grand Bali Beach* hotel in north Sanur (Mon–Fri 8.30am–4.30pm, Sat 8.30am–1.30pm; ☎0361/288449), Poste Restante, c/o American Express, Room 1111, *Grand Bali Beach* hotel, Sanur, Bali. For fax restante dial ☎0361/287917 and state clearly that it's for the Amex office. Post is kept for one month. Amex also acts as a Moneygram agent. There are Cirrus/MasterCard ATMs dotted all over the resort, and the one at Bank Central Asia (BCA), Jl Danau Tamblingan 154, just south of the Hotel Santai in south-central Sanur, takes Visa cards as well.

Hospitals and clinics The tourist-oriented Legian Clinic 2, near Hotel Santai on central Jl Danau Tamblingan (☎0361/287446) is open 24 hours, has English-speaking staff, and does emergency call-outs. All the big hotels provide 24hr medical service; try the *Grand Bali Beach* (☎0361/288511) or the *Bali Hyatt* (☎0361/288271). The nearest hospitals are in Denpasar; see p.312 for details.

Internet access Available at half a dozen places for Rp500/min, from 8am–11pm, including: Go Network, opposite *Besakih* hotel on central Jl Danau Tamblingan; the Environmental Information Centre (PIL) in the lobby of the *Hotel Santai*, Jl Danau Tamblingan 148; and *Café Bawana* on Jl Hang Tuah, north Sanur. The *Grand Bali Beach* charges US$5/10 min.

Pharmacies There are several pharmacies on Jl Danau Tamblingan, as well as one inside the Alas Alarum Supermarket on central Jl Danau Tamblingan.

Police The police station is on the Ngurah Rai Bypass in north Sanur, just south of the *Radisson* hotel.

Post office Sanur's main post office is on Jl Danau Buyan, north-central Sanur. There are postal agents next to Diwangkara hotel on Jl Hang Tuah in north Sanur; opposite Respati hotel at Jl Danau Tamblingan

66 in central Sanur; and inside the Trophy Centre at the southern end of the same road. You can receive poste restante c/o Agen Pos, Jl Danau Tamblingan 66, Sanur 80228 (Mon–Fri 8.30am–5.30pm, Sat 8.30am–1pm).

Telephone services Direct-dial public telephones in the basement shopping arcade of the Grand Bali Beach in north Sanur.

Benoa Harbour (Pelabuhan Benoa)

If you arrive in Bali on the *Bounty* boat from Gili Meno or Lombok, on the *Mabua Express* from Lombok, or on a Pelni ship from elsewhere in Indonesia, you'll dock at **Benoa Harbour** (Pelabuhan Benoa), located off the end of a long causeway that juts out into the sea 5km southwest of southern Sanur. The easiest way to get to and from Benoa Harbour is by metered taxi; it's a short ride of about Rp10,000 into Sanur, or about Rp15,000 to Kuta. To enquire about Pelni boats to other islands, call the Pelni office (Mon–Fri 8am–4pm, Sat 8am–12.30pm; ☎0361/721377). *Bounty* and *Mabua Express* boats can be booked through almost any tour agent in the main tourist resorts, but you'll need to arrange your own transport to the port.

Batubulan

Barely distinguishable from the northeastern suburbs of Denpasar, **BATUBULAN** acts as the capital's public transport interchange for all bemos heading east and northeast, but it's also an important village in its own right, home of the most famous barong dance troupes, and respected across the island for its superb stonecarvers. The northern stretch of the village, known as Tegaltamu, is the most interesting, and it's here that you'll find the shops selling Batubulan's finest stonecarvings. Local sculptors specialize in images made either from the rough grey lava stone known as paras, or from smooth grey, yellow or pink sandstone.

Every morning of the year, the **barong** is performed (9.30–10.30am; Rp20,000) on a stage 200m east off the main road in the north of the village. You can get here by public bemo and buy tickets on the door, but most people come on all-inclusive tours from Kuta or Sanur. Batubulan dancers also put on nightly performances of the kecak dance in a double bill with the fire dance (6.30–8.00pm; Rp20,000) at a stage a few hundred metres further south down the road to Denpasar.

About 500m west of the Tegaltamu intersection, or 3km northwest of Batubulan bemo terminal, the landscaped grounds of the **Bali Bird Park** (daily 8am–6pm; US$8) are home to an impressive menagerie, including birds of paradise and Bali starlings; in the adjacent **Bali Reptile Park** (daily 8am–6pm; US$8) the star attraction is the eight-metre-long reticulated python. Any bemo running between Batubulan and Ubud or Gianyar will drop you at the intersection.

Batubulan's **bemo station** is at the far southern end of the village and runs chocolate-brown bemos to Ubud, some of which continue to Kintamani. Destinations east of Batubulan are served by dark-blue-and-fawn-coloured bemos, which head for Amlapura via Gianyar, Klungkung, the turn-off for Padang Bai, and Candi Dasa. Buses also depart from Batubulan bemo station to Amlapura and Singaraja.

Ubud

Ever since the German artist Walter Spies arrived here in 1928, **UBUD** has been a magnet for any tourist with the slightest curiosity about Balinese arts. The people of Ubud and adjacent villages really do still paint, carve, dance and make music, and hardly a day goes by without there being some kind of festival in the area. However, although it's fashionable to characterize Ubud as the real Bali, especially in contrast with Kuta, it actually bears little resemblance to a typical Balinese village. Cappuccino cafés, riverside losmen and woodcarving

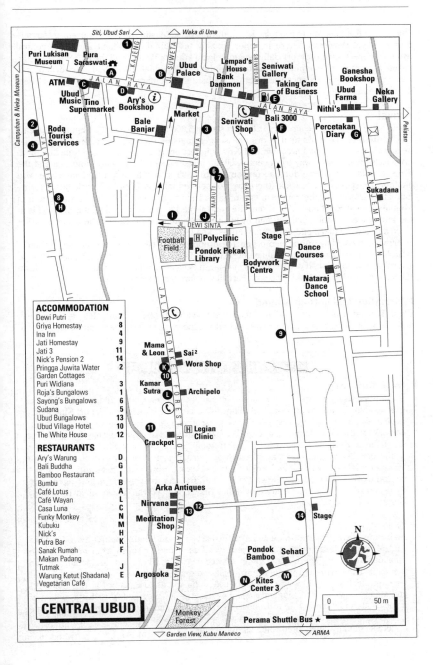

Siti, Ubud Sari △   △ Waka di Ume

Puri Lukisan Museum
Pura Saraswati
ATM
Ubud Music
Tino Supermarket
Ary's Bookshop
Bale Banjar
Roda Tourist Services

JL KAJENG
JL SUWETA
JALAN RAYA
Ubud Palace
Lempad's House
Bank Danamon
Market
JL SRIWEDARI
Seniwati Gallery
Taking Care of Business
Ganesha Bookshop
Ubud Farma
Neka Gallery
Nithi's
Bali 3000
Seniwati Shop
Percetakan Diary
Campuhan & Neka Museum
JALAN BISMA
JALAN KARNA
JALAN MARUTI
JALAN GAUTAMA
JALAN HANOMAN
JALAN SUGRIWA
JALAN JEMBAWAN
Sukadana

JL. DEWI SINTA
Football Field
Polyclinic
Pondok Pekak Library
Stage
Dance Courses
Bodywork Centre
Nataraj Dance School

ACCOMMODATION

Dewi Putri	7
Griya Homestay	8
Ina Inn	4
Jati Homestay	9
Jati 3	11
Nick's Pension 2	14
Pringga Juwita Water Garden Cottages	2
Puri Widiana	3
Roja's Bungalows	1
Sayong's Bungalows	6
Sudana	5
Ubud Bungalows	13
Ubud Village Hotel	10
The White House	12

RESTAURANTS

Ary's Warung	D
Bali Buddha	G
Bamboo Restaurant	I
Bumbu	B
Café Lotus	A
Café Wayan	L
Casa Luna	C
Funky Monkey	N
Kubuku	M
Nick's	H
Putra Bar	K
Sanak Rumah	F
Makan Padang	J
Tutmak	J
Warung Ketut (Shadana)	E
Vegetarian Café	

JALAN MONKEY FOREST ROAD

Mama & Leon
Sai²
Wora Shop
Kamar Sutra
Archipelo
Legian Clinic
Crackpot

JL. WANARA WANAI

Arka Antiques
Nirvana
Meditation Shop
Argosoka
Stage
Pondok Bamboo
Sehati
Kites Center 3
Perama Shuttle Bus ★

CENTRAL UBUD

N

0   50 m

Monkey Forest

▽ Garden View, Kubu Maneco   ▽ ARMA

△ Peliatan

shops crowd its central marketplace and, during peak season, foreigners seem to far out-number local residents. There is major (mostly tasteful) development along the central Monkey Forest Road (now officially renamed Jalan Wanara Wana), and the peripheries of the village have merged so completely into its neighbouring hamlets that Ubud now covers some nine square kilometres, encompassing Campuhan, Penestanan, Nyuhkuning, Peliatan, Pengosekan and Padang Tegal.

Arrival

A fixed-fare taxi from the airport to Ubud costs Rp65,000 and takes about an hour. The smaller **shuttle-bus** operators tend to drop passengers outside their agent's office, which could be anywhere in the Ubud area, while the two biggest operators, Perama and Simpatik, both drop passengers some way from central Ubud; guesthouse touts usually congregate at the drop-off points and if you don't accompany them you'll either have to negotiate a ride with another transport tout, or walk (there are no metered taxis in Ubud). Perama buses terminate at their office at the southern end of Jalan Hanoman, about 750m from the bottom of Monkey Forest Road and 2.5km from the central market place. The Simpatik drop-off is at the Pura Dalem at the northern end of Jalan Sukma, about 1km east of the central market place and the northern end of Monkey Forest Road.

Arriving in Ubud by **public bemo**, you'll be dropped at the central market, on the junction of Jalan Raya (or main road) and Monkey Forest Road (signed as "Jalan Wanara Wana"), close to central accommodation. If you're planning to stay in Peliatan, any bemo coming from Batubulan (Denpasar) or Kintamani can drop you there first before terminating in central Ubud.

Information and getting around

Ubud **Tourist Information** (daily 10am–8pm; ☎0361/973285) is on Jalan Raya and has noticeboards giving dance-performance schedules, news on special events and a directory of

---

MOVING ON FROM UBUD

By shuttle bus

All shuttle-bus operators run several services a day between Ubud and major tourist centres on Bali, Lombok and Java, including: Kuta, Ngurah Rai airport, Sanur, Kintamani, Lovina, Bedugul, Padang Bai, Candi Dasa, Tirtagangga, Tulamben, Culik, Yeh Sanih, Gilimanuk, the Gili Islands, Senggigi, Tetebatu, Kuta in Lombok, Surabaya, Yogyakarta and Jakarta. **Perama** buses (☎0361/973316) do pick-ups from certain designated points in the centre. Perama ticket agents include Purnama on Monkey Forest Road, Wira Wisata on Jalan Dewi Sita, and Rona on Jalan Sukma. **Simpatik**'s head office is in the central market place on Jalan Raya (☎0361/977364) and their ticket/pick-up agents are Ary's Travel on Jalan Raya, Roda on Jalan Bisma, and Wayan Travel, next to Pertiwi Bungalows on Monkey Forest Road.

By bemo

All **bemos** leave from central Jalan Raya: the east- and southbound bemos leave from the central marketplace, and the north- and westbound ones from in front of the tourist information office. There's a regular service between Ubud and Kintamani (brown bemos usually; 1hr), and frequent turquoise-and-orange bemos go to Gianyar (20 min) via Goa Gajah (10min), where you can make connections to Padang Bai (for Lombok) and Candi Dasa, and to Singaraja and Lovina. Any journey south, to Kuta or Sanur, involves an initial bemo ride to Denpasar's Batubulan station (50min), plus at least one cross-city connection (see p.312). To reach western Bali and Java by bemo, you'll need to take an equally convoluted route via Batubulan.

emergency numbers. If you're planning to do any Ubud walks, buy the Travel Treasure Maps: Indonesia VI – Ubud Surroundings, from any bookstore.

The most enjoyable way of seeing Ubud and its environs is **on foot** or by **bicycle** (available from losmen and tour agencies for Rp15,000 per day). Numerous places on Monkey Forest Road rent out motorbikes and cars – if you're driving up to the Kintamani volcanoes or to the north coast, it's worth splashing out on a more powerful Kijang rather than the cheaper Jimny. The most central Ubud fuel station is on the eastern arm of Jalan Raya, opposite Bali 3000 Internet; it's extremely difficult to get fuel after about 7pm anywhere in the Ubud area.

There are no metered taxis in Ubud, but there are plenty of **transport touts**. You can use the **public bemos** for short hops around the area: to get to Campuhan and the Neka Museum, for example, just flag down any bemo heading west, such as the turquoise ones going to Payangan (Rp500), or ask at the terminal in front of the central market. For Pengosekan or Peliatan, take a brown Batubulan-bound bemo.

Accommodation

There are hundreds of rooms for rent in and around Ubud, and you're almost certain to find that your **accommodation** is set in lush surroundings and that a generous breakfast is included in the price of the room. **Monkey Forest Road** is the most central, but also the most congested, part of town, but accommodation on most of the tiny adjacent roads (eg Jalan Karna, Jalan Maruti, Jalan Gautama, Jalan Kajeng and Jalan Bisma) tends to be more peaceful and low-key. Staying in **Peliatan** or **Penestanan** will be more of a village experience, though Penestanan in particular is a bit of a hike from the main restaurants and shops, as is Campuhan. **Nyuhkuning** is a good in-between option, only a pleasant ten-minute walk from the restaurants of Monkey Forest Road and with lots of uninterrupted paddy-field views; its one drawback is that you need to walk or cycle through the Monkey Forest after dark if you're going into central Ubud in the evening.

CENTRAL UBUD

All **Central Ubud** losmen listed below are marked on the Central Ubud map (see p.325), except for *Gasti's*, shown on the map on pp.328–329.

Dewi Putri, Jl Maruti 8 (☎0361/973304). Large, well-furnished bungalows in a quiet little gang make this place very good value. Run by a family of painters. ②.

Griya Homestay, Jl Bisma (☎0361/975428). The cheapest accommodation on this idyllic hillside gang overlooking the terraced paddies. Large, spruce rooms, with fine views. ③.

Gusti's Garden Bungalows, Jl Kajeng 27 (☎0361/96311). Pleasant, inexpensive rooms set around a pool; convenient and peaceful. ③.

Ina Inn, Jl Bisma (☎0361/973317). Well-maintained and nicely furnished cottages, set in a garden on a small gang surrounded by rice fields. Rooftop swimming pool. ⑤–⑥.

Jati Homestay, Jl Hanoman (☎0361/977781). Ten comfortably furnished bungalows built in a two-storey block facing the rice paddies. Run by a family of painters. ②.

Jati 3, off south-central Monkey Forest Road (☎0361/973249). Recommended place with five pleasant losmen bungalows and four gorgeous split-level bungalows with great river views. ③–⑤.

Nick's Pension 2, Jl Hanoman 57 (☎0361/975526). Seven good-value, clean, whitewashed rooms in a typical losmen-style garden compound. ②.

Pringga Juwita Water Garden Cottages, Jl Bisma (☎0361/975734). Beautifully designed bungalows with traditional-style rooms and garden bathrooms. Peaceful, scenic location and there's a swimming pool too. ⑧–⑨.

Puri Widiana, Jl Karna 5 (☎0361/973406). Good-value basic rooms in a small family compound that's centrally located but peaceful. ②.

Roja's Bungalows, Jl Kajeng 1 (☎0361/975107). Small, friendly, centrally located homestay offering large rooms with character at a range of prices. ②–③.

Sayong's Bungalows, Jl Maruti (☎0361/973305). Seven simply furnished bungalow rooms set around a typical losmen garden at the end of a very quiet residential gang. Swimming pool. ②–③.

Sudana, Jl Gautama 11 (☎0361/976435). A typical homestay: small, friendly and family-run, offering clean if slightly spartan rooms in a small garden. ②.

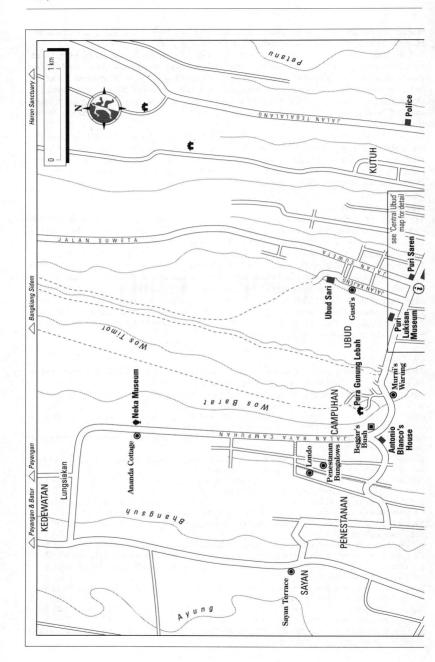

Heron Sanctuary

0   1 km

N

Petanu

JALAN TEGALLANG

Police

KUTUH

see 'Central Ubud' map for detail

Puri Saren

JALAN SUWETA

Bangkiang Sidem

JALAN KAJENG

JALAN SUWETA

Ubud Sari

Gusti's

UBUD

Puri Lukisan Museum

Wos Timor

Neka Museum

Wos Barat

Pura Gunung Lebah

CAMPUHAN

Murni's Warung

Payangan

JALAN RAYA CAMPUHAN

Beggar's Bush

Antonio Blanco's House

Payangan & Batur

KEDEWATAN

Lungsiakan

Ananda Cottage

Bhangsuh

Londo

Penestanan Bungalows

PENESTANAN

Ayung

SAYAN

Sayan Terrace

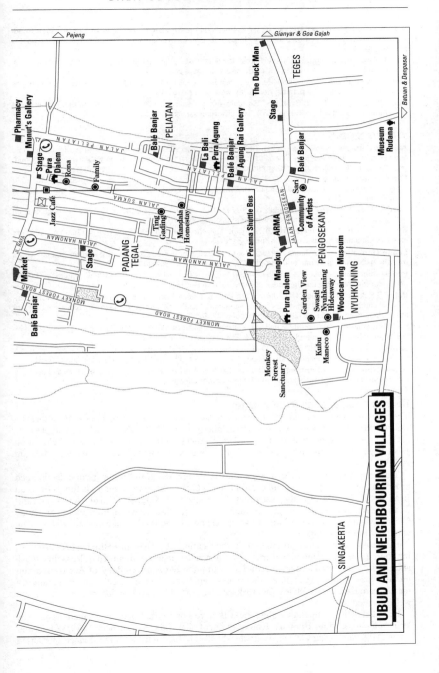

UBUD AND NEIGHBOURING VILLAGES

Swasti (Monkey Forest) Hideaway, far southern end of Monkey Forest Road (☎0361/975354). Good-value, attractively designed bungalows, with some nice views over the lush riverside. A swimming pool is planned. ③–⑤.

Ubud Bungalows, central Monkey Forest Road (☎0361/975537). Comfortable, detached bungalows, some with hot water. Nice garden with attractive swimming pool. ③–⑤.

Ubud Village Hotel, south central Monkey Forest Road (☎0361/975571). Fairly stylish fan-cooled cottages set in their own walled compounds; rice-paddy views and a pool. ⑧–⑨.

The White House (Three Brothers' Bungalows), access from Jl Hanoman and from the southern end of Monkey Forest Road (☎0361/974855). Ten nice rooms, surrounded by rice fields. ③.

THE OUTSKIRTS

Ananda Cottages, Jl Raya, Campuhan (☎0361/975376). Excellent-value cottages with garden bathrooms and verandahs, surrounded by rice paddies; there's a pool and restaurant. 20min walk from central Ubud, but you can rent bicycles, motorbikes and cars. ⑦–⑧.

Family Guest House, Jl Sukma 39, Peliatan (☎0361/974054). Exceptionally friendly place offering a big range of spotless, well-designed bungalows. Famous for its breakfasts. Recommended. 15min walk from central Ubud. ②–⑥.

Garden View Cottages, Nyuhkuning (☎0361/974055). Plush, nicely furnished rooms and bungalows, all with great views. Fan and hot water; swimming pool. ⑥–⑦.

Kubu Maneco, Nyuhkuning (☎0361/974056). The cheapest accommodation in Nyuhkuning, offering clean, well-maintained basic rooms with fine paddy-field views. ②–③.

Londo Bungalows, Penestanan (☎0361/976548). Large, four-person cottages with kitchen, and fine views over the paddies. Run by one of the original "Young Artists", I Nyoman Londo. ③

Penestanan Bungalows, Penestanan (☎0361/975604). Good-value and comfortable mid-range bungalows, with hot water. Swimming pool and some good rice-terrace views. ⑥.

Rona, Jl Sukma 23, Peliatan (☎0361/973229). Recommended, good-value bungalows, with comfortable bamboo beds and armchairs. There's a second-hand bookstore, kids' playroom, bar-restaurant and free pick-up from Ubud area. Deservedly popular. ②–④.

Sari Bungalows, off the southern end of Jl Peliatan, Peliatan (☎0361/975541). Basic bungalows fronted by verandahs which afford superb paddy views. The cheapest rooms in Ubud. ①.

Sayan Terrace, Sayan (☎0361/974384). Awesome location overlooking the Ayung River. Some very good-value, mid-priced cottages plus a few top-notch retreats. A ten-minute drive from central Ubud. ⑥–⑨.

Swasti Hideaway Nyuhkuning, Nyuhkuning (☎0361/974079). Good-value, large, spacious and comfortable rooms, all with hot water and rice-field views. Swimming pool. ⑤–⑥.

Central Ubud and adjacent villages

The major attractions of Ubud and adjacent villages are their **art museums and galleries** – well worth browsing before you buy any paintings yourself. As there are so many impressive art galleries, you'd do well to miss out Ubud's most central museum, the Puri Lukisan on Jalan Raya (daily 8am–4pm; Rp10,000), which is poor in comparison to the Neka Museum and ARMA.

The temple complex of **Pura Saraswati** is set in a delightful water garden, landscaped around a huge lotus pond behind central Ubud's *Café Lotus* – either enter via the gateway on Jalan Raya, or go through the restaurant. A forest of metre-high lotus plants leads you right up to the red-brick entrance gate, through which you'll find a pavilion housing the two huge barong costumes used by villagers for exorcizing rituals: the lion-like Barong Ket and the wild boar Barong Bangkal.

Balinese women feature prominently in the paintings displayed in all the big art museums, but there is barely a handful of works by women artists in any of them. To redress this imbalance, British-born artist Mary Northmore set up the **Seniwati Gallery of Art by Women** on Jalan Sriwedari, off Jalan Raya (daily 9am–5pm; free) which covers the complete range of mainstream Balinese art styles; the works are supported by excellent information sheets and well-informed staff.

Just west of the Campuhan bridge, about 1km west of central Ubud, an ostentatious gateway leads you into **Antonio Blanco's House** and Art Gallery (daily 10am–5pm; Rp10,000), former home of the flamboyant Catalan expatriate who died in 1999 at the age of 88. Blanco specialized in erotic paintings and drawings, particularly portraits of Balinese women in varying states of undress but, whatever you think of his artistic achievements, you'll almost certainly enjoy the exuberance of his works and his gallery space, which is left as it was during his lifetime.

THE NEKA MUSEUM

Boasting the most comprehensive collection of traditional and modern Balinese paintings on the island, the **Neka Museum** (daily 9am–5pm; Rp10,000) is housed in a series of pavilions set high on a hill on the main Campuhan road; either walk, or take any westbound bemo from Ubud Market (Rp500). The first pavilion gives an overview of the three major schools of Balinese painting from the seventeenth century to the present day and includes the lovely Ubud-style painting *The Bumblebee Dance* by Anak Agung Gede Sobrat, and the typically modern Batuan-style *Busy Bali* by I Wayan Bendi's, which takes a wryly humorous look at the effects of tourism on the island. The second pavilion exhibits naive, expressionistic works in the Young Artists style, the third pavilion houses an interesting archive of black-and-white photographs from Bali in the 1930s and 1940s, and the small fourth pavilion is dedicated to local Renaissance man, I Gusti Nyoman Lempad, who produced scores of cartoon-like line drawings inspired by religious mythology and secular folklore. The fifth pavilion focuses on works by artists from other parts of Indonesia, whose style is sometimes labelled "Academic", and the sixth pavilion features the Javanese artist Affandi's bold expressionist portrait of fighting cocks, *Prize Fighters*, and *the Temptation of Arjuna* by the influential Dutch painter Rudolf Bonnet.

MONKEY FOREST SANCTUARY

Ubud's best-known tourist attraction is its **Monkey Forest Sanctuary** (Rp3000, kids Rp1500), which occupies the land between the southern end of Monkey Forest Road (ten minutes' walk south from Ubud's central market) and the northern edge of Nyuhkuning. The focus of numerous day-trips because of its resident troupe of monkeys, the forest itself is actually small and disappointing, traversed by a concrete pathway. Five minutes into the forest, you'll come to Pura Dalem Agung Padang Tegal (donation requested for compulsory sarong and sash), the temple of the dead for the Padang Tegal neighbourhood. Pura dalem are traditionally places of extremely strong magical power and the preserve of evil spirits; in this temple you'll find half a dozen stone-carved images of the witch-widow Rangda, immediately recognizable by her hideous fanged face, unkempt hair, lolling metre-long tongue and pendulous breasts. South from the temple, the track enters the tiny settlement of Nyuhkuning, whose villagers are renowned for their woodcarvings.

THE AGUNG RAI MUSEUM OF ART (ARMA)

Ubud's other major art museum is the **Agung Rai Museum of Art**, usually referred to as **ARMA** (daily 9am–6pm; Rp10,000), in Pengosekan, on the southern fringes of Ubud. ARMA has entrances next to the Kokokan Club restaurant on Jalan Pengosekan as well as on Jalan Hanoman. The upstairs gallery of ARMA's large Balé Daja pavilion gives a brief survey of the development of Balinese art; Anak A Sobrat's *Baris Dance* is a typical example of Ubud-style art, and the contemporary Batuan-style piece by I Wayan Bendi, *Life in Bali*, is crammed with typical Balinese scenes and laced with satirical comments, notably in the figures of long-nosed tourists. Across the garden, the middle gallery of the Balé Dauh reads like a directory of Bali's most famous expats, displaying works by Rudolf Bonnet, Antonio Blanco and Arie Smit and, the highlight, *Calonnarang* by the German artist Walter Spies, a dark portrait of a demonic apparition being watched by a bunch of petrified villagers.

Around Ubud

Thought to be a former hermitage for eleventh-century Hindu priests, the moderately interesting **Goa Gajah**, also known as the Elephant Cave (daily 6am–6pm; Rp3100 plus donation for compulsory sarong and sash), displays impressive carvings around its entranceway and used to serve as meditation cells or living quarters for priests. To get there, either walk or drive the 3km east from Ubud's Jalan Peliatan, or take an Ubud–Gianyar bemo, which goes past the entrance gate.

Chipped away from the sheer rock face, the 25-metre-long series of fourteenth-century rock-cut carvings at **YEH PULU** (daily 6am–6pm; Rp3100, plus donation for sarong and sash) are delightfully engaging, but hardly ever visited. The story of the carvings is uncertain, but scenes include a man carrying two jars of tuak (palm wine), and three stages of a boar hunt. To reach Yeh Pulu, get off the Ubud–Gianyar bemo at the Yeh Pulu signs just east of Goa Gajah or west of the Bedulu crossroads, and then walk 1km south through the hamlet of **BATULUMBANG**. If driving, follow the signs to where the road peters out, a few hundred metres above the stonecarvings.

Balinese people believe **Pura Penataran Sasih** (Rp3100 donation; sarong and sash required), in the village of Pejeng, to be a particularly sacred temple, because this is the home of the so-called Moon of Pejeng – hence the English epithet, Moon Temple. The moon in question is a large hourglass-shaped bronze gong that probably dates from the Balinese Bronze Age (3rd century BC), and at almost 2m long is thought to be the largest such kettledrum ever cast. Etched into its green patina are a chain of striking heart-shaped faces punctured by huge round eyes. To get there from Ubud, take a Gianyar-bound bemo to the Bedulu crossroads and then either wait for a Tampaksiring-bound one, or walk 1km to the temple. The alternative route from Ubud, preferably by motorbike, is the five-kilometre back road that heads off east from the Jalan Raya/Jalan Peliatan T-junction.

Eating, drinking and entertainment

With some 250 **restaurants** to choose from, eating in Ubud is a major pleasure, though prices are higher than elsewhere, and a mandatory ten percent local government tax is added onto all bills. Most places shut at about 10pm.

RESTAURANTS AND CAFÉS

Ary's Warung, Jl Raya, central Ubud. Elegant, pricey Ubud institution, whose menu includes crab fishcakes, duck roasted in Balinese spices, and pomfret fillet with jackfruit. Shuts at 1am.

Bali Buddha, opposite the GPO on Jl Jembawan. Comfortable chairs, delicious juices, filled bagels, tasty cakes and sandwiches. Also a notice board detailing yoga and language courses.

Bamboo Restaurant, Jl Dewi Sita, central Ubud. Inexpensive and authentic Indonesian dishes, with recommended seafood and interesting veggie options.

Bumbu, Jl Suweta, central Ubud. Delicious Indian and Balinese fare such as banana and coconut curry and chilli-fried fish, and lots of veggie dishes. Pleasant water-garden setting. Mid-priced.

Café Lotus, Jl Raya, central Ubud. Long-established Ubud landmark which overcharges for its rather average food, but has a great setting overlooking the Pura Saraswati lotus pond.

Café Wayan, Monkey Forest Road. Good menu of Thai and Indonesian dishes, and scrumptious cakes to eat in and take away.

Casa Luna, Jl Raya, central Ubud. Stylish riverside place specializing in mouthwatering breads and cakes, but also offering great salads, Indonesian and Indian fare. Nightly videos.

Kubuku, southeast of the bottom end of Monkey Forest Rd, central Ubud. Ubud's most laid-back café stands on the edge of the rice fields and serves a limited but delicious vegetarian menu. The perfect place to chill out for an hour or two.

Murni's Warung, Jl Raya, Campuhan. High-class, mid-priced curries, thick home-made soups and Indonesian specialities in a relaxed restaurant built into the side of the Wos River valley.

Nick's, southern end of Jl Bisma, central Ubud. Recommended menu of traditional Balinese food, including fish and rice cooked in banana leaves.

Sanak Rumah Makan Padang, Jl Hanoman, central Ubud. Inexpensive and authentic Sumatran fare, including fried chicken, baked eggs, potato cakes and fish curry.

Tutmak, Jl Dewi Sita. Wholesome mid-priced menu that includes meat, fish and vegetarian nasi campur, delicious breads and cakes, espressos and cappuccinos. Board games and newspapers.

Warung Ketut (Shadana) Vegetarian Café, Jl Raya, central Ubud. Tiny, inexpensive place, which serves the most imaginative Indonesian veggie food in Ubud. Shuts about 8pm.

BARS AND NIGHTLIFE

Beggar's Bush, Jl Raya, Campuhan. Long-running British-style pub and restaurant, owned by the expat author and ornithologist Victor Mason and his Balinese wife.

Funky Monkey (Kafe Kera Lucu), southeast off the southern end of Monkey Forest Road, central Ubud. Small, urban-style disco-bar with trendy decor and reasonably priced drinks. Currently Ubud's main gay venue, though it attracts a mixed crowd. Shuts about 1am.

Jazz Café, Jl Sukma, Peliatan. Rather stylish open-sided café that stages quality live jazz every night from 7.30pm. Check flyers for performance details.

Putra Bar, next to Ubud Village hotel on the central stretch of Monkey Forest Rd, central Ubud. Very lively bar-restaurant that runs themed nights, including frequent reggae evenings, complete with live band. There's a dance floor and a Kuta-ish atmosphere.

TRADITIONAL DANCE PERFORMANCES

The Ubud region boasts dozens of outstanding traditional dance and music groups, and there are up to five different shows performed every night in the area; the tourist office gives details of the regular weekly schedule and also arranges free transport to outlying venues. Tickets cost Rp15,000–20,000 and can be bought either at the tourist office, from touts, or at the door. Performances start between 7pm and 8pm; arrive early for the best seats. If you have only one evening to catch a show, then go for whatever is playing at the Ubud Palace (Puri Saren Agung), opposite the market in central Ubud. The setting of this former raja's home (now a hotel) is breathtaking, with the torchlit courtyard gateways furnishing the perfect backdrop.

Listings

Banks and exchange There is an ATM for Visa, MasterCard and Cirrus next to Casa Luna restaurant on Jl Raya, central Ubud, and a couple of other ATMs for MasterCard and Cirrus further east along Jl Raya. Visa cash advance is available Mon–Fri 8am–1pm from Bank Danamon on Jl Raya. Numerous tour agents on Jl Raya and Monkey Forest Rd offer currency exchange services.

Bookshops English-language books at Ary's Bookshop, Jl Raya and Ganesha Bookshop, Jl Raya. Ganesha also stocks secondhand books, as does Rona Bookshop, Jl Sukma 23 in Peliatan.

Cultural courses Balinese cooking (Rp100,000) at Casa Luna restaurant, Jl Raya (every Mon, Tues & Wed); and Bumbu restaurant, Jl Kajeng (on demand). Batik courses at Crackpot Batik, Monkey Forest Road; Sai2, Monkey Forest Road; and Ubud Batik Centre, Jl Gautama. Music workshops at Ganesha Bookshop, Jl Raya (Tues 6pm); traditional music and dance lessons at Sehati, southeast off the far southern end of Monkey Forest Road (Rp25,000/hr).

Internet access At least a dozen places, including Bali 3000 on Jl Raya (daily 9am–11pm; Rp4000/15min); Roda Tourist Services at Jl Bisma 3 (daily 9am–9pm; Rp5000/15min), and Pondok Pekak Library and Resource Centre on the east side of the football field, off Jl Dewi Sita (Mon–Sat 9am–9pm, Sun 9am–3pm; Rp3000/15min).

Hospitals and clinics For minor casualties go to the Legian Medical Clinic 5 on Monkey Forest Rd (☎0361/976457), or to the Ubud Clinic near the Pura Gunung Lebah on Jl Raya Campuhan (☎0361/974911). Both clinics open 24 hours, are staffed by English-speaking doctors, and will respond to emergency callouts. For anything more serious, the nearest hospitals are in Denpasar: see p.312 for details.

Pharmacies The two central Ubud branches of Ubud Farma on Jl Raya and Monkey Forest Road (daily 8am–9pm) are staffed by helpful English-speaking pharmacists.

Police The police station is on the eastern edge of town, on Jl Tegalalang.

Post office Poste restante (Mon–Thurs 8am–4pm, Fri 8am–2pm, Sat 8am–4pm) at the GPO on Jl Jembawan.

Telephone services The Kantor Telcom (with Home Direct public phone) is at the eastern end of Jl Raya; similar rates at Nomad wartel on Jl Raya (24hr), and Wartel Pertiwi on central Monkey Forest Rd (daily 8.15am–8.45pm). Home Direct phones also outside the GPO and in the central marketplace. Phone cards from the tourist office, Kantor Telcom, and the moneychanger above Ubud Bookshop. All email places also offer fax services.

Klungkung

The bustling trading town of **KLUNGKUNG** (also known as Semarapura) is of most interest for the remains of its royal palace, collectively known as the **Taman Gili** (daily 7am–5.30pm; Rp2000), which stands at the central crossroads and is entered via Jalan Puputan. The Semarapura palace was built around 1710 by the Klungkung rulers, but was largely destroyed in 1908, when the *dewa agung* (literally "Great God", the title of kings of Bali) and his court committed *puputan* (ritual suicide) by marching unarmed into invading Dutch guns rather than submit to foreign rule. Little now remains of the palace, save for a massive red-brick gateway, and the **Kerta Gosa**, an open pavilion on a raised platform, where the king and his ministers probably met and debated. The pavilion's **painted ceiling** is a unique example of the Kamasan style of classical *wayang* painting – strictly two-dimensional, painted with a limited palette and with all figures in three-quarter profile. Nine levels of pictures each describes a specific theme or story. Level one, nearest the floor, shows scenes from the Tantri stories; levels two and three illustrate the Bhima Swarga story from the *Mahabharata*, which is continued in levels six and seven; level five predicts the effects of earthquakes on life and agriculture; and level nine, right at the top of the ceiling, shows a lotus surrounded by four doves symbolizing good luck, enlightenment and salvation. The **Bale Kambung** (Floating Pavilion), almost beside the Kerta Gosa and surrounded by a moat, was the venue for royal tooth-filing ceremonies. Its ceiling is less famous than its neighbour's, but equally interesting. The six levels of paintings cover Balinese astrology, the tales of Pan Brayut (a legendary Balinese figure who produced scores of children) and, closest to the top, the adventures of Satusoma, a Buddhist saint adopted into a Hindu context. The **Museum Daerah Semarapura** in the Taman Gili grounds, houses kris, textiles, and an old royal palanquin.

The main **bus and bemo terminal**, Terminal Kelod, is a fair distance south of the town centre; most public transport stops here. In addition, there is a small terminal just north of the main crossroads, slightly hidden away off Jalan Gunung Rinjani, where bemos depart for Besakih and Padang Bai. Most people prefer to **stay** in Candi Dasa and visit Klungkung as a day-trip, but the *Loji Ramayana* (☎0366/21044; ①), about 500m from the town centre on the road leading down the hill out of town towards Candi Dasa, has simple, clean rooms set back from the road in a courtyard with a small restaurant. If you are really counting the rupiah you might like to consider the *Cahaya Pusaka* (☎0366/22118; ①), slightly closer to the centre of town, on the opposite side of the road but rooms are closer to the main road.

Besakih

The major tourist draw in the east of Bali is undoubtedly the **Besakih** temple complex (daily 8am–5pm; Rp1100; you will also be asked for donations at the entrance to the complex and at individual temples), the island's most venerated site, situated on the slopes of Gunung Agung, Bali's holiest and highest mountain. Besakih is the yardstick by which to measure all Balinese temples, and the stark grandeur of the place makes a lasting impression. Tours start arriving around 10.30am, after which the sheer volume of tourists, traders and self-styled guides make the place pretty unbearable – come early in the morning for the best atmosphere. Tourists are forbidden to enter any of the temples in the complex, but you can see a lot through the gateways and over walls. Bring a sarong, or rent one for Rp1000–2000.

The complex consists of 22 separate temples spread over a site stretching for more than 3km. The central temple is **Pura Penataran Agung**, built on seven ascending terraces, and comprising more than fifty structures and plentiful carved figures. Start here, and then wander at will: the *meru* (multi-tiered shrine roofs) of **Pura Batu Madeg**, rising among the trees in the north of the complex, are particularly enticing; if you feel like a longer walk, **Pura Pengubengan**, the most far-flung of the temples, is a good couple of kilometres through the forest.

Without your own transport, the easiest way of getting to Besakih is to take an organized **bus tour**, but anything offering less than an hour at the temple is hardly worth it. By **public transport**, you have to approach from Klungkung: bemos leave from Terminal Kelod and from the small terminal just north of the main road in the town centre, although you may have to change at Rendang or Menanga, the turn-off for Besakih. There are plenty of bemos in the morning but they dry up in both directions in the afternoon, and after about 2pm or 3pm, you'll have trouble getting back. There are no public bemos beyond Menanga to Penelokan further north, or between Rendang and Bangli.

Accommodation options near Besakih are very limited. The *Lembah Arca* hotel (☎0366/23076; ②), on the road between Menanga and Besakih, a couple of kilometres before the temple complex, has simple rooms in an attractive garden, but it gets chilly at night; the price includes breakfast and blankets. There are also a few unauthorized and unsigned lodgings (①) behind the shops and stalls lining the road from the car park up to the temple; ask at the **tourist office**, on the corner of the car park beside the road at Besakih (no phone; daily 8.30am–3.30pm), for details. These places are very simple, with few private bathrooms, but are useful if you get stranded, if you're climbing Gunung Agung or want to explore the site early or late.

Climbing Gunung Agung

According to legend, **Gunung Agung** was created by the god Pasupati when he split Mount Meru (the centre of the Hindu universe), forming both Gunung Agung and Gunung Batur. At 3014m, the superb conical-shaped Agung is the highest Balinese peak and an awe-inspiring sight. The spiritual centre of the Balinese universe, it is believed that the spirits of the ancestors of the Balinese people dwell on Gunung Agung. Villages and house compounds are laid out in relation to the mountain, and many Balinese people prefer to sleep with their heads towards it. Directions on Bali are always given with reference to Agung, *kaja* meaning "towards the mountain" and *kelod* meaning "away from the mountain".

If you want to **climb** Gunung Agung, there are two routes, both long and hard. While the weather precludes climbing at certain times of the year, it's also forbidden to climb Agung during the myriad religious festivals, effectively ruling out March and April altogether. At any time, you'll have to make offerings at temples at the start and on the way. The dry season (April to mid-October) is the best; don't even contemplate it during January and February, the wettest months. It is essential to take a **guide** with you as the lower slopes are densely forested and it's easy to get lost. Wear strong shoes, and take a torch, water and snacks.

From Pura Pasar Agung, on the southern slope of the mountain, near Selat, it's at least a three-hour climb with an ascent of almost 2000m, so you'll need to set out at 3am or earlier to catch sunrise. This path does not go to the actual summit, but to a point about 100m lower, from where you can see Rinjani, the south of Bali and Gunung Batukau and look down into the 500-metre-deep crater. For this route, you can arrange **guides** at Muncan, 4km east of Rendang, at Tirtagangga, 5km north of Amlapura and also further afield in Toya Bungkah (see p.343). In **Muncan**, contact the highly experienced guide I Ketut Uriada at his small shop in the centre of the village – there's a sign outside – or ask anyone for directions; he may be able to arrange a bemo charter to Pura Pasar Agung and can advise on local accommodation. Expect to pay US$30 for a guide for one person, US$40 for two people, US$50 for three. In **Tirtagangga**, Nyoman Budiarsa arranges transport and food from his small shop, on the right as you head north through the town. He charges US$30–40 per person, depending on numbers.

From Besakih, the climb is longer, taking five to six hours, and you'll need to leave between midnight and 2am. The path starts from Pura Pengubengan, the most distant of the temples in the Besakih complex, and takes you up to the summit of Agung with views in all directions. The descent is particularly taxing and takes four to five hours. **Guides** for this route can be arranged at the tourist office (see above) in the Besakih temple complex; US$50 is the going rate.

Nusa Lembongan

Circled by a mixture of pure white-sand beaches and mangrove swamps, the tiny island of **NUSA LEMBONGAN** (4km by 3km) is sheltered by coral reefs which provide excellent snorkelling and create the perfect conditions for seaweed farming. It is also a major draw for surfers. All the accommodation is in **Jungutbatu** on the west coast and southeast of this in **Chelegimbai** and **Mushroom Bay** (Tanjung Sanghyang). There is no post office on the island, and electricity is currently produced by individual generators, which close down around 10.30pm. You can change money at *Nusa Lembongan Bungalows* or Bank Pembangunan Daerah Bali (Mon–Fri 10am–1pm), both in Jungutbatu, but rates are higher than on the mainland. There is a wartel (4–10pm) attached to *Bunga Lembongan* for local and international calls. The Perama office serves as the **tourist information** service and is in Jungutbatu between *Pondok Baruna* and *Nusa Indah* bungalows; you can book tickets here to destinations on Bali, Lombok and Sumbawa. There are at least daily departures, but all destinations apart from Ubud, Kuta and Sanur require a stop-over on the way. The **surf breaks** are all accessible from Jungutbatu and you can charter boats to take you to the **snorkelling** spots off Mushroom Bay, at Mangrove Corner and Sunfish (prices start at Rp25,000 per person). You can walk around the island in about three hours.

Two scheduled **boats** run daily **from Sanur** to Jungutbatu, departing at 8am and 10am (Rp22,500 one-way) – the ticket office is near the *Ananda Hotel* beachfront; boats return at 8am (from the beachfront office in Jungutbatu). Perama also operates a daily tourist shuttle boat from Sanur (10.30am; Rp27,500), and from Jungutbatu, Lembongan (8.30am); book ahead. You can also get local *prahu* boats, mostly used for cargo, from **Kusamba** to Jungutbatu (Rp5000; 2–3hr). There are no fixed times; boats leave when full (very full) but most go to the islands early in the morning. A charter is approximately Rp400,000 one way.

Jungutbatu

Ranged along the coast for well over 1km, the attractive village of **JUNGUTBATU** is a low-key place, with several losmen and a few shops. The accommodation places at the north end of the beach are grouped close together, spreading out further south.

The only **diving operator** currently based in Nusa Lembongan is World Diving Lembongan (fax ☎0361/288500, *www.world-diving.com*), which operates out of *Pondok Baruna* and runs a range of different courses.

ACCOMMODATION

Bunga Lembongan (☎0361/415185). Next to Bungalow No.7 at the southern end of the beach, with simple rooms behind grandly carved wooden doors. There's an attached wartel. ①.

Bungalow No.7 At the far southern end of the beach, far away from the livelier spots to the north, with an attractive garden and well-furnished rooms with fans. Most are budget rooms with one larger, better furnished room upstairs. There's also a beachside restaurant. ①–③.

Mainski Inn, in the centre of the main accommodation area at the north end of the beach. This is a long-term surfers' favourite with a big choice of accommodation. It is one of the liveliest places, with a busy, breezy upstairs restaurant and videos and table tennis downstairs. More expensive rooms are bigger with hot water. ①–③.

Nusa Lembongan Bungalows Accommodation is in two-storey bamboo-and-thatch buildings set in a spacious compound. The restaurant at the front affords excellent sea views. ②.

Pondok Baruna (fax ☎0361/288500). A few hundred metres south of the main accommodation area, this small, quiet place has clean, tiled rooms looking straight onto the beach and a restaurant. ②.

Mushroom Bay

Just a few kilometres southwest of Jungutbatu, the fabulous white-sand cove of **Mushroom Bay** has long been a favourite snorkelling spot. It's a great place, although don't expect peace once the day-trippers arrive from the mainland. *Bungalows Tanjung Sanghyang* (②–③) has good-quality accommodation in a brilliant location at the northern end of the cove and, a couple of hundred metres inland on the Lembongan road, *Bungalows Panca Dana* (①) has cheaper, adequate rooms, but you'll need to walk to the beach. To get to Mushroom Bay from Jungutbatu, either charter a **boat** (Rp3000–5000 per person) or else it's an hour's hot walk. Take the first turning to the right as you enter Lembongan village on the walk over the hill from Jungutbatu; it's 1km from the turning.

Candi Dasa

At the eastern end of Amuk Bay, **CANDI DASA** is a centre for snorkelling and diving, and a pleasant base from which to explore the east of Bali, including the nearby traditional village of Tenganan (see p.340). However, throughout the 1980s, Candi's offshore reef was crushed to produce lime for the building boom and the beach was left so exposed that it simply washed away. Large sea walls now protect the land, and enormous jetties protrude into the sea in the hope, largely justified, that the beach will build up against them. The tourist developments have spread 8km west around the bay, through the villages of **Senkidu**, **Buitan** and **Manggis**, where the beach is still a respectable size. To get to a decent beach from Candi itself, follow the road past *Bunga Putri* at the end of Forest Road up onto the headland and then down onto the black sand on the other side.

Just off the coast of Candi Dasa, a group of small islands provides excellent spots for experienced divers (currents can be strong), including walls, a pinnacle and the dramatic Tepekong Canyon. Candi Dasa is also an ideal base from which to arrange **diving trips** to Padang Bai, Nusa Penida, Amed and Tulamben (US$55–80) and to take a course. There are many local **dive operators**, including Baruna with a counter in town (☎0363/41185) and one at *Puri Bagus Candidasa* (☎0363/41217); Divelite (☎0363/41660); Maoka Dive Centre (☎0363/41563); Pineapple Divers at *Candi Beach Cottages* (☎0363/41760); Spice Dive at *Balina Beach Resort* (☎0363/41725), the only southern office of this well-regarded north-coast operator; and Stingray Dive Centre in both Senkidu (☎0363/41268) and in central Candi Dasa (☎0363/41063). It is important to follow the guidelines for choosing a dive operator (see "Diving, surfing and trekking" p.199).

Long-distance Denpasar (Batubulan terminal)–Amlapura **buses** and **bemos** all serve Candi Dasa. **Shuttle buses** from the main tourist destinations serve Candi Dasa, and Perama (☎0363/41114; 8am–9pm) has an office with departures three times daily to Kuta and the airport (Rp15,000), Sanur (Rp15,000), Ubud (Rp10,000), Padang Bai (Rp5000) and Senggigi on Lombok (Rp25,000); daily departures to north and east Bali and to other destinations on Lombok. You can also book through to Bima (Rp65,000) and Sape (Rp70,000) on Sumbawa. Simpatik have twice daily departures to Ubud (Rp12,500) and Sanur (Rp19,000). There is a centrally located **tourist office** in the main street close to the lagoon, but it seems to have somewhat erratic opening hours.

Asri Shop provides a **poste restante** service – mail should be addressed c/o Asri Shop, Candi Dasa, PO Box 135, Karangasem, Bali. The **wartel** (daily 6am–11pm) is next to the *Kubu Bali Restaurant*. Several **bookstores** in Candi, including Candidasa Bookstore, sell new and secondhand books.

Accommodation

Most **accommodation** is spread about 1km along the main road running just behind the beach at **Candi Dasa**. East of this central section, **Forest Road** has some quiet guesthouses among coconut palms. To the west, the village of **Senkidu** is about 1km from the centre of Candi Dasa, slightly detached, but still convenient for the main facilities. If you decide to stay any further towards **Buitan** you'll need your own transport to enjoy Candi's nightlife, as public transport stops at dusk.

CANDI DASA
Agung Bungalows (☎0363/41535). Seafront bungalows with good-sized verandahs, fans and attached cold-water bathrooms located in a lush garden complete with ponds. ②.

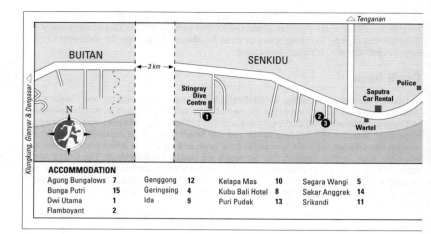

ACCOMMODATION

Agung Bungalows	7	Genggong	12	Kelapa Mas	10	Segara Wangi	5
Bunga Putri	15	Geringsing	4	Kubu Bali Hotel	8	Sekar Anggrek	14
Dwi Utama	1	Ida	9	Puri Pudak	13	Srikandi	11
Flamboyant	2						

Geringsing, (☎0363/41084). Budget bamboo and thatch bungalows set in a small centrally-located compound next to the sea offering excellent value. The real gems are the three bungalows right on the seafront. ①.

Ida (☎0363/41096). Well-furnished, big bungalows in the centre of Candi with huge verandahs, ideal for lounging on, set in a lovely garden stretching down to the sea. Not to be confused with a place with a similar name on Forest Road. ②.

Kelapa Mas (☎0363/41369). Justifiably popular, offering a range of clean bungalows set in a large well-maintained garden on the seafront, centrally located. ②.

Kubu Bali (☎0363/41532). Good value in this price bracket. Bungalows have fan and air-con, hot water but no bath tub, and good-quality furnishings. Set in a lovely garden on the hillside away from the beach, and there's a great swimming pool high on the hillside. ②.

Segara Wangi (☎0363/41159). Excellent-value, clean bungalows, with attached cold-water mandi. It is a bit tucked away, but central, and the seafront places have great verandahs and views. ①.

The Watergarden/Hotel Taman Air (☎0363/41540). On the hillside away from the beach, well-furnished, fan and air-con bungalows with verandahs overlooking pools, set in an atmospheric tropical garden. ②–③.

FOREST ROAD

Bunga Putri (☎0363/41140). At the far eastern end of the bay, the bungalows are nothing special, but are the ultimate in get-away-from-it-all peacefulness in Candi Dasa. ②.

Genggong (☎0363/41105). There are a few bungalows, but most rooms are in a two-storey block with big balconies and verandahs. There is hot water at the top end, but the big plus is the lovely garden and picturesque bit of white-sand beach just over the hill. ③.

Puri Pudak (☎0363/41978). A range of bungalows right beside the beach. The compound isn't brilliant but more expensive bungalows have hot water and are not bad value. ②–③.

Sekar Anggrek (☎0363/41086). The best value on Forest Road with good-quality bungalows, hot water at the top end, in a quiet seafront compound. ②.

Srikandi (☎0363/41972). A neat row of simple, good-value bungalows in an attractive garden with a seaside location. ①.

SENKIDU AND MANGGIS

Amarta Beach Inn (☎0363/41230). Large, tiled bungalows in a row facing the ocean and set in a pretty garden. There is plenty of space for sunbathing and a beachside restaurant. ②.

Dwi Utama (☎0363/41053). A short row of fan rooms with attached cold-water bathroom, simple but adequate, set in a small garden with a restaurant overlooking the beach. ②.

Flamboyant (☎0363/41886). Recently renovated, spotless bungalows in an attractive garden right beside the sea in a quiet spot. Pricier bungalows are right on the seafront. ②–③.

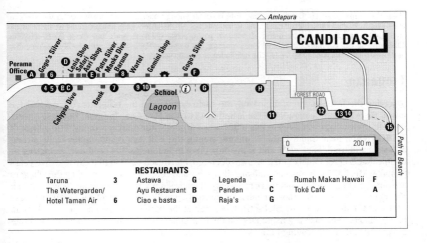

RESTAURANTS

Taruna	**3**	Astawa	**G**	Legenda	**F**	Rumah Makan Hawaii	**F**
The Watergarden/		Ayu Restaurant	**B**	Pandan	**C**	Toké Café	**A**
Hotel Taman Air	**6**	Ciao e basta	**D**	Raja's	**G**		

Taruna (☎0363/41823). A neat row of good-value bungalows in a smart garden with a small seaside bar, in a quiet location next to *Flamboyant*. ①–②.

Eating, drinking and nightlife

Apart from a few late-opening restaurants, things are pretty quiet by 11pm, and **nightlife** is low-key in Candi Dasa. There is no disco scene and live music comes and goes – check out *Legenda*, *Ayu's* and *Ciao e basta*; events are advertised on flyers nailed to trees around town. Videos are the main entertainment at *Raja's*, the *Candi Bagus Pub*, next door, *Ciao e basta* and *Ari Tavern*, but viewing can be frustrating as heavy traffic whizzes past.

Balinese **dance** often accompanies dinner at local restaurants; again, look out for local advertisements. All the places below are marked **on the map** above.

Astawa The most popular of a clutch of places at the eastern end of the main road offering highly competitive prices for good food, well-cooked and attractively presented. This one provides excellent lassis and a wide choice of local dishes and seafood as well as Western options. Also check out *Aditya*, *Ketut*, *Iris* and *Lumbung* nearby.

Ayu's Restaurant This is one of the best-value restaurants on the main street. There's a large menu with all the usual traveller's fare and set menus from Rp15,000 are especially good value. There is regular live music.

Ciao e basta Slightly hidden away off the main road, this two-storey place has an extensive menu of superb and good-value pasta, pizza, salads and home-made ice creams and desserts, plus a good selection of drinks and coffees.

Legenda, centrally located on the main street. One of the few venues in Candi Dasa for live music, they also have an extensive menu featuring plenty of western choices, including spaghetti, pizza and steak, along with Indonesian food.

Nyoman Café, on the turning down to the coast from the main road, Buitan. Attractively decorated and furnished with high ceilings, plus a good sound system and selection of recorded music. The menu isn't huge but there's a good choice of Western (lots of Italian) and Indonesian meals at reasonable prices. It's a relaxed spot and a brilliant place to chill out and write those postcards.

Pandan Ignore the breakwater in the foreground and this is a pretty fair spot for a sunset drink. There's a big menu, good seafood and twice-weekly Indonesian/Western buffet for Rp25,000.

Raja's Lots of people come for the nightly videos, but there is also a very big drinks list and plenty of Indonesian and Western dishes, including sausage and mash, pork chops and fillet steak.

Rumah Makan Made There's a huge menu of steaks, pork and seafood featuring Western, local and Chinese cooking, but the baguettes filled with ham, cheese or tuna are especially fine and drinks come with free popcorn.

Toke Café This long-term Candi Dasa favourite is set far enough back from the main road at the western end of central Candi Dasa for the road noise to be minimal. All customers get a non-alcoholic welcome drink and nibbles and there's a vast menu of seafood, pasta, pizza, chicken, pork and steak (Rp10–25,000), although you can eat more cheaply with nasi goreng. Set menus at Rp25–35,000 are excellent value and a blackboard advertises daily specials. The drinks list is equally varied.

Tenganan

Rejecting the Javanization of their land, the caste system and the religious reforms that followed the Majapahit conquest of the island in 1343, the Bali Aga ("original Balinese") withdrew to their village enclaves to live a life based around ritual and ceremony. The village of **TENGANAN**, near Candi Dasa, is unique among the Bali Aga communities in its strong adherence to traditional ways, and is the only place in Indonesia that produces *geringsing* or double ikat, a ceremonial cloth in brown, deep-red, blue-black and tan that can take five years to make. Most of the complex round of daily rituals and ceremonies observed by the villagers are not open to the public, but there are plenty of festival days: the month-long Usaba Sambah (May/June) is one of the most colourful. The road up to Tenganan is an easy **walk** from the centre of Candi, but, even so, **ojeks** (Rp1000) wait at the bottom to transport you the 3km up to the village. Tenganan is a major stop on the tour-bus circuit, but it's easy to avoid the 11am to 2pm rush if you're staying in the area.

Padang Bai

PADANG BAI, the **port for Lombok** (ferries run to Lembar every 2hr), nestles in a small cove with a white-sand beach lined with fishing boats. The jetty, ferry offices and car park are all at the western end of the bay, and everything is within easy walking distance from here. Increasingly, people are choosing to stay a night or two in Padang Bai, and the village has developed into a small laid-back resort. If you find the main beach a bit busy, the bay of **BIASTUGAL**, to the west, is smaller and quieter. Follow the road past the post office and, just as it begins to climb, take the track to the left. Alternatively, over the headland in the other direction, take the path from Pura Silayukti, to another small, white cove. Several places in Padang Bai rent out **snorkelling** equipment: there's good snorkelling at Blue Lagoon, just around the headland in Amuk Bay, but it's even better to charter a boat (you'll start negotiating at Rp100,000 for 2hr); ask at *Celagi* restaurant or your guesthouse. The dive operation, Geko Dive (☎0363/41516), is a large set-up on Jalan Silayukti with a lot of experience diving in the area and offers the full range of PADI courses (PADI Open Water from US$320 per person) and dives for experienced divers (US$45–70 depending on location, including equipment rental).

Bemos arrive at, and depart from, the port entrance; orange for Candi Dasa (20min) and Amlapura (40min), blue or white for Klungkung (aka Semarapura; 20min). The government **tourist office** (daily 7am–8pm) is 500m further east on the beach road, Jalan Silayukti, and also rents cars and motorbikes. Perama **tourist shuttle buses** to destinations on Bali and Lombok operate from their office near the jetty in *Café Dona*. There is a **post office** near the port entrance, many seafront restaurants **change money** and *Made Homestay* can arrange **car rental** (Rp40,000) and motorbike rental (Rp15–25,000).

Accommodation and eating

There's a choice of **accommodation** in the village and on the road behind the beach; the beach places are generally bigger and airier. Freshly caught **seafood** is the speciality here, served at numerous seafront restaurants; the row of places in front of Geko Dive have great locations and good food.

Bagus Inn (☎0363/41398). An excellent budget choice in the centre of the village offering small rooms with attached bathroom in a friendly family compound. Often full. ③.

Dharma (☎0363/41394). A small family place in the village; the downstairs rooms are dark but the ones upstairs have good sitting areas outside. ②.

Kembar Inn (☎0363/41364). New, clean, tiled place in the village. All rooms have fan and attached cold-water bathroom. The downstairs rooms are rather small and airless but upstairs they are better and there is also a pleasant sitting area. ②–③.

Made Homestay (☎0363/41441). Large, clean, tiled rooms with fan and attached cold-water bathroom in a cosy compound on the seafront. ②.

Mahayani (no phone). Three rooms in a small family compound tucked away off the road at the top of town. Rooms are clean and tiled and have attached bathrooms plus deep verandas. ①.

Pantai Ayu (☎0363/41396). Long-established place in the village up on the hill behind the cemetery with good views and a small attached restaurant. The better, pricier rooms are upstairs. ②.

Serangan Inn (☎0363/41425). This new place is the most expensive in the village, but is built high up on the hill overlooking the village and the bay and has some great views, catches the breeze and has good rooms, all with fan and attached cold-water bathroom. ②.

Tirtagangga

TIRTAGANGGA's main draw is its lovely Water Palace, but the town is also surrounded by beautiful paddy fields offering pleasant walks and glorious views of Gunung Agung and Gunung Lempuyang. The refreshingly cool temperatures make this one of the best day-trips from Candi Dasa (take a bemo to Amlapura then change on to one for Tirtagangga, which takes 10 minutes), and there's accommodation too. The **Water Palace** (daily 7am–6pm; Rp1100, camera Rp1000) was built in about 1947 by Anak Agung Anglurah, the last rajah of Karangasem, and is an impressive terraced area of pools, water channels and fountains set in a garden. You can swim in an upper deeper pool (Rp4000) or a lower, shallower pool (Rp2000).

Nyoman Budiarsa's shop, next to the *Genta Bali Warung*, sells souvenirs plus a printed **map** of local walks (Rp2500), can arrange **guides** for local treks and also arranges **climbs** up Gunung Agung (see p.335). There is a **moneychanger** and a **postal agent** on the track to the Water Palace from the main road.

There is plenty of **accommodation**. *Rijasa* (☎0363/21873; ②–③), across the main road from the track leading to the Water Palace, is a good-value place with a neat row of bungalows in an attractive garden. *Good Karma* (☎0363/22445) has tiled, clean rooms set in a small garden in the paddy fields; take the track on the left of the main road, above *Good Karma* resturant that follows the water-channel, then take the first path to the left. *Prima* (☎0363/21316; ②) is almost 1km north of the village with clean, light rooms and great views of Gunung Lempuyang. *Puri Sawah* (☎0363/21847; ③–④), about 100m beyond the Water Palace, on a track heading left from a sharp turn in the road, has a few well-furnished rooms with verandahs in a small, peaceful garden; more expensive ones have hot water. For **food**, try the tourist menu at *Good Karma*, above the car park, and the *Rice Terrace Coffee Shop*, attached to *Puri Sawah*, with good food in a lovely location in the fields.

Amed and Jemeluk

From **Culik**, 10km beyond Tirtagangga, the junction of the road around the far east and the Amlapura–Singaraja road, it's 3km to the picturesque, sleepy fishing village of **AMED**, with a one-kilometre-long black-sand beach and hills rising up behind. About 2km beyond the village, *Congkang 3 Brothers* (③) has simple bungalows and across the road there is a beach-side restaurant. A few hundred metres further round the coast, *Bamboo Bali* (②) is a good budget choice, although it's a short walk to the beach. There are just three bungalows on the hill in an attractive garden and with great views from the verandahs and a small restaurant.

Less than 1km further on, the village of **JEMELUK** is the **diving** focus of the area: a sloping terrace of coral leads to a wall dropping to a depth of more than 40m and there are plenty of fish. Eco-Dive, attached to *Dharma Samadi* restaurant and bungalows (①), arranges local dives and snorkelling. One kilometre further around the coast, *Amed Beach Cottages* (③) is situated by the beach with various standards of smart bungalows, and a pool. Mega Dive Centre is here (in Denpasar ☎0361/754165), offering introductory dives, dives for certified divers and PADI courses. Just beyond this, the *Kusumajaya Indah* (②) has attractive bungalows in a lovely garden that slopes down to the rocky beach.

The next bay along cradles the small village of **BUNUTAN**, a peaceful and rural spot just behind the local beach. On the climb up out of the village look out for the tiny *Warni's Warung* (②–③) on the cliff side of the road, the perfect spot for a sunset drink. The views to the northwest are stunning and they have a couple of simple bungalows.

LIPAH BEACH, although still very peaceful, is the most developed beach. *Wawa Wewe* (②–③) and *Tiying Petung* (②) stand side by side and are great, relaxed places offering occasional live music, a range of Western and Indonesian dishes and simple accommodation.

There is another headland and several kilometres between here and the bay at **SELANG**, almost 12km from Culik, where *Good Karma* (③–⑤) is currently the easternmost accommodation. It is right on the black-and-white-sand beach, and it offers good snorkelling. There are various standards of accommodation and deep, relaxing verandahs set in a gorgeous garden – an oasis in the midst of a parched landscape.

Tulamben

The small, rather unattractive village of **TULAMBEN**, about 10km west of Culik, is the site of the most famous and most popular dive in Bali, the **Liberty wreck**, which sank during World War II. The wreck lies about 30m offshore, and is completely encrusted with coral, providing a wonderful habitat for over 400 species of reef fish. Parts of the stern are only about 2m below the surface, making this a good snorkelling site, too. Up to a hundred divers a day now visit, so it's worth avoiding the rush hours (11.30am–4pm); night dives are especially good. Most divers come to Tulamben on day-trips from Candi Dasa or Lovina, but you can also dive with local operators: check out *Tauch Terminal Resort*, *Mimpi Resort* and Dive Paradise Tulamben at *Paradise Palm Beach Bungalows*. Expect to pay around US$60 for two dives at Tulamben, US$75 for two dives at Amed or Jemeluk and US$350 for a PADI Open Water course. Snorkelling gear is also available for rent.

Tulamben is easily accessible from either Singaraja or Amlapura by public **bemo** or bus. When it comes to **moving on**, daily tourist shuttle buses leave for all major destinations in Bali and Lombok. There is also a Perama office in *Ganda Mayu* guesthouse. It's worth noting that shuttle buses travelling from Tulamben to Candi Dasa can drop you off at Culik if you are intending to explore the far east of the island. **Accommodation** here is fairly pricey, but *Ganda Mayu* (☎0363/22912; ②) is a good budget choice, just above the main road. *Paradise Palm Beach Bungalows* (☎0363/22910; ②–⑥), centrally located on the coast in the middle of the village, has several standards of rooms in a cosy compound and *Puri Madha* (☎0363/22921; ②) is very near the *Liberty* wreck, which is offshore, at the western end of the village. The biggest place is *Tauch Terminal Resort* (☎0363/22911 or through Kuta reservations office ☎0361/730200; ⑤–⑧), which fronts a long section of the coast and has an attractive pool and a very busy dive centre. The top-end rooms are the best in the area, with high ceilings, huge windows and lovely furnishings.

Gunung Batur and Danau Batur

The centre of Bali is occupied by the awesome volcanic masses of the Batur and Bedugul areas, where dramatic mountain ranges shelter crater lakes, and small, peaceful villages line their shores. The **Batur** area was formed 30,000 years ago by the eruption of a gigantic volcano. The entire area is sometimes referred to as **Kintamani**, although in fact this is just one of several villages dotted along the rim of the ancient crater. More villages are situated around **Danau Batur** (Lake Batur) at the bottom of the crater: **Toya Bungkah** is the start of the main route up Gunung Batur and the chief accommodation centre, although **Kedisan** offers some options, and is the access point for boat trips across the lake to the Bali Aga village of **Trunyan**. At the furthest end of the lake, **Songan** is one of the quietest places to stay in the area. The highest points on the rim are **Gunung Abang** (2153m) on the eastern side, and **Gunung Penulisan** (1745m), on the southwest corner, with Pura Tegeh Koripan perched on its summit. Rising from the floor of the main crater, **Gunung Batur** (1717m) is an active volcano with four craters of its own.

The crater rim

Spread out along the rim of the crater for 11km, the villages of **Penelokan**, **Batur** and **Kintamani** almost merge with each other. If you're planning to stay up here, beware that the mist (and sometimes rain) that obscures the view in late afternoon brings a creeping dampness, and the nights are extremely chilly, so bring warm clothes. There is an **entrance charge** for visiting the crater area (Rp3000 per person); the ticket offices are just south of Penelokan. Getting to the rim is straightforward from any direction, with regular **buses** (every 30min until mid-afternoon) between Singaraja (Penarukan terminal; 1hr 30min) and Denpasar (Batubulan terminal; 1hr 30min), via Gianyar (50min) and Bangli (45min); the route from Ubud is served by brown (Kintamani) **bemos**.

The views from **PENELOKAN** (1450m) are excellent, offering a panorama of enormous scale and majesty. Danau Batur, with its ever-changing colours, lies far below, while Gunung Batur and Gunung Abang tower on either side of the lake. Over 2000 tourists in the low season and 4000 in the high are estimated to pass through Penelokan every day, attracting an entourage of **hawkers** selling all sorts of goods. The only way to really avoid the circus is to come early or late in the day, or stay overnight.

Yayasan Bintang Danu **tourist office** in Penelokan, almost opposite the turning down to Kedisan (daily 9am–3pm; ☎0366/51730), has information about accommodation, transport and walks. The crater rim is packed with plush **restaurants**, but cheaper meals are available at *Ramana* – about 300m towards Kintamani from Penelokan, right on the crater's rim. If you want to **stay** up here and your budget will run to it, *Lakeview Hotel* (☎0366/51464; ⑥), at the junction of the road from the south and the crater rim, has comfortable rooms with attached hot-water bathrooms and verandas that make the most of the views. The **post office** and **telephone office** are 2km north of Penelokan on the road along the rim. There are several places to **change money** on the main road on the rim, though rates are poor.

Danau Batur

Home of Dewi Danu, the goddess of the crater lake, **Danau Batur** is especially sacred to the Balinese, and the waters from the lake, generated by eleven springs, are believed to percolate through the earth and reappear as springs in other parts of the island. Situated 500m below the crater rim, Danau Batur is the largest lake in Bali, 8km long and 3km wide, and one of the most glorious. The most popular road to the lakeside, served by **public bemos**, leaves the crater rim at Penelokan. Bemos, in theory, go as far as Songan on the western side of the lake and Abang on the eastern side, but you'll have to bargain hard to get reasonable fares beyond Toya Bungkah and Buahan; most tourists end up paying Rp5000 or more to get to Toya Bungkah.

Toya Bungkah

TOYA BUNGKAH, 8km from Penelokan, is the accommodation centre of the lakeside area and the main starting point for climbs up Gunung Batur. The stylish hot springs, **Tirta Sanjiwana** (daily 8am–6pm) have a cold-water and hot-water pool (US$5 for both) and a private jacuzzi (US$20). Jero Wijaya (☎0366/51249), Arlina's (☎0366/51165) and the new, enthusiastic Gede Mangun's trekking and tour company (☎0366/51824) provide reliable **information** about the area and operate travel and tour services. They also offer guides for climbs up Batur (US$10–30 per person, Gunung Abang (US$30–35 per person) and Agung (US$50–75 per person). You can **change money** and travellers' cheques at several places in the village. **Places to stay** line the road in Toya Bungkah, with a few more down by the lakeside. *Arlina's* (☎0366/51165; ②) is a friendly, popular setup at the southern end of town, with clean rooms, some en-suite. Close to the hot springs, *Pualam* (②) is small and quiet with good rooms; the lakeside *Tirta Yatra* (①) is more basic; and the nearby *Nyoman Mawa II* (*Under the Volcano II*; no phone; ②) has attractive rooms.

TRUNYAN, KEDISAN AND BUAHAN

Three kilometres from Penelokan, the southernmost lakeside village of **KEDISAN** is convenient for visits to the Bali Aga village of Trunyan but further to the start of the Gunung Batur climb. The Penelokan road splits at Kedisan: the right fork leads to the jetty for boats to Trunyan and continues on to the villages of Buahan and Abang. Public boats to Trunyan are for locals only, so you'll have to charter one: the price for a boat shared by three people is Rp95,000. A couple of hundred metres beyond the village of **BUAHAN**, *Baruna* (☎0366/51221; ①) is one of the quietest places to stay on the lake. It offers basic rooms with cold-water bathrooms and the view is pretty perfect. Public bemos from Penelokan go as far as Buahan; the public price is Rp1500 but tourists usually end up paying more. At the bottom of the hill down from Penelokan, the left fork leads to Toya Bungkah. A few hundred metres from the junction, towards Toya Bungkah, *Hotel Segara* (☎0366/51136; ①–⑤) has a wide range of accommodation. Nearby *Hotel Surya* (☎0366/51139; ②–③) also offers clean rooms with cold or hot water, and good balconies; they have a limited free local pick-up service – telephone for details.

Gunung Batur

With a choice of four main craters, there are several ways to approach **Gunung Batur** (1717m). With your own transport, the easiest way to get to the top is to drive to **SERONG-GA**, west of Songan. From the car park, it's a climb of between thirty minutes and one hour to the largest and highest crater, **Batur I**.

Climbing Batur is best as a dry-season expedition (April–Oct) as paths are unpleasant in the wet season and there are no views. If you're reasonably fit and don't have your own transport, the most common route is to climb up to Batur I from either **Toya Bungkah** or the road near **Pura Jati**. Allow two to three hours to get to the top and about half that time to get back down. **In daylight**, you shouldn't really need a guide for this route, but fewer people climb during the day because of the heat, and the possibility of clouds obscuring the view. From Toya Bungkah, numerous paths head up through the forest – one path starts just south of the car park near *Arlina's* – and after about an hour you'll come out onto the bare slope of the mountain. From here, just follow the paths that head up to the tiny warung perched way up on the crater rim on the skyline. Most people climb **in the dark** to get to the top for the fabulous dawn view over Gunung Abang and Lombok's Rinjani. You'll need to leave early (4–5am), and should take a **guide** as it's easy to get lost in the forest. There are also longer routes on the mountain; for a medium-length trek, climb Batur I, walk around the rim and then descend by another route. The long option involves climbing up to Batur I, walking around the rim to the western side, descending to the rim of crater II and then to the rim of crater III. From here you can either walk down to Toya Bungkah or Yehmampeh (about 8hr in all). You'll need a guide for either of these routes. The **Association of Trekking Guides** have one office in Toya Bungkah (☎0366/52362) and another on the road into Toya Bungkah at Pura Jati. They charge Rp300,000 per climb for a maximum of four people for the short trip, while prices for longer treks are negotiable. Organized trekking services also offer guides (see p.343).

Candikuning and Danau Bratan

Neither as big nor as dramatic as the Batur region, the **Bedugul** and **Danau Bratan** area, nevertheless, has impressive mountains, beautiful lakes, quiet walks and attractive temples.

There is no direct route between the two regions: Bedugul and Danau Bratan lie on a busy parallel road, 53km from Denpasar and 30km from Singaraja, nestling in the lee of Gunung Catur, with the smaller, quieter lakes Buyan and Tamblingan about 5km to the northwest.

The small village of **CANDIKUNING**, situated above the southern shores of Danau Bratan, is the centre for many local sights, including the highly recommended **Bali Botanical Gardens** (Kebun Raya Eka Karya Bali; daily 8am–4pm; Rp1000 per person). The gardens are a short walk south from the market area, along a small side road by a giant corn-on-the-cob statue, and host over 650 different species of tree and more than 400 species of orchids; it's also a rich area for birdwatching. The daily **market**, Bukit Mungsu, is small but extremely diverse and colourful, selling a vast range of spices and plants, including orchids.

Situated at 1200m above sea level and thought to be 35m deep in places, **Danau Bratan** is surrounded by forested hills, with Gunung Catur rising sheer behind. Revered by Balinese farmers as the source of freshwater springs across a wide area of the island, the lake and its goddess, Dewi Danu, are worshipped in the immensely attractive temple of **Pura Ulun Danu Bratan** (daily 7am–5pm; Rp3000), which consists of several shrines, some spread along the shore and others dramatically situated on small islands that appear to float on the surface of the lake.

To the north, the path up **Gunung Catur** (2096m) is easy to find: turn away from the lake just past the third Japanese cave and take the short track that zigzags up onto the ridge, about 20m above. It hits another, bigger path heading along the ridge; turn left onto this path and simply follow it (and the litter) through forest to the top of Catur. Allow two to three hours' unrelenting uphill climb, and 90 minutes for the descent; take plenty of water and some snacks, and don't forget to tell somebody where you are going.

Practicalities

Situated north of Candikuning's market, *Sari Atha Inn* (☎0368/21011; ①–②) has a choice of **rooms** with or without hot water. *Cempaka* (☎0368/21402; ①–②) offers accommodation in a two-storey block behind the road to the Botanical Gardens, and the nearby *Citera Ayu* (no phone; ②) and *Permata Firdaus* (☎0368/21531; ②) are all good-value possibilities. *Ashram Guest House* (☎0368/21450; ②–④) occupies lovely grounds on the lakeside and offers a range of rooms. For good-value **food**, the warung in the temple car park are worth a try, or check out the stalls on the main road as it runs along the lakeside, or the Muslim places on the road to the Botanical Gardens. The Perama **shuttle bus** office is at the *Sari Atha Inn* (see above) and runs daily buses to major destinations on Bali and Lombok. There are **bemo** services to and from Denpasar (Ubung terminal; 1hr 30min) and Singaraja (Sukasada terminal; 1hr 30min). There is a **wartel** (daily 8am–9.30pm) in the market and you can **change money** at the moneychangers in the car park to Pura Ulan Danu.

Singaraja and around

The second largest Balinese city after Denpasar, **SINGARAJA** is a pleasantly spacious harbour on the north coast, of most interest to tourists for its good transport connections. There are three bemo and bus **terminals** in Singaraja. **Sukasada** (locally called Sangket), to the south of the town, serves Danau Bratan and Denpasar; **Banyuasri**, on the western edge of town, serves the west, including Lovina, Seririt and Gilimanuk; and **Penarukan** is for services eastwards along the north coast via Tulamben to Amlapura and along the Kintamani/Penelokan road for the Batur area and on to Bangli. Small bemos (flat rate Rp1000) ply main routes around town.

The **tourist office** is south of the town centre at Jl Veteran 23 (Mon–Thurs 7am–2pm, Fri 7am–noon, Sat 7am–12.30pm; ☎0362/25141). As Lovina is just 6km west of Singaraja, there's little reason to stay, but *Sentral* (☎0362/21896; ①–②), Jl Jen Achmad Yani 48, and *Losmen Darma Setu* (☎0362/23200; ①), Jl Jen Achmad Yani 46A, reached via a small lane to the east of *Sentral*, both offer straightforward rooms, while the *Wijaya*, Jl Sudirman 74 (☎0362/21915; ①–④), has the widest range of rooms and is conveniently close to Banyuasri terminal. The night market is in the Jalan Durian area. Singaraja has several **hospitals**, including Rumah Sakit Umum (the public hospital), Jalan Ngurah Rai (☎0362/22046) and Rumah Sakit Kerta Usada (a private hospital that also has a dentist), Jl Jen Achmad Yani 108 (☎0362/22396).

Temple carvings at Sangsit, Jagaraga and Kubutambahan

To the east of Singaraja lies a string of temples with unusual, sometimes humorous, carvings. They can all be reached by **bemo** from Singaraja's Penarukan terminal. Eight kilometres east of Singaraja, a small road north takes you 200m to the pink sandstone **Pura Beji** of **SANGSIT**, justly famous for the sheer exuberance of its carvings. About 400m to the north-east across the fields from Pura Beji, carvings at the **Pura Dalem** cover the whole range of heavenly rewards and hellish punishments, including a lot of soft pornography that could count as either.

Back on the main road, 500m east of the Sangsit turning, you come to the road that leads 4km to **JAGARAGA** and the famous carvings at **Pura Dalem Jagaraga** temple. The very lively carvings here depict life before and after the Dutch invasion in 1848 – pictures on the left show village life before the Dutch, next to these are the Dutch arriving, and on the right-hand side is the much-photographed carving of two Dutch men driving a Model T Ford, being held up by bandits.

The most spectacular of the temples in the area is **Pura Meduwe Karang** at **KUBU-TAMBAHAN**, 12km east of Singaraja and 500m west of the junction with the Kintamani road. It's built on a huge scale, and supports 34 figures from the Ramayana as well as numerous very human **carvings** of Balinese villagers. In the inner courtyard you'll find one of the most famous carvings on Bali: a cyclist, wearing floral shorts, with a rat about to go under the back wheel, apparently being chased by a dog (possibly the Dutch artist WOJ Nieuwenkamp, who first visited Bali in 1904). The tiny *Sarah and Dewa's Losmen* (no phone; ①) is a homestay with two simple rooms in a family compound, in the village of Bungkulan which joins on to the western edge of Kubutambahan. Look out for a small sign by the Pura Desa pointing south off the main road; it's a hundred metres or so up on the right – you'll probably need to ask.

Lovina

LOVINA stretches along 8km of black-sand beach, the largest resort in Bali outside the Kuta-Legian-Seminyak conurbation. Beginning 6km west of Singaraja, the resort encompasses six villages: Pemaron, Anturan, Tukad Mungga, Kalibukbuk, Kaliasem and Temukus. **Kalibukbuk** is generally accepted as the centre of Lovina and it's here you'll find most tourist facilities.

Many people consider the early-morning **dolphin trips** from Lovina to be the highlight of their stay, but others find them grossly overrated. Boats leave at 6am and cost Rp20,000 per person for the two-hour trip; book directly with the skippers on the beach if you can. The reef off Lovina used to stretch at least 5km along the coast, but anchors and fish-bombs have caused severe damage. The skippers know the best spots for snorkelling and will take you out for about Rp15,000 per person for a one-and-a-half to two-hour trip. Situated between the main **diving** areas on the north coast of Bali – Pulau Menjangan (Deer Island) to the west (see p.352), and Tulamben (p.342) and Amed (p.341) to the east – Lovina is a good place to base yourself for diving. There are plenty of **dive operators** in the resort, offering dive trips (US$40–50) and courses: Baruna, on the main road in Kalibukbuk (☎0362/41084) and at *Puri Bagus Hotel* (☎0362/25542); Malibu Dive next to *Malibu* restaurant (☎0362/41225) and in Bina Ria Street (☎0362/41061; 11am–3pm and 5–9pm); Permai, *Hotel Permai*, Tukad Mungga (☎0362/41471) with another counter in

Bina Ria Street (☎0362/41017); and, probably the best known, **Spice Dive**, at Kaliasem (☎0362/41305) and on Bina Ria Street. **Watersports** are curently in their infancy in Lovina, but Karisma Bahari (☎0362/41969) have a lovely beach location in Kaliasem offering para-sailing (US$12 for one run), as well as wakeboarding, kneeboarding and water-skiing (all US$15 for 15min) and the highly recommended *Café Spice* (see p.350) from where you can watch all the action.

One popular outing ftrom Lovina is to Bali's only Buddhist monastery, the **Brahma Vihara Ashrama**, 10km southwest of Lovina, which can be combined with a visit to the hot springs at Banjar. Catch any westbound bemo to **DENCARIK**, where a sign points inland to the monastery, and ojek wait to take you the last steep 5km. From the temple you can walk to the **hot springs** (daily 8am–6pm; Rp1000). Head back downhill and take the first major left turn. After a few hundred metres you'll reach a major crossroads and marketplace at the village of **BANJAR TEGA**. Turn left and a *kulkul* tower will now be on your right. After about 200m you'll see a sign for the "Holy Hot Springs, Air Panas" (1km).

All inter-island **buses** from Java to Singaraja pass through Lovina, as do Gilimanuk–Singaraja and Amlapura–Gilimanuk services and all buses from the west of the island. From Denpasar and the east of Bali, you'll come via Singaraja. As the accommodation is so spread out, it's worth knowing where you want to be dropped off. **Tourist shuttle** buses also serve the resort. Perama has three offices in the area, at Anturan (☎0362/41161; 8am–9pm), on the main road in Kalibukbuk (☎0362/41104; 8am–8pm) and on Ketapang (☎0362/41161; 7am–10pm). Simpatik (☎0362/41584) offers a daily air-con service to Kintamani (Rp19,000) and Danau Bratan (Rp12,500) and twice daily services to Ubud, Sanu, the airport and Kuta (all Rp25,000).

To **get around** the resort, you can pick up the frequent bemos (4am–9pm) that zip through between Singaraja and Seririt. **Vehicle rental** is widely available: prices start at around Rp70,000 a day. Insurance deals vary and are only available with established compa-nies. Motorbikes are also available for rent (Rp25–35,000 per day), as are bicycles (Rp15000 per day). Established companies include Koperasi Marga Sakti (☎0362/41061), on Bina Ria Street, and Yuli Transport (☎0362/410184), opposite *Rambutan* on Ketapang.

Lovina's **tourist office** (Mon–Sat 8am–8pm) is on the main road at Kalibukbuk and the **police** station is in the same building. The **post office** is about 1km west of Kalibukbuk; get poste restante addressed to you at Post Office, Jalan Raya Singaraja, Lovina, Banjar, Singaraja 81152, Bali, Indonesia. There are also several postal agents in Kalibukbuk who sell stamps. Internet access is available at several places for Rp300–500 a minute; try Outpost or Spice Dive in Bina Ria Street or Planet Lovina at *Arya's Café* on the main road in Kalibukbuk.

There are **wartels** and **moneychangers** dotted throughout the resort. The closest **hos-pitals** are in Singaraja (see opposite), although for anything serious you'll have to go to Denpasar (p.312).

Accommodation

Generally **accommodation** closest to the beach is more expensive, and that on the main road is the cheapest. The busy season is from mid-June until late August and again in December, when accommodation is booked solid, and a lot of people end up spending their first night on the beach.

PEMARON AND TUKAD MUNGGA

Most accommodation in **PEMARON** and **TUKAD MUNGGA** is on side roads leading down to the beach. It's very quiet with minimal hassle, but there are no amenities nearby and the nightlife of Kalibukbuk is several kilometres away.

Happy Beach Inn, aka *Bahagia* (☎0362/41017). Good-value basic rooms close to the beach. Small, pleasant garden and a beachside restaurant. ①–②.

Hepi (☎0362/41020). Fan and air-con rooms, all with cold water, in a quiet garden setting, a short walk from the beach, and with a small pool. ②–⑤.

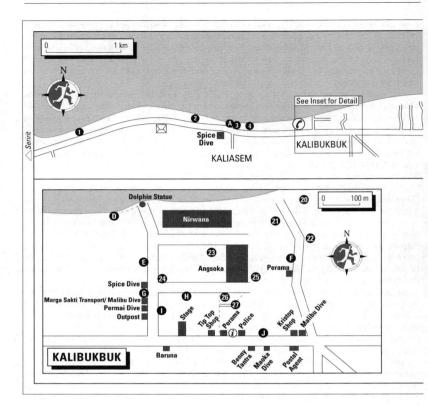

Permai (☎0362/41471). A large, clean, airy place near the beach with a good-sized pool. There's a range of options, with air-con and hot water in the more expensive rooms. The Permai diving centre is based here, so it's fairly lively when courses are going on and if you enrol on a diving course you get free accommodation for the duration. ②–④.

Puri Bedahulu (☎0362/41731). Right next to the beach, the entrance resembles a temple, and there is a restaurant looking across the sand. The bungalows are elegantly carved and comfortable with air-con at the top end. ②–④.

ANTURAN

The main turning to the fishing village of **ANTURAN** is almost opposite the petrol station and Anturan health centre (*Puskesmas*). Coming from the east look out for big signs for *Bali Taman Lovina, Yudha* (*Simon Seaside Cottages*) and *Villa Agung*. If you get to the Perama office you are too far west. From the main road it's a short walk down to the beach where most of the accommodation is grouped quite close together.

Bayu Mantra (☎0362/41930). Clean, tiled fan rooms away from the beach with hot-water showers and big windows looking out onto the garden. ②.

Gede Homestay (☎0362/41526). Close to the beach in a cosy compound, with a range of reasonable bungalows. There's a small beachfront restaurant. ①–②.

Mari (☎0362/41882). One row of rooms near the beach with cold-water bathrooms and fan, although a bit overwhelmed by the bigger places nearby. ②.

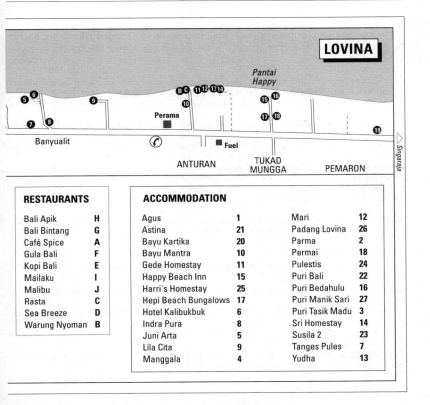

RESTAURANTS

Bali Apik	H
Bali Bintang	G
Café Spice	A
Gula Bali	F
Kopi Bali	E
Mailaku	I
Malibu	J
Rasta	C
Sea Breeze	D
Warung Nyoman	B

ACCOMMODATION

Agus	1	Mari	12
Astina	21	Padang Lovina	26
Bayu Kartika	20	Parma	2
Bayu Mantra	10	Permai	18
Gede Homestay	11	Pulestis	24
Happy Beach Inn	15	Puri Bali	22
Harri's Homestay	25	Puri Bedahulu	16
Hepi Beach Bungalows	17	Puri Manik Sari	27
Hotel Kalibukbuk	6	Puri Tasik Madu	3
Indra Pura	8	Sri Homestay	14
Juni Arta	5	Susila 2	23
Lila Cita	9	Tanges Pules	7
Manggala	4	Yudha	13

Sri Home Stay (☎0362/41135). A small, relaxed place with a row of rooms looking seawards. This is the most easterly and quietest of the Anturan beachside spots and there's a small restaurant and plenty of places to relax. ①–②.

Yudha (*Simon Seaside Cottage*; ☎0362/41183). A long-time favourite just beside the beach with a big choice of comfortably furnished rooms. There's a small pool. ②–⑤.

BANYUALIT

The **BANYUALIT** side road marks the beginning of the developed part of Lovina, with plenty of accommodation and a few restaurants.

Hotel Kalibukbuk (☎0362/41701). In an excellent location at the ocean end of Banyualit. The bungalows at the front have brilliant verandas facing the ocean and there are air-con rooms in the two-storey block. ②.

Indra Pura (☎0362/41560). Straightforward place offering good budget accommodation in bungalows with attached cold-water bathroom set in a garden. *Janur* (☎0362/41056), closer to the beach, is similar. ②.

Juni Arta (☎0362/41885). Reached via a path behind *Hotel Kalibukbuk*, this is a small row of sparkling new, good-quality bungalows in a peaceful spot. ②.

Lila Cita (no phone). Right on the beach at the end of a quiet lane. This is a good budget choice; rooms are in a two-storey block, the ones upstairs have a fan. One of the quietest places along the coast. ①.

Tanges Pules (☎0362/41753). Located 200m west of the Banyualit turning on the main road, this budget place has rooms or bungalows in a shady garden and there's a footpath to the beach. ①.

KALIBUKBUK

Centred around two side roads, Ketapang and Bina Ria Street, **KALIBUKBUK** has most of the tourist facilities. The narrow entrance to Ketapang is across from *Khi Khi Restaurant*.

Astina (☎0362/41187). A big range of options in a large, airy compound quite close to the beach at the end of Ketapang. ①–③.

Bayu Kartika (☎0362/41219). In one of the best positions in Lovina, on the coast at the end of Ketapang. A good range of bungalows, with an attractive pool and a restaurant located to catch the breeze. ②–⑤.

Harri's Homestay (☎0362/41152). A popular little gem tucked away in the back streets off Bina Ria Street – worth searching out. ②.

Puri Manik Sari (☎0362/41089). Accessible from the main road and Bina Ria Street. There are a variety of fan, cold-water bungalows in a pretty garden set far enough back from the road to avoid the noise. ②.

Padang Lovina (☎0362/41302). Straightforward accommodation in a two-storey block just off Bina Ria Street. The downstairs rooms have hot water; all rooms have good balconies or verandas. ②.

Pulestis (☎0362/41035). Through a grand entrance on Bina Ria Street, the small compound has comfortable rooms with fan and cold water and there is a pleasant pool with a fun waterfall feature. ②.

Puri Bali (☎0362/41485). A variety of rooms in an attractive garden with a good-sized pool; more expensive ones, closer to the pool, have air-con and hot water. Quiet location on Ketapang not far from the beach. ②–③.

Susila 2 (☎0362/41080). Good-value, simple accommodation off Bina Ria Street, with rooms off a tiny garden with attached cold-water bathrooms and verandas. ②.

KALIASEM AND TEMUKUS

West of Kalibukbuk, restaurants and accommodation line the roadside in the villages of **KALIASEM** and **TEMUKUS**.

Agus (☎0362/41202). A small place, close to the sea. Clean, tiled rooms with verandas that face the ocean. ②.

Manggala (☎0362/41371). Clean, simple rooms in a quiet family compound tucked between the beach and the road. ②.

Parma (☎0362/41555) The best budget option at this end of Lovina. Simple, fan rooms in a good, quiet location in a pretty garden near the sea. ①.

Puri Tasik Madu (☎0362/41376). Situated right next to the beach, this a a good budget cheapie offering basic rooms with attached bathrooms next to the beach. ①.

Eating and entertainment

There's a high turnover of **restaurants** in Lovina. Aside from *Malibu* and *Café 3*, also in Kalibukbuk, there's not much nightlife here, except for the **Balinese dance shows** at the Yayasan Budaya Den Bukit stage on the main road (Rp12,500), with local performers providing a range of Balinese dances. Several restaurants offer free local dance or gamelan to accompany your dinner; look out for the flyers around town.

Bali Apik Tucked away off Bina Ria Street, this place offers an excellent choice of breakfasts, pizzas, Indo–Chinese, seafood and Western food and lots of "Happy Hour" specials at night.

Bali Bintang Stretching back off Bina Ria Street, with high ceilings and a quiet atmosphere. There's a big drinks list including liqueurs, spirits and cocktails, plus an extensive menu of the usual Indo–Chinese, Western and seafood dishes.

Café Spice (☎0362/41969). Base of the Karisma Bahari watersports set-up, beside the beach at Kaliasem. The menu includes seafood, Western and Indo–Chinese meals, plus plenty of snacks, shakes and juices. Open 8am–8pm. Ring for a free pick-up in the Lovina area.

Gula Bali A quiet, attractive option on Ketapang with low-key taped music, free welcome drink and a good menu of Indonesian and Western food, including pizzas. They also offer a good-value breakfast.

Kopi Bali Popular, good-value place at the ocean end of Bina Ria Street. There's a big, inexpensive menu and everyone gets a free welcome drink and garlic bread with dinner.

Mailaku You'll certainly notice this massive three-storey eye-sore on Bina Ria Street. The second-floor restaurant has standard Lovina fare, and there are nightly videos.

Malibu On the main road in Kalibukbuk. The centre of Lovina nightlife, this large restaurant offers nightly videos and regular live music, free transport within the Lovina area, and is open until about 2am. Also worth a trip during the day for the cakes and bread.

Rasta At the end of the road in Anturan overlooking the beach. The location is the reason for a visit to this tiny place with a standard menu and plenty of reggae music.

Sea Breeze Brilliantly located on the beach, a great spot for a sunset drink – the apple or mango (in season) crumble is one of the culinary highlights of Lovina.

Warung Nyoman Just west of Rasta along the beach at Anturan. Seafood beach barbecues are the speciality, and you can arrange an expedition with them to catch your own dinner beforehand.

Pura Tanah Lot

Dramatically marooned on a craggy wave-lashed rock sitting just off the southwest coast, **Pura Tanah Lot** (Rp3100) really does deserve its reputation as one of Bali's top sights. Fringed by frothing white surf and glistening black sand, its elegant multi-tiered shrines have become the unofficial symbol of Bali, appearing on a vast range of tourist souvenirs. Unsurprisingly, the temple attracts huge crowds every day, particularly around sunset. Tanah Lot is said to have been founded by the wandering Hindu priest Nirartha and is one of the most holy places on Bali. Only bona fide devotees are allowed to climb the stairway carved out of the rock face and enter the compounds; everyone else is confined to the base of the rock.

Though there are occasional bright-blue **bemos** from Denpasar's Ubung terminal direct to Tanah Lot, you'll probably end up having to go via **Kediri**, 12km east of the temple complex on the main Denpasar–Tabanan road. All Ubung (Denpasar)–Gilimanuk bemos drop passengers at Kediri bemo station (30min; Rp1500), where you should change on to a Kediri–Tanah Lot bemo (more frequent in the morning; 25min; Rp1000). Alternatively, join one of the numerous tours to Tanah Lot that operate out of all major tourist resorts.

Gilimanuk and ferries to Java

Situated on the westernmost tip of Bali, less than 3km from East Java, the small, ribbon-like town of **GILIMANUK** is used by visitors mainly as a transit point for boats to and from Java. **Ferries** shuttle constantly between Gilimanuk and Ketapang, near **Banyuwangi** (every 20min day and night; 30min). Tickets (Rp1400) must be bought before boarding from the desks in the terminal buildings. If you're travelling quite a way into Java, to Probolinggo (for Mount Bromo) for example, or to Surabaya, Yogyakarta or Jakarta, the easiest option is to get an all-inclusive ticket from your starting point in Bali. The cheapest **long-distance buses** travel out of Denpasar's Ubung bemo station, but there are also more convenient tourist shuttle buses and bus and train combinations operating from major tourist centres across Bali. Ticket prices always include the ferry crossing.

Getting to Gilimanuk by **bemo** from almost any major town in north, south and west Bali is straightforward. All bemos terminate at the bemo station in the town centre, ten minutes' walk from the ferry terminal or a short *dokar* ride. From Denpasar (128km southwest) and the southern beaches, take either the direct dark-green bemos from Denpasar's Ubung terminal or a Gilimanuk-bound bus. From Singaraja (88km northeast), dark-red bemos run to Gilimanuk, as do a few buses.

Accommodation in Gilimanuk itself is not at all traveller-oriented, and the most appealing places are on the edge of town, about 2km south of the port along the road to Cekik, or 1.5km north of the Bali Barat National Park headquarters. Here, *Pondok Wisata Lestari* (☎0365/61504; ①–③) has a range of losmen rooms and a reasonably good restaurant; 50m north of *Wisata Lestari*, *Sari* (☎0365/61264; ②–③) has decent rooms in two-storey bamboo bungalows. If you want to stay near the port, *Nusantarra 2* (no phone; ②–③) offers shabby rooms about five minutes' walk from the ferry terminal, or more expensive shared bungalows another five minutes' walk around the bay. To get there from the ferry terminal, walk a few metres to your right, then cross the road and take the first turning on your left; if you miss that one there's another access road 50m further on, beside the police station. If

Nusantarra 2 is full, try *Kartika Candra* (①), *Nusantarra 1* (①) or *Surya* (①), which are all on the main road, about fifteen minutes' walk south of the ferry terminal, less than five minutes from the bemo station. You can change money at the bank opposite the bemo terminal.

Bali Barat national park

Nearly the whole of west Bali's mountain ridge is conserved as **Bali Barat national park (Taman Nasional Bali Barat)**, a 760-square kilometre area of savannah, rainforest, monsoon forest and coastal flats, which supports some 160 species of bird, including the endangered **Bali starling**, Bali's one true endemic creature. However, only a few trails are open to the public. Anyone who enters Bali Barat has to go with a guide and must also have a permit, both of which need to be arranged through the **National Park headquarters** (daily 7am–5pm), conveniently located at **CEKIK**, at the Denpasar–Gilimanuk–Singaraja T-junction, 3km south of Gilimanuk itself. **Guides** charge Rp65,000 for a two-hour hike, then Rp35,000 per extra hour. Permits costs Rp2500 per person per day. All dark-green Ubung (Denpasar)–Gilimanuk **bemos** pass the park headquarters, as do all dark-red Singaraja–Gilimanuk bemos; get out at the "Taman Nasional Bali Barat" sign.

There are two major trails through the park. If your main interest is birdspotting, you should opt for the **Tegal Bunder trek** (1–2hr), which takes in the Bali Starling Pre-Release Centre as well as possible sightings of the pinky-brown spotted dove, the black drongo, and the tiny bright-yellow-breasted olive-backed sunbird. The climb up **Gunung Klatakan** (a 5–6hr round-trip) is the most popular and most strenuous of the Bali Barat hikes, most of it passing through moderately interesting rainforest. You're unlikely to spot much wildlife on this trail, but you should certainly hear the black monkeys and might stumble across a wild boar.

The obvious place to stay is the *National Park Guest House* (①) in Cekik; call ☎0365/61060 Mon–Thurs 7am–2pm, Fri 7–11am, Sat 7am–12.30pm to check availability. The next best options are Pondok Wisata Lestari and Sari guest houses, about 1.5km north of the headquarters on the road into Gilimanuk; see p.351 for details. There are no warung or food hawkers inside the park (though a soup and noodle cart does set up outside the Cekik park headquarters every day), so you'll need to take your own supplies for the hikes. The nearest restaurant is at *Pondok Wisata Lestari*.

Pulau Menjangan (Deer Island)

By far the most popular part of Bali Barat is **Pulau Menjangan (Deer Island)**, a tiny uninhabited island just 8km off the north coast, whose shoreline is encircled by some of the most spectacular **coral reefs** in Bali, perfect for snorkelling and diving, with drop-offs of 40–60m, first-class wall dives and superb visibility (though some parts of the reef are showing signs of damage). There's also an old shipwreck which is frequented by sharks and rays.

As the island is part of the national park, you're obliged to go with a guide, but you can arrange both the guide and boat transport at the jetty in Labuang Lalang without first checking in at the Cekik headquarters. The departure point for Pulau Menjangan is **LABUAN LALANG**, 13km east of Cekik, on the dark red Giliminuk–Singaraja bemo route – 25 minutes from Gilimanuk or two hours from Lovina. There's a small national park office here (daily except national holidays 7.30am–3pm), as well as several restaurants. Boats to Pulau Menjangan can be hired at any time of day up to about 3pm; they hold ten people and cost Rp150,000 for a four-hour snorkelling tour – it's thirty minutes to the island. You'll also have to pay Rp60,000 for a guide (one per boat) plus Rp2500 per person for the national park entry fee. You can rent snorkelling equipment at the jetty for Rp20,000 a set. There have been reports of thefts from the boats while snorkellers are underwater, so leave your valuables elsewhere. Pulau Menjangan also features on day- and overnight tours for snorkellers and divers (US$80–180) who are based in Kuta, Sanur, Candi Dasa or Lovina.

LOMBOK AND THE GILI ISLANDS

Thirty-five kilometres east of Bali at its closest point, Islamic **Lombok** (80km by 70km) is populated by Sasak people and differs considerably from its Hindu neighbour. The landscape is much more barren and its tourist facilities are still developing. The island's northern area is dominated by the awesome bulk of **Gunung Rinjani**, until late 1994 believed to be dormant. Trekking at least part of the way up Rinjani is the reason many tourists come to Lombok and most base themselves in the nearby villages of **Senaru** and **Batu Koq** or in the foothills at tiny **Tetebatu**. The other big draw are the beaches: at the developed resort of **Senggigi** on the northwest coast, at the trio of backpacker-friendly **Gili Islands**, just offshore, and at less frantic south-coast **Kuta**, a popular surfing spot. Lombok's capital **Mataram** has little of interest, except for decent transport connections.

Ampenan-Mataram-Cakranegara-Sweta

The **AMPENAN-MATARAM-CAKRANEGARA-SWETA** conurbation comprises four towns and measures over 8km from west to east, but there's a fairly straightforward local transport system and anyway there's not much to see here. The westernmost part of the city is the old port town of **Ampenan**, the jumping-off point for Senggigi a few kilometres up the coast. Merging into Ampenan to the east, **Mataram** is the capital of West Lombok and full of offices and government buildings. East again, **Cakranegara**, usually known as just Cakra (pronounced "Chakra"), is the commercial capital of the island, with shops,

---

JANUARY 2000

On the afternoon of January 17, 2000, **rioting** broke out in Ampenan and Mataram on Lombok. The initial targets were Christian churches, homes and businesses which were set alight, ransacked and destroyed. It is believed that the perpetrators were fundamentalist Muslims. Rioting continued the next day, and that night some businesses in Senggigi were also attacked. In the days following the outbreak of violence, at least 4000 people left the island by sea and air. This included virtually all the tourists who were on the island at the time, expats, Indonesian visitors and Chinese and Balinese businesspeople.

Initial commentary linked the Lombok violence to the ongoing religious conflict in Maluku which had been raging between Christians and Muslims since early 1999, leaving hundreds dead and thousands injured. Later reports linked the sudden and violent explosion on Lombok to outside agitators who had flown to the island with the express purpose of stirring up trouble. More sinisterly, it was speculated that this was just part of a broader plan by the Indonesian military and/or other allies of ex-President Suharto to destabilize the country and provide apparent validity for a military takeover of the democratically elected government. The riot certainly came at a time when the government was rather vulnerable – the President was away on an extensive overseas tour at the time.

Whatever the truth of the matter, fears proved unfounded, and the violence on Lombok ended as quickly as it started. However, it left the **tourist industry** in tatters with zero occupancy of most hotels for several weeks afterwards, chunks of Ampenan reduced to rubble and the Lombok people deeply shocked by the speed with which their burgeoning economic well-being had vanished. An industry that had developed slowly but surely over twenty years was devastated in just two days.

But, fortunately for Lombok, tourist memories are short and within a couple of months visitors started to drift back and bookings were starting to rise again, although it remains to be seen how many businesses will have been unable to ride out the storm.

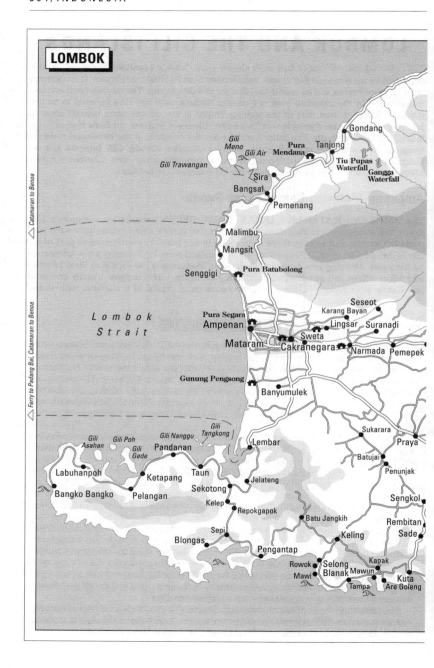

LOMBOK

Gondang

Gili
Meno
Gili Air
Gili Trawangan

Pura
Mendana
Tanjung

Tiu Pupas
Waterfall
Gangga
Waterfall

Sira

Bangsal

Pemenang

Malimbu

Mangsit

Senggigi
Pura Batubolong

Seseot
Karang Bayan

Pura Segara
Ampenan
Lingsar
Suranadi

Mataram
Sweta
Cakranegara
Narmada
Pemepek

*Lombok
Strait*

Gunung Pengsong

Banyumulek

◁ *Catamaran to Benoa*

◁ *Ferry to Padang Bai, Catamaran to Benoa*

Gili
Tangkong
Gili Nanggu

Gili
Asahan
Gili Poh
Gili
Gede
Pandanan
Lembar

Sukarara
Praya

Labuhanpoh
Ketapang
Taun

Batujai

Bangko Bangko
Pelangan
Sekotong
Jelateng
Penunjak

Kelep
Repokgapok
Sengkol

Sepi
Batu Jangkih
Rembitan
Sade

Blongas
Pengantap
Keling

Rowok
Selong
Blanak
Kapak

Mawi
Mawun
Kuta
Are Goleng
Tampa

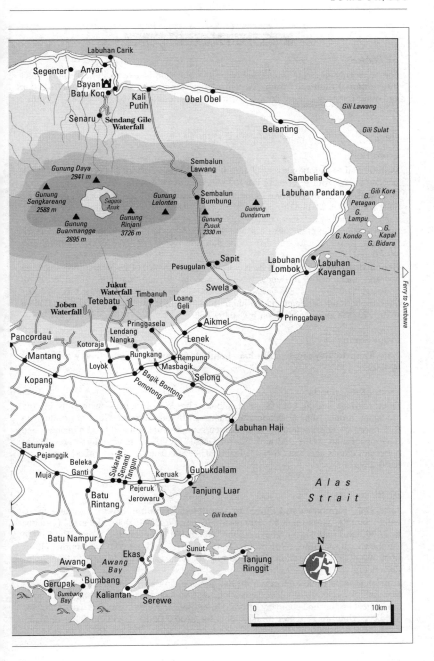

GETTING TO LOMBOK

BY PLANE

Lombok's only airport is Selaparang Airport in Mataram (see opposite). The only direct **international flights** are from Singapore. There are regular **internal flights** from Bali and other points in Indonesia with Garuda, Air Mark and Merpati; see "Travel Details", p.442.

BY BOAT

From Bali

Padang Bai to Lembar (every 90min; 4hr–4hr 30min). Ferry tickets cost Rp16,600 VIP (air-con lounge with soft seats); Rp7100 Ekonomi (hard seats).

Benoa Harbour to Lembar Mabua Express catamaran (one daily increasing to two daily December 23–January 5 and July 1–August 31, and during major local holidays; 2hr). There are two classes costing US$25–30, but none include transport at either end. Some motion sickness sufferers find this a particularly uncomfortable trip. Book through travel agents or direct in Bali on ☎0361/721212, or in Lombok on ☎0370/681195.

Benoa Harbour to Malimbu Bounty Cruise (daily; 2–3hr). This high-speed catamaran operates daily between Benoa Harbour, Gili Meno and Malimbu, 10km north of Senggigi. The fare is US$35 one-way between Bali and Lombok. A shuttle bus (Rp5000) operates between Senggigi and Malimbu. Book through travel agents or direct in Bali on ☎0361/733333, or in Lombok on ☎0370/693666.

From Sumbawa

Poto Tano to Kayangan, Labuhan Lombok (every 45min; 2hr). Ferry tickets cost Rp4000.

From other islands

Pelni services call at Lembar on Lombok. The *KM Awu* calls fortnightly on the Waingapu, Ende, Kupang, Maumere, Makassar, Berau, Tarakan, Nunukan route. The *KM Tilongkabila* calls monthly from Bali en route to Sulawesi and the Philippines. See "Getting around" p.192–193 and "Travel Details" p.442 for more information. Prices between Lembar and Bali (4hr) are Rp14–40,000 and from Lembar to Makassar (48hr) Rp76–254,500.

BY BUS

Java, Bali, Sumbawa and Flores to Mandalika Terminal, Sweta. Several services daily. Sample fares include Denpasar (6–8hr; Rp35–45,000); Jakarta (2 days; Rp97,500–Rp135,000); Surabaya (20hr; Rp65,000); Yogyakarta (26hr; Rp95,000); Sumbawa Besar (6hr; Rp15,000); Bima (12hr; Rp22–44,000); Domphu (10hr; Rp20,500–40,500); Sape (14hr; Rp47,500); Labuhan Bajo (24hr; Rp70,000); Ruteng (36hr; Rp80,000).

Tourist shuttle buses operate from Bali to the main tourist destinations on Lombok: Mataram, Senggigi, Bangsal for the Gili Islands, Tetebatu and Kuta, Lombok. Perama are the longest established company, offering Kuta (Bali) to Kuta (Lombok; 3 daily; 12hr) for Rp55,000; Ubud to Senggigi (3 daily; 8hr) for Rp30,000; and Lovina to Bangsal (daily, involving a stop-over) for Rp55,000.

markets, workshops and hotels all aimed at Indonesian trade but welcoming to tourists as well.

Planes land at **Selaparang Airport**, on Jalan Adi Sucipto at Rembiga, only a few kilometres north of Mataram and Ampenan. There is an exchange counter, open for all international arrivals and a taxi counter with fixed price fares (Mataram Rp9500, Senggigi Rp15,000, Bangsal Rp32,000, Kuta Rp62,000). To get to Bangsal on public transport, turn left on the road at the front of the airport, head 500m to the left to a set of traffic lights on a crossroads, turn left and catch a public bus marked "Tanjung" which will drop you at Pemenang.

If you're coming across the island from the east, from Lembar in the south (see p.359 for details of transport from here) or from the airport on an eastbound bemo, you'll arrive at Mandalika **bus station** in Sweta, at the western extremity of the city area. Most, but not all, of the public transport from the north arrives here as well, and if you're heading on to anywhere except Senggigi, you can pick up a connection here. **Long-distance bus** tickets are available from the numerous ticket counters at Mandalika bus station. From Senggigi and on some of the bemos from Pemenang you'll arrive at the Kebun Roek terminal in **Ampenan**. It's a good idea to have some notion of where you want to stay before you arrive, as accommodation is so widely spread out. The Ampenan places are twenty minutes' walk from the terminal there, and the Cakranegara places are not too far from the main bemo routes, but several kilometres from Sweta.

All **bemo** trips within the four-cities area cost Rp500, and yellow bemos constantly ply to and from Ampenan and Mandalika terminal, Sweta, from early in the morning until late in the evening. The horse-drawn carts here, unlike the ones on Bali, have small pneumatic tyres and are called **cidomo**. They are not allowed on the main streets, but cover instead the back routes that bemos don't work, and are generally used for carrying heavy loads. Always negotiate a price before getting in.

The **Pelni** office for ferry tickets from Lembar is temporarily located at Jl Sriwijaya 1A (Mon–Fri 8am–noon & 2–3pm, Sat 8.30–11am; ☎0370/637212) and due to relocate shortly to Jl Industri 1, Ampenan.

The most helpful **tourist office** is the Provincial Tourist Service for West Nusa Tenggara, which is in Ampenan at Jl Langko 70 (Mon–Thurs & Sat 8am–3pm, Fri 8am–1pm; ☎0370/637828); you can pick up leaflets and an excellent map of Lombok here, and get advice about travel in Lombok and Sumbawa.

Accommodation and eating

Few tourists stay in Mataran, as Senggigi is only just up the road. Most of **Ampenan's backpackers' lodges** have seen better days, but *Hotel Zahir*, Jl Koperasi 9 (☎0370/634248; ①), is a good-value budget cheapie, with basic rooms. There's a better-value clutch of losmen in **Cakranegara**, where *Shanta Puri*, Jl Maktal 15 (☎0370/632649; ①–②), is the most popular travellers' place, offering a range of rooms and some air-con and hot water. Other good Cakra options are *Adiguna*, Jl Nursiwan 9 (☎0370/625946; ①), in a quiet, convenient street, near the bemo routes, and the similarly quiet *Oka*, Jl Repatmaja 5 (☎0370/622406; ①).

For **food in Ampenan**, *Pabean* on Jalan Yos Sudarso does inexpensive Chinese dishes, while *Rainbow Café*, further along the same road, has a small Indonesian menu and cheap beer. In **Cakra**, on Jalan Maktal, *Shanta Puri* and the *Suharti Sate House* are both inexpensive. For good-value Padang food try *Adenna*, Jl Saleh Sungkar 33 in Ampenan, or *Asano*, Jalan Hasanudin in Cakra. The best bakeries in town are *Mirasa Modern Bakery*, Jl AA Gede Ngurah in Cakra, which unfortunately only has take-away, and *Roti Barokah,* Jl Saleh Sungkar 22, in Ampenan, about 100m south of the turning to Kebun Roek terminal, where you can sit in and enjoy the doughnuts, pizza and cakes.

Shopping

Although it doesn't have anywhere near the retail opportunities of the Bali resorts or of Senggigi, just up the coast, shopping in the city can be fun. The **Mandalika market** has an

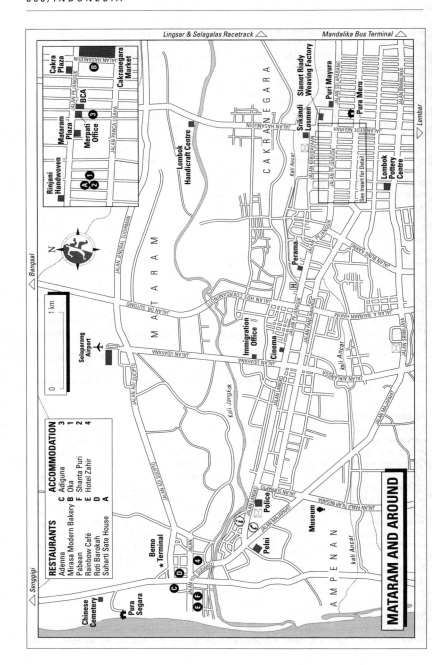

MATARAM AND AROUND

Lingsar & Selagalas Racetrack △

Mandalika Bus Terminal △

△ Bangsal

△ Senggigi

▽ Lembar

Cakra Plaza
Cakranegara Market
Mataram Plaza
BCA
Merpati Office
Rinjani Handwoven
Slamet Riady Weaving Factory
Puri Mayura
Srikandi Losmen
Pura Meru
CAKRANEGARA
Lombok Handicraft Centre
Lombok Pottery Centre
See Insert for Detail
Kali Ancar
Perama
MATARAM
Selaparang Airport
Immigration Office
Cinema
Kali Jangkok
Museum
AMPENAN
Police
Pelni
Bemo Terminal
Chinese Cemetery
Pura Segara
kali Ancar

Jalan Jendral Sudirman
Jalan Adi Sucipto
Jalan HOS Cokroaminoto
Jalan Udayana
Jalan Panca Usaha
Jalan Pejanggik
Jalan Hasanudin
Jalan Gede Ngurah
Jalan Selaparang
Jalan Brawijaya
Jalan Kebudayan
Jalan A. Rahman Hakim
Jalan Bung Karno
Jalan Sriwijaya
Jalan Airin Angga
Jalan Langko
Jalan Panji Tilar Negara
Jalan Majapahit

RESTAURANTS
Adenna   C
Mirasa Modern Bakery   B
Pabean   F
Rainbow Café   E
Roti Barokah   D
Suharti Sate House   A

ACCOMMODATION
Adiguna   3
Oka   1
Shanta Puri   2
Hotel Zahir   4

0   1 km

N

extensive range of crafts scattered amongst the vegetables, fish, meat and plastic household goods. **Ampenan** has a clutch of art and "antique" shops selling **crafts** from Lombok and the islands further east. They are concentrated in Jalan Saleh Sungkar, starting with Yufi, about 200m south from the turning to the bemo terminal, and in the Jalan Yos Sudarso area, north of the bridge across the Jangkok River. A couple of factories also produce **ikat** cloth; Rinjani Handwoven, Jl Pejanggik 44–46, Cakra (daily 9am–9pm), and Slamet Riady, Jl Tanun 10, just off Jl Hasanudin, Cakra, are both worth a look. For Lombok **pottery** visit Lombok Pottery Centre, Jl Sriwijaya 111A, Ampenan (☎0370/640351), which stocks the best quality products of the three main pottery centres on the island, and Sasak Pottery, Jl Koperasi 102 (☎0370/631687) which operates shops in several hotels on the island and is the biggest earthenware showroom in Indonesia, with more than 400 designs on display. An excellent one-stop shopping spot is the **Lombok Handicraft Centre** at Rungkang Jangkok, Sayang Sayang. Just beyond the Jangkok River, about 2km north of Cakranegara on Jalan St Hasanudin, it has numerous small shops selling every type of craftwork imaginable.

Listings

Airlines All the domestic airlines have ticket counters at the airport. There are also some additional offices: Air Mark, Selaparang Airport (☎0370/643564); Bouraq Airlines, *Hotel Selaparang*, Jl Pejanggik 40–42, Mataram (☎0370/627333); Merpati, Jl Pejanggik 69 (☎0370/636745, airport ☎0370/633691); PT Nitour Inc (Merpati and Garuda agents), Jl Yos Sudarso 4 (☎0370/623672); Garuda, *Hotel Lombok Raya*, Jl Panca Usaha 11 (☎0370/637950, airport ☎0370/622987 ext 246). Silk Air is the only international airline office on Lombok – it's in Senggigi (see p.363). For information on international airline offices in Bali, see p.317.

Banks and exchange All the large Mataram and Cakra banks change money and travellers' cheques. The most convenient if you are staying in Cakra is the Bank of Central Asia, Jalan Pejanggik 67, which also has an ATM which accepts Visa cards and is connected to the Cirrus and Maestro networks. For longer hours (Mon–Sat 8.30am–5pm) there are a couple of moneychangers on Jl Saleh Sungkar, just north of the junction with Jl Yos Sudarso. If you are coming from the east of the island and desperate for cash there is a BCA ATM which accepts Visa cards and is connected to the Cirrus and Maestro networks on Jalan Sandubaya, about 500m west of the Mandalika bus terminal. If you are getting money wired from overseas, Western Union use the main branch of Bank Internasional Indonesia (BII), Jl Gede Ngurah 4B, Mataram (see p.23 for more details on getting money wired).

Hospitals Catholic Hospital, Jl Koperasi, Ampenan (☎0370/621397); Muslim Hospital, Jl Pancawarga, Mataram (☎0370/623498); Public hospital, Jl Pejanggik 6, Mataram (☎0370/621354).

Immigration office (Kantor Imigrasi), Jl Udayana 2, Mataram (☎0370/622520).

Internet access Internet A & N, Jl Koperasi 30 (8am–8pm; Rp400 per minute), almost opposite *Hotel Zahir* in Ampenan. The main post office on Jl Sriwijaya offers public Internet access (daily except Sun 8am–4pm, Sun 8am–2pm; Rp2500 per 15 min and then Rp200 per min).

Motorbike rental If you know a bit about bikes and aren't worried about insurance, the main rental place is at the roadside at Jalan Gelantik 21, Cakranegara, a couple of hundred metres west of the *Srikandi* losmen on Jalan Kebudayaan.

Police Jl Langko (☎0370/631225).

Post office, Jl Sriwijaya, Mataram. This is the main post office in Lombok (Mon–Thurs & Sat 8am–2pm, Fri 8–11am, Sun 8am–noon) and also offers public access to the Internet (daily except Sun 8am–4pm, Sun 8am–2pm; Rp2500 per 15 min and then Rp200 per min). For simply sending things, the post office at Jl Langko 21 opposite the tourist office is more accessible, as is the one on Jl Kebudayaan (same hours). For **poste restante** the Senggigi post office is more used to dealing with tourists.

Telephone services The main telephone office is at Jl Langko 23, opposite the tourist office (daily; 24hr), but there are also plenty of wartels in town including Jl Panca Usaha 22B (8am–midnight); Jl Saleh Sungkar 2G (7.30am–midnight); Jl Pejanggik 105 (6.30am–11pm).

Lembar and boats to Bali

Boats to and from Bali dock at **LEMBAR**, 22km south of Mataram (for details of boat services see p.356). The Pelni ferries *KM Tilongkabila* and *KM Awu* also dock here (see "Getting around", pp.192–193, and Travel Details, p.442). **Bemos** run between Mandalika terminal and Lembar. If you're arriving in Lembar from Bali and need transport, you'll find the Lembar bemo drivers hard bargainers; the price should be about Rp1000 to Sweta, but you'll do well to bargain them down to anything respectable. The hassles in Lembar are one good reason to book through to Mataram or Senggigi with Perama or another tourist shuttle company. For **accommodation** around Lembar, the most tourist-oriented option is the *Sri Wahyu* losmen (☎0370/681048; ①), Jl Pusri 1, Serumbung, signposted from the main road about 1.5km north of the port.

Senggigi

With a reputation among travellers for being spoilt by big money and big hotels, it's a pleasant surprise to find that the long sweeping bays of **SENGGIGI** are in reality backed by an attractive, laid-back beach resort. Although parts of the area are packed with hotels, it's perfectly possible to have an inexpensive stay here, and its accessibility to the airport makes it an ideal first- or last-night destination. Plenty of operators here cater for people who want to **dive** in the Gili Islands, but with the comforts of Senggigi. Expect to pay around US$45–60 for two dives, including the boat trip from Senggigi and lunch. You'll need to check whether equipment rental is included in the price. A PADI Open Water course will cost around US$375. Contact Albatross (☎0370/693399), Blue Coral (☎0370/693441), Blue Marlin (☎0370/93045), Dive Indonesia (☎0370/693367), Dream Divers (☎0370/693738) or Manta Diving (☎0370/693139). All have booking offices in central Senggigi.

Senggigi is served by regular **bemos** from Ampenan terminal. The most convenient place to pick them up is on Jalan Saleh Sungkar just north of the turn-off to the bemo terminal in Ampenan. Fixed-price **taxis** also run direct from the airport for Rp15,000. The resort is very spread out, so it's useful to have an idea of where you're heading; the southern end of Senggigi is just 5km north of Ampenan, and there are a few places spread out along the next 4km until the main concentration of hotels stretching for roughly 1km from the *Pondok Senggigi* to the *Sheraton*. Low-density development continues for another 8km to *Hillberon*. Bemos serve all accommodation north of the resort except *Hillberon* but they can be quite infrequent and many terminate at the *Sheraton* or the Pacific Supermarket. Many hotels on this stretch operate free shuttle services to central Senggigi during the day, and many restaurants offer free pick-ups in the evening. Metered blue taxis cost Rp3000–5000 from most places north of the central area.

Several travel agents including Lombok Mandiri (☎0370/693477), on the main road, book **long-distance bus tickets**, and both they and Perama (☎0370/693007) operate **tourist shuttles** to Bali (Kuta, Ubud and Lovina), as well as to Kuta (Lombok). Perama also has shuttles to Tetebatu.

Accommodation

It's still possible to find reasonable budget **accommodation** in the resort, although you'll get more choice the more you can spend. The most attractive part of the coast is in north Senggigi, where there are great views across to Bali when it is clear, and there's the interest of ordinary village life carrying on behind the beachside accommodation. In central Senggigi there's plenty happening, an excellent choice of bars and restaurants and plenty of shopping opportunities, although unless you find a place well off the main road it can be rather noisy. South Senggigi has the advantage of easy accessibility, it's close to the city and there are some good budget options.

NORTH SENGGIGI

Bale Kampung (no phone). Small, peaceful, budget place in Kerandangan village, easily accessible from central Senggigi. The turning is 100m north of *Lombok Coconut* and is just 50m from the main road. Accommodation is in traditional one- and two-storey bungalows, set in a glorious garden. ①.

Lombok Coconut (☎0370/693195). Ranged up the hillside, these are good-value, attractively decorated bungalows with cold water and fans. There's a great little swimming pool too. ③.

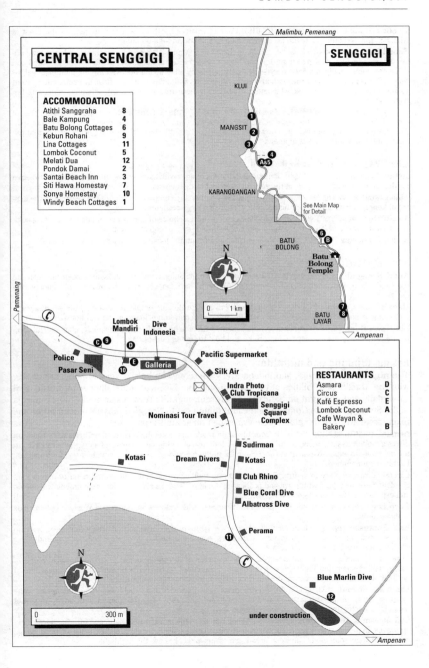

CENTRAL SENGGIGI

SENGGIGI

ACCOMMODATION

Atithi Sanggraha	8
Bale Kampung	4
Batu Bolong Cottages	6
Kebun Rohani	9
Lina Cottages	11
Lombok Coconut	5
Melati Dua	12
Pondok Damai	2
Santai Beach Inn	3
Siti Hawa Homestay	7
Sonya Homestay	10
Windy Beach Cottages	1

Malimbu, Pemenang

KLUI

MANGSIT

A&5

KARANGDANGAN

See Main Map
for Detail

BATU
BOLONG

Batu
Bolong
Temple

N

0   1 km

BATU
LAYAR

Ampenan

Pemenang

Lombok
Mandiri

Dive
Indonesia

Police

Pasar Seni

Galleria

Pacific Supermarket

Silk Air

Indra Photo
Club Tropicana

Senggigi
Square
Complex

Nominasi Tour Travel

RESTAURANTS

Asmara	D
Circus	C
Kafé Espresso	E
Lombok Coconut	A
Cafe Wayan & Bakery	B

Sudirman

Kotasi

Dream Divers

Kotasi

Club Rhino

Blue Coral Dive

Albatross Dive

Perama

N

0   300 m

Blue Marlin Dive

under construction

Ampenan

Pondok Damai, Mangsit (☎0370/693019). Four kilometres north of central Senggigi, on the coast at Mangsit, this is a quiet spot with accommodation in bamboo-and-thatch bungalows. ③.

Santai Beach Inn (☎0370/693038). Right on the coast at Mangsit, these popular thatched bungalows are set in a wonderfully overgrown garden and have a very relaxed atmosphere. Meals can be provided and are eaten communally in a *bale* (open–sided pavilion) lit by oil lamps in the evening; the menu is ideal for fish-eating vegetarians, but they can also cater for vegans and nobody objects if carnivorous guests want to dine outside. All rooms have a fan and cold water but there are a couple of larger family rooms with hot water. ②.

Windy Beach Cottages (*Pondok Taman Windy*) (☎0370/693191). Comfortable bungalows, 5km north of central Senggigi, right on the coast at Mangsit. It does get windy in the afternoons, but it's a lovely spot. The more expensive rooms have hot water. You can book shuttle bus tickets here, organize tours of the island and rent snorkelling equipment. ②–③.

CENTRAL SENGGIGI

Kebun Rohani (☎0370/693018). Bamboo-and-thatch cottages with excellent verandahs, set in an attractive garden on the hillside away from the sea. An excellent budget choice in this area. ②.

Lina Cottages (☎0370/693237). All the bungalows in this tiny compound right on the seafront in the centre of Senggigi have air-con but no hot water. There's a large restaurant too. ②–⑤.

Melati Dua (☎0370/693288). Set in pleasant gardens with a choice of good-value bungalows offering cold-water bathrooms and fan at the bottom end and hot water and air-con at the top. ②–⑤.

Sonya Homestay (☎0370/693447) Budget rooms in a centrally located, cosy, family compound. ①.

SOUTH SENGGIGI

Atithi Sanggraha, Batu Layar (☎0370/693070). Well-built bungalows in a pleasant garden between the road and beach, 4km south of central Senggigi. All rooms have fan, cold-water bathroom and a good veranda. ②.

Batu Bolong Cottages (☎0370/693198). Just north of Batu Bolong temple, these are attractive cottages in pleasant gardens, on both sides of the road; the more expensive ones have air-con and hot water. ②–⑥.

Siti Hawa Homestay (☎0370/93414). Small rooms with attached bathroom in a simple, characterful compound. The family have a bicycle, motorbike and boat to rent to guests. ①.

Eating, drinking and nightlife

The **nightlife** in Senggigi, and indeed everywhere on Lombok, is very low-key, in keeping with the Muslim sensibilities of the local population. Licences generally permit music until 11pm daily and midnight on Saturday. At present, nightlife revolves around Club Tropicana in the Senggigi Square Complex and Club Rhino next to *Senggigi Sunset*'s restaurant on the main street. Most of the places below are open till around 11pm.

Asmara (☎0370/693619). Set back from the main road, this tastefully furnished and relaxed restaurant offers a moderate-sized menu featuring Western, Indonesian and Sasak dishes and a massive drinks list in the moderate to expensive range. Free pick-up throughout Senggigi. Good homemade bread for breakfast. Highly recommended.

Circus Attractive place in central Senggigi, offering mellow music and a moderate menu of Indonesian, Sasak and Western food with pizza and pasta as specialities. There's also a big ice cream menu, cappucino and espresso coffee, plus a good wine list.

Coco Loco One of several seafront places in Pasar Seni with Indonesian, Sasak and Western options plus barbecued fish.

Kafé Espresso This is a clean, friendly place towards the north of the central area, offering cappuccino and espresso coffee, as well as salads, sandwiches, pasta, Indonesian favourites, lassis and an indulgent range of desserts. Prices are moderate.

Lina Large, popular restaurant attached to the cottages of the same name. There's a massive menu of soups, fish, chicken and Indo–Chinese options and the tables on the terrace overlooking the beach are a brilliant place to watch the sunset during Happy Hour. Inexpensive–moderate.

Lombok Coconut (☎0370/693195). Serving pizza, pasta, burgers and salads, as well as Indonesian satay and *gado-gado*, this restaurant is located in a large *bale* just above the road, about 4km north of central Senggigi. There's free transport in the Senggigi area.

Café Wayan & Bakery (☎0370/693098). About 1km from the centre of Senggigi and offering a free pick-up service in the area, they serve excellent moderate to expensive Indonesian dishes, seafood, pizza, pasta, salads and vegetarian food. The fresh bread, croissants and cakes are the highlight.

Listings

Airlines Silk Air (☎0370/693877) has a central office. Other airlines which serve Lombok have offices in Mataram-Ampenan-Cakranegara-Sweta (see p.359). For information on international airline offices in Bali, see the box on p.317.

Car and bike rental There are plenty of places renting vehicles with and without drivers. Kotasi (☎0370/693435) is the local transport co-operative and has two counters (see map on p.361). Prices start at Rp90,000 per day on a self-drive basis. Car rental includes half insurance (the maximum you'll pay in case of an accident is US$500). They also have pushbikes for Rp12,000, but remember that the road north of Senggigi is extremely steep. It is also worth checking at Lombok Mandiri (☎0370/693477), which operates a similar half insurance policy and Nominasi (☎0370/693690) which rents vehicles with full insurance; the maximum you'll pay in case of an accident is Rp200,000. Expect to pay around Rp25,000 for a driver for the day.

Hospitals and clinics Some of the luxury hotels have in-house doctors who can be consulted: *Holiday Inn* (☎0370/693444); *Sheraton* (☎0370/693333) 3–11pm; *Senggigi Beach Hotel* (☎0370/693210). There is also a clinic (☎0370/693210) near *Senggigi Beach Hotel* which operates a 24hr call-out service. For anything serious, you'll have to go to a hospital in the four-cities area (see p.359).

Internet access There are several Internet cafés along the main street: *Bulan Cybercafé* (8.30am–10.30pm) is as good as any and prices are fairly standard at Rp400 per minute.

Post office Located in the centre of Senggigi (daily 8am–5pm). Poste restante is available here; get mail addressed to you at Post Office, Senggigi, Lombok 83355, West Nusa Tenggara, Indonesia.

Telephone services There are a couple of wartels in the centre of Senggigi and one just above the *Sheraton* with longer hours (7am–midnight).

The Gili Islands

Strikingly beautiful, with glorious white-sand beaches lapped by warm, brilliant-blue waters, the trio of **Gili Islands** just off the northwest coast of Lombok have developed rapidly in recent years to cope with the crowds of visitors. Of the three, **Gili Trawangan** best fits the image of "party island", with heaps of accommodation, restaurants and nightlife. The smallest of the islands, **Gili Meno**, has absolutely no nightlife and not much accommodation and, closest to the mainland, **Gili Air** offers a choice, with plenty of facilities in the south, and more peace elsewhere.

Prices on the islands vary significantly according to the season: the same bungalow will cost Rp30,000 in February and Rp50,000 in July, August and December. None of the islands has a particular **crime** problem, but there are no police on the Gilis, so in the event of trouble it is the role of the *kepala desa*, the head man who looks after Gili Air (where he lives), and Gili Meno, and the *kepala kampung* on Gili Trawangan, to deal with the situation and take you to police at Tanjung or Ampenan to make a report. It seems that when problems do arise they are sometimes dealt with poorly.

The **access port** for the Gili Islands is **BANGSAL**, 25km north of Senggigi, which has a few restaurants, some moneychangers and a Perama office (7.30am–4pm). If you get stuck, the losmen *Taman Sari* (no phone; ②) is just by the gate into the harbour. Bangsal is a short *cidomo* (horse-drawn cart) ride or a shadeless 1.5-kilometre walk from **PEMENANG**, 26km beyond the Ampenan-Mataram-Cakranegara-Sweta area and served by **bemos or buses** from Mandalika terminal. There are also some bemos from Ampenan. All transport between Mandalika and points around the north coast passes through Pemenang. There is no public bemo service along the coastal road north from Senggigi to Pemenang. Perama sells **tourist shuttle** tickets to Bangsal from most tourist spots on Bali and Lombok. Sample fares are Rp45,000 from Kuta, Rp35,000 from Candi Dasa, Rp10,000 from Mataram or Senggigi.

Boats leave Bangsal throughout the morning, when full, and take between twenty and forty-five minutes; buy your ticket at the office on the quayside right by the beach. Blue, red and white boats serve Gili Air (Rp1500), yellow and red go to Gili Meno (Rp1900), and red and white to Gili Trawangan (Rp2000). They operate from 7.30am until 4.30pm and leave when full. From **Senggigi**, you can take the daily Sunshine boat to Gili Trawangan, run by Sunshine Tours (☎0370/693232), in central Senggigi, or the daily Perama shuttle (1hr 30min;

SNORKELLING AND DIVING

The **snorkelling and diving** around the islands is some of the best and most accessible in Lombok and, despite a lot of visitors, the reefs remain in reasonable condition. All the islands are fringed by **coral reefs** and visibility is generally around 15m. The **fish** life here is the main attraction and includes white-tip and black-tip reef sharks, sea turtles, manta rays, Napoleon wrasse and bumphead parrotfish. There are good snorkelling spots just off the beaches of all the islands but most of the best **dive sites** involve short boat trips. Away from the shore, the currents are treacherous, so be careful.

There are **dive operations** on all the islands, with most based on Gili Trawangan. Expect to pay around US$45–55 for a two-dive trip, PADI Open Water courses hover either side of US$300. You'll need to check whether the price you are quoted includes equipment rental. The nearest hospital is in Mataram and the nearest decompression chamber is in Denpasar on Bali.

Rp20,000). At both ends of all boat trips you'll get your feet wet, as the boats anchor in the shallows and you have to wade to and fro.

Once on the islands, the "hopping island" boat service is extremely handy for **getting around**. It does one circuit, Air–Meno–Trawangan–Meno–Air, in the morning, and one in the afternoon. It's conveniently timetabled and fast, and makes a day-trip to another island a feasible option. Times from Gili Air are 8.30am and 3pm, from Gili Meno to Gili Trawangan 8.45am and 3.15pm, from Gili Trawangan 9.30am and 3.30pm, and from Gili Meno to Gili Air 9.45am and 4.15pm. Between Gili Trawangan and Gili Air the fare is Rp5000, between Gili Trawangan or Gili Air and Gili Meno, it's Rp4000.

There are a number of **moving on** options from the islands. Several operators on the islands offer shuttle tickets direct to Lombok or Bali destinations. Lombok Mandiri quote Rp16,000 to Senggigi or Mataram, Rp18,000 to Lembar, Rp29,000 to Padang Bai, Rp38,000 to Ubud and Rp40,000 to Kuta, Bali, all from Gili Trawangan; prices are Rp1000–2000 less from the other islands. Perama have counters on Gili Trawangan and Gili Air and sell tickets from Bangsal; there is just one daily departure leaving Bangsal at 9am and fares are Kuta Rp45,000, Ubud Rp40,000, Candi Dasa Rp35000, Padang Bai Rp30,000, Senggigi Rp10,000, Kuta Lombok or Tetebatu Rp25,000.

Gili Trawangan

Furthest from the mainland, the largest of the islands, with a local population of 700, **GILI TRAWANGAN** attracts the greatest number of visitors and has moved upmarket at meteoric speed. The southeast of the island is virtually wall-to-wall bungalows, restaurants and dive shops; even the road has been paved along here. For quieter and less prettified surroundings head to the northeast, northwest or southwest coasts. Island transport is by *cidomo*, or you can rent bicycles (ask at your guesthouse or the stall near the jetty; around Rp20,000 per day), though the tracks around the island are very sandy in parts. A **walk around the island**, less than 3km long by 2km at the widest part, takes three hours or less. Inland, the hundred-metre **hill** is the compulsory expedition at sunset – follow any of the tracks from the southern end of the island for views of Agung, Abang and Batur.

The area towards the northern end of the east coast of the island is very popular for snorkelling, and most people hang out here during the day; you can rent masks and flippers easily. There are plenty of **dive operators** on the island, Albatross (☎0370/638134), Blue Marlin (☎0370/632424), Dream Divers (☎0370/634496), Dive Indonesia (☎0370/642289) and the Vila Ombak Diving Academy (☎0370/642336) all in the southeast corner and Manta Diving (☎0370/643649) further north.

There are several secondhand bookshops and a small art market with a **postal agent**. **Moneychangers** all along the main strip change cash and travellers' cheques. *Blue Marlin*

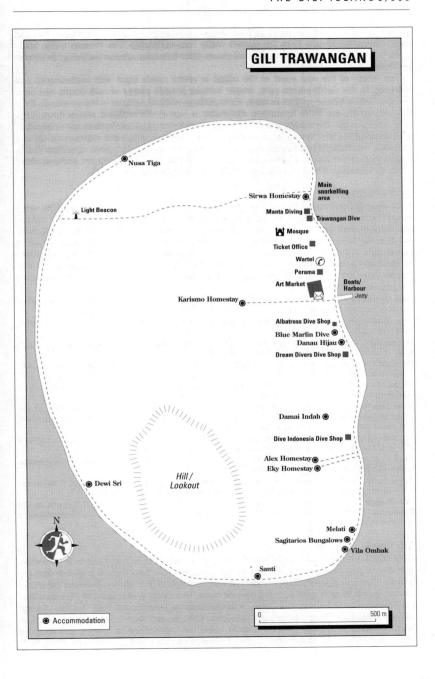

GILI TRAWANGAN

- Nusa Tiga
- Light Beacon
- Sirwa Homestay
- Main snorkelling area
- Manta Diving
- Trawangan Dive
- Mosque
- Ticket Office
- Wartel
- Perama
- Art Market
- Boats/Harbour
- Jetty
- Karismo Homestay
- Albatross Dive Shop
- Blue Marlin Dive
- Danau Hijau
- Dream Divers Dive Shop
- Damai Indah
- Dive Indonesia Dive Shop
- Alex Homestay
- Eky Homestay
- Dewi Sri
- Hill / Lookout
- Melati
- Sagitarios Bungalows
- Vila Ombak
- Santi

N

0   500 m

- Accommodation

guesthouse gives cash advances on Visa cards, but charge a heavy commission. You can make international calls from the **wartel** (daily 7am–midnight). The Perama office (daily 7.30am–9pm) is close to the jetty. Several places offer **Internet access** including *Borobodur* restaurant and Dive Indonesia.

The whole of the east coast of the island is pretty much lined with **restaurants** and **warung**. In the northeastern part, simple warung provide plenty of cold drinks and inexpensive Indo–Chinese options in basic surroundings, while the places in the southeast, from the jetty south, are more upmarket. *Borobodur* is one of the swishest places down here. Wherever you eat, the quality and variety of the food is very good and prices are reasonable, with **seafood** the best option. Many restaurants show two or even three videos each day and there's a surprisingly good range of new films. *Vila Ombak* has the most upmarket dining experience on the island. **Parties** take place on the island nightly, they get going at about 11pm and finish around 2 to 3am. Each night's venue is clearly advertised.

ACCOMMODATION

Accommodation ranges from simple bamboo bungalows, with attached mandi, to more comfortable concrete bungalows, perhaps with Western-style toilets and some newer, upmarket versions with hot water and air-conditioning. The north end of the island is relatively quiet, while the concentration of bungalows at the southern end is more lively and closer to restaurants and discos. Developments around the southern tip and on to the west coast are pleasant and quiet. For simple, good-value accommodation, slightly away from the hustle and bustle, there are a few places springing up behind the warung on the northeast coast and a few places in the village.

Alex Homestay One of several places behind the beach in the village. There is a choice of bamboo and thatch or concrete bungalows. *Eky Homestay* is nearby and *Karisma* further north. ①–②.

Blue Marlin (☎0370/632424). Better quality accommodation than most, with attractive furnishings and air-conditioning and hot water. ⑦.

Danau Hijau Conveniently close to the harbour, these straightforward concrete bungalows are similar to many of the ones nearby, with red-tiled roofs and good verandahs. ①–②.

Dewi Sri Quiet, isolated place on the west coast, thirty minutes' walk from the harbour, with accommodation in traditional bungalows. ①–②.

Melati Modern bungalows in the southeast accommodation area, with cold water bathroom, fan, lockable cupboards and drawers. Pleasant verandahs at the front. ①–②.

Nusa Tiga Up on the peaceful north side of the island. Some traditional thatch-and-bamboo and some more substantial, concrete bungalows. A few of the bungalows have brilliant sea views and there are *bale* where you can sit and admire the scenery at the front. ①–③.

Sagitarios Down towards the southern end of the southeast corner. Bamboo-and-thatch rooms and bungalows in a huge garden. The bungalows face seawards, rare for this part of the island. ①–②.

Santi Near the sea in a shady location at the southern end of the island, these well-built traditional bungalows with a brick mandi are a popular option. ①–②.

Sirwa Homestay One of several new places behind the tiny warung on the northeast coast. A tiny row of four concrete rooms with attached bathroom and small veranda, close to the sea. ①–②.

Vila Ombak (☎0370/642336). In the southeast of the island, this is the most upmarket option on Gili Trawangan. Attractive and well-furnished rooms with some fans and some air-con set in pleasant gardens with a small pool. ⑦–⑧.

Gili Meno

GILI MENO is the most tranquil island of the three, only 2km long and just over 1km wide, with a local population of just 350 and no nightlife, but some solo women travellers find the island's young men particularly persistent. It takes a couple of hours to stroll around the island, and the **snorkelling** is good all along the east coast. There is no postal agent or Perama office, but *Mallia's Child* offers shuttle buses to destinations on Lombok and Bali. You can **change money** at *Mallia's Child*, *Gazebo* and *Casablanca Cottages*, and there's a **wartel** near the harbour. Albatross Dive Shop (☎0370/633847) offers the same range of courses and dives for experienced divers as the operation on Gili Trawangan and is based at *Casablanca Cottages*.

The range of **accommodation** options is pretty wide with several mid-range choices. Most accommodation is spread along the east coast over a fairly small area and each set of bunga-lows has its own generator for electricity except one or two at the northern end, which is where you'll get the best budget value. *Blue Coral, Pondok Meno* and *Pondok Santai* (①–②) are all in the north of the island, and all offer simple, traditional bungalows. *Mallia's Child* (☎0370/622007; ②) is just south of the harbour and has bamboo-and-thatch bungalows in a good location near a fine beach. Just north of the harbour, *Casablanca Cottages* (☎0370/633847; ③–⑦) is one of the better mid-range places with a range of options and a tiny pool set about 100m back from the beach.

The **restaurant** at *Casablanca* is an attractive open *bale* (open-sided pavilion) and serves moderately priced Indonesian, seafood and Western options. If you are walking around the island, *Kafe Lumba-Lumba* and *Good Heart* on the west coast are both worth a stop. The restaurant in front of *Kontiki* has good beach views and a large menu of steak, seafood, rice and noodles, and the two-storey restaurant attached to *Mallia's Child* has an excellent pizza oven. A few beachside warung are springing up around the island; *Lamy's*, north of *Pondok Meno*, has great views across the water, and further south *Café Sentiga* also gets excellent breezes. Eat early as they all stop serving by 9.30pm.

Gili Air

Closest to the mainland, with the largest local population (1000) of the three islands, **GILI AIR** stretches about 1.5km in each direction and takes a couple of hours to walk round. It sits somewhere between lively, social Gili Trawangan and very peaceful Gili Meno. There is a good range of **accommodation** available, from beach huts to luxurious bungalows. The con-glomeration of restaurants and losmen behind the waste ground on the southeast corner is where you'll find most of the action, and the beach here is the most popular, with good snorkelling. Reefseekers **diving operation** (☎0370/641008) is a well-established, highly regarded local company. Dream Divers (☎0370/634547) and Blue Marlin (☎0370/634387), both well-established on Gili Trawangan, also have dive shops here. All dive shops are marked on the map on p.368.

There are plenty of moneychangers around the island, and the **wartel** (7.30am–11pm) is at *Gili Indah*. Tourist shuttle tickets can be booked from Perama (☎0370/637816; 7.30am–7pm), which is just behind *Gili Indah*. There is no **postal agent**, but mail gets taken to the mainland regularly by Perama. There is **Internet access** at *Coconut Cottages* (7am–12noon & 4–10pm) for Rp1000 per minute for the first ten minutes and then Rp500 per minute after that and at *Gili Indah* for Rp800 per minute.

There is a good range of **places to eat**, many of them attached to the accommodation. Most offer a range of Indonesian and Western food at cheap to moderate prices, and Indonesian buffets are laid on by plenty of places – look for the flyers around the island. *Il Pirata*, built in the shape of a pirate ship, has quality furnishings and a small Italian menu at moderate prices. For position, the warung attached to *Bulan Madu* is unbeatable, right on the shoreside, and is a great place for an afternoon drink. *Peanuts* café has an attractive, tra-ditional sitting area and, so far, has not followed the fashion for loud taped music. At the time of writing, **parties** were only allowed twice a week on the island, starting at 9pm or 10pm and finishing fairly strictly at midnight, alternating between *GoGo* and *Legend Warung*. Enquire at your guesthouse for the current situation.

ACCOMMODATION

There's a selection of good-value **accommodation** spread around the island; the quietest spots are the north and west coasts. The island-wide electricity isn't very reliable so the places with their own generators have a bit of an advantage when the cuts occur – keep a torch handy.

Abdi Fantastik (☎0370/641018). In a great location looking seawards on the east coast, the wood and thatch bungalows have fans and mosquito nets. ①

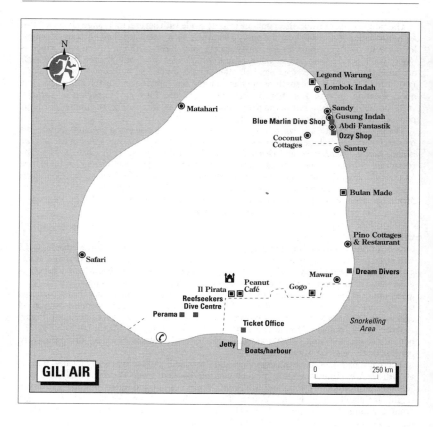

GILI AIR

N

Legend Warung
Lombok Indah

Matahari

Sandy
Gusung Indah
Blue Marlin Dive Shop
Abdi Fantastik
Ozzy Shop
Coconut
Cottages
Santay

Bulan Made

Pino Cottages
& Restaurant

Safari

Mawar
Dream Divers

Peanut
Café
Il Pirata
Gogo
Reefseekers
Dive Centre
Perama
Snorkelling
Area
Ticket Office

Jetty
Boats/harbour

0   250 km

Coconut Cottages (*Pondok Kelapa*; ☎0370/635365). Away from the coast in a coconut grove, with some traditional and some newer bungalows. There's an Internet service, and tours can be arranged. ②–③.

Gusung Indah (no phone). Pleasantly located, close to the east coast, with traditional well-built bungalows facing seaward and larger ones behind. There are great *bale* to sit in and admire the view. ②.

Lombok Indah (no phone). Basic bungalows on a quiet stretch of coast, although the attached *Legends Warung* hosts weekly discos. *Sandy* nearby is quite similar. ①–②.

Matahari (no phone). The bungalows here are close to the quiet north coast with places to sit right beside the beach. Other nearby options are *Pondok Pantai* and *Bunga*. ②.

Mawar (no phone). Well-built cottages with mosquito nets at the southeast corner of the island. You can also check out *Resota* nearby. ①–②.

Pino Cottages (no phone). Good bamboo, thatch and wood cottages in a neat garden just on the edge of the southeast corner with a small restaurant attached. ①.

Safari (no phone). Fan bungalows with attached bathrooms in a lovely spot over on the west coast. Check out *Salabose* and *Lucky's* which are nearby and also good value. ①–②.

Santay (☎0370/641022). Popular, good-quality cottages in a good location set slightly back from the east coast. ②.

BOAT TRIPS TO SUMBAWA, KOMODO AND FLORES

Various travel agencies on Lombok and the Gili Islands run boat trips via Sumbawa and Komodo to Flores. These involve several snorkelling stops, usually some trekking, a beach party, sometimes camping and a visit to see the feeding of the Komodo dragon. Prices average Rp400–750,000 for a five-day/four-night trip, including all meals and mattresses on the deck. Most terminate at Labuhanbajo on Flores, but some travel by road and ferry to Flores and then sail back; round trips are more expensive. Air transport out of Labuhanbajo can be difficult to arrange, so allow plenty of time. The following all organize trips; *Coconut Cottages* on Gili Air (☎0370/635365); Perama – contact any office; Nominasi, *Taman Sari Restaurant* in Bangsal, office in Gili Trawangan (☎0370/644169), Senggigi office (☎0370/693690); and Lombok Mandiri, in Mataram (☎0370/632497), and in Senggigi (☎0370/693477).

Gunung Rinjani and around

From a distance, **Gunung Rinjani** (3726m) appears to rise in solitary glory from the plains, but in fact the entire area is a throng of bare summits, wreathed in dense forest. The most breathtaking feature of the range is **Segara Anak**, the magnificent crater lake, measuring 8km by 6km. The climb up Rinjani is the most energetic and rewarding trek on either Bali or Lombok. You can ascend from **Senaru**, where there is some accommodation, or climb the volcano as part of an organized tour. The trip is only possible in the dry season, from about May to October, is not for the frail or unfit, and should not be attempted without adequate food or water. Although not all the treks need a porter or guide, you should let somebody know where you are going and when you will be back. There are conservation offices at Senaru and Sembalun Lawang to report to when you set off, but they're often deserted. There have been fatal accidents on the mountain and this is an active volcano; Gunung Baru in the crater lake last erupted in 1994.

Although it's easy to go to Senaru or Batu Koq and arrange the climb up Rinjani from there, many companies arrange **inclusive trips**: one-night/two-day trips to the crater rim, three-day trips to the rim and the lake and four-day trips (or longer) that go to the summit from Sembalun Lawang, down to the lake and finish at Senaru. **Operators** include Coconut Cottages, Gili Air (☎0370/635365); Green Belt Lombok Holiday, *Hotel Wisata,* Ampenan (☎0370/626971); Hati Suci in Sapit; Nominasi, Senggigi (☎0370/693690), Gili Trawangan (☎0370/644169); *Taman Sari* Restaurant at Bangsal; and Rainbow, Pringgasela, central Lombok (no phone).

Batu Koq and Senaru

Buses from Mandalika terminal in Sweta terminate at **ANYER**, from where bemos (Rp1500) and ojek (Rp5–6000) run to the neighbouring villages of **BATU KOQ** and **SENARU** (about 86km from Mataram). Both have accommodation spread out for several kilometres along the road: *Segara Anak* is the most northerly and furthest from the mountain, while *Bale Bayan Senaru* lies right at the end of the road where the path up the mountain begins. Places on the east of the road generally have the best views towards the mountain. All will help you arrange your trek, rent out gear, find porters and store your stuff, and most have small restaurants attached. Just to the south of *Pondok Senaru*, a small path heads east to the river and **Sendang Gile waterfall**, where you can bathe, although the water is pretty chilly. The **traditional village** at Senaru, a fenced compound with houses of bamboo and thatch set out in rows, next to the *Bale Bayan Senaru*, is also worth visiting.

ACCOMMODATION

Bale Bayan Senaru This is the place closest to the mountain. Basic bungalows in a small garden. ①.

Bukit Senaru Cottages Bungalows are well spaced in an attractive garden with good verandas. ②.

Gunung Baru Small set-up, not too far from the start of the trail, with a few basic bungalows. ①.

Pondok Achita Bayan Good bungalows and verandahs back and front for mountain and garden views. ①.

Pondok Guru Bakti Basic bungalows with excellent views of the waterfall from the rooms at the back. ①.

Pondok Indah Good bungalows and fine north coast views. ①.

Pondok Senaru The biggest set-up offering best-quality accommodation in the area, all with great verandas, set in a pretty garden with plenty of *bale* to admire the view, and a huge restaurant. ②–④.

Segara Anak The first place on the road from Bayan. There are stunning views from the verandahs of the more expensive bungalows, while the cheaper ones overlook the garden. The restaurant is 100m up the road. ①.

Climbing Gunung Rinjani

The **summit of Rinjani**, the highest point of the region's volcanic mountainous mass, is reached by relatively few trekkers; the majority are satisfied with a shorter, less arduous trip to the crater rim and down to the crater lake. From **the rim** you can see the beautiful turquoise lake, **Segara Anak** inside the massive crater, with the small perfect cone of Gunung Baru rising on the far side. Having lain dormant since 1906, Gunung Baru erupted again in August 1994, closing the mountain for several weeks and raising fears of a major disaster; fortunately all has gone quiet again, and Gunung Rinjani itself has been inactive since 1901.

The simplest trek is from **Senaru**, climbing to the **crater rim**. There's a forestry office at the start of the track in Senaru where you buy your permit (Rp2000) and register. The route takes you from the village at 860m (marked on some maps as Position I), up through the forest to further **rest positions** with small *bale* (open-sided pavilions). Rest Position II is at 1570m and Position III is at 2300m; you then leave the forest for the slog up to the rim at 2634m. It takes most people six to seven hours, not allowing for rests, to get to the rim from Senaru and usually involves a night on the mountain unless you are extremely fit and fast. Sadly the *bale* are in a very poor state of repair and not ideal for sleeping in. A tent is preferable, and vital if you plan to sleep on the actual rim.

A further possibility after climbing to the rim is to descend down into the crater to **the lake** itself, at around 2000m. The path (1hr 30min) into the crater is very steep and rather frightening at the top, but gets better further down. You can bathe in the warm lake or the **hot springs** along its shores. Most people get down to the lake in one day from Senaru, stay by the shore and return the same way in another day's walking. From the lake it's possible to climb out on a different path to a site called Plawangan II at 2900m, and from there up to the **summit** of Rinjani, a seven-hour trek. You'll need a guide for this. The more common alternative if the sumit is your objective, is to climb from Sembalum Lawang on the east of the mountain which is accessible on public transport from Kali Putih, near the north coast, or Aik Mel, on the east–west road across the island and Sapit on the southern slopes of the mountain (see p.372). There is accommodation in Sembalum Lawang at *Cemara Siu* guesthouse (☎0370/621213; ①), where they can help you to arrange your trek. You should try to get to the summit for sunrise or by about 7am as it clouds over and gets very windy by 9am.

PRACTICALITIES

There is spring **water** at Positions II and III during and just after the rainy season, and also around the lakeshore, but check locally before you set out. It's vital to carry adequate water and food for the climb. If you are climbing up from Senaru to the rim or down to the lake you don't need a guide, although a **porter** is a great advantage (Rp30–50,000 a day and you must take food and water for them also). The path leaves to the left just beyond *Bale Bayan Senaru* in Senaru and is difficult to lose. Most of the accommodation near the mountain rents out gear. Sleeping bags are Rp10,000–25,000, mattresses about Rp10,000, tents Rp25,000–40,000 and stoves and cooking stuff Rp10,000–30,000. The price is for each trip and you'll pay this even if you are away just one night; make sure everyone is clear about what is agreed.

Tetebatu

Set high on the southern slopes of Gunung Rinjani, 50km from Sweta, and surrounded by some of the most picturesque scenery in Lombok, the small village of **TETEBATU** is becoming increasingly popular. It's a quiet spot, but developing rapidly, with a moneychanger, a Perama agent (book a day in advance) and transport rental. Enquire at *Green Orry* for bicycles (Rp10,000 a day), motorcycles (Rp25,000), charter transport and exchange. To reach Tetebatu, take a bemo or bus to **Pomotong** (1hr 15min from Sweta's Mandalika Terminal) and either get an ojek straight up to Tetebatu, or a bemo to **Kotaraja** and then a cidomo on to Tetebatu. Perama tourist **shuttle buses** also run here from all over Bali and Lombok. *Green Orry* are the agents.

Accommodation

Most **accommodation** is on the main road leading up to the *Soedjono Hotel* from Kotoraja and on the road to the east, Waterfall Street.

Cendrawasih Accommodation here, in the downstairs part of two-storey traditional *lumbung*-style barns, is some of the most attractive in the area and set in a great garden with an attractive, raised, thatched restaurant. ②.

Danni's Homestay Around 2km from the Kotoraja–Tetebatu road in the hamlet of Penyonggok; the turning is signed a few hundred metres south of the junction with Waterfall Street. There are a couple of small rooms in a family compound; this is about as rural as it gets. ①.

Diwi Enjeni Three brick bungalows with wide verandas set in a large garden. One of the bungalows and the attached restaurant have excellent views. ①.

Green Orry Traditional and modern bungalows in a pleasant compound plus a restaurant with good views. It is also the local Perama agent, has motorbikes and bicycles for rent, can arrange a guide for local treks and charter transport. ②.

Hakiki Set in the middle of rice fields, accommodation is in two-storey traditional-style barns with excellent verandahs upstairs and down. ②.

Mekarsari Pleasant location in the fields behind *Pondok Tetebatu*, this is a small place with accommodation in brick bungalows. The turning is opposite *Pondok Tani* restaurant. ①.

Pondok Bulan Close to the rice fields with good views, there are traditional bamboo-and-thatch lumbung-style bungalows, as well as bigger, less traditional family rooms which are more expensive. ①–②.

Pondok Tetebatu Clean, tiled rooms with good verandas looking onto an attractive garden and a restaurant with fine views. ①.

Rambutan Four hundred metres along a rough track in Kembang Kuning, with traditional bungalows in the middle of a rambutan orchard – the ultimate getaway. ①.

Soedjono Hotel A range of accommodation set in great grounds at the far north end of the village and the most upmarket option in the area. The cheaper rooms are basic but have attractive verandahs and at the top end you get brilliant views and hot water. There is a moderately priced restaurant and a swimming pool. ②.

Lendang Nangka

Developed single-handedly as a tourist destination by local teacher Haji Radiah, **LENDANG NANGKA** is a small farming community 2km north of the main cross-island road, and served by cidomo and ojek from **BAGIK BONTONG**. Although the scenery is not as picturesque as in Tetebatu, the atmosphere is much more welcoming and there's a wealth of walks around the village. Established in 1983, *Radiah's Homestay* (② including three meals), the original **accommodation**, is still the best. You can either stay in rooms in the family compound or in larger, newer rooms in a house in the local fields. It's right in the middle of the village, but tucked away behind the school, so ask for directions. *Radiah* is also a Perama agent (book the day before). A couple of rival losmen are nearby: *Pondok Wira* (② including meals) and

Pondok Sasak (①–②), further from the village centre on the same road. However, the best alternative are the garden bungalows at *Pondok Bambu* (Rp25,000 per person including three meals), 500m north of Lendang Nangka, and signed from the road to Kembang Kuning.

Sapit

Situated high in the hills, at 1400m on the southern slopes of Gunung Pusuk, the small mountain village of **SAPIT** is a quiet retreat with wonderful views. It is accessible from Sembalun Lawang (2–3hr by daily bus) on the northern side of Gunung Pusuk or from the cross-island road, either via **AIK MEL** or **PRINGGABAYA** – it's a fifteen-kilometre drive from either, although there is more public transport from Pringgabaya. In Sapit, there is **accommodation** at *Hati Suci* (③) and the simpler *Balelangga* (☎0370/636545; ②), run by the same people. Staff here will point you in the right direction for walks to the nearby water-falls, monkey forest, canyon and hot springs. They also arrange all-inclusive trekking trips to Gunung Rinjani.

Labuhan Lombok and on to Sumbawa

The port town of **LABUHAN LOMBOK** runs **ferries to Sumbawa**'s Poto Tano (every 45min round the clock; Rp4000) from the ferry terminal, Labuhan Kayangan, at the far end of the promontory, 3km around the south side of the bay or Rp500 by local bemo. **Buses** run regularly between the ferry terminal and the Mandalika terminal at Sweta (2hr); change at Kopang (1hr) for Praya and the route to Kuta. To the north, buses run to and from Obel Obel and Bayan (2hr) on the north coast via Sambelia; this is the way to go if your first stop on Lombok is Gunung Rinjani. The best place to stay is *Lima Tiga*, Jl Kayangan 14 (no phone; ③), about 150m from the town centre on the road to the ferry terminal.

Kuta and around

The peaceful little south-coast fishing village of **KUTA**, 54km from Mataram, has a wide, white-sand beach and is rapidly becoming the favourite choice of Lombok travellers. The big swell here makes the sea good for **surfing** and there are lovely beaches within walking or cycling distance, but no diving or snorkelling.

Coming from the west, **buses and bemos** run to **PRAYA** from Mandalika terminal, Sweta. From Praya, bemos ply either to Sengkol, where you can change, or right through to Kuta (1hr). From the east of Lombok, bemos run to Praya via **KOPANG** on the main cross-island road. Perama also runs **tourist shuttles** to Kuta from all destinations on Bali and Lombok.

There are several **moneychangers** near the losmen. If you want to book tourist shuttle tickets, the **Perama** office (7am–10pm) is attached to *Segare Anak*. They have daily depar-tures to destinations on Bali and Lombok, although some require a stopover. In addition, *Segare Anak* can book Mabua Express or Bounty Cruise tickets to Bali. *Segare Anak* is also a **postal agent** and you can use them for poste restante (get mail addressed to you at Segare Anak, Kuta Beach, Lombok Tengah, Nusa Tenggara Barat 8357, Indonesia), otherwise, the nearest post office is in Sengkol. There is a **wartel** (8am–11pm) in the village offering phone and fax services and **Internet access** (Rp800 per minute). Ask at your accommodation or at Perama if you want to charter transport (Rp60–80,000 for a one-way trip to Lembar, Mataram or Senggigi) or rent motorbikes (Rp25–35,000 per day).

Nearby beaches

The simply glorious **beaches** of Seger and Tanjung Aan are easily accessible from Kuta and, at a push, walkable, though bicycles are a good idea. **Seger** is closest to Kuta (1km east) and is now the location of the luxury *Novotel*. To reach **Tanjung Aan** (5km), follow the road east out of the resort and take the first sealed turning to the right. There are actually two perfect white-sand beaches here, Aan to the west and Pedau to the east, separated by an outcrop. The only facilities are a few drinks stalls.

Along the coast **west of Kuta** you can explore half a dozen or so of the prettiest beaches on the island, but you'll need your own transport. A couple of kilometres out of Kuta you'll pass the "MTM 64" sign; just under 1km west of this, look out for a dirt track heading off to the coast. After 2km it reaches the coastal village of **ARE GOLENG**. The beach here is about 400m long and the seaweed beds in the shallows are clearly visible. The next beach west is **MAWAN**, reached by a sealed road just beyond the "Mataram 66km" sign. The bay is very attractive, and almost semicircular; there are no warung here. Continuing west, access to the beach at **MAWI** isn't easy. Take the next sealed road branching off seaward; after 1500m it degenerates into a track before ending in a plantation with a couple of houses. The people here are well used to keeping an eye on vehicles, as this is a favourite beach with surfers, but you should pay them for it. It's a few hundred metres walk to the lovely white-sand beach, separated from nearby **ROWOK** by a rocky outcrop.

Accommodation, eating and drinking

The **accommodation** here is mostly simple losmen-style, but there are a few upmarket options. In Kuta itself, the road runs about 50m inland from the beach and the accommodation is spread out along the coast for about 500m on the far side, so don't expect cottages on the beach itself. All the losmen have **restaurants** attached. *Segare Anak* and *Anda* both have good quality food, and *Warung Mandalika* in the village is also worth a look. Only the *Mascot Pub* has live music and there is no disco scene here. *Rinjani Agung* shows nightly videos.

Anda (☎ 0370/654836). A range of bungalows in a shady garden setting, located on the road behind the beach. ①–②.

Cockatoo (☎0370/654830). At the far eastern end of the bay, these are good-sized cottages with pleasant verandahs situated in a large compound. ①.

Kuta Indah (☎0370/653781) A short walk from the west end of Kuta beach, this is the newest place in Kuta itself, with good grounds and gleaming bungalows ranged around a pool. Top-end rooms have hot water and air-con. Free transport to neighbouring beaches. ②–⑤.

Lamancha Homestay (☎0370/655186). Nice little place in the village, a short walk from the beach, with one bungalow with attached bathroom and two upstairs rooms with outside mandi. ①.

Matahari Inn (☎0370/655000). Situated in the village, this is an atmospheric place with plenty of accommodation options set in a lush garden. Top-end rooms have air-con and hot water. There's a swimming pool and free transport to Tanjung Aan beach. ②–⑥.

Rinjani Agung (☎0370/654849). A huge range of accommodation on offer, located on the road behind the beach, the most expensive with air-con. ②–③.

Segare Anak (☎0370/654834). Due for renovation, the bungalows, all pretty basic, are set a long way back behind the restaurant in a shady garden on the road behind the beach. ①.

Sekar Kuning (☎0370/654856). A variety of rooms in a garden setting on the road behind the beach. ①.

SUMBAWA

East of Lombok, the scorched, mountainous island of **Sumbawa** is often perceived as an inconvenient but necessary bridge between Lombok and Komodo, but it does hold some fine west-coast **beaches**, as well as spectacular coral just offshore at **Pulau Moyo**. In the east, the exceptional reef breaks at **Hu'u** have become legendary amongst surfers. Sumbawa is a strictly Muslim enclave and both male and female travellers should dress conservatively.

Historically, the Sumbawan people in the western half of the island have always been influenced by the Balinese and the Sasaks of Lombok, while the Bimans in the east share linguistic and cultural similarities with the Makarese of Sulawesi and the peoples of Flores and Sumba. Up until the end of the sixteenth century, Bima Region was still mostly animist, osten-

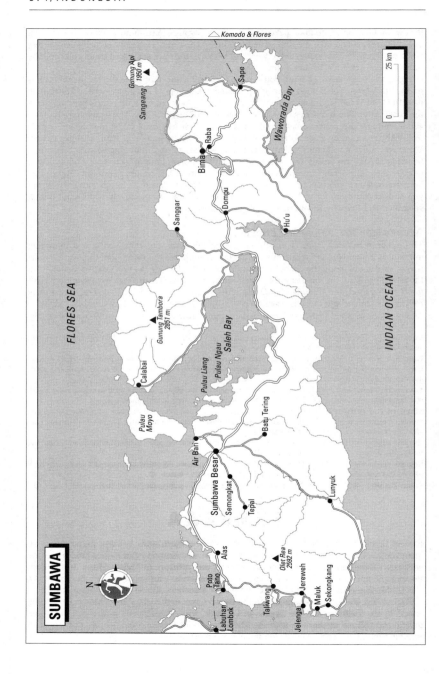

sibly ruled by a succession of Hindu rajahs with Javanese origins but, when the Makarese of Sulawesi took control in the early seventeenth century, they converted the people to **Islam**. The Dutch only really controlled the area at the beginning of the twentieth century, and were ousted by the Japanese in World War II. Soon after, Sumbawa became a part of the modern republic of Indonesia. **Transmigration** and the wholesale reaping of the sappanwood and sandalwood forests have put huge pressure on the little land that is useable and Bima's once illustrious bay is now filling with silt as a result.

Ferries to and **from Lombok** (90min) dock at **POTO TANO**, at the extreme western end of Sumbawa; buses meet all incoming ferries and run south from the harbour to Taliwang (1hr; Rp2000), and north to Alas (45min; Rp2000), Sumbawa Besar (2hr; Rp3000) and sometimes all the way to Bima (9hr; Rp10,000). Ferries to and **from Flores** (9–12hr) use the port at Sape (see p.377). **Pelni** ferries dock at Bima (see p.376).

Sumbawa Besar

SUMBAWA BESAR's open streets are lined with crumbling white plaster buildings, bright-blue wooden doors adorning its many shopfronts. It is now the largest town on the island, and visitors looking to break up the bus-run across the island could do worse than stop here. It's a sprawling place with no particular centre and, apart from a small cluster of losmen on Jalan Hasanuddin near the river, accommodation is also spread across town.

Most buses from the west arrive at **Barang Barat bus terminal** on the east side of town, a fifteen-minute walk south from the centre, but they may drop you at the more central old bus station on Jalan Yos Sudarso. Early-morning buses going east **to Bima** (Rp12,500), Dompu (Rp7500) and Sape (Rp15,000) leave from the Barang Barat terminal from 5.30am until 3.30pm. For Taliwang (Rp3000) and night buses running both east and west, use the **Karang Dima terminal**, 6km northwest of town, reachable by bemo from the town centre. The yellow **bemos**, *bemo kota*, do round-trips of the town and can be flagged down on the street or picked up at the **Seketeng market terminal** on Jalan Setiabudi; they charge a flat rate of Rp400. The **airport** is a short dokar ride into town and a five-minute walk to the *Tambora Hotel*; the Merpati office is on Jalan Yos Sudarso by the post office, and the *Tambora Hotel* is also an agent. The nearest Pelni port is at **Badas**, to the north of the city.

The BNI **bank** at Jl Kartini 10 (Mon–Fri 8.15am–4.15pm) has an ATM. If you're heading east and have currency other than US dollars, then change enough here to see you through. The **post office** is located on Jalan Yos Sudarso, and the **Telkom** opposite has international telephone and fax. The best source of **information** in Sumbawa is a guide called Abdul Muis, who can be contacted through the *Tirtasari Cottages* (☎0371/21987), about 5km west of town at Seliperate. He is the only real choice for a guide to climb Gunung Tambora or visit Sumbawa's only practising animist peoples at Tepal. The **PHPA parks office** is on Jalan Garuda (Mon–Sat 8am–3pm; ☎0371/21358), and can provide information about Pulau Moyo.

Accommodation and eating

Quite a few **hotels** that are not mentioned here double as brothels, and some are renowned for being bug-ridden; always check your room very carefully before signing in. Of the cheaper recommendations, *Dian Losmen*, Jl Hasanuddin 69 (☎0371/22297; ①), is clean, quiet and friendly, and all rooms are en-suite; *Dewi Hotel*, Jl Hasanuddin 60 (☎0371/21170; ①–②), has thirty rooms ranging from good-value ekonomi to plush VIP suites, including breakfast, and *Hotel Tambora*, Jl Kebayan (☎0371/21555; ①–④) has four-bed ekonomi rooms through to luxury suites.

While the majority of **eating places** in Sumbawa Besar are the usual local warung serving goat stews and sate, there are two fantastic options on Jalan Hasanuddin: *Aneka Rasa Jaya*, at no. 14, serves an excellent menu including "insipid rice", "soft corn prawn" and "Chinese bowels cooking"; and *Ingkang Sae Rumah Makan*, two doors down, has the best food in Sumbawa; a full meal with beer is likely to be around Rp25,000.

Pulau Moyo

A few kilometres off the north coast of Sumbawa, the national park island of **Pulau Moyo** (entrance fee Rp2500) is probably the most rewarding destination in Sumbawa, surrounded by beautiful coral reefs and home to wild pig, monitor lizards, 21 species of bat, huge herds of native deer and hordes of crab-eating macaques. The best time to visit is in June and July, though the seas are clear and quiet from April. There are basic private **rooms** at the PHPA post at **Tanjung Pasir** on the south coast, where most boats from the mainland arrive; a Rp5000 donation is expected, and you need to bring your own food. Renting a fishing boat from Tanjung Pasir and going fifteen minutes east to **Stama reef** is very rewarding, with lots of sharks and turtles. There's nowhere on Moyo to rent masks and snorkels so bring your own; fins are advisable due to the strong currents. To hire a PHPA **guide** for trekking from the PHPA post costs Rp30,000 per person a day.

To get to Moyo, take a **bemo** (until 1pm; Rp2500) from beside Seketang Market in Sumbawa Besar to **Air Bari**, a small port settlement to the northeast. From Air Bari, you can charter a **boat** to Moyo for US$15–25 for up to fifteen people. Regular boats are less good value at US$10 per person; they leave infrequently, sometimes three or four times a day, at other times only once or twice a week.

Bima

The rather sleepy port town of **BIMA** is a useful place to break up the otherwise agonizing overland trip to Komodo, but little remains from the days when it served as the most important port in Nusa Tenggara. The town is centred on the market on Jalan Flores; most of the losmen lie to the east of the Sultan's Palace, and the bus terminal is to the south. The Merpati office is at Jl Sukarno Hatta 58; the **Telkom office** is further out on the same road. Change money at the **BRI bank** (Mon–Fri 8am–2.30pm, Sat 8am–11.30pm) by the central square. The main **post office** is a little out of town on Jalan Gajah Mada.

The last word in cheap **accomodation** is *Losmen Vivi* (Rp15,000) on Jalan Sukarno Hatta, but it's a bit grotty and usually full; *Losmen Lila Graha* at Jl Sumbawa 19 (☎0371/42740; ①) is a much more salubrious and friendlier option. By far the most salubrious place in town is *Hotel La'ambitu*, facing the market at Jl Sumbawa 4 (☎0371/43333; ①–③), and offering great value standard rooms with hot water, fan and TV. The **restaurant** of the *Hotel La'ambitu* is equally good, serving Chinese dishes, omelettes, pancakes and fried potatoes. The *Lila Graha* also serves regular Indonesian travellers' cuisine, or try the night stalls at the market.

Most travellers arrive in Bima at the **long-distance bus terminal**, a short dokar ride south of town. Scores of **night-bus agents** on Jalan Pasar offer air-con and standard buses to all major destinations including Mataram and Sumbawa Besar. Kumbe terminal for **buses to Sape** (Rp2000) is in Raba, about 5km out of town. If you want to catch the early-morning bus to Sape to connect with the ferry east, tell your hotel the night before and the bus should pick you up at 4am. **Ferries** including the monthly **Pelni** services *KM Tatamilau* and *KM Tilongkabila* (see "Getting around" pp.192–193 and "Travel Details" p.442) arrive at the harbour, 2km west of Bima and served by dokar. The **airport** is 20km away; buses stop outside the airport and run all the way to the bus terminal.

Hu'u

South of the large but uninteresting town of **Dompu**, on a white-sand coast with swaying palm trees, is the wave rider's Mecca of **HU'U**. The waves break over razor-sharp finger coral, so bring a helmet and first-aid kit. Generally, **surfing** is best between May and August, with the absolute prime in June and July. It's practically impossible to get a bed during these months so bringing a tent is a good idea.

To get to Hu'u village, take a **bus** to Dompu from Sumbawa Besar or Bima, from where it's a one-hour trip south (Rp3000). One bus a day goes there directly from Bima, leaving at around 7.30am. The **accommodation** lies in a cluster on the seafront about 3km from Hu'u village, the longest established being *Mona Lisa Bungalows*, on the beach (①). Next door, *Hotel Amangati* (①) has clean en-suite bungalows. The *Prima Donna Lakey Cottages* (☎0373/21168; ②) takes bookings in advance during high season. All of these losmen are convenient for the famous Lakey Peak and Lakey Pipe breaks. Just over 1km down the beach back towards Hu'u village and by the break of the same name is *Periscopes* (①), a friendly surf camp.

Sape and on to Komodo

More and more travellers are choosing to break their cross-island journey at the port town of **SAPE**. The town itself is no worse than Bima, and staying there means you get a full night's sleep before catching the 8am ferry to Komodo and Flores. Nearby **Gili Banta** is a good day-trip should you get stuck, with nice beaches and a burgeoning turtle population. Many **hotels** in Sape, however, are dirty brothels, infested with bedbugs. The best are probably the reasonably clean *Friendship* and *Mutiara* losmen (both ①), on the single main street that leads down to the port.

At present there are two ferries to **Labuhanbajo** on Flores, stopping in **Komodo** every day except Friday. The larger ferry (Rp17,500) is more spacious and relatively clean, with a tourist-class deck for an extra Rp3000. The other ferry (Rp11,100) is slow and overloaded and some prefer to wait in Sape for an extra day rather than subject themselves to it. The trip from Sape to Labuhanbajo through the tempestuous **Sape** and **Lintah straits** takes nine to twelve hours.

KOMODO

Off the east coast of Sumbawa lies **Komodo national park**, a group of parched but majestic islands that have achieved fame as the home of the Komodo dragon, or *ora* as it is known locally, which lives nowhere else but here and on a few neighbouring islands. The south coast is lined with impressive, mostly dormant volcanoes, the north with mainly dusty plains, irrigated to create rice paddies around the major settlements.

Varanus komodoensis, the **Komodo dragon**, is the largest extant lizard in the world, and there is no evidence that such creatures have existed anywhere other than the Komodo area for well over a million years. Unlike many rare species, the dragon is actually steadily increasing in numbers. The largest recorded specimen was well in excess of 3m long and weighed a mammoth 150kg, but most fully grown males are a more manageable 2m and around 60kg. The dragon usually strikes down prey with its immensely powerful tail or slices the leg tendons with scalpel-sharp fangs. Once the animal is incapacitated, the dragon eviscerates it, feeding on its intestines while it slowly dies. Contrary to popular belief, the dragon has neither poisonous breath or bite, but prey usually die of infected wounds.

At the time of writing, the public **ferry** between Sape in Sumbawa and Labuhanbajo in Flores was not calling at Komodo. As a result, visitors have to charter a boat; this is most easily done from Labuhanbajo. A boat to Komodo takes four hours and costs Rp150,000 per day.

Around the island

Komodo now receives in excess of 40,000 visitors a year, the majority of them offloading at the tiny PHPA camp at **LOH LIANG** in the east of the island, where at least one fully grown dragon is a regular visitor. In the high season, when cruise ships dump tourists here by the hundred, it can seem a bit like an adventure theme park. During the rainy season, however, you can easily find yourself alone: just you and an island full of three-metre flesh-eating predators. The *ora* are in plentiful supply, and the vast majority of tourists who visit see at least one dragon and probably a few juveniles as well. However, there are no guarantees.

The PHPA charges Rp20,000 for both entry into the park and a guide, and Rp25,000 a night for **accommodation** in stilted wooden cabins, surrounded by deer, wild pigs, snakes and dragons. If the cabins are full you'll have to sleep on the floor of the restaurant. The camp also rents out well-used **snorkelling** equipment and is close to setting up a dive facility.

Treks and excursions

The full day's walk to the top of **Gunung Ara** from the PHPA camp, the highest point on the island, doesn't promise dragon sightings, but is absolutely extraordinary. It's an arduous, excruciatingly hot march, but you'll see scores of unusual plants, animals and birdlife, such as sulphur-crested cockatoos, brush turkeys, and the **megapode bird**, which builds huge ground nests where its eggs are incubated in warm dung. Bring water and wear decent boots.

There are also regular walks from the PHPA camp, daily at 11am and 2pm, to **Banunggulung**, the river bed where the dragons used to be fed fresh goats daily, for the benefit of tourists. This practice has been discontinued, and dragons now only get fed weekly, though the forty-minute walk will usually be rewarded with a sighting or two. The guided walk costs Rp2500 per person.

The seas around Komodo, though home to spectacular coral reefs and an abundance of fish, are a far cry from the Gili Islands or Bali, and riptides, whirlpools, sea snakes, sea-wasp jellyfish and a healthy shark population make these waters potentially dangerous, so stick to recommended snorkelling locations such as the excellent **Pantai Merah**. A day's boat trip can be bargained down to around Rp10,000 a day per person if you have a group of six or more; the staff at the PHPA camp restaurant in Loh Liang can usually put you in touch with a boat owner.

FLORES

A fertile, mountainous barrier between the Savu and Flores seas, **Flores** comprises one of the most alluring landscapes in the archipelago. The volcanic spine of the island soars to 2500m and torrential wet seasons result in a lushness that marks Flores apart from its scorched neighbours. It also differs in its religious orientation – 95 percent of islanders are

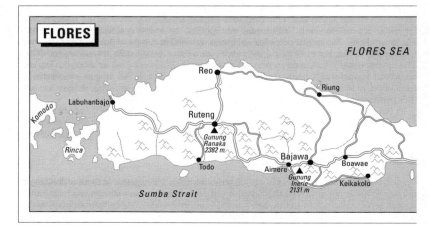

Catholic. The most spectacular natural sight in Flores is magnificent **Keli Mutu**, a unique volcano near Moni, northeast of **Ende**. The three craters of this extinct peak each contain a lake, of vibrantly different and gradually changing colours. In the east of Flores, high-quality **ikat weaving** is still thriving. At the extreme west end of the island, **Labuhanbajo** has some fine **coral gardens** nearby and is also the port for ferries to and **from Sumbawa** (daily except Fri; 9–12hr); see p.377 for prices.

Labuhanbajo and around

The sleepy little port town of **LABUHANBAJO** is the gateway to Flores from the islands of Komodo and Sumbawa, a delightful journey past myriad tiny green islands. **Ferries** arrive late in the afternoon and are met by touts and boats waiting to take you to losmen. You can choose to stay in town or at one of the beach hotels within an hour's boat trip – a pleasant option, as most of these places offer a quiet getaway with unspoilt beaches and decent snorkelling. Whether they're in town or on the beach, most hotels also organize tours to nearby islands for **snorkelling** and sunbathing: the full-day trip to **Pulau Sabolo** (US$45) includes two dives.

Practicalities

The harbour of Labuhanbajo marks the extreme northern end of the main street, on which almost all of the town losmen and restaurants are situated. The **airport** is about 2km out and you'll probably have to charter a bemo; the Merpati office is a fifteen-minute uphill hike east of town. **Bank BNI** at the south end of town is unsure about travellers' cheques, will only take prime-condition bills and gives lousy rates for anything but dollars. The **post office** (Mon–Thurs 7.30am–3pm, Fri 7.30–11am, Sat 7.30am–1pm) is next to the bank, but the PHPA and Telkom offices are a hike out of town: walk south from the harbour, passing most of the hotels, and take the second left up the hill past the market. For most phone calls, the **wartels** in town are just as good a bet.

   Buses heading east to **Ruteng** (4–5hr; Rp7500) start from 6.30am, and tickets can be bought from all the hotels, or you can just hail them from the street; some buses continue to Bajawa (11hr; Rp10,000). Buses meet the ferry for the fourteen-hour trip to **Ende** (Rp30,000). The **ferry** west to Sumbawa leaves at 8am every day except Tuesday; tickets (Rp12,500) are sold right up to departure.

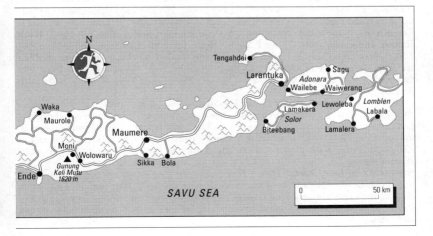

In town, *Gardena Bungalows* (☎0385/41258; ①), on a small hill set back off the main road, a three-minute walk south from the port, is currently the most popular backpackers' **accommodation**, with bungalows overlooking the bay, and breakfast included. A little further up, the *Bajo Homestay* (☎0385/41008; ①) is slightly smarter, though the service leaves something to be desired. Turn left immediately before the market on Jalan Sukarno Hatta and climb for 250m to *Chez Felix* (☎0385/41032; ①), which has tranquil and clean singles, doubles and triples, most en suite. The best **restaurant** in western Flores is *Borobudor Rumah Makan*, next to *Gardena Bungalows*, which serves great, if slightly pricey, seafood, including lobster, as well as steaks and good ice cream. The restaurant at the *Gardena Bungalows* is a good second choice, while next door to the *Borobudur*, *Dewata Rumah Makan* is more basic and serves inexpensive seafood.

All **beach accommodation places** offer regular free boats or bemos to and from the harbour; boatmen meet incoming ferries and the first transport out in the morning is guaranteed to connect with the ferries west or the second bus to Ruteng. Most beach places have only irregular electricity and running water and none have phones. Currently the best of the beach retreats, *Kanawa Hotel* (③) is 45 minutes away by boat and has a great beach and pristine reefs. The hotel also has an agent in Labuhanbajo near the *Bajo Homestay* next to the Waecicu agent. *Waecicu Beach* (①), a twenty-minute boat ride from town, in a beautiful location on the mainland, has attractive cottages ranging from very basic to those with mandi and mosquito nets. The price includes three very square meals a day.

Ruteng

The first large town near Labuhanbajo is **RUTENG**, 140km to the east. Surrounded by stark, forested volcanic hills and rolling rice-paddy plains, it's an archetypal hill town and a cool, relaxing place. The market just to the south is the central meeting point for the local **Manggarai** people, as Ruteng is their district capital. They speak their own language and have a distinctive culture that's most in evidence in villages on the south coast. Their traditional houses are conical and arranged in concentric circles around a round sacrificial arena; even the rice paddies are round, divided up like spiders webs, with each clan receiving a slice. Most of these formations are no longer used, but a good example can still be seen at **GOLO CURU**, a three-kilometre walk uphill from the *Agung* losmen in Ruteng.

Most buses arriving in Ruteng will drop you off at a hotel if you ask. Otherwise the **bus terminal** is relatively central. Buses to Bajawa (5–6hr; Rp5000) and Labuhanbajo start leaving at 7am and continue sporadically until early afternoon. Buses to Ende take ten hours. The **airport** is about 2km out of town, from where most hotels offer free buses. **Bank Rakyat Indonesia** (Mon–Thurs 7.30am–3.45pm, Fri 7.30–11.45am & 1.30–3.45pm, Sat 7.30am–noon) is on Jalan Yos Sudarso opposite the *Sindah* hotel. You'll find the **post office** on Jalan Dewi Sartika (Mon–Thurs 9am–3pm, Fri 9–11.30am, Sat 9am–1pm, Sun 9am–noon), 50m up from the traditional houses. The 24-hour **Telkom office** is on Jalan Achmad Yani.

The most popular travellers' **accommodation** is *Sindah Hotel*, Jl Yos Sudarso (☎0385/21197; ①–②), which has a good range of rooms, from budget singles and doubles to a couple of en-suite rooms, and an especially friendly manager. The en-suite rooms at the sparkling clean *Rima Hotel*, at Jl A Yani 14 (☎0385/22196 or 22195; ①) are superb value. Otherwise, walk fifteen minutes out of town on the road towards Reo to get to **Wisma Agung I**, Jl Waeces 10 (☎0385/21080; ①), which is beautifully set among the rice paddies. As for **food**, *Rumah Makan Pade Doang*, on the first corner as you walk north from the theatre on Jalan Motang Rua, has cold beer and fairly fresh seafood, a rarity this far from the coast. The appealing *Bamboo Den* is almost the next building on your right as you continue north and has a passable selection of Indonesian food, including cold sate and soto ayam.

Bajawa and the Ngada district

The hill town of **BAJAWA** is one of the most popular tourist destinations in Flores, surrounded by lush slopes and striking volcanoes. **Gunung Inerie** is just one of the active volcanoes near Bajawa: it's an arduous but rewarding hike, but you can see all the way to Sumba from the summit if it's clear. Not for the faint-hearted are the local specialities of *moke*, a type of wine that tastes like methylated spirits and *raerate*, dog meat marinated in coconut milk and then boiled in its own blood.

Bajawa is the largest town in the **Ngada district**, an area that maintains its status as the spiritual heartland of Flores. Here, despite the growing encroachment of curious travellers, indigenous animist religions flourish and the villages maintain fascinating houses, megalithic stones and interesting totemic structures. Up to 60,000 people in the Ngada district speak the distinct Ngada language, and a good proportion of the older generation don't understand basic Bahasa Indonesian.

In the centre of most villages in this district stand several **ceremonial edifices** which represent the ancestral protection of, and presence in, the village. These include the **Ngadhu**, which resembles a man in a huge hula skirt, the thatched skirt sitting atop a crudely carved, phallic, forked tree trunk, which is imbued with the power of a male ancestor. The female part of the pairing, the Bhaga, is a symbol of the womb, a miniature house. The symbolic coupling is supplemented by a carved stake called a Peo, to which animals are tied before being sacrificed.

Practicalities

The **airport** lies almost 30km away near Soa, from where you'll have to charter a bemo (US$10). The **bus terminal** is 2km out of town at **Watujaji**. Regular bemos from the terminal to the town cost Rp500. When it comes to **moving on**, most buses come into town to look for passengers, but it's best to be on the safe side and go to them. Buses east to Ende (Rp5000) run pretty much all day from 7am and take four hours. Tourist buses were not running at the time of writing, but were due to start up again soon. When they do resume service, they should run to Moni for Keli Mutu (5hr 30min; Rp7500) and west to Ruteng (5–6hr; Rp7500), starting at 7am but stopping in the early afternoon; the morning buses for Ruteng continue on to Labuhanbajo (11hr; Rp10,000).

The **Merpati office** is next to the market on Jalan Pasar (Mon–Sat 8am–2pm), the **BNI bank** on Jalan Piere Tandeau, a continuation of Jalan Hayamwuruk, and the Bank Rakyat Indonesia on Jalan Sukarno Hatta; they will only change US dollars. The **Telkom** building near the BRI is open 24hr, and the main **post office** is slightly to the west on the same road.

Accommodation in Bajawa is pretty basic, but there are a few decent options. As the road from Watujaji bus terminal reaches the outskirts of the town, it splits at a T-junction and becomes Jalan Achmad Yani, where a small path leads up to *Sunflower Homestay* (☎0383/2123 ①). Its outward-facing rooms have nice views, and well-informed guides congregate here. *Hotel Anggrek* on Jalan Letjend Haryono (☎0383/21172; ①), a few hundred metres beyond the market, has clean rooms, most of them en-suite. The management of the *Nusantara* is notorious for press-ganging travellers at the bus terminal, but the rooms are dirty and to be avoided.

For **food**, try *Restaurant Camellia*, opposite the *Korina* losmen on Jalan Achmad Yani, which does fantastic, reasonably priced guacamole and chips, *kentang goreng* and delicious *lumpiah* (spring rolls). Further up the hill on Jalan Gajah Mada, the *Kasih Bahagia* has a similar, though slightly more expensive, menu plus cold beer. In the market, the local stalls selling snack food are the cheapest places to eat in town.

The Ngada villages

The influx of tourists to the Ngada region has led to a booming **guide** industry in Bajawa. For Rp15,000 a day per person (minimum four people), a guide will arrange transport, entrance to all the villages and often a traditional Bajawan meal. A day-tour should include Langa, Bena, Bela or Luba, which are close by, as well as Wogo and the hot springs at Soa. Most guides speak good English, and among the best are Phillipus, Max and Lukas, who can be contacted at the *Restaurant Camellia*.

From Bajawa, the easiest Ngada village to visit is **LANGA**, which sits under the dramatic shadow of **Gunung Inerie**. Tourists pass through here every day and you'll be asked to sign a visitors' book and pay at least Rp1000 to take photographs, though you're advised to save your film for Bena. If you want to scale Inerie you'll have to set out very early from Bajawa. The guide fee of Rp50,000 (minimum two people) includes a taxi from Bajawa to Langa.

From Langa it's about 10km, mostly downhill, to **BENA** (Rp2500), another village that's very popular with tourists. You'll probably have to walk, though occasional trucks ply the route. Here they have nine different clans, in a village built on nine levels with nine Ngadhu/Bhaga couplings. It's the central village for the local area's religions and traditions, and one of the places to see **festivals** such as weddings, planting and harvest celebrations

Some of the finest megaliths and Ngadhu can be found at the twin villages of **WOGO**. To get here, take one of the regular bemos from Bajawa to **Mataloko** (30min; Rp1000), then walk south along the road for about 1km to Wogo Baru. There are some distinctly eerie megaliths set in a clearing about 1.5km further down the road in Wogo Lama; local kids will lead you to them. On Saturdays, Mataloko has a decent market selling sarongs and Bajawan knives.

The most popular destination near Bajawa is the **hot springs** at **SOA**. The Australian-run *Flores Paradise* bungalows (①) are easily the best place to stay in the area. The springs themselves, set in magnificent surroundings, are a joy, especially in the chilly late afternoon. Buses and **bemos** from Bajawa bemo station run to Soa village (1hr; Rp1000), from where it's a two-kilometre walk to the springs.

Ende

Situated on a narrow peninsula with flat-topped Gunung Meja and the active volcano Gunung Ipi at the sea end, the port of **ENDE** is the largest town on Flores and provides access for Keli Mutu and Moni. Ende suffered severe damage in the 1992 earthquake that razed Maumere and killed several hundred people here. The town still seems shaken by the whole thing – ramshackle, battered and with little to attract the tourist other than banks and **ferries** to other destinations. However, black-sand **beaches** stretch down both east and west coasts: the Bajawa road runs right along the seafront, so just catch a bemo out to Ndao bus terminal and the beach begins right there. The town is also an ideal starting point for exploring villages that specialize in **ikat** weaving. **NGELLA** is a weaving village about 30km east from Wolowaru terminal in Ende, near the coast: take a bemo or truck (Rp1500).

Practicalities

The **airport** at Ende is just north of Ipi harbour on Jalan Jenderal Achmad Yani; any bemos will take you into town. Buses from the west arrive at the **Ndao bus terminal**, which is on the beach, about 2km west of the very centre of town; bemos meet every bus. Buses from the east pull into **Wolowana terminal**, situated at the extreme east of town and a five-kilometre bemo ride from central Ende.

Moving on, a bus for Bajawa, Ruteng and Labuhanbajo leaves the Ndao bus terminal at 6am, with a second bus to Ruteng at 5pm. Buses for Moni (6am–2pm; Rp2500), Maumere (8am–5pm; Rp5000) and Larantuka leave from the Wolowana terminal. There's also usually one passenger truck to Moni from here later in the afternoon.

Ipi harbour on the southeastern coast of the peninsula is used for all long-distance **boats**: the ferry and harbour master's offices are on the road that leads down to the harbour. The **Pelni ferry** *KM Wilis* stops here on its Waingapu–Sabu–Rote–Kupang route; see "Getting around" pp.192–193 and "Travel details" p.442. The Pelni office is at the junction of Jalan Kathedral and Jalan Yos Sudarso. There's also a ferry which does a constant loop:

Ende–Waingapu–Savu–Waingapu–Ende–Kupang–Ende. It leaves from Ipi harbour for Waingapu every Wednesday at 7pm (12hr), and goes to Kupang every Thursday and Saturday (16hr).

The losmen, banks and restaurants are widely dispersed, so you'll probably end up using the **bemo kota** (town bemos) fairly liberally. The best **exchange** rates are available at the BNI, which is past the airport on Jalan Gatot Subroto, a continuation of Jalan Achmad Yani. The more central BRI is next door to the *Dwi Putra Hotel* on Jalan Yos Sudarso, and the Danamon bank (best for credit-card transactions) is behind it on Jalan Sukarno. The **Merpati office** is on Jalan Nangka (closed Wed & Sat).

ACCOMMODATION AND EATING

The majority of **losmen** are spread out along the road that leads from the centre of town to the airport. The original, and still the best as far as travellers are concerned, is *Losmen Ikhlas*, on Jalan Jenderal Achmad Yani heading towards the airport (☎0383/21695; ①). They have dirt-cheap, boxlike rooms through to reasonable en-suite doubles, and lots of travel information is posted on the restaurant walls. Also on the same road, but closer to the town centre, is the comfortable *Nur Jaya* (☎0383/21252; ①), though it's often full. The most central place is *Dwi Putra*, next door to the BRI bank on Jalan Sudarso (☎0383/21685; ①–⑤), which has cheap basic rooms and en-suite ones.

Both the markets provide the best **food**, serving standard *sate murtabak* and *nasi campur*. *Rumah Makan Minang Baru* on Jalan Sukarno near Ende harbour serves simple Padang food, and *Depot Ende* at Jl Sudirman 6 has similar Indonesian fare. *The Losmen Ikhlas* serves travellers' favourites, cold drinks, juices and milkshakes.

Keli Mutu and Moni

Stunning **Keli Mutu** volcano, with its three strangely coloured crater lakes, is without doubt one of the most startling natural phenomena in Indonesia. The nearby village of **Moni**, 40km northeast of Ende, sits close to the mountain's slopes, and is the base for hikes on the volcano. It has a definite lazy charm, nestling among scores of lush rice paddies.

Keli Mutu

The summit of **Keli Mutu** (1620m) is a startling lunar landscape, with, to the east, two vast pools separated by a narrow ridge. The waters of one are a currently luminescent green that seems to be heading for bright-yellow, the other was, a few years ago, a vibrant turquoise, and is now deep magenta. A few hundred metres to the west, in a deep depression, is a pure-black lake. The colours of the lakes are apparently due to the levels of certain **minerals** that dissolve in them. As the waters erode the caldera they lie in, they uncover bands of different compounds and, as the levels of these compounds are in constant flux, so are the colours. In the 1960s, the lakes were red, white and blue, and locals predict that within years they will have returned to these hues.

Every morning at around 4am, an open-sided **truck** takes travellers from Moni up to Keli Mutu, returning at about 7am (Rp10,000 one way, minimum five people, plus Rp1000 park fee). The best view is from the south crater rim, looking north over the two sister lakes; the trails that run around other rims are extremely dangerous – tourists have disappeared up here. A much nicer alternative to returning with the truck is to **walk** back down to Moni, which takes about three hours, with rolling grassy meadows flanking extinct volcanic hills, and views all the way to the sea. Practically the whole walk is downhill, but always bring water and wear good boots. A shortcut by the PHPA post cuts off a good 4km from the road route, takes you through some charming local villages and past the **waterfall** (*air terjun*) less than 1km from central Moni, which is a great spot for a dip after what can be a very hot walk. A little further down is a hot spring, the perfect place to soak weary feet.

Moni

The village of **MONI** is set out along the length of the road that runs from Ende, northeast to Maumere. It's full of losmen and restaurants, but is still a relaxed place to spend a few days, with great walking in the surrounding hills. Behind the *Amina Moe* losmen and opposite the market is a **rumah adat**, where occasional evening dance performances are held (Rp3000) and traders hang around trying to sell ikat. There is no bank, post office or Telkom in Moni.

Buses from Ende (1hr 30min; Rp3000) and Maumere (5hr; Rp7000) stop here about three times a day, the first one at about 11am and the last at about 3pm; ask at the losmen. For such a small isolated village, the **cuisine** in Moni is impressive. The simple but wholesome buffet (Rp10,000) at the *Amina Moe* draws large crowds, but you need to warn the cooks early. The *Mountain View Pub* and *Rumah Makan Sarty*, both a little further up the road, can also arrange buffets and are relaxing places to enjoy an evening beer. The *Sarty* also serves the best food in town.

ACCOMMODATION

The road from Ende comes in from the north of the village and after two sharp turns heads east towards Maumere – all the **accommodation** is laid out along this road. The tourist explosion in Moni has led to rivalry between losmen owners, who may try to persuade you that other places are brothels, or their owners thieves.

Amina Moe, just after *Lelegana*. Still the travellers' favourite, more for the legendary all-you-can-eat evening buffet than for the neglected rooms. ①.

Arwanty, at the top of the village. Largish homestay with some of the best bungalows in the village, including mosquito nets. ①.

Hidayah Bungalows, the first place you see, on the right-hand side as you enter the main part of town. Probably the best value for money in Moni. They offer charming, well-kept bamboo huts, good breakfasts, and the host is very genuine. ①.

Lelegana, aka **John's**. Fair to middling wisma with a friendly host and reasonably clean, though slightly dark rooms. Rp15,000.

Watugana Bungalows, off the road at the bend after *Arwanty* and on the right-hand side. Built to a traditional style and good value; the owner is pleasant. ①.

Maumere and Sikka

On the north coast of Flores, roughly equidistant between Ende and Larantuka, **MAUMERE** was once the visitor centre and best diving resort in Flores. However, since the terrible earthquake of December 1992, it's been a beaten town, still disfigured by heaps of rubble and unrepaired buildings. The majority of the dive sites have been obliterated and those that remain have fairly stunted coral growth. Maumere is the capital of Sikka district, which stretches all the way to the east coast. It's especially renowned for its **weaving**, which characteristically has maroon, white and blue geometric patterns, in horizontal rows on a black or dark-blue background. The village of **SIKKA**, on the opposite coast from Maumere nearly 30km south, is the most-visited weaving village in the area, but the weaving is of poor quality; regular bemos run here from Maumere's Ende terminal (Rp1000).

Practicalities

Maumere has a square and a market at its centre, and much of the town is very close to the seafront. There are two **bus terminals**, both of which are notorious for pickpockets and con artists, so watch your pack. Buses to and from Ende, Moni and other destinations in the west use **Terminal Barat** or **Ende terminal** on the southwest outskirts of town, but may drop you off in the centre. Buses to and from Larantuka and other easterly destinations use the **Terminal Lokaria**, 3km east of the centre. A Rp300 bemo ride will get you into town. When it comes to moving on, most long-distance buses circle town several times before leaving, so ask locally first. Avoid having to **fly** out from Maumere outside of the high season: the unreliable Merpati agent is on Jalan Raja Don Tomas; the best Bouraq agent is PT Garuda on Jalan Moa Toda.

Two **banks** change foreign currency: the BRI is on Jalan Pasar Baru Barat, but the BNI on Sukarno Hatta (Mon–Fri 7.30am–2.30pm, Sat 7.30am–11am) usually has better rates. The 24-hour **Telkom** office stands opposite. The **post office** is on Jalan Jenderal Achmad Yani (Mon–Thurs 7.30am–3pm, Fri 7.30–11.30am, Sat 7.30am–1pm). Toko Harapan Jaya on Jalan Moa Toda is the best **art and weaving store** in Flores, with piles of dusty blankets and sarongs as well as some carvings and jewellery.

ACCOMMODATION AND EATING

Maumere's out-of-town beachside establishments are without exception the best places to stay, and, if you're going east to Larantuka, the beach losmen at **Wodong** are on your way. The black-sand beach here is the most popular place to head to, though people who are interested in **diving** should go to Pantai Waiara, 10km west of town, where Maumere's only dive operators are based. Diving costs US$75 at the *Sea World Club* and US$85 at the *Sao Wisata Hotel* for a full day with two or three dives and food. Alternatively, the *Ankermi* charges just US$60. The only commendable **places to eat** in town are the *Sarinah Chinese Restaurant* on Jalan Raja Centis, right by the market on Jalan Pasar, and the *Golden Fish Restaurant* on Jalan Hasanuddin by the waterfront.

Ankermi Bungalows, on the beach at Wodong. The bungalows are spick and span and the food here is by far the best in Wodong, with regular, fresh barbecued seafood. ③.

Flores Froggies, near Wodong village on the road to Larantuka, about 28km from Maumere. Has a much nicer beach than the places in the east and three slightly run-down bungalows. ②.

Lareska Hotel, next to the Pelni office at Jl Sugio Pranoto 4 (☎0383/21137). The sea-facing rooms have great panoramas and are very clean and good value. Most share a mandi. ①.

Gardena, Jl Patirangga 30 (☎0382/2644). Most popular place in town, with clean and spacious rooms and friendly, informative staff. ①.

Sea World Club, Pantai Waiara (☎0383/21570). Accommodation ranges from clean bungalows with fan and shower through to rooms with air-con and TV. ②.

Wodong Bungalows, in Wodong village close to *Flores Froggies*. An excellent, quiet place to stay, offering free canoe, bike and snorkel rental. ①.

Larantuka and ferries to Timor

LARANTUKA is the port town that serves the Solor and Alor archipelagos and Timor. The main part is centred alongside the road that runs parallel to the coast. The **harbour** lies roughly in the centre of the town, with a small market around the entrance. The harbour master's office, on the left as you enter the jetty, provides information in Bahasa Indonesia on all Pelni ships and ferries leaving from Larantuka area. Only the smaller boats leave from this harbour, however; ferries and Pelni ships leave from the Labuhan Besar pier about 5km south of town. Daily motorboats depart for Lewoleba (4hr; Rp4000) on **Lembata**, leaving at 8am and 2pm; there's also a weekly boat to Lamalera on Lembata (every Fri morning; 8hr; Rp7500). Ferries to **Kupang** leave on Mondays and Wednesdays at noon (12hr; Rp15,000). The **Pelni** ship *KM Tatamilau* calls at Labuhan Besar twice a month, coming from Kupang or Labuhanbajo. The *KM Sirimau* also calls every fortnight, coming from Kupang and going to Makassar and vice versa; see "Getting around" pp.192–193 and "Travel Details" p.442. **Buses** to and from Maumere take four hours.

There is only one place for Westerners to **stay** in Larantuka: *Hotel Rulies* (☎0383/21198; a), southeast of the pier. If you're arriving from the west ask your bus to drop you off here. It's clean and friendly enough, with shared facilities. The *Hotel Tresna* (☎0383/21072; ①), next door, might take you if *Rulies* is full. Several average Padang **warung** line the main road, but by far the best place to eat is the *Nirwhana*, opposite *Hotel Sederhana*. The BNI **bank** is on the unnamed second road back from and parallel to the sea, heading towards Maumere; the BRI is on Jalan Piere Tandeau, around the corner from their disused old building and a short walk southeast of the harbour. Don't count on being able to change currency anywhere east of here except Kupang.

Lembata

East of Flores, the smallish island of **LEMBATA** (also known as Lomblen) is a captivating place, frustrating to travel around but full of friendly people, beautiful landscapes and intriguing culture. Very little English is spoken, and in some places people barely speak Bahasa Indonesian, and there is no Western-standard accommodation. Visitors arrive at the largest town of **Lewoleba** on the west coast, from where there's a weekly boat to the unmissable subsistence whaling village of **Lamalera** on the south coast. The island is also the home of one of the most renowned **weaving** traditions in Indonesia. The best cloths are fashioned in the remote villages on the northern coastal slopes of **Ile Api**, the volcano that looms over Lewoleba. The cloths are an essential part of "the bride price" used by a young man to secure his partner's hand. The island is notoriously **malarial**, so come prepared.

Daily **motorboats** run between Larantuka in **Flores** and Lewoleba (8am & 4pm; 4hr; Rp4000), and there's also a weekly boat from Larantuka to Lamalera (every Fri morning; 8hr; Rp7500). In theory, **flights** to Kupang and Larantuka leave once a week from Lembata; in practice these flights rarely, if ever, run.

Lewoleba

LEWOLEBA is a comatose but picturesque little place, sitting on a palm-lined bay under the shadow of the smoking volcano Ile Api. It comes alive once a week for the Monday **market**, which trades till around midnight. The village is set a little way back from the bay, with the market as its focal point. On the seafront is a beautiful stilted **Bajo fishing village** and a small fish market. About 1km west of town is the harbour, for all boats in and out of Lewoleba and the decrepit **bemo terminal**. The harbour master's office opposite the port is always shut. The **airport** is 3km north of town (charter a bemo), and the *Rejeki* losmen is the **Merpati** agent.

The new **losmen** *Lile Ile* (①), also known as *Mister Jim's*, is exactly halfway between the harbour and the market on the bay side of the road; it's a real gem, with neat cottages, sensational views and superb meals. The losmen *Rejeki* (①) is the first building you encounter by the market when you're coming from the harbour. It's the old standby, a decent place that does terrific food: try the *spesial dengan rusa* (deer meat special). The **bank** in Lewoleba will not change money in any form. The **post office** south of the market is efficient, and the Telkom office about 1km west of the market is open 24hr.

Lamalera

Travellers come to the extremely pleasant south-coast village of **LAMALERA** to participate in the traditional **whale-hunts**, in which local people use only wooden outriggers and bamboo spears. Be warned, though, that this is not a whale-watching pleasure cruise: the people of Lembata are here to kill these magnificent beasts, which can be extremely harrowing to watch, and as a tourist, you will be expected to take up a paddle and help overhaul the animal. Whaling takes place from May to October, never on Sundays as the people are devout Christians. They use extraordinary outrigger prahus – 10m to 12m long, a mere 2m across, and constructed without nails; the sails are woven from palm fronds.

In the peak year of 1969, the Lamalerans took only 56 sperm whales as well as many manta rays, turtles and dolphins. The **World Wildlife Fund** has carried out numerous surveys in the village and decided that their occupation has no effect on world whale stocks, or those of other endangered species. As with certain Inuit peoples, the whaling purely serves the needs of a small community. Lamalera has therefore been declared a protected, subsistence whaling village and is not subject to international charters. Every part of a captured whale is used.

Its meat and blubber are shared out amongst the village people according to ancient lore, and non-edible bits serve as fuel or jewellery.

PRACTICALITIES
Getting to Lamalera can be a real pain. Every Monday night, a crowded **boat** leaves from Lewoleba market, returning at 9am on Tuesday morning (4hr; Rp5000). The only other option is to take an unreliable jeep (daily except Fri; 5–6hr; Rp10,000) along a very rough road. A bemo also goes to **Boto**, which is slightly further north, leaving Lewoleba at around 1pm. From Boto, it's a 45-minute walk uphill to Puor, then a two- or three-hour downhill walk to Lamalera, with sensational views but a rough path.

There are three **accommodation** places in Lamalera, all of comparable quality and all providing three meals a day. The most popular with both travellers and mosquitoes is the *Guru Ben Homestay* (①), on top of the west promontory; take the path that leads to your left coming up from the beach and follow it up about 200m. Owner Ben can arrange boat trips (Rp25,000 a day). If you come into the village by boat, the nearest accommodation is the *White House* (①). This is the villa-like house with a balcony that overhangs the beach at the eastern end. *Adel Beding* homestay (①) is in the centre of the village, by the shaded square. It is well kept and slightly cheaper than the others.

TIMOR

Timor sits at the extreme eastern end of the Sunda Islands, close to Australia, and is extremely mountainous though not volcanic. The island's **indigenous inhabitants** can trace their ancestry back nearly fourteen thousand years, to when a people perhaps related to the modern Atoni tribes roamed over Timor. The Atoni now live mainly in the mountains of **West Timor** and compose nearly half its population. The other major ethnic group in Timor are the Tetum, who originated from migrant peoples from Sulawesi and Flores and probably started to arrive in the fourteenth century. Now the Tetum mainly inhabit areas of **East Timor**, being the most significant ethnic group there. In 1702, Timor was declared a Portuguese colony under the control of Goa, though with little effect on the rule of ascendant native kingdoms. By the mid-eighteenth century, the **Portuguese** had been pushed east and had control of the areas now known as East Timor. The central areas of the island remained independent of colonialism, some of them only falling to foreign rule in the early twentieth century. While the western part of Timor became part of Indonesia upon Independence in 1945, the east remained under Portugal's control right up until World War II; East Timor's turbulent recent history is described on pp.390–391.

West Timor's main city is **Kupang**, a sweaty, noisy maelstrom with everything that's unpalatable in Asian cities alongside the best restaurants and hotels for hundreds of kilometres. From here, most travellers head north to **Soe**, a hill town with fine *ikat* weavings. Close to Soe is the tiny kingdom of **Boti**, a place that maintains ancient traditions and distinctive "beehive"-style houses. In the most intense part of the dry season between June and October, Timor is swept by **monsoon winds** blowing off the deserts of Australia and becomes unbearably hot.

Kupang and around

Dusty, chaotic **KUPANG** is east Nusa Tenggara's biggest city and a major travellers' hub, not least because of the quick, twice-weekly Merpati **flight from Darwin** in Australia. The ferry service on the same route has been promised for a good ten years, and if it ever takes off Kupang will be even more full of backpackers. One of the only real sights in town is the **Museum of Nusa Tenggara Timur** (daily 8am–4pm; donation) out by the bus terminal. It has an excellent collection of *ikat* from the area and a few other artefacts such as a *moko*

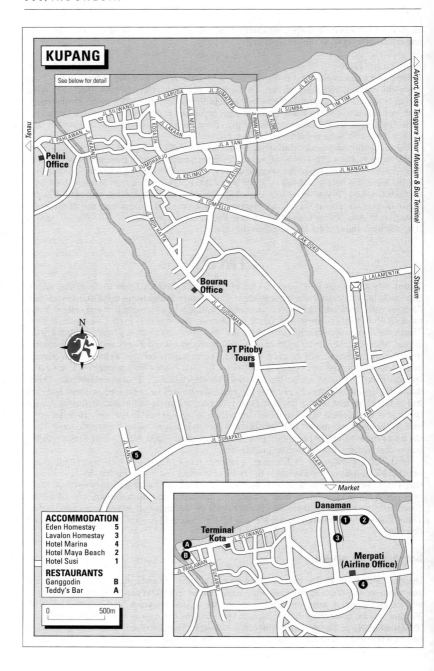

KUPANG

See below for detail

⊳ Tenau

⊲ Airport, Nusa Tenggara Timur Museum & Bus Terminal

⊲ Stadium

Pelni
Office

JL SILIWANGI
JL GARUDA
JL SUMATERA
JL ALOR
JL SUMBA
JL TIM TIM
JL G MUTIS
JL LAKAAN
JL KOSASIH
JL IRIAN JAYA
JL FLORES
JL PAHLAWAN
JL SUKARNO
JL A YANI
JL SUMOHARJO
JL KELIMUTU
JL NANGKA
JL G TALULEU
JL TOMPELLO
JL MOH HATTA
JL CAK DOKO
JL LALAMENTIK

Bouraq
Office

JL J SUDIRMAN

PT Pitoby
Tours

JL PALAPA

JL HEREWILA
JL EL TARI

N

JL SURAPATI
JL J SUHARTO

JL KANCIL
5

▽ Market

Danaman

Terminal
Kota
JL SILIWANGI
A
B
JL PAHLAWAN
JL SUKARNO

1 2
3

Merpati
(Airline Office)

4

ACCOMMODATION
Eden Homestay	5
Lavalon Homestay	3
Hotel Marina	4
Hotel Maya Beach	2
Hotel Susi	1

RESTAURANTS
Ganggodin	B
Teddy's Bar	A

0   500m

drum from Alor and drawings of traditional houses and megaliths. An easy escape from the city itself is the **natural swimming pool** 1km south of town; many travellers choose to stay in one of the nearby losmen.

There are several reasonable **beaches** around Kupang: **Tablalong** is 15km west of town, clean and a better place for a swim than the more popular and closer Lasiana beach. To get to Tablalong, take bemo #3 to the Tabus terminal and Bemo Tablalong goes all the way there. The best beaches are on the **islands** that sit just off Timor's western shore. Pulau Semau is reached by regular boats from Tenau harbour (Rp5000). *Lavalon, Ganggoding Café, Eden, Teddy's Bar* and *Hotel Flobamor* all organize tours to these islands, and you can stay on Semau at *Teddy's Bar* bungalows (④), with three meals a day included.

There is a beautiful **waterfall** at Oenesu with two steps; take bemo #3 to the Tabus terminal and then Bemo Oenesu. Out by Bolok Harbour, where the ferries arrive, 13km west of town, is an **underground cavern** with crystal-clear freshwater springs. It's a little creepy swimming in the pitch darkness; best bring a torch. Take the Bolok bemo and get off as it makes the final right turn down towards the port.

Practicalities

The **Oebolo bus terminal** services all major destinations outside of Kupang, and is the place you're most likely to arrive at. It's 6km east of town in **Walikota** and served by swarms of bemos. The **El Tari Airport** is another 10km to the east; either take a taxi into town, or walk out to the main road and flag down a bemo. The **city bemo** system is complex, but #3 runs to the natural swimming pool and *Eden* losmen; #15 (Baumata) goes to the airport; #24 to Pasar Impres; and #5 and #6 to Oebolo bus terminal. All bemos eventually end up at **Terminal Kota**, right by the waterfront, at the heart of Kupang.

The Danamon **bank** on Jalan Sumatera is efficient for credit-card transactions and advances, while the nearby BNI and the Bank Dagang Negara on Jalan Jenderal Achmad Yani have better exchange rates for travellers' cheques. The main **post office** is quite a way out of town, on Jalan Palapa (Mon–Sat 7am–4pm); take a #3 or #11 bemo from Terminal Kota. They currently have the only public **Internet** facility in West Timor (Rp10,000 per hour).

The **ferry office** is at the **Tenau harbour**. They have timetables here for all the ferries in Nusa Tenggara. The **Pelni office** is at Jl Pahlawan 3, west of the Terminal Kota: head over the river bridge and up the hill and it's on your left-hand side. Pelni services *KM Awu, KM Dobonsolo, KM Tatamailau* and *KM Sirimau* all call here; see "Getting around" pp.192–193 and "Travel Details" p.442. For **tours** or information on travel to Australia, contact Pitoby Tours and Travel Services on Jalan Jenderal Sudirman (☎0380/831044); they can organize scuba-diving tours, island-hopping, and are an agent for all the airlines flying out of Kupang.

ACCOMMODATION

Eden Homestay, on Jl Kencil, out of town by the natural swimming pool (☎0380/821931). Dorms, bungalows and rooms available at reasonable rates. ①.

Lavalon Homestay, off Jl Sumatera and near the Danamon bank (☎0380/832256). The current backpackers' favourite, with excellent information and real characters on the staff. The place is tatty and battered, but very cheap, with all accommodation, be it a dormitory or private room, costing Rp7500 per person. ①.

Hotel Marina, Jl Jenderal Achmad Yani 79 (☎0380/822566). Lovely and clean with delightful staff, the airy and sizable top rooms are especially good value. ①–③.

Hotel Maya Beach, Jl Sumatera 31 (☎0380/832169). Quite plush for the price: has a good restaurant and all the rooms feature air-con and bathtubs. Some have hot water. ②–③.

Hotel Susi, Jl Sumatera 37 (☎0380/822172). A lovely place, clean and quiet with pleasant communal areas and good-value economy rooms, some air-con. ①.

EATING AND DRINKING

Plenty of **night warung** are scattered throughout the city, the largest concentration being around Terminal Kota.

Ganggodin, next to *Teddy's Bar* at western end of seafront. Small, friendly café run by Australian lady, and a favoured haunt of expats. Food is reasonable, beer plentiful and cold.

Nelayan, Jl Mohammed Hatta, on the right-hand side of the road heading south from the centre of town. Not as crowded as the *Palembang*, but almost as good. Around Rp15,000 for a full meal with several different dishes. Daily from 6pm.

Palembang, Jl Mohammed Hatta 54. A terrific option: the king prawns in chilli are excellent; the lobster and grilled fish, quite superb. Everything is cooked at night on woks and barbecues are right out by the pavement.

EAST TIMOR

The foreign offices of most Western states advise against travel in **East Timor**; it is vital to check on the current situation before attempting to visit. A stunningly beautiful place with soaring mountains, immaculate coral reefs and undeveloped coastline, Tim Tim, as the locals call it, remains all but bereft of tourists. There are numerous police posts at the West/East Timor border around the province, and outside of the capital you are always advised to check in with the local police station; they'll probably just check your passport and let you go. Always listen to what the police tell you, and if they say an area is out of bounds then avoid it.

Some history

The modern history of East Timor began in 1904, when the Portuguese and Dutch divided Timor into provinces and East Timor was annexed from the rest of the island. **Portuguese control** continued until the advent of World War II, when the Japanese landed here in great numbers. The allies, fearing for the safety of nearby Australia, sent thousands of ANZAC troops into the hinterlands, where they waged a successful guerrilla war against the Japanese. The Timorese harboured the Australians and many fought with them against the Japanese. Retaliation was savage: an estimated 60,000 East Timorese were killed during the Japanese occupation, about thirteen percent of the population. When the Japanese ceded the land to Portugal at the end of the war, slave labour was reinstated, and only ten percent of the population were educated to basic literacy. There was no electricity or running water anywhere, and malaria was rife. In 1974, following the overthrow of the fascist Caetano regime, the incoming government declared that many of the colonial states were illegally occupied. East Timor was left to face its future alone, without external rule for the first time in nearly three hundred years.

Three parties formed, aspiring to lead the new country. In 1975, the first free general elections in East Timor's history resulted in a landslide victory for the **Fretilin** party, who wanted independence for East Timor, confident that they could at least rely on the support of their wartime ally Australia. They formed a transitional government, while the other two parties formed a coalition opposition. This coalition branded Fretilin as communists, and a small **civil war** followed, from which Fretilin comfortably emerged as victors, claiming independence for the new Democratic Republic of East Timor.

On December 7, 1975, Indonesian president Suharto held talks with US President Ford and Henry Kissinger. Just hours after the talks were completed, **Indonesia invaded** East Timor. In the first year of the conflict, eighty percent of Dili's male population were killed. The UN general assembly and Security Council passed ten resolutions calling on Indonesia to withdraw their troops: all were ignored. The savagery of the invading regime drove the Fretilin members into the highlands, where they fought a protracted guerrilla war. The Indonesian army stifled the independence movement with political executions, imprisonments and kidnappings; Amnesty International reports estimate that, between 1976 and 1986, 200,000 people out of a population of 700,000 were killed.

Savu Fried Chicken, Jl Mohammed Hatta, a small hut on the left-hand side of the road, heading south and before you reach the *Nelayan*. One of the healthiest chunks of chicken you will find for hundreds of kilometres, deep-fried for Rp8000.

Teddy's Bar, on the seafront at the western end of the centre. Serves burgers, pizzas and other Western fare. This is the main expat hangout in Kupang, overpriced but a reasonable spot for a cold beer: they have lots of expensive imported brews. It's a good place to make contacts if you're looking to work your passage on a yacht.

The **Western world** was far from blameless in what has come to be described as the attempted genocide of the East Timorese. The Australian Prime Minister Gough Whitlam told Suharto in 1974 that the dissolution of East Timor was "inevitable", and Australia's largest oil companies were duly given contracts to drill for oil and gas in the Timor strait. Over a ten-year period, America and Britain provided over a billion dollars' worth of **arms** to Indonesia. On November 12, 1991, the East Timor problem was brought to world attention when a massacre at a funeral in Dili's **Santa Cruz cemetery** was captured on film and relayed to the world's press. Around 5000 people had gathered to commemorate Sebastien Gomes, who had been shot by Indonesian troops two weeks earlier. Indonesian troops entered the cemetery and, without provocation, opened fire, killing an estimated 528 people.

The **Indonesian people** had no reports of the 1991 massacre, and are generally told by their media that East Timor is a troublesome, irrelevant little province. However, the 1997 **Nobel peace prize** was awarded to Bishop Carlos Felipe Ximenes Belo and Jose Ramos Horta, the two loudest voices of the East Timorese in their fight for freedom. In another positive move, the jailed East Timorese resistance leader **Jose Alexandre "Xanana" Gusmao** was released from high-security prison in Jakarta and placed under house arrest, in order for him to play a role in bringing peace to the territory. In January 1999, President Habibie promised to grant the province independence if his offer of autonomy was rejected. In the poll that followed later that same year, the Timorese, despite intimidation from pro-Indonesian militia and soldiers, voted overwhelmingly to sever all ties with Indonesia. This led to yet further violence as the pro-Jakarta militias ran rampage throughout the province, creating a wave of unprecedented bloodletting that the Indonesian military did little to stem. The UN were finally forced to step in, with an 8000-strong multinational force charged with the task of restoring the peace. The Indonesian army withdrew in shame the following month, and peace slowly returned to the region.

At the time of writing, East Timor, the world's newest country, still faced a wealth of problems. Before leaving, the pro-Jakarta militia had systematically tried to raze every building to ensure that the East Timorese would have to start from scratch. Consequently, East Timor has no hospitals or schools, and its water, power, transport and communication facilities have all been destroyed. Nor do the East Timorese have any infrastructure to speak of: no police force, no civil service, no laws, no currency or even an official language. The country's largest source of foreign income – the coffee harvest – was also destroyed. And though the international community has pledged US$522 million to help the Timorese rebuild their country, that money has thus far been unforthcoming.

Under the guidance of **the UN**, the Timorese have created a transitional authority, which in turn has established embryo ministries and academies for training judges and policemen. The Timorese also have large natural gas reserves and a promising tourist industry which could help to finance and sustain the long-term growth of Timor. Nevertheless, with unemployment currently running at ninety percent, and with annual per-capita income less than US$100, the imminent future remains bleak for this stunningly beautiful land.

Roti

The island of **Roti**, a short ferry trip from Kupang, is famous for its terrific surf at Nembrala beach on the west coast. Most travellers arrive in Roti at the northern port of Olafulihaa on the daily **ferry** from Kupang. It gets in at about 11am and is met by Nembrala buses (Rp10,000; 4hr). Ferries returning to Kupang leave daily at noon and connecting buses leave Nembrala from 7am to 8am.

The main break at **Nembrala beach** is called T' land, on the reef that runs offshore: it's a long ridable left that's best from April to September. At **Boa**, about an eight-kilometre bike ride from Nembrala, is a right-hander that's worth a go in the morning before the wind picks up. There are presently three **places to stay** and eat in Nembrala: *Losmen Anugurah* (①) is the best, with ice-cold beer and enormous quantities of food. The accommodation is basic but ample. *Homestay Thomas* (①) and *Losmen Ti Rosa* (①) offer similar deals, but fail on the food front. *Nembrala Beach Hotel* (②–④) is a new, overpriced set of bungalows in a good location on the beach.

Soe and Boti

Once a Dutch hill station, **SOE**, 110km north of Kupang, is now a thriving town with many attractive villages in the surrounding hills. People come from miles around to the **market**, to sell everything from *ikat* to betel nut and herbal medicines. The most distinctive feature of the villages around Soe district is the beehive-style **traditional houses** or *lopo*. The Indonesian government actually banned *lopo*, because they considered them unhealthy, and certainly, the acrid, smoky interior feels decidedly noxious. The people of Soe, however, prefer them to their new cold, concrete abodes, and generally still build *lopo* – ostensibly as stores. To visit the villages, rent a motorbike from your losmen.

The kingdom of **BOTI** has become the "must-do" trip in the vicinity of Soe; it lies 45km to the southeast. Boti has remained independent of external influence, owing to its rajah, a proud man who didn't want to see the traditions of old Timor disappear. This has led to a steady influx of curious visitors, and – ironically – the place now feels like a mockup of a traditional village. There's a weaving cooperative, a small thatched workshop, a souvenir shop, traditional houses, and big painted direction signs. It is essential to bring **betel nut** as a gift, and you will also have to pay to enter the village and to see the weaving, and about Rp20,000 to stay overnight and eat with the rajah. The rajah is not very keen on people wandering around Boti and may forbid you to go anywhere without him. To get there, catch a bus to **Oinlassi** and then it's a three-hour walk, only worthwhile if you're overnighting.

Practicalities

Soe is fairly compact: Jalan Diponegoro is the main street, and features a few shops, a wartel, a tourist office (random hours) and the **BNI bank**, which only changes US dollars cash. The souvenir shop next door to the *Losmen Bahagia* has some excellent ikat and genuine antique masks. **Bemos** do a round-trip to the market and then to the out-of-town **bus station**, which lies to the west of town. Buses to and from Kupang take three to four hours.

Most buses into Soe will drop you off on Jalan Diponegro, within walking distance of most **accommodation**. The budget-travellers' favourite is *Losmen Anda*, Jl Kartini 5 (☎0391/21323; ①). The octagenarian owner, Pak Yohannes, is a rare character who speaks five languages and has converted his house and all the rooms so that they resemble battleships and ferries, complete with portholes and steering wheels. *Mahkota Plaza* at Jl Suharto 11 (☎0391/21068; ②) is often closed in low season but has good, clean, en-suite rooms. The Padang **restaurants** by the market dish up some fiery chicken curries and other staples.

SUMBA

Sumba has a genuine reputation in Indonesia for the excesses of its funerals, the wealth of its ikat fabrics and the thrill of the **pasola**, an annual ritual war fought on horseback. One of the main reasons to visit Sumba is to experience first-hand the extraordinary agrarian **animist cultures** in the villages. These villages comprise huge clan houses set on fortified hills, centred around megalithic graves and topped by a totem made from a petrified tree. The most important part of life for the Sumbanese is death, when the mortal soul makes the journey into the spirit world. Sumbanese **funerals** can be extremely impressive spectacles, particularly if the deceased is a person with prestige, inspiring several days' worth of slaughter and feasting, the corpse wrapped in hundreds of exquisite ikat cloths.

The difficulty for **Western visitors** to Sumba is that traditions and taboos in Sumbanese village life are still very powerful and sit ill at ease with the demands of modern tourism. A visitor to a Sumbanese village must first take the time to share *cirih pinang* (**betel nut**) with both the kepala desa (village headman) and his hosts. Betel nut is a sign of peace and of unity; Sumbanese ritual culture sets great store by returning blood to the earth, and the bright-red gobs of saliva produced by chewing *cirih* represent this. Many villages that are on the regular trail for group tours have supplanted the tradition of sharing betel with a simple request for money, but if you come with gifts you will be far more welcome.

The east of the island is rocky, parched and fairly mountainous; the west is contrastingly fertile and green, with rolling hills and a long rainy season. **Waingapu** is well-known for producing the finest ikat in the whole of Indonesia. A little further out at **Rende** and **Melolo** are stone tombs with bizarre carvings, and other villages right out on the east coast offer the chance to see quality weaving and traditional structures near some deserted beaches. On the south coast, **Tarimbang** is an up-and-coming surfers' Mecca with a few waterfalls inland. The main town in the west is **Waikabubak**, where characteristic houses with thatched roofs soar to an apex over 15m above the ground.

Acess to Sumba is either by **ferry** from Ende in Flores to Waingapu or by **air** to either Waingapu or Tambolaka. If you're planning on flying out of Sumba, do it from Waingapu rather than Tambolaka, which has an appalling record for cancellations.

Waingapu

It may be the largest port and town on Sumba, but **WAINGAPU** is still far from a modern metropolis. Pigs and chickens roam the backstreets and locals still walk around barefoot, with ikat tied around their heads and waists. One half of the hourglass-shaped town is centred around the port, and the other around the bus terminal. It's only a fifteen-minute walk between the two, but an endless army of bemos do the circular trip (Rp500). The bay to the west of town has a harbour at the extreme northern point of either shore: the eastern harbour serves ferries and is right at the foot of the town, the western harbour is for larger ships and requires an eight-kilometre journey all around the bay.

PRAILU is the most visited of the local **ikat-weaving villages**, just a ten-minute bemo hop away. After signing in at the large, traditional house (Rp1000), you can inspect weavings that weren't good enough to be bought by the traders. The ikat blankets of East Sumba are ablaze with symbolic dragons, animals, gods and headhunting images. The cloth worn by men is called the **hinggi**, and is made from two identical panels sewn together into a symmetrical blanket. One is worn around the waist and another draped across one shoulder. These are the most popular souvenirs, as they make great wall-hangings. Most pieces retailing at under US$100 will use a *campur* (mix) of traditional vegetable **dyes** and manufactured chemical dyes. Many cloths under US$50 will use only chemical dye. A tight weave, clean precise motifs and sharp edges between different colours are all signs of a good piece. Dealers in the towns will often give you better prices than those in the villages.

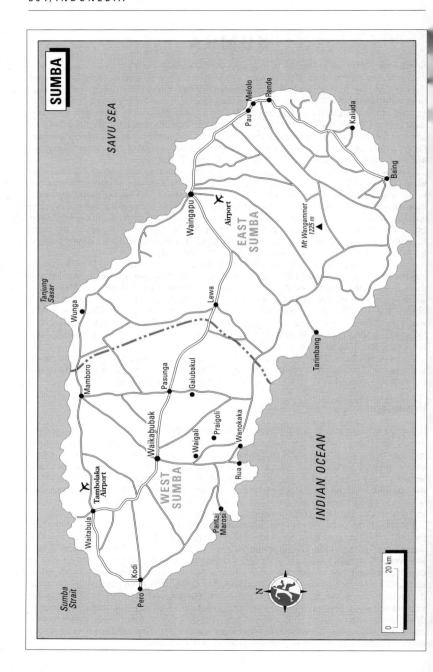

Practicalities

Ferries from Ende on Flores dock at the harbour on the east of the bay, a short walk from town. Pelni ferries arrive about 8km away to the west, and are met by **bemos** running to the hotels in town. The offices for **Pelni** ships and **ferry** services are both down at the bottom of the hill near the east pier, but are unreliable. The *KM Awu* and *KM Wilis* both call in here; see "Getting around" pp.192–193 and "Travel Details" p.442. The **airstrip** is about 10km to the southeast on the road to Rende: if there are no buses waiting, head out to the main road and flag one down. The Merpati office is at Jl Sukarno 4; Bouraq are by Pasar Inpres, behind the bus terminal.

The new **bus terminal** lies 4km to the west of town; catch bemo #3 from Pasar Inpres (Rp450). For buses **to Waikabubak** (Rp6500), don't buy tickets from the touts without first finding out which bus will leave first. Of the three **banks** in town, only the BNI will change travellers' cheques – it's 100m north of the Inpres terminal. The main **post office** with poste restante is at Jl Dr Sutomo 21, the 24-hour **Telkom** on Jalan Tjut Nya Dien.

ACCOMMODATION AND EATING

The cheapest **place to stay** in town is the rather wretched *Lima Saudara*, near the post office on Jalan Wanggameti (☎0387/61083; ①), though you're advised to pay a little more and stay at one of the pleasanter places by the Pasar Inpres. The pick of the bunch is the *Hotel Sandel Wood* at Jl DI Panjaitan 23 (☎0386/61887; ①), where the rooms are large and comfortable. The staff at *Hotel Elvin*, Jl Achmad Yani (☎0386/62097; ③), are friendly and helpful. Easily the plushest place in Waingapu, *Hotel Merlin*, Jl Achmad Yani (☎0386/61300; ①–③), has sparkling rooms, most **with air-con and en suite.**

For **food**, the *Warung Jawa* on Jalan Achmad Yani is one of the most popular places in town, serving large portions of Indonesian staples at rock-bottom prices. The *Nazareth* on Jalan WJ Lala Mentik, south of the Pasar Inpres, is a smart but overpriced little **restaurant** with cold beer and quite a long menu consisting mainly of Chinese cuisine and seafood. On the fourth floor at the top of a Himalayan staircase with fine views of the town, *Hotel Merlin's* restaurant on Jalan Panjaitan is perhaps the most expensive on Sumba: around Rp45,000 for a full Chinese meal with several courses.

The east Sumban villages

The villages of eastern Sumba have made small concessions to modernity, now sporting rusty metal roofs on their houses and using concrete to build their tombs. Most of these villages are used to visitors and will request around Rp1000 as a "signing-in fee". East of Waingapu, and just before the larger town of Melolo, are **PAU** and **UMBARA**. Pau, though tiny, is actually an independent kingdom with its own rajah, an interesting character who is very knowledgeable about Sumba and its traditions. Umbara has a few thatched-roof houses. Buses from Waingapu to Melolo (Rp3000) run until late afternoon and you can ask the driver to stop at Pau or Umbara.

MELOLO, 62km from Waingapu, has three high-roofed houses and a few crudely carved tombs as well as a clean and friendly **losmen** (①). The next major settlement as you head east is **RENDE**. Here the house roofs are all made from tin, but are nevertheless spectacular, and doorways are adorned with huge buffalo horns. Rende is also the site of the finest **tombs** in East Sumba, huge flat slabs topped by animal carvings. There are buses every couple of hours direct to Rende from Waingapu (Rp3500), and occasional trucks; otherwise, catch a bus to Melolo and one of the regular bemos, buses or trucks from there.

About 40km out of Waingapu on the road west to Waikabubak, a turn-off leads down to **TARIMBANG** on the south coast. Here the *Martin Homestay* (① full board), with its rooms fashioned to resemble Sumbanese clan houses, caters for surfers and those looking for quiet beaches and a bit of relaxation.

Waikabubak

Surrounded by lush green meadows and forested hills, tiny **WAIKABUBAK** consists of one dirt road and a few shops, plus several enclosed kampung with slanting thatched roofs and megalithic **stone graves**, where life proceeds according to the laws of the spirits. **Tarung** kampung, on a hilltop just west of the main street, has some excellent megalithic graves and is regarded as one of the most significant spiritual centres on the island. The *ratu* (king) of Tarung is responsible for the annual **wula padu** ceremony, which lasts for a month at the beginning of the Merapu new year in November. The ceremony commemorates the visiting spirits of important ancestors, who are honoured with the sacrifice of many animals and entertained by singing and dancing. **Kampung Praijiang**, a five-tiered village on a hilltop surrounded by rice paddies, is another fine kampung, several kilometres east of town. You can catch a bemo to the bottom of the hill and will be asked for a Rp1500 fee. Waikabubak enjoys an extended rainy season that lasts way into May, when the countryside can be drenched by daily downpours and it can get chilly at night.

Practicalities

The **bus terminal** is in the southeast of the town and serves all areas of western Sumba; trucks and bemos also stop here. Services are erratic, but buses to Waingapu usually stop running around 2pm, and others dry up after late morning. Tambolaka **airport** is a good ninety-minute drive from the north of town; buses and taxis meet arriving planes. Buses leave daily for Tambolaka airport in the early mornings and will pick you up at your hotel door if you go to the bus depot the night before and ask them: the depot is in the back yard of the house opposite the *Hotel Manandang*. Flights out of Tambolaka are often cancelled or severely delayed, especially in the rainy season. In *pasola* season, flights are more reliable but need to be booked months in advance. If you need to rely on leaving Sumba at a precise time then go by ferry from Waingapu. The Merpati office, which is often closed, is on the right-hand side of Jalan Achmad Yani on the second floor of a dusty grain store.

Most things that you will need in Waikabubak are either on the main street of Jalan Achmad Yani, or within several minutes' walk of it. At the southern end, the market and bus terminal are sandwiched together, with the 24-hour **Telkom office** a few hundred metres further south. Opposite the bus-station turn-off is an interesting **art shop** full of old carvings and some jewellery and ikat. The **BRI bank** is a stone's throw west of the bus terminal and will change US dollars cash if the bills are pristine. The **post office** is at the northern end of Jalan Achmad Yani where it meets Jalan Sudirman (Mon–Thurs & Sat 9am–2pm, Fri 9–11.30am).

ACCOMMODATION AND EATING

All **rooms** in Waikabubak must be booked in advance during *pasola* season. The most popular place in town lies just off the road in from Waingapu: *Hotel Artha*, Jl Veteran (☎0387/21112; ①–②), is quite clean, has a reasonable variety of rooms around a central garden, and the staff are wonderful. At *Hotel Aloha*, Jl Gajah Mada (☎0387/21245; ①–②), the beds should have been replaced decades ago and the mandi are brimming with mosquito larvae, but the staff are friendly and there's plenty of information to be had. The clean and comfortable *Hotel Manandang*, Jl Permuda 4 (☎0387/21292 or 21197; ②), offers TV in its most expensive rooms, and its singles are the cheapest in town. *Mona Lisa Cottages*, Jl Adhyaksa (☎0387/21364; ②), is quite upmarket, with bungalows set on a hillside about 2km from town amongst the rice paddies. Some of the cheaper ones are a little grotty and very dark, but the top ones are really lovely. It's usually booked by large tour groups during the *pasola* season.

Probably the best **food** in Waikabubak comes from the warung that set up, particularly at night, along Achmad Yani close to the bus terminal. Otherwise, try *Ronita*, Jl Basuki Rahmat, which has comprehensive karaoke facilities, but is still one of the best places to eat in town. *Rumah Makan Surabaya*, next to the BRI bank, has a limited menu, but the *sate* is pretty good and the proprietor is very friendly. *Hotel Manandang* has the flashiest restaurant in Waikabubak, twice the price of something similar on the street. It is, however, by far the most hygienic option, and their fried *tempe* is excellent.

Kodi and Pero

In the extreme west of Sumba lie the increasingly popular areas of **Kodi** and **Pero**. The Kodi district, with its centre in the village of **BANDOKODI**, is particularly well-known for the towering roofs that top the traditional houses. It is also one of the main *pasola* venues in West Sumba. There is one direct bus a day from Waikabubak to Bandokodi; otherwise, you'll have to take a bus to **Waitabula** in the north and then wait for a bus to fill up for the trip around the coast. As the trip between Bandokodi and Waikabubak takes approximately four hours, and the last bus back to Waitabula is at 2pm, a stopover in Pero is in order.

The Pasola

By far the best-known and most dazzling festival in Nusa Tenggara, the **pasola** is one of those rare spectacles that actually surpasses all expectations. It takes place in Kodi and Lamboya in February and in Wanokaka and Gaura in March; most hotels can give you a rough idea of the date. This brilliant pageant of several hundred colourfully attired, spear-wielding horsemen in a frenetic and lethal pitched battle is truly unforgettable. It occurs within the first two moons of the year, and is set off by the mass appearance of a type of sea worm which, for two days a year, turn the shores into a maelstrom of luminous red, yellow and blue. The event is a rite to balance the upper sphere of the heavens and the lower sphere of the seas. The *pasola* places the men of each village as two teams in direct opposition; the spilling of their blood placates the spirits and restores balance between the two spheres. The proceedings begin several weeks before the main event, with villages hurling abuse and insults at their neighbours in order to get their blood up. The actual fighting takes place on the special *pasola* fields where the battle has taken place for centuries.

Pero

The Waikabubak bus will usually take you all the way to **PERO**, a seaside village with one losmen. The village is not constructed in traditional Sumbanese style, but its rough cobbled street flanked by colourful wooden houses has a certain charm. Numerous kampung with teetering high roofs and mossy stone **tombs** dot the surrounding countryside, only a short walk away. The *Homestay Story* (① full board) is quite clean and provides huge meals, but come prepared for the mosquitoes. To get to the beach, walk down the path outside the losmen and then either head left across the river or right, down to where the most regular offshore surf breaks are. The beach to the left is very sheltered with a narrow stretch of fine sand, whereas the other is far more exposed. Both have dangerous currents – the undertow can be ferocious and even with a surfboard you're not necessarily safe.

KALIMANTAN

Cupped in the palm of an island arc between the Malay peninsula and Sulawesi, **Kalimantan** comprises the southern, Indonesian two-thirds of the vast island of Borneo, whose northern reaches are split between the independent sultanate of Brunei and the Malaysian states of Sabah and Sarawak. Borneo has conjured up sensational images in the outside world ever since Europeans first visited in the sixteenth century and found coastal city-states governed by wealthy sultans and a jungle-cloaked land inhabited by the infamous head-hunting Dayak.

Dayak is an umbrella name for all of Borneo's indigenous peoples, who arrived here from mainland Southeast Asia around 2500 years ago and have since divided into scores of interrelated groups. In Dayak religions, evil is kept at bay by attracting the presence of helpful spirits, or scared away by protective tattoos, carved spirit posts (*patong*), and lavish funerals. Shamans also intercede with spirits on behalf of the living, but, formerly, the most powerful way to ensure good luck was by head-hunting, which forced the victim's soul into the service of its captor. Although these days you'll often find ostensibly Christian communities whose inhabitants dress in shorts and T-shirts, the Dayak are still feared for their jungle skills, abilities with magic, and the way they violently take the law into their own hands if provoked – in 1997, West Kalimantan's Dayak exacted fearsome revenge against Maduran transmigrants, reviving the practice of head-hunting, and killing an estimated 300 to 2000. There's a resurgence in the more acceptable side of tradition, too: communal houses, once banned by the government, are being restored, and public festivals like the annual **Erau Festival**, a massive assembly of Kalimantan's eastern Dayak groups on Sungai Mahakam, provide an assurance that Dayak culture is still very much alive, if being redefined.

Modern Kalimantan has a tough time living up to its romantic tradition, however. In all Kalimantan's 500,000-square-kilometre spread, there are few obvious destinations, and even the provincial capitals of **Pontianak**, **Palangkaraya** and **Samarinda** offer little aside from

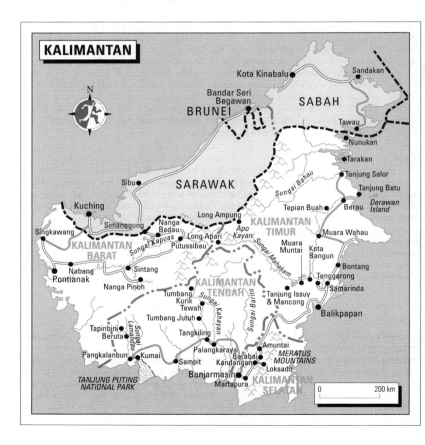

their services. The exception is **Banjarmasin**, which has unusual floating markets, extraordinary street performers and interesting gem mines nearby. However, despite increasingly rapacious logging and catastrophic forest fires, sizeable tracts of the forested interior remain, sporting ancient **longhouses**. With few roads, Kalimantan's waterways are the interior's highways, and cruising up the mighty **Sungai Mahakam** is one of the world's great river journeys. Kalimantan's other big draw is **Tanjung Puting national park**, whose orang-utans and proboscis monkeys alone justify the journey here.

Kalimantan is well connected to the outside world, with **flights from Brunei** to Balikpapan, and **boats from Tewah in Sabah** to northeastern Pulau Nunukan. From elsewhere in Indonesia, there are direct flights from Java, with a half-dozen Pelni vessels stopping off in Kalimantan on their Java–Sulawesi–Maluku runs.

Crossed by the equator, Kalimantan has no real **seasons**. April through to September is the optimum time for a visit: at the height of the rains (Jan–March) you'll find towns isolated by flooding, and planes grounded for weeks on end, while the driest months (Aug–Oct) see boats stranded by low river levels. With only fragmentary infrastructure, Kalimantan's **costs** are higher than in most of the rest of the country, especially for transport in remote areas. **Accommodation** is pricey, too: even simple country losmen charge US$3 a night, and it's rare in cities to find anything under US$7. West and Central Kalimantan operate on Western time, but the south and eastern provinces run on Eastern time.

Pontianak

The capital of West Kalimantan, or Kalbar (short for "Kalimantan Barat"), **PONTIANAK** is a sprawling, grey industrial city of 400,000 lying right on the equator on the confluence of the Landak and Kapuas Kecil rivers. It is hot and noisy, and most travellers stay just long enough to stock up on supplies before heading up the Kapuas or straight on to Kuching. On the western side of Sungai Kapuas Kecil you'll find the Chinese quarter, the commercial heart of the city where most of the hotels, restaurants and travel agents are located. In the centre of this quarter, right on the water's edge, is the **Kapuas Indah bemo terminal**, which is connected to a second bemo terminal in **Siantan**, on the eastern side of the river, by a regular passenger ferry.

The eye-catching **Istana Kadriyah**, built in 1771, and the traditional Javanese four-tiered roof of **Mesjid Jami** stand near each other on the eastern side of the Kapuas Kecil, just to the south of the confluence with the Landak. Small passenger boats from the eastern end of Jalan Mahakam II cost Rp200 for a shared canoe or Rp750 for a rowing boat. But Pontianak's most entertaining attraction is the **Museum Negeri Pontianak** (Mon–Thurs & Sat 8am–1pm, Fri 8–11.30am, Sun 9am–noon; Rp350), a comprehensive collection of Dayak tribal masks, weapons and musical instruments. The museum lies 1.5km south of the town centre on Jalan Jend A Yani; bemos leave from the Kapuas Indah terminal (Rp350) or you can rent a becak (Rp1000). Just round the corner from the museum, on Jalan Sutoyo, is an impressive replica of a **Dayak longhouse**, over 50m long and 15m high, where you're free to wander around. Pontianak's twelve-metre-high **equator monument** stands by the side of Jalan Khatulistiwa on the way to the bus terminal. Catch any bemo to the bus terminal from the Siantan ferry port; the monument stands about halfway along the road on the left-hand side.

Practicalities

Batu Layang bus terminal is inconveniently located 6km north of the centre. Regular white bemos (Rp350) leave from Batu Layang to the Siantan bemo terminal, from where you can catch a ferry (Rp150) to the western side. Nearly every tourist who arrives in Pontianak is looking to catch a bus straight up **to Kuching** in Sarawak – now the easiest way of renewing Indonesian visas. A number of bus companies run the route, and most departures are either early in the morning or late at night; you should be able to pick up your bus from the agent

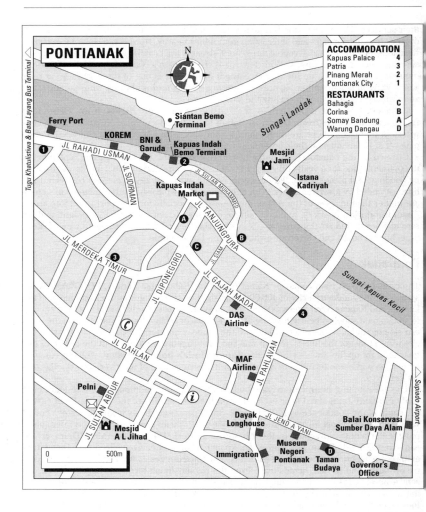

in town. The reliable PT SJS (Setia Jiwana Sakti), Jl Sisingamangaraja 155 (☎0561/34626), runs four buses a day to Kuching, Sibu and Miri. Buses to the **interior** – to Sintang and Putussibau – also leave frequently from these agents.

Supadio Airport lies 20km south of the city centre. Bemos (every 30min; Rp500) run to the Kapuas Indah terminal in the town centre, or you can catch a cab (Rp15,000). The **ferry port** is a few hundred metres north of the Kapuas Indah bemo station in the centre. During the rainy season, weekly passenger ferries travel to and from Putussibau via Sintang. The ferries are extremely basic, though a bed and food are provided for Rp1500. Mitra Kalindo Samudera, Jl Diponegoro 39 (☎0561/49751), sells tickets for the daily 8am *Ketapang Express* to Ketapang, and the *Kapuas Expres* runs twice weekly to Jakarta. At the **Pelni** ferry office, Jl Sultan Abdur Rahman 12 (Mon–Sat 9.30am–noon), you can buy tickets for services to, amongst other places, Jakarta and Kijang on Pulau Batam. The *KM Tilongkabila, KM Bukit Raya, KM Lawit* and *KM Leuser* all call in here; see "Getting around" pp.192–193 and "Travel Details" p.442.

ACCOMMODATION

Addresses in Pontianak can be confusing. Streets often go by two different names (Jalan HOS Cokroaminto is also known as Jalan Merdeka Timur, and Jalan Diponegoro is also known as Jalan Sisingamangaraja), and address numbers do not run in sequence. Despite a far-from-central location, the sprawling *Patria*, Jl Merdeka Timur 497 (☎0561/36063; ①), is the best of the budget **accommodation**, with pleasant en-suite rooms, though watch out for the rats late at night. The best of the two options in the tawdry port area is *Pinang Merah*, Jl Kapten Marsan 51–53 (☎0561/32547; ①),whose English-speaking manager offers a variety of fairly tatty rooms, with TV, air-con and mandi. The excellent-value *Pontianak City*, Jl Pak Kasih 44 (☎0561/32495; ②), is opposite the harbour and has friendly staff and well-appointed rooms (TV and air-con). West Kalimantan's finest hotel, *Kapuas Palace*, Jl Imam Bonjol (☎0561/36122; ⑧), has pools and bars set back from the Jalan Pahlawan junction in the south of the city.

EATING

Street stalls congregate every night on the KOREM Place, a small square by the river beside the Komando Regimen Militer building. Locally grown **coffee** is Pontianak's speciality, and served all over town in warung kopi. Possibly the city's best **warung**, the no-fuss warung *Somay Bandung*, Jl Sisingamangaraja 132, serves basic meals for Rp2500, and free drinking water. *Corina*, Jl Tanjungpura 124, is a clean budget restaurant serving Chinese and Indonesian food, including a particularly tasty crab omelette for Rp4000. One of Pontianak's few vegetarian cafés, *Bahagia*, Jl H. Agus Salim 182, serves unexceptional budget fare. *Warung Dangau*, Jl Jend A Yani, is a highly recommended mid-priced restaurant tucked away in the Taman Budaya and serving fine Indonesian food.

LISTINGS

Airline offices Bouraq, Jl Pahlawan Blok D no. 3 (☎0561/37261); DAS, Jl Gajah Mada 67 (☎0561/32313); Garuda, Jl Rahadi Usman 8a (☎0561/78111); MAF, Jl Supranto 50a (☎0561/30271); MAS, Jl Sidas 8 (☎0561/30069); Merpati, Jl Gajah Mada 210 (☎0561/36568).
Banks and exchange Bank BNI, Jl Rahadi Usman (8am–4pm); PT Safari moneychangers, Jl Nusa Indah III 45.
Consulate Malay consulate, Jl Jend A Yani 42.
Internet access Warposnet at the GPO; Mon–Thurs, Sat & Sun 8am–2pm, Fri 8–11am; Rp2000 for 15min.
Post office Jl Sultan Abdur Rahman 49 (daily 8am–9pm). Poste restante, at the back of the building, closes at 2pm.
Telephone services Telkom, Jl Teuku Umar 15, is open 24hr.

Sintang

As an overnight stop between Pontianak and Putussibau, **SINTANG**, on the confluence of the Kapuas and Melawai rivers, is ideal. Accommodation is clean and fairly inexpensive, and the city is lively and friendly. There are **buses** to and from Pontianak and Putussibau, as well as **boats** to Puttussibau. Sintang's bus and bemo stations, as well as hotels and restaurants, are all within walking distance of each other, on the southern side of the Kapuas to the west of the Melawai. The best-value **hotels** are on the waterfront, 150m due north of the bus station. The *Sesean*, at Jl Brigjen Katamso 1 (☎0565/21011; ①), is cheerful and popular; just behind it, the *Setian*, Jl Brigjen Katamso 78 (☎0565/21611; ①), is one of the cheapest in town, but has no fans. Better value is the *Safary*, a little further south on Jalan Kol Sugiano (☎0565/21776; ①), where doubles come with a fan and TV.

Putussibau

A further 412km east of Sintang, the ramshackle little frontier town of **PUTUSSIBAU** is situated at the point where the Sungai Sibau empties into the Kapuas, and serves as an important base for exploration of the interior. There are also a couple of **Iban longhouses** just a few kilometres upriver from Putussibau that still retain a fairly traditional lifestyle, though they have been receiving tourists for years. The Melapi I longhouse and the Sayut are said to be the most impressive. Boat owners will approach you offering a guided tour of four or five longhouses: Rp50,000 for a day-trip, plus Rp20,000 if you want to stay the night – don't forget to bring presents, and remember that Iban etiquette dictates that you should only enter the longhouse when invited.

Much of Putussibau, including most of the market, stands on stilts on the riverbank. There are a couple of **hotels** here, including the *Gautama* floating hotel (①), where you'll gain an insight into the daily life of the itinerant market traders, fishermen and prostitutes, but don't expect much comfort or privacy. Overlooking the *Gautama*, the *Aman Sentosa* on Jalan Diponegoro (☎0567/21533; ①) is more conventional and comfortable. The centrally located *Marissa Hotel* (①) also has decent rooms.

Nanga Badau and into Malaysia

The ochre-coloured mud-slick running between Putussibau and the ramshackle village of **NANGA BADAU** at the Sarawak border has yet to be sealed, but is served by a daily 8am bemo from Putussibau (7hr). From Nanga Badau, a covered road continues east to **Simanggung**, just over the border in Sarawak. Nanga's **immigration office** (8am–5pm) lies on this road at the eastern end of town. At the moment Nanga Badau is not a designated entry point into Indonesia, though tourists should have no trouble leaving the country from here, and exit formalities are straightforward. There's no public transport to take you into Malaysia, however, and you're not allowed to walk across, so you'll have to try to hitch a lift to the Malaysian border post, where public buses leave regularly for Kuching (9hr). There's no accommodation in Nanga Badau.

Tanjung Puting national park

A wild and beautiful expanse of riverine forest, coastal swamp and peat bogs bursting with wildlife, **TANJUNG PUTING NATIONAL PARK** is Kalimantan at its best. The park's fame rests on the efforts of Dr Birute Galdikas, who in 1971 founded Camp Leakey here as an **orang-utan rehabilitation centre** for animals that had been orphaned or sold as pets and needed to be taught how to forage. Tanjung Puting is also home to *owa-owa*, the vocal, long-armed gibbon, and to troupes of big-nosed proboscis monkeys. Along the rivers, look for monitor lizards and false ghavials, a narrow-nosed crocodile which grows to about 3m, plus scores of birds; on land, hikers need to be aware of potentially dangerous snakes.

Pangkalanbun: park registration

Before heading to Tanjung Puting national park, you must first **register with the police** in the dusty administrative town of **PANGKALANBUN**, which stands on the eastern bank of the modest Sungai Arut. Following the river's southern bank, Jalan Antasari is Pangkalanbun's main street. Orientate yourself by finding the intersection with Jalan Rangga Santrek, marked by the BNI **bank** here (foreign exchange Mon–Thurs 8am–3pm, Fri 8–11am), which runs 70m south to where Jalan Kasamayuda parallels Jalan Antasari. The **police headquarters** are 1km from the centre on Jalan Diponegoro (daily 7am–5pm; catch a bemo from the Jalan Kasamayuda–Jalan Santrek intersection). Registration here is free, but you'll need your passport and a copy of the photo page; the process takes ten minutes and leaves you with a registration certificate to be handed to the park authorities at Kumai.

Arrival points are scattered. **Long-distance buses** stop at bus companies' downtown offices: MP is about 500m west of the BNI on Jalan Antasari, while Yessoe Travel is on the corner of Jalan Santrek and Jalan Kasamayuda. The **airport** is 5km out to the southeast: chartered bemos from here cost a flat Rp10,000. Though the town is small, at Rp500 a ride Pangkalanbun's yellow city **bemos** are a cheap way to get around.

Few of Pangkalanbun's cheaper **lodgings** want foreign custom. Centrally located above a jewellery store in the backstreets off Jalan Antasari, the basic *Losmen Mawar* (①) does, but tidy, simple rooms at the *Thamarin* (②) on Jalan Diponegoro, and *Andika* (☎0532/21218; ②), on Jalan Hasanudin, are a better deal – both are a couple of kilometres from the centre. Closer in on the hill above Jalan Kasamayuda, the *Blue Kecubung* (☎0532/21211; ③) is helpful, overpriced, and also takes bookings for *Rimba Lodge* in Tanjung Puting national park. All hotels serve **meals**, otherwise try the pricey Chinese fare at the *Phoenix* or the good Padang selection at *Beringin Padang*, both on Jalan Antasari.

Leaving, both bus companies operate two daily buses to Palangkaraya (10hr; Rp35,000). Dimendra Travel, at the Jalan Santrek/Kasamayuda junction, makes **airline** bookings to Palangkaraya, Pontianak or Java, and can book **Pelni** tickets out of Kumai. An ojek **to Kumai** costs Rp5000 or, before about 3pm, you can catch a bemo from Pasar Baru to *terminal bis*, then a minibus for the remaining hour-long run – about Rp1500 in all.

Kumai: park permits and boats

After registering in Pangkalanbun, you need to travel 25km east to **KUMAI**, whose small port and couple of streets stand across broad Sungai Kumai from the edge of Tanjung Puting national park. Transport from Pangkalanbun winds up outside the **market** on the kilometre-long strip of Jalan Idris (last bemo back around 3pm); the adjacent *Aloha* and *Cempaka* **losmen** (c) are more welcoming than those in Pangkalanbun. The **Pelni office** across the road at the docks does tickets for the fortnightly *Binaya* to Java and Sulawesi, and the *Lawit*, *Leuser* and *Tilongkabila* also call here; see "Getting around" pp.192–193 and "Travel Details" p.442. Continue up Jalan Idris to organize your **national park permit** from the Departmen Kehutanan Taman Nasional Tanjung Puting (Mon–Thurs & Sat 7am–2pm, Fri 7–11am; ☎0532/61508). Having produced your permit from Pangkalanbun's police and another copy of your passport, you pay Rp2000 a person per day, plus Rp2000 a boat per day.

The next stage is to organize a **boat into Tanjung Puting** – access is by water only. Speedboats are expensive (Rp120,000 a day) and scare wildlife. Slower, quieter *klotok* are six-metre-long hulls powered by an inboard engine, with enclosed mandi, a wooden roof (which makes a fine vantage point), and room for four people plus two crew. Rates are fixed at Rp75,000 a day all-inclusive; sleeping aboard sidesteps the park's pricey accommodation, and the crew will cook for you. National park staff can help find a vessel, or you can head down to the jetties beside their office. Pack walking shoes, sunscreen, a hat and a torch; there are no shops inside the park.

Tanjung Puting practicalities

Tanjung Puting national park covers 4000 square kilometres south of Sungai Sekonyer, though public access, by boat only, is confined to the **ranger posts** at Tanjung Harapan (2hr from Kumai) and Pondok Tanggui (3hr), and the **research stations** at Natai Lengkuas (4–5hr) and Camp Leakey (4–5hr). On arrival at each stopover, you must report with your permit to park staff. Heed their warnings, especially about getting too close to adult male orang-utans, or females with children – and don't carry food, as orang-utans will rip bags apart to find it. Each area has fairly easy paths to explore, the longest of which are at Camp Leakey.

You need at least two full days in the park. If you don't sleep aboard your *klotok*, there are three **places to stay**, all in the vicinity of Tanjung Harapan. The ranger post here has basic cabins (①), which must be booked at Kumai. *Ecolodge* (fax 0532/22991; ②), across the river, has comfortable rooms and, five minutes upstream, there's *Rimba Lodge* "safari camp" (book at *Blue Kecubung* in Pangkalanbun; ⑧). Both lodges have good **restaurants** – the only places to eat in the park – and can arrange **guides**, canoes and *klotoks* for rental. Staff at the two ranger posts and Camp Leakey also offer their guiding services at around Rp50,000 a day.

The park

On leaving Kumai, boats enter the mouth of small Sungai Sekonyer, where an avenue of trunkless nipa palms gradually cedes to patchy forest at **Tanjung Harapan** ranger post. An information hut here has a good rundown on the park's ecology; a few orang-utans move in for feeding at about 3pm; and there's a muddy five-kilometre circuit track into surrounding thickets.

The jungle closes in after Tanjung Harapan – lining the banks are giant lilies, pandanus and gardenia bushes with yellow flowers. Behind them grow dense stands of tall, thin trees with buttressed roots, providing perches for vines, orchids and ferns. The next stop is **Pondok Tanggui**, a good place to moor for the night and watch families of proboscis monkeys. A two-kilometre track leads past the ranger's office to an orang-utan feeding area (milk and bananas at 8am and 4pm).

Past Pondok Tanggui, you veer east off the Sekonyer up Leakey Creek. The water immediately turns clear and deep, and trees eventually give way to grassy marshland, home of triangular-headed false ghavials. At **Camp Leakey**, the local orang-utan population includes two mature males whose overgrown cheek pouches and sheer size – one weighs 100kg – are most imposing. There's another feeding area here, and the camp's rangers can take you on a short hike into the forest proper.

Back on the Sekonyer, a final hour brings you to **Natai Lengkuas**, a research post investigating proboscis monkeys. In fact, this is the last animal you're likely to see here, as trails take you well away from the riverside study areas, but following the orange tags of the ninety-minute "Habitat Walk" through the forest you may see mahogany trees, lizards, bears, wild pigs, scorpions and roosting colonies of short-nosed fruit bats. There are no rangers to act as guides, so read the information notice above the dock and follow all of its instructions.

Palangkaraya

Most travellers only pass through **PALANGKARAYA**, the capital of Dayak-controlled Kalimantan Tengah, or Kalteng, in transit between Pangkalanbun and Banjarmasin. The most interesting part of town surrounds the dock area around Jalan Dharmosugondo, with its day- and night **markets** a good place to pick up locally made bamboo and rattan rain hats (Rp2000) and floormats (Rp3000).

Most of Palangkaraya's services are up in the northeastern end of town off Jalan Yani. **Tjilik Riwut airport** is 1km further east again, Rp5000 by taxi. Arriving by river from Banjarmasin, **speedboats** (Rp25,000) terminate at Rambang Pier at the top of Jalan Dharmosugondo. **Buses** from Banjarmasin (Rp25,000) pull in 2km south across town on Jalan Soedarso, though they generally deliver to hotels first. Buses to Pangkalanbun (Rp30,000) are best booked in advance at the offices near Rambang Pier on Jalan Dharmosugondo. City **bemos** run fixed routes for a flat rate of Rp350.

Change **money** at the BNI on Jalan Dharmosugondo (Mon–Thurs 9am–2pm, Fri 9–11am), which has an ATM for Cirrus/Maestro cards. West along Jalan Yani, the wartel does international phone calls, while Adi Ankassa Travel (☎0514/21480) makes flight bookings. Most of Palangkaraya's budget **accommodation** is set around Rambang Pier, but, like the pleasant-looking *Mina* (①), is generally difficult for foreigners to get into. *Dian Wisata*, Jl Yani 68 (☎0536/21241; ①), offers economy and en-suite doubles; *Yanti*, Jl Yani 82 (☎0536/21634; ④), is also fair value and spotless. *Dandang Tingang*, Jl Yos Soedarso 13 (☎0536/21805; ②), is a little distant from transit points – bemo "C" from Jalan Yani will get you there – but pleasant and spacious. Thick **fish steaks** and fillets are cooked to your order at *Sampurna*, on Jalan Jawa, *Senggol* on Jalan Madura, or *Almuminum* on Jalan Dharmosugondo.

Banjarmasin and around

Set down in southeast Kalimantan, on the closest part of the island to Java, **BANJARMASIN**'s history involves centuries of vigorous dealings with the outside world, and the city has emerged with a strong sense of its own identity. Over ninety percent of residents are Muslim, and Banjarmasin's focus is the marble-and-bronze **Masjid Raya Sabilal Muhtadin**, the Grand Mosque, built in 1981 on the west bank of Sungai Martapura just above the city centre; you can look around outside the main prayer times, provided you dress conservatively.

For real off-the-cuff entertainment head 1.5km east across the river down Jalan Antasari, past the Mitra Plaza and white Masjid Agung, to **Pasar Antasari**, a market and circus rolled into one. You can spend hours here among hawkers and hustlers of every description, though beware of pickpockets. From sunrise, the covered market inside is packed with trays of cheap gems, watches, medicinal spices and trinkets; in the evening, the forecourt fills up with clothing stalls and warung. But the highlight are the **street performers**: musclemen who break coconuts with their heads, chew glass or hammer nails up their noses, and quacks, like the one who piles up cases of poisonous snakes and sits astride a live crocodile while proclaiming the virtues of his reptile oil (a big aid to male virility).

Half of Banjarmasin's population spend their days on wooden porches overlooking the water, and you can catch all this by taking a *klotok* (Rp7000–10,000 an hour from Jalan Hasanuddin bridge) to one of Banjarmasin's famous *pasar terapang*, or **floating markets**. The largest is at Kuin, about 4km northeast of the centre (30 min from Jalan Yani bridge), starting daily at dawn and effectively over by 8am. As you approach the market, you find yourself in a jam of small boats, full of shoppers in *klotok* and dugouts and vendors selling everything from medicines and bricks of fermented prawn *trasi*, to piles of pineapples, beans or watermelons. There are even **floating warung**, where you can have a breakfast of coffee and cakes by tying up alongside and hooking your choice of pastry with a pole-and-nail.

Practicalities

Syamsuddin Noor airport is 25km east, Rp21,000 by taxi, or walk up to the highway and flag down one of the orange Martapura–Banjarmasin bemos (Rp1200). Long-distance **buses** pull into **Terminal Km6**, 6km southeast of the centre on Jalan Yani, Rp1500 by ojek or Rp300 by yellow bemo to Pasar Antasari. **Speedboats** dock close to the Grand Mosque on Jalan Pos, while ocean-going transport ties up at **Trisakti Docks**, about 5km west of the centre, B300 by city bemo.

The only **accommodation** in all Kalimantan solely geared to overseas backpackers, *Borneo Homestay*, Jl Simpang Hasanuddin I, 33 (☎0511/66545; ②), has US$4 dorm beds and a tour office specializing in Loksado trekking. The very friendly *Diamond Homestay*, Jl Simpang Hasanuddin II (☎0511/66100; ②), competes for the backpacker market, with cheaper rooms and tours. *Biuti*, Jl Haryono 21 (☎0511/54493; ②), is a good mid-range option, with both economy rooms and some with fan, TV and soft mattress. The most upmarket place is *Kalimantan*, Jl Lambung Mangkurat (☎0511/66818; ⑧).

Banjarese **food** has characteristic sweet flavours accompanied by unusually hot sambals, like *katupat kandangan*, catfish sate and duck eggs in a spicy coconut sauce. For cheap warung, try Jalan Niaga in the Pasar Baru area, and the area around Pasar Antasar. Otherwise, the low-key *Cak Mentul*, Jl Haryono, specializes in local-style chicken and duck. *Cintoraso*, diagonally across from the *Istana Barito* on Jalan Haryono, serves cheap Padang food, as do the slightly classier *Kaganangan* and *Cendrawasih*, opposite each other at the western end of Jalan Samudra. For Chinese food, check out the recommended *Jakarta*, corner of Jalan Bank Rakyat and Jalan Hasanuddin.

MOVING ON FROM BANJARMASIN

To get to the bus terminal take a bemo from the Jalan Hasanuddin–Jalan Bank Rakyat crossroads. **Buses** to Balikpapan (Rp3500–23,500) and Samarinda (Rp17,000–27,000) start leaving mid-afternoon. There are also daily buses to and from Palangkaraya and frequent services to Martapura.

Speedboats to Palangkaraya (Rp25,000) leave from near the Grand Mosque on Jalan Pos and leave when full until early afternoon. **Pelni**'s *Kelimutu* crosses to Surabaya (24hr) several times a week from Trisakti Docks, and the *KM Sirimau* occasionally calls in on its way to Makassar from Semarang; the Pelni office is about 1km southwest of the centre on Jalan Martadinata.

LISTINGS

Airline offices Bouraq, Jl Yani 343 (☎0511/52445); DAS, Jl Hasanuddin 6 (☎0511/52902); Garuda at *Istana Barito* hotel (☎0511/59063); Merpati, Jl Hasanuddin 31 (☎0511/53885).

Banks and exchange Bank Dayang Negara, near the Grand Mosque on Jl Lambung Mangkurat (Mon–Fri 8am–3.30pm), has the best rates; further down the same road, BCA are also open Saturday (8–11am). Outside banking hours, contact Adi Ankasa Travel.

Hospital The General Hospital is about 1.5km east of the centre on Jl Yani.

Pharmacies Apotik Kasio is diagonally across from the Istana Barito on Jl Haryono, with doctors on call from 5pm to 7pm.

Police Police headquarters are 2.5km out of town along Jl Yani.

Telephone services 24hr wartel at the mosque end of Jl Lambung Mangkurat.

Tourist Information At Kantor Dinas Parawisata, Jl Panjaitan 34 (Mon–Thurs 8am–2pm, Fri 8–11am, Sat 8am–noon; ☎0511/52982). And at *Borneo Homestay*.

Travel agents Adi Ankasa Travel, Jl Hasanuddin 27 (☎0511/53131), can make all accommodation, plane, bus and boat bookings.

Martapura and Cempaka

MARTAPURA, 40km east of Banjarmasin, is famous for **gems**, especially diamonds, mined nearby at the village of Cempaka (except Fri). Orange **bemos** leave Banjarmasin's Terminal Km6 throughout the day (Rp1250) and terminate at Martapura's plaza. Even if you have no intention of buying, it's fascinating to look around the trays of diamonds, turquoise, tiger's-eye, topaz, amethysts and tektites, but don't deal with the hawkers unless you can tell coloured glass from the real thing; the nearby showrooms offer a more reliable place to shop. Martapura's single losmen refuses to take foreigners – the last bemos return to Banjarmasin after dark. Green "Mart-Cemp" minibuses depart regularly from Martapura's plaza for **CEMPAKA** (15min; Rp500), where a muddy, two-kilometre track leads past a monument to the diggings. Most of the excavations are worked entirely by hand: a hole in the ground marks a shaft with a human chain reaching down into the water 10m below.

Balikpapan

Staked out over Kalimantan's richest petroleum deposits, **BALIKPAPAN**'s fortunes wax and wane with international fuel prices: business has boomed since the Gulf War in 1991, and Balikpapan's 350,000 residents currently enjoy a tidy city, with lots of expat oil workers from the US and Australia. There's nothing much to see in this Western-style town, which is best used as a break after a long sojourn in the interior. The city's commercial district surrounds three-kilometre-long Jalan Yani, with the nearest thing to a downtown hub at its southern intersection with Jalan Sudirman.

Practicalities

Sepinggan airport is 8km east of the city (15min by taxi; Rp9000); unless you look like an oil worker, touts here expect you to be heading to Samarinda (2hr; Rp35,000). **Buses** from Banjarmasin (Rp13,500–23,500) use the terminal on the west side of Balikpapan Bay, connected by ferry to the **Kampung Baru dock** on Jalan Mong Insidi (Rp2000). Buses from Banjarmasin continuing to Samarinda, however, cross the bay to the dock at the top of Jalan Somber, then drop off passengers at their offices on Jalan Negara, about 5km north of the centre. Samarinda buses (Rp3500) use **Terminal Antar Kota**, 6km out of town on Jalan Negara, linked to the centre by bemo #3.

Boats from Java, Sumatra and Sulawesi berth at the **Pelni docks**, 2.5km west of the centre on Jalan Sudirman. Pelni's *Kambuna* stops twice a month on a Java–Sulawesi circuit, with the *Kerinci* and *Tidar* also calling at Tarakan and Nunukan, and the *Umsini* running right through to Ternate in Maluku; see "Getting around" pp.192–193 and "Travel Details" p.442. Tickets are available from the Pelni office at the harbour on Jalan Minyak or from tour agents.

City bemos charge a flat fee of Rp350. #3 runs south from Terminal Antar Kota down Jalan Negara and Jalan Yani, before turning west along Jalan Sudirman to the Pelni docks; #6 starts at the Kampung Baru ferry dock, runs south along Jalan Suprato and Jalan Minyak past the Pelni docks, and east along Jalan Sudirman towards the airport. Both #3 and #6 then reverse their routes.

ACCOMMODATION AND EATING

Balikpapan's mainstay budget **accommodation** is the threadbare but acceptable *Aida*, Jl Yani 12 (☎0542/31011; ①). The friendly guesthouse and warung *Citra Rasa Nusantara*, Jl Gajah Mada 76 (☎0542/25366; ②), are down a side street off Jalan Yani and have tiny rooms with shared mandi, and pricier en-suite ones with air-con. *Gajah Mada*, Jl Sudirman 14 (☎0542/34634; ②), offers a good location and a fair price for its clean, spacious rooms, but you must book ahead as otherwise they'll claim to be full. The hilltop *Balikpapan*, Jl Garuda 2 (☎0542/21490; ⑥), has plain, neat air-con rooms, a bar, coffee shop and weekend rates.

There are a string of cheap **warung** opposite Cinema Antasari on Jalan Sutoyo. Terminal Rasa, near the Glora cinema on Jalan Sudirman, is a huge canteen with various stalls. More salubrious **restaurants** include the popular Chinese *New Shangrila*, Jl Yani 29, which serves tasty crab, fried prawn balls and spicy tofu; and *Depot Kawisan Jaya*, just west of the Balikpapan Plaza on Jalan Sudirman, serving the finest goat and venison sates in Kalimantan. At the split-level, open-air courtyard at *Bondy*, Jl Yani, you can eat superbly grilled seafood in real comfort for about Rp45,000 a head. *New Hollan*, Jl Yani, is a bakery, café and restaurant.

LISTINGS

Airline offices Bouraq, Jl Sudirman (☎0542/31475); DAS, Jl Yani 33 (☎0542/24286); Garuda, Jl Yani 19 (☎0542/22300); Merpati, Jl Sudirman 22 (☎0542/24452); Royal Brunei, at the *Hotel Bahtera* (☎0542/26011).

Banks and exchange The BCA, 200m east of *Hotel Bahtera* on Jl Sudirman, only accepts Visa travellers' cheques; otherwise, use the BNI, also on Jl Sudirman, opposite the *Hotel Gadjah Mada*. ATMs outside the Balikpapan Plaza take Cirrus/Maestro cards.

Bookshops Gramedia, 2nd floor, Balikpapan Plaza, is Kalimantan's best-stocked bookshop.

Hospital Public Hospital (Rumah Sakit Umum) is halfway up Jl Yani (☎0542/34181).

Pharmacies Evening consultations at Apotik Vita Farma, at the junction of Jl Yani and Jl Martadinata, and Apotik Dayakindo, further down Jl Yani.

Police Jl Wiluyo (☎0542/21110).

Post The GPO with poste restante and EMS counters is at Jl Sudirman 31.

Telephone services At the wartel opposite *Hotel Altea Benakutai* on Jl Yani.

Samarinda

Some 120km north of Balikpapan, the tropical port town of **SAMARINDA** is 50km upstream from the sea, where the Sungai Mahakam is 1km wide and deep enough to be navigable by ocean-going ships. It has become increasingly prosperous since large-scale logging of Kalimantan Timur's interior began in the 1970s, its western riverfront abuzz with mills. There's not much to see here, but as the source of Sungai Mahakam ferries it's a good place to stock up for trips into Kalimantan's wilds.

Hemmed in by hills, the bulk of Samarinda occupies the north bank of the Mahakam. Most services are near the river in the vicinity of Pasar Pagi, along Jalan Khalid and Jalan Panglima Batur. For an insight into what Samarinda once looked like, head north to **Pasar Sigiri** and Jalan Pernia Gaan, where the canal behind the market remains crowded with rickety wooden housing and boats pulled up on the muddy banks. **Pasar Pagi** is the standard Indonesian maze of overflowing stalls and tight spaces; shops nearby are strangely divided between gold stores and chandlers. Just up the road on Jalan Khalid stands **Mesra Plaza** shopping centre, and east between Jalan Gajah Mada and Jalan Panglima Batur, **Citra Niaga** is a purpose-built bazaar for cheap clothing and souvenir stalls.

Practicalities

The **airport** is 2km north of the centre, Rp8000 by taxi, or you can just turn left at the gates, walk 100m to Jalan Gatot, and wave down a city bemo heading south to Pasar Pagi. **Buses** from the north, including Bontang, terminate 5km northeast of the city at **Terminal Bontang**, from where you catch a brown bemo to the centre; if you're moving on from here, you can get here by brown bemo from Jalan Bhayangkara. Buses from Banjarmasin (Rp17,000–27,000) arrive at **Terminal Banjarmasin** on the south bank of the Mahakam; cross over the road to the pier and catch a boat directly across to Pasar Pagi (Rp500). Terminal Banjarmasin is also the departure point for **minibuses to Tenggarong** (Rp2000); departures are frequent up till mid-afternoon. Buses from Balikpapan (Rp3500) and Kota Bangun (Rp4000) pull into **Terminal Balikpapan**, beyond the bridge, 5km west of the city. Green bemos run between here and Jalan Gajah Mada, outside Pasar Pagi.

The **Mahakam river ferries** use the Sungai Kunjang docks (green bemo into town). All **ocean-going vessels** use the docks east of the centre along Jalan Sudarso: Pelni's *KM Binaiya* runs twice monthly from here to Surabaya via Sulawesi; see "Getting around" pp.192–193 and "Travel Details" p.442.

Samarinda's colour-coded **bemos** cost Rp500 a ride and run between particular areas rather than following strict routes – tell the driver your destination. Jalan Awang Long is a good place to find one heading north, while either side of Pasar Pagi on Jalan Sudirman or Jalan Gajah Mada is where to hail westbound traffic. **Ojeks** wait around Pasar Pagi and the Mesra Plaza; **taxis** can be found west of Pasar Pagi on Jalan Veteran, or at the rank on Jalan Pangalima Batur.

The Dinas Pariwisata or Provincial **Tourist Office** is at Jalan Harmonika 1, off Jalan Suprato (☎0541/41669); ask for Pak Rosihan. Makila, Jl Pirus 168 (☎0541/75121), has Dayak contacts.

ACCOMMODATION AND EATING

Samarinda's best-value **accommodation** is *Pirus*, Jl Pirus 30 (☎0541/41873; ②), which has basic rooms and en-suite air-con ones. The nearby *Hayani*, Jl Pirus 31 (☎0541/42653; ②), is cool, tidy and quiet, and all rooms have a mandi. *Hidayah I* occupies a nice central location at Jalan Mas Temenggung (☎0541/31408; ③), with decent rooms, some air-con, but snotty staff. *Melati*, Jl Sulawesi 4 (☎0541/41043; ③), is modern and comfortable and also has some air-con.

There are cheap **warung** on Jalan Sulawesi, Jalan Jamrud north of Pasar Pagi and Jalan Khalid, opposite Mesra Plaza, with another row on Jalan Awang Long. *CFC*, Jl Sulawesi, is a bakery, coffee shop and fried chicken joint in one. At *Depot Handayani*, Jl Abul Hasan, opposite Jl Diponegoro, order off the main menu for grilled river prawns, and vegetables in peanut sauce with yellow rice. *Istana Iguana*, Jl Awang Long 22, specializes in seafood: prawns cooked with chillies, peanuts and mint is the highlight.

LISTINGS

Airline offices Bouraq, Jl Mulawarman 24 (☎0541/41105); DAS, Jl Gatot Subroto 92 (☎0541/35250); MAF, Jl Rahuia Rahaya, northwest of the airport off Jl Let Jend Parman (☎0541/43628); Merpati, Jl Sudirman 23.

Banks and exchange The BCA on Jl Sudirman has fair rates, with counter no. 2 for foreign exchange. ATMs are on the corner of Jl Sulawesi and Jl Panglima Batur.

Guides You'll need to find a guide in Samarinda if you're heading further upstream than Long Bagun on the Mahakam. The best are accredited by the Dinas Pariwisata so ask there or try at *Hotel Pirus*, where Andi Subagio is recommended, as is Sarkani Gambi (ask at the *Mesra*). Expect to pay Rp35,000 a day plus food and lodgings, or Rp50,000 a day all-inclusive.

Pharmacies Rumah Sakit Bhakti Nugraha on Jl Basuki Rachmat (☎0541/41363).

Police Jl Bhayangkara, 200m south of the cinema (☎0541/41340 or 41516).

Post office Corner of Jl Gajah Mada and Jl Awang Long.

Telephone services 24hr wartel on Jl Awang Long, across from the *Istana Iguana* restaurant, with a smaller office in the Citra Niaga plaza (8pm–midnight).

Travel agents Borneo Kersik Lluwai Tour & Travel, Jl Hasan 3 (☎0541/41486) can arrange most airline (including Royal Brunei, but not MAF) and Pelni tickets and private Mahakam cruises. Also good are Angkassa Travel, Jl Abul Hasan (☎0541/42098), though they don't deal with MAF or DAS.

Sungai Mahakam

Borneo's second longest river, the **Mahakam**, winds southeast for over 900km from its source far inside the central ranges on the Malaysia border, before emptying into the Makassar Straits through a multi-channelled delta. Closest to Samarinda, the Lower Mahakam is the most touristy area, and there's an established three-day circuit taking in the historic town of **Tenggarong** and Benuaq Dayak settlements at **Tanjung Issuy** and adjacent **Mancong**. With a week to spare, scanty forest and less cosmetic communities inland from the Middle Mahakam townships of **Melak** and **Long Iram** are within range; ten days is enough to include a host of Kenyah and Benuaq villages between Long Iram and **Long Bagun**, where the Upper Mahakam begins. Whatever your plans, bring as little as possible with you. A change of clothes, wet-weather gear, decent footwear, a torch and first-aid kit are adequate for the Lower and Middle Mahakam, as there are accommodation and stores along the way. Don't bother with a tent or cooking gear. There are **no banks** on the Mahakam capable of changing money. **Guides** are essential if you can't speak the language; hire one in Samarinda.

Mahakam transport

Crowded **public ferries** are the cheapest way to tackle the Lower and Middle reaches of the Mahakam. Passengers sit on the floor, though night services provide a bedroll on an upper, enclosed, level. Toilets are a simple bucket-and-hole affair at the back; some ferries also serve basic snacks, though hawkers are the main source of food. If you plan to disembark before the boat's ultimate destination, make sure that the pilot, not the ticket collector, knows.

Ferries leave Samarinda's **Terminal Sungai Kunjang** every morning for towns as far upstream as Long Iram; all services pause for half an hour at Tenggarong, a good alternative starting point. As all ferries depart at roughly the same time, if you get out at any stage you'll have to stop over for 24 hours until the next batch arrive. The following **schedule** from Samarinda is a guide only and varies according to the weather and number of stops: Tenggarong (3hr; Rp1000); Melak (24hr; Rp8000); Kota Bangun (10hr; Rp3500); Long Iram (30hr; Rp10,000); Muara Muntai (14hr; Rp5000); and Long Bagun (40hr; Rp15,000). To catch a ferry from smaller settlements you stand on the jetty and hail passing traffic.

A more luxurious option for seeing the Mahakam are **private houseboats**, which can be rented for about Rp150,000 a day through agencies in Samarinda and Balikpapan, and come complete with guides, cooks and private cabins. Away from the water, **buses** link Samarinda to Tenggarong and Kota Bangun, and are a useful shortcut.

Tenggarong

On from Samarinda, the river is broad and slow, with sawmills and villages peppering the banks. **TENGGARONG** is 45km and three hours upstream – or just an hour by road. This small country town was, until 1959, the seat of the Kutai Sultanate, whose territory encompassed the entire Mahakam basin and adjacent coastline. The former palace, just up from the docks, is now **Museum Negeri Mulawarman** (Tues–Thurs, Sat & Sun 8am–4pm, Fri 8–11am & 1.30–4pm; Rp300) on Jalan Diponegoro, and includes statuary from Mahakam's Hindu period (pre-fifteenth century), and replicas of fourth-century conical stone *yupa* which are Indonesia's oldest written records. Dayak pieces include Benuaq weaving, Kenyah beadwork and Bahau *hudoq* masks.

Tenggarong is a far more relaxed – and cheaper – place to stay than Samarinda. The **docks** are at the downstream end of town on Jalan Sudirman, which runs 250m north along the river, over a small canal, and on as Jalan Diponegoro past Seni Tepian Pandan marketplace and the museum. **Minibuses** to Samarinda orbit the roundabout near the docks, and the **tourist information** centre is at the back of the marketplace. **Accommodation** includes the clean and welcoming *Penginapan Anda II*, near the canal at Jalan Sudirman 63 (☎0541/61409; ②), and the more luxurious *Timbau Indah*, 250m south of the docks towards Samarinda at Jl Muksin 15 (☎0541/61367; ③). Overlooking the river about 50m beyond the museum, *Rumah Makan Tepian Pandan* has great Chinese and Indonesian **food**.

Kota Bangun and Muara Muntai

The river narrows perceptibly as it continues to **KOTA BANGUN**, a large, well-supplied town, four hours from Samarinda by bus. Ferries dock on the north bank, where you'll find **meals** and **beds** either off to the left at *Penginapan Mukjizat* (②), or ten minutes' walk along to the right at the comfortable *Sri Bangun Lodge* (③).

Beyond Kota Bangun, there's a definite thickening of the forest along the banks as the river enters the marshy lakelands, and you might see big black hornbills, symbols of the Dayak people. Around four hours from Kota Bangun and fourteen from Samarinda, **MUARA MUNTAI** sits due north of Danau Jempang, the town raised over the swamps on piles and boardwalks. Turn left from the dock and *Penginapan Nita Wardana* is about 50m along on the right, with *Sri Muntai Indah* just a bit further; both have tiny rooms with fans and essential mosquito nets (②). You can visit **Benuaq** settlements across the lake by *ces* speedboat (Rp20,000).

Tanjung Issuy and Mancong

Right out from Muara Muntai, watch for the slate-grey backs of *pesut*, freshwater dolphins and, in the woods, proboscis monkeys, as you pass through the channels into Danau Jempang's hundred square kilometres of reed beds, waterfowl and fishermen. It takes about an hour to reach **TANJUNG ISSUY**, a small township of gravel lanes, timber houses and fruit trees. Turn right off the jetty, past a couple of lumber yards, stores and workshops, and follow the street around to *Losmen Wisata*, a restored Dayak *lamin* (traditional house) maintained as tourist accommodation (②). It's not that "authentic", but the place is surrounded by carved wooden *patong* posts (spirit posts), and tour groups get Benuaq dances performed for them. Out the back is a six-tier mausoleum where Tanjung Issuy's founder was laid to rest in 1984, decorated with carvings of dragons, hornbills and scenes from reburial ceremonies. The *Rumah Makan Jempang Sejahtera* just down the street does chicken curry in the evenings. There's also an unrestored *lamin* with bigger patong to check out near Tanjung

Issuy's mosque, or spend the day a couple of hours' walk or *ces* ride south through farmland at **MANCONG**, a pretty Benuaq village built on boardwalks like Muara Muntai, whose own two-storey *lamin* can house two hundred people. **Continuing your journey** from Tanjung Issuy, you could either return to Muara Muntai, or hire a *ces* to take you across the forested northwest corner of Danau Jempang and back to the Mahakam west at Muara Pahu (Rp30,000).

Bontang

BONTANG is a sprawling township built around Pertamina's huge liquid gas refinery, two twisting hours by road from Samarinda. Bontang's **bus station** is 3km south of the centre. Buses run to and from Samarinda (2hr; Rp3700) until mid-afternoon, and during drier months there are daily kijang from the bus station north to Berau (12–24hr; Rp40,000). If you need to stay, there's the clean *Losmen Rahayu* (②) in rural suburbs about a ten-minute walk down Jalan Mulawarman, or catch a bemo to *Hotel Kartika*, Jalan Yani 37 (☎0548/21012; ③).

Berau

Three hundred kilometres north of Samarinda, the trading port of **BERAU**, alias Tanjung Redeb, is the place to catch marine traffic heading on up the coast to Tarakan. Berau's central core is a small grid of streets running back from riverbank Jalan Yani. **Pelni**'s *Awu* runs fortnightly from the port at Jalan Yani's western end to Tarakan, as part of a huge Sulawesi–Flores–Timor-Sumba loop (see "Getting around" pp.192–193 and "Travel Details" p.442); the Pelni office is here too. Other **boats to Tarakan and Samarinda** leave several times a week from the Jalan Yani waterfront, where owners post departure times on trees; fast craft to Tarakan charge Rp40,000 and take five hours, slower tubs cost Rp25,000 and take ten. If they're running, **buses** to Bontang leave early from the Jalan Guna market, 1km across town; buy tickets at the stop (Rp40,000). The **airport** is a ten-minute bemo or ojek ride to the south. The *Sederhana* and *Citra Indah* hotels can organize all flights. Running off Jalan Yani's western end, Jalan Antasari is where you'll find Berau's **accommodation**: right behind the docks, *Losmen Sederhana* (☎0554/21353; ③) is fine, the *Kartika* is a dive, but cheap (②), and *Hotel Citra Indah* (☎0554/21171; ⑤) has the best rooms. The *Citra Indah* has a restaurant and there are plenty of evening warung on Jalan Yani.

Tarakan, Nunukan and into Malaysia

A 24-kilometre spread of low hills just off the coast northeast of Tanjung Selor, Pulau Tarakan floats above extensive oil reserves: offshore rigs dot the horizon, while the west-coast town of **TARAKAN** is surrounded by smaller-scale "nodding donkey" pumps. It's a surprisingly brisk, busy place, just a stone's throw from **Pulau Nunukan** and the open **border with Malaysia**.

The Jalan Sudarso/Sudirman junction, 2km north of the port, marks the town centre. The **airport** is 2km north of town, Rp5000 by taxi. Wisma Murni Travel at the *Hotel Wisata* (☎0551/21697) can book flights to Samarinda, Nunukan and Balikpapan. All marine traffic docks at the southern end of Jalan Sudarso: **ferries** from Berau (Rp25,000–40,000) and Nunukan (about Rp15,000) use the jetty about 1.5km south of the intersection. The port, 500m further down, is served by **Pelni**'s *Kerinci*, *Tidar* and *Awu* to Balikpapan, Nunukan, Sulawesi and Java; see "Getting around" pp.192–193 and "Travel Details" p.442. The Pelni office is here too. Bemos around town are plentiful and cost Rp300 a ride.

There are numerous **places to stay**, mostly east down Jalan Sudirman within 150m of the centre. *Hotel Wisata*, Jl Sudirman 46 (☎0552/21347; ⑥), is a good standby; the adjacent *Orchid*, Jl Sudirman 171 (☎0551/21664; ④), is cheap and grotty, with Tarakan's best-value rooms a little further along at the tidy *Barito Timur*, Jl Sudirman 129 (☎0551/21181; ⑤). At the intersection on Jalan Sudarso, the *Kartika* is a fine Chinese **restaurant**, as are the *Cahaya* and *Anneka*, both along Jalan Sudirman. Good exchange rates and ATMs can be found at the BNI **bank** just south of the intersection and across from the police station on Jalan Sudarso.

Nunukan and the Malaysian border

Only 100km and half a day north of Tarakan, **NUNUKAN** is a busy, sleazy town on an island of the same name, right up against Malaysian **Sabah**. Crossing is straightforward: Nunukan's Immigration Department, Kantor Imigrasi, is about 200m from the port on the main road into town, and opens at 8am; it can take a few hours to sort out the paperwork, so if you get stuck overnight catch a bemo to the downmarket *Losmen Nunukan* (②) or, slightly better, *Idabus* (②). Once exit formalities are complete, Samudra Expres leaves Nunukan early afternoon for **TAWAU** in Sabah (2hr), where you'll be processed quickly by Malaysian officials.

SULAWESI

Sulawesi sprawls in the centre of the Indonesian archipelago, its bizarre outline resembling a 1000-kilometre letter "K", a foretaste of the many peculiarities that make this one of the country's most compelling regions. Nowhere in Sulawesi is much more than 100km from the sea, though an almost complete covering of mountains not only isolated its four separate peninsulas from one another, but also made them difficult to penetrate individually. Invaders were hard pushed to colonize beyond the coast and, despite echoes of external forces, a unique blend of cultures and habitats developed. By the time the Portuguese first marked Sulawesi as the "Celebes" on their maps during the sixteenth century, the island was ethnically divided much as it is today, with the south split between the highland **Torajans** and the lowland **Bugis**, various isolated tribes in the central highlands, and the Filipino-descended **Minahasans** in the far north. And it wasn't until the late nineteenth century that the Dutch decided to bring the whole island under their thumb.

The most settled part of the island, the south, is home to most of Sulawesi's fifteen million inhabitants, and the energetic capital, the port of **Makassar**. Rich in history, the southern plains rise to the mountain vastness of **Tanah Toraja**, whose beautiful scenery and unusual architecture and festivals are the island's chief tourist attraction. Those after a more languid experience can soak up sun and scenery at **Danau Poso** and the **Togian Islands**, and there's fabulous diving at **Pulau Bunaken**, out from the northern city of **Manado**. In many areas, Sulawesi's roads are well covered by **public transport**, though freelance kijang and minibuses are often faster and cheaper than scheduled buses. Where these fail you'll find ferries, even if services are unreliable. Crossed by the equator, Sulawesi shares its **weather** patterns with western Indonesia, with August through to November the driest time of year, and December to April the wettest. Tourism peaks with the European summer holidays (June–Sept) and Christmas, so April is the best time to see things at their greenest and least crowded.

Makassar

Set down at Sulawesi's southwestern corner and facing Java and Kalimantan, **MAKASSAR** (until recently known as Ujung Pandang) is a large, hot and crowded port city with good transport links between eastern and western Indonesia, and several attractions. More than anything, Makassar offers an introduction to Sulawesi's largest ethnic group, the **Bugis**, who continue to export their goods and presence well beyond Sulawesi in *prahu*, distinctive vessels with steep, upcurved prows. The city has a long and distinguished history as a crucial trading port and coastal defence.

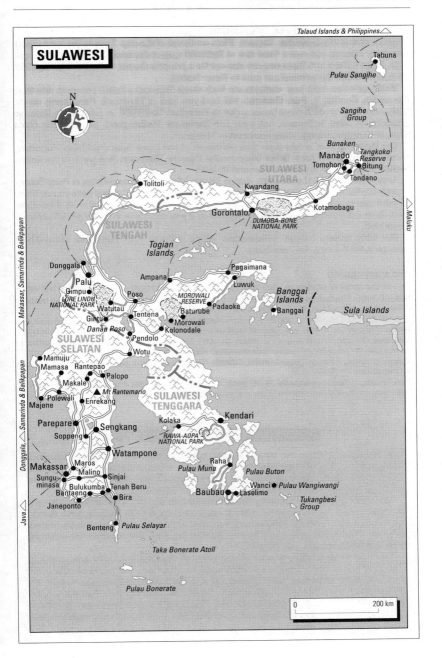

SULAWESI

N

Talaud Islands & Philippines △

Tahuna
Pulau Sangihe

Sangihe Group

Bunaken
Manado *Tangkoko Reserve*
Tomohon Bitung
Tondano

SULAWESI UTARA

Tolitoli
Kwandang
Kotamobagu
Gorontalo
DUMOGA-BONE NATIONAL PARK

△ *Maluku*

SULAWESI TENGAH

Togian Islands

Donggala
Pagaimana
Ampana
Luwuk
Palu
Gimpu
LORE LINDU NATIONAL PARK
Poso
MOROWALI RESERVE
Banggai Islands
Watutau
Padaoke
Sula Islands
Gintu
Tentena
Baturube
Danau Poso
Morowali
Kolonodale
Banggai
Pendolo

SULAWESI SELATAN

Wotu
Mamuju
Mamasa
Rantepao
Palopo
Makale
▲ Mt Rantemario
Polewali
Enrekang
SULAWESI TENGGARA
Majene

Kendari
Parepare
Kolaka
Sengkang
RAWA-AOPA NATIONAL PARK
Soppeng
Watampone
Raha
Makassar
Maros
Pulau Muna
Malino
Sungu-
minasa
Sinjai
Pulau Buton
Bulukumba
Tanah Beru
Wanci ● *Pulau Wangiwangi*
Bantaeng
Bira
Baubau Laselimo
Tukangbesi Group
Janeponto

Benteng *Pulau Selayar*

Taka Bonerate Atoll

Pulau Bonerate

△ *Makassar, Samarinda & Balikpapan*
△ *Donggala, Samarinda & Balikpapan*
△ *Java*

0   200 km

Arrival, getting around and information

Flights arrive at **Hasanuddin Airport**, 25km northeast of the city. Taxis to the town centre take forty minutes and cost a fixed fare of Rp23,000 (pay at the booth on the left of the exit hall). From 6.30am to 6.30pm you can also opt for a *pete-pete* (bemo; Rp700) or bus (Rp1500) from just beyond the terminal car park to Pasar Sentral.

Makassar's two main **bus stations** are both about 5km and a Rp350 pete-pete ride from the centre. Coming in from Rantepao will land you east at **Terminal Panaikang** on the Maros road. Most south-coast buses arrive at **Terminal Tamalate** on Jalan Gowa Raya (an extension of Jalan Sudirman), but some use **Terminal Mallengkeri**, also on Jalan Gowa Raya, or **Sungguminasa**, 10km southeast of Makassar.

The **Pelni** harbour is less than 1km northwest of the Pasar Sentral on Jalan Nusantara, served by becaks and taxis. Other boats dock at **Paotere Harbour**, 3km north of the centre; becaks will take you into town for around Rp1500.

Bemos here are called **pete-pete**, charge Rp350–700, and terminate either at Pasar Sentral or near Medan Karebosi. Shout your destination at drivers, who will either wave you on board or point you to other vehicles. Makassar's **becak** drivers are hard to shake off if you don't want them and often ignorant of your destination if you do; a fare of Rp500 per kilometre is reasonable.

The fairly useless **tourist information office** is inside Fort Rotterdam (Mon–Thurs 7am–2pm, Fri 7–11am, Sat 7am–1pm).

Accommodation

Few of the cheaper **places to stay** take foreigners, but mid-range ③–⑥ rooms are fair value.

Delta, Jl Sultan Hasanuddin 43 (☎0411/312711). Casual hotel recently given a face-lift to attract commercial travellers; comfortable, spacious rooms with all conveniences. ⑦–⑨.

Legend, Jl Jampea 5g (☎0411/328203). The city's budget standby, with basic, sticky dorms and doubles, a good central position, helpful staff, Internet facilities and heaps of information. Rp9500 for dorm-bed. ①.

Makassar Golden, Jl Pasar Ikan 50–52 (☎0411/314408). Makassar's best hotel has finer views and better service than the other luxury places. Accommodation ranges from doubles to seafront cottages. ⑧–⑨.

Makassar Royal, Jl Daeng Tompo 8 (☎0411/328488). Not cheap, but quiet, good-value rooms with air-con, bathrooms and TV. ②–③.

Puri Wisata, Jl Sultan Hasanuddin 36–38 (☎0411/324344). Nicely placed, welcoming and well-run hotel. Older rooms with fans, and doubles in the new wing with air-con. ②–⑤.

MOVING ON FROM MAKASSAR

Hasanuddin **airport** is the busiest in eastern Indonesia, with flights to Irian, Nusa Tenggara, Java, Kalimantan and abroad. To get to the airport from 6am to 6pm, catch the thrice-hourly Maros bus from Jalan Cokroaminoto on the west side of Pasar Sentral and tell the driver you want to be dropped at the airport (Rp1500).

Buses for Sengkang, Parepare, Tanah Toraja and many other destinations right up to Manado leave from Terminal Panaikang; catch a pete-pete from Pasar Sentral. For the south coast use Terminal Mallengkeri, Terminal Tamalate, or Sunguminasa's bus station, all of which can be reached by red pete-pete from the northeast corner of Medan Karebosi on Jalan Sudirman (Rp400).

From the Pelni harbour **ferries** run to ports all over Sulawesi, plus Java, Sumatra, Kalimantan, Bali, Nusa Tenggara, Maluku and Irian. The boats that call here include *KM Awu, KM Bukit Siguntang, KM Ciremai, KM Kambuna, KM Lambelu, KM Rinjani, KM Tatamailau, KM Tidar, KM Tilongkabila* and *KM Umsini*; see "Getting around" pp.192–193 and "Travel Details" p.442. The Pelni office is at Jl Sudirman 38 (☎0411/331401); tickets (Mon–Fri 8am–4pm) on ground level; top floor for timetables. Other boats use Paotere Harbour.

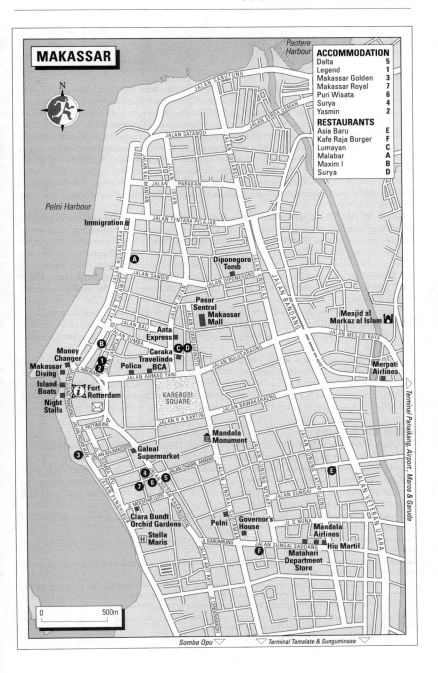

MAKASSAR

N

Paotere Harbour

ACCOMMODATION
Delta	5
Legend	1
Makassar Golden	3
Makassar Royal	7
Puri Wisata	6
Surya	4
Yasmin	2

RESTAURANTS
Asia Baru	E
Kafe Raja Burger	F
Lumayan	C
Malabar	A
Maxim I	B
Surya	D

Pelni Harbour

JALAN SABUTUNG
JALAN SERDA USMAN
JALAN SATANDO
JALAN SUD ARSO
JALAN NUSANTARA
JALAN KALIMANTAN
JALAN THAN
JALAN PARAKAN
JALAN TENTARA PELAJAR

Immigration

A

JALAN SANGIR
JALAN IRIAN
JALAN DIPONEGORO
JALAN ANDALAS
JALAN BANDANG

Diponegoro Tomb

Pasar Sentral
Makassar Mall

Mesjid al Markaz al Islam
JALAN MESJID RAYA

Anta Express
JALAN BALI
JALAN SUMBA
JALAN ANDREA
JALAN DORRIATOTO

B
Money Changer
Makassar Diving
Island Boats
Night Stalls

Caraka Travelindo
BCA
Police
JALAN AHMAD YANI
JALAN RIBURANE
JL RIBURANE

1
2

C D
JALAN BULUSARAUNG
Merpati Airlines

JALAN LILING PANDANG
Fort Rotterdam
i

KAREBOSI SQUARE

JALAN BAWAKARAENG
JALAN PATTIMURA
JALAN R A KARTINI

3
JALAN BALUMASSEP
JALAN PENGHIBUR
JALAN PASAR IKAN

Galeal Supermarket

Mandala Monument

JALAN CHAIRIL ANWAR
JALAN JENDRAL SUDIRMAN
JALAN GUNUNG LATIMOJONG
JALAN GUNUNG MRAPI
JALAN SUNGAI

4
7 6 5

E
JALAN VETERAN UTARA

JL MOCHTAR LUTFI
JALAN HASANUDIN

Clara Bundt Orchid Gardens
Stella Maris
H

Pelni
Governor's House
JL G NONA
Mandala Airlines

JL KARUNRUNG
JALAN SUNGAI SADDANG
F
Hiu Martil

Matahari Department Store

JL CENDRAWASIH
JL ARI FATE

0   500m

Somba Opu   *Terminal Tamalate & Sunguminasa*

Terminal Panaikang Airport, Maros & Garuda

Surya, Jl Daeng Tompo 3 (☎0411/327569). Tiled, pleasant place; all rooms with air-con, hot water and TV. ②.
Yasmin, Jl Jampea 5 (☎0411/320424). Friendly business venue with good new facilities and free airport pick-up. ⑦–⑨.

The City

A monument to Sulawesi's colonial era, **Fort Rotterdam** on Jalan Makassar (daily 7.30am–6pm, donation expected; museum Tues–Thurs 8am–1pm, Fri 8–10.30am, Sat and Sun 8am–noon, Rp750) was established as a defensive position in 1545 and enlarged a century later when the Dutch commander Cornelius Speelman rechristened it in memory of his home town. It remained the regional Dutch military and governmental headquarters until the 1930s. The fort's high, thick walls are its most impressive feature and worth climbing to get a look at the tall, white buildings inside. On the northwest side, Speelman's House – actually dating from after his death in 1686 – is the oldest surviving building, and nestles next to one half of **La Galigo museum** (Rp500), whose most interesting item is a prehistoric megalith from Watampone, and displays on local silk weaving, agriculture and boat-building.

South of Fort Rotterdam, Jalan Makassar runs down along the seafront as Jalan Penghibur, also known as **Pantai Losari**, which is famous for its evening food stalls. Parallel and just east of Jalan Penghibur, **Jalan Somba Opu** is known across Indonesia for its gold shops; other stalls sell silk from Sengkang, intricate silver filigree in the Kendari style, and potentially antique Chinese porcelain, all priced at about three times what you'd pay elsewhere. The street's southern end is crossed by Jalan Mochtar Lufti, down which you'll find the privately owned **Clara Bundt Orchid Gardens** at no. 15a (visitors welcome to look around).

Northwest of Medan Karebosi, and bordered by north-oriented Jalan Nusantara and Jalan Irian (aka Jalan Sudirohusodo), the **Chinese quarter** is worth a look for its half-dozen temples, decked in dragons and brightly coloured decor, which cluster along the lower reaches of Jalan Sulawesi.

From Pasar Sentral, catch a pete-pete heading 3km north up Jalan Sudarso to where Bugis prahu from all over Indonesia unload and embark cargo at **Paotere harbour** (Rp350 admission). Though the smell and lack of sanitation can be a bit much on a hot day, it's quite a spectacle when the harbour is crowded, the red, white and green prahu lined up along the dock wall with much shifting of bales, boxes, barrels and jerry cans on backs and carts.

Eating and drinking

For unequalled atmosphere and the lowest prices, try the after-dark alfresco **stalls** opposite Fort Rotterdam on Jalan Makassar. Another fine evening spot is the sea wall above Pantai Losari along Jalan Penghibur, whose kilometre-long string of mobile food carts sell more seafood, fried rice, noodles and cakes. One **bar** worth patronizing for sunset views and evening atmosphere is the *Taman Safari*, on the corner of Jalan Penghibur and Jalan Haji Bau, south of the Stella Maris hospital.

Asia Baru, Jl Gunung Salahutu 2. Inexpensive fish restaurant, whose menu classes items according to size and quantity of bones. Open daily 11am–2pm & 5–10pm.

Kafe Raja Burger, corner of Jl Merapi and Sungai Saddang. Indonesian versions of pizza and burgers, as well as usual rice-oriented selection.

Lumayan, Jl Samalona 9. Bugis-run restaurant offering well-priced servings of staples such as sate, excellent grilled fish, and nasi campur.

Malabar, Jl Sulawesi 290. Indian restaurant with functional decor and no vegetable, let alone vegetarian, courses. Otherwise, a short but very tasty menu offering crisp, light *martabak*, aromatic sate and curries, and *kebuly* rice specials (usually chicken korma) served noon to midnight on Friday.

Maxim I, Jl Sulawesi 42, corner of Jl Serui. Mid-range, sociable Chinese restaurant doing brisk trade in takeaways, and the finest pineapple chicken in Sulawesi.

Surya, Jl Nusakambangan 16. Nothing but mid-priced shellfish – great crab – and rice here.

Listings

Airline offices Garuda, Jl Pettarani 18b–c, just north of the post office (☎0411/433737); Mandala, Kompleks Latanette Plaza, Jl Sungai Saddang, near the Matahari Plaza (☎0411/325592), to Manado and Surabaya; Merpati, Jl Gunung Bawakareang 109, near *Ramayan Satrya* hotel (☎0411/442474), all destinations in Sulawesi; Silk Air, *Makassar Golden Hotel*, Jl Pasar Ikan 50 (☎0411/326733), to Singapore.

Banks and exchange Most banks in Makassar have ATMs, and many are located along the northern side of Medan Karebosi. BCA have good rates; the BNI, bad. The best moneychanger in town is Haji La Tunrung, in the building by the seafront at the southern end of Jl Nusantara.

Bookshops English-language novels, maps and guidebooks at Promedia, on the top floor of the Matahari Department Store on Jl Sungai Saddang.

Diving Makassar Diving, in the POPSA compound across from the fort at Jl Makassar 3 (☎0411/326056), takes qualified divers on day dives (US$50) and weekend trips to Speermonde.

Hospitals Stella Maris, Jl Penghibur (☎0411/854341). Your best chance in southern Sulawesi for correct diagnosis and treatment by English-speaking staff.

Immigration Jl Seram Ujung 8–12 (☎0411/831531). Not the easiest place in Indonesia to get a visa extended.

Internet access There are dozens of outlets in Makassar. The post office on Jl Slamet Riyadi charges Rp2500 for 15min; the International Net Center, Jl Irian 31/67, charges the same, and the connection is a little faster too.

Police Main office is on Jl Ahmed Yani.

Post office Jl Slamet Riyadi (Mon–Sat 8am–8pm, Sun 9am–3pm).

Telephone services International wartel booths on the western side of Medan Karebosi on Jl Kajaolaliddo, and also on Jl Bali, west of Pasar Sentral.

Travel agents Anta Express, Jl Irian 34a (☎0411/318648), or Sena, Jl Jampea 1a (☎0411/323906).

Bira beach

About 190km southeast from Makassar, tiny Bira is an unassuming group of wooden homes 4km north of **BIRA BEACH**, also known as Paloppalakaya Bay, where the blindingly white sand is fringed by heaps of tourist accommodation. Shallow water off the beach is safe for swimming, ending in a coral wall dropping into the depths about 50m from shore. Snorkellers can see turtles and manta rays here, with exciting diving deeper down featuring strong currents, cold water and big sharks. All accommodation rents out snorkels and fins, and both *Bira Beach* and *Anda Bungalows* have scuba gear and packages for qualified divers starting at US$35. The pick of the cheaper **places to stay** includes *Riswan Guest House* (①), a nice traditional Bugis house on a breezy hilltop with all meals included, and the cabins run by *Riswan Bungalows* (①) and *Anda Bungalows* (☎0413/82125; ②). More upmarket are *Bira Beach Hotel* (☎0413/81515; ③), chic cabins with sea views, with a travel agent and the only international public **telephone** in the area; and *Bira View Inn* (☎0413/82043; ③), bungalows with ocean views. From Makassar's Terminal Mallengkeri, **kijangs** (Rp10,000) to Bulukumba (5hr; Rp10,000) leave early in the morning, from where you can catch a bemo to Bira (Rp3500). There are **no banks** capable of exchanging foreign currency in the region.

Parepare

The port city of **PAREPARE**, four hours and 150km north of Makassar, is a friendly transport hub for buses to Rantepao and Tanah Toraja and boats to multiple destinations in Java and Kalimantan. Jalan Panggir Laut and Jalan Andi Cammi both follow the shore, with Jalan Hasanuddin and Jalan Baumassepe parallel and further inland.

Buses from Rantepao and Makassar arrive 2km south of town on the road to Makassar; catch a "Balai Kota" pete-pete to the centre. Transport from Sengkang draws into the eastern **Mapade terminal**, while the northern **Soreang terminal** serves buses from Polewali. The **port** and **Pelni office** are more central on Jalan Andi Cammi, with ticket agents and blackboard schedules for alternative maritime services on Jalan Baso Patompo. Pelni services *KM*

Kerinci, KM Binaiya and KM Tidar call in here; see "Getting around" pp.192–193 and "Travel Details" p.442.

Parepare's best **accommodation** is in the *Hotel Gandaria*, Jl Baumassepe 395 (☎0421/21093; ①–②), a clean gem; *Hotel Gemini*, Jl Baumassepe 451 (☎0421/21754; ①), is tattier but adequate. There's a popular night market off the northern end of Jalan Panggir Laut, and cheap **warung** dot the area, with excellent chargrilled fish and giant prawns at the black-glassed *Restaurant Asia* and less formal, open-fronted *Warung Sedap*, next to each other and opposite the *Hotel Siswa* on Jalan Baso Patompo. Sort out **money** at the BNI (with a Cirrus/Maestro ATM) on Jalan Veteran, north of the sports field. Your accommodation can advise on onward travel; as an alternative to slogging out to the terminals, some services can be hailed as they pass through the centre, and night buses to Makassar and Tanah Toraja accumulate around the *Hotel Siswa* in the afternoon.

Mamasa and around

Cocooned in a cool, isolated valley 1200m up in the mountains above Polewali, the **Mamasa region** – also known as **Western Toraja** – occupies a landscape of terraced hills with fairly easy hiking to numerous traditional villages, most of which feature extraordinary architecture and noticeably friendly people. Though culturally similar to their eastern neighbours in Tanah Toraja, Western Toraja's heritage is much lower-key; consequently, the hordes of foreigners are absent, and the area is welcoming without catering overly to mass tourism.

The only settlement of any size in the valley is **Mamasa**, reached either along a two- to four-day hiking trail from Tanah Toraja (see p.420) or **by road** from the coast via Polewali, covered by buses from Makassar and Rantepao. Vehicles also originate in **POLEWALI** itself, leaving whenever full; opt for a bus if possible, as minibuses are very cramped and on their last legs (95km; 5hr). If you need to stay in Polewali, the delightful *Hotel Melati* (☎0428/21075; ①) is at Jl Ahmed Yani 71, 300m east of where transport departs for Mamasa.

Mamasa

MAMASA is a spacious village of wooden houses beside Sungai Mamasa, where electricity and telephones are still very recent arrivals. The marketplace and most amenities are on Jalan Ahmed Yani, with everything else scattered around the perimeter of a large football field. A mosque sits in the shadows between the market and river, but Mamasa is predominantly Christian, and a white stone church dominates the slope above town. The twice-weekly market on Thursday and Sunday attracts people from distant hamlets often dragging their wares – including the heavy, boldly coloured **sambu blankets** (Rp70,000–Rp100,000) for which Mamasa is famed – into town on horseback.

Budget **accommodation** in Mamasa includes *Losmen Toraja Church* (①), a nice, bare couple of bungalows down near the river on the northern side of town; and *Losmen Marampan* and *Guesthouse Mini* (both ①), offering cosy rooms in old wooden houses near the market on Jalan Ahmed Yani. Slightly more upmarket, *Mantana Lodge* (①), around the corner from the market on Jalan Emy Salean, is good value with larger rooms. They all serve food and can organize **horses and guides** for the trail to Tanah Toraja.

Mamasa trails

Walking trails surround Mamasa, allowing for hikes of anything from two hours to three days or more. Scenery aside, one of the big attractions here are traditional houses, covered in carvings and adorned with buffalo horns like those in Tanah Toraja. Homemade **maps** available in Mamasa, at *Losmen Marampan*, for instance, show paths between villages, but don't distinguish between easily discernible tracks and those completely invisible without local knowledge. Some trails return to Mamasa, others terminate south of town at various points along the Polewali road, such as the open-air hot springs 3km south of town at **Mese**

Kada. Bemos run in both directions along the Polewali road (not all go as far as Polewali) at least until mid-afternoon. Wear shoes with a good grip, and take a torch, rainwear, food and drink, and a packet of cigarettes to share around.

THE LOKO CIRCUIT

There's a great four-hour **circuit from Mamasa** via **Loko**, involving much cross-country tracking. From Mamasa, aim across the river for **Tusan**, about fifteen minutes from Mamasa's market. Past here are some newish graves and two churches, before **TONDOK BAKARU**, whose wobbly houses are said to be the oldest in the valley. The most interesting is towards the far end of the village, a much-patched home under a twenty-metre roof covered in iron-wood shingles – a sign of status – with elaborate carved panels of buffalo, geometric patterns and birds. Bearing left into a creaking bamboo grove after Tondok Bakaru, follow a path downhill, across a covered bridge, then uphill again to **Rantebonko**. At this point the Loko trail simply vanishes into the fields, and you'll need continual help to know which of the instep-wide tracks to follow. But it's worth the effort: **LOKO** perches like an island on a hill-top, with fields dropping straight off the eastern side into the valley, sacrificial stones fronting its heavily carved houses, buffalo horns adorning their front posts. Continue south to Taupe, but the track is in no way clear and sometimes steep; **TAUPE** itself is not that engrossing. From here, there's a further 5km of cross-paddy weaving to the Polewali road via **Osango**, situated on the Polewali road 2km south of Mamasa, or a direct trail **back to Mamasa** which fizzles out mid-way, leaving you to chose your own path down the river, and into town behind the market.

AROUND RANTE BALLA KALUA

Mamasa's most-celebrated *sambu* weavers live southwest of town around the village of Rante Balla Kalua. Start by taking a bemo 9km down the Polewali road to **RANTE SEPANG**; cross Sungai Mamasa over a good suspension bridge and follow the path uphill for ten minutes to simply ornamented homes at **Sumua**. A kilometre further on, past **Tumangke**, eight house graves face west towards the hills. At this point the path bears right (ignore left fork) to **RANTE BALLA KALUA**, a large village of fifty homes surrounded by tall trees at the upper end of a small valley; among thatched dwellings is a row of three fine old houses and accompanying rice barns adorned with buffalo horns, pig-jaws stacks, and drums. Weavers or their agents will find you, invite you to sit down and start bargaining. A short walk downhill leads to more of the same at **BATARIRAK**, where you can stay in one impressive old building with dozens of ancestor carvings and horns. At this point there are two alternatives to backtracking to Rante Sepang: either spend ninety minutes following the usual obscure rice-field course northeast to **Lumbatu**, where a further hour will take you across to the Polewali road at Osango; or take a similar length of time to cover a nice trail southeast of Batarirak, via more graves and buffalo-horn-bedecked houses at **Buntu Balla**, and get back to the Polewali road some 14km from Mamasa at **Pena**.

RAMBU SARATU AND ON TO TANAH TORAJA

Mamasa's easiest trek follows the vehicle road for 3km north from town to alternative accommodation and a splendid traditional house at Rambu Saratu, past postcard-pretty scenery of vivid green fields and mountain slopes. After about half an hour you'll see a turning west across the river to **Kole** and *Mamasa Cottages* (⑥). Back on the main road, another ten minutes and you're at **RAMBU SARATU** (also known as **Rante Buda**), a name meaning something like "a hundred possibilities", referring to the number of interconnected families in this village. The main building here is magnificent, easily the finest traditional house in the whole Mamasa district: the body is 25m long and the roof extends this considerably, with every possible space on the front wall intricately carved. Visitors are often encouraged to spend the night here by the caretaker and his wife, who speak some English.

Beyond Rambu Saratu, there's a **hiking trail** 70km east **to Bittuang** in **Tanah Toraja**, possible either simply on foot or using ponies to help carry your gear. The walk spreads comfortably over three days, with regularly spaced kampung along the way, the homestays charging around Rp25,000 for room and board. Unfortunately, a road is currently being constructed along the same route, so your pleasant rural trek will probably be marred in places by the noise from heavy industrial machinery.

Following the road north past Rambu Saratu to **Timbaan** (27km from Mamasa), most of the first day is spent climbing steadily through pleasant rural scenes against a backdrop of low terraced hills, though the last 8km after **Pakassasan** feature a pass through the range with patches of forest. The next day follows the trail across two rivers (with a good swimming spot 12km along at the second) before a steep stretch to **Ponding** (40km), a possible first-day destination for the very fit. If you decide to end your trek here you can stay at *Ponding Peningapan* (Rp25,000), then catch the 8am jeep (Rp10,000) to Bituang. If you decide to walk on, 8km above Ponding lies **Paku** (48km), with more accommodation, while the final day enters pine plantations east of Paku, crosses another pass, then descends to the trailhead at **BITTUANG** (66km). Here you'll find more basic accommodation, a further two-day hiking track north to **PANGGALA**, or a bemo for the forty-kilometre run to **Makale** (see below).

Tanah Toraja

Some 250km north of Makassar, a steep wall of mountains marks the limits of Bugis territory and the entrance into the highlands of **Tanah Toraja**, a gorgeous spread of hills and valleys where fat buffalo wallow beside lush green paddy-fields and where the people enjoy one of Indonesia's most confident and vivid cultures. Anthropologists place Torajan **origins** as part of the Bronze Age exodus from Vietnam; Torajans say that their ancestors descended from heaven by way of a stone staircase, which was later angrily smashed by the creator Puang Matua after his laws were broken. These laws became the root of *aluk todolo*, the way of the ancestors, which, at its most basic, divides the world into opposites associated with directions: north for gods, south for humanity, east for life, and west for death. Only a fraction of Torajans now follow the old religion, the strict practice of which was prohibited after head-hunting and raunchy life-rites proved unacceptable to colonial and nationalist administrations. But trappings of the old religion are still an integral part of Torajan life: everywhere you'll see extraordinary **tongkonan** and **alang**, traditional houses and rice-barns, while the Torajan social calendar remains ringed with exuberant ceremonies involving pig and buffalo sacrifices. Torajans are masters at promoting their culture, positively encouraging outsiders to experience their way of life on its own terms. With easy access, Tanah Toraja is planted firmly on the agenda of every visitor to Sulawesi. Tour groups tend to concentrate on key sites, though it's not hard to find more secluded corners.

Tanah Toraja's main towns are the district capital of **Makale** and larger **Rantepao**, 18km further north along the Sungai Sadan valley. Rantepao's range of services makes it the favoured base for tourists, the bulk of whom descend for the major **festival season** between July and September, though the only really quiet time is from February to perhaps May. Expect hot days and cool nights; there is a "dry" season between April and October, but this is relative only to the amount of rain at other times, so bring non-slip walking boots and rainwear.

Tanah Toraja is known as **Tator** in the local idiom, and you should look for this on transport timetables. Daily Merpati **flights** from Makassar to Makale are very unreliable, and the surest way to Tanah Toraja is by **bus**, with Makale and Rantepao connected to points all over Sulawesi. From Makassar buses leave day and night from Terminal Panaikang.

Makale

MAKALE is a small town studded with churches and administrative offices set around a large pond and public square. Jalan Merdeka enters from the south into the square, while Jalan Pong Tiku exits north from the pond towards Rantepao. Every six days, Makale's large **market** fires up after about 9am, drawing people from all over southern Tanah Toraja to buy

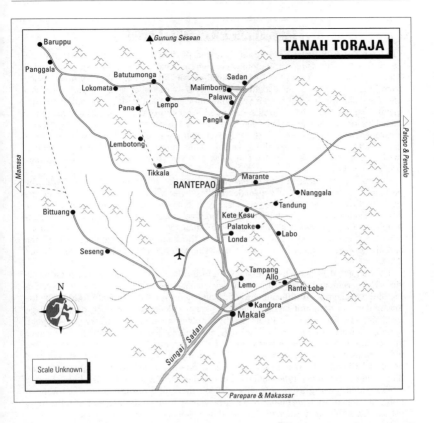

pigs, jerry cans of palm wine and other necessities. Long-distance traffic continues to Rantepao and there's little reason to stop overnight here, but you can **stay** at *Losmen Litha* (①) right on the square on Jalan Pelita (also the agent for buses back south), and better-value *Wisma Bungin* (①) on Jalan Pong Tiku; up near the mosque, the nasi campur-oriented *Idaman* is the cleanest place to eat. Moving on, **bemos** to Rantepao and other destinations – including Bittuang, trailhead for the three-day walk west to Mamasa – leave the square when full between dawn and dusk. Makale's **airport** is 5km northwest at Rantetaya, and taxis for Makale or Rantepao meet flights; Merpati's office is in Rantepao.

Rantepao

RANTEPAO is a prosperous market town on the rocky banks of **Sungai Sadan**, home to both the Sadan Toraja and, for half the year, swarms of foreigners. However unfavourably you view this, Rantepao has excellent facilities and a couple of sites within walking distance. West of the exhibition grounds and away from the couple of main streets, stalls supply locals' day-to-day needs – heavy stone rice mortars, plastic chairs, noodles, fish (couriered up from the coast by motorbike every morning), fresh noodles and tempeh, and chillies, with a warung or two for fried bananas and coffee. Rantepao's main **market** – the biggest in Tanah Toraja and located 2.5km northeast of the centre at Terminal Bolu – is a must: where else could you

TORAJAN FESTIVALS

Although **festivals** have been largely stripped of their religious meaning to become social events, witnessing a traditional ceremony is what draws most visitors to Tanah Toraja, particularly during the "peak festival season" in the agriculturally quiet period from June to September. Take a **gift** for your hosts – a carton of cigarettes, or a jerry can of *balok* (palm wine) – and hand it over when they invite you to sit down with them. Gift-giving is an integral part of Torajan ceremonies, an expression of the reciprocal obligations binding families and friends. Do not sit down uninvited, or take photos without asking; dress modestly, and wear **dark clothing** for funerals – a black T-shirt with blue jeans is perfectly acceptable, as are thong sandals. Most importantly, spend time at any ceremony you attend, drinking coffee and *balok* with your hosts, as too many tourists just breeze in and out.

Ceremonies are divided into *rambu tuka*, or smoke ascending (associated with the east and life), and *rambu solo*, smoke descending (west and death); all *rambu tuka* events begin in the morning, while the sun is rising, and *rambu solo* start after noon, when the sun is falling westwards. A typical *rambu tuka* ceremony is the **dedication of a new tongkonan**. Tongkonan design is credited to Puang Matua, the upcurving roof symbolizing the shape of the sky. They face north, so the front door is a gate between human and divine worlds, and are aligned north–south, defining a borderline between life and death.

The biggest of all Torajan ceremonies are **funerals**, the epitome of a *rambu solo* occasion. The ceremony is held over several days in a special field and starts with the parading of the oval coffin. At the end of the first afternoon you'll see **buffalo fights**. The following day – or days, if it's a big funeral – is spent welcoming guests, who troop village by village into the ceremonial field, led by a noblewoman dressed in orange and gold, bearing gifts of *balok*, pigs trussed on poles, and buffalo. The day after all the guests have arrived, the **major sacrifice** takes place: the nobility must sacrifice at least 24 buffalo, with 100 needed to see a high-ranking chieftain on his way. Horns decorated with gold braid and ribbons, the buffalo are tied one by one to a post and their throats slit, the blood caught in bamboo tubes and used in cooking. Finally, the coffin is laid to rest in a west-oriented house-grave or rockface mausoleum, with a **tau-tau**, a life-sized wooden effigy of the deceased, positioned in a nearby gallery facing outwards, and – for the highest-ranking nobles only – a megalith raised in the village rante ground.

pick up a bargain buffalo then celebrate your purchase with a litre or two of palm wine? It operates on a six-day cycle, and an entry fee of Rp2000 is demanded of foreigners.

An easy hour's **walk from Rantepao** follows Jalan Singki west across the river, and then bears right into the fields along the Sadan's west bank. Across the paddy, hamlets such as **Pa'bontang** are marked by stately tongkonan, but look for where a white mausoleum at **TAMBOLANG** stands below a cliff-side niche sporting rows of tau-tau and coffins. A path leads briefly south from here and then climbs through woodland to the summit of **Bukit Singki** and a view over Rantepao.

ORIENTATION, ARRIVAL AND INFORMATION

Rantepao stretches for 1km along the eastern bank of the Sadan. The central **crossroads** is marked by a miniature tongkonan on a pedestal: north from here, Jalan Mapanyukki is a short run of souvenir shops, bus agents and restaurants; Jalan Ahmed Yani points south towards Makale past more of the same to become Jalan Pong Tiku; east is Jalan Diponegoro and the Palopo road; while westerly Jalan Landorundun heads over to the riverside along the bottom edge of a large exhibition ground.

Long-distance **buses** will either drop you off at accommodation or in the vicinity of the exhibition ground or crossroads; likewise, bemos from the south or Palopo. **Bemos** from northern and northwestern parts of Toraja, however, may terminate either on Jalan Suloara, immediately north of town across the Sadan, or at **Terminal Bolu**, 2.5km northeast from the centre.

Moving on, for Parepare and Makassar, use Litha bus agent, across from the Abadi supermarket on Jalan Andi Mapanyukki, who run basic, comfortable and luxury buses (daily 7.30am–9pm). Departures north to Pendolo, Tentena, Poso and Palu are handled by a small depot just west along Jalan Landorundun. Bemos leave Jalan Ahmed Yani every few minutes for Makale, and just as often from riverside Jalan Mongsidi for Terminal Bolu.

For information, Rantepao's **tourist office** is at Jalan Ahmed Yani 62 (Mon–Fri 8am–4pm; ☎0423/21277), on the Makale side of town. Many tour agents and restaurants with **guide** services (Rp60,000 a day) also give out general information, but don't expect them to divulge festival details unless you've signed up with them.

ACCOMMODATION

Duta 88, Jl Sawerigading 12 (☎0423/23477). Welcoming, beautiful traditional-style bungalows in ideal central location. ②.

Hebron, Jl Pengangunan (☎0423/21519). Bright and friendly hotel with clean, spacious rooms, to the west of the football pitch. ①.

Hotel Indra, Jl Londurundun 63 (☎0423/21163). Chain of three closely grouped mid-range hotels, whose room prices and standards rise the closer you get to the river. *Indra City* offers a good deal (②); *Indra Toraja I* (③) and *Indra Toraja II* (⑥) are overpriced, though the latter has nice riverside rooms and Torajan dance nights.

Wisma Malita, Jl Suloara 110 (☎0423/21011). Extremely tidy, well-run backpackers' haunt; rooms come either with shared mandi, or with their own hot water. ①.

Minda Riska, Jl Niaga 18 (☎0423/25190). New, central place with decent singles and doubles. ①.

Nova, Jl Tappang (☎0423/23312). Rather grubby no-frills place, but cheap and popular with budget travellers. ①.

Pia Poppie's, Jl Pong Tiku 27 (☎0423/21121). One of Rantepao's older upmarket offerings: quiet, comfortable and nicely placed at the southern boundary of town. ①.

Pison, Jl Pong Tiku 8 (☎0423/21221). Across from *Pia Poppie's* and fairly similar; ordinary rooms set behind a nice spacious courtyard with rice barn. ②.

Pondok Pelangi, Jl Pengangunan 11a (☎0423/21753). Central, backstreet homestay, a little bit cramped but fair value. ①.

Surya, Jl Mongsidi (☎0423/21312). Along with neighbouring *Wisma Wisata* – and a fraction better – this is one of the nicest homestays in town and often booked out. ①.

Wisma Wisata, Jl Mongsidi 40 (☎423/21746). Plain cabins overlooking a small garden and stretch of river. ①.

EATING AND DRINKING

Torajans have two favourite beverages: locally grown arabica coffee, and **balok**, or palm wine, sold frothing in bamboo tubes. **Bars** such as the *Tiku Linu*, upstairs above the souvenir shops on Jalan Andi Mapanyukki, have loud music and are popular with Torajan youth, and foreigners who venture in are made welcome.

Indograce, Jl Andi Mapanyukki. Inexpensive Chinese food in spacious and bright surroundings, and the coldest beer in town.

Island Café, 3km north of Rantepao past Tallunglipu ("Pangli" bemo). Riverside open-air restaurant with a mix of Indonesian and pricey Western dishes.

Lisher, Jl Andi Mapanyukki 107. Good food, particularly Torajan items, and some of the lowest restaurant prices in town, but staff regard customers as a nuisance.

Martaallo café, Jl Ahmad Yani. Reasonably-priced place serving Torajan staples and a delicious toffee caramel.

Rainbow, at *Pondok Pelangi*, Jl Pengangunan 11. Slow service, but a fine kitchen; try the garlic beans and chewy buffalo sate.

Rimiko, Jl Andi Mapanyukki 115. Restaurant with small and overpriced Indonesian and Torajan menu, but nevertheless serving some excellent food; their chicken curry is something to write home about.

Setia Kawan, Jl Andi Mapanyukki 32. Slightly pricey Indonesian–Chinese place, but a favourite spot for Westerners to sit for an hour over a coffee or cold drink and peruse the newspapers.

LISTINGS

Airlines Merpati are in a high-rise shack about 1.5km south of Rantepao, the last building on the western side of the road. There's no computer link here, and confirmations are extremely unreliable. Your accommodation place can organize transport to the airport, 13km southwest.

Banks and exchange The BRI and BNI on Jl Ahmed Yani offer good exchange on currency and travellers' cheques. Rantepao's official moneychangers are not reliable, however.

Hospital The best doctors are at Elim Hospital, Jl Ahmed Yani.

Maps Travel Treasure Maps' "Tanah Toraja" sheet shows distances, villages, important sites and heaps of local information. Cheapest at Abadi supermarket and *Setia Kawan* restaurant.

Post office Jl Ahmad Yani. Mon–Thurs 8am–2pm, Fri 8–11am, Sat 8am–1pm.

Telephone services At Jl Ahmed Yani (8am–late). Toraja Permai Tours and Travel, next to the Abadi supermarket on Jl Andi Mapanyukki, have good international phone rates.

Touring Tanah Toraja

There's a morbid attraction to many of Tanah Toraja's sights, which feature ceremonial animal slaughter, decaying coffins and dank mausoleums spilling bones. Fortunately, the people and landscape are very much alive, and there's nothing depressing about spending time here. **Entry fees** of a few thousand rupiah are becoming common at sites around Rantepao. If you speak a little Indonesian, **guides** are seldom necessary for hiking or visiting villages, though outsiders should really have an **invitation** to visit a ceremony, which guides can provide. As more participants means greater honour, however, it's also possible to turn up at an event and hang around the sidelines until somebody offers to act as your host.

Bemos to just about everywhere originate at Rantepao's Terminal Bolu, though those heading south can be hailed on Jalan Ahmed Yani; the further you're going, the earlier you should start looking for transport. Accommodation and tour agents also rent out **bicycles** (Rp20,000 a day), **motorbikes** (Rp50,000), or **minibus/car and drivers** (Rp90,000). Hikers heading off to villages should carry cigarettes, if only to initiate conversations.

RANTEPAO TO MAKALE

Tanah Toraja's most famous sites lie off the eighteen-kilometre Rantepao–Makale road. Just south of Rantepao, a concrete statue of a pied buffalo marks the four-kilometre road east to four much-restored tongkonans at **KETE KESU** (Rp3000). The central one is said to be the oldest in the district. An adjacent rante ground sports a dozen megaliths, the tallest about 3m high, with a path leading up the hill past hanging and no-longer-hanging coffins mortised into the side of the truncated peak.

Back on the Makale road, a signpost at 5km prompts you east towards **Londa** (Rp3000), a twenty-minute walk from the highway. A shaded green well underneath tall cliffs, overhung with a few coffins and a fantastic collection of very lifelike tau-tau, Londa boasts two **caves** whose entrances are piled high with more coffins and bones, all strewn with offerings of tobacco and booze. **Guides** with pressure lamps (Rp7500) are a necessity for venturing inside the labyrinth.

At around 8km from Rantepao, a trail heads up to a **swimming hole** in the forest at **Tilangnga**. Around halfway to Makale, another road runs 1km east to **LEMO** (Rp3000), past a church curiously designed in the shape of a boat. Lemo is famous for the sheer number of its much-photographed tau-tau, set 30m up on a flat cliff-face; they're not as sophisticated as those at Londa but more expressive, mutely staring over the fields with arms outstretched. There are also several dozen square-doored mausoleums bored straight into the rock face.

EAST TO NANGGALA, AND NORTH TO SADAN

If you're pushed for time, you can see almost all the main features of Torajaland at **MARANTE**, a spread-out village 6km east from Rantepao on the Palopo road. Close to the road are a fine row of tongkonan; behind, a path leads to where tau-tau and weathered coffins face out over a river. **NANGGALA**, about 11km along the Palopo road and then 2km south, is a stately village whose dozen brilliantly finished tongkonan are a splendid sight. There's a very pleasant five-hour walk due west to Kete Kesu from here, via **Tandung** village and a couple of small lakes.

For something a bit different, spend a day making the slow haul from Rantepao's bemo terminal **north to Sadan**. Seven kilometres along the way you pass **PANGLI**, famed for its *balok*. Not much further, a rante ground with thirty upright stones marks the short track to **PALAWA**, whose tongkonan are embellished with scores of buffalo horns stacked up their tall front posts, while in the hills beyond the village are babies' graves, wooden platforms in the trees. Five kilometres more brings you to a fork in the road: east is **SADAN** itself, with another market every six days; west is riverside **MALIMBONG**, famous for its ikat.

NORTHWEST TO BATUTUMONGA

The area northwest of Rantepao surrounding Gunung Sesean, the region's highest peak, is quite accessible but not overly explored. There's a smattering of morning traffic about 17km to **LEMPO**, which has a great series of moss-ridden tongkonan. **Accommodation** in the area provides the perfect rural base: before Batutumonga, a sign points to basic bamboo rooms at friendly *Mama Siska's* (① including meals); *Mentirotiku* (②), a little further along, is a smart, pretentious affair with cosy accommodation in tongkonan or cabins. Around the corner is **BATUTUMONGA** itself, where there are further comfortable cabin/tongkonan homestays at *Londurunden* (①) or *Mama Rima's* (①).

Gunung Sesean's 2328-metre **summit** can be reached in a couple of hours from Batutumonga; your accommodation place can point you to the nearest trails. Another fine walk from Batutumonga can take you **back to Rantepao** in under four hours; take the road through Batutumonga until you see about thirty small megaliths in a ring, then follow the footpath opposite downhill. This brings you to a hamlet where you'll have to turn sharp right across the fields to where a broader trail continues down to woodland at **PANA**, the site of some very old, well-camouflaged graves, and a big rante ground with four-metre-high megaliths. From here the track onwards is unmistakable. Not far along the road is **Lembotong**, a kampung famed for its blacksmiths. The remainder of the walk down to the flat fields below is less interesting, and you end up at **TIKKALA**, where you'll find bemos for the seven-kilometre ride back to Rantepao's Jalan Suloara.

The Poso Valley

The hundred-kilometre-long **Poso Valley** is set in the ranges of the Mangkutana Mountains and provides superlative hiking. Domain of the Pomona, a Christianized offshoot of the Torajans, the valley's flooded upper reaches form 35 kilometre-long **Danau Poso**, drained by a river that flows out of the top end of the lake past Tentena and follows the valley north to the coast at Poso town. Set on the lake's sandy southern shore, the tiny village of **PENDOLO** is a practical spot to break your journey. The best places to stay in Pendolo itself are *Pondok Wisata Victory* (①) and *Pondok Masamba* (①), which both enjoy beachside locations on Jalan Pelabuhan; further east, *Pendolo Cottages* (①) has nicer wooden cabins with balconies facing north over the water. All supply filling meals and advice on boat rental and hiking. Moving on, **minibuses** leave early for Mangkutana (where you can find more of the same to Palopo), or Tentena (3hr, Rp10,000). There are also boats plying the route across the lake to Tentena (3hr, Rp20,000). Seasonal water levels dictate which of Pendolo's two **jetties** is in use; one is in the town, the other 2km east near *Pendolo Cottages*.

Tentena and around

Surrounded by clove, cocoa and coffee plantations, scruffy **TENTENA** sits right where the lake empties into Sungai Poso. Exploring the lake is the main pastime, but make sure you also spend half a day at **air terjun Salopa**, an enchanting waterfall (Rp1000) alive with butterflies and birds up against the hills 15km west of town – catch a bemo from the far side of the bridge for the twenty-minute haul to **Tonusu**, then walk the last 4km through fields and groves of fruit trees.

Everything you'll need in Tentena is in a close grid of streets on the eastern side of Pomona Bridge. Most **places to stay** are south of here off Jalan Yos Sudarso, including the basic but clean *Sinar Abadi* (☎0458/21031; ①), at Jl Sudarso 2, and *Moro Seneng* (☎0458/21165; ①), just around the corner on Jalan Diponegoro; in a higher bracket, helpful management and airy rooms make *Hotel Victory* (☎0458/21392; ①), next door, one of the best choices in town, while *Natural Cottages*, at the junction with Jalan Yani and Yos Sudarso (☎0458/21311; ②–③), has unobstructed views over the lake. *Hotel Victory's* **restaurant** has the most hygienic kitchen, but spicy Padang fare at *Moro Seneng* on Jalan Sudarso tastes better and is a touch cheaper. The Ebony Visitor Information, two streets behind *Pondok Remaja* on Jalan Setia Budi, is where to find advice, transport and **guides**, with alternatives offered by *Natural Cottages* and *Hotel Victory*.

Poso is served by a continual stream of minibuses from Tentena's **bus terminal**, 2km north of town. There are also departures at least daily to Pendolo, but for direct services to Rantepao or Makassar, go first to Poso and look for further transport there. **Ferries to Pendolo** leave from the shore off Jalan Yos Sudarso.

Poso

POSO is an orderly port on the south side of Tomini Bay, a vast expanse of water encircled by Sulawesi's eastern and northern peninsulas. It's a major transport hub, but has no attractions to keep you here. On the northern side of Sungai Poso you'll find the port at the end of Jalan Sudarso, which runs south for 500m to a riverside roundabout. Poso runs weekly uncomfortable and unreliable **ferries** to and from Ampana, Gorontalo, Katupat and Wakai; the current schedule is chalked up outside the port, but there are better alternatives from Ampana (for the Togians) and Pagaimana (Gorontalo).

Minibuses from Tentena and some services from the eastern peninsula buses arrive at the **bus depot** about 2km east of the port. Jalan Kalimantan crosses the river into the southern side of town. About 200m down Jalan Kalimantan, Jalan Sumatra branches west for 1km, passing a knot of services before heading out of town past bus company offices and the **main market** – you might get dropped off here if you're coming in from Palu. **Bemos** run between the eastern bus depot and market all through the day (Rp350), as do ojeks.

The most handy **accommodation** is south of the river: *Hotel Alugoro* at Jl Sumatra 20 (☎0452/23736; rooms with fans and mandi Rp20,000 per person) is great value and almost always full, its overflow handled by the slightly less salubrious *Beringin* (☎0452/21851; Rp15,000–45,000) opposite. North of the river on Jalan Agus Salim, *Hotel Kalimantan* (☎0452/21420; Rp17,500–25,000) and *Hotel Bambu Jaya* (☎0452/21570; Rp30,000–100,000) are a little run-down but comfortable, though the *Kalimantan* sits opposite a huge and busy mosque. Poso's **post office** is also north of the river on Jalan Tadulako, as is the Telkom office, round the corner on Jalan Urip Sumoharjo, and moneychanging facilities at Bank Dagang Negara, Jl Hasanuddin 13. **Information** is on hand at the Dinas Pariwisata at the junction of Jalan Sumatra and Jalan Kalimantan (☎0452/21211). **Eating** out, try the *Pemuda*, next to the cinema on Jalan Sumatra, for fine nasi goreng and sweet-and-sour prawns, or the *Pangkep*, on the Jalan Sudarso roundabout, with excellent seafood.

When it comes to **moving on** from Poso, **minibuses** to Tentena (2hr) and **buses** for the east-peninsula towns of Ampana and Pagaimana and all points south to Makassar leave from the eastern bus depot. For Palu, use one of the bus companies on Jalan Sumatra.

Palu

At the base of the northern peninsula and the mouth of the Palu Valley, **PALU** sits in one of the driest areas in Indonesia, surrounded by fields of bleached brown grass and prickly-pear cactus. There's little to do here save getting a connection to the beaches at nearby Donhhala. Palu's centre is a small area on the eastern bank of the river around the junction of Jalan Sudirman and Jalan Hasanuddin, which crosses west over the river into a commercial district along Jalan Gajah Mada and Jalan Bonjol. For an insight into the region, catch a microlet southwest of the centre to the **Museum of Central Sulawesi** (Tues–Sun mornings; Rp200) on Jalan Sapiri, whose front lawn has full-sized concrete copies of Lore Lindu's megaliths. Inside, you'll find ceramics, bark cloth, and some beautiful local silks. There are also wooden coffins and clay burial jars from the Poso Valley's Pamona population.

PRACTICALITIES

Pelni vessels *KM Kambuna, KM Kerinci* and *KM Tidar*, from Makassar, Bitung, Kalimantan and Java dock 30km north of town at **Pantaloan harbour**; see "Getting around" pp.192–193 and "Travel Details" p.442. **Mutiara Airport** is 7km southeast – microlets or taxis will be waiting. Bemos from Donggala use **Terminal Inpres**, on the southwest side of town; buses from destinations between Manado and Makassar use **Terminal Masomba**, 2km southeast of the centre. **Microlets** (bemos) run within the city boundaries for a fixed Rp400.

You'll find cheaper **lodgings** in the city centre, including the convenient *Purnama Raya*, Jl Wahidin 4 (☎0451/23646; ①), a popular budget standby with rather stuffy rooms but English-speaking management. North a little, *Hasanah*, Jl Cut Nyak Dien 19c (☎0451/22225; ①), is a small, friendly, family-run place with simple but roomy doubles and a mostly local clientele. The best mid-range hotels are clustered together 1km southeast of the centre along **Jalan Kartini**, not too far from Terminal Masomba. These include the standard Chinese-owned *Hotel Sentral*, at no. 6 (☎0451/22789; ②), with a booking agent, coffee shop, supermarket and all rooms with air-con, mandi and TV. **Buana**, at no. 8 (☎0451/21475; ②), is a neat hotel where all rooms have air-con and TV; and **Kartini**, at no. 12 (☎0451/21964; ②–③) has old but decent en-suite rooms, some with air-con, off a central courtyard.

To eat with locals it's worth tracking down the nocturnal **grilled-fish stalls** near the cinema on Jalan Heyun and overlooking the bay on Jalan Moili. Otherwise, *Depot Citra*, Jl Hasanuddin Dua, serves *cap cai*, nasi/mie goreng, sate, grilled prawns and iced fruit drinks, *Oriental*, Jl Hasanuddin Dua, does an authentic Chinese menu, and *Ramayana*, Jl Wahidin, serves very good Chinese-Indonesian fare. For snacking, the chocolate and cream cakes at *Golden Bakery* on Jalan Wahidin can't be beaten.

LISTINGS

Airlines Bouraq, Jl Juanda 87 (☎0451/22995), to Makassar, Manado and Kalimantan; Merpati and Garuda at Jl Mongsidi 71 (☎0451/21172), to Makassar. There's also a Merpati agent on Jl Hasanuddin.
Banks and exchange Good rates for cash at Bank Exim, Jl Hasanuddin; and for travellers' cheques, go to the BNI on Jl Sudirman.

MOVING ON FROM PALU

Pelni ferries leave from **Pantaloan harbour**, 30km north of town. The Pelni office in Palu is at Jalan Kartini (☎0451/23237). **Bemos** to Donggala leave from Terminal Inpres; **buses** to destinations between Manado and Makassar use Terminal Masomba, 2km southeast of the centre. You can also go direct to bus companies: Jawa Indah (Jl Hasanuddin, across from Merpati and the Exim bank) for all stops to Rantepao and Makassar; and Alugoro (office 2km north of city on Jalan Sudarso) for Poso, Ampana and Pagaimana.

Hospital Hospital Undata, Jl Suharso 33 (☎0451/21270).
Immigration Jl Kartini (☎0451/21433).
Post office The most central branch is on Jl Sudirman (daily 7am–6pm); the GPO itself is several kilometres southeast of the centre on Jl Mohammed Yamin.
Telephone services The Telkom office is on Jl Ahmed Yani.
Travel agents Avia Tour, Jl Moh Hatta 4 (☎0451/26985), for all airlines and Pelni.

Donggala

The sleepy port of **DONGGALA**, 40km north of Palu, is a peaceful town, and the perfect place to unwind for a few days, checking out the shallow-draft Bugis schooners in the harbour, or enjoying the shallow seas hereabouts. **Minibuses** take under an hour to get here from Palu's Terminal Inpres, dropping you at the bus terminal just short of Donggala, where a dokar or ojek can cart you into town. Alternatively, a **taxi** from Palu can deliver direct to accommodation places, which, excepting no-frills *Losmen Bhakti* (①) on Jalan Samauna, are all about 2km north of town at **Tanjung Karang**, a rocky headland with some gorgeous beaches. If you want to scuba **dive**, *Prince John Dive Resort* (US$122; price includes everything except beer) has all the facilities, and its bungalows overlook the reef; otherwise, there are cheaper, but good options nearby at *Natural Cottages* (① including meals, open to negotiation) and *Harmoni Cottages* (①).

Ampana

Five hours east of Poso along a road crossed by a handful of flood-prone rivers, **AMPANA** is a dusty little hole whose bus station, market and Pertamina fuel storage tanks are the focus of a tumbledown port area from where most transport to the Togian islands departs. There's a private **homestay** (①) around the side of the bus station, or walk about 300m west past the port, market, and over a small bridge to Jalan Kartini, where you'll find reasonable doubles at *Losmen Irama* (①) and *Hotel Oasis* (☎0464/21058; Rp12,500 dorm; ②). On the corner of Jalan Kartini, *Rumah Makan Mekar* (6am–11pm) serves good food. Ask at the port about **ferry schedules** to the Togian islands (see below) – there's transport to Wakai (5hr) most days from here, though some boats to Bomba (5hr) leave from about 3km east of town, best reached by dokar or ojek.

The Togian Islands

The **Togian Islands** form a fragmented, 120-kilometre-long crescent across the shallow blue waters of Tomini Bay, their steep grey sides weathered into sharp ridges capped by coconut palms and hardwoods. The exceptional **snorkelling and diving** around the islands features turtles, sharks, octopus, garden eels, and a mixed bag of reef and pelagic fish species. On the down side, there are also nine depots in the Togians dealing in the live export of seafood to restaurants in Asia; many of these operations employ cyanide sprays, which stun large fish but kill everything else – including coral.

From west to east, **Batu Daka**, **Togian** and **Talata Koh** are the Togians' three main islands. The main settlements here are **Bomba** and **Wakai** on Batu Daka, and **Katupat** on Togian. Wakai is something of a regional hub, with transport out to smaller islands. There are no vehicle roads or widespread electricity in the Togians and, with all travel by boat, you'll find it pays not to be on too tight a schedule; most accommodation places offer day-trips and shared transfers. Tourism in the islands is budget-oriented but good, and prices usually include meals. July through to September are the coolest months, when winds interrupt ferries and make for poor diving.

Even scheduled public **inter-island transport** services are notoriously unreliable. Aside from the weekly Poso–Gorontalo ferry, which stops in Ampana and then travels

Wakai–Katupat–Malenge–Dolong–Gorontalo before returning along the same route, at the time of writing you could (with luck) count on the following: Ampana–Wakai/Wakai–Ampana (5 weekly; Rp11,000); Ampana–Bomba/Bomba–Ampana (daily; Rp11,000); Wakai–Bomba/ Bomba–Wakai (daily; Rp10,000); Wakai–Katupat/Katupat–Wakai (3 or more weekly); Wakai–Kadidiri/Kadidiri–Wakai (daily; free/Rp2500 depending on accommodation at Kadidiri); Wakai–Malenge/Malenge–Wakai (1–2 weekly). Elsewhere, there's bound to be something along eventually if you can afford to wait, or you can **charter** a motorized outrigger at about Rp20,000 an hour.

Around the islands

Three hours from Ampana and at the western end of Batu Daka, **BOMBA** comprises two dozen houses and a mosque facing north across a pleasant bay. There's a long beach 5km west of town, but it's the sea which warrants a visit here, with the Togians' best snorkelling an hour distant at **Catherine reef**. The coast roundabout is interesting, too, with the possibility of seeing crocodiles in remote inlets, and some islets east of Bomba completely covered by villages, their sides reinforced with hand-cut coral ramparts. In Bomba itself, dockside *Losmen Poya Lisa* (①) is a fine **place to stay** with excellent food; immediately offshore on a hump of rock and trees, *Sicilia Bungalows* (①) has friendly management and a monopoly on views; opposite *Sicilia* is a small stretch of sand and cabins (①) on little **Pulau Poya**; or try the unusual *Tandongi Homestay* (①), built out in the bay over a reef. **Ferries** back to Ampana and on to Wakai leave Bomba most mornings.

At the eastern end of Batu Daka, about five hours from Ampana and two from Bomba, **WAKAI** is similar to the dock area at Ampana, though with far better accommodation at the white timber *Togian Islands Hotel* (②). New arrivals from Ampana heading to **KADIDIRI** should go straight to the hotel for transfers. Half an hour by motorized outrigger from Wakai, Kadidiri is one of the nicest of the islands, 3km long and with fine beaches and ample lodgings. The best accommodation is provided by the *Kadidiri Wakai Cottages* (①), whose safety-conscious **scuba** team, led by an English expat, organizes dives to nearby reefs such as Taipi Wall, as well as the submerged wreck of a B-24 fighter plane or volcanic Pulau Una-Una. Nearby is the excellent-value *Lestari Cottages* (①). Just offshore, there are secluded cabins on **Pulau Taipi** (②), run by Wakai's hotel and, if you stay here, transport between Wakai and Kadidiri is free (otherwise, it's Rp2500).

Pagaimana

Five hours east of Ampana lies the small Bajau town of **PAGAIMANA**, a dense collection of houses built over the water next to a busy port. From here the overnight **ferry to Gorontalo** (10hr) departs on alternate days. Buy an ekonomi fare (Rp27,500) at the harbour, and then negotiate a cash donation with the purser for a mattress on the floor of the air-con first-class room. If you've just arrived from Gorontalo, you'll be grabbed and ushered towards a host of minibuses heading to Ampana and Poso.

Gorontalo

GORONTALO is a pleasant, sleepy Muslim city with useful ferry links to Pagaimana and Ampana and buses to Manado. It's centred on the Mesjid Baitur Rahi which stands at a wide crossroads. Jalan Basuki Rahmat runs north of here, though the main road out of town in this direction is parallel Jalan Sam Ratulangi, two blocks further west; Jalan Sultan Botutihe heads east, past a hospital, south are businesses along Jalan Ahmed Yani, while Jalan Hasanuddin points west through Gorontalo's commercial district and over the river.

Weekly **ferries** to and from Poso, Bomba, Wakai and Ampana, and services every other day to and from Pagaimana dock 7km southeast at Gorontalo's port. The nearest **Pelni** port is at Kwandang, two hours' north, which runs a monthly service to Palu, Makassar (two days), Kalimantan and Java on *KM Umsini*; see "Getting around" pp.192–193 and "Travel Details" p.442. The ticket office is at Jl 23 Januari 21, near the Telkom office.

All long-distance **buses**, including those to and from Manado and Makassar, use **Terminal Andalas**, 3km north of the centre. Kijangs, microlets and ojeks service all transport terminals; the city's **microlet terminal** is 1km north at Pasar Sentral on Jalan Sam Ratulangi.

Most **places to stay** are south of the mosque. A favourite is *Hotel Melati* at Jl Gajah Mada 33 (☎0435/822934; ①–②); rooms in the older colonial wing are more charming and cheaper. There are big rooms and aged fittings at *Penginapan Teluk Kau*, Jl Sungai Parman 42 (☎0435/822093; ①), though they occasionally refuse foreigners; and mid-range comforts at friendly *Hotel Saronde*, Jl Walanda Maramis 17 (☎0435/821735; ①–②). All **banks** are on Jalan Ahmed Yani. The **post office** is on the corner of Jalan Ahmed Yani and Jalan 23 Januari, while the **Telkom** office is just west of here at Jl 23 Januari 35. For something **to eat**, night stalls set up south off Jalan Hasanuddin on Jalan Pertiwi, and there's fine sate at the tiny *Warung Kita*, across from the mosque on Jalan Suprator. For something better, head north off Jalan Sultan Botutihe to the *Boulevard* on Jalan Merdeka, with cold beer, juicy grilled fish and karaoke.

Manado

Capital of Sulawesi Utara, **MANADO** is chiefly of interest as the departure point for spectacular **diving and snorkelling** at nearby Bunaken Marine reserve. You can either base yourself in Manado and do day-trips to the reefs, base yourself just outside Manado at one of the dive resorts which offer all-inclusive packages or, the cheapest but least reliable option, base yourself on Pulau Bunaken itself (see p.432). Day-trips from the mainland cost from US$65 for two dives, plus US$30 for full equipment. Blue Banter, Floor 2, Novotel, Jalan Piere Tandeau (☎0431/862135), has good equipment, facilities and dive crew.

Downtown Manado is a couple of blocks of markets, squares and roundabouts on the north side of the city immediately below a shallow, silted **harbour**, with other businesses south of here along the first kilometre of Jalan Sam Ratulangi, which runs parallel to seafront Jalan Piere Tandeau. There's actually little to see here, aside from the fish market at Pasar Bersahati on the north side of the harbour. Manado's **microlets** converge downtown at the top of Jalan Sam Ratulangi at **Pasar 45** ("Pasar Empat Lima"), an area of back-lane stalls, supermarkets and ferry agents next to the dock.

Practicalities

Sam Ratulangi airport is 12km northeast of Pasar 45; taxis and touts meet new arrivals, or take a microlet to Terminal Paal Dua. Long-distance **buses** to and from Gorontalo and Makassar stop on Manado's southern outskirts at **Terminal Malalayang**; Paris Express have air-con and Marina have older buses. Microlets #1, #2, #3 and #4 run between here and Pasar 45. Minibuses to and from the Minahasa highlands arrive southeast at **Terminal Karombasan**; microlets #9, #13, and "Wanea" run from here to Pasar 45. Services to and from Airmadidi, Girian from Bitung (the regional Pelni port) use **Terminal Paal Dua**, from where microlet "Paal II-Pasar 45" runs to Pasar 45.

The **Pelni** office is opposite Telkom on Jalan Sam Ratulangi, and organizes tickets out of Bitung. For tickets and schedules for **boats** from Manado to Tahuna on Sangihe Island, Lirung on Pulau Talaud, and Ambon, try agents in the streets between Pasar 45 and the dock.

ACCOMMODATION

Hotel Celebes, Jl Rumambi 8 (☎0431/870425). Backing onto the harbour, within 100m of Pasar 45, this place has tiny ekonomi singles (Rp25,000), and better en-suite air-con doubles. ①–③.

Hotel Manado Bersahati, Jl Sudirman 20 (☎0431/855022). One of the best budget deals in town, offering bicycle rental and local info. Basic rooms plus some with air-con. ①–②.

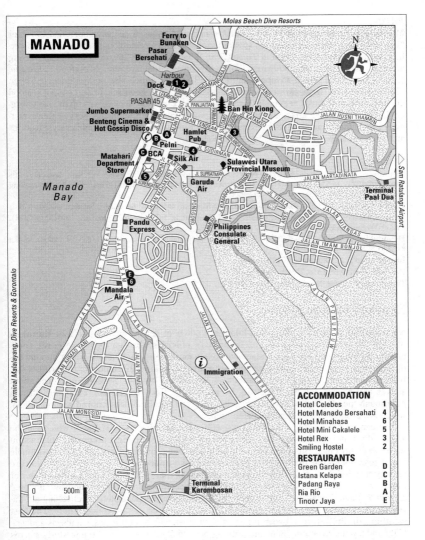

Hotel Minahasa, Jl Sam Ratulangi 199 (☎0431/862059); 1500m south of Pasar 45 on microlet #1, #2, #3 and #4 route. Unusually atmospheric, older hotel with attentive staff. ②–④.

Hotel Mini Cakalele, Jl Korengkeng 40 (☎0431/852942). Old, tidy and friendly, with quieter rooms out the back facing onto the garden. Doubles with mandi. ①–③.

Hotel Rex, Jl Sugiono 3 (☎0431/851136). Very clean and fairly priced, if somewhat cramped. Singles Rp15,000; doubles with fan or air-con. ①–③.

Smiling Hostel, Jl Rumambi 7 (☎0431/868463). Right next to the harbour; helpful, laid-back staff, low prices and an informative noticeboard go some way towards compensating for the dingy rooms and rats. Dorm-bed Rp9500. ①.

EATING
Minahasan cooking features dog (*rintek wuuk* in Minahasan, usually shortened to *rw*, or "airway"), rat (*tikkus*) and fruit bat (*paniki*), generally unceremoniously stewed with blistering quantities of chillies. Try it at *Tinoor Jaya*, Jl Sam Ratulangi 169, or at the cheap warung around Pasar 45 and Jalan Sudirman. For more conventional fare, there's seafood at *Ria Rio*, Jl Sudirman 3 and *Istana Kelapa*, Jalan Pierre Tendean, which also serves imported beer. The Chinese-run *Green Garden*, Jl Sam Ratulangi 52, does good mid-priced soups, seafood and *sayur lohan* (monks' vegetables), while the *News Café* next door serves up the best burgers in the city. *Padang Raya*, across from Telkom on Jalan Sam Ratulangi, serves above-average Padang meals, some of them extremely hot. You can sit down to European-style pastries and coffee at *Bakeri Batavia*, on Jalan Sam Ratulangi.

LISTINGS
Airlines Garuda, Jl Diponegoro 15 (☎0431/851544), to Makassar; Mandala, Jl Sam Ratulangi 206 (☎0431/851324), to Makassar; Merpati, Jl Sudirman 132 (☎0431/864028), to Ternate; Silk Air, Jl Sarapung 5 (☎0431/863744), to Balikpapan and Singapore.
Cash advance BCA, Jl Sam Ratulangi, across from Matahari (Mon–Fri 8am–2pm, Sat 8am–noon).
Consulates Philippines Consulate General, Jl Lumimuut 8, PO Box 1079, Manado (☎0431/862181). Rp250,000 for a sixty-day visa.
Hospital Public hospital 6km south of the city beside Terminal Melalayang (☎0431/853191); take microlet #1–4 from Pasar 45.
Immigration Jl 17 Augustus (☎0431/863491).
Post office GPO Manado, Jl Sam Ratulangi 21.
Telephone services Telkom, Jl Sam Ratulangi 4.

Bunaken Marine Reserve

Northwest of Manado, a 75-square-kilometre patch of sea is sectioned off as **Bunaken Marine Reserve** and promoted as Indonesia's official scuba centre, where **coral reefs** around the reserve's four major islands drop to a forty-metre shelf before falling into depths of 200m and more, creating stupendous reef walls abounding with Napoleon (maori) wrasse, barracuda, trevally, tuna, turtles, manta rays, whales and dolphin. Set aside concerns about snakes and sharks and avoid instead the metre-long Titan triggerfish, sharp-beaked and notoriously pugnacious when guarding its nest; and small, fluorescent-red anemone fish, which are prone to giving divers a painful nip.

You can visit the reserve in two ways, either on day-trips from Manado, which can be arranged privately or through dive operations, or by staying at budget accommodation within the reserve on Pulau Bunaken. If you need any training, qualified assistance or reasonable rental gear, opt for one of the pricier, professional **dive operators** in Manado itself. If you are already certified, have your own equipment and accept that you are not hiring a divemaster or instructor but only a dive guide of unknown competence, then save money by shopping around on Pulau Bunaken. In either case you must assume responsibility for checking out the **reliability** of rental gear and **air quality**, the two biggest causes for concern here. The best **weather conditions** are between June and November, with light breezes, calm seas and visibility underwater averaging 25m and peaking beyond 50m. Try to avoid the westerly storms between December and February and less severe, easterly winds from March until June.

Pulau Bunaken and around
About an hour by ferry out from Manado, **Pulau Bunaken** is a low-backed, five-kilometre-long comma covered in coconut trees and ringed by sand and mangroves. There's a **public ferry** (Rp2500) from the dock behind Manado's Pasar Bersehati daily at 8am (get there 30min early), and plenty of private boat owners (Rp40,000). Either way, you end up at **Bunaken village** on the island's southeastern tip, from where the ferry returns to Manado

at 7.30am. Here you'll be met by pushy homestay touts; places described below draw generally good press and are clustered in two groups within a couple of kilometres of the village, providing rooms with shared mandi (Rp30,000 per person), cottages with own mandi (Rp45,000 per person), all meals and some snorkelling gear. On the east coast, **Pangalisang beach** is quiet and, though some feel that the reef is patchy and the sand compromised by too many mangrove trees, has fine drop-offs; recommended places to stay include *MC's* (the most popular), *Daniel's*, *Lorenzo's* (top food), *Doris* and *Panorama*. Western **Liang beach** is the most popular spot, with fewer trees and Bunaken's best coral 100m offshore; *Papa Boa*, *Yulin*, *Tante Nona* and *Ibu Konda* are the pick of the homestays here.

At the time of writing, the most popular dive schools were Seabreeze, Immannuel, the long-established Froggies (☎0431/3478) and Scubana, whose divemaster, Randi Montalalo, has been diving nearly every day for about twenty years. Two dives start from US$40 all-inclusive, though Froggies charges an exhorbitant US$75. Rental gear on Bunaken is in short supply and bad repair. Off the west beach between Bunaken village and Liang beach, **Lekuan 1, 2** and **3** are exceptionally steep, deep walls, and the place to find everything from gobies and eels to deep-water sharks. Further around on the far western end of the island, there are giant clams and stingrays at **Fukui**, while **Mandolin** is good for turtles and occasional mantas, and **Mike's Point** attracts sharks and sea snakes.

Bitung

The fifty-kilometre highway running east across the peninsula from Manado to Bitung is covered by frequent minibuses from Terminal Paal Dua. These wind up at **Terminal Mapalus**, from where a microlet will carry you the final 5km into **BITUNG**. The **Pelni** port is on Jalan Jakarta, with departures on *KM Ciremai, KM Kambuna, KM Tilongkabila* and *KM Umsini* down Sulawesi's east coast to Makassar and Kadidiri, and further afield to Java, Kalimantan, Maluku, Irian and the Philippines; see "Getting around" pp.192–193 and "Travel Details" p.442. Organize tickets and timetables either in Manado or try the Pandu Express office here at Jl Sukarno 5 (☎0438/30480).

There are a handful of places to **eat** on Jalan Sudarso – the *Remaja Jaya* is a pricey Chinese place serving big portions – but Bitung's accommodation is pretty dire and new arrivals should catch a microlet from Jalan Sukarno back to Terminal Mapalus, where minibuses to Manado await.

To the Sangihe-Talaud Islands and the Philippines

The 500-kilometre straits separating mainland north Sulawesi and the Philippines is dotted with the seventy-odd islands of the Sangihe-Talaud group, which have regular boat connections with both Indonesia and the Philippines. There are two main groups: southernmost are the loosely scattered Sangihe Islands, with the capital of **TAHUNA** on **Pulau Sangihe** itself within a two-hour bemo ride of waterfalls and jungle at Tamako, where you'll find losmen **accommodation** at *Rainbow* or *Fret's*. Northeast of Sangihe, and within about 150km of the Philippines, the Talaud Islands are a compact little group, with the main settlement of **LIRUNG** on central **Pulau Salibau**. Lirung's accommodation places include *Penginepan Sederhana* and the *Chindy*.

There are three passenger boats a week each way between Manado and Tahuna, one a week between Manado and Lirung.

Currently, there are no passenger ferries to the Philippines, though regular **cargo ferries** run between Bitung and **General Santos**, a few hours south of Davao, and will take passengers for around US$30 and take two days. It's an incredibly rough ride: bring a sleeping mat, a tent (if you have one) and plenty of comfort food. Ask at the *Smiling Hostel* in Manado for details. Filipino immigration board the boats on arrival in General Santos and generally hand out three-week visas on the spot.

IRIAN JAYA

The island of **New Guinea**, the second largest in the world, is neatly bisected down its north–south axis, the eastern portion comprising independent Papua New Guinea and the western half, **Irian Jaya**, belonging to Indonesia. From the towering glacial highlands of its spine to the sweaty mangrove swamps of the coast, Irian Jaya is one of the world's last great wildernesses: maps of the area still show stretches as wide as 300km without any relief data at all. Despite numerous attempts by Western explorers to tame Papua, the colossal island all but repelled them right up until the latter part of the twentieth century. On Indonesian **Independence**, it seemed logical that West Papua should itself become independent. After all, the capitals of Jakarta and Jayapura are as far apart as London and Baghdad. However, while the Dutch prepared the island for union with Papua New Guinea, the Indonesians, with the collusion of the US, planned to ensure that every part of the old Dutch East Indies would become Indonesian. On November 19, 1969, the UN passed a resolution to endorse an **Indonesian occupation** of West Papua, on the understanding that a Vote of Free Choice would be held within six years. The vote was stage-managed by the Indonesians and West Papua was ceded entirely to the Indonesians, to be renamed Irian Jaya, or "Victorious Irian". Since then, tribal villages have been bombed and napalmed, and local leaders tortured, executed or dropped out of helicopters. The cleansing, or pacification, of native people in Irian paved the way for the largest **transmigration** scheme the world has ever seen, with four million new inhabitants in little over a decade. An estimated 300,000 Papuans have lost their lives to the Indonesian tyranny, and 15,000 are refugees in New Guinea. The **OPM** (Organisas Papua Merdeka), or Free Papua Movement, is still particularly active in the jungles of the Lorentz reserve and parts of the Bird's Head; kidnapping foreigners is their means of drawing attention to their cause and common sense is your best precaution.

However short, a trip to Irian Jaya requires more **planning** than any other destination in Indonesia. The first complication is the **surat jalan** (travel permit) that must be acquired from the police by every visitor on arrival in Irian, with signed permission for each and every one of the small districts you wish to visit. Apply for every feasible destination, as you can't add places to your *surat jalan* outside of the large towns. **Photography** in Irian is also a different proposition to other parts of Indonesia. No matter what they say, most X-ray machines at airports are not film-safe; take films out and have them searched by hand. Take great care when photographing people; in areas where photography is rare it can cause great distress, and in areas where it is common, permission and cash are expected first. Bring all camera film to Irian with you. **Prices** in Irian are a shock after the rest of Indonesia. There is almost no industry on Irian Jaya and everything but a few foodstuffs is imported at great expense by boat or plane from other areas of Indonesia. A lousy fleapit hotel costs twice as much in Irian as a reasonable guesthouse anywhere else; food and fuel are also expensive as they have to be imported. Chartering transport and hiring guides is likely to be the greatest expenditure: up to US$50 for a day in a canoe, or US$500 in a motorized outboard.

The majority of visitors will arrive, after an eight-hour flight from Java or Bali, via Makassar, in the capital city **Jayapura**, the best place to arrange an onward flight to the **Baliem Valley**, the highland plain that is home to the Dani tribes, and which features the most highly dramatic scenery imaginable.

Sentani and around

The vast majority of visitors to Irian will first arrive at Sentani airport, which also services Irian's capital town of Jayapura. Little more than a cluster of buildings around the airport, **SENTANI** is 30km away from Jayapura and a nicer, quieter place to stay, but travellers will still have to call at the capital to arrange a **surat jalan** (see above), change money and get visas for Papua New Guinea.

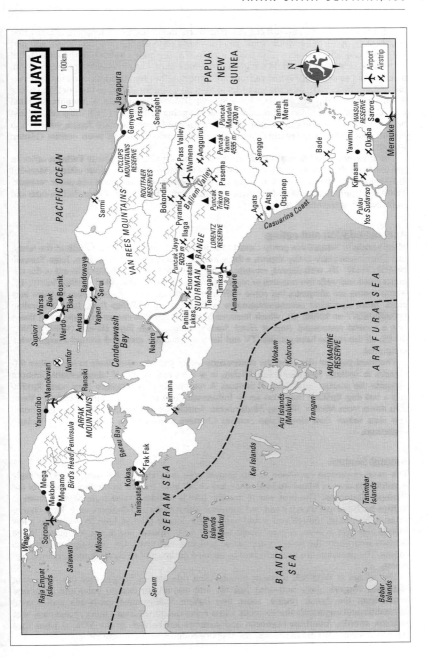

Garuda and Merpati have offices at the **airport**, and though they'll probably insist that you go to Jayapura to buy your ticket, you can check on availability, reserve a seat and find out about cancellations here. The police station is at the main entrance to the airport, but at the time of writing you could not get a *surat jalan* here – worth checking though. If you plan to head straight **to Jayapura** from the airport, either hop in a taxi outside the terminal (35min; Rp25,000), or walk out to Jalan Sentani Chimera (600m to the north) and flag down a minibus (known as *taksi*) heading east. This will terminate at Abepura terminal (30min; Rp800), but if you tell the driver you are going to Jayapura he'll drop you off just before, from where you can catch a taksi on to Entrop (20min; Rp500). Again, you need to get off just before the terminal, and take another taksi into the town centre (15min; Rp350).

The **taksi terminal** lies 1500m to the west of the airport. The 24-hour **Telkom** office in Sentani is on the way north from the airport to the main road. The **post office** (Mon–Sat 8am–5pm) is on the main road to Jayapura, Jalan Sentani Chimera, and has poste restante. There is a **Bank Exim** just east of here on the same road, which will change dollars cash and some brands of travellers' cheques.

Accommodation and eating

Most **hotels** in Sentani are pretty close to the airport and will send staff to wait at the terminal. The closest place to the airport, a three-minute walk east, is *Hotel Semeru*, Jalan Yabasco (☎0967/91447; ②), with decent, en-suite rooms with fan or air-con. Turn right out of the terminal gates and walk five minutes to reach *Mansapur Rani*, Jl Yabaco 113 (☎0967/91219; ①), where rooms are adequate, but come with fan and mandi; this is a good place to leave baggage. More upmarket accommodation is available at *Hotel Ratna Dua*, Jalan Kalurakan (☎0967/92277 or 92496; ⑥), which features beautiful, sizeable rooms with gleaming floors and a central restaurant. And at *Hotel Sentani Indah*, Jalan Raya Hawaii (☎0967/91900; ⑧–⑨), all the rooms have satellite TV and hot water and are arranged around a large swimming pool.

The most popular place and the **restaurant** where you are most likely to meet other foreigners in Sentani, *Rumah Makan Mickey*, is at the western end of Jalan Sentani Chimera opposite the junction with Jalan P Sentani. A reasonable cheeseburger here costs Rp4750 and a hot dog Rp3000; they also serve Indonesian food and some Chinese dishes. About 20m down from *Mickey*, *Warung Madurantna Sentani* serves Javanese deer sate and excellent *ikan bakar*. East along Jalan Sentani Chimera from *Mickey*, *Sederhana* is a Padang restaurant.

Around Sentani

The most rewarding excursion in the Sentani area is to **Danau Sentani**, an exceedingly beautiful expanse of island-studded azure and cobalt blue, framed by the lower slopes of the Cyclops Mountains. The best way to see the lake is to take a taksi from Sentani down to **Yahim harbour** and then try and find someone with a motorized dugout canoe. They charge about $12 an hour, though you would need a little longer than an hour to get out to a few islands and take a swim. A good island to head for is **Apayo**, one of the few places in the Sentani area where the people still practise sculpture and distinctive paintings on bark canvasses. The paintings are characterized by stylized geckos and snakes painted in natural pigments.

The village of **WAENA**, a twenty-minute taksi ride east of Sentani, has the interesting **Museum Negeri** (daily 8am–4pm; Rp200), with several *bisj* (totem) poles and decorated skulls from the Asmat region, some fine Baliem Valley stone axe-heads and several ammonites and mammoth sharks' teeth. Other relics document Irian's more recent past, with samurai swords, American bayonets, and cannons left behind by the VOC (United East Indies Company). To get there, take an Abepura-bound taksi from Sentani.

Jayapura

Huddled in a narrow valley between jungle-covered hills, **JAYAPURA** is Irian Jaya's tiny capital city and major port town. Most people acquire their *surat jalan* at the police station, and all Pelni ferries leave from the harbour. The two main streets of Jalan Achmad Yani and Jalan Percetakan run parallel to each other and at right angles to the seafront. Pretty much every place you will need is within walking distance of here, one exception being the **tourist office** (Mon–Fri 8am–5pm; ☎0967/35923), 3km northwest of the waterfront on Jalan Soa Siu: take a taksi heading northwest from town and ask for Kantor Dinas Parawisata. The **University of Cenderawasih Museum** (Tues–Sat 8am–4pm) between Jayapura and Abepura, has an excellent collection of artefacts from around Irian, with a good deal of *bisj* poles and other carvings from the Asmat region.

Practicalities

It is not necessary to have a **surat jalan** to visit Jayapura, but you can get one for the rest of the country at the **police station** on Jalan Achmad Yani near the Bank Danamon. You need two passport-sized photos (get them from the camera shop 50m southwest on the same street) and about Rp2000; the process rarely takes longer than an hour. Write down every single destination you could conceivably want to visit in Irian. Once the form is processed, photocopy it several times (several nearby shops have copiers); it's much easier to hand in photocopies at the many regional police stations than to risk leaving the original.

The main **post office** is on the waterfront at Jalan Koti, and the 24-hour **Telkom** next door. As there are no **banks** for exchange in the Baliem Valley, you should do any credit-card transactions, ATM and dollar exchange at the Bank Danamon at the sea end of Jalan Achmad Yani, or Bank Exim on the same street. The BNI on Jalan Percetakan may change travellers' cheques in currencies other than US dollars. The hospital, *rumah sakit umum*, is 3km east of town: catch a taksi going northeast round the bay. The **Papua New Guinea consulate** is at Jalan Percetakan 28, by the *Hotel Dafonsoro* (Mon–Fri 8am–9pm). To obtain your three-month **visa** (Rp20,000), you'll need a return plane ticket for PNG, your passport and two photos.

PT Kurera Jaya at Jalan Achmad Yani 39 (☎0967/31583) sell Garuda, Bouraq and Merpati **plane tickets** and are far better for information and tickets for **Pelni** boats than the out-of-town Pelni office. Pelni boats *Ciremai, Dobonsolo, Rinjani* and *Umsini* all call in at Jayapura; see "Getting around" pp.192–193 and "Travel Details" p.442. PT Kurera Jaya also arranges diving (US$55 for two tanks), rafting on the Baliem river, and walking and bird-watching tours. The **Merpati Office** is at Jalan Achmad Yani 15 (Mon–Thurs 8am–3pm, Fri 8am–noon, Sat 8am–1pm, Sun 10am–noon).

ACCOMMODATION AND EATING

Jayapura doesn't have any good-value **accommodation**; even in the larger, smarter hotels it's essential to check your room before signing in. Easily the best place for budget travellers, *Hotel Kartini*, Jl Perintis 2 (☎0967/31557; ①), has friendly staff and clean rooms, but is usually full. *Hotel Sederhana* occupies a good situation close to the seafront at Jl Halmahera 2 (☎0967/31561; ②–④), with very basic doubles through to en-suite air-con options. All rooms at *Hotel Metoa*, Jl Achmad Yani 14 (☎0967/31633; ⑦–⑧), have air-con and hot-water baths.

Night warung along Jalan Irian, at the waterfront and at the end of Jalan Achmad Yani, sell the usual Indonesian snack. Clean, cool *Cafeteria Bahari*, Jl Setiapura 10, provides a variety of dishes such as mixed tofu and fried chicken; the air-con *Pramont Rumah Makan*, Jl Koti 124, has karaoke and hostess girls, and an extensive menu of seafood cooked in Chinese and Javanese styles. *Hotel Metoa*, Jl Achmad Yani 14, stocks a good variety of well-prepared Indonesian foods at high prices plus hamburgers, stuffed tomatoes, steak and seafood. *Prima Gasten* bakery, opposite the *Hotel Metoa*, serves excellent coffee, cakes, puddings and sandwiches.

The Baliem Valley

Today's visitors to the **Baliem Valley** will have their first glimpse of it from the plane, as the undulating jungle-covered mountains abruptly plunge into an unexpected and remarkable landscape. All of a sudden, harsh cliff-faces fall away to a cultivated plain: a chess board of terraced fields, divided by rattan fences to keep the pigs out and the crops segregated. Sprinkled over the valley floor are jumbled assemblies of thatched *honai* huts. Most travellers to Jayawijaya regency, as it is known, come here to encounter the inhabitants of the valley, the **Dani**. These proud people have managed, in the face of continued government and missionary pressure, to maintain a culture of incredible depth and beauty. Whilst the warlike nature of the Dani lives on only symbolically in dance and festival, for the most part they still live by the same methods as have existed in the valley for thousands of years. They mostly shun Western clothes, the men dressing solely in a penis gourd (*horim*), with pig teeth pushed through their noses and their bodies decorated in clay-and-grease warpaint.

The first Western encounter with the peoples of the Baliem Valley didn't happen until **1938**, when the millionaire Richard Archbold saw the cultivations from his seaplane while on a reconnaissance mission for the American Museum of Natural History. He returned and made a successful expedition, but it was not until the 1960s that the missionaries and Indonesian officials started to trickle in. The Indonesians have since made huge logging commissions in Dani areas, which have now almost entirely cleared the Baliem Valley of forests. The summer of 1997 saw the beginning of one of the harshest periods in memory for the peoples of the central highlands. The El Niño weather system was blamed for the terrible destruction all over the island. **Fires** started by slash-and-burn farmers raged out of control, and such a vast amount of smoke poured into the air that for months the haze blocked out the sun, and visibility in Wamena was down to a few hundred metres. By the end of 1997, after four rainless months in the usually lush valley, over five hundred people had starved to death in the Wamena area. Summer smoke haze and its knock-on effects have become quite regular since. Whilst the thickest smoke has been in Kalimantan and northern Sumatra, it's much more of a problem for travellers here, as almost all travel is by air. It may soon be the case that July to September become months when travellers should steer well clear of travel in Irian.

The Tribes of the Baliem

The people of Jayawijaya regency can be subdivided into many different groups, but the three broadest tribes are the Dani, Western Dani or Lani, and the Yali. **Dani** people are instantly recognizable, because they use the thin end of a gourd for their *horim*: the length of the gourd encloses the penis and points it upwards in a permanent erection. Dani headdresses are made of cockerel feathers in a fetching circular crown. Dani women wear knee-length skirts, traditionally made of grass, and usually go bare-chested. All women are considered to be witches in the highlands, with powerful magic that increases with age.

The **Yali**, who come from the east of the Baliem, have a different kind of *horim*. They use the thick end of the gourd but it points straight out at right angles to the body from beneath a rattan skirt. The **Lani** cover their heads in a spray of cassowary feathers, which spills out over the head and hair. Their *horim* are also made from the thick end of the gourd but are secured around the waist by a wide, brightly coloured sash. Often the top of their gourd is used as a pouch for money or tobacco.

Even during freezing cold evenings, valley peoples remain practically naked, coating their bodies with insulating pig fat. The traditional **weapon** of the valley is the bow and arrow. A four-pronged arrow is for shooting birds, three prongs are used to fish, a single bamboo is used on pigs, and a shaft of wood or bone is for people.

Wamena

At first sight, the town of **WAMENA** appears to be the only blot on the wonderful rural landscape of the Baliem Valley, with characterless tin-roofed buildings and slurry-filled drainage trenches. But it's a spacious place, and missionary houses lie on manicured lawns behind white picket fences, amongst the strolling, naked Dani and their ubiquitous pigs. The town rarely suffers the daytime swelter of sea-level towns, and at night you'll need a blanket. The **marketplace** is a real attraction, stocked with snakes, frogs, Baliem river goldfish, cuscus and *horim* penis gourds, and alive with Dani and Lani peoples in traditional dress (expect to pay at least Rp1500 if you want to take a photo of someone).

PRACTICALITIES

There are daily flights to Wamena from Jayapura, and just about all visitors arrive at the **airport** here. Its conspicuous runway is the best landmark for orientation in Wamena: it runs from the northwest to the southeast, and the town spreads away from the runway to the west. The first thing you'll have to do on arrival is have your **surat jalan** stamped by the police officer who runs a small **information office** inside the terminal. He is a great source of information on the Baliem Valley. In his office is a list of all of the qualified guides in Wamena, with their specialities and languages recorded.

The **taksi terminal** is right in front of the main airport buildings, and runs daily battered minibuses and jeep taksis to end-of-the-road destinations such as Bokondini (5hr; Rp15,000), Pit River (6hr; Rp15,000), Pogga (3hr; Rp7000), Tagime (4hr; Rp13,000), and Pondok Yabbagaima for Danau Habbema (4hr; Rp10,000), all of which must be booked a day in advance. Local destinations like Kurima (1hr; Rp2000), Uwosilimo for Jiwika, Waga Waga and Akima are served by hourly taksis. Those to nearby Wesaput and Sinatma leave regularly when full.

The rather unreliable **post office** is next to the terminal on Jalan Timor (Mon–Thurs & Sat 8am–2pm, Fri 8–11am). A fair stroll away is the **Telkom** office, supposedly open 24 hours. Near the huge, sparkling new church is the BRI **bank** on the corner of Jalan Yos Sudarso and Jalan Timor; they change US dollars cash for a lousy rate. The Bank Exim on Jalan Trikora is pretty much the same.

ACCOMMODATION

Because of Wamena's altitude, it can get cold at night, so hot water and heaters are important. **Accommodation** options in town are limited, and an alternative to staying in town is the losmen at Wesaput (see p.440), across the runway.

Baliem Cottages, Jl Thamrin 5 (☎0969/31370). Nicely designed, comfortable traditional houses, arranged around well-kept gardens and a restaurant. ④.

Baliem Palimo, Jl Trikora (☎0969/31043 or 32359). Probably the nicest place to stay in Wamena: the staff are friendly and some speak English. Standard rooms don't have hot water, but the more expensive rooms do, along with TV and their own little private garden. Bathrooms come with a private rainforest, complete with waterfall, the roof open to the stars. ④.

Hotel Nayak, Jl Gatut Sabroto 1 (☎0969/31067). Ensuite rooms have TV and bath, but no hot water; standard rooms are relatively clean but close to the noisy runway. ③–④.

Sri Kandi Hotel, Jl Irian 16 (☎0969/31367). The owners here are friendly and speak a little English, and rooms are reasonable although a little lacking in natural light. ③–④.

Hotel Syriah Jaya, Jl Gatut Subroto (☎0969/31306). About 200m walk south of the airport. The rooms are dark and musty with paper-thin walls, but it's the only budget option in town. ①.

EATING

The rumah makan in Wamena serve almost identical **food**, the choice obviously being limited to what the valley can produce, but wonderful prawns, goldfish and crayfish are plucked daily from Sungai Baliem, and the speciality hot lemon/orange juice is a joy on cold valley evenings. For the cheapest food in town, the market is literally surrounded on all sides by Padang-style warung. The most popular place in town for foreigners, missionaries and wealthier locals is *Mas Budi*, around the corner from the *Hotel Trendy*, whose speciality is prawns and crayfish at Rp10,000–13,000. About 2km out of town out by the tourist office, *Mentari*, Jl Yos Sudarso 46, is easily the best restaurant in the Baliem Valley, serving succulent shrimp sate for Rp10,000, and goldfish for Rp8000–12,000. *Reski*, Jl Trikora next to the *Hotel Trikora*, is a friendly place with sound cooking, cheaper than the *Mas Budi* but with a very similar menu.

Around Wamena: Wesaput and Jiwika

On the other side of the runway from Wamena lies **WESAPUT** village, the turn-off marked by an orange clock tower. There are a few traditional *honai* houses by the end of the road and the locals generally dress traditionally in *horim* and grass skirts, but they're very camera conscious, chanting "seribu, seribu, seribu" (Rp1000, 1000, 1000). On a pleasanter note, Wesaput is an essential trip for its museum, the **Palimo Adat** (Rp1000 donation). It's a beautifully laid-out building, built to resemble a *honai*, and contains a variety of Baliem curiosities such as weapons and traditional clothing. Behind the Palimo Adat is a suspension bridge and a good spot for a swim. Beyond the bridge, a path leads to **Pugima** village. The walk takes about thirty minutes, and, though the scenery isn't as magnificent as in the mountains, it's a good way to view the Dani's agrarian lifestyle. Just off this path is a large spooky cave. **Taksis** come all the way to Wesaput from Wamena, circumnavigating the northwestern end of the runway, and cost Rp400. It's often quicker to walk right across the middle of the runway on the path that starts at the fire station. You can also cut across the fields at the northwestern end of the runway, and then walk down the road. Before you reach Wesaput, you'll come across *Wiosilimo Losmen* (②) on the right-hand side of the road. They have several rooms in reproduction *honai*, all with their own mandi and patio, and the owners will give you transport to and from town in the evenings.

JIWIKA

JIWIKA, 20km northwest of Wamena by regular taksi (1hr; Rp2000), attracts tourists to its nearby showcase villages and strange blackened mummies. Jiwika has one losmen, the *La'uk Inn* (②), a beautifully kept little place with a charming Javanese manager. About 100m further up the road from the losmen and on the right-hand side, is a signpost, pointing up a dirt track to the "momi". In the traditional kampung at the end of this track, an **ancient mummified corpse** is kept, its knees hunched up to its chest and its taut flesh sooty black. The village is a real tourist trap, and it costs about Rp3000 to bring the mummy outside or Rp2000 for you to enter the *honai* and see it inside. Don't believe the guest book, which shows other guests have paid tens or hundreds of thousands to see it; they add extra noughts after you leave.

Trekking in the valley

The Baliem Valley is changing fast, and although Wamena and the nearby villages are still vastly different from anywhere else in Indonesia, you won't experience the really extraordinary aspects of Dani life and culture unless you get off the beaten track. Owing to the paucity of roads and the expense and infrequency of flights, this means a lot of **walking** and significant **planning**. Since the valley opened up to tourists, the most popular way of getting around has been to walk out to a destination with an airfield and then catch a mission **flight** back. But this method is becoming less and less viable and the pioneer and missionary airlines are for the most part pretty sick of tourists using their mercy flights as holiday transport. However, if you're desperate, the missionary airlines, and Pioneers Airfas, Trigana and Manunngal, all have offices in or around Wamena's terminal.

PLANNING A TREK

Apart from a few treks in the Baliem Gorge and along other well-forged trails that can be done alone, a **guide** and **porter** are necessary. Main trails are crisscrossed by side tracks that could take you off into the middle of nowhere, most nights will be spent in tribal villages where nobody speaks Indonesian, let alone English, and you will need more food and water for the trip than you can carry for yourself. All guides who are registered with the police and speak foreign languages are listed in the police office in the airport terminal, so that's a good place to start. A guide should **cost** $10–15 a day, though they may charge more for longer treks, and will expect all food and transport to be paid for. Porters and cooks will usually be found by the guide for about $5 a day.

If you go to one of the many **travel companies** in Wamena or Jayapura and arrange a tour through them, you're likely to get a good guide, but prices are usually higher. Chandra Nusantara Tours and Travel at Jl Trikora 17 (☎0969/31293; Jayapura agent ☎0967/31370) has an excellent reputation and does a range of very interesting tours; sample **prices**, based on seven people participating, are US$360 for five days in Dani country and US$475 for a nine-day encounter with the western Lani.

Anywhere in the valley or around the valley walls you'll need a sleeping bag, fleece, long trousers and a woolly hat. A **water purifier** is a real bonus, as is a bottle of cordial to hide the taste of boiled or iodine-tinged water. Insect repellent with a high percentage of deet, applied all over, will deter fleas, ticks and bed bugs.

AROUND THE VALLEY

The areas to the **east of the valley**, home to the **Yali people**, are becoming increasingly popular for adventure tours. The Yali are renowned for fierce adherence to custom, bizarre traditional dress and ritual war festivals. Some of the tribes here were cannibals right up until the 1970s, and are the only people who still build wooden towers to keep watch over advancing enemy tribes. The Yali region is only accessible by plane and by foot, the usual arrival point being the largest village of **Angguruk**. The village has a mission station, and is quite used to Western faces: the *kepala sekola* (schoolmaster) has a room put aside for tourist guests. From Angguruk, you'll have to walk out to the surrounding villages, and, if a flight can't be arranged, you'll have to walk all the way from Wamena: a minimum of five days.

The **western Baliem Valley** is home to the **Lani people**, and is notable as the place where Sungai Baliem drops underground into a cavern system, to reappear by the town of Tiom. This area boasts some of the most spectacular scenery in Jayawijaya: forested cliffs plunging down to the valley floor, and gullies thick with jungle carving up the hillsides to form razor-edged ridges. The road is passable by taksi through **Pyramid**, where there is a large Protestant missionary set-up, a church and a weekly market held on Saturdays, to Pit River and on to Tiom where the road ends. From Tiom there are two "major" walking paths that skirt the valley edges and head right up to Bokondini and Kelila in the north.

South of the Baliem Valley lies the magnificent **Baliem Gorge**. Here, tumultuous Sungai Baliem leaves the broad flat plain and tears violently into the steep gorge, with waterfalls and scree-covered rock-faces, and villages precariously perched on cliffside promontories. The area is relatively regularly visited, but still retains a raw, natural appeal, especially when you venture beyond the canyon walls. The people who live here are **Dani**, and spending nights in a thatched *honai* to a lullaby of gently grunting pigs is an experience you will not easily forget. Most of the internal Baliem Valley in the south has been deforested with slash-and-burn techniques, and is not as enjoyable to trek through. However, the route into the gorge and surrounding mountains is stunning. The paved road from Wamena now runs all the way to the administrative centre of **KURIMA**: taksis run to the village from 7am until the early evening (Rp2000; 1hr). At Kurima, where the gorge begins, an airstrip and mission have been cut into a precipitous rockface, 300m above the valley floor. Just northwest of Kurima at Sugokmo, you can take a trek uphill and west to **Wulik** village. It's a tough three-hour trek for which you'll be rewarded with a magnificent panorama of the valley and a nearby waterfall. From here you can trek round to **Tangma**, a six-hour walk, mostly through dense forest, for which a guide is a must: the scramble down is extremely steep and difficult. Tangma is arranged around a rarely used airfield where the houses are more modern than the *honai* of nearby settlements. It's wise to stay here with the *kepala sekola*, whose house is at the bottom of the runway. Alternatively, you could push on through **Wamarek** village to areas where several waterfalls tumble down the steep gorge sides. Raging Sungai Baliem is crossed here on a heartstopping suspension bridge, ninety minutes' walk from Tangma.

travel details

JAVA BUSES

Where the bus frequency is not given, buses depart at least once an hour.

Bandung to: Banyuwangi (daily; 24hr); Bogor (4hr 30min); Jakarta (from Leuwi Panjang terminal; 4hr 30min–5hr 30min); Pangandaran (2 daily; 5hr); Yogya (9hr 30min).

Banyuwangi to: Bandung (daily; 24hr); Jakarta (daily; 20–24hr); Madura (Sumenep, hourly; 12hr); Malang (hourly; 7hr); Pasuruan (5 hourly; 6hr); Probolinggo (5 hourly; 5hr); Situbondo (every 20min; 2–3hr); Solo (hourly; 11–13hr); Yogyakarta (hourly; 12–14hr).

Bondowoso to: Denpasar (daily; 8–9hr); Jember (every 20min; 1–2hr); Madura (Sumenep; 7 daily; 9hr); Malang (2 daily; 5–6hr); Situbondo (every 20min; 1hr); Surabaya (hourly; 4hr).

Cilacap to: Wonosobo (4hr); Yogya (5hr)

Jakarta (Pulo Gadung station unless stated otherwise) to: Banda Aceh (60hr); Bandung (from Kampung Rambutan station; 4hr 30min); Bogor (from Kampung Rambutan station; every 15min; 1–2hr); Bukittinggi (30hr); Carita (from Kalideres; 3hr 30min); Denpasar (24hr); Medan (from Pulo Gadung or Kalideres; 2 days); Labuan (from Kalideres; 3hr); Merak (from Kalideres; 3hr); Padang (from Pulo Gadung or Kalideres; 32hr); Pangandaran (12hr); Solo (13hr); Surabaya (15hr); Yogya (12hr).

Magelang to: Wonosobo (2hr)

Malang to: Bandung (daily; 16hr); Banyuwangi (hourly; 7hr); Denpasar (daily; 15hr); Jakarta (daily; 15hr); Pasuruan (hourly; 1–2hr); Probolinggo (hourly; 2–3hr); Situbondo (hourly; 4hr); Solo (7hr); Surabaya (every 20min; 1hr 30min–2hr 30min); Yogyakarta (hourly; 7–9hr).

Pangandaran to: Bandung (3 daily; 5hr); Jakarta (12hr).

Pasuruan to: Banyuwangi (5 hourly; 6hr); Denpasar (daily; 12hr); Jember (hourly; 3hr); Malang (hourly; 2–3hr); Probolinggo (5 hourly; 1hr); Surabaya (5 hourly; 1–2 hr).

Probolinggo to: Banyuwangi (5 hourly; 5hr); Bondowoso (1–2 hourly; 2–3hr); Denpasar (hourly; 11hr); Jakarta (hourly; 24hr); Jember (4 hourly; 2–3hr); Malang (hourly; 2–3hr); Mataram (Lombok, hourly; 16hr); Pasuruan (5 hourly; 1hr); Situbondo (5 hourly; 2–3hr); Solo (hourly; 7hr); Yogyakarta (hourly; 8–9hr).

Purworketo to: Wonosobo (2hr 30min)

Surabaya to: Banyuwangi (every 30min; 5–7hr); Bondowoso (hourly; 4hr); Bukittinggi (daily; 48hr); Denpasar (5 daily; 11hr); Jakarta (20 daily; 14hr); Madura (Sumenep; hourly; 5hr); Mataram (2 daily; 20hr); Medan (daily; 3 days); Padang (daily; 48hr); Pekanbaru (daily; 48hr); Probolinggo (every 30min; 2hr); Solo (every 30min; 5hr); Sumbawa Besar (daily; 26hr); Yogyakarta (every 30min; 7hr).

Wonosobo to: Dieng (1hr).

Yogyakarta to: Bandung (9hr 30min); Bogor (10hr 30min); Borobudur (2hr); Cilacap (5hr); Denpasar (15hr); Jakarta (11hr 30min); Magelang (1hr 30min); Prambanan (45min); Probolinggo (9hr); Solo (2hr); Surabaya (7hr 30min).

JAVA TRAINS

Bandung to: Banjar (hourly; 4hr); Jakarta (hourly; 2hr 20min); Yogyakarta (8 daily; at least 9hr).

Bondowoso to: Jember (2 daily; 2hr); Panarukan (2 daily; 2hr); Situbondo (2 daily; 1hr 30min).

Cilacap to: Jakarta (2 daily; 8hr 10min); Surabaya (daily; 11hr 15min).

Jakarta Gambir to: Bandung (hourly; 2hr 20min); Bogor (every 20min; 1hr 30min); Cilacap (1 daily; 6hr 13min); Cirebon (18 daily; 5hr); Malang (1 daily; 18hr 5min); Solobapan, Solo (4 daily; 7hr–10hr 25min); Surabaya (5 daily; 9hr–14hr 30min); Yogyakarta (6 daily; 6hr 50min–8hr 40min).

Malang to: Banyuwangi (daily; 5–6hr); Jakarta (daily; 12hr 30min–18hr); Surabaya (8 daily; 3hr).

Pasuruan to: Banyuwangi (4 daily; 5hr); Malang (daily; 1hr 40min); Surabaya (daily; 1hr 30min); Yogyakarta (daily; 10hr).

Probolinggo to: Banyuwangi via Jember (4 daily; 5–6hr); Kediri via Malang and Blitar (daily; 5–6hr); Surabaya (3 daily; 2–4 hr).

Solo to: Bandung (5 daily; 8hr 50min); Jakarta (6 daily; 10hr 30min); Malang (1 daily; 6hr 25min); Purworketo (6 daily; 3hr 15min); Surabaya (6 daily; 3hr 20min); Yogya (14 daily; 1hr 30min).

Solobapan to: Jakarta Gambir (3 daily; 7hr 30min); Surabaya (3 daily; 6hr); Yogyakarta (14 daily; 1hr 30min)

Surabaya Kota station to: Bandung (2 daily; 16–18hr); Banyuwangi (3 daily; 6–7hr); Malang (7 daily; 3hr); Jakarta (3 daily; 14–16hr); Yogyakarta (3 daily; 5–6hr).

Surabaya's Pasar Turi station to: Jakarta (6 daily; 12–16hr).

Surabaya's Gubeng station to: Bandung (3 daily; 16–18hr); Banyuwangi (2 daily; 6–7hr); Jakarta (3 daily; 14hr); Pasuruan (daily; 1hr 30min); Probolinggo (3 daily; 2–4 hr); Yogyakarta (daily; 5hr 10min).

Yogyakarta to: Bandung (6 daily; 6hr 30min); Banjar (2 daily; 4–5hr); Jakarta (14 daily; 8hr 45min); Solo (14 daily; 1hr 30min); Surabaya (11 daily; 4hr 50min).

JAVA PELNI FERRIES

For further details see the Map of Pelni routes on pp.192–193.

Banyuwangi Monthly to: Bima (20hr); Denpasar (7hr); Kaimana (6 days); Labuhanbajo (26hr); Larantuka (2 days); Makassar (2 days).

Jakarta (Tanjung Priok) Fortnightly (except where stated) to: Balikpapan (3 days); Banda (4 days); Pulau Batam (every 4 days; 24hr); Belawan, Medan (every 4 days; 2 days); Denpasar (39hr); Jayapura (7 days); Kijang (24–39hr); Kumai (3–4 days); Kupang (5 days); Larantuka (4 days); Nias (2 days); Nunukan (5 days); Padang (29hr); Makassar (2 days); Nias (2 days); Padang (27hr); Pontianak (every 3 days; 11–31hr); Surabaya (24hr); Tarakan (5 days); Ternate (4 days).

Surabaya Fortnightly (except where stated) to: Banda (3 days); Banjarmasin (5 times fortnightly; 24hr); Batulicin (23hr); Denpasar (16hr); Dumai (3 days); Ende (3 days); Jayapura (6–7 days); Kaimana (monthly; 4 days); Ketapang (3 days); Kijang (2 days); Kumai (22hr); Kupang (44hr); Labuanbajo (2 days); Makassar (24hr); Nias (3 days); Nunukan (3 days); Padang (30–42hr); Pontianak (39hr); Rote (3 days); Sabu (3 days); Samarinda (3 days); Sibolga (3 days); Tanjung Priok (16–21hr); Tarakan (weekly; 3 days); Waingapu (2 days).

JAVA OTHER FERRIES

Jakarta (Sunda Kelapa) to: Pontianak (2 weekly; 19hr).

Pangandaran to: Cilacap (4 daily until 1pm; 3hr 30min).

JAVA FLIGHTS

Bandung to: Mataram (daily; 8hr 25min); Singapore (daily; 3hr); Solo (3 weekly; 1hr 30min); Surabaya (3 daily; 1hr 20min); Makassar (daily; 4hr 20min); Yogyakarta (4 weekly; 1hr 20min).

Jakarta to: Banda Aceh (daily; 3hr 45min); Bandung (10 daily; 40min); Banjarmasin (5 daily; 1hr 40min); Pulau Batam (8 daily; 1hr 35min); Denpasar (16 daily; 1hr 50min); Jayapura; (2 daily; 8hr); Makassar (12 daily; 2hr 20min); Manado (4 daily; 4hr 45min); Mataram (6 weekly; 3hr 15min); Medan (16 daily; 2hr 10min); Padang (7 daily; 1hr 40min); Pekanbaru (7 daily; 1hr 40min); Pontianak (9 daily; 1hr 30min); Surabaya (33 daily; 1hr 20min); Solo/Surakarta (4 daily; 1hr 5min); Yogyakarta (14 daily; 1hr 5min).

Surabaya to: Banda Aceh (daily; 10hr); Bandung (4 daily; 1hr–2hr 30min); Banjarmasin (2 daily; 2hr); Denpasar (12 daily; 1hr 10min); Gorontalo (4 weekly; 5hr); Jakarta (22 daily; 1hr 20min); Jayapura (5 daily; 9hr); Kendari (2 daily; 5hr); Kupang (3 daily; 6hr 35min); Makassar (11 daily; 1hr 30min); Manado (daily; 4hr); Mataram (5 daily; 1hr 30min); Medan (5 daily; 7hr); Palangkarya (daily; 5hr); Palu (2 daily; 6hr); Pekanbaru (daily; 6hr); Pontianak (4 daily via Jakarta; 6hr); Pulau Batam (3 daily; 3hr 25min); Samarinda (daily; 7hr); Solo (daily; 1hr 10min); Ternate (daily; 8hr 15min); Waingapu (3 weekly; 3hr 20min–5hr 35min); Yogya (8 daily; 50min).

Solo to: Jakarta (6 daily; 1hr 5min); Singapore (2 weekly; 2hr 20min); Surabaya (2 daily; 1hr 5min).

Yogyakarta to: Bandung (4 weekly; 1hr 15min); Denpasar (6 daily; 2hr 15min); Jakarta (13 daily; 1hr 5min); Surabaya (6 daily; 1hr).

SUMATRA BUSES

Where the bus frequency is not given, buses depart at least once an hour.

Bakauheni to: Bandar Lampung (2–3hr).

Banda Aceh to: Medan (10hr); Jakarta (60hr); Padang (24hr).

Bandar Lampung to: Bakauheni (every 30min; 2–3hr); Banda Aceh (3 daily; 3 days); Bukittinggi (6 daily; 24hr); Denpasar (4 daily; 3 days); Dumai (4 daily; 48hr); Jakarta (20 daily; 8hr); Kalianda (every 30min; 1–2hr); Medan (10 daily; 48hr); Padang (6 daily; 24hr); Parapet (10 daily; 48hr); Pekanbaru (6 daily; 24hr); Yogyakarta (20 daily; 24hr).

Bukittinggi to: Aceh (3 daily; 25hr); Bandar Lampung (5 daily; 24hr); Bandung (5 daily; 34hr); Batusangkar (hourly; 1hr 30min); Bengkulu (4 daily; 16hr); Jakarta (5 daily; 35hr); Maninjau (hourly; 1hr 30min); Medan (5 daily; 18hr); Palembang (4 daily; 15hr); Pekanbaru (6 daily; 6hr); Prapat (5 daily; 14hr); Pulau Batam (daily; 24hr); Sibolga (2 daily; 12hr).

Gunung Sitoli to: Teluk Dalam (every 30min, last at 4pm; 4hr).

Kalianda to: Bandar Lampung (1–2hr).

Kutacane to: Berastagi (6hr); Blangkejeren (10 daily; 3hr); Ketambe (10 daily; 90min); Takengon (daily at 9am; 10hr).

Maninjau to: Bukittinggi (1hr 30min); Padang (2 daily at 7am & 2pm; 3hr); Pekanbaru (1 daily; 8hr).

Medan (Amplas terminal) to: Bukittinggi (hourly; 18hr); Jakarta (hourly; 48hr); Padang (hourly; 20hr); Parapat (hourly, last at 6pm; 3hr); Sibolga (daily at 6pm; 12hr).

Medan (Padang Bulan) to: Berastagi (every 20min; 2hr).

Medan (Pinang Baris terminal) to: Banda Aceh (10hr); Bukit Lawang (every 20min until 6pm; 3hr); Kutacane (12 daily; 8hr).

Padang to: Banda Aceh (4 daily; 30hr); Bandar Lampung (10 daily; 25hr); Bukittinggi (every 20min; 2hr 30min); Jakarta (10 daily; 30–35hr); Medan (10 daily; 20hr); Pekanbaru (10 daily; 8hr); Prapat (10 daily; 18hr); Sibolga (4 daily; 18hr).

Parapat to: Berastagi, via Kabanjahe and Pematangsiantar (1 daily; 6hr); Bukittinggi (2hr 30min); Jakarta (3 days; 43hr); Medan (10 daily, last at 11am; 3hr); Padang (3 daily; 16hr); Sibolga (daily at 10am; 6hr).

Pekanbaru to: Bandar Lampung (10 daily; 24hr); Bukittinggi (10 daily; 6hr); Denpasar (daily; 4 days); Dumai (10 daily; 3hr); Jakarta (10 daily; 34hr); Maninjau (daily; 8hr); Mataram (Lombok, daily; 4 days); Medan (daily; 25–35hr); Padang (10 daily; 8hr); Prapat (daily; 22–30hr); Yogyakarta (4 daily; 42hr).

Sungeipenuh to: Bangko, transit for Palembang, Bandar Lampung and Jakarta (10 daily; 5hr); Bengkulu (daily; 9hr); Dumai (daily; 14hr); Padang (4 daily; 9hr); Painan (2 daily; 7hr); Pekanbaru (daily; 12hr).

SUMATRA TRAINS

Bandar Lampung to: Palembang (3 daily; 6–8hr).

Palembang to: Bandar Lampung (3 daily; 6–8hr).

SUMATRA PELNI FERRIES

For further details see the Map of Pelni routes on pp.192–193.

Medan (Belawan harbour) every 4 days to Pulau Batam (18hr) and Jakarta (42hr); 1 daily to Penang (4hr).

Padang Fortnightly to: Balikpapan (4 days); Makassar (3 days); Nias (9–20hr); Sibolga (13hr–16hr); Surabaya (2 days); Tanjung Priok (30hr).

Parapat to: Ambarita (hourly 8.45am–6.45pm; 45min); Tuk Tuk (hourly 9.30am–7.30pm; 30min).

Pulau Batam Every four days to: Belawan (20hr); Tanjung Priok (28hr).

Pulau Bintan (Kijang) Fortnightly (except where stated) to: Balikpapan (4 days); Banda (5 days); Banjarmasin (4 days); Dobo (monthly; 6 days); Dumai (15hr); Kaimana (monthly; 6 days); Kupang (7 days); Larantuka (7 days); Makassar (3 days); Nunukan (6 days); Pontianak (3 days); Pulau Batam (7hr); Semarang (3 days); Surabaya (3 days); Tanjung Priok (26–38hr); Tarakan (6 days).

Sibolga to: Padang (10 daily).

Tongging to: Tuk Tuk via Ambarita (Mon 9am; 3hr 45min).

SUMATRA OTHER FERRIES

Ambarita to: Haranggaol (Mon 6.30am; 3hr); Parapat (hourly 6.45am–4.45pm; 45min); Tongging (Tues 9am; 3hr 30min).

Bakauheni to: Meraka (every 20min; 40min–2hr).

Bandar Lampung to: Kalianda (every 30min; 1–2hr).

Haranggaol to: Ambarita (Mon 1pm; 3hr); Simanindo (Mon 1pm, Thurs 7pm; 1hr 10min).

Pekanbaru to: Pulau Batam (9–12hr); Pulau Bintan (daily; 12hr).

Pulau Batam to: Dumai (daily; 6–8hr); Pekanbaru (daily; 18hr); Singapore's World Trade Centre (frequent departures daily; 1–2hr); Tanah Merah, Singapore (6 daily 8am–6pm; 1–2hr); Tanjung Pinang, Pulau Bintan (every 15min 8am–5pm; 45min).

Pulau Bintan (Tanjung Pinang) to: Jakarta (Tanjung Priok: daily; 24hr); Johor Bahru (daily; 6hr); Pulau Batam (every 15min; 45min); Pekanbaru (daily; 12hr); Singapore (Tanah Merah; 3 daily; 1hr 30min); Tanjung Balai on Pulau Karimun (2 daily; 2–3hr).

Pulau Karimun (Tanjung Balai) to: Johor Bahru (4 daily; 4–6hr); Pekanbaru (2 daily; 6–7hr); Sekupang on Pulau Batam (8 daily; 3hr); Singapore (9 daily; 1 hr 30min); Tanjung Pinang on Pulau Bintan (4 daily; 3hr).

Sibolga to: Gunung Sitoli (Jambo Jet, daily except Sun 8.30am; 4hr/KM Cucit/Poncan Moale, daily except Sun 8pm; 8hr/Sumber Rezeki, daily except Sun 6pm; 10hr).

SUMATRA FLIGHTS

Bandah Aceh to: Kuala Lumpur (3 weekly; 2hr); Medan (2 daily; 55min).

Gunung Sitoli to: Padang (weekly; 1hr).

Medan to: Banda Aceh (2 daily; 55min); Dumai (weekly; 1hr 25min); Gunung Sitoli (6 weekly; 1hr 10min); Jakarta (15 daily; 2hr 15min); Kuala Lumpur (17 daily; 1hr); Padang (3 daily; 1hr 10min); Pekanbaru (daily; 2hr); Penang (11 weekly; 40min); Pulau Batam (3 daily; 1hr 15min); Sibolga (6 weekly; 1hr); Singapore (2 daily; 1hr 30min).

Padang to: Bandung (daily; 2hr–3hr 30min); Jakarta (4 daily; 45min); Medan (1–2 daily; 1hr 10min); Pekanbaru (3 weekly; 50min); Pulau Batam (daily; 1hr).

Pekanbaru to: Jakarta (6 daily; 1hr–1hr 40min); Kuala Lumpur (4 weekly; 1hr); Melaka (4 weekly; 40min); Medan (daily; 1hr 20min); Padang (3 weekly; 40min); Pulau Batam (3–4 daily; 45min); Tanjung Pinang (4 weekly; 50min).

Pulau Batam to: Balikpapan (9 weekly; 4hr 25min); Bandung (2 daily; 3hr 20min); Banjarmasin (daily; 6hr); Denpasar (daily; 4hr 20min); Jakarta (5 daily; 1hr 35min); Makassar (9 weekly; 6hr 30min); Manado (daily; 7hr 40min); Mataram (2 weekly; 3hr 55min); Medan (daily; 1hr 20min); Padang (daily; 1hr); Pekanbaru (daily; 45min); Pontianak (5 weekly; 3–4hr); Semarang (daily; 3hr 10min); Surabaya (3 daily; 3hr 30min); Yogyakarta (2 daily; 2hr 5min).

Pulau Bintan (Kijang) to: Jakarta (6 weekly; 1hr 45min); Pekanbaru (6 weekly; 55min).

BALI BEMOS AND BUSES

Denpasar (Batubulan terminal) to: Amlapura (2hr 30min); Candi Dasa (2hr); Gianyar (1hr); Kintamani (1hr 30min); Klungkung (1hr 20min); Padang Bai (1hr 40min); Peliatan (45min); Singaraja (Penarukan terminal; 3hr); Ubud (50min).

Denpasar (Kereneng terminal) to: Sanur (15–25min).

Denpasar (Tegal terminal) to: Kuta (25min); Ngurah Rai Airport (35min); Sanur (25min).

Denpasar (Ubung terminal) to: Antosari (1hr); Bedugul (1hr 30min); Cekik (3hr); Gilimanuk (3hr 15min); Jakarta (24hr); Kediri (30min); Singaraja (Sukasada terminal; 3hr); Solo (15hr); Surabaya (10hr); Tabanan (35min); Yogya (15hr).

Gilimanuk to: Antosari (2hr 15min); Cekik (10min); Denpasar (Ubung terminal; 3hr 15min); Kediri (2hr 45min); Labuan Lalang (25min); Lovina (2hr 15min); Singaraja (Banyuasri terminal; 2hr 30min).

Klungkung to: Besakih (45min); Candi Dasa (40min); Denpasar (Batubulan terminal; 1hr 20min); Padang Bai (20min).

Lovina to: Bromo (8hr); Gilimanuk (2hr 10min); Jakarta (24hr); Probolingo (7hr); Solo (17hr); Surabaya (11hr); Yogyakarta (17hr).

Singaraja (Banyuasri terminal) to: Gilimanuk (2hr 30min); Lovina (20min); Seririt (40min).

Singaraja (Penarukan terminal) to: Amlapura (2hr); Denpasar (Batubulan terminal; 3hr); Gianyar (2hr 20min); Penelokan (1hr 30min); Kubutambahan (20min); Sawan (30min).

Singaraja (Sukasada terminal) to: Bedugul (1hr 30min); Denpasar (Ubung terminal; 3hr).

BALI PELNI FERRIES

For further details see the Map of Pelni routes on pp.192–193.

Benoa Harbour Fortnightly services to: Jayapura (5 days); Kupang (26hr); Surabaya (15hr); Tanjung Priok (39hr).

BALI OTHER FERRIES

Benoa Harbour to: Lembar (1–2 daily; 2hr).

Sanur to: Jungutbatu (2 daily; 1hr 30min).

LOMBOK BEMOS AND BUSES

Ampenan to: Senggigi (every 20min; 20min).

Sweta (Mandalika terminal) to: Bayan (for Rinjani; 2hr 30min); Bima (Sumbawa; 12hr); Dompu (Sumbawa; 10hr); Jakarta (Java; 48hr); Labuhan Lombok (2hr); Labuhanbajo (Flores; 24hr); Lembar (30min); Pemenang (50min); Pomotong (for Tetebatu; 1hr 15min); Praya (for Kuta; 30min); Ruteng (Flores; 36hr); Sape (Flores; 14hr); Sumbawa Besar (Sumbawa; 6hr); Surabaya (20hr); Yogyakarta (26hr).

LOMBOK PELNI FERRIES

For further details see the Map of Pelni routes on pp.192–193.

Lembar monthly to: Bima (24hr); Bitung (5 days); Gorontola (4 days); Kendari (3 days); Labuhanbajo (31hr); Lirung, Philippines (6 days); Makassar (48hr); Raha (3 days).

LOMBOK OTHER FERRIES

Labuhan Lombok to: Poto Tano (Sumbawa; every 45min; 2hr).

LOMBOK FLIGHTS

Mataram, Selaparang Airport to: Bima (daily; 45min); Denpasar (connecting to Jakarta; 9 daily;

30min); Kupang (daily; 5hr); Maumere (3 weekly; 3hr 30min); Singapore (daily; 2hr 30min); Sumbawa (daily; 40min); Surabaya (connecting to Jakarta; 3 daily; 45min); Waingapu (4 weekly; 3hr).

SUMBAWA BUSES

Bima to: Mataram (Bima terminal 11hr); Sape (Kumbe terminal 2hr); Sumbawa Besar (Bima terminal 7hr).

Sumbawa Besar to: Bima (daily; 7hr); Dompu (daily; 4hr 30min); Sape (daily; 8hr 30min); Taliwang (daily; 3hr).

SUMBAWA PELNI FERRIES

For further details see the Map of Pelni routes on pp.192–193.

Badas (Sumbawa Besar) Monthly to: Denpasar (16hr); Labuhanbajo (3 days); Larantuka (4 days); Makassar (22hr).

Bima Monthly to: Denpasar (31hr); Labuhanbajo (7hr); Lembar (7hr); Makassar (1 day); Surabaya (2 days).

SUMBAWA FLIGHTS

Bima to: Bajawa (2 weekly; 1hr 15min); Denpasar (2 daily; 1hr 15min); Ende (daily; 1hr 30min); Kupang (2 daily; 2hr 10min); Labuhanbajo (4 weekly; 55min); Mataram (daily; 1hr 10min); Ruteng (daily; 1hr 10min); Surabaya (4 weekly; 2hr 20min); Waingapu (3 weekly; 1hr 30min).

Sumbawa Besar to: Denpasar (6 weekly; 1hr 55min); Mataram (6 weekly; 45min).

FLORES BUSES

Ende to: Bajawa (Ndao terminal; daily; 5hr); Maumere (Wolowana terminal; daily; 6hr); Moni (Wolowana terminal; daily; 1hr 30min).

Maumere to: Ende (Terminal Barat/Ende terminal; 6hr); Larantuka (Terminal Lokaria; 4hr); Moni (Terminal Barat/Ende terminal; 3hr 30min).

FLORES PELNI FERRIES

For further details see the Map of Pelni routes on pp.192–193.

Ende fortnightly to: Badas (33hr); Kupang (20hr); Makassar (2 days); Sabu (8hr); Waingapu (Sumba; 8hr).

Labuanbajo to: Badas (13hr); Bima (7hr); Denpasar (2 days); Kupang (40hr); Makassar (15hr–4 days); Sabu (30hr); Surabaya (36hr); Waingapu (10hr).

Larantuka fortnightly to: Bima (24hr); Denpasar (36hr); Kupang (9hr).

Maumere to: Denpasar (3 days); Kupang (24hr); Waingapu (2 days).

FLORES OTHER FERRIES

Ende to: Waingapu (Sumba; daily in dry season; 10hr).

FLORES FLIGHTS

Ende to: Bajawa (3 weekly; 45min); Bima (5 weekly; 1hr 30min); Kupang (6 weekly; 1hr 10min); Labuhanbajo (4 weekly; 1hr 5min).

Labuhanbajo to: Bajawa (weekly; 2hr 45min); Nima (4 weekly; 45min); Ende (4 weekly; 1hr); Ruteng (3 weekly; 25min).

Maumere to: Denpasar (6 weekly; 2hr 20min); Kupang (4 weekly; 55min); Surabaya (5 weekly; 3hr).

TIMOR BUSES

Kupang to: Camplang (1hr); Soe (3–4hr).

Waingapu to: Melolo (1hr 30min); Rende (2hr); Waikabubak (4hr 30min).

TIMOR PELNI FERRIES

For further details see the Map of Pelni routes on pp.192–193.

Kupang fortnightly to: Denpasar (1 day); Ende (12hr); Larantuka (9hr); Sabu (10hr).

TIMOR FLIGHTS

Kupang to: Jakarta (3 weekly; 3hr 25min); Labuhanbajo (2 weekly; 2hr 45min); Larantuka (weekly; 1hr 5min); Lewoleba (1 weekly; 1hr 50min); Maumere (3 weekly; 55min); Roti (weekly; 55min); Ruteng (daily; 1hr 45min); Sabu (weekly; 1hr 35min); Surabaya (2 daily; 2hr 5min); Tambulaka (4 weekly; 2hr 50min); Waingapu (4 weekly; 1hr 35min).

SUMBA PELNI FERRIES

For further details see the Map of Pelni routes on pp.192–193.

Waingapu monthly to: Denpasar (26hr); Ende (10hr); Labuhanbajo (11hr); Makassar (3 days).

SUMBA FLIGHTS

Waikabubak to: Bima (weekly; 40min); Waingapu (3 weekly; 40min).

Waingapu to: Bima (weekly; 1hr); Denpasar (5 weekly; 1hr 40min); Kupang (4 weekly; 1hr 15min); Surabaya (3 weekly; 2hr 40min).

KALIMANTAN BUSES

Banjarmasin to: Balikpapan (10 daily; 12–14hr); Martapura (frequent; 1hr 30min); Palangkaraya (several daily; 5–7hr); Samarinda (10 daily; 14–16hr).

Bontang to: Samarinda (several daily; 2hr)

Palangkaraya to: Pangkalanbun (4 daily; 10hr).

Pontianak to: Kuching (7 daily; 12hr); Putussibau (12hr); Sintang (8 daily; 8hr).

Putussibau to: Nanga Badau (daily; 8am; 7hr); Pontianak (8 daily from 8am; 12 hr); Sintang (8 daily from 8am).

Samarinda to: Balikpapan (10 daily; 2hr 30min); Kota Bangun (several daily; 3hr).

Sintang to: Pontianak (8 daily; 8hr); Putussibau (daily 6am; 6hr).

KALIMANTAN PELNI FERRIES

For further details see the Map of Pelni routes on pp.192–193.

Balikpapan fortnightly to: Makassar (16–19hr); Pantoloan (14hr); Parepare (19hr); Surabaya (24–45h); Tanjung Priok, Jakarta (2–3 days); Ternate (41hr).

Banjarmasin to: Semarang (weekly; 24hr); Surabaya (3–4 weekly; 24hr).

Berau fortnightly to: Nunukan (14hr); Tarakan (24hr).

Kumai fortnightly to: Semarang (24hr); Surabaya (24hr); Tanjung Pandang (3 days).

Nunukan fortnightly to: Balikpapan (28hr); Tarakan (5–12hr).

Pontianak to: Natuna (monthly; 31hr); Semarang (fortnightly; 34hr); Tanjung Priok, Jakarta (every 3 days; 11hr).

Samarinda to: Parepare (20hr); Surabaya (fortnightly; 3 days).

Tarakan fortnightly to: Balikpapan (20hr); Makassar (35–51hr); Nunukan (7hr); Pantoloan (15hr).

KALIMANTAN OTHER FERRIES

Banjarmasin to: Palangkaraya (frequent; 5hr).

Berau to: Tarakan (3 weekly; 10hr).

Nunukan to: Tarakan (about 2 daily; 6–12hr).

Pontianak to: Jakarta (twice weekly; 19hr); Ketanpang (daily 8am; 6hr); Putussibau (*Kapal Bandung*, weekly; 5 days); Sintang (*Kapal Bandung*, weekly; 2 days).

Samarinda to: Kota Bangun (several daily; 10hr); Long Bagun (seasonally 1 daily; 3–4 days); Long Iram (1–2 daily; 30hr); Melak (several daily; 24hr); Muara Kaman (several daily; 6hr); Muara Muntai (several daily; 14hr); Tenggarong (several daily; 3hr).

Sintang to: Putussibau (*Kapal Bandung*, weekly; 2days; *Bunut Utama* speedboat 3–4 weekly; 6hr).

KALIMANTAN FLIGHTS

Balikpapan to: Banjarmasin (daily; 40min); Brunei (2 weekly; 1hr 30min); Jakarta (3 daily; 2hr); Makassar (daily; 2hr); Palu (daily; 45min); Pontianak (6 weekly; 4hr); Samarinda (2 daily; 40min); Surabaya (3 daily; 1hr 15min); Tarakan (2 daily; 2hr).

Banjarmasin to: Balikpapan (daily; 40min); Jakarta (4 daily; 1hr 45min); Palangkaraya (daily; 40min); Pangkalanbun (6 weekly; 2hr); Surabaya (4 daily; 1hr 10min).

Berau/Tanjung Redeb to: Balikpapan (2 daily; 2hr); Samarinda (2 daily; 1hr 30min); Tarakan (2 daily; 40min).

Palangkaraya to: Balikpapan (daily; 2hr); Banjarmasin (daily; 40min); Pangkalanbun (daily; 2hr); Surabaya (2 daily; 1hr 50min).

Pangkalanbun to: Banjarmasin (6 weekly; 2hr); Palangkaraya (daily; 2hr); Pontianak (daily; 2hr); Semarang (daily; 3hr).

Pontianak to: Balikpapan (4 weekly; 2hr 35min); Ketapang (3 daily; 1hr); Kuching (3 weekly; 1hr 45min); Medan (3 weekly; 3hr 35min); Pekanbaru (3 weekly; 2hr 50min); Putussibau (5 weekly; 1hr 25min).

Samarinda to: Balikpapan (2 daily; 40min); Berau (2 daily; 1hr 30min); Melak (3 weekly; 55min); Tarakan (3 daily; 2hr).

Tarakan to: Balikpapan (3 daily; 2hr 40min); Berau (2 daily; 40min); Samarinda (3 daily; 2hr); Tewau (3 weekly; 40min).

SULAWESI BUSES

daily departures

Ampana to: Makassar (26hr); Pagaimana (5hr); Palu (15hr); Poso (5hr).

Gorontalo to: Makassar (2–4 days); Manado (12hr).

Makassar to: Ampana (26hr); Bira (5hr); Mamasa (15hr); Manado (2–4 days); Palu (29hr); Parepare (4hr); Polewali (7hr); Poso (21hr); Rantepao (8hr); Tentena (19hr).

Palu to: Ampana (15hr); Makassar (29hr); Pagaimana (20hr); Poso (10hr); Rantepao (24hr).

Parepare to: Makassar (daily; 5hr); Rantepao (daily; 4hr); Polewali (daily; 2hr); Sengkang (daily; 2hr 30min).

Poso to: Ampana (5hr); Makassar (21hr); Pagaimana (10hr); Palu (10hr); Pendolo (5hr); Rantepao (13hr).

Rantepao to: Makassar (8hr); Palu (21hr); Parepare (4hr); Pendolo (9hr); Poso (13hr); Tentena (11hr).

SULAWESI PELNI FERRIES

For further details see the Map of Pelni routes on pp.192–193.

Bitung monthly, except where stated, to: Balikpapan (fortnightly; 36–48hr); Lirung (12–24hr); Pantaloan/Palu (fortnightly; 34hr); Makassar (fortnightly; 2 days); Surabaya (4 days); Tahuna (10–24hr); Ternate (fortnightly; 9hr).

Gorontalo monthly to: Bitung (11hr); Denpasar (4–5 days); Java (3 days); Kalimantan (30hr); Kolonodale (24hr); Makassar (2 days); Palu (18hr).

Makassar fortnightly to: Balikpapan (16–21hr); Banda (2 days); Bitung (48hr); Denpasar (2 days); Gorontalo (monthly; 3 days); Jayapura (4–6 days); Kupang (3 days); Maumere (30hr); Nias (4–5 days); Nunukan (60hr); Padang (3–4 days); Parepare (60hr); Surabaya (frequent; 24hr); Tanjung Priok (frequent; 40–48hr); Tarakan (50hr).

Pantaloan/Palu fortnightly to: Balikpapan (11hr); Bitung (34hr); Makassar (17–30hr); Parepare via Kalimantan (3 days); Surabaya (56hr); Tarakan (4 monthly; 24hr).

Parepare fortnightly to: Balikpapan (3 days); Makassar (50hr); Pantaloan (4 monthly; 14hr–3 days); Samarinda (24hr); Surabaya (24–41hr); Tarakan (2 days).

SULAWESI OTHER FERRIES

Gorontalo to: Ampana (1 weekly; 18hr); Bomba (1 weekly; 12hr); Pagaimana (3 weekly; 10hr); Wakai (1 weekly; 13hr).

Manado to: Lirung on Pulau Talaud (1 weekly; 20hr); Tahuna on Sangihe Island (3 weekly; 12hr).

Poso to: Ampana (1 weekly; 6hr); Gorontalo (1 weekly; 24hr); Katupat (1 weekly; 14hr); Wakai (1 weekly; 12hr).

SULAWESI FLIGHTS

Kendari to: Makassar (1 daily; 1hr).

Makale to: Makassar (1–3 daily; 1hr).

Makassar to: Balikpapan (6 weekly; 1hr 10min); Denpasar (2–4 daily; 1hr 20min); Jakarta (5–7 daily; 1hr 10min); Kendari (1 daily; 1hr); Makale (1–3 daily; 1hr); Manado (1–3 daily; 1hr 35min); Singapore (3 weekly; 3hr).

Manado to: Makassar (1–3 daily; 1hr 35min); Palu (1 daily; 1hr 20min); Singapore (3 weekly; 5hr).

Palu to: Balikpapan (1 daily; 40min); Makassar (2 daily; 2hr); Manado (1 daily; 1hr 20min).

IRIAN JAYA PELNI FERRIES

For further details see the Map of Pelni routes on pp.192–193.

Jayapura fortnightly to: Banda (60hr); Denpasar (5 days); Kupang (4 days); Makassar (5 days); Surabaya (6 days); Tanjung Priok, Jakarta (7 days); Ternate (3 days).

Kaimana monthly to: Banda (12hr); Makassar (60hr); Surabaya (4 days); Tanjung Priok (5 days).

CHAPTER FIVE

LAOS

Introduction

Less than a decade ago, **Laos** (pop. 5.25 million) was largely unknown to Western travellers. Other than a brief period during the 1960s, when the former French colony became a player in the **Vietnam War**, it has been largely ignored by the West – a situation that only intensified after the 1975 revolution and the years of xenophobic communist rule that ensued. However, since the Lao People's Democratic Republic reluctantly reopened its doors in the 1990s, a steady flow of visitors has trickled into this poverty-stricken, old-fashioned country, and a few traveller-oriented services have begun to emerge. For many, a journey through Laos consists of a whistlestop tour through the two main towns of Vientiane and Louang Phabang, with perhaps a brief detour to the mysterious Plain of Jars or ancient Wat Phou. However, those willing to explore further and brave difficult roads and basic, candlelit accommodation will be rewarded with sights of a rugged natural landscape and ethnically diverse people not much changed from those that greeted French explorers more than a century ago.

Laos's life-line is the **Mekong River**, which runs the length of the landlocked country and in places serves as a boundary with Thailand. Set on a broad curve of the Mekong, **Vientiane** is perhaps Southeast Asia's most modest capital city, and provides a smooth introduction to Laos, offering a string of cosmopolitan cafés to compensate for a relative lack of sights. From here, most tourists dash north, usually by plane, to **Louang Phabang**, though it's worth taking more time and doing the journey by bus, stopping off en route at the town of **Vang Viang**, set in a spectacular landscape of rice paddies and karsts. Once the heart and soul of the ancient kingdom of **Lane Xang**, tiny, cultured Louang Phabang is Laos's most enticing destination, with a spellbinding panoply of gilded temples and weathered shop-houses. The wild highlands of the **far north** aren't the easiest to get around, but the prospect of trekking to nearby hilltribe villages has put easy-going **Muang Sing** on the map. From here, you can travel to the Burmese border at **Xiang Kok**, and then down the Mekong River to **Houayxai**, an entry point popular with travellers arriving from Thailand in search of a slow boat for the picturesque journey south to Louang Phabang. Lost in the misty mountains of the far northeast, the provincial capital of **Xam Nua** gives access to **Viang Xai**, where the Pathet Lao directed their resistance from deep within a vast cave complex. Following Route 6 south brings you to the ramshackle town of **Phonsavan**, set beside the **Plain of Jars**, a moonscape of bomb craters dotted with very ancient funerary urns. In the south, the vast majority of travellers zip down Route 13, stopping off in the three major southern towns: uninteresting **Thakhek**, the genial and cultural **Savannakhet** – also a handy border crossing with Thailand, and offering buses to Vietnam too – and the important transport hub of **Pakxe**. Further south, near the former royal seat of **Champasak**, lie the ruins of **Wat Phou**, the greatest of the Khmer temples outside Cambodia. South again, the countless river islands of **Si Phan Don** lie scattered across the Mekong, boasting scores of traditional fishing communities and the chance to spot the rare Irawaddy dolphin.

November to January are the **pleasantest months** to travel in lowland Laos, when daytime temperatures are agreeably warm and evenings slightly chilly; at higher elevations temperatures can drop to freezing point. In February, temperatures begin to climb, reaching a peak in April, when the lowlands are baking hot and humid. Generally, the rains begin in May and last until September, rendering many of Laos's roads impassable.

Overland routes into Laos

Laos has **land borders** with Thailand, Vietnam, Cambodia and China.

■ From Burma

Western tourists are not officially permitted to cross between **Burma** and Laos at Xiang Kok, the lone border point between the two countries.

■ From Cambodia

At the time of writing, Western tourists were not allowed to cross between **Cambodia** and Laos at the far southern end of Champasak province, although the crossing may open to foreigners in the near future.

■ From China

Buses travel from **Jinghong** in China's southwestern Yunnan province to Oudomxai or Louang Namtha. The last town on the Chinese side is the village of Mo Han and the first Lao village you come to is Boten.

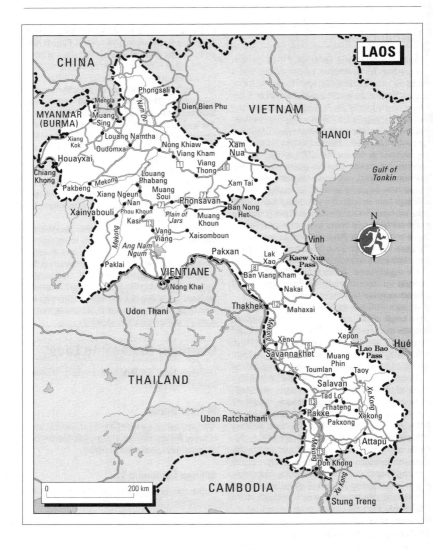

■ From Thailand

There are currently five points along the **Thai border** where it's permissible to cross into **Laos**: Chiang Khong (see p.898) to Houayxai; Nong Khai (p.919) to Vientiane; Nakhon Phanom (p.921) to Thakhek; Mukdahan (p.922) to Savannakhet; and Chong Mek (p.915) to Pakxe. For visa information see opposite.

■ From Vietnam

There are now two border crossings open to foreigners between Vietnam and **Laos**: the most popular is from **Lao Bao** (see p.1037) to Daen Sawan and Savannakhet, as the crossing from **Cau Treo** (see p.1037) to Lak Xao is more difficult to get to.

Entry requirements, visa extensions and reporting in

Visas are required for all foreign visitors to Laos. A fifteen-day visa on arrival can be bought for $30 (US dollars cash only, plus one photo), but is only available to travellers entering Laos at Wattay Airport in Vientiane, Louang Phabang Airport or at the Friendship Bridge between Thailand's Nong Khai and Vientiane. If entering Laos from Chiang Khong in Thailand's Chiang Rai province, you can obtain fifteen-day visas through Chiang Khong guesthouses and travel agencies: processing takes 24 hours and costs the baht equivalent of $50. Thirty-day visas can also be arranged here for much the same price but take three to four days to process; see p.899.

If you want to enter Laos via somewhere other than these border points, or if you want a longer visa, you will have to apply for an advance visa at a Lao embassy (see "Basics" p.21) or a tour agency. Many visitors opt to do this while staying in Bangkok or Hanoi. **In Bangkok**, you can obtain thirty-day visas directly from the embassy (see p.861) for B750–1050, depending on nationality, plus an additional B300 "fax" charge; fifteen-day visas cost the same. You need one passport photo, and processing takes two days (or 12 hours for an extra B300). An alternative option is to go through one of the travel agents in Bangkok's Khao San area, who charge B1200–2000 for a fifteen-day visa, and twice as much for a thirty-day visa; allow three working days for processing. The Lao consulate in Khon Kaen in northeast Thailand (see p.915) can also issue visas, though fees and processing times are variable.

Travellers from Vietnam can get visas for Laos at the Lao embassy in **Hanoi** or at the consulate in **Da Nang**. The embassy in Hanoi charges $25–35 for thirty-day visas, depending on nationality. **In Da Nang**, a thirty-day visa costs around $50 and takes two days; for an extra $13 you can get it on the spot. A seven-day transit visa costs $30 (two days), but you must exit to Thailand from Savannakhet. The Lao Embassy **in Hanoi** does one-month "visit visas" ($50–70; seven days). Transit visas ($25–40; four days), are only valid for five days and for one

province (so not an option if you're travelling via Cau Treo). The one-day express service costs an extra $20.

Transit visas, good for only ten days and non-extendable ($25–30; allow three working days), are offered at the Lao embassy in Hanoi for travellers to Bangkok who wish to make a short stopover in Vientiane, and are also offered by the consulate in Kunming, China.

In Vientiane, you can apply for **visa extensions** at the immigration office on Hatsady Road. Most travellers are charged $3 per day, but you could pay as little as $1 per day; similarly, the length of your visa extension is up to the official on duty. Officially, only the immigration office in Vientiane can issue visa extensions, but it's always worth trying in other towns. Both airport and border immigration offices generally charge $5 per day for overstays.

■ Reporting in

As recently as the early 1990s, you had to get special permission to visit any province other than Vientiane, **reporting to immigration** on arrival in every new province and getting the required rubber stamp. This "reporting in" procedure – *jaeng khao* – has now been officially done away with throughout the country. However, there is no telling if and when word from above will bring new vigour to the old rubber-stamp game, so always check with other travellers. If in doubt, seek out the local immigration office, if there is one, or the police station.

AIRPORT DEPARTURE TAX

When leaving Laos by air or via the Friendship Bridge, you'll have to pay a departure tax equivalent to US$5, payable in US dollars, Thai baht or kip. At other border points, officials may levy small "fees" for arriving or departing during lunch, late in the day or at weekends.

Money and costs

Lao **currency** is the kip and is available in 5000K, 2000K, 1000K, 500K, 100K and 50K notes. There are no coins in circulation. In addition, the Thai baht and American dollar operate parallel to the kip. Although a 1990 law forbids the use of foreign currencies to pay for local goods and services, many hotels and tour operators quote their prices in **dollars** or **baht**, and accept payment in either. The government-owned airline, Lao Aviation, only accepts payment in American dollars cash.

The **Asian financial crisis** in 1997 badly affected the kip. Between June 1997 and early 1999, the kip, which is not freely convertible, fell more than eighty percent against the dollar. The banks are currently broke and inflation is running at around a hundred percent a year (up from 7.3 percent a few years before). Many Lao are suffering real hardship, as prices have gone up while salaries have remained the same.

A **black market** (*talat meut*) in foreign currencies exists and until recently was more or less tolerated. However, the government has started a campaign against the "illegal changing of money", urging tourists to use banks and official exchange kiosks. The difference between the official and black-market rate is now so little that it hardly seems worth the risk of being caught. At the time of writing, the official **exchange rate** was 7600 kip to the US dollar, 195 kip to the Thai baht and 12,054 kip to the pound stirling.

Travellers' cheques are a convenient and safe way to carry your money, although it's wise to have a decent supply of American dollars and Thai baht **in cash**, especially if you intend to spend time in some of the remoter parts of the country. Before travelling into smaller towns, change enough money to get you through until the next major town, but bear in mind that you cannot change your kip back into dollars or baht when leaving the country – and that duty-free shops only accept dollars and baht. Major **credit cards** are accepted at many hotels, upmarket restaurants and shops in Vientiane. **Cash advances** on Visa cards, and less frequently MasterCard, are possible in Louang Phabang, Vientiane, Savannakhet and Pakxe. At present, you can't withdraw cash from ATMs in Laos.

■ **Costs**

Given the volatility of the kip, **prices** for accommodation, river travel and car hire in this chapter have been given in their more stable dollar equivalents. Indeed, many hotels and guesthouses have opted to fix their rates to the dollar. The prices quoted in kip for transport, museum entrance fees, etc were correct at the time of research and have been retained to give a relative idea of costs, though in practice many of these prices will be higher.

By eating at noodle stalls and cheap restaurants, taking local transport and opting for basic accommodation, you can travel in Laos on a **daily budget** of less than \$10. Food and accommodation tend to be slightly more expensive in Vientiane.

While restaurants and some shops have fixed prices, you should always **bargain** in markets and when chartering transport (fares on passenger vehicles are fixed). Room rates can be bargained for in low season. As the Lao in general – with the exception of some tourist businesses in Vientiane and Louang Phabang – are less out to rip off tourists than their counterparts in Thailand and Vietnam, they start off the haggling by quoting a fairly realistic price and expect to come down only a little. **Price tiering** does exist in Laos, with foreigners paying more than locals for airfares, bus fares, speedboat tickets and entry to museums and famous sites. Tipping isn't a Lao custom, although upmarket Vientiane restaurants expect a gratuity of around ten percent.

Information and maps

The **National Tourism Authority of Laos** (NATL) operates offices in a few places, including Vientiane, but staff are generally untrained and speak little English. Two privately owned companies, Sodetour and Diethelm, can provide reliable information. Word-of-mouth information from other travellers is often the best source, as conditions in Laos change with astonishing rapidity.

Nelles 1:1,500,000 **map** of Vietnam, Laos and Cambodia or its Southeast Asia "Road Atlas" of the same scale are adequate for orientation but can be misleading.

Getting around

With Laos's road conditions improving at long last, buses have begun displacing river travel, the traditional means of getting around. However, passenger boats still regularly ply the Mekong, Southeast Asia's ancient highway, and many roads are still potholed. Indeed, in some cases, they're downright dangerous because of local bandit activity. You only need to travel for a week or two in Laos before you realize that timetables are irrelevant, and estimated times of arrival pointless – wherever you go, the journey seems to take all day. For a guide to the frequency and duration of journeys between major destinations in Laos, see "Travel Details" on p.529.

■ Buses

Cramped, overloaded and often extremely uncomfortable, Lao **buses** are profound tests of endurance and patience. Breakdowns are commonplace and in the rainy season, unpaved roads dissolve into rivers of mud, slowing buses to a crawl. On some buses, the driver permits male passengers to ride on the roof, but women should defer to Lao customs and refrain from doing the same (see "Cultural Hints" p.462). As there are no public toilets in Laos, it's perfectly acceptable for passengers to relieve themselves in the open during breaks on long journeys – Lao women usually bring along a sarong for such occasions. However, keep in mind that many areas are still plagued by unexploded ordnance (See p.463), so it's not wise to make a lone dash for the trees.

Ordinary buses run between major towns and link provincial hubs with their surrounding districts. Operating out of Vientiane, a fleet of slightly more comfortable blue, **government-owned buses** caters mostly to the capital's outlying districts, although it does provide a service to Vang Viang and Pakxe. Buses plying long-distance routes tend to be in worse shape and can be either classic buses or souped-up tourist vans. Throughout the south and along the Vientiane–Louang Phabang route, the transport mainstay is a converted Russian flat-bed truck.

Except for buses out of Vientiane, Savannakhet and Louang Phabang, when you should buy a ticket from the bus station before boarding, it's common practice to **pay on board**. **Timetables** only exist in Vientiane, Louang Phabang and Savannakhet; elsewhere it's best to go to the bus station the night before to find out the schedule for the next day. Where there is no information, you should get to the bus station between 6 and 7am, as that is when most Lao passengers prefer to travel. Very few buses leave **after midday**. Even though they're scheduled, long-distance buses won't depart if empty. Route 13, however, sees a steady flow of bus traffic and it's usually possible to flag down a vehicle during daylight hours.

■ Sawngthaews

In rural areas, particularly in the north, the bus network is often replaced by **sawngthaews** – converted pick-up trucks – into which drivers stuff as many passengers as they can onto two facing benches in the back. Pick-up trucks also ply routes between larger towns and their satellite villages, charging roughly the same as buses. They usually depart from the regular bus station, but will only leave when there are enough passengers to make the trip worthwhile. Some drivers try to sweat a few extra kip out of passengers by delaying departure – your fellow passengers may cave in to this extortion, but most often they grudgingly wait. In some situations, you may be forced to flat-out hire the driver to take you where you want to go. To catch a pick-up truck in between stops simply flag it down from the side of the road and tell the driver where you're headed. The fare is usually paid at the end of the ride.

■ Jumbos and tuk-tuks

Transport within Lao towns and cities is by two types of motorized *samlaw* (literally, "three wheels"), more commonly known as **jumbos** and **tuk-tuks**, which function as share taxis for four or five passengers. Jumbos are the original Lao vehicle, a homemade three-wheeler consisting of a two-wheeled carriage soldered to the front half of a motorcycle. Tuk-tuks are really just bigger, sturdier jumbos, and Lao tend to refer to these vehicles interchangeably. To catch one, flag it down as it passes, tell the driver where you're going, and pay at the end of the ride. Payment is per person according to the distance travelled and your bargaining skills. Rates vary, but figure on around 500K per kilometre. In some towns, tuk-tuks run set routes to the surrounding villages and leave from a stand, usually near the market, once full.

■ Boats

With roughly 4600km of navigable waterways, rivers are the ancient highways of mountainous Laos. The main routes link Houayxai to Louang Phabang and Pakxe with Si Phan Don, all of them along the Mekong River. Smaller **boats** regularly cruise up the wide Nam Ou River, linking Louang Phabang to Nong Khiaw and Phongsali, and a weekly vessel still manages the trickier Louang Phabang-to-Vientiane route, a journey that can take nearly a week.

The long, narrow diesel-chugging **slow boats** (*heua sa*) that ply these routes are built to fit the maximum amount of cargo and do not have any seats, leaving passengers to grab any spot they can find on the floor. Male passengers often opt to sit on the roof – an option not available to women because of Lao customs (see "Cultural Hints" p.462). You can never be guaranteed that there'll be a boat on a certain day, so show up early in the morning and ask around. Given fluctuations in current, and lengthy stops to load cargo, boats sometimes don't make their final destination during the daytime, forcing passengers to sleep in the nearest village or aboard the boat. Such stops will take you off the tourist track, so it's a good idea to bring extra water and food. Travel by slow boat can be dangerous and reports of boats sinking are not uncommon. The Mekong has some particularly tricky stretches, with narrow channels threading through rapids and past whirlpools, and can be particularly rough late in the rainy season.

On the northern routes, tickets are sold and ports overseen by a local government official. Foreigners pay significantly more than locals, but fares are generally posted. Buy your ticket the day you leave. **Southern routes** are more haphazard: prices are not posted and it's unlikely that you'll need to buy a ticket in advance.

Pesky, fire-engine red **speedboats** (*heua wai*) are Laos's version of adventure travel, and a riskier, more expensive alternative to the plodding cargo boats. Connecting towns along the Nam Ou and the Mekong from Vientiane to the Chinese border, these five-metre-long terrors can accommodate up to eight diminutive passengers. They can shave hours or days off a river journey, but cost as much as two to three times the slow-boat fare. Crash helmets are handed out before journeys: the headgear is meant to spare your hearing from the overpowering screech of the engine – not your head. However, you should still consider bringing along earplugs. Some drivers also provide life jackets. It's by no means safe, of course, although captains swear by their navigational skills. In one particularly nasty accident in 1998, two boats collided head-on, killing all on board.

■ Planes

Lao Aviation is the sole carrier servicing the country's internal flight network. With demand for domestic flights soaring in recent years, its tiny fleet of Chinese Yun-12 and Yun-7s and its lone ATR 72 have come under severe strain and, as of 1999, several Western embassies had travel advisories warning against flying Lao Aviation. Expats familiar with the airline claim that it is safe to fly the ATR; check with Western embassies in Vientiane for an update before you fly.

As with other forms of transport in Laos, you'll need to be extremely **flexible**. When booking a flight, don't count on the plane leaving at the appointed time or on the scheduled day. You may well turn up at the airport for your scheduled flight and find that the plane left the day before and that there isn't another one for a week. Reliability, however, increases on key routes: Vientiane–Louang Phabang, Vientiane–Pakxe and Vientiane–Phonsavan. Reconfirm your flight early and often at the Lao Aviation office.

Lao Aviation only accepts **US dollars cash**. In the provinces, if you do not have dollars, you'll need to get a letter from Lao Aviation informing the local bank that you need to exchange a travellers' cheque for dollars. Some banks may be able to give you a cash advance on Visa in dollars. **Sample one-way fares** are: Vientiane to Phonsavan $44; Vientiane to Xam Nua $70; Phonsavan to Louang Phabang $35; Louang Phabang to Vientiane $55; Vientiane to Pakxe $95.

■ Vehicle rental

Self-drive is an option, but it's usually easier and cheaper to hire a **car and driver**. Tour agencies will rent out air-conditioned vans and 4WD pick-up trucks as well as provide drivers. Prices can be as much as $80–100 per day. Always clarify who pays for the driver's food and lodging, fuel and repairs and be sure to ask what happens in case of a major breakdown or accident. A cheaper alternative for short distances and day-trips is to charter a tuk-tuk or pick-up truck.

Renting a **motorbike** ($8–10 per day) is only an option in Vientiane and Vang Viang, and even then you'll be restricted to 100cc step-throughs such as the Honda Dream; a licence is not required. Insurance is not available, so it's a good idea to make sure your travel insurance covers you for any potential accidents. Before zooming off, check the bike thoroughly for any scratches and damage and take it for a test run. Few rental places will have a helmet on offer, as it's not against the law to ride without one. Sunglasses are essential in order to fend off the glare and keep dust and bugs out of your eyes. Proper shoes, long trousers and a long-sleeved shirt will provide a thin layer of protection if you take a spill. **Bicycles** can sometimes be rented from guesthouses and tourist-oriented shops for around $1 per day.

Accommodation

Cheap **accommodation** can be found in larger towns all over Laos: for the most basic double room, prices start at around $2 in the provinces and $8 in

Vientiane. Moving up the scale to $20 lands you a cosy room in a restored French villa. Expect to find higher standards of accommodation, as well as the greatest variety, in larger Mekong River towns. Upcountry towns, with the exception of a few popular stopovers on the backpacker route such as Vang Viang and Muang Sing, lag far behind.

Always ask to see several rooms before choosing one, as **standards and room types can vary widely** within the same establishment. Many towns have **electricity** for only a few hours in the evening, so you should weigh the added cost of an air-con room against the number of hours you'll have power. Electrical wiring in budget guesthouses is usually an accident waiting to happen so exercise caution when fiddling with light switches. Electricity is supplied at 220 volts AC. Two-pin sockets are the norm.

En-suite showers and flush toilets are the norm in only mid-range and top-end hotels. At cheaper hotels, showers and toilets will probably be of the **traditional Asian** sort (see "Basics" p.38). In some places, villagers bathe at the river, the men in their underwear, women in sarongs.

The distinction between a **guesthouse and a budget hotel** is rather blurry in Laos. Either can denote anything ranging from a bamboo-and-thatch hut to a multi-storey concrete monstrosity. There are no youth hostels as yet, though some government-owned flophouses operate as dorms, charging by the bed, and some guesthouses also offer **dorm accommodation**. In peak season, finding a cheap room in Louang Phabang, Vang Viang and Vientiane can be tricky. It helps to check in by noon, just after people begin checking out. Guesthouses and budget hotels rarely take advance booking unless they know you already.

Once you've crossed the **$20 threshold**, you enter a whole new level of comfort. In the former French outposts on the Mekong this translates into an atmospheric room in a restored colonial villa or recently built accommodation with cable TV, fridge, air-conditioning and a hot-water shower. These places usually only have a limited number of rooms, so book ahead – well in advance if you plan to visit during the peak months (Dec–Jan).

If you find yourself **stuck in a village overnight**, locals are usually kind enough to put you up in the absence of a local guesthouse. In this situation you should either make yourself known at the police station, or ask permission from the village headman. Before leaving, you should offer to remunerate your host with a small sum of cash.

Food and drink

Fiery and fragrant, with a touch of sour, Lao **food** owes its distinctive taste to fermented fish sauces, lemon grass, coriander leaves, chillies and lime juice and is closely related to Thai cuisine. Eaten with the hands along with the staple sticky rice, much of Lao cuisine is roasted over an open fire and served with fresh herbs and vegetables. Pork, chicken, duck and water buffalo all end up in the kitchen, but freshwater fish is the main source of protein. An ingredient in nearly every recipe is *nâm pa*, or fermented fish sauce, and its thicker variation, *pa dàek*, which contains chunks of fermented fish (and carries the risk of liver flukes, except in Vientiane and Louang Phabang). Use of monosodium glutamate (MSG) is also quite common; if you'd prefer to avoid MSG, try saying *baw sai phõng sú lot* when ordering your food. Vientiane and Louang Phabang are the country's culinary centres, boasting excellent Lao food and international cuisine, but in many places outside the Mekong corridor, you'll be lucky to find anything more than a bowl of noodles.

Very few people in Laos are **vegetarian**, but it's fairly easy to ask for a vegetable-only rice or vegetable dish – in many places that may be your only option unless you eat fish. Most Lao cooking calls for fish sauce so you may want to add *"baw sai nâm pa"* ("without fish sauce").

Hygiene is an important consideration when eating anywhere in Laos. As a rule, noodle stalls and restaurants that do a brisk business are safe bets, though this is not much of a guide in smaller towns and villages, as so few people eat out. Dishes containing raw meat or fish are considered a delicacy, but people who eat them risk ingesting worms and other parasites. Cooked food that has been left standing should also be treated with suspicion. While the communal nature of Lao dining makes it difficult to do so, you should avoid sharing glasses and utensils.

■ Where to eat

The **cheapest places** for food are markets, food stalls and noodle shops. Found in most towns throughout Laos, **morning markets** (*talat sâo*) remain open all day despite their name and provide a focal point for noodle shops (*hân khãi fõe*), coffee vendors, fruit stands and sellers of crusty loaves of French bread. In Louang Phabang and Vientiane, vendors hawking pre-made dishes gather in **evening markets** known as *talat láeng* towards late afternoon. Takeaways such as grilled chicken (*pîng kai*), spicy papaya salad (*tam màk hung*) and, sometimes, dishes ranging from minced pork salad (*làp mu*) to stir-fried vegetables (*khùa phák*), are all available.

Noodle shops and some food stalls feature a makeshift kitchen surrounded by a handful of tables and stools, inhabiting a permanent patch of pavement or even an open-air shophouse. Most stalls will specialize in only one general food type, or even only one dish, for example a stall with a mortar and pestle, unripe papayas and plastic bags full of pork rinds will only offer spicy papaya salads. Similarly, a noodle shop will generally only prepare noodles with or without broth – they won't have meat or fish dishes that are usually eaten with rice. A step up from street stalls and noodle shops are *hân kin deum*, literally "eat–drink shops", where you'll find a somewhat greater variety of dishes, as well as beer and whisky. Outside the major tourist centres, street stalls and noodle shops rarely stay open beyond 8pm.

Most proper **restaurants** (*hân ahãn*) are open-air establishments of dubious hygiene. Ethnic Vietnamese and Chinese dominate the restaurant scene in Laos, as many Lao simply don't eat out. A Lao-food restaurant is identifiable by a bowl of water placed on a stool near the entrance – for diners to wash their hands – and, of course, the *típ khào* (lidded wicker basket for sticky rice) on the tables next to diners. Many of these basic eateries won't have any menus – in Lao or English – so it's a good idea to memorize a few stock dishes. Restaurants catering more to foreigners usually have an English menu and offer fried noodles and fried rice as well as a variety of Lao, Chinese and Thai dishes. Vientiane has a range of more expensive gourmet Lao restaurants, as well as some of the best international food in Southeast Asia. A meal in one of these places won't cost more than $10.

■ Lao food

Most **Lao meals** are enjoyed with **sticky rice** (*khào niaw*), which is served in a lidded wicker basket and eaten with the hands. Typically, rice will be accompanied by a fish or meat dish and soup, with a plate of fresh vegetables such as string beans, lettuce, basil and mint served on the side. Grab a small chunk of rice from the basket, roll it into a firm ball and then dip the ball into one of the dishes. At the end of your meal, it's thought bad luck not to replace the lid of the *típ khào*. Plain steamed white rice (*khào jâo*) is eaten with a fork and spoon; chopsticks (*mâi thu*) are reserved for noodles.

So that a variety of tastes can be enjoyed during the course of a meal, Lao meals are eaten **communally**, with each dish, including the soup, being served at once, rather than in courses. If you're eating a meal with steamed white rice, only put a small amount of one dish onto your rice at a time. If the meal is accompanied by sticky rice, it's normal to simply dip a ball of rice into the main servings. If there are two of you it's common to order two or three dishes, plus your own rice.

If Laos were to nominate a **national dish**, a strong contender would be *làp*, a "salad" of minced meat or fish mixed with garlic, chillies, shallots, eggplant, galingale, fried rice and fish sauce. *Làp* is either eaten raw (*díp*) – a culinary experience you may want to avoid – or *súk* (cooked). Another quintessentially Lao dish is *tam màk hung* (or *tam sòm*), a spicy papaya salad made with shredded green papaya, garlic, chillies, lime juice, *pa dàek* and, sometimes, dried shrimp and crab juice. Each vendor will have their own particular recipe, but it's also acceptable to pick out which ingredients – and how many chilli peppers – you'd like. Usually not too far away from any *tam màk hung* vendor, you'll find someone selling *pîng kai*, basted grilled chicken. Fish, *pîng pa*, is another grilled favourite, with whole fish skewered and barbecued.

When the Lao aren't filling up on glutinous rice, they're busy eating *fõe*, the ubiquitous **noodle soup** that takes its name from the Vietnamese soup *pho*. Although primarily eaten for breakfast, *fõe* can be enjoyed at any time of day, and, outside the tourist centres, may well be the mainstay of your diet. The basic bowl of *fõe* consists of a light broth to which is added thin rice noodles and slices of meat (usually beef, water buffalo or grilled chicken) and is served with a plate of lettuce, mint and coriander leaves and bean sprouts. Also on offer at many noodle shops is *mi*, a yellow wheat noodle served in broth with slices of meat and a few vegetables. It's also common to eat *fõe* and *mi* without broth (*hàeng*), and at times fried (*khùa*).

The best way to round off a meal is with **fresh fruit** (*màk mâi*), as the country offers a wide variety, including guavas, lychees, rambutans, mangosteen and pomelos. Sweets don't figure on many restaurant menus, although some offer desserts such as banana in coconut milk (*nâm wãn màk kûay*). Markets often have a food stall specializing in inexpensive **coconut-milk desserts**, generally called *nâm wãn*. Look for a stall displaying a dozen bowls, containing everything from water chestnuts to fluorescent green and pink jellies, from which one or two items are selected and then added to a sweet mixture of crushed ice, slabs of young coconut meat and coconut milk.

■ Drinks

The Lao don't **drink water** straight from the tap and nor should you; contaminated water is a major cause of sickness (see "Basics" p.27). Plastic bottles of drinking water (*nâm deum*) are sold countrywide for around 1000K, even in smaller towns. Noodle shops and inexpensive restaurants generally serve free pitchers of weak tea or boiled water (*nâm tóm*) which is fine, although perhaps not as foolproof. Most **ice** in Laos is produced in large blocks under hygienic conditions, but it can become less pure in transit or storage, so be wary. Brand-name soft drinks are widely available for around 2000K per bottle. More refreshing are the **fruit shakes** (*màk mâi pan*) available in larger towns, which consist of your choice of fruit blended with ice, liquid sugar and sweetened condensed milk. Freshly squeezed fruit juices, such as lemon (*nâm màk nao*) and coconut juice (*nâm màk phao*) are a popular alternative, as is sugar-cane juice (*nâm oi*).

Twenty thousand tonnes of **coffee** are produced in Laos annually, nearly all of it grown on the Bolaven Plateau, outside Pakxong in southern Laos. The Lao drink very strong coffee, or *kafeh hâwn*, which is served with sweetened condensed milk and sugar. If you prefer your coffee black, and without sugar, ask for *kafeh dam baw sai nâm tan*. Black tea is available at most coffee vendors and is what you get, mixed with sweetened condensed milk and sugar, when you request *sá hâwn*.

Many foreign beers are available in Laos, although **Beer Lao** (*Bia Lao*) is by far the most popular and the cheapest. In Vientiane and Louang Phabang, draft Beer Lao known as *bia sót* and sometimes labelled "Fresh Beer", is available at bargain prices by the litre. There are dozens of *bia sót* outlets in the capital, most of which are outdoor beer gardens with thatch roofs. Drunk with equal gusto is *lào-láo*, a clear **rice alcohol** with the fire of a blinding Mississippi moonshine. Although the government distils its own brand, Sticky Rice, which is sold nationally, most people indulge in local brews. *Lào-láo* is usually sold in whatever bottle the distiller had around at the time (look twice before you buy that bottle of Fanta) and sells at drink shops and general stores for around 2000K per 750ml. Drunk from a large earthenware jar with thin bamboo straws, the rice alcohol *lào hái* is fermented by households in the countryside and is weaker than *lào-láo*, closer to a wine in taste. Drinking *lào hái*, however, can be a bit risky as unboiled water is sometimes added during fermentation. Several brand-name rice whiskies, with a lower alcohol content than *lào-láo*, are available for around $1 at local general stores.

FOOD AND DRINK GLOSSARY

USEFUL PHRASES

Do you have a menu?	*khāw laikan ahān dae?*	No sugar	*baw sai nâm tan*
Do you have...?	*mi...baw?*	No ice	*baw sai nâm kâwn*
Not spicy...	*baw phét*	Bon appétit	*soen sàep*
I am vegetarian	*khói kin te phák*	Delicious	*sàep*
I would like...	*khói ao...*	Fork	*sawm*
Can I have the bill?	*khāw sek dae?*	Noodle shop	*hān kāi fōe*
Without fish sauce	*baw sai nâm pa*	Spoon	*buang*
I can't eat meat	*khói kin sîn baw dâi*	Restaurant	*hân ahān*

STAPLES

jeun khai	omelette	*màk mo*	watermelon	*pa*	fish
kai	chicken	*màk muang*	mango	*pa dàek*	fish paste
khai dao	egg, fried	*màk náo*	lime/lemon	*pét*	duck
khào jāo	rice, steamed	*màk nat*	pineapple	*phák*	vegetables
khào ji	bread	*màk phét*	chilli	*phõng sú lot*	MSG
khào niaw	rice, sticky	*mu*	pork	*pu*	crab
kûng	shrimp	*nâm pa*	fish sauce	*sîn ngúa*	beef
màk kûay	banana	*nâm tan*	sugar	*tâo hû*	bean curd
màk len	tomato	*nóm sòm*	yoghurt		

NOODLES

fõe	rice noodle soup	*khào pûn*	flour noodles with sauce
fõe hàeng	rice noodle soup without broth	*mi hàeng*	yellow wheat noodles without broth
fõe khùa	fried rice noodles		
khào piak sèn	rice noodle soup, served in chicken broth	*mi nâm*	yellow wheat noodle soup

EVERYDAY DISHES

khào ji pateh	bread with Lao-style pâté and vegetables	*mu phát bai hólapha*	pork with basil over rice
khào ji sai boe	bread with butter	*pîng kai*	grilled chicken
khào khùa or *khào phát*	fried rice	*pîng pa* or *jeun pa*	grilled fish
khào khùa sai kai	fried rice with chicken	*tam màk hung*	spicy papaya salad
khùa khing kai	chicken with ginger	*tôm yam pa*	spicy fish soup with lemongrass
khùa phák baw sai sîn	stir-fried vegetables	*yam sìn ngúa*	spicy beef salad
làp mu	minced pork	*yáw díp*	spring rolls, fresh
man falang jeun	chips	*yáw jeun*	spring rolls, fried

DRINKS

bia	beer	*màk mai pan*	fruit shake
bia sót	beer, draught	*nâm deum*	water
kafeh	coffee	*nâm kâwn*	ice
kafeh dam	black coffee	*nâm màk phào*	coconut juice
kafeh nóm hawn	hot Lao coffee (with milk and sugar)	*nâm sá*	tea
		nâm soda	soda water
kafeh nóm yén	iced coffee (with milk and sugar)	*nâm yén*	water, cold
		nóm	milk
lào-láo	rice whisky	*sá jin*	tea, Chinese
màk kuay pan	banana shake		

Communications

Mail takes seven to fourteen days in or out of Laos. Express Mail Service operates to most Western countries and certain destinations within Laos; the service cuts down on delivery time and automatically registers your letter. When sending **parcels**, leave the package open for inspection. However, it is not advisable to ship anything of value home from Laos; if you're going to Thailand, wait and send it from there. Incoming parcels are also subject to inspection.

Poste restante services are available in Vientiane and Louang Phabang; always address mail using the country's official name, Lao PDR, rather than "Laos". See "Basics" p.39 for further information on poste restante.

The best place to make **overseas telephone calls** is the Telecom Office in Vientiane. A few towns have similar offices (8am–9pm); elsewhere, international calls can be placed at the post office, until 11pm. To **call abroad from Laos**, dial ☎00 and then the relevant country code (see "Basics" p.40 for a list). Calls to the UK and North America cost approximately $3 per minute, $1.50 to New Zealand and less than $1 to Australia. There's no facility to collect or **reverse-charge calls**, but you can almost always get a "call back" for a small fee: ask the operator for the minimum call abroad and get the phone number of the post office you're calling from. International **fax** services are available at upmarket hotels in Vientiane and Louang Phabang and at most provincial post offices.

Public **card-phones** are wired for both domestic and international calls, but at the moment aren't much use for the latter. Phone booths are usually stationed outside post offices in provincial capitals, and occasionally elsewhere in larger towns. Phone cards (*bat tholasap*) are sold at post and telephone offices in denominations of 100 and 500 units; these are units of time rather than money. When the cards first came out they offered a relatively good deal for international calls, but by late 1999 it was impossible to make an overseas call that lasted for more than three minutes. You can also place domestic and local calls at hotels and guesthouses for a small fee. **Regional codes** are given throughout the chapter: the "0" must be dialled before all long-distance calls.

The emergence of an Internet Service Provider (ISP) in Laos has drastically reduced the price and increased the availability of access to the Web. Currently you'll find **email and Internet** services at cybercafés, computer shops and some hotels in

---

TIME DIFFERENCES

Laos is seven hours ahead of London (GMT), twelve hours ahead of US Eastern Standard Time, fifteen hours ahead of US Pacific Time, three hours behind Sydney and five hours behind Auckland.

Vientiane, Louang Phabang, Vang Viang and Pakxe, although it won't be long before these services spring up in other tourist centres around the country. **Charges** range from 500K to 2000K per minute, depending on how far you are from the capital, where the lone ISP – Laonet – is based. If you plan to do a lot of emailing or Websurfing, contact Laonet, Samsenthai Road, mezzanine floor of the *Lao Hotel Plaza* (☎021/218841–2; *services@laonet.net*), about setting up a temporary account ($20 for 21 hours of usage). For details on using email as an alternative to poste restante, see "Basics" p.39.

Opening hours and festivals

In 1998, the official **working hours** of all government offices were adjusted. The two-hour lunch break was shortened to one, and government workers were given Saturday off. Old habits die hard though, which means that while official hours for **government offices** are 8am–12pm and 1–5pm Monday to Friday, very little gets done between 11am and 2pm. **Post offices** are generally open 8am–5pm Monday to Friday, 8am–4pm on Saturday and 8am–noon on Sunday. **Banking hours** are usually 8.30am–3.30pm, Monday to Friday nationwide; exchange kiosks keep longer hours but are rare. The hours of private **businesses** vary, but almost all are closed on Sunday. During the heat of the day many

---

PUBLIC HOLIDAYS

January 1: New Year's Day
January 6: Pathet Lao Day
January 20: Army Day
March 8: Women's Day
March 22: Lao People's Party Day
April 15–17: Lao New Year
May 1: International Labour Day
June 1: Children's Day
August 13: Lao Isara
August 23: Liberation Day
October 12: Freedom from France Day
December 2: National Day

shop owners will partly close their doors and snooze, but it is perfectly acceptable to wake them up. All government businesses close on public holidays, though some shops and restaurants should stay open. The only time when many private businesses do close – for three to seven days – is during Chinese New Year (new moon in late Jan to mid-Feb), when the ethnic-Vietnamese and Chinese populations of Vientiane, Thakhek, Savannakhet and Pakxe celebrate with parties and temple visits.

■ Festivals

All major **festivals**, whether Buddhist or animist, feature parades, music and dancing, not to mention the copious consumption of *lào-láo*. Because the Lao calendar is dictated by both solar and lunar rhythms, the dates of festivals change from year to year. Tourists are usually welcome to participate in the more public Buddhist festivals, but at hilltribe festivals you should only watch from a distance.

Festivals of most interest to tourists include **Lao New Year**, *pi mai lao* (April 15–17), which is most stunningly observed in Louang Phabang, where there's a big procession, and sand stupas are erected in monastery grounds; in Vientiane, there's a parade led by a white elephant; and anywhere in the country you may be ambushed by young people carrying pails of water and armed with squirt guns. Also known as the rocket festival, **Bun Bang Fai** (May) is a rain-making ritual that predates Buddhism in Laos, and involves launching crude rockets accompanied by plenty of bawdy jokes and props. **Lai Heua Fai** (full moon in October) is a festival of lights, most magically celebrated in Louang Phabang, where each neighbourhood builds a large float, festoons it with lights and parades it first through the streets and then on the Mekong. In the days leading up to the **That Louang Festival** (full moon in November), Vientiane's great stupa becomes the centrepiece of a fairground, where vendors, musicians and other performers gather for the annual celebrations.

Cultural hints

Laos by and large shares the same **attitudes to dress and social taboos** as other Southeast Asian cultures; see "Basics" p.41 for details.

One additional taboo applies to **women sitting on the roof** of anything – including a bus or a boat. The Lao believe that a woman has the power to ruin the potency of a man's amulets simply by placing herself physically above him. Furthermore, boats are thought to possess a guardian spirit, and a woman riding on the roof offends this spirit, which is to invite dire consequences for passengers and crew.

The **lowland Lao traditionally greet each other** with a *nop* – bringing their hands together at the chin in a prayer-like gesture. The status of the persons giving and returning the *nop* determines how they will execute it, so most Lao prefer to shake hands with Westerners. If you do receive a *nop* as a gesture of greeting or thank you, it is best to reply with a smile and nod of the head, the customary way for strangers to show that they mean well.

Crime and safety

Laos is a **relatively safe country** for travellers, although certain areas remain off-limits because of banditry and unexploded ordnance. The recent economic woes have pushed crime rates up slightly in Vientiane, but petty crime remains on a small scale. As a visitor, however, you're an obvious target for thieves (who may include your fellow travellers), so keep your wits about you.

If you do have **anything stolen**, you'll need to get the police to write up a report for your insurance: bring along a Lao speaker if you can. **Police** generally keep their distance from foreigners, but in some larger Mekong River towns you may be stopped at night and "fined". With patience, you should be able to resolve most problems, and perhaps even bargain down the "fines", easier to do if you always have your passport with you. **Officials at border crossings** routinely levy small "fines"; there's little you can do in such cases. To alleviate unnecessary suspicion in remoter corners of Laos, it never hurts to check in with the police, especially in small towns in the north and near the Vietnamese border in the south.

■ Banditry

Banditry is a very real threat in Laos, although you can greatly reduce the risks by planning your route wisely and heeding local warnings. During the past two decades, buses, motorcyclists and private vehicles on certain highways have been held up, their passengers robbed and, in some instances, killed. Check with local guesthouse owners and bus drivers before setting out.

Security has improved greatly along **Route 13** between Kasi and Louang Phabang since the mid-1990s, but, as of 1998, many expats were still discouraged by their employers from travelling on this stretch.

Bandits are still active east of Route 13 along Route 7, so travel between Muang Phoukhoun and Muang Soui is not advised; at the time of writing, buses were not covering this section and vehicles without military escorts were not permitted on the road. If you plan on travelling by road to Phonsavan, the safest route is via Nong Khiaw, along Routes 1, 6 and 7.

South of Route 7 lies the **Xaisomboun Special Zone**, a new administrative district carved out of Xiang Khouang and Bolikhamxai provinces, also considered unsafe. The eastern part of this district, where Route 6 connects Muang Khoun with Pakxan, is another troubled area that should be avoided. Caution should be exercised in the far south along the Cambodian border as well, particularly the section of the Mekong between the Lao island of Don Khon and the Cambodian right bank.

■ Unexploded ordnance

The Second Indochina War left Laos with a legacy of bombs, **landmines** and mortar shells that will haunt the country for decades to come, despite the efforts of de-mining organizations. Round, tennis-ball sized anti-personnel bomblets, known as *bombi*, are the most common type of **unexploded ordnance** (UXO), and large bombs, ranging in size from 100kg to 1000kg, also proliferate. Ten provinces have one or more districts severely contaminated with UXO; listed in order of impact they are: Savannakhet, Xiang Khouang, Salavan, Khammouan, Xekong, Champasak, Saisomboun, Houa Phan, Attapu and Louang Phabang. Another five provinces have at least one district with significant contamination: Louang Namtha, Phongsali, Bolikhamxai, Vientiane Province, Vientiane Prefecture.

Although most towns and tourist sites are free of UXO, **25 percent of villages remain contaminated** and accidents continue at a rate of two hundred per year. As accidents often occur while people are tending their fields, the risk faced by the average visitor is relatively limited. Nonetheless, the number one rule is: don't be a trailblazer. When in rural areas, always stay on well-worn paths, even when passing through a village, and don't pick up or kick at anything if you don't know what it is. Take special care in areas known to be heavily contaminated, such as the districts surrounding the former Ho Chi Minh Trail.

■ Drugs

Officially it's illegal to smoke ganja but some travellers carry on discreetly. **Opium** use among tourists has increased dramatically in recent years, despite a new law against possession, distribution and trafficking. Opium is not as addictive as heroin, but withdrawal is painful.

EMERGENCY NUMBERS

In Vientiane dial the following numbers: fire ☎190, ambulance ☎195, police ☎191. There are no emergency numbers for the rest of the country.

Medical care and emergencies

You'll find pharmacies in the major cities. Pharmacists in Vientiane and Louang Phabang are quite knowledgeable and have a decent supply of medicines.

Health care in Laos is so poor as to be virtually nonexistent. The nearest **medical care** of any competence is in neighbouring Thailand, and if you find yourself afflicted by anything more serious than travellers' diarrhoea, it's best to head for the closest Thai border crossing and check into a hospital. A clinic attached to the Australian embassy in Vientiane is mainly for embassy personnel, but can be relied upon in extreme emergencies.

History

Laos as a unified state within its present geographical boundaries has only existed for little more than one hundred years. Its national history stretches back six centuries to the legendary kingdom of Lane Xang, once a rival to the powerful empires of mainland Southeast Asia.

■ The beginnings

The earliest known **indigenous culture** in Laos was an iron-age megalithic people that lived on the Plain of Jars, at the centre of trade routes to China, Vietnam and points south. The early inhabitants of Laos and the surrounding parts of central and southern Indochina spoke Austroasiatic languages such as Mon and Khmer, while the ancestors of the lowland Lao spoke proto-Tai languages, and were still living in the river valleys of southeastern China.

With the lowlands to the east and northeast densely settled by Vietnamese and Chinese populations, the **Tai** peoples slowly migrated west and southwest into northern Laos and southern Yunnan, displacing the sparse indigenous population of

Austronesian and Austroasiatic groups and forcing them into the less desirable upland areas – where their descendants still live today. This migration of the Tai is reflected in the Lao legend of **Khoun Borom**, the heavenly first ancestor, a version of which dates this event in 698 AD.

■ Early influences

The cultural roots of the present-day Lao lie in **Indian civilization**, not Chinese. From the first century AD, Indian traders began introducing Buddhism to Southeast Asia, and between the sixth and ninth centuries upper Laos, along with central and north-eastern Thailand, was dominated by the Theravada Buddhist culture of the Mon people, known as **Dvaravati**.

As the ninth century drew to a close, Dvaravati's influence was rapidly being eclipsed by the **Khmer Empire** of Angkor. At its height, the mostly Hindu Khmer Empire extended from its core of Cambodia and lower northeastern Thailand into Vietnam, central Thailand and Laos, where it built dozens of Angkor-style temple complexes.

■ The rise of Lane Xang

By the thirteenth century, Louang Phabang had emerged as one of the chief Tai centres of the Upper Mekong, an area settled by people who called themselves **Lao**. A century later, though still significant, Louang Phabang, then known as Xiang Dong Xiang Thong, had become but one of many small Lao principalities on the fringes of two larger Tai states: Lan Na, centred on Chiang Mai, and Sukhothai.

Lao legends tell of a young prince called **Fa Ngum** who was cast out of Xiang Dong Xiang Thong principality, only to be taken in by the Khmer court at Angkor, where he married a Khmer princess. Provided with an army by the Khmer king, Fa Ngum fought his way up the Mekong valley in 1351 – subduing the principalities of the lower Mekong valley, capturing Muang Phuan, the capital of Xiang Khouang principality, and then ascending the throne in Xiang Dong Xiang Thong in 1353. Fa Ngum called his new kingdom **Lane Xang Hom Khao**, the Kingdom of a Million Elephants and the White Parasol, and during his reign expanded its borders south into northeastern Thailand and north into present-day Xishuangbanna in China.

Fa Ngum's son, Oun Heuan (1373–1417), ruled peacefully for 43 years, but then followed a turbulent period culminating in a major Vietnamese invasion in 1479, which destroyed Xiang Dong Xiang Thong. But Lane Xang recovered quickly, coalescing in particular under Visoun (1500–1520), who reinforced the role of Buddhism in Laos by bringing the golden Buddha image, the **Pha Bang,** to Xiang Dong Xiang Thong from Vientiane in 1512 and establishing it as the symbol of a unified kingdom.

■ The Burmese invasions

By the time Visoun's grandson, Setthathilat (1548–1571), came to power, Burma was becoming an increasing threat to Lane Xang, so he officially moved his capital to the more strategically sited **Vientiane** in 1563; the revered Pha Bang was left in Xiang Dong Xiang Thong, and the city renamed after it. Despite the relocation, Burmese warrior-kings still managed to reduce Lane Xang (along with Lan Na and Ayutthaya) to vassalage within a decade.

■ The division of Lane Xang

The decisive character who returned stability to the kingdom and eventually ushered in the **Golden Age** of Lane Xang was Sourinyavongsa (1637–1694). He aligned Lane Xang through marriage with neighbouring powers, invaded Xiang Khouang, forged a border treaty with Vietnam, and confirmed the watershed line between the Mekong and the Chao Phraya rivers as the frontier with Ayutthaya.

Following Sourinyavongsa's death in 1694, however, the three regions of the country went their separate ways. Sourinyavongsa's grandson Kingkitsalat became the first ruler of an **independent Louang Phabang kingdom**, while another prince, who called himself Setthathilat II, ruled over **Vientiane**.

Meanwhile, the kingdom was further divided by the emergence of a new ruling house in the south, at **Champasak**, under a long lost son of Sourinyavongsa, King Soi Sisamut. Thus the new ruling lines of each of the three major principalities could claim, however tenuously, some link to Fa Ngum and by extension, to Khoun Borom. Rivalry between Louang Phabang and Vientiane was bitter, however, and when a second wave of Burmese invasions swept across the Tai world in the 1760s, forces from Vientiane aligned with the invaders and helped sack Louang Phabang.

■ The rise of Siam

In 1767, the Burmese also razed Ayutthaya, but the **Siamese** quickly rebuilt their kingdom downriver from Ayuthaya near Bangkok, and within a decade had retaken its territory, and were preparing to expand eastwards. 20,000 Siamese soldiers set out for Vientiane in 1778, devastating the city and dragging hundreds of prisoners back to Thailand, as well as the kingdom's precious Pha Bang image. Champasak and Vientiane were reduced to vassal states and Louang Phabang brought into an unequal alliance.

Over the next century, Siam and Vietnam jockeyed for control over the fragmented Lao *muang*, with the Lao territories eventually forming a buffer zone between the two powers. This balancing act was upset, however, by the arrival of the French.

■ French rule

France's initial interest in Laos stemmed from a belief that the Mekong River would provide a backdoor route to China and the resource-rich Yunnan region. Although the Mekong Exploration Commission of 1867–1868 soon discovered that significant stretches of the river were unnavigable, enthusiasm for Laos was rekindled by explorer **Auguste Pavie**, who conducted a "conquest of hearts" in the name of France in the 1880s and 1890s. As vice-consul in Louang Phabang, Pavie persuaded the northern kingdom to pay tribute to France instead of Siam, and by 1893 Siam had relinquished its claim to all territory east of the Mekong River.

For half a century, Laos was ruled as a **French colony**, with Vientiane as their administrative capital. But the French interest was halfhearted and Laos was in reality a neglected backwater of France's other Southeast Asian acquisitions.

■ World War II

The fall of France to Germany in 1940 suddenly changed the political landscape. The Japanese occupied Laos, and Siam, renamed Thailand in 1939, seized the west-bank territories of Xainyabouli and Champasak. In April 1945, the Japanese forced Sisavang Vong, the pro-French Lao king, to declare independence. Phetsarath became prime minister and an independent-minded Lao elite formed a government which became known as the **Lao Issara**, literally "Free Laos". Phetsarath wanted the Kingdom of Louang Phabang and the territory of Champasak to be a single, independent Kingdom of Laos, and King Sisavang Vong was deposed.

The **Potsdam Agreement**, which marked the end of World War II, failed to recognize the Lao Issara government. In March 1946, French reoccupation forces, along with their Lao allies, recaptured Vientiane and Louang Phabang. Thousands of Lao Issara supporters fled to Thailand, where Phetsarath established a government-in-exile in Bangkok, as the French reasserted their control over Laos.

■ The Pathet Lao

By early 1947, the Kingdom of Laos had begun to take shape as Laos – under French political, military and economic control – became unified under the royal house of Louang Phabang.

The French, however, were increasingly bogged down in their struggle with Vietnam's nationalist **Viet Minh**, which had erupted in December 1946 and was to become known as the First Indochina War. The Viet Minh were also active in Laos, participating in Lao Issara guerilla raids on French convoys and garrisons. In July 1949, France appealed to the more moderate elements of the Lao Issara by conceding greater authority and independence to the Vientiane government. The Lao Issara announced its dissolution.

While the moderate members of the dissolved Lao Issara joined the new Royal Lao Government (RLG) in 1950, Souphanouvong (younger brother of Phetsarath) founded the resistance group **"Pathet Lao"**, literally "the Land of the Lao", which called for a truly independent Laos to be governed by a coalition government with the RLG. They immediately set about recruiting for the Lao People's Party and the Liberation Army.

■ The First Indochina War

By the early 1950s, the **First Indochina War** had engulfed the region. Chinese military aid flowed to the Viet Minh, while the United States supported France. For the Viet Minh, Laos was an extension of their battle against the French. Twice in 1953 they staged major invasions of Laos, seizing large areas of the country and turning them over to the Pathet Lao. By the time full independence was granted in October 1953, Laos was a divided country, with large areas controlled by the Pathet Lao and the rest of the country under the Royal Lao Government. Eventually the French surrendered on May 7, 1954.

At the **Geneva Conference**, which convened on May 8, Laos was reaffirmed as a unitary, independent state with a single government. The Royal Lao agreed not to pursue a policy of aggression or to allow a foreign power to use its soil for hostile purposes. And the Pathet Lao were allotted the provinces of Phongsali and Houa Phan in which to regroup.

■ America intervenes

After the 1954 Geneva Accords, which the US did not sign, strengthening the anti-communist governments of Indochina became a priority for President Dwight Eisenhower's administration. For the US, Laos, not South Vietnam, was the key to Indochina; their policies were motivated by the fear of the **Domino Effect** that could follow in Southeast Asia were Laos to turn communist.

As of 1955, the US was **bankrolling** the Royal Lao Army, countering the Viet Minh, which was financing the Pathet Lao's army. For the next eight years, the US spent more on foreign aid to Laos per capita than it did on any other Southeast Asian country, including South Vietnam.

When the **elections** of May 58 gave leftist candidates 21 seats in the National Assembly, the United States got worried and engineered the collapse of the government led by the moderate Prince Souvannaphouma (half-brother of Souphanouvong) and the arrest of Pathet Lao leaders, including Souphanouvong. Power in Vientiane had shifted to the American Embassy, and civil war in Laos seemed inevitable.

With help from the US-backed Committee for the Defence of National Interests (CDNI), General Phoumi staged a coup in December, and when new elections were held, a rigged ballot left the leftists without a seat. As a result, national **support for the Pathet Lao** increased, and by 1960, roughly twenty percent of the population was no longer under government control. Meanwhile, all fifteen Pathet Lao prisoners, including Souphanouvong, escaped from jail.

■ The Laotian crisis

In August 1960, self-proclaimed "neutralist" Kong Le seized control of Vientiane, and invited Souvannaphouma to lead a new government. Phoumi, who refused to join Souvannaphouma's government, gained the backing of the CIA and in November began marching forces on Vientiane. The Soviet Union responded by airlifting supplies to Kong Le's neutralist forces. Laos was now at the centre of a **Cold War** showdown. By the time Phoumi's troops reached Vientiane in December, the neutralists had allied themselves with the Pathet Lao and the Viet Minh.

Meanwhile, the CIA recruited a clandestine army of ethnic **Hmong**, under the command of Vang Pao, a brilliant Hmong lieutenant-colonel. The Hmong were naturals as guerila soldiers; determined to defend their homeland, they knew the terrain. But by 1968, Vang Pao's forces were no longer fighting for their homeland, they were fighting for the United States, pawns of the war in Vietnam.

■ The Second Indochina War

Despite the 1962 accords of a second Geneva conference, Laos was being drawn increasingly into the **Second Indochina War**, as North Vietnam and the United States undermined the country's neutrality in the pursuit of their agendas in Vietnam.

Lao territory was a crucial part of the North Vietnamese war effort. They needed to control the mountainous eastern corridor of southern Laos in order to move soldiers and supplies to South Vietnam along the **Ho Chi Minh Trail**. The US saw no option but to challenge North Vietnam's strategy. So the right-wing Lao, the Americans and the Thais on the one side and the Pathet Lao, the North Vietnamese and their Chinese and Soviet backers on the other all tacitly agreed to pretend to abide by the accords, "guaranteeing Laos's neutrality" while in reality keeping the country at war.

In 1964, a new phase of the war in Laos began. With the US pushing hard for an **escalation of the bombing**, Souvannaphouma (kept in power with help from the US) gave the go-ahead for so-called "armed reconnaissance" flights over Laos, which essentially meant the US could bomb wherever it pleased.

The war took place in **total secrecy**. US ground troops were kept out and military planes had to take off outside the country. As journalist Christopher Robbins wrote, "There was another war even nastier than the one in Vietnam, and so secret that the location of the country in which it was being fought was classified." From 1964 until the ceasefire of February 1973, United States planes flew 580,944 sorties – or 177 a day – over Laos and dropped **2,093,100 tons of bombs** – equivalent to one planeload of bombs every eight minutes around the clock for nine years – making Laos the most heavily bombed country per capita in the history of warfare.

When Nixon became US president in 1969, he initiated a policy of "Vietnamization" in which South Vietnam troops would gradually replace US ground forces, backed up by further escalation of the air war. This proved disastrous two years later, for operation **Lam Son 719** (see p.516), in which South Vietnamese troops invaded Laos in an attempt to sever the Ho Chi Minh Trail near Xepon in the south, the largest remaining communist stronghold after Cambodia. Five thousand South Vietnamese were killed or wounded, and more than one hundred US army helicopters shot down.

■ The Lao People's Democratic Republic

The US, North Vietnam, South Vietnam and the Viet Cong at last signed the **Paris Accords** on January 27, 1973, and a ceasefire was established. In April 1974, a coalition government was formed, with Souvannaphouma as prime minister and Souphanouvong heading the National Political Consultative Council.

When Phnom Penh and then Saigon fell to communist forces in April 1975, a complete communist takeover in Laos appeared inevitable. "Liberating" towns as they went, Pathet Lao forces reached Vientiane on August 23. On December 2, 1975, the **Lao People's Democratic Republic** was proclaimed and the abdication of King Sisavang Vatthana accepted. Kaysone was named prime minister, and Souphanouvong president.

Although the Pathet Lao took power in a bloodless coup, they sent as many as fifty thousand royalists to **re-education camps**, which turned out to be malaria-ridden labour camps. On their release, many lowland Lao left the country, and by the mid-1980s Laos had lost ten percent of its population – including an overwhelming majority of its educated class. The communist government, fearful that the populace would rally around the dethroned king, arrested him and the royal family in 1977 and exiled them to a cave in Houa Phan province near the Vietnamese border where they died of hunger and exposure – effectively extinguishing the centuries-old Lao monarchy.

The new government took over a country stripped of resources, and with an economy in shambles. Intent on ushering in a socialist state, the Pathet Lao followed **Eastern bloc models**, collectivizing farms, centralizing control of prices and nationalizing what little industry there was. Long-haired teenagers were obliged to get haircuts, women had to wear traditional skirts, and prostitutes and petty thieves were shipped off to re-education camps. Gradually a less rigid form of socialism was adopted, but Laos remained one of the world's poorest countries, with a per capita income of $100.

■ The new thinking

In November 1986 Kaysone implemented the **New Economic Mechanism**, essentially a market economy, which resulted in less government intrusion in people's lives and an abundance of material goods on the markets. Political changes did not accompany the economic reforms, however, and dissenters were still arrested. But by the late 1980s, Lao refugees were returning from Thailand, and Western tourists began to visit the country. The government improved ties with Thailand, ambassadorial relations were re-established with the US in 1992, and in 1997 Laos became a member of the Association of Southeast Asian Nations.

Unfortunately, the 1997 **Asian economic crisis** proved a major setback for Laos. The Lao currency lost eighty percent of its value between June 1997 and early 1999; inflation soared to a hundred percent; direct investment plummeted, and infrastructure projects were put on hold. The crisis has brought many of the weaknesses of the Lao economy to the surface, including the country's heavy reliance on foreign aid, which accounts for fifteen percent of Laos's GDP. The party appears to have few answers for the current economic dilemma – something which could ultimately threaten its hold on power and the unity of the country.

On 26 October 1999, a number of students and teachers attempted to hold a demonstration in front of the Presidential Palace in Vientiane to protest against the desperate state of the Lao nation. In a rare show of defiance against the government, the protesters passed out a list of reforms and urged their leaders to loosen their grip on the economy and to institute more freedoms. Predictably, the government cracked down hard on the demonstrators and several were arrested and imprisoned. The Lao government was successful in suppressing news of this event and reports that did reach the outside world were brief and vague.

On 1 January 2000, the Lao government held an exorcism ceremony at the former royal palace in Louang Phabang in an attempt to placate the spirits of the dead royals which, the old communists believe, are avenging their own murders by ruining the Lao economy. Twenty five years after the revolution, the government is still attempting to blame the monarchy for its woes.

Religions of Laos

Theravada Buddhism is the majority religion in Laos, practised by approximately two thirds of the population, followed by animism and ancestor worship. The remainder practise Mahayana Buddhism and Taoism, and a small percentage follow Christianity or Islam. As with many Buddhists of Southeast Asia, most Lao also make offerings to animist spirits and certain Hindu deities. For an introduction to all these faiths, see "Basics" p.47.

Lao-style **Theravada Buddhism** is a blend of indigenous and borrowed beliefs and rituals that owes much to the practices of neighbouring Thailand. In particular, the Hindu deities Brahma and Indra (who were adopted by Siam after the sacking of Angkor) have become icons in the Theravada Buddhist pantheon. Chinese and Vietnamese immigrants brought Mahayana Buddhism with them and today you may well see alongside images of the Buddha a representation of a Hindu god such as Ganesh or a Mahayana Buddhist deity such as Kuan Yin.

Following the Revolution, the communists banned alms-giving, effectively making it impossible to live as a monk, as it's against Buddhist precepts for monks to cultivate plants or raise animals for food. But popular outcry forced the government to rescind these measures, and Lao Buddhism has made a strong comeback.

The Buddhist Lao still harbour vestiges of **animist** beliefs, building "**spirit houses**" (miniature dolls-house- or temple-style buildings on a pedestal) on their property to provide a dwelling for the spirits who have been displaced from the land by humans. Some midland and highland tribal peoples in Laos are exclusively animist, and **ancestor worship** in different forms is also practised by many of the highland tribes that emigrated from China, including the Akha, Hmong and Mien.

The peoples of Laos

Laos is one of the last countries in Southeast Asia whose **minorities** have not been totally assimilated into the culture of the majority. The Lao government officially divides the population into three brackets, according to the elevation at which they live, though there is often no link between peoples in these brackets as many unrelated ethnic groups may reside at any one elevation.

■ The lowland Lao

The so-called **Lao Loum** (or lowland Lao) live at the lowest elevations and on the land best suited for cultivation. For the most part, they are the **ethnic Lao**, a people related to the Thai of Thailand and the Shan of Burma. The lowland Lao make up the majority in Laos, between 50 percent and 60 percent. They pre-

fer to inhabit river valleys and practise Theravada Buddhism as well as some animist rituals. Of all the ethnicities found in Laos, the culture of the lowland Lao is dominant, mainly because it is they who hold political power. Their language is the official language, their religion is the state religion and their holy days are the official holidays.

Akin to the ethnic Lao are the **Tai Leu, Phuan** and **Phu Tai**, found in the northwest, the northeast and mid-south respectively. They are all Theravada Buddhists and, like the Lao, also placate animist spirits. Most have assimilated into Lao culture.

Other Tai peoples related to the Lao are the so-called "**tribal Tai**", who are mostly animists. These include the Tai Daeng (Red Tai), Tai Khao (White Tai) and Tai Dam (Black Tai). **Tai Dam** women wear long-sleeved, tight-fitting blouses in bright colours with a row of butterfly-shaped silver buttons down the front plus a long, indigo-coloured skirt and an indigo bonnet.

■ Mon–Khmer groups

The ethnic Lao believe themselves to have originally inhabited an area that is present-day Dien Bien Phu in Vietnam. As they moved southwards they displaced the original inhabitants of the region, forcing them to resettle at higher elevations. The **Khamu** of northern Laos, speakers of a Mon–Khmer language, are the most numerous of the indigenes, but have assimilated to a high degree. A large spirit house located outside the village gates attests to the Khamu belief in animism.

Another Mon–Khmer-speaking group which inhabits the north, particularly Xainyabouli province, are the **Htin**. Owing to a partial cultural ban on the use of any kind of metal, the Htin excel at fashioning bamboo baskets and fish traps.

The Bolaven Plateau in southern Laos is named for the **Laven** people, yet another Mon–Khmer-speaking group whose presence predates that of the Lao. The Laven were very quick to assimilate the ways of the southern Lao. Other Mon–Khmer-speaking minorities found in the south, particularly in Savannakhet and Salavan include the **Bru**, who are skilled builders of animal traps; the **Gie-Trieng**, who are expert basket weavers; the **Nge**, who produce textiles featuring stylized bombs and fighter planes; and the **Katu**, said to be a very warlike people.

■ Highland groups

The **Lao Soung** (literally the "high Lao") live at the highest elevations, having migrated from China at the beginning of the nineteenth century. This group includes the Hmong, Mien, Lahu and Akha.

Of these the **Hmong** are the most numerous, with a population of approximately 200,000. They migrated from China to escape persecution and found relative freedom in Laos until the arrival of the French, who sought to tax them. This led to a number of bloody revolts. Later, an incident caused a schism between two Hmong clans, and the French backed one side, causing the other side to become allied with the fledgling Lao communist movement. The communists promised the Hmong their own independent state if they were victorious. After the French defeat, their Hmong allies were recruited by the CIA to form a "secret army" against the communists. With the communist victory in 1975, the promise of an independent homeland was conveniently forgotten and many Hmong were severely persecuted. Tens of thousands of Hmong fled to refugee camps in Thailand for eventual resettlement in the United States and France. Today, Hmong bandits (or patriots, depending on whom you talk to) continue to make some roads in northeastern Laos dangerous. Hmong apparel is among the most colourful to be found in Laos and their silver jewellery is prized by collectors. Their written language uses Roman letters and was devised by Western missionaries.

The **Mien** are linguistically related to the Hmong and also emigrated from China, but they write in Chinese characters and worship Taoist deities. Like the Hmong, they cultivate opium, which they trade for salt and other necessities. Mien women wear intricately embroidered pantaloons with a coat and turban of indigo blue and a woolly red boa. It is estimated that nearly half the population of Mien fled Laos after the communist victory.

Speakers of a Tibeto–Burman language, the **Akha** began migrating south from China's Yunnan province in the mid-nineteenth century. In Laos they are found mainly in Phongsali and Louang Namtha provinces. Their villages are easily distinguished by the elaborate "spirit gate" hung with woven bamboo "stars" that block spirits, as well as talismanic carvings of helicopters, aeroplanes and even grenades, and crude male and female effigies. The Akha are animists and rely on a village shaman to help solve problems of health, fertility or protection against malevolent spirits. They use opium to soothe aches and pains. The Akha women's distinctive headgear is covered with rows of silver baubles and coins.

The **Lahu** inhabit areas of northwestern Laos, as well as Thailand and Burma. A branch of the Lahu tribe known as the Lahu Na, or Black Lahu, are known first and foremost for their hunting skills. Formerly they used crossbows but now manufacture their own muzzle-loading rifles which they use to hunt birds and rodents.

Books

As Laos is one of the least-known countries in Southeast Asia, it should come as no surprise to find that **books on Laos** are hard to come by. With the demand for books on Laos very limited, you might have more luck searching for many of the titles listed below at an online bookstore such as *www.amazon.com* than you would wandering the aisles of your local bookstore. The abbreviation "o/p" means "out of print".

Area Handbook Series, *Laos: a country study* (Federal Research Division, Washington DC). This comprehensive (though somewhat outdated) study provides in-depth background and analysis of Laos's economic, social and political institutions, as well as the cultural and historical factors shaping them. Also available online.

Marthe Bassenne, *In Laos and Siam* (White Lotus, Bangkok). The beautifully evocative account of a French woman's 1909 journey up the Mekong River to Louang Phabang.

Tom Butcher and Dawn Ellis, *Laos* (Pallas Athene). A rambling wrap-up of the country's customs, religion and history.

Sucheng Chan (ed), *Hmong Means Free* (Temple University Press). Fascinating personal narratives by three generations of Hmong refugees from five different families, which describe their lives as farmers on the hilltops of Laos, as refugees in the camps of Thailand and as immigrants in the United States.

Patricia Cheesman Naenna, *Costume and Culture: Vanishing Textiles of some of the Tai Groups in Lao PDR* (published by the author). A breakdown of the myriad of textiles to be found in Laos including detailed descriptions of Lao weaving and dyeing techniques.

Grant Evans, *The Politics of Ritual and Remembrance: Laos Since 1975* (University of Hawaii Press). A provocative collection of anthropological essays focusing on the rituals and social structures of Laos yesterday and today and the attempts by the post-1975 government to reinvent "Laos".

Betty Gosling, *Old Luang Prabang* (Oxford University Press). Describing the history, geography and culture of the former royal capital.

LANGUAGE

The main language of Laos is **Lao**, which belongs to the Tai family of languages, which includes Thai, Shan (Tai Yai), spoken in Burma; Phuan, spoken in Laos and parts of Thailand; and Tai Leu, spoken by the Dai minority of southern China's Yunnan province. The spoken Thai of Bangkok and the spoken Lao of Vientiane are very similar, as akin as Spanish is to Portugese, though there are pockets of Laos where no dialect of Lao, much less the Vientiane version, will be heard. Since economic liberalization, **English** has become the preferred foreign tongue, and it's quite possible to get by without Lao in the towns. But once out in the countryside, you'll need some Lao phrases.

The **Lao script** was based on an early version of written Thai. Official governement maps of Laos use a modified form of the old French transliteration system. This can create problems for English speakers, but if you keep in mind for example, that the Lao "ou" rhymes with the French "vous" not the English "noun" – reading Lao place names shouldn't be a problem. The transliteration of place names in this book follows the modified French system used by the Lao National Geographic Service. For the transliteration of Lao words in the following section, a simplified version of the same system is used. However, the Lao are quite cavalier when it comes to consistency in transliteration. In Vientiane, for instance, it is possible to see the Arch of Victory monument transliterated as "Patouxai", "Patousai", "Patuxai" and "Patusai".

TONES AND MARKERS

Lao is a tonal language, which means that the tone a speaker gives to a word will determine its meaning. The dialect of Lao spoken in Vientiane, which has been deemed the official language of Laos, has six tones. Thus, depending on its tone, the word *sang* can mean either "elephant", "craftsman", "granary", "laryngitis", a species of bamboo, or "to build". Since it is impossible to learn the six tones properly without actually hearing them, try getting a speaker of Vientiane Lao to recite numbers one to nine in Lao to you, since all six tones feature in these numbers (see p.472). Number one is a mid tone (unmarked) and since the mid and low tones are so similar, the beginner may pronounce these two tones identically. Number two is a rising tone (~), number five is a low-falling tone (`), number six is a high tone (´), and number nine is a high-falling tone (^).

KEY TO PRONUNCIATION

Consonants:

B as in "big"
D as in "dog"
F as in "fun"
H as in "hello"
J (or CH) as in "jar"
K as in "skin" (unaspirated)
KH as the K in "kiss"
L as in "luck"
M as in "more"
N as in "now"
NG as in "singer" (this combination sometimes appears at the beginning of a word)
NY as in the Russian "nyet"
P as in "speak" (unaspirated)
Ph as the P in "pill"
S (or X) as in "same"
T as in "stop" (unaspirated)
Th as the T in "tin"
W (or V) as in "wish"
Y as in "yes"

Vowels:

A as the AH as in "autobahn"
AE as the A in "cat"
AI as in "Thai"
AW as in "jaw"
AO as in "Lao"
E as in "pen"
EU as in French "fleur"
I as in "mimi"
IA as in "India"
O as in "flow"
OE as in "Goethe"
U (or OU) as the OU in "you"
UA (or OUA) as the UA in "truant"

WORDS AND PHRASES IN LAO

Questions in Lao are not normally answered with a yes or no. Instead the verb used in the question is repeated for the answer. For example: "Do you have a room?", would be answered "Have" in the affirmative or "No have" in the negative.

GREETINGS AND SMALL TALK

Hello	*sabai di (said with a smile)*	Where are you from?	*jâo má tae sãi*
How are you?	*sabai di baw*	I'm from England/ America/Australia/ New Zealand	*khói má tae angkit/ amelika/awsteli/nyu silaen*
I'm fine	*sabai di*		
Can you speak English?	*jâo wâo phasã angkit dâi baw*	What's your name?	*jâo seu nyãng*
No I can't	*wâo baw dâi*	My name is...	*khói seu...*
I only speak a little Lao	*khói wâo phasã láo dâi nói neung*	Are you married yet?	*jâo taeng ngan léu baw*
		Yes, I'm married	*taeng ngan lâewu*
		No, I'm not married	*yáng baw taeng ngan*
Do you understand?	*jâo khào jai baw*	Goodbye	*lá kawn*
I don't understand	*khói baw khào jai*	Goodbye (in reply)	*sok di*

GETTING AROUND

Where are you going?	*pai sãi (often used as a familiar greeting)*	Pharmacy	*hân kãi ya*
		Post Office	*paisani*
To the market	*pai talat*	Police station	*sathani tamluat*
To the guesthouse	*pai bân phak*	Thai embassy	*sathanthut thai*
One thousand kip per person	*phù la phán kip*	Vietnamese embassy	*sathanthut wiatnam*
		Go straight	*pai sêu sêu*
Where is the...?	*...yu sãi*	Turn right	*lîaw khwã*
Where is the guest house?	*bân phak yu sãi*	Turn left	*lîaw sâi*
Where is the boat launch/pier?	*thà heuá yu sãi*		

ACCOMMODATION

Do you have a double room?	*mí hàwng sãwng tiang baw*	Can I see the room?	*khãw beung hàwng kawn dâi baw*
Does the room have a fan?	*hàwng mí phat lóm baw*	How much per night?	*khéun la thao dai*
		Can you discount the price?	*lút lakha dâi baw*
Mosquito net	*mûng*		
Bathroom	*hàwng nâm*	Where is the toilet?	*hàwng suam yu sãi*
Toilet	*suam*	I will stay two nights	*si phak sãwng khéun*
Air-conditioning	*ae yen*	Do you have a laundry service?	*mí bawlikan sak phà baw*
Blankets	*phà hom*		
Hot water	*nâm hâwn*	Do you have bicycles for rent?	*mí lot thip hâi sao baw*

SHOPPING

How much is this?	*an nî thao dai*	Washing powder	*sabu fun*
I'd like to buy...	*khói yak sêu...*	Toilet paper	*jîa hàwng nâm*
Medicine	*ya*	Candles	*thian*
Do you have...?	*mí...baw*	Mosquito coils	*ya kan nyung baep jút*
Do you have soap?	*mí sabu baw*	I only have kip	*khói mí tae ngóen kip*
Toothpaste	*yã si khâew*		

Continued overleaf

LANGUAGE CONTINUED

ON THE ROAD

Does this vehicle go to...?	*lot nî pai... baw*	How much to hire the vehicle/boat outright?	*māo lot/héua thao dai*
How much is it to go to...?	*pai...thao dai*	Do you agree to the price?	*tók lóng lakha baw*
How many hours will it take?	*sai wela ják sua móng*	I agree	*tók lóng*
		I don't agree	*baw tók lóng*
What time will the bus depart?	*lot si awk ják móng*	Please stop here	*jàwt nî dae*
What time will we arrive?	*si hâwt ják móng*	Please stop so I can urinate	*jàwt thai bao dae*

NUMBERS

0) *sun*	14) *síp si*	60) *hók síp*
1) *neung*	15) *síp hà*	70) *jét síp*
2) *sãwng*	16) *síp hók*	80) *pàet síp*
3) *sãm*	17) *síp jét*	90) *kâo síp*
4) *si*	18) *síp pàet*	100) *hôi*
5) *hà*	19) *síp kâo*	200) *sãwng hôi*
6) *hók*	20) *sao*	1000) *phán*
7) *jét*	21) *sao ét*	2000) *sãwng phán*
8) *pàet*	22) *sao sãwng*	10,000) *síp phán*
9) *kâo*	30) *sãm síp*	100,000) *sãen*
10) *síp*	31) *sãm síp ét*	200,000) *sãwng sãen*
11) *síp ét*	32) *sãm síp sãwng*	1,000,000) *lân*
12) *síp sãwng*	40) *si síp*	2,000,000) *sãwng lân*
13) *síp sãm*	50) *hà síp*	

DAYS OF THE WEEK AND TIME

Sunday	*wán thít*	Today	*mêu nî*	Late evening	*tawn khám*
Monday	*wán jan*	Yesterday	*mêu wan nî*	Midnight	*thiang khéun*
Tuesday	*wán angkhán*	Tomorrow	*mêu eun*	Next week	*athit nà*
Wednesday	*wán phut*	Morning	*tawn sâo*	Now	*tawn nî*
Thursday	*wan phahát*	Noon	*thiang wán*	Later	*theua nà*
Friday	*wán súk*	Afternoon	*tawn bai*		
Saturday	*wán sāo*	Early evening	*tawn láeng*		

EMERGENCIES AND HEALTH

Help!	*suay dae*	Please take me to the hospital	*song khói pai hong māw dae*
There's been an accident	*mí ubatihet*	I lost my passport	*pâm doen thang khāwng khói siã hãi*
I need a doctor	*khói tâwng kan hã māw*		
I'm not well	*khói baw sabai*	My pack is missing	*kheuang khāwng khói siã hãi*
I have a fever	*khói pen khai*		
I have diarrhoea	*thâwng khói baw di*		

COMMON ANSWERS TO QUESTIONS

I don't know	*baw hû*	It cannot be done	*baw dâi*
There isn't/aren't any	*baw mí*	It's uncertain	*baw nàe*

Jane Hamilton-Merritt, *Tragic Mountains: the Hmong, the Americans, and the Secret Wars for Laos, 1942–1992* (Indiana University Press). This impressive account, written by a correspondent during the Second Indochina War, follows the Hmong from the battlefields to life after the war.

FJ Harmand, *Laos and the Hilltribes of Indochina* (White Lotus, Bangkok). A cultural barbarian by today's standards, the French explorer's report on his late-nineteenth-century journey through southern Laos is liberally sprinkled with amusing anecdotes.

Christopher Kremmer, *Stalking the Elephant Kings: In Search of Laos* (University of Hawaii Press). An at times self-righteous account of a journalist's search for the monarch who went missing shortly after the communists assumed power in 1975.

Christopher Robbins, *The Ravens: Pilots of the Secret War of Laos* (o/p). Many of the details of America's secretive Laos operations during the Second Indochina War didn't come out until this gripping work by a British journalist was published in 1987. Based on interviews with American pilots who fought in Laos, this hard-to-find book is well worth tracking down.

Phia Sing et al, *Traditional Recipes of Laos* (Prospect Books). One of the rare books explaining how to prepare Lao cuisine.

Martin Stuart-Fox, *A History of Laos* (Cambridge University Press). Written by an Australian scholar who covered the Second Indochina War as a foreign correspondent, this is the best available overview of Laos's history.

Roger Warner, *Shooting at the Moon: The Story of America's Clandestine War in Laos* (Steerforth Press). This prizewinning, thoroughly researched and crisply written account of American involvement reads like an adventure novel.

VIENTIANE AND AROUND

Hugging a bend of the Mekong River, the low-rise capital of Laos is a quaint and easygoing place compared to Southeast Asia's other frenetic capitals, looking more like a rambling collection of villages than a city. However, in the mere decade since Laos reopened its doors to

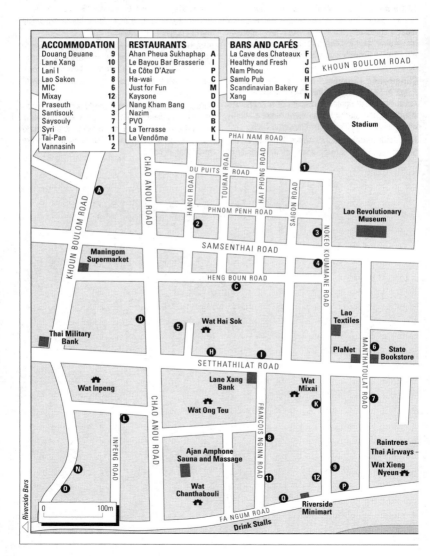

ACCOMMODATION	
Douang Deuane	9
Lane Xang	10
Lani I	5
Lao Sakon	8
MIC	6
Mixay	12
Praseuth	4
Santisouk	3
Saysouly	7
Syri	1
Tai-Pan	11
Vannasinh	2

RESTAURANTS	
Ahan Pheua Sukhaphap	A
Le Bayou Bar Brasserie	I
Le Côte D'Azur	P
Ha-wai	C
Just for Fun	M
Kaysone	D
Nang Kham Bang	O
Nazim	Q
PVO	B
La Terrasse	K
Le Vendôme	L

BARS AND CAFÉS	
La Cave des Chateaux	F
Healthy and Fresh	J
Nam Phou	G
Samlo Pub	H
Scandinavian Bakery	E
Xang	N

foreign visitors, **VIENTIANE** has changed with dizzying rapidity: new businesses are popping up all over the place, and scores of old shade trees have been cut down to accommodate an ever-multiplying number of cars and motorbikes. The city's **history** has been a turbulent one, as its meagre collection of structures from the past suggests. It had been occupied and subsequently abandoned by the Mon and then the Khmer long before the Lao king Setthathilat moved his capital here from Louang Phabang in 1560. After that, the city was

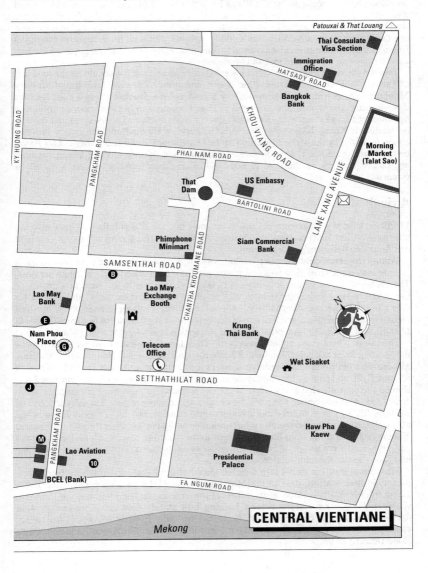

CENTRAL VIENTIANE

overrun or occupied several times by the Burmese, Chinese and, most spectacularly, by the Siamese who levelled the entire place in 1828. By the end of the nineteenth century, the French controlled most of what is now Laos, Cambodia and Vietnam and had rebuilt Vientiane as an administrative capital. As with other urban centres in the region, the majority of modern Vientiane's merchant class are ethnic Chinese and Vietnamese, whose forefathers immigrated to Laos during the French era. Though the city was left relatively unscathed by the Second Indochina War, a large percentage of Vientiane's population found it necessary to escape across the Mekong after the formation of the Lao People's Democratic Republic; they were replaced by immigrants from the former "liberated zone" in northeastern Laos, further changing Vientiane's ethnic make-up. Not until the collapse of the Soviet Union in 1991 was the government forced to rethink its opinions of capitalism, paving the way for the explosion of new ventures and businesses.

Two days is sufficient to see Vientiane's sights. High on your list should be the museum of Lao art, housed at the **Haw Pha Kaew**, and the socialist-era **Lao Revolutionary Museum**. The placid Buddhist monastery known as **Wat Sisaket** offers a good half-day diversion, and you should take a ride out to **That Louang**, Laos's most important religious building, to admire the effects of a sunset on its golden surface. The most popular day-trip destination is **Xiang Khouan** or the "Buddha Park", a Hindu–Buddhist fantasy in ferro-concrete on the banks of the Mekong. Off the beaten track is the eco-resort of **Lao Pako**, on the Nam Ngum River, while further afield, the laid-back town of **Vang Viang**, set amid spectacular scenery on the road to Louang Phabang, has recently become a travellers' favourite.

Arrival

Vientiane, located at the centre of Laos, is the main hub for all domestic travel and also has a very convenient land crossing into Thailand. All Vientiane taxi drivers will accept Thai baht and American dollars as well as Lao kip.

Wattay International Airport is 6km west of downtown Vientiane. Airport facilities include **visa-on-arrival** ($30 plus one photo; see p.453 for details) and exchange services. The cheapest way of getting into town is to take a shared taxi in the form of a tuk-tuk or *jumbo*, a three-wheeled motorized taxi ($1), although unmetered car taxis run the route for only a few dollars more. Alternatively, walk out to Louang Phabang Avenue, a few hundred metres from the terminal, and hail one of the buses or sawngthaews coming from the north (2000K), which will drop you off at the main bus station next to the Morning Market.

The primary land crossing into Laos is the **Thai–Lao Friendship Bridge**, which spans the Mekong River at a point 5km west of Nong Khai in Thailand, and 20km east of Vientiane. **Minibuses** from Nong Khai shuttle passengers across the bridge (every 15min from 8am to 5.30pm; B10), stopping at Thai immigration control before continuing on to **Lao immigration** on the opposite side of the river. At the Lao terminal, you can get a fifteen-day visa-on-arrival ($30 plus one photo; see p.453 for details), and change money. Tuk-tuks (B150) and car taxis (B200) run from here into the city centre (30min), but the cheapest option is bus #14, which stops at the bridge every forty minutes on its run between the old ferry pier at Thadua (600K) and the main bus station next to the Morning Market. Motorcycles are not permitted across the bridge, although sawngthaews can be hired ($10) to transport your bike into Laos – ask at the minibus ticket counter.

Most buses from the south, including Savannakhet and Pakxe, arrive at Vientiane's compact main **bus station**, next to the Morning Market (Talat Sao) on Khou Viang Road, 1.5km from Nam Phou Place. Most transport from the north, including Louang Phabang, via Vang Viang, arrives at the **Khoua Louang bus stand** (*Khiw Lot Khua Luang*), 4km northwest of the city centre, around the corner from the Evening Market (Talat Laeng, sometimes known as Talat Nong Douang), on Khoua Louang Road near its junction with Nong Douang Road.

MOVING ON FROM VIENTIANE

By plane

The easiest way to get to Wattay International Airport is by tuk-tuk ($1); if you want to take a taxi you'll have to walk or take a tuk-tuk to the taxi rank outside the Morning Market. See "Listings" p.483 for addresses of airline offices in Vientiane.

By bus

Most **buses to the south**, including Savannakhet and Pakxe, leave from Vientiane's main bus station (see opposite). Book a day ahead if you want to take an express, air-con bus to Savannakhet via Pakxan and Thakhek. The service is operated by two companies, Angkham (☎021/414848) and Senesabay (☎021/218052 or 217318). Senesabay's office is located next to the Odeon Rama Theatre, near Talat Thong Khan Kham; the bus leaves from opposite the office and stops at the main bus station in Savannakhet. Angkham's office is at Kilometre 5 on Route 13 South, next to Angkham Toyota, and buses leave from next door.

Most transport **to the north**, including Louang Phabang, via Vang Viang, leaves from the Khoua Louang bus stand (see opposite). In addition, sawngthaews to **Vang Viang** operate from a stand on Khou Viang Road near the main station and three daily blue government buses also go there from the main bus station itself.

By boat

Speedboats and occasional slow **boats to the north** leave from Tha Hua Kao Liaw pier, located on the Mekong River, 10km west of the centre of Vientiane; tuk-tuks are $2–3 from the centre. Speedboats depart here for Paklai, 217km upriver from Vientiane and cost $10 per person. You can also hire a speedboat for $60. Slow boats leave only once a week and take four to five days to get to Louang Phabang ($21 per person), while speedboats can make it in a day ($21 per person or $126 to hire the boat). There's no regular boat service between here and points south.

By train

Overnight **trains to Bangkok** leave between 5 and 7pm from Nong Khai, Thailand. Take Bus #14 or hire a taxi to the Friendship Bridge; once on the Thai side hire a shared taxi to the train station (B50–70).

Speedboats and occasional slow boats from the north dock at **Tha Hua Kao Liaw pier**, located on the Mekong River 10km west of the centre of Vientiane. The only way to get to the city centre from the landing is by tuk-tuk ($2–3).

Information and orientation

The fairly unhelpful **Lao National Tourism Authority** (NTAL) operates out of an imposing building on Lane Xang Avenue, near the Morning Market (Mon–Fri 8am–5pm; ☎021/212248 or 212251). Phimphone minimarkets, *Scandinavian Bakery* and *Le Croissant d'Or* maintain more useful noticeboards, displaying information on everything from language classes to motorbikes for sale. Two widely available city **maps** are *The Vientiane Tourist Map*, and the newer hand-drawn *Map of Vientiane*, which gives a detailed and accurate 3-D perspective of the city.

Finding an **address** in Vientiane can be something of a challenge, as street signs are confined to the centre, road names can bleed into one another and house numbers are generally useless. As elsewhere in Laos, local inhabitants often use monasteries as landmarks to identify parts of town: for example, Ban Wat Phaxai ("Wat Phaxai district") refers to the area around Wat Phaxai. When showing addresses in this chapter, we have given the road name, but have omitted the house number, using landmarks instead.

City transport

Vientiane is a very walkable city, but **bicycles** are also handy and can be rented for $1 per day (with $30 deposit) at many guesthouses and other places, including *Douang Deuane Hotel*, Nokeo Koummane Road (☎021/222301–3), and a no-name coffee shop near the *MIC* on Manthatoulat Road. 150cc **motorbikes** are also easy to find ($8 per day); try *Douang Deuane Hotel*, Nokeo Koummane Road (☎021/222301–3) or *PVO*, Samsenthai Road, near Pangkham Road (☎021/214444).

Tuk-tuks and **jumbos** (see "Getting Around" p.455) operate as private or shared taxis within the city (picking up people heading in vaguely the same direction), and charge about 2000K per person for distances of 1–2km, adding a few hundred kip per kilometre beyond that. Shared tuk-tuks generally ply frequently travelled routes, such as Lane Xang Avenue between the Morning Market and That Louang and along Louang Phabang Avenue heading out from the city centre; they charge a flat fee of 500K. Pedal-powered *samlaw* – essentially motorless jumbos – can carry one or two smaller passengers for short distances. A fleet of unmetered **taxis**, consisting of banged-up old Toyotas, gathers outside the Morning Market, in the car park on the Khou Viang Road side of the market. Prices are negotiable and usually quoted in Thai baht, but drivers will accept Lao kip and American dollars.

Accommodation

Most **accommodation** places are conveniently located within a kilometre of Nam Phou Place. Some establishments have also sprung up near Lane Xang Avenue in the vicinity of Patouxai, and on Louang Phabang Avenue, both within walking distance of the city centre.

City centre: around Nam Phou

Douang Deuane, Nokeo Koummane Road, near Wat Mixai (☎021/222301–3). A newish gloss and location near the Mekong make this standard mid-range hotel a worthy option. All rooms en-suite with air-con, TV and phone. Motorbike and bicycle rental, as well as airport pick-up. ④–⑤.

Lane Xang, Fa Ngum Road (☎021/214102). Laos's first post-revolutionary luxury hotel has a pool and spacious grounds along the quay, and 109 tremendously good-value rooms. ⑤–⑦.

Lani I, Setthathilat Road, opposite Wat Ong Teu (☎021/216103). Supremely pleasant accommodation in a centrally located house, decorated with antiques and handicrafts. All twelve rooms have air-con, hot water and phone. Reservations recommended. ⑥.

Lao Sakon, François Nginn Road, near Wat Mixai (☎021/216571). Rooms here improve the higher up you go: top-storey options have air-con, hot showers, TVs and refrigerators. Motorbike rental available. ②–④.

MIC (Ministry of Information and Culture), Manthatoulat Road, near Setthathilat Road (☎021/212362). This budget travellers' favourite guesthouse has reasonably clean en-suite rooms and does visa extension and laundry; solo backpackers often share the three-bed rooms. It's often full, but there's a waiting list. Slight price increases at the weekend. ②.

Mixay, Nokeo Koummane Road, near Wat Mixai (☎021/217023). A friendly, good budget bet with fourteen spartan rooms ranging from cheap fan singles to en-suite triples. ①–②.

Praseuth, Samsenthai Road, near the Revolutionary Museum (☎021/217932). A friendly establishment offering large basic rooms with clean shared facilities. ②.

Santisouk, Nokeo Koummane Road, near the Revolutionary Museum (☎021/215303). Situated above the *Santisouk Restaurant*, with nine clean air-con rooms and an upstairs balcony. ②.

Saysouly, Manthatoulat Road, near Setthathilat Road (☎021/223757). A very friendly guesthouse that offers large, comfortable rooms, some en suite, visa extension and laundry. Car, motorbike and bicycle rental is also available. ③.

Sihom, Sihom Road, near the Thai Military Bank (☎021/214562). Eleven tastefully decorated rooms, fitted out with rattan double beds, air-con and satellite TV. ②–③.

Syri, Saigon Road (☎021/212682). A large house on a quiet lane in the Chao Anou residential district, with spacious double and triple air-con rooms and a nice balcony. Motorbikes and bikes for rent. ③.

Tai-Pan, François Nginn Road, near the Mekong (☎021/216906–9; Bangkok bookings ☎02/260 9888). Vientiane's best-value business hotel, with all mod cons including Internet access and gym. ⑦–⑧.

Vannasinh, Phnom Penh Road, near Chao Anou Road (☎021/218707). Popular, well-run establishment with cheap fan doubles and more spacious air-con doubles, all en suite. ②–④.

Off Louang Phabang Avenue

Auberge du Temple, Sikhotabong Road (☎021/214844). Down a quiet lane off Louang Phabang Avenue, this French-owned guesthouse has eight attractive air-con rooms, some with baths. It's west of the city centre, but close to some restaurants and bars. Motorbikes and bikes for rent. ②–③.

Novotel Belvedere Vientiane, Louang Phabang Avenue, Kilometre 2 (☎021/213570). All 200 rooms have air-con and TV, and there's a pool, email service and beer garden. ⑨.

Riverview, on the corner of Fa Ngum and Sithan Nua roads (☎021/216231–2; Bangkok bookings 02/281 9543). Near riverside bars, a few kilometres west of the town centre, with 32 air-con rooms, all with hot water. ④.

Around Patouxai

Agriculture & Forestry, Hatsady Road, opposite the Immigration Office (☎021/217184). Government-run place boasting the cheapest beds in town, with photos of old comrades taped to the walls. $1.50 per bed.

Lani II, off Sailom Road, near Lane Xang Avenue (☎021/213022 or 216095). On a quiet lane off Sailom Road, the *Lani II* has all the mellow atmosphere of the *Lani I* for slightly less. The seven tasteful air-con rooms, some with hot water, are only a brisk walk to the town centre. ⑤.

Le Parasol Blanc, Sibounheuang Road (☎021/215090 or 216091). Quiet, elegant hotel. Some rooms are a bit dark, but there's a free laundry service, a pool and a good restaurant. ⑥.

East of the city centre

Heuan Lao, off Samsenthai Road, near Wat Simuang (☎021/216258 or 216236). Friendly guesthouse on a quiet lane, offering singles, doubles and triples all with en-suite bathrooms. Bicycles are also available for rent. ②–③.

Villa Manoly, Ban Simuang, next to Honour International School (☎021/218907). Decorated with antiques and boasting a pleasant terrace, this villa stands in spacious grounds close to the river. The singles ($20) and doubles all have en-suite hot showers. ⑤.

The City

A humble fountain in the middle of **Nam Phou Place** marks the heart of downtown Vientiane, where you'll find the greatest concentration of accommodation, restaurants and shops catering to visitors. North of Nam Phou, on Samsenthai Road, the **Lao Revolutionary Museum** (opening hours variable; 700K) deals primarily with the events, both ancient and recent, that led to the "inevitable victory" of the proletariat in 1975. Inside, scenes portray Lao patriots liberating the motherland from Thai and Burmese feudalists and French colonialists bullwhipping villagers. Black-and-white photographs tell the story of the struggle against "the Japanese fascists" and "American imperialists".

Towards the eastern end of Setthathilat Road, the attractive street that runs parallel to and just south of Samsenthai Road, stands **Wat Sisaket** (daily except Mon & public holidays 8am–noon & 1–4pm; 1000K), the oldest wat in Vientiane. Constructed by King Anouvong (Chao Anou) in 1818, it was the only monastery to survive the Siamese sacking ten years later. Surrounded by a tile-roofed cloister, the *sim* (building housing the main Buddha image) contains some charming, though badly deteriorating, murals. A splendidly ornate candle holder of carved wood situated before the altar is a fine example of nineteenth-century Lao woodcarving. Outside, the cloister holds countless niches from which peer diminutive Buddhas.

Opposite Wat Sisaket stands the **Presidential Palace**, an impressive French Beaux Arts-style building, built to house the French colonial governor, and nowadays used mainly for government ceremonies. Just west of the palace, the **Haw Pha Kaew** (daily except Mon & public holidays 8am–noon & 1–4pm; 1000K), once the king's personal Buddhist temple, now functions as a **museum of art and antiquities**. The temple is named for the Emerald Buddha, or Pha Kaew, which was pilfered by the Siamese in 1779 and carried off to their capital, where it remains today (see p.853). The museum houses the finest collection of Lao art in the country, one of the most striking works being a Buddha in the "Calling for Rain" pose (standing with arms to the sides and fingers pointing to the ground) and sporting a jewel-encrusted navel. Also of note are a pair of eighteenth-century terracotta *apsara*, or celestial dancers, and a highly detailed "naga throne" from Xiang Khouang that once served as a pedestal for a Buddha image. Sheltered under an adjacent pavilion is a rather poor-quality sample stone urn from the Plain of Jars.

It has been said that, along with coffee and baguettes, the Lao inherited a taste for pompous town-planning from the French. Seedy **Lane Xang Avenue**, leading off north from Setthathilat Road, was to be Vientiane's Champs Elysées and **Patouxai** its Arc de Triomphe. Popularly known as *anusawali* (Lao for "monument"), this massive ferro-concrete Arch of Victory (8am–6pm daily; 500K; 300K to park your bike), 1km from the Presidential Palace, was built in the late 1950s to commemorate casualties of war on the side of the Royal Lao Government. Said to have been completed with concrete donated by the US government for the construction of an airport, the structure has been jokingly referred to as "the vertical runway". The view of Vientiane from the top is worth the climb. A handful of hawkers are sheltered by a ceiling adorned with reliefs of the Hindu deities; the walls depict characters from the *Ramayana,* the epic Hindu story of battles between good and evil.

One and a half kilometres east of Patouxai stands the Buddhist stupa, **That Louang**, Laos's most important religious building and its national symbol (daily except Mon & public holidays 8am–noon & 1–4pm; 1000K). The original That Louang is thought to have been built in the mid-sixteenth century by King Setthathilat, whose statue stands in front, and was reported to have looked like a gold-covered "pyramid". Today's structure dates from the 1930s: the tapering golden spire of the main stupa is 45m tall and rests on a plinth of stylized lotus petals; it's surrounded on all sides by thirty short, spiky stupas. Within the cloisters are kept a collection of very worn Buddha images, some of which may have been enshrined in the original Khmer temple that once occupied the site.

Buddha Park

Located some 25km from downtown Vientiane on the Mekong River, Xiang Khouan or the "**Buddha Park**" (daily 8am–6pm; 1000K), is surely Laos's quirkiest attraction. This collection of massive ferro-concrete sculptures, which lie dotted around a wide riverside meadow, was created under the direction of Luang Phu Boonlua Surirat, a self-styled holy man who claimed to have been the disciple of a cave-dwelling Hindu hermit in Vietnam. Upon returning to Laos, Boonlua began the sculpture garden in the late 1950s as a means of spreading his philosophy of life and his ideas about the cosmos. Besides the brontosaurian reclining Buddha that dominates the park, there are concrete statues of every conceivable deity in the Hindu–Buddhist pantheon. After the revolution, Boonlua was forced to flee across the Mekong to Nong Khai, Thailand, where he established an even more elaborate version of his philosophy in concrete at Sala Kaeo Kou, also known as Wat Khaek (see p.820). To **get to the park**, either take bus #14 from Vientiane's main bus station (every 40min), or get a shared tuk-tuk from near the Morning Market to Thadua, from where it's a three-kilometre walk or a short hop by tuk-tuk.

Eating

The influx of tourists and a solid foreign community have given rise to restaurants catering to virtually every taste, from Korean BBQ to sauerkraut. The city's Western cuisine in particular is said to be the best in Southeast Asia. **Riverside food stalls** line the Mekong's bank from Nokeo Koummane Road to Khoun Boulom Road, with most offering Lao staples like *tam màk hung* (spicy papaya salad), *pîng kai* (grilled chicken) and fruit shakes from morning until nearly midnight. A **night market** sets up on Khoun Boulom Road near the intersection with Heng Boun Road in the early evening, and there's a more extensive version at Dong Palane Market on Ban Fai Road near Wat Ban Fai. Most of Vientiane's **restaurants** open for lunch and then again for dinner; no-frills eateries are usually open throughout the day, closing around 9pm. In most restaurants you'll pay on average $2 for a meal, and even in more upmarket Western restaurants you'll rarely spend more than $10.

Breakfast, bakeries and cafés

Healthy and Fresh, Setthathilat Road, just west of Nam Phou Place. Does the best sandwiches in town, using freshly baked bread, as well as pretty good quiches and coffee.

Scandinavian Bakery, Nam Phou Place. Bread of the day, sandwiches, a wide selection of pastries and cookies, but very average "America" brand Thai coffee and slow service.

Xang, Khoun Boulom Road, near Wat Inpeng. Run by a young Englishman, *Xang* captures the spirit of a university café, with good coffee, sandwiches, salads and excellent cheeseburgers, plus newspapers and magazines to browse through. Highly recommended. Closed Tues.

Lao

Bounmala, Khou Viang Road, near Wat Phaxai. Classic, inexpensive Lao-beer-and-roast-chicken joint under a tin roof. Also worth sampling is the roast beef, served with *khào pun* (flour noodles in a sauce), star fruit and lettuce.

Nang Kham Bang, Khoun Boulom Road. Excellent no-frills family-run establishment serving delicious *tôm yam pa* (spicy fish soup with lemon grass) and Lao sausage, *sai-ua*.

Riverside Km 4, Thadua Road, Kilometre 4, near Wat Phoxai. Good, mid-priced Lao food served in a clean, comfortable restaurant, but the waterfront setting is really this place's drawing card.

Tham Mak Hung Wat Phaxai, Thadua Road, Kilometre 4. Widely considered the best place in town for spicy papaya salad.

Thai, Vietnamese and Indian

Ha-wai, Heng Boun Road. An excellent French and Vietnamese menu, including recommended kebabs, served with beans smothered in a garlic sauce, and watercress soup.

Kaysone, Chao Anou Road. A man and his wok serving *phat thai* and a selection of fine stir-fried dishes over rice for next to nothing out of a small shop-house on Bakery Street.

Nazim, Fa Ngum Road, between Nokeo Koummane Road and François Nginn Road. Cheap, popular Indian joint strong on vegetarian dishes; meat dishes tend to be a bit greasy.

Phikun, Louang Phabang Avenue, west of Khoun Boulom Road. Excellent, buffet-style Thai food including delicious curries and crispy fried bananas.

PVO, Samsenthai Road. Fantastic spring rolls, *nâm neuang* and *baw bun* served to a cha-cha beat. Great-value, full-flavour food. Highly recommended.

Western

Le Bayou Bar Brasserie, Setthathilat Road, opposite Wat Ong Teu. Reasonable prices with a menu offering pizzas, rôtisserie chicken, pasta, salads, good couscous, as well as terrific *flan au caramel* and mousse. The quality bar has Beer Lao on tap and you can also sit outside.

Le Côte D'Azur, Fa Ngum Road, near Nokeo Koummane Road. One of Vientiane's better restaurants, offering terrific service and a great menu, featuring Provençal-style seafood and pasta, plus a large selection of excellent pizzas. Closed Sun lunchtime.

Golden Horse, Fa Ngum Road, a few streets east of *Lane Xang Hotel*. Seafood restaurant, run by an American expat, and boasting the best fish in town, mostly imported from Thailand.

La Terrasse, Nokeo Koummane Road, near Wat Mixai. Outstanding steaks, pizza, a fair approximation of Mexican food and salads at prices lower than most of the other Western joints. Nightly BBQ from 7.30pm. Highly recommended. Closed Sun.

Le Vendôme, Inpeng Road, near Wat Inpeng. Cosy restaurant in an old house serving French and Thai food, good pizzas and very tasty calzone. Closed Sat & Sun lunchtime.

Vegetarian

Ahan Pheua Sukhaphap, Khoun Boulom Road, just north of Samsenthai Road. Strict health-food joint serving outstanding plates of mixed veggies over rice and inspired tofu-based satay. Yellow sign out front simply reads "Vegetarian Food."

Ahan Thammasat, in the alley behind Khouadin Market. Buffet-style, cheap veggie food and tasty, filling bowls of *fŏe* served out of a narrow shop-house.

Just for Fun, Pangkham Road. Time your meal at this tiny, clean vegetarian-friendly restaurant to avoid the lunchtime crowds, as the tasty over-rice dishes are very good value. Also does some of the best chocolate cake in town and a great selection of herbal teas. Closed Sun.

Beer gardens, bars and clubs

Vientiane's location along an east–west stretch of the Mekong positions it for spectacular sunsets, and makeshift stalls selling bottles of **Beer Lao** and **fruit shakes** line the riverbank from Nokeo Koummane Road to Khoun Boulom Road; 2km upriver along Fa Ngum Road, a long row of **beer gardens** with wooden terraces hang over the riverbank in the vicinity of the *Riverview Hotel*.

Many of Vientiane's **nightclubs** feature live music, $2 cans of beer, dim lighting, deep couches and absurdly overdressed hostesses; the *Anou Cabaret* at the *Anou Hotel* is the long-time favourite. A newer set of **dance clubs** playing Thai pop and international dance mixes, catering to well-heeled teenagers, has cropped up along Louang Phabang Avenue, just beyond the *Novotel*. They don't usually get hopping until after 9pm, and are unplugged by midnight at the latest. There's no cover charge, but you'll have to fork out more than $2 for a can of Beer Lao. Sadly, Vientiane's **live music** scene is largely derivative, with popular taste being bullied into submission by the barrage of bland pop ballads churned out in Thailand.

City centre bars and clubs

La Cave des Châteaux, Nam Phou Place. Excellent little French wine bar, which also offers plates of meats and cheeses.

Chess Café, Sakkalin Road. Buzzing club a step above the teenage clubs, with a live band and mish-mash of foreign covers and Thai pop.

Gecko Club, *Royal Dokmaideng Hotel*, Lane Xang Avenue. A good place to come and get a cocktail and play pool. Popular hang-out for the twenty-something expat crowd.

Marina, Louang Phabang Avenue, 3km west of the centre. Hottest nightspot in town for Lao teenagers to shake their groove thang, with a good dance floor and a separate bar.

Nam Phou, Nam Phou Place. Popular outdoor café with overpriced bottled beer and cocktails, but reasonable pitchers of *bia sot* and tasty "Jimmy's Road Kill Burgers".

Samlo Pub, Setthathilat Road, opposite Wat Ong Teu. Centrally located pub, with darts and a solid wooden bar to lean your elbows on. Gin and tonic costs $2, draft beer is cheaper.

Watcharaporn Night Club, Kilometre 6, Thadua Road. Young Lao pack this dimly lit, Thai-managed nightclub on weekends to hear house band Smile Black Dog. Beer Lao for $1.50.

Riverside venues

Bia Sot Hua Muang, Fa Ngum Road. Lively pub packed with teenagers; the only place on the strip with draught beer.

Bia Sot Sakon, Fa Ngum Road. Casual beer garden, across from Mahosot's International Clinic, with bamboo furniture and the standard pitchers of Beer Lao.

Sala Snake, Fa Ngum Road. Owned by a musician from Louang Phabang who sometimes puts together jam sessions on classical Lao instruments.

Sala Sunset Khounta, Fa Ngum Road. Known to some simply as "The End of the World" and others as "The Sunset Bar", the original spot for sundowners in Vientiane has recently expanded owing to its immense popularity with expats and tour groups, but it still ends up overcrowded and short of food. Get here early to sample the *tam kûay tani*, a spicy salad of green bananas, eggplant and chillis.

Sunset II, off Fa Ngum Road. On its own patch of riverbank west of the competition, the son of the *Sala Sunset Khounta* offers the seclusion of being off the strip, though it is difficult to find.

Shopping

On the whole, silver-work and textiles are more expensive in Vientiane than in Louang Phabang, where they're produced, and Vientiane is no bargain hunters' paradise. However, the Morning Market (Talat Sao) has good bargains in homespun **cotton** clothing ($2–5), lengths of **silk** and handicrafts; shoulder bags (*nyam*) are cheap and functional, hand-woven *pha biang*, a long, scarf-like textile, and chequered *pha khao ma*, the knee-length men's sarong, are also good buys. The Lao Women's Union runs a shop called The Art of Silk, located on Manthatoulat Road near Wat Xieng Nyeun, featuring good deals on plain silk and cotton cloth from all over the country.

Check the antique stores of the Morning Market and the downtown area for old or rare **baskets** made by the tribal peoples of Laos. These may sell for as much as $50. Sticky rice baskets and mats costing $1–3 can be found on Chao Anou Road beyond the Thong Khan Kham Market. The T'Shop Lai Gallery on Inpeng Road next to *Le Vendôme Restaurant* specializes in unique mosaics and other **handicrafts** made from coconut shell; prices are fixed and a bit steep.

Besides the Morning Market, most textile, souvenir and antique shops are found on Samsenthai and Setthathilat roads and along the lanes running between them. Antique brass weights, sometimes referred to as "**opium weights**", are usually seen in antique stores but may also be found in upscale textile shops. They cost two to five times more than in Louang Phabang and the other provinces. **Opium pipes** can be found in the antique shops on Samsenthai Road; real antique pipes may go for $100 or more, but new-made Vietnamese pipes cost as little as $10. Keep in mind that the customs officers in your home country may find a reason or two to confiscate such a purchase. Most antique and curio shops have a small stash of **stamps**, **coins** and **banknotes** from present and previous regimes. A no-name philatelic shop near the corner of Samsenthai and Pangkham roads has a wide selection.

Raintrees on Nokeo Koummane Road, near *La Terrasse Restaurant*, has the best selection of English-language **books** in the city. Smaller branches are located on Pangkham Road, next to the *Thai Airways* office, and in the lobby of the *Novotel* and *Lao Hotel Plaza*. The government-run State Bookstore, on the corner of Manthatoulat and Setthathilat roads, has a small selection of English-language books and even a few dusty titles from the Soviet era.

Listings

Airlines Lao Aviation, Pangkham Road (☎021/212051) or at Wattay International Airport, Louang Phabang Avenue (☎021/512000); Thai Airways International, Pangkham Road (☎021/216143); Vietnam Airlines, Samsenthai Road, mezzanine floor of the *Lao Hotel Plaza* (☎021/217562).

American Express Representative agent in Laos is Diethelm Travel, on the corner of Setthathilat Road and Nam Phou Place (☎021/213833).

Banks and Exchange Banque pour le Commerce Extérieur Lao (BCEL), Pangkham Road; Bangkok Bank, Hatsady Road and Siam Commercial Bank, Lane Xang Avenue, exchange travellers' cheques and do cash advances on Visa and Mastercard; Lao May Bank maintains an exchange booth (Mon–Fri 8.30am–5pm, Sat & Sun 8.30am–3.30pm) on Samsenthai Road that handles cash and travellers' cheques only.

Embassies and consulates Australia, Nehru Road (☎021/413610 or 413805); Cambodia, near That Khao, Thadua Road (☎021/314952 or 315251); China, near Wat Nak Noi, Wat Nak Road (☎021/315100 or 315103); France, Setthathilat Road (☎021/215253 or 215257–9); Germany, Sok Pa Louang Road (☎021/312110–3); India, near Wat Phaxai, That Louang Road (☎021/413802); Indonesia, Phon Kheng Road, Ban Phon Sa-at (☎021/413909 or 413910); Malaysia, near Wat Phaxai, That Louang Road (☎021/414205 or 414206); Philippines, near Wat Nak, Salakoktane Road (☎021/315179); Sweden, near Wat Nak, Sok Pa Louang Road (☎021/315018); Thailand (visa section), across from the Lao National Tourism Authority building, Lane Xang Avenue (☎021/214582); United States, near That Dam, Bartholonie Road (☎021/213966 or 212581); Vietnam, near Wat Phaxai, That Louang Road (☎021/413400–4).

Emergencies Dial ☎190 in case of fire, ☎195 for an ambulance, or ☎191 for police. In the event of an accident dial ☎413306 for the Friendship Hospital Trauma Centre.

Hospitals and clinics Australian Clinic, Nehru Road (☎021/413603), by appointment only, with vaccinations on Thursdays; International Clinic, Mahosot Hospital Compound, Fa Ngum Road (☎021/214022), open 24hr; Mahosot Hospital, Mahosot Road (☎021/214018); Setthathilat Hospital, Phon Sa-at Road (☎021/413720); Swedish Clinic, near Swedish Embassy, near Wat Nak, Sok Pa Louang Road (☎021/315015).

Immigration department Hatsady Road near junction with Lane Xang Avenue (☎021/212520); open Mon–Fri 8am–noon & 1–4pm.

Internet access PlaNet CyberCentre, on the corner of Manthatoulat and Setthathilat roads (☎021/218972–4), $2 per 25 minutes, open Mon–Sat 8.30am–10pm & Sun 9am–8pm; KPL: Internet & Email, Setthathilat Road (☎021/212450), 600K per minute, open daily 8.30am–10.30pm; Intercom Computer, Samsenthai Road (☎021/219222), 500K per minute, open daily 8am–7pm.

Language Courses Centre de Langue Française, Lane Xang Avenue (☎021/215764); Lao–American Language Center, Phon Kheng Road, Ban Phon Sa-at (☎021/414321).

Massage and herbal sauna Massage at $1.50–3 per hour and saunas for $0.50–1.50 at: Ajan Amphone, next to Wat Chanthabouli, Chao Anou Road (Mon–Fri 2–5pm, Sat & Sun 10am–7pm); Hôpital de Médicine Traditionnelle, near Wat Si Amphon; Wat Sok Pa Louang, Wat Sok Pa Louang Road.

Pharmacies The best pharmacies are on Mahosot Road in the vicinity of the Morning Market.

Post office The GPO is on the corner of Khou Viang Road and Lane Xang Avenue. Poste restante is held for up to three months (Mon-Fri 8am–5pm, Sat 8am–4pm, Sun 8am–noon).

Telephone services International calls and faxes at Telecom, Setthathilat Road (daily 7am–10pm).

Tour agencies Diethlem, Nam Phou Place (☎021/215920); Inter-Lao Tourisme, Setthathilat Road (☎021/214832); Lane Xang, Pangkham Road (☎021/213198); Lao Tourism, Lane Xang Avenue (☎021/216671); Lao Travel Service, Lane Xang Avenue (☎021/216603-4); Phudoi Travel, Phonxai Road (☎021/413888); Sodetour, Fa Ngum Road (☎021/216314).

Lao Pako

LAO PAKO, an environmentally friendly resort on the Nam Ngum River, 50km northeast of Vientiane, makes a good trip out of the capital. You could easily spend two days here, swimming, bird-watching and hiking to nearby villages. The resort also hosts monthly full moon parties with a BBQ and *lào hai* rice wine. **Accommodation** ranges from doubles ($13) and dorm beds ($2.60) to a two-room bungalow ($18.50). It's also possible to camp on a bamboo platform ($1.50) in the woods. Call ahead for reservations (☎021/312234 or radio phone ☎222925). Catch the blue Pakxap-bound government **bus** at Vientiane's Morning Market, and get off at Somsamai, where boatmen will ferry you downriver (25 min; 8000K).

Vang Viang and around

Travelling by road from Vientiane to Louang Phabang takes you through the spectacular limestone karst forest of **VANG VIANG**, 155km north of the capital, which, with its beautiful caves and nearby ethnic minority villages, makes an ideal point for a stopover. The friendly town reclines on the east bank of the Nam Xong River, and offers plenty of backpacker-oriented guesthouses and services.

Floating down the Nam Xong on huge tractor inner **tubes** is a good way to take in the view, with enough rapids and tiny islands to keep things interesting. A good launching point is near the village of Pakpok, 4km north of Vang Viang, which makes for a two- to three-hour trip. Tubes (2000K per day), **bicycles** (5000K per day) and **motorcycles** ($10 per day) can be rented at many places around town. A few guides feature tubing on their organized **tours** to the caves – signs are posted in restaurants and guesthouses – but groups can comprise as many as twenty people.

The caves

If you decide to visit the **caves** alone, you'll find the locals are more than happy to point you in the right direction or lead the way for a small tip. **Buses** and sawngthaews ply Route 13, or you could hire a tuk-tuk from near the market. Across the river from the town proper, Chinese-made tractors act as shared taxis; just flag them down like a bus.

Six kilometres west of Vang Viang, **Tham Phou Kham** makes a rewarding half-day trip that takes in some fine scenery. Cross the river by the bamboo footbridge near the *Nam Song Hotel* and follow the road to Na Thong, 4km west. Hop the fence at the bend in the road just past the village school house (if you're on a bike, leave it at the *tam màk hung* stall here) and walk through the rice fields towards the cliff face, 1km away. Cross the bizarrely arched bamboo bridge to reach the path leading to the cave. It's a short steep climb to the entrance, extremely slippery in the rainy season. In the main cavern reclines a bronze Buddha; bring a torch if you want to explore the tunnels branching off the main gallery. Outside the cave, the perfectly blue stream is a great spot for a swim; you can buy cool drinks and fruit nearby.

A descent into **Tham Pha Thao** is the most satisfying caving trip you can make from Vang Viang. Stretching for more than 2km, the tunnel-like cave is pitch-black and filled with huge stalactites and stalagmites. It's best visited near the end of the rainy season, when the water level is perfect for a swim in the subterranean swimming pool 800m into the cave. Bear in mind that you'll be up to your chest in water at times – so travel light and don't bring anything valuable. In the height of the dry season, it's possible to go beyond the pool and explore the full length of the cave. Finding the cave is a matter of getting to the Hmong village of **Pha Thao**, which lies 13km north of Vang Viang. Turn left after the bridge just beyond the Km10 marker on Route 13 – a road sign points the way to the "Nam Xong–Pha Thao Irrigation Project" – and either ford the river or hail a pirogue for a few thousand kip. (This is a good launching point for tubing.) Once across, head for the village at the base of the cliff, where you'll find a few simple restaurants. The villagers will point the way to the cave mouth.

Practicalities

Pick-ups and buses from Vientiane arrive at the **bus station** near Vang Viang's centrally located market, which is close to all accommodation. Buses from Louang Phabang stop just outside of town on Route 13, also close to the guesthouses.

There's a small **bank** (Mon–Sat 8am–noon & 1–4pm) on the town's main street, which changes sterling and dollar travellers' cheques. Nearby is the telecom office (Mon–Fri 8am–noon & 1–5pm) which handles international calls. The **post office** is near the market. Three colourful, hand-drawn **maps** of the Vang Viang area ($0.80) are available from the noodle shop next to *Siripanga* guesthouse near the market. Websurfers should head for **PlaNet CyberCentre** (daily 8.30am–10pm; $2 for 25min), next to *Dok Khoune I* guesthouse.

ACCOMMODATION

This small town is now one of the best-value spots for **accommodation** in the country; it's possible to find a perfectly decent en-suite double for under $3.

Bungalow Thavonsouk, on the banks of the Nam Xong River, near the footbridge. Superbly located en-suite bamboo bungalows. Price depends on the size of the bungalow. ③–⑤.

Dok Khoun I, near the market (☎021/219362). Clean rooms, all en suite and with hot water, in a modern house with second-floor balcony eyeballing karsts across the river. ③.

Dok Khoun II, down a small lane near the airstrip, beyond the bank (☎021/219393). A friendly guesthouse offering a range of rooms housed in two modern buildings. ①.

Kien Thong, down a street off the river road, between the hospital and the school (☎023/511069). Popular two-storey guesthouse with twenty spotlessly clean doubles, most with attached hot-water showers. ③.

Nam Song, near *Bungalow Thavonsouk* (☎023/511016; Louang Phabang bookings 071/252400). This green-roofed ranch-style building occupies a superb location on the river with a magnificent view of the karsts. There's a restaurant, and caving equipment. Reservations are recommended on weekends and holidays. ⑥.

Nana, near *Dok Khoun II* (☎023/511036). Five clean, en-suite doubles, all with hot water and air-con, and a sitting area on the second floor terrace. Management makes an extra effort at friendliness. ③.

Pany, near *Dok Khoun II*. Roomy en-suite doubles in a modern two-storey house, with a friendly owner who is always ready to give tips on day-trips off the beaten path. ①.

Phoubane, on the river road, south of the market. A pleasant, leafy compound, with plenty of outdoor seating, basic but decent rooms, some en suite, and fairly good breakfasts. ①.

Phoukham, in the middle of town. Two-storey house with gaudy pillars and en-suite bathrooms. Several of the upstairs rooms have good views of the karsts. ①.

Sivixay, main road, near Wat Kang. Two modern buildings set in a large compound. Decent en-suite doubles, some with hot water. ①.

Vang Vieng Resort, south end of town (☎023/511050). Standard en-suite bungalows with decent facilities and hot shower. A fifteen-minute walk south along the river from the market. ⑤–⑥.

EATING AND DRINKING

Most of the town's **eateries** seem to be using the same photocopied menu of uninspired noodle and rice dishes. *Nang Bot* on the main road, next to *Vang Vieng* guesthouse, is a popular choice with backpackers – which means you have to wait twice as long for average fare – but it's a good place to find out about hiking and caving in the area. Nearby *Khamphanh* offers better food and service, as well as fresh beer and ice cream. *Viengkeo*, just beyond the bank on the way to Wat Sisuman, is a friendly family-run establishment, away from the main throng. For an excellent bowl of **noodles**, try the *khào biak sen*, served with Lao-style pâté and chicken, at the tiny shop next to the *Siripanga* guesthouse, near the market; the sign reads "soupe de pâté Lao". If you're in the mood for something different, head for *Le Pavot*, across the street from the hospital, overlooking the Nam Xong, where you can choose from an extensive selection of **French** and **Italian** dishes or specialities such as "stewed fatted pullet with bamboo". A great place for a **drink** is the *Sunset*, next to *Bungalow Thavonsouk* on the riverbank: the Beer Lao is cheap and there's a million-dollar view.

LOUANG PHABANG AND AROUND

Nestling in a slim valley shaped by lofty, green mountains and cut by the swift Mekong and Khan rivers, **LOUANG PHABANG** exudes remote tranquillity and casual grandeur. A tiny mountain kingdom for more than a thousand years and designated a World Heritage site in 1995, Louang Phabang is endowed with a legacy of ancient red-roofed temples and French–Indochinese architecture, not to mention some of the country's most refined cuisine, its richest culture and its most sacred Buddha image. The very name Louang Phabang conjures up the classic image of Laos – streets of ochre colonial houses and swaying palms, lines of saffron-robed monks gliding through the morning mist, and, of course, longtail boats racing down the Mekong. This is where the first proto-Lao nation took root. It is the most Lao city in Laos, the only one where ethnic Lao are in the majority and where the back streets and cobblestoned lanes have a distinctly village-like feel. It's the birthplace of countless Lao rituals and the origin of a line of rulers. Conveniently, Louang Phabang is also the **transport** hub of northern Laos, with road, river and air links – both domestic and international – all leading to the city.

The earliest Lao settlers made their way down the Nam Ou Valley, sometime after the tenth century, absorbing the territory on which the city lies and naming it **Xiang Dong Xiang Thong**. But it wasn't until legendary Lao warrior Fa Ngum captured the town in 1353 that it emerged as the heart of a thriving, independent kingdom in its own right. He founded the kingdom of **Lane Xang Hom Khao** – the Land of a Million Elephants and the White Parasol – and established the line of kings that was to rule Laos for six centuries. With Fa Ngum came monks, artisans and learned men from the Khmer court, a legal code, and Theravada Buddhism. Striking temples were built, epic poems composed and sacred texts copied, and in 1512, King Visoun brought the very sacred Pha Bang Buddha image to the city, a hugely significant event. Lane Xang was, for the moment, a major power on the Indochinese peninsula, but by 1563 the fear of encroaching Burmese led to the capital being moved to Vientiane. The Pha Bang was left behind and the city renamed after the revered image. From then on, Louang Phabang had a roller-coaster ride, invaded first by the Burmese and then by the Siamese, until King Oun Kham finally agreed to co-operate with France, and the city's French period began. During the two Indochina wars, Louang Phabang fared better than most towns in Laos. However, the Second Indochina War ultimately took its toll on Louang Phabang's ceremonial life, which lost its regal heart when the Pathet Lao ended the royal line by forcing King Sisavang Vatthana to abdicate in 1975.

Arrival

Louang Phabang **airport** is 2km northeast of the city. If you're arriving on an international flight, you can get a fifteen-day **visa on arrival** here (see p.453). There are also exchange facilities and an immigration checkpoint, where you'll need to get your passport stamped. Tuk-tuks (4000K) and guesthouse touts will ferry you into town.

Louang Phabang has three **bus stations**, all served by shared tuk-tuks which round up passengers heading to similar destinations in town (2000K). Buses from Vientiane, Vang Viang and other points south along Route 13 pull into the **Southern Bus Station**, 3km south of the centre, while buses from Xainyabouli terminate at the nearby Pakkhon depot. Buses and sawngthaews from Oudomxai, Nong Khiaw and all other points north arrive at the **Northern Bus Station**, 4km north of town.

Slow boats dock at the Navigation Office landing behind the former Royal Palace in the old city, an easy walk from most guesthouses. **Speedboats** dock at a separate landing in the village of Ban Don, 7km north of the city (6000K by tuk-tuk).

MOVING ON FROM LOUANG PHABANG

By plane
The easiest way to get to the airport is by tuk-tuk (4000K per person). Lao Aviation's office is on Visounalat Road (☎071/212172).

By bus or sawngthaew
Buses heading **to Vientiane and Vang Viang** and points south along Route 13 use the Southern Bus Station, 3km south of the centre, best reached by tuk-tuk (2000K). Buses to the capital leave hourly from dawn until just after noon. Tickets are sold at the bus station. Buses **to Xainyabouli** and Muang Nan pull out of the Pakkhon depot, near the Southern Bus Station (3000K by tuk-tuk). Buses and sawngthaews **to Oudomxai, Nong Khiaw** and all other points north use the Northern Bus Station, 4km north of town. Almost all north-bound buses depart in the morning, but there's no need to buy your ticket in advance. Tuk-tuks to the station cost around 4000K.

By boat
Slow boats leave from the Navigation Office landing behind the former Royal Palace in the old city, an easy walk from most guesthouses. Departures for Vientiane, Pakbeng and Nong Khiaw are usually posted on a chalk board here, but check with boat captains the evening before and arrive at the pier early. **Speedboats** leave from a separate landing in the village of Ban Don, 7km north of the city (6000K by tuk-tuk). Eight-seat speedboats depart for points north and south along the Mekong River, as well as for destinations along the Nam Ou River from a queue when full. Arrive early to get a seat, although there's no guarantee that every destination is served every day; enquire the day before you plan to travel. Alternatively, you can hire a speedboat.

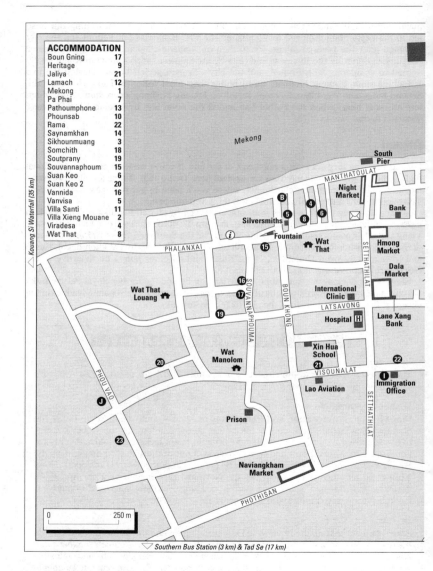

ACCOMMODATION

Boun Gning	17
Heritage	9
Jaliya	21
Lamach	12
Mekong	1
Pa Phai	7
Pathoumphone	13
Phounsab	10
Rama	22
Saynamkhan	14
Sikhounmuang	3
Somchith	18
Soutprany	19
Souvannaphoum	15
Suan Keo	6
Suan Keo 2	20
Vannida	16
Vanvisa	5
Villa Santi	11
Villa Xieng Mouane	2
Viradesa	4
Wat That	8

Southern Bus Station (3 km) & Tad Se (17 km)

Information, orientation and getting around

The Louang Phabang **tourist information office** (Mon–Fri 8am–5pm; ☎071/212487) is on Phalanxai Road, about 140m downriver from the Silversmiths Fountain. The hand-drawn 3D **map** of the town is quite useful and available free at Louang Phabang and Vientiane airports.

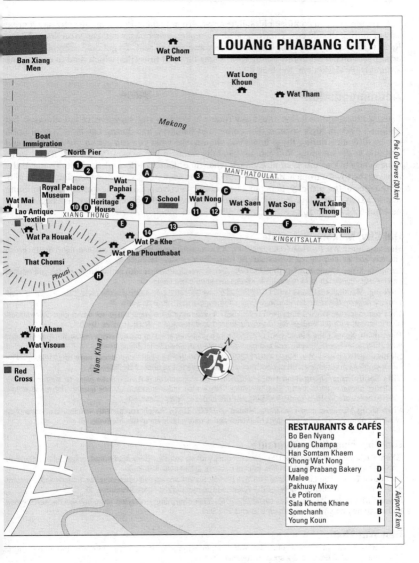

Beyond having multiple spellings for each **street name**, some streets have as many as four different names, while other roads switch names as they wind through the city. For clarity's sake, we've chosen one street name and stuck with it. But, as elsewhere in Laos, locals prefer to use landmarks, such as monasteries, to identify parts of town: thus Ban Wat That ("Wat That district"), refers to the area south of Setthathilat Road, between Wat That and the Mekong River.

Although you can comfortably walk everywhere in Louang Phabang, **bicycles** are a great way of touring the old city. They're available at many guesthouses and shops on Xiang Thong Road ($1 per day). Motorbikes are no longer available to rent. To get out to the bus stations or airport you'll have to rely on the town's small fleet of **tuk-tuks**, which tend to congregate around Dala Market and the boat pier.

Accommodation

Louang Phabang has heaps of unfussy rooms in characterful, inexpensive guesthouses, but finding a place in **high season** (December and January), and during Lao New Year in April, can be difficult – during these times you should take what you can get on the first night and upgrade in the morning. You can get good discounts in low season (May–Oct). It's an early-to-bed-early-to-rise town, so always ask what time doors are locked at night. To make the most of the town's tropical daydream atmosphere, seek out accommodation among the gilded temples of the **old city**, home to a host of inexpensive options. The former silversmithing district, **Ban Wat That**, located between Wat That and the Mekong River, has become the new hot-spot for cheap guesthouses and has just as much character.

Old City: Mekong Riverside

Heritage, near Wat Pa Phai (☎071/252537). A lovely two-storey house with wooden floorboards, green shutters and an informal bar downstairs. All rooms have en-suite facilities. ②.

Lamach, Xiang Thong Road (☎071/252079). A cosy wooden house, with an informal terrace and garden and a tasty vegetarian food restaurant. Rooms are simple but clean. ①.

Mekong, Manthatoulat Road (☎071/212752). This well-located guesthouse is the pick of the bunch of inexpensive digs on the river, harbouring seven rooms including some en suite. ①.

Pa Phai, opposite Wat Pa Phai (☎071/212752). A charming little guesthouse set on an especially atmospheric street, with ten budget rooms, clean shared facilities and a pleasant patio. ①–②.

Phounsab, Xiang Thong Road (☎071/212595). In a prime location on the old city's restaurant and souvenir strip, this hotel has high-ceilinged rooms, with or without en-suite facilities. ①–②.

Sikhounmuang, near Wat Nong (☎071/252065). On a charming old city street near the Mekong. The small singles and doubles with paper-thin walls can prove noisy; shared facilities. ①.

Villa Santi, Xiang Thong Road (☎071/212267). This elegant colonial villa is *the* place to stay in Louang Phabang: it was once home to King Sisavang Vong's wife and is still run by her family. The most atmospheric rooms are in the original building, not the annexe. Book ahead. ⑦.

Villa Xieng Mouane, near Wat Xiang Mouan (☎071/252152). Stately rooms with wooden floors in a pretty white colonial-style villa with light-blue trim and a walkway down to the Mekong. ⑤.

Old City: Nam Khan Riverside

Kheme Khane, Latsavong Road. Spacious rooms with en-suite facilities set behind a riverside restaurant. The management are geared to offer Internet access in the near future. ①.

Pathoumphone, Kingkitsalat Road (☎071/212946). Rooms are spread out across two houses and most are great value considering the views of the river and the mountains; shared facilities. ①.

Saynamkhan, Kingkitsalat Road (☎071/212976). This charmingly restyled shop-house is a well-located mid-range bet. Rooms come with air-con and TV. ⑤.

Ban Wat That

Suan Keo 2, just off Xiang Thong, Ban Wat That. Fifteen rooms in a pretty, white two-storey house with blue shutters, tiled floors and a spacious terrace. ①.

Vanvisa, Ban Wat That (☎071/212925). Mustard-coloured Sixties villa in the former silversmithing district with a distinctly homey feel. Rooms are clean, and some are en suite. ②.

Viradesa, Ban Wat That (☎071/252026). Set on a charming lane, with a wide range of rooms, including two dorms (under $1 per bed). If full, try *Viradesa 2* across the street. ①.

Wat That, Ban Wat That (☎071/212913). This tiny wooden house contains four basic, but surprisingly spacious, rooms with clean shared facilities. There's a restaurant in the garden that serves up pancakes, sandwiches and great fruit shakes. ①.

Ban That Louang, Visounalat Road and Phou Vao

Boun Gning, Souvannaphouma Road (☎071/212274). Although lacking the charm of nearby *Vannida*, this is a well-run backpacker's joint with good rooms and helpful management. ①.

Jaliya, Visounalat Road (☎071/252154). Across from Lao Aviation, rooms in this drab shop-house are perfectly comfortable. ①.

Rama, Visounalat Road (☎071/212247). An old budget stand-by that feels past its prime. Plenty of biggish en-suite rooms, which, although somewhat rundown, are good value. ①.

Somchith, Latsavong Road (☎071/212522). Wooden house with perfectly decent rooms plus a slim, communal balcony. Guests have access to a washing machine and free spring water. ①.

Soutprany, on the corner of Souvannaphouma and Latsavong roads (☎071/213028). A gorgeous two-storey colonial-style villa surrounded by a leafy garden. Basic rooms with shared facilities. ①.

Souvannaphoum, Phalanxai Road (☎071/212200). Two dozen handsomely appointed rooms in Prince Souvannaphouma's former home, set among spacious gardens. Breakfast included. ⑦.

Suan Keo, behind Wat Manolom (☎071/212965). Budget option away from the more touristed neighbourhoods. Set among swaying palms, this friendly ten-room guesthouse is a gem. ①.

Vannida, Souvannaphouma Road (☎071/212374). Run by super-friendly staff, this is the most charming of the inexpensive guesthouses, occupying a fifty-year-old cream-coloured villa in a hilltop garden on a quiet street. The rooms are fine but nothing special. ①–②.

The Old City

Louang Phabang's **old city** is largely concentrated on a tongue of land, approximately 1km long and 0.25km wide, with the confluence of the Mekong and Nam Khan rivers at its tip. This peninsula is dominated by a steep and forested hill, **Phou Si** ("Holy Hill"), crowned with a Buddhist stupa that can be seen for miles around. Most of Louang Phabang's architecture of merit – monasteries and French-influenced mansions – is to be found on the main thoroughfare, **Xiang Thong**, between the tip of the peninsula and Setthathilat Road. Beyond Setthathilat Road, near the Mekong, lies the old silversmithing district, **Ban Wat That**, centred on its monastery, Wat That.

A good place to start your tour of the old city is the dry goods market, **Dala Market**, on Setthathilat Road. Wild chicken calls, resembling tin whistles, are on display beside bags of saltpetre and sulphur which, when mixed with ground charcoal, produce a homemade gunpowder. Stalls selling gold and silver jewellery double as pawn shops and usually display royalist regalia — brass buttons, badges and medals decorated with the Hindu iconography of the old kingdom. This is also a popular haunt of black market currency dealers. Near Dala Market, a small **Hmong Market** occupies a vacant lot on the corner of Setthathilat and Xiang Thong roads, selling traditional hats, bags and clothes.

Further along Xiang Thong, Wat Mai Suwannaphumaham, or **Wat Mai**, dates from the late eighteenth or early nineteenth century, but it is the *sim*'s relatively modern facade with its gilt stucco reliefs that is the main focus of attention. Depicting the second-to-last incarnation of the Buddha set amidst traditional Lao scenes, the facade was created in the 1960s and recently restored, but is already starting to deteriorate.

The Royal Palace

Centrally located between Phou Si Hill and the Mekong River, the former **Royal Palace** (Mon–Fri 8.30am–noon & 1–4pm; 5000K) is now a museum preserving the paraphernalia of Laos's recently extinguished monarchy. It was constructed in 1904 by the French and displays a tasteful fusion of European and Lao design. The pediment over the main entrance is decorated with the symbol of the Lao monarchy: Airavata, the three-headed elephant, being sheltered by the sacred white parasol. This is surrounded by the intertwining bodies of the fifteen guardian naga of Louang Phabang; the naga is a sacred water serpent, both a symbol of water and its life-giving properties and a protector of the Lao people.

At the far end of the gallery to the right of the main entrance is a small, barred room that once served as the king's personal shrine room. It is here that the **Pha Bang**, the most sacred Buddha image in Laos, is being kept until the completion of the Haw Pha Bang — the temple in the eastern corner of the palace compound. The Pha Bang is believed to possess miraculous powers that safeguard the country. According to legend, it was crafted in the heavens and then delivered, via Sri Lanka and Cambodia, to the city of Xiang Dong Xiang Thong, later renamed Louang Phabang (the Great Pha Bang) in its honour. In the early eighteenth century the Pha Bang was moved to Vientiane, whence it was stolen twice by the Siamese (who always returned it, believing it to be bad luck); since 1867, the Pha Bang has been kept in Louang Phabang.

The most impressive room inside the palace is the dazzling **Throne Hall**, its high walls spangled with mosaics of multi-coloured mirrors. On display here are rare articles of royal regalia: swords of hammered silver and gold, an elaborately decorated fly-whisk and even the king's own howdah (elephant saddle). Also on exhibit are a cache of small crystal, silver and bronze Buddha images taken from the inner chamber of the "Watermelon Stupa" at Wat Visoun. Other rooms show theatrical masks and musical instruments used by the royal dance troupe in their performances of the *Ramayana,* diplomatic gifts presented to the people of Laos by a handful of nations, and larger-than-life portraits of King Sisavang Vattana, his wife and their son, painted by a Soviet artist.

Chinatown, Wat Pa Phai and Wat Saen

The neighbourhood encompassing the section of Xiang Thong Road just north of the former Royal Palace is known to locals as "Ban Jek" or **Chinatown**, and contains some fine examples of Louang Phabang shop-house architecture, a hybrid of French and Lao features superimposed on the South Chinese style that was once prevalent throughout urban Southeast Asia. A left-turn at the end of the row of shop-houses will take you to **Wat Pa Phai**, the Bamboo Forest Monastery, whose *sim* is painted and lavishly embellished with stylized naga and peacocks.

Doubling back up to the corner, turn left to continue down Xiang Thong Road as far as **Wat Saen**, where an ornate boat shed houses the monastery's two **longboats**, used in the annual boat race festival. Held at the end of the rainy season, the boat races are believed to lure Louang Phabang's fifteen guardian naga back into the rivers after high waters and flooded rice paddies have allowed them to escape. The boathouse is decorated with carved wooden images of these mythical serpents.

Wat Xiang Thong

Probably the most historic and enchanting Buddhist monastery in the entire country, **Wat Xiang Thong**, the Golden City Monastery (daily 8am to dusk; 3000K), near the northernmost tip of the peninsula, should not be missed. The wonderfully graceful main temple or *sim* was built in 1560 by King Setthathilat and, unlike nearly every other temple in Louang Phabang, was neither razed by Chinese marauders or over-enthusiastically restored. You'll need to stand at a distance to get a view of the roof, the temple's most outstanding feature. Elegant lines curve and overlap, sweeping nearly to the ground, and evoke a bird with outstretched wings or, as the locals say, a mother hen sheltering her brood.

The **walls** of the *sim* are decorated inside and out with stencilled gold motifs. Many of these depict a variety of tales, including the Lao version of the *Ramayana* – the *Pha Lak Pha Lam* – and scenes from the *jataka* (stories about the lives of the Buddha), as well as graphic scenes of punishments doled out in the many levels of Buddhist hell. Such depictions were meant to give a basic education in religion to illiterate laypeople. In one of these punishment scenes, on the wall to the right of the main entrance, an adulterous couple is being forced to flee a pack of rabid dogs by climbing a tree studded with wicked thorns. In the branches above perch a flock of crows, awaiting the chance to peck out the sinners' eyes. Other unfortunate souls are being cooked in a copper cauldron of boiling oil (for committing murder) or are suspended by a hook through their tongues (guilty of telling lies).

In the rafters above and to the right of the main entrance runs a long wooden **aquaduct** in the shape of a mythical serpent. During Lao New Year, lustral water is poured into a receptacle in the serpent's tail and spouts from its mouth, bathing a Buddha image housed in a wooden pagoda-like structure situated near the altar. A drain in the floor of the pagoda channels the water under the floor and out of the mouth of a mirror-spangled elephant's head on the exterior wall. The water is considered to be highly sacred and the faithful will use it to anoint themselves or to ritually bathe household Buddhas. To the left of the *sim*, as you face it, stands a small brick-and-stucco **shrine** containing a standing Buddha image. The intricate purple and gold mirrored mosaics on the pediments are probably the country's finest example of this kind of ornamentation, which is thought to have originated in Thailand and spread to Burma as well. Directly behind the shrine, the Red Chapel enshrines a sixteenth-century **reclining Buddha** image, one of Laos's greatest sculptures in bronze.

On the other side of the monastery grounds is the **Funerary Carriage Hall** (daily 8am to dusk) or *haw latsalot*. Built in 1962, the hall's wide teakwood panels are deeply carved with depictions of Rama, Sita, Ravana and Hanuman, characters from the Lao version of the *Ramayana*. Check out the carved window shutters on the building's left side where Hanuman, the King of the Monkeys, is depicted in pursuit of the fair sex. Inside, the principal article on display is the *latsalot*, the royal funerary carriage, used to transport the mortal remains of King Sisavong Vong to cremation. The vehicle is built in the form of several bodies of parallel naga, whose jagged fangs and dripping tongues heralded the king's final passage through Louang Phabang. Atop the carriage are three gilded urns in which the royal corpse was kept in foetal position until the cremation.

Phou Si – the Holy Hill

Phou Si ("holy hill") is both the geographical and spiritual centre of the city, a miniature Mount Meru, the Mount Olympus of Hindu–Buddhist cosmology. The hill's peak affords a stunning panorama of the city, and can be reached by three different routes. The first and most straightforward is via the stairway directly opposite the main gate of the Royal Palace Museum. A small entrance fee must be paid before ascending and this is when you should ask to be let into the adjacent *sim* which is normally padlocked shut. Known as **Wat Pa Houak**, this fine little temple contains the city's most fascinating murals, which depict Lao, Chinese, Persian and European inhabitants of Louang Phabang. From the *sim* it is a steep but shady climb to the peak. The second approach, on the other side of the hill, is up a zigzag stairway flanked by whitewashed naga, but is only recommended if you want to dodge the entrance fee.

The third and most rambling but atmospheric approach is via **Wat Pha Phoutthabat** near Phou Si's northern foot (across from *Saynamkhan Guest House*). There are actually three monasteries in this compound, and the most interesting structure is the *sim* of **Wat Pa Khe**, a tall, imposing building with an unusual inward-leaning facade. Most noteworthy here are a pair of carved shutters to the left of the main entrance, said to depict seventeenth-century Dutch traders. Behind and to the left of the *sim* is a stairway leading to the **"Buddha's footprint"**, a larger-than-life stylized footprint complete with the 108 auspicious marks after which Wat Pha Phoutthabat was named. The shrine housing the footprint is usually locked. The path meanders up past stone monks' quarters and the remains of an old anti-aircraft gun, to the summit, crowned by the stupa **That Chomsi**.

Beyond the old city

The older parts of the city may have a higher concentration of monasteries and old buildings, but there is plenty to see beyond Setthathilat Road. **Wat That**, officially known as Wat Pha Mahathat, is situated on a rise next to the *Phou Si Hotel* and is reached via a stairway flanked by some impressive seven-headed naga. At the top of the stairs is perhaps the most photographed window in all of Louang Phabang. Framed in ornately carved teak, it's a blend of Lao, Chinese and Khmer design. Other elements of the wat suggest influence from northern Thailand, namely the gold-topped *that* for which the monastery was named.

Wat Visoun and Wat Aham share a parcel of land on the opposite side of Phou Si from the Royal Palace Museum. The *sim* of the former was once lavishly decorated but was razed in 1887, and the bulbous, finial-topped stupa, known as *that makmo* – the Watermelon Stupa – was destroyed as well. The looters made off with many treasures stored within, but what they left behind is now on display in the throne room of the Royal Palace Museum. Wat Visoun's reconstructed *sim* is an unremarkable mix of Louang Phabang and Vientiane styles, but the Watermelon Stupa is still quite unique. Neighbouring Wat Aham features a delightfully diminutive *sim* and a couple of mould-blackened *that*. A small fee is sometimes collected from foreign visitors for access to these monasteries.

Eating, drinking and nightlife

Louang Phabang prides itself on its **food**. At the top of your list should be *aw lam*, a bittersweet soup, heavy on aubergines and mushrooms. Other local specialities include *jaew bong*, a condiment of red chillis, shallots, garlic and dried buffalo skin, and *phak nâm*, a type of watercress particular to the area and widely used in salads.

If you're looking for something lively, head over to the popular *Rama* **disco** (daily 9–11.30pm), on Visounalat Road, a fun, upcountry club attached to the hotel of the same name with a live band and a laid-back dance floor, where both Lao and foreign clientele are welcome. The best **bar** in town is at the French-owned *Duang Champa* (see below), which tends to stay open later than other spots in town at the weekend. Across town in the *Souvannaphoum* (see p.491), *Le Rendez-Vous* benefits from the regal atmosphere of a hotel that was once home to former prime minister Prince Souvannaphouma. If you're looking for a bar on the Lao hipster scene, check out the dimly lit no-name bar across from the *Rama*, run by a cool Lao returnee who spent ten years in Tennessee. Most venues close by midnight.

Noodles and street stalls

A **night market** sets up in the evenings between the post office and the river.

Khao Biak Sen, Xiang Thong Road. Great bowls of round rice noodles served at punishingly low tables outside a gorgeously unrestored French villa built in 1926.

Khao Soi Ban That Louang, Xiang Thong Road. A few blocks south of Nam Phou, this small shop-house serves up excellent, spicy bowls of hard-to-find northern-Lao-style noodles.

Mi Bet, on the corner of Visounalat and Setthathilat roads. Yellow noodles loaded with slices of roast duck. *Nâm whân*, the obscenely-coloured yet delicious dessert, is also available.

Cafés

Bo Ben Nyang, Xiang Thong Road, Ban Khili. Situated in a mulberry paper gallery, *Bo Ben Nyang* serves a range of teas. The upstairs balcony, which affords a wraparound temple view, is the perfect spot to be at 4pm, when the wats' call to meditation is often transformed into a ten-minute drum-and-gong concert.

Luang Prabang Bakery, Xiang Thong Road. The sandwiches are light and tasty and the fruit shakes thick at this place run by a Hmong woman who studied pastry cooking in Bangkok.

Restaurants

Most of Louang Phabang's **restaurants** open daily for lunch and stop serving food by 9pm. With the exception of the restaurants at the *Phou Vao* and *Souvannaphoum* hotels, where dining is very civilized, but pricey by Lao standards, the average meal at a restaurant costs $2.50 and nowhere will you spend more than $6.

Duang Champa, Kingkitsalat Road. Lao and French meals are served in a spacious, stylishly low-key dining area in a colonial house. Investigate the $4 set meals and impressive sundaes.

Han Somtam Khaem Khong Wat Nong, near Wat Nong. Tiny white shop-house serving the town's best spicy papaya salad, and intriguing bowls of boiled rice cubes and spicy sauce, called *feun*. There's no sign: look for the green doors hung with bags of pork skin crisps.

Lamach, Xiang Thong Road. Vegetarian restaurant with outdoor tables and all dishes made without fish sauce. The mango shake here is the dean of Louang Phabang fruit shakes.

Malee, Phou Vao Road. Something of a local legend if still decidedly no frills, this is a good spot to try local specialities such as *aw lam* and *khai phaen*, and an interesting turkey *làp*.

Pakhuay Mixay, near Wat Xiang Mouan. The Lao cuisine served here is perfectly good, but the main draw is the garden atmosphere, in a quiet residential corner of the old city.

Le Potiron, Xiang Thong Road. With full-flavour pâtés, a fine pepper steak for $3.50 and mouth-watering pizzas, it's hard not to satisfy a hankering for Western food at this good-value eatery.

Le Saladier, Xiang Thong Road, next door to *Le Potiron*. An extensive menu of very tasty salads as well as less leafy meals. Equally important, it has draught Beer Lao.

Sala Kheme Khane, Kingkitsalat Road. High on the bank of the Nam Khan River behind Phou Si, this is the classiest of the riverside restaurants. The *keng kai màk nao*, a soup served with chicken, and the *sai-ua Louang Phabang*, or Lao-style sausages, are standouts on this menu of traditional Lao food.

Somchanh, Ban Wat That. Lao food in the old silversmiths' quarter, with good views of the Mekong. The duck is recommended, or try *Kai Sawan*, "heavenly chicken".

Villa Santi, Xiang Thong Road. The best Lao food in town, cooked by the daughter of the legendary Phia Sing, the last chef to cook for the Lao royal family. Very moderately priced.

Young Koun, Visounalat Road. This old backpacker favourite, located across from the *Rama*, offers an extensive selection of Chinese and Lao food with an emphasis on vegetarian dishes.

Shopping

As the royal capital of Laos, Louang Phabang was traditionally a magnet for skilled **artisans** from around the former kingdom and the traditional arts have been experiencing a revival since the tourism boom. Most of the town's souvenir shops are on **Xiang Thong Road**, especially in the neighbourhood known as Ban Jek, between the Royal Palace and the secondary school. The other good place to look is **Talat Dala**, the dry goods market on Setthathilat Road.

Although Thai antique dealers have made off with quite a bit of old Lao **silver**, items still worth looking out for are paraphernalia for betel chewing: round or oval boxes for storing white lime, cone-shaped containers for betel leaves and miniature mortars used to pound areca nuts. Hilltribe silver jewellery is usually bold and heavy – the better to show off one's wealth – and most is the handiwork of the Hmong tribe. The antique brass weights known as **"opium weights"** are also well represented in the silver shops. Weights cast as birds, elephants and lions are an established collectable and can command high prices, but simpler designs are more reasonably priced. New silver of superior quality should be bought directly from Louang Phabang's expert **silversmiths**. The best-known of these is Thithpeng Maniphone, whose workshop is located just down the small lane opposite Wat That. Other silversmiths are located near the Royal Palace and opposite Wat Aham.

Lao Antique Textiles Collection (on Xiang Thong Road, opposite Wat Mai) has an excellent selection of unusual and antique **textiles**, starting at $20. New textiles are cheapest at Talat Dala where *nyam* – shoulder bags – and the all-purpose *pha khao ma*, a chequered, wrap-around sarong used by Lao men, are almost given away. Lao **woodcarving** is traditionally religious in nature, and Buddha images can be found everywhere, but these are now supplemented by souvenirs such as carved wooden hangers for displaying textiles. Ban Khili (opposite Wat Sop) offers a good selection of originally designed traditional mulberry **paper lanterns**, including collapsible models.

Listings

Banks and exchange Lane Xang Bank on Xiang Thong Road changes travellers' cheques for a two per-cent charge; cash advances on Visa are possible; Lane Xang Bank maintains an exchange bureau (daily 8.30am–4pm) on Latsavong Road; cash and travellers' cheques only.

Boat charters Mr Thongdi speaks excellent English and has two boats. You can contact him at Bouchane Rice Shop, Manthatoulat Road (☎071/212910), next to the *Auberge Calao*.

Hospitals and clinics The main hospital is on Setthathilat Road; a new International Clinic (☎071/252049) is around the corner on the hospital's western side. In case of a serious illness, fly to Chiang Mai, Thailand, where there are several good hospitals.

Internet access PlaNet CyberCentre, Xiang Thong Road (daily 8am–8pm; $2 for 10 min); New Computer Center, Latsavong Road (daily 8am–8pm; $2 for 10min or 2000K per min).

Massage and herbal sauna The Red Cross (daily 5–7.30pm) on Visounalat Road (☎071/212303) has traditional Lao massage at 25,000K per hour (reserve ahead) and an excellent sauna for 10,000K (bring a sarong).

Post office The GPO (Mon–Fri 8am–noon & 1–5pm, Sat 8am–noon) is located on the corner of Xiang Thong and Setthathilat roads. Poste restante is kept for three months.

Telephone services International calls and faxes at Telecom (daily 8am–9pm), behind the GPO. No collect calls, but a callback service is available.

Tour agencies Sodetour, Manthatoulat Road (☎071/212092); Lane Xang, Visounalat Road (☎071/212793); Lao Travel Service, Xiang Thong Road (☎071/212725); Diethelm, Xiang Thong Road (☎071/212277); Inter-Lao Tourisme, Setthathilat Road (☎071/212034).

Around Louang Phabang

You haven't seen Louang Phabang until you **cross the Mekong** to Xiang Men and climb up to Wat Chompet, a hilltop monastery which offers superior views of the city's gilded temples at sunset. The popular **Pak Ou caves** trip gets you out on the water, a worthwhile journey if you've not already travelled along the Mekong by boat from Pakbeng. The nearby Kouang Si **waterfall** is a good spot for splashing around in turquoise waters.

Across the river

Surprisingly few tourists bother to cross the Mekong and explore the sleepy village of **XIANG MEN**, but it makes a good half-day trip and gives you a chance to view Louang Phabang from across the river. A passenger ferry operates between Louang Phabang and Xiang Men and leaves from the landing west of the Royal Palace Museum. You could also strike a deal with one of the many boats to be found along the riverbank: the five-minute journey should cost around 5000K per person. Ask to be let off at **Wat Long Khoun**, once used by Louang Phabang's kings as a pre-coronation retreat, which involved ritual baths, meditation and reflection. Of note are the two Chinese door guardians painted either side of the main entrance to the *sim* and the murals within. An easy climb to the top of the hill behind Wat Long Khoun brings you to the *sim* and stupas of **Wat Chom Phet**, a disused monastery best visited at dusk, when the views of the sunset are spectacular.

Kouang Si

The best day-trip from Louang Phabang is the picturesque, multi-level **Kouang Si** waterfall (entry 2000K), which tumbles 60m before spilling through a series of crystal-blue pools – a great spot for a picnic and a swim. The "no swimming" signs posted at the upper pool appear to be intended simply to dissuade you from spoiling photo opportunities, which is not an issue during the week. Vendors near the lower pool sell *tam màk hung*, fruit and drinks. The steep path on the opposite side of the falls leads to a grassy meadow filled with brilliantly coloured butterflies. The path can get quite slippery, and several barefoot trampers have broken a leg here.

Since foreigners are no longer able to rent **motorbikes** in Louang Phabang, visitors to Kouang Si are forced to rely on other forms of transportation to reach the waterfall situated 35km southwest of Louang Phabang. The most pleasant option is by **boat** down the Mekong River – many of the same boat drivers running trips to the Pak Ou caves will also offer to take you to the falls. This entails taking a tuk-tuk for the last portion of the journey, something which is handled by the boat driver and usually worked into his fee: check when negotiating your fare. Boatmen hang out along the Mekong riverside and charge $20 for a boat that can accommodate up to ten people and a further $4 for the tuk-tuk. You can also do the whole journey by **tuk-tuk**; if you can assemble a group this works out quite cheap ($10 return). Drivers, who can be found at the Hmong market, will wait for you while you visit the falls.

A few kilometres before the village of Ban Tha Pene and the waterfall, a small **elephant camp** offers hour-long rides to the waterfall (daily 8am–noon & 2–5pm; $2 per hour).

Accommodation near the waterfall is available at a charming guesthouse (②) in the idyllic lowland Lao village of Ban Tha Pene. It's run by the owners of the *Vanvisa* in Louang Phabang and offers six basic en-suite rooms. Turn right before the hill leading out of the village, cross the footbridge over the stream and you'll see it on the left.

The Buddha Caves and Whisky Village

A popular river excursion, some 25km out of Louang Phabang, is centred around the confluence of the Mekong and Nam Ou rivers, known as Pak Ou. Numerous caves punctuate the limestone cliffs here, the best-known of which are the "**Buddha Caves**", Tham Ting and Tham Phoum. These caves have been used for centuries as a repository for old and unwanted Buddha images that can no longer be venerated on an altar, and the hundreds upon hundreds of serenely smiling images covered in dust and cobwebs make an eerie scene. **Tham Ting**, the lower cave, just above the water's surface, is more of a large grotto and is light enough to explore without artificial light. The upper cave is unlit so bring a torch, or better still, a handful of candles to enhance the spooky effect. A small entrance fee is collected at the lower cave.

On the opposite bank of the river is a village that for thousands of years produced stoneware jars but has now found that distilling liquor is more lucrative. The inhabitants of Ban Xang Hai, referred to by English-speaking boatmen as the **Whisky Village**, are quite used to thirsty visitors stopping by for a pull on the bamboo straw. The liquor is made from fermented sticky rice and pots filled with the hooch are lined up on the beach awaiting transport up or down the river. Both sites can be seen in a couple of hours, and boatmen hired in Louang Phabang usually treat it as a package, assuming that after you've seen a cave-full of Buddhas you'll be ready for a good, stiff drink. Boats are easily arranged in Louang Phabang and should cost $20 to hire for the trip there and back. The ride upriver takes less than an hour.

THE NORTHEAST

Difficult to reach and short on proper tourist sites, the remote **northeast** is one of the least-visited parts of Laos. This area was heavily bombed during the Second Indochina War, and much of the bombing was directed at the strategic **Plain of Jars**, which takes its name from the fields of ancient, giant funerary urns that are the northeast's main tourist draw. Indeed, for most visitors a trip to the region means a flying visit to the town of **Phonsavan** to see the nearby Jar sites. The region's other significant sight are the dozens of **caves** at **Viang Xai**, close to the Vietnam border, which served as the homes and headquarters for the Pathet Lao during their Thirty Year Struggle; very few travellers make it here however, and those who do face a long and convoluted journey via the town of **Xam Nua**.

At present, the only way to get to the region is by **flying** to Xam Nua or Phonsavan, or travelling the circuitous overland route through Louang Phabang province; none of the northeast's four principal borders with Vietnam are yet open, and **Route 7** between Muang Phoukhoun and Phonsavan remains unpaved and unsafe because of bandits. An upgrade of this 140-kilometre stretch of road, however, is currently underway, which will dramatically reduce travel times from Louang Phabang and Vientiane. For the time being, however, you'll need to allow two to three days to get from Louang Phabang to Phonsavan or Xam Nua **by road**: always try to leave on the earliest possible vehicle, bring extra water and food, and be prepared for breakdowns.

Louang Phabang to Nong Khiaw

The six-hour **boat trip** up the Nam Ou from Louang Phabang to Nong Khiaw is wildly scenic, especially the last part. Approximately four hours into the trip, the deforestation of the vertical limestone peaks stops and the river washes onto miniature beaches of pristine white sand. Normally there is only one very crowded passenger boat per day, which leaves before 8am and costs around $5. The alternative is to charter a boat (*mao heua*) for $30 or more. The **road route** from Louang Phabang to Nong Khiaw takes about two and a half hours along well-maintained Route 13. Many Nong-Khiaw buses may dump you off at the junction town of **PAKMONG**, which straddles the junction of Route 1 (connecting Oudomxai and Houa Phan provinces) and Route 13 and is a little way short of Nong Khiaw itself.

Resting at the foot of a striking red-faced cliff, amid towering blue–green limestone escarpments, the dusty, ramshackle town of **NONG KHIAW** lies smack in the middle of some of the most dramatic scenery in Indochina. Local entrepreneurs are gradually realizing that there's money to be made from the backpackers using the town as a hub, and the level of service here has been improving steadily. Arriving by road you'll first pass *Pho Sai* (①), about 600m from the bridge, opposite the school. **Beds** fill up quickly in this friendly establishment, conveniently located next to a little **restaurant** that serves simple fried noodle and rice dishes and mouth-watering banana fritters. The owners of the restaurant also **guide** groups to caves and waterfalls in the area ($15 for a group comprising no more than ten people). On the main road, next to the trail leading to the boat landing is *Vandy* (①), with comfortable doubles and outside bath. A little further upriver is *Somgnot* (①), offering the cheapest deal in town – 3000K for a bamboo "cage" suspended above the ground. The friendly owners also serve food – decent omelettes, fried rice and noodles – and good Lao coffee. If you're in the mood for a little entertainment, there's a tiny "cinema", which shows *Kung Fu* movies between 6 and 9pm, when the town's **electricity** is on the go.

Viang Thong

Route 1 is the main road east from Nong Khiaw and takes you all the way to Viang Thong, though it's in poor condition. You'll probably have to change vehicles at **Viang Kham**, on the banks of the Nam Xeng River. Few travellers tarry here, however, preferring to push on to the first major town of Houa Phan province, **VIANG THONG**, also known by its old name, Muang Hiam. A key northeastern transport hub, Viang Thong sits in the centre of the Louang Phabang–Xam Nua–Phonsavan triangle, and is the launching point for buses heading north to Xam Nua or south to Phonsavan.

The better options out of Viang Thong's three **accommodation** places are the handful of rooms with shared bathroom at the *Phu Kae* (①), a white house on a hill just west of the river, and the friendly *Santisouk* (①), a rickety two-storey building, about 400m west of the market, which stuffs tour groups and truck-drivers into its tiny, thin-walled rooms and communal bathing facilities. There's little to choose from among the handful of restaurants clustered at the heart of town.

Moving on, it's imperative that you track down your bus early, as vehicles depart from the bus stand next to the market between 6.30am and 7.30am each morning. If there's no direct Phonsavan bus, catch a bus to Nam Neun, a gruelling two to three hours to the east along a hilly, potholed road, where connections on to Phonsavan can be made. A direct bus also leaves daily from Viang Thong for Xam Nua; if you miss this, or the bus is cancelled owing to a lack of passengers, take a bus to Nam Neun where you can get a connection north, although you'll need to arrive in Nam Neun by noon lest you wind up stuck there as well.

Nam Neun

The winding road from Viang Thong grinds through Sam Yaek Kaw Hing (appearing on some maps as Houa Phou) – the uninviting cluster of huts scratched onto a hillside that marks the junction of Route 1 and Route 6 – before slipping down into a narrow river valley to the village of **NAM NEUN**. Steep valley walls and a churning river make Nam Neun a diamond in the rough, and for many it's a welcome break from a long day on the road. Drivers chugging along Routes 6 and 7 between Xam Nua and Phonsavan tend to break up the long 240-kilometre haul by stopping here for an hour or more before making the final 140-kilometre run to Phonsavan. If you're stuck, a few beds are available at the *Nam Neun* guesthouse (①), a low wooden building located near the village's restaurants.

Xam Nua

You could be forgiven for thinking that you'd crossed the Vietnamese border on descending into **XAM NUA**, one of the few Lao outposts east of the Annamite Mountains. Flung out across the narrow Nam Xam River valley, Xam Nua's low-slung houses and dreary, institutional-looking buildings, bear the unmistakeable mark of the Vietnamese, who cobbled this town back together after the war. There's little to occupy the traveller here, but it's a departure point for Viang Xai and the Pathet Lao caves.

Buses offload in the dirt lot on the town's main street, just beyond the junction where Route 6 swings sharply east to cross the river en route to Viang Xai and the town's airport. If you've arrived at the **airport**, 3km away, one of the town's two taxis (2000K) will most likely be on hand to shuttle you to a hotel. There's an English-speaking staff member in the provincial **tourist office** (Mon–Fri 8am–noon & 1–4pm), located in the small building at the front of the government compound. **Exchange** services are available at Alounmay Bank's Xam Nua branch, further up the street towards the wat, near the bend in the road.

The two best **hotels** are located around the corner from the bus station, near the bridge over the Nam Xam River. The *Lao Houng* (☎064/312028; ①), a large, squat, grey building, has some rooms with hot shower. Better value is the newer and friendly *Khaem Xam* (①), a narrow three-storey building, with six rooms and hot showers, some en suite. Most **restaurants** shut down or are out of food by 8pm. The *Khaem Xam*, next to the hotel of the same name, is the best restaurant in town, with a range of dishes and an English-language menu.

Viang Xai and the Pathet Lao caves

Sprawled across a valley surrounded by the cave-riddled karst formations used by the Pathet Lao (see "History" p.465) as their wartime headquarters, **VIANG XAI** was cobbled together by comrades from Russia, North Korea and Vietnam as well as labourers from Houa Phan's notorious re-education camps. In 1973, at the end of the war, there were plans to make Viang Xai the heart of a new socialist nation, but in the end, the Pathet Lao leadership moved out and decided to keep Vientiane as the country's capital. Today, a victory arch made of oil drums is the gateway to this wax museum of empty kerbed streets, lined with broken, sci-fi street lamps.

Aside from the two **noodle shops** in the bare-bones market, satisfying meals, even fruit, can be hard to come by in Viang Xai. If you're planning to stay for more than one night you may want to bring supplies from Xam Nua. A little less than 2km from the market, on the northwestern edge of town, the large rooms at the faded, institutional-looking *Viang Xai* (①), surrounded by karsts and pine trees, is the most decent **place to stay** here.

The thrice-daily **pick-up** from Xam Nua (1hr) offloads in the dirt lot in front of the market. A hassle-free way of **getting to Viang Xai** is to hire a taxi ($3) in Xam Nua, which allows you to check into your hotel and order dinner and then get dropped off at Viang Xai's **tourist office** (daily, 8am–noon & 1–4pm), where you must register to tour the caves and pay a 1500K entrance fee. Coming from the town's entrance, pass the market, bear left at the stupa, and the tourist office is in the middle of the second block on the right. A guide will be assigned to you here for no extra charge, though none speaks English.

The Pathet Lao caves

Like Vang Viang in central Laos and Mahaxai in the south, the limestone karst formations in the valleys east of Xam Nua are pockmarked with **caves** and crevices – a perfect hideout for

SAFETY IN XIANG KHOUANG PROVINCE

Occasional attacks by **bandits** have made it dangerous to travel in certain places in Xiang Khouang province, particularly in the area west of Muang Soui. They have been known to attack vehicles, and on one occasion in the mid-1990s even bombed a bus in downtown Phonsavan. Because of this situation, **travelling west to Route 13 along Route 7 and south to Pakxan via Tha Thom is not recommended**, nor are these routes plied by regular public transport. That said, hundreds of tourists visit the area each month without incident.

Of more immediate danger are the **mines, bombis and bombs** littering the province. The Jar sites have been cleared of Unexploded Ordnance (UXO), but there's no telling what the hard rains of the monsoon will unearth. The usual precautions apply: see "Crime and safety" p.463 for details.

the Pathet Lao's parallel government. Viet Minh army units began using the caves in the early 1950s and were soon joined by Lao leftists so that by the mid-1960s the Viang Xai area had become a troglodyte city of thousands living in the more than one hundred caves. The inhabitants of the caves would sleep by day and work at night in the fields or in the caves themselves: caverns held weaving mills, printing presses and workshops where American bombs and worn-out trucks were upgraded into farming tools and appliances. On Saturdays, adults would take a break and attend classes of professional, cultural and political courses. After the Paris peace accords were signed in 1973, a few of the cave-dwelling Pathet Lao leaders built houses outside their caves, where they lived until moving to Vientiane in 1975 to take up government office. After 1975, the caves became a "re-education camp" for the soldiers of the Royal Lao government.

Viang Xai has long been regarded as a national treasure and a symbol of revolutionary resolve along the lines of Mao's Long March, and recently five caves have been opened up to foreigners. Each of these caves, named after the Pathet Lao leaders who lived there, had multiple exits, an office and sleeping quarters, as well as an emergency chamber for use in case of chemical weapons attacks, kitted out with a Soviet oxygen machine and a metal door. The two-hour **tours** of the caves usually begin with **Tham Than Kaysone**, the cave of Kaysone Phomvihane, who led the Lao communist movement from its formation in 1955, and remained head of the Lao People's Democratic Republic from 1975 until his death in 1992. It's around the corner from the tourist office and now has a large brown house and a meeting hall in front of it. Northwest of the tourist office, **Tham Than Souphanouvong** was Prince Souphanouvong's cave, with a garage grotto for his car and an outdoor kitchen on a natural patio. Considered for years by the West to be the Pathet Lao's most important leader, the Red Prince lived here with his wife and ten children from 1963 to 1973; in 1975 he became president of the new government. Beyond the decrepit grandstand on the north side of town, you'll come to **Tham Than Khamtay**, the cave of Khamtay Siphandone, now Prime Minister of Laos. It features a kilometre-long secret tunnel – now shoulder-deep in water – that leads to a cavernous chamber, formerly used as a meeting hall and bizarrely, for the odd circus performance.

Phonsavan

With sections of Route 7 deemed unsafe because of bandits, travellers journeying overland from Vientiane and Louang Phabang through Xiang Khouang province to its provincial capital **PHONSAVAN** are obliged to do a lengthy detour via Route 1 and Route 6. Faced with this prospect, many visitors opt for a **flight** into Phonsavan, which also gives an unforgettable view of the treeless flatlands and crater-ridden moonscape of the Plain of Jars.

It's readily apparent that Phonsavan, located on the vast expanse of the Plain of Jars and hastily rebuilt in the aftermath of decades of fighting, fared little better than anywhere else on the Plain during the war. Since 1975, Phonsavan has, however, emerged as the centre of life in Xiang Khouang province, a magnet for people displaced by years of bombing, scrap-metal merchants from Vientiane and tourists curious to see the nearby Plain of Jars. The downside though, is that Phonsavan has begun to feel a bit of a tourist trap.

Bomb casings and other hunks of rusted steel stacked against shacks that pass for houses on the main street are grim galleries reflecting the area's tragic past. So many bombs were dropped on the area that the Lao are still recycling the ordnance into cash and everyday goods three decades later. In the town's **dry goods market**, across from the GPO, a few stalls sell hoes, shovels and other hardware crafted out of sturdy US steel. Although selling scrap is officially illegal, many people in this poorest of nations continue to plunder the wreckage of war. Nearby, several shops on the eastern flank of the market sell Hmong textiles.

Practicalities

Landing at the **airport**, you'll need to catch a tuk-tuk (3000K) for the four-kilometre hike into town, or go with one of the hotel touts. Arriving from the north by **bus**, from Nam Neun or Xam Nua, you'll be dropped off on the main street near the dry goods market and the GPO, an easy walk to most of the cheap guesthouses. In the lot next to the dry goods market, you'll find trucks, buses and share taxis headed **for Muang Soui** and points north and northeast along routes 6 and 7. **Share taxis**, mostly funky old Soviet Volgas, bound for Muang Khoun and Phaxai, leave from another bus station, about 3.5km away, at Talat Nam Ngum, to the southwest of town on the road heading to the Plain of Jars. They're also good value for hiring out to nearby sites, although many of the roads in the province demand a more rugged vehicle, especially during the rainy season. Four-wheel-drive pick-ups can be arranged through guesthouses and hotels, as well as at Lane Xang Travel (at the *Daophouan Hotel*) and Sousath Tourism (at the *Maly Hotel*). **For getting around** town, you'll find tuk-tuks (2000K), which gather near the dry goods market, especially handy.

Lao Aviation's office is located off the main road, east of the dry goods market. If you're planning to buy a ticket to Louang Phabang or Vientiane here, note that opening hours are random, tickets must be bought in dollars (cash only) and flights are routinely scheduled only hours before the plane takes off.

There is an **exchange** kiosk at the airport, which will change only cash into kip. In town, Alounmay Bank (Mon–Fri 8am–noon & 1–4pm), 700m south of the GPO across from the *Phudoi Hotel*, exchanges US dollars into kip and may accept travellers' cheques, preferring to change them into kip. Sometimes the bank will reluctantly change cheques into US dollars if you persuade them that you need the money to buy a plane ticket – it's worth a try if you're desperate.

ACCOMMODATION

Phonsavan has a healthy roster of basic **guesthouses**, most of which line the road from Muang Kham, east of the dry goods market. Think twice before shelling out extra money for hot water: electricity only runs from 6pm to 11.30pm.

Daophouan (☎061/312171). Above Lane Xang Travel, across from the GPO and fresh goods market. The rooms here are a notch above others in the same category, and all are en suite. ④.

Dokkhoun (☎061/312189). This two-storey white house on Route 7 has clean en-suite doubles with good balconies and bombs used as interior decorations. ③.

Hay Hin, Route 7. *Hay Hin*'s simple, two-bed rooms (with or without bathroom) are the first choice for those on a tight budget. ③.

Maly (☎061/312156). Around the corner from the bank, 1km from the town centre, this well-managed guesthouse has pleasant rooms, hot-water showers and a good restaurant. ③.

Phu Chan (☎061/312264). Roughly 2km southeast of town, this friendly Thai-owned resort has five wooden cabins, each with two large rooms, a common area and striking views. ⑥.

Phu Pha Daeng (☎061/312044). On a hill southeast of town, the *Phu Pha Daeng* offers two-room cabins, each with fireplace and private bathrooms. Good views from the restaurant. ⑦.

EATING
Although there's plenty of decent **places to eat** up and down the main drag, travellers gravitate to the *Sangah*, near the dry goods market, where you can refuel on steak and chips or spicy Lao-style tofu. Across the street, the *Phonekeo* serves good noodles, but if you're a true fan of *fõe*, join the local lunch crowds in making the trek to *Nang Sila*, 600m west of the dry goods market on the left, in a two-storey grey house. For a good morning coffee, head to the northwest corner of the dry goods market – along the back row of shops – where there's a perfect Phonsavan institution, the sort of coffee shop where the owner pours a strong wake-up call while having a chat with the regulars about the intricacies of last night's card game.

The Plain of Jars

The 15km-wide stretch of grassy meadows and low rolling hills around Phonsavan takes its name from the clusters of chest-high funerary urns found there. Scattered across the **Plain of Jars** and on the hills beyond, the ancient jars, which are thought to be around two thousand years old, testify to the fact that Xiang Khouang province, with its access to key regional trade routes, its wide, flat spaces and temperate climate, has been considered prime real estate in Southeast Asia for centuries. The largest jars measure 2m in height and weigh as much as ten tonnes. Little is known about the iron-age megalithic civilization that created them, but in the 1930s bronze and iron tools as well as coloured glass beads, bronze bracelets and cowrie shells were found at the sites, leading to the theory that the jars were funerary urns, originally holding cremated remains. More recent discoveries have also revealed underground burial chambers. During the **Second Indochina War**, the region was bombed extensively between 1964 and 1973. American planes levelled towns and forced villagers to take to the forest, as the two sides waged a bitter battle for control of the Plain of Jars, which represented a back door to northern Vietnam. The Plain was transformed into a moonscape, the treeless flatlands and low rolling brown hills pockmarked with craters leaving a lasting impression on those who fly over it into Phonsavan.

Exploring the Jar Sites
For all the hype, the Plain of Jars is very underwhelming. Of the many Jar sites, three have become entrenched on the tourist route, largely because they are accessible and have a greater concentration of jars. The more atmospheric sites 2 and 3 are 24km and 30km from the centre of Phonsavan respectively. All three Jar sites and old Xiang Khouang (see opposite) can be seen in a day, with guesthouses and tour companies generally pitching the four spots as a **package** ($30–35, plus an extra $10 if you want an English-speaking guide). A less expensive way to go is to negotiate a day rate (generally $20) with one of the share taxi drivers at the dry goods market. Cheaper still, limit yourself to a tuk-tuk tour of Site 1 (15,000K return) or catch a share taxi out to Phaxai, just over 30km south from Phonsavan, and hike up to Site 3. Guesthouses discourage travellers from this do-it-yourself technique, but it never hurts to try. Lane Xang Travel (at the *Daophouan Hotel*), Sodetour (on Route 7, near *Vinh Thong* guesthouse), Phudoi (at the *Phudoi Hotel*), Sousath (at the *Maly Hotel*) and Inter-Lao (across from the *Maly Hotel*) all have branches in town, but can be booked up with tour groups. One good local English-speaking guide, Mr Manopet, can be contacted at the *Sangah Restaurant* (see above).

With more than two hundred jars, **Site 1**, 1.8km southwest of town, known as **Thong Hai Hin** (literally, "Stone Jar Plain"), is the most visited. An entrance fee is requested at one of two pavilions. From here a path leads to Hai Cheaum ("Cheaum Jar"), a massive jar, 2m high and named after a Tai–Lao hero. Walk downhill a little way to find another group of jars, one of which has a crude human shape carved onto it. In the hill off to the left is a large cave which the Pathet Lao used during the war – and which, according to local legend, was used as a kiln to cast the jars. Erosion has carved two holes in the roof of the cave – natural chimneys that make the cavern a worthy kiln of sorts. It may also have been used as a crematorium.

Back on the Phonsavan–Muang Khoun road, the turn-off for more scenic **sites 2 and 3** is 3km further on at the market village of Lat Houang. Ten kilometres on from the turn-off, take a left along a dirt track, following it for 2km through a village until you wind up at two adjacent hills, one on either side of the road. Nearly a hundred jars stretch across the twin humps of Phou Salato, lending the site the name **Hai Hin Phou Salato** ("Salato Hill Stone Jar Site"). The gateway to Site 3, the most atmospheric of these sites, lies in the next village, Ban Xiang Di, 4km up the Phaxai road on the left. Large Lao Phuan houses line the way to Wat Xiang Di, a simple wooden monastery 1km from the turn-off where you'll find the path leading to **Hai Hin Lat Khai**, also known as Hai Hin Xiang Di. Buddha images shattered by bombs have been brought to the wat and placed in a pile in the grounds. Pick up the path at the back corner of the monastery compound, which hops a stream and cuts uphill through several fields before arriving at a clearing with more than a hundred jars and sweeping views.

Muang Khoun (Xiang Khouang)

A ghost of its former self, **MUANG KHOUN**, old Xiang Khouang, 35km southeast of Phonsavan, was once the royal seat of the minor kingdom Xiang Khouang, renowned in the sixteenth century for its 62 opulent stupas, whose sides were said to be covered in treasure. Years of bloody invasions, pillaging and a monsoon of bombs that lasted nearly a decade during the Second Indochina War taxed this town so heavily that, by the time the air raids stopped, next to nothing was left of the kingdom's exquisite temples. Although the town has been rebuilt and renamed, all that remains of the kingdom's former glory are a few evocative ruins, usually visited as part of a day-trip to the Jar sites. A path alongside the market leads up to the blackened hilltop stupa of **That Dam**, the base of which has been tunnelled straight through by treasure seekers. Continuing on the main road beyond the market, you'll pass the ruins of a villa, the only reminder that this town was once a temperate French outpost of ochre colonial villas and shop-houses, and arrive at the ruins of sixteenth-century **Wat Phia Wat**. Brick columns reach skywards around a seated Buddha of impressive size, a mere hint at the temple architecture for which the city was renowned.

THE FAR NORTH

Decades of war and neglect have done their part to keep this isolated region in far northern Laos from developing and have unwittingly preserved a way of life that has virtually vanished in neighbouring countries. The hills and mountains up here have long been the domain of a scattering of **animist tribal peoples**, including the Hmong, Mien and Akha, and it is largely the chance to experience first-hand these near-pristine cultures that is drawing visitors to the region today. See pp.468-469 for an introduction to these tribes.

By far the most popular route out of Louang Phabang is the road through **Oudomxai** and **Louang Namtha** to **Muang Sing**, a laid-back Tai Leu town that lies within the borders of the Golden Triangle, the world's most notorious opium-producing zone. Of late, Muang Sing has become a popular base for trekking, owing to its decent accommodation and easy access to Akha, Mien and Tai Dam villages. Travellers en route to **China** are allowed to cross at **Boten**, reached by bus from Louang Namtha or Oudomxai. From Muang Sing the road leads southwest to the village of **Xiangkok** on the Mekong, the launching point for speedboats to **Houayxai**, an official border crossing with **Thailand**. Many travellers exit Laos here after completing their trip around the north, but it's also possible to come full circle and return to Louang Phabang via a memorable **Mekong-boat journey**. The usual direction of the loop is counter-clockwise (Louang Phabang–Oudomxai–Muang Sing–Xiangkok–Houayxai), but a clockwise route, heading north up the Mekong to Xiangkok first, could offer a more "Lao" experience.

Oudomxai

Most travellers heading north to Muang Sing via Oudomxai and Louang Namtha begin their journey in Louang Phabang and head up Route 13 to the junction town of **Pakmong** (see p.498). Here, a change of vehicle takes you northwest along Route 1 to **OUDOMXAI**, also known as Muang Xai, an important transport hub at the junction of Route 1 and Route 4. **Buses** and pick-ups run in all directions – see "Travel Details", p.529. All vehicles leave early (between 6am and 9am) and by noon the vacant lot that serves as a bus station, in the middle of the town on the main road, is all but empty.

Oudomxai is a popular springboard into Laos for Chinese tourists as well as traders, and the town's hotels and karaoke lounges readily accept Chinese yuan. The town has few sights, but makes a perfect rest-stop between Louang Phabang and Muang Sing, with 24-hour electricity, laundry service, hot water, fruit smoothies and frozen yoghurt. There's even traditional **massage** (10,000K per hour) and a **herbal sauna** (5000K) available at a little shop on the main road, across from the Kaysone monument (Mon–Fri 4–8pm, Sat & Sun 8am–8pm; bring a sarong). The Lane Xang **Bank** is 0.5km north of the market. Dollars, yuan and dollar travellers' cheques are easily converted into kip, but credit card advances are not possible.

Accommodation and eating

Most travellers stay in one of the decent **guesthouses** east of the river, handily located opposite the town's best restaurant. Places to avoid are the two overpriced hotels north of the market that seem to dabble in the flesh trade (*Fu San Lao* and *Singthong*) and a couple of unspeakably dirty hostels catering to Chinese truckers, west of the market (*Saixi* and *Yanglu*). Of the three reasonable hotels opposite the petrol station east of the river, *Seuannalat* (①) is probably the best; housed in a modern shop-house, it offers everything from doubles with hot-water bath to dorm beds. Nearby *Dong Saghuane* (①) has simple doubles with fan and shared bathroom, while the glitzy looking *Linda* (①) has doubles with shared bath and cramped singles, some en suite. Located 500m down the lane next to the petrol station, *Si Wan Kham* (①) is a genuine guesthouse, offering basic rooms in a family home.

One **restaurant** stands out, a no-name place next to a small motorcycle repair shop, located directly opposite *Dong Saghuane* guesthouse, which serves up excellent Chinese dishes – particularly good are the pork fried in ginger and the pork fried with basil leaves – and passable European fare. This place is also renowned locally for its frozen yoghurt and does great fruit smoothies. *Nang Vilai Phone*, across from the market, turns out tangy bowls of *fŏe*, while a few metres west towards the post office, a friendly no-name restaurant prepares good Lao meat and vegetable dishes.

Louang Namtha

Straddling Route 3, four hours' drive northwest of Oudomxai, **LOUANG NAMTHA** was heavily contested during Laos's civil war, which is to say that it was razed to the ground. Once the fighting stopped, the surrounding hills were stripped of their trees and the mammoth logs were trucked away to China. Slowly, the depopulated town was reborn, largely with Chinese money and assistance, but there is very little to see here. The town's only real sight is the **Louang Namtha Provincial Museum** (Mon–Fri 8am–noon & 1–4pm; 500K), housed in a greenroofed building, behind the Kaysone monument, about 200m north of the post office. There are displays of traditional hilltribe costumes and artefacts, a model depicting battle manoeuvres that took place in the area during the civil war and a rusty collection of weaponry.

Most Western travellers, on their way to or from Muang Sing, get a connection here and pass on through, although a few hang out for a day or two arranging to pirogue down the Nam Tha River to Houayxai. To this end, the town has adequate food and lodging. LNT Travel (☎086/312047), a local company that claims to be gearing up to guide treks into nearby Hmong and Leten villages, is located in a large white building across from the museum. A branch of the Lane Xang **Bank** is situated just north of the *Dalasavath Guest House* and can exchange US dollars, baht and yuan, as well as dollar travellers' cheques. Louang Namtha has **electricity** from 6pm to 9pm.

Sawngthaews **for Muang Sing** leave from Louang Namtha's bus station, next to the morning market. Travellers with a valid visa for **China** can take a Chinese-operated bus in the morning from Louang Namtha bus station to the border crossing at Boten and on to Jinghong in China. Sawngthaews only go as far as the border.

Travellers heading for **Houayxai** can go by road or by boat (one and a half days, with a night spent in Na Lae), depending on the time of year. The Nam Tha is only navigable from about July until January. Unless you have unlimited time to wait around, it's most convenient to hire a **boat** outright ($100 for a boat that holds five people). Boatmen will only go as far as **Paktha**, where the Nam Tha meets the Mekong. You'll need to get a speedboat for the 36km stretch along the Mekong from Paktha to Houayxai (1hr; B130 per person). There have been reports of some boatmen demanding more money en route, threatening to maroon passengers in Na Lae if they don't pay up. The way to avoid this situation is to write down the fare on a piece of paper, show it to the boatman during initial negotiations, and keep it handy on the trip. The trip by truck to Houayxai is one of those wild Lao journeys that are fast disappearing with the ongoing road-paving programme. This particular road has been under construction since the mid-Nineties and old Soviet cargo trucks continue to ply the route, taking approximately twelve hours ($7). The beds of the trucks are open to the sky, affording unobstructed views of the thick forest, though during the monsoon season passengers get wet and the mire is sometimes impassable. The trucks are often loaded with Chinese cigarettes and cookies and passengers are left to jostle for any remaining space. If the ride gets too much, there is a basic guesthouse in the village of Phou Kha, at about the halfway point. Once the upgrading of the road has been completed the journey should take under six hours.

Accommodation and eating

Food and **lodging** are much more limited here than in Oudomxai just four hours away, so it's worth opting for the latter if you can. On the main road, across from the dry goods market, friendly *Many Chan* (①) has clean doubles and triples with shared facilities plus a popular restaurant. Also on this road are *Dalasavath* (①), with en-suite rattan bungalows set around a small pond and an atmospheric restaurant, serving the best **food** in town; and *Singsavanh* (①), a pleasant, friendly wooden house with basic two-bed rooms and shared bath. Food in town is expensive by Lao standards, almost double what you pay in Muang Sing, for example. About the only restaurants in town not attached to a guesthouse are located a short walk apart. The *Phonexai*, opposite the post office, stays open fairly late; the menu includes stir-fry Chinese dishes and noodles and they can even rustle up a pancake for breakfast. Nearby, the *Saikhonglongsak*, across from the telephone exchange, also serves stir-fry Chinese, as well as Lao food and has the better coffee of the two. If you're in the mood for a **drink**, try *Phané Jhon Pub*, opposite the Kaysone monument, about 50m west of the main road. It's a cosy little place with good music and reasonable prices.

Muang Sing and around

In a short space of time, **MUANG SING**, located some 60km northwest of Louang Namtha, has progressed from a quaint, middle-of-nowhere Tai Leu village to a talked-about-on-three-continents backpacker haven, and the explanation is simple: **opium**. Just five years ago, barely a trickle of travellers made it to Muang Sing, but since then its residents have opened guesthouses and restaurants to cater to the opiate-seeking visitors. Opium addicts hover around the restaurants at a discreet distance, stoically waiting to be noticed by their potential customers. Travellers tend to ignore their desperate stares until well into the evening, when, alone or in groups, the curious leave the restaurants to follow one of the addicts to an impromptu "den" in the dark.

In the first half of the twentieth century Muang Sing was a weigh station and market for the French government's opium monopoly, Opium Régie, which suppressed **cultivation of the poppy** among local Hmong and Mien tribals in order to tax and control the supply of opium to the licensed dens of Indochina. By the beginning of World War II, taxes on the sale of opium throughout French Indochina made up fifteen percent of the colonial government's revenues. When global war disrupted the traditional maritime route of opium into Indochina, Opium Régie started to encourage local Hmong farmers, resulting in an 800 percent increase in Hmong opium production within four years. Two decades later, America's CIA operatives trained the Hmong guerrillas that had previously sided with the French, using their cash crop to fund their operations. A Byzantine alliance between the Royal Lao Government, opium warlords and the CIA was formed. The CIA co-ordinated the collection of opium, which was transported to refineries in the **Golden Triangle**, the resulting heroin eventually finding its way to markets all over the globe. By the war's end, the production of opium in the Golden Triangle, which overlaps into Burma and Thailand (see p.897), had reached epic proportions. While eradication programmes in Thailand have had limited success in curtailing cultivation of the opium poppy there, Burma and Laos continue to produce significant amounts of the crop. Cultivating, trafficking and using opium is **illegal** in Laos, but the authorities have so far chosen to ignore the present state of affairs. If you have come to indulge, you should be aware that this situation can change at any time. It's also important to realize that by partaking you are also encouraging a vice that creates poverty and shortens lives.

Although Muang Sing has recently started attracting increasing numbers of tourists, it is still an agreeable and friendly little town where great, sway-backed sows drag their teats down the main road and young novice monks play *kataw* and ride bicycles around the monastery grounds. The ancient-looking **Wat Sing Jai**, hidden behind the *Muangsing Guest House*, has a wonderfully rustic *sim* (temple housing the main Buddha image) that has recently been painted in festive Caribbean hues. The Deutsche Gesellschaft für Technische Zusammenarbeit or **GTZ**, a German non-govermental organization which runs an opium detoxification programme for local addicts, has its headquarters on the western edge of town. A small, but informative, free exhibition there (Mon–Fri 9am–4pm) documents their efforts. Muang Sing's **morning market** is well known for its colourfully dressed vendors and shoppers, yet nowadays the camera-toting tourists almost outnumber the locals. If you want to take a photo of a vendor, it's only polite to buy something first and try to have a little conversation. The market convenes very early, just before sunrise, and winds down by seven, though a few stragglers hang around until mid-morning.

Practicalities

Pick-ups to Xiangkok (2hr) and **Louang Namtha** (2hr) wait in the station in front of the market and leave when full. Most vehicles depart in the morning but it's still possible to find one leaving at around 2pm.

You can exchange cash and travellers' cheques at a hole-in-the-wall branch of the Lane Xang **Bank** (Mon–Sat 8.30am–4pm) in the concrete building next to the market. The **post office** is west of the main road, on the street running parallel to the stream. Traditional Lao **massage** (10,000K per hour) and **herbal sauna** (5000K) can be found on the main road, about 100m south of the market. A colourful **map** of the hilltribe villages in the area is available from the little **bookstore** situated on the main road, a few metres north of the stream.

ACCOMMODATION AND EATING

All the accommodation places are friendly and offer pretty much the same basic amenities: bed with mosquito net and shared bath for $2 or less. Electricity is only available from 6pm to 10pm. Tasty, inexpensive bowls of *fŏe* can be found at the little shop-house next to *Singthong* guesthouse. If you get tired of the **food** at *Viengxay* and *Vieng Phone,* try *Anousone,* just south of the stream, which serves the best omelettes in town and has Chinese beer.

Bouachan, behind the market, near the bank. Two- and three-bed rooms with shared bath in a quiet two-storey building.

Muangsing, on the main road, near Wat Sing Jai. Very friendly place and the sitting area on the roof is good for sunsets. One- and two-bed rooms with shared bath.

Sengkhatiyavong, main road, near the market. The lofty three-bed room on the roof of this friendly, clean guesthouse is possibly the best in town. Noodles are served in the restaurant.

Singthong, main road, just south of the stream. Chinese-style concrete building with clean shared facilities and a balcony good for people-watching.

Singxai, behind the market. Probably the quietest lodging in town, the *Singxai* has three-bed rooms with attached bath and a few comfortable bungalows.

Vieng Phone, main road, near Wat Sing Jai. The *Vieng Phone* has basic three- and four-bed rooms and a popular restaurant downstairs, with an extensive menu and good Lao coffee.

Viengxay, main road. Almost indistinguishable from the *Vieng Phone,* this guesthouse offers basic two- and three-bed rooms and good stir-fry dishes in the restaurant downstairs.

Villages and treks around Muang Sing

Approximately 8km northeast of town, on the road to the Chinese border, lie two easily reached **hilltribe villages**: one Akha and one Mien. Both villages are quite used to receiving foreign visitors and are well acquainted with the outsiders' passion for the pipe. The Akha village, by far the poorer of the two, has a fairly high rate of addiction as a result of the demand created by travellers. The Mien village is a good place to visit if you are interested in acquiring a pair of fantastically embroidered traditional pantaloons.

Other hilltribe villages in the vicinity of Muang Sing, including Hmong and Tai Dam settlements, are best reached with the assistance of a local guide. As of yet, **treks** are very informal and there is nothing like the organized trekking that exists in Thailand. Enquire at one of the guesthouses and, if a willing guide is found, you'll have to plan a route and negotiate a price. In a group of four or more, $4–5 per person should be a reasonable rate. Take lunch, as villagers can't be expected to provide food for everyone who passes through.

If you decide to do a trek independently, always trek **in groups**, as there have been assaults on Western tourists in rural areas. If you are approached by armed men and robbery is clearly their intent, do NOT resist. Most hilltribe peoples are animists. **Offerings** to the spirits, often bits of food, left in what may seem like an odd place, should never be touched or tampered with. The Akha are known for the elaborate **gates** which they construct at the entrances to their villages. These gates have special meaning to the Akha and should also be left alone. Many hill folk are willing to be **photographed**, but old women, particularly of the Hmong and Mien tribes, are not always keen, so ask first. Passing out sweets to village kids is a sure way to generate mobs of young beggars. Likewise, the indiscriminate handing out of **medicine**, particularly antibiotics, does more harm than good. Unless you are a trained doctor, you should never attempt to administer medical care.

Xiangkok and Muangmom

The road from Muang Sing to Xiangkok passes through one of Laos's more remote and, at times, lawless corners. While the peaceful scenery of forest-covered hills belies it, the history of this region is tied to the production of illicit drugs: opium, heroin and, more recently, amphetamines. Travellers are unlikely to see any indication of this activity from the road though. While the Lao government has mundanely designated this 75-kilometre stretch of road **Route 322**, a more apt designation might be the Akha Road, given the high density of **Akha villages** through which it passes. This is one of the few areas in Laos where you will see Akha men still wearing their traditional headgear: disk-shaped red turbans or tall hats festooned with seed-beads and even the colourful wrappers from cakes of Thai soap – so rare in these parts that they are used for ornamentation.

A glorified village on the banks of the Mekong, **XIANGKOK** has become something of a curse-word among travellers. Most arrive in the village with precious little time left on their visas and have given themselves a day to get a speedboat down to **Houayxai** and exit into **Thailand**, a fact not lost on the boatmen. What should be a ride costing roughly $20 can cost $30 or more and no amount of haggling, pleading or tears will bring the price down. Time, it seems, is on the boatman's side. In consolation, the Upper Mekong scenery fully lives up to its name, studded with islets of craggy stone. Nearest the boat landing is the worn but accommodating *Singsavanubkeo Guest House* (①), which has two-bed **rooms** with shared bath and an eatery downstairs. The newer *Siathong Guest House* (①), on the village's eastern outskirts, has a similar set-up. There is no **electricity** in Xiangkok.

Mynanmar (Burma), across the river, announces its presence with a thicket of Buddhist pagodas marching up a hillside opposite the Lao village of **MUANGMOM**, a sight best viewed in the early morning when the first rays of the sun illuminate the stupa's mirrored mosaic surfaces. If you happen to find yourself stuck here, the village has a newish no-name guesthouse with two-bed rooms and shared bath ($4.20 per room or $1.40 per bed) and there is one hut down the road from which a Chinese resident offers *khào soi*, a spicy Shan–Yunnanese noodle concoction. Be sure to bring some Thai baht with you, as locals seem reluctant to accept any other currency. The boat also blows past Sop Ruak, Thailand's Golden Triangle tourist-trap (see p.897) before reaching Houayxai.

Houayxai: the Thai border and boats to Louang Phabang

The settlement of **HOUAYXAI**, sandwiched between the Mekong and a range of hills, is a popular **border crossing with Thailand**. Non-extendable thirty-day Thai visas are available on arrival in Chiang Khong (see p.899) on the Thai side. Once you're across the Mekong and past immigration (daily 8am–5.30pm), you can get one of the regular buses to Chiang Rai or Chiang Mai.

Houayxai's only real sight is hilltop **Wat Chom Khao Manilat**, boasting a tall, Shan-style building of picturesquely weathered teakwood, now used as a classroom for novice monks. The most popular of the town's **hotels** is *Manilat Hotel* (①), which is located at the top of the road leading from the ferry landing and has clean two- and three-bed rooms, with fan and attached hot-water bath. The downstairs restaurant does decent Chinese stir-fries. Twenty metres downriver, on the same side of the street, *Houei Sai Hotel* (①–②) offers similar rooms and has a balcony overlooking the Mekong. Newer, but lacking in character, is *Thaweesinh Hotel* (②–⑤), which sits on the opposite side of the street some 50m upriver, offering en-suite doubles, some with air-con. Nearby *Savanh Bokeo* (①) offers the cheapest deal in town, with its large two-, three- and four-bed rooms and shared facilities. Keep going another 500m in the same direction to find *Arimid Guest House* (①–③), a collection of sturdy huts with en-suite bathroom and hot water. The food here is quite good and many travellers reckon it's the best value in town if you plan on staying a few days. Opposite *Thaweesinh Hotel*, the no-frills *Mouang Neua* **restaurant** dishes out decent Lao and Chinese meals – the vegetable omelette is a must. The lively *Nutpop*, a few blocks north, does stir-fry dishes to order, cold beer and delicious fruit smoothies, while nearby *Ban Midtapab* offers excellent **fish** and views across the Mekong.

Down the Mekong to Louang Phabang

Slow boats take two days to complete the journey from Houayxai **to Louang Phabang**, stopping overnight at the village of **Pakbeng** (see opposite). You can also do the trip by speedboat in just over six hours, but this is less atmospheric.

Despite deafening engine noise and a general lack of comfort, most travellers agree that the two-day journey by **slow boat** (*heua sa*) to the old royal capital is one of those once-in-a-lifetime experiences. Most mornings, slow cargo boats leave from the **slow-boat pier**, 1km upriver from the ferry landing, and arrive at Pakbeng in the late afternoon. The following morning the boat continues on to Louang Phabang, arriving around dusk. Fares are payable in Thai baht, dollars or kip, but baht is preferred: B180 to Pakbeng or B360 to Louang Phabang. Passengers must bring their own food and water, as none is provided. Once the cargo has been loaded, passengers lounge on plastic mats or sacks of rice or wherever else they can find space. The **roof of the boat is off-limits** to women because the Lao believe that the guardian spirit of the boat is offended by women sitting up there and that this also renders the captain's amulets impotent – both of which could have dire consequences for captain and passengers on such an unpredictable river. A closed-in area on the stern serves as the toilet.

Speedboats (*heua wai*) also make the journey to Louang Phabang (B860), with a break in Pakbeng (B430); mandatory crash helmets are provided. As with the slow boats, baht is preferred on this route. The **speedboat landing** is located 2km downriver for boats going in that direction. Speedboats going upriver to Xiangkok leave from another landing approximately 2km north of town. It's best to arrive at the landings as early as possible to ensure a seat. If there are no other passengers going, it may be necessary to hire the boat outright. The ride isn't so bad really: while scrunched into the cramped seats your body's circulation is soon cut off and this, combined with the perpetual howl of the engine, makes everything numb. You arrive in Louang Phabang shaken, but alive, though you may find that even after a few drinks your ears won't stop ringing.

Pakbeng and beyond

Hugging a winding road carved up the side of a mountain, the teeming settlement of wood-scrap, corrugated tin and hand-painted signs that constitutes **PAKBENG** is the halfway point between Houayxai and Louang Phabang. As slow boats are unable to navigate the Mekong after dark, a night spent here is unavoidable if you're travelling this way – a taste of back-country Laos complete with hilltribes and rustic accommodation. Follow Pakbeng's only road up to one of the town's few concrete structures, the revamped, package tour-oriented *Sarika* (①). The rooms are pricey by Pakbeng standards, but they do come with fan and attached bath. All the other **guesthouses** in the town have very basic rooms with shared facilities and cost less than $1.50. Continuing up the hill, you'll find *Monsavan*, offering singles and doubles in a quaint wooden house and *Dock Khoune Fang Kong*, with cramped doubles and a small restaurant. A little further along, *Phanthavong* has decent doubles, dorm beds (5000K) and a balcony overlooking the street. Cheap bowls of *fõe* can be found at stalls in and around the market. Otherwise there are two decent **restaurants**, *Bounmy* and *Kham Niaw*, at the bottom of the hill. **Electricity** in Pakbeng is from 6pm until 9pm.

If you have booked a passage clear **through to Louang Phabang**, you should be down at the boat landing before 9am to avoid being left behind. Some captains offer to stop briefly near Louang Phabang at the **caves at Pak Ou** (see p.497), charging each passenger who takes him up a couple of thousand kip extra. This works out cheaper than chartering a boat from Louang Phabang, but leaves little time to explore.

Trucks from Pakbeng to Oudomxai park at the foot of the hill and usually leave between 8am and 9am. The wreck of a road passes through Hmong and Tai Leu villages, and it's possible to break the eight-hour journey with a night at the very basic guesthouse in **MUANG HOUN**, a small town about two hours from Pakbeng.

SOUTH CENTRAL LAOS

Many travellers see very little of **south central Laos**, spending just a night or two in the town of Savannakhet before pressing on to the far south or crossing the border into Vietnam. The two principal settlements of south central Laos – Thakhek and Savannakhet – both lie on the Mekong River, and both offer straightforward **border crossings into**

Thailand. Not all that interesting in itself, **Thakhek** is within day-tripping distance of some awesome limestone tunnels and caverns. **Savannakhet** has been described as southern Laos's equivalent of Louang Phabang, its inhabitants living comfortably among the architectural heirlooms handed down by the French, and is certainly a pleasant enough place. East from Savannakhet, Route 9 climbs steadily and eventually bisects another route of more recent vintage: the **Ho Chi Minh Trail**. Actually a series of parallel roads and paths, the trail was used by the North Vietnamese Army to infiltrate and finally subdue its southern neighbour. The area is still littered with lots of war junk, some of it highly dangerous. The safest way to view these rusting relics is to use the town of **Xepon** as a base. Journeying further east leads to the **Vietnam border crossing** at Daen Sawan, popularly known as "Lao Bao". There's a less frequently used crossing into Vietnam on Route 8, at Cau Treo.

Route 8: east to Lak Xao and the Vietnam border

Tourists journeying through central Laos to the south usually keep to Route 13, which hugs the river, skipping Pakxan and stopping only for a night in Thakhek. However, the area to the east of Route 13 gives you access to one of two border crossings into Vietnam. The road splits at **BAN VIANG KHAM**, 88km south of Pakxan: Route 13 carries on south (see opposite), but **Route 8** strikes eastwards towards the **Lak Xao–Vinh border crossing**, tracing a centuries' old trading route to Vietnam and zigzagging through ruggedly beautiful, hilly countryside, punctuated by black-topped limestone pillars.

Lak Xao

One hundred kilometres east of Ban Viang Kham, Route 8 passes through the sprawling boom town of **LAK XAO**, which was carved out of the hills by the logging company, Phudoi, in the 1980s, to facilitate border trade with Vietnam. For the few travellers who pass through Lak Xao, it's little more than a launching pad for trips into Vietnam, 35km to the east, though its market does have some interesting gold and silver stalls, selling jewellery from minority tribes and old silver bars etched with Chinese characters. You might also see villagers from remote hilltribes, dressed in their finest traditional clothes.

The rag-tag **buses** that make the trip to Lak Xao from Thakhek and Vientiane grind to a dusty halt in the dirt lot outside the market, 3km from the town's only **hotel**, the *Phudoi* (①). Tuk-tuks (1500K) are on hand to ferry you down the main road, Route 8B, to the hotel complex, whose most easily identifiable building is an odd bluish A-frame. For food, go to the *Thiphavongsay* **restaurant**, near the market, which has a range of traditional Lao dishes. Next door, a newly constructed bank **exchanges** American dollars and Vietnamese dong.

The Lak Xao–Vinh border crossing

The Vietnamese **border**, known as **Kaew Nua Pass** (or **Nam Phao** in Lao), is 35km from Lak Xao and best reached by hiring a tuk-tuk (20,000K) from outside the market. Shared tuk-tuks (3000K) can be had, but are often overcrowded and leave infrequently – except when the border market's open (from the 15th to the 20th of each month). For those crossing into Laos from Vietnam, there's usually a tuk-tuk on hand for hire into Lak Xao.

Crossing the border is generally hassle-free, but the crossing (daily 7.30am–5pm) is one of the least-used border points in Laos and has even fewer amenities than the more southerly Lao Bao crossing. Start your journey early to ensure you don't end up stuck at the border: transport on both sides is sparse and neither is near a town of any size. A small **exchange** kiosk sits in the Lao terminal, but don't expect to change large amounts or get a decent rate. The settlement on the Vietnamese side of the border is **Cau Treo**, 105km west of **Vinh** on Highway 8; see p.1037 for details.

Route 13: Thakhek and the Thai border

Route 13 continues south from the Ban Viang Kham junction, passing through **NAM THONE**, 4km further on, which is set amid rice fields and blue mountains and has the only **guesthouse** before Thakhek, 98km to the south – the basic *Phimachak* (①), in the town centre.

The least visited of the Mekong towns, **THAKHEK**, 360km south of Vientiane, still lies in the shadow of Savannakhet and has yet to develop much of a tourist infrastructure. For many visitors it is simply an entry point into Laos from Nakhon Phanom in Thailand, but it does make a good base from which to explore the **Mahaxai caves** in the nearby karst formations. A wander round the streets leading out from the tiny **town square** reveals French villas and shop-houses, crumbling into overgrown gardens, and too-wide streets. This tranquil air of neglect is shattered nightly by club-hopping teenagers who buzz about town on brand-new motorcycles, the inheritors of a tradition only half buried by the revolution in 1975. During the Second Indochina War, Thakhek was a sort of Havana on the Mekong, with visiting Thais flocking to its riverbank casino. These days, budding punters have to content themselves with homemade dart boards and crude pinball games set up along the riverbank.

The **ferry to Nakhon Phanom** (see p.921), across the Mekong from Thakhek in Thailand, runs daily during daylight hours (B50), making crossings every half hour or so, and leaves from the Immigration Office at the north end of Thakhek. Near the ferry landing, an **exchange** kiosk changes cash only. From Nakhon Phanom bus terminal, about half a kilometre west of the centre, buses leave for Ubon Ratchathani, Mukdahan, Khon Kaen and Nong Khai.

Practicalities

Passengers disembark from southbound **buses** at a market, known as Kilometre 2 Market, because it's 2km from the riverbank. Other buses arrive just up the road at the main bus station, located near the larger Souksomboun Market. **Tuk-tuks** serve both markets. For Visa **cash** advances and exchange of travellers' cheques, head for BCEL on Kouvolavong Road, just east of Nong Bua Kham Road. The town **tourist office** (Mon–Fri 8–11am & 2–4pm) is in the *Phudoi Hotel*.

Known locally as the *See Sahn* on account of its four storeys, *Khammuan*, Setthathilat Road (☎051/212216; ③–④), is Thakhek's most popular **hotel**, offering great sunset views from the balcony. Two blocks inland from the Immigration Office, *Tha Khaek May*, Vientiane Road (☎051/212043; ①–②), is the only budget option in town, with drab air-con and fan rooms, some en suite. *Souksomboun*, formerly the *Sikhot*, Setthathilat Road (☎051/212225; ③–④), is housed in an old French police station and boasts air-con rooms with a Seventies interior and cheaper fan rooms; staff are friendly, but do a sideline in arranging liaisons with local women for guests.

Food options are limited to a few noodle shops and one indoor restaurant, the *Kulap Daeng*, behind the *Khammuan* on Chao Anou Road, open daily 8am–10pm, and serving an array of Thai, Chinese and Lao dishes. At the southwest corner of the town square, a noodle shop, *Phawilai*, serves up noodles with grilled chicken, and *mu yáw*, a local sausage, all washed down with cold beer, while east of the square on the left, you'll find a stall selling *mi* (yellow noodles) and superb sapodilla shakes.

Around Thakhek

East of Thakhek, potholed Route 12 is swallowed up by a surreal landscape of karst formations. Hidden among the sea of jagged limestone hills are scores of caves, known as the **Mahaxai caves**, a handful of which are popular tourist spots. The easiest way to get to them is by hiring a tuk-tuk ($16 per day), but more than a few visitors prefer to take in the area as a longish walk, catching one of the Mahaxai-bound buses to the caves and then exploring on foot. Public transport can be tricky, however: though pick-ups and buses travel the road frequently enough in the morning, you can't count on catching one back late in the afternoon. A good point to start a **walking tour of the caves** is Tham Ban Tham, 7km from Thakhek, on the road to Mahaxai. From here you can walk to Tham En, taking in other caves en route, a twelve-kilometre walk in all. Even if you don't bother with the caves, the scenery provides a stunning backdrop for a walk.

To find the first cave, after getting off the bus, turn right down the dirt road that peels off Route 12 towards **BAN THAM**, a small village at the base of the first limestone escarpment. Cut through the village to find the concrete stairs leading up to **Tham Ban Tham**, which contains a shrine, centred around a sizeable Buddha image. From Ban Tham, follow the road cutting north to get back on the main road. A few hundred metres after the second wooden bridge along this road, roughly 17km from Thakhek, drink vendors set up shop in the recesses of two cliffs, signposting the path leading to **Tham Sa Pha In**, which is the best of the caves and only a short walk from the main road. Look for the bamboo gate to find the cave entrance. The cave was renamed for the Hindu god Indra after the Second Indochina War, when villagers claimed to see the Hindu deity's image reflected in the pool. Illuminated by an inaccessible opening in the ceiling of the cave, the sacred pool glows emerald green, the colour of Indra's skin.

The most visited of Mahaxai's caves, **Tham En** (entry 500K) is named for the large number of sparrows that are said to inhabit it and lies another 1.5km up the road. It gets packed at weekends. A concrete stairway takes you deep into the tunnel mouth, but there is still plenty of room to clamber on the rocks and climb up to one of the several cave mouths that offer commanding views of the forest outside.

Savannakhet and the Thai border

The town of **SAVANNAKHET**, known locally as "Sawan", is southern Laos's most visited provincial capital. Its popularity is due in part to its location on the overland route between Thailand and Vietnam and the presence of both a **Thai and a Vietnamese consulate**. Laos's two neighbours are linked to each other, via Sawan, by the 240-kilometre-long Route 9, a popular overland route for travellers doing the "Indochina loop" – through Cambodia, Vietnam, across Laos and into Thailand. But Sawan also has its own appeal, with impressive architecture inherited from the French colonial period and narrow streets and shop-houses of ochre-coloured stucco that are reminiscent of parts of Hanoi. A large percentage of the town's population is ethnic Vietnamese, though most have been living here for generations and consider themselves to be Lao in habits and temperament.

Arrival and information

Most **buses** offload at the station on the north side of Sawan. Air-con buses from Vientiane disgorge passengers at a separate stand nearby, known locally as *khiw Sensabai*. **Tuk-tuks** make the two-kilometre run from the bus stations into the city centre. If you've arrived on one of Lao Aviation's rare flights to Savannakhet, the **airport** is on the southeastern side of the town, a few blocks from the centre, off Makaweha Road. Flights are listed as daily, but are usually cancelled. The **slow-boat service** to Vientiane has been indefinitely cancelled, now that Route 13 has been upgraded.

As Savannakhet is more sprawling than most Lao towns, you may find that tuk-tuks offer a decent alternative to walking the long blocks outside the old quarter. **Bicycles** ($1 per day) can be rented at *Sensabay* restaurant and at a no-name restaurant opposite the *Savanhthy Food Garden*. The *Nanhai Hotel* has a **van** (price dependent on destination and mileage) for hire. You can also hire a car plus driver at Savanbanhao Tourism (☎041/212202), on Senna Road, three blocks north of the church. Self-drive at either place is not an option. The **Tourism Authority** is at the corner of Latsaphanit and Chaleumit roads (☎041/212755).

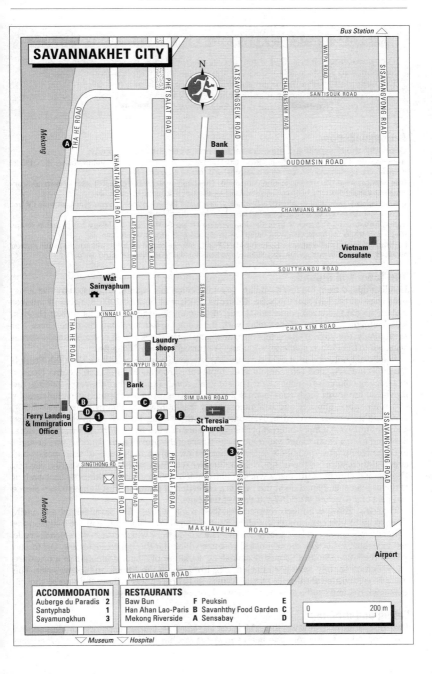

SAVANNAKHET CITY

Bus Station △

N

Mekong

THA HE ROAD

PHETSALAT ROAD

LATSAVONGSEUK ROAD

WATPA ROAD

CHALEUNSINH ROAD

SISAVANGVONG ROAD

SANTISOUK ROAD

Bank

OUDOMSIN ROAD

KHANTHABOULI ROAD

LATSAPHANIT ROAD

KOUVOLAVONG ROAD

CHAIMUANG ROAD

**Vietnam
Consulate**

SOUTTHANOU ROAD

**Wat
Sainyaphum**

SENNA ROAD

KINNALI ROAD

CHAO KIM ROAD

THA HE ROAD

**Laundry
shops**

PHANYPUI ROAD

Bank

SIM UANG ROAD

**Ferry Landing
& Immigration
Office**

B
D
F

C

1

2 E

3

**St Teresia
Church**

SAYAMUNGKHUN ROAD

LATSAVONGSEUK ROAD

SISAVANGVONG ROAD

SINGTHONG RD

KHANTHABOULI ROAD

LATSAPHANIT ROAD

KOUVOLAVONG ROAD

PHETSALAT ROAD

MAKHAVEHA ROAD

Mekong

Airport

KHALOUANG ROAD

ACCOMMODATION
Auberge du Paradis 2
Santyphab   1
Sayamungkhun   3

RESTAURANTS
Baw Bun   **F** Peuksin   **E**
Han Ahan Lao-Paris **B** Savanhthy Food Garden **C**
Mekong Riverside   **A** Sensabay   **D**

0   200 m

▽ Museum ▽ Hospital

CROSSING INTO THAILAND: SAVANNAKHET–MUKDAHAN

The **passenger ferry** that runs across the Mekong between Savannakhet and Mukdahan in Thailand (B40) docks at the Immigration Office in Sawan's town centre. The ferry departs roughly every thirty minutes on weekdays, less frequently at weekends. Near the ferry landing, an **exchange** kiosk changes cash only. Frequent buses leave here for That Phanom and Ubon Ratchathani.

Accommodation

Generally, the cheapest and most convenient area to stay is in the old city.

Auberge du Paradis, Kouvolavong Road (☎041/212445). A handful of welcoming rooms in a 1920s' French villa. Upstairs rooms lead onto a balcony, and there's a garden. ④.

Bus Station Motel, in the bus station compound. This dingy motel is the cheapest joint in town and convenient for early morning buses. Air-con and fan rooms available, none en suite. ①.

Phonepaseud, Santisouk Road (☎041/212158). Quiet, motel-like rooms set in a courtyard, all with TV, hot shower and IDD. There's a large pool, but it's a hike from the old quarter. ⑤.

Santyphab, around the corner from the Immigration Office (☎041/212277). Dingy but passable rooms which are strictly for those on a tight budget, with especially cheap air-con rooms. ③.

Sayamungkhun, Latsavongseuk Road (☎041/212426). A large house near the old quarter, with sixteen spacious, en-suite, air-con rooms. Excellent value. Look for the "guest house" sign. ①–②.

The Town and around

Heading inland from the ferry landing, you soon come to a square, dominated by the octagonal spire of **St Teresia Catholic Church**, which was built in 1930. Objects of interest include an old teakwood confessional and, high up on the walls, a set of hardwood plaques, with Vietnamese mother-of-pearl inlay work, depicting the fourteen Stations of the Cross. Not surprisingly, the biblical characters have distinctly Asian faces: Christ resembles a Confucian sage, while the Roman soldiers look more like turban-wearing Mongols.

Roads laid out on a neat grid surrounding the town square constitute the **Old French Quarter**, and are lined with some fine examples of European-inspired architecture. Housed in a peeling colonial-era mansion on Tha He Road, about 1km south of the ferry landing, the provincial **museum** (daily 8am–noon & 2–4pm; 500K) is given over primarily to photographs of former prime minister and communist party leader Kaysone Phomvihane (1920–1992), Savannakhet's most revered native son, and to the events leading up to the communist takeover in 1975. Of more interest perhaps is a venerable bronze Buddha on display upstairs. Salvaged from a bombed-out wat in the eastern part of the province, the Buddha was brought to the museum after the abbots of local monasteries, fearing the ghosts of slain monks had attached themselves to the image, declined to give it a place on their altars. Nearby, you can view an assortment of the many types of unexploded ordnance which litter the eastern half of the province, and lined up in the yard is a collection of captured RLA light artillery pieces and part of a wrecked World War II-era fighter plane.

That Ing Hang is a much revered Buddhist stupa, just outside Savannakhet and easily reached by bicycle or motorcycle. Follow Route 13 north for 13km until you see a sign on the right and follow this road for a further 3km. The stucco work which covers the stupa is crude yet appealing, especially the whimsical rosettes which dot the uppermost spire. Off to one side of the stupa stands an amusing sandstone sculpture of a lion, grinning like a Cheshire cat, which could only have been hauled here from one of the Khmer ruins downriver. The stupa is best visited during its annual festival in February when thousands make the pilgrimage here, and can be a bit of a let-down during the rest of the year.

Eating and drinking

Two local **noodle** dishes worth seeking out are *baw bun* (Vietnamese rice noodles served with chopped-up spring rolls and beef) and *ap-jao* (a Chinese dish loaded with stir-fried veggies and slices of beef, served in a tangy sauce). Savannakhet's **fruit shakes** are in a class of their own, and can be found throughout the city – look for the blenders. In the evening, shops selling soft drinks and a few *tam màk hung* vendors crop up on the riverbank in front of Wat Sainyaphum, a pleasant spot to catch the sunset over Thailand and mingle with the locals.

Baw Bun, fourth shop-house from the river, behind *Santyphab Hotel*. If it's *baw bun* you're after, this is the place. It's open daily 11.30am–2pm, but often sells out sooner.

Han Ahan Lao-Paris, Tha He Road, near the Immigration Office. Travellers flock to this riverfront shop-house, whose Vietnamese owners serve "Lao–French Food", ranging from spaghetti and steak to Korean BBQ and sukiyaki, as well as a superb Lao beef salad.

Mekong Riverside, north of Immigration Office on Tha He Road. Tables on a wooden terrace supply an excellent sunset view to season mediocre Thai–Lao dishes.

Peuksin, south of the church on Phetsalat Road. The superior ice coffees and a basic breakfast are a treat in this shop-house, frequented by Vietnamese men, who gather to enjoy *boules* and the Vietnamese board game *co thoung. Mi kati,* noodles in coconut milk, is served 11am–4pm.

Savanhthy Food Garden, in the town square. Collection of stalls hawking tasty Chinese and Lao noodle dishes and a few average rice dishes. The house speciality is *ap-jao,* and the tasty *mi haeng* – yellow noodles – comes fried with red pork, green onions and peanuts.

Sensabay, next to *Santyphab* guesthouse. Popular backpacker joint sporting menus in both English and Japanese. Cheap fried noodle and rice dishes, spring rolls and ice cream.

Listings

Airlines Lao Aviation (☎041/212140), at the airport, southeast of the city centre.

Banks and exchange Lao May Bank, near the town square on Khanthabouli Road, can change travellers' cheques; for cash advances on Visa and Mastercard go to BCEL on Oudomsin Road.

Consulates Thailand: at the *Nanhai Hotel* on Santisouk Road (Mon–Fri 8.30am–noon & 2–3.30pm; ☎041/212373); the visa costs B300, requires two photos and takes three working days. Vietnam: on Sisavang Vong Road (Mon–Fri 7.30–11am & 1.30–4.30pm; ☎041/212418); visas cost $50, require two photos and take five working days.

Hospitals and clinics A newly built hospital is located on Khanthabouli Road, near the museum; a 24-hour clinic operates on Phetsalat Road, a block south of the *Hoongthip Hotel*. The biggest pharmacy is on the corner of Oudomsin and Senna roads.

Laundry Fast and cheaply at the shops on Kouvolavong Road, north of the town square.

Post and telephone The GPO is on Khanthabouli Road, a few blocks south of the town square (Mon–Fri 8am–noon & 1–5pm, Sat & Sun 8–11am). The overseas phone and fax service building (daily 8am–10pm) is just behind it.

Route 9: the Ho Chi Minh trail and into Vietnam

Route 9 cuts east from Savannakhet through a series of drab towns, ultimately forming the link between Thailand and Vietnam.The road ends its Lao journey at the Lao Bao pass, the primary land crossing between Vietnam and Laos, before heading on to Dong Ha, where it connects with Vietnam's Highway 1. The Thais have recently shown an interest in Route 9 as a possible trade corridor across to the Vietnamese port of Da Nang, but for the moment the road is still a bumpy track, deteriorating daily under the weight of Vietnamese and Lao trucks.

Xepon

A picturesque village in the foothills of the Annamite Mountains, 40km from the Vietnamese border, **XEPON** is a pleasant rural stopover between Vietnam and Savannakhet. The old town of Xepon was obliterated during the war – along with every house in the district's two hundred villages – and was later rebuilt here 6km west of its original location, on the opposite bank of the Xe Banghiang River. The old city had been captured by communist forces in 1960 and became an important outpost on the Ho Chi Minh Trail. As such it was the target of a joint South Vietnamese and American invasion in 1971, Operation Lam Son 719 (see below), aimed at disrupting the flow of troops and supplies headed for communist forces in South Vietnam.

Buses from Daen Sawan/Lao Bao and Savannakhet drop you off in front of the market, from where it's a short walk uphill to the government **guesthouse** ($1 per bed), a long wooden structure with blue trim, which offers dormitory-style accommodation and an outdoor pump for a shower. If you don't mind a brisk 1.5km walk, the forestry department runs a somewhat nicer dorm-style guesthouse ($1 per bed) at the edge of town. There's no water, so be prepared to bathe in the nearby stream. To get here, take a left at the second road west of the market and follow the road to the foot of the hill. There's an excellent noodle shop on the western side of the market complex, which makes a hearty bowl of *főe*. A second option is the small **restaurant** across from the market (with an English sign) which offers noodles, omelettes and stir-fries. There are no official **exchange services** in Xepon, but you can try your luck at one of the town's restaurants.

East to Ban Dong and the Ho Chi Minh Trail

Heading east out of Xepon, the highway gradually climbs through the foothills of the Annamite Mountains, passing bomb craters – often obscured by brush – and unexploded ordnance, dragged to the roadside by villagers clearing their land. Women squat by the road selling bamboo shoots – a local speciality. The area's abundant bamboo crop is in fact partially a by-product of the spraying of defoliants by American forces who hoped to expose the arteries of the Ho Chi Minh Trail: hardy bamboo is quick to take root in areas of deforestation.

Rows of bamboo-and-thatch drink shops signal your arrival in **BAN DONG**, the site of one of America's most ignominious defeats during the war, and a popular stop on any tour of the Ho Chi Minh Trail. If you're travelling by public transport, the best time to visit Ban Dong is in the morning, as there are no late-afternoon **buses** plying this stretch of Route 9, and Ban Dong has no accommodation. For getting back in the afternoon, check to see if another bus

---

OPERATION LAM SON 719

In 1971, US President Nixon ordered an attack on the **Ho Chi Minh Trail** to cut off supplies to communist forces. Although US ground troops were prohibited by law from crossing the border from Vietnam into Laos and Cambodia, the US command saw this as a chance to test the strengths of Vietnamization, the policy of turning the ground war over to the South Vietnamese. For the operation, code-named **Lam Son 719**, it was decided that ARVN (Army of the Republic of Vietnam) troops were to invade Laos and block the trail with US air support. The objective was Xepon, a town straddled by the Trail, which was 30–40km wide at this point. In early February 1971, ARVN troops and tanks pushed across the border at Lao Bao and followed Route 9 into Laos. Like a caterpillar trying to ford a column of red ants, the South Vietnamese troops were soon engulfed by superior numbers of North Vietnamese (NVA) regulars. ARVN officers stopped halfway to Xepon and engaged the NVA in a **series of battles** that lasted over a month. US air support proved ineffectual, and by mid-March scenes of frightened ARVN troops retreating were being broadcast around the world. In an official Lao account of the battle, a list of "units of Saigon puppet troops wiped out on Highway 9" include four regiments of armoured cavalry destroyed between the Vietnam border and Ban Dong.

The most tangible relic of Operation Lam Son 719 are two rusting **American tanks** that sit on the outskirts of Ban Dong, on Route 9. The tank that's easiest to find lies five minutes' walk off the road that cuts south out of town towards Taoy, and which was once a crucial artery of the Ho Chi Minh Trail. Shaded by a grove of jack fruit trees, it rests atop a small hill east of the road, partially dismantled for its valuable steel. As of 1998, UXO–Lao (the Lao National Unexploded Ordnance Programme) has cleared Ban Dong of unexploded war debris, but it's still a good idea to ask a villager to show you the way, as you should always take extra care when leaving a well-worn path.

will swing through town to pick you up, otherwise you'll have to hitch a ride from a Vietnamese trucker.

Daen Sawan and the Lao Bao border crossing

The road quality takes a dive east of Ban Dong. Gaping potholes and long stretches of dirt (or mud) slow vehicles as they make the final push to the border pass at Lao Bao, cutting through ethnic minority villages and past more bomb craters obscured by thick vegetation. Route 9 ends its journey through Laos in **DAEN SAWAN**, a small village which is more tourist-friendly than most remote border towns. *Friendly* **guesthouse** (①) has utilitarian rooms with shared bathrooms and a helpful owner. Attached to the guesthouse is the popular *Loung Aloune* **restaurant**; baguettes are on offer at another shop nearby. Young Vietnamese girls wander the street offering **exchange services** in all the currencies that drive trade along Route 9, but you're better off swapping bank notes at the Lao May Bank in town or at the branch at the Lao Immigration Office: travellers entering Laos from Vietnam have complained of being shamelessly fleeced by freelance currency traders. $20 is more than enough to get you to Savannakhet.

LAO BAO BORDER CROSSING

Lao Bao border crossing, open round the clock, is the main route used by foreigners to travel overland between Vietnam and Laos. It's a scenic ride up from Xepon, but the road is rough and the crossing not always hassle-free. Vietnamese officials will send you back if your visa is not stamped for "Lao Bao". Motorcyclists have also reported problems, with officials unwilling to allow larger bikes to enter.

The only way to reach the border **from Xepon** is by catching one of the slow buses to Daen Sawan, where you can hire a **motorcycle taxi** for the final one-kilometre ride to the immigration post. On the Vietnamese side, buses leave for the nineteen-kilometre journey to **Khe Sanh** every thirty minutes, with some going straight through to **Dong Ha** on Route 1, where bus or train connections can be made to Hanoi and Hué; see p.1035 for details.

Entering Laos from Vietnam, two buses to Savannakhet leave from Daen Sawan in the morning, the second at 10am. There's also an early afternoon bus to Xepon. Accommodation is available on both sides of the pass for those who miss their bus connections or have visa problems.

THE FAR SOUTH

Bordered by Thailand, Cambodia and Vietnam, the far south conveniently divides into two regions, with **Pakxe**, the most important market town and the access point for the Chong Mek border **crossing into Thailand**, as the hub. In the west, the Mekong River corridor is scattered with dozens of ancient Khmer temples, including **Wat Phou**, the most impressive Angkorian ruin outside Cambodia, and the main tourist attraction in southern Laos. From the nearby town of **Champasak**, it makes sense to go with the flow of the river south to **Si Phan Don**, where the Mekong's 1993-kilometre-journey through Laos rushes to a thundering conclusion in a series of tiny riverine islands at the Cambodian border; the waters here are home to a dwindling number of very rare Irrawaddy **dolphins**. The border with Cambodia is currently only open to Lao and Cambodians. In the east of the region, the fertile highlands of the **Bolaven Plateau** separate the Mekong corridor from the Annamite Mountains that form Laos's border with Vietnam. Much of the area east of the Mekong lies off the beaten track and involves long and gruelling journeys on hard wooden seats along bumpy roads. One city well worth making the effort for is **Attapu**, known as the garden city for its pleasant atmosphere and undemanding pace.

Pakxe and the Thai border

Capitalizing on its location at the confluence of the Xe Don and the Mekong rivers, roughly halfway between the Thai border and the fertile Bolaven Plateau, **PAKXE** is the far south's biggest city, and its commercial and transport hub. For the traveller, however, it is little more than a dull stopover en route to Laos's southernmost tip or via the Thai–Lao border at Chong Mek, though it makes a more comfortable base than Champasak for visits to the Khmer ruins at Wat Phou.

The city's main sight is the **Champasak Provincial Museum** (Mon–Fri 8–11.30am & 2–4pm; 1000K), 1.5km east of the town centre on Route 13 and easily reached by tuk-tuk. It houses some fine examples of ornately carved pre-Angkorian sandstone lintels taken from sites around the province, now on show in the rear gallery. Upstairs, there's a selection of local tribes' costumes and jewellery. Heading back into town along Route 13, you'll pass **Champasak Palace Hotel**, a majestic eyesore resembling a giant cement wedding cake. Legend has it that the late Prince Boun Oum na Champasak, a colourful character who was the heir to the Champasak kingdom and one of the most influential southerners of the twentieth century, needed a palace this size so that he could accommodate his many concubines. The palace, left incomplete after the one-time prime minister wound up on the wrong side of history and left for France in the 1970s, has now been converted into a hotel.

Practicalities

The **airport** lies 2km northeast of the city on Route 13, and is served by tuk-tuks. The Lao Aviation office (☎031/212252) is on No. 11 Road, near BCEL bank. Pakxe has two bus stations, both of which are served by tuk-tuks to hotels (2000K). **Buses** to and from the north

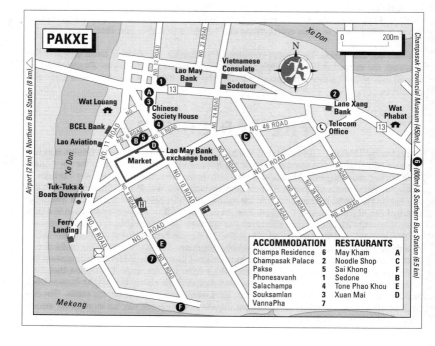

ACCOMMODATION		RESTAURANTS	
Champa Residence	6	May Kham	A
Champasak Palace	2	Noodle Shop	C
Pakse	5	Sai Khong	F
Phonesavanh	1	Sedone	B
Salachampa	4	Tone Phao Khou	
Souksamlan	3	Xuan Mai	D
VannaPha	7		

THE LAO–THAI BORDER AT CHONG MEK

To get to the **Lao–Thai border crossing at Chong Mek**, you'll first need to cross the Mekong from Pakxe to **Ban Muang Kao**. Ferries leave regularly from the ferry landing at the southwestern corner of the city centre (2000K) or you can get a motorized pirogue, which departs when full (2000K) or can be hired (20,000K for up to ten people) for the trip. This service will run its course once a **new bridge**, under construction at the time of writing, is open to traffic. Jury-rigged jalopies whip along the forty-kilometre route from Ban Muang Kao to the **border crossing** (daily 8.30am–4pm), taking around forty-five mintues. These taxis can be hired (90,000K) or shared (9000K). Sawngthaews also ply the route (1hr 15min; 3000K). Drivers will accept Thai baht or kip. The expansive market that straddles the border thrives on weekends. After tipping the immigration officers to exit Laos (it's always a weekend or lunchtime as far as they are concerned), cross into Thailand to find pick-ups to Phibun Mangsahan, where you can transfer to buses to Ubon Ratchathani, with plentiful road and rail links (see p.913). There are also two direct Chong Mek-to-Bangkok air-conditioned buses that leave from the market at 4pm and 5pm respectively.

use the **Northern Bus Station**, 7km north of the city on Route 13. Passengers arriving late from Savannakhet and Vientiane may be forced to pay a little extra to get from the deserted terminal into the town centre. The best way to get to the Northern Bus Station is to catch a pick-up from the ferry landing stand; get to the bus station early in the morning as there are a limited number of departures.

Buses to and from points south and east use the **Southern Bus Station**, 8km east of town on Route 13. Some bus drivers briefly stop short of the southern station, giving you the chance to avoid the chaotic bus station which also doubles as a market. Tuk-tuks leave regularly for the Southern Bus Station (2000K) from the stand on the Xe Don River near the ferry landing; alternatively, flag down any tuk-tuk or sawngthaew headed east. Most towns in the south are served by one or two buses a day, which tend to leave early in the morning. If you're headed to Muang Khong and other points along Route 13 South be prepared for some of the most crowded bus conditions in the country. An express van departs for Attapu from the Southern Bus Station daily in the early afternoon – arrive early as seating is limited.

Ferries to and from Ban Muang Kao, the terminus for taxis and sawngthaews from the border crossing at Chong Mek, and **passenger boats** to and from from Champasak and Si Phan Don dock at the Xe Don landing on No. 11 Road, an easy walk to most hotels. Boats to Champasak (5000K) and Muang Sen (12,000K) in Si Phan Don leave daily in the mornings; arrive early.

ACCOMMODATION AND EATING

The majority of **places to stay** are scattered around the central market, a short walk from the ferry landing. While *Pakse*, above the city's old cinema on No. 5 Road (☎031/212131; ①), undergoes a facelift, budget travellers should head for *Phonesavanh*, on the corner of Route 13 and No. 12 Road (☎031/202842; ①–②). The staff are friendly, but the showers and toilets could do with a clean. Just beyond the hospital from the market, *VannaPha*, No. 9 Road (☎031/212502; ①–②), is a quiet guesthouse set back from the road, with a few clean rooms and a café in the garden. At *Salachampa*, No. 10 Road, near the market (☎031/212273; ③), you should spurn the cheaper modern cottages and opt for one of the spacious rooms with high ceilings in the elegant restored French villa, with teak floors and breezy verandas. The top choice in Pakse, though inconveniently far out on Route 13, is the professionally run *Champa Residence* (☎031/212120; ⑤).

Pakse has the best range of **restaurants** in the south, most of which open for breakfast and operate well into the evening. Easily the best restaurant in town, *May Kham*, on the corner of Route 13 and No. 12 Road, offers an extensive array of reasonably priced Chinese dishes. The most popular with travellers is *Sedone*, close to the central market on No. 5 Road, which offers cheap Chinese, Lao and Thai dishes as well as solid breakfasts, fruit shakes and decent chips. The other travellers' magnet is the nearby *Xuan Mai*, No. 5 Road, a hit-and-miss Vietnamese eatery, run out of a dirty corner shop-house (closed Sun mornings). The *Noodle Shop*, No. 46 Road, is recommended for its big, zesty bowls of *fõe* served with beef and fresh vegetables out of a small store front, and *Tone Phao Khou*, No. 9 Road, near *VannaPha* guesthouse, is the place to go if you want to sample Mekong River fish and bottles of *lào ya*, medicinal whisky. The two **bars** in the town proper – *Sai Khong*, on No. 9 Road near the Mekong River, and *Sengtawan Cabaret*, above the ferry landing – both offer live bands and taxi dancing. A more peaceful spot for a beer is the stall under the shady trees directly above the ferry landing.

Listings

Airlines Lao Aviation's booking office (☎031/212252) is on No. 11 Road, near BCEL bank.

Banks and exchange BCEL, on No. 11 Road, and Lao May Bank, on Route 13, change travellers' cheques and advance cash on Visa and Mastercard; Lao May Bank also has an exchange kiosk (daily 8am–4pm) on No. 5 Road, opposite *Sedone* restaurant, for cash and travellers' cheques only.

Consulates Vietnam, on No. 24 Road (Mon–Fri 8–11am & 2–4.30pm; ☎031/212058); visas cost $50, require two photos and take five working days.

Internet *Pakse Internet Café*, No. 34 Road, opposite the school (☎031/213422); 2000K per minute, open daily 7am–9pm.

Post Office At the corner of No. 8 Road and No. 1 Road (daily 7.30am–9pm).

Telephone services International calls and faxes at Telecom, on the corner of No. 1 and No. 38 roads (daily 8am–9pm).

Tour agencies Sodetour, corner of Route 13 and No. 24 Road (☎031/212122), is at the cutting edge of travel in the area and has a very knowledgeable staff; Lane Xang Travel, No. 10 Road, next to the *Souksamlan Hotel* (☎031/212002); Inter-Lao Tourisme, in the lobby of the *Champasak Palace Hotel* (☎031/212778).

Champasak Town

From Pakxe, daily passenger boats ply the forty-kilometre stretch of the Mekong south, past misty green mountains and riverbanks loaded with palm trees, to the drowsy rural town of **CHAMPASAK**. Of little interest in itself, Champasak is best-known as the gateway to **Wat Phou** and the **Khmer ruins**, though some people prefer to base themselves at Pakxe, which has better facilities, and take in Wat Phou as a day-trip in a hired car. Meandering for 4km along the right bank of the Mekong, Champasak is now an unassuming town, but was once the capital of an important kingdom, whose territory stretched from the Annamite Mountains into present-day Thailand. Scrap metal taken from wartime airstrips and crafted into fences encircles the emerald gardens of the former **palace of Prince Boun Oum na Champasak**, the scion of the royal family of Champasak and a one-time prime minister. As is the case with the naga in front of Boun Oum's house, which were taken from Wat Phou, the area's most exquisite **pre-Angkorian relics** have unfortunately wound up in the late prince's private collection. There is talk, however, of incorporating the collection into a public exhibition in the near future.

Practicalities

Buses will let you off at Champasak town's roundabout, where you'll find almost everything you need, including a **post office** (open until 9pm weekdays for phone calls), and a tiny wooden **bank**, which can exchange cash and travellers' cheques. *Salawatphou* (☎031/213280; ⑥), across from the bank, offers tastefully decorated air-con and fan **rooms** and a moderately priced restaurant. Opposite the roundabout, on the riverside, *Saythong* (③) has basic rooms with shared facilities in an old wooden house, above a restaurant overlooking the Mekong. Across the street, *Kham Phouy* (①) has roomy doubles and triples and a thatched en-suite bugalow in the garden. *Dok Champa* **restaurant**, just west of the round-about, offers the best selection of Lao dishes in town and also rents **bicycles** (5000K per day).

Tuk-tuks can be hired for the eight-kilometre journey to Wat Phou. Drivers, who usually charge 30,000K to take up to four passengers, will wait for you while you visit the ruins. When it comes to moving on, three **buses** pass through Champasak each morning en route to Pakxe (1hr 30min) from Ban Dontalat and can be hailed from the town's main road. For connections to Si Phan Don you'll have to cross the river to Ban Muang and wait for a bus heading south on Route 13, or wait for the **boat** from Pakxe which calls at around 9am at the Ban Phapin ferry landing, located at the northernmost end of Champasak.

Wat Phou

Easily the most evocative Khmer ruin outside Cambodian borders, **Wat Phou** (daily 8.30am–4.30pm; 2000K), 8km southwest of Champasak, should be at the top of your southern Laos must-see list. A romantic and rambling complex of pre-Angkorian temples dating from the sixth to the twelfth centuries, Wat Phou occupies a setting of unparalleled beauty in a lush river valley dominated by an imposing mountain. Unlike ancient Khmer sites of equal size or importance found in neighbouring Thailand, Wat Phou has yet to be overenthusiastically restored, so walking among the half-buried pieces of sculpted sandstone gives an idea of what these sites once looked like. The pristine state of the environment was a major factor in UNESCO's decision to propose the area as a World Heritage site.

Wat Phou, which in Lao means "Mountain Monastery", is actually a series of ruined temples and shrines at the foot of Lingaparvata Mountain. Although the site is now associated with Theravada Buddhism, sandstone reliefs indicate that the ruins were once a **Hindu place of worship**. When viewed from the Mekong, it's clear why the site was chosen. A phallic stone outcropping is easily seen among the range's line of forested peaks: this would have made the site especially auspicious to worshipers of Shiva, a Hindu god that is often symbolized by a phallus.

Some history

Archeologists tend to disagree on who the original founders of the site were and when it was first consecrated. The oldest parts of the ruins are thought to date back to the sixth century and were most likely built by the ancient Khmer, although some experts claim to see a connection to Champa, a Hinduized kingdom once centred in what is now south-central Vietnam. Whatever the case, the site is still considered highly sacred to the ethnic Lao and is the focus of an annual festival that attracts thousands of pilgrims.

The **Khmer**, ancestors of modern-day Cambodians, were the founders of a highly sophisticated culture, whose influence stretched north to Vientiane in Laos and as far west as the present-day border of Thailand and Burma. From its capital, located at Angkor in what is now northwestern Cambodia, a long line of kings reigned with absolute authority, each striving to build a monument to his own greatness which would outdo all previous monarchs. With cultural trappings inherited from earlier Khmer kingdoms, which in turn had borrowed heavily from India, the Khmer rulers at Angkor venerated deities from the **Hindu** and **Buddhist** pantheons. Eventually, a new and uniquely Khmer cult was born, the *devaraja* or god-king, which propagated the belief that a Khmer king was actually an incarnation of a certain Hindu deity on earth.

In 1177, armies from the rival kingdom of **Champa**, taking advantage of a period of political instability, were able to sack Angkor, leaving the empire in disarray. Convinced that the old state religion had somehow failed to protect the kingdom from misfortune, the new Khmer leader Jayavarman VII embraced Mahayana Buddhism and went on to expand his empire to include much of present-day Thailand, Vietnam and Laos. But after his death the empire began to decline and by 1432 was so weak that the **Siamese** were also able to give Angkor a thorough sacking. They pillaged the great stone temples of the Angkorian god-kings and force-marched members of the royal Khmer court, including classical dancers, musicians, artisans and astrologers, back to Ayuthaya, then the capital of Siam. To this day, much of what Thais perceive as Thai culture, from the sinuous moves of classical dancers to the flowery language of the royal Thai court, was actually acquired from the Khmer. Much of the Khmer culture absorbed by the Siamese was passed on to the Lao, including the gracefully curving lines of written Lao.

Exploring the site

Approaching from the east, a **stone causeway** – once lined with low stone pillars – leads up to the first set of ruins. On either side of the causeway there would have been reservoirs which probably represented the oceans that surrounded the mythical Mount Meru, home of the gods of the Hindu pantheon. Just beyond the causeway, on either side of the path, stand two megalithic structures of sandstone and laterite, which may have served as segregated **palaces**, one for men and the other for women. The structure to the right displays a carved relief of Shiva and his consort Uma riding the sacred bull Nandi.

Continuing up the stairs, you come upon a ruined temple containing the finest examples of **decorative stone lintels** in Laos. Although much has been damaged or is missing, sketches done at the end of the nineteenth century show the temple to have changed little since then. The Khmer artisans' depictions of deities, divinities, characters and events from Hindu and Buddhist mythology are some of the most exquisite art ever created; the earliest examples date from around the twelfth century. Some of the most significant include a depiction of the god **Krishna** defeating the naga Kaliya, to the left of the main entrance; the god **Vishnu** riding the bird-man Garuda, on the right of the main entrance; two versions of the god **Indra** riding the three-headed elephant Airavata; seven different images of the temple guardian **Kala**, usually depicted with two stylized garlands spewing from the corners of his mouth, each time supporting a different deity, including Shiva and Vishnu; and a gruesome depiction of **Krishna** tearing his uncle Kamsa in half, on the west wall. On the altar, inside the sanctuary, stand four Buddha images, looking like a congress of benevolent space aliens. Originally, this altar would have supported a *Shivalinga*, or phallic stone, representing Shiva.

Just behind the temple is a relief carved into a half-buried slab of stone depicting the Hindu trinity. A multi-armed, multi-headed Shiva (standing) is flanked by Brahma (left) and Vishnu (right). Continuing up the hill behind the temple you'll come to a **shallow cave**, the floor of which is muddy from the constant drip of water that collects on its ceiling. This water is considered highly sacred, as it has trickled down from the peak of Lingaparvata. In former times, a system of stone pipes directed the run-off to the temple, where it bathed the enshrined *Shivalinga*. Even today, Lao pilgrims will dip their fingers into a cistern located in the cave and ritually anoint themselves. Foreign visitors should resist the temptation to wash with this water, which would be akin to having a clean-up in the baptismal font.

If you follow the base of the cliff in a northerly direction, a bit of sleuthing will lead you to the enigmatic **crocodile stone**, which may or may not have been used as an altar for pre-Angkor period human sacrifices. A few metres away to the north is the **elephant stone**, a huge, moss-covered boulder carved with the face of an elephant, probably dating from the nineteenth century.

Si Phan Don

In Laos's deepest south, just above the border with Cambodia, the muddy stream of the Mekong is shattered into a fourteen-kilometre-wide web of rivulets, creating a landlocked archipelago. Known as **Si Phan Don**, or Four Thousand Islands, this labyrinth of islets, rocks and sandbars has acted as a kind of bell jar, preserving traditional southern lowland Lao culture from outside influences. Island villages were largely unaffected by the French or

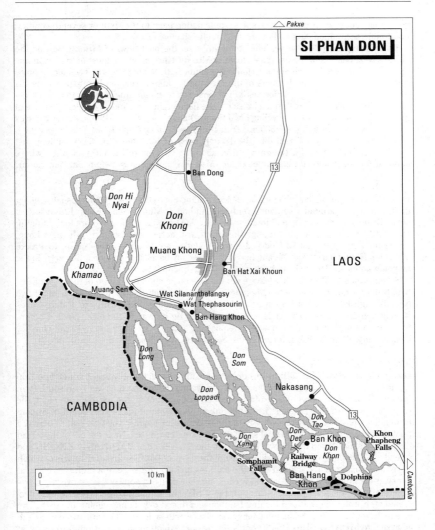

American wars and the islanders' folk ways have been passed down uninterrupted since ancient times. The archipelago is also home to rare flora and fauna, including a species of freshwater dolphin. Southeast Asia's largest, and what many consider to be most spectacular, waterfalls are also located here.

Don Khong

The largest of the Four Thousand Islands group, **Don Khong** draws a steady stream of visitors, most of whom use it as a base to explore other attractions in Si Phan Don. It boasts a venerable collection of Buddhist temples, some dating back to the sixth or seventh century, good-value accommodation and interesting fresh-fish cuisine.

Don Khong has only two settlements of any size, the port town of **Muang Sen** on the island's west coast, and the east-coast town of **Muang Khong**, where most of the accommodation and food are. Like all Si Phan Don settlements, both Muang Sen's and Muang Khong's homes and shops cling to the bank of the Mekong for kilometres, but barely penetrate the interior, which is reserved for rice fields. The best way to explore the island is to rent a **bicycle** and set off along the path that circles it – the flat terrain and almost complete absence of motor vehicles make for ideal cycling conditions. Muang Khong's guesthouses offer bicycles for rent: try *Villa Kang Khong* (5000K per day) or *Done Khong Guest House* (7000K per day).

In Muang Khong you'll find the island's only **post office**, above the ferry landing, just south of the bridge, and a **telecom** office, about 200m west of the ferry landing, where national and international calls can be made (Mon–Fri 8am–noon & 1–4pm; Sat 8am–noon).

ARRIVAL

Boats to Don Khong leave daily from Pakxe around 8am (10,000–12,000K), usually calling in at Champasak around 10am and eventually landing at Muang Sen on Don Khong's west coast. Bring your own water and food for the trip. At Don Khong most visitors hire a tuk-tuk (15,000K) or motorcycle for the eight-kilometre trip across the island to Muang Khong, where the better selection of food and accommodation are located. **Boats going to Pakxe** from Don Khong leave from Muang Sen on a semi-daily basis; get to Muang Sen early in the morning and ask. If there is no boat, get the Pakxe-bound bus.

Seven **buses to Don Khong** leave from Pakxe's bus station daily. Two of these go directly to Muang Khong, crossing the Mekong by ferry from Ban Hat Xai Khoun. The other five pass through Ban Hat Xai Khoun on their way to Nakasang. A daily **bus to Pakxe** leaves Muang Sen around 8am and calls at Muang Khong on its way to the ferry landing before heading north up Route 13. It may also be possible to get a ride to Pakxe by private boat or vehicle: enquire at *Pon's Restaurant* or the *Souksan Guest House* (see opposite).

AROUND THE ISLAND

Doing a **loop of roughly 20km** through the chain of picturesque villages which line Don Kong's south coast makes a very pleasant day's cycling. Following the river road south from Muang Khong, you soon cross a rotting wooden bridge: stick to the narrow path along the river, not the road that parallels it slightly inland. A couple of kilometres south of Muang Khong lies the village of **BAN NA**, where the real scenery begins. The trail snakes between thickets of bamboo, past traditional southern Lao wooden houses. Near the tail of the island the path forks: a veer to the left will lead you to the tiny village of **BAN HANG KHONG** and a dead end. Keeping to the right will put you at the gates of Wat Thephasourin, parts of which were constructed in 1883. From here the path soon skirts the edge of a high riverbank, at intervals opening up views of the muddy Mekong. The dense canopy of foliage overhead provides welcome shade as you pass through **BAN SIW**, with quaint gingerbread houses, decorated with wood filigree, and inviting bamboo-and-thatch drink shops lining the path. The village monastery, Wat Silananthalangsy, is also worth a look. The path widens at the approach to **MUANG SEN**, Don Khong's sleepy port, which makes a welcome stop for rest and refreshment before heading east via the unshaded eight-kilometre stretch of road that leads back to Muang Khong.

For another interesting excursion, head due west from Muang Khong, on the road that bisects the island. Just before reaching the town of **MUANG SEN** on the western side of the island, turn right at the crossroads and head north. Follow this road up and over a low grade and after about 4km you'll cross a bridge. Keep going another 1.5km and you'll notice large black boulders beginning to appear off to the left. Keeping your eyes left, you'll see a narrow trail which leads up to a ridge of the same black stone. Park your bike at the foot of the ridge, and, following the trail up another 200m to the right, you'll spot the teak buildings of **Wat**

Phou Khao Kaew, an evocative little forest monastery situated atop a stone bluff overlooking the Mekong. A fractured pre-Angkorian stone lintel sits at the base of its central stupa, which possibly dates the whole structure to the middle of the seventh century. Nearby sits a charming miniature *sim*, flanked by plumeria trees. A curious collection of carved wooden deities, which somehow found their way downriver from Burma, decorate the ledges.

ACCOMMODATION

Most of the accommodation is concentrated in **Muang Khong**, which has 24-hour electricity and provides a good launching point for excursions to Don Khon and Don Det. Highly recommended is *Villa Kang Khong* (☎031/213539; ②), 100m west of the Muang Khong ferry landing, where the helpful French-speaking owner, Mr Thongleuam, offers five-star service at bargain prices in his colonial-era teak house. The newly built *Done Khong II* (①–②), about 300m from the ferry landing on the road to Muang Sen, is a good alternative. Set in an airy teak house with verandas offering commanding views of the countryside, its accommodation ranges from dorm beds (15,000K) to comfortable en-suite doubles. The *Done Khong Guest House* (☎031/214010; ②), adjacent to the ferry landing, is a reasonable second-best, offering basic rooms with shared facilities, and a popular restaurant. For a smarter option, try *Auberge Sala Done Khong*, south of the ferry landing (☎031/212077; ⑥), whose nicely restored French-era villa has air-con and hot water, catering largely to package-tour clientele.

Choice in **Muang Sen** is currently limited to two guesthouses. *Say Khong* (②), directly above the ferry landing, has spacious fan doubles and triples and a balcony, excellent for viewing Mekong sunsets. A little further east, on the road to Muang Khong, you'll find *Muong Sene Guest House* (①), whose roomy doubles are the cheapest on the island.

EATING AND DRINKING

As you might expect, **fish** is Don Khong's staple, and the islanders have dozens of good recipes – from the traditional *làp pa* (a Lao-style salad of minced fish mixed with garlic, chillies, shallots and fish sauce) to the tropical fish steamed in coconut milk. Be sure to try the island speciality, *mók pa*, which is steamed in banana leaves, has the consistency of custard and takes an hour to prepare. For this and just about anything else, *Mr Pon's* stands out as the best **restaurant** in Muang Khong, serving tasty, plentiful dishes in a relaxed shop-house 200m north of the ferry landing. But if it's Chinese food and a perfect river view you're after, head for the *Souksan's* restaurant, which stands on stilts above the Mekong.

The people of Si Phan Don are very proud of their *lào-láo*, which has gained a reputation nationally as one of the best **rice whiskies** in Laos. For those who haven't taken a liking to Lao white lightning, Muang Khong has devised a gentler blend known as the "Lao cocktail", a mix of wild honey and *lào-láo* served over ice.

Don Khon and Don Det

Tropical islands in the classic sense, **DON KHON** and **DON DET** are fringed with swaying coconut palms and planted with jade- and emerald-coloured rice paddies. Besides being a picturesque little haven, they also offer some leisurely trekking. Linked by a bridge and traversed by a trail, Don Khon and Don Det can be easily explored on foot – there are as of yet no motor vehicles on the islands.

A delightfully sleepy place with a timeless feel about it, **BAN KHON**, located on Don Khon at the eastern end of the bridge, is the islands' largest settlement and has the most comfortable accommodation, plus a near-monopoly on eateries. A short walk south of the bridge stands the village monastery, Wat Khon Tai. Taking the southerly path behind the wat for 1.5km, you'll come to a low cliff overlooking **Somphamit Falls**, a series of high rapids that crashes through a jagged gorge.

If you're interested in exploring the remnants of Laos's **old French railroad**, retrace your steps back to the bridge. There, on the southern side of the foot of the bridge, back behind some houses, lie the rusting remains of the locomotive that once hauled French goods and passengers between piers on Don Khon and Don Det, bypassing the rapids that block this stretch of the river.

Another hike involves crossing the bridge from Don Khon to **Don Det** and following the three-kilometre elevated trail to the small village at the northern end of the island. A Stonehenge-like structure that was used for hoisting cargo from the train onto awaiting boats is all that remains of the railroad's northern terminus.

DOLPHIN-SPOTTING

From Ban Khon, follow the easterly former railroad trail adjacent to the high school through rice paddies and thick forest and eventually, after 4km, you'll reach the village of **BAN HANG KHON**, the jumping-off point for **dolphin-spotting excursions**. The April–May dry season, when the Mekong is at its lowest, is the best time of year to catch a glimpse of this highly endangered species (early mornings and late afternoons are said to be best), and boats can be hired out from the village to see them. During the rest of the year, chances of seeing the dolphins decrease, as deeper water allows them more range. Visitors should also bear in mind that there have been incidents in the recent past in which Cambodian bandits from the opposite riverbank have robbed foreign tourists at gunpoint. If boatmen refuse to shuttle you out to see the dolphins, don't insist: they will know what the current situation is. Boats cost $4 and can carry up to three passengers; you're obliged to pay for the boatman's services whether or not any dolphins are actually sighted.

The bluish–grey freshwater **Irrawaddy dolphin** (*orcaella brevirostris*) known as *pa kha* in Lao, grows to a length of 2.5m and lives in coastal waters stretching from the Bay of Bengal to the northern Australian coast, and inhabits the Irrawaddy River in Burma, the Mahakam in Kalimantan and the Ganges in India. The dolphins are rare in Lao waters, as most are unable to swim beyond the Khone Falls near the Lao–Cambodian border. Over the past century their numbers in the Mekong have dwindled dramatically, from thousands to little more than one hundred today. The present dolphin population off Ban Hang Khon is only ten, down from thirty in 1993. Gill-net fishing and, across the border, the use of poison, electricity and explosives are to blame. In the past, fishermen were reluctant to cut costly nets to free entangled dolphins, but Lao villagers are now compensated for their nets – part of an initiative begun by the Lao Community Fisheries and Dolphin Protection Project.

KHON PHAPHENG FALLS

Despite its reputation as the largest waterfall in Southeast Asia, **Khon Phapheng**, to the east of Don Khon, just off the Mekong shore, is rather disappointing. Indeed, it's best described as a low but wide rock shelf that just happens to have a huge volume of water running over it. The vertical drop is highest during the March–May dry season and becomes much less spectacular when the river level rises during the rainy season. The Niagara Falls it is not. Still, the sight and sound of all that water crashing about is quite mesmerizing and a pavilion situated just above the falls provides an ideal place to sit and enjoy the view.

PRACTICALITIES

Many people opt to do Don Khon–Don Det–Khon Phapheng as a day-trip from Don Khong, which is a shame, since ideally at least two days are needed to absorb the atmosphere on Don Khon. If time and money are not too limited, the best way to do this itinerary is by **boat** from Muang Khong; ask at guesthouses or restaurants. A boat seating ten should cost no more than $15, and you can see both waterfalls and the defunct railroad in one day. It's not possible to go directly to Khon Phapheng Falls by boat, but the boatman will take you to the mainland town of **NAKASANG**, where a tuk-tuk ($7) or motorcycle taxi ($2–3) can be hired for the thirty-kilometre round-trip to the falls. Your boatman will then take you on to Don Khon or back to Don Khong. A cheaper option is to take the **ferry** from Muang Khong across the river to Ban Hat Xai Khoun and then board the **bus** to Nakasang. From here boats to Don

Khon can also be hired. Boats from here to Don Khon and Don Det ($1–2) depart from the landing a short walk from the market.

Accommodation on both Don Khon and Don Det is easily found within walking distance of the old railway bridge. While Don Khon has more to offer than Don Det, those seeking more rustic accommodation should base themselves on the latter. Just over the bridge in **Don Khon** is *Pon's River Resort* (①), a collection of stilted bamboo huts with shared facilities and a decent restaurant. A little further along the trail on the right is the red-roofed *Somphamit* (①), owned by a former US army serviceman who speaks English and French and is full of interesting stories about his travels abroad. *Mr Bounh's* (①) offers simple bungalows with clean shared facilities in a quiet compound close to the river. Next door is the more upscale *Sala Don Khone* (③–⑤), whose over-priced rooms in the former hospital are nothing special. The beautifully built wooden bungalows in the garden, with fan and attached cold-water bath, are better value.

Mr Tho's Bungalows (①) on **Don Det**, about 2km along the trail from the bridge, has three basic bamboo-and-thatch huts and hammocks from which you can idly watch river life passing by. If they're full try *Souksan Bungalow* (①), on the northern tip of the island, where you have the choice between a straw mat in a shared hut (5000K) and your own little shack next to the river.

Good, inexpensive bowls of *fŏe* can be had at a number of stands around **Ban Khon**. It should come as no surprise that **fish** is a big part of the islanders' diet, and one noodle stand, *Lung Jun's*, can do excellent *làp pa* with a few hours' advance notice; morning omelettes and coffee are also done with some flair here. *Phonepasak*, next to the ticket booth on the bridge, offers an extensive array of Lao and Chinese dishes in a relaxed setting. A few metres past *Somphamit* guesthouse, you'll find a few wooden tables under a thatch roof and a genial old lady, whose delicious spicy chicken curry and fresh spring rolls are worth the twenty-minute wait.

Tad Lo and the Bolaven Plateau

Two hours' bus journey northeast of Pakxe and 30km short of Salavan, ten-metre-high **Tad Lo Waterfall**, on the banks of the Xe Set River, draws a steady stream of foreign visitors, providing the perfect setting for a few days' relaxation and the opportunity to ride an elephant along the breezy western flank of the fertile Bolaven Plateau. In the hot season, the pools surrounding Tad Hang, the lower falls, are a refreshing escape from the heat; be sure to clear the water before 8pm, however, when the floodgates of a dam upstream unleash a torrent of water without warning. **Elephant treks** ($4 for 2hr) through the forested hills around Tad Lo are easy to arrange through any of the guesthouses.

The turn-off for Tad Lo is 88km northeast of Pakxe, a few minutes beyond the village of Lao Ngam; **buses** will drop you at the turn-off, from where it's a 1.5-kilometre **tuk-tuk** ride (1000K per person) along a dirt road to Tad Hang. When leaving, find a driver to take you back to the highway, where you can pick up a morning bus to Salavan or Pakxe. High on a hill overlooking Tad Hang perches the *Tad Lo Resort* (☎031/212105 ext 3325; ⑤–⑥), with thirteen **rooms** in an assortment of bungalows. Across the river, *Saise* guesthouse has a handful of rooms with shared facilities in a raised house (②), plus some very pleasant en-suite ones in a "green house", a few hundred metres upstream (②). Beds fill up quickly at both establishments, so reserve ahead; the Sodetour office in Pakxe (see p.520) can do this. The *Tad Lo Resort* has a relaxed open-air **restaurant**, with commanding views and a range of moderately priced French and Lao dishes. For cheaper fare, head down the hill to the *Little Shop*.

Xekong

In 1984, a wide expanse of jungle was cleared of trees and graded flat and the town of **XEKONG** was born. Founded partly because nearby Ban Phon was deemed no longer habitable owing to unexploded ordnance (UXO), Xekong has something of a frontier feel about it, but it is the departure point for a very scenic journey downriver to Attapu. Three major branches of the Ho Chi Minh Trail snaked through the jungle surrounding Xekong, making this area one of the most heavily bombed in Laos, and an astonishing amount of **UXO** still blankets this province, so you shouldn't go off exploring here (see p.463 for more on the dangers of UXO). In addition, there is a disturbing beasty lurking in Xekong's waterways: the *pa pao* is a **blowfish** with a piranha-like appetite and, according to locals, a particular fondness for lopping off the tip of the male member.

Practicalities

Buses from Pakxe grind to a halt in a dirt lot outside the morning market, about 1km from the main market (2000K by tuk-tuk). Heading into town, you'll pass a branch of the Lao May Bank, where you can exchange cash and travellers' cheques, and the **post office** and the **telecom** building, where international calls can be made. A daily **bus** plies the route south along the Xe Kong River to Attapu; it leaves the morning market at 7am, arriving in Attapu about two hours later, and departs for the trip back to Xekong at noon. A pleasant alternative is to hire a **boat to Attapu** (see below).

Cockroaches rule the day at the *Sekong Souksamlane* (☎031/212022; ②–③), 500m downriver from the market, but as it's the one **hotel** at the end of a long highway, the decent enough rooms cost twice what they should. Cheap **restaurants** surround the hotel, but the hotel restaurant cooks rather good Thai food too.

Xe Kong River to Attapu

If you've made it as far as Xekong, the scenic **Xe Kong River**, which meanders through little-visited countryside, provides a strong incentive to hire a boat for the journey south to **Attapu**. Emerging from the mountains of Vietnam, the Xe Kong meanders south by southwest until it eventually joins the Mekong River north of Stung Treng in Cambodia. Motorized pirogues make the four-hour journey through gentle rapids and past lushly forested riverbanks. At around $40 per boat, it's expensive, but well worth the trip. Late in the dry season, the trip can take seven hours, and the shallow waters require passengers to walk some short stretches – at this time of year, captains will only take two passengers, thereby increasing the price per person. To find a captain, follow the road from the *Sekong Souksamlane* hotel south for 1km until you reach a boat landing.

A cosy settlement of almost 20,000 people, most of whom are Vietnamese, Chinese or Lao Loum, remote **ATTAPU** occupies a bend in the Xe Kong River and is one of the gems of the far south. Coconut palms and banana trees shade spacious wooden houses with generous balconies, high on stilts, and the town is known throughout southern Laos as the "garden city". Although it was near this distant outpost that the Ho Chi Minh Trail diverged, with one artery running south towards Cambodia and the other into South Vietnam, Attapu somehow eluded the grave effects of war and remains an easygoing place that's ideal for leisurely wandering. It can be difficult to reach, however, especially in the rainy season, but it's well worth the journey. It also registers the country's highest rate of malaria, so heed the advice in "Basics" p.25.

Practicalities

Arriving in Attapu by **bus**, you'll wind up in a dirt field on the southwestern outskirts of the city, 2km from the centre. If you're on the express bus from Pakxe, don't get off here, as the driver will usually drop you in front of a guesthouse. Arriving by **boat** from Xekong, walk up the ramp and follow the road into town to Attapu's only **bank**, a branch of Lao May Bank, which is a good point of orientation, but doesn't offer good rates.

Attapu has two **guesthouses**, the better of which is *Souksomphone* (①–②), which has seven clean, spacious rooms. Look for the modern building opposite the bank. Near the post office, the *Tawiwan* (①) has rooms with shared bathrooms in a cluster of two-storey houses set back from the road. At the eastern end of this compound is the town's most popular **restaurant**, where you'll find good, moderately priced noodle and rice dishes; service, however, is terribly slow. Walking two blocks towards the ferry landing from the bank, and turning right, you'll find *Boualipham*, a shop-house restaurant that serves frosty 333 beers from Vietnam and an inexpensive range of fruit and rice dishes. The main area for **food stalls** lies along the same east–west road that the *Souksomphone* is on, with hawkers setting up between the bank and the wat.

Moving on from Attapu, the **bus** to Xekong leaves at noon, arriving at the town's morning market at around 2pm. The **express bus** to Pakxe leaves Attapu at 6am, taking just four hours. Otherwise you're stuck with the gruelling regular bus, which can take twice as long (2 daily; 7hr). At the moment, no public buses and very few private vehicles travel Route 18, the shortcut to Si Phan Don, which shadows the southern edge of the Bolaven, although there are plans to upgrade the road as far as Vietnam in the near future. **Boats** up the Xe Kong River to Xekong ($40) can be arranged through the *Souksomphone*.

travel details

Buses and Sawngthaews

Daen Sawan/Lao Bao to: Savannakhet (2 daily; 7hr 30min); Xepon (4 daily; 1hr 15min).

Lak Xao to: Thakhek (1 daily; 5hr); Vientiane (3 daily; 8hr).

Louang Namtha to: Boten (3hr); Houayxai (12hr); Jinghong, China, via Boten (11hr); Muang Sing (2hr); Oudomxai (4hr).

Louang Phabang to: Muang Nan (5 daily; 3hr); Nam Bak (2 daily; 2hr 10min); Nong Khiaw (2 daily; 2–3hr); Oudomxai (3 daily; 5–7hr); Pakmong (5 daily; 2hr); Vang Viang (6 daily; 6–7hr); Viang Kham (1 daily; 4hr 40min); Vientiane (7 daily; 10–12hr).

Muang Sing to: Louang Namtha (2hr); Xiangkok (2hr).

Nam Neun to: Phonsavan (1–2 daily; 6hr); Viang Thong (1 daily; 2–3hr) and Xam Nua (1 daily; 5–6hr).

Nong Khiaw to: Louang Phabang (2 daily; 2–3hr)

Oudomxai to: Boten (4hr); Jinghong, China, via Boten (12hr); Louang Namtha (4hr); Louang Phabang (3 daily; 5hr); Muang Khoua (5hr); Muang Sing (6hr); Pakbeng (8hr); Phongsali (11hr).

Pakxe to: Attapu (3 daily; 4–7hr); Champasak (3 daily; 1hr 30min); Chong Mek (hourly; 1hr); Muang Sen (2 daily; 5hr30min); Nakasang (5 daily; 3hr 30min); Pakxong (hourly; 2hr); Salavan (3 daily; 3hr 30min); Savannakhet (7 daily; 8–9hr); Thakhek (3 daily; 10–11hr); Vientiane (3 daily; 18–20hr); Xekong (3 daily; 4–5hr).

Phonsavan to: Muang Kham (4–5 daily; 1hr 30min); Muang Khoun (2–3 daily; 1hr); Muang Soui (1–2 daily; 3hr); Nam Neun (1–2 daily; 6hr); Nong Het (1 daily; 5hr); Phaxai (2–3 daily; 40min); Xam Nua (1 daily; 11–12hr).

Savannakhet to: Daen Sawan/Lao Bao (2 daily; 7hr 30min); Da Nang (5 weekly; 15hr); Dong Ha (5 weekly; 10hr); Hué (5 weekly; 15hr); Pakxe (7 daily; 8–9hr); Thakhek (9 daily; 2hr); Vientiane (8 daily; 8–10hr); Xepon (2 daily; 6hr 15min).

Thakhek to: Lak Xao (3 daily; 4hr); Mahaxai (5 daily; 2hr 30min); Pakxe (3 daily; 10–11hr); Savannakhet (9 daily; 2hr); Vientiane (10 daily; 6hr).

Viang Kham to: Louang Phabang (1 daily; 4h 40min); Nong Khiaw (2–3 daily; 2hr); Viang Thong (1–2 daily; 4hr).

Viang Thong to: Nam Neun (1 daily; 2–3hr); Viang Kham (1–2 daily; 4hr); Xam Nua (1 daily; 6–7hr).

Vientiane to: Friendship Bridge (every 45min; 45min); Lak Xao (3 daily; 8hr); Lao Pako (3 daily; 1hr); Louang Phabang (6 daily; 10–12hr); Oudomxai (1 daily; 19hr); Pakxan (12 daily; 2hr); Pakxe (3 daily; 18–20hr); Savannakhet (8 daily; 8–10hr); Somsamai (3 daily; 1hr); Thakhek (10 daily; 8hr); Vang Viang (10 daily; 3hr 30 min); Xam Nua (6 monthly; 30hr).

Xam Nua to: Muang Et (1 daily; 7hr); Nam Neun (1–2 daily; 5–6hr); Phonsavan (1 daily; 11–12hr); Viang Thong (1 daily; 6–7hr); Viang Xai (3 daily; 1hr); Vientiane (6 monthly; 30hr); Xiang Kho (1 daily; 6hr).

Xepon to: Daen Sawan/Lao Bao (4 daily; 1hr 15min); Savannakhet (2 daily; 6hr 15min).

Boats

Houayxai to: Louang Namtha (2.5 days); Louang Phabang (slow boat: 2 days; speedboat: 6hr); Pakbeng (slow boat: 1 day; speedboat: 3hr); Xiangkok (4hr).

Louang Phabang to: Houayxai (slow boat: 2–3 days; speedboat: 6hr); Nong Khiaw (4–5 weekly; 7–8hr); Pakbeng (slow boat: 1–2 days; speedboat: 3hr); Vientiane (1 weekly; 3–5 days).

Pakxe to: Champasak (3 daily; 1hr 30min); Muang Sen (1 daily; 8–10hr).

Vientiane to: Louang Phabang (1 weekly; 4–5 days); Paklai (2 daily; 4hr).

Flights

Louang Phabang to: Houayxai (1 daily; 50min); Louang Namtha (2 weekly; 35min); Oudomxai (5 weekly; 35min); Phonsavan (4 weekly; 35min); Vientiane (2–3 daily; 40min).

Pakxe to: Savannakhet (3 weekly; 45min); Vientiane (1 daily; 1hr 20min).

Phonsavan to: Louang Phabang (4 weekly; 35min); Vientiane (1–2 daily; 40min).

Savannakhet to: Pakxe (2 weekly; 45min); Vientiane (1 daily; 1hr 5min).

Vientiane to: Bangkok (2 daily; 1hr); Chiang Mai (1 weekly; 2hr); Hanoi (1 daily; 1hr10min); Ho Chi Minh City (1 weekly; 2hr 40min); Houayxai (4 weekly; 1hr 20min); Kunming (1 weekly; 3hr); Louang Namtha (3 weekly; 1hr 10min); Louang Phabang (3 daily; 40min); Oudomxai (2 weekly; 50min); Pakxe (1 daily; 1hr 20min); Phnom Penh (2 weekly; 3hr 20min); Phonsavan (1–2 daily; 40min); Savannakhet (1 daily; 1hr 5min); Xam Nua (1 daily; 1hr 10min).

Xam Nua to: Vientiane (1 daily; 1hr 10min).

CHAPTER SIX

MACAU

Introduction

Sixty kilometres west across the Pearl River estuary from Hong Kong lies the former Portuguese enclave of **Macau**. A mere sliver of mainland and a couple of islands covering just twenty-three square kilometres in total, the territory is geographically and economically a midget compared to its booming cousin across the water. The transfer of Macau's administration (Portugal gave up any claims to sovereignty in the 1970s) to China in 1999 – two years after Hong Kong's – had none of the drama or controversy that surrounded that of Hong Kong. As in its larger neighbour, the majority of Macau's population of 430,000 are Cantonese-speaking Chinese. But this has not prevented the territory from developing an atmosphere distinct not only from Hong Kong but from other parts of southern China. With a colonial past predating that of Hong Kong by nearly three hundred years, Macau's **historic buildings** – from old fortresses to Baroque churches to faded mansion houses – are still plentiful, while the crumbling backstreets around the port are reminiscent of Hong Kong as it might have been fifty years ago. And Macau can even boast its own indigenous population, the **Macanese**, a tiny mixed-blood minority, whose origins in the colony date back centuries and who are often bilingual in Portuguese and Cantonese and still maintain the traditions of both cultures.The cheap Portuguese wine and Macanese cooking – an interesting marriage of Chinese and Mediterranean influences – are further reminders of colonial heritage, as is the faintly Latin lifestyle, altogether less hectic and mellower than in other parts of southern China. South of the main city, on the tiny islands of **Taipa** and **Coloane** (now linked to the peninsula by bridges and land reclamation), are beaches and quiet villages where you can eat fish and drink Portuguese rum or port in relative peace.

However, by the millions of gambling fanatics living in nearby Hong Kong (and increasingly Shenzhen and Guangzhou as well), Macau, with its liberal gambling laws, is seen as little more than one giant **casino**. It is largely as a spin-off from the colossal gambling trade that money is being pumped in, allowing large-scale construction to take off, including that of Macau's own (underused) **airport** on the island of Taipa. New high-rise hotels, highways and bridges are appearing, and Hong Kong-style land reclamation has begun in earnest.

Considering that costs are a good deal lower here than in Hong Kong, and the ease of travel between Guangzhou, Hong Kong and Macau, it's a great pity not to drop in on the territory if you are in the region. A day-trip from Hong Kong is very easy (tens of thousands do it every weekend), though you need a couple of nights really to do the place justice.

Macau's **climate** is the same as Hong Kong's. Between June and September conditions are hot and humid – above 30°C – with frequent rainstorms, as well as a danger of typhoons. Between October and April conditions are cooler and much pleasanter, and while it can rain a lot in January and February, the temperature rarely falls below 14°C.

Air and sea routes into Macau

Access to Macau is chiefly by **boat from Hong Kong**; see p.540 for details. There are also many **flights** from neighbouring Southeast Asian countries.

Entry requirements and visa extension

Citizens of **Britain**, **Ireland**, **Australia**, **New Zealand**, **Canada**, **USA** and most Western European countries need only a valid passport to enter Macau, and can stay up to twenty days. The simplest way to **extend your stay** is to go to Hong Kong and re-enter Macau at a later date.

> **AIRPORT DEPARTURE TAX**
> Airport departure tax in Macau is $10 for China and $16.25 for all other destinations.

Money and costs

The unit of **currency** in Macau is the pataca (abbreviated to ptca in this book; also sometimes seen as M$), in turn broken down into 100 avos. **Notes** come in denominations of 20, 50, 100, 500 and 1000ptca; **coins** come as 10, 20 and 50 avos, and 1, 5 and 10ptca. The pataca is worth fractionally less than the HK dollar. The current **rate of exchange** is US$1 = 7.96ptca and £1 = 12ptca. HK dollars are freely accepted as currency in Macau, and a lot of visitors from Hong Kong don't bother changing money at all. Like the Hong Kong dollar the pataca is set to continue its status as a separate currency for the foreseeable future.

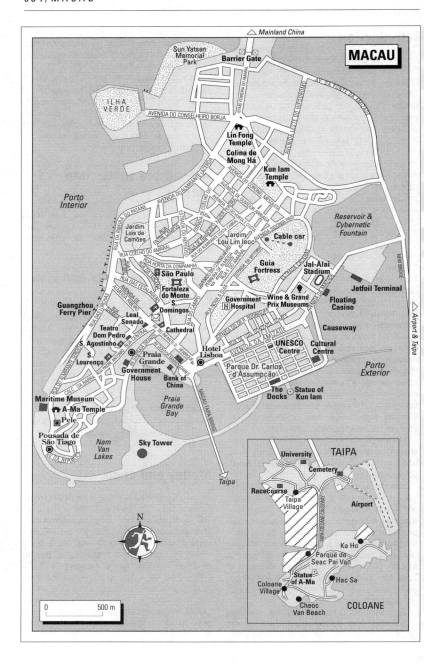

Food and accommodation are more expensive in Macau than most other Southeast Asian destinations, although they are generally cheaper than in Hong Kong. You may pay slightly more than in Hong Kong for the very cheapest beds, but will get much better value in the larger hotels – which drop their prices even further in midweek. An excellent three-course Portuguese meal with wine and coffee can be had for as little as £10/$15. Buses and taxis are in any case extremely cheap. All in all, you could live on about £13/$20 a day if you took the cheapest accommodation and ate frugally. A more comfortable room and better meals will raise your **daily budget** to a more realistic £20–25/$31–38.

All the **major credit cards** are accepted in the larger hotels, but most guesthouses and restaurants want cash. If you need to get money, some ATMs in the centre of town will accept foreign credit cards. If you want to get money sent from overseas you'd be better off doing it in Hong Kong, where they are more efficient and experienced.

Information and maps

The **Macau Government Tourist Office (MGTO)** has offices in Hong Kong at the Macau Ferry Terminal, Room 1303, Shun Tak Centre (Mon–Fri 9am–1pm & 2–6pm, Sat 9am–1pm; ☎2549 8884); at the Visitor Information Centre (daily 9am–6pm; ☎5726 416) in Macau's Jetfoil Terminal; and at Largo do Senado 9 in Macau (daily 9am–6pm; ☎315566). They also have a web page: *www.macau.tourism.gov.mo*. Look out for two useful, free news sheets, *Macau Travel Talk* and *Macau Magazine*, both of which contain decent maps of the main areas of interest.

Accommodation

Accommodation is generally cheaper in Macau than in Hong Kong – at least midweek. For the same money that would get you a tiny box in Hong Kong's Chungking Mansions, you can find quite a spacious room with private shower and a window here. Be warned, however, that at weekends **prices** shoot up everywhere.

Food and drink

The territory's native cuisine, **Macanese food**, is a fascinating blend of Portuguese and Asian elements. The Portuguese elements include fresh bread, cheap imported wine and coffee, as well as an array of dishes ranging from *caldo verde* (vegetable soup) to *bacalao* (dried salted cod). Macau's most interesting Portuguese colonial dish is probably **African chicken**, a concoction of Goan and east African influences, comprising chicken grilled with peppers and spices. Straightforward **Cantonese restaurants**, often serving *dim sum* for breakfast and lunch, are also plentiful, though you'll find wine on the menus even here. Alongside the local dumplings and noodles, Macau's numerous snack bars often sell fresh-milk products such as fruit milkshakes and milk puddings, unusual for China.

The **water** meets European health standards, though you may prefer bottled water. Restaurant **menus** are not always available in English – just Portuguese and Cantonese.

Communications

Airmail sent from Macau to Europe and North America takes between five days and a week. **Poste restante** is delivered to Macau's main post office (see "Listings", p.549). Local calls are free from private **phones**, 1ptca from payphones. Cardphones work with CTM cards, issued by the Macau State Telecommunication Company, on sale in hotels or at the back of the main post office (open 24hr), where you can also make direct calls. **Macau phone numbers** have no area codes; just dial the five- or six-figure number given. Instructions on most phones are in

---

ACCOMMODATION PRICE CODES

All **accommodation** reviewed in this guide has been graded according to the following price codes, in US dollars, which represent the cost of the cheapest double room available in high season. Where a price range is indicated, this means that the establishment offers rooms with varying facilities – as explained in the write-up. In cases where an establishment charges per bed the actual price is given.

① under $5	④ $15–20	⑦ $40–60
② $5–10	⑤ $20–25	⑧ $60–80
③ $10–15	⑥ $25–40	⑨ $80 and over

FOOD AND DRINK GLOSSARY

BASICS AND SNACKS

Arroz	Rice	*Manteiga*	Butter	*Prego*	Steak roll
Batatas fritas	French fries	*Ovos*	Eggs	*Sal*	Salt
Legumes	Vegetables	*Pimenta*	Pepper	*Sandes*	Sandwiches

SOUPS

Caldo verde	Green cabbage and potato soup	*Sopa de mariscos*	Shellfish soup
Sopa álentejana	Garlic and bread soup with a poached egg	*Sopa de peixe*	Fish soup

MEAT

Almondegas	Meatballs	*Cordoniz*	Quail	*Galinha*	Chicken
Bife	Steak	*Costeleta*	Chop	*Pombo*	Pigeon
Chouriço	Spicy sausage	*Dobrada*	Tripe	*Porco*	Pork
Coelho	Rabbit	*Figado*	Liver	*Salsicha*	Sausage

FISH AND SEAFOOD

Ameijoas	Clams	*Camarões*	Shrimps	*Linguado*	Sole
Bacalhão	Dried and salted cod	*Carangueijo*	Crab	*Lulas*	Squid
		Gambas	Prawns	*Meixilhões*	Mussels

SPECIALITIES

Cataplana	Pressure-cooked seafood stew with bacon, sausage and peppers	*Galinha á Portuguesa*	Chicken with eggs, potatoes, onion and saffron in a mild, creamy curry sauce
Cozido á Portuguesa	Boiled casserole of mixed meats, eg pig's trotters, rice and vegetables	*Feijoada*	Brazilian bean, pork, sausage and vegetable stew
Galinha á Africana	Chicken rolled or marinated in a pepper and chilli paste	*Pasteis de bacalhão*	Deep-fried cod fishcakes
		Porco á álentejana	Pork and clam stew

DESSERTS

Arroz doce	Portuguese rice pudding	*Pudim flán*	Crème caramel
Nata	Egg tart		

DRINKS

Água mineral	Mineral water	*Sumo de laranja*	Orange juice
Café	Coffee	*Vinho*	Wine
Chá	Tea	*Vinho do Porto*	Port (both red and white)
Cerveja	Beer	*Vinho verde*	A slightly sparkling white wine.

English as well as Portuguese. For **calls to Hong Kong**, dial ☎01 followed by the eight-digit number. You can make **international calls** from public phones or from the telephone office at the back of the main post office in Largo do Senado. Dial ☎00 + IDD country code (see p.40) + area code minus first 0 + subscriber number. There's also a **Home Direct** service (*Pais Directo*), which gives you access to an operator in the country you're calling, who can either charge calls collect or to your overseas phone card (see "Basics", p.39). For international calls to Macau the prefix is ☎853.

Most of the bigger hotels have business centres which will offer **internet access**. Alternatively, try the cybercafé in the UNESCO centre just off Avenida da Amizade, or those in the new Docks entertainment area, near the Kun lam statue in the Outer Harbour (see p.543).

Opening hours and festivals

Government offices **open** Monday–Friday 9am–1pm and 3–5/5.30pm, Saturday 8.30/9am–1pm. Shops and businesses are usually open for longer and don't close for lunch. **Banks** generally open Monday to Friday from 9am until 4 or 4.30pm, but close by lunchtime on Saturdays.

The normal Chinese **holidays** are celebrated in Macau, plus some Catholic **festivals** introduced

from Portugal, such as the procession of Our Lady of Fatima from São Domingos church annually on May 13. However, this may change in the future, now that Macau has reverted to Chinese rule. Two of the most important Chinese festivals celebrated in Macau and other Chinese communities across the world are **Chinese New Year** (Jan/Feb) and the Mid-Autumn (Moon Cake) Festival (**Sept**). Many of the festivals are highly symbolic and are often a mixture of secular and religious displays and devotions. As the Chinese use the **lunar calendar** and not the Gregorian calendar, many of the festivals fall on different days, even different months, from year to year.

Cultural hints

Macau shares many of the social taboos of other **Southeast Asian cultures**, described in "Basics" on p.41, though, as in Hong Kong, there is less emphasis on modest clothing. Topless bathing, however, is illegal.

Crime and safety

Macau is a **very safe place** for tourists. Although you may have read about some dramatic crimes in the papers – shootings, robberies, arson – what crime there is mostly Triad-organized, and hence not directed against foreigners. In addition, there has been a crackdown on the Triads since China took

---

over, so generally things are very quiet. The main police station is listed on p.549. It is very unwise to have anything to do with **drugs** of any description.

Medical care and emergencies

Pharmacies (daily 9am–6pm) can help with minor injuries or ailments and will prescribe basic medicines: they're all registered, and may employ English speakers. For a **doctor**, contact the reception desk in the larger hotels or go straight to the 24-hr emergency department at the Centro Hospitalar Conde São Januario. Casualty visits cost 200ptca. You'll have to pay for a consultation and any medicines that are prescribed; be sure to get a receipt so that you can make an insurance claim when you get home.

History

For more than a thousand years, all **trade** between China and the West had been carried out by land along the Silk Road through Central Asia, but in the fifteenth century the growth in European seafaring, pioneered by the **Portuguese**, finally led to the demise of the land route. Henceforth, sea trade and control of sea ports were what the European powers looked for in Asia.

Having gained toeholds in India (Goa) and the Malay Peninsula (Malacca) in the early sixteenth century, the Portuguese finally managed to persuade local Chinese officials, in 1557, to rent them a strategically well-placed peninsula at the mouth of the Pearl River Delta with fine natural harbours, known as **Macao** (A-Ma-gao, or bay of A-Ma, A-Ma being the goddess of the sea). Owing to their important trade links with Japan, as well as with India and Malaya, the Portuguese soon found themselves in the delightful position of being sole agents for merchants across a whole swathe of east Asia. Given that the Chinese were forbidden from going abroad to trade themselves, and that other foreigners were not permitted to enter Chinese ports, their trade boomed and Macau grew immensely wealthy. With the traders came **Christianity**, and among the luxurious homes and churches built during Macau's brief

half-century of prosperity was the Basilica of St Paul, whose facade can still be seen today.

By the beginning of the seventeenth century, however, Macau's fortunes were already on the wane, and a slow decline, which has continued almost ever since, set in. A combination of setbacks for the Portuguese, including defeats in war against the Spanish back home, the loss of trading relations with both Japan and China, and the rise of the Dutch as a trading power, saw Macau almost wiped off the map by mid-century.

In the eighteenth century, fortunes looked up somewhat, as more and more non-Portuguese European traders came looking for opportunities to prise open the locked door of China. For these people, Macau seemed a tempting base from which to operate, and eventually they were permitted to settle and build homes in the colony. The British had greater ambitions than to remain forever as guests in someone else's colony and when they finally seized their own piece of the shore to the east in 1841, Macau's status – as a backwater – was definitively settled. Despite the introduction of **licensed gambling** in the 1850s, as a desperate means of securing some kind of income, virtually all trade was lost to Hong Kong.

During the twentieth century, Macau's population increased massively to over half a million, as repeated waves of **immigrants** flooded the territory, whether fleeing Japanese invaders or Chinese Communists, but, unlike in Hong Kong, this growth was not accompanied by the same spectacular economic development. Indeed, in 1974, with the end of the fascist dictatorship in Portugal, the Portuguese attempted unilaterally to hand Macau back to China, the offer was refused. Only after the 1984 agreement with Britain over the future of Hong Kong did China agree to negotiate the formal return of Macau as well. In **1999**, the final piece of Asian soil still in European hands was surrendered. The Chinese mainland was united under a central government for the first time since the Ming dynasty, and Macau became, like Hong Kong, a semi-democratic capitalist enclave, subject to Beijing and classed as a "Special Administrative Region of China".

Religions of Macau

The three main Chinese religions – **Taoism**, **Confucianism** and **Buddhism** – dominate in Macau (see "Basics", p.47, for an introduction to these religions), though there are dozens of **Catholic** churches here too. The whole picture is further confused by the importance attached to superstition and **ancestor worship**.

Books

Austin Coates, *City of Broken Promises* (OUP East Asia, UK). An entertaining novel which offers a colourful picture of eighteenth century Macau, when the enclave was still a centre for China-related trade and intrigue. Coates was Assistant Colonial Secretary in Hong Kong in the 1950s.

Jill McGivering, *Macau Remembers* (OUP). The reminiscences of some of Macau's most notable residents, offering a colourful insight into life in colonial Macau.

Language

The vast majority of people in Macau speak **Cantonese** and many also speak Portuguese and **English**.

MACAU

Macau comprises three distinct parts: the **peninsula**, which is linked by bridge to the island of **Taipa**, which is in turn linked by bridge to a second island, **Coloane**. The peninsula of Macau, where the original old city was located and where most of the historic sights still are (as well as the city amenities), is entirely developed right up to the border with China in the north, though the islands, Coloane in particular, contain some quiet rural patches.

The peninsula is not large and it's possible to get around much of it on foot, though you'll need buses for the longer stretches. The most important road, **Avenida Almeida Ribeiro**, cuts across from east to west, taking in the *Hotel Lisboa*, one of Macau's most famous landmarks, and exits on its western end at the Inner Harbour, near the docking point for ferries from Guangzhou. The western part of Almeida Ribeiro is also the budget-hotel area.

Arrival

Access to Macau is chiefly by **boat from Hong Kong**. Every day, large numbers of competing vessels make the one-hour journey between Hong Kong's Shun Tak Centre and Macau's **Jetfoil Terminal** (Nova Terminal in Portuguese), in the southeast of town, by Avenida da Amizade. The terminal is connected to the *Hotel Lisboa* and the budget-hotel area on Almeida Ribeiro by several buses, including #3A and #10. The boat services include a 24-hour jetfoil service (frequent; 55min), catamarans and high-speed ferries (cheap, but infrequent and slow). There are also less frequent catamaran services from the China Ferry Terminal on Canton Road in Tsimshatsui. **Ticket prices** vary; reckon on paying HK$100–150 each way, less than that for the high-speed ferry. Simply show up at the terminal, purchase a ticket for the next sailing, clear passport control and board.

Planes arrive at the **airport** on Taipa Island, connected by airport bus #AP1 to the *Hotel Lisboa* and the Jetfoil Terminal.

MOVING ON FROM MACAU

By ferry
Advance tickets for the **ferry to Hong Kong** are available from the Jetfoil Terminal in the Outer Harbour. Otherwise, simply show up at the terminal, purchase a ticket for the next sailing, clear passport control and board.

By plane
Planes fly from Taipa Island airport to Beijing (daily; 3hr), Shanghai (daily; 2hr), Xiamen (daily; 1hr), Taiwan (daily; 1hr 30min), Bangkok (3 weekly; 2hr), Manila (2 weekly; 2hr), Seoul (2 weekly; 3hr), Pyongyang (1 weekly; 3hr) and Singapore (2 weekly; 4hr), as well as an increasing number of other Chinese cities.

By bus to China
By land, you can **walk** across the border (daily 7am–9pm) at the Barrier Gate in the far north of the peninsula, into the Zhuhai Special Economic Zone; buses #5 and #9 connect the Barrier Gate with Almeida Ribeiro and Rua da Praia Grande. Alternatively, there are hourly **bus** services which go direct to Guangzhou (6hr) from near the *Peninsula Hotel* in the Inner Harbour. The MGTO (see p.535) can give details; tickets are available at the bus terminal, opposite the Guangdong Ferry terminal, in the Inner Harbour.

Getting around

Many, if not all, places in Macau can be reached on foot. **Taxis** are cheap, although don't expect the drivers to speak English. It's best to get someone to write your destination in Chinese characters. Trips to Coloane or the international airport on Taipa or Coloane will attract a surcharge on top of the meter reading of 5ptca, and there is a 2ptca surcharge between the two islands. Otherwise, hop onto one of the many very inexpensive **buses** (exact fare only). Some important bus interchanges include the Jetfoil Terminal (Nova Terminal), the *Hotel Lisboa*, Almeida Ribeiro, Barra (near the A-Ma Temple), Praça Ponte e Horta (near the Guangzhou Ferry Pier on the Inner Harbour), Barra (near the Maritime Museum on the Inner Harbour), the Barrier Gate (usually referred to by its Portuguese name, Portas do Cerco, and the islands Taipa and Coloane. Useful routes include:

#3 and #3A from the Jetfoil Terminal to *Hotel Lisboa* and Almeida Ribeiro.
#5 and #9 from Barra to Almeida Ribeiro and the Barrier Gate.
#21, #21A and #25 from Almeida Ribeiro to Taipa Village and/or Coloane.
#28B from the Jetfoil Terminal to *Hotel Lisboa* and Rua da Praia Grande.

Finally, **cycling** is a possibility, on the islands at least, though note that you are not allowed to cycle over the causeway from the mainland to Taipa. For details on rental, see p.547.

Accommodation

The densest concentration of **hotels** occurs around the western end of Almeida Ribeiro, spreading out from the inner harbour, though one or two places can be found in remote, tranquil places such as the island of Coloane. Note that addresses are written with the number after the name of the street.

East Asia, Rua da Madeira 1A (☎922 433; Hong Kong reservations ☎2540 6333). A couple of blocks north from the western end of Almeida Ribeiro. One of Macau's oldest hotels, and a very smart, comfortable place, with great views and friendly staff. Very good value. ⑤–⑦.
Hotel London, Praça de Ponte e Horta 4 (☎937 761). A nice, modern place offering single, double and triple rooms. ④–⑥.
Ko Wah, Rua da Felicidade 71 (☎375 599). A reasonably pleasant hotel on one of Macau's most interesting and historic streets. A bit run down, but the rooms are large, making this one of the most attractive budget choices. ④–⑦.
Mandarin Oriental, 956–1110 Avenida da Amizade (☎576 888). A ritzy spa and health facility, complete with enormous, landscaped swimming pool, makes this an attractive choice if you want a bit of pampering. They have good inclusive deals and mid-week discount rates. ⑨.
Pousada de Mong-Ha, Colina de Mong-Ha (☎561 252). This place in the quieter northern Macau area is also used as a hotel-and-restaurant training school. Although the rooms are quite spartan local residents recommend it as good value. ⑦–⑧.
Pousada de São Tiago, Avenida da República (☎378 111; Hong Kong reservations ☎2739 1216). Constructed from an old fortress on the southern tip of the peninsula, with walled stairways lined with gushing streams, huge stone archways and delightfully furnished rooms. ⑨.
Vila Universal, Rua da Felicidade 73 (☎573 247). Next door to the *Ko Wah*, this is a fairly large place, clean and comfortable, with spacious rooms. Numerous interesing eating places nearby. Highly recommended. ④–⑤.

Macau Peninsula

The town of Macau was born in the south of the peninsula, around the bay-front road known as the **Praia Grande**, and grew out from there. Sadly, these days, a stroll on the seafront is not what it was, with the bay now being enclosed and reclamation work underway. More rewarding is the main road that cuts the Praia from east to west, called **Avenida do Infante** d'Henrique to the east and **Avenida de Almeida Ribeiro** to the west. At the eastern end of the road rises the extraordinarily garish *Hotel Lisboa*, though most of the interest lies in the section west of the Praia, particularly in the beautiful **Largo do Senado** (Senate Square), which marks the downtown area and bears the unmistakeable influence of southern Europe, not only in its architecture, but also in its role as a place for people to stroll, sit and chat.

At the northern end of Largo do Senado, away from the main road, is the beautiful seventeenth-century Baroque church, **São Domingos**, while to the south, facing the square from across the main road, stands the **Leal Senado** (Mon–Sat 1–7pm; free), generally considered the finest Portuguese building in the city. Step into the interior courtyard here to see wonderful blue-and-white Portuguese tiles around the walls, while up the staircase from the courtyard, you reach first a formal garden and then the richly decorated **senate chamber** itself. In the late sixteenth century, all of the colony's citizens would cram into this hall to debate issues of importance. The senate's title *leal* (loyal) was earned during the period when Spain occupied the Portuguese throne and Macau became the final stronghold of those loyal to the true king. Today, the senate chamber is still used by the municipal government of Macau. Adjacent to the chamber is the wood-carved **public library**, whose collection includes many fifteenth- and sixteenth-century books which visitors are free to browse.

West from Largo do Senado, Almeida Ribeiro emerges on to the so-called **Inner Harbour**, which overlooks the mainland just across the water and is used by ferries to and from Guangzhou. Some of the streets immediately inland from here, especially those just north of Almeida Ribeiro, are worth poking around. Streets such as Rua da Felicidade have been nicely restored and are now full of small hotels and friendly restaurants, serving local specialities such as snake. South of the Guangzhou Ferry Pier, the seafront road Rua das Lorchas is lined with old arcades and characterful shops.

São Paulo and around

A few hundred metres north of Largo do Senado stands Macau's most famous landmark, the church of **São Paulo**, once hailed as the greatest Christian monument in east Asia, but today surviving as no more than a facade. Constructed at the beginning of the seventeenth century, it dominated the city for two hundred years until its untimely destruction by fire in 1835. Luckily, however, the facade, which had always been considered the highlight of the building, did not collapse – richly carved and laden with statuary, the cracked stone still presents an imposing sight from the bottom of the steps leading up from the Rua de São Paulo. The former crypt and nave have become a **museum** (9am–6pm daily, except Tues; free), detailing the building and design of the church.

Immediately east of São Paulo looms another early seventeenth-century monument, the **Fortaleza do Monte**, which also houses the **Macau Museum** (Tues–Sun 10am–6pm; 15ptca). The fort is an impressive pile, though it was only once used in a military capacity: to repel the Dutch in 1622, when it succeeded in blowing up the Dutch magazine with a lucky shot from a cannon ball.

Negotiating the roads a few hundred metres northwest of São Paulo brings you to perhaps the nicest part of Macau, around **Praça Luís de Camões** (also accessible on buses #17 from the *Hotel Lisboa* and #18 from the Barrier Gate and Inner Harbour). North, facing the square, is the **Jardim Luís de Camões** (6am–9.30pm), a delightful shady park built in honour of the great sixteenth-century Portuguese poet, Luís de Camões, who is thought to have been banished here for part of his life. There is also a museum, the **Museu de Luís de Camões**, in the park (10am–7pm), which is housed in an eighteenth-century villa, known as the **Fundacão Oriente**, and has some attractive historical prints of the enclave.

Immediately east of the square, though, is the real gem, the **Old Protestant Cemetery**, where all the non-Catholic traders, visitors, sailors and adventurers who happened to die in Macau in the early part of the nineteenth century were buried. The gravestones have all been restored and are quite legible. In this quiet, shady garden, the last testaments to these mainly British, American and German individuals, including the painter George Chinnery, make poignant reading.

The east

About 1km northeast of the Fortaleza do Monte is another area worth walking around (buses #12 and #22 run up here from near the *Hotel Lisboa* along the Avenida do Conselheiro Ferreira de Almeida). At the junction with Estrada de Adolfo Loureiro, the first site you'll reach, screened off behind a high wall, is the scenic **Jardim Lou Lim Ioc** (daily dawn–dusk; 1ptca), a formal Chinese garden full of bamboos, pavilions, birds in cages and old men playing mahjong. A couple of minutes' walk around the corner from here you'll find the **Sun Yatsen Memorial Home** (daily except Tues 10am–5pm; free), at the junction of Avenida de Sidonia Pais and the Rua de Silva Mendes. There isn't that much to see – basically, it's an attractive, rambling old mansion scattered about with mementoes of Sun Yatsen, who spent some time living in Macau in the years before he turned to revolutionary activities.

The sharp hill to the east of here is Macau's highest, and its summit is crowned by the seventeenth-century **Guia Fortress**, the dominant feature of which is a charming whitewashed lighthouse, added in the nineteenth century and reputed to be the oldest anywhere on the Chinese coast. You can take a leisurely hike along a path up to the fort in about an hour, or at the other end of the Colina da Guia there's a **cable car** which connects to the Flora Garden below. At the top there are some superb views over the whole peninsula, including, on a clear day, a glimpse of Lantau Island far to the east. There's a tourist information counter and coffee bar (daily 9am–5.30pm) up here as well. In the harbour below the Colina da Guia you'll see the **Floating Casino**, a rickety but atmospheric wooden structure, packed with hard-faced Chinese gamblers. Nearby is the so-called **Tourist Activity Centre** containing the **Grand Prix Museum** (daily 10am–6pm; 10ptca), and the **Wine Museum** (daily 10am–6pm; 15ptca), which offers tastings. To the south, another feature of the Outer Harbour is the twenty-metre-high bronze statue of Kun Iam, the Goddess of Mercy. It stands on a small artificial island, linked to the seafront by a short causeway. The seafront area in front of the statue, along Avenida Marginal da Baia Nova, has become Macau's newest entertainment area, **The Docks**, with dozens of bars and restaurants open until the small hours.

The north

The northern part of the peninsula up to the border with China is largely residential, though it has a couple of points of interest. It's possible to walk the 3km from Almeida Ribeiro to the border, but the streets at this end of town are not particularly atmospheric, so it makes sense to resort to the local buses.

On Avenida do Coronel Mesquita, cutting the peninsula from east to west about 2km north of Almeida Ribeiro, is the enchanting **Kun Iam Temple** (daily 7am–6pm), accessible on bus #12 from the *Hotel Lisboa*. The complex of temples here, dedicated to the Goddess of Mercy, is around four hundred years old. In 1844, the United States and China signed their first treaty of trade and co-operation here – you can still see the granite table they used. Around the central statue of Kun Iam, to the rear of the main temple, is a crowd of statues representing the eighteen wise men of China, among whom, curiously, is Marco Polo (on the far left), depicted with a curly beard and moustache. The worshippers you'll see here shaking bamboo sticks in cylinders are trying to find out their fortunes.

To the west of the temple, near Rua do Padre João Climaco, there is an interesting daily market, known locally as the Red Market. Alternatively, you can catch bus #18 directly from the Kun Iam Temple to the **Portas do Cerco**, or Barrier Gate, the nineteenth-century stuccoed archway marking the border with China. These days, people actually cross the border through a customs and immigration complex to one side. A short walk to the west of the gate is **Sun Yatsen Memorial Park**, which gives interesting views over Zhuhai in the People's Republic, immediately across a small canal. Buses #3 or #10 will get you back to Almeida Ribeiro and the *Hotel Lisboa* from the gate.

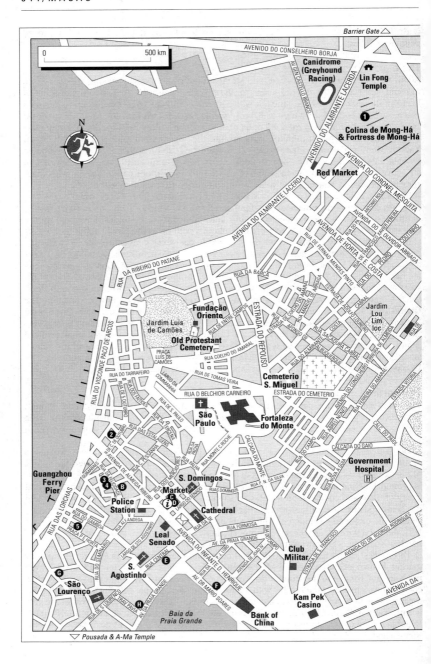

Barrier Gate △

AVENIDO DO CONSELHEIRO BORJA

Canidrome
(Greyhound
Racing)

Lin Fong
Temple

Colina de Mong-Há
& Fortress de Mong-Há

Red Market

Fundação
Oriente

Jardim Luis
de Camões

Old Protestant
Cemetery

Jardim
Lou
Lim
Ioc

Cemeterio
S. Miguel

São
Paulo

Fortaleza
do Monte

Government
Hospital

Guangzhou
Ferry
Pier

S. Domingos
Market

Police
Station

Cathedral

Leal
Senado

Club
Militar

S.
Agostinho

São
Lourenço

Kam Pek
Casino

Baia da
Praia Grande

Bank of
China

▽ Pousada & A-Ma Temple

0   500 km

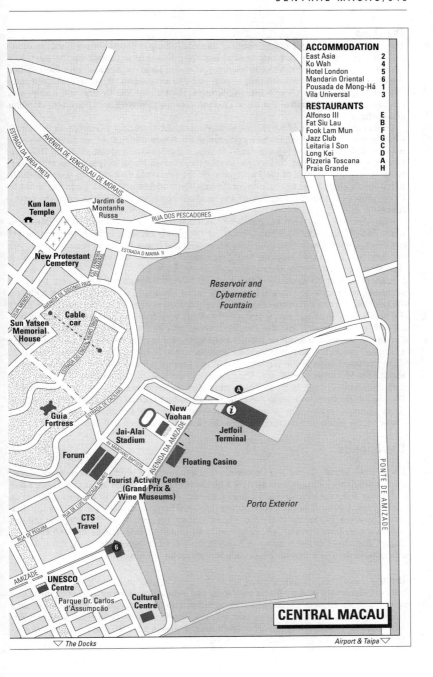

ACCOMMODATION

East Asia	2
Ko Wah	4
Hotel London	5
Mandarin Oriental	6
Pousada de Mong-Há	1
Vila Universal	3

RESTAURANTS

Alfonso III	E
Fat Siu Lau	B
Fook Lam Mun	F
Jazz Club	G
Leitaria I Son	C
Long Kei	D
Pizzeria Toscana	A
Praia Grande	H

ESTRADA DA AREIA PRETA

AVENIDA DE VENCESLAU DE MORAIS

Kun Iam
Temple

Jardim de
Montanha
Russa

RUA DOS PESCADORES

New Protestant
Cemetery

ESTRADA D MARIA II

RUA FERREIRA

SILVA

Reservoir and
Cybernetic
Fountain

AVENIDA DE SIDONIO PAIS

SILVA MENDES

Sun Yatsen
Memorial
House

Cable
car

ESTRADA DO ENGENHEIRO TRIGO

Guia
Fortress

ESTRADA DE CACILHAS

New
Yaohan

Jai-Alai
Stadium

AVENIDA DA AMIZADE

Jetfoil
Terminal

A

i

Forum

AV MARCIANO BAPTISTA

Floating Casino

AVENIDA DE LUIS GONZAGA GOMES

Tourist Activity Centre
(Grand Prix &
Wine Museums)

RUA DE LUIS GONZAGA GOMES

Porto Exterior

RUA DE PEQUIM

CTS
Travel

6

PONTE DE AMIZADE

AMIZADE

UNESCO
Centre

Parque Dr. Carlos
d'Assumpção

Cultural
Centre

CENTRAL MACAU

▽ *The Docks*

Airport & Taipa ▽

The south

The small but hilly tongue of land south of Almeida Ribeiro is dotted with colonial mansions and their gardens. The best way to start exploring this area is to walk up the steep Rua Central leading south from Almeida Ribeiro, just east of Largo do Senado. After five minutes you can detour off down a small road to your right, which contains the pastel-coloured early nineteenth-century church of **Santo Agostinho**. Back along Rua Central will lead you to another attractive church of the same era, the cream-and-white **São Lourenço**, standing amid palm trees.

Continuing several hundred metres farther south, you'll reach the seafront on the south-western side of the peninsula, which is known as the **Barra district**. As you face the sea, the celebrated **A-Ma Temple** is immediately to your right. Situated underneath Barra Hill over-looking the Inner Harbour, this temple may be as old as six hundred years in parts, and certainly predates the arrival of the Portuguese on the peninsula. Dedicated to the goddess A-Ma, whose identity blurs from Queen of Heaven into Goddess of the Sea (and who seems to be the same as Tin Hau in Hong Kong), the temple is an attractive jumble of altars among the rocks.

Immediately across the road from here, on the seafront, stands the **Maritime Museum** (daily except Tues 10am–5.30pm; 10ptca), an excellently presented collection covering old explorers, seafaring techniques, equipment, models and boats. For an additional charge, you can even join an English-language boat tour around the Inner Harbour (daily except Tues; 10ptca) on one of the junks moored just outside the museum.

A short walk south along the shore from the museum brings you to the very tip of the peninsula, which is today marked by the *Pousada de São Tiago*, an incredible hotel built into the remains of the seventeenth-century Portuguese fortress, the **Fortaleza de Barra**. Enter the hotel's front door and you find yourself walking up a stone tunnel running with water – it's well worth dropping into the *Pousada*'s verandah café for a drink overlooking the sea. Continuing the walk around the southern headland, and back to the north again, you'll pass a beautiful cream colonial-style building high up on the headland. This used to be the *Bela Vista*, the finest hotel in the territory, but at the handover it was given to Portugal's representative in Macau as a residence. The futuristic tower built on reclaimed land on your right is the Sky Tower, 338m high, and containing restaurants, offices and an observation deck. The road north from here up to the Praia Grande, near the *Hotel Lisboa*, takes about another ten minutes on foot. The wonderful pink building on your left shortly before the *Praia Grande* is the nineteenth-century **Palácio do Governo**, not open to visitors.

The islands

Macau's two islands, **Taipa** and **Coloane**, are just dots of land which traditionally supported a few small fishing villages, though now, with the opening of the new airport on Taipa, a second bridge from the mainland and a large reclamation programme, that old tranquillity is on the way out. Indeed, Taipa is fast acquiring the characteristics of a city suburb. For the time being, however, life seems to remain relatively quiet, particularly on Coloane, and the two islands are well worth a visit, either by bus or by rented bicycle. **Buses** #11 and #33 go to Taipa Village from different stops on Almeida Ribeiro, while buses #21, #21A, #26 and #26A stop outside the *Hyatt Regency* on Taipa before going on to Coloane.

Taipa

Until the eighteenth century **Taipa** used to be two islands separated by a channel, the silting up of which subsequently caused the two to merge into one. The same fate is now befalling Taipa and Coloane, except that this time it is not silt which is the culprit, but land reclamation – the two islands are being deliberately fused into one, to make space for new development.

Although Taipa's northern shore is hardly worth a stop, now that it is being subsumed into the general Macau conurbation, **Taipa Village** on the southern shore, with its old colonial promenade, makes a pleasant stop for an extended lunch. There isn't much more than a few streets to the modern village, where the buses stop, though there are some great restaurants (see p.548) along the central north–south alley, Rua do Cunha, and, to the west – on the right as you face the shore – a couple of temples in the vicinity of a quiet old square. Next to the Pak Tai Temple you can **rent bicycles** for around 15ptca an hour.

The island's real interest lies a few minutes' walk to the east of Taipa Village, in the former waterfront area. Here, as though frozen in time, is a superb old colonial promenade, the **Avenida da Praia**, complete with its original houses, public benches and street lamps. The beautifully restored mansions overlook what was the sea – sadly, reclamation has pushed the shoreline almost out of sight. The mansions are now being opened to the public; one houses the **Taipa House Museum** (Tues–Sun 9.30am–1pm & 3–5.30pm; free), which gives you some idea of what bourgeois domestic life was like at the beginning of the twentieth century. Plans for the others include exhibitions of regional Portuguese culture, aspects of traditional island life, and a restaurant and piano bar.

Coloane

Coloane is considerably bigger than Taipa, and, although it has no outstanding attractions, it's a pleasant place to spend a few hours. After crossing the bridge from Taipa, the buses pass the **Parque de Seac Pai Van** (daily except Mon 8am–6pm; free), a large park with pleasant walks. On top of the hill is a white marble statue of the goddess A-Ma, at almost twenty metres high the tallest in the world. Once past the park, the buses all stop at the roundabout in **Coloane Village** on the western shore, overlooking mainland China just across the water. There's no beach, just mud, in which you'll see old men fishing with nets. To the north are a few junk-building sheds, while the street leading south from the village roundabout, one block back from the shore, contains a couple of interesting old shops and the unexpected yellow-and-white **St Francis Xavier Chapel**, where a relic of the saint's armbone is venerated. A couple of hundred metres beyond this is the **Tam Kong Temple**, housing a metre-long whale bone, carved into the shape of a dragon boat.

On the north side of the village roundabout there's a small shop where you can rent bicycles for 12ptca an hour. Cycling is a good way to travel the 3km farther round to **Hac Sa Beach** on the eastern shore (otherwise, take bus #21A, #25, #26 or #26A), perhaps dropping in on **Cheoc Van Beach** to the south on the way as well. The beach at Hac Sa, tree-lined and stretching far off round the bay, is without doubt the best in Macau, despite the black colour of its sand, and has good facilities including showers and toilets, as well as some fine restaurants nearby (see p.548). There's also a sports and swimming pool complex here (daily 8am–9pm, Sun until midnight; 15ptca).

Eating, drinking and nightlife

Most restaurants here don't open as late as they do in Hong Kong – although bars do. If you want to get a meal served much after 10pm you'll probably end up either in a hotel or in the new bar/restaurant area, The Docks. Costs, however, are nearly always lower, with bills even in smart venues usually not exceeding 150–250ptca per head.

The range of **bars and nightlife** has improved enormously in the last year or so, and a whole new area of late-night bars and cafés, known as **The Docks** (follow signs to NAPE or ZAPE reclamation) has opened up in a colonnade on the seafront, near the statue of Kun Iam.

Restaurants and cafés

Alfonso III, Rua Central 11 (☎586 272). Genuine and excellent Portuguese food in a Portuguese environment, though the waiters speak English. Central, and not far from Largo do Senado.

Club Militar de Macau, Avenida da Praia Grande 795 (☎714 009). The dining room and bar of this beautifully restored club is open to the public, giving you a taste of the way the Portugese elite lived. A great selection of ports, fascinating atmosphere and reasonable prices.

Fat Siu Lau, Rua da Felicidade 64 (☎573 580). A very popular, traditional old restaurant in a busy restaurant area. Pigeon is the speciality.

Fook Lam Mun, Avenida Dr Mario Soares 259 (☎786 622). Excellent, though expensive, Cantonese seafood.

Leitaria I Son, Largo do Senado 7. Virtually next door to *Long Kei*, this is an excellent milk bar offering milk with everything – fruit, chocolate, eggs, ice creams, puddings and breakfasts.

Long Kei, Largo do Senado 7B (☎573 970). A 100-year-old traditional but inexpensive Cantonese restaurant, on the left as you face the square from Almeida Ribeiro. *Dim sum* available.

Pizzeria Toscana, Grand Prix Building, Avenida da Amizade (☎726 637). Right by the Jetfoil Terminal. Genuine Italian food and not just pizzas – though these are superb, as is the coffee.

Praia Grande, Praça Lobo D'Avila 10A, Avenida da Praia Grande (☎973 022). One of Macau's best restaurants, just outside the city centre. Pleasant staff, excellent food, good value.

TAIPA

O Galo, Rua da Cunha 45 (☎827 423). Low-priced, basically international menu. Just inland from the main bus stop on Rua Correa da Silva in Taipa Village.

Moçambique, Rua dos Clerigos 28 (☎827 471). Probably the most popular restaurant in Taipa Village, serving tasty Portuguese colonial food alongside various dishes from Goa and Africa.

Pinocchio II, Rua da Cunha 33 (☎827 128). On the corner with Rua do Sol. Good Macanese food, including fish cakes, crab, prawns and crispy roast duck. On the square opposite the fire station in Taipa Village.

Restaurante Panda, Rua Carlos Eugenio 4 (☎827 338). On a tiny alley leading east from the southern end of Rua da Cunha in Taipa Village. Reasonably priced Portuguese place, with outdoor tables in good weather.

COLOANE

Caçarola, Rua das Gaivotas 8 (☎882 226). Off the main village square, a welcoming and deservedly popular restaurant with excellent daily specials and very affordable prices.

Fernando's, Hac Sa Beach (☎882 531). Not far from the bus stop. An institution amongst local expats, *Fernando's* has the casual, cheerful atmosphere of a Mediterranean bistro and great Portuguese food. Advance booking recommended, especially at weekends.

Lord Stow's Bakery, Coloane Town Square. One of the best places to eat Macau's creamy egg tarts, or *natas*.

La Torre, Cheoc Van Beach (☎880 170). Good Italian food, on the seafront.

Bars and nightlife

Crazy Paris Show, Mona Lisa Hall, *Hotel Lisboa*, Avenida da Amizade (☎577 666). Something of a Macau institution now, this vaguely naughty cabaret-style show of scantily clad dancing girls can be seen nightly at 8pm and 9.30pm (also 11pm Sat; 250ptca).

Casablanca Café, Avenida Dr Calos Assumpção, Ed Vista Magnifica (☎751 281). Overlooking the sea and the Kun Iam stature, this place has a 1930's Hollywood theme. A covered colonnade and wicker chairs outside mean it's protected from the weather, as well as being a good place to watch the world go by. Things don't really get going until around midnight.

Jazz Club, Rua das Alabardas 9 (☎596 014). Behind St Lawrence's Church, this is a real late-night place – midnight and after. Brazilian and African music as well as the jazz, and live bands at the weekend.

Opiarium, Avenida Marginal Da Baia (☎750 975). One of the first of the bars to open on this seafront strip, west of the Kun Iam statue in the outer harbour. They have live jazz some evenings and funk on others. The outside seating gives a nice, slightly Mediterranean feel; inside, you can lounge on cushions, opium-den style.

Listings

Airlines The airline situation in Macau is likely to develop fast, though as yet airline representation in the territory is thin. Air Macau is at Avenida da Praia Grande 639 (☎396 555). Other airlines operating from Macau include Singapore Airlines (☎711 728) and EVA Airways of Taiwan (☎726 866); call the airport flight enquiries (☎861 111) or contact a travel agency.

Banks and exchange In addition to the banks, there are also licensed moneychangers which exchange travellers' cheques (and which open seven days a week), including a 24-hour one in the basement of the *Hotel Lisboa*, and one near the bottom of the steps leading up to São Paulo.

Bookshops Don't bother looking for English-language books here – go to Hong Kong.

Hospitals There's a 24-hour emergency department at the Centro Hospitalar Conde São Januário, Calçada Visconde São Januário (☎313 731; English spoken).

Pharmacy Largo do Senado.

Police The main police station is at Avenida Dr Rodrigo Rodrigues (☎573 333). In an emergency call ☎999.

Post office Macau's General Post Office is in Largo do Leal Senado, on the east side (Mon–Fri 9am–5.30pm, Sat 9am–12.30pm). Small red booths all over the territory also dispense stamps from machines.

Travel agencies CTS, Rua de Nagasaki (☎700 888), can sort out China visas and tickets, as can most other tour operators.

CHAPTER SEVEN

MALAYSIA

Introduction

Malaysia does not have the grand, ancient ruins of neighbouring Thailand, but its rich cultural heritage is apparent, both in its traditional kampung (village) areas and in its commitment to religious plurality. The dominant cultural force has undoubtedly been Islam, but the country's diverse population of indigenous Malays, Chinese and Indians has spawned a fabulous juxtaposition of mosques, temples and churches, a panoply of festivals and a wonderful mixture of cuisines. In addition, Malaysia boasts fine beaches, as well as some of the world's oldest tropical rainforest and most spectacular cave systems.

Your first impressions of Malaysia's hi-tech, fast-growing west-coast capital, **Kuala Lumpur** (KL), are likely to be of a vibrant and colourful, if crowded, place. Traditionally, people have stayed just long enough to think about their next destination, but there are good reasons to stay a little longer: accommodation is plentiful and cheap, the food is excellent and its streets safe and friendly. Less than three hours' journey south lies the birthplace of Malay civilization, **Melaka**, a must on anybody's itinerary, while north up the coast is the first British settlement, the island of **Penang**, and its very appealing capital, Georgetown. For a taste of Old England and lots of walks, head for the hill station of the **Cameron Highlands**.

North of Penang, the premier tourist destination is **Pulau Langkawi**, a popular duty-free island. Routes down the Peninsula's east coast are more relaxing, with stops at the sleepy mainland kampung like Cherating and the stunning islands of Pulau Perhentian and Pulau Tioman. The state capitals of **Kota Bharu**, near the northeastern Thai border, and **Kuala Terengganu**, further south, are showcases for the best of Malay crafts and performing arts, while the unsullied tropical rainforests of **Taman Negara National Park** offer trails, animal hides, a high canopy walkway and waterfalls.

Across the sea from the Peninsula are the Bornean states of **Sarawak** and **Sabah**. For most travellers, their first taste of Sarawak is Kuching, the old colonial capital, and then the Iban longhouses of the Batang Ai and Batang Lupar river systems, or the Bidayuh communities closer to the Kalimantan border. The best time to visit is in late May-early June when the Iban and the Bidayuh celebrate their harvest festivals with ribald parties to which everyone is invited. Sibu, much further to the north, is another starting point for more visits to other Iban longhouses and the idyllic Pelagus Rapids region. In the north of the state, **Gunung Mulu National Park** is the principal destination, its extraordinary razor-sharp limestone needles providing demanding climbing and its deep, cathedral-shaped caves awe-inspiring.

The main reason for a trip to Sabah is to conquer the 4101-metre granite peak of **Mount Kinabalu**, though the lively modern capital **Kota Kinabalu** and its offshore islands have their moments, too. Beyond this, Sabah is worth a visit for its wildlife, including turtles, orang-utans, proboscis monkeys and hornbills, while oceanic **Pulau Sipadan** has a host of sharks, fish and turtles, as well as one of the world's top coral reef dives.

Temperatures in Malaysia constantly hover around 30°C (22°C in highland areas), and humidity is high all year round. The major distinction in the seasons is marked by the arrival of the monsoon, which brings heavy and prolonged downpours to the east coast of Peninsular Malaysia, the northeastern part of Sabah, and the western end of Sarawak from November to February; boats to most of the islands do not run during the height of the monsoon. The Peninsula's west coast experiences fewer major thunderstorms during the months of April and May. The ideal time to visit is between April and October, avoiding the worst of the rains.

Overland and sea routes into Malaysia

Malaysia has land borders with Thailand, Singapore, Brunei and Indonesian Kalimantan. Aside from the options detailed below, there are regular boats from Bandar in **Brunei** to Lawas and Limbang in Sarawak and to Pulau Labuan in Sabah. Weekly boats from Zamboanga in the **Philippines** run to Sandakan in Sabah. Below is an outline of overland and sea routes: full details are given in the accounts of relevant departure points.

■ From Indonesia

A variety of ferries and speedboats departs **from Indonesia** to Malaysia. **Boats** run from Tanjung Balai (see p.301), in Sumatra, to **Port Klang**, just outside Kuala Lumpur; from Medan (see p.272), in north Sumatra, to **Penang**; from Dumai (see p.299), south of Medan, to **Melaka**; from Pulau Batam (see p.301), in the Riau Archipelago, to **Johor Bahru**; from Nunukan and Tarakan (see p.411) in northeastern Kalimantan, to **Tawau**; and from Tanjung Balai (see p.301) to **Kukup**, 200km south of Melaka.

There is a **land border** at Entikong, 100km southwest of Kuching; buses run from Pontianak in south-

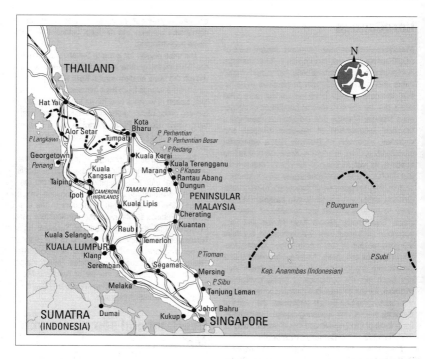

ern Kalimantan through here to Kuching. You can also cross from Nanga Badau (see p.402) into Sarawak.

■ From the Philippines

There are several weekly sailings from Zamboanga (see p.770), in the southern Philippines, to Sandakan, in Sabah.

■ From Thailand

Travelling **from Thailand** to Malaysia is straightforward and a very commonly used route. Most Western tourists can spend thirty days in Malaysia and fourteen days in Singapore without having bought a visa beforehand, and the transport connections between the three countries are excellent. This makes it an ideal route for tourists and expats needing to renew their Thai visas; there are Thai consulates in Kuala Lumpur, Georgetown (Penang) and Kota Bahru.

Most people choose to travel by long-distance **train** or bus to Malaysian cities such as KL or Butterworth, either from Bangkok, Krabi, Surat Thani

or Hat Yai; see individual city accounts and "Travel Details". However, you can also travel by more local transport, as there are a number of **border crossings** between Thailand and Malaysia – from Satun (see p.953) to Kuala Perlis and Langkawi; Padang Besar (see p.953) to Kuala Perlis and Alor Setar; Betong (see p.957) to Sungei Petani; Sungai Kolok (see p.957) to Kota Bharu; Ban Taba (see p.957) to Kota Bharu, Sadao and Wang Prachan.

Plenty of **buses** also cross the Thai–Malaysian border every day. The southern Thai town of Hat Yai (see p.953) is the major transport hub for international bus connections to Butterworth (5hr), Penang (6hr), Kuala Lumpur (12hr) and Singapore (18hr).

Entry requirements and visa extension

Most nationalities do not need a **visa** for stays of fewer than two months in Malaysia, but passports must be valid for three months beyond your date of departure, and for six months if you're going to

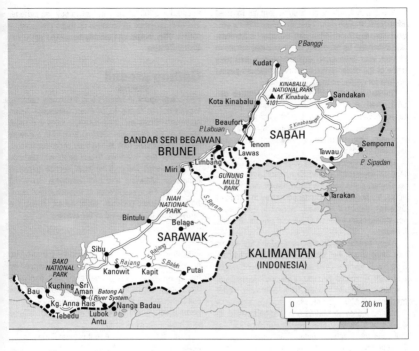

Sabah or Sarawak. To **extend your visa**, go to an immigration department office (eg in KL, Penang or Johor Bahru), or simply cross into Singapore and back. A one-month extension should be no problem, and a three-month extension may be possible.

Tourists travelling from the Peninsula **to Sarawak** and Sabah must be cleared again by immigration. Visitors **to Sabah** can remain as long as their original two-month stamp is valid. Visitors to Sarawak – whether from Sabah or the Peninsula – receive a new, one-month stamp which is rarely extendable. If you start your trip in Sarawak and then fly to the mainland, be sure to get your passport stamped by immigration with the usual two-month pass. If an officer isn't available to do this then go to the Immigration Office in Kuching at the first opportunity to get it stamped there.

Money and costs

Malaysia's unit of **currency** is the Malaysian ringgit, divided into 100 sen. You'll also see the ringgit written as "RM", or simply as "$" (M$), and often hear it called a "dollar". Notes come in $1, $5, $10, $20, $50, $100, $500 and $1000 denominations; coins are minted in 1 sen, 5 sen, 10 sen, 20 sen, 50 sen and $1 denominations. At the time of writing, the **exchange rate** was around RM5.80 to £1, RM3.50 to US$1. There is no black market.

If entering Malaysia from Thailand, you will find your **daily budget** remains pretty much unchanged, but approaching from Indonesia, costs will take a step up. **In Peninsular Malaysia**, if you stay in basic accommodation, use local transport and eat at roadside stalls, you can manage on £10/US$14 a day. With air-conditioned rooms, decent restaurants and the occasional beer, your daily budget becomes a more realistic £20/US$28.

AIRPORT DEPARTURE TAX

Departure tax is RM5 for domestic flights and flights to Brunei and Singapore, and RM40 on international flights. If you're buying your ticket from a discounted agent in, say, the UK, tax will usually be included in the overall price.

You'll find living costs roughly similar **in East Malaysia**, though room rates are around thirty percent more expensive. Moreover, transport in Sarawak and Sabah can be expensive, since you may decide to charter your own boat, and adequately exploring some of the major national parks can require paying upfront for guides or tours.

Sterling and US dollar **travellers' cheques** can be cashed at Malaysian banks, licensed money-changers and some hotels. Ban Hin Lee Bank (BHL) doesn't charge any commission for changing American Express travellers' cheques, but can only be found in major cities.

Licensed moneychangers' kiosks in bigger towns tend to open until around 6pm, and sometimes at weekends; some hotels will **exchange** money at all hours. It's not difficult to change money in Sabah or Sarawak, though if travelling by river in the interior, you should carry a fair bit of cash, in smallish denominations.

Major **credit cards** are accepted in most hotels and large shops, but beware of illegal surcharges. Banks will advance cash against major credit cards, and with American Express, Visa and MasterCard, you can withdraw money from automatic teller machines (ATMs) in big cities.

Wiring money to Malaysia is straightforward. In KL, the best banks to use are Bank of America, 1st Floor, Wisma Stephens, galan Raja Chulan, Golden Triangle (☎03/202 1133) and the Hongkong and Shanghai Bank, 2 Lebuh Ampang, Little India (☎03/230 0744). For more details on wiring money see "Basics" p.23.

Information and maps

The Malaysian Tourism Promotion Board (MTPB) operates a **tourist office** in most major towns (Mon–Fri 8am–12.45pm & 2–4.15pm, Sat 8am–12.45pm), but is not that useful for areas off the beaten track. Locally run **Visitor Centres**, found in most major towns, are more geared up to independent travellers' needs. You can also book permits and accommodation for the **national parks** at these centres.

The best general **maps** of Malaysia are Macmillan's 1:2,000,000 Malaysia Traveller's Map and the more detailed Nelles 1:650,000 West Malaysia (not including Sabah and Sarawak). The best detailed relief map of Sarawak is the Land and Survey Department's 1:500,000 issue, available in the bookshop at the Kuching *Holiday Inn;* also good is the Periplus 1:1,000,000 Sarawak map – it was updated in 2000, so be sure not to buy the old one. The best coverage of Sabah is on maps produced by Nelles. **City maps** can usually be picked up in the Visitor Centres.

Getting around

Public **transport** in Malaysia is extremely reliable, though not as cheap as in other Southeast Asian countries. Buses and long-distance taxis are most useful on the Peninsula. Getting around in Sarawak has become easier with the sealing of the coast road, though you may still have to use boats and perhaps the odd plane. There is no boat service between Peninsular Malaysia and East Malaysia, so you'll have to fly. For a rough idea of frequency and duration of transport between major towns, check the "Travel details" at the end of the chapter.

■ Buses

Inter-state destinations are covered by comfortable, air-conditioned **express buses**, operated either by the government's Transnational, or by state or private bus companies; each company has an office at the bus station which is where you buy your ticket. Since prices are fairly similar on all routes, it matters little which company you opt for.

Buses for long-distance routes (over 3hr) typically leave in clusters in the early morning and late evening, while shorter routes are served throughout the day. In most cases you can just turn up, though on popular routes like KL to Penang (8hr; RM18.50), or Kuantan to Singapore, you should reserve ahead. Local buses usually operate from a separate station, serve routes within the state, and are cheaper, but also slower, less comfortable and without air-conditioning; buy your ticket on the bus.

Several buses run across Sabah, but they are outnumbered by the more uncomfortable, and seldom faster, **minibuses** that leave when full, from the same terminals; Kota Kinabulu to Sandakan will cost RM15 by bus and RM20 by minibus. Landcruisers, outsized jeeps, are also common; they take eight passengers and cost less than a taxi but more than a bus. Modern air-con buses in Sarawak ply the trans-state coastal road between Kuching and the Brunei border, via Sibu (RM30), Bintulu and Miri (RM70).

■ Long-distance taxis

Most towns in Peninsular Malaysia have a **long-distance taxi** rank. The four-seater taxis are generally very reliable and a lot quicker than the buses; they charge fixed-price fares which are 50–100 percent more than the regular bus fare (KL to Butterworth costs RM30, KL to Kota Bharu RM35). You have to wait until the car is full, but this is rarely long in big towns. As a foreigner you may be pressured to charter the whole car (at four times the one-person fare).

■ Trains

The Peninsula's **train** service, operated by Keretapi Tanah Melayu (KTM), is limited, relatively expensive and very slow. However, it is the best way to reach some of the more interesting places in the interior. A free timetable for the whole country is available from major train stations.

There are only **two main lines** through Peninsular Malaysia, both originating in Thailand at the southern town of Hat Yai. The west coast route from Thailand via Padang Besar on the Malaysian border runs south through Butterworth (for Penang), Ipoh, Tapah Road (for the Cameron Highlands) and KL, where you usually have to change trains before continuing on to Singapore. Between KL and Singapore the train route splits at Gemas, 58km northeast of Melaka, from where a second line runs north through the mountainous interior – a section known as the jungle railway – via Kuala Lipis and skirting Kota Bharu to the northeastern border town of Tumpat. East Malaysia's only rail line is the bone-shaking 55-kilometre link between Kota Kinabalu and Tenom in Sabah; only the stretch between Beaufort and Tenom is worth considering (see p.659).

Express trains run on the west coast line only and stop at principal stations; ordinary trains, labelled *M* on the timetables, run on both lines and stop at virtually every station. Both trains have three classes: second-class is fine for most journeys, and the only real advantage of first-class travel is the air-conditioning; third-class is more crowded. On overnight sleepers, there's only first- and second-class available, though you can opt for air-con or not in second class. From KL to Butterworth costs RM67/34/19 for 1st/2nd/3rd class travel on an express train and RM58/25/14 on an ordinary train. Seat reservations must be made at the station, not by phone.

Eurotrain International offers an **Explorer Pass** to all under 26 years, students and 30s with an ISIC, HI or Young Scot card, but you'll have to travel almost exclusively by train to get your money's worth. This is valid for unlimited second-class train travel on KTM in Peninsular Malaysia and Singapore, but not in

Sabah, for 7 (£25/US$40), 14 (£33/US$52) or 21 (£41/US$66) days. It's available from Campus Travel in London, or from student-oriented travel agents in Kuala Lumpur and Singapore.

■ Ferries and boats

Ferries sail to all the major islands off Malaysia's east and west coasts, but during the monsoon (Nov–Feb), east-coast services are vastly reduced. There are no ferry services from the Peninsula to East Malaysia, so you'll have to fly. Once you're **in Sarawak**, the most usual method of travel is by turbo-charged express boat along the river systems; they run to a fairly regular timetable. On the smaller tributaries, travel is by longboat, which you may have to charter. This mode of travel can get very expensive, as diesel prices multiply alarmingly the further into the interior you travel. Increasingly, however, longboat travel is becoming obselete as isolated riverside longhouse communities are getting connected to the road network – mostly by way of logging tracks hacked out of the jungle by timber concessionaires. This makes them accessible by 4WD and trucks, if not yet by buses, taxis and cars. **Sabah** has no express boats, but regular ferries connect Pulau Labuan with its west-coast towns. Ferries **to Indonesia and the Philippines** from eastern Sabah ports are being increasingly used by travellers.

■ Planes

The Malaysian national airline, MAS, operates a wide range of **domestic flights**: from KL to Langkawi (RM135) takes just 55 minutes, thus saving an eleven-hour bus journey followed by an hour's ferry ride. Night tourist flights can reduce the price of a flight from KL to Alor Setar from RM113 to RM57. Also, between Peninsular Malaysia and East Malaysia and between Sabah and Sarawak, three or more passengers travelling together get a fifty percent discount; for other routes in Malaysia, a 25 percent discount applies (book seven days ahead). Blind or disabled passengers can get a fifty percent discount; only students studying in Malaysia get reductions.

If you buy an international MAS flight, you can get a **Discover Malaysia Pass**: £62/US$99 for up to five free flights within one of Malaysia's three sectors (Sarawak, Sabah and the Peninsula) and £125/US$199 for five flights in any of these three. The passes are valid for 28 days; dates can be changed for free and you can alter the route for US$25. Flights to East Malaysia operate mainly out of Kuala Lumpur, with Johor Bahru providing additional services to Kuching and Kota Kinabalu. Within Sarawak and Sabah, there are numerous nineteen-seater Twin-Otter and Fokker flights from Miri to other towns in the state's northern interior, like Bario, Ba Kalalan, Lawas and Limbang. Small aircraft also fly from Kota Kinabalu to Kudat, Sandakan and Tuwau.

■ Vehicle rental

The condition of the roads in Peninsular Malaysia is generally excellent, making **driving** there a viable prospect for tourists, though not so in Sabah and Sarawak where the roads are rougher and susceptible to flash flooding.

Malaysians drive on the left, and wearing seat belts in the front is compulsory. Malaysian drivers flash their headlights when they are claiming the right of way, *not* the other way around, as is common practice in the West. The **speed limit** is 110km/hr on highways, 90km/hr on trunk roads, and 50km/hr in built-up areas; speed traps are common and fines are RM200. **Fuel** costs just over RM1 (25p/38 sen) a litre. The North–South Highway is the only toll road – you can reckon on paying approximately RM1 for every 7km travelled.

To rent a vehicle, you must be 23 or over and have held a clean driving licence for at least a year; a national driving licence should be sufficient. Avis, Budget, Hertz and National have offices in major towns and at the airports (book two days ahead). **Rates** start at RM165 (£42/US$68) per day or RM700 (£175/US$262) per week; local companies charge the same.

Motorbike rental is more informal, usually offered by guesthouses and shops in touristy areas (RM20–30 per day). You may need to leave your passport as a deposit, but it's unlikely you'll have to show any proof of eligibility – officially you must be over 21 and have an appropriate driving licence. Wearing helmets is compulsory. **Bicycles** can be rented for about RM4 a day.

Accommodation

Accommodation in Malaysia is not the cheapest in Southeast Asia, but double rooms for under RM25 (£4.50/US$7) are common. East Malaysia is a little more expensive: Sabah is the pricier of the two states – you'll often have to pay RM40 (£7/US$11) for a very ordinary place there. Official **youth hostels** in Malaysia are often hopelessly far-flung and

no cheaper than the guesthouses, and there are few official campsites.

A single room usually contains one double bed, while a double has two double beds or two single beds. Room rates can rise dramatically during the major holiday periods – Christmas, Easter and Hari Raya – but as a general rule it's always worth bargaining. At the budget end of the market you'll have to share a bathroom. Older places sometimes have mandi (see "Basics" p.38) instead of showers.

The mainstay of the travellers' scene in Malaysia are the **guesthouses**, now increasingly being called "backpackers'", located in popular tourist areas and usually good places to meet other people and pick up information. They can range from simple beachside A-frame huts to modern multistorey apartment buildings. Almost all offer dormitory beds (RM7) and basic double rooms (from RM15). Prices on the east coast can drop to as little as RM10 for a double room, but on the islands you'll get nothing for less than RM25.

The **cheapest hotels** in Malaysia are usually Chinese-run and cater for a predominantly local clientele. They're generally clean and there's never any need to book in advance, but they can be noisy and some of the cheapest ones double as brothels (especially those called *Rumah Persinggahan*). Ordinary rooms start at RM20 and will have a wash-basin, fan and a hard mattress; there's usually an air-con option too. Bathrooms are shared.

Mid-range hotels have sprung mattresses, en-suite bathrooms, air-con and TV. Prices range from RM40 to RM100, but a genuine distinction is made between single rooms and doubles. Also in the mid-range category are the excellent-value Government Resthouses (*Rumah Rehat*): rooms are large, en suite and well equipped. In many towns they have been replaced by *Seri Malaysia* hotels, which offer a uniformly good standard for RM100 per night.

High-class hotels are as comfortable as you might expect. Prices can be as reasonable at RM100–150, but rates in popular destinations such as Penang can rocket to RM300. They're always cheaper if booked as part of a package. Prices often include an all-you-can eat buffet breakfast. Since the economic slump of the late 1990s many large hotels are finding it hard to reach capacity, so it's worth asking if any promotions are going – you can pick up a great room officially priced at around RM250 for as little as RM70.

The most atmospheric accommodation in Malaysia is in the stilted **longhouses**, found on the rivers of Sarawak and Sabah. These can house dozens of families, and usually consist of three elevated sections reached by a simple ladder. The snag is that it's getting increasingly hard to stay in them as an independent traveller – most tourists can only stay at longhouses as part of an organized tour. Also, the traditional, wooden longhouse design is fast disappearing and being replaced by more utilitarian concrete – although still long – structures.

Electricity in Malaysia is supplied at 220 volts, and plugs have three prongs like British ones.

Food and drink

Malaysian cuisine is inspired by its three main communities, Malay, Chinese and Indian. The standard of cooking is extremely high and food everywhere is remarkably good value. Basic noodle- or rice-based meals at a street stall will cost just a few dollars, and a full meal with drinks in a reputable restaurant will seldom cost more than RM40 a head.

■ The cuisines

Malay cuisine is based on rice, often enriched with *santan* (coconut milk), which is served with a dazzling variety of curries, vegetable stir-fries and sambals, a condiment of chillies and shrimp paste.

The most famous dish is **satay** – virtually Malaysia's national dish – which is skewers of barbecued meat dipped in spicy peanut sauce. The classic way to sample Malay curries is to eat **nasi campur**, a buffet (usually served at lunchtime) of steamed rice supplemented by any of up to two dozen accompanying dishes, including *lembu* (beef), *kangkong* (greens), fried chicken, fish steaks and curry sauce, and various vegetables. Ather popular dish is **nasi goreng** (mixed fried rice with meat, seafood and vegetables). For breakfast, the most popular Malay dish is **nasi lemak**, rice cooked in coconut milk and served with *sambal ikan bilis* (tiny fried anchovies in hot chilli paste).

In Sabah, there's the Murut speciality of *jaruk* – raw wild boar fermented in a bamboo tube, but the most famous Sabah dish is *hinava*, or raw fish pickled in lime juice. **In Sarawak**, you're most likely to eat with the Iban, sampling wild boar with jungle ferns and sticky rice. A particular favourite in Kuching are bamboo clams, small pencil-shaped slivery delicacies which only grow in the wild in mangrove-dense riverine locations. These are called "monkey's penises" by the locals.

Typical **Nonya dishes** incorporate elements from Chinese, Indonesian and Thai cooking. Chicken, fish and seafood form the backbone of the cuisine, and unlike Malay food, pork is used. Noodles (*mee*) flavoured with chillies, and rich curries made from rice flour and coconut cream, are common. A popular breakfast dish is *laksa*, noodles in spicy coconut soup served with seafood and beansprouts, lemon grass, pineapple, pepper, lime leaves and chilli. Other popular Nonya dishes include *ayam buah keluak*, chicken cooked with Indonesian "black" nuts; and *otak-otak*, fish mashed with coconut milk and chilli and steamed in a banana leaf.

Chinese food dominates in Malaysia – fish and seafood is nearly always outstanding, with prawns, crab, squid and a variety of fish on offer almost everywhere. Noodles, too, are ubiquitous, and come in wonderful variations – thin, flat, round, served in soup (wet) or fried (dry). Malaysians eat *mee* any time of the day or night, and a particular favourite is a dish called *hokkien mee*: fat, white noodles with tempe in a rich soy sauce whipped up in three minutes flat by a wok chef at the side of the road. The dominant style is Cantonese and the classic lunch is *dim sum*, a variety of steamed and fried dumplings served in bamboo baskets. Standard dishes include chicken in chilli or with cashew nuts; buttered prawns, or prawns served with a sweet and sour sauce; spare ribs; and mixed vegetables with tofu (beancurd) and beansprouts. For something a little more unusual, try a steamboat, a Chinese-style fondue filled with boiling stock in which

A FOOD GLOSSARY

GENERAL TERMS

Menu	*Menu*	Hot (temperature)	*Panas*
Fork	*Garpu*	Hot (spicy)	*Pedas*
Knife	*Pisau*	I don't eat meat or	*Saya tak makan daging*
How much is it?	*Berapa harga?*	fish	
Cold	*Sejuk*	I want to pay	*Saya nak bayar*

NOODLES (*MEE*) AND NOODLE DISHES

Bee hoon	Thin rice noodles, like vermicelli	*Laksa*	Noodles, beansprouts, fish-cakes and prawns in a spicy coconut soup
Char kuey teow	Flat noodles with prawns, sausage, fishcake, egg, vegetables or chilli	*Mee*	Standard round yellow noodles made from wheat flour
Foochow noodles	Steamed and served in soy and oyster sauce	*Mee suah*	Noodles served dry and crispy
Hokkien fried mee	Yellow noodles fried with pork, prawn and vegetables	*Wan ton mee*	Roast pork, noodles and vegetables served in a light soup containing dumplings
Kuey teow	Flat noodles, like tagliatelle		

RICE (*NASI*) DISHES

Claypot	Rice topped with meat, cooked in an earthenware pot over a fire	*Nasi goreng*	Fried rice with diced meat and veg
Daun pisang	Banana-leaf curry, a southern Indian meal with chutneys and curries	*Nasi lemak*	A Malay classic: fried anchovies, cucumber, peanuts and fried or hard-boiled egg slices served on coconut rice
Nasi campur	Rice served with several meat, fish and vegetable dishes	*Nasi puteh*	Plain boiled rice

MEAT, FISH AND BASICS

Ayam	Chicken	*Garam*	Salt	*Ikan*	Fish
Babi	Pork	*Goreng*	Fried	*Kambing*	Mutton
Daging	Beef	*Gula*	Sugar	*Kepiting*	Crab

you cook meat, fish, shellfish, eggs and vegetables; or a claypot – meat, fish or shellfish cooked over a fire in an earthenware pot.

North Indian food tends to rely more on meat, especially mutton and chicken, and breads – *naan*, *chapatis*, *parathas* and *rotis* – rather than rice. The most famous style of north Indian cooking is *tandoori* – named after the clay oven in which the food is cooked. A favourite breakfast is *roti canai* (pancake and *daal*) or *roti kaya* (pancake spread with egg and jam). **Southern Indian** food tends to be spicier and more reliant on vegetables. Its staple is the *dosai* (pancake), often served at breakfast time as a *masala dosai*, stuffed with onions, vegetables and chutney. Indian Muslims serve the similar *murtabak*, a grilled *roti* pancake with egg and minced meat. Many south Indian cafés serve *daun pisang* at lunchtime, usually a vegetarian meal where rice is served on banana leaves with vegetable curries. It's normal to eat a banana-leaf meal with your right hand, though restaurants will always have cutlery.

■ Where to eat

To eat inexpensively go to **hawker stalls**, traditionally simple wooden stalls on the roadside, with a few stools to sit at. They serve standard Malay noodle and rice dishes, satay, Indian fast food like *roti canai*, plus more obscure regional delicacies. Most are scrupulously clean, with the food cooked in front of

Makan	Food	Sotong	Squid	Telor	Egg
Minum	Drink	Sup	Soup	Udang	Prawn
Sayur	Vegetable	Tahu	Tofu (beancurd)		

OTHER SPECIALITIES

Char siew pow	Cantonese steamed bun stuffed with roast pork in a sweet sauce		and steamed in a banana leaf
Chay tow kueh	An omelette made with white radish and spring onions	Popiah	Chinese spring rolls; sometimes known as *Lumpia*
Gado gado	Malay/Indonesian salad of lightly cooked vegetables, boiled egg, slices of rice cake and a crunchy peanut sauce	Rendang	Dry, highly spiced coconut curry with beef, chicken or mutton
		Rojak	Indian fritters dipped in chilli and peanut sauce
Murtabak	Thick Indian pancake, stuffed with onion, egg and chicken or mutton	Roti canai	Layered Indian pancake served with curry sauce or *daal*; also called *roti pratha*
Otak-otak	Fish mashed with coconut milk and chilli paste	Steamboat	Raw vegetables, meat or fish dunked into a steaming broth

DESSERTS

Bubor cha cha	Sweetened coconut milk with pieces of sweet potato, yam and tapioca balls	Es kachang	Shaved ice with red beans, jelly, sweetcorn, rose syrup and evaporated milk
Cendol	Coconut milk, palm syrup and pea-flour noodles poured over shaved ice	Pisang goreng	Fried banana fritters
		Pisang murtabak	Banana pancake

DRINKS

Air minum	Water	Kopi susu	Coffee with milk	Teh susu	Tea with milk
Bir	Beer	Lassi	Sweet or sour yoghurt	Teh tarik	Sweet, frothy, milky tea
Jus	Fruit juice				
Kopi	Coffee	Teh	Tea		
Kopi-o	Black coffee	Teh-o	Black tea		

you. Avoid dishes that look as if they've been standing around, or have been reheated, and you should be fine. Hawker stalls don't have menus and you don't have to sit close to the stall you're patronizing: find a free table, and the vendor will track you down when your food is ready. You may find that the meal should be paid for when it reaches your table, but the usual form is to pay at the end. Most outdoor stalls open at around 11am, usually offering the day's nasi campur selection; prices are determined by the number of dishes you choose on top of your rice, usually about RM2–3 per portion. Hawker stalls generally close well before midnight.

Few streets exist without a *kedai kopi*, a **coffee house or café**, usually run by Chinese or Indians.

Most open at 7am or 8am; closing times vary from 6pm to midnight. Basic Chinese coffee houses serve noodle and rice dishes all day, as well as cakes. The culinary standard might not be very high, but a filling one-plate meal costs a couple of dollars. If available, full meals of meat, seafood and vegetables cost about RM5.

On the whole, proper **restaurants** are places to savour particular delicacies found nowhere else, like shark's-fin dishes, bird's-nest soup, and high-quality seafood. In many restaurants, the food is not necessarily superior to that served at a good café or hawker stall – you're just paying for air-con and tablecloths. Tipping is not expected and bills arrive complete with service charge and government tax. In the main, restaurants are open from 11.30am to 2.30pm and from 6 to 10.30pm.

■ Drinking

Tap water is safe to drink in Malaysia, though it's wise to stick to bottled water (RM2 a litre) in rural areas, and in Sarawak and Sabah. Using ice for drinks is generally fine, too, making the huge variety of seasonal fresh fruit drinks, available in hawker centres and street corners, even more pleasant. You'll often find that sweet condensed milk is added to tea and coffee unless you ask for it without. In city centres look out for the sweetened soy milk and sugar cane juice touted on street corners.

Only in certain places on the east coast of the Malaysian Peninsula is drinking alcohol outlawed. Elsewhere, despite the Muslim influence, alcohol is available in bars, restaurants, Chinese *kedai kopi*, supermarkets and sometimes at hawker's stalls. Anchor and Tiger **beer** (lager) are locally produced and are probably the best choice, although Carlsberg and Heineken are being marketed heavily. Locally produced whisky and rum are cheap enough, too, though pretty rough. The **brandy**, which is what some local Chinese drink, tends to be better. **Wine** is becoming more plentiful and competitively priced too. There is a thriving bar scene in KL, Kuching and Penang; less so in other towns. Fierce competition keeps happy hours a regular feature (usually 5–7pm), bringing the beer down to around RM5.00 a glass. Some bars open all day (11am–11pm), but most tend to double as clubs, opening in the evenings until 2 or 3am. All night clubs are a relatively new development, and again liberal licencing seems to apply.

Communications

Overseas **mail** takes four to seven days to reach its destination. Packages are expensive to send, with surface/sea mail taking two months to Europe, longer to the USA, and even air mail taking a few weeks. There's usually a shop near the post office which will wrap your parcel for RM5 or so. If you leave your letter or package unsealed, the postage will be cheaper. Each Malaysian town has a General Post Office, with a poste restante/general delivery section, where mail is held for two months. GPOs also forward mail (for one month), free of charge, if you fill in the right form. See "Basics" p.39 for advice on poste restante.

There are **public telephone boxes** in most towns in Malaysia; local calls cost 10 sen for an

> **TIME DIFFERENCES**
> Malaysia is eight hours ahead of GMT, sixteen hours ahead of US Pacific Standard Time, thirteen ahead of Eastern Standard Time, and two hours behind Sydney.

unlimited amount of time. For long-distance calls, it makes sense to use a **card phone**, either the ubiquitous Uniphone (yellow), the green Cityphone, or the widespread government Kadfon (blue). Cards of RM5, RM10, RM20 and RM50 are sold at Shell and Petronas stations, newsagents and most *7-Elevens*. Note that the Uniphone only takes RM20 or RM50 cards. Check for an international logo on the phone booth before dialling overseas. To **call abroad** from Malaysia, dial ☎007 + IDD country code (see "Basics" p.40) + area code minus first 0 + subscriber number.

You can also use your BT or AT&T chargecard in Malaysia. **Collect (reverse charge) calls** can be made from hotels or from a **Telekom** office (open office hours), though these are found only in larger towns. In KL, Penang and Kota Kinabalu there are also **Home Country Direct** phones – press the appropriate button and you'll be connected with your home operator, who can either arrange a collect call or debit you. Many businesses in Malaysia have mobile phone numbers; they are prefixed ☎011 or 010 and are expensive to call.

Internet cafés are plentiful and often found in smaller places, as well as major towns. Many hostels and guesthouses also provide internet access, as do top-of-the-range hotels. Prices are very competitive, ranging between RM3 and RM10 per hour. Connections are invariably excellent.

Opening hours and festivals

Shops are open daily 9am–7pm and shopping centres 10am–11pm. **Government offices** work Mon–Thurs 8am–12.45pm & 2–4.15pm, Fri 8am–12.15pm & 2.45–4.15pm, Sat 8am–12.45pm; however, in the states of Kedah, Kelantan and Terengannu, on Thursday the hours are 8am–12.45pm, they're closed on Friday and open on Sunday. **Banking hours** are generally Mon–Fri 10am–3pm and Sat 9.30–11.30am. **Post offices** are open Mon–Sat 8am–6pm. During major holiday periods it can be difficult to get a seat on public transport or a room in a hotel, particularly over Ramadan and during Chinese New Year.

■ Festivals

Three great religions – Islam, Buddhism and Hinduism – are represented in Malaysia, and they play a vital role in the everyday lives of the population. Some **religious festivals** are celebrated at home or in the mosque or temple. During Ramadan, Muslims fast during the daytime for a whole month, but others are marked with great spectacle. Most of the festivals have no fixed dates, but change annually according to the lunar calendar.

Festivals of interest to tourists include: **Chinese New Year**, when Chinese operas and lion and dragon dance troupes perform in the streets (Jan–Feb); **Thaipusam**, during which entranced Hindu penitents carry elaborate steel arches, attached to their skin by hooks and skewers (especially at KL's Batu Caves; Jan/Feb); **Gawai Dayak**, when Sarawak's Iban and Bidayuk people hold extravagant feasts to mark the end of the harvest, best experienced at the Iban longhouses on the Ai, Skrang and Lemanak rivers near Kuching (June) and in Bidayuh communities around Bau; the **Dragon Boat Festival** in Penang, Melaka and Kota Kinabalu (June/July); the **Festival of the Hungry Ghosts**, Yue Lan, when there are many free performances of Chinese opera and wayang, or puppet shows (late Aug); **Navarathiri**, when Hindu temples devote nine nights to classical dance and music in honour of the deities (Sept–Oct); and the **Kota Belud Tamu Besar**, Sabah's biggest annual market, which features cultural performances (Oct/Nov).

Cultural hints

Malaysia shares the same attitudes to dress and social taboos as other **Southeast Asian cultures**; see "Basics" p.41 for details.

Diving and trekking

The crystal-clear waters of Malaysia and its abundance of tropical fish and coral make **snorkelling and diving** a must for any underwater enthusiast. This is particularly true of East Sabah's islands, which include Sipadan and Mabul, and the Peninsula's east coast islands of Perhentian, Redang, Kapas and Tioman. Pulau Tioman offers the most choice for schools and dive sites. Dive courses cost from RM650 for a five-day open water course, to RM1200 for a fourteen-day dive master course. Make sure that the dive operator is registered with PADI (Professional Association of Diving Instructors) or

---

PUBLIC HOLIDAYS

January 1: New Year's Day.
January/February: Chinese New Year (2 days).
February/March: Hari Raya Haji.
February: Thaipusam.
March/April: Maal Hijrah (the Muslim New Year).
May: Pesta Kaamatan (Sabah only).
May 1: Labour Day.
May/June: Birthday of the Prophet Mohammed.
June: Gawai Dayak (Sarawak only).
June 4: Yang di-Pertuan Agong's birthday.
August 31: National Day.
November: Deepavali.
December: Hari Raya Puasa.
December 25: Christmas Day.

---

equivalent. Increasingly, it's possible to get a day's worth of diving for a competitive price of around RM80–100, which includes basic training.

The majority of **treks**, either on the Malaysian Peninsula or in Sarawak and Sabah, require some forethought and preparation, and you should be prepared for trails and rivers to become much more difficult to negotiate when it rains. That said, although the rainy season (Nov–Feb) undoubtedly slows your progress on some of the trails, conditions are less humid and the parks and adventure tours not oversubscribed. Most visitors trek in the large national parks to experience the remaining primary jungle and rainforest at first hand. For these you often need to be accompanied by a guide, which can either be arranged through tour operators in Kuala Lumpur, Kuching, Miri and Kota Kinabulu, or at the parks themselves. For inexperienced trekkers, Taman Negara (see p.604) is probably the best place to start, while Sarawak's Gunung Mulu (see p.650) offers sufficient challenges for most tastes, and few people who make it across to Sabah forego the chance of climbing Mount Kinabalu, not a task to be undertaken lightly, however. Details of essential trekking equipment are given in each relevant account.

Crime and safety

If you lose something in Malaysia, you're more likely to have someone running after you with it than running away. Nevertheless, muggings have been known, and **theft** from dormitories by other tourists is a common complaint In the more remote parts of Sarawak or Sabah there is little crime, and you needn't worry unduly about carrying more cash than usual. If you do need to report a crime in Malaysia, head for the nearest **police station**, where there'll be someone who speaks English – you'll need a copy of the police report for insurance purposes. In many major tourist spots, there are specific tourist police stations. It is very unwise to have anything to do with **drugs** of any description in Malaysia. The penalties for trafficking drugs in or out of either country are extreme – foreigners have been executed in the past.

Medical care and emergencies

The levels of hygiene and **medical care** in Malaysia are higher than in much of the rest of Southeast Asia; staff almost everywhere speak good English and use up-to-date techniques. There's always a pharmacy in main towns, which is well stocked with brand-name drugs. They also sell oral contraceptives and condoms over the counter. Pharmacists can help with simple complaints, though if you're in any doubt, get a proper diagnosis. Opening hours are usually Mon–Sat 9.30am–7pm; pharmacies in shopping malls stay open later. **Private clinics** are found even in the smallest towns; a visit costs around RM30, excluding medication. The **emergency department** of each town's General Hospital will see foreigners for the token fee of RM1, though costs rise rapidly if continued treatment or overnight stays are necessary. See the "Listings" sections at major towns for addresses of pharmacies and hospitals.

History

Malaysia only gained full independence in 1957. Before that, its history was inextricably linked with events in the larger Malay archipelago, from Sumatra, across Borneo to the Philippines.

■ Srivijaya

The development of the Malay archipelago owed much to its location on the shipping route between India and China. The shipping trade flourished as

early as the first century AD, introducing Hindu and Buddhist practices, along with *wayang kulit* (shadow plays), to the region.

The calm channel of the Melaka Straits provided a refuge for ships which were forced to wait several months for a change in the monsoon winds, and from the fifth century onwards a succession of entrepôts (storage ports) was created to cater for the needs of passing vessels.

The mightiest of these entrepôts was **Srivijaya**, whose empire was eminent from the beginning of the seventh century until the end of the thirteenth, eventually encompassing all the shores and islands surrounding the Straits of Melaka. Srivijaya itself (Palembang, in Sumatra) became an important centre for Mahayana Buddhism.

■ The Melaka sultanate

With the collapse of the Srivijayan empire in the thirteenth century came the establishment of the **Melaka Sultanate** by a Palembang prince named Paramesvara.

Melaka was well endowed with a deep, sheltered harbour and grew into an international marketplace. The sultanate forged crucial trading and political agreements with China, Ayutthaya and Majapahit, and, by the sixteenth century, had expanded to include the west coast of the Peninsula as far as Perak, Pahang, Singapore, and most of east-coast Sumatra.

Arab merchants brought Islam to the sultanate and this was adopted as the dominant religion. Meanwhile, the Melaka Sultanate refined Malay into a language of the elite, and it soon became the most widely used language in the archipelago.

■ The Portuguese conquest of Melaka

At the beginning of the sixteenth century, the **Portuguese** set about gaining control of crucial Eastern ports. They attacked Melaka in 1511; Sultan Mahmud Shah fled and was replaced by a colonial administration of 800 Portuguese officers. Despite frequent attacks from upriver Malays, the Portuguese controlled Melaka for the next 130 years, during which period they built numerous churches and converted many locals to Catholicism.

■ The kingdom of Johor

Fleeing Melaka, Sultan Mahmud Shah made for Pulau Bentan in the Riau archipelago, south of Singapore, where he established the first court of **Johor**. When, in 1526, the Portuguese attacked and razed the settlement, Mahmud fled once again, and

---

EMERGENCY PHONE NUMBERS

Police/Ambulance ☎999
Fire Brigade ☎994

it was left to his son, Alauddin Riayat Shah, to found a new court on the upper Johor river, though the capital of the kingdom then shifted repeatedly, during a century of assaults by Portugal and Aceh.

The arrival of the Dutch in Southeast Asia towards the end of the sixteenth century marked a distinct upturn in Johor's fortunes. The court aligned itself firmly with the new European arrivals, and was the supreme Malay kingdom for much of the seventeenth century. But by the 1690s, its empire was fraying under the irrational rule of another Sultan Mahmud, who was eventually murdered in 1699. This marked the end of the Melaka dynasty. In 1721, Bugis People from Sulawesi captured Johor, now based in Riau, installed a Malay puppet sultan, and ruled for over sixty years.

■ The Dutch in Melaka

Already the masters of Indonesia's valuable spice trade, the Vereenigde Oostindische Compagnie (VOC), or Dutch East India Company, successfully laid seige to **Melaka** in 1641. Instead of ruling from above as their predecessors had tried to do, the **Dutch** ensured that each racial group was represented by a *Kapitan*, a respected figure from the community who mediated between his own people and the new administrators.

■ The arrival of the British

At the end of the eighteenth century, Dutch control in Southeast Asia was more widespread than ever, but the VOC's coffers were empty and it faced the superior trading and maritime skills of the **British**. High taxes in Melaka were forcing traders to more economical locations such as the newly established British port of Penang, whose foundation in 1786 heralded the awakening of British interest in the Straits.

When the British East India Company (EIC) moved in on Melaka and the rest of the Dutch Asian domain in 1795, the VOC barely demurred. The British soon founded Singapore as their own regional entrepôt, signing an agreement with the Sultanate of Riau-Johor in 1819. The strategic position and free-trade policy of Singapore instantly threatened the viability of both Melaka and Penang, forcing the Dutch finally to relinquish their hold on the former to the British, and leaving the latter to decline.

The **Anglo-Dutch Treaty** of 1824, which divided territories between the two countries using the Straits of Melaka as the dividing line, split the Riau-Johor kingdom. This was followed in 1826 by the unification of Melaka, Penang and Singapore into one administration, known as the Straits Settlements, with Singapore replacing Penang as its capital in 1832.

The Anglo-Dutch Treaty did not include Borneo, however, and though the EIC discouraged official expansion, British explorer James Brooke (1803–68) managed to persuade the Sultan of Brunei to award him his own area – Sarawak – in 1841, becoming the first of a line of "White Rajahs" that ruled the state until the start of World War II.

■ The Pangkor Treaty

Although settlers had trickled into the Peninsula since the early days of Melaka, new plantations, and the rapidly expanding tin mines, attracted floods of willing **Chinese** workers eager to escape a life of poverty. By 1845, the Chinese formed over half of Singapore's population, while principal towns along the Peninsula's west coast as well as Sarawak's capital, Kuching, became predominantly Chinese.

Struggles between Chinese clan groups were rife, and Malay factions frequently became involved too, causing a string of civil wars, often about control of the tin trade or tax claims. This was not good for trade, and finally the British intervened, at the request of a Perak Malay chief, Rajah Abdullah. On January 20, 1874, the **Pangkor Treaty** was signed between the British and Abdullah, formalizing British intervention in the political affairs of the Malay people.

■ British Malaya

By 1888 the name **British Malaya** had been brought into use. Over subsequent decades, the Malay sultans' powers were gradually eroded, while the introduction of rubber estates made British Malaya one of the most productive colonies in the world.

Each state soon saw the arrival of a Resident, a senior British civil servant whose main function was to act as advisor to the local sultan, but who also oversaw the collecting of local taxes. Agreements along the lines of the Pangkor Treaty were drawn up with Selangor, Negeri Sembilan and Pahang states in the 1880s, and in 1896, these three became bracketed together under the title of the Federated Malay States, with the increasingly important town of Kuala Lumpur made the regional capital.

By 1909, the northern Malay states of Kedah, Perlis, Kelantan and Terengganu – previously under Thai control – were brought into the colonial fold: along with Johor (which joined in 1914) they were grouped together as the Unfederated Malay States and by the outbreak of World War I, British political control was more or less complete. The seat of power was split between Singapore and Kuala Lumpur. Borneo, too, had been brought under British control: the three states of Sarawak, Sabah and Brunei had been transformed into protectorates in 1888.

■ Ethnic rivalries

In the first quarter of the twentieth century hundreds of thousands of immigrants from China and India were encouraged by the British to emigrate to sites across Peninsular Malaysia, Sarawak, North Borneo and Singapore. They came to work as tin miners or plantation labourers, and Malaya's population in this period doubled to four million.

This recruitment drive fuelled resentment among the Malays, who believed that they were being denied the economic opportunities advanced to others. A further deterioration in Malay–Chinese relations followed the success of the mainland Chinese revolutionary groups in Malaya. The educated Chinese, who joined the Malayan Communist Party (MCP) from 1930 onwards, formed the backbone of the politicized Chinese movements after World War II, which demanded an end to British rule and to what they perceived as special privileges extended to the Malays. In response, the Malays established the Singapore Malay Union, which gradually gained support in Straits Settlement areas where Malays were outnumbered by Chinese. It held its first conference in 1939 and advocated a Malay supremacist line.

■ Japanese occupation

By February 1942, the whole of Malaya and Singapore was in **Japanese** hands and most of the British were POWs. The Japanese regime brutalized the Chinese, largely because of Japan's history of conflict with China: up to fifty thousand people were tortured and killed in the two weeks immediately after the British surrender of Singapore. Allied POWs were rounded up into prison camps, and many were sent to build the infamous "Death Railway" in Burma and Thailand.

In Malaya, the occupiers ingratiated themselves with some of the Malay elite by suggesting that after the war the country would be given independence. Predictably, it was the Chinese activists in the MCP, more than the Malays, who organized resistance during wartime.

The Japanese invaded Sarawak in late 1941, and, once again, the Chinese were the main targets. In North Borneo, the Japanese invaded Pulau Labuan on New Year's Day, 1942, and over the next three years the main suburban areas were bombed by the Allies. By the time of the **Japanese surrender** in September 1945, most of Jesselton (modern-day KK) and Sandakan had been destroyed.

The Japanese surrender on September 9, 1945 led to a power vacuum in the region, with the British initially left with no choice but to work with the Chinese activisits, the **Malayan People's Anti-Japanese Army** (MPAJA), to exert political control. Violence occurred between the MPAJA and Malays, particularly towards those accused of collaborating with the Japanese.

■ The federation of Malaya

Immediately after the war, the British updated the idea of a **Malayan union** – a position halfway towards full independence – which would make the Chinese and Indian inhabitants full citizens and give them equal rights with the Malays.

This quickly aroused **opposition** among the Malays, with Malayan nationalists forming the United Malays National Organization (UMNO) in 1946. Its main tenet was that Malays should retain their special privileges, largely because they were the region's first inhabitants.

The idea of union was subsequently replaced by the **Federation of Malaya**, established in 1948, which upheld the power of the sultans and brought all the regional groupings together under one government, with the exception of Chinese-dominated Singapore, whose inclusion would have led to the Malays being in a minority. Sarawak and North Borneo were made Crown Colonies of Britain.

■ The emergency

In Peninsular Malaya many **Chinese** were angered by the change of the status of the country from a colony to a federation, in which they effectively became second-class citizens. According to the new laws, non-Malays could only qualify as citizens if they had lived in the country for fifteen out of the last twenty-five years, and they also had to prove they spoke Malay or English.

More Chinese began to identify with the **MCP**, which, under its new leader, **Chin Peng**, wanted to set up a Malayan republic. Peng established guerrilla cells deep in the jungle, and, from June 1948, launched sporadic attacks on rubber estates, killing planters and employees, and spreading fear among rural communities.

The period of unrest, which lasted from 1948 to 1960, was referred to as the **Emergency**, rather than a civil war, which it undoubtedly was. The

British were slow to respond until lieutenant-general Sir Harold Briggs enacted the resettlement of 400,000 rural Chinese – mostly squatters who had moved to the jungle borders to escape the Japanese – as well as thousands of Orang Asli seen as potential MCP sympathizers in 400 "New Villages", scattered across the country. This made both Chinese and Orang Asli more sympathetic to the idea of a Communist republic replacing British rule.

The **violence** peaked in 1950 with ambushes and attacks on plantations near Ipoh, Kuala Kangsar, Kuala Lipis and Raub, and the assassination of the British high commissioner to Malaya. In 1956, Peng and most of the remaining cell members fled over the border to Thailand where they received sanctuary; some still live there and only formally admitted defeat in 1989.

■ Towards independence

Although UMNO stuck to its "Malays first" policy, in 1955 the new leader, Tunku Abdul Rahman, forged a united position between UMNO, the moderate Malayan Chinese Association (MCA) and the Malayan Indian Association. This merger was called the Alliance, and it was to sweep into power under the rallying cry of **Merdeka** (Freedom) for an **independent Malaya**.

With British backing, Merdeka was promulgated on August 15, 1957. The first Prime Minister was Tunku Abdul Rahman. The **new constitution** allowed for the nine Malay sultans to alternate as king, and established a two-tier parliament – a house of elected representatives and a Senate with delegates from each of the states. Although the system was, in theory, a democracy, the Malay-dominated UMNO remained by far the most influential party. Rahman committed the country to economic expansion and full employment, and foreign investment was encouraged.

After full self-government was attained by **Singapore** in 1959, its leader Lee Kuan Yew wanted Singapore and Malaya to be joined administratively. Rahman initially agreed, although he feared the influence of pro-Communist extremists in Singapore's ruling People's Action Party (PAP). He campaigned hard for the inclusion of Sarawak and North Borneo in a revised federation, to act as a demographic balance to the Chinese in Singapore.

■ Federation and the Konfrontasi

In September 1963, North Borneo (quickly renamed Sabah), Sarawak and Singapore joined Malaya in the **Federation of Malaysia**. Both Indonesia, which laid claim to Sarawak, and the Philippines, which argued it had jurisdiction over Sabah, reacted angrily. Although the Philippines backed down, Indonesia didn't, and border skirmishes known as the **Konfrontasi** ensued. Indonesian soldiers crossed the border, and only the arrival of British and Gurkha troops averted a wider war.

Differences soon developed between Lee Kuan Yew and the Malay-dominated Alliance party over the lack of egalitarian policies. Tensions rose in Singapore and ugly racial incidents developed into full-scale riots in 1964. Rahman decided it would be best if Singapore left the Federation, and Singapore duly acquired full independence on August 9, 1965.

The **exclusion of Singapore** from the Malaysian Federation was not enough to quell the ethnic conflicts. Resentment built up among the Chinese over the principle that Malay be the main language taught in schools and over unfair job opportunities.

In 1969, the UMNO (Malay)-dominated Alliance lost regional power in parliamentary elections, and Malays in major cities reacted angrily to a perceived increase in power of the Chinese. Hundreds of people, mostly Chinese, were killed and injured in the **riots** which followed. Rahman kept the country under a state of emergency for nearly two years, using the draconian Internal Security Act (ISA) to arrest and imprison activists, as well as many writers and artists.

■ The New Economic Policy

Rahman resigned in 1971, handing over to the new Prime Minister, Tun Abdul Razak, also from UMNO, who took a less authoritarian stance – although still implementing the ISA. He brought the parties in Sarawak and Sabah into the political process and initiated a broad set of directives, called the **New Economic Policy** (NEP). This set out to restructure the management of the economy so that it would be less reliant on the Chinese. **Ethnic Malays** were classed as *bumiputras* (sons of the soil) and given favoured positions in business, commerce and other professions.

■ Contemporary Malaysia

For the last two decades, Malaysian politics has been dominated by the present prime minister, **Dr Mahathir Mohammed**, who, like all previous PMs, leads the UMNO party; he has triumphed at every election since winning his party's nomination in 1981. **UMNO** is the dominant party in a coalition, the

Barisan National (BN), which includes representatives from the other mainstream Chinese and Indian parties.

Many Malays have got richer through the NEP's blatantly racist system of opportunities, such as tax, educational and financial breaks, but their share of the economy still stands at just twenty percent. In 1991, the supposedly less iniquitous **New Development Policy** succeeded the NEP, though it still favours *bumiputras*.

The main voice of opposition has been the **Islamic Fundamentalist Party**, PAS, which wants to bring strict Islamic law into force in **Kelantan**. In a Muslim country, Mahathir cannot be seen to be too un-Islamic in opposing PAS outright. Instead, he has done little to assist the economy of Kelantan, which remains the poorest state in Malaysia. The **1999 general election** re-asserted BN's strong grip over the nation, but PAS made some significant gains, most notably taking Terengganu, a state which previously had been solidly behind the BN. The economic hardship that many Malaysians endured during the Southeast Asian **financial crisis** of 1997 is cited by some observers as the reason why voters turned away from the ruling party.

Mahathir may not have met with any substantial internal opposition, but some of Malaysia's **economic policies** have been condemned internationally. **Logging** and development projects, such as the now-ditched Bakun Dam hydro-electric scheme, in particular, have brought severe criticism. Currently, logging is actually on the decrease, but critics say that within thirty years forests will cover less than twenty percent of the surface of the country, instead of the current sixty percent.

The issue which has harmed Mahathir most, however, concerns his personal dealings with his former second-in-command, deputy prime minister **Anwar Ibrahim**. Dr Mahathir began to see Anwar as a threat, and, in a manner which shocked many Malaysians and much of the democratic world, Anwar was imprisoned in 1998, awaiting trial on charges of homosexual misconduct and political mismanagement. By early 2000, he had not been proved conclusively guilty of either, but still remained behind bars. His wife Azizah Wan Ismail leads the Keadilan Reform Party, which made a minor impact in the 1999 election, winning a handful of seats. The Anwar issue has succeeded in rallying some disparate opposition forces, but not to any potent effect. Now that the Malaysian economy is regaining its strength, Mahathir's hold on the political scene looks for the time being unassailable.

The mid-Nineties' government plan to turn Malaysia into a fully developed country by the year 2020 is now back as a viable policy after the eonomic worries of the last four years; to all intents and purposes, Malaysia is already a Newly Industrialized Economy. But many observers wonder how Malaysia can continue to expand its economy *and* maintain full employment, and suspect that certain skeletons in the closet, particularly the ethnic distrust which has characterized the country's recent past, will return to haunt it when factors such as the likelihood of recession start to bite.

Religions of Malaysia

The vast majority of Malaysians are Muslims, but there are also significant numbers of Hindus, Buddhists, Confucianists and animists among the population. For an introduction to all these faiths, see "Basics" p.47.

Islam in Malaysia today is a mixture of Sufi and Wahabi elements and as such is relatively liberal. Although most Muslim women wear traditional costume, especially headscarves, very few adopt the veil, and some taboos, like not drinking alcohol, are ignored by a growing number of Malays. There are stricter, more fundamentalist Muslims – in Kelantan the local government is dominated by them – but in general Islam here has a modern outlook, blending a vibrant, practising faith with a business-minded approach.

Hinduism arrived in Malaysia long before Islam, and Sufi Islam integrated some of its beliefs, including the tradition of pluralist deity worship, which accounts for the strong cultural importance of festivals like Deepavali and Thaipusam. Malaysian Chinese usually consider themselves either Buddhist, Taoist or Confucianist, although in practice they are often a mixture of all three.

Although many of Malaysia's ethnic groups are now nominally Christian or Muslim, many of their old **animist beliefs and ceremonies** still survive. Birds, especially the hornbill, are of particular significance to the Iban and the Kelabit peoples in Sarawak. Many Kelabit depend upon the arrival of migrating flocks to decide when to plant their rice crop, while Iban hunters still interpret sightings of the hornbill and other birds as good or bad omens. For the Orang Asli groups in the interior of the Peninsula, most of their remaining animist beliefs centre on healing and funeral ceremonies.

Peoples of Malaysia

Largely because of its pivotal position on the maritime trade routes between the Middle East, India and China, present-day Malaysia has always been a cultural melting-pot, attracting Malays from what is now Sumatra, Indians, and Chinese. But the region already contained many indigenous tribes, **Orang Asli** ("the first people"), thought to have migrated here around 50,000 years ago from the Philippines, which was then connected by a land bridge to Borneo and Southeast Asia.

On the Peninsula, the Malays still form just over fifty percent of the population, the Chinese number nearly 38 percent, Indians ten percent and the Orang Asli around one percent; in Sarawak and Sabah, on the other hand, the indigenous tribes account for around fifty percent of the population, the Chinese 28 percent, with the other 22 percent divided amongst Malays, Indians and Eurasians.

■ The Malays

The **Malays**, a Mongoloid people believed to have originated from the meeting of Central Asians with Pacific islanders, first moved to the west coast of the Malaysian Peninsula from Sumatra in early times. But it was the growth in power of the Malay sultanates from the fifteenth century onwards – coinciding with the arrival of Islam – that established Malays as a significant force. They developed an aristocratic tradition, courtly rituals and a social hierarchy which still have an influence today.

The main contemporary change for Malays in Malaysia was the introduction, some time after independence, of the *bumiputra* policy, which was designed to make it easier for the Malays, the Orang Asli of the Peninsula, and the Malay-related indigenous groups in Sarawak and Sabah, to compete in economic and educational fields against the high-achieving Chinese and Indians. But as the policy has developed, it's only really been the Malays who have gained, taking most of the top positions in government and in state companies.

■ The Chinese and Straits Chinese

It was in Melaka in the fifteenth century that the first significant **Chinese** community established itself. However, the ancestors of the majority of Chinese now living in Peninsular Malaysia emigrated from southern China in the nineteenth century to work in the burgeoning tin-mining industry. In Sarawak and Sabah, Chinese played an important part in opening up the interior. Chinatowns developed throughout the region, and Chinese traditions became an integral part of a wider Malayan culture. The Malaysian Chinese are well represented in parliament and occupy around a quarter of the current ministerial positions.

One of the few examples of regional intermarrying is displayed in the Peranakan or "Straits-born Chinese" heritage of Melaka and Penang. When male Chinese immigrants married local Malay women, their male offspring were termed "Baba" and the females "Nonya". Baba–Nonya society, as it became known, adapted elements from both cultures to create its own traditions: the descendants of these sixteenth-century liaisons have a unique culinary and architectural style. Most follow Chinese Confucianism and speak a distinct Malay dialect.

■ The Indians

The first large wave of **Tamil** labourers arrived in the nineteenth century to build the roads and railways and to work on the rubber estates. But an embryonic entrepreneurial class from **north India** soon followed and set up businesses in Penang; because most were Muslims, they found it easier to assimilate with the Malay community than the Hindu Tamils did. Although Indians comprise only ten percent of Malaysia's population their impact is felt everywhere. The festival of Deepavali is a national holiday, and Indians dominate certain professional areas like medicine and law. Despite this, in general Indians are second to the bottom of the economic ladder, higher only than the Orang Asli.

■ The Orang Asli

The **Orang Asli** – the indigenous peoples of Peninsular Malaysia – mostly belong to three distinct groups, within which there are various tribes. Though most tribes retain some cultural traditions, government drives have encouraged many tribespeople to settle and work within the cash economy.

The largest of the groups is the **Senoi** (pop. 40,000), who live in the forested interior of Perak, Pahang and Kelantan states, and divide into two main tribes, the Semiar and the Temiar. They follow animist customs and practise shifting cultivation. The dark-skinned, curly haired **Semang** (or Negritos; pop. 2000) live in the northern areas of the Peninsula and share a traditional nomadic, hunter-gatherer culture. The so-called **Aboriginal Malays** live south of the Kuala Lumpur–Kuantan road. This group includes the Jakun, who live around Tasek Chini, and the Semelais of Tasek Bera, both of which have retained their animist religion and artistic traditions and are among the easiest of the Orang Asli to approach, since some work in the two lakes' tourist industries.

■ Sarawak's peoples

Nearly fifty percent of **Sarawak's population** is made up of various indigenous Dayak and Orang Ulu groups – including the Iban, Bidayuh, Kayan, Kenyah, Kelabit and Penan tribes, many of whom live in longhouses and maintain a rich cultural legacy.

The **Iban**, a stocky, rugged people, make up nearly one-third of Sarawak's population. They originated in the Kapuas valley in Kalimantan, and migrated north in the sixteenth century. Nowadays, Iban longhouse communities are found in the Batang Ai river system in the southwest, and along the Rajang, Katibas and Baleh rivers. These communities are quite accessible, their inhabitants always hospitable and keen to show off their traditional dance, music, textile-weaving, blow-piping, fishing and game-playing. In their time, the Iban were infamous head-hunters, but, these days, this tradition has been replaced by that of *berjelai*, or "journey", whereby a young man leaves the community to prove himself in the outside world – returning to his longhouse with television sets, generators and outboard motors, rather than heads.

The southernmost of Sarawak's indigenous groups are the **Bidayuh**, who traditionally lived away from the rivers, building their longhouses on the sides of hills. Culturally, they are similar to the Iban.

Most of the other groups in Sarawak are classed as **Orang Ulu** (people of the interior). They inhabit the more remote inland areas, on the upper Rajang, Balui, Baram and Linau rivers. The most numerous, the **Kayan** and the **Kenyah**, are longhouse-dwellers, animists and shifting cultivators. They are also considered to be the most artistic of Sarawak's people, with many excellent painters and musicians among them.

The **Kelabit** people live in longhouses on the highland plateau which separates north Sarawak from Kalimantan and are Christian. The semi-nomadic **Penan** live in the upper Rajang and Limbang areas and rely on hunting and gathering. They are lighter skinned, largely because they live within the shade of the forest, rather than on the rivers and in clearings. The state government's resettlement programme – a controversial policy not entirely unconnected with the logging industry – is now largely complete, and few Penan still live their traditional lifestyle.

■ Sabah's peoples

The **Dusun**, or Kadazan/Dusun, account for around a third of Sabah's population. Traditionally agriculturists, they inhabit the western coastal plains and the interior. Although most Dusun are now Christians, remnants of their animist past are still evident, most obviously in the harvest festival. The mainly Muslim **Bajau** tribe drifted over from the southern Philippines some two hundred years ago, and now constitute ten percent of Sabah's population, living in the northwest. They are agriculturists and fishermen, noted for their horsemanship and their rearing of buffalo. The **Murut** inhabit the area between Keningau and the Sarawak border, in the southwest. They farm rice and cassava by a system of shifting cultivation, and, at times, still hunt using blowpipes and poison darts.

Books

Malaysia has for over one hundred years offered a vivid subject for writers. Below is a selection of the most entertaining and informative works available. Publishers' details for books published in the UK and US are given in the form "UK publisher/US publisher" where they differ; if books are published in one of these countries only, this follows the publisher's name. "O/p" means "out of print".

Charles Allen, *Tales from the South China Seas* (Futura/David Charles, o/p). Memoirs of the last generation of British colonists, in which predictable Raj attitudes prevail, though some of the drama of everyday lives is evinced with considerable pathos.

Barbara Watson Andaya and Leonard Andaya, *The History of Malaysia* (Macmillan/St Martin's Press, o/p in UK). This standard text on the region takes a fairly even-handed view of Malaysia, and finds time for cultural coverage.

Noel Barber, *War of the Running Dogs* (Arrow, UK, o/p). Illuminates the Malayan Emergency with a novelist's eye for mood.

Odoardo Beccari, *Wanderings in the Great Forests of Borneo* (OUP, o/p in US). Vivid turn-of-the-century account of the natural and human environment of Sarawak.

Isabella Bird, *The Golden Chersonese* (OUP/Century, o/p). Delightful epistolary romp through old Southeast Asia, penned by the intrepid Bird, whose adventures in the Malay states in 1879 included elephant-back rides and encounters with alligators.

Margaret Brooke, *My Life in Sarawak* (OUP, UK, o/p). Engaging account of nineteenth-century Sarawak by White Rajah Charles Brooke's wife, which reveals a sympathetic attitude to her subjects and an unprejudiced colonial eye.

Anthony Burgess, *The Long Day Wanes* (Minerva/Norton). Burgess's Malayan trilogy – *Time for a Tiger*, *The Enemy in the Blanket* and *Beds in the East* – published in one volume, provides a witty and acutely observed vision of 1950s Malaya, underscoring the racial prejudices of the period.

Iskandar Carey, *The Orang Asli* (OUP, o/p). The only detailed anthropological work on the indigenes of Peninsular Malaysia.

Spencer Chapman, *The Jungle is Neutral* (Mayflower/Royal Publications, o/p). This riveting first-hand account of being lost, and surviving, in the Malay jungle during World War II reads like a breathless novel.

Mark Cleary & Peter Eaton, *Borneo Change and Development* (Penerbit Fajar Bakti, Malaysia). A very readable composite of Bornean history, economy and society, that's rounded off by a section dealing with issues such as logging, conservation and the future of the Penan.

GWH Davison & Chew Yen Fook, *A Photographic Guide to Birds of Peninsular Malaysia and Singapore* (New Holland/ R.Curtis). Well-keyed and user-friendly, these slender volumes carry oodles of glossy plates that make positive identifying a breeze. The companion volume, *A Photographic Guide to Birds of Borneo*, is also excellent.

Peter Dickens, *SAS The Jungle Frontier* (Lionel Leventhal). Gripping account of British special forces involvement in the Malayan Emergency.

CS Godshalk, *Kalimantaan* (Abacus). Recent novel based around the life of James Brooke, the first White Rajah. A brilliantly written story very faithful to the cultural facts of nineteenth-century Sarawak.

Eric Hansen, *Stranger In The Forest* (Abacus/Houghton Mifflin o/p). A gripping book, the result of a seven-month tramp through the forests of Sarawak and Kalimantan in 1982, that almost saw the author killed by a poison dart.

Tom Harrisson, *A World Within* (OUP, US, o/p). The only in-depth description of the Kelabit peoples of Sarawak, and a cracking good World War II tale courtesy of Harrisson, who parachuted into the Kelabit Highlands to organize resistance against the Japanese.

Victor T King, *The Best of Borneo Travel* (OUP Blackwell). Compendium of extracts from Bornean travel writing since the sixteenth century; an interesting travelling companion.

Dennis Lau Penans, *The Vanishing Nomads of Borneo* (Lee Ming Press, Malaysia) and *Borneo – A Photographic Journey* (Travelcom Asia). Two brilliant photographic journeys with descriptive texts on Sarawak's indigenous peoples.

Andro Linklater, *Wild People* (John Murray/Grove-Atlantic). As telling and as entertaining a glimpse into the lifestyle of the Iban as you could pack, depicting their age-old traditions surviving amidst the baseball caps and rock posters.

KS Maniam, *The Return* (Skoob, UK); *In A Far Country* (Skoob, UK); *Haunting the Tiger*. The purgative writings of this Tamil-descended Malaysian author are strong, highly descriptive and humorous – essential reading.

W Somerset Maugham, *Short Stories Volume 4* (Mandarin/Penguin). Peopled by hoary sailors and colonials wearing mutton chop whiskers and topees, Maugham's short stories resuscitate turn-of-the-century Malaya; quintessential colonial literature graced by an easy style and a steady eye for a story.

Redmond O'Hanlon, *Into The Heart of Borneo* (Picador/Vintage). A hugely entertaining yarn recounting O'Hanlon's refreshingly amateurish romp through the jungle to a remote summit on the Sarawak/Kalimantan border, partnered by the English poet James Fenton.

Ambrose B Rathborne, *Camping and Tramping in Malaya* (OUP, o/p). Lively nineteenth-century account with insights into the colonial personalities and working conditions of the leading figures of the day.

James Ritchie, *Bruno Masser, The Inside Story* (Summer Times Publishing, Malaysia). Detailed account on the self-styled hero of the Penan in the early years of the 1990s when indigenous people manned barricades in a vain attempt to stop loggers ruining parts of Sarawak.

Spenser St John, *Life in the Forests of the Far East* (OUP, UK). A description of an early ascent of Mount Kinabalu is a highlight of this animated nineteenth-century adventure, written by the personal secretary to Rajah Brooke.

Vinson H Sutlive, *The Iban of Sarawak* (Waveland Press, Malaysia). Academic work exploring the recent history of the largest and most influential of Malaysia's indigenous peoples, after the Malays themselves.

C Mary Turnbull, *A Short History of Malaysia, Singapore & Brunei* (Graham Brash, Singapore). Decent, informed introduction to the region.

Alfred Russel Wallace, *The Malay Archipelago* (OUP/Dover, o/p). Wallace's peerless account of the flora and fauna of Borneo, based on travels made between 1854 and 1862 – during which time he collected over one hundred thousand specimens. Still required reading for nature lovers.

LANGUAGE

The national language of Malaysia is *Bahasa Malaysia*. It's an old language, with early roots in the central and south Pacific, and simple enough to learn. In practice, you'll be able to get by with English in all but the most remote areas. As a general rule, older Malaysians speak better English than younger ones, as English used to be on the curriculum in schools, but is rarely these days.

Nouns have no genders and don't require an article, while the plural form is constructed just by saying the word twice; thus "child" is *anak*, while "children" is *anak anak*. Doubling a word can also indicate "doing"; for example, *jalan jalan* is used to mean "walking". Verbs have no tenses either. Sentence order is the same as in English, though adjectives usually follow the noun.

PRONUNCIATION

The pronunciation of *Bahasa Malaysia* is broadly the same as the English reading of Roman script, with a few exceptions:

a as in c**u**p
c as in **ch**eap
e as in **e**nd
g as in **g**irl
i as in bout**i**que
j as in **j**oy
k hard, as in English, except at the end of the word, when you should stop just short of pronouncing it.

o as in g**o**t
u as in b**oo**t
ai as in f**i**ne
au as in h**ow**
sy as in **sh**ut

GREETINGS AND BASIC PHRASES

Selamat is the all-purpose greeting derived from Arabic, which communicates general goodwill.

Good morning	*Selamat pagi*	Sorry/excuse me	*Maaf*
Good afternoon	*Selamat petang*	No worries/never mind	*Tidak apa-apa*
Good evening	*Selamat malam*	Yes	*Ya*
Good night	*Selamat tidur*	No	*Tidak*
Goodbye	*Selamat tinggal*	What is your name?	*Siapa nama anda?*
Bon Voyage	*Selamat jalan*	My name is...	*Nama saya...*
Welcome	*Selamat datang*	Where are you from?	*Dari mana?*
Bon Appetit	*Selamat makan*	I come from...	*Saya dari...*
How are you?	*Apa kabar?*	Do you speak English?	*Bisa bercakap bahasa*
Fine/ok	*Baik*		*Inggris?*
See you later	*Jumpa lagi*	I don't understand	*Saya tidak mengerti*
Please	*Tolong*	What is this/that?	*Apa ini/itu?*
Thank you	*Terima kasih*	Can you help me?	*Bolekah anda tolong*
You're welcome	*Sama sama*		*saya?*

GETTING AROUND

Where is the...?	*Dimana...?*	Right	*Kanan*
I want to go to...	*Saya mahu naik ke...*	Left	*Kiri*
How far?	*Berapa jauh?*	Straight	*Terus*
How long will it take?	*Berapa lama?*	North	*Utara*
When will the bus leave?	*Bila bas berangkat?*	South	*Selatan*
		East	*Timur*
What time does the train arrive?	*Jam berapa keratapi sampai?*	West	*Barat*
		Street	*Jalan*
Stop	*Berhenti*	Train station	*Stesen keratapi*

Bus station	*Stesen bas*	Restaurant	*Restoran*
Airport	*Lapangan terbang*	Shop	*Kedai*
Ticket	*Tiket*	Market	*Pasar*
Hotel	*Hotel/rumah penginapan*	Taxi	*Teksi*
Post office	*Pejabat pos*	Trishaw	*Becak*

ACCOMMODATION

How much is...?	*Berapa...?*	I'm staying for one night	*Saya mahu tinggal satu hari*
I need a room	*Saya perlu satu bilik*		
Cheap/expensive	*Murah/mahal*	Can I store my luggage here?	*Bisa titip barang?*

GENERAL ADJECTIVES AND NOUNS

Good	*Bagus*	Toilet	*Tandas*
A lot/very much	*Banyak*	Man	*Lelaki*
A little	*Sedikit*	Woman	*Perempuan*
Hot	*Panas*	Water	*Air*
Sweet	*Manis*	Money	*Wang/duit*
Big	*Besar*	Food	*Makan*
Small	*Kecil*	Drink	*Minum*
Closed	*Tutup*	Boyfriend/girlfriend	*Pacar*
Ill/sick	*Sakit*	Husband	*Suami*
Entrance	*Masuk*	Wife	*Istri*
Exit	*Keluar*	Friend	*Kawan*

NUMBERS

0	*Nul*	8	*Lapan*	143	*Seratus empatpuluh tiga*
1	*Satu*	9	*Sembilan*		
2	*Dua*	10	*Sepuluh*	200	*Duaratus*
3	*Tiga*	11	*Sebelas*	1000	*Seribu*
4	*Empat*	12	*Duabelas*	1 million	*Sejuta*
5	*Lima*	20	*Duapuluh*	A half	*Setengah*
6	*Enam*	21	*Dua puluh satu*		
7	*Tujuh*	100	*Seratus*		

TIME AND DAYS OF THE WEEK

What time is it?	*Jam berapa?*	Year	*Tahun*
It's...		Today	*Hari Ini*
three o'clock	*Jam tiga*	Tomorrow	*Besok*
ten past four	*Jam empat lewat sepuluh*	Yesterday	*Kemarin*
quarter to five	*Jam lima kurang seperempat*	Now	*Sekarang*
		Not Yet	*Belum*
six-thirty	*Jam setengah tujuh* (lit. "half to seven")	Never	*Tidak Perna*
7am	*Tujuh pagi*	Monday	*Hari Isnin*
8pm	*Lapan malam*	Tuesday	*Hari Selasa*
Minute	*Menit*	Wednesday	*Hari Rabu*
Hour	*Jam*	Thursday	*Hari Kamis*
Day	*Hari*	Friday	*Hari Jumaat*
Week	*Minggu*	Saturday	*Hari Sabtu*
Month	*Bulan*	Sunday	*Hari Ahad/minggu*

KUALA LUMPUR AND AROUND

Founded in the mid-nineteenth century, **KUALA LUMPUR**, or KL as it's popularly known, is the youngest Southeast Asian capital and the most economically successful after Singapore – and it's still growing: building sites abound and the city is awash with stunning examples of modern architecture, not least the famous Petronas Towers and the recently opened Museum of Islamic Arts. It's not one of Malaysia's most charming cities perhaps: it doesn't have, for example, the narrow alleys, bicycles and mahjong games of Melaka or Kota Bharu or the atmospheric waterfront of Kuching. But it's safe and sociable, and with a population of nearly two million, it's usually exciting in the day and always buzzing with energy at night. From a cultural standpoint, it certainly has enough interesting monuments, galleries, markets and museums to keep visitors busy for at least a week.

KL began life as a swampy staging post for Chinese tin miners in 1857 – Kuala Lumpur means "muddy estuary" in Malay – and blossomed under the competitive rule of pioneering merchants. But as fights over tin concessions erupted across the country, the British used gunboat diplomacy to settle the Selangor Civil War and the British Resident, Frank Swettenham, took command of KL, making it the capital of the state and, in 1896, the capital of the Federated Malay States. Swettenham imported British architects from India to design suitably grand buildings, and thousands of Tamil labourers poured in to build them; development continued steadily through the first quarter of the twentieth century. The Japanese invaded in December 1941, but although they bombed the city, they missed their main targets. Following the Japanese surrender in September 1945, the British were once more in charge in the capital, but Nationalist demands had replaced the Malays' former acceptance of the colonizers, and Malaysian independence – Merdeka – finally came in 1957.

Arrival

KL is at the hub of Malaysia's transport systems. It has the country's main international airport, where you'll have to change if you're flying on to Sarawak or Sabah; buses from all over Peninsular Malaysia converge on one of four bus stations, the train station has connections with Thailand and Singapore, and there are ferries to Sumatra in Indonesia.

By air

The ultra-modern **Kuala Lumpur International Airport** (KLIA) at Sepang is 60km south of the centre. **Airport coaches** (6am–midnight; every 30min; RM25) leave from the bus station on level 1 and take an hour and a half to get to the centre. Follow the clearly marked signs from the arrivals area at Level 4 to the escalators down to the concourse. The coach will drop you directly at your accommodation. Alternatively, from the same concourse take the **local bus** to Nilai train station (6.30am–10pm; every 30min; 40min; RM1.50) and change onto the Komuter Train line (6.30am–10.30pm; 1hr; RM4.70), which terminates at KL train station. From here it's only a short walk north to Chinatown. For both the coach and bus routes buy tickets from the counter in the concourse.

Taxis into the centre cost around RM65 – you'll need to buy a coupon at the taxi counter in the arrivals hall; it's best to avoid the taxi touts, who may charge upwards of RM140, and have been known to demand payment in US, rather than Malaysian, dollars. All the major car rental firms have offices at the airport and there are money exchange outlets here, too.

In 2002, a high-speed rail link should be finished, whisking people from the airport into the heart of KL in 35 minutes and providing an efficient connection with the city's LRT (Light Rail Transit) system.

MOVING ON FROM KUALA LUMPUR

Airport

The easiest way to get to the airport is to call a taxi from your hotel (RM65); taxis flagged down on the street tend not to want to go out that far. Most of the larger hostels can help arrange transport to the airport for around the same price. Otherwise, call the airport coach service (☎03/653 3154), preferably giving a day's notice, to ensure you're picked up from your hotel in good time. Or thirdly, do the Nilai route in reverse: enter KL railway station from Jalan Sambathan; take the Komuter Train from platform 3B (end station Seramban), getting off at Nilai, then change onto the local airport bus from directly outside the station.

Trains

The station's information kiosk (daily 8am–8pm) has up-to-date train timetables; ☎03/274 7443 or 273 8000 for information and reservations. You must book, preferably at least three days ahead, for the night sleeper to Singapore or Butterworth; most large hotels can do this for you.

Buses and long-distance taxis

For long-distance **bus** route information, call the English-speaking Infoline (☎03/230 0300). Most long-distance buses leave from Pudu Raya bus station (☎03/230 0145) on Jalan Pudu, just to the east of Chinatown. The buses leave from ground-floor bays, and ticket offices are on the floor above, along with a left-luggage office (daily 8am–10pm; RM2). Some buses also operate from outside the terminus – these are legitimate, but may only leave when full. **Long-distance taxis** also use Pudu Raya, arriving and departing from the second floor above the bus ticket offices.

For some departures you'll need one of the other bus stations: Putra (☎03/442 9530), near the Putra World Trade Centre, for the east coast; Klang (☎03/230 7694) on Jalan Sultan Mohammed Services for Klang and Port Klang; and Pekeliling (☎03/442 1256) at the northern end of Jalan Raja Laut, for Kuantan and the interior.

Ferries

Ferries to Tanjung Balai, in Sumatra, depart from Port Klang, 38km southwest of KL. Take the Komuter train or a bus from the Klang bus station on Jalan Sultan Mohammed to the port (see p.578).

Trains

Chinatown is ten minutes' walk north of the main **train station**. There are two exits: the west-side one on Jalan Sultan Hishamuddin and the east-side one on Jalan Sambathan. The covered walkway on the east side leads down from the station and ends across from Central Market.

Buses and long-distance taxis

Most long-distance buses pull into **Pudu Raya bus station** (☎03/230 0145) on Jalan Pudu, just to the east of Chinatown. Long-distance taxis also arrive at Pudu Raya, on the second floor above the bus ticket offices.

Some buses from the east coast arrive at **Putra bus station** (☎03/442 9530), to the northwest of the city centre, beside the Putra World Trade Centre. This is handy for the budget hotels on Jalan Raja Laut and in the Chow Kit area. To head downtown, walk down Jalan Putra to The Mall shopping centre, where you should either catch a bus to Central Market on Jalan Hang Kasturi or walk a little further south to the Putra Komuter Station, for trains to Bank Negara and the main train station.

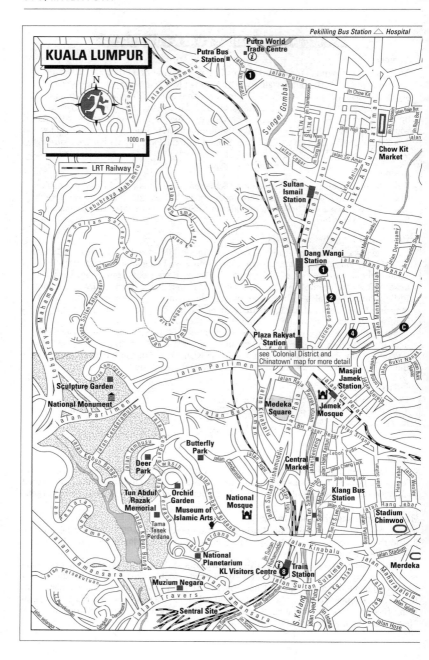

KUALA LUMPUR

N

0   1000 m

━━━ LRT Railway

Pekililing Bus Station △ Hospital

Putra World Trade Centre
Putra Bus Station

Jalan Mahameru

Sungei Gombak

Jin Chow Kit

Chow Kit Market

Jalan Kuching

Sultan Ismail Station

Lebuhraya Mahameru

Dang Wangi Station

Jalan Dang Wangi

Plaza Rakyat Station

see 'Colonial District and Chinatown' map for more detail

Masjid Jamek Station

Sculpture Garden

National Monument

Jalan Parlimen

Medeka Square

Jamek Mosque

Jalan Bukit

Butterfly Park

Deer Park

Central Market

Tun Abdul Razak Memorial

Orchid Garden

Museum of Islamic Arts

National Mosque

Klang Bus Station

Stadium Chinwoo

Taman Tasek Perdana

National Planetarium

KL Visitors Centre

Train Station

Merdeka

Muzium Negara

Sentral Site

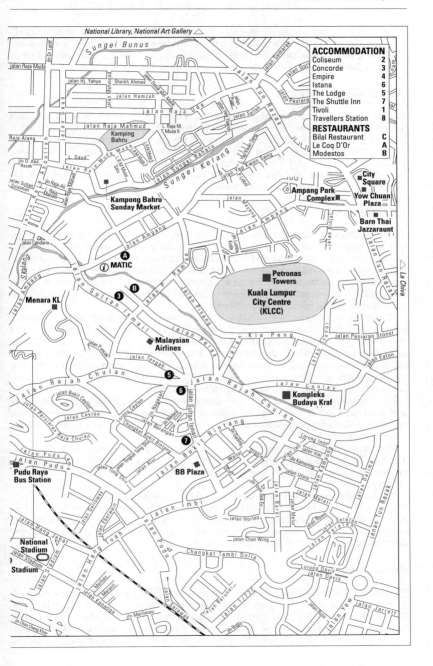

National Library, National Art Gallery △

ACCOMMODATION

Coliseum	2
Concorde	3
Empire	4
Istana	6
The Lodge	5
The Shuttle Inn	7
Tivoli	1
Travellers Station	8

RESTAURANTS

Bilal Restaurant	C
Le Coq D'Or	A
Modestos	B

Services from Kuantan and the interior arrive at **Pekeliling bus station** (☎03/442 1256), at the northern end of Jalan Raja Laut; from here, regular buses head south to Chinatown. The **Klang bus station** (☎03/230 7694) on Jalan Sultan Mohammed, just south of Central Market, is used by Klang Valley buses to and from Klang and Port Klang.

Information and maps

KL has lots of **tourist information centres**, each of which hands out excellent free maps and bus route details. The biggest is MATIC (Malaysian Tourist Information Complex) at 109 Jl Ampang (daily 9am–9pm; ☎03/264 3929), east of the centre, close to the junction with Jalan Sultan Ismail, where you can also book for Taman Negara National Park. The KL Visitor Centre, however (Mon–Fri & Sun 8am–5pm, Sat 8am–12.45pm; ☎03/274 6063), outside the train station's west-side entrance, has a better selection of leaflets and more knowledgeable staff who can also help with accommodation.

City transport

The latest attempt to ease KL's chronic traffic problem is the **Light Rail Transit** (LRT) system, a 29-kilometre, mostly elevated, metro network. There are two lines. LRT1, also known as Star, runs from Ampang, east of the centre, through the Masjid Jamek hub to Sentul Timur in the north of town and Komonwel in the south. LRT2, aka Putra, has the longest stretch of automated metro in the world runnning from west of the centre to the northeast, intersecting with the Star system at Masjid Jamek. Trains on both lines operate every five to fifteen minutes from 6am to midnight (from 75 sen).

KL **city buses** run from 6am to midnight. Costs range from 90 sen on the larger, municipal-owned Intrakota buses to 60 sen on the privately run City Liner ones. Fares go up to just above RM2 depending on the length of the journey; for example, you'll be paying RM2.20 to go to the Batu Caves, which, although outside KL, still comes under the city bus system. If the bus has no conductor, you'll need the exact change. The main depots are Central Market, the Jalan Sultan Mohammed terminus (opposite Klang bus station), 100m south of the market, and Lebuh Ampang, on the northern edge of Chinatown.

If you're planning to stay in KL for more than a week it's worth getting an **integrated bus and train card**, called Touch And Go, available from the main LRT stations. The minimum price is RM20; each fare is eletronically deducted from the sum on your card when you go through the turnstiles.

Taxi fares start at RM1.50 and rise 30 sen per kilometre. To call a cab, use Comfort Radio Taxi Service (☎03/733 0507); Koteksi (☎03/781 5352) or Radio Teksi (☎03/442 0848). Many taxi drivers can't speak English, and some don't know their way around the city, so it's best to carry a map.

The **Komuter train** is of limited use in central KL, but is handy for sights outside the city. There are two lines – one from Rawang to Seremban (for Nilai), the other from Sentul to Port Klang (for Sumatra). Both connect at the central KL stations of Putra, Bank Negara and Kuala Lumpur Railway Station. Trains run at least every 30min and tickets start at RM1; a RM5 day ticket (valid Mon–Fri after 9.30am) allows unlimited travel.

Accommodation

Most travellers head for the **hotels** of Chinatown, though Little India has become a valid budget and mid-range alternative. There are a few inexpensive places close to the Pudu Raya bus station and around Jalan Pudu. Further east, the Golden Triangle is where the first-class hotels are situated. Many of these hotels offer excellent deals, and are worth checking out. West and north of Little India and Chinatown, the hotels along the two-kilometre stretch of

Jalan TAR include some of the sleaziest and most infamous in town. Suffice to say, there's no need to book in advance.

Around Chinatown

Backpackers Travellers Inn, 2nd Floor, 60 Jl Sultan (☎03/238 2473). Centrally located, with small, clean rooms, some air-con, and a dorm (RM15 per bed). Its roof-top bar is a highly convivial spot. There's a book exchange and Internet access too. ②.

Backpackers Travellers Lodge, 1st Floor, 158 Jl Tun HS Lee (☎03/201 0889). Recommended sister operation, with a range of clean rooms, some air-con, and RM15 dorms. Also Internet access. Owner Stevie also runs excellent, inexpensive tours to see the fireflies in Selangor (see p.586). ②.

Furama, Kompleks Selangor, Jl Sultan (☎03/230 1777). Modern air-con hotel with small but comfortable, well-equipped rooms. ⑥.

Leng Nam, 165 Jl Tun HS Lee (☎03/230 1489). In the heart of the quarter, this traditional Chinese hotel has a great atmosphere. Small rooms have two large beds and shared facilities. ②.

Lok Ann, 113a Jl Petaling (☎03/238 9544). Neat, good-value hotel, with full facilities, though the rooms are rather charmless. ④.

Sun Kong, 210 Jl Tun HS Lee (☎03/230 2308). A small, friendly, family-run Chinese hotel. ②.

Travellers Moon Lodge, 36b Jl Silang (☎03/230 6601). Just south of Jl Tun Perak, this popular lodge includes a rather grotty dorm, small rooms and a roof terrace. ②.

Travellers Station, KL train station, Jl Sultan Hishamuddin (☎03/273 5588). Superb, spacious, switched-on backpackers place with Internet access, notice board, washing machines and plenty of information on other parts of Malaysia and South East Asia in general. Owner Indy also does a night tour which takes in Chinese and Indian temples and clubs. ②.

YWCA, 12 Jl Hang Jebat (☎03/230 1623). Delightful, good-value, peaceful hostel which only rents its clean, comfortable singles and doubles to women, couples and families. ②.

Little India and Jalan TAR

Coliseum, 98 Jl TAR (☎03/292 6270). KL's most famous old-style hotel can be a bit noisy, but it oozes atmosphere. ③.

Empire, 48b Jl Masjid India (☎03/293 6890). A good deal, with well-equipped rooms and discounts for longer stays. ③.

Tivoli, 136 Jl TAR (☎03/292 4108). Budget place with clean rooms and shared facilities. ②.

Around Pudu Raya

Kawana Tourist Inn, 68 Jl Pudu Lama (☎03/238 6714). Neat, small, very good-value rooms in a modern place only ten minutes' walk from Pudu Raya bus station. ③.

KL City Lodge, 16 Jl Pudu (☎03/230 5275). Convenient, but can be noisy. Dorms and air-con rooms; laundry service and free lockers. Dorms RM12. ③.

The Golden Triangle

Concorde, 2 Jl Sultan Ismail (☎03/244 2200). The trendiest of the area's hotels, housing the *Hard Rock Café* and fashionable boutiques. Large rooms with full facilities. Price includes breakfast and pick-up from airport. ⑧.

Istana, 73 Jl Raja Chulan (☎03/244 1445). One of KL's best hotels. Palace-like decor, tropical plants, swimming pool and high quality rooms. Price includes breakfast. ⑦.

The Lodge, Jl Sultan Ismail (☎03/242 0122). One of the best-value deals in the Triangle area, with motel-style rooms and swimming pool. ⑤.

The Shuttle Inn, 112b Jl Bukit Bintang (☎03/245 0828). The cheapest, most central decent hotel in the area, with small, but clean, en-suite air-con rooms. ④.

The City

Despite much modernization, much of Kuala Lumpur's appeal – markets, temples and historic mosques – remains untouched. The city centre is quite compact, with the **Colonial District** centred on Merdeka Square; close by, across the river and to the south, **Chinatown** and **Little India** are the two main traditional commercial districts. One of the most promi-

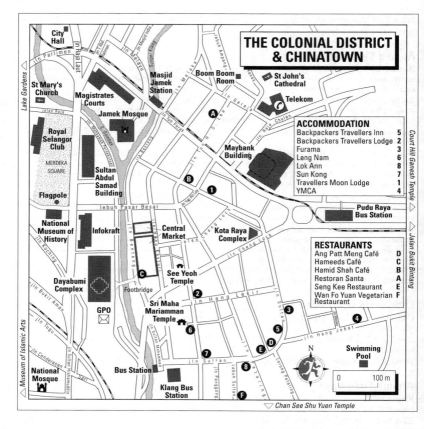

THE COLONIAL DISTRICT & CHINATOWN

ACCOMMODATION

Backpackers Travellers Inn	5
Backpackers Travellers Lodge	2
Furama	3
Leng Nam	6
Lok Ann	8
Sun Kong	7
Travellers Moon Lodge	1
YMCA	4

RESTAURANTS

Ang Patt Meng Café	D
Hameeds Café	C
Hamid Shah Café	B
Restoran Santa	A
Seng Kee Restaurant	E
Wan Fo Yuan Vegetarian Restaurant	F

⬇ Chan See Shu Yuen Temple

nent (and busiest) of KL's central streets, Jalan Tunku Abdul Rahman, or **Jalan TAR**, as it's often known, runs due north from Merdeka Square for 2km to Chow Kit Market; closer in, west of the square, are the **Lake Gardens**, while to the south lie the **Masjid Negara** (National Mosque), the new **Islamic Arts Museum**, the landmark Railway Station and the Muzium Negara (National Museum). From Merdeka Square, the congested Jalan Tun Perak leads southeast to the Pudu Raya bus station, a kilometre further east of which is the **Golden Triangle**. This fashionable consumer sector is delineated by three main roads – Jalan Bukit Bintang, Jalan Imbi and Jalan Sultan Ismail – and contains most of the city's expensive hotels, nightlife locations, modern malls, and the lofty Menara and Petronas Towers which, at just over 490m high, is currently the tallest building in the world.

South and West of Merdeka Square

The small **Colonial District** is centred on the beautifully tended **Merdeka Square** on the west bank of the Klang: Malaysian Independence (*merdeka*, or freedom) was proclaimed here on August 31, 1957. Nearby, to the south, the **National Museum of History** (daily 9am–6pm; free), on the corner of Jalan Raja, provides an informative romp through the main points of the nation's history, from the geological formation of the Peninsula to Prime Minister Mahathir's Vision 2020. South along Jalan Sultan Hishamuddin, the 35-storey Dayabumi Complex is home to the national oil company, Petronas, which maintains the excellent Galeri Petronas, on the ground floor, displaying contemporary Malaysian art.

Continuing south down Jalan Sultan Hishamuddin, you'll see the impressive seventy-metre-high minaret and geometric lattice work of the **Masjid Negara**, the National Mosque (daily 9am–6pm except Fri 2.45–6pm). To enter, you need to be properly dressed: robes can be borrowed from the desk at the entrance. Behind the mosque on Jalan Perdana is the ultra-modern **Museum of Islamic Arts** (Tues–Sun 10am–6pm; RM8). This fascinating collection of textiles, metalwork and ancient Korans is a must-see, as it's the first of its type in the world. Check out the calligraphic section, which includes handwritten sections of the Koran, some dating back a thousand years, and many of them intricate and beautiful.

A hundred metres south, the spires, minarets, domes and arches of the 1911 **train station** is probably the city's most famous building. Ten minutes' walk west along Jalan Damansara brings you to the extensive ethnographic and archeological exhibits of the **Muzium Negara**, Malaysia's National Museum (daily 9am–6pm; RM1). Alongside dioramas of traditional Malaysian life, from simple *kampung* (village) activities to elaborate wedding and circumcision ceremonies, you see wayang kulit (shadow play) puppets, *kris* daggers, and traditional musical instruments.

Once at the National Museum you're only a short walk from the extensive **Lake Gardens** and the interesting **National Planetarium** (Tues–Sun 10am–7pm; RM1), where displays illuminate the Islamic origins of astronomy as well as Malaysia's modern-day thrust for the stars. Also in the park, close to the Orchid Garden, you'll find the excellent **Bird Park** (daily 9am–6pm; RM3), whose walkways loop around streams to take in the habitats of indigenous species such as hornbills and the Brahminy Kite. There are many entrances into the park, but the main one is a thirty-minute walk due west of Merdeka Square along Jalan Parlimen, or you can take bus #21 or #48 from Jalan Sultan Mohammed.

Jamek Mosque, Chinatown and Little India

East of Merdeka Square, on a promontory at the confluence of the Klang and Gombak rivers, stands KL's most attractive devotional building, the **Jamek Mosque**. The mosque was completed in 1909, its pink brick walls, arched colonnades, oval cupolas and squat minarets inspired by Moghul architecture. The main entrance is on Jalan Tun Perak.

Bordered by Jalan Tun Perak to the north and Jalan Petaling to the east, **Chinatown**'s narrow lanes still reveal dilapidated shop-houses and Chinese pharmacies. After 6pm, Jalan Petaling is closed to vehicles and the entire area is transformed into a *pasar malam* (night market). The area's largest temple, **Chan See Shu Yuen** stands at the far southern end of Jalan Petaling and displays an ornately painted inner shrine covered in scenes of mythical creatures battling with warriors. The intricately carved roof depicts monumental events in Chinese history and mythology.

KL's main Hindu focus, **Sri Maha Mariamman Temple**, is also located in the heart of Chinatown, on Jalan Tun HS Lee, between the two main Buddhist temples. First built in 1873, it was radically renovated in the 1960s with a profusion of statues on and around the five-tiered gate tower. The temple is free and always open. One hundred metres due west of Jalan Tun HS Lee lies the Art-Deco **Central Market** (daily 9am–10pm). Over a hundred stalls here sell everything from textiles to stationery, fine art to tee shirts. On the first floor is one of KL's best food courts, which serves excellent Indian and Malay food.

Just to the north of Chinatown, compact Little India is the commercial centre for KL's Indian community. Turning into Jalan Masjid India from Jalan Tun Perak, it's soon clear you've entered the Tamil part of the city, with *poori* and *samosa* vendors and cloth salesmen vying for positions on the crowded streets.

Chow Kit and Jalan Tun Razak

Two kilometres due north of Central Market along Jalan TAR lies **Chow Kit**, a daily market which sells anything and everything. There are excellent hawker stalls here, a great variety of textiles and clothes, as well as fish, meat and vegetables. Close by on the orbital highway, Jalan Tun Razak, you'll find the National Art Gallery (daily 10am–6pm; free), recently relocated here, which houses a disappointing permanent collection of Malaysian artists alongside temporary exhibitions of fine art and mixed media from a wider net of Southeast Asian artists.

Eating

All the **restaurants** listed below are open daily from 10am until midnight, unless otherwise stated. Phone numbers are given where you need to book ahead. Most **Malay** restaurants in KL serve a limited range of dishes, so for a wider selection you'll need to dine out at one of the big hotels, many of which offer special buffets. Finding good **Chinese** or **Tamil** and **North Indian** food is much easier: it's served in cafés and restaurants in both Chinatown and Little India. In Little India especially, the cafés and hawker stalls do a manic trade at lunchtime in excellent banana-leaf curries, *murtabak*, *dosai* and *roti*. The trendiest area in KL to eat and drink in the evening is **Bangsar**, around 4km west of the centre, with over a dozen top-notch restaurants, two hawkers' areas – one inside a giant hangar, the other in the adjoining street.

Chinatown and Little India

Ang Patt Meng Café, 97 Jl Petaling, Chinatown. Typical cheap Chinese café, serving morning noodles and, after midday, *nasi campur* with meat, fish and vegetable dishes.

Bilal Restaurant, 33 Jl Ampang. At the city-centre end of Jl Ampang, this north Indian restaurant is particularly popular for its chicken and mutton curries. About RM20 for two.

Central Market, 1st and 2nd Floors, Jl Hang Kasturi. Best are the superb Malay stalls on the top floor where plates of *nasi campur* cost just RM2.

Hameeds Café, Ground Floor, Central Market, Jl Hang Kasturi, Chinatown. Superb, busy, north Indian café serving tandoori chicken, curries and rice dishes.

Hamid Shah Café, 30 Jl Silang, Chinatown. Excellent, busy café for Malay and North Indian curries and *roti*. Very good value at around RM10–12 for two. Open 8am–6pm.

Lakshmi Villas, Lebuh Ampang, Little India. On the edge of Chinatown, this is the best south Indian café in KL. The ground floor serves various delicious *dosais*; the first floor specializes in banana-leaf curries, a bargain at around RM6 for two. Daily 7am–7pm.

Restoran Santa, 7 Jl Tun HS Lee (Little India end). Nicknamed the "chapati house", a lively place, best at midday to mid-afternoon, with delicious chapatis and curries for around RM5.

Seng Kee Restaurant, 100 Jl Petaling, Chinatown. Frenetically busy restaurant with great prawn and duck dishes; well priced at around RM25 for two.

Wan Fo Yuan Vegetarian Restaurant, Jl Panggong, Chinatown. The area's best-known vegetarian restaurant serving excellent tofu and vegetable dishes.

Golden Triangle

Le Coq D'Or, 121 Jl Ampang (☎03/242 9732). Housed in a converted tin *towkay*'s mansion. It's worth coming for a drink on the verandah, even if you don't want to sample the French, Malay and Chinese cuisine (RM40 a head). Dress smartish.

Modestos, Lorong Perak, just off Jl P Ramlee (☎03/248 9924). Sprawling pizza and pasta joint with a lively bar.

Rasa Utara, BB Plaza, Jl Bukit Bintang. Northern Malay menu: try the *ayam percik*, a hot, sour chicken dish from the state of Kelantan. Moderately priced.

Seri Angkasa, Menara KL (☎03/208 5055). Revolving restaurant which serves an excellent lunch, high tea and dinner buffets atop KL's landmark tower. Smart dress (no shorts and sandals) essential for dinner, which costs around RM55 a head.

Bangsar

Alexis Bistro, 29 Jl Telawi Tiga (☎03/284 2880). Big helpings of designer food for KL's growing cappuccino class. Excellent pastries at a buzzy hangout.

Annalakshmi, 46 Jl Maarof (☎03/282 3799). Sensational Indian restaurant with a very wide choice of dishes from across the sub-continent.

Kah Koh Seafood, Jl Telawi 5 (opposite Bangsar Seafood Village). Busy Chinese favourite and an institution among *metsallehs* ("foreigners") and KL foodies. The chilli and cashew chicken dishes are a must.

Nightlife and entertainment

Most **bars** are open from noon until midnight. The music played at **clubs** is mostly US house and the lighter styles of techno. Entrance charges of around RM20 include one drink. The best place to see **traditional theatre** and **music** is at the Malaysian Tourist Information Complex (MATIC), 109 Jl Ampang (☎03/243 4929), which does costumed shows (Tues, Thurs, Sat & Sun at 3.30pm; RM2).

Bars and live music

Barn Thai, 370b Jl Tun Razak (☎03/244 6699). Spicy Thai food followed by some of the best live jazz that KL offers.

Bull's Head, Central Market, Jl Benteng. A very busy bar, popular with expats, tourists and business people alike. Closes at midnight.

La Chiva, 1b Jl Utara. If you're into lively South American and Caribbean music, this is the top dance spot in KL. Also serves salsa-type food.

Echo, Jl Telawi 2, Bangsar. Neon, quite minimal, but with comfortable sofas, this is a great bar for mid-evening through to the early hours. Local DJs provide a hopping soundtrack with jazz earlier and house music later on.

Hard Rock Café, *Concorde Hotel*, 2 Jl Sultan Ismail. Features well-known rock bands and gets packed on Friday and Saturday nights – cover charge if not eating. Open 11am–midnight.

Riverbank, Central Market, Jl Benteng. Well-placed bar, opposite the river; occasional music.

Clubs

Backroom, Lorong Shangri-La, behind the *Shangri La Hotel*, Golden Triangle. Although a poor venue, international DJs play house, techno and drum 'n bass here to a packed mixed bohemian crowd. Thurs–Sat 10pm–6am.

Baze-2, Yow Chuan Plaza, Jl Tun Razak. Happening club frequented by KL's well-heeled youth; soul, reggae and funk played. Open 9pm–3am.

Blue Moon, *Hotel Equatorial*, Jl Sultan Ismail (opposite the MAS Building). Popular with KL's gay crowd, the only place where you'll hear Malaysian golden oldies from the 1950s, French schmaltz and the golden-voiced P Ramlee. Open 7pm–midnight.

Boom Boom Room, 11 Lebuh Ampang. Another gay hangout, where thumping house music and a twice-nightly drag show create a winning combination. Probably KL's most popular mainstream night club. Daily 8pm–3am.

Liquid, Central Market annexe. With its young, gay and friendly weekend crowd, this superb, small atmospheric club is a must for house music fans in town. Open Fri & Sat 10pm–3am.

Markets and shopping

Most of KL's malls are open daily from 10am to 10pm; elsewhere, shops are usually open daily from 9am to 6pm. However, most locals do their shopping at the **markets**. The Central Market is among the most popular (see p.581); the nearby Jalan Petaling market (daily 9am–10pm) is equally crowded and lively; and the sprawling Chow Kit on Jalan Haji Hussein, off Jalan TAR (daily 9am–5pm), is quite an experience, with its warren of stalls selling everything from animals' brains to quality batik textiles. There's a good weekly night market at Pasar Minggu, Jalan Raja Muda Musa, Kampung Bharu (Sat 6pm–1am).

Recommended outlets for **handicrafts and batiks** include Aked Ibu Kota on Jalan TAR, opposite the Coliseum; Central Market on Jalan Hang Kasturi, where you can see the craftsmen at work; Infokraft, Jalan Sultan Hishamuddin, which deals in work by government-sponsored craftmakers; Kompleks Budaya Kraf, Jalan Conlay, which offers all of Malaysia's crafts under one roof, beside the museum; and Wisma Batek, Jalan Tun Perak, where shirts, sarongs, bags and paintings are inexpensive. More upmarket is Peter How, 2 Jl Hang Lekir, a stone's throw from Central Market, with beautiful bags, batik shirts and sarongs, as well as locally made and Indonesian crafts.

For English-language **books** try Berita Book Centre, Bukit Bintang Plaza; MPH, Jalan Telawi Lima, Bangsar; Times Books, Yow Chuan Plaza, Jalan Ampang; Minerva Book Store, 114 Jl TAR; and Yaohan Book Store, second floor, The Mall, Jalan Putra. KL is full of **shopping malls**, especially in the Golden Triangle, where you'll find BB Plaza on Jalan Bukit Bintang, which has excellent deals on cameras, electronic equipment, shoes and much else besides. Lot 10 Shopping Centre, junction of Jalan Bukit Bintang and Jalan Sultan Ismail, specializes in designer clothes, sportswear and music.

Listings

Airlines Most airlines have offices in and around the Golden Triangle. Major airlines include: Aeroflot, Ground Floor, 1 Jl Perak (☎03/261 3331); American Airlines, Angkasa Raya Building, 123 Jl Ampang (☎03/242 4311); Bangladesh Airlines, Subang Airport (☎03/248 3765); British Airways, Wisma Merlin, Jl Sultan Ismail (☎03/242 6177); Cathay Pacific, UBN Tower, 10 Jl P Ramlee (☎03/238 3377); China Airlines, Level 3, Amoda Building, 22 Jl Imbi (☎03/242 7344); Delta Airlines, UBN Tower, 10 Jl P Ramlee (☎03/291 5490); Garuda, 1st Floor, Angkasa Raya Building, 123 Jl Ampang (☎03/262 2811); Japan Airlines, 20th Floor, Jl Ampang, Menara Lion (☎03/261 1728); KLM, Shop 7, Ground Floor, President House, Jl Sultan Ismail (☎03/242 7011); MAS, MAS Building, Jl Sultan Ismail (☎03/261 0555); Pelangi Air, c/o MAS (☎03/262 4448); Qantas, UBN Tower, 10 Jl P Ramlee (☎03/238 9133); Royal Brunei, 1st Floor, Wisma Merlin, Jl Sultan Ismail (☎03/230 7166); Singapore Airlines, Wisma SIA, 2 Jl Sang Wangi (☎03/292 3122); Thai International, Kuwasa Building, 5 Jl Raja Laut (☎03/293 7100); United Airlines, MAS Building, Jl Sultan Ismail (☎03/261 1433).

Banks and exchange Main branches are: Bank Bumiputra, Menara Bumiputra,Jl Melaka (☎03/298 8011); Bank of America, 1st Floor, Wisma Stephens, Jl Raja Chulan (☎03/202 1133); Hongkong and Shanghai Bank, 2 Lebuh Ampang, Little India (☎03/230 0744); Maybank, 100 Jl Tun Perak (☎03/230 8833); Standard Chartered Bank, 2 Jl Ampang (☎03/232 6555). Almost all of their branches change money (Mon–Fri 10am–4pm, Sat 9am–12.30pm), but you get better rates from official moneychangers, of which there are scores in the main city areas; the kiosk below the General Post Office, on Jl Sultan Hishamuddin, also gives good rates.

Car rental All main companies have offices at the airport; or contact Avis, 40 Jl Sultan Ismail (☎03/241 7144); Budget, 29 Jl Yap Kwan Seng (☎03/242 5166); Hertz, International Complex, Jl Sultan Ismail (☎03/243 3433); National Car Rental, 9th Floor, Menara Bausted, 69 Jl Raja Chulan (☎03/248 0522); Pacific, Wisma MCA, Jl Ampang (☎03/263 7748).

Embassies and consulates Australia, Menara Baustead, 69 Jl Raja Chulan (☎03/2465555); Brunei, 113 Jl U Thant (☎03/261 2820); Cambodia, 83-JKR 2809 Lingkungan U Thant (☎03/457-3711); Canada, 7th Floor, Osk Plaza, 172 Jl Ampang (☎03/261 2000); China, 229 Jl Ampang (☎03/242 8495); Indonesia, 233 Jl Tun Razak (☎03/984 2011); Japan, 11 Persiaran Stonor (☎03/242 7044); Laos, 108 Jl Damai (☎03/248 3895); Netherlands, 4 Jl Mesra, off Jl Damai (☎03/248 5151); New Zealand, 193 Jl Tun Razak (☎03/238 2533); Philippines, 1 Jl Changkat Kia Peng, (☎03/248 4233); Thailand, 206 Jl Ampang (☎03/248 8333); UK, 185 Jl Ampang (☎03/248 2122); USA, 376 Jl Tun Razak (☎03/216 5000); Vietnam, 4 Persiaran Stonor (☎03/248 4036).

Emergencies Dial ☎999 for ambulance, police or fire. For the Tourist Police Unit call ☎03/241 5522 or ☎03/241 5243.

Hospitals and clinics General Hospital, Jl Pahang (☎03/292 1044); Assunta Hospital, Petaling Jaya (☎03/778 3433); Pantai, Jl Pantai, off Jl Bangsar, Bangsar (☎03/282 5077); Tung Shin Hospital, Jl Pudu (☎03/232 1655). There are 24-hour casualty wards at all of the above.

Immigration 3rd Floor, Jl Pantai Bahru, off Jl Damansara (Mon–Fri 9am–4.30pm; ☎03/757 8155). This is where you come for visa extensions.

Internet access Adamz Cyber Café, Lot 2, Annexe, Central Market; Cheng Lock Internet, Jl Cheng Lock, Chinatown; Dataran Cyber Café, Ground Gloor, Medan Mara Building, Jl Raja Laut; Easy Access, 146a Jl Bukit Bintang (in front of Planet Hollywood); Golden Date Internet Zone, 1st Floor, City One Plaza, Jl Musha Abdullah; Star Surf, 105 Jl Sultan (opp Rex Cinema); Traveller's E Mail Centre, Room 6, 3rd Floor, Wisma Kwong Siew, 147 Jl Tun HS Lee. In Bangsar, 7km west of the city centre (take any Bangsar bus from Central Market): Poem, 38a Jl Telawi 5; Surf, 54 Jl Maarof.

Pharmacy Kota Raya Pharmacy, 1st Floor, Kota Raya Plaza, Jl Cheng Lock, Chinatown.

Police The Chinatown police station is at the southern end of Jl Tun HS Lee (☎03/232 5044). The main Tourist Police station, where you must report stolen property and claim your insurance form, is 1PK, Jl Hang Tuah (☎03/2302222, ext 259). It's opposite the old Pudu Jail.

Post office Poste restante at the GPO on Jl Sultan Hishamuddin, opposite Central Market (Mon–Fri 8am–4pm, Sat 8am–2pm).

Telephone services The cheapest places to make international calls are the Telekom Malaysia offices; the largest branch is in *Wisma Jothi*, Jl Gereja (daily Mon–Sun 8.30am–9pm).

Travel agencies Reliance Travel, 3rd Floor, Sungei Wang Plaza (☎03/248 6022); STA, 5th Floor, Magnum Plaza, 128 Jl Pudu (☎03/248 9800); Tina Travel, 30 Jl Mamarda, Ampang Point (☎03/457 8877).

Around KL

The biggest attractions **around KL** are north of the city, where limestone peaks rise up out of the forest and the roads narrow as you pass through small kampungs. There is dramatic scenery as close as 13km from the city, where the Hindu shrine at the **Batu Caves** attracts enough visitors to make it one of Malaysia's main tourist attractions. Further north, the Orang Asli Museum offers a fascinating insight into the Peninsula's native inhabitants, and the **Forest Institute of Malaysia** encompasses the nearest portion of primary rainforest to the capital. Southwest of KL, the most alluring place is **Klang**, Selangor's first capital, location of a fascinating tin museum. **Ferries to Sumatra** leave from Port Klang, 8km southwest of Klang. A little further north along the coast, **Kuala Selangor Nature Park** and the fireflies at Kuala Kuantan are worth a visit.

The Batu Caves

Long before you reach the entrance to the **Batu Caves**, you can see them ahead: small, black holes in the vast limestone hills, 13km north of the city centre. Since 1891, the caves have sheltered Hindu shrines, and today they're surrounded by shops selling religious paraphernalia. The caves are always packed with visitors, never more so than during the three-day Thaipusam festival held at the beginning of every year. To the left of the staircase up to the main Temple Cave, a small path strikes off to the Art Gallery (daily 8.30am–7pm; RM1), which contains dozens of striking multicoloured statues and murals, portraying scenes from the Hindu scriptures. At the top of the main staircase, Subramaniam Swamy Temple (daily 8am–7pm) is set deep in a huge cave, its walls lined with idols representing the six lives of Lord Subramaniam. To get to the caves, catch bus #11 from Central Market.

The Orang Asli Museum

Located 24km north of the city, KL's **Orang Asli Museum** (Mon–Thurs & Sun 9am–5.30pm; free) provides a fine illustration of the cultural richness of the Orang Asli ("the first people"), Malaysia's indigenous inhabitants. Orang Asli groups are found in just about every part of the region, many of them maintaining a virtually pre-industrial lifestyle, and pursuing their traditional occupations in some isolation. Bus #174 leaves from Lebuh Ampang in Little India (every 30min; 50min); the museum stop is beside two run-down shops, but ask the driver to tell you when you've arrived.

The Forest Institute of Malaysia

If you don't make it out to Taman Negara and its canopy walkway, you can stroll through the tree-tops at the **Forest Institute of Malaysia**, or FRIM (daily 8am–6.30pm; ☎03/635 9578). Bus #143 from next to the Bangkok Bank takes you there in about an hour (RM1.60). The canopy walkway, ten minutes' walk from the Institute's main building, takes about twenty minutes to cross and provides a unique view of KL's skyscrapers through the trees. As with all hikes into Malaysia's forests, bring plenty of drinking water, insect repellent and decent shoes. There are plenty of other treks within FRIM's fifteen square kilometres, as well as a museum.

Port Klang and on to Indonesia

You can catch a ferry to Tanjung Balai in Sumatra, Indonesia, from **PORT KLANG**, 38km southwest of KL in Selangor State. The six times weekly sailing is at 11am and takes three and a half hours (RM150 plus RM15 dep tax). At Tanjung Balai you can get a free, non-extendable sixty-day visa on arrival. The best way to get to Port Klang is on the Komuter train (every 30min) from KL's train station which stops directly opposite the main jetty. Buses #51, #58 and #225 from Klang bus station in KL (hourly; 1hr) stop 200m further along the road. The jetty complex has a small café and moneychanger.

Kuala Selangor Nature Park and the fireflies

North of Klang is the small **Kuala Selangor Nature Park** (☎03/889 2294), set in partial primary rainforest; the trails are short but lead to hides which are perfect spots to view birds. The park is accessible by bus #14 from KL's Klang bus station (hourly; RM3.90). Three-bed chalets in the park are available for RM45, and there is also accommodation in nearby Kuala Selangor town at *Hotel Kuala Selangor*, 88 Main St (☎03/889 2709; ②).

Ten kilometres away (no bus; RM20 return by taxi from Kuala Selangor) lies Kuala Kuantan, famous for its luminous **fireflies**. It costs RM10 to take a ride in a sampan (small boat) along the river, Sungei Kuantan, at around 8pm, to see the thousands of flies glowing on the river bank.

THE WEST COAST

The west coast of the Malaysian Peninsula, from Kuala Lumpur north to the Thai border, is the most industrialized and densely populated part of the country. Chinese towns punctuate the route north, many of them founded on the tin economy, and this is also the area in which the British held most sway, attracted by the political prestige of controlling such a strategic trading region. Most visitors are too intent on the beckoning delights of Thailand to bother stopping at anything other than the major destinations, and there are plenty of ways to **cross into Thailand**, by boat, bus or train (see p.593 and p.603). You can get Thai visas in **Georgetown**, the vibrant and stimulating capital of the island of **Penang**, which rewards a few days' stay and is a magnet for travellers of all budgets. But before you leave Malaysia, you can chill out happily at the **Cameron Highlands** hill station, or sun yourself on the pretty white-sand shores of popular **Pulau Langkawi**, a large and increasingly upmarket island.

Cameron Highlands

Amid the lofty peaks of Banjaran Titiwangsa, the various outposts of the **CAMERON HIGH-LANDS** (1524m) form Malaysia's most extensive hill station, used as a weekend retreat since the 1920s and still – despite hotels and luxury apartments – quintessentially English in character, its rolling green fields dotted with country cottages, farms and a golf course. Weekenders flock here in their thousands to cool down and go walking in the hills and forests. The highlands encompass three small towns: **Ringlet**, site of the famous tea plantations; 13km beyond and 300m higher, **Tanah Rata**, the principal settlement of the highlands; and 5km further north, **Brinchang**, renowned for its farms. Tours of the whole region are organized by various hostels in Tanah Rata (3hr; RM15). Tanah Rata and Brinchang have the best accommodation, but prices shoot up at peak holiday times. Temperatures drop dramatically at night, so bring warm clothes.

The Cameron Highlands trails take in some of the most spectacular scenery in Malaysia. They are often badly signposted and maintained, though you can get sketch maps at some shops and hostels in Tanah Rata. The best is the black-and-white sketch map ($1), though some of its trails no longer exist. If you want to attempt any unofficial routes, you must go with a guide from the tourist office and you must get a permit from the District Office, just north of Tanah Rata (Mon–Fri 8am–1pm & 3pm–4.30pm, ☎05/491 1105). To get there, go north towards Brinchang, and take the first major right after about 1km. Always inform someone, preferably at your hotel, where you are going and what time you expect to be back. On longer trips take warm clothing, water, a torch and a cigarette lighter or matches for basic survival should you get lost. If someone else doesn't return as expected, inform the District Office.

Getting to the Cameron Highlands

The main access point for the Cameron Highlands is **TAPAH**, which has good **bus links** with major towns (see "Travel Details", p.668). The **train station** is on Tapah Road, a few kilometres west of town and served by hourly local bus or by taxi (RM7) into Tapah. Tapah's **bus station** is on Jalan Raja, off the main street, and is the departure point for buses up to Tanah Rata in the Cameron Highlands (hourly 8.15am–6.15pm; 2hr). When leaving, you can buy long-distance bus tickets, including to Hat Yai in Thailand, from any express-bus agency in town, including Kah Mee, 10 Jl Raja (☎05/412 973), opposite the bus station. If you need a **hotel** in Tapah, try the clean *Hotel Bunga Raya*, 6 Jl Besar (☎05/401 1436; ②) on the corner of the main street and Jalan Raja, or the good-value *Timuran*, 23 Jl Stesen (☎05/401 1092; ②) where you'll pay an extra RM5 or so for a standard double, but will get hot water.

Ringlet

There's not much to **RINGLET**, the first settlement you come to in the Cameron Highlands. The best-known is the **Boh Tea Estate** (Tues–Sun 11am–3pm), 8km northeast of town, which has free tours. Here you can see the whole process, from the picking to the packing of the tea. There are buses from Ringlet to Habu – the junction for the Boh Tea Estate – daily at 6.30am, 11.30am, 3.15pm and 5.15pm, with return journeys at 7.20am, 12.20pm, 3.45pm and 6pm. It's easy enough to get to Ringlet from Tanah Rata: there are four buses a day, starting at 8.30am, with the last service at 1.30pm.

Tanah Rata

Since many of the Cameron Highlands' **walks** start from nearby, the genteel town of **TANAH RATA**, the highlands' main development, is an ideal base. A couple of waterfalls and three reasonably high mountain peaks are all within hiking distance, and the town itself is festooned with white balustraded buildings, flowers and parks. It comprises little more than one street (officially called Jalan Pasar, but usually known as "Main Road"), the location of most hotels, banks and restaurants.

Buses from Tapah terminate at the **bus station** about halfway along the main road, where you'll have to change for local buses to Brinchang and Kampung Raja, the furthest point north. CS Travel, Main Road (☎05/491 1200), sells tickets for express buses from Tapah to all major destinations. You can collect poste restante at the **post office** on Main Road; the **police station** (☎05/491 1222) is on Main Road, opposite the *Garden Inn*; the **hospital** is at the north end of Main Road (☎05/491 1966), and there's a clinic at 48 Main Road (8.30am–12.30pm, 2–5.30pm & 8–10pm). There are a few **Internet** places behind Jalan Perisan Camellia; the best is *Mix House Net* at 76b.

ACCOMMODATION

Cameronian Inn, 16 Jl Mentigi (☎05/491 1327). Friendly, clean and well informed with Internet access and a library. There's a small dorm (RM6) and some double rooms. Trekkers set off from here at 9.30am most mornings, non-guests are welcome at no charge. ①.

Cool Point, just off the main road behind the Shell station (☎05/491 4914). A new hotel in a quiet location, but the large rooms tend to be dark and damp. ⑥.

Father's Guest House (☎05/491 2484). The best of the budgets set on a quiet hill in the outskirts. There are doubles in a stone house and dorm beds (RM7) in funky, tunnel-like aluminium outhouses. There's a large collection of books, a few Internet terminals and very friendly staff. ②.

Heritage, Jl Gereja (☎05/491 3888). Set on a hill near the approach road from Ringlet, the most upmarket hotel in Tanah Rata is very comfortable and has several good restaurants. ⑧.

Orient, 38 Main Rd (☎05/491 1633). Very good value with thoughtfully furnished airy rooms, although it can be noisy during holiday periods. ②.

Seah Meng, 39 Main Rd (☎05/491 1618). Clean, well-kept rooms, very similar to the *Orient* next door. ②.

Twin Pines, 2 Jl Mentigi (☎05/491 2169). Set back from the main road, this blue-roofed building has small doubles, a garden and books full of travellers' tips. There are dorms (RM6), a café and online facilities. ①.

EATING

At night, **food stalls** set up on the main road. Many restaurants serve the local steamboat, which involves dipping raw fish, meat, noodles and vegetables in a steaming broth until cooked.

Bunga Suria, Jl Perisan Camellia. The best south Indian restaurant in Tana Rata and a haven for vegetarians as well as meat eaters.

Excellent Food Centre, on the main road opposite the post office. Lives up to its name with a large, inexpensive menu of Western and Asian dishes – it's great for breakfast. Open during the day only. In the adjacent *Fresh Milk Corner*, you can get wonderful shakes and *lassis* (yoghurt drinks).

Jasmine Restoran, 45 Main Rd. Popular with German and Dutch travellers for its *rijstafel* set meals. It has karaoke in the evenings, which can get a bit rowdy.

Little Grasshopper, 57b Persiran Camellia 3. On the second floor above the new shop-houses. Excellent-value steamboats, starting at just RM6, served by friendly staff in a tasteful setting. Also has traditional Chinese tea.

Orient Restoran, 38 Main Rd. Standard Chinese food in the restaurant below the hotel. The set meals are reasonable value, as are the steamboats.

Restoran Kumar, Main Road. Along with *Thanam* next door, the *Kumar* specializes in clay-pot rice.

Rich Bake Café, Main Road. Bright jazzy spot on the corner, which sometimes has live music; serves good pancakes.

Ye Olde Smokehouse (☎05/491 1215). Halfway to Brinchang from Tanah Rata, just south of the golf course. The hotel opens its restaurant to non-residents, and provides intimate surroundings for a romantic splash-out. The traditional English menu features a choice of roast meat dinners for around RM70, and other dishes start at RM20. You'll need to book in advance. Afternoon tea is RM11.

Brinchang and around

BRINCHANG, 5km north of Tanah Rata, lacks its neighbour's charm, but some of the walks are easily approached from here too, and it's closer to the farms and tea estates further north. You can also hike to the summit of Gunung Brinchang (2032m), a steep two-to-three hour climb along a sealed road, with wonderful views. To get to Brinchang, get a local bus from Tanah Rata (approximately hourly 6.40am–6pm) or a taxi (RM4).

The Sungai Palas Tea Estate (Tues–Sun 8.30am–3pm, tours every 10min; free) is set high in the hills and doesn't attract crowds of people. The tea leaves here are no longer hand-picked, but cut with shears, after which they go to the factory (which you'll be guided round) to be withered, sifted, rolled, fermented and then fired. Buses for the estate leave from Brinchang's bus station, just south of the square, at 9.30am, 11.45am, 1.45pm and 4.15pm. You can also get back by making your own way to the main road (a 20min walk) and picking up one of the more regular Brinchang-bound buses from Kampung Raja. The last bus back from Sungai Palace leaves around 4.40pm.

Most of the **hotels** in Brinchang line the east and west sides of the central square. The only real budget accommodation is *Rafflesia Inn*, Lot 30 Main Road (☎05/491 2859; ②), but the dorm beds (RM10) are a bit hard. The *Silverstar*, 10 Main Rd (☎05/491 1387; ③), is one of the few places in Brinchang where you won't pay over the odds for clean sheets. *Pines and Roses* (☎05/491 2203; ⑤) offers comfortable, clean en-suite accommodation, all with TV. *Kowloon*, 34–35 Main Rd (☎05/491 1366; ⑤) has small, comfortable rooms with TV and bathroom. The *Equatorial Resort*, Kea Farm (☎05/496 1777; ⑧), a luxury resort about 2km north of Brinchang, is the plushest place in the region with lovely views and great-value rooms. As for **food**, *Restoran Sakaya* on Main Road is one of three good budget Chinese eating houses (along with *You ho* and *Kuan Kee*), doing buffet lunches (RM3 for three dishes).

Ipoh

Eighty kilometres north of Tapah in the Kinta Valley, **IPOH** grew rich on the tin trade and is now the third biggest city in Malaysia. The muddy **Sungei Kinta** cuts the centre of Ipoh neatly in two; most of the hotels are situated east of the river, whilst the **old town** is on the opposite side between Jalan Sultan Idris Shah and Jalan Sultan Iskander. Some of Ipoh's old colonial street names have been changed in favour of something more Islamic, though the signs haven't always caught up; hence, Jalan CM Yusuf instead of Jalan Chamberlain, Jalan Mustapha Al-Bakri for Jalan Clare and Jalan Bandar Timar for Jalan Leech.

Many Ipoh buildings show the influence of colonial and Straits Chinese architecture, the most impressive of which is the white stucco **Hong Kong Bank** north of the Birch Memorial Clocktower on Jalan Dato' Maharaja Lela. Turning right from the bank into Jalan Sultan Yusuf, you're on the outskirts of **Chinatown**, many of whose pastel-coloured nineteenth-century shop-houses are now looking rather tatty. The **Perak Museum** (daily 9am–5pm; free) is housed in an elegant former tin miner's mansion, 400m north of the padang on Jalan Panglima Bukit Gantang Wahab, and displays photos of Ipoh's glory days during the tin boom.

The most prominent reminder of Ipoh's economic heyday, the **train station** was built in 1917, a typical example of the British conception of "East meets West", with its Moorish turrets and domes and a 200-metre-long verandah. It's on Jalan Panglima Bukit Gantang Wahab, west of the old town, with the **GPO** practically next door. The **local bus station** is just south of the train station, at the junction with Jalan Tun Abdul Razak. Opposite you'll find the taxi stand. **Express buses** operate from behind the ticket booths across the road. Local buses to **Lumut** (the departure point for Pulau Pangkor; see below) leave from a separate forecourt, beside a row of shops, a little further along Jalan Tun Abdul Razak; get a ticket from Perak Roadways under the bill hoardings. The Sultan Azlan Shah **airport** is 5km from the city (☎05/312 2459). The best **tourist office** is in the State Economic Planning Unit close to the train station on Jalan Tun Sambanthan (Mon–Thurs 8am–1pm & 2pm–4.30pm; closed Fri and first & third Sat of every month; ☎05/241 2959). The main **banks** are on Jalan Sultan Idris Shah and Jalan Yang Kalsom, and there is **Internet** access at *Triple Net*, 41 Jl CM Yusuff (☎05/254 4725).

The best budget **accommodation** with private bathroom is the *Embassy*, Jalan CM Yusuf (☎05/254 9496; ②); all rooms are clean and have hot water. The cheaper *West Pool Hotel*, 74 Clare St (☎05/254 5042; ①), is also clean and has communal hot-water showers. The best mid-range choice is the *Central*, 20–26 Jl Ali Pitchay (☎05/242 4777; ④), where all the rooms have TV, balcony and bathrooms that you'd usually only see at twice the price. A close second is the *Ritz Garden*, CM Yusuf (☎05/254 7777; ④). For a taste of the old colonial style, check into the *Majestic* (☎05/255 5605; ⑤), on the third floor of the train station, off Jalan Panglima. You'll get a roomy en-suite opening onto a huge tiled veranda where you'll be served afternoon tea on wicker chairs (RM120).

Many of Ipoh's **restaurants** close in the evenings, but there are excellent hawker stalls at the southern end of Jalan Greenhill, east of the *Shanghai Hotel*. Nearly a hundred stalls stay open well into the night, serving just about anything you care to name. Jalan CM Yusuf has the *Grand Cathay* restaurant which is very popular with Chinese locals, and the *Rahman*, an extremely friendly Indian restaurant. Around Jalan Bandar Timar in the old town are several Chinese restaurants, the oldest and best-known of which is the *Kedai Kopi Kong Heng* (lunchtime only) where you wander round the bustling stalls and pick your dish.

Pulau Pangkor

PULAU PANGKOR is one of the west coast's more appealing islands, with some of the best beaches to be found on this side of the Malay Peninsula, and it's only a thirty-minute ferry ride from the port of Lumut (85km southwest of Ipoh). The island is a mere 3km by 9km, but attracts a lot of weekenders, who have inevitably brought the odd concrete highrise with them, particularly In Pasir Bogak. There's already an airport here (daily flights from Singapore and KL) and several international-standard hotels. But the inhabitants still live largely by fishing rather than tourism. Most villages lie along the east coast, while tourist accommodation and the best beaches are on the west side of the island at Pasir Bogak and Teluk Nipah.

Express ferries to Pulau Pangkor run from **LUMUT** approximately every half hour (daily 6.45am–8pm; RM2 one way), calling at Kampung Sungei Pinang Kecil before reaching the main jetty at Pangkor Town. You can also catch a catamaran from the same spot for an extra ringgit which will get you to the island in half the time. **Buses** arrive at Lumut's bus station a minute's walk south of the jetty. There's a **Tourism Malaysia office** (Mon–Sat 9am-5pm; ☎05/683 4057) just left, past the petrol pumps on Jalan Sultan Idris Shah itself. Should you have to spend the night, *The Indah* at 208 Jl Iskandar Shah (☎05/683 5064; ④), a little way northwest along the waterfront from the jetty, has comfortable en-suites, as does the *Harbour View*, Jalan Titi Panjang (☎05/683 7888; ④) which is visible from the bus station. To get there, walk to the service station and take a hairpin right onto the shore road. Just past the *Harbour View* is Lumut's least expensive option, the clean and basic *Phin Lum Hooi*, 93 Jl Panjang (☎05/683 5641; ②).

The Lumut ferry docks at **Pangkor Town**, the island's principal settlement, from where buses and taxis will ferry you to the beaches. A sealed road runs right round the island, and across it from Pangkor Town to Pasir Bogak, 2km away on the west coast. The best way to explore is by motorbike (RM35) or pushbike (RM15), available from Pangkor Town and from guesthouses. Otherwise, there are **minibus taxis** (RM4 to Pasir Bogak, RM10 to Teluk Nipah and RM24–30 for a round-island trip), and infrequent **local buses** from Pangkor Town to Pasir Bogak (hourly 8am–6pm).

Pasir Bogak

PASIR BOGAK is the biggest and most upmarket development on the island, but has a disappointingly narrow strip of grubby sand. Only a few of the chalets front the beach itself; most line the road that continues north along the west coast, but they're all reasonably close to the sea. *Pangkor Standard Camp* (☎05/685 1878; ②) is the best deal for those on a budget, sleeping three at a squeeze. A step up is *Beach Hut* (☎05/685 1159; ④), with pleasant beachfront chalets and simple double rooms. *Khoo's Holiday Resort* (☎05/685 2190; ③) is a large complex of tasteful doubles perched on the hillside. The views are fantastic, there are air-con options and the rate includes breakfast. *Sri Bayu Beach Resort* (☎05/685 1929; ⑨) is by far the most characterful outfit on the beach. The carved wood and antique-strewn lobby leads onto a well-landscaped garden and chalets. The best value of the resort **restaurants** is *Ye Lin*, on the cross-island road, which offers huge plates of excellent Chinese food. The finest view belongs to the *Pangkor Paradise Village* up a dirt track to the south of the main strip, whose beachfront restaurant – on stilts over the water – is great for a beer at sunset. Back in the thick of things, there are some stalls clustered around the inexpensive *Pantai Beach Seafood Restaurant* on the seafront just north of the *Standard Camp*.

Teluk Ketapang and Teluk Nipah

Much better beaches than those at Pasir Bogak are to be found about 2km north of here at **TELUK KETAPANG**, whose broad, clean, white-sand shores are edged by palm trees, and at **TELUK NIPAH**, another few kilometres further on. The best beach at Teluk Nipah is Coral Bay – a perfect cove with crystal-clear sea and smooth white sand. The bay is inaccessible by road and to reach it you have to climb over the rocks at the northern end of Teluk Nipah (watch the tide). You can't actually stay at Teluk Ketapang, but there are plenty of options at Teluk Nipah.

ACCOMMODATION
Joe Fisherman Village (☎05/685 2389). One of the first set-ups and still the backpacker's spiritual home on Pangkor. With A-frames (RM20), chalets and a small, very friendly café. ②.

Nazri Nipah Camp (☎05/685 2014). Laid-back traveller place with kitchen facilities, a dorm (RM10), some A-frames and chalets with shower. ②.

Nipah Bay Villa (☎05/685 2198). One of the best choices if you're going for air-con, satellite TV and hot water. Professionally run with an Internet terminal open to non-guests. ⑦.

Palma Beach Resort (☎05/685 3693). Well designed, sturdy chalets with air-con, TVs and an efficient management. ⑤.

Pangkor Bayview Resort (☎05/685 3540). Nicely designed, spacious chalets with all facilities. A good choice if you're spending a bit more than the average. ⑥.

Purnama Beach Resort (☎05/685 3530). Package deal development with a good range of accommodation from comfortable dorms ($20) to plush chalets. There's an Internet terminal open to non-guests. ⑤.

TJ Restoran and Bungalows (☎05/685 3477). The best-value accommodation along this stretch, boasting double chalets with shower at half the price you'll find elsewhere. The café is a good deal too. ②.

Butterworth

The industrial town of **BUTTERWORTH** is the port for the island of Penang and its capital, Georgetown, and of no interest except as a transport hub. The **bus station**, port complex, taxi stand and **train station** (☎04/331 2796) are all next door to each other on the quayside. All but one of the daily north–south trains stop here. The 24-hour passenger and car **ferry service** runs three times an hour from the port complex to Pengkalan Weld in Georgetown and takes twenty minutes. If necessary, you can **stay** near the port at *Sin Tong Ah* (04/323 9679; ④). To get there, walk northeast from the bus station along the main road for a minute or so and follow it left past a huge intersection; the hotel is on the other side of the road.

Penang

PENANG, 370km from Kuala Lumpur on Malaysia's northwestern coast, is a confusing amalgam of state and island. Everything of interest in Penang State is on Penang Island, **Pulau Penang**, a large island of 285 square kilometres which is connected to the mainland by a bridge and by round-the-clock ferry services from Butterworth. Confusingly, the island's capital and Malaysia's second-largest city, **Georgetown**, is also often referred to as "Penang". Most visitors make day-trips out from Georgetown to the island's north-coast beaches of **Batu Ferringhi** and **Tanjung Bungah**, though you can also stay in both these resorts.

Until the late eighteenth century, Pulau Pinang was ruled by the Sultans of Kedah. In 1771, Sultan Mohammed J'wa Mu'Azzam Shah II took a shine to Captain Francis Light, who worked for a European trading company, and thought it expedient to accept military protection in exchange for offering the British the use of densely forested Penang as a port. By 1791, the island, then inhabited by less than a hundred indigenous fishermen, had become the **first British settlement** in the Malay Peninsula and quickly evolved into a major colonial administrative centre. Francis Light was made superintendent and declared the island a free port, with Georgetown the capital of the newly established Straits Settlements (incorporating Melaka and Singapore). But the founding of Singapore in 1819 was the beginning of the end for Georgetown, and Penang's fortunes rapidly began to wane. However, the strategic significance of Singapore proved to be Penang's saving grace, and there was little or no bomb damage to the island during World War II.

Georgetown

GEORGETOWN is Malaysia's most fascinating city and retains more of its cultural history than virtually anywhere else in the country. It is a magnet for budget travellers, a place not only to renew Thai visas, but to relax and observe street life in between trips to the beach. The most confusing thing about finding your way around Georgetown is the fact that many **streets** have several names – Penang Road has become Jalan Penang, Penang Street is Lebuh Penang, Weld Quay has become Pengkalan Weld, and Beach Street is now Lebuh Pantai. Lebuh Cinta is almost universally known as Love Lane, and Jalan Mesjid Kapitan Kling is often referred to as Lebuh Pitt.

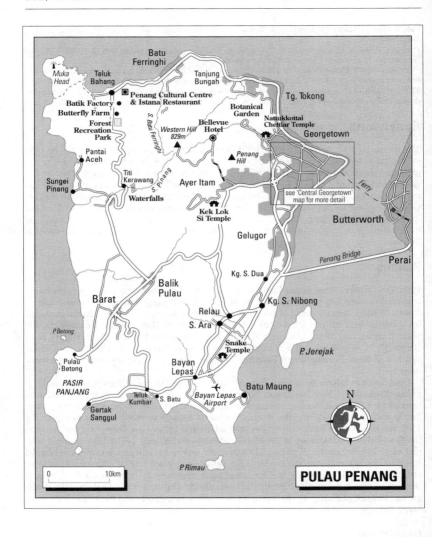

PULAU PENANG

ARRIVAL AND INFORMATION

The most convenient approach from the mainland is the 24-hour passenger-and-car **ferry service from Butterworth**, which takes twenty minutes and docks at the centrally located terminal on Pengkalan Weld (60 sen return). **Long-distance taxis** from the Peninsula use the thirteen-kilometre-long Penang Bridge (RM7 toll), which crosses from just south of Butterworth at Perai to a point on Jalan Udini, 8km south of Georgetown on the east coast. The nearest **airport** is at Bayan Lepas (☎04/643 0373), on the southeastern tip of the island. Yellow bus #83 (hourly on the hour, 6am–9pm) takes about 45 minutes to get into Georgetown, dropping you next to the Pengkalan Weld ferry terminal. A taxi costs RM20 – buy a coupon inside the terminal building.

Arriving at either the bus station, taxi stand or ferry terminals on Pengkalan Weld or near-by Swettenham Pier, puts you at the eastern edge of Georgetown, a twenty-minute walk from the hotels. On arrival, the most convenient tourist office is the **Penang Tourist Association** (Mon–Thurs 8.30am–1pm & 2–4.30pm, Fri 8.30am–12.30pm & 2.30–4.30pm, Sat 8.30am–1pm; ☎04/261 6663), on the ground floor of the Penang Port Commission building on Jalan Tun Syed Sheh Barakbah, which produces an excellent island and city **map** (RM1). Better, however, is the **Tourist Information Centre** (daily 10am–6pm; ☎04/261 4461) on the third floor of the huge KOMTAR Centre shopping complex in the centre of town, which is really clued up on local information and can also arrange half-day tours of the city, from around RM30 – not a bad way to see Penang if your time is limited.

GETTING AROUND

The city centre is small enough to get around on foot. For longer journeys to the outskirts or to other parts of the island there is an excellent bus service. From the station next to the ferry terminal on Pengkalan Weld, blue **buses** service the north of the island, and yellow buses the south and west, while red-and-white Transit Link buses – the most common of the lot – run on most routes through the island. A few buses are also run by the small Sri Negara company and there are a number of minibuses. All buses eventually stop at (and leave from) the station by the KOMTAR Centre on Jalan Ria and most stop at the Pengkalan Weld station too. **Fares** are rarely more than a dollar and services are frequent, though by 8pm in the evening they become more sporadic, and stop completely at 10pm.

A traditional way of seeing the city is by **rickshaw**: drivers tout for custom outside the major hotels and all along Lebuh Chulia. Negotiate the price in advance; a ride from the ferry

---

MOVING ON FROM GEORGETOWN/PENANG

Airport

To get to **Bayan Lepas International Airport** (☎04/643 0373) take a taxi (RM20) or the Yellow bus #83 (hourly on the hour, 6am–9pm; 45min) from Pengkalan Weld or the KOMTAR Centre. There are daily flights to Medan, Singapore, Bangkok, Phuket and Madras.

Ferries

Ferries to **Butterworth** are frequent and take twenty minutes (see p.591). Ferries to **Medan** and **Langkawi** depart twice daily from Swettenham Pier. Tickets for either route can be purchased in advance from the office next to the Penang Tourist Association and from the tourist information office at the KOMTAR Centre. Tickets for Langkawi are sold from the Kuala Perlis–Langkawi Ferry Service (☎04/262 5630) and Langkawi Ferry Service (☎04/264 2088), both at the PPC Shopping Complex. Travel agencies on Lebuh Chulia will also book for you.

Trains and buses

The nearest **train** station is in Butterworth, but there is a booking office in the Pengkalan Weld ferry terminal (☎04/261 0290). Although some **buses** to destinations on the Peninsula depart from Pengkalan Weld, most use the terminal at Butterworth; any travel agency on Lebuh Chulia will book seats for you.

To Thailand

For travel **to Thailand**, there are trains from Butterworth to Hat Yai, Surat Thani and Bangkok; several hostels (like the *New China* on Lebuh Leith) and travel agents on Lebuh Chulia run long-distance taxis to Hat Yai, though it's uneconomical unless there are four of you.

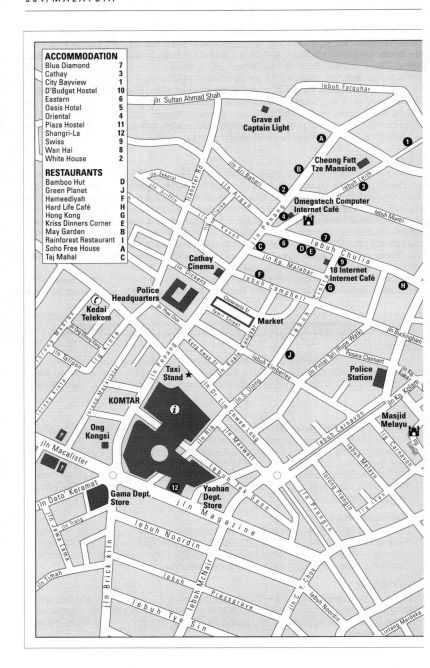

ACCOMMODATION

Blue Diamond	7
Cathay	3
City Bayview	1
D'Budget Hostel	10
Eastern	6
Oasis Hotel	5
Oriental	4
Plaza Hostel	11
Shangri-La	12
Swiss	9
Wan Hai	8
White House	2

RESTAURANTS

Bamboo Hut	D
Green Planet	J
Hameediyah	F
Hard Life Café	H
Hong Kong	G
Kriss Dinners Corner	E
May Garden	B
Rainforest Restaurant	I
Soho Free House	A
Taj Mahal	C

Grave of Captain Light

Cheong Fatt Tze Mansion

Omegatech Computer Internet Café

jln Sultan Ahmad Shah

lebuh Farquhar

jln Sekerat

jln Ariffin

jln Transfer Rd

jln Sri Bahari

jln Argyll

jln Clarke

jln Penang

jln Koyah

lebuh Leith

lebuh Muntri

lebuh Chulia

jln Kg. Malabar

jln Cintra

Cathay Cinema

jln Dickens

lebuh Campbell

18 Internet Internet Café

Police Headquarters

Kedai Telekom

jln Phee Chon

Chowrasta St

Tamil Street

Market

lebuh Buckingham

lorong Madras

jln Ong Chong Leng

trg Kinta

jln Kinta

jln Penang

Keng Kwee St

jln Kuala Kangsar

lebuh Kimberley

lebuh Kuala Kangsar

Pesara Claimant

jln Pintal Tali (Rope Walk)

Police Station

jln Kg. Kaka

jln Kg. Kolam

lorong Kinta

lorong Macalister

Taxi Stand

KOMTAR

Ong Kongsi

jln Macalister

jln Dr. Lim Chwee Long

jln Ria

jln Maxwell

jln S. Ujong

lebuh Carnavon

lebuh Melayu

lorong Prangin

Masjid Melayu

trg Carnavon

trg Tumit

jln Dato Keramat

jln Jawa Lama

jln Trang

Gama Dept. Store

lebuh Tek Soon

Yaohan Dept. Store

jln Magazine

jln Prangin

trg Ikan

jln Timah

jln Brick Kiln

lebuh Noordin

lebuh McNair

lebuh Pressgrave

lebuh Tye Sin

jln C.Y. Choy

lebuh Noordin

Lintang Merdeka

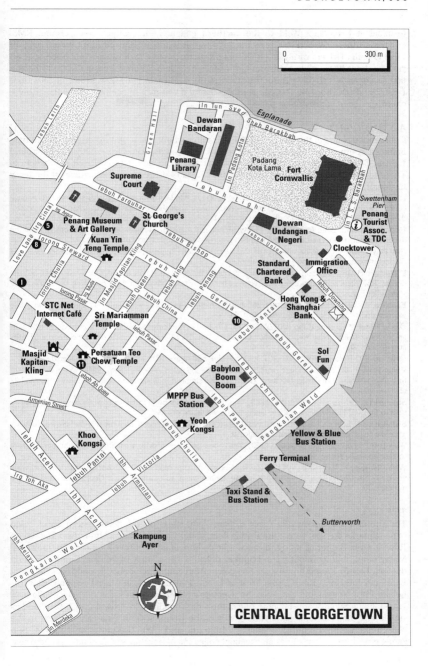

CENTRAL GEORGETOWN

terminal at Pengkalen Weld to the northern end of Lebuh Chulia costs around RM3. Otherwise, there are **taxi** stands by the ferry terminal and on Jalan Dr Lim Chwee Long, off Jalan Penang. Drivers rarely use their meters, so fix the fare in advance – a trip across town runs to about RM5, while a ride out to the airport or Batu Feringghi costs RM20. To book a taxi in advance, call Jade Auto (☎04/226 3015), CT Taxis (☎04/229 9467), or JRI Taxis (☎04/229 0501). For **bike or car rental** – useful if you plan to see the rest of the island – check the list of addresses on p.598.

ACCOMMODATION

Georgetown is one of the few places in the country where you might experience difficulty in finding a **room**, so arrive early or book ahead. The budget places are mostly on and around **Lebuh Chulia**; most have dorm beds as well as rooms, and many will sell bus tickets to Thailand and obtain Thai visas. No. 1 Lebuh Chulia is at the eastern end (nearest the ferry terminal).

Blue Diamond, no. 422 Lebuh Chulia (☎04/261 4117). Modern frontage but with an interesting inner courtyard and a grand staircase. The large, scruffy rooms with shower have luxurious sprung mattresses, there's a dorm (RM8) and a friendly café outside. ②.

Cathay, 15 Lebuh Leith (☎04/262 6271). Stylish colonial mansion dating from 1910. The cool greys of the decor, spacious rooms and courtyard fountain make for a tranquil environment. ⑤.

City Bayview, 25a Lebuh Farquhar (☎04/263 3161). Modern four-star, with a pool and fantastic views over the bay from the rooftop revolving restaurant. ⑦.

D'Budget Hostel, 9 Lebuh Gereja (☎04/263 4794). The long corridors are a bit claustrophobic, but the dorms (RM7) and rooms are clean and secure. There are shared bathrooms with hot showers and Western-style toilets. ②.

Eastern, no. 509 Lebuh Chulia (☎04/261 4597). Small, clean rooms with fan or air-con and saloon-style wooden doors. More solidly built than most. ②.

Oasis Hotel, 23 Lorong Cinta (☎04/261 6778). The best of the budgets, clean rooms and a dorm (RM8) in an attractive stone house with a shady, tranquil garden. There are communal hot showers and a friendly atmosphere. ②.

Oriental, 105 Jl Penang (☎04/263 4211). Good-value mid-range hotel with helpful, professional staff. ⑤.

Plaza Hostel, 32 Lebuh Ah Quee (☎04/263 0560). The top dorm in Georgetown (RM8) with a balcony, sitting area, washing facilities and lockers. There are also simple doubles, a good café, online services and lots of travel info. ②.

Shangri-La, Jl Magazine (☎04/262 2622). The most luxurious hotel in Georgetown, conveniently placed next to the KOMTAR Centre. All the facilities you would expect. ⑨.

Swiss, no. 431 Lebuh Chulia (☎04/262 0133). Standard hostel that sees a lot of the traveller crowd. Set back from the road with parking and an airy café. ②.

Wan Hai, 35 Lorong Cinta (☎04/261 6853). The rooms and dorm (RM8) are a little dingy, but there's a roof terrace and bike rental. ②.

White House, 72 Jl Penang (☎04/263 2385). Very clean, large rooms – all with hot showers – for half what you'd pay elsewhere. The fan rooms are among the best-value accommodation in Georgetown, and can sell out early. ②.

THE CITY

The site of **Fort Cornwallis** (daily 8.30am–7pm; RM1) on the northeastern tip of Pulau Penang marks the spot where the British fleet, under Captain Francis Light, disembarked on July 16, 1786. But for all its significance it holds little of interest save a replica of a traditional Malay house and an underground bunker detailing the history of Penang. Southwest from the fort, **Lebuh Pantai** holds some fine colonial buildings, including the Standard Chartered Bank and the Hong Kong Bank. West of Lebuh Pantai, on Jalan Masjid Kapitan Kling (or Lebuh Pitt), stands the Anglican **St George's Church** (Tues–Sat 8.30am–12.30pm & 1.30–4.30pm, Sun 8.30am–4.30pm), one of the oldest buildings in Penang (1817–1819) and as simple and unpretentious as anything built in the Greek style in Asia can be. Next to the church on Lebuh Farquhar, **Penang Museum and Art Gallery** (Sat–Thurs & Sun 9am–5pm, closed Fri; free) has an excellent collection of rickshaws, press cuttings and black-

and-white photographs. The area east of here, enclosed by parallel Lebuh King and Lebuh Queen, forms Georgetown's compact **Little India** district, full of saree and incense shops, banana-leaf curry houses, and the towering **Sri Mariamman Temple** (open early morning to late evening) on the corner of Lebuh Queen and Lebuh Chulia, a typical example of Hindu architecture.

To the south, in a secluded square at the end of an alleyway off Lebuh Acheh, stands the **Khoo Kongsi** (Mon–Fri 9am–5pm, Sat 9am–1pm; free – closed at the time of writing for refurbishment), one of many *kongsi,* or traditional "clan-houses" in Penang where Chinese families gather to worship their ancestors. The original building was started in 1894 and meticulously crafted by experts from China. Its central hall is dark with heavy, intricately carved beams and pillars and bulky mother-of-pearl inlaid furniture. The hall on the left is a richly decorated shrine to Tua Peh Kong, the god of prosperity; the right-hand hall contains the gilded ancestral tablets. Connecting all three halls is a balcony minutely decorated in carvings of folk tales.

On the western edge of Georgetown, on the corner of Lebuh Leith, is the stunning **Cheong Fatt Tze Mansion**, whose outer walls are painted in a striking rich blue. It's the best example of nineteenth-century Chinese architecture in Penang, built by Thio Thiaw Siat, a Cantonese businessman. The elaborate halls of ceremony, bedrooms and libraries, separated by courtyards and gardens, have been restored and are privately owned. Tours are infrequent and by appointment only (☎04/261 6301).

Bedecked with flags, lanterns, statues and pagodas, the sprawling and exuberant **Kek Lok Si Temple** (open morning to late evening; free) is supposedly the largest Buddhist temple complex in Malaysia and a major tourist spot. The "Million Buddhas Precious Pagoda" is the most prominent feature of the compound, with a tower of simple Chinese saddle-shaped eaves and more elaborate Thai arched windows, topped by a golden Burmese stupa. It costs RM2 to climb the 193 steps to the top, where there is a great view of Georgetown and the bay. Getting there involves a thirty-minute bus ride west on Transitlink #1, 101, 130, 351, 361, yellow bus #85 or minibus #21.

EATING

A local favourite is Penang *laksa*, noodles in thick fish soup, garnished with vegetables, pineapple and *belacan* (shrimp paste). The main travellers' hang-outs around Lebuh Chulia serve Western breakfasts, banana pancakes and milkshakes, for less than a couple of dollars each; they usually open from 9am to 5pm. There are also hawker stalls on Lebuh Kimberley and Lebuh Cintra.

Bamboo Hut, Lebuh Chulia. Good for all-day breakfasts and Indian dishes. Also has great milkshakes in bamboo cups.

Green Planet, 63 Lebuh Cintra. This café serves international veggie food, with some ingredients organically grown, and wonderful baguettes and wholemeal bread. Also has a book exchange. Open 9.30am–3pm & 6pm–midnight.

Hameediyah, 164 Lebuh Campbell. Great Indian food at reasonable prices; around RM4 a head for a full meal.

Hard Life Café, 363 Lebuh Chulia. Bob Marley and co plastered across the walls and the sound system make this a laid-back spot for drinks, snacks and beers.

Hong Kong, 29 Lebuh Cintra. Although this looks like any number of *kedai kopis* in the area, the food is of much better quality than usual, something reflected in the prices; portions are huge.

Kashmir, basement of *Oriental Hotel*, 105 Jl Penang. Very popular high-class north Indian restaurant; you'll need to book at weekends. Expensive but chic.

Kriss Dinners Corner, Lebuh Chulia. Tasty and surprisingly well-priced buffet of Chinese and Malay food. Shows films and football in the evenings.

May Garden, 70 Jl Penang. Plush, but affordable Cantonese restaurant with excellent food.

Rainforest Café, 294a Lebuh Chulia. Run by the friendly Mr Tan who also owns the *Green Planet*. Similar set-up, with good food and drinks, a book exchange system and Internet terminal.

Revolving Restaurant On the fourteenth floor of the *City Bayview Hotel*, serving Western and Oriental dishes, with a colourful all-you-can-eat lunchtime buffet for around RM30.

Soho Free House, Jl Penang. A pub that might have been transported straight from England, with authentic fish and chips, pies and draught Guinness.

Taj Mahal, Jl Penang. Near the junction with Lebuh Chulia, this busy and very inexpensive north Indian eatery is popular with the locals and open well into the night.

DRINKING AND NIGHTLIFE

Most of Georgetown's **bars** are comfortable places to hang out, but when the fleet arrives, a good many turn into rowdy meat markets, so choose carefully. Usual opening hours are 6pm–2am. In Georgetown's **discos** you're unlikely to hear the latest Western club sounds, and there's usually a cover charge of around RM10.

Babylon Boom Boom, Lebuh China Ghaut. A fun gay and straight disco and café, whose main attraction is the twice-nightly drag cabaret show.

No name bar, Lebuh Chulia. Further up from the *Hong Kong Bar* by the bus stop, this basic place always hosts a steady stream of travellers.

Polar Café, 48a Jl Penang. Family-run sing-along bar with organist and music machine, bright lighting and TV. A hamburger stall operates outside at night.

Rock World, In a yard off Lebuh Campbell. A spangle of neon, featuring the local Bon Jovis every weekend. Very 80's.

Sol Fun, Pengkalan Weld. Techno makes it to Penang at this gay disco in a converted warehouse. There's also a nightly "Funky Divas" show.

Tai Wah, Lebuh Chulia. This daytime café turns into a lively bar in the evening with the cheapest beer in town. The resident Tom Waits impersonator provides musical diversion until the small hours.

20 Lebuh Leith. This renovated 1930s Straits-style mansion is littered with film memorabilia; it has a large video screen and a beer garden. Slightly pricey, but interesting.

LISTINGS

Airlines Cathay Pacific, Menara PSCI, Jl Sultan Ahmed Shah (☎05/226 0411); Malaysia Airlines, ground floor, KOMTAR, Jl Penang (☎04/262 0011); Singapore Airlines, Wisma Penang Gardens, Jl Sultan Ahmed Shah (☎04/226 3201); Thai International, Wisma Central, Jl Macalister (☎04/226 6000).

American Express Care of Mayflower Tours, 274 Lebuh Victoria (Mon–Fri 8.30am–5.30pm, Sat 8.30am–1pm; ☎04/262 8198). Credit-card- and travellers' cheque-holders can use the office as a poste restante/general delivery address.

Banks and exchange Major banks (Mon–Fri 10am–3pm, Sat 9.30–11.30am) are along Lebuh Pantai, including Standard Chartered and the Hong Kong Bank, but since they charge a hefty commission, the licensed moneychangers on Lebuh Pantai, Lebuh Chulia and Jl Kapitan Kling (daily 8.30am–6pm) are preferable – they charge no commission and the rate is often better.

Bike rental Outlets on Lebuh Chulia rent out motorbikes and pushbikes: RM20 a day for a motorbike (you need a valid driving licence – in practice, you'll rarely be asked to show it); RM8 for a pushbike.

Bookshops United Books Ltd, Jl Penang, has a large selection of English-language books, including travel books. There are several outlets in the KOMTAR Centre, including Popular Books on the second floor. Times Books in the lifestyle department store also has a good selection. In addition, there are a few secondhand bookshops on Lebuh Chulia; the best is HS Sam Bookstore at no. 144 near the junction with Lebuh Queen.

Car rental Avis, at the airport (☎04/643 9633) and Batu Ferringhi (☎04/881 1522); Hertz, 38 Lebuh Farquhar (☎04/263 5914) and at the airport (☎04/643 0208); National, at the airport (☎04/643 4205).

Consulates Australia, care of Denis Mark Lee, 1c Lorong Hutton (☎05/263 3320); Bangladesh, 15 Lebuh Bishop (☎04/262 1085); Denmark, Standard Chartered Bank Chambers, Lebuh Pantai (☎04/261 1457); France, care of *Jumaboy and Sons*, Wisma Rajab, 82 Lebuh Bishop (☎04/262 9707); Indonesia, 467 Jl Burma (☎04/227 4686); Japan, 2 Jl Biggs (☎04/226 8222); Netherlands, c/o Algemene Bank Nederland, 59 Lebuh Pantai (☎04/261 6471); Norway, Standard Chartered Bank Chambers, Lebuh Pantai (☎04/262 5333); Sweden, Standard Chartered Bank Chambers, Lebuh Pantai (☎04/248 5433); Thailand, 1 Jl Tunku Abdul Rahman (☎04/226 9484); Turkey, no. 1, 1st floor, Nutrajaya shipping, 7 Pengkalan Weld (☎04/261 5933); UK, Standard Chartered Bank Chambers, Lebuh Pantai (☎04/262 5333). There is no representation for citizens of the USA, Canada, Ireland or New Zealand – KL has the nearest offices (see p.584).

Hospitals Adventist Hospital, Jl Burma (☎04/226 1133) – take blue bus #93, minibus #26, 31, 88 or Transitlink #202, 212; General Hospital, Jl Utama (☎04/229 3333) – Sri Negara bus #136, 137.

Immigration office Pejabat Imigresen, Lebuh Pantai, on the corner of Lebuh Light (☎04/261 5122). For on-the-spot visa renewals.

Internet access As well as a few places in the KOMTAR centre, you'll find no shortage of Internet terminals in Lebuh Chulia. The *18 Internet Café* (18 Lebuh Cintra (☎04/264 4902) has the best equipment, but you'll have to pay for a minimum of one hour. *STC Net Café* (☎04/264 3378) is friendlier and you can be as brief as you like, but the rates are a little higher.

Pharmacy There are several pharmacies along Jl Penang (10am–6pm).

Police In emergencies dial ☎999; the police headquarters is on Jl Penang.

Post office The GPO is on Lebuh Downing (Mon–Fri 8.30am–5pm, Sat 8.30am–4pm). The efficient poste restante/general delivery office is here, and parcel-wrapping is available from shops on Lebuh Chulia.

Sport You can play golf at Bukit Jambul Country Club, 2 Jl Bukit Jambul (☎04/644 2255; green fees RM100, RM150 weekends), or the Penang Turf Club Golf (☎04/226 6701; green fees RM84); there's racing at the Penang Turf Club, Jl Batu Gantung (☎04/3226 6701) – see the local paper for fixtures and you can swim at the Pertama Sports Complex, Paya Terubong, near Ayer Atam (9–11am & 4–9pm; RM4).

Telephone services Calls within Penang made from public telephone booths cost a flat rate of 10 sen and can be dialled direct. For international calls you can buy a phone card or use the Telekom office at the GPO on Lebuh Downing, open 24 hours.

Travel agencies Try MSL Travel, *Angora Hotel*, 202 Jl McAllister, for student and youth travel. There are a large number of other agencies on Lebuh Chulia.

Batu Ferringhi

BATU FERRINGHI, a thirty-minute bus ride west of Georgetown on Transitlink #202 or Transitlink air-con #93 (but not the standard #93), has a decent beach and several guesthouses, albeit filthy sea. The road runs more or less straight along the coast for 3km, on which all the hotels and restaurants are lined up side by side. The bus stops in the centre, where you'll find the Telekom office, post office, police station and clinic.

Towards the western end of Batu Ferringhi there's a small enclave of similar standard **budget guesthouses** facing the beach – take the road by the *Guan Guan Café*. Here you'll find the homely *Ah Beng* (☎04/881 1036; ②), the spotless *Baba's* (☎04/881 1686; ②), and the best place, *Ali's* (☎04/881 1316; ②), has a relaxing open-air café and garden, and better rooms than most. The most popular of the expensive places is the grand *Park Royal* (☎04/881 1133; ⑧), with lavish rooms and five-star restaurants.

Set just back from the main cluster of beachfront hotels, *Jewel of the North* serves very tasty north Indian **food** at around RM15 per dish, while *Oasis*, on the main road, does Malay dishes from as little as RM3. On the beachfront, *Restaurant Vibration* has snacks and drinks and in the middle of the beach you'll find *Eden Seafood Village*, a huge place whose boast is "Anything that swims, we cook it." At the western end of the main strip, *Happy Garden* is set just off the road in a colourful flower garden and serves cheapish Chinese and Western food.

Teluk Bahang

Five kilometres west of Batu Ferringhi, the small fishing kampung of **TELUK BAHANG** is the place to come to escape the development. The long spindly pier towards the far end of the village with its multitude of fishing boats is the focus of daily life. Beyond the pier, a small path disappears into the forest and it's a two-hour trek west to the lighthouse at **Muka Head**. The beaches around this rocky headland are better than the ones at Teluk Bahang itself, but since the big hotels run boat trips out here, it's unlikely that you'll have them to yourself.

Accommodation is somewhat limited. The friendly *Rama's Guest House* (☎04/885 1179; ①) is the cheapest place, a hippy homestay with basic dorm beds (RM8) and rooms; take the right (beachward) turn at the roundabout coming from Georgetown and it's about 20m down the road on the right. There's also *Miss Loh's* (②), a longhouse and garden in the kampung a little back from the sea. To get there from the direction of Georgetown, turn left at the roundabout and carry on for 100m passing the batik factory and mosque. After the telecom tower, turn right, cross the bridge and you'll see the hostel on your left. You can book at the Kwong Tuck Hing shop on the main road. At the other end of the price scale is the beautifully decorated

Penang Mutiara at the eastern end of the main road (☎04/885 2828; ⑨). Tanjung Bungah's real attraction is its plethora of inexpensive **places to eat** on the little stretch of main road, including an excellent seafood restaurant by the pier, called *End of the World I* (dinner only).

Alor Setar

ALOR SETAR, the tiny state capital of Kedah, is the last major stop before the Thai border. It's a city that is keen to preserve its heritage – witness the many royal buildings and museums – and since Alor Setar has useful transport links to the east coast as well as to Thailand, you might as well spend at least a short time here. The main sights are located to the west of the town around the padang, whose west side is dominated by Masjid Zahir. Behind the elegant Istana Balai Besar (Royal Audience Hall) stands the old royal palace, now serving as the **Muzium Di Raja** (daily 10am–5pm; Fri closed noon–2.30pm; free) where some rooms have been kept exactly as they were when used by the sultan and his family. On the south side of the square, the grandiose, white stucco art gallery, **Balai Seni Negeri** (same hours as Muzium Di Raja), displays largely uninspiring works showing the influence of traditional Malay culture on contemporary artists.

South of the padang, across the Sungei Kedah, at 18 Lorong Kilang Ais, **Rumah Kelahiran Mahathir** (Tues–Sun 10am–5pm; Fri closed noon–3pm; free) is the birthplace of Dr Mahathir Mohammed; it's now a museum, documenting the life of the local doctor who became the most powerful Malaysian prime minister of modern times. The **Pekan Rabu** market, held every day from morning to midnight on Jalan Tunku Ibrahim, is a good place to buy handicrafts and sample local foods. North of the padang, beside the roundabout on Jalan Telok Wanjah, the **Nikhrodharam Buddhist Temple** is a glittering complex with numerous statues, mosaics and paintings, that shows the continuing influence of Thai culture.

Practicalities

Long-distance buses arrive at Alor Setar's huge **express bus station** (*Sharap Perdana*), 6km north of the centre, well connected to the city by municipal buses (60 sen) and taxis (RM7). The **local bus station**, on Jalan Langar, runs services to the express terminal and is also the place to catch the #106 to Kuala Kedah for the Langkawi ferry. The **train station** is behind the Jalan Langar terminus, a five-minute walk east of the centre on Jalan Stesyen. The domestic **airport** (MAS office; ☎04/721 1186), 11km north of town, is served by the hourly "Kepala Batas" bus from the express bus station and by taxi (RM10).

The **State Tourist Office** (Tues–Sun 8am–4.15pm, closed Fri and first & third Sat of every month; ☎04/730 1957) is in the State Secretariat Building on Jalan Sultan Badlishah. Most of the major **banks** are on Jalan Raja, and there are a few places in town where you can get **online**: of the cybercafés in the Citypoint shopping centre, *MCC Internet* on the third floor is the cheapest (☎04/732 4439). Most **budget hotels** are close to the southbound bus station on Jalan Langgar. Furthest away from the station, but by far the best value, is the *Lim Kung* (☎04/732 8353; ①), with simple, clean and very inexpensive rooms. The *Sing Tak Sing Hotel*, right above the bus station (☎04/732 5482; ②), is a slightly seedy, cavernous alternative at a higher price, while the best mid-range place is the *Hotel Regent*, 1536-G Jl Sultan Badlishah (☎04/731 1900; ④), which looks a lot more expensive than it is, both inside and out. Alor Setar is known for its Thai **food** – try *Hajjah* opposite Citypoint on Jalan Tungku Ibrahim, for Thai seafood. One of the best-value Indian places is the *Yashmeen*, on Jalan Sultan Badlishah, which serves excellent and filling food. For a variety of dishes under one roof head for the Pekan Rabu market.

Pulau Langkawi

Situated 30km off the coast at the very northwestern tip of the Peninsula is a cluster of 104 tropical islands, the largest of which is **PULAU LANGKAWI**. Pulau Langkawi has seen unparalleled development in recent years: some of the country's most luxurious hotels are here, and there's a new airport, but the mountainous interior, white sands, limestone outcrops and lush vegetation have remained relatively unspoiled. The principal town on Pulau Langkawi is **Kuah**, a boom town of hotels and shops in the southeast of the island. The main tourist development has taken place around two bays on the western side of the island, at **Pantai Tengah** and **Pantai Cenang**. Of these, Cenang is by far the most commercialized, but has some budget accommodation. The best beach on the island is at Pantai Kok in the west, though there is no budget accommodation here.

Arrival and information

All boat services to Langkawi dock at the jetty on the southeastern tip of the island, two minutes' taxi drive (RM4) from Kuah. The most common approach is by ferry **from Kuala Perlis**, adjacent to the Thai border (hourly; 45min; RM13), but ferries also operate **from Kuala Kedah** (9 daily, 7am–7pm; 1hr 15min; RM15 one-way), 8km from Alor Setar, **from Satun in Thailand** (3 daily; 1hr 30min; RM19), and **from Penang** (2 daily, 5pm & 5.30pm; 2hr 30min; RM35). The **airport** (☎04/955 1311) is 20km west of Kuah, near Pantai Cenang; a taxi will cost less than RM16 to Kuah. There's an MAS office (☎04/966 6622) on the ground floor of the Langkawi Shopping Complex, 400m from the main jetty.

There is basically one circular road around the island, with the other main road connecting north and south, and some minor roads. There are no bus routes, so you'll have to get around by **taxi**: a journey to Pantai Cenang from the jetty will cost you RM14. Many of the chalets and motels offer **motorbike rental** (RM35 per day). The Langkawi **tourist office** (Sat–Thurs 9am–5pm; ☎04/966 7789), next to the mosque on the way into Kuah, is very helpful and there's also an information booth at the airport, open daily.

Kuah

Lining a large sweep of bay in the southeastern corner of the island, **KUAH** is easily the largest town on Langkawi, and has a ferry terminal, hotels and shopping complexes. Beside the ferry terminal is Dataran Lang (Eagle Square) and **Lagenda Langkawi Dalan Taman** (daily 9am–9pm; RM5), a landscaped "theme park" of giant sculptures based around the legends of the islands. Most of the hotels are further around the bay.

You'll find the post office (Sat–Thurs 9am–5pm, closed Fri) and police station (☎04/966 6222) on the main road, Jalan Kisap Kuah. The General Hospital is at Jalan Bukit Tekoh 07000, 7km from Kuah (☎04/966 3333). Behind the MAYA shopping complex, also on the main road, are three parallel streets with all the banks (virtually the only places to change money on the island) and the Telekom centre. There's an Internet café – *IT Base* – at 6–7 Banguan Chempaka on the corner of the main road and Jalan Pandak Maya 1. Kuah is not an unattractive place, but despite the multitude of hotels it's not somewhere you're likely to want to stay. If you need to, the *Hotel Langkawi*, at 6–8 Pekan Kuah (☎04/966 6248; ②) and *JB Motel*, 19 Jl Pandak Maya 4 (☎04/966 8545; ③) near the banks, are budget possibilities. The huge *City Bayview* (☎04/966 1818; ⑥), on Jalan Pandak Mayah 1, is the luxury option. There are numerous eating options, from the hawker stalls – past the post office heading towards the jetty – to the pricier seafood restaurants on the front.

Pantai Tengah

Heading 18km west from Kuah, a clearly signed junction takes you to the first of the western beaches, **PANTAI TENGAH**, 6km away. It's a quiet beach and the sand isn't bad, but the water is murky. There are also jellyfish, so take local advice before you swim. **Accommodation** is limited to a couple of smart resorts and a handful of low-key chalet places. Best of the budgets is *Tanjung Malie* (☎04/955 1891; ③) with comfortable fan or aircon chalets set in a garden, closely followed by the similar *Sugary Sands Motel* (☎04/955 3473; ③); both are at the northern end of the beach. A good upmarket option is the *Sunset*

Beach Resort (☎04/955 1751; ⑥), a cluster of luxury chalets set amongst shady trees, a little further south. For **eating**, the Chinese restaurants by the junction with Jalan Pantai Tengah have the best atmosphere. *Moody's* place on the junction is a good place for Western break-fasts though it's a little pricey and portions are small. Later in the day, *Charlie's* has beach-front barbecues, and next-door *Oasis* has the best bar. Further south, the *White Sands Restaurant* has very good Malay seafood at around RM17 a dish.

Pantai Cenang

Five hundred metres north of Tengah, the development at **PANTAI CENANG** is the most extensive on the island, with cramped chalet sites side by side. The bay forms a large sweep of wide, white beach with crisp, sugary sand, but again the water here won't win any prizes for cleanliness. Plenty of places offer **watersports** and **boat rental**, including Langkawi Marine Sports (☎04/955 1389), where you can expect to pay around RM200 per boat (for eight people) for a round-island boat tour, RM110 for a day's fishing or RM25 for ten minutes' waterskiing. The main attraction on Pantai Cenang is the huge **Underwater World** (daily 10am–6pm; RM12), where the highlight is a walk-through aquarium.

ACCOMMODATION AND EATING
Delta Motel (☎04/955 2253; ③), just north of the Underwater World, has pleasant and inex-pensive wooden chalets in a well-planned, shady garden; *Langkapuri Beach Resort* (☎04/955 1202; ⑥), next door, is a little plusher with a range of sturdy brick chalets on a leafy patch of beach, and further north still, the *AB Motel* (☎04/955 1300; ③) is a good budget choice with hammocks and a terrace restaurant. Two minutes' walk further, back from the road on the land-ward side, the very simple, clean cabins of the *Yahok Homestay* (☎04/955 8120; ②) and *Yeti Beach Motel* (☎017/477 1678; ②) are priced as low as you'll find on Langkawi. Most of the resorts also have attached restaurants: the ones at *AB Motel* and *Delta* are good value, though the latter doesn't serve alcohol. The *Beach Garden Resort Bistro*, across from the track leading to the *Yeti*, is a pretty beachside operation serving up pizzas, pasta and beer, while opposite the *AB Motel*, the pricey *Champor Champor*, which combines Western and Oriental influence to successful effect in an enchanted grove atmosphere, is well worth the splurge.

Pantai Kok and Telaga Tujuh

PANTAI KOK lies on the far western stretch of Langkawi and is the best beach on the island, a large sweep of powdery white sand with relatively clear and shallow water – quieter and more secluded than Cenang and more intimate in feel. Accommodation, however, is lim-ited to a few big resorts, only one of which – the *Baru Bay* – is actually on the beach.

The road after the turn-off to the *Berjaya Resort* leads up to the island's most wonderful natural attraction, **Telaga Tujuh** or "Seven Pools", where the mossy rocks enable you to slide from one pool to another, before the fast-flowing water disappears over the cliff to form the ninety-metre waterfall. It's a steep 200-metre climb to the pools from the base of the hill – in total, it's about a 45-minute walk from the road near the *Burau Bay Resort*.

ACCOMMODATION AND EATING
Heading north from Cenang, the first **acccommodation place** you'll come to is the *Langkasuka Resort* (☎04/955 6888; ⑦), a luxurious place on a lovely beach on the way to Pantai Kok that's very good value. Continue past Pantai Kok and you'll reach the *Burau Bay Resort* (☎04/959 1061; ⑦) at the western end of the beach where the facilities are up to scratch but the metallic and plastic chalets are a little tacky. A little further is the *Berjaya Langkawi Beach and Spa Resort* (☎04/959 1888; ⑧), which is luxurious and a little kitsch, but the Japanese massages, facials and forest-spa are the real attraction. Last up, and least expen-sive by far is the *Seven Wells Motel and Seafood Restaurant* (☎04/959 3842; ③), with a few double rooms with showers on a quiet spot west of the *Berjaya*.

The best **food** around also happens to be the cheapest, at the tiny *7 Wells Restoran*, just before you reach Telaga Tujuh, on the corner of the road to Datai, which has wonderful home cooking. Other than here, you're limited to the big resort restaurants.

Kuala Perlis and overland into Thailand

Boats to and from Langkawi (hourly; 45min) dock at the little town of **KUALA PERLIS**, 45km north of Alor Setar, and although it's the second largest settlement in the state it only has two streets. Buses drop you next to the jetty, from where a wooden footbridge connects with the older, more interesting part of town, a ramshackle collection of buildings on stilts. While express buses to Padang Besar, Alor Setar and Butterworth are fairly frequent, there are a couple of **hotels** if you need to stay, the cheapest of which is the *Asia*, 18 Taman Sentosa (☎04/985 5392; ②), a signposted right turn after a short five-minute walk, keeping the water on your left, right through town. There's also a restaurant downstairs.

You can reach Satun in Thailand directly from Kuala Perlis: small boats leave from the jetty en route from Langkawi as soon as they're full and charge RM4 for the thirty-minute journey. This is the quickest cross-border option if you're coming from Langkawi, otherwise, you have to cross by bus or train; see below. At weekends you'll be charged an additional RM1 for the immigration officers' overtime payment.

The nearest train station is at **ARAU**, 16km east of Kuala Perlis, where you can catch the **daily train to Hat Yai and Bangkok** (though the train doesn't stop here on the return journey); there are also less convenient daily connections to Butterworth, Alor Setar, Sungei Petani, Taiping, Ipoh, Tapah Road and Kuala Lumpur. The northbound train comes to a halt at **PADANG BESAR**, where a very long platform connects the Malaysian service with its Thai counterpart. You don't change trains here, although you must get off and go through customs at the station. You can also do the journey by **bus**: there are frequent services from the local bus station (1km north of the express terminal) at **KANGAR**, 12km east of Kuala Perlis, to the border at Padang Besar. The crossing is open from 6am to 10pm. Buses also ply the North–South Highway, which runs to the Thai border at **BUKIT KAYU HITAM**, from where it is about a five-hundred-metre walk to Danok on the Thai side. Once you've passed through immigration, there are regular bus connections from both places with Hat Yai, 60km away – southern Thailand's transport hub (see p.953).

THE INTERIOR

Banjaran Titiwangsa (Main Range) forms the western boundary of the interior; to its east is an H-shaped range of steep, sandstone mountains and luxuriant valleys where small towns and kampung nestle. The rivers which flow from these mountains – Pahang, Tembeling, Lebir, Nenggiri and Galas – provide the northern interior's indigenous peoples, the Negritos and Senoi, with their main means of transport. Visitors, too, can travel by boat to perhaps the most stunning of all Peninsular Malaysia's delights, **Taman Negara National Park**. Bordering Taman Negara to the south, **Kenong Rimba** is a smaller, quieter, less visited national park, but none the worse for that. And what better way to get from the coasts to these wilderness places, than by the **Jungle Railway**, which chugs leisurely through the scenic interior from **Gemas** in the south to **Kota Bharu** on the northwest coast.

The Jungle Railway

Unless you're in a real hurry to get to either coast, consider a trip on the **jungle railway** which winds through the valleys and round the sandstone hills from Mentakab in southern Pahang to Kota Bharu, 500km to the northeast, with useful stops at Jerantut and Kuala Tembeling (see p.606), both access points for Taman Negara, and at Kuala Lipis (p.609), close to Kenong Rimba park. The line was completed in 1931 and runs at a snail's pace (it is seldom less than two hours behind schedule) along valley floors where trees and plants almost envelop the track. It's a great way to encounter rural life, as for the Malays, Tamils and Orang Asli who live in these remote areas, the railway is the only alternative to walking.

The most common approach to the jungle railway from KL is to take a bus to **MENTAKAB** (every 30min from Pudu Raya; 2hr 30min), less than 100km east of KL. To reach the train station walk from the bus station south onto the main road, Jalan Temerloh, and bear left for 50m to a big junction. Turn right, walk another 200m and watch for a narrow road on your right, marked to the train station – a fifteen-minute walk. There are numerous budget **hotels** on Jalan Temerloh which you'll reach if you carry on walking eastwards. The cleanest is the *London Café and Hotel*, 71 Jl Temerloh (☎09/277 1119; ②), which has neat, basic doubles with attached bathrooms. A few doors away on a side street leading south is the *Hotel Hoover*, 25 Jl Moh Hee Kiang (☎09/277 1622; ②), which has smaller and more expensive doubles than the *London*, but also offers single-room rates.

Taman Negara

Peninsular Malaysia's largest and most popular national park is **TAMAN NEGARA**, 250km northeast of KL. Numerous rewarding trails snake through some of the oldest rainforest in the world and there are resorts, hides and campsites to stay in. To see any sizeable mammal, including the resident elephants, you really have to make a three- or four-day trek, or journey upriver to remote Kuala Keniam. Staying overnight in the hides (tree houses beside salt licks) might give you sightings of mouse deer, tapir and wild ox – and the park has over three hundred species of birds. The busiest place in the park is **Kuala Tahan**, where you'll find most of the accommodation and the park headquarters. For a quieter experience, there's the more basic **Nusa Camp**, 2km upstream, and the upriver camps at **Kuala Keniam** and **Kuala Trenggan**. The best time to **visit** the park is between February and October, during the "dry" season, although it still rains even then. In the wet season (mid-Oct to Feb), there may be restrictions on the trails and boat trips.

Access to the park

The usual approach to the park is by bus to **Tembeling jetty**, from where it's a three-hour boat trip (9am & 2pm except Fri; RM19) to the accommodation and park headquarters at **Kuala Tahan**. This is 10km from the town of **Jerantut**, or thirty minutes' walk from the village of **Kuala Tembeling** – both these places are stops on the Jungle Railway. There's no accommodation at Kuala Tembeling, so many stay the night at Jerantut, from where you can also take a bus into the park.

FROM KL AND THE EAST COAST

In KL, at the *Istana Hotel* (see p.579), you can book accommodation for the *Taman Negara Resort* at Kuala Tahan and get a shuttle bus direct to Tembeling jetty (8am; RM25). By **public bus from KL**, first take the bus to Jerantut from Pekeliling station (4 daily; 3hr 30min; RM9), then either a **taxi** (RM16), or a **local bus** (8am, 11am & 1.30pm; 40min; RM3) to Tembeling jetty (the 1.30pm bus doesn't get to the jetty in time for the 2pm boat). Alternatively, join the *Hotel Sri Emas* **bus trip** which leaves Jerantut at 8.30am and gets to Kuala Tahan at 10.30am (RM23; same as the combined cost of a shared taxi and boat). The **train from KL** involves travelling to Gemas (trains leave KL at 8am & 2.45pm), where you change to the jungle train, which leaves Gemas at 2.20am, getting to **Jerantut** at 5.30am and to tiny **Kuala Tembeling** at 6am (Kampung Tembeling is an unscheduled stop, so you'll need to tell the guard you want to get off). From here it's a two-kilometre walk west to the jetty. The total price for the train trip from KL is around RM15.

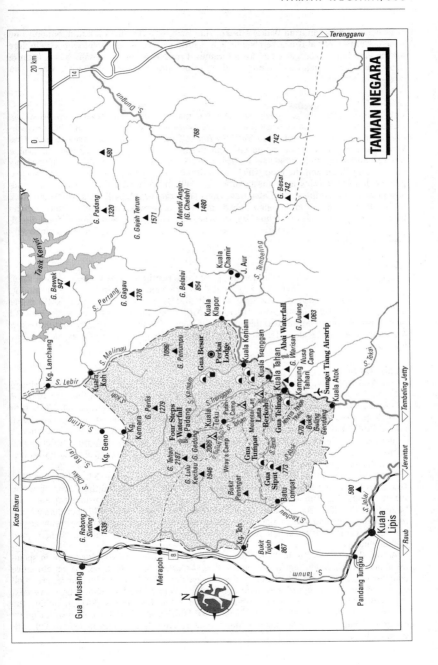

TAMAN NEGARA

Two daily trains run from **Wakaf Bharu**, 7km from Kota Bharu, to Jerantut, but only one – the 6.30am – stops at Kuala Tembeling. The 8.10am train might get you to the jetty in time for the 2pm boat if you get a taxi from Jerantut. **From Kuantan**, two daily buses (8am & noon; RM12) go straight to Jerantut, or there's an hourly service to Temerloh, where you change for Jerantut.

JERANTUT

JERANTUT is a small, busy town with only one major street, Jalan Besar. From Jerantut's **bus station** it's a five-minute walk south to Jalan Besar and the centre of town. The **train station** is off Jalan Besar, just behind *Hotel Sri Emas*. There are plenty of **places to stay**. One kilometre west of the train station on Jalan Besar is the large, rambling and good-value *Jerantut Resthouse* (☎09/266 6200; ③). The *Hotel Sri Emas* (☎09/266 4499; ①), at the junction of Jalan Besar and the road which leads to the train station, has a dorm (RM7), inexpensive doubles and air-con rooms and offers a wealth of information on the park. The friendliest place in town is the small *Chong Heng Hotel* (*Traveller's Inn*), 24 Jl Besar (☎09/266 3693; ①), south of the *Emas* on the opposite side of the road. Between the train and bus stations there are plenty of stalls and mini-restaurants serving Thai, Malay and Chinese **food**, usually open until 3am. Near the train station itself, at 4 Jl Stesen Kertapi, you'll find Jerantut's only **cybercafé** – the *AZM*.

TEMBELING JETTY

Many motorized sampans depart for the park from **Tembeling jetty** (daily 9am & 2pm, except Fri 2.30pm; 3hr; RM19 one-way), and there are shops and cafés clustered around it. When here, you must buy a park entry **permit** (RM1) and a camera licence (RM5) at the nearby *Taman Negara Resort* ticket office. The *Nusa Camp* kiosk is to the left of the jetty. All boats leave at the same time, travelling along the Sungei Tembeling either to *Taman Negara Resort* and the park headquarters at Kuala Tahan, or to the private *Nusa Camp*, 2km further upriver.

Kuala Tahan

At **KUALA TAHAN**, visitors can stay either at the *Taman Negara Resort* or in the village itself on the other side of the river; the shuttle boat will ferry you across here for 50 sen. *Taman Negara Resort* office has an excellent free site and park **map** and deals with all park queries, regardless of where you're staying. Behind the office is the official **Parks and Wildlife Department** headquarters where you can book sampans and hides. There's a minimart next door selling basic provisions. The nearby **camping shop** rents trekking and camping gear, including backpacks and lightweight jungle boots. You can also store your luggage at the camping shop (RM1 per day).

For accommodation at the *Taman Negara Resort* you need to book in KL, either at MATIC (see p.578) or at the *Istana Hotel* office (see p.579). Alternatively, call the *Resort* direct on ☎09/266 3500. Accommodation consists of twin-bed chalets (⑧) and luxurious two-bedroom bungalows (RM600). You can also camp 300m from the resort office (RM2 per person) and tents can be rented for RM8 a night – the RM40 dormitory isn't worth bothering with, as you can get the same standard at half the price across the river. The resort will also prepare good packed lunches.

Across the river **in Kuala Tahan** itself, the best place to stay if you don't want to spend too much, is the *Tembeling Riverview Hostel and Chalets* (☎09/266 6766; ③), an attractive complex of thatched, timber chalets and a café–garden. The doubles with shower are good value and the two dormitories (RM10) are the best around by a long shot. The *Liana* next door (☎03/266 9322) is a barracks-style corridor of four-bed dorms (RM10). Behind the *Riverview*, the *Ekotan Chalets* (☎09/266 9897; ⑥) is the best mid-range option with slightly overpriced but comfortable air-conditioned chalets. There's also a dorm (RM15–20) with good facilities.

Nusa Camp

Nusa Camp is 2km further upstream on Sungei Tembeling. Boats from Tembeling jetty will take you straight there, stopping briefly at Kuala Tahan first. Although accommodation and food is a little cheaper than at the resort, the disadvantage of staying here is that you are dependent on the sampans to ferry you around. For **accommodation**, it's best to book in advance at MATIC (☎03/264 3929) in KL, or call SPKG Tours (☎09/266 2369) in Jerantut. There's also an office for Nusa Camp by the jetty at Kuala Tembeling (☎09/266 3043). The twin-bed "Malay Houses" (⑤) are much more basic chalets than the ones at the resort, but have attached bathrooms. You can also stay in tiny tepee-like pyramid buildings for two people (③), which have an external toilet and shower, or four-bed dorm rooms (RM10.35). Nusa Camp has one small **cafeteria** (daily 8am–10pm) which does cheap set meals.

The hides

Spending a night in one of the park's **hides** beside a salt lick doesn't guarantee sightings of large mammals, but it'll be a memorable experience, and you may catch sight of deer, tapir, elephant, leopard or wild ox. The hides offer very basic bunk accommodation for six to eight people and must be booked at the wildlife office in the resort (RM5 per person). They have no washing or cooking facilities, and no electricity, so bring a torch. Also take rain gear, hat and sleeping bag, and all the food and drink you will need – and bring all your rubbish back. It's best to go in a group and take turns keeping watch for animals. The closest hide to the resort is the **Bumbun Tahan**, just south of the junction with the Bukit Teresek trail. Much more promising are the **Bumbun Tabing**, on the east bank of Sungei Tahan, and the **Bumbun Cegar Anjing**, an hour further, on the west bank of Sungei Tahan. The most distant hide to the north of the resort is the six-bed **Bumbun Kumbang**, an eleven-kilometre walk from Kuala Tahan, and the best place to catch sight of animals.

Exploring the park

There are numerous hiking possibilities in Taman Negara, the most popular of which are the day-treks out of Kuala Tahan, described here. For these, T-shirts, shorts and strong trainers are adequate, but always have a hat, mosquito repellent and water to hand. Binoculars are a good idea. Always **inform park staff** first, so they know where you are if you get into any difficulty. Although the trails are well marked, people do sometimes get lost.

Transport around the park is by sampan. Staff at the *Taman Negara Resort* office can arrange a trip for you, or you can speak to the boatmen at the jetty, and sort out a (cheaper) price with them. Always book your return trip at the same time, since the boatmen only operate out of Kuala Tahan and Nusa Camp. For trips to upriver sites or Lata Berkoh on Sungei Tahan, expect to spend at least RM80 a day per boat one-way.

BUKIT TERESEK

Although heavily used, the route to **Bukit Teresek** is an excellent starter. Follow the path between the chalets east of the resort office, beyond which a trail heads northeast away from the river. It's wide and easy to follow, hitting primary jungle almost immediately; after around twenty minutes the trail divides, straight on to Bukit Teresek and left for the Tabing hide and Bukit Indah (see p.607). The climb up 342-metre high Bukit Teresek (1hr) offers marvellous views. Along the trail you might hear gibbons or hill squirrels in the trees. Back at the base of the hill, the canopy walkway (see below) is just 300m to the north along a clearly marked path.

THE CANOPY WALKWAY

About thirty minutes' walk east from Kuala Tahan along the riverside Bukit Indah trail is the **canopy walkway**. Only a small group of people can gain access to the walkway (daily 11am–2.45pm, except Fri 9am–noon; RM5) at any one time, so you may have to wait. The walkway is a 450-metre swaying bridge made from aluminium ladders bound by rope and set 30m above the ground. It's reached by climbing a sturdy wooden tower and takes thirty minutes to cross. Once you've got used to the swaying, it's a pleasurable experience taking in the fine views of Sungei Tembeling and observing the insect life and tree parasites which abound at that height. Other species usually visible include the grey banded leaf monkey, and the white-eyed dusky leaf monkey.

THE BUKIT INDAH TRAIL

Past the canopy the route divides, north and slightly uphill to the Tabing hide, another 1km further on, or northeast along the lovely **Bukit Indah trail**, a three-hour round-trip from the resort office. Initially, this follows the riverbank, and you are bound to see monkeys, plenty of bird life, squirrels, shrews, a multitude of insects and perhaps tapir or wild ox. The path to Bukit Indah itself leaves the main riverside trail (which continues to Kuala Trenggan, 6km away) and climbs at a slight gradient for 200m to give a lovely view over Sungei Tembeling.

GUA TELINGA AND KEMAH KELADONG

Another major trail leads south alongside the river, with branches to Gua Telinga and the campsite at Kemah Keladong. From the jetty by the *KT Restoran*, take a sampan across Sungei Tahan. On the other side, follow the trail through a small *kampung* into the trees. After 3km, follow the sign north for a further 200m to reach **Gua Telinga**, a small but deceptively deep limestone cave. In theory it's possible to follow a guide rope through the eighty-metre cave, but you have to be pretty small to get yourself through the narrow cavities. Thousands of tiny roundleaf and fruit bats live in the cave, along with giant toads, black-striped frogs and whip spiders (which aren't poisonous). From Gua Telinga, it's another 500m to the noisy Belau hide, and another 1km to that at Yong, where the trail divides, north to Kemah Rentis and left to the tranquil **Keladong campsite**, 1km further on. Given an early start, it's quite possible to reach this point, have a swim, and get back to the resort before dusk; bring at least a litre of water each and lunch.

LATA BERKOH

Most people visit the "roaring rapids" of **Lata Berkoh** by boat, but you could walk the trail there and arrange for a boat to pick you up for the return journey. **Sampans** from Kuala Tahan cost around RM80 for four people and take half an hour. The **trail** from the resort (8km; 3hr) starts at the campsite and leads through dense rainforest, passing Lubok Lesong campsite (3km), then crossing gullies and steep ridges, before reaching the river, which must be forded. The final part of the trail runs north along the west side of Sungei Tahan before reaching the falls. The **waterfall** itself is 50m north of *Berkoh Lodge*. There's a deep pool for swimming, and you may see kingfishers, large fish eagles, *bulbul* birds and monitor lizards.

TRENGGAN AND KENIAM LODGES

The upriver lodges are set in tranquil surroundings, and make excellent bases for exploring less visited parts of the park. You should pre-book all lodges with the park wildlife office at the resort. The closer lodge, at **KUALA TRENGGAN**, is 11km upstream from *Taman Negara Resort,* reached either by boat (30min; RM80 per boat), or by one of two trails (6–8hr). The shorter and more direct trail runs alongside Sungei Tembeling (9km), but can be quite hard going; the easier inland route (12km) runs north past the campsite at Lubok Lesong. *Trenggan Lodge* (10 beds; ⑤) has wooden chalets and a café.

A further 20km north along Sungei Tembeling (2hr from the resort; RM140 per boat), *Keniam Lodge* (10 beds; ⑥) comprises several chalets and a small café. From here, the **Perkai trail** (3km; 2hr) is rich with banded and dusky leaf monkeys, long-tailed macaques and white-handed gibbons. The more popular hike from here is the **Keniam–Trenggan trail** (13km), a major highlight, combining the possibility of seeing elephants with visits to three caves. It's generally a tough, full day's hike, but can be done in around six hours; there are innumerable streams to wade through and hills to circumvent.

Kuala Lipis

KUALA LIPIS, 170km northeast of KL, was once a vibrant tin-town and from 1898 to 1955 served as the state capital of Pahang, but today it's an inconsequential place, of interest to tourists mainly as a **transit point** en route to Kenong Rimba State Park. Both train and bus stations are very central, close to the town's inexpensive hotels. The jetty – from where boats leave on Saturdays for Kenong Rimba State Park – lies 50m northeast of the market on Jalan Jelai. There are two **tourist information offices**, both offering much the same services. One is a private concern (☎09/312 3277; Mon–Fri 9am–5pm, Sat 9am–1pm), tucked away on the left of the train station exit, opposite the ticket booth; the other is just outside the station (Mon–Fri 9am–5pm, Sat 9am–1pm; ☎09/312 5032). The most atmospheric **place to stay** is the *Government Rest House*, on Jalan Bukit Residen (☎09/312 7284; ③), which has twenty en-suite rooms with air-con or fan; the furniture is a bit old, but all the rooms are large and clean and the surrounds are stately. The budget options are in the town centre, mostly on Jalan Besar heading east from the bus station. Try *Gin Loke* at 64 Jl Besar (☎09/312 1388; ①) or next-door *Hotel Lipis* (☎09/312 3142; ①), run by Appu, a trekking guide; there's a spotless dorm (RM7), a range of rooms with shared showers and Internet facilities.

Kenong Rimba State Park

KENONG RIMBA STATE PARK is one of the best reasons to travel the jungle railway into the interior and makes a good stop-off between KL and Kota Bharu. It offers a compact version of the Taman Negara experience – jungle trails, caves, riverside camping, mammal-spotting and excellent bird-watching – at much reduced prices and without the hype. No special equipment is needed, other than a tent and blanket for sleeping. Take lots of mosquito repellent and always carry at least one litre of water with you on the trails. You can organize a **tour** of the park from Kuala Lipis (4 days; RM180) at either of the tourist information offices (see above). *The Gin Loke* hotel and the *Hotel Lipis* also organize tours. It's not possible to visit without a guide.

Practicalities

The easiest way to get to the park is to travel **from Kuala Lipis** on Saturday, when a sampan (RM16) leaves the Jalan Jelai jetty at 2pm, arriving at the Tanjung Kiara jetty at around 4pm. On other days of the week, you can charter a sampan directly from Kuala Lipis, at around RM70 per boat. However, it's cheaper to take the 6.30am local train to **BATU SEMBILAN** (30min; RM1), just a few stops to the south of Kuala Lipis, where you walk left (east) along a narrow road 50m to the jetty on Sungei Jelai. Here, sampans take you on the thirty-minute trip downstream (RM20 per person) to the **Tanjung Kiara jetty**. From the jetty it's then a thirty-minute walk along a road through Kampung Dusun, past a small store on your right to a bridge where the park proper begins. After a further hour along a forest path, you reach the **park headquarters** and chalets at **GUNUNG KESONG**.

The caves and trails

The first of the six **caves** in Rimba is outside the park proper, close to the Tanjung Kiara jetty. About ten minutes' walk from the jetty along the road look out for a path on your left (west) which leads to **Gua Batu Tinggi**. Inside, there's a surprising variety of plant life – including orchids and fig trees. **Gua Batu Tangga** can be reached direct from the camp at Gunung Kesong, though you can also get there from Tinggi by returning on the same trail and crossing the road, following the path to the left of a house – there's a sign pointing to the cave, another twenty minutes' walk further on. It has a wide, deep chamber and in the northwest corner a row of rocks forms ledges or steps. Two smaller caves, **Gua Batu Tangkup** and **Gua Batu Telahup**, are just a few hundred metres beyond Tangga on the same trail. **Gua Hijau** is five minutes' walk from headquarters and home to thousands of bats.

The main trail in the park, the Kesong trail, leads to Seven Steps Waterfall (10km; 4hr one-way), which heads north from the headquarters along Sungei Kesong. Around 250m before the waterfall you cross Sungei Kesong for the final time to reach the Kenong campsite. From here, the trail continues through high forest to a set of rapids, with jungle closing in all around. Returning on the southeastern loop of the trail takes longer – around twelve hours walking – and is harder going as it traverses small hills and follows a less well-defined path. You need at least a one-night stop. The first leg of the return trail is a six-hour walk to Gunung Putih (cave camp). After a further three hours or so, you pass close to a Batek village, where you can pitch a tent near the huts, if you ask. From here you could climb Bukit Agong (1800m; 2hr each way), a stiff ascent along an unmarked and overgrown track. Returning to headquarters from the village takes around another two hours on the main trail. Most people take four days to complete the circuit.

THE EAST COAST

The four-hundred-kilometre stretch from the northeastern corner of the Peninsula to Kuantan, roughly halfway down the east coast, is the most "Malay" region in Malaysia, with strong cultural traditions – particularly in **Kota Bharu**, the last major town before the Thai border, whose inhabitants still practise ancient Malay crafts such as kite-making and top-spinning. The casuarina-fringed beaches and coral reefs on two of the most beautiful islands in the South China Sea, **Pulau Perhentian** and **Pulau Kapas**, are the greatest attraction, but there are some appealing places on the mainland too, not least the laid-back backpackers' resort of **Cherating**, and **Rantau Abang**, one of only five places in the world where giant leatherback turtles come to nest between May and September. Many of the east-coast islands are virtually out of bounds between November and February because of the annual monsoon.

Kota Bharu

At the very northeastern corner of the Peninsula, close to the Thai border, **KOTA BHARU** is the capital of Kelantan State and one of the most important cultural centres in Malaysia. The town is a showcase for skills and customs little practised elsewhere in Malaysia, with an impressive Cultural Centre and lots of craft workshops. It is also one of only three towns in Malaysia (together with Kuala Terangganu and Dungun) to have a Malay majority. Foreign women sometimes complain about feeling uncomfortable in Kota Bharu, but while it's not a place to sport beach wear, there's a relaxed air about the town which belies its political conservatism and mitigates its male-dominated outlook. During the month of **Ramadan**, early in the year, strongly Muslim Kota Bharu virtually shuts up shop.

Arrival and information

Long-distance **buses** arrive at one of the two **bus stations**, inconveniently situated on the southern outskirts of the town. The state bus company, SKMK, operates from the Langgar bus station on Jalan Pasir Puteh, as does the MARA company, which runs buses to KL and Singapore; other companies use the larger bus station on Jalan Hamzah, which also has a left-luggage facility. If you arrive at night, you're at the mercy of the unofficial taxis at the stations, whose drivers can charge up to RM15 for the two-kilometre drive to the centre: the daytime charge is around RM4. The **local bus station**, where buses from Kuala Terengganu arrive,

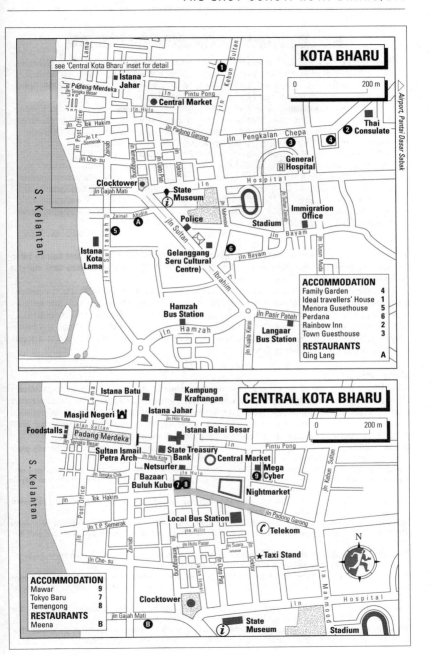

KOTA BHARU

0   200 m

Airport, Pantai Dasar Sabak

see 'Central Kota Bharu' inset for detail

Istana Jahar

Padang Merdeka

Jln Tengku Besar

Jln Pintu Pong

Central Market

Jln Padong Garong

Jln Pengkalan Chepa

Thai Consulate

General Hospital

Jln Post Office

Jln T.P Semerak

Jln Che-su

Jln Tok Hakim

Hospital

Clocktower

Jln Gajah Mati

State Museum

Police

Jln Zainal Abidin

Istana Kota Lama

S. Kelantan

Gelanggang Seru Cultural Centre)

Jln Bayam

Immigration Office

Stadium

Jln Sultan Zainab

Jln Dusun Muda

Hamzah Bus Station

Jln Pasir Pateh

Jln Hamzah

Langaar Bus Station

ACCOMMODATION
Family Garden   4
Ideal travellers' House   1
Menora Gusethouse   5
Perdana   6
Rainbow Inn   2
Town Guesthouse   3

RESTAURANTS
Qing Lang   A

CENTRAL KOTA BHARU

0   200 m

Istana Batu

Kampung Kraftangan

Masjid Negeri

Istana Jahar

Jln Hilir Kota

Istana Balai Besar

Foodstalls

Padang Merdeka

Jln Tengku Besar

Sultan Ismail Petra Arch

State Treasury Bank

Jln Hulu Kota

Central Market

Pintu Pong

Netsurfer

Jln Hulu

Mega Cyber

Jln Tengku Chik

Bazaar Buluh Kubu

Nightmarket

S. Kelantan

Jln Padong Garong

Local Bus Station

Jln Hilir

Telekom

Jln Post Office

Jln Tok Hakim

Jln Hulu Pasar

Jln Suara Muda

Taxi Stand

Jln T.P Semerak

Jln Che-su

N

Clocktower

ACCOMMODATION
Mawar   9
Tokyo Baru   7
Temengong   8
RESTAURANTS
Meena   B

Jln Gajah Mati

State Museum

Hospital

Stadium

CROSSING THE BORDER INTO THAILAND

From Kota Bharu, you can cross the Thai border by river or by land. If you're going to stay in Thailand for more than a month, you'll need a **visa**, easily obtainable from the town's consulate (see "Listings", p.614). Both **border posts** are open daily 6am–6pm; remember that Thai time is one hour behind Malaysian time.

The coastal access point is at **Pengkalan Kubor**, 20km northwest of Kota Bharu, which connects with the small town of Tak Bai on the Thai side. Take bus #27 or #43 from the local bus station for the thirty-minute journey (RM1.70), then the car ferry (50 sen).

More convenient however is the land crossing at **Rantau Panjang**, 30km southwest of Kota Bharu. Bus #29 departs from the local bus station in Kota Bharu every thirty minutes (6.45am–6.30pm) for the 45-minute trip (RM2.60), or you can take a shared taxi from Kota Bharu for RM3.50 each; from Rantau Panjang, it's a short walk across the border to Sungai Kolok on the Thai side. Trains depart from here at noon and 3pm for the 23-hour trip to Bangkok via Hat Yai and Surat Thani; if you want to be sure of a seat, tickets can be booked for RM30 at the *Town Guesthouse* (see below). Buses to Bangkok leave at 9am and 12.30pm; buses to Hat Yai take four hours.

is on Jalan Padong Garong; SKMK also operates some services from here and has an information counter (daily 8am–9pm; closed Fri 12.45pm–2pm). The **long-distance taxi** stand is behind the bus station on Jalan Doktor.

The nearest **train station** to Kota Bharu is 7km to the west at Wakaf Bharu, the penultimate stop on the jungle railway (see p.603). From here it's a twenty-minute ride into town on bus #19 or #27. The **airport** is 9km northeast of the centre; a taxi into town costs RM15 – buy a coupon from the taxi counter in the airport. Tours to local craft workshops and homestays can be booked at the **Tourist Information Centre** (Sun–Thurs 8am–1pm & 2–4.45pm; ☎09/748 5534) on Jalan Sultan Ibrahim.

Accommodation

Kota Bharu has some of the cheapest **accommodation** in Malaysia; nearly all guesthouses have dorms as well as ordinary rooms, and the rates often include breakfast. An alternative option is the **homestay programme** run by Roselan Hanafiah at the Tourist Information Centre, which offers the chance to stay with a family, often expert in a particular craft (RM220 per person, minimum 2 people for 2 nights/3 days, including all meals).

Family Garden, 4945d Lorong Islah Lama (☎09/747 5763). Near the Thai consulate, this homely place offers free breakfast and transport to the out-of-town bus stations. ②.

Ideal Travellers' House, 3954f Jl Kebun Sultan (☎09/744 2246). Friendly and quiet despite its very central location, this budget hostel with a peaceful beer garden and dorm (RM6) is the most pleasant retreat you'll find in Kota Bharu. ①.

Mawar, Jl Parit Dalam (☎09/744 8888). A Baroque lobby and small but comfortable rooms. It has its own café, and is situated right by the pasar malam. ⑦.

Menora Guesthouse, 3338d Jl Sultanah Zainab (☎09/748 1669). Accommodation consists of a dorm (RM6) and large, brightly painted rooms with or without shower and toilet; there's also a café and roof garden with a river view. ①.

Perdana, Jl Mahmood (☎09/748 5000). A concrete monstrosity on the outside, but a good-value, high-end hotel indoors with swimming pool, squash courts, gym and in-house movies. ⑦.

Rainbow Inn, 4423a Jl Pengkalan Chepa (☎09/743 4936). Clean rooms in a hundred-year old wooden house east of the centre. Laid-back and friendly with a garden, batik workshop, dorms (RM6) and bikes for rent. ①.

Tokyo Baru, 3945 Jl Tok Hakim (☎09/744 4511). Top-floor rooms have great balconies overlooking the town centre and the simple, clean doubles with fan or air-con are good value. ②.

Temenggong Hotel, Jl Tok Hakim 15000 (☎09/748 3481). Spotless mid-range choice in the centre. The modern rooms complete with bathtub, fridge, TV and air-con are excellent value. ⑤.

Town Guesthouse, 286 Jl Pengkalan Chepa (☎09/748 3207). A warm and welcoming, family-run guesthouse with a communal lounge, rooftop café and Internet facilities. ①.

The Town

Small Padang Merdeka in the north part of town is Kota Bharu's historical heart. Near here, the **Istana Jahar** (daily except Fri 8.30am–4.45pm; RM2) houses the Royal Customs Museum whose ground floor is given over to a display of exquisite *ikat* and *songket* textiles and ornate gold jewellery; upstairs you'll see life-size reconstructions of various traditional royal ceremonies, from weddings to circumcisions. Behind the istana, a **Weapon's Gallery** (RM1) displays an impressive collection of spears, daggers and *kris*.

As you leave the museum, turn the corner to your left and after a few metres you'll see the sky-blue **Istana Batu** (daily 8am–4.45pm, closed Fri; RM2), now the Kelantan Royal Museum, with the Sultan's rooms left in their original state. Directly opposite, the **Kampung Kraftangan** (daily except Fri 8am–4.45pm), or "Handicraft Village", comprises gift shops, a café and a museum (RM1).

Situated on the corner of Jalan Hospital and Jalan Sultan Ibrahim, the **State Museum** (Sat–Thurs 8am–4.45pm; RM2) houses an odd collection of paintings and pots, as well as some more interesting musical instruments, such as the *kertok*, a large coconut with its top sliced off and fitted with a sounding board – one of the percussion instruments peculiar to Kelantan. To see these in action, visit the **Gelanggang Seni**, Kota Bharu's Cultural Centre, on Jalan Mahmood. Free performances here (March–Oct Mon, Wed & Sat except during Ramadan) feature many of the traditional pastimes of Kelantan, including the vigorous sport of top-spinning, and the playing of giant 100kg *rebana* drums. On Wednesday evenings there are wayung kulit (shadow play) performances, and on Saturday nights, shows combine singing, dancing and comedy, derived from nineteenth-century court entertainments.

For a chance to watch local crafts being made, and to buy them direct, visit the **workshops** (daily 9am–5pm) that line the road north from Kota Bharu to the coast. Kampung Penambang is particularly good for *songket* weaving and **batik** (many workshops here will allow you to create your own designs), while Kampung Kijang specializes in kite-making; both villages are barely beyond the town suburbs on the #10 bus, which leaves from beside the Central Market.

Eating

Easily the most exciting place to eat at is Kota Bharu's **night market** (daily 6.30pm–midnight; closed for evening prayers 7.30–8pm), with an amazing variety of food – although vegetarians could find themselves limited to vegetable *murtabaks*. Try the local speciality *ayam percik* (barbecued chicken with a creamy coconut sauce) or the delicious *nasi kerabu* (purple, green or blue rice with a dash of vegetables, seaweed and grated coconut), finish off with a filling *pisang murtabak* (banana pancake), and you won't have parted with much more than RM5. The town's **restaurants** are a letdown after the night market, but *Meena* on Jalan Gajah Mati does excellent, inexpensive banana-leaf curries and *Qing Lang* on Jalan Zainal Abidin serves a totally meat-free menu at RM3 per dish.

Listings

Airlines MAS, Komplek Yakin, Jl Gajah Mati (☎09/744 7000).

Banks and exchange Bank Bumiputra, Jl Kebu Sultan; Hong Kong Bank, Jl Padong Garong; Standard Chartered Bank, Jl Tok Hakim.

Hospital The General Hospital is on Jl Hospital (☎09/748 5533).

Immigration On-the-spot visa renewals are available at the Immigration Office, second floor, Wisma Persekutuan, Jl Bayan (daily 8am–4pm except Thurs 8am–12.45pm; ☎09/748 2120).

Internet access It's not hard to find an Internet café in Kota Bharu; most are clustered around the central market. Good choices include *Net Surfer Café* on Jl Hulu and *Mega Cyber*, Jl Parit Dalam.

Police Headquarters on Jl Sultan Ibrahim (☎09/748 5522).

Post office The GPO is on Jl Sultan Ibrahim (Mon–Thurs & Sun 8am–4.30pm; ☎09/748 4033). Efficient poste restante/general delivery at counter 20.

Telephone services The Telekom centre is on Jl Doktor (daily 8am–4.30pm).

Thai visas From the Royal Thai Consulate, 4426 Jl Pengkalan Chepa (☎09/748 2545; Sun–Thurs 9am–12pm & 2–3.30pm, closed Fri & Sat). Two-month tourist visas (RM33) are issued within 24 hours.

Pulau Perhentian

PULAU PERHENTIAN, just over 20km off the northeastern coast, is actually two islands – **Perhentian Kecil** (Small Island) and **Perhentian Besar** (Big Island). Both are textbook tropical paradises, neither more than 4km in length. Not surprisingly, they are a popular getaway for KL and Singaporean weekenders (especially in August), and see a regular stream of backpackers. Life here is delightful, with only flying foxes, monkeys and lizards for company. Neither island boasts a raging nightlife, as there's no alcohol in most places, but local people seem to have no objection to you bringing your own. Don't be tempted to bring drugs, though – there are frequent police road checks on the way to the islands. Activities include snorkelling trips around the islands (RM30 – though you can hire your own gear for RM15 a

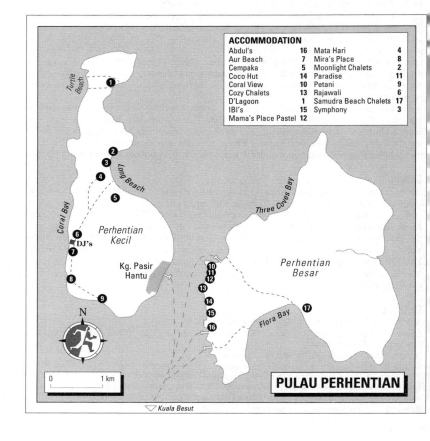

ACCOMMODATION			
Abdul's	16	Mata Hari	4
Aur Beach	7	Mira's Place	8
Cempaka	5	Moonlight Chalets	2
Coco Hut	14	Paradise	11
Coral View	10	Petani	9
Cozy Chalets	13	Rajawali	6
D'Lagoon	1	Samudra Beach Chalets	17
IBI's	15	Symphony	3
Mama's Place Pastel	12		

PULAU PERHENTIAN

day) and dive courses (RM750 four-day open water course, fun dives RM85). The harsh east-coast **monsoon** means that the islands, reached by slow and unsophisticated fishing boats from Kuala Besut, are frequently inaccessible between November and January.

Getting there: Kuala Besut

The ragged little town of **KUALA BESUT**, 45km south of Kota Bharu, is the departure point for Pulau Perhentian. It's reached by taking bus #3 from Kota Bharu's local bus station to Pasir Puteh (every 15min; 1hr), and then bus #96 (every 30min; 30min) to Kuala Besut. Most guesthouses in Kota Bharu also organize share taxis (RM25) direct to Kuala Besut. There are no banks in Kuala Besut, or on the islands, so **change money** before you go. In season, many companies – most of them pretty unscrupulous – run **boats** from the Kuala Besut quay-side, just behind the bus station (every 2hr; 9am–5pm; 1hr 30min). Morning departures are preferable, since the weather tends to be more reliable. Tickets (buy one on the boat) cost RM20 one-way, but don't get a return because it may well not be honoured by a rival boat taking you back. Boats stop at most of the jetties, but perhaps check with the skipper first.

Perhentian Kecil

On the southeastern corner of **PERHENTIAN KECIL** lies the island's only village, **Kampung Pasir Hantu**, with a jetty, police station, school and clinic – but the littered beach doesn't encourage you to stay. The west-facing coves have the advantage of the sunsets: **Coral Bay** is the most popular. East-facing **Long Beach** has been the target of most development on Kecil, not surprisingly, since it boasts a wide stretch of white beach and good coral nearby. However, it's much more exposed to the elements, the crashing surf forcing many of the chalet owners to close up from the end of October to April.

CORAL BAY ACCOMMODATION

Aur Beach (no phone). Basic but popular chalets with showers. ④.

Mira's Place (☎011/976603). Located on its own sandy bay a 25-minute walk from Coral Bay, this popular place is a cluster of rustic chalets with a communal TV and radio. ②.

Petani (☎01/881 2444). Fifteen minutes around the headland from *Mira's* on a superb beach, this has clean, well-built chalets with shower. The easiest way to get here is by boat, otherwise it's a rough 45-minute walk from Coral Bay. ⑤.

Rajawali (☎010/980 5244). Perched high up on the rocky headland, these chalets take mainly package bookings. ②.

Sunset View (☎012/938 8083). Slightly overpriced but smartly furnished chalets with showers, well placed on the southern end of the bay. (③).

LONG BEACH ACCOMMODATION

Cempaka (☎010/985 3729). A mishmash of basic A-frames without electricity, and double chalets with shower. There are also some less expensive doubles in a longhouse. ②–④.

D'Lagoon. Set in a tiny cove at the very northeast tip of the island 1km from Long Beach, with tents, rooms and chalets. From here, you can clamber across the narrow neck of the island to the turtle-spotting beach on the other side. ②.

Mata Hari (☎019/956 8726). Simple but well-designed chalets in a garden, hammocks and a good restaurant. ②.

Moonlight Chalets (☎010/982 8135). A wide range of good-value chalets set at the northern end of the beach ranging from basic A-frames with no electricity to doubles with attached bathrooms. This is also the best place for food, and the upstairs restaurant has a good view across the beach. ①–②.

Symphony, no phone. Some of the least expensive accommodation on the island; hurricane lamps, thatched roofs and very friendly staff who try hard. ①.

Perhentian Besar

The best place on the islands for turtle-watching is undoubtedly Three Coves Bay on the north coast of **PERHENTIAN BESAR**. A stunning conglomeration of three beaches, separated from the main area of accommodation by rocky outcrops and reached only by speedboat, it provides a secluded haven between May and September for green and hawksbill turtles to come ashore and lay their eggs. Most of the accommodation on Perhentian Besar is on the western half of the island and tends to be more upmarket than on Kecil. The beach improves as you go further south and the atmosphere is slightly more laid-back than at Long Beach. The best snorkelling beach (and it's *not* privately owned despite signs up saying "only patrons can use our facilities") is just to the north in front of the *Perenthian Island Resort*. There is more accommodation on Flora Bay, the island's south beach, reached via a trail from *Abdul's*.

Abdul's (☎010/983 7303). Fronting one of the best strips of beach, with some basic rooms in a longhouse as well as some costlier ones with shower. This is one of the best places at the low end of the price spectrum. ②.

Coco Hut (☎019/910 5019). Inexpensive, waterless A-frames on the beach front. ②.

Coral View (☎010/903 0943). Located on a rocky outcrop, these tastefully designed and very well furnished chalets are the best accommodation on either island, ranging from well-designed doubles with shower to hotel-style en-suites with air-con, minibar and hot water. The restaurant is also worth the outlay. ⑥–⑧.

Cozy Chalets (☎09/697 7703). Built on a headland which separates the beach north and south, this has smart, carpeted chalets built two by two up on the rocks. There's also a scenic restaurant. ③.

IBI's (☎010/910 6244). Large, clean but slightly ramshackle chalets set on an excellent beach in semi-detached pairs, two to a bathroom. There's a book exchange, a good restaurant and email facilities, but the rooms themselves are a little better at *Abdul's*. ②.

Mama's Place Pastel-coloured chalets by the beach and cheaper ones behind. Rather regimented, this large operation, the only inexpensive option north of *Cozy Chalets*, has decent doubles, with or without plumbing ②–④.

Paradise Chalets (☎010/981 0930). Similar and nextdoor to *Mama's*, the double chalets here are functional enough but a little expensive and rather crudely laid out. ④.

Samudra Beach Chalets (☎010/983 4929). Pleasant bungalows and smaller, less expensive A-frames, all with plumbing, set on the remote Flora Bay. ③.

Kuala Terengganu

The tiny Muslim metropolis, **KUALA TERENGGANU**, 160km south of Kota Bharu, is a traditional place set on an estuary, with dozens of craft workshops and an exceptional cultural museum complex, the new **Istana Tengku Long Museum** (daily 9am–5pm; Fri closed noon–3pm; RM5), which is set in landscaped gardens 3km west of the centre. The main building displays exquisite fabrics and crafts, and details the history of Terengganu. Elsewhere in the compound, you'll find a fine exhibit of Koranic calligraphy, two traditional sailing boats, a small Maritime Museum and some reconstructed ancient timber palaces. The supreme example of these is the Istana Tunku Long, originally built in 1888 with a high pointed roof and wooden gables fitted with twenty gilded screens, intricately carved with Koranic verses. The museum is easily reached by the regular Losong minibus (20min; 50 sen) from the local bus station.

At the west end of Kuala Terengganu, Jalan Bandar forms the centre of **Chinatown**, where you'll find the excellent *Teratai*, no.151, selling local arts and crafts. Kuala Terengganu's **Central Market** (daily 6am–6pm), a little further down on the right, close to the junction with Jalan Kota, also deals in batik, *songkets* and brassware. For other good craft buys, check out the small **brassware** workshop (daily 8.30am–6pm) on Jalan Ladang in the east of town. *Ky Enterprises*, about 3km due south of the centre on Jalan Panji Alam, is a good place to watch the *mengkuang* style of **weaving**, using pandanus leaves to make bags, floor mats and fans; take minibus #12, #15, #26 or #13c (60sen) for the fifteen-minute ride from the local bus station. In neighbouring Pasir Panjang, about 500m west of Jalan Panji Alam, Abu Bakar bin Mohammed Amin on Lorong Saga, is a **kris** maker (call to make an appointment; ☎09/622 7968); take minibus #12 from the local bus station and get off at the sign marked "Sekolah Kebangsaan Psr. Panjang". You can catch **traditional dance** shows at the Gelanggang Seni cultural centre, a two-kilometre walk or trishaw ride southeast from the centre, facing the town's beach, Pantai Batu Buruk (Fri & Sat 5–7pm & 9–11pm, except during Ramadan; free).

Practicalities

The **local bus station** is opposite the taxi stand on Jalan Masjid Abidin, and the **express bus station** is across town on Jalan Sultan Zainal Abidin. Sultan Mohammed **airport** is 13km northeast of the centre (☎09/666 4500), a RM15–20 taxi ride to the centre; the city bus marked "Kem Seberang Takir" picks up from the road directly outside and runs to the local bus station. The MAS office is at 13 Jl Sultan Omar (☎09/624 5618).

There's a **Tourist Information Centre** (8am–5pm; ☎09/622 1553) near the GPO on Jalan Sultan Zainal Abdin. There are plenty of inexpensive **Internet** places on Jalan Tok Lam, including the *Goldenwood Café* at number 59 (☎09/626 5282) and *Teman Cyber*, no. 18b (☎09/623 4446).

ACCOMMMODATION AND EATING

The pleasantest **place to stay** is *Awi's Yellow House* (☎09/624 7363; ①–②), a delightful complex of stilted huts built over the water, with basic cabins and a spacious dorm (RM6). If you arrive by boat, follow the river south as closely as possible – *Awi's* is known to all the locals. From the bus station take minibus #16 or 20 (60 sen) or a taxi (RM5), and get off at the base of the Sultan Mahmud Bridge, from where *Awi's* is a short walk. Buses across the bridge are infrequent, and the ferries stop running at around 6pm. Back in town, the *Ping Anchorage Travellers' Homestay*, 77a Jl Dato Isaac (☎09/626 2020; ②) is a budget hostel with basic rooms, a dorm (RM6) and a travel agency. The *KT Mutiara*, 67 Jl Sultan Ismail (☎09/622 2655; ②),has small, spotless rooms with air-con, but it's a touch overpriced.

There are excellent **food stalls** on Jalan Tok Lam and behind the express bus station, serving the usual Malay dishes (11.30am–midnight). Otherwise *MD Curry house*, 19c Jl Tok Lam, has some of the best south Indian *thali*s you'll find in Malaysia. *Restoran Golden Dragon*, Jalan Bandar, is the best Chinese, while *kedai kopi* and a wide range of dishes and Western fare – as well as beer – can be had at *Travellers Café* on Jalan Dato Isaac.

Marang

The tiny coastal village of **MARANG**, 17km south of Kuala Terengganu, has long attracted a steady trickle of foreign visitors, drawn to the place by the promise of "old Malaysia", as well as the delights of nearby Pulau Kapas, 6km offshore. There's a handful of guesthouses and batik shops here, but nothing much else. Any Dungun- or Rhu Muda-bound **bus** (every 30min) from Kuala Terengganu will drop you on the main road at Marang, from where the centre is a short walk down one of the roads towards the sea. The **ferry companies** running boats over to Pulau Kapas (RM15 return) have their offices on the main road. Mid-morning is the usual departure time but there is no service during the monsoon (Nov–Feb). One of the best **places to stay** is the *Green Mango Inn* (☎09/618 2040; ①), a real traveller's hangout a little south of town, with a dorm (RM6) and very basic A-frame doubles. The *Island View Resort* (☎09/618 2006; ①–③) has a range of rooms, including air-con doubles, while the *Marang Guest House* up on the hill (☎09/618 1976; ②–③) has nice cabins, and some A-frames with an excellent vantage point over the ocean.

Pulau Kapas

A thirty-minute ride by fishing boat from Marang takes you to **PULAU KAPAS**, less than 2km in length and one of the nicest islands off the east coast. Coves on the western side are accessible only by sea or by clambering over rocks, but you'll be rewarded by excellent sand and aquamarine water. Like many of its neighbours, Kapas is a designated marine park, the best snorkelling being around rocky Pulau Gemia, just off the northwestern shore, while the northernmost cove is ideal for turtle-spotting. The only **accommodation** is at the two western coves that directly face the mainland. The best value is *Zaki Beach Chalet* (☎010/619

5258; ②), which has comfortable A-frames, and its restaurant is definitely the place to be in the evenings. Close by, the welcoming *Pulau Kapas Garden Resort* (☎010/984 1686; ③) has more luxurious rooms and a dive shop (courses start from RM950). A wooden walkway over the rocks leads to the jetty in the next bay and to the *Kapas Island Resort* (☎09/623 6110; ⑥), exclusive Malay-style chalets with a swimming pool and extensive watersports facilities. Next along is the ramshackle *Beauty Island* (☎011/971958; ③). The *Le Village* (☎09/624 6090; ⑥) is a much better operation, and the most basic place is the *Lighthouse* (☎09/618 1529; ③), which has dorm beds (RM10) with only a well shower.

Rantau Abang

The village of **RANTAU ABANG**, 43km from Marang, is no more than a collection of guest-houses strung out along two kilometres of dusty road, but it has made its name as one of a hand-ful of places in the world where the increasingly rare **giant leatherback turtle** comes to lay its eggs, returning year after year between May and September to the same beaches. Specific nest-ing areas and hatcheries have been established on the beach, fenced off from the curious human beings. When the hatchlings have broken out of their shells, they are released at the top of the beach (4–6am), and their scurry to the sea is supervised to ensure their safe progress. Visitors are asked to keep at least 5m away and not to use torches and camera flashes. The guesthouses will arrange for you to be woken during the night if one is sighted, for a fee of RM3. For inter-esting background, visit the **Turtle Information Centre** (May–Aug daily 8am–12.45pm, 2–6pm & 8–11pm, except Fri 9am–noon & 3–11pm; Sept–April Sat–Wed 8am–12.45pm & 2–4pm, Thurs 8am–12.45pm, Fri closed; free), to the north of the central two-kilometre strip.

Local **buses** from Kuala Terengganu and Marang run every thirty minutes (7.30am–6pm; 1hr) to Rantau Abang. If you're coming by express bus from the south, you have to change at Dungun, 13km to the south, from where you can easily get a local bus for the remainder of the journey. Buses drop you on the main road, at the R&R Plaza, just a short walk from all the accommodation.

There are surprisingly few **accommodation** options, all of them close to the beach. Prices rise dramatically when the turtles are in town (May–Sept), and the price codes refer to the high-season rate. *Dahimah's Guest House* (☎09/845 2843; ①–⑤), 1km south of the informa-tion centre, offers a range of rooms, from comfortable fan doubles to riverside air-con family rooms. *Awang's* (☎09/844 3500; ②–③), right by the information centre, is friendly and has a variety of simple rooms, but is a little rundown and the air-con chalets are overpriced. *Ismail's* (☎019/983 6202; ②), next door, is very basic and not as clean. All guesthouses have their own **restaurants** (closed Nov–Jan). In addition, there are **food stalls** near *Awang's*, and the excellent *Kedai Makan Rantau Abang*, 750m further south.

Cherating

The fast-expanding travellers' hangout of **CHERATING**, 47km north of Kuantan, hugs the northern end of a windswept bay, protected from the breeze by the shelter of a rocky cliff. Although most of the locals have long since moved to a small village further south, the set-tlement still tries to reflect kampung life. It's a good place in which to unwind, with a nightlife that comes as close as the east coast gets to raging. Cherating is ideal for **windsurfing**, and you can rent equipment for RM15 an hour. Clambering over the rocks at the eastern end of the bay brings you to a tiny secluded cove, though the beach isn't as good as that belonging to the exclusive *Club Med* over the next outcrop.

Any express or local **bus** between Kuala Terengganu and Kuantan will drop you off at Cherating – tell the driver beforehand. Two rough tracks lead from the road down into the main part of the village, about five minutes' away, although the one nearest the bridge is the most direct. The main drag is a tiny surfaced road that runs roughly parallel to the beach, and this is where you'll find most of the restaurants and bars, as well as the provisions stores and Travel Post (☎09/581 9825), which acts as a travel agency where you can book bus tickets for destinations in Malaysia and to Singapore, as well as local river and snorkelling trips (RM15 including equipment). They also have **Internet** terminals, an international fax line, and money changing services.

Accommodation

Cherating Cottage (☎09/581 9273). A sturdily built bar and restaurant surrounded by chalets for every budget, from RM10 dorms to air-con en-suites with hot water. ②–③.

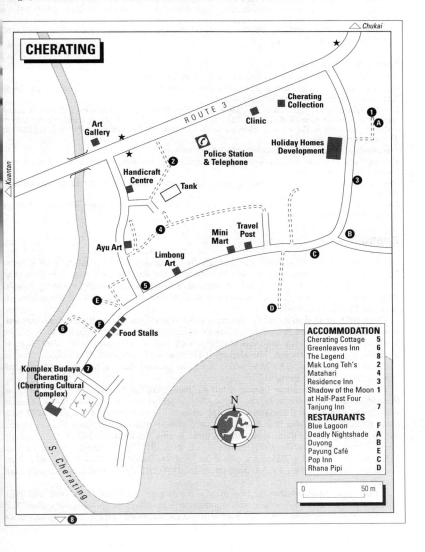

CHERATING

△ Chukai

ROUTE 3

△ Kuantan

Art Gallery

Cherating Collection

Clinic

Police Station & Telephone

Handicraft Centre

Holiday Homes Development

Tank

Ayu Art

Mini Mart

Travel Post

Limbong Art

Food Stalls

Komplex Budaya Cherating (Cherating Cultural Complex)

S. Cherating

N

ACCOMMODATION
Cherating Cottage	5
Greenleaves Inn	6
The Legend	8
Mak Long Teh's	2
Matahari	4
Residence Inn	3
Shadow of the Moon at Half-Past Four	1
Tanjung Inn	7

RESTAURANTS
Blue Lagoon	F
Deadly Nightshade	A
Duyong	B
Payung Café	E
Pop Inn	C
Rhana Pipi	D

0   50 m

Greenleaves Inn (☎09/581 9825). A vividly coloured, new-age, riverside den in the jungle – every loft, veranda and cabin crafted and painted by Iggy, an artist from KL. ②.

Mak Long Teh's (☎09/581 9290). Set back from the main road, this budget, ramshackle place offers home cooking in a warm family environment. ①.

Matahari, no phone. Spacious, sturdy chalets each with a fridge and large verandah, as well as a separate communal area with a TV room, cooking facilities and a batik studio. ①.

Residence Inn (☎09/581 9333). The most upmarket place within the village, this hotel has large and well-equipped rooms arranged around a pleasant swimming pool and lobby area. ⑤.

The Shadow of the Moon at Half-Past Four (☎09/581 9186). Well-designed timber chalets with attached bathroom, hot water and hand-crafted furniture, tucked away in a beautiful wooded area. There's also a dorm (RM10). ③.

Tanjung Inn (☎09/581 9081). An attractive range of chalets and family rooms set in a scenic, landscaped garden with a lake. ②–③.

Eating and drinking

The following restaurants and bars are marked on the map.

Blue Lagoon Busy bar and restaurant whose Chinese-based menu attracts the expat crowd from the oil refineries up the coast; averages RM8 per dish.

Deadly Nightshade, at the *Shadow of the Moon at Half Past Four*. One of the most imaginatively designed bars you'll come across in all of Malaysia. Fairy lights, piles of books, chess sets and homemade furniture add to the atmosphere. There are excellent set meals for around RM7 and banana-leaf curries and BBQ on Thursdays and Fridays.

Duyong Good, inexpensive Chinese food with a beach view.

Payung Café. Inexpensive Italian food, in a riverside setting. Also open for breakfast and lunch, with Western dishes and goulash.

Pop Inn Pub-style steak house, also serving snacks by the beach. Stays open late and has the odd live band and DJ.

Rhana Pipi On the beach opposite *Ranting Beach Resort*. Laid-back bar which keeps late hours and serves decent Western food.

Kuantan

It's virtually inevitable that you'll pass through the dull, concrete town of **KUANTAN** at some stage, since it's the region's transport hub, lying at the junction of Routes 2 (which runs across the Peninsula to KL), 3 and 14. Kuantan's one real sight is the stunning **Masjid Negeri** on Jalan Makhota, boasting an impressive pastel exterior (green for Islam, blue for peace and white for purity).

The **local bus station** is on Jalan Basar, beside Sungei Kuantan, and the **express bus station** is on Jalan Stadium, in front of the Darulmakmur stadium. **Taxis** (☎09/513 4478) can be found between Jalan Besar and Jalan Makhota, while long distance taxis (☎09/504478) leave from the express bus station. The **airport** is 15km west of town (☎09/538 1291) – a taxi to the centre costs RM20. The MAS office is on the ground floor of the Wisma Bolasepak Pahang, Jalan Gambut (☎09/515 7055).

The **Tourist Information Centre** (Mon–Fri 9am–5pm, Sat 9am–1pm; ☎09/513 3026), at the end of Jalan Makhota facing the playing fields, can help you out with accommodation in and around Kuantan, and also organizes **day-trips** to the surrounding area. The **GPO**, with poste restante, is on Jalan Haji Abdul Aziz; the Telekom office is next door (9am–4.15pm), and the **Immigration Office** is on the first floor, Wisma Persekutuan, Jalan Gambut for on-the-spot visa renewals (Mon–Fri 9am–4.15pm; ☎09/521373). **Internet** options include *Cyberpoint*, 3rd Floor, 152 Jl Besar, opposite the local bus station (☎09/513 7685); and *Surfers Paradise*, Premiun Lanes, level 4, Kuantan Plaza (☎09/515 0888), which is expensive but open until 1am.

For cheap **accommodation** the best place is the *Meian*, 78 Jl Teluk Sisek (☎09/552 0949; ①–②), which is basic and spotless with a communal hot shower for the simplest rooms. The *Embassy*, 60 Jl Telok Sisek (☎09/552 7486; ②), is a similar second choice. In ascending price order: the *Oriental Evergreen*, 157 Jl Haji Abdul Rahman (☎09/513 0168; ②), tucked down a side street off the main road, has air-con rooms; the *Suraya*, 55 Jl Haji Abdul Aziz (☎09/555 4266; ④), is a comfortable mid-range place, and the *Holiday Inn*, Jalan Beserah (☎09/555 5899), is very reasonably priced for what you get, with a swimming pool and a *dim sum* restaurant. ⑦.

For **food**, the stalls near the mosque on Jalan Makhota behind the Ocean Shopping Complex on Jalan Tun Ismail are the best bet. Otherwise, try *Restoran E & E*, 219 Jl Tun Ismail, which does Malay versions of Western food: steaks in cashew sauce, pizzas and Cantonese spaghetti for example. *New Yee Mee*, Jalan Aziz, a large busy, budget Chinese restaurant has a far-ranging menu, while *Restoran Beryani*, Jalan Bukit Ubi, is one of the few Indian restaurants in town.

THE SOUTH

The south of the Malaysian Peninsula, below Kuala Lumpur and Kuantan, has some of the most historically and culturally significant towns in the country. The west-coast city of **Melaka**, two hours by bus south from KL, still displays an interesting heritage of cultures from its Portuguese, Dutch and British colonists, not to mention its unique Chinese–Malay community of Peranakans. There's plenty to see here, and the city is also just a short boat ride from **Sumatra**. There's little to recommend **Johor Bahru** (or JB) at the tip of the Peninsula, save for its speedy transport links into Singapore, just across the causeway. It's also handy for heading a little way up the east coast to **Pulau Tioman**, a large island with several nice beaches, good diving opportunities and plenty of budget accommodation.

Melaka

When Penang was known only for its oysters and Singapore was just a fishing village, **MELA-KA** had already achieved worldwide fame. Under the auspices of the Melaka Sultanate, founded in the early fifteenth century, political and cultural life flourished, helping to define what it means to be Malay. The town grew rich by **trading spices** from the Moluccas in the Indonesian archipelago and textiles from Gujarat in northwest India. A levy on all imported goods made it one of the wealthiest kingdoms in the world and it gradually expanded its territory to include Singapore and most of east-coast Sumatra. Yet, beginning in 1511, a series of takeovers and botched administrations by the Portuguese, Dutch and British, caused the subjugation of the Malay people; Melaka's modern-day authorities are still working towards reversing the city's decline.

Legacies of all phases of Melaka's past remain in the city, constituting the main tourist sights. Of these, the most interesting are the ancestral homes of the **Baba-Nonya community**, a new racial mix also known as Peranakan that evolved from the sixteenth-century Chinese merchants who settled here and married Malay women. For a one-stop introduction to the city's history, watch the English-language **Sound and Light Show** on Padang Pahlawan (daily 9.30pm, 8.30pm during Ramadan; 1hr; RM5 – closed for renovations at the time of writing).

Arrival

Most people arrive by the daily ferry from Dumai in Sumatra, which docks at **Shah Bandar jetty** on Jalan Merdeka, close to the historical centre and the budget hostel area. There are two bus stations, both located on the northern outskirts of the city, off Jalan Hang Tuah. Buses from Singapore arrive at the **local bus station**. The chaotic **express bus station** is beyond the **taxi station**, a block to the south. From either, it's just a ten-minute walk over the bridge to the town centre. **Batu Berendam Airport** is 9km from the city centre (RM10 by taxi). There's no **train station** in Melaka itself, the nearest being at Tampin, 38km north; buses from Tampin drop you at the local bus station.

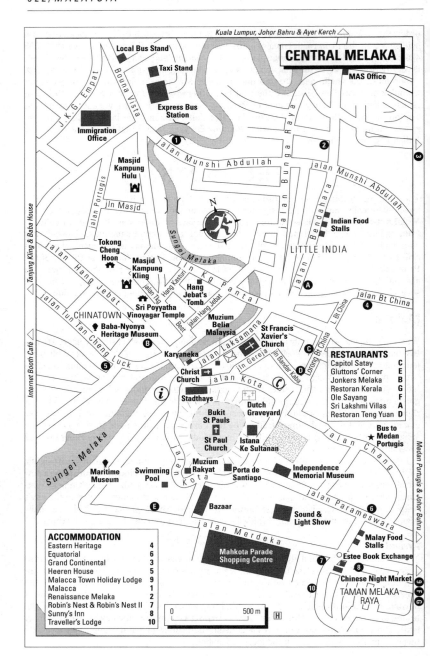

Kuala Lumpur, Johor Bahru & Ayer Kerch △

CENTRAL MELAKA

Local Bus Stand

Taxi Stand

MAS Office

Express Bus Station

Immigration Office

Masjid Kampung Hulu

Jalan Munshi Abdullah

Jln Masjid

jalan Portugis

Jalan Hang Jebat

Tanjung Kling & Baba House △

jalan Munshi Abdullah

Indian Food Stalls

LITTLE INDIA

Tokong Cheng Hoon

Masjid Kampung Kling

Sri Poyyatha Vinoyagar Temple

CHINATOWN

Jalan Tun Tan Cheng Luck

Internet Booth Café △

Baba-Nyonya Heritage Museum

Hang Jebat's Tomb

Muzium Belia Malaysia

Karyaneka

St Francis Xavier's Church

Christ Church

Jalan Laksamana

Jln Gereja

Jalan Kota

Stadthays

Dutch Graveyard

Bukit St Pauls
St Paul Church

Istana Ke Sultanan

Maritime Museum

Swimming Pool

Muzium Rakyat

Porta de Santiago

Independence Memorial Museum

Bus to Medan Portugis

Bazaar

Sungei Melaka

Jalan Chang

Jalan Parameswara

Sound & Light Show

Malay Food Stalls

Medan Portugis & Johor Bahru →

RESTAURANTS

Capitol Satay	C
Gluttons' Corner	E
Jonkers Melaka	B
Restoran Kerala	G
Ole Sayang	F
Sri Lakshmi Villas	A
Restoran Teng Yuan	D

ACCOMMODATION

Eastern Heritage	4
Equatorial	6
Grand Continental	3
Heeren House	5
Malacca Town Holiday Lodge	9
Malacca	1
Renaissance Melaka	2
Robin's Nest & Robin's Nest II	7
Sunny's Inn	8
Traveller's Lodge	10

Jalan Merdeka

Mahkota Parade Shopping Centre

Estee Book Exchange

Chinese Night Market

TAMAN MELAKA RAYA

0   500 m

MOVING ON FROM MELAKA

By plane
Batu Berendam Airport, 9km from the city centre, caters only for small aircraft. Pelangi Air (☎06/282 2648) runs a service to both Singapore (RM150 one-way) and Ipoh (RM120 one-way) from Monday to Saturday, and there are Tuesday and Saturday flights to Pekan Baru (RM145) and Medan (RM258), both in Sumatra. For tickets contact MAS, on the first floor of the *City Bayview Hotel*, Jalan Bendahara (☎06/283 5722), Pelangi Air (☎06/317 4175) at the airport, or Atlas Travel, 5 Jl Hangjebat (☎06/282 0777).

By ferry
A daily boat (RM80) leaves for Dumai in Sumatra. Contact Madai Shipping at 321a Jl Tun Ali (☎06/284 0671), near the bus station, and Tunas Rupat at 17a Jl Merdeka (☎06/283 2506).

By bus
Melaka runs buses to all points on the Peninsula. There are frequent departures from the express bus station to KL, Ipoh, Butterworth and Alor Setar, while most express services to Singapore leave from the local bus station.

By train
Trains run to Singapore from the train station at Tampin, 38km north of Melaka (☎06/411 1034).

Information and city transport

You should be able to get a **trishaw** from the Dutch Square and outside the Mahkota Parade Shopping Centre. A sightseeing tour costs around RM25 for two. **Taxis** are quite hard to find on the street, but you can always get one from the taxi stand near the express bus station. The very helpful **Tourist Information Centre** is on Jalan Kota (Mon–Thurs & Sat 8.45am–5pm, Fri 8.45am–12.15pm & 2.45–5pm, Sun 9am–5pm; ☎06/283 6538), 400m from the Shah Bandar jetty. The information board outside displays the times of the river trips to Kampung Morten (see p.625).

Accommodation

Hotel prices are a little higher than in other Malaysian towns, but so are standards. Most budget hostels are in the south of the city, in the Taman Melaka Raya area; take town bus #17 from the local bus station, or a taxi or trishaw (RM5).

Baba House, 125 Jl Tun Tan Cheng Lock (☎06/281 1216). These beautifully restored Peranakan houses have been turned into an atmospheric hotel, though the rooms are a little on the small side. ⑥.

Eastern Heritage, 8 Jl Bukit China (☎06/283 3026). Set in an imaginatively decorated house that makes the best of its original architectural features. The dorms (RM6) and rooms are spotless and there are some nice touches such as a plunge pool and a batik workshop. The only drawback is that there's only one bathroom. ②.

Equatorial, Jl Bandar Hilir (☎06/628 28333). Has a wide range of restaurants and comes a close second to the *Renaissance* in terms of grandeur. ⑦.

Grand Continental, 20 Jl Tun Sri Lanang (☎06/284 0048). Standard hotel that is very reasonably priced. Its facilities include a pool and coffee house. ⑦.

Heeren House, 1 Jl Tun Tan Cheng Lock (☎06/281 4241). The tasteful rooms, some with four-poster beds, makes this the best choice for a small upmarket hotel. ⑥.

Malacca Town Holiday Lodge, 148b Taman Melaka Raya, above the large *Kingdom* restaurant (☎06/284 8830). A guesthouse offering simple, clean rooms. ①.

Malacca, 27a Jl Munshi Abdullah (☎06/282 2252). Housed in an elegant old building, the large, well-furnished rooms are a little old but good for the price. The drawback is the noisy road. ②.

Renaissance Melaka, Jl Bendahara (☎06/284 8888). The town's major luxury hotel, with an imposing lobby complete with huge chandeliers, and elegant, well-furnished rooms. ⑨.

Robin's Nest & Robin's nest II, 205b & 202 Taman Melaka Raya (☎06/282 9142). These two friendly hostels, almost next to each other, have small rooms and dorms (RM8), but pleasant lounges, video, hot showers and kitchen. ②.

Sunny's Inn, 270a Taman Melaka Raya (☎06/283 7990). As pleasant a hostel as you'll find in Malaysia, with Japanese-style sanded floorboards, roof terrace and a raised lounging area, complete with books and board games. There's home cooking and the wide range of rooms from dorms (RM8) to basic fan doubles to air-con en-suites are all great value. The small sign makes it hard to spot. ②–③.

Traveller's Lodge, 214b Taman Melaka Raya (☎06/281 4793). Small and homely family hostel, which has cable TV, a cosy, floor-cushioned lounge and roof garden. Dorms RM7.

The City

The centre of Melaka is split in two by the murky **Sungei Melaka**, the western bank of which is occupied by **Chinatown** and **Kampung Morten**, a small collection of stilted houses. On the eastern side of the river lies the colonial core with **Bukit St Paul** at its centre, encircled by Jalan Kota. Southeast of here, **Taman Melaka Raya** is a new town with a giant shopping centre and most of the budget hotels, restaurants and bars. A relaxing 45-minute **boat trip** up Sungei Melaka takes you past "Little Amsterdam", the old Dutch quarter of red-roofed *godowns*, which back directly onto the water. Boats leave from the jetty behind the Tourist Information Centre (hourly, depending on the tide, 10am–2pm; RM7).

AROUND BUKIT ST PAUL

The imposing dark timber palace of **Istana Ke Sultanan** (daily 9am–6pm; closed Fri 12.15–2.45pm; RM2) on Jalan Kota is a reconstruction of the original fifteenth-century istana, complete with sharply sloping, multi-layered roofs. Inside, you'll find re-creations of scenes from Malay court life, as well as costumes and local crafts. East of here, the **Independence Memorial Museum** (Tues–Thurs, Sat & Sun 9am–6pm, Fri 9am–noon & 3–6pm; free – closed for renovation at the time of writing) charts the events surrounding the lead-up to independence in 1957, but unfortunately it's poorly laid out.

The **Muzium Rakyat** on Jalan Kota (daily 9am–6pm; Fri closed 12.15–2.45pm; RM1.50) houses several displays, but its most interesting is the **Museum of Enduring Beauty** on the third floor, which shows the many ways in which people have sought to alter their appearance, including head deformation, dental mutilations, tattooing, scarification and foot-binding.

St Paul's Church – roofless, desolate and smothered in ferns – was constructed in 1521 by the Portuguese, and visited by the Jesuit missionary St Francis Xavier, whose body was brought here for burial; and a brass plaque on the south wall of the chancel marks the spot. A winding path beside the church brings you to the sturdy **Stadthuys**, a collection of buildings that dates from 1660 and was used as a town hall during the Dutch and British administrations. It boasts typically Dutch interior staircases and high windows, and now houses the **Museum of Ethnography** (Wed, Thurs, Sat–Mon 9am–6pm; Fri 9am–12.15pm & 2.45–6pm; RM2), which displays Malay and Chinese ceramics and weaponry and a blow-by-blow account of Melakan history.

The **Maritime Museum** (daily 9am–9pm; closed Fri 12.15–2.45pm; RM2), on the quayside to the south of Stadthuys, is housed in a replica of a Portuguese cargo ship that sank here in the sixteenth century. Model ships and paintings chart Melaka's maritime history. Heading north of Stadthuys up Jalan Laksamana, skirting the busy junction with Jalan Temenggong and taking Jalan Bendahara directly ahead, you're in the centre of Melaka's tumbledown **Little India**, a rather desultory line of saree shops, interspersed with a few eating houses. East along Jalan Temenggong brings you to **Bukit China** (RM6 by taxi or trishaw), the ancestral burial ground of the town's Chinese community; it dates from around 1409 but is now used as a park.

CHINATOWN

Melaka owed a great deal of its nineteenth-century economic recovery to its Chinese community, many of whom settled in what became known as **Chinatown**, across Sungei Melaka from the colonial district. Turn left after the bridge by the Tourist Information Centre, then first right, and you'll come to Jalan Tun Tan Cheng Lock, whose elegant townhouses are the ancestral homes of the Baba-Nonya community, descendants of the original Chinese pioneers who married local Malay women. The wealthiest and most successful built long, narrow-fronted houses, and minimized the "window tax" by incorporating several internal courtyards. At nos. 48–50, the **Baba-Nonya Heritage Museum** (daily 10am–12.30pm & 2-4.30pm; RM7), is an amalgam of three adjacent houses belonging to one family, and an excellent example of the Chinese Palladian style. Typically connected by a common covered footway, decorated with hand-painted tiles, each front entrance has an outer swing door of elaborately carved teak. Two red lanterns hang either side of the doorway, and a canopy of Chinese tiles frames the shuttered windows. Inside, the homes are filled with gold-leaf fittings, blackwood furniture inlaid with mother-of-pearl and delicately carved lacquer screens.

Seven hundred metres to the north of Chinatown, on the west bank of the Sungei Melaka, the village of **Kampung Morten** is a surprising find in the heart of the city. To get there, take the footbridge down a small path off Jalan Bunga Raya, one of the principal roads leading north out of town. The wooden stilted houses here are distinctively Melakan, with their long, rectangular living rooms and kitchens, and narrow verandahs approached by ornamental steps. On the left as you cross the footbridge you'll find the **Villa Sentosa** (daily 9am–5pm; voluntary donation), whose welcoming family will gladly show you their artefacts and heirlooms.

TAMAN MINI MALAYSIA

Fourteen kilometres north of central Melaka, in the recreational park area of Ayer Keroh, **Taman Mini Malaysia** and mini **ASEAN** (Mon–Fri 10am–6pm, Sat & Sun 9.30am–6.30pm; RM5) holds full-sized reconstructions of typical houses from all thirteen Malay states and from Brunei, Indonesia, the Philippines, Singapore and Thailand. Cultural shows are regularly staged here too. Town buses #19 and #105 run every thirty minutes to Ayer Keroh from the local bus station.

Eating

Sampling the spicy dishes of Nonya cuisine is a must in Melaka, with its emphasis on sour herbs like tamarind, tempered by creamy coconut milk. Usual opening hours are 9am–11pm unless otherwise stated.

Capitol Satay, Jl Bukit China. Experience *satay celup*, where you take your pick of assorted fish, meat and vegetables skewered on sticks and cook them in a spicy peanut sauce at your table.

Restoran D'Nolasco, Medan Portugis. A Mediterranean atmosphere with oriental food such as crabs in tomato and chilli sauce with soy. Around RM20 a head.

Gluttons' Corner, Jl Merdeka. More a collection of permanent restaurants than food stalls, this is the city's highest profile eating area. Prices are high, however, and service poor. One of the better restaurants is *Bunga Raya*, whose local seafood is popular with the locals.

Heeren House, 1 Jl Tun Tan Cheng Lock. This stylish, air-conditioned café offers Nonya lunches the weekends for RM15 and very reasonably priced local Portuguese food.

Jonkers Melaka, 17 Jl Hang Jebat. In a beautiful Peranakan house, this café is also a gift shop and art gallery. Good for vegetarians – set meals, including Nonya cuisine and desserts, start at RM16. Open 10am–5pm.

Restoran Kerala, 668 Taman Melaka Raya. Cheap and cheerful South Indian food in a sparkling clean establishment. Excellent banana-leaf curries as well as tandoori set meals for about RM5.

Long Feng Chinese Restaurant, *Renaissance Melaka Hotel*, Jl Bendahara. Excellent Cantonese and Szechuan dishes in a classy setting. It's not cheap, though, at around RM25 per dish.

Ole Sayang, 198–199 Jl Taman Melaka Raya (☎06/283 4384). A moderately priced Nonya restaurant, with Peranakan decor. Try the beef *goreng lada*, in a rich soya-based sauce, or the *ayam lemak pulut*, a spicy, creamy chicken dish; both cost around RM7. Open 11.30am–2.30pm & 6–9.30pm, closed Wed.

Sri Lakshmi Villas, 2 Jl Bendahara & *Sri Krishna Bavan* next door have reliable south Indian *thali*s with as many top-ups as you can eat for RM4 a go. Good for vegetarians.

Restoran Teng Yuan, corner of Lorong Bukit China and Jl Banda Kaba. Vegetarian Chinese restaurant with inexpensive tofu and bean dishes in a buffet.

Shopping

Melaka is famed for its **antiques**, and there are many specialist outlets along Jalan Hang Jebat and Jalan Tun Tan Cheng Lock. If it's a genuine antique, check that it can be exported legally and fill in an official clearance form. Interesting places to browse on Jalan Hang Jabat include Abdu Co at no. 79 for china and glass, Wah Aik at no. 92, which sells silk shoes like the ones that used to be made to bind feet (RM75), and Dragon House at no. 65 for old coins and banknotes. For modern **crafts** and souvenirs, Tribal Arts Gallery at 10 Jl Hang Rebat specialises in Sarawakian crafts; and Orang Utan, 59 Lorong Hang Jebat, is the outlet for local artist Charles Cham's witty cartoon T-shirts and paintings. Estee Book Exchange, Taman Melaka Raya, has a good selection of English-language **books**, as does MPH in Mahkota Parade.

Listings

Banks and exchange Bank Bumiputra, Jl Kota; Hong Kong Bank, 1a Jl Kota; Overseas Chinese Banking Corporation, Jl Hang Jebat. Moneychangers are often more convenient and offer as good rates as the banks: Malaccan Souvenir House and Trading, 22 Jl Tokong; Sultan Enterprise, 31 Jl Laksamana.

Car rental Avis, 124 Jl Munshi Abdulla (☎06/284 6710).

Hospital The Straits Hospital is at 37 Jl Parameswara (☎06/283 5336).

Immigration The Immigration Office is on the second floor, Bangunan Persekutuan, Jl Hang Tuah (☎06/282 4958) for on-the-spot visa renewals.

Internet access *Cempaka Technology Shop*, 155 Jl Melaka Raya; *Internet Booth Café*, 3a Jl Kota Laksamana.

Police The tourist police office (☎06/282 2222) is on Jl Kota and is open 24 hours.

Post office The GPO is inconveniently situated on the way to Ayer Keroh on Jl Bukit Baru – take town bus #19. A minor branch on Jl Laksamana sells stamps and aerograms.

Telephone services The Telekom building is on Jl Chan Koon Cheng (daily 8am–5pm).

Travel agents Try Atlas Travel at 5 Jl Hang Jebat (☎06/282 0777) for plane tickets.

Kukup: travel to Indonesia

About 200km south of Melaka and almost right at the tip of the Peninsula, the small fishing community of **KUKUP** is a little-known exit point from Malaysia to **Tanjung Balai in Indonesia**, a 45-minute ferry ride leaving from the jetty (Mon–Thur & Sat 11am and 3pm, Sun 3pm). You don't need to arrange a visa in advance for this trip. The problem with **arriving** in Kukup from Indonesia is that onward travel connections are sketchy – you'll have to catch a ferry or taxi ($4) to Pontian Kecil, 19km away, which has regular buses to Johor Bahru. Kukup's main attraction is its **seafood**. The town's single tumbledown street is packed with restaurants, from the enormous *Makanan Laut*, closest to the jetty, where you can see the food being prepared in a vast array of woks, to the more modest *Restoran Zaiton Hussin* immediately opposite. Expect to pay RM13 for fish, RM12 for prawns.

Johor Bahru

The southernmost Malaysian city of any size, **JOHOR BAHRU** – or simply **JB** – is the gateway into Singapore, linked to the city-state by a 1056-metre causeway, which is crossed by around 50,000 people a day. It also has good links to KL and Melaka, so there's little to detain you whichever direction you're travelling in. JB's one interesting attraction is the **Istana Besar**, the former residence of Johor's royal family. Surrounded by extensive gardens, it is a magnificent building set on a hillock overlooking the Johor Straits. To the right of the building is the ticket booth of the **Museum Di Raja Abu Bakar** (daily 9am–5pm; RM18), which displays gifts from foreign dignitaries, including stuffed tigers and daggers.

The **bus station** is 3km away from the centre of JB on Jalan Geruda. Plenty of buses run from here to the causeway or you can catch a taxi for around RM5. The **train station** is slightly east of the city centre, off Jalan Tun Abdul Razak. Flights to JB land at **Senai airport**, 25km north of the city, from where a regular bus service (RM1.40) runs to the bus station. Heading out to the airport, MAS passengers can take the RM4 shuttle bus from outside the Tourist Information Centre. Alternatively, you can get a taxi to the airport for about RM25. The **MAS** office is at Level 1, Menara Pelangi, Jalan Kuning Taman Pelangi (☎07/334 1001). To **rent a car** (cheaper than in Singapore) contact either Avis, at the *Tropical Inn* (☎07/223 7971), or Hertz, 1 Jl Trus (☎07/223 7520).

The main **Tourist Information Centre (JOTIC)** (Mon–Fri 8am–4.15pm, Sat 8am–12.45pm, Sun 10am–4pm; ☎07/222 3392) is on Jalan Air Molek, and there is also an office on the causeway (Mon–Fri 8am–4.15pm, Sat 8am–12.45pm, Sun 10am–4pm; ☎07/222 3591). There are **moneychangers** in the main shopping centres, or try Maybank, 11 Jl Selat Tebrau; Bank Bumiputra, 51 Jl Segget or OCBC, Jalan Ibrahim. There is also a brace of cash-points on the south side of the Merlin Tower. To get **online**, try the *Pussat Internet Café* on the second floor of the Kotaruya shopping centre or the *ABC Café*, next to the *Hawai Hotel* on Jalan Meldrum (open 24hr).

JB attracts more businessmen than tourists, but the best of the budget **accommodation** is *Footloose Homestay*, 4h Jl Ismail (☎07/224 2881; ②), with a basic dorm (RM14) and double rooms. If you can't get a bed here, try the grim but reasonably clean *Hawaii*, 21 Jl Meldrum (☎07/224 0633; ③). At mid-wallet, the *Rasa Sayang*, Jalan Datok Dalam (☎07/224 8600; ⑤), is comfortable enough, while the plushest place by far is the luxury *Puteri Pan Pacific*, Kotaraya, Jalan Trus (☎07/223 3333; ⑨) – ask for promotions. The liveliest of the **places to eat** in JB is the large night market across the footbridge from the train station beside the Indian Temple.

Travelling from Johor Bahru to Singapore and Indonesia

Two bus services run throughout the day between **Singapore** and JB. The air-con Singapore–JB Express (every 10min, 6.30am–11.30pm; RM2.20) is the most comfortable, though the #170 is cheaper (RM1.20) and runs every ten minutes 6am–11.30pm from Larkin bus station in JB to the Queen Street terminal in central Singapore. You can also catch the bus into Singapore from just outside the train station on the main road at the border. There's also an MAS bus service (RM10) from JB's Senai airport to Singapore's *Novotel Orchid*. Taxis between JB and Singapore departing from the KOMTAR car park, Jalan Wong Ah Fook, cost RM6–7 per person, and leave only when they are full.

The buses drop passengers outside the immigration points at each end of the cause-way and immigration procedures take around ten minutes. If you want to stay in JB *don't* get back on the bus, just walk into town. Similarly, it is possible to board the buses to Singapore at the causeway terminal instead of trekking out to the bus station. The bus will drop you off at the border for the Immigration procedures; they won't wait for you, but if you hold onto your ticket you can board any bus of the same number on the other side of the border. To avoid this hassle, you can make the journey by train, as the for-malities are carried out on board, though at RM8 for a second-class seat, this is more expensive.

You can also take a ferry to Tanjung Pinang and Pulau Batam – both in **Indonesia** – from Sriwani Tours and Travel (☎07/221 1677) in the Bebas Cukai shopping centre, 2km east of the border crossing.

Mersing

The east-coast fishing port of **MERSING**, 130km north of Johor Bahru, is the main gateway to **Pulau Tioman** and the smaller islands of the Seribuat archipelago. The town is grouped around two main streets, Jalan Abu Bakar and Jalan Ismail, fanning out from a roundabout on Route 3.

Express buses drop you off just before the roundabout, and at the R&R Plaza near the jetty. Buses depart from the R&R Plaza. You can buy tickets from Restoran Malaysia and offices at R&R Plaza Itself. The local bus station is on Jalan Sulaiman, close to the riverfront. The Mersing Tourist Information Centre (Mon–Fri 8am–12.45pm & 2–6.30pm, Sat 8am–12.30pm; ☎07/799 5212), on Jalan Abu Bakar, is very helpful and offers impartial advice on the many different island deals.

The **jetty** is about ten minutes' walk from the roundabout along Jalan Abu Bakar. Inside the R&R Plaza near the jetty, a large signboard shows which of the thirteen companies' boats sail when to Tioman (the last one is about 4pm; see below for details). For the other islands, it's best to book ahead, either at the particular island office itself, around the jetty, or at one of the travel agencies on Jalan Abu Baker or Jalan Ismail. Make sure that you **change money** before you leave, as rates on the islands are lousy.

Omar's Backpackers' Hostel, Jalan Abu Bakar (☎07/799 5096; ②), is one of the cheapest **places to stay** in Mersing, with clean dorm beds (RM8) and excellent-value double rooms. A step up, the *Country*, 11 Jl Sulaimen (☎07/799 1799; ③), is more upmarket than its price suggests, while the spic-and-span *Embassy*, 2 Jl Ismail (☎07/799 3545; ②–③), does the best-value budget doubles in town. If you're after real comfort, there's a *Seri Malaysia* on Jalan Ismail (☎07/799 1876; ⑤), opposite the hospital, a ten-minute walk from the jetty. The food stalls near the roundabout are particularly good, but there are plenty of great **restaurants** too. *Al Arif*, Jalan Ismail, opposite the *Parkson Ria* supermarket, serves cheap, good quality Indian food, as does *Zam Zam* on Jalan Abu Bakar.

Pulau Tioman

PULAU TIOMAN, 30km east of Mersing, has long been one of Malaysia's most popular holiday islands. Thirty-eight kilometres long and nineteen kilometres at its widest point, it is the largest island in the Seribuat archipelago and has an inaccessible mountainous spine down its centre. Ever since the 1970s, when Tioman was voted one of the ten most beautiful islands in the world by *Time* magazine, crowds have been flocking to its palm-fringed shores. Now, noisy express boats travel here in less than two hours and several daily flights arrive from Singapore and other parts of the Peninsula. Damage has been inflicted on the surrounding coral and marine life, but Pulau Tioman displays a remarkable resilience, and to avoid it is to miss out. Most of the habitation on Tioman is along the west coast, with the popular budget places being in the main village of **Tekek** and the bay of **Air Batang**; the east coast's sole settlement, **Juara**, is less developed. **Salang** is a noisy, more upmarket resort, but **Nipah** and **Mukut** are just opening up to tourism.

Many of Tioman's nearby islets provide excellent opportunities for snorkelling, and most of the chalet operations offer day-trips (RM35) to nearby reefs. Many **dive centres** on Tioman offer the range of PADI certificates, from the four-day Open Water course (RM750) through to the fourteen-day "Dive Master" (RM1200); always check that qualified English-speaking instructors are employed, and that the cost includes equipment.

Like the rest of the Peninsula's east coast, Tioman is affected by the **monsoon**, making the island hard to reach by sea between November and February. July and August are the busiest months, when prices increase and accommodation should be booked in advance.

Getting there

Express boats from Mersing (see above) take roughly two hours, depending on the tide; tickets are RM25 for the one-way trip. You'll have to decide in advance which bay you want

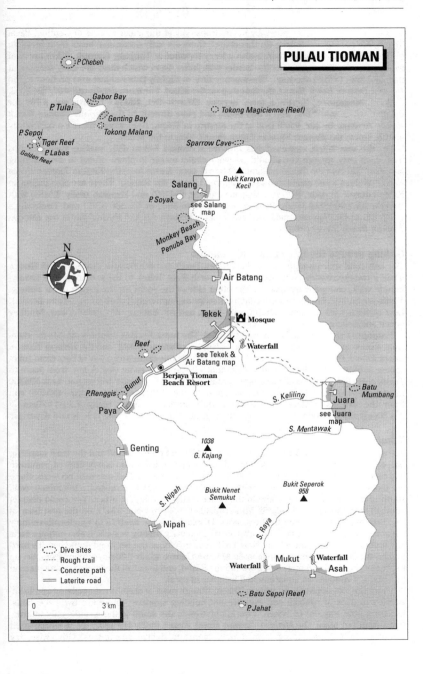

PULAU TIOMAN

P. Chebeh

P. Tulai

Gabor Bay

Genting Bay

Tokong Magicienne (Reef)

Tokong Malang

P. Sepoi

Tiger Reef

P. Labas

Golden Reef

Sparrow Cave

N

Salang

P. Soyak

see Salang map

Bukit Kerayon Kecil

Monkey Beach

Penuba Bay

Air Batang

Tekek

Mosque

Waterfall

Reef

see Tekek & Air Batang map

Bunut

Berjaya Tioman Beach Resort

P. Renggis

Paya

S. Keliling

Juara

Batu Mumbang

see Juara map

S. Mentawak

Genting

1038

G. Kajang

S. Nipah

Bukit Nenet Semukut

Bukit Seperok

958

S. Raya

Nipah

Waterfall

Mukut

Waterfall

Asah

Dive sites

Rough trail

Concrete path

Laterite road

0   3 km

Batu Sepoi (Reef)

P. Jahat

to stay in, since the boats generally make drops only at the major resorts of Genting, Paya, Tekek, Air Batang and Salang (in that order); there are only occasional boats from Mersing to Juara on the east coast. There's also a ferry terminal at **Tanjong Gemuk**, 38km north of Mersing on the Pahang side of the border with Johor, from which there are daily services at 9am and 2pm (RM25 one-way). The journey time is slightly faster at just over an hour to the *Berjaya Tioman Beach Resort*, the first stop on the island. For more details call ☎07/794 2053.

From **Singapore**, there's a ferry service (March–Oct; RM143 return; see p.789 for details), which takes four and a half hours and runs directly to the *Berjaya Tioman Beach Resort*. Arriving **by air**, you'll land at the airstrip in Tekek, from where there's a half-hourly shuttle bus to the *Berjaya Tioman Beach Resort*, 2km to the south.

On the way back, express boats all leave at around 7–8am daily, making their pick-ups from each jetty, though you should ask your chalet owner to phone ahead to avoid getting stranded. The ferry to Tanjung Gemuk (11am & 4pm) leaves from the *Berjaya Tioman Beach Resort*, as does a fast catamaran to Singapore (1.30pm; 4hr 30min). There are also **flights** to Kuala Lumpur (4 daily; RM146), Singapore (daily; RM192) and Kuantan (daily; RM84) with Berjaya Air (☎03/244 1718), Pelangi Air (☎03/746 3000 or 02/336 6777) and Tradewinds (☎02/225 4488). You can make reservations for Berjaya Air and Pelangi Air at the *Berjaya Tioman Beach Resort* (☎09/445445).

Getting around the island and information

The only road wide enough for cars is between Tekek and the *Berjaya Tioman Beach Resort*, while a two-metre-wide concrete path runs north from Tekek to the promontory, a twenty-minute walk, commencing again on the other side of the rocks for the length of Air Batang. **Trails** are limited, but there's a decent track as far as Juara from Tekek (see p.632 for details). Less obvious trails connect Genting with Paya, and Air Batang with Penuba Bay, Monkey beach and Salang.

Transport on the island is somewhat limited. The Juara Sea Bus operates outside the monsoon season and takes two hours to visit Salang, Air Batang, Tekek, and the *Berjaya Tioman Beach Resort*. It's very unreliable, but there is usually one departure a day at 3pm from Juara calling at Salang, Air Batang and Tekek, and returning the same way. A fare from Juara to Tekek costs RM10. You could also hire a small boat, but a five-seater will set you back RM200 for the same journey. Lastly, you could hop onto one of the round-island trips (RM55) run from the various chalets. The **Tourist Information Centre** (daily 7.30–11.30am & 2–4.30pm), right beside the jetty at Air Batang, can help you with boat tickets and day-trips.

Tekek

The sprawling village of **TEKEK** is the main settlement on the island and the least inspiring part of Tioman. It has been overdeveloped and much of the seafront is now littered, rundown and fenced in, but it's the only place on the island where you'll find essential services: there are moneychangers in the new Terminal Complex next to the airstrip and, a ten-minute walk south of the main jetty, you come to the police station and a post office. You could distract yourself with the **Tioman Island Museum** (daily 9.30am–5pm; RM1), on the first floor of the Terminal Complex next to the airport. Displaying some twelfth- to fourteenth-century Chinese ceramics, which were lost overboard from early trading vessels, it also outlines facts and myths concerning the island. North of the main jetty, at the very end of the bay, it's hard to miss the large government-sponsored **Marine Centre** (daily 9.30am–4.30pm; free). Set up to protect the coral and marine life around the island, and to patrol the fishing taking place in its waters, it contains an aquarium and samples of coral.

There are lots of **places to stay** in Tekek, though most of them are dilapidated and located next to piles of rubbish and ever-present building supplies. There are two exceptions, located a little way out of Tekek. Two kilometres to the south is the island's only international-standard place, the *Berjaya Tioman Beach Resort* (☎09/419 1000; ⑨), a village-sized complex offering everything from double rooms to deluxe apartments. Otherwise, try

Samudra Swiss Cottage (☎07/419 1843; ②), the first place north of the resort, in a shady jungle setting, with a dive shop and small restaurant. One of Tekek's nicest **restaurants**, *Liza*, is at the far southern end of the bay, with a wide-ranging menu specializing in seafood and Western snacks at RM20 a meal.

Air Batang

Despite its ever-increasing popularity, **AIR BATANG**, 2km north of Tekek (jetty to jetty), is still one of the best areas on Tioman, and gets most of the budget market. Although there's plenty of accommodation, it feels spacious, and development tends to be relatively taste-ful and low-key. A jetty divides the bay roughly in half; the beach is better at the southern end of the bay. A fifteen-minute **trail** leads over the headland to the north, which – after an initial scramble – flattens out into an easy walk, ending up at secluded **Penuba Bay**. From here, it's an hour's walk to Monkey beach, beyond which is Salang (see p.632).

ACCOMMODATION AND EATING

As you get off the boat, a signpost help-fully lists the direction of the numerous **places to stay** in the bay. Air Batang likes to keep its nightlife low-key, unlike Salang, which can get rowdy. Most of the chalets have **restaurants**.

ABC (☎09/419 1154). At the far northern end of the bay and among the best in Air Batang. A little quieter than most with its location on the far end of the beach, the very inexpensive, pretty chalets are set in a well-tended garden with its own freshwater stream. ①.

Bamboo Hill Chalets (☎09/419 1339). The best accommodation on Air Batang, these beautiful, wooden chalets on stilts, perched on the northern headland, are well equipped and enjoy stunning views. ④.

Johan's (☎09/419 1359). A good choice, with well-spaced standard chalets and new, larger ones up the hill on a pleasant lawn. There is also a dorm (RM10) and rooms have air-con as an option. ②–④.

Nazri's II (☎09/419 1375). A great outfit with large, air-con chalets set in spacious grounds, and some ordinary, cheaper ones. ②–④.

Penuba Chalets (☎011/952963). The only place to stay in Penuba Bay. Its stilted chalets,

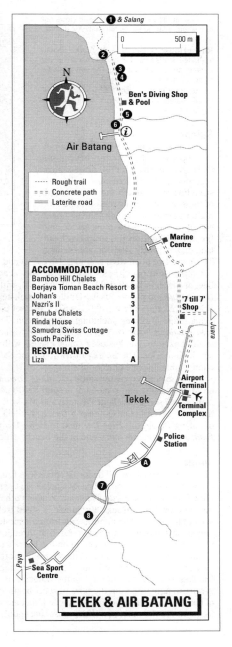

ACCOMMODATION
Bamboo Hill Chalets	2
Berjaya Tioman Beach Resort	8
Johan's	5
Nazri's II	3
Penuba Chalets	1
Rinda House	4
Samudra Swiss Cottage	7
South Pacific	6

RESTAURANTS
Liza	A

Map labels: & Salang · 0 500 m · N · Ben's Diving Shop & Pool · Air Batang · Rough trail · Concrete path · Laterite road · Marine Centre · '7 till 7' Shop · Juara · Airport Terminal · Tekek · Terminal Complex · Police Station · Paya · Sea Sport Centre · **TEKEK & AIR BATANG** high up on the rocks, have fantastic views out to sea and a far better beach than Air Batang. ③–④.

Rinda House (☎09/419 1157). A good spot in a shaded setting at the northern end of Air Batang, perfect for watching the sun go down from one of the hammocks. ①.

South Pacific (no phone). Close to the jetty. Clean chalets with bathrooms, some right on the beach. ②.

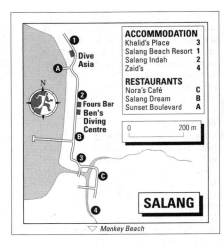

ACCOMMODATION
Khalid's Place	3
Salang Beach Resort	1
Salang Indah	2
Zaid's	4

RESTAURANTS
Nora's Café	C
Salang Dream	B
Sunset Boulevard	A

0   200 m

SALANG

▽ *Monkey Beach*

Salang

North of Air Batang, **SALANG** is a quieter option with a better beach, but there has been a lot of development recently and the string of hostels stretches pretty much the whole length of the seafront; prices tend to be a little higher than at Air Batang. The southern end of the beach is the most scenic, and the small island off the southern headland has a pretty reef for snorkelling. There are two good **dive schools**, Dive Asia and Ben's Diving Centre.

On the right (south) as you leave the jetty is a little cluster of budget **places to stay**, the best of which is *Zaid's* (☎09/415 9020; ③–⑥), with attractive hillside and beachfront chalets. *Nora's Café* (no phone; ③) is friendly with well-kept en-suite chalets, behind the little lagoon. Friendly *Khalid's Place* (☎09/419 5317; ③), set back from the beach in landscaped gardens, has a range of rooms, including some air-con. The largest outfit, towards the centre of the bay, is *Salang Indah* (☎09/419 5015; ③–⑦), with a range of well-appointed chalets, from sea-facing boxes to double-storey family chalets with air-con and hot shower; they also arrange snorkelling trips. The *Salang Beach Resort* or *Salang Sayang Resort* (☎09/419 5019; ③) has comfortable, hillside chalets ($50).

At the expensive **restaurants** of *Salang Dream* and *Salang Beach Resort* the emphasis is on Malay cuisine and seafood at around RM10 per dish, while the more informal *Zaid's* and *Nora's Café* serve excellent Western and Malay dishes for no more than RM3. For **nightlife**, there are several choices: *Four S Bar*, a candlelit bar with a good range of beers, just south of Salang Indah, the *Dive Bar* next to Ben's Diving Centre, and the more upmarket *Sunset Boulevard*, at the northern end of the beach, which has the best views of the bay.

Juara

Life is simple on **Juara**. The locals speak less English and are much more conservative than elsewhere on the island: officially alcohol isn't served. There's only one sea bus to the kampung from the east coast of Tioman, so at any other time the journey to this isolated bay must be made **on foot** through the jungle, a steep trek that takes three hours from Tekek. The start of the trail (a five-minute walk from the airstrip) is easy enough to identify since it's the only concrete path that heads off in that direction, passing the local mosque before hitting virgin jungle after about fifteen minutes. There's no danger of losing your way: cement steps climb steeply through the greenery, tapering off into a smooth, downhill path once you're over the ridge. After 45 minutes, there is a **waterfall** – it's forbidden to bathe here, since it supplies Tekek with water. From the waterfall, it's another hour or so to Juara village. Juara is refreshingly free from the buzz of speedboats and motorbikes, while its lovely wide sweep of beach is far cleaner and less crowded than anywhere on the other side. The bay, however, facing out to the open sea, is the most susceptible on the island to bad weather.

Juara in fact consists of two bays; the northern has a jetty, opposite which the cross-island path emerges. Most of the accommodation and restaurants are here too, although the southern bay does have a few chalets.

ACCOMMODATION AND EATING

Starting at the northern end, you'll find the best options are *Paradise Point* (①), about 100m down the beach from the jetty, which has the cheapest **chalets** with shower. *Atan's* (②), past the cross-island path, has double-storey guest-houses, rather like Swiss chalets, while *Mutiara* (☎07/799 4833; ②–④) is the biggest operation, with a wide variety of room types and prices. These are also the people to see if you want to arrange a boat trip. A little further south, *Basir* (②) has good sea-facing chalets, with some cheaper huts as well, while at the very end of the strip, *Sunrise* and *Rainbow* (both ②) have characterful, painted A-frames right on the beach. If you follow the path round to the even quieter southern bay you'll find several cheap places to stay, including *Mezanie Chalet* (☎09/547 8445; ③), which has its own restaurant.

While there's less choice for **eating**, portions tend, on the whole, to be larger and the menus more imaginative than on the west coast. *Paradise Point* does good *rotis* and unusual dishes, such as fish with peanut sauce and fried rice with coconut. *Ali Putra* and *Beach Café*, by the jetty, both have a huge range of local and Western dishes. At night try *Bushman's*, a shack next to *Sunrise*, and the only place serving alcohol at Juara.

Mukut

MUKUT, a tiny fishing village on the south coast, lies in the shadow of granite outcrops. Shrouded by dense forest, and connected to the outside world by a solitary card phone, it's a wonderfully peaceful and friendly spot to unwind, though be warned that this is still a conservative place, unused to Western sunbathing habits. The nicest position is occupied by *Chalets Park* (④), with secluded **chalets** shaded by trees. Those at *Sri Tanjung Chalets* (②) at the far western end of the cove overlook a patch of beach – ask at the house in the village where the name of the chalets is painted on a tyre. The places to **eat** are few and basic. The *Sri Sentosa* is a bit on the dingy side, though popular with the locals, while the views from *Mukut Coral Resort* and the *7-Eleven* café just by the jetty make up for their lack of variety.

Nipah

For almost total isolation, head to **NIPAH** on Tioman's southwest coast. Comprising a clean, empty beach of coarse, yellow sand and a landlocked lagoon, there's no village to speak of here, but there is a Dive Centre and canoeing. You might be lucky enough to get a ferry from the mainland to drop you here since there is an adequate jetty, but it's more likely that you'll have to come by sea taxi from Genting, costing around RM30 per person.

There's only one **place to stay**: the *Nipah Resort* (☎011/764184; ③), offering basic chalets and more expensive A-frames, as well as a nicely designed restaurant; the food can get a little monotonous. The air-con longhouse, *Nipah Paradise*, at the far end, caters only for pre-booked packages from Singapore.

Pulau Sibu

PULAU SIBU is the most popular – if the least scenic – of the islands after Tioman, though the huge monitor lizards and the butterflies here make up for the lack of mountains and jungle. Like the rest of the islands, Sibu boasts fine beaches, though the sand is yellower and the current more turbulent than some. Shaped like a bone, the island's narrow waist can be crossed in only a few minutes, revealing a double bay known as Twin Beach. Many of the coves have good offshore coral. Most of the resorts on Sibu operate their own boats **from Tanjung Leman**, a tiny village about 30km down the coast from Mersing and an hour's boat ride from the island. It's not an established route, so you must ask the resort in advance to pick you up. *O&H*'s boat runs the one-hour journey to and from Tanjung Leman daily (RM16).

Halfway along the eastern coast, *O&H Kampung Huts* (☎011/354 322; ②–④) is the best **place to stay** on the island if you're on a budget, a friendly and relaxed set-up of A-frames and chalets. Nearby, the *Sea Gypsy Village Resort* (☎07/222 8642; ⑦) is much more exclusive, aiming for the diving market, with all-inclusive packages costing around US$100 per night for two people. Over the small ridge in the centre of the island is *Twin Beach Resort* (☎03/948 8966; ④), the only place with sunrise *and* sunset viewing; its A-frames and pricier chalets are rundown, but you can also camp here.

Eating on Pulau Sibu is a pleasure. *O&H* has excellent fish and chicken curries with rice, vegetables and salad, as well as Western options, at around RM15 for a full meal. *Sea Gypsy* also offers great cuisine, but for resort guests only. The restaurant at *Twin Beach* specializes in reasonably priced Chinese food.

SARAWAK

Six hundred kilometres across the South China Sea from Peninsular Malaysia, the two East Malaysian states of Sarawak and Sabah occupy the northwest flank of the island of Borneo (the rest of which, save the enclave of Brunei, is Indonesian Kalimantan). **Sarawak** is the larger of the two states, and a more different place to Peninsular Malaysia is hard to imagine. Clear rivers spill down the jungle-covered mountains and the surviving rainforest, plateaux and river communities are inhabited by indigenous peoples – traditionally grouped as Land Dayaks, Sea Dayaks or Orang Ulu. They make up around half of the state's population and some still live in massive longhouses. A typical longhouse is made from brick or timber and might have one hundred doors – representing the number of families living there. Visits to these longhouses are one of the highlights of a trip to Sarawak. However, don't expect these longhouse communities to be living some kind of "primitive" lifestyle: almost all longhouses

---

GETTING TO SARAWAK

Most people fly to **Kuching**, either from Kuala Lumpur (RM262 one-way), Johor Bahru (RM170), Kota Kinabalu (RM230), Pontianak (RM170), or Bandar Seri Begawan (RM250). There are also direct flights to Miri in the north from KL (RM422) and Kota Kinabalu (RM100).

There are daily **boat** services from Brunei to both Lawas and Limbang in north Sarawak (see Brunei p.65). The main overland route into Sarawak is by bus from Kuala Belait in Brunei to Miri, a very straightforward crossing involving a ferry across the Belait River; see p.70. The other main crossing is via Sipitang in Sabah (see p.660) to Lawas, either by local bus or taxi or by the daily Lawas Express from Kota Kinabalu. From Indonesian Kalimantan, the easiest overland route is from Pontianak (see p.399) into southwest Sarawak, crossing via Entikong to Tebedu, 100km south of Kuching.

have electricty now and that of course means radio, televisions, if not yet computers. Few of the inhabitants wear traditonal dress, but this takes nothing away from the enjoyment of being among these people; their warmth, hospitality and humour remain legendary despite the passing of many traditions.

Most people start their exploration of Sarawak in the capital **Kuching**, from where you can visit **Iban longhouses** on the Batang Ai river system, **Bidayuh dwellings** near the Indonesian border, and **Bako National Park**. A four-hour boat ride north of Kuching, **Sibu** marks the start of the popular route along Batang Rajang, Sarawak's longest river. Most people stop at **Kapit** and from there visit longhouses on the Katibas and Baleh tributaries. North of Sibu, **Niah National Park** boasts a vast cave system and accessible forest hikes. On its way north to the Brunei border, the road goes to **Miri**, from where you either fly, or take a boat, via Marudi, to the spectacular **Gunung Mulu National Park**, Sarawak's chief natural attraction, which features astonishing limestone pinnacles, numerous caves and undiscovered passageways.

Travelling in Sarawak can be expensive: flights from Peninsular Malaysia are costly, although three-flight deals around the state are an appealing option (see p.557). Also, accommodation and internal travel – much of it by boat – are pricier than on the mainland.

Kuching

On the whole, **KUCHING** – the capital of Sarawak – is underrated by visitors. Most unfortunately only stay for a day or two to organize trips to Bako National Park, the longhouses and the interior. It may be long enough to pick up on Kuching's appeal but not to fall for its special magic. It is a highly attractive place: the courthouse and Astana (palace) still serve their original purpose, while the commercial district – in the heart of the old town – is a warren of crowded lanes and home to Kuching's Chinese community. Main Bazaar, the city's oldest street, sports the remains of its original godowns, now converted into shops but still overlooking Sungei Sarawak, Kuching's main supply route since the city's earliest days when the Rajah Brookes ran the territory. The city is culturally as well as architecturally exciting and has one of the finest museums in Southeast Asia. The city keeps late hours too: the area around the *Hilton Hotel* and *Holiday Inn* is full of bars, pubs and plazas. But what's really unique about Kuching is its atmosphere. It is at once both buzzy and laid back, vibrant and mellow: a town where no one's ever too busy to introduce themselves to you and ask you where you're from. It's quite a unique place in fact, even for friendly Malaysia.

Arrival

Kuching airport (☎082/457373) is 11km south of the city and has a currency exchange (daily 8am–8pm). From the airport, either take a taxi into the centre ($16.50 coupons from a booth outside the Arrivals hall) or the #12a bus, which runs from directly outside the terminal to the station on Lebuh Jawa, taking half an hour (daily 7am–6pm; every 40min; 90 sen). For flight routes, see p.668.

Long-distance buses from Sibu and further north, as well as Pontianak, arrive at the Jalan Penrissen bus station, 5km south of downtown Kuching. Walk 100m to the main road, Jalan Penrissen, where buses #17 and #19 run to Main Bazaar and the nearby bus station at Jalan Masjid (half-hourly 6am–11pm; 30min; 60 sen); and buses #3 or #3a (half-hourly 6.30am–6pm; 50 sen) travel to the waterfront Lebuh Jawa. A taxi costs RM10.

Information and tours

Sarawak Tourist Association (STA) is next to the Sarawak Steamship Building on Main Bazaar, at the junction with Jalan Tun Haji Openg (Mon–Thurs 8.00am–12.45pm & 2–4.15pm, Fri 8.00–11.30am & 2.30–4.45pm, Sat 8am–12.45pm; ☎082/240620). Sarawak Visitor Centre (Mon–Thurs 8am–4.15pm, Fri 8am–4.45pm, Sat 8am–12.45pm; ☎082/410942), overlooking the

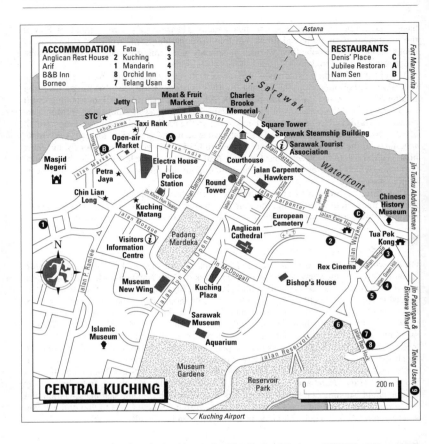

CENTRAL KUCHING

ACCOMMODATION
Anglican Rest House **2**
Arif **1**
B&B Inn **8**
Borneo **7**

Fata **6**
Kuching **3**
Mandarin **4**
Orchid Inn **5**
Telang Usan **9**

RESTAURANTS
Denis' Place **C**
Jubilee Restoran **A**
Nam Sen **B**

padang at Jalan Mosque, has the booking desk of the National Parks and Wildlife Office, which issues permits for Semengoh, Bako, Gading and Kubah parks (☎082/248088).

Many Kuching **tour operators** run tours to Iban longhouses on the Lupar, Lemanak and Skrang rivers, 200km east of Kuching, for around RM100 a day per person, although reductions are available, depending on the size of the group. They will also arrange trips in other parts of the state, including Gunung Mulu Park. Recommended operators include Asian Overland, 286a first floor, Westwood Park, Jalan Tubuan (☎082/251163), which does good longhouse trips near Kuching and on the Batang Ai river system, as well as treks in Mulu National Park; Borneo Adventure, 55 Main Bazaar (☎082/245175), whose main plus is a visit to a great jungle lodge near Batang Ai; Tour Exotica, 1st Floor, 1–3 Jl Temple (☎082/254607), which runs one-day tours to a Bidayuh longhouse (RM140 for two); and Tropical Adventure, 17 Main Bazaar (☎082/413088), which organizes trekking around Bario, exploring Mulu and trips to Iban longhouses.

Accommodation

On the whole, **accommodation** is more expensive than in Peninsular Malaysia; you'll pay around RM30 for a double room if the budget places are full.

Anglican Rest House, Jl McDougall (☎082/240188). Kuching's best deal is set in the gardens of the Anglican Cathedral and has comfortable doubles with shared bathrooms. It's often full, so book ahead. ②.

Arif, Jl Haji Taha (☎082/241211). A snug and friendly place, handily positioned for the night market. A variety of rooms are available, with fan, air-con and bath. ②.

B&B Inn, first floor, 30–31 Jl Tabuan (☎082/237366). Kuching's only backpacker-oriented address has RM14 dorm beds and a handful of bare but tidy private rooms sharing facilities. ②.

Borneo, 30 Jl Tabuan (☎082/244122). A comfortable hotel – Kuching's oldest – whose lovely rooms have polished wooden floors, air-con, bath or shower, and TV. ⑤.

Fata, junction of Lebuh Temple and Jl MacDougall (☎082/248111). Excellent location close to Reservoir Park. The small rooms have air-con, showers and TV. ③.

Kuching, 6 Jl Temple (☎082/413985). About the best budget option after the *Anglican Rest House*, though very basic, spartan and a bit dirty, with one shower and toilet on each floor. ②.

Mandarin, 6 Jl Green Hill (☎082/418269). One of the nicest places in Green Hill. Full facilities – air-con, shower, toilet and TV – but most rooms are rather small. ③.

Merdeka Palace, Jl Tun Abang Openg (☎082/258000). Top-of-the-range, palatial hotel overlooking the padang. Although expensive, it quite often has a promotion on. ⑥.

Orchid Inn, 2 Jl Green Hill (☎082/411417). Run by friendly staff, this is a fairly comfortable place, close to some excellent cafés. ③.

Telang Usan, Jl Ban Hok (☎082/415588). A snugly positioned real gem of a hotel, with superb art by Tusan Padan adorning the walls. A meeting point for most of Kuching's cognoscenti and all Orang Ulu people living in and visiting the city. It has an excellent restaurant and bar too. ④.

The City

The central area, sandwiched between Jalan Courthouse to the west, Jalan Temple to the east and Reservoir Park to the south, is usually referred to as colonial Kuching. Set just below the padang on Jalan Tun Haji Openg, is Kuching's prime tourist attraction, the **Sarawak Museum** (daily except Fri; free), whose main building dates from the 1890s and is set in love-

---

MOVING ON FROM KUCHING

By plane

Take a taxi or the #12a bus from the station on Lebuh Jawa out to the **airport** (flight enquiries ☎082/457373). For flight routes, see "Travel Details" p.668.

By bus

Long-distance buses to points north, and also to Pontianak in Indonesia, leave from the Jalan Penrissen bus station 5km south of downtown Kuching. Buses #3 or #3a (half-hourly 6.30am–6pm; 50 sen) travel between waterfront Lebuh Jawa and Jalan Penrissen; a taxi costs RM10. Larger express-bus companies operating out of the Jalan Penrissen terminal include Biaramas Express (☎082/452139); PB Express (☎082/461277), whose downtown agent is Natural Colour, in Lebuh Khoo Hun Yeng's Electra House; and Borneo Highway Express (☎082/453190), for whose services tickets are available at Yong Ngee Loong, 43 Jl Gambir (☎082/243794).

There are four **local bus services**. The Sarawak Transport Company's green-and-red buses run from the western end of Lebuh Jawa to the airport and Sri Aman. Chin Lian Long's blue-and-white buses start at Jalan Mosque and run to the Indonesian consulate, the immigration office and Bintawa Express Wharf. Petra Jaya Transport runs north from below the open-air market on Lebuh Market to Damai and Bako. Matang Transport Company buses (for Matang and Kubah) depart from the north end of Jalan P Ramlee.

By boat

Express Bahagia, 50 Jl Padungan (☎082/421948), runs daily direct trips to Sarikei ($29) and Sibu ($33), departing at 12.30pm from Bintawa Wharf (also known as the Express Association Wharf), 5km east of the city centre in the suburb of Pending.

ly gardens. Part of the museum displays the diverse natural history collection of the nineteenth-century naturalist Alfred Russell Wallace, who spent two years in Sarawak in the 1850s. Upstairs, the excellent ethnographic section includes an authentic wooden Iban longhouse, a Penan hut, some fearsome Iban war totems, and woodcarvings from the Kayan and Kenyah ethnic groups. Across the road, in the new wing, there's an unparalleled collection of antique Chinese storage jars, brass kettles and cannons from Brunei, plus prehistoric relics and early trading goods. Behind the new wing of the museum, the **Islamic Museum** (daily except Fri 9am–6pm; free) exhibits diverse aspects of Islamic culture, from architecture to weaponry and textiles to prayer.

The grid of streets running eastwards from Jalan Tun Haji Openg to the main Chinese temple, Tua Pek Kong, constitutes Kuching's **Chinatown**. On busy Main Bazaar and, one block south, on Jalan Carpenter, there are numerous stores and restaurants operating out of renovated two-storey shop-houses, built by Hokkien and Teochew immigrants who arrived in the 1890s. Overlooking the river on Jalan Temple, **Tua Pek Kong** is the oldest Taoist temple in Sarawak (1876) and attracts a stream of people wanting to pay their respects to Tua Pek Kong, the patron saint of business. You can learn about the history of Sarawak's Chinese community at the **Chinese History Museum** (daily except Fri 9am–6pm; free) across the road.

Boats cross to the north side of Sungei Sarawak from several jetties on the waterfront, itself a pleasant esplanade, with cafés, bars and seating. One boat leaves from opposite the courthouse on Main Bazaar (every 15min, daily 6am–10pm; 20 sen) to Sapi jetty, close to the Astana, formerly the Brookes residence and now the home of the Head of State of Sarawak. Another route takes you closer to Fort Margherita, 1km east of the Astana; the only one of Sarawak's twenty historic river forts that's open to the public. It now houses a **Police Museum** (Tues–Sun 10am–6pm; free but take your passport), which features old weapons and uniforms, and a reconstructed opium den. From the fort, it's easy to thread your way eastwards and down to the atmospheric **Malay kampung** over which it stands guard: Kampung Boyan segues into Kampung Gersik, which in turn is assimilated by Kampung Sourabaya Ulu. From this side of the fort, boats will deposit you near the *Riverside Majestic Hotel* on the east side of the city centre.

Eating and nightlife

Local **specialities** such as wild boar and deer sometimes crop up on Chinese menus; in addition, Kuching has its own *laksa*, a rich soup where rice vermicelli is combined with shredded chicken, prawns and beansprouts in a spicy coconut gravy. The city's best **bar** is *De Tavern*, a Kayan-run watering-hole opposite the *Hilton* on Jalan Borneo. Should you develop a taste for *tuak* (rice wine), try the range at the *Telang Usan Hotel*'s *Dulit Terrace and Tuak Bar*.

Choon Hui Café, Jl Ban Hock. Storming *laksa* and filling *kolok mee* (noodles, Kuching-style) make this plain coffee shop near Kuching's Hindu temple a huge breakfast-time hit.

Denis' Place, 80 Main Bazaar. Western-style café–bar with superb international cuisine, coffee and pastries.

Jubilee Restoran, 49 Jl India. Excellent Malay restaurant serving tasty *kacang goreng* (peanuts in fish paste) and *sayur* (green beans in chilli and lemon). Full meals from RM8 for two.

Minangkabau, 168 Jl Chan Chin Ann. Excellent Indonesian restaurant with a range of unusual dishes like chilli-hot fish curries and beef *rendang*. RM10–15 for two.

Nam Sen, 17 Jl Market. Lovely old coffee shop, complete with marble tables and "No spitting" signs. Handy for snatching an early-morning coffee or noodle soup before catching a bus.

National Islamic Café, Jl Carpenter. Serves halal (Islamic) food, curries and unleavened bread from mid-morning until about 9pm. Very popular and inexpensive at RM3–4 a head.

Red Eastern Seafood, Jl Ban Hock. Popular steamboat place.

See Good, Jl Ban Hock, beside Telang Usan Hotel. Fantastic Chinese restaurant; don't shirk the bamboo clams. It has the best selection of wine in Kuching, and although it's slightly pricier than some (RM60 for two) it's worth every sen.

Shopping

Kuching is the best place in Sarawak to buy just about anything, although it would be unwise to stock up on tribal textiles and handicrafts here before visiting Sibu, Kapit or the longhouses in the interior. For **handicrafts and souvenirs**, check out Sarakraf, 14 Main Bazaar, for baskets, textiles and ironwork; Sarawak Batik Art Shop, 1 Jl Temple, for fine Iban pua kumbu textiles; Tan Brothers, Jalan Padungan, close to the junction with Jalan Mathies, for baskets, carvings and bags; Talan Usan, Jalan Ban Hock, for superb Penan and Orang Ulu crafts; and Yeo Hing Chuan, 46 Main Bazaar, for interesting carvings and other handicrafts. Adventure Images, 55 Main Bazaar, has the best postcards in Sarawak. Mohamad Yahiah & Sons, with branches in the Holiday Inn and Bell Books in Sarawak Plaza, offers the biggest range of **books** in Sarawak, and also stock the best **maps** of the state. Sky Book Store, 57 Jl Padungan, and Star Books, 30 Main Bazaar, are good for geographical, cultural and anthropological material.

For a typical local shopping experience head out to the weekend **market** at the Jalan Satok/Jalan Palm junction in the southwest of the city. Stalls here sell everything from rabbits to knives, and one alley is dedicated to Dayak produce and handicrafts. The market runs from Saturday afternoon until 2am, then from 6am to noon on Sunday; beware of pickpockets. Take bus #4a or #4b from the Matang Transport Company bus station, or from outside the post office (5min).

Listings

Airlines MAS, Lot 215, Jl Song Thian Cheok (☎082/246622); Merpati, c/o Sin Hwa Travel Service, 8 Lebuh Temple (☎082/246688); Royal Brunei Airlines, 1st Floor, Rugayah Bldg, Jl Song Thian Cheok (☎082/243344); Singapore Airlines, Wisma Bukit Maja Kuching, Jl Tunku Abdul Rahman (☎082/247777).

Banks and exchange Majid & Sons, 45 Jl India and Mohamad Yahia & Sons, in the basement of Jl Abell's Sarawak Plaza, offer good rates.

Hospitals Sarawak General Hospital, Jl Ong Kee Hui (☎082/257555), charges RM1 for A & E consultations; for private treatment, go to Norman Medical Centre, Jl Tun Datuk Patinggi (☎082/440055), or the Timberland Medical Centre, Jl Rock Road (☎082/234991).

Immigration 1st Floor, Bangunan Sultan Iskander, Jl Simpang Tiga (Mon–Fri 8am–noon & 2–4.30pm; ☎082/245661), for visa extensions; take Chin Lian Long bus #11. Get there by 3.30pm if you want service the same day. Indonesian consulate at 5a Jl Pisang (Mon–Thurs 8.30am–noon & 2–4pm; ☎082/241734) – take bus #5a or #6 from Jl Mosque. Visas cost RM10; allow at least two working days – though you may no longer need one to cross at Entikong (see p.641).

Internet access *Cyber Café*, Medan Pelita; *Cyber City*, Block D, off Jl Borneo (behind Riverside Majestic); *Cyber Café*, Abell Road, opposite and down from *Pizza Hut*.

Police Central Police Station on Jl Khoo Hun Yeang (☎082/241222).

Post office The main post office on Jl Tun Haji Openg (Mon–Sat 8am–6pm, Sun 10am–1pm) keeps poste restante.

Telephone services International calls can be made at the Telekom office, Jl Batu Lintang (Mon–Fri 8am–6pm, Sat 8am–noon), from most public card phones, and from all major hotels.

Bako National Park

BAKO NATIONAL PARK, a two-hour bus and boat journey northeast of Kuching, occupies the northern section of the Muara Tebas Peninsula at the mouth of Sungei Bako. It's a beautiful area and the best place to see wildlife in Sarawak. Many people come on a day-trip and then end up staying longer, taking picnics to one of the seven beaches, relaxing at the park headquarters area, or following the trails. You'll see plenty of flora and fauna, including the strange pitcher plants, whose deep, mouth-shaped lids open to trap water and insects which are then digested in the soupy liquid. The best time to see wildlife on the trails is at night or in the early morning; you'll almost definitely catch sight of proboscis, macaque and silver leaf monkeys, snakes, wild boar, giant monitor lizards, squirrels, bearded pigs, otters and mouse deer. The park headquarters and the open paths in the *kerangas* (sparse forest) are the best places for bird-watching: 150 species have been recorded in Bako, including two rare species of hornbills.

The park map clearly shows the sixteen trails, which all start from park headquarters and are colour-coded with paint splashes every twenty metres. Carry a litre of water per person (you can refill your bottle from the streams), a light rainproof jacket, mosquito repellent and sunscreen. Wear good shoes and a sunhat. Don't forget your swimming gear either, as cool streams cut across the trails, and beaches and waterfalls are never far away. Probably the most popular trail is the hike to **Tajor Waterfall** (3.5km; about 2hr), which climbs up the forested cliff, through *kerangas* with plentiful pitcher plants, through peat bog and, eventually to the waterfall itself, a lovely spot for swimming. If you leave the main trail at the wooden hut and viewpoint just after the *kerangas*, and turn west, a path descends to two beautiful beaches, **Telok Pandan Kecil** and **Telok Pandan Besar** (30min). The longest beach on the peninsula is **Telok Sibur beach**. To get there, continue past Tajor Waterfall, following the main trail for around forty minutes, before turning west on the black-and-red trail. The demanding descent to the beach takes anything from twenty minutes to an hour to accomplish. You'll have to drop down the cliff face using creepers and roots to help you, and at the bottom you have to tread carefully through the mangrove swamp. After wading across a river, you reach the beach – not surprisingly, seldom visited.

Practicalities

Before going to Bako you need to get a **permit** and reserve your accommodation at the Visitor Centre in Kuching (see p.635), though day-trippers can get their permits in Kampung Bako. Once at the park, you can extend your stay.

To get to the park, take the Petra Jaya #6 bus (RM3.80 return) from the open-air market beside Electra House, which runs hourly to the jetty at Kampung Bako. From here you can get a motorized boat to the park headquarters (RM30 per boat for ten people; 30min) which leaves when it's full. Once at the park headquarters you need to pay the park fee (RM3), sign in and collect the informative map of the park.

At park headquarters, you can stay at the **hostel** (RM10.50) or one of the lodges (③), all of which provide bed linen, fridge and cooking facilities. Some hikers prefer to camp on the trails – tents can be rented from the headquarters for RM4. There's a simple café at headquarters and a provisions shop.

The Kalimantan border: Anna Rais, Bau and Gunung Penrissen

The mountains straddling the **border with Kalimantan**, 100km south of Kuching, are inhabited by Bidayuh, the only remaining Land Dayaks in Sarawak. Unlike other ethnic groups, the Bidayuh built their multi-levelled, elevated longhouses at the base of hills rather than on rivers, and, as a consequence, endured violent attacks during the nineteenth century from other more aggressive groups, especially the Iban. But the Bidayuh weren't exactly passive victims: traditional communities always had a head-house, where the heads of their enemies were kept and which served as a focus for male activities and rituals. Nowadays, only one traditional Bidayuh longhouse community remains – at **Anna Rais**. Although quite an introverted group, the Bidayuh welcome sensitive visitors.

If you are in Sarawak during late May and early June it's well worth going to the **Bau** area, near Kuching, deep in Bidayuh country. Over this period the Bidayuhs celebrate **Gawai Padi**, a shamanistic ritual, in which people give thanks to the Rice Goddess for an abundant harvest. Each village has a slightly different kind of celebration, but it usually involves dancing and making offerings. Contact Diweng Bekir (☎082/492726) at the Ministry of Tourism for further details about Gawai Padi. **Buses** leave from Jalan Masjid in Kuching for Bau every hour from 7am to 6pm.

The longhouses

From Kuching's Lebuh Jawa, STC bus #9 (6.40am–5.55pm; every 30min; 2hr) goes to **ANNA RAIS**, the largest Bidayuh settlement in the area. The community is used to visitors, and everybody is greeted warmly. You'll be escorted around by a member of the community which consists of two longhouses on either side of a river, Sungei Penrissen, and many separate dwellings. The best time to go is at the weekend, when the longhouse-based women are over with their farming duties, the children are in from school and the wage-earners back from work in the oil-palm plantations or in Kuching. As you wander around, you'll be offered food and drink, possibly even betel nut, and invited to watch and participate in craft demonstrations. Most visitors stay a couple of hours, returning to Kuching the same day, but you can stay the night. If you do, remember to bring some gifts for the children. Alternatively, you can sleep in the community hall (token donation of around RM10) at **KAMPUNG ABANG** (ask at the longhouse whether there is room), a ten-minute drive beyond Anna Rais, and a useful overnight stop if you want to trek up nearby Gunung Penrissen the next day.

Gunung Penrissen

The most accessible of the mountains on the Malaysia/Kalimantan border is the spectacular 1300-metre **Gunung Penrissen**, the hike up which involves tough walking along narrow paths and crossing fast-flowing streams which descend from the source of Sungei Sarawak; vertical ladders help you on the last section. You will need a guide, as the trails aren't easy to follow. Unless you go with a tour operator in Kuching the only way to find a guide is through Anna Rais longhouse. You will have to negotiate a price (expect to pay RM50–100). Although the ascent and descent of Penrissen can be done in one hard day, you may prefer to set up camp at the foot of the summit, so bring a tent and food. From the summit, you can gaze over the rainforest into Kalimantan to the south and east, and to the South China Sea over the forests to the north.

Serian and the border crossing

Some 20km southeast of Gunung Penrissen is the border crossing at **TEBEDU**. Buses to Tebedu leave from **SERIAN**, a workaday town on the main Kuching–Sri Aman road. You'll need to set off first thing, as local buses from Tebedu which run south across the border to the Indonesian town of **ENTIKONG** and on to Pontianak stop running in the early afternoon. Tebedu is little more than an administrative centre, with a couple of dispiriting hotels. The border crossing at Entikong is open 6am–6pm. No visa is needed.

Batang Ai Region

The **Batang Ai** river system lies 200km east of Kuching; this is where the Skrang, Lemanak and Engkari rivers flow into the Batang Ai Lake. The area, designated a national park, is the most popular destination for longhouse visits from the capital. Many of the tour operators in Kuching have established good relations with the Iban communities here (RM300 for a three-day tour; see p.636), but it's quite possible to travel here independently. Access is via the size-able town of **SRI AMAN**, which sits upriver on Sungei Lupar, 150km southeast of Kuching. It's reached either by STC bus from Kuching's Lebuh Jawa (7.30am, 9.30am, noon, 3pm & 7.30pm; RM15), or on the Biramas Express (1pm; RM15) from the Penrissen Road terminal; the journey takes three or four hours. There are several hotels in town: the *Champion Inn*, 1248 Main Bazaar (☎083/320140; ②), is the most central, and *Hoover Hotel*, 139 Jl Club (☎083/321985; ③), the best in town. Batang Ai is around 40km southeast of Sri Aman.

Visiting the longhouses

All the longhouses on the Skrang, Lemanak and Engkari rivers are Iban and it is here that the Iban culture is most concentrated. It's especially visible during the harvest festival, or Gawai Padi, in late May/early June, when traditional dress is encouraged and age-old rituals enacted, including wedding, christening and circumcision ceremonies. At other times of the year, it might be stretching the point to say that they still follow a traditional lifestyle (many have "good" jobs in Kuching, or live abroad, and televisions and music systems are in evidence). However, the gregarious, highly hospitable Iban will make a trip at any time of year an enjoyable one, and you'll find that just going fishing, eating delicious fish and jungle vegetables, and sitting on the longhouse veranda makes for a memorable experience.

The longhouses are fairly accessible from Sri Aman. Head for one of the jetties and get talking to the locals who ply the rivers and with any luck you'll get an invitation to a longhouse. It might be wiser, though, not to leave things to chance and join an organized tour.

The Skrang is reached by taking a Betong bus from Sri Aman, and getting off just short of Entabau, at the **PAIS** jetty. Of all the tributaries in this region, the Skrang is the most touristy, and you may find that longhouses won't take you in unless you've booked through the operator which has "adopted" them. To reach either the Lemanak or the Batang Ai and its tributaries you'll need to take an STC bus from Sri Aman southeast to **LUBOK ANTU**, 50km away. Here, you'll need to ask for the local shuttle (RM1.50) down to the Batang Ai Lake jetty, about 10km to the northeast, in order to explore the tributaries of the Batang Ai; this is not a very regular service, and if you get to Lubok Antu late, you can overnight at the *Kelingkang Inn* (☎083/584331; ③), on the main street, and get dinner at *Oriental Café*, beside the bus station.

Sibu

SIBU, 60km from the coast up Batang Rajang, is Sarawak's second largest city and the state's biggest port. Most of the local population are Foochow Chinese (the town is known locally as New Foochow), and its remarkable modern growth is largely attributed to these enterprising immigrants. Most travellers treat Sibu as the first stage of an expedition upriver and, beyond simply soaking up the town's vibrant atmosphere, there's not much to do.

The town's most striking landmark is the towering, seven-storey **pagoda** at the back of Tua Pek Kong Temple beyond the western, waterfront end of Jalan Khoo Peng Loong. Two large concrete lions guard the entrance to the temple, to the left of which stands a statue of the deity, Tua Pek Kong, a prominent Confucian scholar. The roof and columns are decorated with traditional dragon and holy bird statues, and murals depict the signs of the Chinese zodiac. Across the way, in the network of streets between Jalan Market, Jalan Channel and Jalan Central, is **Chinatown** with its plethora of hardware shops, newspaper stalls, rowdy cafés, food vendors and hotels. The central artery, **Jalan Market**, runs from Jalan Pulau beside the temple, and forms the hub of possibly the most vibrant *pasar malam* in Sarawak. Beside Jalan Channel, the daily Lembangan Market opens before dawn and closes around 5pm; there are hundreds of stalls here, selling anything from edible delicacies like flying fox, snake and jungle ferns, to rattan baskets, beadwork and charm bracelets.

Two kilometres north of the town centre, the modern Civic Centre contains in its **Cultural Exhibition Hall** (Tues–Sun 10.30am–5.30pm; free) a small but high-quality collection of photographs, artefacts and paraphernalia describing the varied peoples of the Rajang. These include costumes, backpacks, musical instruments, and a scale model of an Iban longhouse. To get there, take the Jalan Tun Abang Haji Openg bus from the bus terminal and ask for the Civic Centre.

Practicalities

Flights from Kuching, Bintulu and Miri use the **airport** (☎084/334351), 25km east of the city centre. Taxis cost RM20 into the centre, but the #3a bus (every 40min, daily 7am–6pm; RM2) stops on the main road outside the terminal, and runs to the **bus and taxi station** on Jalan Khoo Peng Loong, 200m west of Chinatown and close to many budget hotels. MAS is at 61 Jl Tunku Osman (☎084/326166). For onward journeys by bus, you can book seats through bus company offices on Jalan Khoo Peng Loong and Jalan Maju.

Boats dock at the **upriver boat wharf**, 100m northwest of the bus terminal. This is where you come to catch the express boat on to Kanowit (RM7), Song (RM12) and Kapit (RM15); they run at least hourly from 5.30am until mid-afternoon. From the **downriver wharf**, 100m further northwest, just beside the Chinese temple, Express Bahagia, 20a Jl Tukang Besi (☎084/319228), runs a daily service to Kuching at 11.30am, and Concorde Marine, 1 Jl Bank (☎084/331593) runs one at 8.15am. The trip takes four hours, costs RM35 and usually involves changing boats at Sarikei, one hour downriver.

You can pick up a good map of the town at Sibu's **Visitor Centre** (Mon–Fri 8am–12.45pm & 2–4.15pm, Sun 8am–12.45pm; ☎084/340980), 32 Jl Cross, at the back of the *Sarawak Hotel*, off Ramin Way. Ibrahim Tourist Guide, 1 Lane One, Jalan Bengkel (☎084/318987; Mon–Sat 9am–5.30pm), does an overnight **tour** to a nearby Iban longhouse (RM200 for two), and Frankie Ting at Sazhong Trading, 4 Jl Central (Mon–Sat 8am–4.40pm; ☎084/336017), does a similar trip to nearby Rumah Sawai. The main **post office** is on Jalan Kampung Nyabar (Mon–Fri 8am–6pm, Sat 8am–noon); the **police** are on Jalan Kampung Nyabor (☎084/336144); and the nearest **hospital** is Lau King Hoe, Jalan Pulau, next to the RPA building (☎084/343333). **Internet** access is available at *My Net*, in the quadrangle behind *Tanahmas Hotel*, and *Forever Link Computers*, 2nd Floor, Wisam Sanyan, Jalan Morshidi Sidek.

ACCOMMODATION AND EATING

The best of the budget **accommodation** is the very clean *Hoover Lodging House*, close to the bus station on 34 Jl Tan Sri (☎084/334490; ②); over in the west of town, *Hoover House Methodist Guesthouse* (☎084/332973; ②) occupies a quiet spot on Jalan Pulau, with basic double rooms (book ahead); *Malaysia*, Jalan Kampung Nyabor (☎084/332299; ②) is a popular, but fairly shabby place on a busy main road. Otherwise, you should go for the quality *Zuhra*, Jalan Kampung Nyabor (☎084/310711; ③), which has modern en-suite rooms with air-con and TV; the pricey but comfortable *Government Rest House*, fifteen minutes' walk from the wharf at the far end of Jalan Pulau (☎084/330406; ③); or the *Premier* (☎084/323222; ⑦), at the junction of Jalan Kampung Nyabor and Jalan Tinggi, a top-class hotel which occasionally does bargain promotions.

Throughout town there are Chinese **cafés** selling Sibu's most famous dish, Foochow noodles – steamed and then served in a soy and oyster sauce with spring onions and dried fish. Other local favourites include *kang puan mee* (noodles cooked in lard) and *kong bian* (oriental bagels, sprinkled with sesame seed). **Hawker stalls** at the Lembangan Market are the busiest place in the morning, but in the evening everyone congregates at the *pasar malam* in the town centre, though you can't sit down and eat here. For a good **restaurant** experience, try the well-known Foochow restaurant *Hock Chu Leu Restoran*, 28 Jl Tukan Besi, which does great baked fish and fresh vegetables (RM25 for two, including beer; or the *Balkis Islamic Café*, near the post office at 69 Jl Osman, which serves good North Indian staples like *roti canai*, *murtabak* and curries (RM3 a head). Top-of-the-league is *The New Capitol Restoran*, beside the *Premier* hotel, the kind of Chinese restaurant where you can get shark's fin and other "delicacies" at around RM60 for two.

Up the Rajang: Kanowit, Song and Sungei Katibas

The 560-kilometre-long **Batang Rajang** – *batang* (big river) rather than *sungei*, because of its great width and length – lies at the very heart of Sarawak. This is the world of isolated colonial forts, and of longboat trips to busy longhouse communities. Note that unlike the longhouses at Batang Ai, the communities here are not used to tourists. The best thing to do is to turn up and see what kind of reception you get. The chances are you'll be offered somewhere to stay. The express boat from Sibu (daily, at least hourly 5.30am–2.30pm; RM15) takes two-and-a-half to three hours to reach Kapit, stopping first at **Kanowit** and then at the little town of **Song**, from where Iban longhouses on the **Katibas** and **Baleh** tributaries become easily accessible.

Kanowit

An hour from Sibu, the boat reaches the sleepy settlement of **KANOWIT**. There are two hotels on waterfront Jalan Kubu, the *Kanowit Air Con* (☎084/752155; ②) and the *Harbour View Inn* (☎084/753188; ②), plus a few cafés. The only real sight here is Fort Emma, which was built in 1859 of timber and bamboo and remains impressive, despite years of neglect. It's just a couple of hundred metres to the west of the jetty in front of the town's two hotels – en route you'll pass the lurid green mosque.

Song and Sungei Katibas

The next stop is at **SONG**, another hour upstream, at the head of one of the Rajang's major tributaries, Sungei Katibas, which winds and narrows as it runs south towards the mountainous border region with Kalimantan. The place is little more than a few blocks of waterfront shop-houses, a jetty, a small Chinese temple and two waterfront hotels: the *Capital Hotel* (☎084/777252; ②) and the much smarter *Katibas Inn* (☎084/777323; ②). On the riverside are the usual Chinese stores, plus several coffee shops.

To explore **Sungei Katibas**, you need to catch the passenger longboat which leaves Song twice each morning; departure times change so ask at the jetty. On the Katibas are several Iban longhouses worth visiting, including the large community at the junction of the Katibas and one of its own small tributaries, Sungei Bangkit. It takes between two and three hours to reach **Nanga Bangkit**, which comprises an impressive fifty-door longhouse and a dozen smaller dwellings on the opposite bank. It's best to get the earliest boat you can to give yourself time to meet people and maximize your chances of getting invited to stay overnight. If no offers are forthcoming you should be in time to get the longboat back to Song. The longhouse women are excellent weavers, and you can buy a wall hanging here for around RM300, which sounds a lot, but you won't be able to find these *ikat* weavings anywhere else.

Kapit and Sungei Baleh

KAPIT, around three hours east of Sibu by express boat, is a fast-growing timber town with a frontier atmosphere, where karaoke lounges, snooker halls and brothels are all much in evidence. Although most travellers stay just one night, waiting for boats along the Rajang or for connecting longboats along Sungei Baleh, there are lots of good cafés and a decent museum, and this is also a good place to organize trips to local Iban communities with one of the tour operators based in town.

Close to the jetty is Kapit's main landmark, **Fort Sylvia**. It was built in 1880 in an attempt to prevent the warring Iban attacking smaller groups such as the upriver Ukit and Bukitan. Kapit's main square, simply called **Kapit Square**, is surrounded by shops selling everything from noodles to rope. The walk west along Jalan Temenggong, which forms the square's northern edge, leads to the day market. Back from the jetty, near the pond, the **Civic Museum** (Mon–Fri 2–4.30pm; free) has a collection of interesting exhibits on the tribes in the Rajang basin, including a well-constructed longhouse and a mural painted by local Iban.

Express boats dock at the town jetty, close to the town centre. There is no information office in Kapit, but you can get leaflets on tours and surrounding attractions from Tan Teck Chuan, whose office is at 11 Jl Sit Leong. The **Maybank**, beside the *Hotel Meligai*, changes travellers' cheques. **Internet** access is available in the town library on Jalan Selinik (Mon–Fri 9am–4.30pm, Sat 9am–12.30pm, Sun closed).

You need a permit (free of charge) to **travel beyond Kapit**, available from the Resident's Office (Mon–Fri 8am–12.30pm & 2.15–4.15pm), on the first floor of the State Government Complex which is 100m north of the jetty on Jalan Selinik. You'll need to take your passport with you.

Accommodation and eating

Rajang, 28 Jl Temenggoh, New Bazaar (☎084/796709; ②), is one of Sarawak's best-known travellers' **hotels**, and many of the large en-suite rooms overlook the river. All eighteen rooms at *Fully Inn*, Jalan Temenggong (☎084/797366; ②), are inexpensive and appealing, and some have river views. *Kapit Longhouse*, 21 Jl Berjaya (☎084/796415; ①), is the cheapest hotel in town and although grubby and basic, remains popular. *New Rajang Inn*, 104 Jl Teo Chow Beng (☎084/796600; ②), has small, en-suite air-con rooms.

The **food** from hawker stalls and markets is good, particularly at the Covered Market on Jalan Airport, where a dozen stalls serve Chinese, Malay and Dayak dishes, and at the day market on Jalan Teo Chow Beng. Of the proper restaurants, try *Hock Bing Seafood Café*, west of the temple, which serves the best prawn dishes in Kapit (RM20 for two, including beer), or the *Ah Kau Restoran*, Jalan Berjaya, which specializes in local recipes: wild boar, steamed fish, jungle vegetables (RM25 for two with beer). Beside the jetty there's *Chuong Hin Café*, a must for breakfast with a fine selection of sweet and savoury cakes.

Sungei Baleh and the Pelagus Rapids

Sungei Baleh branches off from the Rajang 10km east of Kapit. Several boats leave Kapit for Sungei Baleh between 7am and noon. Some ply only the 20km to **NANGA BALEH** (90min; RM8), a large, modern longhouse, where there is also a logging camp; some push on to the junction with the tributaries of Sungei Gaat and Sungei Merirai, two and a half hours from Kapit (RM10); while others follow the shorter stretch to the Sungei Mujong junction (1hr; RM6) – a large tributary closer to Kapit. The express boat ends its route at **PUTAI**, four hours from Kapit, where there is another logging camp.

There are Iban longhouses on the **Gaat and Merirai tributaries**, which can only be reached by renting a longboat (around RM100 return). The longhouse wharves at the junctions of the Baleh and these smaller rivers are the places to ask for advice on how to travel further, and to find out which longhouses are good to visit. One place to make for on the upper Baleh is the river's only Kenyah longhouse, established by a group of Indonesian Kenyah, two hours beyond Putai by longboat. Although the longhouse is not a large wooden beauty, the people here are friendly and the location breathtaking. You're close here to the Kalimantan border and within sight of the remote peak, Batu Tiban.

Just beyond the Baleh turn on Batang Rejang (1hr from Kapit) are the **Pelagus Rapids**, a 800- metre stretch of rock-strewn shallow water which in dry season can be so lethal the express boats are unable to operate. At the most attractive point of the rapids, as the river twists north, lies **the Pelagus Rapids Resort** (RM50 return speedboat from Kapit; call the resort, ☎082/799050, to arrange pick up time). It's a beautiful longhouse-shaped hideaway tucked in between the rapids and the jungle-covered Bukit Pelagus behind. Exquisite rooms with bathroom attached and verandah go from RM63 a night. The resort's resident guide Nyaring leads excursions (RM100) to an Iban longhouse nearby, as well as a fascinating two-hour boat trip to visit a Punan community where you can see rare *Klirieng* burial poles of elaborate design, with a dug-out chamber for storing the bones of aristocrats.

Bintulu

Most people only linger long enough in **BINTULU** to catch a bus connection to Niah National Park. It's a boom town, grown rich on offshore gas. The only sights worth visiting are the **markets**: the day market, housed in two large, open-sided circular buildings overlooking the river at the west end of Main Bazaar, the adjacent *pasar tamu* and, across town, the *pasar malam*, which starts up at around 6pm in the long-distance bus station. The town's compact rectangle of streets is bordered by the airfield to the east and Sungei Kemena to the west, with nothing much of interest in between. The main **post office** is also on Jalan Tun Razak, and the **Telekom** office is at the western end of Jalan Sommerville (Mon–Sat 8.30am–4.30pm). There are two **banks** on Jalan Keppel, the **police** are on Jalan Sommerville (☎086/331129), and the **hospital** is on Jalan Abang Galau (☎086/331455). Similajau Adventure Tours, on the lobby floor of the *Plaza Hotel* (☎086/331552), can arrange **hiking trips** to the nearby national parks, plus boat excursions along Sungei Kemena.

Practicalities

The **airport** (☎086/331963) is, incredibly, right in the town centre, within 100m of most of the hotels and restaurants. MAS is at 129 Jl Masjid (☎086/331554). The long-distance **bus station** is 5km out of town at Medan Jaya. A taxi to the centre will cost RM10 or you can get bus #29 to the local bus station on Lebuh Ray Abang Galau (70 sen). The long-distance bus station serves Batu Niah, Kuching, Sibu and Miri. Borneo Highway Express (☎086/339855) runs a daily 5.30pm service to Pontianak (RM86.50). The town's main **taxi** rank is at the junction of Main Bazaar and Lebuh Queen. **Boats** up Sungei Kemena to Tubau, 60km east, dock at the jetty, in the centre of town.

The most popular budget **accommodation** in Bintulu is the basic and noisy *Capital* on Jalan Keppel (☎086/331167; ②). The more appealing rooms at *Fata Inn*, 113 Jl Masjid (☎086/332998; ③), are en suite and have air-con, or you could try the similar *King's Inn*, Jalan Masjid (☎086/337337; ③). Best choice, however, is the popular *Kemena Inn*, 78 Jl Keppel (☎086/331533; ④), which has spacious, comfortable rooms.

For **eating**, there are hawker stalls at both the day market and the *pasar malam*, though this is take-away only. At *Popular Corner* on Lebuh Raya Abang Galau, several outlets under one roof sell claypots, seafood, chicken rice and juices. *Ama Restoran* on Jalan Keppel serves excellent curries, and *Sea View Restoran*, 254 Esplanade, is an atmospheric Chinese café, overlooking Sungei Kemena and serving quality food (RM15 a head, including beer).

Niah national park

Visiting **NIAH NATIONAL PARK**, 131km north of Bintulu, is a highly rewarding experience – in less than a day you can see one of the largest caves in the world, as well as prehistoric rock graffiti in the remarkable Painted Cave, and hike along primary forest trails. In the outer area of the present park, deep excavations have revealed human remains, including skulls which date back forty thousand years, and artefacts like flake stone tools, mortars and shell ornaments – the first evidence that people had lived in Southeast Asia that long ago.

The park is roughly halfway between Bintulu and Miri, 11km off the main road and close to the small town of Batu Niah, which you can reach by regular Syarikat Bus Suria services from either Bintulu or Miri. There are a few Chinese cafés here, and the *Niah Cave Inn* (☎085/737332; ④) is the best accommodation option. The caves are 3km north of Batu Niah, and reached either by a half-hour walk, by longboat (daily 8am–4pm; RM10) or taxi (RM10).

The path from Batu Niah leads straight to the **park headquarters** on the western bank of Sungei Niah. Here, you can sleep in four-berth hostel rooms ($10) or in chalets (④); there's no need to book ahead, except at weekends. Contact the Visitor Centre in Miri (☎085/434181) to book or check availability of accommodation. There's a shop (daily 7am–10pm) which stocks basic foodstuffs, a canteen (daily 7.30am–10pm) and a small inter-pretation centre covering the geology of the caves and the economy of birds' nest collecting.

The caves and trails

From the park headquarters it's a thirty-minute walk to the caves: take a sampan across the river and then follow a wooden walkway through dense rainforest where you are likely to see monkeys, hornbills, birdwing butterflies, tree squirrels and flying lizards. Some distance along the walkway, a clearly marked path branches off to an Iban longhouse, Rumah Chang, where you can buy drinks and snacks. The main walkway continues, heading up through the Trader's Cave (early nest-gatherers would congregate here to sell their harvests) to the mind-blowing, west mouth (60m by 250m) of the Great Cave. From within the immense, draughty darkness you can hear the voices of the bird's nest collectors who collect swiftlet nests for use in the famous bird's-nest soup; their thin beanstalk poles snake up from the cave floor. Once inside, the walkway continues on, via Burnt Cave and Moon Cave, to the Painted Cave, thirty minutes' walk away. Here, early Sarawak communities buried their dead in boat-shaped coffins, arranged around the cave walls; dating of the contents has proved that the caves had been used as a cemetery for tens of thousands of years. One of these wooden coffins is still perched on an incline, its contents long since removed to the Sarawak Museum. It's hard to distinguish the wall paintings behind the coffin – a thirty-metre-long tableau depicting boats on a journey, the figures apparently either jumping on and off, or dancing. This image fits various Borneo mythologies where the dead undergo challenges en route to the afterlife.

There are two other trails in the park. Jalan Madu splits off the main walkway around 800m from the park headquarters and cuts first east, then south, across a peat swamp forest, where you see wild orchids, mushrooms and pandanus. The trail crosses Sungei Subis and then fol-lows its south bank to its confluence with Sungei Niah, from where you'll have to hail a pass-ing boat to cross over to Batu Niah ($1). The more spectacular trail to Bukit Kasut starts at the confluence of these two rivers. After crossing the river, the clearly marked trail winds through forest, round the foothills of Bukit Kasut and up to the summit – a hard one-hour slog, at the end of which there's a view both of the forest canopy and Batu Niah.

Miri

MIRI is another fast-growing town, with a significant expat community and a strong Chinese character. For tourists it's the main departure point for independent and organized trips into Gunung Mulu National Park (see p.650) and the route north to Brunei and Sabah. Miri's old town around Jalan China in the west of town is the most enjoyable area to wander around. It's packed with cafés and shops, and there's a wet fish market and a Chinese temple at the top of Jalan China. The wide road running east from here and parallel to the river, Jalan Bendahara, is the simplest route into the new town area. The shopping centre Wisma Pelita, south of the old town on Jalan Padang, includes the Pelita Book Centre, on the first floor, which has English-language books on Sarawak, and Longhouse Handicraft Centre, on the top floor, which sells rattan bags, *pua kumbu* (tie-died) textiles and carvings. Directly south of the adjacent bus station is the padang, on whose border lies **Tamu Muhibbah** (daily 6am–4pm), the town's jungle produce market, where Orang Ulu come downriver to sell rattan mats, tropical fruits, rice wine and even jungle animals.

Practicalities

The **airport** (☎085/414242) is 8km west of the town centre: bus #9 (every 45min, daily 6.15am–8pm; RM1) runs from outside the terminal to the **bus station** on Jalan Padang, a five-minute walk from Jalan China and the old town.

Next to the bus station you'll find the **Visitor Centre** (☎085/434181), which handles all accommodation bookings for the local national parks. Pick up the excellent Sarawak Tourism Board **map** here. Several **tour operators** organize trips and treks to Gunung Mulu and other destinations. Seridan Mulu, Lobby Arcade, *Righa Royal Hotel*, 2km west of the centre (☎085414300), is a very professional outfit run by Gracie Geikie, a mine of information on Mulu and other national parks. Also there's Borneo Adventures, ninth floor, Wisma Pelita (☎085/414935); Tropical Adventures, ground floor, *Mega Hotel* (☎082/419337); and Borneo Overland (☎082/430255), beside the Standard Chartered Bank on Jalan Merpati. If you're going independently, contact Endayang Enterprise, second floor, Judson Clinic, 171a Jl Brooke (☎085/438740), to arrange accommodation, boat transfers and guides in the park, although as long as you're not arriving at Mulu at the weekend you'll have no trouble finding a bed.

There is a **moneychanger** in the Magnum 4-digit shop at 12 Jl China. The **post office** and **Telekom** office (daily 7.30am–10pm) are both on Jalan Post. The **immigration office** on Jalan Kipas (Room 3; Mon–Fri 8am–noon & 2–4.15pm) will only extend your Sarawak visa by a few days. Miri's General **Hospital** is on the airport road (☎085/420033). **Internet** access can be found at *WWW Café*, Lot 943, Jalan Post (back of Imperial Mall) and *Fantasy Net Café*, 1st Floor, Bendarlan Plaza, Jalan Bendarlan.

ACCOMMODATION AND EATING

Lodging houses with dorm beds offer the cheapest deal, but these are really basic and none too clean: *Tai Tong Lodging House*, at the jetty end of Jalan China in the old part of town, has men-only dorms ($8) and private rooms (②). More salubrious places include the excellent *Fairland Inn*, Jalan Raja, at Raja Square (☎085/413981; ②), which has well-equipped rooms and is very popular with travellers on not so tight a budget. In the next category up, try the recommended *Brooke Inn*, Jl 14 Brooke (☎085/412881; ③), where all rooms have TV, air-con and bathrooms.

MOVING ON FROM MIRI

By plane

There are four daily flights to Mulu from the airport (☎085/414242), but seats are limited so book ahead (RM70). For other flights see "Travel Details", p.668. MAS is on Jalan South Yu Seng (☎085/414144).

By bus

All buses leave from the bus station. Bus Suria (☎085/412173) operates services to Bintulu and other locations south, including Kuching and Pontianak; Miri Belait Transport (☎085/419129) runs a daily service at 7am to Limbang (RM26) and to Kuala Belait in Brunei (RM12) – the last departure from Belait to BSB in Brunei is around 3.30pm, so you'll need to set off early. You can also get to Mulu by bus and boat – this involves taking an early bus (RM3) or taxi (RM20) from Miri to Kuala Baram (every 15min; 45min); see p.668 for details of the various connections.

As for **food**, the *Apollo Seafood Centre*, 4 Jl South Yu Seng Road, does exquisite grilled stingray and pineapple rice (RM40 for two, including beer), *Maxim Seafood Centre*, Lot 342, Blk 7, Jl Miri-Pujut, serves great grilled fish, and *Bilal Restoran*, Lot 250, Persiaran Kabor, Beautiful Jade Centre, does superb North Indian food (RM6 per dish). At night you can dine at the stalls in the market at the junction of Jalan Entiba and Jalan Begia. At the *Danish Hot Bread* bakery, next to the *Cosy Inn* on Jalan South Yu Seng, you can buy a cream cake to round off your meal.

From Miri to Brunei and Sabah

The trip by road from Sarawak **to Brunei** is quite straightforward, but if you're heading straight on **to Sabah**, the journey can take up to two days; many people prefer to fly straight from Miri to Kota Kinabalu. Heading straight for Brunei from Miri, the trunk road north runs a few kilometres in from the coast to **KUALA BARAM**, 30km away, a small town situated at the mouth of Batang Baram. After crossing the river by ferry (every 20min, daily 6am–8pm) you soon arrive at the border at the Bruneian town of Kuala Belait (see Brunei p.70), another 6km further on. At Kuala Belait, you hop on board a Bruneian bus which runs to Seria, for connections to Bandar Seri Begawan. All stages of the journey from Miri to Kuala Belait are included in the price of a Miri Belait Transport Company ticket. The last bus from Seria that will get you to the Bruneian capital the same day leaves at around 3.30pm, and the first bus from there to the capital leaves at 7am, after which the service is very regular.

Lawas

Boxed in between Sabah and Brunei, **LAWAS TOWN** sits on Sungei Lawas. There's little to see here, but it's an important transit point. Daily **boats** arrive here from Muara in Brunei, Sabah's Pulau Labuan and Limbang. There are also daily departures for these places (see "Travel Details" p.668); tickets cost RM20. The jetty is beside the old mosque, 400m east of the town. A daily **express bus** from Kota Kinabalu calls in here via the Sabah border town of Sipitang and then goes on to Brunei's little-known Temburong District before terminating in Limbang. The fare from Kota Kinabalu is RM30. Lawas **airport** is around 3km south of town – a bus usually meets the daily flights from Kota Kinabalu, Limbang, Bario and Ba Kelalan. The MAS agent is Eng Huat Travel Agency, 455 Jl Law Siew Ann (☎085/285570). The *Mee Yan Hotel* (②), at the bottom of the town, offers adequate **accommodation** or you can go more upmarket and make for the *Federal Hotel* (③) on Jalan Punang. For inexpensive **food**, try the upper floor of the market, where you can get delicious *nasi kampur* (daily 9am–4pm). Otherwise, most of the best eating places cluster around the *Mee Yan Hotel*. Lawas is online too: make for the *Techno Train IT Centre*, Lot 326, Bawah, Jalan Trusan.

Marudi

MARUDI, 80km southeast of Miri on Batang Baram, is the only sizeable town in the whole Baram watershed, and the jetty is the centre of the community. For travellers, there is a useful boat from here to Long Terawan, where there's a connection for Gunung Mulu National Park (8.30am, 10am & 2.30pm; RM15) and west to Kuala Baram, where numerous buses wait to take passengers to Miri or Brunei. Marudi runs a daily nineteen-seater flight to Mulu (RM40), which must be booked ahead. It only takes a few minutes to walk from the town to the airport.

If you have a few hours between boats, you can walk to **Fort Hose**, past the main Bazaar Square, west of the jetty, and along Jalan Fort to the top of the hill, which was built in 1901, and is still in good condition. The fort is now a government office, and also houses a Penan handicraft centre (Mon–Fri 9am–2pm).

The main **hotel**, the *Grand* (☎085/55712; ②), is just off the airport road, Jalan Cinema, and only five minutes' walk south of the jetty. It's a massive place, with clean, quiet rooms, and has information on Gunung Mulu tours. The *Alisan*, on Jalan Queen, off Jalan Cinema (☎085/55601; ③), is also a good deal. For **food**, try the Indian *Restoran Koperselara*, just past the *Alisan* hotel on Jalan Cinema, or *Boon Kee Restoran*, behind the main street in Jalan Newshop.

Gunung Mulu national park

GUNUNG MULU NATIONAL PARK is Sarawak's premier national park, located deep in the rainforest; at the last count, it featured 20,000 animal species and 3500 plant species. Quite apart from the park's primary rainforest, which is characterized by clear rivers and high-altitude vegetation, there are three dramatically eroded mountains, including fifty-metre-high limestone spikes known as the **Pinnacles**. The park also has the largest **limestone cave system** in the world, much of which is still being explored. The two major hikes, to the Pinnacles on **Gunung Api** and to the summit of **Gunung Mulu**, are daunting, but you're rewarded with stupendous views of the rainforest, stretching as far as Brunei.

Although you can arrive unannounced and book into the park hostel, many visitors come to Mulu **as part of a tour** group from Kuching, Miri or Kuala Lumpur – a four-day trip to climb the Pinnacles and see the caves costs about RM600 per person, but covers all incidentals, including permits and guides. **Going independently**, allow yourself an extra day at the beginning to negotiate with the mandatory guides at the park headquarters, who cost, per group, at least RM80 for the Pinnacles (three days), RM110 for the Mulu summit (three days), and RM80 for adventure caving in Sarawak Chamber. Guides, however, are not needed to visit the show caves; you just tag on to the back on the first group you see, which guarantees you entry. For the longer trips, a porter, if so required, will cost an extra RM25 for a day and a night.

Boat travel to the caves is easy to organize from the hostel; the official price is RM85 to hire a boat to get you to Clearwater Cave, a mere 4km upstream, but in practice this is easy to undercut if you ask around. No permits are required anymore to visit the park; just **register** at the Park Headquarters when you arrive, or, if it's after 5.30pm, the following day, where you pay the RM3 park fee.

Among the **equipment** you'll need is a large water bottle, walking shoes, sun hat and swimming gear, a poncho/rain sheet, torch, mosquito repellent, salt solution, ointment for bites, a basic first aid kit and a thin mat. Wear shorts and T-shirts on the trails (it'll be easier to spot leeches), and bring long trousers and long-sleeved shirts for the dusk insect assault at the Pinnacles, Mulu and Headhunter's Trail.

Practicalities

To **fly** to Mulu from Miri (RM70) or Marudi (RM40) you must book ahead, as the small Twin-Otters only have twenty seats. You touch down at the airport, 2km east of park headquarters, and longboats and minibuses meet the planes to take you to the headquarters or accommodation. Return flights to Miri leave the park three times daily, and there are also two weekly flights to Marudi.

Reaching Mulu **by boat** from Miri involves four separate stages and takes all day. The first step is to take an early bus (RM3) or taxi (RM20) to Kuala Baram (30min). From there, take the 7am or 8am express boat upriver to Marudi (2hr 30min; RM12) to connect with the noon express to Long Terawan (3hr; RM20). When the river is low, this boat may only go as far as Long Panai-Kuala Apoh (RM12), though you can then take a longboat (RM10) from there to Long Terawan. From Long Terawan, a longboat (RM25–50 per person, depending on numbers; 2hr) will take you to the park. For the return trip by boat you have to arrange with the park headquarters for the longboat to pick you up at 6am. This connects with the express or longboat at Long Terawan at 7.15am, which gets you to Marudi between 10.30am and 11am, in time to get the noon boat to Kuala Baram.

Near the park headquarters there's a **hostel** with cooking facilities. Dorm beds are RM10 and five-bed rooms cost RM15 per person. Four-person chalets in two price ranges (RM63 or RM90) are close by. There's also a café (daily 8am–8pm) and a provisions shop. Across the bridge over Sungei Melinau, the *Buyun Sipan Lounge* sells meals, packed lunches and beer. Further up the river, the lodges owned by the tour operators sometimes have spare rooms, where independent travellers can often stay cheaply (②); get back on the longboat and ask

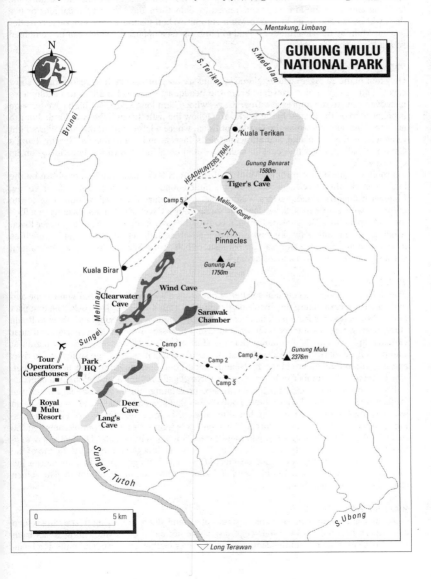

to be dropped off at *Endayang Inn* (☎085/438740; ②), which is one of the best, or *Melinau Canteen* (☎011/291641), which has dorm beds for RM10, both close to the Park HQ. Further downstream is the park's last word in comfort, the *Royal Mulu Resort* (☎085/790100; ⑧).

The park

It is quite possible to see the main caves in a day. If you want to see the caves, do some trekking and scale the Pinnacles you'll need to allow three days. An additional four or five days will be needed to do justice to Mulu summit. When planning your itinerary, consider leaving Mulu by the Headhunter's Trail to Limbang (see opposite), which can be combined with a trip to the Pinnacles.

THE SHOW CAVES

Only four of the 25 caves so far explored in Mulu are open to visitors; they're known as "show caves" and can get quite crowded. From the headquarters, a well-marked three-kilometre plankway runs to the impressive **Deer Cave**, whose 2km long and 174m high cave passage is believed to be the largest in the world. You follow the path through the cave for an hour to an incredible spot known as the Garden of Eden, where a large hole in the roof allows light to penetrate, feeding plants, and attracting birds, insects and leaf monkeys. Nearby, **Lang's Cave** is small, but has fine curtain stalactites and coral-like growths – helictites – on its curved walls.

Probing some 107km through Mulu's substratum, **Clearwater Cave**, thought to be the longest in Southeast Asia, is reached by a fifteen-minute longboat journey along Sungei Melinau from Park Headquarters. Visitors can only explore the small section close to the entrance, where a 300m walkway leads to Young Lady's Cave, which ends abruptly in a fifty-metre-deep pothole. Deep inside the main body of the cave is subterranean Clearwater River, which flows through a five-kilometre passage reaching heights and widths of as much as 90m. En route to Clearwater Cave, most visitors halt at the **Wind Cave**, which contains a great variety of stalactites and stalagmites.

THE PINNACLES

Five million years ago, a constant splatter of raindrops dissolved Gunung Api's limestone and carved out the razor-sharp fifty-metre-high pinnacles from a solid block of rock. The first part of the **Pinnacles** trek from park headquarters is by longboat along Sungei Melinau to Kuala Birar, from where it's a three-hour walk to Camp 5, close to the Melinau gorge, and near Gunung Api (1750m) and Gunung Benarat (1580m). Most climbers spend two nights at Camp 5, where there's a large sleeping hut and cooking facilities. A bridge straddles the river and the path on the other side is the Headhunter's Trail (see opposite). It's a beautiful spot, which, despite the number of hikers passing through, still retains a wild, elemental edge.

It's quite a taxing ascent up the south face of Gunung Api to get a good view of the Pinnacles (7hr there and back), but no one doubts that it is one of the wonders of the Asian world. Bring at least a litre of water, but otherwise travel light. After two hours' climb, a striking vista opens up over the rainforest. The climb gets tougher as you scramble between the rocks, and the high trees give way to moss forest, full of pitcher plants. The last thirty minutes is almost a sheer vertical manoeuvre up ladders, thick pegs and ropes. At the top of the ridge there's a stunning view of the dozens of fifty-metre-high grey limestone pinnacles, jutting out from their perch in an unreachable hollow on the side of the mountain. The return slog takes two to three hours.

WALKS FROM CAMP 5

Once back at the camp, most people rest, swim, eat and sleep, preferring to start the return trip to park headquarters the following day. There are some other interesting walks from here, however. A path from the camp follows the river further upstream and ends at a beautiful spot below the **Melinau Gorge** (2hr return), where a vertical wall of rock rises 100m above the vanishing river. A much longer option from Camp 5 is to follow the so-called **Headhunter's Trail**, a route once traced by Kayan war parties. Cross the bridge, turn left and walk along a wide trail passing a large rock (around 4km). From here a clearly marked flat trail to **Kuala Terikan**, a small Berawan settlement on the banks of Sungei Terikan, takes four hours (11km). You can stay at basic hut accommodation. From here the trail continues for two hours to Sungei Medalam, where you can take a longboat to the Iban longhouse at Bala. It's best to stay here and then continue next day down Sungei Medalam in a longboat into Sungei Limbang and on up to **Limbang Town**, an all-day trip. This is a good way of getting to Brunei from Mulu, as boats run frequently from Limbang to Bandar (hourly until 6pm; RM15). In Limbang Town, the best place to stay is the *Muhibbah Inn* (☎085/212488; ③) on Jalan Banking, although the *Royal Hotel* (☎085/215690; ②), on Jalan Tarap, is cheaper.

GUNUNG MULU

The route to the summit of **Gunung Mulu** (2376m) is a straightforward climb, though very steep, and any reasonably fit person can complete it. The first stage is from park headquarters to Camp 3, an easy three-hour walk on a flat trail. The first night is at the open hut at Camp 3, which has cooking facilities. Day two comprises a hard, ten-hour, uphill slog, some of it along the southwest ridge, a series of small hills negotiated by a narrow, twisting path. The hut at Camp 4 is at 1800m; it can be cool here, so bring a sleeping bag. Most climbers set off well before dawn for the hard ninety-minute trek to the summit, to arrive at sunrise. Near the top you have to haul yourself up by ropes onto the cold, windswept, craggy peak. From here, the view is exhilarating, looking down on Gunung Api. It's just possible to do the whole return trip from the summit to park headquarters in one day. This takes around twelve hours and cuts out the last night at Camp 4. The red-and-white trail marks are easy to see, so you shouldn't lose your way.

SABAH

Bordering Sarawak on the northwestern flank of Borneo, **SABAH**'s beauty lies in its natural resources, wildlife and intriguing mix of ethnic peoples. Until European powers began to gain a foothold here in the nineteenth century, the northern tip of this remote landmass was inhabited by tribal groups who had only minimal contact with the outside world, so that their costumes, traditions and languages were quite unique to the region. Today, the peoples of the Kadazan/Dusun tribes constitute the largest indigenous racial group, along with the Murut of the southwest, and Sabah's so-called "sea gypsies", the Bajau. Latterly, many economic migrants from the southern part of the Philippines and from neighbouring Kalimantan in Indonesia have made Sabah their home, further contributing to the state's rich ethnic mix.

Since joining the Malaysian Federation in 1963, Sabah has undergone rapid, if patchy modernization, not least because of the logging industry and oil palm plantation expansion, which together are substantially eating away at the remaining forests in the state. But environmentalists are optimistic, as plans are on the drawing board to protect a larger proportion of Sabah's remaining forests. The two most ecologically important areas which will gain from this policy are the Maliau Basin in the south of the state and much of the Kinabatangan river catchment to the east.

This is good news, as Sabah's swampy coasts, rainforests and spectacular high mountains host an astounding range of **wildlife**, the region's chief draw. Here, you can watch turtles hatch on **Turtle Islands Park**, see baby orang-utans at the **Sepilok Orang-utan Rehabilitation Centre**, and marvel at forest-dwelling proboscis monkeys along the lower reaches of the Kinabatangan. And then there are the turtles, sharks, barracuda and reefs of **Pulau Sipadan**, which is rated as one of the top diving destinations in the world. Sabah's other huge attraction is the climb up the awesome granite shelves of 4101-metre-high **Mount Kinabalu**, its challenging but manageable slopes seemingly tailor-made for amateur climbers.

GETTING TO SABAH

There are frequent **flights** to Kota Kinabalu (KK) from Kuala Lumpur (11 daily; RM437), Johor Bahru (5 daily; RM347), Kuching (5 daily; RM230), Bandar Seri Begawan (3 weekly; RM117), Manila (3 weekly; RM450), and Hong Kong (3 weekly; RM940). You can also fly to Tawau from Tarakan in Kalimantan (3 weekly; RM185).

Daily **boats** from Brunei (4 daily; 1hr 30min), and from Lawas and Limbang in northern Sarawak, run to Pulau Labuan, which has good connections to KK. There's a ferry from Tarakan and Nunukan in Kalimantan to Tawau (daily) and from Zamboanga in the Philippines (twice weekly) to Sandakan. The only overland route is from Lawas, which is a short bus ride away from the border at Merapok.

Like Sarawak, **travel** in Sabah is pricey, not least because of the expensive flight from the mainland. But increasingly, travellers are getting to Sabah from the other direction. Indonesia's extensive ferry system now makes travelling from Sulawesi to Kalimantan easy and from there it's only a short step to the vibrant Sabah town of Tawau. Getting from Zamboanga in the southern Philippines to Sandakan by boat is also straightforward.

Kota Kinabalu and around

Since 1946, Sabah's seat of government has been based at **KOTA KINABALU**, or KK as it's universally known. Although not pretty architecturally, it's got a unique buzz to it and is the liveliest city in Malaysia after KL, with a plethora of markets, cafés and bars. Most travellers grow fond of KK, not least as its bright lights and excellent eating are gratefully received after a spell roughing it on Mount Kinabalu or at Uncle Tan's Jungle Sanctuary. Aside from the State Museum, KK's major highlight is offshore **Tunku Abdul Rahman Park**, whose five unspoilt islands are just ten minutes by speedboat from the city centre.

Arrival

KK's **airport** is 6km south of the centre. Yellow-and-red Luen Thung Company buses run from the airport to the GPO on Jalan Tun Razak (6 daily 6.30am–5.30pm; 15min; 65 sen). Otherwise, walk out to the main road and catch a minibus (RM1–1.50) into town; or take a taxi (buy a RM12 coupon in the arrival hall). **Trains** arrive at Tanjung Aru Station, which is beside Jalan Kepayan, the main road to points south of KK, so you'll have no trouble catching a bus heading into town. **Buses** stop between Jalan Tunku Abdul Rahman and Jalan Padang, from where it's a five-to-ten minute walk to the central hotels. **Ferries** dock in front of the *Hyatt Hotel*, on Jalan Tun Fuad Stephens.

Information and tours

Sabah Tourism Promotion Corporation or STPC (Mon–Fri 8am–4.15pm, Sat 8am–12.45pm; ☎088/212121) is at 51 Jl Gaya; Tourism Malaysia (Mon–Fri 8am–12.45pm & 2–4.15pm, Sat 8am–12.45pm; ☎088/211732) is across the road in the EON CMG Building.

If you're travelling to Tunku Abdul Rahman Park, Mount Kinabalu or Poring, book your accommodation at the **Kinabalu Gold Resorts office**, 3rd Floor, Block C, Kompleks Karamunsing (Mon–Fri 8am–5am; Sat 8am–2am; ☎088/257941), fifteen minutes' walk south of the centre along Jalan Tunku Abdul Rahman.

All the following **tour operators** charge about RM100 for day-trips to Tunku Abdul Rahman Park, the Rafflesia Centre or Kinabalu National Park, RM180 for a day's white-water rafting, and RM600 upwards for extended tours into the forested interior: Api Tours, 13 Jl Punai Kedut, Mile 5 Jl Tuaran (☎088/421963), for rafting, longhouse tours and the Mount Trusmadi Trek; Borneo Wildlife Adventure, Block L, Sinsuran Complex (☎088/213668), for

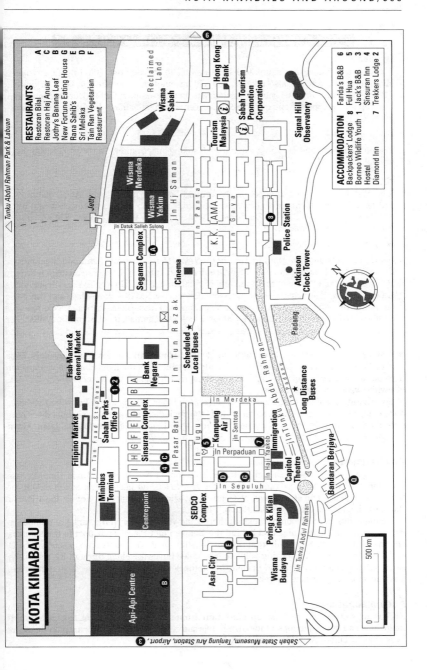

KOTA KINABALU

RESTAURANTS
Restoran Bilal	A
Restoran Haj Anuar	C
Jothy's Banana Leaf	B
New Fortune Eating House	G
Rana Sahib's	E
Sri Melaka	D
Tain Ran Vegetarian Restaurant	F

ACCOMMODATION
Farida's B&B		6
Backpackers' Lodge	8	Full Hua	5
Borneo Wildlife Youth	1	Jack's B&B	3
Hostel		Sinsuran Inn	4
Diamond Inn	7	Trekkers Lodge	2

△ Tunku Abdul Rahman Park & Labuan

▽ Sabah State Museum, Tanjung Aru Station, Airport,

Reclaimed Land

Hong Kong Bank

Wisma Sabah

Tourism Malaysia (i)

Sabah Tourism Promotion Corporation

Signal Hill Observatory

Wisma Merdeka

Wisma Yakim

jln Datuk Salleh Sulong

jln Hj Saman

jln Pantai

jln Gaya

K.K. LAMA

Segama Complex

Cinema

Police Station

Atkinson Clock Tower

Jetty

Fish Market & General Market

Filipino Market

Bank Negara

jln Tun Razak

Scheduled Local Buses ★

Padang

Sabah Parks Office

Sinsuran Complex

jln Pasar Baru

jln Tun Fuad Stephens

jln Merdeka

Kampung Air

jln Sentosa

Long Distance Buses ★

jln Abdul Rahman

jln Pidang

Minibus Terminal

Centrepoint

jln Tugu

jln Perpaduan

jln Hai Yakob

Immigration

Capitol Theatre

Bandaran Berjaya

jln Tunku Abdul Rahman

jln Sepuluh

SEDCO Complex

Poring & Kilan Cinema

Wisma Budaya

Asia City

Api-Api Centre

500 km

0

N

MOVING ON FROM KOTA KINABALU

By plane

A taxi is the fastest and simplest way of getting to the **airport** (RM10). Taxi ranks abound in KK. You can also take a Luen Thung bus from opposite the GPO (6 daily 6.30am–5.30pm; 15min; 65 sen) or a Putatan- or Petagas-bound minibus from behind the Centrepoint Shopping Centre and tell the driver your destination – he might charge an extra RM1.

By train

Trains to Tenom and Beaufort leave from Tanjung Aru Station. Call ☎088/252536 for timetables.

By bus

Long-distance **buses** congregate on the ground between Jalan Tunku Abdul Rahman and Jalan Padang. Generally buses leave when full; turn up by 7am to ensure a seat to, say, Mount Kinabalu Park or Sandakan. The daily Lawas Express (1pm; RM30) runs from here to Lawas in Sarawak.

By ferry

Ferries to Labuan leave from in front of the *Hyatt Hotel*, on Jalan Tun Fuad Stephens. The Ming Hai departs from KK at 8am, returning at 1pm; the Express Kinabalu leaves at 10am, returning at 3pm; and the Duta Muhibbah and the Hoover Express leave for Labuan on alternate days, at 1pm. One-way tickets cost RM28 second class and can be bought at the jetty or at Jasa Samudra Shipping, 1st Floor, Block E, Segama Complex (☎088/219810), or Rezeki Murni, 1st Floor, Block D, Segama Complex (☎088/236835).

tailor-made adventure tours along the Sarawak and Kalimantan borders; and Travellers' Rest Hostel, Block L, Sinsuran Complex (☎088/240625), which has the most competitive rates for trips out of Sandakan. Borneo Expeditions, Shangri-La Tanjung Aru Resort (☎088/222721), is a white-water rafting specialist.

For **diving** expeditions, Sipadan Dive Centre, 10th Floor, Wisma Merdeka (☎088/240584), do two-day dive excursions to Sipadan for RM1495, including all transport, six boat dives plus unlimited shore dives; and Borneo Divers, 9th Floor, Menara Jubili, Jalan Gaya (☎088/222226), does a three-day Sipidan dive trip for US$700.

City transport

The city centre is compact enough to traverse on foot in half an hour. **Taxis** should cross town for RM6, and there are ranks outside the *Hyatt Hotel* on Jalan Datuk Salleh Sulong, at the GPO on Jalan Tun Razak, and at Centrepoint shopping centre on Lebuh Raya Pantai Baru. Book a taxi on either ☎088/52113 or 51863.

Taking a **bus** is more complicated, as there is no visible order in the ranks of minibuses which gather on a patch of gravel behind the Centre Point Plaza. Transport to the suburbs and the airport leave when full from this minibus terminal. The bus stop opposite the GPO on Jalan Tun Razak is the starting point for scheduled buses travelling through KK's suburbs as far as Tuaran in the north and Penampang in the south; they are cheaper than minibuses leave at set times, but take longer.

Accommodation

KK has an excellent range of **accommodation**, from spacious guesthouses to efficient mid range inns and beyond to top-of-the-range hotels and resorts. You can also **camp** on the near by islands in Tunku Abdul Rahman Park (see p.658).

Backpackers' Lodge, Lot 25 Lorong Dewan, Australia Place (☎088/261495). Friendly, popular dorms-only operation below Signal Hill; breakfast included. Dorms RM18.

Bilal, Lot 1, Block B, Segama Complex (☎088/256709). A respectable establishment, offering basic but clean rooms, some en-suite. ②.

Borneo Wildlife Youth Hostel, Lot 4 Block L, Siswan Complex (☎088/213668). Dormitory-class house, next door to *Trekkers Lodge,* but not quite as well equipped. RM15 with YHA or student card; RM20 others.

Diamond Inn, 37 Lot 7, Kampung Air (☎088/261222). A great deal of effort has gone into this comfortable hotel. Rooms have bathrooms, TVs and air-con. ③.

Farida's B&B, 413 Jl Saga, Mile 4.5, Kampung Likas (☎088/428733). A delightful family-run concern, fifteen minutes from the minibus terminal – catch a "Kg Likas" bus. Dorms RM12. ②.

Full Hua, 14 Jl Tugu, Kampung Air (☎088/234950). Smart hotel with high-quality, spotlessly clean rooms, air-con and TV. ④.

Jack's B&B, no. 17, Block B, Jl Karamunsing (☎088/232367). Spotless and friendly dorms-only place 1km southwest of the minibus terminus (take a Sembulan bus). Breakfast is included. The owner organizes island and fishing trips. Dorms RM18.

Sinsuran Inn, Lot 1, Block I, Sinsuran Complex (☎088/255985). Spartan rooms are capacious and clean, and have TV, bathroom and air-con. ③.

Trekkers Lodge, Lot 5/6, Block L, Sinsuran Complex (☎088/252263). The city's best budget choice: dorms and rooms are small but clean and cheery. Under its new ownership the place has had a new lick of paint and facilities have been expanded. Dorms RM12. ②.

The City

Downtown KK was almost obliterated by World War II bombs, and only in the northeastern corner of the city centre – an area known as KK Lama, or old KK – are there even the faintest remains of its colonial past. Jalan Gaya in particular is an attractive street lined with colourful and popular Chinese *kedai kopis*.

The most diverting of the waterfront markets is the **Filipino Market**, opposite blocks K and M of the Sinsuran Complex, which sells Sabahan ethnic wares as well as Filipino baskets, shells and trinkets. Next door is the dark and labyrinthine general market and, behind that, the manic waterfront fish market.

KK's most rewarding cultural experience, though, is the **Sabah State Museum** (Mon–Thurs 10am–6pm, Sat & Sun 9am–6pm; free), twenty minutes' walk west of the town centre along Jalan Tunkul Abdul Rahman (or take a bus from opposite the GPO), and housed in Murut- and Rungus-style longhouses. Its highlight is the ethnographic collection, which includes human skulls from Sabah's headhunting days, and totems. Photographs trace the development of Kota Kinabalu, and there's also a natural history section, an archeology gallery and an Islamic Civilization Gallery. Fronting the museum is an **Ethnobotanic Garden** (daily 6am–6pm), whose huge range of tropical plants is best experienced on one of the free guided tours (9am & 2pm except Fri). Exquisitely crafted, traditional houses representing all Sabah's major tribes border the garden, in the Kampung Warisan.

Eating and drinking

You'll find good **hawker stalls** on the upper floor of the General Market, Jalan Tun Fuad Stephens, and at the night market, behind the Filipino Market, Jalan Tun Fuad Stephens. For nightime **drinking**, check out *Crash*, below *New Sabah Inn*, Jalan Pantai, a lively enough place which has a midweek bikini parade, and *Rocky Fun Pub & Café*, Lot 52, Jalan Gaya (until 2am), a good-time bar favoured by expats and *Yaaha Cowboy Lounge*, Block C, Asia City Complex, which, despite the hick name, is a superb bar with a food court alongside. Pick of the bunch, however, must be the no-frills Chinese and Filipino drinking hole, *Fun Sen*, a few doors down from the *Diamond Inn*. Guinness Stout is the staple here for a friendly, boozy, let-it-all-hang-out clientele.

Restoran Bilal, Block B, Segama Complex. A classic North Indian Muslim eating house, with a buffet-style range of tasty and inexpensive curries. Daily 6am–9pm.

Restoran Haj Anuar, Block H, Sinsuran Complex. Cosy, open-fronted place with a Malay menu including *soto, nasi lemak* and *nasi campur*. Daily 7am–7pm.

Jothy's Banana Leaf, 1/G9 Api Api Centre (☎088/261595). Mountainous *daun pisang* (banana leaf) meals, *biriyanis* and curries. Daily 10am–10pm.

New Fortune Eating House, Block 36, Jl Laiman Diki, Kampung Air. A busy place housing several stalls, the best of which serves superb *dim sum*. 6am–7pm.

Rana Sahib's, Block G, Asia City Complex (☎088/231354). Tasty North Indian food experience marred by high prices and over-fussy owner. However, its *sag gost* and *chicken kashmir* are wonderful. 11.30am–2.30pm & 6.30–10.30pm.

SEDCO Square, SEDCO complex. Restaurant-lined square, with outdoor tables; a fine place for barbecued meat and fish.

Sri Melaka, 9 Jl Laiman Diki, Kampung Air. Exquisite Malay and Nonya food at one of KK's best and most fashionable places; try the excellent *assam fishhead* (RM12 portion feeds two). Open 11am–10.30pm.

Tain Ran Vegetarian Restaurant, Block A, Ruang Singgah Mata 1, Asia City Complex. Coffee shop with a mouthwatering array of veggie dishes. 9am–7pm.

Listings

Airlines Dragon Air, ground floor, Block C, Kompleks Kuwasa, Jl Karamunsing (☎088/254733); MAS, Kompleks Karamunsing, Jl Tuaran (☎088/213555); Philippine Air, Kompleks Karamunsing, Jl Tuaran (☎088/239600); Royal Brunei, ground floor, Block C, Kompleks Kuwasa, Jl Karamunsing (☎088/242193); Singapore Airlines, ground floor, Block C, Kompleks Kuwasa, Jl Karamunsing (☎088/255444); Thai Airways, ground floor, Block C, Kompleks Kuwasa, Jl Karamunsing (☎088/232896).

American Express Lot 3.50 & 3.51, 3rd Floor, Kompleks Karamunsing (Mon–Fri 8.30am–5.30pm; ☎088/241200). Credit-card- and travellers' cheque-holders can use the office as a poste restante/general delivery address.

Banks and exchange Moneychangers (Mon–Sat 10am–7pm) in Wisma Merdeka include Ban Loong Money Changer and Travellers' Money Changer, both on the ground floor; there's also an office in the Taiping Goldsmith, Block A, Sinsuran Complex.

Bookshops For an unparalleled array of books on Southeast Asia, head for Borneo Crafts (Wisma Merdeka), or to their branch at the Sabah State Museum.

Hospital Queen Elizabeth Hospital is beyond the Sabah State Museum, on Jl Penampang (☎088/218166). In an emergency, dial ☎999.

Immigration Office fourth floor, Wisma Dang Bandang, Jl Hj Yaakob (Mon–Fri 8am–12.30pm & 2–4.15pm, Sat 8am–12.45pm; ☎088/216711). Visa extensions up to a month are available for RM2.

Internet access *City Internet Café*, Lot 41, ground floor, City Parade, Jl Centre Point; *Cyber Café Centre*, Lot 4, Wisma Butaya; *Eat & Chat*, 63 Jl Gaya; *Vision de Net Café*, first floor, 91 Jl Gaya.

Laundry Meba Laundry Services, Lot 5, Block D, Sinsuran Complex.

Police Balai Polis KK (☎088/258191 or 088/258111) is below Atkinson Clocktower on Jl Padang.

Post office The GPO (Mon–Sat 8am–5pm, Sun 10am–1pm) on Jl Tun Razak keeps poste restante.

Shopping Borneo Handicraft (first floor, Wisma Merdeka) has a good choice of woodwork, basketry and gongs; Borneo Handicraft & Ceramic Shop (ground floor, Centre Point) stocks ceramics, antiques and primitive sculptures.

Telephone services There are IDD facilities at Kedai Telekom (daily 8am–10pm), in Kompleks Sadong Jaya. Phone cards, available at the GPO, can be used for international calls in orange, but not yellow, public phone booths – there are some in Centre Point.

Tunku Abdul Rahman Park

Situated within an eight-kilometre radius of downtown KK, the five islands of **Tunku Abdul Rahman Park** (TAR Park) represent the most westerly ripples of the undulating Crocker Mountain Range. Largest of the park's islands is Pulau Gaya, where a twenty-kilometre system of trails snakes across the lowland rainforest. Most of these trails start on the southern side of the island at Camp Bay, which also offers pleasant enough swimming, but a more alluring alternative is Police Beach, on the north coast. Boatmen demand extra for circling round to this side of Gaya, but it's money well spent: the dazzling white-sand bay is idyllic. Wildlife on Gaya includes hornbills, wild pigs, lizards, snakes and macaques – which have been known to swim over to nearby Pulau Sapi, a 25-acre islet off the northwestern coast of Gaya that's popular with swimmers, snorkellers and picnickers. Though far smaller than Gaya, Sapi too is ringed by trails.

The park's three other islands cluster together 2.5km west of Gaya. The park headquarters is situated on crescent-shaped Pulau Manukan, the most developed of all the park's islands, but boasting fine beaches and coral. Across a narrow channel is tiny Pulau Mamutik, which can be crossed on foot in fifteen minutes and has excellent sands on either side of its jetty. Pulau Sulug is the most remote of the islands and consequently the quietest. Its good coral makes it popular with divers.

PRACTICALITIES

The Sabah Parks **boat** service leaves KK at 8am, 9am, 10am, 11am, noon, 2pm and 4.30pm, returning at 7.30am, 9.30am, 10.30am, 11.30am, 3pm and 4pm (RM10 return); it calls at all five islands. Chartering a boat to go island-hopping costs RM20 a head (minimum six people). Contact Sabah Parks (☎088/211585) at Block K, Kompleks Sinsuran, for details, or make directly for the waterfront behind the *Hyatt*. Otherwise, numerous speedboats gather daily behind the *Hyatt* – they won't leave for less than RM40–50, but you should only pay when you're safely back in KK. The boatmen rent snorkelling gear for RM5 a day.

A RM2 **entry fee** is charged on landing at Sapi, Manukan and Mamutik. **Accommodation** is available in the park at attractive chalets on Pulau Manukan (RM230 for a four-person unit), which must be booked through Kinabalu Gold Resorts (see p.654). Contact Sabah Parks (see above) to find out details about camping on any of the other islands. The only **place to eat** on the islands is the restaurant serving the chalets on Manukan.

The Rafflesia Complex

Ten kilometres out of KK, paddy fields give way to the rolling foothills of the Crocker Mountain Range, and Tembunan-bound buses (11 daily) start the long haul up to the 1649-metre-high Sinsuron Pass. You'll have views of Mount Kinabalu, weather permitting. Should you wish to dally for a little longer in the bracing chill of the Sinsuron Pass, you can stay at the *Gunung Emas Highlands Resort* (☎011/811562), which has dorms (RM20), rooms (③), treetop cabins (③) and suites (⑤) at the 52km mark of the KK–Tambunan road.

A few kilometres beyond the pass, the **Rafflesia Complex** (Mon–Fri 8am–12.45pm & 2–5pm, Sat & Sun 8am–5pm; free) houses examples of the rafflesia flower, a parasitic plant whose rubbery, liver-spotted blooms can reach up to one metre in diameter – making it the world's largest flower. It was first catalogued in Sumatra in 1818, by Sir Stamford Raffles and the naturalist Dr Joseph Arnold. There's no need to hire one of the guides (RM20) from the Visitor Centre, as the park's paths are simple to follow; someone at the centre should be able to direct you to a plant that's in bloom, though you could phone the Visitor Centre's hotline (☎011/861499) before leaving KK as each flower only lasts a few days before dying.

Tenom

The small town of **TENOM** was once the bustling headquarters of the Interior District of British North Borneo, but today it's a peaceful backwater that's best-known for the impressive train journey to Beaufort (2hr 30min). **Three types of train** ply the Tenom–Beaufort route daily – diesel (Mon–Sat 7.30am & 1.40pm; Sun 7.55am, 12.10pm & 3.05pm; RM2.75); cargo (Mon–Sat 8am; RM2.75); and railcar (Mon–Sat 6.40am & 4pm, Sun 7.20am; RM8.35). The fastest and most comfortable of these is the railcar, but you must book ahead for this on ☎087/4735514 or at the station. Tenom Station is on the southern edge of the padang.

Buses north to Keningau (RM5), from where you can continue on to KK, and south to Kuala Tomani (RM4), circle around Tenom all day long; you can pick one up on the main street, at the western edge of the padang. Shared taxis to Keningau also cost RM5 and leave from the main street. If friendly *Hotel Kim San* (☎087/735485; ②) at the southwestern end of town is full, try the simpler *Hotel Sabah* (☎087/735534; ②), off a side road by the market.

Places to eat are plentiful, with a clutch of coffee shops and restaurants in the area around the *Hotel Kim San*.

Beaufort

BEAUFORT is an uneventful town, normally only used by tourists on their way to the white-water rafting on nearby Sungei Padas or those doing the spectacular **train ride** from Beaufort to Tenom. Although the line runs all the way from KK to Tenom, it's only the two-and-a-quarter-hour journey through dramatic jungle from Beaufort to Tenom that's really worth making. Three types of train run from Beaufort – diesel (Mon–Sat 10.50am & 1.55pm; Sun 6.45am, 10.50am & 2.30pm; RM2.75); cargo (Mon–Sat noon; RM2.75); and railcar (Mon–Sat 8.25am & 3.50pm, Sun 4.05pm; RM8.35). The fastest and most comfortable of these is the railcar, but you must book ahead on ☎087/221518. The **train station** is next to Sungei Padas at the southern side of town, from where it's a minute's walk up the road opposite the station forecourt into the town centre.

Buses stop in the centre itself, beside the market, while taxis congregate outside the train station. Beaufort's two **hotels** are the *Beaufort* (☎087/211911; ②), east of the market, and the slightly nicer *Mandarin Inn* (☎087/212798; ②), ten minutes' walk across the river. *Christopher's Corner Parking*, across from the train station, will rustle you up a really good Western breakfast and there are plenty of hawker stalls upstairs in the town market and next to the bridge.

Pulau Labuan

The small island of **PULAU LABUAN**, around 10km west of the Klias Peninsula, is a duty-free port, used mainly by Bruneians and Sabahans in search of prostitutes and cheap beer. For travellers it's most useful as a transit point between KK and Brunei, though the offshore shipwrecks are popular dive spots – Borneo Divers on Jalan Tun Mustapha in Labuan Town (☎087/415867) charges RM185 for two wreck dives. Also in town, you'll find a Hong Kong Bank and the **tourist information office** (☎087/423445) on Jalan Merdeka, the main street along the seafront. Running north from the middle of Jalan Merdeka, and effectively splitting the town in two, is Jalan Tun Mustapha.

Ferries to Kota Kinabalu (RM28), Limbang (RM20), Lawas (RM20) and Bandar Seri Begawan (RM24) dock at the ferry terminal, below Jalan Merdeka. Plenty of speedboats also run from here to Menumbok (RM10), from where it's a two-hour bus ride to Kota Kinabalu. Tickets can be bought from Duta Muhibbah Agency (☎087/413827) and Sin Matu Agency, at 52 and 55 Jl Merdeka. Labuan's **airport** is 3km north of town and served by minibuses, which run from the eastern end of Jalan Bunga Melati; there's a MAS office in the *Federal Hotel*, on Jalan Bunga Kesuma (☎087/412263).

The best **accommodation** deal in town is a room with a fan in the Indian-run *Pantai View Hotel*, Jalan Bunga Tanjung (☎087/411339; ②), or try *Melati Inn* (☎087/416307; ②), right opposite the ferry terminal, which has en-suite rooms with TV and air-con. On Jalan Merdeka and Jalan OKK Awang Besar you'll find a number of no-frills, Chinese and Indian **restaurants**: particularly good for *rotis*, *murtabaks* and curries is *Restoran Farizah*, next to the *Pantai View*. At night, make a beeline for the stalls west of the town cinema, above Jalan Muhibbah.

To Sarawak: Sipitang

On the bumpy gravel road 47km southwest of Beaufort, **SIPITANG** is a sleepy seafront town worth bearing in mind if you need a place to stay en route to Sarawak. Approaching from the north, a bridge marks the start of town, and there's a jetty here from where a boat leaves for

Labuan (daily 7am; RM20); 250m beyond that, you're in the town centre. Buses for Beaufort, KK and Lawas congregate in the centre of town; the taxi stand is next door. There's nothing much to do here except eat – try the *Kami* and the *Rina*, which occupy pretty west-facing positions on Brunei Bay or, across the main road, *Restoran Bismillah*, which does good curries. Of the hotels on the main road, the *Hotel Asanol* (☎087/821506; ②) is the friendliest and most affordable.

The easiest way to travel from Sipitang to Lawas in Sarawak is to take a minibus or taxi from the centre of town (both RM10; 1hr). The Lawas Express (RM6) passes through Sipitang (on its way from KK) at around 4pm and gets to Lawas after 5pm; or you can catch a RM2 minibus to Sindumin, on the Sabah side of the border, and then connect with a Sarawak bus. Whichever you choose, the driver will wait while you pass through the passport controls flanking the border – one in Sindumin, the other a couple of hundred metres away at Merapok in Sarawak.

Kota Belud Sunday market

KOTA BELUD, 75km northeast of KK on the road to Kudat, springs to life each Sunday, as hordes of villagers from the surrounding countryside congregate at its weekly market, said to be the biggest in Sabah, ten minutes' walk out of town along Jalan Hasbollah. Tribes represented include the Rungus, Kadazan/Dusun and Bajau, who occasionally ride in on horseback and in traditional apparel. Kota Belud's popularity among KK's tour operators means it always has tourists, but you're far more likely to see dried fish, chains of yeast beads (used to make rice wine), buffalo and betel nut for sale, than souvenirs. The annual *tamu besar*, or "big market", usually takes place in November and also features cultural performances.

To catch the weekly *tamu* at its best, plan to leave KK around 7am. Buses leave from the far side of the Shell garage near the GPO (RM5), or catch a Kudat-bound bus (RM5) from the long-distance station; it's a scenic ninety-minute trip. Buses stop beside the district office in the centre of town, and with onward connections so good, it's a fine jumping-off spot for Kinabalu National Park (see below), which can be reached via Tamparuli.

Kinabalu national park

There's no more astounding sight in Borneo than the cloud-encased summit of **Mount Kinabalu** – at 4101m, half the height of Everest – shooting skywards from the 750 square kilometres of **KINABALU NATIONAL PARK**. Plainly visible from Sabah's west coast and 85km northeast of KK, Kinabalu's jagged peaks look impossibly daunting, but in fact, the mountain is a relatively easy, if exhausting, climb. The well-defined, 8.5-kilometre path weaves up the mountain's southern side to the bare granite of the summit where a mile-deep gully known as Low's Gully cleaves the peak in two. Limbs that are weary from the climb will welcome the sulphurous waters of the **Poring Hot Springs**, 43km away. If you get stuck en route to the park, you can stay in **Ranau**, 19km further south.

You'll need at least two days and two nights to climb Mount Kinabalu – three if you want to carry on by bus to Poring – though you'll be glad of a spare day or two, in case cloud cover spoils the view from the summit. Midweek, you should have no problem getting a dorm bed in one of the park's hostels, but it's a good idea to book a few days in advance if you're going on a weekend or want some more upmarket accommodation. Bookings can be made at the Kinabalu Gold Resorts office in KK (see p.654); you can make a telephone booking first and pay upon arrival. You'll also need to get a climbing permit (RM50) from the park headquarters, pay for a guide (RM25–30 for up to eight people) and individual insurance (RM3.50).

Most people spend their first night at the **accommodation** in the park headquarters area, either at the basic *Old* or *New Fellowship* hostels (RM12), or in nearby cabins (④), four-person annexe rooms (RM92 per room), or at the swish *Kinabalu Lodge* (RM311 for a unit which sleeps 11). You can **eat** at *Kinabalu Balsam* (daily 6am–10pm, Sat until 11pm), near reception, which also has a provisions shop, and at *Liwagu Restaurant* (daily 6am–10pm, Sat until 11pm). Alternatively, you can base yourself in another part of the park, the much quieter, higher altitude, *Mesilau Nature Resort*, 27km northeast of the park headquarters. Again contact Kinabalu Gold Resorts for accommodation details (dorm RM30; four-bed chalet units RM350; eight-bed lodge, RM320). There is no public transport to Mesilau, though Kinabalu Gold Resorts will take you there from KK (RM50) or provide minibus transport (RM10) from the park HQ.

Scaling the mountain from either location gets you on the second night to the basic huts at *Gunting Lagadan*, *Panar Laban* or *Waras* (all RM10), which have electricity and cooking facilities, or at the more comfortable *Laban Rata Rest House* (RM25 per person), which has central heating, hot water and a restaurant (daily 7am–8pm). *Sayat-Sayat Hut* (RM10) is an hour further up the mountain, but has no electricity. The advantage of making it as far as this camp on the first day, however, is that you won't need to get up so early the following morning to reach the summit by sunrise.

A bus leaves KK's long-distance terminal for the park daily at 7.30am, after which minibuses depart when they're full. Buses stop about 50m from the park reception office (daily 7am–7.30pm), which is the check-in point for accommodation near the park headquarters. Staff here will provide you with useful maps and can also arrange charter buses (RM40) to Poring.

Climbing Mount Kinabalu

You should aim to be at the park reception by 7am. (Note, however, that hikers staying at the *Mesilau Nature Resort* meet their guides at the Resort Office and strike off from there.) You can hire a porter at the park reception (RM25 a day for loads of up to 24lb), though the lockers and saferoom at reception make this an unnecessary expense. Useful things to take with you include a torch, headache tablets (for altitude sickness), suntan lotion, strong shoes, warm clothes for the summit, and raincoats (sold at the park's souvenir shop). It's over an hour's walk from the reception to the power station at the start of the mountain trail, so many people prefer to take the shuttle bus (RM10).

Climbing to your first night's accommodation, at around 3350m, takes three to six hours, depending on your fitness. Two or three hours into the climb, incredible views of the hills, sea and clouds below you start to unfold. The end of your first day's climbing is heralded by the appearance of the mighty granite slopes of the Panar Laban rock face. You'll spend the night at one of the resthouses at the foot of Panar Laban (see above), from where views of the sun setting over the South China Sea are exquisite. Plan to get up at 2.30am the next morning to join the procession to the top for sunrise. Although ropes have been strung up, none of the climbing is really hairy. That said, the air is quite thin, so headaches, nausea and breathlessness are a possibility. After sunrise on the peak, it's back down to Panar Laban for a hearty breakfast before the two-hour amble to park headquarters.

Poring Hot Springs

Sited 43km from park headquarters on the park's southeastern border, the hot (48–60°C) sulphurous waters of **Poring Hot Springs** (RM2) are a great place to soak your hiking pains away. The baths are close to the main park gates, and there's a plunge pool and two enclosed baths (RM15 an hour). A fifteen-minute walk beyond the baths brings you to Poring's canopy walk (daily 10.30am–3.30pm, RM2; 6pm–6am, RM30 for 1–3 people; 6–10.30am, RM60 1–3 people), where five tree huts connected by suspended walkways 60m above ground afford you a monkey's-eye view of the surrounding lowland rainforest. A trail strikes off to the right of the baths, reaching 150-metre-high Langanan Waterfall about ninety minutes later. On its way, the trail passes smaller Kepungit Waterfall – whose icy pool is ideal for swimming. If it's been raining, there'll be leeches on the trail – you can burn them off with a cigarette.

If you're in a group, it's best to charter a minibus to take you from Kinabalu Park headquarters to Poring (30min). There's a café at the springs, and two restaurants just outside the gates. No permit is needed to visit Poring, though you'll have to book your accommodation at Kinabalu Gold Resorts office in KK (see p.654) or at the park headquarters. Accommodation in Poring is backpacker-oriented. Camping is RM6 per person and the dorm beds in the hostels RM12. Cabin units are RM92 for six people, and chalet units RM207 for six people.

Ranau

The small town of **RANAU** sits on the south side of the main KK–Sandakan road, 20km from Kinabalu National Park, and is a handy stopping point if it's too late to travel the extra 19km to Poring. Minibuses stop at the eastern edge of town, on a patch of land beside Block A. At present, long-distance buses from KK to Sandakan stop briefly across town, on Jalan Kibarambang, also the site of Ranau's shared taxi stand, though they may both move to the minibus terminus. The best hotel is the quiet, six-room *View Motel* (☎088/876445; ③) in Block L, but *Hotel Ranau* (☎088/875661; ③), next to the *Bank Bumiputra* at the top of the square, is cheaper. There's **internet** access at Cyber Station, ground floor, Block B, Jalan Taman Ranau.

Sandakan

Sandwiched between sea and cliffs on the northern lip of Sandakan Bay, **SANDAKAN** isn't an immediately appealing city, but does make a good base for day-trips to the **Turtle Islands Park**, the **Sepilok Orang-utan Rehabilitation Centre** and the **Gomantong Caves**. Stretching west of the dense downtown area is Jalan Leila, while to the east, running up round the bay, is Jalan Buli Sim-Sim. The heart of the town is the colourful market along the harbour's edge: here stalls sell baskets, fruits, scaly fish, clothing and much else besides. A fifteen-minute walk east of the town centre, along Jalan Buli Sim-Sim, brings you to Sandakan's modern mosque. Beyond this is Kampung Buli Sim-Sim, the water village around which Sandakan expanded in the nineteenth century, its countless photogenic shacks spread like lilies out into the bay. Sandakan's less central addresses are pinpointed according to their distances out of the downtown area, hence "Mile 1 1/2", "Mile 3", and so on.

Practicalities

The long-distance **bus station** is on the airport road, 5km from the city centre. Local buses provide a connection from here to the bus station in town. There are frequent buses to and from KK (RM25), Ranau and Tawau (RM20). Long-distance taxis and land cruisers also operate from this area. Sandakan's two local bus stations are within a couple of minutes' walk of each other, in the centre of town. The scheduled services of the Labuk Road Bus Company leave from the waterfront Labuk Road Station – blue-and-white buses travel up Labuk Road itself, while those with red, yellow and green stripes go west, along Jalan Leila. A short walk west along Jalan Pryer brings you to the minibus area. The two stations have many destinations in common, so it's worth checking both to find the earliest departure. The **airport** is 11km north of town and served by minibuses (RM1.50) from the southern end of Jalan Pelabuhan, and by taxis (RM12). MAS is in the Sabah Building, Jalan Pelabuhan, formerly Jalan Edinburgh (☎089/273966).

Boats for Zamboanga in the Philippines leave from Karamunting Jetty, 3km west of town. Departures are at 5pm on Tuesdays and Thursdays; tickets (RM58-150 one-way) should be bought at the jetty at least a day before departure. There's also an office at Timmarine Sdn. Bhd., Lot 22B, Ground Floor, Block A, Hsiang Garden, Jalan Leila (☎089/212063). Tourists are currently issued a three-week visa upon arrival, but check this by phoning the Filipino embassy in KL.

To be able to be in Turtle Islands Park in the early evening – the best time to watch the turtles – you'll need to be on an official tour run by Crystal Quest (☎089/212711), twelfth floor, Wisma Khoo Siak Chiew, Sandakan. This tour company is the only one actually allowed to stay overnight in the park. The *Travellers Rest Hostel* and *Uncle Tan's* (see below) also run trips to the islands but these independent outfits aren't permitted to stay overnight within the park.

Sandakan's **GPO** is five minutes' walk west of town, on Jalan Leila (Mon–Fri 8am–5pm, Sat 10am–1pm). There's a **Telekom** office on the 6th Floor, Wisma Khoo (daily 8.30am–4.45pm). The main **police station** is on Jalan Sim Sim (☎089/211222). **Internet** access is on hand at *Internet Cyber Café*, 2nd Floor, Lot 219, Wisma Sandakan, and *Infokom Cyber Shop*, Block 21, Lot 1A, 2nd Floor, Jalan Tiga.

Accommodation and eating

As Sandakan is mainly used as a base from which to explore the Orang-utan centre and Turtle Islands, many travellers choose to bypass the town altogether and stay instead at *Uncle Tan's* popular **guesthouse** (☎089/531639), around 28km west of Sandakan and quite near the Orang-utan Centre (coming from KK by bus, ask to be dropped outside *Uncle Tan's*). The guesthouse is actually at Mile 17 1/2 Labuk Road, a thirty-minute bus ride from town. The owner, known as "Uncle", charges RM20 for a bed in a basic hut and the price includes three meals. The knowledgeable and courteous Tan also arranges trips to his jungle camp on Sungei Kinabatangan. If you want to stay in Sandakan itself, the equally traveller-oriented *Travellers' Rest Hostel*, second floor, Apartment 2, Block E, Bandar Ramai-Ramai (☎089/221460; ②) offers clean, bargain-priced dorms (RM10) and rooms, with breakfast included. Owner Chris Perez also has a jungle camp. For more upmarket alternatives, try the clean but spartan rooms at *Mayfair*, 24 Jl Pryer (☎089/219855; ③), or mid-range *Ramai*, Mile 1 1/2 Jl Leila (☎089/273222; ④), whose en-suite rooms all have TV and air-con.

For hawker stalls, the market on Jalan Pryer is unbeatable. Otherwise, check out the popular Muslim Indian **restaurant** *Haji*, on Second Avenue, south of the padang (8.30am–9.30pm), *SRC Deluxe Restaurant* (11.30am–2pm & 5–10pm), at the *Sandakan Recreation Club*, Jalan Singapore, which serves good Cantonese dishes, or *Supreme Garden Vegetarian Restaurant*, Block 30, Bandar Ramai-Ramai, Jalan Leila (10am–2pm & 5.30–9pm).

Sepilok Orang-utan Rehabilitation Centre

One of only three orang-utan sanctuaries in the world, the **Sepilok Orang-utan Rehabilitation Centre** (daily 9–11am & 2–3.30pm; feeding times 10am & 3pm; RM10; ☎089/531180), 25km west of Sandakan, trains young and domesticated orang-utans (tailless, red-haired apes) to fend for themselves. Close to feeding time, a warden leads you to Station A, passing the nursery, where baby orang-utans are taught elementary climbing skills – a thrilling sight. There's a better chance of seeing semi-mature and more independent orangs a thirty-minute hike from the Visitor Centre at Station B, though this feeding station isn't always open. Buses leave for the centre daily at 9.20am, 11.30am, 1.30pm and 3pm from Sandakan's Labuk Road Station, but for an earlier start, head for the minibus area and take a "Batu 14" bus; the first bus is at 7.30am and they run every half-hour. The Centre's *Rest House* has a few rooms (③), but most people stay at *Uncle Tan's* (see above) or in Sandakan. There are two other excellent options: *Sepilok B & B* (☎089/532288; dorms RM15; ③) is 500m before the Centre's entrance, and *Labuk B & B* (☎089/533190; ②), 2km further back on the KK road.

Turtle Islands National Park

Peeping out of the Sulu Sea some 40km north of Sandakan, three tiny islands comprise Sabah's **Turtle Islands National Park**, the favoured egg-laying sites of the green and hawksbill turtles, varying numbers of which haul themselves laboriously above the high-tide mark to bury their clutches of eggs. All three of the park's islands (Pulau Selingaan, Pulau Bakkungan Kechil and Pulau Gulisaan) have a hatchery – though only Selingaan has amenities for tourists.

Introduction

The **Philippines** has suffered in the tourism stakes because of its position on the map. Imelda Marcos once said it was "hamburgered" geographically. What she meant was that the Philippines receives fewer visitors than other Southeast Asian countries – about two million a year compared to Thailand's six million – because it is not part of the Southeast Asian mainland. Travellers on the traditional Asian trails tend to get as far as Thailand or Hong Kong, but ignore the Philippines because it involves an extra flight, albeit it a short one, across the South China Sea.

Perversely, it is this very lack of mass tourism that makes the Philippines such an appealing destination. If you want to explore, and if you are ready to cope with some eccentric infrastructure and a distinctly laid-back attitude towards the passage of time, the Philippines has more to offer than many of its neighbours.

The Philippines is a big country in a small package. It is the second largest archipelago in the world, with **7107 islands** (sixty percent of them uninhabited) and 58,390km of coastline, all in a land mass no bigger than Arizona. Filipinos refer to it as their string of pearls. Your biggest problem is likely to be deciding which of the pearls to see first.

Most flights from outside the country land in the capital, **Manila**, which is choked with traffic and dilapidated, but also has some of the ritziest shopping malls and most spectacular nightlife in Asia. JM Nakpil Street in Malate on a Friday night is a sight to behold. Beatnik poets mingle with film stars, models, swaggering transvestites and a smattering of expats to create a good-natured outdoor rave that makes all other raves look tame by comparison.

For connoisseurs of beaches, the central **Visayan region** is an island-hoppers' paradise, with white sand everywhere and unspoiled fishing *barrios* where there's nothing to do at night except watch the fireflies, listen to the geckos, and perhaps share a bottle of local Tanduay rum. **Palawan**, one hour to the southwest of Manila by plane or an overnight journey by ferry, is an unforgettable wilderness of diamond-blue lagoons, volcanic lakes and first-rate scuba diving. In the **Cordillera Mountains** of the far north live tribes who make propitiatory offerings to rice gods and whose way of life has barely changed since they first settled there around 500BC. One of the few concessions they have made to modernity is to give up headhunting.

The Philippines will turn every notion you ever had of Asia on its head. Centuries of **colonial rule** have resulted in a delightfully schizophrenic country of potent but conflicting influences. When Magellan placed a sovereign hand on the Philippines on behalf of King Philip of Spain in 1521, he brought with him Catholicism, European architecture and the *manana* ethic. When monsoon rains swamp the streets, or when volcanoes erupt, a Filipino's usual reaction is to smile, throw up their hands, and say *bahala-na* – "what will be will be".

Three centuries after Magellan, in 1898, there was another bizarre twist in the country's colonial history when **America** bought the Philippines from Spain for US$20 million, part of the booty from a war the two powers had fought over Cuba. It was from America that the Philippines got its town planning, its constitution, and its passion for basketball, beauty pageants and pizza. Independence was finally granted on July 4, 1946, making the Philippines Asia's first real democracy, a fact most Filipinos remain fiercely proud of.

But it was the events of the 1980s that brought the Philippines to the general attention of the rest of the world. In 1972, **President Ferdinand Marcos** decided to overstay his welcome in Malacanang Palace by declaring martial law. When Marcos's lifelong political rival, **Ninoy Aquino**, was assassinated at Manila airport in August 1983, patience with the dictator ran out. What followed was nothing short of momentous: a "people power" revolution to kick out Marcos and his ambitious wife Imelda. In February 1986, they fled to Hawaii, where Ferdinand died in exile. Imelda's famous shoe collection was turned into a museum exhibit, but has since been boxed up and put into storage.

Then, of course, there are the **Filipinos** themselves. It has become hackneyed to describe the Philippines as the land where Asia wears a smile, but there's no denying it's true. Filipinos are a gregarious and accommodating lot. Graciousness and warmth seem to be built into their genes. English is widely spoken, even in the provinces, and everywhere you go you will be greeted with the honorific "ma'am" or "sir".

Filipinos are also passionate, sometimes hotheadedly so. They love food, they love life and they love romance. The Philippines is a passion play writ large and nowhere is this more evident than in the hundreds of **fiestas** and religious ceremonies that are held every year. Some are flamboyant and theatrical, like the **Ati-Atihan** in Kalibo and the **Parade of Pigs** in Batangas. Others have their origins in the Scriptures and are solemn. One of the most famous religious events, and one of the most controversial, is

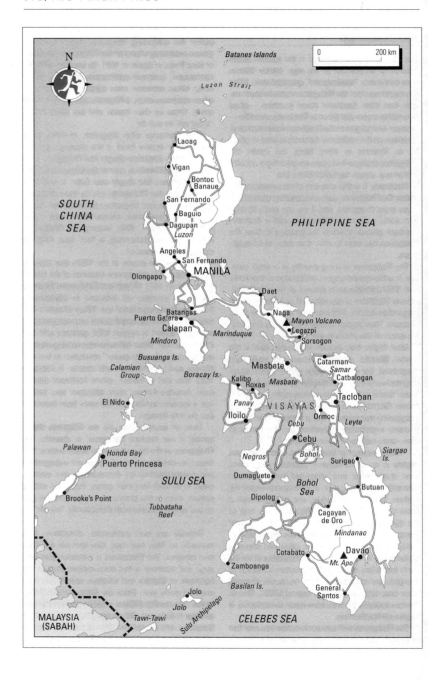

N

Batanes Islands

Luzon Strait

Laoag

Vigan

Bontoc
Banaue

San Fernando

SOUTH
CHINA
SEA

Baguio

Dagupan

Luzon

PHILIPPINE SEA

Angeles

San Fernando

Olongapo

MANILA

Daet

Batangas

Naga

Puerto Galera

Mayon Volcano

Calapan

Marinduque

Legazpi

Mindoro

Sorsogon

Busuanga Is.

Catarman

*Calamian
Group*

Boracay Is.

Masbate

Samar

Catbalogan

Kalibo

Masbate

El Nido

Roxas

Tacloban

Panay

VISAYAS

Iloilo

Ormoc

Leyte

Cebu

Palawan

Honda Bay

Cebu

*Siargao
Is.*

Puerto Princesa

Negros

Bohol

Surigao

SULU SEA

Dumaguete

*Bohol
Sea*

Butuan

Brooke's Point

Dipolog

*Tubbataha
Reef*

Cagayan
de Oro

Mindanao

Cotabato

Davao

Zamboanga

Mt. Apo

Basilan Is.

Jolo

General
Santos

Jolo

MALAYSIA
(SABAH)

Tawi-Tawi

Sulu Archipelago

CELEBES SEA

0   200 km

the **crucifixion of flagellants** held every Easter at San Fernando in Pampanga. Holy Week is a sacred holiday for Filipinos and tens of thousands head north from Manila to hill stations like Baguio.

There are **two distinct seasons** in the Philippines, the wet (southwest monsoon) and the dry (northeast monsoon). The **wet season** runs from May to October and the dry from November to April. The wet season is best avoided, as the country is hit by an average of seven typhoons and affected by fifteen. These cyclonic storms are more of an inconvenience than an outright threat, with flights cancelled and roads made impassable by floodwaters, even in the capital. **November and December** are the coolest months, with daytime temperatures of around 28°C, while March, **April and May** are very hot: expect temperatures to peak at 35°C. Watch out for **Christmas and Easter** when the whole of the Philippines hits the road and getting a seat on a bus or plane can be difficult.

Air and sea routes to the Philippines

Most major Southeast Asian airlines have regular **flights** to Ninoy Aquino International Airport in Manila, with a few also flying to Cebu. **Hong Kong** is the best gateway to the Philippines because Cathay Pacific has five flights a day and Philippine Airlines has three. British Airways, Emirates and Gulf Air all fly to Manila through Hong Kong and it is possible to get good fares because they are keen to fill seats for the last leg of the journey.

Thai Airways has one or two flights a day **from Bangkok**, depending on the day of the week. Garuda flies twice weekly **from Indonesia** and Malaysia Airlines flies **from Kuala Lumpur** to Manila and Cebu.

Every week or so a **cargo boat** leaves Bitung (see p.433) in northern **Sulawesi** for General Santos, the Philippines' southernmost city. Boats also sail from **Sandakan** (see p.663) in Sabah to Zamboanga twice weekly.

Entry requirements and visa extension

Bureaucracy is less of a problem than it used to be, with visitors entitled to an automatic **21-day visa** when they arrive. Make sure you have an onward ticket and a passport that is valid for at least six months. If you get a visa beforehand you will be entitled to 59 days, or you can simply get an **extension**

of up to 59 days at immigration offices in Manila and many provincial towns (P510). Don't forget to take your passport and return airline ticket. Many resorts in the more popular areas will arrange extensions for you for a fee. Extensions beyond 59 days take more time and can usually only be arranged through Manila, although some cities, like Cebu, can process the forms on site.

AIRPORT DEPARTURE TAX

Philippine airport departure tax is currently P550 for international flights.

Money and costs

The Philippine **currency** is the *piso*, although it is almost always spelt "peso". It is divided into 100 centavos, with bills in denominations of P10, 20, 50, 100, 500 and 1000. Coins come in 25 centavos and P1 and P5. Apart from the **peso**, the only currency that's likely to get you anywhere in the Philippines is the **US dollar**. Most banks will not change pounds sterling, euros or anything else. Many hotels will, but you'll get a low rate. In rural areas you may have trouble changing **travellers' cheques**, so it's best to bring a ready supply of cash, both dollars and pesos. The current **exchange rate** is P40 to US$1 and P60 to £1.

Visa, MasterCard and, to a lesser extent, American Express are widely accepted throughout Manila and other major cities, and also in popular tourist destinations such as Boracay. You can withdraw cash from 24-hr ATMs (in the Visa, Plus, Mastercard and Cirrus networks) in all cities and even many smaller towns. Most banks will advance cash against cards (generally Visa and MasterCard) for a commission. If you use credit cards to pay for airline tickets and hotels, there is sometimes an extra charge of around 2.5 percent.

If you need to get **money wired** to you in the Philippines it's best to go to one of the banks in the business district of Makati, such as Cocobank or Bank of the Philippine Islands. They will ask you to open an account, which can be done over the counter in a matter of minutes, as long as you have two forms of identification, each with your photo. A transfer will take at least five working days. Overseas banks with branches in Manila are limited. Citibank and Hong Kong & Shanghai Bank are both in Makati. See "Basics" p.23 for more details on wiring money.

The Philippines is said to be about thirty percent more expensive than Thailand for travel, but depending on where you go and what you do this is not true. Getting around by bus is cheap, with the longest bone-crunching journeys costing less than P150, and an air ticket from Manila to Davao and back can cost considerably less than P4000 depending on who you fly with and how far in advance you book. You should be able to **get by on P600 a day** if you are willing to shop around and bargain hard. In out-of-the-way places you can live like a king for well under P1000 a day, eating fresh fish and washing it down with San Miguel beer bought from a local sari-sari store for P12 a bottle. When it comes to accommodation it's always worth haggling. If a beach hut is P300 a night, you could try and get them to let you stay for five days for P200 a night.

Information and maps

The Department of Tourism's **tourist information** hotlines are ☎02/524 1703 and ☎02/524 2384. There are many government tourist offices throughout the country, particularly in major tourist destinations. Off the beaten track, however, good information can be harder to find.

United Tourist Promotions publishes a basic range of **maps** called E–Z Map, covering Manila and other destinations such as Baguio, Batangas, Palawan, Angeles and Davao. These are sold through hotel bookshops for P80. Road maps and country maps can be bought at National Bookstore in Manila. Nelles Verlag publishes two good maps – a country map and a Manila map – which you can buy at home before you travel.

Getting around

The number of flights and ferry services between major destinations makes it easy to cover the archipelago, even when you're on a tight budget. Local road transport is mostly limited to buses and jeepneys, although in cities such as Manila, Cebu and Davao it's still relatively cheap to get around by taxi.

■ Planes

Air travel is a godsend for island-hoppers in the Philippines, with a number of airlines both large and small linking Manila to most of the country's major destinations. Philippines Airlines has a comprehensive domestic schedule, while two newer airlines, Air Philippines and Cebu Pacific, are catching up fast and

offering competitive rates, particularly if you book in advance. Asian Spirit, Air Ads and Pacific Airways are among some of the smaller airlines. Pacific Airways has a bad reputation regarding delays, but Asian Spirit and Air Ads are generally both reliable.

To give you some idea of **prices**, Philippine Airlines charges P2098 from Manila to Kalibo (for Boracay) if you purchase your ticket in the Philippines. A return ticket is P4196. From Manila to Puerto Princesa in Palawan is P2368 (P4736 return). Manila to Kalibo with Cebu Pacific is P1899 and Manila to Cebu is the same.

■ Buses

Travelling around the Philippines is part of the experience and nowhere is this truer than on the **buses**. Dilapidated contraptions with no air-conditioning compete with bigger bus lines with all mod cons on hundreds of routes that span out from Manila. Fares are cheap, but journeys can be long. Manila to Baguio, for instance, costs P120 on an air-conditioned bus, but takes anything up to nine hours. Many hardened travellers prefer to make these epic journeys at night when traffic is light.

■ Ferries

Boats are the bread and butter of Philippine travel, with wooden outrigger boats, known as *bancas*, and luxury ferries ready to take you from one destination to the next in varying degrees of comfort and safety. Remember that even in the dry season the open ocean can get rough, so think carefully about using small boats that look ill-equipped or overcrowded. Ferry disasters are not unknown in the Philippines. Regulations are gradually improving, but you can make extra sure by sticking to the major lines such as **WG&A**, which has daily sailings throughout the country from Manila Port. On less popular routes you might have to take your chances with smaller lines. Ferries are cheap but often crowded. On overnight journeys you can always keep away from the mass of humanity in the downstairs dormitories by sleeping on the deck. WG&A has cabins for those who want privacy and comfort.

Fares from Manila to Cebu in economy class cost P890, P1230 with a cabin. Manila to Davao is P1200 economy, P1750 cabin class.

■ Taxis

Before you get in a **taxi** make sure the driver will use his meter or that you have negotiated a reasonable fare. From the Manila Bay area to the business district of Makati the metered fare will be about P100. Never use a taxi if the driver has companions. You stand more chance of getting a taxi if you use them at off-peak times. Few taxi drivers will leap at the chance to take you to the airport at five o'clock on a Friday afternoon in a monsoon downpour, so you'll need to be flexible and allow yourself time.

■ Local transport

The workhorse of the transport system is the fabled **jeepney**, a legacy of World War II when American soldiers left behind army jeeps; these were converted by ingenious locals into vehicles, carrying everything from produce to people. Over the years they evolved into today's colourful workhorses of the road, with their fairy lights and cheesy decor. They ply particular routes, indicated on the side of the vehicle. Provincial jeepneys charge as little as P2.50 a ride, while in Manila, prices range up to P20 for longer distances. Jeepneys stop anywhere, so simply flag one down and hop on. When you want to get off bang on the roof or shout "para!"

In Manila and other cities, **Toyota FX Tamaraws** are a popular way to get around. Owners of these functional air-conditioned vehicles, which can seat up to ten passengers at a squeeze, hang signs in their windows with the name of the destination. FX's, as they are affectionately known, have become a common sight, with many office workers using them because they are cheaper than taxis and more comfortable than jeepneys or buses. The minimum fare is P10.

Tricycles are the Filipino equivalent of the Thai tuk-tuk, and while they are not allowed on major roads they can be useful for getting from a bus station to a beach and back again. Fares tend to increase dramatically when a tourist approaches, so always reach agreement beforehand. P30–40 is a reasonable fare for a five-minute journey.

ADDRESSES

It is common in the Philippines for buildings to give an **address** as 122 Legaspi cor. Velasco Streets. This means the place you are looking for is at the junction of Legaspi Street and Velasco Street. Streets are sometimes renamed in honour of new heroes or because old heroes have been discredited or boundaries moved. Pasay Road in Makati is now Arnaiz Avenue, but confusingly everyone still calls it Pasay Road.

■ Vehicle rental

It's easy and relatively cheap to **rent a self-drive car** in the Philippines. The question is whether or not you would want to. Most Filipino drivers seem to have a very relaxed attitude towards the rules of the road. Swerving is common, as is changing lanes suddenly and driving with one hand permanently on the horn, particularly for bus and jeepney drivers. If you do rent a car you'll require nerve and patience. If you need to get somewhere quickly and have money to spare you can always hire a **car with a driver** for about P2000 a day, depending on distance (plus a tip for the driver if he gets you there in one piece). Major car rental firms are listed in the Yellow Pages under Automobile Renting and Leasing. They include Avis (☎02/525 2206), Budget (☎02/831 8256) and Filcar (☎02/843 3530).

Accommodation

There is **accommodation** for everyone in the Philippines, from swanky private resorts, where Hollywood stars chill out, to humble huts on a stretch of deserted beach. On the outlying islands you can find nipa huts, made from indigenous palms, ranging in price from P250 for a simple room with a shower to P1000 for something a bit more refined with aircon or fan. The top-end luxury resorts charge up to US$350 a night.

ACCOMMODATION PRICE CODES

All **accommodation** reviewed in this guide has been graded according to the following price codes, in US dollars, which represent the cost of the cheapest double room available in high season. Where a price range is indicated, this means that the establishment offers rooms with varying facilities – as explained in the write-up. In cases where an establishment charges per bed the actual price is given.

① under $5	④ $15–20	⑦ $40–60
② $5–10	⑤ $20–25	⑧ $60–80
③ $10–15	⑥ $25–40	⑨ $80 and over

In the poorer areas of the country there is no running **water**. Even in the rich enclaves of Manila you'll find that water can be a problem. The water authorities pump water only twice a day into residential areas – many households save it in a purpose-built tank with a small electric pump attached so they can use it when they need it. Households without tanks often keep water in a large plastic dustbin and shower by scooping it over their heads with a plastic scoop known as a *tabo*. In the provinces this is the normal way to bathe.

Electricity is usually supplied at 220 volts, although you may come across 110 volts. Plugs are two pins with the pins flat and rectangular, as opposed to round. Power cuts ("brownouts") are common, especially in the more rural areas.

Food and drink

The high esteem in which Filipinos hold their **food** is encapsulated by the common greeting "Let's Eat!"

Filipino cuisine has not been accepted worldwide in the way Indian or Thai has, but those willing to experiment will discover it has more going for it than its detractors suggest. In fact, Filipino food is undergoing something of a nationalist revival, with intellectuals and cookery writers espousing the virtues of traditional home-and-hearth dishes such as Bicol Express and *sinigang*. Coconut, soy, vinegar and fish sauce are widely used to add flavour. The **national dish**, if there is one, is *adobo*, which is either chicken or pork, or both, cooked in soy and vinegar. At special celebrations Filipinos are passionate about their *lechon*, roasted pig stuffed with pandan leaves and cooked so the skin turns to crackling. *Lechon de leche* is roasted suckling pig. **Fish dishes** are also good, although fish is fresher in the provinces than it is in Manila. The king of Filipino aphrodisiacs is the *balut*, a half-formed duck embryo eaten with beak, feathers and all. You can buy *balut* from street vendors who advertise their proximity with a distinctive baying cry.

FOOD AND DRINK GLOSSARY

GENERAL TERMS AND REQUESTS

I am vegetarian	*Vegetarian ako*	With/without	*Meron/owala*
Can I see the menu?	*Asan yung menu?*	Can I have the bill please?	*Pahingi nung bill?*
I would like . . .	*Gusto ko . . .*		

MAIN DISHES

Adobo	Chicken and/or pork simmered in soy sauce and vinegar, with pepper and garlic	*Lechon de leche*	Roast whole suckling pig
		Lechon	Roast whole pig
		Lengua	Tongue
Beef tapa	Beef jerky	*Longganiza*	Small sausage of either beef or pork, with a lot of garlic
Bicol Express	Fiery dish of pork ribs cooked in coconut milk, soy, vinegar, fish paste and hot chillies	*Lumpia*	Spring rolls
		Sinigang	Sour soup cooked with meat and/or vegetables and tamarind
Kare-kare	Oxtail with heart of banana and peanut sauce		
		Sisig	Baked pig's knuckle

FISH

Adobong pusit	Squid cooked adobo style	*Lapu-lapu*	Popular fish, similar to a grouper
Bagoong	Fermented fish paste, the "caviar of the Philippines", often served with sour mango as a snack	*Panga ng tuna*	Tuna jaw
		Patis	Fish sauce, an all-purpose dip often placed on the table as a condiment
Bangus	Native milkfish, best eaten (with the bones removed) and then dipped in a sauce of vinegar and garlic	*Pusit*	Squid
fried		*Tilapia*	Small freshwater fish often grilled or fried

The **beer** of choice in the Philippines is San Miguel, but with meals many Filipinos tend to stick to soft drinks such as iced tea. Fresh *buko* (coconut) juice is a refreshing alternative on a hot day. If you fancy something stronger there are plenty of cheap Philippine-made spirits such as Tanduay rum and San Miguel Ginebra (gin). For something authentically native, try the strong and pungent *Tapuy* (rice wine).

Communications

Letters from the Philippines take at least five days to reach other countries by air, sometimes significantly longer. For incoming mail, major post offices in Manila have a counter for **poste restante**. See "Basics" p.39 for general advice on poste restante.

The country's **telephone** system has improved dramatically in recent years, although outside urban centres it can still be temperamental. Public **payphones** are not common, but can be found in many malls (where there are often long queues to use them) and hotel lobbies. They take P1 and P5 coins. Many payphones take only Philippine Long Distance Telephone (PLDT) cards only, known as **Fonkards**. These are available in P100, P200, P300 and P500 denominations and can be bought from convenience stores such as 7–11 and hotels. **Long-distance domestic calls** are known as NDD (National Direct Dialling). **Regional codes** are given throughout the chapter; you'll need to dial the "0" before all long-distance national calls within the Philippines. To check a phone code, dial ☎112. Manila to Baguio costs P5 a minute, or P4 during the off-peak hours of 7pm–7am and all day Sunday. For local directory assistance call ☎114.

Rates for **international IDD calls** are fixed and charged in US dollars by the "pulse". A pulse is equivalent to six seconds. To Australia the first ten pulses (60 seconds) cost 19 cents and every additional pulse cost 15 cents. For the UK it's 19 cents then 16 cents. Calls are cheaper 9pm–8am and all day

SNACKS ('MERIENDA')

Aroz caldo	Rice porridge with chicken	*Pancit bihon*	Thin vermicelli noodles with shrimp and vegetable
Balut	Half-formed duck embryo, eaten as a snack	*Pancit canton*	Thick noodles with shrimp and vegetable
Chicken Mami	Chicken noodle soup		
Ensaimada	Sweet cheese rolls		

VEGETABLES

Abong Bambo	Bamboo shoots	*Kamote*	Sweet potato	*Sili*	Chilli pepper
Ampalaya	Bitter melon	*Pechay*	Spinach	*Talong*	Eggplant

FRUIT AND DESSERTS

Bibingka	Rice cake with coconut	*Lanzones*	Similar to lychees
Buko	Coconut	*Leche*	Flan caramel custard
Cassava cake	Made from a root crop similar to sweet potato	*Mangga*	Mango
		Pina	Pineapple
Halo-halo	Literally "mix-mix", a sweet concoction made from ice cream, shaved ice, jelly, beans and tinned milk	*Puto-bumbong*	Made using *ube* (yam) and eaten with brown sugar

DRINKS

Buko juice	Coconut juice	*Lambanog*	Alcoholic drink made from fermented fruit
Calimansi	Small native citrus fruit diluted in soda as a drink	*Tapuy*	Rice wine
Ginebra	Gin		

Sunday. To **call abroad** from the Philippines, dial ☎00 + IDD country code + area code (minus the first 0) + number. The international operator is ☎108. PLDT also has a service for making **overseas collect calls**. If you dial ☎105 plus the country access code you will be connected to the operator of the country you are calling. These calls can be billed to your credit card.

Internet cafés are springing up all over Manila and an increasing number of the more popular resorts and dive centres have email facilities you might be able to use for a small charge.

Opening hours and festivals

Most government offices are **open** Monday to Friday 8.30am–5.30pm. Businesses generally keep the same hours, with some also open for half a day on Saturday from 9am until noon. **Post offices** in major cities are open Mon–Fri 8.30am–5.30pm. Off the beaten track the hours are less regular. **Banks** open Monday to Friday 9am–3pm, while **shops** in major shopping centres are open 10am–8pm.

■ Festivals

Every year, hundreds of **fiestas** are celebrated in the Philippines and it's well worth timing your journey to see one of the major ones. It's at these festivals that you get a chance to see legendary Filipino hospitality at its best. The beer flows, pigs are roasted and there's dancing in the streets for days

on end. More solemn fiestas, usually religious in nature, are a mixture of devotion, drama, passion and reaffirmation of faith. The **crucifixions** held every Good Friday in Pampanga draw tourists who come to see penitents being flogged then nailed to a cross. Other major festivals include the **Ati-Atihan** every third week of January in Kalibo, the **Flores de Mayo** held throughout May in honour of the Virgin Mary, and the **Lanzones** festival every October in Camiguin celebrating the island's favourite fruit.

Entertainment and sport

Entertainment in the Philippines is synonymous with **live music**. Everyone is a singer or a musician, from the humblest farmer to the richest politician. Bands play in the seediest bars and the ritziest hotels, while popular local groups like *The Eraserheads* grace MTV and give regular concerts in clubs and shopping malls. Filipinos are Asia's troubadours, so you won't have to go far to find live entertainment, whether your taste is for sultry lounge singers or hard rock.

Filipinos are enamoured of America and love the **cinema**. Standard fare in the Philippines is either the

Hollywood blockbuster or the Pinoy (slang for "Filipino") blockbuster. You won't find much in the way of alternative cinema. Pinoy films usually have plots revolving around love, violence, sex or all three. Seeing a film in the Philippines isn't always a memorable experience because of the bizarre ticket system. You can't usually book a specific seat in advance, so you have to turn up and take potluck. Limitless tickets are sold, so you might end up standing at the back or sitting in an aisle. To make matters worse, films are screened continuously and you can enter the cinema at any time. All this makes for an endless number of disturbances that can drive even the most patient film lover to distraction. For more on the cinema industry in the Philippines, see p.683.

By far the number one sport – again thanks to America – is **basketball**, with two hugely popular leagues playing games throughout the country. Matches in Manila are played at the Cuneta Astrodome on Roxas Boulevard.

Cockfighting might not be everyone's idea of fun, but there's no denying it's part of the Filipino psyche. National hero Jose Rizal said Filipino men love their roosters more than their children, and sometimes it seems he wasn't far wrong. Cockfights take place every Sunday in barangays (villages) throughout the archipelago, with farmers winning (or losing) the equivalent of a week's wages in what amounts to a two-minute explosion of feathers and blood. In Manila there are highly publicized "cock derbies" on which thousands, sometimes millions, of pesos are wagered.

Outdoor activities

The Philippines' third-world status has limited most people's exposure to the kind of leisure activities that are taken for granted in the West. Facilities are poor and for rural families there are more important considerations than sporting excellence. That said, even the most isolated barangay has some sort of rudimentary basketball court where villagers gather to play in the cool of the late afternoon. **Trekking** is becoming popular among young professionals, with a number of clubs organizing regular trips up famous peaks such as Mount Apo, Mount Makiling and Mayon Volcano. The best organized clubs include the Association of Philippine Mountaineers (Jules Calagui ☎02/922 5760), PLDT Mountaineering Club (Mike Salalila ☎02/813 7851), or the Metropolitan Mountaineering Society (president Romulo Henson ☎02/890 5136). Caving, rock climbing, kayaking and mountain biking are all developing a respectable following. **Surfing** is also taking off, with major international competitions held regularly in Siargao, northeast Mindanao.

■ Scuba diving

Of the two million tourists who visit the Philippines every year many come for the **scuba diving**. It's hardly surprising that in a nation made up of 7107 islands there are dive sites all over the place, with the exception perhaps of the far north. Two hours from Manila by road you can dive on the reefs of **Batangas**. An hour from Batangas City by ferry is the hugely popular area around **Puerto Galera**, home to many dive schools and fine beaches. Around the **Visayas** in the central Philippines are Boracay, Apo Island (near Dumaguete), Cebu and Bohol. A one-hour flight or twelve-hour ferry journey from the capital takes you to the "last frontier" of **Palawan**, where you can dive on World War II Japanese wrecks in the company of dolphins and manta rays. On the southernmost island of Mindanao there is excellent diving around **Davao** and on the northeast coast at laid-back **Siargao Island**. **Tubbataha Reef** in the Sulu Sea is said to offer some of the best diving in the world, but the only way you can reach it is by liveaboard from Puerto Princesa. In short, you can slip into a wet suit just about anywhere.

The Professional Association of Dive Instructors, better known as **PADI**, organizes most scuba tuition in the Philippines. Always pick a PADI dive centre and ask to see their certification. If you haven't been diving before and fancy your chances you can start with a "discovery dive" to see if you like it. The full PADI Open Water Diver course takes around four days. You might want to consider doing a referral course with PADI at home. This involves doing the pool sessions and written tests before you travel, then doing the open water checkout dives with a PADI resort in the Philippines. It saves time and means you don't have to slave over homework in the heat. You'll need to bring your PADI referral documents with you, as your instructor in the Philippines will want to see them.

Cultural hints

Filipinos are outgoing people who are not afraid to ask **personal questions** and certainly don't consider it rude. Prepare to be interrogated by everyone you meet. Filipinos will want to know where you are from, why you are in the Philippines, how old you are, whether you are married, if not why not and so on and so forth. They pride themselves on their hospitality and are always ready to share a meal or a few drinks. Don't offend them by refusing outright.

A sense of *delicadeza* is also important to Filipinos. This is what you might refer to as propriety, a simple sense of good behaviour, particularly in the presence of elders or women. Filipinos who don't speak good English will often answer any question you ask them with a smile and a nod. Be careful: a smile and a nod doesn't always mean "yes". It can also mean "no", "maybe" or "I have no idea what you are talking about". Colonization by America left its mark on the national psyche, so don't be offended if everyone in the provinces thinks you are a *'kano*. Protestations that you are from Britain, France or Australia will often be greeted with the response, "Is that in America?"

Children appreciate gifts of sweets, the kind you can buy from street vendors for a couple of pesos. It's not advisable to **lose your temper** in the Philippines. Filipinos hate to be embarrassed in front of others and the culture of revenge is strong, so you might end up being the one that is sorry.

Filipinos share the same attitudes to **dress** as other Southeast Asian countries; see "Basics" p.4 for details.

Crime and safety

The Philippines is a **safe** place to travel as long as you exercise discretion and common sense. You'll find the same con artists and hustlers here that you'll find anywhere else, but most Filipinos are friendly and helpful. One of the most common scams is for foreigners to be approached by well-dressed young men or women who offer to buy you a coffee or a beer. The next day you wake up from a deep drug-induced sleep to find you have been relieved of your personal belongings. If you have a theft to report, you will have to file a complaint with the police to stand any chance of making an insurance claim. If it's a potentially serious problem, contact your embassy in Manila.

It is generally accepted that **police** in the Philippines are not Asia's finest. Successive government administrations have made some headway in cleaning up the force, but it is still plagued by accusations of corruption, collusion and an alleged willingness to shoot first and ask questions later. Part of the problem is the low pay police officers receive. In 1999, new recruits were being offered the equivalent of US$120 a month. This makes some of them – a tiny minority, according to senior officers – willing to

supplement their income with payoffs from anyone from the humblest motorist to the most notorious drug king.

Medical care and emergencies

There are **pharmacies** everywhere in the Philippines, so if you have a minor ailment and need to buy medicine over the counter, finding one should not be a problem. The biggest chain is Mercury, which has branches all over the place, but even the smallest village tends to have some sort of store where you can buy the basics.

In Manila and other major tourist centres, **hospitals** are generally well equipped and staffed by English-speaking doctors. Hotels and resorts sometimes have their own doctor on duty, or can at least point you in the direction of a local clinic. In case of

---

EMERGENCY PHONE NUMBERS

The 24-hour number for **emergency services** (police, fire and ambulance) throughout the Philippines is ☎166, but bear in mind it doesn't always work in the provinces, where ambulances and fire stations are few and far between. Even in Manila the emergency services are not known for their efficiency.

---

serious illness you will need to be evacuated, either to Manila or your home country, so make sure you have arranged health insurance before you leave home.

History

Filipinos have often been accused of not having a sense of history and even of not knowing who they really are, a result perhaps of the many diverse influences – Malay, Chinese, European, American – that have collided randomly down the centuries.

In fact, human fossil remains found in Palawan suggest the country's "modern" history goes back 50,000 years when humans first migrated across land bridges formed to mainland Asia and Borneo during the Ice Age. The islands were eventually inhabited by different groups, the first of which was the Aeta or **Negritos**, a tribe that arrived around 25,000 years ago from the Asian continent. Many historians believe the Negritos are the true aboriginal inhabitants of the Philippines.

Archeological evidence shows a rich **pre-colonial culture** that included skills in weaving, shipbuilding, mining and goldsmithing. Contact with Asian neighbours dates back to at least 500BC in the form of trade with the powerful Hindu empires in Java and Sumatra. Trade ties with China were extensive by the tenth century, while contact with Arab traders reached its peak in the twelfth century. In 1380, the Arab scholar Makdam arrived in the Sulu Islands, and in 1475, the Muslim leader Sharif Mohammed Kabungsuwan, from Johore, married a native princess and declared himself the first sultan of Mindanao. By the time the Spaniards arrived, Islam was well established in Mindanao and had started to influence groups as far north as Luzon.

■ Spanish rule

The country's turbulent modern history began on April 24, 1521 when Ferdinand Magellan, a Portuguese seafarer in the service of Spain, arrived in Cebu and claimed the islands for **Spain**. Days later he waded ashore on nearby Mactan Island with 48 men in full armour and was promptly killed in a skirmish with warriors led by chief Lapu-Lapu.

Spanish conquistador Ruy Lopez de Villalobos tried once again to claim the islands for Spain in 1543, but was driven out by natives a year later after naming the Philippines in honour of King Philip II. It wasn't until 1565 that serious Spanish colonization of the archipelago began. **Miguel Lopez de Legaspi** left Spain with orders from King Philip to conquer the islands. He duly did so, establishing a colony in Bohol and then moving on to Cebu where he erected the first Spanish fort in the Philippines. The conquest moved further north in 1571 when Legaspi conquered Manila and a year later the whole country. He never managed to bring the Islamic Sulu Islands and Mindanao under Spanish control, but felt nevertheless that he had done his job well and left for home with a cargo of cinnamon.

In his absence, the Spanish conquistadors and friars zealously set about building churches and propagating Catholicism. They imposed a feudal system, concentrating populations under their control into towns and estates and there were numerous small revolts. Until 1821, the Philippines was administered from Mexico, and attempts by the Dutch, Portuguese and Chinese to establish a presence in the archipelago were successfully repelled. The British managed to occupy Manila for a few months in 1762, but handed it back to Spain under the conditions of the Treaty of Paris, signed in 1763.

With the opening of the Suez Canal in 1869, young Filipinos left their country to study in Europe and returned with liberal ideas and talk of freedom. A small revolt in Cavite in 1872 was quickly put down, but the anger and frustration Filipinos felt about colonial rule would not go away. Intellectuals like Marcelo H del Pilar and Juan Luna were the spiritual founders of the independence movement, but it was the critical writings of a diminutive young doctor from Laguna Province, **Jose Rizal**, that provided the spark for the flame. His novel *Noli Me Tangere* (Touch Me Not) was written while he was studying in Spain, and portrayed colonial rule as a cancer and the Spanish friars as fat, pompous fools. It was promptly banned by the Spanish, but distributed underground along with other inflammatory essays by Rizal and, later, his second novel, *El Filibusterismo*.

In 1892, Rizal returned to Manila and founded the reform movement **Liga Filipina**. He was arrested four days later and exiled to Dapitan on Mindanao. Andres Bonifacio took over the reigns by establishing the secret society known as the Katipunan or KKK. Its full name was Kataastaasan, Kagalanggalang na Katipunan nang mga Anak ng Bayan, which means "Honorable, respectable sons and daughters of the nation". In August, 1896, the armed struggle for independence broke out, and Rizal was accused of masterminding it. He was found guilty at a pig circus of a trial and executed by firing squad in what is now known as Rizal Park on December 30, 1896. The night before he died he wrote *Mi Ultimo Adios*, a moving valedictory poem to the country he loved.

■ The US

When independence finally arrived in 1898, it was short-lived. As a result of a dispute over Cuba a war broke out between the **US** and Spain, and the Spanish fleet was soundly beaten in Manila Bay by ships under the command of Commander Dewey, later promoted to Admiral. The Filipinos fought on the side of the US and when the battle was over General Aguinaldo declared the Philippines independent. The US, however, had other ideas and paid Spain US$20 million for its former possession. Having got rid of one colonizing power, Filipinos were now answering to another, the US.

The **Filipino–American War** lasted for more than ten years, resulting in the death of more than 600,000 Filipinos. This little-known war has been described as the "first Vietnam". US troops used tactics such as strategic hamleting and a scorched-earth policy to pacify the natives.

It was only when President Roosevelt recognized a new Philippine constitution that the archipelago celebrated partial independence and Manuel Quezon was sworn in as first President of the Philippine Commonwealth.

■ World War II

The Philippines, especially Manila, underwent heavy bombardment during **World War II** and casualties were high. Japanese troops landed on Luzon and conquered Manila on January 2, 1942. Battles on the island of Corregidor and the Bataan Peninsula were particularly brutal and when the Japanese finally won they subjected the country to harsh military rule. In 1944, the Philippines was liberated by General Douglas MacArthur and US forces. MacArthur had abandoned his base on Corregidor when it became clear the situation was hopeless, but after arriving in Darwin, Australia, he promised Filipinos "I Shall Return". He kept the promise, wading ashore at Leyte and recapturing the archipelago from retreating Japanese forces. Presidential advisers later suggested he revise the wording of his famous statement to "We shall return", so the rest of the army and the White House could bathe in his reflected glory. He refused. MacArthur later said of Corregidor: "It needs no epitaph from me. It has sounded its own story at the mouth of its guns."

The Philippines was granted full **independence** from the US on 4 July 1946, when Manuel Roxas was sworn in as the first president of the republic.

■ The Marcos years

The post-war period in the Philippines was marked by prevarication in America over what official US policy was towards the archipelago, and by the re-emergence of patronage and corruption in Philippine politics. It was in these rudderless years, that Ferdinand Marcos came to power, promoting himself as a force for unification and reform.

Ferdinand Edralin Marcos (1917–1989) was born in Sarrat, Ilocos Norte. A brilliant young lawyer who had successfully defended himself against a murder charge, he was elected to the Philippine House of Representatives in 1949 and to the Senate in 1959. He was elected president in 1965. Marcos' first term as president was innovative and inspirational. He invigorated both populace and bureaucracy, embarking on a huge infrastructure programme and unifying scattered islands with a network of roads, bridges, railways and ports. First Lady Imelda busied herself with social welfare and cultural projects that complemented Marcos' work in economics and foreign affairs.

Marcos was returned to a **second term** – the first Filipino President to be re-elected – with the highest majority in Philippine electoral history. The country's problems, however, were grave. Poverty, social inequality and rural stagnation were rife. They were made harder to bear by the rising expectations Marcos himself had fostered. Marcos was trapped between the entrenched oligarchy, which controlled Congress, and a rising communist insurgency, fuelled mostly by landless peasants who had grown disenchanted with the slow speed of reform.

On September 21, 1972, Marcos declared **martial law**, arresting Senator Benigno Aquino Jr and other opposition leaders. A curfew was imposed and Congress was suspended. Eight years later, in 1980, **Aquino** was released from jail and left for the US for heart surgery. When he returned from exile on August 21, 1983, he was assassinated at the airport and the country was outraged. At a snap election called on February 7, 1986, the opposition united behind Aquino's widow, Cory, and her running mate Salvador Laurel. On February 25, both Marcos and Cory claimed victory and were sworn in at separate ceremonies. Cory became a rallying point for change and was backed by the Catholic Church in the form of Archbishop Jaime Cardinal Sin, who urged people to take to the streets. When Marcos's key allies saw which way the wind was blowing and deserted him, the game was up. Defence Minister Juan Ponce Enrile and Deputy Chief of Staff of the Armed Forces, General Fidel Ramos, later to become President, announced a **coup d'état**. Ferdinand and Imelda fled into exile in Hawaii and the people stormed through the gates of Malacanang Palace.

■ The return of democracy

The presidency of **Cory Aquino** was plagued by problems because she never managed to bring the powerful feudal families or the armed forces under her control. **Land reform** was eagerly awaited by the country's landless masses, but when Aquino realized reform would also involve her own family's haciendas in Tarlac, she quietly shelved the idea. She survived seven coup attempts and made little headway in improving life for the majority of Filipinos who were – still are – living below the poverty line. The communist **New People's Army** (NPA) emerged once again as a threat and human rights abuses continued. Her legacy was that at least she maintained some semblance of a democracy, which was something for her successor, Fidel Ramos, to build on.

President Ramos took office on July 1, 1992 and announced plans to create jobs, revitalize the economy and reduce the burdensome foreign debt of US$32 billion. But the first thing he had to do was establish a **reliable electricity supply**. The country was being paralyzed for hours every day by power cuts, and no multinational companies wanted to invest their hard-earned money under such difficult conditions. Ramos's success in revitalizing the ailing energy sector laid the foundations for a moderate influx of foreign investment, for industrial parks and new manufacturing facilities. The **economy** picked up, but the problems were still huge. The foreign debt was crippling and tax collection was so lax that the government had nothing in the coffers to fall back on. **Infrastructure** improved marginally and new roads and transit systems began to take shape. Ramos also liberalized the banking sector and travelled extensively to promote the Philippines abroad. Most Filipinos view his years in office as a success, although when he stepped down at the end of his six-year term in 1998, poverty and crime were rife.

His successor, former vice-president **Joseph Estrada**, is a former tough-guy film actor who is known universally as Erap, a play on the slang word *pare*, which means friend or buddy. Filipinos joke that Estrada has a poor command of English and often gets his words mixed up. He was once said to have told a reporter: "I learn quickly because I have a pornographic memory". Estrada has a folksy, macho charm that appeals to the masses. He has been more than happy to confirm rumours of his legendary libido by admitting to a string of extra-marital affairs with leading ladies. "Bill Clinton has the sex scandals, I just have the sex," he once said.

Estrada was elected to the Presidency against politicians of greater stature on a pro-poor platform. His rallying cry was *Erap para sa mahirap*, or "Erap for the poor". He has promised food security, jobs, mass housing, education and health for all. Whether these big promises can be kept remains to be seen. His presidency got off to a rocky start, plagued by various tawdry scandals that he swept aside and more serious accusations of a lack of direction and a return to the cronyism of the Marcos years. Many are worried that if Estrada fails to deliver on his bold – some say reckless – campaign promises, the poor will quickly grow disenchanted.

Religions of the Philippines

The Philippines is the only predominantly **Catholic** nation in Asia. Ninety-five percent of the population are Catholic, with the rest either Protestant or animist. Indigenous tribes have beliefs that combine elements from a number of religions with the worship of their own gods such as the *Bulul*, or rice god.

In recent years, a number of charismatic sub-religions have been born, the largest of which is **El Shaddai**, headed by lay preacher Mike Velarde, a real estate developer who found God when his business failed. Velarde is known to his followers as Brother Mike and has captured the imagination of the country's poor Catholics, many of whom feel isolated from the mainstream church, apart from at life's three critical moments: baptism, marriage and death. To make the polarization worse, priests preach in English, a language most barrio folk only have a rudimentary knowledge of. Velarde has bridged this gap by preaching in colloquial and heavily-accented Tagalog at huge open-air gatherings every weekend near the *Manila Hotel*, Manila Bay. He wears screamingly loud made-to-measure suits and outrageous bow ties, but his message is straightforward: give to the Lord and He will return it to you tenfold. He now has eight million followers, most of whom suffer from *sakit sa bulsa*, or "ailment of the pocket", but are nevertheless happy to pay ten percent of their income to become card-carrying members of Brother Mike's flock. Brother Mike's relationship with the mainstream Catholic Church, headed by Manila Archbishop Jaime Cardinal Sin, is uneasy. His relationship with politicians is not. With eight million followers hanging on his every word, Brother Mike is a potent political ally and few candidates for high office are willing to upset him. In the last election, Brother Mike backed Joseph Estrada, a significant factor in the former movie actor's ultimate success.

The Philippines cinema industry

You can't miss them in the Philippines: iconoclastic hand-painted billboards advertising so-called *bomba* movies, made in a couple of days on the kind of budget that wouldn't buy a Caesar's salad in Hollywood.

Bombas are cheap, histrionic and full of wonderfully crass dialogue ("You're nothing but a second-rate, trying hard to copycat").They endure because they espouse the kind of escapist hopes that preoccupy the country's masses: a bashful barrio hunk takes on witless thugs who victimize a beautiful girl. The endings are frothy. The hunk whips the thugs, the girl falls for the hunk, and then becomes a famous actress in Manila, city of dreams.

The proliferation of Tagalog bodice-busters (many of them shown on the popular cable channel Pinoy Blockbusters) is worrying academics and intellectuals, but their hold over the public shows no sign of slackening. While "Pinoywood" is nowhere near as productive or prodigious as Bombay's Bollywood, it is still a potent popular force. Around two hundred bombas are made every year and stars with unlikely names like Ronnie Ricketts, Tipso Cruz III and Boy Chico are known in every barrio.

But not everybody is a fan. Former president Fidel Ramos got so tired of the interminable diet of guns, goons and breathless maidens that he once summoned Manila's top producers to Malacanang Palace to give them a dressing-down. He told them to start making serious films that showed the Philippines in a positive light. His plea fell on deaf ears, however, and the deluge of bombas continued unabated, as it still does today.

The main reason the industry thrives is money. **Prestige films** are a rarity because of the financial problems associated with producing high-class cinematic art in a third world country where quality education is available only to a few. The margin of profit is shrinking and few producers are willing to take a chance on films that have little chance of a paying audience outside arthouse cinemas in Manila.

One true story illustrates the problem. In 1984, Regal Films produced *Sister Stella L*, a reflective biopic about a Catholic nun working with trade unions. It swept the local awards, but losses were so huge Regal producer Lily Monteverde was too traumatized to make another socially relevant film. The bomba bandwagon rolled on.

The **first filmmakers** came to the Philippines from America at the beginning of the twentieth century, using the islands as a bulk-standard Asian backdrop for any film that required palm trees and heat.

The end of WWII, followed by Filipino independence from the US, saw a cinematic blossoming dominated by four studios modelled after the Hollywood majors.

Most of the films followed reliable genre formats, but the **postwar period** also brought more artistically ambitious works by the likes of Gerardo de Leon, who later tried to break into Hollywood using an unlikely vehicle, *The Mad Doctor of Blood Island*, about an unscrupulous scientist who turns his lab assistant into a green-blooded plant monster.

In the 1960s, as the country descended into political turmoil, things went belly up. The industry collapsed and all the major studios stopped production, with dozens of smaller independents appearing on the scene.

It was here that the bomba was born. Under-capitalized and lacking the clout of the now-defunct majors, the independents turned to sensational projects for quick profit. Guns were drawn and cleavages exposed, although most bombas are in fact rather tame, with the artless cliché of surf crashing on a sandy shore still used regularly as a symbol for sexual gratification.

Serious cinema in the Philippines has flapped but never taken off, handicapped by pitiful budgets and the lack of a moneyed audience. But **in the 70s**, things began to change, with a new generation of filmmakers galvanizing themselves in opposition to the Marcos dictatorship.

This age of censorship was also, ironically, the **golden age of Philippine cinema**, with the late Ishmael Bernal and others like him showing their work at European and American festivals. One of Bernal's most striking films is the noirish *City After Dark*, originally known as *Manila by Night* until Imelda Marcos took exception to the unflattering depictions of life in "her city".

One of the strangest martial law stories concerned director Mike de Leon, scion of one of the oligarch families who bitterly opposed Marcos. He directed *Batch 81*, a thinly disguised allegory about the Marcos dictatorship graphically dramatizing fraternity violence at universities. A brave piece of casting saw the fraternity's sadistic Grand Vizier and chief torturer played by Chito Ponce Enrile, brother of Marcos's defence minister Juan Ponce Enrile. The film ran to packed houses and Marcos made no attempt to ban it.

Philippine cinema today is still in a quandary, torn between the easy profits of bankable bombas and the creeping need to give the country's emerging middle class something more than heaving chests and testosterone. So, worthy productions come and go, but the bombas roll on. The Philippines wouldn't be the Philippines without them, and without the peculiar brand of risqué dialogue they perpetrate. Academics may sneer and pontificate, but who could fail to snigger at a line as memorable as: "You're young, fresh and beautiful. What could you possibly want from a poor farmer like me? Eggplant?"

Books

William Boyd, *The Blue Afternoon* (Penguin/Vintage).

Remarkably, Boyd, who has never been to the Philippines, seems to get early twentieth-century Manila just right, infusing it with an oppressive steaminess that makes tragedy for some of the characters seem preordained. Told in flashbacks, the story travels from 1930s Hollywood to the exotic, violent world of the Philippines in 1902, telling a tale of medicine, the murder of American soldiers, and the creation of a magical flying machine. This is a brooding, intense novel that won't tell you much about contemporary Philippines, but will put some of the more brutal history into perspective, particularly the war with the US.

Alan Berlow, *Dead Season: A Story of Murder and Revenge* (Vintage UK & US).

Prepare to be depressed. This brilliantly atmospheric work of reportage is the story of three murders that took place on the Philippine island of Negros. Impossible to read without feeling intense despair for a country where humble and peaceful people have too often become the tragic pawns in a seedy game of power and money that is played out around them. Even Cory Aquino comes out of it badly. The Church asked her to investigate the murders but she refused, fearful that she might be treading on too many toes.

Alex Garland, *The Tesseract* (Penguin/Riverhead).

Alex Garland, author of *The Beach*, has made no secret of his love for the Philippines. Hardly surprising then that his second novel, a sinister and ingenious exploration of fate and chance, is based there. Garland may get most of his Tagalog wrong (it's *tsismis*, not chismis and *konti* not *conte*), but the rest of his prose is devilishly taut and brought more comparisons by critics to Graham Greene. The story? Well it involves a foreigner abroad, a villainous tycoon called Don Pepe, some urchins and a beautiful girl. The characters may be straight from Cliché Street, but Garland's plot is so intriguing and his observational powers so keen that it's impossible not to be swept along by the bravery of it all.

Jessica Hagedom, *Dogeaters* (Penguin UK & US).

Filipino-American Jessica Tarahata Hagedorn assembles a cast of diverse and dubious characters that comes as close to encapsulating the mania of life in Manila as any writer has ever come. Urchins, pimps, seedy tycoons and corpulent politicos are brought together in a brutal but beautiful narrative that pulls no punches and serves as a jolting reminder of all the country's frailties and woes.

James Hamilton-Paterson, *Ghosts of Manila* (Vintage/Farrar Straus & Giroux).

Hamilton-Paterson's excoriating novel is haunting, powerful and for the most part alarmingly accurate. Much of it is taken from real life: the extra-judicial salvagings, the corruption, the abhorrent saga of Imelda Marcos's infamous film centre. Here is a writer who not only sees the city, but *knows* it. A lucid story that is thriller, morality play and documentary in one. Pretty it's not, but if you want Manila dissected, look no further.

James Hamilton-Paterson, *Playing With Water: Passion and Solitude on a Philippine Island* (Granta/New Amsterdam).

"No money, no honey," says one of the (real-life) characters in Hamilton-Paterson's lyrical account of several seasons spent among the impoverished fishermen of a small barrio in the Visayas. It's the kind of refrain you hear time and again in the Philippines, and one that leads large numbers of young men to turn their backs on provincial life to seek fortune in Manila, where they usually end up hawking newspapers, living in shanties and wishing they were back home. This is a rich and original travel book, which by turns warms and disturbs you.

James Hamilton-Paterson, *America's Boy: The Rise and Fall of Ferdinand Marcos and Other Misadventures of US Colonialism in the Philippines* (Granta/Henry Holt).

A controversial narrative history of the US-supported dictatorship that came to define the Philippines. Hackles were raised by the very plausible claim that the Marcoses were merely the latest in a long line of corrupt Filipino leaders in a country which had historically been ruled by oligarchies. Ferdinand, do not forget, was welcomed at the White House by Lyndon Johnson, Nixon, Reagan and the CIA. In the end, a "democratic revolution" replaced him with Corazon Aquino, who came from another great political and landowning dynasty. She, in turn, was followed by Fidel Ramos, Imelda's cousin. Nothing changed: the world applauded, the shadow play went on. Hamilton-Paterson has gathered astonishing information from senators, cronies, rivals, and Marcos family members, including Imelda. If you buy one book about recent history in the Philippines, buy this one.

Nick Joaquin, *Manila, My Manila* (Bookmark, Philippines).

Veteran Filipino novelist and poet Nick Joaquin's paean to the city of his birth. This is no academic

LANGUAGE

Most Filipinos are unsure how many **languages** and dialects there are in the Philippines, although best estimates put the number at 171, with 168 living and three extinct. The **Tagalog** language is spoken by 46 percent of the population and was made the national language by the government in 1947 as well as the medium of communication in schools, businesses and government. **English** is widely spoken, with most Filipinos moving seamlessly between English and Tagalog, often in the space of the same sentence. Many English words have been cleverly adopted by Filipinos, giving rise to a small canon of slang *patois* known affectionately as Taglish. Why ask someone to take a photograph when you can ask them to do some "kodaking"?

Hello	*Kamusta* (There's no word for hello in Filipino. People usually use Kamusta, which means "how are you?")	Excuse me (to get past)	*Makikiraan lang po*
		Please	No direct equivalent. Instead use the word *paki* before a verb. For example, *upo* means sit, so "please sit" is *paki-upo*
How are you?	*Kamusta ka* or *kamusta?*		
Fine, thanks	*Mabuti. Salamat.*		
Pleased to meet you	*Ikinalulugod kitang makilala* (formal)	Thank you	*Salamat*
	Masaya akong makilala ka (colloquial)	What's your name?	*Anong pangalan mo?*
		My name is . . .	*Ang pangalan ko ay . . .*
		Do you speak English?	*Marunong ka bang mag-Ingles?*
Goodbye	*Bye*		
Good Evening	*Magandang gabi*	I don't understand	*Hindi ko naiintindihan*
Excuse me (to say sorry)	*Ipagpaumanhin mo ako*	Could you repeat that?	*Paki-ulit*

EMERGENCIES

Can you help me?	*Puwede mo akong tulungan?*	Please call a doctor	*Paki-tawag ng duktor*
		Hospital	*Ospital*
There's been an accident	*May aksidente*	Police station	*Istasyon ng pulis*

GETTING AROUND

Where is the . . . ?	*Saan ang . . . ?*	Aeroplane	*Eroplano*
How many kilometres is it to . . . ?	*Ilang kilometro papunta sa . . .?*	Airport	*Airport*
		Bus	*Bus* (pronounced *boos*)
We'd like to go to the airport please	*Gusto naming pumunta sa airport*	Bus station	*Istasyon ng bus*
		Train station	*Istasyon ng tren*
Where do I catch the bus to . . . ?	*Saan puwedeng kumuha ng bus papuntang . . . ?*	Boat	*Banca*, small boat or canoe or boat with outriggers
When does the bus for Manila leave?	*Kailan aalis ang bus papuntang Manila?*	ship	*Barco*
		Taxi	*Taxi*
Can I book a seat?	*Puwedeng bumili kaagad ng ticket para I-reser ba ang upuan?*	Car	*Kotse*
		Filling station	*Gasolinahan*
		Bicycle	*Bisikleta*
How long does it take?	*Gaano katagal?*	Bank	*Banko*
Ticket	*Tiket*	Post office	*Koreo*

Passport	*Pasaporte*	Right	*Kanan*
Hotel	*Hotel*	North	*Hilaga*
Restaurant	*Restoran*	South	*Timog*
Please stop here	*Paki-tigil dito*	East	*Silangan*
Left	*Kaliwa*	West	*Kanluran*

ACCOMMODATION

Do you have any rooms?	*Maroon pa kayong kuwarto?*	Single room	*Kuwarto para sa isa*
How much is it?	*Magkano?*	Double room	*Kuwarto para sa dalawang tao*
Do you have . . . ?	*Meron kang . . . ?*	Air-conditioner	*Aircon*
Could I have the bill please?	*Puwedeng kunin ang bill?*	Fan	*Elektrik fan*
Room with a private bathroom	*Kuwarto na may sariling banyo*	Mosquito net	*Kulambo*
		Toilet paper	*Toilet paper*
		Telephone	*Telepono*
Cheap/expensive	*Mura/mahal*	Laundry	*Labahan*

TIME

What's the time?	*Anong oras na?*	Today	*Ngayong araw*
Noon	*Tanghali*	Tomorrow	*Bukas*
Midnight	*Hatinggabi*	Yesterday	*Kahapon*
Minute	*Minuto*	Now	*Ngayon*
Hour	*Oras*	Morning	*Umaga*
Day	*Araw*	Afternoon	*Hapon*
Week	*Linggo*	Evening	*Gabi*
Month	*Buwan*	Night	*Gabi*
Year	*Taon*		

NUMBERS

Zero	*Zero*	Sixteen	*Labing-anim*
One	*Isa*	Seventeen	*Labing-pito*
Two	*Dalawa*	Eighteen	*Labing-walo*
Three	*Tatlo*	Nineteen	*Labing-siyam*
Four	*Apat*	Twenty	*Dalawampu* or *beinte*
Five	*Lima*	Twenty-one	*Dalawampu't isa* or *beinte isa*
Six	*Anim*	Twenty-two	*Dalawampu't dalawa* or *beintedos*
Seven	*Pito*		
Eight	*Walo*	Thirty	*Tatlumpu* or *trienta*
Nine	*Siyam*	Forty	*Apat napu* or *kwarenta*
Ten	*Sampu*	Fifty	*Limampu* or *singkwenta*
Eleven	*Labing-isa*	One hundred	*Isang daan*
Twelve	*Labing-dalawa*	Two hundred	*Dalawang daan*
Thirteen	*Labing-tatlo*	One thousand	*Isang libo*
Fourteen	*Labing-apat*	Two thousand	*Dalawang libo*
Fifteen	*Labing-lima*		

tome, but an eminently readable odyssey through the centuries from the day the diminutive Kingdom of Namayan was established on the banks of the Pasig River. Joaquin never quite gets round to saying exactly what he thinks of contemporary Manila, but reading between the lines it's not hard to feel his dismay. Fellow journalist Augusto Villalon believes Manila has "an urban death wish", with concrete poured over green spaces and refuse dumped in canals. Joaquin never quite goes that far, but he still leaves you with the sense that this is a tribute to the city that was, not the city that exists today.

F Sionil Jose, *Dusk* (Modern Library, US).

One of the premier novelists in the Philippines, Jose's acclaimed Rosales saga chronicles Filipino struggles and triumphs during the last century. *Dusk*, the fifth book in the saga, takes place at the end of the nineteenth century as the Filipinos, with the aid of the Americans, finally expelled the Spanish after three centuries of often brutal rule. Of course it wouldn't be a quintessential Filipino novel if it didn't touch on the themes of poverty, corruption, tyranny and love. All are on display here, presented within the context of one man, a common peasant, and his search for contentment. *Dusk* was only recently released in America in paperback, but you can always buy it from the bookshop owned by Jose himself, in Padre Faura Street, Ermita.

Stanley Karnow, *In Our Image: America's Empire in the Philippines* (Ballantine UK & US).

This is really a book about America, not about the Philippines, says Karnow. The Philippines is the landscape, but the story is about America going abroad for the first time in its history at the beginning of the twentieth century and becoming a colonial power, what it did in its colony and what it left behind. *In Our Image*, which won the Pulitzer Prize, focuses on the relationship that has existed between the two nations since the United States acquired the country from Spain in 1898, examining how America has sought to remake the Philippines as a clone of itself, an experiment marked from the outset by blundering, ignorance and mutual misunderstanding.

Jose Rizal, *Noli Me Tangere – Touch Me Not* (Bookmark, Philippines).

The book that sparked a revolution and is still required reading for every Filipino schoolchild. It's hard to find outside the Philippines, but worth picking up a copy when you get there. The Noli, a passionate and often elegant exposure of the evils of the friar's rule, was published in 1886 and promptly banned by the Spanish colonial government. It tells the story of barrio boy Crisostomo Ibarra's love for the beautiful Maria Clara, but infuses it with tragedy and significance of almost Shakespearian proportions, documenting the religious fanaticism, the double standards and the rank injustice of colonial rule.

MANILA

The capital of the Philippines is technically known as Metro Manila – a grouping of ten smaller urban areas – but is usually referred to simply as **MANILA**. Today's accepted wisdom is that Manila will never be a serious tourist destination until the authorities deal with the twin evils of traffic and pollution. Most tourists are in the capital because they have a day or two to kill either at the beginning or the end of a trip to the rest of the country. But all is not lost. In its favour, Manila has friendly people, some excellent nightlife, a few sights that are worth the effort, plus some of the biggest and ritziest shopping malls in Asia. At first sight, Manila may seem clamorous, unkempt and a bit rough around the edges, but what it lacks in architectural sophistication it makes up for with an accessible chaotic charm. The way to enjoy it is to step into the fray and go with the flow, which is exactly what *Manilenos* have learned to do.

Manila started life as a tiny settlement around the banks of the Pasig River. The name comes from the words *may* ("there is") and *nilad* (a type of plant that grew near the Pasig). With Spanish colonization, Manila grew into an important port. King Philip II of Spain called it *Insigne y Siempre Leal Ciudad* (Distinguished and Ever Loyal City). Images of the city in the eighteenth century show grand merchants' houses and schooners moored in the Pasig. The area around Bindondo, later to become Chinatown, was alive with mercantile activity. Before World War II, Manila was one of the most elegant and cosmopolitan cities in the Orient. But when the smoke cleared at the end of Japanese occupation in March 1945, it was in ruins, having undergone relentless shelling from American howitzers and been set alight by remaining Japanese troops. The Battle of Manila lasted 29 days and claimed 100,000 civilian lives. Rebuilding was slow and plagued by corruption and government inertia. As a consequence, the city that greets visitors today is one of emotional counterpoints, with areas of extreme poverty and degradation lying cheek by jowl with tower blocks and designer boutiques.

Arrival

Ninoy Aquino International Airport, also known by the acronym NAIA, is in Paranaque, on the southern fringes of the city. In the arrivals hall there's a small 24-hour **Department of Tourism** (DoT) reception desk, where you can get maps. There are two small **banks** in the arrivals hall, but their opening hours are a bit erratic, so it's best to make sure you have enough pesos or US dollars to get to your hotel. Getting from the airport to the city can be a headache. The Manila Bay area is only 7km away, but there are no airport shuttle buses. The best thing is to take an official **airport taxi**; they charge around P350 to the main tourist areas. You pay in advance at a small booth (in the arrivals hall), then present your receipt to the driver. Taking a non-official taxi from the airport is a risk, with many tourists being conned into paying much more than the metered rate. You should never get into a taxi that is unmarked or has other people in it.

Orientation and information

The great urban sprawl of Metro Manila, home to about eleven million people, is actually a grouping of ten areas that have all been conferred city status in their own right. These cities stretch from **Caloocan** in the north to **Pas Pinas** in the south. Tourists tend to see only a few of them, usually **Paranaque** (where the airport is), **Pasay**, **Manila** and **Makati**. Manila is the key tourist district, fronting Manila Bay along Roxas Boulevard, taking in the neighbourhoods of **Ermita** and **Malate**, and stretching north to the old walled city of **Intramuros** and over the Pasig River to **Chinatown**, also known as Bindondo. On **Manila Bay** are land-

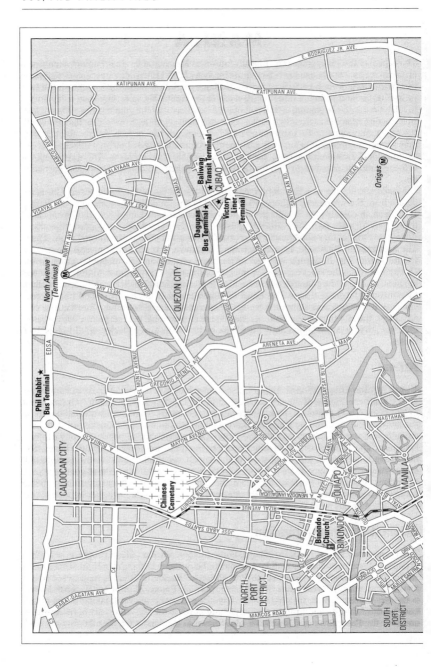

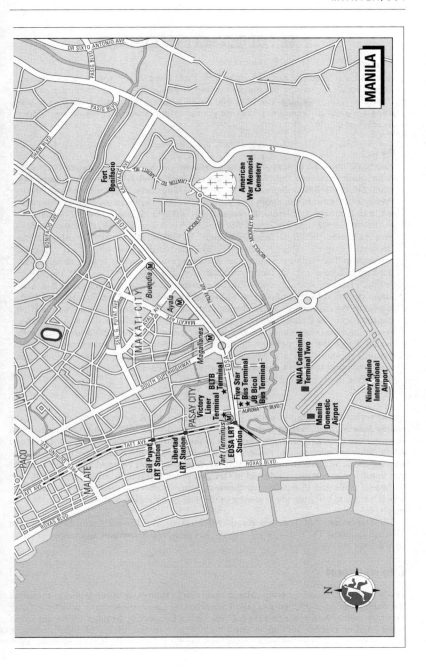

MOVING ON FROM MANILA

By plane

International **flights** and all domestic PAL ones leave from Ninoy Aquino International Airport in Paranaque. Other domestic flights go from the nearby Domestic Airport (☎02/871 0000 or 832 3054), in Domestic Road. Addresses of **airlines** are given in "Listings" p.700. For details of flights from the capital see "Travel Details" on p.772.

By ferry

Nearly all inter-island **ferry** departures sail from the North Harbor, north of Ermita. A taxi from Ermita to the North Harbor will cost about P80. **WG&A Superferry** (☎02/245 0660) has sailings to Cebu, Bohol, Dumaguete, Cagayan de Oro, Puerto Princesa in Palawan, Camiguin and Boracay. The Puerto Princesa service also stops at Coron in northern Palawan. There's a ticket office in Malate at 1105 A Francisco St, on the corner of Singalong Street. You can also buy tickets in the Park Square II shopping mall near the *Hotel Inter-Continental* in Malati, and there's an office at the Domestic Airport (Door 1, Ding Velayo Building, Domestic Road). **Negros Navigation** has sailings to most of the archipelago's major tourist destinations. Booking offices are at 849 Pasay Rd, Makati (☎02/818 4102 or 818 3804) and at Pier 2, North Harbor (☎02/245 0601–12). Other major ferry companies include **Sulpicio Lines** (☎02/241 9701) and **Aleson Shipping Lines** (☎02/712 0507), which sail from Manila to Boracay and on to Zamboanga. For an idea of **fares**, WG&A charges P760 (tourist class) or P1100 (cabin for four people) from Manila to Coron in Palawan. From Manila to Davao latest rates for Negros Navigation are P1425 (tourist class with meals), P1580 (business class with meals), P1790 (deluxe cabin with meals) or P2265 (en-suite cabin with meals). Without meals, the fare is about ten percent cheaper, but remember that some of the journeys last two or three days, depending on stops, so you'll have to pack a lot of food.

marks such as the Cultural Center of the Philippines and, at the north end of the bay, the stately *Manila Hotel*. **Makati** is the central business district (CBD), built around the main thoroughfare of Ayala Avenue, and home to banks, insurance companies, five-star hotels and all the other paraphernalia of modern life. Leaving Makati and heading north through the heaving traffic on **Epifano de los Santos Avenue** (commonly referred to as **EDSA**) brings you to the newer commercial district of **Ortigas**, which is trying to out-Makati Makati, with its hotels, malls and air-conditioned theme restaurants. Beyond Ortigas is **Quezon City**, which has some lively nightlife catering to the nearby University of the Philippines, but not much else.

The **Department of Tourism Head Office** (Mon–Fri 8.30am–5.30pm), Department of Tourism Building, TM Kalaw Street, Ermita, has general **information** and **maps**, although they are not always up-to-date.

City transport

Roads in Manila these days seem to be in a permanent state of advanced gridlock, a result of the capital's rising population and poor infrastructure. There are so many vehicles fighting for every inch of road space that at peak times it can be a sweaty battle of nerves just to get a few hundred metres. Walking is usually out of the question, except for short distances, because buses and jeepneys belch smoke with impunity, turning the air around major thor-

By bus

There is no single unifying **bus** station for Manila. Instead, a number of competing bus companies have terminals either in the **Pasay** area of EDSA, in the south, or at the northern end of EDSA in **Cubao**. Buses from Pasay terminals usually go south, and from Cubao they usually go north.

Baliwag Transit (☎02/364 0778) at 199 Rizal Avenue Extension, Caloocona, operates buses north to Bulacan province, Baliwag, San Jose and Tuguegarao. **BLTB** (☎02/833 5501) has two terminals on EDSA, one at the southern end in Pasay and another at the northern end in Cubao. BLTB buses go south to Nasugbu, Calamba, Batangas, Santa Cruz, Lucena, Naga and Legaspi. BLTB also does epic 28-hour journeys to towns in the Visayas and to Sorsogon in southern Luzon. **Dagupan** (☎02/929 6123) on New York Street, Quezon City, serves the northern destinations of Baguio, Dagupan and Lingayen. **JAM Transit** (☎02/932 2914) is on Taft Avenue in Pasay and serves various destinations in Batangas and Laguna. **Philippine Rabbit** has a nice new terminal at 1240 EDSA, Quezon City, and is popular for destinations in the north such as Angeles, Balanga, Baguio, Vigan, Laoag, San Fernando and Tarlac. Philtranco (☎02/833 5061) is on EDSA at the corner of Apelo Cruz Street, Pasay, and does daily runs as far afield as Quezon, Bicol, Masbate, Camarines, Leyte, Samar and even Davao. **Victory Liner** has terminals at each end of EDSA in Pasay (☎02/833 0293) and Cubao (☎02/727 4534). **Buses go north** to various destinations, including Dau (for Clark), Alaminos, Dagupan, Olongapo, Baguio and Mariveles. If you are staying in the Malate area you can take the LRT from Taft Avenue north to the terminal at Caloocan, where Victory has a third terminal. Buses from here go north.

By train

The government-funded railway has been racked by debt and bad management and only has one line running from Manila to the Bicol region. **Trains** are slow, uncomfortable and are occasionally involved in fatal accidents. At peak times, passengers cling perilously to the carriage roofs, which are sloped to prevent trackside squatters depositing their rubbish on top. This journey is only for the brave. Buses are more frequent, marginally safer and generally faster.

oughfares into a chewable toxic cloud. The new MetroStar light rail system along EDSA does not seem to have eased the snarl.

It's relatively easy to **get around** Manila by **taxi** as long as you don't mind the occasional bout of wearisome haggling. Many taxi drivers are happy to turn on their meters, while others insist on starting even the shortest journey with a long negotiation. Most taxis are air-conditioned and charge an initial P20 plus P1 for every 200 metres. Trips of a couple of kilometres will be about P40 to P50.

The **LRT** (light rail transit) is an elevated railway that runs from Baklaran in the east (near the airport) to Monumento at Caloocan City in the north. Trains run frequently from 5.30am to 9pm and the fare is a standard P10 token. In the Manila Bay area, the LRT runs above Taft Avenue, parallel to Roxas Boulevard. You can use the LRT to get to places in the north of Manila such as Intramuros and the Chinese Cemetery. Another LRT, called **MetroStar**, has just been built along the length of EDSA from North Triangle in Quezon City to Pasay City in the south. The stops include Cubao Station, from where it's a ten-minute walk to bus terminals for the north of the country. Key stations for tourists are Ortigas, from where you can walk to the imposing concrete edifice of Megamall, Cubao, which is close to many of the bus terminals for buses north, and Buendia, which gives access to Makati. MetroStar fares start from P17. From North Triangle to Makati the average journey time is twenty minutes. By bus the same journey could easily take an hour, sometimes more.

Jeepneys go back and forth all over the city. Fares start at P2.50 for the shorter journeys and increase by P0.50 for each kilometre after. A useful route runs the length of Taft Avenue from Baclaran in the south to Bindondo in the north. From Baclaran you can get jeepneys to the bus terminals in Pasay City. Jeepneys heading to Cubao will take you past a number of bus terminals at the northern end of EDSA, where you can get buses to destinations in the north such as Baguio and Vigan.

Local **buses** in Manila bump and grind their way along all major thoroughfares (Taft, EDSA, Senator Gil Puyat Avenue). The destination is written on a sign in the front window and fares start at P8. These "rolling coffins" are in cut-throat competition for your trade because drivers get paid by the number of passengers they carry.

Accommodation

Most of Manila's budget **accommodation** is in the Manila Bay area, specifically in the enclaves of **Ermita** and **Malate**, which also have a high density of restaurants, bars and tourist services. Ermita was once a notorious red-light district, but a former mayor drove out all the "girlie bars" and they have now set up shop in Pasay City where the authorities are more tolerant. In **Makati**, there is some reasonably priced accommodation in and around P Burgos Street at the northern end of Makati Avenue.

Ermita and Malate

Aloha Hotel, 2150 Roxas Blvd (☎02/526 8088). The *Aloha* is a Manila Bay stalwart and is a bit rough around the edges, but popular because of its location. ⑥.

Centerpoint Hotel, 1430 A Mabini St, Ermita (☎02/521 2751). Favoured by many simply because this is the departure point for the Puerto Galera bus every morning at 9am. Rooms are large and air-conditioned. There is a small travel agency in the lobby where you can books tickets and accommodation. ⑥.

Ermita Tourist Inn, 1549 A Mabini St, Ermita (☎02/521 8770–1). Run by helpful staff, with clean and fairly spacious air-con rooms. A popular choice with budget travellers for many years because of its location in Malate. ③.

Hotel Frendy, 1548 A Mabini St, Ermita (☎02/526 4211–14). Spacious air-con rooms in a good location, a short walk from Ermita's nightlife. ⑥.

Joward's Pension House, 1726 Adriatico St, Malate (☎02/521 4845). Cheap but fairly cheerful. ①.

Juen's Place, 1775 D, Adriatico St, Malate (no phone). You can find this simple but clean family-run guesthouse by walking down the dark lane at the side of the *Malate Pensionne*. It's not the *Ritz*, but it represents good value and also has cheap singles. ②.

Kanumayan Tourist Inn, 2317 Leon Guinto St, Malate (☎02/521 1161–66). Good location close to Malate nightlife. Run by friendly management and has a small swimming pool. ⑥.

Mabini Pension, 1337 A Mabini St, Ermita (☎02/524 5404). This has been around a long time and remains a convenient and friendly place to stay. It's safe enough to leave your luggage with the staff, and rooms are usually clean and tidy, though it's best to look before you commit. Rooms range from singles with a fan to doubles with a private bath. ②–⑤.

Malate Pensionne, 1771 Adriatico St, Malate (☎02/523 8304). A popular place furnished in Spanish colonial style and in a good position near Malate's bars and cafés. Rooms have varying facilities. Reservations recommended. ③–⑥.

Pension Natividad, 1690 MH del Pilar St, Malate (☎02/521 0524). This has become a popular place to stay since room rates at the rival *Malate Pensionne* increased. There's a peaceful garden full of bougainvillea and a small coffee shop. Dorm beds are available for P200. ⑤.

Las Palmas Hotel, 1616 A Mabini St, Ermita (☎02/524 5602–17). This place seems to have been about as long as Manila itself. It survived the closure of the nearby red-light district and has transformed itself into a mid-range hotel. It's a little bit rundown, but quiet, clean and safe. ⑥.

Royal Palm Hotel, 1227 A Mabini cor. Padre Faura Street, Ermita (☎02/522 1515). One of a number of mid-range hotels in the area, with large air-conditioned rooms. Breakfast included. ⑥.

Santos' Pension House, 1540 A Mabini St, Ermita (☎02/523 4896). Close to the junction with Pedro Gil Street. The rooms are average and include air-con singles and fan doubles. ②.

The Swagman Hotel, 411 A Flores Street, Ermita (☎02/523 8541). Part of the archipelago-wide Swagman chain of small hotels and travel agents – so staff can help you with everything from visa extensions to bus

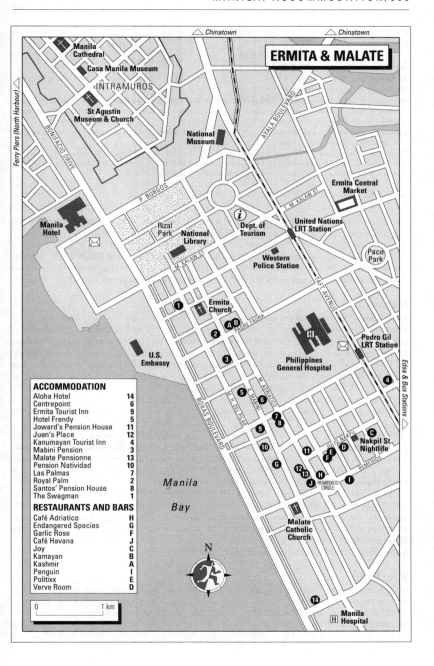

ERMITA & MALATE

Chinatown

Chinatown

Manila Cathedral

Casa Manila Museum

INTRAMUROS

St Agustin Museum & Church

BONIFACIO DRIVE

Ferry Piers (North Harbour)

P. BURGOS

National Museum

AYALA BOULEVARD

Ermita Central Market

M. KALAW ST

United Nations LRT Station

Manila Hotel

Rizal Park

National Library

Dept. of Tourism

M. KALAW ST

Western Police Station

TAFT AVENUE

Paco Park

Ermita Church

PADRE FAURA

A B

U.S. Embassy

ROXAS BOULEVARD

M. H. DEL PILAR

A. MABINI

M. ADRIATICO

Philippines General Hospital

Pedro Gil LRT Station

Edsa & Bus Stations

ACCOMMODATION

Aloha Hotel	14
Centrepoint	6
Ermita Tourist Inn	9
Hotel Frendy	5
Joward's Pension House	11
Juen's Place	12
Kanumayan Tourist Inn	4
Mabini Pension	3
Malate Pensionne	13
Pension Natividad	10
Las Palmas	7
Royal Palm	2
Santos' Pension House	8
The Swagman	1

RESTAURANTS AND BARS

Café Adriatico	H
Endangered Species	G
Garlic Rose	F
Café Havana	J
Joy	C
Kamayan	B
Kashmir	A
Penguin	I
Politixx	E
Verve Room	D

JULIO NAKPIL

Nakpil St. Nightlife

C

D

E F

REMEDIOS

G

12 13 H

J

REMEDIOS CIRCLE

I

Manila Bay

N

Malate Catholic Church

Manila Hospital

0   1 km

tickets and sightseeing tours. Rooms come with air-con, private bath and cable TV, though are somewhat dingy. ⑤.

Makati

El Cielito Inn, 804 Pasay Rd (☎02/815 8951). A small but clean "businessman's hotel" close to Makati's malls. Best to book in advance. ⑤.

Millennium Plaza Hotel, Makati Avenue cor. Eduque Street (☎02/899 4747). A popular hotel at the northern end of Makati Avenue, near P Burgos Street. The *Plaza* has its own coffee shop, and rooms are actually studio apartments. Price includes breakfast. ⑦.

Travelers' Inn Makati, 7880 Makati Ave (☎02/895 7061–70). A clean and comfortable hotel in a good location, managed by a European company. Discount for longer stays. ⑥.

Pensionne Virginia, 816 Pasay Rd (☎02/844 5228 or 843 2546). In a convenient location at the business end of Makati, close to malls and offices. Clean rooms, all with air-con, cable TV, telephone and mini bar. Situated between ACA Video and a branch of the popular bakery, *Goldilocks*. ⑥.

The City

You haven't seen urban sprawl until you've seen Manila. The city seems to get bigger by the day, and to see the major sights you will have to sweat it out in traffic and be prepared for delays. Most visitors base themselves in the bohemian enclave of **Malate**, from where it's a relatively short hop to the fascinating old town of **Intramuros** and **Rizal Park**. Beyond **Chinatown** the gargantuan **Chinese Cemetery** is morbidly interesting, while the business district of **Makati** is a good place to head for shops and yuppie nightlife.

Intramuros

Don't miss a visit to **Intramuros**, the old capital of Manila. It's the one part of the metropolis where you get any real sense of history. It was built in 1571 and remains a monumental, if ruined, relic of the Spanish period in Philippine history. It's a city within a city, separated from the rest of Manila by its crumbling walls. This ancient capital had well-planned streets, plazas, the Governor's Palace, fifteen churches and six monasteries. It also had dozens of cannon that could be used to keep the natives in their place. Many buildings were reduced to rubble in World War II, but Intramuros still lays claim to most of Manila's top tourist sights. **Manila Cathedral**, originally built in 1581, has been destroyed several times down the centuries by a combination of fire, typhoon, earthquake and war. It was last rebuilt between 1954 and 1958. San Agustin Church, with its magnificent baroque interiors and trompe l'oeil murals, dates back to 1599 and is the oldest stone church in the Philippines. It houses a museum of icons and artefacts along with an eighteenth-century Spanish pipe organ that was recently restored. Opposite San Agustin on General Luna Street is the splendid **Casa Manila**, a sympathetically restored colonial-era house (daily 10am–5pm; P50). Next door to Casa Manila is the **Philippine Art, Craft and Cultural Center**, with four floors of antiques, gifts and galleries.

The ruins of **Fort Santiago** stand at the northernmost end of Intramuros, a five-minute walk from the cathedral. Fort Santiago used to be the seat of the colonial powers of both Spain and the US. It was also a dreaded prison under the Spanish regime and the scene of countless military-police atrocities during the Japanese occupation. In the **Rizal Shrine Museum** (daily 8am–10pm; P15) you can see the room where Jose Rizal spent his last hours before his execution on Bagumbayan (now Rizal Park).

Rizal Park

In a city notoriously short on greenery, **Rizal Park** (also known as the Luneta) is everything from early morning jogging circuit to romantic twilight rendezvous for lovers. This was where the colonial-era glitterati use to promenade after church every Sunday. These days, promenading is out and making a fast buck is in. On Sunday afternoons, the park is overrun by hawkers selling everything from balloons to barbecued bananas. Apart from its grassy expanse, the park also has a planetarium, dozens of fountains, an amphitheatre, a children's playground, skating rink and Chinese and Japanese gardens. At the bay end of the park, close to the *Manila Hotel*, is the **Rizal memorial** and Rizal's execution site, where you can walk in his final footsteps – literally – just follow the painted footsteps on the path. At the Taft Avenue end is a gigantic pond with a three-dimensional map of the Philippines.

Makati

Makati was a vast expanse of malarial swampland until the Ayala family, one of the country's most influential business dynasties, started developing it at the turn of the century. It is now Manila's business district and is chock-full of plush hotels, international restaurant chains, expensive condominiums and monolithic air-conditioned malls, containing everything from cinemas and bowling alleys to cacophonous food courts. The main triangle of Makati is bordered by Ayala Avenue, Paseo de Roxas and Makati Avenue, and is where most of the banks, insurance companies and multinational corporations are sited. For sightseers, Makati is something of a wasteland, but for shoppers it's nirvana. The biggest mall by far is **Glorietta**, opposite the Shangri-La Makati. Glorietta heaves with people seeking refuge from the traffic and the heat. All the big brand names are represented, but there aren't many shops with real interest. On the other side of Makati Avenue from Glorietta is **Greenbelt Park** with its pleasant white-domed church. Overlooking the park is the small but interesting **Ayala Museum** (Tues–Sat 8am–6pm; ☎02/812 1191–7), which has a permanent display of Philippine history and rotating exhibitions by artists, photographers and sculptors. It also houses a collection of oils by Amorsolo, the country's most famous painter. Admission is free and there's a nice café and a museum shop. Makati's other main mall is **Greenbelt Mall**, behind the Ayala Museum. It's smaller than Glorietta and has some nice restaurants. The **Filipinas Heritage Library** (☎02/892 1801) on Makati Avenue, opposite *The Peninsula Hotel*, is an interesting little piece of history. It was Manila's first airport. Paseo de Roxas is now where the runway used to be. The library is privately owned (by the Ayalas), but has a bookshop selling Philippine books and a quiet café with Internet access. On the edge of Makati in McKinley Avenue is the **American Cemetery and Memorial** (daily 6.30am–4.30pm; free). The cemetery covers a wide area and contains the largest number of graves of American military dead of World War II, a total of 17,206.

Manila Bay

When Manila was in its heyday **Manila Bay** must have been a sight to behold, with its sweeping panorama across the South China Sea and dreamy sunsets. *Manilenos* still watch sunsets from the harbour wall or the outside bar at the Westin Philippine Plaza, but much of Manila Bay is trading on its romantic past. Its buildings were bombed flat during the war and have been replaced with bulk-standard boxes of poured concrete. Horse-drawn carriages (*calesas*) still tout for business, but the horses look bored and even the palm trees that line Roxas Boulevard are drooping in the face of pollution. A trip along the boulevard heading north from its southern end in Pasay takes you past the *Heritage Hotel* and on towards reclaimed land jutting out into the bay. This is the site of the *Westin Philippine Plaza Hotel*, the Cultural Center of the Philippines and the ruins of Imelda Marcos's infamous Manila Film Center, which she hoped would turn Manila into the Cannes of the east. Construction was rushed to beat tight deadlines and as a result the building collapsed, trapping an unknown number of workers inside. The Marcos government covered up the disaster and continued with the work. Some say bodies are still trapped inside today. A mile or so further on and the US Embassy is on your left followed by Rizal Park on your right. Behind Rizal Park in the Old Congress Building on Padre Burgos Street is the **National Museum** (Mon–Fri 9am–4pm; ☎02/527 1215 or 527 1242; P30), with some dusty but fascinating archeological, botanical and anthropological displays and a priceless selection of Filipino masters, including the renowned *Spolarium* by Juan Luna, an immense oil painting that shows fallen gladiators being dragged from a Roman arena. Another museum in the area is the **Metropolitan**, usually known as the

Met, at the Bangko Sentral ng Pilipinas Complex, Roxas Boulevard (Mon–Sat 10am–6pm; P50). This fine arts museum, a Filipino mini-Guggenheim, also houses the Central Bank's collection of prehistoric jewellery and coins. Roxas Boulevard ends at the *Manila Hotel*, home from home in Manila for the likes of General Douglas MacArthur (who has a suite named after him), Michael Jackson and Bill Clinton.

Ermita and Malate

Two of the city's oldest neighbourhoods, **Ermita and Malate** nestle behind Roxas Boulevard within ten minutes' walk of the Manila Bay seawall. Ermita was infamous up until the late 1980s for its go-go bars and massage parlours until tough guy Mayor Alfredo Lim came along and shut them all down. New bars opened, but the bulk of the tourist trade had moved on and many promptly closed. Ermita is now a ragbag of budget hotels, choked streets and fast-food outlets. A good place to stay it may be, but for anything to see and do you'll have to walk north to Intramuros or east along M Adriatico Street to **J Nakpil Street**, where a lively café society thrives. Indeed, bars have spread like a rash along Nakpil in recent years, and on Friday and Saturday nights this is the place to be seen. Artists, expats, gays and poets all spurn the homogenous air-conditioned yuppiedom of Makati for Nakpil's daring, bohemian hangouts. Don't lose credibility by getting there early. At weekends, things rarely get going before 10pm. There are more cafés and bars in nearby Remedios Circle. A five-minute walk towards the sea from Remedios brings you to the area's major historical site, **Malate Church**, on MH del Pilar Street. British soldiers took refuge inside during Britain's short-lived occupation of the Philippines from 1762 to 1763.

Chinatown

The Chinese and their Chinese-Filipino descendents (known as Chinoys) have found a niche in Philippine society and nowhere is this more apparent than in **Chinatown**, also known as Binondo. It's interesting to wander through the mercantile hubbub of Ongpin Street, past the gold shops and the apothecaries. Urban legend speaks of a special soup you can buy here, enigmatically called Soup Number Five. It is said to cure everything from colds to impotence, but its contents are a mystery. For something Chinese but rather more conventional, try the *mongo hopia* (sweet bean cake) from Eng Bee Tin bakery and deli at 628 Ongpin St. **Binondo Church**, at the west end of Ongpin, is where the first Filipino saint, Lorenzo Ruiz, served as a sacristan. Built in 1614 by Dominicans, it quickly became the hub of the Catholic Chinese community. At the far end of Chinatown, across Rizal Street, you reach the **Quiapo area** and Quiapo Church, where devotees worship the Black Nazarene. Quiapo is a good area for bargain hunters. Several stores that sell handicrafts at local prices are squeezed under Quiapo Bridge, a place known to all Manila's bargain-hunters as *Sa Ilalim ng Tulay* (under the bridge). Outside, the church vendors sell *anting-antings* (amulets). Two kilometres north of Chinatown, a short walk from the JA Santos LRT station, is the impressive **Chinese Cemetery**, established by merchants because the Spanish would not allow foreigners to be buried in Spanish cemeteries. Many of the tombs resemble houses, with fountains, balconies and, in at least one case, a small swimming pool. It has become a sobering joke in the Philippines that this "accommodation" is among the best in the city.

Malacanang Palace

The shoes are gone, but you can still take a tour of the place the President of the Philippines calls home. **Malacanang** was once a stone house, bought by Colonel Luis Miguel Formento in 1802 for the grand sum of P1100. In 1825, the Spanish Government bought it for P5100, and, in 1849, made it the summer residence of the Governor General in the Philippines. Rooms were added and renovations made, but on a number of occasions the building was damaged either by earthquake or typhoon. During the last major renovation in 1978, it underwent extensive interior and exterior changes, and was expanded to its present size. Only a portion now of the basement remains from the original structure. Malacanang will forever be associated with the excesses of the Marcoses. When Cory Aquino became President she didn't want to associate herself with her profligate predecessors and refused to use the palace as a home, keeping it only for official functions. She opened parts of it as a museum for Marcos memorabilia, but when Fidel Ramos took over he severed the Marcos connection and asked that the museum focus only on Philippine presidential history, although the Marcos Room does contain some of the late dictator's personal belongings. Current president Joseph Estrada uses about two-thirds of the palace for his official functions and duties, while the museum takes up about one-third. **Malacanang Museum** (Mon–Fri 9am–3pm; ☎02/733 3721 or 734 7421) is in JP Laurel Street, San Miguel, Manila. A guided tour costs P200 and a non-guided tour P40.

Corregidor

The small tadpole-shaped island of **Corregidor**, which lies in the mouth of Manila Bay and was fought over bitterly during World War II, makes a good day-trip. Sun Cruises (☎02/813 8140, 524 8140 or 524 0333) organizes day-trips from the Cultural Center of the Philippines pier every morning. You can also stay on the island overnight at the *Corregidor Inn*, a former Marcos guesthouse, with a nice restaurant and views towards the Bataan Peninsula. A day-trip package costs P1500 per person and overnight packages start at P1745. It's worth making time for a visit to the **Malinta tunnels**, where General Douglas MacArthur set up temporary headquarters and where vicious hand-to-hand combat took place, a ghostly reminder of the horrors of the war. You can walk on the island's trails, rent mountain bikes or explore the gun batteries. There is also a Japanese cemetery, a museum and a memorial to the thousands who died here.

Eating

Alba, 38-B Polaris St, Makati (☎02/896 6950). Average prices for some of the best Spanish food in Manila.

Barrio Fiesta, Makati Avenue, Makati (☎02/899 4020). There are various branches of this popular and colorful Filipino restaurant dotted around the metropolis, all serving indigenous food such as *adobo* and *lechon* with hefty portions of rice.

Endangered Species, 1834 MH del Pilar, Malate (☎02/524 0167). Fashionable bistro near the *Natividad Pension* serving big portions of continental cuisine at reasonable prices.

Garlic Rose, J Nakpil cor. M Orosa Streets, Malate. Old jazz tunes and the wonderful aroma of fifty dishes, all containing garlic.

Ihaw-Ihaw Kalde Kaldero. You can't go far without seeing the neon lights of this well-known restaurant chain. There's one on Roxas Boulevard and another in Makati Avenue, to name but two. The food is Filipino and the chefs and serving staff give energetic renditions of popular songs. Prices are very reasonable: you'll pay around P250 per person for a good three-course meal.

Kamayan, 532 Padre Faura St, Ermita and 47 Pasay Rd, Makati (☎02/525 1166 or 815 1463). One of the best places for reasonably cheap native Filipino food. The word *kamayan* means "with your hands", which is how you eat, without knife and fork. The staff are dressed in great Filipino costumes and the food ranges from the unorthodox to the delicious. Dudes in shades work the tables singing Spanish ballads and Beatles songs.

Kashmir, Padre Faura Street, Ermita (☎02/524 6851). Long-standing restaurant serving everything from Malaysian and Indonesian to Indian. Some veggie dishes. It's slightly expensive for Manila – P400 a head.

Nightlife and entertainment

Café Adriatico 1900, 1900 M Adriatico St, Malate (☎02/521 6682). A stalwart of the Malate nightlife scene frequented by various trendies throughout the day for coffee and *merienda* (snacks) and in the evening for dinner, drinks and people-watching. 11am–3am.

Conway's, *Shangri-La Makati Hotel*, Makati Avenue, Makati (☎02/813 8888). The most popular happy hour in town, with all-you-can-drink San Miguel for P180 between 6pm and 8pm. 11.30am–1am.

Giraffe, Ground Floor, Ayala Land Building, 6750 Ayala Ave, Makati. Loud music, video screens, expensive drinks and expats on the prowl. *Giraffe* is a horrible cliché, but has nevertheless endured, and on Friday and Saturday nights is still thumping at daybreak. 5pm till late.

Café Havana, 1903 M Adriatico St, Malate (☎02/521 8097). The new kid on the Malate block, and as it's part of the hugely successful LJC Group, is likely to be around for some time. A place to see and be seen. 11am–2am.

In the Mood Dance Bar, 1900 M Adriatico St, Malate (☎02/525 6295). Ballroom dancing is a craze in the Philippines, and this is where you can learn. DIs (dance instructors) are available for a price if you've got two left feet. 11am–1am.

Joy, 1808 Maria Orosa St, Malate. Purple velvet seats, techno music and a tea dance every Sunday at 7pm.

Mondo, The Fort Entertainment Center, Fort Bonifacio (☎02/551 1211). Fort Bonifacio is the raunchy upstart of Metro Manila nightlife, and *Mondo* is one bar among many in the area, ten minutes' walk beyond Makati, near the American Cemetery. 5pm–2am.

Paco Park, San Marcelino Street, Paco. Free Friday night classical concerts at 6pm, performed under the stars in an historic cemetery. Paco Park is just beyond Taft Avenue, twenty minutes by jeepney or taxi from Malate. Rizal Park has similar free concerts every Sunday at 6pm.

Penguin Café and Gallery, 604 Remedios St (☎02/521 2088). Anytime breakfasts for P65, coffee, cocktails, cheap beer and exhibitions and poetry readings to boot. *Penguin* is a senior citizen of Malate. Officially a gay bar, but not really. 11am–3am. Closed Sun.

Politixx, 574 J Nakpil St, Malate. Another of Nakpil's new wave of alternative bars with standup comedy and other live performances throughout the week until the wee hours. 7pm–3am.

Sidebar, 1771 M Adriatico St, Malate. It's the owners' enviable collection of good-taste CDs that brings people to this comfortable and informal little bar in the heart of Malate. If you want to sit back and listen to good sounds over a cold beer, this is your place. The food is wholesome and inexpensive. Happy hour is 5pm to 8pm Monday to Saturday (closed Sunday). 11am–1am. Closed Sun.

Verve Room, 607 J Nakpil St, Malate. Dark, crowded bar that stages offbeat gigs such as poetry readings and serves a cocktail called *calibugan* whose contents are a closely guarded secret. *Calibugan*, roughly translated, means "horniness". 6pm–3am. Closed Sun.

Shopping

There are **shopping malls** everywhere in Metro Manila and hardly anything you can buy in London or New York that you can't buy here, at least as far as chic designer labels and trinkets are concerned. However, the first stop for tourists looking for indigenous gifts and **handicrafts** is usually Balikbayan Handicrafts, which has five branches and sells an inspiring range of products, some to be coveted and some plain bizarre. Native **jewellery**, ethnic carvings and household décor are a bargain. The biggest branch is at 290–298 C Palanca St, Quiapo, with others in Pasay Road, Makati and A Mabini Street, Ermita. There are plenty of other antique and handicraft shops along A Mabini Street, while opposite San Agustin church in Intramuros, is a complex of small art and tribal shops, selling everything from carved rice gods and oil paintings to native basketware and jewellery. For dirt-cheap **clothes** try fighting your way through the crowds at the immense Divisoria Market in CM Recto Street, Binondo. You can hunt down **woodcarvings**, capiz-shell items, buri bags and embroidery under Quezon Bridge in Quiapo. In Baclaran, at the southern tip of Roxas Boulevard, is a flea market selling clothes. Haggling is the operative word in these places. For a small but interesting range of Filipino **books** and environmental videos go to The Filipino Bookstore at G-72, Ground Floor, Glorietta 1, Ayala Center, Makati. On a more prosaic note, **CDs** are excellent value in the Philippines. In Tower Records in Makati new releases cost less than P500. Shops are generally open from 10am until 8pm.

Listings

Airlines Air Ads, Andrews Avenue, Paranaque (☎02/833 3264); Air India, Gammon Center Building, Makati (☎02/815 1280 or 817 5865); Air Philippines, 15th Floor, Multinational Bankcorporation Center, 6805 Ayala Avenue, Makati (☎02/843 7770); American Airlines, Olympia Condominium, Makati (☎02/817 8645); Asian Spirit, LPL Towers, 112 Legaspi St, Makati (☎02/840 3811 to 3816); British Airways, Dela Rosa cor. Legaspi Streets, Legaspi Village, Makati (☎02/817 0361); Canadian Airlines, 168 Salcedo St, Makati (☎02/893 4889); Cathay Pacific, offices in Makati and Manila at 25th Floor Trafalgar Building, Dela Costa Street, Makati (☎02/848 2747) or 2nd Floor Tetra Global Building, 1616 Dr Vasquez cor. Pedro Gil Streets,

Ermita (☎02/525 9367 or 522 3646); Cebu Pacific, Express Ticket Office, Beside Gate 1, Terminal Building 1, Domestic Airport (☎02/636 4938); China Airlines, Ground Floor, Midtown Arcade, M Adriatico Street, Ermita (☎02/523 8021 to 8024); Emirates, Pacific Star Building, Makati Avenue cor. Senator Gil Puyat Avenue, Makati (☎02/811 5278–80); Japan Airlines, Dusit Hotel Nikko, Makati (☎02/812 1591); KLM Royal Dutch Airlines, 160 Alfaro St, Makati (☎02/815 4790); Lufthansa, 134 Legaspi St, Makati (☎02/810 4596); Mindanao Express, 4th Floor, Cargohaus Building, MIA Road, NAIA Complex, Paranaque (☎02/8321541–5); Northwest, Ground Floor, Gedisco Building, 1148 Roxas Blvd (☎02/521 1928 or 819 7341); Philippine Airlines, 24-hour reservations (☎02/855 8888, 816 6691 or 819 1771); Singapore Airlines, 138 HV Dela Costa St, Salcedo Village, Makati (☎02/810 4951 to 4959); Swissair, Zuellig Building, Makati (☎02/818 8351); Thai Airways, Country Space 1 Building, Senator Gil Puyat Avenue, Makati (☎02/817 4044); Qantas, Filipino Merchants Building, Dela Rosa cor. Legaspi Streets, Makati (☎02/812 0607); Vietnam Airlines; Ground Floor, Colonnade Building, 132 Carlos Pelanca St, Makati (☎02/893 7659).

Banks and exchange American Express, Manila Branch, 1810 Mabini St, Malate (☎02/524 8681 or 526 8406); Bank of the Philippine Islands (☎02/818 5541 for details of all branches); Citibank, 8741 Paseo de Roxas, Makati (☎02/813 9177); Hong Kong & Shanghai Banking Corp, Ayala Avenue, Makati (☎02/635 1000); Solidbank, 777 Paseo De Roxas, Makati (☎02/894 8866); Standard Chartered Bank, 6756 Ayala Ave, Makati (☎02/892 0961). Most major bank branches have 24-hour ATMs for Visa and Mastercard cash advances.

Embassies and consulates Australia, Dona Salustiana Building, 104 Paseo de Roxas, Makati (☎02/750 2850); Brunei, 11th Floor, BPI Building, 104 Paseo de Roxas, Makati (☎02/816 2836); Canada, 9–11th Floor, Allied Bank Center, 6754 Ayala Ave, Makati (☎02/867 0001); France, Pacific Star Building, Makati Avenue, Makati (☎02/810 1981); Germany, Solid Bank Building, 777 Paseo de Roxas, Makati (☎02/892 4906); Indonesia, Xanland Center, 152 Amorsolo St, Legaspi Village, Makati (☎02/817 2373); Ireland, Third Floor, 70 Jupiter St, Bel-Air 1, Makati (☎02/896 4668); Laos, 34 Lapu-Lapu St, Magallanes, Makati (☎02/833 5759); Malaysia, 107 Tordesillas St, Salcedo Village, Makati (☎02/817 4581); Myanmar, 4th Floor, Basic Petroleum Condominium, 104 Carlos Palanca Jr St, Legaspi Village, Makati (☎02/817 2373); Netherlands, 9th Floor, King's Court Building, 2129 Pasong Tamo, Makati (☎02/812 5981); New Zealand, 23rd Floor, Far East Bank Center, Sen Gil Puyat Avenue, Makati (☎02/891 5358); Singapore, 6th Floor, ODC International Plaza, 219 Salcedo St, Legaspi Village, Makati (☎02/816 1764); Sweden, PCI Bank Tower II, Makati Avenue cor. Dela Rosa Street, Makati (☎02/819 1951); Switzerland, Solid Bank Building, 777 Paseo de Roxas, Makati (☎02/819 0202); Thailand, Royal Thai Embassy Building, 107 Rada St, Legaspi Village, Makati (☎02/815 4219); UK, 15th–17th Floor, LV Locsin Building 6752 Ayala Ave cor. Makati Avenue, Makati (☎02/816 7116); US, 1201 Roxas Blvd (☎02/523 1001); Vietnam, 554 Vito Cruz St, Malate (☎02/524 0354).

Emergencies The Department of Tourism has two assistance lines (☎02/524 1703 or 524 2384) and two Tourist Hotlines (☎02/524 1728 or 524 1660).

Hospitals and clinics Makati Medical Center, 2 Amorsolo St, Makati (☎02/815 9911), is the largest and one of the most modern hospitals in Manila. It has an emergency department and dozens of specialist clinics. You can't make an appointment for the clinics – you just have to turn up and join the queue. Opening times are 10am–noon and 2–4pm. An initial consultation costs around P350. The HCS Medical Care Center, also in Makati at 3rd Floor, Equitable Bank Building, Senator Gil Puyat Avenue (☎02/897 9111 to 9120), has a rotating team of doctors who deal with ambulant cases. It's a good place to go for basic care and prescriptions, but there are no emergency facilities. A consultation costs P350. In the Manila Bay area, Manila Doctor's Hospital (☎02/524 3011) is at 667 United Nations Ave, and the Medical Center Manila (☎02/523 8131) is at 1122 General Luna St, Ermita.

Immigration Bureau of Immigration and Deportation, Magellanes Drive, Intramuros (☎02/527 3257 or 527 3280). Open 8am–noon & 1–5pm. There is a new Immigration Office in Makati where queues are said to be shorter. It's at 4th Floor, Gotiaco Building, MC Briones Street, opposite Makati City Hall.

Internet access Internet access is increasingly available in Manila and Makati. *Global Café* (☎02/536 8023) is at 3rd Floor, Pedro Gil Wing, Robinson's Place, Ermita. In Makati, the Filipinas Heritage Library in Makati Avenue (☎02/892 1801) charges P100 an hour. Mailstation at 30-A Park Square 1, Ayala Center, Makati (☎02/817 8134 or 817 3135) charges P30 an hour, as do a number of email stations nearby, in the area opposite the Dusit Hotel Nikko.

Pharmacies You are never far from a Mercury Drug outlet in Metro Manila. At the last count there were two hundred of them. In Ermita, there's one at 444 TM Kalaw St and another at the Robinson's Place Complex in M Adriatico. In Makati there's a big branch in Glorietta on the ground floor near Tower Records.

Police Tourist Police, Room 112, Department of Tourism Building, Teodoro Valencia Circle, TM Kalaw Street, Ermita; Western District Police, United Nations Avenue, Ermita.

Post office The closest post office to the Manila Bay area is at Liwasang Bonifacio, Intramuros, near MacArthur Bridge on the Pasig River. The closest LRT station is Central. In Makati, there is a post office at the junction of Senator Gil Puyat and Ayala Avenues, next to Makati Fire Station. Look out also for the numerous Mailstation outlets where you can post letters, make telephone calls and often find email services.

Telephone services Pre-paid PLDT Fonkards are available from 7–11 stores and allow you to make local or international (IDD) calls from PLDT cardphones.

SOUTH OF MANILA AND MINDORO

Leaving the sprawl of Manila behind and heading south takes you along the South Luzon Expressway, known to Filipinos as the South Luzon Distressway, and into the provinces of Cavite, Laguna and Batangas. Traffic heading south can be grim, particularly on weekends and holidays, so try to time your journey for a weekday. **Laguna**, known for hot springs and mountain pools, is the first province south of the capital. It was named after Laguna de Bay, the river that forms its northern boundary and is a major source of sampaguita flowers, orchids, coconuts, rice, sugar, citrus fruits and lanzones. **Cavite** is being touted as a new industrial zone, but will forever be associated with the revolution. In 1872, three Filipino priests – Jose Burgos, Mariano Gomez and Jacinto Zamora – were implicated in the Cavite Revolt, in which two hundred Filipinos rose up in arms against the Spanish forces in the garrisons. The phony revolution was soon cut down, but when the real thing broke out on August 28, 1896, Cavite became a bloody theatre of war, as Emilio Aguinaldo led Cavitenos in a series of daring surprise attacks on Spanish headquarters, soon liberating the whole province. Aguinaldo directed the revolution to its end and the proclamation of the first republic in Asia, the Republic of the Philippines, was made on June 12, 1898 in the small town of Kawit. The town hall where the proclamation was made from a balcony still stands and is the focus of commemoration every June 12. The province of **Batangas** is Manila's weekend playground, with tropical-style beach resorts and **Taal Volcano**. The provincial capital, **Batangas City**, is a polluted port town with little to recommend it except its ferry pier, from where you can escape to the island of **Mindoro** and the beach resorts of **Puerto Galera**.

The best place to get a **bus** from Manila heading south is at one of the many terminals in Pasay. Departures start early, at around 4am and continue at regular intervals until the middle of the evening, with the final departure usually at 8pm. BLTB (on EDSA) and Jam Liner (on Taft Avenue) are two of the most popular services.

Bamboo organ and Sarao jeepney factory

In 1819, the Spanish friar Diego Cera created the world's only organ made from bamboo out of a simple desire to save money. It worked so well that it is still used today, and for a week in February becomes the focal point of the **Las Pinas Bamboo Organ Festival**, which brings together artists from around the world. The organ is in the San Jose Church (Mon–Fri 9–11am & 2–4pm; P10; ☎02/828 1856) in **Las Pinas**, a suburban area about an hour south of Manila depending on traffic. You can reach Las Pinas on buses from Taft Avenue bound for Zapote or Cavite. Ask the conductor to tell you when to get off. It's worth combining a trip to the bamboo organ with a tour of the nearby **Sarao jeepney factory** (tours Mon–Sat 8am–4pm; ☎02/828 1266), on Padre Diego Cerra Avenue, Palanglupa, Las Pinas, about 3km south of San Jose Church. Sarao was one of the first companies to take leftover World War II American jeeps and transmogrify them into the ubiquitous smoke-belching street-art vehicles of today. From San Jose Church it's best to take a jeepney bound for Alabang (20min; P15), from where dozens of buses and jeepneys run back down the South Luzon Expressway to Manila.

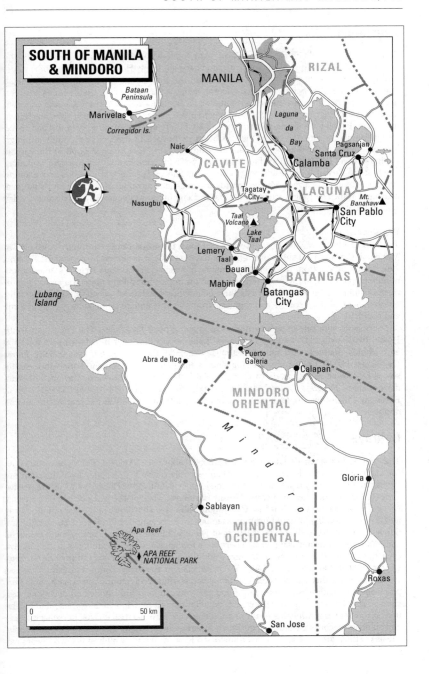

SOUTH OF MANILA & MINDORO

MANILA

RIZAL

Bataan Peninsula

Marivelas

Corregidor Is.

Laguna da Bay

Naic

Pagsanjan

Santa Cruz

CAVITE

Calamba

Tagatay City

LAGUNA

Mt. Banahaw ▲

Nasugbu

San Pablo City

Taal Volcano ▲

Lake Taal

Lemery

Taal

Bauan

BATANGAS

Mabini

Batangas City

Lubang Island

Puerto Galeria

Abra de Ilog

Calapan

MINDORO ORIENTAL

Mindoro

Gloria

Sablayan

MINDORO OCCIDENTAL

Apa Reef

APA REEF NATIONAL PARK ▲

Roxas

0   50 km

San Jose

Pagsanjan Falls

Francis Ford Coppola chose **Pagsanjan**, 80km southeast of Manila, as the location for the final scenes in *Apocalypse Now*. Tourists come here not for its Hollywood memorabilia value, however, but to shoot the fourteen rapids down the Bombongan River from the Magdapio Waterfalls. The local *bangkeros* have become adept at manoeuvering their canoes between the boulders, but have also gained a reputation for being hard-nosed when the time comes to demand a tip. Prices are already rather steep for the seven-kilometre thrill ride, starting at more than P1000 for a single passenger or P580 if there are two or three of you. Tour operators in Manila recently boycotted the falls because they felt charges were too high, although it seems many of them are once again offering day tours that you can book in the capital. Bridges Travel (☎02/867 1186) has a tour for US$55 for a minimum of two people, including lunch at the *Riverside Hotel*. It's best to get to the falls early before the hordes arrive and to avoid weekends if possible. The last rapids trip is usually a couple of hours before sundown, at around 4pm. The rapids are at their most thrilling in the wet season, while during the dry season the ride is much more sedate.

Practicalities
The falls are best reached through the small town of **Santa Cruz**, two hours southeast of Manila on the southern shore of Laguna de Bay. Santa Cruz is served by regular **BLTB and Jam Liner buses** from their Pasay terminals in Manila. From Santa Cruz it's an easy ten-minute jeepney ride to the river, but watch out for touts who will intercept you as you get off the bus and try to guide you towards their boat. Others will offer "special rides" to the falls, but there's no need. Jeepneys run regularly from the little square in the centre of Santa Cruz and cost P10.

There is no shortage of **accommodation** in and around Pagsanjan. The Pagsanjan Youth Hostel (☎049/645 2347; ②), at 237 General Luna St, has basic dorm beds with fan for P150 and singles/doubles with fan. Guesthouses include the simple but clean *Willy Flores Guesthouse* (③), 821 Garcia St, offering singles and doubles with fan and bath. More expensive is *La Corona de Pagsanjan* (☎0912/306 9766; ⑦), on the road towards Cavinti, with standard doubles. *Pagsanjan Falls Lodge and Summer Resort* (☎049/632 7834 or 633 9917; ⑦), in Barangay Pinagsanjan (take a jeepney from General Luna Street) in Pagsanjan, has air-con doubles.

Caliraya

The impressive man-made **Lake Caliraya** is 3050m above sea level and cooler year round than Manila by about eight degrees. The lake can be easily reached by jeepney from the centre of Pagsanjan town (every half hour or when the jeepney is full; P20). The area affords impressive views of **Laguna de Bay** and nearby **Mount Banahaw**, while on the lake you can hire jet-skis, water skis, kayaks and windsurfers. **Pagsanjan Falls** (see above) are only a few minutes away and the neighbouring town of **Lumban** is famous for its beautiful embroidered *barongs*, the traditional Filipino dress shirt. The villagers of Paete sell intricate wood carvings and colourful papier-mâché masks and sculptures. There are a few pensions and guesthouses in the Caliraya area, but the most popular **place to stay** – and the biggest – is the *Lake Caliraya Re-Creation Center* (☎0912/306 0667 or 02/810 9557 in Manila) in Barangay Lewin, Lumban. This is a Christian resort offering "physical, emotional and spiritual recreation". You don't have to be a practising Christian to stay here, but if you are, you can join Bible study and devotional sessions. Cigarettes and alcoholic drinks are not allowed, but to help you take your mind off the unavailability of San Miguel beer there are tennis courts, basketball courts, horseback riding and an obstacle course. P1900 will get you a superior air-con room big enough for four people. Meals cost P95 for breakfast, P135 for lunch and P150 for dinner. Children below 11 years pay half and children below 5 are free. Access to the *Lake Caliraya Re-Creation Center* is from Pagsanjan. Pass through the Pagsanjan Archway and turn left to Lumban, then 500m past Lumban Bridge take the road to your right that goes up the hill to Caliraya Lake. **Jeepneys** from Pagsanjan go to Caliraya every half hour or when they are full (P20).

Tagaytay and Taal Volcano

TAGAYTAY, 70km south of Manila, perches on a 600-metre-high ridge overlooking Taal Volcano, and because of its cool climate – on some days it even gets foggy – is a popular week-end retreat from the heat of the nearby capital. Unfortunately, rash development and abuse of building restrictions have rather turned Tagaytay into the tourist town from hell, with congested roads and menacing shoals of tricycles. Thankfully, you don't actually have to go as far as Tagaytay itself to enjoy spectacular views of the volcano. The views are best if you get off the bus near the *Taal Vista Lodge Hotel*, where you can visit the gardens (free admission) and get a good Filipino buffet lunch. **Taal Volcano** is still active, and there are occasional rumblings that force authorities to issue evacuation warnings to local inhabitants. The volcano last erupted in 1965 without causing major damage, but when it blew its top in 1754, thousands died and the town of Taal was destroyed and had to be moved to a new location on safer ground. The volcano is said to be the smallest active volcano in the world and has the peculiarity of being a lake within an island within a lake within an island: the volcano stands in Lake Taal and in the crater of the volcano is another lake. If you want to climb it, the jumping-off point is the small town of **Talisay** on the shores of Taal Lake. The best way is to hire a boat and guide in Talisay for around P1000. If you make an early start, you can climb to either the new crater or the old crater (both are active) and be back in Talisay in time for a good fish lunch at one of the many native-cuisine restaurants along the shore. There is not much shade on the volcano and it can get hot, so don't go without sunblock, a good hat and plenty of water. You can find out more about Taal Volcano and other volcanoes at the **Taal Volcano Science House**, 5km west of Talisay in **Buco**, next to the *Buco Resort*.

Practicalities

Several BLTB **buses** run daily from Pasay **to Tagaytay** (2hr) on their way to Nasugbu. Hiring a car and driver for the day gives you the flexibility of stopping at one of the pleasant little garden restaurants along the roadside. To get **to Talisay**, take a BLTB bus from Manila marked for Lemery and get off at Tanauan, where you can catch a jeepney at the public market. From Tanauan to Talisay takes thirty minutes along a bumpy road. From Batangas City take a bus marked for Manila, but make sure first that it passes through Tanauan. Alternatively, from Batangas you can take a bus that passes through Tagaytay City, from where there are regular jeepneys to Talisay (40min; P25).

ACCOMMODATION

Villa Adelaide, Foggy Heights, on the main road between Tagaytay City and Talisay (☎046/413 1267). The cheapest rooms are clean and pleasant. There's also a swimming pool and a restaurant. ②.

San Roque Beach Resort, just beyond Talisay on the narrow road to Leynes and close to the shore of Lake Taal (☎046/0918 290 8384). Accommodation is in nipa huts, with room for two or more people. ⑤.

Taal Vista Lodge Hotel, Aguinaldo Highway (☎046/413 1223). A rambling place in a prime position on the ridge. It's a bit on the expensive side, but offers good weekend packages, especially off-peak. As you approach Tagaytay City from Manila it's on your left, overlooking the volcano. ⑦.

EATING AND ENTERTAINMENT

Many Manilenos make the journey from the capital just to have lunch at **Gourmet Café** (Aguinaldo Highway on the left-hand side, 3km before you reach the Tagaytay junction). *Gourmet Café* is a well-known chain of country cottage-style restaurants with outlets in the city, but this one was the first. All the food is organic, produced in a colourful garden. Try also to sample **buko pie**, a delicious coconut pie with crusty pastry that is a speciality of the area and sold by vendors on the ridge above the volcano. The best place to buy hot buko pie is Collette's, a small stall on the road to Talisay. Turn left at the main Tagaytay roundabout and Collette's is 200m on your left.

The Taal area has dozens of other **restaurants**, most of them on the ridge. Sadly, it has also been rather overrun by big chains and fast-food joints. Look out along the ridge for stalls selling *bulalo*, a bone-marrow soup. *Mushroom Burger* is a small roadside restaurant just beyond the *Taal Vista Lodge Hotel* selling – you guessed – burgers made of local mushrooms, which thrive in the cooler climate. Down by the lake shore in Talisay, along Wencislao Road, there are good rustic eateries selling barbecue and fish.

The *Freddie Aguilar Music Lounge and Restaurant* in the Grandview Complex at the Aquino Monument on Tagaytay ridge is owned by the country's most popular singer, the man whose version of *Bayan Ko* ("My Country") became the anti-Marcos anthem in the months leading up to the people power revolution. Freddie still plays there at weekends.

Taal Town

The name Taal is usually associated with the brooding volcano. Most visitors overlook the town of **TAAL** itself, which is a shame because it offers a blast from a glorious past, with faded Spanish colonial architecture, the oldest church in the orient and the house where the first Philippine flag was sewn. The town's *bahay-na-bato* (stone houses) are being preserved by the Taal Heritage Foundation and there's a **Lourdes grotto** with water that is believed to have healing powers. Apart from being the oldest church in the orient, the **Basilica of St Martin de Tours** is also said to be the biggest. The original was built in 1575, but destroyed by volcanic eruption in 1754. The present church was built in 1856 and inaugurated by Augustinian friars in 1865. It has been made a national shrine by Presidential decree. The **market** in Taal is a good place to look for local embroidery. The area is also well known for the manufacture of deadly fan knives.

If you want to **stay** overnight, you could do worse than *Casa Punzalan* (⑤), a pension house in the town square. The Taal Heritage Foundation (☎043/421 1053 or 421 3034) can put you in touch with homestays. From Manila a number of **buses** (BLTB, Tri Tran and Jam) ply the Manila-Taal-Lemery route (P80). From Tagaytay you can catch buses marked for Lemery and get off in Taal. You can also catch jeepneys at the main intersection in Tagaytay City (P15). From Batangas City buses to Manila sometimes pass through Taal, but check first.

Calamba

The small town of **CALAMBA**, built in Spanish colonial style, with a pleasant square in front of a town hall and a church, is at the end of the South Luzon Expressway, about an hour from the southern outskirts of Manila. Its main attraction – in fact its only attraction – is that it was the birthplace on 19 June 1861 of national hero **Jose Rizal**. The house he was born in is a typical nineteenth-century Philippine family home, with floors of narra wood and windows made from capiz shell. It has now been turned into a memorial and museum (Tues–Sun 8am–noon & 1–5pm; P20). Many of Rizal's old belongings are here, including the clothes he was christened in and a suit he wore as a young man. It's incredible to see from his clothes how diminutive he was: a little over five feet. To **get to Calamba** from Manila catch a BLTB bus in Pasay marked for Santa Cruz. From Batangas City some buses going back to Manila pass through Calamba. From Pagsanjan, Manila-bound buses take an hour to reach Calamba.

Laguna hot springs

The area of **Laguna** around Los Banos is famous for **hot springs** and there are a number of resorts that have springs you can bathe in. Most are on the main road between Calamba and

Los Banos. Jeepneys from Calamba (P10–20) head out here from the main square. Many of the resorts have simple accommodation in nipa huts. *Los Banos Lodge and Hot Springs* (☎049/536 0498; ③) is one of the most popular and can get busy at weekends with stressed-out workers from the capital. A bit more upmarket, the *Lakeview Resort Hotel* (☎049/536 0101; ⑦), just outside Los Banos at 728 Lopez St, has air-con rooms with shower. The resorts are easily reached by jeepney or tricycle from the square at Calamba, about twenty minutes' ride away.

Los Banos

LOS BANOS, just south of Calamba heading away from Manila on the South Luzon Expressway, is home to the University of the Philippines Los Banos (UPLB), the forestry campus of the Manila-based university. The campus lies at the foot of **Mount Makiling**. The **rainforest** in this area is unspoiled and there are some nice walking trails. There are a number of other attractions on the campus, including the International Rice Research Institute, which was established to help farmers in developing countries grow more rice on limited land with less water and labour, fewer chemicals, and with less harm to the environment. The IRRI is home to the excellent **Riceworld museum** (Mon–Fri 8am–noon & 1–5pm; ☎049/536 2701), which opened in 1994 with grants from the German government and which gets around 120,000 visitors a year, including heads of state, scientists and schoolchildren. Highlights include a Japanese sculpture of wild rice, microscope viewing of insects, rice products, wild rices, high yielding rice varieties and old implements and clothing. Guided tours are available and if you call in advance you can ask for a short slideshow called *Filling the World's Rice Bowl*. Another museum worth making time for is the **UPLB Museum of Natural History** (Mon–Sat 8am–5pm; P10; ☎049 536 2864), which has more than 200,000 biological specimens of Philippine plants, animals and microorganisms. Sunday visits are possible if you call first.

To **get to the University of Los Banos** take a BLTB bus from Pasay in Manila (90min; P60). Buses are marked for Santa Cruz and the conductor will tell you where to get off. From Calamba take a jeepney from the main square (P15). From Pagsanjan buses going to Manila go through Los Banos (1hr).

Mount Makiling

The dormant volcano of **Mount Makiling** is in Laguna province, half an hour south of Calamba by jeepney or bus. It reaches 1110m and is notable for its unusual shape, rather like a reclining woman. The mountain is named after Mariang Makiling (Mary of Makiling), a young woman whose spirit is said to protect the mountain. On quiet nights, she is said to play music on a harp. Tribespeople say they rarely hear the music any more and believe it is because Makiling is angry about the scant regard paid to the environment by authorities. Mount Makiling is the source of the famous Los Banos hot springs. It has a well established trail, but climbing it alone is not recommended. You can join groups at the nearby University of Los Banos or you can hire a guide, also at the university. The climb to the top can be strenuous because the upper slopes are covered in jungle. To **get to Makiling** from Calamba take a bus or jeepney from the main square heading south (P15). From the university campus take a jeepney marked for the Scout Jamboree Park.

San Pablo

In ancient times, **SAN PABLO**, in Laguna, was known as Sampalok, a large and prospering hamlet in the town of Bay Laguna where sampaloc (tamarind) trees grew in abundance. It was originally inhabited by Aetas, Dumagats and Muslims who migrated from Mindanao.

These days, it is known as the City of Seven Lakes and is a good area for hiking. A five-minute jeepney ride (P15) north of the city lies the largest of the lakes, **Lake Sampalok**, which you can circumnavigate in a few hours. There are floating restaurants along the shore that serve native freshwater fish such as tilapia, bangus, carp and several species of shrimp. The other lakes all lie to the northeast, between San Pablo proper and Rizal. They are Lake Bunot, Lake Calibato, Lake Yambo, Lake Pandin, Lake Palakpakin and Lake Mohicap.

There are plenty of reasonably priced **resorts** in the area. Choose from *Cresta Monte Resort and Countryside Spring Resort* in Barangay Santo Angel, *Star Lake Resort* in Barangay San Buenaventura, *Bato Spring* in Barangay San Cristobal, and dozens of others. These resorts are on the road south of San Pablo heading towards Tiaong and can be reached by jeepney or bus from Lopez Avenue, San Pablo. Most have their own hot springs. Further down the road to Tiaong is *Villa Escudero* (⑦), a former coconut plantation, where you can rent cottages; the price includes all meals. Reservations for Villa Escudero are best made in Manila (☎560/523 2944). The *Tierra De Oro Resort-Hotel* (②), on the Maharlika Highway south of San Pablo, has excellent quad cottages and tree houses for six people, set in expansive tropical gardens. From the BLTB terminal in Pasay, Manila, **buses** leave every hour for San Pablo. There are numerous jeepneys from Los Banos to San Pablo, but only a limited number from Pagsanjan (2hr).

Mount Banahaw

About 130km southeast of Manila, near Dolorez in Quezon province, is 2188-meter Mount Banahaw. Considered a sacred mountain, Banahaw has spawned so many legends and superstitions you would need a lifetime to hear them all. One says that every time a foreigner sets foot on the mountain it will rain. Seventeen religious sects with different beliefs and rituals endow the mountain with mystic qualities. Every year at Easter, thousands of pilgrims flock to the mountain. If you want to climb Banahaw, you can take a jeepney from the town of San Pablo to the jump-off point at Santa Lucia, near Kinabuhayan town. Treat this mountain seriously because although the early part of the trail looks wide and well-trodden it soon peters out into inhospitable rainforest. Even experienced climbers allow three days to reach the summit and get back down safely. You will need to hire a guide in Santa Lucia and sign a logbook before you are allowed to proceed. If you haven't got time to reach the summit you can trek to **Kristalino Falls** (Crystalline Falls) and back in a day. One-and-a-half hours further is a second waterfall, whose surroundings are ideal for a campsite.

Batangas beach resorts

For many hardworking city-dwellers first stop at the weekends is one of the many **beach resorts in Batangas**. In truth, the beaches are nothing to write home about, but they are at least relatively close to Manila. Three hours after leaving the smoke you can be breaking out the suntan oil. When travelling to the beach resorts of Batangas you have two areas to choose from. You can take a bus (BLTB, hourly departures from Pasay terminal) to **NASUGBU** on the west coast. The road that runs north and south through Nasugbu is lined with resorts so the best thing to do is take a jeepney south from Nasugbu and get off where you feel like it. North of Nasugbu the pleasant **White Sands beach** is also home to numerous small resorts. The other area of Batangas province with sea and sand is **ANILAO**, further south, which you reach by taking a bus (BLTB) for Batangas City but asking to be let off at the stop for Bauan. From here you can take a jeepney to the pretty little barrio of **Mabini**, after which you will see dozens of rickety bamboo resorts along the shore. A few kilometres beyond these cheaper resorts and accessible by jeepney are a number of more upmarket ones such as *Aquaventure Reef Club*.

Nasugbu area accommodation

Coral Beach Club, on the main beach in Nasugbu (☎0912/318 4868). A quiet, attractive place with a beachside pool and air-con rooms or deluxe air-con. It claims its white beach is the closest to Manila. ⑥–⑦.

Freddie Reyes Beach Resort, next door to *Maryland*. Has air-con doubles with shower. ⑦.

Maryland Beach Resort, on the coastal road in Nasugbu. Has double cottages and more expensive air-con rooms, a large swimming pool and its own restaurant. ⑥–⑦.

Matabungkay Beach Club (☎043/750 1459). Has basic but clean rooms, some of which are big enough for families and have large balconies. There's a pleasant native-style restaurant and a swimming pool. Take a jeepney from Nasugbu heading south (20 mins; P20). ⑥.

Maya-Maya Reef Resort, north of Nasugbu town. Cottages (for four people) with fan or air-con and bath. You can reach it by jeepney or tricycle from outside Nusugbu's town hall. ⑦.

Swiss House Hotel, Matabungkay. A popular weekend getaway for expats. It's twenty minutes south of Nasugbu by jeepney. ④.

White Sands Beach Resort, Muntingbuhangin Cove, 4km north of Nasugbu by boat or tricycle. Cottages with showers. ⑤.

Anilao area accommodation

Anilao Seasport Center (☎043/807 4570 or 807 4574) has a range of accommodation from doubles sharing verandah rooms to family rooms for five people. ⑥–⑦.

Aquaventure Reef Club. Operated by Manila-based dive outfit Aquaventure (☎02/899 2831) and while it's primarily a scuba resort it also offers island-hopping and snorkelling trips in hired bancas. Buffet-style meals are served in a nice open restaurant overlooking the sea. Double rooms come with fan and bath. ⑥.

Dinky Little Dive Camp, Anilao. The first of many small resorts on the road to Anilao. A good budget base for exploring the coast and perhaps doing some island- or beach-hopping. A cosy lodge has three guest rooms with showers, while meals are served on a veranda overlooking the sea. ⑥.

El Pinoy Dive Inn, on the same main drag as most of the Anilao resorts, a few kilometres past Mabini. It has private detached cottages and deluxe rooms with their own bath, or economy rooms with 2, 3 or 4 beds, with shared facilities. ⑥.

Batangas City

BATANGAS CITY (as opposed to Batangas province) is a transit point for tourists on their way to Puerto Galera. As a destination in its own right it has nothing to offer. As an industrial city there are signs that it is springing into life, with a new pier and talk of numerous industrial zones. If you get stuck overnight in Batangas you can take your pick from a number of poorly-maintained flophouses or you can try the relatively superior *Avenue Pension House* (☎043/725 3720; ③) at 30 JP Rizal Avenue. If you have cash to spare there is a new *Days Inn* (☎043/723 6931 36; ⑦) on the outskirts of the city, fifteen minutes from the pier. BLTB Buses to Batangas City leave from Pasay starting at 5.30am (3hr; P75). They go first to the ferry pier (for Puerto Galera) and then to the terminal in JP Rizal Avenue, near the cathedral. On the way back from Puerto Galera there are numerous buses waiting at the pier for the trip to Manila. Try to take a direct bus marked for Pasay. Some buses go through the barrios, making it a long journey.

Puerto Galera

It may be touristy and the hawkers can wear you down, but there's no denying **PUERTO GALERA** on the northern coast of **Mindoro** has a stunning natural harbour, some quiet coves, cheap accommodation and excellent **scuba diving**. There are dozens of dive outfits in the area making it a good place to strike a deal and get yourself a discount on the going rates. The point of arrival is officially known as Poblacion, though most people refer to it and the surrounding areas as Puerto Galera. From the harbour jeepneys depart for the area's many beaches. **Sabang** is the busiest beach, with a mind-boggling variety of accommodation dotted haphazardly along the shoreline and plenty of choices for eating. Neighbouring **Small La Laguna** and **Big La Laguna** are rather more laid-back and family-oriented. Twenty minutes

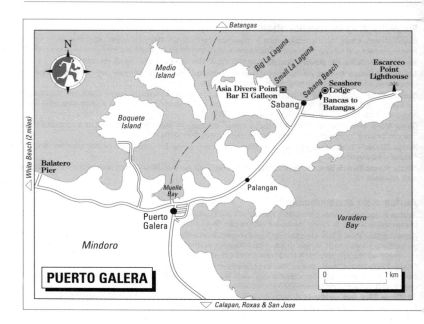

by jeepney the other side of Puerto Galera harbour, to the east, is **White beach**. Accommodation here is strictly of the bamboo-hut variety and for meals you'll have to eat what you are given: it might be catch of the day or a tin of sardines. Five minutes beyond White beach by jeepney is **Talipanan beach**. Both are good bases for **trekking** in the mountains. One of the many locals who earn a little bit extra as guides will gladly take you to Talipanan or Aninuan falls.

Access to Puerto Galera is from **Batangas Pier** on the outskirts of Batangas City. BLTB, Jam and Tritrans **buses** (P80) run regularly from Pasay in Manila to Batangas Pier. Try to avoid travelling on a Saturday morning when city folk are all scrambling to get to the coast and the roads can be choked. Likewise, it's best not to make the return journey on Sunday evening. Once you get to Batangas Pier there are a number of **ferry** options. *MV Super 85* leaves at 10.30am and Si-Kat at midday. Both charge P110 plus P10 terminal fee. Local outriggers (P80) go back and forth to Sabang, leaving Batangas Pier daily at 9.30am, 10.30am, 11.30am, noon, 1.30pm and 2.30pm. Si-Kat operates a joint bus-and-ferry service (P350 one way) that leaves every morning at 9am sharp from the *Centrepoint Hotel* at 1430 A Mabini St, Ermita. The *Royal Palm Hotel* in Ermita has recently launched a rival service (☎02/526 2566 or 521 2814; P695 round-trip) leaving the hotel daily at 8am. Travel time from Manila to Batangas Pier is about three hours by road, then another ninety minutes by boat.

If you take the Si-Kat or the *MV Super 85* you will land at Muelle Pier in Puerto Galera, from where you can hop a jeepney or a small banca to one of the beaches. Jeepneys charge P10 to Sabang and P30 to White beach, but only leave when they are full, meaning packed to the gills with people, baggage, produce and farm animals. It's not unusual on these routes for passengers to be hanging from the sides or sitting on the roof. The jeepney to Sabang no longer departs from the pier itself, so you have to walk up the hill to the left for about 150m.

All boats are met by a welcoming committee of touts offering "special rides" for P200. A banca to Sabang will cost around P150 depending on your negotiating skills. White beach is further and will cost around P200. You can always share the boat with others. On the return journey, the *MV Super 85* leaves Muelle Pier at 8am and the Si-Kat at 9.30am. Outriggers including *Sabang Princess* leave Sabang beach (in front of the *Sunshine Coast Bar and Restaurant*) at 6am, 7am, 8am, 9am and 11.30am. Viva Lines has sailings at 5am, 10.30am and 2pm from Balatero Pier, which is on the eastern outskirts of Puerto Galera town. There are no longer any flights from Manila to northern Mindoro, although if you are feeling flush you can hire a seaplane for US$300 one-way. Call *Atlantis Resort Hotel* in Sabang (☎639/7349 7503) for details. There are also a number of ferries between Batangas and Puerto Galera operated by Blue Diamond Lines. Be careful with these, as they are claustrophobic and often overcrowded.

The **post office** is at the town hall in Puerto Galera, although some resorts will post mail for a charge. There are rudimentary **clinics** in the town, but no hospital. Clinics charge P80 for a consultation, but if in doubt you can always ask the dive shops, who always know where the best doctors are. There are many **telephone stations** in Sabang and Puerto Galera where you can make calls to Manila for P12 a minute or overseas for P130 a minute. Swagman Travel at the western end of Sabang beach offers **exchange**, fax, phone, visa extension and air tickets. Exchange and telephone services are also offered by *Centrum* in Sabang; this used to be a go-go bar until the owner became vice-mayor, and now hosts regular live bands from Manila. To arrange **trekking**, kayaking tours or overnight trips into the tribal hinterland, go to Jungle Trek Adventure Tours opposite *Tropicana* on Sabang's main drag. Motorbikes can be hired at a number of places for around P500 for half a day. Telephones in Puerto Galera are all cellular and there are no landlines, making **Internet** access tricky. Asia Divers lets guests use its email for important messages.

Accommodation

Basic **accommodation** starts from P300 and consists of a small hut with a cramped shower, probably with not much of a view. For something with a balcony overlooking the sea you will pay from P400 upwards.

SABANG

Angelyn Beach Resort, right on the beach at Sabang (☎0912/306 5332 or 043/442 0038). Has double cottages with fan and shower or air-con cottages with comfy sofas on the balcony. There's a small open-air restaurant and a beauty parlour. ③–④.

Gold Coast, close to *Sabang Inn*. Has nice second-storey rooms with shady balconies. ③.

Sabang Inn. At the quieter eastern end of the beach. Has new rooms with refrigerator, air-con or fan. From the main junction in Sabang face the sea and walk to your right. ④.

Seashore Lodge. Almost at the far eastern end of the beach, a five-minute walk from the main road. It has large, airy nipa huts on the beach, most with balconies. ③.

SMALL LA LAGUNA

El Galleon Beach Resort (☎639/7378 2094). One of the nicest places in the area, with tropical-style bamboo rooms and a breezy little restaurant right on its own patch of beach. Next door is the Asia Divers shop and above it a popular bar called the *Point* which is open until midnight and serves some interesting cocktails. From the main road in Sabang it's a ten-minute walk along the beach to the west. ⑤–⑥.

Nick and Sonia's Cottages, at the center of Small La Laguna. Nipa huts with their own cooking facilities and a fridge. ③.

Portofino Beach Resort (☎639/7377 6704). A Mediterranean-style complex with various units ranging from a studio to a two-bedroom apartment overlooking the beach. ⑦–⑨.

Roelyn's Inn, just past *El Galleon*. Has doubles set back from the beach and a small restaurant, which is open until 2am. ③.

BIG LA LAGUNA

El Oro, about half way along the beach (☎0912/306 6642). Offers the usual range of clean but basic nipa huts, either with or without a verandah. The restaurant has a pool table and is open till 11pm. ③.

Paradise Lodge Has standard doubles, and like most places offers discounts for longer stays. ④.

WHITE BEACH

Don't let the touts tie you down. They will try to lead you to their own accommodation but take your time and shop around for the cleanest rooms at the best price. **White beach** is a nice spot for extended R&R, so for longer stays negotiate a discount. *Summer Connection* (④) has cottages with a fan. *White Beach Lodge* (③) and *Pension Natividad* (③) have both been around a long time and have small restaurants attached where you can get food, coffee and beer.

Eating

If you're not sure what to **eat** in PG, eat fish: it comes straight from the sea and is guaranteed fresh. The *Relax Thai Restaurant* in Sabang does brisk business with its P145 Thai curries and lighted joss-stick atmosphere. The *Galley* at *El Galleon* serves Filipino and foreign dishes and bakes its own bread. For tropical charm right on the water try *Tamarind Restaurant* in Sabang where the food fluctuates in quality but the view is wonderful. Opposite *Tamarind* is *Ristorante da Franco* which is part of the *Atlantis Resort Hotel* and does brisk business. On the main road as you come into Sabang is *Tropicana*, a two-storey bamboo edifice which has an eclectic menu but is particularly known for its pizzas. For something exceedingly different, the *Sunshine Coast Bar and Restaurant* (turn right at the main junction and walk for two minutes) has a Feeling Shitty Breakfast (P100) consisting of coffee, Coke, two cigarettes, cornflakes and fresh fruit.

Calapan, Roxas and San Jose

From Poblacion in Puerto Galera it is possible to take a series of jeepneys clockwise around the coast of Mindoro to **Calapan** and onwards to the uninspiring town of **Roxas**, where you can catch cheap local ferries to **Boracay**. The first stage of the journey clockwise is from Poblacion to the coastal town of Calapan, capital of Mindoro Oriental. In Calapan you can stay at the *Traveller's Inn* (②) on Leuterio Street, before taking another jeepney (4hr) to Roxas. It is also possible to do this stage of the journey by bus. One of the few places to stay in Roxas itself is the *Santo Nino Hotel* (②). Further still, is the town of **SAN JOSE**, which also acts as a staging post for ferries to Boracay. The San Jose bus terminal is in Rizal Street and ferries for Boracay leave from the North Pier, a short jeepney ride across the Pandururan River. The main attraction of San Jose is that it is close to **Apo Reef**, a popular **diving spot**. You can rent boats to take you to small islands such as Ambulong or Ilin for **snorkelling**. A good place to organize diving is the *Mina de Oro Beach Resort* (⑦), on Illin. Back in San Jose, the best place to stay is *Sikatuna Beach Hotel* (②), on Airport Road, just north of San Jose, while the *Sikana Town Hotel* (②), on Sikatuna Street, is decent enough.

The journey **anti-clockwise from Puerto Galera** has interesting possibilities. You can hire a banca for about P1500 to take you west along the coast of Mindoro to the village of **Abra de Ilog**. From there jeepneys run south to **Sablayan** where you can catch a water taxi to *Pandan Island Resort* (⑤–⑥), which has budget rooms and deluxe bungalows. The resort runs dive trips to Apo Reef.

NORTHWEST OF MANILA

The provinces of Luzon that lie immediately **northwest of Manila** are so diverse in geographical character that you can go in a day from the volcanic landscape of coastal **Zambales** to the tropical beaches and islands of the **Lingayen Gulf**. The spurs of the **Caraballo Mountains** lie in the east, in Bulacan, the first province you reach travelling north from the capital, and in the west are the fertile lowlands of **Pampanga**, where much of the country's rice and mangoes are produced. Life in this area – known officially as Central Luzon, or Region III – is far from sophisticated, and the kind of upmarket resorts found in the Visayas are conspicuous by their absence. Major attractions include **Mount Pinatubo**, **One Hundred Islands**, and the unspoiled **beaches** of the Luzon west coast.

There's only one way to get out of Manila heading north and that's on the North Luzon Expressway, which starts in the suburb of Cubao and runs north through the provinces of Bulacan and Pampanga. Victory Liner and Philippine Rabbit have dozens of departures daily for all points north of Manila, including Angeles, Dau (for Clark) and Lingayen (for One Hundred islands).

San Fernando

SAN FERNANDO, 50km north of Manila and the capital of Pampanga province, is best known for its controversial **crucifixion of flagellants**. Every year on Good Friday a dozen or so penitents – mostly men but with the occasional woman and sometimes even the odd foreigner – are taken to a rice field in the barrio of San Pedro Cutud, 3km from San Fernando, and nailed to a cross using two-inch stainless steel nails that have been soaked in alcohol to disinfect them. The penitents are taken down seconds later. Other penitents flagellate themselves using bamboo sticks tied to a rope. The blood is real, but the motivation is questionable. The Catholic Church does not approve of the crucifixions and does not endorse them. The media has also turned against the rites, calling them pagan and barbaric but generally admitting they are still a good show. Whatever your opinion, the crucifixions fascinate tourists and social voyeurs.

Bus terminals in Manila are closed on Good Friday, so you'll have to travel to San Fernando the night before. Victory Liner buses leave every hour (P80) from Pasay (see "Moving on from Manila" box on pp.692-693). Make sure you don't confuse San Fernando in Pampanga with San Fernando in La Union, further north. Most buses travel up the North Luzon Expressway and exit at Paskuhan Vilage, a tourist village that sells native handicrafts. Paskuhan is also the site of the **tourist office** (☎045/961 2665) and you can ask the bus driver to let you get off here. San Fernando proper is five minutes away by road and you can reach it by jeepney from Paskuhan (P15). Regular jeepneys connect San Fernando with its northern neighbours of Angeles (15min; P12.50) and Clark (25min; P22).

There is a dearth of good **places to stay** in San Fernando. The best option is *Pampanga Lodge* (①), opposite the church, which has simple fan doubles. Most travellers, however, opt to spend the night in nearby Clark, where there's a much wider choice of rooms. San Fernando's main drag is lined with **fast-food restaurants**.

Angeles

The city of **ANGELES**, a few kilometres north of San Fernando along MacArthur Highway, is a disaster of poor town planning and chaotic traffic, and has little to recommend it, beyond making a handy stop-off point on the way to Clark. The centre of the city is huddled around Henson Sreet, which you reach by turning west off the MacArthur Highway at the busy junction of San Ignacio Street and Angeles Avenue. The Philippine Rabbit bus terminal is at the southern end of Henson Street, close to Mercury Drug Store and PCI Bank. There are a number of other **banks** on Santo Rosario Street and there are two **hospitals**, Saint Catherine's and the Angeles Medical Center, on Rizal Street. Angeles City **post office** is on MacArthur Highway, just north of the city centre. **Jeepneys to Clark** leave from Rizal Street near the market and cost P18.

Clark

Some 70km north of Manila, **CLARK**, formerly the site of an American air base, is popular with visitors for its proximity to the volcanic mountains of **Pinatubo and Arayat**. In 1991,

Clark Air Base became the subject of one of the hottest political debates ever to rage in the Philippines. Many Filipinos, enjoying an era of new nationalism in the wake of the downfall of the Marcos regime, saw no reason for the Philippines, however poor, to depend on the world's greatest superpower for its defence. Senators agreed and voted to end the US Air Force's lease on Clark Air Base. America's undignified departure from the Philippines was hastened somewhat by the catastrophic eruption of Mount Pinatubo, which showered the base in ash. The greatest concern over the withdrawal of 20,000 US air force personnel from the area was the potentially devastating effect it might have on the economy. A decision was taken to turn the base – which is roughly as big as Singapore – into a special economic zone (SEZ) with incentives for companies setting up shop there. The scheme has been a qualified success, with 156 national and international companies taking up the offer. Plans to open a new international airport and high-speed railway links with Manila are, however, like many things in the Philippines, taking a long time to come to fruition.

Inside the former base, there are a number of (expensive) golf courses, one hotel and a few restaurants. The area alongside the base, including Field's Avenue and Don Juico Avenue, is famous for another legacy of the American tenancy, go-go bars. Prostitution is rife in these bars, with many male visitors flying in from Europe for one thing only. Besides climbing mounts Pinatubo and Arayat, there are an increasing number of other activities in and around Clark, including mountain biking, trekking, microlight flying and parachuting. The Tropical Asia Parachute Center at 940 Field's Avenue has been operating at Clark since 1996 and does courses for US$240. For details of a trial microlight flight with an instructor, call the Lite-Flite Flying Club (☎045/599 2120). A flight over Mount Pinatubo's lower slopes costs P600.

Practicalities

The nearest **bus station** is at **Dau**, served by hourly Victory Liner buses from Manila (P80 one-way). From the bus station in Dau you can take a tricycle for the few minutes ride to Field's Avenue or Don Juico Avenue. P30 is a reasonable fare, although some drivers demand P50. Swagman Travel at 411 A Flores St, Ermita (☎02/524 5816), operates buses from the *Centerpoint Hotel* in A Mabini Street, Malate at 7pm and 8pm every day. Return trips depart from the *Premier Hotel* on Don Juico Avenue. The fare is P300 one-way. The main **jeepney station** in Clark is at the MacArthur Highway end of Field's Avenue. You can catch jeepneys from here to the air base and also to Angeles, Pinatubo, Arayat and San Fernando.

Most of the bars, restaurants and tourist facilities in Clark are on Field's Avenue, which turns into Don Juico Avenue. There are dozens of moneychangers on Field's Avenue and there are **banks** on the nearby MacArthur Highway. At the City Airport Terminal (which is no longer an airport terminal), on Field's Avenue, there are convenience stores, ticketing offices and tour operators. *Edelweiss Restaurant*, at 412 21st Sreet (entrance on Fields Avenue), Josefa Subdivision, Barangay Malabanias, Angeles City (☎045/522 3955), acts as a de facto **tourist centre**, offering tour bookings, airline bookings and visa extension services. There is an **Immigration Office** on 7th Street in Dau where you can get your visa extended. Many hotels and tour operators will organize this for you for a fee.

ACCOMMODATION

For comfortable **rooms** in a quiet family home, take a jeepney (P2.50) along Don Juico Avenue to *La Casa Pension* at 511 Tamarind St, Clarkview Subdivision (☎045 322 7984; ②). All rooms have a private bath or shower. There is food next door in the *Blue Boar Inn*, which is owned by the same couple, former US Air Force officer Jim Dale and wife Vina Balala-Dale.

More upmarket choices include the *America Hotel* (☎045/332 1023; ④–⑨), with big, clean rooms ranging from deluxe doubles to a suite with its own whirlpool bath. The *Orchid Inn* (☎045/332 0370; ④–⑤) and *Park Chicago Hotel* (☎045 892 0390; ④–⑤) are both in the busy bar area at the northern end of Don Juico Avenue. The *Clarkton Hotel* (☎045/322 3424; ⑥), further along Don Juico Avenue, away from the hustle and bustle, has a nice swimming pool and a popular bar. The peaceful and secluded *Woodland Park Resort* (☎045/892 1002; ⑤), at Kilometer 87, MacArthur Highway, Dau, five minutes from the bus station by tricycle, offers 54 rooms, a large swimming pool and a restaurant and bar.

If you want the five-star treatment, the only place to stay is the *Holiday Inn Resort Clark Field* (☎045/599 8000; ⑨), which is inside the former US base and has a swimming pool, restaurants and bars.

EATING

Cottage Kitchen Café, 352 Don Juico Ave, Clark View (☎045 322 3366), is owned by a former US Air Force officer and has delicious Creole and Cajun dishes. At the eastern end of Don Juico Avenue, close to where it joins the MacArthur Highway, is the *Jerusalem Restaurant* serving Middle Eastern specialities at reasonable prices. A few hundred yards further along Don Juico on the opposite side of the road, the popular *Salvatore's* (☎045 332 3340) specializes in pizza. In the same area, the trendy *Culture Shack Gallery Café* (☎045/322 2224) was founded by a group of local artists and features live bands, poetry readings and native arte-facts for sale. For home-style Kapampangan food such as *sisig* (pork cheek), *buro* (fermented rice with small shrimps) and *kamaru* (mole crickets sautéed in garlic and onion, then roasted to a crunch) try *Bahay Kubo* (☎045/599 2880) in Acacia Drive, Mimosa Leisure Estate, a short walk from the *Holiday Inn Resort*. Also on the Mimosa Leisure Estate, in Mahogony Drive, is *The Red Crab* (☎045 599 6213), which, as the name suggests, specializes in crab dishes. A popular meeting place for travellers is *Kokomo's*, at the eastern end of Field's Avenue close to its junction with the MacArthur Highway (☎045/892 0509); it offers just about everything a traveller could need, from food and drink to laundry, ticket reservations, tour bookings, moneychanging and email.

Mount Pinatubo

On April 2, 1991, people from the village of Patal Pinto on the lower slopes of **Mount Pinatubo** saw small explosions followed by steaming and the smell of rotten eggs coming from the upper slopes of the supposedly dormant volcano, whose last known eruption was 600 years ago. The Philippine Institute of Volcanology and Seismology (PHIVOLCS) imme-diately installed portable seismometers near the mountain and began recording several hun-dred earthquakes a day. US Geological Survey personnel arrived in the area on April 23. All signals indicated that magma was rising within the volcano and that an eruption was likely. No-one knew quite how big it would be. On June 12, the first of several major explosions took place. The eruption was so violent that shockwaves could be felt in the Visayas. Nearly 20 mil-lion tons of sulfur dioxide gas were blasted into the atmosphere, causing red skies to appear for months after the eruption. A giant ash cloud rose 35km into the sky and red hot blasts seared the countryside. Ash paralyzed Manila, closing the airport for days and turning the capital's streets into an eerie grey post-apocalyptic landscape. Particles from the eruption landed as far away as the United States. By June 16, when the dust had settled, the top of the volcano was gone, replaced by a 2km-wide caldera containing a lake. Lava deposits had filled valleys, buildings had collapsed and 350 people were dead.

Pinatubo is quiet once again, except for tourist activity. **Jeepneys from Clark** to the foothills of Mount Pinatubo take around thirty minutes. It's a hard 1485-metre climb to the crater, through baking valleys of volcanic rock and ash, but you can always limit yourself to a walk through the surreal moonscape of the lower slopes. It takes two days and one night to get to the crater and back. **Tour companies** like Trent Transport (☎045/332 1712) at 222 Field's Avenue, Clark, charge P3500 per person for a package that includes tents, food, guides and transport to the jumping-off point, about thirty minutes from Field's Avenue. One-day crater tours, using a four-wheel-drive vehicle to take you halfway, cost P2500. Trekking the lower slopes costs P650 for six hours with a guide. You can book similar tours at

Swagman Travel (☎045/322 2890), whose office is in the Clark City Terminal Building on Don Juico Avenue (near the bar area). Alternatively, try Rusty at R&J Pinatubo Trek (☎045/602 5231), licenced by the Philippine Department of Tourism. For P500 a day you can hire a Yamaha motorcycle from Trent Transport that will take you through the lahar fields on the lower slopes of the volcano. If you're in the market for something even more memorable, for US$85 per person (minimum two people) you can take an early morning crater flight in a small aircraft. Contact Swagman Travel for details (see above).

Mount Arayat

Mount Arayat, a 1030-metre extinct volcano in Arayat, rises from the lowlands of Pampanga in solitary and dramatic fashion, the only mountain for miles around. Like many mountains in the superstitious Philippines, Arayat is linked to legends. It is said to be inhabited by Mariang Sinukuan (Maria the Abandoned), the sister of Mariang Makiling (Maria of Makiling). When Mariang Sinukuan comes down from the mountain and visits the lowlands her presence can be felt because the air turns fragrant. Some say there is a place on Arayat's wooded slopes where there are many types of fruit, all of which belong to Maria. You can eat as much fruit as you want, but don't take any away from the mountain because an angry Maria will cause you to lose your way. It takes between seven and nine hours to reach the top of Arayat, making it an easier climb than nearby Pinatubo. If you book with one of the growing number of adventure tour companies in the Clark area they will arrange a guide and transport for you; see above for details. At the foot of the mountain is Arayat National Park with picnic sheds and swimming pools. To **get to Mount Arayat** from Clark take a jeepney (45min; P30) from the terminal in Field's Avenue. A taxi will cost about P100.

Olongapo and Subic Bay

Another US base, another withdrawal. **Subic Bay Naval Base**, 12km north of **OLONGAPO** and two hours northwest of Clark, in Zambales province, closed down when US forces left in 1992 and is slowly but surely being turned into a playground for the relatively rich, with the usual golf courses, a yacht club and five-star hotels. There are plenty of small barrios and beaches outside the base, however, where native life goes on. **Barrio Barretto**, north of the naval base, fronts onto Baloy beach, which is one of the best in Luzon. The barrio was another infamous R&R centre for excitable sailors (it featured briefly in the film *An Officer and a Gentleman*), but many of the bars have closed down. The area is popular with budget tourists and there is plenty of accommodation of varying degrees of quality and cleanliness.

There are some good **adventure activities** at Subic. Inside the base, near the airport, you can visit the Jungle Environmental Survival Training Camp (JEST; ☎047/252 4123) and take tours into the area's impressive rainforest with members of the Aeta tribe who trained US marines here for service in Vietnam. Short trips include lectures and demonstrations on basic jungle survival. Overnight trips involve finding your own potable water and setting traps for food. Bat barbecue is a speciality. For **diving** on wrecks (planes as well as ships) try Johan's Adventure Dive Center at Baloy beach.

Practicalities

Victory Liner runs hourly **buses** to Olongapo (P110) from Manila. From Dau and Angeles regular buses start early morning for the bumpy journey to Olongapo. When you get to Olongapo you can take a blue jeepney (P3) for the five-kilometre journey to Barrio Barretto. The naval base is served by jeepneys and taxis from Olongapo. There is a **tourist information office** just north of Palladium Beach Resort in Barrio Barretto.

There are dozens of **banks** in and around Subic and most have ATMs where you can get a cash advance on your Visa card. There's a hospital, the Subic Legend Health and Medical Center (☎047/252 9280–88), inside the naval base at Cubi Point.

ACCOMMODATION
The Pines (②), on Baloy beach, one of the cheapest **places to stay**, is owned by a retired Englishman and has four good rooms. Further along the beach is *ZAB-A* (③), owned by a retired Australian, who offers small studio apartments for P400 a day with a kitchen. *Barts Resort* (☎047/223 4148; ③–⑤) at 117C National Highway, Barrio Barretto, has a swimming pool. Nearby is *By The Sea* (☎047 222 2718; ③–⑧), whose restaurant does the best cheap eats in town. The new *Palmera Garden Beach Resort* (☎047 811 2109; ②–③) is in a lovely position on the beach, off the National Highway, and has nice spacious nipa huts with air-con and fan rooms. *Mango's* beach bar and **restaurant**, in Barrio Barretto, serves both Filipino and European cuisine, while *Mr Pumpernickel*, Baloy beach, also in Barrio Barretto, does fine German food. It's owned by a German, Harry Joost, and his Filipina wife Aida. Harry is also the liaison officer for Baloy beach and a good source of inside information. He can also help with guides and tours to Mount Pinatubo.

Zambales coast

Once you've finished with Subic it's worth taking time to journey north by bus or jeepney along the **Zambales** coastal road. Zambales is a mountainous province that borders the South China Sea to the west, and the coastal road gives you direct access to a number of sweeping beaches that tourists are only just beginning to discover. First stop on the journey is the small town of **SAN ANTONIO**, one hour by road north of Subic, from where you can catch a jeepney at the market square to the fishing village of **PANDAQUIT**, 5km south, which has a nice long beach. In Pandaquit, you can hire bancas for P500 for half a day and explore Camera and Capones islands. By far the best place to stay is the splendid little *Capones Beach Resort* (③), which is right on the sand at Pandaquit and has neatly furnished, clean rooms with fan and shower. The stretch of coastal road immediately north of San Antonio is memorable for the sight of villages that are still buried under tons of hardened ash from Mount Pinatubo. In some areas all you can see are church spires and tin roofs jutting through the ash.

Continuing north, you come to the provincial capital, **IBA** (birthplace in 1907 of popular former President Ramon Magsaysay, who was known as "The Guy"), the small towns of Palauig and Masinioc and **SANTA CRUZ**, with its remarkably expansive saltworks. This also marks the southern end of Dasol Bay, where a handful of resorts have sprung up along beautiful beaches such as **Tambobong**. To get to Tambobong beach take a jeepney (10min; P10) from the plaza in Santa Cruz. There are two islands in **Dasol Bay** that you can reach by hired local banca from the small wharf in Santa Cruz. **Hermana Mayor Island** is generally known as Miss Universe Island because it was where candidates for the Miss Universe title in 1979 had their photographs taken. **Hermana Menor Island** is smaller and totally unspoiled by development. There is no accommodation on either island, so only daytrips are possible.

Victory Liner **buses** run regularly from Olongapo to Iba, a distance of about 85km or two hours, and then on to Alaminos, which takes about another two hours. Jeepneys run from town to town along the Zambales coast, but it can be a slow journey.

One Hundred Islands

It's actually 123, but who's counting? These tiny islands, part of a national park, nestle in the Lingayen Gulf and from the mainland they look as inviting as shining emeralds. None of them, however, has accommodation – the only way to stay overnight is to camp. Many visitors to the islands choose to stay in **Lucap** on the mainland and hop the islands by day (you'll need to take your own food and water), returning to a shower and a comfy bed in the evening. From the pier in Lucap you can arrange a boatman and a boat (around P500 a day). There's a small tourist outpost on the pier where you can arrange camping permits. Most of the accommodation is in this area, some in little resorts and some in private houses. *Ocean View*

Lodge (②), opposite the Lucap pier, has spacious twins and its own restaurant. *Gloria's Cottages* (②) has doubles over the water. Every year in the last week of February Lucap stages The Hundred Islands Festival to drum up support for the preservation and protection of the islands. Highlights include a Mardi Gras and a river parade. The best way **to get to Hundred Islands** is to take a bus to Alaminos and then local transport to Lucap; a tricycle will cost P25. Dagupan, Philippine Rabbit, Five Star and Partas buses leave regularly from Manila and Dau. From Olongapo take Victory Liner.

San Fernando (La Union)

SAN FERNANDO in La Union, as opposed to San Fernando in Pampanga, is the capital of La Union province and a good place to rest up for a few days during a tour of the north. The city itself is the usual jumble of jeepneys and fast-food restaurants. The main road is Quezon Avenue, also known as the National Road, which runs through the city from south to north. **Buses** from Manila heading north stop at the Town Plaza. The **tourist information office** (☎072/412 411) is close by in the Mabang Justice Hall on General Luna Street, and the **post office** is a five-minute walk northeast on P Tavera Street. It's worth taking a walk south along Gapuz Zigzag Road to **Freedom Park**, also known as Heroes' Hill, from where you get good views over the South China Sea. The views from the Provincial Capitol Building, immediately opposite, are arguably even better. Along Quezon Aenue on the northern outskirts of San Fernando is the impressive **Ma-Cho temple**, testament to the influence of the Chinese in the area, many of whose ancestors arrived before the Spanish did.

Philippine Rabbit and Victory Liner **buses** from Manila (P120) are marked for San Fernando, Loaog, Vigan or Abra. You can catch buses from San Fernando to Baguio from the Eso-Nice Terminal in Rizal Street. Buses from Baguio also terminate here.

The best **accommodation** in the area is on the northern outskirts of San Fernando at the *Sea and Sky Hotel* (☎072/415 279; ③–⑤) on Quezon Avenue. It has clean double rooms with air-con and shower plus a number of suites. Centrally located near the Town Plaza is the *Plaza Hotel* (☎072/412 996; ③), offering good singles and doubles with air-con and shower. *Casa Blanca Hotel* (☎072/871 235; ③–④), on Rizal Sreet, is a modern place with functional but well-maintained rooms.

About 10km north of San Fernando is the small town of **SAN JUAN**, which is becoming popular with surfers. Activity seems to centre on the popular *La Union Surf Resort* (☎072/242 4544; ②–④), although there are other resorts nearby. Accommodation ranges from budget rooms with shared bathroom to cottages with fan and fridge. Buses bound for Loaog, Vigan or Abra pass through San Juan; ask the driver to let you off at *Se-Bay Resort*, San Juan, a big place next to *La Union Surf Resort*. They all know where this is. The easiest way here from San Fernando town is by tricycle to *Se-Bay*.

CORDILLERAS AND THE FAR NORTH

To Filipino lowlanders, brought up on a diet of sunshine and beaches, the mountainous north is still seen as a mysterious Shangri-La full of enigmatic tribes and their unfamiliar gods. **Baguio**, the traditional mountain retreat for Manilenos during the fierce heat of Easter week, is about as far north as many southerners get. But it's not until you get beyond Baguio that the adventure really starts. The provinces of Benguet, Ifugao and Mountain Province are the **tribal heartlands** of the northern Philippines, settled first by indigenous Negritos and then during the Spanish regime by hunter-gatherers from neighbouring areas who were on the move looking for food and water. Life for many of these tribal people has changed little in hundreds of years, with traditional ways and values still very much in evidence. If anything is likely to erode these traditions and chip away at the insulation it is the coming of the tourist. Already an increasing number of tribal folk are making more from the sale of handicrafts than they do from the production of rice. One of the challenges faced by the government is to make the highlands accessible to travellers, without causing the breakup of a social and economic structure that is unique to the region.

TRIBES OF THE CORDILLERAS AND TREKKING

There are **tribes** throughout the Philippines, but those of the Central Cordillera are the best-known. The Cordilleras are home to six main indigenous Filipino tribes: the Ibaloy, the Kankanay, the Ifugao, the Kalinga, the Apayao and the Bontoc, collectively known as **Igorots**. There are dozens of smaller, family tribes, including the **Dalicans** and the **Fidelisans**, who recently brandished high-powered weapons at each other in a tiff over water sources. Dalican tribal elders magnanimously proposed a truce, but only because they had run out of bullets. Tribal spats are still commonplace, usually over land, but are rarely resolved these days through headhunting, as they were up until the turn of the twentieth century. The usual method of resolving modern tribal "warfare" is for all tribes from the mountains to be present and help mediate between the two factions. After reaching an agreement for a peace pact, the tribes celebrate by having a huge party, known as a *canao*, a ritual feast during which food, rice wine and blood flow freely. A typical *canao* will involve the slaughter of a carabao, a pig and half a dozen chickens, whose bladders are "read" for signs of good fortune, in much the same way other cultures read tea leaves. A tribe that breaks a peace pact is obliged to pay compensation in the form of livestock or rice.

Tribal communities arose in the Philippines during pre-Spanish times when lowland Filipinos, both Muslim and Christian, expanded into the interiors of Luzon, isolating upland tribes into pockets in which they still exist today. Like other Filipinos, **upland tribes** were a blend of various ethnic origins. Technologically, they ranged from the highly skilled Bontoc and Ifugao to the more primitive groups. Some have intermarried with lowlanders for more than a century, but others, like the **Kalinga**, remain isolated from lowland influences and are happy to remain so. The tribe most visitors to the north are likely to come into contact with is the **Ifugao**, who live in and around Banaue and who built the famous rice terraces.

TREKKING

Trekking is beginning to become a serious activity in the Philippines, and although there are few well-marked trails as yet, there are always local guides available to show you the way. Don't be tempted to wander off into the cordilleran wilderness on your own. Many areas are isolated and medical facilities and rescue services are few and far between. If you get into trouble you could have a long wait before anyone finds you. Most of the challenging trails are around Sagada, Bontoc and Banaue. In all of these towns there is a tourist office that can help arrange **guides**. In smaller barrios a good place to look for a guide is at the barangay (village) hall or town hall. Barangay officials are usually only too eager to help. The guide you are allocated won't have any official certification as a guide, but rest assured he'll know the area like the back of his hand. Rates for a guide start from a few hundred pesos today, but he'll expect a good tip if he gets you home safely. Don't underestimate the **weather** in the mountains. The Philippines may be tropical, but at altitude it can get within inches of freezing at night and cloud can descend fast, resulting in poor visibility. In many places you are likely to be scrambling through inhospitable terrain. If it remains hot and sunny there's the potential problem of dehydration. Take plenty of water and sip it regularly as you walk. Don't wait until you feel thirsty because by then it might be too late. And make sure you have good waterproof clothing, just in case. Many trekking clubs in the Philippines ask potential members to take a fitness test first, an indication that walking through this rugged landscape is not always a walk in the park.

A swing through the north should include visits to the mountain village of **Sagada**, with its caves and hanging coffins, to the riverside town of **Bontoc**, capital of Mountain Province, and the huge **rice terraces at Banaue**. The bucolic **Batanes Islands** off the northern tip of the Philippines are a challenge to reach, but rewarding if you can make the effort. And it isn't all cordilleras and tribes. To the west of Baguio, on the western seaboard, are the provinces of **Ilocos Sur** and **Ilocos Norte**, with miles of beautiful coastline and old Spanish colonial outposts such as **Vigan**. The far northeast is marked by the spectacular **Sierra Madre** range, where few foreigners venture, and the rural provinces of **Isabela** and **Cagayan**.

You can **fly** from Manila to a number of points in the north, including Baguio, Laoag, Cauayan (for Banaue), Ilagan and Tuguegarao in the far northeastern province of Cagayan. Otherwise it's the **bus**. Victory Liner and Philippine Rabbit are two of the most popular services, going to most towns in the north from their terminals in Manila. The journey to Baguio takes around seven hours. You can change buses in Baguio to continue north towards Sagada and Bontoc.

Baguio

BAGUIO, also known as City of Pines or City of Flowers, lies on a plateau 1400m above sea level. It was built by the colonizing Americans as a recreational and administrative centre, from where they could preside over their precious tropical colony without working up too much of a sweat. Baguio is also etched on the Filipino consciousness as the site of one of the country's worst natural disasters, the earthquake of 16 July 1990, in which hundreds died. Most of the damage was to shanty towns, which have either been cleared or rebuilt.

Although for many visitors it's little more than a stopping-off point en route to Sagada and the mountain provinces, Baguio, with its pine trees and rolling hills, has a few secrets worth discovering, such as its parks and bohemian cafés, and the climate is a pleasant respite from the searing heat of the south.

Arrival and information

Loakan Airport is 7km south of the city beyond Camp John Hay. The approach to the airport is not for the faint-hearted, but if you can bear to look you'll be rewarded with panoramic views of the plateau on which Baguio is built. Jeepneys run regularly from the airport to Burham Park and Session Road. **Bus** companies with regular daily services from Manila to Baguio include Victory Liner, Dangwa, Dagupan Bus and Philippine Rabbit. All have terminals in Baguio on Governor Pack Road, a couple of minutes on foot from Session Road. You can also get to Baguio by bus from most other towns in the north, including San Fernando (La Union), Dau (Clark), Angeles, Vigan and Dagupan. These buses also arrive at terminals on Governor Pack Road.

The **tourist information office** (daily 9am–noon & 1–7pm; ☎074/442 6708 or 442 7014) is in the DoT Complex on Governor Pack Road, a ten-minute walk from Session Road. They have maps of Baguio, but not much else, and even the maps aren't great. A good place to go for general advice, guided tours and visa extensions is the ubiquitous **Swagman Travel**, near Rizal Park at 90 Abanao St (☎074/442 5139). There's a **post office**, with a poste restante service, at the junction of Session Road and Governor Pack Road. **Internet cafés** are few and far between, but one of the most popular is Cyberspace, at the *Mount Crest Hotel* in Legarda Road (daily 8am–1am; P100 an hour with free coffee). You can **change** money at the Philippine National Bank at the northern end of Session Road, while Equitable Bank on Magsaysay Avenue (☎074/443 5028) will give cash advances on MasterCard or Visa. Baguio **Medical Center** (☎074/442 4216) is in Governor Pack Road.

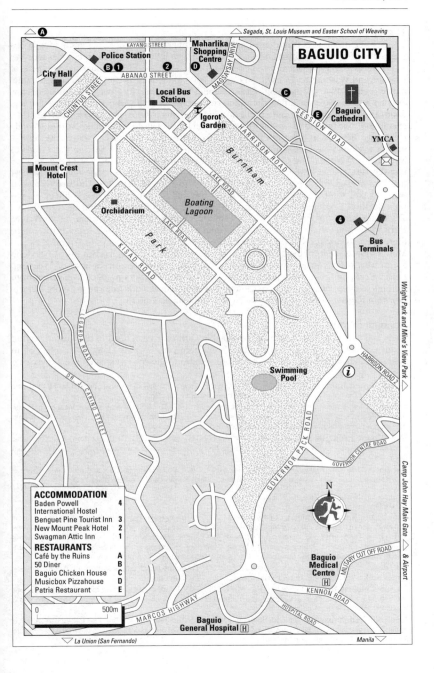

The City

The city's centrepiece is **Burnham Park**, a sort of hilltop version of Rizal Park in Manila. It's a nice place for a stroll, with a boating lake and strange little three-wheeled bicycles for rent. The park area was designed by Daniel Burnham, who was also responsible for parts of Chicago and Washington DC. On the eastern edge of the park is Harrison Road and immediately behind that and running almost parallel to it is the city's congested main artery, Session Road, where you'll find shops and restaurants. Standing imperiously above Session Road, and reached on foot by a flight of a hundred steep steps, is **Baguio Cathedral**, an example of "wedding cake gothic" in an eye-catching shade of rose pink. At the St Louis University Silver Shop, just a few paces away from the cathedral, you can watch silver craftsmen at work and buy the jewellery they make. The southern end of Session Road leads to Magsaysay Drive and the **City Market**, which sells produce from the Cordilleras such as strawberries, peanut brittle, sweet wine, honey, textiles, handicrafts and jewellery. The best museum in Baguio is the **St Louis University Museum of Arts and Culture** (Mon–Sat 9am–4.30pm; ☎074/442 3043), near St Louis Hospital on Bonifacio Street, a fifteen-minute walk north of Session Road. The museum has hundreds of artefacts from the Cordilleras. Travelling out of the city eastwards on Leonard Wood Road for 4km brings you to **Wright Park** where you can hire horses for riding, and a little further to **Mine's View Park**, where there are souvenir stalls, antique shops and some restaurants. Jeepneys to Wright Park and Mine's View leave from the northern end of Session Road. The Baguio **Botanical Gardens** are nearby in Park Road. For some ethnic shopping try the **Easter School of Weaving**, Easter Road, on the northwestern outskirts of the city. Weavers produce everything from clothing to tablecloths and you are allowed to watch them at work. You can get there by jeepney from Kayang Street, at the northern end of Burnham Park.

Accommodation

Taxis and tricycles go from the bus terminal in Governor Pack Road to the western end of Abanao Street, near *Swagman Attic Inn*. From here you can walk along Abanao and on to Session Road, an area full of budget **accommodation**. The cooler climate means there's no need for air-con.

Baden Powell International Hostel, 26 Governor Pack Rd (☎074/442 5836). A big old building visible from the southern end of Session Road. Dorm beds available for P280. ④.

Benguet Pine Tourist Inn, Otek cor. Chanum Street (☎074/442 7325). In a nice quiet location opposite the Orchidarium in Burnham Park. Attractive attic-style doubles with a common bath and balcony or doubles with a private bath. A good breakfast is included in the price. ④.

New Mount Peak Hotel, Abanao Street (☎074/442 3341 or 442 5411). At the bottom of the hill near *Swagman Attic Inn*. Deluxe rooms are big enough for two and are clean and well-furnished. There are also dorm beds (P150), triples and quads. ④–⑤.

Swagman Attic Inn, Abanao Street (☎074/442 5139). Big doubles with cable TV and mod cons. There is also a small but popular restaurant serving fairly standard Filipino and Western dishes. ⑥.

Eating

Café by the Ruins, 25 Chuntog St (☎074/442 4010). Try not to leave Baguio without eating here. It's far and away one of the city's culinary highlights, with excellent organic food prepared with home-grown herbs and spices. There are good vegetarian dishes, or you can try *pinikpikan*, a tribal chicken delicacy that is known by its nickname "killing me softly" because the poor chicken is slowly beaten to death with a hammer to make the meat bloody and tender. Prices for mains start at P80. Open 10am–10pm.

50 Diner, Abanao Street, next to *Swagman Attic Inn*. Does inexpensive bulk-standard chicken and rice dishes, with a smattering of burgers and pizzas. Open 7am to midnight.

Baguio Chicken House, 85 Session Rd (☎074/442 5603). Popular rustic-style place serving just about everything – chicken, steaks, Chinese and Filipino. The set menus are good value and there are some imported wines. Open 24 hours.

Musicbox Pizzahouse, 25 Zandueta St, behind Maharlika Shopping Center. Bustling folk house with live music in the evenings. Pizzas are good and there's a big choice of *pica-pica* (bar snacks). P100 cover charge for live bands. Open 11am to midnight.

Patria Restaurant, 181 Session Rd (☎074/442 4963). Baguio has a number of good Chinese restaurants, but this is a classic. It's old and dusty, but always busy because the food is excellent and there's a great deal of it. Soup and noodle dishes start from P65, while an enormous mound of fried rice with vegetables is P70.

Tam-awan Village

On the outskirts of Baguio heading north towards La Trinidad and best reached by taxi from Baguio (about P50), **TAM-AWAN VILLAGE** is a replica Ifugao tribal villlage established by well-known Filipino artist Ben Cabrera, known as Bencab. If you want to spend the night in a tribal hut, this is your chance. You can stay in wooden huts on stilts and drink rice wine around a traditional Ifugao fire. Food is available from a small kitchen and work by local artists is on sale in the small shop. Staff often perform impromptu ceremonies and dances. There are six huts of varying shapes and sizes. One particular hut, built on stilts like all the rest, is a fertility hut. Carvings of men with impressive sex organs adorn the walls. Higher up on the hill are two large family huts. Tam-awan is hardly the height of luxury, but well worth an overnight stay for the experience. Small huts for two people are P550 a night. Family huts are P800. Toilets and showers are shared. Take a jacket because it can get surprisingly cold.

North to Sagada

The road north from Baguio, known as the Halsema Highway, affords breathtaking views as it snakes up to Sagada. Be prepared for a long, uncomfortable journey, though, as the road is little more than a single lane of rocks and rubble in many places. If you can't face doing the trip in one go you could make an overnight stop at the *Mount Data Hotel* (⑥), at **Mount Data**, about halfway to Sagada. You can make reservations in Manila through Asia Travel (☎02/752 0307 or 752 0308).

The village of **SAGADA**, 160km north of Baguio, has oodles of charm and mystery, much of it attached to the hanging coffins that can be seen perched high in the limestone cliffs, its burial caves and the survival of ancient traditions. The dead are still sometimes positioned outside their house in a chair known as the death chair. This is believed to give the soul a chance to escape before the remains are disposed of. Sagada began to open up as a destination when it got electricity in the early 70s, and intellectuals – internal refugees from the Marcos dictatorship – flocked here to write and paint. They didn't produce anything of note, perhaps because they are said to have spent much of their time drinking the local rice wine, known as *Tapuy*. European hippies followed and so did the military, who thought the *turistas* were supplying funds for an insurgency. Indeed, a 9pm curfew remains in place today. All this artistic activity has left its mark in the form of quaint little cafés and inns and a distinctly bohemian atmosphere.

Most of the village's restaurants and guesthouses are located on the nameless main street, which runs through the town centre past the little market area, the town hall, the police station and the post office. Sagada's forest paths and numerous caves provide some excellent **trekking**, although you must register first with the Sagada Environmental Guides Association (SEGA) at the town hall; the **tourist information office** is here too. A typical five-hour trek for one to four people costs P300 for the group. Tourists have died in Sagada's labyrinth **burial caves**, many of which stretch for miles underground, so don't go alone. One of the best is **Crystal Cave**, on the southern edge of town. Another, **Sumaging Cave**, is a ten-minute walk in the same direction and can take hours to explore. About 500m from the centre of the village heading towards Bontoc is the **Eduardo Masferre Studio** where you can see fascinating old photographs of tribal life in the early twentieth century. At nearby **Sagada Weaving**, fabrics are produced using traditional tribal designs.

Practicalities

Buses from Baguio (Governor Pack Road) to Sagada (P136) terminate close to the town hall on the main street. These buses are rudimentary to say the least, often with uncomfortable seats and no glass in the windows. There are no jeepneys between Baguio and Sagada, but jeepneys do leave Sagada **for Bontoc**, starting at 8.30am (1hr; P30).

Guesthouses in Sagada are extremely cheap. One of the quietest places to stay is the rustic *Masferres Inn* (①), at the far end of Sagada's main street, beyond the town hall, and it also does good chicken curry. Alternatively, try the plain and simple *Sagada Guest House* (①), above the bus station, or the *Country Inn & Café* (①), opposite the town hall, which was once the governor's residence and is famous for its bright-green rooms. Next door is the popular *Green House* (①), while the *Log Cabin Café*, up the hill past the *Sagada Guest House*, does some of the best **food** in town. The *Shamrock Café* and the *Shamrock II Yoghurt House*, on the main street past the town hall heading west, are legendary for their pancakes and home-made yoghurt.

Bontoc

The capital of Mountain Province, **BONTOC** is the first major town in the north beyond Baguio. It lies on the banks of the Chico River, about an hour east of Sagada by jeepney. Jeepneys and buses arrive at the terminal opposite the town plaza, close to the market.

Bontoc is primarily a commercial town used by tourists mainly as a rest-stop on the circuit to Banaue. It is, however, gaining a reputation as a good place for **trekking**; contact the Bontoc Ecological Tour Guides Association at the *Pines Kitchenette and Inn*, behind the market in Rizal Plaza. Guides cost P300–500 for a day. Some of the local tribes can be nervous of foreigners and it would be unwise to confront them without a local guide to help smooth the way. One local tribe, the Kalingas, have been particularly wary of outsiders, and these days, while not outright unfriendly, are still rather standoffish. Don't miss the small but well-run **Bontoc Museum** (Mon–Sat 9.30am–noon & 1–5pm; P20), next to the post office, close to the town plaza. It contains photographs of headhunting victims and of zealous American missionaries trying to persuade incredulous warriors to choose the path of righteousness. *Pines Kitchenette and Inn* (see above; ②–③) is one of the few **places to stay** in Bontoc, with big doubles and private shower or cheaper rooms with shared facilities. Cheaper rooms are available at the *Chico Terrace Inn & Restaurant* (①) on the main street (the streets in Bontoc have no names) near its junction with the "hospital road".

Banaue and the rice terraces

It's a rugged but spectacular four-hour trip from Bontoc to Banaue along a winding road that leads up into the misty Cordilleras, across a mountaintop pass, then down precipitous mountainside. It may only be 300km north of Manila, but Banaue might as well be a world away, 1300m above sea level and far removed in spirit and topography from the beaches and palm trees of the south. This is the heart of rice terrace country. The **rice terraces** at Banaue are one of the great icons of the Philippines. They were hewn from the land 2000 years ago by Ifugao tribespeople using primitive tools, an achievement in engineering terms that ranks alongside the building of the pyramids. Called the "Stairway to Heaven" by the Ifugaos, the terraces would stretch 20,000km if laid out end to end. Not only are they an awesome sight but also an object lesson in what is today known as "sustainability". These vast, layered paddies demonstrate that nature need not be destroyed to satisfy man's needs. The terraces were recently added to the United Nations' World Heritage List, a sign that they will not last forever if they are not protected. Part of the problem is that the walls that link the paddies are beginning to crumble and the lack of local Ifugao labour has resulted in a shortage of young people willing and able to help carry out repairs. The future of the terraces is closely tied to the future of the tribespeople themselves. Part of the problem, it must be said, is tourism. People who would otherwise have been working on the terraces are now making a much easier buck selling reproduction tribal artefacts or rare orchids from the surrounding forests. What's more, rice farming has little allure for the young tribespeople of the

Cordilleras. They are tired of the subsistence livelihood that their parents eked out from the land, and are packing their bags for Manila. The resulting labour shortage means the terraces are producing a mere thirty-five percent of the area's rice needs when they should be producing a hundred percent.

BANAUE itself is a small town centred on a marketplace, where there are a few guesthouses and some souvenir shops. Two kilometres up the road from the marketplace is the main lookout point for the rice terraces. Ifugao in traditional costume will ask for a small fee if you want to take their photograph. A handful of souvenir stalls surrounding the lookout sell carved wooden bowls and woven blankets at bargain prices.

Buses and jeepneys terminate at the marketplace near the town hall and close to the **tourist information office** (Mon–Sat 3–6pm), where you can get maps (P10) of the area for **trekking**. There are half-day treks to local Ifugao communities or longer treks through the rice terraces to isolated communities such as Batad (see below). The tourist information office and most hotels will help you find a guide. There are no banks in Banaue, but most hotels **change** money, usually at a lower rate than banks. The **post office** has poste restante, but it's a ten-minute jeepney ride from the marketplace near the *Banaue Hotel & Youth Hostel*. You can also make **telephone calls** from the post office.

Accommodation and eating

Accommodation in Banaue is generally basic, but clean and friendly, and many places have **restaurants** attached. The best place to stay is *Banaue Hotel and Youth Hostel* (☎074/386 4087 or 4088; dorm beds P75; rooms ⑦), a ten-minute journey from the marketplace by jeepney. It stands on the edge of a ledge with nice grounds, a swimming pool and excellent views across the valley to the terraces. Steep steps lead down from the hotel to Tam-An Village, where you can meet Ifugao and buy handicrafts. If you decide to stay here it's best to book in advance from Manila (☎02/752 0307 or 752 0308). Ask for a room with a view across the terraces: rooms have big balconies and sunrise over the valley is magical.

Back in town, *People's Lodge* (☎074/386 4014; ②) is a popular place, just down the road from the market. More expensive rooms are big with a hot shower and, if you're lucky, you'll have excellent views across the valley. *Jericho Guest House*, above the main market, has dorm beds for P50. Nearby, the quaint *Green View Lodge* (☎074/386 4021; ①–②) offers rooms with varying facilities, some with private shower. In the same marketplace area are *Stairway Lodge* ☎074/386 4053; ①–②) and *Halfway Lodge* (☎074/386 4082; ①–②), where rooms range from the basic to something more spacious with a private shower.

Batad

The strenuous trek from Banaue to the remote little village of **BATAD** has become something of an obligatory pilgrimage for visitors looking for splendid rural isolation and unforgettable rice-terrace scenery. You'll need to take a jeepney from the market in Banaue for the first 12km before starting a tiring walk up a steep trail. Batad nestles in a natural amphitheatre, close to the glorious Tapplya Waterfall, which is 21m high and has a deep, bracing pool for swimming. Village life in Batad has remained virtually unchanged for centuries, although the development of tourism has seen half a dozen primitive guesthouses spring up to cater for the influx. **Rooms** in Batad must be among the cheapest on the planet: P35–50 per head. Choose from the *Foreigner's Inn*, which has a nice balcony restaurant, the wonderful *Hillside Inn*, with its majestic views, and *Simon's Inn*, which has a good cosy café, serving, of all things, pizza.

Vigan

About 135km north of San Fernando (La Union) lies the old Spanish town of **VIGAN**, an obligatory stop on any swing through the northern provinces. It has become a bit of a cliché to describe Vigan as a living museum, but you have to admit it does some justice to the tag. One of the oldest towns in the Philippines, it was called Nueva Segovia in Spanish times and was an important political, military, cultural and religious centre. It still has pavements of cobbled stones and some of the finest **old Spanish colonial architecture** in the country, including some impressive homes that once belonged to friars, merchants and colonial officials. Various governmental and non-governmental organizations have joined forces to preserve the old buildings. Many are still lived in, others are used as curio shops and a few have been converted into museums. Vigan can thank Juan de Salcedo for its glorious architecture. The grandson of conquistador Miguel de Legaspi, he was made ruler of Ilocos province in the late sixteenth century and immediately set about emulating his grandfather's design of Intramuros. Vigan's time-capsule ambience is aided by the decision to close some of the streets to traffic and allow only pedestrians and **carretelas**, one-pony, two-seat traps – a ride in one of these makes for a romantic way to tour the town.

Vigan is one of the easier Philippine towns to negotiate because its streets follow a fairly regular grid pattern. Mena Crisolog Street runs south from Plaza Burgos and is lined with quaint old antique shops and cafés. Running parallel to it is the main thoroughfare, Governor A Reyes Street. Between Plaza P Burgos and Plaza Salcedo, stands the town's **cathedral**, St Paul's, dating back to 1641 – one of the oldest cathedrals in the country. Next to the cathedral, the **Padre Burgos House National Museum** (Mon–Fri 8.30–11am & 1.30–4.30pm) celebrates one of the town's most famous residents, Padre Jose Burgos, whose martyrdom in 1872 galvanized the revolutionary movement. The museum is a captivating old colonial house and houses fourteen paintings by the artist Villanueva, depicting the violent 1807 Basi Revolt, prompted by a Spanish effort to control the production of *basi* (sugar cane wine).

Souvenir-hunters after something more than the usual bulk-produced tourist nick-nacks should head for **Rowilda's Hand Loom**, on Mena Crisologo near the *Cordillera Inn*, which offers the kind of old-style textiles that used to be traded during colonial times. Vigan is also known for its pottery. The massive wood-fired kilns at the **Pagburnayan Potteries** in Rizal Street, at the junction with Liberation Boulevard, turn out huge jars, known as burnay, used by northerners for storing everything from vinegar to fish paste. Carabao (water buffalo) are used to squash the clay under hoof.

Practicalities

From Manila a limited number of **bus** companies make the eight-hour trip north. The best are Philippine Rabbit, Partas Lines or Times Transit (about P300). You can also get buses from San Fernando and Baguio. From Banaue and Bontoc there are no direct buses, so you will have to backtrack to Baguio. Victory Liner goes north from Manila to Laoag, but you can ask the driver to let you get off on the outskirts of Vigan and then take a short ten-peso tricycle ride into town. In Vigan, the Partas and Times Transit terminals are both in Quezon Avenue. The Philippine Rabbit terminal is in General Luna Street, one of the town's major east–west thoroughfares. From here a ten-minute walk north along Governor A Reyes Street will take you to Plaza P Burgos and the **tourist information office** (Mon–Sat 8am–5pm; ☎077/732 5705), housed in the Leona Florentina Building, near *Café Leona*. There are a number of **banks** in Florentino Street and there's a **post office** with poste restante at the junction of Gov. A Reyes and Bonifacio streets. Also on Gov. A Reyes Street is Powernet, where you can send and receive **emails** for P50 an hour. Vigan's main **hospital** is the Gabriela Silang General Hospital (☎077/ 722 2722) on Quirino Boulevard.

ACCOMMODATION

Grandpa's Inn, 1 Bonifacio St (☎077/722 2118). A quaint old place near the river. It's full of curios and has fairly decent rooms from basic singles to doubles with air-con and bath. ②–③.
El Juliana Hotel, Quirino Blvd cor. Liberation Blvd (☎077/722 2994). Rooms come with a toilet and shower. There's a swimming pool, also open to the public. ④.

New Luzon Inn, 31 General Luna St (☎077/722 1458). One of the cheapest places in town and really only an option if you're desperate. ②.

Vigan Hotel, Burgos Street (☎077/722 3001). A dignified colonial building now serving as a hotel. Rooms come with air-con, cable TV and fridge. ④.

Villa Angela, Quirino Boulevard. The most colonial of all the colonial hotels, this is a dusty old museum of a place and the billet of choice if you want to wallow in history. ③–⑤.

EATING

At *Café Leona* in Plaza Burgos you can order **native Ilocano dishes**, all for less than P150; try the Special Vigan Sinanglaw, a dish of pork entrails sautéed with ginger, vinegar, fish sauce, onion and pepper. The *Cool Spot Restaurant* at the back of the *Vigan Hotel* has also acquired a good reputation for its Ilocano cooking. At the pleasant olde worlde *Café Floresita* near the Ancieto Mansion, opposite Plaza P Burgos, native *longganiza* (sausage) features in many dishes. Another of Vigan's specialities is *empanada*, a type of tortilla that you can pick up for a few pesos from one of the many street stalls and small bakeries, where they are freshly baked.

Laoag and Batac

In 1818, the province of Ilocos was divided into two and the city of **LAOAG**, two hours' drive north from Vigan, became the capital of Ilocos Norte. In more recent years, Ilocos Norte has become associated in most Filipino minds with former President Ferdinand Marcos. This was very much his patch, and his son, Bong-Bong, and daughter, Imee, both of whom have entered politics, are still popular in these parts. Marcos was born south of Laoag in Sarrat, while the family seat was 15km southeast of the city in Batac. There's little to see in Laoag itself, though it's worth making time for St William's Cathedral, on FR Castro Avenue, which dates back to 1650. Further east along FR Castro is Ermita Hill, which has nice views across Laoag and out to the South China Sea. It's a thirty-minute walk or you can take a jeepney from outside the cathedral.

In **BATAC**, you can visit the Marcos Mansion, which is full of the dictator's old belongings; you can even see his refrigerated corpse, although many believe it's nothing more than a wax model. The impressive Batac Church, opposite the mansion, is where Imee was married with the kind of pomp and ceremony rarely seen outside royal families. A few kilometres southwest of Batac is the iconoclastic Paoay Chuch, built in a style known as "earthquake baroque", with immense side supports for its walls.

The **bus station** in Laoag is at the eastern end of Primo Lazar Avenue at its junction with General Fidel Segundo Avenue. **Jeepneys for Batac** leave from Jose Rizal Street in Laoag. Laoag isn't a prime tourist destination and **hotels** are few and far between, but the new *Hotel Tiffany* (☎077/770 3550; ③), on General Fidel Segundo Avenue, has small, clean doubles with private shower. The *Texicano Hotel* (☎077/722 0290; ④), on Rizal Street, has bog-standard double rooms with air-con and cable TV. For wholesome Filipino **food**, *Barrio Fiesta* on Manuel Nolasco Street is good value. *La Preciosa Restaurant* on Rizal Street also does cheap native dishes – reckon on P80 per head.

Batanes

Batanes, the smallest province in the country, made up of ten small islands, is the land that time forgot. There are no cinemas, hotels, shops or newspapers and hardly any tourists. It's not easy to get to, but if you persevere you won't regret it. The islands lie off the northernmost tip of the Philippines, 162km north of the Luzon mainland. To say they are different from the rest of the country is an understatement. At times, with its stone houses and windswept hills, Batanes is more reminiscent of the Scottish Highlands than it is of the sunny Philippines. The winter (December–Feb) can indeed get quite cold with temperatures as low as 7°C. However, in summer (April–June) the weather is pleasantly hot.

The most economically important islands in the Batanes group are **Itbayat, Batan** and **Sabtang**. The other islands are Dequey, Siayan, Mabudis, Ibuhos, Diago, North Island and Y'ami, which is closer to Taiwan than it is to the Philippines. The capital, **BASCO**, is on Batan. The Batanes landscape is spectacularly rugged and makes for some great **trekking and exploring**. The province's archetypal stone houses are picturesque in the extreme, as are some of its old colonial churches. Because of its strategic location, the Batanes islands was one of the first points occupied by the invading Japanese imperial forces at the outbreak of the Pacific War.

The native inhabitants of Batanes, the **Ivatan**, trace their roots to prehistoric Formosan immigrants and latter-day Spanish conquistadors. Most still make a living from the cultivation of yam and garlic. Many still wear the suot, a kind of hat made from natural fibres reaching down over the wearer's back, giving protection against both sun and rain. Entertainment is non-existent. Even radio broadcasts from the mainland are garbled. Broadcasts from Taiwan are much clearer, but sadly they are in Chinese. The Ivatan's main dialect is also called Ivatan and includes some pidgin Spanish. It's the only tonal dialect in the Philippines.

The best way **to get to Batanes** is to get on a Laoag International Airways flight to Basco at Laoag International Airport. But don't expect miracles. LIA has just one plane and it only seems to leave if it is full. You could also find yourself hanging around at the airport waiting for the weather to clear. The best time to strike out for Batanes is between December and May. At any other time of year your chances of getting there are slimmer. The only place to stay is *Mama Lily's Inn* (②) in Basco, where rooms are spartan but clean and the price includes full board. If you take a tent, you can camp on the beach.

SOUTH LUZON (THE BICOL REGION)

The region south of Batangas and Quezon is technically known as Region V, but commonly known to Filipinos as **South Luzon** or **Bicol**. The northernmost province of the Bicol region is Camarines Norte. The National Highway meanders south from here to Camarines Sur through the towns of **Daet, Naga, Iriga City** and **Legaspi**, which are typically provincial, with their jumbled traffic, concrete malls and occasional Spanish-era relic. Legaspi is the jumping-off point for active **Mayon Volcano**. Continuing further south still, you reach the coastal town of **Sorsogon**, from where it's a fifty-kilometre ride to the bucolic backwater of **Donsol**. Donsol has seen an increase in tourism recently because of the number of plankton-eating whale sharks that congregate here. From Matnog in Sorsogon province you can take a ferry across the Bernardino Strait to **Samar**, the gateway to the rest of the Visayas.

The Bicol region is easily accessible **by air** from Manila. BLTB also has **buses** that run up and down the National Highway daily, taking you to most major jumping-off points in the area. BLTB even has services that run all the way to Sorsogon, but the journey is a long one. Be prepared to sweat it out for the best part of twenty hours. Many choose to take a bus that leaves Manila in the evening and travels overnight when the roads are quiet, arriving early the next day. Philtranco has a new service that goes all the way from Manila to Davao, using ferries where it has to. It runs through Daet, Naga and Legaspi and on to the port of **Matnog** at the southernmost tip of South Luzon, where it boards a ferry for **Samar**. You can get off at any of these points.

Daet and around

DAET, 200km from Manila, is an unassuming town with little to detain you, but it's a good place to bed down for the night before setting out to explore the rest of the province of

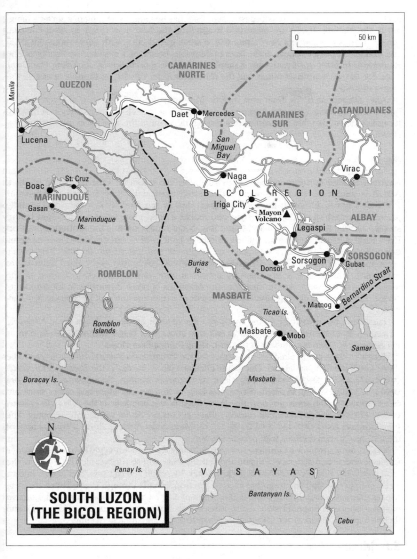

SOUTH LUZON (THE BICOL REGION)

Camarines Norte. It's an area that has been largely overlooked as a tourist destination, but undeservedly so. If it's unspoiled beaches you are after, the coastline to the east of Daet has more than its fair share. One of the most pleasant surprises is **Bagasbas beach**, 4km from Daet and accessible by jeepney and bus from the station on Pimentel Avenue, near the Shell petrol station in Daet. The waves crash in from the Pacific and are sometimes big enough for surfing. In fact, the whole area of coast east of Daet has become something of a surfer's hang-out in the making. If you are interested in **surfing**, the best man to see is Alvin Obsuan, owner of *Alvinos' Pizza and Surf Camp* (②), a small guesthouse, with dorm rooms for P125 and a couple of private rooms, at the back of Bagasbas beach, on a road known simply as The Boulevard. In Daet itself there are a number of simple **guesthouses**, including the *Dolor Hotel* (③–⑤), on Vinzons Avenue, and the *Karilagan Hotel* (②–⑤), on Morena Street, in the centre of town.

Other attractions in the Daet area include **Mananap Falls**, 18km west of Daet. Catch a bus or jeepney from Pimentel Avenue in Daet. The last stretch of the journey is a bracing three-kilometre hike, but you can have a refreshing swim in the falls' deep pools when you arrive.

Naga

Centrally located in the province of Camarines Sur and one hour's journey south of Daet, **NAGA** is one of the country's oldest cities, established in 1578 by Spanish conquistador Pedro de Chavez. Although there's not a great deal to see, the city is a clean and friendly place with a dash of metropolitan style, and makes a good place to spend the night before striking out for the islands of San Miguel Bay. Naga's main sight is the **cathedral**, just off Plaza Rizal, a charming baroque edifice, originally built in 1595, but destroyed several times down the centuries by fire, earthquake and typhoon, and last rebuilt in 1890. The town's other main draw is the annual **Penafrancia Festival**, celebrated every third Saturday of September. The festival is preceded by a novena, nine days of prayer, in honour of the Madonna. On the ninth day, an image of the Madonna is taken downriver in a barge to its shrine. The colourful evening procession consists of numerous boats, lit by thousands of candles.

Naga's **bus terminals** are on the southern edge of town, across the Naga River. A tricycle or jeepney from the terminals into town will cost about P10. **Naga Airport** (also known as Pili Airport) is 12km out of town to the east, along Panganiban Drive.

Hotels in Naga get booked out in advance for the Penafrancia Festival, so if you plan to be there, you'll need to plan ahead. One of the cheapest places to stay is the *Rodson Circle Hotel* (☎054/473 9828; ①–②), which has clean and spartan rooms. *Sampaguita Tourist Inn* (☎054/473 8339; ⑤–⑥), in Abella Street, has long been a popular place and offers small but clean rooms, though some are near the disco. Slightly less monastic is the *Moraville Apartel* (☎054/473 9537; ④), a functional concrete place in Caceres Street with smallish rooms. The *Villa Caracas Hotel* (☎054/473 6532; ②–⑥), on Magsaysay Avenue, in the Pequena area of the city, has air-con doubles with private shower.

Naga is not known for its **cuisine**, but you certainly won't go hungry. There are numerous fast-food outlets and dozens of Filipino-style street stalls, where you can pick up a plate of the local speciality, a fiery concoction of pork, vinegar, soy, chilli and *bagoong* (fish paste), known as Bicol Express, after the train that used to run from Manila through Bicol. There are plenty of restaurants around Plaza Rizal, in the centre of Naga. *Carl's Diner* is a long-standing and popular American fast-food style diner. Most hotels have restaurants or coffee shops and there's a good Chinese place, *Ming Chun Foodhouse*, on Penafrancia Avenue.

San Miguel Bay

Less than 30km northeast of Naga lies **San Miguel Bay**, which has a number of quiet beaches and islands worth exploring and a handful of resorts in the "functional" category. Some of the beaches in this area are as good as anything the Visayas has to offer, and are often deserted because few tourists make the trip. You can hire a banca locally and explore the islands. One of the nicest places to stay is the Swagman-owned resort (④–⑥) on Apuao Grande Island, with its rustic cottages (up to four people) and white-sand beach; you can make reservations through any Swagman office (the Manila number is ☎02/523 8541–45) and they will also help with transport from Manila. You can get to San Miguel Bay through either Naga or Daet. The place to aim for is the fishing village of **Mercedes**, from where the islands are a 45-minute banca ride. Mercedes is 10km southeast of Daet and about 45 minutes by road northeast of Naga. Buses and jeepneys run intermittently from Pimentel Avenue in Daet and the main terminals in Naga.

Legaspi

The port city of **LEGASPI**, also spelt Legazpi, is the place to base yourself if you fancy climbing **Mayon Volcano**. Legaspi is a bustling place, with one main thoroughfare, Rizal Street, that connects the port area with the district of Albay which is where most of the accommodation and restaurants are. The town itself has little in the way of tourist attractions, but one sight that is worth seeing are the **Cagsawa Ruins**, the eerie remains of a church that was buried in the devastating eruption of Mayon in 1814. The best time to see the site is at dawn before the vendors and hawkers stake a claim to it and the clouds roll in and obscure the view of the volcano. The ruins are located fifteen minutes' drive west of Legaspi – take a jeepney from Rizal Street bound for Guinobatan and ask the driver to let you off near the ruins. The nearby **Cagsawa National Museum** (Mon–Sat 8–11.30am & 1–4.30pm) contains exhibits not just about Mayon Volcano, but many other volcanoes in the Philippines. Another good place for viewing Mayon from a safe distance is Kupuntukan Hill in the port area of Legaspi. Also in this area, behind the fish market, is **Victory Village**, a charmingly rustic bamboo village built on stilts over the black sand bay.

Legaspi Airport is 3km northwest of the town centre, off Washington Drive. The BLTB **bus station** is on Penaranda Street near the *Casablanca Hotel*. Buses serving many destinations in the region also run from the JB Bicol Express Line bus terminal in Mabini Street. Philtranco's terminal is on Imperial Street, west of the town centre on the way to the airport.

The **tourist information office** (☎052/214 3215 or 480 6439), 3rd Floor, RCBC Building, Rizal Street, is a good place to set up a Mayon climb. Staff will help with transport, guides and equipment. The **post office** is on Lapu-Lapu Street at the junction with Quezon Avenue, and there are a number of **banks**, mostly on Quezon Avenue, where you can change cash.

The most popular budget **guesthouse** is the modern and clean *Legaspi Tourist Inn* (☎052/480 6147; ③), on Lapu-Lapu Street opposite the post office. The *Casablanca Hotel* (☎052/480 8190; ④), Penaranda Street, is a popular mid-range hotel, with double air-con rooms, some with a balcony. It also has a 24-hour coffee shop and a disco. *Jennifer's Garden Apartelle and Restaurant* (☎052/455 1086; ③), on J Esteves Street in the Albay district, is excellent value, with pool, jacuzzi and Internet access; all rooms have air-con, TV, phone and shower. The *Hotel la Trinidad* (☎052/455 9121; ⑥), on Rizal Street, is in a great location and perhaps the best hotel in town, with a pool, a coffee shop and air-con rooms.

The quaint little café *Old Albay* in the *Hotel Victoria* on Rizal Street is a popular meeting place, serving bulk standard breakfasts, Filipino **food**, sandwiches and snacks. At the *Paayahayan Beer Garden*, Penaranda Street, you can sit in a nipa hut, eat seafood straight from the sea and drink San Miguel beer for P15 a bottle. Further along Penaranda Street, the *Waway* restaurant is big, busy and easy on the pocket. It's a good place for vegetarian dishes and local specialities such as Bicol Express.

Mayon Volcano

The perfectly smooth cone of **Mayon Volcano** (2421m) in Albay province makes it look deceptively benign from a distance, but don't be deceived. Mayon is a devil is disguise and has claimed the lives of a number of climbers in recent years. It is the most active volcano in the country and has erupted more than thirty times since 1616, the date of its first recorded eruption. Recent eruptions occurred in 1984 and 1993, and as recently as the beginning of 2000 it was blowing steam from its crater. It's no wonder the locals spin fearful stories around it. The most popular legend says Mayon was formed when a beautiful native princess eloped with a brave warrior. Her uncle, Magayon, was so possessive of his niece that he chased the young couple, who prayed to the gods for help. Suddenly a landslide buried the raging uncle alive, but he is said to still be inside the volcano, his anger sometimes bursting forth in the form of eruptions.

One of the greatest perils of **climbing Mayon Volcano** is that its slopes are not as silky smooth as they look from a few miles away. You have to work your way slowly through forest, grassland and deserts of rock sand boulders before you reach the summit. A number of accidents on these slopes have been caused by rock avalanches.

The **safest approach** is from the northwestern slope, which starts at 762m above sea level on a ledge where the Philippine Institute of Volcanology and Seismology (PHIVOLCS) research station and the *Mayon Resthouse* are located. You'll need to register at PHIVOLCS. *Mayon Resthouse* is a simple place with dorm beds for P200–300 a night and some rudimentary cooking facilities. Make sure you bring your own food, as the menu is limited. To get there take a public bus or jeepney from Rizal Street in Legaspi and ask to get off near the *Resthouse*. You might have to walk the last few kilometres if the narrow road leading uphill to the guesthouse and PHIVOLCS is impassable. Having arrived at the foot of Mayon, you'll need to allow three days to make a comfortable ascent and descent.

From PHIVOLCS, the **trail** creeps upwards through a tropical secondary forest, then cuts across a wilderness of razor-sharp *talahib* (grass) before turning sharply at approximately 1220m towards Buang Gully, a ravine formed by ancient molten lava flow. On the gully's floor are enormous depressions containing rainwater. At slightly above 1524m, Buang Gully branches out into two canals. This spot is ideal for a campsite since it is near enough to the summit, yet far enough away from the poisonous fumes that can blow down from the crater with a sudden shift in wind direction. Most climbers make camp here the first night and rise before dawn to continue the next morning, which is when the trail gets really hard. After scrambling over rocks and boulders, you reach a cliff system at 2195m. A forty-degree ascent on loose volcanic cinder and lava sand follows, before finally – the summit. You should reach the summit at around 11am, allowing time to descend to the same overnight camp before dark. On the third day, continue your descent to PHIVOLCS, where you must report your arrival.

Most hotels in Legaspi will help you **arrange a climb** and put you in touch with **local guides**. Under no circumstances should you attempt the climb without a guide. If you feel it's worth it, you can hire porters for around P500 a day plus their food. Also, the tourist information office in Legaspi (see p.731) can set up a package for you for P3500 (for two climbers), as long as you notify them before 5pm the day before. The price includes jeepney transfers, tent, climbing ropes (needed for the uppermost slopes) and food. The best time of year to climb the volcano is from March to May.

Sorsogon

On the southeastern tip of the Bicol Peninsula, **SORSOGON**, capital of the same-name province, makes a good base for visiting Donsol and exploring the beaches of the eastern seaboard, where waves hammer in from the Pacific and **surfing** is a growing industry. One of the nicest beaches is **Rizal beach**, in the barrio of Gubat, a twenty-minute jeepney ride from Sorsogon, where you can get an ageing but adequate room at the *Rizal Beach Resort Hotel* (no phone; ③–④). In Sorsogon itself the *Dalisay* Hotel, in VL Peralta Street (☎056/589 1242; ②), is one of your few decent options, with simple doubles. There are two major **festivals** in Sorsogon: the Kasanggayahan Festival on October 24–27 and the Ginubat festival in the Gubat area on June 11–12. Both celebrate the town's history with street parades, banca (boat) races and beauty pageants.

Donsol

DONSOL lies almost equidistant between Legaspi and Sorsogon and you can get here by bus from either in a couple of hours. The area around Donsol is best known for its **whale sharks**, known locally by a number of names including *butanding*, *balilan* and *kulwano*. The whale shark, a timid titan, is a fish, not a mammal, and can grow up to twenty metres in length, making it the largest fish in the seas. Unlike other sharks, they are not carnivorous and feed only on plankton, sucking it through their gills via an enormous vacuum of a mouth. These gentle giants gather here every year around the time of the northeastern monsoon (December or January) to feed on the rich shrimp and plankton streams that flow from the Donsol River into the sea.

The area around Donsol boasts one of the greatest concentrations of whale sharks in the world and the government is trying to protect them by fining fishermen who catch them. It's an uphill battle though, largely because enforcement in a sparsely populated region like this is difficult. Whale sharks were rarely hunted in the Philippines until the 1990s, when demand for their meat from countries such as Taiwan and Japan escalated. Cooks have dubbed it the tofu shark because of the meat's resemblance to tofu. Its fins are in great demand as a soup extender. Tragically, this has led to its near extinction in the Visayas and further south in Mindanao. For poor fishermen, money talks, and a good whale shark can fetch enough to keep a rural family happy for many months.

In Donsol, however, attitudes seem to be changing, with locals beginning to realize that the whale sharks can be worth more alive than dead. Tourists are also subject to new regulations, governing the viewing of the sharks: the number of boats near a shark is limited and scuba gear and flash photography are not allowed. **Boats** for shark-spotting can be hired at the little pier in Donsol for P1000 for half a day, or you can join other boats if space is available. **Accommodation** is limited to *Resty's Guesthouse* (②), opposite the pier.

Masbate

The province of **Masbate** lies in the centre of the archipelago, bounded in the north by the Bicol Peninsula, in the south by the Visayan Sea, in the west by the Sibuyan Sea, and in the east by the Samar Sea. It includes the main island of **Masbate** and a number of smaller islands, including the **Burias Islands** and the large island of **Ticao**, off the northeastern coast. Masbate is the Philippines' wild east. It ranks second only to Bukidnon in Mindanao in cattle production and plays host to a number of **rodeos** which are being touted by the local governnment as a new tourist attraction. Otherwise, Masbate is off the main tourist trail. There are some excellent beaches, including **Dacu beach** in Mobo town, a fifteen-minute jeepney ride from the capital **MASBATE**, on the northeast coast of Masbate Island. **Talisay beach**, famous for its rock formations, on Ticao Island, is 13km south of San Fernando or 30km from Masbate. **Deagan Island** was once famous for being the favourite hideaway of former First Lady Imelda Marcos. These beaches are favoured by the locals and have simple rustic accommodation. In Masbate itself, *Saint Anthony Hotel* (no phone; ②), on Quezon Street, is one of only a few options.

Masbate **airstrip** is only a five-minute jeepney ride (P10) from Masbate City. Asian Spirit flies direct from Manila four times a week. Sulpicio Lines and WG&A both have **ferry** services from Manila leaving once or twice a week. Ferries also connect Masbate to Cebu and Leyte. **Buses** and jeepneys link Masbate City with other places on the island. They leave from the main square, opposite the Provincial Capitol Building.

Marinduque

The heart-shaped island of **Marinduque**, 170km southeast of Manila, is a quiet backwater, chiefly known for its **Moriones Festival**, a unique and animated Easter tradition featuring masked men dressed like Roman soldiers. This week-long celebration starts on Holy Monday and culminates on Easter Sunday, when the story of the centurion Longinus and his links to Christ are re-enacted in pantomime. Celebrated in the capital **Boac**, on the island's west coast, and also in the nearby villages of Mogpog and Gasan, the festival starts with masked men roaming the streets playing pranks on the residents (and tourists), serenading ladies, frightening children and engaging in mock swordfights. The island's people have a unique style of welcoming and honouring friends and visitors, showering them with flowers and coins.

Apart from the Moriones Festival, you can explore the immense **Bathala Caves** in barangay Ipil, on the north coast, twenty minutes from Boac by jeepney. One of the caves is said to be guarded by a python. Another cave has an underground river and one contains human bones which local people believe to be the remains of World War II soldiers. **Tres Reyes Islands**, off the coast of Gasan in the southwest, have some marvellous beaches and coral reefs. To get to Tres Reyes either take a banca from Boac pier or a jeepney to Gasan, where you can hire a boat. Off the small town of Santa Cruz on the northeast coast, 35 minutes from Boac pier by boat, are the islets of **Polo**, **Mompong** and **Maniwaya**, with powdery sand beaches that rival Boracay. There is no accommodation on these tiny islands, so you should take drinking water and tents if you plan to stay. The waters around Marinduque offer excellent diving, with 83 chartered dive sites.

Practicalities

Asian Spirit flies to Boac daily. Jeepneys and tricycles wait at the small **airport**, ten minutes from town, and will ferry you into town for anything from P10 to P50, depending on your bargaining skills. **BLTB buses** depart hourly from their terminal in Pasay in Manila for the port of Dalahican in Lucena City and take three hours. You then transfer to the Lucena-to-Boac ferry, which departs once daily somewhere between 10.30am and 11am (2hr). The ferry often becomes congested, especially at Easter, and in the typhoon season sometimes doesn't sail at all.

There's not much in the way of effective **tourist information** in Boac, although you can get advice and resort information from any of the resorts on the pebbly beach a short tricycle ride immediately south of town. The best **place to stay** in Boac is the *Boac Hotel* (☎322 1121; ②), which has cheap singles and doubles, with a fan and bath. The friendly staff can also give advice on sightseeing. The coast is dotted with rustic beach huts that you can rent for P100–250 a night.

THE VISAYAS

No-one seems entirely sure how many islands there are in **the Visayas**, but the number certainly runs into the thousands. What is clear is that everywhere you turn there seems to be another patch of tropical sand or coral reef awaiting your attention, usually with a ferry to take you there. There are nine major islands – Cebu, Bohol, Guimaras, Samar, Leyte, Panay, Negros, Romblon and Siquijor – but it's the hundreds of others in between that make this part of the archipelago so irresistible. Some are famous for their beaches, some for their mangoes, some for sugar and some for the alleged presence of witches and goblins. No-one can accuse the Visayas, and the Visayans who live here, of being a uniform lot. In some areas they speak Cebuana, while in others it's Ilonggo, Waray Waray or Aklan. Bigger islands have the kind of glitzy shopping malls and hotels that can do serious damage to the most liberal travel budget, while others are enchantingly rustic, the sort of places where even the grasshoppers are slow. A short journey by banca and you can go from air-conditioned ritz to bucolic nirvana.

Rightly or wrongly, the Visayas are considered the cradle of the Philippines. It was here that Ferdinand Magellan laid a sovereign hand on the islands for Spain. The islands were also

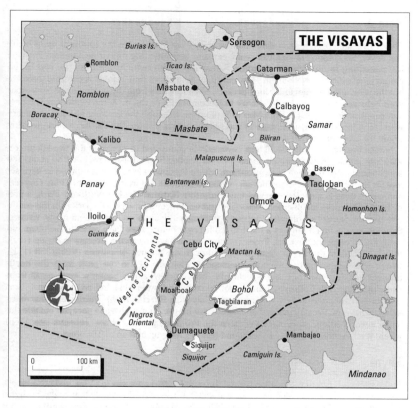

the scene of some of the bloodiest battles fought against the Japanese during World War ll and where General Douglas MacArthur waded ashore to liberate the country after his famous promise, "I shall return". Despite recent efforts to turn **Cebu** into a major international freeport, most of the islands remain lost in their own little world. **Boracay**, off the northern tip of Panay, is representative of the region in topography, but not in atmosphere. Nowhere else will you find the same kind of proliferation of bars and resorts. Vast areas of **Panay**, **Samar** and **Leyte** are still relatively undiscovered, while the "black magic" island of **Siquijor** is said to be home to witches and faith healers. For much of the time in the Visayas you are on your own, free to wander from barrio to barrio and beach to beach. A typical route through the islands would take you from the southern tip of mainland Bicol, across to Samar by ferry, down through Leyte and on to Cebu, Bohol, Negros and Panay, finally ending up on Boracay for R&R. But the beauty of the Visayas is that there's no need to make formal plans. There's always another island, another beach, another place to stay.

Many of the larger Visayan islands have airports with **flights** daily or every few days to Manila Domestic Airport. Boracay, Cebu, Panay, Bohol, Negros, Leyte and Samar are all accessible by air. Island-hopping by plane within the Visayas is harder, with a limited number of flights, but the **ferry network** is so extensive it doesn't really matter. Ferries also ply major routes between Manila and the Visayas. **Cebu** has an international airport with flights to and from Japan, Hong Kong, Kuala Lumpur, Singapore and Taiwan.

Samar

The large island of **Samar**, a short hop by ferry from Matnog, on the southern tip of Bicol, has never, for reasons no-one can really explain, become a big tourist destination. Perhaps it's something to do with the **weather**. Samar has a different climate from the rest of the country, with dry periods only in May and June. Apart from that, rainfall is possible throughout the year, although never for long periods. Most rain falls from the beginning of November until February and from early October to December there can be fierce typhoons. The best and sunniest time to visit is from May to September, although the growing number of surfers who come here to take advantage of the swells that rip in from the Pacific, would probably argue the typhoon season is best.

Samar lies between the Bicol and Leyte and is connected to Leyte by the two-kilometre-long San Juanico Bridge, which spans the San Juanico Strait. It is surrounded by about 180 small islands, one of which is **Homonhon**, where Ferdinand Magellan is reputed to have set foot for the first time on Philippine soil on March 16, 1521, before sailing on to Cebu. One reason not to miss Samar is the marvellous **Sohoton Natural Bridge National Park**, a prehistoric wilderness full of caves, waterfalls and underground rivers. The park is in the southern part of Samar, so quickest access is through Tacloban on Leyte. For many visitors, Sohoton is scheduled only as a day-trip from Leyte before they loop back to Tacloban and continue through the Visayas. From Tacloban you'll have to catch a jeepney to Basey (1hr), then a pedicab to the Department of Environment and Natural Resources (☎055/276 1151), where you can arrange guides and accommodation. To get to the park from the north involves making the long but spectacular bus journey along Samar's west coast from **Catarman** through **Calbayog** (famous for its caves and waterfalls) and on to **Basey**.

There are **airports** at both Catarman and Calbayog. **Ferries from Matnog** are four times a day (6am, 7am, 9am, 10am) and take about two hours. They arrive at a port just outside the small town of **Allen**, on Samar's northern tip. From the port there are jeepneys into Allen, where it is possible to get the southbound bus to Calbayog and on to Tacloban.

Leyte

In the sixteenth century, Magellan passed through **Leyte** on his way to Cebu, making a blood compact with the local chieftain as he did so. But it was World War II that really brought Leyte fame. On October 20, 1944, General Douglas MacArthur landed at Leyte, fulfilling the promise he had made to Filipinos, "I shall return." He brought with him an enormous fleet of transport and warships, and the first President of the Commonwealth, Sergio Osmena.

On the northeast coast, the capital of Leyte, **TACLOBAN**, is associated by most Filipinos with that tireless collector of shoes, Imelda Marcos, who was born here to a humble family called Romualdez. The airport has been renamed Daniel Z Romualdez Airport and numerous streets and buildings bear the same name. In her youth, Imelda was a local beauty queen, and referred to herself in later life as "the rose of Tacloban". There's little to see at Tacloban itself. A climb up to Tacloban Town Hall atop Kanhuraw Hill in front of Santo Nino Church, rewards you with **panoramic views** of Cancabato Bay, San Pedro Bay, San Juanico Strait, Cataisan Point and Samar Island. The **Tacloban Festival** in the last week of June kicks off with the Subiran Regatta, an annual boat race held at the eastern entrance of the San Juanico Strait.

Around Tacloban some of the most memorable sights are the reminders of **World War II** and how fierce it was on Leyte. A memorial marks the spot where MacArthur landed on Red beach, **Palo**, south of Tacloban; you can reach it by jeepney. Just outside Palo, on Hill 522, foxholes still remain. The Battle of Baluarte Marker, 52km away in Barugo, commemorates a hellish battle that saw a small band of Filipinos wipe out a Japanese platoon.

From Tacloban buses travel through the rugged hinterland to the port town of **ORMOC**, where ferries set sail for Cebu. Ormoc is also the starting point for a trail called the **Leyte Mountain Trail**, which winds for 40km through jungle and over mountains to serene Lake

Mahagnao, from where you can catch a jeepney or bus back to Ormoc. The town hall in Ormoc can provide details of the trail.

Practicalities

Jeepneys from Tacloban **airport** to the city centre will cost P5, a taxi about P50. **Buses** arrive at a terminal at the junctions of Quezon Boulevard and Rizal Avenue, on the northeastern edge of the city, close to the coast. Buses leave here daily for Calbayog, Basey, even Davao and Manila. Note that Philtranco buses have their own terminal south of the city. Philtranco serves most major destinations on Leyte. Negros Navigation and Cebu Ferries sail between Tacloban and Manila, but WG&A only operates between Manila and Ormoc. Negros Navigation and Cebu Ferries sail from Tacloban to Manila, but WG&A only operates between Manila and Ormoc.

The **tourist information office** (☎053/321 2048 or 321 4333) is near Children's Park off Magsaysay Avenue. There's a **post office** near the harbour on Tree Martirez Street; the **Philippine National Bank**, and a number of others, are on J Romualdez Street. The *Net Surf Café* at 170 Veteranos St has **Internet** access for P60 an hour.

ACCOMMODATION AND EATING

Cecilia's Lodge at 178 Paterno St (☎053/321 2815; ②) is the place many travellers head for. It has singles and doubles with fan. Also on Paterno Street is *LNU House* (☎053/321 3175 or 321 2170; ③), which has functional but bright **accommodation**, popular with local students. For nutritious **food** the *Alpha Bakery*, at the northern end of Zamora Street, at its junction with Rizal Avenue, is a good place to start. A little further south on Zamora Street is *Chinatown* restaurant, which has rice and vegetarian dishes for P60–120. *Giuseppi's* is a long-standing Italian favourite on Veteranos Avenue, while the newer *Bistro Uno* at 41 Juan Luna St has sandwiches, burgers and traditional Filipino dishes such as *pancit* and *adobo*. The local Waray-Waray cuisine is generally spicy and tasty. *Binagul*, a hot sticky concoction made of coconut and nuts, can be bought freshly made every morning on the street.

Cebu

Like many Philippine cities, **CEBU**, nicknamed the "Queen City of the South", has become something of an urban nightmare in recent decades, with jeepneys taking over the inadequate road network and pedestrians relegated to second-best. There's history and architecture in there somewhere, but you have to look hard for it among the clutter, the exhaust fumes and the malls.

Arrival and information

Planes land at **Mactan International Airport**. Staff at the tourist information counter (Mon–Sat 6am–midnight) in the arrivals hall will help you arrange a taxi (P150) or shuttle to Cebu City itself, 8km away across the suspension bridge that links Mactan island to the main island of Cebu. Public transport from the airport does exist, but is unreliable. An alternative is to take a taxi as far as Lapu-Lapu City on Mactan Island (P40–P50), then switch to public transport. Jeepneys go from here to Cebu City (P10). The arrival point for ferries is the **harbour** area beyond Fort San Pedro. Jeepneys and buses line up along Quezon Boulevard for the short journey into the city. Look for one marked Osmena Boulevard or Colon Sreet.

The main **tourist information office** (Mon–Sat 9.30am–5pm; ☎032/254 2811) is at the corner of Lapu-Lapu and Legaspi streets near Fort San Pedro. There's an **Immigration Office** (8am–noon & 1–5pm; ☎032/253 4339) on the 4th Floor, Ceutiaco Building, MC Briones Street. There is no shortage of places to **change** currency, particularly along the main drag of Osmena Boulevard where you'll also find the Cebu Doctor's Hospital (☎032/253 7511). The **post office**, on Quezon Boulevard close to the port area, offers a poste restante service.

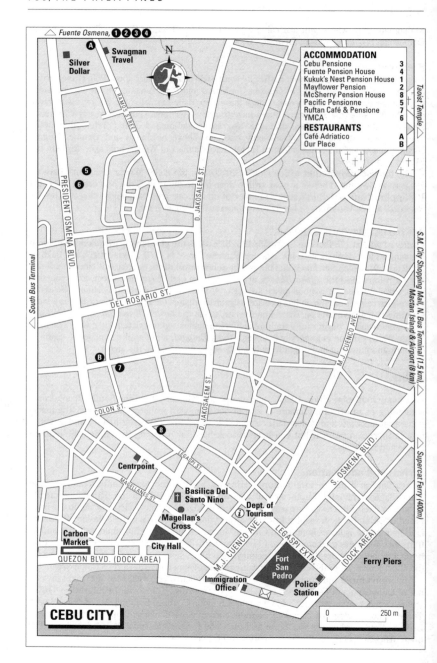

△ Fuente Osmena, ❶❷❸❹

A Swagman Travel

Silver Dollar

N

ACCOMMODATION
Cebu Pensione 3
Fuente Pension House 4
Kukuk's Nest Pension House 1
Mayflower Pension 2
McSherry Pension House 8
Pacific Pensionne 5
Ruftan Café & Pensione 7
YMCA 6
RESTAURANTS
Café Adriatico A
Our Place B

Taoist Temple △

❺
❻

F. RAMOS STREET

PRESIDENT OSMENA BLVD.

D. JAKOSALEM ST.

S.M. City Shopping Mall, N. Bus Terminal (1.5 km),
Mactan Island & Airport (8 km) △

◁ South Bus Terminal

DEL ROSARIO ST.

M.J. CUENCO AVE.

B
❼

Supercat Ferry (400m) ▷

COLON ST.

D. JAKOSALEM ST.

❽

LEGASPI ST.

Centrpoint

MAGELLANES ST.

Basilica Del Santo Nino

Dept. of
ⓘ Tourism

S. OSMENA BLVD.

Magellan's Cross

Carbon Market

City Hall

QUEZON BLVD. (DOCK AREA)

M.J. CUENCO AVE.

LEGASPI EXTN.

Immigration Office

Fort San Pedro

Police Station

(DOCK AREA)

Ferry Piers

CEBU CITY

0   250 m

MOVING ON FROM CEBU

By plane

Major domestic airlines such as Cebu Pacific and Philippine airlines have daily departures to Manila, Davao and Iloilo. The small airline Mindanao Express has a hub at Cebu and offers flights to Bacolod, Cagayan de Oro, Cotabato, Davao, Dipolog, Pagadian, Tawi-Tawi and Zamboanga City. The Philippine airline industry is in a permanent state of flux, so check with the tourist information office for updated schedules and destinations.

By ferry

Leaving Cebu **by ferry** could hardly be easier. The harbour area is in the southeast corner of the city, beyond Fort San Pedro, and is jammed with ferries large and small. The air-conditioned and comfortable Supercats (☎032/232 3455) leave from Pier 4 for Ormoc, Tagbiliran on Bohol and Dumaguete. One-way tickets cost around P275. WG&A Superferry (☎032/232 0490) pulls out of Pier 6. Other ferry companies operating in and out of Cebu include Trans-Asia Shipping Lines (☎032/254 6491), Socor Shipping Lines (☎032/253 6531) and Lite Shipping (☎032/253 7776). A good place to get up-to-date ferry information (schedules and pier numbers often change) is at SM City shopping mall, where the SM Travellers' Lounge (☎032/232 0291) has schedules and a number of offices where you can book tickets.

By bus

There are two **bus terminals** in Cebu, the Northern Bus Terminal just outside the city on the coastal road for buses heading north, and the Southern Bus Terminal in Bacalso Avenue for buses heading south and across the island to destinations on the west coast such as Moalboal.

Internet cafés are proliferating in Cebu. Try *Cybernet Café* (☎032/254 8533) at 151 Junquera St next to the *Elicon Hotel Café* or *Ruftan Internet Café & Pensione* on Legaspi Street. Both charge P50 an hour.

Accommodation

Cebu Mintel Austrian Pension Haus, Irineo Ames Building, Ma. Cristina Street, 53C F Ramos Extension (☎032/254 6200). In a good location ten minutes from Fuente Osmena. Has modern singles and doubles, with private facilities, and a nice coffee shop. ④.

Cebu Pensione, Plaza North Escario Street (☎032/254 6300). Large, clean deluxe rooms, with more than enough room for two. Top-of-the-range suites also available. ④–⑤.

Fuente Pension House, 13 Don Julio Llorente Street (☎032/253-6789). A good variety of rooms, including singles and family rooms. ④–⑤.

Kukuk's Nest Pension House, 157 Gorordo Ave (☎032/412 2026). A hangout for artists and beatniks, offering quaintly furnished rooms, some with air-con, bath and cable TV. Also has a garden restaurant. ①–②.

Mayflower Pension, Villalon Drive (☎032/253 7233). Average rooms with shared facilities. The good news is that it's in a pleasant location near the Capitol Building at the quieter northern end of the city and has a ticket office that can help with travel arrangements, a laundry, a café and a mini-library where you can swap one dog-eared paperback for another. ②–③.

McSherry Pension House, in an alley off Pelaez Street, near the *Mercedes Hotel*. In an excellent location, a short walk from Colon Street and opposite the popular bar *Our Place*, *McSherry's* has been around for years. The rooms are a bit dark and uninspiring, but good value. ②.

Pacific Pensione, 313-A Osmena Blvd (☎032/253 5271). A popular place in a convenient but rather noisy location on Cebu's main drag, which runs from the Fuente Osmena roundabout in the north to Colon Street in the south. ③.

Ruftan Café & Pensione, 61 Legaspi St. A backpacker haven near the Basilica del Santo Nino. Clean rooms, good food, Internet access and a host of travel information from staff and other guests. ①–③.

YMCA, 61 Osmena Blvd (☎032/253 4057). A great range of rooms from cheap singles to quads with fan and shower. Small swimming pool, billiards and an average cafeteria. ②.

The City

Cebu City is defined at its northern limit by **Fuente Osmena**, the large traffic roundabout at the far end of Osmena Boulevard. There are hotels, restaurants, fruit stalls and department stores here, and at night it's the place to be for roller skaters and promenaders. At the other end of Osmena Boulevard – the southern end near the coast – is the city's mercantile heart, with banks, airline offices and yet more department stores. **Osmena Boulevard** is the city's major artery and if you don't fancy the twenty-minute walk from one end to the other, you can always take a jeepney (P10).

The city's spiritual heart is a small crypt opposite the town hall that houses the **Cross of Magellan**. It's actually a modern hollow cross that is said to contain fragments of the original brought by the famous conquistador in 1521 and used in the first conversions of locals to Christianity. Next to the cross on Osmena Boulevard is the dusty and towering **Basilica del Santo Nino** where vendors with tawdry religious icons and amulets offer cures from everything from poverty to infertility. Inside the basilica, built 1735–37, is probably the most famous religious icon in the Philippines, a statue of the Santo Nino (child Christ), said to have been presented to Queen Juana of Cebu by Magellan after her baptism in 1521. The next conquistador, Miguel Lopez de Legaspi, arrived in 1565 and built **Fort San Pedro**, near the port area at the end of Quezon Boulevard, whose shaded garden is today one of the quietest spots in Cebu, away from the choking din of the city centre. For intense local colour and sensory overload take a walk down **Carbon Street**, said to be the oldest street in the country, or struggle through the sweat and bustle of **Carbon Market**, off Magellanes Street, where the range of goods on offer, edible and otherwise, will leave you reeling. A twenty-minute taxi ride from the city takes you to the hills above the city where the **Taoist Temple** and immense houses are testament to the influence and wealth of the Cebuano Chinese, whose forefathers arrived from eastern China as early as the sixteenth century to trade in silks, porcelain and spices.

Eating

Barrio Fiesta, 3rd Level, SM City shopping mall (☎032/232 0640). *Barrio Fiesta*, with its colourful array of native dishes and snacks, is one of dozens of restaurants in the enormous SM City.

Café Adriatico, F Ramos Street (☎032/253 0405). Sister establishment of the hugely popular place of the same name in Malate, Manila. Filipino and European food and *merienda* (snacks) served in a bohemian environment. A good place to cool off with coffee or beer.

Max's Restaurant, Fuente Osmena (☎032/253 4327). This friendly chicken chain is ubiquitous in the Philippines. Fuente Osmena is an interesting area to stroll around at night, with plenty of other restaurants, hotels and bars.

Our Place, Corner of Pelaez Sreet and Sanchiangko (☎032/254 7916). Friendly hangout of the Cebu male expat community. Less popular with women and locals, although that's not to say they won't be made welcome. Steaks, curries and burgers for around P100 and San Miguel for P30. Info from the barflies on everything from diving to collecting seashells.

Visayan Restaurant, 126 V Guillas St (☎032/253 8631). Satisfying and inexpensive native and Chinese dishes, including dim sum, soups, fried rice, bean curd and good fish.

Nightlife and entertainment

Cebu, like its big brother Manila, is a city that never – or rarely – sleeps. You can't walk more than a few metres without passing a pub, a karaoke lounge or a music bar. The colourful and friendly *Jerby's Café and Music Lounge* (9am–2am) is one of many popular **nightspots** on Fuente Osmena. Just south of Fuenta Osmena on Osmena Boulevard is *Harley's* (11am–4am), where the P150 cover charge includes one drink and the chance to listen to female pop singers putting Madonna and Mariah Carey to shame. Close to *Harleys* (look out for *McDonald's*) on Osmena Boulevard is the *Silver Dollar* (5pm–2am), which is popular with expats. The most powerful lure these days for Cebu's pretty young things are the discos and bars of the *Cebu Plaza Hotel*, a ten-minute taxi ride out of town on Cebu Veteran's Drive. The hotel's *Pards* bar hosts good live bands.

Mactan Island

Mactan Island is linked to the main island of Cebu by an impressive suspension bridge and a relatively new road. The small capital of **LAPU-LAPU** has an interesting market and a monument to its eponymous father. The rest of Mactan Island stands as a monument largely to bad taste. Most of its coastline has been colonized by enormous resorts charging hundreds of dollars a night for the pleasure of drinking cocktails on a man-made beach. To get to Mactan from Cebu City take a P10 jeepney ride from SM City shopping mall in J Luna Avenue Extension, close to the *Sheraton Cebu Hotel*. In Lapu-Lapu, jeepneys stop near the small market square, where you can catch a tricycle for the short hop to the beaches.

Maribago beach is ten minutes south of Lapu-Lapu on the island's south coast and has a nice natural beach. One of the cheapest **places to stay** is the *Buyong Hotel and Restaurant* (☎032/492 0118; ③–⑤). In Lapu-Lapu, near Mactan bridge, there are a couple of less expensive hotels, including *Mactan Bridgeside Hotel* (☎032/340 1704; ②–④). Mactan is also famous for its guitar factories, where a steel-stringed acoustic with shell inlay can be picked up for P2000–3000.

Moalboal

Three hours by road and 89km from Cebu City on the southwestern flank of Cebu Island, lies the sleepy coastal village of **MOALBOAL**, for many years a favourite hangout of travellers and scuba divers. Most of the activity in Moalboal is in fact centred around **diving** and it's hardly surprising: the sea is crystal clear, and, while many reefs along the mainland coast were damaged by a typhoon ten years ago, the enigmatic Pescador Island survived, an alluring site a few miles offshore (15min by banca). Divers return from here every day with stories of sharks, mantas and moray eels. Sun-worshippers looking for a Boracay-style sandy beach will be disappointed, though. There isn't one. Moalboal makes up for this in other ways, with a great range of cheap accommodation, a marvellous view of the sunset over distant Negros, and some good discounts on diving and rooms if you hang around long enough.

A number of **bus** companies have regular services from Cebu City's Southern Bus Terminal, but remember that most continue beyond Moalboal so you'll have to make sure the driver knows where you want to get off. ABC and Albines buses are marked for Bato. You'll be dropped off on the main road, from where a tricycle will take you down the dusty track to **Panagsama beach**, where all the resorts are. There's a wide range of **accommodation** and it's all huddled in more or less the same area. Roughly in the middle of the beach is *Pacitas Beach Resort* (cellphone ☎0918/770 9982; ②–③), which has bungalows, while *Emma's Store & Restaurant* (②–③) and *Eve's Kiosk* (②–③) both have rooms at the cheaper end of the scale. For something in the mid-range category, some of the dive outfits offer good rooms. At the southern end of the beach, *Quo Vadis Beach Resort* (cellphone ☎0918/770 8684; ③–⑦) has a range of private bungalows, and *Cora's Palm Court* (③), at the north end, has doubles with fan and a choice of breakfast thrown in. There are as many **places to eat** at Moalboal as there are to stay. *Roxy Music Pub*, near the middle of the beach, has a good menu and the occasional impromptu jam session. *Last Filling Station*, on the main path along the shore, is a Moalboal favourite, with a daily Asian barbecue for a reasonable P135. Besides diving, many dive shops offer other activities such as kayaking, mountain-bike rental and snorkelling. For US$25 you can have a day of horse riding along the shore or through pleasant jungle trails.

Bantayan Island

There's not much to see or do at **Bantayan Island**, just off the northwest coast of Cebu, but this is precisely why people come here – just to lie on its beaches or laze for a few days at one of its sleepy little resorts. It's also a handy stepping stone to Negros and on to Panay and Boracay. Ferries from Cebu arrive at the island's capital **BANTAYAN**, also the departure point for ferries to Negros. Most of the island's resorts and beaches are concentrated in the pretty town of **Santa Fe** on the island's southeast coast.

To **get here** from Cebu City take a Phil-Cebu Bus Lines bus from the Northern Bus Terminal to the northern port town of Hagnaya. It's best to catch an early bus at 5am or 6am. It will take you straight to the pier at Hagnaya where you pay a P2 pier fee and P55 for the one-hour journey to Santa Fe.

For **accommodation**, you could try *Santa Fe Beach Club*, near the police station, though it has been spoiled slightly by the recent erection of oil tanks close to the main building. Bamboo cottages are either P500 or P1000 depending on how much luxury you crave. *Kota Beach Resort* (③–④) has basic fan **rooms** and cottages with fan and bath. It's expensive for what you get, but the **restaurant** is pleasant. *Budyong Beach Resort* (②) next door is better value, with shady rooms, some with air con. On the dusty road from Bantayan to Madridjesos, at the northernmost tip of the island, is the excellent *Moby Dick's Beach Resort* (②–③), with a pool, restaurant and large cottages, with full board. If you have to stay in Bantayan town for the night, try *Namont Pension House* (③) on Osmena Street near Allied Bank.

Malapuscua Island

From Bantayan you can hire bancas to take you to the nearby island of **Malapuscua** for P1500 (one way), about one hour away. Malapuscua is 2.5km long and about 1km wide and tricycles are the only form of transport. **Bounty beach** on the south coast is beautiful and not to be missed. Places to stay on the beach include *BB's Lodging House* (②), which has basic doubles, and the more upmarket *Cocobana Beach Resort* (⑤), which has accommodation in spacious cottages. If you want to go to Malapuscua direct from Cebu City, catch a bus from the Northern Bus Terminal to Maya and then hop on a public banca (45min).

Bohol

It's hard to imagine that **Bohol**, a two-hour hop south of Cebu by fast ferry, has a bloody past. The only reminder of the unpleasantness is a memorial stone in the barrio of Bool, denoting the spot where Rajah Sikatuna and Miguel Lopez de Legaspi concluded an early round of hostilities in 1565 by signing a compact in blood. Even before Legaspi arrived and brought Catholicism with him from Spain, members of the indigenous Bool tribe were using the coves around Panglao and Tagbiliran to hide from vicious Muslim marauders who swept north through the Visayan islands from their bases in Mindanao. These days, however, apart from some mercantile activity in the capital, **Tagbiliran**, Bohol is a dozy sort of place. The only sign of what in other cultures might pass for frenzied activity, is on the beautiful beaches of **Panglao Island**, where scuba divers gather in their incongruous neon wetsuits. Everywhere else, Bohol is on Filipino time and runs at Filipino pace. Even the carabao chew slowly. For most visitors the only obligatory sortie away from Panglao's beaches is to see the island's most iconoclastic tourist attraction, the **Chocolate Hills**. Some geologists believe that these unique forty-meter mounds were formed from deposits of coral and limestone sculpted by centuries of erosion. The locals, however, will tell you the hills are the calcified tears of a giant, whose heart was broken by the death of a mortal lover. The best time to see the Chocolate Hills – there are allegedly 1268 of them – is at dawn, when the rising sun plays spectacular tricks with light, shadow and color. Aficionados recommend the end of the dry season (April or May), when the grass has turned brown, and with a short stretch of the imagination, the hills really do resemble chocolate drops.

More and more people are visiting Bohol for its world-class **scuba diving** – not only at Panglao, but at the lesser-known islands of Pamilacan, Cabilao, Ajo, Mahanay and Lapinin off the northern coast. Away from the water you can visit **Antequera** a twenty-minute bus ride from Tagbilaran, where there's a handicrafts market twice a week on Thursdays and Saturdays. The barrio of **Corolla**, easily accesible by bus, is the start of the Tarsier Trail, a fifteen-kilometre pathway that meanders through the habitat of the Philippine tarsier – tarsius syrichta – the world's smallest primate. This area is a tarsier sanctuary, home to about five hundred of the hand-sized beasts, whose eyes weigh more than their brains. There are a handful of interesting churches in Bohol, also reachable by bus. **Baclayon Church**, built in 1595 in the baroque Jesuit style typical of the central Philippines, is believed to have been the first church in the country. And if you've got half a day to spare you can run out by jeepney to the old Spanish watchtower at **Punta Cruz**, where colonizing garrisons kept their muskets aimed facing west across the Bohol Strait.

Practicalities

Tagbilaran Airport is less than 2km outside the city of Tagbilaran. The only problem is finding an airline to take you there from Manila. Philippine Airlines has dropped Tagbilaran from its schedule, although it might resume flights when its precarious financial situation has improved. The only option at the time of writing was Asian Spirit, which has flights at 5.30am on Tuesdays, Thursdays, Saturdays and Sundays (US$76 one way or US$135 return). Tricycles into town cost P20 and taxis around P50. The **ferry pier** in Tagbilaran is in the northwest of the city off Gallares Street. For **getting around** Bohol by bus all journeys start at the Dao Integrated Bus Terminal in E Butalid Street, twenty minutes outside Tagbilaran by jeepney. Catch any jeepney in Grupo Street marked "Int. Bus Terminal." A bridge links Bohol proper to Panglao Island. Buses and jeepneys are marked for Alona.

The **tourist information office** (Mon–Sat 9am–5pm; ☎038/411 3666) is rather inconveniently situated in the Governor's Mansion, ten minutes by tricycle outside Tagbilaran on the road towards the airport. **Philippine National Bank** is on the junction of CPG Avenue and JA Clarin Street, while the **police station** is near City Hall, behind St Joseph's Cathedral. The **post office** is also near here, at the end of the City Hall car park. The **Internet** has not yet made a significant impact on Bohol. If you desperately need to access your email, try Bohol Quality Megabyte in Grupo Street. A number of the resorts might also be willing to help.

ACCOMMODATION AND EATING

In Tagbilaran itself, not that there's any real reason to stay there, *Traveller's Inn* (☎038/411 3731; ①–②) on CPG Avenue is one of half a dozen pensions in town that offers average **accommodation**. *Everglory Hotel* at 130 C Gallares St (☎038/411 4858; ③) is in a good location close to the pier.

Most of the budget accommodation on **Panglao Island** is at Alona Beach. *Alonaville Beach Resort* (☎038/41 3254; ②–③) has rustic cottages for two, a cosy bar and other tourist facilities such as motorbike rental. *Alona Tropical* (⑤) has a popular restaurant and cottages that sleep two. The more upmarket *Alona Kew White Beach Resort* (⑦) has lush grounds, a stylish restaurant and double cottages with air-con and bath. *Bohol Divers Lodge* (☎038/411 4983; ④) has double cottages; the management is French and there's a good restaurant and bar. A P30 tricycle ride away on Doljo Beach is *Palm Island Beach Resort* (③), with nipa huts and also a nipa dorm with singles for P150.

Negros

The island of **Negros** lies at the heart of the Visayas, between Panay to the west and Cebu to the east. Shaped like a boot, it is split diagonally into the northwestern province of Negros

Occidental and the southeastern province of Negros Oriental. The demarcation came when early missionaries decided the central mountain range was too formidable to cross, even in the name of God. It's an island many tourists miss out and as a result is largely unspoilt: it has miles of untouched coastline, some pleasant towns – **Dumaguete**, the capital of Negros Oriental is one of the stateliest towns in the Philippines – and dormant **volcanoes**. Negros is also "Sugarlandia", producing fifty percent of the country's **sugar**. Around **Bacolod**, the capital of Negros Occidental, authentic 1912 steam locomotives and well-preserved Spanish ancestral homes serve as reminders of the rich sugar barons and Spanish families of the past.

Bacolod and around

The city of **BACOLOD** on the northern coast of Negros is another testament to the wonders you can perform with concrete. It's big, it's hot, it's noisy and there's not much to see or do. The Old Capitol Building is one of the few architectural highlights and houses the excellent **Negros Museum**, which details 5000 years of history. During the third week of October everybody who is anybody attends the flamboyant **Masskara festival**, a mardi gras jamboree of street dancing and beauty pageants. The street-dancing participants wear masks, hence the name Masskara.

MOUNT KANLAON NATIONAL PARK

Mount Kanlaon, two hours from Bacolod by jeepney, is the tallest peak in the central Philippines and offers a potentially dangerous challenge. Climbers have died scaling it, so don't underestimate its fury. It is still one of the thirteen most active volcanoes in the country and locals believe it is home to many spirits. The surrounding forest contains all manner of wonderful fauna, including pythons, monitor lizards, tube-nosed bats and the dahoy pulay, a poisonous green tree snake. There are a number of resorts in the area. It was here that President Manuel Quezon hid from invading Japanese forces during World War II. For up-to-date information about the safety of climbing Kanlaon and for details on accommodation nearby contact the City Tourism Office in Bacolod (☎033/433 2515 or 433 2517).

SILAY AND VICTORIAS

North of Bacolod, **SILAY** is one of the historic centres of the sugar industry. The few tourists that come here do so for the sugar trains and the marvellous ancestral houses. The most interesting aspect of the trains – iron dinosaurs, as they are known – is that they are fuelled by bagasse, a by-product of sugar production. Silay offers a first-rate impression of what life was like in the heyday of the plantations. It's worth making time to spend a few hours at the **Balay Negrense Museum**, 5 Novembre St (daily except Mon & holidays 10am–6pm; free), a lifestyle museum and formerly one of the grandest plantation homes in the area. Silay is a 45-minute ride north of Bacolod by bus or jeepney. In neighbouring **VICTORIAS**, at the Vicmico Public Relations Office on Ossario Avenue, is the Church of St Joseph the Worker, built 1948–50. The church is home to the controversial icon called the Angry Christ, which depicts Jesus sitting in front of the hands of God, straddling a serpent-spewing skull.

Practicalities

Bacolod **Airport** is 5km south of the city on Araneta Street. Turn left outside the airport to pick up a jeepney going to the city (P20). WG&A and Negros Navigation both sail from Manila to Bacolod. There are also regular departures between Bacolod and Iloilo, Cebu City and Cagayan de Oro in Mindanao. Sea Angels runs fast ferries from Bacolod to Iloilo. Ferries arrive at and depart from **Banago Wharf**, north of the city on San Juan street. From the Ceres North Terminal on Lopez Jaena Street in Bacolod there are **local buses** to Dumaguete, Silay, Victorias and other coastal towns on the Negros Coastal Road. It's 313km to Dumaguete and the trip takes about eight hours. Make sure you take an express bus, which avoids many stops at the barrios. There's also a service that travels clockwise around

Negros starting from Bacolod and calling at towns en route before boarding a roll on-roll-off ferry for Toledo on the western coast of Cebu and continuing on to Cebu City.

The **tourist information office** (Mon–Sat 8.30am–5.30pm; ☎033/433 2515 or 433 2517) is in the administrative building of the provincial government complex in City Plaza, San Juan Street. **Immigration** (☎033/708 9502) is on Gatuslao Street and can arrange visa extensions. The **post office** is also on Gatuslao Street, near the junction with Burgos Street. Most of Bacolod's **banks**, including PCI and PNB, are near the city plaza in Araneta and Gonzaga Streets. The trendy *Cyberheads Café* (☎033/434 1604) on the junction of Lacson and 7th Street offers **Internet** access for P60 an hour.

On the relatively peaceful 11th Street is *Pension Bacolod* (①–③), which has a decent restaurant. Also at the budget end of the price range is the *Star Plus Pension House* (②–③), on Lacson Street, with small but clean rooms with air-con. The *King's Hotel* (☎033/433 0574; ③), on Gatusla Street, is slightly more upmarket and great value, with big, clean singles and doubles. For **food** you can nibble ceaselessly on sweet delicacies such as *piyaya* (a hardened pancake with sugar melted inside) and *bay ibayi* (sugar and coconut served in a coconut shell). They are sold all over the city from street stalls and hole-in-the-wall canteens. Don't miss the barbecue chicken at *Chicken House*, Lacson Sreet, at the corner of 24th Street. *Mira's Café* on Locsin Street is a calm and quaint place serving native dishes and local coffee.

Dumaguete and around

The City of Gentle People lives up to its name. **DUMAGUETE**, capital of Negros Oriental, lies on the southeast coast of Negros, within sight of the most southerly tip of Cebu Island. It's off the traditional tourist track, but it's hard to understand why because it has exquisite architecture, mile upon mile of sandy beach, and pleasant piazzas where residents promenade every evening or indulge in a spot of al fresco ballroom dancing. It's close to the marine sanctuary of Apo Island where the scuba diving is superlative. North of the city is the small coastal town of Bais, where you can hire boats to go whale- and dolphin-watching. Dive outfits such as Cocktail Divers, based at Yhalason Beach west of the city, organize scuba courses and trips to Apo.

The small **airport** is a few kilometres northwest of the city centre. Tricycles make the airport-to-city trip for about P30. The alternative is to fly to Cebu and get the fast **ferry** from Cebu City. WG&A Superferry and Negros Navigation both have regular sailings to and from Manila. WG&A also goes from Dumaguete to Cagayan de Oro, while Negros Navigation serves Tagbilaran on Bohol. The pier in Dumaguete is at the end of Rizal Avenue, a few minutes by jeepney or taxi from the city. Delta fast ferries (☎035/225 6358) has daily departures to Cebu, Siquijor and Dapitan. **Buses** arrive at terminals at the far south of Perdices Street, on the far side of the Benica River. A jeepney into the city costs P10. Buses for other destinations on Negros also leave from these terminals.

The **tourist information office** (Mon–Sat 8.30am–6pm; ☎035/225 0549) is in the City Hall complex on Colon Street and the **Immigration Office**, which can arrange visa extensions without going through Manila, is at 38 Dr V Locsin St. The **post office** on Santa Catalina Street offers poste restante, and for **Internet** access the cafés around the Silliman University complex, at the northern end of Hibbard Street, are a good bet; try *Surf Station Internet Café* on Katada cor. Hibbard Avenue. The *Music Box* on Rizal Avenue is Dumaguete's premier expat hangout and a good place to gather intelligence. It offers Internet access and **transport** to local beach resorts.

In Dumaguete there is plenty of budget **accommodation** around the main plaza. *Theresa's Lodge* (☎035/225 4827; ①) on San Juan Street has fairly spartan but clean rooms, with shared facilities. *Vintage Inn* (☎035/225 1076; ②), on Legaspi Street opposite the public market, has singles and doubles, with air con. Overlooking the sea on Rizal Boulevard is *Bethel Guest House* (☎035/225 2009; ④), a tall building with singles, doubles and clean facilities.

South of Dumaguete is beach resort country, with a good range of clean and affordable accommodation close to the sea, often with dive schools attached. **DAUIN** is a popular port of call, twenty minutes' journey by bus or jeepney from Dumaguete. *El Dorado's* beach resort is comfortable, has a good restaurant, a popular bar and offers diving at Apo Island. About 45 minutes' bus ride north of Dumaguete is **BAIS**, a centre for whale- and dolphin-watching. One of the nicest places to stay here is *La Planta* (☎541-5755; ⑤), a colonial-style pension on the hill with wonderful views and a pretty restaurant.

Siquijor

Siquijor, nicknamed "Island of Fire", lying slightly apart from the rest of the Visayas off the southern tip of Cebu and about 22km east of Negros, is so called because of the number of fireflies Spanish sailors used to see as they approached at night. Very little is known about Siquijor and its inhabitants before the arrival of the Spaniards in the sixteenth century. This sense of mystery still persists today, with many Filipinos believing Siquijor to be a centre of witchcraft and black magic. It's a view that's enforced by the annual staging of the Conference of Sorcerers and Healers in the mountain village of San Antonio every Easter. You can circumnavigate Siquijor by bus and jeepney along the bumpy coastal road. **SIQUI-JOR TOWN**, the capital, is twenty minutes by jeepney southwest of Larena, the main port. There are four daily hydrofoil links on Delta Fast Ferries between Dumaguete on Negros and Larena, making it possible to visit Siquijor for a day. Delta also has two journeys a day between Dumaguete and Siquijor Town. There are ferries every other day to and from Cebu, but it's a longer journey (7hr). The most popular beaches on Siquijor are **Sandugan**, half an hour by jeepney north of Larena, and **Paliton** on the west coast, which you can reach by jeepney from San Juan. There is plenty of nipa-type rustic beach **accommodation** in these areas. On Sandugan Beach try *Casa de la Playa*, *Kiwi Dive Resort* or *Paradise Beach Resort*, all offering doubles in the ②–③ range.

Panay

The big heart-shaped island of **Panay** has been largely bypassed by tourism, perhaps because everyone seems to get sucked inexorably towards Boracay off its northern tip instead. Panay comprises four provinces, Antique on the west coast, Aklan in the north, Capiz in the northeast and Iloilo (eel-o-eel-o) running along the east coast to the capital of Iloilo Province, **Iloilo City** in the south. The province that interests most tourists is **Aklan**, whose capital Kalibo is the site of the big and brash **Ati-Atihan Festival**, held every second week of January. Revellers blacken their faces in imitation of their aboriginal forefathers and stage a shuffling dance in the streets amid cries of "hala, bira!" ("go on and fight!"). Most tourists choose to get to Panay by flying from Manila to Kalibo airport. If you have more time on your hands you might choose to take a plane or ferry to Iloilo and there work your way either along the east or west coast by jeepney and bus, though the roads are in poor condition and you should be prepared for delays and some sub-standard accommodation. **Antique** is a bucolic province of beaches and precipitous cordillera mountains, while the northeast coast from **Concepcion** to **Batad** offers access by banca to a number of unspoilt islands, including the conspicuous **Pan de Azucar** (Sugar Loaf). The largest of these islands is **Sicogon**, which measures only 11 square kilometres, fringed by white sandy beaches and home to monkeys, wild pigs and eagles. Most of these islands have few places to stay, so if you want to spend the night take a sleeping bag, water and food. From Iloilo City to Concepcion takes three to four hours by Ceres Liner Bus. You can continue onwards through the city of **Roxas**, capital of Capiz and birthplace of former president Manuel Roxas, then to **Kalibo** and Boracay.

Iloilo City

ILOILO CITY is a useful transit point to northern Panay and other Visayan islands, but otherwise of little interest. There's something hauntingly homogenous about the ramshackle

MOVING ON FROM ILOILO

Iloilo is a big port with numerous ferry services to Manila and other destinations throughout the Visayas. WG&A Superferry and Negros Navigation sail to Manila and other destinations, such as Davao, Cebu, Leyte and Bohol. On the river, near City Hall, you can catch Sea Angels fast ferries (☎033/336 1316) to Bacolod, the capital of Negros Occidental. Buses from two bus stations connect Iloilo to other towns on Panay. The Ceres Bus Terminal on Tanza Sreet is the departure point for Caticlan (for Boracay), Kalibo, Roxas and Estancia. From the 76 Express Ceres terminal in Molo buses run clockwise along the coastal road to San Jose, capital of Antique, and on to Libertad in the north.

nature of Philippine port cities. Apart from some graceful old houses in its side streets and a handful of interesting churches, Iloilo has little to distinguish it from other horrors of urban planning perpetrated throughout the archipelago. You can't help but wonder where all the nice buildings are. The city's handful of sights include the rather threadbare **Museo Iloilo**, behind the Provincial Capitol Building on Bonifacio Drive, which documents the history and traditions of the Western Visayas (Negros and Panay). West of the city in Molo district is a church built of coral blocks. If you are visiting in January the Dinagyang Festival adds some extra frenzy to the city during the fourth weekend.

Iloilo **airport** is about 8km north of the city and a taxi to the centre will cost about P100. A cheaper option is to take a jeepney marked "Iloilo–Mandurriao". Ferries arrive at the wharf at the eastern end of the city, off San Pedro Drive.

The city's **tourist information office** (Mon–Sat 9.30am–6pm; ☎033/337 5411) is on Bonifacio Drive and the Bureau of Immigration is at the Old Customs House on Aduana Street, although visa extensions arranged here take time because they go through Manila. The **post office** is in the same building and has poste restante. For **Internet access** try Global Villagers (☎033/336 9187) on General Luna Street, opposite the provincial Capitol Building.

ACCOMMODATION

Casa Plaza Pension, General Luna cor. Iznart streets. Centrally located opposite the provincial Capitol Building. Offers clean rooms, including singles, with cable TV and private facilities. ④.

Family Pension House, General Luna Street (☎033/335 0070). A helpful travel office with good local information, a pleasant treehouse restaurant and simple singles and doubles with private showers. ②.

La Fiesta Hotel, MH del Pilar Street, Molo (☎033/338 0044). In a good location, ten minutes from the airport and twenty minutes by road from the pier, this new hotel has 29 rooms, car rental, Internet access and all mod cons. ⑥.

Nagarao Pension House, 113 Seminario Street, Jaro (☎033/320 6290). The air-con rooms are clean and comfortable and there's a pleasant restaurant, *Bavaria*, where you can get homemade German bread and wheat beer. ④.

YMCA, Iznart Street (☎033/337 5760). Very basic but adequate accommodation at the junction with general Luna Street. Double rooms with air-con. Dorm beds P120. ②.

EATING

Iloilo is known for a number of delicacies, including Pancit Molo Soup, which is named after the Molo area of the city and is sold at numerous street stalls. La Paz Batchoy, an artery-hardening combination of liver, pork and beef with thin noodles, is also available everywhere you look. For original La Paz Batchoy, go to *Old Ted's* at La Paz market. *Nena's Manokan* on General Luna Street is one of the best places for native fare, along with Marina on Iloilo Diversion Road. *Tatoy's* at Villa Beach is a favourite with locals for fresh oysters (*talaba*) and other seafood.

Kalibo

KALIBO lies on the well-trodden path to Boracay and for most of the year is an uninteresting town, but every second week of January it hosts what is probably the biggest street party in the country, the **Ati-Atihan**. This exuberant festival celebrates the original inhabitants of the area, the Atis, and culminates with choreographed dances through the streets by locals daubed in black paint (Ati-Atihan means "to make like the Atis"). Good accommodation can be hard to find during the Ati-Atihan and prices increase by up to a hundred percent. Direct flights to Kalibo from Manila are often fully booked.

Kalibo's **airport** is ten minutes by road southeast of the city on Roxas Avenue. The cheapest and easiest way to get from airport to town is by tricycle. The official fare is P10, but unwary tourists arriving from Manila will be asked for more. Airlines run shuttle buses to Caticlan, for the short banca ride to Boracay. Alternatively, you can catch a bus to Caticlan (P100; 2hr) from the Ceres Bus Terminal in Kalibo, 1km south of the town centre on C Laserna Street. This terminal also serves other destinations on Panay, including Roxas and Iloilo. WG&A Superferry has three departures a week from Dumaguit, a 45-minute bus ride outside Kalibo, to Manila. Negros Navigation has weekly sailings from Dumaguit to Manila.

Kalibo is a compact place with most city destinations within walking distance. The major thoroughfare is Roxas Avenue and most streets lead off it to the south. **Banks**, including BPI and PNB, are on Martyr's Street and the **post office** is in the provincial Capitol Building. There are three or four **Internet cafés**, the most popular of which is *Webquest* on Roxas Avenue (P90 per hour). The Kalibo Provincial **Hospital** is on Mabini Street.

Apartelle Marietta (☎036/262 3353; ①–②) on Roxas Avenue has fan **rooms** with balconies and shower. Two of the better budget deals in town are *Glowmoon Hotel & Restaurant* (☎036/868 5167; ②–③) on Martelino Street and *Garcia Legaspi Mansion* (☎036/262 5588; ②–③) on the town's main street, Roxas Avenue. Both have monastic but clean rooms. *Gervy's Gourmet & Lodge* (☎036/262 4190; ①) has quiet rooms with fan and bath on R Pastrada Street. *Casa Felicidad* (☎036/268 4320; ④), on Archbishop Reyes Street near the plaza, has an aura of faded luxury about it. Note that the price of accommodation increases drastically during Ati-Atihan, and air-con doubles can cost up to P800–1000. The *Glowmoon Hotel* has a nice **restaurant** with a surprisingly good range of local and continental dishes. *Peking House Restaurant*, on Martyr's Street, is an ever popular place for cheap Chinese food, while the newer *Willhelm Tell Deli & Restaurant*, on Roxas Avenue, has European steaks and pastas from P120.

Guimaras

The small island of **Guimaras** lies a short ferry ride away from Iloilo City and is famous for its mangoes, which not only grow in profusion, but are said to be among the sweetest in the Philippines. It's more than just a day-trip destination. From the ferry pier in the capital, **Jordan**, you can catch a jeepney to the south side of the island around **Cabalagnan** and **San Isidro**, where there are some wonderful, quiet beaches (except at weekends, when the locals converge) and a handful of cheap nipa resorts. The spacious *Raymen Beach Cottages* (②), in Alubihod, **Nueva Valencia**, on the island's southwest coast, are built on a perfect white-sand beach and have large balconies. There's no restaurant or menu, but the owners will make sure there's always a supply of fresh fish, which they will cook for you in their small kitchen and serve under the stars. More upmarket resorts include *Nagarao Island Resort* (☎320 6290; ⑥), 22 native-style bungalows on the tiny island of **Nagarao**, off the southeast coast of Guimaras. Meals are available too, though cost extra. There are no other restaurants on Nagarao, so you are a captive audience. You can make bookings direct or at *Nagarao Pension House* in Iloilo (113 Seminario Street, Jaro).

Several small **ferries** leave Iloilo daily for the short crossing to Jordan, starting at 5am. The best place to catch them is the wharf near the post office, although some also depart from Ortiz Wharf at the southern end of Ortiz Sreet near the market. Ferries arriving in Jordan are greeted by **jeepneys** serving the beaches on the south side of the island.

Boracay

Tourism has arrived on the tiny island of **Boracay** with a vengeance. Where you could once only get catch of the day and local rum you can now sit in marbled luxury with chateaubriand and Cuban cigars. The rapid increase in the number of upmarket resorts has crushed some of the island's free-and-easy spirit, but the beach is still the best in the Philippines and the sunsets alone are worth the journey. Thirty kilometres square and shaped like a dumbbell, Boracay lies at the northwestern tip of Panay Island, 350km south of Manila. It may be only 7km long and 1km wide at its narrowest point, but it's a big tropical island in a small package, with thirty beaches and coves. The most famous is **White beach**, on the island's western shore: 4km of the kind of powder white sand that you thought only existed in Martini adverts. In fact, the word Boracay is said to have come from the local word *borac*, meaning cotton, a reference to the sand's colour and texture. One of the most popular activities in Boracay is doing nothing. Another is sitting on the beach at dusk watching the sun drift towards the horizon, or having an outdoor massage from one of the roaming beach masseuses. You can also go horse riding, rent mountain bikes, motorcycles, kayaks, or go scuba diving with one of the many dive operators. There are 24 official dive sites in and around the island, and because of the calm waters near the shore – although it can get very rough during the rainy season – it's a good place to learn. Other beaches worth exploring include **Puka beach** on the north coast, which is famous for shiny white Puka shells. The best way to get there is to hire a banca from local boatmen on White Beach for half a day (P500) per group. To the north of White Beach sits the little village of **Din-iwid** with its 200-metre beach, accessible from White Beach on a path carved out of the cliffs. At the end of a steep path over the next hill is the tiny **Balinghai beach**, enclosed by walls of rock. On the northeast side of the island **Ilig-Iligan beach** has coves and caves, as well as jungle full of fruit bats.

Practicalities

There are two gateways to Boracay. The nearest **airport** is at Kalibo on the Panay mainland, served by Philippine Airlines and Air Philippines. From here air-con shuttles take passengers the two hours by road to Caticlan, where bancas wait to ferry passengers to Boracay (20min). The bancas will take you to White beach, from where you can walk to the resorts. There's also a small airstrip at Caticlan itself, served by daily Pacific Air and Asian Spirit flights from Manila. From Caticlan it's a five-minute tricycle ride and twenty-minute banca journey to White beach. **WG&A Superferry** has departures every Tuesday, Thursday and Sunday from Manila to Dumaguit in Aklan, from where you can travel by bus to Caticlan. The ferry continues on to Roxas. Negros Navigation also serves Dumaguit, with a weekly sailing from Manila on Tuesdays at 4pm. **Buses** from Kalibo's Ceres Bus Terminal take two hours to get to Caticlan and cost P100. From the Rizal Street terminal in Iloilo catch a Ceres Liner bus or air-conditioned van to Caticlan.

There's a **tourist information office** (Mon–Sat 7am–8pm; ☎036/288 3869), halfway along White beach, where you can get maps, while just south of it, also on the beach, is the Boracay Tourist Centre (Mon–Sat 7am–8pm; ☎036/288 3704), where you can do everything from booking flights to arranging visas and making a long-distance telephone call. The boom in tourism on Boracay means Visa, MasterCard and American Express are widely accepted, although sometimes with a small surcharge. There's even a small branch of Allied Bank on the main road behind White Beach, where you can **change travellers' cheques**, although many resorts also act as de facto currency changers. The **post office** in Balabag, the small community halfway along White beach, is open Mon–Fri 9am–5pm, and you can also post letters at Boracay Tourist Centre. The island has a **hospital** with basic facilities and half a dozen private clinics and pharmacies. A handful of **Internet** coffee shops have sprung up on the island, but connections are not always reliable. You can also try Netcom on the main road

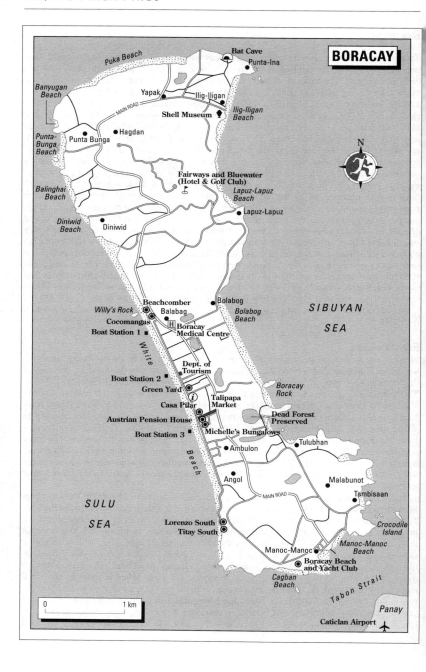

inland near Boat Station 1. The usual charge is P70 an hour or in some cases P1.50 a minute. There are dozens of small sari-sari stores on White beach selling beachwear, T-shirts and souvenirs, and there's a central market, called Talipapa, where you can buy fruit and fish. It's just north of Boat Station 3 behind White beach. The **police** have a small station between Boat Stations 2 and 3.

ACCOMMODATION

There are about two hundred resorts in Boracay, so any selection is only representative. The proliferation of **accommodation**, from the monastic to the luxurious, means that except at peak times (Christmas and Easter), you should be able to find something simply by taking a stroll down White beach from south to north. Whatever you do, don't do business with the irritating "tourist aids" and "commissioners" who try to get a stranglehold on you at Caticlan or Kalibo airports. If it's late and you can't find your dream nipa hut, book for one night and then move on. Prices rise sharply at peak times. All the listed accommodation is on White beach. Beach huts are usually good for two people.

Austrian Pension House & Sundown Restaurant (☎036/288 3406). Clean and quiet rooms, with private shower, at the south end of the beach near Boat Station 3. ②–③.

Casa Pilar, near Boat Station 3. Traditional huts with breezy balconies overlooking quiet gardens. Doubles come with fan and private shower. ⑥.

Fiesta Cottages, at the northern end of the beach near Boat Station 1 and Fisheye Divers (☎036/288 2818). An unbeatable location. Peace and quiet at night, but only a ten-minute walk from other resorts, bars and nightlife. Simple nipa rooms. ②–③.

Green Yard Beach Resort & Seasport Center, halfway down the beach at the rear of Calypso Diving (☎036/288 3748). Good-value huts with fan and shower. As the name suggests, watersports activities can be arranged. ⑤.

Michelle's Bungalows, north of Boat Station 3 (☎036/288 8086). Near the action, but cheaper than many resorts because it is set back from the bustle of the beach in a pleasant courtyard. Quiet, homey and with a small native restaurant. ②.

Mona Lisa White Sand, at the southern end of the beach near Talipapa Market (☎036/288 3012). A relatively new addition to the beachfront skyline with charming gardens and comfortable cottages. ⑥.

Nigi Nigi Nu Noos 'e' Nu Nu Noos, halfway between the Tourist Center and Boat Station 2 (☎288 3101). Long-standing and popular resident of White Beach. The Indonesia-style cottages are almost as impressive as the name. ⑤–⑦.

Seabird Resort Bar & Restaurant, behind the more luxurious *Red Coconut Beach Resort* just before you reach Boat Station 1 (☎036/288 3047). A range of rooms are available, starting from a spartan but comfortable double with fan and shower. Good coffee, pancakes, breakfasts and fish in the restaurant. ③.

Tin-Tin's Cottages, near Boat Station 3 (☎036/288 3051). Another popular place and in a good position right on the beach. Double rooms with fan and shower. ②–③.

Trafalgar Garden & Lodge, close to *Michelle's Bungalows* (☎036/288 3101). Quiet and quaint, with well-kept gardens and excellent little cottages for all budgets. The nipa restaurant serves excellent food. ②–③.

EATING AND NIGHTLIFE

Restaurants and bars come and go in Boracay, but you can eat and drink your way up and down White beach almost 24 hours a day. At the northern end and slightly inland is the *English Bakery and Tea Room*, where, as the name suggests, the fresh bread is excellent, as are the breakfasts and shakes. *Mango-Ray Restaurant*, near Sea World Dive Centre, roughly in the centre of the beach, has pasta, pizza, sandwiches and barbecue, while next door, in the *True Food Restaurant,* you can sit on ethnic cushions (there are no chairs) and eat Indian curry and tandoori chicken. *Nigi Nigi Nu Noos 'e' Nu Nu Noos* (see above) is big on seafood and has interesting cocktails (as do many establishments). *Charlh's Bar* is a small place near *Nigi's* and has a simple menu and late music. On the beach near Boat Station 3, the *Sulu Tha Thai Restaurant* serves spicy Thai dishes such as green curry and red curry, while *Swiss Inn* restaurant has good European dishes, friendly staff and Alp-inspired decor. There are dozens of restaurants around the Boracay Tourist Centre, including the *Diamond Garden* restaurant where native dishes such as adobo and opancit (noodles with shrimps) cost around

P100–P150. Nearby is the 24-hour *Alice in Wonderland Bar & Restaurant*. Some of the best food, however, are the snacks cooked al fresco by the locals, who set up portable barbecues on the beach at sundown and cook everything from fresh lapu-lapu and squid to the tasty local bananas, which are excellent baked with brown sugar.

After dinner, the **nightlife** starts. There are as many bars as there are restaurants. *Moondogs Shooters Bar* in the *Cocomangas Beach Resort* at Balabag (northern end of White beach) is famous – or rather infamous – for its drinking games involving potent cocktails. *Beachcomber* and *Bazura* are Boracay's two major discos. Both are partly al fresco and lively. *Beachcomber* is at the far north end of White beach near *Cocomangas*, and *Bazura* is just north of Boat Station 2, behind the Gem Info Center.

Romblon

Romblon is off the northern coast of Panay, between Mindoro and Bicol, and consists of three main islands, Tablas, Romblon and Sibuyan. Romblon is largely overlooked by visitors, but is well worth the effort. The **beaches** are exceptional and many of the reefs are pristine, making Romblon an excellent off-the-beaten-track destination for scuba diving and snorkelling. Romblon is well-known in the Philippines for its marble, but less well known for anything else. The locals seem to like it that way. They fish, they farm and they maintain their quiet little corner of the archipelago in mint condition. Two of the finest white beaches are at **Lugbung Island** and **Kobrador Island**, off the west coast of Romblon town. Romblon town itself has Spanish forts, a cathedral built in 1726 and some breathtaking views across the Romblon Strait from Sabang Lighthouse.

There's not much in the way of smart **accommodation**, but south of Romblon town there are some pretty nipa huts for rent along the beaches. **Marble beach** has a couple of simple resorts. It's 12km south of Romblon town, a P30 tricycle ride. **Getting to Romblon** has become easier recently with the launching of an Asian Spirit flight to the airport at Tablas on Tablas Island. It departs Manila every Monday, Wednesday, Friday, Saturday and Sunday at 11.30am. From Tablas there are jeepneys to take you to San Agustin on the northeast coast where you can cross by local banca to Romblon town. By **ferry** you can take the *Salve Juliana* from Manila to Romblon town every Sunday at 2pm (16hr). It leaves for the return journey every Friday at 3pm. The *Romblon Bay* leaves Manila for Romblon town every Tuesday at 3pm and Romblon for Manila every Wednesday at 8pm. A good way to fit Romblon into your highland-hopping schedule is to take the big outrigger boat that goes daily from Boracay at 7am to Looc on the southern tip of Tablas Island (2hr).

PALAWAN

If you believe the travel agent clichés, **Palawan** is the Philippine's last frontier. For once it's almost true. Tourism has yet to penetrate this long, sword-shaped island to the southwest of Luzon, and travellers willing to take the rough with the smooth will find a Jurassic landscape of coves, beaches, lagoons and razor-sharp limestone cliffs that rise from crystal clear water. Nature is making its last stand in Palawan, with government officials in the provincial capital, **Puerto Princesa**, declaring war on litterers, loggers and dynamite fishermen. Even in the less populated areas – of which there are many – the battle for the environment is on. Palawan is made up of 1780 islands and islets, most of which have irregular coastlines that make excellent harbours. Thick forests covering these steeply sloped mountains assure adequate watersheds for rivers and streams. Many of the islands are surrounded by a coral shelf that acts as an enormous feeding ground and nursery for marine life. It is sometimes said that Palawan's **Tubbataha Reef** is so ecologically important that if it dies, the Philippines will also die. The area's history can be traced back 22,000 years, as confirmed by the discovery of caveman remains in Quezon, southwest Palawan. Anthropologists believe these early inhabitants came from Borneo across a land bridge that connected the two.

There are several stories regarding the origin of the name Palawan. Some contend that it was derived from the Chinese words "pa lao yu" meaning "Land of the Beautiful Harbours". Popular belief, however, is that "Palawan" is a corrupted form of the Spanish word "Paragua", because the main island is shaped like a closed umbrella. A **typical journey through Palawan** might take you from Puerto Princesa, north to **Honda Bay** and the **Underground River**, then onwards up the coast to **Port Barton, Taytay** and **El Nido**. From El Nido you can take a ferry north to **Busuanga** (Coron) and from there you can fly or take a ferry back to Manila. The southern half of Palawan, from Puerto Princesa downwards, is relatively unexplored.

The main **gateway** to Palawan is the **airport** at Puerto Princesa, but it's by no means the only way to get there. **WG&A** and **Negros Navigation** both sail regularly between Manila and Puerto Princesa, while small airlines such as Pacific Air, Golden Passage and Seair fly to Busuanga in northern Palawan, from where you can island-hop across to the main island and on down the coast to the provincial capital and beyond. **Seair** has a particularly good network of flights from Manila to Palawan and within Palawan itself. Its Let410 aircraft fly two or three times a day to Busuanga. From Busuanga the plane continues to El Nido, Sandoval and finally Puerto Princesa. There are also a limited number of non-stop Seair flights from Manila to Sandoval.

Puerto Princesa

The provincial capital **PUERTO PRINCESA** is the only major urban sprawl in Palawan, with 120,000 residents and an area that actually makes it the second biggest city in the Philippines after Davao. Rural areas 60km north fall under its administration. Puerto Princesa is also clean, green and gun-free, thanks partly to local mayor Edward Hagedorn, a larger-than-life character who has firmly nailed his flag to the environmental mast. Residents and visitors alike are fined for spitting and littering. Throwing your cigarette butt on the pavement brings swift justice in the form of a P200 fine, a small fortune to many locals and therefore a significant deterrent. The town's main artery is the narrow **Rizal Avenue**, which runs from the airport on Puerto's eastern outskirts to the cathedral and the wharf in the west. The distance from end-to-end is only 3km, and tricycles and jeepneys run the length of it, making **transport within the town** easy.

Many see Puerto as a one-night stop on the way to Palawan's coves and coral reefs, but it's not as if there's nothing to see or do. The **Palawan Museum** (Mon, Tues, Thurs & Fri 9am–noon & 2–5pm), in Mendoza Park on Rizal Street, gives a good overview of the history, art and culture of Palawan. At the **Crocodile Farming Institute** (Mon–Sat 10am–5pm) in Barangay Irawan, 12km from the city centre, scientists conduct research into crocodilian ecology, biology, nutrition and biochemistry, pathology and physiology. A visit to the farm will give you a good idea of what makes crocodiles tick. The local name for crocodile is *buwaya*, which means "greedy". To get to the farm take a jeepney (P15) from the terminal in Malvar Street on the northern outskirts of the city. A farm of a rather different kind, a **Butterfly Farm**, owned and operated by Rowell Rodriguez, is located at 27 Bunk House Rd, Santa Monica (☎048/433 5343), and is a haven for hundreds of indigenous species. You can see the stage-by-stage metamorphosis from a caterpillar to a butterfly. Jeepneys go here hourly from Malvar Street.

Don't miss the **Iwahig Penal Colony**, also known as the Prison Without Bars. Prisoners live here as if in a normal village, fishing and cultivating rice and root crops. The "inmates" are identifiable only by their prison T-shirts and ID badges. They return to the prison halls only for meals and sleep. Some long-term residents – those deemed least likely to make a run for it – are allowed to stay in small nipa huts with their families. Tourists are also welcome at the souvenir shop which sells handicrafts made by the prisoners. Prison officials say the rate of recidivism by offenders at Iwahig is significantly lower than among those incarcerated in

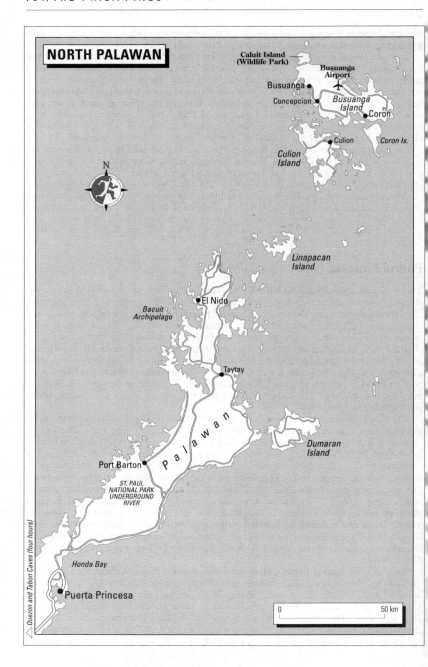

NORTH PALAWAN

Caluit Island
(Wildlife Park)

Busuanga
Airport

Busuanga

Concepcion

*Busuanga
Island*

Coron

Coron Is.

Culion

*Culion
Island*

N

*Linapacan
Island*

*Bacuit
Archipelago*

El Nido

Taytay

P a l a w a n

*Dumaran
Island*

Port Barton

ST. PAUL
NATIONAL PARK
UNDERGROUND
RIVER

Honda Bay

Puerta Princesa

◁ Quezon and Tabon Caves (four hours)

0   50 km

the country's traditional jails. Iwahig is 23km from Puerto Princesa. Jeepneys leave Valencia Street every day at 9.30am.

Just ten minutes by tricycle from Puerto is the **Vietnamese Refugee Centre**, where refugees from Vietnam have established a community away from home, supported by the United Nations. Some choose to earn a living baking the excellent bread which is sold in the city. You can visit the camp anytime free of charge but with clearance from the guards, so take your passport for identification.

Practicalities

There are direct daily **flights** to Puerto Princesa from Manila. By **ferry**, Negros Navigation's Santa Ana leaves Manila every Thursday at 2pm and sails direct to Puerto Princesa, arriving at noon on Friday. It returns on Fridays at 7pm, arriving at Manila on Saturday at 5pm. The *Don Julio* leaves Bacolod every Wednesday at 10am and sails to Puerto Princesa via Iloilo. It leaves Iloilo at 3pm and arrives in Puerto Princesa on Thursday at 8am. This service makes it possible to reach Palawan from the Visayas without backtracking to Manila. WG&A's Superferry 9 leaves Manila North Harbour every Friday at 4pm for Coron in Busuanga (arriving 6am Saturday) before sailing on to Puerto Princesa. For **jeepney rides** to Honda Bay, Quezon and other parts of the island, the main departure point is Valencia Street. There are three **bus terminals** on Malvar Street near the Public market for buses to most other points in Palawan.

The Provincial **Tourism Office** (Mon–Sat 9am–5pm; ☎048/433 2968) is in the Capitol Building on Rizal Avenue, close to the airport, and has good maps for P50. There's also a small Tourist Information Centre (☎048/433 2983) at the airport itself, but most travellers seem to head for *Backpackers Café* at 112 Valencia St, which has become a repository for the latest travel information and transport schedules. The **post office** is on Burgos Street at its junction with Rizal Avenue. Almost next door is the *Hexagon Café*, one of a growing number of **Internet** cafés in town that offers access for P45 an hour. Rizal Avenue is also the best place to look for **banks** and moneychangers. PNB is at the western end, just beyond Mendoza Park. There are two good **hospitals**, the Palawan Adventist Hospital on the National Highway, ten minutes north of the city centre, and the Provincial Hospital on Malvar Street, opposite Jeshiela Pension.

ACCOMMODATION

There are more than fifty pension houses and small **hotels** dotted around Puerto Princesa. Many of them are on Rizal Avenue opposite the airport, while another group is based in and around the city centre, within walking distance of Mendoza Park.

Abelardo's Pension House, 63 D Manga St. Average air-con rooms. Good location in the western part of the city, close to the wharf and the cathedral. ③.

Amelia Pension, 420 Rizal Ave. Close to the airport and offering a good range of rooms, from basic "Mabuhay" doubles with air-con and bath to "Deluxe" doubles. ③–⑨.

Asiaworld Resort Hotel, Barangay San Miguel, Puerto Princesa (☎048/433 2111). Longstanding luxury-standard edifice on National Road heading out of town to the north. Cavernous marble lobby, restaurants, health club and disco. ⑨.

Bachelor's Inn, PEO Road. Near the airport. Six rooms all with air-con. The owners say it's the cleanest inn in Puerto. ③.

Backpackers Café, Bookshop & Inn, 112 Valencia St. Not only accommodation, food and books, but travel information from resident sages and other guests. It's a few minutes past the Palawan Museum on the left heading south towards Abad Santos Street. ②.

Casa Linda Tourist Inn, Trinidad Road (☎048/433 2606). Pleasant courtyard garden and large rooms ranging from basic singles to nice air-con doubles. ③.

Duchess Pension House, 107 Valencia St (☎048/433 2873). Give the claustrophobic singles a miss, but consider the doubles, which have fan and private shower. ③.

Trattoria Inn & Swiss Bistro, 353 Rizal Ave (☎048/433 2719 or 433 4985). Clean, simple and convenient, with the bonus of good European food. Rooms with shower, hot water and air-con. Some doubles have a shared bath. ②–③.

EATING AND NIGHTLIFE

Kamarikutan Cape in Rizal Avenue Extension, Bancao-Bancao, Puerto Princesa (☎048/433 5132), is an incredibly quaint native **restaurant** built almost entirely from indigenous materials such as nipa, bamboo, stone and cogon, a wild grass. Even the salt-and-pepper holders are carved from bamboo by local artists. There's a gallery for art exhibitions and frequent performances by ethnic musical groups. As for the food, there are half a dozen choices of breakfast, good vegetarian dishes, and ten types of coffee. *Ka Lui's*, another bamboo paradise, on the eastern end of Rizal Avenue near the airport, is also an excellent place to fill your stomach without emptying your wallet. Try sweet-and-sour *mameng* (fortune fish), steamed ginger, or spicy squid and grilled prawns. Steamed lobster costs P150 for 200 grams. Vietnamese food is popular in the town because of the number of refugees who made a home here. *Pho Vietnamese Restaurant* (☎048/433 3576), a five-minute tricycle ride beyond the airport, on Rizal Avenue, does good soups, vegetarian dishes and seafood. A huge bowl of beef or chicken noodles is P75. *Vegetarian House* (on the corner of Burgos and Manalo streets, just south of Mendoza Park) is another place for Vietnamese food. Next door is a small *carinderia* (canteen) selling freshly made baguettes with Vietnamese fillings.

For a lively night out, head for *Spice Bar & Disco* on Rizal Street or *Culture Shack*, also on Rizal Street, two rather ethnic **clubs** where you can drink and dance with the trendies.

Honda Bay

Picturesque **Honda Bay** is 10km north of Puerto Princesa by road and makes a good daytrip, though you can also stay overnight. There are seven islands in the bay, and you can visit them all by hiring a boat from Santa Lourdes Wharf. **Snake Island** has a good reef for snorkelling and **Starfish Island** has a rustic restaurant where the seafood is as fresh as it comes. Look out for **Bat Island**: in the late afternoon scores of bats leave here on their nocturnal hunting trips.

Any **jeepney or bus** going north from Puerto Princesa will take you to Honda Bay. You'll need to get off at Santa Lourdes Wharf (this may involve a tricycle ride from where the bus or jeepney leaves you) and sign in at the little tourist office and book your banca. A boat will cost anything from P200 to P500 depending on which island you plan to visit and for how long. Some islands ask visitors to pay a fee (P20).

Accommodation in Honda Bay is limited, but you can always take a sleeping bag and tent. On Starfish Island the *Starfish Sandbar Resort* has rustic huts that sleep four (P500–800), but remember to bring your own tinned food because the small restaurant often runs out. *Meara Marina* claims to be the only island resort in Honda Bay without entrance fees. There are cottages (③) on the beach, and you can book in Puerto Princesa at *Trattoria Inn*.

The Underground River

The **Underground River**, or to give it its proper name, St Paul's Subterranean Cave, is the sight most visitors to Palawan want to see. It's a little way out of Puerto Princesa – more than two hours north by road and another twenty minutes by banca – but it's well worth the trip. The cave meanders underground for more than 8km, making it the longest underground river in the world. It's full of a bewildering array of stalactites, stalagmites, caverns, chambers and pools. Your boatman will take a kerosene lamp to light the way, making the formations appear even more eerie because of the shadows that are cast. You pay a P150 fee at the Visitors Assistance Centre in Sabang to enter the cave, plus another P400–500 (for a group) for the boat. Look out in the area for the famous residents, large monitor lizards (*bayawak*) that are tame enough to take food from your hand.

All **buses and jeepneys** going north from Puerto Princesa pass through **Sabang**, which is the jumping-off point for the Underground River. You can also club together and hire your own jeepney for the three-hour trip (about P1000) and then catch a private banca or wait until

1pm for the daily resort boat which leaves from the pier. The other alternative is to take the air-con van (P250) that leaves *Trattoria Inn* every morning at 7.30am.

Sabang Pier has beaches stretching either side of it. If you walk to the left you will come to *Robert's Beach Cottages and Native Food Palace* (③), where you can **stay** and arrange trips to other parts of Palawan such as El Nido and Port Barton. Next are *Coco Slab* (②–③) and *Villa Sabang* (②–③), both with average nipa rooms and cottages. Ten minutes further, the beach ends at *Mary's Cottages* (②–③). *Panaguman Beach Resort* (③), 2km to the right of Sabang Pier, has three cottages and four rooms with shared shower and toilet.

Port Barton

On the northwest coast of Palawan, roughly half way between Puerto Princesa and El Nido, **Port Barton** has become something of a travellers' rest stop. There are several white-sand islands in the bay and Port Barton itself has a short stretch of beach that is home to half-a-dozen resorts. Buses and jeepneys from Puerto Princesa arrive at Port Barton along Rizal Street and the beach is facing you. If you turn right at Rizal Street and walk along the narrow coastal road you come to the village centre and the church.

Accommodation choices include *Swissippini* (④), which offers nipa huts by the water, *Elsa's Beach Cottages* (③), which are small but okay for the price, and *Mantaray Resort* (③–④). Set apart at the far northern end of the beach is *Shangri-La*, ② part of *Scandinavia beach Resort*, which has cheap huts for two.

Taytay

Half a day north of Port Barton by road on the east coast is **TAYTAY**, the former capital of Palawan. The village is stretched out along a pleasant bay and has a stone fort built by the Spaniards in 1622, a sign of its important trading history. Taytay is also a jumping-off point for a number of **offshore islands** which you can reach by hiring a banca. This quaint and sleepy little coastal town makes a good stop on the journey north from Puerto Princesa towards El Nido. **Buses** leave Port Barton every morning at 5.30am, 6.30am and 7.30am (P54) and arrive in Taytay at the market. There is a small airstrip at Sandoval on the northern edge of Taytay Bay, served by Seair flights from Manila. For **accommodation**, the only real option in Taytay itself is *Pem's Pension House* (③) on Taytay Bay near the fort, which has cottages with fan and bath.

Bacuit archipelago and El Nido

In the far northwest of Palawan is the small coastal town of **EL NIDO**, which is the departure point for trips to the many islands of the Bacuit archipelago. This is limestone island country, with spectacular formations rising from the sea everywhere you look. Its beauty has not gone unnoticed by developers, who have established a number of exclusive and expensive resorts on some of the islands. If US$200 a night for a taste of corporate-style paradise is too much for you, then you can stay in rustic El Nido itself – where electricity cuts off at midnight – and island-hop by day.

Buses and jeepneys from Taytay arrive in El Nido along Rizal Sreet, which terminates at the shore. You'll find a **tourist information** counter at the post office, beyond the church, on Calle Real. Tourism has resulted in the establishment of a few **moneychangers** and the friendly El Nido Boutique & Art Shop in Palmera Street is a good place to drop in for unsolicited advice on where to stay and what to do. There's no shortage of **accommodation**. *Lally and Abett Beach Cottages* (⑥), at the northern end of town on Calle Hama, has beachfront cottages. Cheaper options include *Bayview Inn, Marina Garden Resort* and *Tandikan Cottages*, all in the ②–③ range and all on the beach within walking distance of each other. Roughly in the middle of the beach, *Marina Garden Beach Resort* (③) has some of the nicest nipa huts many with a balcony.

El Nido is at the northern tip of mainland Palawan, but it is possible to **continue north** from here across Linapacan Strait to Culion and then to Busuanga. A ferry leaves El Nido pier every morning at 6am (P200) for the four-hour trip, weather permitting. It arrives in Busuanga at the pier in Coron town.

Busuanga

Busuanga is the largest island in the beautiful little **Calamian Group**, which lies off the northern tip of mainland Palawan. The other two main islands in the group are Culion and Coron, but there are hundreds of other small islands in the area that you can explore by boat Access to the Calamian Group is through the rickety little fishing town of **CORON**, which confusingly is on Busuanga, not Coron. The presence of several Japanese World War II wrecks in the bays near Coron has led to an increase in the number of scuba divers making a pilgrimage to the area. There is no beach in Coron town and most accommodation is geared towards divers. To find your own patch of sand you can hire a banca and hie off for a day, or longer, to the island of your choice. Coron town is also an excellent base for more adventurous pursuits. The precipitous limestone cliffs of **Coron Island**, twenty minutes by boat from Coron town, are spectacular. It's only when you get close to them in a banca that they reveal dozens of perfect little coves, hidden in the folds of the mountains. The volcanic **Cayangan Lake** is a short, steep climb into the hinterlands, but not to be missed. Coron Island is still inhabited by the Tagbanua tribe, who are friendly but shy. If they see visitors, the chances are they will melt back into the forest. You could spend a lifetime in Coron and still not get to see every hot spring, hidden lake or pristine cove. South of Coron town is the large island of **Culion**, home to a former leper colony and a fascinating **museum**, which is open to visitors. Off the northwest tip of Busuanga itself is **Calauit Island**, where non-carnivorous African animals including giraffe, zebra, impala, waterbuck, gazelle, elands and topis are being raised alongside indigenous Philippine fauna as part of an experiment that began in 1977. Visitors are welcome and most resorts in the area will arrange trips. From Coron you can also catch a bus or jeepney to take you west along the **south Busuanga coast** to the villages of Concepcion, Salvacion and Old Busuanga, where there are a number of resorts and piers with bancas for hire.

Practicalities

There are two small **airstrips** on Busuanga, the YKR Airport in the north of the island, 45 minutes along a rocky road from Coron town, and the airstrip near Coron town itself, which is known for its inspiring approach and is used only by Pacific Air. Seair operates at least two departures a day during peak season from Manila to YKR Airport. From YKR you'll have to catch a jeepney into Coron (P50), although many resorts have private vans and will collect you. *WG&A Superferry 9* leaves Manila every Friday at 4pm and arrives in Coron town on Saturday at 7am before continuing to Puerto Princesa. It leaves Coron town for the return journey at 10pm on Sunday, arriving in Manila at noon on Monday. The other regular **ferry** between Manila and Coron is the *M/V Salve Juliana*, which leaves Manila every Monday at noon and returns every Wednesday at 4pm. It is also possible to catch a ferry from Coron town to Culion and then on to El Nido.

Coron town is not short of tourist facilities, most of them no more than a short walk or tricycle ride away. The centre of Coron is huddled around the pier, were you can hire bancas for island trips. Overlooking the pier is **Bayside Divers Lodge**, a good place to get advice from staff on where to go and what to see. They can direct you to the **WG&A ticket office**, which is a short tricycle ride along the National Highway heading east out of town. The ticket office for the *M/V Salve Juliana* is also near here. Below Bayside is a small Agfa shop where you can make telephone calls to Manila. And opposite is Sea Canoe, an eco-minded firm that offers kayaking and camping trips around the islands. Heading west from Bayside on foot (a left turn at the junction) you come to a number of dive shops and, at the next junction, Swagman Travel. Near Swagman is Pascual Video, which has **email** access.

ACCOMMODATION AND EATING

In Coron town most of the **accommodation** is around the pier and can be noisy. The locals perform some ear-bending karaoke at night and the cockerels start their dawn chorus well before dawn. *Bayside Divers Lodge* (③–④) is a good landmark, right on the water's edge. It offers spartan but clean doubles, and upstairs there's a comfortable restaurant with marvellous views across the bay to Coron Island. Also near the pier are *L&M Pe Lodge* (②), which has simple, small rooms and a popular bar and restaurant, where divers gather in the evening to swap stories. Slightly inland in a quiet part of town is *Kalamayan Inn* (⑤), which has two deluxe rooms downstairs and four standard rooms upstairs; prices include breakfast. A little further out of town (five minutes on foot) to the east is the excellent *Darayonan* (④), a rambling bamboo house that has seven twin rooms with shared facilities, nicely furnished in native style. *Darayonan* also has an al fresco restaurant serving breakfast, lunch and dinner. In the opposite direction along the National Highway, a fifteen-minute tricycle ride brings you to *KokusNuss Resort* (③–④), which has bungalows built around a pleasant garden. Even more rustic is the isolated Popototan Island, two hours by banca at the western end of Coron Bay. There are rarely more than a few guests on Popototan, where nipa huts are around P1300 a night including all meals. You can book for Popototan in Manila (☎02/751 6279).

Southern Palawan

A journey through **southern Palawan** represents one of the last great travel challenges in the Philippines. This is country that has so far been almost untouched by tourism. Much of the area is sparsely populated, with limited accommodation and nothing in the way of dependable transport, communications or electricity. About the only noted tourist attraction in the southern half of Palawan are the **Tabon Caves**, 157km southwest of Puerto Princesa in Quezon. It's a five-hour trip by jeepney or bus from Puerto Princesa to Quezon Wharf, where you can hire a banca to take you to the caves. It was here that fossils and crude tools of ancient man dating some 22,000 years back were unearthed. A large quantity of Chinese pottery was also found, most of which was transferred to the National Museum in Manila for preservation. The main entrance to the caves, measuring 18m high and 16m wide, overlooks a beautiful bay studded with white sand beach islands. Of the two hundred caves in the Tabon Caves Complex, only seven are open to visitors. Continuing south down the west coast by bus or jeepney brings you to the village of **Rizal**, from where the road crosses the island west to east, bringing you to **Batarza**, one of the few places with recognized accommodation in the form of the *Bonbon Lodging House* (③). The journey north brings you back to Puerto Princesa via **Brooke's Point**, a trading post, 25km from Mount Matalingahan, Palawan's highest peak at 2086m. Further north between Narra and Aborlan there are some quiet resorts on **Tigman beach**. From Aborlan it's 69km back to Puerto Princesa.

Tubbataha Reef Marine Park

Located in the middle of the Central Sulu Sea, 181km southeast of Puerto Princesa, **Tubbataha Reef Marine Park** was inscribed on the World Heritage List in 1993. It has become a magnet for **scuba divers**, who sail to it every year during high season (March to June) on liveaboard dive boats anchored mostly in Puerto Princesa. Dive operators in Manila can arrange packages, which cost around US$1200 for one week, including flights to Puerto, all food and unlimited diving. The reef is one of the best in the world, with sightings of sharks and mantas a daily occurrence. But its ecological importance should not be forgotten. Sixty percent of Filipinos' animal protein comes from fish, and fishermen rely on reefs such as this for their livelihood and as nurseries that regenerate stocks. Around 2000 divers visit the reef every year and many islanders support themselves by catering to visitors and by selling shells and handicrafts fashioned from reef materials. Both these industries have taken their toll. Overfishing, repeated anchoring on the fragile coral, and a fishing practice called "blasting" – which literally dynamites fish in the water – are all highly destructive. The good news is that scientists have been monitoring the reef and say that in recent years the situation has improved.

Independent travel to Tubbataha is impossible and even licenced dive boats need a permit. For details of liveaboards visiting the reef try Dive Buddies in Manila (☎02/521 9168 or 521 9169), Aquaventure Manila (☎02/899 2831) or Queen Ann Divers in Puerto Princesa (☎048/4332 719)

MINDANAO

The signals **Mindanao** sends to the rest of the Philippines and the rest of the world, are nothing if not mixed. This massive island at the foot of the archipelago is in many ways the cultural and artistic heart of the country, a place where tribalism and capitalism clash head on, and where refugees from Manila's pollution have fled in search of cleaner air and greener pastures. This has led to something of a cultural and economic boom in cities such as **Davao**, Mindanao's de facto capital. Yet Mindanao has also been a nagging thorn in the side of successive governments, with repeated attempts by the island's Muslims to break away from the governance of Manila and establish their own autonomous regions on the island. Mindanao's Muslim (or Moro) and indigenous Lumad peoples, now outnumbered by majority Filipinos – the largely Christian descendants of twentieth-century settlers from the northern and central Philippines – are asserting rights to their traditional lands and to self-determination. The Moro National Liberation Front (MNLF) resorted to a war for independence in the 1970s. Meanwhile, a communist-led rebellion spread from the northern Philippines to Mindanao, drawing many majority Filipinos, particularly among the rural poor, and some Lumads into the New People's Army (NPA). In 1996, the Philippine Government signed a peace pact with the MNLF granting a certain degree of autonomy to four provinces on condition of a plebiscite. But this peace is by no means final or universal, and splinter groups are still engaged in conflict. Tourists are generally safe, but those who venture towards Muslim strongholds in the south should be aware that there have been a number of kidnappings in recent years. Most of the major tourist activities are based around the north and east coasts of Mindanao where there have been few problems. Davao is the gateway to Mindanao, but from **Cagayan de Oro** in the north you can also explore **Bukidnon**, the country's only landlocked province, as well as **Camiguin**, a small island of white beaches and brooding volcanoes.

Access by plane to Mindanao is usually through one of five airports on the island: Davao, Cagayan de Oro, General Santos, Cotabato and Zamboanga City. Philippine Airlines has daily flights to all five and also has a daily flight between Cebu and Davao. Mindanao Express has flights from Cebu and Davao to various destinations on Mindanao, though the airline's schedules are soon set to change and new flights are being added (and old ones dropped), so check with its Manila office for an update. It's a long journey to Mindanao **by ferry** from Manila, with some services stopping off at other ports of call on the way. When you book a ferry ticket it's worth checking if it's direct or not: direct voyages take about eighteen hours, but if the ferry calls at other ports, you will find yourself at sea for a couple of days. WG&A Superferry sails to the following places in Mindanao: Davao, Cagayan de Oro, General Santos, Zamboanga, Dipolog, Iligan, Ozamis, Surigao, Nasipit and Cotabato. Negros Navigation serves the same routes, with the exception of Dipolog. There are numerous ferry services, big and small, connecting Mindanao to other provincial destinations in the Visayas.

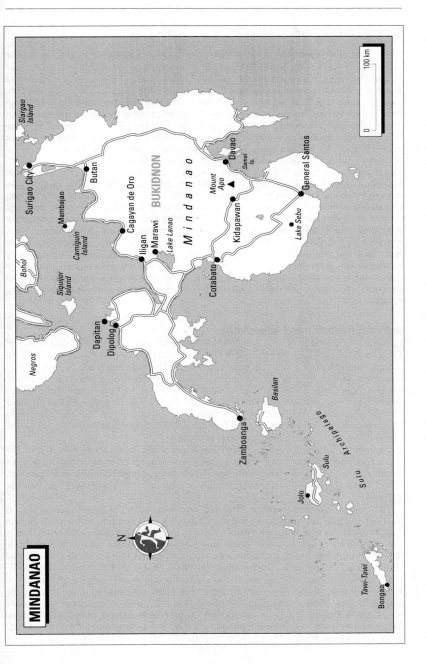

Davao and around

There is more cultural diversity in **DAVAO** than anywhere else in the Philippines. This immense city – one of the largest in the world in terms of land area – is home to the ethnic Bagobo, Mandaya, Manobo, Tiboli, Mansaka and B'laan tribes, whose ancestors were first to arrive in Mindanao across land bridges from Malaysia. Catholics mix freely with Muslims, and churches stand alongside mosques. The name Davao was derived from the word "babadaba", which evoked images of fire-breathing mythical figures and rituals of fire carried out before tribal wars. Other early settlers on the banks of the Davao River were tribes from the neighbouring provinces of Kotabato, Zamboanga and Jolo. Conquest by the Spaniards failed repeatedly until the mid-nineteenth century, when invaders were finally able to overrun the Muslim enclaves. Christian settlers arrived soon afterwards and the heady mix of cultures and beliefs was complete. The city was no stranger to armed struggle, but the violence that took place in the 1980s almost brought Davao to its knees economically. This black decade, marked by violence from the MNLF and the NPA, earned Davao the notorious title of "Gun Capital of the Philippines." Davao became a haven for the underground movement and a laboratory for urban guerilla warfare. The emergence of an anti-communist group known as the Alsa Masa (Rise of the Masses) began in Davao. This military-backed civilian defence force drove the NPA and MNLF away from the city. Davao today is a peaceful city, home to one million people and growing in stature as an investment and tourist destination. It's the gateway to **Mount Apo**, at 2954m the highest mountain in the Philippines and a magnet for trekkers and climbers. Sun, sand and sea are also on the city's doorstep at the many islands just off the coast. The biggest and most popular of these is **Samal Island**, where there are many resorts.

Arrival, orientation and information

Davao is well served by air and ferry from Manila. Philippine Airlines, Air Philippines and Cebu Pacific all have daily flights, while WG&A Superferry and Negros Navigation both have at least two departures a week, depending on season. The **airport** is north of Davao. Taxis, charging a flat fare of P100, will take you into the city. **Ferries** dock either at the northeastern end of the city at Santa Ana Wharf, near Magsaysay Park, or further out of town at Sasa Wharf. There are jeepneys from both to the city. Ferries also leave these piers for other Visayan destinations, including Cebu and Iloilo and to other cities on Mindanao. **Buses** to other parts of Mindanao leave from the Ecoland Terminal in Quimpo Boulevard, across the Davao River on the southwestern oustkirts of the city.

Davao is significantly less polluted and congested than Manila. On the western edge of the city is **San Pedro Street**, where there is a big choice of budget accommodation. San Pedro is linked to Quezon Boulevard, which heads northeast to Magsaysay Park and Santa Ana Wharf. From Magsaysay Park, Leon Garcia Street heads northeast out of the city towards the airport.

The **tourist information office** (Mon–Sat 8am–6pm; ☎082/222 1956) is on the second floor of City Hall, San Pedro Street, and there's another, smaller tourist office in Magsaysay Park, at Santa Ana wharf (Mon–Fri 8am–noon & 1–5pm; ☎082/221 6955 or 221 0070); this is the office to come to if you want permission to climb Mount Apo (see p.765 for further details). A third tourist office (Mon–Sat 8am–6pm; ☎082/221 6798) is located next to *Apo View Hotel* in J Camus Street. The **Immigration Office** (☎082/227 4783) is on the third floor, CAM Building, Monteverde Avenue. There are **banks** and moneychangers everywhere in Davao, so access to cash should not be a problem. Many are gathered in the area around University Mall, Roxas Avenue. Equitable Bank is near the **post office** on one of the main drags, Roxas Avenue. PLDT has an office on Clara M Recto Avenue where you can place **long-distance calls**. For **Internet** access a good bet is *WebHaus Internet Café* (☎082/222 4796) in University Mall.

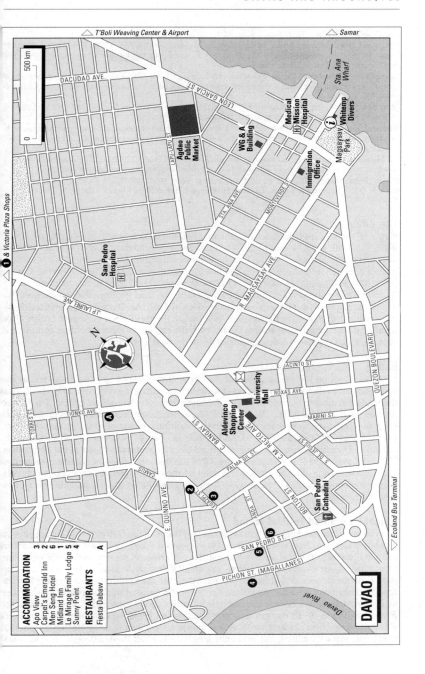

△ T'Boli Weaving Center & Airport

△ Samar

Sta. Ana Wharf

500 km

0

DACUDAO AVE.

LEON GARCIA ST.

Medical
H Mission
Hospital

LAPU-LAPU ST.

WG & A
Building

Agdao Public
Market

i

Magsaysay Whitetip Divers
Park

Immigration
Office

MONTEVERDE ST.

STA. ANA AVE.

◁ ❶ & Victoria Plaza Shops

San Pedro
Hospital
H

R. MAGSAYSAY AVE.

J.P. LAUREL AVE.

N

E. JACINTO ST.

QUEZON BOULEVARD

University
Mall

ROXAS AVE.

TIONKO AVE.

F. TORRES ST.

Aldevinco
Shopping
Center

MABINI ST.

C. BANGOY ST.

CAMUS

C.M. RECTO AVE.

S. DE JESUS ST.

PALMA GIL ST.

E. QUIRINO AVE.

ILUSTRE ST.

❷

❸

ANDA ST.

BOLTON ST.

San Pedro
Cathedral
✝

❺

❻

ACCOMMODATION

Apo View   3
Carpel's Emerald Inn   2
Men Seng Hotel   6
Midland Inn   1
Le Mirage Family Lodge   5
Sunny Point   4

RESTAURANTS

Fiesta Dabaw   A

A

SAN PEDRO ST.

❹

PICHON ST. (MAGALLANES)

Davao River

DAVAO

▽ Ecoland Bus Terminal

Accommodation

Apo View Hotel J Camus Street (☎082/221 6430; Manila office ☎02/893 1288). The hotel of choice in Davao for many travellers with a bit of extra money to spend. Big, comfortable air-con rooms. Sadly, you don't always get a view of Mount Apo. ⑥.

Carpel's Emerald Inn, J Camus Extension (☎082/221 1641–44). This hotel's position close to some of Davao's biggest shopping malls accounts for some of its popularity. The facilities are rudimentary but adequate. ④.

Men Seng Hotel, San Pedro Street (☎082/227 3101). In a good location five minutes' walk north of the cathedral, but rooms are rather dilapidated. Has a small café. ①–②.

Midland Inn, F Inigo Street (☎082/221 1775). Has the distinction of being right in the middle of the main entertainment district, in the north of the city just beyond Victoria Plaza. Range of good rooms with hot water and cable TV. ④–⑥.

Le Mirage Family Lodge, San Pedro Street cor. Anda Street (☎082/226 3811). The wooden floors are a small reminder of the heyday of Filipino architecture. More expensive rooms have air con. ①–③.

Sunny Point Lodge, Magellanes Street cor. Legaspi Street (☎082/221 0155). Clean, quiet rooms in the thick of the city-centre maelstrom. Laundry facilities and free coffee 24 hours a day from the café downstairs. ②–③.

The City

Sights in the city itself include the **Davao Museum** (Tues–Sun 9am–noon & 1–5.30pm; ☎082/235 1876) at 13 Agusan Circle. The museum is dedicated to the area's cultural minorities such as the Mansaka and the Bogobo and has well-maintained displays of their clothes, weapons, as well as anthropological and historical exhibitions. The **T'boli Weaving Center** (☎082/234 3050) at the *Insular Century Hotel Davao* is a good place to buy hand-woven fabric from T'boli tribespeople. This distinctive fabric has bold patterns that symbolize tribal beliefs, in much the same way aborigine art does in Australia. Davao's major **annual festival** is the mardi gras-style Kadayawan, held during the third week of August, which gives thanks for a bountiful harvest. One of the festival's highlights is horsefighting and there is seemingly endless street-dancing, tribal-style, to the sound of drums.

Eating

F Torres Street on the western edge of the city centre is known as Food Street and as the name suggests is home to dozens of **restaurants** specializing in everything from cheap local merienda (snacks) to seafood, Chinese, Japanese and even Mongolian cuisine. On Tionko Avenue, *Fiesta Dabaw* (☎082/224 0006) has Muslim seafaring decor and dishes ranging from fresh lapu-lapu to coconut seafood curry and the delicious *inihaw na panga* (grilled tuna jaw). *Coconut Grove* (☎082/224 2000) on Anda Street is open 24 hours and has excellent fish, shrimp and vegetable dishes. Don't forget that Davao is the **durian** capital of the Philippines. This bright green fruit has a pungent smell that has been described as a subtle combination of old cheese, turpentine and onion, but don't let the slightly noxious perfume put you off. Aficionados say the durian's tender white flesh has a taste suggestive of almonds, sherry, custard and ice cream.

Samal Island and Talikud Island

You can get to **Samal Island**, off the east coast of Davao in the Gulf of Davao, by hopping on a public banca near Sasa Bridge (1hr; P20). Jeepneys marked "Sasa" will take you to within spitting distance of the boat station. You can also get a more expensive ferry (P150) from the pier at the *Insular Century Hotel Davao*, just off JP Cabaguio Avenue, on the road to the airport. Pearl farms once dotted Samal, but these days the main temptation for wealthy tourists are the classy resorts on the west coast. On the northern coast there are some fine beaches and more rudimentary resorts that nevertheless offer good rooms and cheap food. *Paradise Resort* (no phone; ③–④) can get busy at weekends, but has good clean doubles with privet shower and excellent chicken barbecue and tuna jaw. Next door is *Costa Marina* (no phone), which has similar facilities, but is usually less crowded. Off the southwest coast of Samal

Island is **Talikud Island**, which has excellent scuba diving and a handful of quiet but rudimentary beach resorts. Boats for Talikud leave every morning at 6am, 7am and 9am (P30) from Santa Ana Wharf in Davao.

Mount Apo

Mount Apo overlooks Davao and lords it over the Philippines as the highest mountain in the country. No wonder it was called Apo, which means "Grandfather of all Mountains." Apo is actually a volcano, but is certified "inactive" and has no recorded eruptions. What it does have is enough flora and fauna to make your head spin: thundering waterfalls, rapids, lakes, geysers, sulfur pillars, primeval trees, endangered plant and animal species and a steaming blue lake. It is the home of the Philippine Eagle, the tiny falconet and the Mount Apo mynah. Then there are exotic ferns, carnivorous pitcher plants and the Queen of the Philippine orchids, the waling-waling. Revered as a sacred mountain, the people call it Sandawa or "Mountain of Sulfur". The local tribes, the Bagobos, believe the gods Apo and Mandaragan inhabit its upper slopes.

Recently, however, Mount Apo has become something of an **environmental hot potato** and the government is trying to dissuade people from climbing it because of the damage they have done to trails and the litter they have left behind. Small groups of climbers with special interests, such as botany or photography, will still be allowed, but large groups could find they get turned back. The situation is uncertain. The best advice is that visitors go to the tourist information centre in Magsaysay Park (see p.762) to plead their case. Senior Davao tourism officials are based at this office and if anyone can help, they can. If you have a well-prepared case and some documentation to back it up (a letter from your university or employer explaining why you would like to climb Apo, for instance), there's a good chance they'll let you go.

The usual starting point for the climb is **Kidapawan**, a two-hour journey by bus from the Ecoland Bus Terminal in Davao City. There are cheap lodgings in Kidapawan, so you can rest up for a night before starting the climb. Don't attempt Mount Apo alone: **hire a guide** from one of the tourist offices in Davao, where staff will also help you plan the route and get the necessary permits. Also, make sure you go well prepared. Experienced Apo climbers advise allowing four or five days for the climb, averaging four hours of trekking a day with an average load of 40 pounds to supply you with food and shelter for four days in extreme weather. The higher you get the colder it gets. Towards the peak temperatures are as low as 5°C, so don't go without a good sleeping bag, warm clothes and a tent. It's a tough trek, but well worth it. The trail is lined with flowers and on the first day you should reach **Mainit Hot Spring**, where you can take a refreshing dip. Day two brings you to the dramatic **Lake Venado**, which looks like a scene from the Jurassic age, with giant trees, vines and a fine fog floating above the lake itself. At the end of the third day you can make camp below the summit and rise at 5am to get to the top in time for sunrise. The views are nothing short of spectacular. This is the highest point in the Philippines, and the whole of Mindanao is spread before you.

Philippine Eagle Foundation

The **Philippine Eagle Foundation** (daily 8am–5pm; ☎082/224 3021; P12), just outside Davao in Malagos, is known for its excellent work breeding the Philippine Eagle, or monkey-eating eagle, a majestic beast with a fearsome beak and two-meter wingspan. The Philippine Eagle (*pithecophaga jeffryi*) is extremely elusive and its existence was documented only in 1896, a century after most other bird species. That first known sighting was by the intrepid British bird collector John Whitehead in Samar, who gave the eagle its Latin name *jeffryi* after his father, Jeffrey, who financed his expedition. Sadly, the eagle is now officially on the endangered species list, with only one hundred to three hundred believed to be living in the wilds of Mindanao, Samar and Leyte. But there is hope: the Foundation has a captive breeding programme that focuses on developing a viable gene pool for the species by propagating the eagles in captivity. The goal is to reintroduce the eagles back into their natural habitat. Two eagles, named Pag-Asa (Hope) and Pagkakaisa (Unity) were bred in 1992. To **get to the Foundation**, take a bus to Calinan (45min) from the Annil Transport Terminal next to Ateneo de Davao University, then a short tricycle ride.

General Santos

GENERAL SANTOS, southwest of Davao on Sarangani Bay, has the distinction of being the Philippines' southernmost city, which for many travellers means it's one bus journey too far. You can reach "Gensan" by air from Manila and Cebu or by bus on the Davao–Gensan Highway (3hr). It is possible to continue westwards by bus from General Santos to the isolated and beautiful **Lake Sebu**, in an area inhabited by the T'boli tribe. There is some reasonably good accommodation around Lake Sebu and it's a great place to see **T'Boli culture** at first hand. The best place to stay are the cottages at *Lakeside Tourist Lodge* (①) near the market. The *Bao Ba-ay Village Inn* (③), five minutes' walk north from the marketplace, has marvellous lake views and cottages with balconies. The weekly **Saturday market** itself is worth the trip. You can buy brassware, tribal weavings and other local handicrafts. The annual Lem-Lunay T'boli Festival is held every year on the second Friday of November and concludes with traditional horsefights. From Lake Sebu the road meanders west to **Cotabato City**, four hours away by Mintranco Bus, which you can catch from the Lake Sebu marketplace. Cotabato has been the scene of a number of recent bombings and kidnappings, so check the security situation with your embassy. Lake Sebu is usually as far as most tourists go along this road.

Accommodation

The National Highway in General Santos is a good place to look for reasonable accommodation.

757 Inn & Restaurants J Catolico Street Sr (☎083/552 2969 or 552 3212). Twenty-seven clean and well-maintained air-con rooms, all with private facilities. ④–⑤.

Anahaw Village Inn Laurel Avenue cor. Quirino Avenue. Seven air-con rooms and six non-air-con rooms, all with private bath and some with TV. ③–④.

Clara's Lodge Salazar Street (☎083/552-3016). Neat and tidy singles and doubles either with fan or air-con, some with private shower. ②–③.

Hotel Sansu Pioneer Avenue (☎083/552 7219). There are cheap singles and better doubles with air-con, fridge and cable TV. ⑤.

T'Boli Hotel National Highway (☎083/552 3042). At the eastern end of the highway. Air-con doubles with TV and fridge and a good restaurant. ⑤–⑥.

Tropicana Resort Hotel Cabu, Tambler. Fifteen minutes from the city by taxi, the *Tropicana* has air-con cottages and enchanting views of Sarangani Bay. Its restaurant has Filipino dishes and excellent fresh tuna. ④.

Cagayan de Oro

CAGAYAN DE ORO, 785km south of Manila is on the north coast of Mindanao, on the opposite coast of the island to Davao. Cagayan is the starting point for trips to Camiguin and the wild countryside of Bukidnon, and also gives overland access to Siargao in the far northeast of Mindanao. Because of its position below the typhoon belt, Cagayan is generally sheltered from strong winds. What's more, it has no record of major earthquakes, something of a rarity for the Philippines. The city itself is of bulk standard Philippine design, with malls and concrete dominating. There are few memorable sights, apart from **San Agustin Cathedral**, which stands in the south of the city next to the Cagayan River. The **Museo de Oro** (Tues–Sun 9am–5pm; P20 minimum donation) at Xavier University gives an interesting overview of local culture stretching back thousands of years. As you pass through the eastern suburbs of Cagayan on the road to Balingoan (for Camiguin), you'll notice a sweet smell of pineapple in the air. Pineapples from enormous plantations inland, mostly owned by Del Monte, are brought to Cagayan for canning.

Practicalities

Cagayan de Oro is served by daily flights from Manila on Air Philippines, Philippine Airlines and Cebu Pacific. Mindanao Express has daily flights from Davao and Cebu. The **airport** is 10km outside the city and a taxi ride into Cagayan will cost at least P80. WG&A Superferry and Negros Navigation both have regular services from Manila. The Macabalan Wharf is 5km north of the city centre, with regular jeepneys back and forth. Ceres Liner and bachelor buses from Davao stop at the **bus terminal** on the outskirts of the city next to Agora Market. The journey from Davao to Cagayan by road takes about ten hours. Jeepneys connect the terminal with the town. When leaving Cagayan for the terminal, look for jeepneys marked "Agora".

The Provincial **Tourism Office** (Mon–Sat 8am–noon & 1–5pm; ☎08822/727 275 or 726 394) is in the Provincial Capitol Building. There's a **post office** in T Chavez Street, while one of the best places for **Internet** access is *Cyberpoint Café* (☎08822/557 2320) in RN Abejuela Street cor. Pabayo Street (2nd Floor of R&M Building); access is P55 an hour and there's a snack bar.

ACCOMMODATION AND EATING

The area around Tiano Brothers Street in the south of the city, near Golden Friendship Park, is home to most of the town's budget **accommodation**. Check the rooms before you make a commitment, because some places are airless and dank. *Parkview Lodge* (☎08822/723 223; ②–③), in a quiet area right next to the park on Tirso Neri Street, is one of the better options, with adequate rooms with air-con or fan. *Sampaguita Inn* (☎08822/722 640; ②–③), on Borja Street, has very average rooms with fan and shower. A little more cheerful, the *Philtown Hotel* (☎08822/726 295; ⑤–⑥), on Velez Street, is very clean and in a great location. The best hotel in town, though it's not cheap, is *Pryce Plaza* (☎08822/726685–6; ⑧) at Carmen Hill on the road from the airport.

For **food** there are some decent restaurants at the north end of Velez Street, near the Provincial Capitol Building. *Caprice Steakhouse* not surprisingly specializes in steak, while *Salt & Pepper Restaurant* has nondescript but adequate Asian and European fare. Right at the other end of Velez Street, at its junction with Gaerlan Street, is *Paulo's Ristorante*, which has a candlelight ambience and an incredible range of pasta, pizza and Asian dishes.

Camiguin

Filipino modesty is forgotten on the tiny island of **Camiguin** during the annual Lanzones festival in the fourth week of October. Revellers dressed only in lanzones leaves stomp and dance in the streets as a tribute to the humble lanzones fruit, one of the island's major sources of income. The festival is one of the liveliest and friendliest in the country, and this on an island that is already renowned for the friendliness of its people. It's hard to walk more than a few metres without having someone strike up conversation with you. Camiguin (cam-ee-gin) is roughly pear-shaped and lies off the northern coast of Mindanao, bounded on the north by the Bohol Sea, in the east by the northwestern part of Gingong Bay and in the south by the northern part of Majalar Bay. Old Spanish documents indicate that Ferdinand Magellan and Miguel Lopez de Legaspi passed this way in 1521 and 1565 respectively, but it was not until 1598 when the first Spanish settlement was established here and the natives – mostly from nearby Surigao – converted to Catholicism.

Camiguin is a big island in a small package (229.8 square kilometres, to be precise). Apart from the Lanzones Festival, it has seven **volcanoes** (some still active), a multitude of hot springs, a sunken cemetery, ivory-white beaches, offshore islands, a spring that gushes natural soda water, and 35 resorts, most with affordable accommodation and restaurants.

Ferries from mainland Mindanao dock at Benoni on Camiguin's southeast coast, from where several jeepneys run every day to **MAMBAJAO** (30min; P15), the capital, on the north coast, and a good place to start your tour. The last jeepney leaves around 6pm, but you can always negotiate a special ride for P150. **Cabu-An beach** is the closest beach to Mambajao proper and has some nice coral close to the shore. You can swim at **Ardent Hot Springs**, a one-hour trek inland from Mambajao. **Agohay beach**, 7km west from Mambajao (heading anti-clockwise) is more popular than the beaches around the capital and has the benefit of being within striking distance of **Mount Hibok-Hibok**, an active volcano that is a worthwhile but challenging day's climb. The views from the top are nothing short of dramatic, with the coast of Mindanao in the distance. Continuing anti-clockwise you come to the barrio of Bonbon, the site of a sunken cemetery where snorkellers can see gravestones at low tide. The cemetery sank during a volcanic eruption in 1871. The brooding ruins of Guiob Church, another casualty of volcanic activity, are also here. There are a number of good resorts and beaches in Catarman, on the island's southwest coast, 24km from Mambajao. Six kilometres north of Catarman are Tuasan Falls and nearby are the Santo Nino Cold Springs. Both have deep pools that are good for swimming. On the southern coast near Guinsiliban, fifteen minutes east by jeepney from Catarman, is a 300-year-old Moro Watchtower. Off the eastern coast is Mantique Island, which is fringed by nice beaches and has a steep drop-off on the far side for snorkelling. One of Camiguin's most popular attractions is White Island, which sits off the northern coast and is only visible at low tide. It's less of an island and more of an extended sandbar. The views and the water are lovely, but there's no shade, so make sure you take your own. Camiguin has a circumference of 65km and to circumnavigate it by jeepney would take about three hours, although connections between some of the remoter towns on the west coast (Yumbing and Catarman, for example) are unreliable. Alternatively, you could **rent a motorcycle** in Mumbajao.

Practicalities

The usual route to Camiguin is to take a **bus** from the terminal at Agora Market in Cagayan De Oro east along the coast to Balingoan (88km). From the pier at Balingoan there are hourly (sometimes half-hourly) ferries daily to Benoni from 5am until 4pm. Not all of them are by any means luxurious and at peak times there can be hordes of people trying to get on board. There are also three or four ferries a day to Benoni from Cagayan De Oro itself.

There is a **tourist information office** (Mon–Sat 8.30am–5pm; ☎08822/871 014) in the Capitol Compound in Mumbajao where you can enquire about accommodation and climbing Hibok-Hibok. There are six **banks** in Mumbajao and you can change travellers' cheques at most of them, also service is slow and rates are low. As always, it's best to make sure you have enough cash, either in pesos or dollars. Camiguin Authorized Ticket Agent (☎08822/387 4000), in the Negros Navigation Office in Benoni, will help you arrange tours, make long-distance telephone calls and book ferry tickets for Manila, Bacolod, Iloilo, Palawan and Bacolod.

ACCOMMODATION AND EATING

Most of the best beachfront **accommodation** on Camiguin is due west of Mumbajao on Agoho, Yumbing and Naasag. Agoho is popular because it gives quickest access to White Island. You can reach these villages either by jeepney or tricycle from the capital. *Paras Beach Resort* (☎08822/387 9008 or 387 9081; ⑦), in Yumbing, was a private beach house belonging to the Paras family until they decided to add eighteen air-con rooms and open it to the public. It's in a spectacular position on the shore and the staff are efficient organizers of tours. A banca from Paras to White Island and back costs P250 or you can hire your own private jeepney and driver for a day for P1450 – an authentic way to tour the island. Accommodation closer to Mumbajao includes the cheap but cheerful *Turtle's Nest Beach Cottages* (③), ten minutes west by road at Kuguita, and, ten minutes inland, the more upmarket *Ardent Hot Springs* resort (④) in Tagdo, offering spacious doubles. On Airport Road, near

Mumbajao, are *Tia's Beach Resort* (☎08822/871 045; ③) and *Tree House* (☎08822/871 044; ③), both overlooking the sea. *Camiguin Seaside Lodge* (③) is one of half a dozen reasonably priced places in Agoho, giving easy access to White Island. Another is *Payag Beach Resort* (③), where accommodation is in nipa cottages.

Eating on Camiguin is mostly limited to your resort or one of a few nipa-style restaurants dotting the beaches. In Mumbajao itself there are some local eateries near the Capitol Compound, including the *Pachada Café* and *Parola* by the sea. On the beach at Agoho, the *Paradise Bar and Restaurant* is popular.

Siargao Island

Off the northeastern tip of Mindanao lies the little island of **Siargao**, an undeveloped backwater with Boracay-type beaches and dramatic coves and lagoons. It's off the tourist trail and few venture this way, but it won't be long before they do. Already an upmarket resort has sprung up catering to tourists from Europe. Some of the first tourists to step this way were surfers, who discovered a surfing "break" at Tuason Point that was so good they called it Cloud Nine. Kayaking is a great way to explore the area, paddling through mangrove swamps or into hidden coral bays. There are some cheap resorts on the southeast of Siargao Island near the rustic town of **General Luna**. *Siargao Pension House* (⑦), opposite the municipal building, in General Luna, has doubles, meals included. Places to stay at Tuason Point, which is just north of General Luna and can be reached on foot or by banca, include *Surf Camp*, *Green Room*, and *Tuason Point Resort*, all in the ③–⑥ category. The *Pirate's Anchorage Bar and Restaurant* organizes good tours around Siargao Island (P500 for half a day). Surf lessons are available at resorts in Tuason Point and there's a big annual surf competition in September that attracts competitors from around the world.

One of the reasons Siargao is still relatively undiscovered is that getting here can be a bit of a headache. The only airline that serves the small **airport** at Surigao is Mindanao Express, but you will have to check for latest schedules. Another way is to fly to Cebu then take the 8am Waterjet fast ferry to Surigao City, on mainland Mindanao, where you can connect with a local ferry (P55) from the pier on Borromea Street to **Napa**, the biggest town on Siargao. From Napa there are jeepneys that serve most parts of Siargao Island. Jeepneys to General Luna take 45 minutes (P20). From General Luna take a tricycle to Cloud Nine or Tuason Point. Philtranco Bus has a service from Manila to Surigao taking three days. WG&A sails to Surigao City twice a week, usually via Cebu. From Camiguin you will have to backtrack to Cagayan de Oro and take a bus heading east along the coastal road to Surigao City via Butuan City. The bus terminal in Butuan City is near Langihan market on Montilla Street. Cagayan to Butuan takes five hours and Butuan to Surigao City takes two hours. If you have to stay in Butuan, try the *Embassy Hotel* (☎086/3737; ②) on Montilla Street, which is convenient for the bus station and has decent fan rooms. In Surigao City, accommodation includes *Flourish Lodge* (③) on Borromeo Street in the port area, and the nearby *Tavern Hotel* (☎086/87300; ③), whose owners will arrange a boat for island-hopping.

Marawi and Lake Lanao

MARAWI, on the shores of Lake Lanao, three hours' bus journey southwest of Cagayan de Oro, was renamed the Islamic City of Marawi on April 15, 1980. Ninety-two percent of the people are Muslims and the city is the centre of the Islamic religion in the Philippines. The annual Kalilang festival, April 10–15, is dominated by Koran reading competitions and colourful Muslims singing and dancing. The best place to stay is the *Marawi Resort Hotel* (☎063/520 981; ④) on the Mindanao State University campus. Also on the campus is the Aga Kahn Museum, which has an interesting collection of indigenous art from Mindanao, Sulu and Palawan. Sacred Mountain is close to the city and gives nice views across Lake Lanao, the second largest in the country. There are daily **buses** from Cagayan de Oro west along the coast to **Iligan** (1.5hr; P70). In Iligan you can change for a bus south to Marawi (1hr; P65). The bus station in Iligan is on Roxas Avenue at its junction with Zamora Street.

Zamboanga City

ZAMBOANGA CITY, on the southernmost tip of the Zamboanga Peninsula, 700km south of Manila, makes an interesting day-stop on your way to the Sulu archipelago. It's closer to both Malaysia and Indonesia than it is to the capital of the Philippines, a fact that has contributed to its cosmopolitan makeup. More than seventy percent of the population is Catholic and the other thirty percent Muslim. But the Muslim inhabitants are further divided into tribal groups, the most conspicuous of which are the Tausugs of Sulu, the Yakans of Basilan, the Badjaos of the sea, the Samals of Tawi-Tawi, and the Subanons of Zamboanga Peninsula. In addition to the city itself, which sprawls over 1600 square kilometres, the principality of Zamboanga also includes 28 offshore islands. The most popular island for trips is Santa Cruz Island, with its eye-catching pink sand. You can reach it in 25 minutes by ferry from the wharf at the *Lantaka Hotel*. Fort Pilar, an old Spanish fort on the waterfront, south of the city, was built in 1635 and has walls made of coral. There are marvellous views of the coast and across to Rio Hondo, a Muslim village on stilts. The village of **Taluksangay**, 19km east of Zamboanga City, is home to the Samal tribe, who live in huts on stilts. Jeepneys for Taluksagay leave from Zamboanga market. **Yakan Village**, 7km from the city, is where the Basilans live. Families here weave traditional cloth and sell it to visitors. Buses for Yakan leave Zamboanga from Governor Lim Avenue. All these villages have lovely mosques. The one in Taluksangay, built in 1885, is the oldest in the city.

Practicalities

Philippine Airlines, Air Philippines and Cebu Pacific all have more than one departure daily from Manila to Zamboanga. Mindanao Express **flies** to Zamboanga from Cebu and Davao. **WG&A Superferry and Negros Navigation** both sail to Zamboanga Port from Manila, usually via other cities such as Cotabato, Iloilo or Davao. There are also regular sailings to Zamboanga from Davao, Cagayan de Oro, General Santos, Dipolog and Cotabato. Buses link Zamboanga City to Cagayan De Oro (15hr), but bear in mind buses have occasionally become terrorist targets. From Marawi your best bet is to backtrack to Iligan and catch either a Fortune Liner or Almirante Bus. The **tourist office** is in the *Lantaka Hotel*, on the waterfront in Mayor Velderrosa Street.

The *Lantaka Hotel* (☎991 2033; ⑦) is the best **place to stay** in Zamboanga and has a good terrace restaurant with breakfast, lunch and dinner buffets for P220–300. Budget options include *L'Mirage Pension House* (②), in Mayor Jaldon Street, with air-con doubles, or *Paradise Pension* (☎991 1054; ③) on Barcelona Street, offering air-con doubles with cable TV.

It's possible to get a **ferry from Zamboanga to Sandakan** in Malaysia. Aleson Shipping Lines' *M/V Lady Mary Joy* departs Mon at 2pm and Wed at 4pm, and the journey takes sixteen hours. A cabin for two costs P1600 and an economy bed P600. You can get tickets from 172–174 Veteran's Avenue (☎991 4258; port office ☎991 5874). Sampaguita Shipping Corp also runs a service and leaves every Monday and Thursday at noon. A cabin costs P850 per person. Contact them at Zaragosa cor Alvarez Streets (☎991 1784 or 993 1591–93).

Sulu Islands

The volcanic **Sulu Islands** are a group of about 870 islands off southwest Mindanao between the Sulawesi and Sulu seas. They cover an area of 2700 square kilometres and are home to a surprisingly large population of around twelve million. The capital is **JOLO**, on the island (the largest) of the same name. The area around Jolo has some unspoiled beaches and the town itself has a busy market where goods are brought (perhaps smuggled) from Malaysia and

Indonesia. At the southern end of the peninsula lies the island of Tawi-Tawi, whose capital **BONGAO** is a commercial fishing centre and where rice and tubers are produced and coconuts exported. Bongao is slightly smaller than Jolo, but has a cinema, a lively market, banks and a provincial capital building shaped like a mosque. Tawi-Tawi was the seat of Islam in the Philippines, and the first mosque, the Sheik Makdum Mosque, was built here by Arab missionaries during the fourteenth century. From Bongao's harbour you can catch small boats to the tiny islands of Bilitan, Simunul and Manuk Mankaw.

Among the most important cultural minorities in the area are the **Badjao**, who live on boats throughout the archipelago. There is **continued strife** between the various tribes that inhabit the islands and there have been kidnappings of foreigners in the area by Muslim militants. Piracy is also a problem. Up until the late 70s, the archipelago was out of bounds to tourists, but it is now possible to visit the islands. Remember, however, that Muslims in the area are still fighting for independence, and skirmishes and bombings still occur, so **check with your embassy** before you travel.

There's a small **airstrip** at Bongao, but the only airline that uses it is Mindanao Express, which flies from Davao and Cebu, usually via Zamboanga and General Santos. Most of your travel through these islands will have to be by **local banca or ferry**. The *M/V Mary Joy* leaves Zamboanga every night arriving in Bongao the next morning. An increasing number of **liveaboard dive boats** are venturing into the area because of the excellent coral reefs.

travel details

Buses

Angeles to: Baguio (5–6 daily 5–6hr); Olongapo (frequent; 2hr).

Baguio to: Sagada (6–7 daily; 4–8hr); San Fernando; La Union (4–5 daily; 3–4hr).

Cauayan to: Banaue (2–3 daily; 3hr).

Cebu City Southern Bus Terminal to: Moalboal (5–6 daily; 3–4 hr).

Cebu City Northern Bus Terminal to: Hagnaya (2–3 daily; 3–4hr); Maya (2–3 daily; 4hr).

Daet to: Naga (daily; 1–2hr).

Dagupan to: Baguio (5–6 daily; 4hr).

Dau (Clark) to: Baguio (5–6 daily; 5–6hr); Olongapo (frequent; 2hr).

Davao to: Cagayan de Oro (2–3 daily; 5hr); Cebu (1 daily; 39 hr); Cotabato (2–3 daily; 3hr); General Santos (2–3 daily; 3hr); Manila (1 weekly; 36hr); Surigao (1 daily; 8hr); Zamboanga City (1 daily; 9hr).

Iloilo to: Caticlan (2–3 daily; 4hr).

Kalibo to: Caticlan (5–6 daily; 2hr).

Legaspi to: Donsol (2–3 daily; 3hr); Naga (daily; 2hr); Sorsogon (2–3 daily; 3–4 hr).

Manila to: Angeles/Dau (12–15 daily; 2hr); Aparri (3–4 daily; 13hr); Baguio (12–15 daily; 6–8hr); Banaue (5–6 daily; 7–9hr); Bangued (4–5 daily; 8–10hr); Batangas City (18–20 daily; 3hr); Bolinao (3–4 daily; 6–7hr); Bulan (2–3 daily; 18–20hr); Cabanatuan (6–8 daily; 4hr); Calamba (1–12 daily; 2hr); Daet (6–8 daily; 7–8hr); Dagupan (8–10 daily; 6–7hr); Iba (3–4 daily; 6hr); Laoag (6–8 daily; 8–10hr); Lingayan (8–10 daily; 6–7hr); Legaspi (8–10 daily; 8–10hr); Lucena (1–12 daily; 3hr); Naga (6–8 daily; 6–8hr); Nasugbu (6–8 daily; 3hr); Olongapo (8–10 daily; 4–5hr); San Fernando, La Union (4–6 daily; 6–8hr); San Fernando, Pampanga (8–10 daily; 2–3hr); San Pablo (10–12 daily; 3hr); Santa Cruz (6–8 daily; 2–3hr); Pagsanjan (10–12 daily; 3hr); Sorsogon (2–3 daily; 24hr); Taal (10–12 daily; 2–3hr); Tagaytay (10–12 daily; 2–3hr); Tuguegarao (1–2 daily; 10–12hr); Vigan (6–8 daily; 8–10hr).

Olongapo to: Alaminos (frequent; 4hr); Iba (frequent; 2hr).

San Fernando (La Union) to: Baguio (4–5 daily; 3–4hr); Vigan (5–6 daily; 3–4 hr).

Sorsogon to: Donsol (3–4 daily; 1hr).

Tacloban to: Calbayog (hourly; 4hr); Davao (1 weekly; 22hr); Manila (1 weekly; 28hr); Ormoc (1 daily; 5hr).

Vigan to: Laoag (3–4 daily; 3hr).

Trains

Manila (Tayuman Station, Tondo) to: Ragay City, south of Daet in the Bicol Region (daily at 4.15pm; 8hr).

Ferries

It's not uncommon for ferry services to be suspended at short notice, so it's always best to check in advance with the ferry companies that services are running.

Bacolod to: Cagayan de Oro (1 daily; 7hr); Cebu (1 daily; 5hr); Iloilo (2 daily; 2hr).

Cagayan de Oro to: Bacolod (1 daily; 7hr); Dumaguete (3 weekly; 6hr).

Cebu to: Cagayan de Oro (daily; 10hr); Dumaguete (daily; 6hr); Iloilo (daily; 14hr); Manila (1–2 daily; 21 hr); Masbate (2–3 weekly; 14hr); Ormoc (daily; 5hr); Tacloban (daily; 13hr); Tagbilaran (1–2 daily; 3hr); Zamboanga (daily; 12hr).

Dumaguete to: Cagayan de Oro (3 weekly; 6hr); Cebu (1 daily; 6hr); Dapitan (1 daily; 5hr); Siquijor (2–3 daily; 1hr); Tagbilaran (1 daily; 3hr).

Hagnaya to: Santa Fe (2–3 daily; 1hr).

Iloilo to: Bacolod (2 daily; 2hr); Davao (3 weekly; 30–34hr); Jordan (3–4 daily; 1hr); Leyte (Ormoc; 2–3 weekly; 18hr); Tagbilaran (1 weekly; 11–13hr).

Manila to: Bacolod (3–4 week; 22hr); Bohol (1–2 daily; 28–36hr); Butuan (1–2 weekly; 32hr); Cagayan de Oro (1–2 daily; 32hr); Catbalogan (4–5 weekly; 24hr); Caticlan (3–4 weekly; 22hr); Cebu (1–2 daily; 21hr); Coron (2–3 weekly; 12hr); Cotabato (2–3 weekly; 44hr); Damaguit (3–4 weekly; 17hr); Davao (1–2 daily; 46hr); Dipolog (1–2 weekly; 38hr); Dumaguete (5–6 weekly; 22hr); Estancia (1 weekly; 20hr); General Santos (2 weekly; 43hr); Iligan (2–3 weekly; 34hr); Iloilo (1–2 daily; 18–25hr); Masbate (2 weekly; 19hr); Nasipit (2–3 weekly; 26–53hr); Ormoc (Tues & Fri at noon; 18hr); Ozamis (1–2 weekly; 32hr); Palompon (2 weekly; 18hr); Puerto Princesa (1–2 daily; 24hr); Romblon (2–3 weekly; 15hr); Roxas (1–2 daily; 16hr); San Carlos (1 weekly; 28hr); Surigao (2–3 weekly; 26–53hr); Tacloban (Tues & Fri at noon; 26 hr); Tagbilaran (3–4 weekly; 28hr); Zamboanga (1–2 weekly; 28hr).

Flights

Cagayan de Oro to: Cebu (5 weekly; 50min); Davao (5 weekly; 40min); General Santos (1 weekly; 55min).

Cebu to: Bacolod (2 daily; 1hr15); Butuan (1 weekly; 50min); Cagayan de Oro (5 weekly; 50min); Cotabato (2 weekly; 40min); Davao (3 daily; 1hr); Dipolog (1 weekly; 50min); General Santos (1 weekly; 4hr 15min); Iloilo (2 daily; 50min); Kalibo (2 weekly; 1hr); Pagadian (2 weekly; 1hr 5min); Tawi-Tawi (4 weekly; 2hr); Zamboanga (4 weekly; 1hr 40min).

Davao to: Cagayan de Oro (5 weekly; 40–75min); Cebu (3 daily; 1hr); Zamboanga (3 weekly; 1hr 10min).

Iloilo to: Cebu (2 daily; 50min).

Manila to Bacolod (up to 9 daily; 1hr 10min); Baguio (1–2 daily; 1hr 10min); Busuanga (daily; 1hr); Butuan (daily ex Wed; 1hr 30min); Cagayan de Oro (8 daily; 1hr 25min); Calbayog (4 weekly; 1hr 30min); Catarman (5 weekly; 1hr 30min); Caticlan (5 daily; 1hr); Cauayan (daily; 1hr); Cebu (up to 21 daily; 1hr 10min); Cotabato (1–2 daily; 1hr 40min); Davao (up to 10 daily; 1hr 40min); Dipolog (five weekly; 1hr 20min); Dumaguete (up to 3 daily; 1hr 10min); General Santos (2 daily; 1hr 40min); Iloilo (10 daily; 1hr); Kalibo (7–8 daily; 50min); Laoag (daily; 1hr); Legaspi (3–4 daily; 1hr 10min); Marinduque (5 weekly; 40min); Masbate (2 daily; 1hr 20min); Naga (2–3 daily; 1hr); Puerto Princesa (2–3 daily; 1hr 10min); Romblon (five a week; 1hr); Roxas (2 daily; 1hr); San Fernando (4 weekly; 1hr); San Jose (1–2 daily; 1hr); Tablas (five weekly; 1 hr); Tacloban (6–7daily; 1hr 10min); Tagbilaran (daily; 2hr); Tuguegarao (3 weekly; 1hr); Virac (2 daily; 1hr 20min); Zamboanga (4–5 daily; 1hr 30min).

CHAPTER NINE

SINGAPORE

Introduction

Conveniently linked by a kilometre-long causeway to the southern tip of Malaysia, the tiny city-state of **Singapore** (just 580 square kilometres) makes a gentle gateway for many first-time travellers to Asia, providing Western standards of comfort and hygiene alongside traditional Chinese, Malay and Indian enclaves. Its downtown areas are dense with towering skyscrapers and gleaming shopping malls, yet the island retains an abundance of nature reserves and lush, tropical greenery.

Singapore is a wealthy nation compared to the rest of Southeast Asia, with an average per capita income of over US$15,000. At the core of this success story is an unwritten bargain between Singapore's paternalistic **government** and acquiescent population, which stipulates the loss of a certain amount of personal freedom, in return for levels of affluence and comfort that would have seemed unimaginable thirty years ago. Outsiders often bridle at this, and it's true that some of the **regulations** can seem extreme: neglecting to flush a public toilet, jaywalking, chewing gum and eating on the subway all carry sizeable fines. Yet the upshot is that Singapore is a clean, safe place to visit, its amenities are second to none and its public places are smoke-free and hygienic.

Of more relevance to the millions of visitors Singapore receives each year is the fact that improvements in living conditions have been shadowed by a steady loss of the state's **heritage**, as historic buildings and streets are bulldozed to make way for shopping centres. Singapore undoubtedly lacks the personality of some southeast Asian cities, but its reputation for being sterile and sanitized is unfair. Much of the country's fascination springs from its **multicultural population**: of the 3.87 million inhabitants, 77 percent are Chinese (a figure reflected in the predominance of Chinese shops, restaurants and temples across the island), 14 percent are Malay, and 7 percent are Indian, the remainder being from other ethnic groups.

The entire state is compact enough to be explored exhaustively in just a few days. Forming the core of downtown Singapore is the **Colonial District**, around whose public buildings and lofty cathedral the island's British residents used to promenade. Each surrounding enclave has its own distinct flavour, from the aromatic spice stores of **Little India** to the tumbledown backstreets of **Chinatown**, where it's still possible to find calligraphers and fortune tellers, or the **Arab Quarter**, whose cluttered stores sell fine cloths and silks.

Beyond the city, you'll find **Bukit Timah Nature Reserve**, the splendid **Singapore Zoological Gardens**, complete with night safari tours, and the oriental Disneyworld attractions of **Haw Par Villas**. Offshore, you'll find **Sentosa**, the island amusement arcade which is linked to the south coast by a short causeway (and cable car), and **Pulau Ubin**, off the east coast, where the inhabitants continue to live a traditional *kampung* (village) life.

Singapore is just 136km north of the equator, which means that you should be prepared for a hot and sticky time whenever you go; **temperatures** hover around 30°C throughout the year. November, December and January are usually the coolest and the wettest months, but rain can fall all year round. July usually records the lowest annual rainfall.

Overland routes into Singapore

Singapore is connected by a causeway to Johor Bahru at the southern tip of Peninsular Malaysia and has excellent road and rail connections with numerous **Malaysian cities**, as well as even longer-distance connections by road and rail to **Thailand**. In addition, there are daily ferries from Malaysia to Singapore, and from **Indonesia**. Full details of all these options are given in on p.19 and at the relevant chapters.

Entry requirements and visa extension

Citizens of Western Europe, the USA and Commonwealth countries don't need a visa to enter Singapore. Check with the relevant embassy before departure (see "Basics" p.20). Unless you specify how long you intend staying, you'll normally be stamped in for **fourteen days**.

Entering from anywhere other than Malaysia (with which there are no **duty-free** restrictions), you can bring in 1 litre each of spirits, wine and beer duty-free; duty is payable on all tobacco. Other duty-free goods in Singapore include electronic and electrical items, cosmetics, cameras, clocks, watches, jewellery, and precious stones and metals.

Extending your visa for up to three months is possible, at the discretion of the Singapore

---

AIRPORT DEPARTURE TAX

Airport departure tax is $15 on all flights.

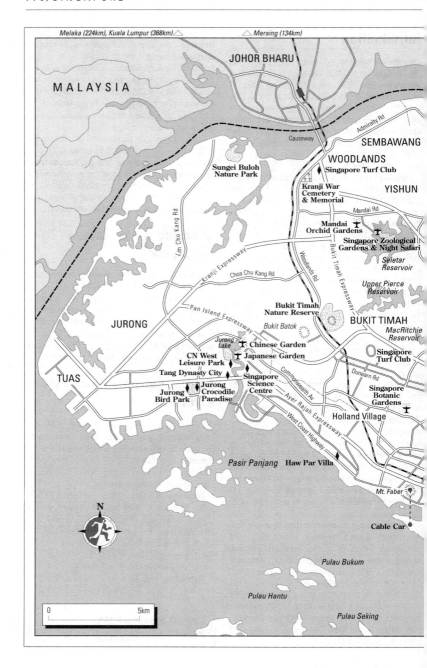

Melaka (224km), Kuala Lumpur (368km) △   △ Mersing (134km)

JOHOR BHARU

MALAYSIA

Admiralty Rd

Causeway

SEMBAWANG

WOODLANDS

Singapore Turf Club

Sungei Buloh
Nature Park

Kranji War
Cemetery
& Memorial

YISHUN

Mandai Rd

Mandai
Orchid Gardens

Singapore Zoological
Gardens & Night Safari

Lim Chu Kang Rd

Kranji Expressway

Choa Chu Kang Rd

Woodlands Rd

Bukit Timah Expressway

Seletar
Reservoir

Upper Pierce
Reservoir

Pan Island Expressway

JURONG

Bukit Timah
Nature Reserve

Bukit Batok

BUKIT TIMAH

MacRitchie
Reservoir

Jurong
Lake

Chinese Garden

Japanese Garden

CN West
Leisure Park

Tang Dynasty City

Singapore
Turf Club

Dunearn Rd

TUAS

Singapore
Science
Centre

Jurong
Bird Park

Jurong
Crocodile
Paradise

Commonwealth Av

Ayer Rajah Expressway

Singapore
Botanic
Gardens

West Coast Highway

Holland Village

Pasir Panjang   Haw Par Villa

Mt. Faber

N

Cable Car

Pulau Bukum

Pulau Hantu

Pulau Seking

0   5km

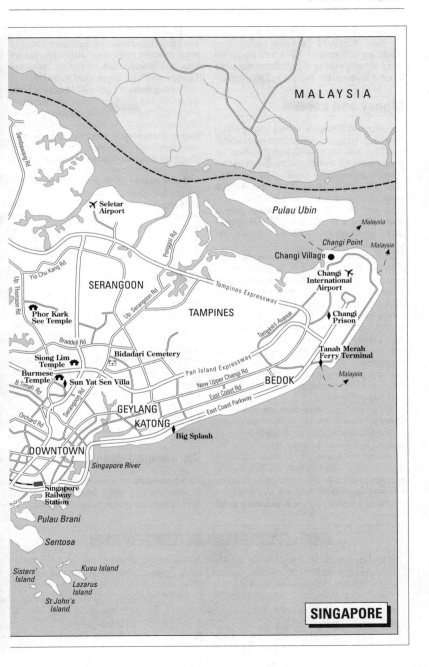

MALAYSIA

Seletar
Airport

Pulau Ubin

Malaysia

Changi Point *Malaysia*

Changi Village ●

Pongol Rd

Sembawang Rd

Yio Chu Kang Rd

Up. Thomson Rd

SERANGOON

Up. Serangoon Rd

Tampines Expressway

TAMPINES

Changi
International
Airport

Phor Kark
See Temple

Braddell Rd

Tampines Avenue

Changi
Prison

Siong Lim
Temple

Bidadari Cemetery

Tanah Merah
Ferry Terminal

Burmese
Temple

B.Timah Rd

Sun Yat Sen Villa

Serangoon Rd

Pan Island Expressway

New Upper Changi Rd

Malaysia

BEDOK

East Coast Rd

GEYLANG

Orchard Rd

East Coast Parkway

KATONG

Big Splash

DOWNTOWN

Singapore River

Singapore
Railway
Station

Pulau Brani

Sentosa

Sisters'
Island

Kusu Island

Lazarus
Island

St John's
Island

SINGAPORE

Immigration and Registration Department (Mon–Fri 9am–5pm; ☎3916100). Extensions beyond three months are less common, but there's always the option of taking a bus up to Johor Bahru, across the border in Malaysia, and then coming back in again.

Money and costs

The currency is **Singapore dollars**, usually written simply as $, though throughout the chapter we have used S$ in order to distinguish from US dollars. The Singapore dollar is divided into 100 cents. **Notes** are issued in denominations of S$1, S$2, S$5, S$10, S$20, S$50, S$100, S$500, S$1000 and S$10,000; **coins** are in denominations of 1, 5, 10, 20 and 50 cents, and S$1. The current **exchange rate** is around S$2.50 to £1, S$1.65 to US$1. Singaporean dollars are not accepted in Malaysia, but are legal tender in Brunei.

Daily necessities like food, drink and travel are marginally more expensive in Singapore than in Malaysia. But with budget dormitory accommodation in plentiful supply, and both food and internal travel cheap in the extreme, you'll find it possible to live on a **daily budget** of less than £10/US$16. Upgrading your lodgings to a private room in a guest house, eating in a restaurant and having a beer or two gives a more realistic budget of £20/US$32 a day. **Bargaining** is *de rigueur* in Singapore, especially when shopping or renting a room for the night – it's always worth trying to haggle, though note that you don't bargain for meals.

Sterling or US dollar **travellers' cheques** can be cashed at Singaporean banks, licenced moneychangers and some hotels. Major **credit cards** are widely accepted in the more upmarket hotels, shops and restaurants, but beware of the illegal surcharges levied by some establishments. Banks will often **advance cash** against major credit cards; moreover, with American Express, Visa and Mastercard, it's possible to withdraw money from **automatic teller machines** (ATMs) in Singapore – get details from your card company before you leave home. For lost or stolen travellers cheques or credit cards contact: **Visa and Master Card** ☎345-1345; **American Express** ☎2998133; **Diners Card** ☎2944222.

Banking hours are generally Monday to Friday 10am–3pm and Saturday 11am–1pm, outside of which you'll have to go to a moneychanger in a shopping centre (see p.817 for locations), or to a hotel. No black market operates in Singapore, nor are there any restrictions on carrying currency in or out of the state. This means that rates at moneychangers are as good as you'll find at the banks.

Wiring money – which can take anything from two to seven working days – incurs a small fee in Singapore and a larger one back home. You'll need, first, to supply your home bank with details of the local branch to which the money should be sent, after which it'll be issued to you upon presentation of some form of ID. For information on wiring money see "Basics" p.23.

Getting around

Getting from A to B is a doddle in diminutive Singapore. The island's impressive bus service and slick underground rail network system – the MRT (Mass Rapid Transport) – have got all corners of the island covered. Bus and MRT fares are extremely reasonable, though if you aren't having to watch the pennies you might consider hailing a taxi in order to buy yourself some time. Singaporean taxis are ubiquitous and so affordable as to make car rental hardly worthwhile, unless you are planning to push up into Malaysia. For more details of getting around Singapore, see "City Transport" p.785.

Accommodation

The **accommodation** scene in Singapore caters to all tastes and all pockets. Downtown guesthouses cater for travellers on tight budgets, and in these you

---

ACCOMMODATION PRICE CODES

All **accommodation** reviewed in this guide has been graded according to the following price codes, in US dollars, which represent the cost of the cheapest double room available in high season. Where a price range is indicated, this means that the establishment offers rooms with varying facilities – as explained in the write-up. In cases where an establishment charges per bed the actual price is given.

① under $5	④ $15–20	⑦ $40–60
② $5–10	⑤ $20–25	⑧ $60–80
③ $10–15	⑥ $25–40	⑨ $80 and over

can get a simple but secure room with access to shared facilities for as little as S$20 a night – or you can crash in a dormitory for around S$10 a night. Another S$10–20 will buy you air-con and a private bathroom. In Singapore's mid-range hotels, you can expect to pay S$60–90 a night for a double room with all mod-cons; while at the upper end of the accommodation scale, you'll find that Singapore has an enormous range of hotels of varying levels of splendour.

Electricity is supplied at 220 volts, so any equipment which uses 110 volts will need a converter.

Food and drink

Eating is the most profound pleasure that Singapore affords its visitors. The island's multicultural make-up translates into a mouth-watering array of cuisines, of which Chinese, Malay and Indian are, predictably enough, the best represented. Dining out in Singapore needn't break the bank. It's possible to eat like a king for S$5 at one of the island's many hawker centres or food courts, where Asian specialities are served, fast-food style. And even in restaurants, you'll be hard-pressed to spend more than S$30–40 a head, including drinks, unless you opt for one of the island's more exclusive addresses. Note that **tap water** is drinkable throughout Singapore.

Communications

Singapore's **postal system** is predictably efficient, with letters and cards often reaching their destination within three days. You can receive **poste restante** beside Paya Lebar MRT (see p.817); see "Basics" p.39 for general advice on poste restante. There are other post offices across the state, with usual hours of Monday to Friday 8.30am–5pm and Saturday 8.30am–1pm, though postal services are available until 9pm at the Comcentre on Killiney Road.

Local calls from public phones cost 10c for three minutes, with the exception of Changi Airport's free courtesy phones. Singapore has **no area codes** – the only time you'll punch more than seven digits for a local number is if you're dialling a toll-free (☎1800-) number. Many businesses have **mobile phone numbers** – usually prefixed ☎011 or 010 – these are very expensive to call. **Card phones** are taking over from payphones in Singapore: cards, available from the **Comcentre** (see p.817) and post offices, as well as *7-Elevens*, stationers and bookshops, come in denominations of S$2 upwards.

TIME DIFFERENCES

Singapore is eight hours ahead of GMT, sixteen hours ahead of US Pacific Standard Time, thirteen ahead of Eastern Standard Time, and two hours behind Sydney.

International calls can be made from all public cardphones. Otherwise, use a credit-card phone. IDD calls made from hotel rooms in Singapore carry no surcharge. To call abroad, dial ☎001 + IDD country code (see "Basics" p.40) + area code minus first 0 + subscriber number. Some booths are equipped with **Home Country Direct** phones – see "Basics" p.40 for the procedure. Or you can use your BT or AT&T **chargecard**.

If you want to **email** somone, you'll have no problem in Singapore. Cybercafés are sprouting up across the island – see p.817 for a selection of the most central ones.

Opening hours and festivals

Shopping centres open daily 10am–7.30pm; **banks** open at least Monday to Friday 10am–3pm, Saturday 9.30am–1pm; while **offices** generally work Monday to Friday 8.30am–5pm and sometimes on Saturday mornings. In general, Chinese **temples** open daily from 7am to around 6pm, Hindu temples from 6am to noon and 5 to 9pm and **mosques** from 8.30am to noon and 2.30pm to 4pm.

■ Festivals

With so many ethnic groups and religions represented in Singapore, you'll be unlucky if your trip doesn't coincide with some sort of **festival**, either secular or religious. Most of the festivals have **no fixed dates**, but change annually according to the lunar calendar;

PUBLIC HOLIDAYS

January 1: New Year's Day
January/February: Chinese New Year (two days)
February/March: Hari Raya Haji
March/April: Good Friday
May 1: Labour Day
May: Vesak Day
August 9: National Day
November: Deepavali
December: Hari Raya Puasa
December 25: Christmas Day

check with the tourist office. Bear in mind that the major festival periods may play havoc with even the best-planned travel itineraries. Over the month of **Ramadan** (between Jan & April) in particular, transport networks and hotel capacity are stretched to their limits, as countless Muslims return to their family homes; during Ramadan, Muslims fast during the daytime. Many hotels and restaurants shut for up to a week over Chinese New Year (early springtime). Some festivals are also public holidays (when everything closes); check the list on p.779.

Not all religious festivals are celebrated in public, but some are marked with truly spectacular parades and street performances. In springtime, during **Chinese New Year**, Chinese operas and lion and dragon dances are performed in the streets, and colourful parades process along Orchard Road. And at **Thaipusam**, entranced Hindu penitents pierce their own flesh with elaborate steel arches, and process from the Sri Srinivasa Perumal Temple to the Chettiar Hindu Temple. Similar feats are executed by mediums on the occasion of the **Birthday of the Monkey God** (summer), best witnessed at the Monkey God Temple on Seng Poh Road. Every year, the whole island goes into an eating frenzy for the month-long **Singapore Food Festival** (July), with almost every food outlet staging events, tastings and special menus. The **Festival of the Hungry Ghosts** (summer) is a good time to catch a free performance of a Chinese opera, or *wayang*, in which characters act out classic Chinese legends, accompanied by cymbals, gongs and singing; a few weeks later, the **Moon Cake Festival**, or Mid-Autumn Festival, is celebrated with children's lantern parades after dark in the Chinese Gardens. For the nine nights of **Navarathiri** (autumn), Chettiar Temple stages classical Hindu dance and music, and at the Sri Mariamman Temple, the Hindu firewalking ceremony of **Thimithi** (autumn) is marked by devotees running across a pit of hot coals. **Deepavali** (Oct/Nov), the Hindu festival celebrating the victory of Light over Dark, is marked by the lighting of oil lamps outside homes.

Cultural hints

Singapore shares the same attitudes to dress and social taboos as other Southeast Asian cultures; see "Basics" p.41.

Crime and safety

Singapore is a **very safe place** for travellers, though you shouldn't become complacent – muggings have

been known to occur and theft from dormitories by other tourists is a common complaint.

Singapore is known locally as a "**fine city**". There's a fine of S$500 for smoking in public places such as cinemas, trains, lifts, air-conditioned restaurants and shopping malls, and one of S$50 for "jaywalking" – crossing a main road within 50m of a pedestrian crossing or bridge. Littering carries a S$1000 fine, with offenders forced to do litter-picking duty, while eating or drinking on the MRT could cost you S$500. Other fines include those for urinating in lifts (some lifts are supposedly fitted with urine detectors), not flushing a public toilet and chewing gum (which is outlawed in Singapore). It's worth bearing all these offences in mind, since foreigners are not exempt from the various Singaporean punishments – as American Michael Fay discovered in 1994, when he was given four strokes of the cane for vandalism.

In Singapore, the possession of **drugs** – hard or soft – carries a hefty prison sentence and trafficking is punishable by the death penalty. If you are caught smuggling drugs into or out of the country, at the very best you are facing a long stretch in a foreign prison; at worst, you could be hanged.

Singapore's **police**, who wear dark blue, keep a fairly low profile, but are polite and helpful when approached. For details of the main police station, see "Listings", p.817.

> ### EMERGENCY PHONE NUMBERS
> Police ☎999 (toll-free)
> Ambulance and Fire Brigade ☎995 (toll-free).

Medical care and emergencies

Medical services in Singapore are excellent, with staff almost everywhere speaking good English and using up-to-date techniques. **Pharmacies** (Mon–Sat 9am–6pm) are well stocked with familiar brand-name drugs, and pharmacists can recommend products for skin complaints or simple stomach problems, though if you're in any doubt, it always pays to get a proper diagnosis. Pharmacists also stock oral contraceptives, spermicidal gels and condoms.

Larger hotels have **doctors** on call at all times. **Dentists** are listed in the *Singapore Buying Guide* (equivalent to the *Yellow Pages*) under "Dental Surgeons", and "Dentist Emergency Service". For details of **hospital casualty departments**, see Listings p.817.

History

What little is known of Singapore's ancient history relies heavily upon legend and supposition. In the late thirteenth century, Marco Polo reported seeing a place called Chiamassie, which could also have been Singapore: by then the island was known locally as Temasek – "sea town" – and was a minor trading outpost of the Sumatran Srivijaya empire. The island's present name – from the Sanskrit **Singapura**, meaning "Lion City" – was first recorded in the sixteenth century.

Throughout the fourteenth century, Singapura felt the squeeze as the Ayutthaya and Majapahit empires of Thailand and Java struggled for control of the Malay Peninsula. Around 1390, a Sumatran prince called **Paramesvara** threw off his allegiance to the Javanese Majapahit Empire and fled from Palembang to present-day Singapore. There, he murdered his host and ruled the island until a Javanese offensive forced him to flee north, up the Peninsula, where he and his son, Iskandar Shah, subsequently founded the Melaka Sultanate.

With the rise of the **Melaka Sultanate**, Singapore evolved into an inconsequential fishing settlement; a century or so later, the arrival of the Portuguese in Melaka forced Malay leaders to flee southwards to modern-day Johor Bahru for sanctuary. A Portuguese account of 1613 described the razing of an unnamed Malay outpost at the mouth of Sungei Johor to the ground, an event which marked the beginning of two centuries of historical limbo for Singapore.

■ Raffles and the British

By the late eighteenth century, with China opening up for trade with the West, the British East India Company felt the need to establish outposts along the Straits of Melaka to protect its interests. Penang was secured in 1786, but with the Dutch expanding their rule in the East Indies (Indonesia), a port was needed further south. Enter **Thomas Stamford Raffles**. In 1818, the governor-general of India authorized Raffles, then lieutenant-governor of Bencoolen (in Sumatra), to establish a **British colony** at the southern tip of the Malay Peninsula; early the next year, he stepped ashore on the northern bank of the Singapore River accompanied by Colonel William Farquhar, former resident of Melaka

and fluent in Malay. Despite living and working in a period of imperial arrogance, Raffles maintained an unfailing concern for the welfare of the people under his governorship, and a conviction that British colonial expansion was for the general good. Today he is the man whom history remembers as the founder of modern Singapore.

At the time of his first landing there, inhospitable swampland and tiger-infested jungle covered Singapore, and its population is generally thought to have numbered around 150, although some historians suggest it could have been as high as a thousand. Raffles recognized the island's potential for providing a deep-water harbour, and immediately struck a treaty with **Abdul Rahman**, *temenggong* (chieftain) of Singapore, establishing a British trading station there. The Dutch were furious at this British incursion into what they considered their territory, but Raffles – who still needed the approval of the Sultan of Johor for his outpost, as Abdul Rahman was only an underling – disregarded Dutch sensibilities. He approached the sultan's brother, Hussein, recognized him as the true sultan, and concluded a second treaty with both the *temenggong* and **His Highness the Sultan Hussein Mohammed Shah**. The Union Jack was raised, and Singapore's future as a free trading post was set.

With its strategic position at the foot of the Straits of Melaka, and with no customs duties levied on imported or exported goods, Singapore's expansion was meteoric. The population had reached ten thousand by the time of the first census in 1824, with Malays, Chinese, Indians and Europeans arriving in search of work as coolies and merchants. In 1822, Raffles set about drawing up the **demarcation lines** that divide present-day Singapore. The area south of the Singapore River was earmarked for the Chinese; a swamp at the mouth of the river was filled and the commercial district established there. Muslims were settled around the Sultan's Palace in today's Arab Quarter.

■ Nineteenth-century boom

In 1824, Sultan Hussein and the *temenggong* were brought out, and Singapore ceded outright to the British. Three years later, the fledgling state united with Penang and Melaka (now under British rule) to form the **Straits Settlements**, which became a British crown colony in 1867. For forty years the island's *laissez-faire* economy boomed, though life was chaotic, and disease rife. More and more immigrants poured onto the island; by 1860 the population had reached eighty thousand, with each ethnic community bringing its attendant cuisines, languages and architecture. Arabs, Indians, Javanese and Bugis all came, but most populous of all were the **Chinese** from the southern provinces of China, who settled quickly, helped by the clan societies (*kongsis*) already establishing footholds on the island. The British, for their part, erected impressive Neoclassical theatres, courts and assembly halls, and in 1887 Singapore's most quintessentially British establishment, the *Raffles Hotel*, opened for business.

By the end of the nineteenth century, the opening of the Suez Canal and the advent of the steamship had consolidated Singapore's position at the hub of international trade in the region, with the port becoming a major staging post on the Europe–East Asia route. In 1877, Henry Ridley began his one-man crusade to introduce the **rubber plant** into southeast Asia, a move which further bolstered Singapore's importance as the island soon became the world centre of rubber exporting. This status was further enhanced by the slow but steady drawing of the Malay Peninsula under British control – a process begun with the Treaty of Pangkor in 1874 and completed in 1914 – which meant that Singapore gained further from the mainland's tin- and rubber-based economy.

Between 1873 and 1913 trade increased eight-fold, a trend which continued well into the twentieth century. Singapore's Asian communities found their **political voice** in the 1920s. In 1926, the Singapore Malay Union was established, and four years later, the Chinese-supported Malayan Communist Party (MCP). But grumblings of independence had risen to no more than a faint whisper before an altogether more immediate problem reared its head.

World war II

The bubble burst in 1942. In December 1941, the Japanese had bombed Pearl Harbour and invaded the Malay Peninsula. Less than two months later they were at the top of the causeway, safe from the guns of "Fortress Singapore", which pointed south from what is now Sentosa island. The inhabitants of Singapore had not been prepared for an attack from this direction and on February 15, 1942, the **fall of Singapore** (which the Japanese then renamed Syonan, or "Light of the South") was complete. Winston Churchill called the British surrender "the worst disaster and the largest capitulation in British history"; cruelly, it later transpired that the Japanese forces had been outnumbered and their supplies hopelessly stretched immediately prior to the surrender.

Three and a half years of brutal **Japanese** rule ensued, during which thousands of civilians were executed in vicious anti-Chinese purges and Europeans were either herded into **Changi Prison**, or marched up the Peninsula to work on Thailand's infamous "'Death Railway". Less well-known is the vicious campaign, known as Operation Sook Ching, mounted by the military police force, or *Kempeitai*, during which upwards of 25,000 Chinese males between 18 and 50 years of age were shot dead at Punggol and Changi beaches as enemies to the Japanese.

■ Towards independence

Following the atomic destruction of Hiroshima and Nagasaki in 1945, Singapore was passed back into British hands, but things were never to be the same. Singaporeans now wanted a say in the government of the island, and in 1957 the British government agreed to the establishment of an elected, 51-member legislative assembly. Full internal **self-government** was achieved in May 1959, when the **People's Action Party** (PAP), led by Cambridge law graduate **Lee Kuan Yew**, won 43 of the 51 seats. Lee became Singapore's first prime minister, and quickly looked for the security of a merger with neighbouring Malaya. For its part (despite reservations about aligning with Singapore's predominantly Chinese population), anti-Communist Malaya feared that extremists within the PAP would turn Singapore into a Communist base, and accordingly preferred to have the state under its wing.

In 1963, Singapore combined with Malaya, Sarawak and British North Borneo (modern-day Sabah) to form the **Federation of Malaysia**. The alliance, though, was an uneasy one, and within two years Singapore was asked to leave the federation, in the face of outrage in Kuala Lumpur at the PAP's attempts to break into Peninsular politics in 1964. Hours after announcing Singapore's **full independence**, on August 9, 1965, a tearful Lee Kuan Yew went on national TV and described the event as "a moment of anguish". One hundred and forty-six years after Sir Stamford Raffles had set Singapore on the world map, the tiny island, with no natural resources of its own, faced the prospect of being consigned to history's bottom drawer of crumbling colonial ports.

■ Contemporary Singapore

Instead, Lee's personal vision and drive transformed Singapore into an Asian economic heavyweight, a position achieved at a price. Heavy-handed **censor-**

ship of the media was introduced, and even more disturbing was the government's attitude towards **political opposition**. When the opposition Worker's Party won a by-election in 1981, the candidate, JB Jeyaretham, found himself charged with several criminal offences, and chased through the Singaporean law courts for the next decade.

The archaic **Internal Security Act** still grants the power to detain without trial anyone the government deems a threat to the nation, which has kept political prisoner Chia Thye Poh under lock and key since 1966 for allegedly advocating violence. Population policies, too, have brought criticism from abroad. These began in the early 1970s, with a birth control campaign which proved so successful that it had to be reversed.

At other times, Singapore tries so hard to reshape itself that it falls into self-parody. "We have to pursue this subject of fun very seriously if we want to stay competitive in the twenty-first century" was the reaction of former Minister of State George Yeo, when confronted with the fact that some foreigners find Singapore dull. The government's annual courtesy campaign, which in 1996 urged the population to hold lift doors open for neighbours and prevent their washing from dripping onto passers-by below, appears equally risible to outsiders.

However, adults beyond a certain age remember how things were before independence and, more importantly, before the existence of the Mass Rapid Transit (MRT) system, housing projects and saving schemes. But their children and grandchildren have no such perspective, and telltale signs – presently nothing more extreme than feet up on MRT seats and jaywalking – suggest that the government can expect more **dissent** in future years. Already a substantial brain drain is afflicting the country, as skilled Singaporeans choose to move abroad in the pursuit of heightened civil liberties.

The man charged with leading Singapore into the new millennium is **Goh Chok Tong**, who became prime minister upon Lee's retirement in 1990. Goh has made it clear that he favours a more open form of government. Certainly, he has the mandate to make whatever changes he wishes.

Religions of Singapore

In Singapore – where three quarters of the population are Chinese – **Buddhism** is the main religion, though many Singaporean Chinese consider themselves specifically **Taoist** or **Confucianist**. There's also a smaller, but significant, **Hindu** Indian pres-

ence, as well an **Islamic** congregation. Buddhism, Hinduism and Islam all play a vital role in the everyday lives of the population. Indeed, some religious festivals, like Muslim Hari Raya and Hindu Thaipusam, have been elevated to such stature that they are among the main cultural events in the calendar. For an introduction to all these faiths, see "Basics" p.47.

Books

In the selection of **books** below, where a book is published in the UK and the US, the UK publisher is given first, followed by the US one; the abbreviation o/p means out of print.

Noel Barber, *Sinister Twilight* (Arrow, UK). Documents the fall of Singapore to the Japanese by re-imagining the crucial events of the period.

James Clavell, *King Rat* (Hodder/Dell). Set in Japanese-occupied Singapore, a gripping tale of survival in the notorious Changi Prison.

Maurice Collis, *Raffles* (Century, o/p). The most accessible and enjoyable biography of Sir Stamford Raffles on the market – very readable.

Tan Kok Seng, *Son Of Singapore* (Heinemann, US, o/p). Tan Kok Seng's candid and sobering autobiography on the underside of the Singaporean success story, telling of hard times spent as a coolie.

Maya Jayapal, *Images of Asia: Old Singapore* (OUP). Concise volume that charts the growth of the city-state, drawing on contemporary maps, sketches and photographs to engrossing effect.

C Mary Turnbull, *A Short History of Malaysia, Singapore & Brunei* (Graham Brash, Singapore). Decent, informed introduction to the region.

Michael Wise (ed), *Travellers' Tales of Old Singapore* (In Print Publishing, UK). A catholic and engrossing collection of vignettes.

Language

The national language of Singapore is **Bahasa Malaysia**, which is outlined, together with an introductory vocabulary, in the Malaysia chapter on p.572-3. As well as Bahasa, Mandarin, Tamil and English all have the status of official languages, which means you should have no problem getting by in **English**. One intriguing by-product of Singapore's ethnic melting pot is **Singlish**, or Singaporean English, a patois which blends English with the speech patterns, exclamations and vocabulary of Chinese and Malay.

SINGAPORE

The diamond-shaped island of Singapore is 42km from east to west at its widest points, and 23km from north to south. The downtown city areas huddle at the southern tip of the diamond, radiating out from the mouth of the **Singapore River**. Two northeast–southwest roads form a dual spine to the central area, both of them traversing the river. One starts out as **North Bridge Road**, crosses the river and becomes **South Bridge Road**; the other begins as **Victoria Street**, becomes Hill Street and skirts Chinatown as **New Bridge Road**.

At the very heart of the city, on the north bank, the **Colonial District** is home to a cluster of buildings that recall the days of early British rule – Parliament House, the cathedral, the Supreme Court, the Cricket Club and, most famously, *Raffles Hotel*. Moving west, the fringes of **Fort Canning Park** has several attractions, including Singapore's National Museum. From here, it's a five-minute stroll to the eastern end of **Orchard Road**, the main shopping area in the city. North from Fort Canning Park you soon enter **Little India**, whose main drag – Serangoon Road – is around fifteen minutes' walk from *Raffles Hotel*. Ten minutes southeast from Little India, Singapore's traditional **Arab Quarter** squats at the intersection of North Bridge Road and Arab Street.

South, across the river, the monolithic towers of the **Financial District** cast long shadows over **Chinatown**, whose row of shop-houses stretches for around one kilometre, as far as Cantonment Road. Singapore's **World Trade Centre** is a fifteen-minute walk southwest of the outskirts of Chinatown, and from there cable cars run across to **Sentosa**.

The **rest of the island** is crossed by expressways, of which the main ones are the east–west **Pan Island Expressway** and the **East Coast Parkway/Ayer Rajah Expressway**, both of which run from Changi to Jurong, and the **Bukit Timah Expressway**, which branches off north from the Pan Island Expressway at Bukit Timah new town, running north to Woodlands. At Woodlands, a causeway links Singapore with Malaysia.

Arrival

Singapore is linked to Johor Bahru in Malaysia by a 1056-metre-long **causeway** which runs across the Strait of Johor to Woodlands town, in the far north of the island. All buses and trains **from Malaysia** currently pass over the causeway, though there is talk of a second connection being constructed further east.

By air

Changi Airport (toll-free ☎1800/542 4422) is at the far eastern end of Singapore, 16km from the city centre. Facilities include duty-free shops, moneychanging and left-luggage services, hotel reservations counters and, in Terminal One's basement, a cheap food centre. Since Singapore's underground train system doesn't yet extend as far as the airport, you'll have to take either a taxi or a public bus into the centre. The **bus** departure points in the basements of both terminals are well signposted: get hold of the exact fare before you leave the terminal. Take the **#36** (every 10min, 6am–midnight; S$1.50), which heads west to Stamford Road (ask the driver to give you a shout at Stamford Road's Capitol Building for Beach Road, and at the YMCA stop if you plan to cross over Bras Basah Park to Bencoolen Street) before skirting the southern side of Orchard Road. Another option is to take a MaxiCab shuttle into town. These six-seater taxis depart every fifteen minutes, or when full, and will take you to any hotel in the city for a flat fare of S$7. MaxiCabs are equipped to take wheelchairs. **Taxis** from the airport cost around S$15 into downtown Singapore (20min); pick-up points are well signposted.

By bus

Singapore has three bus terminals. Local buses **from Johor Bahru** (JB) arrive at **Ban San Terminal** at the junction of Queen and Arab streets, from where a two-minute walk along

Queen Street, followed by a left along Rochor Road takes you to Bugis MRT station. Buses from elsewhere in **Malaysia** and **from Thailand** terminate at one of two sites, **Lavender Street Terminal** and the **Golden Mile Complex**. Lavender Street Terminal is at the corner of Lavender Street and Kallang Bahru, five minutes' walk from Lavender MRT. Alternatively, walk a short way in the other direction to the end of Jalan Besar and hop on bus #139, if you're heading for the guesthouses of Bencoolen Street. Bus #145 passes the Lavender Street Terminal on its way down North Bridge and South Bridge roads. From outside the Golden Mile Complex, buses run up Beach Road towards City Hall MRT.

By train

Trains to and from Malaysia use the **Singapore Railway Station** on Keppel Road, southwest of Chinatown. From Keppel Road, bus #97 travels past Tanjong Pagar MRT and on to Selegie and Serangoon roads.

By sea

Boats from the Indonesian Riau Archipelago (through which travellers from **Sumatra** will approach Singapore) dock at the **World Trade Centre**, off Telok Blangah Road, roughly 5km east of the centre. From Telok Blangah Road, bus #97 runs to Tanjong Pagar MRT, the #65 goes to Selegie and Serangoon roads via Orchard Road, or for Chinatown take bus #166.

Bumboats from Kampung Pengerang on the southeastern coast of Johor Bahru (daily when full, 7am–4pm; 45min; S$5 one-way) moor at **Changi Village**, beyond the airport. Bus #2 travels from Changi Village (see p.808) into the centre, via Geylang, Victoria and New Bridge roads. Newer, more reliable Ferrylink ferries from Tanjung Belungkor, also in Johor, dock at the **Changi ferry terminal**, a little way east of Changi Village. You need to take a taxi from the Changi ferry terminal to the nearest #2 bus stop. Ferries from Tioman Island arrive at the **Tanah Merah Ferry Terminal**, connected to Bedok MRT station by bus #35.

Information

The Singapore Tourism Board (STB) maintains three **Tourist Information Centres**. One is at Tourism Court, 1 Orchard Spring Lane (Mon–Fri 8.30am–5pm, Sat 8.30am–1pm; toll-free ☎1-800/736 2000); another at Liang Court Shopping Centre, Level 1, 177 River Valley Rd (daily 10.30am–9.30pm; ☎336 2888); and the third at 01-35 Suntec City Mall, 3 Temasek Boulevard (daily 8am–8pm; toll-free ☎1-800/332 5066). The most useful of their free handouts is the *Singapore Official Guide*. The best **what's on** listings publications are the weekly *8 Days* magazine ($1.50), and the newer *IS*, a free paper published fortnightly. Recommended **maps** include the *Nelles Singapore*, and the *Singapore Street Directory*, though, again, the STB has free maps.

With so many of Singapore's shops, restaurants and offices located in vast high-rise buildings and shopping centres, deciphering **addresses** can sometimes be tricky. #02-15 means room number 15 on the second floor; #10-08 is room number 8 on the tenth floor. Bear in mind that in Singapore, ground level is referred to as #01, or the first floor.

City transport

All parts of the island are accessible by bus or MRT – the underground rail network – and fares are reasonable; consequently, there's little to be gained by renting a car. However you travel, it's best to avoid rush hour (8–9.30am & 5–7pm) if at all possible; outside these times, things are relatively uncongested. A Transitlink Guide ($1.50), available from bus interchanges, MRT stations and major bookshops, outlines every bus and MRT route on the island in exhaustive detail. Singapore also has thousands of **taxis** which are surprisingly affordable. Getting around **on foot** is the best way to do justice to the central areas.

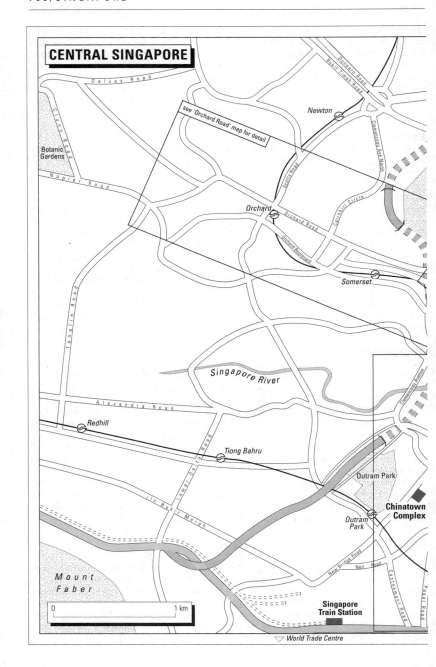

CENTRAL SINGAPORE

Dalvey Road

Duneam Road

Bukit Timah Road

see 'Orchard Road' map for detail

Newton

Botanic
Gardens

Cluny Road

Napier Road

Scotts Road

Clemenceau Ave North

Orchard

Orchard Road

Cairnhill Circle

Orchard Boulevard

Somerset

Tanglin Road

Singapore River

Alexandra Road

Clemenceau Avenue

Redhill

Tiong Bahru

Lower Delta Road

Jln Bukit Merah

Outram Park

Chinatown
Complex

Outram
Park

New Bridge Road

Neil Road

Cantonment Road

Pagar Road

Mount
Faber

0   1 km

Singapore
Train Station

▽ World Trade Centre

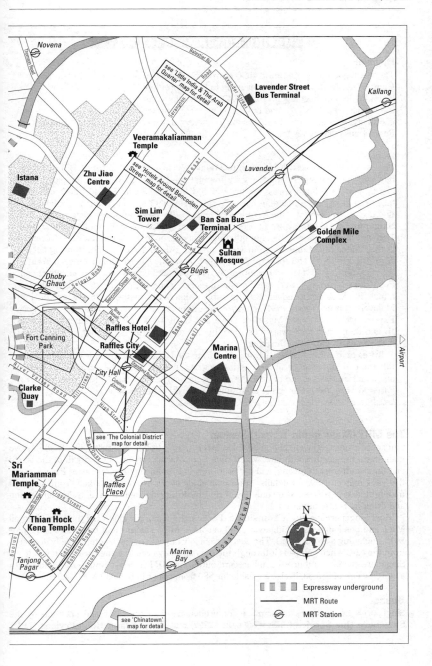

Balestier Rd

Lavender Street
Bus Terminal

Kallang

Veeramakaliamman
Temple

see 'Little India & The Arab
Quarter' map for detail

Istana

Zhu Jiao
Centre

see 'Hotels Around Bencoolen
Street' map for detail

Lavender

Sim Lim
Tower

Ban San Bus
Terminal

Golden Mile
Complex

Sultan
Mosque

*Dhoby
Ghaut*

Bugis

Raffles Hotel

Fort Canning
Park

Raffles City

Marina
Centre

City Hall

Coleman Street

Clarke
Quay

Airport

see 'The Colonial District'
map for detail

Sri
Mariamman
Temple

Raffles
Place

Thian Hock
Keng Temple

*Tanjong
Pagar*

*Marina
Bay*

East Coast Parkway

N

see 'Chinatown'
map for detail

▨▨▨▨▨ Expressway underground

────── MRT Route

⊖ MRT Station

MOVING ON FROM SINGAPORE

By plane

There are good deals on **plane tickets** from Singapore to Australia, Bali, Bangkok and Hong Kong. However, if you're planning to head for either Malaysia or Indonesia by air, it might be worth going to JB (p.627), across the causeway, or Batam, the nearest Indonesian island (p.301), and buying a flight from there. To get to Changi Airport, bus #36 (daily 6am–midnight; S$1.50) runs frequently, down Orchard Road and Brah Basah Road. Taxis costs S$12–15.

By bus

The easiest way across the causeway **to Malaysia** is to get the #170 **Johor Bahru**-bound bus from the Ban San Terminal (every 15min, 6am–12.30am; S$1.20) or the plusher air-con Singapore–Johor Express (every 10min, 6.30am–11.30pm; S$2.40), both of which take around an hour (including border formalities); both stop at JB bus terminal. From the taxi stand next to the terminal, a car to JB (seating four) costs S$30. The **Singapore–Kuala Lumpur** Express leaves from the Ban San Terminal daily at 9am, 1pm, 5pm and 10pm (6hr; 23). For other destinations, go to the Lavender Street Terminal or the Golden Mile Complex, from where buses to **Butterworth** (S$29), **Penang** (S$30), **Kota Bharu** (S$30) and **Ipoh** (S$27) tend to leave in the late afternoon; those to **Melaka** (S$11), **Mersing** (S$11) and **Kuantan** (S$17) depart in the early morning and afternoon. For **Kuala Lumpur** (S$17) there are both morning and night departures from this terminal. Book as far in advance as possible – operators at the terminal include Pan Malaysia Express (☎294 7034), Hasry Ekoba Express (☎292 6243), Malacca–Singapore Express (☎293 5915) and Masmara Travel (☎294 7034). It's slightly cheaper to travel to JB and then catch an onward bus from the bus terminal there – though it still pays to make an early start from Singapore.

Buses **to Thailand** leave early morning from the Golden Mile Complex at 5001 Beach Rd. You can buy a ticket all the way to Bangkok (though it may be cheaper just to buy one as far as Hat Yai and pay for the rest of the journey in Thai currency once there). Fares to **Hat Yai** (16hr) start at around S$30, while **Bangkok** costs S$70. Try Phya

The MRT (Mass Rapid Transit) System

Singapore's clean, efficient and good value **MRT** system (toll-free; ☎1-800/336 8900) has two main lines: the north–south line, which runs from Marina Bay up to the north of the island and then southwest to Jurong, and the east–west line, connecting Boon Lay to Pasir Ris; see the MRT map on p.790 for details. Trains run about every five minutes, daily from 6am until midnight, and cost 60c–S$1.60 one-way. A **no-smoking** rule applies on all trains, and eating and drinking is also outlawed.

Most Singaporeans buy a **Transitlink Farecard** – a stored-value card that's valid on all MRT and bus journeys in Singapore, and is sold at MRT stations and bus interchanges for S$12 (including a S$2 deposit). The cost of each journey you make is automatically deducted from the card when you pass it through the turnstile; any credit on the card when you leave Singapore can be reimbursed at a Farecard outlet. An **MRT Tourist Souvenir Ticket**, with a stored value of S$5.50, is also available for S$6 from major hotels and MRT stations.

Buses

Singapore's **bus** network is far more comprehensive than the MRT and operated by the **Singapore Bus Service** (SBS; ☎1-800/287 2727) and **Trans-Island Bus Services** (TIBS;

Travel Service (☎294 5415) or Sunny Holidays (☎292 7927), and don't forget to allow two working days for securing a Thai visa (needed for stays of over fifteen days).

By train

You can make free seat reservations up to one month in advance of **departure** at the information kiosk (daily 8.30am–2.30pm & 3.00–7pm; ☎222 5165) in the train station. The 10pm Express Senandung Malam gets into **Kuala Lumpur** early the next morning; the 7.30am Express Rakyat arrives in the early afternoon – this continues to **Butterworth**, arriving at 10pm. Unfortunately, none of the trains to Butterworth connect conveniently with the **international express to Bangkok**, involving either an overnight stop in Butterworth or, at best, a six-and-a-half-hour wait. It's a tiring journey done in one go, particularly if you don't book a berth on the overnight leg between Butterworth and Bangkok, but it is the quickest way (other than flying) to travel right through Malaysia.

By boat

Boats to **Batam** in **Indonesia**'s Riau Archipelago depart throughout the day from the World Trade Centre (7.30am–7pm; S$17 one-way), docking at Sekupang, from where you take a taxi to Hangnadim airport for internal Indonesian flights. There are also four boats a day (S$49 one-way) from the Tanah Merah Ferry Terminal (bus 35 from Bedok MRT) to Tanjung Pinang on **Pulau Bintan**, also in the Riau Archipelago; info and tickets from Dino Shipping (☎276 9722), or Bintan Resort Ferries (☎542 4369). From Kijang Port, south of Tanjung Pinang, there are boat services to **Jakarta**.

It's also possible to travel betweeen Singapore and **Malaysia** by boat. Bumboats to **Kampung Pengerang** on the southeastern coast of Johor Bahru (daily when full, 7am–4pm; 45min; S$5 one-way) leave from Changi Village, beyond the airport. Newer, more reliable Ferrylink ferries depart from Changi ferry terminal for **Tanjung Belungkor**, in Johor, a little way east of Changi Village, departing here daily at 7.30am, 11.30am, 4pm and 8pm (45min; S$32 return; ☎545 3600); check in one hour before departure. Ferries to **Tioman Island** run from the **Tanah Merah Ferry Terminal** (March–Oct daily except Wed at 8.30am; S$140 return). Information and tickets from Auto Batam (☎271 4866); check-in is one hour beforehand.

☎482 5433). Most buses charge distance-related fares, ranging from 60c–S$1.20 (70c–S$1.50 for air-con buses); others charge a flat fare, displayed on the front of the bus. Tell the driver where you want to go, and he'll tell you how much money to drop into the metal chute. Change isn't given, so make sure you have coins. If you are in town for a while, buy a **Transitlink Farecard** (see "The MRT System"), which you insert into the validator as you board; press the button to select your fare. Another ticket option is the **Tourist Day Ticket** (S$10), though you'd have to do an awful lot of travelling to make this ticket pay.

Taxis

Taxis are all metered, the fare starting at S$2.40 for the first kilometre, then rising 10c for every 240m. However, there's a fifty percent **surcharge** on journeys between midnight and 6am, a S$3 surcharge from Changi airport, a S$3 surcharge for taxis booked over the phone. The Singaporean government has introduced an Electronic Road Pricing programme (ERP) in order to relieve congestion within the city's **Central Business District** (CBD) at peak times, and these electronic tolls will be reflected in your bill, depending upon the time of day. Singaporean taxi drivers don't always speak good English, so it's a good idea to have your destination written down on a piece of paper. If a taxi displays a red destination sign on its

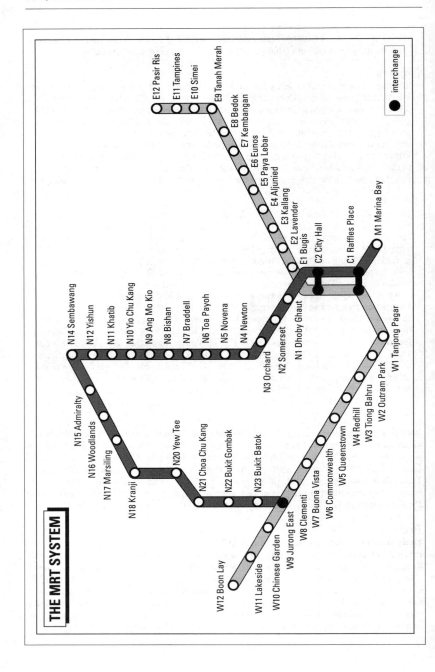

THE MRT SYSTEM

- interchange

USEFUL BUS ROUTES

Note that many of the services from the Orchard Road area actually leave from Penang Road or Somerset Road.

#2 passes along Eu Tong Sen Street (in Chinatown) and Victoria Street (past the Arab Quarter) en route to Changi Prison and Changi Village.

#7 runs along Orchard Road, Bras Basah Road and Victoria Street; its return journey takes in North Bridge Road, Stamford Road, Penang Road and Somerset Road en route to Holland Village.

#36 loops between Orchard Road and Changi Airport.

#65 terminates at the World Trade Centre, after passing down Jalan Besar, Bencoolen Street, Penang Road and Somerset Road.

#97 runs along Stamford Road to Little India, then on to Upper Serangoon Road; returns via Bencoolen Street and Collyer Quay.

#103 runs between New Bridge Road Terminal (Chinatown) and Serangoon Road (Little India).

#124 connects Scotts Road, Orchard Road and North Bridge Road with South Bridge Road, Upper Cross Street and New Bridge Road in Chinatown; in the opposite direction, travels along Eu Tong Sen Street, Hill Street, Stamford Road and Somerset Road.

#139 heads past Tai Gin Road, via Dhoby Ghaut, Selegie Road, Serangoon Road and Balestier Road.

#167 passes down Scotts Road, Orchard Road and Bras Basah Road, Collyer Quay, Shenton Way and Neil Road (for Chinatown).

#170 starts at the Ban San Terminal at the northern end of Queen Street, passing Bukit Timah Nature Reserve and Kranji War Cemetery on its way to JB in Malaysia.

#190 is the most direct service between Orchard Road and Chinatown, via Scotts Road, Orchard Road, Bras Basah Road, Victoria Street, Hill Street and New Bridge Road; returns via Eu Tong Sen Street, Hill Street, Stamford Road, Penang Road, Somerset Road and Scotts Road.

dashboard, it means the driver is changing shift and will accept customers only if they are going in his direction. TIBS Taxis (☎481 1211) have ten **wheelchair**-accessible cabs.

Renting cars and bikes
The Singapore government has introduced huge disincentives to driving in order to combat traffic congestion, making it expensive and tiresome to **rent a car**. **Bicycle rental** (S$4–8 an hour, with ID) is possible along the East Coast Parkway, where a cycle track skirts the seashore. The dirt tracks on Pulau Ubin, off Changi Point (see p.808), are ideal for biking, and there's a range of bikes available for rent next to the ferry terminal on Sentosa Island (S$2–5 an hour), providing by far the best way to see the island.

Singapore river, island and harbour cruises
Fleets of **cruise boats** ply Singapore's southern waters every day and night. The best of these, the Singapore River cruises (☎336 6111), cast off from North Boat Quay, Raffles' Landing Site, Riverside Point Landing Steps and Clarke Quay (every 10 min 9am–11pm) for a S$10 cruise on traditional bumboats, passing the old *godowns* (warehouses) upriver where traders once stored their merchandise. Several cruise companies also operate out of Clifford Pier and the World Trade Centre, offering everything from luxury catamaran trips around Singapore's southern isles to dinner on a Chinese sailing boat. A straightforward cruise costs about S$20, and a dinner special S$35–50.

Accommodation

Room rates take a noticeable leap when you cross the causeway from Malaysia into Singapore, but good deals still abound if your expectations aren't too high or, at the budget end of the scale, if you don't mind sharing. Advance booking is only necessary at Chinese New Year (usually Jan/Feb) and Hari Raya (March/April). The **Singapore Hotel Association** has booking counters at Changi Airport, though they only represent Singapore's official hotels. Touts at the airport also hand out flyers advertising rooms, but things can get embarrassing if you arrive and then don't like the place they represent.

The cheapest beds are in the communal **dormitories** of many resthouses, where you'll pay S$10 or less a night. The next best deals are at **guesthouses**, most of which are situated along Bencoolen Street and Beach Road, with an increasing number in nearby Little India and some also south of the river, in Chinatown. Singapore's classic guesthouse address is *Peony Mansions* on Bencoolen Street, where a cluster of establishments is shoehorned into several floors of a decrepit apartment building, though the Bencoolen area is becoming less fashionable. Guesthouses aren't nearly as cosy as their name suggests: costing S$20–30, the rooms are tiny, bare, and divided by paper-thin partitions, toilets are shared, and showers are cold. However, another S$10–20 secures a bigger, air-con room, and often TV, laundry and cooking facilities, lockers and breakfast are included. Always check that the room is clean and secure, and that the shower and air-con work before you hand over any money. It's always worth asking for a discount, too. Finally, since guesthouses aren't subject to the same safety checks as official hotels, without sounding alarmist, it's a good idea to check for a fire escape. The appeal of Singapore's **Chinese-owned hotels**, similar in price to guesthouses, is their air of faded grandeur, but sadly only a few of these now remain. In more modern, **mid-range hotels**, an en-suite room for two with air-con and TV will cost around S$60–90.

Bencoolen Street and around

Bencoolen Street has long been the mainstay of Singapore's backpacker industry, and is handy for all parts of central Singapore.

City Bayview, 30 Bencoolen St (☎337 2882). One of Bencoolen Street's posher hotels, with very comfortable rooms, a compact rooftop swimming pool and a friendly, modern café. ⑨.

Goh's Homestay, 4th Floor, 169d Bencoolen St (☎339 6561). The smartest guesthouse in town (at the top of its price category), with fresh and inviting rooms, pricier dorm beds than usual, laundry service, and great breakfasts. Recommended. Dorms S$14. ⑥.

Hawaii Hostel, 2nd Floor, 171b Bencoolen St (☎338 4187). Small, tidy, air-con rooms; breakfast included. Dorms S$10. ④.

Lee Boarding House, 07-52 Peony Mansions, 46–52 Bencoolen St (☎338 3149). The brightest place in Peony Mansion: clean, simple dorms and rooms, a pleasant breakfast area and laundry facilities. Dorms S$9. ③.

Peony Mansions Travellers' Lodge, second floor, 131a Bencoolen St (☎334 8697). Lots of clean featureless rooms (some en-suite) but no dorm beds. ④.

South East Asia Hotel, 190 Waterloo St (☎338 2394). Spotless doubles with air-con, TV and phone. Downstairs is a vegetarian restaurant serving Western breakfasts. ⑦.

Strand Hotel, 25 Bencoolen St (☎338 1866). An excellent-value hotel with clean, welcoming rooms and a variety of services. ⑦.

Sun Sun Hotel, 260–262 Middle Rd (☎338 4911). Housed in a splendid 1928 building, with decent rooms, plenty of communal bathrooms, some air-con, and the wonderful *L.E. Café & Confectionery*. ⑤.

Beach Road to Victoria Street

A few blocks east of Bencoolen Street, **Beach Road** boasts a mixture of charismatic old Chinese hotels and smart new guesthouses.

Ah Chew Hotel, 496 North Bridge Rd (☎837 0356). Simple but characterful rooms crammed with period furniture. Despite its address, it's just around the corner from North Bridge Rd, on Liang Seah Street. ④.

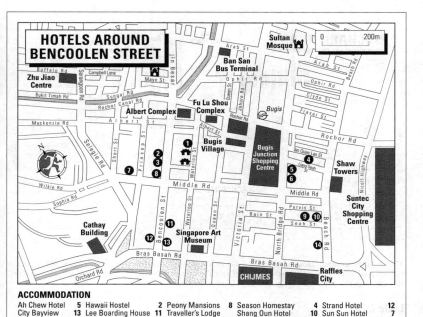

ACCOMMODATION

Ah Chew Hotel		**5**	Hawaii Hostel	**2**	Peony Mansions	**8**	Season Homestay	**8**	Strand Hotel	**12**
City Bayview	**13**	Lee Boarding House	**11**	Traveller's Lodge		Shang Onn Hotel	**10**	Sun Sun Hotel	**7**
Goh's Homestay	**3**	Metropole Hotel	**9**	Raffles Hotel	**14**	South East Asia Hotel	**1**	Waffles Home Stay	**6**

Metropole Hotel, 41 Seah St (☎3363611). Friendly, great-value establishment just across the road from *Raffles*, with roomy lodgings served by the intriguing *Imperial Herbal Restaurant*. ⑧.

Raffles Hotel, 1 Beach Rd (☎3371886). The flagship of Singapore's tourism industry, *Raffles* takes shameless advantage of its reputation but is still a beautiful place, dotted with frangipani trees and palms, and the suites (there are no rooms) are as tasteful as you would expect at these prices. ⑨.

Season Homestay, 26a Liang Seah St (☎3372400). Occupying one of the last few shop-houses on Liang Seah not to have been turned into a trendy café, the *Season* has dorm beds for S$9, plus a modest range of private rooms, all sharing only two common bathrooms. Breakfast is free. ④.

Shang Onn Hotel, 37 Beach Rd (☎3384153). Set in a quaint old building sporting attractive green shutters, the *Shang Onn* has reasonable rooms and a friendly manager/owner. ④.

Waffles Home Stay, 3rd Floor, 490 North Bridge Rd (☎3341608). Recommended crashpad. Breakfast included, and discounts if you introduce new guests. Good noticeboards. Dorms S$8. ④.

Orchard Road and around

Sumptuous hotels abound in the **Orchard Road** area, with most double rooms at least S$80.

Cavenagh Garden, 03-376, Block 73 Cavenagh Rd (☎7374600). A genuine homestay: various rooms are dotted around a family home. At the end of Cuppage Road, cross the Expressway bridge and walk to the left for 300m. Dorms S$10. ⑤.

Holiday Inn Park View, 11 Cavenagh Rd (☎7338333). Smart hotel with all the trimmings, across the road from Singapore's presidential residence. ⑨.

Lloyd's Inn, 2 Lloyd Rd (☎7377309). Motel-style building boasting attractive rooms and a fine location, just five minutes from Orchard Road. ⑦.

Mitre Hotel, 145 Killiney Rd (☎7373811). Reasonable old Chinese hotel, set amid overgrown grounds, and with an endearingly shabby air about it; there's a great lobby bar downstairs. ④.

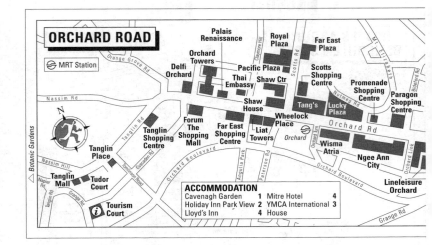

YMCA International House, 1 Orchard Rd (☎336 6000). Plush but overpriced rooms and dorms, a rooftop pool, and free room service from *McDonald's*. There's a first-day charge of S\$5 for non-members. Bus #36 from the airport stops right outside. Dorms \$25. ⑦.

Little India

Little India's hotels and guesthouses are attracting an increasing number of backpackers. Buses along Jalan Besar connect Little India with the rest of central Singapore.

Fortuna Hotel, 2 Owen Rd (☎295 3577). Mid-range hotel offering brilliant value for money; facilities include a health centre and secretarial services. ⑧.

Kerbau Hotel, 54–62 Kerbau Road (☎2976668). Friendly place, if somewhat vault-like, with spruce and welcoming rooms; discounts for stays of three days or more. ⑦.

Little India Guest House, 3 Veerasamy Rd (☎294 2866). A smart guesthouse with excellent, fresh-looking rooms and spotless toilets. ⑤.

Perak Lodge, 12 Perak Rd (☎296 9072). One of the new breed of upper-bracket guesthouses, in a back street behind the Little India arcade. The rooms are secure, well-appointed and welcoming, and the price includes breakfast. Downstairs there's an airy, residents-only living area. Recommended. ⑦.

Chinatown and around

Despite being such a big tourist draw, **Chinatown** isn't very well furnished with budget accommodation.

Chinatown Guest House, 5th Floor, 325d New Bridge Rd (☎220 0671). This friendly, no-frills place is a popular choice, offering varied rooms, free breakfast and luggage storage. However, the cheapest rooms are tiny, the dorms pretty cramped and there are just three bathrooms. Dorms S\$12. ④.

Dragon Inn, 18 Mosque St (☎222 7227). Sizeable, comfortable double rooms in the middle of Chinatown, all with air-con, TV, fridge and bathroom, and set in attractive shop-houses. ⑧.

Majestic Hotel, 31–37 Bukit Pasoh Rd (☎222 3377). Scrupulously clean and enormously friendly hotel. All rooms have air-con and private bathrooms, while those at the front boast little balconies. ⑦.

Downtown Singapore

Ever since Sir Stamford Raffles first landed on its northern bank, in 1819, the area around the Singapore River, which strikes into the heart of the island from the island's south coast, has formed the hub of Singapore. All of Singapore's central districts lie within a three-kilometre

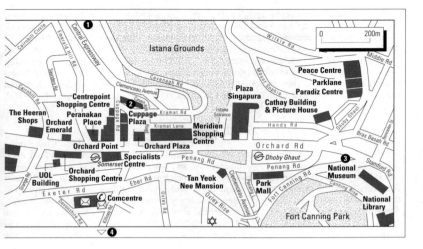

radius of the mouth of the river – which makes **Downtown Singapore** an extremely convenient place to tour.

The Colonial District

As the colony's trade grew in the last century, the **Singapore River** became its main artery, clogged with traditional cargo boats known as bumboats, which ferried coffee, sugar and rice to the *godowns*. A recent campaign to clean up the river relocated the bumboats to the west coast, though a handful still remain and offer trips downriver and around Marina Bay. From Raffles Place MRT it's just a couple of minutes' walk past the former GPO, to the elegant suspension struts of **Cavenagh Bridge** – a good place to start a tour of Singapore's colonial centre. Stepping off the bridge, you're confronted by **Empress Place Building**, a robust Neoclassical structure named for Queen Victoria and completed in 1865. Currently under renovation, it will reopen with a permanent **Asian Civilization** collection. Further inland, along North Bank Quay, a statue of Sir Stamford Raffles, the man who is credited as the founder of Singapore, marks the **landing site** where, in January 1819, he apparently took his first steps on Singaporean soil. The Singapore River cruise boats (see p.791) depart from a tiny jetty a few steps along from Raffles' statue. North of the statue up Parliament Lane, the dignified white Victorian building on the left ringed by fencing is **Parliament House**, built as a private dwelling for a rich merchant in 1833.

THE PADANG

The **Padang** is the very essence of colonial Singapore and was earmarked by Raffles as a recreation ground shortly after his arrival. The brown-tiled roof, whitewashed walls and dark green blinds of the **Singapore Cricket Club**, at the southwestern end of the Padang, have a nostalgic charm. Founded in the 1850s, the club was the hub of colonial British society and still operates a "members only" rule. Just to the west, Singapore's Neoclassical **Supreme Court** was built between 1937 and 1939, and sports a domed roof of green lead and a splendid, wood-panelled entrance hall – which is as far as you'll get unless you're appearing in front of the judges, as it's not open to the public. Next door is older **City Hall**, whose uniform rows of grandiose Corinthian columns reflect its role in recent Singaporean history. Wartime photographs show Lord Louis Mountbatten (then Supreme Allied Commander in southeast

Asia) on the steps announcing Japan's surrender to the British in 1945. Fourteen years later, Lee Kuan Yew chose the same spot from which to address his electorate at a victory rally celebrating self-government for Singapore. The final building on the west side of the Padang, **St Andrew's Cathedral** on Coleman Street, was built in high-vaulted, Neo-Gothic style, using Indian convict labour, and was consecrated in 1862. Its exterior walls were plastered using Madras *chunam* – an unlikely composite of eggs, lime, sugar and shredded coconut husks which shines brightly when smoothed – while the small cross behind the pulpit was crafted from two fourteenth-century nails salvaged from the ruins of England's Coventry Cathedral, razed to the ground during World War II.

RAFFLES CITY AND RAFFLES HOTEL

Immediately north of St Andrew's Cathedral, across Stamford Road, is **Raffles City**, a huge development comprising two enormous hotels, a multi-level shopping centre and floor upon floor of offices. Completed in 1985, the complex was designed by Chinese–American architect IM Pei – the man behind the glass pyramid which fronts the Louvre in Paris. The **Westin Stamford** holds an annual vertical marathon, in which hardy athletes attempt to run up to the top floor in as short a time as possible: the current record stands at under seven minutes. Elevators transport lesser mortals to admire the view from the *Compass Rose* bar and restaurant on the top floor. On the open land east of Raffles City stands the imposing **Civilian War Memorial**. Comprising four seventy-metre-high white columns, it's known locally as "the chopsticks".

The lofty halls, restaurants, bars and peaceful gardens of the legendary **Raffles Hotel** are almost a byword for colonialism. The hotel opened for business on December 1, 1887, and quickly began to attract some impressive guests, including Joseph Conrad, Rudyard Kipling, Herman Hesse, Somerset Maugham, Noël Coward and Günter Grass. It was the first building in Singapore with electric lights and fans, and in 1915, the "Singapore Sling" cocktail was created here by bartender Ngiam Tong Boon. During World War II, the hotel became a Japanese officers' quarters, and then a transit camp for liberated Allied prisoners. Postwar deterioration ended with a S$160-million facelift in 1991, which retains much of its colonial grace, but suffers from a rather tacky attached shopping arcade. Non-guests are welcome to visit the free **museum** (daily 10am–9pm) located upstairs, at the back of the hotel complex, which is crammed with memorabilia. Otherwise, a Singapore Sling in one of the hotel's several bars will cost you around S$17.

CHIJMES, THE SINGAPORE ART MUSEUM AND THE NATIONAL MUSEUM

Brah Basah Road cuts west from *Raffles*, crossing North Bridge Road and then passing Singapore's newest and most aesthetically pleasing eating place, the **CHIJMES** complex. Based around the Neo-Gothic husk of the former Convent of the Holy Infant Jesus (from whose name the complex's acronymic title is derived), CHIJMES is a rustic version of London's Covent Garden, with lawns, courtyards, waterfalls, fountains and sunken forecourt; the shops here open from 9am to 10pm, the restaurants and bars from 11am to 1am. Northwest of CHIJMES, at 71 Bras Basah, the new **Singapore Art Museum** (Tues & Thurs–Sun 9am–5.30pm, Wed 9am–9pm; S$3) is housed in the venerable St Joseph's Institution, Singapore's first Catholic school, many of whose original rooms survive. The Art Museum's strength lies in its contemporary local and southeast Asian exhibitions, mapping the modern Asian experience – from Bui Xian Phai's *Coalmine*, an unremittingly desolate memory of his labour in a Vietnam re-education camp, to Srihadi Sudarsono's *Horizon Dan Prahu*, in which traditional Indonesian fishing boats ply a Mark Rothko-esque canvas. Boonma's *The Pleasure of Being, Crying, Dying and Eating* comprises a tall stack of ceramic bowls decorated with jawbones and fronted by a scattering of broken pottery. Guides conduct free **tours** (Tues–Fri 11am & 2pm, Sat & Sun 11am, 2pm & 3.30pm) around the museum's major works.

An eye-catching dome of stained glass tops the entrance to the **Singapore History Museum** (same times as Art Museum), on Stamford Road. Following a recent shake-up, the

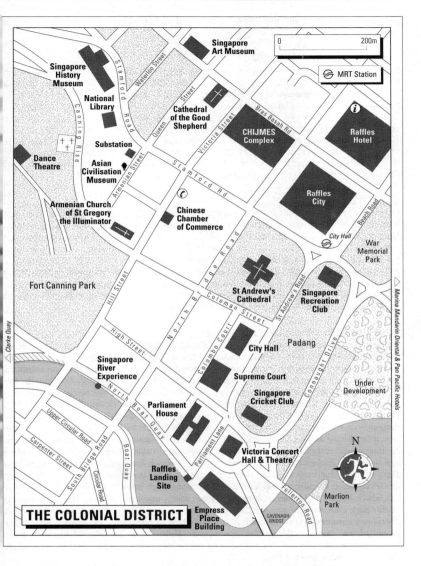

only permanent exhibitions are now the History of Singapore Gallery, which features twenty dioramas depicting formative events in the state's history – from the arrival of Raffles in 1819 up to the first session of parliament in 1965, and the Rumah Baba, or Peranakan House, where the lifestyle and culture of the Straits Chinese is brought to life. Free **guided tours** start downstairs at the ticket counter (same times as Art Museum), and the free film shows in the AV Theatrette (daily at 10am, noon, 2pm & 4pm), examining subjects like old

Chinatown and Little India, the Singapore River and traditional kampung life, are also worth catching.

ASIAN CIVILIZATION MUSEUM

Housed in a spectacular colonial-era mansion fronted by two black eagles, the **Asian Civilization Museum** (same times as Art Museum; ☎3323015), at 39 Armenian St, features ten permanent galleries which together provide a cultural and historical context to Singapore's Chinese population. After kicking off with a breakdown of the Middle Kingdom's various Imperial dynasties, the museum's galleries walk visitors through the architecture, religions, arts and crafts of the Chinese. There is much to be learnt here. The Symbolism Gallery, for instance, explains the bats, dragons and other auspicious motifs featured in Oriental art. There is also much of beauty – nowhere more so than in the Ceramics Gallery, which yields some exquisite cobalt-blue Ming pieces. Free guided tours of the museum start downstairs at the ticket counter (same times as Art Museum).

BUGIS VILLAGE

One block east of Waterloo Street's shops and temples, at the junction of Rochor Road and Victoria Street sits **Bugis Village** – a rather tame manifestation of infamous Bugis Street. Until it was demolished to make way for an MRT station, Bugis Street embodied old Singapore: after dark it was a chaotic place, crawling with rowdy sailors, transvestites and prostitutes – anathema to a Singapore government keen to clean up its country's reputation. Singaporean public opinion demanded a replacement, though when Bugis Village opened in 1991 with its beer gardens, seafood restaurants and pubs, it was a shadow of its former self. The transvestites are notable only by their absence, the sole reminder of their heritage a weak cabaret show in the *Boom Boom Room* nightclub.

FORT CANNING PARK AND CLARKE QUAY

When Raffles first caught sight of Singapore, **Fort Canning Park** was known locally as Bukit Larangan (Forbidden Hill). The five ancient kings of Singapura were said to have ruled the island from here six hundred years ago, and archeological digs have proved it was inhabited as early as the fourteenth century. The last of the kings, Sultan Iskandar Shah, reputedly lies here, and a *keramat*, or auspicious place, on the eastern slope of the hill marks the supposed site of his grave. When the British arrived, Singapore's first British Resident, William Farquhar, displayed typical colonial tact by promptly having the hill cleared and building a bungalow on the summit. The bungalow was replaced in 1859 by a fort, but of this only a gateway, guardhouse and adjoining wall remain. An early European **cemetery** survives, however, upon whose stones are engraved intriguing epitaphs to nineteenth-century sailors, traders and residents. There's a "back entrance" to the park which involves climbing the exhausting flight of steps that runs between the Hill Street Building and Food Centre, on Hill Street. Once you reach the top, there's a brilliant view along High Street towards the Merlion. The hill, which houses two theatres, is ringed by two walks, signs along which illuminate aspects of the park's fourteenth- and nineteenth-century history. What's more, the underground operations complex, from which the Allied war effort in Singapore was masterminded, has recently been opened to the public. Known as the **Battle Box** (Tues–Sun 10am–6pm; S$8), the complex uses audio and video effects and animations to bring to life the last hours before the Japanese occupation in February, 1942.

On the other side of River Valley Road, which skirts the southwestern slope of Fort Canning Park, a chain of nineteenth-century *godowns* has been renovated into the attractive **Clarke Quay** shopping and eating complex. A river taxi for Clarke Quay (daily 11am–11pm; S$2 return) departs every five minutes from the quayside above the Standard Chartered Bank, two minutes' walk from Raffles Place MRT.

Orchard Road

Orchard Road is synonymous with shopping – indeed, tourist brochures refer to it as the "Fifth Avenue, the Regent Street, the Champs Elysées, the Via Veneto and the Ginza of Singapore". Huge **malls**, selling everything you can imagine, line the road, including the dependable, all-round Centrepoint; CK Tang's, Singapore's most famous department store; Lucky Plaza and Orchard Plaza, which are both crammed with tailors and electronics; and Ngee Ann City, which houses a wealth of good clothes shops. The road runs northwest from Fort Canning Park and is served by three **MRT stations** – Dhoby Ghaut, Somerset and Orchard; Orchard MRT is the most central for shopping expeditions.

Three minutes' walk west along Orchard Road from Dhoby Ghaut MRT, at its eastern extremity, takes you past Plaza Singapura and the gate of the **Istana Negara Singapura**, the official residence of the president of Singapore – currently SR Nathan. The changing of the guard ceremony takes place at 5.45pm every first Sunday of the month. Continuing west, **Emerald Hill Road** holds a number of exquisitely crafted houses built in the late nineteenth century by members of the Peranakan community, which evolved in Malaya as a result of the intermarriage between early Chinese settlers and Malay women. A walk up Emerald Hill Road takes you past a number of exquisitely crafted houses dating from this period, built in a decorative architectural style known as Chinese Baroque, typified by highly coloured ceramic tiles, carved swing doors, shuttered windows and pastel-shaded walls with fine plaster mouldings.

By the time you reach the western end of Orchard Road, you'll be glad of the open space afforded by the **Singapore Botanic Gardens** (Mon–Fri 5am–midnight; free) on Cluny Road. Founded in 1859, it was here, in 1877, that the Brazilian seeds from which grew the great rubber plantations of Malaysia were first nurtured. The fifty-odd hectares of land feature a mini-jungle, rose garden, topiary, fernery, palm valley and lakes. There's also the **National Orchid Garden** (daily 8.30am–7pm; S$2) with sixty thousand plants, and orchid jewellery, made by plating real flowers with gold (S$100 per piece). You can pick up a free **map** of the grounds at the ranger's office, to the right of the main gate. The Botanic Gardens are a ten-minute walk from the western end of Orchard Road, or catch **bus** #7, #106 or #174 from Orchard Boulevard. The #106 passes down Bencoolen Street before heading on towards the gardens, while the #174 originates in New Bridge Road in Chinatown.

Chinatown

The two square kilometres of **Chinatown**, bounded by New Bridge Road to the west, Neil and Maxwell roads to the south, Cecil Street to the east and the Singapore River to the north, once constituted the focal point of Chinese life and culture in Singapore. Nowadays the area is on its last traditional legs, scarred by the wounds of demolition and dwarfed by the Financial District. Even so, a wander through the surviving nineteenth-century streets unearths aged craft shops and provision stores, and restaurants unchanged in forty years.

The area was first earmarked for settlement by the Chinese community by Sir Stamford Raffles himself, who decided on his second visit to the island in June 1819 that the ethnic communities should live separately. As increasing numbers of immigrants poured into Singapore, Chinatown became just that – a Chinese town, where new arrivals from the mainland, mostly from the Kwangtung (Canton) and Fukien provinces, would have been pleased to find temples, shops and, most importantly, *kongsi* (clan associations), which helped them to find food and lodgings and work, mainly as small traders and coolies. By the mid-twentieth century, the area was rich with the imported cultural heritage of China, but the government regarded the tumbledown slums of Chinatown as an eyesore and embarked upon a catastrophic **redevelopment campaign** that saw whole roads bulldozed to make way for new shopping centres, and street traders relocated into organized complexes. Only recently did public opinion finally convince the Singaporean authorities to restore, and not redevelop, Chinatown.

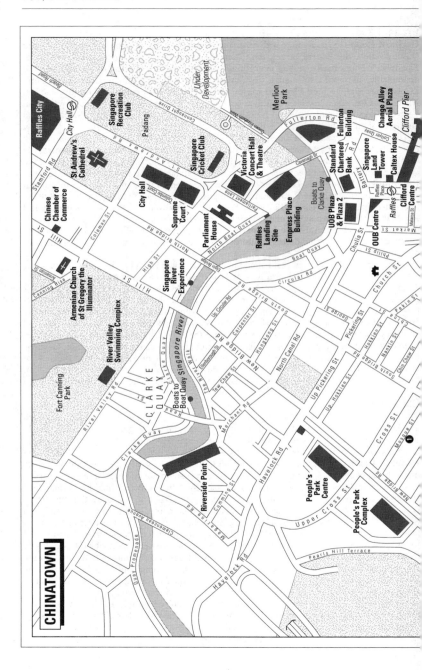

CHINATOWN

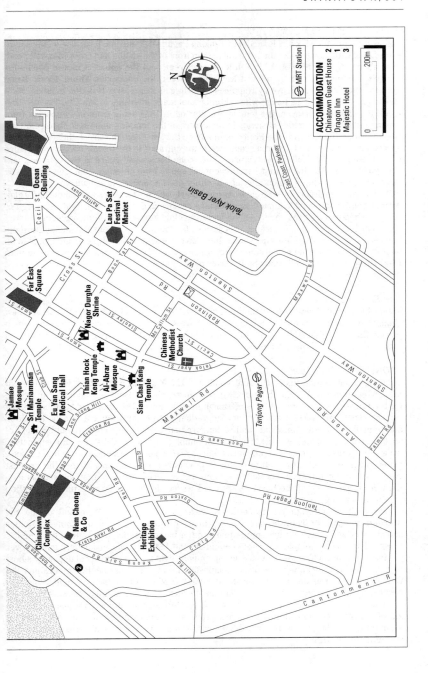

N

ACCOMMODATION
Chinatown Guest House 2
Dragon Inn 1
Majestic Hotel 3

MRT Station

0   200m

Ocean Building

Cecil St

Raffles Quay

Lau Pa Sat Festival Market

Telok Ayer Basin

East Coast Parkway

Cross St

Far East Square

Boon Tat St

Shenton Way

Maxwell Rd

Amoy St

Nagor Durgha Shrine

Stanley St

Boon Tat St

Robinson Rd

McCallum St

Shenton Way

Jamae Mosque

Sri Mariamman Temple

Club St

Eu Yan Sang Medical Hall

Thian Hock Keng Temple

Al-Abrar Mosque

Ann Siang Hill

Erskine Rd

Sian Chai Kang Temple

Telok Ayer St

Cecil St

Chinese Methodist Church

Maxwell Rd

Tanjong Pagar

Ann Siang Rd

Palmer Rd

Pagoda St

Temple St

Smith St

Trengganu St

Sago St

Banda St

Neil Rd

Murray St

Peck Sean St

Duxton Rd

Shenton Way

Chinatown Complex

Nam Cheong & Co

Kreta Ayer Rd

Heritage Exhibition

Keong Saik Rd

Craig Rd

Neil Rd

Tanjong Pagar Rd

Eu Tong Sen St

2

Cantonment Rd

ALONG TELOK AYER STREET

Follow the signs for Maxwell Road out of Tanjong Pagar MRT and you'll surface on the southern edge of Chinatown. Take the left-hand path in front of the station and cross Maxwell Road; after about fifty metres you'll hit **Telok Ayer Street**, and the square Chinese Methodist Church. Further up, shortly beyond McCallum Street, the enormous **Thian Hock Keng Temple**, the Temple of Heavenly Happiness, is a hugely impressive Hokkien building. Built on the site of a small joss house where immigrants made offerings to Ma Chu Por (or Tian Hou), the Queen of Heaven, the temple was started in 1839 using materials imported from China. A statue of the goddess stands in the centre of the temple's main hall, flanked by the God of War on the right and the Protector of Life on the left. From the street, the temple looks spectacular: dragons stalk its broad roofs, while the entrance to the temple compound bristles with ceramic flowers, foliage and figures. Two stone lions stand guard at the entrance, and door gods, painted on the front doors, prevent evil spirits from entering. Look out, too, for the huge ovens, always lit, in which offerings to either gods or ancestors are burnt.

A block west of Telok Ayer Street is **Amoy Street**, which – together with China and Telok Ayer streets – was also designated as a Hokkien enclave in the colony's early days. Long terraces of shop-houses flank the street, all featuring characteristic **five foot ways**, or covered verandahs, so called simply because they jut five feet out from the house. Some of the shop-houses are in a ramshackle state, while others have been marvellously renovated, only to be bought by companies in need of some fancy office space. It's worth walking down to the **Sian Chai Kang Temple**, at 66 Amoy St, its eaves painted a shade of red every bit as fiery as the dragons on its roof.

FAR EAST SQUARE

Meanwhile, Telok Ayer Street continues north over Cross Street to Far East Square, a new shopping-cum-dining centre which taps Chinatown's heritage for its inspiration, and which boasts the Fuk Tak Ch'I Street Museum (daily 10am–10pm; free), housed in one of Singapore's oldest Chinese temples.

ALONG SOUTH BRIDGE ROAD

Turn right out of Ann Siang Hill and you'll see **Eu Yan Sang Medical Hall** (Mon–Sat 8.30am–6pm) at 267–271 South Bridge Rd, first opened in 1910 and geared up, to an extent, for the tourist trade – some of the staff speak good English. The shop has been beautifully renovated and sells a weird assortment of ingredients, from herbs and roots to various dubious remedies derived from exotic and endangered species. The ground-up gall bladders of snakes or bears apparently work wonders on pimples; monkey's gallstones aid asthmatics; while deer penis is supposed to provide a lift to any sexual problem. Antlers, sea horses, scorpions and turtle shells also feature regularly in Chinese prescriptions, though the greatest cure-all of Oriental medicine is said to be ginseng, a clever little root that will combat anything from weakness of the heart to acne and jet lag. If you need a pick-me-up, the shop administers free glasses of ginseng tea.

Across the road from the front doors of *Eu Yan Sang*, the compound of the **Sri Mariamman Hindu Temple** bursts with primary coloured, wild-looking statues of deities and animals, and there's always some ritual or other being attended to by one of the temple's priests. The present temple was completed in around 1843 and boasts a superb gopura over the front entrance. Once inside, you'll see splendidly vivid friezes on the roof depicting a host of Hindu deities, including the three manifestations of the Supreme Being: Brahma the Creator (with three of his four heads showing), Vishnu the Preserver, and Shiva the Destroyer (holding one of his sons). The main sanctum, facing you as you walk inside, is devoted to Goddess Mariamman, who's worshipped for her powers to cure disease. To the left of the main sanctum there's a patch of sand which, once a year during the festival of Thimithi (see p.780), is covered in red-hot coals, which male Hindus run across to prove the strength of their faith.

WEST: CHINATOWN COMPLEX AND BEYOND

After crumbling Telok Ayer and China streets, much of the section of Chinatown west of South Bridge Road seems far less authentic. This is tour-bus Chinatown, heaving with gangs of holidaymakers plundering souvenir shops. The hideous concrete exterior of the **Chinatown Complex**, at the end of Sago Street, belies the charm of the teeming market it houses. Walk up the front steps, past the garlic, fruit and nut hawkers, and once inside, the market's many twists and turns reveal stalls selling silk, kimonos, rattan, leather and clothes. There are no fixed prices, so you'll need to haggle.

Sago Street skirts to the right of the Chinatown Complex, and its name changes to **Trengganu Street**, packed with shops selling Singapore Airlines uniforms, presentation chopstick sets and silk hats with false pony tails – plus a few relics of Chinatown's old trades and industries.

The Financial District

Raffles Place forms the nucleus of the **Financial District** – the commercial heart of the state, home to many of its 140 banks and financial institutions – and is ringed by buildings so tall that pedestrians crossing the square feel like ants in a canyon. The most striking way to experience the giddy heights of the Financial District is by surfacing from Raffles Place MRT – follow the signs for Cecil Street out of the station. To your left is the soaring metallic triangle of the OUB Centre (Overseas Union Bank), and, right of that, the rocket-shaped UOB Plaza 2 (United Overseas Bank); in front of you are the rich brown walls of the Standard Chartered Bank, and to your right rise sturdy Singapore Land Tower and the almost Art Deco Caltex House. The three roads that run southwest from Raffles Place – Cecil Street, Robinson Road and Shenton Way – are all choc-a-bloc with more highrise banks and financial houses; to the west is Chinatown. Just north of Raffles Place, and beneath the "elephant's trunk" curve of the Singapore River, the pedestrianized row of shop-houses known as **Boat Quay** is Singapore's most fashionable hang-out, sporting a huge collection of restaurants and bars.

Branching off the second floor of the Clifford Centre, on the eastern side of Raffles Place, Change Alley Aerial Plaza leads you to Clifford Pier, from where it's just a short walk to the south along Raffles Quay to Telok Ayer Market, recently renamed **Lau Pa Sat Festival Market**. This octagonal cast-iron frame has been turned into Singapore's most tasteful food centre (daily 24hr), which offers a range of southeast Asian cuisines, as well as laying on free entertainment such as local bands and Chinese opera performances. After 7pm, the portion of Boon Tat Street between Robinson Road and Shenton Way is closed to traffic, and traditional hawker stalls take over the street.

Little India

A tour around **Little India**, just fifteen minutes from the colonial district, amounts to an all-out assault on the senses. Indian pop music blares out from gargantuan speakers and the air is heavily perfumed with sweet incense, curry powder and jasmine garlands. Hindu women promenade in bright sarees; and a wealth of "hole-in-the-wall" restaurants serve up superior curries. The enclave grew when a number of **cattle and buffalo yards** opened in the area in the latter half of the nineteenth century, and more Hindus were drawn in search of work. Indians featured prominently in the development of Singapore, though not always out of choice: from 1825 onwards, convicts were transported from the subcontinent and by the 1840s there were over a thousand Indian prisoners labouring on buildings such as St Andrew's Cathedral and the istana.

The district's backbone is the north–south **Serangoon Road**, whose southern end is alive with shops, restaurants and fortune-tellers. To the east, stretching as far as Jalan Besar, is a tight knot of roads that's ripe for exploration, while parallel to Serangoon Road, **Race Course Road** boasts a clutch of fine restaurants and some temples. Little India is only a fifteen-minute walk from Bencoolen Street and Beach Road. From Orchard Road, take bus #65 or

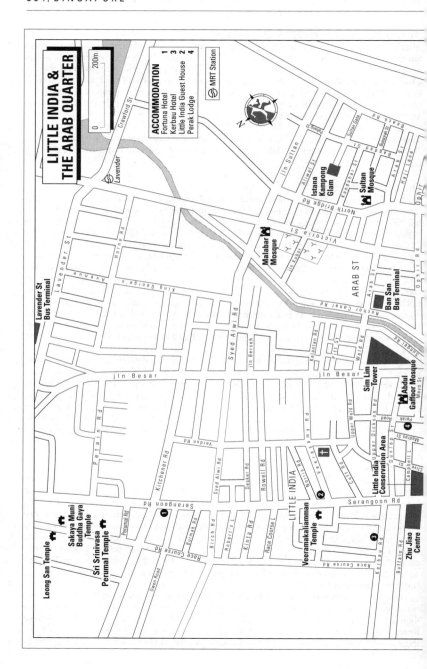

LITTLE INDIA & THE ARAB QUARTER

0   200m

ACCOMMODATION
Fortuna Hotel	1
Kerbau Hotel	3
Little India Guest House	2
Perak Lodge	4

MRT Station

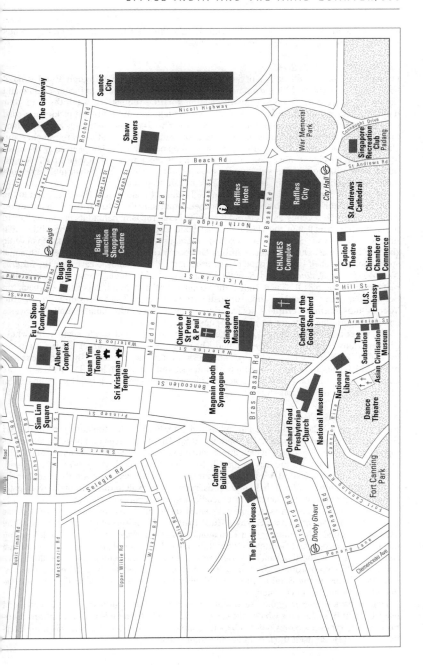

#111 and ask for Serangoon Road. Alternatively, take the MRT to Dhoby Ghaut, hop on bus #65 or #111 and, again, get off at Serangoon Road.

ALONG SERANGOON ROAD

Dating from 1822 and hence one of the island's oldest roadways, **Serangoon Road** is lined with shops selling everything from nostril studs and ankle bracelets to incense sticks and Indian newspapers. Look out for parrot-wielding **fortune-tellers** – you tell the man your name, he passes your name on to his feathered partner, and the bird then picks out a card with your fortune on it. At the southwestern end, the **Zhu Jiao Centre** houses a ground-floor food centre, a wet market and, on the second floor, Indian fabrics, leatherware, watches and cheap electronic goods. Little India's remaining shop-houses are being pleasingly restored; in particular, check out those along Kerbau Road, one block north of Buffalo Road. (A right turn from Kerbau Road takes you onto Race Course Road, whose fine restaurants serve both north and south Indian food; several specialize in fish-head curry.)

Bounded by Serangoon to the west, Campbell Lane to the north and Hastings Road to the south, the lovingly restored block of shop-houses comprising the **Little India Conservation Area** was opened recently as a sort of Little India in microcosm: behind its cream walls and green shutters you'll find the Hastings Road Food Court (see p.812) and the Little India Arcade, where you can purchase textiles, religious statuary and traditional ayurvedic (herbal) medicines. Dunlop Street's **Abdul Gaffoor Mosque** (at no. 41) bristles with small spires, and Campbell Lane is a good place for buying Indian sandals. Nearby are the *Madras New Woodlands Restaurant* and *Komala Villas*, two of Little India's best southern Indian restaurants (see p.813). Turn right when Upper Dickson Road deposits you back on Serangoon Road. Further up, opposite the turning to Veerasamy Road, the **Veeramakaliamman Temple** – dedicated to the ferocious Hindu goddess, Kali – features a fanciful gopura that's flanked by majestic lions on the temple walls.

You won't find **Pink Street** – one of the most incongruous and sordid spots in the whole of clean, shiny Singapore – on any city map. The entire length of the "street" (in fact it's merely an alley between the backs of Rowell and Desker roads) is punctuated by open doorways, inside which gaggles of bored-looking prostitutes sit knitting or watching TV. Stalls along the alley sell sex toys, blue videos and potency pills, while con-men work the "three cups and a ball" routine on unwary passers-by.

NORTH OF DESKER ROAD

Each year, on the day of the Thaipusam festival (Jan/Feb), inside the courtyard of the **Sri Srinivasa Perumal Temple**, at 397 Serangoon Rd, Hindu devotees don huge metal frames topped with peacock feathers, which are fastened to their flesh with hooks and prongs. The devotees then parade all the way to the Chettiar Temple on Tank Road, off Orchard Road. Even if you miss the festival, it's worth a trip to see the five-tiered gopura with its sculptures of the manifestations of Lord Vishnu the Preserver. On the wall to the right of the front gate, a sculpted elephant, its leg caught in a crocodile's mouth, trumpets silently.

Just beyond the Sri Srinivasa temple complex, a small path leads northwest to Race Course Road, where the slightly kitsch **Sakaya Muni Buddha Gaya Temple** (or the Temple of the Thousand Lights), built entirely by a Thai monk, is on the right at no. 366. On the left as you enter is a huge replica of Buddha's footprint, inlaid with mother-of-pearl; beyond sits a huge Buddha ringed by the thousand electric lights from which the temple takes its alternative name, and 25 scenes from the Buddha's life decorate the pedestal on which he sits. It is possible to walk inside the Buddha, through a door in his back; inside is a smaller representation, this time of Buddha reclining.

Double back onto Serangoon Road and a five-minute walk southeast along Petain Road leads to Jalan Besar, a route which takes in some immaculate examples of **Peranakan shophouses**, their facades covered with elegant ceramic tiles; there's more Peranakan architecture on Jalan Besar itself (turn right at the end of Petain Road).

The Arab Quarter

Before the arrival of Raffles, the area of Singapore west of the Rochor River housed a Malay village known as Kampung Glam, after the Gelam tribe of sea gypsies who lived there. Raffles allotted the area to the newly installed "Sultan" Hussein Mohammed Shah and designated the land around it as a Muslim settlement. Soon the zone was attracting Arab traders, as the road names in today's **Arab Quarter** – Baghdad Street, Muscat Street and Haji Lane – suggest. Just outside the quarter, Beach Road still maintains shops which betray its former proximity to the sea – ships' chandlers and fishing tackle specialists – and you should also take the time to walk southwest from Arab Street to see the two logic-defying office buildings that together comprise **The Gateway**. Designed by IM Pei, they rise magnificently into the air like vast razor blades and appear two-dimensional when viewed from certain angles. The Arab Quarter is no more than a ten-minute walk from Bencoolen Street. To get there from Orchard Road, take **bus** #7 to Victoria Street and get off when you spot the *Landmark Mercure Hotel* on your right; alternatively, head for Bugis MRT.

The pavements of **Arab Street** are an obstacle course of carpets, cloths, baskets and bags. Most of the shops have been renovated, though one or two still retain their original dark wood and glass cabinets. Textile stores are most prominent, along with shops dealing in leather, basketware, gold, gemstones and jewellery. The quarter's most evocative patch is the stretch of **North Bridge Road** between Arab Street and Jalan Sultan. Here, the men sport long sarongs and Abe Lincoln beards, the women fantastically colourful shawls and robes, while the shops and restaurants are geared more towards locals than tourists.

Squatting between Kandahar and Aliwal streets, the **Istana Kampong Glam** was built as the royal palace of Sultan Ali Iskandar Shah, son of Sultan Hussein who negotiated with Raffles to hand over Singapore to the British; the sultan's descendants live here to this day. A few steps further on, Baghdad Street crosses pedestrianized Bussorah Street, from where you get the best initial views of the golden domes of the **Sultan Mosque** or Masjid Sultan (Sat–Thur 9am–1pm). The present building was completed in 1925, according to a design by colonial architects Swan and MacLaren: if you look carefully at the glistening necks of the domes, you can see that the effect is created by the bases of thousands of ordinary glass bottles. Steps at the top of Bussorah Street lead into a wide lobby, where a digital display lists current prayer times; all visitors must cover shoulders and legs.

It's only a five-minute walk on to the **Golden Mile Complex** at 5001 Beach Rd, which attracts so many Thai nationals that locals refer to it as "Thai Village". Numerous bus firms selling tickets to Thailand operate out of here, while inside, the shops sell Thai foodstuffs, and cafés and restaurants sell Singha beer and Mekong whisky.

Around the island

Beyond the downtown area, Singapore still retains pockets of greenery in between its sprawling new towns. Most rewarding are the **Bukit Timah Nature Reserve**, and the excellent **Singapore Zoological Gardens**, both in the north of the island. Dominating the eastern tip of the island is Changi Airport and, beyond that, **Changi Village**, in whose prison the Japanese interned Allied troops and civilians during World War II. From Changi Point, it's possible to take a boat to picturesque **Pulau Ubin**, a small island with echoes of pre-development Singapore. Although western Singapore has developed into the manufacturing heart of the state, it remains remarkably verdant, and is the location of fascinating **Jurong BirdPark** and the garish theme park **Haw Par Villa**. There are theme rides aplenty too on the island of **Sentosa**, just off southern Singapore, as well as some nice beaches.

Bukit Timah Nature Reserve

Bukit Timah Road shoots northwest from the junction of Selegie and Serangoon roads, arriving 8km later at the faceless town of **BUKIT TIMAH**, and then on to Singapore's last remaining pocket of primary rainforest, which now comprises **Bukit Timah Nature Reserve** (daily 7am–7pm; free). Tigers roamed the area in the mid-eighteenth century, but now the 81-hectare reserve provides a refuge for the dwindling numbers of species still extant in Singapore – only 25 types of mammal now inhabit the island. Creatures you're most likely to see here are long-tailed macaques, butterflies, insects, and birds like the dark-necked tailorbird, which builds its nest by sewing together leaves. Scorpions, snakes, flying lemurs and pangolins (anteaters) can be found here too. Four well signposted, colour-coded **paths** lead out from the informative **Visitor Centre** (daily 8.30am–6pm) to the top of Bukit Timah Hill. **Bus** #171 passes down Somerset and Scotts roads en route to Bukit Timah Reserve, while the #181 can be picked up on North Bridge Road, South Bridge Road or New Bridge Road; a third option is to take the #170 from the Ban San Terminal on Queen Street.

Singapore Zoological Gardens and Night Safari

The **Singapore Zoological Gardens** (daily 8.30am–6pm; S$10.30) on Mandai Lake Road is one of the world's few open zoos, where moats are preferred to cages. It manages to approximate the natural habitats of the animals it holds, and though leopards, pumas and jaguars still have to be kept behind bars, this is a thoughtful, humane place. There are over two thousand animals here, representing more than 240 species, so it's best to allow a whole day for your visit. A **tram** (S$2) circles the grounds on a one-way circuit. Highlights include the Komodo dragons, the polar bears (which you view underwater from a gallery) and the primate kingdom. Two **animal shows** are featured daily – a primate and reptile show (10.30am & 2.30pm) and an elephant and sea lion show (11.30am & 3.30pm). Kids tend to get most out of these shows, and **Children's World** offers them the chance to ride a camel, hold young chicks and see a milking demonstration; at 9am and 4pm daily they can even share a meal with an **orang-utan**. It's also possible to go on a **Night Safari** here (daily 7.30pm–midnight; S$15.45), which means you watch as over a hundred species of animals – among them elephants, rhinos, giraffes, leopards, hyenas, otters, and incredibly cute fishing cats – play out their nocturnal routines under a forest of standard lamps. Only five of the safari's eight zones are walkable – to see the rest you'll need to take a fifty-minute Jurassic Park-style tram ride (S$3).

Buy the S$1 *Guide to S'pore Zoo* on arrival: besides riding and feeding times and a map, the booklet suggests itineraries which take in all the major shows and attractions. To get to the zoo, take **bus** #171 from either Stamford Road or Orchard Boulevard to Mandai Road, then transfer to #138. Alternatively, take the MRT to Ang Mo Kio and connect with the #138.

Changi

Bus #2 from Victoria Street, or from Tanah Merah MRT, drops you right outside **Changi Prison**, the infamous site of a World War II POW camp in which Allied prisoners were subjected to the harshest of treatment by their Japanese jailers. The prison itself is still in use (drug offenders are periodically executed here), but on its north side, through the outer gates, is the hugely moving prison **museum** (Mon–Sat 10am–5pm, Sun 5.30pm religious service only; free), where sketches and photographs plot the Japanese invasion of Singapore and the fate of the soldiers and civilians subsequently incarcerated here and in nearby camps. Beyond the museum is a replica of a simple wooden chapel, typical of those erected in Singapore's wartime prisons; its brass cross was crafted from spent ammunition casings, while the north wall carries poignant messages, penned by former POWs and relatives.

Journey's end for bus #2 is at the terminal at **CHANGI VILLAGE**, ten minutes further on from the prison. There's little to bring you out here, save to catch a boat from **Changi Point**, behind the bus terminal, for Pulau Ubin (see opposite), or to the coast of Johor in Malaysia (see box on pp.788-789). The left-hand jetty is for Ubin, the right-hand one for bumboats to Johor.

Pulau Ubin

Pulau Ubin, 2km offshore, gives visitors a pretty good idea of what Singapore would have been like fifty years ago. A lazy backwater tucked into the Straits of Johor, it's a great place to head for when you get tired of shops, highrises and traffic, and it's almost worth coming for the boat trip alone, made in an old oil-stained bumboat which departs from Changi Point throughout the day, leaving when full (10min; S$1.50). The last boat back to Changi may leave as late as 10pm, but plan to be at the jetty by 8.30pm at the latest. The boats dock at **Ubin Village**, where Malay stilt houses teeter over the sludgy, mangrove beach.

The best, and most enjoyable, way to explore the dirt tracks of Ubin is by **mountain bike**, which can be rented for S$5–15/day from Universal Adventure on the left-hand side of the road leading west from the jetty. You'll be given a baffling map of the island's labyrinthine network of tracks, though it's more fun to strike off and see where you end up – Ubin is only a small island (just 7km by 2km) so you won't get lost. Ride through the village until you come to a basketball court, where a **right turn** takes you past raised kampung houses and rubber trees to the eastern side of the island. Turning left instead takes you to the centre of the island, past a quarry, to a rather incongruous **Thai Buddhist Temple**, complete with portraits of the King and Queen of Thailand, and murals telling the story of the life of Buddha. If you follow the **left track** out of Ubin Village for twenty or thirty minutes, you'll come to a steep slope: a right turn at the top takes you straight to the temple, just beyond which is another quarry, where you can swim. Ignoring the right turn to the temple at the top of the steep slope and continuing straight ahead takes you towards the island's best restaurant, the *Ubin Restaurant*; it's a bit tricky to find, though – you'll have to look out for a taxi taking Singaporean diners there, to discover which track to turn down.

Telok Blangah, the World Trade Centre and Mount Faber

A twenty-minute walk west of Chinatown is the area known as **Telok Blangah** in which stands Singapore's **World Trade Centre**, itself a splendid shopping centre-cum-marine terminal, where boats depart Singapore for Indonesia's Riau Archipelago. Lots of buses come this way; #97 and #166 travel down Bencoolen Street; from Scotts and Orchard roads, take bus #143. You'll know when to get off, because you'll see cable cars rocking across the skyline in front of you, on their way to and from Mount Faber.

Once called Telok Blangah, **Mount Faber** – 600m north of the WTC – was renamed in 1845 after Government Engineer Captain Charles Edward Faber; the top of the "mount" (hillock would be a better word) commands fine views of Keppel Harbour and, to the northeast, central Singapore – views which are even more impressive at night, when the city is lit up. It's a long, steep walk from Telok Blangah Road up to the top of Mount Faber – it's better to take the **cable car** from the World Trade Centre complex (daily 8.30am–9pm; S$6.90 return).

Haw Par Villa

As an entertaining exercise in bad taste, **Haw Par Villa** has few equals. Located 7km west of downtown, at 262 Pasir Panjang Rd (daily 9am–6pm; S$5), it's a gaudy parade of over a thousand grotesque statues inspired by Chinese legends and mythologies. Previously known as **Tiger Balm Gardens**, the park now takes its name from its original owners, the Aw brothers, Boon Haw and Boon Par, who made a fortune early this century selling Tiger Balm – a cure-all unction created by their father. When the British government introduced licensing requirements for the possession of large animals, the private zoo which the brothers maintained on their estate here was closed down and replaced by statues. To get there, take the **MRT** to Buona Vista and change on to a #200 **bus** to Pasir Panjang Road. Bus #51 trundles down North Bridge Road on its way to the park, while the #143 can be picked up on Scotts, Orchard and New Bridge roads.

Jurong Bird Park

The twenty hectares of land which comprise the **Jurong Bird Park** (Mon–Fri 9am–6pm, Sat & Sun 8am–6pm; S$10.30), on Jalan Ahmad Ibrahim in the Jurong Lake area, has more than eight thousand birds from over six hundred species, ranging from Antarctic penguins to New Zealand kiwis. This makes it one of the world's largest bird collections, and the biggest in southeast Asia. A ride on the **Panorail** (S$2.50) is a good way to get your bearings, the running commentary pointing out the attractions. Be sure at least to catch the **Waterfall Walk-in Aviary**, which allows visitors to walk amongst 1500 free-flying birds in a specially created tropical rainforest, dominated by a thirty-metre-high waterfall. Other exhibits to seek out are the colourful **Southeast Asian Birds**, where a tropical thunderstorm is simulated daily at noon; the **Penguin Parade** (feeding times 10.30am & 3.30pm); and the **World of Darkness**, a fascinating exhibit which simulates night for its nocturnal residents. The best of the **bird shows** is undoubtedly the "Kings of the Skies" (4pm) – a *tour de force* of speed-flying by a band of trained eagles, hawks and falcons. Entrance to this, and to the similar "World of Hawks" show (10am) and "All Star Bird Show" (11am & 3pm), is free. To get to the BirdPark, take either **bus** #194 or #251 from the bus interchange outside Boon Lay MRT station, a ten-minute ride.

Sentosa

Heavily promoted for its beaches, sports facilities, hotels and attractions, and ringed by a speeding monorail, the theme-park island of **SENTOSA** is a contrived but enjoyable place. The 3km by 1km island is linked to the southern shore of downtown Singapore by a five-hundred-metre causeway and a necklace of cable cars. Avoid coming at the weekend, and don't even think about visiting on public holidays.

Two attractions outshine all others on Sentosa. At the **Underwater World** (daily 9am–9pm; S$13) near monorail station 2, a moving walkway carries you along a tunnel between two large tanks: sharks lurk menacingly on all sides, huge stingrays drape themselves languidly above you, and immense shoals of gaily coloured fish dart to and fro. This may not sound all that exciting, but the sensation of being engulfed by sea life is breathtaking. The other major-league attraction is the **Images of Singapore Exhibition** (daily 9am–9pm; S$5), near monorail station 2. Here, life-sized dioramas present the history and heritage of Singapore from the fourteenth century through to the surrender of the Japanese in 1945. The highlight is the Surrender Chambers, where audio-visuals and dioramas recount the events of World War II.

A trip up to **Fort Siloso** (monorail station 3), on the far western tip of the island, ties in nicely with a visit to the Surrender Chambers. The fort – actually a cluster of buildings and gun emplacements above a series of tunnels bored into the island – guarded Singapore's western approaches from the 1880s until 1956, but was rendered obsolete in 1942, when the Japanese moved down into Singapore from Malaysia. Today, the recorded voice of Battery Sergeant Major Cooper talks you through a mock-up of a nineteenth-century barracks, complete with living quarters, laundry and assault course. The rest of Sentosa is crammed with less interesting options. **The Asian Village** (daily 10am–9pm; free), next to the ferry terminal, is essentially a complex of Asian restaurants and craft shops, with cultural shows staged four times daily at the **Thai Pavilion Theatre** (10.15am & 4pm: S$5; 6.30pm & 7.15pm; S$18 including dinner). Otherwise, you might consider **Volcanoland** (daily 10am–7pm; S$12), with a simulated eruption and trip to the earth's core; **Fantasy Island** (daily 10am–6.30pm; S$16), with hi-tech water rides; or **Wondergolf** (9am–9pm; S$8), with 45 crazy holes.

Probably the best option, though, after a trip on the monorail and a visit to one or two attractions, is to head for the three **beaches** (monorail station 2 or 5, or take bus A or bus M) on Sentosa's southwestern coast. Created with thousands of cubic metres of imported white sand and scores of coconut palms, they offer canoes, surf boards and aqua bikes for rent. The water here is great for swimming and Singapore does not demand the same modesty on its beaches as Malaysia, although topless and nude bathing are out.

By 7pm, many of Sentosa's attractions are closed, but not so the **Musical Fountain** (shows at 5pm, 5.30pm, 7.30pm, 8.30pm & 9.30pm), which dances along to such classics as the *1812 Overture*, with colourful lights and lasers adding to the effect. Recently, the display has been overlooked by a new, 37-metre-high statue of Singapore's tourism totem, the **Merlion**, which itself takes centre-stage in the laser-illuminated "Rise of the Merlion" portions of the shows.

PRACTICALITIES
Basic **admission** to Sentosa costs S$5, though this doesn't include the cost of actually reaching the island. From the **World Trade Centre** at 1 Maritime Square (buses #65, #97, #143 and #166), **ferries** depart every fifteen minutes (9am–9pm; S$1.30 return). However, the most spectacular way there is by one of the **cable cars** (daily 8.30am–9pm) which travel on a loop between mainland Mount Faber (see p.809) and Sentosa. A one-station trip (from the WTC to Sentosa, for instance) costs S$5, two stations costs S$5.50, and for a round trip – from the WTC up to Mount Faber, across to Sentosa and back to the WTC, you'll pay S$6.50, not including the basic S$5 admission fee.

Crossing the bridge to Sentosa costs nothing if you walk, though you still have to pay the admission fee. **Bus A** operates out of the WTC bus terminal, running across the bridge every ten to fifteen minutes (7am–12.30am; S$6). Service C, meanwhile, shuttles between Tiong Bahru MRT station and the ferry terminal on Sentosa (7am–12.30am; S$6), while bus E runs from Orchard Road to Sentosa's Gateway station (10am–10.45pm; S$7). All bus tickets include entry to the island.

Sentosa's basic admission fee gives unlimited rides on Sentosa's **monorail and bus systems** – bus #2 circles the island between 9am and 7pm and services A, C and M are often handy too, while the monorail runs from 9am until 10pm. But the best way to get about is to **rent a bike** for the day (S$4–8 an hour) from the kiosk beside the ferry terminal. The *Rasa Sentosa Food Centre*, beside the ferry terminal is the cheapest **eating** option; otherwise, try the nearby *Sentosa Riverboat* for fast food, or monorail station 5's *Sweetimes Café*.

Eating

Along with shopping, **eating** ranks as the Singaporean national pastime. An enormous number of food outlets cater for this obsession, and strict government regulations ensure that they are consistently hygienic. The mass of establishments serving **Chinese** food reflects the fact that Chinese residents account for more than three quarters of the population. **North and South Indian** cuisines give a good account of themselves too, as do restaurants serving **Malay**, **Indonesian**, **Korean**, **Japanese** and **Vietnamese** food. The closest Singapore comes to an indigenous cuisine is **Nonya**, a hybrid of Chinese and Malay food that developed following the intermarrying of nineteenth-century Chinese immigrants with Malay women. Several specialist Chinese restaurants and a number of Indian restaurants serve **vegetarian food**, but otherwise vegetarians need to tread very carefully: chicken and seafood will appear in a whole host of dishes unless you make it perfectly clear that you don't want them.

By far the cheapest and most fun place to dine in Singapore is in a **hawker centre** or **food court**, where scores of stalls let you mix and match dishes at really low prices. Otherwise there's a whole range of **restaurants** to visit, ranging from no-frills, open-fronted eating houses and coffee shops to sumptuously decorated establishments. Most open 11.30am–2.30pm and 6–10.30pm daily.

Breakfast, brunch and snacks
Western breakfasts are available, at a price, at all bigger hotels, most famously at the *Hilton* or *Raffles*. For a really cheap fry-up you can't beat a Western food stall in a hawker centre, where S$8 buys steak, chops and sausage. The classic **Chinese breakfast** is *congee*, a watery

rice porridge augmented with strips of meat, though *dim sum* tend to be more palatable to Western tastes. An abiding favourite among Malays is *nasi lemak*, rice cooked in coconut milk and served with *sambal ikan bilis* (tiny crisp-fried anchovies in hot chilli paste), fried peanuts and slices of fried or hard-boiled egg.

Breakfast With An Orang-Utan, Singapore Zoo, 80 Mandai Lake Rd, Northern Singapore (☎360 8509). A bumper American-style spread, shared with whichever orang is on duty, costs S$15.50. Daily 9–10am.

Breakfast With The Birds, Jurong BirdPark, Jalan Ahmad Ibrahim, Western Singapore (☎265 0022). A buffet of local and Western breakfast favourites, eaten alongside caged songbirds; S$12. Daily 9am–11am.

Champagne Brunch At The Hilton, *Hilton Hotel*, 581 Orchard Rd (☎737 2233). Around S$60 buys a superb free flow of delicacies – oysters, salmon, curry and cakes – washed down with litres of champagne and orange juice. Reservations are essential. Sun 11.30am–2.30pm only.

De Boa (HK) Restaurant, 42 Smith St. Right opposite the Chinatown Complex, a smashing little coffee shop offering *dim sum, pau* and Chinese tea. Daily 7.30am–5pm.

Mr Bean's Café, 30 Selegie Rd, Colonial District. Based in the same wedge-shaped colonial building as the *Selegie Arts Centre*, *Mr Bean's Café* draws an interesting crowd with its muffins, croissants, toast and coffee.

Spinelli Coffee Company, 01–15 Bugis Junction, 230 Victoria St, Colonial District. San Francisco-based outfit that's riding on the local mania for fresh coffee; the narrow bar is ideal for a quick expresso.

Tiffin Room, *Raffles Hotel*, 1 Beach Rd, Colonial District (☎337 1886). Have your buffet breakfast here and you won't eat again until dinner; S$25 per person. Daily 7.30–10am.

Yasinn Restaurant, 127 Bencoolen St, Colonial District. Does a roaring trade in *roti prata* (fried bread) and curry sauce each morning.

Hawker centres and food courts

Although **hawker centres** are kept scrupulously clean, they are often housed in functional buildings which tend to get extremely hot, so an increasing number of smaller, air-conditioned **food courts** are popping up, where eating is a slightly more civilized, if less atmospheric affair. Hawker centres and food courts are open from lunchtime through to dinner time and sometimes beyond. Avoid the peak lunching (12.30–1.30pm) and dining (6–7pm) periods, and you should have no problems in finding a seat.

Chinatown Complex, Smith St, at the end of New Bridge Road, Chinatown. A huge range of dishes with a predictably Chinese bias.

Food Junction, B1, *Seiyu Department Store*, Bugis Junction, 200 Victoria St, Colonial District. Happening food court where Thai, Japanese, *nasi padang* and claypot cusines are all represented.

Hastings Road Food Court, Little India Arcade, Serangoon Rd, Little India. Diminutive food court whose handful of stalls are labelled by region – Keralan, Mughlai, Sri Lankan and so on.

Lau Pa Sat Festival Market, 18 Raffles Quay, Financial District. The smartest hawker stalls in Singapore, and now open round the clock.

Orchard Emerald Food Court, Basement, Orchard Emerald, 218 Orchard Rd. Smart food court, bang in the centre of Orchard Road, where the Indonesian buffet is great value.

Picnic Food Court, Scotts Shopping Centre, 6 Scotts Rd, Orchard Road District. Slap bang in the middle of Orchard Road, squeaky clean, and with lots of choice.

Satay Club, Clarke Quay, Singapore River. A Singapore institution not to be missed, serving inexpensive chicken and mutton satay. Open evenings only, from around 7pm.

Restaurants

Below is a representative selection of the thousands of **restaurants** that span Singapore.

CHINESE

The majority of the **Chinese** restaurants in Singapore are Cantonese (from Guandong) in southern China, though you'll also come across northern Beijing (or Peking) and western Szechuan cuisines, as well as the Hokkien specialities of the southeastern province of Fukien; and Teochew dishes from the area east of Canton. Whatever the region, it's undoubtedly the real thing – Chinese food as eaten by the Chinese – which means it won't always sound particularly appealing to foreigners: the Chinese eat all parts of an animal, from its lips to its undercarriage. Fish and seafood is nearly always outstanding, but for something a little more unusual, try a **steamboat**, a Chinese-style fondue filled with boiling stock in which you cook meat, fish, shellfish, eggs and vegetables; or a **claypot** – meat, fish or shellfish cooked over a fire in an earthenware pot. The other thing to note is that in many Cantonese restaurants (and in other regional restaurants, too), lunch consists of **dim sum** – steamed and fried dumplings served in little bamboo baskets. See "Hong Kong" p.146 for a Chinese cuisine menu reader.

Ban Seng, B1-44 The Riverwalk, 20 Upper Circular Road (☎533 1471). Traditionally prepared Teochew dishes, including steamed crayfish, braised goose and stuffed sea cucumber; mid-priced. Daily 12–2.30pm & 6–10pm.

Fut Sai Kai, 147 Kitchener Rd, Little India (☎298 0336). Old-fashioned vegetarian Cantonese restaurant, where beancurd is shaped to resemble meat or fish. S$20 is sufficient for two. Open Tues–Sun 10am–9pm.

Happy Realm Vegetarian Food Centre, 03-16 Pearls Centre, 100 Eu Tong Sen St, Chinatown (☎2226141). Tasty and reasonably priced vegetarian dishes. Daily 11am–8.30pm.

Hillman, 01-159, Block 1, Cantonment Rd, Chinatown (☎221 5073). Extremely popular for its flavoursome Cantonese meat and seafood stews; small pots (S$10) fill two. Daily 11.30am–2.30pm & 5.30–10.30pm.

Kwan Yim Vegetarian Restaurant, 190 Waterloo St, near Bencoolen Street (☎338 2394). A huge display of sweet and savoury *pow* is the highlight of this unfussy veggie establishment. Daily 8am–8.30pm.

Mitzi's, 24–26 Murray Terrace, Chinatown (☎222 0929). The cracking Cantonese food in this simple place, situated in a row of restaurants known as "Food Alley", draws crowds, so be prepared to wait in line. Two can eat for S$30, drinks extra. Daily 11am–3pm & 6–10pm.

Moi Kong Hakka, 22 Murray St, Chinatown (☎221 7758). Hakka food relies heavily on salted and preserved ingredients and dishes here, in the best Hakka food outlet in Singapore, encompass abacus yam starch beads (S$6) and stewed pork belly with preserved vegetables. Daily 10.30am–2.30pm & 6–10pm.

Swee Kee, *Damenlou Hotel*, 12 Ann Siang Rd, Chinatown (☎221 1900). A Cantonese restaurant that's been serving *ka shou* fish-head noodles for over sixty years. Daily 11am–2.30pm & 5.30–11pm.

Top Flight Mongolian BBQ, 04-01 Park Mall, 9 Penang Rd, off Orchard Road (☎334 4888). Create your own combination from an array of meats, vegetables and sauces. Unlimited visits to the food bar cost under S$20 (lunchtime) and S$25 (dinner), and include starters and desserts. Daily 11.30am–2.30pm & 6–11pm.

Yet Con Chicken Rice Restaurant, 25 Purvis St, Colonial District (☎337 6819). Cheap and cheerful, old-time Hainanese restaurant: try "crunchy, crispy" roast pork with pickled cabbage and radish, or for S$10 chicken rice, washed down with barley water, for two people. Daily 10.30am–9.30pm.

INDIAN

Annalakshmi, *Excelsior Hotel* & Shopping Centre, 5 Coleman St, Colonial District (☎339 9993). Terrific North and South Indian vegetarian food, with all profits going to an Indian cultural association. Many of the staff are volunteers from the Hindu community, so your waiter might just be a doctor or a lawyer. Dishes from S$10. Daily 11.30am–3pm & 6–9.30pm.

Banana Leaf Apolo, 54–58 Race Course Rd, Little India (☎293 8682). Pioneering fish-head curry restaurant (S$30 for two people) where South Indian dishes are all served on banana leaves. Daily 10.30am–10pm.

Islamic Restaurant, 791–797 North Bridge Rd, Arab Quarter (☎298 7563). Muslim restaurant serving the best traditional chicken *biriyani* in Singapore. S$10 for two. Open 9.30am–9.30pm; closed Fri.

Komala Villas, 76–78 Serangoon Rd, Little India (☎293 6980). A cramped, popular vegetarian establishment specializing in fifteen varieties of *dosai*. The "South Indian Meal" is great value at S$4.50. Daily 7am–10pm.

Madras New Woodlands, 12–14 Upper Dickson Rd, Little India (☎297 1594). Recommended, canteen-style place serving up decent vegetarian food at bargain prices. Thali set meals from S$4. Daily 8am–11pm.

SOUTHEAST ASIAN

Blue Ginger, 97 Tanjong Pagar Rd, Chinatown (☎222 3928). Trendy Peranakan restaurant offering *ikan masal assam gulai* (mackerel simmered in a tamarind and lemongrass gravy), and *ayam buah keluak* – braised chicken with Indonesian black nuts. Daily 11.30am–3pm & 6.30–11pm.

Cuppage Thai Food Restaurant, 49 Cuppage Terrace, off Orchard Road (☎734 1116). Cheap and cheerful restaurant serving quality Thai dishes at around the $8 mark. Daily 11am–3pm & 6–11pm.

House of Sundanese Food, 55 Boat Quay, Singapore River (☎534 3775) and 218 East Coast Rd (☎345 5020). Spicy salads and barbecued seafood characterize the cuisine of Sunda (West Java). Try the tasty *ikan sunda* (grilled fish) – an $18 fish serves two to three people. Open Tues–Sun 11am–2.30pm & 5–10pm.

Nonya & Baba, 262 River Valley Rd, Colonial District (☎734 1382). Respected Nonya restaurant where *otak otak* (fish mashed with coconut milk and chilli paste, wrapped in banana leaf) and *ayam buah keluak* (chicken with black nuts) are both terrific; other dishes cost around S$7. Daily 11.30am–10pm.

Pornping Thai Seafood Restaurant, 01-96/98 Golden Mile Complex, 5001 Beach Rd, Arab Quarter (☎298 5016). Set in a complex known locally as "Thai Village" and always full of Thais. All the standard dishes at cheap prices – S$25 buys a meal for two, washed down with Singha beer. Daily 10am–10pm.

Rendezvouse Restaurant, 02-02 Hotel Rendezvous, 9 Bras Basah Rd (☎3397508). Revered nasi padang joint that still turns out lip-smacking curries, rendangs and sambals. Daily 11am–9.30pm.

Rumah Makam Minang, 18a Kandahar St, Arab Quarter. Fiery nasi padang – highly spiced Sumatran cuisine – in the heart of the Arab Quarter; S$4 ensures a good feed. Daily noon–2.30pm & 6–10.30pm.

Viet Café, 01-76 UE Square, Unity Street (☎3336453). The heady aromas of Vietnamese *pho* (soup) – mint, basil and citrus – hang heavy in the air at this sleek café. Daily noon–3am.

US AND INTERNATIONAL

Cha Cha Cha, 32 Lorong Mambong, Holland Village (☎46216509). Classic Mexican dishes from S$10 to 22. Daily 11.30am–10pm.

Milano's, Funan Centre, North Bridge Rd, Colonial District. Their "All you can eat – all day, every day" policy makes *Milano's* unbeatable value: choose from soups, pizzas, pastas and salad. S$11 a head.

Ponderosa, 02-20 Raffles City Shopping Centre, 252 North Bridge Rd (☎3344926). Chicken, steak and fish set meals come with baked potato, sundae, and as much salad as you can eat, at a bargain S$12.50. Daily 11am–10pm.

Seah Street Deli, *Raffles Hotel*, 1 Beach Rd, Colonial District (☎3371886). New York-style deli boasting the most mountainous sandwiches in Asia, at around S$10 each. Daily 11am–10pm, Fri & Sat until 11pm.

Drinking and nightlife

Singapore's burgeoning **bar and pub** scene means there is now a wide range of drinking holes to choose from, with the Colonial District, Boat Quay and Orchard Road areas offering particularly good pub crawl potential. With competition hotting up, more and more bars are turning to **live music** to woo punters, though this is usually no more than cover versions performed by local bands. **Clubs** also do brisk business; glitzy yet unpretentious, they feature the latest imported pop, rock and dance music, though don't expect anything like a rave scene – Ecstasy isn't in the Singaporean dictionary.

Bars and pubs

It's possible to buy a small glass of beer in most **bars and pubs** for around S$5, but prices can be double or treble that, especially in the Orchard Road district. During Happy Hour in the early evening, bars offer local beers and house wine either at half price, or "one for one" – you get two of whatever you order, but one is held back for later. Most places close around midnight (a bit later on Friday and Saturday nights).

Anywhere, 04-08/09 Tanglin Shopping Centre, 19 Tanglin Rd, near Orchard Rd. Tania, Singapore's most famous covers band, plays nightly to a boozy roomful of expats that's at its rowdiest on Friday nights. Happy Hour Mon–Fri 6–8pm; open Mon–Sat 6pm–2am.

Bernie Goes to Town, 82a/b Boat Quay (☎536 3533). Reggae, blues and R&B are the preferred sounds at this laid-back, roadhouse-style joint. Mon–Thurs & Sun 11am–1am, Fri & Sat 3pm–3am.

Bar and Billiards Room, *Raffles Hotel*, 1 Beach Rd. A Singapore Sling (S$17), in the colonial elegance of the hotel where it was invented in 1915, is required drinking on a visit to Singapore. Daily 11.30am–midnight.

Crazy Elephant, 01-07 Trader's Market, Clarke Quay. Clarke Quay's best bar, playing decent rock music on the turntable between live sessions by the house band. Try to nab a table out by the water's edge. Mon–Thur & Sun 5pm–1am, Fri & Sat 5pm–2am.

Compass Rose Bar, 70th Floor, *Westin Stamford Hotel*, 2 Stamford Rd. Tasteful bar from whose floor-to-ceiling windows you can see as far as southern Malaysia. Happy Hour 5.30–8.30pm; minimum charge S$15 after 8.30pm. Daily 11am–12.30am.

Excalibur Pub, B1-06 Tanglin Shopping Centre, 19 Tanglin Rd, near Orchard Rd. Wonderfully cluttered and cramped British-style pub that's full of weatherbeaten expats. Daily 11am–10.30pm.

Harry's Quayside, 28 Boat Quay (☎5383029). Live jazz Wednesday to Saturday, and a blues jam on Sunday evening.

Ice Cold Beer, 9 Emerald Hill, off Orchard Road. Noisy, hectic and happening place; the lamentable upstairs den is best avoided; Happy Hour daily 5–9pm, and there are regular promotions. Daily 5pm–midnight.

Lot, Stock and Barrel Pub, 29 Seah St, Colonial District. Frequented by an early office crowd and a late backpacker crowd (Beach Road's homestays are just around the corner), who come for the rock classics on the jukebox. Happy Hour 4–8pm; open 4pm-midnight.

Saxophone, 23 Cuppage Rd, near Orchard Road. The coolest address in town, and a magnet for the beautiful people, who relax on the terrace to the sounds of the house jazz band. Expensive. Happy Hour (6–8pm). Daily 6pm–2am.

The Yard, 294 River Valley Rd. Busy English pub with bar snacks available with a 3–8pm Happy Hour. Daily 3pm–midnight.

Clubs

Unlike their London and New York counterparts, Singaporean **clubs** are refreshingly naive, their customers more intent on enjoying themselves than on posing. European and American dance music dominates, and many feature live cover bands. Clubs tend to open around 9pm, and most have a **cover charge** of S$10–30, at least on weekends. Singapore also has a plethora of extremely seedy, extortionately priced hostess clubs, worked by aged Chinese hostesses.

Boom Boom Room, 02-04, 3 New Bugis St (☎339 8187). The comedy and dance on show every night is tame by old Bugis Street standards, though still well attended and enjoyed by locals and tourists. Cover charge Tues–Sat; 9pm–2am.

Fire Disco, 04-19 Orchard Plaza, 150 Orchard Rd (☎235 0155). A mixed bag: downstairs is teenybopper paradise; upstairs, cult Singapore covers band Energy plays nightly. Daily 8pm–3am.

Sparks Disco, seventh floor, Ngee Ann City, 391 Orchard Rd (☎735 6133). Soccer pitch-sized and multi-chambered nightspot aimed at the yuppie market. Live bands play jazz, pop and Canto-pop. Daily Mon–Sat 6pm–3am.

Sugar, 13 Mohamed Sultan Rd (☎836 8010). Currently one of Singapore's coolest nightspots: most of the dancing goes on out back, where Singapore's beautiful people get down to house and garage. Mon–Sat 8pm–3am.

Sultan of Swing, 01-01 Central Mall, 5 Magazine Rd (☎557 0828). Singapore's trendiest and most talked about disco, drawing a large enough crowd of young executives to fill the huge dance floor that lies behind the quieter wine bar out front. Daily 5pm–2am.

Zouk, 17–21 Jiak Kim St (☎738 2988). Singapore's trendiest club, where world-renowned DJs like Paul Oakenfold guest occasionally. Happy Hour 8–9pm; open Mon–Sat 6pm–3am.

Traditional entertainment

If you walk around Singapore's streets for long enough, you're likely to come across some sort of streetside **cultural event**, most usually a **wayang**, or Chinese opera, played out on tumbledown outdoor stages that spring up overnight next to temples and markets, or just at the side of the road. Wayangs are highly dramatic and stylized affairs, in which garishly made-up and costumed characters enact popular Chinese legends to the accompaniment of the crashes of cymbals and gongs. Wayangs take place throughout the year, but the best time to catch one is during the Festival of the Hungry Ghosts (see p.780), when they are held to entertain passing spooks, or during the Festival of the Nine Emperor Gods. The STB may also be able to help you track down a wayang, and as usual the local press is worth checking, or you could pop along to the Chinese Opera Teahouse, 5 Smith St (☎323 4862), where S$15 buys you Chinese tea and an opera performance with English subtitles. Another fascinating traditional performance, **lion dancing**, takes to the streets during Chinese New Year, as do **puppet theatres**.

Shopping

For many stopover visitors, Singapore is synonymous with **shopping**, though contrary to popular belief prices are not rock bottom across the board, due to the consistently strong

Singaporean dollar and a rising cost of living. Good deals can be found on watches, cameras, electrical and computer equipment, fabrics and antiques, and cut-price imitations – Rolexes, Lacoste polo shirts and so on – are rife, but many other articles offer no substantial saving. Choice and convenience though, make the Singapore shopping experience a rewarding one. What's more, come during the **Great Singapore Sale** (usually in June or July), and you'll find seriously marked-down prices in many outlets across the island. The free monthly, Where Singapore, has plenty of suggestions as to what you can buy and where, and the STB publishes a Merchants of the Gold Circle brochure, which lists those shops deemed courteous and reliable enough to display the 'Gold Circle Promise of Excellence' logo in their windows.

If you have any complaints to lodge, contact the Retail Promotions Centre on ☎450 2114 or, better still, go to Singapore's **Small Claims Tribunal**, Subordinate Courts, Apollo Centre, 2 Havelock Rd (☎535 6922), which has a fast-track system for dealing with tourists' complaints; to have your case heard costs S$10.

A goods and services **tax** (GST), introduced in 1994, has added a three percent sales tax to all goods and services, but tourists can claim a refund on purchases of S$300 or over at retailers displaying a blue and grey **Tax Free Shopping** sticker. Ask retailers to draft you a Tax Free Shopping Cheque, which you can then redeem subsequently at the airport. Usual **shopping hours** are daily 10am–9pm, though some shopping centres, especially those along Orchard Road, stay open until 10pm (except the Christian-owned *C K Tang's*, which closes on Sunday).

For designer clothes, tailor-made suits, sports equipment, electronic goods or antiques, head for the shopping malls of **Orchard Road** (see p.799). At **Arab Street** (p.807), you'll find exquisite textiles and batiks, and some good deals on jewellery. From here, make a beeline for the silk stores and goldsmiths of **Little India** (see p.803), via the intersection of **Bencoolen Street and Rochor Road**, known for its electrical goods. As well as its souvenir shops, **Chinatown** (see p.799) boasts some more traditional outlets.

Books Times bookshops at 04-08/15 Centrepoint, 175 Orchard Rd, and 02-24/25 Raffles City Shopping Centre, 252 North Bridge Rd. Books Kinokuniya, 03-10/15 Ngee Ann City, 391 Orchard Rd, is the island's biggest bookshop. MPH shops are also well stocked, especially the flagship store on Stamford Road. Select Books, 03-15 Tanglin Shopping Centre, 19 Tanglin Rd, has a huge array of books on Southeast Asia.

Camping equipment Campers' Corner, 01-13 Paradiz Centre, 1 Selegie Rd.

Computers and software Funan Centre, 109 North Bridge Rd.

Electronic equipment Sim Lim Tower, 10 Jalan Besar, Lucky Plaza, 304 Orchard Rd.

Fabrics and silk Jim Thompson Silk Shop, 01-07 Raffles Hotel Arcade, 328 North Bridge Rd. Aljunied Brothers, 91 Arab St. Dakshaini Silks, 164 Serangoon Rd.

Jewellery The entire first floor of the Pidemco Centre, 95 South Bridge Rd, is a jewellery mart.

Music Beethoven Record House, 03-41 Centrepoint, 176 Orchard Rd, for classical sounds; Lata Music Centre, 42 Race Course Rd, for Indian music on tape; Roxy Records, 03-36 Funan Centre, 109 North Bridge Rd, for new releases; Supreme Record Centre, 03-28 Centrepoint, 175 Orchard Rd; Tower Records, fourth floor, Pacific Plaza, Orchard Rd, for a wide choice of music on CD.

Souvenirs Chinese Mec, 03-31/32 Raffles City Shopping Centre, 250 North Bridge Rd; Eng Tiang Huat, 284 River Valley Rd, for Oriental musical instruments, wayang costumes and props; Funan Stamp and Coin Agency, 03-03 Funan the IT Mall, 109 North Bridge Rd; Selangor Pewter, 02-38 Raffles City Shopping Centre, 252 North Bridge Rd, for fine pewterwork; Singapore Handicraft Centre, Chinatown Point, 133 New Bridge Rd, gathers around fifty souvenir shops under one roof; Zhen Lacquer Gallery, 17 Duxton Rd.

Listings

Airlines Aeroflot, 01-02/02-00 Tan Chong Tower, 15 Queen St (☎336 1757); Air Canada, 02-43/46 Meridien Shopping Centre, 100 Orchard Rd (☎732 8555); Air India, 17-01 UIC Building, 5 Shenton Way (☎225 9411); Air Lanka, 13-01a/b, 133 Cecil St (☎225 7233); also PIL Building, 140 Cecil St (☎223 6026); Air New Zealand, 24-08 Ocean Building, 10 Collyer Quay (☎535 8266); American Airlines, 04-01 Middle Rd (☎339 0001); British Airways, 01-56 United Square, 101 Thomson Rd (☎253 8444); Cathay Pacific, 16-01 Ocean Building, 10 Collyer Quay (☎533 1333); Garuda, 01-68 United Square, 101 Thomson Rd (☎250 5666); KLM, 12-06

Ngee Ann City Tower A, 391a Orchard Road (☎737 7622); Lufthansa, 05-07 Palais Renaissance, 390 Orchard Rd (☎737 9222); MAS, 02-09 Singapore Shopping Centre, 190 Clemenceau Ave (☎336 6777); Pelangi Air, 02-09 Singapore Shopping Centre, 190 Clemenceau Ave (☎336 6777); Philippine Airlines, 01-10 Parklane Shopping Mall, 35 Selegie Rd (☎336 1611); Qantas, 04-02 The Promenade, 300 Orchard Rd (☎737 3744); Royal Brunei, 01-4a/4b/5 *Royal Holiday Inn Crowne Plaza*, 25 Scotts Rd (☎235 4672); Royal Nepal Airlines, 09-00 SIA Building, 77 Robinson Rd (☎225 7575); Singapore Airlines, 77 Robinson Rd (☎223 8888), and also at *Mandarin Hotel*, 333 Orchard Rd (☎229 7293) and Raffles City Shopping Centre, 252 North Bridge Rd (☎229 7274); Thai Airways, 02-00 The Globe, 100 Cecil St (☎224 9977); Silkair, see Singapore Airlines (☎221 2221); United Airlines, 01-03 Hong Leong Building, 16 Raffles Quay (☎220 0711).

American Express Travel services at 18-01 The Concourse, 300 Beach Rd (☎299 8133), and 01-04/05 Winsland House, 3 Killiney Rd (☎235 5788).

Banks and exchange All Singapore's banks change travellers' cheques. Licensed moneychangers abound on Arab Street, Serangoon Road's Mustafa Centre, and the Orchard Road shopping centres, and offer more favourable rates.

Embassies and consulates Australia, 25 Napier Rd (☎737 9311); Brunei, 235 Tanglin Hill (☎733 9055); Canada, 14-00 IBM Towers, 80 Anson Rd (☎325 3200); France, 5 Gallop Rd (☎466 4866); Germany, 14-00 Far East Shopping Centre, 545 Orchard Rd (☎737 1355); India, 31 Grange Rd (☎737 6777); Indonesia, 7 Chatsworth Rd (☎737 7422); Ireland, 08-06 Tiong Bahru Rd (☎276 8935); Laos, 179b Gold Hill Centre, Thompson Rd (☎250 6044); Malaysia, 301 Jervois Rd (☎235 0111); New Zealand, 15-06, Ngee Ann City Tower A, 391a Orchard Rd (☎235 9966); Philippines, 20 Nassim Rd (☎737 3977); Sri Lanka, 13-07/13 Goldhill Plaza, 51 Newton Rd (☎254 4595); Thailand, 370 Orchard Rd (☎737 2644); UK, Tanglin Rd (☎473 9333); USA, 30 Hill St (☎338 0251); Vietnam, 10 Leedon Park (☎462 5938).

Hospitals Singapore General, Outram Road (☎222 3322); Alexandra Hospital, Alexandra Rd (☎473 5222); and National University Hospital, Kent Ridge (☎779 5555). All are state hospitals and all have casualty departments.

Internet access Cyberian City, 01-01 Hotel Rendezvous, 9 Bras Basah Rd (☎883 2383). Travel Café, 50 Prinsep St (☎338 9001). PICity@Capitol, 01-09 Capitol Building, 11 Stamford Rd (☎338 9289).

Laundry Washington Dry Cleaning, 02-22 Cuppage Plaza, 5 Koek Rd (Mon–Sat 9am–7.45pm); Washy Washy, 01-18 Cuppage Plaza, 5 Koek Rd (Mon–Sat 10am–7pm).

Pharmacy Guardian Pharmacy has over forty outlets, including ones at Centrepoint, 176 Orchard Rd, and Raffles City Shopping Centre, 252 North Bridge Rd.

Police Tanglin Police Station, 17 Napier Rd, off Orchard Road (☎733 0000); come here to report stolen property. In an emergency, dial ☎999.

Postal services Poste restante at the GPO, beside Paya Lebar MRT (Mon–Fri 8am–6pm, Sat 8am–2pm).

Telephone services There are IDD, fax and telex services at the Comcentre, 31 Exeter Rd; otherwise, IDD calls can be made from any public card phone or credit card phone; see p.779.

Travel agents The following agents are good for discounted air fares and buying bus tickets to Malaysia and Thailand: Airpower Travel, 131a Bencoolen St (☎334 6571); Harharah Travel, first floor, 171a Bencoolen St (☎337 2633); STA Travel, Cuppage Terrace (☎737 7188).

CHAPTER TEN

THAILAND

Introduction

With over six million foreigners flying into the country each year, **Thailand** has become Asia's primary holiday destination and is a useful and popular first stop on any overland journey through Southeast Asia. The influx of tourist cash has played a significant part in the country's recent development, yet Thailand's cultural integrity remains largely undamaged. In this country of fifty-three million people, over ninety percent are practising Theravada Buddhists, and King Bhumibol is a revered figure across his nation. Tiered temple rooftops and saffron-robed monks dominate every vista, and, though some cities and beach resorts are characterized by high-rises and neon lights, the typical Thai community is the traditional farming village: ninety percent of Thais still earn their living from the land.

Most journeys start in **Bangkok**. Thailand's huge, noisy, polluted capital can be an overwhelming introduction to Southeast Asia, but there are traveller-oriented guesthouses aplenty here, and heaps of spectacular temples to visit. It's also the best place for arranging onward travel and visas for neighbouring countries. A popular side-trip from the city takes in the raft houses of Kanchanaburi, the infamous site of the Bridge over the River Kwai. After Bangkok, most travellers head north, sometimes via the ancient capitals of **Ayutthaya** and **Sukhothai**, to the enjoyably laid-back city of **Chiang Mai**, where they organize treks to nearby hilltribe villages. There's tranquil countryside in bucketloads up in the northern highlands around Mae Hong Son and along the Mekong River in Thailand's northeast (Isaan), where you can stay in village guesthouses and hop across the border into Laos. The northeast is the least visited area of Thailand, but holds two fine ancient **Khmer ruins** at Phimai and Phanom Rung, and the country's most popular national park, **Khao Yai**.

After trekking and rural relaxation, most visitors want to head for the **beach** – and Thailand's eastern and southern coasts are lined with gorgeous white-sand shores, aquamarine seas and kaleidoscopic reefs. The most popular of these are the east coast backpackers' resorts of Ko Samet and Ko Chang, the Gulf Coast islands of Ko Samui, Ko Pha Ngan and Ko Tao, and the Andaman coast idylls of Laem Phra Nang, Ko Phi Phi, Ko Lanta and Ko Tarutao. The southern island of Phuket and the east coast resort of Pattaya are more expensive, package-tour oriented spots. In the deep south, Thailand merges almost seamlessly with Malaysia, and there are plenty of border crossing points here; the city of **Hat Yai** in particular offers convenient long-distance bus and rail links to many Malaysian towns. Getting into Cambodia overland is not so easy, but there are two crossings currently open, Poipet and Trat.

The **climate** of most of Thailand is governed by three seasons: rainy (roughly June to October), caused by the southwest monsoon; cool (November to February); and hot (March to May). The cool season is the pleasantest time to visit and the most popular. Christmas is peak season, when accommodation gets booked way ahead and prices rise significantly. In the hot season, temperatures can rise to 40°C. The rainy season hits the Andaman coast (Phuket, Krabi, Phi Phi) harder than anywhere else in the country – heavy rainfall usually starts in May and persists at the same level until October. The Gulf coast (Ko Samui, Ko Pha Ngan and Ko Tao) gets hardly any rain between June and September, but is hit by the northeast monsoon, which brings rain between October and January. This area also suffers less from the southwest monsoon, getting a relatively small amount of rain.

Overland routes into Thailand

Thailand has **land borders** with Burma, Laos, Cambodia and Malaysia, and all these countries have embassies in Bangkok. If you need a visa for China or India, you might want to apply at their consulates in Chiang Mai, which are less busy than their Bangkok embassies. Laos and Vietnam have consulates in Khon Kaen as well as in Bangkok.

■ From Burma

At the time of writing, Western tourists were not allowed to cross between **Burma** and Thailand at Three Pagodas Pass near Kanchanaburi, at Myawaddy near Mae Sot, or at Mae Sai (except for a day-trip and a fresh thirty-day stamp for your Thai visa when you return). However, foreign nationals should be able to cross in and out of Burma via Victoria Point and Ranong on the Andaman Coast: see p.935. Burma now issues four-week tourist visas for B300–400 – apply to the embassy and you should be able to collect the same day.

■ From Cambodia

There are currently **two legal border** crossings between **Cambodia** and Thailand. Be sure to check with other travellers before opting for either crossing, as border regulations can vary. The most commonly used crossing is at **Poipet** (see p.118), which

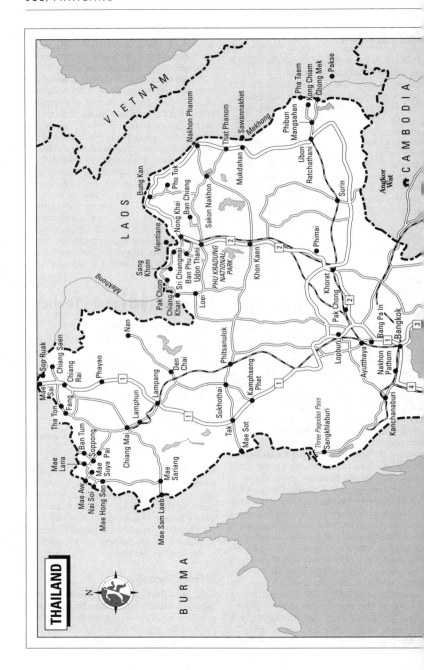

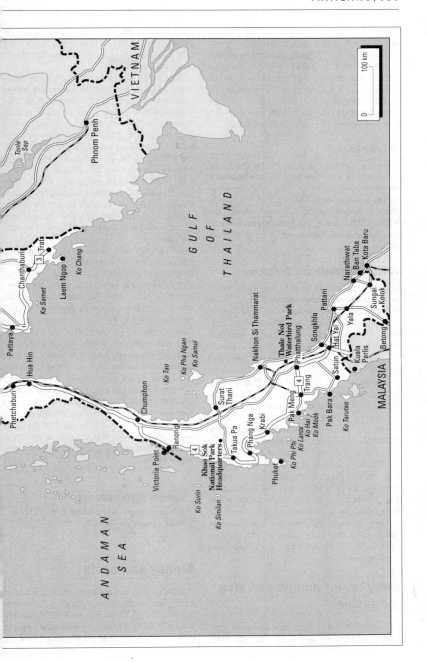

lies just across the border from the Thai town of Aranyaprathet; buses and trains run between Aranyaprathet and Bangkok. Increasingly popular with travellers is the border crossing in Thailand's Trat province, involving a convoluted route via **Hat Lek** and Krong Koh Kong: see p.129 for details. The speedier alternative is to make use of the daily flights operated by Bangkok Airways between Phnom Penh and Bangkok and Siem Reap and Bangkok.

■ From Laos

There are currently five points on the Lao border where tourists can cross overland **into Thailand**: Vientiane (see p.477) to Nong Khai; Houayxai (p.508) to Chiang Kong; Thakhek (p.511) to Nakhon Phanom; Savannakhet (p.512) to Mukdahan; and Pakxe (p.518) to Chong Mek. Non-extendable thirty-day Thai visas are available on arrival at all these points.

■ From Malaysia and Singapore

Most people choose to travel by long-distance train or bus **from Malaysian cities** such as KL or Butterworth to either Bangkok, Krabi, Surat Thani or Hat Yai; see individual city accounts and "Travel Details". However, you can also travel by more local transport, as there are eight border crossings between Malaysia and Thailand – from Kuala Perlis (see p.603) and Langkawi to Satun; from Kuala Perlis (see p.603) and Alor Setar (p.600) to Padang Besar; from Sungai Petani to Betong; from Kota Bahru (p.612) to Sungai Kolok; from Kota Bahru (p.612), Sadao and Wang Prachan to Ban Taba.

The train journey **from Singapore** to Bangkok (1943km) via Malaysia involves several changes, but can be done in around fifty hours at a cost of about £60/$90; trains leave at least once a day from both ends. The most straightforward route is along the west coast line, via Kuala Lumpur and Butterworth (22hr). The east-coast route involves a short taxi ride across the actual border, as the lines don't quite connect.

Plenty of buses also cross the Thai–Malaysian border every day. Buses arrive at Hat Yai from Butterworth (5hr), Penang (6hr), Kuala Lumpur (12hr) and Singapore (18hr).

Entry requirements and visa extension

For stays of up to thirty days, most foreign passport holders automatically get a free non-extendable

transit visa when passing through immigration at Don Muang Airport, at the Malaysian border or at the Laos border, but may have to show proof of onward travel arrangements.

These transit visas are absolutely non-extendable, so you might want to apply for a **sixty-day tourist visa** instead, obtainable in advance from Thai embassies (see p.21 for a list of Thai embassies abroad). In the UK, sixty-day visas take two working days to process if you go in person (Mon–Fri 9.30am–12.30pm), or ten days if you apply by post, and cost £8. In the US, it costs $15 and takes 24 hours in person, or five days by post. In Canada it costs CAN$16.50 and is processed in three working days to a week; in Australia it costs A$18 and takes three to five days. New Zealanders (and nationals of South Korea, Sweden, Denmark, Norway and Finland) with a valid onward ticket get a free ninety-day visa.

All sixty-day tourist visas can be **extended** in Thailand for a further thirty days, at the discretion of officials; visa extensions cost B500 and are issued over the counter at immigration offices (*kaan khao muang*) in nearly every provincial capital – most offices ask for one or two extra photos as well, plus two photocopies of the first four pages and latest Thai visa page of your passport. If you use up the three-month quota, the quickest and cheapest way of extending your stay for a further sixty days is to head down to Malaysia and apply for another tourist visa at the embassy in Kuala Lumpur.

Immigration offices also issue **re-entry permits** (B500) if you want to leave the country and come back again within sixty days. If you overstay your visa limits, expect to be fined B100 per extra day when you depart Don Muang Airport, though an overstay of a month or more could land you in trouble with immigration officials.

AIRPORT DEPARTURE TAX

Airport departure tax on international flights is B500, on domestic flights B30.

Money and costs

Thailand's unit of **currency** is the baht (abbreviated to "B"), which is divided into 100 satang. Notes come in B10, B20, B50, B100, B500 and B1000 denominations. At the time of writing, the **exchange rate** was B40 to US$1 and B60 to £1. **Banking hours** are

Monday to Friday 8.30am–3.30pm, but exchange kiosks in the main tourist centres are often open till 10pm, and upmarket hotels will change money 24 hours a day. The Don Muang airport exchange counters also operate 24 hours, so there's little point arranging to buy baht before you arrive. If you have a PIN number for your credit/debit card, you should also be able to withdraw cash from hundreds of 24-hour **cashpoint machines** around the country.

In a country where the daily minimum wage is under B150 a day, it's hardly surprising that Western tourists find Thailand an extremely cheap place to travel. At the bottom of the scale, you could manage on a **daily budget** of about B300–400 if you're willing to opt for basic accommodation and eat, drink and travel as the locals do, spending B80–120 for a room (less if you share), around B100–150 on three meals, and the rest on travel and incidentals. With extras like air conditioning in rooms and on buses, taking tuk-tuks rather than buses for cross-town journeys, and a meal and a couple of beers in a more touristy restaurant, a day's outlay will rise to a minimum of B800. Staying in expensive hotels and eating in the more exclusive restaurants, you should be able to live in extreme comfort for around B2000 a day.

If you need **money wired** to you in Thailand (see "Basics", p.23), you can pick it up from the following agents in Bangkok: American Express at Bangkok Bank, 33 Tha Silom, Bangkok (☎02/236 8970); any Bangkok branch of Siam Commercial Bank, including the centrally located one at 1060 Tha Phetchaburi, Bangkok (☎02/256 1220); Thomas Cook at Bangkok Bank, 33 Tha Silom, Bangkok (☎02/236 8970); Western Union at any Bangkok branch of the Metropolitan Bank – call ☎02/224 3727 for addresses.

Information and maps

For impartial **information** on local attractions and transport, call in at the efficient Tourism Authority of Thailand (TAT) (*www.tat.or.th*), which has offices in Bangkok and 22 regional towns, all open daily 8.30am–4.30pm. Independent tour operators and information desks crop up in tourist spots all over the country, but be on the lookout for self-interested advice. The best **map** of the country is Bartholomew's 1:1,500,000 map of Thailand.

Getting around

The wide range of efficient **transport** options makes travelling around Thailand easier than elsewhere in Southeast Asia, and it is usually just as inexpensive. For a rough idea of frequency and duration of transport between major towns, check the "Travel Details" at the end of the chapter.

■ Buses

Orange-coloured ordinary **buses** (*rot thammadaa*) are state-run, incredibly inexpensive and cover most short-range routes between main towns (up to 150km) very frequently during daylight hours. They can get very packed and are usually quite slow because they stop frequently and often wait until they have enough passengers to make the journey worthwhile. The state-run blue **air-conditioned buses** (*rot air*) are faster and more comfortable, but cost up to twice as much, depart less frequently, and don't cover nearly as many routes. In a lot of cases the misleadingly named **tour buses** (*rot tua*) – which are privately owned, air-conditioned and ply the most popular long-distance routes, with no tours involved – operate out of the government bus terminals and are indistinguishable from air-conditioned ones. But some, such as Nakorn Chai and Win Tour, do offer a distinctly better service, with reclining seats and plenty of leg room. However, many smaller private tour bus companies have a poor reputation for service and comfort, attracting their customers with bargain fares and convenient timetables. Travellers have reported a frightening lack of safety awareness and occasional thefts on these routes, too, particularly on the overnight buses. **Tickets** for all buses can be bought from the departure terminals, but for ordinary buses it's normal to buy them on board. Air-conditioned buses often operate from a separate station, and tickets for the more popular routes should be booked a day in advance. As a rough indication of prices, a trip from Bangkok to Chiang Mai should cost B307 by state-run air-conditioned bus, and B600 by tour bus.

In rural areas, the bus network is supplemented or replaced by **songthaews**, open-ended vans with two facing benches for passengers. In most towns you'll find the songthaew "terminal" near the market; to pick one up between destinations just flag it down, and to indicate to the driver that you want to get out, either shout, or rap hard with a coin on the ceiling. In the deep south, **share taxis**, often clapped-out old limos, connect all the major towns. Government-run air-con **minibuses** are also the norm on certain routes in the deep south and the central plains.

■ Trains

Managed by the State Railway of Thailand (SRT), the **rail network** consists of four main lines and a few branch lines, and is comfortable and reasonably fast. Fares depend on the class of seat, whether or not you want air conditioning, and on the speed of the train. Hard wooden third-class seats cost about the same as an ordinary bus (Bangkok–Chiang Mai B151); in second class you can choose between reclining seats or berths on long journeys (Bangkok–Chiang Mai B321/421); and in first class (B1193) you automatically get a private two-person air-conditioned compartment. All long-distance trains have dining cars. The speed supplements are as follows: Special Express (B70 extra), Express (B50), Special Diesel Railcars (B50) and Rapid (B30), and you always pay extra for berths. **Advance booking** of at least one day is strongly recommended for second-class and first-class seats on all lengthy journeys, and for sleepers needs to be done as far in advance as possible. It should be possible to make bookings at the station in any major town. The SRT publishes two clear and fairly accurate free **timetables** in English; the best place to get hold of them is over the counter at Bangkok's Hualamphong Station.

■ Planes

The domestic arm of Thai Airways dominates the internal **flight network**, which extends to all parts of the country, using a total of 22 airports. Bangkok Airways plies seven additional routes. All towns served by an airport have at least one Thai Airways booking office; reserve early if possible. To give an idea of **fares**, Bangkok to Chiang Mai costs $50, Chiang Mai to Phuket is $106.

■ Local transport and taxis

Most sizeable towns have some fixed-route transport network of local buses, songthaews or even longtail boats, with set fares and routes, but not rigid timetabling; in most cases vehicles leave when they're full – generally at ten- or twenty-minute inter-vals during the busiest time of day (from about 6am until noon) – and then at least once an hour until 5pm or 6pm.

Named after the noise of its excruciatingly unsilenced engine, the three-wheeled open-sided **tuk-tuk** is the classic Thai vehicle and is basically a cheap taxi. They are fast, fun and inexpensive: fares start at B10 (B20 in Bangkok) regardless of the number of passengers. With all the types of taxi, always establish the fare before you get in. Tuk-tuks are also sometimes known as samlors (literally "three wheels"), but the real **samlors** are tricycle rickshaws propelled by pedal power alone. Samlors operate pretty much everywhere, except in Bangkok, and drivers usually charge a minimum B10 fee and add B10 per kilometre, possibly more for a heavy load. Even faster and more precarious than tuk-tuks, **motorbike taxis** feature both in big towns and out-of-the-way places. Air-conditioned **car taxis** are generally available only in the biggest towns, and resorts such as Bangkok and Phuket have metered taxis; the minimum fare in Bangkok is B35.

Accommodation

Thailand is stuffed full of traveller-oriented **guesthouses** (see "Basics", p.37), offering simple double rooms with shared bathrooms for B100–250. If you're travelling on your own, expect to pay anything between sixty and one hundred percent of the double-room price. You'll find these guesthouses in their dozens in Bangkok, Chiang Mai and all the main backpacker beach resorts, where they're also called bungalows, and even in the most unlikely back-country spots. In the main towns they tend to be concentrated in cheek-by-jowl "farang" ("foreigner") enclaves, but even if you baulk at the world travellers' scene that often characterizes these places, guesthouses make great places to stay, with attached cafeterias, clued-up English-speaking staff

---

ADDRESSES

Property is often numbered twice, firstly to show which real estate lot it stands in, and then to distinguish where it is on that lot. Thus 154/7–10 Thanon Rajdamnoen means the building is on lot 154 and occupies numbers 7–10. "Thanon" means "road". Also, in large cities a minor road running off a major road is often numbered as a soi ("lane" or "alley", though it may be a sizeable thoroughfare), rather than given its own street name. Thanon Sukhumvit for example has minor roads numbered Soi 1 to Soi 103, with odd numbers on one side of the road and even on the other; so a Thanon Sukhumvit address could read something like 27/9–11 Soi 15 Thanon Sukhumvit, which would mean the property occupies numbers 9–11 on lot 27 on minor road number 15 running off Thanon Sukhumvit.

and informative noticeboards. Check-out time is usually noon, so during high season (roughly Nov–Feb & July–Aug) you should arrive to check in at about 11.30am: few places will draw up a "waiting list" and they rarely take advance bookings. With fewer than ten officially registered **youth hostels** in the whole country, it's not worth becoming a YHA member just for your trip to Thailand. There's little point in lugging a tent around Thailand either, unless you're planning an extensive tour of national parks: accommodation everywhere else is too inexpensive to make **camping** a necessity, and anyway there are no campgrounds inside town perimeters; camping is allowed on nearly all islands and beaches, but few people bother.

Few Thais use guesthouses, opting instead for Chinese–Thai-run **budget hotels**, with rooms in the B100–450 range. Beds in these places are large enough for a couple, and it's quite acceptable for two people to ask and pay for a single room (*hong diaw*). You'll find these three- or four-storey places in every sizeable town, often near the bus station. They're generally clean and usually come with fan and attached bathroom, but they can be grim and unfriendly, and generally lacking in any communal area, which makes them lonely places for single travellers. Advance bookings are accepted over the phone, but are rarely necessary. **Mid-range hotels** – priced between B450 and B1000 – can sometimes work out to be good value, with TV, fridge, air-conditioning and pool. Many of Thailand's **upmarket hotels** belong to international chains like *Hilton*, *Holiday Inn*, *Le Meridien* and *Sheraton*, maintaining top-quality standards in Bangkok and major resorts at prices of B3000 and upward for a double; some of the best upmarket Thai hotels are up to B1000 cheaper. Upmarket hotels add ten percent tax and a ten percent service charge to your bill, which we've included in the price codes explained above.

Electricity is supplied at 220 volts AC and available at all but the most remote villages and basic beach huts.

Food and drink

Thai **food** is renowned for its fiery but fragrant dishes spiced with lemon grass, basil and chilli, and you can eat well and cheaply even in the smallest provincial towns. Hygiene is a consideration when eating anywhere in Thailand, but there's no need to be too cautious: wean your stomach gently by avoiding excessive amounts of chillies and too much fresh fruit in the first few days and by always drinking either bottled or boiled water. You can be pretty sure that any noodle stall or curry shop that's permanently packed with customers is a safe bet. Broad price categories are given in restaurant listings throughout this section: "inexpensive" means you can get a main course for under B50, "moderate" means B50–100, and "expensive" over B100.

Throughout the country most inexpensive Thai restaurants specialize in one general food type or preparation method – a "noodle shop", for example, will do fried noodles and noodle soups, plus a basic fried rice, but nothing else; a restaurant displaying whole roast chickens and ducks will offer these sliced or with chillies and sauces served over rice; and "curry shops" serve just that. As often as not, the best and most entertaining places to eat are the local **night markets** (*talaat yen*), where thirty-odd "specialist" pushcart kitchens congregate from about 6pm to 6am on permanent patches in most towns, often close to the fruit and vegetable market or the bus station. Each stall is fronted by tables and stools and you can choose your food from wherever you like.

■ What to eat

Thais eat **noodles** (*kway tiaw or ba mii*) when Westerners would dig into a sandwich – for lunch, as a late-night snack or just to pass the time – and at B15–30 they're the cheapest hot meal you'll find anywhere. They come in assorted varieties (wide and flat, thin and transparent, made with eggs, soy-bean flour

FOOD AND DRINK GLOSSARY

GENERAL TERMS AND REQUESTS

I am vegetarian	*Phŏm (male)/diichăn (female) kin jeh*	With/without	*Sài/mâi sai*
Can I see the menu?	*Khăw duù menu?*	Can I have the bill please?	*Khăw check bin?*
I would like...	*Khăw...*		

NOODLES

Ba mìi	Egg noodles	*Kwáy tiăw/ba mìi rât nâ (mŭu)*	Rice noodles/egg noodles fried in gravy-like sauce with vegetables (and pork)
Kwáy tiăw	White rice noodles		
Ba mìi kràwp	Crisp fried egg noodles		
Kwáy tiăw/ba mìi haêng	Rice noodles/egg noodles fried with egg, meat and vegetables	*Pàt thai*	Thin noodles fried with egg, beansprouts and tofu, topped with ground peanuts
Kwáy tiăw/ba mìi nám (mŭu)	Rice noodle/egg noodle soup, made with chicken broth (and pork balls)	*Pàt siyú*	Wide or thin noodles fried with soy sauce, egg and meat

RICE DISHES

Khâo	Rice	*Khâo niăw*	Sticky rice
Khâo man kài	Chicken served over marinated rice	*Khâo pàt kài/ mŭu/kûng/phàk*	Fried rice with chicken/ pork/shrimp/vegetables
Khâo nâ kài/pèt	Chicken/duck with sauce over rice	*Khâo rât kaeng*	Curry over rice
		Khâo tôm	Rice soup

STIR-FRIES, CURRIES AND SOUPS

Hâwy thâwt	Omelette stuffed with mussels	*Pàt phàk lăi yàng*	Stir-fried vegetables
Kaeng kài/néua/ pèt/plaa dùk/sôm	Chicken/beef/duck/catfish/ fish and vegetable curry	*Plaa (mŭu) prîaw wăan*	Sweet and sour fish (pork)
Kài pàt nàw mái	Chicken with bamboo shoots	*Plaa nêung páe sá*	Whole fish steamed with vegetables and ginger
Kài pàt mét mámûang	Chicken with cashew nuts	*Plaa rât phrík*	Whole fish cooked with chillies
Kài pàt khĭng	Chicken with ginger	*Plaa thâwt*	Fried whole fish
Kûng chúp paêng thâwt	Prawns fried in batter	*Sôm Tam*	Spicy papaya salad
		Thâwt man plaa	Fish cakes
Pàt phàk bûng	Morning glory fried in garlic and bean sauce	*Tôm khàa kài*	Chicken coconut soup
		Tôm yam kûng	Hot and sour prawn soup

DRINKS (KHREÛANG DEÙM)

Bia	Beer	*Nám plaò*	Drinking water (boiled or filtered)
Chaa ráwn	Hot tea		
Chaa yen	Iced tea	*Nom jeùd*	Milk
Kaafae ráwn	Hot coffee	*Ohlíang*	Iced coffee
Nám klûay	Banana shake	*Sohdaa*	Soda water
Nám mánao/sôm	Fresh, bottled or fizzy lemon/ orange juice		

or rice flour) and get boiled up as soups (*kway tiaw nam*), doused in sauces (*kway tiaw rat na*), or stir-fried (*kway tiaw haeng* or *kway tiaw pat*). The usual practice is to order the noodle dish with extra chicken, beef, pork or shrimps. The most popular noodle dish is *kway tiaw pat thai*, usually abbreviated to *pat thai*, a delicious combination of fried noodles, beansprouts, egg and tofu, sprinkled with ground peanuts and lime juice. Fried rice (*khao pat*) is the other faithful standby. Although very few Thais are **vegetarian**, you can nearly always ask for a vegetable-only fried rice or noodle dish – though in rural spots this is often your only option unless you eat fish. All traveller-oriented restaurants are veggie-friendly.

Aside from fiery curries (*kaeng*) and stir-fried chicken pork or fish, more upmarket restaurant menus often include spicy **Thai soup** (*tom yam*), which is eaten with other dishes, not as a starter. Two favourites are *tom kha khai*, a creamy coconut chicken soup, and *tom yam kung* (a prawn soup without coconut milk). Food from the northeastern Isaan region is popular throughout the country, particularly **sticky rice** (*khao niaw*), which is rolled up into balls and dipped into chilli sauces and other side dishes, such as the local dish *som tam*, a spicy green-papaya salad with garlic, raw chillies, green beans, tomatoes, peanuts and dried shrimps. Barbecued chicken on a stick (*kai yang*) is the classic accompaniment. Raw minced pork is the basis of another popular Isaan and northern dish called *larb*, subtly flavoured with mint and served with vegetables.

Sweets (*khanom*) don't really figure on most restaurant menus, but a few places offer bowls of *luk taan cheum*, a jellied concoction of lotus seeds floating in a syrup, and coconut custard (*sangkaya*) cooked inside a small pumpkin. Cakes are sold on the street and tend to be heavy, sticky affairs made from glutinous rice and coconut cream pressed into squares and wrapped in banana leaves.

Thais don't drink **water** straight from the tap, and nor should you: plastic bottles of drinking water (*nam plao*) are sold countrywide, even in the smallest villages. Night markets, guesthouses and restaurants do a good line in freshly squeezed **fruit juices** and shakes, as well as fresh coconut milk (*nam maprao*) and freshly squeezed sugar-cane juice (*nam awy*), which is sickeningly sweet.

Beer (*bia*) is expensive at B60 for a 330ml bottle; the most famous beer is the slightly acrid locally brewed Singha, but Kloster and Chang, which are also brewed locally, are more palatable. At about B60 for a 375ml bottle, the local **whisky** is a lot better value and Thais think nothing of consuming a bottle

a night. The most drinkable and widely available of these is the 35 percent proof Mekong. Sang Thip is an even stronger rum. Bars aren't an indigenous feature, as Thais rarely drink out without eating, but you'll find some in Bangkok and the resorts.

Communications

Mail takes around a week to get from Bangkok to Europe or North America, longer from more isolated areas. Almost all main post offices across the country operate a **poste restante** service (generally Mon–Fri 8am–4pm, Sat 8am–noon) and will hold letters for two to three months (see "Basics" p.39). American Express in Bangkok and Phuket also offers a poste restante facility to holders of Amex credit cards or travellers' cheques. All parcels must be officially boxed and sealed at special counters within main post offices – you can't just turn up with a package and buy stamps for it. Surface packages take three months, air-mail parcels take about a week.

Payphones are straightforward enough and generally come in three colours. Red phones are for **local calls** and take the medium-sized one-baht coins. Blue-and-stainless steel ones are for **long-distance calls** within Thailand, but they gobble up B5 coins and are generally unreliable, so you're better off buying a phonecard (B25 to B240 available from hotels, post offices and some shops) and using a green cardphone.

The least costly way of making an **international call** is to use a government telephone centre – there's usually one located within or adjacent to the town's main post office, open daily from about 7am to 10pm (24hr in Bangkok and Chiang Mai). If you call between 9pm and 5am you get up to 33 percent off standard rates. See "Basics" p.40 for how to call abroad from Thailand. **Collect or reverse charge calls** and home direct calls can be made free of charge at government phone centres.

It's also possible to call internationally at government rates on the green public cardphones, but only with cards of B500 and above. (You can use any public phone, including the blue ones, to call Laos and Malaysia, with cards of less than B500.) In tourist areas public yellow cardphones can be used for international calls only (cards start from B300). Private international call offices are more expensive, and you have to pay a user's fee for collect calls. For **international directory enquiries** call ☎100. For directory assistance in English dial ☎13 (inside Bangkok) or ☎183 (elsewhere).

Most major post offices offer a domestic and international **fax service**. Private phone centres will also send faxes, but charge up to fifty percent more. Many also offer "fax restante".

Internet access is available almost everywhere in Thailand, and at the time of writing there were tourist-friendly cybercafés in Bangkok, Chiang Mai, Chiang Rai, Nong Khai, Pattaya, Phuket, Ko Tao, Ko Pha Ngan, Ko Samui and Krabi; most charge between B1 and B5 per minute online and will receive emails at the cybercafé's email address.

Opening hours and festivals

Most shops **open** at least Monday to Saturday from about 8am to 8pm, while department stores operate daily from around 10am to 9pm. Private office hours are generally Monday to Friday 8am–5pm and

Saturday 8am–noon, though in tourist areas these hours are longer, with weekends worked like any other day. Government offices work Monday to Friday 8.30am–noon and 1–4.30pm, and national museums tend to stick to these hours, too, but some close on Mondays and Tuesdays rather than at weekends. Most shops and tourist-oriented businesses, including TAT, stay open on national holidays.

Thais use both the Western Gregorian calendar and a Buddhist calendar – the Buddha is said to have died (or entered Nirvana) in the year 543 BC, so Thai dates start from that point: thus 2000 AD becomes 2543 BE (Buddhist Era). Dates for religious festivals are often set by the lunar calendar, so check specifics with TAT.

The most spectacular religious **festivals** include **Songkhran** (usually April 13–15), when the Thai New Year is welcomed in with massive public water-fights in the street (most exuberant in Chiang Mai); the **Rocket Festival** in Yasothon (weekend in mid-May), when painted wooden rockets are paraded and fired to ensure plentiful rains; the **Candle Festival** in Ubon Ratchathani (July, three days around the full moon), when enormous wax sculptures are paraded to mark the beginning of the annual Buddhist retreat period; the **Vegetarian Festival** in Phuket and Trang (Oct), when Chinese devotees become vegetarian for a nine-day period and then parade through town performing acts of self-mortification; and **Loy Krathong** (late Oct or early Nov), when baskets of flowers and lighted candles are floated on rivers, canals and ponds nationwide (best in Sukhothai and Chiang Mai) to celebrate the end of the rainy season. The two main tourist-oriented festivals are the **Surin Elephant roundup** (third weekend of Nov), when two hundred elephants play team games, and parade in battle dress; and the **River Kwai Bridge festival** in Kanchanaburi (last week of Nov and first week of Dec), which includes a spectacular son et lumière at the infamous bridge.

Cultural hints

Tourist literature has so successfully marketed Thailand as the "Land of Smiles" that a lot of tourists arrive in the country expecting to be forgiven any outrageous behaviour. This is just not the case: there are some things so universally sacred in Thailand that even a hint of disrespect will cause deep offence. The worst thing you can possibly do is to bad-mouth the universally revered royal family.

Thais very **rarely shake hands**, using the *wai*, a prayer-like gesture made with raised hands, to greet and say goodbye and to acknowledge respect, gratitude or apology. The *wai* changes according to the relative status of the two people involved: as a farang (foreigner) your safest bet is to go for the "stranger's" *wai*, raising your hands close to your chest and placing your fingertips just below your chin.

Thailand shares the same attitudes to dress and social taboos, described in "Basics" on p.41, as other Southeast Asian cultures.

Traditional drama and sport

Drama pretty much equals dance in Thai theatre, and many of the traditional dance-dramas are based on the Hindu epic the Ramayana (in Thai, Ramakien), a classic adventure tale of good versus evil which is known across Southeast Asia.The most spectacular form of traditional Thai theatre is *khon*, a stylized drama performed in masks and elaborate costumes by a troupe of highly trained classical dancers. All the movements follow a strict choreography that's been passed down through generations, and each graceful, angular gesture depicts a precise event, action or emotion which will be familiar to educated *khon* audiences. The story is chanted and sung by a chorus, accompanied by a classical *phipat* orchestra.

Serious and refined, *lakhon* is derived from *khon*, but is used to dramatize a greater range of stories, including Buddhist Jataka tales, local folk dramas and of course the Ramayana. The form you're most likely to come across is *lakhon chatri*, which is performed at shrines like Bangkok's Erawan and Lak Muang as entertainment for the spirits and as a token of gratitude from worshippers. Dancers wear decorative costumes but no masks, and dance to the music of a *phipat* orchestra.

Likay is a much more popular derivative of *khon*, with lots of comic interludes, bawdy jokes and over-the-top acting. Most *likay* troupes adapt pot-boiler romances or write their own, and costumes are often a mixture of traditional and Western. Likay troupes travel around the country doing shows on makeshift outdoor stages and at temple fairs.

Thai boxing (*muay Thai*) enjoys a following similar to football in Europe: every province has a stadium and whenever it's shown on TV you can be sure that large noisy crowds will gather round the sets in streetside restaurants and noodle shops. The best place to see live Thai boxing is at one of Bangkok's two stadiums. There's a strong spiritual and ritualistic dimension to *muay Thai*, adding grace to an otherwise brutal sport. Any part of the body except the head may be used as an offensive weapon in *muay Thai*, and all parts except the groin are fair targets. Kicks to the head are the blows which cause most knockouts. As the action hots up, so the orchestra speeds up its tempo and the betting in the audience becomes more frenetic.

Meditation centres and retreats

Of the hundreds of **meditation** temples in Thailand, a few cater specifically for foreigners by holding meditation sessions and retreats in English. The meditation taught is mostly Vipassana or "insight", which emphasizes the minute observation of internal physical sensation. Novices and practised meditators alike are welcome. To join a short session in Bangkok, drop in at Wat Mahathat (see p.854). Longer retreats are for the serious-minded only. Days are dominated by meditation; there's no talking at all; tobacco, alcohol, drugs and sex are forbidden; and conditions are spartan. The most popular foreigner-oriented retreat takes place the first ten days of every month at Wat Suan Mokkh near Surat Thani (see p.924). Frequent ten-day retreats (Vipassana meditation) led by foreign teachers are also held at Wat Khao Tham, Surat Thani (see p.924).

Trekking and diving

The vast majority of travellers' itineraries take in a few days' trekking in the north and a stint snorkelling or diving off the beaches of the south. **Trekking** is concentrated in the north and is described on pp.879-883, but there are smaller, less touristy trekking operations in Kanchanaburi (see p.863), Sangkhlaburi (p.867) and Umpang (p.878), all of which are worth considering.

The major **dive centres** are on the east coast in Pattaya, on the Andaman coast at Phuket, Khao Lak, Ao Nang, Ko Phi Phi, Ko Lanta, and on the Gulf Coast on Ko Tao, Ko Samui and Ko Pha Ngan. You can organize dive expeditions at all these places, rent out equipment and do a certificated diving course (B7500–11,000 for a four-day Open Water course). Phuket dive centres offer the cheapest courses. You can dive all year round in Thailand, as the coasts are subject to different monsoon seasons: the diving seasons are from November to April along the Andaman coast, from January to October on the Gulf coast, and all year round on the east coast. There are currently two decompression chambers in Thailand, one in

Sattahip on the east coast near Pattaya (see p.899), the other on Ao Patong in Phuket (see p.939).

Crime and safety

As long as you keep your wits about you and follow the precautions outlined in "Basics" on p.42, you shouldn't encounter much trouble in Thailand. **Theft** and **pickpocketing** are the main problems. Be wary of accepting food or drink from strangers, especially on long overnight bus or train journeys: it may be drugged so as to knock you out while your bags are stolen. Violent crime against tourists is not common but it does occur. There have been several serious attacks on women travellers in the last few years, but bearing in mind that six million tourists visit the country every year, the statistical likelihood of becoming a victim is extremely small.

TAT has a special department for **tourist-related crimes** and complaints called the Tourist Assistance Center (TAC), which is based in the TAT headquarters on Rajdamnoen Nok Avenue, Bangkok (daily 8.30am–4.30pm; ☎02/281 5051).

> **EMERGENCY PHONE NUMBERS**
>
> In any emergency, contact the English-speaking tourist police who maintain a toll-free nation-wide line (☎1699) and have offices within many regional TAT offices.

Medical care and emergencies

Thai **pharmacies** (*raan khai yaa*; daily 8.30am–8pm) are well stocked with local and international branded medicaments. Pharmacists are highly trained and most speak English. All provincial capitals have at least one **hospital** (*rong phayaabahn*). Cleanliness and efficiency vary, but generally hygiene and health-care standards are good; most doctors speak English. In the event of a major health crisis, get someone to contact your embassy (see p.861) or insurance company – it may be best to get yourself flown home.

History

The region's first distinctive civilization, **Dvaravati**, was established around two thousand years ago by

an Austroasiatic-speaking people known as the Mon. One of its mainstays was Theravada Buddhism, which had been introduced to Thailand during the second or third century BC by Indian missionaries. In the eighth century, peninsular Thailand to the south of Dvaravati came under the control of the Srivijaya empire, a Mahayana Buddhist state centred on Sumatra which had strong ties with India.

From the ninth century onwards, however, both Dvaravati and Srivijaya Thailand succumbed to invading **Khmers** from Cambodia, who took control of northeastern, central and peninsular Thailand. They ruled from Angkor and left dozens of spectacular temple complexes throughout the region. By the thirteenth century, however, the Khmers had over-reached themselves and were in no position to resist the onslaught of a vibrant new force in Southeast Asia, the Thais.

■ The earliest Thais

The earliest traceable history of the **Thai people** picks them up in southern China around the fifth century AD, when they were squeezed by Chinese and Vietnamese expansionism into sparsely inhabited northeastern Laos. Their first significant entry into what is now Thailand seems to have happened in the north, where, some time after the seventh century, the Thais formed a state known as Yonok. Theravada Buddhism spread to Yonok via Dvaravati around the end of the tenth century, which served not only to unify the Thais themselves, but also to link them to the wider community of Buddhists.

By the end of the twelfth century, they formed the majority of the population in Thailand, then under the control of the Khmer empire. The Khmers' main out-post, at Lopburi, was by this time regarded as the administrative capital of a land called "Syam".

■ Sukhothai

Some time around 1238, Thais in the upper Chao Phraya valley captured the main Khmer outpost in the region at **Sukhothai** and established a kingdom there. When the young Ramkhamhaeng came to the throne around 1278, he seized control of much of the Chao Phraya valley, and over the next twenty years gained the submission of most of Thailand under a complex tribute system.

Although the empire of Sukhothai extended Thai control over a vast area, its greatest contribution to the Thais' development was at home, in cultural and political matters. A famous inscription by Ramkhamhaeng, now housed in the Bangkok

National Museum, describes a prosperous era of benevolent rule, and it is generally agreed that Ramkhamhaeng ruled justly according to Theravada Buddhist doctrine. A further sign of the Thais' growing self-confidence was the invention of a new script to make their tonal language understood by the non-Thai inhabitants of the land.

■ The growth of Ayutthaya

After the death of Ramkhamhaeng around 1299, however, his empire quickly fell apart, and **Ayutthaya** became the capital of the Thai empire. Soon after founding the city in 1351, the ambitious king Ramathibodi united the principalities of the lower Chao Phraya valley, which had formed the western provinces of the Khmer empire. When he recruited his bureaucracy from the urban elite of Lopburi, Ramathibodi set the style of government at Ayutthaya, elements of which persist to the present day. The elaborate etiquette, language and rituals of Angkor were adopted, and, most importantly, the concept of the ruler as *devaraja* (divine king): when the king processed through the town, ordinary people were forbidden to look at him and had to be silent while he passed.

The site chosen by Ramathibodi for an international port was the best in the region, and so began Ayutthaya's rise to prosperity, based on exploiting the upswing in trade in the middle of the fourteenth century along the routes between India and China. By 1540, the Kingdom of Ayutthaya had grown to cover most of the area of modern-day Thailand. Despite a 1568 invasion by the Burmese, which led to twenty years of foreign rule, Ayutthaya made a spectacular comeback, and in the seventeenth century its foreign trade boomed. In 1511, the Portuguese had become the first Western power to trade with Ayutthaya, and a treaty with Spain was concluded in 1598; relations with Holland and England were initiated in 1608 and 1612 respectively. European merchants flocked to Thailand, not only to buy Thai products, but also for the Chinese and Japanese goods on sale there.

In the mid-eighteenth century, however, the rumbling in the Burmese jungle to the north began to make itself heard again. After an unsuccessful siege in 1760, in February 1766, the **Burmese** descended upon the city for the last time. The Thais held out for over a year, but finally, in April 1767, the city was taken. The Burmese savagely razed everything to the ground, led off tens of thousands of prisoners to Burma and abandoned the city to the jungle.

■ Taksin and Thonburi

Out of this lawless mess emerged **Phraya Taksin**, a charismatic general, who was crowned king in December 1768 at his new capital of **Thonburi**, on the opposite bank of the river from modern-day Bangkok. Within two years, he had restored all of Ayutthaya's territories and, by the end of the next decade, had brought Cambodia and much of Laos into a huge new empire.

However, by 1779 all was not well with the king. Taksin was becoming increasingly irrational and sadistic, and in March 1782 he was ousted in a coup. Chao Phraya Chakri, Taksin's military commander, was invited to take power and had Taksin executed.

■ The early Bangkok empire: Rama I

With the support of the Ayutthayan aristocracy, Chakri – reigning as **Rama I** (1782–1809) – set about consolidating the Thai kingdom. His first act was to move the capital across the river to what we know as Bangkok, on the more defensible east bank. Borrowing from the layout of Ayutthaya, he built a new royal palace and impressive monasteries in the area of Ratanakosin – which remains the city's spiritual heart – within a defensive ring of two (later expanded to three) canals. In the palace temple, Wat Phra Kaeo, he enshrined the talismanic Emerald Buddha, which he had snatched during his campaigns in Laos. Trade with China revived, and the style of government was put on a more modern footing: while retaining many of the features of a *devaraja*, he shared more responsibility with his courtiers, as a first among equals.

■ Rama II and Rama III

The peaceful accession of Rama I's son as **Rama II** (1809–24) signalled the establishment of the Chakri dynasty, which is still in place today. This Second Reign is best remembered as a fertile period for Thai literature; indeed, Rama II himself is renowned as one of the great Thai poets.

By the reign of **Rama III** (1824–51), the Thais were starting to get alarmed by British colonialism in the region. In 1826, Rama III was obliged to sign the Burney Treaty, a limited trade agreement with the British, by which the Thais won some political security in return for reducing their taxes on goods passing through Bangkok.

■ Mongkut

Rama IV, more commonly known as **Mongkut** (1851–68), had been a Buddhist monk for 27 years when he succeeded his brother. But far from leading a cloistered life, Mongkut had travelled widely throughout Thailand, and had taken an interest in Western learning, studying English, Latin and the sciences.

Realizing that Thailand would be unable to resist the military might of the British, the king reduced import and export taxes, allowed British subjects to live and own land in Thailand and granted them freedom of trade. Within a decade, agreements similar to the Bowring Treaty had been signed with France, the United States and a score of other nations. Thus, by skilful diplomacy the king avoided a close relationship with just one power, which could easily have led to Thailand's annexation.

■ Chulalongkorn

Mongkut's son, **Chulalongkorn**, took the throne as Rama V (1868–1910) at the age of only fifteen, but he was well prepared by an excellent education which mixed traditional Thai and modern Western elements – provided by Mrs Anna Leonowens, subject of *The King and I*. One of his first acts was to scrap the custom by which subjects were required to prostrate themselves in the presence of the king. In the 1880s, he began to restructure the government to meet the country's needs, setting up a host of departments – for education, public health, the army and the like – and bringing in scores of foreign advisors to help with everything from foreign affairs to rail lines.

Throughout this period, however, the Western powers maintained their pressure on the region. The most serious threat to Thai sovereignty was the Franco–Siamese Crisis of 1893, which culminated in the French sending gunboats up the Chao Phraya River to Bangkok. Flouting numerous international laws, France claimed control over Laos and made other outrageous demands, which Chulalongkorn had no option but to agree to. During the course of his reign, the country was obliged to cede almost half of its territory, and forewent huge sums of tax revenue in order to preserve its independence; but by Chulalongkorn's death in 1910, the frontiers were fixed as they are today.

■ The end of absolute monarchy

Chulalongkorn was succeeded by a flamboyant, British-educated prince, Vajiravudh (Rama VI, 1910–25). By the time the young and inexperienced Prajadhipok – seventy-sixth child of Chulalongkorn – was catapulted to the throne as Rama VII (1925–35),

Vajiravudh's extravagance had created severe financial problems.

On June 24, 1932, a small group of middle-ranking officials, led by a lawyer, Pridi Phanomyong, and an army major, Luang Phibunsongkhram (Phibun), staged a coup with only a handful of troops. Prajadhipok weakly submitted to the conspirators, and a hundred and fifty years of **absolute monarchy** came to a sudden end. The king was sidelined to a position of symbolic significance, and in 1935 he abdicated in favour of his ten-year-old nephew, Ananda, then a schoolboy living in Switzerland.

■ Up to World War II

Phibun emerged as prime minister after the decisive elections of 1938, and a year later officially renamed the country Thailand ("Land of the Free") – Siam, it was argued, was a name bestowed by external forces, and the new title made it clear that the country belonged to the Thais rather than the economically dominant Chinese.

The Thais were dragged into **World War II** on December 8, 1941, when, almost at the same time as the assault on Pearl Harbour, the Japanese invaded the east coast of peninsular Thailand, with their sights set on Singapore to the south. The Thais at first resisted fiercely, but realizing that the position was hopeless, Phibun quickly ordered a ceasefire.

The Thai government concluded a military alliance with Japan and declared war against the United States and Great Britain in January 1942, probably in the belief that the Japanese would win. However, the Thai minister in Washington, Seni Pramoj, refused to deliver the declaration of war against the US, and, in cooperation with the Americans, began organizing a resistance movement called Seri Thai. Pridi Phanomyong, now acting as regent to the young king, secretly coordinated the movement, smuggling in American agents and housing them in Bangkok. By 1944, Japan's defeat looked likely, and in July, Phibun, who had been most closely associated with them, was forced to resign by the National Assembly.

■ Postwar upheavals

With the fading of the military, the election of January 1946 was for the first time contested by organized political parties, resulting in Pridi's becoming prime minister. A new constitution was drafted, and the outlook for democratic, civilian government seemed bright. Hopes were shattered, however, on June 9, 1946, when King Ananda was found dead in his bed, with a bullet wound in his forehead. Three palace servants were hurriedly tried and executed, but the murder has never been satisfactorily explained. Pridi resigned as prime minister, and in April 1948, Phibun, playing on the threat of communism, took over the premiership.

As **communism** developed its hold in the region with the takeover of China in 1949 and the French defeat in Indochina in 1954, the US increasingly viewed Thailand as a bulwark against the red menace. Between 1951 and 1957, when its annual state budget was only about $200 million a year, Thailand received a total $149 million in American economic aid and $222 million in military aid.

Phibun narrowly won a general election in 1957, but only by blatant vote-rigging and coercion. After vehement public outcry, General Sarit, the commander-in-chief of the army, overthrew the new government in September 1957. Believing that Thailand would prosper best under a unifying authority, Sarit set about re-establishing the monarchy as the head of the social hierarchy and the source of legitimacy for the government. Ananda's successor, Bhumibol (Rama IX), was pushed into an active role, while Sarit ruthlessly silenced critics and pressed ahead with a plan for economic development.

■ The American (Vietnam) War

Sarit died in 1963, whereupon the military succession passed to General Thanom. His most pressing problem was the **Vietnam War**. The Thais, with the backing of the US, quietly began to conduct military operations in Laos, to which North Vietnam and China responded by supporting anti-government insurgency in Thailand. By 1968, around 45,000 US military personnel were on Thai soil, which became the base for US bombing raids against North Vietnam and Laos. The effects of the American presence were profound. The economy swelled with dollars, and hundreds of thousands of Thais became reliant on the Americans for a living, with a consequent proliferation of prostitution – centred on Bangkok's infamous Patpong district – and corruption. Moreover, the sudden exposure to Western culture led many to question traditional Thai values and the political status quo.

■ The democracy movement and civil unrest

Poor farmers in particular were becoming increasingly disillusioned with their lot, and many turned against the Bangkok government. At the end of 1964, the Communist Party of Thailand and other groups formed a broad left coalition which soon had the support of several thousand insurgents in remote areas of the northeast and the north. By 1967, a separate threat had arisen in southern Thailand, involving Muslim dissidents and the Chinese-dominated Communist Party of Malaysia.

Thanom was now facing a major security crisis, and in November, 1971, he imposed repressive **military rule**. In response, student demonstrations began in June 1973, and in October as many as 500,000 people turned out at Thammasat University in Bangkok to demand a new constitution. Clashes with the police ensued but elements in the army, backed by King Bhumibol, prevented Thanom from crushing the protest with troops. On October 14, 1973, Thanom was forced to resign.

In a new climate of openness, Kukrit Pramoj formed a coalition of seventeen elected parties and secured a promise of US withdrawal from Thailand, but his government was riven with feuding. In October 1976, the students demonstrated again, protesting against the return of Thanom to Bangkok. This time there was no restraint: supported by elements of the military and the government, the police and reactionary students launched a massive assault on Thammasat University. On October 6, hundreds of students were brutally beaten, scores were lynched and some even burnt alive; the military took control and suspended the constitution.

■ Premocracy

Soon after, the military-appointed prime minister, Thanin Kraivichien, forced dissidents to undergo anti-communist indoctrination, but his measures seem to have been too repressive even for the military, who forced him to resign in October 1977. General Kriangsak Chomanand took over, and began to break up the insurgency with shrewd offers of amnesty. He in turn was displaced in February 1980 by General Prem Tinsulanonda, backed by a broad parliamentary coalition.

Untainted by corruption, Prem achieved widespread support, including that of the monarchy. Overseeing a period of rapid economic growth, Prem maintained the premiership until 1988, with a unique mixture of dictatorship and democracy sometimes called **Premocracy**: although never standing for parliament himself, Prem was asked by the legislature after every election to become prime minister. He eventually stepped down because, he said, it was time for the country's leader to be chosen from among its elected representatives.

■ The 1992 demonstrations

The new prime minister was indeed an elected MP, Chatichai Choonhavan. He pursued a vigorous policy of economic development, but this fostered widespread corruption. Following an economic downturn and Chatichai's attempts to downgrade the political role of the military, the armed forces staged a bloodless coup on February 23, 1991, led by Supreme Commander Sunthorn and General Suchinda, the army commander-in-chief, who became premier.

When Suchinda reneged on promises to make democratic amendments to the constitution, hundreds of thousands of ordinary Thais poured onto the streets around Bangkok's Democracy Monument in **mass demonstrations** between May 17 and 20, 1992. Suchinda brutally crushed the protests, leaving hundreds dead or injured, but was then forced to resign when King Bhumibol expressed his disapproval in a ticking-off that was broadcast on world television.

■ Chuan, Banharn and Chavalit

In the elections on September 13, 1992, the Democrat Party, led by **Chuan Leekpai**, a noted upholder of democracy and the rule of law, gained the largest number of parliamentary seats. Despite many successes through a period of continued economic growth, he was able to hold onto power only until July 1995, when he was forced to call new elections.

Chart Thai and its leader, **Banharn Silpa-archa**, emerged victorious, but allegations of corruption soon followed and in the following year he was obliged to dissolve parliament. In November 1996, **General Chavalit Yongchaiyudh**, leader of the New Aspiration Party (NAP), just won what was dubbed as the most corrupt election in Thai history, with an estimated 25 million baht spent on vote-buying in rural areas.

■ The economic crisis

At the start of Chavalit's premiership, the Thai **economy** was already on shaky ground. In February 1997, foreign-exchange dealers began to mount speculative attacks on the baht, alarmed at the size of Thailand's private foreign debt – 250 billion baht in the unproductive property sector alone, much of it accrued through the proliferation of prestigious skyscrapers in Bangkok. The government valiantly defended the pegged exchange rate, spending $23 billion of the country's formerly healthy foreign-exchange reserves, but at the beginning of July was forced to give up the ghost – the baht was floated and soon went into free-fall.

Blaming its traditional allies, the Americans, for neglecting their obligations, Thailand sought help from Japan; Tokyo suggested the IMF, who in August 1997 put together a rescue package for Thailand of $17 billion. Among the conditions of the package, the Thai government was to slash the national budget, control inflation and open up financial institutions to foreign ownership.

Chavalit's performance in the face of the crisis was viewed as inept, and in November, he was succeded by **Chuan Leekpai**, who took up what was widely seen as a poisoned chalice for his second term. Businesses unable to pay their debts were looking to lay off hundreds of thousands of employees and the IMF has been keeping the squeeze on the government to implement its austerity measures. In October 1998, the Chuan Leekpai administration was strengthened by the Chat Patana Party joining the government coalition.

During the first half of 1999, the Thai economy gradually showed signs of improvement, both in terms of price stability and growth. Tourism too has shown a steady increase, with more than eight and a half million visitors to the kingdom in 1999.

Religions of Thailand

Over ninety percent of Thais practise **Theravada Buddhism**, one of the two main schools of Buddhism in Asia. The other ten percent are Mahayana Buddhists, Muslims, Hindus, Sikhs and Christians; see "Basics" p.47 for an introduction to all these faiths.

While regular Buddhist merit-making insures a Thai for the next life, there are certain **Hindu gods** and animist spirits that most Thais also cultivate for help with more immediate problems, such as passing an exam, becoming pregnant or winning the lottery. Even the Buddhist King Bhumibol employs Brahmin priests to officiate at certain royal ceremonies, and, like his royal predecessors of the Chakri dynasty, he also associates himself with the Hindu god Vishnu by assuming the title Rama IX – Rama, hero of the Hindu epic the Ramayana, having been Vishnu's seventh manifestation.

Whereas Hindu deities tend to be benevolent, **animist spirits** (or *phi*) are not nearly as reliable and need to be mollified more frequently. So that these *phi* don't pester human inhabitants, each building has a special spirit house in its vicinity, as a dwelling for spirits ousted by the building's construction. Usually raised on a short column and designed to look like a temple or a traditional Thai house, these spirit houses are generally about the size of a dolls' house, but their ornamentation is supposed to reflect the status of the humans' building – thus if that building is enlarged or refurbished, then the spirit house should be improved accordingly.

Traditional art and architecture

Aside from pockets of Hindu-inspired statuary and architecture, the vast majority of Thailand's cultural monuments take their inspiration from Theravada Buddhism, and so it is temples and religious images that constitute the kingdom's main sights.

The **wat** or Buddhist temple complex serves both as a community centre and a shrine for holy images. The most important wat building is the *bot*, or "ordination hall", which is only open to monks, and often only recognizable by the eight *sema* (boundary stones) surrounding it. Often almost identical to the *bot*, the *viharn* (assembly hall) is for the lay congregation, and usually contains the wat's principal Buddha image. Thirdly, there's the *chedi*, a stupa which was originally conceived to enshrine relics of the Buddha, but has since become a place to contain the ashes of royalty – and anyone else who can afford it.

In the **early days of Buddhism**, image-making was considered inadequate to convey the faith's abstract philosophies, but gradually images of the Buddha were created, construed chiefly as physical embodiments of his teachings rather than as portraits of the man. Of the four postures in which the Buddha is always depicted, the seated Buddha, which represents him in meditation, is the most common in Thailand. The reclining pose symbolizes the Buddha entering Nirvana at his death, while the standing and walking images both represent his descent from Tavatimsa heaven. Hindu images tend to be a lot livelier than Buddhist ones: the most commonly seen in Thailand are Vishnu, the "Preserver" who often appears in his manifestation of Rama, the epitome of ideal manhood and superhero of the epic story the Ramayana. Shiva (the Destroyer) is commonly represented by a lingam or phallic pillar; he is the father of the elephant-headed boy Ganesh.

In the 1920s, art historians compiled a classification system for Thai art and architecture which was modelled along the lines of the country's historical periods. The first really significant period is known as the **Khmer and Lopburi era** (tenth to fourteenth centuries), when the Hindu Khmers of Angkor built hundreds of imposing stone castle-temples, or *prasat*, across their newly acquired "Thai" territory – blueprints for the even more magnificent Angkor Wat. Almost every surface of these sanctuaries was adorned with intricate carvings of Hindu deities, incarnations and stories. The very finest of the remaining *prasat* are at Phimai and Phanom Rung in Thailand's northeast. During the Khmer period the former Theravada Buddhist principality of Lopburi produced a distinctive style of broad-faced, muscular Buddha statue, wearing an ornamental headband – a nod to the Khmers' ideological fusion of earthly and heavenly power.

The **Sukhothai period** (thirteenth to fifteenth centuries) is considered the acme of Thai artistic endeavour, and is particularly famous for its elegantly sinuous Buddha sculptures, instantly recognizable by their slim oval faces and slender curvaceous bodies. Sukhothai-era architects also devised the equally graceful lotus-bud chedi, a slender tower topped with a tapered finial that was to become a hallmark of the era. Examples of Sukhothai art and architecture can be seen across the country, but the finest are found in the old city of Sukhothai itself.

Though essentially Theravada Buddhists, the **Ayutthayan kings** (fourteenth to eighteenth centuries) also adopted some Hindu and Brahmin beliefs from the Khmers. Their architects retained the concentric layout of Khmer temples, elongated the prang – central tower – into a corncob-shaped tower, and adapted the Sukhothai-style chedi. Like the Lopburi images, early Ayutthayan Buddha statues wear crowns to associate kingship with Buddhahood; as the court became ever more lavish, so these figures became increasingly adorned, with earrings, armlets, anklets and coronets. When Bangkok emerged as Ayutthaya's successor, the new capital's founder was determined to revive the old city's grandeur, and the **Ratanakosin** (or Bangkok) period (eighteenth century to present) began by aping what the Ayutthayans had done. Since then, neither wat architecture nor religious sculpture has evolved much further.

THAI LANGUAGE

Most Thais who deal with tourists speak some English, but off the beaten track you'll probably need at least a few words in **Thai**. Being tonal, Thai is extremely difficult for Westerners to master. Five different tones are used – low (syllables marked `` ` ``), middle (unmarked), high (marked ´), falling (marked ^), and rising (marked ~) – by which the meaning of a single syllable can be altered in five different ways. Thus, using four of the five tones, you can make a sentence from just one syllable: mái mài mâi mãi – "New wood burns, doesn't it?"

Thai script has 44 consonants to represent 21 consonant sounds and 32 vowels to deal with 48 different vowel sounds. However, street signs in touristed areas are nearly always written in Roman script as well as Thai. Because there's no standard system of transliteration of Thai script into Roman, the Thai words and proper names in this book will not always match the versions written elsewhere. A town such as Ubon Ratchathani, for example, could come out as Ubol Rajatani, while Ayutthaya is synonymous with Ayudhia.

A few essential phrases are given below; for more help, try *Thai: A Rough Guide Phrasebook* (Rough Guides).

PRONUNCIATION

VOWELS
a as in dad.
aa is pronounced as it looks, with the vowel elongated.
ae as in there.
ai as in buy.
ao as in now.
aw as in awe.
e as in pen.
eu as in sir, but heavily nasalized.
i as in tip.

ii as in feet.
o as in knock.
oe as in hurt, but more closed.
oh as in toe.
u as in loot.
uay: "u" plus "ay" as in pay.
uu as in pool.

CONSONANTS
r as in rip; in everyday speech, it's often pronounced like "l".

kh as in keep.
ph as in put.
th as in time.
k is unaspirated and unvoiced, and closer to "g".
p is also unaspirated and unvoiced, and closer to "b".
t is also unaspirated and unvoiced, and closer to "d".

GREETINGS AND BASIC PHRASES

Whenever you speak to a stranger in Thailand, it's polite to end your sentence in *khráp* if you're a man, *khâ* if you're a woman – especially after *sawàt dii* (hello/goodbye) and *khàwp khun* (thank you). *Khráp* and *khâ* are also often used to answer "yes" to a question, though the most common way is to repeat the verb of the question (preceded by *mâi* for "no").

Hello	*sawàt dii*	What's your name?	*khun chêu arai ?*
Where are you going? (not always meant literally, but used as a general greeting)	*pai nãi?*	My name is . . .	*phõm (men)/ diichãn (women) chêu . . .*
		I come from . . .	*phõm/diichãn maa jàak . . .*
I'm out having fun /I'm travelling	*pai thîaw* (answer to pai nãi, almost untranslatable pleasantry)	I don't understand	*mâi khâo jai*
		Do you speak English?	*khun phûut phasãa angkrìt dâi mãi?*
Goodbye	*sawàt dii/la kàwn*	Do you have . . . ?	*mii . . . mãi?*
Good luck/cheers	*chôk dii*	Is . . . possible?	*. . . dâi mãi?*
Excuse me	*khãw thâwt*	Can you help me?	*chûay phõm/diichãn dâi mãi?*
Thank you	*khàwp khun*	(I) want . . .	*ao . . .*
How are you?	*sabai dii rêu ?*	(I) would like to . . .	*yàak jà . . .*
I'm fine	*sabai dii*	(I) like . . .	*châwp . . .*

GETTING AROUND

Where is the . . . ?	*. . . yùu thîi nãi?*	Where is this bus going?	*rót níi pai nãi?*
How far?	*klai thâo rai?*	When will the bus leave?	*rót jà àwk mêua rai?*
I would like to go to . . .	*yàak jà pai . . .*		

Stop here	*jàwt thîi nîi*	Ticket	*tŭa*
Here	*thîi nîi*	Hotel	*rohng raem*
Over there	*thîi nâan /thîi nôhn*	Post office	*praisanii*
Right	*khwăa*	Restaurant	*raan ahăan*
Left	*sái*	Shop	*raan*
Straight	*trong*	Market	*talàat*
Street	*thanŏn*	Hospital	*rohng pha-yaabaan*
Train station	*sathàanii rót fai*	Motorbike	*rót mohtoesai*
Bus station	*sathàanii rót meh*	Taxi	*rót táksîi*
Airport	*sanăam bin*	Boat	*reua*

ACCOMMODATION

How much is . . . ?	*. . . thâo rai/kìi bàat?*	Can I store my bag here?	*fàak krapăo wái thîi nîi dâi măi?*
How much is a room here per night?	*hâwng thîi nîi kheun lá thâo rai?*	Cheap/expensive	*thùuk/phaeng*
Do you have a cheaper room?	*mii hâwng thùuk kwàa măi?*	Air-con room	*hâwng ae*
		Bathroom/toilet	*hâwng nám*
Can I/we look at the room?	*duu hâwng dâi măi?*	Telephone	*thohrásàp*
I/We'll stay two nights	*jà yùu săwng kheun*	Fan	*phát lom*

GENERAL ADJECTIVES AND NOUNS

Bad, no good	*mâi dii*	Delicious	*aròi*	Friend	*phêuan*	Open	*pòet*
		Dirty	*sokaprok*	Fun	*sanùk*	Very	*mâak*
Big	*yài*	Food	*ahăan*	Hot (spicy)	*pèt*		
Closed	*pìt*	Foreigner	*fàràng*	Ill	*mâi sabai*		

NUMBERS

Zero	*sŭun*	Nine	*kâo*	Thirty, forty, etc	*săam sìp, sìi sìp . .*
One	*nèung*	Ten	*sìp*		
Two	*săwng*	Eleven	*sìp èt*	One hundred, two hundred, etc	*nèung rói, săwng rói . .*
Three	*săam*	Twelve, thirteen, etc	*sìp săwng, sìp săam . .*		
Four	*sìi*			One thousand	*nèung phan*
Five	*hâa*	Twenty	*yîi sìp/yiip*	Ten thousand	*nèung mèun*
Six	*hòk*	Twenty-one	*yîi sìp èt*		
Seven	*jèt*	Twenty-two, twenty-three, etc	*yîi sìp săwng, yîi sìp săam . . .*		
Eight	*pàet*				

TIME

The commonest system for telling the time, as outlined below, is actually a confusing mix of several different systems. The State Railway and government officials use the 24-hour clock (9am is *kâo naalikaa*, 10am *sìp naalikaa*, and so on), which is easier.

1–5am	*tii nèung–tii hâa*	Week	*aathít*
6–11am	*hòk mohng cháo–sìp èt mohng cháo*	Month	*deuan*
Noon	*thîang*	Year	*pii*
1pm	*bài mohng*	Today	*wan níi*
2–4pm	*bài săwng mohng–bài sìi mohng*	Tomorrow	*phrûng níi*
5–6pm	*hâa mohng yen–hòk mohng yen*	Yesterday	*mêua wan*
7–11pm	*nèung thûm–hâa thûm*	Now	*dĭaw níi*
Midnight	*thîang kheun*	Next week	*aathít nâa*
What time is it?	*kìi mohng láew?*	Morning	*cháo*
Minute	*naathii*	Afternoon	*bài*
Hour	*chûa mohng*	Evening	*yen*
Day	*waan*	Night	*kheun*

Books

The following **books** should be available in the UK, US, or more likely, in Bangkok. Publishers' details for books published in the UK and US are given in the form "UK publisher/US publisher" where they differ; if books are published in one of these countries only, this follows the publisher's name. "O/p" means out of print.

Steve van Beek, *The Arts of Thailand* (Thames and Hudson). Lavishly produced introduction to the history of Thai architecture, sculpture and painting, with fine photographs by Luca Invernizzi Tettoni.

Botan, *Letters from Thailand* (DK Books, Bangkok). Probably the best introduction to the Chinese community in Bangkok, presented in the form of letters written by a Chinese emigrant to his mother.

Vatcharin Bhumichitr, *The Taste of Thailand* (Pavilion/ Collier). The author runs a Thai restaurant in London and provides about 150 recipes adapted for Western kitchens, plus plenty of background detail.

Pierre Boulle, *The Bridge Over the River Kwai* (Mandarin/ Bantam). The World War II novel which inspired the David Lean movie and kicked off the Kanchanaburi tourist industry.

Ashley J Boyd and Collin Piprell, *Diving in Thailand* (Times Editions/ Hippocrene). A thorough guide to 84 dive sites, detailing access, visibility, and marine life for each.

Karen Connelly, *Touch the Dragon* (Black Swan/ Silkworm Books, Chiang Mai). The humorous journal of an impressionable Canadian teenager, sent on an exchange programme to Den Chai in northern Thailand for a year.

John R Davies, *A Trekkers' Guide to the Hilltribes of Northern Thailand* (Footloose Books). Bite-sized but well-informed insight into hilltribe cultures, including some practical information and a small dictionary of hilltribe languages.

Sanitsuda Ekachai, *Behind the Smile* (Thai Development Support Committee, Bangkok). Collected articles of a *Bangkok Post* journalist highlighting the effect of Thailand's economic growth on the rural poor.

Alex Garland, *The Beach* (Penguin/Riverhead). Gripping and hugely enjoyable cult thriller about a young Brit who gets involved with a group of travellers living a utopian existence on an uninhabited Thai island.

Oliver Hargreave, *Exploring Chiang Mai: City, Valley and Mountains* (Within Books, Chiang Mai). Thorough guide to the city and surrounds.

Khammaan Khonkhai, *The Teachers of Mad Dog Swamp* (Silkworm Books, Chiang Mai). The engaging story of a progressive young teacher who is posted to a remote village school.

Chart Korpjitti, *The Judgement* (Thai Modern Classics). Sobering modern-day tragedy about a good-hearted Thai villager who is ostracized by his hypocritical neighbours.

Elaine and Paul Lewis, *Peoples of the Golden Triangle* (Thames and Hudson). Hefty, exhaustive work describing every aspect of hilltribe life.

Nitaya Masavisut and Matthew Grose, *The SEA Write Anthology of Thai Short Stories and Poems* (Silkworm Books, Chiang Mai). Interesting contemporary short stories and poems by eleven Thai writers who have won Southeast Asian Writers' Awards.

Charles Nicholl, *Borderlines* (Picador/Viking Penguin). Entertaining adventures and dangerous romance in the "Golden Triangle" form the core of this slightly hackneyed traveller's tale, interwoven with stimulating cultural diversions.

Cleo Odzer, *Patpong Sisters* (Arcade Publishing). An American anthropologist's funny and touching account of her life with the bar girls of Bangkok's notorious red light district.

James O'Reilly and Larry Habegger (eds.), *Travelers' Tales: Thailand* (Travelers' Tales). This volume of collected contemporary writings from experts, social commentators, travel writers and enthusiastic tourists makes perfect background reading.

Denis Segaller, *Thai Ways and More Thai Ways* (Asia Books, Bangkok). Fascinating collections of short pieces on Thai customs.

Khamsing Srinawk, *The Politician and Other Stories* (Oxford University Press). Anthology of brilliantly satiric short stories which capture the vulnerability of peasant farmers in the modern world.

Pira Sudham, *People of Esarn* (Shire Books, Bangkok). Wry and touching real-life stories of villagers from the poverty-stricken northeast.

David Unkovich, *A Motorcycle Guide to the Golden Triangle* (Silkworm Books, Chiang Mai). Detailed pocket manual to motorbiking in the far north of Thailand, but very useful to any independently mobile traveller.

William Warren, *Jim Thompson: the Legendary American of Thailand* (Jim Thompson Thai Silk Co,

Bangkok). The engrossing biography of the ex-OSS agent, art collector and Thai silk magnate whose disappearance in Malaysia in 1967 has never been satisfactorily resolved.

David K Wyatt, *Thailand: A Short History* (Yale University Press). An excellent treatment, scholarly but highly readable, with a good eye for witty details.

BANGKOK

The headlong pace and flawed modernity of **BANGKOK** (called "Krung Thep" in Thai) match few people's visions of the capital of exotic Siam. Spiked with scores of high-rise buildings of concrete and glass, it's a vast flatness which holds a population of at least nine million, and feels even bigger. But under the shadow of the skyscrapers you'll find a heady mix of frenetic markets and hushed golden temples, of glossy cutting-edge clubs and early-morning almsgiving ceremonies. Most budget travellers head for the **Banglamphu** district, which is just a short walk from the dazzling **Grand Place** and **Wat Phra Kaeo** and the very worthwhile **National Museum**. For livelier scenes, explore the dark alleys of **Chinatown's bazaars** or head for the water: the great **Chao Phraya River** is the backbone of a network of canals and a useful way of crossing the city.

Bangkok is a relatively young capital, established in 1782 after the Burmese sacked Ayutthaya, the former capital. A temporary base was set up on the western bank of the Chao Phraya, in what is now Thonburi, before work started on the more defensible east bank. The first king of the new dynasty, Rama I, built his palace at **Ratanakosin**, within a defensive ring of two (later expanded to three) canals, and this remains the city's spiritual heart. Initially, the city was largely amphibious: only the temples and royal palaces were built on dry land, while ordinary residences floated on thick bamboo rafts on the river and canals, and even shops and warehouses were moored to the river bank. In the late nineteenth century, Rama IV and Rama V modernized their capital along European lines, building roads and constructing a new royal residence in Dusit, north of Ratanakosin.

Since World War II, and especially from the mid-1960s onwards, Bangkok has seen an explosion of modernization, leaving the city without an obvious centre. Most of the canals have been filled in, to be replaced by endless rows of concrete shophouses, sprawling over a built-up area of 330 square kilometres. The benefits of the economic boom of the 1980s and early 1990s were concentrated in Bangkok, which attracted mass migration from all over Thailand and made the capital ever more dominant: Bangkokians now own four-fifths of the nation's cars and the population is forty times that of the second city, Chiang Mai.

Arrival and information

Most travellers' first sight of the city is the International Terminal at **Don Muang Airport**, 25km to the north of the city. Once you're through immigration, you'll find 24-hr exchange booths, a TAT information desk (daily 8am–midnight), an accommodation booking desk and a left-luggage office (B40 per day). The domestic terminal at Don Muang is 500m from Terminal 2, connected by a walkway and a free shuttle bus (daily 5am–11pm; every 20min).

The easiest way of getting into the city is to take one of the three **airport buses** (5am–11pm; every 30min; B70), which pick up from outside each terminal, and, traffic permitting, take about ninety minutes to the end of the line. Route A1 runs along to the west end of Thanon Silom, via Pratunam and Thanon Rajdamri; route A2 goes to Sanam Luang, via Victory Monument, Democracy Monument, Thanon Tanao (for Thanon Khao San), Thanon Phra Sumen and Thanon Phra Athit (Banglamphu); route A3 runs along Thanon Sukhumvit to Soi Thonglor via the Eastern Bus Terminal. **Public buses** are cheaper, but slower and crowded; the bus stop is on the main highway just outside the northern end of Arrivals. Ordinary buses run frequently all day and night, with a reduced service after 10pm; the air-conditioned buses stop around 8.30pm. The **train** (55min; B5–50) to Hualamphong Station is the quickest way into town, and ideal if you want to stay in Chinatown, but services are irregular; follow the signs from Arrivals in Terminal 1. Never take an unlicensed taxi from the airport, as robberies and even murders of new arrivals are not unknown. Licensed **taxis** are operated from clearly signposted counters outside Terminal 1: you can choose either a predetermined fare in an unmetered cab (B250 plus, depending on your destination), or a metered cab, which is usually less expensive, though in both cases you'll have to pay an extra B50 in expressway tolls, plus a B50 booking fee.

If you need to **stay** near the airport, try the upmarket *Amari Airport Hotel* (☎02/566 1020; ⑨), just across the road from the international terminal, or call the *We-Train* guesthouse

---

MOVING ON FROM BANGKOK

Trains

All **trains** depart from Hualamphong Station except the twice-daily service to Kanchanaburi, and a couple of the Hua Hin trains, which leave from Bangkok Noi Station in Thonburi. Tickets for overnight trains should be booked at least a day in advance, and are best bought from Hualamphong, at the advance booking office (daily 8.30am–4pm), or ticket counters #1 and #3 (daily 5–8.30am & 4–10pm). You can also buy train tickets through travel agents and guesthouses for a booking fee of about B50.

Buses

The **Southern Bus Terminal**, on Thanon Pinklao in Thonburi, close to the junction with Thanon Nakhon Chaisi, handles services to all points south of the capital, including Hua Hin, Chumphon (for Ko Tao), Surat Thani (for Ko Samui), Phuket and Krabi (for Ko Phi Phi and Ko Lanta), as well as departures for destinations west of Bangkok, such as Nakhon Pathom and Kanchanaburi.

Services to the north and northeast – including Chiang Mai, Chiang Rai, Nong Khai, Pak Chong (for Khao Yai), as well as Ayutthaya and Sukhothai – use the new **Northern Bus Terminal**, Moh Chit 2 (*sathaanii moh chit song*), on Thanon Kamphaeng Phet 2, near Chatuchak Weekend Market in the far north of the city. Moh Chit 1 (the old northern bus terminal) is across from the market on Thanon Phaholyothin, and only serves Pattaya on the east coast.

The **Eastern Bus Terminal** (*sathaanii ekamai*), at Soi 40, Thanon Sukhumvit, serves east-coast destinations such as Pattaya, Ban Phe (for Ko Samet) and Trat (for Ko Chang). Since the opening of the BTS Skytrain both the Eastern and Northern Terminals have become quickly accessible from many parts of the city, though not from Thanon Khao San. From here you'll need at least an hour and a half (outside rush hour) to get to the Eastern Bus Terminal, and a good hour to get to the Northern or Southern terminals. Regular buses don't need to be booked in advance, but air-conditioned ones should be **reserved** ahead, either at the relevant bus station or through guesthouses.

Budget transport

Many Bangkok outfits offer **budget transport** on small and large buses to major tourist destinations such as Chiang Mai, Surat Thani, Krabi, Ko Samet and Ko Chang. In many cases this works out cheaper than the equivalent fare on a public air-con bus, and departures are usually from Khao San. The main drawbacks are the comfort and safety of the transport: many of the buses are cramped and airless, and drivers often race. Security on large buses is also a problem, so keep your luggage locked or within view. The best advice is to consult other travellers before booking any budget transport and be prepared for a not particularly comfortable ride.

Crossing the border to Cambodia

Trains leave from Hualamphong Station twice a day for Aranyaprathet, near the Poipet border crossing. From Poipet it's a two-hour pick-up ride to Sisophon (see p.117). You can obtain a visa on arrival at the border; you'll need $20 and two photos. The border officials will also ask to see a medical card to check your vaccinations. It's a scam of course, but if you don't have your card, you'll be forced to swallow unidentified pills and pay 200B for the "medication".

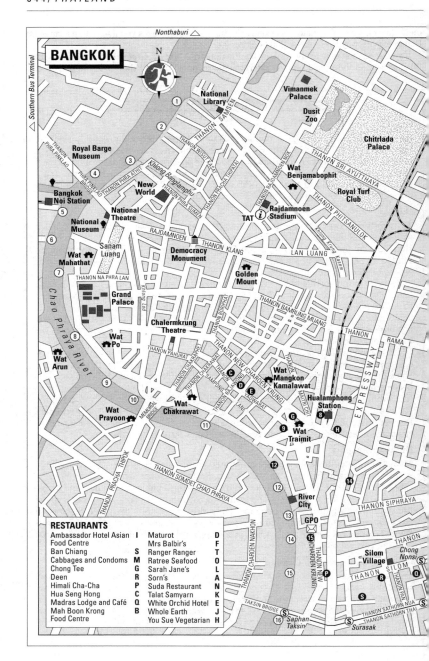

BANGKOK

Nonthaburi △

N

△ Southern Bus Terminal

National Library

Vimanmek Palace

Dusit Zoo

Chitrlada Palace

THANON SRI AYUTTHAYA

Royal Barge Museum

THANON PHRA ATHIT

PHRA PINKLAO BRIDGE

THANON WISUT KASAT

THANON SAMSEN

THANON PRACHA THIPATAI

THANON RAJDAMNOEN NOK

Wat Benjamabophit

Royal Turf Club

New World

THANON PHRA SUMEN

Khlong Banglamphu

Bangkok Noi Station

THANON PHITSANULOK

National Theatre

National Museum

RAJDAMNOEN

THANON KLANG

TAT 🛈

Rajdamnoen Stadium

Khlong Krung Kasem

Wat Mahathat

Sanam Luang

Democracy Monument

LAN LUANG

THANON NA PHRA LAN

Chao Phraya River

Grand Palace

Bunsi rd

Golden Mount

THANON BAMRUNG MUANG

THANON

RAMA I

Wat Po

Chalermkrung Theatre

THANON PAHURAT

THANON NEW (CHAROEN KRUNG)

THANON CHAKRAPHET

SAMPENG LANE

Wat Mangkon Kamalawat

EXPRESSWAY

Wat Arun

Wat Chakrawat

YAOWARAT

METRI CHIT

Hualamphong Station

Wat Prayoon

MEMORIAL BRIDGE

THANON SOMDET CHAO PHRAYA

Wat Traimit

PRACHA THIPOK

River City

GPO

THANON SIPHRAYA

THANON CHAROEN NAKHON

THANON NEW (CHAROEN KRUNG)

Silom Village

Chong Nonsi

SILOM

THANON

TAKSIN BRIDGE

Saphan Taksin

THANON SATHORN NUA

THANON SATHORN THAI

Surasak

RESTAURANTS

Ambassador Hotel Asian Food Centre	**I**	Maturot	**D**
Ban Chiang	**S**	Mrs Balbir's	**F**
Cabbages and Condoms	**M**	Ranger Ranger	**T**
Chong Tee	**G**	Ratree Seafood	**O**
Deen	**R**	Sarah Jane's	**L**
Himali Cha-Cha	**P**	Sorn's	**A**
Hua Seng Hong	**C**	Suda Restaurant	**N**
Madras Lodge and Café	**Q**	Talat Samyarn	**K**
Mah Boon Krong Food Centre	**B**	White Orchid Hotel	**E**
		Whole Earth	**J**
		You Sue Vegetarian	**H**

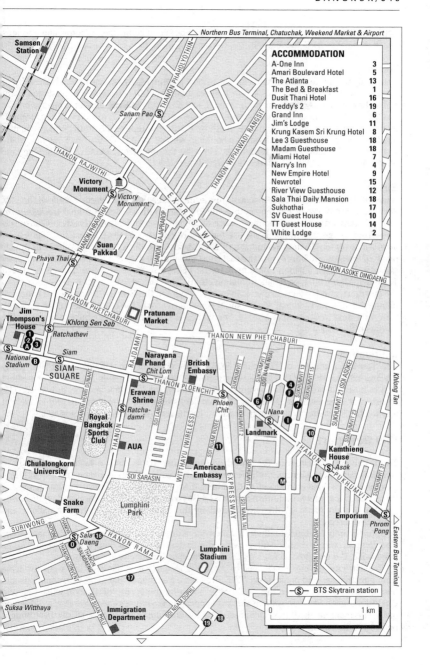

△ Northern Bus Terminal, Chatuchak, Weekend Market & Airport

ACCOMMODATION

A-One Inn	3
Amari Boulevard Hotel	5
The Atlanta	13
The Bed & Breakfast	1
Dusit Thani Hotel	16
Freddy's 2	19
Grand Inn	6
Jim's Lodge	11
Krung Kasem Sri Krung Hotel	8
Lee 3 Guesthouse	18
Madam Guesthouse	18
Miami Hotel	7
Narry's Inn	4
New Empire Hotel	9
Newrotel	15
River View Guesthouse	12
Sala Thai Daily Mansion	18
Sukhothai	17
SV Guest House	10
TT Guest House	14
White Lodge	2

Samsen Station

Sanam Pao Ⓢ

THANON RAJWITHI

THANON PHAHOLYOTHIN

THANON WIPHAWADI RANGSIT

Victory Monument

Ⓢ Victory Monument

EXPRESSWAY

THANON PIRANJAWIT

THANON RAJAPRAROP

Suan Pakkad

Phaya Thai Ⓢ

THANON ASOKE DINDAENG

THANON PHETCHABURI

Pratunam Market

Khlong Sen Seb

Jim Thompson's House

❶❷Ⓐ❸

Ⓢ Ratchathevi

THANON NEW PHETCHABURI

Ⓢ

National Stadium Ⓑ

Ⓢ Siam

SIAM SQUARE

Narayana Phand

Chit Lom

British Embassy

RAJDAMRI

SUKHUMVIT 1

SUKHUMVIT 3 (SOI NANA NUA)

SUKHUMVIT 13

SUKHUMVIT 15

SUKHUMVIT 21 (SOI ASOKE)

THANON HENRI DUNANT

THANON PLOENCHIT

Erawan Shrine

Ⓢ Ratchadamri

Phloen Chit

❹ Ⓕ

❻ ❺ ❼

Ⓢ Nana

❶

Royal Bangkok Sports Club

SOI LANGSUAN

AUA

Landmark

❿

Chulalongkorn University

WITTHAYU (WIRELESS)

SOI RUAM RUDEE

SUKHUMVIT 2

THANON SUKHUMVIT

Kamthieng House

Ⓢ Asok

SUKHUMVIT 31

❶❶

❶❸

American Embassy

SOI SARASIN

Lumphini Park

EXPRESSWAY

SOI NANA TAI

Ⓜ

Ⓝ

SUKHUMVIT 23

THANON RATCHADAPISEK

Snake Farm

SURIWONG

PATPONG

THANON CONVENT

Ⓢ Sala ❶❻ Daeng

Ⓞ

THANON SALADAENG

THANON RAMA IV

Lumphini Stadium

Emporium Ⓢ

△ Khlong Tan

△ Eastern Bus Terminal

Phrom Pong

❶❼

Suksa Witthaya

Immigration Department

SOI NGAM DUPHI

SOI SUAN PHLU

❶❾ ❶❽

-Ⓢ- BTS Skytrain station

0		1 km

△

(☎02/929 2301–10; ④), which has dorms (B140 a bed) and comfortable rooms, and operates a pick-up service from the airport.

Trains

Nearly all **trains** to Bangkok, including services from Malaysia, arrive at Hualamphong Station, which is served by bus #53 to Banglamphu (from the east side of the station), and #25 and #40 to Thanon Sukhumvit. A longtail boat also runs to Banglamphu, from the bridge just 30m to the right of the main station entrance (daily 6.15am–7pm every 20min; 15min). Station facilities include an exchange booth by Platform 8 (open daily until 5pm), cashpoint machines and a free accommodation-booking service at PC & C travel agents (daily 5am–8pm; ☎02/226 5711) in Room 100, close by the newspaper stands. The left-luggage office (daily 4am–10.30pm) charges a hefty B40 per day.

Buses

Bangkok has three main long-distance **bus** terminals, each in a different corner of the city. Services from Malaysia and the south come in at the Southern Bus Terminal (*sathaanii sai tai*), on Thanon Pinklao in Thonburi, close to the junction with Thanon Nakhon Chaisi; services from the north and northeast use the new Northern Terminal, Moh Chit 2 (*sathaanii moh chit song*), on Thanon Kamphaeng Phet 2, near Chatuchak Weekend Market in the far north of the city; and buses from the east coast pull into the Eastern Bus Terminal (*sathaanii ekamai*), at Soi 40, Thanon Sukhumvit (some Pattaya services also use the old Northern Terminal, Moh Chit 1, on Thanon Phaholyothin). The easiest way to get to the centre from the Northern and Eastern terminals is by BTS Skytrain: the Eastern Terminal is a couple of minutes' walk from Ekkamai Station and the northern arm of the Skytrain terminates in Moh Chit right next to Chatuchak Market. See pp.848-849 for details of city buses that serve the Southern Bus Terminal.

Information

The Tourism Authority of Thailand (TAT) has its city office at 4 Rajdamnoen Nok (daily 8.30am–4.30pm; ☎02/281 0422), a twenty-minute stroll from Thanon Khao San, or a short ride in air-con bus #3, and has plenty of handouts about Bangkok and the provinces. The monthly listings magazine, *Metro*, available in bookstores and hotel shops (B100) is the best way to check out the very latest on restaurants, cinemas, nightlife and the gay scene.

City transport

There can be few cities in the world where **transport** is such a headache as it is in Bangkok. Bumper-to-bumper vehicles create fumes so bad that some days the city's carbon monoxide emissions come close to the international danger level. However, the opening of the elevated train network known as the **BTS Skytrain** has radically improved public transport in certain parts of the city, including the Siam Square, Chatuchak, Silom and Sukhumvit areas.

Unfortunately for tourists, the Skytrain system does not stretch as far as Ratanakosin or Banglamphu where **boats** still provide the fastest means of hopping between sights. Otherwise, the cheapest, albeit slow form of transport in the city are still **buses**.

To get around the city, you'll need to buy the blue and yellow Bangkok bus **map**, available from guesthouses and book shops. TAT gives out a free map of Bangkok with some bus and boat routes (available from the TAT/police booth on the corner of Thanon Khao San and Chakra Bongse). Skytrain stations don't yet appear on most maps – we have marked them on ours. The most detailed accurate street map is GeoCenter's *Bangkok 1:15000*, best bought before you leave home.

Buses

There are three types of **bus** service in the city: ordinary (non-air-con), which come in various colours and sizes, cost B3 or B5, and run day and night; the more comfortable and less congested blue air-con buses (B6–16), which stop at around 8.30pm; and the small, commuter-oriented air-conditioned microbuses (B20–30). See p.825 for more detailed explanations of Thailand's bus system. A list of Bangkok's most useful bus routes is given on pp.848-849.

Boats

Bangkok was built around the Chao Phraya River and its network of canals (*khlongs*) and **boats** are still the fastest and most comfortable way of getting around the city. The **Chao Phraya Express** runs large, numbered water buses between Krung Thep Bridge in the south and Nonthaburi in the north, stopping at piers (*tha*) all along its course; boats (6am–7pm; every 15 min) do not necessarily stop at every landing, but will pull in if people want to get on or off. During rush hours (Mon–Fri 6–9am & 4–7pm), there are limited-stop services on set routes: a coloured flag sign on each pier shows which service stops there. The important central Chao Phraya Express stops are outlined in the box below and marked on our city map (see pp.844-845). The less frequent and less useful boats of **Laemthong** for the most part use the same piers, but don't stop at Banglamphu's Phra Athit pier.

Longtail boats (*reua hang yao*) run frequently along Khlong Sen Seb canal from the Phanfa pier at the Golden Mount (handy for Banglamphu, Ratanakosin and Chinatown), and head way out east, with useful stops at Thanon Phrayathai, Pratunam, Soi Chitlom, Thanon Witthayu (Wireless), and Soi Nana Neva (Soi 3), Soi Asoke (Soi 21), Soi Thonglo (Soi 55) and Soi Ekamai (Soi 63), all off Thanon Sukhumvit. This is your quickest and most interesting way of getting across town, if you can stand the stench of the canal. Another very useful longtail service travels along Khlong Krung Kasem between Hualamphong Station and Banglamphu, depositing passengers near the New World department store before terminating at a tiny pier off Thanon Phra Athit (every 20–30min; 15min; B6). It's also possible to get a longtail from Hualamphong to Phanfa pier.

Taxis

Licensed **taxi cabs** have yellow-and-black numberplates and are no more expensive than the (less reliable) unlicensed ones, which have white-and-black plates. Fares in Bangkok's

---

CENTRAL STOPS FOR THE CHAO PHRAYA EXPRESS BOAT

Numbers correspond to those on the map on pp.844-845.

1 Thewes – for National Library and guesthouses.

2 Wisut Kasat – for Thanon Samsen guesthouses.

3 Phra AthitBanglamphu – for Banglamphu guesthouses.

4 Phra Pinklao Bridge – for city buses to the Southern Bus Terminal.

5 Bangkok Noi – for trains to Kanchanaburi.

6 Wang Lang – for Siriraj Hospital.

7 Chang – for the Grand Palace.

8 Thien – for Wat Po, and the cross-river ferry to Wat Arun.

9 Ratchini – for Pak Khlong Talad market.

10 Saphan Phut (Memorial Bridge) – for Pahurat.

11 Rachavongse – for Chinatown.

12 Harbour Department.

13 Si Phraya – for River City.

14 Wat Muang Kae – for GPO.

15 Oriental – for Thanon Silom.

16 Sathorn – for Thanon Sathorn.

USEFUL BUS ROUTES

#2 (air-con): Oriental Hotel– Thanon Silom– Thanon Rajdamri (for Siam Square)–Victory Monument–Chatuchak Weekend Market–Moh Chit 1 (old Northern Bus Terminal)–Lard Phrao–Minburi.

#3 (air-con): Moh Chit 1 (old Northern Bus Terminal)–Chatuchak Weekend Market–Victory Monument–Thanon Sri Ayutthaya (for National Library and guest-houses)–Wat Benjamabophit–Rajdamnoen Nok (for TAT and boxing stadium)–Democracy Monument–Rajdamnoen Klang (for Banglamphu guesthouses)–Sanam Luang–Rajdamnoen Nai–Southern Bus Terminal.

#4 (air-con): Airport–Thanon Rajaprarop–Thanon Silom–Thonburi.

#7 (air-con): Southern Bus Terminal–Sanam Luang (for Banglamphu guesthouses)–Thanon Yaowarat (for Chinatown and Wat Traimit)–Hualamphong Station– Thanon Rama IV– Thanon Sukhumvit.

#8 (air-con): Samut Prakan (for Ancient City)–Eastern Bus Terminal– Thanon Sukhumvit–Siam Square–Grand Palace–Wat Po.

#9 (air-con): Nonthaburi–Moh Chit 1 (old Northern Bus Terminal)–Chatuchak Weekend Market–Democracy Monument–Rajdamnoen Klang (for Banglamphu guest-houses)–Thonburi.

#10 (air-con): Airport–Moh Chit 1 (old Northern Bus Terminal)–Chatuchak Weekend Market–Victory Monument–Dusit Zoo–Thanon Rajwithi (for National Library and guesthouses)–Thonburi.

#11 (air-con): Samut Prakan (for Ancient City)–Eastern Bus Terminal– Thanon Sukhumvit–Democracy Monument–Rajdamnoen Klang (for Banglamphu guesthous-es)–Phra Pinklao–Southern Bus Terminal.

#13 (air-con): Airport–Moh Chit 1 (old Northern Bus Terminal)–Chatuchak Weekend Market–Victory Monument–Thanon Rajaprarop–Thanon Sukhumvit– Eastern Bus Terminal–Sukhumvit 62.

---

metered, air-conditioned taxis start at B35, but it can be hard to get the driver to use the meter. If that's the case, establish a fare first. The noisy, three-wheeled, open-sided buggies known as **tuk-tuks** are the standard way of making shortish journeys and are cheaper and nippier, if less comfortable than taxi cabs; there have been cases of attacks on solo women in tuk-tuks late at night. Cheaper and faster still are **motorbike taxis**, which can only carry one passenger and generally do shortish local journeys. The riders wear numbered, coloured vests; crash helmets are now compulsory on all main thoroughfares in the capital.

The BTS Skytrain

In December 1999, the long-awaited **elevated railway** known as the BTS (Bangkok Transit System) Skytrain began operating in Bangkok, providing a much faster alternative to the bus. There are currently two Skytrain lines in operation, both running daily every few minutes from 6am to midnight.

The **Sukhumvit Line** runs from Mo Chit (stop N8, right next to Chatuchak Market) in the northern part of the city to the interchange, Siam Central Station (CS), at Siam Square, and then east along Sukhumvit, via Ekkamai (stop E7, a couple of minutes' walk from the Eastern Bus terminal) to Soi On Nut (stop E9).

The **Silom Line** runs from the National Stadium (stop W1) through Siam Central Station, and then south and west along Thanon Rajdamri, Silom and Sathorn to Saphan Taksin Bridge (stop S6) on the Chao Phraya River.

#15 (air-con and ordinary): Thanon Phra Athit–National Museum–Sanam Luang–Democracy Monument (for Banglamphu guesthouses)–Phanfa (for TAT office)–Siam Square– Thanon Rajdamri– Thanon Silom–Charoen Krung (New Road)–Krung Thep Bridge.

#25 (ordinary): Samut Prakan (for Ancient City)–Eastern Bus Terminal– Thanon Sukhumvit– Thanon Rama 1 (for Siam Square)–Hualamphong Station– Thanon Yaowarat (for Chinatown)–Tha Thien (for Wat Po and the Grand Palace)– Tha Chang.

#29 (air-con and ordinary): Airport–Moh Chit 1 (old Northern Bus Terminal)–Victory Monument–Siam Square–Hualamphong Station.

#38 (ordinary): Moh Chit 1 (old Northern Bus Terminal)– Thanon Rajaprarop–Eastern Bus Terminal.

#39 (ordinary): Airport–Moh Chit 1 (old Northern Bus Terminal)–Democracy Monument–Rajdamnoen Klang (for Thanon Khao San guesthouses)–Sanam Luang.

 # 40 (ordinary): Thanon Sukhumvit– Thanon Rama 1 (for Siam Square)–Hualamphong Station– Thanon Yaowarat (for Chinatown)–Thonburi.

#53 (ordinary): Hualamphong Station– Thanon Krung Kasem– Thanon Samsen and Thanon Phra Athit (for Banglamphu)–Sanam Luang (National Museum and Wat Mahathat)–Thanon Mahathat (Grand Palace and Wat Po)–Pahurat–Thanon Krung Kasem.

#56 (ordinary): Thanon Chakraphet (for Chinatown)– Thanon Mahachai–Democracy Monument–Thanon Tanao (for Thanon Khao San guesthouses)– Thanon Sri Ayutthaya (for National Library guesthouses).

#59 (ordinary): Airport–Moh Chit 1 (old Northern Bus Terminal)–Victory Monument–Phanfa–Democracy Monument (for Banglamphu)–Sanam Luang.

#124 and **#127** (ordinary): Southern Bus Terminal–Tha Pinklao (for ferry to Phra Athit and Banglamphu guesthouses).

There are two ways of buying **tickets**. All Skytrain stations have vending machines that sell single-fare tickets. Next to the ticket dispenser a map indicates which fare zones you'll cross to get to your destination. There are seven zones, with fares ranging from B10 to B40. Note that the machines only take B5 and B10 coins. After going through the gates to the platforms, hold on to your ticket as you need it to exit the station at the other end. Alternatively, if you are planning on a few journeys, want to avoid queues and save time, you can buy a stored-value card from the ticket office (B30 deposit, B300 minimum charge) which can be charged again and again. Don't count on getting your deposit back though, as this requires much form-filling and reimbursement is only by post.

Accommodation

If your time in Bangkok is limited, you should think carefully about what you want to do in the city before deciding which part of town to stay in. The capital's traffic jams are so appalling that you may find yourself not wanting to explore too far from your hotel. Unless you pay a cash deposit in advance, bookings of any kind are rarely accepted by budget guesthouses; from November to February you may have difficulty getting a room after noon.

Thanon Khao San and Banglamphu

Nearly all backpackers head straight for the legendary Thanon Khao San in Banglamphu, Bangkok's long-established travellers' ghetto and location of the least expensive accommo-

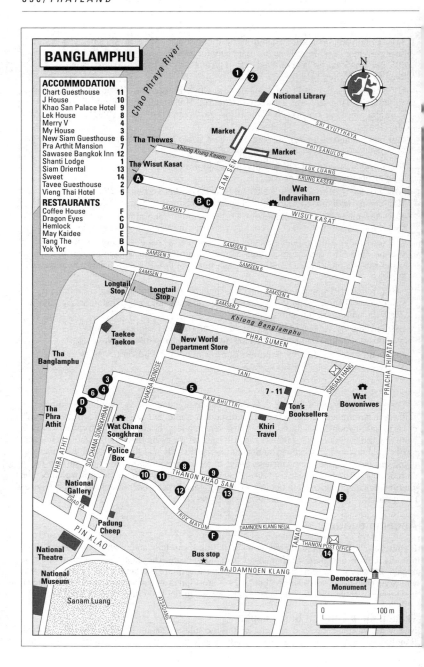

BANGLAMPHU

ACCOMMODATION
Chart Guesthouse	11
J House	10
Khao San Palace Hotel	9
Lek House	8
Merry V	4
My House	3
New Siam Guesthouse	6
Pra Arthit Mansion	7
Sawasee Bangkok Inn	12
Shanti Lodge	1
Siam Oriental	13
Sweet	14
Tavee Guesthouse	2
Vieng Thai Hotel	5

RESTAURANTS
Coffee House	F
Dragon Eyes	C
Hemlock	D
May Kaidee	E
Tang The	B
Yok Yor	A

dation in the city. Banglamphu is within easy reach of the Grand Palace and other major sights in Ratanakosin, and is served by plenty of public transport. All the guesthouses listed lie only a few minutes' walk from one of two Chao Phraya Express boat stops (see p.847), and public longtail boats also ply the three khlongs in the area (see p.847). Useful bus routes in and out of Banglamphu include air-con #11 from both the Eastern and the Southern Bus Terminals, #53 (ordinary) to Hualamphong Station and Airport Bus #A2. Bus route details are given on pp.848-849.

Chart Guesthouse, 58–60 Th Khao San (☎02/282 0171). Clean, comfortable enough hotel in the heart of backpacker land; rooms in all categories are a little cramped, but they all have windows. Most have attached bathroom and some have air-con. ②–③.

J House, 1 Trok Mayom (☎02/281 2949). Simple rooms – some with private bathroom – in a traditional wooden house in a narrow alley. ②–③.

Khao San Palace Hotel, 139 Th Khao San (☎02/282 0578). A clean and well-appointed smallish hotel: all rooms come with attached bathrooms, some have air-con and TV. ②–③.

Lek House, 125 Th Khao San (☎02/282 4927). Classic Khao San guesthouse: old-style with small, basic rooms and shared facilities. ②.

Merry V, 35 Soi Chana Songkhram (☎02/282 9267). Large, efficiently run and scrupulously clean guesthouse, with slightly cramped, basic rooms, all with shared bathrooms. ①.

My House, 37 Soi Chana Songkhram (☎02/282 9263). Popular place offering a range of basic but exceptionally clean rooms, including some with attached bathrooms, and some with air-con. ②–③.

New Siam Guesthouse, 21 Soi Chana Songkhram (☎02/282 4554). Comfortably kitted out, modern and well-maintained hotel-style rooms; all with fans and windows; some private bathrooms and air-con. ②–③.

Pra Arthit Mansion, 22 Th Phra Athit (☎02/280 0744). Mid-range place that offers very good rooms with air-con, TV, hot water and mini-bar. Friendly staff and quiet, convenient location. ④–⑤.

Sawasdee Bangkok Inn, on a tiny soi connecting Thanon Khao San with the parallel Trok Mayom (☎02/280 1251). Popular mini-hotel, with a range of comfortable rooms, though the cheapest are a bit cramped and have no bathroom. ②–③.

Shanti Lodge, Soi 16, Th Sri Ayutthaya (☎02/281 2497). Quiet, attractively furnished and comfortable rooms, some with attached bathrooms, make this the most popular place in the National Library area, 25 minutes' walk from Thanon Khao San. ②–③.

Siam Oriental, 190 Th Khao San (☎02/629 0311). Hotel-style guesthouse right in the middle of Thanon Khao San, offering smallish but good-value en-suite rooms. Some air con. ②–③.

Sweety, 49 Rajdamnoen Klang, opposite new post office (☎02/280 2191). Popular place away from the fray, but convenient for Thanon Khao San. Rooms are very small, but they all have windows, and some are en suite. ①–②.

Tavee Guesthouse, Soi 14, 83 Th Sri Ayutthaya (☎02/282 5983). Good-sized rooms in this quiet, friendly place in the National Library quarter, 25 minutes' walk from Thanon Khao San. Fan and air-con rooms available, plus B80 dorm beds. ②.

Vieng Thai Hotel, Th Ram Bhuttri (☎02/280 5392). This is the best of the options in the upper price bracket: all rooms have air con and TV, and there's a big pool here. ⑥.

Downtown: south of Thanon Rama IV

South of Thanon Rama IV, the left bank of the river contains a full cross-section of places to stay. At the eastern edge there's Soi Ngam Duphli, a ghetto of budget guesthouses with prices on Soi Saphan Khu comparing well with Banglamphu.

Dusit Thani Hotel, 946 Th Rama IV, on the corner of Thanon Silom (☎02/236 0450–9). Central, top-class hotel, famous for its restaurants. ⑨.

Freddy's 2, 27/40 Soi Sri Bamphen (☎02/286 7826). Popular, clean, well-organized, though rather noisy, guesthouse with a café and a beer garden at the rear. ①.

Lee 3 Guesthouse, 13 Soi Saphan Khu (☎02/286 3042). The best of the Lee family guesthouses (1–4), spread around this and adjoining sois. Decent and quiet, the more expensive rooms have air-con. ②.

Madam Guesthouse, 11 Soi Saphan Khu (☎02/286 9289). Cleanish, though often cramped rooms, some en suite, in a warren-like wooden house. Friendly. ①–②.

Newrotel, 1216/1 Charoen Krung (New Road), between the GPO and the *Oriental Hotel* (☎02/630 6995). Smart, clean, prettily decorated and very good value, with air-con, hot water and cable TV; breakfast included. ④.

Sala Thai Daily Mansion, 15 Soi Saphan Khu (☎02/287 1436). The pick of the area. A clean and efficiently run place at the end of this quiet alley; a roof terrace makes it even better. ②.

Sukhothai, 13/3 Th Sathorn Thai (☎02/287 0222). The most elegant of Bangkok's top hotels, its low-rise accommodation coolly furnished in silks, teak and granite. ⑨.

Downtown: Siam Square and Thanon Ploenchit

Siam Square and nearby Thanon Ploenchit are handy for all kinds of shopping, nightlife and Hualamphong Station and are easily reached from the Northern and Eastern Bus Terminals by BTS Skytrain. There's no budget accommodation here, but a few scaled-up guesthouses have sprung up in their own "ghetto" on Soi Kasemsan 1, all of them offering air-con and en-suite bathrooms.

A-One Inn, 25/13 Soi Kasemsan 1, Th Rama I (☎02/215 3029). The original upscale guesthouse and still justifiably popular, with helpful staff, satellite TV and a café. ③.

The Bed & Breakfast, 36/42 Soi Kasemsan 1, Th Rama I (☎02/215 3004). Bright, clean, family-run and friendly, though the rooms are a bit cramped. Breakfast is included. ③.

Jim's Lodge, 125/7 Soi Ruam Rudee, Th Ploenchit (☎02/255 3100–3). In a residential area, luxurious international standards at bargain prices; outdoor jacuzzi. ⑥.

White Lodge, 36/8 Soi Kasemsan 1, Th Rama I (☎02/216 8867). Well-maintained, shining white cubicles and a welcoming atmosphere. ②–③.

Chinatown and Hualamphong Station area

Staying in Chinatown (Sampeng) or in one of the sois around the conveniently close Hualamphong Station, can be noisy, but there's always plenty to look at.

Krung Kasem Sri Krung Hotel, 1860 Th Krung Kasem (☎02/225 0132). Excellent-value mid-range Chinese hotel just 50m across the *khlong* from the station. Rooms are spacious and all have air-con and TV. ③.

New Empire Hotel, 572 Th Yaowarat (☎02/234 6990). Medium-sized hotel right in the thick of the Chinatown bustle, offering average rooms with shower and air-con. ③.

River View Guesthouse, 768 Soi Panurangsri, Th Songvad (☎02/235 8501). Large en-suite rooms. Great views over the bend in the river, and handy for Chinatown, Hualamphong Station and the GPO. Head north for 400m from River City shopping centre (on the express-boat line) along Soi Wanit 2, before following signs to the guesthouse to the left. ①–④.

TT Guest House (also sometimes known as TT2), 516 Soi Sawang, off Th Maha Nakorn (☎02/236 2946). The best budget place in the station area. Clean, friendly and well run, with traveller-oriented facilities and left luggage (B7 a day). All rooms share bathrooms, and there are B100 dorm beds. To get there from the station, cross Thanon Rama IV, then walk left for 250m, right down Thanon Maha Nakorn and left again down Soi Sawang and straight on under the flyover, following the signs for TT. About 15-min walk from either the station or the Si Phraya express-boat stop. ②.

Thanon Sukhumvit

Thanon Sukhumvit is not the place to come if you're on a tight budget, but it's a reasonable area for mid-range hotels (which all accept phone bookings) and for restaurants and shops. Although it's a long way from the main sights, it's now well connected to the centre and other parts of the city by the eastern arm of BTS Skytrain.

Amari Boulevard Hotel, Soi 7 (☎02/255 2930). Medium-sized, unpretentious and friendly top-notch accommodation. Rooftop swimming pool and fitness centre. ⑨.

The Atlanta, at the far southern end of Soi 2 (☎02/252 1650). Classic colonial-era hotel with lots of character, welcoming staff, and some of the cheapest accommodation on Sukhumvit. Rooms are simple and a bit scruffy, but all are en suite and some have air-con. ③.

Grand Inn, Soi 3 (☎02/254 9021). Small, very central hotel offering reasonably priced, sizeable air-con rooms with TV and fridge. Good value. ⑤–⑥.

Miami Hotel, Soi 13 (☎02/253 5611). Very popular, long-established budget hotel built around a swimming pool. Large, clean, if slightly shabby rooms, mostly en suite. ④.

Narry's Inn, Soi 11/1 (☎02/254 9184). Cosy small hotel, offering large air-con rooms with TV, bathroom and fridge. ④.

SV Guest House, Soi 19 (☎02/253 1747). Some of the least expensive beds in the area; just about adequate rooms, most of them with shared bathrooms. Some air-con. ②.

The City

Bangkok is sprawling, chaotic and exhausting: to do it justice and to keep your sanity, you need time, boundless patience and a bus map. The place to start is **Ratanakosin**, the royal island on the east bank of the Chao Phraya and location of the **Grand Palace**, **Wat Po** and the **National Museum**. The other main areas of interest are **Chinatown** for its markets, **Thonburi** for its traditional canalside life and boat rides; and several impressive historical residences in downtown Bangkok, including **Jim Thompson's House** and **Suan Pakkad**. If you're here at a weekend, you shouldn't miss the enormous **Chatuchak Weekend Market**.

Wat Phra Kaeo and the Grand Palace

Built as the private royal temple, **Wat Phra Kaeo** is the holiest site in the country and houses the most important image, the Emerald Buddha. The temple occupies the northeast corner of the huge Grand Palace, which dates back to 1785, but is now only used for state functions, as the king resides in Chitrlada Palace in Dusit. The only entrance to the complex is on Thanon Na Phra Lan, within easy walking distance of Banglamphu, and close to the Tha Chang express-boat pier. Admission to Wat Phra Kaeo and the palace is B125 (daily 8.30am–3.30pm), and includes entry to Vimanmek Palace (see p.855). As it's Thailand's most sacred site, there's a dress code (no vests, shorts, sarongs, miniskirts, slip-on sandals or flip-flops), but you can borrow suitable garments and shoes at an office just inside the entrance.

The turnstiles in the west wall open onto the back of the bot (main sanctuary), which contains the **Emerald Buddha** and is encircled by eight boundary stones, each sheltering in a psychedelic fairy castle. The walls of the bot itself, sparkling with coloured glass, are supported by 112 golden birdmen (garudas), holding mythical serpents (nagas). Inside, a pedestal supports the tiny sixty-centimetre jadeite Emerald Buddha, a hugely sacred figure renowned for its miraculous powers. The king ceremonially changes the statue's costumes according to the season: the crown and ornaments of an Ayutthayan king for the hot season; a gilt monastic robe for the rainy season retreat; and a full-length gold shawl to wrap up in for the cool season. (The spare outfits are displayed in the Coins and Decorations Pavilion.)

North of the bot is a scale model of Angkor Wat, the Cambodian temple complex which was under Thai rule during the reign of Rama IV. At the western end of the terrace, dazzlingly gold **Phra Si Ratana Chedi** enshrines a piece of the Buddha's breastbone. Extending for over a kilometre in the arcades which run inside the wat walls, the surreal murals of the Ramayana depict every blow of this ancient Hindu story of the triumph of good over evil. The story is told in 178 panels, labelled and numbered in Thai only, starting in the middle of the northern side. Panel 109 shows the climax of the story, when Rama, the hero, kills the ten-headed demon Totsagan.

Coming out of the exit in the southwest corner of Wat Phra Kaeo, you'll pass a beautiful Chinese gate before reaching the grand residential complex and its main audience hall, **Phra Thinang Amarin Winichai**, which centres on an open-sided throne with a spired roof, floating on a boat-shaped base. On the western side of the courtyard, the delicately proportioned **Dusit Maha Prasat**, another audience hall, epitomizes traditional Thai architecture with the soaring tiers of its red, gold and green roof culminating in a gilded spire. Inside, you can still see the original throne, a masterpiece of mother-of-pearl inlaid work.

Wat Po

Bangkok's oldest temple, the seventeenth-century **Wat Po** (daily 8am–5pm; B20) is most famous for housing the enormous statue of a reclining Buddha. It lies south of the Grand Palace, close to the Tha Thien express-boat pier. In 1832, Rama turned the temple into "Thailand's first university" by decorating the walls with diagrams on subjects such as history, literature and animal husbandry. The wat is still a centre for traditional medicine, notably

Thai massage: a massage here costs B200 per hour. The elegant bot at the centre of the compound has beautiful teak doors decorated with mother-of-pearl, showing stories from the Ramayana, but it is the chapel of the Reclining Buddha, in the northwest corner of the courtyard, that draws the crowds. The image in question is a 45-metre-long gilded statue of plaster-covered brick, depicting the Buddha entering Nirvana. The beaming smile is five-metres wide, the vast black feet are beautifully inlaid with mother-of-pearl showing the 108 lakshanas or auspicious signs which distinguish the true Buddha.

Wat Mahathat

On the western side of the huge grassy area of Sanam Luang, with its main entrance on Thanon Maharat, **Wat Mahathat** (daily 9am–5pm; free) houses the Mahachulalongkorn Buddhist University and hosts a daily herbal medicine market. Situated in Section Five of the wat is its International Buddhist Meditation Centre (☎02/222 6011) where English-language meditation sessions are held on the second Saturday of the month (4–6pm). Outside, along the pavements of Maharat and surrounding roads, vendors set up stalls to sell some of the city's most reasonably priced amulets.

The National Museum

The **National Museum** (Wed–Sun 9am–4pm; B40), on Thanon Na Phra That, houses a colossal hoard of Thailand's chief artistic riches, and offers worthwhile free guided tours in English (Wed & Thurs 9.30am). Among its numerous attractions are King Ramkhamhaeng's stele (displayed in the information office), a black stone inscription from Sukhothai which dates back to the thirteenth century and is thought to be the earliest record of the Thai alphabet. The main collection boasts a fine chronological survey of the developing styles of religious sculpture in Thailand, from Dvaravati era (sixth to eleventh centuries) stone and terracotta Buddhas through to the more naturalist style of the modern Bangkok era.

Elsewhere in the museum compound, **Wang Na**, a former palace, contains a fascinating array of Thai objets d'art, including an intricately carved ivory howdah, some fine theatrical masks, and a collection of traditional musical instruments. The second holiest image in Thailand, after the Emerald Buddha, is housed in the beautifully ornate **Buddhaisawan Chapel**, the vast hall in front of the eastern entrance to the Wang Na. On the south side of the Buddhaisawan Chapel, the sumptuous Ayutthaya-style house, **Tamnak Daeng**, is furnished in the style of the early Bangkok period.

The Golden Mount

Five minutes' walk southeast of Democracy Monument stands a dirty yellow hill crowned with a gleaming gold chedi, which is grandiosely named **Golden Mount**, or Phu Khao Tong. It rises within the compound of Wat Saket, a dilapidated late eighteenth-century temple built by Rama I just outside his new city walls to serve as the capital's crematorium. The temple became the dumping ground for some sixty thousand plague victims, most of whom were left to the vultures. The Golden Mount was a late addition to the compound and dates back to the early nineteenth century. To reach the base of the mount, follow the renovated crenellations of the old city wall. Climb to the top for good views of the city. Wat Saket hosts an enormous annual temple fair in the first week of November.

Chinatown and the Golden Buddha

The sprawl of narrow alleyways, temples and shophouses packed between Charoen Krung (New Road) and the river is Bangkok's **Chinatown** (Sampeng). Easiest access is to take the Chao Phraya Express boat to Tha Rajavongse (Rajawong) at the southern end of Thanon Rajawong; or get a longtail boat from Banglamphu to Hualamphong (see p.847), then walk. Any Hualamphong-bound bus is also useful, as is #56 from Banglamphu (see box on pp.848-849).

Just west of Hualamphong Station, Wat Traimit (daily 9am–5pm; B20) boasts the world's largest solid-gold Buddha. Over 3m tall and weighing five and a half tons, the **Golden Buddha** gleams as if coated in liquid metal and is a fine example of the curvaceous grace of Sukhothai art. Cast in the thirteenth century, the image was brought to Bangkok completely encased in stucco – a common ruse to conceal valuable statues from would-be thieves. The disguise was so good that no one guessed what was underneath until 1955, when the image was accidentally knocked in the process of being moved to Wat Traimit. The discovery launched a country-wide craze for tapping away at plaster Buddhas, but Wat Traimit's is still the most valuable – it's valued, by weight alone, at $14 million. Sections of the stucco casing are now on display alongside the Golden Buddha.

Turn right outside Wat Traimit onto Thanon Yaowarat, then left onto Thanon Songsawat, to reach Sampeng Lane (also signposted as Soi Wanit 1), which stretches southeast–northwest for about 1km, and is packed full of tiny shops selling everything at bargain-basement rates. About halfway down Sampeng Lane, take a right into Soi Issaranuphap (also signed in places as Soi 16) for tiny shops selling more unusual fare, like ginseng roots, fish heads, cockroach-killer chalk and the like. Soi Issaranuphap finally ends at the Thanon Plaplachai intersection with a knot of shops specializing in paper funeral art: Chinese people buy miniature paper replicas of necessities (like houses, cars, suits and money) to be burned with the body. Wat Mangkon Kamalawat, 10m up New Road from the Soi Issaranuphap junction, is a lovely example of a much-used Mahayana Buddhist Chinese temple. It's dotted with undulating Chinese dragons, statues of bearded sages and saffron-clad Buddha images, and centres on an open-sided room of gold paintwork, red-lacquered wood, and panels inlaid with mother-of-pearl.

Wat Arun, the Royal Barge Museum and Thonburi canal tours

Almost directly across the river from Wat Po, in the Thonburi district, rises the enormous five-pranged **Wat Arun** (daily 7am–5pm; B10), the Temple of Dawn, probably Bangkok's most memorable landmark. To get there, just take a cross-river ferry from Tha Thien. The temple has been reconstructed numerous times, but the Wat Arun that you see today is a classic prang (tower) structure of Ayutthayan style, built as a representation of Mount Meru, the home of the gods in Khmer mythology. The prangs are decorated with polychromatic flowers made from bits of broken porcelain donated by local people. Statues of mythical figures support the different levels, and on the first terrace there are statues of the Buddha at the four most important stages of his life. Climbing the two tiers of the square base that supports the central prang, you get a good view of the river and beyond.

Until over twenty years ago, the king would make an annual procession down the Chao Phraya River to Wat Arun in a flotilla of 51 ornate royal barges. The three intricately lacquered and gilded vessels at the heart of the ceremony are now moored in the **Royal Barge Museum** on the north bank of Khlong Bangkok Noi (daily 9am–5pm; B30). To get there, cross the Phra Pinklao Bridge and take the first left (Soi Wat Dusitaram), which leads, along stilted walkways, to the museum. Alternatively, take a ferry to Bangkok Noi Station, then follow the tracks to the bridge over Khlong Bangkok Noi, from where the museum is signed. Either way it's about a ten-minute walk.

One of the most popular ways of seeing Wat Arun and the other Thonburi sights is to embark on a **canal tour** by chartering a longtail boat (B250 per person) from Tha Chang, in front of the Grand Palace. A less expensive alternative is to use the public longtails that run along back canals from central Bangkok-side piers, departing every ten to thirty minutes and charging B10–30 a round trip. The most accessible ones include the Khlong Bangkok Noi service from Tha Chang; the Khlong Mon service from Tha Thien; and the Khlong Bang Waek service from Tha Saphan Phut.

Vimanmek Palace and Wat Benjamabophit

Vimanmek Palace (daily 9am–4pm; compulsory free guided tours every 30min, last tour 3pm; B50, or free if you have a Grand Palace ticket, which remains valid for one month) stands at the end of Rajdamnoen Nok in the leafy royal district of Dusit. It was built for Rama V and is constructed entirely of golden teak, without a single nail; gardens and lotus ponds encircle it. On display inside is Rama V's collection of artefacts from all over the world, including bencharong ceramics, European furniture and bejewelled Thai betel-nut sets. Considered progressive in his day, Rama V introduced many newfangled ideas to Thailand: the country's first indoor bathroom is here, as is the earliest Thai typewriter. Note that the same dress rules apply here as to the Grand Palace (see p.853).

Ten minutes' walk southeast from Vimanmek along Thanon Sri Ayutthaya, **Wat Benjamabophit** (daily 7am–5pm; B10) is the last major temple to have been built in Bangkok. It's an interesting fusion of classical Thai and nineteenth-century European design, with its Carrara marble walls – hence the touristic tag "The Marble Temple" – complemented by unusual stained-glass windows. The courtyard behind the bot houses a gallery of Buddha images from all over Asia. This is also a very good place to see the early-morning ritual alms-giving ceremony. Between about 6 and 7.30am every day, Wat Benjamabophit's monks line up with their bowls on Thanon Nakhon Pathom, awaiting donations from local citizens – a sight that's well worth getting up early to witness.

Jim Thompson's House

Even now, over thirty years after his death, Jim Thompson remains Thailand's most famous farang (foreigner). A former American OSS (CIA) agent, Thompson was involved in clandestine operations in the Far East, before settling in Bangkok at the end of the war and eventually disappearing mysteriously in Malaysia's Cameron Highlands in 1967. But he is most famous for introducing Thai silk to the world and for his collection of traditional art, much of which is now displayed in his home at **Jim Thompson's House** (Mon–Sat from 9am; last tour 4.30pm; B100, under-25s B40), just off Siam Square at 6 Soi Kasemsan 2, Thanon Rama I. The grand, rambling house is a kind of Ideal Home in elegant Thai style, constructed – without nails – from six 200-year-old teak houses which Thompson shipped to Bangkok from all over the kingdom. The tasteful interior has been left as it was during Thompson's life and displays dozens of fine Southeast Asian artefacts.

The Erawan Shrine

Marking the horribly congested corner of Ploenchit and Rajdamri roads, the luridly ornate **Erawan Shrine** is essentially a huge spirit house for the neighbouring *Grand Hyatt Erawan Hotel*, but also serves any Bangkokian who feels the need to pray – or offer thanks – for good luck. The shrine is dedicated to Brahma, the Hindu creation god, and Erawan, his elephant, and is always garlanded in offertory flowers and incense. The shrine's group of classical dancers are frequently hired by devotees to perform offertory routines here too.

Suan Pakkad Palace Museum

The **Suan Pakkad Palace Museum** (daily 9am–4pm; B80), 352–4 Thanon Sri Ayutthaya, comprises a private collection of Thai artefacts displayed in six traditional wooden houses, which were transported to Bangkok from all corners of Thailand. The highlight is the renovated Lacquer Pavilion, an amalgam of two temple buildings set on stilts whose interior is beautifully decorated with Ramayana panels in gilt on black lacquer. The Ban Chiang House has a fine collection of pottery and jewellery from the tombs at the Bronze Age settlement in Ban Chiang, and elsewhere you'll find Thai and Khmer sculptures, ceramics and teak carvings.

Ban Kamthieng

Another reconstructed traditional Thai residence, **Ban Kamthieng** (Mon–Sat 9am–5pm; B100) was moved from Chiang Mai to 131 Soi Asoke (Soi 21), off Thanon Sukhumvit, and set up as an ethnological museum by the Siam Society. Unlike Suan Pakkad and Jim Thompson's

House, it is the home of a commoner, and the objects on display represent rural life in northern Thailand. Next door to Kamthieng House, in the same compound, Sangaroon House houses the folk-craft collection of Thai architect and lecturer Sangaroon Ratagasikorn, which includes baskets, fishing pots and rattan balls used for *takraw* (Thai volleyball).

Chatuchak Weekend Market

With six thousand open-air stalls to peruse, the enormous **Chatuchak Weekend Market** (Sat & Sun 7am–6pm) is Bangkok's most enjoyable shopping experience. Best buys here include antique amulets and lacquerware, unusual sarongs, northern crafts, jeans, musical instruments, jewellery, basketware and ceramics. The market also contains a controversial wildlife section and is renowned for its role in the international trade of endangered species. The market occupies a huge patch of ground near the old Northern Bus Terminal on the far northern edge of the city. The quickest way to get there from Thanon Sukhumvit, Siam Square and Thanon Silom is to take a BTS Skytrain to nearby Mo Chit Station. Buses also run from Banglamphu: take air-con buses #3 or #9 from Rajdamnoen Klang (1hr). *Nancy Chandler's Map of Bangkok*, available in shops in tourist areas, shows the location of all the specialist sections within the market. TAT have also produced a free map of Chatuchak, and they have a counter in the market building on the southwest edge of the market, across the car park. You can change money (7am–7pm) in the market building too.

Eating

The **restaurants** listed below are graded by three general price categories based on the cost of a main dish: inexpensive (under B50), moderate (B50–100) and expensive (over B100).

Banglamphu and Democracy area

Coffee House, east end of Trok Mayon, tiny stall that serves a wide selection of real coffees and other drinks. Moderate. Open 10am–midnight.

Dragon Eyes, Th Sam Sen, on the corner of Th Wisut Kasat. Small restaurant serving stylish renditions of standard Thai dishes – try the chilli-fried chicken with cashews. Open 6.30pm–midnight, closed Sun. Moderate.

Hemlock, 53 Th Phra Athit, opposite the express-boat pier. Recommended small restaurant with an interesting menu of unusual Thai dishes, including banana-flower salad, and coconut and mushroom curry. Good veggie selection too. Open Mon–Sat 5pm–2am. Moderate.

May Kaidee, across Th Tanao from the eastern end of Khao San, down the soi with the "Royal Fashion" sign. Simple, soi-side foodstall plus tables, serving the best vegetarian food in Banglamphu. Try the green curry with coconut. Shuts about 9pm. Inexpensive.

Tang Teh, corner of Samsen and Wisut Kasat roads. Unusual, quality Thai restaurant: fried catfish with cashews and chilli sauce and steamed sea bass with Chinese plum sauce are recommended; decent veggie menu too. Opens daily noon–2.30pm & 6–11pm. Moderate.

Yok Yor, Tha Wisut Kasat, Th Wisut Kasat. Riverside restaurant in two sections, which sends a boatload of diners down to Rama IX Bridge and back every evening: departs 8pm, returns 10pm. The food is nothing special, but the floodlit views of Wat Arun, Wat Phra Kaeo and others are worth the B50 cover charge. Moderate.

Chinatown

Chong Tee, 84 Soi Sukon 1, Th Traimit, between Hualamphong Station and Wat Traimit. Delicious pork satay and sweet toast. Inexpensive.

Hua Seng Hong, 371 Th Yaowarat. Not too hygienic, but the food is good. Sit outside for delicious egg noodle soup or good-value shark's fin soup; fish and seafood inside. Moderate.

Maturot, Soi Texas, Th Yaowarat. In a soi famous for its seafood stalls, the fresh, meaty prawns and *tom yam kung* stand out. Evenings only, until late. Inexpensive to moderate.

White Orchid Hotel, 409–421 Th Yaowarat. Recommended for its dim sum of prawn dumplings, spare ribs and stuffed beancurd, served 11am–2pm & 5–10pm. Fairly expensive.

You Sue Vegetarian, 75m east of Hualamphong Station at 241 Th Rama IV; directly across the road from the *Bangkok Centre Hotel* sign. Cheap and cheerful Chinese vegetarian café, where Thai curries and Chinese one-pot dishes are made with high-protein meat substitutes.

Downtown: Siam Square and Thanon Ploenchit

Mah Boon Krong Food Centre, 6th Floor of MBK shopping centre, corner of Rama I and Phrayathai roads. Dishes from all over the country served at specialist stalls. Inexpensive.

Sarah Jane's, Ground Floor, Sindhorn Tower 1, 130–132 Th Witthayu (☎02/650 9992–3). Long-standing restaurant serving excellent, simple northeastern food. Moderate.

Sorn's, 36/8 Soi Kasemsan 1, Th Rama I. A laid-back hangout serving delicious Thai and Western dishes, varied breakfasts, good coffee and draught Amarit beer. Moderate.

Talat Samyarn (Samyarn Market), set back on the west side of Th Phrayathai, near the corner of Rama IV. Good range of inexpensive foodstalls, always busy with students.

Whole Earth, 93/3 Soi Langsuan. The best veggie restaurant in Bangkok, serving interesting and varied Thai and Indian-style food (plus some dishes for carnivores). Moderate.

Downtown: south of Thanon Rama IV

Ban Chiang, 14 Th Srivieng, between Silom and Sathorn roads (☎02/236 7045). Fine Thai cuisine in an elegant wooden house. Moderate to expensive.

Deen, 761 Th Silom (although the sign indicates that it is 786), almost opposite Silom Village. Small Muslim café serving Thai and Chinese dishes, as well as Indian-style curries. Mon–Sat 11am–9.30pm. Inexpensive to moderate.

Himali Cha-Cha, 1229/11 Charoen Krung (New Road), south of GPO (☎02/235 1569). Fine north Indian restaurant founded by a character who was chef to numerous Indian ambassadors, and now run by his son; good vegetarian selection. Moderate.

Madras Lodge and Café, 31/10–11 Trok Vaithi (soi 13), opposite the *Narai Hotel*, Thanon Silom. A five-minute walk off the south side of Thanon Silom down Soi 13, this simple café offers a long menu of delicious food from the subcontinent, including south Indian dosas. Inexpensive.

Ranger Ranger, Mahamek Driving Range, south end of Soi Ngam Duphli, by the Ministry of Aviation compound. Unusual location in a golf driving range, but the restaurant itself is on platforms above a lotus pond. Specialities include *yam hua pree*, delicious banana-flower salad with dried shrimp and peanuts; some veggie dishes are available. Moderate.

Ratree Seafood, opposite Thaniya Plaza, Soi 1, Th Silom. Famous street stall, with twenty or so tables serving up all manner of fresh seafood and noodle soup. Evenings only. Inexpensive.

Sui Heng, just north of Soi 65, Charoen Krung (New Road). In a good area for stall-grazing, a legendary Chinese street vendor who has been selling one dish for over seventy years: *khao man kai*, tender boiled chicken breast, served with delicious broth and garlic rice. Evenings only, until late. Inexpensive.

Thanon Sukhumvit

Ambassador Hotel Asian Food Centre, inside the *Ambassador Hotel* complex, between sois 11 and 13. Street-level canteen with about thirty stalls selling Asian and regional Thai dishes. Food bought with coupons, sold (and refunded) from a booth at the entrance. Inexpensive.

Cabbages and Condoms, Soi 12. Run by the Planned Parenthood Association of Thailand: good, authentic Thai food in the Condom Room, relaxed scoffing of barbecued seafood in the beer garden, and free condoms available to all. Moderate.

Lemongrass, Soi 24. Scrumptious Thai nouvelle cuisine in a converted traditional house; vegetarian menu on request. Moderate to expensive.

Mrs Balbir's, Soi 11/1. Deservedly popular Indian restaurant run by TV cook Mrs Balbir. Specialities include the spicy dry chicken and lamb curries and the daily veggie buffet.

Nipa, 3rd Floor of Landmark Plaza, between sois 6 and 8. Tasteful, traditional Thai-style place with a classy menu of adventurous dishes, including spicy fish curry and several masaman and green curries; sizeable vegetarian selection. Last orders at 10.15pm. Moderate to expensive.

Seafood Market, 89 Soi 24. More a pink-neon supermarket than a restaurant: you pick your fish off the racks ("if it swims, we have it") and then choose how you want it cooked. Moderate.

Suda Restaurant, Soi 14. Unpretentious locals' hangout, open till midnight. Standard rice and noodle dishes, plus some fish: fried tuna with cashews and chilli recommended. Moderate.

Nightlife and entertainment

More than a thousand sex-related businesses operate in Bangkok: they dominate Thanon Sukhumvit's Soi Cowboy (between sois 21 and 23) and Nana Plaza (Soi 4), but most are concentrated in **Patpong**, the city's most norious zone between the eastern ends of Silom and Suriwong roads. Here, girls cajole passers-by in front of lines of go-go bars, with names like *French Kiss* and *Love Nest*, while insistent touts proffer printed menus detailing the degradations on show. If you do venture inside one, be warned that you'll be charged exorbitant prices for drinks, and will have to face a scary bouncer if you refuse to pay. In amongst the bars there's a night market which mainly sells fake designer clothes – and attracts all sorts to the strip after dark, including demure tourists of both sexes.

But Bangkok's nightlife is not all seedy and depressing: Silom 4 (ie Soi 4, Thanon Silom), just east of Patpong 2, hosts the capital's hippest **bars** and **clubs**, and nearby Silom 2 is the centre of the city's gay scene. For a more casual drink, join the Thai youth and yuppy couples who pack out the music bars concentrated around Soi Langsuan and Soi Sarasin on the north side of Lumphini Park.

Bars and clubs

In **Banglamphu** bars tend to be backpacker-orientated or style-conscious student hangouts, while many of the **downtown** music bars attract both farang and Thai drinkers.

BANGLAMPHU AND HUALAMPHONG

Banana Bar and Easy Bar, Trok Mayom/Damnoen Klang Neua. Half a dozen tiny cubbyhole bars open up on this alley every night, each with just a handful of alleyside chairs and tables, loud music on the tape player, and a trendy bartender.

Bayon, Th Khao San, second-floor air-con trance dance club. Mixed Thai and farang clientele.

Boh, Tha Thien, Th Maharat. Not quite in Banglamphu, but close to Ratanakosin. When the Chao Phraya express boats stop running around 7pm, this bar takes over the pier with its great sunset views across the river. Beer and Thai whisky with loud Thai pop music.

Buddy Beer, Th Khao San. Huge backpackers' pub with pool tables and streetside seating that makes this the perfect place for watching the action on Khao San. Closes at 2am.

Grand Guesthouse, middle of Th Khao San. Cavernous place lacking in character, but popular because it stays open 24 hours a day. Videos are shown non-stop.

Gypsy Pub, west end of Th Phra Sumen. Friendly, medium-sized bar that attracts a youthful and predominantly Thai clientele with its nightly live music (of varying quality). Closed Sun.

No Name Bar, Th Khao San. Small, low-key drinking-spot at the heart of the backpackers' ghetto. Dim lighting, a more varied than average tape selection and competitively priced beer.

DOWNTOWN

Blue's Bar, 231/16 Soi Sarasin. Long-standing, friendly haunt where creative types drink to British indie sounds.

Brown Sugar, 231/19–20 Soi Sarasin. Chic, pricey but lively bar, acknowledged as the capital's top jazz venue.

Dallas Pub, Soi 6, Siam Square. Typical dark, noisy "songs for life" hangout – buffalo skulls, American flags – but a lot of fun: singalongs to decent live bands, dancing, and friendly staff.

Deeper, Soi 4, Th Silom. Long-running hardcore dance club, done out to give an underground feel, all metal and black. Free.

DJ Station, Soi 2, Th Silom. Highly fashionable but unpretentious gay disco, packed at weekends, attracting a mix of Thais and farangs; midnight cabaret show. B100 including one drink (B200 including two drinks Fri & Sat).

Hyper, Soi 4, Th Silom. Long-standing Soi 4 people-watching haunt, with laid-back music and a fun crowd.

Icon – The Club, 90–96 Soi 4, Th Silom. Once the city's leading gay nightclub, now one of its most fashionable mixed venues (except gay night on Thurs). Slick drag show every midnight, good sounds, and a large dance floor. B100 including one drink (B200 including two drinks Fri & Sat). Closed Tues.

Old West, 231/17 Soi Sarasin. Slightly expensive, but buzzing, saloon with nightly live music from local bands; popular with Thai yuppies.

Om, Soi 4, Thanon Silom. Opposite Hyper, smallish, dark club, playing contemporary trance.

Peppermint, Patpong 1. No-nonsense chart-sound dance club, popular with travellers and Thais. Free moderate drink prices.

Saxophone, 3/8 Victory Monument (southeast corner), Thanon Phrayathai. Lively bar that hosts nightly blues, folk and rock bands and attracts a mix of Thais and farangs; reasonable prices.

Culture shows and Thai boxing

Some of the best traditional **culture shows**, featuring classical Thai music, dance and costumes, can be enjoyed at *Baan Thai* restaurant on Soi 32, Thanon Sukhumvit (performance at 9pm), and the outdoor restaurant in Silom Village on Thanon Silom (8pm). The *Vieng Thai Hotel* on Thanon Ram Bhuttri in Banglamphu (☎02/280 5392) stages classical Thai music performances in its restaurant on Mondays, Wednesdays and Fridays. **Thai boxing matches** can be very violent, but are also very entertaining (see p.831). Sessions usually feature ten bouts of five three-minute rounds and are held in the capital every night of the week at the Rajdamnoen Stadium, next to the TAT office on Rajdamnoen Nok (Mon & Wed 7pm, Thur 5pm & 9pm, Sun 2pm & 6pm), and at Lumphini Stadium on Thanon Rama IV (Tues & Fri 6pm, Sat 5pm). Tickets go on sale one hour beforehand and start at B230.

Shopping

Department stores and tourist-oriented shops in the city open at 10 or 11am and close at about 9pm. The Central department store (two branches: one on Thanon Silom, the other on Thanon Ploenchit) is probably the city's best, but Robinson's (on Sukhumvit Soi 19, Thanon Rajdamri and at the Silom/Rama IV junction) is also good. The massive Chatuchak Weekend Market is a marvellous **shopping** experience – see p.857.

The government souvenir centre, Narayana Phand, 127 Thanon Rajdamri, stocks a huge assortment of reasonably priced **handicrafts** from all over the country; Silom Village, 286/ Thanon Silom, just west of Soi Decho, has some classier stuff, but for more unusual crafts go to the pricey Rasi Sayam (Mon–Sat 9am–5.30pm), a ten-minute hike down Sukhumvit Soi 23, opposite *Le Dalat* Vietnamese restaurant. Come Thai, second floor of the Amarin Plaza on Thanon Ploenchit (no English sign, but has a carved doorframe), holds an impressive range of unusual handwoven silk and cotton fabrics, much of it made up into traditional-style clothes.

Thai **silk** is noted for its thickness and sheen; prices start at about B350 per yard for two-ply silk, B500 for four-ply. Jim Thompson's Thai Silk Company at 9 Thanon Suriwong is a good place to start looking. Inexpensive silk and tailoring shops crowd Silom, Sukhumvit and Khao San roads, but be wary of places offering ridiculous deals – when you see a dozen garments advertised for a total price of less than $200, you know the quality will be poor. If you can't decide, try the reputable Ambassador Fashions, Sukhumvit Soi 11.

Bangkok has some excellent English-language **bookstores**: Asia Books has branches on Thanon Sukhumvit between sois 15 and 19 and between sois 4 and 6; in Peninsula Plaza on Thanon Rajdamri; in Siam Discovery Centre on Thanon Rama I; and in Thaniya Plaza near Patpong. DK (Duang Kamol) Books has branches in MBK shopping centre, on the corner of Rama I and Phrayathai roads; at 244–6 Soi 2, Siam Square; and on Thanon Sukhumvit between sois 8 and 10. Also recommended is Tek Heng Books on Thanon Charoen Krung just north of the turn-off for Thanon Silom. For second-hand books, you can't beat Shaman Books, which has two branches on Thanon Khao San, Banglamphu; all books are displayed alphabetically and logged on the computer, but don't expect bargains.

Bangkok is the place to buy cut and uncut **stones** such as rubies, blue sapphires and diamonds. Recommended outlets include Johnny's Gems at 199 Thanon Fuang Nakhon, Merlin et Delauney at 1 Soi Pradit, off Thanon Suriwong, and Uthai Gems, at 28/7 Soi Ruam Rudee off Thanon Ploenchit. Be extremely wary of touts and the shops they recommend: it's common to charge a lot more than what the gem is worth based on its carat weight. Get the stone tested on the spot, and ask for a written guarantee and receipt. Unless you're an experienced gem trader, don't even consider buying gems in bulk to sell elsewhere: many a gullible traveller has invested thousands of baht on a handful of worthless multi-coloured stones.

Listings

Airlines Aeroflot, Regent House, 183 Th Rajdamri (☎02/251 0617–18); Air France, Unit 2002, 34 Vorwat Building, 849 Th Silom (☎02/635 1186–7); Air India, 12th Floor, One Pacific Place, 140 Th Sukhumvit (☎02/235 0557); Bangkok Airways, Queen Sirikit National Convention Centre, Thanon Ratchadaphisek (☎02/229 3456); Biman Bangladesh Airlines, Chongkolnee Building, 56 Th Suriwong (☎02/235 7643–4); British Airways, 14th Floor, Abdullrahim Place, opposite Lumphini Park, 990 Th Rama IV (☎02/636 1747); Canadian Airlines, Maneeya Centre, 518/5 Th Ploenchit (☎02/251 4521); Cathay Pacific, Ploenchit Tower, 898 Th Ploenchit (☎02/263 0606); China Airlines, Peninsula Plaza, 153 Th Rajdamri (☎02/253 4242–3); Finnair, 6th Floor, Vorawat Building, 849 Th Silom (☎02/635 1234); Garuda, 27th Floor, Lumphini Tower, 1168/77 Th Rama IV (☎02/285 6470–3); Gulf Air, Maneeya Building, 518/5 Th Ploenchit (☎02/254 7931–4); Kampuchea Airlines, c/o Orient Thai Airlines, 17th Floor, Jewellery Centre, 138/70 Th Nares (☎02/267 3210–2); KLM, 19th Floor, Thai Wah Tower 2, 21/133 Th Sathorn Thai (☎02/679 1100 extn 11); Lao Aviation, Silom Plaza, Th Silom (☎02/236 9822–3); Lauda Air, Wall Street Tower, 33/37 Th Suriwong (☎02/267 0873–9); Lufthansa, 18th Floor, Q-House, Soi 21, Th Sukhumvit (☎02/264 2400); Malaysia Airlines, Ploenchit Tower, 898 Th Ploenchit (☎02/263 0565–71); Myanmar Airlines, 23rd Floor, Jewelry Trade Center Building, Unit H1, 919/298 Th Silom (☎02/630 0338); Philippine Airlines, Chongkolnee Building, 56 Th Suriwong (☎02/233 2350–2); Qantas Airways, 14th Floor, Abdullrahim Place, opposite Lumphini Park, 990 Th Rama 1V (☎02/636 1747); Royal Air Cambodge, 17th Floor, Two Pacific Place Building, Room 1706, 142 Th Silom (☎02/653 2261–6); Royal Nepal, 9th Floor, Phrayathai Plaza Building, 128 Th Phrayathai (☎02/216 5691–5); Singapore Airlines Silom Centre, 2 Th Silom (☎02/236 0440); Thai International, 6th Floor, Th Lan Luang (☎02/280 0060); United Airlines, 14th floor, tower 3, Sindhorn Building, 130–132 Th Witthayu (Wireless) (☎02/253 0558); Vietnam Airlines, 7th Floor, Ploenchit Center Building, Sukhumvit Soi 2 (☎02/656 9056–8).

American Express c/o Sea Tours, 128/88–92, 8th Floor, Phrayathai Plaza, 128 Th Phyathai, Bangkok 10400 (☎02/216 5759). Amex credit card- and travellers' cheque-holders can use the office (Mon–Fri 8.30am–5.30pm, Sat 8.30am–noon) as a poste restante; mail and faxes are only held for sixty days. They will also receive faxes for Amex customers on ☎02/216 5757. To report lost cards or cheques call ☎02/273 0044 (cards, office hours), ☎02/273 5296 (travellers' cheques, office hours), or ☎02/273 0022 (after hours).

Embassies and consulates Australia, 37 Th Sathorn Thai (☎02/287 2680); Brunei, 154 Soi Ekamai, Th Sukhumvit (☎02/515766); Burma, 132 Th Sathorn Nua (☎02/233 2237); Cambodia, 185 Th Ratchadamri, Lumphini (☎02/254 6630 & 253 9851); Canada, 15th Floor, Abdulrahim Building, 990 Th Rama 4 (☎02/636 0560); China, 57/2 Th Rajdapisek (☎02/245 7033); UK, 1031 Th Witthayu (Wireless) (☎02/253 0191–9); India, 46 Soi 23, Th Sukhumvit (☎02/258 0300–6); Indonesia, 600–602 Th Phetchaburi (☎02/252 3135–40); Ireland, United Flour Mill Building, 205 Th Rajawong (☎02/223 0876); Laos, 502 Ramkhamhaeng Soi 39 (☎02/539 6667–8); Malaysia, 3–35 Th South Sathorn (☎02/679 2190–9); Nepal, 189 Soi 71, Th Sukhumvit (☎02/391 7240); Netherlands, 106 Th Witthayu (Wireless) (☎02/254 7701–5); New Zealand, 93 Th Witthayu (Wireless) (☎02/254 2530); Philippines, Soi 30/1, 760 Th Sukhumvit, (☎02/259 0139–40); Singapore, 129 Th Sathorn Thai (☎02/286 2111); US, 120–122 Th Witthayu (Wireless) (☎02/205 4000); Vietnam, 83/1 Th Witthayu (Wireless) (☎02/251 5835–8).

Emergencies For all emergencies, call the tourist police on ☎1699.

Hospitals and clinics Travellers' Medical and Vaccination Centre, 8th Floor, Alma Link Building, 25 Soi Chitlom, Th Ploenchit (☎02/655 1024–5); Bangkok Adventist Hospital, 430 Th Phitsanulok (☎02/281 1422); Bangkok Christian Hospital, 124 Th Silom (☎02/233 6981); Bangkok Nursing Home, 9 Th Convent (☎02/233 2610–9); Clinic Banglamphu, 187 Th Chakrabongse (☎02/282 7479).

Immigration Office About 1km down Soi Suan Plu, off Th Sathorn Thai (Mon–Fri 8am–noon & 1–4pm; ☎02/287 3101–10). Visa extension takes about an hour.

Internet access The most efficient cybercafés in Bangkok include: *Bangkok Internet Café* at the western end of Th Khao San, Banglamphu (24 hr); *Hello Internet Café* at 63 Th Khao San, Banglamphu (daily 10am–2am); *Cybercafé* on the 2nd floor of the Ploenchit Center, Soi 2, Th Sukhumvit (daily 10am–9.30pm); *Cyberia*, cnr of Soi 24, Th Sukhumvit (Sun–Wed 10.30am–11pm, Thurs–Sat 10.30am–midnight).

Pharmacies English-speaking staff at Boots the Chemist, on the corner of Soi 33, Th Sukhumvit (☎02/252 8056), and at most other pharmacies in the capital.

Police There's a Tourist Assistance Centre (TAC) in the TAT headquarters (☎02/281 5051). In an emergency contact the English-speaking tourist police (☎1699).

Post office The GPO is at 1160 Th Charoen Krung (aka New Road), a few hundred metres left of the exit for Wat Muang Kae express-boat stop. Poste restante can be collected Mon–Fri 8am–8pm, Sat, Sun & hols 8am–1pm; letters are kept for three months. The parcel packing service at the GPO operates Mon–Fri 8am–4.30pm, Sat 9am–noon. If staying on or near Th Khao San in Banglamphu, it's more convenient to use the poste restante service at the post office on Soi Sibsam Hang, opposite Wat Bowoniwes (Mon–Fri 8.30am–5pm, Sat 9am–noon). Letters should be addressed c/o poste restante, Banglamphubon PO, Bangkok 10203 and are kept for two months. You can also send and receive faxes there on ☎02/281 1579. If staying on Th Sukhumvit, poste restante can be sent to the Th Sukhumvit post office between sois 2 and 4, c/o Nana PO, Th Sukhumvit, Bangkok 10112.

Telephones services The least expensive places to make international calls are the public telephone offices in or near post offices (see above for location details). The largest and most convenient of these is in the compound of the GPO on Charoen Krung (aka New Road), which is open 24hr and also offers a fax service and a free collect-call service. The post offices at Hualamphong Station, on Sukhumvit and on Soi Sibsam Hang in Banglamphu also have international telephone offices attached, but these close at 8pm. Special international yellow cardphones can be found in tourist areas (cards cost from B300 and are available from tourist-oriented shops).

Travel agents Recommended travel agents include the large Diethelm Travel, in Kian Gwan Building II, 140/1 Th Witthayu (Wireless) (☎02/255 9150), which is particularly good on travel to Indochina; and the international STA Travel, 14th Floor, Wall Street Tower, 33 Th Suriwong (☎02/236 0262). Always check that the travel agent belongs to the Association of Thai Travel Agents (ATTA), and be wary of fly-by-night operators on Th Khao San. Many travel agents can also arrange visas for neighbouring countries.

THE CENTRAL PLAINS

North and west of the capital, the unwieldy urban mass of Greater Bangkok peters out into the vast, well-watered **central plains**, a region that for centuries has grown the bulk of the nation's food and been a tantalizing temptation for neighbouring power-mongers. The riverside town of **Kanchanaburi** has long attracted visitors to the notorious Bridge over the River Kwai and is now well established as a budget-travellers' hangout. Few tourists venture further west except to travel on the Death Railway, but the tiny hilltop town of **Sangkhlaburi** is worth continuing for. On the plains north of Bangkok, the historic heartland of the country, the major sites are the ruined ancient cities of **Ayutthaya**, **Lopburi** and **Sukhothai**. **Mae Sot** makes a therapeutic change from ancient history and is the departure point for the rivers and waterfalls of **Umpang**, a remote border region that's becoming increasingly popular for trekking and rafting.

Nakhon Pathom

NAKHON PATHOM, 56km west of Bangkok, is probably Thailand's oldest town and is thought to be the point at which Buddhism first entered the region, when, over two thousand years ago, it was visited by two Indian missionaries. Although the Buddha never actually came to Thailand, legend has it that he rested in Nakhon Pathom, and the original Indian-style (inverted bowl-shaped) **Phra Pathom Chedi** may have been erected to commemorate this. The chedi (stupa) was rebuilt with a Khmer prang (tower) between the eighth and twelfth centuries, which was later encased in the enormous new plunger-shaped chedi that exists today. At 120m high, it stands as tall as St Paul's Cathedral in London. The inner and outer chambers at the cardinal points each contains a tableau of the life of the Buddha. There are two museums within the chedi compound, both called Phra Pathom Museum. The newer one is clearly signposted from the bottom of the chedi's south staircase (Wed–Sun 9am–noon & 1–4pm; B30) and displays historical artefacts excavated nearby. The other collection, which is halfway up the east steps (Wed–Sun 9am–noon & 1–4pm; free), contains curios.

Arriving at Nakhon Pathom's **train station**, a five-minute walk south across the khlong and through the market will get you to the chedi. Buses from Bangkok, Damnoen Saduak and Kanchanaburi terminate 1km east of the town centre, but most circle the chedi first. The town's quietest budget **hotel** is *Mitrsampant Hotel* (☎034/242422; ②), opposite the west gate of the chedi compound at the Lang Phra/Rajdamnoen intersection. For inexpensive Thai and Chinese **food** head for either *Thai Food* or *Hasang*, just south across the khlong from the train station, on the left. Night-time food stalls set up next to the *Muang Thong Hotel*. You can change money at the exchange booth (banking hours) between the train station and the chedi. If you're just stopping off for a few hours, you can leave your luggage in the controller's office at the train station.

Damnoen Saduak floating markets

To get an idea of what shopping in Bangkok used to be like before all the canals were tarmacked over, make an early-morning trip to the floating markets of **DAMNOEN SADUAK**, 60km south of Nakhon Pathom. Vineyards and orchards here back onto a labyrinth of narrow canals, thick with paddle boats selling fresh fruit and vegetables every morning between 6 and 11am. It's a big draw for tour groups – but you can avoid the crowds if you leave before they arrive, at about 9am. The target for most groups is the main **Talat Khlong Ton Kem**, 2km west of the tiny town centre at the intersection of Khlong Damnoen Saduak and Khlong Thong Lang. The two bridges between Ton Kem and Talat Khlong Hia Kui (a little further south down Khlong Thong Lang) make good vantage points. Touts congregate at the Ton Kem pier to sell boat trips on the khlong network (hourly rates from B40 per person to B300 for the whole boat); a quieter alternative is to explore on foot by using the canalside walkways.

Damnoen Saduak is a 109-kilometre **bus** journey from Bangkok's Southern Bus Terminal; the first air-con buses leave at 6am and 6.30am, the first non-air-con bus (#78) leaves at 6.20am. Buses and songthaews from Nakhon Pathom leave every twenty minutes and take an hour, picking up passengers outside the *Nakorn Inn Hotel* on Thanon Rajvithee; the first one leaves at 6am. From Kanchanaburi, take bus #461 to Ban Phe, then change to the #78. The bus terminal is just north of Thanarat Bridge and Khlong Damnoen Saduak. Songthaews cover the 2km to Ton Kem, but a walkway follows the canal from Thanarat Bridge, or you can cross the bridge and take the road to the right (Thanon Sukhaphiban 1, but unsignposted) through the orchards. The only accommodation in town is *Little Bird Hotel*, also known as *Noknoi* (☎032/241315; ②), visible from the main road and Thanarat Bridge.

Kanchanaburi

Set in a fine landscape of limestone hills 65km northwest of Nakhon Pathom, the peaceful riverside raft houses of **KANCHANABURI** make this a popular and very pleasant travellers' hangout. Aside from the town's main sights – the Bridge over the River Kwai and several moving memorials to the town's role in World War II – there are several caves, waterfalls and historical sites to explore. A commemorative son et lumière River Kwai Bridge Festival is held here for ten days every November; it's very popular so you'll need to book accommodation and transport well ahead.

Arrival and information

Trains connect Kanchanaburi with Bangkok Noi Station via Nakhon Pathom. Coming from Hua Hin and points further south, take the train to Ban Pong and then change on to a Kanchanaburi-bound train (or bus). Kanchanaburi's train station is on Thanon Saeng Chuto, about 2km north of the town centre, so guesthouses usually send free transport. Buses run from Bangkok's Southern Bus Terminal and Nakhon Pathom. Arriving at the **bus station** at the southern edge of the town centre, it's a five-minute walk around the corner to the **TAT**

KANCHANABURI

ACCOMMODATION
Apple's Guesthouse	5
C and C Guesthouse	1
Jolly Frog Backpackers	4
Nita Raft House	7
River Guesthouse	6
Sam's House	2
Sugar Cane Guesthouse	3

RESTAURANTS
Pae Karn	C
River Kwai Park	A
Fast Food Hall	
Sabayjit	B

office (daily 8.30am–4.30pm; ☎034/511200) and a ten-minute samlor ride (B35) to the Soi Rong Heeb and Maenam Kwai guesthouses. From Bangkok the speediest mode of transport is one of the **tourist minibuses** from Thanon Khao San (2hr); they make the return trip to Khao San every afternoon. For transport between the bus station, Maenam Kwai guesthouses and the Bridge, use the **songthaews** that run along Thanon Saeng Chuto via the Kanchanaburi War Cemetery (Don Rak) and then up Thanon Maenam Kwai to the Bridge (every 15min; 15min). They start from outside the Bata shoe shop on Thanon Saeng Chuto, one block north of the bus station. The best way to see Kanchanaburi's sights and the surrounding countryside is by **bicycle** (B20–40 per day), available for rent from AS Mixed Travel, Corner Shop, and *Green Bamboo Restaurant*, all on Thanon Maenam Kwai; some places also rent out motorbikes (B150–250 per day) and jeeps.

There are several **banks** with money changing facilities on the main Thanon Saeng Chuto; outside banking hours contact either *Apple Guesthouse* on Thanon Maenam Kwai, or *Punnee Bar* on Thanon Ban Neua. The **Tourist Police** (☎034/512795) shares the TAT building on Thanon Saeng Chuto. Of the several **internet** cafés in town *CS Internet*, near the bus station, on the corner of Thanon Saeng Chuto and Thanon Lak Muang, has the cheapest email service.

The best places for organizing **trips** from Kanchanaburi are AS Mixed Travel at *Apple's Guesthouse* (see below), which does rafting and elephant-riding trips up to Three Pagodas Pass (two days; B1950); and *C and C Guesthouse* (see below), which does overnight trips to a Karen village (B1200) and more serious two-night jungle hikes (B1500).

Accommodation

The stretch of river alongside Thanon Song Kwai is noisy and over-developed, but several hundred metres upriver, the **accommodation** along Soi Rong Heeb and Thanon Maenam Kwai enjoys a much more peaceful setting.

Apple's Guesthouse, 293 Th Maenam Kwai (☎034/514958). Welcoming place, with spotless en-suite rooms, in a quiet garden location, though not on the river. There's also a restaurant, which does exceptionally delicious traditional Thai food, including mouthwatering meat and veggie massaman curries. ①–②.

C and C Guesthouse, 265/2 Th Maenam Kwai (☎034/624547). Family-run, riverside compound of basic but idiosyncratic huts, set in a garden. ①.

Jolly Frog Backpackers, Soi China, just off the southern end of Th Maenam Kwai (☎034/514579). This large and popular complex of comfortable bamboo huts ranged around a riverside garden is most backpackers' first choice, though it can be noisy at night. ①.

Nita Raft House, Th Song Kwai (☎034/514521). Kanchanaburi's most inexpensive accommodation is set away from the main Thanon Song Kwai fray, near the museum. Offers very basic floating rooms, and some more comfortable ones. ①.

River Guesthouse, Soi Rong Heeb (☎034/512491). Beautifully located set of very simple raft houses moored 30m from the riverbank. ①.

Sam's House, Th Maenam Kwai (☎034/515956). Attractively located huts, most of them floating amongst riverine lotuses; though they look rickety many are comfortably furnished. Some air-con rooms on the riverbank. ①–②.

Sugar Cane Guesthouse, 22 Soi Pakistan, off Th Maenam Kwai (☎034/624520). Peaceful, family-run place with just twelve comfortably furnished huts overlooking the river. ①–②.

The Town

In spite of the almost impenetrable terrain, Japanese military leaders chose the River Kwai basin as the route for the construction of the 415-kilometre Thailand–Burma Railway, which was to be a crucial link between Japan's newly acquired territories in Singapore and Burma. Work began in June 1942, and Kanchanaburi became a POW camp and base for construction work on the railway. About 60,000 Allied POWs and 200,000 conscripted Asian labourers worked on the line. With little else but picks and shovels, dynamite and pulleys, they shifted three million cubic metres of rock and built nine miles of bridges. By the time the line was completed, fifteen months later, it had more than earned its nickname, the Death Railway: an estimated 16,000 POWs and 100,000 Asian labourers died while working on it. The **JEATH**

War Museum (daily 8am–6pm; B30) gives the clearest introduction to this horrifying history, painting a vivid picture of the gruesome conditions suffered by the POWs who worked on the line. JEATH is an acronym of six of the countries involved in the railway: Japan, England, Australia, America, Thailand and Holland. The museum is housed in a reconstructed Allied POW hut beside the Mae Khlong River, about 200m from the TAT office or a fifteen-minute walk southwest of the bus station. Thirty-eight POWs died for each kilometre of track laid on the Death Railway, and many of them are buried in Kanchanaburi's two war cemeteries. Opposite the train station on Thanon Saeng Chuto, the **Kanchanaburi War Cemetery**, also known as Don Rak (daily 8am–4pm; free), is the bigger of the two, with 6982 POW graves laid out in straight lines amidst immaculately kept lawns.

For most people the plain steel arches of the **Bridge over the River Kwai** come as a disappointment: it's commercialized and looks nothing like as awesome as it appears in David Lean's famous film of the same name. The bridge was severely damaged by Allied bombers in 1944 and 1945, but has since been repaired and is still in use today. In fact, the best way to see the Bridge is by taking the train over it: the Bangkok–Kanchanaburi–Nam Tok train crosses it twice a day in each direction (see opposite). Otherwise, take any songthaew heading north up Thanon Saeng Chuto, hire a samlor, or cycle – it's 5km from the bus station. Whilst at the Bridge, you can't fail to see the signs for the nearby **World War II Museum** (daily 8am–6pm; B30), 30m south along Thanon Maenam Kwai, a privately owned collection that cynically uses the war to pull in curious coach parties, but nevertheless worth visiting for the sheer volume and bizarre eclecticism of its contents.

Sights across the river

Several of Kanchanaburi's other sights lie some way **across the river**, and are best reached by bike. For Chungkai Cemetery and Wat Tham Khao Poon, both on the left bank of the Kwai Noi, either take the two-minute ferry ride (for pedestrians and bikes) from the pier at the confluence of the two rivers on Thanon Song Kwai, or cycle over the bridge 1km north of the pier. After about 2km you'll reach **Chungkai Cemetery**, built on the banks of the Kwai Noi at the site of a former POW camp, and final resting place for some 1750 POWs. One kilometre on from Chungkai Cemetery, at the top of the road's only hill, sits the cave temple **Wat Tham Khao Poon** (daily 8am–6pm; donation), a labyrinthine Santa's grotto presided over by a medley of religious icons.

The impressive scenery across on the right bank of the River Kwai Noi makes for an equally worthwhile bike trip, but the cave temple on this side – Wat Tham Mangkon Thong, otherwise known as the "Floating Nun Temple" – is fairly tacky. The attraction here is a Thai nun who will get into the temple pond and float there, meditating – if tourists give her enough money to make it worth her while. Behind the pond, an enormous naga staircase leads up to a cave temple embedded in the hillside behind. To get there by bicycle or motorbike, cross the bridge over the Mae Khlong River at the bottom of Thanon Chukkadon (near the museum) and then follow the road on the other side for about 4km. Alternatively, take bus #8191 (every 30min; 20min) from Kanchanaburi bus station.

Eating

At night, the ever-reliable night market sets up alongside Thanon Saeng Chuto on the edge of the bus station.

Pae Karn, Th Song Kwai. The best of the touristy floating restaurants. Moderate.

River Kwai Park Fast Food Hall, 50m south of the Bridge on Th Maenam Kwai. The cheapest place to eat in the vicinity of the Bridge, this is a collection of curry and noodle stalls where you buy coupons for meals that cost just B25 or B30.

Sabayjit, just north of *River Kwai Hotel* on Th Saeng Chuto. Unsigned in English, but directly opposite the unmistakable *Apache Saloon*, this place boasts a large menu of sweet-and-sour soups, curries, spicy salads, wontons and noodle dishes. Moderate.

Around Kanchanaburi

The best way of getting into the Kanchanaburi countryside is to rent a motorbike, or join one of the day-trips offered by guesthouses.

Erawan National Park

Chances are that when you see a poster of a waterfall in Thailand, you'll be looking at a picture of the seven-tiered falls in **Erawan National Park** (B25 admission), 65km northwest of Kanchanaburi. Each level comprises a waterfall feeding a pool of invitingly clear water, of which the best for swimming are levels two and seven. The falls are a popular day-trippers' destination, and there's a fairly easy trail up to the seventh and final tier (2km). Most Kanchanaburi guesthouses arrange songthaew transport to and from Erawan Falls for B80 per person. Though a little less convenient, local buses also run to Erawan (#8170), leaving Kanchanaburi between 8am and 4.30pm (every 50min; 2hr) and stopping at Srinakarind market, from where it's a one-kilometre walk to the national park headquarters and the trailhead. If you miss the 4pm ride back you'll probably be there for the night. There are food stalls near the trailhead.

The Death Railway to Nam Tok

The two-hour rail journey from Kanchanaburi to Nam Tok (two trains daily in both directions) travels the POW-built Death Railway and is very scenic. Highlights include crossing the Bridge over the River Kwai, squeezing through ninety-foot solid rock cuttings at Wang Sing (Arrow Hill), and the Wang Po viaduct, where a three hundred-metre trestle bridge clings to the cliff face as it curves with the Kwai Noi.

Hellfire Pass

At Konyu, 18km beyond Nam Tok, seven separate cuttings were dug over a three-kilometre stretch. The longest and most brutal of these was Hellfire Pass, which got its name from the hellish lights of the fires the POWs used when working at night. Hellfire Pass has now been turned into a circular, ninety-minute memorial walk, which follows the old rail route through the eighteen-metre-deep cutting and on to Hin Tok creek along a course relaid with some of the original track. Most Kanchanaburi tour operators feature visits to Hellfire Pass, but you can also take any bus bound for Thong Pha Phum or Sangkhlaburi and ask to be dropped off at Hellfire Pass, which is signposted on the west side of Highway 323.

Sangkhlaburi and Three Pagodas Pass

Located right at the northernmost tip of the 73-kilometre-long Khao Laem Reservoir, the tiny hilltop town of **SANGKHLABURI**, 220km north of Kanchanaburi, is a charming if uneventful hangout. You can boat across the reservoir in search of the sunken temple Wat Sam Phrasop in canoes (B250 for four hours) rented from *P Guesthouse*, or join a sunset longtail boat trip, organized by either of the town's guesthouses (B70). The Mon village of **Bsan Waeng Ka**, across the reservoir, grew up in the late 1940s after the outbreak of civil war in Burma forced the country's ethnic minorities to flee across the border. To explore the village, rent a motorbike and cross the lake via the spider's web of a wooden bridge, said to be the longest hand-made wooden bridge in the world. Turn left to reach Wat Wiwekaram, which stands at the edge of the village, its massive, golden chedi modelled on the centrepiece of India's Bodh Gaya, the sacred site of the Buddha's enlightenment. There's a good tourist market in the covered cloisters at the chedi compound.

Three Pagodas Pass

The Burmese border is marked by the 1400-metre-high **Three Pagodas Pass** (Sam Phra Chedi Ong), 18km from Sangkhlaburi and easily reached by songthaew (every 40min; 40

min). All border trade for hundreds of kilometres has to come through here, and over the last half-century it has been fought over by several Burmese factions; it's currently controlled by the Burmese government. The pagodas themselves are tiny whitewashed stupas on the edge of Ban Sam Phra Chedi Ong, a small village comprising just a few food stalls, a wat and a tourist restaurant. Burmese land starts 50m away, at the village of Payathonzu. At the time of writing, foreign nationals were not allowed to cross the border here.

Practicalities

Minibuses depart from Kanchanaburi bus station daily, and terminate behind Sangkhlaburi's market at *Pornpailin Hotel* (seven daily from 7.30am to 4.30pm; 3hr; reserve ahead). There are also two air-con buses a day in both directions (3hr). The four daily regular buses stop on the western edge of Sangkhlaburi. The town is small enough to walk round in an hour, but there are plenty of motorbike taxis and both guesthouses rent out motorbikes (B200). There's an **exchange** counter at the bank, close to the market. Sangkhlaburi has two prettily sited waterside **guesthouses**. The friendly *Burmese Inn* (☎034/595146; ①–③), signed 800m down the hill from both bus terminals, comprises a range of huts and bungalows; a few hundred metres further down the same road (also well signposted), the efficiently run *P Guesthouse* (☎034/595061; ①–②) offers basic huts, better rooms in the main house, and a dorm.

Bang Pa-In Royal Palace

Set in manicured grounds on an island in the Chao Phraya River, the extravagant **Bang Pa-In Royal Palace** (daily 8am–4pm; B50), is an eccentric mélange of European, Thai and Chinese architectural styles, dreamt up by Rama V; many buildings, however, can only be viewed from the outside. It can easily be visited by train on a day-trip from Bangkok, as it's only 60km away and takes an hour; from Bang Pa-In station it's a two-kilometre hike to the palace, or a B30 samlor ride. The easiest route from Ayutthaya is by bus from Thanon Naresuan. Every Sunday, the Chao Phraya Express boat company (☎02/222 5330) runs a B300 river tour to Bang Pa-In and other riverside sights; it leaves Bangkok's Maharat pier at 8am, stopping also at Phra Banglamphu pier, and returns at 5.30pm.

Ayutthaya

The city of **AYUTTHAYA**, 80km north of Bangkok, was founded in 1351, and by the mid-fifteenth century had wrested power from the kingdom of Sukhothai to become the capital of an empire covering most of the area of modern-day Thailand. Ayutthaya grew into an enormous amphibious city, which by 1685 had one million people – roughly double the population of London at the same time – living largely on houseboats in a 140-kilometre network of waterways. In 1767, this 400-year-long golden age of prosperity came to an abrupt end when the Burmese captured and ravaged Ayutthaya, and the city was abandoned to the jungle.

The core of the ancient capital was a four-kilometre-wide island at the confluence of the Lopburi, Pasak and Chao Phraya rivers; a grid of broad roads now crosses the island, and the hub of the small, modern town rests on its northeast bank. The majority of Ayutthaya's ancient remains are spread out across the western half of the island in a patchwork of parkland. Distances are deceptively large, but guesthouses rent out bicycles (B50 per day).

The City

One kilometre west out of the new town centre along Thanon Chao Phrom (which becomes Thanon Naresuan), the overgrown **Wat Phra Mahathat**, on the left (daily 8.30am–4.30pm; B30), is the epitome of Ayutthaya's atmospheric decay. Across the road, the towering **Wat Ratburana** (daily 8.30am–4.30pm; B30) retains some original stucco work, including fine

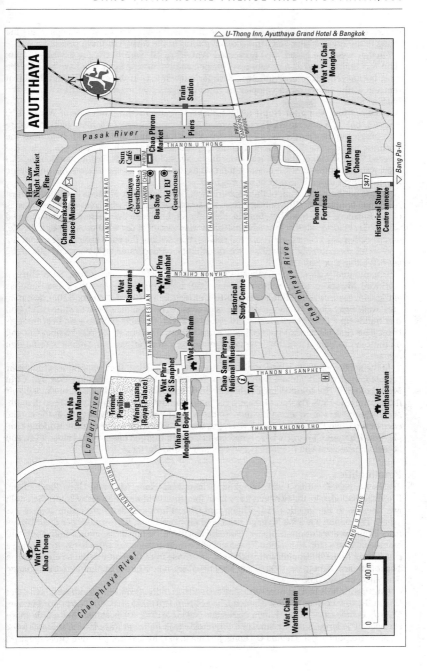

AYUTTHAYA

N

△ U-Thong Inn, Ayutthaya Grand Hotel & Bangkok

Wat Yai Chai Mongkol

Pasak River

Train Station

Chao Phrom Market

Piers

PRIDI DAMRONG BRIDGE

THANON U THONG

▷ Bang Pa-In

3477

Wat Phanan Choeng

Hua Raw Night Market Pier

Chantharakasem Palace Museum

Sun Café

THANON CHAO PHROM

Ayutthaya Guesthouse

Bus Stop

Old BJ Guesthouse

THANON PAMAPHRAO

THANON PATHON

THANON ROJANA

Phom Phet Fortress

Historical Study Centre annexe

Wat Ratburana

Wat Phra Mahathat

THANON CHIKUN

Historical Study Centre

Chao Phraya River

THANON NARESUAN

Wat Phra Ram

Wat Na Phra Mane

Lopburi River

Wat Phra Si Sanphet

Chao Sam Phraya National Museum

TAT

THANON SI SANPHET

H

Wat Phuththaisawan

Trimuk Pavilion

Wang Luang (Royal Palace)

Viharn Phra Mongkol Bopit

THANON KHLONG THO

THANON U THONG

THANON U THONG

Wat Phu Khao Thong

Chao Phraya River

400 m

0

Wat Chai Watthanaram

statues of garudas swooping down on nagas. It's possible to go down steep steps inside the prang to the crypt, where you can make out murals of the early Ayutthaya period.

Further west, the grand, well preserved **Wat Phra Si Sanphet** (daily 8.30am–4.30pm; B30) was built in 1448 as a private royal chapel, and its three grey chedis have become the most hackneyed image of Ayuthhaya. Save for a few bricks in the grass, the wat is all that remains of the huge walled complex of royal pavilions that extended north as far as the Lopburi River.

Viharn Phra Mongkol Bopit (daily 8.30am–4.30pm), on the south side of Wat Phra Si Sanphet, boasts a pristine replica of a typical Ayutthayan viharn (assembly hall), complete with characteristic chunky lotus-capped columns. It was built in 1956, with help from the Burmese to atone for their flattening of the city two centuries earlier, in order to shelter the revered Phra Mongkol Bopit. This powerfully plain statue, with its flashing mother-of-pearl eyes, was cast in the fifteenth century, then sat exposed to the elements from the time of the Burmese invasion until its new home was built.

Across on the north bank of the Lopburi River, **Wat Na Phra Mane** is Ayutthaya's most rewarding temple, as it's the only one from the town's golden age which survived the ravages of the Burmese. The main bot, built in 1503, shows the distinctive outside columns topped with lotus cups, and slits in the walls instead of windows to let the wind pass through. Inside, underneath a rich red-and-gold coffered ceiling representing the stars around the moon, sits a powerful six-metre-high Buddha in the disdainful, overdecorated style characteristic of the later Ayutthaya period.

Ten-minutes' walk south of Viharn Phra Mongkol Bopit, the large **Chao Sam Phraya National Museum** (daily 8.30am–4.30pm; B30) holds numerous Ayutthaya-era Buddhas and gold treasures. The **Historical Study Centre** (daily 8.30am–4.30pm; B100), five minutes' walk away along Thanon Rotchana, is expensive, but contains a worthwhile exhibition that builds up a broad social history of Ayutthaya with the help of videos and reconstructions. The centre's annexe (same times, same ticket), 500m south of Wat Phanan Choeng on the road to Bang Pa-In, tells the fascinating story of Ayutthaya's relations with foreign powers.

In the southeast of the island, cross the river and the rail line, then turn right at the major roundabout, and walk almost 2km to reach the ancient but still functioning **Wat Yai Chai Mongkol** (B20). Its colossal and celebrated chedi was built to mark the decisive victory over the Burmese in 1593. By the entrance, a reclining Buddha, now gleamingly restored in toothpaste white, dates from the same time. To the west of Wat Yai Chai Mongkol, at the confluence of the Chao Phraya and Pasak rivers, stands the city's oldest and liveliest working temple, **Wat Phanan Choeng**, whose nineteen-metre-high Buddha has survived since 1324, and is said to have wept when Ayutthaya was sacked by the Burmese.

Practicalities

Trains connect Ayutthaya with Bangkok, Chiang Mai, Nong Khai and Ubon Ratchathani. From the station, take the two-baht ferry from the jetty 100m west (last ferry 7pm), then walk five minutes to the junction of U Thong and Chao Phrom roads to start your tour of the island. The station has a left-luggage service (daily 5am–10pm; B5 per piece per day). **Buses** from Bangkok are slower and depart from the Northern Terminal. Bangkok, Suphanburi and other local buses stop on Thanon Naresuan, while long-distance services between Ayutthaya and Chiang Mai, Phitsanulok and Sukhothai, and those from Lopburi use the bus terminal on Thanon Rojana, 2km to the west. From Kanchanaburi, take a bus to Suphanburi, then change onto an Ayutthaya bus.

Ayutthaya's best budget **accommodation** is the friendly *Ayutthaya Guesthouse*, on a quiet lane in the town centre at 16/2 Thanon Chao Phrom (☎035/251468; ③). Next door but one, *Old BJ Guesthouse* at 16/7 Thanon Naresuan (☎035/251526; ③) is similar but a little more cramped. The large, simple rooms in the riverside teak house at *Ruenderm Hotel*, 48 Moo 2 Tambon Horattanachai, Thanon U Thong, just north of Pridi Damrong Bridge (☎035/241978;

②) are also a good option. The best place to **eat** is the Hua Raw Night Market, near the northernmost point of Thanon U Thong. The **TAT** office (daily 8.30am–4.30pm; ☎035/246076 or 246077) and **tourist police** are opposite the Chao Sam Phraya National Museum on Thanon Si Sanphet. The *Sun Café* on Thanon Chao Phrom, almost opposite the *Ayutthaya Guesthouse*, offers **internet access** (11am–7pm).

Lopburi and the Buddha's Footprint

LOPBURI, 150km due north of Bangkok, is famous for its historically important but rather unimpressive Khmer ruins, and for the large pack of tourist-baiting monkeys that swarm all over them. The ruins date from around the eleventh century, when Lopburi served for two centuries as the local capital for the extensive Khmer empire. The town was later used as a second capital both by King Narai of Ayutthaya and Rama IV of Bangkok because its remoteness from the sea made it less vulnerable to European expansionists.

The Town

The centre of Lopburi sits on an egg-shaped island between canals and the Lopburi River, with the rail line running across it from north to south. Most of the hotels and just about everything of interest lie to the west of the line, within walking distance of the train station. The main street, Thanon Vichayen, crosses the rail tracks at the town's busiest junction.

Coming out of the train station, the first thing you'll see are the sprawled grassy ruins of **Wat Phra Si Ratana Mahathat** (daily 8.30am–4.30pm; B30), where the impressive centrepiece is a laterite prang in the Khmer style of the twelfth century, decorated with finely detailed stucco work and surrounded by a ruined cloister.

The heavily fortified palace of **Phra Narai Ratchanivet** (free), a short walk northwest of Wat Mahathat, was built by King Narai in 1666 and lavishly restored in 1856. The eastern section of the compound houses the remains of elephant stables and treasure warehouses, but its best feature is the outstanding **Narai National Museum** (Wed–Sun 8.30am–4.30pm; B30), in the central courtyard. The museum exhibits span the whole of Lopburi's existence, from prehistoric pottery to modern Thai abstract painting, including a huge array of Lopburi-style Buddha images. On the south side of the museum lies the shell of the Dusit Sawan Hall, where foreign dignitaries came to present their credentials to King Narai. Inside you can still see the niche, raised 3.5m above the main floor, where the throne was set. The complex in the north part of the palace compound is known as Ban Vichayen (daily 8.30am–4.30pm; B30) and was built by Narai as a residence for foreign ambassadors, complete with a Christian chapel incongruously stuccoed with Buddhist motifs.

Northeast of the palace at the top of Thanon Na Phra Karn, **Phra Prang Sam Yod** seems to have been a Hindu temple, later converted to Buddhism under the Khmers. The three chunky prangs, made of dark laterite with some restored stucco work, are Lopburi's most photographed sight, and a favourite haunt of Lopburi's monkeys. Across the rail line at San Phra Karn, there's even a monkey's adventure playground for the benefit of tourists, beside the ruins of a huge Khmer prang.

Wat Phra Phutthabat (Temple of the Buddha's Footprint)

Seventeen kilometres southeast of Lopburi along Highway 1 stands the most important pilgrimage site in central Thailand, **Wat Phra Phutthabat**, which is believed to house a footprint made by the Buddha when he travelled through Thailand. According to legend, a hunter discovered this foot-shaped trench in 1623 and was immediatly cured of his terrible skin disease. A temple was built on the spot, and a naga staircase leads up to the gaudy mondop which houses the five-foot long footprint. During the dry season in January, February and March, a million pilgrims from all over the country flock to the lively Phrabat Fair. Any of the frequent buses to Saraburi or Bangkok from Lopburi's Sakeo roundabout will get you there in thirty minutes. The souvenir village around the temple, on the western side of Highway 1, has plenty of food stalls.

Practicalities

Lopburi is on the main **train** line from Bangkok via Ayutthaya to Chiang Mai and works best as a half-day stop-off. **Buses** from Bangkok's Northern Terminal also go via Ayutthaya. The long-distance bus terminal is on the south side of the huge Sakeo roundabout, 2km east of the town centre: a city bus or songthaew will save you the walk. **TAT**'s office (daily 8.30am–4.30pm; ☎036/422768–9) is on Thanon Wat Phra That, near Wat Phra Si Ratana Mahathat. Thanon Na Phra Karn is a minefield of seedy **hotels**, but a far better option are the rooms at the clean and friendly *Nett Hotel* at 17/1–2 Soi 2, Thanon Ratchadamnern (☎036/411738; ②).

Phitsanulok

Pleasantly located on the east bank of the River Nan, **PHITSANULOK** makes a handy base for exploring Sukhothai, but only holds a couple of significant sights itself. The fourteenth-century **Wat Phra Si Ratana Mahathat** (aka Wat Mahathat or Wat Yai) is home to the country's second most important Buddha image and stands at the northern limit of town on the east bank of the River Nan (local bus #1 or #3 from the city bus centre); because the image is so sacred, shorts and skimpy clothing are forbidden, and there's an entrance fee of B10. The holy statue itself, Phra Buddha Chinnarat, is a very lovely example of late-Sukhothai style, with a distinctive halo; it is said to have wept tears of blood during a thirteenth-century war.

Across town on Thanon Wisut Kasat, southeast of the train station, the **Sergeant Major Thawee Folklore Museum** (Tues–Sun 8.30am–4.30pm; donation) is one of the best ethnology museums in the country and includes a reconstruction of a typical village house, traditional musical instruments, and weaving paraphernalia. Take local bus #4 to the Wisut Kasat junction with Thanon Ramesuan, then walk five minutes. Cross the road from the museum and walk south about 50m for a rare chance to see Buddha images being forged at the **Buranathai Buddha Bronze-Casting Foundry**, located behind a big green metal gate at 26/43 Thanon Wisut Kasat. The foundry, which also belongs to Dr Thawi (Thawee), is open during working hours and anyone can drop in to watch the stages involved in moulding and casting a Buddha image.

Practicalities

All Bangkok–Chiang Mai **trains** stop in Phitsanulok; the train station is in the town centre. **Buses** are more frequent, but you'll need to catch local bus #1 into town from the regional bus station, 2km east on Highway 12. If you've arrived at Phitsanulok train station and want to make an immediate bus connection **to Sukhothai**, either pick up a Sukhothai-bound bus as it passes the *Topland Plaza Hotel* on Thanon Singawat (local bus #1 stops there), or you can stay on the #1 until it gets to the regional bus station on the eastern edge of town.

City buses all start from Thanon Ekathosarot, 150m south of the train station. Bus #1 heads north up to the *Topland Plaza Hotel* roundabout, then goes west across the Thanon Singawat bridge before doubling back to the regional bus station; #3 also heads west over the river via the Thanon Singawat bridge. Bus #4 goes east along Thanon Ramesuan via the junction with Thanon Wisut Kasat, before turning south along Thanon Sanambin, past the youth hostel, and on to the airport.

On tiny Thanon Sithamtraipidok, you'll find a **TAT** office (daily 8.30am–4.30pm; ☎055/252742), Able Tour and Travel (Mon–Sat 8am–5pm; ☎055/242206), which rents out motorbikes (B200 a day), and Thai Airways (☎055/258020).

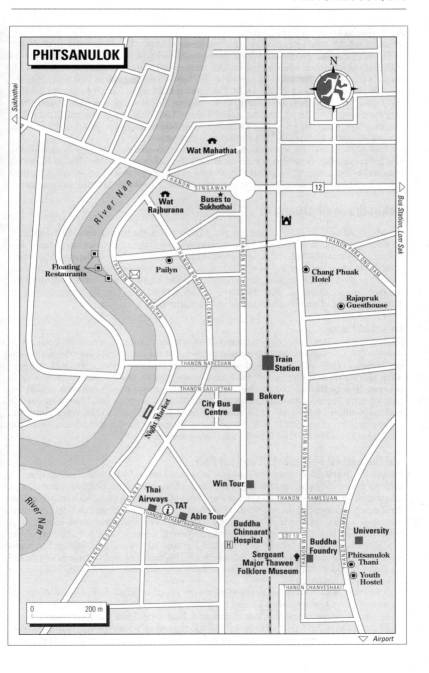

ACCOMMODATION AND EATING

Although not the most central option, the best **place to stay** is the *Phitsanulok Youth Hostel*, 38 Thanon Sanambin (☎055/242060; ②). Recently redeveloped, the wooden buildings are full of character and include a helpful information centre, with free city maps. The hostel is a 1.5-km walk from the centre: take city bus #4 to the *Phitsanulok Thani Hotel* next door; from the regional bus station take a #1, then a #4. The most central of the budget hotels are the relatively good-value *Rajapruk Guesthouse*, which adjoins *Rajapruk Hotel* at 99/9 Thanon Phra Ong Dam (☎055/258788; ②), and the similar *Chang Phuak Hotel*, next to the rail line at 63/28 Thanon Phra Ong Dam (☎055/252822; ②). The luxurious *Pailyn Hotel* at 38 Thanon Boromtrailokanat (☎055/252411; ⑥) offers nice river views.

The lively night market sets up along the east bank of the river at about 6pm: fish and mussels are a speciality. Several **restaurants** around the *Rajapruk Hotel* on Thanon Phra Ong Dam serve "flying vegetables", a strong-tasting morning-glory (*phak bung*), which is stir-fried before being tossed flamboyantly in the air towards the plate-wielding waiter or customer.

Sukhothai and around

For a brief but brilliant hundred and fifty years (1238–1376), the walled city of **SUKHOTHAI** presided as the capital of Thailand. Now an impressive assembly of elegant ruins, Muang Kao Sukhothai (Old Sukhothai), 58km northwest of Phitsanulok, has been designated a historical park. Most travellers stay in "New" Sukhothai, a modern market town 12km to the east, which has good travel links with the old city and is also better for accommodation and long-distance bus connections. For the three nights around the Loy Krathong festival in November, a son et lumière show is held at Old Sukhothai.

New Sukhothai

Straddling the River Yom, **NEW SUKHOTHAI** is a small, friendly town with good guest-houses. There are several **bus terminals** in town, but the usual dropping-off point is near the *Sukhothai Hotel* on Thanon Singhawat. You should go to the relevant terminal, however, when picking up a bus to leave town. Frequent songthaews (every 15min; 15min) shuttle between New Sukhothai and the historical park 12km away; they leave from behind the police box on Thanon Charodvithitong. Most guesthouses organize **local tours**, or you can rent **motorbikes** from *Number 4 Guesthouse* or *Somprasong* (B200) and **bicycles** from *Lotus Village* or *Ban Thai* (B50). CS Internet, on Thanon Chardovithitong opposite Wat Ratchathani (☎055/610621), offers daytime **email** service.

Old Sukhothai: Sukhothai Historical Park

Prior to the thirteenth century, the land now known as Thailand was divided into a collection of petty principalities, most of which owed their allegiance to the Khmer empire and its administrative centre Angkor (in present-day Cambodia). In 1238, two Thai generals ousted the Khmers and founded the kingdom of Sukhothai, with General Intradit as king; soon after, they took control of much of present-day Thailand. The third and most important of Sukhothai's eight kings, Intradit's youngest son Ramkhamhaeng (c.1278–1299), turned the city of Sukhothai into a vibrant spiritual and commercial centre, establishing Theravada Buddhism as the common faith and introducing a Thai alphabet. But his successors lacked his kingly qualities and, by the second half of the fourteenth century, Sukhothai had become a vassal state of Ayutthaya.

In its prime, **Old Sukhothai** boasted some forty separate temple complexes and covered an area of about seventy square kilometres. At its heart stood the walled royal city, protected by a series of moats and ramparts. **Sukhothai Historical Park** (daily 6am–6pm) covers all this area and is divided into five zones: entry to the central zone is B40, plus B10– B50 per vehicle; all other zones cost B30 each, inclusive. Songthaews from New Sukhothai (every

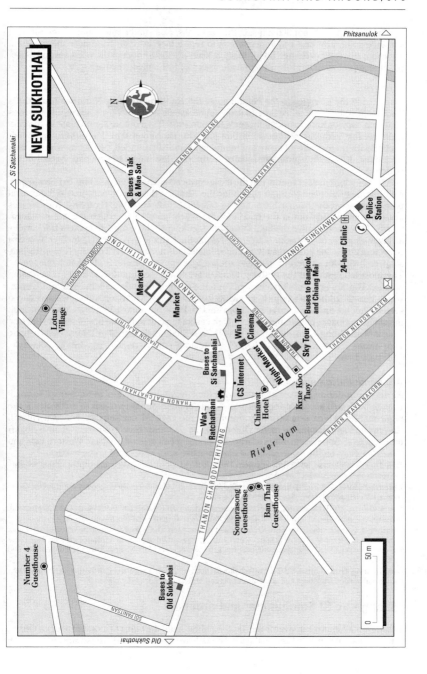

15min; 15min) stop about 300m inside the east walls, close to the museum and central zone entrance point. The best way to explore is to rent a bicycle (B20) from near the museum. There's a currency exchange booth (daily 8.30am–12.30pm) next to the museum and a couple of unappealing and rarely used guesthouses (②) just outside the park gates.

THE RUINS

Just outside the entrance to the central zone, the **Ramkhamhaeng National Museum's** (daily 9am–4pm; B30) collection of locally found artefacts is not very inspiring, but it does include a copy of King Ramkhamhaeng's famous stele. Turn left inside the gate to the central zone for Sukhothai's most important site, the enormous **Wat Mahathat** compound, packed with the remains of scores of monuments and surrounded, like a city within a city, by a moat. It was the spiritual epicentre of the city, the king's temple and symbol of his power.

A few hundred metres southwest, the triple corn-cob-shaped prangs of **Wat Sri Sawai** indicate that this was once a Hindu shrine for the Khmers; the square base inside the central prang supported the Khmer Shiva lingam (phallus). Just west, **Wat Trapang Ngoen** rises gracefully from an island in the middle of the "silver pond" after which the wat is named. North of the chedi, notice the fluid lines of the walking Buddha mounted onto a brick wall – a classic example of Sukhothai sculpture. Taking the water feature one step further, **Wat Sra Sri** commands a fine position on two connecting islands north of Wat Trapang Ngoen; its bell-shaped chedi with a tapering spire and square base shows a strong Sri Lankan influence.
The most interesting of the outlying temples are in the north and east zones. Continuing north of Wat Sra Sri, cross the city walls into the north zone and you'll find **Wat Sri Chum**, which boasts Sukhothai's largest surviving Buddha image. The enormous brick-and-stucco seated Buddha, measuring over 11m from knee to knee and almost 15m high, peers through the slit in its custom-built temple. About 1km east of the city walls, the best temple in the east zone is **Wat Chang Lom**, just off the road to New Sukhothai, near *Thai Village Hotel*. Chang Lom means "Surrounded by Elephants": the main feature here is a large, Sri Lankan-style, bell-shaped chedi encircled by a frieze of elephants.

Accommodation and eating

All **accommodation** gets packed out during the Loy Krathong festival in November, so you'll need to book well ahead during this period. One of the best places to **eat** in Sukhothai is the night market, which sets up every evening in the covered marketplace between Nikhon Kasem and Ramkhamhaeng roads. Otherwise, the *Chinawat Hotel* restaurant (daily 5–10pm) on Thanon Nikhon Kasem offers a large mid-priced menu of good Thai and Western fare, and *Krue Koo Taoy*, on the same road, does inexpensive spicy soups and green curries.

Ban Thai Guesthouse, 38 Th Pravetnakorn (☎055/610163). A comfortable budget option with a few simple rooms and some classier wooden bungalows. ①.

Chinawat Hotel, 1–3 Th Nikhon Kasem (☎055/611031). Popular place offering adequate if rather faded rooms with fan and shower, plus some with air-con. ①.

Lotus Village, 170 Th Ratchathani, but also accessible from Th Rajuthit (☎055/621484). Centrally located, stylish accommodation in a traditional Thai compound of teak houses. Some air-con. ②–③.

Number 4 Guesthouse, 140/4 Soi Khlong Mae Lumpung, off Th Charodvithitong (☎055/610165). Long-established guesthouse in a lovely spot comprising eight rattan bungalows in a tropical garden. Thai cooking courses available. A fifteen-minute walk from the town centre; follow signs from the bus stop for Old Sukhothai. ①.

Somprasong Guesthouse, 32 Th Pravetnakorn (☎055/611709). Large wooden house on the riverfont with sizeable rooms upstairs and some newer air-con bungalows. A friendly place. ①.

Muang Kao Si Satchanalai and around

Fifty-seven kilometres upriver from Old Sukhothai stand the ruins of its satellite town **Old Si Satchanalai**, also now a historical park. Buses leave from opposite the *Chinawat Hotel* sign on Thanon Charodvithitong in New Sukhothai (every 30min; 1hr); the last bus back leaves Old Si Satchanalai at 4.30pm. Most buses drop passengers near a bicycle rental place 2km from the entrance to the historical park. Bikes cost B30 for the day and are the best way of seeing the ruins. Some buses drop passengers 500m further south, in which case you should follow the track southwest over the River Yom for about 500m to another bicycle rental place, conveniently planted at the junction for the historical park (1500m northwest) and Chalieng (1km southeast).

At Muang Kao Si Satchanalai (daily 8am–4pm; B40 plus B10–50 per vehicle), begin your tour with **Wat Chang Lom**, whose centrepiece is a huge, Sri Lankan-style, bell-shaped chedi set on a square base studded with 39 life-sized elephant buttresses. Across the road, **Wat Chedi Jet Taew** has seven rows of small chedis, many of which are copies of famous Thai wats. Following the road southeast, you come to **Wat Nang Phya**, which retains its original stucco reliefs, and one wall is covered with intricate floral motifs. North of Chang Lom, the hilltop ruins of **Wat Khao Phanom Pleung** and **Wat Khao Suan Khiri** afford splendid aerial views of different quarters of the ancient city.

Before Sukhothai asserted control of the region and founded Si Satchanalai, the Khmers governed the area from **Chalieng**, just over 2km to the east of Muang Kao Si Satchanalai, and easily reached by bicycle. All that now remains of Chalieng is a single temple, **Wat Phra Si Ratana Mahathat** (daily 8am–4pm; B10), the most atmospheric of all the sights in the Sukhothai area. Left to sink into graceful disrepair, the wat now serves as grazing land. A huge standing Buddha gazes out from the nearby mondop.

The area around Si Satchanalai – known as Sawankhalok during the Ayutthayan era – commanded an international reputation as a ceramics centre from the mid-fourteenth to the end of the fifteenth century: pieces were glazed in grey-green celadon, and fish and chrysanthemum were popular motifs. More than two hundred kilns have been unearthed in the area and, 2km upstream of Muang Kao Si Satchanalai in Ban Ko Noi, the **Sawankhalok Kiln Preservation Centre** (daily 9am–noon & 1–4pm; B30) showcases an excavated production site.

Tak

The provincial capital of **TAK**, 79km west of Sukhothai, is of little interest to tourists except as a place to change buses for continuing north to Lampang and Chiang Mai, south to Ayutthaya and Bangkok, or west to Mae Sot and the Burmese border. The **bus terminal** is about 3km east of the town centre. **TAT** has an office in the town centre at 193 Thanon Taksin (8.30am–4.30pm; ☎055/514341). If you need a **hotel** in Tak, try the slightly faded *Mae Ping* at 231 Thanon Mahattai Bamroong (☎055/511807; ①).

Mae Sot

Located 100km west of Tak and only 6km from the Burmese border, **MAE SOT** boasts a rich ethnic mix (Burmese, Karen, Hmong and Thai) and a thriving trade in gems and teak. There's little to see in the small town apart from several glittering Burmese-style temples, but it's a relaxed place to hang out before heading down to Umpang, which has gained a reputation as a base for trekking adventures (see p.878). You should change money in one of the exchange booths on Mae Sot's Thanon Prasat Vithi (Mon–Fri 8.30am–3.30pm) as there are currently no exchange facilities in Umpang.

Frequent songthaews ferry Thai traders and a small trickle of tourists the 6km from Mae Sot to the Burmese border at **Rim Moei**, where a large market for Burmese goods has grown up beside the banks of the River Moei. It's a bit tacky, but not a bad place to pick up Burmese handicrafts. At the time of writing, access to the Burmese village of Myawaddy on the opposite bank of the River Moei is only open to farangs for a day's shopping (US$10); visitors are allowed no further into Burma. When coming back through Thai customs you can, if necessary, get a new one-month Thai visa on the spot.

If you have the time, you should try and organize your **trek** through the Umpang region with the local guides who live in Umpang itself (see below), but you can also use a Mae Sot tour operator. SP Tour (☎055/531409) is based at the Mae Sot Travel Centre on the north-ern outskirts of town at 14/21 Asia Highway (Highway 105). It offers rafting, elephant-riding, jungle-walking and bird-watching in the Umpang and Mae Sot region, with nights in Mon or Karen villages (B4500 for three days). Mae Sot Conservation Tour (☎055/532818), next to Pim Hut at 415/17 Thanon Tang Kim Chang, concentrates on the Umpang and Tee Lor Su route, features similar activities and costs about the same. If you're staying at Mae Sot Guesthouse, you can arrange your own trek with the manager, Khun Gree, and, in theory, Number 4 Guesthouse also organizes treks (three to seven days, $80–400), but it can be hard to elicit information from the staff there.

Practicalities

There are frequent direct government minibuses from Tak (1hr 30min) to Mae Sot and some from Sukhothai (2hr 30min), plus several daily long-distance buses to and from Chiang Mai, Bangkok, Mae Sai and Phitsanulok. Songthaews connect Mae Sot with the border towns of Mae Ramat (every 30min; 45min) and Mae Sariang (7 daily; 5hr), and with Umpang (hourly; 3hr 30min–5hr).

The most popular place to stay in the centre of town, the *Bai Fern Guesthouse* (☎055/533343; ④), on 660/2 Thanon Indharakiri, offers simple, clean rooms as well as good Thai and Burmese dishes. Another popular option, though a little haphazard, is *Number 4 Guesthouse* (☎055/544976; ①), at the western end of Thanon Indharakiri, about fifteen min-utes' walk from the bus terminal, offering mattresses on the floor of a nice old teak house. At the other, eastern, end of the road, *Mae Sot Guesthouse* (☎055/532745; ①–②), sometimes referred to as "Number 2", is about ten minutes' walk from the bus terminal and offers both very basic makeshift rooms as well as more comfortable air-con ones. *First Hotel* (☎055/531123; ②–③), just north of Thanon Indharakiri, where Tak-bound songthaews leave from, has better rooms, as does *D.K. Hotel* (☎055/531699; ③) at 298 Thanon Indharakiri. Thanon Prasat Vithi is well stocked with **noodle shops** and night-market stalls, and *Pim Hut* on Thanon Tang Kim Chang offers everything from green curries to pizzas. **Internet** access is available at *Cyberspace*, on Thanon Prasat Vithi, near the police box.

Umpang

Even if you don't fancy joining a trek, it's worth considering making the spectacular trip 160km or so south from Mae Sot to the village of **UMPANG**, both for the stunning mountain scenery and for the buzz of being in such an isolated part of Thailand. Songthaews leave Mae Sot from a spot one block south of Thanon Prasat Vithi (hourly 7.30am–5.30pm). The drive can take anything from three and a half to five hours and the road – dubbed the "Sky Highway" – careers round the edges of endless steep-sided valleys. Umpang is effectively a dead end, so you need to return to Mae Sot to continue anywhere else; songthaews leave hourly throughout the day.

Surrounded by mountains and sited at the confluence of the Mae Khlong and Umpang rivers, Umpang itself is small and sleepy. It has no signed roads, but the two main points of orientation are the river at the far southern end of the village, and the wat – about 500m north of the river – that marks its centre. Most of the shops and restaurants are clustered along the two roads that run parallel to the wat. There's a knot of guesthouses by the river at the south-ern end of the village.

Trekking from Umpang

The focus of all Umpang treks is the three-tiered **Tee Lor Su Waterfall**, which flows all year round and is said to be the sixth highest in the world. During the dry season you can get halfway to the falls by road, but at other times they're reached by a combination of rafting and walking. A variety of other attractions in the area combine to make Umpang treks some of the most genuine organized wilderness experiences in Thailand; there is more emphasis on walking than in the more popular treks around Chiang Mai and Chiang Rai. The three main **trek leaders** operating out of Umpang are Mr Tee, at Trekker Hill (✆055/561090), 700m northwest of the wat; Cocoh, based at BL Tour at *Umpang Guesthouse* (✆055/561021); and Mr Boonchuay, who operates from his home, 500m west of the wat (✆055/561020). They all charge B2500 to 4000 per person (minimum two people) for four-day treks, which include rafting, camping at hot springs, a jungle trek to Tee Lor Su waterfall, an elephant ride and a night in a Karen village. Guides should provide tents, mosquito nets and sleeping bags, plus food and drinking water, though trekkers may be asked to help carry some of the gear. The main drawback with arranging things from Umpang is that you may have to wait for a couple of days for the trek leader to return from his last trip; the best time to contact them is after 6pm. You can usually stay at the trek leader's home for about B50 a night before and after your trek.

Accommodation and eating

Most of the **accommodation** in Umpang is geared either towards groups of trekkers or independent travellers, so many places charge per person rather than per room; the prices listed here are for two people sharing, so expect to pay half if you're on your own. *Umpang Guesthouse* (✆055/561021; ①), also signed as *BL Tour* and *Veera Tourism*, on the north bank of the river at the southern edge of the village, has inexpensive, decent enough en-suite rooms in a large timber house. Across the road, *Boonyaporn Garden Huts* (no English sign, but recognizable from its Carlsberg sign; (✆055/561093; ②) has simple rattan huts in a garden, plus some more comfortable en-suite wooden huts. Across on the south bank of the river, the large, air-conditioned chalets of *Umpang Hill Resort* (✆055/561063; ③) are beautifully set in a flower garden, with fine mountain views. The misleadingly named *Phu Doi Campsite*, about 500m northwest of the wat (✆055/561049; ②), actually comprises a nice set of sparkling en-suite rooms in two wooden houses overlooking a pond. For **meals** try the deservedly popular *Phu Doi*, on the road just north of the temple (recognizable by its big thatched gateway), which has a long English-language menu of noodles, curries and rice dishes, or *Tu Ka Su*, 300m south of the river, which offers a similarly traveller-friendly menu and is usually open till midnight.

THE NORTH

Beyond the northern plains, the climate becomes more temperate, nurturing the fertile land which gave the old kingdom of the **north** the name of **Lanna**, "the land of a million rice fields". Until the beginning of the last century, Lanna was a largely independent region, with its own styles of art and architecture. Its capital, the cool, pleasant city of **Chiang Mai**, is now a major travellers' centre and the most popular base from which to organize treks to nearby hilltribe villages. Another great way of exploring the scenic countryside up here is to rent a motorbike and make the six hundred-kilometre loop over the forested western mountains into **Mae Hong Son** and back. Heading north from Chiang Mai brings you to the increasingly upmarket town of **Chiang Rai**, and then on to the Burmese border settlements of Mae Sai and Sop Ruak – better known as the apex of the "Golden Triangle" (see p.897). You can't enter Burma here for longer than a day-trip, but **Chiang Khong**, on the Mekong River, is an important crossing point to Laos, with same-day but expensive visas available.

Hilltribe treks

Trekking in the mountains of northern Thailand – which is what brings most travellers here – differs from trekking in most other parts of the world, in that the emphasis is not primari-

THE HILLTRIBES

Within the small geographical area of northern Thailand there are at least ten different **hilltribes**, many of them divided into distinct subgroups. Originating in various parts of China and Southeast Asia, the tribes are often termed Fourth World people, in that they are migrants who continue to migrate without regard for established national boundaries. Most arrived in Thailand in the twentieth century, and many have tribal relatives in other parts of Southeast Asia – in Vietnam, for example.

The tribes are mostly pre-literate societies, with sophisticated systems of customs, laws and beliefs. They are predominantly animists, believing all natural objects to be inhabited by spirits, which must be propitiated to prevent harm to the family or village. The base of their economy is slash-and-burn farming, a crude form of shifting cultivation, but many villages have also taken up the lucrative large-scale production of opium, which earns around B500 per kilo at source – much to the horror of the Thai government, who have offered big incentives to change over to more legal cash crops. To learn more about the tribes, visit the library at the Hilltribe Research Institute (see p.883) and its separately located Museum, both in Chiang Mai.

Karen

The **Karen** form by far the largest hilltribe group in Thailand (pop. 350,000), and began to arrive here from Burma and China in the seventeenth century. Most of them live in a broad tract of land west of Chiang Mai, which stretches along the border from Mae Hong Son province all the way down to Kanchanaburi. Karen do not live in extended family groups, so their wooden stilt houses are small. Unmarried Karen women wear loose white or undyed V-necked shift dresses, often decorated with grass seeds at the seams; some subgroups decorate them more elaborately, Sgaw girls with a woven red or pink band above the waist, and Pwo girls with woven red patterns at the hem. Married women wear blouses and skirts in bold red or blue. Men wear blue, baggy trousers, also with red or blue shirts.

Hmong

The **Hmong** (or Meo; pop. 111,000) originated in central China or Mongolia and are now found widely in northern Thailand; they are still the most widespread minority group in south China. There are two subgroups: the Blue Hmong, who live to the west of Chiang Mai; and the White Hmong, who are found to the east. A separate group of White Hmong live in refugee camps along the border with Laos. Hmong villages are usually built at high altitudes, and most Hmong live in extended families in traditional houses with dirt floors and a roof descending almost to ground level. Blue Hmong women wear intricately embroidered pleated skirts decorated with parallel horizontal bands of red, pink, blue and white; their jackets are of black satin, with wide orange and yellow embroidered cuffs and lapels. White Hmong women wear black baggy trousers and simple jackets with blue cuffs. Men of both groups generally wear baggy black pants with colourful sashes and embroidered jackets. All the Hmong are famous for their chunky silver jewellery.

Lahu

The **Lahu** (pop. 82,000) originated in the Tibetan highlands and centuries ago migrated to southern China, Burma and Laos; only since the end of the nineteenth century did they begin to come into Thailand from northern Burma. Their settlements are concentrated close to the Burmese border, in Chiang Rai, northern Chiang Mai and Mae Hong Son provinces. The Lahu language has become the lingua franca of the hilltribes, since the Lahu often hire out their labour. About one-third of Lahu have been converted to Christianity (through exposure in colonial Burma), and many have abandoned their traditional way of life as a result. The remaining animist Lahu believe in a village guardian spirit, who is often worshipped at a central temple that is surrounded by banners and streamers of white and yellow flags. Ordinary houses are built on high stilts and thatched with grass. Some Lahu women wear a distinctive black cloak with diagonal white stripes, decorated in bold red and yellow at the top of the sleeve, but many groups now wear Thai dress. The tribe is famous for its richly embroidered shoulder bags.

Akha

The poorest of the hilltribes, the **Akha** (pop. 50,000) migrated from Tibet over two thousand years ago to Yunnan in China, where many still live. From around 1910, the tribe began to settle in Thailand and are now found in Chiang Rai, Chiang Mai, Lampang and Phrae provinces. Every Akha village is entered through ceremonial gates decorated with carvings of human activities and attributes – even cars and aeroplanes – to indicate to the spirit world that beyond here only humans should pass. To touch any of these carvings, or to disrespect them, is punishable by fines or sacrifices. Akha houses are recognizable by their low stilts and steeply pitched roofs. Women wear elaborate headgear consisting of a conical wedge of white beads interspersed with silver coins, topped with plumes of red taffeta and framed by dangling silver balls. They also sport decorated tube-shaped ankle-to-knee leggings, an above-the-knee black skirt with a white beaded centrepiece, and a loose-fitting black jacket with heavily embroidered cuffs and lapels.

Mien

The **Mien** (or Yao; pop. 42,000) consider themselves the aristocrats of the hilltribes. Originating in central China, they began migrating more than two thousand years ago southwards to southern China, Vietnam, Laos and Thailand. They are now widely scattered throughout the north, especially around Nan, Phayao and Chiang Rai. They are the only people to have a written language, and a codified religion based on medieval Chinese Taoism, although in recent years many have converted to Christianity and Buddhism. Mien women wear long black jackets with lapels of bright scarlet wool, and heavily embroidered loose trousers and turbans. Babies wear embroidered caps with red or pink pom-poms.

Lisu

The **Lisu** (pop. 25,000), who originated in eastern Tibet, first arrived in Thailand in 1921 and are found mostly in the west, particularly between Chiang Mai and Mae Hong Son. They are organized into patriarchal clans which have authority over many villages, and their strong sense of clan rivalry often results in public violence. The Lisu live in extended families at moderate to high altitudes, in bamboo houses built on the ground. The women wear a blue or green parti-coloured knee-length tunic, split up the sides to the waist, with a wide black belt and blue or green pants. Men wear green, pink or yellow baggy pants and a blue jacket.

Lawa

The **Lawa** people (pop. 17,000) have inhabited Thailand since at least the eighth century and they were certainly here when the first Thais arrived eight hundred years ago. As a result, most Lawa villages look no different from Thai settlements and most Lawa speak Thai as their first language. But between Hot, Mae Sariang and Mae Hong Son, the Lawa still live a largely traditional life. Unmarried Lawa women wear strings of orange and yellow beads, white blouses edged with pink, and tight skirts in parallel bands of blue, black, yellow and pink. After marriage, they don a long fawn dress, but still wear the beads. All the women wear their hair tied in a turban, and some men wear light-coloured baggy pants and tunics.

ly on the scenery but on the region's inhabitants. Northern Thailand's hilltribes, now numbering nearly 750,000 people living in around 3500 villages, have so far preserved their way of life with little change over thousands of years; visiting their settlements entails walking for several hours between villages. Around eighty thousand travellers now go trekking each year, the majority heading to certain well-trodden areas such as the Mae Tang Valley, 40km northwest of Chiang Mai, and the hills around the Kok River west of Chiang Rai. Beyond the basic level of disturbance caused by any tourism, this steady flow of trekkers creates pressures for the traditionally insular hilltribes. However, the effects of tourism are minimal in comparison to exploitation of tribes by lowland Thais, their lack of land rights and poor health provision and educational services. Most tribespeople are genuinely welcoming to foreigners, appreciating the contact with Westerners. Nonetheless, it is important to take a responsible attitude when trekking.

Trekking practicalities

The hilltribes are big business in northern Thailand: in Chiang Mai there are over two hundred agencies. Chiang Rai is the second-biggest trekking centre, and agencies can also be found in Mae Hong Son, Pai and Nan. On any trek, you'll need walking boots or training shoes, long trousers (against thorns and wet-season leeches), a hat, a sarong or towel, a sweater or fleece, plus insect repellent and, if possible, a mosquito net. On an organized trek, water, blankets or a sleeping bag, and possibly a small backpack should be supplied.

It's wise not to take anything valuable with you; most guesthouses in Chiang Mai have safes, but check their reputation with other travellers, and sign an inventory – theft and credit-card abuse are not uncommon. Trekkers have occasionally been robbed by bandits, although the Border Patrol Police have recently increased their activities to provide better security. If there is a robbery attempt, don't resist.

Organized treks

Organized treks usually last for three days, have six to twelve people in the group, and follow a route regularly used by the agency. There will be a few hours' walking every day, plus the possibility of an elephant ride and a trip on a bamboo raft. Everybody in the group usually sleeps on the floor of the village headman's hut, and the guide cooks communal meals. A typical three-day trek costs B1500 in Chiang Mai, less in other towns, and much less without rafting and elephant rides.

Recommending particular agencies is difficult, as names change and standards rise and fall; word of mouth is often the best yardstick. If you want to trek with a small group, get an assurance from your agency that you won't be tagged onto a larger group. Meet the guides, who should speak reasonable English, know about hilltribe culture and have a certificate from the Tourism Authority of Thailand. Check how much walking is involved per day, and ask about the menu. Ask about transport from base at the beginning and end of the trek, which sometimes entails a long public bus ride. Before setting off, each trek should be registered with the Tourist Police in case of any trouble.

Independent trekking

The options for **independent trekking** are limited, chiefly by the poor mapping of the area. Royal Thai Survey Department 1:50,000 maps cover a limited area, or try Hongsombud's Guide Map of Chiang Rai (Bangkok Guides) which includes 1:1000 maps of the more popular chunks of Chiang Rai province. You could also consult the maps at Chiang Mai's Research Institute (see opposite), which mark the villages where people can stay. It's possible to find accommodation in hilltribe villages, where you can expect to pay at least B50 per night, possibly including dinner and breakfast (be wary of any food that's not cooked in your presence, as food poisoning is not uncommon). Alternatively, base yourself at one of the guesthouses set deep in the countryside, within walking range of hilltribe villages. These include

Wilderness Lodge near Mae Suya (see p.893); *Mae Lana Guesthouse* at Mae Lana (p.893) and *Cave Lodge* at Ban Tum (p.894).

TREKKING ETIQUETTE
As guests, it's up to farangs to adapt to the customs of the hilltribes and not to make a nuisance of themselves.

• Dress modestly, avoiding skimpy shorts and vests.

• Before entering a hilltribe village, look out for taboo signs of woven bamboo strips on the ground outside the village entrance which mean a special ceremony is taking place and that you should not enter. Be careful about what you touch. In Akha villages, keep your hands off cult structures like the entrance gates and the giant swing. Do not touch or photograph any shrines, or sit underneath them. You'll have to pay a fine for any violation of local customs.

• Most villagers do not like to be photographed. Be particularly careful with pregnant women and babies – most tribes believe cameras affect the soul of the foetus or new-born. Always ask first.

• Taking gifts is dubious practice: writing materials for children are welcome, as are sewing needles, but sweets and cigarettes may encourage begging.

Chiang Mai

Despite recent and rapid economic progress, **CHIANG MAI** – Thailand's second city – manages to preserve some of the atmosphere of an overgrown village. The old quarter, set within a two-kilometre-square moat, has retained many of its traditional wooden houses, and inviting guesthouses, good markets and plenty of sights make it a hugely appealing place to many travellers. Plus, of course, Chiang Mai is the main centre for hilltribe trekking.

Arrival

Most people arrive at the **train** station on Thanon Charoen Muang, just over 2km from the landmark Tha Pae Gate on the eastern side of town, or at the Arcade **bus station** on Thanon Kaeo Nawarat, 3km out to the northeast. Getting from either of these to the centre is easy by songthaew or tuk-tuk. Coming south from Tha Ton, you'll wind up at the Chang Phuak bus station on Thanon Chotana, 500m from the city centre's northern Chang Phuak Gate and 2km northwest of Tha Pae Gate. Beware that many of the low-cost private buses from Bangkok's Thanon Khao San stop on a remote part of the Superhighway, where they "sell" their passengers to various guesthouse touts. Arriving at the **airport**, 3km southwest of the centre, you'll find banks, a TAT office, and taxis (B100 to the city centre). The pink B9 bus (5.30am–10pm) also runs from outside the airport compound into town.

Information

TAT has an office (daily 8.30am–4.30pm; ☎053/235334) at 105/1 Thanon Chiang Mai–Lamphun, on the east bank of the river. An important resource for trekkers is the Hilltribe Research Institute at Chiang Mai University (Mon–Fri 9am–noon & 1–4pm), between Huai Kaeo and Suthep roads, where you can consult detailed maps and get clued up on the cultures of the north.

Nancy Chandler's **map** of Chiang Mai (B80) is very handy for a detailed exploration; and for motorbike trips out of the city you should use Chiang Mai and Thailand North 1:750,000 Map (Berndtson & Berndtson; B145), a complete road map of the region which accurately shows dirt tracks and minor roads.

City transport

Although you can comfortably walk between the most central temples, **bicycles** are handy and can be rented for B30–50 a day at places on the eastern moat. Many places around Tha

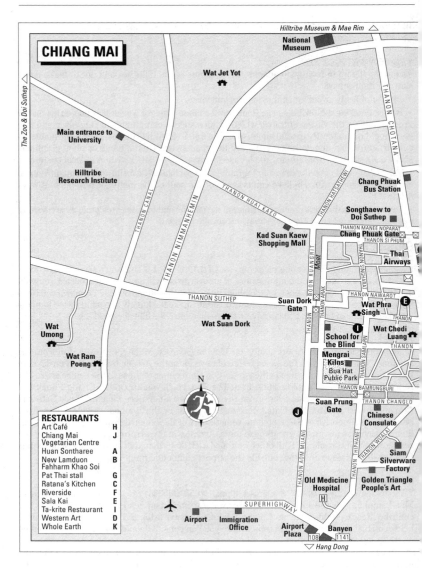

CHIANG MAI

The Zoo & Doi Suthep △

National Museum

Wat Jet Yot

THANON CHOTANA

Main entrance to University

Hilltribe Research Institute

THANON CANAL

THANON NIMMANHEMIN

THANON HUAI KAEO

THANON MAISATHEWI

Chang Phuak Bus Station

Songthaew to Doi Suthep

THANON MANEE NOPARAT

Chang Phuak Gate

THANON SI PHUM

Kad Suan Kaew Shopping Mall

Moat

THANON BOON RUANGRIT

THANON SINGHARAT

THANON ARAK

Thai Airways

THANON SUTHEP

Suan Dork Gate

THANON NAWAROT

Wat Phra Singh E

THANON

Wat Suan Dork

Wat Umong

Wat Ram Poeng

School for the Blind I

Wat Chedi Luang

THANON

THANON SAMLARN

Mengrai Kilns

Bua Hat Public Park

THANON BAMRUNGBURI

Suan Prung Gate

THANON AOM MUANG

Chinese Consulate

THANON CHANGLO

THANON THIPHANET

THANON WUALA

RESTAURANTS	
Art Café	**H**
Chiang Mai Vegetarian Centre	**J**
Huan Sontharee	**A**
New Lamduon Fahharm Khao Soi	**B**
Pat Thai stall	**G**
Ratana's Kitchen	**C**
Riverside	**F**
Sala Kai	**E**
Ta-krite Restaurant	**I**
Western Art	**D**
Whole Earth	**K**

J

Siam Silverware Factory

Old Medicine Hospital H

Golden Triangle People's Art

SUPERHIGHWAY

Airport

Immigration Office

Airport Plaza 108 1141

Banyen

▽ *Hang Dong*

Pae Gate rent out **motorbikes** (from B100); the reliable Queen Bee Travel Service, 5 Thanon Moonmuang (☎053/275525), can also offer limited insurance. Chiang Mai's one **bus**, the pink B9, runs from Khwan Wiang housing estate past the airport and then in a clockwise route around the old city, returning to the airport and the housing estate. Quicker and more efficient are the red **songthaews** (other colours serve outlying villages), which act as shared taxis within the city, picking up people headed in roughly the same direction and taking each

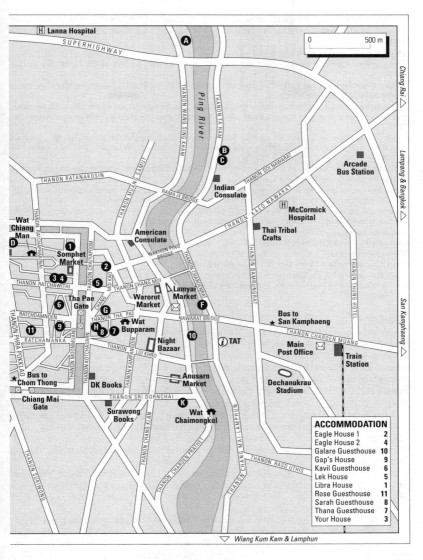

Map legend:

- H Lanna Hospital
- SUPERHIGHWAY
- Ping River
- THANON WANG SING KHAM
- THANON FA HAM
- Chiang Rai ▷
- Lampang & Bangkok ▷
- THANON RATANAKOSIN
- THANON MUANG SAMUT
- RAMA IX BRIDGE
- Ⓑ
- Ⓒ
- Indian Consulate
- THANON DOI NAWARAT
- Arcade Bus Station
- San Kamphaeng ▷
- Wat Chiang Man
- Ⓓ
- THANON RATCHAPAKINAI
- Somphet Market
- ❶
- THANON CHAIYAPOOM
- American Consulate
- NAKHON PING BRIDGE
- THANON KAEO NAWARAT
- McCormick Hospital H
- Thai Tribal Crafts
- THANON BAMRUNGRAT
- THANON THUNG HOTEL
- ❷
- MOI KAO
- THANON CHANG MOI
- THANON RATCHAWITHI
- ❸ ❹
- ❺
- Warorot Market
- Lamyai Market
- Ⓕ
- THANON CHAROENRAT
- Bus to San Kamphaeng ★
- ❻
- RATCHDAMNOEN
- THANON CHANG
- Tha Pae Gate
- Ⓖ
- THANON THA PAE
- Wat Bupparam
- NAWARAT BRIDGE
- ❾
- Ⓗ ❽ ❼
- THANON MOONMUANG
- THANON KOTCHASARN
- THANON KHO MUANG
- Night Bazaar
- THANON LOI KHRO
- ❿
- ⓘ TAT
- Main Post Office ⊠
- Train Station
- ❶❶
- RATCHAMANKA
- THANON PHRA POKKLAO
- Bus to Chom Thong ★
- ⊠
- DK Books
- Anusarn Market
- Dechanukrau Stadium
- Chiang Mai Gate
- THANON SRI DORNCHAI
- Surawong Books
- THANON CHANG KLAN
- Ⓚ
- Wat Chaimongkol
- THANON CHAROEN PRATHET
- THANON CHIANG MAI-LAMPHUN
- THANON RASD UTHIS
- THANON SUWONG

Scale: 0 — 500 m

▽ Wiang Kum Kam & Lamphun

ACCOMMODATION

Eagle House 1	2
Eagle House 2	4
Galare Guesthouse	10
Gap's House	9
Kavil Guesthouse	6
Lek House	5
Libra House	1
Rose Guesthouse	11
Sarah Guesthouse	8
Thana Guesthouse	7
Your House	3

to their specific destination; expect to pay B10 from the train station to Tha Pae Gate. The city is also stuffed with **tuk-tuks** (B30 from the train station to Tha Pae Gate) and **samlors**.

Accommodation

The main concentration of **guesthouses** and restaurants hangs between the moat and the Ping River to the east, centred on the landmark of Pratu Tha Pae (Tha Pae Gate). Many of the least expensive guesthouses make their money from hilltribe trekking, which can be convenient, as a trek often needs a lot of organizing beforehand, but some put pressure on guests to trek.

Eagle House 1, 16 Soi 3, Th Chang Moi Kao and *Eagle House 2*, 26 Soi 2, Th Ratchawithi (☎053/235387). Two guesthouses with garden terraces and spartan en-suite rooms; regularly visited by hill-trek guides. ①–②.

Galare Guesthouse, 7 Soi 2, Th Charoen Prathet (☎053/818887 or 821011). Smart, popular place with a shady riverside lawn; some air-con. ④.

Gap's House, 3 Soi 4, Th Ratchdamnoen (☎053/278140). The best deal in town, with plush air-con rooms and hot showers in a leafy compound. Especially welcoming to lone travellers and has its own friendly bar. ②–③.

Kavil Guesthouse, 10/1 Soi 5, Th Ratchdamnoen (☎053/224740). Smallish, well-run place in a quiet soi with fan and air-con rooms; all have hot-water bathrooms. Internet and fax service; free safe, inventories signed. ①–②.

Lek House, 22 Th Chaiyapoom near Somphet Market (☎053/252686). Central and set back from the road, with clean, en-suite rooms around a garden. ①.

Libra House, 28 Soi 9, Th Moonmuang (☎053/210687). Excellent modern guesthouse with a few traditional trimmings. Hot water en suite or in shared bathrooms. Trekking-oriented. ①.

Rose Guesthouse, 87 Th Ratchamanka (☎053/276574). Reliable, inexpensive place with large but noisy fan rooms and shared bathrooms. Very trek-oriented but no pressure. ①.

Sarah Guesthouse, 20 Soi 4, Th Tha Pae (☎053/208271). A very clean, peaceful, central establishment with a courtyard café and en-suite rooms. ①.

Thana Guesthouse, 27/8 Soi 4, Th Tha Pae (☎053/279794). One of several popular, rowdy hangouts on this soi. Clean rooms with hot showers, some with air con. ②.

Your House, 8 Soi 2, Th Ratchawithi (☎053/217492). Welcoming old-town teak house. Big rooms share hot-water bathrooms; plus some smaller en-suite ones with air con. Free pick-ups from train, bus or airport. Trek-oriented. ①–②.

The City

If you see only one temple in Chiang Mai it should be **Wat Phra Singh**, at the far western end of Thanon Ratchdamnoen in the old town. Its largest structure, a colourful modern viharn fronted by naga balustrades, hides from view the beautiful Viharn Lai Kam, a wooden gem of early nineteenth-century Lanna architecture, with its squat, multi-tiered roof and exquisitely carved and gilded pediment. Inside, sits a portly, radiant and much-revered bronze Buddha in fifteenth-century Lanna style. The walls are enlivened by murals depicting daily life in the north a hundred years ago.

A ten-minute walk east along Thanon Ratchadamnoen brings you to **Wat Chedi Luang** on Thanon Phra Pokklao, where an enormous 60m-high pink-brick chedi presents an intriguing spectacle – especially in the early evening when the resident bats flit around. The oldest temple in Chiang Mai, **Wat Chiang Man**, is fifteen minutes' walk from Chedi Luang on Thanon Wiang Kaeo and houses two dainty and very holy Buddha images.

For a fuller picture of Lanna art and culture, you could head for the **National Museum**, on the northwestern outskirts of Chiang Mai (Wed–Sun 9am–noon & 1–4pm; free), which also houses Buddha images and a weapons collection. To get there, charter a tuk-tuk or songthaew from the centre of town.

Set back from the Superhighway, ten minutes' walk west of the museum, the peaceful garden temple of **Wat Jet Yot** is named after the "seven spires" of its unusual chedi, which lean together like brick chimneys at crazy angles. The temple was built in 1455 by King Tilok, to represent the seven places around Bodh Gaya in India which the Buddha visited in the seven weeks following his enlightenment.

Two kilometres north of the Superhighway off Thanon Chotana, the very worthwhile **Hilltribe Museum** (Mon–Fri 8.30am–4.30pm; free) stands in the artfully landscaped Ratchamangkla Park. The exhibition introduces the major hilltribes with photos, artefacts and models and there's a chance to hear tapes of traditional music. It's about a ten-minute walk from the park gate on Thanon Chotana along the edge of the lake to the museum entrance; songthaews can drop you at the museum, but only pick up from the gate.

More of a park than a temple, **Wat Umong** was built in the 1380s for a brilliant monk who was prone to wandering off into the forest to meditate; the tunnels (*umong*) beneath the chedi were painted with trees, flowers and birds to keep him in one place, and some can still be explored. Above them stands a grotesque black statue of the fasting Buddha, all ribs and veins. The path leading to the chedi is lined with didactic cartoons, and surreal paintings also cover the modern hall nearby. Take a songthaew to the wat, or cycle east along Thanon Suthep for 2km and turn left after Wang Nam Gan then follow the signs. Midway along Thanon Suthep, the brilliantly whitewashed chedi of **Wat Suan Dork** sits next to a garden of smaller, equally dazzling chedis – framed by Doi Suthep to the west, this makes a photogenic sight, especially at sunset.

Shopping

Chiang Mai is a great place for **handicrafts shopping**. The road to San Kamphaeng, which extends due east for 13km from the end of Thanon Charoen Muang, is lined with craft shops and factories. The biggest concentrations are at Bo Sang, the "umbrella village", 9km from town, and at San Kamphaeng itself, dedicated chiefly to silk-weaving. White buses to San Kamphaeng leave Chiang Mai from Lamyai Market (every 30min; 30 min), going via the train station.

The other shopper's playground is the **night bazaar**, around the junction of Chang Klan and Loi Kroa roads, where bumper-to-bumper street stalls sell just about anything produced in Chiang Mai; they open at about 5pm. During the day, the riverside **Warorot market**, north of Thanon Tha Pae, has lots of cheap cotton, linen and ceramics; there's a late-night flower market here too.

Chiang Mai has several non-profit-making shops, which ensure that proceeds go to the hilltribes. These include The Products Foundation, on Thanon Suthep in front of Wat Suan Dork, which sells cotton, silk and hilltribe gear; Thai Tribal Crafts, 204 Thanon Bamrungrat off Thanon Kaeo Nawarat, which has good embroidered shoulder bags; and Golden Triangle People's Art and Handicrafts, 137/3 Thanon Nantharam, which works mainly with Akha women.

For new **books and maps**, try Suriwong at 54/1 Thanon Sri Dornchai and DK Books at 79/1 Thanon Kotchasarn. Second-hand bookshops include The Library Service at 21/1 Soi 2, Thanon Ratchamanka (nearer Thanon Moonmuang) and Lost Bookshop, 34/3 Thanon Ratchamanka.

Eating and drinking

Northern **food** has been strongly influenced by Burmese cuisine, especially in curries such as the spicy *kaeng hang lay* ("Chiang Mai curry"), made with pork, ginger and coconut cream. Another favourite local dish is *khao soi*, a thick broth of curry and coconut cream, with egg noodles and meat. There's a good night market on Thanon Chang Klan.

Art Café, 263/1 Th Tha Pae. Popular farang hangout which exhibits local art. All the café favourites and a big veggie menu. Slow service but there are plenty of mags to browse. Mon 5–10pm, Tues–Sun 10am–10pm. Moderate to expensive.

Chiang Mai Vegetarian Centre, Th Aom Muang. A cavernous traditional pavilion serving good veggie dishes on rice, and desserts. Open Sun–Thurs 6am–2pm only. Inexpensive.

Huan Sontharee, 46 Th Wang Sing Kham. About 2km from the centre and there's no English sign, but well worth the extra distance. This convivial riverfront restaurant is owned by Thai folk singer Sontharee Wechanon, who entertains diners nightly, and serves up northern specialities. Evenings only until 1am. Closed Sun. Moderate.

New Lamduon Fahharm Khao Soi, 352/22 Th Charoenrat. Excellent, inexpensive *khao soi* prepared to a secret recipe. Also satay and *som tam* (spicy papaya salad). Open 9am–3pm.

Pat Thai stall, alleyway on Th Tha Pae, near *Roong Ruang Hotel*. Best *pat thai* in town, prepared with flaming theatricality and worth queuing for. Open 6–9pm. Inexpensive.

Ratana's Kitchen, 350/4 Th Charoenrat. Garden restaurant, run by a travel writer and his Thai wife, specializing in delicious northern dishes like *khao soi* and *gaeng haeng lae*. Moderate.

Riverside, 9 Th Charoenrat (☎053/243239). Archetypal farang bolthole: candlelit terraces by the water, mid-priced Western and Thai food, and inexpensive draught beer.

Sala Kai, 41 Th Nawarot, off Th Phra Pokklao. Delicious and very popular satay and *khao man kai* – boiled chicken served with broth and garlic rice. Open 5am–2pm. Inexpensive.

Ta-krite Restaurant, 17 Soi 1, Th Samlarn, on the south side of Wat Phra Singh. Delicious and varied cuisine, in a maze of rooms around a courtyard. Inexpensive to moderate.

Western Art, 21/3 Th Sri Phum. Darkened hangout for drinking and live music: Chiang Mai's local independent music scene develops here, and there's the usual offering of Western covers.

Whole Earth, 88 Th Sri Dornchai. Mostly veggie dishes from Thailand and India, plus a big fish and seafood selection; occasional live music. Moderate to expensive.

Listings

Airlines Air Mandalay, Room 107, Doi Ping Mansion, 148 Th Charoen Prathat (☎053/818049); Bangkok Airways, Chiang Mai airport (☎053/922258); Lao Aviation, 240 Th Phra Pokklao, behind Thai Airways (☎053/418258–9); Malaysia Airlines, Mae Ping Hotel, 153 Th Sri Dornchai (☎053/276523 or 276538); Silk Air, Mae Ping Hotel, 153 Th Sri Dornchai (☎053/276495 or 276459); Thai Airways, 240 Th Phra Pokklao (☎053/210042).

Consulates Canada, 151 Chiang Mai–Lampang Superhighway (☎053/850147); China, 111 Th Chang Lo (☎053/276125); India, 344 Th Charoenrat (☎053/243066); UK, Grounds of the British Council (☎053/263015); US, 387 Th Witchayanon (☎053/252629–31).

Cookery lessons Chiang Mai Thai Cookery School, 1–3 Th Moonmuang (☎053/206388). Holds one-, two-, three- or four-day courses (B800/B1600/B2300/B3000) covering traditional Lanna, common Thai dishes and vegetarian options. Lessons are held at the cooks' home, 10km northeast of Chiang Mai (free pick-up). Book ahead.

Hospitals 24-hr emergency service at Lanna, 103 Superhighway (☎053/211037–41 or 215020–2), east of Th Chotana; or McCormick on Th Kaeo Nawarat (☎053/240823–5).

Immigration Office 300m east of the airport (☎053/277510).

Internet access Aumnet Internet Service, 65 Th Moonmuang (daily 9am–10pm); Thapae On Line, Th Thapae; Assign Internet at the Chiang Mai Pavilion, 145 Th Chang Klan (daily noon–10.30pm) and at the Huay Kaew Shopping Centre, Th Huay Kaew (daily 11am–8.30pm).

Meditation Month-long Vipassana courses at Northern Insight Meditation Centre, at Wat Ram Poeng (aka Wat Tapotaram) on Th Canal near Wat Umong (☎053/278620). Sunshine House, 24 Soi 4, Th Kaew Nararat (no phone), is a centre for meditation, yoga and t'ai chi.

Police 105/1 Th Chiang Mai–Lamphun (☎053/248974; or nationwide helpline ☎1699).

Post office The GPO, near the train station on Th Charoen Muang, has an overseas phone and fax service (daily until 4.30pm). Poste restante should be addressed to: Chiang Mai Post Office, Th Charoen Muang, Chiang Mai 50000.

Telephone services International phones at the Chiang Mai Telecommunication Center (open 24hr) on the Superhighway, just south of the east end of Th Charoen Muang.

Thai language courses AUA, 24 Th Ratchadamnoen (☎053/211377 or 278407) holds sixty-hour courses (B3500). Thirty-hour courses and single lessons (B250/hour) are also available.

Traditional massage Massages and courses at Old Medicine Hospital, 78/1 Soi Moh Shivagakomarpaj, off Th Wualai near the airport (daily 8.30am–4.30pm; ☎053/2750850); and at International Training Massage behind Wat Santihan at the northwest corner of the moat (☎053/218632).

Doi Suthep

A jaunt up **DOI SUTHEP**, the mountain which rises steeply at Chiang Mai's western edge, is the most satisfying outing you can make from the city, chiefly on account of beautiful **Wat Phra That Doi Suthep**, which dominates the hillside, and, because of a magic relic enshrined in its chedi, is the north's holiest shrine. It is approached by a flight of three hundred steps (or B10 funicular) which leads to the upper terrace, a breathtaking combination of carved wood, filigree and gleaming metal, whose altars and ceremonial umbrellas surround the dazzling gold-plated chedi. Frequent **songthaews** leave the corner of Manee Noparat and Chotana roads for the sixteen-kilometre trip up the mountain (B30 to the wat). The road, although steep in places, is paved all the way and well suited for motor-bikes.

Lampang and the Elephant Conservation Centre

The north's second-largest town and an important transport hub, **LAMPANG**, 100km southeast of Chiang Mai, is best used as a base for visiting the Elephant Conservation Centre, 37km away, as there's little of interest in the town beside the imposing **Wat Phra Kaeo Don Tao** on Thanon Phra Kaeo. If you have a motorbike you might also want to head 15km southwest to **Wat Phra That Lampang Luang**, a grand and well-preserved capsule of beautiful Lanna art and architecture.

The **Elephant Conservation Centre** (shows daily 10am & 11am plus Sat & Sun 1.30pm; B50; ☎054/227051), 37km northwest of Lampang on Highway 11, is the most authentic place to see elephants being trained for forest work; it also cares for abandoned and abused elephants in its elephant hospital. An interpretive centre has exhibits on the history of the elephant in Thailand, elephant rides (B100–200) are available, and daily shows put the elephants through their paces. It's best visited en route from Chiang Mai to Lampang: ask the bus conductor for Suan Pa (Forest Park) Thung Kwian, 70km from Chiang Mai. It's a two-kilometre walk from the gates to the centre. The centre closes during the dry season from March to May and for every religious holiday, so check with TAT first.

Practicalities

From Chiang Mai you can catch any Phayao- or Chiang Rai-bound **bus** to Lampang (2hr) from just south of Nawarat Bridge, or any Nan-bound bus from the Arcade station. Six **trains** a day, in each direction, also stop in Lampang. The train and bus stations lie to the southwest of town, but many buses also stop on Thanon Phaholyothin in the centre. There's a small **tourist information** centre (Mon–Fri 9am–noon & 1–4pm) at the corner of Boonyawat and Pakham roads. The delightful *Riverside Guesthouse*, 286 Thanon Talat Khao (☎054/227005; ②), is a traditional compound of elegant en-suite **rooms**, whose helpful owner rents out motorbikes, and also owns the recommended *Riverside* **restaurant** at 328 Thanon Tipchang. The night market sets up on Thanon Takrao Noi between the clocktower and Thanon Wienglakon.

Nan

Ringed by high mountains, the sleepy provincial capital of **NAN**, 225km east of Lampang, rests on the west bank of the Nan River and comprises a disorientating grid of crooked streets, around a small core of shops, where Mahawong and Anantaworarichides roads meet Thanon Sumondhevaraj. The best place to start an exploration is to the southwest at the **National Museum** (Wed–Sun 9am–noon & 1–4pm; B20) on Thanon Phawang, where informative displays introduce the history and peoples of Nan. Located 150m south along Thanon Phakwang, **Wat Phumin** will grab even the most over-templed traveller. Its 500-year-old centrepiece is an unusual cruciform building, combining both the bot and the viharn, and two giant nagas pass through its base, their tails along the balustrades at the south entrance and their heads at the north, representing the sacred oceans at the base of the central mountain of the universe. The doors have been beautifully carved with animals and flowers, and the restored 1857 murals take you on a whirlwind tour of heaven, hell, the Buddha's previous incarnations and incidents from Nan's history. **Wat Phra That Chae Haeng**, on the opposite side of the river 2km southeast of town, is another must, not least for its setting on a hill overlooking the Nan valley. The wide driveway is flanked by monumental serpents gliding down the slope, and inside the walls stands a slender, 55-metre-high golden chedi, surrounded by four smaller chedis and four carved and gilded umbrellas. The viharn roof has no less than fifteen Lao-style tiers, stacked up like a house of cards.

Shops and tours

There are several good **handicrafts shops** in Nan, most of which are found on Thanon Sumondhevaraj north of the junction with Anantaworarichides. Check out Nan Silverware at the junction, Pha Nan at #21/2 and Thai-Payap Development Association at #288.

When you tire of the town, consider heading into the remote, mountainous countryside around Nan, which runs a close second to the headlong scenery of Mae Hong Son province. Fhu Travel at 453/4 Thanon Sumondhevaraj (☎054/710636) organizes **tours** to Wat Nong Bua (see below) and Doi Phukha (B600), and treks of two days (B1200) or three days (B1500) through thick jungle and high mountains to Hmong and Mien villages.

Practicalities

From Chiang Mai it's a seven-hour bus journey or one-hour flight to Nan. The main **bus station** is on Thanon Anantaworarichides on the west side of town, but Bangkok and Phitsanulok services use a smaller station to the east of the centre on Thanon Kha Luang; both are a manageable walk from hotels. Oversea, at 488 Thanon Sumondhevaraj, rents out bicycles (B30) and mopeds (B150). Nan boasts one very good **guesthouse**, on the north side of town. *Doi Phukha Guesthouse*, 94/5 Soi 1, Thanon Sumondhevaraj (☎054/771422 or 751517; ①), occupies a beautiful wooden house and the simple rooms share hot showers. If *Doi Phukha* is full, try *Nan Guesthouse*, 57/16 Thanon Mahaphom (☎054/771849; ①). The night market and other small Thai **restaurants** line Thanon Anantaworarichides, but Nan's big culinary surprise is *Da Dario* at 37/4 Thanon Rat Amnuay (☎054/750258), which runs west off Thanon Sumondhevaraj, not far north of *Doi Phukha Guesthouse*, and which serves quality Italian and Thai food.

Wat Nong Bua

The most popular day-trip out of Nan is to the village temple of **Wat Nong Bua**, 43km to the north. If you're on a bike, ride 40km up Highway 1080 to the southern outskirts of the town of Tha Wang Pha, where signs point to Wat Nong Bua, 3km away; buses and songthaews from Nan's Thanon Anantaworarichides go to Tha Wang Pha (hourly; 1hr), then take a motorbike taxi, or walk the last 3km. The wat's beautifully gnarled viharn was built in 1862 in typical Lanna style, with low, drooping roof tiers, but its most outstanding features are the remarkably intact late nineteenth-century murals which depict, with much humour and vivid detail, scenes from the Chanthakhat Jataka, the story of one of the Buddha's previous incarnations, as a hero called Chanthakhat.

Doi Inthanon National Park

Covering a huge area to the southwest of Chiang Mai, **Doi Inthanon National Park** (B20 per person, plus B10–30 per vehicle), with its hilltribe villages, dramatic waterfalls and fine panoramas, is a popular destination for naturalists and hikers. The park supports about 380 bird species and, near the summit, the only red rhododendrons in Thailand (in bloom Dec–Feb). Night-time temperatures can drop below freezing, so bring warm clothing. Both the visitor centre, 9km up the main road from **Mae Chaem**, and the park headquarters, a further 22km on, sell detailed park maps.Three sets of waterfalls provide the main roadside attractions on the way to the park headquarters: overrated and overcrowded **Mae Klang Falls**, 8km in; **Vachiratharn Falls**, a long misty drop 11km beyond; and the twin cascades of **Siriphum Falls**, behind the park headquarters. The more beautiful **Mae Ya**, believed to be the highest in Thailand, is accessed by a paved fourteen-kilometre track that heads west off the main park road 2km north of Highway 108. For the most spectacular views in the park, head for the twin chedis on the summit road. Near the chedis, a signpost opposite the helipad marks the trailhead of Gew Mae Pan Trail, an easy two-hour circular walk through forest and savannah around the steep, western edge of Doi Inthanon. Doi Inthanon's summit (2565m), 6km beyond the chedi, is a disappointment. The paved Mae Chaem road skirts yet more waterfalls, 7km after the turnoff: look for a steep, unpaved road to the right, leading down to a ranger station and, just to the east, the dramatic long drop of **Huai Sai Luaeng Falls**. A circular two-hour trail from the ranger station takes in small waterfalls as well as **Mae Pan Falls**.

Practicalities

By **motorbike** or jeep you could do the park justice in a day-trip from Chiang Mai, or treat it as the first stage of a longer trip to Mae Hong Son. The gateway to the park is **Chom Thong**, 58km southwest of Chiang Mai on Highway 108; the main road through the park leaves Highway 108 1km north of here, winding northwestwards for 48km to the top of Doi Inthanon; a second paved road forks left 10km before the summit, reaching the riverside market of Mae Chaem, southwest of the park, after 20km, from where it's 22km to the park headquarters. **Buses** run from the bottom of Thanon Phra Pokklao in Chiang Mai (Chiang Mai Gate) to Chom Thong (every 30 min; 1hr), from where you can catch a songthaew to Mae Chaem, after which you'll have to hitch the last 10km to the summit or charter a whole songthaew (yellow) from Chom Thong's temple (B800 round trip).

You can **stay** in the national park bungalows (B800 for eight people sharing; bookings in Bangkok on ☎02/579 7223 or 579 5734) near the headquarters, or camp near the headquarters and at Mae Pan Falls (B10 per person per night). Tents (B100) and blankets (B15) can be rented at the headquarters. Daytime **food** stalls operate at Mae Klang Falls and at the park headquarters.

Mae Sariang

Apart from admiring the town's Burmese-style wats, there's nothing pressing to do in the outpost of **MAE SARIANG**, 183km from Chiang Mai, but most visitors make a day-trip to the trading post of **Mae Sam Laeb**, 46km to the southwest on the Salween River, on the border with Burma. It's no more than a row of bamboo stores and a riverside gambling den, but the Salween swarms with smuggling traffic and floating teak logs. Sporadic songthaews to Mae Sam Laeb (75min) leave from the bridge over the River Yuam in Mae Sariang.

Buses depart from Chiang Mai's Arcade bus station and enter Mae Sariang from the east along its main street, Thanon Wiang Mai, terminating on Thanon Mae Sariang, one of two north–south streets. The other road, Laeng Phanit, parallels the Yuam River to the west. The bone-rattling 230km south to Mae Sot is covered by songthaews (7 daily; 5hr), which makes a scenic link between the north and the central plains.The best **place to stay** in town is the *See View Guesthouse* (☎053/681556; B200–300), which has nice rooms, dorms and bungalows across the river from the town centre; they also have an office at 70 Thanon Wiang Mai and rent mountain bikes (B40). Rooms in the traditional *River Side Guesthouse*, nicely located at 85 Thanon Laeng Phanit (☎053/681188; B160), are a little cheaper. Don't be put off by the shabby appearance of the *Inthira Restaurant* on Thanon Wiang Mai – it's the locals' favourite, and serves excellent Thai food. **Motorbikes** (B150–300) can be rented from Pratin Kolakan, opposite the bus terminal.

Mae Hong Son and around

Set deep in a mountain valley, **MAE HONG SON** is often billed as the "Switzerland of Thailand" and has become one of the fastest-developing tourist centres in the country. Most travellers come here for trekking and hiking in the beautiful countryside and cool climate, but crowds are also drawn here every April for the spectacular parades of the Poy Sang

Long festival, which celebrates local boys' temporary ordination into the monkhood. Trekking up and down Mae Hong Son's steep inclines is tough, but the hilltribe villages are generally unspoilt and the scenery is magnificent. To the west, trekking routes tend to snake along the Burmese border and can sometimes get a little crowded; the villages to the east are more traditional. Many guesthouses and travel agencies run treks out of Mae Hong Son: the *Mae Hong Son Guesthouse* is reliable (B500 per day/B1500 for three days). Treks from *Sunflower*, 116/115 Soi 3, Thanon Khunlumprapas (☎053/620549) emphasize bird-watching.

Mae Hong Son's main Thanon Khunlumprapas, lined with shops and businesses, runs north to south and is intersected by Singhanat Bamrung at the only traffic lights in the town. Plenty of traditional Thai Yai buildings remain – wooden shop-houses with balconies, shutters and corrugated-iron roof decorations, homes thatched with leaves and fitted with her-ringbone-patterned window panels.

Mae Hong Son's classic picture-postcard view is of its twin nineteenth-century Burmese-style temples from the opposite bank of Jong Kham Lake. In the viharn of **Wat Chong Kham** you'll find a huge, intricately carved sermon throne, decorated with the *dharmachakra* (Wheel of Law) in coloured glass on gold. Next door, **Wat Chong Klang** is famous for its paintings on glass, depicting stories from the lives of the Buddha. It also houses a fabulous collection of humorous and characterful Burmese teak statues. The town's vibrant, smelly morning **market** is a magnet for hilltribe traders and worth getting up for; next door, the many-gabled viharn of **Wat Hua Wiang** shelters the beautiful bronze Burmese-style Buddha image, Chao Palakeng. For a godlike overview of the area, especially at sunset, climb up to **Wat Doi Kong Mu** on the steep hill to the west.

Nai Soi and the Long-Neck Women

The most famous – and notorious – sight in the Mae Hong Son area is its contingent of **"long-neck" women**, members of the Padaung tribe of Burma who have fled to Thailand to escape repression. Though the women's necks appear to be stretched to 30cm and more by a col-umn of brass rings, the pressure of eleven pounds of brass actually squashes the collarbones and ribs; to remove a full stack would cause the collapse of the neck and suffocation. Girls of the tribe start wearing the rings from about the age of six, adding one or two each year up to the age of sixteen. Despite the obvious discomfort, the tribeswomen, when interviewed, say that they're happy to be continuing the tradition. But only half of the Padaung women now lengthen their necks; left to its own course, the custom would probably die out, but the influ-ence of tourism may well keep it alive for some time yet.

The original village of long-neck Padaung women in the Mae Hong Son area, **NAI SOI**, 35km northwest of town, has effectively been turned into a human zoo for snap-happy tourists, with an entrance fee of B250 per person. The "long necks" pose in front of their huts, and visitors click away. At least the entrance fee is used to support the Karenni National People's Party in their fight for the independence of Burma's Kayah state (where the Padaung come from), and the "long necks" themselves get paid a decent wage. Without your own transport, you'll have to join a **tour** (about B650) from town. By motorbike, head north along Highway 1095 for 10km and turn left at the first sign for Pha Sua for 500m, then left again at the army camp and continue for another 25km.

Pha Sua Falls and Mae Aw

North of Mae Hong Son, a trip to **Pha Sua Falls** and the border village of Mae Aw takes in some spectacular and varied countryside, best visited by motorbike or on a Thai Yai tour (see opposite; B400). Head north for 17km on Highway 1095 (ignore the first signpost for Pha Sua, after 10km) and then, after a long, steep descent, turn left onto a side road, paved at first, which passes through the village of Ban Bok Shampae. About 9km from the turn-off you'll reach Pha Sua Falls; take care when swimming, as several people have been swept to their deaths here.

Above the falls, the paved road climbs 11km to the village of Naphapak, then it's another 7km to **MAE AW** (aka Ban Ruk Thai), a Burmese border settlement of Kuomintang anti-communist Chinese refugees. It's the highest point on the border which visitors can reach, and provides a fascinating window on Kuomintang life. Bright-green tea bushes line the slopes and Chinese ponies wander the streets of long bamboo houses. In the marketplace on the north side of the village reservoir, shops sell Oolong and Chian Chian tea, and dried mushrooms.

Practicalities

Buses to Mae Hong Son depart from Chiang Mai's Arcade Bus Station and arrive at the northern end of Thanon Khunlumprapas, close to the guesthouses. Thai Yai, at 20 Singhanat Bamrung (☎053/620105), rents out **motorbikes** (B130–180), and organizes **tours**. Several places on the main street rent out four-wheel drives. The **Tourist Police** are on Thanon Singhanat Bamrung (☎053/611812).

Mae Hong Song has many peaceful, scenic **guesthouses**, of which the lakeside *Friends Guesthouse*, at 21 Thanon Pradit Jongkham (☎053/611674; ①–②), is one of the best, with its smart rooms and nice views. Further east along the lake shore, on Thanon U-domchadnitesh, *Johnnie Guesthouse* (☎053/611667; ①) has basic rooms and herbal saunas in the evening. The clean and friendly *Saban Nga House* (☎053/612280; ①), at 14 Thanon U-domchadnitesh, is more central but less scenic. A little further out, the long-established *Mae Hong Son Guesthouse*, 295 Thanon Makkasandi (☎053/612510; ②) offers a choice of bare wooden rooms, simple huts and large bungalows, and the mid-priced *Rim Nam Klang Doi* (☎053/612142; ⑤–⑦) is a beautifully situated, comfortable resort 5km along the road to Huai Deua.

The night market on Thanon Khunlumprapas does the standard Thai **food**, but for restaurant meals try the very popular *Kai Muk* on Thanon U-Domchaonitesh or the upmarket tourist-oriented *Fern*, at 87 Thanon Khunlumprapas. *Sunflower*, 116/115 Soi 3, Thanon Khunlumprapas, serves home-made bread and filter coffee.

Mae Suya and Mae Lana

Set in wild countryside, 3km east of the Thai Yai/Kuomintang village of **MAE SUYA** (which is 40km from Mae Hong Son), *Wilderness Lodge* (①) is a great place to base yourself for hikes through the mountains to hilltribe villages. It's also within easy reach of two quite significant caves, the 1600-metre-long Tham Nam Pha Daeng, and the dramatic Tham Nam Lang, one of the biggest caves in the world, which has a towering entrance chamber and a spectacular nine-kilometre caving route beyond. To get to *Wilderness Lodge* take the left turning by the police box 3km east of Mae Suya, then continue on a dirt road for 1km.

Another remote guesthouse lies near **MAE LANA**, a Thai Yai village 6km north of Highway 1095, reached by a dirt road which branches off to the left 56km from Mae Hong Son. The clean and cosy *Mae Lana Guesthouse* (①) is by a stream on the edge of the village, from where you can walk to several Lahu villages, as well as the Tham Mae Lana, with its white-water flows and phallic formations. You can also walk to Ban Tum (see below) along an easy-to-follow five-hour track.

Soppong, Ban Tum and Tham Lot

The small, lively market town of **SOPPONG**, 68km from Mae Hong Son, gives access to the area's most famous cave, Tham Lot, 9km north in **BAN TUM** (or Ban Tham). There's no public transport along the paved road to the village, so without a motorbike, you'll have to hitch, walk or rent a motorbike taxi (B50). Turn right in the village for the entrance to the Forestry National Park, where you can hire a guide for B100. A short walk through the forest brings you to the entrance of Tham Lot, where the Lang River begins a 600-metre subterranean journey through the cave, requiring you to wade across the flow half a dozen times, or hire a bamboo raft (B100 per group of one to five). Two hours should allow you enough time for travelling through the broad, airy tunnel, and for climbing up to see the enormous stalagmites and other weird formations in the sweaty caverns in the roof.

The hillside **bungalows** at *Cave Lodge* (①), on the other side of Ban Tum from the cave, make an excellent base for exploring the area. The owners also organize kayak tours through Tham Lot when the water levels are high enough. On the main road at the western end of Soppong, the huts at *Jungle Guesthouse* (☎053/617099; ①) are the most popular in town. A short walk east of Soppong's bus stop, *Lemonhill Guesthouse* (☎053/617039; ②) has chalets in a pretty garden sloping down to the Lang River. All guesthouses give advice on local hikes.

Pai

There's nothing special to do in **PAI**, 43km from Soppong, but the atmosphere is relaxing, the guesthouses pleasant and it's a good place for undemanding valley walks and for trekking to Karen, Lisu and Lahu villages, which can be arranged through the guesthouses (B400 per day). The five-day trek to Mae Hong Son (see p.891) is impressive but quite hard. You can arrange an elephant ride at 5/3 Thanon Rungsiyanon (B400 for two people for 90min) or, from July to the end of January, a two-day rubber-raft trip (B1800) at Thai Adventure Rafting on Thanon Rungsiyanon (☎053/699111).

The small town's traditional buildings spread themselves liberally over the west bank of the Pai River, but everything's still within walking range of the **bus station** at the north end, where buses from Chiang Mai terminate. The most reliable place to rent **motorbikes** is Nop's Bike Shop, by *Rim Nam Restaurant* at 60/3 Thanon Ratchadumrong (☎053/699093); *Duang Guesthouse*, oposite the bus station, has plenty of mountain bikes (B50).

On the river bank east of the bus station, *Golden Hut* (☎053/699024; ①) has simple **rooms** and huts in a quiet spot around a vegetable plot. *Mr Jan's* on Thanon Sukhaphibun 3 (①), one of a mess of small streets behind and to the east of Thanon Rungsiyanon, the main street running south from the bus station, offers simple bamboo bungalows and pricier concrete rooms; good massages (B150/hour) and saunas (B50) are available. In a beautiful setting by the river to the east of the bus station, the log cabins at *Rim Pai Cottage*, 17 Moo 3, Viang Tai (☎053/699133; ②–③) are as posh as Pai gets. *Peter & Vandee's Huts* (B80), 2km east out of town over the bridge, has bamboo huts amongst fruit trees and runs two-, three- and five-day cookery classes (B500/B700/B1000). Best of the travellers' **restaurants** is *Thai Yai* at 12 Thanon Rungsiyanon (Mon–Sat 7.30am–9.30pm, Sun 7.30am–noon). At night, travellers congregate at *Be-Bop*, a small, laid-back bar which hosts live music.

Tha Ton and the Kok River

Leafy **THA TON**, 176km north of Chiang Mai, huddles each side of a bridge over the Kok River, which flows out of Burma 4km upstream. The main attractions here are boat and raft rides, but if you've got a morning to kill, visit the over-the-top ornamental gardens of **Wat Tha Ton** on the south side of the bridge.

Travelling down the hundred-kilometre stretch of the Kok River to Chiang Rai gives you a chance to soak up a rich diversity of typical northern landscapes, through rice fields and orchards, past riverside wats and over rapids. The police have several riverside checkpoints, and at Mae Salak you'll be asked to show your passport. Noisy, canopied longtail boats leave from the south side of the bridge in Tha Ton every day at 12.30pm for the four-hour trip to

Chiang Rai (B200, plus B300 for motorbikes). Boats from Chiang Rai leave at 10.30am. If you have more time, choose the peaceful bamboo rafts which glide downriver to Chiang Rai in two days. They leave at about 8am, take four to six people and the price includes mats, sleeping bags and food. *Thip's Traveller House* organizes the standard two-day raft trips (B1500), with a night spent in a Lahu village and an elephant ride.

Buses between Chiang Mai's northern Chang Phuak bus station and Tha Ton take about four hours, but many buses go only as far as Fang, 23km short of Tha Ton, from where you should take a songthaew. *Thip's Traveller House* (☎053/459312; ①), on the south side of the bridge, is the best budget **place to stay** in Tha Ton, with decent en-suite rooms and good food. Mrs Thip organizes rafting packages to Chiang Rai (see above) and longtail trips to the Burmese border, twenty minutes upstream. On the north side of the river, *Garden Home* (①–②), 300m from the bridge on the north side of the river, has attractive en-suite bungalows in an orchard, and rents bikes.

Chiang Rai

The long arm of the package-tour industry has finally reached **CHIANG RAI**, now a predominantly upmarket resort town of well over two thousand hotel rooms, but also known for its trekking. A walk up to **Doi Tong**, the hummock to the northwest of the centre, offers a fine view up the Kok River. On the highest part of the hill stands a kind of phallic Stonehenge centred on the town's new *lak muang*, representing the Buddhist layout of the universe. The old wooden *lak muang* can be seen in the viharn of **Wat Phra That Chomtong**, the city's first temple, which sprawls shambolically over the eastern side of the hill. Carved in China from 300kg of milky green jade, a beautiful replica of the Emerald Buddha (see p.853), Thailand's most important image, can now be seen here.

There are plenty of handicraft shops in the town, the most authentic selection of which can be found at the non-profit-making **Hilltribe Museum and Shop** at 620/25 Thanon Tanalai. The upstairs museum (Mon–Fri 8.30am–8pm, Sat & Sun 10am–8pm) is a good place to find out about the local hilltribes before going on a trek. It's run by the Population and Community Development Association (PDA), which also organizes treks. A **night bazaar** (7–11pm) sells handicrafts off Thanon Phaholyothin next to the bus station.

The Chiang Rai region offers a range of **treks**, from gentle walking trails near the Kok River to tough mountain slopes further north towards the Burmese border, but the area between Chiang Rai and Mae Salong in particular has become severely over-trekked. All guesthouses in Chiang Rai offer treks – *Chat*, *Chian* and *Mae Hong Son* are responsible and reliable, or try the Museum (see above) – and the tourist office publishes a list of their own recommendations. An average three-day trek, with an elephant ride, costs B2000 each for two people and B1600–1800 each for up to five. For comprehensive and accurate coverage of trails and hilltribe villages in Chiang Rai province, the Guide Map of Chiang Rai by V Hongsombud (Bangkok Guides) is essential.

Arrival and information

Buses arrive at the **bus station** on Thanon Phaholyothin, a long walk to most guesthouses, but served by samlors (around B20) and songthaews. The latter have no set routes, but cost B5 for short hops. **Longtails** from Tha Ton dock at the boat station on the north side of the Mae Fah Luang bridge. The airport, 8km northeast of town, is served by **taxis** (B100). There are two daily **flights** to and from Bangkok. Most guesthouses offer **bike** rental (B30–50). Soon Motorbikes, at 197/2 Thanon Trairat (☎053/714068), has the best choice of **motorbikes** (from B150), and PD Tour at 869/108 Thanon Pemavipat, near the Wiang Come department store (☎053/712829), rents out **jeeps**.

TAT is at 448/16 Thanon Singhakai near Wat Phra Singh (daily 8.30am–4.30pm; ☎053/717433); the 24-hour **tourist police** (☎053/717779) are here, too. **Internet access** is available at the Northern Computer Centre (daily 8am–8pm) on Thanon Phaholyothin, oppo-

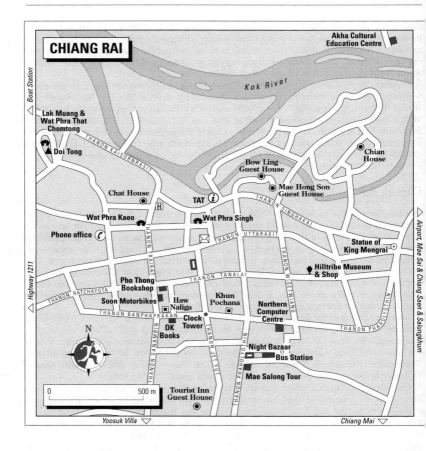

CHIANG RAI

Akha Cultural
Education Centre

Kok River

Boat Station

Lak Muang &
Wat Phra That
Chomtong

Doi Tong

THANON KAISORNRASIT

Chian
House

Bow Ling
Guest House

Chat House

TAT ⓘ

Mae Hong Son
Guest House

THANON SINGHAKAI

Wat Phra Kaeo

H

Wat Phra Singh

Phone office ⓒ

THANON UTTARAKIT

Statue of
King Mengrai

THANON RAIRAY

Hilltribe Museum
& Shop

THANON TANALAI

THANON WISETWIANG

Highway 1211

Pho Thong
Bookshop

Soon Motorbikes

Haw
Naliga

Khun
Pochana

Northern
Computer
Centre

THANON RATCHAYOTA

THANON BANPHAPRAKAN

Clock
Tower

DK
Books

THANON PHAHOLYOTHIN

THANON PHAHOLYOTHIN

Airport, Mae Sai & Chiang Saen & Salungkhum

N

THANON SANAMBIN

THANON JET YOT

Night Bazaar

Bus Station

Mae Salong Tour

0   500 m

Tourist Inn
Guest House

Yoosuk Villa ▽

Chiang Mai ▽

site the *Golden Triangle Inn*, and at KSC Internet, opposite the *Tourist Inn Guest House* on Thanon Jet Yot. The **Thai Airways** office is at 870 Thanon Phaholyothin (☎053/711179).

Accommodation

Many of Chiang Rai's **guesthouses** are clustered on the south bank of the river.

Bow Ling Guesthouse, off Th Singhakai near the *Mae Hong Son Guesthouse* (☎053/712704). A cute, peaceful place in a residential soi, with five en-suite rooms off a fragrant courtyard. ①.

Chat House, 3/2 Soi Sangkaew, Th Trairat (☎053/711481). Chiang Rai's longest-running travellers' hang-out has a laid-back atmosphere and modern en-suite rooms. Does treks, bike rental (B50) and free pick-ups from the bus or airport. ①.

Chian House, 172 Th Sri Boonruang (☎053/713388). Pleasant en-suite rooms and bungalows (all hot water) in a compound around a small pool. Bicycles, motorcycles, and jeeps (B800) for hire, plus treks as well as Internet access. ①.

Mae Hong Son Guesthouse, 126 Th Singhakai (☎053/715367). Friendly courtyard establishment with bar and café in a quiet local street. Decent rooms – some en suite (hot water). Tours and treks offered from B1600 for three days. ①.

Tourist Inn Guesthouse, 1004/4–6 Th Jet Yot (☎053/714682). Immaculately clean hotel-style guesthouse with a bakery, library, and bright en-suite rooms. Free pick-up from bus station. ②.

Eating

The popular, inexpensive, *Khun Pochana*, by the clocktower at 529/4–5 Thanon Banphaprakan, serves tasty Thai and Chinese standards. *Haw Naliga*, west of the clocktower at 402/1–2 Thanon Banphaprakan, offers a more interesting and varied Thai menu, and is a little pricier, but *Salungkhum*, at 843 Thanon Phaholyothin (across from the Cosmo petrol station, between King Mengrai's statue and the river), is rated by locals as serving the best food for the price in town. Another excellent option is the mid-priced *Cabbages and Condoms*, on the Ground Floor of the Museum, 620/25 Thanon Tanalai, which is run by the family planning organization, and does traditional Northern dishes, and plenty of veggie dishes.

Mae Sai

MAE SAI, with its hustling tourist trade and bustling border crossing, is Thailand's northernmost town, 61km from Chiang Rai. Thanon Phaholyothin is the town's single north–south street, which ends at the bridge over the Mae Sai River, the border with Burma. For $5, farangs can make a day-trip across the **border** to Thakhilek (8am–6pm), but you have to leave your passport at the Thai immigration checkpoint on the bridge. On your return you get an extra thirty days on a single-entry visa, sixty days on a multiple-entry visa from the date of re-entry. **Shopping** is the main interest in Thakilek: the huge market on the right after the bridge is an entrepôt for everything from crackers to tigers' intestines, but the Burmese handicrafts are disappointing. There is also a market in the grounds of Mae Sai's Wat Phra That Doi Wao, five minutes' walk from the bridge (behind the *Top North Hotel*), where Burmese and Chinese stuff is sold from 5am to 6pm. Most travellers staying in Mae Sai end up making day-trips out to Sop Ruak (see below).

Frequent **buses** run from Chiang Rai to Mae Sai. You can rent **motorbikes** from Pon Chai, opposite the Bangkok Bank (B150). A handful of **guesthouses** are strung out along the riverbank west of the bridge. The best of these is *Mae Sai* (☎053/732021; ①), a beautifully located set of bungalows, wedged between a steep hill and the river, fifteen minutes from the main road. The welcoming *Chad Guesthouse* on Soi Wiangpan, 1km before the bridge, is the classic travellers' rest (☎053/732054; ①) and also has dorms. Mae Sai's top **eating** place is *Rabieng Kaew*, opposite the Krung Thai Bank, which serves excellent Thai cuisine. The **night market** is across the main road from the *Sri Wattana Hotel*.

Sop Ruak and the Golden Triangle

Opium growing has been illegal in Thailand since 1959, but during the 1960s and 1970s, rampant production and refining of the crop in the lawless region on the borders of Thailand, Burma and Laos earned the area the nickname the **Golden Triangle**. Two "armies" have traditionally operated most of the trade within this area: the Shan United Army from Burma, which is led by the notorious warlord Khun Sa, and the Kuomintang (KMT) refugees from communist China. The Thai government's concerted attempt to eliminate opium growing within its borders has succeeded in reducing the size of the crop to under twenty tonnes per year, but Thailand still has a vital role to play as a conduit for heroin; most of the production and refinement of opium has simply moved over the borders into Burma and Laos.

For the benefit of tourists, "the Golden Triangle" has now been artificially concentrated into the precise spot where the borders meet, at the confluence of the Ruak and Mekong rivers, 57km northeast of Chiang Rai: **SOP RUAK**. Don't expect to run into sinister drugrunners, addicts or even poppy-fields here – instead you'll find souvenir stalls and a huge "Golden Triangle" sign. The green-roofed **Opium Museum** in the centre of town (daily

7am–6pm; B20) is unexpectedly worthwhile, and displays all the paraphernalia of opium growing and smoking. For uninterrupted views of the meeting of the rivers and the lands of Burma and Laos beyond, climb up to **Wat Phra That Phu Khao**, a 1200-year-old temple perched on a small hill above the village.

To get to Sop Ruak you'll have to go via Chiang Saen or Mae Sai first. From Chiang Saen you can go by regular **songthaew** (departing from in front of the school on the west side of the T-junction), rented **bicycle** (an easy 14-km ride on a paved road) or **longtail boat** up the Mekong (B600 round trip). From Mae Sai, songthaews make the 45-minute trip from the side of the *Sri Wattana Hotel* on Thanon Phaholyothin.

Chiang Saen

Combining tumbledown ruins with sweeping Mekong River scenery, **CHIANG SAEN**, 60km northeast of Chiang Rai, makes a rustic haven and a good base camp for the border region east of Mae Sai. Coveted for its strategic location, guarding the Mekong, Chiang Saen was passed back and forth between the kings of Burma and Thailand for nearly three hundred years until Rama I razed the place to the ground in 1804. The present town was resettled in 1881. The **National Museum** (March–Dec Wed–Sun 9am–4pm; Jan & Feb daily 8.30am–4.30pm; B30) makes an informative starting point, housing some impressive locally cast Buddha images and architectural features rescued from the ruins, as well as rural artefacts. **Wat Phra That Chedi Luang**, originally the city's main temple, is worth looking in on next door for its imposing, overgrown octagonal chedi. Beyond the ramparts to the west, **Wat Pa Sak**'s restored brick buildings and laterite columns make this the most impressive of Chiang Saen's many temples (B30). The central chedi owes its eclectic shape largely to the grand temples of Pagan in Burma and displays some beautiful carved stucco decoration.

Practicalities

Buses from Chiang Rai and **songthaews** from Sop Ruak stop just west of the T-junction of Thanon Phaholyothin and the river road; songthaews and the one daily bus from Chiang Khong stop on the river road about 250m south of the T-junction near Wat Pong Sanuk. Longtail boats from Sop Ruak dock just south of the T-junction. By bike, follow Highway 110 north to Mae Chan (30km), then bear northeastwards along Highway 1016 for the last 30km. **Bicycles** (B40) and **motorbikes** (B150) can be rented at *Gin's Guesthouse*.

The best guesthouse is *Gin's Guesthouse* (☎053/650847; ①–②), outside the ramparts, 2km north of the T-junction, which offers large A-frame bungalows in a lychee orchard, or pricier rooms in the main house; the owner can also organize Laos visas, treks and river trips. The **night market** sets up along the riverfront by the cargo pier and Wat Pha Kao Pan.

Chiang Khong and the Laos border

Several routes lead from Chiang Saen to **CHIANG KHONG**, 70km downriver. A peaceful one-street town, Chiang Khong is the only other land **border with Laos**, aside from Nong Khai, where you can turn up and get your Lao visa. The most scenic way to get from Chiang Saen to Chiang Khong is by motorbike; an exciting alternative is to run the rapids on a hired longtail boat (B1200; 3hr). There are two daily buses and several morning-only songthaews (2hr). Frequent buses also ply the route to and from Chiang Rai and Chiang Mai. Chiang Khong's best **guesthouse** is *Ban Tam-Mi-La*, at 113 Thanon Sai Klang (☎053/791234; ①), down a lane immediately in front of Ann Tour, and has tasteful wooden bungalows, a good restaurant, and bike rental. *Orchid Garden Guesthouse* (☎053/655195; ①) is a teakwood house with plain rooms in a quiet local soi running 100m west of the main road from Ann Tour. The best European/Thai **food** is served at nearby *Enjoy Rimkhong*. Opposite Ann Tour, Tawan Tours offers **Internet access** (10am–10pm).

Crossing the border into Laos

Most of Chiang Khong's guesthouses now organize **visas for Laos**, or you can go through Ann Tour, 6/1 Moo 8, Thanon Saiklang (☎053/655198 or 01/950 9691, fax 053/791218; daily 8am–5.30pm). The fifteen-day tourist visas cost US$50 and can be obtained on the same day (not Sat & Sun) if you arrive early enough; a photocopy of your passport is faxed over to Laos at 8am and at noon you can cross. If you hand in the photocopy at 10am, you can cross at 4pm; if you apply the night before you can cross from about 8am. Alternatively, fax a photocopy of your passport a few days in advance to Ann Tour. For the same price you can obtain a thirty-day visa within three to four working days. Note, however, that visa regulations change frequently.

Frequent **longboats (B20) to Houayxai** across the border depart from Chiang Khong's main pier, Hua Wiang, at the north end of town. From Houayxai (see p.508), you can get boats down the Mekong to Louang Phabang.

THE EAST COAST

Thailand's **east coast** is a five-hundred-kilometre string of predominantly dull, grey beaches blotched with expensive, over-packaged family resorts, the largest and most notorious of which is **Pattaya**. Offshore, however, it's a different story: the tiny island of **Ko Samet** attracts backpackers and Bangkokians to its pretty white-sand beaches, while travellers with more time on their hands head east to **Ko Chang**, a large forested island close to the Cambodian border. It is now legal to cross over the border near here.

Pattaya

With its murky sea, narrow, rubbish-strewn beaches and streets packed with high-rise hotels, **PATTAYA** is the epitome of exploitative tourism gone mad. The town swarms with male and female prostitutes, and plane-loads of Western men flock here to enjoy their services in the rash of go-go bars for which "Patpong-on-Sea" is notorious. Yet watersports facilities here are among the best in the country, and it's not a bad place to learn to **dive**, though the reefs off the Andaman Coast are more spectacular. TAT-approved dive shops that run four-day certificate courses (B10,000) and diving expeditions include Dave's Divers Den (☎038/221860) on Soi 6, Thanon Pattaya Beach; Dolphin Diving Centre (☎038/427185) on Soi Post Office; and Seafari Sports Center on Soi 5, Thanon Pattaya Beach (☎038/429253). Be wary of unqualified instructors and dodgy equipment when signing up at any dive centre.

Pattaya comprises three separate bays. At the centre is the four-kilometre **Pattaya beach**, fringed by a sliver of sand and packed with hotels, restaurants, bars and tour operators. The southerly bay, **Jomtien beach**, is cleaner and quieter, but lacks shops and restaurants and is not particularly attractive; it's 14 km long and Thailand's top windsurfing spot. **Naklua Bay**, around the northerly headland from Pattaya beach, is the quietest of the three, but much of the accommodation is inaccessible without private transport, and there's no decent beach.

Arrival and information

Most people arrive in Pattaya by **bus** from Bangkok's Eastern Bus Terminal or the old Northern Bus Terminal, Moh Chit 1. The bus station is just north of Soi 1, off Thanon Pattaya Beach in North Pattaya. Buses from Ban Phe (for Ko Samet) and Trat (for Ko Chang) generally drop passengers on Thanon Sukhumvit. There's a **TAT** office at 609 Thanon Mu Pratamnak, off Jomtien Road, south of Pattaya Beach, daily 8.30am–4.30pm (☎038/428750).

Public **songthaews** in Pattaya Beach follow a standard anti-clockwise route up Thanon Pattaya 2 as far as Thanon North Pattaya and back down Thanon Pattaya Beach (B10). Songthaews to Jomtien leave from the junction between Thanon Pattaya 2 and Thanon South

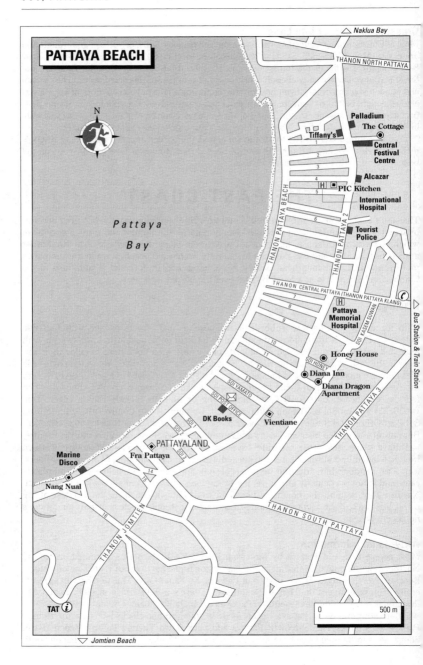

PATTAYA BEACH

△ Naklua Bay

THANON NORTH PATTAYA

N

Pattaya Bay

Palladium
The Cottage
Tiffany's
Central Festival Centre
Alcazar
PIC Kitchen
International Hospital
Tourist Police

THANON PATTAYA BEACH

THANON PATTAYA 2

THANON CENTRAL PATTAYA (THANON PATTAYA KLANG)

Pattaya Memorial Hospital

SOI KASEM SUWAN

Honey House
Diana Inn
Diana Dragon Apartment

SOI HONEY

THANON PATTAYA 3

SOI YAMATO

SOI POST OFFICE

DK Books
Vientiane

PATTAYALAND

Marine Disco
Fra Pattaya
Nang Nual

THANON JOMTIEN

THANON SOUTH PATTAYA

TAT ⓘ

0   500 m

▷ Bus Station & Train Station

▽ Jomtien Beach

Pattaya and cost B10–20. Thanon Pattaya Beach is full of touts offering **motorbikes** (B150–600) and **jeeps** (B1000) for rent.

Accommodation and eating

Really cheap **hotels** are almost impossible to find in Pattaya, but prices in all categories plummet when demand is slack. The best of the cheapies is the small, welcoming *Honey House* on Soi Honey, opposite Soi 10, Thanon Pattaya 2 (☎038/424396; ③), which has large en-suite rooms and some air-con. Nearby *Diana Dragon Apartment*, 198/16 Soi Buakhao, off Thanon Pattaya 2 at the end of the soi opposite Soi 11 (☎038/423928; ②), is also good value, offering enormous rooms and use of the pool at *Diana Inn*, 100m away. Another good deal are the smart and very peaceful garden bungalows of *The Cottage*, Thanon Pattaya 2, North Pattaya (☎038/425660; ③–④), which has two small pools. In Jomtien, *Sea Breeze Hotel* on the central stretch of the beach road (☎038/231056; ④–⑤) offers decent-sized air-con rooms, all with TV, plus a swimming pool and pool table.

PIC Kitchen, Soi 5, North Pattaya, is one of Pattaya's finest traditional Thai **restaurants**, offering a mid-priced menu of elegantly presented curry, seafood and vegetarian dishes. *Dolf Riks*, between sois 12 and 14 on Thanon Naklua, serves high-class Indonesian food – including an 18-dish *rijstaffel*, and *Vientiane*, between sois Yamato and Post Office on Thanon Pattaya 2, also specializes in Indonesian fare and Lao curries. For seafood, check out *Nang Nual* on Thanon Pattaya Beach, South Pattaya, where you choose your fish before eating it on the seafront terrace. Cheapest of the lot is the workaday *Fra Pattaya*, Thanon South Pattaya, which has a big menu of staple Thai and Chinese dishes.

Nightlife

Of the four hundred-odd **bars** in Pattaya, the majority are open-air "bar beers" staffed by hostesses, but not too seedy. For a more subtle drinking environment, try the *Bamboo Bar* at the seafront end of Thanon South Pattaya, or the British-run *Shamrock*, which is on the edge of the gay district in Pattayaland 2, but attracts a mixed clientele. *The Hopf Brew House*, between sois Yamato and Post Office on Thanon Pattaya Beach, is styled on a German beer hall. Drinks are a lot more expensive in the bouncer-guarded go-go bars on the South Pattaya "strip" where live sex shows keep the boozers hooked through the night. Go-go dancers, shower shows and striptease are also the mainstays of the gay scene, centred on Pattayaland Soi 3, South Pattaya. Tour groups constitute the main audience at the clean, family-oriented transvestite cabarets (B400–500), which are performed three times a night at *Alcazar*, opposite Soi 4 on Thanon Pattaya 2, and *Tiffany's*, north of Soi 1 on Thanon Pattaya 2.

Listings

Airlines Bangkok Airways 2nd Floor, Royal Garden Plaza, South Pattaya (☎038/411965); Thai Airways inside the *Dusit Resort*, 240/2 Th Pattaya Beach (☎038/425611–7).

Bookshops Excellent range of books at DK Books on Soi Post Office, and Bookazine in the Royal Garden Plaza, South Pattaya.

Hospitals Pattaya International Hospital (☎038/428374–5) on Soi 4, and Pattaya Memorial Hospital (☎038/429423–4) on Th Central Pattaya. The nearest divers' decompression chamber is at the Apakorn Kiatiwong Naval Hospital (☎038/601185) in Sattahip, 26km south of Pattaya; open 24 hours a day.

Internet access Fast and cheap at *Explorer Internet Café* between Sois 9 and 10 on Th Pattaya Beach.

Police Th Pattaya 2, just south of Soi 6 (☎038/429371).

Ko Samet

Backpackers, package tourists and Thai students flock to the white-sand beaches of the tiny, six-kilometre-long, national park island of **KO SAMET**, 80km southeast of Pattaya. Samet's best beaches are on the east coast, and there are numerous bungalow resorts here. A rough track connects some of them, otherwise it's a question of walking along the beach at low tide or over the low, rocky points at high water. All beaches get packed on weekends and national holidays, when accommodation rates rise by up to fifty percent. Once, Samet was considered to be malarial, but has now been pronounced safe. There's a B20 national park entrance fee on arrival, payable at the checkpoint between Na Dan pier and Hat Sai Kaew.

There is a sporadic **songthaew** service on Ko Samet, which starts at Na Dan pier and continues down the track as far as Wong Deuan. Ko Samet's **health centre** is in Na Dan, and the island's **post office** is run by Naga Bungalows on Ao Hin Kok (see below), who also provide internet access. You can also make international phone calls at Naga, and from every main beach; all Ko Samet's phones are radio phones so the code is always ☎01. The biggest bungalows will also change money, and there are small shops in Na Dan and on Hat Sai Kaew and Ao Wong Deuan. Ao Prao Divers (☎038/616885) are based at Ao Prao Resort on the island's west coast and offer PADI Open Water courses for B10000.

Arrival

The mainland departure point for Ko Samet is the tiny fishing port of **BAN PHE**, about 200km from Bangkok. **Buses** from Bangkok's Eastern Bus Terminal stop at Ban Phe pier, or you can take any Bangkok-to-Rayong bus and then change onto a songthaew for the twenty-minute journey to Ban Phe pier. Tourist **minibuses** run from Thanon Khao San to Ban Phe. Buses from Trat drop you on Thanon Sukhumvit, 5km by songthaew or motorbike taxi from the pier. There are a couple of hotels on the road by the pier: *TN Place* (②), where you can check your email, and *Ban Phe Diamond* (②–③).

In high season, up to nine **boats** a day make the trip from Ban Phe to Ko Samet (every hour from 8am–4pm; 30min; B30–50). Most go to **Na Dan pier** (convenient for Hat Sai Kaew, Ao Hin Kok, Ao Phai, Ao Tub Tim and Ao Nuan). For Ao Wong Deuan, Ao Cho or Ao Thian, it's more convenient to take the boat to Ao Wong Deuan (4 daily; 40min; B50). Boats for all these destinations leave from Ban Phe's Saphaan Nuan Tip pier, opposite the 7–11 shop.

Hat Sai Kaew

HAT SAI KAEW, or Diamond Beach, named for its beautiful long stretch of luxuriant sand, is ten minutes' walk south from Na Dan. The most popular – and congested – beach on Samet, this is the only part of the island where the beachfront is lined with bungalows, restaurants and beachwear stalls. The most appealing bungalow operation here is *Diamond Beach Resort* (☎01/601 6249; ②–③), at the far northern end of the beach, which offers a big range of huts and bungalows comfortably spaced around a garden. Further south along the beach, *Sai Kaew Villa* (☎01/218 6696; ③–⑦) comprises a dozen smart rooms in a block, plus some pricier bungalows.

Ao Hin Kok and Ao Phai

Separated from Hat Sai Kaew by a low promontory on which sits a mermaid statue, **AO HIN KOK** is much smaller and has only three bungalow outfits. The friendly and very popular *Naga* (☎01/218 5732; ①) offers simple huts; *Tok's Little Hut* (①–②) and *Jep's Inn* (②–③) both offer slightly more comfortable bungalows. Ao Hin Kok is particularly strong on food: *Naga* has top veggie dishes, home-made bread and cakes, while *Jep's Inn* serves up fine seafood and travellers' fare on the beach. Songthaews from Na Dan cost B20, or you can walk here in about fifteen minutes. Ko Samet post office is run out of *Naga Bungalows* and offers a phone and fax service, internet access and poste restante; letters are kept for three months and should be addressed c/o Poste Restante, Ko Samet Post Office, Naga Bungalows, Ko Samet.

Beach life gets a little more active around the next collection of rocks on the narrow but pleasant enough **AO PHAI**, with an outdoor bar and weekend disco. *Ao Phai Hut* (☎01/353 2644; ②–③) occupies a lovely position on the rocky divide between Ao Phai and Hin Kok, and offers good en-suite huts, some with air con. *Sea Breeze* (☎01/218 6397; ①–③) has cheap huts with shared facilities, and pricier en-suite ones with air-con. They sell boat trips and

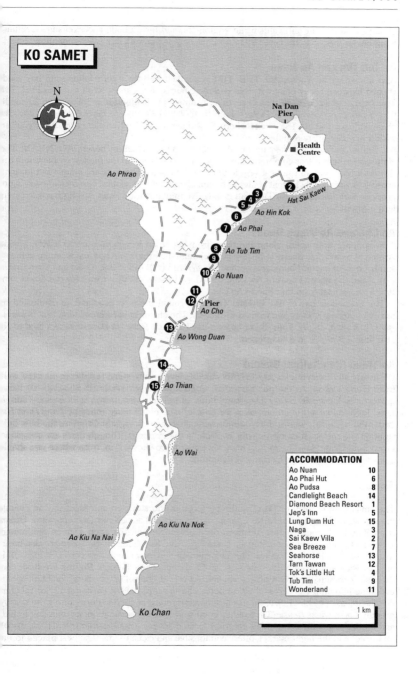

KO SAMET

N

Na Dan
Pier

Health
Centre

Ao Phrao

1

2

Hat Sai Kaew

5 4 3

Ao Hin Kok

6

7 *Ao Phai*

8 *Ao Tub Tim*

9

10 *Ao Nuan*

11

12 *Pier*
Ao Cho

13

Ao Wong Duan

14

15 *Ao Thian*

Ao Wai

Ao Kiu Na Nok

Ao Kiu Na Nai

Ko Chan

ACCOMMODATION

Ao Nuan	10
Ao Phai Hut	6
Ao Pudsa	8
Candlelight Beach	14
Diamond Beach Resort	1
Jep's Inn	5
Lung Dum Hut	15
Naga	3
Sai Kaew Villa	2
Sea Breeze	7
Seahorse	13
Tarn Tawan	12
Tok's Little Hut	4
Tub Tim	9
Wonderland	11

0   1 km

minibus tickets, rent out windsurfing equipment, and have phone and exchange facilities. Songthaews from Na Dan cost B20 to Ao Phai, or you can walk it in twenty minutes.

Ao Tub Tim and Ao Nuan

Also known as Ao Pudsa, **AO TUB TIM** is a small, slightly scruffy white-sand bay sand-wiched between rocky points. It feels secluded, but is only a short stroll from Ao Phai. *Tub Tim* (☎01/218 6425; ②–⑥) has everything from simple bamboo huts through to air-condi-tioned bungalows, while *Ao Pudsa*'s huts (☎01/239 5680; ②) are fairly basic, but you can change money and buy ferry tickets here. Songthaews from Na Dan pier cost B20, or you can walk it in about thirty minutes.

Clamber up over the next headland to reach Samet's smallest beach, **AO NUAN**. The atmosphere here is less commercial than the other beaches, and the mellow restaurant of the *Ao Nuan* has some of the best veggie food on the island. The huts are simple but idiosyn-cratic (②) and usually lamplit at night, though electricity is available. The rocky beach is not great for swimming, but Ao Tub Tim is only five minutes' walk away. A songthaew from Na Dan costs B25.

Ao Cho and Ao Wong Deuan

A five-minute walk south along the track from Ao Nuan brings you to **AO CHO**, a wide stretch of beach that seems to be less popular than the others and has just a couple of pretty similar, decent enough bungalow outfits: *Wonderland* (☎01/438 8409; ①–②) and *TarnTawan* (②). Take the normal boat to Na Dan, then a songthaew (B30), or wait for the direct 2pm White Shark boat from Ban Phe to Ao Cho.

The horseshoe bay of **AO WONG DEUAN**, round the next headland, is dominated by pricey bungalow resorts and fringed with stalls. The cheapest accommodation is at *Seahorse* (☎01/218 5629; ③–④). Four direct boats a day run here from Na Dan; or take a boat to Na Dan then a B30 ride in a songthaew.

Ao Thian (Candlelight Beach)

Off nearly all beaten tracks, **AO THIAN** enjoys a lovely setting and is only ten minutes' walk from Wong Deuan. At the northern end, *Candlelight Beach* (☎01/218 6934; ③–④) has a dozen or so basic and rather dilapidated huts, as well as some newer, solid en-suite bunga-lows. Right down at the other end of the beach is the much more romantic *Lung Dum Hut* (☎01/452 9472; ②), whose thirty simple bungalows are all slightly different, the best built right on the rocks; electricity is only available in the evenings. Though there are occasional direct boats from Ban Phe to Ao Thian, it's easier to go via Na Dan, from where you should get a songthaew to Wong Deuan and then walk.

Trat

The small market town of **TRAT** is the perfect place to stock up on essentials and change money before heading out to Ko Chang, via the port at Laem Ngop (see opposite). **Buses** from Bangkok's Eastern Bus Terminal drop passengers on the main Thanon Sukhumvit, 100m north of the songthaew stop for Laem Ngop and Ko Chang boats. There are also buses to and from Ban Phe and Pattaya. The long-running *Foremost Guesthouse* (☎039/511923; ①) is a short walk southeast of the bus stop, at 49 Thanon Thoncharoen. **Rooms** are basic, but there's a communal area downstairs which has a very useful set of travellers' comment books including info on travel across the Cambodian border. Around the corner at 12 Soi Yai Onn, *NP Guesthouse* (☎039/512270; ①) has nice enough rooms and a B50 dorm, or try the nearby friendly *Cocos Guest House* (①), another good source of information on surrounding islands and border formalities. The more centrally located *Muang Trat Hotel* (☎039/511091; ③–④) on the edge of the night market, offers comfortable and clean rooms. The best **places to eat** in Trat are at the day market, on the ground floor of the Thanon Sukhumvit shopping centre, and the night market, between Soi Vichidanya and Soi Kasemsan, east of Thanon Sukhumvit.

Ban Hat Lek and the Cambodian border

Since 1998, foreigners have been able to cross the **border into Cambodia** from **BAN HAT LEK**, 91km east of Trat. However, it's worth reading the travellers' comment books at *Foremost Guesthouse* in Trat, as the crossing entails a long and complicated journey. The route basically involves taking a motorbike taxi (B20) and short ferry (B20) from Hat Lek to Krong Koh Kong (just across the Cambodian border), then a ferry to Sao Thong, and then a three-hour boat ride to Sihanoukville (Kompong Son). From here it's a four-hour bus ride to Phnom Penh. Alternatively, you can catch a direct boat to Sihanoukville from Ko Kong but it leaves at 8am, meaning you need to leave Trat at 5am. You need a visa from the Cambodian Embassy in Bangkok to cross at this point. The border opens from 7am to 5pm. Public songthaews to Khlong Yai, 74km east of Trat, leave Trat about every thirty minutes from behind the shopping centre; from Khlong Yai you'll have to charter the songthaew to continue on to Ban Hat Lek, about 17km away.

Laem Ngop

The main departure point for Ko Chang and the outer islands is the tiny port of **LAEM NGOP**, 17km southwest of Trat and served by songthaews from Thanon Sukhumvit (every 20min; 20–40min). For details of boat services from here to Ko Chang, see below, and for boat services to the outer islands, see p.909. You can buy ferry tickets, change money and reserve island accommodation (definitely worthwhile in peak season) at the pier. The **TAT office** (daily 8.30am–4.30pm; ☎039/597255) is close by. You can extend your visa at the Laem Ngop Immigration Office, 3km northeast of Laem Ngop pier, on the road to Trat. The friendly, efficient *Chut Kaew* guesthouse (☎039/597088; ①) is close to the bank on the main road, about seven minutes' walk from the pier; you can store luggage here while you're on Ko Chang.

Ko Chang

The focal point of a national marine park archipelago of 52 islands, **KO CHANG** is Thailand's second-largest island (after Phuket) and a popular backpackers' destination. During peak season, accommodation on the west coast tends to fill up very quickly – and things go mad on national holidays – but it gets a lot quieter (and cheaper) from May to October, when fierce storms batter the flimsier huts and can make the sea too rough to swim in.

A wide road runs almost all the way round the island, served by fairly frequent public songthaews; you can also rent motorbikes and mountain bikes on most beaches, and should be able to arrange a motorbike taxi from the same places. There are money-exchange facilities and small shops at Hat Sai Kaew and Hat Kai Bae. Though mosquitoes don't seem to be much in evidence, Ko Chang is one of the few areas of Thailand that's still considered to be malarial, so you may want to start taking your prophylactics before you get here, and bring repellent with you. Ko Chang businesses use radio phones, so the code is ☎01 wherever you call from.

The most convenient **boats to Ko Chang** depart from Laem Ngop (see above) and arrive at either Ao Saparot or, occasionally, at Tha Dan Mai, both on the island's northeast coast. From both points songthaews ferry passengers on to the main beaches. There are six boats a day from Laem Ngop (45min), which, weather permitting, follow the same timetable throughout the year, departing at 9am, 11am, 1pm, 2pm, 3pm and 4pm. From November to April there's also one boat a day (3pm) direct to *White Sand Beach Resort* at Hat Sai Kaew. Tickets cost B80 which includes the songthaew ride to the beach of your choice. It's possible to do the whole Bangkok-to-Ko Chang trip in a day by catching the 8.30am air-con bus from

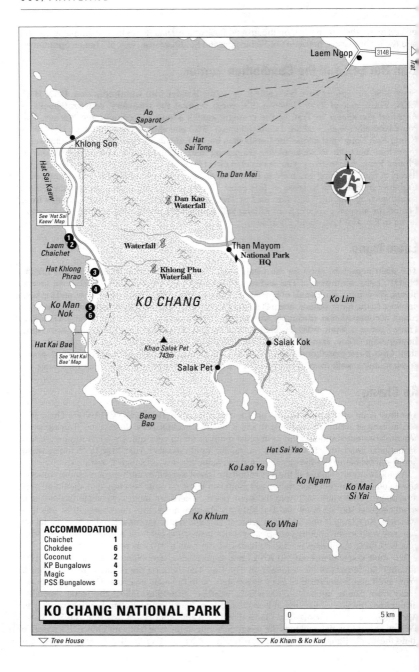

Laem Ngop ● 3148 ▷ Trat

Ao Saparot

Khlong Son ●

Hat Sai Tong

Tha Dan Mai

Hat Sai Kaew

See 'Hat Sai Kaew' Map

N

Dan Kao Waterfall

Laem Chaichet

❶
❷

Waterfall

Than Mayom
National Park HQ

Hat Khlong Phrao

❸

Khlong Phu Waterfall

❹

KO CHANG

Ko Lim

Ko Man Nok

❺
❻

Hat Kai Bae

See 'Hat Kai Bae' Map

▲ Khao Salak Pet 743m

Salak Kok ●

Salak Pet ●

Bang Bao

Hat Sai Yao

Ko Lao Ya

Ko Ngam

Ko Mai Si Yai

Ko Khlum

Ko Whai

ACCOMMODATION

Chaichet	1
Chokdee	6
Coconut	2
KP Bungalows	4
Magic	5
PSS Bungalows	3

KO CHANG NATIONAL PARK

0   5 km

▽ *Tree House*   ▽ *Ko Kham & Ko Kud*

he Eastern Bus Terminal. Tourist minibuses run from Thanon Khao San through to Laem
Ngop (6hr) for B250 (B500 return).

Hat Sai Kaew (White Sand beach)

Framed by a broad band of fine white sand at low tide, **HAT SAI KAEW** (White Sand beach)
is the island's longest beach and, some would argue, its prettiest too. It is also the busiest and
most commercial, with almost twenty different bungalow operations squashed in between
the road and the shore. Be careful when
swimming off Hat Sai Kaew, as currents
are very strong here. Songthaews take
about fifteen minutes to drive from the Ao
Saparot pier to Hat Sai Kaew. You can rent
motorbikes at a couple of roadside stalls
in Hat Sai Kaew for B60 an hour or B400 a
day; the same places will act as a taxi service. Several bungalows run **snorkelling
trips** to nearby islands, and a dive operator (*kcd_werner@hotmail.com*), based at
the *White Sand Beach Resort*, offers Open
Water courses for B9000.

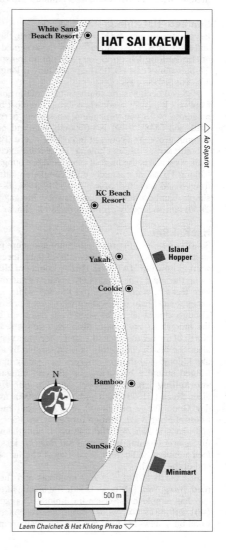

ACCOMMODATION AND EATING

Many of the bungalow restaurants do fish
barbecues at night. Across the road from
the beach, *Ban Nuna* has a menu of Thai
curries, seafood and pizzas; seating is
Thai-style on cushions in a breezy open-
sided *sala*. *Yakah* does pots of real coffee
and home-made bread, as does *Bakery*.

Bamboo. All the huts here are, not surprisingly,
made of bamboo, and though none of them has a
private bathroom or fan, they do all have mosquito nets. ①–②.

Cookie. The best of the mid-range places on this
beach, *Cookie* has smart bungalows, all with
attached tiled bathrooms and fans. ②–③.

KC Beach Resort (☎01/211 5607). The most
popular place in Hat Sai Kaew, and deservedly
so, *KC* has thirty simple bamboo huts strung out
under the palm trees over a long stretch of beach
so that each one feels a little bit private. ①–②.

SunSai (☎01/211 4488). Efficiently run place
with a big range of rooms set in a garden with a
table-tennis table. The cheapest rooms share
facilities, the most expensive have a separate sitting room with TV. ①–⑦.

White Sand Beach Resort (☎01/281 7526).
Located at the far north end of the beach, about
ten minutes' walk along the sand from the next
set of bungalows at Rock Sand, *White Sand*
offers a range of nicely spaced huts, most of
which are still only lit by lamps. Uninterrupted
sea views, some private bathrooms and some
electricity. ①–④.

Yakah. English–Thai run place with a lot of bamboo huts crowded together, some with beach
views, others backing onto the road. ①–②.

Laem Chaichet

LAEM CHAICHET's rocky headland curves round into an attractive and secluded casuari
na-fringed bay. There are just two bungalow operations here: the access track from the main
road leads straight to the cute chalet-style huts at *Coconut* (☎01/219 3432; ③); follow the path
100m to the right, across a small *khlong*, for *Chaichet* (☎01/219 3458; ③), with simple A-frame
huts and bungalows prettily located on the headland. Neither place rents motorbikes, so
you'll either have to get one from Hat Sai Kaew, or rely on songthaews, which take about ten
minutes from Hat Sai Kaew, fifteen minutes to Hat Kai Bae, or 25 minutes from the pier.

Southern Hat Khlong Phrao

Beyond the turn-off for Khlong Phu waterfall, the main road passes signs for *PSS* bungalows
and then for *KP*; take either one of these signed tracks to get down to the southern stretch
of **Hat Khlong Phrao**. If you're on public transport, a songthaew ride from Hat Sai Kaew to
KP bungalows costs B20. The beach here is long, partially shaded by casuarinas and can get
a bit rubbish-strewn.

PSS (①) occupies the southern bank of the northern khlong and a fair length of the shore
front too. It's fairly rundown, offering the most basic bamboo huts on the island (invest in a
mosquito net if you're planning on staying here). Ten minutes' walk down the beach, *KP*
(☎01/863 5448; ①–⑤) is efficiently run and popular, with two dozen bamboo huts in a
coconut grove. You can rent motorbikes here (B500 a day).

South across the next khlong (impassable except by swimming) and round a headland, the
main road skirts the back of a couple more bungalows, which, though technically also in Hat
Khlong Phrao, are actually on a completely different little white sand bay, which is palm
fringed and secluded. *Magic* (☎01/219 3408; ①–⑤) stands right on the beach and has both
simple bamboo huts and larger wood bungalows. The adjacent *Chokdee* (☎01/219 3814;
②–⑥) sits on a rocky promontory and is similar but a bit pricier.

Hat Kai Bae

South of *Chokdee*, the road gets more and more potholed
as it runs through a scenic swathe of palm trees before
veering down to **HAT KAI BAE**, a couple of kilometres
along the coast. The beach here is narrow and overhung
with trees in some places, but the soft white sand and
exceptionally pale blue water make a very pretty scene.
Though almost all of the shorefront has been built on,
the bungalows are mostly discreet, nicely spaced huts.
North of the access track, the shore becomes very rocky,
loses the beach completely as it's dissected by a lagoon-
like khlong, and then re-emerges as a sandy mangrove-
fringed strand a bit further on. Several bungalows do
snorkelling trips (B200–500), and *Kai Bae Hut* organizes **dives** (B1500–2000) and courses (B9000 for a four-
day Open Water certificate). You can rent **mountain
bikes** at *Nang Nual*, **change money** at *Sea View*, and get
provisions at *Kai Bae Hut* minimart. Songthaews from
Ao Saparot (40min) drop you at *Kai Bae Hut*, less than fifteen minutes' walk from *Siam Bay* at the far southern
end of the beach.

Just north of *Kai Bae Hut* minimart and the access
road, *Nang Nual* (①) is set beside the lagoon-like khlong
and has simple huts; cross the khlong to reach *Coral*
(☎01/219 3815; ②), whose large, simple concrete and
wood bungalows are only five minutes' walk from a quiet

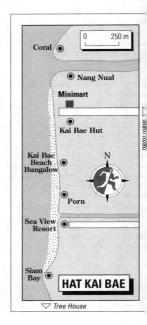

HAT KAI BAE

stretch of sand. Heading south along the beach from the access road and *Kai Bae Hut* mini-mart, *Kai Bae Beach Bungalow* (☎01/219 3861; ①–⑤) is a popular, well-run outfit with lots of bungalows stretching over quite a big patch of the seafront. A few hundred metres further south, *Porn* (①) has simple bamboo bungalows on the beach, with shared bathrooms. Set right at the southern end of the beach, *Siam Bay* (☎01/452 7061; ②–⑤) feels more spacious than the other places on Kai Bae; it has a range of huts set right on the beach, some en-suite. All the Kai Bae bungalows have restaurants, but the best food is served up by *Coral*, north of the access road, which specializes in northeastern dishes.

Ko Mak, Ko Kham and Ko Whai

South of Ko Chang lies a whole cluster of islands, some of which offer tourist accommodation. The most visited and accessible of these is **KO MAK**, which lies off the south coast of Ko Chang, and boasts fine white sand beaches along its south and west coasts. From November to April, one boat a day leaves from Laem Ngop at 3pm, costs B170, and takes about three and a half hours. It's also possible to get here from Ko Chang, on the Island Hopper boat (every Wed). Ko Mak has several bungalow operations: *Lazy Days* (☎02/281 3412; ①), set on a rather rocky stretch of beach, *Bamboo Guesthouse* (①) which offers classic bamboo huts, or try the popular *Fantasia*, with simple bungalows (①).

Miniature **KO KHAM** lies off the northern tip of Ko Mak, and has room for just one set of bungalows, *Ko Kham Resort* (☎039/597114; ②–④), with a restaurant that's not great for vegetarians. There's a daily boat from Laem Ngop at 3pm; it takes three hours and costs B170.

Beaches on **KO WHAI**, east of Ko Kham, tend to be rocky, so the snorkelling is better than the sunbathing. You can stay at *Paradise* (②), which offers cheap bamboo huts, or the more comfortable *Coral Resort* (☎039/512634; ②–③). Boats to Ko Whai depart from Laem Ngop daily at 3pm from November to April, take about two and a half hours, and cost B130. You can also get here from Ko Chang, every Monday, Wednesday and Friday on the Island Hopper boat.

THE NORTHEAST: ISAAN

Bordered by Laos and Cambodia on three sides, the tableland of **northeast** Thailand, known as **Isaan**, is the least-visited region of the kingdom and the poorest, but also its most traditional. Most northeasterners speak a dialect that's more comprehensible to residents of Vientiane than Bangkok, and Isaan's historic allegiances have tied it more closely to Laos and Cambodia than to Thailand. Between the eleventh and thirteenth centuries, the all-powerful Khmers covered the northeast in magnificent stone temple complexes, which can still be admired at **Phimai** and **Phanom Rung**. The mighty **Mekong River** forms 750km of the border between Isaan and Laos, and there are five points along it where foreigners are allowed to cross the border (see p.824). The river makes a popular backpackers' trail, not least because of its laid-back waterfront guesthouses in **Chiang Khan**, **Sri Chiang Mai** and **Nong Khai**. Inland scenery is rewarding too, with good hiking trails at the national parks of **Khao Yai** and **Phu Kradung**.

Khao Yai National Park

Khao Yai National Park offers a realistic chance of seeing white-handed (lar) gibbons, pig-tailed macaques, hornbills, civets and barking deer, plus the possibility of sighting an elephant or a tiger. The park has lots of waterfalls and several undemanding walking trails; it's only 120km northeast of Bangkok, and is Thailand's most popular national park. The best way to see Khao Yai is to stay either in the park itself or just outside in the small town of Pak Chong; you have the choice of exploring the trails yourself or joining a backpackers' tour. Bring warm clothes as it gets cool at night.

Twelve well-worn trails radiate from the area around the visitor centre and park headquarters at kilometre stone 37, and a few more branch off from the roads that cross the park. The main trails are numbered and should be easy to follow, and sketch maps are available at the visitor centre. One of the most popular trails runs from the park headquarters to Nong Pak Chee observation tower (trail 6; 4km; 2hr 30min), passing through forest and grassland and ending at a lakeside observation tower; from the tower it's 1km to the main road, then 2km back to the park headquarters. The trail from Haew Suwat waterfall to the Khao Laem ranger post (trail 5; 3km/2hr each way) features a waterfall and grassland, but is inaccessible in the rainy season; you'll need to hitch or walk the 6km of road from the park headquarters to Haew Suwat. The short walk from Haew Suwat waterfall to the Pha Kluai campsite (trail 4; 2hr round trip), is paved most of the way and offers a good chance of spotting gibbons, macaques, kingfishers and hornbills.

Practicalities

To get to the park, first take a **bus** or **train** to **PAK CHONG**, which is 37km north of Khao Yai's visitor centre and major trailheads. The cheapest way to get from Pak Chong to Khao Yai is to take a songthaew (every 30min from 6.30am–5pm; 30min) from outside the 7–11 shop, 200m west of the footbridge on the north side of Pak Chong's main road, to the park checkpoint, which is about 14km short of the Khao Yai visitor centre, park headquarters and most popular trailheads. At the checkpoint (where'll you'll be asked to pay a B20 entrance fee, B50 per vehicle), park rangers will flag down passing cars and get them to give you a ride up to the visitor centre; this is normal practice and quite safe – public songthaews aren't allowed beyond here. However, if you charter a songthaew from Pak Chong to the park instead (B900 round trip), it's allowed into the park like any private vehicle. Coming back from the park, hitch back to the checkpoint then take a songthaew (last one about 5.30pm).

The cheapest **accommodation** is at the basic and rather chilly national park dorms (B20 per person plus B15 per blanket) next to the park headquarters in the heart of Khao Yai; avoid weekends which get booked out well in advance. There are plenty of hot-food stalls here (daily 7am–6pm). You can also rent a **tent** (B150–B300) at the Pha Kluai campground, 4km east of the park headquarters. Bring your own ground sheet.

Alternatively, you could base yourself in Pak Chong, at the fairly comfortable *Phubade Hotel* (☎044/314964; ②), located just 50m south of the train station on Tesaban Soi 15. If you're doing a tour, you'll stay at the tour operators' accommodation (see below). Pak Chong's exceptionally good **night market** sets up on the edge of the main road, between Tesaban sois 17 and 19. There is a **CS Internet** place on Thanon Thesaban, near soi 15, open till midnight.

Tours and night safaris

The good thing about joining a **tour** of Khao Yai is that you're accompanied by an expert wildlife-spotter, and you have transport between the major sights of the park. There are currently two backpacker-oriented tours running out of Pak Chong, both of which last for a day and a half, with the middle night spent in Pak Chong; book ahead if you can. Tours with Jungle Adventure (☎044/313836), which is based at Soi 1, Thanon Kongvaccine, off Tesaban Soi 16 in central Pak Chong, cost B950 per person and include several hours' trail-walking, plus swimming at the waterfalls and a night safari; you spend the night at the *Jungle Adventure* lodgings (②) in Pak Chong, in either a B70 dorm bed or a basic double room. Some travellers have criticized Jungle Adventure, however, for cutting too many corners, and at the time of writing, it seemed uncertain whether the company would have its guide licence renewed. (Happy Tours, opposite the train station, is run by the same company.) Wildlife Safari (☎044/312922) tours, costing B850 per person, emphasize plant-spotting and animal observation in small groups, and include a night safari. Accommodation is at the Wildlife Safari huts (①–②), behind their office at 39 Thanon Pak Chong Subsanun, Nong Kaja, about 2km north of Pak Chong train station; call for free transport from Pak Chong.

A much touted park attraction are the hour-long **night safaris** ("night lightings") which take truckloads of tourists round Khao Yai's main roads in the hope of sighting deer and civets, or even elephants and tigers. Both tours include a night safari, but if you're on your own, book a place on one of the trucks at the national park headquarters; they leave from there every night at 7pm and 8pm.

Khorat (Nakhon Ratchasima)

KHORAT, 90km from Pak Chong (officially renamed Nakhon Ratchasima), has nothing of interest in itself but can be used as a base for exploring Phimai and Phanom Rung. If you're looking for something to do here, check out the unexceptional **Maha Veeravong Museum** (Wed–Sun 9am–4pm; B10) in the grounds of Wat Suthachinda on Thanon Ratchadamnoen, or take a bus from Khorat's southern city gate to the interesting little pottery village of **DAN KWIAN**, 15km south of Khorat on Route 224.

There are two long-distance **bus terminals** in Khorat, each supposedly serving specific destinations, but there are changes afoot, so check departure points with TAT. Essentially, Bus Terminal 1, which is just off Thanon Suranari, close to the town centre and most hotels, serves the nearest destinations such as Phimai and Pak Chong (for Khao Yai); it also runs some buses to Bangkok. Bus Terminal 2, on the northern edge of the city on Highway 2, is much larger, and is used mainly by the long-distance buses, from Bangkok, Chiang Mai, Surin, Khon Kaen, Nong Khai and Pattaya. Arriving at the **train station** on Thanon Mukkhamontri, you're midway between the commercial centre to the east (1km) and the TAT office to the west (1km).

Local buses and songthaews travel most of the main roads: yellow #1 heads west along Thanon Chumphon, past the train station and out to *Doctor's Guesthouse* and returns east via Thanon Yommarat; #2 runs between the main TAT office in the west, via the train station, and Suranari and Assadang roads, to the east; and #3 also runs right across the city, via Mahathai and Jomsurangyat roads, past the train station, to the TAT office in the west. **TAT** (daily 8.30am–4.30pm; ☎044/213666), on the western edge of town, has free city bus maps.

The best budget **accommodation** in Khorat is the clean, friendly and central *Tokyo Hotel l*, at 329–333 Thanon Suranari, just 30m from Bus Terminal 1 (☎044/242873; ①–②). If that's full, the nearby *Tokyo Guesthouse* and *Tokyo Hotel 2* are similar. *Siri Hotel*, 167–168 Thanon Pho Klang (☎044/242831; ①–③), is also fairly central, quite quiet and spacious. The long-standing backpackers' favourite, *Doctor's Guesthouse* is ten minutes' bus ride out at 78 Soi 4, Thanon Suebsiri, near TAT (☎044/255846; ①). It has a quaint B&B atmosphere with only six rooms and a dorm. Local yellow bus/songthaew #1 stops opposite the soi entrance; #2 passes the Thanon Suebsiri junction (get off when you see Wat Mai Amphawan across the road).

Khorat's small night market, along the *Chomsurang Hotel* end of Thanon Mahathai, is the best place for local northeastern **food**, or there are plenty of roadside noodle stalls opposite the train station. If you're staying at *Doctor's Guesthouse*, try the quality Thai dishes at *C&C*, next to the Soi 4 intersection on Thanon Suebsiri.

Phimai

The tiny modern town of **PHIMAI**, 60km northeast of Khorat, is dominated by the exquisitely restored eleventh-century Khmer temple complex of **Prasat Hin Phimai** (daily 7.30am–6pm; B40). Built mainly of dusky pink and greyish-white sandstone, it was connected by a direct road to the Khmer capital Angkor and follows the classic precepts of Khmer temple design: a series of walls or galleries punctuated by false balustraded windows, surrounding an inner sanctuary containing several prangs (corn-cob-shaped tower), which house important religious images. Phimai's magnificent main prang has been restored to its original cruciform groundplan, complete with an almost full set of carved lintels, pediments and antefixes, and capped with a stone lotus bud. The carvings around the outside of the prang depict predominantly Hindu themes. Shiva – the Destroyer – dances above the main entrance to the southeast antechamber: his destruction dance heralds the end of the world and the creation of a new order. Most of the other external carvings pick out episodes from the Ramayana, starring heroic Rama and his band of faithful monkeys in endless battles against the evil Ravana. By the early thirteenth century, Phimai had been turned into a Buddhist temple and the main prang now houses Phimai's most important image, the Buddha sheltered by a seven-headed naga (snake). Much of the ancient carved stonework discovered at Phimai, but not fitted back into the renovated structure, can be seen at the open-air **museum** (Wed–Sun 8am–4.30pm; free) northeast of the ruins, just inside the old city walls.

Direct **buses** to Phimai depart from Khorat's Bus Terminal 1 every half hour and take one and a half hours; they stop near the ruins. Phimai makes a much more appealing **overnight** stop than Khorat: *Old Phimai Guesthouse* (☎044/471918; ①) is a lovely old wooden house with a roof garden, just off Thanon Chomsudasadet near the ruins. Or you can try the less atmospheric *Phimai Hotel* (☎044/471306; ①), next to the bus station. *Bai Teiy* on Thanon Chomsudasadet serves tasty **Thai dishes**, including fresh fish, and keeps bus timetables. There is an **Internet** place near the *Old Phimai Guesthouse*.

Phanom Rung and Muang Tham

Built during the same period as Phimai, the temple complexes of **Prasat Hin Khao Phanom Rung** and **Prasat Muang Tham** form two more links in the chain that once connected the Khmer capital with the limits of its empire. To get to the ruins, you first need to take a bus to the small town of **Ban Tako**, roughly midway between Khorat and Surin on Route 24; bus #274 travels between the two provincial capitals. From Ban Tako it's 12km south to Phanom Rung and another 8km south to Muang Tham so you'll either have to hitch or rent a motorbike taxi (B60–80 per person to Phanom Rung, plus B50 for the return trip to Muang Tham, plus another B60–80 to Ban Tako). Most people do the ruins as a day-trip from Khorat or Surin, but there's a simple guesthouse, *Honey Inn* (①) in Prakhon Chai, the town closest to Phanom Rung on the eastern stretch of Route 24, between Ban Tako and Surin.

Prasat Hin Khao Phanom Rung

Prasat Hin Khao Phanom Rung (daily 8am–5pm; B50) dates back to the tenth century and stands as the finest example of Khmer architecture in Thailand, its every surface ornamented with exquisite carvings and its buildings so perfectly aligned that on the morning of April's full-moon day you can stand at the westernmost gateway and see the rising sun through all fifteen doors. This day marks Songkhran, the Thai New Year, which is celebrated here with a day-long festival of huge parades.

You approach the temple compound along a dramatic 200-metre-long avenue flanked with lotus-bud pillars, going over the first of three naga (snake) bridges, and past four small purification ponds. This constitutes the symbolic crossing of the abyss between earth and heaven. Part of the gallery which runs right round the inner compound has been restored to its original covered design, with arched roofs, small chambers inside and false windows. Above the entrance to the main prang (corn-cob shaped tower), are carvings of a dancing ten-armed Shiva, and of a reclining Vishnu, who is dreaming up a new universe.

Prasat Muang Tham

Like Phanom Rung, **Prasat Muang Tham** (daily 8am–5pm; B40) was probably built in stages between the tenth and thirteenth centuries, and is based on the classic Khmer design of a central prang which is flanked by minor prangs and encircled by a gallery punctuated with gateways. The four stone-rimmed L-shaped ponds between the gallery and the outer wall may have been used to purify worshippers as they entered the complex.

Surin

Best known for its hugely hyped elephant round-up every November, **SURIN**, 197km east of Khorat, is an otherwise typical northeastern town but makes a good base for Phanom Rung, is an excellent place to buy silk, and has a fine guesthouse. Surin's only official sight is its **museum** (Mon–Fri 8.30am–4.30pm; free), a tiny one-room exhibition on Thanon Chitramboong featuring stacks of carvings and, more interestingly, several sacred elephant ropes formerly used by the local Suay. The best place to buy Surin's famous **silk** weave is from the women who sell their cloth around the Tannasarn–Krungsrinai intersection. Otherwise try the shop opposite the *Ubon Hotel* on Thanon Tannasarn, the Ruen Mai Silk Shop on Thanon Chitramboong, or Netcraft next to *Phetkasem Hotel*.

One of the best reasons for coming to Surin is to take one of the excellent local **tours** organized from *Pirom's Guesthouse* (☎044/515140). Pirom is a highly informed social worker whose day-trips give tourists an unusual glimpse into rural northeastern life. Tours are usually only available on weekends, prices range from B280 to B590 per person, and you can choose from village tours, Khmer ruins, or the Cambodian border market.

The **train station** is on the northern edge of town, ten minutes' walk from the central market area on Thanon Krungsrinai. The **bus terminal** is one block east of the train station. *Pirom's Guesthouse*, one block west of the market at Thanon 242 Krungsrinai (☎044/515140; ①), is one of the friendliest in Isaan. **Rooms** have shared facilities, and there's a B60 dorm; they're planning to relocate to a spot north of the railway tracks, so call first to check. The next best options are *New Hotel*, near the station at Thanon 22 Tannasarn (☎044/511341; ①–②), and the friendly *Nit Diew Hotel*, near the post office at 155–161 Thanon Tannasarn (☎044/512099; ②). For the best in Isaan **food**, head for the traditional *Sai Yen* on Thanon Chitramboong. Surin's lively night market is on the eastern end of Thanon Krungsrinai. The *Worldnet Internet Café* is located on the corner of Thanon Thetsabarn and Thanon Thetsabarn 1.

Ubon Ratchathani

Almost always referred to simply as Ubon – not to be confused with Udon (Udon Thani) to the north – **UBON RATCHATHANI**, east of Surin, is Thailand's fifth-largest city, but only worth stopping at en route to the prehistoric cliff paintings at Pha Taem and the Laos border. If you're here in early July though, drop by for the Ubon Candle Festival, when huge beeswax sculptures are paraded through the streets.

Aside from its confusing number of arrival points, central Ubon is easy enough to negotiate. The main hotel and eating area is between Thanon Sumpasit in the north and the Maenam Mun River in the south. Of the city's eight main wats, **Wat Thung Si Muang**, in the middle of this zone near the post office, is the most noteworthy, mainly for its unusually well-preserved teak library – raised on stilts over an artificial pond to keep book-devouring insects at bay. The murals in the bot, to the left of the library, display lively scenes of everyday nineteenth-century life. Ubon's museum (Wed–Sun 8.30am–4.30pm; B10), housed in the blue-and-grey building opposite the *Ubon Hotel* on Thanon Kaenthani, has decent displays on the region's geology, history and folk crafts.

There's a good northeastern **crafts shop**, called Phanchat, at two locations on Thanon Ratchabut (50m east of the museum, off Thanon Kaenthani). The larger branch is next to a motorbike showroom at no. 158, between the park and Thanon Kaenthani; the smaller branch is off the south side of Thanon Kaenthani. Both specialize in fine-quality regional goods, such as triangular pillows and silk.

Practicalities

The **train station** is in Warinchamrab, a suburb of Ubon which lies just across the Maenam Mun River. White **city bus** #2 runs from the train station across the river into central Ubon, passing along Thanon Kaenthani, location of several hotels and the TAT office. City buses #1, #3, #6 and #7 also cross the river into Ubon. Regular long-distance **buses** from Bangkok and points west, and Kong Chiam to the east, pull into Warinchamrab bus station, one block east of the train station; those from the north – Khon Kaen, Udon Thani – arrive at a terminal north of Ubon's town centre on Thanon Jaengsanit. The several air-conditioned bus companies connecting Ubon with Bangkok, Chiang Mai, Phitsanulok, Khorat, Rayong and Surin have various arrival and departure points near TAT on Thanon Kaenthani and opposite the Monument of Merit on the parallel Thanon Phalorangrit; the terminal for Nakorn Chai, one of the largest air-con bus companies, is just south of the River Mun, on the road to Warinchamrab, and is served by several city buses, including the #2. **When leaving** Ubon, you can only buy your air-con bus tickets from the appropriate terminal; train and air tickets, however, can be bought through TYTS Travel Agent (☎045/246043) on Thanon Chayangkun in the city centre. You can rent **motorbikes** (B200–500) and **cars** (B1200) from Wattana (☎045/242202) at 239/8 Thanon Suriyat, opposite Nikko Massage.

Staff at the **TAT office** on Thanon Kaenthani (daily 8.30am–4.30pm; ☎045/243770) will help with specific queries on bus and train departures. The best and friendliest of Ubon's budget **hotels** is *Tokyo Hotel*, about a five-minute walk north of the museum at 178 Thanon Auparat (☎045/241739; ②–⑤); all rooms have showers, some with air con. Alternatively, the *New Nakorn Luang Hotel* at 84–88 Thanon Yuttaphan (☎045/254768; ②) offers clean, en-suite rooms. The popular and more central *Ratchathani Hotel* at 229 Thanon Kaenthani (☎045/254599; ③–④) has large, good-value rooms with TVs.

Chiokee, across from the museum on Thanon Kaenthani, is a café-style **restaurant** serving inexpensive Thai and Western dishes. Ubon's night market sets up on the north bank of the River Mun, and there are night-time foodstalls on Thanon Ratchabut (north off Thanon Kaenthani), and next to the *Tokyo Hotel*.

East to Kong Chiam, Chong Mek and the Lao border

Transport **east** from Ubon to **Kong Chiam**, **Chong Mek** and the **Lao border** involves a rather convoluted journey via Warinchamrab (see above) and the town of **Phibun Mangsahan** (known locally as Phibun). From Ubon, take city bus #1, #3 or #6 across the river to Warinchamrab bus station, and then change onto a local bus bound for Phibun (every 10min until 4.30pm). These terminate in Phibun's town centre from where it's a ten-minute walk through town to the songthaew stop beside the Kaeng Saphue bridge – the departure point for all public transport to Kong Chiam, Chong Mek and the Lao border. If travelling across to Laos via Chong Mek you should go to Phibun's **Immigration Office** (*kaan khao muang*; ☎045/441108) first to get an exit stamp.

Kong Chiam

Thirty kilometres northeast of Phibun, the small village of **KONG CHIAM** on the banks of the Mekong has no sights of its own, but is the best base from which to explore the impressive prehistoric **Pha Taem cliff paintings**, 18km up the Mekong and clearly signed all the way. Clear proof of the antiquity of the fertile Mekong Valley, the paintings are believed to be 3000–4000 years old and were made by rice-cultivating settlers who lived in huts rather than caves. The bold, red paintings cover a 170-metre stretch of cliff face and include human forms, geometric designs and enormous fish, plus a thirty-metre string of hand prints.

Songthaews to Kong Chiam (60–90min) leave from Phibun's Kaeng Saphue bridge every half-hour in the morning, then hourly until 4.30pm. The best **place to stay** is the convivial *Apple Guesthouse* (☎045/351160; ①–②), opposite the post office on Thanon Kaewpradit, about five minutes' walk from the bus stop and the river bank. Rooms are squeaky-clean with good beds, they rent bicycles and motorbikes, and there's a restaurant. Kong Chiam is well off the beaten track, and rarely do you get the opportunity to stay in such a well-appointed guesthouse in so typical a Thai village.

Chong Mek and the Lao Border

Forty-six kilometres east of Phibun, Highway 217 hits the **Lao border** at **Chong Mek**; hourly songthaews travel this route, leaving from the Kaeng Saphue bridge and taking ninety minutes. If you want to cross into Laos here you need to have a visa which specifies Chong Mek as your entry point (see p.453); the nearest Lao consulate is in Khon Kaen. It's also advisable to get your Thai exit stamp in Phibun Mangsahan's Immigration office (see opposite) before heading on to the border, as some Laos-bound visitors have been sent back when trying to check out at Chong Mek. Though there are currently no hotels in Chong Mek, TAT says there are plans to build accommodation here soon. Once you've walked across the border (daily 8.30am–6pm), you need to take a share taxi or pick-up to the Lao village of Ban Muang Kao (45–75min) and then a boat across the Mekong to Pakxe (soon to be connected by a bridge), Southern Laos's major transport hub; see p.518.

Khon Kaen

The important and burgeoning city of **KHON KAEN**, 188km northeast of Khorat, has a good museum, markets and shops, and makes a decent resting point on the Bangkok–Nong Khai rail line. Crucially, it also has both a Laos consulate and a Vietnamese consulate, the only ones outside Bangkok. In keeping with its status as a university town, Khon Kaen has several fine collections in its **museum** (daily 8.30am–4.30pm; B10), including Bronze Age pots from Ban Chiang, Buddha sculptures, and local folk art. The museum is two blocks north of the bus station on Thanon Lung Soon Rachakarn.

The cavernous **Prathamakant Local Goods Centre** (daily 8am–8.30pm) at the southern end of town at 81 Thanon Ruen Rom stocks hundreds of gorgeous *mut mee* cotton and silk weaves (*mut mee* is the northeastern method of tie-dying bundles of cotton thread before hand-weaving which produces geometrical patterns on a coloured base), as well as clothes, furnishings, triangular axe pillows, *khaen* pipes and jewellery. To get to Prathamakant from the north part of town, take green local bus #6 from anywhere on Thanon Na Muang.

Practicalities

Khon Kaen is easily reached from Bangkok by bus or rail and from most other major towns in the northeast. The **train station** is just off Highway 2 on the southwestern edge of town, about fifteen minutes' walk from the main hotel area. The main **bus station** is on Thanon Prachasamoson, a five-minute walk northwest of the Thanon Klang Muang hotels; the air-conditioned-bus terminal is right in the town centre, at the junction of Ammat and Klang Muang roads. The most useful of the **city buses** and songthaews are **#1** (yellow and red), which travels up Thanon Na Muang from the Si Chan junction, via the regular bus station to the museum; **#3** (yellow and blue) which connects the train station and the regular bus station; **#6** (green) which travels up Thanon Na Muang from the junction with Thanon Ruen Rom, as far as the regular bus station; **#8** (light blue), **#9** (light blue) and **#13** (orange) which all connect the regular bus station with the air-con bus station, via Thanon Klang Muang; and **#11** (white) which connects the air-con bus station with the railway station, via Thanon Si Chan.

The **TAT office** (8.30am–4.30pm; ☎043/244498) is on Thanon Prachasamoson, about five minutes' walk east of the bus station. Khon Kaen's **Lao Consulate** is located at the far southern end of town, about 1.5km east of Beung Kaen Nakhon Lake, at 19/3 Thanon Photisan (☎043/221961 or 223689; Mon–Fri 8.30–11.30am & 1.30–4.30pm). Visas take three working days to process; for more details see p.453. The **Vietnamese Consulate** (Mon–Fri

8.30am–4pm; ☎043/242190) is about 1.5km east of the TAT office, off Thanon Prachasamoson.

ACCOMMODATION AND EATING

Sansumran, at 55 Thanon Klang Muang (☎043/239611; ①), is the most traveller-oriented **hotel** in town, and has a useful noticeboard. *Suksawad*, at 2/2 Thanon Klang Muang (☎043/236472; ①), is less popular, but quiet and fine; all rooms have showers. For good-value, mid-priced rooms, try *Kaen Inn*, at 56 Thanon Klang Muang (☎043/236866; ③), where all rooms are air-conditioned and come with shower, TV and fridge; or the similarly appointed rooms at *Kosa Hotel* at 250 Thanon Si Chan (☎043/225014; ⑤).

Khon Kaen has a reputation for very spicy **food**, particularly sausages, *sai krog isaan*, which are served with cubes of raw ginger, onion, lime chilli at stalls along Thanon Klang

Muang. Steaks, pizzas, Thai curries and huge breakfasts with real coffee are the most popular dishes at *The Parrot*, opposite the *Kosa Hotel* on Thanon Si Chan. There is an Internet place north of Samsumran on Thanon Klang Muang.

Ban Chiang and Udon Thani

The village of **BAN CHIANG** achieved worldwide fame in 1966, when a rich seam of archeological remains was accidentally discovered. Clay pots, uncovered in human graves alongside sophisticated bronze objects, were dated to around 3000 BC, implying the same date for the bronze pieces, and Ban Chiang was immediately hailed as the vanguard of the Bronze Age, seven hundred years before Mesopotamia's discovery of the metal. Although a later, more accurate test set the date at around 2000 BC, Ban Chiang stands as one of the world's earliest bronze producers, its methods of smelting showing no signs of influence from northern China and other neighbouring bronze cultures, which suggests the area was the birthplace of Southeast Asian civilization; in 1992 it was listed as a UNESCO World Heritage site. Ban Chiang's fine **National Museum** (daily except Tues 9am–4pm; ☎042/261351; B30) displays some of the choicest finds from Ban Chiang, including the late-period Ban Chiang clay pots, with their characteristic red whorled patterns on a buff background. In the grounds of **Wat Pho Si Nai**, on the south side of the village, two burial pits (times and price as for the museum) have been exposed to show how and where artefacts were found.

To get to Ban Chiang from Khon Kaen or Nong Khai, you have to go via the charmless grey city of **UDON THANI**. The train station is a couple of kilometres out of town, off Thanon Prayak. A tuk-tuk to any of the bus terminals should be around B20. **Buses** pull into Udon Thani at a variety of locations: Loei, Phitsanulok and Chiang Mai services use the terminal on the town's western bypass; Nong Khai and Ban Phu buses leave from Talat Langsina market on the north side of town; Bangkok, Khorat, Khon Kaen, Nakhon Phanom, Sakhon Nakhon and Ubon Ratchathani services leave from the other main terminal on Thanon Sai Uthit.

Direct **songthaews** to Ban Chiang run from Udon's morning market, Talat Thai Isaan, east of the centre (every 30min until 3.45pm; 1hr 30min), or you could catch a Sakhon Nakhon-bound bus (every 30min) to Ban Palu and then a motorized samlor (B20–30 per person) for the last 5km from the main road to the village. Heading back to Udon the same day by songthaew is problematic, as the service runs only until about 11.30am (every 30min) so you'll have to make do with a samlor and bus combination any later in the day.

Udon's **TAT office** (8.30am–4.30pm; ☎042/325406) is northwest of the town centre on Thanon Mukmontri, and if you need to **stay** in Udon, the clean, fan-cooled rooms at *Prachapakdee Hotel* at 156/7–9 Thanon Prajak (☎042/221804; ①) are your best budget bet. The **night market** sets up on Thanon Makkeng between Saengluang and Srisuk roads. However, the excellent *Lakeside Sunrise Guesthouse* (042/208167; ①) in Ban Chiang itself is a much more appealing option, and you can rent **bikes** here too. Facing the museum, head left then turn right at the first intersection; it's just a few minutes' walk.

Loei

LOEI is really only useful as a transport hub. Buses run here from Udon Thani and Khon Kaen every thirty minutes, from Phitsanulok seven times a day and from Bangkok seventeen times a day, while half-hourly songthaews link the town to Chiang Khan (1hr). They all use the bus terminal on Highway 201, the main north–south road, about 2.5km south of the centre. The best **place to stay** is *Friendship House* (☎042/832408; ①), 257/41 Soi 15, Thanon Charoenrat, just behind and to the north of Wat Sri Boonruang and close to the bus station. The owner can guide you round Phu Kradung and rents **bikes** and motorbikes. The central **night market** is on the east side of Thanon Charoenrat.

Phu Kradung National Park

The most accessible and popular of the parks in Loei province, **Phu Kradung National Park**, about 80km south of Loei, protects a grassy 1300-metre plateau, whose temperate climate supports plant and bird species not normally found in tropical Thailand. Walking trails crisscross much of the plateau and take three days to explore fully; the trip from Loei to the top of the plateau and back can't be done in a day. The park is closed during the rainy season (June–Sept), and October is muddy, though the waterfalls are in full cascade; December brings out the maple leaves, and April is good for the rhododendrons and wild roses. Elephants, sambar deer and gibbons can be seen very occasionally year-round.

Most hikers take at least three hours to do the gruelling main trail from the visitor centre up the eastern side of Phu Kradung (5km). It gets steep and rocky at the end, but the view from the rim is well worth the slog. Several feeder trails fan out from here, including a twelve-kilometre path along the precipitous southern edge. Another trail heads along the eastern rim for 2.5km to Pha Nok An – also reached by a two-kilometre path due east from the park headquarters.

To **get to the park**, take any bus between Loei and Khon Kaen and get off at the village of Phu Kradung (1hr 30min), then hop on a B20 songthaew for the remaining 7km to the visitor centre (daily 7am–3pm), where you can pick up a trail map and pay the B20 admission fee. Leave your gear at the visitor centre, or hire a porter to tote it to the top for B10 per kilo. At park headquarters up on the plateau, 8km from the visitor centre, you can rent out tents for B50–100 per day (or pitch your own for B5–10), and blankets for B10; there are food stalls at park headquarters and at the rim of the plateau. Or you can sleep and eat at the bungalows of *Phu Kradung Resort*, 2–3km from the visitor centre towards Phu Kradung village (☎042/871076; ②).

Chiang Khan

The Mekong route starts promisingly at **CHIANG KHAN**, whose rows of wooden shophouses stretch out in a two-kilometre-long ribbon parallel to the river. The town has only two streets – Highway 211, also known as Thanon Sri Chiang Khan, and the quieter Thanon Sai Khong on the waterfront – with a line of sois connecting them numbered from west to east. Arguably the most enjoyable thing you can do here is to join other travellers for a **boat trip** on the river, organized through one of the guesthouses. Upstream trips (B300–500 per boat; 2–3hr) head west towards the mountains of Khao Laem and Khao Ngu; downstream trips go to Pak Chom (B1200 per boat; 6hr round-trip) through beautiful rural scenery and some dramatic rapids.

Frequent **songthaews** from Loei and Pak Chom stop at the west end of town near the junction of Highway 201 (the road from Loei) and Highway 211. *Friendship Guesthouse* (☎042/821547; ②) offers clean rooms, Internet access, car and motorbike rental; bicycles are free for guests. Across the road, right on the river on Soi 8, *Rimkong Guesthouse* (☎042/821547; ①) offers small, clean **rooms**. The owner is a mine of information and can organize treks and boat trips. The outstanding *Zen Guesthouse* (☎042/821825; ①) has clean, simple wooden rooms and dorms on quiet Soi 12, and offers traditional massage and mountain bikes for rent; smoking is not allowed on the premises. *Poonsawat Guesthouse*, 251/2 Soi 9 (☎042/821114; ①), is Chiang Khan's cheapest, with cleanish rooms in an old wooden building; you can rent motorbikes (B150) or a pick-up (B1000) here. For **food**, try the day market, on the south side of Thanon Sri Chiang Khan between sois 9 and 10, and the night market (6–8pm), between sois 18 and 19 on the same road.

Pak Chom, Sang Khom and Wat Hin Ma Beng

Half-hourly songthaews from Chiang Khan cover the beautiful, winding route to **PAK CHOM**, 41km downriver, where you can pick up a bus from Loei to continue your journey towards Nong Khai via Sang Khom and Sri Chiangmai. If you get stuck, the *Pak Chom Guesthouse* (①), at the west end of town, has primitive bungalows overlooking the river, and offers boat trips (B50 per hour), massages and a communal Thai–Lao dinner. Beyond Pak Chom, the road through the Mekong valley becomes flatter and straighter.

Staying in one of the "backpackers' resorts" in idyllic **SANG KHOM**, 63km east of Pak Chom, puts you in the heart of an especially lush stretch of the river within easy biking distance of several villages and the meditation temple of **Wat Hin Ma Beng**, 19km east. You can rent bicycles (B70; guests only) and motorbikes (B200–300) at *River Huts* (☎042/441012; ①); they also do bicycle repairs, herbal saunas and great food. Further upstream, the bamboo **huts** at *Buoy Guesthouse* (042/441065; ①) enjoy beautiful river views, and you can rent inner tubes, canoes and fishing boats. Next door, *New TXK (Mama's) Guesthouse* (①) has inexpensive but primitive huts, does boat trips (B50–100) and rents canoes and bikes (B40). Just out of town, at 138 Moo Lampuphan Pathang, *Siam Bungalows* (☎042/441399; ②) has new, spacious huts on the river, some en-suite, and offers French and Thai food, a pool table, a small library, laundry service and TV. Motorbikes and mountain bikes can be rented.

Sri Chiangmai

SRI CHIANGMAI, 38km east of Sang Khom, is one of the world's leading manufacturing centres of spring-roll wrappers (200,000 pieces on a good day): if the weather's fine, you can see them drying on bamboo racks around the town. The town also offers the unique opportunity of gazing at the backstreets of Vientiane, directly across the Mekong. Here again, one outstanding guesthouse makes the town accessible to farangs who want to experience its daily life. *Tim Guesthouse* (☎042/451072; ①) has clean, quiet rooms at 553 Moo 2, Thanon Rimkhong (the riverfront road), dishes up tasty Thai and Western food and can arrange herbal saunas, massages, bicycle (B30) and motorbike (B150) rental. The guesthouse is a handy jumping-off point for Ban Phu (see p.920), 40km south, and you can do one-hour sunset **boat trips** (B40) or longer ones past the Vientiane suburbs to Wat Hin Ma Beng (B800 per boat). Frequent buses and songthaews connect Sri Chiangmai with Nong Khai and Pak Chom.

Nong Khai and into Laos

The major border town in these parts is **NONG KHAI**, the terminus of the rail line from Bangkok and the easiest place for overland travel to Laos, whose capital Vientiane is just 24km away. The town is still a backwater, but has been developing fast since the construction of the huge Thai–Australian Friendship Bridge over the Mekong on the west side of town. As with most of the towns along this part of the Mekong, the thing to do in Nong Khai is just to take it easy, enjoying the peaceful settings of the guesthouses.

The town stretches four kilometres along the south bank of the Mekong. Running from east to west, Thanon Meechai dominates activity: the main shops and businesses are plumb in the middle around the post office, with more frenetic commerce to the east at the Po Chai Day Market by the bus station, and to the west at the Chaiyaporn Night Market. To catch the best of life on the river, take the ninety-minute boat trip (B30), which sets out from the *Ruenpae Haisoke* floating restaurant at the top of Thanon Haisoke every evening at 5.30pm. At 1151 Soi Chitapanya, Thanon Prajak, Village Weaver Handicrafts (#786) sells *mut mee* cotton, silk and axe pillows.

Practicalities

From Bangkok, you'll most likely be coming to Nong Khai by night train, arriving at the **train station** 2km west of the centre. The **bus terminal** is on the east side of town off Thanon Prajak. **Motorbikes** (from B150) can be rented at Nana Motorbikes (☎042/411998), 1160

Thanon Meechai, opposite Chaiyaporn Market. Village Weaver Handicrafts (☎042/411236) and Fah Sai Travel rent four-wheel drives (B1000 including insurance), while bicycles are available at *Mut Mee* and *Sawasdee* guesthouses.

You can extend your Thai visa at the **Immigration Office** on the road leading up to the Friendship Bridge. Wasambe Bookshop, near *Mut Mee Guesthouse*, stocks new and second-hand books and offers Internet access, plus a phone and fax service. Bangkok Bank on Thanon Sisaket, off Thanon Meechai, runs a daily currency exchange service until 5pm.

ACROSS THE FRIENDSHIP BRIDGE TO LAOS

The **border crossing** at Nong Khai is the Thai–Australian **Friendship Bridge** (open daily 8am–6pm, but expect to be charged "overtime" if crossing between 2pm and 4pm), and you get a fifteen-day visa on arrival here ($30), extendable in Vientiane only. If you want a longer thirty-day visa, Fah Sai Travel, 1111/1 Thanon Keawworut (☎042/460949), on the soi leading to *Mut Mee Guesthouse*, can get you one in a minimum of two working days (US$80); they also do visas for Vietnam (minimum four-day wait; one month $50).

To cross the border from downtown Nong Khai, take a tuk-tuk to the foot of the Bridge (about B50), then a minibus (B10) across the span itself, before catching a bus or a taxi (about B400 which can be shared between up to four people) to Vientiane, 24km away (see p.474).

ACCOMMODATION AND EATING

The attractive riverside *Mut Mee Guesthouse* at 1111 Thanon Keawworut (no phone, fax 042/460717; ①–②) is a magnet for travellers, offering well-kept **rooms**, bamboo huts and B80 dorm beds, plus yoga, meditation and t'ai chi workshops and a recommended restaurant. The simple, slightly faded rooms at *KC Guesthouse*, next to Wasambe Bookshop on Thanon Thanon Keawworut (no phone; ①), are a cheaper, more intimate alternative, or try *Rimkhong Guesthouse* (☎042/460625; B150) at 815/1-3 Thanon Rimkhong, which has small, clean rooms in a concrete building, with views across the river. *Sawasdee Guesthouse*, 402 Thanon Meechai (☎042/412502; ①–②) is a well-equipped, grand old wooden house, set round a pleasant courtyard with some air-con.

Don't miss the absolutely delicious Vietnamese **food** at *Daeng Naem-Nuang*, 1062/1–2 Thanon Banterngjit (closes 7pm), particularly the *nam nueng* – make-it-yourself fresh spring rolls with barbecued pork. *Udomrod* on Thanon Rimkhong also does Vietnamese and Lao specialities, including *paw pia yuan* (Vietnamese spring rolls), and *kai lao daeng* (Lao-style chicken cooked in red wine). For honest Thai food you won't find anything cheaper than *Thai Thai Restaurant*, Thanon Prajak (daily 1pm–3am).

Sala Kaeo Kou (Wat Khaek)

Just off the main highway, 5km east of Nong Khai and served by frequent songthaews, **SALA KAEO KOU** (aka Wat Khaek; daily 7am–5pm; B30) is best known for its bizarre sculpture garden, which looks like the work of a giant artist on acid. The temple was founded by the unconventional and charismatic Thai holy man, Luang Phu Boonlua Surirat, who died in 1996. The garden bristles with Buddhist, Hindu and secular figures, all executed in concrete with imaginative abandon by unskilled followers under Luang Phu's direction. The religious statues, in particular, are radically modern while others illustrate Thai proverbs. Luang Phu established a similarly weird "Buddha Park" (Xiang Khouan) across the Mekong near Vientiane in Laos (see p.480).

Ban Phu

Deep in the countryside, 61km southwest of Nong Khai, the wooded slopes around **BAN PHU** are dotted with strangely eroded sandstone formations which have long exerted a mystical hold over local people. Many of the outcrops were converted into small temples from the seventh century onwards, and were probably caused by under-sea erosion some fifteen million years ago. The rock formations all fall under the **Phu Phra Bat Historical Park** (daylight hours; free), and a well-signposted network of paths connects 25 of them. Among the most interesting are Tham Wua and Tham Khon, two natural shelters whose paintings of oxen and human figures suggest that the area was first settled at least 6000 years ago. The spectacular Hor Nang Ussa, a mushroom formed by a flat slab capping a five-metre-high rock pillar, is thought to be a Dvaravati-era shrine (seventh to tenth century).

The rocks are hard to reach by public transport. From Nong Khai, take an Udon Thani-bound **bus** for about 35km to Ban Ngoi, and then change onto one of the half-hourly buses from Udon to Ban Phu; from Ban Phu, it's another 13km west to the historical park, which makes a difficult hitch or a hairy ride on a motorbike taxi. The total journey takes a couple of hours.

Wat Phu Tok

The extraordinary hilltop meditation retreat of **Wat Phu Tok**, 170km from Nong Khai, occupies a sandstone outcrop, its fifty or so monks living in huts perched high above breathtaking red cliffs. As you get closer, the horizontal white lines across the cliffs reveal themselves to be painted wooden walkways, built to give the temple seven levels to represent the seven stages of enlightenment. Long wooden staircases take you to the third level, where you fork left for the fifth level and the Sala Yai, which houses the temple's main Buddha image in a dimly lit cavern. The artificial ledges which cut across the northeast face lead to the dramatic northwest tip on level five: on the other side of a deep crevice spanned by a wooden bridge, the monks have built an open-sided Buddha viharn under a huge anvil rock. The flat top of the hill forms the seventh level, where you can wander along overgrown paths through thick forest.

Wat Phu Tok is best reached with your own **transport** from Nong Khai, but can be done by bus if you leave early. From Nong Khai take a bus to Bung Kan, then a Pang Khon-bound bus (every 30min) to Ban Siwilai, from where songthaews make the hour-long, 25-kilometre trip east to Phu Tok (services are more frequent in the morning). There are food stalls just outside the wat, but no accommodation.

Nakhon Phanom and into Laos

NAKHON PHANOM, 313km from Nong Khai, is chiefly of interest for access to Laos, via the town of Thakhek across the Mekong River. The ferry pier is at the northern end of the riverside promenade, opposite the market: boats to **Thakhek** go daily (every 30min; 8.30–11am & 1–3pm; B50), but you need to have a visa already (see p.453). From Thakhek (see p.511) it's a two-hour bus ride to Savannakhet. There's a **TAT office** close to the ferry pier in Nakhon Phanom at 184/1 Thanon Sunthon Vichit, corner of Thanon Salaklang (☎042/513490–1). **Buses** from Ubon Ratchathani, Mukdahan, Khon Kaen and Nong Khai arrive at the bus terminal about half a kilometre west of the centre. The best **place to stay** is *Grand Hotel*, at 210 Thanon Sri Thep (☎042/511526; ①–②), a block back from the river just south of the passenger ferry and market. You can check your **email** at *Jnet Cybercafé*, on Thanon Sri Thep, next to the clock tower.

That Phanom

The riverside village of **THAT PHANOM** sprawls around Wat Phra That Phanom, one of the four sacred pillars of Thai religion, which reputedly dates back to the eighth year after the death of the Buddha (535 BC), when local princes built a simple chedi to house bits of his breastbone. It's a fascinating place of pilgrimage that used to serve both Thais and the Lao, but since 1975, the Lao have only been allowed to cross the river for the annual February festival and the Monday- and Thursday-morning waterfront markets. The white-and-gold chedi looks like a giant upturned table leg. From each of the four sides, an eye stares down, and the whole thing is surmounted by an umbrella made of 16kg of gold. Look out for the brick reliefs above three of the doorways in the base: the northern side shows Vishnu mounted on a garuda; on the western side, the four guardians of the earth are shown putting offerings in the Buddha's alms bowl; and above the south door, there's a carving of the Buddha entering Nirvana.

Frequent **buses** and songthaews connect That Phanom with Nakhon Phanom (every 10min; 1hr), Mukdahan and Ubon Ratachathani, and stop outside the wat. The centre of the village is 200m due east of here, around the pier on the Mekong. That Phanom's outstanding **accommodation** choice is the welcoming *Niyana Guesthouse*, 288 Moo 2, Thanon Rimkhong (☎042/540588; ①), four blocks north of the pier, which has pleasant rooms set in a garden facing the river. The owner rents out bicycles and organizes boat trips.

Mukdahan and into Laos

Fifty kilometres downriver of That Phanom, **MUKDAHAN** is the last stop on the Mekong trail before Highway 212 heads off inland to Ubon Ratchathani, 170km to the south. You may feel as if you're in the Wild East out here, but this is one of the fastest-developing provinces, owing to increasing friendship between Laos and Thailand and the proximity of Savannakhet (see p.512), the second-biggest Lao city, just across the water; a bridge across the Mekong is planned. You can cross the **Lao border** here on the ferry (5 daily Mon–Fri 9am–4pm; 4 daily Sat 9.15am–4pm & Sun 10.30am & 3.30pm; B50). Travellers have been able to get Lao **visas** on arrival at Savannakhet in the past, but it's safer to obtain them first from Bangkok or Khon Kaen; see p.453 for more details.

Half-hourly **buses** from That Phanom and Ubon Ratchathani stop at the bus terminal, about 1km northwest of the centre on Highway 212. The daily market at the main river pier is good for fabrics and Chinese ceramics. The best budget **accommodation** is at *Ban Thom Kasem* (no English sign), a four-storey hotel centrally located at 25–25/2 Thanon Samut Sakdarak (☎042/611235 or 612223; B160). You can access the **Internet** at *CS Internet*, 61 Thanon Songnang Sathet.

SOUTHERN THAILAND: THE GULF COAST

Southern Thailand's Gulf coast is famous chiefly for its three fine islands of the Samui archipelago: the large and increasingly upmarket **Ko Samui**, the laid-back **Ko Pha Ngan**, site of monthly full-moon parties, and the tiny **Ko Tao**, which is encircled by some of Thailand's best dive sites. Other attractions seem minor by comparison, but the typically Thai seaside resort of **Hua Hin** has a certain charm, and the grand old temples in **Nakhon Si Thammarat** are worth a detour.

Phetchaburi

Straddling the River Phet about 120km south of Bangkok, the provincial capital of **PHETCH-ABURI** (aka Phetburi) flourished as a seventeenth-century trading post and retains many fine old historical wats, which make a fairly interesting day-trip from Bangkok or Damnoen Saduak. The **bus station** is on the southwest edge of Khao Wang, about thirty minutes' walk or a ten-minute songthaew ride from the town centre. The **train station** is about 1500m north of the main sight area. The best-placed **hotel** is the basic *Chom Klao* at 1–3 Thanon Phongsuriya, beside Chomrut Bridge (☎032/425398; ①–②).

The town's central sight district clusters around Chomrut Bridge (*saphaan Chomrut*) and the River Phet. About 700m east of the bridge, the still-functioning seventeenth-century **Wat Yai Suwannaram** contains a remarkable set of murals, depicting divinities ranged in rows of ascending importance, and a well-preserved scripture library built on stilts over a pond to prevent ants destroying the precious documents. The five tumbledown Khmer-style prangs of **Wat Kamphaeng Laeng**, ten minutes' walk south from Wat Yai, were built to enshrine Hindu deities, but were later adapted for Buddhist use. Turning west across the river, you reach Phetchaburi's most fully restored and important temple, **Wat Mahathat**, which was probably founded in the fourteenth century. The five landmark prangs at its heart are adorned with stucco figures of mythical creatures, though these are nothing compared with the miniature angels and gods on the roofs of the main viharn and the bot.

Dominating the western outskirts, about thirty minutes' walk from Wat Mahathat, Rama IV's hilltop palace is a stew of mid-nineteenth-century Thai and European styles known as **Khao Wang**; it's reached on foot or by cable car from the base of the hill on Highway 4 (9.30am–6.30pm; B70, includes museum ticket). The wooded hill is littered with wats, prangs, chedis, whitewashed gazebos, as well as the king's summer house and observatory, **Phra Nakhon Khiri**, now a museum.

Hua Hin

The country's oldest beach resort, **HUA HIN** is very popular with Thai families and makes a pleasant enough stop between Bangkok and the south. However, the beach is nowhere near as attractive as those of nearby Ko Samui, Krabi and Ko Samet, and the beachfront is packed with hotels. There's a **tourist information** desk (daily 8.30am–4.30pm; ☎032/532433) on the corner of Thanon Damnern Kasem and Highway 4 (about 50m east of the train station) and an overseas telephone office (daily 8am–midnight) almost next door. You can buy combined bus and boat tickets to Ko Samui (B550), Phuket (B550) and Krabi (B650) from most Hua Hin tour agents.

A night or two at the former Railway Hotel, now the *Hotel Sofitel* (☎032/512021; ⑨) is a reason in itself to visit Hua Hin. It fronts the beach and remains much as it was in 1923, with classic colonial-style architecture and wide sea-view balconies. But it could be almost as fun staying in one of Hua Hin's other equally unusual **accommodation** options – a string of budget guesthouses built on converted squid piers, with rooms strung out along wooden jetties right over the waves: *Bird* (☎032/511630; ②–③), *Karoon Hut* (☎032/530737; ③–④) and *Mod Guesthouse* (☎032/512296; ②–③) are all very near each other on Thanon Naretdamri, and all offer smallish en-suite rooms. Alternatively, try the inland *All Nations* at 10 Thanon Dechanuchit (☎032/512747; ①–④) which has large, spruce rooms with shared facilities and Internet access, or *Phuen Guesthouse* on Soi Binthabat (☎032/512344; ①–③) where small, basic rooms are crammed into a traditional wooden house.

Some of the best places to enjoy the local fish catch are the seafront **restaurants** on Thanon Naretdamri: *Chao Lay*, *Mee Karuna* and *Thanachote* are all recommended. Fish also features heavily at the night market, which sets up at sunset in the streets around the train station and at a spot close to the bus terminal. The biggest concentration of bars is along Soi Bintaban. Check your **email** in the convivial atmosphere of *Cups & Comp Internet Café* on Thanon Naebkehat (9am–12pm).

Chumphon

CHUMPHON is a useful departure point for Ko Tao, but of little other interest. **Buses** from Bangkok arrive at the terminal on Thanon Tha Tapao, one block west of Chumphon's main thoroughfare, Thanon Sala Daeng. **Trains** stop at the station about 500m further north. Most guesthouses sell tickets for **boats to Ko Tao**; otherwise, try Songserm Travel (☎077/502023) or Infinity Travel (☎077/501937), both on Thanon Tha Tapao. There are two departure points for Ko Tao boats, both from the port area at Pak Nam, 14km southeast of Chumphon. Songthaews to the Tha Yang pier leave from Chumpon's Thanon Paramin Manda, but for the Tha Reua Ko Tao pier you'll need to take the taxi arranged by guesthouses. Full details on getting to Ko Tao from Chumphon are given opposite.

Chumphon's **guesthouses** are used to accommodating Ko Tao-bound travellers, so it's generally no problem to check into a room for half a day before catching the night boat. Most places will also store luggage for you until your return to the mainland. *Mayaze's Resthouse*, off Thanon Sala Daeng at 111/35 Soi Bangkok Bank (☎077/504452; ②) is friendly and highly recommended, with nicely maintained rooms. Staff at *New Chumphon Guesthouse* (aka *Miao*), on the quiet, residential Komluang Chumphon Soi 1 (☎077/502900; ①), are also friendly and clued-up; rooms are small, with shared facilities. *Sooksamer Guesthouse* at 118/4 Thanon Sooksamer (☎077/502430; ①) is cheap but rather rundown. The best value of the town's mid-range hotels is *Paradorm Inn* at 180/12 Thanon Paradorm, east off Thanon Sala Daeng (☎077/511597; ②–③); all rooms have air con, TV and there's a pool. The **night market** sets up along both sides of Thanon Sala Daeng. There is an **Internet** service at Ban's Diving offices on Thanon Tha Tapao, a couple of minutes' walk south of Songserm Travel.

Wat Suan Mokkh

The forest temple of **Wat Suan Mokkh** is internationally renowned as a place of meditation, but is also worth visiting in its own right. The temple is centred on the Golden Hill: scrambling up between trees and monks' huts, you'll reach a hushed clearing on top of the hill which is the wat's holiest meeting-place, marked by nothing more than a stone Buddha with the Wheel of Law. At the base of the hill, the outer walls of the Spiritual Theatre are lined with scenes from the life of the Buddha. Inside, every centimetre is covered with colourful didactic painting, executed by resident monks and visitors.

The anapanasati **meditation retreats** are led by farang and Thai teachers over the first ten days of every month at the International Dharma Heritage, 1km from the main temple. These retreats are serious undertakings, intended as a challenging exercise in mental development: conditions are spartan, there is a rule of silence, and the day begins before dawn. Sleeping quarters are segregated and meditators help with chores. The B1200 fee includes two vegetarian meals a day and accommodation; bring a flashlight. Each course has space for about 100 people – enrol at the information desk in Wat Suan Mokkh (☎077/431552 or 431596; *www.suanmokkh.org*) on the last day of the month. Wat Suan Mokkh is on the Chumphon–Surat Thani **bus** route (hourly). **Trains** pull into Chaiya train station, 6km north of the wat; songthaews run from the station to the wat.

Surat Thani

Uninspiring **SURAT THANI**, often shortened to Surat, 54km south of Wat Suan Mokh, is of use only for its long-distance transport connections and as the main jumping-off point for trips to Ko Samui and Ko Pha Ngan; for details on island boats see the box opposite. Most **buses** to Surat Thani arrive at Thanon Taladmai in the centre of town, either at Talat Kaset I on the north side of the road (local buses) or opposite at Talat Kaset II (long-distance buses). Buses from Bangkok and Hua Hin arrive at a terminal 2km southwest of the centre. The **train station** is at Phunphin, 13km to the west, from where buses run every ten minutes between 6am and 7pm and share taxis leave when full (B40 per person or B100 to charter the whole car). You can buy boat tickets to Ko Samui and Ko Pha Ngan from the train station, including a connecting bus to the relevant pier. A minibus (B70) connects Surat Thani airport with the town centre, or you can buy a combination express boat ticket (B280) to Ko Samui; minibuses to the airport leave from the Thai Airways office, south of the centre at

GETTING TO KO SAMUI, KO PHA NGAN AND KO TAO

Getting to Ko Samui

The most obvious way of getting to Ko Samui is on a **boat** from the Surat Thani area. Of these the least expensive is the ferry which leaves Ban Don pier in Surat Thani itself for Na Thon – the main port on Ko Samui – at 11pm every night (7hr); tickets (B60–80) are sold at the pier on the day of departure.

From Tha Thong, 5km east of Surat, Songserm **express boats** run to Na Thon (2 daily; 2hr 30min); the B150 ticket includes bus transport from Surat or Phunphin train station to the pier. **Vehicle ferries**, handled by Samui Tour (see p.926), run between Don Sak pier, 68km east of Surat, and Thong Yang, 8km south of Na Thon (9 daily; 1hr 30min); a combination ticket including the bus trips from Surat or Phunphin to Don Sak and from Thong Yang to Na Thon costs B80 for ordinary buses, B100 for air-conditioned buses. Points of departure from the mainland are sometimes switched around owing to the prevailing weather and tides, but most tickets include bus transport to the boat anyway.

From Bangkok, the State Railway does train–bus–boat packages through to Ko Samui (B380 second-class reclining seat). Government-run overnight bus–boat packages from the Northern Terminal cost B398, and are preferable to the deals offered by the unreliable private companies on Thanon Khao San (from around B250). Bangkok Airways flies to Ko Samui from Bangkok (9–14 daily; 80 min). There are also flights from Phuket (2 daily; 50min), Pattaya (daily; 1hr) and Singapore (4–7 weekly; 1hr 20min). The airport, in the northeastern tip of the island, has a currency exchange and car rental, and is served by minibuses (B100–150) to the main beaches, Choeng Mon, Chaweng, Na Thon and Lamai.

You can also get to Ko Samui **from Ko Pha Ngan**: boats go from Thong Sala to Na Thon (2 daily; 45 min; B95) and from Hat Rin to Bangrak (3 daily; 1 hr; B80). Between January and September, there's sometimes a daily boat from Thong Nai Pan, on Ko Pha Ngan's east coast, to Hat Rin and Maenam.

Getting to Ko Pha Ngan

Boat services **to Ko Pha Ngan** are more changeable than those to Ko Samui and Ko Tao. The least expensive ferry from the mainland runs nightly at 11pm from Ban Don pier in Surat Thani to Thong Sala (7hr); tickets cost B80–B120 and are available from the pier on the day of departure. Songserm express boats run from Tha Thong to Thong Sala (2 daily; 4hr; B120 including transport to the pier) via Ko Samui (45min; B95). Small boats also shuttle between Samui and the eastern side of Pha Ngan (see above).

One ferry boat a day sails to Thong Sala from Ko Tao (3hr; B150). An express boat (2hr; B200) and a speedboat (2hr; B250) also run once daily, but from roughly June to November all these services are occasionally cancelled owing to bad weather.

From Bangkok, bus and train packages similar to those for getting to Ko Samui are available (see above).

Getting to Ko Tao

All services to and from **Ko Tao** are at the mercy of the weather, especially between June and November when travellers can get stranded for several days.

The mainland departure point for Ko Tao is Chumphon (see p.923): boats leave three times daily from Chumpon's port at Pak Nam: the B400 express boat and speedboat depart between 7 and 8am from Tha Yang pier, arriving at Ko Tao's Mae Hat at 9.40am, while the B200 slow boat departs from the Tha Reua Ko Tao pier around midnight, arriving at 6am. Tickets should be bought in Chumphon.

One ferry boat a day, as well as one speedboat and express boat, make the trip to Ko Tao from Ko Pha Ngan; see above. There's also a sporadic direct ferry service from Surat Thani (8–9hr; B300).

3/27–28 Thanon Karoonrat, off Thanon Chonkasem (☎077/272610 or 273355), and the *Wangtai Hotel*, at 1 Thanon Taladmai.

In central Surat, train **tickets** can be booked through Phantip Travel, in front of Talat Kaset I at 293/6–8 Thanon Taladmai (☎077/272230). Boat tickets are available from Songserm Travel, opposite the night-boat pier on Thanon Ban Don (☎077/285124–6), and from Samui Tour at 326/12 Thanon Taladmai (☎077/282352). **TAT** (daily 8am–4pm; ☎077/288818–9) and the **tourist police** (☎077/281300) are at the western end of town at 5 Thanon Taladmai. If you want a **hotel** in Surat, try the inexpensive, pokey rooms at *Surat Hotel* at 496 Thanon Namuang (☎077/272243; ①), or the better ones at *Ban Don Hotel*, above a restaurant at 268/1 Thanon Namuang (☎077/272167; ①). The **night market** sets up between Si Chaiya and Ban Don roads and at Ban Don pier. There is an **Internet** place on Thanon Taladmai, near the bus terminal.

Ko Samui

An ever-widening cross-section of visitors, from globetrotting backpackers to suitcase-toting fortnighters, come to southern Thailand just for the beautiful beaches of **KO SAMUI**, 80km from Surat – and at 15km across and down, Samui is large enough to cope, except during the rush at Christmas and in July and August. The paradisiacal sands and clear blue seas are fringed by palm trees, but development behind the beaches is extensive and often thoughtless. The island is served by frequent ferries: for details, see the box on p.925.

The northeast monsoon blows heaviest here in November, but can bring rain at any time between October and January; January is often breezy, March and April are very hot, and between May and October the southwest monsoon blows mildly onto Samui's west coast and causes a little rain. All the accommodation prices given below are for high-season, but they plummet out of season, in April, May, June, October and November. A fifty-kilometre road encircles the island and is served by songthaews, which set off from between the two piers in Na Thon and run to all the beaches (B30–50). You can rent motorbikes at all main beaches, though note that dozens are killed on Samui's roads each year, so proceed with caution. Ko Samui has a dozen **dive operators**, offering day-trips to Ko Tao reefs (B2800) and courses throughout the year. The most reliable is Samui International Diving School, which has branches in Ban Bophut (☎077/425496), at the *Malibu Resort* on Central Chaweng (☎077/231242), and in central Lamai (☎077/232302).

Na Thon

The island capital, **NA THON** is a frenetic half-built town which most travellers use only for stocking up with supplies en route to the beaches. The two piers come to land at the promenade, Thanon Chonvithi, which is paralleled first by narrow Thanon Ang Thong, then by Thanon Taweeratpakdee, aka Route 4169, the round-island road; the main cross-street is Thanon Na Amphoe, just north of the piers.

The major **travel agents** are Phantip (☎077/421221–2), on Thanon Taweeratpakdee, just north of Thanon Na Amphoe opposite the police station, and Songserm (☎077/420167), on Thanon Chonvithi opposite the piers. Tickets to Surat via Thong Yang and Don Sak can be bought from Samui Tour at *The Bamboo House*, south of the piers on Thanon Chonvithi. **TAT** have a new office (daily 8.30am–4.30pm; ☎077/420504) at the northern end of the promenade, behind the post office (Mon–Fri 8.30am–4.30pm, Sat & Sun 9am–noon), which has poste restante and an international phone service (7am–10pm). **Nathon Book Store**, on Thanon Na Amphoe, is an excellent second-hand bookshop. The **tourist police** are at the main police station, on Thanon Taweeratpakdee just north of Thanon Na Amphoe (☎1699 or 077/421281). **Clinics** operate on Ang Thong and Taweeratpakdee roads, and the island's best hospital (☎077/421230–2 or 421531) is 3km south of town off Route 4169. Tourist visas may

be extended at the **Immigration Office**, 2km south down Route 4169 (☎077/421069). If you really need a **place to stay** in Na Thon, the best budget option is the clean and friendly - *Seaview Guesthouse* at 67/15 Thanon Taweeratpakdee (☎077/420298; ②). *Jimta*, on the promenade, offers cheap and fast **Internet** services (8am–9pm).

Ang Thong National Marine Park

All main beaches sell tickets for boat trips to **Ang Thong National Marine Park** (B450), a gorgeous group of 41 small islands, 31km west of Samui. Boats generally leave Na Thon at 8.30am and return at 5pm. First stop on any boat tour is usually Ko Wua Talab, site of the park headquarters, from where it's a steep 430-metre climb (about 1hr return; bring walking shoes) to the island's peak and fine panoramic views. The feature which gives the park the name Ang Thong, meaning "Golden Bowl", and which was the inspiration for the setting of cult bestseller, *The Beach*, is a landlocked lake, 250m in diameter, on Ko Mae Ko to the north of Ko Wua Talab. A well-made path (30min return) leads from the beach through natural rock tunnels to the rim of the cliff wall which encircles the lake, affording another stunning view of the archipelago and the shallow, blue-green water far below, which is connected to the sea by a natural underground tunnel.

Maenam

The four-kilometre bay at **MAENAM**, 13km from Na Thon, is not the island's prettiest, but it's quiet and offers cheap accommodation, which makes it Samui's most popular destination for shoestring travellers. *Chez Tom*, by the pier, serves excellent, reasonably priced French and Thai **food**, and *Travel Café*, on the road down to the pier, has draught beer and some food, as well as overseas phone and fax facilities. ST Travel, further away from the pier on the same road, provides **Internet** access. Maenam also has a **clinic** and a **post office**, with poste restante facilities.

ACCOMMODATION
The best budget **accommodation** is at the far eastern end of the bay.

Friendly, about 1500m east of the village (☎077/425484). Easy-going place. All the bungalows are very clean and have their own bathrooms. ②.

Maenam Resort, 500m west of the village, just beyond Santiburi Dusit Resort (☎077/247286). Good-value, comfortable rooms and bungalows on the beachfront; some air-con. ④–⑥.

Naplarn Villa, at the far western end, off the access road to Home Bay (☎077/247047). Good value if you don't mind a five-minute walk to the beach: excellent food and clean, well-furnished, en-suite bungalows round a garden. ②–③.

Rose, next door to *Friendly* at the eastern end of the bay. Laid-back old-timer, with basic thatched huts in a shady compound. No fans, and electricity stops at 11pm. ①.

Shangrilah, west of *Maenam Resort*, served by the same access road (☎077/425189). A flower-strewn compound which sprawls onto the nicest, widest stretch of sand along Maenam. Accommodation is in smart, en-suite bungalows and the restaurant serves good Thai food. ②–③.

SR, at the far eastern end of the bay. A quiet, welcoming place with a very good restaurant. Accommodation is in en-suite beachfront bamboo huts. ①.

Bangrak (Big Buddha Beach) and Choeng Mon

BANGRAK is also known as Big Buddha Beach, after the huge but not all that comely Big Buddha statue which gazes down at sunbathers from its island in the bay. A short causeway at the eastern end of the bay leads across to a clump of souvenir shops and food stalls in front of the temple, and ceremonial dragon-steps lead to the terrace around the statue, from where there's a fine view of the sweeping north coast. The beach itself is no great shakes, and the best of its disappointing bungalows is *LA Resort* (☎077/425330; ①–②), a welcoming family-run place set in a colourful garden.

After Bangrak comes the high-kicking boot of the northeastern cape, where quiet, rocky coves, overlooking Ko Pha Ngan and connected by sandy lanes, are fun to explore on a motorbike. Songthaews run along the paved road to the largest and most beautiful bay, **CHO-ENG MON**, whose white sandy beach is lined with casuarina trees. *Choeng Mon Bungalows*, north of Boat House on Choeng Mon (☎077/425372; ②–⑤), occupies a shady compound here with a range of decent en-suite rooms, and offers **Internet** access.

Chaweng

For sheer natural beauty, none of the other beaches can match **CHAWENG**, with its broad, gently sloping strip of white sand sandwiched between the limpid blue sea and a line of palm trees. The six-kilometre bay is framed between the small island of Ko Matlang at the north end and the headland above Coral Cove in the south. The village stretches for two kilometres along the central section and has banks, supermarkets, motorbike rental (B150) and four-wheel drives (B800); for **email**, use *Go Internet Café*, at the south end of Central Chaweng, opposite *Central Samui Beach Resort*. The original village of Ban Chaweng, 1km inland of Central Chaweng beach on the round-island road, has a police station, a post office with poste restante, and a small clinic.

ACCOMMODATION

Over fifty bungalow resorts and hotels at Chaweng are squeezed into thin strips running back from the beachfront.

Blue Horizon, on the hillside above Coral Cove (☎077/422426). One of several resorts clinging to the steep hillside. Some of the sturdy, balconied bungalows have air-con and hot water. The price includes breakfast. ⑤–⑦.

Charlie's Huts, in the heart of Central Chaweng (☎077/422343). The three branches of the Charlie's chain, one of which is also known as *Viking*, offer wooden huts with mosquito nets and fans, some en suite. ①–②.

Dew Drop Huts, at the top end of Central Chaweng (☎077/422238). Secluded among dense trees, with old-fashioned primitive huts and a friendly, laid-back ambience. ②.

IKK, around the point at the far north end of North Chaweng (☎077/422482–3). Comfortable en-suite bungalows on an unusually peaceful stretch of sand. ③.

Matlang Resort, at the top end of North Chaweng (☎077/422172). Shaded wooden en-suite bungalows, each decorated slightly differently, some with air-con. ②–④.

Relax Resort, in the middle of North Chaweng (☎077/422280). Friendly spot with a range of very clean, well-maintained fan-cooled and air-con rooms and chalets, all en suite. ③–⑦.

EATING, DRINKING AND NIGHTLIFE

The beachside **restaurant** at *Relax Resort* serves particularly good seafood, and the upmarket *Budsaba Restaurant* at *Muang Kulaypan* hotel in north Chaweng is also recommended for its unusual Thai dishes, such as banana flower and shrimp salad. The best place to **drink** is at the candlelit tables that materialize on the beach after dark – *Lazy Wave* on North Chaweng is a mellow beach bar which also does good croissants, hams and yoghurt. Also on the beach, *Jah Dub* at *Dew Drop Huts* specializes in reggae, and holds parties, usually on Tuesday and Friday nights. Bang in the heart of Central Chaweng, back from the beach, *The Reggae Pub* is not just a **nightclub**, but a venerable Samui institution, with food and jewellery stalls, a restaurant and a snooker club. Chaweng's other long-standing dance venue is *Green Mango* at the north end of Central Chaweng, but the best and most sophisticated club on the island is *Santa Fe*, at the south end of Central Chaweng.

Lamai

Samui's nightlife is most tawdry at **LAMAI**, which keeps planeloads of European package tourists happy with go-go shows and hostess bars. Running roughly north to south for 4km, the white palm-fringed beach is, fortunately, still a picture, and it's possible to avoid the mayhem by staying at the quiet extremities of the bay, where the backpackers' resorts have a definite edge over Chaweng's. The action is concentrated behind the centre of the beach, where you'll also find supermarkets, clinics, banks and travel agents. The small rock formations on the bay's southern promontory, Hin Yay (Grandmother Rock) and Hin Ta (Grandfather Rock), never fail to raise a giggle with their resemblance to the male and female sexual organs. There's **Internet** access at *Sawadee*, next to the petrol station, on the road between *The Spa Resort* and Ban Lamai.

ACCOMMODATION

Lamai's budget **accommodation** is concentrated around the far southern end of the bay towards the Grandparent Rocks.

Bay View Villa, on the bay's northern headland (☎077/230769). Neat, simple huts with verandahs and en-suite bathrooms. ②.

Lamai Inn 99, on the beach by the tourist village's main crossroads (☎077/424427). Friendly, spacious place, with a variety of bungalows, near the throbbing heart of Lamai's nightlife. ③–⑥.

The Spa Resort, at the far north end of the beach, next to *Weekender Villa* (☎077/230855). Cosy rooms decorated with shells and other bric-a-brac; herbal saunas, massages and delicious food, especially veggie. ②.

Utopia, on the central stretch of Lamai, north of the crossroads (☎077/233113). Good-value, welcoming place with decent en-suite bungalows, some with air-con. ③–④.

Vanchai Villa, at the far southern end of the bay on the access road to White Sand. Quiet, family-run operation set back from the beach, offering a range of very clean, spacious bungalows and excellent, cheap food. ①.

Weekender Villa, between the main road and the beach to the east of Ban Lamai (☎077/424116). Central but quiet spot, with large, well-equipped bungalows in a coconut grove. ②–③.

White Sand, at the far southern end of the bay (☎077/424298). Long-established and laid-back budget place with around fifty simple beachside huts; popular with long-term travellers. ①.

Ko Pha Ngan

In recent years, backpackers have begun moving over to Ko Samui's little sibling, **KO PHA NGAN**, 20km to the north, but the island still has a simple atmosphere, mostly because the lousy road system is an impediment to the developers. With a dense jungle covering its inland mountains and rugged granite outcrops along the coast, Pha Ngan lacks sweeping beaches, but it does have some coral. Full details on getting to Ko Pha Ngan are given on p.925.

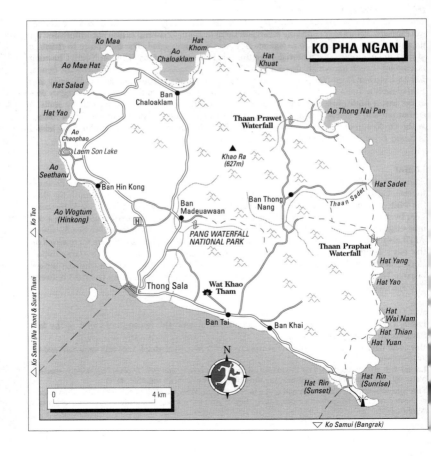

Thong Sala and Wat Khao Tham

THONG SALA is a port of entrance and little more. In front of the pier, transport to the rest of the island (songthaews, jeeps and motorbike taxis) congregates by a dusty row of banks, travellers' restaurants, supermarkets, dive centres and motorbike and jeep rental places. On the west side of the high street, Phangan Batik (daily 10am–8pm) sells batiks and offers **Internet** access. Next door rents out **mountain bikes** (B100) and **motorbikes** (B150–500). Further on, about 500m from the pier, are the **post office** with long-distance phone service (Mon–Fri 8.30am–noon & 1–4.30pm, Sat 9am–noon), and a clinic. The island's **hospital** (☎077/377034) lies 3km north of town, on the road towards Mae Hat. If you need to stay around Thong Sala, walk 800m north out of town to the beachfront bungalows at *Siriphun* (☎077/377140; ②–⑥).

On a quiet hillside above Ban Tai, 4km from Thong Sala, **Wat Khao Tham** holds ten-day meditation retreats most months of the year (B2000 per person to cover food); the farang teachers emphasize compassion and loving kindness as the basis of mental development. Only forty people can attend each retreat, so it's best to pre-register in person, by post or email: Wat Khao Tham, PO Box 18, Ko Pha Ngan, Surat Thani 84280; *www.kohphangan.com*

Hat Rin

The monthly "full moon" parties on **HAT RIN** are famous around the world, attracting up to seven thousand ravers to the beachfront, but there's a more sedate side to Hat Rin's alternative scene, too, with old and new-age hippies packing out the t'ai chi, yoga and meditation classes, and helping consume the drugs that are readily available here. It's not all so chilled-out unfortunately, as dodgy pills and mushroom teas send an average of two farangs a month into psychiatric care, and the local authorities have started instigating roadblocks and bungalow searches.

Hat Rin comprises two back-to-back beaches, joined by transverse roads at the north and south ends. The eastern beach, usually referred to as **Sunrise** or Hat Rin Nok, is a classic curve of fine white sand between two rocky slopes, lined with bars, restaurants and bungalows. **Sunset** beach is usually littered with flotsam, but has plenty of quieter accommodation. The area behind and between the beaches – especially around what's known as Chicken Corner, where the southern transverse road meets the road along the back of Sunrise – is crammed with small shops, clinics, travel agents, a post office, a bank, several Internet cafés and motorbike rental places (from B150). From Thong Sala you can take songthaews or longtail boats to Hat Rin, but from Ko Samui, or even Surat Thani, take one of the direct boats from Samui to Sunset beach; see p.925 for details.

ACCOMMODATION

As there are fewer than three thousand **rooms** on the whole island, around full-moon time you either have to arrive early, forget about sleep altogether, or join one of the many party boats from Ko Samui (B300), which usually leave at 9pm and return around dawn. Even at other times, staying on Sunrise is expensive and noisy.

Blue Hill, at the far northern end of Sunset, a twenty-minute walk from Chicken Corner. Quiet spot with basic, en-suite bungalows and good, cheap food. Catch a songthaew to *Bird Bungalows*, then walk north-west for five minutes along the beach. ①.

Lighthouse Bungalows, on the far southeastern tip of the headland, a twenty-minute walk from the back of *Paradise* on Sunrise. A friendly haven with sturdy wooden bungalows. ①.

Mountain Sea Bungalow, at the quieter northern end of Sunrise. A great spot, bungalows rising up on the rocks at the end of the beach, and set in a garden. ①–②.

Palita, at the northern end of Sunrise (☎01/213 5445). En-suite bungalows give onto the beach, and large, better-value huts stand among the palms behind. The food gets rave reviews. ①–③.

Palm Beach, on and around the tiny head at the centre of Sunset. Clean, sturdy wooden bungalows, most of them fronting the sand. ②–③.

Seaview, at the quieter northern end of Sunrise. On a big plot of shady land, this is similar to next-door *Palita*. Huts with shared bathrooms at the back, en-suite bungalows beachside. ②.

Sun Cliff, high up on the tree-lined slope above the south end of Sunset. Friendly place with bright, smart bungalows, all with cold-water bathrooms. ②–⑥.

The east coast

North of Hat Rin, the rocky, exposed **east coast** stretches as far as Thong Nai Pan, the island's only centre of development. No roads run along this coast, only a rough, steep, fifteen-kilometre trail, which starts from Hat Rin's northern transverse road (signposted). About ninety minutes up the trail, **HAT THIAN**, a shady bay that's good for snorkelling, makes a quiet alternative to Hat Rin. Accommodation is available at *Haad Tien Resort* (contact *Yoghurt Home 3* in Hat Rin, ☎01/725 0919; ①), with en-suite wooden bungalows on the slope above the beach, and at the even mellower *Sanctuary* (①–④), on the southern headland, which also has veggie food and t'ai chi courses.

THONG NAI PAN is a beautiful, semicircular bay backed by steep, green hills, which divide the bay into two parts. The southern half has the better sand and a hamlet, but both are sheltered and good for swimming. A bumpy dirt road winds the 12km from Ban Tai on the south coast. Jeeps connect with boats at Thong Sala every day, but not when it's wet. Half a dozen resorts line the southern half of the bay, where *Pingjun* (②) has a range of large bungalows. The clean, well-maintained bungalows at *Star Huts I* and *II* (☎077/299005; ②) have most of the northern beach to themselves, and are the best budget choice.

The north coast

The village at **CHALOAKLAM**, the largest bay on the **north coast**, is now attracting low-key tourist development, as it can easily be reached by songthaew from Thong Sala, 10km away. *Fanta* (①–②) at the eastern end of the village, has a homely set of bungalows, or walk out to the basic bungalows of *Coral Bay* (①) on the promontory. If the sea is not too rough, longtail boats (2 daily Jan–Sept) run from Chaloaklam to the lovely, secluded **HAT KHUAT** (Bottle Beach); you could also walk there in about ninety minutes along a testing trail from Hat Khom. The nicest of a handful of resorts are the friendly *Bottle Beach* and *Bottle Beach II* (①–②), which have smart beachfront bungalows and tightly packed huts behind.

The west coast

Pha Ngan's **west coast** has almost as much development as the south coast, though most of the bays are enclosed by reefs which keep the sea too shallow for a decent swim, especially between April and October. Motorbike taxis run as far as Hat Yao; songthaews, jeeps and boats cover the rest. Beyond the headland, Laem Son Lake is a beautiful, tranquil stretch of clear water cordoned by pines. Round the next headland on the small bay of **CHAOPHAO**, *Seaflower* (①–②) is quiet and congenial, with great food. You can borrow snorkels here and join their three-day snorkelling trips (B1600) to Ang Thong (see p.927).

Beyond Chaophao, **HAT YAO** offers a long, gently curved beach and a non-stop line of decent bungalows, including the smart *Ibiza* (①) and the friendly *Bay View* (①–③). The only bay to the north of that, **HAT SALAD**, is probably the best of the bunch: it's pretty and quiet, and snorkelling off the northern tip is recommended. *My Way* (①) is the best place for chilling out: the owner brings a boat down to Hat Yao every day to pick up travellers.

Ko Tao

Forty kilometres south of Ko Pha Ngan, small, forested **KO TAO** (Turtle Island) is the last and most remote of the archipelago which continues the line of Surat Thani's mountains into the sea. Famed for its excellent diving and fairly low-key bungalows, it's a popular travellers' destination, especially from December to March. Ko Tao feels the southwest monsoon more than Samui and Pha Ngan, so June to October can have strong winds and rain; some places close from June to August. Full details on getting to Ko Tao are given on p.925.

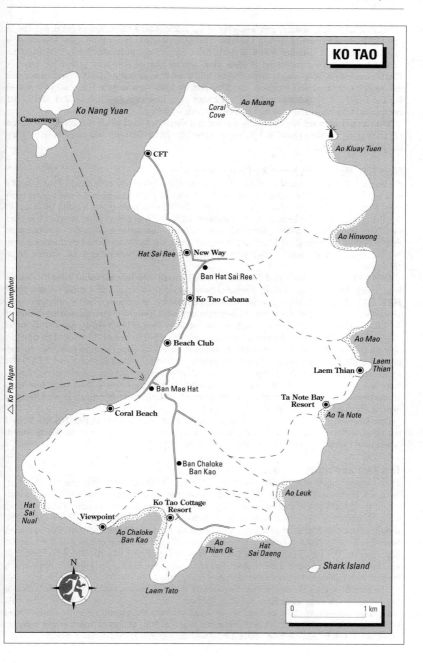

Blessed with clear waters, with visibility of up to 25m and a fair range of coral, Ko Tao is one of Thailand's premier **diving centres**. Diving is possible year-round, but November is the worst time, and visibility is best in April, May, June, September and October. Most of Ko Tao's dive companies are based at **Mae Hat**, and all charge the same prices for four-day **PADI** courses (B7800), single dives (B800), and a ten-dive package (B5400). Recommended companies include Scuba Junction, Big Blue and Buddha View at Mae Hat, Asia Divers and Ko Tao Divers at Hat Sai Ree and Ko Tao Cottage Dive Resort at Ao Chaloke Ban Kao. Some companies take snorkellers along on their dive trips for free.

You can **get around** Ko Tao easily on foot, but there is a road of sorts from the southern beaches along the west coast, and pick-ups, motorbike taxis (B20–40) and mopeds (B150) are available in Mae Hat.

Mae Hat, Hat Sai Ree and Ko Nang Yuan

All boats to the island dock at **MAE HAT**, a small, lively village with most of the island's dive centres, a few restaurants, clinics, and currency exchange, telephone and postal facilities. For somewhere to stay, try *Coral Beach* (②–⑦), which occupies a good position on the lower slopes of the headland, ten minutes' walk south of the village; another ten minutes beyond, there's a sandy, palm-sheltered cove for secluded sunbathing and swimming. Five minutes' walk north of Mae Hat, the quiet and friendly *Beach Club* has thatched huts on the beach, and smart concrete chalets (③–⑦); windsurfers can be rented here (B200/hr).

Beyond the promontory, **Hat Sai Ree**'s two-kilometre strip of white sand is Ko Tao's only long beach. Over twenty bungalow resorts have set up shop here, and a small village, **BAN HAT SAI REE**, with bars, a supermarket and bakery, has evolved at its northern end. Towards the midpoint of the beach, twenty minutes' walk from Mae Hat, **accommodation** at *Ko Tao Cabana* (②) consists of small well-maintained bungalows; nearby *Sai Ree Cottages* (①–②) has primitive huts and sturdy en-suite bungalows by the beach. A hundred metres further up the beach by the village, small, easy-going *New Way* (①) is similar and rents motorbikes (B200). The track north of the village ends beyond the beach at secluded *CFT* (①–②) on the rocky northwest flank of the island, which offers cheap shacks (no electricity) or en-suite bungalows with electricity; there's no beach here, but good views. Most bungalow operations have their own restaurants. There's a branch of **CS Internet** next to Ban's Divers in central Hat Sai Ree (10am–10pm).

One kilometre off the northwest of Ko Tao, the three tiny islands of **KO NANG YUAN** are encircled by a ring of coral, and joined by a causeway of fine white sand. Many round-island boat tours stop off here for snorkelling (5hr; B100).

The east and south coasts

The sheltered inlets of the **east coast**, few of them containing more than one set of bungalows, are best reached by boat, though each is served by at least one path through the forest. In the middle of the east coast, the dramatic tiered promontory of **Laem Thian** shelters a tiny beach and a reef on its south side. With the headland to itself, *Laem Thian* (①) offers simple shacks, decent food and a remote, castaway feel. Laem Thian's coral reef stretches down towards **Ta Note**, a craggy horseshoe bay, with the best snorkelling just north of the bay's mouth. The pick of the resorts here is *Ta Note Bay Resort* (①–②), which has plenty of wooden bungalows and a dive centre. Further south, **Ao Leuk** has a white sandy beach fringed with palms and a handful of primitive huts (①).

The **south coast** is sheltered from the worst of both monsoons, but consequently the main bay here, **Ao Chaloke Ban Kao**, is being developed into a messy, crowded resort. The well-built, clean bungalows at *Viewpoint* (①–②) stand out from the crowd. *Ko Tao Cottage Resort* (☎01/725 0662 or 725 0751; ④) is the island's only real stab at luxury and worth a splurge, especially if you're considering scuba diving with its recommended diving school.

Nakhon Si Thammarat

NAKHON SI THAMMARAT, the south's second-largest town, is an absorbing place, well known for its traditional handicrafts and shadow plays. A huge ten-day festival, Tamboon Deuan Sip, takes place at Sri Nakharin park every September/October and is marked by processions, shadow plays and traditional theatre shows. The town runs 7km from north to south, to either side of Thanon Ratchadamnoen, which is served by frequent songthaews. The south's most important temple, **Wat Mahathat**, is on this road, about 2km south of the train station and town centre. Its courtyard is dominated by the huge Sri Lankan-style chedi, around which are dotted row upon row of smaller chedis. South of Wat Mahathat, the **National Museum** (Wed–Sun 9am–noon & 1–4.30pm; B10) houses a small but diverse collection covering prehistoric finds, Buddha images and ceramics. The best possible introduction to *nang thalung*, southern Thailand's **shadow puppet theatre**, is to head for 110/18 Soi 3, Thanon Si Thammasok, ten minutes' walk east of Wat Mahathat: here Suchart Subsin, one of the south's leading exponents of *nang thalung*, has opened his workshop to the public, and, for a small fee (around B50), will show you scenes from a shadow play. You can also see the puppets being made.

Nakhon's **bus terminal** and **train station** are both centrally placed. The **TAT office** is on Sanam Na Muang park (daily 8.30am–4.30pm; ☎075/346515–6). For inexpensive **accommodation**, *Thai Lee Hotel* at 1130 Thanon Ratchadamnoen (☎075/356948; ①) is the best deal. Nakhon is a great place for **food**. *Khanom Jiin Muangkorn* (10am–3pm) on Thanon Panyom near Wat Mahathat is famous for *khanom jiin*, noodles topped with hot, sweet or fishy sauce. The night market is near the *Bue Loung Hotel* on Thanon Chamroenwithi. Klickzone (8am–10pm), inside Bovorn Bazaar on Thanon Ratchadamnoen, offers **Internet** services.

SOUTHERN THAILAND: THE ANDAMAN COAST

The landscape along the **Andaman coast** is lushly tropical and spiked with dramatic limestone crags, best appreciated by staying in the lovely Khao Sok National Park or taking a boat trip around the bizarre Ao Phang Nga Bay. Most people, however, come here for the beaches and the coral reefs: **Phuket** is Thailand's largest island and the best place to learn to dive, but it's package-tour-oriented, so most backpackers head straight for the beaches off **Krabi**, and the islands of **Ko Phi Phi** and **Ko Lanta**. Unlike the Gulf coast, the Andaman coast is hit by the southwest monsoon from May to October, when the rain and high seas render some of the outer islands inaccessible and litter many beaches with debris; prices drop significantly during this period however.

Ranong and around

Highway 4 hits the Andaman coast at Kraburi, where a signpost welcomes you to the Kra Isthmus, the narrowest part of peninsular Thailand. At this point, just 22km separates the Gulf of Thailand from the southernmost tip of mainland Burma. Seventy kilometres south of the isthmus, the channel widens out at the town of **RANONG**, chiefly of interest for the boats to Victoria Point (Burma) and Ko Chang, which leave from the harbour at Saphan Pla, 5km southwest of the town centre and served by regular songthaews from Thanon Ruangrat.

All buses from Bangkok to Phuket or Krabi pass through Ranong, stopping at the **bus terminal** on Highway 4 (Thanon Phetkasem), 1500m southeast of the centre; a few continue on to Thanon Ruangrat, the town's main street. *Asia Hotel* (☎077/811113; ①–③) at 39/9 Thanon

Ruangrat (the southern end) is clean and has some air-con **rooms**. There's a 24-hour **hot-food market** opposite *Sin Ranong Hotel* on Thanon Ruangrat.

Victoria Point (Kawthaung) and into Burma

The southernmost tip of **Burma** – known as **Victoria Point**, and as **Kawthaung** in Burmese – is easily reached from the Thai side of the border. It is currently quite straightforward for foreign tourists to enter Burma at this point, whether or not they are in possession of a visa. There's nothing much to do in Victoria Point itself, except browse the shops and markets around the port. Longtail boats to Victoria Point (30 min; B50) leave throughout the day from Saphan Pla. Arriving at Victoria Point, you need to pass through immigration where you'll be asked for US$5 hard currency (or B200 in Thai) for a one- to two-day pass into Burma, or US$36 for a thirty-day pass. For stays of over a day you also need to change US dollars into Foreign Exchange Certificates (FECs): $50 for two to three days, or $300 for a month's stay. In theory, you are not allowed to travel beyond Victoria Point unless you have already bought a proper visa from a Burmese embassy to supplement the Victoria Point passes. There's an airport 7km north of Victoria Point, which has flights to Rangoon.

Ko Chang

Not to be confused with the much larger island of Ko Chang on Thailand's east coast (see p.905), Ranong's **Ko Chang** is a forested little island about 5km offshore, with less than great beaches, no coral, but a pleasant laid-back atmosphere. The beaches are connected by tracks through the trees; there are no cars and only sporadic electricity. Several budget **bungalows** operate on the island from November to April only. *Rasta Baby* (☎077/833077; ①–②) has huts on the northernmost beach; further down the west coast is *Sunset* (①), or there's *Sabai Jai* (①), close to the pier. Longtail boats leave Saphan Pla early in the morning, take an hour, and charge B30–B100 per person, depending on numbers.

Khao Sok National Park

Whether you're heading down the Andaman or the Gulf Coast, you should consider veering inland to the exceptionally tranquil guesthouses at **Khao Sok National Park**. Most Surat Thani-bound buses from Phuket and Krabi pass the park entrance, which is located at kilometre stone 109 on Highway 401, less than an hour by bus from **TAKUA PA** or two hours from Surat Thani. Buses run at least every ninety minutes in both directions; ask to be let off at the sliproad to the park and someone will probably give you a lift to the guesthouses, 3km away. Coming by bus from Bangkok, Hua Hin or Chumphon, take a Surat Thani-bound bus, but ask to be dropped off at the junction with the Takua Pa road, about 20km before Surat Thani, and then change onto a Takua Pa bus.

A cluster of very appealing jungle **guesthouses** has grown up along a track to the east of the national park visitor centre and trailheads: just follow the signs. The first guesthouse you reach along the side track is *Bamboo House* (①–④), which has simple bamboo huts and treehouses. Next door, *Nung House* (①–②) has some of the cheapest huts in the park. The most romantically located of Khao Sok's guesthouses are the candlelit cabins and treehouses (no electricity) at *Our Jungle House* (☎076/441068; ②–④), set in a secluded riverside spot beneath the limestone cliffs, about fifteen minutes' walk from *Nung House* (or about an hour from the bus stop on the main road). Continue walking past *Nung House* and when the track forks take the left-hand branch. Further downstream, *Art's Riverview Jungle Lodge* (no phone, fax 076/421613; ②) has wooden cabins and treehouses in a garden next to a good swimming hole.

Nine fairly easy **trails** radiate from the visitor centre (daily 8am–4pm), which sells B5 sketch maps showing their routes. Take plenty of water as Khao Sok is notoriously sticky and humid. The most popular are trail #1 to Ton Gloy Waterfall, 9km from headquarters or about three hours each way; trail #4 to Bang Leap Nam Waterfall, 4.5km from headquarters; and #9 to the eleven-tiered Sip-et Chan Waterfall, which is only 4km from headquarters, but can be difficult to follow and involves some climbing plus half a dozen river crossings – allow three hours each way, and take plenty of water and some food. Longer guided treks including one or two nights' camping in the jungle interior, can be arranged through *Bamboo House*, *Nature Restaurant*, *Our Jungle House* and *Nung House* from about B1000 per person; if you're staying at *Nung House* you can also do a night safari, lasting three hours (B300–500), or longer treks to the stunning lake in the north of the park.

Khao Lak

Thirty kilometres south of Takua Pa and two hours by bus from Khao Sok National Park, Highway 4 passes alongside the scenic strip of bronze-coloured beach at **KHAO LAK**, whose understated ambience and role as a departure point for Ko Similan and Ko Surin now attracts more and more visitors, and is becoming increasingly geared towards package tourism. There's no village to speak of here, just a handful of houses strung out along the main roadside, and a side road through the rubber plantations leading to a growing cluster of beachfront bungalow operations. All the regular **buses** running between Phuket and Ranong, Takua Pa and Surat Thani pass the turn-off to Khao Lak; if you're coming from Krabi or Phang Nga, take a Phuket-bound bus to Khokkloi bus terminal and switch to a Takua Pa or Ranong bus. Whichever bus you're on, get off as soon as you see the big sign for "Sea Dragon Dive Centre"; from here it's a 500-metre walk down the side road to the sea and the bungalows.

The best of Khao Lak's **accommodation** is at *Nang Thong Bay Resort* (☎01/229 2181; ②–④), whose comfortable beachfront bungalows are all en suite. The whitewashed concrete bungalows at neighbouring *Garden Beach Resort* (☎01/229 2179; ②–④) are less attractive, but there are lots of them. Three kilometres north of Khao Lak, *Paradise* (☎01/270 9849; ②–④) has spacious bungalows on Chong Fa Palm Beach, a good restaurant and a pick-up service. Five kilometres south of Khao Lak beach, on a rocky shore, stands *Poseidon Bungalows* (☎076/443258; ②–④; closed May–October), a lovely place to hang out for a few days and also a long-established organizer of snorkelling expeditions to the Similan Islands (see below). To get to *Poseidon*, ask to be dropped off the bus at the village of Laem Kaen; from here it's a **one-kilometre** walk or motorbike-taxi ride to the bungalows. The turn-off is signed between kilometre-stone markers 53 and 54.

The best **places to eat** in Khao Lak are the little beach-shack restaurants squashed together along the shore between *Nang Thong* and *Garden Beach Resort*. There is a **foreign-exchange** booth next door to Sea Dragon Dive Centre. The Nang Thong minimart, across from the dive centre, stocks travellers' essentials.

Diving and snorkelling

Khao Lak is renowned for the **snorkelling** and **diving** trips organized by Sea Dragon Dive Centre (☎076/420420), on the main road, across from the minimart. Their November-to-April programme includes three-day live aboards to the Similan Islands (B11400), and four-night live aboards to the Similans, Surin Islands, Ko Bon, Ko Ta Chai and Richlieu Rock (B15800 for divers, B7900 for snorkellers); if your time is limited, call ahead to book a place. They also offer four-day Padi dive courses (B7800). *Poseidon Bungalows* (see above) also runs recommended three-day trips to the Similans; these are for snorkellers only and cost B4100. Phuket Divers (☎076/215738) have recently opened a branch on the beach in Khao Lak and offer three- and four-day trips to the Similans and Ko Surin (B13500–16500).

Phuket

Thailand's largest island and a province in its own right, **Phuket** (pronounced "Poo-ket") ranks second in tourist popularity only to Pattaya. Thoughtless tourist developments have scarred much of the island, particularly along the west coast, and the trend on all the beaches is upmarket, with very few budget possibilities. As mainstream resorts go, however, those on Phuket are just about the best in Thailand, offering a huge range of watersports and great diving facilities. The sea gets quite rough from May to October. Although the best west-coast beaches are connected by road, to get from one beach to another by public transport you nearly always have to go back into Phuket town.

All direct air-conditioned **buses** from Bangkok travel overnight; book ahead. Some people take the overnight train to Surat Thani, about 290km east of Phuket, and then a bus from there to Phuket. Ordinary buses connect Phuket with Ranong via Takua Pa, and Krabi. All buses arrive at the bus station at the eastern end of Thanon Phang Nga in Phuket town, from where it's a fifteen-minute walk to the Thanon Ranong songthaew stop for the beaches.

Ferries connect Phuket with Ko Phi Phi; minibuses meet the ferries and charge B50 for transfers to Phuket town and the west-coast beaches, or B100 to the airport. You can fly to Phuket from Bangkok, Chiang Mai, Hat Yai, Surat Thani and Ko Samui, and some international destinations. The **airport** is about 32km northwest of Phuket town; there's currently no public transport from the airport, so you have to take a taxi (about B400 to west-coast beaches). The cheapest way of getting to the airport is by Tour Royal Limousine (6.30am, then hourly 7am to 6pm; 45 minutes; B70), but their pick-up point is inconveniently located at 55/3 Thanon Vichitsongkhram (☎076/222062), 4km west of the centre of Phuket town.

Phuket town

Most visitors only remain in **PHUKET TOWN** long enough to jump on a beach-bound songthaew, which run regularly throughout the day from Thanon Ranong in the town centre to all the main beaches (B15–20). If you do want to stay, the *On On Hotel* at 19 Thanon Phang Nga (☎076/211154; ①–②) has basic, just adequate rooms in its attractive, colonial-style 1920s' building; *Talang Guesthouse* at 37 Thanon Talang (☎076/214225; ②) has large, good-value en-suite rooms in an old wooden house in one of Phuket's most traditional streets; and *Wasana Guesthouse* is conveniently located near the songthaew stop for the beaches, opposite Thai Airways at 159 Thanon Ranong (☎076/211754; ①–②). *Suksa Bai Hotel* (076/212287; ②) at 82/9 Thanon Thepkasatri is clean, spacious and quiet. **TAT** (daily 8.30am–4.30pm; ☎076/212213) is located at 73–75 Thanon Phuket.

LISTINGS

Airlines Air Lanka, Emirates & Eva Air, c/o Phuket Centre Tour, 27 Th Rasada (☎076/212892); Bangkok Airways, 158/2–3 Th Yaowarat (☎076/212341); Lauda Air, c/o LTU Asia Tours (☎076/327432); Malaysia Airlines, 1/8 Th Thungka (☎076/216675); Silk Air, 183/103 Th Phangnga (☎076/210849–51); Thai Airways, 78 Th Ranong (☎076/212499).

American Express, c/o Sea Tours, 95/4 Th Phuket (Mon–Fri 8.30am–5pm, Sat 8.30am–noon; ☎076/218417). Poste restante is kept for a month.

Bookshop The Books (daily 11am–9.30pm), near the TAT office on Th Phuket, stocks a phenomenal range of English-language books about Thailand.

Hospitals The best are the private Mission Hospital (aka Phuket Adventist Hospital), about 1km north of TAT on Th Thep Kasatri (☎076/211173), and Phuket International Hospital (☎076/249400, emergencies ☎210935), on the Airport Bypass just outside Phuket town.

Immigration Office At the southern end of Th Phuket, near Ao Makham (☎076/212108; Mon–Fri 8.30am–4.30pm).

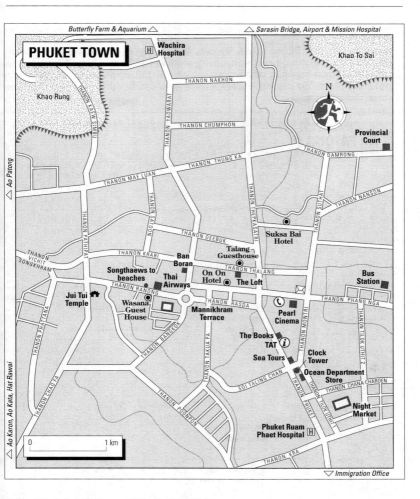

Butterfly Farm & Aquarium △   △ Sarasin Bridge, Airport & Mission Hospital

PHUKET TOWN

[H] Wachira Hospital

Khao To Sai

THANON NAKHON

Khao Rung

THANON KAEW SIMBU

THANON YAOWARAT

THANON CHUMPHON

N

Provincial Court

THANON DAMRONG

THANON THUNG KA

THANON NANSON

THANON MAE LUAN

THANON SUTHAT

Ao Patong

THANON PATHIPAT

THANON SALOON

THANON THEPKASATRI

THANON DEEBUK

Suksa Bai Hotel

THANON VICHIT SONGKHRAM

THANON KRABI

Ban Boran

Talang Guesthouse

THANON THALANG

Bus Station

Songthaews to beaches

Thai Airways

On On Hotel

The Loft

THANON RANONG

THANON PHANG NGA

Jui Tui Temple

Wasana Guest House

THANON RASDA

THANON MONTRI

THANON TILOK UTHIT 2

Mannikhram Terrace

Pearl Cinema

THANON PHATTANA

THANON BANGKOK

The Books

TAT (i)

Clock Tower

Sea Tours

THANON CHAO FA

THANON TAKUA PA

Ocean Department Store

THANON CHANA CHAROEN

SOI TALING CHAN

THANON PHUKET

THANON TILOK UTHIT

Night Market

Ao Karon, Ao Kata, Hat Rawai

THANON POONPON

Phuket Ruam Phaet Hospital [H]

0   1 km

THANON KRA

▽ Immigration Office

Police 24-hr help available on ☎1699 and ☎076/225361.

Post office Th Montri. Poste restante: Mon–Fri 8.30am–4.30pm, Sat 8.30am–3.30pm.

Telephone services International calls from the 24-hr public phone office on Th Phang Nga.

Ao Patong

The most popular and developed of all Phuket's beaches, **AO PATONG**, 15km west of Phuket town, has a broad, three-kilometre beach with good sand and plenty of shade, plus the island's biggest choice of watersports and diving centres. On the downside, high-rise hotels, tour agents and souvenir shops disfigure the beachfront, and the resort is full of hostess bars and strip joints. Patong is strung out along the two main roads – Thavee Wong and Raja Uthit/Song Roi Phi – that run parallel to the beachfront, spilling over into a network of connecting sois, most prominently the nightlife zone of Soi Bangla and the more sedate Soi Post Office.

Songthaews from Phuket town's Thanon Ranong (every 15min 6am–6pm; 20min) approach the resort from the northeast, driving south along Thanon Thavee Wong as far as the *Patong Merlin*, where they usually wait for a while to pick up passengers for the return trip to Phuket town. You can send **emails** at the *Internet Café* in Patong Shopping Centre on Thanon Thavee Wong.

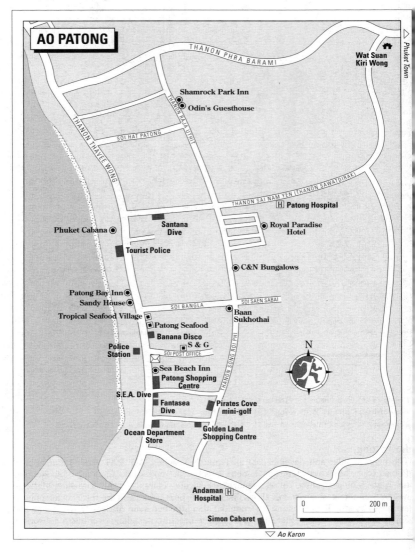

DIVING AND SNORKELLING

The reefs and islands within sailing distance of Phuket rate amongst the most spectacular in the world, and this is where you'll find Thailand's best-value **dive centres**, all of which offer certificated diving courses (B11000 for a four-day Open Water). Always check the equipment and staff credentials carefully and ask whether the dive centre is a member of Divesafe Asia, which runs Phuket's decompression chamber, located at 113/16 Thanon Song Roi Phi on Ao Patong (☎076/342518); non-members need to put down a deposit of B100,000 before they can get treated. Dive centres on Ao Patong include: Fantasea Divers, next to *Holiday Inn* at the southern end of Patong (☎076/340088); Phuket International Diving Centre (PIDC), on Thanon Thavee Wong (☎076/341197); Santana, 6 Thanon Sawatdirak (☎076/294220); Southeast Asia divers, 116/1 Thanon Thavee Wong (☎076/292079).

ACCOMMODATION

There is no budget **accommodation** on Patong, but the best-value mid-range places are at the far northern end of Thanon Raja Uthit, beneath the hill road that brings everyone in from town, a 750-metre walk from the central shopping and entertainment area. Rates quoted here are for November to April, but at Christmas most places charge an extra 25 percent. You get good discounts in low season.

C&N Bungalows, 50/20 Th Raja Uthit (☎076/340745). Good-value, spacious bungalows with fridge, bathroom and air-con, set in a garden (though beware the din from the nearby *Titanic* disco). ④–⑤.

Odin's Guesthouse, 78/59 Th Raja Uthit (☎076/340732). One of several budget options at the far northern end of the resort, with two-storey rows of very acceptable en-suite bungalows; some air-con. ④–⑤.

Phuket Cabana, 94 Th Thavee Wong (☎076/340138). Gorgeous collection of thoughtfully designed bungalows (with air con, TV and fridge) set around a garden swimming pool. Right on the beach and definitely the choice option of its price bracket. ⑨.

Sea Beach Inn, 90/1–2 Soi Permpong 2 (☎076/341616). Huge, good-value, slightly faded rooms, a stone's throw from the beach. Some air-con. ⑤.

Shamrock Park Inn, 17/2 Th Raja Uthit (☎076/340991). Pleasant rooms with shower, many with balconies, in a two-storey complex near *Odin's*. ③.

EATING AND DRINKING

As you'd expect, **seafood** is good on Patong: the open-air *Tropica Seafood Village*, close to the Soi Bangla/Thavee Wong intersection specializes in Phuket lobster, cooked to Thai, Chinese and Western recipes, and *Patong Seafood Restaurant*, on the central stretch of Thanon Thavee Wong at no. 98/2 is another recommended, if rather pricey, option. For a splurge, head to the elegant *Baan Sukhothai*, a hotel restaurant at the eastern end of Soi Bangla, which is known for its fine "Royal Thai" dishes, a sort of nouvelle cuisine. Real coffees and cappuccinos make *S&G Restaurant*, Soi Post Office, a good choice for breakfast, while for cheap evening meals, you can't beat the **night market** between Soi Bangla and Soi Sai Nam Yen on Thanon Raja Uthit. Most of Patong's **nightlife** is packed into the strip of neon-lit open-air "bar-beers" along Soi Bangla and neighbouring sois. The **gay bars** are concentrated around *Paradise Hotel* on Thanon Raja Uthit.

Ao Karon

Twenty kilometres southwest of Phuket town, **AO KARON** is only about 5km south of Patong, but a lot less congested. Although the central stretch of beachfront is dominated by large-capacity hotels, the beach is, as yet, free of developments, and elsewhere you'll only find low-rise guesthouses and bungalows. The beach, while long and sandy, offers very little shade and almost disappears at high tide. Swimming off any part of Karon can be quite dangerous during the monsoon season, when the undertow gets treacherously strong (look out for the red flags).

The resort is encircled by a ring road, called Thanon Patak, which branches off the main access route to Phuket town. Hotels, restaurants, dive shops and minimarts line the northern curve of Thanon Patak, near the *Islandia Hotel*; there are banks, supermarkets and a post office on the beachfront near *Phuket Arcadia*; and spread along Thanon Taina (on the Karon/Kata headland at the southern end of the beach) is a little tourist village – sometimes referred to as Kata Centre – full of minimarts and café–bars, as well as a secondhand bookshop, and the resort's most efficient place to send emails, the *Little Mermaid Hotel* (open to non-guests). **Dive centres** on Ao Karon/Ao Kata include: Dive Asia, at 36/10 Thanon Patak,

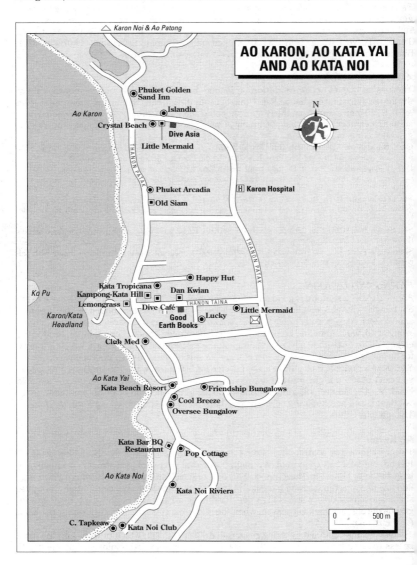

north Karon (☎076/396199) and on the Kata/Karon headland (☎076/330598); and Marina Divers, next to Marina Cottages on the headland between Ao Karon and Ao Kata (☎076/330272).

Songthaews from Phuket's Thanon Ranong (every 20min; 30min) arrive in Karon via the outer stretch of Thanon Patak, hitting the beach at the northern end of Ao Karon and then driving south along the beachfront length of Thanon Patak and continuing over the headland as far as *Kata Beach Resort* on Ao Kata Yai.

ACCOMMODATION

One of the best places for budget **hotels** is on the Karon/Kata headland, particularly along Thanon Taina, which bisects the road to Kata Yai. Rates quoted here are for high season, which runs from November to April, but over Christmas most places charge an extra 25 percent. You can get good discounts in low season.

Crystal Beach Hotel, 36/10 Th Patak (☎076/396580). Decent enough city-style hotel, central for shops and bars. Air-con. ⑥.

Happy Hut, up the hill from *Kata Tropicana* at the southern end of Karon (☎076/330230). Pleasantly located in a grassy dip some 300m from the beach, with simple huts and sturdier bungalows. Some of the cheapest rooms on the island. ②–③.

Kata Tropicana, far southern end of Karon (☎076/330408). Many travellers' first stop, and deservedly popular, though no bargain. Range of well-spaced bungalows on a grassy slope; two minutes from the beach, and within walking distance of Th Taina's bars and restaurants. ④–⑥.

The Little Mermaid, eastern end of Th Taina (☎076/330730). Exceptionally good bungalow rooms, all with air-con and TV, set round a pool. Internet service and motorbike rental. Also some cheaper, city-style fan and air-con rooms in the central hotel block. ②–⑦.

Lucky, Th Taina (☎076/330572). Friendly and relatively inexpensive. Room quality varies a lot, but all are en suite. ②–③.

Phuket Golden Sand Inn, northern end of Ao Karon (☎076/396493). Popular, medium-sized hotel with good-value fan or air-con bungalows. ⑥–⑧.

EATING AND DRINKING

Many of Karon's best **restaurants** and bars are sprinkled along Thanon Taina. Most of the **bars** are small, genial places: *Blue Fin* and *Anchor Bar* are both recommended.

Dan Kwian, Th Taina. Specializes in northeastern fare, but also offers fresh seafood and pizzas. Occasional performances from live bands. Moderate.

Dive Café, Th Taina. Popular, cheap and cheerful restaurant serving a good choice of authentic Thai curries – yellow, green and massaman – plus seafood.

Kampong-Kata Hill Restaurant, Th Taina. Specializes in high-quality Thai dishes. Expensive.

Lemongrass, Kata/Karon headland. Pleasant place that specializes in good-quality Thai food (mainly curries, noodles and seafood) at reasonable prices.

Old Siam, in front of the *Thavorn Palm Beach Hotel*, beachfront road (☎076/396090). Large, teak-wood restaurant, renowned for its traditional Royal Northern Thai cuisine; stages classical Thai dance on Wednesdays and Saturdays. Call for free transport. Moderate to expensive.

Ao Kata Yai and Ao Kata Noi

Tree-lined and peaceful, **AO KATA YAI** (Big Kata Bay) is only a few minutes' drive around the headland from Karon, but both prettier and safer for swimming. The northern stretch of Kata Yai is occupied by the unobtrusive buildings of the *Club Med* resort, and then it's a lengthy trek down to the rest of the accommodation at the southern end. A headland at the southernmost point divides Ao Kata Yai from the much smaller **AO KATA NOI** (Little Kata Bay). Most songthaews from Phuket go first to Karon, then drive south past *Club Med*, terminating at *Kata Beach Resort* on the headland between Kata Yai and Kata Noi. To get to Kata Noi, continue walking over the hill for about ten minutes, or take a tuk-tuk.

There is no budget **accommodation** on Kata Yai. *Friendship Bungalows* (☎076/330499; ④) has very adequate fan and air-con bungalows in a garden, about five minutes' walk from the southern end of the beach, and the nearby *Oversee Bungalow* (☎076/330116; ③–⑥) has decent fan and some air-con rooms. At neighbouring *Cool Breeze* (☎076/330484; ③–⑥) you get the choice between basic huts and bigger rooms with air-con. Located midway between Kata Yai and Kata Noi, the middle-sized hotel known as *Pop Cottage* (☎076/330181; ⑦–⑨) has pleasant enough mid-priced rooms; across the road, *Kata Bar B Q Restaurant* (☎076/330989, ④) offers a few good rooms, right on the beach. The best of Kata Noi's accommodation is at *C. Tapkeaw Bungalow* (☎076/33043; ⑤), where spacious bungalows are ranged up the hillside at the far southern end of the road. The adjacent *Kata Noi Club* (☎076/330194; ⑥–⑦) has some rather spartan bungalows, while the fan rooms at *Kata Noi Riviera* (☎076/330726; ③–⑥) feel box-like but are cheapish.

Ao Phang Nga

Covering some four hundred square kilometres of coast between Phuket and Krabi, the mangrove-lined bay of **AO PHANG NGA** is littered with dramatic limestone karst formations of up to 300m in height. The best and most affordable way of seeing the bay is to join one of the popular longtail **boat trips** arranged from the nearby town of Phang Nga: Sayan Tour (☎076/430348), Mr Kaen Tour (☎076/430619) and James Bond Tours (☎076/440595) have offices inside the bus station and offer the same things. Half-day tours (B200) depart every day at 7.30am and 2pm and last about three hours; full-day tours (B450) last until 4pm. Overnight trips with a stay on the unusual Muslim stilt village of Ko Panyi, built almost entirely on stilts around the rock that supports the mosque, cost B500. All tours leave from Phang Nga bus station. The standard itinerary follows a circular or figure-of-eight route around the bay, passing weirdly shaped karst silhouettes including "James Bond Island" which was Scaramanga's hideaway in *The Man With the Golden Gun*. Most boats return to the mainland via Ko Panyi.

Phang Nga town is served by hourly **buses** to and from Phuket and Krabi, and four air-con buses a day to and from Surat Thani. The bus station is on Thanon Phetkasem, a few minutes' walk from the hotels and restaurants. The staff at Sayan Tour will store your baggage for a few hours; they also sell bus and boat tickets for onward journeys to Krabi, Ko Phi Phi, Ko Lanta and Ko Samui. Phang Nga's best budget **hotel** is *Thawisuk Hotel* (☎076/412100; ①). The *Phing Kan Restaurant* under the *Ratanapong Hotel* (☎076/411247; ①–③) has a decent menu of noodle and rice standards.

Krabi

The small fishing town of **KRABI** is a major transport hub for the islands of Ko Phi Phi and Ko Lanta. During high season, heaps of travellers stop off here and wait for the next boat, but it's a nice spot for a couple of nights too. Although Krabi has no beaches of its own, it's only a 45-minute boat ride to the stunning bays of Laem Phra Nang and about the same time in a songthaew to Ao Nang (both beaches are described below). Every Krabi travel agent sells day-trips to Ao Phang Nga (see above) and snorkelling trips to four or five nearby islands, and many agents also offer interesting tours of Krabi's mangrove swamps.

Overnight air-con **buses** to Krabi leave from Bangkok's Southern Bus Terminal; you'll need to book ahead. See Travel Details on p.956 for details of other bus connections. Only a few buses drop their passengers in central Krabi: most pull in at the bus terminal 5km north of town in the village of Talat Kao, from where there's a frequent songthaew service to Krabi's Thanon Maharat. Ferries from Ko Phi Phi and Ko Lanta dock at Chao Fa pier, but the longtails from Laem Phra Nang often pull in at the pier 300m further north. Most Krabi tour agents can arrange domestic air tickets and bus tickets direct to Malaysia and Singapore. For **accommodation**, hard-core budget travellers tend to head for *Cha Guesthouse* (①–②), opposite the post office on Thanon Utrakit, offering huts set in a garden compound, as well as motorbike rental (B150); *KL Guesthouse* on Maharat Soi 2 (☎075/612511; ①) is a similar no-frills place. *Grand Tower Hotel*, at the corner of Utrakit and Chao Fa roads (☎075/611741; ②–③) is a popular, medium-sized travellers' place with simple but spruce rooms, and *KR Mansion*, a ten-minute walk west along Thanon Chao Fa from the pier (☎075/612761; ②–③) is fairly similar. All the above listed accommodation provides **Internet access**. *Thammachat Restaurant* on Thanon Kong Ka boasts the most adventurous Thai menu in town; *Muslim Restaurant* on Thanon Pruksa Uthit does cheap and filling rotis (flat fried breads) with curry sauces, and the night market sets up around the pier head.

Laem Phra Nang

The stunning headland of **Laem Phra Nang** is accessible only by boat from Krabi (45min), so staying on one of its three beaches can feel like being on an island. The sheer limestone cliffs, pure white sand and emerald waters make it a spectacular spot, but bungalows have now been built on almost every centimetre of available land. Laem Phra Nang's three beaches are all within ten minutes' walk of each other: **Ao Phra Nang** is the prettiest, with luxuriously soft sand, reefs close to shore, and just one discreetly hidden super-luxury hotel. Ao Phra Nang is flanked by **Hat Railae**, technically one bay, but in fact composed of distinct east and west beaches. The least attractive of the cape's beaches, **East Railae** (also known as Nam Mao) is not suitable for swimming because of its fairly dense mangrove growth, a tide that goes out for miles, and a bay that's busy with incoming longtails. Accomodation here is cheaper, and you're never more than ten minutes' walk from the much cleaner sands of West Railae and Ao Phra Nang. Sometimes known as Sunset Beach, West Railae comes a close second to Ao Phra Nang, with similarly impressive karst scenery, crystal-clear water and a much longer stretch of good sand.

Several bungalows on the cape organize **snorkelling trips** (about B200), and Phra Nang Divers on West Railae (☎075/637064) runs **diving** trips and courses (B8000 for the four-day Open Water course). There are at least eighteen rock-climbing sites on the cape alone, and no shortage of places where you can rent equipment and hire guides and instructors. Check with other tourists before choosing a climbing guide, as operators' safety standards vary. A typical half-day introduction costs B500.

Longtail boats to the cape depart from beside the floating restaurant on the Krabi riverfront and from Chao Fa pier (45min), leaving throughout the day as soon as they fill up. From November to April the boatmen pull in at Ao Phra Nang, and can usually be persuaded to continue round to west Railae; during the rainy season they'll only go as far as East Railae. Except during the monsoon season, longtails also run between the mainland beach of Ao Nang (see p.946), and West Railae (10min). Several bungalows change money, but rates are better in Krabi.

Accommodation

During high season, it's essential to arrive on the beaches as early in the morning as possible. Rates can drop by up to fifty percent from May to October. All bungalows have restaurants.

EAST RAILAE

Coco House, in the centre of the beach. Basic but pleasant enough huts in a small garden compound, with some of the cheapest accommodation on the cape. ②.

Diamond 2, at the far eastern end of the beach. Concrete rooms and bamboo huts in a peacefully secluded spot. The cheaper rooms share facilities. ⑤–⑦.

Sunrise Bay Bungalows, towards the western (Laem Phra Nang) end of the beach (☎01/228 4236). Small, en-suite concrete huts. ④.

Viewpoint, at the far eastern end of east Railae (☎01/228 4115). The poshest spot on the beach; many of its glass-windowed bungalows have bay views. ③–⑥.

Ya Ya Bungalows, in the centre of the beach (☎01/476 9077). Dozens of huts and three-storey wooden towers jammed into a small area make this place seem a bit claustrophobic and leave the ground floor rooms rather dark. Internet access. ③–④.

WEST RAILAE

Railae Bay (☎01/722 0112). A big range, from inexpensive rattan constructions through to top-end bungalows with sea views and air-con. ③–⑦.

Railae Village (☎01/228 4366). Decent fan-cooled bungalows similar to the mid-priced ones at *Railae Bay* and *SandSea*, plus some air-con villas. ⑤–⑦.

SandSea (☎01/228 4114). Comfortable bungalows with fan and bathroom, plus deluxe air-con versions with big windows and nice furniture. Breakfast included in the price. ⑥–⑦.

Ao Nang and Hat Nopparat Thara

The scene at **AO NANG** (sometimes confusingly referred to as Ao Phra Nang), 45 minutes by road from Krabi or a ten-minute boat ride from cape Laem Phra Nang, is more sedate than at Laem Phra Nang, but correspondingly friendlier and less claustrophobic. The narrow and unexceptional beach has a road running right along its length, with the resort area stretching back over 1km from the shore along Route 4203. Don't bother coming to Ao Nang between May and October, when the beach gets covered in sea-borne debris and most accommodation is closed. There are a couple of official money exchanges and a shopping centre on the beach road, as well as about ten dive shops: one-day diving trips average B2000, and four-day PADI Open Water courses cost B8000. Ao Nang has some recommended seafood restaurants on its beachfront. Songthaews run from Krabi regularly throughout the day, taking about 45 minutes; from November to May, a daily boat connects Ao Nang with Ko Phi Phi Don (2hr).

Follow the road northwest past *Krabi Resort*, just north of the main beachfront in Ao Nang, for about a kilometre and you come to the eastern end of two-kilometre-long **HAT NOPPA-RAT THARA**. Invariably deserted, this beach is part of the **national marine park** that encompasses Ko Phi Phi, with the park headquarters about halfway along. Krabi–Ao Nang songthaews usually go via the park headquarters.

Accommodation

Rates quoted here are for high season, which in Ao Nang only runs from December to February; during the rest of the year rates can drop by up to fifty percent. Hat Nopparat Thara only has grim national park bungalows (②), but a handful of privately run bungalows have sprung up just across the estuary from the westernmost end of Hat Nopparat Thara on a beach known as Hat Ton Son, and these places are listed below. To get to Hat Ton Son, take any Ao Nang-bound songthaew from Krabi and ask to be dropped at the park's headquarters, then hop in a longtail taxi to cross the estuary to the bungalows on the other side; all Hat Ton Son bungalows shut down for the rainy season, from May to October.

AO NANG

Ao Nang Mountain View, on Route 42303 (☎075/637294), between *Penny's* and *Nongeed*. Clean, new, concrete en-suite bungalows. ②–④.

Ao Nang Orchid, about 80m up Route 4203 (☎075/637116). Basic concrete huts, plus some more comfortable concrete bungalows with hot showers and air-con. ④–⑥.

Green Park Bungalow, 200m up Route 4203 (☎075/637300). Recommended, friendly, family-run place; en-suite bamboo and concrete huts set in a grove of shady trees. ②–④.

Nongeed House, 250m up Route 4203 (☎075/637287). Large, clean rooms in a new concrete building. ②–④.

Penny's, 270m up Route 4203 (☎075/637295). Friendly, family-run place offering very clean, comfortable rooms and some air-con. ②–④.

HAT TON SON AND HAT KHLONG MUANG

Amber Andaman, on a remote stretch of the beach across the estuary from the national park headquarters (☎075/612761). Simple bamboo huts, some en suite. ②.

Andaman Inn, across the estuary from the national park headquarters (☎01/956 5129). Nice collection of comfortable bungalows, some en suite. ②–③.

Emerald Bungalows, across the estuary from the national park headquarters. Good, comfortable traveller-oriented bungalows. ①–⑥.

Ko Phi Phi

One of southern Thailand's most popular destinations, the two spectacular **KO PHI PHI** islands, 40km south of Krabi and 48km east of southern Phuket, recently leapt to international fame as the location for the film *The Beach*. The action is concentrated on the larger **Ko Phi Phi Don**, its fabulous long white beaches packed with bungalow operations and tourist enterprises. Its sister island, **Ko Phi Phi Leh**, is an uninhabited national marine park and can only be visited on day-trips. Inevitably, both islands have started to suffer the negative consequences of their outstanding beauty: some of the beaches are now littered with rubbish, and Phi Phi Don seems to be permanently under construction.

Diving and snorkelling off Ko Phi Phi is exceptionally good, and you can arrange day-dives (B1800) and four-day PADI courses (B9900) at Barrakuda (☎075/620698) and Moskito (☎01/229 2802) in Ton Sai village, and at Long Beach Diving on Hat Yao. Always check the equipment and the staff credentials first and check that the centre is insured to use the nearest decompression chamber, which is on Ao Patong in Phuket (see p.941).

During peak season, **ferries** to Ko Phi Phi Don run at least three times daily from Krabi (1hr 30min–2hr) and up to six times a day from Phuket (1hr 30min–2hr 30min); in the rainy season all services are reduced to once or twice daily. From November to May, there are also once-daily boats to Phi Phi Don from Ao Nang (2hr) and Ko Lanta Yai (1hr 30min).

All boats dock at **Ao Ton Sai**, the busiest bay on Ko Phi Phi Don. From here you can catch a longtail to any of the other beaches or walk – there are no roads or vehicle tracks on Phi Phi Don, just a series of paths across the steep and at times rugged interior. Accommodation on Phi Phi Don costs up to fifty percent more than on the mainland; at Christmas there are surcharges on listed rates and reservations are essential. The island's health centre is at the west end of Ao Ton Sai.

Ao Ton Sai

Ko Phi Phi Don would itself be two islands were it not for the tenuous palm-fringed isthmus that connects the hilly expanses to east and west, separating the stunningly symmetrical double bays of Ao Ton Sai to the south and **Ao Loh Dalum** to the north. The constantly expanding village at **AO TON SAI** is now a full-blown low-rise holiday resort, and it's the liveliest place to stay on the island. Shops, tour operators, restaurants, bars, Internet cafés and dive centres line the main track that parallels the beachfront and runs east as far as *Chao Ko* bungalows. The beach itself is most attractive at the western end, but gets unbearably crowded with day-trippers.

Most of Ton Sai's **accommodation** is packed between the Ao Ton Sai and Ao Loh Dalum beaches. *Twin Palm Guesthouse*, in the thick of the inland scrum, north of *Mama's* restaurant (☎01/477 9251; ②–④), scrapes by with a few dark guesthouse rooms and some nicer bungalows. The pleasanter and more peaceful huts at *Chong Khao Bungalows* (②) stand in a coconut grove behind *Tonsai Village* and *PP Cabana*, at the western end of the village. Ten minutes' walk east of the pier at the edge of the village, *Chao Ko* (☎075/611313; ③–④) fills up fast because it's close to the village action but quiet; it has standard en-suite concrete bungalows. There are dozens of little **restaurants** in the village, the best of which are the French-run *Mama's* and *The Grand Beach* which both specialize in seafood. *Carlito's Wave*, next to *Chao Ko*, has a big cocktails menu, while *Casablanca* and the *Reggae Bar* are lively outdoor rave spots further east along the track.

Laem Hin

East along the coast from *Chao Ko*, about ten minutes' walk from the pier, you come to the promontory known as **Laem Hin**, beyond which is a small stretch of beach that's quieter than Ao Ton Sai and better for swimming. Bungalows here are popular, being only a ten- to fifteen-minute walk from the restaurants and nightlife on Ao Ton Sai. *Gypsy 1* (③), inland, down the track between the mosque and *PP Don,* offers good-value concrete bungalows, all en suite, while its sister operation, *Gypsy 2* (②), 100m north along the track, has simpler bamboo huts. The comfortable bungalows at *Andaman Beach Resort*, east of the mosque (☎01/228 4368; ③–④), all have private bathrooms and are recommended.

Ao Loh Dalum

Just a few minutes' walk north through Ton Sai village, **AO LOH DALUM** is a quieter place for swimming and sunbathing, though the tide goes out for miles here. The viewpoint which overlooks the far eastern edge of the beach affords a magnificent wraparound panorama of both Ao Loh Dalum and Ao Ton Sai: to get there, follow the track inland (south) from beside *Paklong Seaside* and then branch off to your left (eastwards) near the water treatment plant. Loh Dalum's bungalows are all mid-range and upmarket, the cheapest of which is *Charlie Resort*, in the middle of the beach (☎075/620615; ③–⑥), where each bungalow has its own tiny garden area out front. *Paklong Seaside* (⑥) at the easternmost end of the beach is a comfortable guesthouse right on the shore.

Hat Yao

With its deluxe sand and large reefs just 20m offshore, **HAT YAO** (Long Beach) is the best of Phi Phi's main beaches – and the most crowded. Longtail boats do the ten-minute shuttle (B30) between Hat Yao and Ao Ton Sai from about 8am to 8pm, but it's also possible to walk between the two in half an hour. At low tide you can get to Hat Yao along the shore, though this involves some clambering. The alternative route takes you over the hillside and is easier to follow in reverse (from Hat Yao to Ton Sai) because you have to pass through private land belonging to one of the bungalow operations. From the far western end of Hat Yao, follow the path up into the trees from behind one of the last *Paradise Pearl* bungalows and continue to Ao Ton Sai along inland tracks.

The most attractive of Hat Yao's accommodation is the tiny and friendly *Ma Prao* (②–③), in a little cove west of Hat Yao itself, with easy access via a rocky path. The simple bungalows, some with bathrooms, overlook the sea. Of the two budget operations on Hat Yao, most budget travellers head first for *Long Beach Bungalows* (☎075/612410; ①–③), which covers the eastern half of the beach. Some of the cheapest huts here are on the verge of collapse, but the newer, more expensive huts are better value. The larger, better-maintained bungalows at *Paradise Pearl* (☎01/228 4370; ④–⑤) are decently spaced along the western half of the beach.

Ko Lanta Yai

KO LANTA YAI is quiet and offers plenty of fine sandy beaches; development on the 25-kilometre long island is still fairly low-key, and has so far been confined to the six west-coast beaches, so the island still feels like it belongs to its residents. Ko Lanta is even quieter during the rainy season (May to October), when the seas become too rough for boats to travel here from Krabi and the shores suffer from a fair bit of water-borne debris. Some bungalows close during this period, but most places on Hat Khlong Dao, the island's most popular beach, stay open.

From November to May two daily **ferries** run from Krabi to the tiny fishing village of Ban Sala Dan on the northern tip of Ko Lanta Yai (2hr 30min), and there's at least one ferry a day between Ko Phi Phi and Ban Sala Dan (1hr). Bungalow touts always meet the boats at Ban Sala Dan and transport you to the beach of your choice. During the rest of the year (the rainy season), you'll need to arrange overland minivan transport from a Krabi tour agent.

A road runs almost the entire length of Ko Lanta Yai's west coast, but there's no regular songthaew service on the island, so many bungalows rent out **motorbikes**. Most will also change money, and many offer international telephone services. **Tour operators** in Ban Sala Dan can arrange day-trips and onward transport, and there are a couple of tiny shops and a currency exchange (open bank hours) in the village too. This is also where you'll find the island's **dive shops**, including Ko Lanta Diving Centre/Ko Lanta Tauchschule (☎01/723 1103) and Atlantis (☎01/228 4089), which do day-trips ($75) and four-day PADI courses ($295). The diving season only runs from November to April.

HAT KHLONG DAO AND ACCOMMODATION

Lanta Yai's longest, loveliest and most popular beach is **HAT KHLONG DAO**, the northernmost of the west-coast beaches, about half an hour's walk from Ban Sala Dan, or 2–3km by road. The sand here is soft and golden, and palms and casuarinas shade parts of the shore. There's a tiny minimart next to *Lom Thaleh* at the southern end, and all the bungalows have **restaurants**. There is Internet access (10am–10.30pm) at the top of the slip road to *Lanta Villa*. Khlong Dao has the most **accomodation** on the island, but bungalows are still quite well spaced.

Golden Bay Cottages (☎01/229 1879). Occupies an ideal spot in the northern part of the bay, and offers basic bamboo huts and nicely furnished bungalows, some with air-con. ④–⑧.

Kaw Kwang Beach Bungalow, northernmost end of Hat Khlong Dao (☎01/228 4106). Good-value, if simple, bungalows set in a secluded garden. Some concrete bungalows with air-con. ②–⑦.

Lanta Garden Home, far southern end of Hat Khlong Dao. Friendly, family-run place offering a range of large, basic bamboo huts, nearly all with sea view. ②–③.

Lanta Sea House, southern end of the beach (☎01/228 4160). Comfortable wooden chalet-style bungalows in a seafront garden; some air-con too. ③–⑧.

Lanta Villa, middle of the beach (☎075/620629). Decent-sized wooden bungalows, some air-con. ②–⑦.

Lom Taleh, southern end of the beach (☎01/228 3720). Handful of comfortable bungalows in a seafront garden, plus some cheaper ones across the road. ④.

AO PHRA-AE (PALM BEACH)

A couple of kilometres south of Khlong Dao, the exceptionally pleasant **AO PHRA-AE** (also known as Palm Beach) boasts a beautiful long strip of almost deserted white sand, with just a few bungalow operations. At the northern end of the beach, *Lanta Palm Beach* (②–④) is a lovely place to stay, with its good-value bamboo huts spread out in a coconut grove. Three kilometres further south, *Rapala* (☎01/607 6477; ②) has 26 comfortable, idiosyncratically designed huts in a garden; it closes from May to September. Right at the southernmost end of the beach, *Relax Bay Tropicana* (☎01/228 4089; ④–⑤) occupies a fantastic position on a rocky point, and offers tasteful bungalows with verandahs and open-air bathrooms.

HAT KHLONG KHOANG AND HAT KHLONG NIN (PARADISE BEACH)

The rocky shore at **HAT KHLONG KHOANG**, 2km south of *Relax Bay Tropicana*, is not good for swimming or sunbathing, but it's quite rewarding for snorkelling. *Lanta's Lodge* (②) has inexpensive wooden bungalows; neighbouring *Where Else?* (②) has a relaxed, laid-back atmosphere and consists of just fifteen bamboo and coconut-wood bungalows; and, next door, *Lanta Coconut Greenfield* (☎01/4150713; ③) has new, en-suite concrete and bamboo bungalows.

A further 5km on you reach the sands of **HAT KHLONG NIN** (sometimes known as Paradise Beach), where three bungalow operations are clustered together in a rather claustrophobic knot at the centre of the shore, the cheapest of which are *Miami Bungalows* (☎01/228 4506; ②–⑤). *Lanta Paradise* (☎01/228 4488; ②–④) has lots of closely packed but spacious bamboo huts and concrete bungalows.

AO KANTIANG AND AO KHLONG JAAK

Three kilometres south of Khlong Hin, *SeaSun* (①–②) is one of three sets of bungalows on the tiny sandy fishing cove of **AO KANTIANG**. It's still a secluded, almost remote spot, and you have the choice between small bamboo huts and larger concrete affairs. The beach is good for swimming, and you can do snorkelling and fishing trips. The road gets worse and worse as you head south from Ao Kantiang, eventually degenerating into a track that leads to the isolated little **AO KHLONG JAAK**, site of the exceptionally popular *Waterfall Bungalows* (☎01/228 0014; ②–⑥). The huts here are simple but stylish, many with split-level accommodation. Advance booking is essential and the place shuts down from June to September.

Ko Jum

Situated halfway between Krabi and Ko Lanta Yai, **KO JUM** (also known as Ko Pu) has one tiny fishing village and just two small bungalow operations. *Joy Bungalows* (☎01/229 1502; ①–④) are comfortably equipped and lit by paraffin lamps at bedtime. About fifteen minutes' walk from *Joy New Bungalow* (①–③) has a handful of basic bamboo huts, plus a couple of treehouses. Both bungalows send longtails out to meet the Krabi–Ko Lanta ferries as they pass the west coast (1hr 30min from Krabi); in the rainy season, book transport through Krabi tour agents.

THE DEEP SOUTH

As Thailand drops down to meet Malaysia, the cultures of the two countries begin to merge. Many inhabitants of the **deep south** are ethnically more akin to the Malaysians: most of the 1,500,000 followers of Islam here speak Yawi, an old Malay dialect, and many yearn for secession from Thailand. There are eight **border crossings to Malaysia** down here (see p.824), with the most efficient transport connections to Malaysia starting at the ugly, modern city of **Hat Yai**. The nearby old town of **Songkhla** is a more sympathetic spot for sightseeing, but if you're after coastal attractions, either take a boat trip through the **Thale Noi Waterbird Park**, or head for the rarely visited beaches of the **Trang coast** and the spectacular **Ko Tarutao islands**.

Thale Noi Waterbird Park

The beautiful watery landscape of **Thale Noi Waterbird Park** is rich in exotic birds and vegetation and best seen by longtail boat; boats can be hired for about B300 at the pier in Ban Thale Noi for two-hour trips. This bizarre freshwater habitat at the head of the huge lagoon that spills into the sea at Songkhla is dotted with marshy islands, lotus pads and reeds, all of which appeal to the hundreds of thousands of birds which breed here – brown teals, loping purple herons, white cattle egrets, and nearly two hundred other species. Most are migratory, so March and April are the best spotting months, particularly early morning and late evening. Easiest access is via **PHATTHALUNG**, a hot, dusty town halfway between Nakhon Si Thammarat and Hat Yai, where you can stay at the clean and friendly *Thai Hotel*, at 1 Thanon Disara Sakarin, behind the Bangkok Bank on Thanon Ramet (☎074/611636; ①–②). Songthaews depart from Thanon Nivas, which runs north off Thanon Ramet near the station to **BAN THALE NOI** (1hr), the village on the western bank of the lagoon. If you want to get a dawn start, ask in the village souvenir shops about renting a room (①). Coming from Nakhon or points further north by bus, you can save yourself a trip into Phatthalung by getting out at Ban Chai Khlong, 15km from Ban Thale Noi, and waiting for a songthaew there.

Trang and around

TRANG (aka Taptieng) holds an eye-catching **Vegetarian Festival** every October (see p.830), but is chiefly of interest for the string of gorgeous beaches and islands nearby. Most **buses** arrive at the terminal on Thanon Huay Yod, to the north of the centre; buses from Satun and Palian stop on Thanon Ratsada, which runs south from the eastern end of Thanon

Rama VI. Air-con minibuses for Hat Yai have two bases, one at the petrol station on Thanon Phatthalung to the northeast of the centre, the other on Thanon Huay Yod, 200m south of the main bus terminal; those for Nakhon Si Thammarat are based on Thanon Klong Huai Yang, off Thanon Wisetkul about 200m from the clocktower; those for Ko Lanta and for Pak Bara are handled by Trang Tour (see below). The **train station** is at the western end of Thanon Rama VI.

The best budget **hotel** is the *Ko Teng Hotel* at 77–79 Thanon Rama VI (☎075/218622; ③), with large, clean en-suite rooms and a travellers' restaurant. **Night markets** set up in the station square, and around the clocktower on Wisetkul and Rama VI roads. Trang Tour **travel agency**, beside *Thumrin Hotel* on Thanon Rama VI (☎075/214564), books boat trips to the nearby islands (B600) and three-day dive trips (B6500), and arranges rental of motorbikes (B180–250) and cars (B800; B1500 with driver). **Internet** access is also available here.

The Trang coast

From Ban Pak Meng, 40km due west of Trang town, to the mouth of the Trang River runs a thirty-kilometre stretch of gorgeous beaches, best explored by car or motorbike. The beach at **PAK MENG** is typical of the area, a long, gently curving strip strewn with small shells. Air-con minibuses make the one-hour trip here every half hour from Trang's Thanon Tha Klang, the northwesterly continuation of Thanon Ratchadamnoen. Food stalls line the back of the beach.

Of all the Trang islands, **KO HAI** (aka Ko Ngai), 16km southwest of Pak Meng, offers the best combination of accommodation and scenery. From November to May, boats leave Pak Meng at 11am and noon (1hr; B100). The long white-sand beach on the east coast is pretty and ideal for swimming. The huts and bungalows of *Ko Hai Resort* (☎075/211045; Trang office at Tha 112 Rama VI; ☎075/210496; Bangkok reservations ☎02/246 4399; ②–⑦) occupy a sandy cove by the island's jetty.

KO MOOK, about 8km southeast of Ko Hai, is known for Tham Morakhot, the beautiful "Emerald Cave" on the west coast, which can only be reached by boat. At low tide, boats can sail into the cave – at other times it's a short swim – to emerge at an inland beach at the base of a natural chimney whose walls are coated with dripping vegetation. Farang Beach, south of Tham Morakhot and a thirty-minute walk from the island village, is the best strip of sand, good for swimming and snorkelling. On this coast just north of the village, *Ko Mook Resort* (☎075/212613; Trang office at Stone Graphic, 45 Thanon Rama VI, ☎075/222296; ②) has the least expensive bungalows on the Trang islands (fans, mosquito screens and shared bathrooms). The resort's office in Trang has **Internet** facilities and can arrange transport by car and boat (B130), or longtails can be chartered at Pak Meng (B400).

Ko Tarutao National Marine Park

The unspoilt **Ko Tarutao National Marine Park** is probably the most beautiful of all Thailand's accessible beach destinations. The park covers 51 mostly uninhabited islands, of which three – Ko Tarutao, Ko Adang and Ko Lipe – are easy to reach and offer accommodation. The island's forests support langurs, crab-eating macaques and wild pigs, plus reef egrets and hornbills. The park is also the habitat of about 25 percent of the world's fish species, as well as dugong, sperm whale and dolphins. Turtles lay their eggs on Ko Tarutao between September and April.

The park is officially closed to tourists from mid-May to mid-November, but in season, boats to Ko Tarutao leave **PAK BARA**, 60km north of Satun, at 10.30am and 3pm (90 min; B150). The only way to reach Ko Adang and Ko Lipe is on the mail boat which, from December to May, travels from Pak Bara via Ao Pante (daily; 4hr 30min). In low season, private operators organize trips to Ko Tarutao, Ko Adang and Ko Lipe (B700 return). The private boats are notoriously unreliable. Boats for Ko Bulon Lae leave Pak Bara at 2pm from

November to April (1hr 30min; B120), but will sometimes set off in the low season (contact Udom Tours on ☎01/963 6916 in Pak Bara).

To **get to Pak Bara** from Trang, take a Satun-bound bus or share taxi to Langu and change to a red songthaew for the ten-kilometre hop to the port. From Hat Yai three buses a day from the Plaza Cinema (at 7am, 11am & 3pm; 2hr 30min) and faster air-con minibuses from an office on Thanon Prachathipat go all the way through to Pak Bara; otherwise, take a share taxi to Langu, or a Satun-bound bus to Chalung and change onto a Satun–Trang bus to get to Langu. From Satun, frequent buses and taxis travel the 50km to Langu. If you miss the boat, you can **stay** in Pak Bara at *Diamond Beach* (①–②), 500m before the pier, or at *Isra Guesthouse* (☎01/9690956; ①), 150m from the pier along the main road, which has clean rooms, a restaurant, travel agent and Internet access.

Ko Tarutao

Hilly **KO TARUTAO**, the largest of the islands, is covered in rainforest and has perfect beaches all along its 26-kilometre west coast. Boats dock at **Ao Pante**, on the northwestern side, where the admission fee (B20) is collected; here you'll find the park headquarters and visitor centre, a small shop and a restaurant. You can stay in national park bungalows (③–⑥), longhouses (B80 per bed), or tents (B100 a night for two people), or pitch your own tent (B10 per person per night). Behind the settlement, the steep, half-hour climb to To-Boo Cliff is a must, especially at sunset, for its fine views. A half-hour walk south from Ao Pante, the two quiet bays of **Ao Jak** and **Ao Malae** are fringed by coconut palms. Behind the house at the south end of Ao Malae, a road leads over the headland to the three-kilometre sweep of **Ao Sone** (2hr from Ao Pante), whose freshwater stream makes it a good spot for camping.

Ko Adang and Ko Lipe

At **KO ADANG**, a wild island covered in tropical rainforest, the boat pulls in at the Laem Sone park station on the southern shore, where the beach is steep and narrow. There are longhouses (B100 per bed), tents (B100 for two people) and a restaurant here. About 2km west along the coast, there's a small beach lined with coconut palms, and behind an abandoned customs house a trail leads to the small Pirate Waterfall (20min).

KO LIPE, 2km south of Adang, is covered in coconut plantations and inhabited by *chao ley* or sea gypsies (a distinct group scattered around the west coast of the Malay peninsula who speak their own language and follow animistic beliefs). There are shops, a school and a health centre in the village on the eastern side – from where longtail boats come out to meet the mail boat. There are several simple bungalow outfits (①–②) under shady pine trees by the village, and the *chao ley* rent longtail boats to the reefs (B100–150 per person). *Pattaya Son Resort* (①–②), on the other side of the island, is run by the *chao ley* and has en-suite bungalows on the beach and the adjacent headland and the best food on the island. Tiny *Ko Gra*, 200m out to sea, also has a beautiful reef. There are two dive centres on the island offering day-trips from B1600.

Ko Bulon Lae

Tiny **KO BULON LAE**, 20km west of Pak Bara, is not part of the national park, and not quite as beautiful. But a two-kilometre strip of fine white sand runs the length of the east coast and there are good reefs off the east and south shores. Snorkelling gear, as well as boats for island trips can be rented at *Pansand*, the island's largest and best resort (☎01/722 0279; ②–④), where accommodation ranges from simple longhouse rooms to swanky clapboard cottages; two-person tents can also be rented for B80 a night. To book a room or find out about off-season boats, contact First Andaman Travel, opposite *Queens Hotel* at 82–84 Thanon Wisetkul in Trang (☎075/218035). You can also stay at nearby *Moloney/Bulon Resort* (②).

Satun and boats to Malaysia

Remote **SATUN** nestles in the last wedge of Thailand's west coast and is chiefly of interest for its **boat services to Malaysia**. Satun's **bus depot** is at the north end of town, but most buses also make a stop in the centre; share taxis and air-conditioned minibuses are centrally based around the junction of Thanon Saman Pradit, the main east–west thoroughfare, and Thanon Buriwanit. *Rian Thong* (☎074/711036; ①), by the town pier at 4 Thanon Saman Pradit, is the best budget **hotel**.

The **boats** to Malaysia depart from Thammalang pier, 10km south of Satun and served by frequent songthaews (30min). In the morning, frequent longtails run to Kuala Perlis on Malaysia's northwest tip (30min; B40), from where there are plentiful transport connections down the west coast (see p.603). Four ferry boats a day also cross from Thammalang pier to the Malaysian island of Langkawi (90min); buy tickets (B360 return) from Satun Travel and Ferry Service, opposite the *Wangmai Hotel* at 45/16 Thanon Satun Thani (☎074/711453). **Entering Thailand** by sea from Malaysia, you need to get your passport stamped at the immigration office at Thammalang pier.

Hat Yai and transport to Malaysia

HAT YAI, the transport axis of the region, is a concrete mess, but attracts half a million tourists a year, nearly all of them Malaysians who nip across the border to shop and get laid. It's only 50km from the border with Malaysia, and you can get to many destinations from here by direct share taxis, air-con minibuses (tickets available from any Hat Yai travel agent) and trains.The **train station**, on the west side of the centre at the end of Thanon Thamnoon Vithi, has a useful left-luggage office (daily 6am–7pm with an unpredictable break for lunch; B5–10 per piece per day); the **bus terminal** is far to the southeast of town on Thanon Kanchanawanit, but most buses make a stop at the Plaza Cinema on Thanon Petchkasem, on the north side of the centre. Share taxis and air-con minibuses have different ranks around town (marked on the map). Regular **flights** connect Hat Yai with Johor Baru, Kuala Lumpur and Singapore; the airport is 12km from town and served by Thai Airways minibuses, whose office is at 190/6 Thanon Niphat Uthit 2 (☎074/233433). The **TAT office** is at 1/1 Soi 2, Tha Niphat Uthit 3 (☎074/243747) and the **tourist police** have offices at Thanon Sripoovanart on the south side of town (☎074/230972), and near the Odean department store on Niphat Uthit 3; the **immigration office** is on Thanon Petchkasem (☎074/233760). There is an **Internet** office on the corner of Soi 2, Thanon Nipat Uthit 3, next to TAT.

Into Malaysia

Share taxis depart Hat Yai every morning for Penang, **Malaysia** (5–6hr; B250). Air-conditioned **minibuses** run from Hat Yai to Sungai Kolok (3hr), Alor Setar (3hr) and Butterworth (5hr), and VIP buses to Kuala Lumpur (12hr) and Singapore (18hr). Two **trains** make the daily run to Sungai Kolok (see p.956), and one a day heads via the frontier at **PADANG BESAR** to Butterworth (for the ferry to Penang or trains on to Kuala Lumpur). The least expensive but most time-consuming method is to catch a bus to Padang Besar (every 10min; 1hr 40min), walk 800m across the border and take a share taxi to Kuala Perlis (30min) or Alor Setar (1hr) – avoid the obvious route straight down Highway 4 to Sadao, because there's a long stretch between the opposing border posts which there's no inexpensive way of covering.

Accommodation and eating

Hat Yai has a huge range of **hotels**, none of them very good value and most worked by prostitutes. *Cathay Guesthouse* at 93 Thanon Niphat Uthit 2 (☎074/243815 or 235044; ②) is falling apart, but traveller-friendly and has B80 dorm beds. *Hok Chin Hin*, 87 Thanon Niphat Uthit

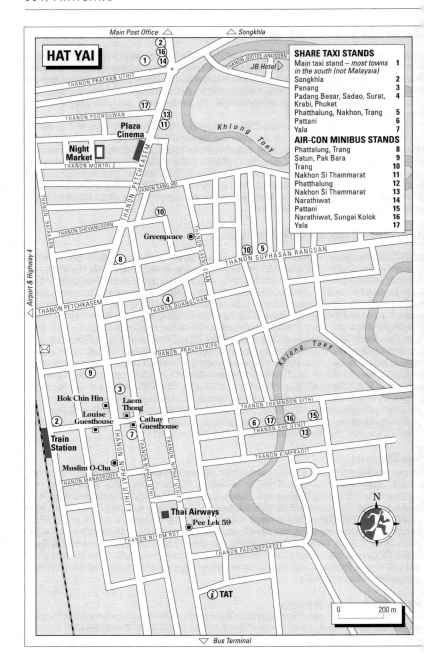

HAT YAI

△ Main Post Office △ Songkhla

THANON JOOTEE-ANUSORN

JB Hotel

THANON PRATHAN UTHIT

THANON POONSUWAN

Plaza Cinema

Night Market

THANON MONTRI 2

THANON PETCHKASEM

THANON SANG SRI

Khlong Toey

THANON RATAKARN

THANON SHEVANUSORN

THANON SAENG CHAN

Greenpeace ⊙

THANON SUPHASAN RANGSAN

THANON PETCHKASEM

THANON DUANGCHAN

THANON PRACHATHIPAT

Khlong Toey

△ Airport & Highway 4

THANON THAMNOON VITHI

Hok Chin Hin

Laem Thong

Louise Guesthouse

Cathay Guesthouse

THANON NIPHAT UTHIT 1

THANON NIPHAT UTHIT 2

THANON NIPHAT UTHIT 3

THANON SHE UTHIT

Train Station

Muslim O-Cha ⊙

THANON MANASRUDEE

THANON KIMPRADIT

Thai Airways

Pee Lek 59

THANON NIYOM ROT

THANON PADUNGPAKDEE

ⓘ TAT

N

0   200 m

▽ Bus Terminal

SHARE TAXI STANDS

Main taxi stand – *most towns in the south (not Malaysia)*	1
Songkhla	2
Penang	3
Padang Besar, Sadao, Surat, Krabi, Phuket	4
Phatthalung, Nakhon, Trang	5
Pattani	6
Yala	7

AIR-CON MINIBUS STANDS

Phattalung, Trang	8
Satun, Pak Bara	9
Trang	10
Nakhon Si Thammarat	11
Phatthalung	12
Nakhon Si Thammarat	13
Narathiwat	14
Pattani	15
Narathiwat, Sungai Kolok	16
Yala	17

1 (☎074/243258; ①–②), has en-suite rooms; the large, efficiently run *Laem Thong*, 46 Thanon Thamnoon Vithi (☎074/352301; ②), also offers air-con, as does the more comfortable *Louise Guesthouse*, by the train station at 21–23 Thanon Thamnoon Vithi (☎074/220966; ③). At the junction with Thanon Niyom Rot, the welcoming **restaurant** *Pee Lek 59*, 185/4 Niphat Uthit 3, does tasty, moderately priced seafood in Thai style. *Muslim O-Cha*, at 117 Niphat Uthit 1 (closes 8.30pm), is a simple place which serves curried chicken and rice. *Greenpeace Restaurant*, at 50 Thanon Saengchan, has a leafy patio and offers a good menu of Thai and Western food. The night market sets up behind the Plaza Cinema on Thanon Montri 2.

Songkhla

The small, sophisticated former trading port of **SONGKHLA** makes a much pleasanter alternative to Hat Yai, 25 km away. It retains many historic buildings, including the graceful Chinese mansion which now houses the **Songkhla National Museum** (Wed–Sun 9am–4pm; B30) – it's on Thanon Jana, the main east–west street, and contains a jumble of folk exhibits, Ban Chiang pottery, Hindu and Buddhist statues. From the museum, you can explore the atmospheric old streets of Nakhon Nai and Nakhon Nawk on your way south to **Wat Matchimawat**, a grand affair set in ornamental grounds on Thanon Saiburi. Every centimetre of its interior is covered with murals, telling of the previous lives of the Buddha, mixed in with vivacious tableaux of nineteenth-century Songkhla life.

Buses from Hat Yai and other main towns arrive at the major junction of Thanon Ramwithi with Jana and Platha roads. Share taxis congregate on the south side of the main bus stop, just off Thanon Ramwithi. *Narai*, at 14 Thanon Chai Khao (☎074/311078; ①), is Songkhla's bottom-end **hotel**, situated in a quiet wooden house at the foot of Doi Tung Kuan. A good alternative is the new *Abritus Guesthouse*, 28/16 Thanon Ramwithi (☎074/326047; ②), which has large, clean rooms and Thai and Western food. Also excellent value is the easygoing *Amsterdam Guesthouse*, at 15/3 Thanon Rong Muang on the north side of the museum (☎074/314890; ②). Songkhla's most famous **restaurant**, *Raan Tae*, at 85 Thanon Nang Ngarm, is justly popular, serving especially good seafood – but it closes at 8pm. The night market sets up south of the post office on Thanon Nakhon Nai. A ghetto of westernized bars and restaurants on Saket, Sisuda and Sadao roads caters to workers from the offshore oil rigs. You can treat yourself to ice cream or milkshakes while surfing the net at *E milk Internet Café* (11am–9.30pm), at 72 Thanon Saiburi.

Ko Yo

KO YO, the small island in the Thale Sap to the west of Songkhla, has long been a destination for day-trippers, and the road link with the land on both sides of the lagoon has accelerated the transformation of **Ban Nok** – the island's main settlement – into a souvenir market. The chief appeal of Ko Yo is the **Southern Folklore Museum** (daily 8am–6pm; B50), which sprawls over twelve acres of hillside on the northern tip of Ko Yo just before the northern bridge. The park is strewn with all kinds of boats and wooden reproductions of traditional southern houses, in which the collections are neatly set out. The exhibits inside, such as the shadow-puppet paraphernalia and the *kris* – long knives with intricately carved handles and sheaths – show the strong influences of Malaysia and Indonesia on southern Thailand. Also on show are elaborate dance costumes and carved wooden coconut-scrapers. One hundred metres south of the museum, a short slip road leads up to the recommended *Suan Kaeo* restaurant. To **get to Ko Yo** from Songkhla, take one of the frequent Ranot-bound buses from Thanon Jana (30 min). From Hat Yai, take a Songkhla-bound bus, but get off on the edge of the suburbs at the junction with Highway 408, and catch a songthaew or bus across the bridge to KoYo.

Betong and the Malay border

Perched on a narrow tongue of land reaching into Malaysia, **BETONG** is of interest only for the taxis that run across the **Malay border** to Keroh, which gives access to Sungai Petani and the west coast. Betong is three hours from Yala by frequent share taxi or air-conditioned minibus, or six hours by the daily bus. You can stay in Yala at *Thepvimarn*, 31 Thanon Sribumrung (☎073/212400; ①–②).

Ban Taba and boats to Malaysia

At the riverside frontier post of **BAN TABA**, a **ferry** (B5) will shuttle you across to the Malaysian town of Pengkalan Kubor, which has frequent taxis and buses to Kota Bahru 20km away (see p.610). There are frequent buses from the provincial capital, **Narathiwat**, to Ban Taba (90min), most of them based at 308/5 Thanon Pichit Bamrung; share taxis hang around further north on the same road. Narathiwat's best budget hotel is the characterful riverside *Narathiwat*, at 341 Thanon Na (☎073/511063; ①); there's nowhere to stay in Ban Taba.

Sungai Kolok and into Malaysia

The seedy brothel town of **SUNGAI KOLOK** is at the end of the rail line from Bangkok, and right on the **Malay border**. The **train station** (☎073/611162) is in the northern part of town and from here you can walk or take a motorbike taxi or samlor to the border. From Rantau Panjang on the other side of the border, frequent taxis and buses head for Kota Bahru, 30km away (see p.610). The budget **hotel** in Sungai Kolok is the *Thanee*, at 4/1 Thanon Cheunmanka (☎073/611046; ②), five minutes' walk south from the train station down Thanon Charoenkhet. **TAT** has an office right beside the frontier checkpoint (daily 8.30am–4.30pm; ☎073/516144).

For those **arriving in Sungai Kolok** from Malaysia, there are trains at noon and 3pm for the 23-hour trip to Bangkok via Hat Yai and Surat Thani. Air-conditioned minibuses to and from Hat Yai park opposite the station.

travel details

Buses

Ayutthaya to: Bang Pa-In (every 30min; 30min); Chiang Mai (5 daily; 12 hr).

Bangkok's Eastern Bus Terminal to: Ban Phe, for Ko Samet (12 daily; 3hr); Pattaya (every 30min; 2hr 30min); Rayong (every 15min; 2hr 30min); Trat, for Ko Chang (23 daily; 6–8hr).

Bangkok's Northern Bus Terminal to: Ayutthaya (every 15min; 2hr); Bang Pa-In (every 20min; 2hr); Chiang Mai (up to 40 daily; 9–10hr); Chiang Rai (19 daily; 12hr); Khon Kaen (31 daily; 6–7hr); Khorat (every 15min; 3–4hr); Lopburi (every 20min; 3hr); Mae Hong Son (8 daily; 18hr); Mae Sot (14 daily; 8hr

30min); Mukdahan (8 daily; 11hr); Nong Khai (2 daily; 10hr); Pak Chong, for Khao Yai National Park (every 15min; 3hr); Phitsanulok (up to 25 daily; 5–6hr) Sukhothai (12 daily; 6–7hr); Surin (up to 25 daily; 8–9hr); Ubon Ratchathani (19 daily; 10–12hr); Udon Thani (36 daily; 9hr).

Bangkok's Southern Bus Terminal to: Chumphon (14 daily; 7hr); Damnoen Saduak (every 20min; 2hr); Hat Yai (12 daily; 14hr); Hua Hin (every 25min; 3hr–3hr 30min); Kanchanaburi (every 15min; 2–3hr); Ko Samui (7 daily; 15hr); Krabi (9 daily; 12–14hr); Nakhon Pathom (every 10min; 40min–1hr 20min) Nakhon Si Thammarat (17 daily; 12hr); Phang Nga (4 daily; 11hr–12hr 30min); Phetchaburi; (every 20min; 2hr–2hr 30min); Phuket (at least 10 daily; 14–16hr); Ranong (7 daily; 9–10hr); Satun (2 daily; 16hr); Sungai Kolok (3 daily; 18hr); Surat Thani (15 daily; 11hr); Trang (7 daily; 14hr).

Ban Phe to: Bangkok (12 daily; 3hr); Pattaya (for Ko Samet; 1hr 30min); Trat (6 daily; 3hr).

Chiang Mai to: Bangkok (19 daily; 10–11hr); Chiang Khong (5 daily; 6hr); Chiang Rai (45 daily; 3–6hr); Fang (every 30min; 3hr 30min); Khon Kaen (10 daily; 12hr); Khorat (8 daily; 11–12hr); Mae Hong Son (9 daily; 8hr); Mae Sariang (8 daily; 4–5hr); Mae Sot (3 daily; 6–7hr); Nan (10 daily; 7hr); Pai (6 daily; 4hr); Phitsanulok (10 daily; 5–6hr); Rayong (7 daily; 15hr); Sukhothai (12 daily; 6hr); Tak (4 daily; 4hr); Tha Ton (7 daily); Ubon Ratchathani (6 daily; 15hr); Udon Thani (12 daily; 12hr).

Chiang Rai to: Chiang Khong (every 45min; 2hr); Chiang Mai (37 daily; 3–6hr); Chiang Saen (every 15min; 1hr 30min); Mae Sai (every 15min; 1hr 30min); Phitsanulok (5 daily; 6–7hr).

Damnoen Saduak to: Nakhon Pathom (every 20min; 1hr).

Hat Yai to: Chumphon (6 daily; 9hr); Ko Samui (1 daily; 7hr); Krabi (13 daily; 4–5hr); Padang Besar (every 10min; 1hr 40min); Pak Bara (10 daily; 2hr 30min); Phuket (11 daily; 7–9hr); Satun (every 15min; 1hr 30min–2hr); Songkhla (every 10min; 30min); Sungai Kolok (5 daily; 4hr); Surat Thani (10 daily; 5hr–6hr 30min); Trang (every 30min; 2hr 30min).

Hua Hin to: Chumphon (daily every 40min; 4hr 30min).

Kanchanaburi to: Ban Phe (every 15min from 5.25am; 1hr 15min); Nakhon Pathom (every 10min; 1hr 20min); Sangkhlaburi (14 daily; 3–5hr); Suphanburi (every 30min; 2hr).

Khon Kaen to: Bangkok (64 daily; 6–7hr); Chiang Rai (5 daily; 12hr); Khorat (hourly; 2hr 30min–3hr); Loei (every 30min; 4hr); Nakhon Phanom (12 daily; 5hr); Nong Khai (10 daily; 2–3hr); Phitsanulok (hourly; 5–6hr); Sri Chiangmai (6 daily; 3hr); Ubon Ratchathani (15 daily; 6hr); Udon Thani (every 20 min; 1hr 30min–2hr).

Khorat to: Chiang Mai (7 daily; 9–11hr); Chiang Rai (2 daily; 13hr); Khon Kaen (hourly; 2hr 30min–3hr); Lopburi (11 daily; 3hr 30min); Nong Khai (7 daily; 6hr); Pak Chong (for Khao Yai) (every 20min; 1hr 30min); Pattaya (4 daily; 5hr); Phitsanulok (7 daily; 5–7hr); Rayong (18 daily; 6hr); Sri Chiangmai (6 daily; 6hr 30min); Surin (every 30min; 4–5hr); Ubon Ratchathani (20 daily; 5hr); Udon Thani (every 45min; 3hr 30min–5hr).

Krabi to: Phuket (hourly; 4hr); Surat Thani (hourly; 3hr 30min–4hr 30min); Trang (14 daily; 3hr).

Lopburi to: Ayutthaya (every 15min; 2hr).

Loei to: Udon Thani (every 30min; 3hr).

Mae Sai to: Mae Sot (2 daily; 12hr).

Mae Sot to: Chiang Rai (2 daily; 11hr); Sukhothai (6 daily; 3hr).

Mukdahan to: Nakhon Phanom (hourly; 2hr); That Phanom (hourly; 1hr 20min).

Nakhon Phanom to: That Phanom (every 10min; 1hr).

Nong Khai to: Bung Kan (17 daily; 2hr); Nakhon Phanom (8 daily; 6hr).

Phang Nga to: Krabi (hourly; 1hr 30min–2hr).

Phetchaburi to: Chumphon (every 2hr; 5–6hr).

Phitsanulok to: Ayutthaya (9 daily; 5hr); Chiang Rai (4 daily; 7hr); Mae Sot (7 daily; 5hr); Sukhothai (every 30min; 1hr); Udon Thani (5 daily; 8hr).

Phuket to: Hat Yai (7 daily; 7–8hr); Krabi (at least hourly; 3–5hr) via Phang Nga (1hr 30min–2hr 30min); Ranong (6 daily; 5–6hr); Surat Thani (10 daily; 5–6hr); Takua Pa (9 daily; 3hr); Trang (12 daily; 6hr).

Ranong to: Chumphon (hourly; 2hr); Krabi (3 daily; 4hr); Phuket (8 daily; 6hr).

Rayong to: Bangkok (every 15min; 2 hr 30min); Ubon Ratchathani (9 daily; 9hr).

Satun to: Krabi (2 daily; 5hr).

Sukhothai to: Ayutthaya (6 daily; 6hr); Chiang Rai (5 daily; 6hr).

Suphanburi to: Ayutthaya (every 30min; 1hr 30min).

Surat Thani to: Chaiya (hourly; 1hr); Chumphon (every 30min; 3–4hr); Hat Yai (10 daily; 5hr); Hua Hin (9 daily; 12hr); Krabi (Phang Nga (6 daily; 4hr); Phuket (6 daily; 5-6hr); Ranong (14 daily; 4hr); Takua Pa (11 daily; 3hr); Trang (2-4 daily; 3hr).

Surin to: Khorat (every 30min; 4hr); Ubon Ratchathani (12 daily; 2hr 30min).

Takua Pa to: Krabi (4 daily; 4hr 30min); Phuket (every 40min; 3hr).

Trang to: Satun (every 30min; 2hr 30min–3hr).

Trat to: Pattaya (for Ko Chang; 6 daily; 4hr 30min); Ban Phe (6 daily; 3hr).

Ubon Ratchathani to: Nakhon Phanom (hourly; 4hr); That Phanom (9 daily; 4hr).

Udon Thani to: Bangkok (36 daily; 9hr); Khon Kaen (every 20min; 2hr); Khorat (every 45min; 4hr 30min); Nong Khai (every 30min; 1hr); Ubon Ratchani (11 daily; 5–7hr).

Trains

Ayutthaya to: Bangkok Hualamphong (20 daily; 1hr 30min); Chiang Mai (5 daily; 12hr); Nong Khai (3 daily; 9hr 30min); Ubon Ratchathani (6 daily; 8hr30min–10hr).

Bangkok Hualamphong Station to: Aranyaprathet (2 daily; 5hr); Ayutthaya (19 daily; 1hr 30min); Butterworth (daily; 22hr); Chiang Mai (6 daily; 10hr 40min–14hr 15min); Chumphon (9 daily; 6hr 45min–8hr 20min); Don Muang Airport (30 daily; 50min); Hat Yai (5 daily; 16hr); Hua Hin (12 daily; 3–4hr); Khon Kaen (3 daily; 7–8hr); Khorat (7 daily; 4–5hr); Lopburi (9 daily; 2hr 30min–3hr); Nakhon Pathom (10 daily; 1hr 20min); Nong Khai (3 daily; 11–12hr); Pak Chong, for Khao Yai National Park (7 daily; 3hr 30min); Padang Besar (1 daily; 17hr); Phitsanulok (10 daily; 5hr 15min–9hr 30min); Sungai Kolok (2 daily; 20hr); Surat Thani (10 daily; 9hr–11hr 30min); Surin (7 daily; 8–10hr); Ubon Ratchathani (6 daily; 10hr 20min–13hr 15min); Udon Thani (3 daily; 10hr).

Bangkok Noi Station to: Hua Hin (2 daily; 4hr 30min); Kanchanaburi (2 daily; 2hr 40min); Nakhon Pathom (1hr 25min).

Chiang Mai to: Ayutthaya (5 daily; 12hr); Bangkok (7 daily; 13hr); Lampang (6 daily; 2hr); Lopburi (5 daily; 11hr); Phitsanulok (4 daily; 7hr 10min–8hr).

Hat Yai to: Butterworth, Malaysia (1 daily; 5hr); Padang Besar (1 daily; 1hr); Sungai Kolok (2 daily; 3hr 30min–5hr); Surat Thani (6 daily; 4hr–6hr 30min).

Khorat (Nakhon Ratchasima) to: Ayutthaya (7 daily; 3hr 30min); Khon Kaen (3 daily; 3hr); Surin (7 daily; 2hr 30min–3hr 40min); Ubon Ratchathani (6 daily; 5hr–6hr 40min); Udon Thani (2 daily; 4hr 30min).

Nong Khai to: Bangkok (3 daily; 11hr), via Udon Thani (1hr), Khon Kaen (3hr) and Ayutthaya (10hr).

Surat Thani to: Butterworth, Malaysia (1 daily; 11hr); Chumphon (9 daily; 4hr); Hat Yai (5 daily; 4–5hr); Nakhon Pathom (10 daily; 9–11hr 30min); Nakhon Si Thammarat (2 daily; 3hr 30min); Sungai Kolok (2 daily; 9hr); Trang (2 daily; 4hr).

Ferries

Phuket to: Ko Phi Phi (1–4 daily; 1hr 30min–2hr 30min).

Flights

Bangkok to: Chiang Mai (14 daily; 1hr 5min); Chiang Rai (4–5 daily; 1hr 25min); Hat Yai (5 daily; 1hr 25min); Khon Kaen (4–5 daily; 55min); Ko Samui (14 daily; 1hr 20min); Phuket (14 daily; 1hr 20min); Sukhothai (1 daily; 1hr); Surat Thani (2 daily; 1hr 10min); Ubon Ratchathani (2 daily; 1hr 5min); Udon Thani (3 daily; 1hr).

Chiang Mai to: Bangkok (10–15 daily; 1hr); Kuala Lumpur (2 weekly); Kunming, China (2 weekly; 3hr); Mandalay (2 weekly; 50min); Nan (3 weekly; 1hr); Phuket (daily; 2hr); Rangoon (2 weekly; 40min); Singapore (4 weekly; 3hr); Sukhothai (1 daily; 1hr); Vientiane (2 weekly; 1hr).

Hat Yai to: Johor Baru, Malaysia (3 weekly; 4hr); Kuala Lumpur (7 weekly; 1hr); Phuket (1 daily; 1hr); Singapore (10–14 weekly; 1hr 30min–4hr); Tapah (daily; 10hr).

Ko Samui to: Phuket (2 daily, 50 min); Singapore (1 daily; 1hr 20min); U-Tapao (Pattaya; daily; 1hr).

Phuket to: Chiang Mai (daily; 1hr 55min); Hat Yai (1 daily; 45min); Ko Samui (2 daily; 50min); Surat Thani (2 daily; 50min); U-Tapao (for Pattaya; 3 weekly; 50min).

CHAPTER ELEVEN

VIETNAM

Introduction

History weighs heavily on **Vietnam**. For more than a decade, reportage of the war that racked the country portrayed it as a savage netherworld, yet, only twenty-odd years after the war's end, this incredibly resilient nation is beginning to emerge from the shadows.

As the number of tourists finding their way here soars, the word is out that this is a land not of bomb craters and army ordnance, but of shimmering paddy fields and sugar-white beaches, full-tilt cities and venerable pagodas. The speed with which Vietnam's population of 77 million has been able to transcend the recent past comes as a surprise to visitors who are generally met with warmth and curiosity rather than shell-shocked resentment and war fatigue.

Inevitably, that's not the whole story. The adoption of a **market economy** has polarized the gap between rich and poor: average monthly incomes for city dwellers remain at about $50, but drops to $15 in the poorest provinces.

For the majority of visitors, the furiously commercial southern city of **Ho Chi Minh City** provides a head-spinning introduction to Vietnam, so a trip out into the rice fields and orchards of the nearby **Mekong Delta** makes a welcome next stop – best explored by boat from **My Tho, Vinh Long** or **Can Tho**. Heading north, the quaint hill-station of **Da Lat** provides a good place to cool down, but some travellers eschew this for the **beaches** of **Vung Tau** and **Phan Thiet**. A few hours' ride further up the coast, the city of **Nha Trang** has become a crucial stepping stone on the Ho Chi Minh–Hanoi run. Next up comes the enticing little town of **Hoi An**, full of wooden shop-houses and close to Vietnam's greatest Cham temple ruins at **My Son**. The temples, palaces and imperial mausoleums of aristocratic **Hué** should also not be missed. One hundred kilometres north, warsites litter the **Demilitarized Zone (DMZ)**, which cleaved the country in two from 1954 to 1975.

Hanoi has served as Vietnam's capital for close on a thousand years and is a small, absorbing city of pagodas and dynastic temples, where life proceeds at a gentler pace than in Ho Chi Minh. From here most visitors strike out east to the labyrinth of limestone outcrops in **Ha Long Bay**, usually visited from the resort town of **Bai Chay**, but more interestingly approached from tiny **Cat Ba Island**.The little market-town of **Sa Pa**, set in spectacular uplands close to the Chinese border in the far northwest, makes a good base for exploring nearby ethnic minority villages.

Vietnam has a tropical monsoon **climate**, dominated by the south or southwesterly monsoon from May to September and the northeast monsoon from October to April. Overall, late September to December and March and April are the **best times** if you're covering the whole country, but there are distinct regional variations. In **southern Vietnam and the central highlands** the dry season lasts from December through April, and daytime temperatures rarely drop below 20°C in the lowlands, averaging 30°C during March, April and May. Along the **central coast** the wet season runs from September through February, though even the dry season brings a fair quantity of rain; temperatures average 30°C from June to August. Typhoons can hit the coast around Hué in April and May and the northern coast from July to November, when flooding is a regular occurence. **Hanoi and Northern Vietnam** are generally hot (30°C) and very wet during the summer, warm and sunny from October to December, then cold and misty until March.

Overland routes into Vietnam

It's possible to cross overland from Cambodia, Laos and China into Vietnam.

■ From Cambodia

You can go by bus from Phnom Penh to **Ho Chi Minh**. Alternatively, you can take a local bus from Phnom Penh to the border at Moc Bai and then continue by shared taxi to Ho Chi Minh; see p.95 for details.

■ From China

At the time of writing, the Chinese border was open to foreigners at three points: at Lao Cai (see p.1058), Mong Cai (see p.1057) and Huu Nghi (see p.1063). There are two **direct train services** between Vietnam and China; they start in Beijing and Kunming and terminate in Hanoi; see p.1040 for more details.

■ From Laos

There are two border points between **Laos** and Vietnam where tourists can cross overland. The **Lao Bao Pass** (see p.1037), roughly 240km from Savannakhet, is the most popular and gives you access to Dong Ha, 80km away. There's also an international bus link between Savannakhet and Da Nang (15hr), although it's cheaper to travel by local buses. Crossing from Lak Xao to the Vietnamese town of Vinh, via the Kaew Nua Pass (usually referred to as Nam Phao in Lao) and **Cau Treo**, can be more difficult; see p.1037.

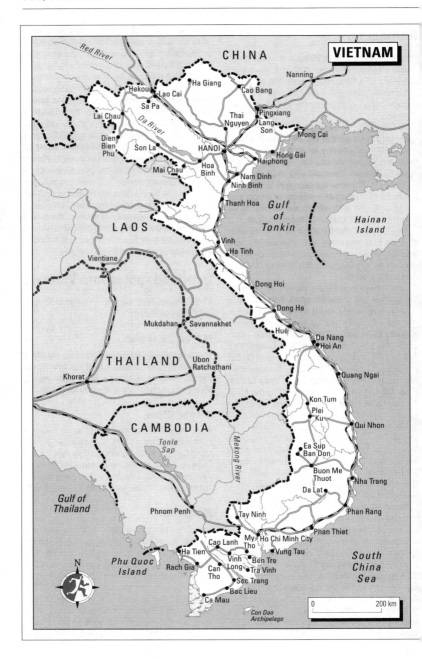

Entry requirements and visa extension

All foreign nationals need a visa to enter Vietnam. **Tourist visas** are generally valid for thirty days, cost $50–100, and take seven to ten days to process. See p.21 for a list of Vietnamese embassies abroad. In Southeast Asia, Bangkok is the most popular place to apply for a Vietnamese visa (four to five working days; $80).

At the time of writing, the majority of visas were being issued with specific start and end **dates** indicating the period of validity within which you can enter and leave Vietnam. However, a number of embassies and consulates, including that in London, are currently issuing visas with just the issue date and an expiry date, allowing greater flexibility; in this case the thirty days start ticking once you pass through Vietnamese immigration and you must have left the country before the visa expires. On arrival, you'll need the copy of your visa application form given to you when you collected your visa, plus a completed Arrival and Departure Card and a Baggage Declaration form. You'll need the **Departure Card** to register at hotels, and you'll need both forms when you eventually leave the country. Get all your shots recorded on an **International Certificate of Vaccination**, as some travellers entering Vietnam from China have been fined if they try to enter without one.

At the time of writing, thirty-day **visa extensions** were being issued through tour agents and travellers' cafés in Ho Chi Minh City, Hanoi and Da Nang ($30–40; three or four days), but the situation changes frequently, so check with the embassy before you leave. The fine for overstaying your visa is at least $50.

AIRPORT DEPARTURE TAX

Airport departure tax is $10 for international flights (payable in dong or dollars) and $1.50 on domestics.

Money and costs

Despite what you might have heard, travelling in Vietnam needn't be much more expensive than in its Southeast Asian neighbours. By eating and sleeping at the simplest places and travelling on local buses, you should be able to manage on a **daily budget** of $12–15. Upgrading to more salubrious lodgings, eating good food followed by a couple of beers in a bar, and signing up for the odd minibus tour would bring it to $25–30.

Vietnam maintains a **two-tier pricing system**, with foreigners paying many times more than locals for transport and accommodation. The system is, however, rumoured to be on its way out, and there are signs of some standardization of prices, though it will probably be a while before two-tier pricing disappears completely. For the moment, it remains something of a grey area and the amount you pay may well depend on the person you happen to be dealing with.

Vietnam's unit of **currency** is the dong, usually abbreviated as "d" (occasionally "VND"). Notes come in denominations of 200d, 500d, 1000d, 2000d, 5000d, 10,000d, 20,000d and 50,000d; there are no coins. The American **dollar** operates in parallel to the dong as unofficial tender and most travellers carry some dollars as back-up for when banks won't change travellers' cheques. Because dong amounts tend to be more volatile, we've given prices in US dollars ($) throughout this chapter. At the end of your trip you can change leftover dong back into dollars if you have an exchange certificate. At the time of writing, the **exchange rate** was 22,000d to £1 and 14,000d to $1.

US dollar travellers' cheques are the easiest method of carrying money around in Vietnam. They can be cashed at major banks (Vietcombank usually charges the lowest rates), but often not at banks in smaller towns. Dong are not available outside the country at present, though if you take in some small-denomination American dollars you'll have no problems getting by until you reach a bank. **Banking hours** are Mon–Fri 8–11.30am and 1–4pm, though in major cities you can change cash outside these hours at registered exchange counters and hotels. A black market of sorts exists in Vietnam, but is best avoided, especially as the markup is tiny.

Major **credit cards** – Visa, Mastercard and, to a lesser extent, American Express – are slowly becoming more acceptable in Vietnam. You can withdraw cash from 24-hr ATMs (in the Visa, Plus, Mastercard and Cirrus networks) in Hanoi and Ho Chi Minh City. Even outside the major cities, banks will now advance cash against cards (generally Visa and Mastercard) for a small commission.

If you need to have **money wired**, contact the Vietcombank in Hanoi or Ho Chi Minh, though some provincial branches can also now handle telegraphic transfers. Vietcombank has arrangements with selected banks across the world, including Lloyd's Bank in London; the Commonwealth Bank in Sydney; the Royal Bank of Canada; and the Chase Manhattan Bank and Citibank in New York (Vietcombank has a full list). Payment can be made to you in dong or dollars, but hefty charges are levied at both ends. Vietcombank and major post offices also accept the faster, but even more expensive, Moneygram; again this has to come from a designated bank, but charges are levied at the sender's end and to collect the money all you need is the sender's eight-digit reference number.

Information and maps

The Vietnamese government maintains a handful of **tourist promotion offices** around the globe (see p.33 for a list), but state-owned tourist offices in Vietnam itself are profit-making concerns and not information bureaux. The biggest of these is Vietnamtourism, with offices in Hanoi, Ho Chi Minh City and other major tourist centres.

The best **maps** of Vietnam are the International 1:1,000,000 "Travel Map" of Vietnam and the Nelles 1:1,500,000 map of Vietnam, Laos and Cambodia. The 1:2,000,000 "Vietnam, Cambodia & Laos World Travel Map" from Bartholomew isn't bad either. All but the Nelles map feature plans of Ho Chi Minh City and Hanoi.

Getting around

Vietnam's main thoroughfare is Highway 1, which runs from Hanoi to Ho Chi Minh, passing through Hué, Da Nang and Nha Trang en route, and is ghosted by the country's main rail line. Though things have been improving, **public transport** remains fairly shambolic: bus timetables are for the most part redundant, and many tourists opt for internal flights or private tours in order to escape the clapped-out buses and snail-slow trains. On buses, never fall asleep with your bag by your side, and never leave belongings unattended. On trains, ensure your money-belt is safely tucked under your clothes before going to sleep and that your luggage is safely stowed (preferably padlocked to an immovable object). For an idea of journey times between major destinations see "Travel Details" on p.1063.

■ Planes

Vietnam Airlines operates a reasonably cheap, efficient and comprehensive network of **domestic**

flights and has offices in all towns with an airport. The two-hour journey between Hanoi and Ho Chi Minh City ($135), for instance, compares favourably with the thirty or more hours you might spend on the train. Book as far ahead as you can.

■ Buses and minibuses

Vietnam's national **bus network** offers daily services between all major towns, but buses can be unbearably cramped, seats are hard, breakdowns frequent, and progress slow. All towns have a bus station, and larger places have both a local and a long-distance station. Most buses depart early, from 5am through to mid-morning, waiting only as long as it takes to get enough passengers. For longer journeys, tickets are best bought a day in advance, since many routes are heavily over-subscribed. Prices at certain tourist hotspots can be over the odds; always try to ascertain the correct price before boarding.

Privately owned **minibuses** compete with public buses on most routes; they sometimes share the local bus station, or simply congregate in the centre of a town. Though generally even more cramped than ordinary buses, they do at least run throughout the day.

Special **"open-tour" buses** shuttling beween major tourist destinations are becoming an increasingly popular way for foreigners to travel in Vietnam. Competition is fierce, so prices are coming down, though they are still way more expensive than local buses. The best thing to do is buy a one-way through ticket, for example from Ho Chi Minh to Hué ($24) or Hanoi ($38), which enables you to stop off at specified destinations en route: heading north, the main stops are Da Lat, Nha Trang, Hoi An, Da Nang, Hué and Vinh. You can either make firm bookings at the outset or opt for an open-dated ticket. Tickets and onward reservations are available from agents in each town.

■ Trains

Though Vietnamese **trains** are slow, travelling on them can be a pleasant experience if you splash out on a soft-class berth or seat, but this can work out quite expensive.

The country's main line shadows Highway 1 on its way **from Ho Chi Minh City to Hanoi** (1726km), passing through Nha Trang, Da Nang and Hué en route. **From Hanoi**, one branch goes northwest to Lao Cai and the border crossing **into China**'s Yunnan Province; another runs north to Dong Dang, and is the route taken by the two weekly trains from **Hanoi to Beijing**; and the third goes to **Haiphong**.

The most popular lines with tourists are the shuttle from Da Nang to Hué, and the overnighters from Hué to Hanoi and from Hanoi up to Lao Cai, for Sa Pa. Four **"Reunification Express"** trains depart each day from Hanoi to Ho Chi Minh and vice versa. They are labelled S1 to S8; odd-numbered trains travel south, even ones north, hence the S2 (32hr), S4 (37hr) and S6 and S8 (41hr) depart daily from Ho Chi Minh City, and the S1 to S7 (same times) make the trip in the opposite direction.

When it comes to choosing which **class** to travel in, it's essential to aim high. Hard seats are bearable for short journeys, but even soft seats are grim for long hauls. On overnight journeys, you should go for a **berth**: cramped hard-berth compartments have six bunks (cheapest at the top) and soft-berths have only four bunks; two-bed super-berth compartments are only available on the S1 and S2 services and are often booked well in advance. Simple meals are included in the price of the ticket on overnight journeys.

Booking ahead is essential; you may need your passport when you buy a ticket. **Fares** vary according to the class and the speed of the train: the following is a guide to fares on the slowest service from Ho Chi Minh to Hanoi (S6). From Ho Chi Minh to Nha Trang costs around $10 for a hard seat, $23 for a soft berth; from HCMC to Da Nang, the same classes cost $23 and $45; from HCMC to Hanoi they cost $42 and $83.

■ Vehicle rental

Although self-drive isn't yet possible in Vietnam, it's easy to hire a **car, jeep or minibus with driver** from tour agencies and tourist offices ($25–60 per day). Check who pays for the driver's accommodation and meals, fuel, tolls, parking fees and repairs and what happens in the case of a major breakdown. Sign a contract showing this and the agreed itinerary, and arrange to pay half before and the balance at the end.

Bicycles are available from hotels and tour agencies in most towns for about $1 a day. **Motorbike** ($6–10 per day) and/or **moped** ($5–7) rental is possible in most major towns, but the appalling road discipline of most Vietnamese drivers means that the risk of an accident is very real. Check everything carefully, especially brakes, lights and horn. Wearing a **helmet** is now a legal requirement at speeds over 40km/hr; they can be bought in Hanoi and Ho Chi Minh for $20–40. Also check the small print on your **insurance** policy, and con-

sider taking out local accident insurance anyway. The biggest local insurer is Bao Viet, with offices in Ho Chi Minh City and Hanoi; their policies cost $10–12 for the basic three-month cover and are easy to obtain. **Repair shops** are fairly ubiquitous – look for a Honda sign or ask for *sua chua xe may* (motorbike repairs) – but you should still carry at least a puncture-repair kit, pump and spare spark plug. Fuel (*xang*) is less than $0.40 per litre and widely available. Always leave your bike in a parking compound (*gui xe*) or pay someone to keep an eye on it.

The theory is that you **drive on the right**, though in practice motorists and cyclists swerve and dodge wherever they want, using no signals and their **horn** as a surrogate brake. **Right of way** invariably goes to the biggest vehicle on the road; note that overtaking vehicles assume you'll pull over onto the hard shoulder to avoid them. Its best to avoid driving after dark, since many vehicles don't use headlights. If you are involved in an **accident** and it was deemed to be your fault, the penalties can involve fairly major fines.

■ Local transport

Taxis are becoming increasingly common in big cities, and there are also some city **bus** services. Elsewhere you'll have to rely upon a host of two- and three-wheeled vehicles. Cheap, ubiquitous and fun, **cyclos** – three-wheeled bicycle rickshaws – can carry one person, or two at a push, and cost 8000–10,000d for a five- or ten-minute hop. Secure a price before setting off, ensuring you know which currency you are dealing in (five fingers could mean 5000d or $5), and whether you're negotiating for one passenger or two.

The motorized version of the cyclo, found in the south, is known as the **cyclo mai**. In the Mekong Delta, the **xe dap loi** is also a variation on the cyclo theme, and the motorized version is known as a **Honda loi**. **Honda oms** or motorbike taxis, known in the north as a **xe oms**, are becoming more common in the main cities; prices are a shade cheaper than a cyclo.

Xe lams (also known as **Lambros**) are three-wheeled, motorized buggies whose drivers squeeze in more passengers than you'd believe possible. These act as a local bus service outside Hanoi and Ho Chi Minh, and rows of them are usually found either at the local bus station, or outside the local market. A typical xe lam ride of a few kilometres costs 3000–4000d.

Accommodation

Compared to other Southeast Asian countries, **accommodation** in Vietnam is poor-quality and pricey, though standards are improving rapidly in the major cities. Expect to pay around £5.50/$8 for the most basic double room with fan and attached bathroom; it's always worth bargaining. Some places add a government **tax** and service charge of fifteen percent.

A "**single**" room could have a single or twin beds in it, while a "double" room could have two, three or four single beds, a single and a twin, and so on. In the cheapest places, rooms are cleaned irregularly and may have cockroaches and even rats roaming free; you can minimize health risks by not bringing foodstuffs or sugary drinks into your room.

Hotel **security** can be a big problem, so never leave valuables in your room, and use your own padlock on the door if possible. **Prostitution** is rife in Vietnam, and in less reputable budget hotels it's not unknown for Western men to be hassled at night.

Not all places are permitted to take foreigners: if the staff merely smile and shake their heads, chances are this is the case. On the whole there's no need to book ahead, except during the festival of Tet (early spring).

> ### ADDRESSES
>
> Where two numbers are separated by a slash, such as 110/5, you simply make for no. 110, where an alley will lead off to a further batch of buildings – you want the fifth one. Where a number is followed by a letter, as in 117a, you're looking for a single block encompassing several addresses, of which one will be 117a.

■ Types of accommodation

The very cheapest form of accommodation in Vietnam is a bed in a dormitory; there are no youth hostels as yet, or camp sites. In the budget **guesthouses** (*nha khach*) and **rooms for rent** in Hanoi and Ho Chi Minh, you can expect to pay $2–3 for either a bed or a mattress on the dorm floor. Otherwise, you'll need to upgrade to a simple fan room sharing washing facilities, in either a room for rent or a state-run **hotel** (*khach san*) or guesthouse, this should cost $4–7. Rooms at this level are generally windowless and decrepit; in the $10–15 price range, you will get a private bathroom too. In major cities, the next rung is either a room for rent or a **mini-hotel** (a modest, privately owned hotel), offering cheerful rooms with air-con, hot water and possibly phone and satellite TV for around $15–30. Elsewhere, you'll probably have to upgrade to the local state-run hotel. Paying $40–75 will get you a room in a middle-range hotel of some repute, with in-house restaurant, bar and room service; while at the top of the range you could easily spend up to $200 a night in international-class hotels.

Electricity is usually supplied at 220 volts, though you may come across 110 volts; plugs are two-pinned, with the pins rounded.

Food and drink

Though closely related to Chinese cuisine, **Vietnamese food** is quite distinct, using herbs and seasoning rather than sauces, and favouring boiled or steamed dishes over stir-fries. The usual basic **health** precautions apply when eating out in Vietnam; see "Basics" p.27 for advice.

■ Where to eat

The cheapest and most fun places to eat are the **street kitchens**, which range from makeshift food stalls set up on the street, to open-fronted eating houses. They are permanent, with an address if not a name, and most specialize in one type of food, generally indicated on a signboard, or offer the

---

ACCOMMODATION PRICE CODES

All **accommodation** reviewed in this guide has been graded according to the following price codes, in US dollars, which represent the cost of the cheapest double room available in high season. Where a price range is indicated, this means that the establishment offers rooms with varying facilities – as explained in the write-up. In cases where an establishment charges per bed the actual price is given.

① under $5	④ $15–20	⑦ $40–60
② $5–10	⑤ $20–25	⑧ $60–80
③ $10–15	⑥ $25–40	⑨ $80 and over

ubiquitous *com pho* rice dishes and noodle soups. **Com binh dan**, "people's meals", comprise an array of prepared dishes like stuffed tomatoes, fried fish, tofu, pickles and eggs, plus rice; expect to pay from around $1 for a good plateful. Outside the major cities, street kitchens rarely stay open beyond 8pm.

Western-style **Vietnamese restaurants** (*nha hang*) have chairs and menus and usually serve a wide range of meat and fish dishes. Menus often don't show prices and overcharging is a regular problem. Peanuts, hot towels and tissues on the table will be added to the bill even if untouched; ask for them to be taken away if you don't want them. A modest meal for two will cost roughly $8–10 (112,000–140,000d). The more expensive restaurants tend to stay open until 9.30 or 10.30pm, have menus priced in dollars and, in some cases, accept credit cards; a meal for two will cost at least $10.

Catering primarily to budget travellers, **travellers' cafés** tend to serve mediocre Western and Vietnamese dishes, from banana pancakes to steak and chips or fried noodles – and usually open from 7am to 11pm. They're mainly found in Hanoi, Ho Chi Minh, Hoi An, Hué, Nha Trang and Da Lat.

■ Vietnamese food

The staple of Vietnamese meals is **rice**, with noodles a popular alternative. Typically, rice will be accompanied by a fish or meat dish, a vegetable dish and soup. Even in the south, Vietnamese food tends not to be overly spicy as chilli sauces are served separately. Vietnam's most popular seasoning is *nuoc mam*, a fermented fish sauce. The use of monosodium glutamate (**MSG**) can be excessive, and what looks like salt on the table may be MSG, so taste it first. You can try asking for no MSG in your food: *khong co my chinh*.

The most famous Vietnamese dish has to be **spring rolls**, known as *cha gio, cha nem, nem ran* or just plain *nem*. Various combinations of minced pork, shrimp or crab, rice vermicelli, onions and beansprouts are rolled in rice-paper wrappers, and then eaten fresh or deep-fried. The other great staple is **pho** (pronounced "fur"), a noodle soup eaten at any time of day but primarily at breakfast. The basic bowl of *pho* consists of a light beef broth flavoured with ginger and coriander, to which are added broad, flat rice-noodles, spring onions and slivers of chicken, pork or beef. *Lau* is more of a main meal than a soup, where the vegetable broth arrives at the table in a **steamboat** (a ring-shaped dish on live coals or,

nowadays, often electrically heated) and you cook slivers of beef or prawns in it, and then afterwards drink the flavourful liquid that's left in the pot.

Most restaurants offer a few meat-free dishes, ranging from stewed spinach or similar greens, to a mix of onion, tomato, beansprouts, various mushrooms and peppers; places used to foreigners may be able to do **vegetarian** spring rolls (*nem an chay*, or *nem khong co thit*). At street kitchens you're likely to find tofu and one or two dishes of pickled vegetables. However, soups are usually made with beef stock, morsels of pork fat sneak into many dishes and animal fat tends to be used for frying. The phrase to remember is *an chay* (vegetarian), or seek out a vegetarian rice shop (*tiem com chay*). On the 1st and 14th/15th days of every lunar month many Vietnamese spurn meat so you'll find more veggie options on these days.

Vietnam is blessed with dozens of tropical and temperate **fruits**. Pineapple, coconut, papaya, mangoes, longan and mangosteen flourish in the south. Da Lat is famous for its strawberries, but a fruit you might want to give a miss is the durian, a spiky, yellow-green football-sized fruit with an unmistakably pungent odour reminiscent of mature cheese and caramel, but tasting like an onion-laced custard.

■ Drinks

Giai khat means "quench your thirst" and you'll see the signs everywhere. The simple rule is don't drink the **water** in Vietnam, and avoid **ice** in your drinks – *dung bo da, cam on* (no ice, thanks). Contaminated water causes diarrhoea, gastroenteritis, typhoid, cholera, dysentery, poliomyelitis, hepatitis A and giardia. Particular care should be taken anywhere where there is flooding as raw sewage may be washed into the water system. However, most guesthouses and hotels provide thermos flasks of boiled water, hot tea is always on offer, and cheap, **bottled water** ($1 or less per litre) and carbonated drinks are widely available. When buying bottled water check the seal is unbroken.

Other good thirst-quenchers include fresh coconut milk, orange and lime **juices**, and sugar-cane juice (*mia da*). Somewhere between a drink and a snack is **chè**, sold in glasses at the markets. It's made from taro flour and green bean, and served over ice with chunks of fruit, coloured jellies and even sweetcorn or potato. Small cups of refreshing, strong, green **tea** are presented to all guests or visitors in Vietnam: the well-boiled water is safe to drink. The Vietnamese drink **coffee** very strong and in small quantities, with

A GLOSSARY OF FOOD AND DRINK

Some names differ between north (N) and south (S).

GENERAL TERMS AND REQUESTS

how much is it?	*bao nhieu tien?*	vegetarian	*nguoi an chay*
cheers!	*can chen* (N); *can ly* (S)	I don't eat meat or fish	*toi khong an thit*
delicious	*rat ngon*		

RICE AND NOODLES

bun	round rice noodles	*chao*	rice porridge
bun bo	beef with bun noodles	*mi xao*	fried noodles
bun ga	chicken with bun noodles	*pho*	flat rice noodles, usually in soup
com	cooked rice	*pho bo tai*	noodle soup with rare beef
com rang (N); *com chien* (S)	fried rice	*pho bo chin*	with medium done beef
com trang	steamed or boiled rice	*pho co trung*	with eggs

FISH, MEAT AND VEGETABLES

ca	fish	*lon* (N); *heo* (S)	pork
ca ran (N); *ca chien* (S)	fried fish	*vit*	duck
cua	crab	*rau co* or *rau cac loai*	vegetables
luon	eel	*ca chua*	tomato
muc	squid	*ca tim*	aubergine
tom	shrimp or prawn	*dau*	beans
tom hum	lobster	*khoai tay*	potato
thit	meat	*mang*	bamboo shoots
bo	beef	*ngo* (N); *bap* (S)	sweetcorn
ga	chicken	*rau xao cac loai*	stir-fried vegetables

MISCELLANEOUS

banh	cake	*mut*	jam
banh mi	bread	*ot*	chilli
bo	butter	*tao pho* (N); *dau hu* (S)	tofu
duong	sugar	*trai cay*	fruit
pho mat, fo mat or *fromage*	cheese	*trung*	egg
lac (N); *dau phong* (S)	peanuts	*trung om let* or *op lep*	omelette
muoi	salt	*trung ran* or *trung op la*	fried eggs

DRINKS

bia	beer	*nuoc cam*	orange juice
ca phé den	black coffee	*nuoc chanh*	lime juice
ca phé sua	coffee with milk	*nuoc dua*	coconut milk
tra	tea	*or choum*	rice alchohol
khong da	no ice	*so da cam*	orange soda
nuoc	water	*sua tuoi*	fresh milk
nuoc khoang	mineral water		

a large dollop of condensed milk at the bottom of the cup.

Several foreign **beers** are brewed under licence in Vietnam, but good local brews include 333 (Ba Ba Ba) and Bivina. **Bia hoi** ("fresh" or draught beer) is served warm from the keg and then poured over ice. Its quality varies, but it's unadulterated with chemicals. *Bia hoi* has a 24-hour shelf life, which means the better places sell out by early evening. There are dozens of *bia hoi* outlets in Hanoi and Ho Chi Minh, ranging from a few ankle-high stools gathered round a barrel on the pavement to beer gardens; most offer snacks of some sort. The stronger, pricier **bia tuoi** comes in a light or dark brew and is served from pressurized barrels. The most common local wine is **rice alcohol**; the ethnic minorities drink stem alcohol (*ruou can*).

Communications

Mail can take anywhere from four days to four weeks in or out of Vietnam; from major towns, eight to ten days is the norm. Most main post offices are open daily 7am–8pm; some may close at lunch while others stay open until 10pm. Rates for all post office services are posted up in the main halls. **Poste restante** services are now available in major towns, including Hanoi, Ho Chi Minh, Da Nang, Hué, Hoi An and Da Lat. Mail is held for between one and two months. If you want to leave a message for someone in poste restante, you have to buy a local stamp. For general info on poste-restante services, see "Basics" p.39.

When **sending parcels** out of Vietnam take everything to the post office unwrapped and keep it small: after inspection, and a good deal of form-filling, the parcel will be wrapped for you. Some parcel counters are only open in the morning and note that you'll need your passport. Surface mail takes between one and four months. **Receiving parcels** is not such a good idea. Some parcels simply go astray; those that do make it are subject to thorough customs inspections and import duty.

International calls are best made from the post office; they cost $3–5 per minute, with cheaper rates from Mon–Sat 11pm–7am, all day Sunday and on public holidays. **To call abroad** from Vietnam, dial ☎00 + country code + area code minus first 0 + number. There's no facility for reversed-charge calls but you can almost always get a **"call-back"** to the post office you're calling from, for the price of a one-minute call.

In theory you can dial abroad direct from a public telephone, but they're usually unbearably noisy.

Calling direct from **hotel** rooms costs at least an extra ten percent and there's a minimum charge even if the call goes unanswered. At a few luxury hotels, and at major post offices, it's now possible to use **chargecards**, such as AT&T Direct, billed to your home account at less extortionate rates, though at present only the USA, Canada, Australia, Singapore and Korea are signed up.

Long-distance domestic calls are best made from the post office; cheap rates apply between 10pm and 5am. There's a three-minute minimum charge for **local calls** made from a post office or phone box, but in theory they're free from private phones (including hotels and restaurants). The better hotels should have up-to-date directories; otherwise, try asking in the post office, or calling general enquiries number (☎108 or 116). **Public phones** (all card phones) are only found in the main cities. Phone cards (international, $15 or $30; domestic, $3–5) can be purchased at the post office.

International and domestic **fax** is available at many hotels, but cheaper at post offices, which charge per page. Both hotels and post offices charge for receiving faxes on your behalf ($0.50–1 per page); post offices will deliver them to your hotel (if specified on the fax) for no extra charge.

In Vietnam you can connect to the **Internet** – and your Hotmail account or equivalent (see "Basics" p.39) – from a growing number of travellers' cafés in major tourist destinations.

TIME DIFFERENCES
Vietnam is seven hours ahead of London, fifteen hours ahead of Los Angeles, twelve hours ahead of New York, one hour behind Perth and three hours behind Sydney – give or take an hour or two when summer time is in operation.

Opening hours and festivals

Basic **hours of business** are 7.30–11.30am and 1.30–4.30pm. Most offices close on Sunday, and many now also close on Saturdays following the recent introduction of a five-day (forty-hour) working week. State-run banks and government offices are adjusting their hours accordingly, and this new law may affect the opening times of certain museums and tourist sights. Most tourist offices and tour agents open all weekend and, on weekdays, may keep going into the evening. Museums usually close one day a week, generally on Mondays, and their core opening

---

PUBLIC HOLIDAYS

January 1: New Year's Day

Late January/mid-February (dates vary each year): Tet, Vietnamese New Year (three days, though increasingly offices tend to close down for a full week)

February 3: Founding of the Vietnamese Communist Party

April 30: Liberation of Saigon, 1975

May 1: International Labour Day

May 19: Birthday of Ho Chi Minh

June: Birthday of Buddha (eighth day of the fourth moon)

September 2: National Day

December 25: Christmas Day

---

hours are 8–11am and 2–4pm. Temples and pagodas occasionally close for lunch but are otherwise open all week and don't close until late evening.

■ Festivals

Most Vietnamese **festivals** are fixed by the lunar calendar: the majority take place in spring, and the days of the full moon (day one) and the new moon (day fourteen or fifteen) are particularly auspicious. All Vietnamese calendars show both the lunar and solar (Gregorian) months and dates.

Tet Nguyen Dan, or simply Tet ("festival"), is Vietnam's most important annual event; it lasts for seven days and falls sometime between the last week of January and the third week of February, on the night of the new moon. This is a time when families get together to celebrate renewal and hope for the new year, when ancestral spirits are welcomed back to the household, and when everyone in Vietnam becomes a year older – age is reckoned by the new year and not by individual birthdays. Everyone cleans their house from top to bottom, pays off debts, and makes offerings to Ong Tau, the Taoist god of the hearth. The eve of Tet explodes into a cacophony of drums and percussion and the subsequent week is marked by feasting on special foods. For tourists, Tet can be a great time to visit Vietnam, but it pays to note that not only does most of Vietnam close down for the week after the new year, but either side of the holiday local transport services are stretched to the limit.

Festivals of interest to tourists include the **Water Puppet Festival** held at Thay Pagoda, west of Hanoi (Feb; see p.1050); the two-week Buddhist full moon festival at the **Perfume Pagoda**, west of Hanoi (March–April; p.1050); **Tet Doan Ngo**, the summer solstice, which is marked by festivities and dragon boat races (late May to early June); and **Trung Thu,** also known as Children's Day, when dragon dances take place and children are given lanterns in the shape of stars, carp or dragons (Sept–Oct).

Cultural hints

Vietnam shares the same **attitudes to dress and social taboos**, described in "Basics" on p.41, as other Southeast Asian cultures. In a pagoda or temple you are also expected to leave a small **donation**. Passing round **cigarettes** (to men only) is always appreciated and is widely used as a social gambit aimed at progressing tricky negotiations, bargaining etc.

Crime and safety

Violent crime against tourists in Vietnam is extremely rare, though Ho Chi Minh City and Nha Trang have a fairly bad reputation for thieves, pickpockets and con-artists. In Ho Chi Minh City, cyclo drivers can sell you **drugs** and then turn you in to the police. A substantial bribe might persuade them to drop the matter; otherwise, you're looking at fines and jail sentences for lesser offences, or the death penalty for smuggling large quantities.

Vietnam is generally a safe country for **women** to travel around alone; most Vietnamese will simply be curious as to why you are on your own. That said, it pays to take the normal precautions, especially late at night, when you should avoid taking a cyclo by yourself in Ho Chi Minh City, Nha Trang or Hanoi; it's wise to use a taxi instead. Asian women travelling with a white man have reported cases of harassment – attributed to the fact that some Vietnamese men automatically label all such women as prostitutes.

If you have anything stolen, get the **police** to write up a report for your insurance company; try to recruit an English speaker to come with you – and be prepared to pay a "fee". Corruption among police and other officials can be a problem: you might be stopped on the road or at border crossings and "fined", and trumped-up fines are often imposed on bus, cyclo or other drivers seen carrying a Westerner – fines *you'll* often be expected to pay. But with patience, plus a few cigarettes to hand round, you should be able to bargain fines down considerably.

Not surprisingly, the Vietnamese authorities are sensitive about **military installations**, border regions, military camps, bridges, airports and train stations. Anyone taking photographs near such sites risks having the film removed from their camera, or the ubiquitous "fine". **Unexploded mines** still pose a serious threat: the problem is most acute in the Demilitarized Zone, where each year a few local farmers are killed or injured. Always stick to well-trodden paths and never touch any shells or half-buried chunks of metal.

Medical care and emergencies

Pharmacies can generally help with minor injuries or ailments and in major towns you may well find a pharmacist who speaks French or even English. Both Ho Chi Minh City and Hanoi now have reasonably well-stocked pharmacies. That said, drugs past their shelf life and even counterfeit medicines are rife, so inspect packaging carefully, check use-by dates – and bring anything you know you're likely to need from home. Condoms (*bao cao su*) are sold in Hanoi and Ho Chi Minh – reliable imported brands to look out for are OK and Trust.

Local **hospitals** will treat minor problems, but in a real emergency your best bet is to head for Hanoi or Ho Chi Minh City, where excellent international medical centres can provide diagnosis and treatment. Hospitals expect immediate cash payment for health services rendered; you will then have to seek reimbursement from your insurance company (hang on to receipts).

EMERGENCY PHONE NUMBERS

Try to get a Vietnamese-speaker to phone for you.

Police ☎113   Fire ☎114   Ambulance ☎115

History

Vietnam as a unified state within its present geographical boundaries has only existed since the early nineteenth century. The national history, however, stretches back thousands of years to a kingdom in the Red River Delta.

■ The beginnings

The most significant period in Vietnam's early history began in about 2000 BC with the emergence of a highly organized society of rice-farmers, the Lac Viet.

Held to be the original Vietnamese nation, this embryonic kingdom, Van Lang, evolved into a sophisticated Bronze Age culture whose greatest creations were the ritualistic **bronze drums**, found near Dong Son.

■ Chinese rule

In 111 BC, the Han emperors annexed the whole Red River Delta and so began a thousand years of Chinese domination. They introduced **Confucianism** and with it a rigid, feudalistic hierarchy dominated by a mandarin class. Mahayana Buddhism first entered Vietnam from China during the second century AD.

The local aristocracy increasingly resented their Chinese rulers and engaged in various insurrections, culminating in the battle of the Bach Dang River in 938 AD, a famous victory for Ngo Quyen, leader of the Vietnamese forces, who subsequently declared himself ruler of **Nam Viet**, heralding what was to be nearly ten centuries of Vietnamese independence.

■ Champa

Meanwhile, in the south of Vietnam it was the Indianized kingdom of **Champa** which dominated the region until the late tenth century. Ruled over by divine kings who worshipped first Shiva and later embraced Buddhism, the Champa people built temples all along the coast of south-central Vietnam, including the magnificent My Son.

By the end of the eleventh century, Champa had lost its territory north of Hué to the Viets, and four centuries later the whole kingdom became a vassal state under Viet hegemony.

■ Independent Vietnam

Back in the Red River Delta, the period immediately following independence from Chinese rule in 939

THE VIETNAMESE DYNASTIES	
Ngo	939–965 AD
Dinh	968–980
Early Le	980–1009
Ly	1009–1225
Tran	1225–1400
Ho	1400–1407
(Ming Chinese	1407–1428)
Later Le	1428–1789
Nguyen and Trinh lords	1592–1788
Tay Son	1788–1802
Nguyen	1802–1945

AD was marked by factional infighting until Dinh Bo Linh finally united the country in 968, securing the country's future by paying tribute to the Chinese Emperor, a system which continued until the nineteenth century.

For the next ten centuries, Dai Viet (Great Viet) was ruled by a sequence of dynasties (see box on p.971), the most important of which were the **Ly dynasty**, who founded the city of Thang Long, the precursor of modern Hanoi, the **Tran dynasty**, who repelled three successive Mongol invasions, and the **Later Le dynasty** who reconstructed the nation after a brief relapse into Chinese rule from 1407 to 1428.

As the Later Le declined in the sixteenth century, two powerful clans took over, splitting the country in two at the Gianh River, near Dong Hoi. The **Trinh** lords held sway in Hanoi and the north, while the **Nguyen** set up court at Hué. The Nguyen lords conquered the Mekong Delta, and by the mid-eighteenth century Viet people occupied the whole peninsula down to Ca Mau.

■ The Nguyen dynasty

In 1771, three disgruntled brothers raised their standard in Tay Son village, west of Qui Nhon, and ended up ruling the whole country. Their **Tay Son rebellion** gained broad support for its message of equal rights, justice and liberty, and by the middle of 1788 had overthrown both the Trinh and Nguyen lords.

One of the few Nguyen lords to survive the Tay Son rebellion was Prince Nguyen Anh who, with the help of a French bishop, Pigneau de Béhaine, raised an army and regained the throne in 1802 as **Emperor Gia Long**.

For the first time **Vietnam**, as the country was now called, fell under a single authority from the northern border all the way down to the point of Ca Mau. Gia Long established his capital at Hué, where he built a magnificent citadel in imitation of the Chinese emperor's Forbidden City. Gia Long and the **Nguyen dynasty** he founded were resolutely Confucian. He immediately abolished the Tay Son reforms, reimposing the old feudal order, and gradually closed the country to the outside world.

■ French rule

In the nineteenth century, French governments began to see Vietnam as a potential route into the resource-rich provinces of southern China and in 1858 an armada of fourteen French ships captured Da Nang. By 1862, they controlled the whole Mekong Delta, and by 1887 had power over the whole country, which they combined with Cambodia and, later, Laos to form the **Union of Indochina**. For the next seventy years Vietnam was once again under foreign occupation.

Paul Doumer, governor-general from 1897 to 1902, launched a massive programme of **infrastructural development**, which was funded by punitive taxes. There was a shift to large-scale rice production for export, which eroded traditional social systems and forced peasants off the land to work as indentured labour.

Up until the mid-1920s, Vietnam's various anti-colonial movements tended to be fragmented. But, over the border in southern China, Vietnam's first Marxist–Leninist organization, the Revolutionary Youth League, was founded in 1925 by **Ho Chi Minh**. Born in 1890, Ho left Vietnam in 1911, became a founding member of the French Communist Party and by 1923 was in Moscow, training as a communist agent.

In 1930 Ho persuaded the various rival anti-colonial movements to unite into one **Indochinese Communist Party** whose main goal was an independent Vietnam governed by workers, peasants and soldiers. In preparation for the revolution, cadres went into rural areas and among urban workers to set up party cells.

■ World War II

The German occupation of France in 1940 overturned the established order in Vietnam and by mid-1941 the region's coal mines, rice fields and military installations were all under Japanese control.

In February 1941, Ho returned to Vietnam after thirty years in exile, joining other resistance leaders at Pac Bo cave, near Cao Bang, where they forged a nationalist coalition, known as the **Viet Minh**. The organization was specifically designed to win broad popular support for independence, followed by moderate social and democratic reforms.

Over the next few years, Viet Minh recruits received military training in southern China and the **Vietnamese Liberation Army** was formed. Gradually the Viet Minh established liberated zones in the northern mountains to provide bases for future guerilla operations.

Meanwhile, Japanese forces seized full control of the country in March 1945. They declared a nominally independent state under Bao Dai, the last Nguyen emperor, and imprisoned most of the French Army. The Viet Minh quickly moved onto the offensive.

■ The August revolution

The Japanese surrender on August 14 left a power vacuum and Ho Chi Minh immediately called for a national uprising. On September 2, 1945, he proclaimed the establishment of the **Democratic Republic of Vietnam**.

The **Potsdam Agreement**, which marked the end of World War II, failed to recognize the new Republic of Vietnam. Instead, Japanese troops south of the Sixteenth Parallel were to surrender to British authority, while those in the north would defer to the Kuomintang. In the south, the British commander proclaimed martial law and Saigon was soon back in French hands.

■ The French war

In the north, the 200,000 Chinese soldiers on Vietnamese soil acted increasingly like an army of occupation, obliging Ho Chi Minh to sign a treaty allowing a limited French force to replace them. In return France recognized the Democratic Republic as a "free state" within the proposed French Union. However, it soon became apparent that the French were not going to abide by the treaty, and skirmishes between Vietnamese and French troops escalated into an all-out conflict.

For the first years of the **war against the French** (also known as the First Indochina War) the Viet Minh kept largely to their mountain bases in northern and central Vietnam, where they could simply melt away into the jungle whenever threatened.

The communist victory in China in 1949 proved to be a turning point. Almost immediately, both China and Russia recognized the Democratic Republic of Vietnam and military aid started to flow across the border. Suddenly Bao Dai's shaky government in the south was seen as the last bastion of the free world and America was drawn into the war, funding the French military with at least $3 billion by 1954.

But by 1953, France was tiring of the war and both sides agreed to peace discussions at the Geneva Conference, due to take place in May the next year. Meanwhile, a crucial battle was unfolding near **Dien Bien Phu**, where French battalions established a massive camp, deliberately trying to tempt the Viet Minh into the open. After 59 days of bitter fighting the Viet Minh forced the French to surrender, on May 7, 1954, the eve of the Geneva Conference.

■ The Geneva conference

The nine delegations attending the **Geneva Conference** succeeded only in reaching a stopgap solution, dividing Vietnam at the Seventeenth Parallel, along the Ben Hai River, pending nationwide free elections to be held by July 1956; a demilitarized buffer zone was established on either side of this military front. France and the Viet Minh agreed to an immediate ceasefire, but crucially neither the United States nor Bao Dai's government endorsed the Accords, fearing that they heralded a reunited, communist-ruled Vietnam.

■ Diem and the south

On July 7, Emperor Bao Dai named himself President, and the vehemently anti-communist **Ngo Dinh Diem** Prime Minister, of South Vietnam. Diem promptly ousted Bao Dai, declared himself President of the Republic of Vietnam, and began silencing his enemies, chiefly members of the Hoa Hao and Cao Dai religious sects and Viet Minh dissidents in the South. Over 50,000 citizens died in his pogrom.

■ Back in Hanoi...

In **Hanoi**, meanwhile, Ho Chi Minh's government set about constructing a socialist society. Years of warring with France had profoundly damaged the country's infrastructure, and now it found itself deprived of the South's plentiful rice stocks. Worse still, the **land reforms** of the mid-1950s saw many thousands of innocents "tried" as landlords by ad hoc People's Agricultural Reform Tribunals, tortured, and then executed or sent to labour camps.

Conscription was introduced in April 1960, cadres and hardware began to creep down the Ho Chi Minh Trail (see box on p.974), and Hanoi orchestrated the creation of the **National Liberation Front** (NLF), which drew together all opposition forces in the South. Diem dubbed its guerilla fighters **Viet Cong**, or VC, Vietnamese Communists, though in reality the NLF represented a united front of Catholic, Buddhist, communist and non-communist nationalists.

■ America enters the fray

In early 1955, the White House began to bankroll Diem's government and the training of his army, the **ARVN** (Army of the Republic of Vietnam). Behind these policies lay the fear of the chain reaction that could follow in Southeast Asia, were South Vietnam to be overrun by communism – the so-called **Domino Effect**.

Diem's brutally repressive government was losing ground to the VC in the battle for the hearts and minds of the population. Buddhists celebrating

THE HO CHI MINH TRAIL

The **Ho Chi Minh trail** was conceived in early 1959 as a safe route by which to direct men and equipment down the length of Vietnam in support of communist groups in the south. By the end of its "working" life, the Ho Chi Minh Trail had grown from a rough assemblage of jungle paths to become a highly effective **logistical network** stretching from near Vinh, north of the Seventeenth Parallel, to Tay Ninh Province on the edge of the Mekong Delta. For much of its southerly route the trail ran through **Laos** and **Cambodia**, always through the most difficult, mountainous terrain.

Initially it took up to six months to walk the trail from north to south, most of the time travelling at night, but by 1975, the trail – comprising at least three main arteries plus several feeder roads and totalling over **15,000km** – was wide enough to take tanks and heavy trucks, and could be driven in just one week. It was protected by anti-aircraft emplacements and supported by fuel depots, ammunition dumps, food stores and hospitals, often located underground.

By early 1965, **aerial bombardment** of the trail had begun in earnest, using napalm and defoliants as well as conventional bombs. In eight years the US Air Force dropped over two million tonnes of bombs, mostly over Laos, in an effort to cut the flow. But the trail was never completely severed.

Buddha's birthday were fired upon by ARVN soldiers in Hué, sparking off riots against religious repression, and provoking **Thich Quang Duc**'s infamous self-immolation in Saigon. America tacitly sanctioned a coup in 1963 that ousted Diem, who was shot.

In August 1964, when two American ships were subjected to allegedly unprovoked attacks from North Vietnamese craft, reprisals followed in the form of 64 **bombing** sorties against Northern coastal bases. US senators empowered Johnson to deploy regular American troops in Vietnam, "to prevent further aggression".

■ The escalation of the war

Early 1965 saw the start of **Operation Rolling Thunder**, a sustained carpet-bombing campaign, which lasted three and a half years and saw twice the tonnage of bombs dropped (around 800 daily) as had fallen on all World War II's theatres of war. Despite this, Rolling Thunder failed either to break the North's sources or their lines of supply. North Vietnamese Army (NVA) troops continued to infiltrate the South in increasing numbers, so that by 1967 over 100,000 a year were making the trek south along the Ho Chi Minh Trail.

By the end of 1965, there were 200,000 GIs in Vietnam – a figure that was to approach half a million by the winter of 1967. Their mission was largely confined to keeping the NVA at bay in the central highlands and neutralizing the guerrilla threat in the Viet Cong power-bases of the South. They also flushed active Viet Cong soldiers out of villages, most infamously at **My Lai** (see p.1022).

■ The Tet Offensive

On January 21, 1968, around 40,000 NVA troops laid siege to a remote American military base at **Khe Sanh**, near the Lao border. They were met with a carpet-bombing campaign that claimed over 10,000 victims. However, Khe Sanh was primarily a decoy to steer US troops and attention away from the **Tet Offensive** that exploded a week later. In the early hours of January 31, a combined force of 70,000 communists violated a New Year truce to launch offensives on over a hundred urban centres across the South. But the campaign failed to spark a hoped-for revolt against the Saigon regime and the VC was left permanently lamed.

However, success *did* register across the Pacific, where the assault on the **US Embassy in Saigon**, during which five Americans died, caused a sea change in popular US perceptions of the war. On March 31, President Johnson announced a virtual cessation of bombing and peace talks began a month later.

■ The fall of the south

In 1969, Richard Nixon's presidency introduced the strategy of "**Vietnamization**", a gradual US withdrawal coupled with a stiffening of ARVN forces and hardware. By the end of 1970 only 280,000 US troops remained, while ARVN numbers topped a million.

Under the terms of the **Paris Accords**, signed on January 27 1973 by the United States, the North, the South and the Viet Cong, a ceasefire was established, and all remaining American troops were repatriated. But the agreements allowed the NVA and ARVN troops to retain whatever positions they held and **renewed aggression** soon erupted. Thieu's ARVN soon set about retaking territory lost to the North and then, over Christmas 1974, an **NVA drive** overran the area north of Saigon now called Song Be Province. Towns in the South fell like ninepins, President Thieu fled to Taiwan, and Saigon fell to the North on April 30.

The **toll** of the American War, in human terms, was staggering. Of the 3.3 million Americans who served in Vietnam between 1965 and 1973, over 57,600 died, and more than 150,000 received wounds which required hospitalization. The ARVN lost 250,000 troops. Hanoi declared that over two million Vietnamese civilians, and one million communist troops, died during the war.

■ Post-reunification Vietnam

Vietnam was once again a unified nation, and in July 1976 the **Socialist Republic of Vietnam** was officially born. However, the North had no industry, a co-operative system of agriculture, and much of its land had been bombed on a massive scale. In stark contrast, American involvement in the South had underwritten what John Pilger describes as "an 'economy' based upon the services of maids, pimps, whores, beggars and black-marketeers", which dried up when the last helicopter left Saigon.

Hanoi was intent on ushering in a rigid socialist state. Privately owned land was confiscated, collectivization of agriculture was introduced, and as the state took control of industry and trade, output dwindled. Vietnam was, until 1993, unable to look to the IMF, World Bank or Asian Development Bank for **development loans**.

Anyone with remote connections with America was interned in a "**re-education camp**", along with Buddhist monks, priests and intellectuals. Hundreds of thousands of southerners were sent to these camps, and some remained for over a decade. Discrimination against those on the "wrong side" in the war continues today, in areas as diverse as health care and job opportunities.

The quagmire Vietnam found itself in after reunification prompted many of its citizens to flee across the oceans; from 1979 until the early 90s alone, an estimated 840,000 of these "**boat people**" arrived safely in "ports of first asylum" (Hong Kong was the prime destination), of whom more than 750,000 were eventually resettled overseas.

■ A return to war

Three weeks before the fall of Saigon in 1975, **Pol Pot**'s genocidal regime had seized power in Cambodia; within a year his troops were making cross-border forays into regions of Vietnam around the Mekong Delta and north of Ho Chi Minh City (as Saigon had been renamed). Finally, on Christmas Day 1978, 120,000 **Vietnamese troops invaded Cambodia** and ousted Pol Pot. They remained there until September 1989.

■ Doi moi... and the future

By the early 1980s the only thing keeping Vietnam afloat was Soviet aid. Finally, in 1986, Nguyen Van Linh introduced sweeping economic reforms, known as **doi moi** or "renovation". Collectivization and central planning were abandoned, a market economy was embraced, agriculture and retail businesses were privatized, and attempts were made to attract foreign capital.

In 1993, the Americans lifted their veto on aid, and Western cash began to flow. By year's end, inflation was down to five percent. Vietnam was admitted into **ASEAN** (the Association of Southeast Asian Nations) in July 1995, and full diplomatic relations with the US were restored.

Revenues from oil, manufacturing and tourism took off and everyone was forecasting Vietnam as **the next Asian tiger**. But by 1997 the honeymoon period was definitely over. Economic growth flagged as foreign companies scaled back, or pulled out altogether, frustrated by an overblown bureaucracy and regulations in a constant state of flux. As the economic crisis in Southeast Asia took hold, Vietnam's state-run industries became increasingly uncompetitive, and smuggling grew at an alarming rate.

National elections in July 1997 ushered in the popular new prime minister, **Phan Van Khai**, who has continued both the economic reforms and the fight against corruption. One of the government's biggest immediate problems is how to speed up the restructuring and privatization of debt-ridden state enterprises. As Vietnam enters the new millennium, there's no doubt a great deal has been achieved in a comparatively short time; perhaps the initial expectations of *doi moi* were just unrealistically high – on all sides.

Religions of Vietnam

The moral and religious life of most Vietnamese people is governed by a mixture of Confucian, Mahayana

Buddhist and Taoist teachings interwoven with ancestor worship and ancient, animistic practices. Vietnam also has small Hindu, Muslim and Theravada Buddhist communities, as well as the second largest Catholic congregation in Southeast Asia, after the Philippines. For an introduction to all these faiths, see "Basics" p.47. After 1975, the Marxist–Leninist government of reunified Vietnam declared the state atheist: churches and pagodas were closed down and religious leaders sent for re-education. Since 1986 the situation has eased, and many Vietnamese are once again openly practising their faith.

No matter what their religion, virtually every Vietnamese household will maintain an ancestral altar for rituals associated with **ancestor worship**, which is based on the principles of filial piety and obligation to the past, present and future generations. Residual **animism** plus a whole host of spirits borrowed from other religions further complicate Vietnam's mystical world, in which the universe is divided into three realms – the sky, earth and man – under the overall guardianship of Ong Troi, Lord of Heaven.

Up to two-thirds of the Vietnamese population consider themselves **Mahayana Buddhists**, while at the same time adhering to a **Confucian** philosophy, whose emphasis on conformity and duty has played an essential role in Vietnam's political, social and educational systems. Many **Taoist** deities have been absorbed into other more mainstream cults, in particular Mahayana Buddhism.

Vietnam in the movies

The embroilment of the US in Vietnam and its conflicts has spawned hundreds of movies, ranging from fond soft-focused colonial reminiscences, to blood-and-guts depictions of the horrors of war.

Even by the mid-1950s, the country was often treated less as a nation with its own unique set of political issues, and more as a generic Asian theatre of war, in which the righteous battle against communism could be played out. **China Gate** (1957) is an early example of this trend. Rather more depth of thought went into the making of **The Quiet American** (1958), in which Michael Redgrave played the British journalist and cynic, Fowler, while Audie Murphy played Pyle, the eponymous "hero" of Graham Greene's novel. To Greene's chagrin, Pyle was depicted not as a representative of the American government, but of a private aid organization – something which the author felt blunted his anti-American message.

With American troops duly deployed by 1965, it was only a matter of time before John Wayne produced his patriotic and monumentally bad **The Green Berets** (1968), which depicts American soldiers in spotless uniforms fighting against no less a threat than total "Communist domination of the world". But the war was a much dirtier affair than *The Green Berets* made it seem, and as popular support for the conflict soured, a raft of exploitation movies was churned out, in which the mental scars of Vietnam provided topical window-dressing to improbable tales of martial arts, motorbikes and mayhem. At best, vets were treated as dysfunctional vigilantes acting beyond the pale of society – most famously in **Taxi Driver** (1976), which has Robert De Niro's disturbed insomniac returnee, Travis Bickle, embarking on a one-man moral crusade to purge the streets of a hellish New York.

Only in 1978 did Hollywood finally pluck up courage enough to confront the war head-on, and so aid the nation's healing process. Movies no longer sought to make sense of past events, but to highlight their futility, and audiences were confronted by disaffected troops seeking comfort in prostitution and drug abuse, along with far more shocking examples of soldiers' fraying moral fibre. **Coming Home** (1978), which cast Jane Fonda as a military career-man's wife who falls in love with a wheelchair-bound veteran (Jon Voight), was significant for its sensitive consideration of the emotional and physical tolls exacted by the war. Similarly concerned was **The Deer Hunter** (1978), in which the conscription of three friends fractures their Russian orthodox community in Pennsylvania. The friends' "one-shot" code of honour, espoused on a last pre-Vietnam hunting trip, contrasts wildly with the moral vacuum of the war, whose random brutality is embodied in the movie's central scenes of Russian roulette. But for all its power, *The Deer Hunter* is marred by overt racist stereotyping of the Vietnamese. Francis Ford Coppola's hugely indulgent but visually magnificent **Apocalypse Now** (1979) rounded off the vanguard of postwar Vietnam combat movies. It was described by one critic as "Film as opera... it turns Vietnam into a vast trip, into a War of the Imagination". Coppola totally mythologizes the conflict, rendering it not so much futile as insane.

The precedent set by *Coming Home* of sympathetic consideration for returning veterans' mindsets spurred many movies along similar lines in subsequent years. These focused on the disillusionment and disorientation felt by soldiers coming back, not to heroes' welcomes, but to indifference and even dis-dain. One of the first was **First Blood** (1982), which introduced audiences to Sly Stallone's muscle-bound super-vet, John Rambo. Alan Parker's **Birdy** (1984) and Oliver Stone's **Born on the 4th of July** (1989) reiterated the message of stolen youth.

During the 1980s, Hollywood attempted, bizarrely, to rewrite the script, in a series of revisionist movies. Richard Gere had made the armed forces hip again in 1982's weepie **An Officer and a Gentleman**; and a year later the first of an intriguing sub-genre of films hit cinemas, in which Americans returned to Vietnam, invariably to rescue MIAs, and "won". **Uncommon Valor** (1983), a rather silly piece about an MIA rescue starring Gene Hackman, kicked things off, closely followed by **Missing in Action** (1983), in which Chuck Norris karate-kicks his way towards the same resolution. The mother of them all, though, was **Rambo: First Blood, Part II** (1985), in which the hero of *First Blood* gets to settle some old scores.

The backlash to the patent nonsense of the revisionist films came in a series of shockingly realistic movies which attempted to reveal the real Vietnam, routine atrocities, indiscipline and all. There are no heroes in these GI's-view movies, only fragile, confused-looking young men in fatigues. In **Platoon** (1986), Oliver Stone, himself a foot-soldier in Vietnam, shows the circumstances under which it was feasible for young American boys to become murderers of civilians. It powerfully conjures the paranoiac near-hysteria spawned by fear, confusion, loss of motivation and inability to discriminate between friend and foe. In **Hamburger Hill** (1987), the image of an entire generation stumbling towards the maws of death is strengthened by the fact that the cast includes no big-name actors – the men who fall are neighbours, sons or brothers, not film stars. Stanley Kubrick's **Full Metal Jacket** (1987) picks up this theme of the war's theft of American youth with a brutal drill-sergeant who sets about expunging the soldiers' humanity.

Vietnamese people have mostly been noticeable by their absence from Hollywood films, or have been viewable only through the filter of blatant stereotyping. **Heaven and Earth** (1993), the final part of Oliver Stone's Vietnam trilogy, went some way towards rectifying this imbalance. Its depiction of a Vietnamese girl's odyssey from idyllic early childhood to the traumas of life as a wife in San Diego acts as a timely reminder that not only Americans suffered during the struggle.

Meanwhile, Tran Anh Hung has emerged as Vietnam's pre-eminent domestic film director. **Cyclo** (1996), his grisly tale of murder and prostitution on Vietnam's mean streets, contrasted hugely with **Scent of Green Papaya** (1993), the nostalgic colonial period piece that made his name.

Books

Mark Baker, *Nam* (Sphere, UK; Berkley, US). Unflinching firsthand accounts of the GI's descent from boot camp into the morass of death, paranoia, exhaustion and tedium.

John Balaban and Nguyen Qui Duc (eds.), *Vietnam: A Traveller's Literary Companion* (Whereabouts Press, UK/US). Entertaining volume of short stories, written by Vietnamese writers based both at home and abroad.

Bao Ninh, *The Sorrow of War* (Minerva, UK; Berkley, US). This is a ground-breaking novel, largely due to its portrayal of communist soldiers suffering the same traumas, fear and lost innocence as their American counterparts.

Maria Coffey, *Three Moons in Vietnam* (Abacus, UK). Delightfully jolly jaunt around Vietnam by boat, bus and bicycle, in which Coffey conspires to meet more locals in one day than most travellers do in a month.

Duong Thu Huong, *Novel Without a Name* (Picador, UK; Penguin, US). A tale of young Vietnamese men seeking glory but finding only loneliness, disillusionment and death, as war abridges youth and curtails loves.

Duong Van Mai Elliot, *The Sacred Willow* (OUP). Mai Elliot brings Vietnamese history to life in this compelling account of her family through four generations.

Marguerite Duras, *The Lover* (Flamingo, UK; HarperCollins, US). The story of a young French girl's affair with a wealthy Chinese from Cholon depicts a dysfunctional French family in Vietnam and provides an interesting slant on expat life.

Bernard Fall, *Hell in a Very Small Place* (Da Capo, UK/US). The classic account of the siege of Dien Bien Phu.

Graham Greene, *The Quiet American* (Penguin, UK/US). Greene's prescient and cautionary tale of the dangers of innocence in uncertain times, which second-guessed America's boorish manhandling of Vietnam's political situation, is still the best single account of wartime Vietnam.

Graham Greene, *Ways of Escape* (Penguin, UK; Pocket Books, US). Greene's global travels in the 1950s took him to Vietnam for four consecutive win-

LANGUAGE

Linguists are uncertain as to the exact roots of **Vietnamese**, though it betrays Thai, Khmer and Chinese influences. It's tonal, and extremely tricky for Westerners to master – luckily, English has now superseded Russian as *the* language to learn in Vietnam. The script is Romanized. Vietnam's minority peoples have their own languages, and may not understand standard Vietnamese. For further phrases, try *Vietnamese: A Rough Guide Phrasebook*.

PRONUNCIATION

The Vietnamese language is tonal, that is, one in which a word's meaning is determined by the pitch at which you deliver it. Six tones are used – the mid-level tone (syllables with no marker), the low falling tone (syllables marked `), the low rising tone (syllables marked ˀ), the high broken tone (syllables marked ˜), the high rising tone (syllables marked ´) and the low broken tone (syllables marked ̣). Depending upon its tone, the word *ba*, for instance, can mean either three, grandmother, poisoned food, waste, aunt or any.

Vowels				**Consonants**	
a	'a' as in father	au	'a-oo'	c	'g'
ă	'u' as in hut (slight 'u' as	âu	'oh' as in oh!	ch	'j' as in jar
	in unstressed English 'a')	ay	'ay' as in hay	d	'y' as in young
â	'uh' sound as above only	ây	'ay-i' (as in 'ay' above	v	'd' as in day
	longer		but longer)	g	'g' as in goat
e	'e' as in bed	eo	'eh-ao'	gh	'g' as in goat
ê	'ay' as in pay	êu	'ay-oo'	gi	'y' as in young
i	'i' as in -ing	iu	'ew' as in few	k	'g' as in goat
o	'o' as in hot	iêu	'i-yoh'	kh	'k' as in keep
ô	'aw' as in awe	oa	'wa'	ng/ngh	'ng' as in sing
ơ	'ur' as in fur	oe	'weh'	nh	'n-y' as in canyon
u	'oo' as in boo	ôi	'oy'	ph	'f'
ư	'oo' closest to French 'u'	ơi	'uh-i'	q	'g' as in goat
y	'i' as in -ing	ua	'waw'	t	'd' as in day
		uê	'weh'	th	't'
		uô	'waw'	tr	'j' as in jar
		uy	'wee'	x	's'
Vowel combinations		ưa	'oo-a'		
ai	'ai' as in Thai	ưu	'er-oo'		
ao	'ao' as in Mao	ươi	'oo-uh-i'		

GREETINGS AND BASIC PHRASES

How you speak to somebody in Vietnam depends on their sex, and on their age and social standing, relative to your own. As a rule, if you address a man as *ông*, and a woman as *bà*, you are being polite. With someone of about your age, you can use *anh* (for a man) and *chi* (for a woman).

Hello	*chào ông/bà*	Excuse me	*xin ông/bà thứ*	I don't	*tôi không hiểu*
How are you?	*ông/bà có khie*	(to get past)	*lỗi*	understand	
	không?	Please	*làm ơn*	Could you	*xin ông/bà lập*
Fine, thanks	*tôi khỏe cám ơn*	Thank you	*cám ơn ông/bà*	repeat that?	*lại?*
Pleased to	*hân hạnh gặp*	What's your	*ông/bà tên gi?*	Yes	*vâng* (north);
meet you	*ông/bà*	name?			*dạ* (south)
Goodbye	*chào, tạm biệt*	My name is...	*tên tôi là...*	No	*không*
Goodnight	*chúc ngủ ngon*	Do you speak	*ông/bà biwt nói*		
Excuse me	*xin lỗi*	English?	*tiếng Anh*		
(to say sorry)			*không?*		

EMERGENCIES

Can you help me?	*ông/bà có thể giúp*	Please call a doctor	*làm ơn gui bác sẹ*
	tôi không?	hospital	*bệnh viện*
There's been an accident	*có một vụ tai nạn*	police station	*don cong an*

GETTING AROUND

Where is the...?	....ở đâu?	Can I book a	tôi có thể đặt	filling station	trạm xăng
How many	bao nhiêu cây	seat?	ghw trước	bicycle	xe đạp
kilometres	số thì		không?	bank	nhà băng
is it to...?	đến...?	How long does	phải tốn bao	post office	sổ bưu đi-n
We'd like to	chúng tôi	it take?	lâu?	passport	hộ chiếu
go to...	muốn đi...	ticket	vé	hotel	khách sạn
To the airport,	làm ơn vđa tôi	aeroplane	máy bay	restaurant	nhà hàng
please	đi sân bay	airport	sân bay	Please stop here	xin dừng lại đây
Where do we	ở vậu vón xe	boat	tàu bè	left/right	bên trái/bên
catch the bus	đi...?	bus	xe buxt		phải
to...?		bus station	bwn xe buxt	north	phía bắc
When does the	khi nào xe Hoi	train station	bwn xe lửa	south	phía nam
bus for Hoi	An chạy?	taxi	tắc xi	east	phía vông
An leave?		car	xe hới	west	phía tây

ACCOMMODATION

Do you have	ông/bà có	room with a	một phòng	mosquito net	cái màn
any rooms?	phòng không?	private	tắm riêng	toilet paper	giấy vệ sinh
How much	bao nhiêu tiền?	bathroom		telephone	viện thoại
is it?		cheap/expensive	rẻ/đắt	laundry	quần ào dơ
Can I have a	xem có đượ́ c	single room	phòng một	blanket	chăn (north)
look?	không?		ngứai		mền (south)
I'd like...	cho tôi xin mot...	double room	phòng hai	open/closed	mở cửa/
Could I have	làm ơn tính		ngứai		vóng cửa
the bill	tiền?	air-conditioner	máy lạnh		
please?		fan (electric)	quạt máy		

NUMBERS

For numbers ending in 5, from 15 onwards, lăm is used in northern Vietnam and nhăm in the south, rather than the written form of năm. Also, an alternative for numbers that are multiples of ten is chục – so, ten can be một chục, twenty can be hai chục, etc.

zero	không	ten	mười	twenty	hai mười
one	một	eleven	mười một	twenty-one	hai mười một
two	hai	twelve	mười hai	twenty-two	hai mười hai
three	ba	thirteen	mười ba	thirty	ba mười
four	bốn	fourteen	mười bốn	forty	bốn mười
five	năm	fifteen	mười lăm /nhăm	fifty	năm mười
six	sáu	sixteen	mười sáu	one hundred	mot trăm
seven	bảy	seventeen	mười bảy	two hundred	hai trăm
eight	tám	eighteen	mười tám	one thousand	mot ngàn
nine	chín	nineteen	mười chín	ten thousand	mười ngàn

TIME

What's the time?	mấy giờ rồi?	week	tuần	now	bây giờ
noon	buổi trưa	month	tháng	morning	buổi sáng
midnight	nửa đêm	year	năm	afternoon	buổi chiều
minute	phút	today	hôm nay	evening	buổi tối
hour	giờ	tomorrow	mai	night	ban đêm
day	ngày	yesterday	hôm qua		

ters; the coverage of Vietnam in this slim autobiographical volume is intriguing, but tantalizingly short.

Anthony Grey, *Saigon* (Pan, UK; Dell OP, US). A rip-roaring narrative, whose Vietnamese, French and American protagonists conspire to be present at all defining moments in recent Vietnamese history, from French plantation riots to the fall of Saigon.

Michael Herr, *Dispatches* (Pan, UK; Random House, US). Infuriatingly narcissistic at times, Herr's spaced-out narrative still conveys the mud, blood and guts of the American war effort in Vietnam.

Henry Kamm, *Dragon Ascending*. Pulitzer prize-winning correspondent Kamm lets the Vietnamese – art dealers, ex-colonels, academics, doctors, authors – speak for themselves, in this convincing portrait of contemporary Vietnam.

Stanley Karnow, *Vietnam: A History* (Pimlico, UK; Penguin, US). Weighty, august tome that elucidates the entire span of Vietnamese history.

Gabriel Kolko, *Vietnam: Anatomy of a Peace* (Routledge, UK). No other recent account of contemporary Vietnam has done a better job of describing the social, political and economic upheavals that the country has suffered over the past few years.

Le Ly Hayslip, *When Heaven and Earth Changed Places* (Pan, UK; NAL-Dutton, US). This heart-rending tale of villagers trying to survive in a climate of hatred and distrust is perhaps more valuable than any history book.

Norman Lewis, *A Dragon Apparent* (Eland, UK; Hippocrene, US). When in 1950 Lewis made the journey that would inspire his seminal Indochina travelogue, the Vietnam he saw was still a land of long-houses and imperial hunts, though poised for renewed conflict.

Michael Maclear, *Vietnam: The Ten Thousand Day War* (Mandarin OP, UK; Avon, US). A detailed yet accessible account of the French and American wars.

Nguyen Du, *The Tale of Kieu* (Yale University Press, UK/US). Vietnamese literature reached its zenith with this tale of ill-starred love.

Nguyen Huy Thiep, *The General Retires and Other Stories* (Oxford University Press, UK/US). These short stories by Vietnam's pre-eminent writer articulate the lives of ordinary Vietnamese.

Tim O'Brien, *The Things They Carried* (Flamingo, UK; Penguin, US). Through a mix of autobiography and fiction O'Brien lays to rest the ghosts of the past in a brutally honest reappraisal of the war.

Robert Olen Butler, *A Good Scent from a Strange Mountain* (Minerva, UK; Penguin, US). Pulitzer prize-winning collection of short stories that ponder the struggles of Vietnamese in America to maintain the cultural ley lines linking them with their mother country, and the gulf between them and their Americanized offspring.

John Pilger, *Heroes* (Pan, UK). Pilger's systematic dismantling of the myth that America's role was in any way a justifiable "crusade" makes his Vietnam reportage required reading.

Neil Sheehan, *A Bright Shining Lie* (Pan, UK; Random House, US). This monumental account of the war, hung around the life of the soldier John Paul Vann, won the Pulitzer Prize for Sheehan; one of the true classics of Vietnam-inspired literature.

Robert Templer, *Shadows and Wind* (Little, Brown & Co). This hard-hitting book casts a critical eye over Vietnam's decade of reform, from corruption and censorship to the emergence of a consumer-oriented youth culture.

Justin Wintle, *Romancing Vietnam* (Penguin, UK; Pantheon OP, US). Wintle's genial but lightweight yomp upcountry was one of the first of its kind, post-doi moi.

Gavin Young, *A Wavering Grace* (Penguin, UK). The poignant tale of a Vietnamese family torn apart by the war and its aftermath, as witnessed by this veteran adventurer.

HO CHI MINH CITY AND AROUND

Washed ashore above the Mekong Delta, some 40km north of the South China Sea, **HO CHI MINH CITY** is a city on the march, a boomtown where the rule of the dollar is absolute. Fuelled by the sweeping economic changes wrought by *doi moi*, this effervescent city, perched on the west bank of the Saigon River, now boasts fine restaurants, immaculate hotels, and glitzy bars among its colonial villas, venerable pagodas and austere, Soviet-style housing-blocks. Sadly, Ho Chi Minh City is also full to bursting with people for whom progress hasn't yet translated into food, lodgings and employment, so begging, stealing and prostitution are all facts of life here.

Ho Chi Minh City started life as a fishing village known as Prei Nokor and, during the Angkor period (until the fifteenth century), it flourished as an entrepôt for Cambodian boats pushing down the Mekong River. By the seventeenth century it boasted a Khmer garrison and a community of Malay, Indian and Chinese traders. During the eighteenth century, Hué's Nguyen Dynasty ousted the Khmers, renamed Prei Nokor **Saigon**, and established a temporary capital here between 1772 and 1802, after which the Emperor Gia Long used it as his regional administrative centre. The French seized Saigon in 1861, and a year later the Treaty of Saigon declared the city the capital of French Cochinchina. They set about a huge public works programme, building roads and draining marshlands, but ruled harshly. After a thirty-year war against the French, Saigon was finally designated the capital of the **Republic of South Vietnam** by President Diem in 1955, soon becoming both the nerve-centre of the American war effort, and its R&R capital, with a slough of sleazy bars catering to GIs on leave of duty. The American troops withdrew in 1973, and two years later the Ho Chi Minh Campaign rolled through the gates of the presidential palace and the communists were in control. Within a year, Saigon had been renamed Ho Chi Minh City.

Arrival

Tan Son Nhat Airport is 7km northwest of the city centre and has banks (daily 8am–9pm) and a Saigontourist booth (daily 7.30–11.30am & 2–6pm) that stocks city maps and can help with accommodation; there are also left-luggage facilities in the arrivals hall. Metered Airport Taxi and Vinataxi **cabs** travel to the city for $5–7, though these are undercut by the vintage – and perfectly legitimate – Peugeots. The cheaper option is to try and gather enough passengers (normally six to eight) to fill an estate car or minibus taxi ($2 per person), or you could get a Honda om or cyclo ($2) from outside the airport gates.

Trains from the north pull in at the **train station**, or Ga Saigon, 3km northwest of town, on Nguyen Thong. Cyclos will take you to the centre for less than $1 (15min), or you can get a taxi ($4). There's also a post office here (daily 6.30am–10pm).

Buses stop at different terminals. Those from the north arrive at **Mien Dong bus station**, 5km north of the city on Xo Viet Nghe Tinh; local buses shuttle between here and central **Ben Thanh bus station**, a five-minute walk from Pham Ngu Lao; or take a cyclo mai ($2–3). Most buses from the south use **Mien Tay bus station**, 10km west of the city centre in An Lac District; local buses shuttle into town from here, passing along Pham Ngu Lao en route. My Tho and most My Thuan buses use **Cholon bus station**, from where Saigon Star Co buses run into the city – walk out of the station and along Huynh Thoai Yen towards Binh Tay Market. Some buses from Tay Ninh pull in at Mien Dong but most arrive at **An Suong bus station**, west of the airport on Highway 22, and linked by bus with Ben Thanh bus station; most arrivals **from Cu Chi town** also end their journeys here, though some continue on to Ben Thanh.

Hydrofoils from Vung Tau, My Tho, Vinh Long, Chau Doc and Can Tho dock at the **Passengers Quay** of Ho Chi Minh City, opposite the end of Ham Nghi. Boats from My Tho and Ben Tre generally moor 1.5km south of the Ho Chi Minh Museum on **Ton That Thuyet**;

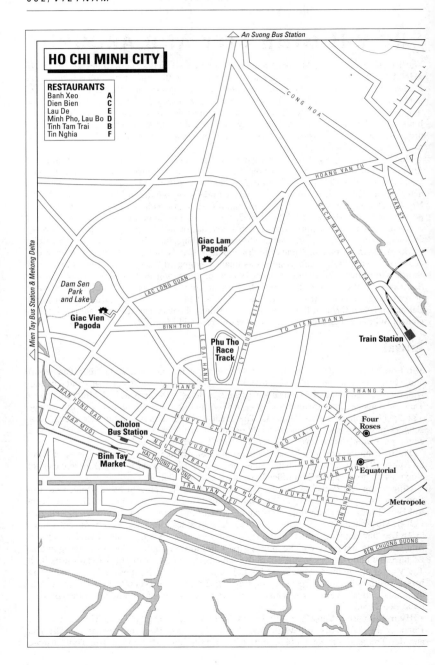

HO CHI MINH CITY

RESTAURANTS

Banh Xeo	A
Dien Bien	C
Lau De	E
Minh Pho, Lau Bo	D
Tinh Tam Trai	B
Tin Nghia	F

An Suong Bus Station

CONG HOA

HOANG VAN TU

LE VAN SY

CACH MANG THANG TAM

Giac Lam Pagoda

Dam Sen Park and Lake

LAC LONG QUAN

Giac Vien Pagoda

BINH THOI

LY THUONG KIET

TO HIEN THANH

Train Station

Phu Tho Race Track

Mien Tay Bus Station & Mekong Delta

3 THANG 2

3 THANG 2

TRAN HUNG DAO

HAI MUOI

NGUYEN CHI THANH

Cholon Bus Station

NGO GIA TU

LY HAI TO

Four Roses

HUNG VUONG

NGUYEN TRAI

Binh Tay Market

HAI THUONG LAN ONG

NGUYEN TRAI

HUNG VUONG

TRAN PHU

Equatorial

TRAN VAN KIEU

TRAN HUNG DAO

NGUYEN TRAI

TRAN BINH TRONG

Metropole

BEN CHUONG DUONG

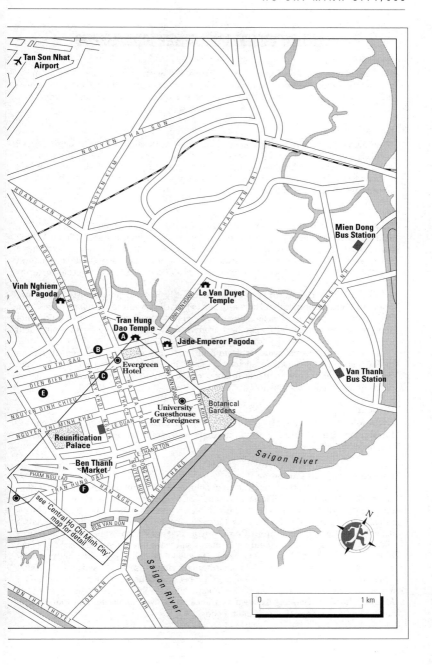

MOVING ON FROM HO CHI MINH CITY

By plane

The easiest way **to get to Tan Son Nhat Airport** is by taxi, but you can also take an airport shuttle from *Sinh Café* or one of the other tour operators in the Pham Ngu Lao area ($2–5). Flight enquiries should be made at the office of the relevant carrier (see "Listings", p.992).

By train

When **leaving by train**, always book as far ahead as possible, either through a travel agent, Saigon Railways Tourist Service, 275c Pham Ngu Lao (☎08/836 7640); or in person at the foreigners' enquiries counter (daily 7.30–11.30am & 1.30–4.30pm; ☎08/843 6527 or 844 0218) at the train station. Opposite the counter, a board details all fares, arrivals and departures in English.

By bus

Buses to points north and also **Vung Tau** leave from Mien Dong bus station. Buy a ticket in advance from opposite the blue one-storey building, marked "Phong Ve Toc Hanh" (daily 5am–5pm), to your left as you enter the terminal. Express air-con buses depart every half hour for Vung Tau from here, but you can pick up a shuttle bus in town at 102, Ky Con, or book a local minibus from *Café 333*, De Tham, as an alternative means of getting to Vung Tau.

Most buses **for the south** (exceptions include My Tho and some for My Thuan) use **Mien Tay bus station**. Either catch a xe lam to Mien Tay or there are hourly buses from Ben Thanh bus station. My Tho and most My Thuan departures are from **Cholon bus station**. Saigon Star Co buses run here from the city (see opposite for the route) and there is also a shuttle service from Ben Thanh bus station.

Open-tour buses mainly depart from Kim Travel and *Sinh Café* in De Tham and run to the main tourist destinations such as Da Lat, Nha Trang, Hoi An, Da Nang, Hué and Hanoi; tickets either open-dated or pre-booked can be one-way with breaks en-route or purchased in separate segments.

By boat

Hydrofoils to Vung Tau, My Tho, Vinh Long, Chau Doc and Can Tho leave from the **Passengers Quay** of Ho Chi Minh City, opposite the end of Ham Nghi. Tickets can be purchased here.

Overland travel to Cambodia

At present the only overland entry and exit point between Cambodia and Vietnam for foreigners is at **Moc Bai**, which is northwest of Ho Chi Minh City, the usual overland departure point for this crossing. The Moc Bai border is open 24 hours a day, but most buses usually cross during day hours. *Sinh Café*, 246–248 De Tham (☎08/836 7338), runs a daily air-con bus ($6) **to Phnom Penh**, which leaves at 8.45am from outside its offices and arrives at 5pm. Buses bound for Phnom Penh leave daily, departing early morning from the garage at 145 Nguyen Du – arrive in good time and buy a ticket on the bus, or contact ☎08/822 2496. You'll need a **Cambodian visa** from the consulate at 41 Phung Khac Khoan (☎08/829 2751; $30; 1–3 days' processing). Another option is to sign up for a **shared taxi** in Pham Ngu Lao ($20–25 for a full car); this will take you as far as the **Moc Bai border crossing**, from where you can walk over the border and connect with an awaiting air-con bus ($5) to Phnom Penh.

while those from further afield terminate behind Cholon's Binh Tay Market, or just below here at the junction of Chu Van An and Tran Van Kieu.

Information

As with the rest of Vietnam, there is no efficient and impartial tourist information office in Ho Chi Minh. Your best sources of **information** are the tour agencies and travellers' cafés. They also offer motorbike and car rental, guide services and day-trips; some also do longer tours and visa services. Popular jaunts include a one-day trip to Tay Ninh and the Cu Chi tunnels ($8); one- to five-day tours of the Mekong Delta; and the ten-day trawl up to Hué, via the central highlands and the coast. For a list of recommended agencies see "Listings" on p.993.

Two publications carry **listings** information in and around Ho Chi Minh City; the *Vietnam Economic Times'* ($5 monthly) supplement *The Guide,* which can also be purchased separately for $1; and the weekly *Vietnam Investment Review's* ($2.50) *Time Out.* A fairly detailed city **map** is available from street hawkers, the GPO or from Vietnamtourism and Saigontourist.

City transport

With over fifty thousand **cyclos** (three-wheeled cycle-rickshaws) operating in Ho Chi Minh City, hailing one is easy and rates are pretty consistent throughout the city. The roads around the central Dong Khoi area are off-limits to cyclos, so your driver may follow a circuitous course. **Taxis** gather outside the *Rex Hotel.* You can also phone for one of the white Airport Taxis (☎08/844 6666) or yellow Vinataxis (☎08/811 0888); a trip within the city centre will cost $3. Cheaper colonial-era Peugeots also operate around the city; you can track them down below Ben Thanh Market, on Pham Ngu Lao, and outside the *Rex.* The two-wheeled motorbike taxis or **Honda om** cost about the same as a cyclo but are faster.

The only time you might use a **city bus** is to get to one of the long-distance bus terminals (see p.981) or to go to Cholon. Saigon Star Co runs buses to Cholon (daily 5am–10pm), looping between the south side of Mei Linh Square and Huynh Thoai Yen, below Binh Tay Market. From Pham Ngu Lao, head down to the eastern end of Bui Vien to pick up the service to Cholon; on the return journey, you'll be dropped at the far side of Tran Hung Dao. **Xe lams** – three-wheeler buggies – function as buses around the city. They're slightly less expensive than buses, but crowded. They gather at Ben Thanh bus station, and at the corner of Pham Ngu Lao and Nguyen Thai Hoc.

Most **bike, moped and motorbike rental** operations are around Pham Ngu Lao; average daily costs are around $1 for a bicycle and $5–7 for a moped or medium-sized motorbike. Try the kiosk outside the *Que Huong-Liberty 3 Hotel,* at 187 Pham Ngu Lao, *Hotel 265,* 265 De Tham, and *Huong Hotel,* 40/19 Bui Vien; for larger motorbikes try *Hotel 211,* 211 Pham Ngu Lao and *Thanh Thanh Guesthouse,* 205 Pham Ngu Lao – both outlets offer long-term rental discounts. *Sinh Café,* 246–248 De Tham, rents out mountain bikes at $2 per day. In the centre, Getrantours, 24 Hai Ba Trung, and 21 Ngo Duc Ke (next to *Restaurant 19,* ask for Mr Tuan) rent out a wide selection of motorbikes and mopeds, including 250cc bikes. Bao Viet at 23–25 Thai Van Lung (☎08/829 4182) does motorbike **insurance**. Pretty much every one of the city's tour operators (see p.993) can arrange **car rental** plus driver ($40–50 per day); self-drive is not an option.

Accommodation

Ho Chi Minh's budget enclave centres on **Pham Ngu Lao**, 1km west of the city centre, where you'll also find travel agencies, restaurants and bars. Room rates here start from $4–5

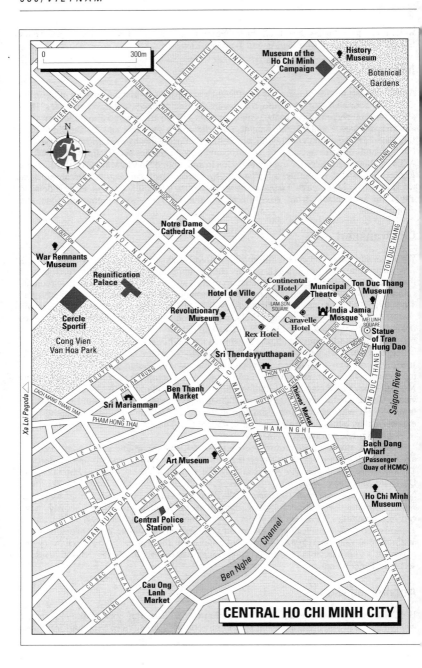

CENTRAL HO CHI MINH CITY

for a grim fan-cooled box with shared bathroom; for a few dollars more however, you'll get a bright, air-con or fan en-suite room. Ho Chi Minh's most pleasant and convenient area in which to stay is the region around **Dong Khoi**, which has mid-range as well as top hotels. Staying in **Cholon** leaves you marooned in the bustle of Ho Chi Minh's Chinatown, but there are some bargains and you're away from the travellers' enclave. There shouldn't be any need to book in advance unless you're hitting town around Tet (usually late Jan/mid-Feb).

Pham Ngu Lao and Ben Thanh Market

Anh Quang, 217/12 De Tham (☎08/836 9906). One of several private homes, offering bargain lodgings down a Dickensian alleyway between 217 and 219 De Tham: others include *Ngoc Yen* (☎08/836 0200), directly opposite, and the genial *Minh* at 199/22 (☎08/836 9816). ①–②.

Bach Cung, 170–172 Nguyen Thai Binh (☎08/821 2777). Gaudy but comfortable, with reasonable room rates and good facilities, including bath, fridge and satellite TV. ④–⑤.

Hong Kong, 22 Bui Vien (☎08/836 4904). Popular mini-hotel, offering clean, modern rooms, with either fan or air-con; staff will also help with tour bookings. ②–③.

Hotel 127, 127 Cong Quynh (☎08/836 8761). The friendly family in charge pay lots of attention to detail, resulting in a range of comfortable rooms, some sleeping up to four; free breakfast and airport transfers. Recommended. ③–④.

Lan Anh, 252 De Tham (☎08/836 5197). A relative newcomer, but already a favourite, this is a friendly, family-run mini-hotel, with bright, clean air-con and fan rooms; breakfast is included. ②–③.

Le Le, 171 Pham Ngu Lao (☎08/836 8686). Comfortable and popular mini-hotel. Rooms have hot water and satellite TV; breakfast and airport transfer inclusive. The sister hotel, *Vinh Guesthouse*, 269 De Tham (☎08/836 8585), has cheaper rooms. ④–⑤.

My Man Mini Hotel, 373/20 Pham Ngu Lao (☎08/836 7544). Tucked away down an alley off the western end of Pham Ngu Lao, so quieter than most; ten decent rooms all with hot water; some air-con. ②–③.

Que Huong-Liberty 3, 187 Pham Ngu Lao (☎08/836 9522). Large, budget hotel; the range of down-at-heel, high-ceilinged fan and air-con rooms get cheaper the higher you climb. ②–③.

Room For Rent 70, 70 Bui Vien (☎08/833 9569). A friendly, hugely popular veteran of the scene, offering a choice of air-con and fan rooms, some of them airy and pleasant. Hot drinks, breakfast and vegetarian meal inclusive. ②–③.

Thanh Thanh, 205 Pham Ngu Lao (☎08/837 3595). Friendly and efficient staff, and generously proportioned though slightly dowdy rooms, some air-con; breakfast is inclusive. ②–④.

Thanh Thao, 71 Le Thi Hong Gam (☎08/822 5664). Sparkling, minty-fresh rooms with air-con, fridge, telephone and hot water – a bargain, but it's a long haul to the upper floors. ⑤.

Vien Dong, 275a Pham Ngu Lao (☎08/836 8941). Dependable first-night mid-range option, though rates are negotiable; all rooms have air-con, fridge, satellite TV and complimentary breakfast. ⑧.

Dong Khoi and around

Bong Sen, 117–123 Dong Khoi (☎08/829 1516). Stylish but personable hotel in the heart of Dong Khoi; breakfast is included. The *Bong Sen II* (☎08/823 5818), around the corner at 61 Hai Ba Trung, has newer rooms at lower rates. ⑧.

Grand, 8 Dong Khoi (☎08/823 0163). Painstakingly restored 1930's hotel, whose attractive furnishings and spacious suites have an unabashedly old-world feel. ⑨.

Majestic, 1 Dong Khoi (☎08/829 5517) Historic riverfront hotel, 1929-built and still oozing character. All rooms are charming and include breakfast; staff fall over themselves to be helpful. ⑨.

Rex, 141 Nguyen Hue (☎08/829 2185). The *Rex* shamelessly milks its fame, with ashtrays, slippers and other fittings for sale, but its rooms are extremely comfortable and well-equipped, and the main lobby is stunning. ⑧.

Riverside, 18–20 Ton Duc Thang (☎08/822 4038). Grand colonial pile, proudly eyeing the river from the base of Dong Khoi; recently modernized rooms are stylish but functional. ⑦.

University Guesthouse for Foreigners, 10 Dinh Tien Hoang (☎08/829 8686). Meant for visiting professors, but also accepts tourists; TV, air-con and en-suite bathroom in good-value rooms; bicycle rental also available. ③.

Cholon and around

Four Roses, 790/5 Nguyen Dinh Chieu (☎08/832 5895). Located in no-man's land between Cholon and the city centre, this is a peaceful, family-run delight: ten pleasant rooms with balconies and a garden. ④.

Hanh Long 2, 1115 Tran Hung Dao (☎08/838 1173). The good-value, functional tiled rooms are far more inviting than the run-down exteriors in this somewhat noisy hotel; some air-con rooms. ②–③.

Tan Da, 22–24 Tan Da (☎08/855 5711). Fairly quiet mini-hotel, with reasonably well-appointed rooms, bearing in mind the price. Staff can be surly, however. ②–③.

The City

Ho Chi Minh City is divided into eighteen districts, though tourists rarely travel beyond districts One, Three and Five, unless it's to visit the tunnels at Cu Chi (see p.994). The city proper hugs the west bank of the Saigon River, and its central area, District One, nestles in the hinge formed by the confluence of the river with the silty Ben Nghe Channel; traditionally the **French Quarter** of the city, this area is still widely known as Saigon. Dong Khoi is its backbone, and around the T-shape it forms along with Le Duan Boulevard are scattered most of the city's museums and colonial remnants, including the late nineteenth-century Notre Dame Cathedral, the *Hotel Continental*, once a bastion of French high society, and the ostentatious former Hotel de Ville, which now houses the People's Committee. But, except for **Cholon**, Ho Chi Minh's frenetic Chinatown, the city doesn't carve up into homogeneous districts, so visitors have to do a dot-to-dot between sights. These are almost invariably places that relate to the American War, such as the **War Remnants Museum**, the **Revolutionary Museum** and the **Presidential Palace**. But there are many religious sights too, most notably the **Jade Emperor Pagoda**.

The Revolutionary Museum

Of all the stones of empire thrown up in Vietnam by the French, few are more eye-catching than the former **Gia Long Palace** at 65 Ly Tu Trong, built in 1886 for the governor of Cochinchina. Diem decamped here in 1962, and it was in the tunnels under the building that he spent his last hours of office, before fleeing to the church in Cholon, near which he met his death. Nowadays it houses the **Revolutionary Museum** (daily 7.30am–noon & 1–4.30pm; $1), which uses photos, documents and artefacts to trace the struggle of the Vietnamese people against France and America. This is one of the city's most engaging museums, although it lacks English-language signs. Downstairs, the years of French rule come under the microscope, and there are some interesting photos of old Saigon. Upstairs, the focus turns to the war with America, and the best exhibits showcase the ingenuity of the Vietnamese – bicycle parts made into mortars, the inner tubes of a motorbike used to smuggle documents into Saigon, and so on. There's also a model of the Cu Chi tunnels.

The Reunification Palace

Five minutes' stroll through the parkland northwest of the Revolutionary Museum, a red flag billows proudly above the **Reunification Palace** (daily 7.30–11am & 1–4pm; $4 including guided tour; entrance on Nguyen Du), which occupies the site of a colonial mansion erected in 1871 to house the governor-general of Indochina. With the French departure in1954, Ngo Dinh Diem commandeered this extravagent monument as his presidential palace, but after the February 1962 assassination attempt, the place had to be pulled down. The present building was labelled the Independence Palace in 1966, only to be retitled the Reunification Hall when the South fell in 1975. Spookily unchanged from its working days, much of the building's interior is a veritable time-capsule of Sixties and Seventies kitsch: pacing its airy rooms, it's as if you've strayed into the arch-criminal's lair in a James Bond movie. Most interesting is the third floor with its presidential library, projection room and entertainment lounge complete. The basement served as the former command centre and displays archaic radio equipment and vast wall maps.

The War Remnants Museum

One block northwest of the palace, at 28 Vo Van Tan, the **War Remnants Museum** (daily 7.30–11.45am & 1.30–4.45pm; $1) is probably the city's most popular attraction. Its exhibits speak for themselves, a distressing compendium of the horrors of modern warfare. Some of the perpetrators of these horrors are on display in the courtyard outside, including a 28-tonne howitzer, a ghoulish collection of bomb parts, and a renovated Douglas Skyraider plane. A series of halls present a grisly portfolio of photographs of mutilation, napalm burns and torture. One gallery details the effects of the 75 million litres of defoliant sprays dumped across the country, including hideously malformed foetuses preserved in pickling jars; another looks at international opposition to the war as well as the American peace movement. The museum rounds off with a grisly mock-up of the tiger cages, the prison cells of Con Son Island. There's a **water puppetry theatre** (daily 9–11am & 2–4pm; $2) opposite the souvenir shop. A minimum of five people are required for a performance.

The History Museum

A pleasing, pagoda-style roof crowns the city's **History Museum** (Mon–Sat 8–11.30am & 1.30–4.30pm; Sun 8.30am–4.30pm; $1), whose main entrance is tucked just inside the gateway to the Botanical Gardens. If you want to visit the museum only, use the side entrance on Nguyen Binh Khiem to avoid paying the extra $1 for the gardens. The museum houses a train of galleries illuminating Vietnam's past from primitive times to the end of French rule by means of a decent if unastonishing array of artefacts and pictures. Other halls focus on ceramics, Buddha images from around Asia, Champa art and Vietnam's ethnic minorities. There's also a **water puppetry theatre** ($1).

Jade Emperor Pagoda

After ten minutes' walk northwest from the Botanical Gardens up Nguyen Binh Khiem, you'll reach the spectacular **Jade Emperor Pagoda** (daily 6am–6pm) on Mai Thi Luu, built by the city's Cantonese community around the turn of the century, and still its most captivating pagoda. If you visit just one temple in town, make it this one, with its exquisite panels of carved gilt woodwork, and its panoply of Taoist and Buddhist deities beneath a roof that groans under the weight of dragons, birds and animals. A statue of the Jade Emperor lords it over the main hall's central altar, sporting an impressive moustachio. The Jade Emperor monitors entry into Heaven, and his two keepers – one holding a lamp to light the way for the virtuous, the other wielding an ominous-looking axe – are on hand to aid him. A rickety flight of steps in the chamber to the right of the main hall runs up to a balcony, behind which is set a neon-haloed statue of Quan Am. Left out of the main hall stands Kim Hua, to whom women pray for children, and in the larger chamber behind you'll find the Chief of Hell alongside ten dark-wood reliefs depicting all sorts of punishments.

Cholon

The dense cluster of streets comprising the Chinese ghetto of **CHOLON** is linked to the city centre by five-kilometre-long Tran Hung Dao and best reached by Saigon Star Co bus to Huynh Thoai Yen, on Cholon's western border. The full-tilt mercantile mania here is breathtaking, and from its beehive of stores, goods spill exuberantly out onto the pavements. The ethnic Chinese, or Hoa, first began to settle here around the turn of the nineteenth century and Cholon is now the biggest Hoa community in the country. Residents tended to gravitate towards others from their region of China, and each congregation built its own places of worship and clawed out its own commercial niche – thus the Cantonese handled retailing and groceries, the Teochew dealt in tea and fish, the Fukien were in charge of rice, and so on. By the 1950s, Cholon was also thriving with vice industries, including numerous opium dens or fumeries.

If any one place epitomizes Cholon's vibrant commercialism, it's **Binh Tay Market** on Thap Muoi Binh Tay, near the bus terminus. The market's corridors are abuzz with stalls offering everything from dried fish and chilli paste to pottery and bonnets. To the north, Tran Chanh Chieu is given over to a poultry market, with cereals and pulses at its eastern end, where you'll also see the slender pink spire of **Cha Tam Church**, though its entrance is on Hoc Lac. It was in this unprepossessing little church that President Ngo Dinh Diem and his brother Ngo Dinh Nhu holed up on November 1, 1963, during the coup that had chased them out of the Gia Long Palace; as they drove into town next morning to surrender, they were both shot dead by ARVN soldiers.

Northeast of the church on tiny Lao Tu, **Quan Am Pagoda** has ridged roofs encrusted with "glove-puppet" figurines and gilt panels at the doorway depicting scenes from tradition-al Chinese court life. A Pho, the Queen of Heaven, stands in the centre of the main hall, and in the courtyard behind her are two statues of Quan Am. Nearby, **Phuoc An Hoi Quan Temple** displays menacing dragons and sea monsters on its roof, and a superb wood carv-ing of jousters and minstrels over the entrance. In the sanctuary sits Quan Cong with his blood-red face and two attendant storks. The chambers to either side are crammed with rose-wood furniture and old photographs.

Eating

Ho Chi Minh City offers an extensive scope of culinary options, ranging from streetside stalls, cafés to sophisticated restaurants. Expats, tourists and foreign influences have somewhat fuelled the global choices now available, with French establishments arguably comprising the largest contingent, but flavoursome, good value Vietnamese cuisine can be found almost everywhere. Where phone numbers are given, it's advisable to book ahead.

Around Pham Ngu Lao

Bao, 132 Nguyen Thai Hoc. Try barbecued beef wrapped in rice paper with mint leaves and noodles, or the terrific *lau* (steamboat). 11am–1am.

Kim Café, 270 De Tham. Besides breakfasts and veggie meals galore, there's guacamole, garlic bread, mashed potatoes, and a fantastic Malay-style chicken curry ($2). 7am–2am.

Pho 2000, 01–03 Phan Chu Trinh. Next to Ben Thanh Market, big bowls of delicious noodle soup for around $1 in spotless surroundings. 6am–2am.

Saigon Café, 195 Pham Ngu Lao. Always busy at breakfast owing to its fine croissants, and eggs with pork chop for just over $1. 7am–1am.

Sinh Café, 246 De Tham. The big daddy of the traveller scene, doling out average but affordable meals. 6am–midnight.

Thu Thuy, 26 Cach Mang Thanh Tam. Banana-leaf parcels of cured pork hang along the frontage of this excellent *nem* specialist, a short walk north of Pham Ngu Lao. 5am–10pm.

Tin Nghia, 9 Tran Hung Dao. Mushrooms and tofu provide the backbone to the inventive menu in this genial "pure vegetarian" restaurant. 7am–2pm & 4–8.30pm.

Zen, 175/18 Pham Ngu Lao. One of the few really authentic eating options along Pham Ngu Lao. Bargain-priced, imaginative veggie dishes including pancakes, wild red rice, and coconut and pumpkin soup. 7am–11.30pm.

Around Dong Khoi and Thi Sach

Ashoka, 17a/10 Le Thanh Ton. Smart Indian restaurant with authentic moghul Indian dishes like *cho cho tikka* (chicken marinated in yoghurt). 11.30am–2pm & 5–10pm.

Cay Xoai, 15a Thi Sach. One of several charismatic restaurants along this strip; cracking seafood is guar-anteed. There's a second outlet at no. 29. 10am–11pm.

Continental Palace Restaurant, *Hotel Continental*, 132–134 Dong Khoi (☎08/829 9201). Stylish restau-rant in the hotel's charming courtyard. Imaginative dishes such as shrimp paste on sugar cane, followed by baked seabass with sweet-and-sour sauce shouldn't cost more than $10. 6am–10pm.

Givral, 169 Dong Khoi. A Ho Chi Minh institution, facing the *Continental,* now refurbished as a restaurant with a light Western and Asian menu, plus an adjoining patisserie. 6am–10pm.

Madame Dai's Bibliotheque, 84a Nguyen Du (☎08/823 1438). The food (either French or Vietnamese set meals; $12 a head) is perfectly satisfying, but it's the ambience you pay for: guests dine in the library of the home of Madame Dai, a lawyer and ex-member of Thieu's National Assembly, who floats around like royalty. Performances of traditional music and dance follow weekend sittings. Book ahead. 7–10pm.

Quan An 39, 39 Nguyen Trung Truc. Hectic streetside operation, dishing up tasty and remarkably good-value set lunches – grilled pork on rice, veggies, soup and iced tea – all around $1. 11am–1pm.

Saigon Floating Restaurant, Ton Duc Thang. One of four boats offering dinner cruises on the Saigon River. Choose between set meals ($5 a head) or the à la carte menu; boats return by 10pm. Daily 8.30pm.

Tan Nam, 60–62 Dong Du (☎08/829 8634). Top-notch Vietnamese meat and fish dishes, plus one or two veggie alternatives, in traditional surroundings. 10am–10pm.

Vietnam House, 93–95 Dong Khoi (☎08/829 1623). Occupying a splendid louvred colonial building, this is a cracking introduction to Vietnamese food, with a pianist on the ground floor or traditional folk music upstairs each night; set lunches from $4. 11am–2pm & 5–10pm.

Around Dien Bien Phu

Banh Xeo, 46a Dinh Cong Trang. Cheap, filling Vietnamese pancakes, stuffed with shrimps, pork, beans and egg at around $1, are the speciality at this streetside place off Hai Ba Trung. 10am–10pm.

Dien Bien, 165 Dien Bien Phu. Cheap and cheerful soup kitchen and *com* shop, dishing out flavoursome *pho* and rice dishes in workaday surroundings. 6am–11pm.

Lau De, 20 Truong Dinh. Goat meat – boiled, fried or barbecued – is the order of the day at this charismatic and hugely popular two-storey restaurant. 11am–9pm.

Minh Pho, Lau Bo, 107/12 Truong Dinh. *Lau* (steamboat) and *pho* are the staples at this streetside, no-frills restaurant. Optional extras include oxtails and bone marrow. 6am–10pm.

Tinh Tam Trai, 170a Vo Thi Sau. No-frills veggie restaurant where you choose your meal from the front window. 6am–1pm & 3–9pm.

Nightlife and entertainment

Ho Chi Minh's **nightlife** is developing in direct proportion to the number of foreigners hitting town. The main listings supplements, *Time Out* and *The Guide* (see p.985), catalogue new venues.

Bars and clubs

The Dong Khoi area is predictably well-endowed with **bars** and pubs, while another boozy enclave has developed around Le Thanh Ton, Hai Ba Trung and Thi Sach; most places are shut by 1am. A BGI beer at a streetside café won't come to more than $1, but you can multiply that by four in a more upmarket bar. If you can't afford a BGI, try a **bia hoi bar**, spit-and-sawdust bars where locals glug cheap local beer over ice by the jug-full. All **clubs** and discos levy a cover charge (normally $4–5) entitling you to your first drink free.

Allez-Boo, 187 Pham Ngu Lao. Pham Ngu Lao's largest bar, heaving most nights and popular for its loud music, bar food and good selection of cocktails in a Polynesian ambience. Open 24hr.

Apocalypse Now, 2c Thi Sach. Always rowdy and sweaty at weekends, though can be dull during the week. Sandbags, *Apocalypse Now* posters and murals create a suitably Nam-ish atmosphere, but there's upfront prostitution here too. 7pm–late.

Backpackers Bar, 169 Pham Ngu Lao. A long established faithful, attracting a decent mix of drinkers; there are bar snacks and billiards but staff can be surly. Open 24hr.

Bia Hoi Nguyen Chat, 159 Pham Ngu Lao. Streetside drinking, with simple snacks, at this *bia hoi* bar, at the eastern end of Pham Ngu Lao.

Bia Hoi Thanh Nha, 6 Hai Ba Trung. Right down at the junction of Hai Ba Trung and Mac Thi Buoi, modestly located in converted garage space, but still well patronized by locals.

Club Monaco, 651 Tran Hung Dao. Huge pulsating dance area with impressive laser show brings Saigon's club scene bang up to date; new but already one of the coolest clubs in town. 8pm–2am.

Gecko Bar, 74/1a Hai Ba Trung. Themed and party nights, plus good music makes this small bar a huge favourite with expats and tourists. 5pm–late.

Gossip, 79 Tran Hung Dao. Upmarket nightclub, a hit with younger locals and tourists. A giant video screen and elevated bar look down on a large dance floor. 8pm–2.30am.

Long Phi Café, 163 Pham Ngu Lao. Stylish, slightly more expensive bar than its neighbours, but relaxing and popular, with small bistro upstairs. 11.30am–late.

Planet Europa, Saigon Superbowl, 43 Truong Son. Club that draws a young and moneyed crowd with mostly Western sounds. 6pm–2am.

Saigon–Saigon Rooftop Bar, *Caravelle Hotel*, 19 Lam Son Square. Stunning views of the city plus nightly live music in this elegant and lofty hotel bar compensate for the pricey drinks list. 4.30pm–1am.

333 Bar, 201 De Tham. Translates as the *Ba Ba Ba Bar*. No frills, but easily one of the most pleasant bars around Pham Ngu Lao, with a great choice of CDs and relaxed, friendly atmosphere. 6am–late.

Traditional entertainment

There are regular performances of modern and traditional **Vietnamese music** at 3 Thang 2's Hoa Binh Theatre (☎08/865 5199), as well as traditional theatre and dance. The only real tourist-oriented venue in the city is the *Binh Quoi Village*, whose regular programmes ($5) of folk music, traditional dancing and **water puppetry**, organized by Saigontourist, can be coupled with a Saigon River dinner-cruise. The village is at 1147 Xo Viet Nghe Tinh (☎08/899 1831) – or contact Saigontourist (☎08/829 8914). Other places to see water puppetry include the History Museum, Le Duan (on the hour; $1); and the War Remnants Museum, 28 Vo Van Tan ($2).

Shopping

Generally speaking, **shops** open daily 10am to dusk, with some larger stores staying open beyond 8pm. For lacquerware, ceramics and other **handicraft souvenirs**, try Art Arcade at 151 Dong Khoi, Precious Oil at 27 Dong Khoi, Bich Lien at 125 Dong Khoi, or MIV, 26b Le Thanh Ton. Pure **silk ao dais** can be purchased at Nap, 63 Le Thanh Ton; they also specialize in embroidered wares as do Kim Phuong, 77 Le Thanh Ton, and Minh Huong at 85 Mac Thi Buoi. For **tailoring**, try Albert at 22 Vo Van Tan or Zakka at 134 Pasteur. For **paintings on silk** and **rice paper**, try Workshop Hai, 239 and 241 De Tham. Recommended picture galleries are Hoang Hac, 73 Ly Tu Trong, and Nam Phuong, 156 Dong Khoi. Phung Dinh, 120 Le Thi Hong Gam, specializes in Vietnamese musical **instruments**. Check out the booths inside the GPO and on Dong Khoi itself for old **coins**, **stamps**, notes and greetings cards featuring typical Vietnamese scenes. Ho Chi Minh's best **bookshops** are found on Dong Khoi – Bookazine at no. 28 and Xuan Thu at no. 185; Lao Dong, opposite the *Rex* at 104 Nguyen Hue, stocks a wide range of magazines and newspapers. The city's biggest **market** is Ben Thanh, at the junction of Tran Hung Dao, Le Loi and Ham Nghi, where you can find everything from conical hats, basketware bags, Da Lat coffee and Vietnam T-shirts to buckets of eels and heaps of pigs' ears and snouts. Cholon's equivalent is Binh Tay Market (p.989), below Thap Muoi. If you're looking for American and Vietnamese army surplus, try Dan Sinh Market at 336 Nguyen Cong Tru.

Listings

Airlines Air France, 130 Dong Khoi (☎08/829 0981); British Airways, Jardine House, 58 Dong Khoi (☎08/829 1288); Cathay Pacific, Jardine House, 58 Dong Khoi (☎08/822 3203); China Airlines, 132–134 Dong Khoi (☎08/825 1388); China Southern Airlines, 52b Pham Hong Thai (☎08/829 1172); Garuda, 132–134 Dong Khoi (☎08/829 3644); Japan Airlines, Sun Wah Tower, 115 Nguyen Hue (☎08/821 9098); KLM, 2A-4A Ton Duc Thang (☎08/823 1990); Lao Aviation, 93 Pasteur (☎08/822 6990); Lufthansa, 132–134 Dong Khoi (☎08/829 8529); Malaysia Airlines, 132–134 Dong Khoi (☎08/829 2529); Pacific Airlines, 177 Vo Thi Sau (☎08/820 0978); Philippine Airlines, 132–134 Dong Khoi (☎08/823 0502); Qantas, Saigon Centre, 65 Le Loi (☎08/821 4660); Royal Cambodia Airlines, 343 Le Van Sy (☎08/844 0126); Singapore Airlines, Saigon Tower, 29 Le Duan (☎08/823 1588); Thai Airways, 65 Nguyen Du (☎08/829 2810); United Airlines, Jardine House, 58 Dong Khoi (☎08/823 4755); Vietnam Airlines, 116 Nguyen Hue (☎08/829 2118) and 20 Tran Hung Dao (☎08/836 0789).

Banks and exchange Most banks and exchanges can now arrange cash advances on Visa and Mastercard, some on JCB (usual fee is 3–4 percent) and electronic money transfers from abroad. 24-hour cash dispensers (ATMs) can be found at HSBC and ANZ; both accept Cirrus, Plus, Visa and Mastercard, with a small fee automatically deducted. HSBC, New World Hotel Building, 75 Pham Hong Thai Street (Mon–Thurs

8.30am–4.30pm, Fri 8.30am–5pm), will only change cash and travellers' cheques for HSBC members, but do cash advances against credit cards at good rates for non-members. ANZ, 11 Me Linh Square (Mon–Fri 8.30am–4pm) charges slightly higher rates for travellers' cheques and cash exchange. Vietcombank, main branch at 17 & 29 Chuong Duong, also at 132–134 Dong Khoi (Mon–Fri 7.30–11.30am & 1–4pm), offers marginally better rates, as do Vietincombank, 79a Ham Nghi (Mon–Fri 7.30–11am & 1–4pm) and Tacombank, 31 Bui Vien (Mon–Sat 7.30–11.30am & 1.30–4.30pm). Outside normal banking hours, try the Vietcombank bureaux within Fiditourist, 195 Pham Nhu Lao (Mon–Sat 7.30–11.30am & 1.30–9pm), the airport exchanges (daily 8am–9pm) or Sacombanks foreign exchange annexe on the corner of Pham Ngu Lao at 211 Nguyen Thai Hoc (Mon–Fri 7.30–11.30am & 1–7.30pm, Sat 7.30am–noon, Sun 8–11.30am & 1.30–4.30pm). Otherwise, foreign exchange kiosks on Nguyen Hue and Le Loi have extensive daily opening times.

Embassies and consulates Australia, Landmark Building, 5b Ton Duc Thanh (☎08/829 6035); Cambodia, 41 Phung Khac Khoan (☎08/829 2751); Canada, 235 Dong Khoi (☎08/824 5025); China, 39 Nguyen Thi Minh Khai (☎08/829 2457); France, 27 Nguyen Thi Minh Khai (☎08/829 7231); Germany, 126 Nguyen Dinh Chieu (☎08/829 1967); India, 49 Tran Quoc Thao (☎08/823 1539); Indonesia, 18 Phung Khac Khoan (☎08/822 3799); Italy, Room 903-904 17 Le Duan (☎08/829 8721); Japan, 13–17 Nguyen Hue (☎08/822 5314); Laos, 93 Pasteur (☎08/829 7667); Malaysia, 53 Nguyen Dinh Chieu (☎08/829 9023); Netherlands, 29 Le Duan (☎08/823 5932); New Zealand, 41 Nguyen Thi Minh Khai (☎08/822 6907); Russia, 40 Ba Huyen Thanh Quan (☎08/829 2936); Singapore, Saigon Centre, 65 Le Loi (☎08/822 5173); Sweden, 8A/11 Thai Van Lung (☎08/823 6800); Switzerland, 270A, Bach Dang (☎08/841 2211); Thailand, 77 Tran Quoc Tuan (☎08/822 2637); UK (and British Council), 25 Le Duan (☎08/823 2604); USA, 4 Le Duan (☎08/822 9433).

Emergencies Dial ☎113 for the police, ☎114 in case of fire or ☎115 for an ambulance; it's advisable to get a Vietnamese-speaker to call on your behalf.

Hospitals and clinics Oscat/AEA International Clinic, 65 Nguyen Du (☎08/829 8520), has international doctors with a standard consultation fee of $80 and upwards; they can also arrange vaccinations and emergency evacuation; Columbia Asia International Clinic, 1 No Trang Long (☎08/803 0678), has multinational doctors, charging $48 and upwards for consultations; Cholon's Cho Ray Hospital, at 201 Nguyen Chi Thanh (☎08/855 4137), has an outpatients' room for foreigners ($4 per consultation) and foreigners' ward ($20 per night); St Paul Hospital, 280 Dien Bien Phu (☎08/829 8732), is an eye specialist, charging around $6 per consultation.

Immigration Department The Ministry of the Interior, 254–258 Nguyen Trai, at the junction with Nguyen Cu Trinh.

Internet access Many hotels have business centres; there are numerous Internet and email outlets on and around De Tham and Pham Ngu Lao. Most prominent is SaigonNet, offering Internet access at 400d a minute, and computer use at 4000d an hour; at 220 De Tham, SaigonNet have a scanner and web-designing facilities. Viet Quang Public Internet, 271 Pham Ngu Lao, has the same rates, with scanner and hourly computer use. Downtown, try the Saigon Business Centre, 41–47 Dong Du, or *Tin Café,* 2a Le Duan, which has mail-box addresses and hourly computer rental.

Pharmacies There are several around Pham Ngu Lao area, including 214 De Tham and 81 Bui Vien. Downtown, there are pharmacies at 197–199 Dong Khoi, 199 and 205 Hai Ba Trung and 14a Nguyen Dinh Chieu.

Post offices The GPO (daily 6am–10pm) is beside the cathedral at the head of Dong Khoi. Poste restante is kept here, but incoming faxes (☎08/829 8540) are held nearby at 230 Hai Ba Trung, and there's a 50¢ pick-up fee. There are also post offices at 125 Cong Quynh and 199–205 Nguyen Thai Hoc, serving the Pham Ngu Lao area, and one at Ga Saigon (Railway station) – all of which have poste restante.

Telephone services There are IDD, fax and telex facilities at the GPO and numerous IDD telephone kiosks around De Tham and Pham Ngu Lao, plus IDD facilities at most hotels.

Travel agencies Ann's Tourist, 58 Ton That Tung (☎08/833 2564); Sinh Café, 246–248 De Tham (☎08/835 5601); Kim Travel, 270 De Tham (☎08/836 9859); Peace Tours, 60 Vo Van Tan (☎08/822 6909); Cam On Tours, Unit 63, 6th Floor, 7 Phung Khac Khoan (☎08/825 6074); Fidi Tourist, 195 Pham Ngu Lao (☎08/836 1922); Tomateco Pro Tour, 40 Bui Vien (☎08/837 3716). Larger, more upmarket outfits include Saigontourist, 49 Le Thanh Ton (☎08/829 8914); Vietnamtourism, Room 101, Mondial Centre, 203 Dong Khoi (☎08/824 2000) and 234 Nam Ky Khoi Nghia (☎08/829 0776); Diethelm Travel, International Business Centre, 1a Me Linh Square (☎08/829 4932) and Exotissimo Travel, Saigon Trade Centre, 37 Ton Duc Thang (☎08/825 1723).

Around Ho Chi Minh City

The single most popular trip out of the city takes in two of Vietnam's most memorable sights: the **Cu Chi tunnels**, for twenty years a bolt hole, first for Viet Minh agents, and later for Viet

Cong cadres; and the weird and wonderful **Cao Dai Holy See** at Tay Ninh, the fulcrum of the country's most charismatic indigenous religion.

The Cu Chi tunnels

During the American War, the villages around the district of Cu Chi supported a substantial VC presence. Faced with American attempts to neutralize them, they quite literally dug themselves out of harm's way, and the legendary **Cu Chi tunnels** were the result. Today, the tunnels have been widened to allow passage for Western tourists but it's still a dark, sweaty, claustrophobic experience. The most popular site is **Ben Dinh** (daily 7.30am–5pm; $4), 40km from Ho Chi Minh City and best visited on a tour, but also accessible by bus from **Ben Thanh** and **An Suong** stations in Ho Chi Minh. Buses stop in **CU CHI**, from where you'll need to take a Honda om for the final 10km to the site; on a motorbike, turn right off the highway when you reach Cu Chi post office.

Anti-colonial Viet Minh dug the first **tunnels** here in the late 1940s and over a decade later, Viet Cong (VC) activists controlling this staunchly anti-government area went to ground. By 1965, 250km of tunnels criss-crossed Cu Chi and surrounding areas. Tunnels could be as small as 80cm wide and 80cm high, and were sometimes four levels deep; there were latrines, wells, meeting rooms and dorms here, as well as rudimentary hospitals, where operations were carried out by torchlight using instruments fashioned from shards of ordnance. At times it was necessary to stay below ground for weeks on end: inhabitants often had to lie on the floor in order to get enough oxygen to breathe. American attempts to flush out the tunnels proved ineffective. They evacuated villagers into strategic hamlets and then used defoliant sprays and bulldozers to rob the VC of cover, in "scorched earth" operations. GIs known as tunnel rats would go down themselves, but faced booby traps and bombs. Finally they sent in the B52s to level the district with carpet bombing.

The Cao Dai Holy See at Tay Ninh

Northwest of Cu Chi, signed 10km off Highway 22 at **Tay Ninh**, a grand gateway marks the entrance to the grounds of the fantastical confection of styles that is **Cao Dai Cathedral**; buses to Tay Ninh depart from Ho Chi Minh City's An Suong or Mien Dong bus stations, but a tour is preferable. The Cathedral is the Holy See of the Cao Dai religion, a faith that was founded in October 1926 as a fusion of oriental and occidental religions, propounding the concept of a universal god. Cao Daism borrowed the structure and terminology of the Catholic Church, but is primarily entrenched in Buddhism, Taoism and Confucianism. By following its five commandments, Cao Daists look to hasten the evolution of the soul through reincarnation. Tay Ninh became the Cao Daists' Holy See in 1927 and the first pope was Le Van Trung, a reformed mandarin from Cholon.

The Cathedral's central portico is topped by a bowed, first-floor balcony and a Divine Eye, the most recurrent motif in the building. A figure in semi-relief emerges from the towers to either side: on the left is Cao Daism's first female cardinal, Lam Huong Thanh, and on the right, Le Van Trung, its first pope. Men enter the cathedral through an entrance in the right wall, women by a door to the left, and all must take off their shoes. The eclectic ideology of Cao Daism is mirrored in the **interior**, and tourists are welcome to wander through the nave, as long as they remain in the aisles, and don't stray between the rows of pink pillars, entwined by green dragons, that march up the chamber. The papal chair stands at the head of the chamber, its arms carved into dragons. Dominating the chamber, though, and guarded by eight scary silver dragons, a vast, duck-egg-blue sphere, speckled with stars, rests on a polished, eight-sided dais. The ubiquitous Divine Eye peers through clouds painted on the front. **Services** are held daily at 6am, noon, 6pm and midnight and are well worth attending. A traditional band plays as robed worshippers chant, pray and sing.

THE MEKONG DELTA

The orchards, paddy fields and swamplands of the **MEKONG DELTA** stretch from Ho Chi Minh's city limits southwest to the Gulf of Thailand, crisscrossed by nine tributaries of the Mekong River. By the time it reaches Vietnam, the mighty Mekong has already covered more than 4000km from its source high up on the Tibetan Plateau, via southern China, Burma, Laos, Thailand and Cambodia – a journey that ranks it as Asia's third-longest river, after the Yangtse and Yellow rivers. Here at its delta not only does it water "Vietnam's rice bowl", but it also serves as a crucial transportation artery, teeming with rowing boats, sampans, ferries and floating markets. In fact, the most enjoyable way to experience delta-life is by boat: most people hire boats in **My Tho**, but from here a ferry crosses the uppermost strand of the Tien Giang to laid-back **Ben Tre**. You can cross the main body of the Tien Giang on the My Thuan ferry, or the soon-to-be-opened My Thuan bridge nearby, both convenient for visiting the flower markets of **Sa Dec** and bustling **Vinh Long**, which are situated on the "island" between Tien Giang and Hau Giang. **Can Tho**, on the west bank of the Hau Giang, holds the delta's most famous floating markets; access to the city is by ferry or via the Can Tho bridge, due for completion in this edition's lifetime. From here, a road runs via **Long Xuyen** to the Cambodian border towns of **Chau Doc** and **Ha Tien**. At the time of writing, it was not possible to cross into Cambodia from either point; however future plans include the border crossing opening to foreigners at Chau Doc and hydrofoils running from Chau Doc to Phnom Penh. Hydrofoils now operate between Ho Chi Minh City and My Tho, Can Tho, Vinh Long and Chau Doc.

My Tho

Seventy kilometres southwest of Ho Chi Minh City, **MY THO** sits on the north bank of Tien Giang, the Mekong River's northernmost strand, and attracts crowds of tourists because of its boat trips. The town is ringed by waterways, and the main tourist-oriented hotels, businesses and restaurants are on the waterfront streets of 30 Thang 4, which runs east–west along the town's southern edge, and Trung Trac, which runs northeast–southwest, round the corner from 30 Thang 4, along the west bank of Bao Dinh canal. The lower of the two bridges spanning Bao Dinh canal deposits you at the start of waterfront Phan Thanh Gian, home to My Tho's modest **Chinese Quarter**, where shopfronts are piled to the rafters with sugar-cane poles, watermelons and fish awaiting transportation up to Ho Chi Minh. A cyclo journey east of Phan Thanh Gian, Nguyen Trung Truc's attractive **Vinh Trang Pagoda** (daily 7.30am–noon & 2–5pm), with its Rajah's palace-style front facade, has become rather a tourist trap. It's said that VC soldiers hid here in the Sixties, but today it's home only to monks. The main chamber has formidable darkwood pillars and tons of gilt woodwork, and the pagoda boasts classical pillars, Grecian-style mouldings and glazed tiles.

Boat trips on the delta

Taking a **boat trip** on the Mekong is the undoubted highlight of a stay in My Tho. Of the four nearby islands, Tan Long Island, Phung Island and Thoi Son Island are all regularly visited by tourist boats, though you'll get more time on the water if you ask to explore the labyrinthine north coastline of Ben Tre Province, or just to idle along the river – in which case the **Dong Tam snake farm** (daily 7am–5pm; $1) provides an interesting enough focus. Whatever you do, it's worth making an early start to catch the river at its mistiest. Beyond its chaotic shoreline of stilthouses and boatyards, **Tan Long** ("Dragon Island") boasts bounteous sapodilla, coconut and banana plantations. **Phung Island** (daily 7am–5pm) is famed as the home of an offbeat religious sect set up three decades ago by the eccentric Coconut Monk, Ong Dao Dua, but only the skeleton of the open-air complex he established remains.

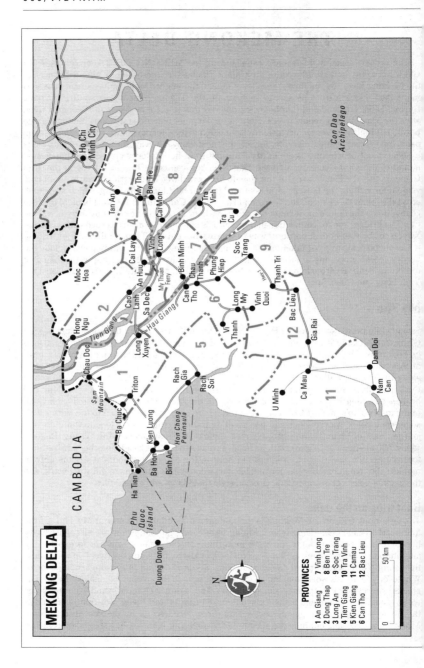

MEKONG DELTA

Ho Chi Minh City

Con Dao Archipelago

Tan An

My Tho
Ben Tre

8

Cai Lay
Vinh Long
Cai Mon

Tra Vinh

10

3

4

Binh Minh

Tra Cu

Moc Hoa

An Huu

Chau Thanh

Soc Trang

7

Cao Lanh

My Thuan Ferry

Can Tho

Phung Hiep

Thanh Tri

9

2

Sa Dec

Hau Giang

Long My

Hong Ngu

Tien Giang

Long Xuyen

Vinh Quoi

Bac Lieu

Chau Doc

Vi Thanh

12

Sam Mountain

1

Triton

Rach Gia

5

Gia Rai

Ba Chuc

Rach Soi

Dam Doi

CAMBODIA

Kien Luong

Hon Chong Peninsula

U Minh

Ca Mau

Nam Can

11

Ba Hon
Binh An

Ha Tien

Phu Quoc Island

Duong Dong

N

PROVINCES
1 An Giang	7 Vinh Long
2 Dong Thap	8 Ben Tre
3 Long An	9 Soc Trang
4 Tien Giang	10 Tra Vinh
5 Kien Giang	11 Camau
6 Can Tho	12 Bac Lieu

0   50 km

Beyond the compound stretch acres of orchards, whose fruits can be sampled at the several cafés dotted around the island. **Thoi Son** ("Unicorn Island") is the largest of the four islands and most tours out of Ho Chi Minh stop here for lunch. Slender canals, their banks shaded by water coconut trees, allow boats to weave through its interior.

The cheapest way of getting onto the water is to take a **public ferry** to one of the islands. For services to Phung Island, you'll need to get across to Ben Tre by public ferry from the **Ben Tre Ferry Terminal**, 300m west of Vong Nho Market, and from there take another boat to the island; those to Tan Long leave from opposite the *Huong Duong* hotel on Trung Trac, while Thoi Son ferries leave from either Vong Nho or Binh Duc markets.

However, for a full-on tropical river experience, you should **charter** a boat. Tien Giang Tourist, with three offices along 30 Thang 4, and Ben Tre Tourist Company, at 4/1 Le Thi Hong Gam, both offer boat trips to the islands, but touts for private companies will undercut them, offering three-hour trips for $5–7.

Practicalities

Buses terminate at Tien Giang bus station, 3km northwest of town, from where cyclos shuttle into the centre. Onward departures are from the same place, though with direct connections leaving before 7am, you'll probably need to take a bus to the My Thuan ferry and transfer onto a service along the highway. **Hydrofoils** from Can Tho, Ho Chi Minh, Vinh Long and Chau Doc disembark at the jetty next to the *Cuu Long Restaurant*, from where onward tickets can be purchased. Cargo/passenger **boats** heading to My Thuan (for Vinh Long) and Chau Doc use the jetty below Vong Nho Market, 200m west of the foot of Tran Hung Dao (daily at noon, 1pm & 5pm). Vietnam Airlines have a branch next to the *Chuong Duong Hotel*.

Cyclos are plentiful, and Honda oms await custom at the junction of Trung Trac and Thu Khoa Huan. **Bicycles** can be rented ($1) from the *Hung Vuong Hotel*, and a car plus driver is available from either Tien Giang or Ben Tre tourist companies on the river. The **State Bank**, at Thu Khoa Huan's western end, changes travellers' cheques and advances cash against Visa and Mastercard; the Agribank on the corner of Le Loi and Thu Khoa Huan changes dollars. **Internet** facilities are found at Vinh Tan Computer, 203 Le Dai Hanh.

The *Cong Doan* (☎073/8724324; ②–③), beside the GPO on the waterfront 30 Thang 4, has spartan but light double **rooms**; the *Rang Dong* (☎073/874410; ②), 300m west along the street, has slightly smarter rooms, all with air-con; the *Hung Vuong* (☎073/876868; ⑤), one block above the church in the north of town, is friendly and quiet, but overpriced. The smartest place in town, the brand-new *Chuong Duong* (☎073/870875; ⑤) opposite the GPO, boasts an impressive riverside location.

The well-cooked Vietnamese **food** at no-frills *Chi Thanh*, 56 Trung Trac, draws nightly crowds, or further along, the *Viet Hai* at 50 Trung Trac serves great breakfasts and affordable shrimps and oysters on a terrace built out over the channel on stilts. Out along the Tien Giang, the *Cuu Long Restaurant* is reasonable, but the open-air riverside terrace found at the *Chuong Duong Hotel* restaurant takes some beating, with an affordable and extensive menu.

Ben Tre and Cai Mon

The few travellers who push on beyond My Tho into riverlocked **Ben Tre Province** are rewarded with breathtaking scenery of fruit orchards and coconut groves. Ben Tre town itself is a pleasant place, a world away from touristed My Tho. **Ferries** from My Tho disgorge their passengers 11km north of Ben Tre, from where a Honda loi will take you into town. You could also catch a bus – buses either terminate at the bus station 2km out of town, or nearer the centre at Truc Giang Lake. Near here, on Dong Khoi, Ben Tre Tourism (☎075/829618) can help with **tours** and car-rental.

Once you've scanned Ben Tre's buzzing **market** in the centre of town, you'll want to pass over the quaint bridge leading to Ben Tre River's more rustic south bank, where scores of boats moor in front of thatch houses. With a bicycle (bring one from My Tho, or ask at your hotel), you can explore the maze of dirt tracks and visit the riverside **wine factory**, 450m west of the bridge, where *ruou trang* (rice wine) fizzes away in earthenware jars.

Honda oms congregate outside the GPO in the centre of Ben Tre, and for $3.50 they'll whisk you off on a three-hour round-trip to the fruit orchards of **CAI MON**. Ten minutes' ride west of town you cross a river on the Ham Luong Ferry, then head off into waxy green paddy fields to the coconut village of Ba Vat (20min). Twenty-five minutes later, the road reaches Cai Mon, a sleepy community whose residents make a living by cultivating fruit in the vast plain of orchards, veined by miles of canals and paths.

The riverside *Hung Vuong* (☎075/822866; ②–③) has the poorest rooms but the best location of Ben Tre's **hotels**; *Ben Tre* (☎075/822223; ②–③) is better value, but at the wrong end of town. The *Ben Tre Floating Restaurant*, near the bridge, has seen better days, but is a good spot for a sunset drink and more enticing than the hotel restaurants.

Vinh Long

Ringed by water and besieged by boats and tumbledown stilthouses, the island that forms the heart of **VINH LONG** has the feel of a medieval fortress. Waterfront hotels, restaurants and cafés conjure up a riviera atmosphere far quainter and more genuine than My Tho's, from where you can watch life on the Co Chien River roll by. There's not much else to see in town, aside from a few war relics and a handful of colonial buildings, but the chief attraction is the trip to An Binh Island. Cuu Long Tourist at the top of 1 Thang 5 can also arrange leisurely, though pricey, **boat trips** on the Co Chien River; the boat-owners themselves charge less and can be contacted on the waterfront; theoretically, they're not supposed to take tourists, but their boats usually set off from the back of the market on 1 Thang 5.

An Binh Island

A five-minute ferry ride across the Co Chien River from the top of town accesses a patch of the delta's most breathtaking scenery. Known by locals as **An Binh Island**, in fact it's a jigsaw of bite-sized pockets of land, skeined by a fine web of channels and criss-crossed by dirt paths, making it ideal for a morning's rambling. A grove of longan trees a few paces north of the jetty shades sandy, century-old **Tien Chau Pagoda**. Inside, monks sup tea against the ghoulish backdrop of a mural depicting sinners being trampled by horses and devoured by snakes in the ten Buddhist hells. As an alternative to following the island's narrow tracks and single-log bridges, you could rent a **boat** out of Vinh Long. With a vessel at your disposal, it's also possible to tootle along the river or, provided you set out early enough, head upriver to the floating market at Cai Be (5–11am).

Practicalities

Long-distance **buses** pull in at the provincial bus station, 2km southwest of Vinh Long on Nguyen Hue. You'll have to return here when you leave, unless you're off to Sa Dec, which is served by the local station in the centre of town. If you're coming from My Tho, take a bus to An Huu (1hr), then a xe lam for the 4km to the **My Thuan ferry** across the Mekong. Buses marked Vinh Long or Tra Vinh sometimes meet the ferry, otherwise you can share a Honda loi or take a xe lam for the 9km into town. Coming from the north, some buses may take you direct to My Thuan and across the river, dropping you just outside town en-route for onward destinations. Once the My Thuon bridge is completed this should make travel a lot simpler. If you've battled across from Ben Tre, you'll need to take a ferry from An Binh Island, which will drop you 3km east of central Vinh Long. A daily hydrofoil service operating between Chau Doc, My Tho and Ho Chi Minh arrives at and departs from the Vinh Long jetty, 1, 1 Thang 5.

Most of Vinh Long's **accommodation** options are near the waterfront 1 Thang 5. The down-at-heel *Long Chau*, or *Cuu Long C* (☎070/823611; ②–③), boasts the cheapest river views in town, but the nearby *Cuu Long 'A' Hotel* (☎070/822494; ③–⑥) has homely, better-value rooms. The recently upgraded *Cuu Long 'B'* (☎070/823656; ⑤–⑦) has smart though pricey rooms, also with fine views of the Vinh Long Riviera. Away from the water, the gloomy *An Binh* at 3 Hoang Thai Hieu (☎070/823190; ③–⑥) has a range of somewhat overpriced quarters, but for the best deal in town, head for the *Phuong Hoang Guesthouse* on Hung Vuong (☎070/825185; ③), with immaculate, sparkling rooms, which are cheaper if you don't use air-con.

For **food**, the *Com Binh Dan* restaurant next door to the *Long Chau* serves cheap and wholesome Vietnamese and Western dishes from an English menu. East of the market, the *Chieu Ky* doles out rice and noodle staples, while further along, both the *Lan Que* and *Tu Hai*, opposite each other on 2 Thang 9, serve good fish dishes. The Incombank at the three-way roundabout west of town changes travellers' cheques; for straight US **currency** transactions its Hoang Thai Hieu branch is more central.

Sa Dec

A cluster of brick and tile kilns announces your arrival in the charming town of **SA DEC**, 20km upriver of Vinh Long. French novelist Marguerite Duras lived here as a child, and the town's stuccoed shop-houses, riverside mansions and remarkably busy stretch of the Mekong provided the backdrop for the movie adaptation of her novel *The Lover*.

Buses terminate 300m southeast of the town centre: turn left out of the station and continue straight across the bridge. The town's three main arteries – Nguyen Hue, Tran Hung Dao and Hung Vuong – branch off to your right. Duck straight down into Nguyen Hue to find Sa Dec's extensive riverside market. Half-way up the street, ferries cross to the childhood **home of Marguerite Duras**, a crumbling old colonial villa (now a police station) that's the nearest of the two villas to the place where boats drop you.

Across the metal bridge that runs over the top of Nguyen Hue and across the river, climb down the steps to your left and follow the river road west and past Sa Dec's Cao Dai temple: after twenty-five minutes, a gaggle of cafés tells you that you've hit **Qui Dong**, Sa Dec's famed flower village, where over a hundred farms cultivate ferns, fruit trees, shrubs and flowers. The 6000 hectares of Tu Ton Rose Garden cultivate over 580 species of plants and get the lion's share of tourists visiting the village (it's especially crowded on Sundays).

The only tourist **hotel** in town at present is Hung Vuong's reasonably appealing, but jaded *Sa Dec* (☎067/861430; ②–⑤). When it's time for **eating**, the friendly *My Restaurant* and the nearby family-run *Chanh Ky* both serve up cheap and tasty rice and noodle staples from English menus; both are on Quoc Lo 80 near the GPO. Otherwise, the *Quan Com Cay Sung* on the crossroads below the *Sa Dec Hotel* is a popular local *com* shop.

Can Tho

Sited at the confluence of the Can Tho and Hau Giang rivers, **CAN THO** is the delta's biggest city (pop. 310,000), a major trading centre and transport interchange. However, abundant rice fields are never far away, and boat trips along the canals and rivers, through memorable floating markets, are undoubtedly Can Tho's star attraction. Broad Hoa Binh is the city's backbone, and the site of the new **Ho Chi Minh Museum** (Tues, Thurs & Fri 8–11am & 1.30–4.30pm, Sat & Sun 8–11am & 7–9pm), where yet more photographs and army ordnance are displayed. Can Tho was the last city to succumb to the North Vietnamese Army, a day after the fall of Saigon, on May 1, 1975 – the date that has come to represent the absolute reunification of the country. The city's **central market** swallows up the entire central segment of waterfront Hai Ba Trung. North of the market on Hai Ba Trung, **Ong Pagoda** is a prosperous place financed and built late last century by a wealthy Chinese townsman, Huynh An Thai. Inside, a ruddy-faced Quan Cong presides, flaunting Rio Carnival-style headgear. On his right is Than Tai, to whom a string of families come on the first day of every month, asking, not unreasonably, for money and good fortune.

Boat trips and floating markets

Every morning an armada of boats takes to the web of waterways spun across Can Tho Province, and makes for one of its **floating markets**. Lacking the almost staged beauty and charm of Bangkok's riverine markets, as snapshots of Mekong life these tableaux are still unbeatable. Everything your average villager could ever need is on sale, from haircuts to coffins, though predictably fruit and vegetables make up the lion's share of the wares on offer. Each boat's produce is identifiable by a sample hanging off a bamboo mast in its bow.

Of the three major markets in the province, two are west of the city. First up, 7km out of Can Tho, is the busiest of the three, **Cai Rang**, sited under Cai Rang Bridge. Another 10km west and you're at the modest **Phong Dien**. Both see relatively few tourists and are correspondingly friendly. **Phung Hiep**, 32km south of Can Tho, on the road to Soc Trang, is a shadow of its former self, but its floating market is still an interesting sight. Best viewed from Phung Hiep Bridge, which carries the main road across the river, dozens of boats jostle and bump along the water's edge, whilst their owners shout out to advertise their wares.

It's possible to visit Cai Rang, Phong Dien and Phung Hiep by boat, but with the round-trip to Phong Dien (passing Cai Rang) taking around five hours, and getting to Phung Hiep and back more like eight, you'd be wiser to go by **road**, and rent a sampan (approximately $2–3 an hour) on arrival. A Honda om ($3–4 return) is the safer bet for Phong Dien, while Phung Hiep is served by xe lams from Ly Tu Trong. However you travel, you'll need a really **early start**: any boat-owner who tells you the spectacle is just as impressive throughout the day is lying. Most organized tours take in one of the above markets and return to Can Tho via the maze of surrounding canals.

Practicalities

Long-distance buses take you across the Hau Giang estuary and into the Mekong's transportational hub, Can Tho's **bus station**, 1200m northwest of town at the junction of Cach Mang Thang Tam and Hung Vuong. Most buses terminate here, though local services from Vinh Long dump you on the north bank of the Hau Giang River at **Binh Minh**, from where you'll have to take a short ferry ride. The Can Tho Bridge, presently under construction, should make travel across the Hau Giang easier. **Hydrofoils** from Ho Chi Minh and My Tho arrive at the Ninh Kieu jetty, at the top end of Hai Ba Trung. The Can Tho Tourist Company, at 20 Hai Ba Trung, has a Vietnam Airlines branch and can help with **car rental** and **boat tours**, though for the latter, you'll do better to book an unofficial boat ($2–3 per hour) through a tout on Hai Ba Trung.

Most **hotels** are on Hai Ba Trung and Chau Van Liem. Delightful, cottagey little *Tay Ho*, 36 Hai Ba Trung (☎071/823392; ②–③), sits in an aged row of shop-houses and has rooms ranging from basic to comfortable. The salubrious *Hau Giang 'B'*, 27 Chau Van Liem (☎071/821636; ②–③), has light, fairly spacious rooms and some air-con, and *Huy Hoang*, 35 Ngo Duc Ke (☎071/825833; ②) is also well-maintained, with pleasant enough rooms that are popular with tour groups. For more upmarket accommodation, try the agreeable and smart *Quoc Te*, 12 Hai Ba Trung (☎071/822080; ⑤), or the attractive and well-appointed *Ninh Kieu*, 2 Hai Ba Trung (☎071/824583; ⑤) next to the boat jetty; some of the rooms have great river views. Rates at both hotels include breakfast.

Mekong Restaurant, 38 Hai Ba Trung (24hr) is hard to top for cheap, flavoursome Vietnamese and Chinese **meals** – fried fish in sour sauce ($1.50) comes highly recommended. *Ninh Kieu*, 2 Hai Ba Trung (6am–10pm), is stylishly set on a riverside terrace and serves steamboat for two at less than $4, whilst the *Nambo Café*, 50 Hai Ba Trung (9am–11pm) serves French-influenced dishes in colonial-style elegance and has a pleasant balcony overlooking the riverfront. For simpler, less expensive fare, head for the hole-in-the-wall *Vinh Loi*, 42 Hai Ba Trung (5am–2am), which has a good reputation for *banh bao* and pork satty, or *Thien Hoa*, 26 Hai Ba Trung (9am–2pm & 5pm–midnight), where you get huge portions of sour soups and other local food.

Vietcombank at 7 Hoa Binh will **change** cash and travellers' cheques and arrange cash advances against Visa and Mastercard, while further along, the **GPO** has IDD, fax and poste restante services. **Internet** facilities can be found at Nhat Minh Internet Service, 26–28 Ly Tu Trong.

Long Xuyen

The dull town of **LONG XUYEN**, 60km northwest of Can Tho, is of interest only as a transport hub and location at the junction of the two main routes to the delta's northwestern corner. If you do need to while away a few hours, you could visit the birthplace of Ton Duc Thang, successor to Ho Chi Minh as president of the Democratic Republic of Vietnam, on My Hoa Hung Island (Tues–Sun 7.30–11am & 1–5pm). The **An Giang Museum** (Tues & Thurs 8–10.30am, Sat & Sun 8–10.30am & 2–4pm; $1), at 77 Thoai Ngoc Hau, also displays artefacts from the ancient port of Oc Eo.

Buses from Can Tho and Chau Doc stop a few hundred metres south of town, on Tran Hung Dao – coming from Chau Doc, yell for the driver to stop as you pass the cathedral. From Sa Dec and Cao Lanh you'll reach town via the An Hoa **ferry** at the end of Ly Thai To; services from Ho Chi Minh City come either through Can Tho or – more usually – Cao Lanh, and pick up passengers for the return journey at either the ferry terminal, or the intersection of Tran Hung Dao and Hung Vuong – express buses to Chau Doc also pass through here. Passenger/cargo **boats** for Sa Dec, Chau Doc, Rach Gia and Choi Moi depart from Long Xuyen's other ferry station, east of the bridge on Le Thi Nhieu – enquire locally for times and costs. Vietcombank, 1 Hung Vuong, changes **travellers' cheques** – something none of Chau Doc's banks do yet.

The best place to **stay** are the cheap and cheery rooms at the *An Long* (076/843298; ①–②). If full, its neighbour, the family-run *Thoai Chau 2*, 283a Tran Hung Dao (☎076/843882; ①–③) is also a good bet. Pleasant and good-value rooms are found at the An *Giang*, 40 Hai Ba Trung (☎076/841297; ②–③), the *Xuan Phuong*, 68 Nguyen Trai (☎076/841041; ②–③) or the smart and central *Long Xuyen* (☎076/841927; ②–③). When it's time to **eat**, the spotless *com* shops *Tiem Com Huynh Lai* on 252/1 Nguyen Trai and the nearby *Thang Loi* come recommended for their tasty, cheap rice and *pho* dishes.

Chau Doc

Snuggled against the west bank of the Hau Giang River, next to the Cambodian border, **CHAU DOC** was under Cambodian rule until the mid-eighteenth century and still sustains a large Khmer community. Forays by Pol Pot's genocidal Khmer Rouge into this corner of the delta led to the Vietnamese invasion of Cambodia in 1978, but today Chau Doc is a bustling, friendly town that's worth visiting. First stop should be the town's **market**, located roughly between Quang Trung, Doc Phu Thu, Tran Hung Dao and Nguyen Van Thoi. A few colonial relics are on parade in nearby Doc Phu Thu, some of whose grand shop-house terraces flaunt arched upper-floor windows and decorous wrought-iron struts. A grand, four-tiered gateway deep in the belly of the market announces **Quan Cong Temple**, ornamented with two rooftop dragons and some vivid murals. Inside, Quan Cong sports a green robe and bejewelled crown.

Northwest up Tran Hung Dao, long boardwalks lead to sizeable stilthouse communities, and from here, at the junction with Thuong Dang Le, you can get a ferry across the Hau Giang River to the stilthouses of **Con Tien Island**. Opposite the GPO, downriver from the first jetty, a second jetty runs boats out to Cham-dominated **Chau Giang District**. Turn right when you dock, and you'll discover kampung-style wooden houses, sarongs and white prayer caps that betray the influence of Islam, as do the twin domes and minaret of the Mubarak Mosque. Just beyond the mosque, another ferry delivers you back to the west bank, setting you down just below the *Victoria Chau Doc Hotel*.

Sam Mountain

Arid, brooding **Sam Mountain** rises dramatically from an ocean of paddy fields 5km south-west of Chau Doc, and Vietnamese tourists flock here to worship at its clutch of pagodas and shrines. From town, a road runs straight to the foot of the mountain, covered by xe dap lois and xe lams, or easily done by a rented bicycle. As you approach from town, you'll see the kitsch, 1847-built **Tay An Pagoda**, its frontage awash with portrait photographers, beggars, joss stick vendors and bird-sellers. Inside, there are over two hundred gaudy statues of deities and Buddhas, including a goddess with a thousand eyes and a thousand hands, on whose mound of heads teeters a tiny Quan Am. A track leads **up the mountain** from beyond a large, mustard-coloured school, 1km around Sam in a clockwise direction. After fifteen minutes, an observatory affords fine views of the patchwork of fields below. It's another twenty minutes to the top, where "military zone no picture" is daubed in red on a boulder at the peak and Vietnamese soldiers keep a sharp eye on the Cambodian border.

Practicalities

Buses offload southeast of town, on Le Loi, from where xe dap lois run into town; some minibuses also offload in the centre on Thu Khoa Nghia. Bring plenty of **cash** with you, as the Incombank at 70 Nguyen Huu Canh doesn't change cheques. Around 400m up Tran Hung Dao, heading north from the Con Tien jetty, a narrow concrete path marked "Ben Tau Ha Tien" signals the departure point for the passenger/cargo boat along the Vinh Te Canal, which defines the border with Cambodia, **to Ha Tien** (three times weekly 5am; $5) and Kien Luong, 15km south of Ha Tien (daily 9am; $5). Hydrofoils from Vinh Long, My Tho and Ho Chi Minh City disembark at the jetty in front of the **Victoria Chau Doc Hotel**, from where onward tickets are sold. Hydrofoils from Chau Doc to Phnom Penh are also in the pipeline, once border restrictions are lifted. With your own motorbike, or on a Honda om, you could negotiate the Chau Doc–Ha Tien road, which runs more or less parallel to the Vinh Te Canal. It's a very rough and tiring ride, but the stunning scenery more than compensates. Several buses a day ply this route, although sometimes during the wet season, if the road gets impassable, the bus may re-route.

For somewhere to **stay**, the best deal in town is the waterfront *Thuan Loi Guesthouse*, 18 Tran Hung Dao (☎076/8661340; ②–③), with its prime views of the river and stilt restaurant; the choice of comfortable, clean rooms includes bargain fan quarters. The *Thanh Tra*, 77 Thu Khoa Nghia (☎076/866788; ②), also gets a steady flow of guests and standards are fair for the price range. *My Loc*, 51 Nguyen Van Thoai (☎076/866455; ①–②), is a bit faded, but is friendly and geared to tourists. Cheapest of the lot is the *Nha Khach 44*, 44 Doc Phu Tru (☎076/866540; ①), with basic, gloomy, but sizeable rooms with attached bathrooms. Finally, the *Nui Sam Hotel* (☎076/861666; ⑤) is clinically clean and characterless, but it's ideally situated at the base of Sam Mountain.

For **food**, *Lam Hung Ky*, 71 Chi Lang, serves the town's most imaginative menu, featuring dishes like beef with bitter melon and black beans, while the *Thanh* and its near neighbour *Truong Van*, on Quang Trung, serve tasty, inexpensive Vietnamese dishes and are popular with both tourists and locals.

Rach Gia

RACH GIA teeters precariously over the Gulf of Thailand and is home to a farming and fishing community of almost 150,000 people and is also the gateway to the outlying Phu Quoc Island. A small islet in the mouth of the Cai Lon River forms the hub of town, its central area shoehorned tightly between Le Loi and Tran Phu, but the urban sprawl spills over bridges to the north and south of it and onto the mainland. Once you've seen the wartime souvenirs and Oc Eo relics – shards of pottery, coins and bones – of the pedestrian **museum** at 21 Nguyen Van Troi (Mon–Fri 7–11am &1.30–5pm) and dived through the lively markets, you've pretty uch bled Rach Gia town dry of sights. Walk west along **Bach Dang** for a few hundred etres, though, and the town springs spectacularly to life. To your right is the upper channel f the Cai Lon River, choked by blue fishing boats, and the shoreline is a hive of activity: men nd women darn nets, charcoal sellers hawk their wares to ships' captains and roadside cafés eave with fishermen.

Of Rach Gia's handful of pagodas, only the **Nguyen Trung Truc Temple**, at 18 Nguyen ong Tru, is worth making the effort for. From 1861 to 1868, Nguyen Trung Truc spear-eaded anti-French guerrilla activities in the western region of the delta (his statue stands in ie centre of Rach Gia). The riotous colour scheme of the temple roof, with its lurid pink tiles sing to powder-blue crests that are stalked by dragons, is plainly visible from a distance. side there's a portrait of Nguyen in black robe and hat.

racticalities

uses from points north pull up 500m above town, at 30 Thang 4's Noi Tinh station. Arrivals om Long Xuyen and beyond hit the coast at Rach Soi, 7km southeast of Rach Gia. Some con-nue into town, dropping you outside the *Palace Hotel*; others terminate at Rach Soi bus sta-on, from where a xe lam or Honda om will get you to the centre. Arriving at the **airport** lights from Ho Chi Minh and Phu Quoc Island), you'll need to catch a xe lam to Rach Soi, 1d then another into Rach Gia.

When you're ready to **move on**, xe lams heading back to Rach Soi can be picked up on ran Phu; if you're heading for Ha Tien or Hom Chong you'll leave from the 30 Thang 4 bus ation. If you're taking one of the couple of nightly express buses **to Ho Chi Minh**, you'll pard in town: buy tickets in advance from the booth marked "Toc Hanh" in front of the ietcombank or the *Binh Minh Hotel* in the centre of town. From the "Ben Tau Rach Meo" rminal, 5km south of town on Ngo Quyen, passenger/cargo **boats** leave for destinations in ie delta. Boats bound for Phu Quoc Island depart daily from Ben Tau Khach Bien Quay,)0m west of Nguyen Trung temple. Kien Giang Tourism at 12 Ly Tu Trong (☎077/862081) in arrange **tours** and car hire around Rach Gia. Vietcombank exchanges travellers' ieques, **cash** and can advance cash against Visa and Mastercard – a priority if you're push-g on to Ha Tien or the Hon Chong Peninsula. As far as **accommodation** goes, the cheery *alace Hotel* (☎077/863049; ④) has smart refurbished rooms, but its endearing top-floor gar-•ts sharing communal bathrooms are only $5 a piece. Otherwise, the central *Binh Minh* ☎077/862154; ②) is a very reasonable budget option and all rooms have attached bath-»oms; the nearby *To Chau* (☎077/863718; ②–④) has a range of rooms; while the riverside *oa Binh* (☎077/861523; ①) offers basic but clean doubles with fan, some with private facil-es. Two popular seafront **restaurants**, the *Vinh Hong* and *Son Bien*, claim the best location town and are both known for their seafood. Nearer to the town centre, the *Tay Ho* also 1joys a good reputation as does the *Vinh Hong 1* by the river on Tran Hung Dao, where the gredients of its seafood dishes eye you warily from tanks mounted on the walls.

on Chong Peninsula

ie calm waters and palm-fringed beaches of **Hon Chong Peninsula** are best reached by king a bus from Rach Gia to **BINH AN** (daily at 10am; return bus from Binh An at 4am). ie bulk of the area's **accommodation** lies a couple of kilometres south of Binh An: *Binh n Guesthouse* (☎077/854332; ②–④) has rooms to suit all pockets, while the *Hon Trem uesthouse* (☎077/854331; ③) is in a better location, though its musty beach-side cabins are ther overpriced; bike rental is available here. Perched on the hillside at the other end of the rip, the *Green Hill Guesthouse* (☎077/854369; ②–③) has a few immaculate rooms with sea ews. The **beach** in front of the *Binh An Guesthouse* is fine for sunbathing, but the most pic-resque beach lies 1.5km further south. After passing cacti, tamarind and *thot not* trees, the •astal track peters out at a towering cliff, into which Sea and Mountain Pagoda ("Hai Son 1") has been hewn: a low doorway leads from its outer chamber to a grotto with statues of

Quan Am and several Buddhas. The cramped stone corridor that runs on from here makes as romantic an approach to a beach as you could imagine. As you hit the sand, the twin peaks of Father and Son Isle ("Hon Phu Thu") rear up in front of you. The beach itself is a little gem, although sadly it's rather overrun with cafés and restaurants.

Ha Tien

Many visitors find **HA TIEN**, with its shuttered terraces, crumbling colonial buildings and seafood drying in the sun, the quaintest and most beautiful town in the delta. Lapped by the Gulf of Thailand, 93km northwest of Rach Gia and only a few kilometres from the Cambodian border, the town has a real end-of-the-line feel. Once you've dipped into Ben Tran Hau's lively waterfront **market** and examined the fishing boats unloading below the common land to the west of it, you've pretty much exhausted the sights of Ha Tien. Walk up Mac Thien Tich and west along Mac Cuu, though, and a temple dedicated to **Mac Cuu** stands at the foot of the hill, where he and his relatives lie buried in semicircular Chinese graves. Mac Cuu's grave is uppermost on the hill, daubed with a yin and yang symbol, and guarded by two swordsmen, a white tiger and a blue dragon. From this vantage point, there are good views down to the river. Further up Mac Thien Tich, **Tam Bao Pagoda** is set in tree-lined grounds dominated by a huge statue of Quan Am. In the rear chamber of the pagoda, a statue of the goddess with a thousand hands and a thousand eyes sits on a lurid pink lotus. Behind her are photos and funerary tablets remembering the local dead.

Biking around Ha Tien

A full day can be spent **biking** through the countryside around Ha Tien, with a convenient circular route northwest of town meaning you won't need to backtrack; bikes can be rented at the *Dong Ho* and *To Chau* hotels. Strike off west along Lam Son, through rice fields, coconut groves and water palm, past a war cemetery (2.5km from town), from where it's 1.5km to the first of two marked turnings to **Mui Nai** peninsula, a peaceful, dark-sand cove. Several hundred metres further on is the second Mui Nai turning, from which a track marked by a toll gate (less than $1) leads to the best stretch of beach in the area, a 400-metre curve of sand, shaded by coconut palms and backed by lush green hills. A handful of cafés and restaurants means you can spend a full day here. Follow the track around the southern promontory and you'll find an almost identical but more secluded beach.

You'll see the 48-metre-high granite outcrop housing **Thach Dong** cave, long before you reach it; 3–4km past Mui Nai, the track hits a sealed road, and a right turn deposits you at its base. A monument shaped like a clenched fist and commemorating the 130 people killed by the Khmer Rouge near here in 1978 marks the entrance (daily 7am–6pm) to Thach Dong, beyond which steps lead up to a cave-pagoda that's home to a colony of bats. To your right is Cambodia. From here, another 3km brings you back to Ha Tien.

Practicalities

Buses terminate below the southern end of the pontoon bridge that links Ha Tien with the rest of Vietnam, from where it's a short walk up to town. The most important street is waterfront Ben Tran Hau, from where passenger/cargo boats for Chau Doc and Phu Quoc Island depart daily at 6am and 9am respectively. Local regulations concerning Westerners constantly change, so it's best to check beforehand if you are allowed on these boats; Phu Quoc bound vessels are alarmingly small and decrepit.

Across the street at the southern end of To Chau, the *To Chau* (☎077/852148; ②) has spartan, though adequate fan and air-con **rooms**, while the nearby *Dong Ho* (☎077/852141; ②) is another reliable and inexpensive option. Further along the waterfront, two friendly guest houses – the *Hoa Mai* (☎077/852670; ②) and *Thanh Mai* (☎077/852213; ②) – have comfortable rooms, all with en-suite bathrooms. In the same price range, the imposing *Phao Dai*

Hotel (☎077/851849; ②), at the end of Mac Thien Tich, boasts a spectacular location overlooking the bay, and its upper fan rooms with balcony are a bargain. Although set back from the main selection, the convivial *Hai Van* (☎077/852872; ②) at 646a Lam Son seems more geared up to taking foreigners than most.

The cheery *Xuan Thanh* on the waterfront is the town's best **restaurant** serving cheap Western and Vietnamese dishes, or the *Huong Bien* round the corner on Bach Dang has a good range of reliable staples averaging around $1.50. Kien Giang Tourist Company is located inside the *Dong Ho* and is the only place which **exchanges** cash currencies into dong.

THE SOUTHERN AND CENTRAL HIGHLANDS

After a hot and sticky stint labouring across the coastal plains, the little-visited **southern and central highlands**, with their host of ethnic minorities, mist-laden mountains and crashing waterfalls, can provide an enjoyable contrast. Many of the highlands' 2.5 million inhabitants are *montagnards* ("mountain folk") from Bahnar, Ede, Jarai, Sedang, Koho and Mnong **ethnic minorities**, but visiting their villages independently can be difficult and is best done by basing yourself at the highland towns of **Buon Me Thuot** and **Kon Tum**, from where you can either book a tour or take a Honda om. For most tourists up here, the main target is **Da Lat**, a former French mountain retreat that unfortunately is not as idyllic as it sounds (dreary architecture and drearier tourist trappings), though it does have its charms, among them some beguiling colonial buildings, picturesque bike rides and a market overflowing with fruit and vegetables.

Da Lat and around

Nestled at an elevation of around 1500m among the hills of the Lang Bian Plateau, the city of **DA LAT** is Vietnam's premier hill station, a beguiling amalgam of mazy cobbled streets and picturesque churches, spliced unfortunately with dingy East European-style constructions and touristic kitsch. In 1897, the Governor-General of Indochina ordered the founding of a convalescent hill station here, where Saigon's hot-under-the-collar *colons* could recharge their batteries, enjoy the bracing alpine chill, and perhaps even partake in a day's game-hunting. By tacit agreement during the American War, both Hanoi and Saigon refrained from bombing the city and it remains much as it was half a century ago, a great place to chill out, literally and metaphorically.

Arrival, information and getting around

Buses from Ho Chi Minh, Nha Trang and elsewhere arrive at Da Lat Bus Station, 1.5km south of the city on 3 Thang 4, from where Honda oms trundle into the centre. **Lien Khuong Airport** (☎063/843373) is 29km below the city, off the road to Ho Chi Minh: Vietnam Airlines Buses ($3) depart from here to their offices at 40, Ho Tung Mau (☎063/822895), while a taxi or Honda om will cost $15 and $6 respectively.

Local officials insist that all tourists leaving Da Lat for Ho Chi Minh City or Nha Trang by bus should do so on the **open-tour buses**, priced $7–8, and ticket sellers at the public bus station enforce the rule. To get around this, simply wait outside the station gate, flag down a **local bus** going in the direction you want and pay the local fare. Should you decide to comply and pay extra, tickets for open-tour buses are on sale at most hotels and tourist cafés; Huy Hung Hotel, 54 Bui Thi Xuan for Sinh Café buses and Dalat Tourism Service Company, Kim Café 2, 9 Le Dai Hanh for those operated by Kim Travel. In both cases, buses depart from

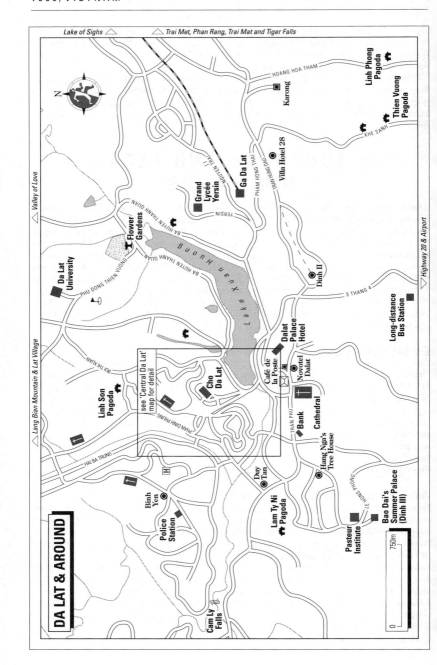

DA LAT & AROUND

Lake of Sighs △   △ *Trai Met, Phan Rang, Trai Mat and Tiger Falls*

Valley of Love ◁

◁ *Lang Bian Mountain & Lat Village*

▽ *Highway 20 & Airport*

HOANG HOA THAM

Linh Phong Pagoda

Thien Vuong Pagoda

Karong

KHE SANH

Ga Da Lat

Villa Hotel 28

PHAM HONG THAI

NGUYEN TRAI 11

TRAN HUNG DAO

Grand Lycée Yersin

YERSIN

BA HUYEN THANH QUAN

Flower Gardens

Da Lat University

PHU DONG THIEN VUONG

BA HUYEN THANH QUAN

Lake Xuan Huong

Dinh II

3 THANG 4

Long-distance Bus Station

Dalat Palace Hotel

Café de la Poste

Novotel Dalat

see 'Central Da Lat' map for detail

Cho Da Lat

BUI THI XUAN

Linh Son Pagoda

PHAN DINH PHUNG

TRAN PHU

Bank

Cathedral

Hang Nga's Tree House

HAI BA TRUNG

Duy Tan

Binh Yen

Police Station

Lam Ty Ni Pagoda

Pasteur Institute

HONG PHONG 37

Bao Dai's Summer Palace (Dinh III)

Cam Ly Falls

0   750m

outside the relevant office (Kim Travel can also arrange hotel pick-ups) with daily departures to Ho Chi Minh City and Nha Trang.

Several hotels rent **bicycles** and moutainbikes ($2–3). **Honda om** drivers with the best English tend to hang around the budget hotels and charge $8–10 for a day-long tour to local pagodas, waterfalls and ethnic villages. **Taxis** congregate beside the food market at the base of Le Dai Hanh, and two blocks above the cinema; they charge $12 upwards for a day-long tour. The following **tourist offices** can organize tours, guides and car plus driver ($27) – Da Lat Travel Service, at 7, 3 Thang 2 (☎063/822125), Dalat Tourist Travel Service, at *Thuy Tien Hotel*, 2 Nguyen Thai Hoc (☎063/822520), Travel Centre, Cam Do Hotel, 81 Phan Dinh Phung (☎063/822482) and Dalat Tourism Service Company, Kim Café 2, 9 Le Dai Hanh (☎063/822479). The **post office** at 14 Tran Phu (daily 6.30am–9pm) has poste restante, IDD, fax and DHL courier services. Lam Dong **Hospital** is at 4 Pham Ngoc Thach (☎063/822154), and the **police** are at 9 Tran Binh Trong (☎063/822032). Vietincombank, 46–48 Khu Hoa Binh, and Agribank, 216 Tran Phu, can **change** travellers' cheques, foreign cash and can arrange Visa and Mastercard advance payments. The Cam Do Hotel has a foreign exchange desk and can arrange credit card cash advances, but expect rates to be higher than normal. There are **Internet** facilities at Dalat Travel Service at the Thuy Tien Hotel and Kim Café 2.

Accommodation

The densest concentrations of **budget hotels** lie on the web of roads around the cinema and along Phan Dinh Phung; check that prices include hot water – a necessity in Da Lat.

Binh Yen, 7/2 Hai Thuong (☎063/823631). Nicely tucked away at the top of Hai Thuong, offering functional rooms, all with hot water and TV and mountain bikes for rent $8. Three-bed room for $12.

Cam Do, 81 Phan Dinh Phung (☎063/822482). Salubrious rooms, all with hot water and private facilities, some with bathtubs. There's bike-rental, a travel centre and foreign exchange, plus a café. ②.

Chau Au-Europa, 76 Nguyen Chi Tanh (☎063/822870). Popular, professionally run mid-range hotel; rooms are homely and dazzlingly clean, some with balcony; breakfast is included, staff are helpful and there's Internet access. ④.

Hang Nga's Tree House, 3 Huynh Thuc Khang (☎063/822070). Childhood fantasy construction shaped to resemble the knotted trunks of huge trees with themed *Alice in Wonderland*-style rooms. ⑥.

Hoa Binh I, 64 Truong Cong Dinh (☎063/822787). Friendly, budget hotel popular with backpackers. Great value rooms have hot water and a café and mountain bikes for rent. An identical set-up is found at *Hoa Binh ll* at no. 67. ②.

Hoang Hau Villa, 8a Ho Tung Mau (☎063/821431). Just below the GPO, an appealing mini-hotel with well-appointed rooms, some overlooking city gardens. Breakfast is included. ④.

Ngoc Lan, 42 Nguyen Chi Thanh (☎063/822136). Soccer pitch-sized rooms in this central hotel offer "every modern comfort" and bird's-eye views of Lake Xuan Huong. ⑤.

The City

Cho Da Lat market is housed in a charmless reinforced concrete structure, but offers the usual entertainment in its staggering range of fruit and vegetables as well as some interesting souvenirs such as watergourds, lacquerware, and hilltribe backpacks and fabrics on its upper level, linked by a raised walkway to the top of Le Dai Hanh.

Cycling or walking round glassy, man-made **Lake Xuan Huong** is a pleasant pastime and takes in Da Lat's **flower gardens** (daily 6.30am–6pm) at its northeastern corner, from where you continue south down Ba Huyen Thanh Quan, with the option of striking east up Nguyen Trai to **Ga Da Lat**, the city's Art Deco train station, built in 1938. Only two trains are kept operational, running a shuttle service ($4 per person; 16 round trips daily, but trains leave according to demand) through market gardens to the village of **Trai Mat**, a few kilometres away; the train idles for thirty minutes – time enough to take a look at **Linh Phuoc Pagoda** – before returning to Da Lat. Back at the southwest corner of the lake, the splendidly restored **Dalat Palace Hotel** stands on Tran Phu; now part of the *Sofitel Hotel* empire, the original was the social heart of colonial-era Da Lat. Across the road, Da Lat's dusty pink

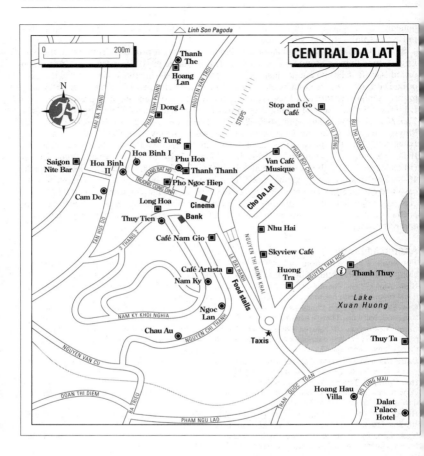

cathedral, completed in 1942, is dedicated to Saint Nicholas, protector of the poor; its seventy stained-glass windows were mostly crafted in Grenoble.

The nautical portholes punched into its walls, and the mast-like pole sprouting from its roof give **Dinh III** (daily 7am–5pm), erstwhile summer palace of Emperor Bao Dai, the distinct look of a ship's bridge. Reached by bearing left onto Le Hong Phong 500m west of the cathedral, and then left again when you see the wide mansion housing the Pasteur Institute to your right, the palace was erected between 1933 and 1938 to provide Bao Dai with a bolt hole between elephant-slaughtering sessions. Once inside, you have the chance to nose into his working room, festivities room and imperial bedrooms.

Dropping in at **Lam Ty Ni Pagoda** at the western edge of town, north of Le Hong Phong on Thien My, represents one of the unlikeliest and most delightful attractions of a stay in Da Lat. The pagoda is home to Vien Thuc, the so-called "mad monk" of Da Lat, who is also a poet, gardener, builder and artist. His studio is stacked with over 100,000 abstract watercolours, all for sale, and Vien Thuc relishes visitors, for whom he gives a full conducted tour in English. His paintings flank the walls of the pagoda too, and the canopy around the altar depicting birds carrying Buddhist *sutras* is also his handiwork.

Eating and drinking

Most of Da Lat's **restaurants** are on Phan Dinh Phung and near the cinema. *Pho* and *com* are bashed out at the covered food market at the base of Le Dai Hanh, where there are also one or two vegetarian stalls, signposted as *com chay*. The city now boasts a number of **bars**, some of which have copied Ho Chi Minh City's winning formula of loud music and pool tables.

Café Tung, 6 Khu Hoa Binh. Leather upholstery, dark varnished wood and covers of old 45s by Nancy Sinatra and Jacques Brel on the walls: truly a café lost in time. 4pm–midnight.

Hoang Lan, 118 Phan Dinh Phung. Next door to the *Thanh The* hotel, a bare but reputable restaurant where Vietnamese and Chinese cuisines share top billing. 7am–9pm.

Huong Tra, 1 Nguyen Thai Hoc. Popular lakeside restaurant. Rice dishes cooked in a claypot are a speciality, and the menu also runs to rabbit and deer. 6am–9pm.

Karong, 6b Yen The (☎063/831334). The full-on *montagnard* dining experience: seated on cushions in grass-roof huts, guests choose from bat, deer, snake and wild boar, washed down with copious amounts of *ruou can*, the local rice wine, drunk in the traditional way from a communal jar. Phone ahead. Open 24hr.

Long Hoa, 3 Thang 2. French-style ambience, with decent and filling Vietnamese food and steaks, where two can dine for $7. 8am–10pm.

Nhu Hai, 40–41 Nguyen Thi Minh Khai. Meals are filling and affordable in this terrific open-fronted joint, but it's the range of exotic fruits that's outstanding. 5.30am–11.30pm.

Sky View Café, *Golf 3 Hotel*. Perched on the top floor of the *Golf 3 Hotel*, a fine venue for relaxing over a beer and watching the city unfurl below. 1–11pm.

Thanh Thanh Restaurant, 4 Tang Bat Ho (☎063/821836). Refined, friendly and popular; sugarcane prawns are tasty, and the special salad (shrimps, peanuts, lotus gourd, pork and herbs) is superb. 11am–10.30pm.

Around Da Lat

Five kilometres south of Da Lat, halfway down the dramatic Prenn Pass, are the **Datanla Falls** (6am–4pm), signposted on the right of the road as "Thac Datanla". The falls are unthrilling, but a popular photo-opportunity. A couple of hundred metres before Datanla is the right turn to **Lake Tuyen Lam** (6am–4pm), whose northern shore is presently being turned into a tacky tourist park, though fortunately, large areas of the lake remain unspoilt and Phuong Nam Adventure Tourism (6 Ho Tung Mau; ☎063/822781) organize trekking tours, elephant rides and rice-wine feasts in the forests nearby.

None of the Koho residents of **Chicken Village** (ask Honda drivers for *Lang Con Ga*), 18km from Da Lat, seem sure of the origins of the five-metre-high cement cockerel that stands proudly on a plinth in the midst of their dwellings. Some say praying to it is supposed to ensure a good harvest; others attach the inevitable love story to the edifice. Whatever the truth, strolling around this hamlet gives visitors a taste of the daily life of a minority community. Approaching from Da Lat, rows of golden thatched barns used for cultivating mushrooms to your right tell you you're nearing the village. A kilometre later, a group of Koho women by the roadside sell traditional textiles, which they weave on a rudimentary loom. From here, it's a ten-minute stroll through the village to the infamous chicken, beyond which you can take a walk up into the layered hills casing the village.

Buon Me Thuot and around

Sited 160km west of Ninh Hoa, **BUON ME THUOT** is chiefly of interest for its outlying minority Ede villages of **Tour** and **Ban**. The town itself is the western highlands' unofficial capital, and, during French colonial times, developed on the back of the coffee, tea, rubber and hardwood crops that grew so successfully in its fertile red soil; coffee is still the backbone of the local economy. If you need to while away a few hours in town, try the Dak Lak Museum (Mon–Fri 7–11am & 1.30–4.30pm; $1), which comprises the **History Museum** on Le Duan, chronicling the struggles against both the French and the Americans, and the more interesting **Ethnographic Museum**, a little further down the road on the opposite side, (entrance on Nguyen Du) with its display of exhibits pertaining to local minority peoples, among them a scale model of an Ede longhouse, rice-wine jars, and instruments for taming elephants. You could also check out **BUON KO SIER**, an Ede community 2km beyond the *Saigon Moi* eating-house. Now effectively no more than a district of Buon Me Thuot, it's still a convenient way of witnessing a longhouse community going about its daily routines.

Tour village and the Dray Sap Falls
The splendid **Dray Sap Falls** are accessed by heading southwest out of Buon Me Thuot along Doc Lap. Before them, 14km out of town, a track to the left of the road runs into serene **TOUR VILLAGE**, one of the biggest minority villages in the area, where four hundred Edes share fifteen stilted wooden longhouses and live very much as they have done for centuries, sustained by their maize, corn, peanut, cashew and sugarcane crops. Visitors are often invited to take tea with the village's **headman**, a French-speaking gentleman called Enor. While Tour's residents are more than happy to let you look inside their longhouses, a token gift is much appreciated – cigarettes, sweets, salt and stationery will all be well received. The Honda om return trip to Tour costs $3 but you'll need to double that to continue on to crescent-shaped **Dray Sap Falls** (7am–5pm), 20km from Buon Me Thuot. Almost 15m high and over 100m wide, the "waterfall of smoke" can be reached by clambering through bamboo groves and over rocks to the right of the pool formed by the falls.

Yok Don National Park and Ban Don
Exit west out of Buon Me Thuot along Phan Boi Chau, and 37km later, you'll arrive at the entrance to Vietnam's largest wildlife reserve, the **Yok Don National Park**, whose 58,000 hectares lie nestled into the hinge of the Cambodian border and the Serepok River. Over sixty species of animals, including tigers, leopards and bears, and around two hundred types of birds, from peacocks to hornbills, populate Yok Don Park, but **elephant rides** are the park's main attraction ($20 an hour for two people). There are also one-day walking tours available and two-day, one-night ($180) safaris for two, the latter best in the dry season when wildlife is more visible. Longer tours penetrating deeper into the forest where animals still preside are also available. For enquiries, phone the park HQ (☎050/789149) and ask for Mr Chuong or Mr Nghia.

The three sub-hamlets that comprise the village of **BAN DON** lie 2km beyond Yok Don's park HQ on the bank of the crocodile-infested Serepok River. Khmer, Thai, Lao, Jarai and Mnong live in the vicinity, though it's the **Ede** who are in the majority. They adhere to a matriarchal social system, and build their houses on stilts. As you explore, you are bound to be welcomed in somewhere to share tea or rice wine ($5 a jar). If you get invited to a party, bear in mind that the women drink first, then the village elder, and finally the other guests.

Ban Don Tourist Centre (☎050/789119), in the centre of the village, organizes elephant rides and guided tours of Ban Don and surrounding areas ($14, plus $5 village entrance fee). Dak Lak Tourist (see opposite) also arranges tours here, but you could just as well hire a Honda om ($8–10) and guide ($5 for a half-day) from Buon Me Thuot. You can also reach Ban Don by getting a **bus** from Buon Me Thuot beside 200 Phan Boi Chau (7am & 2pm) to **EA SUP**. Both the Ban Don Tourist Centre and the Yok Don Park HQ can organize three-hour cultural programmes of Ede dance, music and wine ($60–80 per group) with the option of spending the night in a nearby longhouse (extra $5 per person); there's also accommodation available at both the Park HQ and the Ban Don Tourist Centre.

Dak Lake and Jun Village
About 60km south of Buon Me Thuot, Highway 27 passes **Dak Lake**, a beautiful and peaceful spot that's amongst the top tourist destinations in Vietnam. Along the lake's shoreline, the ruined remains of Emperor Bao Dai's palace enjoys a prime spot; beyond this sits **JUN VILLAGE**, a thriving Mnong community, whose impressive longhouses have remained little

unchanged. Dak Lak Tourist have a branch office here and a couple of longhouses (①), where it's possible to overnight; there is also a simple stilt restaurant built out on the lake, which offers magnificent views. You can also arrange to stay at a Jun longhouse in the village (around $5), partake in organised rice wine feasts ($60 per group), guided treks or elephant rides around the lake ($30 for two per hour); there are also dug-out canoe excursions ($10 per hour for two). Although Dak Lake is mostly geared towards organised tour groups, it's possible to arrive here independently, but you should ring ahead first: either by Honda om, or the twice daily local buses from Buon Me Thuot. Coming from either Buon Me Thuot or Da Lat, some sections of the route are as yet unsealed, something to bear in mind in the rainy season, when the road resembles porridge. For bookings and enquiries, contact the Dak Lak office (☎050/886184) and ask for Miss Loan – French-speaking – or Mr Liem, who speaks English.

Practicalities

Buon Me Thuot's **bus station** (☎050/852603) is 2km above town on Nguyen Chi Tranh; from here several air-con express buses ($3) depart daily to Nha Trang and to Ho Chi Minh ($5–6). The **airport** is a few kilometres back off the road towards Ninh Hoa: Vietnam Airlines (☎050/855055), at 67 Nguyen Tat Thanh, has an airport shuttle to and from the city ($1.50). **Dak Lak Tourist** is at 3 Phan Chu Trinh (☎050/852108) and Vietcombank, on Y-Jut, can **change** travellers' cheques, foreign currencies and advance cash on Visa, Mastercard and JCB cards.

The cheapest beds in town are at Le Hong Phong's *Hoang Gia* (☎050/852161; ②), which has passable rooms for the price, all en suite; or there are somewhat lacklustre rooms at Hai Ba Trung's *Hong Kong* (☎050/852630; ②–③), but at least it's fairly quiet. The *Agribank Hotel,* at 111, Le Hong Phong (☎050/857828; ⑤) has spacious doubles with TV and air-con. Pick of the crop is the smart *Thang Loi* (☎050/857615; ⑥), across from the Victory Monument, whose well-equipped rooms include satellite TV; breakfast is inclusive.

When it's time to **eat**, *Saigon Moi,* a no-frills roadside eating house on Hung Vuong, serves stuffed tofu and prawns as well as flavoursome *com suon* and excellent *thit kho tau* (slow-boiled pork and eggs). The *Ninh Hoa* on Ly Thuong Kiet is famed locally for its fine *nem* (spring rolls). Hai Ba Trung's *Ngoc Lanh* cooks tasty food from its simple menu, and beef dishes at *Quan Bo Ne* next door are popular. In the evenings, local males converge on Nguyen Duch Canh to consume platefuls of seafood and vast quantities of Tiger beer. Most of the restaurants along here are simply called *Bia Lanh* (cold beer), followed by the street number.

Kon Tum and the Bahnar villages

Some 246km north of Buon Me Thuot, northbound Highway 14 crosses the Dakbla River and runs into the southern limits of diminutive **KON TUM**, a sleepy, friendly town which serves as a springboard for jaunts to its outlying **Bahnar villages**. Phan Dinh Phung forms the western edge of town; running east above the river is Nguyen Hue, and between these two axes lies the town centre. Kon Tum had a hard time of it during the American War, and yet a stroll along Nguyen Hue still reveals some red-tile terraces of shophouses left over from the French era. At the base of Tran Phu stands the grand, white-washed bulk of Tan Huong Church. Further east is the so-called **Wooden Church**, built by the French in 1913, and recently revarnished. A statue of Christ stands behind glass over the front entrance; below him, a stained-glass window neatly fuses the classic Christian symbol of the dove with images of local resonance – a Bahnar village and an elephant. In the grounds, there's a scale model of a communal house.

Kon Kotu

There are dozens of Bahnar villages encircling Kon Tum, but one of the most fascinating and accessible is **KON KOTU**, a relatively timeless community only 5km east of Kon Tum. A kilometre or so east of the bus station, Nguyen Hue veers northeast; another 500m later, and a cluster of cafés at a crossroads is your signal to turn right onto Tran Hung Dao. This dwindles to a track, striking past stilt villages and sugarcane; eventually, you'll cross over a bridge where on the opposite bank of the river, you should veer left (east) for 3–4km to reach the village. Although there has been some outside influence here, many of the dwellings in Kon Kotu are still made of bamboo and secured with rattan string, but it's the village's immaculate *rong*, with its impossibly tall thatch roof, that commands the most attention. The *rong* is used as a venue for festivals and village meetings, and as a village court at which anyone found guilty of a tribal offence has to ritually kill a pig and a chicken, and must apologize in front of the village. No nails were used in the construction of this lofty communal hall made from bamboo.

Practicalities

Kon Tum's **bus station** is on your left, as you cross the bridge into town. From there, it's a 250-metre walk east along Nguyen Hue to the foot of Le Hong Phong, and another 150m to Tran Phu; both run up into the town centre. Agribank on Tran Phu does **currency exchange**. Until the rumoured improvements to the Kon Tum–Quang Ngai road materialize, most visitors to Kon Tum are backtracking to Plei Ku and dropping down to Qui Nhon in order to continue their tour. Actually, onward travel **from Kon Tum to Da Nang** along Highway 14 is possible with your own transport, but a good motorcycle or four-wheel-drive jeep is essential; Highway 14 eventually rejoins Highway 1 20km south of Da Nang, at Dien Ban.

There's a choice of just two **hotels** in Kon Tum – the first of these as you approach town is the riverside *Dakbla* (☎060/863333; ④–⑥), a large, modern place with rooms that have satellite TV, bath and hot water; Kon Tum Tourist (☎060/861626) is also located here and can offer tailor-made tours and good information on the area. The endearing *Quang Trung* (☎060/862249; ②–③), north of the centre on Ba Trieu, has relatively cheaper air-con and fan rooms, all with hot water. Both hotels rent **bicycles** and motorbikes.

As for **food**, the *Dakbla Restaurant*, 100m east of the bus station, serves surprisingly sophisticated local and Western dishes, whilst the *Hiep Thanh* at 129 Nguyen Hue is a reliable alternative for simple food. The *Dakbla Hotel Restaurant* enjoys idyllic river views from its stilt wooden terrace and the extensive menu is reasonably priced.

THE SOUTH-CENTRAL COAST

Extending from the wetlands of the Mekong Delta right the way up to the central provinces, Vietnam's south-central coast was, from the seventh to the twelfth century, the domain of the Indianized trading empire of Champa. A few communities of Cham people still live in the area, around Phan Thiet and Phan Rang, and there are some fine relics of their ancestors' temple complexes near **Nha Trang**, which also happens to boast an attractive municipal beach and some good snorkelling trips to nearby islands. The **Vung Tau** peninsula also offers a couple of fairly decent beaches, though nothing compared to the high dunes and aquamarine waters of **Mui Ne**, a short hop from the fishing town of **Phan Thiet**. The scars of war tend not to intrude too much along this stretch of the country, except at the village of Son My near Quang Ngai, sombre site of the notorious **My Lai massacre**.

Vung Tau and around

With every passing day, a little more of the charm ebbs from **VUNG TAU**, "The Bay of Boats", located some 125km southeast of Ho Chi Minh City on a hammerheaded spit of land jutting into the mouth of the Saigon River. Once a thriving riviera-style beach resort, the city is now a shadow of its former, quaint self. Today, Western oil-workers nurturing the city's bur-

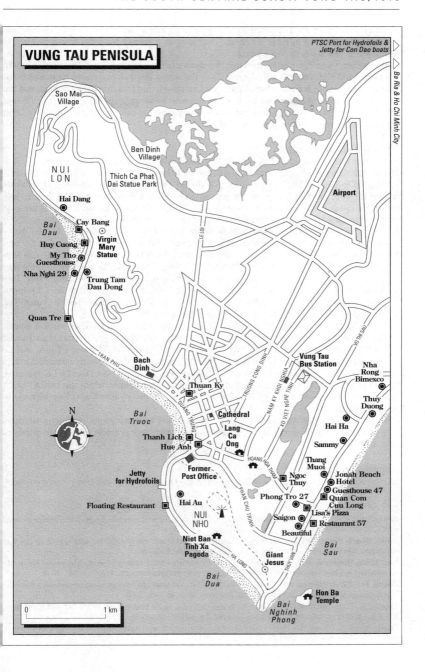

VUNG TAU PENISULA

PTSC Port for Hydrofoils &
Jetty for Con Dao boats

Ba Ria & Ho Chi Minh City

Sao Mai
Village

Ben Dinh
Village

Thich Ca Phat
Dai Statue Park

N U I
L O N

Airport

Hai Dang

Bai
Dau

Cay Bang

Huy Cuong

My Tho
Guesthouse

Nha Nghi 29

Virgin
Mary
Statue

Trung Tam
Dau Dong

Quan Tre

LE LOI

TRAN PHU

Bach
Dinh

Thuan Ky

Vung Tau
Bus Station

Nha
Rong
Bimexco

TRUONG CONG DINH

NAM KY KHOI NGHIA

XO VIET NGHE TINH

VO THI SAU

Thuy
Duong

Bai
Truoc

GIANG TRUNG

Cathedral

Lang
Ca
Ong

Hai Ha

Thanh Lich

Hue Anh

HOANG HOA THAM

Sammy

Thang
Muoi

Former
Post Office

PHAN CHU TRINH

Ngoc
Thuy

Jonah Beach
Hotel

Guesthouse 47

Jetty
for Hydrofoils

Phong Tro 27

Quan Com
Cuu Long

Floating Restaurant

Hai Au

NUI
NHO

Saigon

Lisa's Pizza

Restaurant 57

Beautiful

Niet Ban
Tinh Xa
Pagoda

HA LONG

Giant
Jesus

Bai
Sau

THUY VAN

Bai
Dua

Hon Ba
Temple

Bai
Nghinh
Phong

N

0   1 km

geoning oil industry are a common sight around town, and a slather of bars and massage parlours have sprung up to cater for them. That said, as a retreat from the frenzy of Ho Chi Minh, Vung Tau is worth considering.

Downtown Vung Tau nestles between two diminutive peaks, Nui Lon ("Big Mountain") to the north, and Nui Nho ("Small Mountain") to the south. Roads loop around both, and these circuits take in all of the city's **beaches** – quiet, northerly Bai Dau, blustery Bai Dua, and Bai Sau, or "Back Beach", which has the city's best sands. Between them runs Bai Truoc ("Front Beach"), Vung Tau's skinny municipal beach. Many prefer to push on to more intimate Long Hai, just 20km around the coast (see p.1016).

Arrival and information

Public **buses** terminate at Vung Tau bus station, at the northeastern end of Nam Ky Khoi Nghia; **Minibuses** drop passengers in the square below the cathedral on Tran Hung Dao – moving on to Ho Chi Minh, mini-buses ($3) depart every half hour from here. **Hydrofoils** from Ham Nghi (Ho Chi Minh) use the jetty opposite *Hai Au Hotel*, just south of the city centre on Ha Long, or during the rainy season, the PTSC terminal, 12km northeast of the city; free shuttle buses to and from the jetty are provided. Hydrofoils to Ho Chi Minh City ($10) have six to seven departures daily; tickets can be bought at the jetty opposite the *Hai Au*.

Cyclos and honda om are ubiquitous, and there are taxis in the central areas. *Dai Loc* and *Quan Com Cuu Long* restaurants have the best rates for **bicycles** ($1.50) and both can supply motorbikes and mopeds ($4–7). *Thuang Moi, Song Hong, Hai Au* and *Royal* hotels also do bike rental. **Car** rental plus driver can be arranged at Vicarrent, 54 Tran Hung Dao (☎064/852400). Vietcombank, 27 Tran Hung Dao (Mon–Fri 7–11.30am & 1.30–4pm), changes travellers' cheques and advances cash on Visa and Mastercard; Vung Tau Commercial Bank, 43, Tran Hung Dao, can **exchange** dollars.

The **GPO** at 408 Le Hong Phong has IDD, fax, poste restante and DHL services. Vietnam Airlines is at 29 Tran Hung Dao (☎064/856099). Adjoining this office is Vung Tau Tourist (☎064/856446), which can arrange tours and car rental, as can OSC Vietnam Tours, at 2 Le Loi (☎064/852008). **Internet** access is available at business centres at many upmarket hotels such as the *Palace* and *Hai Au*. There's a **pharmacy** at 70 Tran Hung Dao; Le Loi Hospital, 22 Le Loi (☎064/852667), has an outpatients' **clinic** for foreigners, while the OSCAT/AEA International Clinic at 1 Le Ngoc Han (☎064/858776) is a twenty-four-hour clinic with multinational doctors.

Future planned developments in Vung Tau have led to a somewhat confusing situation with **street numbers**, especially along Back beach. Wherever possible, new street numbers have been quoted.

Accommodation

Bai Sau offers the biggest range of lodgings and the best beach, but Bai Dau is more peaceful.

BAI SAU (BACK BEACH)

Beautiful Hotel, 57–59 Thuy Van (☎064/852177). Friendly place with appealingly fresh and modern rooms with IDD and satellite TV. ⑦.

Jonah Beach Hotel, 29 Thuy Van (☎064/853481). Relaxed beachside guesthouse with simple air-con and fan rooms, where the owners are friendly and helpful to a fault. ①–③.

Nha Rong Bimexco, Thuy Van (☎064/859916). Peacefully sited in the pine groves up at the far north-eastern end of Thuy Van, the fifty tidy and solid huts here get good reports; some air-con. ②–③.

Phong Tro 27, 170 Hoang Hoa Tham (☎064/858124). Good-value, friendly guesthouse, set back from the beach; rooms are spacious, though spartan, and some have air-con. ①–②.

Saigon, 85 Thuy Van (☎064/852317). Not blessed with Bai Sau's best strip of beach but still good value given the quality of the rooms, which are cheaper the higher you go. ②–⑤.

Thang Muoi, 127 Thuy Van (☎064/852665). Motel-style with a wide range of clean and capacious rooms, with garden restaurant and pool. ②–④.

BAI TRUOC (FRONT BEACH), THE CITY CENTRE AND BAI DUA

Song Hong, 3 Hoang Dieu (☎064/852137). Competitively priced, set back from the beach; the comfortable rooms all boast air-con, bathtubs and satellite TV. ⑥.

Tu Hai, 17 Ly Thuong Kiet (☎064/852702). One of the very few budget options in the centre. Air-con and fan rooms are basic but reasonable and all have en-suite facilities. ③.

BAI DAU

Hai Dang, 164 Tran Phu (☎064/838563). Out on a limb, but tranquil and friendly, with good size air-con and fan rooms, some of which gaze out to sea.

My Tho Guesthouse, 43 Tran Phu (☎064/832035). A gem of a place run by a charming couple. Offers big an rooms looking onto the beach, and smaller, internal rooms with air-con; plus there's a sun terrace. ②.

Trung Tan Dau Dung, 84 Tran Phu (☎064/832625). Presently under construction, but expect the 38 rooms in this villa-style hotel to be in the $15–20 bracket when it opens.

Around the Peninsula

The skinny strip of litter- and rubble-strewn town beach, **Bai Truoc** or **Front Beach** is ribbed by souvenir shops, bars and restaurants and of most interest at dawn and dusk when fishermen dredge its shallows. Imposing late-nineteenth century **Bach Dinh** (daily 7am–5pm), on the southern slope of Nui Lon above the northern extent of Quang Trung, has long served as a holiday home to Vietnam's political players and now exhibits "valuable antique items" excavated from a seventeenth-century shipwreck, and Cambodian Buddhist statuary.

The foot of Quang Trung is the starting-block for the six-kilometre circuit of **Nui Nho**. From there, the exposed coastal road, Ha Long, loops around the southside of the mountain. Not far past the former post office, a pretty pink villa marked "53/2 Ha Long" signposts the left turn up to Vung Tau's **lighthouse**, which affords panoramic views of the peninsula. The most noteworthy of several pagodas strung along this stretch of coastline is **Niet Ban Tinh Xa Pagoda** (daily 7am–5pm), a modern and multi-level complex fronted by a structure resembling a high-rise dovecote. **Bai Dua**, south of the pagoda, is a composite of shingle, dark sand and rocks, so if you want a swim or a sunbathe, hold on until you round the promontory. Meanwhile, a gruelling fifteen-minute hike from the southwestern tip of Nui Nho brings you to Vung Tau's own little touch of Rio, its 33-metre-high **Giant Jesus** (daily 7.30–11.30am & 1.30–5pm). Climb the steps inside the statue and you'll enjoy giddying views. Immediately around the headland is the sweet, sandy cove of **Bai Nghinh Phong**, and beyond that, **Hon Ba Temple** marooned a little way out to sea on a tiny islet, accessible only at low tide.

Despite its ugly block-buildings and proposed development, **Bai Sau**, or **Back Beach**, is far and away Vung Tau's widest, longest (8km) and best beach. Hoang Hoa Tham cuts round the north side of Nui Nho to reach the city centre. En route, you might check out **Lang Ca Ong**, or Whale Temple. According to Cham folklore, the whale was a sacred creature, and protector of seafarers; three glass cabinets behind the altar are filled with the bones of whales washed up on the shore.

North of Bach Dinh, sleepy **Bai Dau** is the most hassle-free of all Vung Tau's beaches. Barring the odd restaurant, there's very little action here, but heavy stone walls and blue-shuttered buildings lend it a Mediterranean ambience. The actual beach is short, dark and slightly pebbly, but still suitable for swimming. With a bicycle you could continue north from Bai Dau to the leaf-roofed stilthouses of the delightful fishing village of **Sao Mai**. Further clockwise, Sao Mai blends into the busy quayside of bigger **Ben Dinh**.

Eating and drinking

FRONT BEACH AND BAI DUA

Floating Restaurant, 150 Ha Long (☎064/856577). The emphasis is squarely on seafood in this upmarket Vietnamese/Chinese restaurant housed right on the sea, though the menu still yields many affordable dishes; there's a music club downstairs. 9am–9.30pm.

Hue Anh, 15/a Truong Cong Dinh. Chicken with plum is boney but delicious and the diced beef is also good, but big-boy portions are guaranteed at this popular place; two eat for $10. 9am–9.30pm.

Thanh Lich, 11 Quang Trung. One of the cheapest options in central Vung Tau; meals on rice start at $1 and there are filling breakfasts – the *pho ga* is recommended. 6am–midnight.

Thuan Ky, 23–25 Trung Nhi. Huge and hugely popular *com* and *pho* shop, slap-bang in the centre of the city. 5am–10pm.

Whispers/BB Bar, 13–15 Nguyen Trai. The two main expat hang-outs in Vung Tau. *Whispers*, the more refined, has a restaurant-cum-bar serving traditional roasts and good-quality Western fare; the adjoining *BB Bar* shares the same menu but resembles a fun-pub. Mon–Sat 11am–2pm & 4.30pm–midnight, Sun 11am–midnight.

BACK BEACH

Dai Loc, 170 Hoang Hoa Tham. Attached to the *Phong Tro 27* guesthouse, this is an excellent-value restaurant, serving tasty Western and Vietnamese dishes. 5am–late.

Quan Com Cuu Long, 57 Thuy Van. Fortifying breakfasts and cheap and cheerful dishes in this friendly roadside restaurant. 6am–10pm.

BAI DAU

Cay Bang, 93 Tran Phu. Pricey, but popular with locals who come out of town for seafood overlooking the beach at sunset. Weekends are busy, though restaurants either side cater for the overspill. 10am–9pm.

Quan Tre Bamboo, 7 Tran Phu. The glorious setting of candle-lit, open-air terraced dining area beside the sea could have been lifted straight from the South of France; the reasonably-priced extensive menu ranges from grilled kangaroo with soya cheese, to red clam salad. 9am–10pm.

Long Hai

Modest **LONG HAI**, 20km around the coast from Vung Tau, is a drowsy and relaxing holiday resort. Sands here are arguably more enticing than those at Vung Tau; dunes fringe the town's eastern extreme; while to the west stands a fishing village, complete with stilt-houses and a huge flotilla of fishing boats. Long Hai is served by **buses** from Ho Chi Minh's Mien Dong Station; coming from Vung Tau, you'll need to take a bus to Ba Ria and then change at the bus station for another bus into Long Hai. A huge, domed mansion, set amid frangipanis, the *Palace Hotel* (☎064/868364; ②) is a gem of a place **to stay**, with a range of good-value, spacious quarters. There are similar rooms at the nearby *Rang Dong* (☎064/868356; ③); or if money is tight, there are box-like rooms, some sharing facilities, at the *Ngoc Minh* (☎064/868429; ①). At the other end of the scale, try the *Long Hai (Kach San Du Lich)* (☎064/868010; ④–⑥), where all rooms have hot water and air-con; its location is set further up from the other three hotels, which are on the main drag parallel to the beach.

Phan Thiet and Cape Mui Ne

More and more foreigners are discovering **PHAN THIET**'s hidden charms, and this friendly fishing port now looks set to become one of the stepping stones between Ho Chi Minh and Hanoi, not least because of its proximity to wonderful **Cape Mui Ne**, a 21-kilometre-long arc of fine sand. Quaint colonial villas season Phan Thiet's main streets, some decorated with glazed ceramic tiles, most with louvred windows and colonnaded facades. Turn left off the southwestern end of Tran Hung Dao Bridge, and stroll along Trung Trac, and you'll soon plunge into the wharfside **fish market**. Back in the other direction, Trung Trac skirts the city centre en route to the riverside **Ho Chi Minh Museum** (Tues–Sun 7.30–11am & 1.30–4.30pm; $1), rather a flat museum, but with some nicely quaint memorabilia. A couple of hundred metres south on Tran Phu, **Ong Pagoda** also merits a browse. Over Tran Hung Dao Bridge, Vo Thi Sau strikes off to the right and to the city **beach** which, 700m northeast opens out into a nice pine-shaded spot.

East to Mui Ne

At the head of every Phan Thiet itinerary should be the jaunt out east along Thu Khoa Huan towards **Cape Mui Ne** – a trip rewarded by mile after mile of palm-shaded golden sand, lapped by clear waters. The beach commences soon after you've crossed Ke Bridge and passed the Phu Hai Cham towers, but the best stretch starts around 12km out of Phan Thiet, after which the coconut trees give way to the impressive red dunes for which this area is famous. Open-tour buses now run through Mui Ne en route from Nha Trang or Ho Chi Minh, stopping at Ha Phuong Tourist Company office (Hanh café), located at Km14, Ham Tien. Alternatively, a Honda om from Phan Thiet should cost around $2 each way. A range of accommodation choices have recently sprung up on the main drag. The more tasteful of the luxury options is the French-run *Hai Duong* (also known as *Coco Beach*; ☎062/84711; ⑨), with well-equipped wooden thatched bungalows. There's also low-key *Bamboo Village Seaside Resort* (☎062/847007; ⑦), set in coconut and banana gardens with attractive, simply furnished bamboo bungalows. At the far end of the beach are three guesthouses, including *The Full Moon* (☎062/847008; ④–⑥), with a choice of fan rooms with shared bathroom, or bamboo quarters on stilts – rates are negotiable. Some of the resorts have provision for wind-surfing, sailing, mountainbiking and motorbiking.

Practicalities

Buses terminate at the **bus station** a couple of kilometres north of Phan Thiet. Coming from Ho Chi Minh, you can save yourself a cyclo fare by getting off as the bus passes through the city centre. Traveller cafés' open-tour buses depart and arrive at either *Hoang Yen Restaurant* (☎062/821614), up towards the bus station; or *My Thuan Restaurant* (☎062/822908); both are situated on Tran Hung Dao and sell onward bus tickets. The nearest **train station** is Ga Muong Man (☎062/868814), 10km from Phan Thiet; it's not the most welcoming of places, there's no public transport from here and it's not the place to find yourself stranded at any hour. Alighting here, jump on a Honda Om (if you can find one), or arrange a car in advance with Binh Thuan Tourist, 82 Trung Truc (☎062/816821); alternatively ring for a taxi (☎062/821614 or 822646). If you're staying in **Mui Ne** (see above), some of the resorts can arrange shuttle transfers in advance.

Vietnam Airlines has a branch office in Phan Thiet at 15, Nguyen Du; you can change US dollars at the Incombank on Tran Hung Dao; for traveller's cheques and cash advances on Visa, MasterCard and JCB, you'll need to go to the larger branch on Nguyen Tat Thanh, just off Victory Monument.

Of the several **places to stay** in Phan Thiet, local government-run *Nha Khach Uy Ban*, over the river from the water tower, on Trung Trac (☎062/818858; ②–③), has a range of simple but well-equipped rooms. Also low-priced is the spartan *Nha Nghi Cong Duan* (☎062/821395; ②), just off the grubbier end of the city beach at the base of Vo Thi Sau. For a few dollars extra, there are good-value, spacious rooms, with hot water, TV and air-con at the friendly *Phan Thiet Hotel*, 276 Tran Hung Dao (☎062/821694; ③). If you want to be near the sea, there are a couple of higher-priced hotels situated at the southern end of Nguyen Tat Thanh on the best section of beach, as well as a choice of luxury resorts or guesthouses at Mui Ne (see above).

The *Ca Ty* floating **restaurant**, moored opposite the water tower, gets the bulk of the passing tourist trade, whilst across the road, the *Kim Anh Quan* serves cheap and wholesome Vietnamese staples in no-fuss surroundings. On the square, the bright *Nam Thanh Lau* restaurant serves great seafood and generous portions of a variety of dishes.

Nha Trang and around

Nestled below the bottom lip of the Cai River, some 260km north of Phan Thiet, **NHA TRANG** has earned its place on Vietnam's tourist mainline partly on merit and partly owing

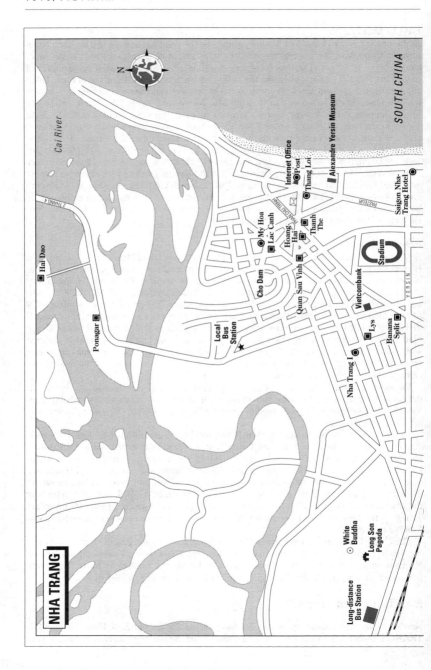

NHA TRANG

SOUTH CHINA

Cai River

2 THANG 4

Hai Dao

Ponagar

Local Bus Station

Cho Dam

My Hoa
Lac Canh

Hoang Hai

Quan Sau Vinh

Thanh The

Internet Office
Post
Thang Loi

Alexandre Versin Museum

THAN DUC THANG

PASTEUR

Saigon Nha-Trang Hotel

Stadium

Vietcombank

YERSIN

Lys

Banana Split

Nha Trang I

White Buddha

Long Son Pagoda

Long-distance Bus Station

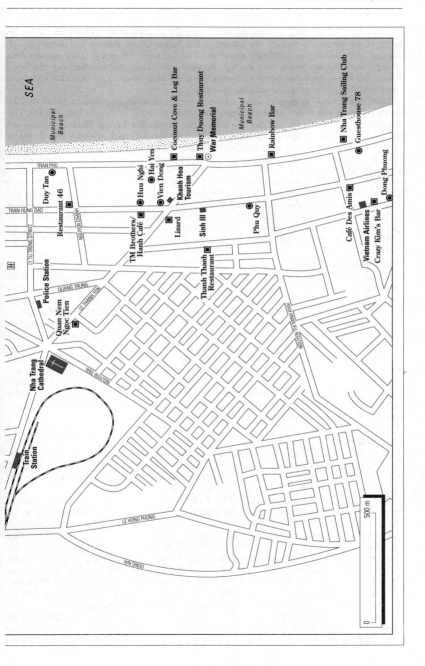

to its location. By the time the Nguyen lords wrested this patch of the country from Champa in the mid-seventeenth century, the intriguing **Po Nagar Cham towers** had already stood, stacked impressively on a hillside above the Cai, for over 700 years. They remain Nha Trang's most famous image, yet it's the coastline that brings tourists flocking: the town boasts the finest municipal beach in Vietnam, scuba-diving courses are available here, and there are plenty of day-trips to outlying islands too.

Most new arrivals in the city make a beeline for the **municipal beach**, a grand six-kilometre scythe of soft yellow sand that's only five minutes' stroll east of Cho Dam market. The Pasteur Institute at the top of Tran Phu houses the **Alexandre Yersin Museum** (Mon–Sat 8–11am & 2–4.30pm; $2), which profiles the life of the Swiss-French scientist who settled in Nha Trang in 1893 and became a local hero, thanks not to his greatest achievement – the discovery of a plague bacillus – but rather to his educational work in sanitation and agriculture, and to his ability to predict typhoons and thus save the lives of fishermen. Yersin's desk is here, with his own French translations of Horace still slotted under its glass top; so, too, are the barometers and telescope he used to forecast the weather, and his phenomenal library. The huge **White Buddha** seated on a hillside above Long Son Pagoda in the northwest of town is Nha Trang's major landmark. It was crafted in 1963 to symbolize the Buddhist struggle against the repressive Diem regime, and around its lotus-shaped pedestal are carved images of the monks and nuns that set fire to themselves in protest.

The Po Nagar Cham towers

One and a half kilometres north of the city centre along 2 Thang 4 stands Nha Trang's most gripping attraction, the **Po Nagar Cham Towers** (daily 6am–6pm). The Hindu Chams probably built ten towers or *kalan* here on Cu Lao Hill between the seventh and twelfth centuries, but only four remain. The largest and most impressive of these is the 23-metre-high northern tower, built in 817 and dedicated to Yang Ino Po Nagar, Goddess Mother of the Kingdom and a manifestation of Uma, Shiva's consort. Time has taken its toll on this square-shaped tower, but the lotus-petal and spearhead motifs are still intact, as is the lintel over the outer door, on which four-armed Shiva dances. Inside, the main chamber holds a headless black stone statue of ten-armed Uma. The central tower is dedicated to the god Cri Cambhu and popular with childless couples praying for fertility. Beneath the boat-shaped roof of the northwest tower, half-formed statues in relief are still visible, and the frontal view of an elephant is just about discernible on the western facade. The on-site museum (daily 7.30am–5pm) holds a dreary display of statues and photographs.

The islands

Perhaps the single greatest pleasure of a stay in Nha Trang is a day-trip to one of the nearby **islands**, best reached on one of the popular day-trips organized by the tour operators listed opposite. It's also possible, though pricey, to charter your own boat from Cau Da Wharf, 6km south of Nha Trang; prices start at $50 per boat per day.

The closest of the islands to Cau Da, **HON MIEU**, is served by a local ferry (15min; $1 return) which docks at Tri Nguyen, a fishing village, from where it's a few minutes' walk to Tri Nguyen Aquarium, a series of saltwater ponds constructed for breeding and research purposes and a small indoor aquarium. Southeast of the aquarium there's a shingly beach at the fishing village at Bai Soai. The shallows that ring **HON TAM**, 2km southeast of Mieu, are good for snorkelling. **HON TRE**'s cliffs lend a welcome dash of drama to this, the largest of Nha Trang's islands, and offset the fine white sand of its beach, Bai Tru. Two smaller isles hover off Hon Tre's southern coast: **HON MOT** has a stony beach but good snorkelling; **HON MUN** harbours caves where sea swifts' nests are harvested and sold at thousands of dollars per kilo for use in birds' nest soups. There's no beach to speak of on Mun, but some great coral.

A pricier boat excursion ($20) takes in some of the above islands before finishing up at the resort area of **Con Se Tre**, fifteen minutes by boat from Nha Trang beach, on Hon Tre. The resort attempts to "recreate the atmosphere of a Vietnamese village" with its thatched huts, bamboo bridges and traditional activities. Information and tickets are available from the Con Se Tre office at 100/16 Tran Phu (☎ 058/811163). On some of the islands there is a range of accommodation available; the tour operators (see below) can give details.

Practicalities

Nha Trang's **long-distance bus station** sits 1km west of the city centre at 58, 23 Thang 10; if you're moving on to Buon Me Thuot, four air-con express minibuses ($3, journey time four hours), leave daily from here. **Open-tour buses** will usually drop you at a selection of hotels in town, before terminating at their respective offices (see below). The **train station** (ticket office daily 7.30–11am & 1.30–9pm; ☎058/822113) is a few hundred metres east along Thai Nguyen. The **airport** is just below town, a short cyclo ride from hotels. Vietnam Airlines is at 91 Nguyen Thien Thuat.

Bicycles can be rented from most hotels ($1) and there are **cyclos** and **Honda oms** aplenty. The following **tour operators** can arrange car rental ($30–35 per day), tours of the region and further afield, open-tour buses to Ho Chi Minh, Da Lat, Hoi An, Phan Thiet and Da Nang, as well as **boat trips** to nearby islands ($7 a head): Mama Linh, 2a Hung Vuong (☎058/826693); Khanh Hoa Tourism, 1 Tran Hung Dao (☎058/822753); My A Tours, 10 Hung Vuong (☎058/826195); TM Brothers Café, 22 Tran Hung Dao (☎058/814556); Hanh Café, 22 Tran Hung Dao (☎058/829014).

Vietcombank, 17 Quang Trung, changes **cash** and travellers' cheques, and can also advance cash against Visa, Mastercard and JCB cards. The GPO, 2 Tran Phu (daily 7am–9pm), has fax, **poste restante**, DHL courier and **IDD** facilities; IDD is also available at the smaller post office opposite the *Vien Dong*, at 50 Le Thanh Ton (24hr) or at 23, Biet Thu (daily 6.30am–9pm). **Internet** access is available at Internet Services at 2 Le Loi opposite the main GPO, and at the post office (24hr access) on Le Thanh Ton. Nha Trang's **hospital** is below the city stadium, at 19 Yersin (☎058/822168) and there's an English-speaking pharmacy at 12 Tran Quy Cap, in the centre.

Petty crime has become something of a problem in Nha Trang. Due attention should be taken at all times with your belongings not only on the beach, but also on cyclos and around the streets after dark.

ACCOMMODATION

Ana Mandara Resort, Beachside Tran Phu (☎058/829829). Luxurious resort with top facilities, attractive bungalow suites and a scuba-diving school. ⑨.

Bai Duong, Hon Chong Beach (☎058/831015). Sleepy seaside hotel signposted 300m north of the turning to Hon Chong Promontory. Bargain-priced en-suite doubles and several smarter rooms. ②–④.

Dong Phuong, 103 Nguyen Thien Thuat (☎058/825896). Hugely popular, family-run hotel, one of many budget options clustered around this area. Functional, but spacious rooms, some with air-con. Discounts negotiable and free transfer shuttles. ②–④.

Guesthouse 78, 78 Tran Phu (☎058/826342). Motel-style place offering characterless but pristine doubles with air-con, no-frills fan rooms in a grungier annexe and good-value four-bed rooms – all come with private bathroom. ②–⑥.

Hai Yen, 40 Tran Phu (☎058/822828). Rooms are well fitted and comfy, and there are a handful of budget rooms. Shares swimming pool with *Vien Dong*. ③–⑥.

Huu Nghi, 3 Tran Hung Dao (☎058/822246). Perennial backpackers' stamping ground; bright, good-value choice of en-suite rooms, recently upgraded. ②–④.

My Hoa, 7 Hang Ca (☎058/810111). Smart, family-run, centrally located mini-hotel with tidy, reasonably priced en-suite rooms. ②–③.

Nha Trang I, 129 Thong Nhat (☎058/823764). Ageing budget hotel, but en-suite rooms are clean and reasonably well maintained; some air-con. ②–③.

Phu Quy, 54 Hung Vuong (☎058/810609). Friendly, new family-run mini-hotel; air-con and fan rooms are small, but reasonably priced and clean; extra dollars secure a balcony and there's a roof-top terrace. ②–④.

Vien Dong, 1 Tran Hung Dao (☎058/821606). Professionally run operation with a pool, tennis courts and nightly traditional music. Rooms in the main building are welcoming, but those in the poolside annexe are less polished. ⑥.

EATING AND DRINKING

Café des Amis, 13 Biet Thu. Perennial favourite run by two former academics from Hué; well-prepared Vietnamese and Western dishes, with local artwork for sale. 7.30am–late.

Hai Dao, 304, 2 Thang 4. Secluded restaurant perched on an isle in the Cai River; grilled cuttlefish with citronella and pimento comes recommended, traditional music performed here three times a week. 10am–10pm.

Hoan Hai, 6 Phan Chu Trinh. Busy seafood restaurant, with a good vegetarian selection. 8am–11pm.

Lac Canh, 11 Hang Ca. Charismatic joint, locally renowned for its mouth- and eye-watering cooked-at-table barbecues. 8am–9.30pm.

Lizard/Zippo Bar, 2 Hung Vuong. One of Nha Trang's trendiest bar–restaurants. Gorge on shrimps in coconut milk or barbecued beef, then shift to the bar with its stack of CDs. 6am–10pm (food); 6pm–3am (bar).

Nha Trang Sailing Club, 72–74 Tran Phu. Draws a well-heeled expat crowd and hordes of tourists to its refined beachfront bar which gets less refined as the night wears on; make sure you keep an eye on your drinks bill. There are laser disc films shown daily and fairly decent Italian and Japanese restaurants in the club compound. Noon–3am.

Rainbow Bar, 52 Tran Phu. Hugely popular with the backpacker set; beachside bar with lively dance floor, deadly cocktails, billiards and regular beach barbecues. 7am–late.

Thanh The Restaurant, 3 Phan Chu Trinh. Bright, open-fronted seafood restaurant where the shrimps grilled with garlic won't disappoint. 7.30–10.30pm.

Quang Ngai and Son My Village

The area around **QUANG NGAI**, 130km south of Da Nang, had a long tradition of resistance against the French, which found further focus during American involvement. In response, this region suffered some of the most extensive bombing meted out during the war: by 1967, seventy percent of villages in the town's surrounding area had been destroyed. A year later, the Americans turned their sights on Son My Village, site of the infamous **My Lai massacre**, which is now remembered in a moving memorial garden and museum.

Son My Village

The massacre of civilians in the hamlets of **Son My Village**, the single most shameful chapter of America's involvement in Vietnam, began at dawn on March 16, 1968. US Intelligence suggested that the 48th Local Forces Battalion of the NVA was holed up in Son My and the task force assembled to flush them out included Charlie Company, whose First Platoon was assigned to sweep through My Lai 4 (Tu Cung). Charlie Company had suffered casualties and losses from snipers and booby traps and had come to feel frustrated and impotent, so Son My offered the chance to settle some old scores. At a briefing, GIs were glibly told that all civilians would be at the market by 7am and that anyone remaining was bound to be an active VC sympathizer. A massacre ensued. Five hundred Son My villagers were killed, 347 of them from Tu Cung. Not one shot was fired at a GI in response. The My Lai massacre is remembered at the **Son My Memorial Park** (daily 7am–6pm; $1), 12km east of Quang Ngai in Son My's sub-hamlet of Tu Cung. The garden retains its scars – bullet holes in trees; foundations of homes burnt down, each with a stone tablet recording its family's losses. Inside the second of two buildings on its western flank, there's a memorial plaque recording the names of the dead, and a grisly photograph gallery documenting the events of that day.

Buses for Son My leave occasionally from the bus station in Quang Ngai, but the most efficient means of reaching the village is by Honda om. In stark contrast, secluded **My Khe Beach**, 3km east of My Lai, is several kilometres long and very good for swimming.

Practicalities

The junction of Quang Trung (Highway 1) with westward-pointing Hung Vuong effectively forms central Quang Ngai. **Trains** arrive 3km west of town along Hung Vuong, while the **bus station** is 500m south of the centre, and 50m east of Quang Trung on Le Thanh Ton. Quang

Ngai Tourist is 150m north of Hung Vuong at 310 Quang Trung; the post office is 300m west of the highway, on Hung Vuong. At the far western end of the same, Vietcombank changes travellers' cheques and dollars and can arrange cash advances on Visa, MasterCard and JCB cards. The more central Vietincombank at 89 Hung Vuong and the *My Tra Hotel* can also change travellers' cheques and dollars.

First choice among the handful of **places to stay** in town is one of the twenty-three rooms, some spacious with balcony, in Hung Vuong's clean and friendly *Kim Thanh Hotel* (☎055/823471; ①–③); a few metres west, the *Vietnam* (☎055/823610; ②) is rather grimier, but still adequate. The more upmarket *My Tra Hotel* (☎055/842985; ⑥), just across the bridge, enjoys a prime riverside location — its well-appointed rooms all have balconies. The hotel's open-air terrace **restaurant** looks out across the river and its selection of local dishes are reasonable; otherwise head for two decent *com* shops – the *Mimosa* and the *Bac Son* – next door to the *Kim Thanh* in town.

THE CENTRAL PROVINCES

Vietnam's narrow waist comprises a string of provinces squeezed between the long, sandy coastline and the formidable barrier of the Truong Son Mountains, which mark the border between Vietnam and Laos. For foreigners, there are just two **overland crossings into Laos** here: the straightforward and accessible Lao Bao, along Highway 9 from Dong Ha (see p.1037), and the more remote Cau Treo, on Highway 8 from Vinh (see p.1037). Lao visas can be obtained in the city of **Da Nang**, a useful transport hub but not much more. However, there's plenty to occupy you before heading off to Laos, not least the much visited riverside town of **Hoi An**, renowned for its traditional Chinese merchants' houses and temples, and its crafts, and as a base for exploring the fine ruins of the Cham temple complex at nearby **My Son**. The former Vietnamese capital of **Hué** is equally impressive, and its nineteenth-century palaces, temples and royal mausoleums constitute one of Vietnam's highlights. In 1954 Vietnam was divided at the Seventeenth Parallel, only 100km north of Hué, where the **Demilitarized Zone (DMZ)** marked the border between North and South Vietnam until reunification in 1975. The desolate battlefields of the DMZ and the extraordinary complex of residential **tunnels** nearby are a poignant memorial to those, on both sides, who fought here and to the civilians who lost their lives in the bitter conflict.

Hoi An

The ancient core of seductive, charming **HOI AN** is a rich architectural fusion of Chinese, Japanese, Vietnamese and European influences dating back to the sixteenth century. In its heyday the port town attracted vessels from the world's great trading nations, and many Chinese merchants stayed on. Somehow the town escaped damage during both the French and American wars and its charming 200-year-old wooden-fronted shop-houses are among its chief tourist sights. Not surprisingly, Hoi An is now firmly on the tourist agenda and for some is already too much of a trap, with its proliferating souvenir stalls, art galleries and hotels.

Arrival, information and getting around

Most people arrive in Hoi An by car, or by Honda om from Da Nang airport or train station (30km); local **buses** drop you 1km west of the town centre. Bicycles (less than $1) and motorbikes ($4–6 a day) are available for rent from Mr My at the stall opposite Kin Kin fabric shop. He can also organize day-trips for $6–8 including motorbike and driver; large motorbikes are prohibited from Tran Phu, Nguyen Thai Hoc and Bach Dang.

Hoi An has plenty of **tour agencies** offering tours, transport, rail and air tickets: try Hoi An Booking Office (also known as *Hai's Café*; ☎0510/861947) at 23 Tran Hung Dao, or *Hoi An Hotel* at 6 Tran Hung Dao. They all do cars and tourist **minibuses to Hué** ($5 per per-

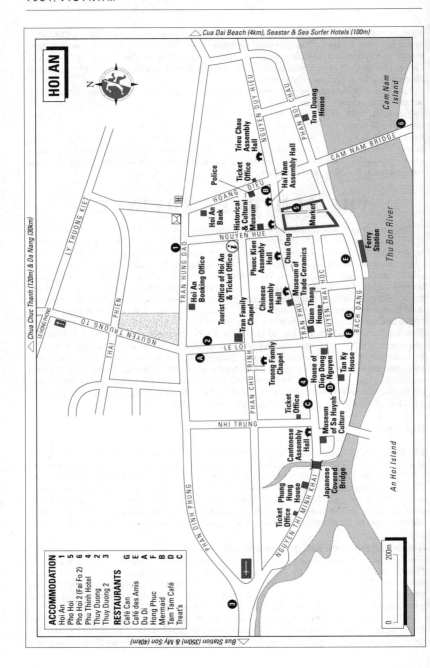

HOI AN

Cua Dai Beach (4km), Seastar & Sea Surfer Hotels (100m)

Chua Chuc Thanh (120m) & Da Nang (30km)

Bus Station (350m) & My Son (40km)

Cam Nam Island

Thu Bon River

An Hoi Island

Cam Nam Bridge

Tran Duong House

Hai Nam Assembly Hall

Trieu Chau Assembly Hall

Police

Ticket Office

Historical & Cultural Museum

Hoi An Bank

Market

Chua Ong

Phuoc Kien Assembly Hall

Tourist Office of Hoi An & Ticket Office

Hoi An Booking Office

Tran Family Chapel

Chinese Assembly Hall

Museum of Trade Ceramics

Quan Thang House

Ferry Station

Truong Family Chapel

House of Diep Dong Nguyen

Tan Ky House

Ticket Office

Museum of Sa Huynh Culture

Cantonese Assembly Hall

Phung Hung House

Japanese Covered Bridge

Ticket Office

HOANG DIEU
NGUYEN DUY HIEU
PHAN BOI
CHAU
NGUYEN HUE
TRAN HUNG DAO
LY THUONG KIET
LE HONG PHONG
NGUYEN TRUONG TO
THAI PHIEN
LE LOI
PHAN CHU TRINH
TRAN PHU
NGUYEN THAI HOC
BACH DANG
NHI TRUNG
PHAN DINH PHUNG
NGUYEN THI MINH KHAI

ACCOMMODATION
Hoi An	1
Pho Hoi	5
Pho Hoi 2 (Fai Fo 2)	6
Phu Thinh Hotel	4
Thuy Duong	2
Thuy Duong 2	3

RESTAURANTS
Café Can	G
Café des Amis	E
Du Di	A
Hong Phuc	F
Mermaid	B
Tam Tam Café	D
Treat's	C

N

200m

son) and Nha Trang ($10–15 per person); for transport **to Da Nang** hire a car ($8–10) or Honda om ($2–3), as local buses from Hoi An bus station (every 3hr until 4 or 5pm; 2hr; $1–2) take ages and are always overcrowded.

Hoi An Bank, at 4 Hoang Dieu, and *Hoi An Hotel*, **exchange** dollar notes and travellers' cheques; and the **GPO** at 5 Tran Hung Dao keeps poste restante. **Internet** access is available at a number of places: the cheapest are Bao Anh, 2 Phan Chu Trinh, and Ho Van Dan booking office, 35 Le Loi (both charge 400d per min). The **Police** are located at 8 Hoang Dieu.

Accommodation

Cua Dai, 18a Cua Dai (☎0510/862231). The best address in town aims for a notch above the backpacker standard. Friendly service, Internet access and a full complement of tours, ticketing and transport arrangements make it well worth a little extra. ③–④.

Dong Xanh aka *Green Field*, 1c Cua Dai (☎0510/863484). A new and well appointed hotel, with comfortable rooms, tour information and Internet. ③–④.

Hoi An, 6 Tran Hung Dao (☎0510/861373). Large, state-run, colonial-style hotel, with simple en-suite doubles, spacious suites and a pool. Also has a restaurant, exchange, bike rental, information, onward travel and Internet. The swimming pool is also open to non-residents. ②–③.

Pho Hoi aka *Fai Fo*, 7/2 Tran Phu (☎0510/861633). Two neighbouring hotels under the same owner, located down an alley beside the *Coconut Milk Café*. The newer *Pho Hoi 2* is just beside the exit from the bridge on Cam Nam Island, and quieter than guesthouses in town. ②–③.

Phu Thinh, 144 Tran Phu (☎0510/861297). Very centrally located and reasonably priced, though rooms are basic. ②.

Thuy Duong, 11 Le Loi (☎0510/861574). Clean four-berth rooms and a central location make this popular with budget travellers. Its new annexe at 68 Huynh Thuc Khang (☎0510/861394) is a fair walk from town. ②.

The Town

The **historic core** of Hoi An consists of just three short streets: Tran Phu is the oldest and even today is the principal commercial street, with plenty of crafts shops and galleries; one block south, Nguyen Thai Hoc has many wooden townhouses and some galleries; and riverfront Bach Dang holds the ferry station and several waterside cafés. A **combined ticket** ($3) covers Hoi An's more famous sights and allows access to four places: the temple on the Japanese Covered Bridge; the Historical and Cultural Museum (including Chua Ong), the museum of trade ceramics, or the museum of Sa Huynh culture; one of the participating Chinese Assembly Halls; and one of the participating merchants' houses or family chapels. Extra tickets are available for less than $1 per sight. Tickets are on sale at the Tourist Office of Hoi An at 12 Phan Chu Trinh, at 52 Nguyen Thi Minh Khai (☎0510/861982), 19 Nhi Trung and 5 Hoang Dieu; all offices and relevant sights are open daily from 6am to 6pm.

JAPANESE COVERED BRIDGE

The western end of Tran Phu is marked by a small, red bridge known as the **Japanese Covered Bridge**, which has been adopted as Hoi An's emblem. It has been reconstructed several times since the mid-sixteenth century to the same simple design. Inside the bridge's narrow span are a collection of stelae and four statues, two dogs and two monkeys, usually said to record that work began in the year of the monkey and ended in that of the dog. All motorbikes are forbidden on the Japanese bridge, and pedal bikes must be pushed across it.

THE CHINESE ASSEMBLY HALLS

Historically, Hoi An's ethnic Chinese population organized themselves according to their place of origin (Fujian, Guangdong, Chaozhou or Hainan), and each group maintained its own Assembly Hall as both community centre and house of worship. The most populous group hails from Fujian, and their **Phuoc Kien Assembly Hall**, at 46 Tran Phu, is an imposing edifice with an ostentatious, triple-arched gateway. The hall is dedicated to Thien Hau, Goddess of the Sea and protector of sailors. She stands, fashioned in 200-year-old papier mâché, on the main altar flanked by her green- and red-faced assistants, who between them can see or hear any boat in distress over a range of a thousand miles.

Trieu Chau Assembly Hall, on the far eastern edge of town at 157 Nguyen Duy Hieu, was built in 1776 by Chinese from Chaozhou and has a remarkable display of woodcarving. In the altar-niche sits Ong Bon, a general in the Chinese Navy, surrounded by a frieze teeming with bird, animal and insect life; the altar table also depicts life on land and in the ocean.

THE MERCHANTS' HOUSES

Most of Hoi An's original wooden buildings are on Tran Phu and south towards the river, which is where you'll see the best-known merchants' house, at 101 Nguyen Thai Hoc. The **Tan Ky House** is a beautifully preserved example of a two-storey, late eighteenth-century shop-house, with shop space at the front, a tiny central courtyard and access to the river at the back. It is wonderfully cluttered with the property of seven generations grown wealthy from trading silk, tea and rice and boasts two exceptionally fine hanging poem-boards. The house gets very crowded and is best visited early or late in the day.

Just up from the covered bridge at 4 Nguyen Minh Khai, **Phung Hung House** has been home to the same family for eight generations since they moved from Hué in about 1780 to trade cinnamon and hardwoods from the central highlands. The large two-storey house is Vietnamese style although its eighty ironwood columns and small glass skylights denote Japanese influence. An upstairs living area features a shrine to the ancestors as well as a large shrine to the protector deity Thien Hau, suspended from the ceiling.

Phan Chu Trinh, one block north of Tran Phu, hides two captivating "family chapels". On Phan Chu Trinh itself is the 200-year-old **Tran Family Chapel** within a walled compound on the junction with Le Loi. Over home-made lotus flower tea you learn about the family, going back thirteen generations (300 years) to when the first ancestor settled in Hanoi. Family portraits are displayed in the reception room, and oblong wooden funerary boxes contain a name-tablet and biographical details of deceased family leaders. The smaller but more elaborate **Truong Family Chapel** is hidden down an alley beside *Pho Hoi Restaurant* at 69 Phan Chu Trinh (not covered by ticket scheme; 7.30am–noon & 2–5pm; small donation expected). The Truong ancestors fled China in the early eighteenth century following the collapse of the Ming dynasty. The four finely carved wooden partitions in the sanctuary room come from Fujian and gifts from the Hué court are on display.

MUSEUMS AND THE MARKET

Housed in a traditional timber residence-cum-warehouse, the **Museum of Trade Ceramics** at 80 Tran Phu showcases the history of Hoi An's ceramics trade, which peaked in the fifteenth and sixteenth centuries. The smaller **Museum of Sa Huynh Culture** at 149 Tran Phu displays artefacts found in Sa Huynh, 130km south of Hoi An, which flourished between the second century BC and the second century AD. Hoi An **market** at the east end of Tran Phu retains the atmosphere of a typical, traditional country market despite the number of tourists. This is a good place to buy **silk** (which is cheaper than in Hanoi or Ho Chi Minh City) and to get clothes made – rows of tailors will knock up beautiful garments in a matter of hours.

Eating

Hoi An has excellent food of all kinds, including local **specialities** such as *cao lau*, thick rice-flour noodles, beansprouts and pork-rind croutons in a light soup topped with thin slices of pork. Also look out for the steamed manioc-flour parcels of finely diced crab or shrimp called *banh bao* (or *banh vac*), and fried wanton (*hoanh thanh chien*).

Café Can, 74 Bach Dang. A welcoming restaurant offering Hoi An specialities and an excellent-value seafood menu – four courses for $3.

Café des Amis, 52 Bach Dang. Renowned for its "Vietnamese cuisine plus imagination" and charismatic host, there's no menu, just four dishes for $3. The veggie and seafood specialities are all great. Try the Vietnamese set menu to sample a bit of everything. Open till late.

Du Di, 12 Le Loi. A popular backpacker haunt, serving standard traveller-friendly fare.

Hong Phuc, 86 Bach Dang. A friendly, good-value eatery in a great waterside location, run by two multi-lingual female cousins who niftily fillet your fish at the table. Happy hour drinks 5–6.30pm get a twenty per-cent reduction.

Mermaid aka *Nhu Y*, 2 Tran Phu. Run by the owner of the *Cua Dai* hotel, the restaurant shares the hotel's strong reputation for service and value. The speciality is marinated fish grilled with saffron in banana leaf, or try the set dinner – choice of two starters and mains plus dessert for under $5.

Tam Tam Café, 110 Hguyen Thai Hoc. Stylish French-run bar/eatery open late with music, pool, happy hour beers 6–9pm and an upscale international cuisine restaurant.

Treat's Same Same Café, 158 Tran Phu. Bar–restaurant with a popular happy hour 7–9pm daily which enigmatically promises to be "same same but different."

My Son

The mouldering, overgrown ruins of Vietnam's most evocative Cham site, **MY SON** (daily 6.30am–4.30pm; $4 includes transport 2km from the ticket office to the ruins), lie 40km southwest of Hoi An, in a bowl of lushly wooded hills. The track out to the site strikes west from Highway 1 at Duy Xuyen and is quite treacherous so most visitors come on a tour from Hoi An or Da Nang ($7) rather than on a rented motorbike.

Excavations at My Son show that Cham kings were buried here as early as the fourth century, but the ruined sanctuaries you see today were erected between the seventh and thirteenth centuries. My Son was considered the domain of gods and god-kings, and in its prime, comprised some seventy buildings. The sanctuaries weathered well until the Sixties when the Viet Cong based themselves here and were pounded by American B52s. There are **unexploded mines** in the area, so don't stray from main paths.

Group B is regarded by archeologists as the spiritual epicentre of My Son. Of the central *kalan* (sanctuary), **B1**, only the base remains; but stone epitaphs reveal that it was dedicated to the god-king Bhadresvara, a hybrid of Shiva and King Bhadravarman, and erected in the eleventh century. **B5**, the impressive **repository room**, boasts a bowed, boat-shaped roof still in reasonably good nick. The outer walls support ornate columns and statues of deities, and, on the western side, a bas-relief depicting two elephants with their trunks entwined around a coconut tree. Next door in **Group C**, the central *kalan*, **C1**, is fairly well preserved; statues of gods stand around the walls and a carved lintel runs across the entrance.

East of B and C, the two long, windowed meditation halls that comprise **Group D** have now both been converted into modest galleries. **D1** contains a lingam, the remains of a carving of Shiva, and a statue of Nandi, Shiva's Bull; while in **D2** you'll see a fine frieze depicting many-armed Shiva dancing, and, below the steps up to its eastern entrance, a statue of Garuda. Bomb damage was particularly cruel in the vicinity of **Group A**, reducing the once-spectacular *kalan*, **A1**, to a heap of toppled columns and lintels. Within, a huge lingam base is ringed by a number of detailed, 15cm-high figures at prayer.

Da Nang

Central Vietnam's dominant port and its fourth largest city, **DA NANG** harbours few sights beyond the exceptional Cham Museum, but is an unexpectedly amiable place and a major transport hub with air connections as well as road and rail links. In the American War it served as a massive South Vietnamese airbase and played host to thousands of US troops as well as refugees searching for work. But walking around today, it's the earlier, French presence which is more apparent in the leafy boulevards and colonial-style houses.

Two blocks south of Cho Han market, past the soft, salmon-mousse cathedral, colonial Da Nang is represented by a few wooden and stucco houses at the eastern end of Tran Quoc Toan. From here turn right along the river for 750m to reach the **Cham Museum**, at the south end of Bach Dang (daily 7am–5pm; $2), the most comprehensive display of Cham art

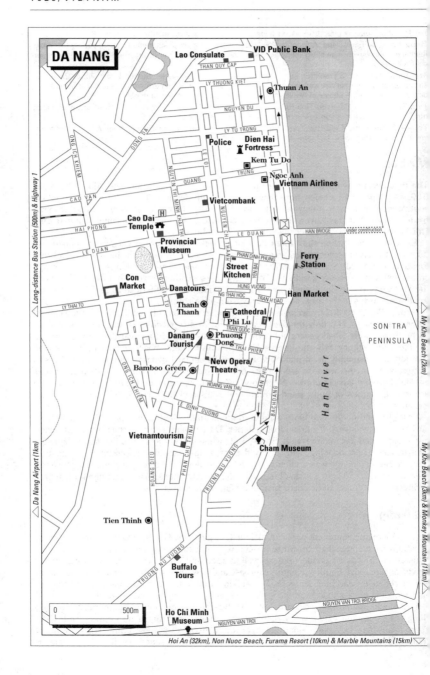

DA NANG

VID Public Bank
Lao Consulate
THAN QUY CAP
LY THUONG KIET
Thuan An
NGUYEN DU
LY TU TRONG
Police
Dien Hai
Fortress
Kem Tu Do
TRUNG
Ngoc Anh
Vietnam Airlines
QUANG
Vietcombank
Cao Dai
Temple
Provincial
Museum
LE DUAN
HAN BRIDGE   under construction
PHAN DINH PHUNG
Street
Kitchen
Ferry
Station
Con
Market
Danatours
HUNG VUONG
NG THAI HOC
TRAN H DAO
Han Market
Thanh
Thanh
Cathedral
Phi Lu
TRAN QUOC TOAN
Danang
Tourist
Phuong
Dong
THAI PHIEN
SON TRA
PENINSULA
New Opera/
Theatre
Bamboo Green
HOANG VAN THU
LE DINH DUONG
Vietnamtourism
Cham Museum
Tien Thinh
Buffalo
Tours
0   500m
Ho Chi Minh
Museum
NGUYEN VAN TROI
NGUYEN VAN TROI BRIDGE

DONG DA
ONG ICH KHIEM
CAO VAN
HAI PHONG
LE DUAN
NGO GIA TU
LY THAI TO
ONG ICH KHIEM
HOANG DIEU
PHAN CHI TRINH
TRUONG NU VUONG
NGUYEN THI MINH KHAI
NGUYEN CHI THANH
YEN BAI
TRAN PHU
BACH DANG
TRUONG NU VUONG

Han River

◁ Long-distance Bus Station (500m) & Highway 1

◁ Da Nang Airport (1km)

▷ My Khe Beach (2km)

▷ My Khe Beach (3km) & Monkey Mountain (11km) ▷

Hoi An (32km), Non Nuoc Beach, Furama Resort (10km) & Marble Mountains (15km) ▽

in the world. Its display of graceful, sometimes severe, terracotta and sandstone figures gives a tantalizing glimpse of an artistically inspired culture that ruled most of southern Vietnam for a thousand years. Exhibits are grouped according to their place of origin: My Son (4–11C), Tra Kieu (Simhapura; 4–10C), Dong Duong (Indrapura; 8–10C), and Binh Dinh (11–15C).

Da Nang's **Cao Dai Temple**, at 63 Hai Phong opposite the hospital, was built in 1956 and is Vietnam's second most important after Tay Ninh (see p.994). An elderly archbishop, assisted by seventeen priests, ministers to a congregation here said to number 50,000. The temple is a smaller, simpler version of Tay Ninh, dominated inside by the all-seeing eye of the Supreme Being and paintings of Cao Dai's principal saints, Lao-tzu, Confucius, Jesus Christ and Buddha. Adherents gather to worship four times a day (6am, noon, 6pm, midnight).

Practicalities

Da Nang's **airport** is 3km southwest of the city and served by taxis ($5) and Honda om ($1–2). The **train station** lies 2km west of town at 122 Hai Phong. Long-distance **buses** arrive 1km further out at Lien Tinh bus station, 33 Dien Bien Phu. To get into town take a cyclo or a xe om (less than $1). Most hotels and tour agents offer **bicycle** rental ($1), **car** rental ($20–30) and self-drive **motorbikes** ($5–7).

For tours and **information**, contact Danatours at 95 Hung Vuong (☎0511/823993), Danang Tourist, at 92a Phan Chu Trinh (☎0511/821423) or Vietnamtourism at 274 Phan Chu Trinh (☎0511/822990). More reliable is the branch of Hanoi's Buffalo Tours at 103a Trung Nu Vuong (☎0511/872909). **Exchange facilities** are available at Vietcombank, 104 Le Loi, including credit-card transactions and travellers' cheques. The main **post office** is at 60 Bach Dang, but cross the Le Duan junction to find poste restante (6.30am–9.30pm) at no. 62. Vietnam Airlines is at 35 Tran Phu (☎0511/821130), the **immigration police** are at 78 Le Loi, and the city **hospital** is at Benh Vien C, 76 Hai Phong, opposite the Cao Dai Temple (☎0511/821118). You can get **tourist visas for Laos** at the Lao Consulate, 12 Tran Quy Cap (☎0511/821208; Mon–Fri 8–11.30am & 2–4.30pm), in two days for $50; see p.451 for details on Laos visas and border crossings. **Internet** access is expensive in Da Nang; try the *Bamboo Café* at 5 Bach Dang (1000d per min).

Da Nang has plenty of **hotels**, but you'll still find better value and choice in Hoi An. The best of the cheapies is probably *Thuan An* (☎0511/820527; ①), at 14 Bach Dang, which has en-suite though rather dark rooms on the riverfront. The *Tien Thinh*, 310 Hoang Dieu (☎0511/834566; ③–④), is a good-value mini-hotel with twenty clean rooms offering satellite TV, private bathroom and IDD telephone as standard. Transport and ticketing can be

---

MOVING ON FROM DA NANG

Heading to Hué, you can take the train (6am train is fastest), the bus, a Honda om ($10) or a hire car ($20–30). Local buses for Hué leave from the main Lien Tinh bus station; a tourist bus ($6) leaves daily at 9am and 3pm and will collect you from your hotel. Motorbikes wait outside Da Nang train station to whisk you off to Hoi An (45min; $4–5); by taxi or hire car it's about $15. Local buses run there from opposite Lien Tinh bus station (every 3hr; 1hr30min–2hr; $1–2). A more comfortable option is the tourist bus, with daily departures ($3). Tourist buses also leave daily at 7am for Nha Trang ($15) and Ho Chi Minh ($25). The Tien Thinh Hotel at 310 Hoang Dieu can help organize tickets for trains and tourist buses.

An overnight bus service runs from Da Nang direct to Savannakhet on the Laos/Thai border (Mon, Wed, Thurs and Sun; departs 7.30pm and can take up to 24 hours owing to long delays at the border; $23).

arranged via the reception. *Thanh Thanh* (☎0511/830684; ②–③), 50 Phan Chu Trinh, has reasonable rates for the city centre. Rooms are clean while the bathrooms are run-down but adequate. The *Bamboo Green* (☎0511/822996; ⑥–⑧), 158 Phan Chu Trinh, caters mainly for tour groups and businessmen, but does have some cheaper rooms.

Fruitful hunting grounds for local **restaurants** and foodstalls are along Ly Tu Trong, the southern end of Nguyen Thi Minh Khai, and streets around the *Phuong Dong Hotel* crossroads. *Ngoc Anh*, at 30 Tran Phu, serves generous portions of seafood dishes in a charming garden setting. *Phi Lu*, 225 Nguyen Chi Thanh, is a Chinese eatery popular with locals; try and get there around 8pm. The street kitchen at 42 Phan Dinh Phung is actually set in a garden and has excellent food at cheap prices, while the *Kem Tu Do* at 20 Quang Trung is the place for ice creams.

Hué

Unlike Hanoi, Ho Chi Minh and most other Vietnamese cities, **HUÉ** somehow seems to have stood aside from the current economic frenzy and, despite its calamitous history, has retained a unique cultural identity. It's a small, peaceful city, full of lakes, canals and lush vegetation and some magnificent historical sights – including the nineteenth-century walled citadel, the remnants of its once-magnificent Imperial City and seven palatial Royal Mausoleums. With all this to offer, Hué is inevitably one of Vietnam's pre-eminent tourist destinations. It's also the main jumping-off point for day-tours of the DMZ (see p.1035).

In 1802, Emperor Gia Long, founder of the **Nguyen dynasty**, moved the capital from Hanoi and built his Imperial City in Hué. From then on, the Nguyen dynasty ruled Vietnam from Hué until the abdication of Emperor Bao Dai in 1945, though the French seized the city in 1885, leaving them as nominal rulers only. During the 1968 **Tet Offensive** the North Vietnamese Army (NVA) held the city for 25 days, and in the ensuing counter-assault the city was all but levelled. Seven years later, on March 26, 1975, the NVA were back to liberate Hué, the first big town south of the Seventeenth Parallel. The huge task of rebuilding received a boost in 1993 when UNESCO listed Hué as a World Heritage Site.

Arrival, information and getting around

Flights into Hué's **Phu Bai Airport**, 15km southeast of the city, are met by an airport bus (less than $1) which goes to central hotels, and by metered taxis ($7). When it comes to moving on, the airport bus leaves from the MASCO office at 12 Ha Noi (☎054/825640), or arrange a pick-up from your hotel reception. Vietnam Airlines is in the *Thuan Hoa Hotel* at 7 Nguyen Tri Phuong (7–11am & 2–5pm). The train station lies about 1500m from the centre of town at the far western end of Le Loi, a boulevard running along the south bank of the Perfume River. Note that trains out of Hué get quickly booked up, so make onward travel arrangements as early as possible (ticket office open daily 7.30–11am & 1.30–4pm). Hué has two long-distance **bus stations**: services from the south pull into An Cuu station, 1km southeast of the centre, while buses from Hanoi and the north dump you at An Hoa station, 4km northwest on Highway 1: cyclos are on hand to take you into the centre. **Bicycles** (less than $1), **motorbikes** ($5–10) and **cars** ($20–30) can be rented from hotels, guesthouses and cafés. These will also help arrange onward transport by tourist minibus or hired car to Hoi An, Da Nang and Hanoi. The *Mandarin Café* (☎054/82128112), 12 Hung Vuong, is home to the Sinh Café's **open-tour** booking desk.

The main **post office** has temporarily relocated to 14 Ly Thong Kiet and offers the usual poste restante facilities. Vietcombank, near An Cuu bus station at 46 Hung Vuong, **exchanges** cash and travellers' cheques. **Internet** access is available from Giba Computer and Napeco Computers, both located on Tran Cao Van (400–500d per min). Hué Central **Hospital** is at 16 Le Loi (☎054/822325) and the **immigration police** are at 45a Ben Nghe.

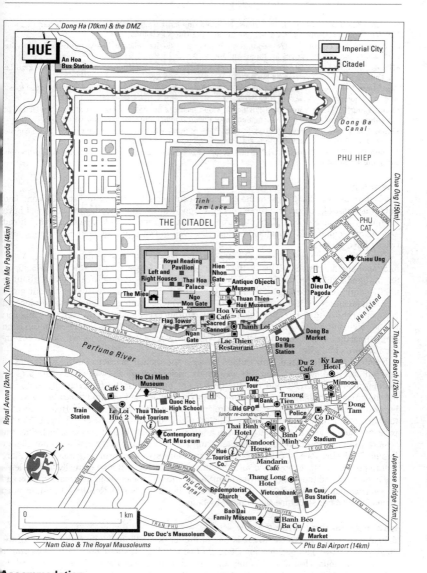

HUÉ

An Hoa Bus Station

Imperial City

Citadel

Dong Ha (70km) & the DMZ

Dong Ba Canal

PHU HIEP

Chua Ong (150m)

PHU CAT

Chieu Ung

Dieu De Pagoda

THE CITADEL

Tinh Tam Lake

Royal Reading Pavilion

Left and Right Houses

Thai Hoa Palace

Hien Nhon Gate

Antique Objects Museum

The Mieu

Ngo Mon Gate

Thuan Thien-Hué Museum

Hoa Viên

Café

Flag Tower

Sacred Cannons

Thanh Loi

Ngan Gate

Lac Thien Restaurant

Dong Ba Bus Station

Dong Ba Market

Perfume River

Thien Mu Pagoda (4km)

Royal Arena (2km)

Ho Chi Minh Museum

Café 3

Le Loi Hué 2

Train Station

Quoc Hoc High School

Thua Thien-Hué Tourism

Contemporary Art Museum

Hué Tourist Co.

Du 2 Café

Ky Lan Hotel

Mimosa

DMZ Tour

Bank

Truong Tien

Old GPO (under re-construction)

Police

Co Do

Dong Tam

Thai Binh Hotel

Tandoori House

Binh Minh

Stadium

Mandarin Café

Thang Long Hotel

Redemptorist Church

Vietcombank

An Cuu Bus Station

Bao Dai Family Museum

Banh Béo Ba Cu

An Cuu Market

Duc Duc's Mausoleum

Phu Cam Canal

Thuan An Beach (12km)

Hen Island

Japanese Bridge (7km)

Nam Giao & The Royal Mausoleums

Phu Bai Airport (14km)

0   1 km

N

Accommodation

There's always a room shortage in July and August when given rates may increase by up to a third.

Binh Minh aka *Sunrise*, 12 Nguyen Tri Phuong (☎054/825526). Bright, popular hotel with facilities ranging from rooms with fan and no window to TV, IDD phone and balcony. ④–⑤.

Ky Lan, 58 Le Loi (☎054/826556). A smart hotel offering large, well-decorated rooms, a decent range of facilities, including satellite TV and a restaurant serving Hué specialities. ③–④.

Le Loi Hué 2, 2 Le Loi (☎054/824668). A big hotel of unattractive concrete blocks but the closest to the train station and with fair prices for rooms and tours. ②–③.

Mimosa, 46/6 Le Loi (☎054/828068). One of several rather grotty guesthouses on an alley leading off Le Loi. Only for those on a very strict budget. ①.

Thai Binh, 10 Nguyen Tri Phuong (☎054/828058). A decent-value mini-hotel with standard facilities located down a quiet alleyway next to *Binh Minh*. ③.

Thang Long, 16 Hung Vuong (☎054/826462). Good facilities, homely rooms plus a decent selection of tours ($8 city tours) and tourist information make this new mini-hotel a good option. ③–④.

Thanh Loi, 7 Dinh Tien Hoang (☎054/824803). One of the few hotels north of the river located near the Citadel. Its top-floor rooms offer the best value, affording views of the flag tower. ②.

Truong Tien, 8 Hung Vuong (☎054/823127). A spruce hotel offering well-priced rooms, all with bathrooms and some with air-con. Tour booking office. ②.

The citadel

Hué's days of glory kicked off in the early nineteenth century when Emperor Gia Long laid out a vast **citadel**, comprising three concentric enclosures. In its heyday the city must have been truly awe-inspiring, a place of glazed yellow and green roof tiles, pavilions of rich red and gilded lacquer, and lotus-filled ponds. However, out of the original 148 buildings, only twenty have survived.

Ten gates pierce the citadel wall: enter through Ngan Gate, east of the flag tower. A second moat and defensive wall inside the citadel guard the **Imperial City** (daily 6am–5.30pm; $3; optional guide costs $3), which follows the same symmetrical layout about a north–south axis as Beijing's Forbidden City. By far the most impressive of its four gates is south-facing **Ngo Mon**, the Imperial City's principal entrance and a masterpiece of Nguyen architecture. The gate itself has five entrances: the central one for the emperor; two for civil and military mandarins, and two for the royal elephants. Perched on top is an elegant pavilion called the **Five Phoenix Watchtower** as its nine roofs are said to resemble five birds in flight.

North of Ngo Mon, **Thai Hoa Palace** boasts a spectacular interior glowing with sumptuous red and gold lacquers, and this was where major ceremonies were held. The present building dates from 1833, and was the only major building in the Imperial City to escape bomb damage. Nevertheless, the throne room's eighty ornate ironwood pillars, each weighing two tonnes, had to be painstakingly relacquered in 1991. North of Thai Hoa Palace, the ten-hectare **Forbidden Purple City**, enclosed by a low wall, was reserved for residential palaces, many of which were destroyed in a fire in 1947, but a handful remain, including the restored **Left House** and **Right House** facing each other across a courtyard immediately behind Thai Hoa Palace. Civil and military mandarins would spruce themselves up here before proceeding to an audience with the monarch. The Right House (actually to your left – the names refer to the emperor's viewpoint) is the more complete with its ornate murals and two gargantuan framed mirrors. Northeast from here, the **Royal Reading Pavilion** is an appealing, two-tier structure surrounded by bonsai.

Boat trips on the Perfume River

A boat trip on the **Perfume River** is one of the city's highlights, puttering in front of the citadel, past row-boats heading for Dong Ba market. The standard **boat trip** takes you to Thien Mu Pagoda, Hon Chen Temple and the most rewarding Royal Mausoleums, and it's usually possible to take a bicycle on the boat and cycle back to Hué. Most tour agents and hotels offer river tours starting at $3 per person. The same agents can arrange charter boats at $20–25 for the day, or go direct to the boatmen beside the Dap Da causeway, where the going rate should be $2–3 per hour.

Founded in 1601 by Nguyen Hoang, **Thien Mu Pagoda** is the oldest in Hué and has long been a focus for Buddhist protest against repression. In 1963 it hit international headlines when one of its monks, the Venerable Thich Quang Duc, burned himself to death in Saigon, in protest at the excesses of President Diem's regime. The monk's powder-blue Austin car is now on display here, with a copy of the famous photograph that shocked the world. The seven tiers of the octagonal, brick stupa each represent one of Buddha's incarnations on earth. Thien Mu Pagoda is also within **cycling** distance of Hué (6km; 30min). Follow Le Duan (Highway 1) south from the citadel as far as the train tracks and then just keep heading west along the river.

Hon Chen Temple ($2) is most memorable for its scenery of russet temple roofs among towering trees. Of several shrines and temples that populate the hillside, the most interesting is the main sanctuary, Hue Nam, up from the landing stage and to the right, with its unique nine-tier altar table and small, upper sanctuary room accessible via two steep staircases. Hon Chen Temple is 9km from Hué and is only accessible from the river. If you don't want to take a **tour**, hire a sampan either from the ferry station opposite the temple (accessible from the riverside road), or from Minh Mang pier; $2 return).

A more unusual way to enjoy the Perfume River is to attend a traditional **folksong performance** on its waters. Under the Nguyen emperors Hué was the cultural as well as political capital of Vietnam, and artists would entertain the gentry with poetry and music from sampans on the river. These days, the kiosk next to *Song Huong Floating Restaurant*, just east of Trang Tien Bridge, organizes boats most evenings; an hour's performance costs $30, which includes a boat for up to ten people, plus six musicians. Minh-Hai boat company (☎054/845060 after 9pm) can also organize dinner cruises with traditional music.

The Royal Mausoleums

The Nguyens built themselves magnificent **Royal Mausoleums** in the valley of the Perfume River among low, forested hills to the south of Hué. Each one is a unique expression of the monarch's personality, usually planned in detail during his lifetime to serve as his palace in death. Once an auspicious site was found, artificial lakes, waterfalls, hills and garden settings were added. Though the details vary, all the mausoleums consist of three elements. The main **temple** is dedicated to the worship of the deceased emperor and his queen and houses their funeral tablets and possessions. A large, stone **stele** records details of his reign, in front of which spreads a paved courtyard, where ranks of stone mandarins line up to honour their emperor. The royal **tomb** itself is enclosed within a wall.

The contrasting mausoleums of Tu Duc, Khai Dinh and Minh Mang are the most attractive and well preserved, as well as being easily accessible. These are also the three covered by the boat trips, so they can get crowded; everywhere gets packed at weekends. **Entry** to the mausoleums (daily 6.30am–5.30pm) is $5 each for the main three and $2 each for the best of the rest. To **get to the mausoleums** you can either rent a bicycle or motorbike, or take a Perfume River boat trip, which entails a couple of longish walks; a good compromise is to take a bike on board a tour boat and cycle back to Hué from the last stop.

The Mausoleum of Tu Duc

Emperor Tu Duc was a romantic poet and a weak king, who ruled Vietnam from 1847 to 1883. The **Mausoleum of Tu Duc** is the most harmonious of all the mausoleums, with elegant pavilions and pines reflected in serene lakes. It took only three years to complete (1864–67), allowing Tu Duc a full sixteen years here for boating and fishing, meditation, and composing some of the 4000 poems he is said to have written. Entering by the southern gate, brick paths lead beside a lake and a couple of waterside pavilions, from where steps head up through a triple-arched gateway to a second enclosure containing the **main temple**, Hoa Khiem, which Tu Duc used as a palace before his death. Behind the temple stands the colourful royal theatre. The second group of buildings, to the north, is centred on the **emperor's tomb**, preceded by the salutation court and stele-house. Tu Duc's Mausoleum is 7km from central Hué by road. From the boat jetty, it's a 2km walk from the river, or there might be a Honda om waiting on the river bank.

The Mausoleum of Khai Dinh

By way of a complete contrast the **Mausoleum of Khai Dinh** is a monumental confection of European Baroque and ornamental Sino-Vietnamese style, set high up on a wooded hill. Khai Dinh was the penultimate Nguyen emperor and his mausoleum has neither gardens nor living quarters. Though he only reigned for nine years (1916–1925) it took eleven (1920–31) to complete his mausoleum. The approach is via a series of dragon-ornamented stairways leading first to the salutation courtyard and the stele-house. Climbing up a further four terraces brings you to the **principal temple**, built of concrete with slate roofing imported from France, whose walls, ceiling, furniture, everything is decorated to the hilt, in glass and porcelain mosaic that writhes with dragons and is peppered with symbolic references and classic imagery. A life-size statue of the emperor holding his sceptre sits under the canopy. Khai Dinh's Mausoleum is 10km from Hué by road. Arriving by boat, it's a 1500-metre walk on a paved road, heading eastwards with a giant Quan Am statue on your right until you see the mausoleum on the opposite hillside.

The Mausoleum of Minh Mang

Court officials took fourteen years to find the location for the **Mausoleum of Minh Mang** and then only three years to build (1841–43), using 10,000 workmen. Minh Mang, the second Nguyen emperor (1820–1841), was a capable, authoritarian monarch who was passionate about architecture, and he designed his mausoleum along traditional Chinese lines, with fifteen hectares of superb landscaped gardens and plentiful lakes to reflect the red-roofed pavilions. Inside the mausoleum a processional way links the series of low mounds bearing all the main buildings. After the salutation courtyard and stele-house comes the crumbling principal temple where Minh Mang and his queen are worshipped. Continuing west you reach **Minh Lau**, the elegant, two-storey "Pavilion of Pure Light" standing among frangipani trees, symbols of longevity. To reach Minh Mang's Mausoleum from Khai Dinh's, follow the **road** west until you hit the Perfume River (1500m) and turn left along the bank, looking out on your left for the village post office, opposite which you'll find **sampans** to take you across the river ($2 return per person). The entrance is then 200m walk on the other side. This is also where you'll pick up sampans for the Hon Chen Temple (see p.1033).

Eating and nightlife

The most famous **Hué dish** is *banh khoai*, a small, crispy yellow pancake, fried up with shrimp, pork and bean sprouts, and served with peanut and sesame sauce, starfruit, green banana, lettuce and mint; try it at *Ban Khoai Hanh* at 2 Nguyen Tri Phuong. Hué's two nightspots are the *Apocalypse Now* bar (a less sleazy sister establishment to the Hanoi and Ho Chi Minh branches) and the *DMZ Bar* at 7 Nguyen Tri Phuong and 44 Le Loi respectively. Both are open late and are popular with travellers for beers, pool and dancing.

Banh Beo Ba Cu, 93/5 Phan Dinh Phung. A locally famous establishment where you can sample *banh beo*, special local dumplings, at lunchtime or up until 5pm; walk up the narrow lane opposite 142 Nguyen Hue.

Café 3, 3 Le Loi. A cheap and cheerful streetside café near the train station serving the standard range of Western and Vietnamese dishes. They will help with tour information and tickets.

Co Do, 15a Ben Nghe. Cheap prices and a sorely lacking decor shouldn't put you off sampling the food in this small, no-frills restaurant. Lemongrass and chilli are the predominant flavours accompanying squid, chicken or shrimps.

Dong Tam, 48/7 Le Loi. A vegetarian restaurant, run by a Buddhist family who offer a short menu, including vegetarian *banh khoai* and good-value combination dishes. Best at lunchtime when the food's freshest and you can sit in the garden courtyard.

Hoa Vien, 51 Ong Ich Khiem. This outdoor café is set beside the citadel walls in a beautiful garden belonging to a well-known classical musician. Good for drinks and snacks.

Lac Thien, 8 Dinh Tien Hoang. Probably Hué's friendliest and most interesting eatery, located on the Citadel side. Run by a deaf-mute familly who communicate by a highly developed sign language, the food is excellent, taking in the Hué staples. Not to be confused with the *Lac Thanh* next door.

Mandarin Café, 12 Hung Vuong. The centre of Hué's developing backpacker trade, this unassuming café hosts the Sinh Café's Open Tour booking desk. Boat trips, car/bike hire, tour information and standard backpacker fare make it a staple for travellers arriving in town.

Tandoori House, 10 Nguyen Tri Phuong. Despite its ramshackle appearance this good-value Indian café serves decent vegetarian curries for $2.

Dong Ha

As a former US Marine Command Post and then ARVN base, **DONG HA** was obliterated in 1972 but it has bounced back, thanks largely to its administrative status and location at the eastern end of Highway 9, which leads through Laos to Savannakhet on the Mekong River. As the closest town to the DMZ, Dong Ha also attracts a lot of tourist traffic, though most people choose to stay in nearby Hué.

Dong Ha is a two-street town: Highway 1, known here as Le Duan Avenue, forms the main artery as it passes through on its route north, while Highway 9 takes off inland at a central T-junction. The town's **bus station** is located on this junction, and its **train station** lies 1km south towards Hué and just west of the highway. The market and bridge over the Cua Viet River, 1km beyond the bus station, mark Dong Ha's northern extremity, where a road branches left to the **post office** and the remains of three US tanks. **Information**, expensive car rental and guides can be found at DMZ Tour (☎053/853047), in the *Dong Ha Hotel*, and at the state-owned *Quang Tri Hotel and Tourism Co*, 203 Le Duan (☎053/852927).

The local authorities' reluctance to grant permits to put up foreigners means that the **accommodation** market is dominated by dreary state-run guesthouses. Before the police put the frighteners on them, the *Nha Tro Hai Ly* (no phone; ②), a small place with negotiable prices tucked down a lane right across from the bus station, used to be the best option for budget travellers, and may still be worth a try. Otherwise there's the *Ngan Ha Guesthouse* (☎053/852806; ②–③) at 1a Le Quy Don: walk left out of the bus station onto Le Duan for about 400m and take the first left. Or try the good-value rooms at *Buu Dien Tinh Guesthouse* (☎053/854417; ③–④), 600m south of the bus station on the Hué road. Dong Ha's two best restaurants, the *Hiep Loi* and *Tan Chau*, are on the intersection of Highways 1 and 9.

The DMZ and across to Laos

Under the terms of the 1954 Geneva Accords, Vietnam was split in two along the Seventeenth Parallel, pending elections intended to reunite the country in 1956. The demarcation line ran along the Ben Hai River and was sealed by a strip of no-man's-land 5km wide on each side known as the **Demilitarized Zone**, or DMZ. All communist troops were supposed to regroup north in the Democratic Republic of Vietnam, leaving the southern Republic of Vietnam to non-communists. When the elections failed to take place the Ben Hai River became the de facto border until 1975. In reality both sides of the DMZ were anything but demilitarized after 1965, and anyway the border was easily circumvented – by the Ho Chi Minh Trail to the west and sea routes to the east – enabling the North Vietnamese to bypass a string of American firebases overlooking the river. The North Vietnamese finally stormed the DMZ in 1972 and pushed the border 20km further south. The two provinces either side of the DMZ were the most heavily bombed and saw the highest casualties, civilian and military, American and Vietnamese, during the American War. So much fire power was unleashed over this area, including napalm and herbicides, that for years nothing would grow in the chemical-laden soil, but the region's low, rolling hills are now mostly reforested. In theory you can only visit the DMZ with a local **guide**, but this is recommended anyway as most sites are unmarked and still harbour **unexploded mines**. Tours are best arranged from Da Nang or Hué, and the fee includes a compulsory "permit" ($1–2).

North to the Vinh Moc Tunnels

The American front line comprised a string of firebases set up on a long, low ridge of hills looking north across the DMZ and the featureless plain of the Ben Hai River. The most accessible of these, **Doc Mieu Firebase**, lies just east of Highway 1, 14km north of Dong Ha. A track, marked by a faded concrete sign, leads a few hundred metres to where a number of NVA-built bunkers still stand amid a landscape pocked with craters. Before the NVA overran Doc Mieu in 1972, the base played a pivotal role in the South's defence and for a while, this was the command post for calling in airstrikes along the Ho Chi Minh Trail. Just beyond Doc Mieu, Highway 1 drops down into the DMZ, running between paddy fields to **Hien Luong Bridge** and the Ben Hai River, which lies virtually on the Seventeenth Parallel. It was destroyed in 1967, and reopened in 1975 as a symbol of reunification.

One kilometre north, 22km from Dong Ha, a signpost indicates a right turn to an amazing complex of tunnels where over a thousand people sheltered, sometimes for weeks on end, during the worst American bombardments. A section of the **Vinh Moc Tunnels** has been restored and opened to visitors, with a small museum at the entrance (daily 7am–5pm; $2 including guide and flashlight); the tour takes fifteen minutes. From 1966, villagers spent two years digging more than fifty tunnels here, which were constructed on three levels at 10, 15 and 20–23m deep with good ventilation, freshwater wells and, eventually, a generator and lights. The underground village had a school, clinics, and a maternity room where seventeen children were born. Each family was allocated a tiny cavern, and were only able to emerge at night; the lack of fresh air and sunlight was a major problem, especially for young children. In 1972, the villagers were finally able to abandon their tunnels and rebuild their homes above ground. Vinh Moc is 16km from Highway 1 on a twisting, unmarked route that takes you north beside the coast; the last few unpaved kilometres become impassable in heavy rains; there's a small toll for cars and motorbikes.

Con Thien Firebase and the Truong Son Cemetery

The largest American installation along the DMZ was **Con Thien Firebase** which, in the lead-up to the 1968 Tet Offensive, became the target of prolonged shelling. The Americans replied with everything in their arsenal, but the NVA finally overran the base in the summer of 1972. In the last twenty years the pulverized land has struggled back to life and now has a veneer of green. From the ruined lookout post on Con Thien's highest point you get a great view over the DMZ and directly north to former enemy positions on the opposite bank of the Ben Hai River. To get there, drive west on Highway 9 from Dong Ha as far as Cam Lo town (11km) and then turn north on Highway QL15, following signs to the Truong Son Cemetery. The base is roughly 12km out of Cam Lo and 1km east of the road on an unmarked, winding path which is best travelled with a guide.

Eight kilometres further along the same road you come to the **Truong Son War Martyr Cemetery**, dedicated to the estimated 25,000 men and women who died on the Truong Son Trail, better known in the west as the Ho Chi Minh Trail. Many bodies were never recovered, but a total of 10,036 graves lie in the fourteen-hectare cemetery. Graves are arranged in five geographical regions, and each headstone announces *liet si* ("martyr").

Khe Sanh

The **battle of Khe Sanh** attracted worldwide media attention and, along with the simultaneous Tet Offensive, demonstrated the futility of America's efforts to contain their enemy. In late 1967, skirmishes around Khe Sanh increased as intelligence reports indicated a massive build-up of North Vietnamese Army (NVA) troops, possibly as many as 40,000, facing 6000 Marines together with a few hundred South Vietnamese and Bru. Both the Western media and American generals were soon presenting the confrontation as a crucial test of America's credibility in South Vietnam. The NVA attack began in the early hours of January 21, 1968 and the battle lasted nine weeks, during which time the US pounded the area with nearly 100,000 tonnes of bombs, averaging one airstrike every five minutes, backed up by napalm and defoliants. The NVA were so well dug in that they continued to return fire, despite horrendous casualties. By the middle of March the NVA had all but gone, having successfully diverted American resources away from southern cities prior to the Tet Offensive. Three months later the Americans also withdrew, leaving a plateau that resembled a lunar landscape, contaminated for years to come with chemicals and explosives; white phosphorus continues to smoulder here in the summer sun.

The town of **KHE SANH** (now officially rechristened **Huang Hoa**) is a bleak, one-street settlement, its frontier atmosphere reinforced by the smugglers' trail across the border to Laos, only 19km away. To find **the base**, fork right beside a three-legged monument on the town's eastern outskirts, follow the road for 2km and then turn right beside a house onto an unmarked path. There are two basic **guesthouses** on Khe Sanh's dusty main street (Highway 9): *Mien Nui Guesthouse* (☎053/880237; ②) in the centre of town under the radio mast has bigger rooms; 1km further west find the slightly cheaper but more run-down *Huong Hoa Guesthouse* (☎053/880563; ②). Opposite the *Mien Nui*, and about 20m west, are a few wooden shacks which serve as pretty good **restaurants**. The bank next to the *Huong Hoa* will change dollar notes but at poor rates. **Buses** either stop on the highway or leave from Khe Sanh bus station, an open field across from the *Mien Nui*, with frequent departures for Lao Bao and the **Lao border**, and for Dong Ha in the opposite direction; change in Dong Ha for Hué.

The Lao Bao border crossing to Laos

Nineteen kilometres from Khe Sanh, the **Lao Bao border crossing**, open round the clock, is the most popular of Vietnam's two overland routes into Laos. To reach the border gate, take a local bus from Dong Ha or Khe Sanh as far as Lao Bao village, where you can pick up a Honda om for the final 3km. At the crossing you just walk 1km between inspection posts. On the Lao side of the border, you can stay at **Daen Sawan**, 1km away (see p.517), or catch a bus for the transport hub of Savannakhet (see p.512), which is also on the Thai border. Two buses to Savannakhet leave from Daen Sawan in the morning, the second at 10am.

The Cau Treo border crossing into Laos

Although Lao Bao is by far the most popular land crossing into Laos, it is also possible, though still tricky, to cross the border at **CAU TREO**, 105km west of the city of Vinh on Highway 8; the biggest hurdle is getting the exit point on your Vietnamese visa changed. There's a daily bus (6am) from Vinh bus station as far as Trung Tam (formerly known as Huong Son), the last settlement of any size before the border. From here you'll either have to pick up a motorbike taxi for the last 35km to Cau Treo or, better still, hitch a ride on a truck heading all the way to **Lak Xao**, 35km across the border in Laos (see p.510). Alternatively, hotels and travel agents in Vinh can arrange a car all the way to the border (105km) for a princely $80. Thus far, facilities at Cau Treo amount to about half a dozen *pho* stalls, so sort out money and anything else you need before leaving Vinh. In **VINH**, you can stay at the ostentatious *Hong Ngoc*, just north of the bus station at 99 Le Loi (☎038/841314; ③–④), or at *Railway Station Guesthouse* (☎038/853754; ②), a basic guesthouse above a café in the northeast corner of the station forecourt.

HANOI AND AROUND

The Vietnamese nation was born among the lagoons and marshes of the Red River Delta around 4000 years ago and for most of its independent existence has been ruled from **HANOI**, Vietnam's small, elegant capital lying in the heart of the northern delta. Given the political and historical importance of Hanoi and its burgeoning population of one million, it's a surprisingly low-key city, with the character of a provincial town – quite unlike brash, young Ho Chi Minh City. It still retains buildings from the eleventh-century court of its founding father King Ly Thai To, most notably the **Temple of Literature**, and some of the streets in the **Old Quarter** still trade in the same speciality goods they dealt in 500 years ago. In 1887, the French turned Hanoi into the centre of government for the entire Union of Indochina, replacing ancient monuments with grand colonial residences, many of which survive today. Hanoi finally became the capital of independent Vietnam in 1954, with Ho Chi Minh its first president: **Ho Chi Minh's Mausoleum** is now the city's biggest crowd-puller. The city sustained serious damage in the American War, particularly the infamous Christmas Bombing campaign of 1972, much of it lucidly chronicled in the **Army Museum**. Until recently, political isolation together with lack of resources preserved what was essentially the city of the 1950s. However, since the advent of tourism in 1993, the city has seen an explosion in traveller cafés, mini-hotels and cybercafés. Indeed, Hang Bac, one of the Old Quarter's main drags which is home to a large number of traveller hang-outs, is starting to resemble a little piece of Bangkok's Khao San Road in Hanoi. The big question now is how much of central Hanoi will survive the onslaught of modernization.

Arrival and information

It's a 45-minute ride into central Hanoi from **Noi Bai airport**, 35km away. An airport minibus service operates until the last flights ($3), dropping off passengers at Vietnam Airlines, Quang Trung. Airport **taxis** (☎04/873 3333) now have a standardized price of $10 for the ride into town. You need to fill in a form at the airport taxi desk and collect a receipt and sticker before going through customs. The taxis wait outside at the entrance after you've gone through the baggage reclaim. As neither of the airport's two **exchange** bureaux offer particularly good rates, it's best to pay the fare in dollars and change your money in Hanoi.

Arriving by **train** from Ho Chi Minh City and all points south or from China you exit the main station onto Le Duan Avenue. However, trains from the east and north (Haiphong, Lang Son and Lao Cai) pull into platforms at the rear of the main station, bringing you out onto Tran Quy Cap. There's a left-luggage office opposite ticket counter number 1 ($1 per day). There are a few hotels nearby that are useful if you arrive late or have an early start; otherwise pick up a cyclo or xe om (motorbike taxi) for under $1 to the Old Quarter.

Long-distance **buses** from the south use **Giap Bat station**, 6km south of town on Giai Phong Avenue; a xe om to the centre will cost less than $1. Services from the northeast arrive at **Gia Lam station**, 4km away on the east bank of the Red River; a xe om to the centre costs less than $1. Buses to and **from the northwest** use **Kim Ma station**, located at the junction of Giang Vo and Kim Ma, 2km west of the centre. However, some buses, particularly **private services**, drop passengers at more central spots in the city. Buses **from Hoa Binh** sometimes terminate in Ha Dong, 10km from the centre; jump on one of the waiting city buses into town (40min). Always check at the station a day or two before you want to travel, especially for destinations north and west of Hanoi where public services are crumbling in the face of independent operators.

State-run **tourist offices** such as Vietnamtourism and Vinatour are unreliable; it's best to go to one of the reliable travellers' cafés, such as *Love Planet* or *Green Bamboo* (see "Listings" on p.1050) for information on visas, tours and transport. Many cafés also arrange walking tours of the city ($10 for the morning including lunch).

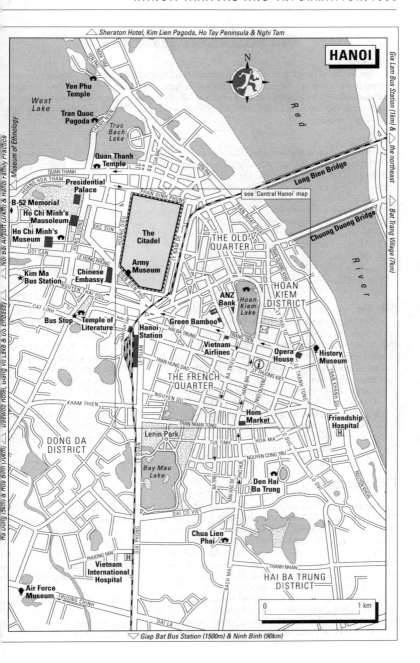

Sheraton Hotel, Kim Lien Pagoda, Ho Tay Peninsula & Nghi Tam

HANOI

Gia Lam Bus Station (1km) & the northeast

Bat Trang Village (7km)

Museum of Ethnology

Noi Bai Airport (3km) & Hanoi Family Practice

Daewoo Hotel, Giang Vo Lake & US Embassy

Ha Dong (3km) & Hoa Binh (10km)

West Lake

Yen Phu Temple

Tran Quoc Pagoda

Truc Bach Lake

Quan Thanh Temple

Presidential Palace

B-52 Memorial

Ho Chi Minh's Mausoleum

Ho Chi Minh's Museum

Kim Ma Bus Station

Chinese Embassy

Bus Stop

Temple of Literature

The Citadel

Army Museum

PHAN DINH PHUNG

Red

River

Long Bien Bridge

Chuong Duong Bridge

THE OLD QUARTER

see 'Central Hanoi' map

ANZ Bank

Hoan Kiem Lake

HOAN KIEM DISTRICT

Green Bamboo

Hanoi Station

Vietnam Airlines

Opera House

History Museum

THE FRENCH QUARTER

Hom Market

Friendship Hospital

Lenin Park

Bay Mau Lake

DONG DA DISTRICT

KHAM THIEN

Den Hai Ba Trung

Chua Lien Phai

Vietnam International Hospital

Air Force Museum

TRUONG CHINH

DAI LA

PHUONG MAI

GIAI PHONG

BACH MAI

THANH NHAN

HAI BA TRUNG DISTRICT

0   1 km

Giap Bat Bus Station (1500m) & Ninh Binh (90km)

MOVING ON FROM HANOI

By plane

To get to the airport, take the airport minibus from Vietnam Airlines, 1 Quang Trung. Departures are every half hour from 5.30am to 5pm: buy your tickets from the Vietnam Airlines office at 112 Cau Go near Hoan Kiem lake ($3). Alternatively, you could organize a car from your hotel ($12–20), or sign up at one of the travellers' cafés for a shared car ($4–5 per person).

By train

Tickets and **information** are available at the window marked "Booking Office for Foreigners" (daily 7.30am–noon & 1.30–4.30pm; to 9pm for Express trains) in the main station building facing onto Le Duan. Book early, especially for sleeping berths to Hué and Ho Chi Minh City. Services **to the east and north**, but not China-bound trains leave from the back station. There have been an increasing number of thefts on the night train between Hanoi and Lao Cai, so keep bags locked when you're asleep.

There are two direct train services from Hanoi **to China**. Tickets should be booked well in advance and you'll need your passport with a valid China visa when you buy them. The **Hanoi–Beijing** service (54hr) leaves Hanoi on Tuesdays and Fridays at 2pm and goes via Dong Dang, but cannot be boarded anywhere other than Hanoi; in China you can get off at Pingxiang just across the border, or at Nanning, Guilin and so on. The twice-weekly **Hanoi–Kunming** service (17hr 30min) leaves at 9.30pm on Sundays and Fridays, and goes via Lao Cai, where it's also possible to board the train.

By bus

Long-distance **buses** to the south use **Giap Bat station**, 6km south of town on Giai Phong Avenue. Services **to the northeast** (Haiphong, Bai Chay/Ha Long Bay and Cao Bang) arrive at **Gia Lam station**, 4km away on the east bank of the Red River. Buses **to the northwest** (Son La, Mai Chau and Lao Cai) use **Kim Ma station**, located at the junction of Giang Vo and Kim Ma, 2km west of the centre. Always check at the station a day or two before you want to travel, especially for destinations north and west of Hanoi where public services are crumbling in the face of independent operators.

Tourist minibuses organized by the traveller cafés run out to Bai Chay for Ha Long Bay early every morning from the north end of Hoan Kiem Lake ($5). The ubiquitous Sin Café Open Tour bus makes the trek down to Hué nearly every night (details available from Hanoi tour agencies), but it's a long, uncomfortable journey and well worth forking out a bit extra for a sleeper on the train.

City transport

Cyclos are banned from many roads in central Hanoi, notably around Hoan Kiem Lake (Dinh Tien Hoang and Le Thai To) and in the Old Quarter, so don't be surprised if you seem to be taking a circuitous route. **Taxis** wait outside the more upmarket hotels and at the north end of Hoan Kiem Lake and cost just over $1 per 2km.

Bicycles can be rented for under $1 a day from many hotels and traveller cafés in the Old Quarter. It's best to pay the minuscule charge at a supervised bike park (*gui xe dap*), rather than run the risk of a stolen bike. Parking is banned on Trang Tien and Hang Khay; elsewhere it's only allowed within designated areas.

Motorbikes are available from guesthouses and small tour agencies (see p.1050), and also from the *Meeting Café*, 59b Ba Trieu and *Memory Café*, 33b Tran Hung Dao. Prices start from $5 per day, including use of a helmet. You'll be required to leave your passport as a deposit. Park in supervised motorbike parks (*gui xe may*). Bao Viet at 15c Tran Khanh Du (☎04/934

0289) does motorbike insurance. For motorbike repairs, try Phu Doan, just behind the cathedral, or along Thinh Yen at the south end of Pho Hué. Any tour agency will rent you a **car with driver** (from $30 per day).

Hanoi's snail-paced **city buses** are mainly useful for transport between the long-distance bus stations (every 15min 5am–5.30pm; flat fare of 2000d). Bus stops are marked by missable white signs, sometimes with the route numbers written in blue, but corresponding numbers displayed on the buses aren't necessarily accurate. The most useful route, **#3**, runs between Gia Lam and Giap Bat with stops on Tran Quang Khai, Phan Chu Trinh (or Phan Huy Chu, heading north), Tran Hung Dao and outside the train station. From the centre of town, it's about 30min to either Gia Lam or Giap Bat. Route **#2** (Bat Co–Ha Dong) serves the Temple of Literature (10 min) and Ha Dong (40 min); there are stops at the northwest corner of Hoan Kiem Lake and on Trang Thi opposite Vietnam Airlines.

Accommodation

Most of the budget **hotels** are found in the Old Quarter, and there are now some excellent bargains to be had, though generally rooms are more expensive than in Ho Chi Minh. Several hotels adopt the same name (there are multiple *Camellia* and *Prince* hotels), so you'll need an exact address if arriving by cyclo or taxi.

The Old Quarter and west of Hoan Kiem Lake

Anh Dao, 37 Ma May (☎04/826 7151). Popular, well-run budget hotel on one of the Old Quarter's most interesting streets. More expensive rooms have balconies and bathtubs. Price includes breakfast. ③–④.

Binh Minh, 50 Hang Be (☎04/826 7356). Popular old hotel with a range of rooms – getting lighter and better as you climb higher. ②–③.

Camellia 2, 31 Hang Dieu (☎04/828 5704). Probably the best-deal budget hotel in the Old Quarter, the *Camellia 2* has excellent, clean rooms with TV, phone and bathtub at very reasonable prices. A restaurant and Internet access are available downstairs. ③.

Fortuan Hotel, 68 Hang Bo (☎04/828 1324). A good-value mini-hotel tastefully decorated and well-located opposite the *Red River Café* in the heart of the Old Quarter. ④.

Nam Phuong, 26 Nha Chung (☎04/824 6894). This little hotel located in the increasingly trendy Cathedral area has bright, airy rooms at good prices. ②–③.

North 2, 5 Tam Thuong (☎04/828 5030). One of two family-run hotels offering basic but perfectly adequate accomodation with TV, fridge and phone as standard. *The North 1* at 15 Hang Ga (☎826 7242) has similar facilities. ②.

Prince 2, 51 Luong Ngoc Quyen (☎04/828 0155). A very smart hotel with huge rooms and excellent facilities, including a video in each room. ③.

Saljut, 7 Hang Dau (☎04/825 8003). A new and very smart hotel located between Hoan Kiem Lake and the Old Quarter. Rooms are comfortable and well equiped with chic marble-effect bathrooms. Prices include breakfast served at downstairs café. ④–⑤.

Sinh Handspan, 116 Hang Bac (☎04/828 1996). Popular on the backpacker circuit for its cheap and cheerful dorms. Similar accommodation can be found at *Queen Café* (65 Hang Bac; ☎04/826 0860). Dorms $6–8.

Thu Giang, 5a Tam Thuong (☎04/828 5734). A spotless, welcoming family hotel in a good location, with basic no-frills rooms. ②.

Win Hotel, 34 Hang Hanh (☎04/288 7371). Best of the mini-hotels on the ultra-cool Hang Hanh café strip. Rooms are large, airy and have all mod cons, although the price is rather high. ④.

French Quarter

Ben Luc, 30 Ly Thai To (☎04/825 3167). An older hotel built around a tree-filled courtyard; the cheapest rooms face outwards. ④.

Hoaman, 83a Ly Thong Kiet (☎04/822 2800). A business hotel in neo-colonial style with tastefully decorated rooms and upscale facilities. ⑧.

Hilton Hanoi Opera, 1 Le Thanh Tong (☎04/933 0500). The new smart address in town has five-star accommodation with IDD, satellite TV and data ports in every room, while in-house services include a business centre, two executive floors, fitness centre and outdoor swimming pool. ⑥–⑧.

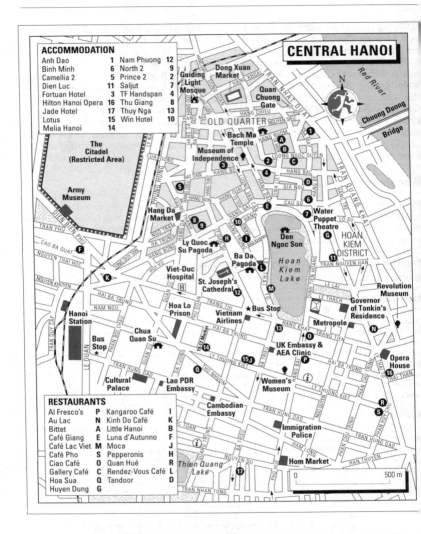

CENTRAL HANOI

ACCOMMODATION

Anh Dao	1	Nam Phuong	12
Binh Minh	6	North 2	9
Camellia 2	5	Prince 2	2
Dien Luc	11	Saljut	7
Fortuan Hotel	3	TF Handspan	4
Hilton Hanoi Opera	16	Thu Giang	8
Jade Hotel	17	Thuy Nga	13
Lotus	15	Win Hotel	10
Melia Hanoi	14		

RESTAURANTS

Al Fresco's	P	Kangaroo Café	I
Au Lac	N	Kinh Do Café	K
Bittet	A	Little Hanoi	B
Café Giang	E	Luna d'Autunno	F
Café Lac Viet	M	Moca	J
Café Pho	S	Pepperonis	H
Ciao Café	O	Quan Hué	R
Gallery Café	C	Rendez-Vous Café	L
Hoa Sua	Q	Tandoor	D
Huyen Dung	G		

Jade Hotel, 73 Ba Trieu (☎04/826 5669). A quiet location to the south of Ba Trieu and better-than-average rooms make this mini-hotel worth seeking out. Decent facilities and a friendly welcome from the French speaking owner. ④.

Lotus, 42v Ly Thuong Kiet (☎04/826 8642). One of the original dorm-style guesthouses in Hanoi, w dingy shared rooms. The rooms with private bathroom are better. There's a downstairs café with Interr access. It's showing its age but remains popular for its prime location in the quieter and calmer Frer Quarter. Best to book ahead. ②–③.

Melia Hanoi, 44b Ly Thong Kiet (☎04/934 3343). The newest upscale property in town pitches its pri lower while providing international-class accommodation. Luxurious rooms, a rooftop swimming pool well as fitness and business centres make this a good option for the business traveller. ⑥–⑧.

Thuy Nga, 4 Ba Trieu (☎04/934 1256). A very smart hotel, with tastefully decorated rooms and in a great location near Hoan Kiem Lake. All mod cons offered for a reasonable price. ⑥.

The City

At the heart of Hanoi lies **Hoan Kiem Lake**, around which you'll find the banks, airlines and GPO, plus many hotels, restaurants, shopping streets and markets. The lake lies between the cramped and endlessly diverting **Old Quarter** in the north, and the tree-lined boulevards of the **French Quarter** to the south. West of this central district, across the rail tracks, some of Hanoi's most impressive monuments occupy the wide, open spaces of the former **Imperial City**, grouped around Ho Chi Minh's Mausoleum on Ba Dinh Square and extending south to the ancient, walled gardens of the Temple of Literature. A vast body of water confusingly called **West Lake** sits north of the city, harbouring a number of interesting temples and pagodas.

Around Hoan Kiem Lake

Hoan Kiem Lake itself is small – you can walk round it in thirty minutes – and not particularly spectacular, but to Hanoians this is the soul of their city. A squat, three-tiered pavilion known as the **Tortoise Tower** ornaments a tiny island in the middle of Ho Hoan Kiem, "Lake of the Restored Sword". The names refer to a legend of the great fifteenth-century Vietnamese hero, Le Loi, whose miraculous sword was swallowed by a golden turtle/tortoise in this lake. Cross the red-lacquered Huc Bridge to a second island on which stands **Den Ngoc Son** (daily 8am–7pm; $1), founded in the fourteenth century and rebuilt in the 1800s in typical Nguyen dynasty style. National hero General Tran Hung Dao, who defeated the Mongols in 1288, sits on the principal altar, above which you'll see dragon heads, carved with bulbous noses and teeth bared in manic grins. A preserved giant turtle, caught in the lake in 1968, is displayed in a room off the first sanctuary hall.

The neo-Gothic **St Joseph's Cathedral** at the far end of Nha Tho Street, west of the lake, was constructed in the early 1880s, and boasts an impressive interior featuring an ornate altar screen and French stained-glass windows. Enter the cathedral through a small door on the south side. If it's closed ring the bell. North of the cathedral on Ly Quoc Su, the small thirteenth-century **Ly Quoc Su Pagoda** houses a statue of the Buddhist teacher and healer Ly Quoc Su, the man credited with curing the hallucinating King Ly Than Tong from believing he was a tiger.

The Old Quarter

An ugly office block with turtles pinned to its sides dominates the northern end of Hoan Kiem Lake. Walk behind this onto Cau Go and suddenly you're in the congested square kilometre known as the **Old Quarter**. Hanoi is the only city in Vietnam to retain its ancient, merchants' quarter, and its street names date back five centuries to when the area was divided among 36 artisans' guilds, each gathered around a temple or a *dinh* (communal house) dedicated to the guild's patron spirit. Even today a surprising number of streets are still dedicated to the original craft or its modern equivalent: Hang Quat remains full of bright red banners and lacquerware for funerals and festivals, and at Hang Ma, paper votive objects have been made for at least five hundred years.

The aptly named fifteenth-century **tube-houses** evolved from market stalls into narrow shops of a single storey. Some are just 2m wide, the result of taxes levied on street-frontages and of subdivision for inheritance, while behind stretches a succession of storerooms, living quarters and courtyards up to 60m in length. The range of building styles along Hang Bac and Ma May are typical, and Ma May even retains its own **dinh**, or communal house (no. 64), which served as both meeting hall and shrine to the neighbourhood's particular patron spirit. From here, walk north and along Hang Buom, past an attractive row of tube-houses at nos. 10–14, to reach the quarter's oldest and most revered place of worship, **Bach Ma Temple** (daily 8–11.30am & 2.30–5.30pm). The present structure dates from the eighteenth century and shelters a pair of charismatic, red-cloaked guardians.

The city's largest covered market, **Dong Xuan**, occupies a whole block behind its original, 1889 facade, but its half-empty halls contrast vividly with the bustling street market to the rear. One block east, two ramps take bikes and pedestrians up onto **Long Bien Bridge** which, until the 1980s, was the Red River's only bridge and therefore of immense strategic significance. During the American War this was one of Vietnam's most heavily defended spots. Cutting back southwards, it was at 48 Hang Ngang that Ho Chi Minh drafted the Declaration of Independence for the Democratic Republic of Vietnam in 1945. The house where he lived for those heady months is now the **Museum of Independence** (Mon–Sat 8am–4pm; no charge), and upstairs you can see where he slept, wrote and debated.

The French Quarter

The first French concession was granted in 1874, and gradually elegant villas filled plots along the grid of tree-lined avenues to the south and east of Hoan Kiem Lake. The jewel in the crown was the stately **Opera House** (now known as the Municipal Theatre), at the eastern end of Trang Tien, which was based on the Neo-Baroque Paris Opéra, complete with Ionic columns and tiles imported from France. After ten years in the making, it was finally opened in 1911; in 1945, the Viet Minh proclaimed the August Revolution from its balcony.

One block east of the Opera House, Hanoi's **History Museum**, at 1 Trang Tien (Tues–Sun 8.30–11.30am & 1.30–4.30pm; $1) is a fanciful blend of Vietnamese palace and French villa which came to be called "Neo-Vietnamese" style. Inside, exhibits include arrowheads and ceremonial bronze drums from the Dong Son culture, a sophisticated Bronze Age civilization which flourished in the Red River Delta from 1200 to 200 BC. Upstairs, there are eye-catching ink-washes depicting Hué's Imperial Court in the 1890s, along with sobering evidence of royal decadence and French brutality. The story continues at the **Museum of Vietnamese Revolution**, one block north at 25 Tong Dan (Tues–Fri & Sun 8–11.30am & 1.30–4pm; Sat 8–11.30am; $1), which catalogues the "Vietnamese people's patriotic and revolutionary struggle" from the first anti-French movements of the late nineteenth century to post-1975 reconstruction. Much of the tale is told through original documents, including revolutionary tracts penned by Ho Chi Minh.

South of **Trang Tien**, the main artery of the French Quarter, you enter French Hanoi's principal residential quarter, whose distinguished villas run the gamut of styles from elegant Neoclassical through to 1930s Modernism and Art Deco. To take a swing through the area, drop down Hang Bai onto Ly Thuong Kiet and start heading west. Just round the corner, the revamped **Museum of Vietnamese Women**, at 36 Ly Thuong Kiet (Tues–Sun 8.30–11.30am & 1.30–4pm; $1), puts a different perspective on national history. Further west, the French-built **Hoa Lo Prison** (Tues–Sun 8–11am & 1.30–4.30pm; $1) only deals with the pre-1954 period when the French incarcerated many nationalist leaders here. As yet there's little to see beyond a few, grim cells – which were still in use up to 1994.

At the next junction west, turn left down Quan Su to find the arched entrance of **Chua Quan Su**, the Ambassadors' Pagoda (daily 8.30–11.30am & 1.30–4pm), one of Hanoi's most active pagodas. A magnificent iron lamp hangs over the crowded prayer-floor and ranks of crimson-lacquered Buddhas glow through a haze of incense.

Around Ho Chi Minh's Mausoleum

The wide, open spaces of **Ba Dinh Square**, 2km west of Hoan Kiem Lake, are the nation's ceremonial epicentre. It was here that Ho Chi Minh read out the Declaration of Independence to half a million people on September 2, 1945, and here that Independence is commemorated each National Day with military parades. Cyclos and xe om will bring you here from the centre for less than $1. The square's west side is dominated by **Ho Chi Minh's Mausoleum** (summer Tues–Sat 7.30–10.30am, Sun 7.30–11am; winter Tues–Sat 8–11am, Sun 8–11.30am; closed Mon), where, in the tradition of great communist leaders, Ho Chi

Minh's embalmed body is displayed under glass in a cold, dark room. Huge crowds come here to pay their respects to "Uncle Ho", especially at weekends: sober behaviour is required, and there's talk of reimposing the dress code (no shorts or vests). Every year the mausoleum closes for two months while Ho undergoes "maintenance", usually in October and November.

Follow the crowd on leaving Ho's mausoleum and you pass the grand Presidential Palace, constructed in 1901 for the governor-general of Indochina, en route to **Ho Chi Minh's House** (Tues–Sun 8–11am & 1.30–4.30pm). After Independence in 1954 President Ho Chi Minh built a modest dwelling for himself behind the palace, modelling it on an ethnic minority stilthouse. The ground-level meeting area was used by Ho and the politburo; upstairs, his study and bedroom are sparsely furnished and unostentatious.

Close by Ho's stilthouse, the tiny **One Pillar Pagoda** rivals the Tortoise Tower as a symbol of Hanoi and represents a flowering of Vietnamese art. Founded in the eleventh century (and reconstructed in 1954), it is supported on a single column rising from the middle of a lake, the whole structure designed to resemble a lotus blossom, the Buddhist symbol of enlightenment. **Ho Chi Minh's Museum** (Tues–Sun 8–11am & 1.30–4.30pm), the gleaming white building just 200m west of the One Pillar Pagoda, celebrates Ho Chi Minh's life and the pivotal role he played in the nation's history. Exhibits focus on Ho's life and the "Vietnamese Revolution", in the context of socialism's international development.

Around 500m from Ba Dinh Square on Dien Bien Phu, Lenin's statue still stands opposite a white, arcaded building housing the **Army Museum** at 28a Dien Bien Phu (Tues–Sun 8–11.30am & 1.30–4.30pm; $1). If you visit only one museum in Hanoi, then this should be it. While ostensibly tracing the story of the People's Army from its foundation in 1944, in reality the museum chronicles national history from the 1930s to the present day, a period dominated by the French and American wars.

Across busy Nguyen Thai Hoc Avenue at 66 Nguyen Thai Hoc is the **Temple of Literature** or **Van Mieu**, Vietnam's principal Confucian sanctuary and its historical centre of learning (Tues–Sun 9am–5pm; $1). The temple is one of the few remnants of the Ly kings' original eleventh-century city and consists of five walled courtyards, modelled on that of Confucius's birthplace in Qufu, China. Entering the third courtyard, via an imposing double-roofed gateway, you'll see the central Well of Heavenly Clarity (a walled pond), flanked by the temple's most valuable relics: 82 stone **stelae** mounted on tortoises. Each stele records the results of a state examination held at the National Academy between 1442 and 1779, and gives biographical details of successful candidates. Passing into the fourth courtyard brings you to the **ceremonial hall**, a long, low building whose sweeping, tiled roof is crowned by two lithe dragons bracketing a full moon. Here the king and his mandarins would make sacrifices before the altar of Confucius. These days recitals of traditional music echo among the ironwood pillars (daily 9am–5pm, according to demand; $1). Directly behind the ceremonial hall lies the temple sanctuary, where Confucius sits with his four principal disciples. The fifth courtyard used to house the National Academy, Vietnam's first university, but was destroyed by French bombs in 1947.

Around West Lake

North of the city, **West Lake** is a shallow lagoon left behind as the Red River shifted course eastward to leave a narrow strip of land. In the seventeenth century villagers built a causeway across the lake's southeast corner, creating a small fishing lake, still in use today and now called **Truc Bach**. The eleventh-century **Quan Thanh Temple** (daily 8am–4pm) still stands on the lake's southeast bank, and is dedicated to the Guardian of the North, Tran Vo, whose statue, cast in black bronze in 1677, is nearly 4m high and weighs 4 tonnes. The shrine room also boasts a valuable collection of seventeenth- and eighteenth-century poems and parallel sentences (boards inscribed with wise maxims and hung in pairs). The gate of Quan Thanh is just a few paces south of the causeway, Thanh Nien Street, which leads to Hanoi's oldest religious foundation, **Tran Quoc Pagoda**, occupying a tiny island in West Lake (daily 7–11.30am & 1.30–6pm; no shorts allowed). The pagoda probably dates back to the sixth century and the sanctuary's restrained interior is typical of northern Vietnamese pagodas but contains nothing of particular importance.

Museum of Ethnology

After thirteen years in the planning, the **Museum of Ethnology**, *Bao Tang Toc Hoc Viet Nam* (Tues–Sun 8.30–11.30am & 1.30–5.30pm; $1 plus extra for cameras and English-speaking guide), was finally opened in 1997 on the western outskirts of Hanoi in the Cai Giay district; though a bit of a trek it's worth the effort, as it offers a fair amount of information on all the major ethnic groups. Musical instruments, games, traditional dress and other items of daily life fill the showcases, alongside recordings, photos and videos of festivals and rites. To get there, follow Thuy Khue Avenue along the southern edge of West Lake and then keep heading west to find the museum 6km out of town, signposted left off Hoang Quoc Viet Street (also known as Nghia Do). A cab from the Old Quarter will cost around $5.

On the way back into central Hanoi, you could make a detour to Ngoc Ha village, where the mangled undercarriage of an American **B-52 bomber** lies half-submerged in a small lake. The plane was one of twenty-three shot down in December 1972 and now serves as a memorial to those who died during intensive raids known as the "Christmas Bombing". Huu Tiep Lake lies just off Hoang Hoa Tham Avenue at its eastern end, where a red sign announcing "B-52" points 100m down a narrow road.

Eating

For sheer value for money and atmosphere it's hard to beat the rock-bottom, stove-and-stools **food stalls** or the slightly more upmarket street kitchens; try streets such as Ma Hac De, Hang Dieu and Duong Thanh. At conventional restaurants you'll need to **get there early**: local places stop serving around 8pm, while Western-style restaurants and top hotels tend to allow an extra hour or two. We've given phone numbers for places where it's advisable to make reservations. Look out for two Hanoi **specialities**: the ubiquitous *pho* noodle soup and *bun cha*, small barbecued pork burgers served with a bowl of rice noodles.

THE OLD QUARTER AND WEST OF HOAN KIEM LAKE

Bittet, 51 Hang Buom. Hidden down a long, dark passage, this small and bustling restaurant probably represents the best bargain in the Old Quarter. $2 will buy you a plate of *bittet* – a Vietnamese corruption of traditional French *bifteck* and chips served with lashings of garlic, a salad, crusty bread and beer. Open 5–8pm daily.

Café Giang, 7 Hang Gai. A café famous for its Vietnamese take on cappuccino, *café trung* – delicious and extremely rich coffee frothed up with whipped egg. Alternatively, this little hole-in-the-wall café offers *cocao trung* or even *bia trung* for a few thousand dong.

Café Lac Viet, 46 Le Thai To. A quiet and comfy spot for coffees. Head for the sofas on the second floor, browse the bookshelves or catch one of the film screenings each Sunday, Monday and Thursday at 8pm.

Gallery Café, 35 Luong Ngoc Quyen. Unpretentious and friendly backstreet café, with snacks and drinks at reasonable prices. A permanent exhibition of stills by local photographer Cat Vi adds a nice touch.

Huyen Dung, 4 Ly Thai To. This small streetside café is another hidden treasure in the *Bittet* vein. The sizzling hot plates of steak, eggs and chips for $1 are the closest you'll get to a decent fry-up in Hanoi. Open all day, it's a great place for a filling breakfast or hangover lunch.

Kangaroo Café, 18 Bao Khanh. This Australian-run traveller café is a great place to come for travel advice and to organize tours, visas and tickets. It also serves a mean bacon buttie with lashings of Tommy K for less than $2, and has a fine selection of vegetarian food prepared in a germ-free kitchen. Try the pumpkin and sweet potato patties with salad ($1.50) and a fruit shake. Open 8am–11pm.

Little Hanoi, 25 Ta Hien. A small, friendly and great-value restaurant on a quiet side street, serving traditional Vietnamese fare. Try the fried tofu in tomato sauce ($1) and the pork with lemon and chilli.

Love Planet, 25 Hang Bac. A welcoming traveller café in the heart of the old quarter serving better than average fare at reasonable prices. Try the fresh spring rolls, sweet-and-sour salad and noodle dishes, and check out the rooftop eating area known as the "Garden of Eden".

Luna d'Autunno, 11b Dien Bien Phu. Excellent pizzas at reasonable prices make this Italian restaurant a good-value option despite its being rather a trek from the Old Quarter. The downstairs snack bar has breakasts while the upstairs dining room has main meals, and every weekend the garden hosts a jazz set menu $7) with live jazz music. Pizza delivery service ☎04/8237338. Open 7.30am–midnight.

Moca, 14–16 Nha Tho. Located in the hippest part of town near the cathedral, *Moca* used to be something of a favourite with travellers and expats, with its colonial-style decor and Western-friendly menu. Recently, though, reports of falling standards have sullied its reputation, leaving neighbouring cafés to absorb its clientele. They still change money at a rate of 14,000d to $1.

Pepperonis, 29 Ly Quoc Su. Relocated to the up-and-coming cathedral area, this Western-style pizza chain from Hong Kong has excellent pasta ($2), salads ($1.50) and vegetarian specials ($2) for those craving a break from the noodles. Aim for a seat on the upstairs balcony. Free Pizza delivery service ☎04/9285246.

Rendez-Vous Café, 136 Hang Trong. A bright and airy café–bistro next to the lake. Best at lunchtimes when they serve an Asian set lunch for $2 and a Western set menu for around $3. Live music nightly. Open 7am–midnight.

Tandoor, 24 Hang Be. A well-established Indian restaurant popular with tourists. Simple decor but cracking curries: fish tikka, tandoori chicken and plenty of vegetarian dishes; the thali set lunch is a good deal at $4. 11am–2pm & 5–10pm.

Whole Earth, *TF Handspan*, 116 Hang Bac. Good-value vegetarian restaurant housed inside the Handspan traveller café. Try the cheap set menus.

THE FRENCH QUARTER

Al Fresco's, 23 Hai Ba Trung (☎04/826 7782). The sister restaurant to *Pepperonis* is a relaxed, expat-run place with a pleasant balcony on the first floor. The menu includes good-quality American and international fare (ribs, salads, nachos and pizzas), all served in hefty portions. Prices are $5–7.

Au Lac, 57 Ly Thai To. A popular upmarket café with a strong reputation. It claims to brew Hanoi's best coffee, but prices don't always reflect quality. Still, it's a relaxing spot to sup your cappuccino and snack on a sandwich. Live jazz Tues & Thurs 5.30–7.30pm, Sun 8–10pm.

Café Pho, 15 Ly Thong Kiet. A delightful garden café similar in layout to *Au Lac*, but there are more locals, fewer hawkers and cheaper prices. Serves possibly the best cup of tea in Hanoi using fresh milk, not the sickly condensed gloop prevalent around town.

Ciao Café, 2 Hang Bai. A Western-style menu including sandwiches, pasta ($2.50) and pizza make this another favourite for travellers and expats seeking tastes from home and prepared to pay a little extra. Try the ice creams.

Com Chay Nang Tam, 79a Tran Hung Dao (☎04/826 6140). Small, elegant vegetarian restaurant down a quiet alleyway off Tran Hung Dao and named after a Vietnamese Cinderella character. *Goi bo*, a main-course salad of banana flower, star fruit and pineapple, is recommended, or try one of the well-priced set menus. There's always one non-vegetarian dish among the daily specials, and no MSG is used. 11am–1.30pm & 5–10pm.

Hoa Sua, 81 Tho Nhuom (☎04/824 0448). Excellently presented food with a heavy French influence, served on a delightful garden patio or in refined, airy dining rooms; reserve to sit outside at lunchtime. *Hoa Sua* is part of a non-profit-making vocational training school giving disadvantaged children a start in the restaurant trade, hence prices are above the norm. Try the Vietnamese combo plate ($1.50) or one of the superb desserts. Open till 9pm.

Kinh Do Café, 252 Hang Bong. "Café 252" became famous after Catherine Deneuve complimented the patron on his yoghurts. The fresh yoghurts are indeed good; also serves pastries. 7am–10pm.

Quan Hué, 6 Ly Thuong Kiet. The only restaurant in Hanoi serving Hué cuisine. Don't miss the banana flower salad, and pep it up with eel fried in chilli and lemongrass. Open-air seating and reasonable prices make this a popular spot. 7am–2pm & 5–10pm.

Salsa, 25 Nha Tho. The most recent and one of the smartest openings in town in a great location at the heart of the buzzy cathedral area. Western fare, great wines, delicious tapas and cooked breakfasts have made this a new expat favourite. Open late.

Van Anh Thai Food, 5a Tong Duy Tan. Popular with locals for its authentic Thai cuisine prepared by a Thai chef, this place has hiked prices lately but quality remains good. Try the tofu curry for $2.

Nightlife and entertainment

For a capital city, Hanoi doesn't have a great choice of **bars**, and venues open and close quickly so check the English-language press such as *The Guide* for the latest listings information. Pool halls are more numerous and popular with young Vietnamese, although they tend to be a male preserve. The best are found in-between the cafés on Hang Hanh or try the *Super Club* at 31 Trang Thi. For drinking, you could start off at the *Polite Pub*, 5 Bao Khanh, a relaxed spot, with a full-sized snooker table, music and cocktails, open till late. Also open late is *Le Maquis Bar*, 2a Ta Hien, which is popular with the Francophile community and sells Rizzlas. The *Jazz Club* by Quyen Van Minh, 31 Luong Van Can, has live jazz music every night led by the charismatic Mr Minh. For clubbing, *Zouk*, 78 Hang Chieu, is the newest nightspot in town. Admission is 25,000d, beers 22,000d and there's a sushi bar at the rear. Finally, Hanoi's best-known nightspot, *Apocalypse Now*, 5c Hoa Ma, with its dark, apocalyptic decor, sleazy reputation and loud music, gets seething on Friday and Saturday nights; open 7pm till late.

Serious beer drinking tends to be an all-male preserve in Vietnam, but don't be put off as the local **bia hoi** outlets are fun, friendly and extremely cheap. The best-known one is at 59 Ly Thuong Kiet, which sells the more alcoholic, pressurized beer, *bia tuoi*. The *bia hoi* at 167 Nguyen Thai Hoc, down from Kim Ma bus station, is busy all day serving good vegetarian food, while 89 Pho Hue – known as the "bunny bia hoi" – is a garden café serving excellent food, while rabbits play at your feet. The best *bia hoi* for lunch are at 72 Ma May, where you choose from the range of dishes displayed in a large case, and at 24 Tong Dan, which has a more unusual menu than most, featuring such specialities as pig's ear and goat meat.

Most people don't leave Hanoi without seeing a performance by the traditional **water puppets**, *mua roi nuoc* – literally, puppets that dance on the water – a uniquely Vietnamese art form which originated in the Red River Delta. Traditional performances consist of short scenes depicting rural life or historic events accompanied by musical narration. Puppeteers stand waist-deep in water, manipulating the heavy wooden puppets attached to long under water poles. The Thang Long Water Puppet Troupe gives nightly tourist-oriented performances of their up-dated repertoire at Kim Dong Theatre, 57 Dinh Tien Hoang (☎04/825 5450; 6.30pm, 8pm & 9pm; $2–3, extra for cameras and videos). Check the English-language press for information about other venues.

Ballroom dancing is still popular with the Vietnamese. You can take a turn or two at Palace Dancing, 40 Nha Chung (Tues, Thurs, Sat & Sun 8.30–10.30pm; $1) or contact The Sophie Martin Ballet School (room 203/04 UN Apartments, 2E Van Phuc; ☎04/943 2701), a dance studio with lessons in ballroom and latin dancing for $9 per session.

Shopping and markets

The best areas to browse are Hang Gai in the Old Quarter and around the southeastern edge of Hoan Kiem Lake. Compared with Thailand, Vietnamese **silk** is slightly inferior quality, but prices are lower and the tailoring is great value. So many silk shops are concentrated on Hang Gai, at the southern edge of the Old Quarter, that it's now known as "Silk Street". The best-known is Khai Silk at no. 96 Hang Gai, but try also Thanh Ha at no. 114, and Kenly at no 102. Tailoring Shop Co, 18 Nha Tho, has the best hand-made clothes in town. For **embroideries** and drawn threadwork Song, 7 Nha Tho, is probably Hanoi's most famous shop, while Tan My, at 16 Hang Trong, stocks delicate pillow cases and covers.

The non-profit Craft Link, at 43 Van Mieu, sells traditional **crafts** made by ethnic minorities, including lacquerware, paper goods, basketry and clothes. Most ordinary souvenir shops also stock ethnic minority crafts, particularly the Hmong and Dao bags, coats and jewellery that are so popular in Sa Pa, though many are actually factory-made. For more unusual mementoes, have a look at the traditional Vietnamese **musical instruments** on sale at 11 Hang Non or 1a or 1c Hang Manh. Several small shops on Hong Bong supply Communist Party **banners and badges** and Vietnamese flags. Hanoi also has a flourishing art scene and any exploration should start with the Apricot Gallery, 40b Hang Bong, a well-established gallery with a range of works by local artists; open 8am–8pm.

Hanoi has over fifty **markets**, selling predominantly foodstuffs: Cho Dong Xuan on Dong Xuan Street is Hanoi's biggest covered fresh- and dried food market, but for greater variety try Cho Hom, on Pho Hué, which has clothing upstairs, and a supermarket. All around Hom market are specialist shopping streets: Tran Nhan Tong focuses on shirts and jackets, while Phung Khac Khoan, off Tran Xuan Soan, is a riot of colourful fabrics. Hanoi's wholesale flower market is held each dawn beside Nghi Tam Avenue at its most northerly junction with Yen Phu; action starts around 5am (6am in winter), and lasts an hour.

Listings

Airlines Aeroflot, 4 Trang Thi (☎04/825 6742); Air France, 1 Ba Trieu (☎04/825 3484); Cathay Pacific, 49 Hai Ba Trung (☎04/826 7298); China Airlines, 18 Tran Hung Dao (☎04/824 2688); China Southern Airlines, 27 Ly Thai To (☎04/826 9233); Emirates, 330 Ba Trieu (☎04/974 0040); Japan Airlines, 1 Ba Trieu (☎04/826 5693); Lao Aviation, 41 Quang Trung (☎04/822 9951); Malaysia Airlines, 15 Ngo Quyen (☎04/826 8820); Pacific Airlines, 100 Le Duan (☎04/518 1503); Scandinavian Airlines System (SAS), 49 Hai Ba Trung (☎04/934 2626); Singapore Airlines, 17 Ngo Quyen (☎04/826 8888); Thai International, 44b Ly Thuong Kiet (☎04/826 6893); Vietnam Airlines, 1 Quang Trung for domestic and international services (☎04/825 0888), and with sales agents at 112 Cau Go (☎04/825 9811) and 30a Ly Thuong Kiet (☎04/826 9130).

Banks and exchange Vietcombank head office is at 23 Phan Chu Trinh, for all services including cash withdrawals on credit cards and telegraphic transfers. Branch at 78 Nguyen Du with agents all over town. ANZ Bank, 14 Le Thai To, boasts Hanoi's first 24-hr ATM which dispenses both US$ and dong for Visa, Visa Plus and MasterCard holders. They also offer a safety deposit service from $10 per month. Other banks with counter facilities are: Citibank, 2nd Floor, 17 Ngo Quyen (Citibank card-holders can use the ATM to access US$ for no charge); Standard Chartered, 8th Floor, 49 Hai Ba Trung; VID Public Bank, 2 Ngo Quyen and Vietincombank at 10 Le Loi. Money changers in and around the GPO offer higher rates than banks, but will try to befuddle you with stacks of small denominations – watch out for notes folded to count twice. You can also change money at the *Mocca Café*, in gold shops and at the currency exchange at 25 Luong Ngoc Quyen.

Books and bookshops Apart from small outlets in top-class hotels, Trang Tien is the main area for books. Otherwise try The Foreign Language Bookshop at 61 Trang Tien; Tien Phong at 175 Nguyen Thai Hoc; Hanoi Bookshop, 34 Trang Tien; Fahasa, 22b Hai Ba Trung and Xunhasaba, 32 Hai Ba Trung.

Embassies and consulates Australia, 8 Dao Tan, Van Phuc (☎04/831 7755); Austria, 104 Tran Hung Dao (☎04/822 4005); Belgium, Daeha Business Centre, 360 Kim Ma (☎04/831 5240); Burma, A3 Van Phuc (☎04/845 3369); Cambodia, 71 Tran Hung Dao (☎04/825 3788); Canada, 31 Hung Vuong (☎04/823 5500); China, 46 Hoang Dieu (☎04/845 3736); Denmark, 19 Dien Bien Phu (☎04/823 1888); Finland, 31 Hai Ba Trung (☎04/826 6788); France, 57 Tran Hung Dao (☎04/825 2719); Germany, 29 Tran Phu (☎04/845 3836); India, 58–60 Tran Hung Dao (☎04/824 4989); Indonesia, 50 Ngo Quyen (☎04/825 7969); Israel, 68 Nguyen Thai Hoc (☎04/843 3140); Italy, 9 Le Phung Hieu (☎04/825 6256); Japan, 27 Lieu Giai (☎04/846 3000); Lao PDR, 22 Tran Binh Trong (☎04/825 5476); Malaysia, Fortuna Hotel, 6b Lang Ha (☎04/831 3400); Netherlands, 360 Kim Ma (☎04/831 5650); New Zealand, Daeha Business Centre, 360 Kim Ma (☎04/824 1481); Norway, 7th Floor, Metropole Centre, 56 Ly Thai To (☎826 2111); Philippines, 27b Tran Hung Dao (☎04/825 7948); Russia, 58 Tran Phu (☎04/845 4632); Singapore, 41–43 Tran Phu (☎04/823 3966); Spain, Daeha Business Centre, 360 Kim Ma (☎04/771 207); Sweden, 2 Nui Truc, Van Phuc (☎04/845 4825); Switzerland, 77b Kim Ma (☎04/823 2019); Thailand, 63–65 Hoang Dieu (☎04/823 5092); UK, 5th Floor, 31 Hai Ba Trung (☎04/825 2510); USA, 7 Lang Ha (☎04/843 1500).

Emergencies Dial ☎113 for police, ☎114 for fire service and ☎115 for an ambulance.

Hospitals and clinics Vietnam International Hospital, 1 Phuong Mai, offers international-class facilities at their outpatients clinic (☎04/574 0740; Mon–Fri 8am–5.30pm, Sat am only; $35–60 consultation fee), plus dental and optical care, surgery and a 24-hr emergency and ambulance service (☎04/574 1111). Hanoi Family Practice in Van Phuc (Building A1, 109–112 Kim Ma) has an outpatients clinic (☎04/843 0748; Mon–Fri 8.30am–6pm, Sat am only; $50 standard consultation fee) and 24-hr emergency service (☎09040 9919). The emergency assistance company, AEA International at 31 Hai Ba Trung, also provides routine care to travellers (☎04/934 0555; Mon–Fri 8.30am–7pm, Sat am only; $55–65 consultation fee). Of the local hospitals, your best bet is the Vietnam–Korea Friendship Hospital at 12 Chu Van An (☎04/843 7231), which has some English-speaking doctors and charges around $15–30 initial fee. The Institute of Acupuncture is at H3, Vinh Ho, Thai Thinh (☎04/853 3881).

Immigration Office 40 Bang Hai with a branch office at 89 Tran Hung Dao.

Internet access *Tony's Oldstreet Café*, 118 Hang Bac (300d per min).

Post offices The GPO occupies a whole block at 75 Dinh Tien Hoang. International postal services, including parcel dispatch (8am–noon & 1–4pm) and poste restante (Mon–Sat 7.30am–noon & 1–4pm; $10 yearly and 500d per letter), are located in the southernmost hall; next entrance up is for telephone and fax services 6.30am–10pm; fax 24-hr; $3.5 per minute to call the UK; $3 per minute to Australia and the US; prices fall by 50 percent 7pm–7am Sun). The main entrance leads to general mail services. To collect a parcel, tak your passport and 3000d to the poste restante section. Useful sub-post offices are at 66 Trang Tien, 6 Luong Van Can, 18 Nguyen Du, D2 Giang Vo and at Hanoi train station.

Travel agencies Many travellers' cafés organize similar bargain-basement tours to the Perfume Pagod ($17), Ha Long Bay (2–3 days; $20–40) and Sa Pa (4 days; $40). They also do car rental, visa services an airport transport. Recommended agencies include: *Love Planet*, 18 Hang Bac (☎04/828 4864), *Red Rive Tours*, 73 Hang Bo (☎04/826 8427), *Lonely Planet*, 33 Hang Be (☎04/825 0974), *Real Darling*, 33 Hang Qua (☎04/826 9386), and *Green Bamboo*, at 42 Nha Chung (☎04/826 8752).

Around Hanoi

Around Hanoi, the fertile and densely populated landscape of the Red River Delta is criss crossed with massive ancient dykes and studded with temples, pagodas, family graves, com munal houses and all the other leftovers of successive generations. It's worth venturing int by motorbike or car, or with a tour from Hanoi, for the chance to visit the dramatic Perfume Pagoda, and a couple of other interesting religious sites.

The Perfume Pagoda

Sixty kilometres southwest of Hanoi, a forested spur shelters north Vietnam's most famou pilgrimage site, the **Perfume Pagoda**, Chua Huong, said to be named after spring blossom that scent the air. The easiest and most popular way to visit the pagoda is on a day tour ou of Hanoi ($12) or in a hired car. Alternatively, it's a two- to three-hour motorbike ride: follow Highway 6 through Ha Dong as far as the fourteen-kilometre marker where the highway crosses the rail tracks, then turn left on the D426 heading due south, through Thanh Oai an Van Dinh, to Duc Khe village and the Suoi Yen (Yen River) boat station. There's a sightsee ing **fee** of $8 to visit the pagoda, though this does include the return boat trip; tickets are sol at the entrance to the village beside the post office (*buu dien*). There are some overpriced **food stalls** at the boat station and at the start of the walk to Chua Thien Chu.

The Perfume Pagoda occupies a spectacular grotto over 50m high; the journey there begins with an appealing, half-hour sampan ride up a flooded valley among karst hills, then a path brings you to the seventeenth-century Chua Thien Chu ("Pagoda Leading to Heaven") in front of which stands a magnificent, triple-roofed bell pavilion. Quan Am, Goddess o Mercy, takes pride of place on the pagoda's main altar. To the right of the pagoda, a three kilometre path leads steeply uphill (1–2hr) to the Perfume Pagoda, also dedicated to Quar Am. The walk is rewarded when the gaping cavern is revealed beneath the inscription "supreme cave under the southern sky". A flight of 120 steps descends into the Dragon's mouth-like entrance, where gilded Buddhas emerge from dark recesses wreathed in clouds of incense (bring a torch). Note that long trousers and long-sleeve shirts are required for entry to Chua Thien Chu (shorts are considered disrespectful). You should also wear shoes with good grips and take a waterproof.

Thay Pagoda (the Master's Pagoda) and Tay Phuong Pagoda

Thay Pagoda (Chua Thay) or the **Master's Pagoda** was founded in the reign of King Ly Nhan Tong (1072–1127) and is an unusually large complex overlooking a lake in the lee of a limestone crag. The Master was the ascetic monk and healer Tu Dao Hanh, an accomplished water puppeteer – hence the lake's dainty theatre-pavilion – and the pagoda is dedicated to the cult of Tu Dao Hanh in his three incarnations as monk (the Master), Buddha, and king Nearly a hundred statues fill the prayer halls, including two seventeenth-century giant guardians made of clay and papier mâché, which weigh a thousand kilos apiece. The highest altar holds a Buddha trinity, dating from the 1500s, and a thirteenth-century, wooden statue of the Master as a bodhisattva, dressed in yellow and perched on a lotus throne. On a sepa rate altar to the left he appears again as King Ly Than Tong, also in yellow, with two Cambodian slaves. In front of the pagoda are two covered bridges with arched roofs built in

602 and dedicated to the sun and moon: one leads to an islet where spirits of the earth, water and sky are worshipped in a tiny Taoist temple; the second takes you to a flight of steps up the limestone hill. Thay Pagoda lies 30km from Hanoi in Sai Son village, between Ha Dong and Son Tay, and is best visited by car, motorbike or xe om. The easiest route is via Highway , taking a right turn in front of Ha Dong post office (*buu dien*) onto the TL72/TL80 to Quoc Oai, where the pagoda is signed 4km off to the right. The entry fee ($1.50) includes an English-speaking guide; Sundays are very crowded.

Tay Phuong Pagoda

Six kilometres west of the Thay Pagoda, the much smaller **Tay Phuong Pagoda** perches atop a fifty-metre-high limestone hillock and was one of the first pagodas built in Vietnam. It's renowned for its fine collection of jackfruit-wood **statues**, particularly the eighteen *arhats*, disturbingly life-like representations of Buddhist ascetics, grouped around the main altar (bring a torch). As Tay Phuong is also an important Confucian sanctuary, disciples of the sage are included on the altar, each carrying a gift to their master, some precious object, a book or a symbol of longevity, alongside the expected Buddha effigies. From the Thay Pagoda, backtrack to Quoc Oai to rejoin the road heading northwest to Son Tay; after the 8km marker, look out on the left for an unsigned, paved road running a short distance across the paddy to the pagoda entry gate ($1.50).

HA LONG BAY AND THE NORTHERN SEABOARD

The mystical scenery of **Ha Long Bay**, peppered with thousands of evocatively craggy limestone outcrops, is what draws people to the northeast coast of Vietnam, and there are plenty of tourist boats and accommodation in nearby **Ha Long City** to facilitate your visit. **Cat Ba Island**, accessible from the port city of **Haiphong**, makes a less touristy base for bay trips. If you still haven't tired of karst scenery, head inland, south of Hanoi, for the city of Ninh Binh and make a day-trip to **Tam Coc**. Vietnam borders China 150km up the coast from Ha Long Bay, and foreigners in possession of the right visa can **enter China** at Mong Cai.

Ninh Binh and around

The dusty provincial capital of **NINH BINH**, 90km south of Hanoi, has little to detain you, but the surrounding hills shelter **Tam Coc**, where sampans slither through the limestone tunnels of "Ha Long Bay on land", and dynastic temples from the ancient capital, **Hoa Lu**. Two radio masts provide convenient landmarks in town: the taller stands over the post office at the south, while the shorter signals the northern extremity 2km away up Highway 1 (Tran Hung Dao). Exactly halfway between the two, Le Hong Phong shoots off east at a major junction, taking traffic to join the Nam Dinh road. To the east, a dismembered church spire bears witness to American bombing raids of the late 1960s, while 1km to the north a picturesque little pagoda nestles at the base of Non Nuoc Mountain.

Ninh Binh's **bus station** lies 100m south of the post office, across the small Lim Bridge and beside a busy crossroads. To find the **train station**, head one block north on Le Dai Hanh, turn right opposite the *Huong Gia Hotel* and walk 200m east. From either station, the centre" of town is a one-kilometre xe om ride away. For advice on booking tours and transport it's best to ask your hotel or guesthouse. Mr Da, owner of the *Thuy Anh*, is particularly knowledgeable about the area. You can **exchange** cash at Agribank, immediately south of the *Hoa Lu Hotel*, and at Vietcombank, located on the main strip on Tran Hung Dao (they also take travellers' cheques).

The best **place to stay and eat** is the *Thuy Anh Hotel* at 55a Truong Han Sieu (☎030/871602 ③), which has a panoramic roof terrace restaurant (open only in summer) and spotless, newl refurbished rooms. Its owner, Mr Da, is a good source of local tourist information. Otherwise there's the small, popular *Queen*, a mini-hotel just 30m straight in front of the train station at 2 Hoang Hoa Tham (☎030/871874; ②–③), or the central *Star*, 267 Tran Hung Da (☎030/871522; ②–③), a clean mini-hotel with en-suite, air-con rooms and Internet access.

Tam Coc and Bich Dong

The film *Indochine* put the **Tam Coc region**, 9km southwest of Ninh Binh, firmly on the map for French tour groups and it's hard not to be won over by the mystical, watery beauty of the area, which is a miniature landlocked version of Ha Long Bay. The three-hour sampan-ride through the flooded landscape is a definite highlight, and journey's end is **Tam Coc**, three long, dark tunnel-caves eroded through the limestone hills with barely sufficient clearance for the sampan in places. **Boats** leave the dock in Van Lam village between 6.30am and 5pm (go early or late to avoid the crowds), and cost $3.50 per person.

Follow the road another 2km beyond the boat dock to visit the cave-pagoda of **Bich Don** ($1.50), where stone-cut steps, entangled by the thick roots of banyan trees, lead up a clif face peppered with shrines to the cave entrance. Three Buddhas sit unperturbed on their lotus thrones beside a head-shaped rock which bestows longevity if touched. A second entrance opens out higher up the cliff, from where steps continue to a viewpoint.

The easiest and most enjoyable way to reach Tam Coc is to rent a **bicycle** or **motorbik** from a Ninh Binh guesthouse ($1 and $6 respectively for a day); the turning, signed t "Bich Dong", is 4km south of the Lim Bridge on Highway 1, before the cement factory. / **xe om** from Ninh Binh will cost about $4 all-in. If your next stop is Hoa Lu (see below), yo could take a roughish back road for a spectacular ten-kilometre-ride through rice fields and karst scenery. To pick up the road, heading back from Tam Coc towards the Highway, look out for the left turn after about 2km, opposite a banyan tree, which leads through a smal village.

Hoa Lu

Thirteen kilometres northwest of Ninh Binh stands **Hoa Lu** (entrance $2), site of the tenth century capital of an early, independent Vietnamese kingdom called Dai Co Viet. The fort fied royal palaces of the Dinh and Le kings are now in ruins, but their dynastic temples, sev enteenth-century copies of eleventh-century originals, still rest quietly in a narrow valle surrounded by hills. First stop at the site should be the more imposing **Den Dinh Tien Hoang**, furthest from the ticket barrier, dedicated to King Dinh Tien Hoang who seize power in 968 AD and moved the capital south from Co Loa in the Red River Delta to thi secure valley far from the threat of Chinese intervention. Dinh Tien Hoang's gilded effig can be seen in the temple's second sanctuary room, flanked by his three sons. The secon temple, **Den Le Dai Hanh**, is dedicated to the army commander who succeeded Dinh Tie Hoang in 980. He is enshrined in the temple's rear sanctuary with his eldest son and queen The roof beams of the temple porch are decorated with polychrome carvings of dragons an lotus flowers. Opposite the temples, steps lead up "Saddle Mountain" for a panoramic view of Hoa Lu. It's also possible to take a **boat trip** (2–3hr; $1.50 per person) along the Sao Kh River.

The quickest way out to Hoa Lu is by xe om ($4–5 round-trip), but going by **bicycle i** more fun. After the first five unnerving kilometres on Highway 1, it's a pleasant ride on pave back roads west of the highway, following signs to Truong Yen village and Hoa Lu (13km i total). You can then cycle back along the Sao Khe River: take the paved road heading eas directly in front of the temples, turn right over the bridge and follow the dirt track for abou 4km to the first village. Here, a left turn leading to a concrete bridge will take you to Nin Binh, while the road straight ahead continues for another 6km to Tam Coc; in either cas allow at least one hour for the journey.

Haiphong

Located 100km east of Hanoi on the Cua Cam River, one of the main channels of the Red River Estuary, **HAIPHONG** has long been North Vietnam's principal port, and its history runs the gamut from major seventeenth-century trading centre through bombardment by both the French and the Americans. These days it's a small, orderly city of broad avenues and subtle, cosmopolitan charms, with good ferry links to Cat Ba Island and Hong Gai (for Ha Long Bay), but not much else of interest. The city's crescent-shaped nineteenth-century core lies between the curve of the Tam Bac River and the loop of the train tracks. To the north of the main artery, **Dien Bien Phu**, you'll find broad avenues and colonial architecture. To the south is the merchants' quarter, these days a dilapidated area of street markets between Tran Trinh Street and Cho Sat. Opposite Cho Sat on the south side of Tam Bac Lake, no. 124 Nguyen Duc Canh houses **Hang Kenh Carpet Factory**, where you can watch the carpets being hand-woven on old wooden looms (Mon–Sat 7–11.30am & 1–5pm, Sun 7–11.30am). The temple of **Den Nghe**, about ten minutes' walk east of the factory along Me Linh, is noted for its carvings, particularly on the massive stone table in the first courtyard.

Practicalities

Haiphong **train station** is on the southeast side of town, close to the centre. The station has left-luggage lockers in a "reception room" off the main ticket hall, where you can also buy ferry tickets for Cat Ba Island. The **ferry station**, serving both Hong Gai and Cat Ba, is on the Cua Cam River about 500m north of the city centre along Ben Binh. **Buses** from the south and west usually pitch up at Niem Nghia bus station, about 3km from the centre. Some Hanoi services use Tam Bac bus station, near the west end of Tam Bac Lake and Sat market. Buses from Bai Chay and the northeast arrive at Binh bus station on the north bank of the Cua Cam River, 300m from the cross-river ferry, but if you're coming from this direction the Hong Gai–Haiphong **ferry** (4 daily; 3hr 30min) is a more scenic alternative. **Hanoi-bound** minibuses hang around the ferry station and Tam Bac bus station, where you'll also find public buses to Hanoi; all other buses to the south and west depart from Niem Nghia bus station. Haiphong's **Cat Bi airport** (flights to Ho Chi Minh City and Da Nang only) is 7km southeast of the city, $5 by taxi (☎031/841999). Vietnam Airlines is at 30 Tran Phu, next to the *Cat Bi Hotel* (daily 8–11.30am & 1.30–5pm).

You can rent **cars** through Vietnamtourism ($35) at 15 Le Dai Hanh (Mon–Sat 7am–noon & 1.30–5pm; ☎031/842989), or 57 Dien Bien Phu (☎031/842432). All the following **banks** change currency and travellers' cheques: Incombank, 36 Dien Bien Phu; Indovina Bank, 30 Tran Phu; Maritime Bank, 25 Dien Bien Phu; Vietcombank, 11 Hoang Dieu. The **GPO** is at the junction of Nguyen Tri Phuong and Hoang Van Thu, with a sub-post office at 36 Quang Trung. Ben Vien Viet–Tiep **hospital** is at 1 Nha Thuong (☎031/846236).

Budget **accommodation** is in short supply and tends to fill up early, but the clean cell-like rooms and decrepit bathrooms in the old block at *Hoa Binh*, 104 Luong Khanh Thien (☎031/859029; ②), are the cheapest in town. Right in the station courtyard at 19 Luong Khanh Thien, *Phuong Dong (Orient*; ☎031/855391; ③) is small and sparklingly new and rooms have TV and phone. Close by, *Cat Bi* at 30 Tran Phu (☎031/846306; ③) has spacious, comfortable rooms. The large new *Military Zone Guesthouse* (also known as *Nha Khach Quanh Khu*), opposite the GPO at 2 Hoang Van Thu (☎031/842492; ④), has clean, bright rooms, all with TV and air-con. The *Atlantic* **restaurant** at 30 Dinh Tien Hoang is recommended for its inexpensive home-cooking, or try the slightly more expensive *Lucky* at 22 Minh Khai.

Cat Ba Island

Dragon-back mountain ranges mass on the horizon 20km out of Haiphong as the ferry approaches **Cat Ba Island**, the largest member of an archipelago sitting on the west of Ha

Long Bay. The island's main settlement is Cat Ba Town, from where the only road heads 30km across a landscape of forested peaks to tiny Phu Long village. **Cat Ba Town** is in two sections, separated by a small headland: the tourist facilities are grouped around the new ferry pier, and 800m to the west lies the original fishing village and market. A steep road just east of the waterfront leads to a small, sandy **beach** (small entrance fee), with showers, toilets and an overpriced restaurant.

In 1986, almost half the island and adjacent waters were declared a **national park** ($1), the entrance to which is 16km along the road from Cat Ba Town. It's worth hiring a guide to explore the park ($5 for up to one day), as people have got seriously lost on the unmarked paths. You'll need good boots, lots of water, potent mosquito repellent, and a compass. The going can be quite tough and paths slippery in wet weather.

Most Cat Ba hotels can help arrange **boat tours** and treks in the National Park. The most popular option is a full-day trip with a trek through the National Park, lunch in a village, boat trip back to Cat Ba town via Lan Ha Bay, with a swimming stop and visit to a pearl farm. Hanoi's *Red River Café* and *TF Handspan* travel companies both have a representative in Cat Ba, based at the *Giang Son Hotel* (☎031/888214), on the waterfront, offering a trek/boat trip package for $12 per person. A half-day boat trip into Lan Ha Bay with snorkelling, swimming and pearl farm visit costs around $7. Other boat trips venture up into Ha Long Bay itself, or to one of the bay's more dramatic caves, **Ho Ba Ham** ($50 for a full day).

Practicalities

The most convenient way of **getting to Cat Ba** is the Jet Cat service **from Haiphong**'s old ferry station (9am daily; 1hr 10min; $6), with a return sailing at 4pm. Two ordinary ferries also depart Haiphong twice daily at 6.30am and 1.30pm (3hr; $5). Some terminate at the adjacent island of Cat Hai, from where you should take the small ferry over to Phu Long village and then get a bus (1hr; $2) or motorbike for the last 30km to Cat Ba Town. You can also get to Cat Ba **from Hong Gai** ferry station (daily; 2hr 30min; $2), but the return is only serviced by expensive tourist boats. Tours from Hanoi often combine Cat Ba and Ha Long Bay for $30. For most of the year, ferries use Cat Ba's new harbour pier, but from May to August, and during strong winds, they sail round to the island's east side, from where a bus brings you to the hotels (10min). Two island buses run daily from Cat Ba Town to Phu Long village (1hr; $2). Hotels and restaurants will change money, but cash only and at poor rates.

Officially all **hotels** must charge $10 per room (up to three beds) in winter and $15 in summer. Most are a stone's throw from the new pier and pretty similar: try *Van Anh* (☎031/888201; ③) or *Huong Cang* (☎031/888399; ②). The *Flightless Bird Café* towards the market is a joint venture between Vietnamese and New Zealand owners. Staff speak good English and can help arrange tours and boat trips. International calls can be made from the **post office** (7am–noon & 12.30–9pm), located on the opposite corner to the *Hoang Hung Hotel*, on the waterfront. **Internet access** is available at the *Duc Thuan* (*Sunflower*) on the waterfront and the *Pacific* (☎031/888331; ③), set one street back; they both offer Internet access for 2000d per minute as well as accommodation.

Ha Long Bay

An estimated 1600 bizarrely shaped limestone outcrops jut out of the emerald **Ha Long Bay**, its hidden bays, echoing caves and needle-sharp ridges providing the inspiration for dozens of local legends and poems, and frequently referred to as the eighth natural wonder of the world. Navigating the silent channels and scrambling through caves is a hugely popular activity, but with so much hyperbole, some find Ha Long disappointing: this stretch of coast is an industrialized region, and views in February and March can be poor. The epicentre of tourism in Ha Long Bay is **Bai Chay**, a resort on the north shore, which offers rather mediocre accommodation and overpriced restaurants plus hordes of boatmen. A more low-key base is **Hong Gai**, a short hop away by ferry across a narrow channel east of Bai Chay.

Hong Gai provides only basic tourist facilities, but has a more workaday atmosphere. The other option is to base yourself on quieter Cat Ba Island (see p.1053).

Boat trips

The vast majority of visitors to Ha Long Bay come on organized tours from Hanoi and stay in Bai Chay, but it's not difficult to **charter a boat** locally, though it works out more expensive than a tour unless you can share costs. Most hotels and some restaurants in Bai Chay can help with boat hire, as can Quang Ninh Tourism (☎033/846274), beside the entrance to the *Ha Long Hotel*. Alternatively, go direct to the boatmen at the tourist wharves, 2km out of town to the west, or around the harbour in Hong Gai. **Rates** range from $4 to 7 per hour (maximum ten people). Always agree the itinerary in advance and pay at the end. As it takes about an hour to get in among the islands, a **full** day's boat tour (6–8hr) is preferable to two half-days. You could also try and arrange to overnight on board (take warm clothes) but officially a permit is required. Every **meal** on board costs an extra $2–4 per person. There have been occasional reports of thefts, so either have someone stay on the boat all the time or leave valuables in your hotel safe. A few caverns are still unlit, so take a **torch**, and wear shoes with a good grip.

The caves and islands

Ha Long Bay is split in two by a wide channel running north–south: the larger, western portion contains the most dramatic scenery and best caves, while to the east lies an attractive area of smaller islands, known as Bai Tu Long. Before exploring the caves, you need to buy an entrance ticket ($1) from the Bai Chay boat station. This allows entrance to a maximum of five caves and includes a coracle to ferry you from your main boat. The bay's most famous cave is the closest to Bai Chay: **Hang Dau Go** ("Grotto of the Wooden Stakes") is where General Tran Hung Dao amassed hundreds of stakes deep inside the cave's largest chamber prior to the Bach Dang River battle of 1288. The same island also boasts the beautiful **Hang Thien Cung** cave, whose rectangular chamber, 250m long and 20m high, holds a textbook display of sparkling stalactites and stalagmites. Continuing south, you should single out Ho Dong Tien ("Grotto of the Fairy Lake") and the enchanting Dong Me Cung ("Grotto of the Labyrinth").

Of the far-flung sights, **Hang Hanh** is one of the more adventurous day-trips from Bai Chay: the tide must be exactly right (at half-tide) to allow a coracle ($10 extra) access to the two-kilometre-long tunnel-cave; a powerful torch is very useful. Dau Bo Island, on the southeastern edge of Ha Long Bay, encloses **Ho Ba Ham** ("Three Tunnel Lake"), a shallow lagoon wrapped round with limestone walls and connected to the sea by three low-ceilinged tunnels that are only navigable by sampan at low tide. This cave is sometimes included in two-day excursions out of Bai Chay but is easiest to arrange from Cat Ba (see opposite).

Bai Chay and Hong Gai

In 1994 Hong Gai and Bai Chay were amalgamated into **Ha Long City**, but locals still stick to the old names – as do ferry services and minibuses – since this is a useful way to distinguish between the two towns, which lie on either side of the narrow Cua Luc channel. Neon signs blaze out at night along the **BAI CHAY** waterfront, advertising north Vietnam's most developed resort, whose main business is boat tours around the bay. **HONG GAI**, on the other hand, is a bustling working harbour.

The **accommodation** in Hong Gai may be basic, but the atmosphere of the town has a certain charm and the welcoming, family-run *Hien Cat* guesthouse, conveniently located right by the ferry pier at 252 Ben Tau (☎033/827417; ②–③), has the most scenic bathrooms in Ha Long City. **Bai Chay** has a bigger choice of hotels, most located along the two main drags, Ha Long Avenue and Vuon Dao, but quality is variable. *Hoa Binh* (☎033/846009; ③) is one of

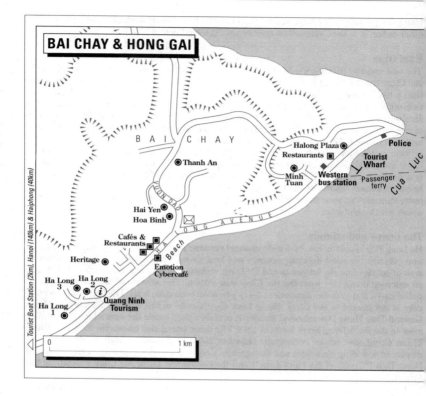

the better mini-hotels on Vuon Dao, and has boats for hire. The *Thang Loi* (☎033/845092; ③) is a spotless new hotel tucked away down a dusty sidestreet, while *Hai Yen*, 57 Vuon Dao (☎033/846126; ③), has standard rooms and Internet access for 600d a minute. *Minh Tuan* on Ho Xuan Huong (☎033/846200; ②) has the only cheap beds near the bus station; rooms are small but clean.

The larger hotels in Bai Chay and both post offices **change cash**, but the only place to handle travellers' cheques is Hong Gai's Vietcombank, at the east end of Le Thanh Tong. Fresh seafood is the natural speciality of Ha Long Bay, with excellent lobster, crab and fish on offer at the **restaurants**. The restaurants on Ha Long Avenue tend to cater for mass tourist groups, but the *Van Song* and *Binh Minh* restaurants are worth a try, while the best eating in Hong Gai is at the market food stalls. A welcome addition is a branch of Hanoi's *Emotion Cybercafé* on Ha Long Ave (☎033/847 354), which has fast food and drinks, as well as **Internet** access.

The frequent **buses** between Hanoi, Haiphong and Bai Chay use the Western bus station, at the far end of Ha Long Avenue. Hang around the tourist bus stop near the *Emotion Cybercafé* at lunchtime and you can often get a seat on an air-con bus ($5) returning to Hanoi by negotiating direct with the driver. Buses from Mong Chai and the north use the Eastern bus station; from here, Hong Gai centre is 1km back down Le Thanh Tong, or you can cross

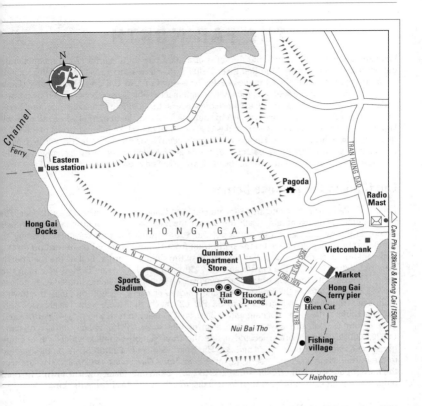

over to Bai Chay on the passenger ferry that shuttles between the two bus stations. A slower and more expensive, but far more scenic approach is to take the **train** from Hanoi to Haiphong and then the public **ferry** to Hong Gai (4 daily; 3hr 30min), for a total cost of around $9. One ferry a day departs for Cat Ba, at 12.30pm.

Mong Cai and the Chinese border

Since the border reopened for trade in 1992, **MONG CAI** has been booming and its markets are stuffed with Chinese goods. Highway 18 enters the town from the west across a bridge and then peters out in a large, open area, with the public **minibus station** straight ahead and the post office on the south side. A rooftop clock identifies Mong Cai's focal point, the covered market. The **Chinese border** is just 1km away to the north; walk from the bridge through the goods-only bus stand and then follow the river, past the bank, to reach the border gate (7am–5pm). There's not much to choose between Mong Cai's **hotels**, all of which offer air-con, hot water, TV and telephone. Best value is the *Huu Nghi* (✆033/881408; ③–④), down a sidestreet near the post office. Alternatively, try the *Dong A* (✆033/881151; ③–④), opposite the minibus station. Streets near the covered market turn into open-air restaurants in the evening.

THE FAR NORTH

Vietnam fans out above Hanoi like the head of a giant pin, the majority of it a mountainous buffer zone wrapped around the Red River Delta. Two arteries carry road and rail links north from the capital towards the **Chinese border crossings** of Lao Cai and Dong Dang (Lang Son), and the rest of the region is mostly wild and inaccessible, sparsely populated by a fascinating mosaic of **ethnic minorities**, whose presence is the chief tourist attraction around here. The former hill station of **Sa Pa** has become famous for its weekend market when minority villagers trek in to buy, sell and gossip, and is also the main departure point for treks to their settlements. **Mai Chau** and **Bac Ha** are less touristy centres for walks to minority villages. Note that changing travellers' cheques north of Hanoi is problematic and cash exchanges garner poor rates, so make sure you have all the **cash** you need before you leave the capital.

Lao Cai and the Chinese border

Follow the Red River Valley northwest from Hanoi and after 300km, pushing ever deeper into the mountains, you eventually reach the border town of **LAO CAI**, of little interest in itself except as the railhead for Sa Pa and a popular **route into China** for travellers heading to Kunming. Most people arrive off the night train from Hanoi at Lao Cai **train station** on the east bank of the Red River, just 3km due south of the Chinese border. Follow the road north from the station towards the border and after 2km you reach Coc Leu Bridge, spanning the river to link up with the bulk of Lao Cai town over on the opposite bank. Immediately across the bridge, turn left for the **bus station** and market, or carry straight on along the town's main axis, Hoang Lien. A tourist bus **to Sa Pa** ($2) meets the Hanoi train. Local buses only run this route in the early morning and at 3pm, so it's easier to take a jeep ($4–5 per person) or a xe om ($5) all the way from the train or bus station. The Tulico tourist company (☎020/832788) has an office located inside the train station complex which can arrange transport as well as trips to Sa Pa and Bac Ha. Nearly all Lao Cai's **hotels** are on the road up to the border, Nguyen Hue. Best of the lot is *Song Hong Guesthouse* (☎020/830004; ②), near the border gate, or try the *Hanoi* (☎020/832486; ①), 100m or so back towards town. The road outside the train station is lined with food stalls, of which the *Thai Du* is the best.

Into China: Hekou Bridge

The border crossing from Lao Cai **into China** is via the **Hekou Bridge border gate** (7.30am–5pm), on the east bank of the Red River. Queues at emigration are longest in the early morning. Next to the emigration office you'll find an exchange desk (7.30am–3pm), which deals in dong, dollars and yuan, but not travellers' cheques. Across on the Chinese side, turn right and Hekou **train** station is only five minutes' walk away, where a direct train to **Kunming** departs at 1.30pm every day (Chinese time). At least two regular bus services leave Hekou each day (12hr; 520km). Travellers **entering Vietnam** at Lao Cai may have to pay a small "fee" for paperwork.

Sa Pa and around

Forty kilometres from Lao Cai, the small market town of **SA PA** perches dramatically on the western edge of a high plateau and enjoys a refreshing climate (bring warm clothes) set in magnificent scenery, with plenty of walks out to **minority villages** of Hmong, Dao and Giay peoples. Sa Pa itself is ethnically Vietnamese, but the weekend market, which runs from noon on Saturday to noon on Sunday, draws in minority villagers from all around and has become a major tourist attraction, not least for the chance to see minority women clad in their colourful finery (always ask permission before taking photographs); in peak season, however, tourists can outnumber minorities.

THE ETHNIC MINORITIES

Historically, all the peoples of northern Vietnam migrated from southern China at various times throughout history: those who arrived first, notably the Tay and Thai, settled in the fertile valleys where they now lead a relatively prosperous existence, whereas late arrivals, such as groups of Hmong and Dao, were left to eke out a living on the inhospitable higher slopes. Around five million minority people (nearly two-thirds of Vietnam's total) now live in the northern uplands, mostly in isolated villages. The largest ethnic groups are Thai and Muong in the northwest, Tay and Nung in the northeast, and Hmong and Dao dispersed throughout the region. Despite government efforts to integrate them into the Vietnamese community, minorities in these remote areas continue to follow a way of life little changed over the centuries. For an insight into their cultures, visit Hanoi's Museum of Ethnology (see p.1046).

Visiting minority villages

For many people, one of the highlights of travelling in the far north of Vietnam is the experience of visiting minority villages. This is easiest with your own transport. If you're reliant on public services, you'll need to allow more time but, basing yourself in the main towns, it's still possible to get out to traditional villages – notably around Sa Pa, Son La, Mai Chau and Cao Bang. A popular, hassle-free alternative is to join an organized trip from a Hanoi tour agency, whose usual destinations are Sa Pa for the weekly market (4 days; from $40 per person), and Mai Chau (2 days; from $25). The standard package includes guided walks to at least two different minority villages and, in the case of Mai Chau, a night in a stilthouse. You'll need strong boots or training shoes, long trousers (against thorns and leeches), a hat, sunblock and warm clothing; take plenty of water. You might also want a sleeping bag, mosquito net and food – though these may be provided. Carry a strong stick against the dogs. Otherwise, you could try and arrange an individual programme through a Hanoi tour agent or provincial tourist offices, but English-speaking guides who know the area may be hard to find; the guesthouses in Sa Pa are probably your best source. Don't turn up at a village and expect to find accommodation, as your hosts may get in trouble with the authorities and crime is becoming a problem.

It's preferable to visit the minority villages as part of a small group, ideally four people or fewer, as this causes least disruption and allows for greater communication. There's a whole debate about the ethics of cultural tourism and its negative impact on traditional ways of life. Most villagers are genuinely welcoming, appreciating contact with Westerners and the material benefits which they bring; tourism may also help to protect the minorities against enforced Vietnamization, at least in the short term, by encouraging greater respect for cultural diversity. Nonetheless, it's important to take a responsible attitude, and try not to cause offence. Dress modestly (no shorts or vests), never take photographs without asking and only enter a house when invited, removing your shoes first. Small gifts, such as fresh fruit, are always welcome. However, there is a view that even this can foster begging, and that you should only ever give in return for some service or hospitality. A compromise is to buy craftwork produced by the villagers. Take litter back to the towns and be frugal if burning local wood. Growing and using opium is illegal and is punished with fines or prison.

Walks to surrounding villages

There are several Hmong villages within easy walking distance of town, of which the most popular is **CAT CAT** village, roughly 3km away. Follow the track west from the market square, past the steeple-shaped building, then turn left onto a path that drops steeply down to the river. Cat Cat, a huddle of wooden houses, hides among fruit trees and bamboo. Look out for tubs of indigo dye, used to colour the hemp cloth typical of Hmong dress. Cat Cat waterfall is just below the village. For a longer walk, instead of cutting down to Cat Cat, continue on the main track, turning right at the last bend before a river to follow a footpath up the valley. After 4km you'll reach **SIN CHAI** village, a much larger Hmong settlement.

One of the most enjoyable treks is to follow the main track from the *Auberge* south down the Muong Hoa Valley for 12km to a wooden suspension bridge and **TA VAN** village, on the opposite side of the river. Ta Van actually consists of two villages: immediately across the bridge is a Giay community, while further uphill to the left is a Dao village. From here, it's possible to walk back towards Sa Pa on the west side of the river, as far as another Hmong village, **LAO CHAI**, before rejoining the main track. If you don't want to walk all the way back up to Sa Pa, you can pick up a motorbike taxi at one of the huts along the track ($2).

Following the main road another 3km south from the turnoff to Ta Van, a track leads to the Dao settlement of **GIANG TA CHAI**, or **CHAI MAN**. The path branches off to the right, just after a stream crosses the road and before a small shop. After crossing a suspension bridge, take the left fork, directly across a stream, after which it's 1km to the village. From the last turnoff the road deteriorates rapidly for another 6km, then dwindles to a footpath just after **SU PAN**, an unprepossessing collection of huts which is being developed as a commercial centre. From here, heading 4km straight down into the valley, bearing right at each fork, brings you to the Tay village of **BAN HO**, which straddles the river at a suspension bridge. Ban Ho is the staging point for longer treks in the next valley.

New villages are being explored all the time as more tourists arrive seeking out ever more remote spots. Of these, **BANG KHOANG** and **TA GANG PHINH** are best explored by jeep in a day-trip from Sa Pa. *The Cha Pa* restaurant in Sa Pa town can organize treks from $15 a day. The *Auberge* runs some unusual excursions to remote markets and a "Conquer Fan Si Pan" trip for $65 per person, while the *Friendly Café* has a Sunday day-trip to Muong Hum market, 1km from the Chinese border, for $15.

Practicalities

The most popular routing is a **train** to Lao Cai (see p.1058), and then the connecting **tourist bus** ($2) up to Sa Pa, which drops you at Sa Pa's main post office on the eastern edge of town. Heading **back to Lao Cai**, both local and air-con buses leave from outside the church early in the morning. Guesthouses can also organize a jeep back to Lao Cai for $2, as well as train tickets. Buy tickets a day ahead from *La Rose* or the sub-post office, opposite the *Sunrise Hotel*. The sub-post office also sells **train tickets**; tickets for the night train are in short supply at Lao Cai, so book in Sa Pa. **Local buses** leave from a junction 2km east of town: between 8 and 9 in the morning there are a couple to Lao Cai. **Motorbike taxis** can be arranged through your guesthouse or near the market; you need to be an experienced biker to tackle the stony mountain tracks yourself. Guesthouses also rent **jeeps** ($40) and provide **information** on walks to minority villages; guides are available for around $20 per day. The *Auberge* sells area maps and the useful *Sa Pa* guidebook ($3). The bank and most guesthouses **change money** (US dollars only) but rates are better in Hanoi.

In the summer, rooms in Sa Pa can be in short supply, and prices rise by up to fifty percent. The two best **guesthouses** are the *Cat Cat* (☎020/871387; ①–②), off the main drag and behind the market, and the *Auberge Dang Trung* (☎020/871243; ②–③), on the main street, both of which have Sa Pa's accommodation, food and tourist information sewn up. The *Cha Pa Restaurant* (☎020/871245) also has a good reputation for its menu and its tours working with Hanoi's TF Handspan travel company. Other guesthouses offering budget accommodation include the *Queen Hotel* (☎020/871301; ③), which is well kept and friendly, and the newly-opened *Flying Banana* (☎020/871580; ②). The rather pricey rooms at *Green Bamboo* (☎020/871214; ④) come with TVs and fridges. Closer to the town centre, *The Rose* (☎020/871263; ②) offers clean rooms and Internet access, as does the *Viet Hung* aka *Friendly Café* (☎020/871313; ②). To the north of town the *Forestry Guesthouse* (☎020/871230; ③) is quieter and set among pine trees with great views, while, for those looking to splash out, the

Victoria Hotel (☎020/871522; ⑧–⑨) boasts a pool, tennis courts, sauna and jacuzzi on site. Note that the hotel drops its prices drastically midweek and offers a $5 day pass to non-residents wanting to use its leisure facilities.

Bac Ha and around

The small town of **BAC HA**, nestling in a high valley 40km northeast of Highway 7, makes a popular day excursion from Sa Pa on Sundays, when villagers of the Tay, Dao, Nung, Giay and above all Flower Hmong ethnic minorities trek in for the dawn-to-dusk **market**. The town is much less touristy than Sa Pa and worth lingering in – if you're here on a Saturday, you could take in the livestock market at Can Cau as well. The road which leads in from Pho Lu forms the **main street** of Bac Ha. Buses stop outside the post office, where a bend in the road marks the centre of town before leading on for another 2km to the local People's Committee headquarters and onwards in the direction of Can Cau. A road branching off to the right immediately beside the post office leads to the market and a couple of guesthouses. The building that is temporarily housing the People's Committee headquarters is an unmissable wedding cake folly known as **Vua Meo**, or Cat King House, built in 1924 by the French as a palace for a Hmong leader, Vuong Chiz Sinh, whom they had installed as the local "king". Visitors are free to wander through the courtyard.

Trips to surrounding villages

Recently Bac Ha has attempted to emulate Sa Pa's success by developing its own trekking business focused around the nearby rural markets. The picturesque Hmong hamlet of **BAN PHO**, 3km from town, makes a pleasant stroll. Take the road half left at the hammer and sickle sign and head down past the *Sao Mai Hotel*, turning left immediately after the next big building, which is the local hospital. The road continues up the hill for 2km after the village, and affords good views of the valley.

The village of **CAN CAU**, 18km north of Bac Ha, hosts a market each Saturday which is well worth the effort if you can organize transport out there. The market has an emphasis on livestock, especially buffalo, with traders trekking in from as far afield as China in search of bargains. Relatively few visitors get there so the fair retains much of its authenticity. Other than this there's nothing at all to see in Can Cau, but the ride, across a high, empty range with panoramic views on either side, is glorious: simply follow the main road north out of town. The route is passable only by motorbike or four-wheel drive, and after heavy rain is impossible for any vehicle. The *Hoang Vu Hotel* in Bac Ha organizes a day-trip to Can Cau for $10 per person.

Practicalities

Coming **from Hanoi**, get off the bus or train at Pho Lu, from where there are several buses a day to Bac Ha (2hr) from the bus station on the highway, just across from the railway station. About an hour from Pho Lu, you'll have to alight briefly to cross a damaged suspension bridge and change on to another bus on the other side. Coming **from Lao Cai**, you can either take the one daily bus to Bac Ha, at 1pm, or go via Pho Lu. If you're coming **from Sa Pa** on a Sunday, take a tour ($7), organized by your guesthouse, which will include the market and a short trek. A motorbike from Sa Pa takes three hours and costs about $8. Returning from Bac Ha, buses leave for Lao Cai via Pho Lu at 5am and 1pm (4hr; $3) and direct to Pho Lu at 7am and 11am (2 hrs; $2). A jeep or motorbike to Lao Cai takes two hours.

Places to stay in Bac Ha are basic. The pick of the bunch is the *Hoang Vu Hotel* (☎020/880264; ③), where the rooms are dark but adequate. To find it, go past the post office on your right along the main street and walk up the hill until you come to a road leading off half left at a hammer and sickle sign, and the hotel is immediately on your left. Further down the same street the *Sao Mai Hotel* (☎020/880288; ③) has rather overpriced rooms in a wooden stilthouse design. Bac Ha has two main eateries, *Tran Sin Guesthouse* (☎020/880240; ②), located next to the market entrance, is superior and has adequate double rooms. The *Cong Phu Restaurant*, just off the main road where the first street leads off to the right as you come up the hill from the post office, is popular with the Sunday tourists.

Mai Chau and around

The minority villages of the **Mai Chau Valley**, inhabited mainly by Thai people, are close enough to Hanoi (150km) to make this a popular destination, particularly at weekends. The valley itself, however, is still largely unspoilt, a peaceful scene of rice fields and jagged mountains. **MAI CHAU** is the valley's main village, a friendly, quiet place which suddenly bursts into life for its Sunday **market** when minority people trek in to haggle over buffalo meat, starfruit, sacks of tea or groundnuts. Unlike in Sa Pa, the minorities here have largely forsaken their traditional dress, but there's plenty of colour on the road outside the market where freshly dyed yarn hangs up to dry. On the south side of Mai Chau, the *Mai Chau Guesthouse* (☎018/867262; ②) has nine basic but comfortable rooms.

The most accessible village in the fertile Mai Chau Valley is **BAN LAC**, a White Thai settlement of seventy houses where you can buy hand-woven textiles, watch performances of traditional dancing and sleep overnight. The village receives a fair number of tourists and visits can feel overly organized, but this is one of the easiest places to stay in a stilthouse. To reach Ban Lac, follow the road south of the *Mai Chau Guesthouse* for about 500m, to find the turning signed to the right. No one speaks English, but houses displaying cloth outside are most likely to offer accommodation. Expect to pay $5 per person per night, plus $1 per meal.

Most people visit the Mai Chau Valley on an organized tour out of Hanoi, and it's not the easiest place to get to by **public transport**: from Son La take any bus heading east to Hoa Binh or Hanoi and ask the driver to let you off at the Mai Chau junction, around 65km after Moc Chau; at the junction pick up one of the waiting xe om for the final 6km up the valley. From Hanoi, in theory there's a daily bus (5am) from Kim Ma bus station to Mai Chau, though you may have to change in Hoa Binh; alternatively, take any bus going west on Highway 6 and get off at the Mai Chau junction to pick up a motorbike for the last stretch. You have to pay a small sightseeing fee at a barricade at the bottom of the road. A very overcrowded bus **leaving Mai Chau** passes the *Mai Chau Guesthouse* each day around noon on its way down to Hoa Binh, from where you can pick up a Hanoi bus. Alternatively, take a xe om to the junction with Highway 6 and flag down a bus going in your direction.

Lang Son and the Chinese border

For most people, **LANG SON** is merely an overnight stop on the journey through the northeast or en **route to China**, only 18km away to the north. The Ky Cung River splits the town in two, leaving the main bulk on the north side of the Ky Lua Bridge and provincial offices to the south. Highway 1, the town's main north–south artery, is called Tran Dang Ninh, and along here you'll find **Ky Lua market**, which is well worth investigating in the early morning when Tay, Nung and Dao women come to trade. Chinese imports dominate alongside an amazing array of local produce, from freshwater fish to silkworm larvae. The post office lies near the Ky Lua Bridge, 200m east of the highway down Le Loi Street. Next door is the provincial **bus station**, though most long-distance buses will drop you on the main road. Most hotels exchange dollars and yuan. Budget travellers should head straight for the clean, friendly and well-priced **rooms** at *Hoa Phuong Guesthouse* (☎025/871233; ②) on the highway between the bridge and Ky Lua market. A few hundred metres further north, opposite the market entrance, the *Tam Thanh* (☎025/870979; ③–④) is a well-kept older hotel with large, comfortable rooms. For **food**, try street kitchens on Tran Dang Ninh – no. 28 is recommended, opposite the junction with Tam Thanh.

The Chinese border: Huu Nghi and on to Nanning

The road crossing known as the **Huu Nghi (Friendship) border gate** is 18km north of Lang Son and 4km from Dong Dang at the end of Highway 1. If you're travelling by local bus, spend the night in Lang Son and then take a motorbike to the border gate (less than $1). Otherwise, **minibuses** shuttle between Lang Son's Le Loi Street and Dong Dang town, but you'll then have to hop on a motorbike for the last leg. Local **trains** from Hanoi (hard seat only) terminate at Dong Dang station, 800m south of the main town, from where you can take a xe om up to the border (less than $1). At the Huu Nghi border gate (daily 7am–6pm) there's a walk of less than 1km between the two checkpoints. On the Chinese side, take a minibus to **Pingxiang** (15km), for the nearest accommodation and the daily mid-afternoon train to Nanning. Depending on your mode of transport, you must have the correct exit (or entry) point on your Vietnam visa – Dong Dang checkpoint for the train crossing, Huu Nghi for the road.

travel details

Buses

*It's almost impossible to give the **frequency** with which buses run, though scheduled, long-distance public buses won't depart if empty. Moreover, private services, often mini-buses or pick-ups, ply more popular routes, and depart only when they have enough passengers to make the journey worthwhile. Highway 1 sees a near-constant stream of buses passing through to various destinations, and it's possible to flag something down at virtually any time of the day. Off the highway, to be sure of a bus, it's advisable to start your journey early – most long-distance departures leave between 5 and 9am, very few run after midday. **Journey times** can also vary; figures below show the normal length of time you can expect the journey to take.*

Buon Me Thuot to: Da Nang (12hr); Ho Chi Minh City (3 daily; 7hr 30min); Nha Trang (4 daily; 4hr).

Can Tho to: Bac Lieu (4hr); Chau Doc (3hr 40min); Ha Tien (7hr); Ho Chi Minh City (5hr); Long Xuyen (2hr); My Tho (3hr).

Chau Doc to: Can Tho (3hr 40min); Ho Chi Minh City (8hr 40min); Long Xuyen (1hr 40min).

Da Lat to: Buon Me Thuot (10hr 30min); Da Nang (21hr); Ho Chi Minh City (7hr 30min); Nha Trang (5hr).

Da Nang to: Da Lat (two weekly; 1hr 15min); Dong Ha (5hr); Hoi An (1hr 30min–2hr); Hué (3–4hr); Nha Trang (16hr); Quang Ngai (5hr).

Dong Ha to: Hué (2hr 30min); Khe Sanh (2hr 30min).

Haiphong to: Bai Chay (3hr); Hanoi (2hr 30min); Ninh Binh (5hr 30min).

Hanoi to: Bai Chay (4hr); Haiphong (2hr 30min); Hué (19hr); Lang Son (5hr); Mai Chau (7hr); Ninh Binh (3hr); Son La (12hr).

Ha Tien to: Can Tho (7hr); Ho Chi Minh City (13hr); Long Xuyen (6hr); Rach Gia (4hr).

Ho Chi Minh City to: Buon Me Thuot (16hr); Ca Mau (10hr); Can Tho (4hr); Chau Doc (8hr); Da Lat (8hr); Da Nang (26hr); Hanoi (49hr); Ha Tien (10hr); Hué (28hr); My Tho (1hr 30min); Nha Trang (11hr); Phan Thiet (5hr); Qui Nhon (18hr); Vung Tau (2hr).

Hoi An to: Da Nang (1hr 30min–2hr); Quang Ngai (4hr).

Hué to: Da Nang (3–4hr); Dong Ha (2hr 30min); Hanoi (1–2 daily; 1hr 10min–1hr 30min).

Khe Sanh to: Dong Ha (2hr 30min); Lao Bao (40min).

Lao Cai to: Sa Pa (1hr 30min–2hr).

Long Xuyen to: Chau Doc (1hr 40min); Ha Tien (6hr); Ho Chi Minh City (7hr).

Mai Chau to: Hoa Binh (4hr).

Mong Cai to: Hanoi (9hr); Hong Gai (5hr).

My Tho to: Can Tho (3hr); Cholon, Ho Chi Minh City (2hr); My Thuan Ferry (1hr 30min).

Nha Trang to: Buon Me Thuot (5hr 30min); Da Lat (7hr); Da Nang (16hr); Hanoi (38hr); Ho Chi Minh City (11hr); Hué (17hr).

Ninh Binh to: Haiphong (5–6hr); Hanoi (3hr).

Phan Thiet to: Ho Chi Minh City (4hr); Nha Trang (6hr 30min).

Quang Ngai to: Da Nang (4hr); Nha Trang (12hr).

Vinh to: Dong Ha (9hr); Dong Hoi (6hr); Hué (11hr); Ninh Binh (6hr); Thanh Hoa (4hr).

Vinh Long to: Sa Dec (1hr).

Vung Tau to: Ba Ria (40min); Da Lat (8hr 30min); Ho Chi Minh City (2hr); Hué (29hr); Nha Trang (12hr).

Trains

Da Lat to: Trai Mat (up to 16 daily; 40min).

Da Nang to: Hanoi (3 daily; 17–21hr); Ho Chi Minh City (3–4 daily; 19–26hr); Hué (3–4 daily; 3–4hr); Nha Trang (3–4 daily; 10–14hr).

Dieu Tri to: Da Nang (4 daily; 5hr 45min–7hr 30min); Ho Chi Minh City (4 daily; 12hr 50min–16hr); Hué (4 daily; 9–11hr); Nha Trang (4 daily; 4hr 40min–5hr 30min).

Dong Ha to: Hanoi (2 daily; 15–16hr); Hué (2 daily; 1hr 30min).

Hanoi to: Da Nang (3 daily; 16hr 40min–22hr); Dong Dang (2 daily; 8–10hr); Dong Ha (2 daily; 14hr–16hr 30min); Haiphong (5–6 daily; 2hr–2hr 30min); Ho Chi Minh City (3 daily; 34–44hr); Hué (3 daily; 13hr 30min–18hr); Lao Cai (2 daily; 10–11hr); Nha Trang (3 daily; 27hr–33hr 30min); Ninh Binh (4 daily; 2hr 20min–4hr).

Ho Chi Minh City to: Da Nang (4 daily; 18hr 30min–25hr 10min); Dieu Tri (4 daily; 12hr 12min–16hr); Hanoi (3 daily; 40–44hr); Hué (4 daily; 22hr–29hr 30min); Muong Man (4 daily; 4hr 10min–4hr 50min); Nam Dinh (3 daily; 37hr 30min–41hr 30min); Nha Trang (4 daily; 8hr–11hr 10min); Ninh Binh (3 daily; 37–41hr); Quang Ngai (3 daily; 19hr 40min); Vinh (3 daily; 33–36hr).

Hué to: Da Nang (3–4 daily; 3–4hr); Dong Ha (2 daily; 1hr 30min); Hanoi (3 daily; 14–17hr); Ho Chi Minh City (3–4 daily; 22–31hr); Nha Trang (3–4 daily; 13–19hr); Ninh Binh (2 daily; 13–15hr).

Lao Cai to: Hanoi (2 daily; 10–11hr).

Muong Man to: Da Nang (4 daily; 20hr 50min–22hr 30min); Ho Chi Minh City (4 daily; 4hr 10min–4hr 50min); Hué (4 daily; 24hr 20min–26hr 50min); Nha Trang (4 daily; 5hr–5hr 40min).

Nha Trang to: Da Nang (4 daily; 10hr 30min–12hr 10min); Hanoi (3 daily; 28hr–33hr 30min); Ho Chi Minh City (4 daily; 8hr–11hr 10min); Hué (4 daily; 13hr 40min–16hr 30min).

Ninh Binh to: Hanoi (4 daily; 2hr 30min–4hr 30min); Hué (2 daily; 13–15hr); Vinh (2 daily; 4hr 30min).

Vinh to: Dong Ha (2 daily; 7hr–8hr 30min); Hanoi (3 daily; 7hr–8hr 30min); Hué (2 daily; 8hr 30min–10hr); Ninh Binh (2 daily; 4hr 30min).

Hydrofoils and Boats

Can Tho to: Ho Chi Minh City (1 daily, 4hr); My Tho (1 daily, 2hr).

Chau Doc to: Ho Chi Minh City (1 daily, 5hr); My Tho (1 daily, 3hr); Vinh Long (1 daily, 2hr).

Ho Chi Minh City to: Can Tho (1 daily, 4hr); Chau Doc (1 daily, 5hr); My Tho (2 daily, 2hr); Vinh Long (1 daily; 2 hr 20min); Vung Tau (Mon–Fri 6 daily, Sat–Sun 7 daily; 1hr 15min).

My Tho to: Can Tho (1 daily, 2hr); Chau Doc (1 daily, 3hr 40min); Ho Chi Minh City (2 daily, 2hr); Vinh Long (1 daily, 1hr).

Rach Gia to: Phu Quoc Island (1 daily, 9hr).

Vinh Long to: Chau Doc (1 daily, 2hr 40min); Ho Chi Minh City (1 daily, 3hr); My Tho (1 daily, 1hr).

Vung Tau to: Ho Chi Minh City (Mon–Fri 6 daily, Sat–Sun 7 daily; 1hr, 15min).

Flights

Buon Me Thuot to: Da Nang (3 weekly; 1hr 10min); Hanoi (8 weekly; 4hr 15min); Ho Chi Minh City (1 daily; 50min).

Da Lat to: Hanoi (1 daily; 5hr 30min); Ho Chi Minh City (3 weekly; 50min).

Da Nang to: Buon Me Thuot (3 weekly; 1hr 10min); Haiphong (2–3 weekly; 1hr 20min); Hanoi (2 daily; 1hr 10min); Ho Chi Minh City (4 daily; 1hr 15min); Nha Trang (3 weekly; 1hr 20min); Plei Ku (1 daily; 50min).

Hanoi to: Da Nang (2 daily; 1hr 10min); Dien Bien Phu (5 weekly; 1hr); Ho Chi Minh City (6 daily; 2hr); Hué (1–2 daily; 1hr 10min–1hr 30min); Nha Trang (1 daily; 2hr 40min).

Ho Chi Minh City to: Buon Me Thuot (2 daily; 50min); Da Lat (2 daily; 1hr 50min); Da Nang (5 daily; 1hr); Haiphong (2–3 daily; 2hr); Hanoi (9 daily; 2hr); Hué (3 daily; 1hr 40min); Nha Trang (2 daily; 50min).

Hué to: Ho Chi Minh City (1–2 daily; 1hr 50min).

Nha Trang to: Da Nang (2 weekly; 1hr); Hanoi (5 weekly; 2hr 30min); Ho Chi Minh City (1 daily; 50min).

Rach Gia to: Ho Chi Minh City (2 weekly; 2hr).

INDEX

Stay in touch with us!

ROUGH*NEWS* **is Rough Guides' free newsletter. In four issues a year we give you news, travel issues, music reviews, readers' letters and the latest dispatches from authors on the road.**

ROUGH GUIDES: Travel

Alaska
Amsterdam
Andalucia
Argentina
Australia
Austria

Bali & Lombok
Barcelona
Belgium &
  Luxembourg
Belize
Berlin
Brazil
Britain
Brittany &
  Normandy
Bulgaria
California
Canada
Central America
Chile
China
Corsica
Costa Rica
Crete
Croatia
Cuba
Cyprus
Czech & Slovak
  Republics

Dodecanese &
  the East Aegean
Devon &
  Cornwall
Dominican
  Republic
Dordogne & the
  Lot
Ecuador
Egypt
England
Europe
Florida
France
French Hotels &
  Restaurants
  1999
Germany
Goa
Greece
Greek Islands
Guatemala
Hawaii
Holland
Hong Kong &
  Macau
Hungary

Iceland
India
Indonesia
Ionian Islands
Ireland

Israel & the
  Palestinian
  Territories
Italy
Jamaica
Japan
Jordan
Kenya
Lake District
Languedoc &
  Roussillon
Laos
London
Los Angeles
Malaysia,
  Singapore &
  Brunei
Mallorca &
  Menorca
Maya World
Mexico
Morocco
Moscow
Nepal
New England
New York
New Zealand
Norway
Pacific
  Northwest
Paris
Peru
Poland
Portugal
Prague
Provence & the
  Côte d'Azur
The Pyrenees
Romania
St Petersburg
San Francisco

Sardinia
Scandinavia
Scotland
Scottish
  highlands and
  Islands
Sicily
Singapore
South Africa
South India
Southeast Asia
Southwest USA
Spain
Sweden
Switzerland
Syria

Thailand
Trinidad &
  Tobago
Tunisia
Turkey
Tuscany &
  Umbria
USA
Venice
Vienna
Vietnam
Wales
Washington DC
West Africa
Zimbabwe &
  Botswana

AVAILABLE AT ALL GOOD BOOKSHOPS

Turtles visit the park every day of the year, but the peak nesting time falls between July and October. They begin to come ashore around 7.30pm, then dig a nesting pit and lay upwards of a hundred eggs. With hatchings a nightly event, you're almost guaranteed the stirring sight of scores of determined little turtles wriggling up through the sand. In the meantime, Selingaan's quiet beaches are good for swimming and sunbathing, or you can go snorkelling off nearby Bakkungan Kechil (RM15 per person, minimum four people; details from park headquarters).

As mentioned above, the only way to stay overnight on Selingaan is to come on a tour with Crystal Quest. Sabah Parks allows no more than twenty visitors a night onto Selingaan, all of whom are put up in the island's four comfortable chalets. *Uncle Tan's* and the *Travellers' Rest Hostel* visit Selingaan during the day and then take you to other islands, which are not in the park, for the night. *Roses' Café* inside the visitor centre provides meals for the limited number of people in the evening and for extra visitors during the day.

Gomantong Caves

Further afield, the **Gomantong Caves**, south of Sandakan Bay, are inspiring enough at any time of the year, though you'll get most out of the trip when the edible nests of their resident swiftlets are being harvested (Feb–April & July–Sept). Bird's-nest soup has long been a Chinese culinary speciality and Chinese merchants have been coming to Borneo to trade for birds' nests for at least twelve centuries. Of the two major caves, Simud Hitam is easiest to visit: follow the trail from behind the staff quarters to the right of the reception building, taking a right fork after five minutes, and continue for a further ten minutes. Simud Hitam supports a colony of black-nest swiftlets, whose nests – a mixture of saliva and feathers – sell for US$40 a kilogram. Above Simud Hitam, the larger but less accessible Simud Putih is home to the white-nest swiftlet, whose nests are of pure, dried saliva and can fetch prices of over US$500 a kilogram. To reach Simud Putih, take the left fork, five minutes along the trail behind reception, and start climbing.

It's easiest to go with a tour agency (from RM80 per person), but under your own steam, regular minibuses leave daily from Jalan Pryer in Sandakan for Sukau (6am onwards), 20km beyond the turning to Gomantong. This drops you 5km from the caves on a former logging road. Be sure to bring a torch.

Sungei Kinabatangan

East of the entrance to Sandakan Bay, Sabah's longest river, the 560-kilometre **Kinabatangan**, ends its northeasterly path from the interior to the Sulu Sea. Elephants, orang-utans, gibbons, macaques and crocodiles all dwell in the forest flanking the river, and the resident bird life is equally impressive. With luck, you'll glimpse hornbills, Brahminy kites, crested serpent eagles, egrets, exquisite kingfishers and oriental darters. The Kinabatangan's greatest assets, however, are its proboscis monkeys, found beside the water's edge each afternoon. The best way to appreciate the river is to stay in one of the several jungle camps or lodges on its banks. The camps, run by *Uncle Tan's* and the *Travellers' Rest Hostel* in Sandakan (see opposite), charge RM145 and RM150 respectively for two nights' accommodation and travel, plus RM15 per day for meals. About two hours downstream from the camps, in Sukau, *Sukau Rainforest Lodge* (⑦) is more upmarket, but well worth the extra cost, as its location is breathtaking and the chalets lovely. The *Lodge* is run by Borneo Eco Tours in KK (☎088/220210), who will get you from Sandakan to Sukau free of charge.

Semporna

The Bajau fishing town of **SEMPORNA**, 108km east of Tawau, is the departure point for Pulau Sipadan. Chances are that the company taking you to Sipadan will have booked you in at *Dragon Inn Hotel* (☎089/781088; ⑤). If not, one economical option, the adequate *Hotel Semporna* (☎089/781378; ③), sits right in the centre of town. Borneo Divers, Sipadan Dive Centre and Borneo Sea Adventures all have offices at the Semporna Ocean Tourism Centre (SOTC) on the waterfront causeway, as does Today Travel Service, Semporna's MAS agent.

Pulau Sipadan

The waters around tiny **Pulau Sipadan**, 30km south of Semporna in the Celebes Sea, teem with turtles, moray eels, sharks, barracuda, vast schools of tropical fish, and a huge diversity of coral. Not surprisingly, it's a mecca for divers. The diving highlights include a network of marine caves, White-tip Avenue and Barracuda Point and Hanging Gardens of soft coral. Snorkellers accompanying divers to the island can expect to see reef sharks and white-tips, lion fish, barracudas and scores of turtles, without having to leave the surface. The island itself is carpeted by lush forest, and fringed by white sand beaches, used by green turtles to lay their eggs.

The only way to stay on Pulau Sipadan is by booking through a tour operator – all but one of the companies selling diving trips operate out of Kota Kinabalu (see p.654), the exception being *Pulau Sipadan Resort*, which is based in Tawau (see below). It is possible to make independent day-trips to the island; locals with boats (and snorkelling equipment) for rent are plentiful on the SOTC causeway in Semporna. Expect to pay around RM100 for the boat and RM80 for diving equipment.

Tawau and on to Indonesia

TAWAU, Sabah's southernmost town of any size, is a major departure point for Kalimantan. There's not a great deal to see or do here, though the **market** beside *Soon Yee* hotel is worthy of a browse. Long-distance **buses** terminate below the eastern end of Jalan Dunlop, with land cruisers to Keningau leaving from the same site; the local bus station is on Jalan Stephen Tan to the west of the centre of town, sharing the same patch of ground as the minibuses.

The **airport** is just 5km northwest of town – take one of the hotel courtesy buses waiting there, or hail a taxi (RM10). The sole Sipadan **dive operator** not based in KK is *Pulau Sipadan Resort*, Block F, Bandar Sabindo (☎089/765200). **Ferries to Indonesia** depart from Customs Wharf, 150m south of Jalan Dunlop's Shell station. As well as several **banks**, the commercial estate known as the Fajar Centre, east of Jalan Masjid, houses both the Telekom building in Block 35, and the MAS office in Wisma Sasco; you'll find the post office across the southern side of Jalan Dunlop.

The best bargain **accommodation** in town is the friendly Chinese hotel *Soon Yee*, on Jalan Stephen Tan (☎089/772447; ②), while the *Belmost Marco Polo* on Jalan Clinic is the top hotel in town (☎089/777888; ⑥). Two blocks below Jalan Dunlop in the Sabindo Complex, the two-hundred-metre stretch of open-air restaurants and stalls collectively known as *Taman Selera* sets up daily. You'll find several good Indian Muslim **restaurants** on Jalan Chen Fook to the south edge of the town centre. Internet access is available at *Datcom Cyber Café*, on the second floor of the Suhindo Plaza, off Jalan Dunlop.

Transport into Indonesia

Tawau is the main stepping stone for onward travel to Kalimantan (no visa needed). Presently, two ferries ply the route daily: the Samudra Express leaves early in the morning, and the Samudra Indah in the early afternoon – though you should check at the ticket booth north of the jetty on Jalan Pelabuhan. Nunukan (RM25) is an hour from Tawau, after which it's a further two hours to Tarakan (RM65). There are two weekly flights on MAS from Tawau to Tarakan in Indonesia, on Thursday and Sundays.